Baseball America
2024 ALMANAC

Editor
J.J. Cooper

Associate Editors
King Kaufman, Josh Norri

Contributing E
Ben Badler, Teddy Cahill, Carlos Collazo,
Savannah McCa

Database and Applicatio
Mark Taylor

Design & Prod
Seth Mates

Programming & Technical Development
Mark Taylor

Cover Photo
MAIN PHOTO: Ronald Acuña Jr.
PHOTO BY: Patrick Smith/Getty Images

For additional copies, visit our Website at
BaseballAmerica.com or call 1-800-845-2726 to order.
US $34.95 / CAN $45.95, plus shipping and handling per order. Expedited shipping available.
Distributed by Simon & Schuster.
ISBN-13: 979-8-9869573-4-0
Statistics provided by Major League Baseball Advanced Media and Compiled by Baseball America.

EDITOR'S NOTE: Major league statistics are based on final, unofficial 2023 averages.

» The organization statistics, which begin on Page 45, include all players who participated in at least one game during the 2023 season.

» Pitchers' batting statistics are not included, nor are the pitching statistics of position players who pitched in fewer than five games.

» For players who played with more than one team in the same league, the player's cumulative statistics appear on the line immediately after the player's statistics with each team. DSL stats have been combined into one team listing.

TABLE OF CONTENTS

Shohei Ohtani

ROB TRINGALI

MAJOR LEAGUES 8

Baseball America

2024 ALMANAC

BASEBALL AMERICA INC. · DURHAM, N.C.

Baseball America

ESTABLISHED 1981
P.O. BOX 12877, DURHAM, NC 27709 • PHONE (800) 845-2726

EDITOR IN CHIEF J.J. Cooper *@jjcoop36*
EXECUTIVE EDITOR Matt Eddy *@MattEddyBA*
CHIEF INNOVATION OFFICER Ben Badler *@benbadler*
VICE PRESIDENT, DESIGN & STRATEGY Seth Mates *@sethmates*
HEAD OF AUDIENCE DEVELOPMENT Mark Chiarelli *@Mark_Chiarelli*
DIRECTOR OF FINANCE AND REVENUE Mike Stewart

EDITORIAL

SENIOR EDITOR Josh Norris *@jnorris427*
SENIOR WRITER Kyle Glaser *@KyleAGlaser*
NATIONAL WRITERS Teddy Cahill *@tedcahill*
Carlos Collazo *@CarlosACollazo*
Peter Flaherty *@PeterGFlaherty*
PROSPECT WRITER Geoff Pontes *@GeoffPontesBA*
SENIOR EDITOR, DIGITAL & SOCIAL Kayla Lombardo *@KaylaLombardo11*
CONTENT PRODUCER Savannah McCann *@savjaye*
SPECIAL CONTRIBUTOR Tim Newcomb *@tdnewcomb*

BUSINESS

MARKETING/OPERATIONS COORDINATOR Angela Lewis
CUSTOMER SERVICE Melissa Sunderman

STATISTICAL SERVICE

MAJOR LEAGUE BASEBALL ADVANCED MEDIA

BASEBALL AMERICA ENTERPRISES

CHAIRMAN & CEO Gary Green
PRESIDENT Larry Botel
GENERAL COUNSEL Matthew Pace
DIRECTOR OF OPERATIONS Joan Disalvo
PARTNERS Stephen Alepa
Jon Ashley
Martie Cordaro
David Geaslen
Glenn Isaacson
Sonny Kalsi
Peter R. Riguardi
Ian Ritchie
Brian Rothschild
Beryl Snyder
Tom Steiglehner

PJL MEDIA

PRESIDENT Jonathan Segal
VICE PRESIDENT, OPERATIONS B.J. Schecter

BASEBALL AMERICA is published monthly, 12 issues per year, by Baseball America Enterprises, LLC, 650 Fifth Avenue, Suite 2400, New York, NY 10019. Subscription rate is $109.99 for one year; Canada $112.99 (U.S. funds); all other foreign $125.99 per year (U.S. funds). Periodicals postage paid at New York NY, & additional mailing offices. Occasionally our subscriber list is made available to reputable firms offering goods and services we believe would be of interest to our readers. If you prefer to be excluded, please send your current address label and a note requesting to be excluded from these promotions to Baseball America Enterprises, LLC, PO Box 12877, Durhan, NC 27709, Attn: Privacy Coordinator. POSTMASTER: Send all UAA to CFS (See DMM 707.4.12.5); NONPOSTAL & MILITARY FACILITIES: send address corrections to Baseball America, P.O. Box 420235, Palm Coast, FL 32142-0235. CANADA POST: Return undeliverable Canadian addresses to IMEX Global Solutions, P.O. Box 25542, London, ON N6C 6B2. Please contact 1-800-381-1288 to start carrying Baseball America in your store.

BA COVERS 2023

JANUARY
CORBIN CARROLL

FEBRUARY
TOMMY WHITE, PAUL SKENES AND DYLAN CREWS

MARCH
GUNNAR HENDERSON

APRIL
TREA TURNER

MAY
IMAGE GENERATED BY ARTIFICIAL INTELLIGENCE

JUNE/JULY
PAUL SKENES AND DYLAN CREWS

AUGUST
JACKSON HOLLIDAY

SEPTEMBER
ELLY DE LA CRUZ

OCTOBER
SHOHEI OHTANI

NOVEMBER
JACKSON CHOURIO

DECEMBER
EVAN CARTER

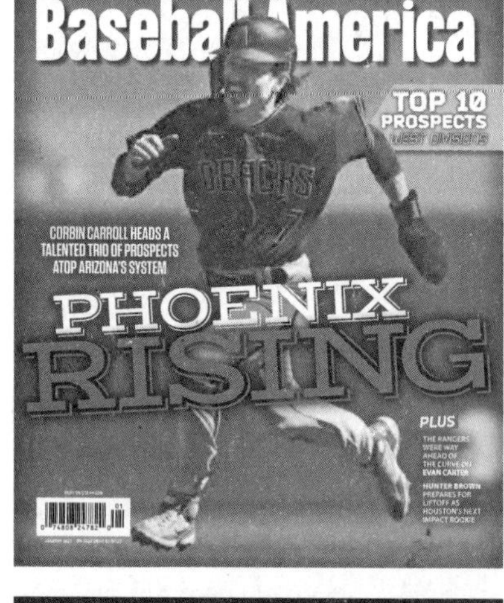

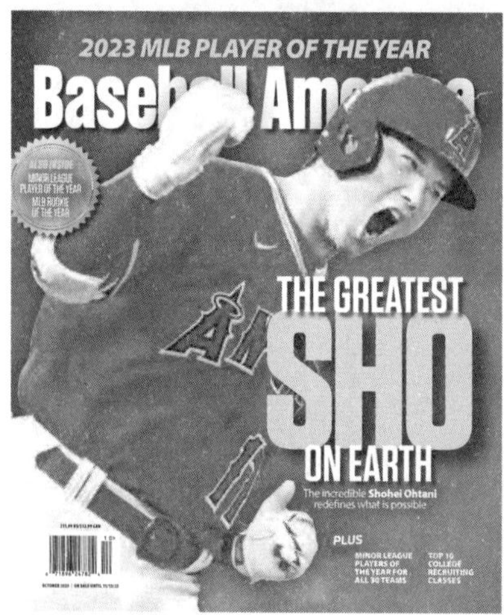

COLLEGE PREVIEW
AN INSIDE LOOK AT HOW LSU BUILT ITS STACKED ROSTER
PURPLE REIGN

TOP 100 PROSPECTS
GUNNAR HENDERSON AND THE ORIOLES' PROSPECT COHORT WILL BRING THE CHARM BACK TO BALTIMORE
YEAH!
PLUS WORLD BASEBALL CLASSIC PREVIEW | FANTASY: SEE WHO THE EXPERTS DRAFT IN DYNASTY STARTUP

DRAFT PREVIEW
LSU TEAMMATES PAUL SKENES & DYLAN CREWS COULD MAKE DRAFT HISTORY
GOLD
STANDARD
EVERYTHING YOU NEED TO KNOW FOR DRAFT DAY!

TOP 100 PROSPECTS: SUMMER UPDATE
LAST YEAR'S NO. 1 PICK IS NOW BASEBALL'S NO. 1 PROSPECT
JACKSON HOLLIDAY FOLLOWS THE LEAD OF ADLEY RUTSCHMAN & GUNNAR HENDERSON TO BALTIMORE
HOLLIDAY SEASON
PLUS
NEXT UP
EARLY 2024 DRAFT PREVIEW: WAKE FOREST EYES HISTORY
WAY-TOO-EARLY MOCK: LACK OF DEFINITION CLOUDS TOP PICKS

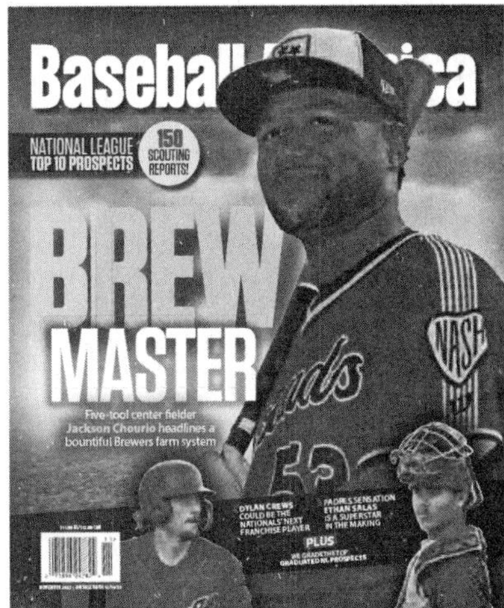
NATIONAL LEAGUE TOP 10 PROSPECTS
150 SCOUTING REPORTS!
BREW
MASTER
Five-tool center fielder Jackson Chourio headlines a bountiful Brewers farm system
DYLAN CREWS COULD BE THE NATIONALS' NEXT FRANCHISE PLAYER
PADRES SENSATION ETHAN SALAS IS A SUPERSTAR IN THE MAKING

Baseball America
150 SCOUTING REPORTS!
AMERICAN LEAGUE TOP 10 PROSPECTS
TEXAS TOAST
ALSO INSIDE
BEST OF 2023 AWARDS

MAJOR LEAGUES

A New Era Arrives

JESS RAPFOGEL

All hitters, including the Orioles' Adley Rutschman, had to keep an eye on the new pitch clock.

BY KYLE GLASER

As much as Major League Baseball is revered for its consistency and tradition, the game's history is one of distinct eras ushered in by seismic rules changes.

The Dead Ball era began in 1901 when the size of home plate was changed from a 12-inch square to a 17-inch pentagon and foul balls started counting as strikes. Strikeouts increased more than 50%, batting averages, slugging percentages, home runs and scoring plummeted, and low-scoring affairs became the norm.

That gave way to the Live Ball era, which was facilitated by new rules changing the ball itself. The spitball and use of emery boards were outlawed. For the first time, new, pearl-white baseballs were introduced after every foul ball or home run. With balls newly visible and playing true, offense skyrocketed, highlighted by Babe Ruth breaking the single-season home record of 11 by hitting 29 in 1919, then 54 the next year.

The Integration Era, starting in 1947, expanded the pool of players eligible to play in MLB, bringing Black players into the fold for the first time and leading to a surge of offense and athleticism. Pitchers briefly retook control until the height of the mound was lowered from 15 to 10 inches in 1969, launching another offensive explosion.

The DH was introduced in the American League in 1973, ending nearly 100 years of pitchers batting in both leagues. The proliferation of artificial turf in that decade tilted the game toward speedy players with lightning-quick reflexes. That lasted until the steroid era of the late 1980s through early 2000s, when performance-enhancing drugs made previously unthinkable home run totals a regular occurrence. Just twice in the first 120 years of major league history did a player hit 60 home runs in a season. It happened six times in four seasons between 1998 and 2001.

Despite that history, the narrative of baseball's purity has long made its stakeholders—fans, players, executives, owners—resistant to change. Inevitably, though, change becomes part of the fabric of the game.

That was truer than ever in 2023. MLB implemented sweeping rules changes before the season to quicken the game's pace and increase the number of balls in play. The changes, which MLB tested in the minors in 2021-22, came against the backdrop of increasing game times and rising rates of walks and strikeouts, a combination of less action and more time that did not bode well for baseball's future.

The commissioner's office introduced four key rules changes for the 2023 season.

The first, and most significant, was a pitch clock that gave pitchers 15 seconds to deliver the ball with the bases empty and 20 seconds with runners on base. Batters had to be in the box ready to hit with eight seconds remaining or a strike would be called.

The second change limited pitchers to two pickoff attempts per plate appearance, with a third attempt ruled a balk if it failed to record an out.

The third rule change dictated two infielders had to remain on either side of second base with both feet on the dirt when a pitch was delivered, effectively banning defensive shifts that had gained prominence in recent years.

The final change increased the size of the bases from 15 to 18 inches square, shortening the distance between bases and creating more space for fielders to work without risk of colliding with a runner.

The changes were adopted after a majority vote by the league's 11-person competition committee, made up of six representatives from the commissioner's office, four representatives from the MLB Players Association and one umpire. The vote to increase the size of the bases was unanimous, but all four player representatives voted against the pitch clock and shift restrictions.

Over the players' objections, the changes were implemented.

"Players live the game—day in and day out," the MLBPA said in a statement issued following the announcement of the changes. "On-field rules and regulations impact their preparation, performance, and ultimately, the integrity of the game itself. Player leaders from across the league were engaged in on-field rules negotiations through the Competition Committee, and they provided specific and actionable feedback on the changes proposed by the Commissioner's Office.

"Major League Baseball was unwilling to meaningfully address the areas of concern that Players raised, and as a result, Players on the Competition Committee voted unanimously against the implementation of the rules covering defensive shifts and the use of a pitch timer."

Spring training began on time and played out uninterrupted for the first time since 2019 after the coronavirus pandemic shortened the 2020-21 Cactus and Grapefruit League schedules and the owners' lockout delayed the start of 2022 spring training. With the rules changes being tried out for the first time by major leaguers, however, spring training games were anything but normal.

On the first day of Cactus League play, Padres third baseman Manny Machado became the first player to be called for a pitch clock violation when he failed to step into the box on time against Mariners lefthander Robbie Ray. The next day, a Grapefruit League contest between the Red Sox and Braves ended in a 6-6 tie when Braves shortstop Cal Conley was called for a pitch clock violation with a full count and the bases loaded in the bottom of the ninth inning. Conley's game-ending strikeout gave rise to concerns that games could be decided by the clock, instead of the players, in critical late-game situations.

"The umpire said I was looking down," Conley told the Atlanta Journal-Constitution. "I was looking down at the catcher as he was standing up. Not really sure if the pitcher was ready to go, the catcher definitely wasn't. I was just trying to go with the rhythm of them, kind of wasn't looking at the clock. Next time, should've called time in that situation, I guess, is what the umpire said. I guess learn from it and move on."

The adjustment period carried into the start of the regular season.

On Opening Day, Red Sox third baseman Rafael Devers became the first player to strike out on a pitch clock violation when he failed to get in the batter's box on time against Orioles righthander Bryan Baker. Just over a week later, Machado became the first player ejected for arguing a pitch clock violation when he was issued a third strike by umpire Ron Kulpa for not being in the box on time against the Diamondbacks. Machado argued that he'd called timeout, but Kulpa ruled that he'd called it too late and ejected him during the ensuing argument.

"I called it at eight seconds," Machado said. "He did not give it to me. Now I got struck out. Hurt my team by coming out of the game and getting tossed there. I feel like I didn't do anything wrong."

The early hiccups fueled fears that the changes, particularly the pitch clock, would wreak havoc on the game.

In time though, the fears proved unfounded. As the season progressed, the players slowly adapted. In time, the changes became not just a part of the game, but a central part of its post-Covid resurgence.

Whole New Ballgame

From Opening Day, it was clear the rules changes would alter the way the game was played.

ROB CARR/GETTY IMAGES

Reds shortstop Elly De La Cruz was one of eight Reds to reach double digits in steals.

Gone were the sluggish contests lasting nearly four hours. Gone was the station-to-station baseball that had teams dependent on walks and home runs to score. In their place emerged a faster, more kinetic game that changed the fan—and player—experience.

Games on Opening Day averaged 2 hours, 45 minutes, a 26-minute decrease from the average Opening Day game in 2022. Ten of the 15 games lasted under three hours.

The Dodgers and D-backs played a game that featured 10 runs, 16 hits, 20 strikeouts, four mid-inning pitching changes and a lengthy delay after a controversial pitch clock violation was called. The game lasted just 2:35.

"It's great," Dodgers manager Dave Roberts said. "That was front of mind, actually, looking at (our) game and going, 'Man, we played 2:35 tonight.' Last year it was probably 3:35."

The games only got faster as players acclimated further. By the all-star break, the average game time had dropped to 2:38. Most notably, violations dropped from nearly one per game at the start of the season to less than one every four games by midseason, allaying fears that violations and ensuing arguments would become a daily occurrence.

Most importantly, not a single game was determined by a violation in a late-and-close situation.

"The biggest thank you goes to the players," Commissioner Rob Manfred said. "I understand how important routines are to players. When you say to a professional athlete, 'You've done this a certain way your whole life and we're going to change it because we're going to have a rule change,' that's a big deal. Our players, the game's players, have adjusted quickly and effectively." By the end of the season, the average time of a nine-inning game was 2:40, the shortest since 1985 and a decrease of 30 minutes from the all-time high of 3:10 in 2021.

Just nine games the entire season lasted longer than three-and-a-half hours. In 2021, there were 390 games that took at least that long.

"I think it's gone smoothly," Dodgers catcher Will Smith said. "It's nice for you to get home a bit earlier. You don't have the four-hour games anymore."

While the pitch clock received most of the focus, it wasn't the only rule to alter play. Stolen bases skyrocketed with pitchers limited to just two pickoffs per plate appearance, opening the door for young, athletic teams and players to flourish.

Teams attempted 4,369 stolen bases in 2023, more than 1,000 more than in 2022. It was the highest number of stolen base attempts in a season since 1987, and the league's 80.2% success rate was the highest of all-time.

Braves superstar Ronald Acuña Jr. hit 41 home runs and led the majors with 73 stolen bases, becoming the first player to ever go 40-70 in a season (or 40-50 or 40-60, for that matter). D-backs outfielder Corbin Carroll hit 25 home runs and stole 54 bases, becoming the first rookie ever to record a 25-50 season. Athletics outfielder Esteury Ruiz stole 67 bases despite missing a month with a shoulder injury. Royals shortstop Bobby Witt Jr., Nationals shortstop CJ Abrams and Cubs second baseman Nico Hoerner all recorded at least 40 steals, marking the first time six players notched 40 steals in a season since 2012.

Led by their running games, the youthful D-backs and Reds surged up the standings and into wild card contention. The Reds led the majors with 190 steals, the most by a team since the 2009 Rays (194). Fueled by the midseason callup of rookie Elly De La Cruz, the Reds ran wild over opponents, with eight players reaching double-

PLAYER OF THE YEAR

Ohtani Keeps Raising The Bar

BY KYLE GLASER

No matter what happens next, Shohei Ohtani has redefined what is possible in Major League Baseball.

Ohtani put the capper on one of the greatest three-year stretches in baseball history in 2023. The Angels' two-way star didn't pitch after Aug. 23 due to a torn ulnar collateral ligament in his right elbow and discontinued batting after straining his right oblique on Sept. 4.

Despite that, he still hit a career-best .304/.412/.654, led the American League with 44 home runs and led the majors with a 1.066 OPS. On the mound, he went 10-5 with a 3.14 ERA with 167 strikeouts in 132 innings. Opponents hit just .184, lowest in the AL among pitchers with at least 100 innings.

Already baseball's preeminent talent, Ohtani found a way to raise his game yet again. He set new career highs in batting average, on-base percentage, slugging percentage, OPS and total bases.

He was, simultaneously, the most dangerous hitter in baseball and the hardest pitcher to hit in his league, a level of dominance even he had never achieved.

For yet another transcendent, precedent-shattering season, Ohtani is the 2023 Major League Player of the Year.

"Really, it's crazy," Rangers manager Bruce Bochy said. "I never thought we'd see it in the major leagues that a guy could do what he's been doing. Obviously he's an outlier. Goes back to Babe Ruth. That's what he's been, and it really is amazing."

RONALD MARTINEZ/GETTY IMAGES

Shohei Ohtani led the American League in home runs despite missing a month

The very notion that Ohtani, 29, could keep getting better seems preposterous. After all, this is the player whose two-way exploits were already unmatched in MLB history, even by Ruth. Yet, he kept raising the bar.

In 2021, he hit 46 home runs, posted a .965 OPS and logged a 3.18 ERA on the mound en route to becoming the unanimous AL MVP. In 2022, he raised his batting average by 16 points, lowered his ERA to 2.33, increased his strikeout rate and lowered his rates of walks, hits and home runs allowed.

And in 2023, he raised his batting average another 31 points and led the AL in homers, walks, OBP, slugging percentage, OPS and total bases for the first time. Simultaneously, he was the hardest to hit that he's ever been on the mound.

"I mean, he got better at everything, honestly, which shows a lot to his work ethic and determination to do it," said Angels shortstop David Fletcher.

"I will probably remember just him having fun doing it and obviously putting all the work in. When the game came, whether he failed or succeeded, he always had confidence that he would bounce back if he failed." ■

LAST 10 WINNERS

2013: Mike Trout, OF, Angels
2014: Clayton Kershaw, LHP, Dodgers
2015: Bryce Harper, OF, Nationals
2016: Mike Trout, OF, Angels
2017: Jose Altuve, 2B, Astros
2018: Mike Trout, OF, Angels
2019: Justin Verlander, RHP, Astros
2020: Freddie Freeman, 1B, Braves
2021: Shohei Ohtani, DH/RHP, Angels
2022: Aaron Judge, OF, Yankees

Full list: search "Baseball America awards"

digit steals.

De La Cruz's signature moment came when he stole second, third and home in a span of two pitches against the Brewers on July 9, the steal of home on a throw back to the mound.

"It's so much fun to watch, so much fun to be part of," Reds manager David Bell said. "It's one of those plays that's so rare, especially on two pitches to steal a base like that. The speed is obvious, just elite speed like maybe we've never seen, but also how heads-up it was."

While the Reds couldn't maintain their momentum down the stretch, the Diamondbacks did. Led by Carroll, Arizona finished second in the majors with 166 steals and wreaked havoc by taking extra bases when opposing defenses least suspected. The young, high-flying D-backs used their athleticism to surge into first place in the National League West by the end of June and into the NL's final wild card spot at the end of the season, their first postseason appearance since 2017.

It was a stark turnaround for a team that lost 110 games only two years earlier.

"I think a lot of the emotion you see is that a lot of these guys were here the last few years," first baseman Christian Walker said the night the D-Backs clinched, "and we feel like we really earned this. We pulled ourselves out of a [tough] situation and turned ourselves into some winners."

The other rules changes had less of an effect. The league-wide batting average increased from .243 to .248 with the ban on defensive shifts, but a five-point increase is in the normal range of variance from year to year. (The leaguewide batting average also increased five points from 2018 to 2019 without any rules changes). The hope that opening up the field for hitters would encourage them to focus on contact and strike out less also did not come to fruition. The league-wide strikeout rate was 22.7%, a slight increase from 22.4% in 2022.

The increased base size added little, to the point that most people forgot about it over the course of the year.

But while offense did not spike, more stolen bases and shorter game times gave MLB the more dynamic product and increased fan appeal it desired.

Attendance rose 9.6% in 2023 and the league crossed the 70 million attendance mark for the first time since 2017. The league witnessed the largest per-game spike in attendance in 30 years. Seventeen teams drew at least 2.5 million fans, tied for most in a season in MLB history. Overall, 26 of the 30 teams saw attendance increase from 2022 to 2023.

The rules changes, by and large, were a hit for fans, owners and league officials. By the end, even the players who had once been skeptical were on board with the new brand of baseball.

"It took some getting used to, but once you get used to it the game's a lot faster," Twins shortstop Carlos Correa said. "There's not wasted time. The pace was great, so I think it's here to stay."

Money Isn't Everything

The Padres' transformation from low-payroll penny-pinchers into one of baseball's biggest spenders under owner Peter Seidler had been

AMERICAN LEAGUE STANDINGS

East	W	L	PCT	GB	Manager	PBO/GM	Attendance	Average	Last Penn.
Baltimore Orioles	101	61	.623	—	Brandon Hyde	Mike Elias	1,936,798	23,911	1983
Tampa Bay Rays	99	63	.611	2	Kevin Cash	Erik Neander	1,440,301	17,781	2020
Toronto Blue Jays	89	73	.549	12	John Schneider	Mark Shapiro	3,021,904	37,307	1993
New York Yankees	82	80	.506	19	Aaron Boone	Brian Cashman	3,269,016	40,863	2009
Boston Red Sox	78	84	.481	23	Alex Cora	Chaim Bloom	2,672,130	32,989	2018
Central	**W**	**L**	**PCT**	**GB**	**Manager**	**PBO/GM**	**Attendance**	**Average**	**Last Penn.**
Minnesota Twins	87	75	.537	—	Rocco Baldelli	Derek Falvey	1,974,124	24,372	1991
Detroit Tigers	78	84	.481	9	A.J. Hinch	Scott Harris	1,612,876	20,946	2012
Cleveland Guardians	76	86	.469	11	Terry Francona	Chris Antonetti	1,834,068	23,514	2016
Chicago White Sox	61	101	.377	26	Pedro Grifol	Rick Hahn	1,669,628	21,405	2005
Kansas City Royals	56	106	.346	31	Matt Quatraro	J.J. Picollo	1,307,052	16,136	2015
West	**W**	**L**	**PCT**	**GB**	**Manager**	**PBO/GM**	**Attendance**	**Average**	**Last Penn.**
Houston Astros	90	72	.556	—	Dusty Baker	Dana Brown	3,052,347	37,683	2022
Texas Rangers	90	72	.556	—	Bruce Bochy	Chris Young	2,533,044	31,272	2023
Seattle Mariners	88	74	.543	2	Scott Servais	Jerry Dipoto	2,690,418	33,215	Never
Los Angeles Angels	73	89	.451	17	Phil Nevin	Perry Minasian	2,640,575	32,600	2002
Oakland Athletics	50	112	.309	40	Mark Kotsay	David Forst	832,352	10,276	1990

Wild Card Series: Twins defeated Blue Jays 2-0; Rangers defeated Rays 2-0 in best-of-3 series. **Division Series:** Astros defeated Twins 3-1 and Rangers defeated Orioles 3-0 in best-of-5 series. **Championship Series:** Rangers defeated Astros 4-3 in best-of-7 series.

ROOKIE OF THE YEAR

Carroll Finds Stardom As Rookie

BY ZACH BUCHANAN

After his first taste of the majors in 2022, Diamondbacks outfielder Corbin Carroll entered the offseason on a mission.

Called up for a 32-game audition at the end of that season, Carroll had certainly justified the hype. He batted .260 with an .830 OPS. His sprint speed had immediately placed him in the 100th percentile of big leaguers.

Yet, after zooming from Double-A Amarillo to the majors in just five months, there had also been weaknesses. Known for his plate discipline, Carroll struck out 27% of the time in 115 MLB plate appearances. The young lefthanded hitter struggled against lefthanders, leading D-backs manager Torey Lovullo to sit him or hit for him in those situations.

After the season, Carroll made a promise to his manager—and to himself.

"I'm going to work as hard as I can to hit lefthanded pitching," Carroll told Lovullo, "so you never have to pinch-hit for me ever again."

Mission more than accomplished.

In 2023, Carroll achieved far more than the sanding down of his weaknesses and the rounding out of his game. He fashioned one of the best rookie seasons ever.

Heading into the final series of the season, he hit .287/.362/.509, including a .283 average versus lefties. He showed a tantalizing combination of speed and power packed into a wiry frame by blasting the ball to all fields and wreaking havoc on the basepaths.

Carroll clubbed 25 homers and stole 52 bases, becoming just the ninth player ever to record a 20-50 season. On that list, he keeps company with the likes of Barry Bonds, Rickey Henderson, Joe Morgan and Ronald Acuña Jr. Carroll, who turned 23 in August, is the only one of them to accomplish the feat as a rookie.

Just where Carroll ranks in the pantheon of great rookies makes for a stirring debate, but where he ranks among rookies this season isn't all that difficult to determine. For that reason, Carroll is crowned the 2023 Baseball America Rookie of the Year.

CHRISTIAN PETERSEN/GETTY IMAGES

Corbin Carroll's amazing rookie season included a trip to the World Series

"He's quite possibly the best young player I've ever played with," said D-backs veteran Evan Longoria, who won the American League Rookie of the Year award in 2008. "I could probably say that pretty easily."

Teammates and coaches rave about Carroll's work ethic. He is such a fiend for hitting off the pitching machine, said assistant hitting coach Rick Short, that he can tell when the speed or spin isn't set to his preferences.

That's one of the many reasons that, before the 2023 season even started, the D-backs eagerly locked Carroll up to an unprecedented extension worth at least $111 million over eight years, a record amount of money to guarantee a player with less than 100 days of major league service time. ■

LAST 10 WINNERS

2013: Jose Fernandez, RHP, Marlins
2014: Jose Abreu, 1B, White Sox
2015: Kris Bryant, 3B, Cubs
2016: Corey Seager, SS, Dodgers
2017: Aaron Judge, OF, Yankees
2018: Shohei Ohtani, RHP/DH, Angels
2019: Pete Alonso, 1B, Mets
2020: Tony Gonsolin, RHP, Dodgers
2021: Jonathan India, 2B, Reds
2022: Julio Rodriguez, OF, Mariners

Full list: search "Baseball America awards"

one of the sport's most polarizing developments in recent years. Fresh off the heels of a National League Championship Series appearance in 2022, the Padres took their spending to yet another level in 2023.

The Padres delivered the shock of the Winter Meetings when they signed shortstop Xander Bogaerts to an 11-year, $280 million contract. They followed up by awarding third baseman Machado an 11-year, $350 million deal to avoid him opting out after the season and extending righthander Yu Darvish for six years and $108 million. They brought back setup man Robert Suarez on a five-year, $46 million deal and swingman Nick Martinez on a three-year, $26 million contract, and they signed free agent starters Seth Lugo and Michael Wacha for a combined $41 million. Shortly after Opening Day, they signed two-time all-star infielder Jake Cronenworth to a seven-year, $80 million extension.

Those outlays and others brought the Padres payroll to an astounding $249 million, third highest in MLB behind only the Mets and Yankees. With their spending, they switched from a revenue sharing recipient to a revenue sharing payer.

"Look, I think there's real positives in the Padres story," Manfred said at a February press conference. "I think that the investment that the club has made in talent has allowed them to grow their revenue to the point that they will be a payer under the revenue-sharing system this year.

"The trick for the smaller markets has always been sustainability. Hats off to Peter Seidler. He's made a massive financial commitment, personally, to make this all happen. And the question becomes, how long can you continue to do that?"

Seidler, for his part, dismissed the skepticism from the commissioner and fellow owners.

"I don't spend too much time, if any, thinking about what other people are thinking," Seidler said at the start of spring training. "Truly, I care about what we're thinking in this room in San Diego. To me, it just feels great.

"We believe we have a great chance to go after that trophy and to deliver San Diego its first parade."

The Padres were hardly the only team to spend big. With free-spending owner Steve Cohen opening up his wallet even more than ever before, the Mets re-signed center fielder Brandon Nimmo to an eight-year, $162 million contract and closer Edwin Diaz to a five-year, $102 million deal, the largest contract ever for a closer. They grabbed two of the best free agent pitchers on the market, signing future Hall of Famer Justin Verlander to a two-year, $86.6 million contract and Japanese righthander Kodai Senga for five years and $75 million. They tried to go one step further, agreeing with Correa on a 12-year, $315 million deal before backing out after a physical raised concerns about the health of Correa's surgically repaired right ankle.

Even without Correa, the Mets began the season with a $331 million payroll, highest in major league history.

"What you're really trying to do is just fill out the roster, and the market's going to dictate where you have to go with that," general manager Billy Eppler said. "It's something that we consider, something that we're aware of, something that

NATIONAL LEAGUE STANDINGS

East	W	L	PCT	GB	Manager	PBO/GM	Attendance	Average	Last Penn.
Atlanta Braves	104	58	.642	—	Brian Snitker	Alex Anthopoulos	3,191,505	39,401	2021
Philadelphia Phillies	90	72	.556	14	Rob Thomson	Dave Dombrowski	3,052,605	38,158	2022
Miami Marlins	84	78	.519	20	Skip Schumaker	Kim Ng	1,162,819	14,356	2003
New York Mets	75	87	.463	29	Buck Showalter	Billy Eppler	2,573,555	32,577	2015
Washington Nationals	71	91	.438	33	Dave Martinez	Mike Rizzo	1,865,832	23,035	2019
Central	**W**	**L**	**PCT**	**GB**	**Manager**	**PBO/GM**	**Attendance**	**Average**	**Last Penn.**
Milwaukee Brewers	92	70	.568	—	Craig Counsell	Matt Arnold	2,551,347	31,498	1982 (AL)
Chicago Cubs	83	79	.512	9	David Ross	Jed Hoyer	2,775,149	34,261	2016
Cincinnati Reds	82	80	.506	10	David Bell	Nick Krall	2,038,302	25,164	1990
Pittsburgh Pirates	76	86	.469	16	Derek Shelton	Ben Cherington	1,630,624	20,131	1979
St. Louis Cardinals	71	91	.438	21	Oliver Marmol	John Mozeliak	3,241,091	40,013	2013
West	**W**	**L**	**PCT**	**GB**	**Manager**	**PBO/GM**	**Attendance**	**Average**	**Last Penn.**
Los Angeles Dodgers	100	62	.617	—	Dave Roberts	Andrew Friedman	3,837,079	47,371	2020
Arizona Diamondbacks	84	78	.519	16	Torey Lovullo	Mike Hazen	1,961,182	24,212	2023
San Diego Padres	82	80	.506	18	Bob Melvin	A.J. Preller	3,271,554	40,390	1998
San Francisco Giants	79	83	.488	21	Gabe Kapler/Kai Correa	Farhan Zaidi	2,500,153	30,866	2014
Colorado Rockies	59	103	.364	41	Bud Black	Bill Schmidt	2,607,935	32,197	2007

Wild Card Series: D-backs defeated Brewers 2-0 and Phillies defeated Marlins 2-0 in best-of-3 series. **Division Series:** D-backs defeated Dodgers 3-0 and Phillies defeated Braves 3-1 in best-of-5 series. **Championship Series:** D-backs defeated Phillies 4-3 in best-of-7 series.

Steve and I talk about regularly. But ultimately, he made a commitment to the fans, and he and his wife are completely supportive in providing the resources for us."

All across the sport, teams threw money around. The Yankees signed reigning AL MVP Aaron Judge to a nine-year, $360 million contract, the largest ever signed in free agency. The Red Sox, facing a fan revolt after trading Mookie Betts and losing Bogaerts in free agency in a span of less than three years, gave Devers an 11-year, $331 million extension. The Phillies, fresh off a World Series appearance, signed shortstop Trea Turner to an 11-year, $300 million deal. Correa eventually landed a six-year, $200 million contract to re-sign with the Twins, the Rangers signed righthander Jacob deGrom for five years, $185 million, and the Cubs brought in Gold Glove shortstop Dansby Swanson on a seven-year, $177 million deal.

It was the most expensive offseason in major league history, with teams shelling out a combined $3.7 billion in guaranteed contracts.

Once the season began, however, reality set in that money doesn't always equal success.

The Padres fell below. 500 on May 12 and remained there until the final days of the season. They lost early-season home series to the last-place Royals and Nationals, playing in such uninspired fashion that they were booed off the field after their May 17 loss to Kansas City. Even the return of Fernando Tatis Jr., who missed the 2022 season because of a wrist injury and PED suspension, couldn't jolt the team out of an offensive slumber that lasted throughout the year. Only a 13-2 surge to end the season pushed them over .500 for an 82-80 finish.

"It's something that, looking back on when we're all old, it's going to be one that stings," lefthander Blake Snell said, "because I don't know if I'll ever play on a team this talented and this good."

As ugly as the Padres' season was, it was still better than the Mets' fate.

Early-season injuries to Verlander and Max Scherzer exposed the Mets' lack of pitching depth and sent their season spiraling. The Mets were in fourth place in the NL East by May 15, fell under .500 for good on June 6 and played some of the worst baseball of the summer, committing an MLB-high 22 errors in June. With nothing improving even after Verlander and Scherzer returned, the Mets pulled the plug at the trade deadline, sending Verlander to the Astros, Scherzer to the Rangers, closer David Robertson to the Marlins and veteran contributors Tommy Pham (D-backs) and Mark Canha (Brewers) out of town as well.

RICH SCHULTZ/GETTY IMAGES

Manager Buck Showalter was let go by the Mets after a disappointing 75-87 season.

With their attention turned to the future following the deadline, the Mets finished 75-87 and in fourth place in the NL East after fielding the most expensive roster in baseball history.

"We were obviously a good team," Canha said. "We had a lot of talent. And we just didn't have that magic, and that was frustrating. Because we all liked playing so much. We wanted it to work so bad. And it just didn't."

The rest of baseball's biggest spenders didn't fare much better. The Yankees stumbled on both sides of the ball to finish 82-80, their worst record since 1992. The Angels, with the sixth-highest payroll in MLB, tried to contend in Shohei Ohtani's final guaranteed season with the team by acquiring Lucas Giolito, Reynaldo Lopez, C.J. Cron and Randal Grichuk at the trade deadline. The attempt flopped and the Angels spiraled to a 73-89 record and another playoff-less season with Ohtani and Mike Trout. The Red Sox, after handing out nearly $500 million in contract extensions and free agent deals, finished in last place in the AL East for the third time in four years.

In all, the teams with the three-highest Opening Day payrolls—the Mets, Yankees and Padres—all missed the playoffs.

There was a price to pay for such failures. The Mets fired manager Buck Showalter after the final game of the season. Eppler resigned shortly after the Mets announced they were hiring former Brewers executive David Stearns to rank above him

ALL-ROOKIE TEAM 2023

Pos	Player, Team	AVG	OBP	SLG	AB	R	H	2B	3B	HR	RBI	BB	SO	SB	CS
C	Yainer Diaz, Astros	.282	.308	.538	355	51	100	22	0	23	60	11	74	0	0
1B	Triston Casas, Red Sox	.263	.367	.490	429	66	113	21	2	24	65	70	126	0	0
2B	Matt McLain, Reds	.290	.357	.507	365	65	106	23	4	16	50	31	115	14	5
3B	Josh Jung, Rangers	.266	.315	.467	478	75	127	25	1	23	70	30	151	1	3
SS	Gunnar Henderson, Orioles	.255	.325	.489	560	100	143	29	9	28	82	56	159	10	3
OF	Corbin Carroll, D-backs	.285	.362	.506	565	116	161	30	10	25	76	57	125	54	5
OF	Nolan Jones, Rockies	.297	.389	.542	367	60	109	22	4	20	62	53	126	20	4
OF	James Outman, Dodgers	.248	.353	.437	483	86	120	16	3	23	70	68	181	16	3
DH	Spencer Steer, Reds	.271	.356	.464	582	74	158	37	3	23	86	68	139	15	3

Pos.	Player, Team	W	L	ERA	G	GS	SV	IP	H	R	ER	HR	BB	SO	WHIP
SP	Andrew Abbott, Reds	8	6	3.87	21	21	0	109	100	47	47	16	44	120	1.32
SP	Tanner Bibee, Guardians	10	4	2.98	25	25	0	142	122	49	47	13	45	141	1.18
SP	Bobby Miller, Dodgers	11	4	3.76	22	22	0	124	105	53	52	12	32	119	1.10
SP	Eury Perez, Marlins	5	6	3.15	19	19	0	91	72	35	32	15	31	108	1.13
SP	Kodai Senga, Mets	12	7	2.98	29	29	0	166	126	60	55	17	77	202	1.22
RP	Yennier Cano, Orioles	1	4	2.11	72	0	8	73	60	19	17	4	13	65	1.00

as president of baseball operations.

Padres manager Bob Melvin was allowed to interview with the Giants and ultimately left to become their manager. The Red Sox fired chief baseball officer Chaim Bloom with two weeks remaining in the season.

The Yankees fired hitting coach Dillon Lawson at midseason, though they opted to retain manager Aaron Boone.

Still, owner Hal Steinbrenner vowed that the Yankees weren't satisfied with the status quo.

"We're going to be making some changes," Steinbrenner said. "Some may be more subtle than others. But I think we've uncovered certainly things we can do better."

Rise of the Small Markets

While some of baseball's biggest spenders scuffled, some of the lowest payroll teams experienced great success.

The Orioles, with the second-lowest payroll in MLB, emerged from their rebuild with a thrilling 101-win season and their first American League East title since 2014. Led by franchise catcher Adley Rutschman and star rookie infielder Gunnar Henderson, the Orioles became the AL's fourth-highest scoring offense and one of baseball's most exciting teams throughout the summer.

"I've got to imagine this is a top moment in the recent history of the franchise," Orioles GM Mike Elias said after the Orioles clinched the division. "One hundred wins, AL East, it's an incredible achievement for this group."

The Orioles' main competition in the division were the Rays, owners of the MLB's third-lowest payroll, who got off to a 27-6 before being hit by a spate of injuries and player losses.

The Rays lost starting pitchers Jeffrey Springs and Drew Rasmussen for the year with arm injuries early in the season and spent extended stretches without aces Tyler Glasnow and Shane McClanahan. Their lineup suffered a brutal blow, and the franchise an overall embarrassment, when star shortstop Wander Franco was placed on administrative leave Aug. 22 as the league and Dominican police investigated allegations he engaged in an inappropriate relationship with an underage girl.

Despite the setbacks, the Rays went 99-63 and secured the AL's top wild card for their sixth straight playoff berth. Ten different players reached double-digit home runs as their offense ranked second in the AL in scoring. Seventeen different pitchers started a game for the Rays, and they still finished with the AL's second-lowest ERA.

"It's taken a lot to get here," Rays manager Kevin Cash said. "I think everybody realizes that. Really commend this group and happy that we're in (the postseason)."

The Rays (28th) and Orioles (29th) were hardly alone among teams with bottom-10 Opening Day payrolls to have success. The Marlins (23rd) overcame a season-ending elbow injury to ace Sandy Alcantara to win a wild card and reach the playoffs in a full season for the first time since 2003. The Diamondbacks (21st) led the NL West most of the first half before securing a wild card berth. The Brewers (20th) led the NL Central nearly wire-to-wire to win the division and reach the playoffs for the fifth time in six years.

But not all was positive for low-payroll teams. Early in the season, the lowest-payroll team of all delivered a gut-punch to the city it has called home for 55 years.

A's Make Their Move

For most of the previous three years, A's ownership systematically dismantled the team's roster to lower payroll. They failed to make franchise shortstop Marcus Semien a competitive offer before the 2021 season, traded cornerstones Matt Olson, Matt Chapman, Chris Bassitt, Sean Manaea and Frankie Montas in a six-month span in 2022 and traded Gold Glove-winning catcher Sean Murphy and burgeoning closer A.J. Puk before the 2023 season.

What remained was one of the worst teams in modern major league history playing in the dilapidated Oakland Coliseum, a combination that led to historic attendance lows.

The A's started the season 3-16 and averaged less than 10,000 fans per home game. The sight of a nearly empty Coliseum combined with a terrible on-field product only furthered the notion that remaining in Oakland was becoming a less likely option for the franchise.

On April 19, the A's announced they had signed a binding agreement to purchase land in Las Vegas for a future ballpark site, cementing their intent to relocate. After 20-plus years of trying to reach a deal for a new stadium in the East Bay, the franchise appears to be on its way out of town.

"For a while we were on parallel paths, but we have turned our attention to Las Vegas to get a deal here for the A's to find a long-term home," Athletics president Dave Kaval told the Las Vegas Review-Journal. "Oakland has been a great home for us for over 50 years, but we really need this 20-year saga completed and we feel there's a path here in Southern Nevada." The A's initially agreed to purchase a plot of vacant land along the Las Vegas Strip before pivoting to a new agreement with Bally Resorts Co. to build a $1.5 billion, 30,000-seat stadium on the current site of the Tropicana Hotel.

In mid-June, the Nevada Legislature passed a bill allocating $380 million in public money to help fund the A's new stadium. Nevada Gov. Joe Lombardo signed the bill, SB1, one day later.

"I'm excited to officially sign SB1 this afternoon," Lombardo said in a statement. "This is an incredible opportunity to bring the A's to Nevada, and this legislation reflects months of negotiations between the team, the state, the county, and the league. Las Vegas' position as a global sports destination is only growing, and Major League Baseball is another tremendous asset for the city."

As the relocation process unfolded, A's fans did not go quietly. On June 13, the day the Nevada legislature voted to approve the bill partially fund-

MICHAEL ZAGARIS

A's fans held a reverse boycott to protest the team's efforts to move to Las Vegas.

ing the A's stadium in Las Vegas, Oakland fans staged a "reverse boycott" intended to show owner John Fisher and MLB that the team still had a passionate fan base and should remain in the East Bay. With giant banners saying "Sell the team" plastered throughout the stadium, a season-high crowd of 27,759 turned out to watch the A's beat the Rays 2-1, with chanting and buzzing filling the ballpark from start to finish. Thousands of fans wore shirts with the word "SELL" across the chest and, after the game, threw trash on the field to protest Fisher and the relocation.

The fans continued to show their support beyond just the bounds of the Coliseum. A small contingent of A's fans showed up at the All-Star Game in Seattle with "Sell the Team" banners and protested the proposed relocation at the home plate gate. Fan clubs dedicated to keeping the team in Oakland popped up and rapidly gained thousands of members.

While inspired, though, it was all for naught.

Manfred quashed any notion that the reverse boycott had changed minds when he dismissively said, "It's great to see what is, this year, almost an average Major League Baseball crowd in the facility for one night. That's a great thing."

On the field, meanwhile, the A's struggled to compete at the level expected of a major league team. They lost 23 of 28 games to start the year, had a 10-45 record at roughly the one-third mark of the season and were 30-80 by Aug. 3. They rallied to finish 50-112, the worst record in MLB and the franchise's worst record since 1919, when they were the Philadelphia Athletics.

All the while, Fisher stayed out of sight.

"It's hard to talk about the season positively and not have it sound a little fake," A's general manager David Forst said. "Let's be honest: It was a really challenging year in a lot of ways. When you finish with the worst record in baseball, it's clear that things didn't go the way you expected."

While the A's relocation will not be finalized until owners vote to approve it, the team has made its intentions clear. The proposed Las Vegas stadium will not be ready to open until 2028, meaning the A's still have some time remaining in Oakland.

Barring an unexpected turn of events, however, the team is in its final days in the East Bay.

The Good, the Bad, and the End

The gap between the best and worst teams continued to expand in 2023. The Braves won 104 games, tied for the second-most in franchise history, on the strength of a historic offense that became the first to hit 300 home runs and steal 100 bases in a season. They hit .276/.344/.501 as a team, the first club to ever post a .500 slugging percentage over a full season, and had five players hit at least 30 home runs, led by Olson's National League-leading 54 homers.

The youthful Orioles won 101 games as part of their emergence from the rebuild, while the Dodgers won 100 games behind MVP-caliber seasons from Betts and Freddie Freeman. The Rays fell one win shy of becoming the fourth 100-win team, which would have tied the record for one season.

On the flip side, the A's (52-110), Royals (56-106), Rockies (59-103) and White Sox (61-101) all lost at least 100 games, tying the record for most 100-loss teams in a season. From 1904-2018, there was only one season in which four teams lost at least 100 games.

It has now happened in each of the last four full seasons.

On an individual level, the good mostly outweighed the bad. Two-way sensation Ohtani capped a transcendent three-year stretch with his best season yet for the Angels. He hit .304/.412/.654, all career-highs, and led the American League with 44 home runs, a 1.066 OPS and 325 total bases. On the mound he went 10-5, 3.14 with 167 strikeouts and 55 walks in 132 innings and held opponents to a .184 batting average, lowest in the AL. He authored one of the greatest single-day performances in MLB history on July 27: In a doubleheader against the Tigers, he threw a one-hit shutout in the first game and hit two home runs in the nightcap.

But it all came to a crushing end when he left

AMERICAN LEAGUE BEST TOOLS

A Baseball America survey of American League managers, conducted at midseason 2023, ranked players with the best tools.

Best Hitter
1. Shohei Ohtani, Angels
2. Corey Seager, Rangers
3. Bo Bichette, Blue Jays

Best Power
1. Shohei Ohtani, Angels
2. Aaron Judge, Yankees
3. Luis Robert Jr., White Sox

Best Bunter
1. Andres Gimenez, Guardians
2. Daulton Varsho, Blue Jays
3. Esteury Ruiz, Athletics

Best Strike-Zone Judgment
1. Yandy Diaz, Rays
2. Jose Ramirez, Guardians
3. Ryan Noda, Athletics

Best Hit-And-Run Artist
1. Steven Kwan, Guardians
2. Andres Gimenez, Guardians
3. Whit Merrifield, Blue Jays

Best Baserunner
1. Esteury Ruiz, Athletics
2. Bobby Witt Jr., Royals
3. Daulton Varsho, Blue Jays

Fastest Baserunner
1. Bobby Witt Jr., Royals
2. Esteury Ruiz, Athletics
3. Jorge Mateo, Orioles

Most Exciting Player
1. Shohei Ohtani, Angels
2. Luis Robert Jr., White Sox
3. Julio Rodriguez, Mariners

Best Pitcher
1. Gerrit Cole, Yankees
2. Kevin Gausman, Blue Jays
3. Framber Valdez, Astros

Best Fastball
1. Jhoan Duran, Twins
2. Felix Bautista, Orioles
3. Gerrit Cole, Yankees

Best Curveball
1. Framber Valdez, Astros
2. Tyler Glasnow, Rays
3. Jhoan Duran, Twins

Best Slider
1. Shohei Ohtani, Angels
2. Dylan Cease, White Sox
3. Matt Brash, Mariners

Best Changeup
1. Shane McClanahan, Rays
2. Pablo Lopez, Twins
3. Trevor Richards, Blue Jays

Best Control
1. George Kirby, Mariners
2. Zach Eflin, Rays
3. Framber Valdez, Astros

Best Pickoff Move
1. Taylor Clarke, Royals
2. Tanner Bibee, Guardians
3. Zack Greinke, Royals

Best Reliever
1. Felix Bautista, Orioles
2. Matt Brash, Mariners
3. Ryan Pressly, Astros

Best Defensive C
1. Jonah Heim, Rangers
2. Adley Rutschman, Orioles
3. Jose Trevino, Yankees

Best Defensive 1B
1. Nathaniel Lowe, Rangers
2. Anthony Rizzo, Yankees
3. Yandy Diaz, Rays

Best Defensive 2B
1. Marcus Semien, Rangers
2. Andres Gimenez, Guardians
3. Taylor Walls, Rays

Best Defensive 3B
1. Matt Chapman, Blue Jays
2. Jose Ramirez, Guardians
3. Alex Bregman, Astros

Best Defensive SS
1. Wander Franco, Rays
2. Bobby Witt Jr., Royals
3. Javier Baez, Tigers

Best Infield Arm
1. Matt Chapman, Blue Jays
2. Carlos Correa, Twins
3. Eugenio Suarez, Mariners

Best Defensive OF
1. Kevin Kiermaier, Blue Jays
2. Julio Rodriguez, Mariners
3. Daulton Varsho, Blue Jays

Best Outfield Arm
1. Adolis Garcia, Rangers
2. Alex Verdugo, Red Sox
3. Kevin Kiermaier, Blue Jays

Best Manager
1. Bruce Bochy, Rangers
2. Kevin Cash, Rays
3. Dusty Baker, Astros

ORGANIZATION OF THE YEAR

Rangers Cap Remarkable Turnaround

BY JEFF WILSON

The 2020 Rangers entered the shortened, 60-game season with hopes of contending for the American League playoffs.

They were built on pitching, or so they thought, and would need some veteran bats to help eke out just enough runs. By mid-August, with the trade deadline looming, the Rangers were an average club.

Average, with the postseason expanded, was good enough for club brass to weigh if acquiring help would get the Rangers into the postseason. The team made the decision easy by collapsing in the week before the deadline.

Rather than retooling for next season, though, president of baseball operations Jon Daniels decided it was time, past time, really, to blow the whole thing up.

The Rangers weren't good enough, their farm system wasn't good enough and they hadn't played well enough for four seasons running to convince ownership that the World Series was just a free agent or two away.

It was time to rebuild, starting immediately and with no deadline to complete the project.

As of Nov. 1, it's finished. The Rangers won the 2023 World Series, four games to one over the Diamondbacks, just two years removed from losing 102 games.The Rangers are the Baseball America Organization of the Year.

The executive who brought it across the finish line, general manager Chris Young, wasn't even with the organization when Daniels created the blueprint. Young didn't tear it up. Instead, he followed it to a T: rebuild the farm system, add talent through under-the-radar acquisitions and eventually spend the big bucks.

BEN LUDEMAN

Chris Young proved a quick study as the head of the Rangers' front office.

"It started way before me," Young said. "There are people in our organization who have made great decisions for a period of time. And I came in at a moment in time where things were, in my opinion, on the up. It may not have shown record-wise, but there was a foundation built by Jon Daniels, commitment from ownership with Ray Davis and many others within the organization."

The splashy signings always grab the spotlight, but the Rangers' 2023 success is also built on player development and some savvy work by their professional scouts.

Young followed the blueprint he inherited when he joined the organization late in 2020. There is much more to the Rangers franchise than payroll. They are built to last with a strong farm system, a belief in player development and a trust in the scouting department.

"It's not about the high-dollar signings," Young said. "It's all about all the other players that often are role players that are also winning pieces that have come in trades, they've come in player development, international signings, stuff like that. There's not one way to do it." ■

LAST 10 WINNERS

2013: St. Louis Cardinals
2014: Kansas City Royals
2015: Pittsburgh Pirates
2016: Chicago Cubs
2017: Los Angeles Dodgers
2018: Milwaukee Brewers
2019: Tampa Bay Rays
2020: Los Angeles Dodgers
2021: Tampa Bay Rays
2022: Seattle Mariners
Full list: search "Baseball America awards"

ACTIVE LEADERS

Career leaders among players who played in a game in 2023. Batters require 3,000 plate appearances and pitchers 1,000 innings to qualify for percentage titles.

BATTERS			PITCHERS		
AVG	Jose Altuve	.307	**ERA**	Clayton Kershaw	2.48
OBP	Juan Soto	.421	**SO/9**	Chris Sale	11.06
SLG	Aaron Judge	.586	**BB/9**	Kyle Hendricks	1.99
OPS	Mike Trout	.993	**HR/9**	Clayton Kershaw	0.75
R	Miguel Cabrera	1,551	**W**	Justin Verlander	259
H	Miguel Cabrera	3,174	**L**	Zack Greinke	156
2B	Miguel Cabrera	627	**SV**	Kenley Jansen	420
3B	Charlie Blackmon	63	**IP**	Zack Greinke	3,389
HR	Miguel Cabrera	511	**SO**	Max Scherzer	3,367
RBI	Miguel Cabrera	1,881	**BB**	Justin Verlander	925
BB	Joey Votto	1,365	**AVG**	Jacob deGrom	.208
SO	Miguel Cabrera	2,105	**G**	Kenley Jansen	817
XBH	Miguel Cabrera	1,155	**GS**	Zack Greinke	541
SB	Elvis Andrus	347	**HR**	Zack Greinke	367

his Aug. 23 start with an elbow injury that eventually required surgery. His season as a hitter ended Sept. 4, when he injured his oblique during batting practice.

Ohtani, who had Tommy John surgery after the 2018 season, will not pitch in 2024 after the unspecified procedure, but he will hit. He is expected to resume pitching as well as hitting in 2025.

Marlins second baseman Luis Arraez made an early run at becoming the first .400 hitter since Ted Williams in 1941 and sported a .401 batting average on June 24. He slowed down the stretch but still hit .354 to win the NL batting title. The 2022 AL batting champion with the Twins, he became the first player to win a batting title in back-to-back years in different leagues.

Rays first baseman Yandy Diaz hit .330 and won the AL batting title from the bench on the last day of the regular season. Diaz began the day percentage points behind Rangers shortstop Corey Seager, but he sat with the Rays resting their starters for the postseason while Seager went 0-for-4. Diaz became the first Rays player to win a batting title.

Freeman hit 59 doubles for the Dodgers, tied with Todd Helton in 2000 for the most in a season since 1936. Olson led the majors with 54 home runs and 139 RBIs to power the Braves offense, while Acuña's 73 steals led the majors.

Amid a disappointing Padres season, Snell provided a bright spot by going 14-9 and leading the majors with a 2.25 ERA. He allowed just 18 earned runs in his final 23 starts in one of the most dominant stretches in recent major league history.

In the AL, Gerrit Cole provided a similar bright spot in an otherwise dismal Yankees season. The veteran righthander went 15-4 with an AL-leading 2.63 ERA. He led the AL with 209 innings pitched and allowed the fewest hits per nine innings (6.8) among qualified starters.

Braves righthander Spencer Strider was the majors' lone 20-game winner with a 20-5 record,

NATIONAL LEAGUE BEST TOOLS

A Baseball America survey of National League managers, conducted at midseason 2023, ranked players with the best tools.

Best Hitter
1. Ronald Acuña Jr., Braves
2. Freddie Freeman, Dodgers
3. Luis Arraez, Marlins

Best Power
1. Matt Olson, Braves
2. Ronald Acuña Jr., Braves
3. Pete Alonso, Mets

Best Bunter
1. TJ Friedl, Reds
2. Corbin Carroll, D-backs
3. Geraldo Perdomo, D-backs

Best Strike-Zone Judgment
1. Juan Soto, Padres
2. Luis Arraez, Marlins
3. Freddie Freeman, Dodgers

Best Hit-And-Run Artist
1. Luis Arraez, Marlins
2. Nico Hoerner, Cubs
3. Jeff McNeil, Mets

Best Baserunner
1. Corbin Carroll, D-backs
2. Trea Turner, Phillies
3. Christian Yelich, Brewers

Fastest Baserunner
1. Elly De La Cruz, Reds
2. Corbin Carroll, D-backs
3. Trea Turner, Phillies

Most Exciting Player
1. Ronald Acuña Jr., Braves
2. Elly De La Cruz, Reds
3. Corbin Carroll, D-backs

Best Pitcher
1. Zac Gallen, D-backs
2. Spencer Strider, Braves
3. Clayton Kershaw, Dodgers

Best Fastball
1. Spencer Strider, Braves
2. Zack Wheeler, Phillies
3. Camilo Doval, Giants

Best Curveball
1. Blake Snell, Padres
2. Charlie Morton, Braves
3. Clayton Kershaw, Dodgers

Best Slider
1. Alexis Diaz, Reds
2. Clayton Kershaw, Dodgers
3. Spencer Strider, Braves

Best Changeup
1. Devin Williams, Brewers
2. Logan Webb, Giants
3. Sandy Alcantara, Marlins

Best Control
1. Logan Webb, Giants
2. Zac Gallen, D-backs
3. Aaron Nola, Phillies

Best Pickoff Move
1. Max Fried, Braves
2. Taijuan Walker, Phillies
3. David Peterson, Mets

Best Reliever
1. Josh Hader, Padres
2. Alexis Diaz, Reds
3. Devin Williams, Brewers

Best Defensive C
1. Patrick Bailey, Giants
2. Sean Murphy, Braves
3. JT Realmuto, Phillies

Best Defensive 1B
1. Christian Walker, D-backs
2. Paul Goldschmidt, Cardinals
3. Freddie Freeman, Dodgers

Best Defensive 2B
1. Ha-Seong Kim, Padres
2. Nico Hoerner, Cubs
3. Ozzie Albies, Braves

Best Defensive 3B
1. Nolan Arenado, Cardinals
2. Manny Machado, Padres
3. Ke'Bryan Hayes, Pirates

Best Defensive SS
1. Dansby Swanson, Braves
2. Francisco Lindor, Mets
3. Willy Adames, Brewers

Best Infield Arm
1. Elly De La Cruz, Reds
2. Casey Schmitt, Giants
3. Manny Machado, Padres

Best Defensive OF
1. Fernando Tatis Jr., Padres
2. Joey Wiemer, Brewers
3. Mookie Betts, Dodgers

Best Outfield Arm
1. Ronald Acuña Jr., Braves
2. Fernando Tatis Jr., Padres
3. Nolan Jones, Rockies

Best Manager
1. Craig Counsell, Brewers
2. Brian Snitker, Braves
3. Torey Lovullo, D-backs

MAJOR LEAGUE ALL-STARS

SELECTED BY BASEBALL AMERICA

ADAM HAGY

The Braves' Ronald Acuña Jr. became the first member of the 40-70 club.

JOE SARGENT

The Yankees' Gerrit Cole led the American League in ERA and innings.

FIRST TEAM

Pos.	Player, Team	AVG	OBP	SLG	AB	R	H	2B	3B	HR	RBI	BB	SO	SB	CS
C	William Contreras, Brewers	.289	.367	.457	540	86	156	38	1	17	78	63	126	6	1
1B	Matt Olson, Braves	.283	.389	.604	608	127	172	27	3	54	139	104	167	1	0
2B	Mookie Betts, Dodgers	.307	.408	.579	584	126	179	40	1	39	107	96	107	14	3
3B	Austin Riley, Braves	.281	.345	.516	636	117	179	32	3	37	97	59	172	3	1
SS	Corey Seager, Rangers	.327	.390	.623	477	88	156	42	0	33	96	49	88	2	1
OF	Ronald Acuña Jr., Braves	.337	.416	.596	643	149	217	35	4	41	106	80	84	73	14
OF	Julio Rodriguez, Mariners	.275	.333	.485	654	102	180	37	2	32	103	47	175	37	10
OF	Kyle Tucker, Astros	.284	.369	.517	574	97	163	37	5	29	112	80	92	30	5
DH	Shohei Ohtani, Angels	.304	.412	.654	497	102	151	26	8	44	95	91	143	20	6

Pos.	Player, Team	W	L	ERA	G	GS	SV	IP	H	R	ER	HR	BB	SO	WHIP
SP	Gerrit Cole, Yankees	15	4	2.63	33	33	0	209	157	64	61	20	48	222	0.98
SP	Zac Gallen, D-backs	17	9	3.47	34	34	0	210	188	87	81	22	47	220	1.12
SP	Sonny Gray, Twins	8	8	2.79	32	32	0	184	156	59	57	8	55	183	1.15
SP	Blake Snell, Padres	14	9	2.25	32	32	0	180	115	47	45	15	99	234	1.19
SP	Spencer Strider, Braves	20	5	3.86	32	32	0	187	146	85	80	22	58	281	1.09
RP	Felix Bautista, Orioles	8	2	1.48	56	0	33	61	30	14	10	4	26	110	0.92

SECOND TEAM

Pos.	Player, Team	AVG	OBP	SLG	AB	R	H	2B	3B	HR	RBI	BB	SO	SB	CS
C	Adley Rutschman, Orioles	.277	.374	.435	588	84	163	31	1	20	80	92	101	1	2
1B	Freddie Freeman, Dodgers	.331	.410	.567	637	131	211	59	2	29	102	72	121	23	1
2B	Marcus Semien, Rangers	.276	.348	.478	670	122	185	40	4	29	100	72	110	14	3
3B	Jose Ramirez, Guardians	.282	.356	.475	611	87	172	36	5	24	80	73	73	28	6
SS	Bobby Witt Jr., Royals	.276	.319	.495	641	97	177	28	11	30	96	40	121	49	15
OF	Corbin Carroll, D-backs	.285	.362	.506	565	116	161	30	10	25	76	57	125	54	5
OF	Luis Robert Jr., White Sox	.264	.315	.542	546	90	144	36	1	38	80	30	172	20	4
OF	Juan Soto, Padres	.275	.410	.519	568	97	156	32	1	35	109	132	129	12	5
DH	Luis Arraez, Marlins	.354	.393	.469	574	71	203	30	3	10	69	35	34	3	2

Pos.	Player, Team	W	L	ERA	G	GS	SV	IP	H	R	ER	HR	BB	SO	WHIP
SP	Luis Castillo, Mariners	14	9	3.34	33	33	0	197	160	81	73	28	56	219	1.10
SP	Kevin Gausman, Blue Jays	12	9	3.16	31	31	0	185	163	72	65	19	55	237	1.18
SP	Justin Steele, Cubs	16	5	3.06	30	30	0	173	167	71	59	14	36	176	1.17
SP	Logan Webb, Giants	11	13	3.25	33	33	0	216	201	83	78	20	31	194	1.07
SP	Zack Wheeler, Phillies	13	6	3.61	32	32	0	192	168	82	77	20	39	212	1.08
RP	Devin Williams, Brewers	8	3	1.53	61	0	36	59	26	13	10	4	28	87	0.92

EXECUTIVE OF THE YEAR

MITCHELL LAYTON
Mike Elias

When the Orioles hired Mike Elias to lead their front office after the 2018 season, they expected that at some point he'd lead a turnaround.

But that doesn't make what the Orioles did in 2023 any less surprising. Just two years after losing 110 games, Baltimore won 101, topping the century mark for the first time since 1980. And the Orioles did it with a homegrown lineup. They've hit on top draft picks like Adley Rutschman and Gunnar Henderson. They've developed pitchers like Kyle Bradish, Felix Bautista and Grayson Rodriguez.

But there's more on the way. After producing the No. 1 prospects in 2022 (Rutschman) and 2023 (Henderson), they have the 2023 Minor League Player of the Year Jackson Holliday next up.

LAST 10 WINNERS

2013: Billy Beane, Athletics
2014: Dan Duquette, Orioles
2015: Sandy Alderson, Mets
2016: Chris Antonetti, Indians
2017: Brian Cashman, Yankees
2018: Dave Dombrowski, Red Sox
2019: Mike Rizzo, Nationals
2020: Andrew Friedman, Dodgers
2021: Farhan Zaidi, Giants
2022: Alex Anthopoulous, Braves

Full list: search "Baseball America awards"

MANAGER OF THE YEAR

ROB TRINGALI/MLB PHOTOS VIA GETTY IMAGES
Torey Lovullo

In his first year as D-backs manager, Torey Lovullo led the team to a 93-69 record and a spot in the NL Division Series.

It was a sign of what Lovullo could do as a manager, which was important, because it would be a long while before Lovullo would get to experience anything like that again. The D-backs slowly down the NL West standings in 2018, 2019 and 2020 before falling apart to go 52-110 in 2021.

But Lovullo kept grinding and he never lost the trust of the team or the front office. In a brutally tough NL West, Arizona snuck into the playoffs, but once the young D-backs got there, they found their footing. With Lovullo masterfully handling the starting rotation and bullpen, Arizona made its second World Series appearance.

LAST 10 WINNERS

2013: Clint Hurdle, Pirates
2014: Buck Showalter, Orioles
2015: Joe Maddon, Cubs
2016: Terry Francona, Indians
2017: A.J. Hinch, Astros
2018: Bob Melvin, Athletics
2019: Craig Counsell, Brewers
2020: Brian Snitker, Braves
2021: Dusty Baker, Astros
2022: Brandon Hyde, Orioles

Full list: search "Baseball America awards"

and he struck out 281 batters, 44 more than anyone else.

Guardians closer Emmanuel Clase led the AL with 44 saves, while David Bednar of the Pirates and Camilo Doval of the Giants tied for the NL lead with 39.

Yankees righthander Domingo German delivered the best game of the year in the non-Ohtani division, throwing a perfect game against the A's on June 28. German struck out nine and threw just 99 pitches en route to the 24th perfect game in major league history, the first since Felix Hernandez's in 2012.

Tigers Matt Manning (6.2 IP), Alex Lange (1) and Jason Foley (1.1) pitched a combined no-hitter in a 2-0 win over the Blue Jays on July 8, while Astros lefthander Framber Valdez and Phillies righthander Michael Lorenzen threw no-hitters eight days apart in August against the Guardians and Nationals, respectively. Amazingly, Lorenzen went from throwing a no-hitter to being moved to the bullpen in a few weeks.

The game said goodbye to Miguel Cabrera, Adam Wainwright and Nelson Cruz, all of whom retired after the season.

Cabrera, a certain first-ballot Hall of Famer, finished his career with 3,174 hits and 511 home runs. Wainwright, poetically, pitched seven scoreless innings against the Brewers on Sept. 18 to pick up career win No. 200 in his final career start. His final appearance came in a pinch-hit at-bat against the Reds on Oct. 1. He struck out.

Astros manager Dusty Baker also announced his retirement after the season, bringing his 26-year managerial career to a close. Baker retired seventh all-time with 2,183 career wins, and he left in style, having won a World Series in Houston in 2022 to add to an incredibly impressive resume.

Diaz Home Run Leads NL To Rare Win

BY KYLE GLASER

SEATTLE —Three and a half years ago, Elias Diaz was non-tendered by the second-worst team in the National League.

Elias signed with the Pirates out of Venezuela in 2008 and spent seven years climbing their system. He made his major league debut in 2015, didn't get even semi-regular playing time until 2017 and played 100 games for the first time in 2019. Known as a talented defender with a light bat, he hit .241 with two home runs that season and was not tendered a contract by the 69-93 Pirates. When they let him go, he had a career .656 OPS over five partial seasons.

Nothing in Diaz's performance or pedigree suggested an all-star berth was in his future. And yet, he not only stood among baseball's best players as the Rockies' lone all-star representative, but delivered the game's signature moment.

Diaz hit the go-ahead two-run home run in the eighth inning to lift the National League to a 3-2 win over the American League in the 93rd All-Star Game at T-Mobile Park. His home run snapped a nine-game losing streak for the NL and gave the Senior Circuit its first All-Star Game victory since 2012. Diaz, the unlikeliest of all-stars, was named MVP.

"I mean, it's incredible," Diaz said through interpreter Danny Sanchez. "Obviously when that happened, when (the Pirates) let me go, I didn't allow myself to feel defeated. I maintained my confidence and stayed positive. And now I'm just happy to be here and happy to have this experience."

Diaz was the first Rockies catcher to be an all-star and now is the first Rockies player to win an All-Star Game MVP award. For a franchise whose history includes perennial all-stars like Larry Walker, Todd Helton, Matt Holliday, Troy Tulowitzki and Nolan Arenado, among others, it's nothing short of a stunning and remarkable achievement.

The game was a showcase of pitching and defense for most of the night, with runs hard to come by.

ALL-STAR GAME

Elias Diaz

DUSTIN BRADFORD

2023 ALL-STAR GAME

JULY 11, 2023
NATIONAL LEAGUE 3, AMERICAN LEAGUE 2

National	AB	R	H	RBI	American	AB	R	H	RBI
Acuña Jr., RF	2	0	0	0	Semien, 2B	2	0	0	0
Soto, J, PH-RF	3	0	1	0	Merrifield, 2B	2	0	1	0
Freeman, F, 1B	1	0	0	0	Ohtani, DH	1	0	0	0
Olson, 1B	1	0	0	0	Perez, S, PH-DH	2	1	1	0
Alonso, PH-1B	2	0	0	0	Arozarena, LF	2	0	1	0
Betts, CF	2	0	0	0	Rooker, LF	2	0	1	0
Castellanos, N, CF	2	1	1	0	Seager, SS	1	0	0	0
Martinez, J, DH	2	1	2	0	Bichette, SS	1	0	0	1
Soler, PH-DH	1	0	0	0	Franco, SS	1	0	0	0
Díaz, E, PH-DH	2	1	1	2	Díaz, Y, 1B	2	1	1	1
Arenado, 3B	2	0	0	0	Guerrero Jr., 1B	2	0	0	0
Riley, A, 3B	2	0	1	0	García, Ad, RF	2	0	0	0
Arraez, 2B	2	0	2	1	Tucker, RF	1	0	0	0
Albies, 2B	2	0	0	0	Hays, CF	2	0	1	0
Murphy, S, C	2	0	0	0	Rodríguez, Ju, CF	1	0	0	0
Smith, W.D., C	1	0	0	0	Jung, 3B	2	0	0	0
Carroll, LF	2	0	0	0	Ramírez, Jo, 3B	2	0	1	0
Gurriel Jr., LF	2	0	1	0	Heim, C	2	0	0	0
Arcia, Or, SS	2	0	0	0	Rutschman, C	1	0	0	0
Perdomo, SS	1	0	0	0					
Totals	**36**	**3**	**9**	**3**	**Totals**	**31**	**2**	**7**	**2**

2B: Rooker (1, Díaz, A); Ramírez, Jo (1, Doval). **HR:** Díaz, Y (1, 2nd inning off Keller, M, 0 on, 1 out). **TB:** Arozarena; Díaz, Y 4; Hays; Merrifield; Perez, S; Ramírez, Jo 2; Rooker 2. **RBI**: Bichette (1); Díaz, Y (1). Runners left in scoring position, 2 out: Rutschman; Díaz, Y; Heim; Guerrero Jr.; Ramírez, Jo. **SF:** Bichette. **Team RISP:** 0-for-7. **Team LOB:** 6. **CS:** Arozarena (1, 2nd base by Gallen/Murphy, S). **E:** Guerrero Jr. (1, throw).

Time of Game: 3:03. **Attendance:** 47,159.

National	IP	H	R	SO	American	IP	H	R	SO
Gallen	1	1	0	1	Cole	1	0	0	0
Keller, M	1	1	1	1	Eovaldi	1	2	0	1
Gray, Js	1	0	0	1	Gray, So	1	0	0	2
Cobb	1	0	0	1	Kirby	1	2	1	0
Steele	1	1	0	1	Estévez	1	0	0	2
Díaz, A	1	2	1	0	Cano	1	1	0	2
Doval (W, 1-0)	1	1	0	1	Romano	0.1	0	0	0
Hader	1	1	0	0	Lorenzen	0.2	1	0	1
Kimbrel (S, 1)	1	0	0	2	Bautista, F (L, 0-1)	0.2	1	2	1
					Jansen	0.1	0	0	1
					López, P	1	2	0	2
Totals	**9**	**7**	**2**	**8**	**Totals**	**9**	**9**	**3**	**12**

ARIZONA DIAMONDBACKS
Carlos Vargas........Mar 30
Dominic Fletcher.. Apr 30
Brandon Pfaadt..... May 3
Justin Martinez.........Jul 7
Dominic Canzone......Jul 8
Slade Cecconi..........Aug 2
Bryce Jarvis ....Aug 15
Andrew Saalfrank... Sep 5
Jordan Lawlar......... Sep 7

ATLANTA BRAVES
Jared Shuster.......... Apr 2
Dylan Dodd............ Apr 4
Braden Shewmake May 5
AJ Smith-Shawver.. Jun 4
Forrest Wall ....Jul 22
Allan Winans ....Jul 22
Daysbel Hernández.Jul 23
Darius Vines..........Aug 30

BALTIMORE ORIOLES
Grayson Rodriguez . Apr 5
Joey Ortiz .... Apr 27
Jordan Westburg ...Jun 26
Chris Vallimont ....Jul 3
Colton Cowser...........Jul 5
Heston Kjerstad .... Sep 14

BOSTON RED SOX
Masataka Yoshida.Mar 30
Enmanuel Valdez.. Apr 19
Chris Murphy.......... Jun 7
Joe Jacques...........Jun 12
David Hamilton .....Jun 21
Brandon Walter .....Jun 22
Wilyer Abreu.........Aug 22
Ceddanne Rafaela Aug 28

CHICAGO WHITE SOX
Oscar Colás ....Mar 30
Jesse Scholtens....... Apr 7
Sammy Peralta ...... May 4
Zach Remillard ......Jun 17
José Rodriguez ......Jun 20
Declan Cronin ....Jul 30
Edgar Navarro.........Jul 30
Lane Ramsey ....Aug 6

CINCINNATI REDS
Casey Legumina ... Apr 15
Levi Stoudt .... Apr 19
Matt McLain .... May 15
B. Williamson...........May 16
Eduardo Salazar... May 24
TJ Hopkins .... Jun 3
Andrew Abbott....... Jun 5
Elly De La Cruz .... Jun 6
Ricky Karcher.........Jun 12
Randy Wynne ....Jun 25
Jake Wong ....Jun 26
C.Encarnacion-Strand Jul 17
Lyon Richardson .....Aug 6
Noelvi Marte.........Aug 19
Carson Spiers.......... Sep 3
Connor Phillips .... Sep 5

CLEVELAND GUARDIANS
Tim Herrin .... Apr 2
Peyton Battenfield. Apr 12
Logan Allen .... Apr 23
Tanner Bibee .... Apr 26
David Fry .... May 1
Brayan Rocchio.... May 16
Gavin Williams.......Jun 21
José Tena ....Aug 5

COLORADO ROCKIES
Brenton Doyle ...... Apr 24
Riley Pint............ May 17
Karl Kauffmann ... May 19
Blair Calvo .... May 30
Coco Montes ....Jun 11
Connor Kaiser ....Jun 19
Evan Justice ....Aug 26
Hunter Goodman..Aug 27
Victor Vodnik .... Sep 9

DETROIT TIGERS
Mason Englert......Mar 30
Reese Olson .... Jun 2
Brendan White ......Jun 14
Parker Meadows...Aug 21
Andre Lipcius.......... Sep 1
Sawyer Gipson-Long..Sep 10
Brenan Hanifee..... Sep 21

HOUSTON ASTROS
Corey Julks............Mar 31
César Salazar .... Apr 2
J.P. France .... May 6
Grae Kessinger........ Jun 7
Shawn Dubin.........Jun 19

KANSAS CITY ROYALS
Austin Cox................. May 4
Samad Taylor............Jun 17
James McArthur.......Jun 28
Alec Marsh................Jun 30
John McMillon.........Aug 17
Steven Cruz..............Aug 29
Nick Loftin .... Sep 1
Logan Porter............ Sep 12
Tyler Cropley............ Sep 19
Anthony Veneziano. Sep 26
Jonathan Bowlan.... Sep 27

LOS ANGELES ANGELS
Zach Neto .... Apr 15
Sam Bachman ..... May 26
Ben Joyce .... May 29
José Soriano .... Jun 3
Kolton Ingram ....Jun 17
Victor Mederos ......Jun 30
Trey Cabbage ....Jul 14
Jordyn Adams.........Aug 2
Nolan Schanuel ....Aug 18
Kyren Paris.............. Sep 1
Davis Daniel............ Sep 7
Kelvin Caceres....... Sep 27

LOS ANGELES DODGERS
Michael Busch ...... Apr 25
Gavin Stone .... May 3
Bobby Miller........ May 23
Jonny Deluca .... Jun 7
Nick Robertson .... Jun 7
Emmet Sheehan....Jun 16
Bryan Hudson........Jun 17
Kyle Hurt .... Sep 12

MIAMI MARLINS
Jeff Lindgren .... Apr 3
George Soriano..... Apr 16
Xavier Edwards...... May 2
Eury Pérez............ May 12
Jacob Amaya ....Jun 18
Dane Myers ....Jul 4
Robert Garcia..........Jul 14
Enmanuel De Jesus... Sep 9

MILWAUKEE BREWERS
Brice Turang..........Mar 30
Gus Varland ....Mar 30
Joey Wiemer........... Apr 1
Blake Perkins........ Apr 19
A. Monasterio.........May 28
Clayton Andrews ......Jul 1
Abner Uribe ....Jul 8
Sal Frelick ....Jul 22
Caleb Boushley..... Sep 29

MINNESOTA TWINS
Edouard Julien...... Apr 12
Brent Headrick...... Apr 19
Jordan Balazovic....Jun 18
Kody Funderburk..Aug 28

NEW YORK METS
Kodai Senga .... Apr 2
Zach Muckenhirn... May 3
Josh Walker .... May 16
Grant Hartwig ....Jun 19
Ronny Mauricio ...... Sep 1

NEW YORK YANKEES
Anthony Volpe......Mar 30
Jhony Brito .... Apr 2
Randy Vásquez .... May 26
Matt Krook ....Jun 16
Everson Pereira.....Aug 22
Jasson Domínguez.. Sep 1
Austin Wells............ Sep 1
Yoendrys Gómez... Sep 28

OAKLAND ATHLETICS
Ryan Noda............Mar 30
Shintaro Fujinami... Apr 1
Hogan Harris .... Apr 14
Mason Miller .... Apr 19
Luis Medina .... Apr 26
Garrett Acton....... May 14
Lucas Erceg .... May 19
Angel Felipe ....Jul 7
Zack Gelof...............Jul 14
Tyler Soderstrom ....Jul 14
Lawrence Butler ...Aug 11
Easton Lucas........... Sep 8
Joe Boyle .... Sep 17
Joey Estes .... Sep 20

PHILADELPHIA PHILLIES
McKinley Moore.... Apr 10
Johan Rojas ....Jul 15
Weston Wilson........Aug 9
Orion Kerkering .... Sep 24

PITTSBURGH PIRATES
Jose Hernandez ...... Apr 1
Drew Maggi........... Apr 26
Cody Bolton .... Apr 29
Osvaldo Bido ....Jun 14
Carmen Mlodzinski Jun 16
Henry Davis ....Jun 19
Nick Gonzales ....Jun 23
Jared Triolo ....Jun 28
Quinn Priester ....Jul 17
Endy Rodríguez ......Jul 17
Alika Williams.........Jul 25
Colin Selby..............Aug 9
Hunter Stratton ...... Sep 5
Kyle Nicolas .... Sep 19

ST. LOUIS CARDINALS
Jordan Walker.......Mar 30
Guillermo Zuñiga... May 2
Luken Baker............ Jun 4
José Fermín ....Jul 7
Kyle Leahy ....Jul 7
Masyn Winn..........Aug 18
Drew Rom ....Aug 21
Irving Lopez.......... Sep 23

SAN DIEGO PADRES
Brett Sullivan........ Apr 18
Tom Cosgrove .... Apr 29
Matt Waldron ....Jun 24
Alek Jacob ....Jul 15
Taylor Kohlwey ....Jul 19
Jackson Wolf...........Jul 22
Nick Hernandez .... Sep 12
Jose Espada .... Sep 24
Chandler Seagle ... Sep 30

SAN FRANCISCO GIANTS
Blake Sabol...........Mar 30
Brett Wisely..........Mar 30
Tristan Beck .... Apr 20
Casey Schmitt........ May 9
Patrick Bailey....... May 19
Ryan Walker .... May 21
Keaton Winn..........Jun 13
Luis Matos ....Jun 14
Marco Luciano ....Jul 26
Wade Meckler.......Aug 14
Kyle Harrison ....Aug 22
Tyler Fitzgerald..... Sep 21

SEATTLE MARINERS
José Caballero....... Apr 15
Bryce Miller .... May 2
Juan Then .... May 6
Bryan Woo.............. Jun 3
Ty Adcock...............Jun 12
Isaiah Campbell........Jul 7
Devin Sweet ....Jul 19
Cade Marlowe ....Jul 20
Prelander Berroa ....Jul 21
Emerson Hancock ...Aug 9
Ryder Ryan.............Aug 11

TAMPA BAY RAYS
Kevin Kelly.............. Apr 1
Taj Bradley............ Apr 12
Braden Bristo........ Apr 13
Joe La Sorsa......... May 29
José Lopez ....Jun 10
Curtis Mead ....Aug 4
Osleivis Basabe.....Aug 13
Jacob Lopez ....Aug 14
Tristan Gray .... Sep 16
Junior Caminero ... Sep 23

TEXAS RANGERS
Cody Bradford...... May 15
Grant Anderson ... May 30
Owen White...........Jun 13
Alex Speas ....Jul 19
Jonathan Ornelas ...Aug 7
J.P. Martínez ....Aug 11
Evan Carter .... Sep 8

TORONTO BLUE JAYS
Nathan Lukes........Mar 30
Spencer Horwitz....Jun 18
Davis Schneider......Aug 4
Hagen Danner ......Aug 11
Mason McCoy ....Aug 30
Cam Eden .... Sep 21

WASHINGTON NATIONALS
Hobie Harris............ Apr 1
Thaddeus Ward....... Apr 1
Jake Irvin .... May 3
Jake Alu................. May 9
Amos Willingham..Jun 28
Jose Ferrer ....Jul 1
Blake Rutherford ....Aug 4
Jacob Young..........Aug 26
Drew Millas ....Aug 28
Jackson Rutledge.. Sep 13

MAJOR LEAGUES

AMERICAN LEAGUE 2023 STATISTICS

CLUB BATTING

	AVG	G	AB	R	H	2B	3B	HR	RBI	BB	SO	SB	OBP	SLG
Texas	.263	162	5595	881	1470	326	18	233	845	599	1416	79	.337	.452
Tampa Bay	.260	162	5511	860	1432	282	24	230	827	514	1420	160	.331	.445
Houston	.259	162	5567	827	1441	280	22	222	799	550	1241	107	.331	.437
Boston	.258	162	5562	772	1437	339	19	182	734	486	1372	112	.324	.424
Toronto	.256	162	5562	746	1423	292	19	188	705	550	1303	99	.329	.417
Baltimore	.255	162	5495	807	1399	309	28	183	780	512	1370	114	.321	.421
Cleveland	.250	162	5513	662	1379	294	29	124	622	471	1142	151	.313	.381
Los Angeles	.245	162	5489	739	1346	248	26	231	708	518	1524	72	.317	.426
Kansas City	.244	162	5428	676	1325	258	43	163	651	411	1396	163	.303	.398
Minnesota	.243	162	5489	778	1336	264	24	233	745	594	1654	86	.326	.428
Seattle	.242	162	5500	758	1332	283	12	210	728	548	1603	118	.321	.413
Chicago	.238	162	5501	641	1308	264	13	171	617	377	1424	86	.291	.384
Detroit	.236	162	5478	661	1292	245	29	165	635	508	1473	85	.305	.382
New York	.227	162	5323	673	1207	221	15	219	650	557	1427	100	.304	.397
Oakland	.223	162	5311	585	1187	225	21	171	563	498	1496	149	.298	.370

CLUB PITCHING

	ERA	G	CG	SHO	SV	IP	H	R	ER	HR	BB	SO	AVG
Seattle	3.74	162	2	18	44	1449.1	1300	659	602	184	421	1459	.237
Toronto	3.78	162	1	15	51	1451.2	1326	671	610	198	488	1528	.241
Tampa Bay	3.86	162	0	14	45	1442.0	1258	665	618	177	439	1507	.231
Minnesota	3.87	162	2	12	38	1451.1	1294	659	624	194	443	1560	.236
Baltimore	3.89	162	0	12	49	1453.2	1334	678	629	177	473	1431	.242
Houston	3.94	162	2	7	42	1445.1	1312	698	632	201	537	1460	.241
Cleveland	3.96	162	1	13	47	1444.0	1352	697	635	173	534	1311	.246
New York	3.97	162	3	8	44	1439.2	1272	698	635	195	508	1439	.234
Detroit	4.24	162	0	15	41	1442.1	1320	740	680	187	476	1374	.240
Texas	4.28	162	3	13	30	1436.1	1330	716	683	198	491	1351	.245
Boston	4.52	162	0	5	43	1430.0	1416	776	718	208	497	1423	.256
Los Angeles	4.64	162	1	9	43	1431.2	1394	829	738	209	636	1445	.252
Chicago	4.87	162	2	7	28	1431.2	1372	841	774	214	654	1470	.249
Kansas City	5.17	162	3	6	28	1409.0	1429	859	809	207	553	1270	.262
Oakland	5.48	162	0	5	29	1419.2	1464	924	865	213	694	1300	.266

CLUB FIELDING

	PCT	PO	A	E	DP
Texas	.990	4309	1423	57	143
Minnesota	.988	4354	1286	66	116
Baltimore	.988	4361	1444	71	140
Toronto	.988	4355	1307	71	125
Seattle	.987	4348	1379	73	123
Tampa Bay	.987	4326	1401	75	114
Kansas City	.986	4227	1391	80	123
Houston	.986	4336	1346	81	144

	PCT	PO	A	E	DP
Cleveland	.986	4332	1418	83	119
New York	.984	4319	1427	96	113
Los Angeles	.983	4295	1284	95	124
Chicago	.983	4295	1249	95	117
Detroit	.983	4327	1403	100	129
Boston	.982	4290	1429	102	137
Oakland	.982	4259	1269	102	124

INDIVIDUAL BATTING LEADERS

	AVG	G	AB	R	H	2B	3B	HR	RBI	BB	SO	SB
Yandy Díaz, Rays	.330	137	525	95	173	35	0	22	78	65	94	0
Corey Seager, Rangers	.327	119	477	88	156	42	0	33	96	49	88	2
Bo Bichette, Blue Jays	.306	135	571	69	175	30	3	20	73	27	115	5
Shohei Ohtani, Angels	.304	135	497	102	151	26	8	44	95	91	143	20
Masataka Yoshida, Red Sox	.289	140	537	71	155	33	3	15	72	34	81	8
Kyle Tucker, Astros	.284	157	574	97	163	37	5	29	112	80	92	30
Jose Ramírez, Guardians	.282	156	611	87	172	36	5	24	80	73	73	28
Adley Rutschman, Orioles	.277	154	588	84	163	31	1	20	80	92	101	1
Bobby Witt Jr., Royals	.276	158	641	97	177	28	11	30	96	40	121	49
Marcus Semien, Rangers	.276	162	670	122	185	40	4	29	100	72	110	14

INDIVIDUAL PITCHING LEADERS

	W	L	ERA	G	GS	CG	SV	IP	H	R	ER	BB	SO
Gerrit Cole, Yankees	15	4	2.63	33	33	2	0	209	157	64	61	48	222
Sonny Gray, Twins	8	8	2.79	32	32	0	0	184	156	59	57	55	183
Kyle Bradish, Orioles	12	7	2.83	30	30	0	0	169	132	54	53	44	168
Kevin Gausman, Blue Jays	12	9	3.16	31	31	0	0	185	163	72	65	55	237
Luis Castillo, Mariners	14	9	3.34	33	33	0	0	197	160	81	73	56	219
George Kirby, Mariners	13	10	3.35	31	31	1	0	191	179	74	71	19	172
Framber Valdez, Astros	12	11	3.45	31	31	2	0	198	166	86	76	57	200
Zach Eflin, Rays	16	8	3.50	31	31	0	0	178	158	69	69	24	186
Chris Bassitt, Blue Jays	16	8	3.60	33	33	1	0	200	176	88	80	59	186
Jose Berríos, Blue Jays	11	12	3.65	32	32	0	0	190	173	82	77	52	184

AWARD WINNERS

Selected by Baseball Writers Association of America

MOST VALUABLE PLAYER

Player	1st	2nd	3rd	Total
Shohei Ohtani, Angels	30			420
Corey Seager, Rangers		24	6	264
Marcus Semien, Rangers		5	8	216
Julio Rodríguez, Mariners			8	197
Kyle Tucker, Astros		1	4	178
Yandy Díaz, Rays			4	137
Bobby Witt Jr., Royals				83
Gunnar Henderson, Orioles				77
Adley Rutschman, Orioles				50
José Ramírez, Guardians				40
Gerrit Cole, Yankees				30
Luis Robert Jr., White Sox				21
Yordan Alvarez, Astros				16
Adolis García, Rangers				14
Aaron Judge, Yankees				7
Bo Bichette, Blue Jays				5
J.P. Crawford, Mariners				5
Cal Raleigh, Mariners				2
Rafael Devers, Red Sox				2
Isaac Paredes, Rays				2
Sonny Gray, Twins				2
Alex Bregman, Astros				1
Josh Naylor, Guardians				1

CY YOUNG AWARD

Player	1st	2nd	3rd	Total
Gerrit Cole, Yankees	30			210
Sonny Gray, Twins		20	6	104
Kevin Gausman, Blue Jays		7	15	82
Kyle Bradish, Orioles			6	39
Luis Castillo, Mariners		2		23
Zach Eflin, Rays		1	2	19
Pablo López, Twins				11
George Kirby, Mariners				8
Framber Valdez, Astros				6
Chris Bassitt, Blue Jays			1	4
Félix Bautista, Orioles				3
Chris Martin, Red Sox				1

ROOKIE OF THE YEAR

Player	1st	2nd	3rd	Total
Gunnar Henderson, Orioles	30			150
Tanner Bibee, Guardians		20	7	67
Triston Casas, Red Sox		6	7	25
Josh Jung, Rangers		3	7	16
Yainer Diaz, Astros		1	3	6
Masataka Yoshida, Red Sox			3	3
Edouard Julien, Twins			2	2
Anthony Volpe, Yankees			1	1

MANAGER OF THE YEAR

Player	1st	2nd	3rd	Total
Brandon Hyde, Orioles	27	3		144
Bruce Bochy, Rangers	3	12	10	61
Kevin Cash, Rays		13	13	52
Rocco Baldelli, Twins		1	5	8
Dusty Baker, Astros		1	1	4
John Schneider, Blue Jays			1	1

GOLD GLOVE WINNERS

Selected by AL Managers

C: Jonah Heim, Rangers; **1B:** Nathaniel Lowe, Rangers; **2B:** Andres Gimenez, Guardians; **3B:** Matt Chapman, Blue Jays; **SS:** Anthony Volpe, Yankees; **LF:** Steven Kwan, Guardians; **CF:** Kevin Kiermaier, Blue Jays; **RF:** Adolis Garcia, Rangers; **UT:** Mauricio Dubon, Astros; **P:** Jose Berrios, Blue Jays.

AMERICAN LEAGUE DEPARTMENT LEADERS

BATTING

GAMES
Marcus Semien, Texas	162
Eugenio Suarez, Seattle	162
Nathaniel Lowe, Texas	161
Alex Bregman, Houston	161
Teoscar Hernandez, Seattle	160

AT-BATS
Marcus Semien, Texas	670
Julio Rodriguez, Seattle	654
Bobby Witt, Kansas City	641
Steven Kwan, Cleveland	638
Teoscar Hernandez, Seattle	625

PLATE APPEARANCES
Marcus Semien, Texas	753
Alex Bregman, Houston	724
Nathaniel Lowe, Texas	724
Steven Kwan, Cleveland	718
Julio Rodriguez, Seattle	714

RUNS
Marcus Semien, Texas	122
Adolis Garcia, Texas	108
Alex Bregman, Houston	103
Shohei Ohtani, LA Angels	102
Julio Rodriguez, Seattle	102

HITS
Marcus Semien, Texas	185
Julio Rodriguez, Seattle	180
Bobby Witt, Kansas City	177
Bo Bichette, Toronto	175
Yandy Diaz, Tampa Bay	173

TOTAL BASES
Shohei Ohtani, LA	325
Marcus Semien, Texas	320
Julio Rodriguez, Seattle	317
Bobby Witt, Kansas City	317
Corey Seager, Texas	297
Kyle Tucker, Houston	297

DOUBLES
Corey Seager, Texas	42
Anthony Santander, Balt.	41
Marcus Semien, Texas	40
Matt Chapman, Toronto	39
Nathaniel Lowe, Texas	38

TRIPLES
Bobby Witt, Kansas City	11
Gunnar Henderson, Balt.	9
Shohei Ohtani, Los Angeles	8
Steven Kwan, Cleveland	7
3 tied	6

EXTRA-BASE HITS
Shohei Ohtani, Los Angeles	78
Luis Robert, Chicago	75
Corey Seager, Texas	75
Marcus Semien, Texas	73
Kyle Tucker, Houston	71
Julio Rodriguez, Seattle	71

HOME RUNS
Shohei Ohtani, Los Angeles	44
Adolis Garcia, Texas	39
Luis Robert, Chicago	38
Aaron Judge, New York	37
Rafael Devers, Boston	33
Corey Seager, Texas	33

RUNS BATTED IN
Kyle Tucker, Houston	112
Adolis Garcia, Texas	107
Julio Rodriguez, Seattle	103
Marcus Semien, Texas	100
Rafael Devers, Boston	100

Marcus Semien

SACRIFICES
Martin Maldonado, Houston	12
Tony Kemp, Oakland	7
Nick Allen, Oakland	6
Myles Straw, Cleveland	6
2 tied	5

SACRIFICE FLIES
Eugenio Suarez, Seattle	11
Kyle Tucker, Houston	10
Maikel Garcia, Kansas City	10
3 tied	8

HIT BY PITCHES
Ty France, Seattle	34
Andres Gimenez, Cleveland	20
Isaac Paredes, Tampa Bay	20
Luke Raley, Tampa Bay	18
Randy Arozarena, Tampa Bay	18

WALKS
J.P. Crawford, Seattle	94
Nathaniel Lowe, Texas	93
Adley Rutschman, Baltimore	92
Alex Bregman, Houston	92
Shohei Ohtani, Los Angeles	91

STOLEN BASES
Esteury Ruiz, Oakland	67
Bobby Witt, Kansas City	49
Julio Rodriguez, Seattle	37
Willi Castro, Minnesota	33
Josh Lowe, Tampa Bay	32
Jorge Mateo, Baltimore	32

STOLEN BASE PERCENTAGE
Taylor Walls, Tampa Bay	95.7
Travis Jankowski, Texas	95.0
Jarren Duran, Boston	92.3
Josh Lowe, Tampa Bay	91.4

STRIKEOUTS
Eugenio Suarez, Seattle	214
Teoscar Hernandez, Seattle	211
Adolis Garcia, Texas	175
Julio Rodriguez, Seattle	175
Brent Rooker, Oakland	172
Luis Robert, Chicago	172

Zach Eflin

STRIKEOUT PERCENTAGE
Steven Kwan, Cleveland	10.4
Jose Ramirez, Cleveland	10.6
Alex Bregman, Houston	12.0
Kyle Tucker, Houston	13.6
Masataka Yoshida, Boston	14.0

DOUBLE PLAYS
Carlos Correa, Minnesota	30
Ty France, Seattle	25
Vladimir Guerrero, Toronto	23
Alex Bregman, Houston	22
Nathaniel Lowe, Texas	22

MULTI-HIT GAMES
Julio Rodriguez, Seattle	55
Marcus Semien, Texas	53
Yandy Diaz, Tampa Bay	43
Bobby Witt Jr., Kansas City	52
Bo Bichette, Toronto	52

ON-BASE PERCENTAGE
Shohei Ohtani, Los Angeles	.412
Yandy Diaz, Tampa Bay	.410
Corey Seager, Texas	.390
J.P. Crawford, Seattle	.380
Adley Rutschman, Balt.	.374

ON-BASE PLUS SLUGGING
Shohei Ohtani, LA	1.066
Corey Seager, Texas	1.013
Yandy Diaz, Tampa Bay	.932
Kyle Tucker, Houston	.886
Triston Casas, Boston	.857

PITCHING

WINS
Zach Eflin, Tampa Bay	16
Chris Bassitt, Toronto	16
Kyle Gibson, Baltimore	15
Gerrit Cole, New York	15
Luis Castillo, Seattle	14

LOSSES
Jordan Lyles, Kansas City	17
Zack Greinke, Kansas City	15
Lucas Giolito, LA/Cle./Chi.	15
JP Sears, Oakland	14
Hunter Brown, Houston	13
Joey Wentz, Detroit	13
Patrick Sandoval, LA	13

GAMES
Matt Brash, Seattle	78
Emmanuel Clase, Cleveland	75
Justin Topa, Seattle	75
Yimi Garcia, Toronto	73
Bryan Abreu, Houston	72
Yennier Cano, Baltimore	72

GAMES STARTED
Dylan Cease, Chicago	33
Gerrit Cole, New York	33
Luis Castillo, Seattle	33
Kyle Gibson, Baltimore	33
Chris Bassitt, Toronto	33
Lucas Giolito, LA/Cle./Chi.	33

GAMES FINISHED
Emmanuel Clase, Cleveland	65
Ryan Pressly, Houston	56
Carlos Estevez, Los Angeles	49
Jordan Romano, Toronto	49

DANIEL SHIREY (TOP)/ JULIO AGUILAR (BOTTOM)

AMERICAN LEAGUE DEPARTMENT LEADERS

Felix Bautista, Baltimore	46

COMPLETE GAMES

Jordan Lyles, Kansas City	3
Gerrit Cole, New York	2
Nathan Eovaldi, Texas	2
Framber Valdez, Houston	2
Mike Clevinger, Chicago	2

SHUTOUTS

Gerrit Cole, New York	2
Framber Valdez, Houston	2
7 tied	1

SAVES

Emmanuel Clase, Cleveland	44
Jordan Romano, Toronto	36
Felix Bautista, Baltimore	33
Carlos Estevez, Los Angeles	31
Ryan Pressly, Houston	31

INNINGS PITCHED

Gerrit Cole, New York	209
Chris Bassitt, Toronto	200
Framber Valdez, Houston	198
Luis Castillo, Seattle	197
Pablo Lopez, Minnesota	194

HITS ALLOWED

Kyle Gibson, Baltimore	198
Brady Singer, Kansas City	182
George Kirby, Seattle	179
Chris Bassitt, Toronto	176
Pablo Lopez, Minnesota	176
Jordan Lyles, Kansas City	176

RUNS ALLOWED

Jordan Lyles, Kansas City	130
Lucas Giolito, LA/Cle./Chi.	110
Brady Singer, Kansas City	102
Kyle Gibson, Baltimore	101
Dylan Cease, Chicago	98

HOME RUNS ALLOWED

Lucas Giolito, LA/Cle./Chi.	41
Jordan Lyles, Kansas City	39
JP Sears, Oakland	34
Joe Ryan, Minnesota	32
Logan Gilbert, Seattle	29
Michael Kopech, Chicago	29

WALKS ALLOWED

M. Kopech, Chicago	91
Dylan Cease, Chicago	79
Patrick Sandoval, Los Angeles	74
Lucas Giolito, LA/Cle/Chi.	73
Ken Waldichuk, Oakland	71

Emmanuel Clase

RON SCHWANE

LOWEST WALKS PER NINE

George Kirby, Seattle	0.90
Zach Eflin, Tampa Bay	1.22
Logan Gilbert, Seattle	1.70
Gerrit Cole, New York	2.07
Pablo Lopez, Minnesota	2.23

HIT BATTERS

JP Sears, Oakland	16
Reid Detmers, Los Angeles	13
Chris Bassitt, Toronto	12
Michael Kopech, Chicago	11
Clarke Schmidt, New York	11
Shohei Ohtani, Los Angeles	11

STRIKEOUTS

Kevin Gausman, Toronto	237
Pablo Lopez, Minnesota	234
Gerrit Cole, New York	222
Luis Castillo, Seattle	219
Dylan Cease, Chicago	214

STRIKEOUTS PER NINE

Kevin Gausman, Toronto	11.5
Dylan Cease, Chicago	10.9
Pablo Lopez, Minnesota	10.9
Luis Castillo, Seattle	10.0
Lucas Giolito, LA/Cle/Chi.	10.0

STRIKEOUTS PER NINE (Relievers)

Felix Bautista, Baltimore	16.2
Aroldis Chapman, KC/Texas	15.9
Matt Brash, Seattle	13.6
Trevor Richards, Toronto	13.0
Bryan Abreu, Houston	12.5

DOUBLE PLAYS

Kyle Gibson, Baltimore	24
Brayan Bello, Boston	23
Framber Valdez, Houston	22
Dane Dunning, Texas	20
2 tied	19

PICKOFFS

Zack Greinke, Kansas City	5
Enyel De Los Santos, Cle.	4
Taylor Clarke, Kansas City	4
11 tied	3

WILD PITCHES

Dylan Cease, Chicago	14
Shohei Ohtani, Los Angeles	12
Clarke Schmidt, New York	11
Matt Brash, Seattle	11
Tyler Glasnow, Tampa Bay	11
Luis Medina, Oakland	11

WALKS PLUS HITS PER INNING

Gerrit Cole, New York	0.98
Zach Eflin, Tampa Bay	1.02
George Kirby, Seattle	1.04
Kyle Bradish, Baltimore	1.04
Logan Gilbert, Seattle	1.08

OPPONENT AVERAGE

Gerrit Cole, New York	.206
Kyle Bradish, Baltimore	.215
Luis Castillo, Seattle	.218
Sonny Gray, Minnesota	.226
Framber Valdez, Houston	.228

WORST ERA

Jordan Lyles, Kansas City	6.28
Lucas Giolito, LA/Cle/Chi.	4.88
Kyle Gibson, Baltimore	4.73
Dylan Cease, Chicago	4.58
Cristian Javier, Houston	4.56

FIELDING

PITCHER

PCT	9 players	1.000
PO	Nathan Eovaldi, Texas	22
A	Jose Berrios, Toronto	26
DP	6 tied	3
E	Ken Waldichuk, Oakland	4

CATCHER

PCT	Salvador Perez, Kansas City	.999
PO	Cal Raleigh, Seattle	1083
A	Martin Maldonado, Houston	51
DP	Christian Vazquez, Minnesota	10
E	Connor Wong, Boston	11
CS	Shea Langeliers, Oakland	38
PB	Martin Maldonado, Houston	12

FIRST BASE

PCT	Ty France, Seattle	.999
PO	Nathaniel Lowe, Texas	1221
A	Nathaniel Lowe, Texas	106
DP	Nathaniel Lowe, Texas	128
E	Spencer Torkelson, Detroit	11

SECOND BASE

PCT	Michael Massey, Kansas City	.993
PO	Marcus Semien, Texas	270
A	Andres Gimenez, Cleveland	401
DP	Marcus Semien, Texas	109
E	Gleyber Torres, New York	15

THIRD BASE

PCT	Josh Jung, Texas	.988
PO	Eugenio Suarez, Seattle	115
A	Alex Bregman, Houston	281
DP	Matt Chapman, Toronto	38
E	Rafael Devers, Boston	19

SHORTSTOP

PCT	Carlos Correa, Minnesota	.987
PO	Jeremy Peña, Houston	200
A	Jeremy Peña, Houston	362
DP	Jeremy Peña, Houston	89
E	Javier Baez, Detroit	19

OUTFIELD

PCT	4 players	1.000
PO	Luis Robert, Chicago	370
A	Teoscar Hernandez, Seattle	12
	Alex Verdugo, Boston	12
DP	Teoscar Hernandez, Seattle	7
E	MJ Melendez, Kansas City	8
	Esteury Ruiz, Oakland	8

NATIONAL LEAGUE 2023 STATISTICS

CLUB BATTING

	AVG	G	AB	R	H	2B	3B	HR	RBI	BB	SO	SB	OBP	SLG
Atlanta	.276	162	5597	947	1543	293	23	307	916	538	1289	132	.344	.501
Miami	.259	162	5497	666	1423	258	23	166	633	430	1287	86	.316	.405
Los Angeles	.257	162	5524	906	1422	303	20	249	877	644	1359	105	.340	.455
Philadelphia	.256	162	5541	796	1417	291	29	220	771	539	1481	141	.327	.438
Chicago	.254	162	5504	819	1399	269	30	196	786	570	1391	140	.330	.421
Washington	.254	162	5522	700	1401	279	26	151	665	423	1149	127	.314	.396
Arizona	.250	162	5436	746	1359	274	44	166	706	540	1247	166	.322	.408
St. Louis	.250	162	5510	719	1376	264	12	209	697	570	1326	101	.326	.416
Cincinnati	.249	162	5499	783	1371	268	37	198	747	556	1500	190	.327	.420
Colorado	.249	162	5496	721	1368	305	31	163	685	447	1543	76	.310	.405
San Diego	.244	162	5401	752	1316	273	14	205	719	653	1311	137	.329	.413
Milwaukee	.240	162	5386	728	1290	257	16	165	696	591	1412	129	.319	.385
Pittsburgh	.239	162	5406	692	1293	287	31	159	662	556	1464	117	.315	.392
New York	.238	162	5363	717	1276	221	21	215	692	525	1331	118	.316	.407
San Francisco	.235	162	5412	674	1271	256	13	174	651	544	1492	57	.312	.383

CLUB PITCHING

	ERA	G	CG	SHO	SV	IP	H	R	ER	HR	BB	SO	AVG
Milwaukee	3.71	162	1	16	46	1443	1218	647	595	198	493	1425	.226
San Diego	3.73	162	0	16	36	1441	1270	648	598	174	557	1445	.236
San Francisco	4.02	162	4	11	50	1435	1395	719	641	173	403	1359	.253
Philadelphia	4.03	162	1	4	45	1442	1318	715	646	185	470	1454	.240
Los Angeles	4.06	162	0	15	44	1446	1284	699	652	200	454	1388	.236
Chicago	4.08	162	1	13	35	1435	1328	723	651	179	513	1377	.244
Atlanta	4.14	162	1	15	52	1440	1341	716	662	187	534	1516	.245
Miami	4.21	162	3	9	43	1435	1340	723	672	191	514	1490	.246
New York	4.30	162	1	7	34	1416	1331	729	676	190	595	1397	.247
Arizona	4.48	162	1	9	44	1435	1375	761	714	197	525	1351	.251
Pittsburgh	4.60	162	2	10	47	1430	1380	790	731	179	596	1363	.251
St. Louis	4.79	162	0	10	36	1428	1549	829	760	179	530	1215	.276
Cincinnati	4.83	162	0	6	53	1439	1426	821	772	222	613	1381	.257
Washington	5.02	162	0	3	42	1428	1512	845	797	245	592	1225	.273
Colorado	5.67	162	0	6	32	1414	1599	957	891	234	586	1129	.288

CLUB FIELDING

	PCT	PO	A	E	DP		PCT	PO	A	E	DP
Arizona	.990	4306	1399	56	134	New York	.985	4249	1394	88	142
St. Louis	.989	4285	1592	67	154	Chicago	.984	4306	1490	92	137
San Diego	.988	4323	1444	73	130	Philadelphia	.984	4327	1385	91	117
Los Angeles	.987	4339	1406	76	139	Pittsburgh	.984	4290	1403	91	135
Milwaukee	.987	4329	1407	77	117	Cincinnati	.984	4318	1283	91	125
Colorado	.986	4242	1516	81	169	Miami	.983	4306	1412	98	144
Atlanta	.986	4320	1339	82	133	San Francisco	.981	4304	1606	117	143
Washington	.985	4285	1505	90	158						

INDIVIDUAL BATTING LEADERS

	AVG	G	AB	R	H	2B	3B	HR	RBI	BB	SO	SB
Luis Arraez, Marlins	.354	147	574	71	203	30	3	10	69	35	34	3
Ronald Acuña Jr., Braves	.337	159	643	149	217	35	4	41	106	80	84	73
Freddie Freeman, Dodgers	.331	161	637	131	211	59	2	29	102	72	121	23
Cody Bellinger, Cubs	.307	130	499	95	153	29	1	26	97	40	87	20
Mookie Betts, Dodgers	.307	152	584	126	179	40	1	39	107	96	107	14
Bryce Harper, Phillies	.293	126	457	84	134	29	1	21	72	80	119	11
Michael Harris II, Braves	.293	138	505	76	148	33	3	18	57	25	101	20
William Contreras, Brewers	.289	141	540	86	156	38	1	17	78	63	126	6
Seiya Suzuki, Cubs	.285	138	515	75	147	31	6	20	74	59	130	6
Xander Bogaerts, Padres	.285	155	596	83	170	31	2	19	58	56	110	19

INDIVIDUAL PITCHING LEADERS

	W	L	ERA	G	GS	CG	SV	IP	H	R	ER	BB	SO
Blake Snell, Padres	14	9	2.25	32	32	0	0	180	115	47	45	99	234
Kodai Senga, Mets	12	7	2.98	29	29	0	0	166	126	60	55	77	202
Justin Steele, Cubs	16	5	3.06	30	30	0	0	173	167	71	59	36	176
Logan Webb, Giants	11	13	3.25	33	33	2	0	216	201	83	78	31	194
Merrill Kelly, D-backs	12	8	3.29	30	30	0	0	178	143	71	65	69	187
Corbin Burnes, Brewers	10	8	3.39	32	32	0	0	194	141	77	73	66	200
Zac Gallen, D-backs	17	9	3.47	34	34	1	0	210	188	87	81	47	220
Jesus Luzardo, Marlins	10	10	3.58	32	32	0	0	179	162	79	71	55	208
Zack Wheeler, Phillies	13	6	3.61	32	32	0	0	192	168	82	77	39	212
Charlie Morton, Braves	14	12	3.64	30	30	0	0	163	150	70	66	83	183

AWARD WINNERS

Selected by Baseball Writers Association of America

MOST VALUABLE PLAYER

Player	1st	2nd	3rd	Total
Ronald Acuña Jr., Braves	30			420
Mookie Betts, Dodgers		30		270
Freddie Freeman, Dodgers			17	227
Matt Olson, Braves			13	223
Corbin Carroll, Diamondbacks				165
Juan Soto, Padres				106
Austin Riley, Braves				68
Luis Arraez, Marlins				67
Francisco Lindor, Mets				52
Cody Bellinger, Cubs				49
William Contreras, Brewers				39
Bryce Harper, Phillies				36
Blake Snell, Padres				16
Fernando Tatis Jr., Padres				5
Ha-Seong Kim, Padres				5
Ozzie Albies, Braves				4
Logan Webb, Giants				3
Pete Alonso, Mets				3
Marcell Ozuna, Braves				2
Devin Williams, Brewers				2
Dansby Swanson, Cubs				2
Kyle Schwarber, Phillies				2
Zac Gallen, Diamondbacks				1
Christian Walker, Diamondbacks				1
TJ Friedl, Reds				1
Nick Castellanos, Phillies				1

CY YOUNG AWARD

Player	1st	2nd	3rd	Total
Blake Snell, Padres	28	2		204
Logan Webb, Giants	1	17	1	86
Zac Gallen, Diamondbacks	1	3	11	68
Spencer Strider, Braves		6	9	64
Justin Steele, Cubs		1	2	31
Zack Wheeler, Phillies			4	28
Kodai Senga, Mets			3	16
Corbin Burnes, Brewers		1		13

ROOKIE OF THE YEAR

Player	1st	2nd	3rd	Total
Corbin Carroll, Diamondbacks	30			150
Kodai Senga, Mets		22	5	71
James Outman, Dodgers		5	5	20
Nolan Jones, Rockies		2	11	17
Matt McLain, Reds		1	2	5
Spencer Steer, Reds			4	4
Eury Perez, Marlins			1	1
Elly De La Cruz, Reds			1	1
Patrick Bailey, Giants			1	1

MANAGER OF THE YEAR

Player	1st	2nd	3rd	Total
Skip Schumaker, Marlins	8	8	8	72
Craig Counsell, Brewers	5	7	5	51
Brian Snitker, Braves	8	2	2	48
Torey Lovullo, Diamondbacks	4	5	7	42
Dave Roberts, Dodgers	4	5	6	41
David Bell, Reds	1	2	2	13
David Ross, Cubs		1		32

GOLD GLOVE WINNERS

Selected by NL Managers

C: Gabriel Moreno, Diamondbacks; **1B:** Christian Walker, Diamondbacks; **2B:** Nico Hoerner, Cubs; **3B:** Ke'Bryan Hayes, Pirates; **SS:** Dansby Swanson, Cubs; **LF:** Ian Happ, Cubs; **CF:** Brenton Doyle, Rockies; **RF:** Fernando Tatis Jr., Padres; **UT:** Ha-Seong Kim, Padres; **P:** Zack Wheeler, Phillies.

NATIONAL LEAGUE DEPARTMENT LEADERS

BATTING

GAMES
Matt Olson, Atlanta 162
Juan Soto, San Diego 162
Freddie Freeman, Los Angeles 161
Francisco Lindor, New York 160
Kyle Schwarber, Philadelphia 160

AT-BATS
Ronald Acuña Jr., Atlanta 643
Trea Turner, Philadelphia 639
Freddie Freeman, LA 637
Austin Riley, Atlanta 636
Lane Thomas, Washington 628

PLATE APPEARANCES
Ronald Acuña Jr., Atlanta 735
Freddie Freeman, LA 730
Kyle Schwarber, Philadelphia 720
Matt Olson, Atlanta 720
Austin Riley, Atlanta 715

RUNS
Ronald Acuña Jr., Atlanta 149
Freddie Freeman, LA 131
Matt Olson, Atlanta 127
Mookie Betts, Los Angeles 126
Austin Riley, Atlanta 117

HITS
Ronald Acuña Jr., Atlanta 217
Freddie Freeman, LA 211
Luis Arraez, Miami 203
Mookie Betts, Los Angeles 179
Austin Riley, Atlanta 179

TOTAL BASES
Ronald Acuña Jr., Atlanta 383
Matt Olson, Atlanta 367
Freddie Freeman, LA 361
Mookie Betts, Los Angeles 338
Austin Riley, Atlanta 328

DOUBLES
Freddie Freeman, Los Angeles 59
Mookie Betts, Los Angeles 40
Jeimer Candelario, Chi./Wash. 39
William Contreras, Milwaukee 38
3 tied 37

TRIPLES
Corbin Carroll, Arizona 10
Ketel Marte, Arizona 9
TJ Friedl, Cincinnati 8
Will Benson, Cincinnati 8
3 tied 7

EXTRA-BASE HITS
Freddie Freeman, Los Angeles 90
Matt Olson, Atlanta 84
Ronald Acuña Jr., Atlanta 80
Mookie Betts, Los Angeles 80
Austin Riley, Atlanta 72

HOME RUNS
Matt Olson, Atlanta 54
Kyle Schwarber, Philadelphia 47
Pete Alonso, New York 46
Ronald Acuña Jr., Atlanta 41
Marcell Ozuna, Atlanta 40

RUNS BATTED IN
Matt Olson, Atlanta 139
Pete Alonso, New York 118
Ozzie Albies, Atlanta 109
Juan Soto, San Diego 109
Mookie Betts, Los Angeles 107

Matt Olson

SACRIFICES
Geraldo Perdomo, Arizona 14
Austin Hedges, Pittsburgh 9
TJ Friedl, Cincinnati 8
Corbin Carroll, Arizona 6
Johan Rojas, Philadelphia 6

SACRIFICE FLIES
Will Smith, Los Angeles 12
Cody Bellinger, Chicago 12
Austin Riley, Atlanta 11
J.D. Martinez, Los Angeles 9
4 tied 8

HIT BY PITCHES
Pete Alonso, New York 21
Jeff McNeil, New York 18
Sean Murphy, Atlanta 18
Mark Canha, New York/Mil. 17
Freddie Freeman, Los Angeles 16
Jonathan India, Cincinnati 16

WALKS
Juan Soto, San Diego 132
Kyle Schwarber, Philadelphia 126
Matt Olson, Atlanta 104
Ian Happ, Chicago 99
Mookie Betts, Los Angeles 96

STOLEN BASES
Ronald Acuña Jr., Atlanta 73
Corbin Carroll, Arizona 54
CJ Abrams, Washington 47
Nico Hoerner, Chicago 43
Ha-Seong Kim, San Diego 38

STOLEN BASE PERCENTAGE
Trea Turner, Philadelphia 100
Freddie Freeman, LA 95.8
C.J. Abrams, Washington 92.2
Bryson Stott, Philadelphia 91.2
Xander Bogaerts, San Diego 90.5

STRIKEOUTS
Kyle Schwarber, Philadelphia 215
Ryan McMahon, Colorado 198
Nick Castellanos, Philadelphia 185
James Outman, Los Angeles 181
Lane Thomas, Washington 176

STRIKEOUT PERCENTAGE
Luis Arraez, Miami 5.5
Jeff McNeil, New York Mets 10.0
Keibert Ruiz, Washington 10.3
Ronald Acuña Jr., Atlanta 11.4
Nico Hoerner, Chicago 12.1

Luis Arraez

DOUBLE PLAYS
Alec Bohm, Philadelphia 23
William Contreras, Milwaukee 23
Nolan Arenado, St. Louis 21
Xander Bogaerts, San Diego 21
3 tied 20

MULTI-HIT GAMES
Ronald Acuña Jr., Atlanta 69
Freddie Freeman, Los Angeles 62
Austin Riley, Atlanta 56
Luis Arraez, Miami 55
Nico Hoerner, Chicago 51

ON-BASE PERCENTAGE
Ronald Acuña Jr., Atlanta .416
Juan Soto, San Diego .410
Freddie Freeman, LA .410
Mookie Betts, Los Angeles .408
Bryce Harper, Washington .401

ON-BASE PLUS SLUGGING
Ronald Acuña Jr., Atlanta 1.012
Matt Olson, Atlanta .993
Mookie Betts, Los Angeles .987
Freddie Freeman, LA .977
Juan Soto, San Diego .929

PITCHING

WINS
Spencer Strider, Atlanta 20
Zac Gallen, Arizona 17
Justin Steele, Chicago 16
Taijuan Walker, Philadelphia 15
3 tied 14

LOSSES
Patrick Corbin, Washington 15
Rich Hill, Pittsburgh/SD 14
Kyle Freeland, Colorado 14
Johan Oviedo, Pittsburgh 14
3 tied 13

GAMES
Miguel Castro, Arizona 75
Ian Gibaut, Cincinnati 74
Tanner Scott, Miami 74
Hoby Milner, Milwaukee 73
Alexis Diaz, Cincinnati 71
Buck Farmer, Cincinnati 71
Craig Kimbrel, Philadelphia 71

GAMES STARTED
Miles Mikolas, St. Louis 35
Zac Gallen, Arizona 34
Logan Webb, San Francisco 33
9 tied 32

GAMES FINISHED
Camilo Doval, San Francisco 60
David Bednar, Pittsburgh 57
Josh Hader, San Diego 52
Alexis Diaz, Cincinnati 51
Raisel Iglesias, Atlanta 50

COMPLETE GAMES
Sandy Alcantara, Miami 3
Alex Cobb, San Francisco 2
Logan Webb, San Francisco 2
8 tied 1

SHUTOUTS
10 tied 1

SAVES
Camilo Doval, San Francisco 39
David Bednar, Pittsburgh 39

MATTHEW GRIMES JR. (TOP)/ RICH STORRY (BOTTOM)

NATIONAL LEAGUE DEPARTMENT LEADERS

Alexis Diaz, Cincinnati	37
Devin Williams, Milwaukee	36
Josh Hader, San Diego	33
Raisel Iglesias, Atlanta	33

INNINGS PITCHED

Logan Webb, San Francisco	216
Zac Gallen, Arizona	210
Miles Mikolas, St. Louis	201
Mitch Keller, Pittsburgh	194
Corbin Burnes, Milwaukee	193
Aaron Nola, Philadelphia	193

HITS ALLOWED

Miles Mikolas, St. Louis	226
Patrick Corbin, Washington	210
Logan Webb, San Francisco	201
Zac Gallen, Arizona	188
Kyle Freeland, Colorado	187
Mitch Keller, Pittsburgh	187

RUNS ALLOWED

Patrick Corbin, Washington	113
Miles Mikolas, St. Louis	110
Aaron Nola, Philadelphia	105
Rich Hill, Pittsburgh/SD	98
Trevor Williams, Washington	97
Mitch Keller, Pittsburgh	97

HOME RUNS ALLOWED

Trevor Williams, Washington	34
Patrick Corbin, Washington	33
Aaron Nola, Philadelphia	32
Kyle Freeland, Colorado	29
MacKenzie Gore, Washington	27
Jameson Taillon, Chicago	27

WALKS ALLOWED

Blake Snell, San Diego	99
Charlie Morton, Atlanta	83
Johan Oviedo, Pittsburgh	83
Josiah Gray, Washington	80
Kodai Senga, New York	77

LOWEST WALKS PER NINE

Logan Webb, San Francisco	1.29
Miles Mikolas, St. Louis	1.74
Zack Wheeler, Philadelphia	1.83
Justin Steele, Chicago Cubs	1.87
Zac Gallen, Arizona	2.01

HIT BATTERS

Johan Oviedo, Pittsburgh	13
Charlie Morton, Atlanta	12
Mitch Keller, Pittsburgh	12
Braxton Garrett, Miami	11
4 tied	10

Blake Snell

STRIKEOUTS

Spencer Strider, Atlanta	281
Blake Snell, San Diego	234
Zac Gallen, Arizona	220
Zack Wheeler, Philadelphia	212
2 tied	210

STRIKEOUTS PER NINE

Spencer Strider, Atlanta	13.6
Blake Snell, San Diego	11.7
Freddy Peralta, Milwaukee	11.4
Kodai Senga, New York Mets	10.9
Jesus Luzardo, Miami	10.5

STRIKEOUTS PER NINE (Relievers)

Josh Hader, San Diego	13.6
Fernando Cruz, Cincinnati	13.4
Devin Williams, Milwaukee	13.4
Pierce Johnson, Colo./Atl.	12.9
A.J. Puk, Miami	12.4

DOUBLE PLAYS

Logan Webb, San Francisco	30
Bryce Elder, Atlanta	26
Graham Ashcraft, Cincinnati	21
Merrill Kelly, Arizona	19
Tylor Megill, New York	19

PICKOFFS

Patrick Corbin, Washington	7
David Peterson, New York	6
Ryan Weathers, SD/Miami	6
Taijuan Walker, Philadelphia	6
3 tied	4

WILD PITCHES

Kodai Senga, New York	14
Blake Snell, San Diego	13
Bryce Elder, Atlanta	11
Camilo Doval, San Francisco	10
Corbin Burnes, Milwaukee	10
Bobby Miller, Los Angeles	10

WALKS PLUS HITS PER INNING

Corbin Burnes, Milwaukee	1.07
Logan Webb, San Francisco	1.07
Zack Wheeler, Philadelphia	1.08
Spencer Strider, Atlanta	1.09
Freddy Peralta, Milwaukee	1.12

OPPONENT AVERAGE

Blake Snell, San Diego	.181
Corbin Burnes, Milwaukee	.200
Kodai Senga, New York	.208
Spencer Strider, Atlanta	.210
Freddy Peralta, Milwaukee	.212

WORST ERA

Patrick Corbin, Washington	5.20
Miles Mikolas, St. Louis	4.78
Aaron Nola, Philadelphia	4.46
Taijuan Walker, Philadelphia	4.38
Johan Oviedo, Pittsburgh	4.31

FIELDING

PITCHER

PCT	6 players	1.000
PO	Corbin Burnes, Milwaukee	29
A	Patrick Corbin, Washington	36
DP	4 tied	4
E	Sandy Alcantara, Miami	5

CATCHER

PCT	J.T. Realmuto, Philadelphia	.998
PO	J.T. Realmuto, Philadelphia	1190
A	Gabriel Moreno, Arizona	55
DP	Elias Diaz, Colorado	9
E	Francisco Alvarez, New York	13
	Patrick Bailey, San Francisco	13
CS	Patrick Bailey, San Francisco	25
PB	3 tied	8

FIRST BASE

PCT	Freddie Freeman, Los Angeles	.999
PO	Matt Olson, Atlanta	1194
A	Dominic Smith, Washington	143
DP	Dominic Smith, Washington	134
E	Lamonte Wade, San Francisco	10

SECOND BASE

PCT	Luis Arraez, Miami	.993
PO	Bryson Stott, Philadelphia	235
A	Ozzie Albies, Atlanta	368
DP	Luis Arraez, Miami	93
E	Jonathan India, Cincinnati	9

THIRD BASE

PCT	Ke'Bryan Hayes, Pittsburgh	.984
PO	Austin Riley, Atlanta	95
	Ryan McMahon, Colorado	95
A	Austin Riley, Atlanta	287
DP	Austin Riley, Atlanta	38
E	Max Muncy, Los Angeles	16

SHORTSTOP

PCT	Geraldo Perdomo, Arizona	.989
PO	CJ Abrams, Washington	245
A	Francisco Lindor, New York	396
DP	CJ Abrams, Washington	100
E	Trea Turner, Philadelphia	23

OUTFIELD

PCT	Nick Castellanos, Phila.	1.000
PO	Brenton Doyle, Colorado	370
A	Nolan Jones, Colorado	21
DP	3 tied	4
E	Fernando Tatis Jr., San Diego	6

EZRA SHAW

CHRISTIAN PETERSEN

Josh Sborz finished a dominating postseason by recording the final out of the World Series

Rangers Slug Their Way To First World Series Win

BY KYLE GLASER

As with any change, the expansion of the postseason field from 10 to 12 teams in 2022 led to unexpected consequences.

The top two teams in each league earn byes through the Wild Card Series under the new format, and thus are off for five days between the end of the regular season and the start of the Division Series. So baseball's best teams enter their opening series cold against lower-seeded teams that are fully in rhythm, a dynamic that appears to make it more difficult for top seeds to win. The 111-win Dodgers and 101-win Braves struggled to score and were unceremoniously dumped in the Division Series in the first year under the expanded format, while the 99-win Yankees needed all five games to dispatch an inferior Guardians team.

The 2023 playoffs provided evidence that those outcomes weren't a fluke. For the second time in as many years under the new setup, the best teams in baseball saw their championship ambitions come to a premature end.

The MLB-best Braves boasted a historic offense but scored just eight runs in four games as they fell to the rival Phillies in the NLDS for the second straight year. The 100-win Dodgers never led at any point in their Division Series while being swept by the upstart Diamondbacks. The 101-win Orioles were blown out twice and swept by the Rangers in the ALDS. Only the defending champion Astros managed to withstand the bye and advance to the next round.

"I don't think we need five (days off), but we did need a few," Orioles manager Brandon Hyde said. "Whether that affected us in this series or not, I'm not going to speculate. But it's a long time off. That's the bottom line."

By the time the Division Series wrapped up, the four remaining teams had 90 wins (Astros, Phillies and Rangers) and 84 wins (Diamondbacks) during the regular season. The teams with the five-highest regular season win totals—the Braves (104), Orioles (101), Dodgers (100), Rays (99) and Brewers (92)—had all been eliminated.

"It's only year two," Commissioner Rob Manfred said during the Braves-Phillies NLDS. "I'm sort of of the view you need to give something a chance to work out. I know some of the higher-seeded teams didn't win. I think if you think about where some of those teams were, there are other explanations than a five-day layoff. But I think we'll reevaluate in the offseason like we always do and think about if we have the format right."

While the early elimination of baseball's best teams led to frustration and criticism of the expanded postseason format, it also gave rise to compelling underdog stories.

HARRY HOW

Ketel Marte came up big repeatedly for the Diamondbacks in the postseason.

Underdogs Have Their Day

The D-backs, just two years removed from a 52-110 season, clinched the NL's final wild card spot on the penultimate day of the season and became an unexpected contender with their youthful energy and penchant for comeback wins.

It began in the Wild Card Series against the Brewers. The D-backs fell behind 3-0 early in Game 1 and faced a daunting task with ace Corbin Burnes on the mound for Milwaukee, but Corbin Carroll, Ketel Marte and Gabriel Moreno all homered to chase Burnes from the game after four innings and fuel a 6-3 win. The D-backs did it again in Game 2, falling behind 2-0 in the first inning before rallying against standout righthander Freddy Peralta in the middle innings for a 5-2 victory that eliminated the Brewers.

As it turned out, the D-backs were just getting started.

In Game 1 of the NLDS at Dodger Stadium, they jumped on Clayton Kershaw for five runs before he recorded an out. They chased him from the game after just eight batters, the shortest outing of Kershaw's career, and piled on against the Dodgers bullpen for an 11-2 rout.

In Game 2, they scored three runs in the first inning against rookie standout Bobby Miller to jump out to a lead they would not relinquish in a 4-2 win. And in Game 3, their first home game of the playoffs, the D-backs became the first team ever to hit four homers in an inning in the postseason when Geraldo Perdomo, Marte, Christian Walker and Moreno all went deep against Lance Lynn in the third inning. The historic barrage fueled a 4-2 victory that eliminated the Dodgers and sent the D-backs to the NLCS for the first time since 2007.

"We're here," center fielder Alek Thomas said. "This is a different Diamondbacks team than in the past. We're just gonna keep on playing our brand of baseball and try to get this thing done."

Meanwhile, the Phillies upset the Braves for the second straight year in the NLDS as Citizens Bank Park cemented its place as the most difficult road environment in baseball.

After the Phillies took Game 1 in Atlanta, the Braves trailed 4-0 before rallying for five runs in the final four innings of Game 2, capped by Austin Riley's two-run homer in the bottom of the eighth to give the Braves a 5-4 lead. The game ended in thrilling fashion in the top of the ninth when center fielder Michael Harris II made a leaping catch at the wall to rob Nick Castellanos of extra bases, then threw the ball back toward the infield, where Riley picked it up off the grass and fired a bullet to just get a retreating Bryce Harper at first base for a game-ending double play.

Instead of using the thrilling victory to swing the momentum of the series, however, the Braves committed a fatal faux pas.

In the postgame clubhouse celebration, shortstop Orlando Arcia yelled, "Ha ha, atta boy Harper" in front of a large media contingent, mocking the Phillies star for getting doubled off first to end the game. While it was hardly an offensive outburst, Harper, the Phillies and their fans nonetheless framed it as disrespectful and used it as motivation. Afterward, Arcia said about Harper, "He wasn't supposed to hear it."

With a rabid sellout crowd at Citizens Bank Park mercilessly heckling Arcia and the Braves in Game 3, the Phillies pounded six home runs in a 10-2 rout to take the series lead. Harper put the Phillies in front with a tiebreaking three-run homer into the second deck in the third inning and stared down Arcia as he rounded second base. For good measure, Harper launched another towering home run to center field in the fifth and stared Arcia down again.

"I mean, anytime anybody says something, right?" Harper said when asked if Arcia's comment motivated him. "I mean, that's what it's all about."

The Phillies wrapped it up in Game 4 with two solo home runs by Castellanos and a solo shot by Trea Turner providing all the scoring in a 3-1 win. Castellanos, who also homered twice in Game 3, became the first player to hit two home runs in back-to-back postseason games.

On the other side, Arcia lost his composure and repeatedly yelled at the crowd from the visitor's dugout after they once again targeted him for jeers.

In the postgame victory celebration, Phillies players donned custom T-shirts that read "Atta Boy Harper" on the front and "He wasn't supposed to hear it" on the back.

"You disrespect one of the great players in the game, it just adds fuel to his fire," Phillies right-hander Zack Wheeler said. "Those guys a lot of times don't need more fuel to the fire. Because it's dangerous."

The two American League Division Series lacked similar drama or subplots. The Rangers, fresh off steamrolling the Rays in the Wild Card Series, pounded the Orioles for 30 hits and 21 runs in three games for an emphatic sweep to secure their ticket to the ALCS. The Twins ended an 18-game postseason losing streak by beating the Blue Jays in the first game of the AL Wild Card Series and beat them again the next day to win their first playoff series since 2002, but the defending champion Astros dispatched them in four games in the ALDS. Yordan Alvarez hit four homers in as many games and Jose Abreu homered three times as the Astros advanced to their record seventh-straight ALCS, setting up a Lone Star

AMERICAN LEAGUE CHAMPIONS, 1998-2023

American League postseason results from 1998 to present, where (*) denotes wild card playoff entrant.

YEAR	CHAMPIONSHIP SERIES	ALCS MVP	DIVISION SERIES	DIVISION SERIES
2023	Texas 4, Houston 3	Adolis Garcia, OF, Texas	Houston 3, Minnesota 1	Texas* 3, Baltimore 0
2022	Houston 4, New York 0	Jeremy Peña, SS, Houston	Houston 3, Seattle* 0	New York 3, Cleveland 2
2021	Houston 4, Boston 2	Yordan Alvarez, OF, Houston	Houston 3, Chicago 1	Boston* 3, Tampa Bay 1
2020	Tampa Bay 4, Houston 3	Randy Arozarena, OF, Tampa Bay	Tampa Bay 3, New York* 2	Houston* 3, Oakland 1
2019	Houston 4, New York 2	Jose Altuve, 2B, Houston	Houston 3, Tampa Bay* 2	New York 3, Minnesota 0
2018	Boston 4, Houston 1	Jackie Bradley Jr., OF, Boston	Boston 3, New York* 1	Houston 3, Cleveland 0
2017	Houston 4, New York 3	Justin Verlander, RHP, Houston	New York* 3, Cleveland 2	Houston 3, Boston 1
2016	Cleveland 4, Toronto 1	Andrew Miller, LHP, Cleveland	Toronto* 3, Texas 0	Cleveland 3, Boston 0
2015	Kansas City 4, Toronto 2	Alcides Escobar, SS, Kansas City	Kansas City 3, Houston* 2	Baltimore 3, Texas 2
2014	Kansas City 4, Baltimore 0	Lorenzo Cain, OF, Kansas City	Kansas City 3, Los Angeles 0	Baltimore 3, Detroit 0
2013	Boston 4, Detroit 2	Koji Uehara, RHP, Boston	Boston 3, Tampa Bay* 1	Detroit, 3, Oakland 2
2012	Detroit 4, New York 0	Delmon Young, OF, Detroit	New York 3, Baltimore* 2	Detroit 3, Oakland 2
2011	Texas 4, Detroit 2	Nelson Cruz, OF, Texas	Detroit 3, New York 2	Texas 3, Tampa Bay* 1
2010	Texas 4, New York 2	Josh Hamilton, OF, Texas	Texas 3, Tampa Bay 2	New York* 3, Minnesota 0
2009	New York 4, Los Angeles 2	C.C. Sabathia, LHP, New York	New York 3, Minnesota 0	Los Angeles 3, Boston* 0
2008	Tampa Bay 4, Boston 3	Matt Garza, RHP, Tampa Bay	Boston* 3, Los Angeles 1	Tampa Bay 3, Chicago 1
2007	Boston 4, Cleveland 3	Josh Beckett, RHP, Boston	Boston 3, Los Angeles 0	Cleveland 3, New York* 1
2006	Detroit 4, Oakland 0	Placido Polanco, 2B, Detroit	Detroit* 3, New York 1	Oakland 3, Minnesota 0
2005	Chicago 4, Los Angeles 1	Paul Konerko, 1B, Chicago	Chicago 3, Boston* 0	Los Angeles 3, New York 2
2004	Boston 4, New York 3	David Ortiz, DH, Boston	Boston* 3, Anaheim 0	New York 3, Minnesota 1
2003	New York 4, Boston 3	Mariano Rivera, RHP, New York	New York 3, Minnesota 1	Boston* 3, Oakland 2
2002	Anaheim 4, Minnesota 1	Adam Kennedy, 2B, Anaheim	Anaheim* 3, New York 1	Minnesota 3, Oakland 2
2001	New York 4, Seattle 1	Andy Pettitte, LHP, New York	Seattle 3, Cleveland 2	New York 3, Oakland* 2
2000	New York 4, Seattle 2	David Justice, OF, New York	New York 3, Oakland 2	Seattle* 3, Chicago 0
1999	New York 4, Boston 1	Orlando Hernandez, RHP, New York	Boston* 3, Cleveland 2	New York 3, Texas 0
1998	New York 4, Cleveland 2	David Wells, LHP, New York	Cleveland 3, Boston* 1	New York 3, Texas 0

RICH GRAESSLE/ICON SPORTSWIRE VIA GETTY IMAGES

Bryce Harper made a point of sending a message to Orlando Arcia after both of his Game 3 homers

NATIONAL LEAGUE CHAMPIONS, 1998–2023

National League postseason results from 1998 to present, where (*) denotes wild card playoff entrant.

YEAR	CHAMPIONSHIP SERIES	NLCS MVP	DIVISION SERIES	DIVISION SERIES
2023	Arizona 4, Philadelphia 3	Ketel Marte, 2B, Arizona	Philadelphia* 3, Atlanta 1	Arizona* 3, Los Angeles 0
2022	Philadelphia 4, San Diego 1	Bryce Harper, OF, Philadelphia	Philadelphia* 3, Atlanta 1	San Diego* 3, Los Angeles 1
2021	Atlanta 4, Los Angeles 2	Eddie Rosario, OF, Atlanta	Atlanta 3, Milwaukee 1	Los Angeles* 3, San Francisco 2
2020	Los Angeles 4, Atlanta 3	Corey Seager, SS, Los Angeles	Los Angeles 3, San Diego* 0	Atlanta 3, Miami* 0
2019	Washington 4, St. Louis 0	Howie Kendrick, 2B, Washington	Washington* 3, Los Angeles 2	St. Louis 3, Atlanta 2
2018	Los Angeles 4, Milwaukee 3	Cody Bellinger, 1B/OF, Los Angeles	Los Angeles 3, Atlanta 1	Milwaukee 3, Colorado 0*
2017	Los Angeles 4, Chicago 1	Justin Turner, 3B/Chris Taylor, CF, L.A.	Los Angeles 3, Arizona* 0	Chicago 3, Washington 2
2016	Chicago 4, Los Angeles 2	Javier Baez, 2B/Jon Lester, LHP, Chicago	Chicago 3, San Francisco* 1	Los Angeles 3, Washington 2
2015	New York 4, Chicago 0	Daniel Murphy, 2B, New York	New York 3, Los Angeles 2	Chicago* 3, St. Louis 1
2014	San Francisco 4, St. Louis 1	Madison Bumgarner, LHP, San Francisco	San Francisco 3, Washington 1	St. Louis 3, Los Angeles 1
2013	St. Louis 4, Los Angeles 2	Michael Wacha, RHP, St. Louis	St. Louis 3, Pittsburgh* 2	Los Angeles 3, Atlanta 1
2012	San Francisco 4, St. Louis 3	Marco Scutaro, 2B, San Francisco	St. Louis* 3, Washington 2	San Francisco 3, Cincinnati 2
2011	St. Louis 4, Milwaukee 2	David Freese, 3B, St. Louis	St. Louis* 3, Philadelphia 2	Milwaukee 3, Arizona 2
2010	San Francisco 4, Philadelphia 2	Cody Ross, OF, San Francisco	Philadelphia 3, Cincinnati 0	San Francisco 3, Atlanta* 1
2009	Philadelphia 4, Los Angeles 1	Ryan Howard, 1B, Philadelphia	Los Angeles 3, St. Louis 0	Philadelphia 3, Colorado* 1
2008	Philadelphia 4, Los Angeles 1	Cole Hamels, LHP, Philadelphia	Los Angeles 3, Chicago 0	Philadelphia 3, Milwaukee* 1
2007	Colorado 4, Arizona 0	Matt Holliday, OF, Colorado	Arizona 3, Chicago 0	Colorado* 3, Philadelphia 0
2006	St. Louis 4, New York 3	Jeff Suppan, RHP, St. Louis	New York 3, Los Angeles* 0	St. Louis 3, San Diego 1
2005	Houston 4, St. Louis 2	Roy Oswalt, RHP, Houston	St. Louis 3, San Diego 0	Houston* 3, Atlanta 1
2004	St. Louis 4, Houston 3	Albert Pujols, 1B, St. Louis	St. Louis 3, Los Angeles 1	Houston* 3, Atlanta 2
2003	Florida 4, Chicago 3	Ivan Rodriguez, C, Florida	Florida* 3, San Francisco 1	Chicago 3, Atlanta 2
2002	San Francisco 4, St. Louis 1	Benito Santiago, C, San Francisco	San Francisco* 3, Atlanta 2	St. Louis 3, Arizona 0
2001	Arizona 4, Atlanta 1	Craig Counsell, SS, Arizona	Atlanta 3, Houston 0	Arizona 3, St. Louis* 2
2000	New York 4, St. Louis 1	Mike Hampton, LHP, New York	St. Louis 3, Atlanta 0	New York* 3, San Francisco 1
1999	Atlanta 4, New York 2	Eddie Perez, C, Atlanta	Atlanta 3, Houston 1	New York* 3, Arizona 1
1998	San Diego 4, Atlanta 2	Sterling Hitchcock, LHP, San Diego	Atlanta 3, Chicago* 0	San Diego 3, Houston 1

ROB CARR/GETTY IMAGES

Adolis Garcia was an easy choice as ALCS MVP after he hit five home runs and drove in 15

Showdown with the rival Rangers.

High Drama

For all the excitement of the early rounds, no series went the distance. None of the eight contests in the Wild Card Series and Division Series went to a winner-take-all game.

Any criticism that the 2023 playoffs lacked tension, however, fell by the wayside with the AL and NL Championship Series. Both went to seven games, with the underdogs prevailing as they had so often during the postseason.

The marquee intrastate showdown between the Astros and Rangers lived up to its billing. The Rangers won the first two games in Houston, but the defending champion Astros fought back to win the first two games in Arlington to tie the series at two games apiece.

That set the stage for a tense, dramatic, thrilling Game 5. The Astros led 2-1 in the bottom of the sixth when Rangers right fielder Adolis Garcia launched a mammoth three-run homer off Justin Verlander to put the Rangers in front, 4-2. Garcia walked slowly down the first-base line, admiring his home run as it sailed over the fence, then banging his chest heartily with his left hand and slamming his bat to the ground in celebration. After he rounded the bases, he stepped on home plate with an emphatic stomp.

The Astros took exception to the celebration. The next time Garcia stepped to the plate in the eighth inning, Astros reliever Bryan Abreu drilled him in the ribs with a 99 mph fastball.

Garcia immediately turned to Astros catcher Martin Maldonado and began yelling at him and trying to push him. Both benches cleared and a minor fracas ensued as Garcia tried to get around the crowd of players to confront Maldonado and Abreu, but in the end no punches were thrown.

"It was just the heat of the moment," Garcia said. "I just reacted to being hit by the pitch. I just reacted toward Maldonado as soon as I felt the hit. It was just a thing that happened in that instant."

Abreu, Garcia and Astros manager Dusty Baker were all ejected, a decision Baker vociferously objected to as he refused to leave the dugout. After a 12-minute delay, Baker finally left and the game resumed.

The Astros, invigorated by the series of events, rallied in the top of the ninth. After pinch-hitters Yainer Diaz and Jon Singleton reached against Rangers closer Jose Leclerc on a single and walk, respectively, to lead off the inning, Altuve hammered a Leclerc changeup into the left-field stands for a stunning, go-ahead three-run homer. The Rangers tried to rally in the bottom of the ninth and had two on with none out, but Astros closer Ryan Pressly retired the next three batters in order to end the wild contest.

The Astros won that battle, but they lost the war, and Garcia led the way in making them pay. With the Astros one win away from returning to the World Series and back at home in Houston, Garcia—who had struck out his first four times—crushed a grand slam in the ninth inning to complete a Rangers rout and force a Game 7. In the winner-take-all game, Garcia mashed two more homers to lead an 11-4 rout, sending the Rangers to the World Series.

In all, Garcia hit five home runs and set a record for RBIs in a postseason series with 15, winning ALCS MVP.

"He's a bad man, isn't he?" Rangers shortstop Corey Seager said. "To be able to come into this atmosphere and get booed every at-bat and do what he did was really special. It was really fun to watch."

In the NLCS, the Phillies looked to be on their way to a repeat World Series appearance after taking the first two games in Philadelphia and holding late leads in Games 3 and 4 in Arizona. But each time, the D-backs rallied, giving rise to the "Snakes Alive" and "Answerbacks" rallying cries that defined their postseason run.

In Game 3, Lourdes Gurriel Jr. hit a game-tying double in the seventh and Marte won it with a walk-off single off Craig Kimbrel in the ninth.

In Game 4, the Phillies led 5-3 in the bottom of the eighth before Thomas hit a game-tying two-run homer off Kimbrel and Moreno added an RBI single to give the D-backs a 6-5 lead, which they would hold.

The Phillies once again appeared in control when Wheeler held the D-backs to one run over seven innings in a dominant performance to give them a 3-2 series lead heading back to Philadelphia, where they hadn't lost a game all postseason. But against all odds, the D-backs went into Citizens Bank Park and took both games without much drama.

Tommy Pham and Gurriel hit back-to-back home runs off Aaron Nola in the third inning of Game 6 to put the D-backs up for good en route to a 5-1 win. The Phillies took an early 2-1 lead in Game 7, but RBI singles by Carroll and Moreno in the fifth put the D-backs in front, and they held on for a 4-2 win to shock the Phillies and return to the World Series for the first time since 2001.

"Watching them prior to this series, I don't think anything scared that team," Harper said. "I don't think they had any doubt in their minds of coming back here and playing in Philadelphia. They did it to the Brewers, they did it to the Dodgers and then they were able to do it to us as well. I just don't think that team is scared of any situation or any spot."

Texas Hold 'Em

The World Series matchup between the Rangers and Diamondbacks wasn't what anyone expected, but both teams proved their worth in getting there.

In the end, it was the Rangers who had enough left in the tank to become champions.

The D-backs led nearly the entire way in Game 1 before Seager hit a game-tying two-run homer in the ninth off Paul Sewald and Garcia hit a walk-off solo homer in the 11th to give the Rangers a thrilling 6-5 win.

The D-backs took out their frustrations on the Rangers pitching staff the following night, pounding out 16 hits in a 9-1 rout to send the series back to Arizona tied 1-1.

The Rangers, sniffing the first World Series title in franchise history, left no doubt who the better team was once they arrived in Phoenix. They never trailed in Game 3 as Marcus Semien hit a two-out RBI single and Seager smashed a two-run homer to give the Rangers a 3-1 victory.

Jon Gray pitched three critical innings of emergency relief after Max Scherzer left with a back injury.

In Game 4, with Arizona forced to throw a bullpen game, the Rangers smashed the D-backs relief corps and led 10-0 by the third inning on the way to an 11-7 victory.

In Game 5, D-backs ace Zac Gallen pitched no-hit ball through six innings, but the Rangers jumped on him with three consecutive hits to open the seventh and broke a scoreless tie on Mitch Garver's RBI single.

With the Rangers looking for insurance in the ninth, Thomas misplayed Jonah Heim's ground single to center field to allow two runs to score, and Semien belted a two-run homer that made it 5-0 Texas and all but assured the Rangers their first World Series title.

Josh Sborz retired the side in the bottom of the ninth, punctuated by striking out Marte looking at a curveball to end it, giving the Rangers the first World Series title in their 63-year franchise history.

"The wait is over," general manager Chris Young said. "Our history has changed. I just am so happy for so many people that have waited a long time for this."

Seager was named World Series MVP after hitting .286 with three home runs in the series. Rangers manager Bruce Bochy, lured out of retirement before the season, won his fourth World Series title and became just the third manager ever to win a World Series in both leagues.

THE WORLD SERIES YEAR-BY-YEAR

Year	Winner	Loser	Result
1903	Boston (AL)	Pittsburgh (NL)	5-3
1904	NO SERIES		
1905	New York (NL)	Philadelphia (AL)	4-1
1906	Chicago (AL)	Chicago (NL)	4-2
1907	Chicago (NL)	Detroit (AL)	4-0
1908	Chicago (NL)	Detroit (AL)	4-1
1909	Pittsburgh (NL)	Detroit (AL)	4-3
1910	Philadelphia (AL)	Chicago (NL)	4-1
1911	Philadelphia (AL)	New York (NL)	4-2
1912	Boston (AL)	New York (NL)	4-3-1
1913	Philadelphia (AL)	New York (NL)	4-1
1914	Boston (NL)	Philadelphia (AL)	4-0
1915	Boston (AL)	Philadelphia (NL)	4-1
1916	Boston (AL)	Brooklyn (NL)	4-1
1917	Chicago (AL)	New York (NL)	4-2
1918	Boston (AL)	Chicago (NL)	4-2
1919	Cincinnati (NL)	Chicago (AL)	5-3
1920	Cleveland (AL)	Brooklyn (NL)	5-2
1921	New York (NL)	New York (AL)	5-3
1922	New York (NL)	New York (AL)	4-0
1923	New York (AL)	New York (NL)	4-2
1924	Washington (AL)	New York (NL)	4-3
1925	Pittsburgh (NL)	Washington (AL)	4-3
1926	St. Louis (NL)	New York (AL)	4-3
1927	New York (AL)	Pittsburgh (NL)	4-0
1928	New York (AL)	St. Louis (NL)	4-0
1929	Philadelphia (AL)	Chicago (NL)	4-1
1930	Philadelphia (AL)	St. Louis (NL)	4-2
1931	St. Louis (NL)	Philadelphia (AL)	4-3
1932	New York (AL)	Chicago (NL)	4-0
1933	New York (NL)	Washington (AL)	4-1
1934	St. Louis (NL)	Detroit (AL)	4-3
1935	Detroit (AL)	Chicago (NL)	4-2
1936	New York (AL)	New York (NL)	4-2
1937	New York (AL)	New York (NL)	4-1
1938	New York (AL)	Chicago (NL)	4-0
1939	New York (AL)	Cincinnati (NL)	4-0
1940	Cincinnati (NL)	Detroit (AL)	4-3
1941	New York (AL)	Brooklyn (NL)	4-1
1942	St. Louis (NL)	New York (AL)	4-1
1943	New York (AL)	St. Louis (NL)	4-1
1944	St. Louis (NL)	St. Louis (AL)	4-2
1945	Detroit (AL)	Chicago (NL)	4-3
1946	St. Louis (NL)	Boston (AL)	4-3
1947	New York (AL)	Brooklyn (NL)	4-3
1948	Cleveland (AL)	Boston (NL)	4-2
1949	New York (AL)	Brooklyn (NL)	4-1
1950	New York (AL)	Philadelphia (NL)	4-0
1951	New York (AL)	New York (NL)	4-2
1952	New York (AL)	Brooklyn (NL)	4-3
1953	New York (AL)	Brooklyn (NL)	4-2
1954	New York (NL)	Cleveland (AL)	4-0
1955	Brooklyn (NL)	New York (AL)	4-3
1956	New York (AL)	Brooklyn (NL)	4-3
1957	Milwaukee (NL)	New York (AL)	4-3
1958	New York (AL)	Milwaukee (NL)	4-3
1959	Los Angeles (NL)	Chicago (AL)	4-2
1960	Pittsburgh (NL)	New York (AL)	4-3
1961	New York (AL)	Cincinnati (NL)	4-1
1962	New York (AL)	San Francisco (NL)	4-3
1963	Los Angeles (NL)	New York (AL)	4-0
1964	St. Louis (NL)	New York (AL)	4-3
1965	Los Angeles (NL)	Minnesota (AL)	4-3
1966	Baltimore (AL)	Los Angeles (NL)	4-0
1967	St. Louis (NL)	Boston (AL)	4-3
1968	Detroit (AL)	St. Louis (NL)	4-3
1969	New York (NL)	Baltimore (AL)	4-1
1970	Baltimore (AL)	Cincinnati (NL)	4-1

Commissioner's Trophy

Year	Winner	Loser	Result
1971	Pittsburgh (NL)	Baltimore (AL)	4-3
1972	Oakland (AL)	Cincinnati (NL)	4-3
1973	Oakland (AL)	New York (NL)	4-3
1974	Oakland (AL)	Los Angeles (NL)	4-1
1975	Cincinnati (NL)	Boston (AL)	4-3
1976	Cincinnati (NL)	New York (AL)	4-0
1977	New York (AL)	Los Angeles (NL)	4-2
1978	New York (AL)	Los Angeles (NL)	4-2
1979	Pittsburgh (NL)	Baltimore (AL)	4-3
1980	Philadelphia (NL)	Kansas City (AL)	4-2
1981	Los Angeles (NL)	New York (AL)	4-2
1982	St. Louis (NL)	Milwaukee (AL)	4-3
1983	Baltimore (AL)	Philadelphia (NL)	4-1
1984	Detroit (AL)	San Diego (NL)	4-1
1985	Kansas City (AL)	St. Louis (NL)	4-3
1986	New York (NL)	Boston (AL)	4-3
1987	Minnesota (AL)	St. Louis (NL)	4-3
1988	Los Angeles (NL)	Oakland (AL)	4-1
1989	Oakland (AL)	San Francisco (NL)	4-0
1990	Cincinnati (NL)	Oakland (AL)	4-0
1991	Minnesota (AL)	Atlanta (NL)	4-3
1992	Toronto (AL)	Atlanta (NL)	4-2
1993	Toronto (AL)	Philadelphia (NL)	4-2
1994	NO SERIES		
1995	Atlanta (NL)	Cleveland (AL)	4-2
1996	New York (AL)	Atlanta (NL)	4-2
1997	Florida (NL)	Cleveland (AL)	4-3
1998	New York (AL)	San Diego (NL)	4-0
1999	New York (AL)	Atlanta (NL)	4-0
2000	New York (AL)	New York (NL)	4-1
2001	Arizona (NL)	New York (AL)	4-3
2002	Anaheim (AL)	San Francisco (NL)	4-3
2003	Florida (NL)	New York (AL)	4-2
2004	Boston (AL)	St. Louis (NL)	4-0
2005	Chicago (AL)	Houston (NL)	4-0
2006	St. Louis (NL)	Detroit (AL)	4-1
2007	Boston (AL)	Colorado (NL)	4-0
2008	Philadelphia (NL)	Tampa Bay (AL)	4-1
2009	New York (AL)	Philadelphia (NL)	4-2
2010	San Francisco (NL)	Texas (AL)	4-1
2011	St. Louis (NL)	Texas (AL)	4-3
2012	San Francisco (NL)	Detroit (AL)	4-0
2013	Boston (AL)	St. Louis (NL)	4-2
2014	San Francisco (NL)	Kansas City (AL)	4-3
2015	Kansas City (AL)	New York (NL)	4-1
2016	Chicago (NL)	Cleveland (AL)	4-3
2017	Houston (AL)	Los Angeles (NL)	4-3
2018	Boston (AL)	Los Angeles (NL)	4-1
2019	Washington (NL)	Houston (AL)	4-3
2020	Los Angeles (NL)	Tampa Bay (AL)	4-2
2021	Atlanta (NL)	Houston (AL)	4-2
2022	Houston (AL)	Philadelphia (NL)	4-2
2023	Texas (AL)	Arizona (NL)	4-1

CATO CATALDO

WORLD SERIES BOX SCORES

GAME ONE *October 27, 2023*

TEXAS RANGERS 6, ARIZONA D-BACKS 5 (11)

	1	2	3	4	5	6	7	8	9	10	11	R	H	E
ARIZONA	0	0	3	1	1	0	0	0	0	0	0	5	8	0
TEXAS	2	0	1	0	0	0	0	0	2	0	1	6	9	0

ARIZONA	AB	R	H	RBI	BB	SO	LOB	AVG
Carroll, RF	5	1	1	2	0	1	1	.286
Marte, K, 2B	5	0	1	2	0	0	0	.345
Moreno, C	5	0	0	0	0	3	2	.250
Walker, C, 1B	4	0	0	0	1	3	1	.163
Pham, DH	5	1	1	1	0	2	2	.213
Gurriel Jr., LF	5	0	1	0	0	2	0	.245
Thomas, A, CF	5	1	2	0	0	1	1	.237
Longoria, 3B	4	1	1	0	0	2	1	.146
Rivera, E, 3B	0	0	0	0	0	0	0	.167
Perdomo, SS	3	1	1	0	0	0	1	.282
Gallen, P	0	0	0	0	0	0	0	.000
Thompson, R, P	0	0	0	0	0	0	0	.000
Mantiply, P	0	0	0	0	0	0	0	.000
Ginkel, P	0	0	0	0	0	0	0	.000
Sewald, P	0	0	0	0	0	0	0	.000
Nelson, K, P	0	0	0	0	0	0	0	.000
Castro, P	0	0	0	0	0	0	0	.000
TOTALS	**41**	**5**	**8**	**5**	**1**	**14**	**9**	**.195**

2B: Marte, K (6, Eovaldi). **3B:** Carroll (1, Eovaldi). **HR:** Pham (3, 4th inning off Eovaldi, 0 on, 0 out).**TB:** Carroll 3; Gurriel Jr.; Longoria; Marte, K 2; Perdomo; Pham 4; Thomas, A 2. **RBI:** Carroll 2 (8); Marte, K 2 (9); Pham (3). Runners left in scoring position, 2 out: Walker, C; Pham 2; Perdomo. **SAC:** Perdomo. **SB:** Marte, K (3, 2nd base off Eovaldi/Heim); Perdomo (2, 2nd base off Eovaldi/Heim); Walker, C (5, 2nd base off Dunning/Heim); Thomas, A (2, 2nd base off Bradford/Heim). **DP:** 2 (Longoria-Marte, K-Walker, C; Perdomo-Marte, K-Walker, C).

TEXAS	AB	R	H	RBI	BB	SO	LOB	AVG
Semien, 2B	6	0	1	0	0	2	2	.190
Seager, SS	4	3	1	2	2	1	2	.327
Carter, LF	6	1	2	1	0	2	0	.311
García, Ad, RF	4	1	3	2	1	0	0	.357
Garver, DH	3	0	0	1	2	1	2	.270
Heim, C	2	0	0	0	2	0	3	.235
a-Smith, J, PR	0	0	0	0	0	0	0	.000
Hedges, C	1	0	0	0	0	1	2	.000
Lowe, N, 1B	4	0	0	0	1	0	3	.208
Jung, 3B	5	0	2	0	0	1	3	.300
Taveras, CF	3	1	0	0	2	2	3	.227
Eovaldi, P	0	0	0	0	0	0	0	.000
Dunning, P	0	0	0	0	0	0	0	.000
Bradford, P	0	0	0	0	0	0	0	.000
Gray, Jn, P	0	0	0	0	0	0	0	.000
Smith, W, P	0	0	0	0	0	0	0	.000
Leclerc, P	0	0	0	0	0	0	0	.000
TOTALS	**38**	**6**	**9**	**6**	**10**	**10**	**20**	**.237**

a-Ran for Heim in the 8th. **2B:** Carter 2 (8, Gallen, Gallen). **HR:** Seager (4, 9th inning off Sewald, 1 on, 1 out); García, Ad (8, 11th inning off Castro, 0 on, 1 out). **TB:** Carter 4; García, Ad 6; Jung 2; Seager 4; Semien. **RBI:** Carter (6); García, Ad 2 (22); Garver (12); Seager 2 (8).2-out **RBI:** Garver. Runners left in scoring position, 2 out: Jung; Hedges; Seager; Heim 2; Taveras. **GIDP:** Garver; Jung. **SB:** García, Ad (2, 2nd base off Sewald/Moreno).

ARIZONA	IP	H	R	ER	BB	SO	HR	ERA
Gallen	5.0	4	3	3	4	5	0	5.27
Thompson, R (H, 5)	1.0	1	0	0	1	0	0	2.31
Mantiply (H, 1)	1.0	0	0	0	0	1	0	4.26
Ginkel (H, 6)	1.0	1	0	0	1	1	0	0.00
Sewald (BS, 1)	1.0	1	2	2	2	3	1	2.00
Nelson, K	1.1	1	0	0	2	0	0	2.70
Castro (L, 0-1)	0.0	1	1	1	0	0	1	7.20
TOTALS	**10.1**	**9**	**6**	**6**	**10**	**10**	**2**	**5.23**

TEXAS	IP	H	R	ER	BB	SO	HR	ERA
Eovaldi	4.2	6	5	5	1	8	1	3.52
Dunning	1.0	1	0	0	0	0	0	6.35
Bradford	1.0	0	0	0	0	0	0	1.35
Gray, Jn	1.2	1	0	0	0	4	0	3.38
Smith, W	0.2	0	0	0	0	0	0	6.75
Leclerc (W, 1-1)	2.0	0	0	0	0	2	0	3.65
TOTALS	**11.0**	**8**	**5**	**5**	**1**	**14**	**1**	**4.09**

Castro pitched to 1 batter in the 11th. **WP:** Ginkel. **IBB:** Garver (by Sewald). **HBP:** García, Ad (by Sewald). **Pitches-strikes:** Gallen 99-61; Thompson, R 17-10; Mantiply 15-11; Ginkel 28-18; Sewald 22-15; Nelson, K 24-11; Castro 5-2; Eovaldi 89-57; Dunning 14-10; Bradford 11-7; Gray, Jn 26-19; Smith, W 7-4; Leclerc 26-19. **Batters faced:** Gallen 22; Thompson, R 5; Mantiply 3; Ginkel 5; Sewald 7; Nelson, K 6; Castro 1; Eovaldi 22; Dunning 4; Bradford 3; Gray, Jn 6; Smith, W 2; Leclerc 6. **Inherited runners-scored:** Dunning 2-0; Bradford 1-0. **Umpires: HP:** D.J. Reyburn. **1B:** Alfonso Marquez. **2B:** David Rackley. **3B:** Brian Knight. **LF:** Vic Carapazza. **RF:** Bill Miller. **Official Scorer:** Steve Weller. **Weather:** 73 degrees, Roof Closed. **Wind:** 0 mph, None. **First pitch:** 7:07 PM. **T:** 4:02. **Att:** 42,472. **Venue:** Globe Life Field

GAME TWO *October 28, 2023*

ARIZONA D-BACKS 9, TEXAS RANGERS 1

	1	2	3	4	5	6	7	8	9	R	H	E
ARIZONA	0	0	0	2	0	0	2	3	2	9	16	0
TEXAS	0	0	0	0	1	0	0	0	0	1	4	0

ARIZONA	AB	R	H	RBI	BB	SO	LOB	AVG
Marte, K, 2B	5	0	1	2	0	0	3	.333
Carroll, RF	5	0	2	2	0	0	1	.296
Moreno, C	4	1	1	1	1	1	2	.250
Walker, C, 1B	5	0	1	0	0	0	2	.167
Pham, DH	4	2	4	0	0	0	0	.275
b-Peterson, PH-DH	1	1	0	0	0	0	1	.000
Gurriel Jr., LF	3	1	2	1	1	0	1	.268
Thomas, A, CF	5	1	2	0	0	1	4	.256
Longoria, 3B	2	1	1	1	0	0	0	.163
Smith, P, PH	0	0	0	0	0	0	0	.333
a-Rivera, E, PH-3B	1	1	1	2	1	0	0	.231
Perdomo, SS	2	1	1	0	1	0	1	.293
Kelly, M, P	0	0	0	0	0	0	0	.000
Saalfrank, P	0	0	0	0	0	0	0	.000
Frías, P	0	0	0	0	0	0	0	.000
TOTALS	**37**	**9**	**16**	**9**	**4**	**2**	**15**	**.308**

a-Walked for Smith, P in the 8th. **b-**Grounded into a forceout for Pham in the 9th. **2B:** Pham 2 (2, Montgomery, Montgomery); Thomas, A (1, Montgomery). **HR:** Moreno (4, 4th inning off Montgomery, 0 on, 1 out). **TB:** Carroll 2; Gurriel Jr. 2; Longoria; Marte, K; Moreno 4; Perdomo; Pham 6; Rivera, E; Thomas, A 3; Walker, C. **RBI:** Carroll 2 (10); Gurriel Jr. (7); Longoria (4); Marte, K 2 (11); Moreno (10); Rivera, E 2 (3).
2-out **RBI:** Gurriel Jr.; Rivera, E 2; Marte, K 2; Carroll 2. Runners left in scoring position, 2 out: Walker, C; Moreno; Marte, K; Carroll. SAC: Gurriel Jr.; Longoria; Perdomo. **GIDP:** Gurriel Jr. **SB:** Perdomo (3, 2nd base off Montgomery/Heim). **PO:** Pham (2nd base by Montgomery).

TEXAS	AB	R	H	RBI	BB	SO	LOB	AVG
Semien, 2B	4	0	1	0	0	2	0	.194
Seager, SS	4	0	0	0	0	1	1	.302
Carter, LF	3	0	1	0	0	2	0	.313
a-Grossman, PH	1	0	0	0	0	1	1	.105
García, Ad, RF	3	0	0	0	1	1	1	.339
Garver, DH	4	1	1	1	0	0	2	.268
Heim, C	3	0	0	0	0	1	0	.222
Lowe, N, 1B	3	0	0	0	0	1	0	.196
Jung, 3B	3	0	1	0	0	0	0	.302
Taveras, CF	3	0	0	0	0	1	1	.213
Montgomery, P	0	0	0	0	0	0	0	.000
Heaney, P	0	0	0	0	0	0	0	.000
Dunning, P	0	0	0	0	0	0	0	.000
Stratton, C, P	0	0	0	0	0	0	0	.000
Pérez, M, P	0	0	0	0	0	0	0	.000
TOTALS	**31**	**1**	**4**	**1**	**1**	**10**	**6**	**.188**

a-Struck out for Carter in the 9th. **HR:** Garver (3, 5th inning off Kelly, M, 0 on, 0 out). **TB:** Carter; Garver 4; Jung; Semien. **RBI:** Garver (13). Runners left in scoring position, **2 out:** Garver. **Outfield assists:** Carter (Rivera, E at 2nd base). **Pickoffs:** Montgomery (Pham at 2nd base). DP: (Semien-Seager-Lowe, N).

ARIZONA	IP	H	R	ER	BB	SO	HR	ERA
Kelly, M (W, 3-1)	7.0	3	1	1	0	9	1	2.25
Saalfrank	1.1	1	0	0	0	0	0	3.86
Frías	0.2	0	0	0	1	1	0	2.08
TOTALS	**9.0**	**4**	**1**	**1**	**1**	**10**	**1**	**3.26**

TEXAS	IP	H	R	ER	BB	SO	HR	ERA
Montgomery (L, 3-1)	6.0	9	4	4	1	0	1	2.90

Heaney	0.2	1	0	0	0	0	0	6.00
Dunning	0.1	0	0	0	1	0	0	6.00
Stratton, C	0.2	1	1	1	0	1	0	8.10
Pérez, M	1.1	5	4	4	2	1	0	9.64
TOTALS	**9.0**	**16**	**9**	**9**	**4**	**2**	**1**	**6.30**

Montgomery pitched to 2 batters in the 7th. **IBB:** Gurriel Jr. (by Montgomery). **Pitches-strikes:** Kelly, M 89-63; Saalfrank 17-11; Frías 14-7; Montgomery 75-50; Heaney 6-5; Dunning 9-4; Stratton, C 19-13; Pérez, M 39-23. **Batters faced:** Kelly, M 24; Saalfrank 5; Frías 3; Montgomery 26; Heaney 3; Dunning 2; Stratton, C 3; Pérez, M 10. **Inherited runners-scored:** Frías 1-0; Heaney 1-1; Dunning 1-0; Pérez, M 1-1. **Umpires: HP:** Quinn Wolcott. **1B:** David Rackley. **2B:** Brian Knight. **3B:** Vic Carapazza. **LF:** Bill Miller. **RF:** D.J. Reyburn. **Official Scorer:** Will Rudd. **Weather:** 74 degrees, Roof Closed. **Wind:** 0 mph, None. **First pitch:** 7:05 PM. **T:** 2:59. **Att:** 42,500. **Venue:** Globe Life Field

GAME 3 *October 30, 2023*

TEXAS RANGERS 3, ARIZONA D-BACKS 1

	1	2	3	4	5	6	7	8	9	R	H	E
TEXAS	0	0	3	0	0	0	0	0	0	3	5	0
ARIZONA	0	0	0	0	0	0	0	1	0	1	6	0

TEXAS	**AB**	**R**	**H**	**RBI**	**BB**	**SO**	**LOB**	**AVG**
Semien, 2B	4	1	1	1	0	0	1	.197
Seager, SS	4	1	1	2	0	1	0	.298
García, Ad, RF	3	0	0	0	1	1	0	.323
Jankowski, RF	0	0	0	0	0	0	0	.500
Carter, LF	3	0	2	0	1	0	0	.333
Garver, DH	4	0	0	0	0	1	4	.244
Heim, C	4	0	0	0	0	1	3	.207
Lowe, N, 1B	3	1	1	0	1	0	1	.203
Jung, 3B	3	0	0	0	0	2	2	.286
Taveras, CF	3	0	0	0	0	0	2	.200
Scherzer, P	0	0	0	0	0	0	0	.000
Gray, Jn, P	0	0	0	0	0	0	0	.000
Sborz, P	0	0	0	0	0	0	0	.000
Chapman, P	0	0	0	0	0	0	0	.000
Leclerc, P	0	0	0	0	0	0	0	.000
TOTALS	**31**	**3**	**5**	**3**	**3**	**6**	**13**	**.180**

2B: Lowe, N (2, Pfaadt). **HR:** Seager (5, 3rd inning off Pfaadt, 1 on, 2 out). **TB:** Carter 2; Lowe, N 2; Seager 4; Semien. **RBI:** Seager 2 (10); Semien (3).2 - o u t **R B I :** Semien; Seager 2. Runners left in scoring position, 2 out: Heim. **GIDP:** Garver. **Outfield assists:** Garcia, Ad (Walker, C at home). **DP:** 2 (Jung-Semien-Lowe, N; Seager-Semien-Lowe, N).

ARIZONA	**AB**	**R**	**H**	**RBI**	**BB**	**SO**	**LOB**	**AVG**
Carroll, RF	3	0	0	0	1	2	1	.281
Marte, K, 2B	3	0	1	0	1	0	2	.333
Moreno, C	4	0	0	0	0	1	2	.232
Walker, C, 1B	4	0	1	0	0	1	0	.173
Pham, DH	4	0	2	0	0	1	0	.291
Gurriel Jr., LF	3	0	0	0	0	1	2	.254
Thomas, A, CF	3	0	0	0	0	1	2	.239
Longoria, 3B	2	0	0	0	0	1	0	.156
Smith, P, PH	0	0	0	0	0	0	0	.333
a-Rivera, E, PH-3B	1	1	1	0	0	0	0	.286
Perdomo, SS	3	0	1	1	0	1	0	.295
Pfaadt, P	0	0	0	0	0	0	0	.000
Castro, P	0	0	0	0	0	0	0	.000
Nelson, K, P	0	0	0	0	0	0	0	.000
Frías, P	0	0	0	0	0	0	0	.000
Saalfrank, P	0	0	0	0	0	0	0	.000
TOTALS	**30**	**1**	**6**	**1**	**2**	**9**	**9**	**.278**

a-Doubled for Smith, P in the 8th. **2B:** Walker, C (4, Scherzer); Pham (3, Sborz); Rivera, E (1, Chapman). **TB:** Marte, K; Perdomo; Pham 3; Rivera, E 2; Walker, C 2. **RBI:** Perdomo (4). Runners left in scoring position, **2 out:** Thomas, A 2; Marte, K. **GIDP:** Marte, K; Moreno. **DP:** (Pfaadt-Marte, K-Walker, C).

TEXAS	**IP**	**H**	**R**	**ER**	**BB**	**SO**	**HR**	**ERA**
Scherzer	3.0	2	0	0	2	1	0	6.52
Gray, Jn (W, 1-0)	3.0	1	0	0	0	3	0	1.59
Sborz (H, 5)	1.0	1	0	0	0	2	0	0.93
Chapman (H, 5)	1.0	2	1	1	0	1	0	2.45
Leclerc (S, 4)	1.0	0	0	0	0	2	0	3.38
TOTALS	**9.0**	**6**	**1**	**1**	**2**	**9**	**0**	**4.66**

ARIZONA	**IP**	**H**	**R**	**ER**	**BB**	**SO**	**HR**	**ERA**
Pfaadt (L, 0-1)	5.1	4	3	3	2	4	1	3.27
Castro	0.2	1	0	0	0	0	0	6.35
Nelson, K	1.0	0	0	0	0	0	0	2.08
Frías	1.2	0	0	0	1	2	0	1.50
Saalfrank	0.1	0	0	0	0	0	0	3.60
TOTALS	**9.0**	**5**	**3**	**3**	**3**	**6**	**1**	**3.18**

WP: Scherzer. **Pitches-strikes:** Scherzer 36-21; Gray, Jn 30-25; Sborz 16-11; Chapman 16-10; Leclerc 16-10; Pfaadt 87-55; Castro 11-7; Nelson, K 12-6; Frías 20-11; Saalfrank 4-3. **Batters faced:** Scherzer 11; Gray, Jn 10; Sborz 4; Chapman 4; Leclerc 3; Pfaadt 21; Castro 3; Nelson, K 3; Frías 6; Saalfrank 1. **Inherited runners-scored:** Castro 1-0; Saalfrank 1-0. **Umpires: HP:** Alfonso Marquez. **1B:** Brian Knight. **2B:** Vic Carapazza. **3B:** Bill Miller. **LF:** D.J. Reyburn. **RF:** Quinn Wolcott. **Official Scorer:** Jason Johnson. **Weather:** 78 degrees, Clear. **Wind:** 1 mph, Varies. **First pitch:** 5:03 PM. **T:** 2:51. **Att:** 48,517. **Venue:** Chase Field

GAME 4 *October 31, 2023*

TEXAS RANGERS 11, ARIZONA D-BACKS 7

	1	2	3	4	5	6	7	8	9	R	H	E
TEXAS	0	5	5	0	0	0	0	1	0	11	11	0
ARIZONA	0	0	0	1	0	0	0	4	2	7	12	1

TEXAS	**AB**	**R**	**H**	**RBI**	**BB**	**SO**	**LOB**	**AVG**
Semien, 2B	5	2	2	5	0	1	0	.211
Seager, SS	5	1	2	2	0	2	0	.306
a-Smith, J, PR-SS	0	0	0	0	0	0	0	.000
Garver, DH	4	0	0	0	1	3	1	.224
Carter, LF	4	0	0	0	0	0	1	.309
Jung, 3B	5	2	3	0	0	0	2	.311
Lowe, N, 1B	4	1	1	0	0	1	2	.206
Heim, C	4	2	1	1	0	1	3	.210
Taveras, CF	3	1	0	0	1	1	3	.189
Jankowski, RF	4	2	2	2	0	0	0	.500
Heaney, P	0	0	0	0	0	0	0	.000
Dunning, P	0	0	0	0	0	0	0	.000
Bradford, P	0	0	0	0	0	0	0	.000
Burke, P	0	0	0	0	0	0	0	.000
Stratton, C, P	0	0	0	0	0	0	0	.000
Smith, W, P	0	0	0	0	0	0	0	.000
Leclerc, P	0	0	0	0	0	0	0	.000
TOTALS	**38**	**11**	**11**	**10**	**2**	**9**	**12**	**.210**

a-Ran for Seager in the 9th. **2B:** Jung (4, Mantiply); Jankowski (1, Frías); Seager (6, Nelson, R). **3B:** Semien (1, Castro). **HR:** Seager (6, 2nd inning off Nelson, K, 1 on, 2 out); Semien (1, 3rd inning off Frías, 2 on, 2 out); Heim (3, 8th inning off Nelson, R, 0 on, 0 out). **TB:** Heim 4; Jankowski 3; Jung 4; Lowe, N; Seager 6; Semien 7. **RBI:** Heim (7); Jankowski 2 (2); Seager 2 (12); Semien 5 (8). 2-out **RBI:** Jankowski 2; Semien 5; Seager 2. **GIDP:** Jung. **DP:** (Seager-Semien-Lowe, N).

ARIZONA	**AB**	**R**	**H**	**RBI**	**BB**	**SO**	**LOB**	**AVG**
Marte, K, 2B	5	0	2	0	0	1	3	.338
Carroll, RF	5	1	1	0	0	2	5	.274
Moreno, C	4	2	2	2	1	1	1	.250
Walker, C, 1B	5	1	3	0	0	0	1	.211
Pham, DH	3	0	1	1	0	1	2	.293
Gurriel Jr., LF	3	1	2	4	0	0	2	.274
Thomas, A, CF	4	0	0	0	0	1	2	.220
Rivera, E, 3B	3	0	0	0	0	0	0	.235
Smith, P, PH	0	0	0	0	0	0	0	.333
a-Lawlar, PH	0	1	0	0	1	0	0	.000
Perdomo, SS	3	1	1	0	1	0	0	.298
Mantiply, P	0	0	0	0	0	0	0	.000
Castro, P	0	0	0	0	0	0	0	.000
Nelson, K, P	0	0	0	0	0	0	0	.000
Frías, P	0	0	0	0	0	0	0	.000
Nelson, R, P	0	0	0	0	0	0	0	.000
Saalfrank, P	0	0	0	0	0	0	0	.000
TOTALS	**35**	**7**	**12**	**7**	**3**	**6**	**16**	**.294**

a-Walked for Smith, P in the 9th. **2B:** Marte, K (7, Heaney); Walker, C (5, Heaney). **HR:** Gurriel Jr. (3, 8th inning off Stratton, C, 2 on, 2 out). **TB:** Carroll; Gurriel Jr. 5; Marte, K 3; Moreno 2; Perdomo; Pham; Walker, C 4. **RBI:** Gurriel Jr. 4 (11); Moreno 2 (12); Pham (4). 2-out **RBI:** Gurriel Jr. 3; Moreno 2. **SF:** Gurriel Jr.; Pham. GIDP: Gurriel Jr. **CS:** Marte, K (1, 2nd base by Heaney/Heim). E: Walker, C (1, fielding). **DP:** (Perdomo-Marte, K-Walker, C).

TEXAS	**IP**	**H**	**R**	**ER**	**BB**	**SO**	**HR**	**ERA**
Heaney (W, 1-0)	5.0	4	1	1	2	3	0	4.09
Dunning	1.0	2	0	0	0	0	0	5.14
Bradford	1.0	0	0	0	0	1	0	1.17
Burke	0.1	3	3	3	0	0	0	67.50

TEXAS	IP	H	R	ER	BB	SO	HR	ERA
Stratton, C	0.2	1	1	1	0	0	1	9.00
Smith, W	0.2	1	2	2	1	2	0	10.80
Leclerc	0.1	1	0	0	0	0	0	3.29
TOTALS	**9.0**	**12**	**7**	**7**	**3**	**6**	**1**	**5.21**

ARIZONA	IP	H	R	ER	BB	SO	HR	ERA
Mantiply (L, 2-1)	1.1	1	1	1	1	1	0	4.70
Castro	0.1	2	3	3	1	0	0	10.50
Nelson, K	0.2	3	3	1	0	0	1	3.60
Frías	0.2	2	3	0	0	2	1	1.35
Nelson, R	5.1	3	1	1	0	6	1	5.68
Saalfrank	0.2	0	0	0	0	0	0	3.18
TOTALS	**9.0**	**11**	**11**	**6**	**2**	**9**	**3**	**3.86**

WP: Castro. **HBP:** Carter (by Saalfrank). **Pitches-strikes:** Heaney 80-47; Dunning 16-10; Bradford 13-10; Burke 14-8; Stratton, C 15-12; Smith, W 18-13; Leclerc 10-6; Mantiply 28-19; Castro 18-10; Nelson, K 19-9; Frías 17-12; Nelson, R 68-45; Saalfrank 2-1. **Batters faced:** Heaney 20; Dunning 4; Bradford 3; Burke 4; Stratton, C 3; Smith, W 4; Leclerc 2; Mantiply 6; Castro 4; Nelson, K 5; Frías 5; Nelson, R 19; Saalfrank 2. **Inherited runners-scored:** Stratton, C 3-3; Leclerc 2-2; Castro 1-1; Nelson, K 1-1; Frias 2-2; Saalfrank 1-0. **Umpires:** HP: David Rackley. **1B:** Vic Carapazza. **2B:** Bill Miller. **3B:** D.J. Reyburn. **LF:** Quinn Wolcott. **RF:** Alfonso Marquez. **Official Scorer:** Patrick Lagreid. **Weather:** 78 degrees, Clear. **Wind:** 5 mph, L To R. **First pitch:** 5:04 PM. **T:** 3:18. **Att:** 48,388. **Venue:** Chase Field

GAME 5 *November 1, 2023*

TEXAS RANGERS 5, ARIZONA D-BACKS 0

	1	2	3	4	5	6	7	8	9	R	H	E
TEXAS	0	0	0	0	0	0	1	0	4	5	9	0
ARIZONA	0	0	0	0	0	0	0	0	0	0	5	1

TEXAS	AB	R	H	RBI	BB	SO	LOB	AVG
Semien, 2B	5	1	2	2	0	1	0	.224
Seager, SS	4	1	2	0	1	0	0	.318
Carter, LF	5	0	1	0	0	4	4	.300
Garver, DH	4	0	1	1	0	1	3	.226
Jung, 3B	4	1	1	0	0	1	2	.308
Lowe, N, 1B	3	1	1	0	1	0	2	.212
Heim, C	4	1	1	1	0	1	3	.212
Taveras, CF	4	0	0	0	0	1	1	.175
Jankowski, RF	3	0	0	0	1	0	1	.333
Eovaldi, P	0	0	0	0	0	0	0	.000
Chapman, P	0	0	0	0	0	0	0	.000
Sborz, P	0	0	0	0	0	0	0	.000
TOTALS	**36**	**5**	**9**	**4**	**3**	**9**	**16**	**.218**

2B: Carter (9, Gallen). **HR:** Semien (2, 9th inning off Sewald, 1 on, 2 out). **TB:** Carter 2; Garver; Heim; Jung; Lowe, N; Seager 2; Semien 5. **RBI:** Garver (14); Heim (8); Semien 2 (10). **2-out RBI:** Semien 2. Runners left in scoring position, **2 out:** Garver 2; Heim.

ARIZONA	AB	R	H	RBI	BB	SO	LOB	AVG
Carroll, RF	4	0	1	0	1	0	0	.273
Marte, K, 2B	2	0	0	0	3	1	1	.329
Moreno, C	3	0	0	0	0	2	3	.238
Walker, C, 1B	3	0	1	0	1	1	3	.217
Pham, DH	3	0	0	0	1	1	4	.279
Gurriel Jr., LF	4	0	1	0	0	0	3	.273
Thomas, A, CF	4	0	1	0	0	0	1	.222
Longoria, 3B	3	0	1	0	0	1	1	.167
a-Smith, P, PH	1	0	0	0	0	1	1	.300
Rivera, E, 3B	0	0	0	0	0	0	0	.235
Perdomo, SS	4	0	0	0	0	3	2	.275
Gallen, P	0	0	0	0	0	0	0	.000
Ginkel, P	0	0	0	0	0	0	0	.000
Sewald, P	0	0	0	0	0	0	0	.000
TOTALS	**31**	**0**	**5**	**0**	**6**	**10**	**19**	**.270**

a-Struck out for Longoria in the 8th. **2B:** Longoria (3, Eovaldi). **TB:** Carroll; Gurriel Jr.; Longoria 2; Thomas, A; Walker, C. Runners left in scoring position, 2 out: Pham 3; Gurriel Jr. 2; Perdomo 2. SAC: Moreno. **SB:** Carroll (5, 2nd base off Eovaldi/Heim); Walker, C (6, 2nd base off Eovaldi/Heim). **E:** Thomas, A (1, fielding).

TEXAS	IP	H	R	ER	BB	SO	HR	ERA
Eovaldi (W, 5-0)	6.0	4	0	0	5	5	0	2.95
Chapman (H, 6)	0.2	0	0	0	1	1	0	2.25
Sborz (S, 1)	2.1	1	0	0	0	4	0	0.75
TOTALS	**9.0**	**5**	**0**	**0**	**6**	**10**	**0**	**4.21**

ARIZONA	IP	H	R	ER	BB	SO	HR	ERA
Gallen (L, 2-3)	6.1	3	1	1	1	6	0	4.54
Ginkel	1.2	1	0	0	2	1	0	0.00
Sewald	1.0	5	4	4	0	2	1	5.40
TOTALS	**9.0**	**9**	**5**	**5**	**3**	**9**	**1**	**4.08**

Pitches-strikes: Eovaldi 97-60; Chapman 10-4; Sborz 31-20; Gallen 83-57; Ginkel 32-15; Sewald 20-14. **Batters faced:** Eovaldi 27; Chapman 3; Sborz 8; Gallen 23; Ginkel 8; Sewald 8. **Inherited runners-scored:** Sborz 1-0; Ginkel 2-0 **Umpires: HP:** Brian Knight. **1B:** Bill Miller. **2B:** D.J. Reyburn. **3B:** Quinn Wolcott. **LF:** Alfonso Marquez. **RF:** David Rackley. **Official Scorer:** Jason Johnson. **Weather:** 79 degrees, **Clear Wind:** 1 mph, Varies. **First pitch:** 5:06 PM. **T:** 2:54. **Att:** 48,511. **Venue:** Chase Field

AMERICAN LEAGUE WILD CARD

TEXAS RANGERS VS. TAMPA BAY RAYS

TEXAS	AVG	G	AB	R	H	2B	3B	HR	RBI	BB	SO	SB
Evan Carter	.750	2	4	2	3	2	0	1	2	3	1	1
Corey Seager	.625	2	8	2	5	3	0	0	2	2	2	0
Josh Jung	.375	2	8	2	3	2	1	0	2	0	3	0
Leody Taveras	.333	2	9	1	3	0	0	0	0	0	3	2
Jonah Heim	.250	2	8	0	2	0	0	0	0	1	1	0
Adolis García	.200	2	10	1	2	0	0	1	1	0	3	0
Nathaniel Lowe	.200	2	10	1	2	0	0	0	1	0	3	0
Robbie Grossman	.111	2	9	0	1	0	0	0	0	1	4	0
Marcus Semien	.111	2	9	2	1	1	0	0	1	1	1	0
Totals	**.293**	**2**	**75**	**11**	**22**	**8**	**1**	**2**	**9**	**8**	**21**	**3**

TEXAS	W	L	ERA	G	GS	SV	IP	H	R	ER	BB	SO
Josh Sborz	0	0	0.00	1	0	0	1.1	0	0	0	0	1
Jordan Montgomery	1	0	0.00	1	1	0	7	6	0	0	0	5
José Leclerc	0	0	0.00	2	0	0	2	2	0	0	1	3
Aroldis Chapman	0	0	0.00	1	0	0	1	0	0	0	0	1
Nathan Eovaldi	1	0	1.35	1	1	0	6.2	6	1	1	0	8
TOTALS	**2**	**0**	**0.50**	**2**	**2**	**0**	**18**	**14**	**1**	**1**	**1**	**18**

TAMPA BAY	AVG	G	AB	R	H	2B	3B	HR	RBI	BB	SO	SB
Randy Arozarena	.375	2	8	0	3	1	0	0	0	0	2	0
Isaac Paredes	.375	2	8	0	3	1	0	0	0	0	2	0
Curtis Mead	.333	2	6	0	2	0	0	0	1	0	2	0
Taylor Walls	.333	2	6	0	2	0	0	0	0	0	1	0
Josh Lowe	.250	2	4	1	1	0	0	0	0	1	0	0
Manuel Margot	.167	2	6	0	1	0	0	0	0	0	2	0
Yandy Díaz	.125	2	8	0	1	0	0	0	0	0	1	0
Harold Ramírez	.125	2	8	0	1	0	0	0	0	0	2	0
Jonathan Aranda	.000	1	1	0	0	0	0	0	0	0	1	0
Junior Caminero	.000	2	2	0	0	0	0	0	0	0	1	0
René Pinto	.000	2	5	0	0	0	0	0	0	0	4	0
Jose Siri	.000	1	3	0	0	0	0	0	0	0	0	0
TOTALS	**.215**	**2**	**65**	**1**	**14**	**2**	**0**	**0**	**1**	**1**	**18**	**0**

TAMPA BAY	W	L	ERA	G	GS	SV	IP	H	R	ER	BB	SO
Zack Littell	0	0	0.00	1	0	0	2	0	0	0	0	4
Andrew Kittredge	0	0	0.00	1	0	0	1	1	0	0	0	1
Jake Diekman	0	0	0.00	1	0	0	1	1	0	0	1	2
Chris Devenski	0	0	0.00	1	0	0	2	1	0	0	0	0
Shawn Armstrong	0	0	0.00	1	0	0	1	1	0	0	0	1
Tyler Glasnow	0	1	5.40	1	1	0	5	6	4	3	5	8
Zach Eflin	0	1	9.00	1	1	0	5	9	5	5	2	3

	W	L	ERA	G	GS	SV	IP	H	R	ER	BB	SO
Colin Poche	0	0	18.00	1	0	0	1	3	2	2	0	2
TOTALS	**0**	**2**	**5.00**	**2**	**2**	**0**	**18**	**22**	**11**	**10**	**8**	**21**

SCORE BY INNINGS

TEXAS	**0**	**1**	**0**	**4**	**2**	**4**	**0**	**0**	**0**	**11**
TAMPA BAY	**0**	**0**	**0**	**0**	**0**	**0**	**1**	**0**	**0**	**1**

TORONTO BLUE JAYS VS. MINNESOTA TWINS

TORONTO	AVG	G	AB	R	H	2B	3B	HR	RBI	BB	SO	SB
Santiago Espinal	1.000	1	2	0	2	0	0	0	0	0	0	0
Bo Bichette	.500	2	8	1	4	0	0	0	0	0	2	0
Kevin Kiermaier	.400	2	5	0	2	0	0	0	1	1	2	0
Alejandro Kirk	.333	2	6	0	2	0	0	0	0	1	1	0
George Springer	.222	2	9	0	2	0	0	0	0	0	0	0
Matt Chapman	.143	2	7	0	1	0	0	0	0	1	3	0
Vladimir Guerrero Jr.	.143	2	7	0	1	1	0	0	0	1	0	0
Cavan Biggio	.125	2	8	0	1	0	0	0	0	0	3	0
Brandon Belt	.000	2	8	0	0	0	0	0	0	0	5	0
Whit Merrifield	.000	2	1	0	0	0	0	0	0	1	0	0
Daulton Varsho	.000	2	5	0	0	0	0	0	0	0	3	0
Totals	**.227**	**2**	**66**	**1**	**15**	**1**	**0**	**0**	**1**	**5**	**19**	**0**

TORONTO	W	L	ERA	G	GS	SV	IP	H	R	ER	BB	SO
Erik Swanson	0	0	0.00	2	0	0	1.1	0	0	0	3	2
Jordan Romano	0	0	0.00	1	0	0	1.1	1	0	0	0	1
Tim Mayza	0	0	0.00	1	0	0	0.1	1	0	0	0	0
Jordan Hicks	0	0	0.00	1	0	0	1	1	0	0	2	2
Chad Green	0	0	0.00	1	0	0	1.1	0	0	0	0	1
Yimi García	0	0	0.00	1	0	0	1.1	0	0	0	1	3
Génesis Cabrera	0	0	0.00	1	0	0	0.2	0	0	0	0	2
José Berríos	0	1	3.00	1	1	0	3	3	1	1	1	5
Yusei Kikuchi	0	0	5.40	1	0	0	1.2	3	1	1	1	0
Kevin Gausman	0	1	6.75	1	1	0	4	3	3	3	3	5
TOTALS	**0**	**2**	**2.81**	**2**	**2**	**0**	**16**	**12**	**5**	**5**	**11**	**21**

MINNESOTA	AVG	G	AB	R	H	2B	3B	HR	RBI	BB	SO	SB
Carlos Correa	.429	2	7	0	3	0	0	0	1	0	1	0
Royce Lewis	.333	2	6	3	2	0	0	2	3	2	1	0
Jorge Polanco	.286	2	7	0	2	0	0	0	0	1	3	1
Willi Castro	.250	2	4	0	1	0	0	0	0	0	2	0
Max Kepler	.250	2	8	1	2	0	0	0	0	0	3	0
Edouard Julien	.167	2	6	1	1	0	0	0	0	1	2	0
Michael A. Taylor	.167	2	6	0	1	0	0	0	0	0	4	0
Kyle Farmer	.000	2	1	0	0	0	0	0	0	0	1	0
Ryan Jeffers	.000	2	6	0	0	0	0	0	0	2	2	0
Alex Kirilloff	.000	2	2	0	0	0	0	0	0	1	1	0
Donovan Solano	.000	2	2	0	0	0	0	0	0	3	0	0
Matt Wallner	.000	2	3	0	0	0	0	0	0	1	1	0
TOTALS	**.207**	**2**	**58**	**5**	**12**	**0**	**0**	**2**	**4**	**11**	**21**	**1**

MINNESOTA	W	L	ERA	G	GS	SV	IP	H	R	ER	BB	SO
Louie Varland	0	0	0.00	2	0	0	0.2	2	0	0	0	1
Caleb Thielbar	0	0	0.00	2	0	0	1.2	1	0	0	0	0
Brock Stewart	0	0	0.00	1	0	0	1	0	0	0	0	2
Griffin Jax	0	0	0.00	2	0	0	2	1	0	0	0	2
Sonny Gray	1	0	0.00	1	1	0	5	5	0	0	2	6
Jhoan Duran	0	0	0.00	2	0	2	2	1	0	0	1	5
Pablo López	1	0	1.59	1	1	0	5.2	5	1	1	2	3
TOTALS	**2**	**0**	**0.50**	**2**	**2**	**2**	**18**	**15**	**1**	**1**	**5**	**19**

SCORE BY INNINGS

MINNESOTA	**2**	**0**	**1**	**2**	**0**	**0**	**0**	**0**	**0**	**5**
TORONTO	**0**	**0**	**0**	**0**	**0**	**1**	**0**	**0**	**0**	**1**

AMERICAN LEAGUE DIVISION SERIES

MINNESOTA TWINS VS. HOUSTON ASTROS

MINNESOTA	AVG	G	AB	R	H	2B	3B	HR	RBI	BB	SO	SB
Carlos Correa	.400	4	15	1	6	3	0	0	3	1	4	0
Edouard Julien	.364	4	11	1	4	2	0	1	2	4	6	0
Kyle Farmer	.333	1	3	1	1	0	0	1	2	0	1	0
Max Kepler	.200	4	15	0	3	2	0	0	0	1	7	0
Royce Lewis	.188	4	16	3	3	0	0	2	2	2	7	0
Willi Castro	.182	4	11	1	2	0	0	0	1	2	4	0
Ryan Jeffers	.154	4	13	1	2	0	0	0	0	0	6	0
Jorge Polanco	.143	4	14	2	2	0	0	1	3	3	5	0
Michael A. Taylor	.143	3	7	1	1	0	0	0	0	0	1	0
Donovan Solano	.125	3	8	1	1	0	0	0	0	0	4	0
Byron Buxton	.000	1	1	0	0	0	0	0	0	0	0	0
Alex Kirilloff	.000	3	7	0	0	0	0	0	0	1	3	0
Matt Wallner	.000	3	5	1	0	0	0	0	0	2	4	0
TOTALS	**.198**	**4**	**126**	**13**	**25**	**7**	**0**	**5**	**13**	**16**	**52**	**0**

MINNESOTA	W	L	ERA	G	GS	SV	IP	H	R	ER	BB	SO
Emilio Pagán	0	0	0.00	2	0	0	2	0	0	0	1	1
Chris Paddack	0	0	0.00	2	0	0	3.2	1	0	0	0	6
Pablo López	1	0	0.00	1	1	0	7	6	0	0	1	7
Griffin Jax	0	0	0.00	2	0	0	1.2	0	0	0	0	3
Jhoan Duran	0	0	0.00	2	0	0	3	1	0	0	0	1
Joe Ryan	0	0	4.50	1	1	0	2	2	1	1	0	1
Kenta Maeda	0	0	6.75	2	0	0	4	6	3	3	3	4
Brock Stewart	0	0	9.00	2	0	0	2	1	2	2	1	2
Sonny Gray	0	1	9.00	1	1	0	4	8	5	4	1	6
Bailey Ober	0	1	12.46	2	1	0	4.1	8	6	6	1	4
Caleb Thielbar	0	1	20.25	2	0	0	1.1	3	3	3	1	2
TOTALS	**1**	**3**	**4.89**	**4**	**4**	**0**	**35**	**36**	**20**	**19**	**9**	**37**

HOUSTON	AVG	G	AB	R	H	2B	3B	HR	RBI	BB	SO	SB
Yordan Alvarez	.438	4	16	7	7	2	0	4	6	1	5	0
Mauricio Dubón	.400	3	5	0	2	0	0	0	0	0	1	0
Chas McCormick	.364	4	11	0	4	0	0	0	1	0	3	0
José Abreu	.313	4	16	3	5	0	0	3	8	1	2	0
Michael Brantley	.273	3	11	1	3	0	0	1	1	1	3	1
Jeremy Peña	.267	4	15	1	4	1	0	0	0	1	1	0
Jose Altuve	.235	4	17	2	4	0	0	1	1	0	2	0
Alex Bregman	.200	4	15	4	3	0	0	1	2	1	6	0
Martín Maldonado	.167	4	12	0	2	0	0	0	0	1	4	0
Kyle Tucker	.143	4	14	2	2	1	0	0	1	3	6	0
Yainer Diaz	.000	2	6	0	0	0	0	0	0	0	4	0
Totals	**.261**	**4**	**138**	**20**	**36**	**4**	**0**	**10**	**20**	**9**	**37**	**1**

HOUSTON	W	L	ERA	G	GS	SV	IP	H	R	ER	BB	SO
Justin Verlander	1	0	0.00	1	1	0	6	4	0	0	3	6
Ryan Pressly	0	0	0.00	2	0	2	2	0	0	0	0	5
Rafael Montero	0	0	0.00	2	0	0	2.2	1	0	0	1	5
Phil Maton	0	0	0.00	2	0	0	1.2	0	0	0	1	2
Cristian Javier	1	0	0.00	1	1	0	5	1	0	0	5	9
Bryan Abreu	0	0	0.00	3	0	0	3.1	2	0	0	0	7
José Urquidy	1	0	3.18	1	1	0	5.2	3	2	2	1	6
Hunter Brown	0	0	4.50	2	0	0	2	2	1	1	1	2
Ryne Stanek	0	0	6.75	1	0	0	1.1	2	1	1	0	0
Framber Valdez	0	1	10.38	1	1	0	4.1	7	5	5	3	5
Hector Neris	0	0	18.00	2	0	0	2	3	4	4	1	5
Totals	**3**	**1**	**3.25**	**4**	**4**	**2**	**36.0**	**25**	**13**	**13**	**16**	**52**

SCORE BY INNING

MINNESOTA	**2**	**2**	**0**	**0**	**2**	**2**	**5**	**0**	**0**	**13**
HOUSTON	**5**	**1**	**2**	**2**	**3**	**1**	**1**	**2**	**3**	**20**

TEXAS RANGERS V. BALTIMORE ORIOLES

TEXAS	AVG	G	AB	R	H	2B	3B	HR	RBI	BB	SO	SB
Josh Jung	.417	3	12	4	5	1	0	1	1	1	2	0
Mitch Garver	.400	2	10	3	4	1	0	1	7	0	1	0
Adolis García	.357	3	14	2	5	1	0	1	4	0	7	0
Corey Seager	.333	3	6	4	2	0	0	1	1	9	0	0
Evan Carter	.300	3	10	1	3	1	0	0	1	3	2	0
Jonah Heim	.231	3	13	0	3	0	0	0	2	0	2	0
Marcus Semien	.214	3	14	2	3	1	0	0	1	1	3	0
Robbie Grossman	.200	1	5	0	1	1	0	0	0	0	4	0
Leody Taveras	.200	3	10	3	2	1	0	0	2	3	1	0
Nathaniel Lowe	.167	3	12	2	2	0	0	1	1	1	6	0
Totals	**.283**	**3**	**106**	**21**	**30**	**7**	**0**	**5**	**20**	**18**	**28**	**0**

TEXAS	W	L	ERA	G	GS	SV	IP	H	R	ER	BB	SO
Will Smith	0	0	0.00	1	0	0	0.1	0	0	0	0	1
Josh Sborz	0	0	0.00	2	0	0	1.1	0	0	0	1	2
Aroldis Chapman	0	0	0.00	2	0	0	1.2	1	0	0	4	2
Cody Bradford	1	0	0.00	1	0	0	3.2	3	0	0	0	4
Nathan Eovaldi	1	0	1.29	1	1	0	7	5	1	1	0	7

	W	L	ERA	G	GS	SV	IP	H	R	ER	BB	SO
Andrew Heaney	0	0	2.45	1	1	0	3.2	2	1	1	1	1
José Leclerc	0	0	3.00	3	0	1	3	2	1	1	0	3
Dane Dunning	1	0	4.50	1	0	0	2	2	1	1	1	1
Jordan Montgomery	0	0	9.00	1	1	0	4	9	5	4	1	2
Brock Burke	0	0	54.00	1	0	0	0.1	1	2	2	1	0
TOTALS	**3**	**0**	**3.33**	**3**	**3**	**1**	**27.0**	**25**	**11**	**10**	**9**	**23**

BALTIMORE	AVG	G	AB	R	H	2B	3B	HR	RBI	BB	SO	SB
Jorge Mateo	.800	3	5	1	4	2	0	0	1	0	1	0
Gunnar Henderson	.500	3	12	3	6	0	0	1	2	1	4	0
Ramón Urías	.500	1	2	0	1	0	0	0	0	0	0	0
Austin Hays	.273	3	11	1	3	1	0	0	0	2	3	0
Anthony Santander	.273	3	11	2	3	0	0	1	1	2	0	0
Aaron Hicks	.250	3	8	1	2	0	0	1	5	2	1	0
Jordan Westburg	.222	3	9	2	2	1	0	0	0	0	4	0
Ryan O'Hearn	.200	3	5	0	1	0	0	0	0	0	1	0
Ryan Mountcastle	.182	3	11	1	2	1	0	0	2	1	4	0
Adley Rutschman	.083	3	12	0	1	1	0	0	0	1	2	0
Adam Frazier	.000	2	5	0	0	0	0	0	0	0	0	0
Cedric Mullins	.000	3	12	0	0	0	0	0	0	0	3	0
TOTALS	**.243**	**3**	**103**	**11**	**25**	**6**	**0**	**3**	**11**	**9**	**23**	**0**

BALTIMORE	W	L	ERA	G	GS	SV	IP	H	R	ER	BB	SO
Tyler Wells	0	0	0.00	3	0	0	3.1	1	0	0	0	3
Cionel Pérez	0	0	0.00	2	0	0	1.2	1	0	0	1	4
DL Hall	0	0	0.00	2	0	0	3.1	1	0	0	1	6
Danny Coulombe	0	0	0.00	2	0	0	1	0	0	0	1	1
Kyle Gibson	0	0	3.00	1	0	0	3	1	1	1	1	1
Kyle Bradish	0	1	3.86	1	1	0	4.2	7	2	2	1	9
Jack Flaherty	0	0	4.50	1	0	0	2	2	1	1	3	1
Yennier Cano	0	0	6.75	2	0	0	1.1	2	1	1	1	0
Jacob Webb	0	0	9.00	2	0	0	2	2	2	2	1	1
Grayson Rodriguez	0	1	27.00	1	1	0	1.2	6	5	5	4	2
Dean Kremer	0	1	32.40	1	1	0	1.2	7	6	6	1	0
Bryan Baker	0	0	81.00	1	0	0	0.1	0	3	3	3	0
TOTALS	**0**	**3**	**7.27**	**3**	**3**	**0**	**26.0**	**30**	**21**	**21**	**18**	**28**

SCORE BY INNINGS

TEXAS	**1**	**10**	**4**	**2**	**1**	**2**	**0**	**0**	**1**	**21**
BALTIMORE	**2**	**0**	**0**	**3**	**2**	**1**	**0**	**0**	**3**	**11**

AMERICAN LEAGUE CHAMPIONSHIP SERIES

TEXAS RANGERS VS. HOUSTON ASTROS

TEXAS	AVG	G	AB	R	H	2B	3B	HR	RBI	BB	SO	SB
Travis Jankowski	.500	4	2	0	1	0	0	0	0	0	0	0
Adolis García	.357	7	28	7	10	0	0	5	15	0	6	1
Nathaniel Lowe	.259	7	27	4	7	1	0	2	4	2	11	0
Corey Seager	.258	7	31	6	8	2	0	2	3	1	5	0
Mitch Garver	.250	7	24	4	6	1	0	1	4	3	5	0
Jonah Heim	.250	7	28	2	7	0	0	2	4	2	3	1
Evan Carter	.240	7	25	5	6	3	0	0	2	3	8	2
Leody Taveras	.227	7	22	2	5	0	1	1	1	4	4	2
Marcus Semien	.207	7	29	4	6	0	0	0	0	4	2	0
Josh Jung	.200	7	25	4	5	0	0	2	5	2	10	0
Robbie Grossman	.000	3	4	1	0	0	0	0	0	0	1	0
Josh Smith	.000	1	0	0	0	0	0	0	0	0	0	0
TOTALS	**.249**	**7**	**245**	**39**	**61**	**7**	**1**	**15**	**38**	**21**	**55**	**6**

TEXAS	W	L	ERA	G	GS	SV	IP	H	R	ER	BB	SO
Jordan Montgomery	2	0	1.29	3	2	0	14	13	2	2	3	10
Josh Sborz	0	0	1.50	5	0	0	6	2	1	1	3	4
Aroldis Chapman	0	0	2.45	4	0	0	3.2	4	1	1	0	1
Martín Pérez	0	0	2.70	2	0	0	3.1	4	1	1	1	1
Nathan Eovaldi	2	0	3.65	2	2	0	12.1	10	5	5	4	13
Cody Bradford	0	0	4.50	2	0	0	2	1	1	1	0	0
José Leclerc	0	1	6.75	5	0	2	5.1	4	4	4	5	4
Chris Stratton	0	0	6.75	2	0	0	2.2	2	2	2	2	2
Jon Gray	0	0	9.00	1	0	0	1	2	1	1	1	1
Max Scherzer	0	1	9.45	2	2	0	6.2	9	7	7	3	6
Dane Dunning	0	1	10.13	1	0	0	2.2	3	3	3	3	4
Will Smith	0	0	10.80	2	0	0	1.2	2	2	2	2	1
Andrew Heaney	0	0	16.20	2	1	0	1.2	4	3	3	1	0
TOTALS	**4**	**3**	**4.71**	**7**	**7**	**2**	**63**	**60**	**33**	**33**	**28**	**47**

HOUSTON	AVG	G	AB	R	H	2B	3B	HR	RBI	BB	SO	SB
Yordan Alvarez	.481	7	27	5	13	0	1	2	9	3	9	0
Jose Altuve	.313	7	32	9	10	3	0	3	5	2	2	1
Mauricio Dubón	.300	5	20	3	6	0	0	0	2	0	3	0
Jose Abreu	.286	7	28	3	8	1	0	1	5	3	6	1
Chas McCormick	.235	6	17	1	4	0	0	1	2	2	2	1
Alex Bregman	.231	7	26	6	6	1	1	3	5	6	4	0
Jeremy Peña	.160	7	25	0	4	0	0	0	1	0	5	0
Kyle Tucker	.154	7	26	2	4	2	0	0	0	5	4	0
Yainer Diaz	.125	5	8	1	1	0	0	0	0	0	1	0
Martin Maldonado	.125	7	16	2	2	0	0	0	2	3	7	0
Michael Brantley	.118	5	17	0	2	1	0	0	1	3	3	0
Grae Kessinger	.000	2	0	1	0	0	0	0	0	0	0	0
Jonathan Singleton	.000	2	1	0	0	0	0	0	0	1	1	0
Totals	**.247**	**7**	**243**	**33**	**60**	**8**	**2**	**10**	**32**	**28**	**47**	**3**

HOUSTON	W	L	ERA	G	GS	SV	IP	H	R	ER	BB	SO
Phil Maton	0	0	0.00	4	0	0	4.1	1	0	0	0	5
Ryan Pressly	1	0	0.00	3	0	1	4	2	0	0	2	5
Hunter Brown	0	0	1.80	2	0	0	5	4	1	1	0	4
Hector Neris	0	0	2.84	5	0	0	6.1	3	2	2	4	3
Justin Verlander	0	1	4.38	2	2	0	12.1	12	6	6	3	8
Ryne Stanek	1	0	6.75	3	0	0	2.2	2	2	2	0	1
Bryan Abreu	0	0	7.20	6	0	0	5	4	4	4	2	7
Cristian Javier	1	1	7.50	2	2	0	6	7	5	5	2	3
Rafael Montero	0	0	7.71	3	0	0	2.1	1	3	2	2	3
Framber Valdez	0	2	8.22	2	2	0	7.2	12	8	7	3	12
José Urquidy	0	0	8.31	2	1	0	4.1	7	4	4	1	2
J.P. France	0	0	12.00	2	0	0	3	6	4	4	2	2
Totals	**3**	**4**	**5.29**	**7**	**7**	**1**	**63**	**61**	**39**	**37**	**21**	**55**

SCORE BY INNINGS

HOUSTON	**6**	**4**	**2**	**6**	**0**	**3**	**5**	**5**	**4**	**33**
TEXAS	**7**	**4**	**3**	**6**	**4**	**5**	**2**	**3**	**5**	**39**

NATIONAL LEAGUE WILD CARD

ARIZONA D-BACKS VS. MILWAUKEE BREWERS

ARIZONA	AVG	G	AB	R	H	2B	3B	HR	RBI	BB	SO	SB
Corbin Carroll	.571	2	7	3	4	1	0	1	2	2	0	0
Christian Walker	.375	2	8	1	3	1	0	0	2	1	2	1
Ketel Marte	.250	2	8	1	2	0	0	1	3	1	3	0
Geraldo Perdomo	.250	2	4	2	1	0	0	0	0	3	1	0
Gabriel Moreno	.200	2	5	1	1	0	0	1	1	1	1	0
Lourdes Gurriel Jr.	.125	2	8	0	1	0	0	0	1	0	4	0
Evan Longoria	.125	2	8	0	1	0	0	0	0	0	3	0
Tommy Pham	.125	2	8	2	1	0	0	0	0	1	3	1
Alek Thomas	.125	2	8	1	1	0	0	1	1	0	4	0
Jose Herrera	.000	1	2	0	0	0	0	0	0	1	0	0
Totals	**.227**	**2**	**66**	**11**	**15**	**2**	**0**	**4**	**10**	**10**	**21**	**2**

ARIZONA	W	L	ERA	G	GS	SV	IP	H	R	ER	BB	SO
Ryan Thompson	0	0	0.00	2	0	0	2.2	1	0	0	1	2
Paul Sewald	0	0	0.00	2	0	2	2	1	0	0	0	3
Andrew Saalfrank	0	0	0.00	1	0	0	0.2	0	0	0	0	0
Ryne Nelson	0	0	0.00	1	0	0	0.1	3	0	0	0	1
Joe Mantiply	1	0	0.00	1	0	0	0.2	0	0	0	1	0
Kevin Ginkel	0	0	0.00	2	0	0	2.1	4	0	0	0	5
Miguel Castro	0	0	0.00	1	0	0	0.2	0	0	0	1	0
Zac Gallen	1	0	3.00	1	1	0	6	5	2	2	3	4
Brandon Pfaadt	0	0	10.13	1	1	0	2.2	7	3	3	1	4
TOTALS	**2**	**0**	**2.50**	**2**	**2**	**2**	**18.0**	**21**	**5**	**5**	**7**	**19**

MILWAUKEE	AVG	G	AB	R	H	2B	3B	HR	RBI	BB	SO	SB
Willy Adames	.571	2	7	0	4	1	0	0	1	1	2	0
Christian Yelich	.500	2	8	2	4	1	0	0	0	2	1	1
Mark Canha	.375	2	8	0	3	0	0	0	0	0	2	0

William Contreras	.333	2	9	0	3	0	0	0	0	1	3	0
Josh Donaldson	.286	2	7	1	2	0	0	0	0	0	0	0
Carlos Santana	.286	2	7	1	2	0	0	0	1	2	2	0
Sal Frelick	.250	2	8	0	2	0	0	0	1	0	3	0
Tyrone Taylor	.125	2	8	1	1	0	0	1	2	0	2	0
Andruw Monasterio	.000	2	1	0	0	0	0	0	0	0	1	0
Brice Turang	.000	2	3	0	0	0	0	0	0	1	2	0
Jesse Winker	.000	2	2	0	0	0	0	0	0	0	1	0
TOTALS	**.309**	**2**	**68**	**5**	**21**	**2**	**0**	**1**	**5**	**7**	**19**	**1**

MILWAUKEE	W	L	ERA	G	GS	SV	IP	H	R	ER	BB	SO
Bryse Wilson	0	0	0.00	1	0	0	0.1	0	0	0	0	0
Elvis Peguero	0	0	0.00	2	0	0	1.2	1	0	0	0	2
Joel Payamps	0	0	0.00	1	0	0	1.2	1	0	0	1	2
Hoby Milner	0	0	0.00	2	0	0	2.1	2	0	0	0	2
Trevor Megill	0	0	0.00	1	0	0	1	0	0	0	0	3
Abner Uribe	0	0	6.75	2	0	0	1.1	2	1	1	2	1
Freddy Peralta	0	1	7.20	1	1	0	5	3	4	4	2	5
Corbin Burnes	0	1	9.00	1	1	0	4	5	4	4	2	5
Devin Williams	0	0	27.00	1	0	0	0.2	1	2	2	3	1
TOTALS	**0**	**2**	**5.50**	**2**	**2**	**0**	**18.0**	**15**	**11**	**11**	**10**	**21**

SCORE BY INNINGS

ARIZONA	0	0	3	1	1	4	0	0	2	11
MILWAUKEE	3	2	0	0	0	0	0	0	0	5

PHILADELPHIA PHILLIES VS. MIAMI MARLINS

PHILADELPHIA	AVG	G	AB	R	H	2B	3B	HR	RBI	BB	SO	SB
Trea Turner	.571	2	7	0	4	2	0	0	1	1	1	2
J.T. Realmuto	.375	2	8	2	3	1	0	1	1	0	0	0
Alec Bohm	.250	2	8	1	2	2	0	0	1	0	1	0
Nick Castellanos	.250	2	8	1	2	2	0	0	1	0	2	0
Kyle Schwarber	.250	2	8	1	2	1	0	0	1	0	5	0
Bryson Stott	.250	2	8	2	2	0	0	1	5	0	5	0
Cristian Pache	.200	2	5	1	1	0	0	0	1	1	2	0
Bryce Harper	.167	2	6	2	1	0	0	0	0	2	3	0
Johan Rojas	.167	2	6	1	1	0	0	0	0	0	3	0
Brandon Marsh	.000	1	2	0	0	0	0	0	0	0	0	0
Totals	**.273**	**2**	**66**	**11**	**18**	**8**	**0**	**2**	**11**	**4**	**22**	**2**

PHILADELPHIA	W	L	ERA	G	GS	SV	IP	H	R	ER	BB	SO
Aaron Nola	1	0	0.00	1	1	0	7	3	0	0	1	3
Craig Kimbrel	0	0	0.00	1	0	1	1	1	0	0	0	0
Orion Kerkering	0	0	0.00	1	0	0	1	0	0	0	0	1
Jeff Hoffman	0	0	0.00	1	0	0	0.1	0	0	0	0	0
José Alvarado	0	0	0.00	1	0	0	1	1	0	0	0	2
Zack Wheeler	1	0	1.35	1	1	0	6.2	5	1	1	0	8
Gregory Soto	0	0	9.00	1	0	0	1	2	1	1	0	2
TOTALS	**2**	**0**	**1.00**	**2**	**2**	**1**	**18.0**	**12**	**2**	**2**	**1**	**16**

MIAMI	AVG	G	AB	R	H	2B	3B	HR	RBI	BB	SO	SB
Xavier Edwards	1.000	1	1	1	1	0	0	0	0	0	0	0
Josh Bell	.500	2	8	1	4	2	0	0	1	0	1	0
Jake Burger	.286	2	7	0	2	0	0	0	0	0	0	0
Jon Berti	.200	2	5	0	1	1	0	0	0	0	3	0
Jesús Sánchez	.200	2	5	0	1	0	0	0	0	0	1	0
Bryan De La Cruz	.167	2	6	0	1	0	0	0	1	1	0	0
Luis Arraez	.125	2	8	0	1	0	0	0	0	0	0	0
Jorge Soler	.125	2	8	0	1	0	0	0	0	0	5	0
Jazz Chisholm Jr.	.000	2	8	0	0	0	0	0	0	0	4	0
Nick Fortes	.000	1	2	0	0	0	0	0	0	0	1	0
Yuli Gurriel	.000	1	1	0	0	0	0	0	0	0	1	0
Garrett Hampson	.000	1	1	0	0	0	0	0	0	0	0	0
Jacob Stallings	.000	2	2	0	0	0	0	0	0	0	0	0
TOTALS	**.194**	**2**	**62**	**2**	**12**	**3**	**0**	**0**	**2**	**1**	**16**	**0**

MIAMI	W	L	ERA	G	GS	SV	IP	H	R	ER	BB	SO
George Soriano	0	0	0.00	1	0	0	1	0	0	0	0	1
Tanner Scott	0	0	0.00	1	0	0	1	0	0	0	0	1
A.J. Puk	0	0	0.00	1	0	0	1	1	0	0	0	1
JT Chargois	0	0	0.00	1	0	0	0.2	1	0	0	1	0
Huascar Brazoban	0	0	0.00	1	0	0	1	0	0	0	1	2
Braxton Garrett	0	1	6.00	1	1	0	3	3	2	2	1	5
Jesús Luzardo	0	1	6.75	1	1	0	4	8	3	3	0	5
David Robertson	0	0	9.00	1	0	0	2	2	2	2	0	4
Steven Okert	0	0	9.00	1	0	0	1	2	1	1	0	1
Andrew Nardi	0	0	13.50	1	0	0	1.1	1	3	2	1	2
TOTALS	**0**	**2**	**5.63**	**2**	**2**	**0**	**16.0**	**18**	**11**	**10**	**4**	**22**

SCORE BY INNINGS

MIAMI	0	0	0	0	0	0	1	0	1	2
PHILADELPHIA	0	0	3	3	0	4	0	1	0	11

NATIONAL LEAGUE DIVISION SERIES

ARIZONA D-BACKS VS. LOS ANGELES DODGERS

ARIZONA	AVG	G	AB	R	H	2B	3B	HR	RBI	BB	SO	SB
Tommy Pham	.429	3	14	4	6	0	0	1	1	0	2	1
Ketel Marte	.357	3	14	3	5	1	0	1	1	0	3	1
Lourdes Gurriel Jr.	.308	3	13	1	4	1	0	1	3	0	0	0
Corbin Carroll	.300	3	10	3	3	0	0	1	2	4	3	2
Gabriel Moreno	.273	3	11	2	3	0	0	2	5	0	4	0
Alek Thomas	.273	3	11	2	3	0	0	1	1	2	3	0
Christian Walker	.222	3	9	3	2	1	0	1	3	3	3	1
Evan Longoria	.200	3	10	0	2	1	0	0	2	0	5	0
Geraldo Perdomo	.125	3	8	1	1	0	0	1	1	1	3	0
Jose Herrera	.000	1	1	0	0	0	0	0	0	0	0	0
Jace Peterson	.000	2	1	0	0	0	0	0	0	0	0	0
TOTALS	**.284**	**3**	**102**	**19**	**29**	**4**	**0**	**9**	**19**	**11**	**26**	**5**

ARIZONA	W	L	ERA	G	GS	SV	IP	H	R	ER	BB	SO
Paul Sewald	0	0	0.00	2	0	2	2	1	0	0	0	2
Andrew Saalfrank	0	0	0.00	2	0	0	0.2	1	0	0	1	1
Brandon Pfaadt	0	0	0.00	1	1	0	4.1	2	0	0	0	2
Joe Mantiply	1	0	0.00	2	0	0	2	0	0	0	0	2
Merrill Kelly	1	0	0.00	1	1	0	6.1	3	0	0	2	5
Kevin Ginkel	0	0	0.00	2	0	0	2	0	0	0	2	3
Luis Frías	0	0	0.00	1	0	0	1	0	0	0	0	1
Zac Gallen	1	0	3.38	1	1	0	5.1	5	2	2	2	4
Ryan Thompson	0	0	7.71	2	0	0	2.1	4	2	2	0	2
Miguel Castro	0	0	18.00	1	0	0	1	1	2	2	2	1
TOTALS	**3**	**0**	**2.00**	**3**	**3**	**2**	**27**	**17**	**6**	**6**	**9**	**23**

LOS ANGELES	AVG	G	AB	R	H	2B	3B	HR	RBI	BB	SO	SB
Will Smith	.417	3	12	1	5	1	1	0	2	0	1	0
Enrique Hernández	.375	3	8	0	3	0	0	0	2	0	0	0
Miguel Rojas	.333	3	6	0	2	0	0	0	0	0	0	0
J.D. Martinez	.200	3	10	1	2	0	0	1	1	2	4	0
Max Muncy	.182	3	11	2	2	0	0	0	0	1	4	0
David Peralta	.167	3	6	0	1	1	0	0	0	0	1	0
Chris Taylor	.167	3	6	0	1	0	0	0	1	1	2	0
Freddie Freeman	.100	3	10	1	1	0	0	0	0	2	2	0
Austin Barnes	.000	1	1	0	0	0	0	0	0	0	0	0
Mookie Betts	.000	3	11	1	0	0	0	0	0	1	2	0
Jason Heyward	.000	3	7	0	0	0	0	0	0	0	4	0
James Outman	.000	3	5	0	0	0	0	0	0	1	3	0
Kolten Wong	.000	3	3	0	0	0	0	0	0	1	0	0
TOTALS	**.177**	**3**	**96**	**6**	**17**	**2**	**1**	**1**	**6**	**9**	**23**	**0**

LOS ANGELES	W	L	ERA	G	GS	SV	IP	H	R	ER	BB	SO
Evan Phillips	0	0	0.00	2	0	0	2.1	2	0	0	1	3
Shelby Miller	0	0	0.00	1	0	0	2	1	0	0	0	3
Joe Kelly	0	0	0.00	1	0	0	1.2	2	0	0	1	3
Brusdar Graterol	0	0	0.00	2	0	0	3	1	0	0	1	2
Caleb Ferguson	0	0	0.00	2	0	0	2.1	0	0	0	1	2
Ryan Brasier	0	0	3.86	1	0	0	2.1	1	1	1	0	3
Alex Vesia	0	0	4.50	2	0	0	2	1	1	1	0	2
Michael Grove	0	0	4.50	2	0	0	2	1	1	1	2	2
Emmet Sheehan	0	0	7.36	1	0	0	3.2	4	3	3	2	4
Lance Lynn	0	1	13.50	1	1	0	2.2	6	4	4	0	1
Bobby Miller	0	1	16.20	1	1	0	1.2	4	3	3	2	1
Clayton Kershaw	0	1	162.00	1	1	0	0.1	6	6	6	1	0
TOTALS	**0**	**3**	**6.58**	**3**	**3**	**0**	**26**	**29**	**19**	**19**	**11**	**26**

SCORE BY INNINGS

ARIZONA	9	3	0	3	0	1	1	1	0	19
LOS ANGELES	0	0	0	1	0	1	2	2	0	6

PHILADELPHIA PHILLIES VS. ATLANTA BRAVES

PHILADELPHIA	AVG	G	AB	R	H	2B	3B	HR	RBI	BB	SO	SB
Trea Turner	.471	4	17	5	8	2	0	2	2	1	3	2
Nick Castellanos	.467	4	15	5	7	0	0	4	4	2	1	1
Bryce Harper	.462	4	13	5	6	0	0	3	5	5	2	1
Brandon Marsh	.417	4	12	2	5	1	0	1	1	1	5	1
Bryson Stott	.231	4	13	1	3	0	0	0	2	2	5	1
J.T. Realmuto	.214	4	14	1	3	1	0	1	5	1	5	0
Alec Bohm	.154	4	13	1	2	0	0	0	1	4	5	0
Kyle Schwarber	.118	4	17	0	2	1	0	0	0	1	5	0
Cristian Pache	.000	1	2	0	0	0	0	0	0	1	1	1
Johan Rojas	.000	4	15	0	0	0	0	0	0	1	6	0
TOTALS	**.275**	**4**	**131**	**20**	**36**	**5**	**0**	**11**	**20**	**19**	**38**	**7**

PHILADELPHIA	W	L	ERA	G	GS	SV	IP	H	R	ER	BB	SO
Matt Strahm	0	0	0.00	3	0	1	2.1	2	0	0	1	1
Gregory Soto	0	0	0.00	2	0	0	0.2	1	0	0	1	0
Michael Lorenzen	0	0	0.00	1	0	0	1	1	0	0	1	0
Craig Kimbrel	0	0	0.00	2	0	1	2	0	0	0	1	1
Orion Kerkering	0	0	0.00	2	0	0	2	1	0	0	1	0
Seranthony Domínguez	0	0	0.00	3	0	0	2.2	4	0	0	0	4
José Alvarado	0	0	0.00	3	0	0	3	1	0	0	2	2
Ranger Suárez	1	0	1.04	2	2	0	8.2	4	1	1	1	6
Zack Wheeler	0	0	2.84	1	1	0	6.1	3	3	2	1	10
Aaron Nola	1	0	3.18	1	1	0	5.2	6	2	2	1	9
Jeff Hoffman	1	1	27.00	2	0	0	0.2	1	2	2	1	1
Totals	**3**	**1**	**1.80**	**4**	**4**	**2**	**35**	**24**	**8**	**7**	**11**	**34**

ATLANTA	AVG	G	AB	R	H	2B	3B	HR	RBI	BB	SO	SB
Austin Riley	.353	4	17	2	6	0	0	2	3	0	6	0
Sean Murphy	.286	2	7	0	2	0	0	0	0	0	2	0
Ozzie Albies	.267	4	15	0	4	0	0	0	1	2	3	0
Matt Olson	.250	4	16	1	4	0	0	0	0	1	1	0
Orlando Arcia	.154	4	13	0	2	0	0	0	1	1	4	0
Marcell Ozuna	.154	4	13	1	2	0	0	0	0	2	4	0
Ronald Acuna Jr.	.143	4	14	3	2	1	0	0	0	2	2	2
Travis d'Arnaud	.143	3	7	1	1	0	0	1	2	1	2	0
Eddie Rosario	.143	4	7	0	1	0	0	0	0	0	3	0
Vaughn Grissom	.000	1	1	0	0	0	0	0	0	0	1	0
Michael Harris II	.000	4	13	0	0	0	0	0	0	0	3	0
Kevin Pillar	.000	4	5	0	0	0	0	0	0	2	3	0
Forrest Wall	.000	2	1	0	0	0	0	0	0	0	0	0
TOTALS	**.186**	**4**	**129**	**8**	**24**	**1**	**0**	**3**	**7**	**11**	**34**	**2**

ATLANTA	W	L	ERA	G	GS	SV	IP	H	R	ER	BB	SO
Kirby Yates	0	0	0.00	1	0	0	1	1	1	0	1	2
Michael Tonkin	0	0	0.00	1	0	0	0.2	2	0	0	0	1
A.J. Minter	1	0	0.00	3	0	0	2.1	3	1	0	2	1
Pierce Johnson	0	0	0.00	3	0	0	2.2	2	0	0	2	4
Joe Jiménez	0	0	0.00	1	0	0	1	1	0	0	1	1
Raisel Iglesias	0	0	0.00	3	0	1	2.1	0	0	0	0	2
Daysbel Hernández	0	0	0.00	1	0	0	1	0	0	0	1	0
Spencer Strider	0	2	2.84	2	2	0	12.2	12	5	4	5	15
Max Fried	0	0	6.75	1	1	0	4	6	3	3	4	3
Brad Hand	0	0	9.00	1	0	0	1	1	1	1	1	2
AJ Smith-Shawver	0	0	10.13	1	0	0	2.2	3	3	3	1	3
Bryce Elder	0	1	20.25	1	1	0	2.2	5	6	6	1	4
TOTALS	**1**	**3**	**4.50**	**4**	**4**	**1**	**34**	**36**	**20**	**17**	**19**	**38**

SCORE BY INNINGS

ATLANTA	0	0	1	1	1	3	2	4	0	8
PHILADELPHIA	1	0	8	2	2	2	0	1	0	20

NATIONAL LEAGUE CHAMPIONSHIP SERIES

ARIZONA D-BACKS VS. PHILADELPHIA PHILLIES

ARIZONA	AVG	G	AB	R	H	2B	3B	HR	RBI	BB	SO	SB
Ketel Marte	.387	7	31	2	12	4	1	0	3	1	10	1
Gerardo Perdomo	.333	7	24	4	8	0	0	1	2	1	8	1
Pavin Smith	.333	6	9	1	3	0	0	0	0	0	2	0
Gabriel Moreno	.296	7	27	0	8	1	0	0	3	3	7	0
Lourdes Gurriel Jr.	.259	7	27	2	7	2	0	1	2	1	6	2
Corbin Carroll	.222	7	27	3	6	0	0	0	2	1	5	2
Alex Thomas	.214	7	14	4	3	0	0	2	4	2	2	1
Emmanuel Rivera	.167	5	12	1	2	0	0	0	1	0	2	0
Evan Longoria	.105	7	19	1	2	1	0	0	1	3	9	0
Tommy Pham	.100	6	20	1	2	0	0	1	1	0	9	0
Christian Walker	.091	7	22	2	2	1	0	0	2	7	9	2
Jordan Lawlar	.000	1	1	0	0	0	0	0	0	0	0	00
TOTALS	**.236**	**7**	**233**	**21**	**55**	**9**	**1**	**5**	**21**	**19**	**69**	**9**

ARIZONA	W	L	ERA	G	GS	SV	IP	H	R	ER	BB	SO
Slade Cecconi	0	0	0.00	2	0	0	2	2	0	0	0	1
Kevin Ginkel	1	0	0.00	4	0	0	4.2	2	0	0	0	5
Paul Sewald	1	0	0.00	4	0	2	4	1	0	0	1	6
Ryan Thompson	1	0	1.59	4	0	0	5.2	5	1	1	2	4
Brandon Pfaadt	0	0	1.86	2	2	0	9.2	6	2	2	2	16
Miguel Castro	0	0	2.70	3	0	0	3.1	2	1	1	1	3
Luis Frías	0	0	3.38	3	0	0	2.2	1	1	1	1	2
Merrill Kelly	1	1	4.22	2	2	0	10.2	6	5	5	6	14
Kyle Nelson	0	0	4.50	2	0	0	2	2	1	1	0	1
Zac Gallen	0	2	7.36	2	2	0	11	14	9	9	4	5
Andrew Saalfrank	0	0	9.00	5	0	0	2	1	3	2	7	1
Joe Mantiply	0	0	10.13	4	1	0	2.2	5	4	3	2	2
Ryne Nelson	0	0	40.50	1	0	0	0.2	4	3	3	1	0
TOTALS	**4**	**3**	**3.98**	**7**	**7**	**2**	**61**	**51**	**30**	**27**	**27**	**60**

PHILADELPHIA	AVG	G	AB	R	H	2B	3B	HR	RBI	BB	SO	SB
Kyle Schwarber	.364	7	22	8	8	2	0	5	5	8	7	0
Jake Cave	.333	3	3	0	1	1	0	0	0	0	1	0
Brandon Marsh	.333	7	24	0	8	3	0	0	3	3	10	1
Alec Bohm	.280	7	25	3	7	1	0	1	4	2	3	0
J.T. Realmuto	.259	7	27	4	7	2	0	1	6	0	8	0
Bryson Stott	.240	7	25	2	6	1	0	0	2	2	4	4
Bryce Harper	.217	7	23	7	5	0	0	2	3	6	6	2
Trea Turner	.200	7	25	4	5	1	0	1	2	3	4	0
Johan Rojas	.136	7	22	1	3	1	1	0	0	0	6	0
Nick Castellanos	.042	7	24	1	1	0	0	1	2	2	11	0
Christian Pache	.000	1	0	0	0	0	0	0	0	1	0	0
Edmundo Sosa	.000	2	1	0	0	0	0	0	0	0	0	0
Garrett Stubbs	.000	1	0	0	0	0	0	0	0	0	0	0
TOTALS	**.231**	**7**	**221**	**30**	**51**	**12**	**1**	**11**	**27**	**27**	**60**	**7**

PHILADELPHIA	W	L	ERA	G	GS	SV	IP	H	R	ER	BB	SO
Seranthony Domínguez	0	0	0.00	3	0	0	2.2	2	1	0	3	3
Jeff Hoffman	0	0	0.00	5	0	0	6	4	0	0	0	8
Michael Lorenzen	0	0	0.00	1	0	0	1.2	1	0	0	1	1
Matt Strahm	0	0	0.00	4	0	0	3	1	0	0	1	4
Zack Wheeler	2	0	1.84	3	2	0	14.2	9	3	3	2	17
José Alvarado	0	0	2.25	4	0	0	4	5	1	1	1	2
Ranger Suárez	0	1	2.70	2	2	0	10	9	3	3	1	13
Aaron Nola	1	1	3.48	2	2	0	10.1	9	4	4	2	11
Cristopher Sánchez	0	0	3.86	1	1	0	2.1	2	2	1	1	1
Gregory Soto	0	0	6.75	2	0	0	1.1	2	1	1	1	1
Orion Kerkering	0	0	7.71	4	0	0	2.1	6	2	2	2	4
Craig Kimbrel	0	2	12.00	4	0	1	3	5	4	4	4	4
TOTALS	**3**	**4**	**2.79**	**7**	**7**	**1**	**61.1**	**55**	**21**	**19**	**19**	**69**

SCORE BY INNINGS

ARIZONA	1	4	1	0	3	2	6	3	1	21
PHILADELPHIA	5	3	2	2	2	8	6	2	0	30

ORGANIZATION STATISTICS

Arizona Diamondbacks

SEASON SYNOPSIS: Arizona had one of the best 84-win seasons in MLB history. After earning the last wild card spot in the National League, the D-backs got hot and won the NL pennant.

HIGH POINT: Arizona shocked the Phillies by winning back-to-back games in Philadelphia with a spot in the World Series on the line. Five D-backs relievers combined for five scoreless innings in Game 7.

LOW POINT: The D-backs went 11-17 in May and looked like they were headed for the cliff, especially after righthander Luke Weaver went on the shelf with a forearm injury on May 31.

NOTABLE ROOKIES: Corbin Carroll had an exceptional rookie season, as he immediately became a spark plug for the team's offense, Carroll stole 54 bases in 59 attempts while also hitting 25 home runs and 65 extra-base hits. He wasn't the only contributor. Righthander Brandon Pfaadt had a rough introduction to the majors, but after a demotion to regroup, he became a fixture in Arizona's rotation. He went 0-1, 3.27 in five postseason starts. Reliever Andrew Saalfrank made 11 postseason appearances. Outfielder Dominic Fletcher hit a productive .301/.350/.441 in a 28-game stint.

KEY TRANSACTIONS: Arizona made a bold move during the offseason by trading Daulton Varsho to Toronto for catcher Gabriel Moreno and outfielder Lourdes Gurriel Jr. Moreno immediately became one of the better young catchers in the National League, while Gurriel was a productive outfielder. The midseason addition of Tommy Pham from the Mets paid off in the postseason. The outfielder hit three home runs in the playoffs, and his 10 runs scored was tied for second most on the team.

DOWN ON THE FARM: Shortstop Jordan Lawlar put a slow start behind him to earn a promotion to Triple-A Reno and eventually a spot on the MLB roster. While he struggled in his brief time in the majors, the D-backs were impressed enough to carry him on the postseason roster. Triple-A Reno was one of the winningest teams in the minors, but its 88 wins weren't enough to earn a playoff spot in a very top-heavy Pacific Coast League. Double-A Amarillo won the Texas League title, as Kristian Robinson homered twice in six games. The ACL D-backs Reds lost in the league's championship game.

OPENING DAY PAYROLL: $116,471,292 (21st).

PLAYERS OF THE YEAR

MAJOR LEAGUE

Corbin Carroll
OF

.285/.362/.506
25HR
116 R, 54 SB in 59 Att.

MINOR LEAGUE

Jordan Lawlar
SS

(AA/AAA)
.278/.378/.496,
20 HR, 36 SB

ORGANIZATION LEADERS

Batting		*Minimum 250 AB
MAJORS		
*AVG	Corbin Carroll	.285
* OPS	Corbin Carroll	.868
HR	Christian Walker	33
RBI	Christian Walker	103
MINORS		
* AVG	Ryan Bliss, Amarillo/Reno	.332
* OBP	Buddy Kennedy, Reno	.444
* SLG	Ivan Melendez, Hillsboro/Amarillo	.578
* OPS	Ryan Bliss, Amarillo/Reno	.947
R	Phillip Evans, Reno	107
H	Phillip Evans, Reno	150
TB	A.J. Vukovich, Amarillo	221
2B	Diego Castillo, Reno	33
3B	4-tied	8
HR	Ivan Melendez, Hillsboro/Amarillo	30
RBI	A.J. Vukovich, Amarillo	96
BB	Diego Castillo, Reno	96
SO	Alvin Guzman, ACL D-backs Black & Red/Visalia	154
SB	Wildred Patino, ACL D-backs Black/Hillsboro	54

Pitching		#Minimum 75 IP
MAJORS		
W	Zac Gallen	17
# ERA	Merrill Kelly	3.29
SO	Zac Gallen	220
SV	Paul Sewald	13
MINORS		
W	Blake Walston, Reno	12
L	3-tied	10
# ERA	Ricardo Yan, Visalia/Hillsboro	3.65
G	2-tied	51
GS	Blake Walston, Reno	30
SV	Kyle Backhus, Amarillo/Reno	10
IP	Blake Walston, Reno	149
BB	Blake Walston, Reno	93
SO	Yiber Diaz, Hillsboro/Amarillo	140
	Yu-Min Lin, Hillsboro/Amarillo	140
# AVG	Ricardo Yan, Visalia/Hillsboro	.184

2023 PERFORMANCE

General Manager: Mike Hazen. **Farm Director:** Josh Barfield. **Scouting Director:** Ian Rebhan.

Class	Team	League	W	L	PCT	Finish	Manager
Majors	Arizona Diamondbacks	National	84	78	.519	5 (15)	Torey Lovullo
Triple-A	Reno Aces	Pacific Coast	88	62	.587	3 (10)	Blake Lalli
Double-A	Amarillo Sod Poodles	Texas	77	61	.558	1 (10)	Shawn Roof
High-A	Hillboro Hops	Northwest	56	76	.424	6 (6)	Ronnie Gajownik
Low-A	Visalia Rawhide	California	50	82	.379	8 (10)	Dee Garner
Rookie	ACL D-backs Black	Arizona Complex	22	34	.393	14 (17)	Gift Ngoepe
Rookie	ACL D-backs Red	Arizona Complex	34	21	.618	2 (17)	Jorge Cortes
Rookie	DSL Arizona Black	Dominican Sum.	30	25	.545	16 (50)	Izzy Alcantara
Rookie	DSL Arizona Red	Dominican Sum.	21	33	.389	40 (50)	Luis Alen
Overall 2023 Minor League Record			378	394	.490	18th (30)	

ORGANIZATION STATISTICS

ARIZONA DIAMONDBACKS

NATIONAL LEAGUE

Batting	B-T	Ht.	Wt.	DOB	AVG	OBP	SLG	G	PA	AB	R	H	2B	3B	HR	RBI	BB	HBP	SH	SF	SO	SB	CS	BB%	SO%
Ahmed, Nick	R-R	6-2	201	3-15-90	.212	.257	.303	72	210	198	14	42	10	1	2	17	12	0	0	0	52	5	1	5.7	24.8
Canzone, Dominic	L-R	5-11	190	8-16-97	.237	.293	.368	15	41	38	4	9	2	0	1	8	2	1	0	0	8	0	0	4.9	19.5
2-team (44 Seattle)					.220	.258	.399	59	182	173	23	38	13	0	6	21	8	1	0	0	32	1	0	4.4	17.6
Carroll, Corbin	L-L	5-10	165	8-21-00	.285	.362	.506	155	645	565	116	161	30	10	25	76	57	13	6	4	125	54	5	8.8	19.4
Castillo, Diego	R-R	5-10	185	10-28-97	.000	.000	.000	1	1	1	0	0	0	0	0	0	0	0	0	0	0	0	0	0.0	0.0
Fletcher, Dominic	L-L	5-6	185	9-02-97	.301	.350	.441	28	102	93	10	28	5	1	2	14	7	0	2	0	22	0	2	6.9	21.6
Gurriel, Lourdes	R-R	6-4	215	10-10-93	.261	.309	.463	145	592	551	65	144	35	2	24	82	33	6	0	2	103	5	0	5.6	17.4
Herrera, Jose	B-R	5-10	217	2-24-97	.208	.296	.257	43	120	101	15	21	5	0	0	7	13	0	5	1	30	1	0	10.8	25.0
Kelly, Carson	R-R	6-2	212	7-14-94	.226	.283	.298	33	92	84	6	19	3	0	1	6	7	0	0	1	23	1	0	7.6	25.0
2-team (19 Detroit)					.206	.278	.287	52	151	136	13	28	5	0	2	13	14	0	0	1	40	1	0	9.3	26.5
Kennedy, Buddy	R-R	5-9	190	10-05-98	.167	.310	.208	10	29	24	1	4	1	0	0	1	4	1	0	0	6	0	0	13.8	20.7
Lawlar, Jordan	R-R	6-1	190	7-17-02	.129	.206	.129	14	34	31	2	4	0	0	0	0	2	1	0	0	11	1	1	5.9	32.4
Lewis, Kyle	R-R	6-4	222	7-13-95	.157	.204	.255	16	54	51	2	8	2	0	1	2	3	0	0	0	21	0	0	5.6	38.9
Longoria, Evan	R-R	6-1	213	10-07-85	.223	.295	.422	74	237	211	25	47	9	0	11	28	23	0	0	3	73	0	0	9.7	30.8
Marte, Ketel	B-R	6-1	210	10-12-93	.276	.358	.485	150	650	569	94	157	26	9	25	82	71	5	0	5	109	8	2	10.9	16.8
McCarthy, Jake	L-L	6-2	215	7-30-97	.243	.318	.326	99	312	276	37	67	7	5	2	16	26	5	4	1	62	26	4	8.3	19.9
Moreno, Gabriel	R-R	5-11	195	2-14-00	.284	.339	.408	111	380	341	33	97	19	1	7	50	29	3	0	7	75	6	2	7.6	19.7
Perdomo, Geraldo	B-R	6-2	203	10-22-99	.246	.353	.359	144	495	407	71	100	20	4	6	47	64	6	14	4	86	16	4	12.9	17.4
Peterson, Jace	L-R	6-0	215	5-09-90	.183	.276	.258	41	106	93	5	17	3	2	0	9	11	1	1	0	24	4	1	10.4	22.6
2-team (93 Oakland)					.211	.304	.307	134	430	374	35	79	10	4	6	37	47	4	2	3	101	15	2	10.9	23.5
Pham, Tommy	R-R	6-1	223	3-08-88	.241	.304	.415	50	217	195	26	47	12	2	6	32	18	1	0	3	50	11	2	8.3	23.0
2-team (79 Mets)					.256	.328	.446	129	481	426	55	109	27	3	16	68	47	2	0	6	106	22	3	9.8	22.0
Rivera, Emmanuel	R-R	6-2	225	6-29-96	.261	.314	.358	86	283	257	32	67	13	0	4	29	22	0	0	4	56	1	0	7.8	19.8
Rojas, Josh	L-R	6-1	207	6-30-94	.228	.292	.296	59	216	189	23	43	13	0	0	26	18	1	2	4	51	6	0	8.3	23.6
2-team (46 Seattle)					.245	.303	.338	105	350	314	47	77	17	0	4	40	27	1	2	4	81	12	0	7.7	23.1
Smith, Pavin	L-L	6-2	208	2-06-96	.188	.317	.325	69	228	191	26	36	5	0	7	30	35	1	0	0	45	1	1	15.4	19.7
Thomas, Alek	L-L	5-11	175	4-28-00	.230	.273	.374	125	402	374	51	86	17	5	9	39	19	4	2	3	86	9	1	4.7	21.4
Walker, Christian	R-R	6-0	208	3-28-91	.258	.333	.497	157	661	582	86	150	36	2	33	103	62	8	0	8	127	11	0	9.4	19.2
Zavala, Seby	R-R	5-11	205	8-28-93	.357	.471	.429	7	17	14	2	5	1	0	0	2	2	1	0	0	2	0	0	11.8	11.8
2-team (66 White Sox)					.171	.230	.314	73	193	175	17	30	4	0	7	18	12	2	2	2	70	1	0	6.2	36.3

Pitching	B-T	Ht.	Wt.	DOB	W	L	ERA	G	GS	SV	IP	Hits	Runs	ER	HR	BB	SO	AVG	OBP	SLG	SO%	BB%	BF
Adams, Austin	R-R	6-3	220	5-05-91	0	1	5.71	24	0	0	17	16	12	11	1	8	22	.235	.358	.294	27.2	9.9	81
Bumgarner, Madison	R-L	6-4	240	8-01-89	0	3	10.26	4	4	0	17	25	20	19	4	15	10	.347	.456	.625	11.1	16.7	90
Castro, Miguel	R-R	6-7	201	12-24-94	6	6	4.31	75	0	7	65	51	32	31	8	25	60	.213	.296	.360	22.4	9.3	268
Cecconi, Slade	R-R	6-4	219	6-24-99	0	1	4.33	7	4	0	27	27	13	13	4	4	20	.260	.297	.471	18.0	3.6	111
Chafin, Andrew	R-L	6-2	235	6-17-90	2	3	4.19	43	0	8	34	31	17	16	3	18	49	.235	.327	.394	32.7	12.0	150
Crismatt, Nabil	R-R	6-1	220	12-25-94	0	1	0.00	1	0	0	2	2	1	0	0	0	3	.250	.250	.375	37.5	0.0	8
Davies, Zach	R-R	6-0	180	2-07-93	2	5	7.00	18	18	0	82	98	67	64	10	39	72	.295	.370	.461	19.1	10.3	377
Frias, Luis	R-R	6-3	245	5-23-98	1	0	4.06	29	0	0	31	30	14	14	3	17	26	.250	.353	.417	18.7	12.2	139
Gallen, Zac	R-R	6-2	189	8-03-95	17	9	3.47	34	34	0	210	188	87	81	22	47	220	.238	.284	.382	26.0	5.6	846
Gilbert, Tyler	L-L	6-3	223	12-22-93	0	2	5.19	11	0	0	17	21	10	10	2	5	19	.313	.361	.537	26.4	6.9	72
Ginkel, Kevin	L-R	6-4	235	3-24-94	9	1	2.48	60	0	4	65	41	24	18	3	23	70	.181	.260	.288	27.6	9.1	254
Henry, Tommy	L-L	6-3	205	7-29-97	5	4	4.15	17	16	0	89	86	42	41	12	35	64	.251	.328	.418	16.8	9.2	381
Herrera, Jose	B-R	5-10	217	2-24-97	0	0	9.00	2	0	0	2	4	2	2	0	0	0	.400	.400	.500	0.0	0.0	10
Jameson, Drey	R-R	6-0	165	8-17-97	3	1	3.32	15	3	1	41	40	15	15	6	18	37	.260	.339	.416	21.3	10.3	174
Jarvis, Bryce	L-R	6-2	195	12-26-97	2	1	3.04	11	1	0	24	14	9	8	3	9	12	.171	.250	.305	13.0	9.8	92
Kelly, Carson	R-R	6-2	212	7-14-94	0	0	9.00	2	0	0	2	5	2	2	0	1	0	.455	.500	.455	0.0	8.3	12
Kelly, Merrill	R-R	6-2	202	10-14-88	12	8	3.29	30	30	0	178	143	71	65	20	69	187	.222	.300	.371	25.9	9.6	722
Mantiply, Joe	R-L	6-4	219	3-01-91	2	2	4.62	35	3	0	39	35	22	20	4	9	28	.236	.280	.405	17.8	5.7	157
Martinez, Justin	R-R	6-3	180	7-30-01	0	0	12.60	10	0	1	10	13	14	14	2	11	14	.295	.456	.523	24.6	19.3	57
McGough, Scott	R-R	5-11	190	10-31-89	2	7	4.73	63	1	9	70	60	40	37	14	30	86	.226	.306	.440	28.6	10.0	301

Misiewicz, Anthony	R-L	6-1	196	11-01-94	1	0	5.63	7	0	0	8	11	5	5	1	3	6	.333	.378	.606	16.2	8.1	37
Nelson, Kyle	L-L	6-1	175	7-08-96	7	4	4.18	68	2	0	56	59	30	26	12	14	67	.267	.314	.484	28.0	5.9	239
Nelson, Ryne	R-R	6-3	184	2-01-98	8	8	5.31	29	27	0	144	159	87	85	24	46	96	.284	.334	.515	15.5	7.4	619
Pfaadt, Brandon	R-R	6-4	220	10-15-98	3	9	5.72	19	18	0	96	109	63	61	22	26	94	.282	.329	.534	22.3	6.2	421
Rojas, Josh	L-R	6-1	207	6-30-94	0	0	18.00	2	0	0	2	6	4	4	0	1	1	.500	.538	.583	7.7	7.7	13
Ruiz, Jose	R-R	6-1	245	10-21-94	2	1	4.43	34	1	0	41	44	22	20	7	17	36	.277	.357	.478	19.8	9.3	182
Saalfrank, Andrew	L-L	6-3	205	8-18-97	0	0	0.00	10	0	0	10	7	2	0	0	4	6	.189	.268	.189	14.6	9.8	41
Sewald, Paul	R-R	6-3	219	5-26-90	0	1	3.57	20	0	13	18	16	8	7	3	10	20	.235	.342	.412	25.0	12.5	80
Solomon, Peter	R-R	6-4	211	8-16-96	0	0	12.15	5	0	0	13	17	18	18	2	11	6	.309	.433	.600	9.0	16.4	67
Strzelecki, Peter	R-R	6-2	216	10-24-94	0	0	0.00	1	0	0	1	1	0	0	0	2	0	.200	.429	.200	0.0	28.6	7
Sulser, Cole	R-R	6-1	190	3-12-90	0	0	6.75	4	0	0	5	5	4	4	2	3	4	.250	.348	.600	17.4	13.0	23
Thompson, Ryan	R-R	6-5	210	6-26-92	0	0	0.69	13	0	1	13	6	1	1	1	1	9	.140	.178	.233	20.0	2.2	45
Vargas, Carlos	R-R	6-4	210	10-13-99	0	0	5.79	5	0	0	5	5	3	3	2	4	7	.294	.455	.647	31.8	18.2	22
Zavala, Seby	R-R	5-11	205	8-28-93	0	0	0.00	1	0	0	1	0	0	0	0	0	0	.000	.000	.000	0.0	0.0	2

Fielding

Catcher	PCT	G	PO	A	E	DP	PB
Herrera	.990	40	295	12	3	4	3
Kelly	1.000	31	217	12	0	1	0
Moreno	.997	104	821	55	3	3	1
Zavala	.973	6	35	1	1	0	0

First Base	PCT	G	PO	A	E	DP
Gurriel	1.000	1	1	1	0	0
Peterson	1.000	1	3	0	0	1
Rivera	.984	12	57	4	1	8
Smith	1.000	10	63	8	0	5
Walker	.998	152	1075	77	2	106

Second Base	PCT	G	PO	A	E	DP
Kennedy	1.000	1	1	0	0	0
Marte	.986	145	226	355	8	84
Perdomo	1.000	28	30	45	0	10
Peterson	1.000	1	4	1	0	1
Rojas	1.000	6	11	11	0	4

Third Base	PCT	G	PO	A	E	DP
Kennedy	1.000	6	2	9	0	0
Longoria	.977	41	25	60	2	4
Perdomo	1.000	16	0	12	0	0
Peterson	1.000	35	12	34	0	0
Rivera	.974	65	34	80	3	9
Rojas	.963	47	29	75	4	7

Shortstop	PCT	G	PO	A	E	DP
Ahmed	.963	65	75	133	8	26
Lawlar	.977	13	15	27	1	6
Marte	.000	1	0	0	0	0
Perdomo	.989	116	126	240	4	62

Outfield	PCT	G	PO	A	E	DP
Canzone	1.000	4	4	1	0	0
Carroll	.996	182	293	5	1	2
Fletcher	.992	30	64	4	1	1
Gurriel	1.000	95	152	8	0	0
Lewis	1.000	3	1	0	0	0
Marte	.000	2	0	0	0	0
McCarthy	.991	96	197	1	3	0
Pham	.969	30	49	3	1	1
Rojas	.000	2	0	0	0	0
Smith	1.000	22	33	1	0	1
Thomas	.993	117	278	5	2	4

RENO ACES

TRIPLE-A

PACIFIC COAST LEAGUE

Batting	B-T	Ht.	Wt.	DOB	AVG	OBP	SLG	G	PA	AB	R	H	2B	3B	HR	RBI	BB	HBP	SH	SF	SO	SB	CS	BB%	SO%
Alcantara, Sergio	B-R	6-4	151	7-10-96	.264	.392	.372	34	148	121	23	32	5	1	2	19	25	1	0	1	35	0	0	16.9	23.6
Alexander, Blaze	R-R	5-11	160	6-11-99	.291	.408	.457	73	305	247	45	72	13	2	8	52	42	10	1	5	83	2	2	13.8	27.2
Barrosa, Jorge	B-L	5-5	165	2-17-01	.274	.394	.456	120	502	412	91	113	20	8	13	65	80	3	4	3	82	15	7	15.9	16.3
Beer, Seth	L-R	6-0	225	9-18-96	.200	.266	.314	19	79	70	5	14	2	0	2	12	6	1	0	2	23	0	0	7.6	29.1
Bliss, Ryan	R-R	5-6	165	12-13-99	.196	.274	.357	13	62	56	6	11	2	2	1	4	5	1	0	0	12	5	3	8.1	19.4
2-team (45 Tacoma)					.239	.339	.441	60	288	247	43	59	9	4	11	39	34	4	1	2	64	25	7	11.8	22.2
Canzone, Dominic	L-R	5-11	190	8-16-97	.354	.431	.634	71	304	257	61	91	18	3	16	71	39	1	0	7	40	2	3	12.8	13.2
Carrion, Julio	R-R	6-2	185	12-29-98	.333	.333	.333	1	3	3	0	1	0	0	0	0	0	0	0	0	2	0	0	0.0	66.7
Castillo, Diego	R-R	5-10	185	10-28-97	.313	.431	.410	124	556	454	94	142	33	1	3	72	97	0	1	4	79	13	10	17.4	14.2
Dalesandro, Nick	R-R	5-11	175	10-03-96	.207	.303	.241	9	33	29	4	6	1	0	0	2	4	0	0	0	10	2	0	12.1	30.3
Del Castillo, Adrian	L-R	5-9	208	9-27-99	.248	.340	.350	37	159	137	18	34	6	1	2	23	20	0	0	2	46	0	0	12.6	28.9
Duzenack, Camden	R-R	5-7	170	3-08-95	.217	.333	.304	6	27	23	5	5	2	0	0	2	4	0	0	0	2	0	1	14.8	7.4
English, Tristin	R-R	6-0	208	5-14-97	.293	.380	.514	84	371	321	60	94	20	0	17	73	40	7	0	3	82	1	3	10.8	22.1
Evans, Phillip	R-R	5-10	210	9-10-92	.312	.424	.439	128	590	481	107	150	24	2	11	88	92	8	0	9	75	2	2	15.6	12.7
Fletcher, Dominic	L-L	5-6	185	9-02-97	.291	.399	.500	66	334	278	71	81	18	5	10	45	42	10	1	3	62	5	2	12.6	18.6
Hager, Jake	R-R	6-1	170	3-04-93	.245	.301	.415	56	209	188	29	46	13	5	3	30	14	2	3	2	47	1	3	6.7	22.5
Herrera, Jose	B-R	5-10	217	2-24-97	.257	.364	.376	28	119	101	19	26	4	1	2	14	15	2	1	0	20	0	0	12.6	16.8
Higgins, P.J.	R-R	5-10	195	5-10-93	.317	.407	.473	58	263	224	50	71	15	1	6	46	33	3	0	3	49	1	0	12.5	18.6
Kelly, Carson	R-R	6-2	212	7-14-94	.345	.412	.448	8	34	29	5	10	3	0	0	4	3	1	0	1	8	0	0	8.8	23.5
Kennedy, Buddy	R-R	5-9	190	10-05-98	.318	.444	.481	90	417	337	76	107	24	8	5	46	70	8	0	2	68	3	3	16.8	16.3
2-team (11 Las Vegas)					.307	.436	.455	101	463	374	82	115	24	8	5	50	76	9	0	4	81	3	3	16.4	17.5
Lawlar, Jordan	R-R	6-1	190	7-17-02	.358	.438	.612	16	80	67	18	24	0	1	5	19	9	2	0	2	12	3	1	11.3	15.0
Lewis, Kyle	R-R	6-4	222	7-13-95	.371	.457	.641	63	293	248	55	92	16	0	17	80	39	3	0	3	58	0	0	13.3	19.8
Longoria, Evan	R-R	6-1	213	10-07-85	.000	.333	.000	3	12	8	1	0	0	0	0	0	4	0	0	0	3	0	0	33.3	25.0
Martin, David	L-R	6-1	185	10-28-00	.250	.231	.250	3	13	12	0	3	0	0	0	2	0	0	0	1	2	0	0	0.0	15.4
McCarthy, Jake	L-L	6-2	215	7-30-97	.360	.416	.594	45	221	197	42	71	13	3	9	36	17	4	0	3	29	15	4	7.7	13.1
Miroglio, Dominic	R-R	5-10	205	3-10-95	.265	.342	.397	21	76	68	10	18	6	0	1	16	7	1	0	0	12	0	0	9.2	15.8
Moreno, Gabriel	R-R	5-11	195	2-14-00	.500	.625	.667	2	8	6	2	3	1	0	0	2	1	1	0	0	0	0	0	12.5	0.0
Munoz, Yairo	R-R	5-11	200	1-23-95	.304	.389	.391	12	54	46	8	14	4	0	0	5	6	1	0	1	11	0	0	11.1	20.4
Rivera, Emmanuel	R-R	6-2	225	6-29-96	.330	.395	.598	28	129	112	23	37	9	3	5	25	12	2	0	3	18	1	0	9.3	14.0
Rojas, Josh	L-R	6-1	207	6-30-94	.255	.321	.373	12	56	51	9	13	0	0	2	8	5	0	0	0	10	1	0	8.9	17.9
Sanchez, Ali	R-R	6-1	200	1-20-97	.311	.375	.492	67	267	238	37	74	10	0	11	43	26	0	0	3	42	0	3	9.7	15.7
Smith, Pavin	L-L	6-2	208	2-06-96	.318	.428	.506	62	290	239	45	76	14	2	9	49	46	2	0	3	47	2	0	15.9	16.2
Thomas, Alek	L-L	5-11	175	4-28-00	.348	.409	.518	26	128	112	24	39	6	2	3	31	12	1	1	2	20	2	0	9.4	15.6
Walters, Jean	B-R	5-11	155	8-13-01	.000	.000	.000	1	4	4	0	0	0	0	0	0	0	0	0	0	1	0	0	0.0	25.0

Pitching	B-T	Ht.	Wt.	DOB	W	L	ERA	G	GS	SV	IP	Hits	Runs	ER	HR	BB	SO	AVG	OBP	SLG	SO%	BB%	BF
Adams, Austin	R-R	6-3	220	5-05-91	1	0	2.84	12	0	3	13	9	5	4	0	6	20	.191	.296	.234	37.0	11.1	54
Backhus, Kyle	L-L	6-4	185	1-31-98	0	1	3.29	11	0	0	14	11	5	5	1	6	12	.224	.298	.347	21.1	10.5	57

Barnes, Zach	R-R	6-0	180	4-10-99	1	0	18.00	1	0	0	1	2	2	2	0	1	0	.400	.500	.600	0.0	16.7	6
Biddle, Jesse	L-L	6-5	220	10-22-91	0	1	14.29	8	0	0	6	9	9	9	1	13	6	.375	.600	.625	15.0	32.5	40
Brice, Austin	R-R	6-4	238	6-19-92	0	0	24.00	5	0	0	3	6	12	8	1	9	3	.375	.630	.750	11.1	33.3	27
Briceno, Endrys	R-R	6-5	175	2-07-92	0	0	4.80	12	0	0	15	9	10	8	3	11	13	.173	.338	.423	19.1	16.2	68
Cecconi, Slade	R-R	6-4	219	6-24-99	5	9	6.11	23	23	0	116	124	81	79	24	36	118	.268	.327	.496	23.3	7.1	507
Chatwood, Tyler	R-R	5-11	200	12-16-89	0	0	1.69	5	0	0	5	3	1	1	0	1	2	.167	.200	.222	10.0	5.0	20
Crismatt, Nabil	R-R	6-1	220	12-25-94	4	3	6.85	14	9	0	47	59	38	36	10	18	44	.303	.361	.528	20.4	8.3	216
Davies, Zach	R-R	6-0	180	2-07-93	1	0	8.78	3	3	0	13	22	13	13	1	7	6	.386	.446	.561	9.2	10.8	65
Ferguson, Tyler	R-R	6-4	225	10-05-93	5	2	5.49	51	3	2	79	79	50	48	6	58	86	.258	.380	.399	23.2	15.7	370
Frias, Luis	R-R	6-3	245	5-23-98	3	0	3.13	27	0	4	32	21	11	11	3	9	36	.188	.254	.330	29.3	7.3	123
Gilbert, Tyler	L-L	6-3	223	12-22-93	7	3	5.30	30	7	0	75	89	47	44	10	26	88	.292	.351	.456	26.1	7.7	337
Ginkel, Kevin	L-R	6-4	235	3-24-94	1	0	0.00	4	0	1	5	4	0	0	0	0	11	.211	.211	.263	57.9	0.0	19
Green, Josh	R-R	6-3	211	8-31-95	6	1	6.75	18	0	0	35	42	27	26	5	12	26	.290	.356	.448	16.3	7.5	160
Gustave, Jandel	R-R	6-3	220	10-12-92	0	2	16.43	9	0	1	8	17	15	14	1	6	5	.447	.533	.605	10.6	12.8	47
Hager, Jake	R-R	6-1	170	3-04-93	0	0	4.50	2	0	0	2	1	2	1	1	0	0	.125	.125	.500	0.0	0.0	8
Hendrix, Ryan	R-R	6-3	215	12-16-94	0	0	3.00	3	0	0	3	2	1	1	1	1	2	.182	.250	.545	16.7	8.3	12
Henry, Tommy	L-L	6-3	205	7-29-97	1	0	6.33	4	4	0	21	23	15	15	3	8	22	.288	.356	.450	24.2	8.8	91
Jameson, Drey	R-R	6-0	165	8-17-97	4	0	5.79	5	5	0	28	29	18	18	2	11	24	.271	.344	.421	19.5	8.9	123
Jarvis, Bryce	L-R	6-2	195	12-26-97	7	5	5.26	24	16	0	92	92	60	54	10	46	96	.256	.344	.415	23.4	11.2	411
Mantiply, Joe	R-L	6-4	219	3-01-91	1	0	7.30	11	1	0	12	18	11	10	2	4	11	.340	.379	.528	19.0	6.9	58
Martinez, Justin	R-R	6-3	180	7-30-01	2	1	4.20	47	0	9	49	33	26	23	3	48	67	.190	.372	.287	29.6	21.2	226
McAllister, Zach	R-R	6-6	240	12-08-87	1	2	4.93	37	0	3	38	41	24	21	4	20	54	.268	.360	.412	30.3	11.2	178
Melancon, Mark	R-R	6-1	215	3-28-85	0	1	40.50	1	1	0	1	2	3	3	0	1	0	.500	.600	.500	0.0	20.0	5
Misiewicz, Anthony	R-L	6-1	196	11-01-94	2	0	2.84	10	0	0	13	12	4	4	1	5	14	.250	.321	.396	26.4	9.4	53
Nelson, Ryne	R-R	6-3	184	2-01-98	0	1	3.74	4	4	0	22	19	10	9	3	7	9	.247	.330	.377	10.2	8.0	88
Nogosek, Stephen	R-R	6-2	205	1-11-95	3	0	6.55	27	0	2	33	30	25	24	2	28	32	.238	.380	.325	20.1	17.6	159
Otanez, Michel	R-R	6-4	218	7-03-97	1	0	11.25	4	0	0	4	2	5	5	1	7	6	.143	.429	.429	28.6	33.3	21
Perez, Adonys	L-L	6-3	185	10-10-03	0	0	0.00	1	0	0	0	4	3	3	0	1	0	1.000	1.000	1.250	0.0	20.0	5
Pfaadt, Brandon	R-R	6-4	220	10-15-98	6	2	3.71	12	12	0	61	59	27	25	11	16	69	.251	.303	.455	27.1	6.3	255
Pilkington, Konnor	L-L	6-3	240	9-12-97	2	4	8.46	22	14	0	61	71	58	57	14	52	63	.290	.414	.535	20.7	17.1	304
Pope, Austin	R-R	6-3	210	10-26-98	4	0	2.45	19	0	3	22	26	10	6	1	8	28	.302	.358	.395	29.2	8.3	96
Ruiz, Jose	R-R	6-1	245	10-21-94	0	1	4.10	17	4	1	26	24	12	12	3	13	33	.238	.330	.376	28.7	11.3	115
Saalfrank, Andrew	L-L	6-3	205	8-18-97	4	2	2.35	23	0	1	31	22	10	8	2	15	48	.196	.291	.304	37.5	11.7	128
Sanchez, Aaron	R-R	6-4	212	7-01-92	0	1	6.61	4	4	0	16	23	15	12	3	10	11	.319	.393	.542	13.1	11.9	84
Solomon, Peter	R-R	6-4	211	8-16-96	1	7	10.00	18	10	0	54	94	67	60	11	35	57	.378	.455	.586	19.7	12.1	289
Strzelecki, Peter	R-R	6-2	216	10-24-94	0	1	8.76	13	0	0	12	12	12	12	0	16	16	.255	.462	.362	24.6	24.6	65
Stumpo, Mitchell	R-R	6-2	205	6-17-96	0	2	16.55	12	0	1	10	17	19	19	5	15	4	.386	.550	.773	6.7	25.0	60
Sulser, Cole	R-R	6-1	190	3-12-90	0	0	9.00	2	0	0	2	2	2	2	0	3	3	.286	.500	.429	30.0	30.0	10
Thompson, Ryan	R-R	6-5	210	6-26-92	0	0	0.00	2	0	0	3	0	0	0	0	0	4	.000	.000	.000	50.0	0.0	8
Vargas, Carlos	R-R	6-4	210	10-13-99	1	1	7.02	38	0	2	42	57	42	33	3	32	36	.322	.425	.435	17.0	15.1	212
Vizcaino, Raffi	R-R	6-0	237	12-02-95	2	2	6.59	14	0	0	14	13	10	10	1	15	20	.250	.426	.346	29.4	22.1	68
Walston, Blake	L-L	6-5	175	6-28-01	12	6	4.52	30	30	0	149	142	81	75	9	93	104	.254	.367	.366	15.6	14.0	666
Zuber, Tyler	R-R	5-11	195	6-16-95	0	1	5.23	16	0	0	21	21	12	12	3	10	18	.266	.344	.430	20.0	11.1	90

Fielding

Catcher	PCT	G	PO	A	E	DP	PB
Del Castillo	.992	29	241	17	2	0	6
Herrera	.992	24	224	12	2	1	1
Higgins	.989	30	250	14	3	0	2
Kelly	1.000	7	67	1	0	0	0
Miroglio	.984	13	117	6	2	1	3
Moreno	1.000	1	2	0	0	0	0
Sanchez	.998	53	429	30	1	6	2

First Base	PCT	G	PO	A	E	DP
Beer	.979	6	43	3	1	3
Canzone	1.000	1	8	0	0	0
English	.995	49	344	21	2	45
Evans	1.000	36	248	22	0	31
Higgins	1.000	16	98	9	0	10
Miroglio	1.000	1	9	1	0	3
Munoz	1.000	6	40	4	0	6
Rivera	1.000	5	17	2	0	1
Sanchez	1.000	1	7	1	0	0
Smith	.996	32	233	23	1	23

Second Base	PCT	G	PO	A	E	DP
Alcantara	.938	12	18	27	3	8
Alexander	1.000	8	13	22	0	2
Bliss	1.000	13	21	38	0	11
Castillo	.962	31	60	92	6	34
Duzenack	1.000	3	4	12	0	4
Evans	1.000	25	40	48	0	12
Hager	1.000	2	1	3	0	1
Kennedy	.969	57	116	134	8	34
Walters	1.000	1	3	2	0	0

Third Base	PCT	G	PO	A	E	DP
Alcantara	.840	16	6	15	4	0
Alexander	1.000	4	1	0	0	0
Castillo	.923	6	5	7	1	1
Duzenack	1.000	1	0	2	0	0
Evans	.928	60	44	110	12	14
Hager	.909	5	1	9	1	1
Higgins	.750	1	1	2	1	1
Kennedy	.957	23	11	33	2	3
Lawlar	1.000	1	0	1	0	0
Longoria	1.000	1	0	1	0	0
Munoz	.818	5	2	7	2	1
Rivera	.926	25	9	41	4	4
Rojas	.935	9	8	21	2	3

Shortstop	PCT	G	PO	A	E	DP
Alcantara	.963	8	9	17	1	3
Alexander	.982	60	74	148	4	40
Castillo	.973	24	29	43	2	7
Duzenack	1.000	1	3	2	0	2
Hager	.981	46	47	108	3	27
Lawlar	.952	15	24	36	3	11

Outfield	PCT	G	PO	A	E	DP
Barrosa	.972	120	304	2	4	0
Canzone	.981	61	101	5	2	1
Castillo	.988	63	76	6	1	1
Dalesandro	1.000	8	11	0	0	0
Del Castillo	.000	1	0	0	0	0
Duzenack	1.000	1	3	0	0	0
English	1.000	24	43	1	0	0
Fletcher	.995	66	162	3	1	0
Hager	1.000	1	1	0	0	0
Kennedy	.000	1	0	0	0	0
Lewis	.947	19	35	1	2	0
McCarthy	.922	44	85	1	2	1
Smith	1.000	28	49	2	0	1
Thomas	.981	22	57	0	2	0

AMARILLO SOD POODLES

DOUBLE-A

TEXAS LEAGUE

Batting	B-T	Ht.	Wt.	DOB	AVG	OBP	SLG	G	PA	AB	R	H	2B	3B	HR	RBI	BB	HBP	SH	SF	SO	SB	CS	BB%	SO%
Beer, Seth	L-R	6-0	225	9-18-96	.290	.387	.482	83	359	307	58	89	20	0	13	54	34	16	0	2	81	0	0	9.5	22.6
Bliss, Ryan	R-R	5-6	165	12-13-99	.358	.414	.594	68	324	293	67	105	25	4	12	47	24	5	0	2	55	30	8	7.4	17.0
Carrion, Julio	R-R	6-2	185	12-29-98	.500	.667	1.000	1	3	2	2	1	1	0	0	2	0	1	0	0	1	0	0	0.0	33.3
Castillo, Neyfy	R-R	6-1	175	3-02-01	.239	.317	.448	98	391	348	61	83	16	3	17	63	35	6	0	2	128	19	6	9.0	32.7
Centeno, Juan	L-R	5-9	195	11-16-89	.271	.324	.327	68	273	251	25	68	11	0	1	23	20	0	1	1	72	4	1	7.3	26.4
Chen, Sheng-Ping	L-R	5-9	165	10-27-00	.233	.340	.442	18	50	43	7	10	1	1	2	7	7	0	0	0	12	0	0	14.0	24.0
Cintron, Jancarlos	R-R	5-8	170	12-01-94	.225	.257	.268	20	74	71	6	16	3	0	0	4	3	0	0	0	14	2	1	4.1	18.9
D'Orazio, J.J.	R-R	6-1	170	12-28-01	.217	.236	.297	37	145	138	12	30	6	1	1	13	4	0	1	2	33	0	0	2.8	22.8
Dalesandro, Nick	R-R	5-11	175	10-03-96	.221	.299	.285	58	194	172	28	38	4	2	1	12	18	2	0	2	48	17	4	9.3	24.7
De Los Santos, Deyvison	R-R	5-11	185	6-21-03	.254	.297	.431	113	481	452	73	115	16	2	20	61	25	3	0	1	125	4	1	5.2	26.0
Del Castillo, Adrian	L-R	5-9	208	9-27-99	.273	.386	.505	63	265	220	36	60	13	1	12	45	40	2	1	2	67	2	2	15.1	25.3
Duzenack, Camden	R-R	5-7	170	3-08-95	.320	.392	.502	67	291	253	43	81	16	0	10	47	23	9	3	3	54	4	5	7.9	18.6
English, Tristin	R-R	6-0	208	5-14-97	.333	.436	.712	18	78	66	14	22	7	0	6	20	12	0	0	0	21	1	0	15.4	26.9
Enriquez, Roby	L-L	6-0	210	3-21-97	.258	.364	.335	48	184	155	19	40	12	0	0	16	24	3	0	2	32	5	1	13.0	17.4
Guzman, Jonathan	R-R	5-11	156	8-17-99	.310	.375	.414	9	32	29	5	9	0	0	1	7	3	0	0	0	9	1	0	9.4	28.1
Lawlar, Jordan	R-R	6-1	190	7-17-02	.263	.366	.474	89	410	350	77	92	23	3	15	48	47	11	0	2	89	33	4	11.5	21.7
Melendez, Ivan	R-R	6-3	225	1-24-00	.275	.335	.556	38	170	153	29	42	5	1	12	33	10	5	0	2	60	0	2	5.9	35.3
Roberts, Caleb	L-R	5-11	195	2-09-00	.278	.382	.523	97	434	367	72	102	23	8	17	66	58	6	0	3	114	11	3	13.4	26.3
Robinson, Kristian	R-R	6-3	190	12-11-00	.250	.294	.688	5	17	16	4	4	1	0	2	6	1	0	0	0	7	0	1	5.9	41.2
Tawa, Tim	R-R	5-10	196	4-07-99	.256	.338	.461	116	497	434	76	111	21	1	22	75	55	2	0	6	121	11	7	11.1	24.3
Valdez, Jesus	R-R	5-9	175	12-29-97	.400	.400	.600	7	20	20	4	8	1	0	1	4	0	0	0	0	4	1	1	0.0	20.0
Vicuna, Kevin	R-R	6-0	140	1-14-98	.255	.348	.418	32	115	98	19	25	4	0	4	11	11	3	2	0	19	1	0	9.6	16.5
Vukovich, A.J.	R-R	6-2	210	7-20-01	.263	.333	.485	115	507	456	84	120	19	5	24	96	46	3	0	2	144	20	9	9.1	28.4
Watkins, Jarrod	L-R	5-10	180	4-25-97	.231	.231	.462	5	13	13	2	3	1	1	0	3	0	0	0	0	4	0	0	0.0	30.8

Pitching	B-T	Ht.	Wt.	DOB	W	L	ERA	G	GS	SV	IP	Hits	Runs	ER	HR	BB	SO	AVG	OBP	SLG	SO%	BB%	BF
Albright, Luke	R-R	6-4	215	12-13-99	8	5	5.46	25	25	0	112	118	74	68	11	69	136	.270	.372	.430	26.5	13.4	514
Backhus, Kyle	L-L	6-4	185	1-31-98	5	4	3.76	40	0	10	55	56	25	23	6	26	64	.257	.341	.408	26.0	10.6	246
Bain, Jeff	R-R	6-4	200	3-03-96	1	3	7.16	19	7	0	55	73	53	44	17	17	48	.323	.382	.664	18.8	6.7	255
Barnes, Zach	R-R	6-0	180	4-10-99	0	0	6.75	2	0	0	4	5	3	3	0	3	2	.313	.421	.438	10.5	15.8	19
Briceno, Endrys	R-R	6-5	175	2-07-92	0	0	13.50	2	0	0	1	3	1	1	0	1	1	.600	.667	.600	16.7	16.7	6
Centeno, Juan	L-R	5-9	195	11-16-89	0	0	0.00	1	0	0	1	0	0	0	0	0	0	.000	.000	.000	0.0	0.0	3
Chen, Sheng-Ping	L-R	5-9	165	10-27-00	0	0	0.00	1	0	0	1	2	0	0	0	0	1	.333	.333	.333	16.7	0.0	6
Dalesandro, Nick	R-R	5-11	175	10-03-96	0	0	3.38	4	0	0	3	1	1	1	1	0	2	.111	.111	.444	22.2	0.0	9
Davies, Zach	R-R	6-0	180	2-07-93	0	0	0.00	1	1	0	5	3	0	0	0	1	7	.176	.222	.235	38.9	5.6	18
Diaz, Yilber	R-R	6-0	190	8-19-00	1	0	3.60	3	3	0	15	12	6	6	1	9	16	.222	.328	.296	25.0	14.1	64
Fisher, Hugh	R-L	6-6	210	2-11-99	0	1	10.80	9	0	0	8	10	14	10	3	15	9	.278	.509	.583	17.0	28.3	53
Goddard, Jackson	R-R	6-3	220	12-12-96	1	2	6.93	18	0	0	25	25	20	19	4	15	30	.253	.351	.434	26.1	13.0	115
Grammes, Conor	R-R	6-1	200	7-13-97	5	2	3.55	30	6	0	46	40	26	18	5	35	65	.240	.377	.359	31.4	16.9	207
Green, Josh	R-R	6-3	211	8-31-95	1	0	2.05	21	0	5	31	19	7	7	2	9	26	.178	.256	.290	21.5	7.4	121
Groen, Gunnar	R-R	6-6	220	7-01-97	0	1	10.80	2	2	0	5	12	7	6	1	1	3	.480	.481	.640	11.1	3.7	27
Hill, Jamison	R-R	6-1	180	3-28-99	7	6	4.35	26	25	0	118	95	60	57	13	74	104	.218	.344	.361	20.0	14.2	521
Jarvis, Bryce	L-R	6-2	195	12-26-97	2	1	3.86	3	3	0	14	8	8	6	0	7	17	.170	.273	.213	30.9	12.7	55
Larsen, Dillon	R-L	6-5	230	7-09-98	0	0	5.72	16	0	0	28	19	18	18	3	32	26	.192	.391	.354	19.4	23.9	134
Lin, Yu-Min	L-L	5-11	160	7-12-03	5	2	4.28	11	11	0	61	49	34	29	7	26	64	.221	.323	.351	24.7	10.0	259
Mabrey, Will	L-L	6-0	185	9-23-00	4	0	3.20	16	2	2	25	16	9	9	4	18	20	.190	.340	.381	19.2	17.3	104
Mantiply, Joe	R-L	6-4	219	3-01-91	2	0	0.00	2	0	0	3	2	0	0	0	0	3	.200	.200	.300	30.0	0.0	10
Meza, Carlos	L-L	6-1	155	2-10-01	0	0	15.19	5	0	0	5	10	10	9	0	4	7	.417	.452	.500	22.6	12.9	31
Montes De Oca, Chr.	R-R	6-4	230	8-30-99	2	3	4.28	42	0	9	61	51	33	29	8	26	55	.227	.311	.382	21.5	10.2	256
Montilla, Emailin	L-L	4-4	255	10-02-95	0	1	6.00	11	1	0	15	20	16	10	0	9	15	.313	.392	.438	20.3	12.2	74
Norris, Liam	L-L	6-4	215	8-13-01	0	2	16.88	4	0	0	3	5	6	5	1	6	4	.417	.611	.833	22.2	33.3	18
Ogando, Gerald	R-R	6-2	180	7-28-00	1	2	9.82	9	0	1	11	16	13	12	1	11	13	.364	.482	.568	23.2	19.6	56
Olivero, Deyni	R-R	6-1	165	1-07-98	5	5	9.53	17	17	0	68	108	77	72	15	38	38	.367	.441	.609	11.2	11.2	338
Otanez, Michel	R-R	6-4	218	7-03-97	4	2	5.45	28	0	1	33	30	21	20	2	21	55	.238	.364	.349	36.2	13.8	152
Patrick, Chad	R-R	6-1	205	8-14-98	4	7	4.71	19	19	0	92	91	49	48	11	36	90	.260	.332	.417	22.9	9.2	393
Pope, Austin	R-R	6-3	210	10-26-98	2	0	4.23	29	0	1	45	43	22	21	5	15	56	.256	.321	.417	29.3	7.9	191
Rashi, Taylor	R-R	6-4	220	1-15-96	3	0	0.73	8	0	1	12	4	1	1	0	1	17	.098	.119	.171	40.5	2.4	42
Ray, Dylan	R-R	6-3	230	5-09-01	1	2	8.36	3	3	0	14	17	14	13	3	8	15	.309	.403	.564	22.4	11.9	67
Rice, Jake	L-L	6-1	220	7-19-97	5	0	7.50	40	0	3	42	37	35	35	5	34	58	.234	.390	.380	28.9	16.9	201
Rincon, Hansel	R-R	6-1	160	8-23-02	0	0	4.50	1	0	0	2	4	3	1	0	3	1	.400	.538	.600	7.7	23.1	13
Saalfrank, Andrew	L-L	6-3	205	8-18-97	4	0	2.70	21	0	1	33	23	11	10	0	20	45	.195	.312	.237	31.9	14.2	141
Saul, Eli	L-R	6-5	215	8-16-01	0	0	3.86	2	0	0	2	2	1	1	0	1	2	.250	.300	.250	20.0	10.0	10
Solomon, Peter	R-R	6-4	211	8-16-96	0	2	4.17	7	7	0	37	36	22	17	6	10	38	.252	.303	.420	24.5	6.5	155
Sosa, Listher	R-R	6-4	208	9-06-01	1	0	12.46	3	0	0	4	6	6	6	3	4	5	.316	.435	.947	21.7	17.4	23
Stumpo, Mitchell	R-R	6-2	205	6-17-96	1	4	6.95	30	0	0	34	36	30	26	6	31	54	.269	.408	.455	32.0	18.3	169
Tineo, Marcos	R-R	6-0	165	3-14-97	0	3	15.30	4	4	0	10	15	20	17	1	18	6	.341	.532	.545	9.7	29.0	62
Valdez, Jesus	R-R	5-9	175	12-29-97	0	0	0.00	1	0	0	1	0	0	0	0	1	0	.000	.250	.000	0.0	25.0	4
Vizcaino, Raffi	R-R	6-0	237	12-02-95	1	1	4.63	27	2	4	35	29	22	18	7	22	48	.225	.340	.450	31.2	14.3	154
Workman, Blake	R-R	6-3	195	10-08-97	1	0	6.90	17	0	0	30	33	25	23	11	9	32	.277	.338	.630	24.2	6.8	132

Fielding

Catcher	PCT	G	PO	A	E	DP	PB
Centeno	.993	41	400	29	3	1	4
D'Orazio	.993	27	261	23	2	1	3
Dalesandro	.923	1	11	1	1	0	0
Del Castillo	.988	41	372	28	5	1	7
Roberts	.990	30	272	19	3	2	8

First Base	PCT	G	PO	A	E	DP
Beer	.996	66	451	21	2	41
Castillo	1.000	5	29	1	0	2
De Los Santos	.992	35	234	16	2	27
English	.976	11	75	5	2	5
Melendez	.984	10	58	4	1	7
Roberts	.981	8	51	1	1	2
Vukovich	.979	7	42	5	1	4

Second Base	PCT	G	PO	A	E	DP
Bliss	.973	55	69	114	5	19
Chen	.935	13	19	24	3	9
Cintron	1.000	7	8	13	0	2
Duzenack	.911	14	24	27	5	5
Tawa	.975	47	75	119	5	29
Valdez	1.000	2	3	4	0	1
Vicuna	.952	5	11	9	1	2

Third Base	PCT	G	PO	A	E	DP
Cintron	.889	2	2	6	1	1
De Los Santos	.932	74	48	116	12	5
Duzenack	.960	12	9	15	1	0
Melendez	.933	24	19	37	4	5
Tawa	.867	5	6	7	2	0
Valdez	.857	4	2	4	1	1
Vicuna	1.000	7	4	6	0	1
Vukovich	.955	15	11	31	2	4

Shortstop	PCT	G	PO	A	E	DP
Bliss	1.000	10	11	24	0	5
Chen	1.000	1	4	1	0	1
Cintron	.947	13	16	38	3	11
Duzenack	.976	24	31	50	2	14
Lawlar	.976	84	128	195	8	35
Vicuna	.889	9	10	22	4	7

Outfield	PCT	G	PO	A	E	DP
Carrion	1.000	1	1	0	0	0
Castillo	.968	83	152	10	4	4
Dalesandro	1.000	53	85	5	0	3
Duzenack	.980	19	30	2	1	0
English	1.000	3	2	0	0	0
Enriquez	.993	42	74	4	1	0
Guzman	1.000	9	21	1	0	0
Roberts	.961	48	85	7	1	0
Robinson	.775	4	7	0	2	0
Tawa	1.000	60	121	5	0	1
Vicuna	1.000	10	15	1	0	0
Vukovich	.991	91	209	4	2	0
Watkins	1.000	4	4	1	0	0

HILLSBORO HOPS

HIGH CLASS A

NORTHWEST LEAGUE

Batting	B-T	Ht.	Wt.	DOB	AVG	OBP	SLG	G	PA	AB	R	H	2B	3B	HR	RBI	BB	HBP	SH	SF	SO	SB	CS	BB%	SO%
Carrion, Julio	R-R	6-2	185	12-29-98	.176	.222	.235	5	18	17	0	3	1	0	0	2	1	0	0	0	3	0	0	5.6	16.7
Cerda, Christian	R-R	6-0	190	12-27-02	.236	.411	.425	40	168	127	24	30	6	0	6	21	38	1	0	2	35	0	0	22.6	20.8
Chen, Sheng-Ping	L-R	5-9	165	10-27-00	.207	.296	.298	59	227	198	21	41	6	0	4	18	25	1	1	2	59	4	2	11.0	26.0
Conticello, Gavin	L-R	6-4	195	6-11-03	.263	.282	.500	10	39	38	4	10	3	0	2	9	1	0	0	0	11	0	0	2.6	28.2
Corniel, Juan	B-R	5-11	150	10-02-02	.225	.280	.297	42	150	138	16	31	4	0	2	10	10	1	0	1	24	1	6	6.7	16.0
D'Orazio, J.J.	R-R	6-1	170	12-28-01	.308	.380	.488	67	296	260	41	80	17	3	8	37	31	1	0	3	56	2	0	10.5	18.9
Day, Joshua	R-R	6-2	200	3-25-00	.197	.283	.303	82	337	300	32	59	10	2	6	29	25	11	1	0	93	3	3	7.4	27.6
Franco, Junior	L-L	5-9	165	9-13-02	.230	.304	.351	58	247	222	28	51	11	2	4	23	21	3	0	1	56	9	6	8.5	22.7
Graham, Kevin	L-R	6-1	195	8-12-99	.252	.328	.354	63	256	226	27	57	11	3	2	29	24	3	0	3	63	7	4	9.4	24.6
Groover, Gino	R-R	6-2	212	4-16-02	.264	.340	.379	23	100	87	13	23	5	1	1	14	8	3	0	2	9	1	1	8.0	9.0
Guzman, Jonathan	R-R	5-11	156	8-17-99	.219	.352	.260	19	88	73	9	16	0	0	1	9	13	2	0	0	23	4	1	14.8	26.1
Hurley, Jack	L-R	6-0	185	3-13-02	.293	.341	.415	20	88	82	12	24	5	1	1	6	5	1	0	0	25	6	1	5.7	28.4
Johnson, Brett	L-R	5-11	195	1-06-00	.172	.317	.273	30	121	99	11	17	5	1	1	7	21	0	1	0	38	4	1	17.4	31.4
Logan, Gavin	L-R	5-9	212	1-14-00	.144	.301	.216	54	206	167	16	24	4	1	2	14	35	3	0	1	62	2	2	17.0	30.1
Malave, Ramses	R-R	5-11	175	9-29-00	.136	.224	.182	15	49	44	4	6	2	0	0	2	5	0	0	0	15	0	0	10.2	30.6
Martin, David	L-R	6-1	185	10-28-00	.287	.412	.352	37	148	122	14	35	2	0	2	16	22	4	0	0	18	0	0	14.9	12.2
Mattis, Gary	R-R	5-11	175	2-01-98	.260	.325	.451	47	192	173	24	45	9	3	6	24	13	4	1	1	59	3	1	6.8	30.7
Melendez, Ivan	R-R	6-3	225	1-24-00	.270	.352	.593	58	256	226	36	61	17	1	18	43	21	8	0	1	86	4	0	8.2	33.6
Muntz, Shane	R-R	6-4	240	2-23-99	.233	.333	.377	62	252	215	25	50	11	1	6	28	26	8	0	3	66	3	1	10.3	26.2
Ortiz, Channy	B-R	5-10	165	4-11-99	.237	.305	.322	67	273	245	33	58	7	4	2	21	22	3	1	2	54	6	3	8.1	19.8
Patino, Wilderd	R-R	6-1	175	7-18-01	.259	.370	.338	99	449	382	73	99	13	1	5	33	45	22	0	0	126	47	10	10.0	28.1
Pena, Manuel	L-R	6-1	170	12-05-03	.242	.301	.381	57	237	215	25	52	10	4	4	24	17	2	1	2	59	5	5	7.2	24.9
Pintar, Andrew	R-R	6-2	190	3-23-01	.241	.299	.348	37	157	141	17	34	7	1	2	14	11	2	0	3	36	4	6	7.0	22.9
Roberson, Jacen	L-L	6-1	192	5-23-00	.117	.281	.189	38	140	111	11	13	2	0	2	11	25	1	1	2	45	5	2	17.9	32.1
Robinson, Kristian	R-R	6-3	190	12-11-00	.265	.359	.441	10	39	34	6	9	0	0	2	6	4	1	0	0	13	2	3	10.3	33.3
Troy, Tommy	R-R	5-10	197	1-17-02	.247	.343	.447	23	99	85	13	21	5	0	4	16	12	1	0	1	26	8	0	12.1	26.3
Valdez, Jesus	R-R	5-9	175	12-29-97	.222	.247	.412	70	292	279	33	62	12	4	11	41	7	3	0	3	76	5	2	2.4	26.0
Vicuna, Kevin	R-R	6-0	140	1-14-98	.286	.333	.357	4	16	14	0	4	1	0	0	0	0	1	1	0	4	1	0	0.0	25.0
Walters, Jean	B-R	5-11	155	8-13-01	.179	.207	.250	11	29	28	2	5	2	0	0	4	1	0	0	0	8	0	0	3.4	27.6
Watkins, Jarrod	L-R	5-10	180	4-25-97	.086	.179	.143	10	39	35	2	3	0	1	0	3	2	2	0	0	9	1	1	5.1	23.1

Pitching	B-T	Ht.	Wt.	DOB	W	L	ERA	G	GS	SV	IP	Hits	Runs	ER	HR	BB	SO	AVG	OBP	SLG	SO%	BB%	BF
Alcantara, Jose	R-R	6-2	180	8-03-99	3	2	4.87	11	0	0	20	19	14	11	1	17	21	.250	.387	.395	22.3	18.1	94
Barnes, Zach	R-R	6-0	180	4-10-99	4	4	4.21	39	0	0	58	61	32	27	5	31	52	.270	.370	.403	19.8	11.8	263
Cabrera, Jose	R-R	6-3	190	5-30-02	0	3	6.81	8	8	0	37	40	31	28	3	24	29	.270	.382	.432	16.3	13.5	178
Clayton, Logan	R-R	6-5	188	5-02-00	2	2	6.19	24	1	3	32	45	27	22	3	21	32	.331	.420	.522	19.6	12.9	163
Corcoran, Billy	R-R	6-8	220	8-21-99	1	4	4.76	19	5	1	40	36	26	21	4	15	43	.240	.308	.393	25.4	8.9	169
Diaz, Yilber	R-R	6-0	190	8-19-00	2	10	5.03	22	22	0	88	68	54	49	13	49	124	.215	.324	.391	33.0	13.0	376
Elbis, Joe	R-R	6-1	150	9-24-02	1	7	4.84	14	14	0	74	69	46	40	9	37	60	.244	.348	.428	18.3	11.3	328
Fisher, Hugh	R-L	6-6	210	2-11-99	2	0	3.68	5	0	0	7	5	3	3	1	3	10	.179	.281	.321	31.3	9.4	32
Giesting, Spencer	L-L	6-4	200	7-02-01	7	6	4.00	24	24	0	117	100	58	52	9	71	124	.227	.341	.352	23.7	13.6	523
Grammes, Conor	R-R	6-1	200	7-13-97	0	1	3.38	10	0	1	13	7	5	5	0	10	17	.159	.351	.159	29.8	17.5	57
Groen, Gunnar	R-R	6-6	220	7-01-97	3	0	1.00	5	0	0	9	10	3	1	0	4	10	.270	.333	.297	23.8	9.5	42
Kelly, Levi	R-R	6-4	205	5-14-99	0	0	11.05	7	0	0	7	8	10	9	0	12	2	.276	.476	.517	4.8	28.6	42
Larsen, Dillon	R-L	6-5	230	7-09-98	1	4	4.54	25	0	0	42	41	23	21	0	38	55	.258	.411	.308	27.1	18.7	203
Lin, Yu-Min	L-L	5-11	160	7-12-03	1	3	3.43	13	13	0	60	47	26	23	3	22	76	.223	.305	.322	32.1	9.3	237
Linskey, Matthew	R-R	6-7	245	4-19-02	0	0	0.00	1	0	0	1	0	0	0	0	0	2	.000	.000	.000	66.7	0.0	3
Mabrey, Will	L-L	6-0	185	9-23-00	1	1	2.33	18	0	2	27	19	8	7	1	5	31	.194	.238	.286	29.5	4.8	105
Malave, Ramses	R-R	5-11	175	9-29-00	0	0	11.57	2	0	0	2	4	3	3	1	3	0	.364	.500	.727	0.0	21.4	14
Mendez, Eric	R-R	6-0	175	12-03-99	0	2	18.90	7	0	0	10	21	21	21	6	6	10	.412	.483	.863	17.2	10.3	58

Meza, Carlos	L-L	6-1	155	2-10-01	3	4	4.94	35	0	1	47	44	37	26	3	31	61	.238	.364	.362	27.1	13.8	225
Mieses, Junior	R-R	6-1	168	10-15-99	1	0	6.46	21	0	1	24	14	18	17	5	28	32	.175	.427	.375	27.4	23.9	117
Montilla, Emailin	L-L	4-4	255	10-02-95	0	0	2.45	5	0	0	7	4	2	2	2	1	10	.160	.185	.400	37.0	3.7	27
Morillo, Alfred	R-R	6-3	190	11-14-01	0	0	7.71	8	0	1	9	18	14	8	1	6	15	.383	.473	.596	27.3	10.9	55
Norris, Liam	L-L	6-4	215	8-13-01	2	2	2.50	15	0	2	18	7	6	5	2	12	34	.113	.276	.226	44.7	15.8	76
Ogando, Gerald	R-R	6-2	180	7-28-00	2	1	4.25	22	0	1	30	24	23	14	3	20	36	.216	.348	.333	26.7	14.8	135
Ortiz, Channy	B-R	5-10	165	4-11-99	0	0	0.00	3	0	0	1	0	0	0	0	1	0	.000	.250	.000	0.0	25.0	4
Otano, Peniel	R-R	6-4	190	10-07-00	3	5	6.91	39	0	4	56	50	51	43	2	39	58	.234	.365	.313	22.3	15.0	260
Ray, Dylan	R-R	6-3	230	5-09-01	7	6	3.81	22	22	0	99	84	43	42	8	32	123	.229	.297	.343	30.4	7.9	404
Russell, Zane	R-R	6-2	196	6-12-02	2	0	0.00	3	0	0	7	4	0	0	0	4	8	.190	.320	.190	32.0	16.0	25
Saul, Eli	L-R	6-5	215	8-16-01	2	1	5.46	38	7	3	59	64	41	36	6	34	45	.281	.387	.404	16.4	12.4	275
Short, Avery	R-L	6-1	205	3-14-01	1	4	5.40	11	10	0	45	55	28	27	9	17	36	.306	.372	.550	18.1	8.5	199
Sierra, Diomede	L-L	6-2	170	9-11-01	0	0	4.50	5	0	0	6	5	3	3	1	5	9	.227	.370	.364	33.3	18.5	27
Sosa, Listher	R-R	6-4	208	9-06-01	4	2	4.67	36	1	3	69	69	44	36	8	23	62	.258	.348	.427	20.3	7.5	305
Tineo, Marcos	R-R	6-0	165	3-14-97	0	1	5.14	2	2	0	7	6	4	4	0	4	8	.214	.313	.321	25.0	12.5	32
Vasquez, Armando	L-L	5-11	160	5-04-01	0	1	2.89	6	0	0	9	10	6	3	2	3	12	.294	.351	.471	32.4	8.1	37
Walters, Jean	B R	5 11	155	8 13 01	0	0	0.00	1	0	0	1	0	0	0	0	0	0	.000	.000	.000	0.0	0.0	2
Yan, Ricardo	R-R	6-4	180	11-14-02	1	0	1.19	5	3	0	23	10	3	3	1	11	33	.133	.270	.187	37.1	12.4	89

Fielding

Catcher	PCT	G	PO	A	E	DP	PB
Cerda	.992	33	325	28	3	2	6
D'Orazio	.993	43	409	38	3	5	9
Logan	.981	35	338	22	7	3	7
Malave	1.000	7	59	14	0	2	3
Martin	.993	16	138	8	1	0	7
Muntz	1.000	2	8	1	0	0	0

First Base	PCT	G	PO	A	E	DP
Conticello	1.000	6	34	5	0	7
Day	1.000	4	40	1	0	3
Logan	.977	10	77	7	2	6
Malave	.943	4	31	2	2	7
Martin	.987	22	134	17	2	12
Melendez	.995	26	197	14	1	16
Muntz	.990	53	378	22	4	41
Valdez	1.000	5	31	4	0	4
Vicuna	1.000	3	24	3	0	2
Walters	1.000	3	5	2	0	0
Watkins	1.000	2	19	0	0	1

Second Base	PCT	G	PO	A	E	DP
Chen	.982	35	76	91	3	20
Corniel	.962	13	24	27	2	5
Day	.963	20	46	59	4	13
Guzman	1.000	2	6	8	0	3
Ortiz	.984	14	18	45	1	10
Pena	.952	43	87	110	10	31
Pintar	.821	7	14	9	5	5

Third Base	PCT	G	PO	A	E	DP
Conticello	.800	3	1	3	1	1
Corniel	.889	3	2	6	1	3
Day	.918	29	16	40	5	2
Groover	.918	18	7	38	4	2
Melendez	.948	33	19	73	5	7
Ortiz	.909	3	2	8	1	0
Pena	.895	8	7	10	2	2
Valdez	.931	39	21	73	7	11
Walters	1.000	1	2	2	0	1

Shortstop	PCT	G	PO	A	E	DP
Chen	.973	15	16	20	1	6
Corniel	.956	26	27	59	4	13
Day	.989	27	28	58	1	14
Guzman	.929	5	5	8	1	1
Ortiz	.990	25	27	74	1	11
Troy	.944	18	19	49	4	6
Valdez	.947	18	19	52	4	11
Walters	1.000	3	5	11	0	3

Outfield	PCT	G	PO	A	E	DP
Carrion	.909	5	9	1	1	0
Chen	1.000	1	3	1	0	1
Franco	.974	50	76	0	4	0
Graham	.995	58	106	2	1	1
Guzman	.933	11	21	4	1	0
Hurley	1.000	16	30	1	0	0
Johnson	.963	30	49	3	1	0
Malave	1.000	1	1	0	0	0
Mattis	.974	26	31	1	1	0
Ortiz	.979	26	33	3	1	0
Patino	.953	99	198	6	6	1
Pena	1.000	1	1	0	0	0
Pintar	.976	22	41	3	1	1
Roberson	.990	40	50	6	1	0
Robinson	1.000	10	20	0	0	0
Vicuna	1.000	1	2	0	0	0
Walters	1.000	2	9	0	0	0
Watkins	.882	8	15	0	2	0

VISALIA RAWHIDE

LOW CLASS A

CALIFORNIA LEAGUE

Batting	B-T	Ht.	Wt.	DOB	AVG	OBP	SLG	G	PA	AB	R	H	2B	3B	HR	RBI	BB	HBP	SH	SF	SO	SB	CS	BB%	SO%
Benitez, Johan	B-R	6-3	170	8-07-03	.231	.294	.308	56	216	195	19	45	9	0	2	15	18	0	2	1	65	5	3	8.3	30.1
Boyd, Jermiah	R-R	5-10	225	7-01-00	.190	.227	.262	12	44	42	3	8	3	0	0	7	1	1	0	0	14	0	0	2.3	31.8
Cabral, Riquelmin	B-R	5-10	165	5-12-03	.183	.255	.279	56	216	197	25	36	9	2	2	14	19	0	0	0	70	4	1	8.8	32.4
Carrion, Julio	R-R	6-2	185	12-29-98	.239	.289	.366	41	152	142	16	34	7	1	3	13	7	3	0	0	61	0	0	4.6	40.1
Castillo, Kenny	R-R	6-2	170	5-13-04	.207	.247	.264	23	93	87	10	18	3	1	0	4	4	1	0	1	22	0	0	4.3	23.7
Cerda, Christian	R-R	6-0	190	12-27-02	.252	.397	.382	68	302	238	35	60	14	1	5	32	55	5	0	4	61	1	0	18.2	20.2
Conticello, Gavin	L-R	6-4	195	6-11-03	.216	.314	.408	100	427	370	50	80	20	3	15	49	45	9	0	3	95	12	5	10.5	22.2
Corniel, Juan	B-R	5-11	150	10-02-02	.237	.328	.309	66	272	236	35	56	7	5	0	21	28	5	1	2	52	14	4	10.3	19.1
Feltner, Jackson	R-R	6-2	225	9-19-01	.208	.406	.250	8	32	24	4	5	1	0	0	1	6	2	0	0	11	0	0	18.8	34.4
Fernandez, Jose	R-R	6-3	165	9-22-03	.262	.320	.377	95	394	355	50	93	18	4	5	44	31	2	0	6	92	9	2	7.9	23.4
Franco, Junior	L-L	5-9	165	9-13-02	.222	.286	.278	5	21	18	0	4	1	0	0	3	2	0	0	1	10	1	0	9.5	47.6
Gutierrez, Sergio	B-R	6-1	195	1-18-01	.147	.286	.373	24	91	75	13	11	2	0	5	10	14	1	0	1	38	2	0	15.4	41.8
Guzman, Alvin	R-R	6-1	166	10-20-01	.223	.312	.360	94	382	336	49	75	11	4	9	49	41	3	1	1	148	32	5	10.7	38.7
Hurley, Jack	L-R	6-0	185	3-13-02	.265	.405	.471	9	42	34	3	9	4	0	1	5	7	1	0	0	13	3	0	16.7	31.0
Johnson, Brett	L-R	5-11	195	1-06-00	.226	.380	.383	42	167	133	29	30	10	1	3	16	31	2	1	0	53	6	2	18.6	31.7
Jones, Druw	R-R	6-4	180	11-28-03	.252	.366	.351	29	131	111	19	28	3	1	2	9	20	0	0	0	34	6	2	15.3	26.0
Logan, Gavin	L-R	5-9	212	1-14-00	.258	.388	.530	20	80	66	12	17	4	1	4	9	12	2	0	0	28	0	1	15.0	35.0
Luis, Jansel	B-R	6-0	170	3-06-05	.257	.310	.417	36	155	144	19	37	5	3	4	15	8	3	0	0	35	7	2	5.2	22.6
Martin, David	L-R	6-1	185	10-28-00	.294	.414	.373	53	220	177	32	52	11	0	1	25	34	5	0	4	26	1	3	15.5	11.8
Ortiz, Francisco	R-R	6-0	160	9-15-99	.200	.286	.200	2	7	5	0	1	0	0	0	1	1	0	0	1	2	0	0	14.3	28.6
Pena, Manuel	L-R	6-1	170	12-05-03	.248	.314	.345	52	229	206	22	51	9	4	1	24	19	2	0	2	58	8	5	8.3	25.3
Pintar, Andrew	R-R	6-2	190	3-23-01	.241	.328	.370	14	61	54	7	13	4	0	1	5	5	2	0	0	12	2	0	8.2	19.7
Polanco, Ronny	R-R	5-11	180	8-23-03	.153	.216	.241	34	148	137	13	21	4	1	2	13	8	3	0	0	48	2	0	5.4	32.4
Robinson, Kristian	R-R	6-3	190	12-11-00	.288	.407	.538	43	189	156	29	45	6	3	9	26	24	8	0	1	58	20	3	12.7	30.7
Rojas, Anderdson	L-R	5-10	150	3-08-04	.249	.285	.346	93	419	393	45	98	20	6	2	51	13	8	2	3	69	12	5	3.1	16.5
Rubio, Luis	R-R	5-10	155	1-10-02	.094	.256	.094	11	39	32	2	3	0	0	0	0	7	0	0	0	10	1	0	17.9	25.6

Sanabria, Danyer	L-L	6-1	155	3-07-02	.238	.303	.360	58	191	172	29	41	9	3	2	24	16	0	3	0	55	2	1	8.4	28.8
Sim, Kevin	R-R	6-2	210	2-07-02	.255	.333	.400	29	123	110	14	28	7	0	3	14	10	3	0	0	31	1	2	8.1	25.2
Torin, Cristofer	R-R	5-10	155	5-26-05	.236	.314	.300	39	156	140	16	33	1	1	2	11	14	2	0	0	30	6	4	9.0	19.2
Torres, Daniel	R-R	5-9	150	1-10-02	.222	.293	.250	12	42	36	6	8	1	0	0	3	4	0	1	1	13	3	1	9.5	31.0

Pitching	B-T	Ht.	Wt.	DOB	W	L	ERA	G	GS	SV	IP	Hits	Runs	ER	HR	BB	SO	AVG	OBP	SLG	SO%	BB%	BF
Abner, Philip	L-L	6-1	220	5-05-02	1	0	5.40	4	0	0	7	5	5	4	0	4	6	.200	.310	.200	20.7	13.8	29
Alvarez, Jhosmer	R-R	6-1	155	6-29-01	0	0	8.31	3	0	0	4	7	6	4	2	5	6	.333	.462	.619	23.1	19.2	26
Amendt, Kyle	R-R	6-5	237	4-05-00	1	0	0.00	9	0	3	11	3	0	0	0	9	21	.088	.279	.088	48.8	20.9	43
Anderson, Casey	R-R	6-4	185	8-31-00	1	2	10.38	5	4	0	9	14	11	10	1	7	8	.341	.460	.439	16.0	14.0	50
Andueza, Axel	R-R	6-0	163	10-27-98	2	1	5.51	32	0	0	49	43	37	30	6	27	50	.234	.355	.370	22.6	12.2	221
Baker, Alec	R-R	6-3	202	12-04-99	0	1	6.08	8	1	1	13	12	10	9	3	3	17	.226	.281	.453	29.8	5.3	57
Benitez, Johan	B-R	6-3	170	8-07-03	0	0	0.00	1	0	0	1	1	0	0	0	0	0	.250	.250	.500	0.0	0.0	4
Cabrera, Jose	R-R	6-3	190	5-30-02	4	6	4.48	15	15	0	70	81	44	35	10	32	67	.287	.366	.443	20.7	9.9	323
Carrion, Julio	R-R	6-2	185	12-29-98	0	0	27.00	1	0	0	1	3	3	3	0	1	1	.500	.571	.833	14.3	14.3	7
Cerda, Junior	R-R	5-11	170	6-15-00	2	0	6.26	10	2	0	23	30	17	16	2	8	30	.306	.358	.429	27.5	7.3	109
Clayton, Logan	R-R	6-5	188	5-02-00	0	0	2.04	10	0	0	18	14	5	4	0	6	20	.215	.274	.292	27.4	8.2	73
Corcoran, Billy	R-R	6-8	220	8-21-99	2	1	3.68	11	2	0	29	27	13	12	2	10	32	.252	.336	.364	26.2	8.2	122
Del Pozo, Gustavo	R-R	6-5	190	12-17-99	0	1	5.14	29	0	3	42	27	31	24	3	32	39	.184	.353	.299	20.5	16.8	190
Elbis, Joe	R-R	6-1	150	9-24-02	3	2	1.76	10	10	0	41	34	15	8	1	14	37	.219	.307	.290	21.0	8.0	176
Encarnacion, Lorenzo	R-R	5-11	175	11-09-01	0	8	7.92	15	15	0	64	73	62	56	10	29	56	.286	.378	.463	18.7	9.7	300
Fisher, Hugh	R-L	6-6	210	2-11-99	0	0	2.35	6	0	0	8	7	4	2	0	5	9	.233	.368	.233	23.7	13.2	38
Fitzgibbons, Jake	L-L	5-11	175	3-21-02	0	0	4.91	5	0	0	7	3	4	4	1	7	10	.120	.313	.240	31.3	21.9	32
Gil, Miguel	R-R	6-1	160	5-12-01	0	0	37.13	4	0	0	3	6	12	11	2	5	0	.462	.652	1.000	0.0	21.7	23
Groen, Gunnar	R-R	6-6	220	7-01-97	1	2	6.11	22	0	0	28	40	23	19	1	17	25	.333	.423	.458	17.6	12.0	142
Jones, Brock	L-L	5-11	180	6-14-01	1	6	7.94	19	9	0	51	60	50	45	11	33	44	.286	.392	.529	17.6	13.2	250
Larrondo, Denny	R-R	6-2	180	5-31-02	0	1	6.17	3	1	0	12	8	12	8	2	10	14	.190	.370	.333	25.9	18.5	54
Mabrey, Will	L-L	6-0	185	9-23-00	2	0	3.95	9	0	0	14	14	6	6	1	7	13	.292	.397	.479	22.0	11.9	59
Mendez, Eric	R-R	6-0	175	12-03-99	1	0	0.00	4	0	0	7	5	2	0	0	2	11	.185	.258	.185	34.4	6.3	32
Montilla, Emailin	L-L	4-4	255	10-02-95	1	0	8.79	9	0	0	14	23	14	14	2	4	17	.383	.422	.533	26.6	6.3	64
Morillo, Alfred	R-R	6-3	190	11-14-01	4	2	3.72	32	0	7	39	32	18	16	1	28	47	.221	.369	.338	26.3	15.6	179
Norris, Liam	L-L	6-4	215	8-13-01	3	0	3.86	23	0	0	35	26	20	15	2	20	55	.210	.320	.290	37.4	13.6	147
Perdomo, Yaifer	L-L	5-10	160	8-16-01	2	1	7.63	21	0	0	31	34	28	26	2	28	46	.274	.408	.379	30.1	18.3	153
Pimentel, Yoscar	R-R	6-2	160	11-03-01	3	3	5.40	10	10	0	43	45	28	26	6	26	39	.269	.385	.419	19.4	12.9	201
Russell, Zane	R-R	6-2	196	6-12-02	1	0	1.86	6	0	1	10	4	2	2	0	1	17	.125	.152	.219	51.5	3.0	33
Sanabria, Danyer	L-L	6-1	155	3-07-02	0	0	13.50	4	0	0	4	9	6	6	1	3	3	.429	.500	.619	12.5	12.5	24
Saul, Eli	L-R	6-5	215	8-16-01	0	0	1.29	4	0	1	7	8	3	1	0	1	8	.267	.290	.300	25.8	3.2	31
Sims, Landon	R-R	6-2	227	1-03-01	0	3	6.89	7	7	0	16	16	14	12	3	8	19	.262	.356	.475	26.0	11.0	73
Smith, Caswell	R-R	6-3	210	1-26-01	1	1	5.06	13	0	0	16	17	10	9	1	10	20	.262	.368	.323	26.3	13.2	76
Steinmetz, Jacob	R-R	6-5	220	7-19-03	1	10	6.19	19	16	0	73	77	57	50	8	44	62	.280	.396	.455	18.5	13.1	335
Swales, Josh	R-R	6-2	195	10-28-01	2	5	6.99	49	0	2	66	88	60	51	9	36	63	.326	.403	.496	20.4	11.7	309
Tejeda, Luis	R-R	5-10	170	2-14-01	4	4	6.08	35	0	0	67	72	51	45	9	42	69	.274	.383	.445	22.0	13.4	313
Vasquez, Armando	L-L	5-11	160	5-04-01	2	3	4.81	30	1	3	58	51	36	31	6	41	78	.233	.358	.370	29.0	15.2	269
Wendell, Wyatt	R-R	6-5	215	2-11-00	4	10	5.40	22	21	0	90	96	65	54	6	46	92	.272	.373	.397	22.1	11.1	416
Yan, Ricardo	R-R	6-4	180	11-14-02	1	9	4.33	18	18	0	81	58	42	39	5	34	105	.198	.310	.314	30.6	9.9	343

Fielding

Catcher	PCT	G	PO	A	E	DP	PB
Boyd	1.000	12	109	13	0	1	4
Castillo	.990	17	182	13	2	2	2
Cerda	.976	53	524	45	14	5	9
Gutierrez	1.000	8	67	3	0	0	3
Logan	1.000	14	127	13	0	2	4
Martin	.996	29	240	23	1	0	4
Ortiz	1.000	2	8	0	0	0	0

First Base	PCT	G	PO	A	E	DP
Benitez	.984	8	61	2	1	3
Cabral	.976	22	149	12	4	17
Carrion	.985	8	60	4	1	4
Conticello	.984	47	338	20	6	35
Feltner	1.000	6	34	5	0	2
Gutierrez	.972	10	62	8	2	9
Logan	.000	1	0	0	0	0
Polanco	.965	13	72	10	3	10
Sanabria	.986	15	68	5	1	5
Sim	1.000	7	42	4	0	4
Torres	1.000	5	31	1	0	3

Second Base	PCT	G	PO	A	E	DP
Benitez	.000	1	0	0	0	0
Cabral	1.000	1	1	1	0	0
Corniel	.988	15	38	47	1	10
Fernandez	.961	17	35	38	3	9
Luis	1.000	16	20	29	0	7
Pena	.927	38	77	89	13	23
Pintar	1.000	8	15	13	0	3
Polanco	1.000	4	8	11	0	3
Rojas	.957	8	20	24	2	6
Rubio	1.000	2	0	1	0	0
Sim	.931	6	11	16	2	3
Torin	.962	19	35	40	3	12
Torres	1.000	1	2	2	0	1

Third Base	PCT	G	PO	A	E	DP
Benitez	.833	8	2	8	2	0
Cabral	.900	28	17	37	6	5
Conticello	.906	47	33	82	12	5
Corniel	.765	5	1	12	4	2
Fernandez	.767	19	10	23	10	1
Polanco	.861	15	7	24	5	5
Sim	.931	14	8	19	2	0
Torres	.000	1	0	0	0	0

Shortstop	PCT	G	PO	A	E	DP
Corniel	.940	40	57	99	10	19
Fernandez	.956	53	80	139	10	29
Luis	.946	15	18	35	3	9
Pena	.935	8	7	22	2	4
Torin	.947	18	24	47	4	9

Outfield	PCT	G	PO	A	E	DP
Benitez	.822	36	39	4	2	0
Carrion	.475	29	31	7	2	2
Franco	.500	4	1	0	1	0
Guzman	.902	94	200	11	11	4
Hurley	1.000	9	19	0	0	0
Johnson	.986	44	59	5	1	0
Jones	.984	23	62	1	1	0
Martin	1.000	1	1	0	0	0
Robinson	.967	40	51	1	1	0
Rojas	.977	86	164	8	6	1
Rubio	1.000	9	12	1	0	0
Sanabria	.986	37	70	5	1	2
Torres	.417	4	4	1	1	0

AZL D-BACKS BLACK

ROOKIE

ARIZONA COMPLEX LEAGUE

Batting	B-T	Ht.	Wt.	DOB	AVG	OBP	SLG	G	PA	AB	R	H	2B	3B	HR	RBI	BB	HBP	SH	SF	SO	SB	CS	BB%	SO%
Alcala, Moises	B-R	5-9	155	2-10-03	.000	.286	.000	3	7	5	0	0	0	0	0	0	2	0	0	0	2	0	0	28.6	28.6
2-team total (9 ACL D-backs Red)					.120	.353	.200	12	34	25	5	3	0	1	0	0	9	0	0	0	11	0	0	26.5	0.0
Alexander, Blaze	R-R	5-11	160	6-11-99	.364	.417	.727	3	12	11	2	4	1	0	1	3	0	1	0	0	2	0	0	0.0	16.7
2-team (3 ACL D-backs Black)					.273	.304	.636	6	23	22	4	6	2	0	2	6	0	1	0	0	5	0	0	0.0	0.0
Aparicio, Juan	R-R	6-0	165	9-25-02	.000	.143	.000	2	7	6	0	0	0	0	0	0	1	0	0	0	1	0	0	14.3	14.3
2-team (37 ACL D-backs Red)					.240	.338	.289	39	139	121	14	29	3	0	1	18	14	4	0	0	18	2	1	10.1	12.9
Baez, Franyel	B-R	6-3	170	3-01-03	.153	.267	.200	32	101	85	10	13	4	0	0	7	12	2	0	2	46	0	1	11.9	45.5
Benua, Alexander	R-R	6-2	185	10-19-03	.175	.309	.281	18	68	57	8	10	1	1	1	6	8	3	0	0	19	3	3	11.8	27.9
2-team (4 ACL D-backs Red)					.214	.317	.314	22	82	70	12	15	2	1	1	8	8	3	1	0	20	3	3	9.8	24.4
Boyd, Jermiah	R-R	5-10	225	7-01-00	.233	.425	.433	11	40	30	8	7	3	0	1	7	9	1	0	0	6	0	1	22.5	15.0
Cabeza, Diosfran	B-R	5-10	155	5-13-03	.179	.347	.333	15	49	39	8	7	3	0	1	7	8	2	0	0	11	0	2	16.3	22.4
2-team (6 ACL D-backs Red)					.191	.356	.319	21	59	47	8	9	3	0	1	8	10	2	0	0	12	0	2	16.9	20.3
Caicuto, Luis	R-R	5-10	160	3-05-03	.063	.304	.125	8	23	16	3	1	1	0	0	2	5	1	0	1	6	0	0	21.7	26.1
2-team (1 ACL D-backs Red)					.105	.346	.158	9	27	19	4	2	1	0	0	2	6	1	0	1	7	0	0	22.2	25.9
Caldera, Ricardo	R-R	6-1	175	4-06-02	.238	.319	.262	17	47	42	2	10	1	0	0	4	4	1	0	0	15	1	0	8.5	31.9
2-team (1 ACL D-backs Red)					.244	.320	.267	18	50	45	2	11	1	0	0	4	4	1	0	0	17	1	0	8.0	34.0
Castillo, Kenny	R-R	6-2	170	5-13-04	.339	.420	.492	17	69	59	10	20	6	0	1	10	7	2	0	1	7	0	0	10.1	10.1
Chen, Sheng-Ping	L-R	5-9	165	10-27-00	.250	.458	.375	6	24	16	1	4	0	1	0	2	7	0	0	1	6	1	0	29.2	25.0
2-team (3 ACL D-backs Red)					.357	.486	.500	9	36	28	1	10	2	1	0	4	7	0	0	1	9	1	0	19.4	25.0
Cintron, Jancarlos	R-R	5-8	170	12-01-94	.313	.476	.313	6	21	16	5	5	0	0	0	1	4	1	0	0	1	0	0	19.0	4.8
2-team (5 ACL D-backs Red)					.323	.462	.419	11	39	31	8	10	0	0	1	5	5	3	0	0	2	0	0	12.8	5.1
Crenshaw, Wyatt	L-R	6-0	180	4-21-00	.241	.353	.345	11	34	29	5	7	0	0	1	6	4	1	0	0	7	5	0	11.8	20.6
2-team (7 ACL D-backs Red)					.235	.350	.353	18	61	51	9	12	3	0	1	11	8	1	0	1	16	6	1	13.1	26.2
Crisantes, Demetrio	R-R	6-0	178	9-05-04	.347	.417	.465	29	115	101	24	35	7	1	1	14	11	2	0	1	21	2	2	9.6	18.3
De La Cruz, Abdias	R-R	6-3	175	11-03-04	.279	.413	.459	22	75	61	13	17	2	0	3	13	13	1	0	0	20	3	3	17.3	26.7
2-team (3 ACL D-backs Red)					.236	.360	.389	25	86	72	13	17	2	0	3	13	13	1	0	0	26	3	3	15.1	30.2
Estrada, Deivi	B-R	5-10	155	1-17-01	.000	.500	.000	1	2	1	0	0	0	0	0	0	1	0	0	0	0	0	0	50.0	0.0
2-team (19 ACL D-backs Red)					.156	.321	.178	20	57	45	6	7	1	0	0	6	10	1	0	1	8	4	0	17.5	14.0
Graham, Kevin	L-R	6-1	195	8-12-99	.200	.200	.400	1	5	5	1	1	1	0	0	0	0	0	0	0	2	0	0	0.0	40.0
2-team (3 ACL D-backs Red)					.400	.526	.533	4	19	15	3	6	2	0	0	1	4	0	0	0	3	0	0	21.1	15.8
Grice, Caden	L-L	6-6	240	6-15-02	.273	.429	.545	4	14	11	3	3	0	0	1	3	3	0	0	0	4	1	0	21.4	28.6
Groover, Gino	R-R	6-2	212	4-16-02	.500	.500	.500	1	2	2	0	1	0	0	0	0	0	0	0	0	1	0	0	0.0	50.0
2-team (3 ACL D-backs Red)					.417	.417	.500	4	12	12	2	5	1	0	0	2	0	0	0	0	1	0	0	0.0	8.3
Guzman, Alvin	R-R	6-1	166	10-20-01	.000	.000	.000	1	4	4	0	0	0	0	0	0	0	0	0	0	1	0	0	0.0	25.0
2-team (5 ACL D-backs Red)					.381	.480	.429	6	25	21	3	8	1	0	0	2	4	0	0	0	6	3	0	16.0	24.0
Johnson, Brett	L-R	5-11	195	1-06-00	.227	.452	.318	8	31	22	3	5	2	0	0	0	8	1	0	0	9	5	0	25.8	29.0
2-team (1 ACL D-backs Red)					.208	.457	.292	9	35	24	4	5	2	0	0	0	10	1	0	0	10	5	0	28.6	28.6
Jones, Druw	R-R	6-4	180	11-28-03	.111	.200	.333	3	10	9	1	1	0	1	0	1	1	0	0	0	4	0	0	10.0	40.0
2-team (9 ACL D-backs Red)					.194	.310	.250	12	42	36	9	7	0	1	0	3	6	0	0	0	11	3	1	14.3	26.2
Josepha, Jakey	L-R	6-2	135	5-15-04	.400	.625	.600	2	8	5	1	2	1	0	0	0	2	1	0	0	3	0	1	25.0	37.5
2-team (32 ACL D-backs Red)					.315	.430	.450	34	137	111	25	35	4	1	3	16	22	1	1	2	35	8	4	16.1	25.5
Lopez, Cristian	R-R	6-2	175	3-12-02	.220	.311	.310	53	193	168	16	37	9	3	0	12	18	5	0	2	53	11	3	9.3	27.5
Luis, Jansel	B-R	6-0	170	3-06-05	.297	.381	.495	25	105	91	18	27	7	1	3	12	9	4	0	1	15	9	2	8.6	14.3
2-team (1 ACL D-backs Red)					.287	.374	.479	26	108	94	18	27	7	1	3	12	9	4	0	1	16	9	2	8.3	14.8
Marte, Modeifi	R-R	6-1	200	7-31-02	.305	.406	.494	52	197	164	29	50	10	3	5	29	25	5	0	3	28	4	1	12.7	14.2
2-team (2 ACL D-backs Red)					.314	.420	.503	54	204	169	30	53	11	3	5	31	25	6	0	4	28	4	1	12.3	13.7
Nin, Yerald	L-R	6-0	170	8-18-05	.211	.275	.273	49	183	161	18	34	4	3	0	21	14	2	1	5	51	7	4	7.7	27.9
Patino, Wilderd	R-R	6-1	175	7-18-01	.250	.423	.600	6	26	20	8	5	1	0	2	6	5	1	0	0	7	7	0	19.2	26.9
Pernalete, Marco	R-R	6-4	175	9-12-02	.098	.196	.098	17	46	41	4	4	0	0	0	2	5	0	0	0	17	0	0	10.9	37.0
Pintar, Andrew	R-R	6-2	190	3-23-01	.200	.429	.200	2	7	5	1	1	0	0	0	0	0	2	0	0	1	0	0	0.0	14.3
2-team (5 ACL D-backs Red)					.263	.417	.263	7	24	19	4	5	0	0	0	1	3	2	0	0	5	0	1	12.5	20.8
Polanco, Ronny	R-R	5-11	180	8-23-03	.000	.000	.000	2	6	6	0	0	0	0	0	0	0	0	0	0	1	0	0	0.0	16.7
2-team (39 ACL D-backs Red)					.295	.392	.447	41	154	132	30	39	5	0	5	28	16	5	0	1	29	1	0	10.4	18.8
Roberts, Cole	R-R	5-9	165	10-09-00	.375	.500	.375	3	10	8	3	3	0	0	0	0	2	0	0	0	3	0	0	20.0	30.0
2-team (16 ACL D-backs Red)					.400	.492	.564	19	68	55	14	22	3	0	2	11	9	1	0	3	7	4	1	13.2	10.3
Rubio, Luis	R-R	5-10	155	1-10-02	.205	.337	.256	31	96	78	9	16	2	1	0	11	14	2	1	1	20	3	1	14.6	20.8
2-team (4 ACL D-backs Red)					.212	.340	.259	35	104	85	9	18	2	1	0	13	15	2	1	1	22	3	1	14.4	21.2
Santana, Ruben	R-R	6-0	190	2-16-05	.316	.389	.487	52	211	187	33	59	12	4	4	35	17	6	0	1	50	7	1	8.1	23.7
Santos, Oscar	R-R	5-9	175	9-24-00	.154	.333	.615	4	18	13	3	2	0	0	2	4	4	0	0	1	5	0	1	22.2	27.8
2-team (17 ACL D-backs Red)					.194	.306	.403	21	74	62	10	12	2	1	3	14	10	0	0	2	17	0	1	13.5	23.0
Suero, Luis	R-R	6-2	165	5-25-03	.300	.300	.300	3	11	10	3	3	0	0	0	2	0	0	1	0	3	0	0	0.0	27.3
2-team (12 ACL D-backs Red)					.222	.275	.278	15	40	36	8	8	0	1	0	5	2	1	1	0	8	0	1	5.0	20.0
Torres, Daniel	R-R	5-9	150	1-10-02	.235	.278	.353	5	18	17	3	4	2	0	0	2	1	0	0	0	9	0	0	5.6	50.0
2-team (26 ACL D-backs Red)					.233	.320	.349	31	97	86	15	20	4	3	0	7	7	4	0	0	34	0	2	7.2	35.1

Pitching	B-T	Ht.	Wt.	DOB	W	L	ERA	G	GS	SV	IP	Hits	Runs	ER	HR	BB	SO	AVG	OBP	SLG	SO%	BB%	BF
Almonte, Lisandro	R-R	6-1	170	6-11-02	1	0	0.00	2	1	0	7	2	0	0	0	3	8	.095	.296	.095	29.6	11.1	27
Angelo, Roman	R-R	6-5	220	5-17-00	0	0	2.35	5	2	0	8	7	3	2	0	5	6	.233	.343	.233	17.1	14.3	35
Basora, Victor	R-R	6-3	170	2-04-02	2	0	6.66	18	0	0	24	32	24	18	4	13	29	.314	.408	.480	24.2	10.8	120
Caldera, Ricardo	R-R	6-1	175	4-06-02	0	0	0.00	1	0	0	1	2	0	0	0	1	0	.667	.750	1.000	0.0	25.0	4
Casihis, Rolando	L-L	6-1	170	9-02-01	0	3	6.90	10	5	0	30	40	29	23	1	23	25	.342	.439	.462	16.9	15.5	148

Cerda, Junior	R-R	5-11	170	6-15-00	0	0	1.74	4	1	0	10	6	2	2	0	6	11	.162	.295	.216	25.0	13.6	44
Chatwood, Tyler	R-R	5-11	200	12-16-89	0	0	0.00	1	1	0	1	0	0	0	0	0	2	.000	.000	.000	66.7	0.0	3
De Dios, Fredely	R-R	6-2	165	11-03-00	0	2	15.43	8	0	0	9	14	17	16	0	15	13	.341	.533	.463	21.7	25.0	60
Diaz, Luis	R-R	6-5	230	3-09-01	0	0	8.14	19	0	1	21	23	22	19	0	19	26	.277	.455	.349	23.2	17.0	112
Fisher, Hugh	R-L	6-6	210	2-11-99	0	0	1.59	4	0	0	6	2	2	1	1	2	5	.105	.217	.263	21.7	8.7	23
Fuerte, Abel	R-R	6-2	175	1-01-05	2	4	9.00	10	4	0	31	41	35	31	4	26	30	.325	.459	.492	18.8	16.3	160
Gil, Miguel	R-R	6-1	160	5-12-01	1	0	5.40	4	0	0	5	6	4	3	1	3	9	.261	.414	.391	31.0	10.3	29
Herrera, Jean	R-R	6-0	178	11-14-00	0	0	18.00	1	0	0	1	1	2	2	1	1	1	.250	.400	1.000	20.0	20.0	5
Isea, Edgar	R-R	6-3	185	8-20-02	5	1	6.00	17	0	1	21	14	17	14	2	23	34	.187	.390	.360	34.0	23.0	100
Jimenez, Jesus	R-R	6-2	185	10-02-02	0	0	4.50	1	0	0	2	0	1	1	0	2	1	.000	.286	.000	14.3	28.6	7
Liebano, Alexis	R-R	6-1	175	3-08-03	4	1	7.80	14	1	0	30	31	30	26	2	29	26	.265	.416	.376	17.3	19.3	150
Linares, Jose	R-R	6-0	170	12-12-01	0	1	5.40	17	0	6	18	23	12	11	1	8	19	.315	.373	.466	22.9	9.6	83
Linskey, Matthew	R-R	6-7	245	4-19-02	0	0	3.60	4	3	0	5	3	2	2	1	4	11	.167	.318	.333	50.0	18.2	22
Lira, Moises	R-R	6-1	160	10-18-04	0	1	10.38	5	2	0	13	21	15	15	3	6	10	.368	.422	.596	15.6	9.4	64
Mantiply, Joe	R-L	6-4	219	3-01-91	0	0	0.00	1	0	0	2	0	0	0	0	1	3	.000	.143	.000	42.9	14.3	7
Mendez, Teofilo	R-R	5-11	170	10-08-01	0	0	3.10	12	0	0	20	15	7	7	2	7	31	.197	.262	.355	36.9	8.3	84
Misiewicz, Anthony	R-L	6-1	196	11-01-94	0	0	0.00	1	1	0	1	1	0	0	0	0	2	.333	.333	.333	66.7	0.0	3
Montilla, Emailin	L-L	4-4	255	10-02-95	0	0	0.00	1	0	1	2	0	0	0	0	0	5	.000	.000	.000	71.4	0.0	7
Morel, Osvaldo	R-R	6-3	195	6-17-01	0	0	2.70	3	2	0	3	2	2	1	0	1	5	.167	.231	.250	38.5	7.7	13
Ogando, Gerald	R-R	6-2	180	7-28-00	1	0	2.45	2	0	1	4	2	1	1	0	0	8	.154	.154	.231	61.5	0.0	13
Paredes, Wilkin	L-L	6-2	180	9-19-03	0	2	7.36	4	4	0	15	19	15	12	1	8	20	.302	.375	.429	27.8	11.1	72
Perdomo, Yaifer	L-L	5-10	160	8-16-01	0	1	27.00	1	0	0	1	4	4	3	0	0	1	.500	.500	.750	12.5	0.0	8
Pimentel, Yoscar	R-R	6-2	160	11-03-01	0	1	9.39	2	2	0	8	9	10	8	1	4	3	.300	.405	.467	8.1	10.8	37
Rashi, Taylor	R-R	6-4	220	1-15-96	0	1	27.00	3	3	0	2	3	7	6	0	4	1	.273	.500	.273	6.3	25.0	16
Rey, Carlos	L-L	6-2	180	5-19-02	0	0	4.76	5	0	0	6	3	5	3	0	6	6	.176	.417	.235	25.0	25.0	24
Reynoso, Erick	R-R	6-4	185	11-21-02	2	4	7.16	11	7	0	33	35	28	26	3	24	24	.294	.422	.521	15.6	15.6	154
Rincon, Hansel	R-R	6-1	160	8-23-02	0	0	0.00	1	0	0	1	2	0	0	0	0	1	.500	.500	.500	25.0	0.0	4
Rubio, Luis	R-R	5-10	155	1-10-02	0	0	0.00	2	0	0	1	1	0	0	0	1	3	.167	.286	.167	42.9	14.3	7
Santa, Gemil	R-R	5-11	160	11-26-02	3	1	7.29	17	1	1	33	43	33	27	4	28	36	.303	.435	.486	20.3	15.8	177
Santana, Sebastian	R-R	6-4	185	7-31-01	0	1	72.00	2	0	0	1	3	9	8	2	4	1	.429	.692	1.429	7.7	30.8	13
Sims, Landon	R-R	6-2	227	1-03-01	0	1	4.50	5	4	0	6	5	3	3	0	3	5	.238	.333	.238	20.8	12.5	24
Sulser, Cole	R-R	6-1	190	3-12-90	0	1	4.50	2	2	0	2	1	1	1	1	0	5	.143	.143	.571	71.4	0.0	7
Telfer, Shane	L-L	6-1	185	7-17-01	1	2	8.71	7	3	0	10	21	11	10	0	7	14	.412	.492	.510	23.7	11.9	59
Valdez, Vitico	R-R	6-4	175	11-06-03	0	0	2.45	1	0	0	4	2	1	1	0	3	5	.143	.294	.214	29.4	17.6	17
Veloz, Juan	R-R	6-0	155	10-21-04	0	6	17.50	8	6	0	18	26	35	35	1	18	25	.342	.490	.461	24.5	17.6	102
Vizcaino, Raffi	R-R	6-0	237	12-02-95	0	0	0.00	2	1	0	2	3	0	0	0	0	3	.300	.300	.400	30.0	0.0	10

Fielding

C: Castillo 17, Caldera 15, Boyd 11, Cabeza 9, Alcala 3, Caicuto 2, Santos 2. **1B:** Marte 44, Santana 7, Santos 2, Cabeza 2, Torres 1, Pernalete 1. **2B:** Nin 26, Luis 13, De La Cruz 3, Cabeza 2, Chen 2, Cintron 2, Pintar 2, Polanco 2, Roberts 2, Torres 2, Rubio 1, Aparicio 1. **3B:** Santana 45, Marte 8, Rubio 2, Torres 1, Groover 1. **SS:** Nin 21, De La Cruz 19, Luis 10, Alexander 3, Rubio 2, Chen 2, Aparicio 1. **OF:** Lopez 54, Baez 32, Rubio 26, Pernalete 15, Benua 13, Crenshaw 11, Johnson 8, Patino 6, Suero 3, Jones 3, Josepha 2, Estrada 1, Graham 1, Cabeza 1, Chen 1, Roberts 1.

AZL D-BACKS RED — *ROOKIE*

ARIZONA COMPLEX LEAGUE

Batting	B-T	Ht.	Wt.	DOB	AVG	OBP	SLG	G	PA	AB	R	H	2B	3B	HR	RBI	BB	HBP	SH	SF	SO	SB	CS	BB%	SO%
Alcala, Moises	B-R	5-9	155	2-10-03	.150	.370	.250	9	27	20	5	3	0	1	0	0	7	0	0	0	9	0	0	25.9	33.3
2-team total (3 ACL D-backs Black)					.120	.353	.200	12	34	25	5	3	0	1	0	0	9	0	0	0	11	0	0	26.5	0.0
Alexander, Blaze	R-R	5-11	160	6-11-99	.182	.182	.545	3	11	11	2	2	1	0	1	3	0	0	0	0	3	0	0	0.0	27.3
2-team (3 ACL D-backs Black)					.273	.304	.636	6	23	22	4	6	2	0	2	6	0	1	0	0	5	0	0	0.0	0.0
Aparicio, Juan	R-R	6-0	165	9-25-02	.252	.348	.304	37	132	115	14	29	3	0	1	18	13	4	0	0	17	2	1	9.8	12.9
2-team (2 ACL D-backs Black)					.240	.338	.289	39	139	121	14	29	3	0	1	18	14	4	0	0	18	2	1	10.1	12.9
Barriga, Alberto	R-R	5-9	155	11-15-04	.414	.457	.586	10	35	29	8	12	0	1	1	7	4	0	0	2	5	3	3	11.4	14.3
Benua, Alexander	R-R	6-2	185	10-19-03	.385	.385	.462	4	14	13	4	5	1	0	0	2	0	0	1	0	1	0	0	0.0	7.1
2-team (18 ACL D-backs Black)					.214	.317	.314	22	82	70	12	15	2	1	1	8	8	3	1	0	20	3	3	9.8	24.4
Cabeza, Diosfran	B-R	5-10	155	5-13-03	.250	.400	.250	6	10	8	0	2	0	0	0	1	2	0	0	0	1	0	0	20.0	10.0
2-team (15 ACL D-backs Black)					.191	.356	.319	21	59	47	8	9	3	0	1	8	10	2	0	0	12	0	2	16.9	20.3
Cabral, Riquelmin	B-R	5-10	165	5-12-03	.372	.391	.767	12	46	43	12	16	7	2	2	7	1	1	0	1	6	1	0	2.2	13.0
Caicuto, Luis	R-R	5-10	160	3-05-03	.333	.500	.333	1	4	3	1	1	0	0	0	0	1	0	0	0	1	0	0	25.0	25.0
2-team (8 ACL D-backs Black)					.105	.346	.158	9	27	19	4	2	1	0	0	2	6	1	0	1	7	0	0	22.2	25.9
Caldera, Ricardo	R-R	6-1	175	4-06-02	.333	.333	.333	1	3	3	0	1	0	0	0	0	0	0	0	0	2	0	0	0.0	66.7
2-team (17 ACL D-backs Black)					.244	.320	.267	18	50	45	2	11	1	0	0	4	4	1	0	0	17	1	0	8.0	34.0
Chen, Sheng-Ping	L-R	5-9	165	10-27-00	.500	.500	.667	3	12	12	0	6	2	0	0	2	0	0	0	0	3	0	0	0.0	25.0
2-team (6 ACL D-backs Black)					.357	.486	.500	9	36	28	1	10	2	1	0	4	7	0	0	1	9	1	0	19.4	25.0
Cintron, Jancarlos	R-R	5-8	170	12-01-94	.333	.444	.533	5	18	15	3	5	0	0	1	4	1	2	0	0	1	0	0	5.6	5.6
2-team (6 ACL D-backs Black)					.323	.462	.419	11	39	31	8	10	0	0	1	5	5	3	0	0	2	0	0	12.8	5.1
Crenshaw, Wyatt	L-R	6-0	180	4-21-00	.227	.333	.364	7	27	22	4	5	3	0	0	5	4	0	0	1	9	1	1	14.8	33.3
2-team (11 ACL D-backs Black)					.235	.350	.353	18	61	51	9	12	3	0	1	11	8	1	0	1	16	6	1	13.1	26.2
De La Cruz, Abdias	R-R	6-3	175	11-03-04	.000	.000	.000	3	11	11	0	0	0	0	0	0	0	0	0	0	6	0	0	0.0	54.5
2-team (11 ACL D-backs Black)					.236	.360	.389	25	86	72	13	17	2	0	3	13	13	1	0	0	26	3	3	15.1	30.2
De Leon, Adrian	R-R	5-7	180	2-09-04	.328	.459	.414	39	146	116	22	38	2	1	2	20	20	9	0	1	40	0	1	13.7	27.4
Estrada, Deivi	B-R	5-10	155	1-17-01	.159	.309	.182	19	55	44	6	7	1	0	0	6	9	1	0	1	8	4	0	16.4	14.5
2-team (1 ACL D-backs Black)					.156	.321	.178	20	57	45	6	7	1	0	0	6	10	1	0	1	8	4	0	17.5	14.0

Feltner, Jackson	R-R	6-2	225	9-19-01	.232	.286	.357	16	63	56	6	13	4	0	1	9	5	0	0	2	18	0	0	7.9	28.6
Gonnella, Dominic	L-R	5-11	205	9-16-01	.282	.391	.513	12	46	39	9	11	1	1	2	7	4	3	0	0	16	2	0	8.7	34.8
Graham, Kevin	L-R	6-1	195	8-12-99	.500	.643	.600	3	14	10	2	5	1	0	0	1	4	0	0	0	1	0	0	28.6	7.1
2-team (1 ACL D-backs Black)					.400	.526	.533	4	19	15	3	6	2	0	0	1	4	0	0	0	3	0	0	21.1	15.8
Groover, Gino	R-R	6-2	212	4-16-02	.400	.400	.500	3	10	10	2	4	1	0	0	2	0	0	0	0	0	0	0	0.0	0.0
2-team (1 ACL D-backs Black)					.417	.417	.500	4	12	12	2	5	1	0	0	2	0	0	0	0	1	0	0	0.0	8.3
Guzman, Alvin	R-R	6-1	166	10-20-01	.471	.571	.529	5	21	17	3	8	1	0	0	2	4	0	0	0	5	3	0	19.0	23.8
2-team (1 ACL D-backs Black)					.381	.480	.429	6	25	21	3	8	1	0	0	2	4	0	0	0	6	3	0	16.0	24.0
Hurley, Jack	L-R	6-0	185	3-13-02	.182	.471	.182	4	17	11	6	2	0	0	0	0	4	2	0	0	6	1	0	23.5	35.3
Johnson, Brett	L-R	5-11	195	1-06-00	.000	.500	.000	1	4	2	1	0	0	0	0	0	2	0	0	0	1	0	0	50.0	25.0
2-team (8 ACL D-backs Black)					.208	.457	.292	9	35	24	4	5	2	0	0	0	10	1	0	0	10	5	0	28.6	28.6
Jones, Druw	R-R	6-4	180	11-28-03	.222	.344	.222	9	32	27	8	6	0	0	0	2	5	0	0	0	7	3	1	15.6	21.9
2-team (3 ACL D-backs Black)					.194	.310	.250	12	42	36	9	7	0	1	0	3	6	0	0	0	11	3	1	14.3	26.2
Josepha, Jakey	L-R	6-2	135	5-15-04	.311	.414	.443	32	129	106	24	33	3	1	3	16	20	0	1	2	32	8	3	15.5	24.8
2-team (2 ACL D-backs Black)					.315	.430	.450	34	137	111	25	35	4	1	3	16	22	1	1	2	35	8	4	16.1	25.5
Luis, Jansel	B-R	6-0	170	3-06-05	.000	.000	.000	1	3	3	0	0	0	0	0	0	0	0	0	0	1	0	0	0.0	33.3
2-team (25 ACL D-backs Black)					.287	.374	.479	26	108	94	18	27	7	1	3	12	9	4	0	1	16	9	2	8.3	14.8
Marte, Modeifi	R-R	6-1	200	7-31-02	.600	.571	.800	2	7	5	1	3	1	0	0	2	0	1	0	1	0	0	0	0.0	0.0
2-team (52 ACL D-backs Black)					.314	.420	.503	54	204	169	30	53	11	3	5	31	25	6	0	4	28	4	1	12.3	13.7
Moreno, Gabriel	R-R	5-11	195	2-14-00	.333	.333	.667	1	3	3	0	1	1	0	0	0	0	0	0	0	1	0	0	0.0	33.3
Ortiz, Francisco	R-R	6-0	160	9-15-99	.259	.344	.333	10	32	27	5	7	2	0	0	9	4	0	0	1	3	0	0	12.5	9.4
2-team (16 ACL Rockies)					.278	.373	.375	26	84	72	15	20	4	0	1	16	8	3	0	1	22	0	0	9.5	26.2
Pena, Jefferson	R-R	5-8	160	1-13-04	.351	.438	.481	43	178	154	32	54	11	3	1	27	18	6	0	0	43	15	2	10.1	24.2
Pintar, Andrew	R-R	6-2	190	3-23-01	.286	.412	.286	5	17	14	3	4	0	0	0	1	3	0	0	0	4	0	1	17.6	23.5
2-team (2 ACL D-backs Black)					.263	.417	.263	7	24	19	4	5	0	0	0	1	3	2	0	0	5	0	1	12.5	20.8
Polanco, Ronny	R-R	5-11	180	8-23-03	.310	.405	.468	39	148	126	30	39	5	0	5	28	16	5	0	1	28	1	0	10.8	18.9
2-team (2 ACL D-backs Black)					.295	.392	.447	41	154	132	30	39	5	0	5	28	16	5	0	1	29	1	0	10.4	18.8
Roberts, Cole	R-R	5-9	165	10-09-00	.404	.466	.596	16	58	47	11	19	3	0	2	11	7	1	0	3	4	4	1	12.1	6.9
2-team (3 ACL D-backs Black)					.400	.492	.564	19	68	55	14	22	3	0	2	11	9	1	0	3	7	4	1	13.2	10.3
Robinson, Kristian	R-R	6-3	190	12-11-00	.296	.296	.519	7	27	27	3	8	1	1	1	4	0	0	0	0	8	1	0	0.0	29.6
Rodriguez, Adrian	R-R	6-0	170	10-21-03	.259	.360	.273	46	173	143	28	37	2	0	0	20	21	4	1	4	38	6	1	12.1	22.0
Rojas, Josh	L-R	6-1	207	6-30-94	.333	.333	.667	1	3	3	0	1	1	0	0	0	0	0	0	0	0	0	0	0.0	0.0
Rubio, Luis	R-R	5-10	155	1-10-02	.286	.375	.286	4	8	7	0	2	0	0	0	2	1	0	0	0	2	0	0	12.5	25.0
2-team (21 ACL D-backs Black)					.212	.340	.259	35	104	85	9	18	2	1	0	13	15	2	1	1	22	3	1	14.4	21.2
Santos, Oscar	R-R	5-9	175	9-24-00	.204	.286	.347	17	56	49	7	10	2	1	1	10	6	0	0	1	12	0	0	10.7	21.4
2-team (4 ACL D-backs Black)					.194	.306	.403	21	74	62	10	12	2	1	3	14	10	0	0	2	17	0	1	13.5	23.0
Sim, Kevin	R-R	6-2	210	2-07-02	.533	.500	.600	4	16	15	5	8	1	0	0	7	0	0	0	1	2	1	0	0.0	12.5
Suero, Luis	R-R	6-2	165	5-25-03	.192	.276	.269	12	29	26	5	5	0	1	0	3	2	1	0	0	5	0	1	6.9	17.2
2-team (3 ACL D-backs Black)					.222	.275	.278	15	40	36	8	8	0	1	0	5	2	1	1	0	8	0	1	5.0	20.0
Torin, Cristofer	R-R	5-10	155	5-26-05	.320	.437	.427	26	126	103	31	33	3	1	2	13	21	1	0	1	9	15	0	16.7	7.1
Torres, Daniel	R-R	5-9	150	1-10-02	.232	.329	.348	26	79	69	12	16	2	3	0	5	6	4	0	0	25	0	2	7.6	31.6
2-team (5 ACL D-backs Black)					.233	.320	.349	31	97	86	15	20	4	3	0	7	7	4	0	0	34	0	2	7.2	35.1
Troy, Tommy	R-R	5-10	197	1-17-02	.455	.563	.636	4	16	11	4	5	0	1	0	5	4	0	0	1	2	1	0	25.0	12.5
Walters, Jean	B-R	5-11	155	8-13-01	.341	.401	.492	36	147	132	26	45	10	2	2	28	13	1	0	1	21	2	1	8.8	14.3

Pitching	**B-T**	**Ht.**	**Wt.**	**DOB**	**W**	**L**	**ERA**	**G**	**GS**	**SV**	**IP**	**Hits**	**Runs**	**ER**	**HR**	**BB**	**SO**	**AVG**	**OBP**	**SLG**	**SO%**	**BB%**	**BF**
Almonte, Lisandro	R-R	6-1	170	6-11-02	2	1	4.71	10	5	0	29	24	19	15	3	24	41	.224	.382	.374	30.1	17.6	136
Alvarez, Jhosmer	R-R	6-1	155	6-29-01	0	0	1.80	4	4	0	5	2	1	1	1	2	3	.133	.235	.333	17.6	11.8	17
Amendt, Kyle	R-R	6-5	237	4-05-00	0	0	0.00	1	0	0	1	0	0	0	0	0	4	.000	.000	.000	100.0	0.0	4
Anderson, Casey	R-R	6-4	185	8-31-00	0	0	0.00	2	2	0	2	0	0	0	0	1	1	.000	.286	.000	14.3	14.3	7
Baker, Alec	R-R	6-3	202	12-04-99	0	0	1.29	5	0	2	7	3	1	1	0	2	11	.125	.192	.167	42.3	7.7	26
Cerda, Junior	R-R	5-11	170	6-15-00	1	1	10.32	6	0	0	11	18	13	13	0	12	13	.360	.492	.460	20.6	19.0	63
Chalas, Yordin	R-R	6-3	175	2-22-04	2	3	3.18	14	0	2	17	16	7	6	2	10	18	.242	.351	.348	23.4	13.0	77
Dominguez, Eric	L-L	6-3	180	1-12-03	1	1	2.93	4	3	0	15	14	6	5	1	9	25	.241	.371	.310	35.7	12.9	70
Durke, Hayden	R-R	6-1	206	5-01-02	1	0	9.72	7	0	0	8	11	9	9	0	10	10	.344	.500	.375	23.8	23.8	42
Fitzgibbons, Jake	L-L	5-11	175	3-21-02	0	1	5.40	2	1	0	2	4	1	1	0	1	3	.444	.500	.667	30.0	10.0	10
Fuerte, Abel	R-R	6-2	175	1-01-05	1	1	11.05	5	0	0	7	13	10	9	0	7	8	.419	.526	.484	21.1	18.4	38
Gil, Miguel	R-R	6-1	160	5-12-01	4	1	7.20	14	0	0	20	22	19	16	2	17	34	.265	.402	.398	33.3	16.7	102
Groen, Gunnar	R-R	6-6	220	7-01-97	2	0	3.65	8	0	0	12	13	6	5	1	4	11	.271	.333	.375	20.4	7.4	54
Herrera, Jean	R-R	6-0	178	11-14-00	1	0	4.26	4	0	0	6	6	3	3	2	1	8	.250	.333	.542	29.6	3.7	27
Isea, Edgar	R-R	6-3	185	8-20-02	0	0	0.00	1	0	0	1	1	0	0	0	0	3	.250	.250	.250	75.0	0.0	4
Jimenez, Jesus	R-R	6-2	185	10-02-02	1	1	5.00	6	0	0	9	10	7	5	0	9	5	.278	.426	.361	10.6	19.1	47
Larrondo, Denny	R-R	6-2	180	5-31-02	2	0	4.01	12	12	0	49	44	23	22	4	30	54	.235	.356	.353	24.3	13.5	222
Linares, Jose	R-R	6-0	170	12-12-01	0	0	10.80	4	0	1	5	5	6	6	1	5	7	.263	.417	.474	29.2	20.8	24
Linskey, Matthew	R-R	6-7	245	4-19-02	1	0	0.00	1	0	0	1	1	0	0	0	0	2	.250	.250	.250	50.0	0.0	4
Lira, Moises	R-R	6-1	160	10-18-04	1	3	7.46	7	4	0	25	29	21	21	7	10	19	.290	.351	.540	16.7	8.8	114
Mendez, Teofilo	R-R	5-11	170	10-08-01	4	0	1.15	9	0	0	16	11	7	2	2	2	19	.196	.237	.357	32.2	3.4	59
Montes De Oca, Christian	R-R	6-4	230	8-30-99	0	0	54.00	1	0	0	1	4	4	4	1	0	1	.667	.667	1.167	16.7	0.0	6
Morel, Osvaldo	R-R	6-3	195	6-17-01	0	0	0.00	1	0	0	1	0	0	0	0	0	1	.000	.333	.000	33.3	0.0	3
Paredes, Wilkin	L-L	6-2	180	9-19-03	2	1	4.34	5	3	0	19	27	10	9	2	2	11	.351	.383	.481	13.6	2.5	81
Perdomo, Yaifer	L-L	5-10	160	8-16-01	0	0	0.00	1	0	0	1	0	0	0	0	1	2	.000	.200	.000	40.0	20.0	5
Perez, Adonys	L-L	6-3	185	10-10-03	3	1	4.31	10	8	0	40	33	24	19	0	21	30	.228	.329	.269	18.0	12.6	167
Polanco, Sarlin	R-R	6-1	190	2-23-02	2	0	6.23	17	0	2	22	17	19	15	1	23	23	.213	.394	.275	21.9	21.9	105
Rey, Carlos	L-L	6-2	180	5-19-02	0	0	0.00	2	0	0	1	0	0	0	0	1	0	.000	.200	.000	0.0	20.0	5
Reynoso, Erick	R-R	6-4	185	11-21-02	0	0	0.00	1	0	0	1	0	0	0	0	2	1	.000	.400	.000	20.0	40.0	5

	B-T	Ht.	Wt.	DOB	W	L	ERA	G	GS	SV	IP	Hits	Runs	ER	HR	BB	SO	AVG	OBP	SLG	SO%	BB%	BF
Rincon, Hansel	R-R	6-1	160	8-23-02	3	2	3.58	16	0	2	33	28	13	13	1	15	35	.231	.319	.273	24.8	10.6	141
Russell, Zane	R-R	6-2	196	6-12-02	0	0	0.00	1	0	0	1	0	0	0	0	0	2	.000	.000	.000	66.7	0.0	3
Sanchez, Vince	R-R	6-0	185	8-25-04	0	1	5.40	6	4	0	13	16	10	8	2	10	17	.296	.424	.444	25.8	15.2	66
Sims, Landon	R-R	6-2	227	1-03-01	0	0	0.00	3	2	0	3	2	1	0	0	1	4	.182	.250	.182	33.3	8.3	12
Smith, Caswell	R-R	6-3	210	1-26-01	0	0	3.00	7	0	2	12	6	5	4	0	7	18	.150	.286	.200	36.7	14.3	49
Sulser, Cole	R-R	6-1	190	3-12-90	0	1	21.60	2	2	0	2	2	4	4	2	4	3	.286	.545	1.143	27.3	36.4	11
Torres, Daniel	R-R	5-9	150	1-10-02	0	0	0.00	1	0	0	0	0	0	0	0	0	1	.000	.000	.000	100.0	0.0	1
Valdez, Vitico	R-R	6-4	175	11-06-03	0	2	5.53	10	5	1	28	25	19	17	2	20	19	.245	.378	.382	14.8	15.6	128
Vizcaino, Raffi	R-R	6-0	237	12-02-95	0	0	27.00	1	0	0	1	1	2	2	0	3	2	.333	.667	.333	33.3	50.0	6

Fielding

C: De Leon 23, Ortiz 10, Barriga 9, Santos 8, Alcala 8, Cabeza 6, Caldera 1, Moreno 1. **1B:** Polanco 22, Feltner 15, Aparicio 6, Walters 6, Santos 3, Torres 2, Josepha 2, Marte 2, Cabral 1. **2B:** Rodriguez 16, Roberts 13, Torin 8, Walters 6, Polanco 5, Pintar 3, Aparicio 2, Chen 2, Cintron 2, Torres 1, Rubio 1. **3B:** Aparicio 27, Cabral 11, Polanco 9, Sim 4, Groover 3, Rodriguez 1, Chen 1, De La Cruz 1. **SS:** Rodriguez 29, Torin 18, Troy 4, Rubio 2, Alexander 2, De La Cruz 2, Luis 1, Aparicio 1. **OF:** Pena 46, Josepha 31, Walters 26, Torres 22, Estrada 16, Jones 8, Suero 8, Crenshaw 7, Robinson 5, Benua 4, Hurley 4, Graham 3, Roberts 3, Guzman 2, Gonnella 2, Johnson 1, Rubio 1, Polanco 1.

DSL D-BACKS — ROOKIE

DOMINICAN SUMMER LEAGUE

Batting	B-T	Ht.	Wt.	DOB	AVG	OBP	SLG	G	PA	AB	R	H	2B	3B	HR	RBI	BB	HBP	SH	SF	SO	SB	CS	BB%	SO%
Alejos, Eliesbert	R-R	6-0	175	6-09-06	.223	.303	.257	53	202	179	25	40	4	1	0	16	15	6	1	1	30	6	5	7.4	14.9
Alpuria, Jose	B-R	6-2	160	2-12-05	.248	.356	.321	51	194	165	39	41	4	1	2	12	14	14	0	1	50	22	8	7.2	25.8
Antigua, Ronal	R-R	6-1	180	1-27-03	.230	.384	.299	36	112	87	16	20	3	0	1	14	18	5	0	2	36	3	1	16.1	32.1
Araujo, Gabriel	R-R	6-0	175	9-07-04	.274	.381	.326	48	161	135	21	37	4	0	1	12	16	8	1	1	20	16	4	9.9	12.4
Belen, Harlem	R-R	6-0	165	3-30-05	.179	.337	.269	31	83	67	13	12	3	0	1	4	16	0	0	0	22	4	1	19.3	26.5
Bonalde, Cesar	L-L	6-2	160	3-18-05	.269	.336	.317	36	116	104	13	28	2	0	1	15	10	1	0	1	25	2	0	8.6	21.6
Carpio, Albert	R-R	5-9	150	8-12-05	.160	.266	.193	47	140	119	19	19	4	0	0	16	12	6	1	2	19	4	3	8.6	13.6
Catuy, Pedro	R-R	6-1	150	2-03-06	.288	.361	.441	48	192	170	30	49	10	2	4	24	15	5	1	1	33	18	2	7.8	17.2
Colmenarez, Anderson	B-R	5-8	145	1-12-04	.248	.399	.295	48	163	129	23	32	1	1	1	15	30	3	0	1	28	4	4	18.4	17.2
Colmenarez, Jose	R-R	6-1	170	9-04-04	.248	.318	.305	41	157	141	20	35	5	0	1	22	7	8	0	1	22	4	1	4.5	14.0
De La Cruz, Abdias	R-R	6-3	175	11-03-04	.270	.378	.419	23	90	74	18	20	6	1	1	14	14	0	0	2	19	5	2	15.6	21.1
De La Cruz, Lewin	B-R	5-10	160	8-07-03	.228	.439	.366	49	172	123	25	28	5	3	2	14	46	1	1	1	35	13	10	26.7	20.3
Encarnacion, Andy	R-R	6-1	160	1-18-05	.206	.281	.275	48	179	160	25	33	6	1	1	15	14	3	1	1	31	6	3	7.8	17.3
Gallardo, Leo	L-R	6-0	185	11-02-05	.211	.309	.282	26	81	71	9	15	2	0	1	4	8	2	0	0	16	0	1	9.9	19.8
Gonzalez, Dauwin	R-R	6-1	170	2-19-06	.221	.343	.310	43	138	113	14	25	4	0	2	21	21	1	1	2	34	6	2	15.2	24.6
Lara, Jorge	B-R	5-6	145	10-24-05	.295	.410	.432	42	161	132	20	39	9	0	3	16	21	6	0	2	17	18	3	13.0	10.6
Martinez, Luis	L-R	6-1	190	9-19-05	.189	.322	.284	27	90	74	9	14	5	1	0	7	13	2	0	1	18	1	2	14.4	20.0
Moya, Omar	R-R	5-10	165	5-06-05	.227	.255	.364	17	47	44	4	10	3	0	1	9	2	0	0	1	9	0	0	4.3	19.1
Perez, Enyervert	R-R	5-11	180	10-20-05	.309	.356	.515	21	73	68	12	21	5	0	3	7	2	3	0	0	20	1	1	2.7	27.4
Perez, Miguel	R-R	6-0	155	6-01-06	.000	.000	.000	1	2	2	0	0	0	0	0	0	0	0	0	0	1	0	0	0.0	50.0
Rios, Alejandro	R-R	5-11	150	3-30-05	.158	.282	.193	23	71	57	7	9	2	0	0	10	7	4	0	3	15	0	1	9.9	21.1
Rodriguez, Jeremy	L-R	6-0	170	7-04-06	.246	.363	.377	38	146	122	24	30	6	2	2	18	22	1	0	1	27	12	5	15.1	18.5
Santos, Kevin	L-L	6-0	180	1-09-04	.243	.417	.419	32	96	74	20	18	4	0	3	11	20	2	0	0	35	3	2	20.8	36.5
Soler, Yassel	R-R	5-11	185	1-26-06	.252	.363	.358	37	146	123	23	31	7	0	2	16	14	8	0	1	18	1	1	9.6	12.3
Suarez, Brayan	R-R	6-0	175	4-30-04	.000	.000	.000	18	2	1	0	0	0	0	0	0	0	0	1	0	1	0	0	0.0	50.0
Surun, Ezequiel	R-R	6-0	150	7-07-04	.275	.348	.325	52	182	160	20	44	8	0	0	16	9	10	1	2	41	16	8	4.9	22.5
Urbina, Jose	R-R	5-11	195	5-14-06	.240	.366	.310	36	123	100	15	24	7	0	0	11	15	6	0	2	22	1	2	12.2	17.9
Virahonda, Carlos	R-R	5-11	180	12-12-05	.304	.401	.482	38	139	112	15	34	13	2	1	18	5	16	2	4	18	3	4	3.6	12.9
Vizcaino, Yeral	L-R	6-2	185	10-05-04	.203	.370	.328	26	81	64	10	13	2	0	2	9	16	1	0	0	31	3	2	19.8	38.3
Zabala, Bernardo	R-R	5-11	190	8-24-03	.258	.395	.366	34	119	93	15	24	4	0	2	18	16	7	0	3	16	1	0	13.4	13.4
Zapata, Gian	L-L	6-4	195	9-13-05	.254	.364	.522	44	165	134	26	34	9	0	9	31	19	7	0	5	48	5	4	11.5	29.1

Pitching	B-T	Ht.	Wt.	DOB	W	L	ERA	G	GS	SV	IP	Hits	Runs	ER	HR	BB	SO	AVG	OBP	SLG	SO%	BB%	BF
Aguilar, Luis	R-R	5-11	150	2-18-05	1	0	9.16	15	0	0	19	23	23	19	1	16	19	.311	.465	.365	19.2	16.2	99
Aguirre, Jose	R-R	6-1	170	10-11-03	5	1	3.71	17	0	0	34	25	18	14	2	17	48	.200	.327	.288	32.0	11.3	150
Amparo, Jeffrey	R-R	6-3	175	9-24-04	0	1	15.75	4	4	0	4	4	7	7	0	9	5	.286	.556	.429	18.5	33.3	27
Brea, Victor	L-L	6-4	170	10-08-02	1	0	10.80	13	0	0	15	17	21	18	0	17	17	.279	.464	.361	20.2	20.2	84
Calvo, Jeison	R-R	6-2	200	10-31-05	2	3	6.10	11	6	0	31	24	24	21	1	28	32	.214	.397	.321	21.2	18.5	151
Cardenas, Anderson	R-R	6-2	160	6-21-06	0	1	2.48	13	12	0	36	32	13	10	2	15	38	.241	.322	.323	25.5	10.1	149
Chalas, Yordin	R-R	6-3	175	2-22-04	2	0	3.68	6	0	2	7	6	3	3	0	1	9	.214	.241	.286	31.0	3.4	29
Ciprian, Junior	R-R	6-3	180	6-02-05	0	0	9.00	3	1	0	3	2	5	3	0	4	2	.167	.421	.167	10.5	21.1	19
De Aza, Luis	R-R	6-4	190	10-21-04	2	2	4.26	17	0	1	25	21	18	12	0	17	15	.223	.359	.330	12.8	14.5	117
De Jesus, Eskoly	L-L	6-2	185	9-07-03	0	1	4.58	17	0	0	20	17	14	10	0	21	16	.239	.444	.310	16.2	21.2	99
De Los Santos, Greudis	R-R	6-4	175	11-22-05	1	3	3.60	10	4	0	25	14	20	10	1	26	30	.159	.361	.227	25.2	21.8	119
Diaz, Francis	R-R	6-2	180	12-26-04	0	1	18.00	5	1	0	6	11	14	12	0	12	5	.393	.571	.464	11.6	27.9	43
Digon, Jairon	R-R	6-0	165	11-07-05	0	3	4.00	12	5	0	27	16	12	12	1	24	41	.168	.347	.221	33.6	19.7	122
Duarte, Rancel	R-R	6-2	195	11-30-02	3	2	5.92	19	0	1	24	20	24	16	2	18	17	.227	.369	.432	15.3	16.2	111
Elias, Berny	R-R	6-3	185	4-03-05	0	2	4.30	12	0	0	15	6	8	7	1	17	13	.133	.354	.200	20.0	26.2	65
Escobar, Jesus	R-R	6-0	150	2-28-06	3	2	3.48	12	7	0	34	27	15	13	5	19	21	.231	.350	.368	14.5	13.1	145
Fell, Mervin	R-R	6-1	215	2-22-03	0	0	3.46	7	3	0	13	11	5	5	0	6	17	.224	.321	.306	30.4	10.7	56
Frias, Frederic	R-R	6-3	180	6-24-04	3	4	7.33	19	1	1	23	27	25	19	2	21	17	.297	.458	.418	14.2	17.5	120
Garcia, Jan Pierre	R-R	6-1	165	4-22-03	1	0	4.50	3	0	0	6	6	5	3	0	3	5	.261	.346	.304	19.2	11.5	26
Gonzalez, Joangel	R-R	6-4	210	7-01-04	0	1	4.91	7	4	1	11	11	6	6	2	2	11	.262	.319	.476	23.4	4.3	47
Jimenez, Cesar	R-R	6-1	170	7-18-05	2	0	1.27	15	4	2	28	22	6	4	1	4	28	.214	.243	.301	25.2	3.6	111
Jimenez, Onias	R-R	6-1	170	5-23-04	4	0	1.50	15	0	4	18	7	5	3	0	10	24	.117	.274	.150	32.4	13.5	74

Lozoya, Cristhofer	R-R	5-11	198	2-09-05	2	0	4.66	18	0	2	19	19	10	10	1	17	21	.288	.449	.364	23.6	19.1	89
Mena, Walvin	R-R	6-1	195	9-30-05	0	2	2.22	8	7	0	28	26	11	7	2	12	10	.241	.336	.324	8.0	9.6	125
Minyety, Jorge	R-R	6-1	170	1-04-03	3	0	3.86	12	3	0	35	29	16	15	1	14	30	.232	.322	.312	21.0	9.8	143
Monegro, Cristian	R-R	6-3	170	4-11-05	1	1	23.28	16	0	0	10	10	26	25	0	25	10	.263	.608	.395	13.5	33.8	74
Otero, Amauri	L-L	6-1	175	2-19-05	1	3	7.71	11	1	0	21	30	21	18	0	20	25	.337	.468	.371	22.5	18.0	111
Paredes, Wilkin	L-L	6-2	180	9-19-03	0	1	3.55	3	3	0	13	6	8	5	0	5	18	.128	.226	.191	34.0	9.4	53
Parra, Nixon	R-R	6-2	170	1-07-04	0	2	4.61	17	4	0	27	25	15	14	1	15	19	.255	.362	.316	16.4	12.9	116
Pascual, Saul	R-R	6-4	190	9-29-05	0	0	7.20	5	0	0	5	4	11	4	1	10	5	.235	.517	.529	17.2	34.5	29
Peralta, Hamlet	R-R	6-7	210	7-26-02	1	0	9.24	15	0	2	13	15	15	13	2	17	11	.288	.519	.423	14.1	21.8	78
Ramirez, Gregori	R-R	6-3	170	9-12-04	1	1	6.53	16	0	0	21	15	18	15	0	22	22	.208	.408	.306	22.4	22.4	98
Rodriguez, Brayan	R-R	6-3	175	3-06-05	1	0	5.40	8	0	0	7	7	7	4	0	10	3	.259	.459	.333	8.1	27.0	37
Rosario, Kelvin	L-L	6-2	140	8-28-06	0	3	5.01	12	8	0	32	26	19	18	1	17	33	.217	.319	.333	23.9	12.3	138
Rubio, Alexis	R-R	5-9	190	8-09-02	0	3	2.66	19	0	5	24	20	15	7	1	13	18	.227	.330	.295	17.0	12.3	106
Sanchez, Junior	R-R	5-10	175	9-16-05	2	2	2.76	11	9	0	42	28	17	13	0	17	39	.187	.297	.213	22.2	9.7	176
Sanchez, Vince	R-R	6-0	185	8-25-04	0	0	6.23	3	1	0	4	2	3	3	0	3	3	.143	.294	.214	17.6	17.6	17
Santana, Sandro	L-L	5-10	150	3-07-05	2	3	4.71	10	3	0	29	25	21	15	0	17	36	.236	.376	.311	27.1	12.8	133
Serda, Dawel	R-R	6-3	165	10-13-04	2	4	4.15	12	10	0	39	37	21	18	2	22	43	.257	.372	.354	24.9	12.7	173
Serrano, Maicor	R-R	6-2	180	2-03-04	2	1	6.05	15	0	0	19	24	15	13	3	13	19	.312	.430	.455	20.2	13.8	94
Suarez, Brayan	R-R	6-0	175	4-30-04	2	3	7.77	16	0	0	24	27	27	21	4	19	17	.297	.430	.462	14.9	16.7	114
Vasquez, Daury	R-R	6-2	170	4-17-06	1	2	4.67	10	8	0	27	20	15	14	1	24	13	.211	.400	.284	10.3	19.0	126

Fielding

C: Urbina 34, Virahonda 31, Rios 23, Martinez 20, Moya 10, Zabala 5, Gallardo 1. **1B:** Colmenarez 38, Zabala 30, De La Cruz 27, Gallardo 11, Belen 9, Surun 5, Moya 4, Araujo 2, Vizcaino 1. **2B:** Lara 40, Colmenarez 24, Alejos 22, Carpio 16, Perez 10, De La Cruz 5, Surun 3, Belen 1. **3B:** Soler 33, Colmenarez 24, De La Cruz 20, Surun 19, Belen 11, Carpio 10. **SS:** Rodriguez 33, Alejos 30, Carpio 21, Surun 21, De La Cruz 12, Perez 3. **OF:** Alpuria 53, Encarnacion 52, Araujo 50, Catuy 45, Gonzalez 43, Zapata 39, Antigua 35, Bonalde 27, Santos 21, Vizcaino 14, Surun 5, Suarez 1, Perez 1, Carpio 1.

Atlanta Braves

SEASON SYNOPSIS: Atlanta was home to baseball's best regular-season team, with 104 victories, and one of the best offenses in MLB history, which tied a record with 307 home runs and a .501 team slugging percentage. But for the second straight season, the Braves faltered in the first round against the Phillies, winning only one postseason game.

HIGH POINT: Two Braves had incredible seasons, starting with leadoff-hitting right fielder Ronald Acuña Jr. He finished with 41 homers and 73 stolen bases, the first 40-70 season in MLB history. First baseman Matt Olson, playing for the franchise of Henry Aaron, set the Braves' single-season home run record with 54, and also led MLB with 139 RBIs and playing 162 games. He led a parade of a record-tying five Braves who hit at least 30 homers.

LOW POINT: Atlanta's pitching health deteriorated as the year progressed, putting a large burden on righthander Spencer Strider, MLB's leader in wins (20) and strikeouts (281). He pitched well against the Phillies in the Division Series, allowing five runs (four earned) in 12.2 IP, but the Braves didn't score to back him. Baseball's best offense scored three runs in its three losses, including being shut out by seven Phillies pitchers in the series opener.

NOTABLE ROOKIES: The veteran-laden Braves didn't need many rookie bats, but five rookie arms combined to make 29 starts for Atlanta. Lefty Jared Shuster (5.81 ERA) seized a spot out of spring training but made nine of his 11 starts before the all-star break. Righties A.J. Smith-Shawver, Darius Vines and Allan Winans and lefty Dylan Dodd also got their shots but none of them thrived consistently.

KEY TRANSACTIONS: Shortstop Dansby Swanson left as a free agent in the offseason, with veteran Orlando Arcia replacing him well and cheaply. Charlie Morton returned on a one-year, $20 million deal with a team option for '24 and made 30 starts before faltering with a late finger injury that kept him off the Division Series roster. Righty Joe Jimenez, an offseason trade pickup, contributed a 3.04 ERA in 56.1 relief innings.

DOWN ON THE FARM: The system has thinned, but A.J. Smith-Shawver's speedy ascent reminded everyone that this organization can still produce pitching.

OPENING DAY PAYROLL: $203,077,500 (8th).

PLAYERS OF THE YEAR

MAJOR LEAGUE

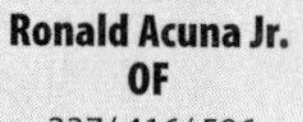

Ronald Acuna Jr.
OF
.337/.416/.596
41 HR, 73 SB

MINOR LEAGUE

A.J. Smith-Shawver, RHP
(HiA/AA/AAA)
4-2, 2.76, 15 GS,
62 IP, 33 BB, 79 SO

ORGANIZATION LEADERS

Batting		*Minimum 250 AB
MAJORS		
*AVG	Ronald Acuna Jr.	.337
*OPS	Ronald Acuna Jr.	1.012
HR	Matt Olson	54
RBI	Matt Olson	139
MINORS		
*AVG	Vaughn Grissom, Gwinnett	.330
*OBP	Vaughn Grissom, Gwinnett	.419
*SLG	Drew Lugbauer, Mississippi/Gwinnett	.545
*OPS	Vaughn Grissom, Gwinnett	.920
R	Braden Shewmake, Gwinnett	79
H	Vaughn Grissom, Gwinnett	131
TB	Vaughn Grissom, Gwinnett	199
2B	Vaughn Grissom, Gwinnett	36
3B	Kevin Kilpatrick Jr., Rome	7
HR	Drew Lugbauer, Mississippi/Gwinnett	25
RBI	David McCabe, Augusta/Rome	75
BB	Yolmer Sanchez ,Gwinnett	89
SO	Ambioris Tavarez, Augusta	196
SB	Forrest Wall, Gwinnett	52

Pitching		#Minimum 75 IP
MAJORS		
W	Spencer Strider	20
# ERA	Max Fried	2.55
SO	Spencer Strider	281
SV	Raisel Iglesias	33
MINORS		
W	Jorge Bautista, Augusta/Rome	10
L	Alan Rangel, Mississippi/Gwinnett	16
# ERA	Allan Winans, Gwinnett	2.85
G	Grant Holmes, Gwinnett	50
GS	Luis De Avila, Mississippi/Gwinnett	25
SV	Grant Holmes, Gwinnett	13
IP	Domingo Robles, Mississippi/Gwinnett	129
BB	Luis De Avila, Mississippi/Gwinnett	65
SO	Alan Rangel, Mississippi/Gwinnett	140
# AVG	Jhancarlos Lara, Augusta/Rome	.202

2023 PERFORMANCE

General Manager: Alex Anthopoulos. **Farm Director:** Ben Sestanovich. **Scouting Director:** Ronit Shah.

Class	Team	League	W	L	PCT	Finish	Manager
Majors	Atlanta Braves	National	104	58	.642	1 (15)	Brian Snitker
Triple-A	Gwinnett Stripers	International	70	78	.473	12 (20)	Matt Tuiasosopo
Double-A	Mississippi Braves	Southern	62	75	.453	6 (8)	Kanekoa Texeira
High-A	Rome Braves	South Atlantic	64	68	.485	8 (12)	Angel Flores
Low-A	Augusta GreenJackets	Carolina	63	68	.481	9 (12)	Cody Gabella
Rookie	FCL Braves	Florida Complex	30	24	.556	4 (15)	Nestor Perez
Rookie	DSL Braves	Dominican Sum.	15	36	.294	48 (50)	Maikol Gonzalez
Overall 2023 Minor League Record			304	349	.466	27th (30)	

ORGANIZATION STATISTICS

ATLANTA BRAVES

NATIONAL LEAGUE

Batting	B-T	Ht.	Wt.	DOB	AVG	OBP	SLG	G	PA	AB	R	H	2B	3B	HR	RBI	BB	HBP	SH	SF	SO	SB	CS	BB%	SO%
Acuna, Ronald	R-R	6-0	205	12-18-97	.337	.416	.596	159	735	643	149	217	35	4	41	106	80	9	0	3	84	73	14	10.9	11.4
Adrianza, Ehire	B-R	6-1	198	8-21-89	.000	.091	.000	5	11	10	0	0	0	0	0	0	1	0	0	0	4	0	0	9.1	36.4
Albies, Ozzie	B-R	5-8	165	1-07-97	.280	.336	.513	148	660	596	96	167	30	5	33	109	46	8	0	8	107	13	1	7.0	16.2
Arcia, Orlando	R-R	6-0	187	8-04-94	.264	.321	.420	139	533	488	66	129	25	0	17	65	39	3	0	3	102	1	0	7.3	19.1
Culberson, Charlie	R-R	6-1	200	4-10-89	1.000	1.000	1.000	1	1	1	0	1	0	0	0	0	0	0	0	0	0	0	0	0.0	0.0
d'Arnaud, Travis	R-R	6-2	210	2-10-89	.225	.288	.397	74	292	267	31	60	13	0	11	39	21	3	0	1	67	0	0	7.2	22.9
Grissom, Vaughn	R-R	6-2	210	1-05-01	.280	.313	.347	23	80	75	5	21	3	1	0	9	2	2	0	1	15	0	1	2.5	18.8
Harris, Michael	L-L	6-0	195	3-07-01	.293	.331	.477	138	539	505	76	148	33	3	18	57	25	5	1	3	101	20	4	4.6	18.7
Hilliard, Sam	L-L	6-5	236	2-21-94	.236	.295	.431	40	78	72	15	17	5	0	3	6	6	0	0	0	33	4	0	7.7	42.3
Lopez, Nicky	L-R	5-11	180	3-13-95	.277	.333	.369	26	72	65	13	18	3	0	1	12	5	1	0	1	10	2	0	6.9	13.9
2-team (68 Kansas City)					.231	.326	.307	94	262	225	32	52	8	3	1	25	26	6	4	1	40	6	2	9.9	15.3
Murphy, Sean	R-R	6-3	228	10-04-94	.251	.365	.478	108	438	370	65	93	21	0	21	68	49	18	0	1	98	0	0	11.2	22.4
Olson, Matt	L-R	6-5	225	3-29-94	.283	.389	.604	162	720	608	127	172	27	3	54	139	104	4	0	4	167	1	0	14.4	23.2
Ozuna, Marcell	R-R	6-1	225	11-12-90	.274	.346	.558	144	592	530	84	145	29	1	40	100	57	3	0	2	134	0	0	9.6	22.6
Pillar, Kevin	R-R	6-0	200	1-04-89	.228	.248	.416	81	206	197	29	45	10	0	9	32	6	0	0	3	50	4	1	2.9	24.3
Riley, Austin	R-R	6-3	240	4-02-97	.281	.345	.516	159	715	636	117	179	32	3	37	97	59	9	0	11	172	3	1	8.3	24.1
Rosario, Eddie	L-R	6-1	180	9-28-91	.255	.305	.450	142	516	478	64	122	24	3	21	74	34	1	1	2	122	3	4	6.6	23.6
Shewmake, Braden	L-R	6-3	190	11-19-97	.000	.000	.000	2	4	4	0	0	0	0	0	0	0	0	0	0	1	0	0	0.0	25.0
Solak, Nick	R-R	5-9	185	1-11-95	--	--	--	1	0	0	1	0	0	0	0	0	0	0	0	0	0	0	0	--	--
2-team (1 Detroit)					.000	.000	.000	2	0	0	1	0	0	0	0	0	0	0	0	0	0	0	0	--	--
Tromp, Chadwick	R-R	5-8	221	3-21-95	.125	.125	.188	6	16	16	1	2	1	0	0	1	0	0	0	0	7	0	0	0.0	43.8
Wall, Forrest	L-R	6-0	195	11-20-95	.462	.533	.846	15	15	13	6	6	2	0	1	2	2	0	0	0	4	5	1	13.3	26.7
White, Eli	R-R	6-2	195	6-26-94	.071	.235	.071	6	17	14	1	1	0	0	0	0	2	1	0	0	7	0	0	11.8	41.2
Williams, Luke	R-R	6-0	186	8-09-96	.000	.000	.000	7	9	9	1	0	0	0	0	0	0	0	0	0	4	3	0	0.0	44.4
2-team (4 Los Angeles Dodgers)					.053	.053	.053	11	19	19	1	1	0	0	0	0	0	0	0	0	7	4	0	0.0	36.8

Pitching	B-T	Ht.	Wt.	DOB	W	L	ERA	G	GS	SV	IP	Hits	Runs	ER	HR	BB	SO	AVG	OBP	SLG	SO%	BB%	BF
Allard, Kolby	L-L	6-1	195	8-13-97	0	1	6.57	4	3	0	12	16	9	9	2	4	13	.308	.357	.481	23.2	7.1	56
Anderson, Nick	R-R	6-4	205	7-05-90	4	0	3.06	35	0	1	35	30	14	12	3	9	36	.229	.277	.366	25.5	6.4	141
Chavez, Jesse	R-R	6-1	175	8-21-83	1	0	1.56	36	1	1	35	26	10	6	2	12	39	.203	.285	.297	27.1	8.3	144
Chirinos, Yonny	R-R	6-2	225	12-26-93	1	1	9.27	5	5	0	22	33	23	23	5	7	22	.344	.390	.552	21.0	6.7	105
Dodd, Dylan	L-L	6-2	210	6-06-98	2	2	7.60	7	7	0	34	53	29	29	9	12	15	.351	.402	.616	9.1	7.3	164
Elder, Bryce	R-R	6-2	220	5-19-99	12	4	3.81	31	31	0	175	160	79	74	19	63	128	.245	.316	.390	17.5	8.6	732
Fried, Max	L-L	6-4	190	1-18-94	8	1	2.55	14	14	0	78	70	24	22	7	18	80	.242	.290	.343	25.7	5.8	311
Hand, Brad	L-L	6-3	224	3-20-90	2	2	7.50	20	0	1	18	19	15	15	2	6	18	.279	.355	.456	22.8	7.6	79
Hearn, Taylor	L-L	6-6	230	8-30-94	0	0	108.00	1	0	0	0	2	4	4	1	2	0	.667	.800	1.667	0.0	40.0	5
Heller, Ben	R-R	6-3	210	8-05-91	0	0	3.86	19	0	0	19	16	9	8	2	11	16	.232	.354	.362	19.5	13.4	82
Hernandez, Daysbel	R-R	5-10	220	9-15-96	1	0	7.36	4	0	0	4	6	3	3	1	3	6	.353	.450	.529	30.0	15.0	20
Iglesias, Raisel	R-R	6-2	190	1-04-90	5	4	2.75	58	0	33	56	51	23	17	7	15	68	.238	.286	.379	29.4	6.5	231
Jimenez, Joe	R-R	6-3	277	1-17-95	0	3	3.04	59	0	0	56	51	22	19	9	14	73	.233	.284	.420	30.7	5.9	238
Johnson, Pierce	R-R	6-2	202	5-10-91	1	1	0.76	24	0	0	24	16	6	2	3	5	32	.190	.236	.333	36.0	5.6	89
Lee, Dylan	L-L	6-3	214	8-01-94	1	0	4.18	24	1	0	24	24	14	11	4	8	24	.264	.323	.429	23.8	7.9	101
Lopez, Nicky	L-R	5-11	180	3-13-95	0	0	7.71	2	0	0	2	4	2	2	1	2	0	.364	.462	.636	0.0	15.4	13
Luetge, Lucas	L-L	6-4	205	3-24-87	1	0	7.24	12	0	0	14	17	11	11	2	7	14	.304	.385	.429	21.5	10.8	65
McHugh, Collin	R-R	6-2	191	6-19-87	4	1	4.30	41	1	0	59	70	34	28	5	22	47	.293	.362	.397	17.5	8.2	268
Minter, A.J.	L-L	6-0	215	9-02-93	3	6	3.76	70	0	10	65	56	28	27	6	21	82	.236	.296	.354	31.5	8.1	260
Morton, Charlie	R-R	6-5	215	11-12-83	14	12	3.64	30	30	0	163	150	70	66	14	83	183	.244	.344	.371	25.6	11.6	716
Rodriguez, Dereck	R-R	6-0	208	6-05-92	0	0	15.43	3	0	0	5	8	8	8	2	4	1	.364	.462	.818	3.8	15.4	26
Shuster, Jared	L-L	6-3	210	8-03-98	4	3	5.81	11	11	0	53	53	34	34	7	26	30	.264	.348	.438	13.0	11.3	230
Smith-Shawver, AJ	R-R	6-3	205	11-20-02	1	0	4.26	6	5	0	25	17	14	12	7	11	20	.183	.276	.419	19.0	10.5	105
Soroka, Michael	R-R	6-5	225	8-04-97	2	2	6.40	7	6	0	32	36	23	23	9	12	29	.281	.361	.555	20.0	8.3	145
Stephens, Jackson	R-R	6-2	220	5-11-94	0	0	3.00	5	0	0	12	13	4	4	1	5	11	.283	.353	.370	21.2	9.6	52
Strider, Spencer	R-R	6-0	195	10-28-98	20	5	3.86	32	32	0	187	146	85	80	22	58	281	.210	.279	.355	36.8	7.6	763
Tonkin, Michael	R-R	6-7	220	11-19-89	7	3	4.28	45	0	1	80	64	41	38	13	23	75	.217	.276	.380	23.1	7.1	325

Pitching	B-T	Ht.	Wt.	DOB	W	L	ERA	G	GS	SV	IP	Hits	Runs	ER	HR	BB	SO	AVG	OBP	SLG	SO%	BB%	BF
Vines, Darius	R-R	6-1	190	4-30-98	1	0	3.98	5	2	0	20	15	10	9	3	7	14	.203	.274	.419	16.7	8.3	84
Winans, Allan	R-R	6-2	165	8-10-95	1	2	5.29	6	6	0	32	37	19	19	5	8	34	.287	.333	.481	24.1	5.7	141
Wright, Kyle	R-R	6-4	215	10-02-95	1	3	6.97	9	7	0	31	40	26	24	5	17	34	.303	.396	.485	21.9	11.0	155
Yates, Kirby	L-R	5-10	205	3-25-87	7	2	3.28	61	0	5	60	35	22	22	9	37	80	.167	.304	.314	31.5	14.6	254
Young, Danny	L-L	6-3	200	5-27-94	0	0	1.08	8	0	0	8	7	1	1	0	2	11	.233	.343	.267	31.4	5.7	35

Fielding

Catcher	PCT	G	PO	A	E	DP	PB
d'Arnaud	.991	63	563	12	5	1	1
Murphy	.990	102	919	30	10	2	3
Tromp	1.000	6	53	0	0	0	0

First Base	PCT	G	PO	A	E	DP
Lopez	1.000	2	6	0	0	0
Olson	.994	162	1194	96	8	124
Williams	1.000	1	5	0	0	0

Second Base	PCT	G	PO	A	E	DP
Albies	.986	148	211	368	8	79
Grissom	1.000	4	2	3	0	0
Lopez	1.000	14	19	35	0	12

Third Base	PCT	G	PO	A	E	DP
Lopez	1.000	2	1	1	0	0
Riley	.972	159	95	287	11	38
Williams	1.000	2	0	3	0	0

Shortstop	PCT	G	PO	A	E	DP
Adrianza	.800	3	2	2	1	1
Arcia	.977	139	184	322	12	69
Grissom	.905	19	20	37	6	8
Lopez	.952	6	6	14	1	2
Shewmake	1.000	2	1	1	0	0

Outfield	PCT	G	PO	A	E	DP
Acuna	.983	156	281	10	5	1
Harris	.994	138	306	8	2	2
Hilliard	.667	32	38	0	0	0
Ozuna	1.000	2	3	0	0	0
Pillar	.996	80	102	1	1	0
Rosario	.983	130	223	4	4	1
Wall	1.000	9	8	0	0	0
White	1.000	5	9	0	0	0
Williams	.000	1	0	0	0	0

GWINNETT STRIPERS — *TRIPLE-A*

INTERNATIONAL LEAGUE

Batting	B-T	Ht.	Wt.	DOB	AVG	OBP	SLG	G	PA	AB	R	H	2B	3B	HR	RBI	BB	HBP	SH	SF	SO	SB	CS	BB%	SO%
Adrianza, Ehire	B-R	6-1	198	8-21-89	.143	.200	.214	8	30	28	1	4	2	0	0	0	2	0	0	0	3	0	0	6.7	10.0
Aguilar, Jesus	R-R	6-3	277	6-30-90	.271	.373	.379	56	241	203	26	55	7	0	5	34	34	1	0	3	49	0	0	14.1	20.3
Baldwin, Drake	L-R	6-0	210	3-28-01	.333	.333	.583	3	12	12	2	4	0	0	1	2	0	0	0	0	3	0	0	0.0	25.0
Casteel, Ryan	R-R	5-11	205	6-06-91	—	—	—	1	0	0	0	0	0	0	0	0	0	0	0	0	0	0	0	—	—
Clementina, Hendrik	R-R	6-2	250	6-17-97	.317	.326	.463	11	43	41	2	13	3	0	1	6	1	0	0	1	12	0	0	2.3	27.9
Culberson, Charlie	R-R	6-1	200	4-10-89	.204	.234	.255	27	107	98	7	20	2	0	1	10	5	0	0	4	35	3	1	4.7	32.7
d'Arnaud, Travis	R-R	6-2	210	2-10-89	.000	.200	.000	3	10	8	1	0	0	0	0	0	2	0	0	0	3	0	0	20.0	30.0
Dean, Justin	R-R	5-8	185	12-06-96	.164	.307	.270	62	199	159	25	26	3	1	4	19	32	3	0	5	67	13	3	16.1	33.7
Dunand, Joe	R-R	6-1	205	9-20-95	.268	.362	.481	95	403	347	49	93	19	2	17	52	45	8	0	3	107	3	2	11.2	26.6
Fuentes, Joshua	R-R	6-0	209	2-19-93	.227	.300	.339	65	260	233	27	53	7	2	5	29	20	5	0	2	52	3	0	7.7	20.0
Grissom, Vaughn	R-R	6-2	210	1-05-01	.330	.419	.501	102	468	397	74	131	36	4	8	61	56	8	0	4	66	13	2	12.0	14.1
Guthrie, Dalton	R-R	5-11	160	12-23-95	.271	.363	.345	49	205	177	21	48	5	1	2	22	20	6	1	1	45	3	1	9.8	22.0
2-team (22 Lehigh Valley)					.274	.370	.386	71	301	259	32	71	11	3	4	31	31	9	1	1	67	6	3	10.3	22.3
Harris, Michael	L-L	6-0	195	3-07-01	.143	.333	.143	2	9	7	0	1	0	0	0	0	2	0	0	0	3	1	0	22.2	33.3
Hilliard, Sam	L-L	6-5	236	2-21-94	.308	.438	.308	4	16	13	2	4	0	0	0	2	3	0	0	0	5	0	0	18.8	31.3
Hudson, Joe	R-R	5-11	210	5-21-91	.232	.371	.395	69	272	220	39	51	9	0	9	37	44	6	0	2	79	4	0	16.2	29.0
Lugbauer, Drew	L-R	6-3	220	8-23-96	.225	.276	.348	25	98	89	5	20	2	0	3	15	6	1	0	2	44	0	0	6.1	44.9
Luplow, Jordan	R-R	5-11	195	9-26-93	.300	.429	.300	3	14	10	2	3	0	0	0	3	2	1	0	1	2	0	1	14.3	14.3
Miroglio, Dominic	R-R	5-10	205	3-10-95	.250	.524	.583	6	21	12	4	3	1	0	1	3	7	1	0	1	2	0	0	33.3	9.5
Pabst, Arden	R-R	6-1	205	3-14-95	.400	.600	.800	4	15	10	3	4	1	0	1	1	5	0	0	0	1	0	0	33.3	6.7
Park, Hoy	L-R	6-0	200	4-07-96	.262	.385	.379	101	389	317	49	83	15	2	6	42	60	4	2	1	86	16	2	15.4	22.1
Pearson, Jacob	L-R	5-10	185	6-01-98	.300	.417	.300	3	12	10	1	3	0	0	0	0	2	0	0	0	2	0	0	16.7	16.7
Pinder, Chad	R-R	6-2	210	3-29-92	.323	.344	.548	7	32	31	2	10	1	0	2	3	1	0	0	0	6	0	0	3.1	18.8
2-team (16 Rochester)					.256	.319	.395	23	94	86	8	22	3	0	3	7	8	0	0	0	21	0	0	8.5	22.3
Robertson, Daniel	R-R	5-11	210	3-22-94	.220	.336	.316	54	211	177	25	39	6	1	3	20	24	8	0	2	37	0	0	11.4	17.5
Sanchez, Yolmer	B-R	5-8	210	6-29-92	.236	.381	.350	117	481	377	55	89	15	2	8	62	89	5	1	9	106	4	3	18.5	22.0
Shewmake, Braden	L-R	6-3	190	11-19-97	.234	.298	.407	122	526	474	79	111	28	3	16	69	39	7	0	6	104	27	1	7.4	19.8
Sierra, Magneuris	L-L	5-11	178	4-07-96	.218	.293	.295	61	216	193	26	42	5	2	2	21	21	0	1	1	55	11	1	9.7	25.5
Solak, Nick	R-R	5-9	185	1-11-95	.272	.364	.444	38	173	151	23	41	8	0	6	28	17	5	0	0	27	2	2	9.8	15.6
2-team (54 Toledo)					.244	.358	.373	92	394	332	49	81	15	2	8	48	50	9	0	3	74	4	3	12.7	18.8
Tromp, Chadwick	R-R	5-8	221	3-21-95	.210	.336	.384	65	268	224	32	47	9	0	10	33	43	0	0	1	54	0	0	16.0	20.1
Velazquez, Andrew	R-R	5-9	170	7-14-94	.217	.266	.250	14	64	60	4	13	2	0	0	4	4	0	0	0	25	1	1	6.3	39.1
Waddell, Luke	L-R	5-7	180	7-13-98	.221	.346	.279	29	131	104	16	23	2	2	0	10	20	2	0	4	15	3	1	15.3	11.5
Wall, Forrest	L-R	6-0	195	11-20-95	.280	.372	.427	90	411	354	62	99	16	6	8	43	52	2	0	3	90	52	8	12.7	21.9
White, Eli	R-R	6-2	195	6-26-94	.254	.363	.450	43	201	169	30	43	4	1	9	23	30	0	0	2	58	14	1	14.9	28.9
Williams, Luke	R-R	6-0	186	8-09-96	.251	.343	.396	48	216	187	31	47	5	2	6	24	26	1	0	2	42	17	4	12.0	19.4

Pitching	B-T	Ht.	Wt.	DOB	W	L	ERA	G	GS	SV	IP	Hits	Runs	ER	HR	BB	SO	AVG	OBP	SLG	SO%	BB%	BF
Allard, Kolby	L-L	6-1	195	8-13-97	0	0	2.70	2	2	0	7	6	2	2	0	2	8	.231	.286	.269	28.6	7.1	28
Anderson, Ian	R-R	6-3	170	5-02-98	0	0	54.00	1	1	0	1	4	6	4	3	2	1	.571	.667	1.857	11.1	22.2	9
Anderson, Nick	R-R	6-4	205	7-05-90	0	1	11.57	3	0	0	2	5	3	3	0	2	1	.455	.500	.455	7.1	14.3	14
Burrows, Beau	R-R	6-2	210	9-18-96	3	5	5.67	36	10	0	73	72	47	46	13	34	71	.256	.342	.438	22.0	10.6	322
Chavez, Jesse	R-R	6-1	175	8-21-83	0	0	0.00	3	1	0	3	2	0	0	0	1	6	.167	.231	.167	46.2	7.7	13
Culberson, Charlie	R-R	6-1	200	4-10-89	0	0	4.91	4	0	0	4	8	5	2	0	2	5	.400	.455	.400	22.7	9.1	22
De Avila, Luis	L-L	5-9	215	5-29-01	0	0	2.45	1	1	0	4	4	2	1	0	4	3	.250	.429	.250	14.3	19.0	21
Dodd, Dylan	L-L	6-2	210	6-06-98	4	6	5.91	16	14	0	75	86	50	49	14	30	67	.291	.357	.497	20.4	9.1	329
Elder, Bryce	R-R	6-2	220	5-19-99	0	0	6.00	1	1	0	6	5	4	4	1	1	4	.227	.261	.364	17.4	4.3	23
Elledge, Seth	R-R	6-3	240	5-20-96	4	2	4.83	25	0	0	32	33	20	17	6	9	36	.273	.323	.488	27.7	6.9	130
Fried, Max	L-L	6-4	190	1-18-94	0	2	5.00	3	3	0	9	12	5	5	2	4	10	.353	.410	.588	25.6	10.3	39
Gordon, Tanner	L-R	6-5	215	10-26-97	1	4	8.28	6	5	0	29	38	30	27	3	10	21	.328	.380	.466	16.2	7.7	130
Harvey, Joe	R-R	6-2	236	1-09-92	2	1	5.64	24	0	1	30	20	19	19	3	18	28	.189	.323	.311	22.0	14.2	127

Heller, Ben	R-R	6-3	210	8-05-91	2	0	2.16	14	0	0	17	9	4	4	0	7	23	.158	.273	.193	34.8	10.6	66
Hernandez, Daysbel	R-R	5-10	220	9-15-96	0	0	1.69	5	0	0	5	2	1	1	0	3	11	.125	.286	.250	52.4	14.3	21
Holmes, Grant	L-R	6-0	226	3-22-96	7	3	3.54	50	0	13	61	53	27	24	5	26	74	.232	.310	.346	28.7	10.1	258
Iglesias, Raisel	R-R	6-2	190	1-04-90	0	0	3.00	3	0	0	3	2	1	1	0	0	5	.182	.182	.273	45.5	0.0	11
Johnstone, Connor	R-R	6-1	195	10-04-94	0	1	14.40	3	0	0	5	12	8	8	2	3	3	.462	.517	.769	10.3	10.3	29
Kingham, Nolan	R-R	6-4	210	8-18-96	0	4	4.56	20	7	0	51	55	29	26	6	25	41	.284	.369	.448	18.5	11.3	222
Kolarek, Adam	L-L	6-3	215	1-14-89	2	0	9.82	7	0	0	7	9	9	8	3	10	7	.321	.500	.679	18.4	26.3	38
Lee, Dylan	L-L	6-3	214	8-01-94	1	1	6.14	7	0	0	7	8	5	5	3	3	4	.296	.367	.667	13.3	10.0	30
Lovelady, Richard	L-L	6-0	185	7-07-95	0	1	7.20	4	0	0	5	4	4	4	0	2	4	.222	.318	.278	18.2	9.1	22
Luetge, Lucas	L-L	6-4	205	3-24-87	2	1	3.75	21	0	0	24	26	13	10	4	9	26	.265	.327	.408	24.3	8.4	107
Margevicius, Nick	L-L	6-5	225	6-18-96	3	2	7.13	14	8	0	48	63	40	38	7	14	33	.332	.373	.505	15.6	6.6	211
McHugh, Collin	R-R	6-2	191	6-19-87	0	1	15.43	2	0	0	2	4	4	4	0	3	5	.364	.500	.455	35.7	21.4	14
Minter, A.J.	L-L	6-0	215	9-02-93	0	0	0.00	2	0	0	2	2	0	0	0	1	2	.286	.375	.429	25.0	12.5	8
Moran, Brian	L-L	6-4	225	9-30-88	2	1	3.21	38	0	2	48	41	17	17	6	20	58	.227	.317	.376	28.3	9.8	205
Morin, Mike	R-R	6-4	220	5-03-91	0	0	5.09	16	1	0	18	18	11	10	3	11	16	.269	.378	.433	19.5	13.4	82
Munoz, Roddery	R-R	6-2	210	4-14-00	2	2	4.28	16	0	0	27	23	16	13	3	19	27	.228	.361	.396	22.0	15.4	123
Olczak, Jon	R-R	6-0	180	11-14-93	0	0	27.00	4	0	0	3	12	12	10	1	4	3	.522	.621	.783	10.3	13.8	29
Ramirez, Roel	R-R	6-0	235	5-26-95	0	0	6.20	16	0	0	20	25	14	14	3	12	18	.301	.381	.482	18.6	12.4	97
Rangel, Alan	R-R	6-2	170	8-21-97	1	1	4.20	3	2	0	15	12	7	7	2	9	12	.214	.318	.429	18.2	13.6	66
Rios, Yacksel	R-R	6-3	215	6-27-93	1	2	2.49	22	0	7	25	14	9	7	2	8	30	.163	.237	.256	30.3	8.1	99
Robertson, Daniel	R-R	5-11	210	3-22-94	0	0	18.00	1	0	0	1	3	2	2	1	0	0	.500	.500	1.167	0.0	0.0	6
Robles, Domingo	L-L	6-2	170	4-29-98	0	2	10.24	3	2	0	10	17	11	11	1	6	12	.405	.481	.548	23.1	11.5	52
Rodriguez, Dereck	R-R	6-0	208	6-05-92	1	4	6.17	24	4	1	47	53	33	32	6	23	44	.290	.365	.464	21.0	11.0	210
Sanchez, Yolmer	B-R	5-8	210	6-29-92	0	1	9.00	1	0	0	1	1	2	1	1	2	0	.250	.500	1.000	0.0	33.3	6
Sheffield, Justus	L-L	5-10	224	5-13-96	2	5	6.63	13	11	0	54	57	41	40	7	34	56	.275	.377	.425	23.0	13.9	244
Shuster, Jared	L-L	6-3	210	8-03-98	5	6	5.01	16	16	0	79	88	49	44	10	45	64	.289	.374	.461	17.9	12.6	357
Smith-Shawver, AJ	R-R	6-3	205	11-20-02	2	2	4.17	10	10	0	41	26	20	19	4	26	47	.179	.304	.310	27.5	15.2	171
Soroka, Michael	R-R	6-5	225	8-04-97	4	4	3.41	17	17	0	87	65	35	33	6	28	92	.205	.285	.303	25.9	7.9	355
Stephens, Jackson	R-R	6-2	220	5-11-94	1	1	3.28	12	4	0	25	23	9	9	1	4	26	.256	.320	.367	26.0	4.0	100
Swarmer, Matt	R-R	6-5	195	9-25-93	2	4	8.07	19	1	0	32	36	30	29	5	24	30	.288	.392	.448	19.6	15.7	153
Tice, Ty	L-R	5-9	185	7-04-96	3	0	7.94	20	1	0	23	35	28	20	4	17	35	.337	.437	.510	27.8	13.5	126
Tonkin, Michael	R-R	6-7	220	11-19-89	0	0	0.00	1	0	0	1	0	0	0	0	0	2	.000	.000	.000	66.7	0.0	3
Vines, Darius	R-R	6-1	190	4-30-98	3	2	2.36	6	5	0	34	29	11	9	5	13	28	.234	.309	.387	20.1	9.4	139
Waldrep, Hurston	R-R	6-2	205	3-01-02	0	0	0.00	1	1	0	4	4	0	0	0	3	5	.235	.350	.235	25.0	15.0	20
Whitley, Kodi	R-R	6-3	220	2-21-95	0	0	6.43	14	0	0	14	17	10	10	2	11	10	.298	.412	.456	14.7	16.2	68
Wilcox, Kyle	R-R	6-3	195	6-14-94	1	0	4.26	12	0	2	13	6	7	6	0	12	8	.150	.333	.175	14.8	22.2	54
Wilson, Brooks	L-R	6-2	205	3-15-96	0	0	9.00	2	0	0	2	1	2	2	0	4	2	.143	.455	.143	18.2	36.4	11
Winans, Allan	R-R	6-2	165	8-10-95	9	4	2.85	23	17	1	126	101	45	40	11	36	113	.218	.279	.343	22.3	7.1	506
Wright, Kyle	R-R	6-4	215	10-02-95	0	2	6.35	3	3	0	11	11	8	8	1	5	14	.268	.375	.439	29.2	10.4	48
Young, Danny	L-L	6-3	200	5-27-94	0	0	6.32	16	0	1	16	22	12	11	4	11	18	.333	.450	.606	22.5	13.8	80

Fielding

Catcher	PCT	G	PO	A	E	DP	PB
Baldwin	1.000	2	25	2	0	0	0
Casteel	1.000	1	1	0	0	0	0
Clementina	1.000	10	78	2	0	1	2
d'Arnaud	1.000	2	9	1	0	0	0
Hudson	.992	68	551	48	5	2	1
Miroglio	1.000	6	44	2	0	0	0
Pabst	1.000	4	34	2	0	0	0
Tromp	.993	63	540	21	4	3	6

First Base	PCT	G	PO	A	E	DP
Aguilar	.975	14	105	13	3	14
Culberson	.989	10	83	3	1	11
Dunand	1.000	36	262	18	0	32
Fuentes	.989	61	440	28	5	47
Lugbauer	.987	20	135	18	2	22
Pinder	1.000	2	14	1	0	3
Robertson	1.000	8	49	4	0	5
Williams	1.000	2	2	0	0	0

Second Base	PCT	G	PO	A	E	DP
Adrianza	1.000	3	2	6	0	1
Grissom	.992	31	53	65	1	19
Park	.967	12	9	20	1	4
Sanchez	1.000	34	58	74	0	22
Shewmake	.990	63	126	177	3	53
Waddell	.968	14	33	28	2	11

Third Base	PCT	G	PO	A	E	DP
Adrianza	1.000	2	5	5	0	0
Culberson	.923	4	3	9	1	2
Dunand	.951	31	30	48	4	12
Fuentes	.875	3	0	7	1	3
Park	.957	9	7	15	1	2
Robertson	.918	31	13	43	5	10
Sanchez	.971	69	59	110	5	8
Williams	.833	3	2	3	1	2

Shortstop	PCT	G	PO	A	E	DP
Adrianza	1.000	1	1	1	0	0
Grissom	.967	73	71	192	9	38
Sanchez	1.000	4	5	11	0	6
Shewmake	.978	60	73	150	5	35
Waddell	.956	15	15	50	3	8

Outfield	PCT	G	PO	A	E	DP
Adrianza	1.000	2	1	0	0	0
Culberson	1.000	2	5	1	0	0
Dean	1.000	58	101	1	0	0
Dunand	1.000	7	7	1	0	0
Guthrie	1.000	49	98	4	0	1
Harris	1.000	2	5	0	0	0
Hilliard	1.000	2	3	0	0	0
Luplow	1.000	3	3	0	0	0
Park	1.000	53	95	4	0	0
Pearson	.928	3	8	0	1	0
Pinder	1.000	4	5	0	0	0
Sanchez	.800	4	12	0	3	0
Sierra	.986	59	110	6	2	1
Solak	1.000	34	50	2	0	0
Velazquez	1.000	14	29	0	0	0
Wall	1.000	89	175	4	0	0
White	1.000	40	97	6	0	1
Williams	.992	43	70	4	1	0

MISSISSIPPI BRAVES — *DOUBLE-A*

SOUTHERN LEAGUE

Batting	B-T	Ht.	Wt.	DOB	AVG	OBP	SLG	G	PA	AB	R	H	2B	3B	HR	RBI	BB	HBP	SH	SF	SO	SB	CS	BB%	SO%
Baldwin, Drake	L-R	6-0	210	3-28-01	.321	.390	.396	14	59	53	4	17	1	0	1	5	6	0	0	0	11	0	0	10.2	18.6
Bunnell, Cade	L-R	5-11	190	5-14-97	.201	.313	.368	113	467	399	46	80	17	1	16	50	62	4	0	2	179	7	2	13.3	38.3
Campbell, Drew	L-L	5-11	180	11-10-97	.254	.307	.404	78	300	272	31	69	14	0	9	30	14	8	4	2	77	10	9	4.7	25.7
Clarno, Nick	R-R	6-0	205	6-25-98	.000	.000	.000	3	10	10	0	0	0	0	0	0	0	0	0	0	4	0	0	0.0	40.0
Clementina, Hendrik	R-R	6-2	250	6-17-97	.212	.328	.288	16	61	52	6	11	4	0	0	6	6	3	0	0	15	0	0	9.8	24.6
Conley, Cal	B-R	5-8	185	7-17-99	.219	.298	.286	135	599	535	67	117	21	3	3	24	53	8	2	1	133	32	13	8.8	22.2

Dean, Justin	R-R	5-8	185	12-06-96	.228	.366	.332	55	236	193	40	44	3	1	5	14	39	3	1	0	72	22	5	16.5	30.5
Franklin, Jesse	L-L	6-1	215	12-01-98	.232	.315	.419	94	387	341	55	79	17	1	15	46	32	11	0	3	115	21	4	8.3	29.7
Fuentes, Joshua	R-R	6-0	209	2-19-93	.357	.357	.429	4	14	14	1	5	1	0	0	1	0	0	0	0	3	0	0	0.0	21.4
Horne, Bryson	L-R	5-10	220	3-06-99	.299	.330	.448	23	91	87	5	26	8	1	1	10	4	0	0	0	21	0	0	4.4	23.1
Lugbauer, Drew	L-R	6-3	220	8-23-96	.279	.385	.635	69	273	233	40	65	13	2	22	58	37	3	0	0	94	2	0	13.6	34.4
Milligan, Cody	L-R	5-9	170	12-23-98	.280	.377	.414	69	308	261	49	73	16	5	3	22	38	5	0	4	67	23	4	12.3	21.8
Moritz, Andrew	L-R	5-9	180	12-22-96	.221	.309	.303	37	139	122	14	27	3	2	1	14	14	2	0	1	31	3	2	10.1	22.3
Pabst, Arden	R-R	6-1	205	3-14-95	.129	.257	.247	28	101	85	6	11	1	0	3	6	13	2	0	1	35	0	1	12.9	34.7
Parker, Brandon	R-R	6-0	205	5-27-99	.161	.350	.194	11	40	31	3	5	1	0	0	4	9	0	0	0	11	1	1	22.5	27.5
Pearson, Jacob	L-R	5-10	185	6-01-98	.152	.235	.283	28	102	92	8	14	2	2	2	7	10	0	0	0	37	3	0	9.8	36.3
Philip, Beau	R-R	5-11	200	10-23-98	.199	.307	.301	70	264	226	26	45	9	1	4	19	31	5	0	2	91	2	2	11.7	34.5
Potts, Hudson	R-R	6-2	205	10-28-98	.160	.258	.311	72	271	238	21	38	12	0	8	27	30	2	0	1	116	0	0	11.1	42.8
Stephens, Landon	R-R	6-1	204	3-15-98	.199	.319	.431	103	404	341	46	68	16	0	21	59	53	8	0	2	151	2	3	13.1	37.4
Tolman, Mitchell	L-R	5-10	195	6-08-94	.182	.308	.182	3	13	11	1	2	0	0	0	1	2	0	0	0	4	0	0	15.4	30.8
Tolve, Tyler	L-R	6-0	200	7-16-00	.238	.304	.394	50	217	193	28	46	9	0	7	32	20	0	0	4	59	2	0	9.2	27.2
Valdes, Javier	R-R	5-10	205	11-19-98	.234	.379	.402	73	298	239	33	56	14	1	8	26	46	11	0	2	63	1	2	15.4	21.1
Waddell, Luke	L-R	5-7	180	7-13-98	.290	.395	.403	101	446	372	57	108	16	1	8	64	65	3	0	6	57	26	9	14.6	12.8
Worrell, Bryson	B-R	6-2	226	11-07-98	.100	.182	.200	3	11	10	0	1	1	0	0	0	1	0	0	0	4	0	0	9.1	36.4

Pitching	B-T	Ht.	Wt.	DOB	W	L	ERA	G	GS	SV	IP	Hits	Runs	ER	HR	BB	SO	AVG	OBP	SLG	SO%	BB%	BF
Barger, Alec	R-R	6-2	201	3-24-98	3	2	3.29	30	0	5	38	31	15	14	2	21	48	.223	.325	.309	29.3	12.8	164
Blewett, Scott	R-R	6-6	245	4-10-96	3	4	4.21	17	13	0	73	59	37	34	7	29	76	.217	.296	.382	24.7	9.4	308
Burrows, Beau	R-R	6-2	210	9-18-96	0	0	0.00	1	1	0	3	3	0	0	0	2	5	.214	.353	.286	29.4	11.8	17
De Avila, Luis	L-L	5-9	215	5-29-01	6	10	3.28	25	25	0	123	99	53	45	8	61	125	.223	.324	.329	24.0	11.7	521
Deal, Hayden	L-L	6-4	210	11-04-94	3	1	3.56	29	5	0	48	46	22	19	2	22	41	.251	.349	.322	19.3	10.4	212
Gonzalez, Domingo	R-R	6-0	185	9-27-99	3	5	4.19	40	1	1	54	45	31	25	2	33	76	.220	.351	.307	30.5	13.3	249
Gordon, Tanner	L-R	6-5	215	10-26-97	4	5	4.61	11	11	0	57	54	34	29	7	15	55	.243	.289	.414	22.9	6.3	240
Hackenberg, Drue	R-R	6-2	220	4-01-02	0	0	13.50	1	1	0	1	0	1	1	0	4	1	.000	.667	.000	16.7	66.7	6
Halligan, Patrick	R-R	6-6	230	10-04-99	0	1	1.00	7	1	0	9	6	4	1	0	2	11	.188	.229	.250	31.4	5.7	35
Harris, Hayden	L-L	6-0	186	3-02-99	3	2	2.83	23	0	0	35	27	13	11	1	17	50	.213	.310	.307	34.2	11.6	146
Hernandez, Daysbel	R-R	5-10	220	9-15-96	1	0	0.00	12	0	2	14	4	0	0	0	5	19	.089	.180	.089	38.0	10.0	50
Howard, Nick	R-R	6-4	215	4-06-93	1	0	3.46	11	0	0	13	14	5	5	1	12	9	.275	.422	.333	14.1	18.8	64
Huntley, Coleman	R-R	6-4	225	3-10-93	3	0	2.88	18	0	1	25	34	14	8	0	9	31	.318	.375	.346	25.8	7.5	120
Kingham, Nolan	R-R	6-4	210	8-18-96	4	2	4.11	7	6	0	35	38	18	16	1	12	22	.279	.347	.324	14.6	7.9	151
Luetge, Lucas	L-L	6-4	205	3-24-87	0	0	0.00	1	0	0	2	0	0	0	0	0	3	.000	.167	.000	50.0	0.0	6
Lugbauer, Drew	L-R	6-3	220	8-23-96	0	0	0.00	1	0	0	1	0	0	0	0	0	1	.000	.000	.000	50.0	0.0	2
Margevicius, Nick	L-L	6-5	225	6-18-96	0	1	6.10	7	4	0	21	20	14	14	4	4	16	.253	.286	.481	18.8	4.7	85
Martinez, Daniel	L-R	5-11	190	7-28-98	1	2	4.71	6	6	0	29	26	16	15	0	18	37	.243	.352	.346	28.9	14.1	128
McSteen, Jake	R-L	6-0	215	3-12-96	1	2	4.13	40	0	1	57	61	30	26	10	18	51	.272	.328	.469	20.6	7.3	248
Montilla, Jose	R-R	6-1	235	6-04-98	1	2	6.80	21	6	0	46	54	41	35	8	20	36	.290	.356	.457	17.2	9.6	209
Munoz, Roddery	R-R	6-2	210	4-14-00	0	1	6.75	1	1	0	4	3	3	3	0	4	3	.214	.368	.214	15.8	21.1	19
Owens, Tyler	R-R	5-10	185	1-09-01	0	1	4.21	14	4	3	26	31	14	12	2	13	25	.290	.369	.411	20.5	10.7	122
Pena, Miguel	L-R	6-1	190	11-26-98	0	0	3.97	9	0	0	11	11	10	5	2	14	10	.250	.424	.409	16.9	23.7	59
Rangel, Alan	R-R	6-2	170	8-21-97	3	15	4.66	23	23	0	112	104	62	58	16	41	128	.240	.307	.408	26.6	8.5	482
Riley, Trey	L-R	6-3	205	4-21-98	2	3	4.07	42	0	2	49	42	28	22	2	41	59	.237	.390	.299	26.1	18.1	226
Robles, Domingo	L-L	6-2	170	4-29-98	9	7	3.39	23	22	0	119	109	53	45	9	32	119	.241	.296	.342	24.1	6.5	494
Segal, Alex	L-L	6-4	190	3-18-98	1	0	5.74	17	0	0	16	13	14	10	1	16	20	.210	.402	.290	24.4	19.5	82
Sheffield, Justus	L-L	5-10	224	5-13-96	0	0	9.00	1	1	0	1	1	1	1	0	1	0	.250	.400	.750	0.0	20.0	5
Smith-Shawver, AJ	R-R	6-3	205	11-20-02	1	0	0.00	2	2	0	7	5	0	0	0	3	9	.192	.276	.346	31.0	10.3	29
Smith, Austin	R-R	6-4	210	6-22-99	0	0	13.50	1	0	0	1	0	1	1	0	1	0	.000	.333	.000	0.0	33.3	3
Tice, Ty	L-R	5-9	185	7-04-96	0	2	5.23	25	1	3	31	35	18	18	2	14	48	.271	.345	.357	33.1	9.7	145
Vodnik, Victor	R-R	6-0	200	10-09-99	3	1	3.10	30	0	4	41	26	14	14	2	25	56	.183	.316	.282	32.6	14.5	172
Waldrep, Hurston	R-R	6-2	205	3-01-02	0	1	2.70	3	3	0	10	8	3	3	1	7	11	.216	.356	.324	24.4	15.6	45
Wilcox, Kyle	R-R	6-3	195	6-14-94	4	4	2.13	36	0	3	42	21	11	10	2	23	64	.145	.266	.221	37.0	13.3	173
Williams, Peyton	R-R	6-1	180	5-06-98	0	1	7.56	11	0	0	17	19	14	14	4	7	20	.292	.368	.615	26.3	9.2	76
Wilson, Brooks	L-R	6-2	205	3-15-96	2	0	1.08	6	0	1	8	1	1	1	1	2	12	.038	.107	.154	42.9	7.1	28

Fielding

Catcher	PCT	G	PO	A	E	DP	PB
Baldwin	1.000	9	89	4	0	1	1
Clarno	.923	3	36	0	3	0	0
Clementina	.993	15	140	12	1	0	3
Pabst	.983	26	221	11	4	2	2
Tolve	.984	43	406	25	7	0	4
Valdes	.988	42	385	27	5	0	8

First Base	PCT	G	PO	A	E	DP
Bunnell	.989	13	83	8	1	8
Fuentes	1.000	2	12	2	0	2
Horne	.993	17	134	7	1	12
Lugbauer	.992	48	325	31	3	20
Potts	1.000	37	264	16	0	31
Stephens	.989	13	89	4	1	6
Valdes	1.000	10	91	2	0	7

Second Base	PCT	G	PO	A	E	DP
Bunnell	.973	22	36	35	2	8
Conley	.967	64	97	164	9	36
Milligan	.968	12	10	20	1	4
Philip	.987	18	39	38	1	13
Tolman	1.000	1	1	3	0	1
Waddell	.971	23	36	66	3	6

Third Base	PCT	G	PO	A	E	DP
Bunnell	.928	59	31	98	10	7
Fuentes	.875	2	1	6	1	0
Philip	.925	40	28	58	7	8
Potts	.915	28	17	37	5	2
Tolman	1.000	1	1	1	0	0
Waddell	.964	10	8	19	1	1

Shortstop	PCT	G	PO	A	E	DP
Bunnell	1.000	2	1	7	0	0
Conley	.943	69	89	158	15	27
Waddell	.968	66	79	190	9	42

Outfield	PCT	G	PO	A	E	DP
Bunnell	1.000	5	7	0	0	0
Campbell	.996	75	142	4	1	0
Dean	.995	55	99	2	1	1
Franklin	.993	84	145	2	2	0
Lugbauer	.000	1	0	0	0	0
Milligan	.910	60	114	4	3	1
Moritz	1.000	31	44	0	0	0
Parker	1.000	7	8	0	0	0
Pearson	.967	25	48	1	1	0
Potts	1.000	2	2	0	0	0
Stephens	.658	79	132	8	3	2
Worrell	1.000	2	2	0	0	0

ROME BRAVES

HIGH CLASS A

SOUTH ATLANTIC LEAGUE

Batting	B-T	Ht.	Wt.	DOB	AVG	OBP	SLG	G	PA	AB	R	H	2B	3B	HR	RBI	BB	HBP	SH	SF	SO	SB	CS	BB%	SO%
Acton, Cory	L-R	5-11	175	3-22-99	.208	.378	.260	30	99	77	10	16	1	0	1	7	19	2	1	0	36	5	3	19.2	36.4
Adrianza, Ehire	B-R	6-1	198	8-21-89	.316	.417	.421	7	24	19	3	6	2	0	0	4	4	0	0	1	2	1	0	16.7	8.3
Alvarez, Ignacio	R-R	5-11	190	4-11-03	.284	.395	.391	116	501	419	62	119	24	0	7	66	66	13	0	3	87	16	5	13.2	17.4
Baldwin, Drake	L-R	6-0	210	3-28-01	.260	.385	.466	92	405	335	57	87	25	1	14	54	61	8	0	1	84	0	0	15.1	20.7
Cerrato, Wiston	B-R	5-8	170	4-09-99	.200	.200	.200	4	5	5	2	1	0	0	0	0	0	0	0	0	2	0	0	0.0	40.0
Horne, Bryson	L-R	5-10	220	3-06-99	.189	.247	.296	76	299	270	21	51	11	0	6	30	22	1	0	6	101	3	0	7.4	33.8
Janas, Justin	L-R	6-2	205	9-18-00	.233	.307	.307	41	166	150	18	35	6	1	1	11	9	7	0	0	35	3	0	5.4	21.1
Keck, Andrew	R-R	6-2	225	12-12-99	.125	.250	.125	8	28	24	2	3	0	0	0	0	3	1	0	0	11	3	0	10.7	39.3
Kilpatrick, Kevin	R-R	5-10	186	11-25-00	.226	.333	.333	120	551	469	75	106	21	7	5	30	68	9	1	4	140	32	5	12.3	25.4
McCabe, David	B-R	6-3	230	3-25-00	.281	.388	.428	81	348	292	37	82	16	0	9	50	53	0	0	3	66	9	1	15.2	19.0
Mezquita, Brandol	R-R	6-0	170	7-14-01	.155	.221	.264	39	141	129	18	20	4	2	2	9	10	1	0	0	51	5	0	7.1	36.2
Morton, Kadon	R-R	6-1	195	11-19-00	.173	.267	.265	80	281	249	28	43	9	1	4	18	28	4	0	0	110	16	1	10.0	39.1
Oqans, Keshawn	R-R	5-8	180	8-26-01	.265	.360	.397	113	454	388	43	103	22	1	9	67	46	14	1	5	87	10	8	10.1	19.2
Pabst, Arden	R-R	6-1	205	3-14-95	.000	.103	.000	7	29	26	0	0	0	0	0	0	3	0	0	0	13	0	0	10.3	44.8
Paolini, Stephen	L-L	6-1	195	11-23-00	.208	.346	.315	71	241	197	24	41	8	2	3	18	37	5	1	1	91	6	2	15.4	37.8
Parker, Brandon	R-R	6-0	205	5-27-99	.250	.331	.410	47	175	156	27	39	8	1	5	21	16	3	0	0	59	10	2	9.1	33.7
Quintero, Geraldo	B-R	5-5	155	10-10-01	.251	.345	.325	112	472	406	54	102	11	5	3	41	55	4	1	1	88	29	13	11.7	18.6
Stevens, Eliezel	L-R	5-9	185	10-08-00	.220	.290	.286	30	100	91	9	20	3	0	1	5	7	2	0	0	35	2	0	7.0	35.0
Workinger, Ethan	R-R	6-0	185	10-19-01	.221	.254	.305	52	201	190	15	42	13	0	1	24	9	0	0	2	64	0	0	4.5	31.8
Worrell, Bryson	B-R	6-2	226	11-07-98	.136	.286	.136	7	28	22	3	3	0	0	0	2	4	1	0	1	13	1	0	14.3	46.4
Zebrowski, Adam	R-R	6-0	230	9-28-00	.203	.307	.376	95	381	330	33	67	16	1	13	38	44	6	0	1	119	1	0	11.5	31.2

Pitching	B-T	Ht.	Wt.	DOB	W	L	ERA	G	GS	SV	IP	Hits	Runs	ER	HR	BB	SO	AVG	OBP	SLG	SO%	BB%	BF
Alesandro, Ronaldo	R-R	6-0	170	5-07-98	0	1	2.70	20	0	5	27	24	11	8	2	13	32	.238	.336	.307	27.4	11.1	117
Bautista, Jorge	R-R	6-0	155	12-10-00	4	2	5.95	9	7	0	39	39	29	26	4	21	46	.255	.350	.412	25.8	11.8	178
Braun, Lucas	R-R	6-0	185	8-26-01	0	0	5.59	2	2	0	10	8	6	6	2	3	13	.229	.289	.429	34.2	7.9	38
Burgess, Brent	R-R	6-0	200	5-02-97	0	1	4.15	3	0	0	4	3	2	2	1	6	8	.188	.409	.375	36.4	27.3	22
De Grandpre, Cedric	R-R	6-2	210	1-25-02	2	5	5.13	12	12	0	54	64	35	31	4	15	48	.290	.344	.403	19.9	6.2	241
Dum, Benjamin	L-R	6-0	215	9-30-96	1	1	5.14	13	0	1	14	17	9	8	1	11	16	.315	.431	.426	22.2	15.3	72
Fried, Max	L-L	6-4	190	1-18-94	0	0	0.00	1	1	0	3	2	0	0	0	0	3	.222	.222	.222	33.3	0.0	9
Griswold, Rob	R-R	6-1	185	7-13-98	2	4	3.65	33	0	7	44	43	20	18	3	10	40	.254	.308	.331	21.6	5.4	185
Halligan, Patrick	R-R	6-6	230	10-04-99	5	5	4.45	21	9	1	63	64	36	31	6	28	68	.264	.347	.401	24.5	10.1	278
Harris, Hayden	L-L	6-0	186	3-02-99	2	1	3.94	10	0	1	16	10	8	7	2	4	26	.182	.258	.327	41.9	6.5	62
Harvey, Joe	R-R	6-2	236	1-09-92	0	0	0.00	3	0	0	3	1	0	0	0	1	5	.100	.182	.100	45.5	9.1	11
Hernandez, Daysbel	R-R	5-10	220	9-15-96	2	0	8.44	6	0	0	5	5	6	5	1	5	6	.238	.385	.429	23.1	19.2	26
Howard, Nick	R-R	6-4	215	4-06-93	1	0	4.70	5	0	0	8	10	4	4	0	1	7	.323	.344	.387	21.9	3.1	32
Hughes, Jonathan	R-R	6-2	196	1-08-97	3	6	3.08	35	0	5	53	48	26	18	5	20	50	.241	.315	.372	22.2	8.9	225
Johnson, Jared	R-R	6-2	225	3-15-01	1	1	2.63	10	0	3	14	7	6	4	1	6	11	.156	.250	.244	21.2	11.5	52
Jones, Ryder	L-R	6-2	221	6-07-94	0	1	7.53	13	0	0	14	16	12	12	3	9	20	.281	.391	.526	29.0	13.0	69
Lara, Jhancarlos	R-R	6-3	190	1-15-03	0	1	4.82	2	2	0	9	5	6	5	2	4	18	.156	.263	.375	47.4	10.5	38
Martinez, Daniel	L-R	5-11	190	7-28-98	3	5	3.07	18	14	0	82	74	37	28	8	18	79	.235	.294	.368	23.0	5.2	343
McHugh, Collin	R-R	6-2	191	6-19-87	0	0	0.00	2	1	0	5	3	0	0	0	1	4	.176	.222	.294	22.2	5.6	18
Mejia, Ian	R-R	6-3	205	1-31-00	4	11	4.69	23	23	0	121	121	71	63	16	28	110	.260	.306	.430	21.8	5.6	504
Montilla, Jose	R-R	6-1	235	6-04-98	2	0	2.66	10	0	1	24	20	8	7	0	0	18	.235	.227	.306	20.5	0.0	88
Munoz, Roldy	R-R	6-2	183	4-14-00	4	1	2.29	20	7	0	59	47	19	15	1	32	60	.217	.325	.267	23.4	12.5	256
Murphy, Owen	R-R	6-1	190	9-27-03	0	1	4.76	3	3	0	17	21	10	9	1	4	16	.313	.342	.448	21.9	5.5	73
Niekro, J.J.	R-R	6-0	185	1-28-98	4	4	4.89	31	7	0	85	93	52	46	11	36	75	.292	.364	.456	20.5	9.8	366
Owens, Tyler	R-R	5-10	185	1-09-01	0	5	2.27	15	11	1	40	35	16	10	3	9	42	.232	.287	.344	25.6	5.5	164
Pena, Miguel	L-R	6-1	190	11-26-98	6	1	3.15	27	0	3	34	26	13	12	3	12	46	.200	.283	.315	31.7	8.3	145
Ramirez, Roel	R-R	6-0	235	5-26-95	0	0	6.23	4	0	0	4	6	3	3	0	0	7	.316	.316	.421	36.8	0.0	19
Riggins, Hunter	R-R	6-3	205	8-10-98	7	4	5.13	27	10	0	81	86	51	46	8	36	67	.277	.349	.402	19.0	10.2	353
Rodriguez, Estarlin	R-R	6-0	180	10-24-99	1	0	5.79	9	0	1	14	12	9	9	2	15	11	.240	.433	.360	16.4	22.4	67
Schanaman, Shay	R-R	6-0	195	8-12-99	0	1	2.45	5	0	1	7	8	3	2	0	4	6	.276	.364	.345	18.2	12.1	33
Schwellenbach, Spencer	R-R	6-1	200	5-31-00	1	0	1.98	3	3	0	14	4	3	3	0	1	14	.091	.130	.114	30.4	2.2	46
Smith-Shawver, AJ	R-R	6-3	205	11-20-02	1	0	0.00	3	3	0	14	6	0	0	0	4	23	.125	.192	.167	44.2	7.7	52
Stephens, Jackson	R-R	6-2	220	5-11-94	1	0	3.00	2	0	0	3	3	1	1	0	2	2	.273	.385	.273	15.4	15.4	13
Strickland, Samuel	R-L	6-2	218	3-26-99	0	2	14.46	4	2	0	9	19	15	15	7	6	12	.422	.490	.911	23.5	11.8	51
Thompson, Tyree	R-R	6-4	165	6-12-97	3	0	4.43	10	0	3	22	17	12	11	0	15	31	.210	.350	.284	31.0	15.0	100
Vargas, Luis	R-R	5-11	196	5-02-02	4	3	4.37	14	9	0	60	55	29	29	5	28	57	.253	.344	.387	22.2	10.9	257
Vines, Darius	R-R	6-1	190	4-30-98	0	0	4.00	2	2	0	9	6	4	4	2	3	14	.188	.257	.406	40.0	8.6	35
Waldrep, Hurston	R-R	6-2	205	3-01-02	0	0	0.75	3	3	0	12	4	3	1	0	5	17	.100	.200	.125	37.8	11.1	45
Williams, Peyton	R-R	6-1	180	5-06-98	0	1	4.15	26	0	8	35	30	18	16	4	15	52	.231	.324	.377	34.9	10.1	149
Wilson, Brooks	L-R	6-2	205	3-15-96	0	0	4.50	2	0	0	2	3	1	1	0	1	3	.333	.400	.444	30.0	10.0	10
Wright, Kyle	R-R	6-4	215	10-02-95	0	0	0.00	1	1	0	3	1	0	0	0	0	4	.100	.100	.100	40.0	0.0	10

Fielding

Catcher	PCT	G	PO	A	E	DP	PB
Baldwin	.989	63	563	54	7	6	2
Cerrato	.000	1	0	0	0	0	1
Keck	1.000	1	1	0	0	0	0
Pabst	.973	6	68	3	2	0	1
Zebrowski	.992	65	550	47	5	4	5

First Base	PCT	G	PO	A	E	DP
Acton	.976	6	40	0	1	4
Horne	.985	76	572	34	9	67
Janas	.997	37	285	15	1	18
Stevens	1.000	15	85	7	0	11

Second Base	PCT	G	PO	A	E	DP
Acton	.952	11	11	9	1	3

Adrianza	1.000	2	2	5	0	1
Ogans	.967	36	41	76	4	15
Quintero	.975	80	125	184	8	38
Stevens	.958	11	21	25	2	8

Third Base	PCT	G	PO	A	E	DP
Acton	.867	9	6	7	2	3
Adrianza	.000	1	0	0	0	0
Alvarez	1.000	1	1	0	0	0
McCabe	.904	70	41	91	14	9

Ogans	.928	44	30	47	6	9
Quintero	.882	13	3	12	2	1

Shortstop	PCT	G	PO	A	E	DP
Adrianza	.857	2	4	2	1	1
Alvarez	.965	107	144	268	15	54
Ogans	.958	29	32	60	4	10

Outfield	PCT	G	PO	A	E	DP
Kilpatrick	.978	118	264	6	6	2
Mezquita	.972	37	68	1	2	0
Morton	.945	78	118	7	10	2
Paolini	.961	63	97	1	1	0
Parker	.924	37	58	4	5	0
Quintero	1.000	20	30	0	0	0
Workinger	.976	52	93	4	1	2
Worrell	1.000	6	7	0	0	0

AUGUSTA GREENJACKETS

LOW CLASS A

CAROLINA LEAGUE

Batting	B-T	Ht.	Wt.	DOB	AVG	OBP	SLG	G	PA	AB	R	H	2B	3B	HR	RBI	BB	HBP	SH	SF	SO	SB	CS	BB%	SO%
Acton, Cory	L-R	5-11	175	3-22-99	.252	.356	.325	45	177	151	25	38	5	0	2	22	24	1	0	1	38	19	5	13.6	21.5
Backstrom, Mahki	L-L	6-5	220	10-10-01	.179	.273	.359	12	44	39	3	7	0	2	1	6	4	1	0	0	19	0	1	9.1	43.2
Boucher, Pier-Olivier	L-R	6-2	185	12-03-99	.183	.256	.220	23	90	82	10	15	3	0	0	5	6	2	0	0	38	4	1	6.7	42.2
Casanova, Jair	R-R	5-11	170	11-14-03	.199	.307	.327	67	261	226	28	45	6	1	7	35	30	5	0	0	77	4	0	11.5	29.5
Ceballos, Sabin	R-R	6-3	225	8-17-02	.281	.343	.375	9	35	32	3	9	0	0	1	6	3	0	0	0	11	0	0	8.6	31.4
Celedonio, Jeremy	R-R	6-1	183	12-26-01	.188	.331	.386	87	356	293	41	55	7	0	17	46	56	7	0	0	155	11	5	15.7	43.5
Clarno, Nick	R-R	6-0	205	6-25-98	.149	.285	.240	66	249	208	25	31	7	0	4	18	34	6	0	1	74	4	3	13.7	29.7
Collins, Tyler	L-R	5-9	180	3-06-03	.201	.289	.255	91	344	298	38	60	14	1	0	46	38	1	1	6	85	33	9	11.0	24.7
Compton, Drew	B-R	6-2	212	3-25-01	.243	.346	.342	31	130	111	18	27	6	1	1	16	17	1	0	1	27	1	0	13.1	20.8
Dilone, Jose	L-R	5-10	165	10-09-00	.236	.353	.264	23	85	72	10	17	2	0	0	4	12	1	0	0	29	3	1	14.1	34.1
Dimon, Dawson	R-R	6-0	185	5-17-99	.153	.272	.206	55	202	170	18	26	6	0	1	17	27	2	0	3	70	2	0	13.4	34.7
Exposito, E.J.	R-R	5-11	190	5-04-01	.208	.323	.328	110	449	375	51	78	19	1	8	55	61	6	0	7	136	23	5	13.6	30.3
Floyd, Francisco	R-R	5-11	167	5-25-02	.189	.310	.305	57	197	164	26	31	3	2	4	14	30	0	0	3	74	13	5	15.2	37.6
Godman, Jacob	R-R	6-2	200	5-07-00	.162	.313	.243	13	48	37	7	6	0	0	1	7	9	0	0	2	15	0	0	18.8	31.3
Grady, Jace	B-R	5-11	182	5-25-01	.242	.336	.374	28	116	99	15	24	7	0	2	17	15	0	0	2	31	10	2	12.9	26.7
Janas, Justin	L-R	6-2	205	9-18-00	.310	.394	.412	77	325	284	47	88	16	2	3	32	29	11	0	1	44	6	4	8.9	13.5
Keck, Andrew	R-R	6-2	225	12-12-99	.202	.377	.309	35	122	94	13	19	4	0	2	8	19	8	0	1	30	4	0	15.6	24.6
Kern, Kade	R-R	6-0	200	9-18-01	.242	.337	.374	27	104	91	13	22	3	0	3	15	13	0	0	0	31	7	3	12.5	29.8
Magee, Cam	L-R	6-1	190	6-01-02	.184	.271	.289	30	129	114	18	21	6	0	2	14	10	4	0	1	39	11	3	7.8	30.2
McCabe, David	B-R	6-3	230	3-25-00	.267	.381	.493	42	176	146	26	39	7	1	8	25	27	1	0	2	47	1	1	15.3	26.7
Moreno, Luis	R-R	5-11	160	12-09-02	.000	.167	.000	4	12	10	0	0	0	0	0	0	2	0	0	0	7	1	0	16.7	58.3
Potts, Hudson	R-R	6-2	205	10-28-98	.000	.000	.000	1	4	4	0	0	0	0	0	0	0	0	0	0	2	0	0	0.0	50.0
Stevens, Eliezel	L-R	5-9	185	10-08-00	.300	.391	.550	7	23	20	4	6	3	1	0	2	3	0	0	0	6	0	0	13.0	26.1
Tavarez, Ambioris	R-R	5-11	168	11-12-03	.216	.319	.337	108	480	416	61	90	19	5	7	34	44	19	0	1	196	21	20	9.2	40.8
Then, Alexander	B-R	5-9	156	12-11-01	.045	.192	.045	8	26	22	2	1	0	0	0	0	4	0	0	0	9	0	0	15.4	34.6
Verdung, Will	R-R	6-2	200	6-08-03	.237	.303	.247	26	109	97	10	23	1	0	0	9	9	1	0	2	30	3	3	8.3	27.5
Workinger, Ethan	R-R	6-0	185	10-19-01	.289	.380	.507	61	258	225	41	65	10	3	11	33	31	2	0	0	46	5	4	12.0	17.8
Worrell, Bryson	B-R	6-2	226	11-07-98	.209	.326	.378	56	237	201	30	42	8	4	6	25	32	3	0	0	81	17	1	13.5	34.2

Pitching	B-T	Ht.	Wt.	DOB	W	L	ERA	G	GS	SV	IP	Hits	Runs	ER	HR	BB	SO	AVG	OBP	SLG	SO%	BB%	BF
Alesandro, Ronaldo	R-R	6-0	170	5-07-98	1	1	1.93	13	0	1	19	14	5	4	1	7	18	.212	.293	.303	24.0	9.3	75
Austin, Zack	R-R	6-2	190	7-17-01	0	0	2.19	9	0	1	12	6	4	3	0	10	17	.154	.353	.154	33.3	19.6	51
Baumann, Garrett	L-R	6-8	245	8-15-04	0	0	4.50	1	1	0	2	1	1	1	0	2	1	.143	.333	.143	11.1	22.2	9
Bautista, Jorge	R-R	6-0	155	12-10-00	6	4	2.93	13	8	1	68	50	27	22	8	20	65	.207	.265	.339	24.4	7.5	266
Braun, Lucas	R-R	6-0	185	8-26-01	0	2	1.04	4	4	0	17	14	3	2	0	2	19	.212	.235	.258	27.9	2.9	68
Bryant, Chad	R-R	6-0	210	8-03-99	4	3	6.18	27	0	1	44	44	32	30	6	29	49	.262	.386	.440	24.3	14.4	202
De Grandpre, Cedric	R-R	6-2	210	1-25-02	1	1	1.95	7	5	0	32	23	10	7	1	7	40	.202	.258	.272	32.0	5.6	125
Diaz, Giomar	R-R	6-2	190	11-23-02	0	0	4.43	11	0	2	20	26	11	10	0	10	23	.313	.389	.398	24.2	10.5	95
Farris, Mitch	L-L	6-2	187	2-14-01	0	0	3.52	2	2	0	8	8	3	3	0	4	14	.267	.353	.267	41.2	11.8	34
Florentino, Darling	R-R	6-0	210	5-25-01	0	0	5.51	14	0	1	16	19	13	10	0	13	15	.275	.393	.377	17.9	15.5	84
Franks, Jason	R-R	6-3	200	1-23-99	1	3	4.67	30	0	4	35	33	23	18	3	13	45	.243	.309	.426	29.6	8.6	152
Frey, Riley	L-L	6-1	185	4-19-02	1	1	6.50	5	5	0	18	22	13	13	2	5	24	.306	.354	.486	30.4	6.3	79
Fuentes, Didier	R-R	6-0	170	6-17-05	0	4	7.27	10	7	0	26	32	22	21	6	12	27	.330	.389	.598	23.7	10.5	114
Gowens, Riley	R-R	6-3	220	10-18-99	1	0	1.04	2	1	0	9	3	1	1	0	3	13	.107	.194	.107	41.9	9.7	31
Griswold, Rob	R-R	6-1	185	7-13-98	0	0	0.00	5	0	1	5	4	0	0	0	3	5	.222	.333	.278	23.8	14.3	21
Gutierrez, Rolando	L-L	6-2	190	4-06-02	0	0	27.00	1	0	0	1	4	5	4	1	1	0	.444	.500	.778	0.0	10.0	10
Hackenberg, Drue	R-R	6-2	220	4-01-02	0	0	0.00	2	2	0	6	3	1	0	0	2	12	.143	.217	.190	52.2	8.7	23
Harper, Landon	R-R	6-1	176	4-08-01	6	3	3.34	31	0	5	73	69	33	27	6	11	69	.245	.280	.379	23.2	3.7	297
Harris, Hayden	L-L	6-0	186	3-02-99	0	1	9.72	7	0	1	8	11	9	9	2	3	15	.314	.385	.543	38.5	7.7	39
Johnson, Jared	R-R	6-2	225	3-15-01	2	3	4.24	18	9	1	51	41	26	24	7	40	72	.214	.348	.385	30.8	17.1	234
Joseph, Elison	R-R	6-0	170	1-24-01	3	2	5.72	38	0	10	46	40	35	29	7	31	66	.225	.355	.388	30.7	14.4	215
Keller, Seth	R-R	5-10	180	5-26-04	2	4	6.26	16	7	0	46	44	33	32	1	27	32	.260	.406	.325	15.0	12.7	213
Kuehler, Cade	R-R	6-0	215	5-24-02	0	0	0.00	2	2	0	7	1	0	0	0	4	8	.045	.192	.045	30.8	15.4	26
Lara, Jhancarlos	R-R	6-3	190	1-15-03	4	7	4.00	18	13	0	72	55	40	32	4	38	96	.210	.318	.305	31.4	12.4	306
Martinez, Nolan	R-R	6-2	165	6-30-98	7	1	6.06	28	2	3	68	88	52	46	7	27	66	.315	.379	.470	21.0	8.6	315
McDonough, LJ	R-R	6-4	200	4-02-00	1	2	6.75	4	0	0	5	6	6	4	0	5	6	.261	.414	.261	20.7	17.2	29
Murphy, Owen	R-R	6-1	190	9-27-03	6	3	4.71	18	18	0	73	62	43	38	8	28	97	.227	.303	.388	31.4	9.1	309
Ritchie, JR	R-R	6-2	185	6-26-03	0	1	5.40	4	4	0	13	11	9	8	0	3	25	.220	.264	.280	47.2	5.7	53
Rodriguez, Estarlin	R-R	6-0	180	10-24-99	2	4	7.55	21	0	1	31	45	30	26	5	12	32	.333	.393	.504	21.3	8.0	150
Schanaman, Shay	R-R	6-0	195	8-12-99	0	0	0.00	4	0	1	7	2	0	0	0	1	9	.087	.160	.130	36.0	4.0	25
Schwellenbach, Spencer	R-R	6-1	200	5-31-00	4	2	2.63	13	13	0	51	44	17	15	3	15	41	.234	.295	.319	19.6	7.2	209

Shoemaker, Adam	L-L	6-6	205	8-24-02	2	7	6.06	22	14	1	68	67	56	46	9	52	67	.259	.393	.421	21.0	16.3	319
Strickland, Samuel	R-L	6-2	218	3-26-99	5	2	2.76	20	5	4	62	58	26	19	4	13	68	.249	.295	.348	26.7	5.1	255
Thompson, Tyree	R-R	6-4	165	6-12-97	0	2	2.86	18	2	0	44	27	16	14	2	17	47	.182	.271	.284	28.3	10.2	166
Vargas, Luis	R-R	5-11	196	5-02-02	2	3	5.35	8	6	0	37	35	28	22	4	14	36	.246	.317	.387	22.2	8.6	162
Waldrep, Hurston	R-R	6-2	205	3-01-02	0	0	3.00	1	1	0	3	3	2	1	0	1	8	.250	.308	.333	61.5	7.7	13
Wall, Cory	R-R	6-4	230	3-14-00	2	2	4.30	9	0	0	15	13	8	7	0	4	15	.232	.290	.268	24.2	6.5	62

Fielding

Catcher	PCT	G	PO	A	E	DP	PB
Clarno	.983	66	617	66	12	6	9
Dimon	.975	54	512	36	14	4	11
Godman	.979	12	127	10	3	1	2
Keck	1.000	2	18	1	0	0	0

First Base	PCT	G	PO	A	E	DP
Acton	.889	1	8	0	1	0
Backstrom	.966	7	54	3	2	4
Compton	.988	24	157	7	2	13
Dilone	.993	20	142	9	1	7
Exposito	.936	6	40	4	3	4
Janas	.994	68	471	35	3	38
McCabe	1.000	1	1	0	0	0
Stevens	.984	7	56	4	1	5

Second Base	PCT	G	PO	A	E	DP
Acton	.971	19	22	45	2	6
Exposito	.962	65	84	143	9	29
Floyd	.924	18	31	30	5	5
Moreno	.900	4	2	7	1	1
Then	.900	3	2	7	1	1
Verdung	.944	24	39	62	6	10

Third Base	PCT	G	PO	A	E	DP
Acton	.939	23	14	32	3	4
Ceballos	1.000	5	3	7	0	1
Dilone	.000	1	0	0	0	0
Exposito	.906	14	5	24	3	1
Floyd	.921	33	29	53	7	5
Magee	.909	14	4	26	3	2
McCabe	.907	39	24	54	8	5
Potts	1.000	1	0	4	0	3
Then	1.000	5	2	8	0	0

Shortstop	PCT	G	PO	A	E	DP
Exposito	.950	26	41	55	5	6
Floyd	1.000	6	9	6	0	2
Magee	.961	13	17	32	2	7
Tavarez	.932	91	122	208	24	34

Outfield	PCT	G	PO	A	E	DP
Acton	1.000	1	2	0	0	0
Backstrom	1.000	4	5	0	0	0
Boucher	.967	19	26	3	1	0
Casanova	.947	63	107	9	7	2
Celedonio	.905	57	65	2	7	0
Collins	.995	88	185	5	2	1
Dilone	.000	2	0	0	0	0
Grady	.963	26	27	3	3	0
Keck	.500	5	4	0	1	0
Kern	.986	25	48	3	1	1
Workinger	.961	54	101	2	4	0
Worrell	.981	52	83	5	2	0

FCL BRAVES

ROOKIE

FLORIDA COMPLEX LEAGUE

Batting	B-T	Ht.	Wt.	DOB	AVG	OBP	SLG	G	PA	AB	R	H	2B	3B	HR	RBI	BB	HBP	SH	SF	SO	SB	CS	BB%	SO%
Aguilar, Jesus	R-R	6-3	277	6-30-90	.364	.364	.545	3	11	11	3	4	2	0	0	4	0	0	0	0	3	0	0	0.0	27.3
Benitez, Diego	R-R	6-0	180	11-19-04	.261	.332	.392	46	196	176	22	46	11	3	2	19	17	2	0	1	44	3	3	8.7	22.4
Boucher, Pier-Olivier	L-R	6-2	185	12-03-99	.235	.350	.235	5	20	17	3	4	0	0	0	4	3	0	0	0	3	2	0	15.0	15.0
Callez, Leonel	R-R	5-10	165	1-25-01	.188	.316	.375	10	19	16	4	3	0	0	1	5	3	0	0	0	5	0	0	15.8	26.3
Ceballos, Sabin	R-R	6-3	225	8-17-02	.375	.667	.375	5	15	8	4	3	0	0	0	2	6	1	0	0	3	2	0	40.0	20.0
Clementina, Hendrik	R-R	6-2	250	6-17-97	.200	.250	.400	2	8	5	1	1	1	0	0	2	1	0	0	2	1	0	0	12.5	12.5
Compton, Drew	B-R	6-2	212	3-25-01	.263	.300	.684	6	20	19	3	5	2	0	2	5	1	0	0	0	6	0	0	5.0	30.0
Cortorreal, Elian	B-R	5-10	160	11-08-04	.220	.439	.322	25	82	59	17	13	3	0	1	7	20	3	0	0	15	3	1	24.4	18.3
Dilone, Jose	L-R	5-10	165	10-09-00	.412	.535	.735	10	43	34	9	14	1	2	2	14	8	1	0	0	12	2	0	18.6	27.9
Drake, Isaiah	L-R	5-10	185	7-15-05	.221	.312	.279	18	77	68	9	15	0	2	0	8	8	1	0	0	29	9	2	10.4	37.7
Figueroa, Leiker	R-R	5-10	155	1-12-05	.215	.335	.295	45	176	149	27	32	7	1	1	19	22	5	0	0	42	7	3	12.5	23.9
Floyd, Francisco	R-R	5-11	167	5-25-02	.250	.375	.300	7	24	20	5	5	1	0	0	1	4	0	0	0	10	2	0	16.7	41.7
Glod, Douglas	R-R	5-9	185	1-20-05	.224	.386	.398	47	207	161	29	36	9	2	5	25	38	6	0	2	64	6	3	18.4	30.9
Godman, Jacob	R-R	6-2	200	5-07-00	.000	.375	.000	3	8	5	0	0	0	0	0	0	2	1	0	0	1	0	0	25.0	12.5
Gonzalez, Robert	L-R	5-10	175	12-22-04	.241	.316	.295	46	187	166	19	40	5	2	0	14	17	2	0	2	44	11	2	9.1	23.5
Graciano, Wilfrank	R-R	5-8	155	2-18-03	.154	.267	.231	7	15	13	2	2	1	0	0	3	0	2	0	0	5	1	0	0.0	33.3
Grady, Jace	B-R	5-11	182	5-25-01	.250	.500	.417	6	20	12	3	3	2	0	0	5	7	0	0	1	2	4	1	35.0	10.0
Jackson, Christian	R-R	6-2	185	10-23-03	.116	.250	.116	18	53	43	2	5	0	0	0	2	6	2	0	1	15	3	0	11.3	28.3
Kern, Kade	R-R	6-0	200	9-18-01	.200	.294	.400	6	17	15	4	3	1	1	0	5	1	1	0	0	2	4	1	5.9	11.8
King, Will	R-R	5-9	190	9-02-03	.310	.405	.448	11	37	29	7	9	1	0	1	5	6	0	0	2	6	1	0	16.2	16.2
Lugbauer, Drew	L-R	6-3	220	8-23-96	.125	.222	.125	2	9	8	0	1	0	0	0	0	1	0	0	0	4	0	0	11.1	44.4
Magee, Cam	L-R	6-1	190	6-01-02	.286	.474	.286	6	19	14	6	4	0	0	0	0	5	0	0	0	3	4	0	26.3	15.8
Maria, Maximo	R-R	6-2	185	10-01-04	.140	.241	.220	19	58	50	4	7	1	0	1	6	6	1	0	1	32	4	0	10.3	55.2
Martinez, Alexander	R-R	5-11	170	11-16-04	.171	.272	.194	37	147	129	22	22	3	0	0	8	17	1	0	0	38	0	0	11.6	25.9
Milligan, Cody	L-R	5-9	170	12-23-98	.429	.429	.857	2	7	7	2	3	0	0	1	1	0	0	0	0	1	1	0	0.0	14.3
Moreno, Luis	R-R	5-11	160	12-09-02	.286	.464	.333	10	29	21	6	6	1	0	0	5	5	2	0	0	8	1	0	17.2	27.6
Nieves, Yorfran	R-R	6-0	145	2-26-03	.130	.231	.152	15	52	46	2	6	1	0	0	2	3	3	0	0	13	3	1	5.8	25.0
Olsavsky, Joe	R-R	6-1	180	3-29-02	.500	.667	.500	1	3	2	0	1	0	0	0	0	1	0	0	0	0	0	0	33.3	0.0
Owen, Harry	R-R	6-1	225	3-07-02	.228	.400	.263	20	75	57	6	13	2	0	0	11	12	5	0	1	16	1	0	16.0	21.3
Parker, Brandon	R-R	6-0	205	5-27-99	.286	.421	.429	4	19	14	2	4	2	0	0	2	4	0	0	1	3	0	0	21.1	15.8
Pineda, Alen	R-R	5-10	180	11-04-04	.161	.239	.210	25	71	62	7	10	1	1	0	4	5	2	0	2	22	1	1	7.0	31.0
Sanchez, Luis	R-R	5-7	165	1-16-04	.240	.385	.313	46	187	150	28	36	4	2	1	22	34	2	0	1	28	7	4	18.2	15.0
Then, Alexander	B-R	5-9	156	12-11-01	.091	.200	.091	8	25	22	2	2	0	0	0	1	2	1	0	0	13	0	0	8.0	52.0
Verdung, Will	R-R	6-2	200	6-08-03	.250	.382	.464	9	34	28	5	7	3	0	1	4	5	1	0	0	6	1	0	14.7	17.6
Williams, Noah	B-R	6-1	180	4-12-04	.165	.304	.198	32	112	91	10	15	3	0	0	8	16	3	0	2	24	4	2	14.3	21.4

Pitching	B-T	Ht.	Wt.	DOB	W	L	ERA	G	GS	SV	IP	Hits	Runs	ER	HR	BB	SO	AVG	OBP	SLG	SO%	BB%	BF
Almonte, Genderson	R-R	6-2	170	12-13-03	1	1	4.97	6	4	0	13	16	9	7	1	7	8	.333	.421	.458	14.0	12.3	57
Austin, Zack	R-R	6-2	190	7-17-01	0	1	0.00	1	0	0	1	1	1	0	0	0	2	.200	.200	.200	40.0	0.0	5
Bourassa, Ryan	R-R	6-0	230	12-18-99	2	0	1.80	5	0	0	5	1	2	1	0	4	7	.059	.238	.118	33.3	19.0	21
Chavez, Jose	R-R	6-0	185	12-23-03	2	0	4.80	7	2	0	15	23	8	8	2	6	14	.359	.423	.563	19.7	8.5	71
Corona, Reibyn	R-R	5-11	175	11-13-01	0	1	4.05	11	10	0	20	19	9	9	2	10	14	.260	.365	.479	16.5	11.8	85
Diaz, Giomar	R-R	6-2	190	11-23-02	1	1	2.45	6	0	0	11	10	3	3	0	4	13	.238	.347	.238	26.5	8.2	49
Dilone, Adel	R-R	6-3	207	10-07-00	2	1	2.95	8	3	0	18	13	7	6	0	11	22	.203	.333	.281	27.8	13.9	79
Dodd, Dylan	L-L	6-2	210	6-06-98	0	0	0.00	1	1	0	3	0	0	0	0	0	4	.000	.000	.000	40.0	0.0	10

Pitching	B-T	Ht.	Wt.	DOB	W	L	ERA	G	GS	SV	IP	Hits	Runs	ER	HR	BB	SO	AVG	OBP	SLG	SO%	BB%	BF
Farris, Mitch	L-L	6-2	187	2-14-01	1	0	1.00	3	0	0	9	3	1	1	1	2	7	.103	.161	.276	22.6	6.5	31
Frey, Riley	L-L	6-1	185	4-19-02	0	0	0.00	1	1	0	3	0	0	0	0	1	4	.000	.111	.000	44.4	11.1	9
Gallegos, Isaac	R-R	6-3	215	9-17-02	0	0	0.00	1	0	0	1	2	0	0	0	0	1	.500	.500	.500	25.0	0.0	4
Gowens, Riley	R-R	6-3	220	10-18-99	0	0	1.29	3	2	0	7	6	2	1	0	3	9	.222	.300	.296	30.0	10.0	30
Gutierrez, Rolando	L-L	6-2	190	4-06-02	4	2	4.30	13	8	0	52	47	29	25	3	19	41	.246	.318	.403	18.9	8.8	217
Guzman, Wellington	R-R	5-10	170	12-29-04	1	0	4.87	12	0	0	20	20	11	11	1	11	14	.274	.386	.384	15.7	12.4	89
Hernandez, Miguel	R-R	6-0	174	10-01-02	2	0	3.81	18	0	5	26	36	12	11	2	8	30	.327	.388	.427	24.8	6.6	121
Long, Justin	R-R	6-1	180	3-04-02	0	0	54.00	1	0	0	0	1	2	2	0	1	1	.500	.750	1.000	25.0	25.0	4
Martinez, Jhonny	R-R	5-10	172	10-17-04	2	0	5.49	14	0	0	20	16	15	12	0	21	12	.232	.415	.275	12.8	22.3	94
McDonough, LJ	R-R	6-4	200	4-02-00	0	0	0.00	2	0	0	2	3	3	0	0	0	2	.300	.300	.300	20.0	0.0	10
Moreno, Cesari	R-R	6-4	214	12-21-01	1	2	6.16	18	0	0	19	17	16	13	0	19	16	.233	.423	.315	16.5	19.6	97
Munoz, Roddery	R-R	6-2	210	4-14-00	1	0	1.13	5	3	0	8	4	2	1	0	3	10	.160	.276	.240	34.5	10.3	29
Ojeda, Jose	R-R	5-10	170	5-15-05	1	0	2.54	16	0	5	28	22	10	8	1	21	23	.208	.333	.302	17.8	16.3	129
Patino, Marco	R-R	6-0	175	11-17-04	3	1	4.32	14	0	1	25	22	16	12	3	6	22	.234	.291	.394	21.4	5.8	103
Perez, Kelvin	R-R	6-3	175	9-09-00	2	0	5.50	15	0	3	18	24	11	11	2	3	15	.308	.333	.462	18.5	3.7	81
Pirela, Yorvi	R-R	6-0	160	1-03-05	0	1	11.85	12	0	0	14	18	18	18	4	13	12	.310	.452	.603	16.4	17.8	73
Polanco, Efrain	R-R	5-10	165	2-23-03	1	2	6.05	14	0	0	19	15	14	13	2	13	14	.234	.346	.422	17.3	16.0	81
Polo, Davis	R-R	6-1	150	10-27-04	1	4	4.40	13	9	0	45	37	23	22	6	14	32	.226	.295	.390	17.3	7.6	185
Rivas, Albert	R-R	6-0	155	2-18-03	1	1	4.26	5	1	1	19	16	11	9	2	4	19	.222	.278	.375	24.1	5.1	79
Sanchez, Jeuan	R-R	6-2	180	5-21-03	0	2	11.68	10	5	0	12	11	18	16	1	19	13	.229	.449	.333	18.8	27.5	69
Schanaman, Shay	R-R	6-0	195	8-12-99	0	0	0.00	1	0	0	1	0	0	0	0	0	1	.000	.000	.000	33.3	0.0	3
Stephens, Jackson	R-R	6-2	220	5-11-94	0	0	0.00	4	1	0	6	2	0	0	0	1	6	.095	.136	.095	27.3	4.5	22
Taveras, Jhonly	R-R	6-1	180	12-16-04	1	4	9.89	14	2	1	24	21	29	26	2	25	13	.244	.433	.360	10.8	20.8	120
Vines, Darius	R-R	6-1	190	4-30-98	0	0	0.00	2	2	0	6	3	0	0	0	0	7	.150	.150	.150	35.0	0.0	20
Wilson, Brooks	L-R	6-2	205	3-15-96	0	0	0.00	1	0	0	1	0	0	0	0	0	1	.000	.000	.000	33.3	0.0	3

Fielding

C: Martinez 29, Owen 13, Pineda 10, King 7, Callez 4, Godman 3, Clementina 2. **1B:** Nieves 15, Cortorreal 14, Pineda 10, Dilone 8, Compton 6, Callez 5, Aguilar 2, Lugbauer 2, Moreno 2. **2B:** Sanchez 18, Figueroa 15, Cortorreal 11, Verdung 9, Graciano 6, Moreno 5, Floyd 3, Milligan 1, Then 1. **3B:** Sanchez 27, Figueroa 19, Then 5, Ceballos 5, Floyd 4, Magee 1, Moreno 1. **SS:** Benitez 41, Figueroa 11, Magee 5, Olsavsky 1, Sanchez 1. **OF:** Glod 43, Gonzalez 43, Williams 28, Maria 18, Drake 17, Jackson 16, Grady 7, Kern 6, Boucher 5, Parker 4, Milligan 2.

DSL BRAVES — *ROOKIE*

DOMINICAN SUMMER LEAGUE

Batting	B-T	Ht.	Wt.	DOB	AVG	OBP	SLG	G	PA	AB	R	H	2B	3B	HR	RBI	BB	HBP	SH	SF	SO	SB	CS	BB%	SO%
Baez, Mario	R-R	5-9	175	8-25-06	.311	.393	.422	47	206	180	36	56	7	2	3	31	20	5	0	1	25	24	5	9.7	12.1
Baez, Michael	R-R	5-11	195	10-03-04	.364	.500	.636	6	16	11	2	4	0	0	1	2	3	1	0	1	3	0	0	18.8	18.8
Cordero, Carlos	B-R	6-0	170	9-11-05	.230	.347	.294	41	150	126	13	29	3	1	1	15	21	2	0	1	31	2	0	14.0	20.7
Estevez, John	L-R	6-3	190	5-17-06	.198	.359	.322	49	224	177	28	35	9	2	3	21	42	3	0	1	42	4	4	18.8	18.8
Garcia, Elian	L-L	5-10	175	10-31-04	.179	.293	.218	27	92	78	12	14	3	0	0	3	13	0	0	1	17	1	2	14.1	18.5
Garcia, Junior	L-R	6-2	190	7-13-05	.232	.372	.357	32	137	112	17	26	7	2	1	13	22	3	0	0	26	2	0	16.1	19.0
Gil, John	R-R	6-1	175	5-14-06	.285	.409	.386	48	199	158	33	45	9	2	1	28	33	3	1	4	34	20	3	16.6	17.1
Guanipa, Luis	R-R	5-11	188	12-15-05	.238	.361	.384	46	208	172	34	41	11	1	4	17	23	11	0	2	42	20	6	11.1	20.2
Hernandez, Hojans	R-R	5-11	175	3-07-06	.176	.211	.176	8	20	17	0	3	0	0	0	2	1	0	1	1	6	0	0	5.0	30.0
Monteverde, Carlos	L-L	6-1	177	12-10-05	.219	.325	.320	48	209	178	20	39	12	0	2	22	25	4	0	2	45	5	2	12.0	21.5
Niazoa, Roiber	R-R	6-0	175	12-23-04	.174	.284	.244	32	103	86	13	15	6	0	0	9	12	2	1	2	33	4	0	11.7	32.0
Nieblas, Angel	R-R	5-8	170	9-04-05	.256	.340	.346	41	150	133	19	34	5	2	1	9	13	4	0	0	28	8	2	8.7	18.7
Orellana, Josnaider	R-R	5-11	175	9-26-04	.317	.397	.366	39	141	123	19	39	6	0	0	19	14	3	0	1	23	3	0	9.9	16.3
Parababire, Luis	R-R	5-10	195	4-08-06	.255	.381	.404	29	113	94	15	24	8	0	2	19	13	6	0	0	25	2	1	11.5	22.1

Pitching	B-T	Ht.	Wt.	DOB	W	L	ERA	G	GS	SV	IP	Hits	Runs	ER	HR	BB	SO	AVG	OBP	SLG	SO%	BB%	BF
Abreu, Cristobal	R-R	6-1	165	2-02-06	4	2	5.60	11	2	0	27	29	18	17	0	14	20	.271	.373	.346	15.9	11.1	126
Antonio, Rayven	R-R	6-1	190	3-02-06	3	0	1.16	10	2	1	31	19	6	4	1	10	22	.174	.242	.220	18.3	8.3	120
Arestigueta, Luis	R-R	6-3	175	10-14-05	2	2	3.48	11	8	0	34	25	20	13	1	17	25	.202	.313	.266	17.4	11.8	144
Beltran, Jeiki	R-R	5-11	170	10-11-03	0	2	9.82	10	0	1	15	12	17	16	1	12	8	.231	.388	.365	11.9	17.9	67
Carmona, Kelvin	R-R	6-1	170	8-20-06	0	1	9.15	14	0	0	20	23	22	20	2	23	11	.311	.500	.514	10.8	22.5	102
Cedano, Edward	R-R	6-1	165	11-14-05	1	2	7.59	10	6	0	21	17	22	18	0	29	12	.233	.467	.260	11.2	27.1	107
Estiven, Sebastian	R-R	6-4	220	12-18-01	0	1	9.00	9	1	0	13	15	13	13	0	14	10	.283	.457	.321	14.3	20.0	70
Frias, Yonathan	L-L	6-0	175	9-22-05	0	0	8.31	14	0	0	22	34	22	20	1	17	19	.362	.470	.479	16.5	14.8	115
Garcia, Enderson	R-R	6-3	185	1-12-04	0	0	27.00	2	0	0	2	2	5	5	1	5	2	.250	.538	.625	15.4	38.5	13
Guerra, Whilmer	R-R	6-2	160	10-14-05	1	5	4.91	11	3	0	33	39	25	18	3	9	15	.289	.347	.437	10.1	6.0	149
Gutierrez, Jean F.	R-R	6-1	170	10-25-05	0	1	2.79	6	1	0	10	7	4	3	0	10	3	.226	.422	.290	6.7	22.2	45
Marcano, Jose	R-R	6-3	170	1-04-05	0	3	3.33	16	0	6	24	15	13	9	1	6	22	.170	.235	.227	22.4	6.1	98
Marine, Yansel	L-L	6-2	160	6-11-05	0	0	11.48	13	0	0	13	23	23	17	0	13	10	.377	.481	.508	12.5	16.3	80
Orozco, Bernie	R-R	6-3	205	7-25-04	0	2	10.50	12	0	0	12	13	15	14	1	21	12	.302	.522	.442	17.4	30.4	69
Paez, Styven	R-R	5-11	170	10-29-04	0	3	5.34	11	5	0	32	31	23	19	2	16	30	.252	.345	.415	20.7	11.0	145
Pina, Rudit	R-R	6-3	170	3-20-06	0	5	7.90	11	5	0	27	28	26	24	1	27	18	.280	.436	.390	13.5	20.3	133
Pineda, Jose	R-R	5-11	150	1-07-05	2	0	4.80	8	4	0	15	13	9	8	0	14	15	.250	.406	.308	21.7	20.3	69
Ramos, Johan	R-R	5-11	192	7-17-06	0	0	8.10	6	1	0	3	3	4	3	0	2	2	.250	.333	.333	13.3	13.3	15
Reyes, Jeremy	R-R	6-1	170	1-11-06	0	2	5.40	5	4	0	8	9	8	5	0	6	7	.281	.425	.313	17.5	15.0	40
Rodriguez, Jesus	R-R	6-1	170	12-20-04	0	1	23.14	3	1	0	2	0	8	6	0	9	3	.000	.588	.000	17.6	52.9	17
Rossis, Elvin	R-R	6-4	200	1-20-01	0	0	13.50	6	0	0	6	7	11	9	0	12	2	.280	.537	.440	4.9	29.3	41
Sifontes, Lewis	L-L	5-9	155	2-07-06	0	2	7.39	11	6	0	28	32	26	23	4	22	25	.281	.397	.474	18.4	16.2	136
Vicioso, Francisco	R-R	6-0	175	11-28-04	0	2	351.00	3	2	0	0	0	14	13	0	11	1	.000	.882	.000	5.9	64.7	17
Zapata, Daury	R-R	6-1	170	11-08-02	2	0	4.88	17	0	0	24	22	19	13	3	24	18	.244	.425	.400	15.0	20.0	120

Fielding

C: Orellana 26, Parababire 23, Hernandez 5, Baez 4. **1B:** Niazoa 19, Monteverde 12, Orellana 11, Gil 10, Parababire 5, Garcia 1. **2B:** Cordero 32, Nieblas 18, Baez 5, Niazoa 2. **3B:** Gil 31, Nieblas 20, Niazoa 6. **SS:** Baez 41, Gil 8, Niazoa 4. **OF:** Garcia 46, Estevez 43, Guanipa 40, Monteverde 30, Hernandez 1.

Baltimore Orioles

SEASON SYNOPSIS: Two years after losing 110 games, the Orioles won 101—their first 100-win season since 1980—and earned their first AL East Division title since 2014. Even a sweep in the Division Series—their first sweep of the season—couldn't take all the shine off the club's best season in more than 40 years.

HIGH POINT: After trailing Tampa Bay by 6.5 games entering July, the Orioles got hot, winning eight in a row sandwiched around the all-star break. They took the division lead, though, by winning three of four July 20-23 in St. Petersburg, passing the Rays. Closer Felix Bautista won the first game and saved the last two, striking out Wander Franco with two on and two out in the finale to grow the division lead to two. Baltimore never looked back.

LOW POINT: Waiver pickup Jacob Webb gave up home runs in the first two games of the Division Series and Texas jumped Dean Kremer for six runs in the first two innings of Game 3 as the Orioles were swept in a series for the first time since catcher Adley Rutschman was promoted to the majors in May 2022.

NOTABLE ROOKIES: Ranked No. 1 on the Top 100 Prospects entering 2023, infielder Gunnar Henderson was a 6-WAR player in a .255/.325/.489 season that included a team-best 28 home runs. Top pitching prospect Grayson Rodriguez was sent back to the minors to make adjustments, which paid off in a stellar second half. He went 7-4, 4.35 overall as one of the majors' hardest-throwing starters. Reliever Yennier Cano didn't give up a hit until May 2 or a run until May 19. Jordan Westburg, a 2020 first-round pick, held his own in 208 at-bats, batting .260/.311/.404 while playing second and third base.

KEY TRANSACTIONS: GM Mike Elias traded for Cole Irvin in the offseason and signed free agent Kyle Gibson to bolster the rotation in the regular season. Then he traded with St. Louis to acquire impending free-agent righthander Jack Flaherty in July. None started a postseason game, however.

DOWN ON THE FARM: Even with so many graduations, there's more talent to come. Shortstop Jackson Holliday sped through four levels while winning BA's Minor League Player of the Year award. Catcher Samuel Basallo had a very impressive full-season debut.

OPENING DAY PAYROLL: $60,722,300 (29th).

PLAYERS OF THE YEAR

MAJOR LEAGUE

Gunnar Henderson
SS/3B
.255/.325/.489
29 2B, 28 HR
100 R, 82 RBIs, 10 SB

MINOR LEAGUE

Jackson Holliday
SS
(LoA/HiA/AA/AAA)
.323/.442/.499,
113 R, 24 SB

ORGANIZATION LEADERS

Batting		*Minimum 250 AB
MAJORS		
* AVG	Ryan O'Hearn	.275
* OPS	Gunnar Henderson	.801
HR	Anthony Santander	28
RBI	Anthony Santander	89
MINORS		
* AVG	Cesar Prieto, Bowie/Norfolk	.349
* OBP	Jackson Holliday, 4-levels	.442
* SLG	Jordan Westburg, Norfolk	.567
* OPS	Coby Mayo, Bowie/Norfolk	.979
R	Jackson Holliday, 4-levels	113
H	Connor Norby, Norfolk	164
TB	Ryan Mountcastle, Norfolk	274
2B	Coby Mayo, Bowie/Norfolk	45
3B	Jackson Holliday, 4-levels	9
HR	Coby Mayo, Bowie/Norfolk	29
RBI	Coby Mayo, Bowie/Norfolk	99
BB	Jackson Holliday, 4-levels	101
SO	Jud Fabian, Aberdeen/Bowie	169
SB	Luis Valdez, Delmarva/Aberdeen	47

PITCHING		#Minimum 75 IP
MAJORS		
W	Kyle Gibson	15
# ERA	Kyle Bradish	2.83
SO	Kyle Bradish	168
SV	Felix Bautista	33
MINORS		
W	Garrett Stallings, Bowie/Norfolk	11
L	Juan De Los Santos, Delmarva	10
# ERA	Alex Pham, Aberdeen/Bowie	2.57
G	Morgan McSweeney, Norfolk	42
GS	Cade Povich, Bowie/Norfolk	28
SV	Wandisson Charles, Bowie/Norfolk	11
IP	Garrett Stallings, Bowie/Norfolk	127
BB	Chayce McDermott, Bowie/Norfolk	68
SO	Cade Povich, Bowie/Norfolk	171
# AVG	Chayce McDermott, Bowie/Norfolk	.165

2023 PERFORMANCE

General Manager: Mike Elias. **Farn Director:** Matt Blood. **Scouting Director:** Brad Ciolek.

Class	Team	League	W	L	PCT	Finish	Manager
Majors	Baltimore Orioles	American	101	61	.623	1 (15)	Brandon Hyde
Triple-A	Norfolk Tides	International	90	59	.604	1 (20)	Buck Britton
Double-A	Bowie Baysox	Eastern	67	70	.489	7 (12)	Kyle Moore
High-A	Aberdeen IronBirds	South Atlantic	66	63	.512	6 (12)	Roberto Mercado
Low-A	Delmarva Shorebirds	Carolina	56	74	.431	12 (12)	Felipe Alou
Rookie	FCL Orioles	Florida Complex	22	32	.407	13 (15)	Christian Frias
Rookie	DSL Orioles Orange	Dominican Sum.	35	19	.648	8 (50)	Chris Madera
Rookie	DSL Orioles Black	Dominican Sum.	20	35	.364	41 (50)	Elvis Morel
Overall 2023 Minor League Record			356	352	.503	13th (30)	

ORGANIZATION STATISTICS

BALTIMORE ORIOLES

AMERICAN LEAGUE

Batting	B-T	Ht.	Wt.	DOB	AVG	OBP	SLG	G	PA	AB	R	H	2B	3B	HR	RBI	BB	HBP	SH	SF	SO	SB	CS	BB%	SO%
Bemboom, Anthony	L-R	6-2	195	1-18-90	.182	.308	.182	6	13	11	0	2	0	0	0	0	2	0	0	0	2	0	0	15.4	15.4
Cowser, Colton	L-R	6-2	220	3-20-00	.115	.286	.148	26	77	61	15	7	2	0	0	4	13	2	0	1	22	1	0	16.9	28.6
Frazier, Adam	L-R	5-10	180	12-14-91	.240	.300	.396	141	455	412	59	99	21	2	13	60	32	4	4	2	68	11	4	7.0	14.9
Hays, Austin	R-R	5-11	200	7-05-95	.275	.325	.444	144	566	520	76	143	36	2	16	67	38	3	0	5	141	5	1	6.7	24.9
Henderson, Gunnar	L-R	6-3	220	6-29-01	.255	.325	.489	150	622	560	100	143	29	9	28	82	56	3	0	3	159	10	3	9.0	25.6
Hicks, Aaron	B-R	6-1	205	10-02-89	.275	.381	.425	65	236	200	35	55	7	1	7	31	35	0	0	1	49	6	0	14.8	20.8
2-team (76 New York Yankees)					.253	.353	.383	93	312	269	44	68	9	1	8	36	42	0	0	1	69	6	0	13.5	22.1
Kjerstad, Heston	L-R	6-3	205	2-12-99	.233	.281	.467	13	33	30	3	7	1	0	2	3	2	0	0	0	10	0	0	6.1	30.3
Lester, Josh	L-R	6-3	180	7-17-94	.182	.217	.182	11	23	22	0	4	0	0	0	4	1	0	0	0	7	0	0	4.3	30.4
Mateo, Jorge	R-R	6-1	200	6-23-95	.217	.267	.340	116	350	318	58	69	14	2	7	34	22	1	5	3	82	32	5	6.3	23.4
McCann, James	R-R	6-3	235	6-13-90	.222	.269	.377	70	226	207	25	46	14	0	6	26	9	5	3	2	57	3	1	4.0	25.2
McKenna, Ryan	R-R	5-11	195	2-14-97	.254	.316	.361	89	139	122	23	31	7	0	2	18	9	3	3	2	40	5	0	6.5	28.8
Mountcastle, Ryan	R-R	6-4	220	2-18-97	.270	.328	.452	115	470	423	64	114	21	1	18	68	37	3	0	7	107	3	1	7.9	22.8
Mullins, Cedric	L-L	5-9	175	10-01-94	.233	.305	.416	116	455	404	51	94	23	3	15	74	43	1	3	4	101	19	3	9.5	22.2
O'Hearn, Ryan	L-L	6-3	220	7-26-93	.289	.322	.480	112	368	346	48	100	22	1	14	60	15	3	1	3	82	5	1	4.1	22.3
Ortiz, Joey	R-R	5-9	190	7-14-98	.212	.206	.242	15	34	33	4	7	1	0	0	4	0	0	0	1	9	0	0	0.0	26.5
Rutschman, Adley	B-R	6-2	230	2-06-98	.277	.374	.435	154	687	588	84	163	31	1	20	80	92	2	0	5	101	1	2	13.4	14.7
Santander, Anthony	B-R	6-2	230	10-19-94	.257	.325	.472	153	656	591	81	152	41	1	28	95	55	6	0	4	152	5	1	8.4	23.2
Stowers, Kyle	L-L	6-3	215	1-02-98	.067	.152	.067	14	33	30	1	2	0	0	0	0	3	0	0	0	12	0	0	9.1	36.4
Urias, Ramon	R-R	5-10	185	6-03-94	.264	.328	.375	116	396	360	45	95	22	3	4	42	27	8	0	1	101	3	1	6.8	25.5
Vavra, Terrin	L-R	6-0	185	5-12-97	.245	.315	.245	27	56	49	9	12	0	0	0	5	5	0	2	0	12	1	0	8.9	21.4
Westburg, Jordan	R-R	6-2	210	2-18-99	.260	.311	.404	68	228	208	26	54	17	2	3	23	16	1	0	3	56	4	1	7.0	24.6

Pitching	B-T	Ht.	Wt.	DOB	W	L	ERA	G	GS	SV	IP	Hits	Runs	ER	HR	BB	SO	AVG	OBP	SLG	SO%	BB%	BF
Akin, Keegan	L-L	6-0	240	4-01-95	2	2	6.85	24	1	0	24	35	22	18	2	7	27	.337	.375	.490	24.1	6.3	112
Baker, Bryan	R-R	6-6	235	12-02-94	4	3	3.60	46	0	0	45	33	19	18	4	24	51	.210	.314	.338	27.4	12.9	186
Baumann, Mike	R-R	6-4	240	9-10-95	10	1	3.76	60	0	0	65	52	29	27	7	33	61	.221	.320	.370	22.3	12.1	273
Bautista, Felix	R-R	6-8	285	6-20-95	8	2	1.48	56	0	33	61	30	14	10	4	26	110	.144	.245	.215	46.4	11.0	237
Bazardo, Eduard	R-R	6-0	190	9-01-95	0	0	15.43	3	0	0	2	6	4	4	0	0	1	.462	.462	.692	7.7	0.0	13
Bradish, Kyle	R-R	6-3	215	9-12-96	12	7	2.83	30	30	0	169	132	54	53	14	44	168	.215	.275	.330	25.0	6.6	671
Cano, Yennier	R-R	6-4	245	3-09-94	1	4	2.11	72	0	8	73	60	19	17	4	13	65	.226	.270	.331	23.0	4.6	283
Coulombe, Danny	L-L	5-10	190	10-26-89	5	3	2.81	61	0	2	51	45	17	16	4	12	58	.231	.282	.323	27.6	5.7	210
Flaherty, Jack	R-R	6-4	225	10-15-95	1	3	6.75	9	7	0	35	46	27	26	7	12	42	.311	.376	.514	25.5	7.3	165
Fujinami, Shintaro	R-R	6-6	180	4-12-94	2	0	4.85	30	0	2	30	21	17	16	3	15	32	.193	.302	.358	25.4	11.9	126
Garrett, Reed	R-R	6-2	195	1-02-93	0	0	10.13	2	0	0	3	7	3	3	0	1	0	.467	.500	.600	0.0	6.3	16
Gibson, Kyle	R-R	6-6	200	10-23-87	15	9	4.73	33	33	0	192	198	101	101	23	55	157	.270	.322	.437	19.5	6.8	807
Gillaspie, Logan	R-R	6-2	215	4-17-97	0	1	6.00	11	0	0	9	14	7	6	2	5	8	.350	.435	.725	17.4	10.9	46
Givens, Mychal	R-R	6-0	250	5-13-90	0	1	11.25	6	0	0	4	4	6	5	0	6	2	.286	.500	.357	9.1	27.3	22
Hall, DL	L-L	6-2	210	9-19-98	3	0	3.26	18	0	0	19	18	8	7	2	5	23	.237	.284	.382	28.4	6.2	81
Irvin, Cole	L-L	6-4	225	1-31-94	1	4	4.42	24	12	0	77	78	42	38	11	21	68	.256	.315	.420	20.2	6.3	336
Krehbiel, Joey	R-R	6-3	250	12-20-92	1	0	1.80	6	0	0	5	2	1	1	1	2	5	.118	.211	.353	26.3	10.5	19
Kremer, Dean	R-R	6-2	210	1-07-96	13	5	4.12	32	32	0	173	171	85	79	27	55	157	.254	.314	.416	21.4	7.5	735
Lester, Josh	L-R	6-3	180	7-17-94	0	0	0.00	1	0	0	1	1	0	0	0	1	1	.250	.400	.500	20.0	20.0	5
Lopez, Jorge	R-R	6-3	200	2-10-93	0	0	5.25	12	0	0	12	13	7	7	4	2	14	.271	.300	.563	28.0	4.0	50
McCann, James	R-R	6-3	235	6-13-90	0	0	0.00	1	0	0	1	2	0	0	0	0	0	.400	.400	.600	0.0	0.0	5
McKenna, Ryan	R-R	5-11	195	2-14-97	0	0	18.00	1	0	0	1	4	2	2	0	0	0	.667	.667	.833	0.0	0.0	6
Means, John	L-L	6-4	230	4-24-93	1	2	2.66	4	4	0	24	13	7	7	4	4	10	.159	.205	.354	11.4	4.5	88
Perez, Cionel	R-L	6-0	175	4-21-96	4	2	3.54	65	0	3	53	56	30	21	2	27	44	.264	.357	.340	17.8	10.9	247
Rodriguez, Grayson	L-R	6-5	230	11-16-99	7	4	4.35	23	23	0	122	121	62	59	16	42	129	.259	.321	.418	25.0	8.2	515
Vallimont, Chris	R-R	6-5	240	3-18-97	0	0	0.00	1	0	0	1	1	0	0	0	0	1	.500	.500	1.000	50.0	0.0	2
Vespi, Nick	L-L	6-3	235	10-10-95	1	0	4.30	9	0	0	15	16	7	7	2	2	9	.286	.322	.500	15.3	3.4	59
Voth, Austin	R-R	6-2	215	6-26-92	1	2	5.19	25	0	0	35	39	22	20	6	15	34	.279	.358	.457	21.3	9.4	160
Webb, Jacob	R-R	6-2	210	8-15-93	0	0	3.27	25	0	0	22	16	8	8	0	10	23	.203	.304	.278	25.0	10.9	92

Pitching	B-T	Ht.	Wt.	DOB	W	L	ERA	G	GS	SV	IP	Hits	Runs	ER	HR	BB	SO	AVG	OBP	SLG	SO%	BB%	BF
Wells, Tyler	R-R	6-8	260	8-26-94	7	6	3.64	25	20	1	119	83	50	48	25	34	117	.193	.257	.413	24.9	7.2	470
Zimmermann, Bruce	L-L	6-1	220	2-09-95	2	0	4.73	7	0	0	13	17	8	7	3	0	14	.293	.311	.500	23.0	0.0	61

Fielding

Catcher	PCT	G	PO	A	E	DP	PB
Bemboom	1.000	6	38	1	0	0	0
Kolozsvary	1.000	1	1	0	0	0	0
McCann	.994	59	472	22	3	2	2
Rutschman	.994	110	932	45	6	5	0

First Base	PCT	G	PO	A	E	DP
Lester	1.000	5	25	1	0	1
McCann	.000	2	0	0	0	0
Mountcastle	.997	90	647	67	2	79
O'Hearn	.996	70	475	22	2	38
Santander	1.000	12	69	3	0	4
Urias	1.000	13	56	3	0	6

Second Base	PCT	G	PO	A	E	DP
Frazier	.987	130	143	244	5	56
Ortiz	1.000	7	7	9	0	3
Urias	1.000	22	22	48	0	15
Vavra	1.000	1	1	1	0	1
Westburg	1.000	50	49	115	0	22

Third Base	PCT	G	PO	A	E	DP
Henderson	.962	84	43	110	6	14
Lester	.000	1	0	0	0	0
Ortiz	1.000	4	0	3	0	0
Urias	.967	92	46	130	6	15
Vavra	1.000	2	0	1	0	0
Westburg	.977	29	10	32	1	1

Shortstop	PCT	G	PO	A	E	DP
Henderson	.969	83	87	164	8	34
Mateo	.970	110	113	242	11	60
Ortiz	1.000	3	8	6	0	4

Outfield	PCT	G	PO	A	E	DP
Cowser	.958	29	40	2	1	0
Frazier	1.000	10	12	1	0	0
Hays	1.000	149	256	4	0	0
Hicks	.977	69	106	1	2	0
Kjerstad	.500	4	4	0	0	0
Lester	.000	1	0	0	0	0
Mateo	1.000	4	5	0	0	0
McKenna	.986	95	96	2	1	1
Mullins	.989	110	255	4	3	3
O'Hearn	.977	29	25	0	1	0
Santander	.998	98	194	5	1	1
Stowers	.950	10	18	1	1	0
Vavra	1.000	19	23	0	0	0

NORFOLK TIDES — *TRIPLE-A*

INTERNATIONAL LEAGUE

Batting	B-T	Ht.	Wt.	DOB	AVG	OBP	SLG	G	PA	AB	R	H	2B	3B	HR	RBI	BB	HBP	SH	SF	SO	SB	CS	BB%	SO%
Bellony, Isaac	B-R	6-2	220	12-15-01	--	1.000	--	1	1	0	0	0	0	0	0	0	1	0	0	0	0	0	0	100.0	0.0
Bemboom, Anthony	L-R	6-2	195	1-18-90	.288	.365	.417	38	148	132	19	38	4	2	3	17	15	1	0	0	28	1	1	10.1	18.9
Cameron, Daz	R-R	6-2	185	1-15-97	.268	.346	.452	110	446	385	62	103	23	0	16	67	43	8	1	9	95	23	6	9.6	21.3
Cowser, Colton	L-R	6-2	220	3-20-00	.300	.417	.520	87	399	323	72	97	18	1	17	62	64	5	1	6	107	9	3	16.0	26.8
Cullen, Greg	L-R	5-9	190	11-13-96	.207	.324	.310	10	34	29	6	6	0	0	1	4	4	1	0	0	6	2	0	11.8	17.6
DeLuzio, Ben	R-R	6-3	200	8-09-94	.203	.266	.339	18	65	59	7	12	2	0	2	5	4	1	1	0	22	1	0	6.2	33.8
Diaz, Lewin	L-L	6-2	225	11-19-96	.268	.362	.442	118	483	414	64	111	21	0	17	64	60	4	0	5	95	2	0	12.4	19.7
Fontana, Shayne	L-L	6-1	195	6-21-97	.279	.382	.416	58	227	190	28	53	10	2	4	26	26	7	2	2	43	12	1	11.5	18.9
Glendinning, Robbie	R-R	6-0	196	10-06-95	.248	.331	.476	33	118	105	15	26	6	0	6	16	12	1	0	0	41	0	0	10.2	34.7
Godoy, Jose	L-R	5-11	200	10-13-94	.266	.363	.342	25	91	79	13	21	3	0	1	7	11	1	0	0	14	1	0	12.1	15.4
2-team (11 Scranton/Wilkes-Barre)					.267	.356	.397	36	132	116	19	31	3	0	4	14	15	1	0	0	22	2	1	11.4	16.7
Grenier, Cadyn	R-R	5-8	188	10-31-96	1.000	1.000	1.000	1	5	3	1	3	0	0	0	1	2	0	0	0	0	0	0	40.0	0.0
Handley, Maverick	R-R	5-10	210	3-10-98	.236	.373	.329	69	264	216	39	51	8	0	4	30	38	9	1	0	65	7	2	14.4	24.6
Haskin, Hudson	R-R	6-0	200	12-31-98	.268	.368	.463	23	95	82	14	22	5	1	3	13	6	7	0	0	34	5	1	6.3	35.8
Hicks, Aaron	B-R	6-1	205	10-02-89	.125	.125	.125	2	8	8	1	1	0	0	0	0	0	0	0	0	3	0	0	0.0	37.5
Holliday, Jackson	L-R	6-0	185	12-04-03	.267	.396	.400	18	91	75	18	20	4	0	2	9	16	0	0	0	17	1	1	17.6	18.7
Kjerstad, Heston	L-R	6-3	205	2-12-99	.298	.371	.498	76	337	295	57	88	19	5	10	32	27	9	0	3	69	2	1	8.0	20.5
Kolozsvary, Mark	R-R	5-7	185	9-04-95	.162	.250	.265	20	76	68	9	11	1	0	2	7	5	3	0	0	26	1	0	6.6	34.2
2-team (6 St. Paul)				.171	.253	.305	26	91	82	11	14	2	0	3	11	6	3	0	0	31	1	0	6.6	34.1	
Lara, Gilbert	R-R	6-4	198	10-30-97	.150	.190	.150	6	21	20	2	3	0	0	0	0	1	0	0	0	5	0	0	4.8	23.8
Lester, Josh	L-R	6-3	180	7-17-94	.257	.307	.475	110	470	432	62	111	21	2	23	87	31	2	0	4	122	2	0	6.6	26.0
Mantecon, Michael	R-R	5-11	192	2-02-02	.000	.000	.000	2	3	3	0	0	0	0	0	0	0	0	0	0	1	0	0	0.0	33.3
Mayo, Coby	R-R	6-5	230	12-10-01	.267	.393	.512	62	267	217	36	58	15	1	12	55	42	5	0	3	62	1	0	15.7	23.2
McKenna, Ryan	R-R	5-11	195	2-14-97	.182	.262	.418	15	61	55	14	10	2	1	3	7	6	0	0	0	21	2	0	9.8	34.4
Mountcastle, Ryan	R-R	6-4	220	2-18-97	.222	.276	.296	12	58	54	6	12	1	0	1	6	4	0	0	0	17	0	0	6.9	29.3
Mullins, Cedric	L-L	5-9	175	10-01-94	.100	.182	.400	3	11	10	1	1	0	0	1	2	1	0	0	0	1	0	0	9.1	9.1
Norby, Connor	R-R	5-9	180	6-08-00	.290	.359	.483	138	633	565	104	164	40	3	21	92	57	6	0	5	137	10	4	9.0	21.6
O'Hearn, Ryan	L-L	6-3	220	7-26-93	.354	.404	.729	11	52	48	11	17	4	1	4	13	4	0	0	0	14	0	0	7.7	26.9
Ortiz, Joey	R-R	5-9	190	7-14-98	.321	.378	.507	88	389	349	66	112	30	4	9	58	32	3	0	5	69	11	4	8.2	17.7
Placencia, Erison	R-R	6-1	170	12-31-01	.000	.000	.000	1	1	1	0	0	0	0	0	0	0	0	0	0	0	0	0	0.0	0.0
Prieto, Cesar	L-R	5-9	175	5-10-99	.317	.365	.471	27	115	104	16	33	8	1	2	20	8	1	0	2	10	2	1	7.0	8.7
2-team (38 Memphis)					.288	.337	.419	65	291	267	40	77	13	2	6	40	15	5	1	3	35	4	1	5.2	12.0
Rodriguez, Ramon	R-R	6-0	210	10-30-98	.282	.383	.333	12	48	39	4	11	2	0	0	3	7	0	1	1	3	1	0	14.6	6.3
Romero, Noelberth	R-R	6-0	183	12-05-01	.000	.000	.000	1	2	2	0	0	0	0	0	0	0	0	0	0	0	0	0	0.0	0.0
Rosa, Joseph	B-R	5-10	165	3-06-97	.276	.364	.362	33	121	105	18	29	9	0	0	12	13	2	0	1	28	3	1	10.7	23.1
Stowers, Kyle	L-L	6-3	215	1-02-98	.245	.364	.511	68	283	233	42	57	9	1	17	49	40	6	0	4	76	3	2	14.1	26.9
Susnara, Tim	L-R	5-10	185	4-17-96	.000	.250	.000	1	4	3	0	0	0	0	0	0	1	0	0	0	2	0	0	25.0	50.0
Vavra, Terrin	L-R	6-0	185	5-12-97	.333	.382	.524	14	68	63	12	21	4	1	2	9	3	2	0	0	13	2	1	4.4	19.1
Viloria, Meibrys	L-R	5-11	225	2-15-97	.375	.375	.375	2	8	8	0	3	0	0	0	1	0	0	0	0	1	0	0	0.0	12.5
Westburg, Jordan	R-R	6-2	210	2-18-99	.295	.372	.567	67	301	268	57	79	15	2	18	54	29	4	0	0	64	6	0	9.6	21.3

Pitching	B-T	Ht.	Wt.	DOB	W	L	ERA	G	GS	SV	IP	Hits	Runs	ER	HR	BB	SO	AVG	OBP	SLG	SO%	BB%	BF
Akin, Keegan	L-L	6-0	240	4-01-95	0	0	1.13	5	1	0	8	1	1	1	1	1	14	.040	.077	.160	53.8	3.8	26
Armbruester, Justin	R-R	6-4	235	10-21-98	3	4	4.70	14	13	0	59	55	34	31	9	32	66	.238	.328	.424	24.9	12.1	265
Baker, Bryan	R-R	6-6	235	12-02-94	1	1	6.75	13	0	0	13	17	14	10	2	8	18	.293	.379	.483	27.3	12.1	66
Baumann, Mike	R-R	6-4	240	9-10-95	0	0	0.00	6	0	1	6	1	0	0	0	5	9	.056	.261	.056	39.1	21.7	23
Bazardo, Eduard	R-R	6-0	190	9-01-95	4	1	3.05	27	1	2	38	31	14	13	1	11	43	.218	.291	.296	27.2	7.0	158
Cano, Yennier	R-R	6-4	245	3-09-94	0	0	0.00	3	0	1	3	3	0	0	0	1	4	.250	.308	.250	30.8	7.7	13
Charles, Wandisson	R-R	6-4	250	9-07-96	5	3	5.70	28	0	8	30	20	20	19	2	28	40	.190	.356	.276	29.2	20.4	137
Conroy, Ryan	R-R	6-3	190	12-31-96	0	0	22.50	2	0	0	2	6	5	5	0	4	2	.500	.625	.583	12.5	25.0	16
Coulombe, Danny	L-L	5-10	190	10-26-89	0	0	0.00	1	0	0	1	0	0	0	0	0	2	.000	.000	.000	66.7	0.0	3

Denoyer, Noah	B-R	6-5	250	2-17-98	3	0	5.61	25	5	1	51	50	36	32	9	38	63	.249	.372	.433	25.8	15.6	244
Dowdy, Kyle	R-R	6-1	210	2-03-93	8	4	4.38	39	0	1	64	66	37	31	4	35	74	.262	.355	.373	25.4	12.0	291
Garrett, Reed	R-R	6-2	195	1-02-93	5	1	1.59	19	0	3	23	19	5	4	2	10	27	.226	.309	.333	28.4	10.5	95
Gillaspie, Logan	R-R	6-2	215	4-17-97	3	3	4.71	34	0	5	36	38	20	19	6	16	34	.266	.340	.476	21.4	10.1	159
Givens, Mychal	R-R	6-0	250	5-13-90	0	0	7.27	8	0	0	9	7	7	7	2	4	7	.219	.342	.406	18.4	10.5	38
Gomez, Ofreidy	R-R	6-3	240	7-06-95	0	1	8.72	19	0	0	22	25	24	21	1	23	31	.278	.442	.389	25.6	19.0	121
Hall, DL	L-L	6-2	210	9-19-98	1	2	4.22	17	11	1	49	38	23	23	7	30	70	.209	.336	.346	32.3	13.8	217
Hernandez, Darwinzon	L-L	6-2	255	12-17-96	2	1	2.96	27	0	1	27	13	10	9	3	19	37	.144	.325	.244	32.2	16.5	115
Hoffman, Nolan	R-R	6-4	190	8-09-97	0	0	3.00	3	0	0	3	4	1	1	0	2	0	.333	.467	.500	0.0	13.3	15
Irvin, Cole	L-L	6-4	225	1-31-94	6	3	4.38	9	9	0	49	54	25	24	8	9	30	.274	.316	.437	14.2	4.2	212
Krehbiel, Joey	R-R	6-3	250	12-20-92	1	1	3.89	35	0	3	39	37	17	17	7	25	32	.247	.358	.420	18.2	14.2	176
Lester, Josh	L-R	6-3	180	7-17-94	0	0	0.00	2	0	0	1	0	0	0	0	0	0	.000	.000	.000	0.0	0.0	5
Loeprich, Conner	R-R	6-3	215	9-13-97	0	0	0.00	1	0	0	0	0	0	0	0	2	0	.000	.667	.000	0.0	66.7	3
Lucas, Easton	L-L	6-4	180	9-23-96	0	0	4.61	10	0	1	14	10	8	7	4	9	14	.196	.317	.529	23.3	15.0	60
Mantecon, Michael	R-R	5-11	192	2-02-02	0	0	21.60	1	0	0	2	4	4	4	2	0	0	.444	.444	1.111	0.0	0.0	9
McDermott, Chayce	L-R	6-3	197	8-22-98	3	2	2.49	10	8	0	51	27	15	14	3	24	64	.156	.268	.266	31.2	11.7	205
McFarland, T.J.	L-L	6-3	200	6-08-89	3	0	1.80	21	0	1	30	22	6	6	0	11	30	.206	.301	.271	24.4	8.9	123
McSweeney, Morgan	R-R	6-4	210	9-21-97	2	0	5.48	42	0	0	46	39	32	28	7	30	46	.227	.340	.436	22.2	14.5	207
Means, John	L-L	6-4	230	4-24-93	1	0	2.51	3	3	0	14	11	4	4	1	6	12	.216	.310	.314	20.7	10.3	58
Povich, Cade	L-L	6-3	185	4-12-00	2	3	5.36	10	10	0	45	32	30	27	6	29	53	.194	.315	.327	26.9	14.7	197
Rodriguez, Grayson	L-R	6-5	230	11-16-99	4	0	1.96	8	8	0	41	26	12	9	4	19	56	.178	.274	.295	33.1	11.2	169
Rom, Drew	L-L	6-2	215	12-15-99	7	6	5.34	19	18	0	86	100	53	51	7	46	100	.291	.386	.410	25.1	11.5	399
Roth, Houston	R-R	6-3	220	3-09-98	1	0	9.00	1	0	0	2	2	2	2	0	2	2	.250	.400	.250	20.0	20.0	10
Sanders, Phoenix	R-R	5-10	205	6-05-95	1	0	2.00	9	0	0	9	6	2	2	2	3	11	.188	.257	.406	31.4	8.6	35
Stallings, Garrett	R-R	6-2	200	8-08-97	8	4	5.47	15	12	1	74	85	47	45	10	25	80	.291	.350	.479	24.7	7.7	324
Tate, Dillon	R-R	6-2	190	5-01-94	0	1	13.50	8	0	0	7	12	10	10	0	8	6	.400	.550	.500	15.0	20.0	40
Uvila, Cole	R-R	6-3	205	1-30-94	0	0	2.25	3	0	0	4	3	1	1	1	3	3	.214	.353	.500	17.6	17.6	17
Vallimont, Chris	R-R	6-5	240	3-18-97	2	5	5.02	14	8	2	57	50	37	32	8	30	64	.234	.335	.397	25.8	12.1	248
Vespi, Nick	L-L	6-3	235	10-10-95	4	0	2.33	36	0	7	39	31	11	10	3	13	41	.225	.284	.362	26.5	8.4	155
Voth, Austin	R-R	6-2	215	6-26-92	0	0	5.28	9	3	0	15	20	10	9	1	9	20	.313	.397	.438	27.4	12.3	73
Watkins, Spenser	R-R	6-2	195	8-27-92	2	1	7.27	8	6	0	26	33	23	21	1	17	20	.311	.417	.396	15.7	13.4	127
Watson, Ryan	R-R	6-5	225	11-15-97	4	5	5.95	34	12	0	88	94	62	58	13	46	82	.279	.365	.457	20.9	11.7	393
Wells, Tyler	R-R	6-8	260	8-26-94	0	0	9.00	7	0	1	6	7	6	6	1	4	7	.280	.379	.520	24.1	13.8	29
Zimmermann, Bruce	L-L	6-1	220	2-09-95	4	7	4.42	21	21	0	100	115	56	49	5	39	110	.283	.349	.401	24.6	8.7	448

Fielding

Catcher	PCT	G	PO	A	E	DP	PB
Bemboom	.990	31	283	21	3	5	2
Godoy	.987	24	228	6	3	0	2
Handley	.986	64	590	34	9	1	4
Kolozsvary	.985	19	183	12	3	4	0
Mantecon	1.000	1	10	0	0	0	0
Rodriguez	1.000	11	112	5	0	0	0
Susnara	1.000	1	13	1	0	0	0
Vavra	1.000	2	4	1	0	0	0
Viloria	1.000	1	12	0	0	0	0

First Base	PCT	G	PO	A	E	DP
Diaz	.993	83	631	37	5	58
Glendinning	1.000	2	7	1	0	0
Kjerstad	1.000	22	157	8	0	11
Lester	.979	15	86	9	2	18
Mayo	.979	19	135	5	3	19
Mountcastle	.982	7	51	3	1	3
O'Hearn	.950	4	36	2	2	2

Second Base	PCT	G	PO	A	E	DP
Cullen	1.000	1	1	4	0	1
Glendinning	1.000	1	1	2	0	0
Holliday	1.000	4	5	9	0	0
Lara	1.000	1	4	5	0	1
Norby	.960	105	143	240	16	62
Ortiz	.981	12	18	33	1	5
Prieto	1.000	6	3	9	0	2
Romero	1.000	1	1	2	0	1
Rosa	.911	13	14	27	4	4
Vavra	1.000	5	7	7	0	2
Westburg	1.000	7	8	19	0	4

Third Base	PCT	G	PO	A	E	DP
Cullen	.909	7	2	8	1	1
Glendinning	.927	17	6	32	3	6
Lara	.000	1	0	0	0	0
Lester	.975	49	23	96	3	12
Mayo	.925	39	29	69	8	6
Ortiz	1.000	9	7	15	0	6
Prieto	.944	9	8	9	1	2
Vavra	1.000	4	2	8	0	0
Westburg	.956	20	15	28	2	4

Shortstop	PCT	G	PO	A	E	DP
Glendinning	.750	1	1	2	1	0
Grenier	1.000	1	3	1	0	0
Holliday	.936	14	4	40	3	5
Lara	1.000	4	3	11	0	0
Norby	1.000	1	1	1	0	0
Ortiz	.984	69	81	172	4	35
Prieto	.971	12	13	21	1	3
Rosa	.977	16	13	30	1	7
Westburg	.990	33	38	62	1	8

Outfield	PCT	G	PO	A	E	DP
Bellony	.000	1	0	0	0	0
Bemboom	.000	1	0	0	0	0
Cameron	.992	98	206	0	1	0
Cowser	.948	77	149	3	7	1
DeLuzio	.988	18	33	1	1	0
Fontana	.989	54	91	2	1	0
Haskin	1.000	18	35	1	0	0
Hicks	1.000	1	2	0	0	0
Kjerstad	.970	45	65	3	1	2
Lester	.970	28	43	2	2	1
McKenna	1.000	15	28	0	0	0
Mullins	1.000	2	2	1	0	0
Norby	.989	32	52	0	1	0
O'Hearn	1.000	4	2	0	0	0
Stowers	.981	61	102	6	3	2
Vavra	1.000	5	6	0	0	0
Westburg	.438	6	7	0	1	0

BOWIE BAYSOX

DOUBLE-A

EASTERN LEAGUE

Batting	B-T	Ht.	Wt.	DOB	AVG	OBP	SLG	G	PA	AB	R	H	2B	3B	HR	RBI	BB	HBP	SH	SF	SO	SB	CS	BB%	SO%
Ardoin, Silas	R-R	6-0	215	9-19-00	.286	.359	.410	28	117	105	16	30	4	0	3	10	11	1	0	0	35	2	0	9.4	29.9
Basallo, Samuel	L-R	6-3	180	8-13-04	.467	.500	.667	4	16	15	2	7	1	1	0	2	1	0	0	0	1	0	0	6.3	6.3
Beavers, Dylan	L-R	6-4	206	8-11-01	.321	.417	.478	34	157	134	29	43	9	3	2	12	20	2	0	0	32	5	4	12.7	20.4
Bellony, Isaac	B-R	6-2	220	12-15-01	.364	.417	.364	3	12	11	0	4	0	0	0	1	1	0	0	0	0	0	0	8.3	0.0
Bowens, TT	R-R	6-4	235	5-27-98	.226	.317	.402	47	186	164	24	37	8	0	7	15	22	0	0	0	57	0	0	11.8	30.6
Burns, Collin	L-R	5-11	187	5-20-00	.206	.270	.235	9	38	34	3	7	1	0	0	2	3	0	1	0	8	3	0	7.9	21.1
Cook, Billy	R-R	6-1	200	1-07-99	.251	.320	.456	120	501	447	64	112	16	2	24	81	42	6	1	5	125	30	3	8.4	25.0
Costes, Maxwell	R-R	6-1	215	7-30-99	.210	.289	.259	24	97	81	8	17	4	0	0	11	8	3	0	5	16	1	0	8.2	16.5
Cullen, Greg	L-R	5-9	190	11-13-96	.272	.420	.388	47	189	147	14	40	8	0	3	20	35	4	1	2	46	2	0	18.5	24.3

Fabian, Jud	R-L	6-1	195	9-27-00	.176	.314	.399	64	288	238	36	42	6	1	15	31	44	4	1	1	108	12	2	15.3	37.5
Florentino, Randy	L-R	5-11	182	7-05-00	.111	.207	.125	25	82	72	3	8	1	0	0	2	8	1	0	1	12	0	0	9.8	14.6
Fontana, Shayne	L-L	6-1	195	6-21-97	.240	.344	.364	39	151	129	22	31	7	0	3	14	15	6	0	1	20	8	4	9.9	13.2
Handley, Maverick	R-R	5-10	210	3-10-98	.267	.353	.533	4	17	15	1	4	1	0	1	3	2	0	0	0	8	1	0	11.8	47.1
Haskin, Hudson	R-R	6-0	200	12-31-98	.333	.364	.381	5	22	21	3	7	1	0	0	2	0	1	0	0	6	1	0	0.0	27.3
Holliday, Jackson	L-R	6-0	185	12-04-03	.338	.421	.507	36	164	142	28	48	9	3	3	15	21	0	0	1	34	3	1	12.8	20.7
Kjerstad, Heston	L-R	6-3	205	2-12-99	.310	.383	.576	46	206	184	30	57	10	3	11	23	15	7	0	0	31	3	3	7.3	15.0
Kolozsvary, Mark	R-R	5-7	185	9-04-95	.211	.250	.421	5	20	19	2	4	1	0	1	2	1	0	0	0	8	0	0	5.0	40.0
Lara, Gilbert	R-R	6-4	198	10-30-97	.192	.236	.279	28	110	104	9	20	3	0	2	11	6	0	0	0	25	1	1	5.5	22.7
Mantecon, Michael	R-R	5-11	192	2-02-02	.000	.000	.000	1	3	3	0	0	0	0	0	0	0	0	0	0	2	0	0	0.0	66.7
Mayo, Coby	R-R	6-5	230	12-10-01	.307	.424	.603	78	347	287	48	88	30	2	17	44	51	8	0	1	86	4	1	14.7	24.8
McCann, James	R-R	6-3	235	6-13-90	.000	.000	.000	2	9	9	0	0	0	0	0	1	0	0	0	0	2	0	0	0.0	22.2
Mullins, Cedric	L-L	5-9	175	10-01-94	.150	.150	.150	4	20	20	1	3	0	0	0	1	0	0	0	0	2	0	1	0.0	10.0
Pavolony, Connor	R-R	6-1	195	10-25-99	.164	.233	.239	20	73	67	6	11	2	0	1	4	4	2	0	0	26	1	0	5.5	35.6
Placencia, Erison	R-R	6-1	170	12-31-01	.167	.286	.167	2	7	6	0	1	0	0	0	1	1	0	0	0	1	0	0	14.3	14.3
Prieto, Cesar	L-R	5-9	175	5-10-99	.364	.406	.476	58	249	231	33	84	12	1	4	29	15	2	0	1	17	5	6	6.0	6.8
Rhodes, John	R-R	6-0	200	8-15-00	.228	.323	.422	108	468	408	60	93	22	3	17	69	53	5	0	2	123	8	1	11.3	26.3
Rodriguez, Ramon	R-R	6-0	210	10-30-98	.219	.324	.342	37	137	114	13	25	5	0	3	11	19	0	1	3	14	1	1	13.9	10.2
Romero, Noelberth	R-R	6-0	183	12-05-01	.145	.203	.203	22	74	69	6	10	1	0	1	5	5	0	0	0	24	0	0	6.8	32.4
Rosa, Joseph	B-R	5-10	165	3-06-97	.235	.368	.369	46	185	149	23	35	4	2	4	19	28	5	0	3	55	8	1	15.1	29.7
Servideo, Anthony	L-R	5-10	175	3-11-99	.201	.278	.279	71	274	244	27	49	11	1	2	21	25	2	1	2	109	7	3	9.1	39.8
Susnara, Tim	L-R	5-10	185	4-17-96	.208	.319	.396	33	113	96	13	20	6	0	4	17	11	5	0	1	33	0	0	9.7	29.2
Teter, Jacob	L-L	6-6	225	2-26-99	.190	.270	.238	38	141	126	12	24	3	0	1	8	14	0	0	1	33	1	0	9.9	23.4
Wagner, Max	R-R	6-0	215	8-19-01	.252	.303	.414	27	119	111	16	28	7	1	3	18	7	1	0	0	34	1	1	5.9	28.6
Watson, Zach	R-R	5-10	160	6-25-97	.209	.265	.396	52	208	187	25	39	9	1	8	31	12	3	1	2	56	11	0	5.8	26.9
Williams, Donta'	L-L	5-10	185	6-30-99	.194	.328	.322	103	408	335	50	65	17	1	8	44	57	11	1	3	115	23	11	14.0	28.2

Pitching	B-T	Ht.	Wt.	DOB	W	L	ERA	G	GS	SV	IP	Hits	Runs	ER	HR	BB	SO	AVG	OBP	SLG	SO%	BB%	BF
Armbruester, Justin	R-R	6-4	235	10-21-98	3	2	2.47	12	12	0	62	52	21	17	5	19	43	.228	.295	.355	17.1	7.5	252
Bradish, Kyle	R-R	6-3	215	9-12-96	0	1	5.40	1	1	0	5	3	4	3	1	1	5	.150	.190	.300	23.8	4.8	21
Bright, Trace	R-R	6-4	199	10-26-00	1	0	2.12	4	3	0	17	13	7	4	1	8	20	.213	.310	.279	28.2	11.3	71
Brnovich, Kyle	L-R	6-2	190	10-20-97	0	2	7.71	4	2	0	14	14	12	12	5	5	19	.255	.333	.564	30.2	7.9	63
Burch, Tyler	R-R	6-2	190	9-02-97	2	3	3.07	26	0	1	41	40	15	14	5	21	34	.253	.346	.418	18.6	11.5	183
Charles, Wandisson	R-R	6-4	250	9-07-96	2	1	2.35	13	0	3	15	7	5	4	2	5	26	.127	.226	.273	41.9	8.1	62
Elliott, Jensen	R-R	6-6	231	4-08-97	0	1	0.66	10	0	1	14	6	2	1	1	5	7	.143	.234	.214	14.6	10.4	48
Feliz, Ignacio	R-R	6-1	180	10-23-99	1	1	9.86	13	0	0	21	30	26	23	4	13	29	.330	.427	.549	26.4	11.8	110
Gillies, Keagan	R-R	6-8	255	1-27-98	2	1	3.75	18	0	2	24	17	12	10	2	10	34	.195	.287	.356	33.7	9.9	101
Gillispie, Connor	R-R	5-11	185	11-10-97	7	4	3.89	27	14	2	116	96	55	50	14	37	99	.224	.296	.382	20.5	7.7	482
Givens, Mychal	R-R	6-0	250	5-13-90	0	2	6.75	6	1	0	5	4	5	4	0	4	5	.200	.320	.300	20.0	16.0	25
Gomez, Ofreidy	R-R	6-3	240	7-06-95	0	0	2.61	7	0	4	10	8	3	3	1	4	10	.229	.333	.343	23.8	9.5	42
Hammer, Dan	R-R	6-2	210	9-10-97	0	1	6.75	6	0	0	8	5	6	6	0	11	12	.172	.415	.172	29.3	26.8	41
Heid, Dylan	R-R	6-1	180	5-18-98	1	0	1.50	3	0	0	6	1	1	1	0	2	5	.059	.190	.059	22.7	9.1	22
Hennen, Ryan	R-L	6-0	180	9-30-97	2	0	0.00	7	0	1	12	10	1	0	0	3	14	.222	.271	.244	29.2	6.3	48
Hoffman, Nolan	R-R	6-4	190	8-09-97	1	2	3.05	29	0	7	41	40	17	14	1	12	34	.253	.313	.310	19.3	6.8	176
Johnson, Seth	R-R	6-1	205	9-19-98	0	0	3.00	1	1	0	3	3	2	1	1	2	4	.250	.357	.500	28.6	14.3	14
Loeprich, Conner	R-R	6-3	215	9-13-97	4	2	4.91	34	0	2	51	47	34	28	6	17	55	.239	.312	.411	24.7	7.6	223
Long, Ryan	R-R	6-6	240	10-19-99	3	3	6.51	12	6	1	47	52	34	34	8	17	42	.283	.343	.484	20.4	8.3	206
Lucas, Easton	L-L	6-4	180	9-23-96	1	0	1.59	11	0	0	17	9	3	3	2	4	24	.155	.210	.293	38.7	6.5	62
McDermott, Chayce	L-R	6-3	197	8-22-98	5	6	3.56	16	14	1	68	42	29	27	6	44	88	.175	.303	.292	30.7	15.3	287
McGough, Trey	L-L	6-3	195	3-29-98	1	1	4.50	2	0	0	4	3	3	2	0	4	6	.214	.389	.357	33.3	22.2	18
Means, John	L-L	6-4	230	4-24-93	0	1	6.14	3	3	0	7	6	5	5	1	2	10	.214	.290	.393	32.3	6.5	31
Moore, Xavier	R-R	6-2	175	1-07-99	2	0	6.37	26	0	0	30	26	24	21	3	35	44	.234	.420	.333	29.1	23.2	151
Perez, Cionel	R-L	6-0	175	4-21-96	0	0	0.00	1	0	0	2	0	0	0	0	1	3	.000	.167	.000	50.0	16.7	6
Pham, Alex	R-R	5-11	165	10-10-99	0	2	2.67	14	9	1	61	43	20	18	5	17	54	.197	.255	.294	23.0	7.2	235
Pinto, Jean	R-R	5-11	175	1-09-01	2	1	3.72	9	4	0	29	32	20	12	4	12	28	.269	.341	.412	21.2	9.1	132
Povich, Cade	L-L	6-3	185	4-12-00	6	7	4.87	18	18	0	81	74	46	44	12	37	118	.240	.327	.412	33.4	10.5	353
Richmond, Nick	R-R	6-4	195	4-02-98	2	1	5.95	16	0	3	20	26	14	13	3	9	21	.329	.396	.481	22.6	9.7	93
Roth, Houston	R-R	6-3	220	3-09-98	7	3	5.01	25	4	2	79	70	44	44	17	44	82	.239	.344	.457	24.0	12.9	341
Stallings, Garrett	R-R	6-2	200	8-08-97	3	2	4.73	13	7	0	53	48	29	28	8	19	53	.238	.300	.401	23.8	8.5	223
Strowd, Kade	R-R	6-2	200	9-17-97	4	1	5.20	35	0	2	55	54	42	32	7	32	67	.251	.357	.381	26.3	12.5	255
Tate, Dillon	R-R	6-2	190	5-01-94	0	1	21.00	4	0	0	3	7	9	7	1	3	3	.389	.476	.667	14.3	14.3	21
Tavera, Carlos	R-R	6-1	195	10-06-98	3	7	4.86	23	17	0	80	70	57	43	15	58	89	.231	.354	.419	24.2	15.8	368
Van Loon, Peter	R-R	6-5	210	2-18-99	2	7	6.04	18	11	1	54	57	37	36	12	23	70	.271	.347	.500	29.0	9.5	241
Velez, Antonio	L-L	6-1	195	3-31-97	0	1	7.71	3	0	0	7	9	7	6	3	3	4	.300	.364	.633	12.1	9.1	33
Voth, Austin	R-R	6-2	215	6-26-92	0	0	4.50	1	1	0	2	2	1	1	1	0	2	.250	.250	.750	25.0	0.0	8
Wells, Tyler	R-R	6-8	260	8-26-94	0	0	3.12	3	3	0	9	6	3	3	2	3	7	.194	.257	.419	20.0	8.6	35
Young, Brandon	R-R	6-6	210	8-19-98	0	3	4.26	6	6	0	25	28	12	12	4	6	23	.298	.350	.489	22.1	5.8	104

Fielding

Catcher	PCT	G	PO	A	E	DP	PB
Ardoin	.996	26	224	16	1	3	1
Basallo	1.000	2	18	2	0	1	0
Florentino	.982	23	214	7	4	0	3
Handley	1.000	3	26	2	0	0	0
Kolozsvary	1.000	4	31	1	0	0	0
Mantecon	1.000	1	4	0	0	0	0
McCann	.955	2	21	0	1	0	0
Pavolony	.983	17	162	12	3	3	1
Rodriguez	.988	34	326	15	4	3	2
Susnara	.997	33	299	4	1	0	4

First Base	PCT	G	PO	A	E	DP
Basallo	1.000	1	8	0	0	2
Bowens	.986	35	203	11	3	16
Cook	1.000	8	55	2	0	2
Costes	.994	22	155	7	1	11
Cullen	1.000	2	7	0	0	0

	PCT	G	PO	A	E	DP
Fontana	1.000	14	92	2	0	8
Kjerstad	.965	16	103	7	4	12
Mayo	1.000	9	52	7	0	3
Teter	.988	34	229	14	3	16

Second Base	PCT	G	PO	A	E	DP
Burns	.944	4	10	7	1	1
Cook	.971	36	71	94	5	17
Cullen	1.000	11	7	21	0	1
Holliday	1.000	3	2	4	0	1
Prieto	.973	23	38	69	3	10
Romero	.909	18	22	38	6	8
Rosa	.932	16	20	35	4	7
Servideo	.965	25	27	55	3	15
Wagner	.952	5	10	10	1	1

Third Base	PCT	G	PO	A	E	DP
Burns	.667	1	1	1	1	0
Cullen	1.000	27	11	26	0	2
Holliday	1.000	1	2	0	0	0
Lara	1.000	5	2	3	0	0
Mayo	.914	63	43	85	12	9
Prieto	1.000	13	12	15	0	1
Romero	1.000	1	2	0	0	0
Rosa	1.000	9	7	10	0	1
Servideo	.000	2	0	0	0	0
Wagner	.977	19	7	36	1	3

Shortstop	PCT	G	PO	A	E	DP
Burns	.909	4	5	5	1	0
Holliday	.981	30	41	61	2	10
Lara	.926	23	32	56	7	10
Prieto	.950	18	18	39	3	3
Romero	.000	1	0	0	0	0
Rosa	.961	19	21	28	2	6
Servideo	.940	44	50	75	8	21
Wagner	1.000	1	0	4	0	1

Outfield	PCT	G	PO		A	E	DP
Beavers	.978	28	64	1	1	0	0
Bellony	1.000	2	5	1	0	0	0
Bowens	1.000	2	5	0	0	0	0
Cook	.985	66	143	8	4	1	0
Fabian	1.000	55	123	7	0	3	0
Fontana	.939	16	37	2	3	1	0
Haskin	1.000	4	9	0	0	0	0
Kjerstad	.928	20	36	0	1	0	0
Mullins	1.000	3	12	0	0	0	0
Rhodes	.991	90	150	8	2	3	0
Romero	.000	1	0	0	0	0	0
Watson	.995	44	97	1	1	1	0
Williams	.655	87	185	1	3	0	0

ABERDEEN IRONBIRDS

HIGH CLASS A

SOUTH ATLANTIC LEAGUE

Batting	B-T	Ht.	Wt.	DOB	AVG	OBP	SLG	G	PA	AB	R	H	2B	3B	HR	RBI	BB	HBP	SH	SF	SO	SB	CS	BB%	SO%
Ardoin, Silas	R-R	6-0	215	9-19-00	.215	.369	.336	68	268	214	31	46	11	0	5	28	50	3	0	1	86	4	5	18.7	32.1
Basallo, Samuel	L-R	6-3	180	8-13-04	.333	.443	.688	27	115	96	21	32	6	2	8	24	19	0	0	0	20	5	2	16.5	17.4
Beavers, Dylan	L-R	6-4	206	8-11-01	.273	.369	.463	85	369	311	46	85	26	3	9	48	50	1	0	7	84	22	6	13.6	22.8
Bellony, Isaac	B-R	6-2	220	12-15-01	.190	.265	.307	44	155	137	10	26	8	1	2	12	10	5	0	3	68	2	0	6.5	43.9
Bemboom, Anthony	L-R	6-2	195	1-18-90	.200	.429	.200	2	7	5	0	1	0	0	0	0	2	0	0	0	1	0	0	28.6	14.3
Bencosme, Frederick	L-R	6-0	160	12-25-02	.246	.338	.319	114	476	414	60	102	18	3	2	49	55	3	2	2	67	28	6	11.6	14.1
Bowens, TT	R-R	6-4	235	5-27-98	.188	.235	.438	5	17	16	4	3	1	0	1	3	0	1	0	0	6	0	0	0.0	35.3
Bradfield, Enrique	L-L	6-1	170	12-02-01	.118	.286	.118	5	21	17	3	2	0	0	0	0	4	0	0	0	4	4	0	19.0	19.0
Burns, Collin	L-R	5-11	187	5-20-00	.265	.358	.373	22	95	83	14	22	2	2	1	7	10	2	0	0	20	7	0	10.5	21.1
Costes, Maxwell	R-R	6-1	215	7-30-99	.242	.363	.508	45	157	132	24	32	6	1	9	28	16	9	0	0	32	4	1	10.2	20.4
Craig, Trendon	R-R	6-1	195	7-11-00	.194	.306	.226	20	73	62	4	12	2	0	0	3	10	0	0	0	18	5	4	13.7	24.7
De Leon, Isaac	R-R	6-3	209	11-07-01	.202	.316	.305	102	393	331	41	67	15	2	5	30	48	8	4	2	124	9	3	12.2	31.6
Etzel, Matthew	L-R	6-2	211	4-30-02	.267	.421	.400	5	19	15	2	4	2	0	0	2	4	0	0	0	3	3	0	21.1	15.8
Fabian, Jud	R-L	6-1	195	9-27-00	.281	.392	.490	56	237	192	35	54	13	0	9	43	37	2	0	6	61	19	6	15.6	25.7
Florentino, Randy	L-R	5-11	182	7-05-00	.286	.318	.381	6	22	21	2	6	2	0	0	2	1	0	0	0	7	1	0	4.5	31.8
Guerrero, Kevin	R-R	6-3	165	4-17-04	.143	.294	.286	5	17	14	3	2	0	1	0	0	2	1	0	0	6	0	0	11.8	35.3
Hall, Adam	R-R	5-11	165	5-22-99	.059	.273	.118	6	22	17	1	1	1	0	0	1	5	0	0	0	3	2	0	22.7	13.6
Haskin, Hudson	R-R	6-0	200	12-31-98	.333	.550	.417	5	20	12	3	4	1	0	0	5	4	3	0	1	4	2	0	20.0	20.0
Higgins, Ryan	R-R	6-1	200	1-25-00	.217	.305	.358	66	260	226	32	49	12	1	6	35	20	10	1	3	74	10	5	7.7	28.5
Hodo, Douglas	R-R	6-0	185	9-25-00	.098	.213	.171	15	47	41	5	4	1	1	0	3	5	1	0	0	12	3	0	10.6	25.5
Holliday, Jackson	L-R	6-0	185	12-04-03	.314	.452	.488	57	259	207	52	65	11	5	5	35	50	2	0	0	54	17	7	19.3	20.8
Horvath, Mac	R-R	6-1	195	7-22-01	.235	.435	.647	5	23	17	9	4	1	0	2	3	6	0	0	0	6	5	0	26.1	26.1
Mantecon, Michael	R-R	5-11	192	2-02-02	.000	.000	.000	3	6	6	0	0	0	0	0	0	0	0	0	0	1	0	0	0.0	16.7
McCann, James	R-R	6-3	235	6-13-90	.571	.625	.571	2	8	7	1	4	0	0	0	1	1	0	0	0	0	0	0	12.5	0.0
Placencia, Erison	R-R	6-1	170	12-31-01	.122	.143	.195	16	42	41	3	5	0	0	1	1	1	0	0	0	19	1	0	2.4	45.2
Prado, Elio	R-R	6-0	160	11-29-01	.239	.323	.423	41	162	142	21	34	7	2	5	13	12	6	1	1	37	6	2	7.4	22.8
Retzbach, Adam	R-R	6-4	220	11-13-00	.222	.304	.378	26	102	90	7	20	4	2	2	12	10	1	0	1	42	2	0	9.8	41.2
Romero, Noelberth	R-R	6-0	183	12-05-01	.261	.292	.391	6	24	23	1	6	3	0	0	0	1	0	0	0	6	1	0	4.2	25.0
Servideo, Anthony	L-R	5-10	175	3-11-99	.135	.224	.173	15	58	52	2	7	2	0	0	4	5	1	0	0	21	0	1	8.6	36.2
Stowers, Kyle	L-L	6-3	215	1-02-98	.500	.550	1.056	4	20	18	7	9	1	0	3	8	2	0	0	0	2	0	0	10.0	10.0
Susnara, Tim	L-R	5-10	185	4-17-96	.152	.278	.326	13	54	46	5	7	2	0	2	2	6	2	0	0	16	0	0	11.1	29.6
Teter, Jacob	L-L	6-6	225	2-26-99	.228	.322	.381	60	230	197	21	45	12	0	6	32	28	1	0	4	59	2	0	12.2	25.7
Trimble, Reed	B-R	6-0	180	6-06-00	.167	.298	.250	16	57	48	9	8	2	1	0	1	8	1	0	0	13	6	0	14.0	22.8
Urias, Ramon	R-R	5-10	185	6-03-94	.167	.444	.167	2	9	6	2	1	0	0	0	0	3	0	0	0	3	0	0	33.3	33.3
Valdez, Luis	B-R	5-11	165	1-22-00	.197	.258	.285	83	276	249	46	49	12	2	2	20	20	2	1	4	77	43	5	7.2	27.9
Wagner, Max	R-R	6-0	215	8-19-01	.234	.356	.401	80	360	299	60	70	14	3	10	36	51	7	0	3	90	26	5	14.2	25.0
Welk, Toby	R-R	6-0	205	5-02-97	.190	.320	.190	6	25	21	1	4	0	0	0	1	4	0	0	0	5	0	0	16.0	20.0
Willems, Creed	L-R	6-0	225	6-04-03	.192	.267	.319	75	311	276	22	53	8	0	9	47	26	4	0	5	86	0	1	8.4	27.7
Young, Carter	B-R	6-0	180	1-24-01	.293	.344	.397	15	64	58	8	17	4	1	0	7	5	0	0	1	25	4	1	7.8	39.1

Pitching	B-T	Ht.	Wt.	DOB	W	L	ERA	G	GS	SV	IP	Hits	Runs	ER	HR	BB	SO	AVG	OBP	SLG	SO%	BB%	BF
Beck, Jared	L-L	7-0	225	7-01-00	1	1	5.82	7	2	1	17	17	14	11	1	13	20	.270	.422	.397	24.1	15.7	83
Bright, Trace	R-R	6-4	199	10-26-00	2	6	4.35	22	18	0	83	62	50	40	8	48	127	.203	.323	.338	35.0	13.2	363
Brnovich, Kyle	L-R	6-2	190	10-20-97	0	0	1.29	2	2	0	7	6	1	1	0	0	11	.222	.222	.333	40.7	0.0	27
Carter, Carson	R-R	6-4	212	8-06-97	2	5	4.30	30	0	3	38	37	25	18	4	24	46	.257	.376	.403	26.4	13.8	174
Chandler, Cooper	R-R	6-2	200	8-12-98	5	8	3.84	23	13	0	89	85	57	38	8	31	89	.246	.312	.403	23.1	8.1	385
Federman, Daniel	L-R	6-1	205	9-18-98	2	1	4.71	10	6	0	36	32	19	19	4	11	47	.235	.303	.404	30.9	7.2	152
Feliz, Ignacio	R-R	6-1	180	10-23-99	1	5	9.28	15	0	0	21	22	23	22	3	10	30	.262	.364	.417	30.3	10.1	99
Firoved, Graham	R-R	6-1	185	9-26-99	0	3	7.28	32	0	3	38	46	32	31	4	27	46	.299	.421	.442	24.2	14.2	190
Gillies, Keagan	R-R	6-8	255	1-27-98	3	0	0.54	15	0	2	17	2	3	1	1	4	27	.038	.107	.096	48.2	7.1	56
Hammer, Dan	R-R	6-2	210	9-10-97	2	2	3.28	23	0	2	25	17	14	9	1	20	44	.195	.363	.299	38.9	17.7	113
Heid, Dylan	R-R	6-1	180	5-18-98	4	2	2.75	29	0	4	39	29	14	12	1	18	63	.200	.291	.290	38.2	10.9	165
Hennen, Ryan	R-L	6-0	180	9-30-97	2	0	3.86	17	0	2	21	16	9	9	3	8	25	.216	.302	.392	29.1	9.3	86

Johnson, Seth	R-R	6-1	205	9-19-98	0	1	8.31	2	2	0	4	4	4	4	0	3	7	.235	.350	.353	35.0	15.0	20
Kemlage, Joe	B-L	6-1	220	1-19-99	0	0	2.70	2	0	0	3	5	1	1	1	2	5	.357	.438	.643	31.3	12.5	16
Lloyd, Daniel	R-R	6-3	232	8-08-00	5	5	3.24	25	15	2	103	102	46	37	9	32	108	.262	.326	.396	25.2	7.5	429
Long, Ryan	R-R	6-6	240	10-19-99	3	3	2.52	15	6	0	61	43	21	17	4	18	71	.205	.267	.314	30.1	7.6	236
Lyons, Jake	R-R	6-5	280	8-19-98	6	3	4.16	21	6	2	63	65	35	29	6	20	71	.264	.324	.455	26.1	7.4	272
McGough, Trey	L-L	6-3	195	3-29-98	0	1	3.86	3	2	0	12	5	5	5	2	4	9	.128	.209	.359	20.9	9.3	43
Nierman, Hayden	B-R	6-2	170	1-27-00	0	1	5.23	14	0	0	10	6	7	6	0	3	11	.167	.250	.194	26.8	7.3	41
Nunez, Juan	R-R	5-11	190	12-07-00	0	2	3.99	13	9	1	50	40	23	22	5	32	53	.223	.350	.374	24.4	14.7	217
Peek, Zach	R-R	6-3	190	5-06-98	0	1	6.23	3	3	0	9	5	8	6	0	8	10	.172	.342	.276	26.3	21.1	38
Pham, Alex	R-R	5-11	165	10-10-99	3	3	2.45	12	10	0	51	29	17	14	5	25	76	.163	.266	.281	36.7	12.1	207
Pinto, Jean	R-R	5-11	175	1-09-01	1	1	2.75	13	13	0	52	40	17	16	4	18	73	.204	.284	.337	33.3	8.2	219
Portes, Edgar	R-R	6-2	165	10-02-02	0	0	4.91	4	0	1	4	3	2	2	1	2	4	.214	.333	.429	22.2	11.1	18
Richmond, Nick	R-R	6-4	195	4-02-98	1	0	0.73	11	0	1	12	8	1	1	0	5	11	.178	.260	.178	21.2	9.6	52
Rinehart, Logan	R-R	6-3	185	9-21-97	1	0	0.95	8	1	1	19	9	2	2	1	8	21	.138	.243	.215	28.4	10.8	74
Rivera, Yaqui	R-R	6-2	150	7-19-03	3	1	1.45	9	0	1	19	7	4	3	0	15	25	.117	.303	.183	32.9	19.7	76
Sharp, Reese	R-R	6-3	220	8-07-00	6	3	4.97	22	0	1	38	33	25	21	3	24	42	.241	.353	.431	24.7	14.1	170
Tate, Dillon	R-R	6-2	190	5-01-94	0	0	9.00	1	0	0	1	2	1	1	0	0	2	.400	.400	.800	40.0	0.0	5
Velez, Antonio	L-L	6-1	195	3-31-97	4	1	4.91	17	0	1	26	27	16	14	4	6	27	.265	.297	.529	24.3	5.4	111
Virbitsky, Kyle	R-R	6-7	235	10-08-98	6	1	3.83	25	15	1	103	81	47	44	10	40	103	.215	.299	.351	24.4	9.5	422
Weston, Cameron	R-R	6-2	215	8-27-00	3	1	2.68	12	3	0	40	38	15	12	1	12	49	.250	.311	.296	29.2	7.1	168
Young, Brandon	R-R	6-6	210	8-19-98	0	2	7.45	3	3	0	10	13	8	8	2	0	10	.342	.333	.632	25.6	0.0	39

Fielding

Catcher	PCT	G	PO	A	E	DP	PB
Ardoin	.990	56	552	34	6	2	3
Basallo	.969	15	145	13	5	1	1
Bemboom	1.000	2	16	2	0	0	0
Florentino	.980	4	44	4	1	0	0
Mantecon	1.000	2	24	0	0	0	0
McCann	1.000	1	13	0	0	0	0
Retzbach	.974	15	177	13	5	1	4
Willems	.986	42	391	35	6	3	2

First Base	PCT	G	PO	A	E	DP
Basallo	.964	6	49	4	2	5
Bowens	1.000	2	6	1	0	1
Costes	.989	17	88	6	1	5
De Leon	.983	42	210	22	4	18
Higgins	.974	11	64	12	2	4
Retzbach	.983	9	52	7	1	4
Susnara	1.000	4	28	2	0	2
Teter	.995	34	203	14	1	20
Willems	1.000	14	78	3	0	7

Second Base	PCT	G	PO	A	E	DP
Bencosme	.987	45	71	81	2	18
Burns	.973	8	18	18	1	4
De Leon	.800	2	1	3	1	0
Hall	1.000	2	3	6	0	1
Holliday	.957	8	4	18	1	2
Horvath	1.000	2	2	5	0	0
Placencia	1.000	14	18	11	0	4
Romero	1.000	2	2	2	0	1
Servideo	.967	9	9	20	1	0
Valdez	.889	21	19	37	7	3
Wagner	.975	24	44	34	2	9
Young	.889	3	3	5	1	0

Third Base	PCT	G	PO	A	E	DP
Bencosme	.875	10	8	6	2	2
Burns	1.000	2	2	2	0	0
Costes	1.000	3	1	3	0	0
De Leon	.911	49	22	60	8	8
Higgins	1.000	2	1	6	0	1
Holliday	1.000	1	1	0	0	0
Horvath	1.000	2	1	2	0	0
Romero	1.000	3	1	6	0	1
Servideo	1.000	4	1	3	0	1
Urias	1.000	1	1	1	0	0
Wagner	.950	58	46	68	6	6
Young	1.000	3	1	7	0	0

Shortstop	PCT	G	PO	A	E	DP
Bencosme	.911	58	62	102	16	15
Burns	1.000	12	15	28	0	8
Holliday	.961	46	55	92	6	18
Placencia	1.000	1	5	1	0	0
Romero	1.000	1	0	2	0	0
Servideo	.900	3	3	6	1	1
Young	.959	10	18	29	2	7

Outfield	PCT	G	PO	A	E	DP
Beavers	.990	77	136	2	2	0
Bellony	.901	36	43	0	6	0
Bowens	1.000	1	1	0	0	0
Bradfield	1.000	5	11	0	0	0
Costes	1.000	7	9	0	0	0
Craig	1.000	19	33	2	0	0
De Leon	1.000	7	6	1	0	0
Etzel	1.000	4	6	0	0	0
Fabian	.980	51	95	4	1	0
Guerrero	.900	5	8	1	1	0
Hall	.667	4	9	0	0	0
Haskin	1.000	3	9	1	0	0
Higgins	.986	47	79	1	1	0
Hodo	.934	12	34	0	2	0
Horvath	1.000	1	2	0	0	0
Mantecon	.000	1	0	0	0	0
Prado	.971	34	76	0	5	0
Stowers	1.000	3	11	0	0	0
Teter	1.000	14	17	2	0	0
Trimble	.980	11	24	0	1	0
Valdez	.953	59	117	6	8	2
Welk	1.000	5	3	0	0	0

DELMARVA SHOREBIRDS

LOW CLASS A

CAROLINA LEAGUE

Batting	B-T	Ht.	Wt.	DOB	AVG	OBP	SLG	G	PA	AB	R	H	2B	3B	HR	RBI	BB	HBP	SH	SF	SO	SB	CS	BB%	SO%
Acevedo, Stiven	R-R	6-4	185	8-02-02	.239	.304	.411	102	434	394	52	94	18	4	14	52	35	3	0	2	130	33	11	8.1	30.0
Basallo, Samuel	L-R	6-3	180	8-13-04	.299	.384	.503	83	352	308	52	92	19	4	12	60	41	2	0	1	73	7	3	11.6	20.7
Bellony, Isaac	B-R	6-2	220	12-15-01	.246	.299	.464	19	77	69	7	17	6	3	1	12	6	0	0	2	29	0	1	7.8	37.7
Bowens, TT	R-R	6-4	235	5-27-98	.240	.321	.240	7	28	25	3	6	0	0	0	1	2	1	0	0	12	0	0	7.1	42.9
Bradfield, Enrique	L-L	6-1	170	12-02-01	.302	.494	.340	17	77	53	15	16	2	0	0	6	19	3	0	2	9	20	2	24.7	11.7
Burns, Collin	L-R	5-11	187	5-20-00	.286	.286	.429	3	14	14	1	4	0	1	0	2	0	0	0	0	3	1	0	0.0	21.4
Costes, Maxwell	R-R	6-1	215	7-30-99	.368	.435	.526	6	23	19	5	7	0	0	1	3	2	1	0	1	8	0	0	8.7	34.8
Craig, Trendon	R-R	6-1	195	7-11-00	.302	.398	.453	39	168	139	21	42	10	1	3	21	21	3	0	3	36	18	3	12.5	21.4
Crampton, Adam	R-R	6-1	183	5-24-01	.196	.272	.256	111	411	367	49	72	13	3	1	25	33	6	1	2	105	17	7	8.0	25.5
Cruz, Rolphy	B-R	5-11	164	9-21-02	.139	.190	.215	23	84	79	6	11	3	0	1	8	5	0	0	0	31	2	2	6.0	36.9
Cullen, Greg	L-R	5-9	190	11-13-96	.250	.455	.313	5	22	16	0	4	1	0	0	1	5	1	0	0	3	0	0	22.7	13.6
Cunningham, Jake	R-R	6-4	205	7-03-02	.229	.386	.343	12	44	35	7	8	1	0	1	10	9	0	0	0	10	3	1	20.5	22.7
De Los Santos, Anderson	R-R	5-11	185	1-11-04	.228	.288	.339	104	419	378	42	86	20	2	6	47	31	3	0	5	104	10	10	7.4	24.8
Etzel, Matthew	L-R	6-2	211	4-30-02	.314	.444	.486	21	91	70	16	22	4	1	2	19	14	4	0	2	17	16	3	15.4	18.7
Florentino, Randy	L-R	5-11	182	7-05-00	.289	.348	.454	33	112	97	21	28	4	0	4	19	11	0	0	4	14	2	1	9.8	12.5
Gonzalez, Luis	L-L	6-4	185	11-02-02	.139	.264	.212	55	193	165	20	23	5	2	1	15	25	3	0	0	94	0	2	13.0	48.7
Gonzalez, Victor	R-R	5-10	155	10-08-02	.219	.306	.219	12	36	32	2	7	0	0	0	2	0	4	0	0	12	0	2	0.0	33.3
Hernandez, Brayan	L-R	6-1	225	11-11-01	.195	.286	.432	37	134	118	17	23	6	2	6	11	12	3	0	0	41	0	0	9.0	30.6
Higgins, Ryan	R-R	6-1	200	1-25-00	.222	.333	.444	5	21	18	2	4	4	0	0	4	2	1	0	0	8	0	0	9.5	38.1
Hodo, Douglas	R-R	6-0	185	9-25-00	.255	.403	.349	34	134	106	16	27	6	2	0	12	24	3	0	1	42	6	3	17.9	31.3

Holliday, Jackson	L-R	6-0	185	12-04-03	.396	.522	.660	14	67	53	15	21	6	1	2	16	14	0	0	0	13	3	0	20.9	19.4
Horvath, Mac	R-R	6-1	195	7-22-01	.308	.422	.500	14	64	52	11	16	4	0	2	5	10	1	0	1	17	9	0	15.6	26.6
Josenberger, Tavian	B-R	6-0	185	10-23-01	.256	.390	.308	22	102	78	14	20	2	1	0	12	19	0	1	3	22	7	2	18.6	21.6
Lara, Gilbert	R-R	6-4	198	10-30-97	.000	.000	.000	4	16	16	0	0	0	0	0	0	0	0	0	0	3	0	0	0.0	18.8
Mantecon, Michael	R-R	5-11	192	2-02-02	.286	.545	.286	4	11	7	2	2	0	0	0	0	3	1	0	0	3	0	0	27.3	27.3
Martinez, Roberto	B-R	6-0	145	1-16-03	.176	.333	.176	7	21	17	2	3	0	0	0	0	4	0	0	0	9	1	0	19.0	42.9
Mordan, Aneudis	R-R	6-1	175	6-10-04	.364	.417	.727	3	12	11	1	4	1	0	1	3	1	0	0	0	3	0	0	8.3	25.0
Pavolony, Connor	R-R	6-1	195	10-25-99	.000	.200	.000	2	10	8	2	0	0	0	0	0	2	0	0	0	4	0	0	20.0	40.0
Placencia, Erison	R-R	6-1	170	12-31-01	.231	.320	.275	33	103	91	8	21	4	0	0	9	10	2	0	0	35	1	2	9.7	34.0
Prado, Elio	R-R	6-0	160	11-29-01	.251	.354	.389	65	280	239	41	60	8	2	7	27	32	7	0	2	46	7	7	11.4	16.4
Retzbach, Adam	R-R	6-4	220	11-13-00	.125	.300	.125	6	20	16	0	2	0	0	0	1	4	0	0	0	8	0	1	20.0	40.0
Rodriguez, Carlos	R-R	5-11	195	10-14-03	.000	.400	.000	3	5	3	1	0	0	0	0	0	1	1	0	0	0	0	0	20.0	0.0
Rodriguez, Ramon	R-R	6-0	210	10-30-98	.263	.263	.316	5	19	19	3	5	1	0	0	2	0	0	0	0	2	0	0	0.0	10.5
Romero, Noelberth	R-R	6-0	183	12-05-01	.220	.283	.361	64	251	227	26	50	11	0	7	30	18	3	0	3	48	13	5	7.2	19.1
Servideo, Anthony	L-R	5-10	175	3-11-99	.147	.396	.265	11	48	34	10	5	1	0	1	3	13	1	0	0	17	0	1	27.1	35.4
Tejada, Angel	R-R	5-10	160	1-30-04	.249	.315	.366	85	292	265	39	66	17	1	4	26	16	10	0	1	65	6	5	5.5	22.3
Urman, Cole	R-R	6-1	195	7-28-01	.316	.350	.368	6	20	19	0	6	1	0	0	1	1	0	0	0	8	0	0	5.0	40.0
Valdez, Luis	B-R	5-11	165	1-22-00	.333	.360	.375	6	25	24	4	8	1	0	0	1	1	0	0	0	8	4	1	4.0	32.0
Vasquez, Jalen	L-R	6-0	175	1-18-02	.267	.409	.413	24	93	75	14	20	5	3	0	5	17	1	0	0	19	3	2	18.3	20.4
Vavra, Terrin	L-R	6-0	185	5-12-97	.167	.286	.167	2	7	6	1	1	0	0	0	2	1	0	0	0	2	0	0	14.3	28.6
Welk, Toby	R-R	6-0	205	5-02-97	.286	.375	.286	4	16	14	0	4	0	0	0	0	2	0	0	0	6	0	0	12.5	37.5
Willems, Creed	L-R	6-0	225	6-04-03	.302	.442	.615	30	120	96	20	29	6	0	8	28	20	4	0	0	29	2	0	16.7	24.2
Young, Carter	B-R	6-0	180	1-24-01	.236	.325	.319	85	388	339	53	80	13	3	3	30	45	1	0	3	104	7	2	11.6	26.8

Pitching	B-T	Ht.	Wt.	DOB	W	L	ERA	G	GS	SV	IP	Hits	Runs	ER	HR	BB	SO	AVG	OBP	SLG	SO%	BB%	BF
Alcantara, Darlin	R-R	6-3	180	9-20-01	3	4	8.04	16	0	0	31	52	30	28	3	13	26	.374	.436	.604	16.6	8.3	157
Alvarez, Cesar	R-R	6-1	175	9-11-02	2	0	5.92	28	0	0	38	45	28	25	5	24	43	.300	.421	.507	23.5	13.1	183
Barnhart, Zane	R-R	5-10	190	5-30-02	0	0	0.00	4	0	1	5	3	0	0	0	6	6	.188	.409	.188	27.3	27.3	22
Barroso, Luis	R-R	6-3	165	9-07-98	0	0	3.52	4	0	0	8	8	4	3	1	2	7	.267	.324	.400	20.6	5.9	34
Baumler, Carter	R-R	6-2	195	1-31-02	1	0	5.00	3	2	0	9	6	5	5	0	6	10	.188	.333	.281	25.6	15.4	39
Beck, Jared	L-L	7-0	225	7-01-00	2	3	3.86	16	10	0	58	54	32	25	3	34	78	.241	.345	.353	29.5	12.9	264
Beltran, Hugo	R-R	6-1	190	6-13-00	3	1	2.73	16	0	3	26	27	13	8	2	7	30	.262	.319	.340	26.5	6.2	113
Beriguete, Randy	R-R	6-4	221	11-02-02	0	4	9.76	25	0	2	28	39	34	30	4	18	25	.339	.420	.548	18.1	13.0	138
Bragg, Braxton	R-R	6-2	207	10-28-00	1	0	6.75	4	0	1	7	7	5	5	1	3	6	.292	.345	.417	20.7	10.3	29
Brehmer, Bradley	R-R	6-6	205	2-12-00	2	3	4.61	16	14	0	70	82	44	36	6	25	61	.295	.365	.432	19.7	8.1	310
Brnovich, Kyle	L-R	6-2	190	10-20-97	0	0	0.00	1	1	0	3	1	0	0	0	2	2	.100	.250	.100	16.7	16.7	12
Chace, Moises	R-R	6-1	213	6-09-03	5	2	4.50	21	9	2	68	47	37	34	8	53	100	.198	.350	.384	33.1	17.5	302
Cheney, Wyatt	R-R	6-0	185	1-10-01	2	8	6.02	17	9	0	52	61	42	35	6	32	49	.284	.379	.414	19.8	12.9	248
Costes, Maxwell	R-R	6-1	215	7-30-99	0	0	0.00	1	0	0	1	0	0	0	0	0	0	.000	.000	.000	0.0	0.0	1
Cruz, Deivy	L-L	5-11	154	2-13-04	8	4	3.62	25	16	0	97	74	40	39	7	50	103	.218	.332	.338	25.4	12.3	405
De Leon, Luis	L-L	6-3	168	4-14-03	3	1	2.39	9	5	0	26	17	12	7	0	16	31	.177	.301	.188	27.4	14.2	113
De Los Santos, Juan	R-R	6-3	250	5-25-02	1	10	4.60	24	15	1	90	90	60	46	2	49	89	.264	.365	.337	22.0	12.1	405
Johnson, Seth	R-R	6-1	205	9-19-98	0	0	0.00	1	1	0	2	1	0	0	0	0	1	.143	.143	.286	14.3	0.0	7
Kemlage, Joe	B-L	6-1	220	1-19-99	1	1	5.27	6	0	0	14	8	9	8	2	7	11	.174	.273	.304	20.0	12.7	55
LaRoche, Kelvin	R-R	5-11	170	7-31-99	1	0	2.57	5	0	1	7	5	2	2	1	4	9	.185	.313	.296	28.1	12.5	32
Maruskin, Jack	R-R	6-2	200	12-15-99	0	0	8.44	4	0	0	5	1	5	5	0	6	8	.059	.304	.059	34.8	26.1	23
McGough, Trey	L-L	6-3	195	3-29-98	0	0	0.00	1	1	0	3	3	0	0	0	1	3	.273	.333	.273	25.0	8.3	12
Mendez, Alejandro	R-R	6-5	254	2-28-01	3	1	4.73	25	0	0	32	17	21	17	2	36	42	.159	.384	.262	27.8	23.8	151
Money, Blake	R-R	6-7	240	11-14-01	0	0	3.38	5	0	1	8	8	3	3	0	0	8	.250	.250	.281	25.0	0.0	32
Nordmann, Trey	R-R	6-5	220	2-13-01	0	0	0.00	4	0	0	4	1	0	0	0	7	4	.083	.421	.083	21.1	36.8	19
Nunez, Juan	R-R	5-11	190	12-07-00	0	4	3.93	13	10	1	55	44	28	24	3	26	72	.218	.316	.332	31.2	11.3	231
Peek, Zach	R-R	6-3	190	5-06-98	0	0	0.00	1	1	0	1	3	0	0	0	1	2	.429	.556	.571	22.2	11.1	9
Portes, Edgar	R-R	6-2	165	10-02-02	5	6	4.24	23	11	0	81	71	43	38	6	35	106	.234	.310	.366	31.0	10.2	342
Rangel, Raul	R-R	6-4	200	10-09-02	2	1	4.50	8	2	0	26	28	15	13	0	10	10	.280	.354	.330	8.8	8.8	113
Rivera, Yaqui	R-R	6-2	150	7-19-03	1	5	3.16	20	2	6	31	22	17	11	2	18	43	.200	.338	.282	31.6	13.2	136
Rodriguez, Eris	R-R	6-3	188	9-10-01	1	1	6.28	9	0	1	14	20	13	10	1	7	10	.323	.394	.403	13.9	9.7	72
Rojas, Juan	L-L	6-0	165	1-31-04	1	3	6.39	8	4	0	25	25	22	18	3	14	21	.258	.357	.433	18.3	12.2	115
Sanchez, Brayner	R-R	6-4	189	6-02-01	0	1	4.66	14	0	1	19	15	11	10	0	9	25	.211	.318	.225	29.4	10.6	85
Sanchez, Luis	R-R	6-0	167	3-04-03	0	3	4.43	15	0	1	22	18	15	11	0	15	30	.217	.369	.289	29.1	14.6	103
Sharkey, Teddy	R-R	5-11	215	8-01-01	1	0	0.00	4	1	2	8	4	0	0	0	2	13	.143	.200	.143	43.3	6.7	30
Sharp, Reese	R-R	6-3	220	8-07-00	1	0	1.13	9	0	3	16	4	2	2	0	20	25	.080	.352	.100	34.7	27.8	72
Showalter, Zack	R-R	6-2	195	1-23-04	0	2	3.10	6	5	0	20	19	8	7	1	10	25	.253	.360	.387	28.1	11.2	89
Stauffer, Adam	R-R	6-7	240	1-13-99	0	0	2.25	5	0	0	8	4	3	2	1	4	7	.148	.294	.259	20.6	11.8	34
Vargas, Angel	R-R	6-1	173	12-01-01	1	1	3.31	10	0	1	16	9	8	6	0	12	21	.161	.319	.214	29.2	16.7	72
Vega, Alfred	R-R	6-1	169	1-19-01	4	5	6.72	23	10	1	66	88	56	49	6	37	46	.322	.408	.451	14.6	11.8	314
Weatherly, Ty	L-R	6-6	200	9-19-00	1	0	2.89	5	0	0	9	5	3	3	1	2	12	.152	.200	.333	34.3	5.7	35
Young, Brandon	R-R	6-6	210	8-19-98	0	0	0.00	1	1	0	3	1	0	0	0	0	2	.100	.100	.100	20.0	0.0	10

Fielding

Catcher	PCT	G	PO	A	E	DP	PB
Basallo	.988	51	499	58	7	5	6
Florentino	.986	25	191	16	3	1	6
Hernandez	.989	26	244	24	3	3	2
Mantecon	1.000	4	34	1	0	0	0
Mordan	.968	3	26	4	1	0	0
Pavolony	1.000	1	9	3	0	0	1
Retzbach	.867	1	9	4	2	0	0
Rodriguez	.978	3	41	4	1	0	1
Urman	.969	5	28	3	1	1	0
Willems	.987	16	138	15	2	2	3

First Base	PCT	G	PO	A	E	DP
Basallo	.982	21	158	6	3	17
Bowens	1.000	4	23	2	0	4
Costes	1.000	3	24	1	0	1
Crampton	.974	6	37	0	1	1
De Los Santos	1.000	11	72	6	0	8
Florentino	1.000	2	4	0	0	0
Gonzalez	.909	3	9	1	1	1
Hernandez	.959	8	44	3	2	9

Higgins	1.000	2	16	0	0	1
Lara	1.000	2	13	0	0	1
Martinez	1.000	2	8	3	0	3
Placencia	.993	18	131	6	1	9
Retzbach	.909	2	9	1	1	1
Rodriguez	.667	2	2	0	1	1
Romero	.984	26	173	10	3	15
Tejada	1.000	24	162	7	0	9
Willems	1.000	9	69	1	0	7

Second Base	PCT	G	PO	A	E	DP
Burns	1.000	1	1	4	0	0
Crampton	.980	36	58	88	3	19
Cruz	.944	8	3	31	2	3
Cullen	1.000	2	8	3	0	2
Gonzalez	1.000	2	2	6	0	1
Holliday	1.000	5	7	9	0	2
Horvath	.902	8	19	18	4	4
Josenberger	1.000	3	5	5	0	1
Martinez	.882	4	4	11	2	2
Placencia	.917	4	7	4	1	0
Romero	.962	15	19	32	2	3
Servideo	1.000	3	4	8	0	2
Tejada	.958	15	24	22	2	5

Valdez	1.000	3	5	11	0	0
Vasquez	.968	7	13	17	1	4
Vavra	.500	1	1	0	1	0
Young	.973	22	37	73	3	19

Third Base	PCT	G	PO	A	E	DP
Crampton	.875	12	9	19	4	2
Cullen	1.000	1	1	2	0	1
De Los Santos	.911	91	64	100	16	5
Gonzalez	.818	7	2	7	2	2
Horvath	.833	4	3	2	1	1
Lara	1.000	2	2	2	0	0
Placencia	.000	3	0	0	1	0
Romero	.813	12	3	10	3	1
Tejada	1.000	3	3	1	0	0
Young	1.000	5	2	6	0	0

Shortstop	PCT	G	PO	A	E	DP
Burns	1.000	2	2	3	0	0
Crampton	.979	55	71	113	4	27
Holliday	.974	8	14	24	1	5
Servideo	.917	3	3	8	1	2
Vasquez	.939	16	23	39	4	6
Young	.929	47	77	105	14	27

Outfield	PCT	G	PO	A	E	DP
Acevedo	.958	93	148	6	6	3
Bellony	.857	18	29	0	4	0
Bowens	1.000	1	1	0	0	0
Bradfield	.970	17	39	2	2	1
Costes	1.000	1	1	0	0	0
Craig	.983	36	36	3	1	0
Crampton	1.000	2	1	0	0	0
Cruz	1.000	12	15	0	0	0
Cunningham	1.000	10	12	3	0	1
Etzel	1.000	19	35	0	0	0
Gonzalez	.961	49	64	5	4	2
Higgins	1.000	1	2	0	0	0
Hodo	.982	34	51	2	1	1
Horvath	1.000	2	4	0	0	0
Josenberger	1.000	17	41	1	0	1
Prado	.992	59	119	9	2	3
Romero	1.000	1	2	0	0	0
Tejada	.920	25	46	4	4	1
Valdez	1.000	3	3	0	0	0
Welk	1.000	3	6	0	0	0

FCL ORIOLES — *ROOKIE*

FLORIDA COMPLEX LEAGUE

Batting	B-T	Ht.	Wt.	DOB	AVG	OBP	SLG	G	PA	AB	R	H	2B	3B	HR	RBI	BB	HBP	SH	SF	SO	SB	CS	BB%	SO%
Amparo, Edwin	B-R	6-0	165	10-14-04	.203	.384	.284	25	99	74	12	15	6	0	0	11	21	2	0	2	18	11	5	21.2	18.2
Arias, Leandro	B-R	6-1	155	2-05-05	.271	.370	.414	44	162	140	17	38	7	2	3	19	20	2	0	0	20	12	2	12.3	12.3
Baez, Kenny	R-R	5-11	185	9-26-02	.107	.242	.107	11	33	28	4	3	0	0	0	1	1	4	0	0	5	0	0	3.0	15.2
Benavides, Cristian	R-R	6-0	155	5-11-05	.171	.271	.268	32	96	82	14	14	2	0	2	8	12	0	0	2	29	3	1	12.5	30.2
Bradfield, Enrique	L-L	6-1	170	12-02-01	.556	.667	.667	3	12	9	4	5	1	0	0	0	3	0	0	0	3	1	0	25.0	25.0
Bucce, Yasmil	B-R	5-11	168	8-13-04	.302	.405	.444	23	74	63	11	19	4	1	1	8	10	1	0	0	20	0	0	13.5	27.0
Burns, Collin	L-R	5-11	187	5-20-00	.061	.220	.061	10	41	33	5	2	0	0	0	3	5	2	0	1	10	3	0	12.2	24.4
Castillo, Eruviel	R-R	6-1	150	12-10-03	.130	.310	.130	12	29	23	1	3	0	0	0	2	5	1	0	0	10	0	0	17.2	34.5
Cortorreal, Teudis	L-L	6-1	170	12-15-03	.203	.284	.322	27	67	59	4	12	5	1	0	3	7	0	0	1	20	1	0	10.4	29.9
Craig, Trendon	R-R	6-1	195	7-11-00	.250	.308	.250	3	13	12	2	3	0	0	0	1	1	0	0	0	4	1	0	7.7	30.8
Cruz, Rolphy	B-R	5-11	164	9-21-02	.500	.594	1.192	8	32	26	8	13	2	2	4	9	6	0	0	0	3	3	0	18.8	9.4
Cullen, Greg	L-R	5-9	190	11-13-96	.429	.636	.571	4	11	7	0	3	1	0	0	0	4	0	0	0	0	0	0	36.4	0.0
Cunningham, Jake	R-R	6-4	205	7-03-02	.500	.667	.500	2	9	6	3	3	0	0	0	2	3	0	0	0	2	1	0	33.3	22.2
Estrada, Aron	B-R	5-8	142	1-13-05	.206	.383	.365	23	81	63	16	13	3	2	1	6	15	3	0	0	11	5	0	18.5	13.6
Etzel, Matthew	L-R	6-2	211	4-30-02	.455	.571	.818	4	14	11	4	5	2	1	0	4	3	0	0	0	3	2	0	21.4	21.4
Gonzalez, Luis	L-L	6-4	185	11-02-02	.222	.300	.222	4	10	9	1	2	0	0	0	0	1	0	0	0	7	0	1	10.0	70.0
Gonzalez, Victor	R-R	5-10	155	10-08-02	.221	.280	.397	26	75	68	5	15	4	1	2	11	3	3	0	1	28	3	0	4.0	37.3
Guerrero, Kevin	R-R	6-3	165	4-17-04	.277	.323	.420	33	130	119	20	33	3	1	4	19	9	0	0	2	38	4	3	6.9	29.2
Hall, Adam	R-R	5-11	165	5-22-99	.238	.304	.381	5	23	21	3	5	1	1	0	1	2	0	0	0	8	0	0	8.7	34.8
Hernandez, Brayan	L-R	6-1	225	11-11-01	.000	.000	.000	2	2	2	0	0	0	0	0	0	0	0	0	0	0	0	0	0.0	0.0
Hernandez, Maikol	R-R	6-3	175	10-04-03	.179	.308	.269	38	159	134	25	24	6	0	2	10	17	8	0	0	33	1	3	10.7	20.8
Higgins, Ryan	R-R	6-1	200	1-25-00	.231	.412	.231	5	17	13	1	3	0	0	0	2	2	2	0	0	5	0	1	11.8	29.4
Horvath, Mac	R-R	6-1	195	7-22-01	.556	.667	1.111	3	12	9	6	5	2	0	1	3	3	0	0	0	3	0	1	25.0	25.0
Josenberger, Tavian	B-R	6-0	185	10-23-01	.000	.400	.000	3	10	6	4	0	0	0	0	1	4	0	0	0	1	2	1	40.0	10.0
Lara, Gilbert	R-R	6-4	198	10-30-97	.278	.316	.333	4	19	18	3	5	1	0	0	5	1	0	0	0	4	0	0	5.3	21.1
Lara, Junior	L-L	5-11	165	1-27-04	.222	.250	.222	11	28	27	2	6	0	0	0	0	0	1	0	0	6	4	2	0.0	21.4
Mantecon, Michael	R-R	5-11	192	2-02-02	1.000	.500	1.000	1	2	1	0	1	0	0	0	2	0	0	0	1	0	0	0	0.0	0.0
Martinez, Roberto	B-R	6-0	145	1-16-03	.296	.424	.407	14	33	27	3	8	3	0	0	3	6	0	0	0	7	1	2	18.2	21.2
Mordan, Aneudis	R-R	6-1	175	6-10-04	.274	.390	.504	38	141	117	25	32	6	0	7	24	19	4	0	1	29	2	0	13.5	20.6
Pavolony, Connor	R-R	6-1	195	10-25-99	.077	.400	.077	5	20	13	2	1	0	0	0	0	6	1	0	0	6	0	0	30.0	30.0
Ramos, Raylin	R-R	6-1	180	12-01-04	.343	.343	.486	11	35	35	7	12	3	1	0	3	0	0	0	0	9	2	1	0.0	25.7
Rodriguez, Carlos	R-R	5-11	195	10-14-03	.222	.367	.286	23	79	63	9	14	1	0	1	8	13	2	0	1	25	2	0	16.5	31.6
Sosa, Thomas	L-L	6-1	160	1-18-05	.290	.385	.492	39	143	124	26	36	7	3	4	25	17	2	0	0	31	5	4	11.9	21.7
Stowers, Kyle	L-L	6-3	215	1-02-98	.714	.778	1.143	3	9	7	2	5	0	0	1	1	1	1	0	0	2	0	0	11.1	22.2
Tavera, Braylin	R-R	6-2	175	2-19-05	.262	.391	.421	35	133	107	15	28	5	0	4	20	22	2	0	2	23	13	5	16.5	17.3
Urman, Cole	R-R	6-1	195	7-28-01	.429	.500	.571	2	8	7	1	3	1	0	0	1	1	0	0	0	1	0	0	12.5	12.5
Vasquez, Jalen	L-R	6-0	175	1-18-02	.200	.333	.200	2	6	5	1	1	0	0	0	0	1	0	0	0	0	2	1	16.7	0.0
Velasquez, Alfredo	R-R	5-11	153	9-30-04	.230	.295	.356	28	95	87	20	20	5	0	2	17	7	1	0	0	16	7	0	7.4	16.8
Vicioso, Carlos	L-R	5-10	160	12-06-02	.042	.258	.042	14	31	24	0	1	0	0	0	0	6	1	0	0	11	1	1	19.4	35.5
Viloria, Meibrys	L-R	5-11	225	2-15-97	.375	.545	.750	3	11	8	2	3	0	0	1	2	3	0	0	0	1	1	0	27.3	9.1

Pitching	B-T	Ht.	Wt.	DOB	W	L	ERA	G	GS	SV	IP	Hits	Runs	ER	HR	BB	SO	AVG	OBP	SLG	SO%	BB%	BF
Akin, Keegan	L-L	6-0	240	4-01-95	0	0	27.00	1	1	0	1	4	3	3	0	0	1	.667	.571	.833	14.3	0.0	7
Alberto, Eddy	R-R	6-2	190	3-10-02	2	4	8.04	14	2	1	28	31	27	25	4	22	25	.292	.414	.453	18.8	16.5	133
Arias, Harol	R-R	6-2	180	11-07-02	0	1	13.50	4	0	1	3	6	7	5	1	2	2	.333	.429	.611	9.5	9.5	21
Barnhart, Zane	R-R	5-10	190	5-30-02	0	1	18.00	1	0	0	1	2	2	2	0	2	2	.400	.571	.600	28.6	28.6	7
Baumler, Carter	R-R	6-2	195	1-31-02	0	0	1.13	4	3	0	8	4	2	1	0	3	11	.138	.219	.241	34.4	9.4	32

Bautista, Bryan	R-R	6-3	175	2-08-04	0	1	3.60	6	6	0	20	19	8	8	1	10	18	.260	.349	.370	21.7	12.0	83
Bello, Anthony	R-R	6-1	209	4-04-99	1	2	5.40	7	0	0	15	10	10	9	2	10	14	.185	.343	.407	20.9	14.9	67
Brnovich, Kyle	L-R	6-2	190	10-20-97	0	0	0.00	1	1	0	2	0	0	0	0	0	2	.000	.000	.000	33.3	0.0	6
Cartaya, Yeiber	R-R	6-5	165	1-20-03	2	2	8.57	10	2	0	21	23	21	20	2	18	25	.277	.410	.434	23.8	17.1	105
Correa, Eccel	R-R	6-0	170	2-01-03	1	2	7.88	8	4	1	24	29	22	21	2	10	27	.290	.385	.460	23.1	8.5	117
Cortorreal, Teudis	L-L	6-1	170	12-15-03	0	0	0.00	1	0	0	1	1	0	0	0	0	0	.250	.250	.250	0.0	0.0	4
Cuevas, Noelin	L-L	6-0	165	5-03-02	0	1	3.86	6	2	1	14	16	8	6	0	12	13	.296	.426	.333	19.1	17.6	68
De Leon, Luis	L-L	6-3	168	4-14-03	2	0	1.65	6	6	0	27	23	8	5	0	14	36	.230	.342	.290	30.8	12.0	117
Figueroa, Pedro	R-R	6-1	202	6-03-02	1	0	5.65	9	0	1	14	18	11	9	1	12	17	.295	.427	.475	22.7	16.0	75
Frias, Harif	R-R	6-4	163	5-19-01	1	4	5.52	21	0	2	31	42	26	19	1	16	31	.321	.401	.427	20.3	10.5	153
Gibson, Trey	R-R	6-5	230	5-18-02	1	0	0.00	1	0	0	2	1	0	0	0	1	2	.143	.250	.143	25.0	12.5	8
Givens, Mychal	R-R	6-0	250	5-13-90	0	0	0.00	1	0	0	1	1	0	0	0	0	2	.250	.400	.250	40.0	0.0	5
Gonzalez, Victor	R-R	5-10	155	10-08-02	0	0	0.00	1	0	0	1	2	0	0	0	0	0	.500	.500	.750	0.0	0.0	4
Hall, DL	L-L	6-2	210	9-19-98	1	0	0.00	2	1	0	3	1	0	0	0	2	8	.100	.250	.100	66.7	16.7	12
Hernandez, Omar	L-L	5-8	155	1-24-04	0	2	27.00	5	0	0	4	5	13	11	1	11	4	.294	.552	.647	13.8	37.9	29
Johnson, Seth	R-R	6-1	205	9-19-98	0	0	0.00	1	1	0	1	1	0	0	0	0	2	.250	.250	.250	50.0	0.0	4
Lara, Junior	L-L	5-11	165	1-27-04	0	0	20.25	1	0	0	1	4	4	3	0	0	0	.500	.444	.625	0.0	0.0	9
LaRoche, Kelvin	R-R	5-11	170	7-31-99	1	0	0.00	2	0	0	3	0	0	0	0	1	2	.000	.100	.000	20.0	10.0	10
Lord, Kiefer	R-R	6-3	195	6-22-02	0	0	0.00	1	0	0	2	0	0	0	0	1	1	.000	.286	.000	14.3	14.3	7
Lowther, Zac	L-L	6-2	235	4-30-96	0	0	9.00	1	0	0	1	2	1	1	0	0	0	.400	.400	.800	0.0	0.0	5
Martinez, Roberto	B-R	6-0	145	1-16-03	0	0	9.00	1	0	0	1	2	1	1	0	2	0	.400	.571	.400	0.0	28.6	7
Maruskin, Jack	R-R	6-2	200	12-15-99	0	1	36.00	2	0	0	2	5	8	8	0	7	2	.556	.765	.667	11.8	41.2	17
McGough, Trey	L-L	6-3	195	3-29-98	0	0	0.00	1	1	0	2	1	0	0	0	2	4	.143	.333	.143	44.4	22.2	9
Mesa, Miguel	R-R	6-2	188	2-05-03	0	0	5.59	4	2	0	10	8	6	6	0	9	6	.229	.391	.229	13.0	19.6	46
Money, Blake	R-R	6-7	240	11-14-01	0	0	5.40	1	1	0	2	3	1	1	0	0	3	.333	.333	.333	33.3	0.0	9
Morillo, Anthony	R-R	6-2	170	2-07-02	1	1	7.30	6	2	0	12	12	11	10	1	11	20	.235	.371	.392	32.3	17.7	62
Morla, Jorge	R-R	6-3	185	4-13-00	0	2	8.41	7	6	0	20	27	20	19	3	17	23	.329	.446	.537	22.8	16.8	101
Nierman, Hayden	B-R	6-2	170	1-27-00	0	0	0.00	1	0	0	1	1	1	0	0	1	2	.250	.400	.250	40.0	20.0	5
Parra, Andres	L-L	5-11	160	3-19-05	2	0	3.12	4	0	0	9	5	3	3	1	5	7	.172	.294	.345	20.6	14.7	34
Peek, Zach	R-R	6-3	190	5-06-98	0	0	13.50	1	1	0	1	2	4	1	0	0	1	.333	.333	.667	16.7	0.0	6
Pina, Junior	R-R	6-4	170	12-19-02	0	1	6.23	17	0	0	26	17	25	18	1	32	19	.189	.429	.278	14.3	24.1	133
Pineda, Yonatan	R-R	6-1	196	12-07-01	0	1	9.39	11	0	0	15	16	18	16	2	17	11	.286	.449	.482	14.1	21.8	78
Polanco, Elvis	L-L	5-10	165	9-16-03	0	0	108.00	1	0	0	0	0	4	4	0	4	0	.000	.833	.000	0.0	66.7	6
Rangel, Raul	R-R	6-4	200	10-09-02	1	3	4.39	10	5	0	27	27	21	13	2	14	26	.243	.325	.342	20.6	11.1	126
Rodriguez, Eris	R-R	6-3	188	9-10-01	4	1	0.82	7	0	0	11	5	2	1	0	9	8	.139	.311	.194	17.8	20.0	45
Rojas, Juan	L-L	6-0	165	1-31-04	1	0	2.70	3	1	0	7	3	2	2	0	6	6	.150	.346	.250	23.1	23.1	26
Salazar, Grabiel	R-R	6-0	165	2-19-01	0	0	5.06	17	0	1	27	21	21	15	1	20	27	.214	.378	.327	21.3	15.7	127
Sanchez, Brayner	R-R	6-4	189	6-02-01	0	0	4.15	5	0	0	9	7	6	4	1	2	12	.189	.231	.270	30.8	5.1	39
Sharkey, Teddy	R-R	5-11	215	8-01-01	0	0	0.00	1	0	0	2	0	0	0	0	1	3	.000	.143	.000	42.9	14.3	7
Showalter, Zack	R-R	6-2	195	1-23-04	0	0	0.90	3	3	0	10	7	1	1	0	4	16	.194	.275	.222	40.0	10.0	40
Solano, Issac	R-R	6-6	195	10-23-01	0	1	3.52	4	1	0	8	8	6	3	1	6	6	.267	.410	.367	15.4	15.4	39
Stauffer, Adam	R-R	6-7	240	1-13-99	0	0	0.00	2	0	0	1	0	1	0	0	3	2	.000	.444	.000	22.2	33.3	9
Vargas, Angel	R-R	6-1	173	12-01-01	0	1	11.57	2	0	0	2	5	4	3	0	5	5	.417	.588	.667	29.4	29.4	17
Vicioso, Carlos	L-R	5-10	160	12-06-02	0	0	108.00	1	0	0	0	2	4	4	1	2	0	.667	.800	1.667	0.0	40.0	5
Voth, Austin	R-R	6-2	215	6-26-92	0	0	0.00	1	1	0	1	0	0	0	0	0	0	.000	.000	.000	0.0	0.0	3
Weatherly, Ty	L-R	6-6	200	9-19-00	0	0	0.00	1	0	0	2	1	0	0	0	1	2	.143	.250	.143	25.0	12.5	8
Weston, Cameron	R-R	6-2	215	8-27-00	0	0	13.50	1	0	0	3	5	4	4	0	1	1	.385	.429	.615	7.1	7.1	14
Young, Brandon	R-R	6-6	210	8-19-98	0	0	0.00	1	1	0	2	2	0	0	0	0	5	.250	.333	.250	55.6	0.0	9

Fielding

C: Mordan 19, Bucce 18, Rodriguez 13, Baez 10, Pavolony 3, Hernandez 2, Viloria 2, Urman 1, Mantecon 1. **1B:** Mordan 16, Gonzalez 11, Castillo 10, Rodriguez 9, Martinez 8, Cruz 6, Bucce 5, Baez 2, Benavides 1, Higgins 1. **2B:** Arias 15, Estrada 14, Amparo 11, Velasquez 10, Martinez 5, Benavides 4, Hall 3, Hernandez 2, Cullen 2, Gonzalez 1, Burns 1, Cruz 1. **3B**: Benavides 19, Arias 12, Hernandez 11, Velasquez 8, Amparo 6, Horvath 3, Lara 3, Higgins 1, Burns 1, Cullen 1. **SS:** Hernandez 25, Arias 15, Velasquez 7, Amparo 5, Burns 5, Benavides 2, Lara 2, Vasquez 2, Hall 1. **OF:** Sosa 34, Guerrero 30, Tavera 28, Cortorreal 26, Gonzalez 13, Vicioso 12, Lara 9, Benavides 6, Estrada 5, Josenberger 4, Ramos 4, Velasquez 3, Etzel 3, Bradfield 3, Craig 2, Cruz 2, Higgins 2, Martinez 1, Stowers 1, Cunningham 1.

DSL ORIOLESROOKIE

DOMINICAN SUMMER LEAGUE

Batting	B-T	Ht.	Wt.	DOB	AVG	OBP	SLG	G	PA	AB	R	H	2B	3B	HR	RBI	BB	HBP	SH	SF	SO	SB	CS	BB%	SO%
Almeyda, Luis	R-R	6-2	180	4-17-06	.190	.290	.310	19	69	58	6	11	1	0	2	14	8	1	0	2	14	2	2	11.6	20.3
Amparo, Felix	R-R	5-10	180	2-27-06	.257	.312	.316	52	206	187	33	48	7	2	0	13	7	9	1	2	40	15	2	3.4	19.4
Aybar, Junior	L-R	6-0	145	7-14-06	.217	.336	.292	40	126	106	15	23	6	1	0	6	19	0	1	0	37	0	5	15.1	29.4
Campos, Edrei	L-R	6-1	165	5-08-05	.199	.296	.322	49	170	146	18	29	8	2	2	21	20	1	1	2	34	9	4	11.8	20.0
Celedonio, Victor	B-R	5-11	150	12-16-03	.230	.274	.345	28	95	87	9	20	7	0	1	9	5	1	0	2	20	2	0	5.3	21.1
Cohen, Abraham	L-L	6-1	175	6-15-06	.211	.375	.421	7	25	19	4	4	1	0	1	1	5	0	1	0	6	1	0	20.0	24.0
Cuevas, Elis	B-R	5-11	150	11-08-04	.305	.401	.455	54	217	187	41	57	14	4	2	28	23	7	0	0	41	17	5	10.6	18.9
De Los Santos, Sebastian	B-R	5-10	145	6-16-06	.243	.400	.311	30	96	74	18	18	3	1	0	6	20	0	1	1	23	4	4	20.8	24.0
Feliciano, Wilmer	L-R	6-3	190	4-06-04	.167	.286	.167	16	49	42	2	7	0	0	0	1	6	1	0	0	20	2	0	12.2	40.8
Frias, Wander	B-L	5-10	155	9-05-05	.200	.333	.400	6	18	15	4	3	1	1	0	3	2	1	0	0	5	2	0	11.1	27.8
Guevara, Luis	B-R	5-8	167	2-06-06	.318	.444	.380	44	160	129	29	41	6	1	0	21	28	2	0	1	24	16	5	17.5	15.0
Jimenez, Hector	R-R	5-11	155	2-08-04	.174	.335	.220	46	167	132	19	23	6	0	0	13	20	13	0	2	35	9	7	12.0	21.0
Leonte, Raul	L-L	6-1	170	5-07-06	.212	.342	.258	24	79	66	10	14	0	0	1	9	13	0	0	0	22	4	1	16.5	27.8
Liranzo, Joshua	R-R	6-3	180	8-25-06	.244	.393	.400	50	201	160	30	39	6	2	5	23	31	9	0	1	48	7	1	15.4	23.9
Martinez, Juan	R-R	6-4	175	9-19-04	.213	.342	.369	43	146	122	27	26	3	2	4	17	24	0	0	0	41	1	2	16.4	28.1

Mata, Jean	R-R	5-11	158	9-09-04	.261	.354	.291	46	159	134	25	35	2	1	0	16	18	3	1	3	24	6	7	11.3	15.1
Mejia, Adriander	R-R	6-0	165	8-29-06	.277	.362	.355	47	178	155	19	43	9	0	1	22	19	2	1	1	27	1	2	10.7	15.2
Mejia, Jose	R-R	5-11	175	9-29-05	.346	.500	.385	10	34	26	8	9	1	0	0	1	6	2	0	0	3	7	2	17.6	8.8
Noguera, Jose	R-R	6-2	189	2-24-05	.176	.250	.206	25	76	68	8	12	2	0	0	6	7	0	0	1	18	0	0	9.2	23.7
Nolaya, Andres	R-R	6-1	185	3-27-05	.293	.366	.415	39	142	123	21	36	8	2	1	25	16	0	0	3	33	9	4	11.3	23.2
Ortega, Juan	R-R	5-8	177	4-10-06	.268	.375	.415	13	49	41	9	11	2	2	0	6	5	2	1	0	13	1	1	10.2	26.5
Ortiz, Diorky	R-R	5-10	145	11-15-05	.222	.296	.306	31	81	72	10	16	3	0	1	10	6	2	0	1	13	5	5	7.4	16.0
Peguero, Fernando	B-R	5-9	145	12-27-04	.333	.423	.475	52	217	183	54	61	12	4	2	27	29	1	2	2	28	20	11	13.4	12.9
Perez, Jose	L-R	5-10	150	5-15-05	.194	.295	.295	43	149	129	15	25	1	0	4	10	18	1	0	1	44	7	3	12.1	29.5
Ramirez, Breiny	L-L	6-4	180	5-19-06	.193	.317	.235	46	142	119	21	23	1	2	0	13	18	4	0	1	41	14	6	12.7	28.9
Robain, Jhonanderson	R-R	6-0	176	1-14-06	.180	.226	.220	20	53	50	4	9	2	0	0	4	3	0	0	0	15	2	1	5.7	28.3
Rodriguez, Miguel	R-R	5-11	160	12-29-05	.323	.489	.385	40	131	96	21	31	6	0	0	17	24	9	0	2	13	6	4	18.3	9.9
Rojas, Elvis	L-L	6-3	175	9-25-05	.248	.351	.293	45	154	133	19	33	6	0	0	23	20	1	0	0	33	7	3	13.0	21.4
Ruiz, Yirber	B-R	6-1	160	10-08-04	.273	.442	.485	29	87	66	16	18	4	2	2	13	17	3	1	0	14	4	2	19.5	16.1
Sandoval, Jonaiker	R-R	6-0	188	3-09-04	.200	.278	.314	27	79	70	6	14	2	0	2	9	5	3	0	1	30	2	0	6.3	38.0
Santos, Adriam	R-R	5-11	165	10-28-04	.074	.167	.111	13	30	27	2	2	1	0	0	2	2	1	0	0	18	0	0	6.7	60.0
Urbina, Omar	R-R	6-1	175	9-01-05	.000	.000	.000	3	3	3	0	0	0	0	0	0	0	0	0	0	0	0	0	0.0	0.0
Vicioso, Luis	R-R	5-10	188	5-07-03	.314	.376	.436	45	173	156	18	49	10	3	1	28	13	3	0	1	32	2	2	7.5	18.5

Pitching	B-T	Ht.	Wt.	DOB	W	L	ERA	G	GS	SV	IP	Hits	Runs	ER	HR	BB	SO	AVG	OBP	SLG	SO%	BB%	BF
Alvero, Xavier	R-R	6-2	170	12-01-05	0	1	4.13	8	5	1	28	27	19	13	3	20	19	.243	.375	.351	14.0	14.7	136
Batista, Eriner	R-R	5-10	180	1-30-04	2	2	9.31	8	0	1	10	9	10	10	1	8	12	.250	.426	.389	25.5	17.0	47
Bello, Anthony	R-R	6-1	209	4-04-99	0	0	0.00	4	0	1	8	1	0	0	0	1	9	.037	.071	.074	32.1	3.6	28
Beltran, Luis	R-R	6-4	175	4-06-04	2	5	8.03	15	0	1	25	18	23	22	1	30	32	.205	.412	.250	26.9	25.2	119
Bolivar, Angel	R-R	6-1	175	10-01-05	1	0	1.35	2	0	0	7	5	1	1	0	2	3	.227	.320	.273	12.0	8.0	25
Bonilla, Ezequiel	R-R	6-1	160	8-12-05	1	3	3.48	11	11	0	41	35	27	16	3	26	39	.236	.373	.345	21.1	14.1	185
Brito, Carlos	R-R	5-11	160	8-22-02	3	0	0.86	7	3	0	21	8	2	2	1	9	20	.113	.210	.225	24.7	11.1	81
Caballero, Darwin	R-R	6-3	190	7-15-00	0	0	0.00	2	0	0	2	1	0	0	0	2	2	.143	.400	.143	20.0	20.0	10
Cartaya, Yeiber	R-R	6-5	165	1-20-03	0	0	0.79	3	2	0	11	6	2	1	0	8	12	.158	.319	.184	25.0	16.7	48
Correa, Eccel	R-R	6-0	170	2-01-03	2	0	1.69	3	0	0	11	4	2	2	1	5	18	.114	.225	.229	43.9	12.2	41
Crispin, Francisco	R-R	6-6	190	12-09-02	0	1	9.00	6	0	0	7	8	8	7	0	8	7	.308	.472	.500	19.4	22.2	36
Cuevas, Noelin	L-L	6-0	165	5-03-02	1	3	2.17	6	5	0	29	22	12	7	0	10	25	.206	.295	.243	20.5	8.2	122
Delgado, Adrian	R-R	6-3	182	5-12-05	2	1	4.50	13	0	0	20	10	10	10	2	21	18	.167	.393	.283	21.4	25.0	84
Dicent, Esteban	R-R	6-5	185	6-10-03	1	0	4.38	9	0	0	12	10	8	6	0	14	9	.217	.446	.304	13.8	21.5	65
Duran, Juan	R-R	6-0	160	11-25-03	2	2	5.47	10	5	0	25	24	17	15	1	18	31	.258	.389	.355	27.2	15.8	114
Espinal, Cesar	R-R	6-2	165	8-25-05	2	1	3.18	9	8	0	34	29	12	12	2	11	34	.240	.319	.372	25.0	8.1	136
Figueroa, Pedro	R-R	6-1	202	6-03-02	0	1	2.16	6	0	4	8	8	5	2	0	4	7	.235	.333	.294	17.9	10.3	39
Genao, Joldanny	R-R	6-4	168	8-01-02	1	2	4.41	10	0	3	16	13	9	8	1	12	13	.255	.423	.392	18.3	16.9	71
Gonzalez, Javier	R-R	6-0	150	9-22-05	1	3	5.48	11	11	0	43	45	28	26	6	16	42	.280	.355	.472	22.8	8.7	184
Gonzalez, Ledwin	L-L	5-11	160	6-22-06	5	1	3.14	14	3	0	29	29	11	10	1	17	29	.279	.376	.404	23.0	13.5	126
Jimenez, Hector	R-R	5-11	155	2-08-04	0	0	27.00	1	0	0	0	1	1	1	1	0	0	.500	.667	2.000	0.0	0.0	3
Leandro, Alberto	R-R	6-3	171	4-24-02	2	1	4.18	14	0	3	28	29	16	13	0	7	25	.269	.319	.361	21.0	5.9	119
Magallanes, Fermin	R-R	6-7	170	2-17-02	2	1	5.32	17	0	2	22	15	16	13	0	21	26	.197	.384	.263	26.3	21.2	99
Martinez, Francis	R-R	6-5	200	12-27-01	0	1	7.79	13	0	1	17	25	15	15	1	11	6	.362	.465	.449	6.9	12.6	87
Mesa, Miguel	R-R	6-2	188	2-05-03	2	1	3.75	7	5	0	24	14	11	10	1	19	20	.175	.377	.275	18.9	17.9	106
Mora, Jeyderson	R-R	6-0	145	3-13-05	1	0	1.80	2	1	0	5	4	1	1	0	1	5	.222	.263	.222	26.3	5.3	19
Morao, Francisco	L-L	6-2	178	11-15-05	2	3	3.89	11	11	0	39	32	21	17	2	21	52	.218	.335	.299	29.9	12.1	174
Moreta, Oscar	R-R	6-2	180	10-12-03	1	4	5.81	15	2	0	31	32	23	20	2	22	35	.264	.403	.380	23.5	14.8	149
Morfe, Keeler	R-R	5-8	161	6-09-06	1	5	7.01	9	9	0	26	24	25	20	0	21	25	.242	.400	.293	20.0	16.8	125
Moscoso, Elias	R-R	5-11	162	3-27-05	1	1	4.50	11	10	0	34	27	18	17	1	24	38	.216	.373	.280	24.1	15.2	158
Palacios, Jesus	R-R	6-2	167	3-07-05	3	0	1.95	11	11	0	51	37	14	11	0	13	60	.196	.264	.254	28.8	6.3	208
Parra, Andres	L-L	5-11	160	3-19-05	0	1	0.00	5	5	0	14	6	2	0	0	6	16	.128	.241	.149	29.6	11.1	54
Rasquin, Juan	B-R	6-3	165	12-24-05	2	1	5.14	13	0	1	21	14	16	12	0	12	17	.184	.323	.250	18.1	12.8	94
Rombley, Geronimo	R-R	6-5	200	4-20-04	1	3	10.80	10	0	0	10	20	20	12	3	13	6	.408	.547	.694	9.4	20.3	64
Rondon, Wilton	R-R	6-2	185	9-10-02	5	2	2.33	15	0	2	27	19	8	7	0	14	23	.204	.321	.247	20.5	12.5	112
Ruiz, Yirber	B-R	6-1	160	10-08-04	0	0	27.00	1	0	0	1	3	4	3	0	0	0	.500	.500	1.167	0.0	0.0	8
Santana, Mario	R-R	6-1	165	6-30-06	0	0	13.89	12	0	0	12	9	18	18	0	19	18	.200	.455	.289	27.3	28.8	66
Sosa, Raymond	R-R	6-4	185	5-03-06	0	0	5.40	13	0	0	17	13	15	10	0	22	11	.220	.484	.288	11.8	23.7	93
Suero, Rafael	R-R	6-2	180	5-07-06	1	0	1.29	13	0	1	21	11	4	3	1	17	17	.155	.322	.239	18.9	18.9	90
Torres, Eduardo	R-R	6-2	155	12-23-03	0	2	1.86	16	0	1	19	7	5	4	0	21	21	.121	.388	.190	24.4	24.4	86
Vasquez, Jairo	R-R	6-1	160	1-16-02	2	1	5.93	7	0	1	14	18	13	9	1	8	10	.310	.437	.448	14.1	11.3	71
Velasco, Kevin	R-R	6-11	155	1-11-06	3	1	4.68	11	2	0	25	29	13	13	2	6	20	.299	.340	.505	18.7	5.6	107
Yan, Jose	R-R	6-2	200	10-15-00	0	0	21.00	9	0	1	9	14	23	21	0	17	8	.350	.567	.550	13.3	28.3	60

Fielding

C: Rodriguez 36, Mejia 30, Nolaya 28, Robain 13, Noguera 11, Ortega 10. **1B:** Vicioso 42, Cuevas 20, Mejia 19, Noguera 15, Nolaya 11, Rodriguez 6, Martinez 5, Ortega 3, Feliciano 3, Liranzo 1, De Los Santos 1, Perez 1, Robain 1, Celedonio 1, Santos 1, Urbina 1. **2B:** De Los Santos 28, Ortiz 23, Perez 19, Amparo 13, Campos 11, Peguero 10, Mejia 9, Celedonio 7, Aybar 5, Frias 1, Guevara 1. **3B:** Liranzo 45, Peguero 22, Guevara 16, Cuevas 15, Campos 9, Almeyda 5, Celedonio 4, Santos 3. **SS:** Campos 32, Guevara 27, Amparo 23, Peguero 16, Almeyda 13, Aybar 3, Frias 2, Perez 2. **OF:** Jimenez 45, Mata 45, Ramirez 39, Rojas 37, Aybar 37, Cuevas 30, Ruiz 26, Leonte 19, Martinez 18, Perez 17, Sandoval 15, Celedonio 15, Feliciano 10, Ortiz 9, Peguero 7, Cohen 6, Vicioso 5, Robain 4, Frias 1.

Boston Red Sox

SEASON SYNOPSIS: The Red Sox were interesting in spurts but never for long en route to their third last-place finish in the last four seasons. The inability to contend and the lack of improvement cost general manager Chaim Bloom his job in his fourth year at the helm.

HIGH POINT: Boston took care of business against the Yankees all season, winning nine of 13, including a sweep at Yankee Stadium in mid-August that served to vault the Sox ahead of the Yanks in the wild-card standings. Justin Turner was the hero in the finale while another former Dodger, Kenley Jansen, got the save.

LOW POINT: Boston was still contending for the wild card and held a 4-3 lead against the Astros on at Fenway Park on Aug. 28—four days after splitting a four-game series in Houston—when Kyle Barraclough relieved Chris Sale in the fifth. While the journeyman Barraclough escaped the fifth, he gave up six runs in the sixth, but no one was warming up in Boston's bullpen. Manager Alex Cora left him in for the rest of the game as he gave up 10 runs in a 13-5 defeat that kicked off a 9-22 finishing stretch for the Sox.

NOTABLE ROOKIES: DH Masataka Yoshida arrived from Japan as a free agent and hit well enough, but his defense and stamina (he struggled with jet lag from the added travel) will need to improve. First baseman Triston Casas struggled early but caught fire in July and was one of the game's better offensive rookies, batting .263/.367/.490 with 24 homers in 502 plate appearances.

KEY TRANSACTIONS: Jansen (29 saves, 3.63 ERA) and Turner (.800 OPS, 23 HR) were free-agent signees who worked out well, while reliever Chris Martin (1.05 ERA) was an even better one. But veteran Corey Kluber (3-6, 7.04) couldn't contribute, and Bloom didn't do anything at the deadline to bolster a faltering rotation.

DOWN ON THE FARM: Outfielder Roman Anthony showed an excellent batting eye to go with promising power. The Red Sox aggressively moved him to High-A even though he was hitting .228/.376/.316. His underlying metrics were much better than that, which was quickly demonstrated when he became one of the best players in the South Atlantic League. He earned a late-season promotion to Double-A Portland. Shortstop Marcelo Mayer was a very smooth defender, but a shoulder injury hindered his hitting.

OPENING DAY PAYROLL: $181,207,484 (13th).

PLAYERS OF THE YEAR

MAJOR LEAGUE

Rafael Devers
3B
.271/.351/.500
33 HR
34 2B, 100 RBIs, 90 R

MINOR LEAGUE

Roman Anthony
OF
(LoA/HiA/AA)
.272/.403/.466,
14 HR, 14 SB

ORGANIZATION LEADERS

Batting — *Minimum 250 AB

MAJORS		
* AVG	Jarren Duran	.295
* OPS	Tristan Casas	.857
HR	Rafael Devers	33
RBI	Rafael Devers	100
MINORS		
* AVG	Ceddane Rafaela, Portland/Worcester	.302
* OBP	Niko Goodrum, Worcester	.448
* SLG	Bobby Dalbec, Worcester	.557
* OPS	Bobby Dalbec, Worcester	.938
R	Bobby Dalbec, Worcester	82
H	Blaze Jordan, Greenville/Portland	141
TB	Bobby Dalbec, Portland, Pawtucket	217
2B	Blaze Jordan, Greenville/Portland	32
3B	Ryan Fitzgerald, Worcester	8
3B	Bryan Gonzalez, Greenville	8
HR	Bobby Dalbec, Pawtucket	33
RBI	Blaze Jordan, Greenville/Portland	86
BB	Niko Kavadas,Portland/Worcester	98
SO	Niko Kavadas,Portland/Worcester	172
SB	David Hamilton, Worcester	57

Pitching — #Minimum 75 IP

MAJORS		
W	Eduardo Rodriguez	19
# ERA	Josh Winckowski	2.88
SO	Chris Sale	218
SV	Brandon Workman	16
MINORS		
W	Isaac Coffey, Greenville/Portland	11
L	Jose Ramirez, Salem	10
# ERA	Jedixson Paez, Salem	3.31
G	Andrew Politi, Worcester	54
GS	3-tied	25
SV	Luis Guerrero, Portland/Worcester	19
IP	Brian Van Belle, Portland/Worcester	141
BB	Noah Dean, Salem	72
SO	Wikelman Gonzalez, Greenville/Portland	168
# AVG	Wikelman Gonzalez, Greenville/Portland	.190

2023 PERFORMANCE

General Manager: Chaim Bloom. **Farm Director:** Brian Abraham. **Scouting Director:** Mike Rikard.

Class	Team	League	W	L	PCT	Finish	Manager
Majors	Boston Red Sox	American	78	84	.481	9 (15)	Alex Cora
Triple-A	Worcester Red Sox	International	79	68	.537	7 (20)	Chad Tracy
Double-A	Portland Sea Dogs	Eastern	73	63	.537	4 (12)	Chad Epperson
High-A	Greenville Drive	South Atlantic	63	69	.477	9 (12)	Iggy Suarez
Low-A	Salem Red Sox	Carolina	55	72	.433	11 (12)	Liam Carroll
Rookie	FCL Red Sox	Florida Complex	28	25	.528	7 (15)	Tom Kotchman
Rookie	DSL Red Sox Blue	Dominican Sum.	28	26	.519	22 (50)	Amaury Garcia
Rookie	DSL Red Sox Red	Dominican Sum.	26	26	.500	27 (50)	Sandy Madera
Overall 2023 Minor League Record			352	349	.502	14th (30)	

ORGANIZATION STATISTICS

BOSTON RED SOX

AMERICAN LEAGUE

Batting	B-T	Ht.	Wt.	DOB	AVG	OBP	SLG	G	PA	AB	R	H	2B	3B	HR	RBI	BB	HBP	SH	SF	SO	SB	CS	BB%	SO%
Abreu, Wilyer	L-L	5-10	217	6-24-99	.316	.388	.474	28	85	76	10	24	6	0	2	14	9	0	0	0	23	3	1	10.6	27.1
Alfaro, Jorge	R-R	6-3	230	6-11-93	.118	.250	.118	8	20	17	0	2	0	0	0	0	2	1	0	0	3	0	0	10.0	15.0
2-team (10 Colorado)					.146	.212	.292	18	52	48	2	7	4	0	1	4	2	2	0	0	15	0	0	3.8	28.8
Arroyo, Christian	R-R	6-1	210	5-30-95	.241	.268	.369	66	206	195	23	47	16	0	3	24	7	1	1	2	45	1	3	3.4	21.8
Casas, Triston	L-R	6-4	252	1-15-00	.263	.367	.490	132	502	429	66	113	21	2	24	65	70	1	0	2	126	0	0	13.9	25.1
Chang, Yu	R-R	6-1	180	8-18-95	.162	.200	.352	39	112	105	12	17	2	0	6	18	3	2	2	0	34	4	0	2.7	30.4
Crawford, Kutter	R-R	6-1	209	4-01-96	—	—	—	32	0	0	1	0	0	0	0	0	0	0	0	0	0	0	0	—	—
Dalbec, Bobby	R-R	6-4	227	6-29-95	.204	.264	.306	21	53	49	6	10	2	0	1	1	4	0	0	0	28	1	0	7.5	52.8
Devers, Rafael	L-R	6-0	240	10-24-96	.271	.351	.500	153	656	580	90	157	34	0	33	100	62	11	0	3	126	5	1	9.5	19.2
Duran, Jarren	L-R	6-2	212	9-05-96	.295	.346	.482	102	362	332	46	98	34	2	8	40	24	3	0	2	90	24	2	6.6	24.9
Duvall, Adam	R-R	6-1	215	9-04-88	.247	.303	.531	92	353	320	45	79	24	2	21	58	22	6	0	5	110	4	0	6.2	31.2
Hamilton, Caleb	R-R	6-0	185	2-05-95	.000	.167	.000	4	6	5	0	0	0	0	0	0	1	0	0	0	5	0	0	16.7	83.3
Hamilton, David	L-R	5-10	175	9-29-97	.121	.256	.182	15	39	33	2	4	2	0	0	0	6	0	0	0	10	2	1	15.4	25.6
Hernandez, Enrique	R-R	5-11	190	8-24-91	.222	.279	.320	86	323	297	38	66	11	0	6	31	22	2	0	2	68	3	1	6.8	21.1
2-team (54 Los Angeles Dodgers)					.237	.289	.357	140	508	465	57	110	23	0	11	61	34	3	0	6	97	4	1	6.7	19.1
McGuire, Reese	L-R	6-0	218	3-02-95	.267	.310	.358	72	206	187	15	50	12	1	1	16	11	1	2	1	53	2	1	5.3	25.7
Rafaela, Ceddanne	R-R	5-9	152	9-18-00	.241	.281	.386	28	89	83	11	20	6	0	2	5	4	1	0	1	28	3	1	4.5	31.5
Refsnyder, Rob	R-R	6-0	205	3-26-91	.248	.365	.317	89	243	202	31	50	9	1	1	28	33	5	1	1	47	7	2	13.6	19.3
Reyes, Pablo	R-R	5-8	175	9-05-93	.287	.339	.377	64	185	167	27	48	9	0	2	20	14	0	2	2	21	7	2	7.6	11.4
Story, Trevor	R-R	6-2	213	11-15-92	.203	.250	.316	43	168	158	12	32	9	0	3	14	9	1	0	0	55	10	3	5.4	32.7
Tapia, Raimel	L-L	6-3	175	2-04-94	.264	.333	.368	39	97	87	14	23	4	1	1	10	9	0	0	0	19	6	1	9.3	19.6
2-team (5 Tampa Bay)					.271	.346	.365	44	108	96	18	26	4	1	1	10	11	0	0	0	20	8	1	10.2	18.5
Turner, Justin	R-R	5-11	202	11-23-84	.276	.345	.455	146	626	558	86	154	31	0	23	96	51	11	0	6	110	4	1	8.1	17.6
Urias, Luis	R-R	5-10	202	6-03-97	.225	.361	.337	32	109	89	13	20	4	0	2	13	14	5	0	0	26	0	0	12.8	23.9
2-team (20 Milwaukee)					.194	.337	.299	52	177	144	18	28	6	0	3	18	21	10	0	0	41	0	0	11.9	23.2
Valdez, Enmanuel	L-R	5-8	191	12-28-98	.266	.311	.453	49	149	139	17	37	8	0	6	19	8	1	0	0	37	5	1	5.4	24.8
Verdugo, Alex	L-L	6-0	192	5-15-96	.264	.324	.421	142	602	546	81	144	37	5	13	54	45	6	0	5	93	5	3	7.5	15.4
Wong, Connor	R-R	6-1	181	5-19-96	.235	.288	.385	126	403	371	55	87	25	2	9	36	22	6	3	1	134	8	2	5.5	33.3
Yoshida, Masataka	L-R	5-8	176	7-15-93	.289	.338	.445	140	580	537	71	155	33	3	15	72	34	7	0	2	81	8	0	5.9	14.0

Pitching	B-T	Ht.	Wt.	DOB	W	L	ERA	G	GS	SV	IP	Hits	Runs	ER	HR	BB	SO	AVG	OBP	SLG	SO%	BB%	BF
Barraclough, Kyle	R-R	6-3	229	5-23-90	1	1	12.91	3	0	0	8	14	11	11	3	6	4	.400	.522	.743	8.7	13.0	46
Bello, Brayan	R-R	6-1	170	5-17-99	12	11	4.24	28	28	0	157	165	77	74	24	45	132	.270	.324	.453	19.8	6.7	668
Bernardino, Brennan	L-L	6-4	180	1-15-92	2	1	3.20	55	6	0	51	48	19	18	4	18	58	.250	.333	.375	26.9	8.3	216
Bleier, Richard	L-L	6-3	215	4-16-87	1	0	5.28	27	0	0	31	37	20	18	5	5	16	.306	.346	.479	12.1	3.8	132
Brasier, Ryan	R-R	6-0	227	8-26-87	1	0	7.29	20	0	1	21	24	18	17	2	9	18	.286	.368	.417	18.9	9.5	95
Crawford, Kutter	R-R	6-1	209	4-01-96	6	8	4.04	31	23	0	129	107	59	58	17	36	135	.221	.281	.388	25.6	6.8	527
Dermody, Matt	R-L	6-5	190	7-04-90	0	1	6.75	1	1	0	4	4	3	3	2	1	1	.267	.353	.667	5.9	5.9	17
Faria, Jake	R-R	6-4	230	7-30-93	0	0	22.50	1	0	0	2	4	5	5	0	4	3	.444	.571	.667	21.4	28.6	14
Garza, Justin	R-R	5-10	170	3-20-94	0	2	7.36	17	1	0	18	22	17	15	3	12	17	.286	.385	.506	18.7	13.2	91
Houck, Tanner	R-R	6-5	230	6-29-96	6	10	5.01	21	21	0	106	104	61	59	14	41	99	.254	.328	.415	21.4	8.9	463
Jacques, Joe	L-L	6-4	210	3-11-95	2	1	5.06	23	1	1	27	32	17	15	2	10	20	.308	.397	.452	16.4	8.2	122
Jansen, Kenley	B-R	6-5	265	9-30-87	3	6	3.63	51	0	29	45	40	21	18	5	17	52	.237	.314	.379	27.7	9.0	188
Kelly, Zack	R-R	6-3	205	3-03-95	0	0	3.86	8	0	0	9	7	4	4	0	8	6	.219	.405	.375	14.0	18.6	43
Kluber, Corey	R-R	6-4	215	4-10-86	3	6	7.04	15	9	1	55	69	47	43	17	21	42	.297	.366	.603	16.3	8.2	257
Lamet, Dinelson	R-R	6-3	228	7-18-92	0	0	13.50	1	0	0	2	4	3	3	1	1	1	.400	.455	.700	9.1	9.1	11
Littell, Zack	R-R	6-4	220	10-05-95	0	0	9.00	2	0	0	3	3	3	3	0	3	2	.250	.400	.417	13.3	20.0	15
Llovera, Mauricio	R-R	5-11	224	4-17-96	1	3	5.46	25	0	0	30	32	24	18	2	13	24	.264	.353	.364	17.3	9.4	139
Martin, Chris	R-R	6-8	225	6-02-86	4	1	1.05	55	0	3	51	45	6	6	2	8	46	.237	.266	.300	23.1	4.0	199
Murphy, Chris	L-L	6-1	175	6-05-98	1	2	4.91	20	0	1	48	50	27	26	5	17	49	.263	.324	.416	23.1	8.0	212
Ort, Kaleb	R-R	6-4	240	2-05-92	1	2	6.26	21	2	0	23	27	19	16	6	9	24	.290	.356	.548	22.4	8.4	107
Paxton, James	L-L	6-4	227	11-06-88	7	5	4.50	19	19	0	96	93	51	48	18	33	101	.250	.313	.452	24.6	8.0	411

Pivetta, Nick	R-R	6-5	214	2-14-93	10	9	4.04	38	16	1	143	110	69	64	23	50	183	.208	.283	.402	31.2	8.5	587
Reyes, Pablo	R-R	5-8	175	9-05-93	0	0	4.50	2	0	0	2	3	1	1	0	4	0	.333	.538	.333	0.0	30.8	13
Robertson, Nick	R-R	6-6	265	7-16-98	0	0	6.00	9	1	0	12	13	9	8	2	5	13	.265	.327	.490	23.2	8.9	56
Rodriguez, Joely	L-L	6-1	200	11-14-91	0	0	6.55	11	0	0	11	13	9	8	2	6	14	.289	.373	.489	27.5	11.8	51
Sale, Chris	L-L	6-6	183	3-30-89	6	5	4.30	20	20	0	103	87	52	49	15	29	125	.227	.292	.417	29.4	6.8	425
Schreiber, John	R-R	6-2	210	3-05-94	2	1	3.86	46	2	1	47	41	22	20	6	25	53	.237	.343	.399	26.0	12.3	204
Scott, Tayler	R-R	6-3	185	6-01-92	0	0	4.91	4	1	0	4	6	3	2	1	4	2	.400	.550	.733	10.0	20.0	20
Sherriff, Ryan	L-L	6-1	190	5-25-90	0	0	2.70	5	0	0	7	6	2	2	0	2	5	.240	.310	.440	17.2	6.9	29
Walter, Brandon	L-L	6-2	200	9-08-96	0	0	6.26	9	0	1	23	32	17	16	3	7	16	.327	.377	.490	15.1	6.6	106
Weiss, Zack	R-R	6-3	210	6-16-92	0	0	2.08	6	0	0	9	3	3	2	2	4	8	.107	.212	.357	24.2	12.1	33
Whitlock, Garrett	R-R	6-5	225	6-11-96	5	5	5.15	22	10	1	72	82	43	41	13	13	72	.288	.323	.502	23.7	4.3	304
Winckowski, Josh	R-R	6-4	202	6-28-98	4	4	2.88	60	1	3	84	89	34	27	9	31	82	.267	.335	.393	22.3	8.4	367

Fielding

Catcher	PCT	G	PO	A	E	DP	PB
Alfaro	.957	6	39	5	2	0	0
Hamilton	1.000	4	16	1	0	0	0
McGuire	.998	62	451	15	1	1	1
Wong	.989	121	953	45	11	7	7

First Base	PCT	G	PO	A	E	DP
Casas	.995	125	858	95	5	89
Chang	1.000	2	5	2	0	2
Dalbec	1.000	15	80	7	0	7
Reyes	.000	2	0	0	0	0
Turner	.989	41	240	25	3	28

Second Base	PCT	G	PO	A	E	DP
Arroyo	.992	62	105	146	2	45
Chang	1.000	4	1	3	0	0
Dalbec	1.000	1	1	0	0	0
Hamilton	1.000	2	6	4	0	0
Hernandez	.984	21	25	36	1	10
Rafaela	1.000	4	1	2	0	1
Reyes	.943	30	32	34	4	5
Turner	1.000	10	4	13	0	3
Urias	.979	28	40	54	2	14
Valdez	.959	47	54	110	7	21
Wong	1.000	4	1	1	0	0

Third Base	PCT	G	PO	A	E	DP
Arroyo	1.000	4	2	1	0	1
Chang	.000	1	0	0	0	0
Dalbec	1.000	2	1	3	0	1
Devers	.949	151	104	247	19	24
Reyes	1.000	4	0	2	0	0
Turner	.842	7	4	12	3	3
Urias	1.000	8	6	8	0	2

Shortstop	PCT	G	PO	A	E	DP
Arroyo	1.000	4	6	7	0	2
Chang	.991	33	37	74	1	23
Dalbec	.833	1	1	4	1	0
Devers	.000	1	0	0	0	0
Hamilton	.957	13	13	31	2	9
Hernandez	.935	64	69	134	14	28
Rafaela	.923	5	5	7	1	2
Reyes	.972	31	36	67	3	12
Story	.986	36	39	100	2	16
Valdez	1.000	1	0	1	0	0

Outfield	PCT	G	PO	A	E	DP
Abreu	.889	27	40	2	1	1
Duran	.657	103	168	2	1	1
Duvall	1.000	94	152	4	0	3
Hernandez	1.000	14	19	0	0	0
Rafaela	1.000	20	24	0	0	0
Refsnyder	1.000	75	81	5	0	0
Tapia	1.000	29	37	1	0	0
Verdugo	.990	140	293	12	3	4
Yoshida	.977	87	125	5	3	1

WORCESTER RED SOX — *TRIPLE-A*

INTERNATIONAL LEAGUE

Batting	B-T	Ht.	Wt.	DOB	AVG	OBP	SLG	G	PA	AB	R	H	2B	3B	HR	RBI	BB	HBP	SH	SF	SO	SB	CS	BB%	SO%
Abreu, Wilyer	L-L	5-10	217	6-24-99	.274	.391	.538	86	363	299	67	82	11	1	22	65	59	1	0	4	74	8	1	16.3	20.4
Alfaro, Jorge	R-R	6-3	230	6-11-93	.320	.366	.520	43	191	175	22	56	13	2	6	30	9	5	0	2	43	4	0	4.7	22.5
2-team (18 Jacksonville)					.288	.345	.450	61	264	240	25	69	17	2	6	36	14	7	0	3	60	4	0	5.3	1.1
Allen, Greg	B-R	6-0	185	3-15-93	.250	.407	.388	37	151	116	25	29	8	1	2	15	21	11	1	2	29	23	0	13.9	19.2
2-team (4 Scranton/Wilkes-Barre)					.242	.385	.366	49	203	161	32	39	9	1	3	19	25	13	1	3	39	26	2	12.3	19.2
Alvarez, Eddy	L-R	5-8	178	1-30-90	1.000	1.000	1.000	1	2	1	0	1	0	0	0	0	1	0	0	0	0	1	0	50.0	0.0
2-team (63 Nashville)					.286	.402	.476	64	259	206	42	59	14	2	7	31	37	6	5	5	58	17	2	14.3	22.4
Arroyo, Christian	R-R	6-1	210	5-30-95	.138	.211	.169	18	71	65	5	9	2	0	0	2	6	0	0	0	12	1	0	8.5	16.9
Chang, Yu	R-R	6-1	180	8-18-95	.323	.364	.500	16	66	62	10	20	2	0	3	10	4	0	0	0	13	2	0	6.1	19.7
Crook, Narciso	R-R	6-3	220	7-12-95	.216	.335	.392	93	325	273	46	59	14	2	10	36	40	10	0	2	117	11	4	12.3	36.0
Dalbec, Bobby	R-R	6-4	227	6-29-95	.269	.381	.557	114	493	413	82	111	14	3	33	79	64	13	0	3	169	18	2	13.0	34.3
Dearden, Tyler	L-R	6-2	185	7-06-98	.125	.125	.125	2	8	8	0	1	0	0	0	1	0	0	0	0	2	0	0	0.0	25.0
Diaz, Edwin	R-R	6-1	223	8-25-95	.333	.600	1.333	2	5	3	1	1	0	0	1	1	1	1	0	0	2	0	0	20.0	40.0
Duran, Jarren	L-R	6-2	212	9-05-96	.195	.353	.439	11	51	41	8	8	2	1	2	6	10	0	0	0	11	2	0	19.6	21.6
Duvall, Adam	R-R	6-1	215	9-04-88	.208	.345	.500	7	29	24	5	5	1	0	2	3	5	0	0	0	8	0	0	17.2	27.6
Ferguson, Max	L-R	6-0	180	8-23-99	.083	.077	.167	5	13	12	0	1	1	0	0	1	0	0	0	1	6	0	0	0.0	46.2
Fitzgerald, Ryan	L-R	6-0	185	6-17-94	.261	.345	.484	95	369	322	51	84	24	6	12	56	41	2	0	3	99	9	7	11.1	26.8
Goodrum, Niko	B-R	6-3	215	2-28-92	.280	.448	.440	65	286	218	49	61	9	1	8	36	66	1	0	1	60	7	3	23.1	21.0
Hamilton, Caleb	R-R	6-0	185	2-05-95	.167	.270	.304	42	159	138	14	23	7	0	4	14	19	1	0	1	55	0	0	11.9	34.6
Hamilton, David	L-R	5-10	175	9-29-97	.247	.363	.438	103	469	393	74	97	16	4	17	54	71	2	1	2	109	57	14	15.1	23.2
Hernandez, Ronaldo	R-R	6-1	230	11-11-97	.242	.336	.445	99	393	335	49	81	17	0	17	70	41	10	0	7	69	2	0	10.4	17.6
Kavadas, Niko	L-R	5-11	235	10-27-98	.209	.364	.426	48	187	148	27	31	8	0	8	27	35	2	0	2	62	0	0	18.7	33.2
Koss, Christian	R-R	6-1	182	1-27-98	.237	.285	.351	34	124	114	13	27	8	1	1	10	5	3	1	1	26	2	1	4.0	21.0
McDonough, Tyler	B-R	5-8	180	4-02-99	.250	.308	.500	4	14	12	1	3	1	1	0	0	1	0	0	0	3	0	0	7.1	21.4
McGuire, Reese	L-R	6-0	218	3-02-95	.200	.273	.300	3	11	10	0	2	1	0	0	1	1	0	0	0	2	0	0	9.1	18.2
Palka, Daniel	L-L	6-2	230	10-28-91	.233	.309	.410	79	314	283	44	66	12	1	12	48	30	1	0	0	72	3	2	9.6	22.9
2-team (23 Syracuse)					.237	.311	.420	102	412	371	55	88	15	1	17	60	38	2	0	0	96	3	2	9.2	23.3
Rafaela, Ceddanne	R-R	5-9	152	9-18-00	.312	.370	.618	48	219	199	40	62	13	3	14	42	12	7	0	1	48	6	5	5.5	21.9
Rangel, Oscar	L-R	5-11	184	5-27-98	.000	.000	.000	1	1	1	0	0	0	0	0	0	0	0	0	0	1	0	0	0.0	100.0
Reyes, Pablo	R-R	5-8	175	9-05-93	.280	.308	.520	7	26	25	6	7	0	0	2	4	1	0	0	0	2	1	0	3.8	7.7
Rosier, Corey	L-R	5-10	180	9-07-99	.282	.364	.359	12	44	39	6	11	3	0	0	2	4	1	0	0	10	0	1	9.1	22.7
Scott, Stephen	L-R	5-11	207	5-23-97	.228	.339	.470	63	254	215	36	49	11	1	13	44	35	2	0	2	51	2	1	13.8	20.1
Sogard, Nick	B-R	6-1	180	9-09-97	.266	.370	.391	112	460	391	74	104	20	4	7	47	63	3	1	2	79	17	7	13.7	17.2
Story, Trevor	R-R	6-2	213	11-15-92	.313	.421	.719	10	38	32	6	10	4	0	3	6	5	1	0	0	8	1	0	13.2	21.1
Valdez, Enmanuel	L-R	5-8	191	12-28-98	.254	.388	.476	57	232	189	38	48	8	2	10	41	41	1	0	1	48	4	3	17.7	20.7
Wilson, Marcus	R-R	6-2	198	8-15-96	.153	.265	.254	37	68	59	12	9	3	0	1	4	9	0	0	0	32	5	0	13.2	47.1
Zimmer, Bradley	L-R	6-2	185	11-27-92	.199	.321	.340	47	184	156	23	31	3	2	5	17	21	7	0	0	68	11	5	11.4	37.0

Pitching	B-T	Ht.	Wt.	DOB	W	L	ERA	G	GS	SV	IP	Hits	Runs	ER	HR	BB	SO	AVG	OBP	SLG	SO%	BB%	BF
Barraclough, Kyle	R-R	6-3	229	5-23-90	8	1	3.65	14	13	0	74	52	30	30	9	45	62	.204	.330	.357	20.4	14.8	304
Bello, Brayan	R-R	6-1	170	5-17-99	0	0	1.50	1	1	0	6	4	1	1	1	0	4	.190	.227	.381	18.2	0.0	22
Bernardino, Brennan	L-L	6-4	180	1-15-92	1	0	1.80	3	0	0	5	3	2	1	0	3	6	.167	.318	.222	27.3	13.6	22
Bleier, Richard	L-L	6-3	215	4-16-87	0	0	0.00	3	0	0	4	1	0	0	0	0	3	.083	.083	.167	25.0	0.0	12
Booser, Cam	L-L	6-3	225	5-04-92	4	3	4.99	48	0	1	58	54	38	32	11	24	66	.245	.320	.464	26.7	9.7	247
Broadway, Taylor	R-R	5-11	205	4-08-97	1	1	6.34	22	1	0	33	37	28	23	11	16	28	.287	.366	.628	19.3	11.0	145
Crawford, Kutter	R-R	6-1	209	4-01-96	1	0	3.00	1	0	0	3	3	1	1	1	0	4	.250	.250	.583	33.3	0.0	12
Denlinger, Theo	R-R	6-3	240	7-10-96	2	0	6.89	11	0	0	16	11	14	12	2	17	17	.196	.408	.357	22.4	22.4	76
Dermody, Matt	R-L	6-5	190	7-04-90	3	2	4.59	10	9	0	49	56	29	25	7	11	52	.284	.332	.462	24.1	5.1	216
Drohan, Shane	L-L	6-3	195	1-07-99	5	7	6.47	21	19	0	89	103	68	64	19	63	93	.293	.404	.548	21.9	14.9	424
Faria, Jake	R-R	6-4	230	7-30-93	3	2	6.38	21	9	0	61	60	54	43	10	36	53	.254	.365	.449	18.7	12.7	283
Feltman, Durbin	R-R	6-0	208	4-18-97	0	0	6.75	2	0	0	3	2	2	2	2	1	4	.182	.250	.727	33.3	8.3	12
Fernandez, Ryan	R-R	6-0	170	6-11-98	3	3	6.16	26	0	0	31	38	23	21	7	10	35	.302	.348	.548	25.2	7.2	139
Gambrell, Grant	L-R	6-4	225	11-21-97	1	1	1.69	2	2	0	11	7	2	2	1	5	14	.189	.286	.270	33.3	11.9	42
Garza, Justin	R-R	5-10	170	3-20-94	2	1	4.82	24	0	2	28	28	15	15	3	14	28	.269	.358	.385	23.1	11.6	121
Gillaspie, Logan	R-R	6-2	215	4-17-97	0	0	0.00	4	0	1	4	3	0	0	0	1	4	.188	.235	.188	23.5	5.9	17
Gomez, Rio	L-L	6-0	190	10-20-94	0	3	4.45	16	12	0	57	60	30	28	11	32	63	.268	.359	.487	24.3	12.4	259
Gudino, Norwith	R-R	6-2	200	11-22-95	4	4	5.73	22	8	0	55	63	40	35	5	29	33	.275	.360	.424	12.6	11.1	261
Guerrero, Luis	R-R	6-0	215	8-05-00	0	1	7.71	6	0	1	5	4	4	4	1	7	9	.222	.440	.389	36.0	28.0	25
Hagenman, Justin	R-R	6-3	205	10-07-96	2	0	3.26	16	0	1	30	25	11	11	5	14	28	.231	.320	.398	22.6	11.3	124
Houck, Tanner	R-R	6-5	230	6-29-96	0	0	2.08	3	3	0	9	5	2	2	0	3	10	.156	.229	.156	28.6	8.6	35
Jacques, Joe	L-L	6-4	210	3-11-95	1	3	2.54	33	1	1	39	32	15	11	4	13	35	.224	.306	.336	21.6	8.0	162
Kelly, Zack	R-R	6-3	205	3-03-95	0	1	18.00	3	0	0	2	3	4	4	2	1	3	.333	.400	1.000	30.0	10.0	10
Kluber, Corey	R-R	6-4	215	4-10-86	0	1	4.76	3	2	0	6	5	3	3	1	1	5	.227	.261	.364	21.7	4.3	23
Lamet, Dinelson	R-R	6-3	228	7-18-92	0	0	3.72	5	4	0	19	17	8	8	4	7	16	.236	.304	.444	20.0	8.8	80
Martin, Chris	R-R	6-8	225	6-02-86	1	0	0.00	1	0	0	1	2	2	0	0	0	0	.333	.333	.333	0.0	0.0	6
Mata, Bryan	R-R	6-3	238	5-03-99	0	3	6.33	9	7	0	27	29	21	19	1	30	28	.274	.447	.358	19.9	21.3	141
Mosqueda, Oddanier	L-L	5-10	155	5-06-99	4	4	5.31	48	3	0	61	53	41	36	10	39	74	.231	.367	.406	26.2	13.8	282
Murphy, Chris	L-L	6-1	175	6-05-98	2	3	6.32	15	9	0	53	63	41	37	7	31	61	.293	.393	.447	24.2	12.3	252
Nail, Brendan	R-L	6-0	190	10-18-95	2	2	4.85	20	0	3	26	30	15	14	4	16	28	.294	.407	.461	22.6	12.9	124
Nunez, Andres	R-R	6-4	240	9-20-95	1	0	5.31	16	1	1	20	21	12	12	2	15	16	.259	.378	.395	16.3	15.3	98
Ort, Kaleb	R-R	6-4	240	2-05-92	1	2	1.54	13	0	1	12	8	4	2	1	8	16	.182	.321	.295	30.2	15.1	53
Paxton, James	L-L	6-4	227	11-06-88	2	3	6.23	6	5	0	22	18	16	15	2	16	26	.217	.340	.373	26.0	16.0	100
Politi, Andrew	R-R	6-0	195	6-04-96	7	5	4.45	54	0	15	59	57	35	29	6	28	60	.250	.341	.390	22.8	10.6	263
Robertson, Nick	R-R	6-6	265	7-16-98	2	1	4.40	15	0	2	14	14	9	7	3	4	16	.241	.302	.448	25.4	6.3	63
Rodriguez, Joely	L-L	6-1	200	11-14-91	1	0	4.50	7	0	0	6	11	3	3	0	1	9	.407	.429	.481	31.0	3.4	29
Sale, Chris	L-L	6-6	183	3-30-89	0	0	0.00	2	2	0	6	4	0	0	0	2	10	.174	.240	.217	40.0	8.0	25
Schreiber, John	R-R	6-2	210	3-05-94	0	0	2.45	4	0	0	4	2	1	1	1	1	3	.154	.214	.385	21.4	7.1	14
Scott, Tayler	R-R	6-3	185	6-01-92	0	0	3.00	2	0	0	3	5	1	1	1	0	2	.357	.357	.571	14.3	0.0	14
Sherriff, Ryan	L-L	6-1	190	5-25-90	2	1	2.82	21	0	2	22	17	9	7	2	10	24	.207	.301	.366	25.8	10.8	93
Shugart, Chase	L-R	5-10	198	10-24-96	4	1	8.22	40	2	4	46	62	44	42	11	24	39	.320	.393	.567	17.8	11.0	219
Thompson, Jake	R-R	6-0	215	9-22-94	1	0	5.40	8	0	0	10	15	8	6	0	5	6	.349	.444	.465	10.9	9.1	55
Van Belle, Brian	R-R	6-3	185	9-03-96	5	4	6.41	13	12	0	60	69	45	43	18	25	65	.282	.348	.559	23.7	9.1	274
Walter, Brandon	L-L	6-2	200	9-08-96	3	5	4.60	21	18	0	94	99	53	48	10	35	88	.268	.336	.407	21.3	8.5	413
Weiss, Zack	R-R	6-3	210	6-16-92	0	0	0.00	4	0	0	4	2	0	0	0	2	6	.154	.267	.231	40.0	13.3	15
Whitlock, Garrett	R-R	6-5	225	6-11-96	0	0	1.20	4	4	0	15	17	2	2	1	2	17	.293	.328	.448	27.4	3.2	62

Fielding

Catcher	PCT	G	PO	A	E	DP	PB
Alfaro	1.000	27	218	8	0	1	6
Hamilton	.980	38	334	16	7	0	9
Hernandez	.986	52	449	32	7	4	5
McGuire	1.000	3	18	1	0	0	0
Scott	1.000	32	266	8	0	0	6

First Base	PCT	G	PO	A	E	DP
Alfaro	.947	2	16	2	1	2
Chang	1.000	3	13	1	0	0
Crook	.980	9	43	7	1	6
Dalbec	.986	28	201	16	3	23
Fitzgerald	1.000	1	2	0	0	0
Goodrum	.991	30	202	17	2	19
Hamilton	1.000	1	3	0	0	1
Kavadas	.988	46	312	23	4	38
Palka	.977	25	149	18	4	15
Scott	.979	12	87	7	2	9

Second Base	PCT	G	PO	A	E	DP
Alvarez	1.000	1	1	2	0	0
Arroyo	.917	6	6	5	1	2
Chang	1.000	2	3	5	0	2
Ferguson	1.000	4	8	6	0	2
Fitzgerald	1.000	19	23	34	0	7
Goodrum	.990	22	39	56	1	14
Hamilton	1.000	14	21	31	0	9
Koss	.895	3	8	9	2	2
McDonough	.909	3	4	6	1	2
Reyes	.917	5	5	6	1	2
Sogard	.993	37	58	81	1	25
Valdez	.982	50	65	99	3	21

Third Base	PCT	G	PO	A	E	DP
Chavis	.933	7	3	11	1	1
Arroyo	.947	6	4	14	1	1
Chang	1.000	3	2	4	0	0
Dalbec	.928	43	27	76	8	10
Fitzgerald	.966	44	16	69	3	7
Goodrum	.895	12	10	24	4	3
Hamilton	.667	1	0	2	1	0
Koss	.846	6	3	8	2	1
McDonough	.667	1	2	0	1	0
Sogard	.967	42	27	61	3	4
Valdez	.857	2	3	3	1	0

Shortstop	PCT	G	PO	A	E	DP
Arroyo	1.000	5	4	6	0	0
Chang	.880	8	6	16	3	3
Dalbec	.944	6	5	12	1	2
Diaz	1.000	2	1	2	0	0
Fitzgerald	1.000	1	0	1	0	0
Hamilton	.969	85	110	200	10	49
Koss	.952	20	26	54	4	15
Rafaela	1.000	6	5	15	0	1
Sogard	.925	21	23	39	5	9
Story	1.000	7	9	10	0	4

Outfield	PCT	G	PO	A	E	DP
Abreu	.985	80	138	10	2	1
Allen	.991	37	72	0	1	0
Crook	.956	81	153	2	5	0
Dalbec	.949	36	70	4	4	0
Dearden	1.000	2	3	0	0	0
Duran	1.000	10	19	0	0	0
Duvall	1.000	6	13	0	0	0
Ferguson	1.000	1	1	0	0	0
Fitzgerald	.984	34	56	1	1	0
Goodrum	.000	1	0	0	0	0
Hamilton	1.000	6	12	1	0	0
Koss	.833	6	3	0	1	0
Palka	.978	27	43	2	1	0
Rafaela	1.000	41	114	2	0	0
Rosier	.976	12	24	2	1	1
Sogard	.916	19	22	0	2	0
Wilson	.986	29	28	2	1	0
Zimmer	.952	49	88	1	2	0

PORTLAND SEA DOGS

DOUBLE-A

EASTERN LEAGUE

Batting	B-T	Ht.	Wt.	DOB	AVG	OBP	SLG	G	PA	AB	R	H	2B	3B	HR	RBI	BB	HBP	SH	SF	SO	SB	CS	BB%	SO%
Anthony, Roman	L-R	6-2	200	5-13-04	.343	.477	.543	10	44	35	10	12	4	0	1	8	8	1	0	0	6	3	0	18.2	13.6
Binelas, Alex	L-R	6-1	225	5-26-00	.223	.296	.459	82	328	296	47	66	18	2	16	52	30	1	0	1	115	13	2	9.1	35.1
Bonaci, Brainer	B-R	5-10	164	7-09-02	.279	.361	.426	16	72	61	10	17	3	0	2	7	9	0	0	2	17	1	1	12.5	23.6
Chang, Yu	R-R	6-1	180	8-18-95	.071	.133	.071	4	15	14	1	1	0	0	0	0	1	0	0	0	4	0	0	6.7	26.7
Dearden, Tyler	L-R	6-2	185	7-06-98	.270	.361	.411	71	286	248	34	67	12	1	7	41	33	3	1	1	70	0	1	11.5	24.5
Diaz, Edwin	R-R	6-1	223	8-25-95	.091	.167	.295	13	48	44	3	4	1	1	2	7	4	0	0	0	19	0	0	8.3	39.6
Donlan, Matt	R-R	6-3	213	11-09-99	.222	.382	.296	10	34	27	3	6	2	0	0	2	6	1	0	0	7	0	0	17.6	20.6
Erro, Alex	B-R	5-9	182	12-05-97	.286	.382	.429	9	34	28	7	8	1	0	1	9	5	0	0	1	7	0	0	14.7	20.6
Esplin, Tyler	L-R	6-2	230	7-06-99	.265	.296	.441	21	71	68	9	18	7	1	1	18	2	1	0	0	22	0	0	2.8	31.0
Hickey, Nathan	L-R	5-11	210	11-23-99	.258	.352	.474	80	335	291	49	75	18	0	15	56	40	3	0	1	91	3	0	11.9	27.2
Jordan, Blaze	R-R	6-2	220	12-19-02	.254	.296	.402	49	203	189	19	48	10	0	6	31	12	0	0	2	28	0	0	5.9	13.8
Kavadas, Niko	L-R	5-11	235	10-27-98	.204	.386	.430	69	293	221	35	45	8	0	14	42	63	5	0	4	110	2	0	21.5	37.5
Koss, Christian	R-R	6-1	182	1-27-98	.224	.283	.336	38	147	134	18	30	7	1	2	10	10	1	2	0	33	11	1	6.8	22.4
Lugo, Matthew	R-R	6-1	187	5-09-01	.242	.297	.381	83	322	289	37	70	23	1	5	37	19	5	1	4	89	8	4	5.9	27.6
Marrero, Elih	B-R	5-7	185	6-21-97	.269	.397	.370	37	131	108	18	29	8	0	1	10	22	1	0	0	33	8	7	16.8	25.2
Mayer, Marcelo	L-R	6-2	188	12-12-02	.189	.254	.355	43	190	169	20	32	8	1	6	20	15	1	0	4	49	4	3	7.9	25.8
McDonough, Tyler	B-R	5-8	180	4-02-99	.250	.326	.370	97	365	316	50	79	15	4	5	35	35	3	1	5	97	24	7	9.6	26.6
Meidroth, Chase	R-R	5-9	170	7-23-01	.255	.386	.375	91	396	325	59	83	16	1	7	43	59	11	0	1	78	9	1	14.9	19.7
Miller, Ryan	R-R	6-0	180	3-28-96	.000	.000	.000	41	1	1	0	0	0	0	0	0	0	0	0	0	1	0	0	0.0	100.0
Rafaela, Ceddanne	R-R	5-9	152	9-18-00	.294	.332	.441	60	266	245	40	72	18	0	6	37	14	2	1	4	55	30	8	5.3	20.7
Reyes, Pablo	R-R	5-8	175	9-05-93	.222	.364	.370	7	33	27	4	6	1	0	1	3	6	0	0	0	6	3	0	18.2	18.2
Rosier, Corey	L-R	5-10	180	9-07-99	.285	.349	.439	104	400	358	64	102	22	6	7	39	33	4	2	3	86	49	7	8.3	21.5
Scott, Stephen	L-R	5-11	207	5-23-97	.248	.369	.448	37	149	125	23	31	5	1	6	22	24	0	0	0	34	4	1	16.1	22.8
Sikes, Phillip	R-R	6-2	190	4-27-99	.210	.296	.333	111	476	414	69	87	18	3	9	43	44	10	0	8	146	39	7	9.2	30.7
Story, Trevor	R-R	6-2	213	11-15-92	.250	.400	.625	3	10	8	2	2	0	0	1	3	2	0	0	0	5	0	0	20.0	50.0
Teel, Kyle	L-R	6-1	190	2-15-02	.323	.462	.484	9	39	31	3	10	2	0	1	11	8	0	0	0	11	2	0	20.5	28.2
Yorke, Nick	R-R	5-11	200	4-02-02	.268	.350	.435	110	506	444	74	119	25	5	13	61	51	7	0	4	122	18	5	10.1	24.1

Pitching	B-T	Ht.	Wt.	DOB	W	L	ERA	G	GS	SV	IP	Hits	Runs	ER	HR	BB	SO	AVG	OBP	SLG	SO%	BB%	BF
Arias, Skylar	L-L	6-3	204	6-30-97	1	0	4.07	14	1	0	24	20	12	11	2	17	34	.225	.351	.393	30.6	15.3	111
Bastardo, Angel	R-R	6-1	175	6-18-02	0	1	5.06	3	3	0	16	12	9	9	3	9	10	.207	.319	.448	14.5	13.0	69
Bleier, Richard	L-L	6-3	215	4-16-87	0	0	0.00	1	1	0	1	1	0	0	0	0	2	.250	.250	.250	50.0	0.0	4
Broadway, Taylor	R-R	5-11	205	4-08-97	1	0	0.00	3	0	0	4	4	0	0	0	0	4	.250	.250	.313	25.0	0.0	16
Cellucci, Brendan	L-L	6-4	211	6-30-98	1	2	5.29	37	0	0	51	60	36	30	7	33	63	.291	.394	.451	26.1	13.7	241
Coffey, Isaac	R-R	6-1	205	6-21-00	7	4	3.92	12	11	0	57	46	27	25	11	23	72	.215	.313	.407	28.7	9.2	251
Denlinger, Theo	R-R	6-3	240	7-10-96	2	4	4.70	24	0	0	31	25	19	16	1	15	34	.221	.323	.319	25.4	11.2	134
Dobbins, Hunter	R-R	6-2	185	8-30-99	5	5	4.27	13	12	0	72	69	36	34	8	26	78	.250	.320	.377	25.4	8.5	307
Drohan, Shane	L-L	6-3	195	1-07-99	5	0	1.32	6	6	0	34	19	5	5	1	9	36	.161	.227	.186	28.1	7.0	128
Fernandez, Ryan	R-R	6-0	170	6-11-98	2	1	1.77	14	0	1	20	14	5	4	1	8	26	.192	.272	.247	32.1	9.9	81
Gambrell, Grant	L-R	6-4	225	11-21-97	6	3	3.42	15	15	0	84	71	34	32	10	32	84	.227	.296	.377	23.8	9.1	353
Gomez, Rio	L-L	6-0	190	10-20-94	2	2	6.41	10	1	1	20	14	16	14	3	11	25	.194	.326	.361	29.1	12.8	86
Gonzalez, Wikelman	R-R	6-0	167	3-25-02	3	1	2.42	10	10	0	48	27	15	13	2	28	63	.162	.288	.228	31.8	14.1	198
Guerrero, Luis	R-R	6-0	215	8-05-00	3	2	1.81	43	0	18	50	26	14	10	2	30	59	.150	.279	.249	27.8	14.2	212
Hoppe, Alex	R-R	6-1	200	12-17-98	1	1	4.50	12	0	2	14	12	7	7	3	3	16	.226	.263	.415	28.1	5.3	57
Jones, Joe	R-R	6-5	245	7-22-95	2	1	3.79	18	3	2	19	10	8	8	2	13	18	.156	.333	.266	22.0	15.9	82
Kelly, Zack	R-R	6-3	205	3-03-95	0	0	4.50	1	1	0	2	1	1	1	1	0	1	.167	.167	.667	14.3	0.0	7
Kluber, Corey	R-R	6-4	215	4-10-86	0	0	0.00	1	0	0	2	1	0	0	0	0	1	.143	.143	.143	14.3	0.0	7
Kwiatkowski, Robert	R-R	6-1	190	6-08-97	0	0	3.78	8	2	1	17	10	7	7	2	5	12	.179	.242	.357	19.4	8.1	62
Liu, Chih-Jung	B-R	6-0	185	4-07-99	7	8	5.35	26	24	0	114	117	74	68	19	61	145	.268	.366	.437	28.4	12.0	510
Miller, Ryan	R-R	6-0	180	3-28-96	5	3	4.03	41	1	2	60	63	30	27	8	19	67	.269	.331	.415	25.8	7.3	260
Nail, Brendan	R-L	6-0	190	10-18-95	1	1	0.99	14	5	1	27	15	10	3	2	10	26	.161	.266	.258	23.6	9.1	110
Olds, Wyatt	R-R	6-0	183	8-05-99	0	7	8.47	23	8	0	46	42	45	43	4	47	54	.243	.430	.405	22.8	19.8	237
Rodriguez, Joely	L-L	6-1	200	11-14-91	0	0	1.69	5	0	0	5	3	1	1	1	2	6	.167	.250	.333	30.0	10.0	20
Schreiber, John	R-R	6-2	210	3-05-94	0	0	0.00	2	0	0	2	0	0	0	0	0	3	.000	.000	.000	50.0	0.0	6
Scroggins, Cody	R-R	6-0	195	8-17-96	0	1	4.70	5	0	0	8	6	6	4	2	2	7	.200	.294	.400	20.0	5.7	35
Sharp, Sterling	R-R	6-3	182	5-30-95	3	5	5.36	20	18	0	86	95	51	51	12	37	65	.281	.357	.462	17.0	9.7	382
Spacke, Dylan	B-R	6-0	194	3-11-98	1	1	3.46	30	0	0	52	45	20	20	4	27	37	.243	.357	.362	16.7	12.2	221
Troye, Christopher	R-R	6-4	225	2-08-99	0	0	3.77	24	0	0	31	20	17	13	0	27	50	.179	.345	.268	34.7	18.8	144
Van Belle, Brian	R-R	6-3	185	9-03-96	6	3	3.00	14	13	0	81	72	32	27	9	25	69	.242	.312	.391	20.8	7.6	331
Webb, Jacob	L-R	6-5	246	3-23-99	8	3	5.03	41	0	0	59	50	39	33	5	38	65	.227	.343	.341	24.4	14.3	266
Whitlock, Garrett	R-R	6-5	225	6-11-96	1	0	1.50	1	1	0	6	1	1	1	1	1	8	.053	.100	.211	40.0	5.0	20
Zeferjahn, Ryan	R-R	6-5	209	2-28-98	0	4	5.02	34	0	2	43	33	27	24	7	40	68	.210	.387	.382	33.3	19.6	204

Fielding

Catcher	PCT	G	PO	A	E	DP	PB
Donlan	.943	4	32	1	2	0	2
Erro	.963	9	96	7	4	2	1
Hickey	.985	58	596	14	9	4	4
Marrero	.988	35	301	22	4	1	3
Scott	.989	30	262	16	3	3	6
Teel	1.000	4	35	2	0	0	0

First Base	PCT	G	PO	A	E	DP
Binelas	.996	34	211	16	1	18
Dearden	1.000	1	1	0	0	0
Esplin	.982	10	52	4	1	4
Jordan	.984	30	169	14	3	18
Kavadas	1.000	65	453	24	0	4

Second Base	PCT	G	PO	A	E	DP
Bonaci	1.000	1	2	3	0	1
Diaz	.929	8	10	16	2	3
Koss	1.000	2	6	4	0	2
Lugo	1.000	1	0	2	0	0
McDonough	.929	14	26	26	4	7
Meidroth	1.000	16	26	32	0	8

	PCT	G	PO	A	E	DP
Reyes	1.000	1	5	0	0	0
Yorke	.984	96	145	222	6	42

Third Base	PCT	G	PO	A	E	DP
Binelas	.984	28	17	43	1	6
Diaz	1.000	5	8	10	0	0
Jordan	.933	16	10	18	2	1
Koss	1.000	1	2	1	0	1
Lugo	.868	35	19	40	9	4
Mayer	1.000	1	1	3	0	0
McDonough	.500	1	1	0	1	0
Meidroth	.952	55	35	64	5	7

Shortstop	PCT	G	PO	A	E	DP
Bonaci	.944	15	21	30	3	5
Chang	1.000	2	1	6	0	0
Koss	.992	32	42	77	1	14
Lugo	1.000	1	0	2	0	0
Mayer	.978	39	54	80	3	19
McDonough	.942	24	26	39	4	7
Meidroth	.962	18	22	28	2	4
Rafaela	.896	9	13	30	5	4
Reyes	1.000	1	4	1	0	0
Story	1.000	2	1	3	0	1

Outfield	PCT	G	PO	A	E	DP
Anthony	1.000	10	27	1	0	1
Dearden	1.000	51	83	2	0	0
Esplin	1.000	10	9	0	0	0
Koss	1.000	1	2	0	0	0
Lugo	.490	32	46	3	1	1
McDonough	.995	63	116	6	1	3
Rafaela	.974	43	109	3	3	2
Reyes	1.000	4	5	0	0	0
Rosier	.995	105	194	5	2	1
Sikes	.991	111	225	5	2	1

GREENVILLE DRIVE

HIGH CLASS A

SOUTH ATLANTIC LEAGUE

Batting	B-T	Ht.	Wt.	DOB	AVG	OBP	SLG	G	PA	AB	R	H	2B	3B	HR	RBI	BB	HBP	SH	SF	SO	SB	CS	BB%	SO%
Anthony, Roman	L-R	6-2	200	5-13-04	.294	.412	.569	54	245	204	41	60	14	3	12	38	40	1	0	0	75	2	1	16.3	30.6
Bonaci, Brainer	B-R	5-10	164	7-09-02	.301	.353	.473	63	278	256	34	77	15	1	9	38	21	0	0	1	63	6	3	7.6	22.7
Campbell, Kristian	R-R	6-3	191	6-28-02	.267	.400	.422	14	55	45	5	12	2	1	1	3	7	3	0	0	13	1	2	12.7	23.6
Castro, Allan	B-R	6-0	170	5-24-03	.283	.355	.446	43	186	166	23	47	11	2	4	17	17	2	0	1	36	4	1	9.1	19.4
Coffey, Cutter	R-R	6-1	190	5-21-04	.136	.253	.167	18	79	66	8	9	2	0	0	5	11	0	0	2	21	1	1	13.9	26.6
Decker, Nick	L-L	6-0	207	10-02-99	.218	.325	.422	68	246	211	37	46	14	4	7	24	28	6	0	1	83	8	3	11.4	33.7
Diaz, Jonathan	L-R	5-11	170	7-07-99	.250	.400	.406	11	40	32	6	8	2	0	1	7	7	1	0	0	8	0	1	17.5	20.0
Donlan, Matt	R-R	6-3	213	11-09-99	.125	.364	.125	3	11	8	1	1	0	0	0	0	1	2	0	0	3	0	0	9.1	27.3
Erro, Alex	B-R	5-9	182	12-05-97	.250	.325	.364	64	249	220	33	55	10	0	5	32	25	1	0	3	40	7	3	10.0	16.1
Esplin, Tyler	L-R	6-2	230	7-06-99	.176	.300	.235	6	20	17	2	3	1	0	0	0	2	1	0	0	2	0	0	10.0	10.0
Ferguson, Max	L-R	6-0	180	8-23-99	.234	.355	.347	86	366	308	52	72	16	2	5	33	57	1	0	0	102	28	4	15.6	27.9
Gonzalez, Bryan	R-R	6-0	220	9-18-01	.252	.317	.404	110	448	408	68	103	15	7	11	56	35	4	0	1	149	15	8	7.8	33.3
Hickey, Nathan	L-R	5-11	210	11-23-99	.294	.402	.588	18	82	68	13	20	6	1	4	9	12	1	0	1	20	0	0	14.6	24.4
Jimenez, Gilberto	B-R	5-11	212	7-08-00	.221	.256	.352	32	130	122	18	27	8	1	2	18	6	0	1	1	37	7	3	4.6	28.5
Jordan, Blaze	R-R	6-2	220	12-19-02	.324	.385	.533	73	322	287	48	93	22	1	12	55	28	3	0	4	47	2	0	8.7	14.6
Lopez, Eduardo	B-R	5-11	187	5-08-02	.261	.356	.384	79	315	268	48	70	16	1	5	45	42	0	0	5	81	12	2	13.3	25.7
Mayer, Marcelo	L-R	6-2	188	12-12-02	.290	.366	.524	35	164	145	23	42	11	1	7	34	17	1	0	1	37	5	2	10.4	22.6
Meidroth, Chase	R-R	5-9	170	7-23-01	.338	.495	.459	20	97	74	19	25	3	0	2	14	21	2	0	0	20	4	0	21.6	20.6
Meredith, Kier	L-L	5-10	200	9-12-99	.178	.337	.301	26	92	73	11	13	4	1	1	10	11	7	0	1	26	14	3	12.0	28.3
Miller, Tyler	L-R	6-2	193	12-17-99	.263	.315	.422	91	371	339	50	89	21	3	9	51	25	3	0	4	90	19	6	6.7	24.3
Paulino, Eddinson	L-R	5-10	155	7-02-02	.257	.338	.420	115	500	440	68	113	28	4	12	58	50	6	0	4	113	26	8	10.0	22.6
Romero, Mikey	L-R	5-11	175	1-12-04	.100	.100	.100	3	10	10	0	1	0	0	0	0	0	0	0	0	4	0	0	0.0	40.0
Rosario, Ronald	R-R	6-0	175	1-01-03	.260	.344	.377	62	247	215	35	56	12	2	3	33	27	2	0	3	74	1	0	10.9	30.0
Simas, Karson	R-R	5-11	175	6-02-01	.190	.282	.229	46	174	153	20	29	3	0	1	9	18	2	0	1	54	6	2	10.3	31.0
Teel, Kyle	L-R	6-1	190	2-15-02	.377	.485	.453	14	66	53	10	20	4	0	0	9	11	1	0	1	11	1	0	16.7	16.7
Ugueto, Miguel	R-R	5-11	185	9-03-02	.216	.249	.304	51	205	194	20	42	9	1	2	20	8	1	0	2	50	12	3	3.9	24.4

Pitching	B-T	Ht.	Wt.	DOB	W	L	ERA	G	GS	SV	IP	Hits	Runs	ER	HR	BB	SO	AVG	OBP	SLG	SO%	BB%	BF
Altavilla, Dan	R-R	5-11	226	9-08-92	0	0	3.86	4	0	0	7	4	3	3	1	3	4	.167	.250	.292	14.3	10.7	28
Bastardo, Angel	R-R	6-1	175	6-18-02	2	7	4.62	21	21	0	103	86	59	53	11	46	139	.223	.307	.358	31.8	10.5	437
Bell, Brock	R-R	6-4	227	3-18-98	4	1	2.72	24	0	3	36	31	17	11	2	9	35	.228	.270	.309	23.6	6.1	148
Blalock, Bradley	R-R	6-2	200	12-25-00	5	1	2.55	7	7	0	35	31	12	10	3	9	36	.233	.283	.361	24.8	6.2	145
Bolden, Caleb	R-R	6-2	190	12-19-98	0	0	6.75	5	0	0	9	14	9	7	3	3	9	.350	.386	.575	20.5	6.8	44
Campbell, Maceo	R-R	6-1	215	6-17-99	1	1	9.25	25	0	0	36	46	38	37	9	27	51	.307	.426	.560	27.9	14.8	183
Cepeda, Felix	R-R	6-3	170	7-15-00	0	1	1.33	14	0	4	20	10	3	3	1	6	21	.152	.219	.242	28.4	8.1	74
Cobb, Casey	R-R	5-10	200	6-27-96	2	3	5.62	29	1	1	58	68	37	36	11	19	63	.288	.345	.496	24.3	7.3	259
Coffey, Isaac	R-R	6-1	205	6-21-00	4	2	2.83	11	11	0	60	51	23	19	11	10	83	.223	.258	.410	34.4	4.1	241
DiValerio, Jordan	R-R	6-1	200	10-09-97	5	6	5.08	30	5	0	73	85	56	41	19	15	68	.281	.330	.550	20.7	4.6	328
Dobbins, Hunter	R-R	6-2	185	8-30-99	4	1	2.63	7	7	0	41	34	15	12	1	5	44	.222	.261	.281	27.3	3.1	161
Encarnacion, Juan Daniel	R-R	6-2	173	3-30-01	4	9	6.32	24	21	0	100	109	85	70	22	42	101	.270	.347	.501	22.1	9.2	457
Gambrell, Grant	L-R	6-4	225	11-21-97	2	2	4.88	6	6	0	31	35	23	17	6	9	36	.271	.333	.504	25.5	6.4	141
Godman, Jaret	L-R	6-2	187	5-07-00	0	1	8.22	7	0	2	8	15	7	7	0	4	7	.429	.487	.514	17.9	10.3	39
Gonzalez, Wikelman	R-R	6-0	167	3-25-02	6	3	5.14	15	15	0	63	49	41	36	5	42	105	.210	.333	.326	37.6	15.1	279
Hoffman, Graham	R-R	6-3	211	12-26-98	2	2	6.55	23	0	0	33	38	29	24	7	26	37	.306	.425	.492	24.2	17.0	153
Hoppe, Alex	R-R	6-1	200	12-17-98	1	4	3.93	31	0	3	34	40	18	15	3	14	48	.288	.357	.417	31.2	9.1	154
Jackson, Gabriel	R-R	6-2	180	9-07-01	0	1	6.14	4	0	0	7	12	7	5	0	4	7	.353	.436	.500	17.9	10.3	39
Jones, Joe	R-R	6-5	245	7-22-95	3	0	3.86	11	0	0	16	16	7	7	0	5	20	.250	.304	.313	29.0	7.2	69
Kelly, Zack	R-R	6-3	205	3-03-95	0	0	0.00	1	1	0	1	0	0	0	0	1	2	.000	.250	.000	50.0	25.0	4
Kwiatkowski, Robert	R-R	6-1	190	6-08-97	1	1	4.22	26	1	4	43	35	23	20	5	13	38	.217	.273	.360	21.6	7.4	176
Landry, Nathan	R-L	6-2	200	5-04-99	1	1	7.54	19	0	0	23	27	20	19	8	10	22	.297	.373	.626	21.6	9.8	102
Monegro, Yordanny	R-R	6-4	180	10-14-02	1	1	1.80	2	1	0	10	8	2	2	1	5	13	.222	.317	.333	31.7	12.2	41
Penrod, Zach	L-L	6-2	210	6-16-97	2	1	2.18	4	4	0	21	16	5	5	1	11	20	.205	.303	.256	22.5	12.4	89
Perales, Luis	R-R	6-1	160	4-14-03	0	3	4.95	8	8	0	36	39	24	20	8	22	44	.275	.371	.493	26.3	13.2	167
Perry, Aaron	R-R	5-11	175	6-07-99	1	2	9.70	19	0	0	21	34	25	23	3	10	28	.347	.414	.490	25.2	9.0	111
Rogers, Dalton	R-L	5-11	172	1-18-01	2	6	5.52	17	17	0	75	66	49	46	7	48	102	.238	.352	.386	30.9	14.5	330
Sena, Reidis	R-R	5-10	160	4-07-01	0	1	6.14	10	0	0	15	18	11	10	0	7	17	.305	.379	.441	25.4	10.4	67
Song, Noah	R-R	6-4	200	5-28-97	1	2	4.15	7	6	0	22	19	11	10	3	11	15	.232	.344	.427	15.6	11.5	96
Stock, Joey	R-R	6-5	210	9-08-97	1	5	8.31	33	0	6	35	31	37	32	3	27	52	.228	.365	.360	31.0	16.1	168
Tellier, Nate	R-R	5-9	180	6-05-98	6	1	7.13	31	0	0	42	41	37	33	11	29	51	.252	.376	.521	25.9	14.7	197
Troye, Christopher	R-R	6-4	225	2-08-99	2	0	1.96	14	0	0	18	10	4	4	3	9	37	.152	.263	.318	48.7	11.8	76

Fielding

Catcher	PCT	G	PO	A	E	DP	PB
Diaz	.975	8	72	5	2	0	2
Donlan	1.000	3	23	0	0	0	0
Erro	.987	37	359	19	5	2	4
Hickey	.987	17	214	11	3	0	3
Rosario	.982	55	561	47	11	1	10
Teel	.985	13	122	11	2	3	3

First Base	PCT	G	PO	A	E	DP
Erro	.978	27	173	8	4	12
Esplin	1.000	4	20	1	0	1
Gonzalez	.973	17	102	8	3	7
Jordan	1.000	35	231	10	0	19
Lopez	1.000	1	5	0	0	1
Miller	.992	50	326	28	3	27

Second Base	PCT	G	PO	A	E	DP
Bonaci	.958	20	28	40	3	7
Campbell	1.000	10	13	16	0	3
Coffey	1.000	3	3	8	0	1
Decker	.000	1	0	0	0	0
Ferguson	.964	43	77	82	6	17
Meidroth	.971	11	10	24	1	6
Paulino	.972	29	40	64	3	13
Romero	1.000	1	2	4	0	1
Simas	.948	18	28	27	3	6

Third Base	PCT	G	PO	A	E	DP
Bonaci	.714	3	2	3	2	0
Coffey	1.000	8	4	7	0	0
Ferguson	1.000	3	1	1	0	0
Jordan	.936	35	20	53	5	1
Meidroth	.938	8	4	11	1	0
Miller	.922	21	12	35	4	4
Paulino	.927	29	22	29	4	4
Simas	.936	26	31	42	5	5

Shortstop	PCT	G	PO	A	E	DP
Bonaci	.958	33	37	78	5	12
Coffey	.900	8	10	17	3	2
Ferguson	1.000	3	6	7	0	1
Mayer	.929	32	32	60	7	15
Paulino	.939	57	64	121	12	26
Romero	.667	2	0	2	1	0

Outfield	PCT	G	PO	A	E	DP
Anthony	.981	44	104	5	4	1
Bonaci	1.000	1	1	0	0	0
Campbell	1.000	3	9	1	0	1
Castro	.971	38	65	1	3	0
Decker	.954	48	72	5	6	1
Esplin	1.000	1	3	0	0	0
Ferguson	.987	37	77	0	1	0
Gonzalez	.962	60	105	6	6	1
Jimenez	.929	32	47	2	3	1
Lopez	.970	70	127	0	3	0
Meredith	.958	11	15	2	1	1
Miller	.667	20	29	2	0	0
Simas	.000	3	0	0	0	0
Ugueto	.950	40	52	0	2	0

SALEM RED SOX

LOW CLASS A

CAROLINA LEAGUE

Batting	B-T	Ht.	Wt.	DOB	AVG	OBP	SLG	G	PA	AB	R	H	2B	3B	HR	RBI	BB	HBP	SH	SF	SO	SB	CS	BB%	SO%
Alcantara, Marvin	R-R	5-10	157	11-02-04	.203	.277	.257	21	83	74	9	15	1	0	1	7	7	1	0	1	27	6	0	8.4	32.5
Anderson, Antonio	B-R	6-3	205	6-28-05	.185	.214	.222	7	28	27	2	5	1	0	0	1	1	0	0	0	9	0	1	3.6	32.1
Anthony, Roman	L-R	6-2	200	5-13-04	.228	.376	.316	42	202	158	27	36	9	1	1	18	38	2	0	4	38	11	6	18.8	18.8
Asigen, Albertson	R-R	5-10	175	8-27-01	.318	.436	.434	42	156	129	22	41	5	2	2	12	24	3	0	0	42	13	3	15.4	26.9
Bleis, Miguel	R-R	6-0	170	3-01-04	.230	.282	.325	31	142	126	18	29	3	3	1	16	10	1	0	5	38	11	4	7.0	26.8
Brannon, Brooks	R-R	5-11	210	5-04-04	.292	.320	.667	6	25	24	4	7	0	0	3	9	1	0	0	0	8	0	0	4.0	32.0
Castro, Allan	B-R	6-0	170	5-24-03	.247	.376	.378	69	306	251	39	62	20	2	3	29	51	2	0	2	54	15	5	16.7	17.6
Chacon, Juan	R-R	6-1	171	12-04-02	.241	.353	.332	57	235	199	22	48	6	6	0	18	31	4	0	1	52	20	10	13.2	22.1
Coffey, Cutter	R-R	6-1	190	5-21-04	.226	.341	.348	81	349	296	51	67	14	2	6	30	45	7	0	1	79	18	6	12.9	22.6
Feliz, Albert	R-R	6-2	200	4-13-02	.242	.315	.407	90	333	297	39	72	17	1	10	45	29	4	0	3	121	0	0	8.7	36.3
Garcia, Jhostynxon	R-R	5-11	163	12-11-02	.230	.329	.374	73	310	265	46	61	14	6	4	24	37	4	0	4	79	9	2	11.9	25.5
Garcia, Johanfran	R-R	5-10	196	12-08-04	.203	.279	.305	15	68	59	8	12	3	0	1	5	5	2	0	2	24	3	0	7.4	35.3
Hernandez, Alexis	R-R	6-0	170	10-05-02	.252	.345	.364	42	174	151	19	38	8	0	3	21	20	2	0	1	38	11	1	11.5	21.8
James, Lyonell	R-R	6-2	165	10-14-02	.238	.311	.311	92	354	315	35	75	12	1	3	45	27	8	0	4	44	2	4	7.6	12.4
Jimenez, Gilberto	B-R	5-11	212	7-08-00	.229	.263	.314	8	38	35	2	8	0	0	1	6	1	1	0	1	13	1	1	2.6	34.2
Liendo, Ahbram	B-R	5-8	170	2-01-04	.205	.353	.304	71	276	224	43	46	10	3	2	20	45	6	1	0	86	30	6	16.3	31.2
Lira, Enderso	R-R	6-1	185	10-11-03	.238	.269	.287	62	238	223	18	53	8	0	1	26	11	0	0	4	50	0	2	4.6	21.0
McElveny, Daniel	R-R	5-10	190	4-21-03	.208	.296	.375	7	27	24	6	5	1	0	1	3	1	2	0	0	8	0	0	3.7	29.6
Mejicano, Yorberto	R-R	5-11	185	11-21-00	.268	.350	.412	61	223	194	34	52	9	2	5	25	23	3	0	3	42	6	3	10.3	18.8
Montero, Juan	R-R	5-11	180	6-10-02	.247	.321	.342	23	81	73	10	18	7	0	0	8	6	2	0	0	20	0	2	7.4	24.7
Ravelo, Luis	B-R	6-1	187	11-05-03	.217	.311	.303	108	444	383	48	83	15	0	6	47	51	4	0	6	126	6	6	11.5	28.4
Romero, Mikey	L-R	5-11	175	1-12-04	.217	.288	.304	23	105	92	11	20	4	2	0	9	9	1	0	2	17	2	3	8.6	16.2
Rosario, Ronald	R-R	6-0	175	1-01-03	.250	.389	.429	17	72	56	10	14	5	1	1	11	12	2	0	2	22	0	0	16.7	30.6
Salazar, Johnfrank	R-R	6-1	159	8-05-03	.228	.307	.374	34	137	123	13	28	3	0	5	17	14	0	0	0	22	0	2	10.2	16.1
Simas, Karson	R-R	5-11	175	6-02-01	.238	.342	.317	34	120	101	16	24	2	3	0	11	13	4	0	2	28	8	4	10.8	23.3
Simon, Claudio	R-R	5-9	170	12-09-01	.235	.311	.284	30	90	81	6	19	2	1	0	5	7	2	0	0	30	11	4	7.8	33.3
Tucker, Stanley	R-R	5-9	165	4-22-02	.077	.111	.192	8	27	26	2	2	0	0	1	3	1	0	0	0	11	1	0	3.7	40.7
Yuten, Natanael	L-L	6-2	143	10-09-04	.197	.240	.239	18	75	71	13	14	1	1	0	5	3	1	0	0	25	2	1	4.0	33.3
Zanetello, Nazzan	R-R	6-2	190	5-25-05	.500	.500	.500	1	2	2	0	1	0	0	0	1	0	0	0	0	0	0	0	0.0	0.0

Pitching	B-T	Ht.	Wt.	DOB	W	L	ERA	G	GS	SV	IP	Hits	Runs	ER	HR	BB	SO	AVG	OBP	SLG	SO%	BB%	BF
Bell, Brock	R-R	6-4	227	3-18-98	2	1	4.58	11	0	1	20	16	10	10	2	5	15	.229	.295	.371	19.2	6.4	78
Blalock, Bradley	R-R	6-2	200	12-25-00	1	0	1.50	4	4	0	18	10	3	3	1	4	22	.167	.231	.300	33.8	6.2	65
Blanco, Royman	R-R	6-1	170	4-17-01	0	1	8.59	4	0	0	7	13	9	7	2	0	3	.351	.351	.568	8.1	0.0	37
Bolden, Caleb	R-R	6-2	190	12-19-98	1	2	3.67	27	0	4	49	36	21	20	1	26	75	.208	.317	.283	35.9	12.4	209
Brand, Jonathan	R-R	5-9	200	2-20-00	4	2	2.58	29	0	8	38	24	17	11	3	14	47	.183	.263	.305	30.7	9.2	153
Butler, Connor	L-L	6-0	180	4-22-00	0	0	6.75	8	0	0	9	7	10	7	1	15	10	.200	.462	.400	19.2	28.8	52
Cepeda, Felix	R-R	6-3	170	7-15-00	3	3	3.03	19	0	2	33	27	19	11	0	23	39	.216	.347	.288	25.5	15.0	153
Cruz, Nathanael	R-R	6-2	175	2-04-03	3	2	5.14	25	0	0	42	32	29	24	2	36	45	.216	.388	.304	22.6	18.1	199
De La Rosa, Luis	R-R	6-1	170	7-06-02	2	7	2.94	28	6	0	70	53	37	23	4	40	88	.208	.320	.302	28.9	13.2	304
Dean, Noah	L-L	6-2	185	3-10-01	2	8	6.29	21	17	0	63	52	49	44	4	72	86	.233	.430	.336	28.5	23.8	302
Duffy, Matthew	L-R	6-1	185	10-04-01	0	1	13.50	2	2	0	3	4	5	5	2	2	4	.333	.467	.833	26.7	13.3	15
Early, Connelly	L-L	6-3	195	4-03-02	0	0	4.50	1	1	0	2	1	1	1	1	0	4	.125	.125	.500	50.0	0.0	8
Felix, Jhonny	B-R	6-0	180	9-04-98	2	2	6.55	24	1	1	45	41	36	33	5	33	42	.243	.386	.396	20.0	15.7	210
Feliz, Albert	R-R	6-2	200	4-13-02	0	1	9.00	1	0	0	1	0	2	1	0	2	0	.000	.400	.000	0.0	40.0	5
Fernandez, Ryan	R-R	6-0	170	6-11-98	1	0	0.00	2	0	0	3	1	0	0	0	0	6	.100	.100	.100	60.0	0.0	10
Fogell, Zach	L-L	5-11	190	7-23-00	0	0	0.00	2	0	0	4	1	1	0	0	1	3	.083	.154	.083	23.1	7.7	13
German, Franklin	R-R	6-2	195	9-22-97	1	0	2.25	3	0	0	4	3	2	1	0	5	8	.200	.400	.200	40.0	25.0	20
Jackson, Gabriel	R-R	6-2	180	9-07-01	4	1	3.05	25	4	0	62	61	25	21	4	19	40	.264	.327	.381	15.7	7.5	254
Johnson, Marques	R-R	6-2	210	7-04-00	2	2	6.55	28	0	2	34	31	26	25	1	24	43	.242	.364	.297	27.9	15.6	154

Kelly, Zack	R-R	6-3	205	3-03-95	0	2	27.00	2	1	0	1	3	3	3	0	4	1	.600	.700	1.200	10.0	40.0	10
Landry, Nathan	R-L	6-2	200	5-04-99	0	0	0.00	8	0	0	10	6	0	0	0	3	11	.171	.237	.200	28.9	7.9	38
Litwicki, Matt	R-R	6-2	220	8-03-98	0	1	33.75	2	0	0	1	5	5	5	0	3	2	.556	.692	.667	15.4	23.1	13
Monegro, Yordanny	R-R	6-4	180	10-14-02	3	2	2.43	9	9	0	41	33	12	11	0	17	60	.217	.312	.276	34.5	9.8	174
Mullins, Hayden	L-L	6-0	194	9-14-00	0	1	7.36	2	2	0	4	1	3	3	0	3	8	.083	.313	.167	50.0	18.8	16
Nunez, Cristian	R-R	6-5	210	10-22-02	0	1	5.29	5	3	0	17	17	10	10	1	4	14	.270	.338	.413	18.9	5.4	74
Paez, Jedixson	R-R	6-1	170	1-17-04	5	5	3.31	18	16	0	84	73	37	31	7	12	73	.230	.270	.343	21.6	3.6	338
Perales, Luis	R-R	6-1	160	4-14-03	4	4	3.21	13	13	0	53	38	22	19	2	28	71	.197	.299	.285	31.4	12.4	226
Perez, Railin	R-R	6-3	185	9-02-01	2	3	3.70	32	0	3	56	48	31	23	1	34	69	.224	.344	.290	27.0	13.3	256
Ramirez, Jose	R-R	6-0	142	3-28-01	3	10	3.80	21	20	0	90	80	63	38	2	49	78	.237	.352	.332	19.2	12.0	407
Ramsey, Garrett	R-R	6-3	194	10-29-99	0	0	3.00	5	0	0	9	8	8	3	0	5	8	.222	.333	.250	18.2	11.4	44
Rodriguez-Cruz, Elmer	L-R	6-3	160	8-18-03	6	3	2.60	14	14	0	55	43	25	16	4	27	51	.219	.319	.347	22.6	11.9	226
Rogers, Dalton	R-L	5-11	172	1-18-01	0	1	2.49	6	6	0	22	11	7	6	0	13	38	.139	.261	.177	41.3	14.1	92
Scroggins, Cody	R-R	6-0	195	8-17-96	1	0	3.48	6	0	0	10	8	10	4	2	3	7	.200	.273	.400	15.9	6.8	44
Sena, Reidis	R-R	5-10	160	4-07-01	0	1	1.20	11	0	1	15	10	3	2	0	8	18	.196	.300	.235	30.0	13.3	60
Soto, Elvis	R-R	6-0	174	3-02-04	0	3	4.88	7	7	0	24	24	16	13	3	10	25	.264	.343	.418	23.8	9.5	105
Talavera, Luis	R-R	6-3	175	2-06-02	0	2	4.83	28	0	0	54	51	32	29	5	34	37	.262	.369	.379	15.5	14.3	238
Valera, Michael	R-R	6-2	176	2-12-99	2	0	5.93	21	0	0	30	30	23	20	2	19	41	.248	.364	.339	28.7	13.3	143
Zeferjahn, Ryan	R-R	6-5	209	2-28-98	1	0	0.00	2	1	0	3	3	0	0	0	0	2	.250	.250	.250	16.7	0.0	12

Fielding

Catcher	PCT	G	PO	A	E	DP	PB
Brannon	1.000	4	33	2	0	0	1
Garcia	.973	10	100	10	3	1	2
Lira	.975	58	550	72	16	6	11
McElveny	.979	4	42	4	1	1	0
Mejicano	.969	14	108	16	4	1	1
Montero	.972	23	192	17	6	3	3
Rosario	.956	16	165	8	8	0	4

First Base	PCT	G	PO	A	E	DP
Feliz	.984	48	357	19	6	28
Hernandez	1.000	4	37	3	0	2
James	.990	40	285	17	3	29
Mejicano	.991	29	206	15	2	20
Salazar	.986	10	70	3	1	5

Second Base	PCT	G	PO	A	E	DP
Alcantara	.946	8	10	25	2	8
Coffey	.941	6	7	9	1	2
Liendo	.995	43	72	114	1	22
Ravelo	.971	38	46	89	4	17
Romero	1.000	8	10	24	0	3
Salazar	.947	7	8	10	1	1
Simas	.851	11	14	26	7	6
Simon	.949	11	17	20	2	6
Tucker	1.000	2	2	10	0	1

Third Base	PCT	G	PO	A	E	DP
Anderson	1.000	5	2	6	0	0
Coffey	.875	31	26	37	9	4
James	.888	47	32	63	12	9
Liendo	.882	26	16	44	8	0
Ravelo	1.000	5	2	8	0	1
Salazar	.907	16	12	27	4	7
Simon	.800	5	3	1	1	0
Tucker	.000	1	0	0	0	0

Shortstop	PCT	G	PO	A	E	DP
Alcantara	.952	13	16	24	2	3
Coffey	.950	38	47	86	7	24
Liendo	.750	3	2	1	1	1
Ravelo	.941	64	75	132	13	36
Romero	.951	11	14	25	2	5
Simon	1.000	1	2	2	0	0
Zanetello	1.000	1	1	2	0	1

Outfield	PCT	G	PO	A	E	DP
Anthony	.820	34	57	2	2	1
Asigen	.963	42	50	4	3	0
Bleis	.976	24	42	4	1	1
Castro	.990	60	90	4	2	0
Chacon	.971	46	70	2	3	1
Feliz	.979	21	21	3	1	1
Garcia	.963	70	155	5	5	1
Hernandez	.667	37	48	2	0	0
Jimenez	1.000	6	11	0	0	0
Mejicano	1.000	2	4	0	0	0
Simas	.651	26	40	1	2	0
Simon	1.000	12	16	0	0	0
Tucker	.500	5	5	2	0	0
Yuten	.944	15	26	1	2	0

FCL RED SOX — *ROOKIE*

FLORIDA COMPLEX LEAGUE

Batting	B-T	Ht.	Wt.	DOB	AVG	OBP	SLG	G	PA	AB	R	H	2B	3B	HR	RBI	BB	HBP	SH	SF	SO	SB	CS	BB%	SO%
Alcantara, Marvin	R-R	5-10	157	11-02-04	.240	.347	.307	40	176	150	26	36	7	0	1	21	23	2	0	1	35	6	5	13.1	19.9
Anderson, Antonio	B-R	6-3	205	6-28-05	.133	.278	.200	5	18	15	0	2	1	0	0	3	3	0	0	0	6	1	0	16.7	33.3
Asigen, Albertson	R-R	5-10	175	8-27-01	.333	.440	.452	14	50	42	12	14	3	1	0	5	6	2	0	0	5	7	2	12.0	10.0
Avila, Rivaldo	R-R	5-10	172	9-11-02	.219	.342	.313	13	38	32	4	7	1	1	0	1	6	0	0	0	17	0	0	15.8	44.7
Ayubi, Karim	R-R	6-1	165	12-08-03	.200	.435	.246	28	92	65	16	13	3	0	0	7	24	3	0	0	23	3	2	26.1	25.0
Brannon, Brooks	R-R	5-11	210	5-04-04	.250	.294	.542	11	52	48	8	12	3	1	3	14	3	0	1	0	12	0	0	5.8	23.1
Campbell, Kristian	R-R	6-3	191	6-28-02	.391	.517	.565	8	29	23	4	9	2	1	0	2	3	3	0	0	5	2	1	10.3	17.2
De Leon, Fraymi	B-R	5-10	155	9-28-04	.295	.411	.328	29	73	61	17	18	2	0	0	4	9	3	0	0	18	9	2	12.3	24.7
Diaz, Kelvin	R-R	5-11	148	3-17-03	.212	.384	.314	47	178	137	30	29	4	2	2	16	34	5	1	1	49	21	4	19.1	27.5
Ehrhard, Drew	R-R	5-11	185	1-16-99	.286	.286	.429	5	7	7	0	2	1	0	0	0	0	0	0	0	2	0	0	0.0	28.6
Encarnacion, Freili	R-R	6-1	181	1-26-05	.182	.308	.212	8	39	33	4	6	1	0	0	1	2	4	0	0	8	2	0	5.1	20.5
Fitzgerald, Ryan	L-R	6-0	185	6-17-94	.429	.429	.643	4	14	14	1	6	1	1	0	4	0	0	0	0	1	2	0	0.0	7.1
Garcia, Johanfran	R-R	5-10	196	12-08-04	.302	.408	.497	42	179	149	21	45	10	2	5	32	19	9	0	2	37	3	1	10.6	20.7
Hernandez, Alexis	R-R	6-0	170	10-05-02	.500	.722	.600	4	18	10	2	5	1	0	0	3	8	0	0	0	0	2	0	44.4	0.0
Jimenez, Gilberto	B-R	5-11	212	7-08-00	.393	.414	.786	8	29	28	5	11	3	1	2	10	1	0	0	0	6	1	1	3.4	20.7
Jones, Deundre	L-L	5-9	190	12-12-03	.191	.371	.294	28	89	68	11	13	1	0	2	10	19	1	0	1	32	1	0	21.3	36.0
Koss, Christian	R-R	6-1	182	1-27-98	.292	.320	.458	7	25	24	4	7	1	0	1	3	1	0	0	0	6	2	1	4.0	24.0
Martinez, Enmanuel	R-R	5-11	194	5-24-04	.154	.233	.231	12	30	26	1	4	0	1	0	4	3	0	0	1	4	1	0	10.0	13.3
McElveny, Daniel	R-R	5-10	190	4-21-03	.250	.250	.250	2	4	4	1	1	0	0	0	0	0	0	0	0	1	1	0	0.0	25.0
Pierre, Angel	R-R	6-0	170	9-19-03	.239	.415	.348	35	123	92	16	22	6	2	0	9	21	8	0	2	38	8	5	17.1	30.9
Romero, Mikey	L-R	5-11	175	1-12-04	.250	.379	.292	8	29	24	4	6	1	0	0	4	5	0	0	0	4	0	0	17.2	13.8
Salazar, Johnfrank	R-R	6-1	159	8-05-03	.374	.408	.593	25	103	91	22	34	11	0	3	20	5	3	0	4	12	2	0	4.9	11.7
Sierra, Armando	R-R	6-1	189	1-17-04	.265	.363	.398	30	113	98	13	26	7	0	2	12	14	1	0	0	30	0	1	12.4	26.5
Simon, Claudio	R-R	5-9	170	12-09-01	.200	.333	.240	10	30	25	5	5	1	0	0	0	4	1	0	0	7	5	0	13.3	23.3
Teel, Kyle	L-R	6-1	190	2-15-02	.429	.556	.857	3	9	7	2	3	0	0	1	2	2	0	0	0	0	0	0	22.2	0.0
Tucker, Stanley	R-R	5-9	165	4-22-02	.195	.298	.366	12	47	41	6	8	2	1	1	5	6	0	0	0	12	3	0	12.8	25.5
Viloria, Diego	R-R	5-10	165	2-23-03	.293	.369	.362	20	65	58	8	17	4	0	0	5	4	3	0	0	6	0	0	6.2	9.2
Yuten, Natanael	L-L	6-2	143	10-09-04	.336	.396	.483	38	164	149	28	50	9	2	3	32	11	4	0	0	36	8	4	6.7	22.0
Zanetello, Nazzan	R-R	6-2	190	5-25-05	.139	.311	.222	12	45	36	6	5	3	0	0	1	9	0	0	0	15	5	1	20.0	33.3

Batting	B-T	Ht.	Wt.	DOB	AVG	OBP	SLG	G	PA	AB	R	H	2B	3B	HR	RBI	BB	HBP	SH	SF	SO	SB	CS	BB%	SO%
Zayas, Bryant	R-R	5-9	178	10-25-03	.242	.294	.330	31	103	91	16	22	3	1	1	14	8	0	1	3	34	13	3	7.8	33.0
Zimmer, Bradley	L-R	6-2	185	11-27-92	.273	.429	.455	4	14	11	2	3	2	0	0	1	3	0	0	0	5	1	0	21.4	35.7

Pitching	B-T	Ht.	Wt.	DOB	W	L	ERA	G	GS	SV	IP	Hits	Runs	ER	HR	BB	SO	AVG	OBP	SLG	SO%	BB%	BF
Abreu, Wandy	R-R	6-4	238	6-08-02	1	3	4.76	9	7	0	34	32	24	18	2	18	29	.246	.340	.369	19.0	11.8	153
Altavilla, Dan	R-R	5-11	226	9-08-92	1	0	1.80	4	2	0	5	4	1	1	0	2	3	.222	.300	.278	14.3	9.5	21
Blanco, Royman	R-R	6-1	170	4-17-01	3	0	3.86	12	0	0	21	27	12	9	1	1	19	.300	.337	.444	20.0	1.1	95
Burnet, Yizreel	R-R	6-4	210	1-15-04	1	0	0.00	1	0	0	1	0	0	0	0	0	0	.000	.000	.000	0.0	0.0	3
Butler, Connor	L-L	6-0	180	4-22-00	1	0	5.50	15	0	2	18	12	13	11	1	19	23	.185	.384	.277	26.7	22.1	86
Carlson, Max	R-R	6-1	190	9-13-01	0	0	0.00	1	0	0	1	0	0	0	0	0	2	.000	.000	.000	66.7	0.0	3
Cohen, Luis	R-R	6-0	172	5-26-03	3	2	3.46	10	7	1	39	28	18	15	2	14	39	.206	.286	.316	25.3	9.1	154
Colmenares, Willian	R-R	6-0	183	2-03-05	0	2	5.40	4	3	0	10	10	6	6	0	7	6	.263	.391	.342	13.0	15.2	46
De La Cruz, Darlyn	R-R	6-4	210	11-26-02	1	0	6.43	4	0	0	7	6	6	5	1	4	5	.231	.355	.423	16.1	12.9	31
Duffy, Matthew	L-R	6-1	185	10-04-01	0	0	0.00	1	0	0	1	0	0	0	0	0	1	.000	.000	.000	33.3	0.0	3
Feeney, Cade	R-R	6-0	195	7-31-01	0	0	0.00	1	0	0	1	2	0	0	0	0	1	.400	.400	.400	20.0	0.0	5
Fogell, Zach	L-L	5-11	190	7-23-00	0	0	0.00	1	0	0	1	1	0	0	0	1	1	.250	.400	.250	20.0	20.0	5
Garcia, Jogly	R-R	6-1	175	9-08-03	1	3	9.47	13	0	0	19	23	21	20	4	11	16	.291	.380	.494	17.4	12.0	92
German, Franklin	R-R	6-2	195	9-22-97	0	0	3.86	2	0	0	2	1	1	1	0	2	4	.167	.375	.333	50.0	25.0	8
Hernandez, Francis	R-R	6-2	170	9-04-01	3	1	2.30	14	3	0	27	22	9	7	1	11	19	.227	.333	.299	16.7	9.6	114
Litwicki, Matt	R-R	6-2	220	8-03-98	1	0	4.15	4	0	0	4	3	2	2	1	2	3	.214	.313	.429	18.8	12.5	16
Mejias, Alvaro	R-R	6-2	170	9-13-03	0	1	40.50	1	0	0	1	2	3	3	0	2	0	.500	.667	.500	0.0	33.3	6
Monegro, Yordanny	R-R	6-4	180	10-14-02	2	0	1.20	3	3	0	15	5	2	2	0	4	20	.102	.185	.163	37.0	7.4	54
Mullins, Hayden	L-L	6-0	194	9-14-00	0	1	3.38	2	2	0	3	0	1	1	0	2	7	.000	.182	.000	63.6	18.2	11
Nunez, Cristian	R-R	6-5	210	10-22-02	1	1	6.23	7	5	0	17	17	13	12	1	8	17	.262	.377	.385	22.1	10.4	77
Olds, Wyatt	R-R	6-0	183	8-05-99	1	2	5.40	5	4	0	20	23	12	12	1	5	21	.291	.349	.405	24.4	5.8	86
Pacheco, Simon	R-R	5-11	164	6-14-02	0	0	5.40	14	0	7	15	17	12	9	3	14	14	.274	.444	.468	17.3	17.3	81
Polanco, Eybersson	R-R	6-0	170	9-03-03	0	2	5.06	8	7	0	32	36	22	18	3	15	22	.288	.378	.488	15.4	10.5	143
Ramsey, Garrett	R-R	6-3	194	10-29-99	1	3	5.32	17	0	0	24	26	20	14	3	15	29	.289	.409	.489	26.4	13.6	110
Reguillo, Dennis	R-R	5-11	165	9-09-03	1	2	5.11	10	2	0	25	27	16	14	3	10	28	.284	.361	.442	25.9	9.3	108
Rodriguez, Yonfi	R-R	5-10	160	7-30-02	1	0	3.54	16	0	0	20	18	12	8	0	19	18	.237	.402	.250	18.6	19.6	97
Ruiz, Cesar	R-R	6-3	170	6-04-03	0	0	6.75	3	0	0	5	6	7	4	0	4	4	.273	.370	.318	14.8	14.8	27
Soto, Elvis	R-R	6-0	174	3-02-04	1	1	3.70	7	5	0	24	18	11	10	0	11	21	.214	.316	.238	21.4	11.2	98
Valera, Michael	R-R	6-2	176	2-12-99	1	1	2.70	10	0	1	13	7	6	4	1	3	16	.149	.226	.234	30.2	5.7	53
Van Der Schaaf, Stijn	R-R	6-4	185	4-08-04	3	0	4.42	9	1	1	18	10	9	9	0	15	14	.167	.370	.200	17.3	18.5	81
Wehunt, Blake	R-R	6-6	240	11-09-00	0	0	0.00	1	0	0	1	1	0	0	0	0	1	.250	.250	.500	25.0	0.0	4
Weins, CJ	R-R	6-3	223	8-15-00	0	0	0.00	1	0	0	1	0	0	0	0	1	1	.000	.250	.000	25.0	25.0	4
Wu-Yelland, Jeremy	L-L	6-2	210	6-24-99	0	0	9.00	3	2	0	4	4	4	4	1	5	2	.286	.474	.500	10.5	26.3	19

Fielding

C: Garcia 23, Viloria 18, Avila 5, Brannon 5, Martinez 4, Salazar 4, Teel 3, McElveny 1, Ehrhard 1. **1B:** Sierra 28, Garcia 9, Martinez 7, Avila 6, Salazar 3, Hernandez 2, Viloria 1. **2B:** Pierre 18, Zayas 16, De Leon 11, Alcantara 7, Campbell 5, Koss 4, Simon 4, Romero 2, Fitzgerald 2. **3B:** Salazar 18, Pierre 12, Zayas 9, De Leon 7, Encarnacion 5, Anderson 3, Simon 2. **SS:** Alcantara 37, Zanetello 8, De Leon 6, Romero 5, Koss 3, Encarnacion 1. **OF:** Diaz 53, Yuten 36, Jones 26, Ayubi 26, Asigen 11, Tucker 11, De Leon 6, Jimenez 6, Campbell 3, Zimmer 3, Simon 2, Hernandez 2, Fitzgerald 1.

DSL RED SOX — ROOKIE

DOMINICAN SUMMER LEAGUE

Batting	B-T	Ht.	Wt.	DOB	AVG	OBP	SLG	G	PA	AB	R	H	2B	3B	HR	RBI	BB	HBP	SH	SF	SO	SB	CS	BB%	SO%
Arias, Franklin	R-R	5-11	170	11-19-05	.350	.440	.453	37	159	137	32	48	9	1	1	15	19	3	0	0	14	3	2	11.9	8.8
Arredondo, Luis	R-R	6-3	187	3-06-06	.184	.264	.265	31	110	98	10	18	5	0	1	9	11	0	0	1	30	0	0	10.0	27.3
Asencio, Yosander	B-R	5-11	160	11-14-04	.321	.457	.476	28	106	84	17	27	9	2	0	7	21	0	1	0	27	1	1	19.8	25.5
Castillo, Alex	R-R	6-1	179	3-15-06	.220	.281	.329	30	89	82	9	18	1	1	2	9	5	2	0	0	35	3	2	5.6	39.3
Cespedes, Yoeilin	R-R	5-9	181	9-08-05	.346	.392	.560	46	209	191	37	66	15	4	6	38	14	2	0	2	24	1	2	6.7	11.5
Chalas, Albert	L-R	5-11	189	9-30-05	.183	.300	.350	22	70	60	9	11	2	4	0	5	9	1	0	0	30	0	0	12.9	42.9
Cueche, Nixson	R-R	5-11	156	3-06-06	.277	.333	.353	38	132	119	19	33	5	2	0	15	11	0	0	2	13	2	2	8.3	9.8
De Leon, Fraymi	B-R	5-10	155	9-28-04	.274	.413	.298	38	104	84	21	23	2	0	0	7	16	2	0	1	27	14	2	15.3	25.9
De Los Santos, Raimundo	B-R	5-10	147	2-27-05	.221	.340	.235	38	162	136	27	30	2	0	0	10	23	2	0	1	37	12	1	14.2	22.8
Delancey, Chad	R-R	5-11	175	7-12-06	.103	.182	.155	19	66	58	7	6	3	0	0	5	5	1	0	2	29	1	1	7.6	43.9
Eusebio, Natanael	L-L	6-0	160	7-02-05	.218	.307	.269	32	88	78	15	17	4	0	0	4	10	0	0	0	29	3	2	11.4	33.0
Evangelista, Claudio	B-R	5-9	165	11-19-05	.224	.314	.290	38	121	107	18	24	5	1	0	12	11	3	0	0	36	1	0	9.1	29.8
German, Nathanael	R-R	5-9	151	11-04-05	.184	.282	.263	36	131	114	18	21	2	2	1	11	15	1	0	1	33	2	3	11.5	25.2
Jimenez, Frederik	B-R	6-0	178	11-15-04	.256	.354	.396	46	192	164	25	42	12	1	3	30	24	2	0	2	53	6	1	12.5	27.6
Linarez, Yohander	B-R	5-11	160	3-19-05	.272	.317	.366	48	208	191	24	52	10	4	0	32	14	0	0	3	35	0	1	6.7	16.8
Liriano, Jose	L-R	6-2	216	6-26-03	.207	.340	.402	33	106	87	9	18	5	0	4	12	16	2	0	1	22	1	1	15.1	20.8
Marin, Liosward	L-R	5-10	158	5-15-06	.169	.243	.231	21	74	65	6	11	1	0	1	7	7	0	0	2	14	0	1	9.5	18.9
Martinez, Enmanuel	R-R	5-11	194	5-24-04	.184	.256	.263	17	43	38	1	7	1	1	0	5	4	0	0	1	5	1	0	9.3	11.6
Mavarez, Gabriel	R-R	5-9	141	3-15-06	.162	.340	.162	26	94	74	16	12	0	0	0	4	18	2	0	0	19	3	1	19.1	20.2
Musett, Andruw	R-R	5-10	198	11-21-05	.289	.433	.414	44	164	128	23	37	5	1	3	23	30	4	0	2	23	1	0	18.3	14.0
Noria, Franyer	R-R	5-10	135	9-24-04	.221	.327	.290	42	153	131	23	29	7	1	0	15	14	7	0	1	15	6	4	9.2	9.8
Nunez, Starlyn	B-R	6-0	155	10-10-05	.325	.391	.479	49	215	194	32	63	12	3	4	34	17	4	0	0	29	7	5	7.9	13.5
Paniagua, Cristofher	R-R	6-2	170	11-08-04	.269	.387	.344	46	194	160	28	43	7	1	1	22	26	6	0	2	37	10	6	13.4	19.1
Prado, Jesus	R-R	5-11	175	10-22-05	.260	.373	.280	21	59	50	6	13	1	0	0	3	8	1	0	0	18	0	0	13.6	30.5
Rodriguez, Gerardo	R-R	5-10	177	12-08-05	.346	.390	.488	38	136	127	26	44	9	0	3	25	8	1	0	0	13	4	1	5.9	9.6
Romero, Anger	R-R	6-0	185	3-16-05	.104	.254	.104	20	59	48	6	5	0	0	0	1	8	2	0	1	10	0	0	13.6	16.9
Ruiz, Yoiber	R-R	5-7	171	11-11-05	.217	.392	.261	49	209	161	30	35	3	2	0	20	46	1	0	1	41	6	2	22.0	19.6

Salazar, Kleyver	R-R	6-1	187	5-01-06	.240	.377	.347	36	151	121	14	29	10	0	1	18	26	2	0	2	25	0	0	17.2	16.6
Santana, Jancel	B-R	6-0	157	8-17-05	.206	.335	.277	46	188	155	18	32	4	2	1	22	26	5	0	2	40	6	4	13.8	21.3
Semerite, Moises	R-R	6-0	151	5-31-06	.221	.353	.320	38	150	122	19	27	8	2	0	10	23	3	0	2	51	9	4	15.3	34.0
Solarte, Jhoan	R-R	5-11	151	7-04-06	.165	.244	.294	35	124	109	17	18	3	1	3	16	12	0	1	2	32	7	0	9.7	25.8

Pitching	B-T	Ht.	Wt.	DOB	W	L	ERA	G	GS	SV	IP	Hits	Runs	ER	HR	BB	SO	AVG	OBP	SLG	SO%	BB%	BF
Almanzar, Marcos	R-R	6-1	155	3-14-06	0	0	8.76	11	0	0	12	10	13	12	1	24	10	.238	.529	.381	14.3	34.3	70
Arredondo, Breilin	R-R	5-11	151	7-10-05	2	2	5.14	11	3	1	35	45	22	20	4	14	31	.321	.400	.471	19.4	8.8	160
Ascanio, Ali	R-R	6-1	185	11-18-03	3	1	4.18	15	0	3	24	14	12	11	1	19	22	.175	.343	.250	21.6	18.6	102
Balderas, Obed	R-R	6-2	175	7-19-06	1	2	2.54	11	10	0	39	44	17	11	1	10	25	.299	.348	.367	15.5	6.2	161
Bautista, Gilberto	R-R	6-0	165	1-08-05	1	3	3.54	11	9	0	41	34	17	16	3	8	54	.228	.275	.329	33.5	5.0	161
Carta, Enrique	R-R	5-10	180	12-23-03	3	1	3.48	12	1	0	21	21	12	8	1	18	22	.266	.398	.342	22.4	18.4	98
Chirino, Yoelvin	R-R	6-0	161	5-13-05	0	3	7.15	8	0	0	11	9	12	9	1	10	8	.231	.404	.359	15.4	19.2	52
De La Cruz, Darlyn	R-R	6-4	210	11-26-02	6	1	4.08	12	0	0	35	28	18	16	5	16	39	.224	.336	.343	26.3	10.8	148
De La Cruz, Nicolas	L-L	6-4	252	11-18-05	1	3	3.51	11	10	0	33	17	16	13	1	20	22	.153	.287	.198	16.2	14.7	136
De La Cruz, Ruben	R-R	5-10	150	1-14-05	2	2	3.65	16	0	4	25	25	15	10	2	8	31	.255	.330	.347	27.7	7.1	112
De Los Santos, Hanssel	R-R	6-4	175	9-19-04	0	3	15.75	11	0	0	12	9	22	21	0	21	3	.214	.534	.286	4.1	28.8	73
Del Orbe, Allsson	B-R	6-3	185	9-06-01	2	1	1.23	15	0	0	29	16	7	4	0	14	44	.162	.282	.192	37.6	12.0	117
Figueroa, Geiser	R-R	6-4	170	3-24-06	3	3	4.68	11	5	1	33	29	26	17	0	25	32	.250	.393	.293	21.3	16.7	150
Garcia, Jesus	R-R	6-1	191	11-06-05	1	1	3.30	11	10	0	44	41	17	16	3	15	36	.255	.320	.360	20.2	8.4	178
Henriquez, Juan	R-R	6-0	172	6-29-06	2	4	4.68	11	11	0	42	35	22	22	1	21	44	.232	.331	.338	24.7	11.8	178
Jerez, Luis	R-R	6-1	217	8-26-03	1	1	3.21	12	4	1	34	29	15	12	0	9	31	.240	.313	.331	23.1	6.7	134
Jimenez, Andres	R-R	6-2	203	1-04-05	3	2	2.22	14	0	2	24	17	14	6	0	15	31	.187	.308	.220	29.0	14.0	107
Liranzo, Aaron	R-R	6-0	171	2-16-04	1	0	8.80	11	0	1	15	17	16	15	1	13	14	.288	.413	.390	18.7	17.3	75
Martinez, Jose	R-R	6-1	204	1-07-05	2	0	1.80	9	1	0	25	18	6	5	3	4	28	.198	.229	.341	29.2	4.2	96
Nunez, Daniel	L-L	6-2	175	4-05-03	2	1	2.78	10	6	0	32	20	14	10	1	22	44	.177	.329	.274	31.4	15.7	140
Pena, Daury	R-R	5-10	180	10-18-04	1	0	1.00	6	0	0	9	8	1	1	0	3	12	.235	.333	.265	30.8	7.7	39
Polo, Emmanuel	R-R	5-11	192	8-26-01	2	1	10.13	14	0	0	19	26	25	21	4	9	16	.351	.422	.622	17.8	10.0	90
Portes, Ovis	R-R	6-4	167	12-03-04	0	0	12.46	4	4	0	4	2	6	6	0	6	9	.133	.458	.267	37.5	25.0	24
Prado, Jesus	R-R	5-11	175	10-22-05	0	1	54.00	1	0	0	0	1	3	2	1	1	0	.500	.667	2.000	0.0	33.3	3
Reyes, Jean Carlos	R-R	6-2	203	12-17-03	3	1	3.57	15	0	2	23	21	13	9	0	14	17	.259	.394	.346	17.2	14.1	99
Rijo, Brahian	R-R	5-11	180	8-22-06	1	0	10.70	12	0	0	18	22	21	21	1	17	19	.314	.462	.500	20.4	18.3	93
Rodriguez, Ricardo	R-R	6-0	178	12-23-05	0	1	4.15	11	10	0	35	26	19	16	4	24	32	.218	.379	.361	20.8	15.6	154
Rodriguez, Wuilliams	R-R	6-2	199	11-03-05	1	2	2.75	10	10	0	36	34	17	11	4	10	28	.254	.308	.396	19.0	6.8	147
Ruiz, Cesar	R-R	6-3	170	6-04-03	1	1	2.40	16	0	3	30	22	13	8	3	16	33	.198	.295	.292	25.0	12.2	132
Salcedo, Deybi	R-R	6-1	197	7-05-04	1	2	1.35	8	0	1	13	5	3	2	0	2	19	.114	.188	.250	39.6	4.2	48
Sanchez, Argeny	R-R	6-1	150	9-17-05	0	2	7.20	9	0	0	15	17	12	12	2	7	8	.288	.391	.508	11.6	10.1	69
Sanchez, Denison	R-R	6-1	164	8-30-05	3	1	9.00	13	0	0	19	23	24	19	4	22	22	.307	.495	.600	21.2	21.2	104
Sanchez, Oscar	L-L	6-0	180	6-26-03	3	0	5.12	12	0	1	19	21	12	11	0	9	26	.276	.348	.421	29.2	10.1	89
Soriano, Cristofer	R-R	6-1	160	11-23-02	0	0	3.04	17	0	3	27	17	9	9	0	22	25	.195	.368	.218	21.9	19.3	114
Valera, Juan	R-R	6-3	205	5-18-06	3	1	5.93	15	1	0	27	27	22	18	0	20	31	.255	.403	.302	23.1	14.9	134
Vargas, Yeferson	R-R	6-0	177	8-04-04	0	5	6.09	12	11	0	34	41	25	23	0	24	33	.313	.420	.382	21.0	15.3	157

Fielding

C: Musett 29, Salazar 29, Marin 21, Rodriguez 20, Romero 14, Jimenez 8, Martinez 2. **1B:** Jimenez 31, Arredondo 15, Cueche 15, Rodriguez 12, Liriano 12, Musett 11, Salazar 6, Romero 5, Martinez 3, Mavarez 1, De Los Santos 1. **2B:** Santana 34, Nunez 20, Ruiz 20, Linarez 9, De Los Santos 7, Noria 6, German 5, Mavarez 5, De Leon 4, Cueche 3. **3B:** Nunez 25, Linarez 22, Cueche 15, Ruiz 14, Mavarez 12, Noria 7, Santana 7, Arredondo 7, Evangelista 3. **SS:** Cespedes 36, Arias 33, Linarez 18, Ruiz 13, Cueche 7, Mavarez 4, De Leon 2, De Los Santos 2, Santana 2, Castillo 1. **OF:** Paniagua 46, Semerite 37, Evangelista 37, Solarte 34, Eusebio 30, De Los Santos 28, Noria 28, German 26, Castillo 25, Asencio 22, Chalas 18, Prado 13, Delancey 10, De Leon 3.

Chicago Cubs

SEASON SYNOPSIS: After consecutive losing seasons, the 2023 Cubs became the first in club history to go from 10 games under .500 to 10 games over in the same season, but a late September fade dropped the Cubs behind the Marlins and Diamondbacks in the race for the final National League wild-card spot.

HIGH POINT: The Cubs had a positive run differential but couldn't get over the .500 hump until an eight-game win streak in late July. The fact that the victims were the rival Cardinals (six wins) and cross-town White Sox (a two-game sweep) made the streak even sweeter. Righty Adbert Alzolay earned the save in five of the eight wins.

LOW POINT: Alzolay missed most of September with a forearm strain, and the Cubs were 76-64 when the roof caved in. They lost six of seven over two series against Arizona as the D-backs passed them in the standings. A painful sweep in Atlanta included Seiya Suzuki's misplay of a fairly routine fly ball as the Cubs blew a six-run lead and a 10-inning game in which Chicago blew leads of 3-1, 4-3 and 5-4 and lost 6-5. Shortstop Dansby Swanson, in his first series in Atlanta as a visiting player, went 1-for-10 and contributed to the Cubs' sloppy defensive series.

NOTABLE ROOKIES: Righties Javier Assad and Hayden Wesneski contributed nearly 200 innings combined in hybrid starter/bulk-innings roles, with Assad posting a 3.05 ERA. Panamanian catcher Miguel Amaya had his moments down the stretch, hitting .214/.329/.359 as Yan Gomes' main complement. Minor league vet Miles Mastrobuoni contributed 13 steals in a utility role.

KEY TRANSACTIONS: Swanson signed a seven-year, $177 million deal in the offseason and quickly emerged as a clubhouse leader, while hitting 22 homers in a .244/.328/.416 line. Former NL MVP Cody Bellinger rediscovered his swing after shoulder surgery; signed to a one-year, $17 million deal, Bellinger posted a .307/.356/.525 slash line while leading the team with 26 homers and 97 RBIs. Hoping for a lineup boost in July, Chicago re-acquired former farmhand Jeimer Candelario, the biggest-name hitter traded at the deadline. He hit six home runs in 41 games while batting .234.

DOWN ON THE FARM: The Cubs are building better depth in the minors than they have had in several years. Cade Horton tops a talented pitching group, while Owen Caissie improved his contact rate in the second half to go with big power.

OPENING DAY PAYROLL: $184,219,250 (12th).

PLAYERS OF THE YEAR

MAJOR LEAGUE	MINOR LEAGUE
Cody Bellinger	**Owen Caissie**
OF	**OF**
.307/.356/.525	(AA)
26 HR, 20 SB	.289/.399/.519,
29 2B, 95 R	22 HR, 31 2B

ORGANIZATION LEADERS

Batting		*Minimum 250 AB
MAJORS		
* AVG	Cody Bellinger	.307
* OPS	Cody Bellinger	.881
HR	Cody Bellinger	26
RBI	Cody Bellinger	97
MINORS		
* AVG	Jared Young, Iowa	.310
* OBP	Jared Young, Iowa	.417
* SLG	Jared Young, Iowa	.577
* OPS	Jared Young, Iowa	.995
R	Yonathan Peralza, Iowa	100
H	Yonathan Peralza, Iowa	131
TB	Yonathan Peralza, Iowa	246
2B	Yonathan Peralza, Iowa	40
3B	Pete Crow-Armstrong, Tennessee/Iowa	7
HR	Felix Stevens, Myrtle Beach/South Bend	27
RBI	Hayden McGeary, South Bend/Tennessee	88
BB	B.J. Murray Jr., Tennessee	82
SO	Owen Caissie, Tennessee	164
SB	Pete Crow-Armstrong, Tennessee/Iowa	37
Pitching		#Minimum 75 IP
MAJORS		
W	Justin Steele	16
SO	Justin Steele	176
SV	Adbert Azolay	22
MINORS		
W	Walker Powell, Tennessee	11
L	Kohl Franklin, South Bend/Tennessee	12
# ERA	Cade Horton, Myrtle Beach/South Bend/Tennessee	2.65
G	Cam Sanders, Iowa	51
GS	Kohl Franklin, South Bend/Tennessee	26
SV	Manuel Rodriguez, Iowa	13
IP	Caleb Killian,Iowa	120
BB	Cam Sanders, Iowa	69
SO	Ben Brown, Tennessee/Iowa	130
# AVG	Cade Horton, Myrtle Beach/South Bend/Tennessee	.190

2023 PERFORMANCE

President: Jed Hoyer. **Farm Director:** Jared Banner. **Scouting Director:** Dan Kantrovitz.

Class	Team	League	W	L	PCT	Finish	Manager
Majors	Chicago Cubs	National	83	79	.512	7 (15)	David Ross
Triple-A	Iowa Cubs	International	82	65	.558	5 (20)	Marty Pevey
Double-A	Tennessee Smokies	Southern	75	62	.547	3 (8)	K. Graber/M. Ryan
High-A	South Bend Cubs	Midwest	57	73	.438	10 (12)	Lance Rymel
Low-A	Myrtle Beach Pelicans	Carolina	75	55	.577	1 (12)	Buddy Bailey
Rookie	ACL Cubs	Arizona Complex	18	37	.327	17 (17)	Nick Lovullo
Rookie	DSL Cubs Blue	Dominican Sum.	17	37	.315	46 (50)	Enrique Wilson
Rookie	DSL Cubs Red	Dominican Sum.	24	28	.462	32 (50)	Carlos Ramirez
Overall 2023 Minor League Record			347	357	.494	16th (30)	

ORGANIZATION STATISTICS

CHICAGO CUBS

NATIONAL LEAGUE

Batting	B-T	Ht.	Wt.	DOB	AVG	OBP	SLG	G	PA	AB	R	H	2B	3B	HR	RBI	BB	HBP	SH	SF	SO	SB	CS	BB%	SO%
Amaya, Miguel	R-R	6-0	230	3-09-99	.214	.329	.359	53	156	131	17	28	4	0	5	18	12	11	1	1	40	0	0	7.7	25.6
Barnhart, Tucker	L-R	5-11	192	1-07-91	.202	.285	.257	47	123	109	6	22	3	0	1	9	12	1	0	1	42	1	0	9.8	34.1
Bellinger, Cody	L-L	6-4	203	7-13-95	.307	.356	.525	130	556	499	95	153	29	1	26	97	40	5	0	12	87	20	6	7.2	15.6
Canario, Alexander	R-R	5-11	165	5-07-00	.294	.294	.647	6	17	17	1	5	1	1	1	6	0	0	0	0	8	0	0	0.0	47.1
Candelario, Jeimer	B-R	6-2	222	11-24-93	.234	.318	.445	41	157	137	20	32	9	1	6	17	17	1	0	2	39	2	0	10.8	24.8
2-teams (99 Washington)					.251	.336	.471	140	576	505	77	127	39	3	22	70	53	13	0	4	127	8	1	9.2	22.0
Crow-Armstrong, Pete	L-L	5-11	184	3-25-02	.000	.176	.000	13	19	14	3	0	0	0	0	1	3	0	2	0	7	2	2	15.8	36.8
Fulmer, Michael	R-R	6-3	224	3-15-93	.000	.000	.000	58	1	1	0	0	0	0	0	0	0	0	0	0	1	0	0	0.0	100.0
Gomes, Yan	R-R	6-2	212	7-19-87	.267	.315	.408	116	419	382	44	102	20	2	10	63	21	9	0	7	81	1	0	5.0	19.3
Happ, Ian	B-R	6-0	205	8-12-94	.248	.360	.431	158	691	580	86	144	35	4	21	84	99	6	0	6	153	14	3	14.3	22.1
Hoerner, Nico	R-R	6-1	200	5-13-97	.283	.346	.383	150	688	619	98	175	27	4	9	68	49	14	1	5	83	43	7	7.1	12.1
Hosmer, Eric	L-L	6-4	226	10-24-89	.234	.280	.330	31	100	94	7	22	3	0	2	14	6	0	0	0	25	0	0	6.0	25.0
Madrigal, Nick	R-R	5-8	175	3-05-97	.263	.311	.352	92	294	270	34	71	16	1	2	28	10	9	5	0	24	10	2	3.4	8.2
Mancini, Trey	R-R	6-3	230	3-18-92	.234	.299	.336	79	263	235	31	55	12	0	4	28	21	2	0	3	78	0	0	8.0	29.7
Mastrobuoni, Miles	L-R	5-11	185	10-31-95	.241	.308	.301	61	149	133	24	32	5	0	1	5	13	0	3	0	32	13	1	8.7	21.5
Mervis, Matt	L-R	6-2	225	4-16-98	.167	.242	.289	27	99	90	8	15	2	0	3	11	8	1	0	0	32	0	0	8.1	32.3
Morel, Christopher	R-R	5-11	145	6-24-99	.247	.313	.508	107	429	388	62	96	17	3	26	70	36	2	1	2	133	6	2	8.4	31.0
Rios, Edwin	L-R	6-3	220	4-21-94	.071	.235	.214	18	34	28	3	2	1	0	1	2	5	1	0	0	16	0	0	14.7	47.1
Suzuki, Seiya	R-R	5-11	182	8-18-94	.285	.357	.485	138	583	515	75	147	31	6	20	74	59	2	0	7	130	6	7	10.1	22.3
Swanson, Dansby	R-R	6-1	190	2-11-94	.244	.328	.416	147	638	565	81	138	25	3	22	80	66	5	0	2	154	9	1	10.3	24.1
Tauchman, Mike	L-L	6-2	220	12-03-90	.252	.363	.377	108	401	337	64	85	18	0	8	48	56	4	1	3	86	7	1	14.0	21.4
Torrens, Luis	R-R	6-0	217	5-02-96	.250	.318	.300	13	22	20	1	5	1	0	0	3	1	1	0	0	8	0	0	4.5	36.4
2-team (5 Seattle)					.250	.300	.357	18	30	28	1	7	3	0	0	4	1	1	0	0	9	0	0	3.3	30.0
Velazquez, Nelson	R-R	6-0	190	12-26-98	.241	.313	.621	13	32	29	8	7	2	0	3	6	3	0	0	0	8	0	0	9.4	25.0
2-team (40 Kansas City)					.235	.302	.586	53	179	162	35	38	6	0	17	34	14	2	0	1	51	0	0	7.8	28.5
Wisdom, Patrick	R-R	6-2	220	8-27-91	.205	.289	.500	97	302	268	43	55	8	1	23	46	30	2	1	1	111	4	2	9.9	36.8
Young, Jared	L-R	6-0	185	7-09-95	.186	.255	.465	16	47	43	8	8	0	3	2	8	3	1	0	0	13	2	0	6.4	27.7

Pitching	B-T	Ht.	Wt.	DOB	W	L	ERA	G	GS	SV	IP	Hits	Runs	ER	HR	BB	SO	AVG	OBP	SLG	SO%	BB%	BF
Alzolay, Adbert	R-R	6-1	208	3-01-95	2	5	2.67	58	0	22	64	52	23	19	5	13	67	.225	.278	.333	26.5	5.1	253
Assad, Javier	R-R	6-1	200	7-30-97	5	3	3.05	32	10	0	109	93	38	37	13	41	94	.231	.306	.388	20.9	9.1	449
Barnhart, Tucker	L-R	5-11	192	1-07-91	0	0	2.25	4	0	0	4	7	1	1	0	0	0	.368	.368	.368	0.0	0.0	19
Boxberger, Brad	R-R	5-10	211	5-27-88	0	1	4.95	22	0	2	20	15	11	11	3	11	17	.208	.321	.403	20.2	13.1	84
Burdi, Nick	R-R	6-3	225	1-19-93	0	0	9.00	3	0	0	3	3	3	3	0	3	4	.273	.400	.545	26.7	20.0	15
Cuas, Jose	R-R	6-3	195	6-28-94	0	2	3.04	27	1	1	24	17	9	8	2	14	19	.205	.340	.313	19.0	14.0	100
Duffey, Tyler	R-R	6-3	220	12-27-90	0	0	4.50	1	0	0	2	1	1	1	1	0	3	.143	.143	.571	42.9	0.0	7
Estrada, Jeremiah	B-R	6-1	185	11-01-98	0	0	6.75	12	0	0	11	12	8	8	4	12	13	.279	.429	.605	23.2	21.4	56
Fulmer, Michael	R-R	6-3	224	3-15-93	3	5	4.42	58	1	2	57	48	29	28	7	28	65	.235	.329	.402	27.4	11.8	237
Greene, Shane	R-R	6-4	200	11-17-88	0	0	0.00	2	0	0	3	2	0	0	0	2	3	.200	.333	.300	25.0	16.7	12
Hendricks, Kyle	R-R	6-3	190	12-07-89	6	8	3.74	24	24	0	137	138	68	57	13	27	93	.255	.293	.393	16.1	4.7	578
Hughes, Brandon	B-L	6-2	215	12-01-95	0	3	7.24	17	0	0	14	14	11	11	2	8	17	.264	.371	.415	27.0	12.7	63
Kay, Anthony	L-L	6-0	225	3-21-95	0	0	6.35	13	0	0	11	12	8	8	1	8	8	.267	.389	.444	14.8	14.8	54
Kilian, Caleb	R-R	6-4	180	6-02-97	0	1	16.88	3	1	0	5	13	10	10	0	2	5	.481	.576	.593	15.2	6.1	33
Leiter, Mark	R-R	6-0	210	3-13-91	1	3	3.50	69	0	4	64	48	27	25	7	24	77	.206	.299	.365	28.6	8.9	269
Little, Luke	L-L	6-8	220	8-30-00	0	0	0.00	7	0	0	7	5	0	0	0	4	12	.208	.333	.292	40.0	13.3	30
Mastrobuoni, Miles	L-R	5-11	185	10-31-95	0	0	108.00	1	0	0	0	4	4	4	1	0	0	.800	.800	1.600	0.0	0.0	5
Merryweather, Julian	R-R	6-4	215	10-14-91	5	1	3.38	69	0	2	72	58	28	27	8	36	98	.219	.314	.332	32.3	11.9	303
Palencia, Daniel	R-R	5-11	160	2-05-00	5	3	4.45	27	0	0	28	22	16	14	3	14	33	.216	.322	.353	27.7	11.8	119
Rucker, Michael	R-R	6-1	195	4-27-94	2	1	4.91	35	0	0	40	39	22	22	6	19	40	.257	.347	.434	22.7	10.8	176
Smyly, Drew	L-L	6-2	188	6-13-89	11	11	5.00	41	23	0	142	147	89	79	26	56	141	.265	.335	.478	22.5	8.9	626
Steele, Justin	L-L	6-2	205	7-11-95	16	5	3.06	30	30	0	173	167	71	59	14	36	176	.251	.295	.371	24.6	5.0	716
Stroman, Marcus	R-R	5-7	180	5-01-91	10	9	3.95	27	25	0	137	120	68	60	9	52	119	.231	.304	.335	20.7	9.0	575

Pitching	B-T	Ht.	Wt.	DOB	W	L	ERA	G	GS	SV	IP	Hits	Runs	ER	HR	BB	SO	AVG	OBP	SLG	SO%	BB%	BF
Taillon, Jameson	R-R	6-5	230	11-18-91	8	10	4.84	30	29	1	154	156	96	83	27	41	140	.258	.308	.442	21.4	6.3	655
Thompson, Keegan	R-R	6-1	210	3-13-95	2	2	4.71	19	0	1	29	20	15	15	2	19	26	.194	.320	.291	20.8	15.2	125
Wesneski, Hayden	R-R	6-3	210	12-05-97	3	5	4.63	34	11	0	89	82	50	46	20	32	83	.242	.311	.460	21.9	8.4	379
Wicks, Jordan	L-L	6-3	220	9-01-99	4	1	4.41	7	7	0	35	33	17	17	5	11	24	.252	.306	.435	16.3	7.5	147

Fielding

Catcher	PCT	G	PO	A	E	DP	PB
Amaya	.987	41	282	14	4	3	2
Barnhart	.994	42	301	6	2	2	0
Gomes	.993	103	789	54	6	7	4
Torrens	1.000	4	5	0	0	0	0

First Base	PCT	G	PO	A	E	DP
Bellinger	.993	59	405	24	3	29
Candelario	.993	21	131	8	1	13
Hosmer	.985	15	118	17	2	14
Mancini	.994	51	305	24	2	33
Mervis	.991	27	210	10	2	22
Wisdom	.976	14	73	7	2	5
Young	.976	14	78	3	2	6

Second Base	PCT	G	PO	A	E	DP
Hoerner	.988	135	226	363	7	78
Madrigal	1.000	14	14	24	0	6
Mastrobuoni	1.000	7	8	8	0	2
Morel	.987	19	28	50	1	15
Wisdom	.000	1	0	0	0	0

Third Base	PCT	G	PO	A	E	DP
Candelario	.956	19	10	33	2	2
Madrigal	.977	72	45	123	4	9
Mastrobuoni	.967	29	13	45	2	3
Morel	.857	5	2	4	1	0
Rios	1.000	5	0	1	0	0
Wisdom	.927	61	53	87	11	15

Shortstop	PCT	G	PO	A	E	DP
Hoerner	.972	20	21	48	2	12
Mastrobuoni	.857	4	2	4	1	2
Morel	1.000	2	0	3	0	1
Swanson	.981	147	187	382	11	72

Outfield	PCT	G	PO	A	E	DP
Bellinger	.990	84	192	4	2	1
Canario	.667	3	3	0	0	0
Crow-Armstrong	1.000	13	12	0	0	0
Happ	.989	154	253	12	3	4
Mancini	1.000	5	3	0	0	0
Mastrobuoni	.500	7	5	0	0	0
Morel	.970	28	38	2	1	1
Suzuki	.987	132	221	2	3	1
Tauchman	.977	95	166	4	4	1
Torrens	.000	1	0	0	0	0
Velazquez	1.000	8	14	0	0	0
Wisdom	.928	9	7	1	1	0

IOWA CUBS — *TRIPLE-A*

INTERNATIONAL LEAGUE

Batting	B-T	Ht.	Wt.	DOB	AVG	OBP	SLG	G	PA	AB	R	H	2B	3B	HR	RBI	BB	HBP	SH	SF	SO	SB	CS	BB%	SO%
Alcantara, Sergio	B-R	6-4	151	7-10-96	.270	.364	.419	64	255	215	40	58	12	1	6	32	34	0	2	4	59	0	0	13.3	23.1
Amaya, Miguel	R-R	6-0	230	3-09-99	.313	.450	.479	15	60	48	5	15	5	0	1	10	11	1	0	0	14	0	0	18.3	23.3
Bellinger, Cody	L-L	6-4	203	7-13-95	.143	.125	.143	2	8	7	0	1	0	0	0	1	0	0	0	1	2	0	0	0.0	25.0
Bote, David	R-R	6-1	205	4-07-93	.258	.361	.456	99	425	360	61	93	29	0	14	61	53	7	1	4	96	7	1	12.5	22.6
Canario, Alexander	R-R	5-11	165	5-07-00	.276	.342	.524	36	161	145	23	40	12	0	8	35	15	0	0	1	45	2	0	9.3	28.0
Crow-Armstrong, Pete	L-L	5-11	184	3-25-02	.271	.350	.479	34	158	140	30	38	7	2	6	22	15	2	1	0	47	10	2	9.5	29.7
Davis, Brennen	R-R	6-0	210	11-02-99	.187	.296	.279	62	257	219	27	41	8	0	4	26	22	13	0	3	58	9	3	8.6	22.6
Higgins, P.J.	R-R	5-10	195	5-10-93	.285	.333	.480	32	135	123	18	35	9	0	5	21	9	1	0	2	35	0	0	6.7	25.9
Hill, Darius	L-L	5-11	190	8-17-97	.272	.343	.377	90	372	334	48	91	21	4	2	44	33	3	2	0	56	3	1	8.9	15.1
Jordan, Levi	R-R	5-8	170	9-24-95	.179	.295	.358	22	79	67	14	12	2	2	2	10	10	1	1	0	19	2	0	12.7	24.1
Madrigal, Nick	R-R	5-8	175	3-05-97	.424	.514	.678	16	70	59	18	25	6	3	1	7	8	3	0	0	7	0	0	11.4	10.0
Maldonado, Nelson	R-R	5-9	195	8-13-96	.267	.500	.467	5	22	15	2	4	0	0	1	1	7	0	0	0	4	0	0	31.8	18.2
Mastrobuoni, Miles	L-R	5-11	185	10-31-95	.295	.448	.473	39	165	129	35	38	11	3	2	14	36	0	0	0	39	9	0	21.8	23.6
Mervis, Matt	L-R	6-2	225	4-16-98	.282	.399	.533	100	441	362	77	102	23	1	22	78	67	7	0	5	100	2	1	15.2	22.7
Morel, Christopher	R-R	5-11	145	6-24-99	.330	.425	.730	29	134	115	31	38	9	2	11	31	17	2	0	0	41	4	1	12.7	30.6
Nunez, Dom	L-R	5-8	212	1-17-95	.216	.367	.366	45	167	134	29	29	8	0	4	21	29	3	1	0	46	4	0	17.4	27.5
2-team (18 Indianapolis)					.187	.322	.311	63	236	193	35	36	9	0	5	22	36	4	3	0	64	4	0	15.3	27.1
Perlaza, Yonathan	B-R	5-9	170	11-10-98	.284	.389	.534	121	543	461	100	131	40	3	23	85	76	4	0	2	119	13	5	14.0	21.9
Rios, Edwin	L-R	6-3	220	4-21-94	.263	.364	.454	42	176	152	26	40	11	0	6	20	20	4	0	0	54	0	0	11.4	30.7
Roederer, Cole	L-L	5-9	180	9-24-99	.290	.378	.387	10	37	31	4	9	1	1	0	4	5	0	0	1	10	2	0	13.5	27.0
Slaughter, Jake	R-R	6-1	200	10-24-96	.243	.340	.482	104	432	371	59	90	21	1	22	77	46	11	0	4	119	16	6	10.6	27.5
Strumpf, Chase	R-R	6-0	170	3-08-98	.212	.356	.442	67	267	217	40	46	6	1	14	45	44	5	0	1	90	2	1	16.5	33.7
Suzuki, Seiya	R-R	5-11	182	8-18-94	.308	.333	.538	4	15	13	3	4	0	0	1	2	1	0	0	1	2	0	0	6.7	13.3
Tauchman, Mike	L-L	6-2	220	12-03-90	.278	.427	.443	24	103	79	17	22	4	0	3	15	21	1	0	2	21	1	0	20.4	20.4
Vazquez, Luis	R-R	6-0	165	10-10-99	.257	.381	.428	66	270	222	34	57	11	0	9	40	38	8	0	2	56	6	3	14.1	20.7
Velazquez, Nelson	R-R	6-0	190	12-26-98	.253	.333	.469	74	330	292	48	74	15	0	16	44	32	4	0	2	97	7	3	9.7	29.4
2-team (6 Omaha)					.239	.319	.439	80	353	314	49	75	15	0	16	44	33	4	0	2	103	9	3	9.3	29.2
Washer, Jake	R-R	6-0	220	2-23-96	.167	.200	.306	23	75	72	5	12	5	1	1	5	3	0	0	0	19	1	0	4.0	25.3
Windham, Bryce	L-R	5-10	190	9-25-96	.290	.367	.376	61	217	186	25	54	9	2	1	31	25	0	2	4	41	4	2	11.5	18.9
Wisdom, Patrick	R-R	6-2	220	8-27-91	.200	.333	.600	3	12	10	2	2	1	0	1	2	2	0	0	0	5	0	0	16.7	41.7
Young, Jared	L-R	6-0	185	7-09-95	.310	.417	.577	90	376	310	71	96	16	2	21	72	50	10	2	4	84	7	3	13.3	22.3

Pitching	B-T	Ht.	Wt.	DOB	W	L	ERA	G	GS	SV	IP	Hits	Runs	ER	HR	BB	SO	AVG	OBP	SLG	SO%	BB%	BF
Assad, Javier	R-R	6-1	200	7-30-97	0	1	3.68	4	4	0	15	12	7	6	0	7	15	.218	.328	.273	23.4	10.9	64
Bigge, Hunter	R-R	6-1	205	6-12-98	0	0	8.71	11	0	0	10	12	10	10	1	13	12	.300	.455	.450	21.8	23.6	55
Bleier, Richard	L-L	6-3	215	4-16-87	0	0	6.35	5	0	0	6	6	4	4	0	5	2	.273	.393	.455	6.9	17.2	29
Borucki, Ryan	L-L	6-4	210	3-31-94	1	0	12.00	8	0	0	9	13	13	12	1	6	11	.317	.429	.585	22.4	12.2	49
Bote, David	R-R	6-1	205	4-07-93	0	0	27.00	1	0	0	1	3	3	3	0	1	0	.500	.571	.833	0.0	14.3	7
Boxberger, Brad	R-R	5-10	211	5-27-88	0	0	5.40	6	0	0	5	6	3	3	0	4	4	.300	.440	.400	16.0	16.0	25
Brown, Ben	R-R	6-6	210	9-09-99	6	8	5.33	22	15	0	73	60	46	43	9	51	100	.226	.354	.402	31.1	15.8	322
Burdi, Nick	R-R	6-3	225	1-19-93	0	0	3.20	21	0	4	20	16	7	7	1	14	33	.225	.396	.338	36.3	15.4	91
Clarke, Chris	R-R	6-7	215	5-13-98	5	5	4.90	35	11	1	75	87	44	41	5	27	66	.291	.360	.438	19.6	8.0	336
Correa, Danis	R-R	5-11	150	8-26-99	0	0	14.00	8	0	0	9	11	15	14	2	13	9	.324	.538	.588	17.3	25.0	52
Duffey, Tyler	R-R	6-3	220	12-27-90	4	1	3.77	36	2	2	45	27	20	19	7	23	53	.175	.286	.357	29.1	12.6	182
Elias, Roenis	L-L	6-1	205	8-01-88	2	0	5.48	4	4	0	21	16	13	13	6	5	18	.200	.256	.450	20.9	5.8	86
Estrada, Jeremiah	B-R	6-1	185	11-01-98	1	1	5.97	26	0	1	29	24	21	19	8	26	43	.220	.377	.495	31.2	18.8	138
Gonsalves, Stephen	L-L	6-5	218	7-08-94	0	0	6.19	10	5	0	16	12	11	11	1	19	25	.214	.408	.393	32.9	25.0	76
Greene, Shane	R-R	6-4	200	11-17-88	2	1	1.75	9	7	0	26	22	7	5	2	12	27	.229	.327	.323	24.5	10.9	110

Guzman, Carlos	R-R	6-1	210	5-16-98	0	0	13.50	1	0	0	1	1	2	2	0	4	1	.200	.556	.600	11.1	44.4	9
Hendricks, Kyle	R-R	6-3	190	12-07-89	2	1	5.75	5	5	0	20	21	13	13	2	6	20	.273	.333	.442	23.5	7.1	85
Heuer, Codi	R-R	6-5	200	7-03-96	0	1	7.82	15	0	0	13	15	12	11	2	11	15	.288	.413	.462	23.8	17.5	63
Holloway, Jordan	R-R	6-6	230	6-13-96	1	1	10.29	8	0	0	7	10	12	8	2	9	15	.313	.463	.563	36.6	22.0	41
Horn, Bailey	L-L	6-2	210	1-15-98	7	2	4.58	39	0	2	53	52	29	27	5	29	59	.265	.356	.423	24.9	12.2	237
Hughes, Brandon	B-L	6-2	215	12-01-95	2	0	9.00	11	0	0	11	18	11	11	3	9	9	.375	.475	.708	15.3	15.3	59
Jensen, Ryan	R-R	6-0	190	11-23-97	0	2	6.10	16	0	0	21	18	15	14	2	24	26	.222	.422	.370	23.9	22.0	109
Kay, Anthony	L-L	6-0	225	3-21-95	3	1	4.10	30	1	0	37	28	22	17	2	22	50	.209	.325	.306	31.1	13.7	161
Kilian, Caleb	R-R	6-4	180	6-02-97	8	3	4.56	25	24	0	120	123	66	61	17	36	95	.266	.325	.445	18.6	7.0	512
Kobos, Scott	L-L	6-2	200	8-03-97	0	1	9.00	2	0	0	2	3	2	2	0	2	1	.375	.500	.375	10.0	20.0	10
Little, Brendon	L-L	6-2	195	8-11-96	3	3	4.05	50	2	1	73	67	38	33	6	38	73	.251	.348	.375	23.1	12.0	316
Little, Luke	L-L	6-8	220	8-30-00	2	0	1.54	8	0	1	12	8	2	2	0	7	21	.186	.314	.233	41.2	13.7	51
Martin, Riley	L-L	6-1	215	3-19-98	1	1	7.30	14	0	0	12	19	12	10	3	15	17	.352	.486	.593	24.3	21.4	70
Neidert, Nick	R-R	6-1	202	11-20-96	5	7	5.64	27	24	0	107	127	76	67	18	40	86	.292	.357	.513	17.7	8.2	486
Nittoli, Vinny	R-R	6-1	210	11-11-90	1	1	3.48	16	0	0	21	18	12	8	2	7	22	.228	.311	.367	24.4	7.8	90
Palencia, Daniel	R-R	5-11	160	2-05-00	0	0	7.90	13	0	2	14	13	12	12	1	7	18	.232	.348	.393	27.3	10.6	66
Reyes, Samuel	R-R	5-11	180	3-13-96	3	2	3.86	10	5	0	28	23	13	12	4	13	25	.223	.316	.379	21.4	11.1	117
Roberson, Josh	R-R	6-3	175	5-12-96	0	1	20.25	5	0	0	4	7	9	9	2	9	6	.412	.615	.824	23.1	34.6	26
Rodriguez, Manuel	R-R	5-11	210	8-06-96	2	4	4.42	35	0	13	39	40	25	19	2	18	56	.268	.353	.416	32.7	10.5	171
Rucker, Michael	R-R	6-1	195	4-27-94	0	1	1.69	13	2	2	21	12	4	4	2	5	19	.169	.221	.254	24.7	6.5	77
Sampson, Adrian	R-R	6-2	210	10-07-91	0	2	10.17	7	4	0	23	30	31	26	6	15	22	.313	.417	.615	19.1	13.0	115
Sanders, Cam	R-R	6-2	175	12-09-96	7	2	5.15	51	0	5	65	40	40	37	6	69	97	.172	.374	.310	31.2	22.2	311
Taylor, Curtis	R-R	6-6	235	7-25-95	0	0	12.27	3	0	0	4	5	5	5	1	4	7	.357	.474	.643	36.8	21.1	19
Thompson, Keegan	R-R	6-1	210	3-13-95	3	0	8.10	20	0	0	30	34	28	27	8	23	40	.286	.404	.555	27.4	15.8	146
Thompson, Riley	L-R	6-4	210	7-09-96	3	8	5.64	25	19	0	81	77	51	51	15	54	78	.253	.364	.530	21.5	14.9	363
Uceta, Edwin	R-R	6-0	155	1-09-98	0	1	16.20	5	0	0	5	9	9	9	4	6	3	.375	.516	.958	9.7	19.4	31
Wesneski, Hayden	R-R	6-3	210	12-05-97	1	0	1.35	5	5	0	20	12	6	3	2	8	28	.171	.253	.286	35.4	10.1	79
Whitney, Blake	R-R	6-3	185	5-25-96	0	0	10.80	1	0	0	2	2	2	2	1	3	1	.286	.500	.714	10.0	30.0	10
Wick, Rowan	L-R	6-3	234	11-09-92	4	3	8.60	23	1	0	30	34	34	29	9	19	35	.279	.379	.615	24.1	13.1	145
Wicks, Jordan	L-L	6-3	220	9-01-99	3	0	3.82	7	7	0	33	26	14	14	3	13	30	.217	.299	.367	22.2	9.6	135
Young, Jared	L-R	6-0	185	7-09-95	0	0	0.00	2	0	0	2	1	0	0	0	2	2	.167	.444	.333	22.2	22.2	9

Fielding

Catcher	PCT	G	PO	A	E	DP	PB
Amaya	.984	13	118	6	2	2	0
Higgins	.996	30	266	17	1	2	1
Nunez	1.000	43	351	27	0	3	5
Washer	.993	16	139	10	1	0	4
Windham	.984	55	524	27	9	1	5

First Base	PCT	G	PO	A	E	DP
Bellinger	1.000	2	11	2	0	2
Bote	1.000	13	78	5	0	10
Maldonado	1.000	1	6	1	0	0
Mervis	.991	80	510	41	5	56
Rios	1.000	11	70	8	0	8
Slaughter	.943	6	30	3	2	4
Strumpf	1.000	5	38	1	0	4
Windham	1.000	1	0	1	0	0
Wisdom	1.000	1	5	0	0	2
Young	.992	35	240	12	2	21

Second Base	PCT	G	PO	A	E	DP
Alcantara	1.000	8	14	22	0	10
Bote	.985	31	55	75	2	15
Jordan	1.000	12	20	28	0	11
Madrigal	1.000	6	11	13	0	2
Mastrobuoni	.989	22	38	48	1	12
Slaughter	.974	44	69	79	4	23
Strumpf	.974	21	32	43	2	11
Vazquez	1.000	6	17	16	0	5

Third Base	PCT	G	PO	A	E	DP
Bote	.933	9	3	11	1	0
Jordan	.941	6	4	12	1	2
Madrigal	1.000	7	3	16	0	2
Mastrobuoni	.923	6	7	5	1	0
Morel	.958	9	6	17	1	3
Rios	.871	15	10	17	4	4
Slaughter	.971	46	24	78	3	3
Strumpf	.946	34	21	49	4	3
Vazquez	1.000	4	5	4	0	1
Wisdom	1.000	1	2	2	0	0
Young	.893	16	4	21	3	1

Shortstop	PCT	G	PO	A	E	DP
Alcantara	.932	53	59	120	13	24
Bote	.973	37	49	94	4	29
Jordan	1.000	1	1	2	0	0
Mastrobuoni	1.000	1	1	1	0	1
Vazquez	.986	57	85	129	3	28

Outfield	PCT	G	PO	A	E	DP
Bote	1.000	6	7	0	0	0
Canario	.976	37	71	3	3	2
Crow-Armstrong	.881	34	93	2	4	0
Davis	.963	53	93	6	4	1
Hill	.991	82	140	3	1	1
Mastrobuoni	.667	7	9	1	0	0
Morel	1.000	20	31	0	0	0
Perlaza	.958	89	138	4	6	1
Roederer	1.000	9	24	1	0	0
Suzuki	1.000	3	8	0	0	0
Tauchman	1.000	18	46	0	0	0
Velazquez	.996	70	121	1	1	1
Young	1.000	26	43	0	0	0

TENNESSEE SMOKIES — *DOUBLE-A*

SOUTHERN LEAGUE

Batting	B-T	Ht.	Wt.	DOB	AVG	OBP	SLG	G	PA	AB	R	H	2B	3B	HR	RBI	BB	HBP	SH	SF	SO	SB	CS	BB%	SO%
Alcantara, Kevin	R-R	6-6	188	7-12-02	.250	.381	.500	5	21	16	4	4	1	0	1	4	3	1	0	1	7	0	0	14.3	33.3
Aliendo, Pablo	R-R	6-0	170	5-29-01	.231	.332	.458	91	375	321	49	74	23	1	16	61	41	9	2	2	114	5	0	10.9	30.4
Amaya, Miguel	R-R	6-0	230	3-09-99	.273	.411	.659	13	56	44	9	12	5	0	4	8	8	3	0	1	17	1	0	14.3	30.4
Artis, D.J.	L-L	5-9	165	3-20-97	.125	.125	.125	3	8	8	1	1	0	0	0	0	0	0	0	0	2	0	0	0.0	25.0
Ball, Bryce	L-R	6-4	240	7-08-98	.161	.324	.286	16	71	56	9	9	4	0	1	8	14	0	0	1	28	0	0	19.7	39.4
Ballesteros, Moises	L-R	5-7	195	11-08-03	.238	.273	.238	5	22	21	3	5	0	0	0	1	1	0	0	0	3	0	0	4.5	13.6
Beesley, Bradlee	R-R	5-9	180	2-21-98	.228	.364	.411	65	272	224	44	51	12	4	7	22	37	11	0	0	79	22	2	13.6	29.0
Caissie, Owen	L-R	6-3	190	7-08-02	.289	.398	.519	120	528	439	77	127	31	2	22	84	76	7	1	5	164	7	9	14.4	31.1
Crow-Armstrong, Pete	L-L	5-11	184	3-25-02	.289	.371	.527	73	342	298	68	86	19	5	14	60	31	10	0	3	82	27	8	9.1	24.0
Davis, Zach	B-R	5-9	175	6-29-94	.161	.278	.161	21	36	31	6	5	0	0	0	0	4	1	0	0	14	4	1	11.1	38.9
Franklin, Christian	R-R	5-8	195	11-30-99	.200	.333	.400	5	12	10	3	2	0	1	0	2	2	0	0	0	2	1	0	16.7	16.7
Jordan, Levi	R-R	5-8	170	9-24-95	.235	.371	.288	45	210	170	32	40	9	0	0	18	31	7	0	2	39	12	1	14.8	18.6
Knight, Caleb	R-R	5-9	220	1-02-96	.277	.443	.362	17	61	47	10	13	1	0	1	4	11	3	0	0	11	0	0	18.0	18.0
Maldonado, Nelson	R-R	5-9	195	8-13-96	.210	.310	.356	81	310	267	30	56	16	1	7	37	36	4	0	3	60	1	1	11.6	19.4
McGeary, Haydn	R-R	6-4	235	10-09-99	.255	.382	.435	104	442	361	56	92	15	1	16	75	67	10	0	4	105	4	3	15.2	23.8

McKeon, Scott	R-R	5-11	185	10-30-97	.171	.248	.333	38	119	105	20	18	7	2	2	17	11	0	2	1	53	4	0	9.2	44.5
Murray, BJ	B-R	5-10	205	1-05-00	.263	.382	.462	124	542	452	71	119	34	4	16	74	82	6	0	2	129	14	3	15.1	23.8
Nwogu, Jordan	R-R	6-1	230	3-10-99	.194	.273	.370	97	363	324	44	63	7	1	16	41	27	9	1	2	137	15	7	7.4	37.7
Opitz, Casey	B-R	5-9	200	7-30-98	.209	.336	.352	29	110	91	14	19	1	0	4	12	17	1	0	1	41	2	0	15.5	37.3
Pagan, Ezequiel	L-R	5-9	163	7-08-00	.167	.375	.167	2	8	6	1	1	0	0	0	0	0	2	0	0	0	0	0	0.0	0.0
Pertuz, Fabian	R-R	5-11	156	9-01-00	.091	.259	.091	8	27	22	3	2	0	0	0	0	4	1	0	0	7	1	0	14.8	25.9
Roederer, Cole	L-L	5-9	180	9-24-99	.245	.340	.420	83	335	286	39	70	9	1	13	49	40	4	0	5	94	8	2	11.9	28.1
Shaw, Matt	R-R	5-11	185	11-06-01	.292	.329	.523	15	70	65	10	19	4	1	3	9	3	1	0	1	12	6	1	4.3	17.1
Strumpf, Chase	R-R	6-0	170	3-08-98	.258	.401	.500	37	167	132	32	34	11	0	7	21	28	5	0	2	50	3	1	16.8	29.9
Triantos, James	R-R	6-1	195	1-29-03	.333	.385	.417	3	13	12	2	4	1	0	0	2	1	0	0	0	2	0	0	7.7	15.4
Vazquez, Luis	R-R	6-0	165	10-10-99	.284	.340	.483	58	258	232	38	66	13	0	11	40	16	5	2	3	65	4	7	6.2	25.2
Verdugo, Luis	R-R	6-0	160	10-12-00	.105	.175	.140	18	64	57	3	6	2	0	0	3	4	1	1	1	28	0	0	6.3	43.8
Weber, Andy	L-R	5-11	190	7-24-97	.237	.335	.333	106	433	372	62	88	19	1	5	35	50	7	0	4	90	4	1	11.5	20.8

Pitching	B-T	Ht.	Wt.	DOB	W	L	ERA	G	GS	SV	IP	Hits	Runs	ER	HR	BB	SO	AVG	OBP	SLG	SO%	BB%	BF
Bigge, Hunter	R-R	6-1	205	6-12-98	3	1	3.50	31	0	2	44	34	18	17	3	21	56	.211	.310	.335	30.4	11.4	184
Birdsell, Brandon	R-R	6-2	240	3-23-00	1	3	3.95	6	6	0	27	32	15	12	5	5	27	.283	.322	.478	22.3	4.1	121
Brown, Ben	R-R	6-6	210	9-09-99	2	0	0.45	4	4	0	20	13	2	1	1	6	30	.186	.250	.243	39.0	7.8	77
Correa, Danis	R-R	5-11	150	8-26-99	1	1	3.44	18	0	8	18	11	9	7	1	9	26	.172	.280	.266	34.7	12.0	75
Espinoza, Manuel	R-R	5-11	150	11-17-00	2	3	7.06	10	8	0	29	39	26	23	6	15	24	.331	.409	.568	17.5	10.9	137
Franklin, Kohl	R-R	6-4	195	9-09-99	4	10	5.99	21	21	0	86	90	60	57	19	38	86	.271	.359	.497	22.7	10.0	379
Gallardo, Richard	R-R	6-1	180	9-06-01	0	1	8.38	3	3	0	10	12	12	9	1	8	9	.286	.423	.381	17.3	15.4	52
Guzman, Carlos	R-R	6-1	210	5-16-98	6	2	4.86	35	1	0	76	74	46	41	8	43	82	.261	.366	.385	24.4	12.8	336
Hecht, Ben	R-R	6-2	170	5-31-95	3	2	3.77	22	0	3	29	16	15	12	5	25	32	.168	.362	.337	25.0	19.5	128
Herz, DJ	R-L	6-2	175	1-04-01	1	1	3.97	14	14	0	59	47	31	26	4	37	80	.216	.336	.312	30.3	14.0	264
Hodge, Porter	R-R	6-4	230	2-21-01	6	7	5.13	35	12	0	81	64	49	46	3	49	103	.215	.338	.322	28.5	13.6	361
Horn, Bailey	L-L	6-2	210	1-15-98	0	1	2.00	6	0	1	9	3	2	2	0	5	19	.100	.229	.167	54.3	14.3	35
Horton, Cade	R-R	6-1	211	8-20-01	1	1	1.33	6	6	0	27	18	8	4	0	11	31	.188	.269	.229	28.4	10.1	109
Jensen, Ryan	R-R	6-0	190	11-23-97	2	5	5.57	14	6	0	32	36	23	20	4	22	40	.281	.388	.414	26.3	14.5	152
Kachmar, Chris	R-R	6-3	180	9-03-96	3	2	4.84	25	11	0	67	72	39	36	12	21	75	.273	.342	.458	25.3	7.1	296
Knight, Caleb	R-R	5-9	220	1-02-96	0	0	27.00	1	0	0	1	2	3	3	0	3	0	.500	.625	.750	0.0	37.5	8
Kobos, Scott	L-L	6-2	200	8-03-97	0	1	11.81	5	0	0	5	4	8	7	0	14	5	.200	.529	.200	14.7	41.2	34
Laskey, Adam	R-L	6-3	205	3-09-98	0	0	15.19	5	0	0	5	13	11	9	2	4	3	.464	.531	.821	9.4	12.5	32
Leigh, Zac	R-R	6-0	170	11-14-97	3	2	4.11	25	0	2	35	26	17	16	4	16	52	.202	.302	.333	34.7	10.7	150
Little, Luke	L-L	6-8	220	8-30-00	3	2	3.12	23	0	0	35	20	12	12	1	28	63	.169	.357	.212	40.9	18.2	154
Marquez, Brailyn	L-L	6-4	185	1-30-99	1	1	6.56	16	0	0	23	17	19	17	1	34	35	.198	.444	.279	28.2	27.4	124
Martin, Riley	L-L	6-1	215	3-19-98	5	1	3.52	30	0	4	46	32	25	18	3	28	78	.192	.315	.287	39.6	14.2	197
McAvene, Michael	R-R	6-3	207	8-24-97	0	1	11.77	11	0	0	13	19	18	17	3	12	11	.352	.478	.593	16.2	17.6	68
Nahas, Joe	R-R	6-1	185	11-14-99	0	3	10.04	13	4	0	26	33	33	29	6	16	20	.303	.398	.560	15.6	12.5	128
Nunez, Eduarniel	R-R	6-2	170	6-07-99	2	0	3.79	16	0	1	19	14	8	8	1	20	24	.212	.413	.288	26.1	21.7	92
Palencia, Daniel	R-R	5-11	160	2-05-00	0	0	5.87	5	5	0	15	11	10	10	3	9	18	.196	.303	.393	27.3	13.6	66
Pertuz, Fabian	R-R	5-11	156	9-01-00	0	0	9.00	1	0	0	1	2	1	1	1	0	1	.400	.400	1.000	20.0	0.0	5
Powell, Walker	R-R	6-8	210	6-11-96	11	6	3.68	25	21	0	120	105	57	49	23	25	109	.236	.281	.428	22.9	5.3	475
Reindl, Jake	R-R	6-1	190	1-15-97	0	0	0.93	6	0	0	10	4	1	1	0	4	10	.129	.270	.226	27.0	10.8	37
Remy, Peyton	L-R	6-2	170	8-20-96	0	1	36.00	1	0	0	1	2	4	4	0	2	2	.500	.667	.500	22.2	22.2	9
Reyes, Samuel	R-R	5-11	180	3-13-96	3	1	2.72	23	1	1	40	28	13	12	2	19	44	.197	.288	.275	26.8	11.6	164
Scalzo, Frankie	R-R	6-3	185	11-25-99	0	0	2.84	4	1	0	6	2	2	2	0	4	9	.100	.250	.150	37.5	16.7	24
Stambaugh, Dalton	R-L	6-0	195	2-11-97	0	0	5.40	2	0	0	7	9	5	4	2	4	7	.290	.371	.581	20.0	11.4	35
Ueckert, Cayne	R-R	6-3	195	5-28-96	4	3	4.58	36	0	4	39	36	22	20	3	22	50	.250	.355	.361	28.9	12.7	173
Whitney, Blake	R-R	6-3	185	5-25-96	4	0	3.01	38	0	4	69	62	26	23	5	26	80	.238	.310	.360	27.5	8.9	291
Wicks, Jordan	L-L	6-3	220	9-01-99	4	0	3.39	13	13	0	58	49	27	22	9	19	69	.227	.290	.407	29.0	8.0	238

Fielding

Catcher	PCT	G	PO	A	E	DP	PB
Aliendo	.992	86	917	58	8	7	8
Amaya	.970	11	123	7	4	1	0
Knight	.987	16	144	7	2	0	2
Opitz	.981	26	236	21	5	3	0

First Base	PCT	G	PO	A	E	DP
Amaya	1.000	2	17	0	0	0
Ball	1.000	5	31	2	0	2
Ballesteros	1.000	4	39	2	0	2
Maldonado	.993	47	269	22	2	29
McGeary	.979	72	432	42	10	60
Murray	.986	10	67	4	1	9
Strumpf	1.000	2	8	0	0	0

Second Base	PCT	G	PO	A	E	DP
McKeon	.952	30	41	77	6	22
Murray	.429	2	3	0	4	0
Pertuz	.952	5	9	11	1	7
Shaw	.976	8	19	21	1	4
Strumpf	.989	22	31	61	1	13
Triantos	.882	3	3	12	2	1
Vazquez	1.000	1	2	2	0	2
Verdugo	1.000	2	2	1	0	1
Weber	.965	65	75	118	7	33

Third Base	PCT	G	PO	A	E	DP
McKeon	.667	3	0	2	1	0
Murray	.959	97	64	122	8	12
Shaw	1.000	3	5	2	0	1
Strumpf	1.000	11	1	10	0	0
Verdugo	.815	15	5	17	5	2
Weber	.750	9	3	9	4	3

Shortstop	PCT	G	PO	A	E	DP
Jordan	.974	45	61	87	4	27
Pertuz	.833	1	1	4	1	2
Shaw	.909	3	4	6	1	0
Vazquez	.975	57	84	109	5	29
Verdugo	.500	1	1	0	1	0
Weber	.980	30	35	64	2	16

Outfield	PCT	G	PO	A	E	DP
Alcantara	1.000	4	2	0	0	0
Artis	1.000	3	1	0	0	0
Beesley	.994	58	98	2	1	0
Caissie	.994	107	173	10	2	3
Crow-Armstrong	.908	71	162	2	5	1
Davis	1.000	13	19	0	0	0
Franklin	.500	4	8	0	0	0
Maldonado	1.000	9	14	0	0	0
Nwogu	.985	94	170	3	4	0
Pagan	1.000	2	2	0	0	0
Pertuz	1.000	1	2	0	0	0
Roederer	1.000	66	122	4	0	2

SOUTH BEND CUBS

HIGH CLASS A

MIDWEST LEAGUE

Batting	B-T	Ht.	Wt.	DOB	AVG	OBP	SLG	G	PA	AB	R	H	2B	3B	HR	RBI	BB	HBP	SH	SF	SO	SB	CS	BB%	SO%
Alcantara, Kevin	R-R	6-6	188	7-12-02	.286	.341	.466	95	408	371	65	106	25	3	12	66	31	2	0	4	97	15	4	7.6	23.8
Artis, D.J.	L-L	5-9	165	3-20-97	.333	.481	.429	6	27	21	8	7	0	1	0	2	4	2	0	0	6	5	1	14.8	22.2
Avitia, David	R-R	5-9	205	9-20-98	.222	.300	.222	5	10	9	1	2	0	0	0	1	0	1	0	0	4	0	0	0.0	40.0
Ball, Bryce	L-R	6-4	240	7-08-98	.237	.322	.313	36	149	131	11	31	10	0	0	20	16	1	0	1	38	1	1	10.7	25.5
Ballesteros, Moises	L-R	5-7	195	11-08-03	.300	.364	.463	56	231	203	33	61	15	0	6	31	22	1	0	5	45	2	0	9.5	19.5
Beesley, Bradlee	R-R	5-9	180	2-21-98	.302	.383	.491	13	60	53	12	16	5	1	1	5	4	3	0	0	12	8	0	6.7	20.0
Canario, Alexander	R-R	5-11	165	5-07-00	.256	.370	.282	10	46	39	4	10	1	0	0	7	6	1	0	0	14	0	0	13.0	30.4
Chavers, Parker	L-R	5-9	185	7-25-98	.238	.273	.238	8	22	21	3	5	0	0	0	1	1	0	0	0	6	2	0	4.5	27.3
Davis, Brennen	R-R	6-0	210	11-02-99	.208	.208	.417	5	24	24	3	5	2	0	1	3	0	0	0	0	12	0	0	0.0	50.0
Franklin, Christian	R-R	5-8	195	11-30-99	.248	.380	.410	76	288	234	46	58	11	0	9	36	42	9	1	2	74	9	6	14.6	25.7
Granadillo, Dilan	B-R	5-7	175	5-18-01	.000	.000	.000	2	2	2	0	0	0	0	0	0	0	0	0	0	1	0	0	0.0	50.0
Hearn, Ethan	L-R	5-10	200	8-31-00	.156	.236	.224	72	263	237	21	37	6	2	2	18	20	5	0	1	89	6	2	7.6	33.8
Howard, Ed	R-R	6-1	185	1-28-02	.199	.239	.244	45	188	176	15	35	2	0	2	14	8	2	0	2	58	4	1	4.3	30.9
Huma, Josue	B-R	5-11	175	3-17-00	.100	.250	.133	10	36	30	5	3	1	0	0	1	6	0	0	0	8	1	0	16.7	22.2
Made, Kevin	R-R	5-9	160	9-10-02	.240	.328	.355	70	300	262	39	63	17	2	3	25	30	5	1	2	54	3	4	10.0	18.0
McGeary, Haydn	R-R	6-4	235	10-09-99	.368	.467	.592	20	90	76	9	28	8	0	3	13	13	1	0	0	16	3	0	14.4	17.8
McKeon, Scott	R-R	5-11	185	10-30-97	.284	.336	.440	35	126	116	17	33	9	3	1	19	6	3	1	0	36	12	0	4.8	28.6
Mora, Juan	R-R	5-9	176	9-30-99	.115	.233	.154	8	30	26	2	3	1	0	0	1	2	2	0	0	9	0	1	6.7	30.0
Opitz, Casey	B-R	5-9	200	7-30-98	.209	.309	.309	39	162	139	15	29	6	1	2	19	18	3	0	2	46	2	1	11.1	28.4
Pagan, Ezequiel	L-R	5-9	163	7-08-00	.301	.379	.404	97	429	376	57	113	20	2	5	37	39	10	0	3	66	12	10	9.1	15.4
Pertuz, Fabian	R-R	5-11	156	9-01-00	.199	.269	.327	68	279	251	30	50	11	3	5	30	21	4	0	3	64	14	4	7.5	22.9
Pinango, Yohendrick	L-L	5-11	170	5-07-02	.247	.317	.349	104	439	392	46	97	18	2	6	45	40	2	0	5	72	15	6	9.1	16.4
Rivera, Josh	R-R	6-2	215	10-10-00	.250	.320	.402	25	103	92	18	23	8	0	2	12	9	1	0	1	26	1	1	8.7	25.2
Shaw, Matt	R-R	5-11	185	11-06-01	.393	.427	.655	20	89	84	14	33	4	3	4	18	4	1	0	0	12	7	1	4.5	13.5
Spence, Liam	R-R	6-1	195	4-09-98	.213	.346	.303	36	107	89	15	19	5	0	1	10	17	1	0	0	28	2	0	15.9	26.2
Stevens, Felix	R-R	6-4	225	7-30-99	.242	.316	.502	64	256	231	36	56	18	0	14	39	22	3	0	0	84	4	1	8.6	32.8
Triantos, James	R-R	6-1	195	1-29-03	.285	.363	.390	80	350	305	43	87	14	3	4	46	34	6	0	5	37	16	4	9.7	10.6
Verdugo, Luis	R-R	6-0	160	10-12-00	.271	.336	.454	60	244	218	30	59	19	0	7	38	23	0	0	3	36	4	1	9.4	14.8
Wetzel, Jacob	L-L	5-9	215	3-26-00	.211	.298	.309	67	218	194	23	41	10	3	1	13	22	2	0	0	64	9	3	10.1	29.4

Pitching	B-T	Ht.	Wt.	DOB	W	L	ERA	G	GS	SV	IP	Hits	Runs	ER	HR	BB	SO	AVG	OBP	SLG	SO%	BB%	BF
Arias, Michael	R-R	6-0	155	11-15-01	0	6	5.77	11	11	0	39	42	27	25	2	26	46	.278	.394	.391	25.6	14.4	180
Bain, Max	R-R	6-5	240	9-25-97	2	1	6.66	16	0	0	26	21	20	19	3	19	27	.219	.380	.354	22.3	15.7	121
Birdsell, Brandon	R-R	6-2	240	3-23-00	3	5	2.36	18	18	0	80	58	24	21	4	27	70	.201	.273	.284	21.7	8.4	322
Cabrera, Yovanny	R-R	6-2	180	3-22-01	1	1	8.18	7	0	0	11	14	15	10	1	8	11	.304	.400	.435	20.0	14.5	55
Casey, Derek	R-R	6-2	190	2-15-96	2	0	3.12	9	0	0	17	11	6	6	3	9	29	.177	.274	.371	39.7	12.3	73
Cruz, Yovanny	R-R	6-0	180	8-23-99	0	1	1.89	14	0	0	19	14	5	4	0	10	22	.203	.317	.261	26.5	12.0	83
Deppermann, Brad	R-R	6-0	195	6-15-96	0	0	5.93	10	0	0	14	17	9	9	2	5	18	.304	.361	.464	29.5	8.2	61
Devers, Luis	R-R	6-3	178	4-24-00	4	5	5.11	15	14	0	56	49	34	32	4	32	62	.234	.352	.330	24.8	12.8	250
Espinoza, Manuel	R-R	5-11	150	11-17-00	1	3	2.18	9	7	0	33	24	11	8	1	8	36	.203	.266	.322	27.9	6.2	129
Franklin, Kohl	R-R	6-4	195	9-09-99	0	2	2.79	5	5	0	19	13	8	6	2	12	30	.181	.314	.292	34.9	14.0	86
Gallardo, Richard	R-R	6-1	180	9-06-01	5	3	3.93	13	13	0	66	59	36	29	5	13	63	.231	.277	.357	22.9	4.7	275
Gonsalves, Stephen	L-L	6-5	218	7-08-94	1	0	8.53	6	0	0	6	7	6	6	2	1	11	.292	.414	.542	37.9	3.4	29
Gonzalez, Angel	R-R	6-2	175	8-26-02	0	2	9.60	16	0	0	15	15	20	16	1	16	18	.263	.463	.386	21.7	19.3	83
Guzman, Carlos	R-R	6-1	210	5-16-98	0	0	1.93	4	0	2	9	8	2	2	1	1	10	.242	.257	.394	28.6	2.9	35
Horton, Cade	R-R	6-1	211	8-20-01	3	3	3.83	11	11	0	47	35	22	20	6	12	65	.203	.259	.337	35.1	6.5	185
Hull, Nick	R-R	6-0	205	8-21-99	2	0	3.24	5	1	0	17	10	6	6	2	5	11	.179	.277	.304	16.9	7.7	65
Kipp, Grant	R-R	6-6	220	11-11-99	0	3	8.14	5	5	0	21	26	19	19	5	9	25	.292	.376	.494	24.3	8.7	103
Laskey, Adam	R-L	6-3	205	3-09-98	4	1	3.14	33	0	1	49	46	22	17	3	17	59	.242	.311	.342	28.2	8.1	209
Leigh, Zac	R-R	6-0	170	11-14-97	0	0	0.00	4	0	1	4	0	0	0	0	1	6	.000	.071	.000	42.9	7.1	14
Little, Luke	L-L	6-8	220	8-30-00	0	0	0.52	5	4	0	17	12	3	1	0	7	21	.194	.324	.226	28.4	9.5	74
Marquez, Brailyn	L-L	6-4	185	1-30-99	0	0	0.00	2	0	0	2	0	0	0	0	0	3	.000	.000	.000	50.0	0.0	6
McAvene, Michael	R-R	6-3	207	8-24-97	0	1	8.25	8	0	0	12	13	11	11	3	10	12	.271	.397	.542	20.7	17.2	58
McCullough, Brody	R-R	6-4	205	6-30-00	0	3	4.25	9	9	0	36	32	20	17	3	14	34	.235	.307	.397	22.1	9.1	154
Nahas, Joe	R-R	6-1	185	11-14-99	2	1	2.14	23	0	1	46	38	16	11	0	23	39	.228	.326	.299	20.0	11.8	195
Noland, Connor	R-R	6-2	215	7-20-99	1	8	4.08	24	23	0	108	106	58	49	11	22	86	.252	.289	.410	19.2	4.9	447
Nunez, Eduarniel	R-R	6-2	170	6-07-99	1	1	2.63	22	0	0	27	22	8	8	2	12	37	.218	.307	.317	32.5	10.5	114
Oquendo, Johzan	R-R	6-2	180	1-06-01	1	0	2.60	8	0	1	17	13	5	5	0	13	16	.220	.373	.237	21.3	17.3	75
Reed, Sheldon	L-R	6-2	205	7-30-97	6	3	3.38	40	0	5	53	39	24	20	4	26	63	.207	.306	.314	28.9	11.9	218
Reid, Bailey	R-R	6-2	195	7-03-98	0	0	27.00	6	0	0	3	5	10	10	0	10	5	.333	.600	.467	20.0	40.0	25
Santana, Tyler	R-R	6-1	205	5-13-98	7	8	4.07	30	9	0	91	91	51	41	9	35	78	.261	.330	.415	20.0	9.0	390
Scalzo, Frankie	R-R	6-3	185	11-25-99	4	4	2.31	35	0	8	66	51	26	17	5	21	64	.205	.274	.301	23.2	7.6	276
Thoresen, Sam	R-R	6-3	210	9-21-98	1	0	4.50	5	0	0	12	14	9	6	0	13	17	.298	.484	.426	26.6	20.3	64
Vargas, Didier	R-L	6-0	175	3-13-99	3	3	4.68	17	0	0	25	19	14	13	1	13	27	.213	.327	.281	25.2	12.1	107
Watkins, Chase	L-L	6-4	215	10-04-99	0	4	5.23	21	0	0	33	36	20	19	8	15	32	.275	.349	.511	21.5	10.1	149
Wright, Jarod	R-R	6-3	205	12-15-96	3	1	4.10	28	0	2	53	42	29	24	5	18	38	.213	.279	.376	17.2	8.1	221

Fielding

Catcher	PCT	G	PO	A	E	DP	PB
Avitia	1.000	1	2	0	0	0	0
Ballesteros	.977	38	354	24	9	4	5
Granadillo	1.000	1	2	0	0	0	0
Hearn	.975	62	510	27	14	3	3
Opitz	.989	33	326	25	4	1	2

First Base	PCT	G	PO	A	E	DP
Ball	.993	36	263	31	2	26
Ballesteros	.988	9	76	5	1	10
Hearn	.973	6	35	1	1	2
McGeary	.992	16	122	9	1	12
Opitz	1.000	6	34	3	0	5
Spence	.985	11	55	10	1	7
Stevens	.990	52	372	32	4	27
Verdugo	.929	2	11	2	1	2

Second Base	PCT	G	PO	A	E	DP
Howard	.955	17	18	46	3	7
Huma	.971	9	15	18	1	3
Made	1.000	7	12	18	0	6
McKeon	1.000	10	15	10	0	5
Mora	1.000	3	5	7	0	1
Pertuz	.980	11	13	35	1	8
Rivera	1.000	4	5	7	0	2
Shaw	1.000	2	3	2	0	1
Spence	.952	21	30	50	4	10
Triantos	.940	52	62	141	13	23

Third Base	PCT	G	PO	A	E	DP
Made	.833	5	4	6	2	1
McKeon	.968	15	13	17	1	1
Mora	.857	3	1	5	1	1
Pertuz	.929	39	28	63	7	7
Rivera	1.000	6	10	10	0	1
Spence	.667	2	0	2	1	0
Triantos	.950	7	9	10	1	4
Verdugo	.924	57	30	80	9	7

Shortstop	PCT	G	PO	A	E	DP
Howard	.955	19	31	33	3	11
Made	.972	58	81	160	7	38
McKeon	.828	9	7	17	5	2
Pertuz	.979	15	18	29	1	3
Rivera	.983	15	18	39	1	8
Shaw	.865	15	13	19	5	3

Outfield	PCT	G	PO	A	E	DP
Alcantara	.991	86	213	6	2	2
Artis	1.000	4	7	0	0	0
Beesley	.979	12	25	1	1	0
Canario	1.000	8	12	1	0	1
Chavers	.944	7	12	0	1	0
Davis	1.000	4	9	1	0	1
Franklin	.966	66	118	4	4	1
Pagan	.960	85	153	6	5	2
Pinango	.474	67	89	2	5	1
Stevens	.472	6	17	0	1	0
Triantos	1.000	5	10	1	0	0
Wetzel	.991	59	94	4	2	0

MYRTLE BEACH PELICANS

LOW CLASS A

CAROLINA LEAGUE

Batting	B-T	Ht.	Wt.	DOB	AVG	OBP	SLG	G	PA	AB	R	H	2B	3B	HR	RBI	BB	HBP	SH	SF	SO	SB	CS	BB%	SO%
Avitia, David	R-R	5-9	205	9-20-98	.190	.278	.274	28	98	84	13	16	4	0	1	9	8	3	1	2	34	0	1	8.2	34.7
Ballesteros, Moises	L-R	5-7	195	11-08-03	.274	.394	.457	56	241	197	28	54	12	0	8	32	40	1	0	3	30	5	0	16.6	12.4
Bateman, Brett	L-L	5-10	170	3-19-02	.298	.431	.327	29	130	104	23	31	3	0	0	16	24	1	0	1	19	11	1	18.5	14.6
Carico, Michael	L-R	6-0	190	9-04-02	.286	.444	.714	3	9	7	1	2	0	0	1	2	1	1	0	0	1	0	0	11.1	11.1
Chavers, Parker	L-R	5-9	185	7-25-98	.251	.341	.418	76	316	275	49	69	9	2	11	54	33	5	1	1	79	21	5	10.4	25.0
Encarnacion, Jefferson	L-L	6-1	185	8-28-01	.224	.326	.336	37	144	125	21	28	4	2	2	11	18	1	0	0	45	1	0	12.5	31.3
Espinoza, Leonel	R-R	6-0	165	4-07-03	.128	.196	.149	13	52	47	6	6	1	0	0	4	2	2	1	0	15	2	1	3.8	28.8
Fabrizio, Miguel	L-R	5-9	178	9-26-00	.219	.250	.292	27	100	96	8	21	4	0	1	12	3	1	0	0	35	3	2	3.0	35.0
Franklin, Christian	R-R	5-8	195	11-30-99	.238	.373	.429	11	51	42	8	10	3	1	1	7	5	4	0	0	14	4	0	9.8	27.5
Garcia, Reivaj	B-R	5-9	175	8-12-01	.306	.372	.404	92	415	366	72	112	21	3	3	41	41	1	1	6	71	21	8	9.9	17.1
Garriola, Andy	R-R	6-3	235	12-15-99	.225	.280	.380	103	416	382	43	86	23	0	12	60	19	11	1	3	82	11	3	4.6	19.7
Hernandez, Cristian	R-R	6-1	175	12-13-03	.223	.302	.301	106	431	385	46	86	12	3	4	40	39	5	0	2	118	27	5	9.0	27.4
Kalmer, Brian	R-R	6-2	215	8-17-00	.358	.423	.683	32	138	120	22	43	5	2	10	40	13	2	0	2	28	0	1	9.4	20.3
Long, Jonathan	R-R	6-0	210	1-20-02	.260	.380	.532	23	92	77	11	20	3	0	6	12	11	4	0	0	18	0	0	12.0	19.6
Mena, Ismael	L-L	6-3	185	11-30-02	.236	.277	.340	56	226	212	27	50	5	4	3	16	12	0	2	0	54	13	5	5.3	23.9
Mora, Juan	R-R	5-9	176	9-30-99	.278	.335	.403	40	164	144	18	40	7	1	3	26	11	4	0	5	25	8	6	6.7	15.2
More, Cristian	L-L	5-10	170	8-11-01	.175	.266	.175	17	65	57	9	10	0	0	0	4	7	0	1	0	17	6	2	10.8	26.2
Morel, Rafael	R-R	6-0	170	11-22-01	.263	.368	.356	94	391	334	63	88	10	0	7	30	50	6	0	1	94	16	9	12.8	24.0
Olivo, Christian	R-R	5-9	168	10-29-03	.000	.250	.000	1	4	2	0	0	0	0	0	1	1	0	0	1	1	0	0	25.0	25.0
Pabon, Miguel	R-R	5-9	165	8-30-00	.236	.312	.304	83	313	276	36	65	14	1	1	25	27	5	2	3	70	3	1	8.6	22.4
Preciado, Reginald	B-R	6-3	185	5-16-03	.160	.225	.198	27	90	81	8	13	1	1	0	3	5	2	1	1	23	3	0	5.6	25.6
Quintero, Malcom	B-R	5-10	165	7-29-00	.208	.387	.354	21	62	48	10	10	1	0	2	5	11	3	0	0	14	2	0	17.7	22.6
Ramirez, Pedro	B-R	5-8	165	4-01-04	.266	.358	.404	104	414	354	53	94	19	3	8	54	49	5	1	5	71	17	7	11.8	17.1
Rojas, Jefferson	R-R	5-10	150	4-25-05	.268	.345	.404	70	307	272	48	73	14	1	7	31	23	10	0	2	61	13	4	7.5	19.9
Santana, Yeison	R-R	5-11	170	12-07-00	.389	.389	.556	5	19	18	2	7	1	1	0	3	0	0	1	0	4	0	1	0.0	21.1
Stevens, Felix	R-R	6-4	225	7-30-99	.289	.380	.561	55	216	187	30	54	10	1	13	33	24	4	0	1	67	4	2	11.1	31.0

Pitching	B-T	Ht.	Wt.	DOB	W	L	ERA	G	GS	SV	IP	Hits	Runs	ER	HR	BB	SO	AVG	OBP	SLG	SO%	BB%	BF
Aldrich, Jack	L-L	5-11	204	6-12-99	2	0	5.68	6	0	1	6	8	6	4	0	7	9	.320	.486	.360	24.3	18.9	37
Arias, Michael	R-R	6-0	155	11-15-01	1	4	2.55	11	11	0	42	24	12	12	1	25	64	.164	.291	.233	37.2	14.5	172
Armstrong, Sam	R-R	6-2	245	9-26-00	2	0	5.27	8	0	0	14	11	8	8	0	8	10	.224	.367	.286	16.7	13.3	60
Brown, Garrett	L-R	6-7	218	11-06-99	0	0	2.84	4	0	2	6	7	2	2	0	5	10	.280	.400	.360	33.3	16.7	30
Cabrera, Yovanny	R-R	6-2	180	3-22-01	6	3	2.93	27	0	2	61	46	27	20	4	34	69	.215	.331	.318	26.8	13.2	257
Ferris, Jackson	L-L	6-4	195	1-15-04	2	3	3.38	18	18	0	56	35	22	21	1	33	77	.179	.312	.255	32.5	13.9	237
Ginn, Landon	B-R	6-3	200	7-19-01	2	0	4.66	6	0	0	10	11	7	5	0	7	5	.314	.419	.400	11.4	15.9	44
Gonsalves, Stephen	L-L	6-5	218	7-08-94	0	1	3.00	3	0	0	3	1	1	1	0	2	4	.111	.273	.222	36.4	18.2	11
Gonzalez, Angel	R-R	6-2	175	8-26-02	2	1	3.46	20	0	5	26	22	13	10	0	10	35	.224	.304	.265	31.3	8.9	112
Gonzalez, Saul	R-R	6-7	235	12-28-99	2	1	2.67	15	0	7	27	24	8	8	1	6	29	.240	.284	.330	26.6	5.5	109
Gray, Drew	L-L	6-3	190	5-09-03	0	3	4.23	11	11	0	28	19	13	13	0	23	45	.196	.376	.227	36.0	18.4	125
Hambley, Dominic	R-R	6-2	230	4-24-03	0	1	10.29	3	0	0	7	7	10	8	0	11	8	.259	.488	.259	19.5	26.8	41
Hernandez, Angel	L-L	6-2	180	5-06-00	2	2	4.14	32	0	0	54	42	29	25	1	45	79	.220	.366	.267	32.1	18.3	246
Holloway, Jordan	R-R	6-6	230	6-13-96	2	0	1.69	4	0	0	5	2	1	1	0	3	9	.111	.273	.111	40.9	13.6	22
Horton, Cade	R-R	6-1	211	8-20-01	0	0	1.26	4	4	0	14	8	2	2	1	4	21	.157	.218	.235	38.2	7.3	55
Hull, Nick	R-R	6-0	205	8-21-99	6	3	4.30	18	15	1	75	58	42	36	4	34	77	.212	.308	.297	24.4	10.8	315
Kipp, Grant	R-R	6-6	220	11-11-99	3	7	3.24	18	17	0	78	71	35	28	5	26	80	.247	.318	.376	24.9	8.1	321
Kobos, Scott	L-L	6-2	200	8-03-97	1	0	2.79	8	0	1	10	8	3	3	1	3	13	.222	.300	.333	32.5	7.5	40
Lebron, Scarlyn	R-R	6-3	178	1-02-02	3	1	6.36	23	0	2	47	49	35	33	4	22	40	.272	.357	.406	18.8	10.3	213
Marquez, Brailyn	L-L	6-4	185	1-30-99	0	0	0.00	2	0	0	2	1	1	0	0	2	4	.125	.364	.125	36.4	18.2	11
Martinez-Gomez, Luis	R-R	6-2	178	5-27-03	0	1	20.25	3	0	0	4	5	9	9	1	7	4	.313	.542	.625	16.7	29.2	24

McCullough, Brody	R-R	6-4	205	6-30-00	5	2	2.86	12	12	0	50	29	18	16	3	17	74	.166	.239	.257	37.6	8.6	197
Montano, Gregori	R-R	5-11	175	8-18-99	0	0	7.88	7	0	2	8	9	9	7	0	8	10	.273	.467	.303	22.2	17.8	45
Moore, Grayson	B-R	6-3	215	7-09-01	0	1	11.37	4	0	0	6	7	8	8	0	3	6	.280	.379	.400	20.0	10.0	30
Moreno, Koen	R-R	6-2	170	8-01-01	7	2	2.90	26	6	0	71	55	25	23	5	57	79	.224	.379	.347	25.3	18.3	312
Noriega, Branden	L-L	6-2	180	7-09-01	0	1	9.42	7	1	0	14	15	16	15	1	24	21	.273	.512	.455	25.6	29.3	82
Oquendo, Johzan	R-R	6-2	180	1-06-01	5	1	2.19	21	0	5	37	15	10	9	0	27	54	.121	.286	.145	34.8	17.4	155
Paredes, Eligio	R-R	6-1	190	7-10-02	1	0	4.67	6	0	0	17	15	9	9	1	8	24	.234	.338	.344	32.4	10.8	74
Perez, Kenyi	R-R	6-2	165	8-09-01	0	0	11.05	10	0	0	15	12	20	18	2	30	18	.226	.538	.358	19.8	33.0	91
Pichardo, Starlyn	R-R	6-0	175	1-12-04	7	1	4.28	24	0	0	40	30	25	19	2	29	52	.205	.345	.308	29.4	16.4	177
Quintero, Malcom	B-R	5-10	165	7-29-00	0	0	20.25	2	0	0	1	3	3	3	0	3	1	.429	.600	.571	10.0	30.0	10
Rodriguez, Erian	R-R	6-3	190	11-23-01	5	6	6.49	26	3	0	69	71	54	50	5	45	74	.267	.391	.417	23.1	14.1	320
Romero, Jose	R-R	5-10	185	4-20-01	3	1	2.77	28	0	3	49	35	17	15	3	23	68	.193	.311	.293	32.1	10.8	212
Rujano, Luis	R-R	6-4	200	4-22-03	0	4	4.10	19	9	0	53	49	26	24	3	34	56	.246	.371	.362	23.1	14.0	242
Santy, Marino	L-L	5-11	170	3-04-02	3	2	3.12	22	16	0	75	53	38	26	1	59	100	.196	.362	.244	29.2	17.2	343
Stevens, Felix	R-R	6-4	225	7-30-99	0	0	13.50	1	0	0	1	1	1	1	0	1	0	.333	.500	.667	0.0	25.0	4
Valdez, Kevin	R-R	6-4	185	11-13-01	3	3	3.46	12	7	0	39	21	16	15	2	25	37	.157	.309	.224	22.4	15.2	165
Vargas, Didier	R-L	6-0	175	3-13-99	0	0	4.50	1	0	1	2	1	1	1	0	1	3	.143	.250	.429	37.5	12.5	8

Fielding

Catcher	PCT	G	PO	A	E	DP	PB
Avitia	.992	25	234	19	2	5	3
Ballesteros	.986	38	399	38	6	3	5
Carico	1.000	1	6	0	0	0	0
Pabon	.993	61	623	53	5	3	9
Quintero	.991	13	105	9	1	0	3

First Base	PCT	G	PO	A	E	
DPAvitia	1.000	3	18	3	0	4
Ballesteros	.990	13	95	5	1	10
Fabrizio	.990	14	93	10	1	8
Garcia	.989	27	173	11	2	14
Kalmer	.994	19	151	5	1	17
Long	1.000	10	69	5	0	8
Pabon	1.000	21	141	8	0	7
Stevens	.990	25	183	10	2	20

Second Base	PCT	G	PO	A	E	DP
Garcia	1.000	28	37	63	0	16
Hernandez	.980	36	61	83	3	20
Mora	1.000	4	5	12	0	3
Morel	1.000	1	0	2	0	0
Ramirez	.958	53	68	137	9	34
Rojas	1.000	4	5	11	0	1
Santana	.917	5	9	13	2	4

Third Base	PCT	G	PO	A	E	DP
Garcia	.920	18	9	37	4	10
Hernandez	.000	1	0	0	0	0
Kalmer	1.000	1	1	1	0	0
Long	.968	14	12	18	1	2
Mora	.963	26	22	30	2	2
Morel	.947	13	6	12	1	1
Preciado	.933	24	14	28	3	2
Ramirez	.968	38	20	40	2	5

Shortstop	PCT	G	PO	A	E	DP
Hernandez	.932	59	68	124	14	29
Morel	.975	11	18	21	1	3
Preciado	.000	1	0	0	0	0
Ramirez	.833	1	3	2	1	2
Rojas	.939	60	79	122	13	29

Outfield	PCT	G	PO	A	E	DP
Bateman	1.000	29	49	6	0	1
Chavers	.980	68	104	6	2	1
Encarnacion	1.000	35	47	2	0	0
Espinoza	.979	12	24	2	1	1
Franklin	.955	9	20	1	1	1
Garriola	.994	84	121	4	2	0
Mena	.977	57	80	5	5	2
More	.970	18	25	0	1	0
Morel	.958	66	97	8	7	1
Olivo	1.000	1	2	0	0	0
Preciado	.000	1	0	0	0	0
Stevens	1.000	24	38	2	0	0

ACL CUBS — ROOKIE

ARIZONA COMPLEX LEAGUE

Batting	B-T	Ht.	Wt.	DOB	AVG	OBP	SLG	G	PA	AB	R	H	2B	3B	HR	RBI	BB	HBP	SH	SF	SO	SB	CS	BB%	SO%
Alcantara, Kevin	R-R	6-6	188	7-12-02	.250	.500	.250	2	6	4	2	1	0	0	0	1	2	0	0	0	1	0	0	33.3	16.7
Altuve, Brayan	R-R	5-9	160	1-22-03	.186	.245	.326	32	94	86	11	16	3	0	3	8	7	0	0	1	35	4	1	7.4	37.2
Bateman, Brett	L-L	5-10	170	3-19-02	.111	.273	.111	3	11	9	4	1	0	0	0	0	2	0	0	0	0	3	0	18.2	0.0
Beesley, Bradlee	R-R	5-9	180	2-21-98	.222	.300	.556	3	10	9	3	2	0	0	1	2	1	0	0	0	4	1	0	10.0	40.0
Bowser, Drew	R-R	6-4	226	10-02-01	.295	.367	.386	13	49	44	5	13	4	0	0	7	5	0	0	0	21	4	1	10.2	42.9
Canario, Alexander	R-R	5-11	165	5-07-00	.286	.423	.619	7	26	21	6	6	2	1	1	5	4	1	0	0	5	0	0	15.4	19.2
Carico, Michael	L-R	6-0	190	9-04-02	.111	.385	.111	4	13	9	0	1	0	0	0	1	3	1	0	0	3	0	0	23.1	23.1
Collier, Ke'Shun	L-R	5-4	160	12-21-00	.260	.495	.315	30	110	73	16	19	4	0	0	4	30	5	1	1	27	8	4	27.3	24.5
Davis, Brennen	R-R	6-0	210	11-02-99	.455	.500	.636	4	12	11	0	5	2	0	0	1	1	0	0	0	3	0	0	8.3	25.0
Diaz, Jairo	L-R	5-10	180	7-14-04	.263	.371	.386	21	70	57	11	15	2	1	1	6	10	1	0	2	14	1	0	14.3	20.0
Encarnacion, Jefferson	L-L	6-1	185	8-28-01	.296	.366	.418	29	112	98	17	29	5	2	1	14	12	0	0	2	28	3	1	10.7	25.0
Escobar, Jose	L-R	5-10	165	9-13-04	.333	.413	.395	26	92	81	8	27	2	0	1	10	6	5	0	0	13	6	1	6.5	14.1
Espinoza, Leonel	R-R	6-0	165	4-07-03	.339	.420	.446	33	138	121	21	41	9	2	0	13	14	3	0	0	26	8	3	10.1	18.8
Fabrizio, Miguel	L-R	5-9	178	9-26-00	.455	.647	.636	4	17	11	5	5	2	0	0	3	5	1	0	0	3	0	0	29.4	17.6
Franklin, Christian	R-R	5-8	195	11-30-99	.360	.467	.800	7	30	25	10	9	1	2	2	11	5	0	0	0	5	0	1	16.7	16.7
Hernandez, Alexis	R-R	6-0	155	12-27-04	.315	.407	.515	37	150	130	25	41	9	4	3	25	18	2	0	0	50	9	2	12.0	33.3
Hernandez, Frank	R-R	5-9	185	12-10-01	.242	.296	.348	23	71	66	9	16	2	1	1	3	5	0	0	0	12	0	1	7.0	16.9
Hope, Zyhir	L-L	6-0	193	1-19-05	.286	.419	.543	11	43	35	8	10	0	0	3	9	8	0	0	0	13	3	1	18.6	30.2
Kalmer, Brian	R-R	6-2	215	8-17-00	.333	.455	.444	3	11	9	4	3	1	0	0	2	2	0	0	0	2	0	0	18.2	18.2
Long, Jonathan	R-R	6-0	210	1-20-02	.429	.600	1.000	3	10	7	2	3	1	0	1	2	3	0	0	0	0	0	0	30.0	0.0
Lubo, Geuri	R-R	6-2	185	9-24-03	.205	.333	.284	32	105	88	18	18	7	0	0	7	16	1	0	0	28	1	2	15.2	26.7
Melendez, Yahil	L-R	6-2	175	9-05-05	.237	.256	.342	10	39	38	3	9	2	1	0	3	1	0	0	0	16	0	0	2.6	41.0
More, Cristian	L-L	5-10	170	8-11-01	.370	.453	.519	18	64	54	6	20	4	2	0	12	9	0	0	1	8	11	2	14.1	12.5
Olivo, Christian	R-R	5-9	168	10-29-03	.264	.391	.374	34	111	91	22	24	7	0	1	13	16	3	1	0	23	7	3	14.4	20.7
Paciolla, Christopher	R-R	6-0	185	3-16-04	.260	.324	.402	35	142	127	20	33	6	0	4	23	8	5	0	2	31	6	3	5.6	21.8
Preciado, Reginald	B-R	6-3	185	5-16-03	.100	.136	.200	7	22	20	3	2	0	1	0	5	1	0	0	1	9	0	0	4.5	40.9
Rivera, Josh	R-R	6-2	215	10-10-00	.364	.364	.818	3	11	11	3	4	0	1	1	4	0	0	0	0	2	0	0	0.0	18.2
Rojas, Jefferson	R-R	5-10	150	4-25-05	.000	.000	.000	1	3	3	0	0	0	0	0	0	0	0	0	0	1	0	0	0.0	33.3
Rosario, Alfonsin	R-R	6-2	215	6-21-04	.250	.364	.286	9	33	28	3	7	1	0	0	1	4	1	0	0	8	4	0	12.1	24.2
Ruiz, Lizardo	R-R	5-11	165	8-20-02	.267	.333	.333	13	33	30	3	8	2	0	0	1	2	1	0	0	10	0	1	6.1	30.3
Sanchez, Adan	R-R	6-0	205	5-24-05	.232	.356	.250	35	135	112	20	26	2	0	0	12	19	3	0	1	31	1	1	14.1	23.0
Shaw, Matt	R-R	5-11	185	11-06-01	.500	.636	1.000	3	11	8	3	4	1	0	1	1	2	1	0	0	1	2	1	18.2	9.1

Soto, Wally	L-R	5-6	170	1-05-03	.167	.291	.303	23	79	66	8	11	4	1	1	10	9	3	0	1	24	1	1	11.4	30.4
Suriel, Anderson	L-L	5-11	175	4-11-03	.243	.317	.355	32	120	107	16	26	4	1	2	22	10	2	0	1	30	2	4	8.3	25.0
Trice, Carter	R-R	6-0	200	8-23-02	.296	.406	.556	10	32	27	5	8	4	0	1	6	5	0	0	0	11	0	0	15.6	34.4

Pitching	B-T	Ht.	Wt.	DOB	W	L	ERA	G	GS	SV	IP	Hits	Runs	ER	HR	BB	SO	AVG	OBP	SLG	SO%	BB%	BF
Agrazal, Gabriel	R-R	6-1	185	9-10-03	2	1	5.70	19	0	1	24	31	16	15	0	6	21	.316	.343	.429	19.4	5.6	108
Almanzar, Elian	L-R	6-4	210	2-01-00	0	1	18.90	5	1	0	3	5	10	7	1	7	6	.294	.500	.588	25.0	29.2	24
Armstrong, Sam	R-R	6-2	245	9-26-00	0	0	0.00	1	1	0	1	1	0	0	0	0	1	.333	.333	.333	33.3	0.0	3
Bain, Max	R-R	6-5	240	9-25-97	0	0	1.93	3	0	0	5	4	1	1	0	0	8	.222	.222	.444	44.4	0.0	18
Bello, Juan	R-R	6-1	173	4-06-04	0	1	10.38	4	3	0	4	5	5	5	0	4	5	.294	.429	.353	23.8	19.0	21
Boxberger, Brad	R-R	5-10	211	5-27-88	0	1	13.50	2	2	0	1	2	3	2	0	0	1	.286	.375	.286	12.5	0.0	8
Brown, Garrett	L-R	6-7	218	11-06-99	0	1	3.38	3	0	0	3	3	5	1	0	4	1	.300	.467	.300	6.7	26.7	15
Burdi, Nick	R-R	6-3	225	1-19-93	0	0	13.50	2	0	0	1	4	2	2	1	1	2	.500	.556	1.000	22.2	11.1	9
Casey, Derek	R-R	6-2	190	2-15-96	0	1	3.18	5	3	0	6	6	6	2	0	3	5	.250	.345	.500	17.2	10.3	29
Coran, Raino	R-R	6-4	210	5-13-02	0	0	81.00	1	0	0	0	0	3	3	0	2	1	.000	.750	.000	25.0	50.0	4
Cruz, Yovanny	R-R	6-0	180	8-23-99	0	0	0.00	2	0	0	2	1	1	0	0	1	2	.125	.200	.125	20.0	10.0	10
Cunningham, Wilson	L-L	6-8	185	5-19-03	1	1	13.50	13	0	0	11	10	22	17	2	19	13	.222	.470	.378	19.7	28.8	66
Duffey, Tyler	R-R	6-3	220	12-27-90	0	0	0.00	3	0	0	4	2	0	0	0	1	5	.143	.200	.143	33.3	6.7	15
Garcia, Carlos	L-L	6-4	190	7-12-02	0	4	10.44	9	5	0	25	38	33	29	4	21	35	.345	.467	.573	25.5	15.3	137
Ginn, Landon	B-R	6-3	200	7-19-01	0	0	0.00	1	0	0	1	0	0	0	0	0	3	.000	.000	.000	100.0	0.0	3
Gonsalves, Stephen	L-L	6-5	218	7-08-94	0	0	0.00	3	0	0	3	2	0	0	0	0	4	.200	.200	.200	40.0	0.0	10
Gray, Drew	L-L	6-3	190	5-09-03	0	0	5.68	3	3	0	6	3	5	4	0	6	11	.143	.379	.238	37.9	20.7	29
Greene, Shane	R-R	6-4	200	11-17-88	0	0	2.45	3	0	0	4	5	3	1	0	0	4	.313	.313	.313	25.0	0.0	16
Hambley, Dominic	R-R	6-2	230	4-24-03	2	2	6.68	10	2	0	31	31	33	23	3	25	37	.254	.392	.393	24.2	16.3	153
Kobos, Scott	L-L	6-2	200	8-03-97	0	0	4.50	3	0	0	4	3	2	2	1	3	5	.214	.389	.429	27.8	16.7	18
Machado, Joel	L-L	6-1	160	2-09-02	4	1	5.11	17	1	1	25	23	17	14	3	9	17	.253	.317	.385	16.2	8.6	105
Marquez, Brailyn	L-L	6-4	185	1-30-99	0	0	0.00	3	2	0	3	3	0	0	0	2	2	.273	.429	.364	14.3	14.3	14
Martinez-Gomez, Luis	R-R	6-2	178	5-27-03	0	0	27.00	1	0	0	1	2	2	2	0	1	1	.500	.600	.500	20.0	20.0	5
McGwire, Mason	R-R	6-4	190	1-05-04	1	6	9.42	11	10	0	35	48	44	37	5	29	36	.327	.454	.585	19.5	15.7	185
Montano, Gregori	R-R	5-11	175	8-18-99	0	0	7.71	7	0	0	7	8	7	6	1	3	11	.286	.375	.393	34.4	9.4	32
Moore, Grayson	B-R	6-3	215	7-09-01	0	0	0.00	1	0	0	1	0	0	0	0	1	2	.000	.250	.000	50.0	25.0	4
Mora, Wilme	R-R	6-5	180	6-28-03	0	1	9.56	14	0	0	16	15	27	17	0	29	14	.242	.515	.258	14.3	29.6	98
Morales, Gleiber	R-R	5-10	165	9-28-02	0	0	6.75	3	0	0	7	5	5	5	0	8	9	.217	.406	.304	28.1	25.0	32
Noriega, Branden	L-L	6-2	180	7-09-01	1	0	5.40	15	0	0	28	12	20	17	1	30	45	.133	.365	.222	35.7	23.8	126
Paredes, Eligio	R-R	6-1	190	7-10-02	2	0	2.55	12	1	0	25	20	9	7	1	12	33	.230	.337	.322	31.7	11.5	104
Perez, Kenyi	R-R	6-2	165	8-09-01	0	0	1.00	5	0	0	9	5	3	1	0	6	14	.156	.308	.219	35.9	15.4	39
Peters, Mathew	R-R	6-4	215	12-28-00	0	1	16.68	14	0	0	11	12	21	21	1	24	12	.273	.522	.386	17.4	34.8	69
Reyes, Luis A.	R-R	6-3	220	10-23-03	3	4	6.38	16	0	0	24	20	17	17	1	29	26	.235	.432	.329	21.8	24.4	119
Rodriguez, Wilber	R-R	6-4	220	1-09-00	0	0	16.20	13	0	0	12	20	24	21	2	19	20	.385	.584	.615	26.0	24.7	77
Rojas, Yenrri	R-R	6-1	186	11-30-03	1	4	6.94	10	8	0	35	48	30	27	3	17	25	.329	.407	.486	15.0	10.2	167
Romero, Alfredo	R-R	6-3	175	6-27-03	0	1	18.00	2	1	0	3	3	6	6	1	4	4	.273	.500	.545	25.0	25.0	16
Sampson, Adrian	R-R	6-2	210	10-07-91	0	1	5.40	2	2	0	5	7	4	3	0	0	2	.333	.318	.429	9.1	0.0	22
Sanchez, Tomy	R-R	5-8	163	2-09-03	1	0	7.25	14	0	3	22	16	19	18	3	19	25	.200	.377	.363	23.6	17.9	106
Silverio, Freilyn	R-R	6-3	180	1-24-05	0	4	21.71	10	6	0	17	36	43	41	4	21	11	.444	.569	.728	9.5	18.1	116
Valdez, Kevin	R-R	6-4	185	11-13-01	0	1	2.08	5	4	0	9	5	3	2	1	10	8	.200	.429	.360	22.9	28.6	35

Fielding

C: Sanchez 25, Diaz 19, Hernandez 10, Soto 10, Trice 2, Ruiz 2. **1B:** Suriel 21, Soto 10, Hernandez 9, Ruiz 8, Fabrizio 4, Bowser 3, Kalmer 3, Long 2. **2B:** Escobar 16, Lubo 10, Paciolla 10, Hernandez 8, Olivo 8, Bowser 5, Melendez 2, Rivera 1, Altuve 1. **3B:** Paciolla 16, Lubo 13, Escobar 9, Preciado 6, Bowser 5, Hernandez 5, Olivo 4, Long 1, Rivera 1. **SS:** Hernandez 24, Lubo 9, Olivo 9, Paciolla 8, Melendez 7, Shaw 2, Rivera 1, Rojas 1. **OF:** Espinoza 31, Collier 29, Altuve 25, Encarnacion 25, More 17, Olivo 11, Hope 11, Rosario 8, Suriel 8, Bateman 3, Canario 3, Davis 3, Alcantara 2, Beesley 2, Hernandez 2, Franklin 1.

DSL CUBS — *ROOKIE*

DOMINICAN SUMMER LEAGUE

Batting	B-T	Ht.	Wt.	DOB	AVG	OBP	SLG	G	PA	AB	R	H	2B	3B	HR	RBI	BB	HBP	SH	SF	SO	SB	CS	BB%	SO%
Alcala, Henniel	R-R	5-11	175	6-22-06	.188	.266	.319	27	79	69	7	13	3	0	2	6	5	3	0	2	14	0	0	6.3	17.7
Alcantara, Derik	L-R	6-0	160	2-20-05	.265	.344	.372	34	131	113	16	30	8	2	0	12	14	1	0	3	6	7	3	10.7	4.6
Aleksandrov, Yoanis	R-R	6-1	220	7-29-04	.172	.273	.172	10	33	29	3	5	0	0	0	0	3	1	0	0	17	1	2	9.1	51.5
Altuve, Carlos	R-R	5-11	192	1-06-05	.216	.319	.258	37	113	97	9	21	1	0	1	16	12	3	0	1	29	4	1	10.6	25.7
Benschop, Daniel	R-R	6-2	185	5-26-05	.271	.320	.443	22	76	70	14	19	5	2	1	12	3	2	1	0	14	6	2	3.9	18.4
Bonolis, Andres	R-R	6-0	175	5-28-04	.189	.416	.302	43	149	106	18	20	6	0	2	21	33	9	0	1	44	3	0	22.1	29.5
Campos, Daniel	R-R	5-11	170	12-20-05	.185	.274	.200	30	73	65	11	12	1	0	0	3	7	1	0	0	14	2	1	9.6	19.2
Cepeda, Angel	R-R	6-1	170	10-29-05	.286	.427	.429	30	117	91	19	26	4	3	1	14	18	6	0	2	28	5	1	15.4	23.9
Chalas, Elizaul	B-R	5-10	150	1-08-05	.155	.286	.211	27	84	71	12	11	2	1	0	8	8	5	0	0	20	4	3	9.5	23.8
Cruz, Andrws	R-R	5-10	150	12-03-02	.267	.368	.327	35	125	101	20	27	6	0	0	23	17	2	0	5	13	24	8	13.6	10.4
De Leon, Abel	R-R	5-11	180	8-20-04	.254	.384	.322	32	73	59	9	15	2	1	0	9	11	2	0	1	24	0	0	15.1	32.9
De Leon, Darlyn	L-R	5-8	150	2-11-05	.223	.375	.309	33	120	94	15	21	0	4	0	11	17	7	0	2	24	11	4	14.2	20.0
Delgado, Joan	R-R	5-11	165	12-07-04	.274	.337	.465	47	175	157	25	43	12	3	4	27	11	5	0	2	57	9	3	6.3	32.6
Diaz, Yidel	R-R	5-10	203	11-03-04	.245	.392	.394	38	120	94	20	23	5	0	3	17	22	2	0	2	26	2	0	18.3	21.7
Espinoza, Leonel	R-R	6-0	165	4-07-03	.750	.800	1.500	3	10	8	4	6	0	0	2	4	1	1	0	0	0	3	2	10.0	0.0
Espinoza, Ludwing	B-R	5-11	170	12-10-05	.196	.306	.310	45	183	158	20	31	9	3	1	17	19	6	0	0	48	6	4	10.4	26.2
Febrillet, Moises	R-R	6-2	165	11-01-04	.194	.381	.319	34	97	72	12	14	5	2	0	9	19	4	0	2	40	7	5	19.6	41.2
Ferreira, Daniel	R-R	5-10	170	10-02-03	.226	.375	.290	12	40	31	3	7	2	0	0	4	8	0	0	1	12	0	2	20.0	30.0
Ferrera, Omar	L-R	5-10	150	7-09-02	.146	.331	.188	41	127	96	18	14	4	0	0	6	24	4	0	3	21	6	0	18.9	16.5
Gomez, Dilver	R-R	5-10	190	1-15-04	.200	.385	.200	10	13	10	1	2	0	0	0	1	2	1	0	0	4	0	0	15.4	30.8

Gutierrez, Albert	R-R	6-1	195	2-15-04	.247	.357	.392	49	185	158	25	39	7	2	4	18	24	3	0	0	49	0	1	13.0	26.5
Guzman, Raul	L-L	5-11	145	10-18-03	.182	.367	.182	10	30	22	4	4	0	0	0	1	7	0	0	1	7	4	1	23.3	23.3
Hernandez, Oferman	L-R	6-0	160	10-15-03	.154	.200	.231	19	55	52	4	8	4	0	0	6	3	0	0	0	16	0	0	5.5	29.1
Herrera, Jose	R-R	5-11	162	4-03-03	.000	.214	.000	6	14	11	1	0	0	0	0	0	2	1	0	0	6	0	0	14.3	42.9
Jaque, Erbin	R-R	5-9	170	9-07-02	.223	.348	.384	41	135	112	22	25	5	2	3	14	16	6	0	1	47	19	8	11.9	34.8
Lumpuy, Alexey	L-L	6-0	180	2-22-04	.217	.316	.337	29	98	83	10	18	2	4	0	9	7	6	0	2	26	3	2	7.1	26.5
Maza, Luis	L-R	5-10	150	10-10-02	.231	.412	.410	18	51	39	5	9	4	0	1	7	11	1	0	0	11	1	0	21.6	21.6
Nunez, Vicent	R-R	5-10	185	2-28-05	.145	.289	.145	23	76	62	4	9	0	0	0	6	11	2	0	1	13	2	0	14.5	17.1
Pascual, Brailin	R-R	6-2	160	12-02-04	.192	.241	.250	36	112	104	12	20	1	1	1	10	7	0	0	1	45	4	1	6.3	40.2
Ramirez, Josias	R-R	6-0	155	7-08-05	.197	.337	.336	47	166	137	23	27	8	1	3	18	23	6	0	0	54	8	1	13.9	32.5
Ramon, Eriandys	B-R	6-3	170	1-07-03	.222	.355	.356	31	111	90	8	20	5	2	1	6	15	4	0	1	21	3	1	13.5	18.9
Sanchez, Sandy	B-R	5-10	150	7-15-05	.228	.331	.317	38	118	101	20	23	5	2	0	14	16	0	0	1	26	7	1	13.6	22.0
Valdez, Derniche	R-R	5-11	150	3-29-06	.234	.328	.477	35	125	107	17	25	4	2	6	20	15	1	0	2	51	4	4	12.0	40.8
Vargas, Edward	R-R	6-2	165	1-22-04	.307	.355	.457	42	155	140	22	43	8	5	1	15	11	1	0	3	16	6	7	7.1	10.3
Velasquez, Grenyerbert	B-R	5-11	180	9-08-05	.250	.320	.307	31	100	88	14	22	5	0	0	8	10	0	0	2	23	2	2	10.0	23.0

Pitching	**B-T**	**Ht.**	**Wt.**	**DOB**	**W**	**L**	**ERA**	**G**	**GS**	**SV**	**IP**	**Hits**	**Runs**	**ER**	**HR**	**BB**	**SO**	**AVG**	**OBP**	**SLG**	**SO%**	**BB%**	**BF**
Amador, Melvyn	L-L	5-10	172	1-08-04	2	3	8.64	12	2	1	25	30	29	24	4	27	29	.291	.438	.456	22.3	20.8	130
Archbold, Juan	R-R	6-2	180	3-21-04	0	5	5.65	12	12	0	37	39	29	23	2	22	37	.267	.383	.432	21.1	12.6	175
Bracho, David	R-R	6-0	160	2-24-05	0	4	3.68	12	12	0	37	38	18	15	0	21	28	.275	.375	.341	17.5	13.1	160
Camacho, Kevin	R-R	5-11	200	2-10-05	4	1	5.09	14	0	1	23	25	16	13	4	13	22	.275	.377	.505	20.8	12.3	106
Castillo, Eduardo	R-R	6-1	176	9-16-03	1	2	9.37	14	0	0	16	16	19	17	2	18	15	.258	.440	.468	17.9	21.4	84
Cruz, Miguel	L-L	6-4	200	8-03-03	0	5	5.00	13	13	0	36	26	27	20	0	28	35	.200	.359	.254	21.0	16.8	167
Diaz, Brayan	R-R	6-1	190	1-05-01	0	1	4.66	5	0	1	10	10	6	5	0	6	11	.286	.390	.286	26.8	14.6	41
Dugarte, Diego	R-R	6-1	182	11-08-02	0	3	3.21	12	11	0	48	44	23	17	2	10	43	.246	.318	.330	21.7	5.1	198
Florentino, Jostin	R-R	6-0	175	12-01-04	4	1	3.57	13	0	0	35	34	14	14	2	10	35	.256	.306	.398	24.3	6.9	144
Gonzalez, Charbel	R-R	6-2	180	3-13-04	0	1	8.64	14	0	0	25	27	29	24	5	20	24	.270	.392	.510	19.2	16.0	125
Imbriano, Zhiorman	L-L	6-0	180	1-30-03	0	2	2.98	12	11	0	42	39	14	14	1	22	32	.253	.350	.305	18.1	12.4	177
Jimenez, Jair	R-R	6-1	172	4-09-02	0	3	2.45	15	0	2	26	18	11	7	3	20	25	.202	.351	.337	22.5	18.0	111
Landaez, Bryan	R-R	6-1	175	8-03-04	1	0	2.38	6	0	0	11	9	8	3	2	5	9	.214	.333	.357	17.6	9.8	51
Lopez, Ronny	R-R	6-1	185	11-18-02	3	4	5.75	14	4	0	36	24	26	23	2	26	35	.192	.335	.344	22.2	16.5	158
Madeira, Emannoel	R-R	6-3	225	8-20-06	0	0	4.15	13	13	0	30	20	20	14	3	28	35	.190	.370	.305	25.9	20.7	135
Marte, Fraimin	R-R	6-3	170	7-21-01	4	2	3.77	17	3	1	31	21	17	13	2	18	25	.183	.317	.278	18.0	12.9	139
Mosquea, Dalbert	R-R	6-0	185	6-01-05	0	3	3.14	9	0	1	14	12	8	5	0	3	23	.226	.254	.377	39.0	5.1	59
Olivo, David	R-R	6-0	170	9-28-02	2	1	6.26	15	0	0	23	22	20	16	2	19	19	.253	.421	.356	16.7	16.7	114
Pirela, Nestor	R-R	6-1	170	2-26-06	1	1	6.94	8	0	1	12	14	10	9	0	4	7	.304	.421	.435	12.3	7.0	57
Quintero, Welington	R-R	6-0	185	12-17-00	3	4	2.70	16	0	5	27	26	16	8	3	8	31	.255	.315	.441	27.9	7.2	111
Reyes, Luis R.	R-R	6-0	185	10-22-02	1	0	2.79	6	0	0	10	7	4	3	0	6	10	.200	.326	.286	23.3	14.0	43
Reynoso, Francis	R-R	6-5	206	12-26-02	3	0	2.25	20	0	3	28	20	11	7	1	15	42	.192	.306	.240	34.7	12.4	121
Romero, Alfredo	R-R	6-3	175	6-27-03	1	2	2.25	10	10	0	28	27	16	7	0	15	28	.257	.350	.343	22.8	12.2	123
Romero, Jordi	R-R	6-2	185	7-05-02	0	0	1.93	4	0	0	5	3	2	1	0	6	4	.167	.375	.167	16.7	25.0	24
Santana, Adrian	R-R	6-1	165	9-04-03	2	4	3.09	16	1	2	32	23	17	11	0	26	30	.200	.345	.252	20.7	17.9	145
Santana, Welington	R-R	6-3	182	5-20-01	0	1	7.00	7	0	0	9	8	11	7	0	14	5	.267	.560	.333	10.0	28.0	50
Siri, Saul	R-R	6-2	195	12-20-04	2	4	14.04	15	4	0	17	25	37	26	2	36	9	.347	.568	.569	8.1	32.4	111
Toribio, Runelvis	R-R	6-1	155	5-02-03	0	1	9.99	14	0	0	24	27	39	27	2	27	24	.278	.467	.474	17.8	20.0	135
Vasquez, Yafrerlyn	R-R	6-1	190	3-18-04	1	3	5.32	9	6	0	22	18	17	13	2	19	18	.228	.382	.367	17.6	18.6	102
Vazquez, Irving	R-R	6-3	195	7-13-03	3	2	4.03	16	0	1	29	28	18	13	3	11	33	.246	.336	.404	25.2	8.4	131
Vizcaino, Jeral	R-R	6-1	155	1-07-02	3	2	2.38	14	4	0	34	25	11	9	1	14	34	.200	.297	.296	23.4	9.7	145

Fielding

C: De Leon 32, Diaz 31, Campos 24, Alcala 22, Altuve 22, Nunez 15, Gomez 10, Maza 2. **1B:** Gutierrez 36, Febrillet 15, Altuve 15, Diaz 11, Nunez 11, Ferrera 8, Alcala 6, Campos 5, Maza 5, Herrera 4, Aleksandrov 3, Hernandez 2. **2B:** Velasquez 20, Sanchez 18, Chalas 14, Espinoza 14, Pascual 13, De Leon 11, Ferrera 10, Cruz 8, Ramon 6, Cepeda 3, Delgado 1. **3B:** Sanchez 19, Ferrera 16, Febrillet 15, Pascual 14, Delgado 13, Chalas 9, Ramon 9, Cruz 7, Cepeda 6, Velasquez 6, Maza 3. **SS:** Espinoza 32, Valdez 31, Cepeda 17, Ramon 15, Pascual 6, Velasquez 5, Cruz 4, Sanchez 2, Chalas 1, Ferrera 1. **OF:** Ramirez 48, Vargas 41, Jaque 39, Delgado 33, Bonolis 32, Alcantara 28, Lumpuy 24, Cruz 20, De Leon 19, Benschop 17, Hernandez 17, Guzman 9, Ferreira 8, Ferrera 5, Espinoza 2.

Chicago White Sox

SEASON SYNOPSIS: Nothing went according to plan on the South Side of Chicago, where the White Sox racked up more losses than they had since 1970. The disaster led to a shocking shakeup of the front office as owner Jerry Reinsdorf fired team president Kenny Williams and general manager Rick Hahn in August.

HIGH POINT: In a 101-loss season, the highlight highlighted one of the team's biggest issues—the absence of closer Liam Hendriks, who rang the bell after being treated for non-Hodgkin's Lymphoma. He made an emotional return to the mound at home on May 29 against the Angels and picked up two wins and a save in five appearances to give the team a boost. However, Hendriks soon hurt his elbow and wound up having Tommy John surgery.

LOW POINT: Former all-star shortstop Tim Anderson had a forgettable season—a .288 career hitter entering 2023, he batted .245/.286/.296, hit only one home run and posted -2.0 bWAR. But few will forget his fight with Cleveland's Jose Ramirez during an Aug. 5 game. Ramirez slid in with a double and objected to Anderson's hard tag. Anderson squared up, dropped his gloves and put up his dukes ... whereupon Ramirez jolted him with a punch to the jaw.

NOTABLE ROOKIES: Outfielder Oscar Colas jumped from Double-A to the big league Opening Day roster but didn't make it to May before being sent to Triple-A; he came back in July and stayed through the rest of the season. Righty Gregory Santos (3.39 ERA) led the team in relief innings. Righty Jesse Scholtens, a 2016 draftee and minor league free-agent signing, wound up sixth on the team with 85 innings pitched.

KEY TRANSACTIONS: Reinsdorf stayed in-house, promoting Chris Getz to GM; the former big leaguer had served as the Sox' farm director the last seven seasons, including as assistant GM since 2021. Hahn and Williams sold assets prior to being let go, including young third baseman Jake Burger, dealt to Miami for minor league lefty Jake Eder. They added prospects by sending Lance Lynn and Joe Kelly to the Dodgers and Kendall Graveman to the Astros.

DOWN ON THE FARM: The White Sox had the worst win-loss record across the minors. Their Triple-A Charlotte team was particularly disastrous, going 53-96 (.356), but Double-A Birmingham's 51-87 (.370) record wasn't much better.

OPENING DAY PAYROLL: $181,158,666 (14th)

PLAYERS OF THE YEAR

MAJOR LEAGUE

Luis Robert Jr.
OF
.264/.315/.542
36 2B, 38 HR
20 SB, 90 R

MINOR LEAGUE

Terrell Tatum
OF
(HiA/AA)
.248/.397/.367
47 SB in 56 Att.

ORGANIZATION LEADERS

Batting		*Minimum 250 AB
MAJORS		
* AVG	Eloy Jimenez	.272
* OPS	Luis Robert Jr.	.857
HR	Luis Robert Jr.	38
RBI	Luis Robert Jr.	80
	Andrew Vaughn	80
MINORS		
* AVG	Michael Turner, Winston-Salem	.309
* OBP	Colson Montgomery, ACL W-S/W-S/Birmingham/	.455
* SLG	Tim Elko, Kannapolis/W-S/Birming.	.427
* OPS	Colson Montgomery, ACL W-S/W-S/Birmingham/	.940
R	Terrell Tatum, W.-Salem/Birmingham	89
H	Wilfred Veras, W.-Salem/Birmingham	150
TB	Tim Elko, Kannapolis/W-S/Birming.	266
2B	Wilfred Veras, W.-Salem/Birmingham	39
3B	D.J. Gladney, Winston-Salem	6
3B	Loidel Chapelli, Winston-Salem	6
HR	Tim Elko, Kannapolis/W-S/Birming.	28
RBI	Tim Elko, Kannapolis/W-S/Birming.	106
BB	Terrell Tatum, W.-Salem/Birmingham	100
SO	Wes Kath, Winston-Salem	168
SB	Terrell Tatum, W.-Salem/Birmingham	47

Pitching		#Minimum 75 IP
MAJORS		
W	Mike Clevinger	9
# ERA	Mike Clevinger	3.77
SO	Dylan Cease	214
SV	Kendall Graveman	8
MINORS		
W	Manuel Veloz, Kannap./W-S	10
L	Matthew Thompson, Birmingham	15
# ERA	Mason Adams, Kann./W-S/Birming.	3.14
G	Declan Cronin, Charlotte	47
	Bily Seidl, Kannapolis	47
GS	Matthew Thompson, Birmingham	27
	Christian Mena, Birm./Charlotte	27
SV	Bily Seidl, Kannapolis	14
IP	Christian Mena, Birm./Charlotte	133
# BB	Matthew Thompson, Birmingham	74
SO	Christian Mena, Birm./Charlotte	156
AVG	Shane Murphy, Kannapolis	.226

2023 PERFORMANCE

General Manager: Rick Hahn. **Farm Director:** Chris Getz. **Scouting Director:** Mike Shirley

Class	Team	League	W	L	PCT	Finish	Manager
Majors	Chicago White Sox	American	61	101	.377	13 (15)	Pedro Grifol
Triple-A	Charlotte Knights	International	53	96	.356	20 (20)	Justin Jirschele
Double-A	Birmingham Barons	Southern	51	87	.370	8 (8)	Lorenzo Bundy
High-A	Winston-Salem Dash	South Atlantic	60	66	.476	10 (12)	Guillermo Quiroz
Low-A	Kannapolis Cannon Ballers	Carolina	67	64	.511	4 (12)	Pat Leyland
Rookie	ACL White Sox	Arizona Complex	21	35	.375	15 (17)	Danny Gonzalez
Rookie	DSL White Sox	Dominican Sum.	32	22	.593	12 (50)	Anthony Nunez
Overall 2023 Minor League Record			**284**	**370**	**.434**	**30th (30)**	

ORGANIZATION STATISTICS

CHICAGO WHITE SOX

AMERICAN LEAGUE

Batting	B-T	Ht.	Wt.	DOB	AVG	OBP	SLG	G	PA	AB	R	H	2B	3B	HR	RBI	BB	HBP	SH	SF	SO	SB	CS	BB%	SO%
Alberto, Hanser	R-R	5-11	215	10-17-92	.220	.261	.390	30	90	82	11	18	5	0	3	16	4	1	2	1	13	0	0	4.4	14.4
Anderson, Tim	R-R	6-1	185	6-23-93	.245	.286	.296	123	524	493	52	121	18	2	1	25	26	3	0	2	122	13	2	5.0	23.3
Andrus, Elvis	R-R	6-0	210	8-26-88	.251	.304	.358	112	406	374	39	94	20	1	6	44	25	4	1	2	71	12	4	6.2	17.5
Benintendi, Andrew	L-L	5-9	180	7-06-94	.262	.326	.356	151	621	562	72	147	34	2	5	45	52	3	1	3	89	13	2	8.4	14.3
Burger, Jake	R-R	6-2	230	4-10-96	.214	.279	.527	88	323	294	44	63	15	1	25	52	22	5	0	2	102	1	1	6.8	31.6
2-team (53 Miami)					.250	.309	.518	141	540	492	71	123	28	1	34	80	32	12	0	4	149	1	1	5.9	27.6
Colas, Oscar	L-L	5-11	209	9-17-98	.216	.257	.314	75	263	245	32	53	9	0	5	19	12	2	2	2	71	4	3	4.6	27.0
Frazier, Clint	R-R	5-11	212	9-06-94	.197	.303	.242	33	76	66	10	13	1	1	0	3	10	0	0	0	23	4	2	13.2	30.3
Gonzalez, Romy	R-R	6-1	215	9-06-96	.194	.208	.376	44	97	93	11	18	4	2	3	14	2	0	1	1	36	7	0	2.1	37.1
Grandal, Yasmani	B-R	6-2	225	11-08-88	.234	.309	.339	118	405	363	33	85	14	0	8	33	36	4	0	2	86	0	0	8.9	21.2
Hamilton, Billy	B-R	6-0	160	9-09-90	.000	.000	.000	3	2	2	2	0	0	0	0	0	0	0	0	0	1	2	0	0.0	50.0
Haseley, Adam	L-L	6-1	190	4-12-96	.222	.282	.278	28	39	36	6	8	2	0	0	2	3	0	0	0	8	1	0	7.7	20.5
Jimenez, Eloy	R-R	6-4	240	11-27-96	.272	.317	.441	120	489	456	50	124	23	0	18	64	30	1	0	2	93	0	0	6.1	19.0
Lee, Korey	R-R	6-2	210	7-25-98	.077	.143	.138	24	70	65	4	5	1	0	1	3	5	0	0	0	20	0	0	7.1	28.6
Marisnick, Jake	R-R	6-4	220	3-30-91	.000	.000	.000	9	2	2	1	0	0	0	0	0	0	0	0	0	1	0	0	0.0	50.0
3-team (33 Detroit, 4 Los Angeles Dodgers)					.237	.280	.408	46	83	76	10	18	3	2	2	10	3	2	1	1	21	2	3	3.6	25.3
Moncada, Yoan	B-R	6-2	225	5-27-95	.260	.305	.425	92	357	334	39	87	20	1	11	40	20	2	0	1	107	1	0	5.6	30.0
Naquin, Tyler	L-R	6-1	202	4-24-91	.000	.000	.000	5	8	8	0	0	0	0	0	0	0	0	0	0	7	0	0	0.0	87.5
Perez, Carlos	R-R	5-11	205	9-10-96	.204	.264	.347	27	53	49	5	10	4	0	1	3	4	0	0	0	11	0	0	7.5	20.8
Remillard, Zach	R-R	6-0	185	2-21-94	.252	.295	.320	54	160	147	16	37	7	0	1	18	8	1	4	0	48	4	3	5.0	30.0
Robert, Luis	R-R	6-2	220	8-03-97	.264	.315	.542	145	595	546	90	144	36	1	38	80	30	12	0	2	172	20	4	5.0	28.9
Rodriguez, Jose	R-R	5-11	175	5-13-01	.000	.000	.000	1	0	0	1	0	0	0	0	0	0	0	0	0	0	0	0	0.0	0.0
Sheets, Gavin	L-L	6-5	230	4-23-96	.203	.267	.331	118	344	311	24	63	10	0	10	43	28	1	0	4	66	1	0	8.1	19.2
Sosa, Lenyn	R-R	6-0	180	1-25-00	.201	.224	.348	52	173	164	12	33	6	0	6	14	5	0	3	1	40	0	1	2.9	23.1
Thompson, Trayce	R-R	6-3	225	3-15-91	.171	.261	.232	36	92	82	5	14	2	0	1	3	9	1	0	0	40	2	0	9.8	43.5
2-team (36 Los Angeles Dodgers)					.163	.285	.294	72	179	153	17	25	2	0	6	17	24	2	0	0	77	2	0	13.4	43.0
Vaughn, Andrew	R-R	6-0	215	4-03-98	.258	.314	.429	152	615	566	67	146	30	2	21	80	36	11	0	2	129	0	0	5.9	21.0
Zavala, Seby	R-R	5-11	205	8-28-93	.155	.207	.304	66	176	161	15	25	3	0	7	16	10	1	2	2	68	1	0	5.7	38.6
2-team (7 Arizona)					.171	.230	.314	73	193	175	17	30	4	0	7	18	12	2	2	2	70	1		6.2	36.3

Pitching	B-T	Ht.	Wt.	DOB	W	L	ERA	G	GS	SV	IP	Hits	Runs	ER	HR	BB	SO	AVG	OBP	SLG	SO%	BB%	BF
Alberto, Hanser	R-R	5-11	215	10-17-92	0	0	21.60	2	0	0	2	6	4	4	1	1	1	.545	.583	.818	8.3	8.3	12
Banks, Tanner	R-L	6-1	210	10-24-91	1	4	4.43	32	3	1	61	59	32	30	10	16	51	.254	.310	.474	20.0	6.3	255
Bummer, Aaron	L-L	6-3	215	9-21-93	5	5	6.79	61	0	0	58	53	45	44	4	36	78	.236	.352	.347	29.2	13.5	267
Cease, Dylan	R-R	6-2	195	12-28-95	7	9	4.58	33	33	0	177	172	98	90	19	79	214	.250	.332	.405	27.3	10.1	784
Clevinger, Mike	R-R	6-4	215	12-21-90	9	9	3.77	24	24	0	131	121	56	55	16	40	110	.244	.310	.407	20.0	7.3	549
Colome, Alex	R-R	6-2	240	12-31-88	0	1	6.00	4	0	0	3	2	4	2	1	3	2	.167	.333	.500	13.3	20.0	15
Crochet, Garrett	L-L	6-6	230	6-21-99	0	2	3.55	13	0	0	13	12	6	5	1	13	12	.255	.413	.404	18.8	20.3	64
Cronin, Declan	R-R	6-4	225	9-24-97	0	1	9.00	9	0	0	11	11	12	11	3	7	8	.262	.392	.500	15.7	13.7	51
Diekman, Jake	R-L	6-4	195	1-21-87	0	1	7.94	13	0	0	11	11	14	10	1	13	11	.244	.414	.378	19.0	22.4	58
Garcia, Deivi	R-R	5-9	163	5-19-99	0	1	2.89	6	0	0	9	5	8	3	1	8	7	.156	.333	.313	16.7	19.0	42
Giolito, Lucas	R-R	6-6	245	7-14-94	6	6	3.79	21	21	0	121	106	55	51	20	42	131	.232	.304	.430	25.8	8.3	507
Graveman, Kendall	R-R	6-2	200	12-21-90	3	4	3.48	45	0	8	44	33	20	17	6	20	42	.208	.314	.365	22.6	10.8	186
Hendriks, Liam	R-R	6-0	235	2-10-89	2	0	5.40	5	0	1	5	4	3	3	1	1	3	.222	.250	.444	15.0	5.0	20
Honeywell, Brent	R-R	6-2	195	3-31-95	0	0	11.12	4	0	0	6	9	7	7	2	3	3	.346	.433	.654	10.0	10.0	30
Kelly, Joe	R-R	6-1	174	6-09-88	1	5	4.97	31	0	1	29	26	19	16	3	12	41	.228	.313	.404	32.0	9.4	128
Kopech, Michael	R-R	6-3	210	4-30-96	5	12	5.43	30	27	0	129	115	80	78	29	91	134	.238	.368	.470	22.7	15.4	591
Lambert, Jimmy	R-R	6-2	190	11-18-94	2	3	5.26	35	1	1	38	41	26	22	10	20	41	.273	.363	.560	23.8	11.6	172
Lopez, Reynaldo	R-R	6-1	225	1-04-94	2	5	4.29	43	0	4	42	33	21	20	7	22	52	.213	.309	.381	29.2	12.4	178
Lynn, Lance	B-R	6-5	270	5-12-87	6	9	6.47	21	21	0	120	130	94	86	28	45	144	.270	.340	.497	26.9	8.4	535
Middleton, Keynan	R-R	6-3	215	9-12-93	2	2	3.96	39	0	2	36	33	17	16	7	16	47	.239	.323	.413	30.1	10.3	156
Navarro, Edgar	R-R	6-1	180	2-05-98	0	0	7.27	8	0	0	9	11	7	7	2	2	9	.314	.385	.571	23.1	5.1	39
Padilla, Nicholas	R-R	6-2	220	12-24-96	0	1	5.79	3	0	0	5	9	3	3	1	1	6	.409	.435	.682	26.1	4.3	23
Patino, Luis	R-R	6-1	192	10-26-99	0	1	3.57	7	1	0	18	16	8	7	1	12	13	.235	.350	.309	16.3	15.0	80
Peralta, Sammy	L-L	6-2	205	5-10-98	2	0	4.05	16	0	0	20	19	11	9	2	11	18	.241	.333	.392	20.0	12.2	90

Ramirez, Yohan	R-R	6-4	212	5-06-95	0	0	9.00	5	0	0	4	5	4	4	0	3	4	.313	.429	.500	19.0	14.3	21
Ramsey, Lane	R-R	6-9	245	7-16-96	1	0	5.85	21	0	0	20	25	13	13	1	9	18	.313	.374	.400	19.6	9.8	92
Ruiz, Jose	R-R	6-1	245	10-21-94	0	0	22.09	4	0	0	4	8	9	9	3	4	3	.421	.560	.895	12.0	16.0	25
Santos, Gregory	R-R	6-2	190	8-28-99	2	2	3.39	60	0	5	66	69	29	25	2	17	66	.258	.315	.318	22.8	5.9	289
Scholtens, Jesse	R-R	6-4	230	4-06-94	1	9	5.29	26	11	1	85	100	54	50	15	30	58	.292	.350	.458	15.4	8.0	377
Shaw, Bryan	B-R	6-1	226	11-08-87	0	0	4.14	38	0	4	46	39	21	21	3	17	40	.235	.326	.337	21.1	8.9	190
Toussaint, Touki	R-R	6-3	215	6-20-96	4	6	4.97	19	15	0	83	66	46	46	10	52	83	.221	.344	.356	22.7	14.2	365
Urena, Jose	R-R	6-2	208	9-12-91	0	3	4.10	5	5	0	26	23	15	12	4	8	20	.235	.294	.418	18.2	7.3	110

Fielding

Catcher	PCT	G	PO	A	E	DP	PB
Grandal	.995	92	730	30	4	3	4
Lee	.978	23	170	11	4	0	2
Perez	.980	20	91	7	2	2	1
Zavala	.994	65	490	16	3	1	4

First Base	PCT	G	PO	A	E	DP
Alberto	1.000	2	4	0	0	1
Burger	1.000	5	24	0	0	1
Grandal	1.000	6	18	1	0	3
Sheets	.981	22	95	8	2	15
Vaughn	.995	143	950	69	5	87

Second Base	PCT	G	PO	A	E	DP
Alberto	.976	11	18	23	1	7
Anderson	.833	2	3	2	1	0
Andrus	.975	63	92	139	6	29
Burger	1.000	5	5	11	0	2
Gonzalez	1.000	28	23	47	0	8
Remillard	.985	34	53	80	2	18
Rodriguez	1.000	1	0	1	0	0
Sosa	.987	44	64	92	2	19

Third Base	PCT	G	PO	A	E	DP
Alberto	.921	19	16	19	3	1
Andrus	1.000	3	3	4	0	0
Burger	.972	53	33	73	3	13
Gonzalez	.000	1	0	0	0	0
Moncada	.971	90	60	138	6	13
Remillard	1.000	7	5	8	0	0
Sosa	.933	10	4	10	1	4

Shortstop	PCT	G	PO	A	E	DP
Anderson	.966	119	157	239	14	58
Andrus	.961	52	63	86	6	19
Gonzalez	1.000	2	0	3	0	0
Remillard	1.000	4	3	1	0	0

Outfield	PCT	G	PO	A	E	DP
Benintendi	.986	147	271	6	4	1
Colas	.979	77	157	5	6	2
Frazier	.982	35	25	2	1	0
Gonzalez	.600	10	9	0	1	0
Hamilton	.000	1	0	0	0	0
Haseley	.667	25	26	0	0	0
Jimenez	1.000	14	22	0	0	0
Marisnick	.500	8	1	0	0	0
Naquin	.500	3	4	0	0	0
Remillard	.857	12	11	1	2	1
Robert	.992	143	370	7	3	3
Sheets	.995	75	103	2	1	0
Thompson	1.000	34	49	2	0	0

CHARLOTTE KNIGHTS

TRIPLE-A

INTERNATIONAL LEAGUE

Batting	B-T	Ht.	Wt.	DOB	AVG	OBP	SLG	G	PA	AB	R	H	2B	3B	HR	RBI	BB	HBP	SH	SF	SO	SB	CS	BB%	SO%
Alberto, Hanser	R-R	5-11	215	10-17-92	.444	.444	.556	3	9	9	2	4	1	0	0	1	0	0	0	0	0	0	0	0.0	0.0
Anderson, Tim	R-R	6-1	185	6-23-93	.200	.200	.300	3	10	10	1	2	1	0	0	1	0	0	0	0	1	0	0	0.0	10.0
Andrus, Elvis	R-R	6-0	210	8-26-88	.357	.400	.571	4	15	14	2	5	0	0	1	1	1	0	0	0	1	1	0	6.7	6.7
Burger, Jake	R-R	6-2	230	4-10-96	.200	.227	.250	5	22	20	2	4	1	0	0	2	1	0	0	1	3	0	0	4.5	13.6
Cespedes, Yoelqui	R-R	5-7	205	9-24-97	.362	.362	.553	11	47	47	10	17	6	0	1	6	0	0	0	0	7	1	2	0.0	14.9
Claunch, Troy	R-R	6-0	210	9-01-98	.250	.250	.250	2	4	4	0	1	0	0	0	0	0	0	0	0	3	0	0	0.0	75.0
Colas, Oscar	L-L	5-11	209	9-17-98	.272	.345	.465	54	238	213	36	58	14	0	9	29	22	2	0	1	53	2	0	9.2	22.3
Fernandez, Xavier	R-R	5-8	245	7-15-95	.331	.397	.548	36	141	124	19	41	12	0	5	15	15	0	0	2	23	0	0	10.6	16.3
Frazier, Clint	R-R	5-11	212	9-06-94	.231	.363	.442	63	256	208	32	48	9	1	11	30	40	5	0	3	68	5	4	15.6	26.6
Gonzalez, Erik	R-R	6-3	205	8-31-91	.272	.322	.360	131	493	453	47	123	21	2	5	59	32	3	3	2	104	3	4	6.5	21.1
Hackenberg, Adam	R-R	6-1	225	9-08-99	.259	.328	.393	35	125	112	12	29	6	0	3	13	11	1	0	1	30	1	0	8.8	24.0
Hamilton, Billy	B-R	6-0	160	9-09-90	.147	.261	.253	28	89	75	14	11	3	1	1	4	11	1	1	1	29	3	0	12.4	32.6
2-team (8 Durham)					.179	.286	.263	36	113	95	19	17	3	1	1	4	14	1	2	1	35	8	0	12.4	31.0
Haseley, Adam	L-L	6-1	190	4-12-96	.264	.338	.386	72	313	280	39	74	10	3	6	24	28	3	2	0	52	10	4	8.9	16.6
Lee, Korey	R-R	6-2	210	7-25-98	.255	.309	.275	14	55	51	2	13	1	0	0	4	3	1	0	0	22	1	0	5.5	40.0
Marisnick, Jake	R-R	6-4	220	3-30-91	.260	.408	.396	33	120	96	12	25	6	2	1	11	19	5	0	0	28	9	1	15.8	23.3
Matthews, Jason	R-R	6-0	187	4-09-97	.143	.250	.357	4	16	14	2	2	0	0	1	4	2	0	0	0	5	0	0	12.5	31.3
Moncada, Yoan	B-R	6-2	225	5-27-95	.409	.480	.636	13	50	44	7	18	4	0	2	5	6	0	0	0	13	0	0	12.0	26.0
Mondou, Nate	L-R	5-7	205	3-24-95	.270	.379	.434	116	465	389	60	105	23	1	13	61	69	2	1	4	89	7	5	14.8	19.1
Naquin, Tyler	L-R	6-1	202	4-24-91	.216	.294	.371	28	109	97	10	21	6	0	3	9	10	1	0	1	36	0	0	9.2	33.0
2-team (40 Nashville)					.257	.317	.408	68	269	245	31	63	10	0	9	30	19	3	1	1	81	3	0	7.1	30.1
Neslony, Tyler	L-R	5-11	190	2-13-94	.244	.333	.406	48	183	160	23	39	8	0	6	17	21	1	0	1	44	7	3	11.5	24.0
Perez, Carlos	R-R	5-11	205	9-10-96	.240	.295	.408	77	312	287	31	69	12	0	12	34	19	4	0	2	41	0	0	6.1	13.1
Piscotty, Stephen	R-R	6-4	211	1-14-91	.232	.330	.390	51	206	177	27	41	10	0	6	32	24	3	0	2	38	0	0	11.7	18.4
Remillard, Zach	R-R	6-0	185	2-21-94	.235	.342	.355	65	276	234	46	55	11	1	5	28	34	5	1	2	50	16	1	12.3	18.1
Reyes, Victor	B-R	6-5	194	10-05-94	.279	.330	.462	128	546	502	75	140	28	2	20	83	36	4	0	4	124	3	1	6.6	22.7
Rivera, Laz	R-R	5-11	185	9-20-94	.231	.296	.313	52	164	147	15	34	8	2	0	17	11	3	2	1	43	5	1	6.7	26.2
Rivero, Sebastian	R-R	6-1	210	11-16-98	.232	.277	.361	58	213	194	17	45	11	1	4	26	9	5	0	5	42	0	1	4.2	19.7
Rodriguez, Jose	R-R	5-11	175	5-13-01	.253	.270	.379	19	89	87	11	22	2	0	3	8	2	0	0	0	13	3	3	2.2	14.6
Sanchez, Yolbert	R-R	5-9	176	3-03-97	.271	.321	.333	108	445	406	47	110	14	1	3	40	28	4	2	5	75	6	6	6.3	16.9
Shaw, Chris	L-R	6-3	220	10-20-93	.200	.429	.400	2	7	5	1	1	1	0	0	0	2	0	0	0	2	0	0	28.6	28.6
Skoug, Evan	L-R	5-9	200	10-21-95	.171	.299	.325	43	147	123	21	21	7	0	4	15	20	3	0	1	44	0	0	13.6	29.9
Snyder, Taylor	R-R	6-1	165	9-28-94	.000	.000	.000	3	5	5	0	0	0	0	0	0	0	0	0	0	4	0	0	0.0	80.0
Sosa, Lenyn	R-R	6-0	180	1-25-00	.271	.313	.507	71	308	288	41	78	17	0	17	44	18	0	1	1	75	0	1	5.8	24.4
Thompson, Trayce	R-R	6-3	225	3-15-91	.125	.125	.125	2	8	8	0	1	0	0	0	0	0	0	0	0	5	0	0	0.0	62.5
Wong, Kean	L-R	5-9	189	4-17-95	.196	.308	.250	17	65	56	8	11	0	0	1	3	8	1	0	0	14	2	1	12.3	21.5
Zavala, Seby	R-R	5-11	205	8-28-93	.227	.292	.364	8	24	22	2	5	0	0	1	2	2	0	0	0	5	0	0	8.3	20.8

Pitching	B-T	Ht.	Wt.	DOB	W	L	ERA	G	GS	SV	IP	Hits	Runs	ER	HR	BB	SO	AVG	OBP	SLG	SO%	BB%	BF
Alexy, A.J.	R-R	6-4	195	4-21-98	0	3	12.00	16	4	0	21	13	28	28	4	41	21	.188	.504	.449	17.8	34.7	118
Banks, Tanner	R-L	6-1	210	10-24-91	2	0	3.13	13	0	0	23	27	8	8	3	3	30	.303	.323	.483	31.9	3.2	94
Burke, Sean	R-R	6-6	230	12-18-99	1	4	7.61	9	9	0	37	36	33	31	9	27	34	.265	.388	.507	20.5	16.3	166
Colome, Alex	R-R	6-2	240	12-31-88	4	1	3.24	33	0	2	33	38	18	12	2	15	26	.275	.355	.377	16.7	9.6	156

Crochet, Garrett	L-L	6-6	230	6-21-99	0	0	2.84	6	0	0	6	4	2	2	0	2	13	.174	.269	.174	50.0	7.7	26
Cronin, Declan	R-R	6-4	225	9-24-97	3	0	3.83	47	0	2	52	54	28	22	3	20	42	.271	.356	.362	18.7	8.9	225
Davila, Garrett	L-L	6-2	180	1-17-97	2	11	6.68	23	20	0	102	119	78	76	21	53	103	.292	.375	.543	21.9	11.3	470
Dominguez, Johan	R-R	6-4	190	1-18-96	0	3	5.65	8	8	0	29	32	19	18	7	14	24	.283	.364	.504	18.6	10.9	129
Farrell, Luke	L-R	6-6	200	6-07-91	2	3	5.56	37	7	2	55	65	36	34	10	27	52	.286	.367	.485	20.1	10.4	259
Fernandez, Xavier	R-R	5-8	245	7-15-95	0	0	18.00	2	0	0	2	0	4	4	0	7	0	.000	.571	.000	0.0	50.0	14
Fisher, Nate	L-L	6-1	205	5-28-96	5	10	6.51	26	20	0	104	125	86	75	23	49	85	.298	.382	.544	17.6	10.1	483
Freeman, Caleb	R-R	6-1	195	2-23-98	0	2	6.08	12	0	0	13	16	10	9	3	11	15	.296	.415	.537	23.1	16.9	65
Gallagher, Nick	R-R	6-3	200	9-09-95	0	0	13.50	3	0	0	3	2	5	5	0	3	5	.182	.333	.273	33.3	20.0	15
Garcia, Deivi	R-R	5-9	163	5-19-99	0	1	2.00	7	0	0	9	5	2	2	2	6	17	.152	.282	.364	43.6	15.4	39
German, Franklin	R-R	6-2	195	9-22-97	0	0	7.15	9	0	0	11	19	9	9	4	9	16	.388	.483	.735	26.7	15.0	60
Green, Haylen	L-L	5-11	185	8-12-97	1	0	10.13	3	1	0	5	7	6	6	0	5	7	.318	.444	.409	25.9	18.5	27
Hendriks, Liam	R-R	6-0	235	2-10-89	0	0	10.80	6	0	0	5	7	6	6	3	1	5	.350	.364	.800	22.7	4.5	22
Henzman, Lincoln	R-R	6-2	205	7-04-95	1	0	9.00	11	0	0	15	17	15	15	1	10	13	.288	.419	.390	17.6	13.5	74
Holloway, Jordan	R-R	6-6	230	6-13-96	0	2	7.45	25	0	0	19	14	17	16	3	30	30	.197	.447	.352	29.1	29.1	103
Holmes, Ben	L-L	6-1	195	9-12-91	0	2	15.00	6	0	0	6	9	10	10	1	9	6	.375	.541	.667	16.2	24.3	37
Honeywell, Brent	R-R	6-2	195	3-31-95	0	1	7.04	4	4	0	15	16	12	12	4	7	9	.271	.377	.559	13.0	10.1	69
Lambert, Jimmy	R-R	6-2	190	11-18-94	0	1	7.71	15	0	0	16	17	15	14	3	11	12	.266	.382	.516	15.6	14.3	77
Leasure, Jordan	R-R	6-3	215	8-15-98	0	2	6.08	15	0	2	13	16	12	9	3	8	23	.286	.385	.554	35.4	12.3	65
Martin, Davis	L-R	6-2	200	1-04-97	0	0	2.81	3	3	0	16	10	5	5	2	7	20	.179	.281	.321	31.3	10.9	64
Mateo, Alejandro	R-R	6-2	210	1-18-94	1	0	7.51	36	1	0	44	56	41	37	11	29	51	.299	.397	.540	23.3	13.2	219
Mayers, Mike	R-R	6-2	220	12-06-91	1	4	5.29	16	5	0	34	40	24	20	6	17	28	.294	.365	.522	17.9	10.9	156
Mena, Cristian	R-R	6-2	170	12-21-02	1	1	5.95	4	4	0	20	26	13	13	1	9	20	.317	.391	.427	21.7	9.8	92
Middleton, Keynan	R-R	6-3	215	9-12-93	0	0	0.00	3	0	1	3	1	0	0	0	2	3	.111	.273	.222	27.3	18.2	11
Muller, Chris	R-R	6-5	210	4-22-96	0	0	11.88	9	0	0	8	10	15	11	3	13	7	.286	.479	.571	14.6	27.1	48
Nastrini, Nick	R-R	6-3	215	2-18-00	1	2	4.12	4	4	0	20	10	10	9	2	10	23	.154	.278	.323	29.1	12.7	79
Navarro, Edgar	R-R	6-1	180	2-05-98	2	2	4.33	39	0	3	44	35	22	21	1	32	38	.220	.369	.302	19.2	16.2	198
Neslony, Tyler	L-R	5-11	190	2-13-94	0	0	0.00	1	0	0	1	0	0	0	0	2	0	.000	.400	.000	0.0	40.0	5
Olson, J.B.	L-R	6-2	195	2-15-95	1	1	10.99	15	1	0	29	44	35	35	7	12	21	.341	.406	.597	14.7	8.4	143
Padilla, Nicholas	R-R	6-2	220	12-24-96	2	3	5.52	44	0	5	46	49	31	28	5	39	54	.280	.427	.440	24.4	17.6	221
Parke, John	L-L	6-4	220	1-03-95	2	6	6.91	14	8	0	42	57	38	32	5	23	37	.322	.410	.492	18.0	11.2	205
Patino, Luis	R-R	6-1	192	10-26-99	0	1	5.65	5	5	0	14	11	9	9	3	13	12	.220	.375	.480	18.8	20.3	64
Peralta, Sammy	L-L	6-2	205	5-10-98	5	6	5.09	29	6	0	69	71	45	39	9	19	68	.261	.312	.423	23.1	6.4	295
Perez, Andrew	L-L	6-2	215	7-25-97	3	2	9.69	18	0	0	26	37	30	28	5	18	24	.325	.431	.588	17.5	13.1	137
Ponce de Leon, Daniel	R-R	6-3	200	1-16-92	1	4	9.99	8	7	0	24	37	28	27	8	24	19	.359	.469	.650	14.5	18.3	131
Ramirez, Yohan	R-R	6-4	212	5-06-95	0	1	7.71	4	0	0	5	7	4	4	2	3	7	.333	.440	.619	28.0	12.0	25
Ramsey, Lane	R-R	6-9	245	7-16-96	4	4	5.50	32	0	6	36	38	24	22	4	27	48	.275	.395	.471	28.6	16.1	168
Rivera, Laz	R-R	5-11	185	9-20-94	1	0	5.06	4	0	0	5	6	3	3	1	1	0	.300	.318	.450	0.0	4.5	22
Sanchez, Ricardo	L-L	5-10	220	4-11-97	0	0	5.40	3	1	0	7	8	4	4	0	4	8	.308	.387	.308	25.8	12.9	31
Scholtens, Jesse	R-R	6-4	230	4-06-94	2	2	4.44	9	9	0	47	45	23	23	9	13	45	.254	.309	.458	23.4	6.8	192
Shaw, Bryan	B-R	6-1	226	11-08-87	2	1	4.94	23	0	4	24	16	14	13	2	17	26	.193	.340	.277	25.2	16.5	103
Skoug, Evan	L-R	5-9	200	10-21-95	0	0	20.25	2	0	0	1	5	3	3	1	1	0	.625	.700	1.000	0.0	10.0	10
Snyder, Taylor	R-R	6-1	165	9-28-94	0	0	0.00	2	0	0	2	2	0	0	0	0	1	.286	.286	.286	14.3	0.0	7
Solesky, Chase	R-R	6-3	201	9-26-97	2	9	6.35	17	16	0	78	91	59	55	14	42	63	.294	.375	.506	17.6	11.8	357
Stiever, Jonathan	R-R	6-2	210	5-12-97	0	0	6.75	2	2	0	4	5	3	3	1	3	2	.294	.400	.529	10.0	15.0	20
Urena, Jose	R-R	6-2	208	9-12-91	1	1	3.38	4	4	0	21	22	8	8	1	7	20	.262	.333	.333	21.3	7.4	94
Walters, Nash	R-R	6-5	210	5-18-97	0	0	19.89	7	0	0	6	15	15	14	4	6	7	.429	.512	.914	17.1	14.6	41

Fielding

Catcher	PCT	G	PO	A	E	DP	PB
Claunch	1.000	2	4	0	0	0	0
Fernandez	1.000	1	8	1	0	0	0
Hackenberg	.992	30	232	10	2	3	0
Lee	1.000	10	65	1	0	0	2
Perez	1.000	54	445	24	0	3	4
Rivero	.979	38	310	20	7	2	1
Skoug	.988	19	156	6	2	1	0
Zavala	1.000	7	45	0	0	0	2

First Base	PCT	G	PO	A	E	DP
Burger	.947	2	18	0	1	1
Fernandez	1.000	34	234	13	0	34
Mondou	.992	68	469	36	4	59
Perez	.990	15	93	5	1	8
Remillard	.991	18	104	7	1	10
Rivero	.986	19	129	10	2	15

Second Base	PCT	G	PO	A	E	DP
Alberto	1.000	2	4	5	0	2
Andrus	1.000	2	5	1	0	0
Gonzalez	.939	11	12	19	2	3
Hamilton	1.000	1	2	1	0	0
Matthews	1.000	2	4	5	0	1
Mondou	.991	28	41	70	1	21
Remillard	1.000	7	17	14	0	3
Rivera	.927	25	34	42	6	17
Rodriguez	.947	9	14	22	2	9
Sanchez	.992	32	53	79	1	19
Sosa	.964	30	45	62	4	14
Wong	.979	11	22	25	1	8

Third Base	PCT	G	PO	A	E	DP
Alberto	1.000	1	0	1	0	0
Burger	1.000	2	1	3	0	0
Gonzalez	1.000	7	2	6	0	0
Matthews	1.000	1	0	3	0	0
Moncada	.885	10	6	17	3	1
Mondou	.933	11	10	18	2	4
Remillard	.947	20	10	26	2	2
Rivera	.846	6	3	8	2	3
Rodriguez	.963	8	8	18	1	2
Sanchez	.955	72	55	116	8	14
Snyder	1.000	1	0	1	0	0
Sosa	.981	19	14	39	1	6

Shortstop	PCT	G	PO	A	E	DP
Anderson	1.000	2	1	3	0	1
Gonzalez	.966	114	142	282	15	78
Matthews	1.000	1	0	5	0	1
Remillard	.977	12	11	32	1	4
Sanchez	.944	6	11	6	1	3
Sosa	.945	20	27	59	5	9

Outfield	PCT	G	PO	A	E	DP
Cespedes	.931	11	27	0	2	0
Colas	.977	45	91	3	2	0
Frazier	.987	53	125	7	2	2
Hamilton	1.000	27	56	2	0	0
Haseley	.986	71	133	6	3	1
Marisnick	1.000	34	62	0	0	0
Naquin	.988	19	38	4	1	0
Neslony	1.000	37	49	2	0	1
Piscotty	.977	36	55	1	1	0
Remillard	.952	9	24	2	1	1
Reyes	.985	106	190	7	3	3
Rivera	.955	17	21	0	1	0
Thompson	1.000	2	10	0	0	0
Wong	1.000	4	7	0	0	0

BIRMINGHAM BARONS — *DOUBLE-A*

SOUTHERN LEAGUE

Batting	B-T	Ht.	Wt.	DOB	AVG	OBP	SLG	G	PA	AB	R	H	2B	3B	HR	RBI	BB	HBP	SH	SF	SO	SB	CS	BB%	SO%
Atwood, Andy	R-R	6-1	195	11-15-96	.136	.204	.136	14	50	44	5	6	0	0	0	4	3	1	1	1	19	2	0	6.0	38.0
Castillo, Moises	R-R	6-0	170	7-14-99	.225	.314	.308	106	424	373	45	84	16	0	5	39	43	6	0	2	76	3	2	10.1	17.9
Cespedes, Yoelqui	R-R	5-7	205	9-24-97	.214	.315	.326	110	456	393	52	84	15	1	9	31	45	14	2	2	135	15	5	9.9	29.6
Elko, Tim	R-R	6-4	240	12-27-98	.269	.292	.431	34	137	130	17	35	3	0	6	23	3	2	0	2	49	0	0	2.2	35.8
Ellis, Duke	L-L	6-1	180	1-16-98	.157	.317	.216	16	63	51	5	8	1	1	0	4	12	0	0	0	21	3	1	19.0	33.3
Fernandez, Xavier	R-R	5-8	245	7-15-95	.284	.365	.500	63	255	222	29	63	18	0	10	41	26	4	0	3	39	0	1	10.2	15.3
Gonzalez, Ivan	R-R	5-6	190	10-28-96	.100	.163	.125	13	43	40	4	4	1	0	0	0	3	0	0	0	6	0	0	7.0	14.0
Goosenberg, Shawn	R-R	6-1	195	12-05-99	.250	.308	.500	3	13	12	1	3	0	0	1	1	1	0	0	0	3	0	0	7.7	23.1
Hackenberg, Adam	R-R	6-1	225	9-08-99	.276	.384	.386	66	268	228	38	63	10	0	5	25	31	9	0	0	59	2	0	11.6	22.0
Jimenez, Eloy	R-R	6-4	240	11-27-96	.125	.417	.125	3	12	8	0	1	0	0	0	2	4	0	0	0	2	0	0	33.3	16.7
Matthews, Jason	R-R	6-0	187	4-09-97	.209	.320	.372	18	50	43	7	9	1	0	2	6	4	3	0	0	18	1	0	8.0	36.0
Mieses, Luis	L-L	6-3	180	5-31-00	.236	.257	.356	115	485	458	43	108	26	1	9	48	14	2	0	8	113	1	0	2.9	23.3
Mondou, Nate	L-R	5-7	205	3-24-95	.200	.429	.800	2	7	5	1	1	0	0	1	1	2	0	0	0	1	1	0	28.6	14.3
Montgomery, Colson	L-R	6-3	205	2-27-02	.244	.400	.427	37	167	131	27	32	8	2	4	21	25	9	0	0	36	0	1	15.0	21.6
Neslony, Tyler	L-R	5-11	190	2-13-94	.235	.350	.393	49	217	183	27	43	8	0	7	23	32	1	0	1	52	14	3	14.7	24.0
Norman, Ben	L-R	6-2	200	2-15-98	.206	.308	.359	59	201	170	30	35	5	0	7	28	26	1	0	4	68	12	1	12.9	33.8
Osik, Tyler	R-R	5-9	203	11-15-96	.212	.333	.318	18	78	66	8	14	7	0	0	7	10	2	0	0	20	1	0	12.8	25.6
Quero, Edgar	B-R	5-11	170	4-06-03	.277	.366	.393	31	134	112	12	31	4	0	3	22	17	1	0	4	23	0	0	12.7	17.2
2-team (70 Rocket City)					.255	.387	.351	101	455	368	52	94	17	0	6	57	72	7	0	8	76	1	2	15.8	16.7
Ramos, Bryan	R-R	6-2	190	3-12-02	.271	.369	.457	77	342	291	46	79	10	1	14	48	38	8	0	2	75	4	3	11.1	21.9
Rivero, Sebastian	R-R	6-1	210	11-16-98	.167	.259	.188	15	54	48	8	8	1	0	0	2	5	1	0	0	9	0	0	9.3	16.7
Rodriguez, Jose	R-R	5-11	175	5-13-01	.264	.297	.450	87	404	382	63	101	17	0	18	54	18	1	0	3	95	28	6	4.5	23.5
Shaw, Chris	L-R	6-3	220	10-20-93	.197	.329	.426	55	225	188	33	37	7	0	12	28	35	2	0	0	83	1	0	15.6	36.9
Snyder, Taylor	R-R	6-1	165	9-28-94	.186	.296	.309	69	274	236	34	44	6	1	7	29	35	2	0	1	81	13	4	12.8	29.6
Tatum, Terrell	L-L	5-9	167	7-27-99	.230	.361	.315	65	276	222	35	51	9	2	2	22	42	6	2	4	80	15	0	15.2	29.0
Torres, Victor	R-R	6-0	180	7-29-00	.160	.192	.160	13	26	25	2	4	0	0	0	0	0	1	0	0	8	0	0	0.0	30.8
Veras, Wilfred	R-R	6-2	180	11-15-02	.309	.346	.533	38	162	152	23	47	14	1	6	30	8	1	0	1	44	6	0	4.9	27.2
Weaver, Caberea	R-R	6-3	180	12-01-99	.000	.000	.000	1	1	1	0	0	0	0	0	0	0	0	0	0	0	0	0	0.0	0.0
Womack, Alsander	R-R	5-9	205	3-16-99	.258	.362	.345	99	447	380	43	98	12	0	7	46	56	8	0	3	69	7	4	12.5	15.4

Pitching	B-T	Ht.	Wt.	DOB	W	L	ERA	G	GS	SV	IP	Hits	Runs	ER	HR	BB	SO	AVG	OBP	SLG	SO%	BB%	BF
Adams, Mason	R-R	6-0	200	2-23-00	0	2	2.70	3	3	0	13	16	7	4	0	8	13	.291	.385	.418	20.0	12.3	65
Atwood, Andy	R-R	6-1	195	11-15-96	0	0	0.00	1	0	0	2	0	1	0	0	1	1	.000	.222	.000	11.1	11.1	9
Burke, Jeremiah	R-R	6-2	195	5-16-98	2	0	4.97	17	0	1	25	24	14	14	2	16	21	.255	.366	.340	18.6	14.2	113
Bush, Ky	L-L	6-6	240	11-12-99	3	4	6.70	9	9	0	42	48	34	31	10	22	36	.293	.378	.549	19.0	11.6	189
Cannon, Jonathan	R-R	6-6	213	7-19-00	1	4	5.77	11	11	0	48	61	40	31	8	15	39	.298	.344	.473	17.3	6.7	225
Coffey, Adisyn	R-R	6-2	185	1-22-99	1	0	5.26	18	0	0	26	28	17	15	3	14	24	.280	.365	.460	20.7	12.1	116
Cousin, Josimar	R-R	6-3	185	2-18-98	1	1	4.00	2	2	0	9	12	5	4	1	4	6	.324	.390	.432	14.6	9.8	41
Crochet, Garrett	L-L	6-6	230	6-21-99	0	0	6.00	6	0	0	6	6	4	4	0	4	11	.261	.357	.391	39.3	14.3	28
Davila, Garrett	L-L	6-2	180	1-17-97	0	3	6.00	6	4	0	24	26	16	16	2	7	18	.277	.358	.415	17.0	6.6	106
Dollander, Hunter	R-R	6-0	232	11-24-96	0	4	10.08	15	2	0	28	38	34	31	7	28	27	.325	.466	.598	18.2	18.9	148
Eder, Jake	L-L	6-4	215	10-09-98	0	3	11.42	5	5	0	17	27	22	22	3	15	22	.360	.500	.573	22.9	15.6	96
Ellard, Fraser	L-L	6-4	205	11-06-97	0	1	7.45	19	0	2	19	22	17	16	0	12	27	.278	.387	.405	28.7	12.8	94
Ernst, Nick	R-R	6-3	195	8-27-96	0	0	9.82	6	0	0	7	7	8	8	1	7	6	.250	.417	.500	16.7	19.4	36
Freeman, Caleb	R-R	6-1	195	2-23-98	0	0	1.96	20	0	3	18	16	7	4	0	14	22	.229	.368	.300	25.3	16.1	87
Gallagher, Nick	R-R	6-3	200	9-09-95	1	2	5.61	28	0	0	34	27	28	21	2	23	43	.221	.382	.352	27.4	14.6	157
Gonzalez, Ivan	R-R	5-6	190	10-28-96	0	0	3.86	2	0	0	2	6	2	1	0	1	0	.500	.500	.500	0.0	7.1	14
Gosswein, Brooks	L-L	6-2	205	10-09-98	0	2	2.45	4	3	0	11	12	11	3	0	16	7	.286	.492	.333	11.3	25.8	62
Green, Haylen	L-L	5-11	185	8-12-97	1	0	5.56	27	0	5	34	36	22	21	3	16	34	.265	.359	.397	21.8	10.3	156
Henzman, Lincoln	R-R	6-2	205	7-04-95	0	0	0.00	1	0	0	2	2	0	0	0	0	4	.250	.250	.250	50.0	0.0	8
Holmes, Ben	L-L	6-1	195	9-12-91	2	4	3.30	25	0	4	30	24	18	11	6	9	36	.214	.282	.411	29.0	7.3	124
Kelley, Jared	R-R	6-3	230	10-03-01	0	3	11.74	16	0	0	23	34	32	30	3	29	28	.351	.511	.536	21.4	22.1	131
Luna, Gil	L-L	5-10	173	7-29-99	1	3	6.13	40	0	2	40	30	33	27	3	41	51	.224	.413	.396	27.7	22.3	184
Mateo, Alejandro	R-R	6-2	210	1-18-94	2	0	0.84	9	0	2	11	6	1	1	0	3	17	.158	.220	.184	41.5	7.3	41
Matthews, Jason	R-R	6-0	187	4-09-97	0	0	9.00	2	0	0	2	4	2	2	0	0	0	.364	.364	.364	0.0	0.0	11
Mena, Cristian	R-R	6-2	170	12-21-02	7	6	4.66	23	23	0	114	99	64	59	17	55	136	.234	.327	.416	27.9	11.3	488
Nastrini, Nick	R-R	6-3	215	2-18-00	3	0	4.22	4	4	0	21	20	12	10	1	7	31	.235	.301	.329	33.0	7.4	94
Navarro, Edgar	R-R	6-1	180	2-05-98	1	0	0.00	7	0	0	9	3	0	0	0	5	6	.111	.250	.148	18.8	15.6	32
Osik, Tyler	R-R	5-9	203	11-15-96	0	0	4.50	1	0	0	2	2	1	1	0	0	0	.250	.250	.375	0.0	0.0	8
Perez, Andrew	L-L	6-2	215	7-25-97	2	3	4.42	22	1	0	37	32	19	18	2	12	43	.230	.288	.353	28.1	7.8	153
Plymell, Chase	R-R	6-4	205	5-29-98	0	2	8.50	15	1	1	18	28	21	17	3	12	24	.346	.426	.568	25.3	12.6	95
Schoenle, Garrett	L-L	6-5	185	6-21-98	4	7	6.22	34	18	0	103	97	72	71	15	64	117	.253	.364	.445	25.3	13.9	462
Scolaro, Jonah	L-L	5-10	193	8-03-98	3	2	3.72	34	0	0	56	38	24	23	5	32	66	.192	.319	.303	27.6	13.4	239
Shilling, Luke	R-R	6-4	230	11-18-97	0	0	11.08	15	0	0	13	14	18	16	4	17	15	.275	.465	.529	21.1	23.9	71
Silven, Yoelvin	R-R	6-1	176	6-26-99	3	4	7.64	41	0	0	55	67	50	47	12	24	59	.295	.365	.524	23.0	9.4	256
Snyder, Taylor	R-R	6-1	165	9-28-94	0	0	11.57	2	0	0	2	4	3	3	0	3	1	.364	.533	.455	6.7	20.0	15
Solesky, Chase	R-R	6-3	201	9-26-97	3	2	3.23	9	9	0	39	40	14	14	2	13	29	.272	.344	.388	17.8	8.0	163
Sommer, Tommy	L-L	6-4	220	9-25-98	2	4	6.09	16	14	0	68	67	48	46	17	46	57	.259	.373	.502	18.6	15.0	306
Stivors, Tristan	R-R	6-4	220	9-22-98	0	1	3.38	10	0	1	11	9	6	4	0	6	14	.225	.347	.275	28.6	12.2	49
Thompson, Matthew	R-R	6-3	195	8-11-00	6	15	4.85	27	27	0	124	110	78	67	15	85	136	.232	.349	.392	23.9	15.0	568
Torres, Victor	R-R	6-0	180	7-29-00	0	0	0.00	1	0	0	0	0	0	0	0	0	0	.000	.500	.000	0.0	0.0	2

	B-T	Ht.	Wt.	DOB	W	L	ERA	G	GS	SV	IP	Hits	Runs	ER	HR	BB	SO	AVG	OBP	SLG	SO%	BB%	BF
Vannelle, Vince	R-R	5-10	202	12-19-97	1	1	8.86	18	1	0	21	33	29	21	5	19	25	.351	.457	.617	21.6	16.4	116
Walters, Nash	R-R	6-5	210	5-18-97	1	3	6.65	20	0	3	22	20	19	16	5	11	37	.241	.344	.446	38.1	11.3	97
Warner, Austin	L-L	5-11	185	6-27-94	0	1	3.68	3	1	0	7	6	3	3	0	3	8	.222	.323	.333	25.8	9.7	31

Fielding

Catcher	PCT	G	PO	A	E	DP	PB
Fernandez	.993	30	284	18	2	2	5
Gonzalez	1.000	4	35	4	0	0	0
Hackenberg	.978	61	584	49	14	2	9
Quero	.978	27	251	12	6	3	2
Rivero	.961	14	112	12	5	0	2
Torres	.956	9	39	4	2	0	3

First Base	PCT	G	PO	A	E	DP
Elko	.992	33	240	11	2	20
Fernandez	.993	20	128	8	1	11
Gonzalez	1.000	2	16	0	0	5
Hackenberg	1.000	1	4	0	0	1
Mieses	1.000	18	87	9	0	4
Osik	1.000	14	86	4	0	8
Rivero	1.000	1	9	0	0	1
Shaw	.973	13	70	3	2	6
Snyder	1.000	17	104	12	0	14
Womack	.989	28	163	9	2	10

Second Base	PCT	G	PO	A	E	DP
Atwood	.923	9	12	12	2	3
Castillo	.957	29	32	57	4	7
Matthews	.875	3	8	6	2	2
Mondou	.000	1	0	0	0	0
Osik	1.000	1	1	1	0	0
Rodriguez	.968	54	84	126	7	25
Snyder	1.000	2	2	4	0	0
Womack	.976	43	58	103	4	23

Third Base	PCT	G	PO	A	E	DP
Atwood	.875	5	5	2	1	0
Castillo	.917	4	1	10	1	0
Matthews	1.000	7	9	16	0	2
Mondou	1.000	1	1	1	0	0
Osik	.500	1	1	0	1	0
Ramos	.924	64	44	113	13	7
Snyder	.922	45	39	55	8	6
Womack	.900	15	14	13	3	2

Shortstop	PCT	G	PO	A	E	DP
Atwood	1.000	1	1	0	0	0
Castillo	.966	74	104	148	9	34
Matthews	.929	5	5	8	1	0
Montgomery	.918	32	39	73	10	22
Rodriguez	.928	26	28	36	5	5
Snyder	1.000	2	2	5	0	0

Outfield	PCT	G	PO	A	E	DP
Cespedes	.989	108	229	14	6	5
Ellis	1.000	16	30	2	0	1
Goosenberg	.889	3	8	0	1	0
Jimenez	1.000	2	3	0	0	0
Mieses	.989	98	187	3	2	1
Neslony	.979	45	84	7	3	0
Norman	.992	52	107	4	2	1
Shaw	1.000	2	4	0	0	0
Tatum	.972	61	142	4	4	1
Veras	.988	35	52	2	1	0
Weaver	1.000	1	1	0	0	0

WINSTON-SALEM DASH

HIGH CLASS A

SOUTH ATLANTIC LEAGUE

Batting	B-T	Ht.	Wt.	DOB	AVG	OBP	SLG	G	PA	AB	R	H	2B	3B	HR	RBI	BB	HBP	SH	SF	SO	SB	CS	BB%	SO%
Atwood, Andy	R-R	6-1	195	11-15-96	.242	.290	.342	37	132	120	8	29	10	1	0	12	6	3	1	2	30	5	0	4.5	22.7
Baldwin, Brooks	B-R	6-2	175	8-15-00	.327	.375	.495	26	113	101	22	33	2	0	5	19	8	1	1	2	25	8	0	7.1	22.1
Burke, Jacob	R-R	6-1	208	2-26-01	.281	.377	.394	50	236	203	40	57	13	2	2	18	21	11	0	1	52	10	4	8.9	22.0
Camilletti, Mario	L-R	5-9	195	4-19-99	.200	.410	.267	14	62	45	8	9	0	0	1	3	14	2	1	0	9	1	2	22.6	14.5
Chapelli, Loidel	L-R	5-8	187	12-20-01	.254	.361	.411	106	466	394	73	100	20	6	10	57	61	7	0	4	115	26	6	13.1	24.7
Claunch, Troy	R-R	6-0	210	9-01-98	.214	.333	.464	11	37	28	4	6	1	0	2	7	5	1	1	2	4	0	0	13.5	10.8
DeGuzman, Cristopher	B-R	5-11	185	12-01-99	.200	.429	.400	3	7	5	0	1	1	0	0	0	1	1	0	0	2	0	0	14.3	28.6
Elko, Tim	R-R	6-4	240	12-27-98	.319	.374	.569	31	131	116	20	37	8	3	5	26	11	1	0	3	31	0	0	8.4	23.7
Fish, Keegan	L-R	5-11	190	9-19-99	.176	.299	.324	23	87	74	13	13	2	0	3	5	11	2	0	0	34	0	0	12.6	39.1
Gladney, DJ	R-R	6-3	195	7-14-01	.243	.308	.475	96	409	366	59	89	16	6	19	63	27	8	0	2	114	12	2	6.6	27.9
Gonzalez, Ivan	R-R	5-6	190	10-28-96	.260	.382	.300	31	123	100	12	26	2	1	0	9	18	3	0	2	19	2	0	14.6	15.4
Goosenberg, Shawn	R-R	6-1	195	12-05-99	.261	.359	.389	101	421	360	60	94	16	3	8	47	48	9	0	4	91	32	6	11.4	21.6
Kath, Wes	L-R	6-3	200	8-03-02	.193	.275	.311	95	389	347	44	67	13	2	8	31	37	3	0	2	168	7	0	9.5	43.2
Lanzilli, Chris	R-R	6-2	225	6-18-98	.219	.327	.305	38	153	128	13	28	5	0	2	13	20	2	0	3	35	3	2	13.1	22.9
Matthews, Jason	R-R	6-0	187	4-09-97	.171	.320	.220	26	103	82	16	14	1	0	1	9	14	5	0	2	36	5	2	13.6	35.0
Montgomery, Colson	L-R	6-3	205	2-27-02	.345	.537	.552	17	82	58	15	20	3	0	3	10	20	4	0	0	15	0	2	24.4	18.3
Nakawake, Taishi	R-R	5-11	185	6-20-98	.201	.278	.247	81	314	279	30	56	10	0	1	28	25	6	1	3	93	6	5	8.0	29.6
Norman, Ben	L-R	6-2	200	2-15-98	.313	.476	.750	5	21	16	4	5	1	0	2	4	3	2	0	0	4	0	1	14.3	19.0
Sanchez, Wilber	R-R	5-10	160	2-21-02	.000	.000	.000	2	7	7	0	0	0	0	0	0	0	0	0	0	3	0	0	0.0	42.9
Smelley, Colby	R-R	6-2	195	3-15-00	.270	.384	.326	28	112	89	9	24	2	0	1	19	15	4	0	4	21	0	0	13.4	18.8
Tatum, Terrell	L-L	5-9	167	7-27-99	.268	.434	.421	60	276	209	54	56	14	3	4	29	58	4	4	1	69	32	9	21.0	25.0
Turner, Michael	L-R	6-2	205	8-18-98	.309	.430	.441	92	377	304	43	94	26	1	4	41	64	4	0	5	58	0	2	17.0	15.4
Veras, Wilfred	R-R	6-2	180	11-15-02	.277	.316	.438	92	402	372	52	103	25	1	11	63	20	4	0	6	101	18	7	5.0	25.1
Weaver, Caberea	R-R	6-3	180	12-01-99	.252	.297	.374	60	222	206	25	52	7	0	6	29	11	3	0	2	73	11	4	5.0	32.9
Willits, Bryce	L-R	6-2	200	8-25-99	.287	.398	.287	27	114	94	12	27	0	0	0	12	16	2	1	1	19	0	1	14.0	16.7
Womack, Alsander	R-R	5-9	205	3-16-99	.298	.344	.474	14	61	57	6	17	2	1	2	11	4	0	0	0	11	1	0	6.6	18.0

Pitching	B-T	Ht.	Wt.	DOB	W	L	ERA	G	GS	SV	IP	Hits	Runs	ER	HR	BB	SO	AVG	OBP	SLG	SO%	BB%	BF
Adams, Mason	R-R	6-0	200	2-23-00	2	0	2.50	3	3	0	18	12	5	5	2	3	18	.197	.231	.344	27.7	4.6	65
Adler, Eric	R-R	6-2	190	10-12-00	2	0	2.70	16	0	3	20	17	9	6	0	11	23	.227	.333	.307	26.4	12.6	87
Atwood, Andy	R-R	6-1	195	11-15-96	0	0	0.00	1	0	0	1	0	0	0	0	1	2	.000	.250	.000	50.0	25.0	4
Bailey, Brandon	R-R	5-10	195	10-19-94	0	0	0.00	1	0	0	0	0	0	0	0	0	0	.000	.000	.000	0.0	0.0	1
Burke, Jeremiah	R-R	6-2	195	5-16-98	1	1	2.63	11	0	0	24	16	7	7	0	8	27	.193	.261	.277	29.3	8.7	92
Burns, Dylan	R-R	6-1	194	12-29-96	2	3	8.49	21	2	0	41	55	42	39	3	25	31	.316	.408	.477	15.0	12.1	206
Cannon, Jonathan	R-R	6-6	213	7-19-00	5	2	3.59	14	14	0	73	65	31	29	7	24	67	.246	.305	.417	22.9	8.2	292
Carela, Juan	R-R	6-3	186	12-15-01	1	3	3.34	6	6	0	32	30	18	12	5	11	27	.244	.316	.374	19.9	8.1	136
Claunch, Troy	R-R	6-0	210	9-01-98	0	0	0.00	1	0	0	1	0	0	0	0	0	1	.000	.000	.000	25.0	0.0	4
Coffey, Adisyn	R-R	6-2	185	1-22-99	0	2	4.29	22	0	4	21	16	10	10	3	8	29	.205	.276	.385	33.3	9.2	87
Comas, Anderson	L-L	6-3	185	2-10-00	0	0	0.00	1	0	0	3	1	0	0	0	3	1	.111	.333	.111	8.3	25.0	12
Cousin, Josimar	R-R	6-3	185	2-18-98	1	1	5.71	10	10	0	41	46	29	26	5	10	40	.279	.328	.467	22.6	5.6	177
Dalquist, Andrew	R-R	6-1	175	11-13-00	3	6	7.69	22	15	0	62	64	60	53	9	49	60	.270	.398	.464	20.4	16.7	294
Dollander, Hunter	R-R	6-0	232	11-24-96	1	2	4.94	12	1	0	24	21	15	13	4	15	30	.236	.361	.427	27.8	13.9	108
Dominguez, Johan	R-R	6-4	190	1-18-96	0	2	2.45	5	5	0	11	6	4	3	1	5	12	.154	.250	.308	27.3	11.4	44
Duensing, Cole	L-R	6-4	195	6-16-98	1	0	2.16	9	0	0	8	8	2	2	1	5	9	.267	.371	.367	25.0	13.9	36
Gosswein, Brooks	L-L	6-2	205	10-09-98	1	4	5.89	16	9	0	55	53	40	36	7	33	54	.255	.356	.438	21.8	13.3	248

Green, Haylen	L-L	5-11	185	8-12-97	2	1	4.91	13	0	0	15	13	8	8	1	7	17	.245	.355	.434	27.4	11.3	62
Hazelwood, Everhett	R-R	6-2	210	5-12-99	3	2	7.66	33	0	1	49	56	44	42	8	32	59	.286	.395	.474	24.7	13.4	239
Jaquez, Ernesto	R-R	6-2	190	6-11-99	5	0	5.30	21	0	1	37	33	23	22	5	21	31	.244	.352	.467	19.1	13.0	162
Jenkins, Liam	R-R	6-8	225	4-09-97	0	0	0.00	1	0	0	0	2	4	4	1	3	0	1.000	1.000	2.500	0.0	60.0	5
Kelley, Jared	R-R	6-3	230	10-03-01	2	4	5.14	12	5	0	42	36	27	24	2	25	47	.232	.337	.368	26.0	13.8	181
Kincanon, Will	L-R	6-3	215	10-27-95	0	1	94.50	2	0	0	1	5	7	7	1	3	1	.714	.800	1.571	10.0	30.0	10
McCullough, Connor	R-R	6-1	185	10-05-99	5	5	5.33	16	16	0	76	74	47	45	15	18	86	.254	.308	.433	27.3	5.7	315
Mechals, Kade	R-R	5-11	185	10-28-97	0	1	6.35	8	1	1	17	12	12	12	3	5	17	.200	.296	.433	23.9	7.0	71
Mikel, Jordan	R-R	6-5	190	3-24-99	1	0	2.45	12	0	0	18	11	5	5	1	7	25	.175	.288	.270	34.2	9.6	73
Owen, Noah	L-R	6-4	200	10-01-00	1	1	6.07	22	1	0	46	57	35	31	7	19	34	.313	.378	.538	16.3	9.1	209
Palisch, Jake	L-L	6-4	215	8-19-98	1	2	5.31	36	0	3	42	40	28	25	5	13	50	.242	.304	.382	27.3	7.1	183
Plymell, Chase	R-R	6-4	205	5-29-98	4	3	3.26	26	0	0	50	38	19	18	2	22	49	.216	.303	.307	24.3	10.9	202
Ramage, Kole	R-R	6-1	205	9-11-98	1	1	6.95	14	2	0	22	28	23	17	4	20	26	.311	.451	.533	23.0	17.7	113
Ray, Johnny	R-R	6-2	220	10-10-98	1	1	6.97	12	0	2	10	11	9	8	1	14	14	.275	.456	.450	24.6	24.6	57
Schweitzer, Tyler	L-L	6-0	185	9-19-00	0	2	4.08	10	9	0	40	32	23	18	5	24	45	.215	.331	.369	25.6	13.6	176
Scolaro, Jonah	L-L	5-10	193	8-03-98	0	0	9.22	5	1	0	14	23	14	14	5	4	23	.371	.409	.726	34.8	6.1	66
Simas, Kohl	R-R	6-1	190	12-22-99	5	8	6.42	21	17	0	83	93	67	59	12	42	102	.284	.379	.477	26.6	10.9	384
Sommer, Tommy	L-L	6-4	220	9-25-98	1	0	2.57	5	4	0	14	8	6	4	1	8	19	.160	.276	.260	32.8	13.8	58
Stivors, Tristan	R-R	6-4	220	9-22-98	5	3	3.71	23	0	6	27	23	11	11	0	15	40	.232	.350	.303	33.9	12.7	118
Vannelle, Vince	R-R	5-10	202	12-19-97	3	2	5.24	17	0	0	34	45	25	20	3	12	29	.313	.361	.493	18.4	7.6	158
Veloz, Manuel	R-R	6-2	185	1-28-01	0	0	2.25	1	0	0	4	2	1	1	0	2	2	.182	.308	.364	15.4	15.4	13
Vera, Norge	R-R	6-4	185	6-01-00	0	3	10.61	6	6	0	9	10	13	11	1	17	10	.286	.519	.486	19.2	32.7	52
Veras, Frander	L-R	6-5	185	10-08-98	0	0	7.94	6	0	0	6	7	5	5	1	6	2	.304	.448	.522	6.9	20.7	29

Fielding

Catcher	PCT	G	PO	A	E	DP	PB
Claunch	.984	6	51	9	1	2	1
Fish	.990	22	191	16	2	0	3
Gonzalez	.974	18	172	13	5	4	2
Smelley	.994	16	151	6	1	0	2
Turner	.988	67	608	43	8	5	9

First Base	PCT	G	PO	A	E	DP
Elko	.994	24	151	8	1	17
Gladney	.978	15	85	4	2	9
Goosenberg	.989	68	530	28	6	55
Turner	1.000	5	29	0	0	2
Willits	.979	19	128	9	3	20
Womack	1.000	2	15	0	0	1

Second Base	PCT	G	PO	A	E	DP
Atwood	1.000	10	7	18	0	2
Camilletti	1.000	2	6	1	0	1
Chapelli	.982	102	156	229	7	71
DeGuzman	1.000	1	1	1	0	0
Goosenberg	1.000	2	2	2	0	0
Matthews	1.000	2	4	8	0	1
Nakawake	1.000	11	17	32	0	8
Womack	1.000	1	2	1	0	1

Third Base	PCT	G	PO	A	E	DP
Atwood	.929	18	15	24	3	3
Camilletti	1.000	1	1	4	0	1
DeGuzman	.500	1	0	2	2	0
Kath	.922	95	63	149	18	18
Matthews	.667	2	0	2	1	0
Nakawake	.967	10	5	24	1	5
Willits	.000	2	0	0	0	0
Womack	1.000	3	3	4	0	0

Shortstop	PCT	G	PO	A	E	DP
Atwood	.917	8	6	16	2	2
Baldwin	.959	22	24	46	3	15
Matthews	.974	22	17	59	2	8
Montgomery	.949	13	20	36	3	10
Nakawake	.962	61	61	143	8	32
Sanchez	1.000	2	1	7	0	0

Outfield	PCT	G	PO	A	E	DP
Burke	.976	50	122	1	3	1
Camilletti	.938	8	15	0	1	0
Gladney	.987	69	107	4	2	0
Goosenberg	.955	15	20	1	1	0
Lanzilli	.992	38	65	3	1	0
Norman	1.000	5	9	0	0	0
Tatum	.962	60	126	1	5	0
Veras	.971	78	127	8	4	3
Weaver	.969	62	107	2	3	0
Willits	1.000	7	12	0	0	0

KANNAPOLIS CANNON BALLERS — *LOW CLASS A*

CAROLINA LEAGUE

Batting	B-T	Ht.	Wt.	DOB	AVG	OBP	SLG	G	PA	AB	R	H	2B	3B	HR	RBI	BB	HBP	SH	SF	SO	SB	CS	BB%	SO%
Baldwin, Brooks	B-R	6-2	175	8-15-00	.245	.338	.445	67	283	245	41	60	13	3	10	39	34	1	2	1	61	14	5	12.0	21.6
Betancourt, Jhoneiker	R-R	6-1	174	5-02-00	.226	.324	.403	68	275	226	26	51	10	0	10	45	28	10	0	11	64	0	0	10.2	23.3
Burke, Jacob	R-R	6-1	208	2-26-01	.315	.416	.512	35	149	127	23	40	11	1	4	22	15	7	0	0	33	9	3	10.1	22.1
Camilletti, Mario	L-R	5-9	195	4-19-99	.289	.432	.375	97	434	339	64	98	23	0	2	60	84	4	0	4	70	0	1	19.4	16.1
Claunch, Troy	R-R	6-0	210	9-01-98	.194	.300	.291	30	120	103	12	20	4	0	2	13	12	4	0	1	22	0	0	10.0	18.3
DeGuzman, Cristopher	B-R	5-11	185	12-01-99	.175	.283	.225	18	47	40	9	7	2	0	0	3	6	0	1	0	17	5	0	12.8	36.2
Elko, Tim	R-R	6-4	240	12-27-98	.297	.360	.556	66	286	259	43	77	14	1	17	57	24	2	0	1	85	0	1	8.4	29.7
Felix, Edrick	R-R	6-0	198	1-14-02	.227	.292	.364	12	48	44	7	10	1	1	1	5	3	1	0	0	16	0	0	6.3	33.3
Galanie, Ryan	R-R	6-2	215	6-20-00	.282	.341	.418	28	123	110	21	31	5	2	2	12	7	4	0	2	22	3	1	5.7	17.9
Glass, Logan	R-R	6-4	215	4-09-01	.202	.288	.333	56	206	183	28	37	7	1	5	20	18	4	0	0	86	7	0	8.7	41.7
Gonzalez, Jacob	L-R	6-2	200	5-30-02	.207	.328	.261	30	137	111	16	23	3	0	1	13	20	2	0	4	23	1	1	14.6	16.8
Gonzalez, Juan	R-R	5-9	195	2-20-01	.259	.382	.361	34	131	108	20	28	5	0	2	8	15	7	0	1	32	5	0	11.5	24.4
Harris, Calvin	L-R	6-0	205	11-15-01	.241	.362	.315	30	130	108	14	26	3	1	1	19	20	1	0	1	23	0	1	15.4	17.7
Lanzilli, Chris	R-R	6-2	225	6-18-98	.302	.391	.459	56	235	205	26	62	14	0	6	40	22	8	0	0	51	0	1	9.4	21.7
Laureano, Johnabiell	R-R	6-0	180	10-11-00	.197	.335	.299	46	179	147	26	29	3	0	4	14	31	0	0	1	57	1	1	17.3	31.8
Logan, Drake	R-R	6-4	205	9-05-00	.208	.327	.278	98	370	313	44	65	8	1	4	25	48	8	0	1	161	11	2	13.0	43.5
McCarthy, Ryan	L-R	6-3	235	1-13-99	.232	.342	.391	42	161	138	20	32	8	4	2	12	18	5	0	0	34	5	1	11.2	21.1
Mora, Javier	R-R	5-11	170	3-23-03	.203	.257	.219	19	70	64	8	13	1	0	0	5	5	0	0	1	26	0	0	7.1	37.1
Nishida, Rikuu	L-R	5-6	150	5-06-01	.222	.310	.278	19	87	72	12	16	0	2	0	6	8	2	3	2	9	5	2	9.2	10.3
Park, Eddie	L-L	6-1	187	8-22-01	.333	.426	.383	21	94	81	18	27	2	1	0	5	12	1	0	0	19	4	0	12.8	20.2
Pineda, Luis	R-R	6-1	209	3-19-02	.193	.254	.312	29	119	109	10	21	4	0	3	17	7	2	0	0	40	0	0	5.9	33.6
Ramos, Bryan	R-R	6-2	190	3-12-02	.125	.125	.313	4	17	16	3	2	0	0	1	2	0	0	0	0	4	0	0	0.0	23.5
Sanchez, Wilber	R-R	5-10	160	2-21-02	.207	.319	.291	89	309	261	45	54	12	2	2	39	40	4	2	2	72	28	9	12.9	23.3
Smelley, Colby	R-R	6-2	195	3-15-00	.282	.346	.310	19	78	71	6	20	2	0	0	5	6	1	0	0	17	0	0	7.7	21.8
Sprinkle, Jordan	R-R	5-11	180	3-06-01	.228	.307	.309	71	323	285	35	65	10	2	3	32	31	3	1	3	82	17	3	9.6	25.4
Tapia, Layant	R-R	6-1	160	1-04-02	.091	.167	.121	17	72	66	5	6	2	0	0	2	5	1	0	0	28	1	2	6.9	38.9
Torres, Victor	R-R	6-0	180	7-29-00	.000	.250	.000	1	4	3	1	0	0	0	0	0	1	0	0	0	2	0	0	25.0	50.0

Batting	B-T	Ht.	Wt.	DOB	AVG	OBP	SLG	G	PA	AB	R	H	2B	3B	HR	RBI	BB	HBP	SH	SF	SO	SB	CS	BB%	SO%
Weaver, Caberea	R-R	6-3	180	12-01-99	.236	.277	.360	25	94	89	17	21	8	0	1	9	4	1	0	0	28	2	1	4.3	29.8
Willits, Bryce	L-R	6-2	200	8-25-99	.263	.356	.430	88	365	316	45	83	15	1	12	50	46	1	0	2	78	3	4	12.6	21.4

Pitching	B-T	Ht.	Wt.	DOB	W	L	ERA	G	GS	SV	IP	Hits	Runs	ER	HR	BB	SO	AVG	OBP	SLG	SO%	BB%	BF
Adams, Mason	R-R	6-0	200	2-23-00	4	3	3.36	17	7	1	78	74	36	29	6	18	94	.245	.300	.341	28.5	5.5	330
Adler, Eric	R-R	6-2	190	10-12-00	0	0	3.18	12	0	2	11	6	4	4	1	7	19	.158	.289	.263	42.2	15.6	45
Andujar, Horacio	R-R	6-2	161	1-14-99	4	5	4.84	28	0	3	48	44	28	26	4	15	36	.242	.303	.379	17.9	7.5	201
Batista, Aldrin	R-R	6-2	185	5-04-03	0	0	2.66	5	5	0	24	18	7	7	0	7	21	.209	.271	.256	21.9	7.3	96
Beutel, Ben	L-L	6-0	165	9-02-99	7	4	3.12	29	0	2	52	50	21	18	1	15	47	.258	.321	.330	21.8	6.9	216
Burns, Dylan	R-R	6-1	194	12-29-96	0	0	0.00	1	0	0	3	2	0	0	0	3	2	.200	.385	.200	15.4	23.1	13
Cable, Zach	R-R	6-0	215	10-22-97	1	0	7.13	18	0	1	18	21	15	14	4	22	19	.296	.479	.521	19.8	22.9	96
Castro, Oriel	L-L	6-0	175	5-05-01	0	2	6.62	13	1	0	18	14	15	13	2	15	18	.222	.390	.381	21.7	18.1	83
Comas, Anderson	L-L	6-3	185	2-10-00	1	0	1.83	9	0	0	20	21	4	4	1	6	14	.300	.359	.386	17.7	7.6	79
DeGuzman, Cristopher	B-R	5-11	185	12-01-99	0	0	4.50	2	0	0	2	2	1	1	1	0	1	.250	.250	.625	12.5	0.0	8
Franklin, Zach	R-R	6-1	198	10-27-98	0	0	8.64	8	0	0	8	10	9	8	0	4	12	.286	.390	.400	29.3	9.8	41
Gordon, Lucas	L-L	6-1	193	2-13-02	0	0	0.00	2	2	0	5	4	0	0	0	3	6	.222	.333	.278	28.6	14.3	21
Hammerberg, Ethan	L-R	6-5	250	12-18-00	2	3	4.26	23	0	1	32	25	17	15	3	25	48	.214	.352	.342	32.9	17.1	146
Keener, Seth	R-R	6-1	195	10-04-01	0	1	7.11	3	3	0	6	9	5	5	1	2	7	.321	.367	.429	23.3	6.7	30
Krogman, Chase	L-L	5-11	180	2-27-01	0	1	34.71	4	0	0	2	7	9	9	2	7	4	.538	.682	1.154	18.2	31.8	22
Lyle, Logan	L-L	5-11	202	2-01-98	1	1	4.35	12	0	2	21	21	11	10	2	7	16	.259	.318	.383	18.0	7.9	89
McCullough, Connor	R-R	6-1	185	10-05-99	3	3	2.17	7	7	0	37	22	9	9	2	7	44	.168	.216	.229	31.7	5.0	139
McDaniel, Drew	R-R	6-2	185	8-26-00	5	8	4.60	20	17	1	78	88	48	40	7	27	67	.278	.336	.435	19.0	7.7	352
McDougal, Tanner	R-R	6-5	185	4-09-03	0	3	4.15	21	21	0	69	54	35	32	5	43	80	.218	.348	.319	26.7	14.3	300
McLaughlin, Mark	R-R	6-3	205	2-14-01	1	2	14.11	8	1	0	15	25	24	23	1	20	15	.403	.536	.565	17.9	23.8	84
Mechals, Kade	R-R	5-11	185	10-28-97	0	1	5.00	5	0	0	9	7	5	5	2	3	6	.212	.270	.485	16.2	8.1	37
Milto, Pauly	R-R	6-3	245	3-06-97	0	1	9.33	17	0	0	18	20	19	19	1	11	21	.286	.407	.414	24.4	12.8	86
Murphy, Shane	L-L	6-5	210	1-19-01	4	4	3.63	21	21	0	97	81	46	39	13	23	98	.228	.276	.386	25.5	6.0	384
Nolasco, Yohemy	R-R	6-3	160	7-12-03	2	0	1.50	11	0	2	24	25	8	4	1	10	23	.266	.340	.372	21.7	9.4	106
Pallette, Peyton	R-R	6-1	180	5-09-01	0	4	4.13	22	22	0	72	57	40	33	8	41	78	.213	.332	.348	24.4	12.8	320
Pellerin, Connor	R-R	6-4	210	7-22-99	1	2	5.14	16	0	0	21	12	13	12	1	21	28	.176	.404	.221	29.8	22.3	94
Peters, Connery	R-R	6-6	240	2-03-00	0	1	4.50	7	0	1	8	6	4	4	0	4	13	.194	.342	.258	34.2	10.5	38
Ramage, Kole	R-R	6-1	205	9-11-98	2	2	4.35	17	0	0	31	28	16	15	3	11	32	.239	.305	.359	25.0	8.6	128
Ray, Johnny	R-R	6-2	220	10-10-98	2	0	8.44	9	0	0	11	12	10	10	1	10	14	.286	.418	.429	25.5	18.2	55
Schultz, Noah	L-L	6-9	220	8-05-03	1	2	1.33	10	10	0	27	17	7	4	3	6	38	.175	.231	.309	36.5	5.8	104
Schweitzer, Tyler	L-L	6-0	185	9-19-00	7	2	3.86	13	13	0	68	62	31	29	5	21	76	.234	.293	.351	26.5	7.3	287
Seidl, Billy	R-R	6-0	220	11-09-99	5	4	5.06	47	0	14	53	48	35	30	0	29	53	.246	.385	.318	21.7	11.9	244
Talavera, Emerson	R-R	5-10	160	10-01-02	3	2	6.48	32	0	2	50	51	38	36	9	30	42	.264	.368	.466	18.2	13.0	231
Veloz, Manuel	R-R	6-2	185	1-28-01	10	2	3.82	21	1	1	66	68	34	28	5	26	44	.269	.347	.364	15.4	9.1	285
Veras, Frander	L-R	6-5	185	10-08-98	1	1	5.29	11	0	0	17	19	10	10	0	8	14	.292	.405	.400	17.7	10.1	79

Fielding

Catcher	PCT	G	PO	A	E	DP	PB
Betancourt	1.000	7	52	4	0	0	0
Claunch	.985	29	241	20	4	0	3
Gonzalez	.976	29	263	21	7	6	4
Harris	.969	23	173	15	6	3	0
Pineda	.986	28	260	28	4	2	3
Smelley	1.000	18	167	13	0	1	2

First Base	PCT	G	PO	A	E	DP
Baldwin	1.000	2	16	0	0	1
Betancourt	.994	41	284	23	2	31
Elko	.994	48	333	20	2	25
Galanie	.993	18	140	9	1	15
Willits	.990	24	186	14	2	14

Second Base	PCT	G	PO	A	E	DP
Baldwin	1.000	3	8	6	0	2
Camilletti	.968	58	88	126	7	35
DeGuzman	1.000	5	4	9	0	1
Felix	.952	11	16	24	2	9
Mora	.946	15	21	32	3	7
Sanchez	.974	27	44	69	3	12
Smelley	.000	1	0	0	0	0
Sprinkle	.953	15	25	36	3	11

Third Base	PCT	G	PO	A	E	DP
Baldwin	.947	34	30	59	5	7
Camilletti	.941	13	3	13	1	1
DeGuzman	1.000	3	0	3	0	0
Mora	.000	1	0	0	1	0
Ramos	1.000	4	5	7	0	2
Sanchez	.920	10	9	14	2	4
Sprinkle	.963	13	7	19	1	0
Tapia	.941	11	6	10	1	0
Willits	.932	46	30	66	7	7

Shortstop	PCT	G	PO	A	E	DP
Baldwin	1.000	1	1	0	0	0
DeGuzman	.938	8	8	7	1	0
Gonzalez	.958	29	44	94	6	17
Mora	1.000	1	1	1	0	0
Sanchez	.961	47	54	119	7	18
Sprinkle	.973	42	40	104	4	18
Tapia	1.000	6	11	10	0	4

Outfield	PCT	G	PO	A	E	DP
Baldwin	.961	10	22	2	1	0
Burke	.978	33	85	2	2	1
Glass	1.000	55	106	3	0	1
Lanzilli	.977	52	89	2	4	1
Laureano	.965	47	55	1	2	0
Logan	.978	97	171	7	4	2
McCarthy	.992	40	77	5	1	2
Nishida	.977	19	32	2	1	1
Park	.975	20	37	2	1	0
Weaver	1.000	25	48	2	0	1
Willits	1.000	4	4	1	0	0

ACL WHITE SOX — ROOKIE

ARIZONA COMPLEX LEAGUE

Batting	B-T	Ht.	Wt.	DOB	AVG	OBP	SLG	G	PA	AB	R	H	2B	3B	HR	RBI	BB	HBP	SH	SF	SO	SB	CS	BB%	SO%
Aguero, Alvaro	R-R	6-0	160	3-19-03	.265	.303	.406	44	165	155	31	41	8	1	4	18	6	3	0	1	39	13	3	3.6	23.6
Archer, Matt	R-R	5-10	180	8-13-00	.367	.458	.571	17	60	49	10	18	5	1	1	6	6	3	1	1	8	3	0	10.0	13.3
Benavides, Ruben	R-R	6-1	178	8-09-01	.154	.241	.192	12	29	26	1	4	1	0	0	1	3	0	0	0	12	0	0	10.3	41.4
Bennett, Godwin	R-R	6-2	170	10-04-02	.244	.358	.372	25	95	78	10	19	2	1	2	12	13	2	0	2	26	11	1	13.7	27.4
Borrero, Dario	L-L	6-5	190	11-13-03	.250	.286	.313	29	105	96	9	24	6	0	0	10	6	0	0	3	14	0	0	5.7	13.3
Burrowes, Ryan	R-R	6-2	170	8-17-04	.259	.330	.386	43	178	158	24	41	8	3	2	15	12	5	2	1	51	12	5	6.7	28.7
Claunch, Troy	R-R	6-0	210	9-01-98	.000	.286	.000	4	14	10	0	0	0	0	0	1	4	0	0	0	3	0	0	28.6	21.4
Connor, Caden	L-L	6-1	200	8-02-00	.143	.306	.179	9	36	28	4	4	1	0	0	3	7	0	0	1	8	0	0	19.4	22.2
Eberly, Weston	R-R	6-0	195	1-07-01	.087	.192	.087	8	26	23	0	2	0	0	0	0	2	1	0	0	7	0	0	7.7	26.9
Espinoza, Anthony	R-R	5-10	165	9-27-01	.250	.250	.250	3	8	8	2	2	0	0	0	0	0	0	0	0	5	0	0	0.0	62.5
Felix, Edrick	R-R	6-0	198	1-14-02	.409	.536	.727	9	28	22	3	9	1	0	2	6	3	3	0	0	7	1	1	10.7	25.0

Galanie, Ryan	R-R	6-2	215	6-20-00	.231	.286	.308	4	14	13	0	3	1	0	0	0	1	0	0	0	4	1	0	7.1	28.6
Gonzalez, Jacob	L-R	6-2	200	5-30-02	.250	.375	.250	4	16	12	2	3	0	0	0	4	3	0	0	1	2	0	0	18.8	12.5
Gonzalez, Misael	R-R	6-0	175	5-23-01	.194	.293	.361	13	41	36	7	7	1	1	1	4	5	0	0	0	17	5	0	12.2	41.5
Guariman, Manuel	R-R	6-0	196	2-09-04	.278	.366	.333	13	41	36	4	10	2	0	0	3	3	2	0	0	3	1	0	7.3	7.3
Harris, Calvin	L-R	6-0	205	11-15-01	.214	.267	.286	4	15	14	2	3	1	0	0	3	1	0	0	0	5	0	0	6.7	33.3
Hernandez, Arxy	R-R	6-2	170	7-29-03	.243	.341	.278	34	132	115	18	28	4	0	0	12	15	2	0	0	32	6	6	11.4	24.2
Hernandez, Erick	L-L	6-0	170	1-15-05	.145	.295	.210	25	78	62	7	9	2	1	0	4	12	2	0	2	27	2	0	15.4	34.6
Hernandez, Ronny	R-R	6-1	200	11-09-04	.338	.430	.493	45	172	148	20	50	12	1	3	36	22	2	0	0	35	1	0	12.8	20.3
Jimenez, Carlos	L-L	6-4	220	2-03-02	.212	.287	.356	29	115	104	14	22	6	0	3	16	8	3	0	0	22	3	0	7.0	19.1
Jimenez, Enoy	R-R	5-10	160	11-08-00	.086	.179	.086	14	41	35	6	3	0	0	0	0	4	0	2	0	9	2	1	9.8	22.0
Kane, Mikey	R-R	6-3	195	7-11-01	.375	.464	.375	7	28	24	3	9	0	0	0	3	4	0	0	0	4	1	0	14.3	14.3
Mondesi, Randel	R-R	6-3	190	12-04-02	.154	.274	.192	17	62	52	1	8	0	1	0	5	7	2	0	1	32	2	1	11.3	51.6
Montgomery, Colson	L-R	6-3	205	2-27-02	.353	.511	.588	10	45	34	9	12	3	1	1	6	11	0	0	0	5	2	0	24.4	11.1
Mora, Javier	R-R	5-11	170	3-23-03	.360	.467	.440	9	30	25	3	9	2	0	0	3	5	0	0	0	6	0	1	16.7	20.0
Nishida, Rikuu	L-R	5-6	150	5-06-01	.250	.250	.250	1	4	4	1	1	0	0	0	0	0	0	0	0	0	1	0	0.0	0.0
Park, Eddie	L-L	6-1	187	8-22-01	.308	.438	.308	4	16	13	5	4	0	0	0	1	2	1	0	0	1	4	0	12.5	6.3
Pineda, Luis	R-R	6-1	209	3-19-02	.220	.347	.390	15	50	41	5	9	1	0	2	5	8	0	0	0	14	1	3	16.0	28.0
Prado, Arnold	R-R	6-3	194	11-20-04	.182	.273	.219	42	154	137	16	25	5	0	0	9	12	5	0	0	44	6	2	7.8	28.6
Rodriguez, Guillermo	R-R	5-9	156	9-03-04	.189	.333	.253	33	117	95	9	18	3	0	1	9	18	3	0	1	40	3	2	15.4	34.2
Sprinkle, Jordan	R-R	5-11	180	3-06-01	.333	.333	.500	3	12	12	1	4	2	0	0	0	0	0	0	0	4	1	0	0.0	33.3
Tamez, Dominic	R-R	5-10	205	1-12-01	.000	.000	.000	4	16	16	0	0	0	0	0	0	0	0	0	0	5	0	0	0.0	31.3
Tapia, Layant	R-R	6-1	160	1-04-02	.200	.305	.260	17	59	50	7	10	3	0	0	3	7	1	0	1	28	1	3	11.9	47.5
Wolkow, George	L-R	6-7	225	1-11-06	.225	.392	.325	13	51	40	6	9	1	0	1	3	9	2	0	0	17	2	0	17.6	33.3

Pitching	B-T	Ht.	Wt.	DOB	W	L	ERA	G	GS	SV	IP	Hits	Runs	ER	HR	BB	SO	AVG	OBP	SLG	SO%	BB%	BF
Arias, Frankeli	L-L	6-0	170	4-05-03	3	2	4.67	13	10	0	54	55	32	28	6	23	52	.270	.355	.436	22.1	9.8	235
Bailey, Brandon	R-R	5-10	195	10-19-94	0	0	81.00	1	1	0	0	2	3	3	1	1	0	.667	.750	2.000	0.0	25.0	4
Bell, Luke	R-R	6-4	200	8-09-00	0	1	1.69	6	0	0	5	9	1	1	0	2	9	.391	.440	.522	34.6	7.7	26
Bockenstedt, Jacob	R-R	6-1	190	11-15-99	0	0	3.00	5	0	1	6	4	2	2	2	2	6	.182	.250	.455	25.0	8.3	24
Brizuela, Ricardo	R-R	6-3	198	6-30-03	3	4	4.62	14	5	1	51	51	33	26	8	16	55	.258	.311	.460	25.0	7.3	220
Carrion, Brian	R-R	6-2	180	1-01-99	0	1	7.59	8	0	1	11	17	11	9	3	9	17	.370	.464	.674	30.4	16.1	56
Castro, Oriel	L-L	6-0	175	5-05-01	0	0	0.00	2	0	0	2	0	0	0	0	1	2	.000	.143	.000	28.6	14.3	7
Comas, Anderson	L-L	6-3	185	2-10-00	1	0	1.10	7	0	0	16	11	2	2	1	2	15	.183	.222	.250	23.8	3.2	63
Cousin, Josimar	R-R	6-3	185	2-18-98	0	0	7.20	3	3	0	5	4	4	4	1	1	1	.211	.273	.474	4.5	4.5	22
Cuevas, Guillermo	L-L	6-0	180	5-13-99	2	4	7.36	12	3	0	26	34	24	21	1	13	30	.309	.384	.491	23.8	10.3	126
Duensing, Cole	L-R	6-4	195	6-16-98	3	0	4.15	4	0	0	4	2	2	2	0	2	1	.154	.250	.154	6.3	12.5	16
Ellard, Fraser	L-L	6-4	205	11-06-97	0	0	4.50	2	0	0	2	3	1	1	0	0	3	.375	.375	.375	37.5	0.0	8
Franklin, Zach	R-R	6-1	198	10-27-98	0	0	0.00	3	0	0	3	3	0	0	0	2	6	.273	.385	.273	46.2	15.4	13
Freeman, Caleb	R-R	6-1	195	2-23-98	0	0	3.86	3	0	0	2	1	1	1	0	6	1	.125	.563	.125	6.3	37.5	16
Gonzalez, Daniel	L-L	6-3	160	11-27-01	0	3	1.83	16	0	1	20	8	11	4	2	16	31	.118	.302	.206	36.0	18.6	86
Gordon, Lucas	L-L	6-1	193	2-13-02	1	0	1.59	5	0	0	6	5	2	1	0	5	8	.227	.370	.227	29.6	18.5	27
Hammer, Zach	R-R	6-2	165	7-04-00	1	0	15.00	4	0	0	3	6	5	5	0	0	3	.400	.412	.467	17.6	0.0	17
Hildebrand, Eric	R-R	6-0	180	1-04-00	0	0	9.53	11	0	0	11	17	12	12	2	9	8	.347	.459	.592	13.1	14.8	61
Hinestroza, Carlos	R-R	6-1	190	2-04-03	1	3	5.82	14	0	1	22	22	15	14	1	7	29	.259	.319	.400	30.9	7.4	94
Jacobs, Carson	R-R	6-9	215	8-17-01	0	0	1.42	5	0	0	6	4	1	1	0	3	9	.182	.280	.227	36.0	12.0	25
Jimenez, Jose	L-L	6-3	195	8-31-02	1	0	4.86	8	0	0	17	15	10	9	1	12	17	.242	.385	.306	21.5	15.2	79
Jimenez, Juan	R-R	6-2	194	9-11-02	0	1	19.29	4	0	0	2	6	6	5	1	5	3	.462	.611	.846	16.7	27.8	18
Keener, Seth	R-R	6-1	195	10-04-01	1	0	1.50	4	2	0	6	2	1	1	0	2	7	.100	.182	.150	31.8	9.1	22
Kincanon, Will	L-R	6-3	215	10-27-95	1	0	4.50	2	0	0	2	1	1	1	1	1	2	.143	.250	.571	25.0	12.5	8
Krogman, Chase	L-L	5-11	180	2-27-01	0	1	2.03	14	0	3	13	5	5	3	0	10	22	.114	.316	.114	38.6	17.5	57
Lyle, Logan	L-L	5-11	202	2-01-98	0	0	2.08	6	1	0	9	7	2	2	1	7	6	.233	.395	.367	15.8	18.4	38
McLaughlin, Mark	R-R	6-3	205	2-14-01	0	6	10.00	13	8	0	36	56	51	40	0	24	35	.346	.429	.426	18.4	12.6	190
Mendez, Jesus	R-R	5-11	180	7-30-04	0	2	4.11	16	0	5	15	15	8	7	1	12	17	.259	.397	.397	23.3	16.4	73
Mendoza, Jose	R-R	6-2	175	3-15-04	0	0	3.38	3	0	0	3	2	1	1	0	2	2	.200	.333	.200	16.7	16.7	12
Mikel, Jordan	R-R	6-5	190	3-24-99	0	0	5.40	3	2	0	5	7	3	3	2	2	6	.333	.391	.667	26.1	8.7	23
Oppor, Christian	L-L	6-2	175	7-23-04	0	0	1.17	5	1	0	8	6	2	1	0	2	9	.222	.267	.259	30.0	6.7	30
Pellerin, Connor	R-R	6-4	210	7-22-99	0	0	0.00	2	0	0	3	1	0	0	0	1	7	.100	.182	.100	63.6	9.1	11
Peppers, Jake	R-R	6-3	160	12-26-01	0	2	6.35	4	2	0	6	5	4	4	1	3	8	.227	.320	.364	32.0	12.0	25
Perkins, Carlton	R-R	6-3	180	11-09-02	0	2	10.80	6	4	0	8	10	10	10	0	6	6	.286	.390	.286	14.6	14.6	41
Peters, Connery	R-R	6-6	240	2-03-00	0	0	9.00	4	0	0	3	4	4	3	0	3	2	.308	.471	.385	11.8	17.6	17
Ray, Johnny	R-R	6-2	220	10-10-98	0	0	0.00	2	0	0	2	0	0	0	0	0	4	.000	.000	.000	66.7	0.0	6
Robles, Ronny	R-R	6-2	180	11-11-01	0	0	17.36	6	0	0	5	7	9	9	0	7	4	.350	.517	.350	13.8	24.1	29
Rodriguez, Gabriel	R-R	5-11	172	11-20-02	2	1	3.78	14	9	1	48	48	22	20	1	24	61	.259	.363	.351	28.4	11.2	215
Rodriguez, Jose	R-R	6-3	200	7-26-00	1	1	6.52	13	0	0	10	6	7	7	0	13	9	.194	.413	.258	19.6	28.3	46
Shilling, Luke	R-R	6-4	230	11-18-97	0	0	0.00	2	1	0	2	0	0	0	0	0	1	.000	.000	.000	14.3	0.0	7
Stivors, Tristan	R-R	6-4	220	9-22-98	0	0	0.00	1	0	0	1	0	0	0	0	1	2	.000	.250	.000	50.0	25.0	4
Vera, Norge	R-R	6-4	185	6-01-00	0	1	0.00	4	4	0	6	3	2	0	0	4	5	.167	.348	.222	21.7	17.4	23
Veras, Frander	L-R	6-5	185	10-08-98	0	0	0.00	3	0	0	3	1	1	0	0	2	6	.100	.250	.100	50.0	16.7	12

Fielding

C: Hernandez 28, Benavides 10, Guariman 8, Eberly 7, Pineda 6, Harris 3, Claunch 3, Tamez 2. **1B:** Borrero 28, Jimenez 26, Galanie 2, Guariman 1, Connor 1, Espinoza 1. **2B:** Archer 15, Rodriguez 15, Burrowes 9, Felix 9, Mora 6, Tapia 6, Jimenez 5, Espinoza 1, Sprinkle 1. **3B:** Hernandez 33, Tapia 8, Rodriguez 7, Kane 7, Mora 2, Jimenez 2, Galanie 2. **SS:** Burrowes 35, Rodriguez 12, Montgomery 7, Gonzalez 4, Tapia 3, Sprinkle 2, Hernandez 1, Jimenez 1. **OF:** Aguero 44, Prado 41, Bennett 23, Hernandez 22, Mondesi 14, Wolkow 13, Gonzalez 12, Connor 9, Jimenez 4, Park 4, Nishida 1, Tapia 1.

DSL WHITE SOX

ROOKIE

DOMINICAN SUMMER LEAGUE

Batting	B-T	Ht.	Wt.	DOB	AVG	OBP	SLG	G	PA	AB	R	H	2B	3B	HR	RBI	BB	HBP	SH	SF	SO	SB	CS	BB%	SO%
Alberto, Albert	R-R	6-3	190	3-03-06	.205	.391	.313	32	110	83	12	17	6	0	1	13	22	4	0	1	32	2	1	20.0	29.1
Alcala, Marcelo	R-R	6-0	183	3-23-06	.245	.417	.408	42	127	98	28	24	8	1	2	18	20	9	0	0	37	5	1	15.7	29.1
Alsinois, Leandro	R-R	5-10	175	9-06-04	.301	.422	.390	45	185	146	41	44	10	0	1	18	32	2	0	5	25	9	7	17.3	13.5
Alvarez, Rafael	R-R	6-2	190	2-13-05	.215	.461	.333	35	141	93	31	20	5	0	2	11	32	13	0	3	31	5	0	22.7	22.0
Castillo, Ryan	L-R	6-1	170	1-28-05	.259	.370	.422	35	139	116	20	30	7	0	4	20	17	4	1	1	34	0	0	12.2	24.5
D'Oleo, Cesar	R-R	6-0	180	1-05-05	.185	.364	.247	29	110	81	15	15	2	0	1	15	24	1	0	4	23	1	0	21.8	20.9
Flores, Stiven	R-R	5-11	180	12-26-05	.391	.456	.477	37	147	128	15	50	8	0	1	33	15	2	0	2	7	7	0	10.2	4.8
Gil, Adrian	R-R	5-11	195	10-21-03	.000	.333	.000	8	3	2	0	0	0	0	0	0	0	1	0	0	1	0	0	0.0	33.3
Gil, Adrian	R-R	6-0	193	11-17-05	.340	.481	.517	45	190	147	33	50	11	0	5	33	25	15	1	0	21	5	5	13.2	11.1
Hernandez, Angelo	R-R	6-1	200	9-11-05	.232	.436	.304	21	78	56	11	13	4	0	0	8	16	5	0	1	8	2	0	20.5	10.3
Mogollon, Javier	R-R	5-8	160	11-01-05	.315	.417	.582	47	199	165	41	52	10	2	10	42	27	4	0	3	28	11	2	13.6	14.1
Nunez, Abraham	L-R	6-2	175	2-17-06	.299	.427	.442	44	185	147	28	44	8	2	3	29	33	2	0	3	22	12	7	17.8	11.9
Ramos, Edwin	R-R	6-2	194	10-16-04	.167	.400	.222	24	75	54	15	9	3	0	0	3	20	1	0	0	16	0	1	26.7	21.3
Riera, Elias	R-R	6-2	180	4-18-06	.154	.362	.212	22	69	52	11	8	3	0	0	7	6	11	0	0	22	0	0	8.7	31.9
Tejada, D'Angelo	R-R	6-0	160	11-12-05	.255	.324	.309	43	170	149	31	38	6	1	0	18	13	4	0	4	43	7	2	7.6	25.3
Ugueto, Eyke	R-R	5-11	175	3-19-06	.188	.350	.260	36	124	96	24	18	7	0	0	12	16	9	1	2	31	8	1	12.9	25.0
Uribe, Juan	R-R	5-10	160	6-07-06	.131	.384	.180	22	86	61	10	8	1	1	0	7	24	1	0	0	31	0	1	27.9	36.0

Pitching	B-T	Ht.	Wt.	DOB	W	L	ERA	G	GS	SV	IP	Hits	Runs	ER	HR	BB	SO	AVG	OBP	SLG	SO%	BB%	BF
Chirinos, Jordany	R-R	6-3	196	5-04-06	3	1	4.12	12	5	0	39	41	21	18	1	15	43	.258	.320	.371	24.3	8.5	177
Diaz, Reudis	R-R	6-1	180	2-16-06	4	1	6.60	16	2	0	30	35	26	22	2	7	21	.287	.348	.434	15.3	5.1	137
Dishmey, Halan	R-R	6-6	210	11-11-04	1	2	14.46	9	0	0	9	12	16	15	1	11	8	.308	.460	.462	16.0	22.0	50
Gil, Adrian	R-R	5-11	195	10-21-03	0	0	7.36	7	0	0	7	9	6	6	0	5	8	.310	.412	.586	23.5	14.7	34
Gomez, Ricardo	R-R	6-3	158	11-09-04	1	0	5.55	11	4	0	24	24	15	15	4	9	20	.255	.333	.457	18.3	8.3	109
Gonzalez, Jeremy	L-L	6-0	168	4-01-05	0	4	3.75	10	10	0	36	30	24	15	3	13	44	.219	.294	.358	28.8	8.5	153
Hernandez, Oscar	R-R	6-4	190	1-18-06	4	0	6.17	15	0	1	23	19	18	16	2	21	34	.226	.411	.393	30.4	18.8	112
Lima, Denny	R-R	6-0	170	8-30-04	4	2	3.79	13	13	0	55	47	27	23	4	16	44	.232	.298	.350	19.6	7.1	225
Malave, Jose	R-R	6-2	198	4-10-06	0	2	8.64	11	1	0	17	22	18	16	2	16	10	.310	.437	.437	11.4	18.2	88
Mateo, Alexander	R-R	6-5	205	10-28-05	3	0	6.00	10	0	0	18	26	16	12	2	8	16	.347	.437	.520	18.2	9.1	88
Peralta, Edwin	R-R	6-3	175	5-10-01	1	0	6.20	15	0	1	20	22	20	14	1	15	25	.262	.373	.345	24.5	14.7	102
Redman, Pedro	R-R	6-2	190	4-19-04	4	0	2.45	15	0	3	22	14	6	6	0	12	26	.184	.308	.237	28.6	13.2	91
Reyes, Luis	R-R	6-2	190	10-13-05	4	6	7.17	16	9	1	38	38	37	30	6	30	49	.264	.398	.472	27.1	16.6	181
Rodriguez, Luis	R-R	6-2	181	12-29-03	2	1	3.55	15	0	0	33	32	16	13	1	6	45	.248	.297	.357	32.6	4.3	138
Rosario, Emilio	R-R	6-4	190	10-19-04	0	0	12.54	11	0	0	9	12	14	13	2	10	11	.300	.472	.525	20.8	18.9	53
Valladares, Marcelo	R-R	6-4	187	8-28-04	1	0	2.93	13	11	0	46	32	19	15	2	29	43	.195	.316	.287	21.9	14.8	196
Vargas, Fernando	R-R	6-2	185	8-03-02	0	0	29.25	8	0	1	4	3	13	13	1	18	6	.273	.735	.545	17.6	52.9	34
Ysalla, Fabian	R-R	6-0	161	12-14-04	0	3	3.24	9	0	0	17	10	8	6	1	11	12	.175	.319	.228	17.4	15.9	69

Fielding

C: Flores 29, Ramos 19, Hernandez 16, Riera 1. **1B:** Gil 27, Castillo 25, Riera 6, Ramos 2, Alvarez 1. **2B:** Mogollon 28, Ugueto 18, Uribe 12, Gil 5. **3B:** Alvarez 33, Gil 16, Ugueto 8, Riera 1, Castillo 1. **SS:** Tejada 37, Mogollon 15, Ugueto 7. **OF:** Alcala 42, Nunez 42, Alsinois 41, Alberto 31, D'Oleo 27.

Cincinnati Reds

CINCINNATI REDS

SEASON SYNOPSIS: Few teams were as fun as the Reds, who electrified their fans with a young, exciting roster that slugged its way into playoff contention. Their 82-80 finish was a 20-win improvement over 2022 but fell short of the postseason as its pitching fell short.

HIGH POINT: Rookie infielders Matt McLain (May) and Elly De La Cruz (June) burst on the scene and changed the Reds' identity, giving the team energy and dynamic power-speed combos and spurring a 12-game June winning streak, eight of them on the road. An 11-10 win against Atlanta capped it off with De La Cruz hitting for the cycle while the Reds rallied from a 5-0 deficit in front of a raucous crowd of 43,086.

LOW POINT: Cincinnati jumped into first place in late July heading into a series at the contending Cubs. With starters Hunter Greene and Nick Lodolo shelved by injuries, the Reds lost eight of their first nine in August, including consecutive losses to the Cubs in which they gave up 36 runs. A 10-17 month included De La Cruz slumping to .198 with 44 strikeouts in 116 plate appearances.

NOTABLE ROOKIES: De La Cruz and McClain, who missed the season's final month with an oblique strain, ignited the organization. Lefthanders Brandon Williamson (117 IP) and Andrew Abbott (109 IP) proved crucial reinforcements to the rotation, with Abbott leading the team's starters with eight victories. Versatile Spencer Steer led the team with 156 games played, 23 home runs and 37 doubles and batted .271/.356/.464 while starting at five different defensive spots. Reclamation project Will Benson (.275/.365/.498, 19 SB) emerged as a force in a lefty-heavy outfield.

KEY TRANSACTIONS: Cincinnati added Benson in a February trade with the Guardians, whose outfield ranked last in the majors in home runs without him. Cincy boosted its bullpen at the deadline by adding Sam Moll from Oakland. Many of the moves made last year came to fruition, as trade acquisitions like Steer and Christian Encarnacion-Strand paid off.

DOWN ON THE FARM: The Reds graduated more rookies than pretty much anyone, but the system still has hope thanks to Noelvi Marte, a young core in Class A and breakout prospects like outfielder Blake Dunn, who posted a 25-50 year between High-A and Double-A.

OPENING DAY PAYROLL: $83,610,000 (26th).

PLAYERS OF THE YEAR

MAJOR LEAGUE
Matt McLain
2B
.290/.357/.507
23 2B, 16 HR
14 SB, 65 R

MINOR LEAGUE
Blake Dunn
OF
(HiA/AA)
.312/.425/.522
23 HR, 54 SB

ORGANIZATION LEADERS

Batting		***Minimum 250 AB**
MAJORS		
* AVG	Matt McLain	.290
* OPS	Matt McLain	.864
HR	Spencer Steer	23
RBI	Spencer Steer	86
MINORS		
* AVG	Christian Encarnacion-Strand, Louisv.	.331
* OBP	Jacob Hurtubise, Chatt./Louisville	.479
* SLG	Christian Encarnacion-Strand, Louisv.	.637
* OPS	Christian Encarnacion-Strand, Louisv.	1.042
R	Blake Dunn, Dayton/Chattanooga	107
H	Blake Dunn, Dayton/Chattanooga	143
TB	Blake Dunn, Dayton/Chattanooga	239
2B	Matt Reynolds, Louisville	38
3B	Edwin Arroyo, Dayton/Chattnooga	11
HR	Rece Hinds, Chattanooga	23
HR	Blake Dunn, Dayton/Chattanooga	23
RBI	Rece Hinds, Chattanooga	98
BB	Sal Stewart, Dayton/Daytona	84
SO	Austin Hendrick, Dayton	185
SB	Blake Dunn, Dayton/Chattanooga	54

Pitching		**#Minimum 75 IP**
MAJORS		
W	Alexis Diaz	9
# ERA	Ian Gibaut	3.33
SO	Hunter Greene	152
SV	Alexis Diaz	37
MINORS		
W	Carson Spiers, Chatt./Louisville	9
L	Sam Benschoter, Chattanooga	12
# ERA	Julian Aguiar, Dayton/Chattanooga	2.95
G	Ryan Nutof, Louisville	59
GS	Sam Benschoter, Chattanooga	27
SV	Ryan Meisinger, Chatt./Louisv.	10
IP	Julian Aguiar, Dayton/Chattanooga	125
BB	Christian Roa, Chatt./Louisv.	91
SO	Christian Roa, Chatt./Louisv.	170
# AVG	Ryan Cardona, Daytona/Dayton	.197

CINCINNATI REDS

2023 PERFORMANCE

General Manager: Nick Krall. **Farm Director:** Shawn Pender. **Scouting Director:** Brad Meador.

Class	Team	League	W	L	PCT	Finish	Manager
Majors	Cincinnati Reds	National	82	80	.506	8 (15)	David Bell
Triple-A	Louisville Bats	International	75	73	.507	9 (20)	Pat Kelly
Double-A	Chattanooga Lookouts	Southern	70	67	.511	5 (8)	Jose Moreno
High-A	Dayton Dragons	Midwest	67	65	.508	6 (12)	Bryan LaHair
Low-A	Daytona Tortugas	Florida State	56	72	.438	9 (10)	Julio Morillo
Rookie	ACL Reds	Arizona Complex	28	28	.500	10 (17)	Gustavo Molina
Rookie	DSL Reds	Dominican Sum.	28	26	.519	23 (50)	Juan Ballara
Overall 2023 Minor League Record			**324**	**331**	**.495**	**15th (30)**	

ORGANIZATION STATISTICS

CINCINNATI REDS

NATIONAL LEAGUE

Batting	B-T	Ht.	Wt.	DOB	AVG	OBP	SLG	G	PA	AB	R	H	2B	3B	HR	RBI	BB	HBP	SH	SF	SO	SB	CS	BB%	SO%
Bader, Harrison	R-R	6-0	210	6-03-94	.161	.235	.194	14	34	31	4	5	1	0	0	3	3	0	0	0	3	3	1	8.8	8.8
2-team (84 New York Yankees)					.232	.274	.348	98	344	319	44	74	12	2	7	40	17	3	1	4	59	20	3	4.9	17.2
Barrero, Jose	R-R	6-2	211	4-05-98	.218	.295	.323	46	149	133	15	29	8	0	2	17	15	0	0	1	44	3	2	10.1	29.5
Benson, Will	L-L	6-5	230	6-16-98	.275	.365	.498	108	329	287	51	79	15	8	11	31	40	1	0	1	103	19	3	12.2	31.3
Casali, Curt	R-R	6-2	220	11-09-88	.175	.290	.200	40	96	80	8	14	2	0	0	6	11	2	3	0	23	0	0	11.5	24.0
De La Cruz, Elly	B-R	6-5	200	1-11-02	.235	.300	.410	98	427	388	67	91	15	7	13	44	35	2	1	1	144	35	8	8.2	33.7
Encarnacion-Strand, Christian	R-R	6-0	224	12-01-99	.270	.328	.477	63	241	222	29	60	7	0	13	37	14	5	0	0	69	2	0	5.8	28.6
Fairchild, Stuart	R-R	6-0	205	3-17-96	.228	.321	.388	97	255	219	34	50	16	2	5	28	25	6	3	2	69	10	3	9.8	27.1
Fraley, Jake	L-L	6-0	206	5-25-95	.256	.339	.443	111	380	336	41	86	18	0	15	65	37	6	0	1	71	21	5	9.7	18.7
Friedl, TJ	L-L	5-10	180	8-14-95	.279	.352	.467	138	556	488	73	136	22	8	18	66	47	10	8	3	90	27	6	8.5	16.2
Hopkins, TJ	R-R	6-1	195	1-16-97	.171	.227	.171	25	44	41	7	7	0	0	0	1	2	1	0	0	17	1	0	4.5	38.6
India, Jonathan	R-R	6-0	200	12-15-96	.244	.338	.407	119	529	454	78	111	23	0	17	61	52	16	0	7	109	14	2	9.8	20.6
Lopez, Alejo	B-R	5-8	170	5-05-96	.500	.500	1.000	1	2	2	1	1	1	0	0	1	0	0	0	0	1	0	0	0.0	50.0
Maile, Luke	R-R	6-3	225	2-06-91	.235	.308	.391	78	199	179	17	42	10	0	6	25	14	5	1	0	49	2	1	7.0	24.6
Marte, Noelvi	R-R	6-0	216	10-16-01	.316	.366	.456	35	123	114	15	36	7	0	3	15	8	1	0	0	25	6	2	6.5	20.3
Martini, Nick	L-L	5-11	205	6-27-90	.264	.329	.583	29	79	72	10	19	3	1	6	16	5	2	0	0	15	0	0	6.3	19.0
McLain, Matt	R-R	5-8	180	8-06-99	.290	.357	.507	89	403	365	65	106	23	4	16	50	31	7	0	0	115	14	5	7.7	28.5
Myers, Wil	R-R	6-3	207	12-10-90	.189	.257	.283	37	141	127	11	24	3	0	3	12	12	0	1	1	48	2	1	8.5	34.0
Newman, Kevin	R-R	6-1	195	8-04-93	.253	.311	.364	74	253	225	28	57	16	0	3	28	17	4	2	5	34	8	1	6.7	13.4
Ramos, Henry	B-R	6-0	215	4-15-92	.243	.349	.311	23	86	74	9	18	3	1	0	5	11	1	0	0	21	2	1	12.8	24.4
Renfroe, Hunter	R-R	6-1	230	1-28-92	.128	.227	.205	14	44	39	4	5	0	0	1	4	5	0	0	0	12	0	0	11.4	27.3
2-team (126 Los Angeles Angels)					.233	.297	.416	140	548	498	60	116	31	0	20	60	44	3	0	3	125	0	0	8.0	22.8
Reynolds, Matt	R-R	6-1	210	12-03-90	.200	.200	.200	2	5	5	1	1	0	0	0	0	0	0	0	0	3	0	0	0.0	60.0
Senzel, Nick	R-R	6-1	218	6-29-95	.236	.297	.399	104	330	301	49	71	10	0	13	42	26	1	0	2	74	6	2	7.9	22.4
Siani, Michael	L-L	6-1	188	7-16-99	—	1.000	—	3	1	0	1	0	0	0	0	0	1	0	0	0	0	0	1	100.0	0.0
2-team (5 St. Louis)					.000	.167	.000	8	6	5	1	0	0	0	0	0	1	0	0	0	1	1	1	16.7	16.7
Steer, Spencer	R-R	5-11	185	12-07-97	.271	.356	.464	156	665	582	74	158	37	3	23	86	68	11	0	4	139	15	3	10.2	20.9
Stephenson, Tyler	R-R	6-4	225	8-16-96	.243	.317	.378	142	517	465	59	113	20	2	13	56	47	4	0	1	135	0	1	9.1	26.1
Vosler, Jason	L-R	6-1	220	9-06-93	.161	.200	.371	20	65	62	6	10	2	1	3	10	3	0	0	0	25	0	0	4.6	38.5
Votto, Joey	L-R	6-2	220	9-10-83	.202	.314	.433	65	242	208	26	42	6	0	14	38	27	7	0	0	62	0	0	11.2	25.6

Pitching	B-T	Ht.	Wt.	DOB	W	L	ERA	G	GS	SV	IP	Hits	Runs	ER	HR	BB	SO	AVG	OBP	SLG	SO%	BB%	BF
Abbott, Andrew	L-L	6-0	192	6-01-99	8	6	3.87	21	21	0	109	100	47	47	16	44	120	.244	.316	.425	26.1	9.6	459
Antone, Tejay	R-R	6-4	230	12-05-93	0	0	1.59	5	1	0	6	3	1	1	0	2	7	.158	.238	.211	33.3	9.5	21
Ashcraft, Graham	L-R	6-2	248	2-11-98	7	9	4.76	26	26	0	146	148	78	77	23	52	111	.265	.338	.444	17.8	8.3	624
Bracho, Silvino	R-R	5-10	190	7-17-92	0	0	3.68	5	0	0	7	5	3	3	0	6	6	.200	.355	.240	19.4	19.4	31
Busenitz, Alan	R-R	6-1	180	8-22-90	0	0	2.57	6	0	0	7	8	2	2	0	1	5	.286	.310	.357	17.2	3.4	29
Cessa, Luis	R-R	6-0	222	4-25-92	1	4	9.00	7	6	0	26	46	26	26	3	12	11	.397	.450	.603	8.3	9.1	132
Cruz, Fernando	R-R	6-2	237	3-28-90	1	2	4.91	58	2	0	66	52	39	36	6	28	98	.211	.295	.366	35.1	10.0	279
Diaz, Alexis	R-R	6-2	224	9-28-96	9	6	3.07	71	0	37	67	44	30	23	4	36	86	.186	.317	.280	30.1	12.6	286
Duarte, Daniel	R-R	6-0	235	12-04-96	3	0	3.69	31	0	1	32	24	14	13	5	20	23	.211	.331	.360	16.9	14.7	136
Farmer, Buck	L-R	6-4	243	2-20-91	4	5	4.20	71	0	3	75	58	36	35	11	29	70	.214	.296	.402	22.7	9.4	309
Gibaut, Ian	R-R	6-3	250	11-19-93	8	4	3.33	74	0	3	76	69	33	28	8	28	69	.245	.320	.365	21.7	8.8	318
Greene, Hunter	R-R	6-5	242	8-06-99	4	7	4.82	22	22	0	112	111	65	60	19	48	152	.253	.337	.477	30.5	9.6	498
Herget, Kevin	L-R	5-10	185	4-03-91	1	2	5.18	14	0	1	24	26	14	14	4	6	13	.268	.324	.495	12.4	5.7	105
Karcher, Ricky	R-R	6-4	230	9-18-97	0	0	0.00	1	0	1	1	0	0	0	0	1	0	.000	.250	.000	0.0	25.0	4
Kennedy, Brett	R-R	6-0	200	8-04-94	1	0	6.50	5	2	0	18	19	13	13	1	7	9	.275	.354	.478	10.8	8.4	83
Kuhnel, Joel	R-R	6-5	290	2-19-95	0	0	8.10	2	0	0	3	6	3	3	0	2	0	.400	.471	.533	0.0	11.8	17
Law, Derek	R-R	6-3	225	9-14-90	4	6	3.60	54	3	2	55	50	24	22	6	26	45	.239	.332	.364	18.8	10.8	240
Legumina, Casey	R-R	6-2	195	6-19-97	1	0	5.68	11	0	0	13	16	11	8	3	9	11	.308	.410	.596	18.0	14.8	61
Lively, Ben	R-R	6-4	235	3-05-92	4	7	5.38	19	12	0	89	96	53	53	20	25	79	.270	.324	.490	20.6	6.5	383
Lodolo, Nick	L-L	6-6	216	2-05-98	2	1	6.29	7	7	0	34	50	24	24	10	10	47	.340	.406	.605	28.3	6.0	166
Maile, Luke	R-R	6-3	225	2-06-91	0	0	16.62	4	0	0	4	12	8	8	4	0	0	.500	.480	1.125	0.0	0.0	25
Mariot, Michael	R-R	6-0	190	10-20-88	0	0	3.38	1	0	0	3	4	1	1	1	1	2	.333	.385	.667	15.4	7.7	13

Mills, Alec	R-R	6-4	205	11-30-91	0	0	18.00	1	0	0	1	4	5	2	1	1	0	.500	.600	1.125	0.0	10.0	10
Moll, Sam	L-L	5-9	190	1-03-92	2	0	0.73	25	0	0	25	13	2	2	1	11	22	.151	.247	.221	22.4	11.2	98
Overton, Connor	L-R	6-0	205	7-24-93	0	1	11.45	3	3	0	11	19	14	14	3	7	9	.404	.473	.766	16.4	12.7	55
Phillips, Connor	R-R	6-2	209	5-04-01	1	1	6.97	5	5	0	21	18	16	16	5	13	26	.220	.333	.415	27.1	13.5	96
Richardson, Lyon	B-R	6-2	207	1-18-00	0	2	8.64	4	4	0	17	17	16	16	6	15	12	.258	.395	.576	14.8	18.5	81
Salazar, Eduardo	R-R	6-2	177	5-05-98	1	0	8.03	8	0	0	12	16	11	11	0	5	5	.327	.410	.388	8.2	8.2	61
Sanmartin, Reiver	L-L	6-2	160	4-15-96	1	0	7.07	14	0	0	14	17	13	11	2	10	13	.288	.386	.424	18.6	14.3	70
Santillan, Tony	R-R	6-3	285	4-15-97	1	0	2.70	3	0	0	3	4	1	1	0	5	1	.308	.500	.462	5.6	27.8	18
Shreve, Chasen	L-L	6-4	180	7-12-90	0	0	2.70	3	0	0	3	1	1	1	1	2	3	.091	.231	.364	23.1	15.4	13
Sims, Lucas	R-R	6-2	213	5-10-94	7	3	3.10	67	0	3	61	33	23	21	5	39	72	.163	.320	.302	27.9	15.1	258
Spiers, Carson	R-R	6-3	205	11-11-97	0	1	6.92	4	2	1	13	18	12	10	1	7	12	.321	.391	.429	18.8	10.9	64
Stoudt, Levi	R-R	6-1	195	12-04-97	0	1	9.58	4	2	0	10	16	11	11	1	8	9	.348	.436	.543	16.4	14.5	55
Vosler, Jason	L-R	6-1	220	9-06-93	0	0	4.50	2	0	0	2	5	1	1	0	0	0	.455	.455	.455	0.0	0.0	11
Weaver, Luke	R-R	6-2	183	8-21-93	2	4	6.87	21	21	0	97	125	76	74	24	34	85	.306	.362	.574	19.0	7.6	448
Williamson, Brandon	R-L	6-6	210	4-02-98	5	5	4.46	23	23	0	117	111	63	58	18	39	98	.248	.311	.432	20.0	7.9	491
Wong, Jake	R-R	6-2	218	9-03-96	0	0	9.00	1	0	0	3	6	3	3	0	3	0	.500	.600	.583	0.0	20.0	15
Wynne, Randy	R-R	6-1	180	3-09-93	0	1	3.86	1	0	0	2	3	1	1	0	1	0	.300	.364	.500	0.0	9.1	11
Young, Alex	L-L	6-3	220	9-09-93	4	2	3.86	63	0	1	54	53	27	23	10	20	50	.248	.315	.435	21.2	8.5	236

Fielding

Catcher	PCT	G	PO	A	E	DP	PB
Casali	.992	38	235	10	2	0	1
Maile	.991	71	535	27	5	0	4
Stephenson	.994	92	648	18	4	3	3

First Base	PCT	G	PO	A	E	DP
Casali	1.000	2	3	1	0	1
Encarnacion-Strand	.991	35	205	18	2	24
Martini	1.000	4	8	1	0	0
Myers	1.000	13	47	7	0	9
Newman	1.000	9	49	5	0	4
Reynolds	.667	1	1	1	1	0
Steer	.988	73	388	40	5	39
Stephenson	1.000	8	25	3	0	1
Vosler	1.000	18	92	12	0	8
Votto	.997	47	296	18	1	34

Second Base	PCT	G	PO	A	E	DP
India	.977	104	162	219	9	62
Lopez	1.000	1	1	3	0	1
Marte	.000	1	0	0	0	0
McLain	.969	37	45	79	4	15
Newman	1.000	16	17	23	0	9
Senzel	1.000	6	3	7	0	2
Steer	1.000	16	19	24	0	7

Third Base	PCT	G	PO	A	E	DP
Casali	1.000	1	1	0	0	0
De La Cruz	.986	32	25	47	1	5
E'cion-Strand	1.000	9	2	6	0	1
Marte	.926	29	18	45	5	9
Newman	.952	24	13	27	2	3
Reynolds	.000	2	0	0	0	0
Senzel	.951	57	18	79	5	7
Steer	.943	47	24	59	5	3
Vosler	1.000	4	0	2	0	1

Shortstop	PCT	G	PO	A	E	DP
Barrero	.978	26	42	48	2	16
De La Cruz	.953	69	110	154	13	30
Marte	1.000	4	1	5	0	2
McLain	.994	53	55	121	1	25
Newman	.969	19	19	43	2	5

Outfield	PCT	G	PO	A	E	DP
Bader	1.000	12	29	0	0	0
Barrero	.969	19	30	1	1	0
Benson	1.000	104	197	6	0	1
E'cion-Strand	1.000	1	1	0	0	0
Fairchild	.986	102	152	5	2	1
Fraley	.995	84	137	3	1	0
Friedl	.665	151	305	9	1	2
Hopkins	.907	15	22	0	3	0
Martini	1.000	17	14	0	0	0
Myers	.981	27	50	1	1	0
Ramos	1.000	13	25	1	0	0
Renfroe	1.000	6	11	0	0	0
Senzel	1.000	59	69	1	0	1
Siani	1.000	2	2	0	0	0
Steer	1.000	48	76	1	0	0

LOUISVILLE BATS — *TRIPLE-A*

INTERNATIONAL LEAGUE

Batting	B-T	Ht.	Wt.	DOB	AVG	OBP	SLG	G	PA	AB	R	H	2B	3B	HR	RBI	BB	HBP	SH	SF	SO	SB	CS	BB%	SO%
Barrero, Jose	R-R	6-2	211	4-05-98	.258	.333	.540	80	335	291	47	75	17	4	19	57	22	14	1	6	105	20	1	6.6	31.3
Benson, Will	L-L	6-5	230	6-16-98	.206	.406	.402	28	133	97	25	20	6	2	3	9	32	2	0	2	35	11	1	24.1	26.3
Casali, Curt	R-R	6-2	220	11-09-88	.261	.292	.304	6	24	23	2	6	1	0	0	0	0	1	0	0	7	0	0	0.0	29.2
Creal, Ashton	R-R	6-1	205	3-23-99	.000	.000	.000	3	1	1	1	0	0	0	0	0	0	0	0	0	1	0	0	0.0	100.0
De La Cruz, Elly	B-R	6-5	200	1-11-02	.297	.398	.633	38	186	158	38	47	11	3	12	36	26	1	0	1	50	11	6	14.0	26.9
Encarnacion-Strand, Christian	R-R	6-0	224	12-01-99	.331	.405	.637	67	316	278	65	92	21	2	20	62	33	3	0	2	69	2	0	10.4	21.8
Fairchild, Stuart	R-R	6-0	205	3-17-96	.277	.384	.447	24	114	94	19	26	2	1	4	13	11	6	2	1	27	3	1	9.6	23.7
Fraley, Jake	L-L	6-0	206	5-25-95	.125	.125	.125	2	8	8	0	1	0	0	0	0	0	0	0	0	1	0	0	0.0	12.5
Hernandez, Miguel	R-R	6-0	194	4-13-99	.283	.309	.358	22	55	53	8	15	1	0	1	6	1	1	0	0	17	0	0	1.8	30.9
Hopkins, TJ	R-R	6-1	195	1-16-97	.308	.411	.514	94	393	331	63	102	18	1	16	55	55	4	1	2	94	2	3	14.0	23.9
Hurtubise, Jacob	L-R	6-0	180	12-11-97	.390	.537	.460	36	137	100	28	39	4	0	1	10	29	5	1	2	14	12	3	21.2	10.2
India, Jonathan	R-R	6-0	200	12-15-96	.200	.333	.400	2	6	5	2	1	1	0	0	2	1	0	0	0	1	0	0	16.7	16.7
Leyton, Steven	R-R	5-10	165	12-17-98	.200	.200	.400	3	10	10	0	2	2	0	0	1	0	0	0	0	3	0	0	0.0	30.0
Lopez, Alejo	B-R	5-8	170	5-05-96	.292	.401	.410	125	558	466	76	136	30	2	7	43	79	8	0	3	76	18	4	14.2	13.6
Mancini, Trey	R-R	6-3	230	3-18-92	.316	.316	.737	5	19	19	3	6	2	0	2	3	0	0	0	0	5	0	0	0.0	26.3
Marte, Noelvi	R-R	6-0	216	10-16-01	.280	.365	.455	39	167	143	31	40	10	3	3	20	20	1	0	3	31	8	2	12.0	18.6
Martini, Nick	L-L	5-11	205	6-27-90	.275	.393	.481	93	417	345	64	95	20	3	15	65	60	9	0	3	87	0	1	14.4	20.9
McGarry, Alex	L-L	6-1	213	5-11-98	.167	.231	.354	15	52	48	4	8	3	0	2	6	4	0	0	0	20	0	0	7.7	38.5
McLain, Matt	R-R	5-8	180	8-06-99	.340	.467	.688	40	180	144	30	49	12	1	12	40	30	5	0	1	37	10	5	16.7	20.6
Mount, Drew	L-R	5-11	205	3-24-96	.306	.375	.532	20	72	62	17	19	5	0	3	12	4	4	0	2	23	1	1	5.6	31.9
Myers, Wil	R-R	6-3	207	12-10-90	.185	.241	.296	7	29	27	4	5	0	0	1	3	2	0	0	0	7	0	0	6.9	24.1
Newman, Kevin	R-R	6-1	195	8-04-93	.211	.318	.211	11	44	38	6	8	0	0	0	3	5	1	0	0	8	0	0	11.4	18.2
Northcut, Nicholas	R-R	6-1	206	6-13-99	.111	.158	.111	6	19	18	1	2	0	0	0	0	1	0	0	0	6	0	0	5.3	31.6
Pereda, Jhonny	R-R	6-1	202	4-18-96	.325	.405	.468	67	264	231	32	75	15	0	6	36	32	0	0	1	51	0	1	12.1	19.3
Ramos, Henry	B-R	6-0	215	4-15-92	.318	.411	.543	76	327	280	52	89	18	3	13	55	41	4	1	1	65	6	4	12.5	19.9
Rey, Brian	R-R	5-11	170	2-22-98	.185	.214	.259	8	28	27	3	5	2	0	0	1	1	0	0	0	7	0	0	3.6	25.0
Reynolds, Matt	R-R	6-1	210	12-03-90	.266	.351	.514	115	515	444	76	118	38	3	22	90	60	3	0	8	141	8	0	11.7	27.4
Robinson, Chuckie	R-R	6-0	215	12-14-94	.290	.356	.450	101	413	369	57	107	16	2	13	74	32	8	0	4	77	7	2	7.7	18.6
Senzel, Nick	R-R	6-1	218	6-29-95	.224	.348	.362	15	70	58	11	13	3	1	1	3	9	2	0	0	15	4	0	12.9	21.4
Siani, Michael	L-L	6-1	188	7-16-99	.228	.344	.354	108	454	378	63	86	15	3	9	47	69	0	3	4	109	22	4	15.2	24.0

2-team (10 Memphis)					.225	.345	.345	126	499	414	70	93	17	3	9	48	77	1	3	4	118	24	5	15.4	23.6
Urbaez, Francisco	R-R	5-11	195	10-13-97	.265	.342	.353	15	38	34	2	9	1	1	0	2	4	0	0	0	7	0	0	10.5	18.4
Vosler, Jason	L-R	6-1	220	9-06-93	.240	.333	.482	92	363	313	55	75	16	0	20	68	45	1	0	4	94	3	1	12.4	25.9
Votto, Joey	L-R	6-2	220	9-10-83	.185	.340	.346	24	103	81	10	15	4	0	3	13	19	1	0	2	34	0	0	18.4	33.0
Yang, Eric	R-R	5-11	185	3-26-98	.279	.323	.344	19	65	61	4	17	4	0	0	6	4	0	0	0	17	0	0	6.2	26.2
Yerzy, Andy	L-R	6-3	215	7-05-98	.250	.308	.833	5	13	12	3	3	1	0	2	5	1	0	0	0	4	0	0	7.7	30.8

Pitching	B-T	Ht.	Wt.	DOB	W	L	ERA	G	GS	SV	IP	Hits	Runs	ER	HR	BB	SO	AVG	OBP	SLG	SO%	BB%	BF
Abbott, Andrew	L-L	6-0	192	6-01-99	3	0	3.05	7	7	0	38	27	13	13	8	14	54	.193	.271	.393	34.8	9.0	155
Anderson, Chase	R-R	6-1	210	11-30-87	2	1	4.30	5	5	0	23	23	13	11	4	13	19	.271	.370	.471	19.0	13.0	100
Antone, Tejay	R-R	6-4	230	12-05-93	0	0	3.00	12	0	0	12	12	4	4	1	5	11	.261	.346	.370	21.2	9.6	52
Aranguren, Frainger	R-R	6-2	190	3-17-97	0	0	6.00	1	1	0	3	3	2	2	0	2	1	.273	.385	.364	7.7	15.4	13
Bracho, Silvino	R-R	5-10	190	7-17-92	4	3	5.51	47	1	3	51	50	33	31	18	20	52	.258	.329	.588	24.0	9.2	217
Brown, Zack	R-R	6-1	199	12-15-94	3	1	8.05	19	4	0	35	38	31	31	4	22	14	.286	.388	.496	8.8	13.8	160
Busenitz, Alan	R-R	6-1	180	8-22-90	3	4	4.94	47	0	9	51	51	31	28	7	25	50	.254	.342	.443	21.9	11.0	228
Cruz, Fernando	R-R	6-2	237	3-28-90	0	0	16.20	2	0	0	2	2	3	3	0	2	2	.286	.444	.429	22.2	22.2	9
Demurias, Eddy	R-R	6-0	184	8-01-97	0	0	9.00	4	0	0	4	7	4	4	1	0	5	.368	.368	.579	26.3	0.0	19
Duarte, Daniel	R-R	6-0	235	12-04-96	4	0	3.34	32	0	7	35	24	14	13	0	17	39	.192	.318	.248	25.8	11.3	151
Dunn, Justin	R-R	6-2	209	9-22-95	0	0	9.00	1	0	0	1	1	1	1	1	1	0	.250	.400	1.000	0.0	20.0	5
Eveld, Tommy	R-R	6-5	214	12-30-93	0	0	3.00	1	0	0	3	2	2	1	1	0	2	.167	.167	.500	16.7	0.0	12
Garcia, Pedro	R-R	5-11	220	3-21-95	2	1	7.62	10	0	0	13	13	14	11	5	12	14	.271	.435	.583	22.6	19.4	62
German, Franklin	R-R	6-2	195	9-22-97	0	0	8.64	10	0	0	8	10	8	8	2	6	13	.286	.381	.514	31.0	14.3	42
Greene, Hunter	R-R	6-5	242	8-06-99	0	0	3.00	3	3	0	12	6	5	4	2	7	12	.143	.265	.310	24.5	14.3	49
Guerrero, Tayron	R-R	6-8	225	1-09-91	0	4	11.51	20	0	0	23	29	30	29	3	22	20	.326	.466	.562	17.1	18.8	117
Gutierrez, Vladimir	R-R	6-1	205	9-18-95	1	1	8.31	3	0	0	4	3	4	4	1	4	4	.200	.368	.467	21.1	21.1	19
Herget, Kevin	L-R	5-10	185	4-03-91	2	3	5.13	34	5	0	47	52	35	27	8	21	48	.283	.360	.484	22.7	10.0	211
Karcher, Ricky	R-R	6-4	230	9-18-97	7	4	4.77	51	0	2	60	41	39	32	3	72	70	.194	.406	.318	24.1	24.8	290
Kennedy, Brett	R-R	6-0	200	8-04-94	4	4	4.81	17	16	0	79	87	46	42	9	31	72	.282	.350	.442	20.8	9.0	346
Kravetz, Evan	L-L	6-8	240	12-19-96	0	1	6.75	19	2	0	31	36	25	23	5	23	31	.298	.420	.479	20.7	15.3	150
Kuhnel, Joel	R-R	6-5	290	2-19-95	1	2	7.13	21	0	0	24	31	21	19	2	11	15	.316	.402	.469	13.3	9.7	113
Law, Derek	R-R	6-3	225	9-14-90	0	0	0.00	2	0	0	2	3	0	0	0	0	3	.300	.300	.300	30.0	0.0	10
Legumina, Casey	R-R	6-2	195	6-19-97	2	1	4.83	26	1	0	32	40	18	17	3	13	39	.308	.374	.446	26.5	8.8	147
Lively, Ben	R-R	6-4	235	3-05-92	4	0	4.68	7	6	0	33	29	17	17	5	12	22	.244	.316	.429	16.4	9.0	134
Lodolo, Nick	L-L	6-6	216	2-05-98	0	0	7.71	1	1	0	2	3	2	2	0	3	3	.300	.462	.300	23.1	23.1	13
Lopez, Alejo	B-R	5-8	170	5-05-96	0	0	0.00	1	0	0	1	2	0	0	0	1	0	.400	.500	.400	0.0	16.7	6
Mariot, Michael	R-R	6-0	190	10-20-88	5	4	6.49	12	11	0	51	59	37	37	13	22	40	.289	.362	.534	17.5	9.6	229
Martini, Nick	L-L	5-11	205	6-27-90	0	0	4.50	2	0	0	2	4	2	1	0	1	0	.364	.462	.455	0.0	7.7	13
Meisinger, Ryan	R-R	6-4	235	5-04-94	1	1	12.27	10	0	0	11	14	15	15	4	13	11	.311	.466	.644	19.0	22.4	58
Mills, Alec	R-R	6-4	205	11-30-91	0	3	6.58	10	7	0	26	27	19	19	5	16	16	.278	.388	.505	13.7	13.7	117
Murphy, John	R-R	6-4	245	12-11-96	0	0	4.50	1	0	0	2	3	1	1	0	2	0	.333	.455	.444	0.0	18.2	11
Nutof, Ryan	L-R	6-2	190	11-02-95	4	2	5.35	59	0	1	66	58	44	39	6	41	58	.244	.354	.382	20.1	14.2	289
Phillips, Connor	R-R	6-2	209	5-04-01	2	3	4.69	11	10	1	40	33	21	21	1	30	43	.224	.360	.320	24.2	16.9	178
Richardson, Lyon	B-R	6-2	207	1-18-00	0	1	9.42	6	6	0	14	11	15	15	0	15	24	.212	.391	.308	34.8	21.7	69
Roa, Christian	R-R	6-4	220	4-02-99	1	4	5.43	15	12	0	61	61	40	37	12	47	83	.257	.383	.477	28.6	16.2	290
Salazar, Eduardo	R-R	6-2	177	5-05-98	1	1	9.09	27	0	0	33	53	36	33	5	20	27	.379	.470	.564	16.1	11.9	168
Santillan, Tony	R-R	6-3	285	4-15-97	1	2	7.88	35	0	2	32	38	28	28	5	28	40	.297	.431	.492	25.0	17.5	160
Shreve, Chasen	L-L	6-4	180	7-12-90	1	0	2.25	6	0	0	4	2	1	1	1	1	5	.154	.214	.385	35.7	7.1	14
Sims, Lucas	R-R	6-2	213	5-10-94	0	0	0.00	3	0	0	3	1	0	0	0	2	3	.100	.250	.200	25.0	16.7	12
Solomon, Jared	R-R	6-2	219	6-10-97	1	1	10.29	26	0	0	28	32	32	32	5	28	22	.283	.438	.442	15.1	19.2	146
Sousa, Bennett	L-L	6-3	220	4-06-95	0	0	27.00	1	0	0	0	1	1	1	0	1	1	.500	.667	1.500	33.3	33.3	3
Spiers, Carson	R-R	6-3	205	11-11-97	1	0	0.00	1	0	0	2	0	0	0	0	0	0	.000	.000	.000	0.0	0.0	6
Spitzbarth, Shea	R-R	6-1	215	10-04-94	2	1	7.20	12	0	0	15	12	12	12	1	14	10	.222	.391	.370	14.5	20.3	69
Stankiewicz, Teddy	R-R	6-4	215	11-25-93	1	2	9.79	7	7	0	27	29	29	29	5	26	17	.282	.422	.505	12.6	19.3	135
Stoudt, Levi	R-R	6-1	195	12-04-97	5	6	6.23	25	19	0	82	87	60	57	20	50	58	.273	.376	.530	15.1	13.0	384
Strickland, Hunter	R-R	6-3	225	9-24-88	1	1	11.45	12	0	0	11	13	14	14	2	12	8	.302	.466	.558	13.8	20.7	58
Urbaez, Francisco	R-R	5-11	195	10-13-97	0	0	18.00	1	0	0	1	1	2	2	0	3	0	.250	.571	.250	0.0	42.9	7
Vosler, Jason	L-R	6-1	220	9-06-93	0	0	2.45	5	0	0	4	4	1	1	0	0	0	.267	.267	.333	0.0	0.0	15
Weaver, Luke	R-R	6-2	183	8-21-93	0	0	3.00	2	2	0	9	3	3	3	1	4	9	.107	.212	.250	27.3	12.1	33
Williamson, Brandon	R-L	6-6	210	4-02-98	2	4	6.62	8	8	0	34	44	29	25	7	20	27	.310	.400	.535	16.4	12.1	165
Wong, Jake	R-R	6-2	218	9-03-96	1	3	9.58	12	1	0	21	22	22	22	8	17	12	.289	.426	.645	12.8	18.1	94
Wynne, Randy	R-R	6-1	180	3-09-93	3	4	6.57	29	13	0	74	92	62	54	26	19	49	.299	.353	.636	14.5	5.6	337
Yang, Eric	R-R	5-11	185	3-26-98	0	0	36.00	1	0	0	1	5	4	4	1	2	0	.625	.700	1.000	0.0	20.0	10
Young, Alex	L-L	6-3	220	9-09-93	0	0	0.00	2	0	0	2	0	0	0	0	0	4	.000	.000	.000	66.7	0.0	6

Fielding

Catcher	PCT	G	PO	A	E	DP	PB
Casali	1.000	4	29	0	0	0	0
Pereda	.997	34	269	16	1	2	5
Robinson	.991	100	757	45	7	9	7
Yang	.987	16	146	3	2	0	1
Yerzy	1.000	1	1	0	0	0	0

First Base	PCT	G	PO	A	E	DP
Casali	.923	2	10	2	1	1
E'cion-Strand	.989	41	323	22	4	43
Mancini	1.000	2	9	0	0	2
Martini	1.000	17	107	4	0	15
McGarry	.988	11	78	5	1	8
Northcut	1.000	4	19	3	0	3
Pereda	.990	17	93	3	1	13
Reynolds	1.000	17	95	12	0	11
Vosler	.995	30	169	16	1	26
Votto	.986	21	123	18	2	16
Yerzy	1.000	1	3	1	0	0

Second Base	PCT	G	PO	A	E	DP
Hernandez	.978	14	22	22	1	8
India	1.000	2	1	2	0	1
Leyton	.938	3	8	7	1	2
Lopez	1.000	39	55	86	0	22
McLain	.986	14	27	41	1	12
Newman	1.000	3	4	4	0	3
Reynolds	.983	81	131	215	6	61
Urbaez	1.000	4	6	5	0	2
Vosler	.000	1	0	0	0	0

Third Base	PCT	G	PO	A	E	DP
De La Cruz	.957	9	8	14	1	0
'cion-Strand	.913	16	17	25	4	4
Hernandez	.000	1	0	0	0	0

Lopez	1.000	33	26	60	0	7
Marte	.922	37	28	55	7	10
Northcut	1.000	1	0	1	0	0
Reynolds	1.000	4	2	8	0	0
Senzel	1.000	6	3	7	0	1
Urbaez	.000	2	0	0	0	0
Vosler	.974	48	36	75	3	10

Shortstop	PCT	G	PO	A	E	DP
Barrero	.968	57	93	120	7	36
De La Cruz	.977	28	53	72	3	27
Hernandez	1.000	6	2	6	0	3

Lopez	.990	27	37	65	1	18
McLain	.935	25	33	53	6	14
Newman	1.000	7	8	9	0	2
Reynolds	.962	6	7	18	1	5

Outfield	PCT	G	PO	A	E	DP
Barrero	1.000	25	50	0	0	0
Benson	.989	28	64	4	1	1
E'cion-Strand	1.000	2	4	0	0	0
Fairchild	1.000	23	41	0	0	0
Hopkins	.990	84	154	6	2	1
Hurtubise	.971	38	63	3	2	2

Lopez	1.000	28	50	5	0	0
Martini	1.000	72	137	4	0	1
Mount	1.000	19	28	1	0	0
Myers	1.000	6	9	0	0	0
Ramos	.989	24	50	0	1	0
Rey	.500	1	1	0	1	0
Senzel	1.000	9	19	2	0	1
Siani	.997	107	261	5	2	2
Urbaez	1.000	3	3	0	0	0
Vosler	1.000	1	2	0	0	0

CHATTANOOGA LOOKOUTS — *DOUBLE-A*

SOUTHERN LEAGUE

Batting	B-T	Ht.	Wt.	DOB	AVG	OBP	SLG	G	PA	AB	R	H	2B	3B	HR	RBI	BB	HBP	SH	SF	SO	SB	CS	BB%	SO%
Arroyo, Edwin	B-S	6-0	175	8-25-03	.353	.400	.588	4	20	17	2	6	2	1	0	5	1	1	0	1	6	1	0	5.0	30.0
Callahan, Austin	L-R	6-3	215	6-06-01	.188	.202	.241	28	114	112	10	21	3	0	1	9	2	0	0	0	38	1	0	1.8	33.3
Callihan, Tyler	L-R	6-1	205	6-22-00	.310	.396	.460	22	101	87	11	27	10	0	1	11	13	0	0	1	20	4	1	12.9	19.8
Cerda, Allan	R-R	6-3	203	11-24-99	.181	.342	.342	48	193	155	23	28	7	0	6	22	31	7	0	0	71	5	6	16.1	36.8
Creal, Ashton	R-R	6-1	205	3-23-99	.203	.329	.322	22	71	59	11	12	1	0	2	7	10	1	1	0	27	1	0	14.1	38.0
Dunn, Blake	R-R	6-0	210	9-05-98	.332	.433	.556	77	357	295	75	98	13	4	15	52	41	15	1	5	84	35	4	11.5	23.5
Fernandez, Ilvin	R-R	6-1	160	9-08-01	.286	.286	.357	7	15	14	4	4	1	0	0	4	0	0	1	0	5	0	0	0.0	33.3
Free, James	B-R	6-2	205	4-14-98	.268	.364	.456	117	489	421	57	113	24	2	17	69	61	4	0	3	98	1	1	12.5	20.0
Hernandez, Miguel	R-R	6-0	194	4-13-99	.310	.375	.621	9	33	29	9	9	1	1	2	4	3	0	1	0	4	1	0	9.1	12.1
Hinds, Rece	R-R	6-4	215	9-05-00	.269	.330	.536	109	461	412	63	111	29	6	23	98	34	7	0	8	151	20	6	7.4	32.8
Hunter, Cade	L-R	6-2	200	11-29-00	.222	.417	.222	3	12	9	1	2	0	0	0	0	3	0	0	0	3	0	0	25.0	25.0
Hurtubise, Jacob	L-R	6-0	180	12-11-97	.306	.453	.492	83	318	242	74	74	7	10	6	36	48	19	3	2	49	33	6	15.1	15.4
Johnson, Ivan	B-R	6-0	190	10-11-98	.225	.314	.413	93	386	334	57	75	19	1	14	55	35	11	1	5	103	20	2	9.1	26.7
Leyton, Steven	R-R	5-10	165	12-17-98	.154	.313	.385	6	16	13	3	2	1	1	0	0	1	2	0	0	3	0	0	6.3	18.8
Marte, Noelvi	R-R	6-0	216	10-16-01	.281	.356	.464	50	222	196	37	55	10	1	8	25	22	2	0	2	38	10	2	9.9	17.1
McAfee, Quincy	R-R	5-11	185	9-16-97	.240	.361	.454	97	385	317	63	76	18	4	14	54	46	16	3	3	76	10	4	11.9	19.7
McGarry, Alex	L-L	6-1	213	5-11-98	.280	.346	.431	98	416	371	50	104	19	5	9	60	38	2	0	5	107	14	6	9.1	25.7
Mount, Drew	L-R	5-11	205	3-24-96	.281	.324	.375	8	34	32	6	9	1	1	0	7	1	1	0	0	7	0	1	2.9	20.6
Nelson, Matheu	R-R	5-11	209	1-14-99	.297	.469	.568	12	49	37	9	11	1	0	3	5	10	2	0	0	8	0	0	20.4	16.3
Northcut, Nicholas	R-R	6-1	206	6-13-99	.216	.265	.392	69	272	250	27	54	14	0	10	39	14	4	0	4	102	0	0	5.1	37.5
Quintana, Nick	R-R	5-10	180	10-13-97	.135	.292	.243	37	137	111	17	15	6	0	2	14	19	6	0	1	36	0	0	13.9	26.3
Torres, Jose	R-R	6-0	171	9-28-99	.187	.284	.293	89	344	294	50	55	11	1	6	35	34	7	3	3	107	11	3	9.9	31.1
Trautwein, Michael	L-R	6-1	205	9-13-99	.235	.367	.353	49	166	136	26	32	8	1	2	13	23	6	0	1	41	3	2	13.9	24.7
Urbaez, Francisco	R-R	5-11	195	10-13-97	.264	.358	.380	68	293	250	38	66	11	0	6	34	35	4	0	4	55	4	3	11.9	18.8
Vellojin, Daniel	L-R	5-11	160	3-15-00	.198	.312	.308	70	280	237	27	47	12	1	4	19	38	2	1	2	63	3	0	13.6	22.5
Yang, Eric	R-R	5-11	185	3-26-98	.155	.319	.241	22	72	58	9	9	2	0	1	3	12	2	0	0	19	0	0	16.7	26.4
Yerzy, Andy	L-R	6-3	215	7-05-98	.231	.388	.436	12	49	39	8	9	2	0	2	9	9	1	0	0	8	1	0	18.4	16.3

Pitching	B-T	Ht.	Wt.	DOB	W	L	ERA	G	GS	SV	IP	Hits	Runs	ER	HR	BB	SO	AVG	OBP	SLG	SO%	BB%	BF
Abbott, Andrew	L-L	6-0	192	6-01-99	1	0	1.15	3	3	0	16	6	2	2	0	3	36	.113	.161	.151	64.3	5.4	56
Aguiar, Julian	L-R	6-3	180	6-04-01	4	4	4.28	11	11	0	55	57	32	26	6	13	61	.266	.310	.435	26.3	5.6	232
Benoit, Donovan	R-R	6-3	203	1-22-99	0	2	5.40	11	0	1	15	8	10	9	1	14	16	.160	.377	.280	23.2	20.3	69
Benschoter, Sam	R-R	6-3	215	3-17-98	7	12	7.28	27	27	0	124	137	102	100	29	67	140	.279	.377	.532	24.3	11.6	576
Boyle, Joe	R-R	6-7	240	8-14-99	6	5	4.50	19	19	0	84	63	48	42	6	75	122	.211	.377	.318	31.5	19.4	387
Branche, Stevie	R-R	6-4	205	5-18-97	1	4	4.79	31	0	2	41	28	27	22	2	33	60	.194	.362	.285	31.6	17.4	190
Byrne, Michael	R-R	6-3	205	4-16-97	4	1	2.77	31	0	2	52	44	18	16	5	16	63	.219	.279	.348	28.8	7.3	219
Cachutt, Manuel	R-R	6-0	185	6-07-97	2	0	4.32	26	4	0	50	38	26	24	8	27	37	.209	.324	.385	17.1	12.5	216
Correa, Danis	R-R	5-11	150	8-26-99	0	1	11.57	4	0	0	5	9	6	6	0	1	4	.409	.435	.455	17.4	4.3	23
Crawford, Brooks	R-R	6-4	215	8-19-96	0	0	2.25	2	0	0	4	1	1	1	1	1	3	.083	.154	.333	23.1	7.7	13
Curlis, Connor	L-L	6-1	208	11-29-96	0	0	6.23	6	0	0	9	13	6	6	2	3	11	.351	.442	.622	25.6	7.0	43
Demurias, Eddy	R-R	6-0	184	8-01-97	1	0	1.38	11	0	0	13	16	5	2	1	9	14	.296	.397	.370	22.2	14.3	63
Eveld, Tommy	R-R	6-5	214	12-30-93	2	2	5.22	19	0	4	29	34	18	17	3	8	36	.283	.333	.442	27.9	6.2	129
Farr, Thomas	R-R	6-0	203	4-29-99	1	7	7.63	11	11	0	48	59	50	41	8	22	22	.304	.387	.546	9.7	9.7	226
Fisher, Andy	L-L	6-1	185	1-09-96	4	0	2.94	45	0	1	52	37	17	17	4	21	45	.202	.303	.328	21.2	9.9	212
Garcia, Pedro	R-R	5-11	220	3-21-95	4	4	5.84	37	0	6	37	26	24	24	7	28	64	.191	.351	.404	37.4	16.4	171
Glogoski, Kyle	R-R	6-2	183	1-06-99	2	0	8.68	7	0	0	9	10	9	9	0	14	10	.270	.481	.378	19.2	26.9	52
Gozzo, Jake	R-R	6-5	221	1-05-97	0	1	6.66	18	0	0	26	23	20	19	3	25	21	.250	.411	.424	16.8	20.0	125
Heatherly, Jacob	L-L	6-1	215	5-20-98	0	0	2.25	2	0	0	4	2	1	1	0	2	7	.133	.278	.133	38.9	11.1	18
Holt, Owen	R-R	6-3	225	4-22-99	0	0	9.00	1	0	0	2	2	2	2	1	2	2	.250	.400	.750	20.0	20.0	10
Kravetz, Evan	L-L	6-8	240	12-19-96	3	0	2.40	17	0	1	30	20	8	8	3	9	36	.189	.256	.321	30.8	7.7	117
Lodolo, Nick	L-L	6-6	216	2-05-98	0	0	0.00	1	1	0	3	0	0	0	0	2	6	.000	.182	.000	54.5	18.2	11
Meisinger, Ryan	R-R	6-4	235	5-04-94	3	3	4.03	23	0	10	29	22	16	13	2	18	39	.204	.323	.306	30.7	14.2	127
Petty, Chase	R-R	6-1	190	4-04-03	0	0	0.00	2	2	0	8	5	2	0	0	1	5	.167	.194	.233	16.1	3.2	31
Phillips, Connor	R-R	6-2	209	5-04-01	2	2	3.34	14	14	0	65	58	29	24	9	27	111	.232	.320	.388	39.1	9.5	284
Richardson, Lyon	B-R	6-2	207	1-18-00	0	2	2.15	15	15	0	46	35	13	11	2	22	58	.213	.314	.311	30.9	11.7	188
Roa, Christian	R-R	6-4	220	4-02-99	4	5	4.88	13	13	0	59	41	35	32	7	44	87	.199	.353	.340	33.7	17.1	258
Roxby, Braxton	R-R	6-3	215	3-12-99	0	0	7.71	4	0	0	5	3	4	4	2	0	8	.188	.278	.563	44.4	0.0	18
Salazar, Eduardo	R-R	6-2	177	5-05-98	0	0	0.68	9	0	1	13	9	2	1	0	2	22	.176	.222	.176	40.7	3.7	54
Sandridge, Jayvien	L-L	6-5	220	2-11-99	0	1	2.25	3	0	0	4	2	2	1	0	4	7	.143	.333	.286	38.9	22.2	18
Sceroler, Mac	R-R	6-3	215	4-09-95	1	0	7.00	5	0	1	9	8	8	7	2	6	14	.229	.349	.457	32.6	14.0	43

Pitching	B-T	Ht.	Wt.	DOB	W	L	ERA	G	GS	SV	IP	Hits	Runs	ER	HR	BB	SO	AVG	OBP	SLG	SO%	BB%	BF
Spiers, Carson	R-R	6-3	205	11-11-97	8	3	3.69	28	9	0	83	71	37	34	6	41	106	.226	.328	.363	29.2	11.3	363
Stankiewicz, Teddy	R-R	6-4	215	11-25-93	3	2	6.23	11	7	0	43	54	32	30	6	16	32	.300	.365	.483	16.0	8.0	200
Stockton, Spencer	B-R	6-3	210	4-24-96	3	2	3.56	28	0	2	43	37	17	17	6	20	47	.230	.313	.416	25.8	11.0	182
Timpanelli, Vin	R-R	6-2	210	10-02-98	2	2	4.85	23	0	0	26	20	15	14	1	22	31	.206	.374	.278	25.2	17.9	123
Urbaez, Francisco	R-R	5-11	195	10-13-97	0	0	0.00	1	0	0	0	0	0	0	0	0	0	.000	.000	.000	0.0	0.0	1
Wong, Jake	R-R	6-2	218	9-03-96	2	2	5.17	22	1	1	47	43	31	27	9	15	50	.243	.303	.441	25.4	7.6	197
Yerzy, Andy	L-R	6-3	215	7-05-98	0	0	0.00	1	0	0	1	1	0	0	0	0	2	.250	.250	.250	50.0	0.0	4

Fielding

Catcher	PCT	G	PO	A	E	DP	PB
Free	1.000	3	7	1	0	0	0
Hunter	1.000	2	19	0	0	0	0
Nelson	.971	11	94	7	3	2	1
Trautwein	.994	37	308	22	2	1	2
Vellojin	.990	69	713	48	8	4	10
Yang	.982	22	262	12	5	1	2
Yerzy	1.000	2	16	1	0	0	0

First Base	PCT	G	PO	A	E	DP
Fernandez	.000	1	0	0	0	0
Free	.984	54	347	18	6	21
McAfee	1.000	7	34	1	0	6
McGarry	.993	70	418	31	3	38
Northcut	1.000	18	86	7	0	12
Yerzy	1.000	5	21	1	0	2

Second Base	PCT	G	PO	A	E	DP
Callihan	.959	20	32	61	4	15
Fernandez	.000	1	0	0	0	0
Hernandez	1.000	2	2	4	0	1
Johnson	.958	60	68	136	9	24
Leyton	1.000	1	1	0	0	0
McAfee	.981	14	20	33	1	7
Quintana	1.000	15	15	22	0	3
Torres	.900	3	3	6	1	2
Urbaez	.945	28	32	54	5	12

Third Base	PCT	G	PO	A	E	DP
Callahan	.970	26	20	45	2	2
Fernandez	.000	1	0	0	0	0
Hernandez	1.000	3	3	6	0	0
Leyton	1.000	2	0	4	0	0
Marte	.925	17	16	21	3	4
McAfee	.943	16	11	22	2	0
Northcut	.920	49	31	72	9	7
Quintana	.789	19	8	7	4	0
Torres	1.000	1	0	6	0	0
Urbaez	.897	11	7	19	3	1

Shortstop	PCT	G	PO	A	E	DP
Arroyo	.778	4	3	4	2	1
Fernandez	1.000	4	1	2	0	0
Hernandez	1.000	4	8	9	0	4
Leyton	1.000	3	3	4	0	0
Marte	.946	30	51	55	6	15
McAfee	.962	15	15	35	2	4
Quintana	1.000	1	1	2	0	1
Torres	.975	85	102	172	7	37
Urbaez	1.000	1	0	4	0	0

Outfield	PCT	G	PO	A	E	DP
Cerda	.961	48	73	0	2	0
Creal	.985	21	36	0	1	0
Dunn	.949	78	180	6	3	1
Hinds	.972	95	135	14	8	2
Hurtubise	.986	80	122	4	1	1
Johnson	1.000	18	18	2	0	0
McAfee	.993	42	73	3	1	0
McGarry	1.000	16	24	0	0	0
Mount	1.000	7	14	1	0	0
Trautwein	.944	12	17	0	1	0
Urbaez	.833	25	45	1	2	0

DAYTON DRAGONS — HIGH CLASS A

MIDWEST LEAGUE

Batting	B-T	Ht.	Wt.	DOB	AVG	OBP	SLG	G	PA	AB	R	H	2B	3B	HR	RBI	BB	HBP	SH	SF	SO	SB	CS	BB%	SO%
Allen, Jay	R-R	6-2	190	11-22-02	.154	.260	.220	25	105	91	15	14	3	0	1	3	8	5	1	0	40	10	3	7.6	38.1
Arroyo, Edwin	B-S	6-0	175	8-25-03	.248	.321	.427	119	534	475	72	118	26	10	13	55	48	5	1	4	112	28	7	9.0	21.0
Callahan, Austin	L-R	6-3	215	6-06-01	.255	.320	.429	97	403	364	48	93	34	4	7	50	32	4	0	3	116	3	1	7.9	28.8
Callihan, Tyler	L-R	6-1	205	6-22-00	.236	.312	.373	109	447	399	44	94	21	5	8	47	37	7	4	0	104	25	4	8.3	23.3
Cerda, Allan	R-R	6-3	203	11-24-99	.238	.433	.286	8	30	21	4	5	1	0	0	4	7	1	0	1	8	0	0	23.3	26.7
Chevalier, Luis	B-R	5-11	160	1-18-02	.200	.333	.320	10	30	25	2	5	0	0	1	2	5	0	0	0	6	1	0	16.7	20.0
Contreras, Yan	R-R	6-2	185	1-30-01	.143	.238	.161	22	63	56	5	8	1	0	0	2	5	2	0	0	34	3	1	7.9	54.0
Creal, Ashton	R-R	6-1	205	3-23-99	.143	.276	.143	19	60	49	6	7	0	0	0	3	4	5	2	0	25	3	1	6.7	41.7
Dunn, Blake	R-R	6-0	210	9-05-98	.276	.411	.460	47	202	163	32	45	4	1	8	27	21	17	0	1	46	19	3	10.4	22.8
Faltine, Trey	R-R	6-2	198	1-08-01	.103	.231	.181	64	184	155	16	16	3	0	3	13	20	6	2	1	88	4	0	10.9	47.8
Fernandez, Ilvin	R-R	6-1	160	9-08-01	.286	.286	.286	3	7	7	2	2	0	0	0	2	0	0	0	0	3	0	0	0.0	42.9
Hendrick, Austin	L-L	6-0	195	6-15-01	.204	.271	.335	125	516	465	55	95	17	1	14	47	38	7	0	6	185	19	5	7.4	35.9
Hunter, Cade	L-R	6-2	200	11-29-00	.228	.343	.356	43	178	149	26	34	4	0	5	18	23	4	0	2	42	0	1	12.9	23.6
Ibarra, Ruben	R-R	6-5	290	4-26-99	.238	.346	.441	98	402	340	45	81	13	1	18	63	47	11	0	4	98	1	0	11.7	24.4
Jones, Hayden	L-R	6-0	215	4-27-00	.230	.240	.392	25	76	74	4	17	3	0	3	7	1	0	1	0	25	0	0	1.3	32.9
Jorge, Carlos	L-R	5-10	160	9-22-03	.239	.277	.398	23	94	88	8	21	3	1	3	14	5	0	0	1	30	1	2	5.3	31.9
Marrero, Wendell	L-L	6-2	195	11-28-00	.184	.292	.255	38	113	98	11	18	3	2	0	3	11	4	0	0	45	1	0	9.7	39.8
Nelson, Matheu	R-R	5-11	209	1-14-99	.220	.322	.422	89	364	313	50	69	9	0	18	42	39	9	1	2	101	6	0	10.7	27.7
Rodriguez, Hector	L-R	5-8	186	3-11-04	.294	.309	.373	14	55	51	6	15	2	1	0	5	1	1	0	2	10	0	1	1.8	18.2
Rogers, Jack	L-L	6-2	205	4-05-99	.258	.349	.459	107	421	368	49	95	23	6	13	63	44	8	0	1	142	11	9	10.5	33.7
Serrano, Jose	R-R	6-0	180	10-14-03	.172	.200	.207	8	30	29	2	5	1	0	0	3	1	0	0	0	13	0	0	3.3	43.3
Stewart, Sal	R-R	6-3	215	12-07-03	.291	.397	.391	29	131	110	16	32	5	0	2	11	18	2	0	1	18	5	0	13.7	13.7
Thompson, Justice	R-R	6-4	205	7-08-00	.248	.347	.407	104	394	339	54	84	19	4	9	42	48	4	0	1	118	11	3	12.2	29.9
Trautwein, Michael	L-R	6-1	205	9-13-99	.262	.350	.418	38	141	122	17	32	5	1	4	16	15	2	0	1	39	0	0	10.6	27.7

Pitching	B-T	Ht.	Wt.	DOB	W	L	ERA	G	GS	SV	IP	Hits	Runs	ER	HR	BB	SO	AVG	OBP	SLG	SO%	BB%	BF
Abel, Kevin	R-R	6-1	195	2-19-99	1	1	6.32	7	7	0	31	33	22	22	3	15	29	.268	.353	.390	20.9	10.8	139
Acuna, Jose	R-R	6-2	175	10-20-02	7	3	3.93	22	19	0	101	80	49	44	14	44	100	.214	.307	.380	23.4	10.3	427
Aguiar, Julian	L-R	6-3	180	6-04-01	4	1	1.92	14	14	0	70	44	20	15	2	24	77	.174	.258	.233	27.2	8.5	283
Benoit, Donovan	R-R	6-3	203	1-22-99	1	2	1.59	11	0	3	17	11	3	3	0	7	23	.186	.296	.271	31.9	9.7	72
Boatman, Dennis	R-R	6-5	225	11-20-99	1	3	9.73	21	0	1	29	40	34	31	5	29	31	.339	.467	.525	20.5	19.2	151
Cachutt, Manuel	R-R	6-0	185	6-07-97	1	0	1.98	7	0	0	14	8	4	3	0	7	7	.170	.278	.234	13.0	13.0	54
Cardona, Ryan	R-R	6-1	200	5-07-00	0	0	7.00	2	2	0	9	13	7	7	1	2	8	.351	.390	.622	19.5	4.9	41
Cooper, Tanner	R-R	6-3	215	9-08-99	0	0	7.71	4	0	0	12	17	14	10	1	5	8	.327	.379	.500	13.8	8.6	58
Crawford, Brooks	R-R	6-4	215	8-19-96	7	1	3.43	38	0	3	81	62	34	31	10	32	78	.213	.295	.364	23.4	9.6	333
Demurias, Eddy	R-R	6-0	184	8-01-97	1	1	6.55	7	0	0	11	15	8	8	1	5	9	.326	.385	.457	17.3	9.6	52
Farr, Thomas	R-R	6-0	203	4-29-99	1	4	4.05	14	14	0	67	55	40	30	7	21	60	.227	.305	.393	22.2	7.8	270
Gayman, Myles	R-R	6-4	200	2-19-98	7	2	3.20	36	0	1	76	74	31	27	10	12	60	.250	.297	.409	19.0	3.8	316
Gozzo, Jake	R-R	6-5	221	1-05-97	4	2	1.16	21	0	5	31	16	6	4	1	14	30	.157	.279	.216	24.4	11.4	123
Harmon, Johnathan	R-R	6-5	195	9-04-00	0	0	2.25	1	1	0	4	4	1	1	0	2	5	.267	.353	.333	29.4	11.8	17
Heatherly, Jacob	L-L	6-1	215	5-20-98	0	0	2.70	7	0	0	13	9	5	4	1	10	18	.191	.328	.277	31.0	17.2	58
Holt, Owen	R-R	6-3	225	4-22-99	5	6	4.42	36	0	2	59	58	33	29	6	29	73	.254	.338	.417	28.1	11.2	260

	B-T	Ht.	Wt.	DOB	W	L	ERA	G	GS	SV	IP	Hits	Runs	ER	HR	BB	SO	AVG	OBP	SLG	SO%	BB%	BF
Jessee, Brody	R-R	6-4	217	12-01-00	0	0	4.50	1	0	0	2	2	1	1	0	0	5	.286	.286	.286	62.5	0.0	8
Jones, Hayden	L-R	6-0	215	4-27-00	0	0	0.00	1	0	0	0	1	0	0	0	0	0	.500	.500	.500	0.0	0.0	2
Law, Derek	R-R	6-3	225	9-14-90	0	0	0.00	1	1	0	1	0	0	0	0	0	1	.000	.000	.000	33.3	0.0	3
Maxwell, Zach	R-R	6-6	275	1-26-01	3	2	4.56	13	0	1	26	17	16	13	2	15	41	.185	.321	.304	36.6	13.4	112
McElvain, Chris	R-R	6-0	205	9-15-00	2	2	4.53	11	11	0	46	45	25	23	6	22	34	.257	.343	.406	16.7	10.8	203
Moore, Andrew	L-R	6-5	205	8-11-99	1	0	5.52	10	0	0	15	13	10	9	1	10	20	.245	.375	.358	31.3	15.6	64
Murphy, John	R-R	6-4	245	12-11-96	4	3	4.89	26	0	4	46	46	28	25	8	19	44	.261	.337	.455	22.1	9.5	199
Parks, Hunter	R-R	6-4	187	4-28-01	3	7	4.18	22	22	0	80	60	39	37	6	60	88	.211	.366	.330	24.6	16.8	358
Petty, Chase	R-R	6-1	190	4-04-03	0	2	1.95	16	16	0	60	58	16	13	0	14	61	.257	.305	.310	25.1	5.8	243
Rivera, Javier	R-R	6-1	195	11-27-99	0	4	4.01	10	9	0	43	36	23	19	4	18	36	.228	.319	.386	19.4	9.7	186
Roxby, Braxton	R-R	6-3	215	3-12-99	4	4	2.96	37	0	4	55	37	28	18	4	22	67	.183	.283	.287	29.1	9.6	230
Rudd, Carson	R-R	6-5	190	9-17-98	5	8	4.64	21	15	0	66	55	36	34	10	32	77	.224	.318	.394	27.2	11.3	283
Sandridge, Jayvien	L-L	6-5	220	2-11-99	4	3	3.81	36	1	1	59	42	28	25	5	47	84	.205	.365	.322	32.3	18.1	260
Sceroler, Mac	R-R	6-3	215	4-09-95	1	0	8.10	2	0	0	3	5	3	3	0	1	2	.357	.400	.500	13.3	6.7	15
Timpanelli, Vin	R-R	6-2	210	10-02-98	0	4	3.07	20	0	6	29	22	16	10	2	9	29	.202	.270	.321	23.8	7.4	122

Fielding

Catcher	PCT	G	PO	A	E	DP	PB
Hunter	.997	27	269	17	1	0	1
Jones	.993	20	141	9	1	0	6
Nelson	.993	71	655	26	5	1	4
Trautwein	.994	20	168	11	1	1	2

First Base	PCT	G	PO	A	E	DP
Callahan	1.000	3	20	3	0	2
Callihan	.984	12	54	6	1	7
Ibarra	.991	77	528	53	5	58
Marrero	.941	5	15	1	1	2
Rogers	.985	49	299	30	5	23

Second Base	PCT	G	PO	A	E	DP
Callihan	.972	92	145	241	11	39
Contreras	.955	12	17	25	2	11
Faltine	.976	23	27	56	2	14
Fernandez	1.000	1	1	0	0	0
Jorge	.962	12	25	26	2	6
Serrano	.909	5	6	4	1	1

Third Base	PCT	G	PO	A	E	DP
Callahan	.968	87	57	124	6	19
Chevalier	.875	3	1	6	1	0
Contreras	.778	4	3	4	2	0
Faltine	1.000	10	6	16	0	1
Fernandez	1.000	2	1	0	0	0
Serrano	.750	4	1	2	1	0
Stewart	.929	29	12	40	4	5

Shortstop	PCT	G	PO	A	E	DP
Arroyo	.953	112	179	226	20	60
Contreras	1.000	2	1	2	0	0
Faltine	.970	19	25	39	2	11
Serrano	1.000	1	3	1	0	0

Outfield	PCT	G	PO	A	E	DP
Allen	1.000	22	50	0	0	0
Cerda	1.000	8	12	0	0	0
Chevalier	1.000	5	14	0	0	0
Creal	.974	19	29	0	1	0
Dunn	.957	47	82	2	3	0
Hendrick	.990	117	214	7	4	1
Hunter	1.000	5	8	0	0	0
Jorge	.938	12	14	1	1	0
Marrero	.974	27	29	0	1	0
Rodriguez	1.000	11	14	1	0	1
Rogers	.978	50	79	8	2	1
Thompson	.982	103	173	4	4	1
Trautwein	1.000	8	10	0	0	0

DAYTONA TORTUGAS — *LOW CLASS A*

FLORIDA STATE LEAGUE

Batting	B-T	Ht.	Wt.	DOB	AVG	OBP	SLG	G	PA	AB	R	H	2B	3B	HR	RBI	BB	HBP	SH	SF	SO	SB	CS	BB%	SO%
Acosta, Victor	B-R	5-11	170	6-10-04	.251	.364	.354	100	411	347	41	87	20	5	2	31	41	21	2	0	85	12	2	10.0	20.7
Almonte, Ariel	L-L	6-1	170	12-01-03	.203	.298	.299	97	383	335	35	68	15	1	5	33	42	4	0	2	133	4	0	11.0	34.7
Antonia, Donovan	R-R	5-10	182	8-13-03	.213	.339	.319	24	56	47	10	10	2	0	1	3	7	2	0	0	14	1	0	12.5	25.0
Ascanio, Johnny	B-R	5-10	150	7-04-03	.255	.329	.392	63	240	212	24	54	15	1	4	25	23	1	3	1	47	3	1	9.6	19.6
Balcazar, Leonardo	R-R	5-10	190	6-17-04	.324	.427	.471	18	82	68	11	22	5	1	1	11	13	0	0	1	22	2	2	15.9	26.8
Burns, Connor	R-R	6-1	185	12-25-01	.152	.269	.333	19	78	66	9	10	1	1	3	10	11	0	0	1	39	0	0	14.1	50.0
Cabrera, Ricardo	R-R	5-11	178	10-31-04	.316	.519	.316	5	27	19	7	6	0	0	0	2	5	3	0	0	5	3	0	18.5	18.5
Cerda, Allan	R-R	6-3	203	11-24-99	.143	.182	.381	6	22	21	3	3	0	1	1	2	1	0	0	0	7	0	0	4.5	31.8
Collier, Cam	L-R	6-2	210	11-20-04	.246	.349	.356	111	461	390	40	96	21	2	6	68	57	8	0	6	106	5	1	12.4	23.0
Confidan, Yerlin	L-L	6-3	170	12-16-02	.197	.273	.339	74	264	239	28	47	17	4	3	33	23	2	0	0	70	1	3	8.7	26.5
Contreras, Yan	R-R	6-2	185	1-30-01	.412	.524	.647	6	21	17	4	7	4	0	0	6	2	2	0	0	5	3	0	9.5	23.8
Garcia, Juan	R-R	5-11	185	5-03-03	.064	.100	.064	14	50	47	0	3	0	0	0	1	1	1	0	1	18	0	0	2.0	36.0
Graham, Carter	R-R	6-2	232	9-17-01	.194	.350	.226	11	40	31	5	6	1	0	0	3	6	2	0	1	11	2	0	15.0	27.5
Hunter, Cade	L-R	6-2	200	11-29-00	.245	.355	.410	61	251	212	34	52	5	0	10	34	29	8	0	2	75	5	3	11.6	29.9
Jorge, Carlos	L-R	5-10	160	9-22-03	.295	.400	.483	86	356	298	70	88	11	9	9	36	47	7	0	3	70	31	7	13.2	19.7
Marrero, Wendell	L-L	6-2	195	11-28-00	.156	.325	.313	12	40	32	4	5	2	0	1	5	7	1	0	0	11	1	0	17.5	27.5
Miller, Jackson	L-R	6-0	195	1-03-02	.235	.350	.353	5	20	17	2	4	2	0	0	1	3	0	0	0	6	0	0	15.0	30.0
Moss, Jack	L-R	6-5	215	10-30-01	.333	.474	.333	9	38	27	6	9	0	0	0	5	9	0	0	2	7	0	0	23.7	18.4
O'Donnell, Ethan	L-R	6-1	190	3-27-02	.350	.447	.600	23	94	80	15	28	4	2	4	19	10	4	0	0	18	3	0	10.6	19.1
Pino, Yassel	R-R	6-2	200	10-04-01	.227	.315	.358	90	355	313	47	71	19	2	6	40	37	4	0	1	65	3	0	10.4	18.3
Pitelli, Dominic	L-R	5-11	175	1-18-02	.203	.263	.297	21	80	74	9	15	2	1	1	8	6	0	0	0	22	4	1	7.5	27.5
Rodriguez, Hector	L-R	5-8	186	3-11-04	.293	.347	.510	101	444	410	85	120	23	9	16	56	27	7	0	0	84	18	5	6.1	18.9
Salcedo, Andruw	B-R	5-11	175	9-29-02	.162	.179	.189	15	39	37	4	6	1	0	0	2	1	0	0	1	13	0	0	2.6	33.3
Sanchez, Carlos	L-R	6-0	177	1-12-05	.188	.316	.313	4	19	16	2	3	2	0	0	3	3	0	0	0	8	0	0	15.8	42.1
Stewart, Sal	R-R	6-3	215	12-07-03	.269	.395	.424	88	387	316	55	85	19	0	10	60	66	2	0	3	59	10	4	17.1	15.2
Tanner, Logan	R-R	6-0	215	11-10-00	.202	.304	.307	65	258	218	31	44	15	1	2	27	34	0	0	5	65	0	0	13.2	25.2
Triana, Michel	L-R	6-3	230	11-23-99	.149	.230	.236	47	165	148	12	22	8	1	1	16	16	0	0	1	48	3	0	9.7	29.1
Valdez, Malvin	R-R	6-2	178	10-14-03	.144	.233	.240	33	117	104	18	15	5	1	1	6	11	1	1	0	44	3	2	9.4	37.6

Pitching	B-T	Ht.	Wt.	DOB	W	L	ERA	G	GS	SV	IP	Hits	Runs	ER	HR	BB	SO	AVG	OBP	SLG	SO%	BB%	BF
Abel, Kevin	R-R	6-1	195	2-19-99	3	2	4.69	12	7	0	40	35	22	21	4	32	61	.236	.376	.399	33.7	17.7	181
Adcock, Cody	R-R	6-4	210	6-21-02	0	0	6.23	4	0	1	9	6	7	6	2	8	10	.200	.375	.433	25.0	20.0	40
Aguilera, Gabriel	R-R	6-0	165	8-19-00	0	2	5.74	7	7	0	27	20	20	17	4	22	28	.217	.381	.413	23.7	18.6	118
Alfonseca, Pedro	R-R	6-0	178	9-04-97	0	0	10.54	13	0	0	14	9	16	16	1	21	15	.184	.453	.306	20.0	28.0	75
Antonia, Donovan	R-R	5-10	182	8-13-03	0	0	0.00	1	0	0	1	0	0	0	0	0	1	.000	.000	.000	33.3	0.0	3
Aranguren, Frainger	R-R	6-2	190	3-17-97	3	5	2.96	24	1	3	52	45	22	17	4	23	45	.241	.335	.369	20.9	10.7	215
Brutti, Ben	R-R	6-3	200	5-16-03	0	0	10.80	1	0	0	2	2	2	2	0	2	3	.286	.444	.286	33.3	22.2	9
Cardona, Ryan	R-R	6-1	200	5-07-00	2	2	3.10	22	14	2	81	52	31	28	3	48	106	.181	.303	.260	30.8	14.0	344

Cooper, Tanner	R-R	6-3	215	9-08-99	1	3	4.50	8	5	0	26	28	18	13	2	8	17	.272	.319	.456	15.0	7.1	113
Correa, Jean	R-R	6-1	145	2-16-98	1	0	7.68	17	0	0	36	51	31	31	6	23	35	.336	.445	.592	19.1	12.6	183
Fransen, Arij	R-R	6-3	190	5-20-01	3	8	6.09	24	16	0	81	98	64	55	8	36	85	.295	.368	.470	22.5	9.5	378
Harmon, Johnathan	R-R	6-5	195	9-04-00	3	5	3.97	22	15	1	88	81	49	39	8	33	92	.238	.312	.372	24.1	8.6	382
Heatherly, Jacob	L-L	6-1	215	5-20-98	6	3	2.78	27	0	1	36	15	15	11	0	41	66	.127	.354	.161	40.7	25.3	162
Hensey, Rob	L-L	6-4	220	9-29-99	0	2	6.83	12	2	0	29	39	23	22	3	18	35	.328	.420	.504	25.2	12.9	139
Hubbart, Bryce	L-L	6-1	181	6-28-01	1	3	4.96	16	7	3	45	39	27	25	3	49	51	.229	.401	.376	23.0	22.1	222
Huggins, Kenya	R-R	6-3	215	12-12-02	1	2	4.67	14	6	0	35	38	18	18	1	22	43	.271	.372	.421	26.2	13.4	164
Jessee, Brody	R-R	6-4	217	12-01-00	1	0	1.84	17	0	3	29	22	7	6	1	21	43	.214	.367	.282	33.6	16.4	128
Johnson, Alexander	R-R	6-6	220	7-02-00	0	2	7.82	7	0	0	13	7	12	11	1	15	11	.175	.397	.375	18.6	25.4	59
Lockwood, Brett	L-R	6-4	220	4-15-97	0	1	5.79	18	0	0	28	31	23	18	0	28	19	.284	.441	.376	13.3	19.6	143
Lopez, Jefferson	R-R	6-1	185	2-18-01	0	0	6.75	2	0	0	3	3	2	2	1	2	2	.300	.385	.600	15.4	15.4	13
Lorant, Nestor	R-R	6-2	175	5-04-02	1	1	3.86	8	2	0	21	12	9	9	2	17	26	.167	.326	.306	29.2	19.1	89
Lyons, Jared	R-R	6-1	190	9-27-00	3	5	3.69	14	11	0	54	52	30	22	4	31	65	.254	.357	.385	27.2	13.0	239
Martinez, Juan	R-R	6-1	160	12-30-02	1	1	12.27	2	1	0	4	6	5	5	0	3	5	.375	.474	.625	26.3	15.8	19
Maxwell, Zach	R-R	6-6	275	1-26-01	3	2	3.79	21	0	1	36	30	16	15	1	23	55	.227	.340	.348	35.0	14.6	157
McElvain, Chris	R-R	6-0	205	9-15-00	3	3	3.04	12	8	0	50	40	22	17	3	19	53	.212	.281	.365	25.2	9.0	210
Menefee, Joseph	L-L	6-2	220	10-06-99	7	5	5.48	31	0	1	48	46	33	29	3	36	66	.254	.389	.348	29.6	16.1	223
Mey, Luis	R-R	6-2	160	6-24-01	1	3	5.40	14	0	1	17	14	10	10	3	16	18	.233	.403	.417	23.4	20.8	77
Miller, Simon	R-R	6-2	210	9-08-00	0	0	0.00	1	0	0	1	0	0	0	0	1	1	.000	.250	.000	25.0	25.0	4
Montero, Jose	R-R	6-2	180	7-14-03	1	1	0.00	2	1	0	8	5	1	0	0	2	5	.192	.250	.231	17.9	7.1	28
Murphy, John	R-R	6-4	245	12-11-96	1	0	2.19	10	0	3	12	9	5	3	0	3	15	.200	.265	.267	30.6	6.1	49
Osman, Graham	L-L	6-3	183	1-29-01	2	0	1.04	5	0	0	9	3	2	1	0	5	13	.100	.270	.133	35.1	13.5	37
Pelio, Mason	R-R	6-3	230	7-15-00	3	7	5.06	25	20	0	96	84	60	54	14	63	77	.239	.365	.443	18.0	14.7	428
Pinazzi, Nicolo	L-L	6-2	195	10-25-99	1	3	9.82	13	2	0	18	18	21	20	2	26	25	.265	.505	.426	24.3	25.2	103
Richardson, Lyon	B-R	6-2	207	1-18-00	0	0	1.00	3	3	0	9	5	1	1	0	1	18	.167	.212	.200	54.5	3.0	33
Salcedo, Andruw	B-R	5-11	175	9-29-02	0	0	15.43	2	0	0	2	5	5	4	0	3	2	.455	.500	.455	12.5	18.8	16
Sikorski, Easton	R-R	6-0	210	1-12-00	4	1	3.41	17	0	6	29	20	12	11	3	14	33	.200	.310	.320	28.2	12.0	117

Fielding

Catcher	PCT	G	PO	A	E	DP	PB
Burns	.991	19	199	16	2	2	1
Garcia	.992	13	122	9	1	1	3
Hunter	1.000	28	277	19	0	1	2
Salcedo	1.000	7	76	4	0	0	3
Tanner	.990	63	592	31	6	4	4

First Base	PCT	G	PO	A	E	DP
Graham	.985	10	61	4	1	10
Pino	.988	87	560	38	7	58
Triana	.983	35	217	17	4	20

Second Base	PCT	G	PO	A	E	DP
Acosta	1.000	2	1	3	0	1
Ascanio	.963	45	62	92	6	33
Balcazar	1.000	4	4	4	0	2
Contreras	1.000	1	0	3	0	0
Jorge	.983	67	101	134	4	32
Pitelli	.974	9	14	23	1	9
Stewart	1.000	8	13	16	0	2

Third Base	PCT	G	PO	A	E	DP
Ascanio	.875	5	2	5	1	1
Balcazar	1.000	5	2	5	0	0
Cabrera	1.000	1	0	1	0	0
Collier	.941	72	39	105	9	14
Pino	1.000	3	1	11	0	0
Pitelli	1.000	1	1	1	0	0
Sanchez	1.000	2	2	1	0	0
Stewart	.967	45	39	77	4	10

Shortstop	PCT	G	PO	A	E	DP
Acosta	.941	94	110	178	18	45
Ascanio	1.000	10	12	29	0	9
Balcazar	.941	9	10	22	2	2
Cabrera	.923	4	5	7	1	2
Contreras	.889	4	5	11	2	2
Pitelli	.970	10	14	18	1	6

Outfield	PCT	G	PO	A	E	DP
Almonte	.947	97	142	4	6	1
Antonia	.956	17	25	0	2	0
Cerda	1.000	6	13	0	0	0
Confidan	.968	74	112	4	5	0
Hunter	.956	26	42	1	2	0
Jorge	.923	6	10	2	1	1
Marrero	.641	12	13	1	1	0
Moss	1.000	8	9	0	0	0
O'Donnell	.941	20	47	1	3	1
Rodriguez	.975	93	188	6	9	1
Triana	.955	12	20	1	1	0
Valdez	.988	33	56	4	1	1

ACL REDS — ROOKIE

ARIZONA COMPLEX LEAGUE

Batting	B-T	Ht.	Wt.	DOB	AVG	OBP	SLG	G	PA	AB	R	H	2B	3B	HR	RBI	BB	HBP	SH	SF	SO	SB	CS	BB%	SO%
Alcantara, Deivid	R-R	6-2	180	6-14-03	.091	.286	.364	3	14	11	3	1	0	0	1	2	2	1	0	0	9	0	0	14.3	64.3
Allen, Jay	R-R	6-2	190	11-22-02	.231	.583	.462	6	24	13	9	3	0	0	1	1	8	3	0	0	4	6	2	33.3	16.7
Antonia, Donovan	R-R	5-10	182	8-13-03	.423	.531	.731	9	32	26	6	11	2	0	2	6	5	1	0	0	4	1	0	15.6	12.5
Burns, Connor	R-R	6-1	185	12-25-01	.333	.500	.667	4	14	9	4	3	3	0	0	2	3	1	0	1	4	0	0	21.4	28.6
Cabrera, Ricardo	R-R	5-11	178	10-31-04	.350	.469	.559	39	175	143	41	50	7	4	5	21	21	11	0	0	35	21	2	12.0	20.0
Cerda, Allan	R-R	6-3	203	11-24-99	.235	.519	.824	6	27	17	8	4	1	0	3	6	10	0	0	0	8	1	0	37.0	29.6
Chevalier, Luis	B-R	5-11	160	1-18-02	.340	.486	.453	22	70	53	10	18	3	0	1	12	16	0	0	1	10	4	4	22.9	14.3
Chirino, Ray-Jacson	R-R	6-1	175	12-24-02	.177	.224	.290	19	67	62	4	11	4	0	1	7	2	2	0	1	23	1	0	3.0	34.3
Espinoza, Iverson	R-R	5-10	155	1-06-03	.243	.404	.297	17	47	37	9	9	2	0	0	2	10	0	0	0	12	2	2	21.3	25.5
Garcia, Juan	R-R	5-11	185	5-03-03	.244	.351	.436	23	94	78	16	19	6	0	3	16	13	1	0	2	19	2	0	13.8	20.2
Graham, Carter	R-R	6-2	232	9-17-01	.231	.231	.538	4	13	13	2	3	1	0	1	1	0	0	0	0	5	0	0	0.0	38.5
Grullon, Wilkin	R-R	6-0	220	11-28-99	.125	.222	.125	3	9	8	1	1	0	0	0	1	1	0	0	0	5	0	0	11.1	55.6
Henley, Kyle	R-R	6-3	180	12-15-04	.231	.231	.231	4	13	13	0	3	0	0	0	0	0	0	0	0	5	1	0	0.0	38.5
Hernandez, Miguel	R-R	6-0	194	4-13-99	.360	.500	.520	9	32	25	8	9	1	0	1	6	7	0	0	0	2	3	1	21.9	6.3
Inirio, Wencer	R-R	6-3	190	10-28-02	.080	.111	.160	9	27	25	2	2	2	0	0	2	0	1	0	1	15	0	0	0.0	55.6
Isturiz, Eddy	R-R	5-10	182	1-16-04	.222	.488	.593	21	41	27	8	6	4	0	2	4	13	1	0	0	11	1	1	31.7	26.8
Leones, Luis	L-L	5-10	155	6-12-03	.323	.457	.492	32	82	65	21	21	4	2	1	9	14	2	1	0	27	5	0	17.1	32.9
Lin, Sheng-En	L-R	5-11	185	9-01-05	.214	.371	.286	9	35	28	6	6	0	1	0	3	6	1	0	0	16	2	0	17.1	45.7
Marte, Noelvi	R-R	6-0	216	10-16-01	.222	.300	.222	3	10	9	1	2	0	0	0	0	1	0	0	0	1	0	0	10.0	10.0
Miller, Jackson	L-R	6-0	195	1-03-02	.471	.500	.647	6	18	17	3	8	1	1	0	6	1	0	0	0	5	0	0	5.6	27.8
Moon, Bernard	R-R	6-0	185	4-15-05	.360	.429	.480	7	28	25	7	9	1	1	0	6	3	0	0	0	8	5	1	10.7	28.6
Moss, Jack	L-R	6-5	215	10-30-01	.282	.348	.333	12	46	39	7	11	2	0	0	8	5	0	0	2	13	1	0	10.9	28.3
Mount, Drew	L-R	5-11	205	3-24-96	.310	.444	.345	9	36	29	13	9	1	0	0	6	5	2	0	0	6	3	1	13.9	16.7

O'Donnell, Ethan	L-R	6-1	190	3-27-02	.200	.294	.200	4	17	15	3	3	0	0	0	2	2	0	0	0	5	1	0	11.8	29.4
Omana, Diego	R-R	5-11	165	1-10-03	.274	.387	.403	20	75	62	5	17	5	0	1	11	11	1	0	1	21	0	1	14.7	28.0
Pineda, Esmith	R-R	5-10	183	11-13-04	.273	.360	.400	48	197	165	30	45	14	2	1	36	25	1	0	6	41	5	2	12.7	20.8
Pitelli, Dominic	L-R	5-11	175	1-18-02	.154	.214	.154	4	14	13	3	2	0	0	0	2	1	0	0	0	3	2	0	7.1	21.4
Reyes, Luis	R-R	5-11	193	11-15-03	.315	.428	.538	40	159	130	24	41	17	0	4	36	22	5	0	2	31	2	0	13.8	19.5
Rijo, Brayan	R-R	6-0	190	11-24-03	.119	.208	.238	28	97	84	12	10	2	1	2	16	10	0	1	2	40	4	1	10.3	41.2
Salcedo, Andruw	B-R	5-11	175	9-29-02	.174	.259	.304	6	27	23	1	4	1	1	0	2	3	0	0	1	4	0	0	11.1	14.8
Sanchez, Carlos	L-R	6-0	177	1-12-05	.281	.468	.445	40	175	128	42	36	12	3	1	26	44	1	0	0	44	9	4	25.1	25.1
Serrano, Jose	R-R	6-0	180	10-14-03	.227	.345	.362	42	168	141	27	32	5	4	2	25	22	4	0	1	56	2	4	13.1	33.3
Stafura, Sammy	R-R	6-0	188	11-15-04	.071	.212	.190	12	53	42	7	3	2	0	1	6	8	0	1	2	23	0	0	15.1	43.4
Valdez, Malvin	R-R	6-2	178	10-14-03	.225	.362	.401	49	222	182	41	41	11	0	7	32	33	6	0	0	76	19	4	14.9	34.2
Ysabel, Vladimir	B-R	6-0	150	3-07-02	.400	.500	.400	2	6	5	1	2	0	0	0	0	1	0	0	0	2	2	0	16.7	33.3

Pitching	**B-T**	**Ht.**	**Wt.**	**DOB**	**W**	**L**	**ERA**	**G**	**GS**	**SV**	**IP**	**Hits**	**Runs**	**ER**	**HR**	**BB**	**SO**	**AVG**	**OBP**	**SLG**	**SO%**	**BB%**	**BF**
Adcock, Cody	R-R	6-4	210	6-21-02	1	0	0.00	1	0	0	1	0	0	0	0	0	1	.000	.000	.000	33.3	0.0	3
Aguilera, Gabriel	R-R	6-0	165	8-19-00	0	0	5.06	4	4	0	5	5	3	3	0	2	10	.250	.348	.350	43.5	8.7	23
Alfonseca, Pedro	R-R	6-0	178	9-04-97	0	1	3.72	7	0	1	10	8	6	4	0	6	9	.222	.348	.222	19.1	12.8	47
Antone, Tejay	R-R	6-4	230	12-05-93	0	0	20.25	2	2	0	1	3	3	3	1	0	2	.429	.429	.857	28.6	0.0	7
Arellano, Joneiker	R-R	5-11	155	2-20-05	2	2	16.42	12	4	0	25	49	45	45	6	13	21	.415	.478	.678	15.7	9.7	134
Batista, Jonathan	R-R	6-3	195	2-28-02	1	2	8.22	14	0	1	23	28	28	21	7	23	25	.289	.434	.598	20.3	18.7	123
Branche, Stevie	R-R	6-4	205	5-18-97	0	0	0.00	2	0	0	2	1	0	0	0	0	1	.167	.167	.167	16.7	0.0	6
Brutti, Ben	R-R	6-3	200	5-16-03	0	3	4.18	10	6	0	28	25	14	13	0	16	36	.243	.360	.320	28.8	12.8	125
Correa, Jean	R-R	6-1	145	2-16-98	2	1	1.17	5	0	0	8	8	4	1	0	1	12	.258	.294	.387	35.3	2.9	34
Davila, Vladimir	R-R	5-11	158	9-10-02	0	0	45.00	2	0	0	1	3	5	5	0	2	1	.500	.700	1.000	10.0	20.0	10
Demurias, Eddy	R-R	6-0	184	8-01-97	1	0	6.35	6	0	0	6	6	4	4	0	1	7	.273	.333	.409	29.2	4.2	24
Dunn, Justin	R-R	6-2	209	9-22-95	0	0	3.86	2	2	0	2	2	1	1	0	1	5	.222	.300	.222	50.0	10.0	10
Edgington, Brian	R-R	6-0	200	9-02-98	1	0	4.50	3	0	1	8	11	4	4	0	2	12	.333	.371	.394	34.3	5.7	35
Galindo, Cristian	L-L	6-2	150	10-14-02	2	1	8.72	16	0	1	22	27	22	21	0	15	26	.310	.445	.379	23.6	13.6	110
German, Franklin	R-R	6-2	195	9-22-97	0	0	54.00	1	0	0	0	1	2	2	0	1	0	.333	.500	.333	0.0	25.0	4
Greene, Hunter	R-R	6-5	242	8-06-99	0	0	0.00	1	1	0	2	1	0	0	0	0	3	.143	.143	.143	42.9	0.0	7
Gutierrez, Dualvert	R-R	6-0	185	1-25-01	1	1	5.46	12	5	0	30	32	25	18	1	24	36	.269	.399	.387	24.3	16.2	148
Gutierrez, Vladimir	R-R	6-1	205	9-18-95	0	0	0.00	2	1	0	2	0	0	0	0	2	3	.000	.250	.000	37.5	25.0	8
Hensey, Rob	L-L	6-4	220	9-29-99	0	1	3.86	2	1	0	5	4	2	2	0	5	8	.235	.435	.294	34.8	21.7	23
Isturiz, Eddy	R-R	5-10	182	1-16-04	0	0	27.00	1	0	0	0	1	1	1	1	0	0	.500	.500	2.000	0.0	0.0	2
Jessee, Brody	R-R	6-4	217	12-01-00	0	0	0.00	2	0	0	3	1	0	0	0	2	7	.100	.357	.100	50.0	14.3	14
Johnson, Alexander	R-R	6-6	220	7-02-00	2	1	2.41	11	0	2	19	12	8	5	1	13	28	.185	.316	.292	35.4	16.5	79
Lambert, Carson	L-R	6-3	220	9-02-99	1	1	0.00	3	0	0	6	4	2	0	0	1	7	.167	.200	.250	28.0	4.0	25
Laureano, Anyer	R-R	6-2	188	12-29-02	0	1	6.75	10	2	0	12	11	11	9	0	14	12	.262	.448	.333	20.7	24.1	58
Legumina, Casey	R-R	6-2	195	6-19-97	0	0	0.00	1	0	0	1	0	0	0	0	0	1	.000	.000	.000	33.3	0.0	3
Lodolo, Nick	L-L	6-6	216	2-05-98	0	0	0.00	1	1	0	2	1	0	0	0	0	4	.143	.143	.143	57.1	0.0	7
Longstaff, Darcy	R-R	6-0	200	1-22-04	1	4	6.84	11	4	1	25	31	26	19	2	14	27	.310	.387	.500	22.7	11.8	119
Lopez, Jefferson	R-R	6-1	185	2-18-01	1	2	6.35	16	0	1	23	36	25	16	4	9	37	.353	.412	.549	32.5	7.9	114
Lorant, Nestor	R-R	6-2	175	5-04-02	1	0	6.48	6	4	0	17	18	12	12	2	8	17	.269	.342	.478	22.4	10.5	76
Lyons, Jared	R-R	6-1	190	9-27-00	0	0	10.13	3	2	0	5	7	6	6	0	6	7	.318	.464	.455	25.0	21.4	28
Martinez, Juan	R-R	6-1	160	12-30-02	1	0	6.75	10	4	0	27	28	24	20	0	17	27	.262	.372	.336	20.9	13.2	129
Mills, Alec	R-R	6-4	205	11-30-91	0	1	3.60	2	2	0	5	6	3	2	1	0	4	.273	.273	.409	18.2	0.0	22
Montero, Jose	R-R	6-2	180	7-14-03	2	2	4.93	11	3	0	35	46	23	19	4	8	39	.319	.367	.507	24.7	5.1	158
Moore, Andrew	L-R	6-5	205	8-11-99	0	0	0.00	4	0	0	4	0	0	0	0	1	9	.000	.143	.000	64.3	7.1	14
Morellis, Luis	R-R	6-2	165	2-07-04	2	1	5.06	8	2	0	21	21	13	12	3	16	23	.263	.400	.488	22.8	15.8	101
Nierenberg, Leo	R-R	6-0	190	6-05-98	2	1	6.00	4	0	0	3	3	2	2	0	7	4	.273	.556	.364	22.2	38.9	18
Osman, Graham	L-L	6-3	183	1-29-01	0	0	0.00	1	0	0	1	0	0	0	0	0	2	.000	.000	.000	66.7	0.0	3
Payero, Nick	R-R	6-2	200	6-21-00	0	0	10.57	4	0	0	8	15	11	9	2	6	9	.405	.488	.622	20.9	14.0	43
Pinazzi, Nicolo	L-L	6-2	195	10-25-99	2	0	5.60	12	0	1	18	14	11	11	3	15	25	.226	.407	.452	30.9	18.5	81
Quintana, Ricardo	R-R	5-11	160	11-01-02	1	2	9.37	15	0	1	16	27	19	17	0	9	12	.355	.443	.447	13.6	10.2	88
Sceroler, Mac	R-R	6-3	215	4-09-95	1	0	3.00	4	0	0	6	7	4	2	0	1	6	.292	.346	.292	22.2	3.7	27
Serwinowski, Adam	L-L	6-5	190	6-07-04	0	0	3.62	11	6	0	27	13	12	11	1	16	43	.149	.302	.230	40.2	15.0	107

Fielding

C: Garcia 21, Omana 20, Isturiz 12, Salcedo 6, Burns 4, Grullon 1. **1B:** Reyes 33, Chirino 13, Inirio 7, Graham 4, Moss 3, Chevalier 2. **2B:** Serrano 42, Moon 7, Espinoza 5, Hernandez 3, Pitelli 1. **3B:** Cabrera 17, Sanchez 17, Chevalier 14, Espinoza 11, Reyes 6, Marte 2, Pitelli 2. **SS:** Sanchez 23, Cabrera 20, Stafura 11, Hernandez 5, Lin 3, Pitelli 1, Chevalier 1. **OF:** Pineda 48, Valdez 47, Leones 32, Rijo 28, Cerda 6, Chevalier 5, Lin 5, Mount 5, Antonia 5, O'Donnell 4, Allen 4, Henley 4, Alcantara 2, Ysabel 2, Moss 1, Isturiz 1.

DSL REDS — *ROOKIE*

DOMINICAN SUMMER LEAGUE

Batting	**B-T**	**Ht.**	**Wt.**	**DOB**	**AVG**	**OBP**	**SLG**	**G**	**PA**	**AB**	**R**	**H**	**2B**	**3B**	**HR**	**RBI**	**BB**	**HBP**	**SH**	**SF**	**SO**	**SB**	**CS**	**BB%**	**SO%**
Abad, Pablo	R-R	6-2	175	11-05-05	.127	.205	.183	23	78	71	6	9	4	0	0	3	7	0	0	0	38	0	3	9.0	48.7
Alcantara, Alfredo	R-R	5-9	165	10-25-05	.267	.411	.467	35	152	120	25	32	9	0	5	16	24	6	1	1	32	2	1	15.8	21.1
Buten, Anielson	R-R	5-9	155	9-22-05	.251	.321	.374	53	218	195	35	49	7	1	5	32	17	4	0	2	66	10	5	7.8	30.3
Correa, Jesus	B-R	5-8	167	9-08-04	.265	.359	.336	40	131	113	23	30	3	1	1	12	17	0	0	1	33	5	1	13.0	25.2
De La Cruz, Angel	R-R	6-3	160	3-27-06	.059	.158	.088	13	38	34	3	2	1	0	0	1	3	1	0	0	18	0	0	7.9	47.4
Diaz, Brauli	B-R	6-0	149	1-23-06	.139	.244	.167	26	83	72	13	10	2	0	0	4	6	4	1	0	38	5	2	7.2	45.8
Duno, Alfredo	R-R	6-2	210	1-07-06	.303	.451	.493	45	195	152	36	46	9	1	6	41	38	4	0	1	41	6	0	19.5	21.0
Gomes, Gabriel	R-R	5-9	170	3-31-04	.375	.592	.531	14	49	32	9	12	2	0	1	3	15	2	0	0	7	3	0	30.6	14.3
Guerrero, Henry	R-R	6-0	191	10-19-04	.237	.296	.268	27	108	97	10	23	3	0	0	15	5	4	0	2	15	0	2	4.6	13.9

Joseph, Brayan	B-R	5-10	145	9-22-05	.091	.167	.091	4	12	11	0	1	0	0	0	0	1	0	0	0	7	0	0	8.3	58.3
Mora, Angelo	R-R	6-1	195	6-10-05	.203	.356	.254	20	73	59	9	12	3	0	0	7	10	4	0	0	12	1	0	13.7	16.4
Reyes, Adrian	B-R	6-1	215	11-26-04	.201	.366	.383	47	191	149	27	30	12	3	3	21	39	1	0	2	57	1	1	20.4	29.8
Rojas, Gilberto	R-R	6-1	165	1-19-05	.250	.324	.385	30	108	96	16	24	7	0	2	17	10	1	0	1	25	0	0	9.3	23.1
Romero, Yael	L-R	5-11	175	10-15-05	.272	.481	.380	33	131	92	22	25	7	0	1	22	35	3	0	1	29	1	0	26.7	22.1
Soriano, Yeycol	L-L	6-0	150	9-03-05	.273	.388	.427	29	134	110	21	30	9	1	2	23	19	3	0	2	23	6	3	14.2	17.2
Torres, Jesus	R-R	6-0	160	10-02-02	.271	.280	.396	14	50	48	4	13	1	1	1	6	1	0	0	1	11	3	1	2.0	22.0
Torres, Rafhlmil	B-R	5-11	150	9-05-05	.259	.374	.327	45	197	162	41	42	7	2	0	20	27	4	1	2	30	8	3	13.7	15.2
Valencia, Anthuan	R-R	5-8	177	10-14-04	.225	.333	.256	37	153	129	16	29	4	0	0	17	17	5	0	2	37	6	3	11.1	24.2

Pitching	B-T	Ht.	Wt.	DOB	W	L	ERA	G	GS	SV	IP	Hits	Runs	ER	HR	BB	SO	AVG	OBP	SLG	SO%	BB%	BF
Cervantes, Edwin	L-L	6-3	159	9-06-04	3	1	2.78	14	7	0	45	26	18	14	2	26	42	.167	.299	.244	22.2	13.8	189
Colina, Jesus	R-R	5-11	170	3-21-05	3	4	6.20	15	0	0	25	20	19	17	2	13	24	.227	.358	.364	22.4	12.1	107
Colmenares, Mauricio	R-R	6-0	170	11-04-03	0	4	5.34	13	4	0	30	33	22	18	1	16	31	.282	.378	.393	22.8	11.8	136
Diaz, Brauli	B-R	6-0	149	1-23-06	0	0	0.00	1	0	0	1	1	2	0	0	1	1	.200	.333	.200	16.7	16.7	6
Diaz, Bryan	L-L	5-10	140	9-11-03	2	2	10.22	12	0	2	12	15	16	14	1	17	16	.306	.493	.388	23.2	24.6	69
Diaz, Jean	R-R	6-0	170	1-24-03	2	0	2.25	3	0	0	4	3	1	1	0	1	3	.231	.333	.308	20.0	6.7	15
Gaitan, Abraham	R-R	6-2	180	2-06-04	2	1	2.45	13	8	0	51	38	18	14	1	14	36	.204	.270	.253	17.6	6.9	204
Gonzalez, Irvin	R-R	5-10	150	6-09-06	2	0	5.28	15	0	1	15	16	10	9	1	6	17	.254	.314	.365	24.3	8.6	70
Guevara, Khristian	L-L	6-3	150	8-24-04	3	4	4.17	13	9	0	45	44	26	21	2	17	38	.257	.325	.392	19.7	8.8	193
Lantigua, Lisnerkin	R-R	6-0	181	9-01-04	1	2	4.36	12	7	0	33	36	28	16	0	19	30	.265	.358	.346	18.9	11.9	159
Leon, Rafael	R-R	6-1	175	1-11-06	0	0	9.28	10	0	1	11	9	11	11	1	15	9	.237	.444	.395	16.7	27.8	54
Lopez, Christian	L-L	6-2	207	7-06-06	0	0	5.14	5	0	0	7	8	5	4	1	4	9	.267	.371	.500	25.7	11.4	35
Lorduy, David	R-R	6-0	198	10-15-03	5	1	3.60	13	8	0	50	36	20	20	4	11	58	.199	.244	.320	30.1	5.7	193
Morellis, Luis	R-R	6-2	165	2-07-04	1	0	1.80	4	2	0	10	7	2	2	0	2	10	.200	.237	.257	26.3	5.3	38
Payano, Nelfri	R-R	5-10	179	11-09-04	0	0	4.82	14	0	3	19	19	11	10	0	8	25	.264	.365	.403	29.4	9.4	85
Prodanovic, Nicola	R-R	6-0	190	4-05-04	0	2	7.84	7	1	0	10	17	11	9	0	8	6	.378	.473	.467	10.9	14.5	55
Rivera, Cesar	R-R	6-1	198	11-17-03	1	0	3.14	7	1	1	14	15	5	5	0	5	15	.268	.339	.321	24.2	8.1	62
Rodriguez, Edmundo	L-L	6-0	160	10-08-03	1	2	12.00	14	0	0	18	29	27	24	3	17	20	.372	.474	.615	20.6	17.5	97
Talavera, Enmanuel	R-R	6-2	170	10-07-05	1	2	3.09	14	3	1	23	14	9	8	2	13	25	.175	.320	.275	25.8	13.4	97
Vasquez, Andre	R-R	6-2	175	12-27-05	1	1	4.60	14	5	0	31	21	17	16	1	19	32	.191	.308	.291	24.6	14.6	130
Zazueta, Angel	R-R	5-11	176	3-05-04	0	0	4.50	7	0	1	8	7	4	4	1	3	7	.250	.323	.500	21.9	9.4	32

Fielding

C: Guerrero 27, Mora 19, Gomes 8, Rojas 7. **1B:** Romero 33, Rojas 22, Diaz 5. **2B:** Buten 17, Torres 17, Valencia 14, Alcantara 10, Correa 2. **3B:** Valencia 24, Diaz 19, Buten 15, Correa 5, Joseph 2. **SS:** Torres 31, Alcantara 25, Joseph 2, Buten 1. **OF:** Reyes 45, Correa 30, Soriano 29, Buten 27, Abad 24, Torres 15, De La Cruz 11, Diaz 2, Gomes 1.

Cleveland Guardians

SEASON SYNOPSIS: The Guardians, with the youngest roster in the major leagues, led the American League Central at the all-star break. However, their offense never clicked like it did in the second half of 2022 and they faded down the stretch in manager Terry Francona's final season, resulting in a disappointing third-place finish and the worst record of Francona's tenure.

HIGH POINT: Cleveland won six of its first eight in July to take over first place. The 10-6 win against Kansas City that put them into first was an 18-hit barrage—but no homers, in Guardians fashion.

LOW POINT: Cleveland trailed Minnesota by five games but had added waiver claims Lucas Giolito, Matt Moore and Reynaldo Lopez to bolster its pitching staff entering September. With the Twins in town for three games Sept. 4-6, Giolito took the mound to open the series and got pounded for nine runs in three innings. Francona waved the white flag by putting in utilityman David Fry, a position player, to pitch the final four innings in a 20-6 loss that featured six Twins homers.

NOTABLE ROOKIES: Catcher Bo Naylor joined older brother Josh on the big league roster and was one of the team's best bats, hitting 11 homers in just 198 at-bats. With the youngest pitching staff in MLB (average age: 26.1), the Guardians broke in several impact arms. Righty Tanner Bibee led the club with 142 innings pitched while going 10-4, 2.98. Righty Gavin Williams (3-5, 3.29, 81 SO/82 IP) and lefty Logan Allen (7-8, 3.81 in 125.1 IP) joined him as rotation stalwarts, while Xzavion Curry (4.07 ERA) thrived in a hybrid start/relief role. Gabriel Arias became the everyday shortstop in the second half but struggled offensively (.628 OPS).

KEY TRANSACTIONS: In addition to waiver adds Giolito, Lopez and Moore, the Guardians bolstered their lineup with veteran waiver pickups Kole Calhoun and Ramon Laureano, who took over the corner outfield/DH roles when younger players Brennan and Oscar Gonzalez faltered.

DOWN ON THE FARM: The Guardians didn't have a dominant team at any level of the minors, as Lynchburg's .511 winning percentage was the organization's best. They continue to develop and produce contact-oriented hitters and a slew of pitchers. Righthander Daniel Espino is trying to come back from a shoulder injury that has now cost him most of two seasons.

OPENING DAY PAYROLL: $89,424,629 (25th).

PLAYERS OF THE YEAR

MAJOR LEAGUE

Jose Ramirez
3B

.282/.356/.475
36 2B, 24 HR
28 SB, 87 R

MINOR LEAGUE

Juan Brito
SS

(HiA/AA/AAA)
.271/.377/.434
31 2B, 14 HR

ORGANIZATION LEADERS

Batting		*Minimum 250 AB
MAJORS		
* AVG	Josh Naylor	.308
* OPS	Josh Naylor	.842
HR	Jose Ramirez	24
RBI	Josh Naylor	97
MINORS		
* AVG	Oscar Gonzalez, Columbus	.287
* OBP	Nate Furman	.397
* SLG	Johnathan Rodriguez, Akron/Columbus	.529
* OPS	Johnathan Rodriguez, Akron/Columbus	.897
R	Brayan Rocchio, Columbus	81
R	Jhonkensky Noel, Columbus	81
H	Johnathan Rodriguez, Akron/Columbus	142
TB	Johnathan Rodriguez, Akron/Columbus	263
2B	Brayan Rocchio, Columbus	33
3B	Wuilfredo Antunez, Lynchburg	7
HR	Johnathan Rodriguez, Akron/Columbus	29
RBI	Johnathan Rodriguez, Akron/Columbus	88
BB	Juan Brito, Lake Cnty/Akron/Columb.	78
SO	Johnathan Rodriguez, Akron/Columbus	163
SB	Nate Furman	37

Pitching		#Minimum 75 IP
MAJORS		
W	Tanner Bibee	10
# ERA	Aaron Civale	2.34
SO	Tanner Bibee	141
SV	Emmanuel Clase	44
MINORS		
W	Zach Jacobs, Lynchburg	10
L	Hunter Stanley, Akron	11
# ERA	Will Dion, Lake County/Akron	2.39
G	Cade Smith, Akron/Columbus	47
GS	5-tied	24
SV	Cade Smith, Akron/Columbus	15
IP	Alonzo Richardson, Lynchburg	124
BB	Doug Nikhazy, Akron	73
SO	Joey Cantillo, Akron/Columbus	146
# AVG	Will Dion, Lake County/Akron	.214

2023 PERFORMANCE

General Manager: Mike Chernoff. **Farm Director:** Rob Cerfolio. **Scouting Director:** Scott Barnsby.

Class	Team	League	W	L	PCT	Finish	Manager
Majors	Cleveland Guardians	American	76	86	.469	11 (15)	Terry Francona
Triple-A	Columbus Clippers	International	68	79	.463	17 (20)	Andy Tracy
Double-A	Akron RubberDucks	Eastern	65	73	.471	8 (12)	Rouglas Odor
High-A	Lake County Captains	Midwest	65	64	.504	7 (12)	Omir Santos
Low-A	Lynchburg Hillcats	Carolina	67	64	.511	5 (12)	Jordan Smith
Rookie	ACL Guardians	Arizona Complex	22	33	.400	13 (17)	T.J. Rivera
Rookie	DSL Guardians Red	Dominican Sum.	25	27	.481	31 (50)	Jesus Tavarez
Rookie	DSL Guardians Red	Dominican Sum.	25	27	.481	31 (50)	Juan De La Cruz
Overall 2023 Minor League Record			**324**	**331**	**.495**	**15th (30)**	

ORGANIZATION STATISTICS

CLEVELAND GUARDIANS

AMERICAN LEAGUE

Batting	B-T	Ht.	Wt.	DOB	AVG	OBP	SLG	G	PA	AB	R	H	2B	3B	HR	RBI	BB	HBP	SH	SF	SO	SB	CS	BB%	SO%
Arias, Gabriel	R-R	6-1	217	2-27-00	.210	.275	.352	122	345	315	36	66	15	0	10	26	28	1	0	1	113	3	4	8.1	32.8
Bell, Josh	B-R	6-4	261	8-14-92	.233	.318	.383	97	393	347	26	81	19	0	11	48	43	1	0	2	81	0	1	10.9	20.6
2-team (53 Miami)					.247	.325	.419	150	617	547	52	135	28	0	22	74	63	2	0	3	134	0	1	10.2	21.7
Brennan, Will	L-L	6-0	200	2-02-98	.266	.299	.356	138	455	432	41	115	24	0	5	41	16	5	0	2	57	13	5	3.5	12.5
Calhoun, Kole	L-L	5-10	205	10-14-87	.217	.282	.376	43	174	157	18	34	7	0	6	25	13	2	0	2	37	0	1	7.5	21.3
Collins, Zack	L-R	6-3	220	2-06-95	.500	.667	.500	2	6	4	0	2	0	0	0	0	2	0	0	0	2	0	0	33.3	33.3
Freeman, Tyler	R-R	6-0	190	5-21-99	.242	.295	.366	64	168	153	20	37	7	0	4	18	10	2	2	1	30	5	0	6.0	17.9
Fry, David	R-R	6-0	215	11-20-95	.238	.319	.416	58	113	101	12	24	6	0	4	15	8	4	0	0	30	2	0	7.1	26.5
Gallagher, Cam	R-R	6-3	230	12-06-92	.126	.154	.168	56	149	143	6	18	6	0	0	7	4	1	0	1	46	0	0	2.7	30.9
Gimenez, Andres	L-R	5-11	161	9-04-98	.251	.314	.399	153	616	557	76	140	27	5	15	62	32	20	4	3	112	30	6	5.2	18.2
Gonzalez, Oscar	R-R	6-4	240	1-10-98	.214	.239	.312	54	180	173	15	37	7	2	2	12	5	1	0	1	46	0	0	2.8	25.6
Haase, Eric	R-R	5-10	210	12-18-92	.200	.273	.200	3	11	10	0	2	0	0	0	0	1	0	0	0	3	1	0	9.1	27.3
2-team (86 Detroit)					.201	.247	.281	89	293	274	22	55	8	1	4	26	17	0	1	1	81	4	1	5.8	27.6
Kwan, Steven	L-L	5-9	170	9-05-97	.268	.340	.370	158	718	638	93	171	36	7	5	54	70	3	1	6	75	21	3	9.7	10.4
Laureano, Ramon	R-R	5-11	203	7-15-94	.243	.342	.382	41	158	136	22	33	8	1	3	14	16	5	0	1	41	4	1	10.1	25.9
2-team (64 Oakland)					.224	.304	.371	105	404	361	46	81	18	4	9	35	33	9	0	1	114	12	1	8.2	28.2
Naylor, Bo	L-R	6-0	205	2-21-00	.237	.339	.470	67	230	198	33	47	13	0	11	32	30	1	0	1	53	5	0	13.0	23.0
Naylor, Josh	L-L	5-11	250	6-22-97	.308	.354	.489	121	495	452	52	139	31	0	17	97	33	3	0	7	68	10	3	6.7	13.7
Ramirez, Jose	B-R	5-9	190	9-17-92	.282	.356	.475	156	691	611	87	172	36	5	24	80	73	1	0	6	73	28	6	10.6	10.6
Rocchio, Brayan	B-R	5-10	170	1-13-01	.247	.279	.321	23	86	81	9	20	6	0	0	8	4	0	0	1	27	0	0	4.7	31.4
Rosario, Amed	R-R	6-2	190	11-20-95	.265	.306	.369	94	412	385	51	102	19	6	3	40	22	2	0	3	77	9	0	5.3	18.7
2-team (48 Los Angeles Dodgers)					.263	.305	.378	142	545	510	70	134	25	8	6	58	29	3	0	3	99	15	2	5.3	18.2
Straw, Myles	R-R	5-10	178	10-17-94	.238	.301	.297	147	518	462	52	110	18	3	1	29	42	2	6	6	97	20	6	8.1	18.7
Tena, Jose	L-R	5-11	195	3-20-01	.226	.294	.290	18	34	31	2	7	2	0	0	3	3	0	0	0	13	0	0	8.8	38.2
Viloria, Meibrys	L-R	5-11	225	2-15-97	.000	.250	.000	10	4	3	0	0	0	0	0	0	1	0	0	0	0	0	0	25.0	0.0
Zunino, Mike	R-R	6-2	235	3-25-91	.177	.271	.306	42	140	124	11	22	7	0	3	11	15	1	0	0	61	0	0	10.7	43.6

Pitching	B-T	Ht.	Wt.	DOB	W	L	ERA	G	GS	SV	IP	Hits	Runs	ER	HR	BB	SO	AVG	OBP	SLG	SO%	BB%	BF
Allen, Logan	R-L	6-0	190	9-05-98	7	8	3.81	24	24	0	125	127	55	53	16	48	119	.263	.330	.420	22.2	8.9	537
Battenfield, Peyton	R-R	6-4	224	8-10-97	0	5	5.19	7	6	0	35	34	22	20	7	12	27	.256	.315	.474	18.5	8.2	146
Bibee, Tanner	R-R	6-2	205	3-05-99	10	4	2.98	25	25	0	142	122	49	47	13	45	141	.230	.295	.353	24.1	7.7	585
Bieber, Shane	R-R	6-3	200	5-31-95	6	6	3.80	21	21	0	128	124	56	54	14	34	107	.253	.303	.406	20.1	6.4	533
Civale, Aaron	R-R	6-2	215	6-12-95	5	2	2.34	13	13	0	77	58	20	20	5	22	58	.207	.269	.311	19.0	7.2	306
Clase, Emmanuel	R-R	6-2	206	3-18-98	3	9	3.22	75	0	44	73	68	37	26	4	16	64	.242	.282	.327	21.2	5.3	302
Curry, Xzavion	R-R	6-0	195	7-27-98	3	4	4.07	41	9	0	95	98	47	43	12	30	67	.267	.323	.436	16.6	7.4	404
De Los Santos, Enyel	R-R	6-3	235	12-25-95	5	2	3.29	70	0	0	66	50	26	24	4	25	62	.216	.302	.332	23.7	9.5	262
Fry, David	R-R	6-0	215	11-20-95	0	0	12.60	2	0	0	5	10	7	7	3	1	0	.400	.423	.800	0.0	3.8	26
Gaddis, Hunter	R-R	6-6	260	4-09-98	2	1	4.50	11	7	0	42	41	21	21	6	14	24	.255	.324	.447	13.2	7.7	182
Giolito, Lucas	R-R	6-6	245	7-14-94	1	4	7.04	6	6	0	31	30	27	24	11	16	39	.248	.333	.595	28.3	11.6	138
Hentges, Sam	L-L	6-6	245	7-18-96	3	2	3.61	56	0	0	52	53	24	21	2	18	56	.260	.318	.338	25.1	8.1	223
Herrin, Tim	L-L	6-6	230	10-08-96	1	1	5.53	23	0	0	28	29	18	17	3	12	32	.279	.361	.404	26.4	9.9	121
Karinchak, James	R-R	6-3	215	9-22-95	2	5	3.23	44	0	0	39	24	18	14	6	28	52	.178	.322	.356	30.4	16.4	171
Kelly, Michael	R-R	6-4	185	9-06-92	1	0	3.78	14	0	0	17	13	8	7	0	9	16	.210	.310	.258	22.5	12.7	71
Lopez, Reynaldo	R-R	6-1	225	1-04-94	1	0	0.00	12	0	0	11	5	0	0	0	4	12	.143	.231	.143	30.0	10.0	40
McKenzie, Triston	R-R	6-5	165	8-02-97	0	3	5.06	4	4	0	16	12	9	9	1	13	16	.200	.342	.350	21.9	17.8	73
Moore, Matt	L-L	6-3	210	6-18-89	0	0	3.86	5	0	0	5	9	2	2	1	2	8	.391	.440	.565	32.0	8.0	25
Morgan, Eli	R-R	5-10	190	5-13-96	5	2	4.01	61	0	1	67	73	37	30	9	24	75	.267	.328	.414	25.1	8.0	299
Morris, Cody	R-R	6-4	205	11-04-96	0	0	6.75	6	0	0	8	10	6	6	3	6	9	.313	.421	.719	23.7	15.8	38
Norris, Daniel	L-L	6-2	207	4-25-93	0	0	5.68	7	0	0	13	10	11	8	3	12	11	.204	.365	.408	17.5	19.0	63
Pilkington, Konnor	L-L	6-3	240	9-12-97	0	0	0.00	1	0	0	2	1	0	0	0	1	2	.143	.250	.143	25.0	12.5	8
Plesac, Zach	R-R	6-3	220	1-21-95	1	1	7.59	5	5	0	21	37	20	18	3	5	14	.374	.404	.576	13.3	4.8	105
Quantrill, Cal	L-R	6-3	195	2-10-95	4	7	5.24	19	19	0	100	111	59	58	11	35	58	.279	.345	.437	13.1	7.9	444
Sandlin, Nick	R-R	5-11	175	1-10-97	5	5	3.75	61	0	0	60	38	28	25	12	24	66	.182	.270	.388	27.6	10.0	239

Stephan, Trevor	R-R	6-5	225	11-25-95	7	7	4.06	71	0	2	69	63	35	31	6	26	75	.245	.323	.389	25.5	8.8	294
Syndergaard, Noah	L-R	6-6	242	8-29-92	1	2	5.40	6	6	0	33	33	21	20	10	10	18	.252	.324	.519	12.4	6.9	145
Toussaint, Touki	R-R	6-3	215	6-20-96	0	1	4.91	1	1	0	4	3	2	2	0	5	2	.250	.444	.333	10.5	26.3	19
Williams, Gavin	L-R	6-6	250	7-26-99	3	5	3.29	16	16	0	82	66	32	30	8	37	81	.219	.310	.368	23.5	10.7	345

Fielding

Catcher	PCT	G	PO	A	E	DP	PB
Collins	1.000	2	14	2	0	0	0
Fry	.990	28	99	5	1	1	2
Gallagher	.993	56	418	19	3	1	2
Haase	1.000	3	24	0	0	0	0
Naylor	.992	67	486	22	4	2	5
Viloria	1.000	10	21	1	0	0	1
Zunino	.990	42	276	17	3	2	5

First Base	PCT	G	PO	A	E	DP
Arias	1.000	35	134	8	0	6
Bell	.990	30	185	21	2	15
Calhoun	1.000	25	164	11	0	19
Freeman	1.000	1	1	0	0	0
Fry	1.000	19	62	3	0	9
Naylor	.995	91	680	50	4	59

Second Base	PCT	G	PO	A	E	DP
Arias	1.000	1	1	3	0	1
Freeman	.981	17	22	31	1	5
Gimenez	.991	150	259	401	6	87
Tena	.889	3	4	4	1	1

Third Base	PCT	G	PO	A	E	DP
Arias	.920	14	8	15	2	1
Freeman	.960	25	14	34	2	4
Fry	1.000	1	0	1	0	0
Ramirez	.956	125	84	220	14	15
Rocchio	.846	6	5	6	2	0
Tena	.000	3	0	0	0	0

Shortstop	PCT	G	PO	A	E	DP
Arias	.988	53	54	106	2	31
Freeman	.962	11	7	18	1	3
Rocchio	.967	18	21	37	2	9
Rosario	.964	88	87	205	11	33
Tena	.950	10	9	10	1	2

Outfield	PCT	G	PO	A	E	DP
Arias	.943	19	31	2	2	0
Brennan	.969	128	242	9	3	3
Calhoun	1.000	3	7	0	0	0
Freeman	1.000	1	1	0	0	0
Fry	.909	9	16	0	2	0
Gonzalez	1.000	32	57	0	0	0
Kwan	.989	153	344	10	4	2
Laureano	.975	44	76	3	2	1
Naylor	1.000	1	1	0	0	0
Straw	1.000	145	337	6	0	2

COLUMBUS CLIPPERS — *TRIPLE-A*

INTERNATIONAL LEAGUE

Batting	B-T	Ht.	Wt.	DOB	AVG	OBP	SLG	G	PA	AB	R	H	2B	3B	HR	RBI	BB	HBP	SH	SF	SO	SB	CS	BB%	SO%
Brito, Juan	B-R	5-11	162	9-24-01	.214	.450	.286	5	20	14	1	3	1	0	0	1	6	0	0	0	4	1	0	30.0	20.0
Collins, Zack	L-R	6-3	220	2-06-95	.251	.358	.434	116	495	419	66	105	29	0	16	76	70	2	0	4	159	4	1	14.1	32.1
Delgado, Raynel	L-R	6-1	200	4-04-00	.254	.344	.370	104	393	343	56	87	15	2	7	33	47	1	1	1	88	14	7	12.0	22.4
Donovan, Joe	R-R	5-9	180	1-20-99	.400	.400	.400	1	5	5	1	2	0	0	0	0	0	0	0	0	3	0	0	0.0	60.0
Freeman, Tyler	R-R	6-0	190	5-21-99	.319	.457	.462	24	116	91	24	29	5	1	2	17	15	9	0	1	16	10	0	12.9	13.8
Fry, David	R-R	6-0	215	11-20-95	.317	.402	.545	29	117	101	18	32	9	1	4	19	11	4	0	1	21	2	0	9.4	17.9
Gonzalez, Marcos	R-R	5-11	190	10-12-99	.140	.254	.180	18	59	50	6	7	2	0	0	7	4	4	0	1	15	0	0	6.8	25.4
Gonzalez, Oscar	R-R	6-4	240	1-10-98	.287	.323	.496	83	362	335	49	96	23	4	13	64	19	2	0	6	83	2	0	5.2	22.9
Haase, Eric	R-R	5-10	210	12-18-92	.154	.233	.269	8	30	26	1	4	0	0	1	2	3	0	0	1	8	0	0	10.0	26.7
Lavastida, Bryan	R-R	6-0	200	11-27-98	.233	.310	.407	52	218	189	32	44	9	0	8	37	22	1	2	4	47	7	1	10.1	21.6
Leon, Sandy	B-R	5-10	235	3-13-89	.220	.361	.400	16	61	50	6	11	3	0	2	4	10	1	0	0	11	0	0	16.4	18.0
Manzardo, Kyle	L-R	6-0	205	7-18-00	.256	.348	.590	21	92	78	16	20	8	0	6	16	12	0	0	2	14	0	0	13.0	15.2
2-team (73 Durham)					.242	.348	.475	94	405	343	49	83	27	1	17	54	54	2	0	6	79	1	1	13.3	19.5
Martinez, Angel	B-R	6-0	200	1-27-02	.268	.320	.401	37	154	142	17	38	8	1	3	19	10	1	1	0	36	1	0	6.5	23.4
Naylor, Bo	L-R	6-0	205	2-21-00	.253	.393	.498	60	270	217	45	55	12	1	13	48	49	2	0	2	52	2	2	18.1	19.3
Noel, Jhonkensy	R-R	6-3	250	7-15-01	.220	.303	.420	138	585	519	81	114	23	0	27	85	49	14	0	3	145	1	3	8.4	24.8
Palacios, Richie	L-R	5-10	180	5-16-97	.217	.351	.318	56	269	217	42	47	13	0	3	30	41	6	1	4	41	6	4	15.2	15.2
2-team (40 Memphis)					.251	.383	.377	96	464	374	76	94	23	0	8	59	73	8	2	7	61	9	6	15.7	13.1
Pries, Micah	L-R	6-3	210	2-27-98	.232	.328	.424	115	464	401	64	93	27	4	14	43	47	12	0	4	101	3	4	10.1	21.8
Quinn, Roman	B-R	5-10	175	5-14-93	.176	.391	.235	15	48	34	8	6	2	0	0	6	10	2	2	0	19	2	0	20.8	39.6
2-team (10 Nashville)					.149	.326	.194	25	89	67	13	10	3	0	0	9	16	3	3	0	30	7	0	18.0	33.7
Rocchio, Brayan	B-R	5-10	170	1-13-01	.280	.367	.421	116	537	468	81	131	33	6	7	65	60	6	0	3	66	25	7	11.2	12.3
Rodriguez, Eric	R-R	6-0	195	7-28-98	.263	.318	.316	9	22	19	0	5	1	0	0	1	2	0	0	1	4	0	0	9.1	18.2
Rodriguez, Johnathan	R-R	6-3	224	11-04-99	.280	.376	.560	47	202	175	32	49	12	2	11	33	25	2	0	0	66	0	0	12.4	32.7
Roller, Chris	R-R	5-11	190	10-08-96	.222	.373	.412	92	327	257	46	57	13	0	12	47	55	10	0	5	94	13	4	16.8	28.7
2-team (16 Nashville)					.247	.399	.449	108	396	312	55	77	16	1	15	67	68	11	0	5	109	19	6	17.2	27.5
Schneemann, Daniel	L-R	6-0	185	1-23-97	.267	.360	.437	114	484	419	67	112	30	1	13	60	59	3	1	2	100	17	3	12.2	20.7
Tena, Jose	L-R	5-11	195	3-20-01	.350	.394	.667	15	66	60	9	21	5	1	4	11	4	1	0	1	17	0	1	6.1	25.8
Valera, George	L-L	6-0	195	11-13-00	.211	.343	.375	73	312	256	40	54	10	1	10	35	50	3	0	3	85	1	2	16.0	27.2

Pitching	B-T	Ht.	Wt.	DOB	W	L	ERA	G	GS	SV	IP	Hits	Runs	ER	HR	BB	SO	AVG	OBP	SLG	SO%	BB%	BF
Allen, Logan	R-L	6-0	190	9-05-98	0	0	3.10	5	5	0	20	16	7	7	1	9	26	.213	.291	.307	30.2	10.5	86
Arias, Jaime	R-L	6-0	210	1-21-99	0	0	6.14	2	1	0	7	4	5	5	2	1	3	.154	.185	.385	11.1	3.7	27
Baragar, Caleb	R-L	6-3	215	4-09-94	2	1	6.54	23	0	2	32	27	24	23	6	27	41	.227	.367	.437	27.9	18.4	147
Battenfield, Peyton	R-R	6-4	224	8-10-97	0	5	5.66	9	9	0	48	45	31	30	13	21	24	.249	.333	.514	11.8	10.3	204
Bibee, Tanner	R-R	6-2	205	3-05-99	2	0	1.76	3	3	0	15	8	3	3	0	8	19	.151	.262	.170	31.1	13.1	61
Bieber, Shane	R-R	6-3	200	5-31-95	0	0	0.00	1	1	0	4	0	0	0	0	3	7	.000	.214	.000	50.0	21.4	14
Bilous, Jason	R-R	6-2	185	8-11-97	3	2	5.92	38	2	1	49	53	35	32	7	53	56	.282	.447	.484	22.8	21.5	246
Caddell, Seth	R-R	5-9	190	5-29-99	0	0	0.00	2	0	0	1	0	0	0	0	0	0	.000	.000	.000	0.0	0.0	4
Cantillo, Joey	L-L	6-4	225	12-18-99	6	4	4.64	20	18	0	95	89	50	49	16	55	111	.245	.349	.421	26.1	12.9	425
Civale, Aaron	R-R	6-2	215	6-12-95	0	0	4.91	3	3	0	11	13	6	6	2	4	16	.302	.362	.535	34.0	8.5	47
Collins, Zack	L-R	6-3	220	2-06-95	0	0	36.00	1	0	0	1	6	4	4	1	0	0	.667	.667	1.222	0.0	0.0	9
Daniels, Brett	R-R	6-0	208	2-25-96	0	3	7.80	14	1	0	15	18	16	13	3	19	13	.310	.468	.517	16.5	24.1	79
Diehl, Phillip	L-L	6-2	169	7-16-94	3	1	6.89	24	0	0	33	29	30	25	6	20	35	.230	.338	.421	23.6	13.5	148
Eickhoff, Jerad	R-R	6-4	246	7-02-90	1	7	6.92	14	13	0	68	83	53	52	14	32	41	.305	.383	.522	13.1	10.2	313
Enright, Nic	R-R	6-3	205	1-08-97	5	2	5.45	25	0	1	35	35	23	21	9	17	38	.267	.349	.534	25.0	11.2	152
Gaddis, Hunter	R-R	6-6	260	4-09-98	2	10	6.05	20	15	0	74	82	55	50	18	33	65	.276	.359	.532	19.2	9.8	338
Garrett, Amir	R-L	6-5	239	5-03-92	1	1	5.79	5	0	0	5	3	4	3	2	4	4	.188	.333	.563	19.0	19.0	21
Hentges, Sam	L-L	6-6	245	7-18-96	0	0	3.38	3	0	0	3	2	1	1	0	1	2	.200	.273	.300	18.2	9.1	11

Pitching	B-T	Ht.	Wt.	DOB	W	L	ERA	G	GS	SV	IP	Hits	Runs	ER	HR	BB	SO	AVG	OBP	SLG	SO%	BB%	BF
Herrin, Tim	L-L	6-6	230	10-08-96	7	2	3.38	33	0	3	37	21	14	14	3	20	43	.164	.275	.273	28.9	13.4	149
Karinchak, James	R-R	6-3	215	9-22-95	0	0	4.24	24	0	5	23	14	12	11	1	13	42	.175	.281	.325	43.8	13.5	96
Kelly, Michael	R-R	6-4	185	9-06-92	1	3	3.58	32	0	2	38	38	16	15	3	22	58	.262	.363	.400	33.7	12.8	172
Labaut, Randy	L-L	6-2	205	10-01-96	0	2	6.46	16	1	1	24	20	18	17	3	21	14	.233	.385	.372	12.8	19.3	109
Marman, Kyle	R-R	6-3	195	3-03-97	1	0	4.91	4	0	0	4	7	2	2	0	5	5	.467	.591	.467	21.7	21.7	23
McKenzie, Triston	R-R	6-5	165	8-02-97	0	1	5.14	4	4	0	14	12	8	8	5	5	15	.235	.304	.529	26.8	8.9	56
Morris, Cody	R-R	6-4	205	11-04-96	2	1	3.74	18	1	0	34	20	14	14	5	25	40	.171	.326	.308	27.8	17.4	144
Norris, Daniel	L-L	6-2	207	4-25-93	4	5	5.45	22	16	0	68	78	46	41	13	29	62	.291	.364	.507	20.3	9.5	306
Oviedo, Luis	R-R	6-5	250	5-15-99	4	0	4.82	42	0	1	62	53	36	33	4	40	60	.230	.365	.361	21.0	14.0	286
Pilkington, Konnor	L-L	6-3	240	9-12-97	0	2	8.36	4	4	0	14	19	14	13	3	11	14	.339	.456	.625	20.3	15.9	69
Plesac, Zach	R-R	6-3	220	1-21-95	5	6	6.08	19	18	0	95	98	64	64	30	42	71	.268	.345	.584	17.4	10.3	409
Ponticelli, Thomas	R-R	6-1	205	4-15-97	2	7	4.64	44	5	2	64	71	40	33	8	32	57	.281	.369	.470	19.5	10.9	293
Quantrill, Cal	L-R	6-3	195	2-10-95	1	2	9.00	3	3	0	14	17	14	14	3	7	10	.298	.379	.509	15.2	10.6	66
Romero, Jhon	R-R	5-10	195	1-17-95	3	3	4.28	34	1	1	48	42	24	23	5	27	56	.240	.357	.400	27.1	13.0	207
Scott, Adam	L-L	6-4	230	10-10-95	0	1	5.83	23	10	0	46	47	36	30	3	46	45	.263	.446	.380	18.8	19.2	240
Simpson, Caleb	R-R	6-4	231	9-15-91	1	0	7.71	11	1	0	12	11	10	10	3	19	8	.275	.517	.550	13.3	31.7	60
Smith, Cade	R-R	6-5	230	5-09-99	4	3	4.65	30	0	2	41	37	22	21	6	19	66	.236	.326	.414	37.1	10.7	178
Smith, Riley	R-R	6-1	207	1-15-95	0	1	19.80	2	1	0	5	12	13	11	1	12	2	.480	.649	.760	5.4	32.4	37
Toussaint, Touki	R-R	6-3	215	6-20-96	2	1	4.06	20	1	3	38	27	19	17	3	23	48	.206	.333	.344	30.2	14.5	159
Vallimont, Chris	R-R	6-5	240	3-18-97	2	1	6.52	16	1	0	29	31	21	21	6	16	22	.277	.379	.509	16.7	12.1	132
Williams, Gavin	L-R	6-6	250	7-26-99	3	2	2.93	9	9	0	46	29	16	15	6	21	61	.186	.286	.327	33.3	11.5	183
Zapata, Juan	R-R	6-1	198	11-19-98	1	0	4.15	2	0	0	4	1	2	2	0	5	2	.091	.353	.273	11.1	27.8	18

Fielding

Catcher	PCT	G	PO	A	E	DP	PB
Collins	.982	35	308	18	6	4	2
Fry	1.000	2	9	0	0	0	1
Haase	1.000	8	80	7	0	0	0
Lavastida	.987	46	379	15	5	2	2
Leon	.989	10	87	4	1	1	0
Naylor	.987	44	431	24	6	3	3
Rodriguez	.970	5	30	2	1	0	1

First Base	PCT	G	PO	A	E	DP
Collins	.989	13	93	1	1	13
Fry	1.000	8	34	1	0	5
Gonzalez	1.000	2	6	0	0	0
Manzardo	1.000	19	146	17	0	11
Noel	1.000	28	171	18	0	19
Pries	.987	93	563	44	8	66

Second Base	PCT	G	PO	A	E	DP
Brito	.929	5	4	9	1	0
Delgado	.980	82	181	211	8	58
Freeman	.983	13	21	38	1	12
Fry	1.000	1	1	1	0	1
Gonzalez	.952	9	9	11	1	0
Martinez	1.000	12	24	27	0	7
Rocchio	.975	11	18	21	1	6
Schneemann	.981	15	22	31	1	12
Tena	1.000	2	3	3	0	1

Third Base	PCT	G	PO	A	E	DP
Delgado	1.000	19	12	23	0	3
Freeman	1.000	4	1	5	0	1
Fry	.980	23	16	33	1	6
Martinez	1.000	18	8	37	0	3
Noel	.974	20	14	24	1	8
Pries	1.000	1	1	0	0	0
Rocchio	1.000	5	0	5	0	1
Schneemann	.968	66	36	113	5	13
Tena	.750	2	2	1	1	1

Shortstop	PCT	G	PO	A	E	DP
Freeman	.955	7	9	12	1	3
Martinez	1.000	5	4	5	0	1
Rocchio	.971	98	126	237	11	50
Schneemann	.978	30	33	57	2	14
Tena	.900	9	13	32	5	6

Outfield	PCT	G	PO	A	E	DP
Donovan	.000	1	0	0	2	0
Gonzalez	.982	79	123	9	2	0
Noel	1.000	85	126	15	0	3
Palacios	.931	59	104	2	5	1
Pries	1.000	23	37	2	0	1
Quinn	1.000	13	22	1	0	1
Rodriguez	.966	42	78	6	3	1
Roller	.995	90	214	8	3	2
Schneemann	1.000	3	5	0	0	0
Valera	.966	73	147	7	3	3

AKRON RUBBERDUCKS — *DOUBLE-A*

EASTERN LEAGUE

Batting	B-T	Ht.	Wt.	DOB	AVG	OBP	SLG	G	PA	AB	R	H	2B	3B	HR	RBI	BB	HBP	SH	SF	SO	SB	CS	BB%	SO%
Amditis, Michael	R-R	5-10	205	8-14-97	.122	.235	.203	24	85	74	6	9	0	0	2	10	11	0	0	0	34	0	0	12.9	40.0
Ball, Bryce	L-R	6-4	240	7-08-98	.224	.305	.436	43	174	156	22	35	9	0	8	22	18	0	0	0	46	0	0	10.3	26.4
Berglund, Michael	L-R	6-1	195	7-18-97	.161	.309	.284	52	188	155	15	25	4	0	5	21	26	7	0	0	65	1	0	13.8	34.6
Bracho, Aaron	B-R	5-9	193	4-24-01	.245	.340	.441	104	424	367	50	90	14	2	18	59	49	5	0	3	97	3	2	11.6	22.9
Brito, Juan	B-R	5-11	162	9-24-01	.276	.373	.444	87	374	315	46	87	21	1	10	60	48	4	1	6	63	3	7	12.8	16.8
Caddell, Seth	R-R	5-9	190	5-29-99	.333	.333	.333	2	3	3	0	1	0	0	0	1	0	0	0	0	2	0	0	0.0	66.7
DeLauter, Chase	L-L	6-4	235	10-08-01	.364	.464	.409	6	28	22	3	8	1	0	0	4	5	0	0	1	3	0	0	17.9	10.7
Delgado, Raynel	L-R	6-1	200	4-04-00	.148	.207	.296	7	29	27	1	4	1	0	1	2	2	0	0	0	9	1	0	6.9	31.0
Donovan, Joe	R-R	5-9	180	1-20-99	.289	.304	.400	13	46	45	6	13	3	1	0	5	1	0	0	0	13	0	0	2.2	28.3
Escobedo, Julian	L-L	6-0	190	6-10-98	.220	.313	.381	33	135	118	19	26	10	0	3	10	12	4	1	0	36	6	1	8.9	26.7
Gonzalez, Marcos	R-R	5-11	190	10-12-99	.500	.556	.688	5	19	16	2	8	3	0	0	1	2	0	1	0	0	0	0	10.5	0.0
Halpin, Petey	L-R	6-0	200	5-26-02	.243	.312	.372	113	510	452	55	110	23	4	9	38	47	2	1	8	126	12	2	9.2	24.7
Holland, Korey	R-R	5-10	170	1-01-00	.237	.329	.399	80	326	283	35	67	17	4	7	39	37	3	1	2	105	12	3	11.3	32.2
Idrogo, Cesar	B-R	5-11	170	3-26-01	.243	.312	.314	20	77	70	7	17	5	0	0	1	7	0	0	0	16	2	1	9.1	20.8
Kokx, Connor	R-R	6-1	195	2-24-00	.228	.347	.311	104	390	325	52	74	18	0	3	22	47	14	1	3	88	29	5	12.1	22.6
Lavastida, Bryan	R-R	6-0	200	11-27-98	.246	.367	.350	56	247	203	31	50	9	0	4	33	34	6	0	2	38	9	4	13.8	15.4
Martinez, Angel	B-R	6-0	200	1-27-02	.245	.321	.392	99	437	383	55	94	15	4	11	60	37	8	4	5	83	10	3	8.5	19.0
Naranjo, Joe	L-L	5-10	205	5-11-01	.201	.321	.278	89	343	288	29	58	13	0	3	29	45	7	0	3	84	0	0	13.1	24.5
Naylor, Josh	L-L	5-11	250	6-22-97	.444	.444	.444	3	9	9	1	4	0	0	0	2	0	0	0	0	0	0	0	0.0	0.0
Planez, Alexfri	R-R	6-2	180	8-17-01	.261	.320	.348	7	25	23	4	6	2	0	0	1	1	1	0	0	8	0	0	4.0	32.0
Ramirez, Micael	R-R	5-9	170	6-08-99	.184	.288	.219	34	132	114	15	21	4	0	0	3	15	2	0	1	20	0	0	11.4	15.2
Rodriguez, Gabriel	R-R	6-3	215	2-22-02	.192	.312	.288	78	300	250	36	48	8	2	4	23	38	7	2	3	88	2	1	12.7	29.3
Rodriguez, Johnathan	R-R	6-3	224	11-04-99	.289	.364	.512	88	363	322	42	93	14	2	18	55	34	5	0	2	97	3	2	9.4	26.7
Tena, Jose	L-R	5-11	195	3-20-01	.260	.353	.370	81	362	308	44	80	20	1	4	37	41	6	2	5	104	16	7	11.3	28.7
Tolentino, Milan	L-R	6-1	185	11-17-01	.207	.306	.241	32	134	116	15	24	4	0	0	6	15	2	0	1	36	2	0	11.2	26.9

Pitching	B-T	Ht.	Wt.	DOB	W	L	ERA	G	GS	SV	IP	Hits	Runs	ER	HR	BB	SO	AVG	OBP	SLG	SO%	BB%	BF
Aleman, Franco	R-R	6-6	235	6-26-00	2	2	0.00	19	0	7	24	9	5	0	0	5	38	.111	.182	.123	42.2	5.6	90

Arias, Jaime	R-L	6-0	210	1-21-99	0	2	6.46	6	5	0	24	27	19	17	4	14	24	.284	.378	.484	21.6	12.6	111
Battenfield, Peyton	R-R	6-4	224	8-10-97	0	0	1.17	2	2	0	8	4	1	1	0	4	5	.160	.276	.200	17.2	13.8	29
Benton, Trey	R-R	6-4	215	6-18-98	1	4	3.83	42	0	0	47	50	33	20	5	30	65	.267	.374	.401	29.4	13.6	221
Bieber, Shane	R-R	6-3	200	5-31-95	0	0	2.45	1	1	0	4	0	2	1	0	1	4	.000	.200	.000	26.7	6.7	15
Burns, Tanner	R-R	6-0	210	12-28-98	5	3	3.01	29	14	1	87	68	31	29	11	41	86	.217	.315	.350	23.9	11.4	360
Caddell, Seth	R-R	5-9	190	5-29-99	0	0	0.00	1	0	0	1	0	0	0	0	0	0	.000	.000	.000	0.0	0.0	2
Cantillo, Joey	L-L	6-4	225	12-18-99	1	0	1.85	6	6	0	24	14	7	5	2	14	35	.175	.309	.300	36.1	14.4	97
Carver, Ross	R-R	6-2	205	8-27-99	1	5	6.15	19	15	0	72	68	52	49	9	34	81	.248	.339	.420	25.2	10.6	322
Daniels, Brett	R-R	6-0	208	2-25-96	1	1	3.86	2	0	0	2	0	1	1	0	3	2	.000	.400	.000	20.0	30.0	10
Dion, Will	L-L	5-10	180	4-17-00	3	4	2.60	17	15	0	83	67	27	24	6	25	88	.223	.285	.327	26.7	7.6	329
Hanner, Bradley	R-R	6-4	210	2-10-99	8	6	2.78	41	0	8	65	48	24	20	6	34	70	.207	.337	.297	25.0	12.1	280
Hart, Zach	R-R	6-4	235	5-17-97	1	1	5.58	17	1	0	31	32	21	19	6	17	30	.262	.367	.475	20.1	11.4	149
Hentges, Sam	L-L	6-6	245	7-18-96	0	0	0.00	2	0	0	2	3	0	0	0	1	2	.333	.400	.333	20.0	10.0	10
Hickman, Mason	R-R	6-6	228	12-23-98	4	4	3.95	35	0	0	55	46	27	24	9	32	71	.230	.339	.425	30.3	13.7	234
Jones, Jordan	R-R	6-1	210	10-02-97	2	3	2.00	37	0	1	63	33	24	14	7	42	63	.159	.306	.308	24.3	16.2	259
Kelly, Michael	R-R	6-4	185	9-06-92	0	0	0.00	2	0	0	2	1	0	0	0	0	3	.143	.143	.143	42.9	0.0	7
Labaut, Randy	L-L	6-2	205	10-01-96	3	0	1.82	17	0	1	35	23	8	7	2	14	37	.187	.268	.285	26.8	10.1	138
Leftwich, Jack	R-R	6-4	220	9-26-98	6	7	5.19	23	14	0	78	71	48	45	12	25	70	.243	.301	.418	21.5	7.7	326
Mace, Tommy	R-R	6-6	230	11-11-98	4	5	5.49	14	9	1	61	69	40	37	9	36	51	.288	.387	.463	18.3	12.9	279
McCarthy, Shane	R-R	6-2	215	7-29-96	1	1	6.38	9	0	0	18	21	15	13	6	8	15	.280	.345	.573	17.6	9.4	85
McKenzie, Triston	R-R	6-5	165	8-02-97	0	0	3.00	1	1	0	3	1	1	1	0	1	4	.111	.200	.111	36.4	9.1	11
Morris, Cody	R-R	6-4	205	11-04-96	0	0	0.00	3	3	0	5	2	1	0	0	2	5	.125	.250	.125	25.0	10.0	20
Nikhazy, Doug	L-L	6-0	210	8-11-99	4	8	4.94	26	22	0	102	92	65	56	13	73	128	.235	.357	.409	27.0	15.4	474
Quantrill, Cal	L-R	6-3	195	2-10-95	1	0	1.04	2	2	0	9	7	1	1	1	2	7	.226	.294	.323	20.6	5.9	34
Sabrowski, Erik	R-L	6-4	235	10-31-97	4	0	2.49	20	0	0	22	13	6	6	1	18	28	.176	.337	.257	30.4	19.6	92
Sharpe, Davis	R-R	6-4	215	1-30-00	7	5	4.30	41	0	3	61	67	38	29	8	16	64	.276	.332	.457	23.8	5.9	269
Smith, Cade	R-R	6-5	230	5-09-99	1	0	2.86	17	0	13	22	17	9	7	1	9	29	.213	.308	.263	31.5	9.8	92
Stanley, Hunter	R-R	5-11	203	11-25-97	4	11	4.92	26	24	0	119	116	76	65	16	49	108	.248	.318	.418	20.7	9.4	523
Thornton, Tyler	L-R	6-3	200	7-08-00	0	0	2.20	11	0	0	16	8	4	4	2	10	18	.154	.333	.308	27.3	15.2	66
Turner, Matt	L-L	6-4	180	8-04-99	0	1	4.15	14	0	0	30	27	16	14	1	18	26	.243	.358	.306	19.3	13.3	135
Williams, Gavin	L-R	6-6	250	7-26-99	1	0	0.63	3	3	0	14	6	1	1	0	3	20	.120	.170	.160	37.7	5.7	53
Zapata, Juan	R-R	6-1	198	11-19-98	0	0	5.06	2	1	0	5	9	4	3	1	0	1	.360	.360	.600	4.0	0.0	25

Fielding

Catcher	PCT	G	PO	A	E	DP	PB
Amditis	.988	18	155	6	2	1	4
Berglund	.987	46	429	31	6	7	7
Donovan	.991	13	111	3	1	2	1
Lavastida	.974	38	365	15	10	2	4
Ramirez	.982	26	244	23	5	2	5

First Base	PCT	G	PO	A	E	DP
Ball	.974	20	107	7	3	12
Bracho	.983	28	159	14	3	17
Delgado	1.000	1	9	1	0	0
Gonzalez	1.000	2	13	1	0	1
Naranjo	.982	85	509	47	10	42
Naylor	1.000	3	8	0	0	0
Rodriguez	1.000	5	23	2	0	5

Second Base	PCT	G	PO	A	E	DP
Bracho	.991	37	41	71	1	18
Brito	.990	52	80	110	2	27
Delgado	.889	4	9	7	2	1
Martinez	.987	44	76	77	2	23
Rodriguez	1.000	2	3	2	0	0
Tolentino	1.000	1	0	2	0	0

Third Base	PCT	G	PO	A	E	DP
Bracho	.813	21	8	31	9	1
Brito	.944	27	21	46	4	5
Delgado	1.000	2	1	2	0	1
Gonzalez	.833	3	5	5	2	2
Martinez	1.000	20	18	30	0	4
Rodriguez	.919	69	53	94	13	10

Shortstop	PCT	G	PO	A	E	DP
Brito	.923	8	14	10	2	3
Martinez	.964	28	47	59	4	13
Tena	.942	73	95	133	14	34
Tolentino	.949	30	40	54	5	10

Outfield	PCT	G	PO	A	E	DP
DeLauter	1.000	6	11	0	0	0
Escobedo	.970	31	55	3	1	2
Halpin	.984	108	277	10	5	3
Holland	.980	72	135	5	2	1
Idrogo	.949	16	33	0	3	0
Kokx	.986	98	203	5	3	1
Planez	1.000	5	6	0	0	0
Rodriguez	.968	81	151	11	8	3

LAKE COUNTY CAPTAINS

HIGH CLASS A

MIDWEST LEAGUE

Batting	B-T	Ht.	Wt.	DOB	AVG	OBP	SLG	G	PA	AB	R	H	2B	3B	HR	RBI	BB	HBP	SH	SF	SO	SB	CS	BB%	SO%
Bartlett, Will	R-R	6-2	215	2-02-01	.160	.317	.242	79	303	244	33	39	8	0	4	30	55	2	0	2	97	3	1	18.2	32.0
Boyd, Justin	R-R	6-0	201	3-30-01	.140	.290	.200	15	62	50	8	7	0	0	1	5	10	1	0	1	19	1	0	16.1	30.6
Brito, Juan	B-R	5-11	162	9-24-01	.265	.379	.424	35	161	132	29	35	9	0	4	14	24	2	0	3	21	3	1	14.9	13.0
Burgos, Jorge	L-L	5-10	165	12-26-01	.238	.330	.356	94	370	323	40	77	15	1	7	46	42	3	0	2	84	0	3	11.4	22.7
Cairo, Christian	R-R	5-8	170	6-11-01	.239	.376	.351	61	229	188	32	45	6	3	3	13	39	2	0	0	44	10	5	17.0	19.2
DeLauter, Chase	L-L	6-4	235	10-08-01	.366	.403	.549	42	176	164	24	60	18	0	4	31	10	1	0	1	22	3	3	5.7	12.5
Donovan, Joe	R-R	5-9	180	1-20-99	.241	.320	.411	51	178	158	21	38	10	1	5	24	12	7	0	1	49	0	0	6.7	27.5
Fascia, Zac	L-R	6-0	225	9-15-98	.154	.200	.231	16	55	52	3	8	1	0	1	3	1	2	0	0	17	0	0	1.8	30.9
Fox, Jake	L-R	5-11	185	2-12-03	.256	.330	.398	101	453	402	61	103	23	5	8	53	45	1	0	4	103	9	5	9.9	22.7
Frias, Dayan	B-R	5-9	140	6-25-02	.260	.356	.426	100	397	338	43	88	19	2	11	49	51	2	1	5	83	8	3	12.8	20.9
Furman, Nate	L-R	5-8	180	7-23-01	.227	.340	.267	68	266	225	31	51	7	1	0	20	30	9	1	1	35	10	2	11.3	13.2
Greene, Isaiah	L-L	6-0	180	8-29-01	.180	.284	.279	55	211	183	17	33	7	1	3	19	27	0	0	1	74	10	2	12.8	35.1
Idrogo, Cesar	B-R	5-11	170	3-26-01	.238	.312	.321	29	93	84	14	20	1	0	2	6	8	1	0	0	19	2	1	8.6	20.4
Ingle, Cooper	L-R	5-10	185	2-23-02	.288	.464	.385	17	69	52	8	15	5	0	0	10	17	0	0	0	8	2	1	24.6	11.6
Lampe, Joe	L-R	5-11	185	12-05-00	.235	.336	.332	111	459	392	42	92	17	3	5	50	54	8	0	5	89	21	1	11.8	19.4
Paz, Richard	L-R	5-7	150	6-12-01	.000	.000	.000	1	1	1	0	0	0	0	0	0	0	0	0	0	0	0	0	0.0	0.0
Planchart, Victor	B-R	5-6	165	5-17-01	.236	.323	.319	44	164	144	17	34	9	0	1	14	18	1	0	1	36	2	1	11.0	22.0
Ramirez, Micael	R-R	5-9	170	6-08-99	.242	.319	.358	36	135	120	16	29	5	0	3	18	14	0	0	1	18	2	0	10.4	13.3
Sanquintin, Junior	B-R	6-0	172	1-08-02	.172	.231	.254	60	225	209	17	36	8	0	3	22	13	3	0	0	76	1	1	5.8	33.8
Tolentino, Milan	L-R	6-1	185	11-17-01	.260	.336	.406	67	289	254	38	66	16	3	5	25	29	2	0	4	77	12	0	10.0	26.6
Turner, Tyresse	B-R	5-10	170	1-05-00	.267	.371	.533	13	35	30	10	8	1	2	1	2	4	1	0	0	12	4	1	11.4	34.3
Valdes, Yordys	B-R	5-10	170	8-16-01	.236	.291	.325	79	317	292	32	69	15	1	3	30	19	4	1	1	82	16	2	6.0	25.9

Watson, Kahlil	L-R	5-10	178	4-16-03	.233	.306	.442	23	98	86	15	20	3	0	5	16	8	2	0	2	24	11	1	8.2	24.5
2-team (58 Beloit)					.214	.333	.386	81	341	285	41	61	13	0	12	38	43	8	0	5	92	25	3	12.6	27.0

Pitching	B-T	Ht.	Wt.	DOB	W	L	ERA	G	GS	SV	IP	Hits	Runs	ER	HR	BB	SO	AVG	OBP	SLG	SO%	BB%	BF
Abney, Alaska	R-R	6-1	205	5-05-00	1	1	5.77	36	0	1	53	49	37	34	6	28	57	.247	.355	.419	24.4	12.0	234
Aleman, Franco	R-R	6-6	235	6-26-00	2	2	5.52	20	0	2	31	35	26	19	4	13	46	.280	.355	.432	32.2	9.1	143
Arias, Jaime	R-L	6-0	210	1-21-99	1	0	4.70	4	0	0	8	5	4	4	3	1	8	.179	.207	.500	27.6	3.4	29
Boone, Rodney	L-L	6-1	195	4-09-00	6	4	4.95	18	17	0	80	82	47	44	14	32	90	.264	.331	.463	25.9	9.2	348
Davenport, Aaron	R-R	6-0	185	7-25-00	6	10	5.73	24	19	1	115	109	79	73	19	65	95	.251	.349	.472	18.6	12.7	510
Denholm, Trenton	R-R	5-11	180	11-29-99	3	3	3.16	23	6	3	77	70	32	27	4	18	67	.238	.283	.340	21.2	5.7	316
Dion, Will	L-L	5-10	180	4-17-00	3	0	1.87	9	4	0	34	24	9	7	1	10	41	.198	.263	.281	30.8	7.5	133
Ellerts, Magnus	R-R	6-5	225	3-15-01	1	1	5.94	16	0	3	17	12	14	11	3	13	29	.194	.333	.387	38.2	17.1	76
Hajjar, Steve	R-L	6-5	240	8-07-00	3	4	3.61	14	14	0	57	37	23	23	4	52	58	.182	.352	.286	22.6	20.2	257
Hankins, Ethan	R-R	6-6	200	5-23-00	1	7	4.70	15	15	0	46	38	26	24	3	26	50	.224	.332	.353	24.9	12.9	201
Jerez, Elvis	R-R	6-4	185	2-05-00	0	3	6.53	21	0	0	21	18	24	15	4	24	23	.228	.417	.418	21.1	22.0	109
Johnston, Reid	L-R	6-3	218	4-07-99	7	6	3.83	23	15	0	92	72	45	39	11	48	101	.216	.338	.357	25.4	12.1	398
Mace, Tommy	R-R	6-6	230	11-11-98	2	1	3.67	10	8	0	54	48	22	22	4	18	52	.239	.305	.368	23.2	8.0	224
Messick, Parker	L-L	6-0	225	10-26-00	2	4	4.43	13	11	0	65	62	35	32	10	25	75	.249	.344	.430	26.3	8.8	285
Miller, Jake	R-R	6-2	210	7-14-00	0	1	4.76	4	2	1	11	9	8	6	1	8	5	.209	.333	.349	9.8	15.7	51
Morillo, Sergio	R-R	6-3	190	9-13-99	3	4	7.21	33	0	0	49	41	43	39	8	43	53	.237	.391	.451	23.5	19.0	226
Ramirez, Micael	R-R	5-9	170	6-08-99	0	0	0.00	1	0	0	1	1	0	0	0	1	0	.250	.400	.250	0.0	20.0	5
Rapp, Shawn	R-L	6-2	200	7-03-00	0	1	2.63	21	0	2	27	19	8	8	3	8	36	.196	.277	.330	32.1	7.1	112
Thornton, Tyler	L-R	6-3	200	7-08-00	5	1	2.88	29	0	10	34	15	14	11	3	22	61	.130	.297	.226	41.8	15.1	146
Torres, Lenny	R-R	6-1	190	10-15-00	5	2	5.03	34	0	8	39	37	23	22	2	34	53	.247	.399	.320	27.9	17.9	190
Turner, Matt	L-L	6-4	180	8-04-99	0	0	17.18	3	0	1	4	8	7	7	1	2	5	.444	.476	.722	23.8	9.5	21
Webb, Ryan	L-L	6-1	202	4-19-99	3	4	3.29	17	17	0	82	68	33	30	5	34	83	.222	.309	.330	23.8	9.7	349
Wolf, Josh	R-R	6-3	170	9-01-00	6	3	5.52	23	0	0	44	41	28	27	4	36	46	.244	.389	.333	21.8	17.1	211
Zapata, Juan	R-R	6-1	198	11-19-98	5	2	4.28	20	1	0	55	59	27	26	11	10	48	.273	.312	.454	20.8	4.3	231

Fielding

Catcher	PCT	G	PO	A	E	DP	PB
Donovan	.987	43	350	22	5	2	7
Fascia	.992	15	128	3	1	0	0
Ingle	.983	12	107	7	2	0	0
Paz	1.000	1	1	0	0	0	0
Planchart	.969	28	266	13	9	1	6
Ramirez	.984	35	341	22	6	1	4

First Base	PCT	G	PO	A	E	DP
Bartlett	.996	75	456	30	2	41
Donovan	1.000	3	19	1	0	0
Frias	1.000	2	9	2	0	0
Planchart	1.000	1	5	0	0	0
Sanquintin	.984	51	290	19	5	30

Second Base	PCT	G	PO	A	E	DP
Brito	.983	18	22	35	1	7
Cairo	.960	13	17	31	2	5
Fox	1.000	1	3	3	0	0
Frias	1.000	6	11	14	0	3
Furman	.954	53	68	98	8	22
Tolentino	1.000	4	6	5	0	1
Turner	1.000	4	10	10	0	5
Valdes	.971	26	41	58	3	13
Watson	.967	8	18	11	1	6

Third Base	PCT	G	PO	A	E	DP
Brito	.875	4	4	3	1	0
Cairo	.914	29	20	33	5	2
Frias	.938	77	71	127	13	15
Furman	.923	11	6	6	1	1
Sanquintin	.000	1	0	0	0	0
Tolentino	1.000	2	0	4	0	0
Turner	.778	4	3	4	2	0
Valdes	.833	4	0	5	1	0

Shortstop	PCT	G	PO	A	E	DP
Brito	.921	10	15	20	3	2
Cairo	.875	6	3	4	1	1
Frias	.909	7	8	12	2	2
Tolentino	.969	53	67	91	5	16
Valdes	.955	44	55	94	7	17
Watson	.934	14	15	42	4	7

Outfield	PCT	G	PO	A	E	DP
Bartlett	1.000	3	4	0	0	0
Boyd	.974	13	25	3	1	0
Burgos	.987	79	131	5	4	1
Cairo	1.000	2	3	0	0	0
DeLauter	.983	37	82	1	2	0
Fox	.986	92	209	10	4	3
Greene	.986	46	72	1	2	1
Idrogo	.976	29	53	3	1	0
Lampe	.984	103	216	5	3	3

LYNCHBURG HILLCATS

LOW CLASS A

CAROLINA LEAGUE

Batting	B-T	Ht.	Wt.	DOB	AVG	OBP	SLG	G	PA	AB	R	H	2B	3B	HR	RBI	BB	HBP	SH	SF	SO	SB	CS	BB%	SO%
Antunez, Wuilfredo	L-R	6-0	150	5-16-02	.275	.354	.420	89	384	338	47	93	17	7	6	39	39	4	0	3	72	11	6	10.2	18.8
Benjamin, Juan	B-R	5-8	150	4-25-03	.271	.362	.346	98	413	358	53	97	16	1	3	44	49	3	1	2	81	24	10	11.9	19.6
Brown, Jordan	R-R	6-3	185	9-09-01	.181	.281	.333	47	167	144	17	26	5	1	5	14	16	5	0	2	57	2	3	9.6	34.1
Cavenaugh, Pres	L-L	6-0	206	10-31-00	.227	.353	.355	66	266	220	32	50	10	3	4	19	37	7	0	2	60	15	2	13.9	22.6
Chourio, Jaison	B-R	6-1	162	5-19-05	.200	.310	.229	9	42	35	7	7	1	0	0	3	6	0	0	1	15	1	0	14.3	35.7
Collado, Maick	B-R	5-11	160	12-24-02	.279	.367	.348	68	297	244	34	68	12	1	1	40	41	0	0	12	43	11	0	13.8	14.5
Devers, Jose	R-R	6-0	140	5-17-03	.252	.345	.398	111	458	397	65	100	15	5	11	66	48	10	0	3	92	34	11	10.5	20.1
Durango, Luis	L-L	5-10	135	4-08-03	.273	.365	.291	19	63	55	13	15	1	0	0	2	7	1	0	0	11	10	0	11.1	17.5
Fascia, Zac	L-R	6-0	225	9-15-98	.276	.378	.422	52	217	185	17	51	7	7	2	23	24	7	0	1	49	1	0	11.1	22.6
Filia, Marc	R-R	6-1	205	1-06-01	.159	.342	.303	68	257	195	41	31	6	2	6	24	45	12	0	5	75	6	1	17.5	29.2
Furman, Nate	L-R	5-8	180	7-23-01	.328	.486	.375	40	175	128	43	42	4	1	0	12	35	7	0	3	19	27	3	20.0	10.9
Genao, Angel	B-R	5-9	150	5-19-04	.263	.345	.385	72	316	278	44	73	20	1	4	32	34	2	0	2	49	6	3	10.8	15.5
Hernandez, Wilmer	R-R	5-11	165	9-10-02	.208	.321	.250	8	28	24	1	5	1	0	0	2	3	1	0	0	9	0	0	10.7	32.1
Kayfus, C.J.	L-L	6-0	188	10-28-01	.271	.429	.542	17	77	59	13	16	4	0	4	19	15	2	0	1	12	5	2	19.5	15.6
Lipscomb, Guy	L-R	6-2	195	3-11-01	.263	.386	.351	75	321	262	47	69	12	4	1	45	53	2	0	4	56	48	7	16.5	17.4
Lopez, Robert	L-R	5-10	150	1-02-04	.243	.319	.379	67	273	243	27	59	13	1	6	41	27	1	0	2	61	1	0	9.9	22.3
Mejias, Manuel	B-R	5-7	166	6-13-04	.172	.240	.216	30	129	116	7	20	5	0	0	22	10	1	0	2	27	0	0	7.8	20.9
Mooney, Alex	R-R	6-1	195	7-06-02	.152	.263	.212	17	76	66	8	10	4	0	0	4	7	3	0	0	13	4	0	9.2	17.1
Pastrano, Jose	B-R	5-9	145	9-12-02	.184	.305	.252	48	176	147	25	27	5	1	1	10	25	1	1	1	30	2	1	14.2	17.0
Saduy, Lexer	L-L	5-10	148	10-14-02	.221	.327	.323	80	309	263	31	58	14	2	3	35	34	9	0	3	90	14	5	11.0	29.1
Tincher, Johnny	R-R	5-8	170	8-25-01	.200	.333	.200	2	6	5	1	1	0	0	0	0	1	0	0	0	1	0	0	16.7	16.7
Tucker, Carson	R-R	6-2	180	1-24-02	.200	.296	.263	29	108	95	9	19	3	0	1	5	11	2	0	0	42	2	0	10.2	38.9

Batting	B-T	Ht.	Wt.	DOB	AVG	OBP	SLG	G	PA	AB	R	H	2B	3B	HR	RBI	BB	HBP	SH	SF	SO	SB	CS	BB%	SO%
Turner, Tyresse	B-R	5-10	170	1-05-00	.233	.343	.295	52	209	176	36	41	3	1	2	21	24	6	2	1	62	26	4	11.5	29.7
Zarate, Angel	L-L	5-11	190	7-16-99	.261	.355	.341	68	307	261	40	68	11	2	2	50	34	7	0	5	57	16	3	11.1	18.6

Pitching	B-T	Ht.	Wt.	DOB	W	L	ERA	G	GS	SV	IP	Hits	Runs	ER	HR	BB	SO	AVG	OBP	SLG	SO%	BB%	BF
Almonte, Luis	R-R	5-10	184	7-19-99	2	0	5.02	21	0	0	29	25	17	16	2	18	37	.227	.333	.382	28.7	14.0	129
Artiles, Reny	R-R	6-0	160	1-17-02	3	1	7.07	20	0	1	28	41	29	22	2	22	23	.333	.432	.463	15.5	14.9	148
Brito, Abel	R-R	6-1	175	3-04-01	0	3	7.59	10	10	0	32	28	29	27	1	27	27	.228	.389	.341	16.7	16.7	162
Brown, Jordan	R-R	6-3	185	9-09-01	0	1	0.00	1	0	0	0	1	1	0	0	0	0	1.000	1.000	1.000	0.0	0.0	1
Driver, Jay	R-R	6-3	195	2-25-02	0	0	9.82	7	0	1	7	12	9	8	2	11	11	.375	.535	.719	25.6	25.6	43
Ellerts, Magnus	R-R	6-5	225	3-15-01	0	1	2.22	16	0	5	24	19	8	6	1	4	38	.209	.242	.297	40.0	4.2	95
Gervacio, Yeury	L-L	6-1	168	7-01-99	5	2	3.00	20	0	2	36	17	15	12	2	17	40	.137	.257	.226	27.8	11.8	144
Gomez, Yorman	R-R	5-11	167	11-10-02	7	9	4.40	25	22	0	102	96	65	50	4	52	100	.244	.340	.340	21.7	11.3	461
Hernandez, Allan	R-R	6-5	225	1-19-01	1	1	3.18	5	0	0	6	4	2	2	2	2	6	.200	.273	.500	27.3	9.1	22
Humphries, Jackson	R-L	6-1	200	7-20-04	0	1	5.32	6	6	0	24	20	15	14	3	8	24	.225	.320	.360	23.3	7.8	103
Jachec, Matt	R-R	6-0	205	7-25-01	1	0	3.27	7	0	0	11	8	5	4	0	3	14	.186	.239	.186	29.8	6.4	47
Jacobs, Zach	R-R	6-1	170	9-09-01	10	4	4.43	29	3	3	91	89	51	45	4	29	94	.249	.316	.331	23.7	7.3	397
Jasiak, Jack	R-R	6-1	198	3-06-01	2	1	4.46	32	0	1	69	67	36	34	5	37	50	.259	.359	.386	16.3	12.1	307
Messick, Parker	L-L	6-0	225	10-26-00	3	2	3.02	13	13	0	57	48	23	19	1	14	61	.221	.281	.318	26.0	6.0	235
Morehouse, Zane	R-R	6-4	200	11-16-99	0	0	8.22	7	0	4	8	5	8	7	1	7	5	.179	.361	.357	13.9	19.4	36
Munoz, Braunny	R-R	6-1	170	8-20-00	6	1	4.59	21	5	2	69	69	43	35	6	16	59	.256	.295	.393	20.1	5.5	293
Peterson, Austin	R-R	6-6	234	9-19-99	6	8	4.54	24	24	0	117	133	68	59	12	27	102	.286	.331	.434	20.3	5.4	502
Rapp, Shawn	R-L	6-2	200	7-03-00	1	0	1.72	11	0	2	16	11	4	3	0	9	21	.193	.324	.211	30.9	13.2	68
Reyes, Tomas	L-L	5-11	150	9-23-99	1	2	2.53	26	0	10	32	19	10	9	3	14	30	.167	.273	.298	22.7	10.6	132
Richardson, Alonzo	R-R	5-11	165	10-07-02	6	7	4.79	26	24	0	124	129	71	66	10	52	73	.271	.341	.414	13.5	9.6	539
Tulloch, Adam	L-L	6-2	200	7-01-00	5	6	4.89	28	20	0	96	85	59	52	8	50	115	.240	.348	.342	27.4	11.9	419
Vasquez, Samuel	R-R	6-3	170	9-20-99	2	5	4.50	35	0	5	42	35	29	21	2	25	47	.219	.324	.344	25.0	13.3	188
Vasquez, Wardquelin	R-R	6-3	194	7-25-01	3	5	4.63	26	1	0	58	56	40	30	5	32	61	.247	.345	.379	22.8	12.0	267
Vinicio, Miguel	R-R	6-3	170	9-01-99	3	3	5.86	34	0	0	51	65	35	33	12	26	51	.311	.390	.560	21.2	10.8	241
Zapata, Juan	R-R	6-1	198	11-19-98	0	1	3.77	4	3	1	14	19	6	6	2	4	9	.317	.359	.517	14.1	6.3	64

Fielding

Catcher	PCT	G	PO	A	E	DP	PB
Fascia	.965	21	155	12	6	1	4
Filia	.978	16	123	11	3	0	3
Hernandez	.951	4	35	4	2	1	0
Lopez	.986	66	524	45	8	0	6
Mejias	.989	29	263	19	3	2	8
Tincher	1.000	1	8	2	0	0	0

First Base	PCT	G	PO	A	E	DP
Benjamin	1.000	3	13	1	0	1
Brown	.923	2	12	0	1	2
Collado	.993	55	405	20	3	25
Fascia	.984	18	116	5	2	3
Filia	.988	43	298	21	4	32
Hernandez	.925	4	36	1	3	5
Kayfus	.987	11	69	6	1	4

Second Base	PCT	G	PO	A	E	DP
Benjamin	.977	39	59	69	3	17
Furman	1.000	21	28	38	0	6
Genao	.857	5	5	7	2	0
Mooney	.929	3	8	5	1	1
Pastrano	.955	19	27	57	4	15
Tucker	.952	16	27	33	3	6
Turner	.959	33	46	71	5	8

Third Base	PCT	G	PO	A	E	DP
Benjamin	.872	34	16	52	10	1
Collado	.750	6	4	5	3	1
Devers	.979	22	18	29	1	3
Furman	.926	10	7	18	2	1
Genao	.928	30	16	48	5	2
Mooney	.895	5	6	11	2	1
Pastrano	.805	18	7	26	8	4
Tucker	.882	7	7	8	2	0
Turner	.778	4	1	6	2	0

Shortstop	PCT	G	PO	A	E	DP
Benjamin	.889	6	6	10	2	1
Devers	.961	82	140	184	13	35
Furman	.000	1	0	0	0	0
Genao	.893	30	37	63	12	10
Mooney	.909	8	6	14	2	1
Tucker	1.000	2	2	7	0	2
Turner	.923	5	5	7	1	1

Outfield	PCT	G	PO	A	E	DP
Antunez	.982	85	178	8	5	2
Brown	.952	39	54	3	4	0
Cavenaugh	.958	61	131	4	5	0
Chourio	1.000	8	15	1	0	0
Devers	1.000	1	1	0	0	0
Durango	1.000	18	38	1	0	0
Kayfus	.900	4	9	0	1	0
Lipscomb	.952	69	181	3	1	1
Saduy	.976	78	154	6	4	1
Zarate	.970	49	87	4	1	1

ACL GUARDIANS

ROOKIE

ARIZONA COMPLEX LEAGUE

Batting	B-T	Ht.	Wt.	DOB	AVG	OBP	SLG	G	PA	AB	R	H	2B	3B	HR	RBI	BB	HBP	SH	SF	SO	SB	CS	BB%	SO%
Advincula, Jonah	L-R	6-1	197	1-06-01	.250	.519	.563	6	27	16	6	4	1	2	0	4	9	1	0	1	1	3	0	33.3	3.7
Alduey, Fran	B-R	5-7	140	1-07-04	.264	.335	.429	37	158	140	29	37	19	2	0	19	15	1	0	2	38	21	5	9.5	24.1
Aranguren, Nelson	R-R	5-11	183	8-26-03	.236	.319	.370	32	144	127	16	30	7	2	2	27	11	5	0	1	41	0	0	7.6	28.5
Baez, Jose	B-R	5-9	146	8-30-02	.176	.263	.294	5	19	17	2	3	0	1	0	1	2	0	0	0	9	0	0	10.5	47.4
Cedeno, Jose	L-R	5-7	140	3-01-05	.241	.313	.310	8	32	29	4	7	0	1	0	8	2	1	0	0	7	0	0	6.3	21.9
Cedeno, Oscar	B-R	5-7	138	8-02-03	.222	.308	.358	23	91	81	13	18	3	1	2	7	6	4	0	0	18	2	3	6.6	19.8
Chourio, Jaison	B-R	6-1	162	5-19-05	.349	.476	.463	39	189	149	40	52	12	1	1	25	38	0	0	2	37	19	2	20.1	19.6
Clark, Logun	R-R	6-2	195	6-04-03	.200	.286	.292	23	77	65	9	13	3	0	1	14	6	3	0	3	26	2	1	7.8	33.8
DeLauter, Chase	L-L	6-4	235	10-08-01	.286	.447	.500	9	38	28	8	8	3	0	1	4	8	1	0	1	5	3	0	21.1	13.2
Durango, Luis	L-L	5-10	135	4-08-03	.571	.625	.786	4	16	14	6	8	1	1	0	2	2	0	0	0	3	8	1	12.5	18.8
Espinola, Christopher	L-L	5-7	165	9-19-03	.254	.383	.392	36	162	130	33	33	5	2	3	23	28	1	0	3	45	11	2	17.3	27.8
Gomez, Jose	L-L	5-9	142	2-05-05	.245	.314	.415	29	106	94	13	23	4	3	2	16	8	2	1	1	43	5	2	7.5	40.6
Gonzalez, Esteban	L-R	5-8	150	3-19-03	.300	.410	.569	36	156	130	51	39	9	4	6	26	17	8	0	1	38	21	0	10.9	24.4
Hawke, Tommy	L-R	5-6	160	7-07-02	.235	.381	.294	5	21	17	5	4	1	0	0	2	4	0	0	0	6	2	1	19.0	28.6
Hernandez, Wilmer	R-R	5-11	165	9-10-02	.227	.292	.227	9	24	22	2	5	0	0	0	2	1	1	0	0	7	0	1	4.2	29.2
Izturis, Victor	L-R	5-9	165	3-22-05	.264	.389	.306	33	149	121	16	32	2	0	1	18	24	2	0	2	27	0	0	16.1	18.1
Lopez, Miguel	B-R	5-6	135	8-20-04	.211	.268	.211	14	41	38	4	8	0	0	0	4	3	0	0	0	10	2	0	7.3	24.4
Manzardo, Kyle	L-R	6-0	205	7-18-00	.000	.100	.000	3	10	8	1	0	0	0	0	1	1	0	0	1	1	0	0	10.0	10.0
Mejias, Manuel	B-R	5-7	166	6-13-04	.250	.250	.250	1	4	4	0	1	0	0	0	1	0	0	0	0	0	0	0	0.0	0.0
Mendez, Alberto	L-R	5-9	146	11-29-04	.214	.393	.366	38	150	112	22	24	2	0	5	20	31	4	0	3	36	6	4	20.7	24.0
Mercedes, Jeffrey	B-R	5-8	146	10-02-04	.298	.346	.444	32	136	124	17	37	7	1	3	22	8	2	0	2	31	1	0	5.9	22.8

Parra, Samuel	L-L	5-10	155	5-07-03	.226	.344	.415	22	64	53	10	12	2	1	2	8	10	0	0	1	20	2	0	15.6	31.3
Paz, Richard	L-R	5-7	150	6-12-01	.136	.345	.136	7	29	22	6	3	0	0	0	1	6	1	0	0	8	0	0	20.7	27.6
Purroy, Emerson	B-R	5-9	146	2-25-04	.204	.371	.306	17	62	49	12	10	2	0	1	8	13	0	0	0	18	1	0	21.0	29.0
Ramirez, Rafael	L-R	6-0	159	7-22-05	.250	.453	.426	41	190	136	33	34	6	3	4	27	50	2	0	2	54	6	2	26.3	28.4
Riebock, Barrett	L-L	6-2	190	7-30-02	.357	.526	.643	4	19	14	1	5	0	2	0	3	5	0	0	0	2	1	0	26.3	10.5
Rivas, Kevin	B-R	5-7	128	4-07-03	1.000	1.000	4.000	1	2	1	2	1	0	0	1	1	1	0	0	0	0	1	0	50.0	0.0
Valera, George	L-L	6-0	195	11-13-00	.333	.423	.667	6	26	21	5	7	4	0	1	3	4	0	0	1	5	2	0	15.4	19.2
Velazquez, Ralphy	L-R	6-2	220	5-28-05	.348	.393	.739	6	28	23	7	8	3	0	2	8	3	0	0	2	5	1	0	10.7	17.9
Zarate, Angel	L-L	5-11	190	7-16-99	.320	.370	.520	6	27	25	4	8	3	1	0	5	1	1	0	0	6	0	0	3.7	22.2

Pitching	B-T	Ht.	Wt.	DOB	W	L	ERA	G	GS	SV	IP	Hits	Runs	ER	HR	BB	SO	AVG	OBP	SLG	SO%	BB%	BF
Aldeano, Austin	R-R	6-1	180	6-06-04	1	0	6.23	4	0	1	9	6	6	6	1	7	13	.188	.381	.281	31.0	16.7	42
Almanzar, Pedro	R-R	5-10	165	11-05-02	2	3	13.05	17	0	2	20	31	30	29	2	16	32	.360	.453	.535	30.2	15.1	106
Bresnahan, Jacob	L-L	6-3	175	6-27-05	0	1	6.75	3	3	0	4	5	4	3	0	2	3	.333	.421	.400	15.8	10.5	19
Breton, Albert	R-R	6-3	165	10-07-00	3	0	11.31	15	0	0	25	36	32	31	3	22	21	.343	.454	.514	16.2	16.9	130
Brito, Abel	R-R	6-1	175	3-04-01	0	0	8.31	2	2	0	4	3	4	4	0	3	4	.200	.350	.200	20.0	15.0	20
Candelario, Elmson	R-R	6-4	185	11-09-00	0	4	14.73	10	2	1	15	26	27	24	0	16	14	.371	.489	.500	15.6	17.8	90
Carver, Ross	R-R	6-2	205	8-27-99	0	0	14.73	2	2	0	4	7	6	6	1	3	7	.389	.476	.667	33.3	14.3	21
Contreras, Jose	R-R	6-2	175	5-13-02	2	0	10.89	15	0	0	21	21	30	25	0	36	26	.269	.504	.333	21.8	30.3	119
Driver, Jay	R-R	6-3	195	2-25-02	0	0	0.00	2	0	0	2	1	1	0	0	0	5	.125	.125	.125	62.5	0.0	8
Figueroa, Daniel	R-R	6-0	172	9-25-00	0	0	9.95	13	0	2	13	23	18	14	1	10	14	.390	.500	.627	18.9	13.5	74
Garcia, Frederic	R-R	6-4	195	12-17-00	2	2	9.12	15	0	0	26	30	28	26	0	22	36	.297	.425	.396	28.3	17.3	127
Garcia, Jogly	R-R	6-1	170	9-08-03	0	1	5.45	11	9	0	33	33	20	20	1	30	36	.273	.427	.421	22.9	19.1	157
Hajjar, Steve	R-L	6-5	240	8-07-00	1	1	3.86	2	1	0	7	6	3	3	0	6	7	.231	.375	.346	21.9	18.8	32
Harlow, Josh	R-R	6-3	215	4-18-01	1	0	10.50	4	1	0	6	11	7	7	2	1	5	.393	.433	.714	16.7	3.3	30
Hernandez, Allan	R-R	6-5	225	1-19-01	0	2	5.40	11	1	0	13	10	10	8	2	8	20	.200	.305	.400	33.9	13.6	59
Hernandez, Evelio	R-R	5-11	167	9-03-03	1	1	7.40	7	4	0	24	30	21	20	4	13	26	.297	.371	.525	22.4	11.2	116
Humphries, Jackson	R-L	6-1	200	7-20-04	0	6	5.61	9	8	0	34	30	27	21	2	21	48	.244	.362	.390	31.6	13.8	152
Jachec, Matt	R-R	6-0	205	7-25-01	0	0	9.00	2	0	0	3	4	3	3	1	0	4	.308	.308	.615	30.8	0.0	13
Lewis, Justin	R-R	6-7	205	8-10-95	0	0	0.00	2	1	0	2	1	0	0	0	0	1	.143	.143	.286	14.3	0.0	7
Marman, Kyle	R-R	6-3	195	3-03-97	0	0	6.23	5	1	0	4	4	3	3	0	1	7	.222	.263	.333	36.8	5.3	19
Miller, Jake	R-R	6-2	210	7-14-00	0	0	1.04	4	3	0	9	2	1	1	0	1	9	.071	.103	.107	31.0	3.4	29
Morehouse, Zane	R-R	6-4	200	11-16-99	0	0	7.71	2	0	0	2	5	2	2	0	0	3	.455	.417	.455	25.0	0.0	12
Noboa, Darlin	R-R	6-1	175	2-19-00	1	1	3.63	15	0	1	17	16	10	7	0	11	25	.239	.358	.284	30.9	13.6	81
Perez, Steven	L-L	6-0	155	4-21-01	4	1	3.56	17	0	0	30	32	17	12	2	20	42	.269	.371	.395	29.2	13.9	144
Pettway, Zach	R-R	6-2	215	1-29-99	0	0	54.00	1	0	0	0	1	2	2	1	1	0	.500	.667	2.000	0.0	33.3	3
Santos, Felipito	R-R	6-2	180	7-20-99	0	0	10.47	13	0	0	16	12	26	19	1	19	13	.188	.430	.281	14.0	20.4	93
Santos, Javier	L-R	6-0	190	6-02-03	0	0	0.00	1	0	0	0	0	4	4	0	4	0	.000	1.000	.000	0.0	100.0	4
Scott, Kyle	R-R	6-1	220	4-16-02	0	0	2.45	3	1	0	4	3	1	1	0	4	5	.250	.438	.417	31.3	25.0	16
Soteldo, Victor	R-R	6-1	165	8-27-01	3	1	7.50	17	0	2	30	33	27	25	2	25	32	.280	.409	.415	21.3	16.7	150
Turner, Matt	L-L	6-4	180	8-04-99	0	0	18.00	1	0	0	1	1	2	2	1	1	1	.250	.400	1.000	20.0	20.0	5
Vasquez, Wardquelin	R-R	6-3	194	7-25-01	0	0	5.40	4	3	0	10	12	11	6	1	7	11	.293	.400	.415	22.0	14.0	50
Ventimiglia, Tommy	R-R	6-4	205	10-01-03	0	0	16.71	17	0	0	14	17	26	26	0	30	15	.304	.574	.393	16.0	31.9	94
Villalobos, Hugo	R-R	5-10	170	7-27-01	0	1	8.10	6	1	0	7	10	7	6	1	4	9	.333	.412	.500	26.5	11.8	34
Virguez, Kendeglys	R-R	6-2	160	5-06-04	1	5	7.68	11	7	0	39	44	36	33	4	28	40	.289	.423	.421	21.2	14.8	189
Webb, Ryan	L-L	6-1	202	4-19-99	0	1	1.93	2	2	0	5	4	1	1	1	3	4	.250	.368	.563	21.1	15.8	19
Wilkinson, Matthew	R-L	5-11	260	12-10-02	0	0	0.00	1	0	0	1	0	0	0	0	0	3	.000	.000	.000	100.0	0.0	3
Wolf, Josh	R-R	6-3	170	9-01-00	0	1	21.60	1	1	0	2	3	4	4	0	4	1	.429	.636	1.000	9.1	36.4	11
Zinn, Keegan	R-R	6-3	165	3-30-05	0	1	37.80	2	2	0	2	3	7	7	0	6	1	.429	.692	.429	7.7	46.2	13

Fielding

C: Izturis 28, Clark 16, Hernandez 7, Cedeno 7, Paz 5, Rivas 1, Velazquez 1, Mejias 1. **1B:** Aranguren 30, Cedeno 23, Hernandez 2, Manzardo 1, Velazquez 1. **2B:** Mendez 18, Alduey 12, Mercedes 11, Lopez 8, Ramirez 5, Purroy 2, Baez 1. **3B:** Mercedes 20, Mendez 15, Alduey 10, Purroy 4, Ramirez 3, Lopez 3, Baez 2. **SS:** Ramirez 30, Alduey 16, Purroy 8, Mendez 5, Lopez 1. **OF:** Chourio 34, Espinola 33, Gonzalez 32, Gomez 28, Parra 20, DeLauter 8, Zarate 6, Advincula 5, Valera 5, Hawke 5, Riebock 3, Durango 2.

DSL GUARDIANS — *ROOKIE*

DOMINICAN SUMMER LEAGUE

Batting	B-T	Ht.	Wt.	DOB	AVG	OBP	SLG	G	PA	AB	R	H	2B	3B	HR	RBI	BB	HBP	SH	SF	SO	SB	CS	BB%	SO%
Abreus, Jhorvic	B-R	5-7	144	10-27-05	.229	.299	.396	27	107	96	15	22	7	0	3	20	8	2	0	1	17	9	2	7.5	15.9
Aparicio, Luis	L-L	5-9	160	1-11-05	.337	.402	.452	30	117	104	16	35	10	1	0	17	8	4	0	1	5	5	2	6.8	4.3
Arosemena, Pablo	R-R	5-8	154	2-17-06	.178	.327	.233	29	113	90	14	16	3	1	0	13	17	4	0	2	15	1	0	15.0	13.3
Ayala, Yelserth	B-R	5-8	140	6-05-06	.283	.357	.336	32	126	113	16	32	6	0	0	7	11	2	0	0	22	16	6	8.7	17.5
Baptiste, Yanki	B-R	5-11	185	11-18-04	.224	.427	.513	23	103	76	16	17	2	4	4	17	23	4	0	0	36	6	1	22.3	35.0
Bolivar, Mason	L-R	5-10	162	8-18-06	.281	.391	.326	38	161	135	24	38	6	0	0	13	22	3	0	1	16	2	2	13.7	9.9
Borrome, Gueile	L-R	5-10	155	12-18-04	.230	.342	.290	30	117	100	10	23	4	1	0	10	16	1	0	0	25	3	2	13.7	21.4
Cadiz, Sebastian	L-R	5-11	180	2-01-06	.196	.294	.413	29	109	92	19	18	3	4	3	20	12	2	0	3	30	2	0	11.0	27.5
Dalmagro, Pedro	L-R	5-11	170	12-17-05	.361	.425	.528	23	80	72	14	26	5	2	1	12	7	1	0	0	12	2	0	8.8	15.0
Frances, Juan	B-R	5-9	145	9-07-05	.195	.228	.208	40	158	149	17	29	0	1	0	13	7	0	0	2	14	8	3	4.4	8.9
Francisca, Welbyn	B-R	5-8	148	5-17-06	.316	.419	.500	40	179	152	34	48	7	6	3	24	24	3	0	0	35	11	7	13.4	19.6
Guedez, Brayan	L-R	5-8	135	12-07-04	.234	.354	.336	32	127	107	15	25	4	2	1	12	20	0	0	0	26	9	4	15.7	20.5
Gutierrez, Carlos	L-L	5-6	135	6-18-04	.372	.460	.453	29	100	86	21	32	7	0	0	12	14	0	0	0	17	10	1	14.0	17.0
Hernandez, Pedro	R-R	5-7	137	10-17-04	.137	.322	.158	31	121	95	16	13	2	0	0	7	19	7	0	0	30	2	1	15.7	24.8
Herrera, Reiner	L-R	5-11	170	10-20-05	.208	.337	.260	25	92	77	12	16	4	0	0	11	10	5	0	0	26	1	0	10.9	28.3
Hidalgo, Reyden	L-R	5-7	115	5-17-04	.290	.400	.376	34	110	93	19	27	6	1	0	13	15	2	0	0	10	11	0	13.6	9.1

John, Yorfran	B-R	5-10	163	9-14-04	.200	.264	.240	30	110	100	10	20	1	0	1	13	5	4	0	1	12	1	3	4.5	10.9
Leon, David	L-R	5-11	156	2-02-04	.281	.494	.386	27	81	57	15	16	0	3	0	10	22	2	0	0	12	4	2	27.2	14.8
Luis, Yerlin	B-R	5-9	155	9-09-05	.224	.478	.296	39	186	125	36	28	3	3	0	14	54	7	0	0	42	15	4	29.0	22.6
Marcano, Jose	L-R	5-10	155	10-03-05	.188	.269	.256	43	201	176	23	33	10	1	0	18	20	1	0	4	42	3	1	10.0	20.9
Martinez, Jonathan	B-R	5-9	131	8-16-06	.246	.402	.373	40	179	142	29	35	6	3	2	11	30	7	0	0	41	16	4	16.8	22.9
Merejo, Luis	R-R	6-2	185	6-28-06	.321	.441	.485	40	170	134	23	43	6	2	4	32	20	12	0	4	26	1	1	11.8	15.3
Mijares, Yaikel	B-R	5-9	145	12-13-05	.253	.388	.438	41	178	146	41	37	5	5	4	30	27	5	0	0	39	15	2	15.2	21.9
Molero, Moises	L-L	5-9	145	2-19-05	.219	.344	.291	43	180	151	23	33	7	2	0	21	24	5	0	0	37	0	0	13.3	20.6
Pena, Ronald	R-R	6-4	195	8-14-04	.258	.367	.348	28	109	89	15	23	5	0	1	14	17	0	0	3	26	6	2	15.6	23.9
Pirela, Jose	L-R	6-3	181	4-09-06	.270	.395	.480	41	185	148	33	40	11	1	6	34	25	8	0	4	40	8	3	13.5	21.6
Silva, Heribert	L-L	5-9	152	3-31-06	.284	.368	.385	38	171	148	26	42	4	1	3	21	19	2	0	2	24	11	1	11.1	14.0
Taveras, Emilio	R-R	5-10	175	9-18-02	.298	.459	.596	28	74	57	12	17	8	0	3	15	15	2	0	0	22	2	0	20.3	29.7
Taveras, Jonathan	B-R	5-8	146	9-01-05	.179	.246	.255	31	118	106	13	19	4	2	0	9	10	0	0	2	32	4	2	8.5	27.1
Velasquez, Nomar	L-R	5-9	158	5-21-05	.310	.414	.372	35	133	113	27	35	5	1	0	8	19	1	0	0	24	21	3	14.3	18.0

Pitching	**B-T**	**Ht.**	**Wt.**	**DOB**	**W**	**L**	**ERA**	**G**	**GS**	**SV**	**IP**	**Hits**	**Runs**	**ER**	**HR**	**BB**	**SO**	**AVG**	**OBP**	**SLG**	**SO%**	**BB%**	**BF**
Abreu, Javier	R-R	5-11	150	5-24-06	0	1	2.77	4	3	0	13	7	4	4	1	10	10	.163	.327	.256	18.2	18.2	55
Acosta, Neiver	R-R	6-1	184	7-23-03	1	3	14.77	15	0	2	18	21	30	29	3	23	23	.292	.485	.458	23.2	23.2	99
Alcantara, Eudry	R-R	5-11	150	12-27-04	2	5	7.33	11	11	0	43	41	38	35	4	31	34	.258	.386	.459	16.8	15.3	202
Alfaro, Jervis	R-R	5-11	170	10-24-03	5	0	1.74	9	9	0	41	31	15	8	0	12	32	.214	.285	.283	19.4	7.3	165
Batista, Dahan	R-R	6-1	170	3-15-00	2	2	5.11	13	0	1	25	35	22	14	1	6	17	.333	.372	.467	14.9	5.3	114
Betancourt, Joswal	R-R	6-0	170	9-14-05	2	0	8.56	11	0	2	14	14	13	13	2	3	14	.264	.344	.491	23.0	4.9	61
Castillo, Wagner	R-R	6-0	180	9-23-03	1	4	6.84	14	0	3	25	27	20	19	0	18	21	.278	.419	.330	16.8	14.4	125
Castro, Alexandro	L-L	5-11	162	2-06-01	3	0	2.78	14	0	1	23	18	8	7	1	8	19	.217	.295	.349	20.0	8.4	95
Cordones, Miguel	R-R	6-6	180	9-16-99	4	0	3.97	13	1	0	34	29	15	15	0	18	28	.234	.360	.298	18.7	12.0	150
Crisostomo, Yatner	R-R	5-11	155	6-21-03	0	0	0.00	1	1	0	2	0	0	0	0	2	0	.000	.375	.000	0.0	25.0	8
Cruz, Estarlin	L-L	6-7	177	10-05-04	0	1	16.46	13	0	0	14	21	32	25	1	32	16	.344	.574	.508	17.0	34.0	94
Cruz, Robert	R-R	6-3	170	4-11-00	4	3	2.27	11	4	0	44	34	12	11	1	6	36	.213	.272	.281	20.8	3.5	173
Flores, Luis	L-L	6-1	160	10-05-03	1	0	9.00	2	0	0	2	0	3	2	0	5	3	.000	.455	.000	27.3	45.5	11
Garcia, Luis	R-R	6-1	175	8-15-02	1	1	4.87	6	6	0	20	28	14	11	1	3	15	.322	.359	.471	16.3	3.3	92
Garcia, Victor	R-R	6-0	168	2-08-03	2	1	17.76	10	0	0	13	14	26	25	1	15	7	.286	.533	.490	9.3	20.0	75
Garcia, Yonaiker	R-R	5-11	165	12-15-00	1	3	5.23	13	0	2	21	23	13	12	2	13	28	.288	.418	.463	28.0	13.0	100
Hernandez, Daiher	L-L	5-11	141	3-02-06	1	2	7.63	12	0	0	15	11	16	13	0	19	9	.224	.444	.347	12.5	26.4	72
Hernandez, Evelio	R-R	5-11	167	9-03-03	1	0	3.78	4	4	0	17	15	8	7	2	4	26	.227	.292	.394	36.1	5.6	72
Hernandez, Melkis	L-L	6-0	186	1-18-05	1	4	3.71	10	10	0	44	36	21	18	2	19	44	.224	.313	.335	24.2	10.4	182
Jimenez, Ezequiel	R-R	6-1	182	6-10-03	2	1	3.67	11	11	0	42	41	20	17	1	26	45	.265	.375	.316	24.5	14.1	184
Leon, David	L-R	5-11	156	2-02-04	1	0	27.00	1	0	0	1	3	2	2	0	0	1	.750	.750	1.250	25.0	0.0	4
Mariano, Diovel	R-R	6-1	175	2-23-04	1	3	9.00	14	0	1	22	37	25	22	5	12	18	.352	.415	.610	15.3	10.2	118
Mejia, Algeni	L-L	6-4	183	9-13-04	1	1	6.75	13	0	0	17	16	15	13	0	14	28	.246	.373	.308	33.7	16.9	83
Navarro, Diego	R-R	5-11	176	12-29-02	0	2	3.24	13	0	2	25	24	14	9	2	9	19	.250	.315	.406	17.6	8.3	108
Osorio, Manuel	L-L	5-10	170	3-24-06	1	3	4.50	11	9	1	38	31	22	19	4	23	37	.223	.333	.360	22.8	14.2	162
Padilla, Erick	R-R	5-10	145	11-26-03	0	1	8.31	8	0	0	9	10	13	8	0	9	4	.286	.444	.343	8.9	20.0	45
Peraza, Santiago	R-R	5-11	135	5-17-05	2	0	6.00	13	1	1	30	25	25	20	2	27	32	.227	.397	.373	22.7	19.1	141
Perez, Joelvis	R-R	6-3	180	12-08-04	1	2	8.02	9	0	0	21	35	22	19	2	13	11	.376	.464	.538	10.0	11.8	110
Polanco, Felix	L-L	6-2	190	6-26-00	1	2	2.33	11	0	1	27	20	8	7	2	5	29	.206	.257	.278	27.6	4.8	105
Ramirez, Jose	R-R	5-11	155	9-03-04	1	1	3.71	12	0	2	17	12	14	7	2	16	20	.197	.367	.328	25.0	20.0	80
Ramos, Renil	R-R	6-2	143	12-01-05	0	3	4.31	11	6	0	40	26	22	19	0	29	24	.184	.341	.248	13.6	16.5	176
Rivera, Raudy	R-R	5-10	195	5-03-05	1	2	4.42	11	10	0	37	26	22	18	1	43	48	.217	.435	.292	28.2	25.3	170
Ruiz, Harrison	R-R	6-1	192	10-02-03	1	0	1.85	10	7	1	34	26	9	7	1	6	31	.210	.259	.290	23.0	4.4	135
Sosa, Juan	L-L	6-2	200	4-23-03	0	0	17.61	9	0	0	8	7	19	15	1	25	7	.269	.635	.462	13.5	48.1	52
Urena, Dielmon	R-R	6-6	166	5-15-01	1	1	10.80	11	0	0	15	17	20	18	4	20	7	.298	.518	.526	8.2	23.5	85
Vasquez, Eriberto	R-R	5-11	175	3-08-04	2	3	16.20	12	0	0	13	26	29	24	0	21	14	.419	.570	.661	16.1	24.1	87
Vicente, Adauri	R-R	6-2	188	12-18-00	0	1	5.91	4	0	1	11	12	9	7	2	6	10	.273	.385	.455	19.2	11.5	52
Zapata, Julio	R-R	6-1	184	11-22-02	0	1	3.72	12	12	0	46	43	30	19	3	24	47	.239	.354	.378	22.2	11.3	212

Fielding

C: Arosemena 28, Cadiz 24, Herrera 20, Dalmagro 18, Leon 14, Taveras 14. **1B**: Pena 26, Merejo 22, Taveras 18, Baptiste 12, Leon 11, Borrome 9, Hidalgo 7, Abreus 4, John 3, Ayala 2, Dalmagro 2, Hernandez 1. **2B:** Mijares 20, Martinez 17, John 15, Marcano 13, Ayala 13, Guedez 9, Velasquez 9, Taveras 6, Hernandez 4, Francisca 3, Hidalgo 1, Abreus 1**. 3B:** Merejo 17, Velasquez 14, Borrome 14, John 12, Taveras 12, Mijares 8, Baptiste 7, Guedez 7, Hernandez 5, Martinez 5, Abreus 4, Ayala 3, Francisca 3, Hidalgo 2. **SS:** Francisca 28, Marcano 25, Martinez 11, Hernandez 11, Guedez 10, Abreus 9, Mijares 8, Ayala 4, Hidalgo 1. OF: Pirela 41, Molero 40, Bolivar 40, Frances 39, Luis 39, Silva 38, Aparicio 30, Gutierrez 27, Hidalgo 15, Ayala 6, Velasquez 6, Hernandez 4, Abreus 3, Pena 2, Leon 1, Borrome 1.

Colorado Rockies

SEASON SYNOPSIS: The Rockies entered the season with little hope of contending and quickly sank to the bottom of the National League. Their 59-103 record proved to be the worst in franchise history.

HIGH POINT: Nolan Jones was the Rockies' best player by a wide margin with a .931 OPS in 367 at-bats, and he earned a 20-homer, 20-steal season with one of each in Game 162, a 3-2 win over Minnesota. Jones just missed a third 20, as he had 19 assists in only 83 games in the outfield.

LOW POINT: Colorado couldn't keep its starting pitchers healthy, starting when ace German Marquez had to have Tommy John surgery after four April starts. Righty Antonio Senzatela joined him on the shelf in May, and the Rockies' lack of depth was laid bare. Journeymen such as Chase Anderson, Ty Blach and Chris Flexen combined for 42 starts, with Anderson taking the loss in a club-record 25-1 loss to the Angels on June 24—despite Shohei Ohtani going just 1-for-7. The Angels had 28 hits as Anderson gave up three home runs on three pitches for the second time in his career.

NOTABLE ROOKIES: Aside from Jones, the Rockies had rookies shine defensively at two key positions. Shortstop Ezequiel Tovar, who ranked in the 99th percentile in Statcast's range/outs above average metric, started 152 games and hit .253/.287/.408 with 56 extra-base hits but also 166 strikeouts. Center fielder Brenton Doyle also was in the 99th percentile thanks to elite speed and featured the best outfield arm in the majors, averaging 96.1 mph, but you can't steal first base: He hit .203/.250/.343.

KEY TRANSACTIONS: Colorado added Jones in November 2022 from the Guardians, who missed his power, and the Rockies got him to the majors May 26. He and Doyle helped replace Yonathan Daza, who was designated for assignment in May after being the regular in center field in 2021-22. The Rockies added reliever Justin Bruihl from the Dodgers in July, then traded veteran Brad Hand to the Braves for prospect righty Alec Barger at the Aug. 1 deadline.

DOWN ON THE FARM: The Arizona Complex League Rockies were the only domestic minor league team to post a winning percentage above .700. They went 40-15 (.727) but fell in the playoffs to the ACL Brewers. Outfielder Hunter Goodman's 34 home runs were third best in MiLB.

OPENING DAY PAYROLL: $171,108,778 (16th).

PLAYERS OF THE YEAR

MAJOR LEAGUE	MINOR LEAGUE
Nolan Jones	**Hunter Goodman**
OF	**OF**
.289/.389/.542	(AA/AAA)
22 2B, 20 HR	.259/.338/.580
19 OF Assists	34 HR, 30 2B, 111 RBI

ORGANIZATION LEADERS

Batting		***Minimum 250 AB**
MAJORS		
* AVG	Nolan Jones	.297
* OPS	Nolan Jones	.931
HR	Ryan McMahon	23
RBI	Ezequiel Tovar	73
MINORS		
* AVG	Wynton Bernard, Albuquerque	.329
* OBP	Wilie MacIver, Albuquerque	.416
* SLG	Hunter Goodman, Hartford/Albuquerque	.580
* OPS	Zach Kokosa, Spokane	.961
R	Jimmy Herron, Albuquerque	106
H	Coco Montes, Albuquerque	138
TB	Jordan Beck, Spokane/Hartford	245
2B	Jordan Beck,	34
3B	Jake Snider, Fresno	10
HR	Hunter Goodman, Hartford/Albuquerque	34
RBI	Hunter Goodman, Hartford/Albuquerque	111
BB	Grant Lavigne, Hartford	77
SO	Ryan Ritter, Fresno/Spokane/Hartford	152
SB	Jimmy Herron, Albuquerque	33

Pitching		**#Minimum 75 IP**
MAJORS		
W	Austin Gomber	9
# ERA	Justin Lawrence	3.72
SO	Kyle Freeland	94
SV	Piece Johnson	13
MINORS		
L	Case Williams, Hartford	11
ERA	Michael Prosecky, Fresno	2.72
# G	Angel Chivilli, Spokane/Hartford	53
GS	Stephen Jones, Hartford/Alb.	53
SV	Jeff Criswell, Albuquerque	26
SV	Zach Agnos, Fresno	27
IP	Jeff Criswell, Albuquerque	121
BB	Jeff Criswell, Albuquerque	71
SO	Jeff Criswell, Albuquerque	135
# AVG	Michael Prosecky, Fresno	.215

2023 PERFORMANCE

General Manager: Bill Schmidt. **Farm Director:** Chris Forbes. **Scouting Director:** Danny Montgomery.

Class	Team	League	W	L	PCT	Finish	Manager
Majors	Colorado Rockies	National	59	103	.364	15 (15)	Bud Black
Triple-A	Albuquerque Isotopes	Pacific Coast	68	82	.453	7 (10)	Pedro Lopez
Double-A	Hartford Yard Goats	Eastern	57	76	.429	12 (12)	Chris Denorfia
High-A	Spokane Indians	Northwest	62	67	.481	4 (6)	Robinson Cancel
Low-A	Fresno Grizzlies	California	78	54	.591	1 (10)	Steve Soliz
Rookie	ACL Rockies	Arizona Complex	40	15	.727	1 (17)	Fred Ocasio
Rookie	DSL Colorado	Dominican Sum.	34	19	.642	9 (50)	Eugenio Jose
Rookie	DSL Rockies	Dominican Sum.	29	24	.547	15 (50)	Mauricio Gonzalez
Overall 2023 Minor League Record			**368**	**337**	**.522**	**8th (30)**	

ORGANIZATION STATISTICS

COLORADO ROCKIES

NATIONAL LEAGUE

Batting	B-T	Ht.	Wt.	DOB	AVG	OBP	SLG	G	PA	AB	R	H	2B	3B	HR	RBI	BB	HBP	SH	SF	SO	SB	CS	BB%	SO%
Alfaro, Jorge	R-R	6-3	230	6-11-93	.161	.188	.387	10	32	31	2	5	4	0	1	4	0	1	0	0	12	0	0	0.0	37.5
2-team (8 Boston)					.146	.212	.292	18	52	48	2	7	4	0	1	4	2	2	0	0	15	0	0	3.8	28.8
Blackmon, Charlie	L-L	6-3	221	7-01-86	.279	.363	.440	96	413	359	57	100	24	5	8	40	39	11	0	4	55	4	1	9.4	13.3
Bouchard, Sean	R-R	6-3	215	5-16-96	.316	.372	.684	21	43	38	11	12	2	0	4	7	4	0	0	1	14	0	1	9.3	32.6
Bryant, Kris	R-R	6-5	230	1-04-92	.233	.313	.367	80	335	300	36	70	10	0	10	31	29	6	0	0	68	0	0	8.7	20.3
Castro, Harold	L-R	5-10	195	11-30-93	.252	.275	.314	99	270	258	24	65	13	0	1	31	9	0	1	2	66	1	0	3.3	24.4
Cron, C.J.	R-R	6-4	235	1-05-90	.260	.304	.476	56	224	208	31	54	12	0	11	32	13	1	0	2	50	0	0	5.8	22.3
2-team (15 Los Angeles Angels)					.248	.295	.434	71	278	258	38	64	12	0	12	37	17	1	0	2	65	0	0	6.1	23.4
Daza, Yonathan	R-R	6-2	207	2-28-94	.270	.304	.351	24	80	74	8	20	6	0	0	7	3	1	1	1	13	1	0	3.8	16.3
Diaz, Elias	R-R	6-1	223	11-17-90	.267	.316	.409	141	526	486	48	130	25	1	14	72	34	2	0	4	118	1	0	6.5	22.4
Doyle, Brenton	R-R	6-2	200	5-14-98	.203	.250	.343	126	431	399	48	81	16	5	10	48	22	4	3	3	151	22	5	5.1	35.0
Goodman, Hunter	R-R	5-11	210	10-08-99	.200	.247	.386	23	77	70	6	14	4	3	1	17	5	0	0	2	24	1	0	6.5	31.2
Grichuk, Randal	R-R	6-2	216	8-13-91	.308	.365	.496	64	263	240	40	74	19	1	8	27	18	4	0	1	51	2	2	6.8	19.4
2-team (54 Los Angeles Angels)					.267	.321	.459	118	471	434	65	116	31	2	16	44	29	6	0	2	96	2	2	6.2	20.4
Jones, Nolan	L-R	6-4	195	5-07-98	.297	.389	.542	106	424	367	60	109	22	4	20	62	53	3	0	1	126	20	4	12.5	29.7
Kaiser, Connor	R-R	6-3	195	11-20-96	.000	.000	.000	3	4	4	0	0	0	0	0	0	0	0	0	0	2	0	0	0.0	50.0
McMahon, Ryan	L-R	6-2	219	12-14-94	.240	.322	.431	152	627	555	80	133	31	3	23	70	68	1	0	3	198	5	5	10.8	31.6
Montero, Elehuris	R-R	6-3	235	8-17-98	.243	.290	.426	85	307	284	40	69	15	2	11	39	15	5	0	3	111	0	0	4.9	36.2
Montes, Coco	R-R	6-1	200	10-07-96	.184	.244	.316	18	41	38	3	7	2	0	1	3	2	1	0	0	12	0	0	4.9	29.3
Moustakas, Mike	L-R	6-0	225	9-11-88	.270	.360	.435	47	136	115	21	31	7	0	4	17	17	1	0	3	34	0	0	12.5	25.0
2-team (65 Los Angeles Angels)					.247	.293	.392	112	386	352	43	87	15	0	12	48	23	3	0	8	95	0	0	6.0	24.6
Profar, Jurickson	B-R	6-0	184	2-20-93	.236	.316	.364	111	472	415	51	98	25	2	8	39	45	6	0	5	86	1	0	9.5	18.2
2-team (14 San Diego)					.242	.321	.368	125	521	459	55	111	27	2	9	46	50	6	0	5	90	1	0	9.6	17.3
Rodgers, Brendan	R-R	6-0	204	8-09-96	.258	.313	.388	46	192	178	21	46	9	1	4	20	11	3	0	0	41	0	0	5.7	21.4
Serven, Brian	R-R	6-0	207	5-05-95	.130	.130	.174	11	23	23	0	3	1	0	0	1	0	0	0	0	10	0	0	0.0	43.5
Toglia, Michael	B-L	6-5	226	8-16-98	.163	.224	.284	45	152	141	18	23	5	0	4	9	10	1	0	0	50	1	1	6.6	32.9
Tovar, Ezequiel	R-R	6-0	162	8-01-01	.253	.287	.408	153	615	581	79	147	37	4	15	73	25	4	2	3	166	11	5	4.1	27.0
Trejo, Alan	R-R	6-2	205	5-30-96	.232	.288	.343	83	227	207	24	48	11	0	4	26	16	1	1	2	51	5	1	7.0	22.5
Tucker, Cole	B-R	6-3	200	7-03-96	.500	.600	.500	5	10	8	2	4	0	0	0	2	1	1	0	0	2	0	0	10.0	20.0
Wynns, Austin	R-R	6-0	190	12-10-90	.214	.273	.282	45	131	117	11	25	5	0	1	8	8	2	3	1	32	1	0	6.1	24.4
3-team (5 Los Angeles Dodgers, 1 San Francisco)					.208	.268	.277	51	145	130	11	27	6	0	1	10	9	2	3	1	39	1	0	6.2	26.9

Pitching	B-T	Ht.	Wt.	DOB	W	L	ERA	G	GS	SV	IP	Hits	Runs	ER	HR	BB	SO	AVG	OBP	SLG	SO%	BB%	BF
Abad, Fernando	L-L	6-2	235	12-17-85	1	0	4.26	6	0	0	6	11	3	3	2	3	2	.379	.438	.655	6.3	9.4	32
Anderson, Chase	R-R	6-1	210	11-30-87	1	6	5.75	17	17	0	81	88	53	52	17	32	62	.282	.360	.494	17.5	9.0	354
Bard, Daniel	R-R	6-4	215	6-25-85	4	2	4.56	50	0	1	49	35	30	25	5	49	47	.206	.397	.371	20.3	21.1	232
Bird, Jake	R-R	6-3	200	12-04-95	3	3	4.33	70	3	0	89	94	47	43	6	27	77	.276	.336	.396	20.2	7.1	381
Blach, Ty	R-L	6-1	215	10-20-90	3	3	5.54	20	13	0	78	104	51	48	15	24	50	.330	.381	.537	14.2	6.8	352
Bruihl, Justin	L-L	6-2	215	6-26-97	0	0	14.73	7	0	0	4	4	7	6	0	3	3	.286	.421	.429	15.8	15.8	19
Calvo, Blair	R-R	6-3	195	2-27-96	0	0	0.00	1	0	0	1	0	0	0	0	0	0	.000	.000	.000	0.0	0.0	3
Carasiti, Matt	R-R	6-2	205	7-23-91	1	0	6.29	16	0	1	24	28	19	17	3	11	16	.292	.364	.427	14.5	10.0	110
Castro, Harold	L-R	5-10	195	11-30-93	0	0	9.00	2	0	0	2	4	2	2	0	1	0	.444	.545	.556	0.0	9.1	11
Davis, Noah	R-R	6-2	195	4-22-97	0	4	8.70	8	6	0	30	43	30	29	6	15	26	.341	.425	.532	17.8	10.3	146
Doyle, Tommy	R-R	6-6	244	5-01-96	0	1	6.85	15	0	0	24	23	18	18	5	13	18	.256	.350	.500	17.5	12.6	103
Feltner, Ryan	R-R	6-4	190	9-02-96	2	4	5.82	10	10	0	43	45	29	28	2	28	38	.265	.373	.359	18.9	13.9	201
Flexen, Chris	R-R	6-3	219	7-01-94	2	4	6.27	12	12	0	60	74	45	42	14	19	45	.305	.361	.547	16.7	7.0	270
Freeland, Kyle	L-L	6-4	204	5-14-93	6	14	5.03	29	29	0	156	187	96	87	29	42	94	.300	.342	.506	13.9	6.2	677
Gomber, Austin	L-L	6-5	220	11-23-93	9	9	5.50	27	27	0	139	164	88	85	26	43	87	.297	.351	.513	14.4	7.1	603
Hand, Brad	L-L	6-3	224	3-20-90	3	1	4.54	40	0	0	36	35	18	18	4	16	41	.265	.348	.462	26.1	10.2	157
Hollowell, Gavin	R-R	6-7	215	11-04-97	2	0	5.88	26	0	1	34	31	23	22	8	18	32	.238	.357	.477	20.8	11.7	154
Johnson, Pierce	R-R	6-2	202	5-10-91	1	5	6.00	43	0	13	39	47	28	26	7	25	58	.292	.385	.491	30.9	13.3	188
Justice, Evan	L-L	6-4	205	7-07-98	0	0	8.59	9	0	0	7	14	7	7	0	8	7	.438	.561	.500	16.7	19.0	42
Kauffmann, Karl	R-R	6-2	200	8-15-97	2	5	8.23	11	3	0	35	42	34	32	5	16	16	.311	.392	.504	10.1	10.1	158

Pitching	B-T	Ht.	Wt.	DOB	W	L	ERA	G	GS	SV	IP	Hits	Runs	ER	HR	BB	SO	AVG	OBP	SLG	SO%	BB%	BF
Kinley, Tyler	R-R	6-4	220	1-31-91	0	4	6.06	18	0	5	16	21	11	11	3	6	17	.318	.373	.515	22.4	7.9	76
Koch, Matt	L-R	6-3	215	11-02-90	3	2	5.12	39	1	0	39	41	22	22	7	9	27	.272	.319	.450	16.6	5.5	163
Lambert, Peter	R-R	6-2	208	4-18-97	3	7	5.36	25	11	0	87	93	54	52	18	28	71	.273	.336	.534	18.9	7.5	375
Lamet, Dinelson	R-R	6-3	228	7-18-92	1	4	11.57	16	4	0	26	38	35	33	6	22	31	.349	.455	.642	23.1	16.4	134
Lawrence, Justin	R-R	6-3	213	11-25-94	4	7	3.72	69	0	11	75	65	37	31	5	36	78	.235	.334	.354	23.9	11.0	326
Marquez, German	R-R	6-1	230	2-22-95	2	2	4.95	4	4	0	20	19	11	11	4	3	17	.257	.282	.527	21.3	3.8	80
Mears, Nick	R-R	6-2	200	10-07-96	0	1	3.72	16	0	0	19	14	8	8	1	14	21	.194	.333	.319	24.1	16.1	87
Pint, Riley	R-R	6-5	225	11-06-97	0	0	27.00	1	0	0	0	1	1	1	0	3	0	.500	.800	1.000	0.0	60.0	5
Seabold, Connor	R-R	6-2	190	1-24-96	1	7	7.52	27	13	0	87	116	76	73	19	28	67	.317	.372	.563	16.4	6.9	408
Senzatela, Antonio	R-R	6-1	236	1-21-95	0	1	4.70	2	2	0	8	7	4	4	3	2	4	.250	.300	.607	13.3	6.7	30
Suter, Brent	L-L	6-4	213	8-29-89	4	3	3.38	57	2	0	69	65	36	26	3	25	55	.249	.320	.341	18.8	8.6	292
Trejo, Alan	R-R	6-2	205	5-30-96	0	0	13.50	2	0	0	2	4	3	3	2	0	1	.444	.400	1.222	10.0	0.0	10
Urena, Jose	R-R	6-2	208	9-12-91	0	4	9.82	5	5	0	18	27	22	20	9	14	9	.346	.441	.821	9.7	15.1	93
Vodnik, Victor	R-R	6-0	200	10-09-99	1	0	8.31	6	0	0	9	15	9	8	0	3	12	.366	.409	.439	27.3	6.8	44

Fielding

Catcher	PCT	G	PO	A	E	DP	PB
Alfaro	1.000	2	7	0	0	0	0
Diaz	.988	126	807	48	10	9	6
Serven	.969	10	59	3	2	0	0
Wynns	.993	45	285	16	2	4	4

First Base	PCT	G	PO	A	E	DP
Bryant	1.000	7	43	4	0	6
Cron	.993	47	372	26	3	42
Goodman	1.000	8	55	1	0	5
Jones	.986	10	69	3	1	8
Montero	.996	55	424	29	2	55
Moustakas	1.000	24	158	14	0	14
Toglia	1.000	26	186	14	0	25

Second Base	PCT	G	PO	A	E	DP
Castro	.988	68	105	143	3	49
McMahon	.988	22	31	53	1	14
Montes	.979	15	19	27	1	11
Rodgers	1.000	43	71	103	0	28
Trejo	.972	49	64	108	5	24

Third Base	PCT	G	PO	A	E	DP
Castro	1.000	2	3	2	0	0
Jones	1.000	1	0	4	0	1
McMahon	.969	130	95	274	12	28
Montero	.857	12	4	14	3	2
Montes	1.000	2	0	3	0	1
Moustakas	.944	12	6	11	1	0
Trejo	1.000	23	16	34	0	5

Shortstop	PCT	G	PO	A	E	DP
Castro	1.000	4	2	7	0	0
Kaiser	1.000	2	2	4	0	1
Montes	.000	1	0	0	0	0
Tovar	.988	153	179	392	7	95
Trejo	.971	9	11	22	1	9

Outfield	PCT	G	PO	A	E	DP
Blackmon	.983	30	56	1	1	0
Bouchard	.975	16	30	0	1	0
Bryant	.984	47	89	2	3	0
Castro	1.000	19	21	0	0	0
Daza	.500	25	49	0	0	0
Doyle	.997	125	373	10	1	3
Goodman	1.000	10	17	0	0	0
Grichuk	.985	60	103	3	2	0
Jones	.989	99	163	19	3	3
Profar	.975	89	151	3	4	0
Toglia	.488	18	39	0	1	0
Tucker	.375	4	3	0	1	0

ALBUQUERQUE ISOTOPES — TRIPLE-A

PACIFIC COAST LEAGUE

Batting	B-T	Ht.	Wt.	DOB	AVG	OBP	SLG	G	PA	AB	R	H	2B	3B	HR	RBI	BB	HBP	SH	SF	SO	SB	CS	BB%	SO%
Alfaro, Jorge	R-R	6-3	230	6-11-93	.357	.357	.571	3	14	14	2	5	0	0	1	3	0	0	0	0	5	1	0	0.0	35.7
Bernard, Wynton	R-R	6-2	195	9-24-90	.329	.388	.484	66	307	277	56	91	17	1	8	34	26	2	0	2	51	26	4	8.5	16.6
Blackmon, Charlie	L-L	6-3	221	7-01-86	.300	.300	.500	2	10	10	2	3	2	0	0	1	0	0	0	0	1	0	0	0.0	10.0
Boone, Trevor	R-R	6-2	210	9-09-97	.238	.326	.444	42	175	151	24	36	7	6	4	25	18	3	0	3	71	1	1	10.3	40.6
Bouchard, Sean	R-R	6-3	215	5-16-96	.222	.408	.315	16	71	54	11	12	2	0	1	6	17	0	0	0	14	5	0	23.9	19.7
Bryant, Kris	R-R	6-5	230	1-04-92	.250	.400	.250	1	5	4	1	1	0	0	0	0	1	0	0	0	2	0	0	20.0	40.0
Carreras, Julio	R-R	6-1	190	1-12-00	.255	.371	.373	16	62	51	8	13	3	0	1	7	10	0	0	1	14	1	2	16.1	22.6
Cope, Daniel	R-R	6-0	195	6-15-97	.319	.401	.475	42	167	141	22	45	10	0	4	29	20	2	0	4	46	0	0	12.0	27.5
Cordova, Jose	R-R	6-0	180	1-11-00	.200	.200	.400	2	5	5	0	1	1	0	0	2	0	0	0	0	1	0	0	0.0	20.0
Datres, Kyle	R-R	6-0	205	1-05-96	.222	.313	.370	9	32	27	5	6	0	2	0	4	4	0	0	1	14	0	1	12.5	43.8
Daza, Yonathan	R-R	6-2	207	2-28-94	.305	.350	.415	39	181	164	22	50	10	1	2	19	9	4	1	3	24	4	3	5.0	13.3
Doyle, Brenton	R-R	6-2	200	5-14-98	.306	.404	.633	12	57	49	12	15	1	0	5	8	8	0	0	0	19	1	0	14.0	33.3
Fulford, Braxton	R-R	5-10	190	12-09-98	.500	.600	1.125	3	10	8	3	4	2	0	1	4	2	0	0	0	2	0	0	20.0	20.0
Goodman, Hunter	R-R	5-11	210	10-08-99	.371	.418	.903	15	67	62	15	23	6	0	9	33	4	1	0	0	17	0	1	6.0	25.4
Greiner, Grayson	R-R	6-6	238	10-11-92	.186	.269	.286	20	79	70	10	13	4	0	1	8	6	2	1	0	32	0	1	7.6	40.5
Grichuk, Randal	R-R	6-2	216	8-13-91	.091	.167	.121	8	36	33	6	3	1	0	0	3	3	0	0	0	6	0	0	8.3	16.7
Hannah, Jameson	L-L	5-10	185	8-10-97	.267	.348	.283	18	70	60	8	16	1	0	0	11	8	0	1	1	11	4	1	11.4	15.7
Herron, Jimmy	R-L	6-0	195	7-27-96	.296	.395	.498	128	539	456	106	135	27	4	19	83	69	9	0	5	103	33	5	12.8	19.1
Jones, Nolan	L-R	6-4	195	5-07-98	.356	.481	.711	39	187	149	38	53	13	2	12	42	33	4	0	1	43	5	0	17.6	23.0
Kaiser, Connor	R-R	6-3	195	11-20-96	.238	.353	.404	90	363	307	64	73	14	5	9	39	52	3	0	1	96	16	3	14.3	26.4
MacIver, Willie	R-R	6-1	205	10-28-96	.252	.383	.393	49	201	163	32	41	10	2	3	24	32	4	0	2	56	10	4	15.9	27.9
Montano, Daniel	L-R	6-0	204	3-31-99	.237	.350	.426	75	320	270	39	64	13	7	8	46	46	2	0	2	91	2	0	14.4	28.4
Montero, Elehuris	R-R	6-3	235	8-17-98	.359	.411	.718	35	163	142	32	51	6	0	15	48	14	2	0	5	28	0	1	8.6	17.2
Montes, Coco	R-R	6-1	200	10-07-96	.317	.400	.550	107	507	436	96	138	26	5	22	89	59	6	0	6	130	11	6	11.6	25.6
Morales, Jonathan	R-R	5-11	200	1-29-95	.258	.317	.429	93	397	357	44	92	17	1	14	61	33	1	0	6	55	1	0	8.3	13.9
Quinn, Roman	B-R	5-10	175	5-14-93	.219	.326	.397	23	88	73	9	16	5	1	2	15	10	2	2	1	31	9	1	11.4	35.2
Rodgers, Brendan	R-R	6-0	204	8-09-96	.350	.381	.600	5	21	20	3	7	2	0	1	1	1	0	0	0	2	0	0	4.8	9.5
Romo, Drew	B-R	5-11	205	8-29-01	.353	.389	.529	4	18	17	2	6	1	1	0	3	0	1	0	0	4	0	0	0.0	22.2
Schunk, Aaron	R-R	6-1	205	7-24-97	.290	.350	.461	116	508	458	71	133	24	6	14	77	44	1	0	5	122	12	7	8.7	24.0
Serven, Brian	R-R	6-0	207	5-05-95	.199	.241	.331	38	162	151	14	30	5	0	5	20	8	1	0	2	51	0	0	4.9	31.5
Stovall, Hunter	R-R	5-6	170	9-05-96	.278	.347	.408	106	432	385	72	107	18	4	8	51	39	3	2	3	62	15	6	9.0	14.4
Toglia, Michael	B-L	6-5	226	8-16-98	.256	.368	.474	78	367	308	57	79	15	2	16	64	53	3	0	3	82	3	1	14.4	22.3
Torrealba, Yorvis	R-R	6-0	195	7-14-97	.259	.328	.345	20	64	58	7	15	2	0	1	8	4	2	0	0	13	4	1	6.3	20.3
Trejo, Alan	R-R	6-2	205	5-30-96	.370	.463	.565	12	54	46	9	17	4	1	1	4	7	1	0	0	12	2	1	13.0	22.2
Tucker, Cole	B-R	6-3	200	7-03-96	.280	.391	.407	70	321	268	57	75	17	1	5	35	49	1	1	2	67	7	4	15.3	20.9

Pitching	B-T	Ht.	Wt.	DOB	W	L	ERA	G	GS	SV	IP	Hits	Runs	ER	HR	BB	SO	AVG	OBP	SLG	SO%	BB%	BF
Abad, Fernando	L-L	6-2	235	12-17-85	3	2	3.86	26	0	3	30	23	13	13	4	3	32	.205	.226	.384	27.8	2.6	115
Adams, Chance	R-R	6-1	215	8-10-94	2	0	3.86	31	0	1	33	35	15	14	4	10	21	.276	.336	.417	15.0	7.1	140

Allen, Logan	R-L	6-3	200	5-23-97	1	0	7.20	24	0	0	45	66	41	36	8	28	50	.338	.422	.564	22.2	12.4	225
Anderson, Chase	R-R	6-1	210	11-30-87	0	0	4.76	2	2	0	6	7	3	3	1	5	2	.350	.444	.650	7.4	18.5	27
Bard, Daniel	R-R	6-4	215	6-25-85	0	0	0.00	1	0	0	1	1	0	0	0	0	3	.250	.250	.250	75.0	0.0	4
Blach, Ty	R-L	6-1	215	10-20-90	3	1	4.40	11	5	0	31	36	16	15	2	8	27	.290	.331	.379	20.3	6.0	133
Braymer, Ben	L-L	6-2	212	4-28-94	1	7	9.75	16	15	0	60	91	75	65	17	33	42	.342	.422	.620	13.8	10.9	304
Bruihl, Justin	L-L	6-2	215	6-26-97	1	1	5.59	9	1	0	10	7	6	6	1	4	10	.206	.300	.324	25.0	10.0	40
Calvo, Blair	R-R	6-3	195	2-27-96	2	3	7.43	24	0	3	23	29	22	19	3	10	32	.299	.389	.454	28.3	8.8	113
Carasiti, Matt	R-R	6-2	205	7-23-91	2	1	3.33	25	0	2	27	28	10	10	1	12	26	.269	.347	.404	21.8	10.1	119
Cessa, Luis	R-R	6-0	222	4-25-92	0	2	8.44	6	6	0	21	30	20	20	5	10	19	.333	.400	.622	18.8	9.9	101
Criswell, Jeff	R-R	6-4	225	3-10-99	5	10	7.51	29	26	0	121	140	105	101	32	71	135	.286	.380	.558	23.7	12.5	569
Darnell, Dugan	L-R	6-2	205	6-26-97	2	0	6.04	18	0	0	25	31	18	17	7	9	24	.287	.353	.574	20.2	7.6	119
Davis, Noah	R-R	6-2	195	4-22-97	1	4	4.50	14	14	0	60	52	34	30	7	35	45	.242	.374	.405	17.0	13.2	265
Doyle, Tommy	R-R	6-6	244	5-01-96	4	4	3.41	33	0	8	37	29	18	14	5	18	41	.213	.305	.368	26.6	11.7	154
Feltner, Ryan	R-R	6-4	190	9-02-96	0	1	2.45	2	2	0	7	6	2	2	0	4	6	.231	.333	.269	20.0	13.3	30
Flexen, Chris	R-R	6-3	219	7-01-94	1	0	0.96	2	2	0	9	5	1	1	1	5	11	.156	.270	.281	29.7	13.5	37
Gaddis, Will	R-R	6-1	185	3-12-96	0	0	12.66	14	0	0	21	43	33	30	6	23	8	.434	.528	.758	6.4	18.4	125
Gordon, Tanner	L-R	6-5	215	10-26-97	1	1	4.31	6	6	0	31	34	17	15	4	10	34	.264	.312	.403	24.1	7.1	141
Hollowell, Gavin	R-R	6-7	215	11-04-97	0	0	3.47	19	0	2	23	23	9	9	2	10	27	.250	.330	.380	26.2	9.7	103
Johnston, Kyle	R-R	5-11	218	7-17-96	1	0	7.23	13	0	0	19	25	17	15	4	19	14	.342	.463	.589	14.6	19.8	96
Jones, Stephen	R-R	6-4	195	7-30-97	2	3	13.79	29	0	2	31	56	49	48	7	24	34	.389	.477	.708	19.5	13.8	174
Justice, Evan	L-L	6-4	205	7-07-98	0	1	6.23	13	0	0	13	8	9	9	1	12	19	.174	.371	.304	30.6	19.4	62
Kauffmann, Karl	R-R	6-2	200	8-15-97	3	5	6.43	19	19	0	92	125	71	66	11	42	61	.329	.403	.484	14.3	9.8	428
Kennedy, Nick	R-L	6-1	200	6-20-96	2	0	5.65	30	0	1	37	40	24	23	2	28	27	.278	.412	.389	15.3	15.8	177
Kinley, Tyler	R-R	6-4	220	1-31-91	0	0	2.08	4	0	0	4	3	1	1	0	3	7	.188	.316	.188	36.8	15.8	19
Kitchen, Austin	L-L	6-0	200	2-11-97	0	1	54.00	2	0	0	1	5	6	6	1	1	0	.625	.700	1.250	0.0	10.0	10
Koch, Matt	L-R	6-3	215	11-02-90	1	2	7.27	29	1	2	35	45	29	28	7	11	34	.317	.363	.535	21.5	7.0	158
Lambert, Peter	R-R	6-2	208	4-18-97	0	2	4.15	7	7	0	22	20	12	10	0	14	21	.244	.361	.293	21.4	14.3	98
Lamet, Dinelson	R-R	6-3	228	7-18-92	0	0	0.84	3	3	0	11	6	1	1	0	1	11	.171	.194	.171	30.6	2.8	36
Lingos, Eli	L-L	5-11	200	5-21-96	4	2	5.01	32	0	0	50	53	31	28	8	28	37	.283	.378	.535	17.1	12.9	217
McGowan, Bryce	R-R	6-1	205	3-20-00	0	0	9.00	1	0	0	1	2	1	1	0	1	1	.400	.500	.600	16.7	16.7	6
Mears, Nick	R-R	6-2	200	10-07-96	4	1	6.08	24	0	1	24	16	18	16	1	22	39	.193	.364	.277	36.4	20.6	107
Petersen, Michael	R-R	6-7	195	5-16-94	1	1	3.68	22	0	1	22	23	10	9	2	17	21	.280	.412	.402	20.6	16.7	102
Pint, Riley	R-R	6-5	225	11-06-97	3	4	6.12	47	0	0	57	43	44	39	3	57	85	.210	.397	.312	31.1	20.9	273
Poulin, PJ	R-L	6-1	195	7-25-96	3	3	5.44	32	0	0	50	58	36	30	10	33	39	.287	.387	.505	16.4	13.9	238
Rock, Joe	L-L	6-6	200	7-29-00	0	0	10.13	1	1	0	3	3	3	3	1	2	4	.300	.462	.600	30.8	15.4	13
Rogers, Josh	L-L	6-3	211	7-10-94	8	8	8.02	30	13	0	104	141	97	93	31	42	64	.323	.379	.613	13.1	8.6	487
Rolison, Ryan	R-L	6-2	213	7-11-97	0	1	12.60	2	2	0	5	8	7	7	2	3	2	.381	.440	.905	8.0	12.0	25
Seabold, Connor	R-R	6-2	190	1-24-96	1	2	7.47	8	8	0	31	46	27	26	3	8	36	.338	.383	.500	24.2	5.4	149
Senzatela, Antonio	R-R	6-1	236	1-21-95	0	1	9.95	2	2	0	6	13	10	7	0	3	7	.394	.432	.606	18.4	7.9	38
Summers, Luke	R-R	6-0	215	7-11-98	0	0	0.00	1	0	0	1	2	0	0	0	0	0	.400	.400	.400	0.0	0.0	5
Suter, Brent	L-L	6-4	213	8-29-89	0	0	0.00	1	0	0	1	1	0	0	0	0	1	.333	.333	.333	33.3	0.0	3
Valdez, Phillips	R-R	6-2	160	11-16-91	5	7	8.15	22	15	0	67	90	66	61	11	41	49	.325	.425	.534	15.0	12.5	327
Vodnik, Victor	R-R	6-0	200	10-09-99	1	1	7.71	8	0	0	7	11	6	6	3	5	4	.355	.444	.677	11.1	13.9	36

Fielding

Catcher	PCT	G	PO	A	E	DP	PB
Alfaro	1.000	2	20	1	0	0	0
Cope	.993	17	139	7	1	1	3
Cordova	1.000	2	10	1	0	0	0
Fulford	1.000	2	18	1	0	0	0
Goodman	1.000	1	9	2	0	0	1
Greiner	.994	18	155	7	1	1	3
MacIver	.984	46	366	15	6	0	1
Morales	.992	29	241	11	2	0	0
Romo	.955	3	21	0	1	0	2
Serven	.993	35	263	15	2	1	2

First Base	PCT	G	PO	A	E	DP
Bouchard	1.000	1	5	0	0	1
Cope	1.000	1	8	0	0	2
Datres	1.000	7	43	5	0	10
Fulford	1.000	1	4	0	0	0
Goodman	.982	7	56	0	1	5
Herron	1.000	1	8	0	0	0
Jones	1.000	7	47	7	0	4
Montero	1.000	21	180	11	0	24
Morales	.997	45	314	33	1	45
Toglia	.998	55	432	32	1	41
Tucker	.989	11	86	6	1	12

Second Base	PCT	G	PO	A	E	DP
Montes	.982	57	100	169	5	47
Rodgers	1.000	3	5	11	0	3
Schunk	.978	26	35	56	2	14
Stovall	.983	53	93	139	4	47
Tucker	.975	20	25	54	2	11

Third Base	PCT	G	PO	A	E	DP
Jones	.933	17	12	30	3	4
Kaiser	1.000	4	3	5	0	2
Montero	1.000	4	4	9	0	0
Montes	.970	13	5	27	1	3
Morales	1.000	10	4	19	0	1
Schunk	.942	84	48	165	13	20
Stovall	.961	21	14	35	2	4
Trejo	1.000	1	0	2	0	0

Shortstop	PCT	G	PO	A	E	DP
Carreras	1.000	15	25	43	0	13
Kaiser	.984	84	131	250	6	62
Montes	.974	33	36	76	3	17
Stovall	.977	11	10	32	1	6
Trejo	.930	10	16	24	3	7

Outfield	PCT	G	PO	A	E	DP
Bernard	.986	65	146	3	4	1
Blackmon	.667	1	2	0	1	0
Boone	.980	41	66	3	3	0
Bouchard	1.000	11	30	1	0	0
Bryant	1.000	1	5	0	0	0
Datres	1.000	2	1	0	0	0
Daza	.990	38	60	3	1	0
Doyle	1.000	14	31	0	0	0
Goodman	1.000	4	11	1	0	0
Grichuk	1.000	6	11	0	0	0
Hannah	1.000	19	27	0	0	0
Herron	.993	104	206	5	2	1
Jones	1.000	14	21	4	0	0
Montano	.972	51	74	1	2	0
Quinn	.972	20	40	2	1	0
Stovall	.926	14	23	2	2	0
Toglia	.941	15	21	2	2	0
Torrealba	1.000	16	25	0	0	0
Tucker	1.000	41	85	4	0	2

HARTFORD YARD GOATS — DOUBLE-A

EASTERN LEAGUE

Batting	B-T	Ht.	Wt.	DOB	AVG	OBP	SLG	G	PA	AB	R	H	2B	3B	HR	RBI	BB	HBP	SH	SF	SO	SB	CS	BB%	SO%
Amador, Adael	B-R	6-0	160	4-11-03	.143	.244	.229	10	41	35	3	5	0	0	1	2	4	1	0	1	8	3	1	9.8	19.5
Beck, Jordan	R-R	6-3	225	4-19-01	.240	.342	.406	50	223	192	22	46	15	1	5	19	30	0	0	0	71	9	2	13.5	31.8
Bernabel, Warming	R-R	6-1	180	6-06-02	.225	.270	.338	83	322	302	30	68	14	1	6	28	15	4	0	1	68	2	0	4.7	21.1
Blomgren, Jack	R-R	5-10	180	9-27-98	.262	.368	.431	19	78	65	11	17	2	0	3	9	6	5	2	0	31	4	1	7.7	39.7

Boswell, Bret	L-R	5-10	198	10-04-94	.186	.295	.340	66	251	215	27	40	11	2	6	26	33	1	0	2	78	2	0	13.1	31.1
Carreras, Julio	R-R	6-1	190	1-12-00	.235	.316	.334	88	356	311	48	73	14	1	5	31	33	5	4	2	81	13	1	9.3	22.8
Cordova, Jose	R-R	6-0	180	1-11-00	.211	.318	.211	7	22	19	2	4	0	0	0	1	1	2	0	0	6	0	0	4.5	27.3
Datres, Kyle	R-R	6-0	205	1-05-96	.251	.374	.419	89	380	315	53	79	10	2	13	50	53	10	0	2	90	24	3	13.9	23.7
Decolati, Niko	R-R	6-0	215	8-12-97	.225	.380	.313	80	304	240	50	54	10	1	3	16	49	12	1	2	78	12	4	16.1	25.7
Diaz, Eddy	R-R	5-10	175	2-14-00	.152	.252	.182	41	152	132	18	20	4	0	0	5	15	3	0	1	36	1	4	9.9	23.7
Fernandez, Yanquiel	L-L	6-2	198	1-01-03	.206	.262	.362	56	237	218	20	45	10	0	8	25	15	2	0	2	78	0	0	6.3	32.9
Fulford, Braxton	R-R	5-10	190	12-09-98	.219	.331	.381	35	125	105	13	23	8	0	3	6	15	3	1	1	36	2	1	12.0	28.8
Goodman, Hunter	R-R	5-11	210	10-08-99	.239	.325	.523	91	400	348	53	83	24	0	25	78	41	6	0	5	98	0	0	10.3	24.5
Lavigne, Grant	L-R	6-2	220	8-27-99	.227	.350	.398	125	534	445	53	101	19	3	17	51	77	9	0	3	142	4	2	14.4	26.6
Navarro, Cristopher	R-R	6-0	170	6-14-99	.161	.229	.230	37	98	87	9	14	4	1	0	8	8	0	2	1	24	0	0	8.2	24.5
Palma, Ronaiker	R-R	5-8	180	1-02-00	.263	.282	.342	11	39	38	4	10	1	1	0	1	1	0	0	0	7	0	0	2.6	17.9
Restituyo, Bladimir	R-R	5-10	151	7-02-01	.258	.277	.414	108	456	430	61	111	20	1	15	55	8	5	9	4	86	17	6	1.8	18.9
Ritter, Ryan	R-R	6-2	200	11-10-00	.160	.276	.200	8	29	25	4	4	1	0	0	1	3	1	0	0	11	2	0	10.3	37.9
Romo, Drew	B-R	5-11	205	8-29-01	.254	.313	.440	91	368	327	45	83	18	2	13	48	29	2	4	6	67	6	7	7.9	18.2
Simpson, Colin	L-R	5-7	228	7-23-96	.221	.309	.385	66	236	208	25	46	16	0	6	24	27	0	0	1	72	0	0	11.4	30.5
Thompson, Sterlin	L-R	6-4	200	6-26-01	.238	.333	.429	34	144	126	14	30	3	0	7	17	15	3	0	0	32	3	1	10.4	22.2
Veen, Zac	L-R	6-3	190	12-12-01	.209	.303	.308	46	201	172	15	36	7	2	2	24	23	2	0	4	43	22	2	11.4	21.4

Pitching	B-T	Ht.	Wt.	DOB	W	L	ERA	G	GS	SV	IP	Hits	Runs	ER	HR	BB	SO	AVG	OBP	SLG	SO%	BB%	BF
Barger, Alec	R-R	6-2	201	3-24-98	0	2	11.66	13	0	0	15	19	23	19	3	10	15	.311	.425	.525	20.5	13.7	73
Biddy, Jared	R-R	6-2	180	7-25-96	0	0	19.64	5	0	0	7	21	16	16	1	4	4	.500	.563	.690	8.3	8.3	48
Chivilli, Angel	R-R	6-2	162	7-28-02	0	0	2.25	3	0	0	4	4	1	1	0	1	3	.267	.313	.333	18.8	6.3	16
Darnell, Dugan	L-R	6-2	205	6-26-97	6	1	1.55	22	0	7	29	20	7	5	2	14	41	.196	.293	.294	35.3	12.1	116
Del Bonta-Smith, Fineas	R-R	6-0	190	2-02-97	2	2	5.40	35	0	1	45	49	28	27	12	21	55	.275	.361	.562	27.2	10.4	202
Ethridge, Will	R-R	6-5	240	12-20-97	1	0	4.24	12	0	0	17	13	9	8	0	10	15	.206	.346	.238	19.2	12.8	78
Garcia, Nick	L-R	6-4	215	4-20-99	3	9	7.35	26	18	0	94	119	81	77	20	38	83	.308	.382	.534	18.9	8.7	439
Goldsberry, Blake	R-R	6-4	220	5-21-97	3	2	3.86	33	2	1	44	40	21	19	8	20	55	.241	.323	.440	29.1	10.6	189
Gordon, Tanner	L-R	6-5	215	10-26-97	2	2	5.96	4	4	0	23	24	15	15	5	6	21	.273	.326	.511	21.9	6.3	96
Halvorsen, Seth	R-R	6-2	225	2-18-00	0	0	3.00	6	0	0	6	5	2	2	1	3	5	.238	.333	.381	20.8	12.5	24
Hughes, Gabriel	R-R	6-4	220	8-22-01	2	2	7.14	6	6	0	29	34	27	23	7	11	29	.286	.348	.563	22.0	8.3	132
Jones, Stephen	R-R	6-4	195	7-30-97	1	1	1.99	24	0	5	32	24	7	7	2	11	49	.214	.305	.304	37.4	8.4	131
Justice, Evan	L-L	6-4	205	7-07-98	5	0	3.38	15	0	0	16	5	6	6	0	9	25	.096	.250	.173	39.1	14.1	64
Kilkenny, Mitchell	R-R	6-4	206	3-24-97	2	2	6.04	13	0	0	22	31	20	15	0	9	17	.320	.385	.392	15.6	8.3	109
Kitchen, Austin	L-L	6-0	200	2-11-97	6	2	3.62	43	0	3	60	62	27	24	4	15	54	.268	.324	.372	21.3	5.9	253
Kostyshock, Jacob	R-R	6-4	175	1-02-98	0	1	7.07	14	0	0	14	12	11	11	1	11	13	.250	.406	.396	20.0	16.9	65
Kuzia, Nick	R-R	6-4	190	2-07-96	7	1	5.24	45	0	10	55	47	34	32	5	30	51	.236	.351	.367	20.6	12.1	248
Lackey, Shelby	R-R	6-3	190	7-08-97	0	0	7.71	10	0	0	9	5	9	8	1	15	11	.152	.453	.273	20.4	27.8	54
McGowan, Bryce	R-R	6-1	205	3-20-00	0	1	8.04	15	0	0	16	22	16	14	2	14	20	.324	.439	.485	24.4	17.1	82
McKillican, Adam	R-R	6-5	225	1-09-98	3	0	6.21	25	0	1	33	36	26	23	5	14	33	.263	.344	.445	21.3	9.0	155
McMahon, Chris	R-R	6-2	217	2-04-99	2	3	5.91	15	15	0	67	84	48	44	13	25	66	.299	.364	.512	21.1	8.0	313
Mejia, Juan	R-R	6-3	200	7-04-00	1	3	5.74	13	0	1	16	15	11	10	1	9	22	.254	.371	.322	31.4	12.9	70
Navarro, Cristopher	R-R	6-0	170	6-14-99	0	0	0.00	1	0	0	0	0	0	0	0	0	0	.000	.000	.000	0.0	0.0	1
Palmquist, Carson	L-L	6-3	185	10-17-00	0	2	4.43	4	4	0	22	19	11	11	4	9	28	.226	.309	.393	29.8	9.6	94
Petersen, Michael	R-R	6-7	195	5-16-94	1	1	3.20	19	0	1	20	15	9	7	1	8	28	.214	.310	.286	33.3	9.5	84
Quezada, Andrew	L-R	6-1	185	6-28-97	4	8	5.52	25	20	0	106	132	69	65	17	41	85	.310	.376	.481	17.8	8.6	477
Rock, Joe	L-L	6-6	200	7-29-00	1	10	4.50	19	19	0	90	94	53	45	13	32	108	.266	.335	.439	27.3	8.1	395
Ruff, Mike	R-R	6-2	212	3-31-98	0	6	7.75	26	12	0	72	81	63	62	18	42	61	.286	.395	.544	18.1	12.5	337
Schmidt, Colten	L-L	6-0	175	11-25-95	0	1	8.44	9	2	0	16	22	20	15	3	8	14	.306	.393	.528	16.7	9.5	84
Spain, Dylan	R-R	6-6	205	6-21-98	2	2	5.85	22	0	0	32	35	24	21	8	11	31	.278	.365	.524	20.9	7.4	148
Van Scoyoc, Connor	R-R	6-6	234	11-26-99	2	1	5.62	8	8	0	42	47	27	26	7	15	36	.285	.351	.461	19.5	8.1	185
Vodnik, Victor	R-R	6-0	200	10-09-99	0	0	0.00	4	0	2	6	4	0	0	0	1	9	.182	.217	.227	39.1	4.3	23
Williams, Case	R-R	6-3	210	2-16-02	1	11	7.08	23	23	0	102	131	87	80	22	51	79	.316	.395	.566	16.5	10.7	478

Fielding

Catcher	PCT	G	PO	A	E	DP	PB
Cordova	1.000	7	50	3	0	1	0
Fulford	.975	31	269	9	7	0	5
Goodman	.991	12	109	3	1	1	0
Palma	.986	8	64	6	1	1	2
Romo	.982	78	701	44	14	6	8

First Base	PCT	G	PO	A	E	DP
Datres	1.000	2	13	1	0	2
Goodman	.995	24	180	5	1	12
Lavigne	.987	103	710	31	10	71
Simpson	.975	7	36	3	1	5

Second Base	PCT	G	PO	A	E	DP
Amador	.971	9	13	20	1	3
Blomgren	.982	13	21	34	1	9
Boswell	1.000	14	18	26	0	4
Datres	.965	36	56	83	5	19
Diaz	.958	41	67	94	7	25
Navarro	.979	17	24	23	1	7
Simpson	1.000	2	5	6	0	2
Thompson	.980	14	23	26	1	7

Third Base	PCT	G	PO	A	E	DP
Bernabel	.951	80	56	117	9	11
Boswell	.915	28	15	50	6	5
Datres	.966	23	26	31	2	4
Navarro	.938	9	4	11	1	1
Thompson	1.000	3	0	3	0	1

Shortstop	PCT	G	PO	A	E	DP
Amador	1.000	1	1	1	0	1
Blomgren	.917	6	9	13	2	4
Boswell	.987	23	27	47	1	6
Carreras	.949	88	127	229	19	43
Navarro	.950	11	18	20	2	8
Ritter	1.000	8	11	18	0	4

Outfield	PCT	G	PO	A	E	DP
Beck	1.000	48	96	6	0	1
Blomgren	1.000	1	1	0	0	0
Boswell	.667	4	7	0	0	0
Datres	.977	19	32	2	1	1
Decolati	.979	78	135	6	3	0
Fernandez	.977	49	81	4	2	1
Goodman	.922	31	55	4	5	0
Restituyo	.993	108	257	8	2	1
Simpson	.986	23	35	0	1	0
Thompson	1.000	9	15	1	0	0
Veen	.994	45	83	3	1	0

SPOKANE INDIANS

HIGH CLASS A

NORTHWEST LEAGUE

Batting	B-T	Ht.	Wt.	DOB	AVG	OBP	SLG	G	PA	AB	R	H	2B	3B	HR	RBI	BB	HBP	SH	SF	SO	SB	CS	BB%	SO%
Amador, Adael	B-R	6-0	160	4-11-03	.302	.391	.514	54	259	222	46	67	14	3	9	35	31	3	1	2	26	12	4	12.0	10.0
Baylor, Jamari	R-R	5-10	190	8-25-00	.185	.313	.333	18	64	54	10	10	3	1	1	8	9	1	0	0	22	6	0	14.1	34.4
Beck, Jordan	R-R	6-3	225	4-19-01	.292	.378	.566	76	341	295	62	86	19	1	20	72	43	0	0	3	71	11	3	12.6	20.8
Bess, Cuba	L-R	6-2	215	9-29-97	.238	.310	.429	19	71	63	6	15	1	1	3	11	6	1	0	1	24	0	1	8.5	33.8
Bouchard, Sean	R-R	6-3	215	5-16-96	.333	.368	.611	5	19	18	2	6	2	0	1	4	0	1	0	0	5	0	0	0.0	26.3
Cordova, Jose	R-R	6-0	180	1-11-00	.267	.313	.400	5	16	15	1	4	2	0	0	3	1	0	0	0	6	0	0	6.3	37.5
Fernandez, Yanquiel	L-L	6-2	198	1-01-03	.319	.354	.605	58	268	248	47	79	14	3	17	64	14	2	0	4	48	1	1	5.2	17.9
Fulford, Braxton	R-R	5-10	190	12-09-98	.307	.398	.511	37	162	137	33	42	8	1	6	21	15	7	1	2	35	4	2	9.3	21.6
Guerrero, Juan	R-R	6-1	160	9-10-01	.256	.314	.374	112	488	441	62	113	22	6	6	59	32	8	1	6	70	14	7	6.6	14.3
Kelly, Parker	R-R	6-3	220	3-18-99	.217	.341	.406	22	82	69	13	15	3	2	2	7	11	2	0	0	32	5	0	13.4	39.0
Kent, Nic	R-R	6-2	185	4-10-00	.277	.352	.433	112	456	393	59	109	24	2	11	62	41	9	4	9	69	9	5	9.0	15.1
Kokoska, Zach	L-L	6-1	200	10-20-98	.303	.399	.562	76	322	274	47	83	21	1	16	53	35	10	1	2	74	18	7	10.9	23.0
Lewis, AJ	R-R	5-10	195	5-31-98	.203	.367	.350	73	276	217	35	44	12	1	6	24	37	20	1	1	73	3	3	13.4	26.4
MacKenzie, Jake	R-R	5-10	195	5-23-99	.133	.350	.133	5	20	15	2	2	0	0	0	0	4	1	0	0	9	1	0	20.0	45.0
Martin, Robby	L-R	6-3	190	8-17-99	.265	.324	.382	44	148	136	17	36	10	0	2	16	10	2	0	0	39	10	3	6.8	26.4
Montgomery, Benny	R-R	6-4	200	9-09-02	.251	.336	.370	109	497	438	62	110	18	2	10	51	52	5	0	2	135	18	5	10.5	27.2
Navarro, Cristopher	R-R	6-0	170	6-14-99	.222	.276	.296	10	29	27	4	6	2	0	0	1	2	0	0	0	7	0	0	6.9	24.1
Ordonez, Jesus	R-R	5-8	180	12-26-99	.232	.283	.357	16	62	56	5	13	4	0	1	10	4	0	2	0	17	0	0	6.5	27.4
Palma, Ronaiker	R-R	5-8	180	1-02-00	.240	.304	.311	52	206	183	23	44	8	1	1	18	16	2	2	3	21	5	2	7.8	10.2
Perez, Jean	R-R	5-10	178	7-20-02	.333	.389	.364	11	36	33	4	11	1	0	0	0	2	1	0	0	8	0	1	5.6	22.2
Quijada, Bryant	R-R	5-10	167	7-02-99	.144	.300	.178	34	113	90	7	13	3	0	0	5	19	1	3	0	20	0	1	16.8	17.7
Ritter, Ryan	R-R	6-2	200	11-10-00	.265	.367	.441	46	201	170	33	45	10	1	6	26	22	6	2	1	69	12	2	10.9	34.3
Rodgers, Brendan	R-R	6-0	204	8-09-96	.143	.294	.143	5	17	14	1	2	0	0	0	0	2	1	0	0	5	0	0	11.8	29.4
Rodriguez, Aiverson	R-R	6-0	170	4-01-02	.192	.288	.231	18	59	52	6	10	0	1	0	5	7	0	0	0	16	0	1	11.9	27.1
Sems, Benjamin	L-R	6-3	200	2-16-98	.222	.337	.259	76	286	239	18	53	9	0	0	29	32	11	1	3	66	11	5	11.2	23.1
Thompson, Sterlin	L-R	6-4	200	6-26-01	.323	.399	.520	60	263	229	42	74	22	1	7	39	23	8	0	3	42	14	2	8.7	16.0
Ward, Braiden	L-R	5-10	160	1-18-99	.265	.402	.341	80	279	223	63	59	10	2	1	16	27	25	3	1	55	44	7	9.7	19.7

Pitching	B-T	Ht.	Wt.	DOB	W	L	ERA	G	GS	SV	IP	Hits	Runs	ER	HR	BB	SO	AVG	OBP	SLG	SO%	BB%	BF
Adams, Blake	R-R	6-2	215	9-11-00	0	2	6.10	8	8	0	38	45	27	26	5	17	33	.300	.368	.513	19.3	9.9	171
Ahearn, Tyler	R-R	6-2	202	8-25-98	1	3	8.12	39	0	3	38	58	43	34	10	23	40	.345	.427	.583	20.8	12.0	192
Albright, Mason	L-L	6-0	190	11-26-02	2	0	2.88	5	5	0	25	24	13	8	4	12	24	.258	.349	.484	22.4	11.2	107
Amoroso, Luis	R-R	6-1	192	12-12-99	5	1	6.75	44	0	2	57	70	49	43	10	18	41	.300	.363	.536	15.6	6.9	262
Baumgartner, Collin	L-R	6-6	250	9-26-98	0	0	6.75	2	0	0	4	4	3	3	0	2	4	.267	.353	.400	23.5	11.8	17
Bido, Anderson	R-R	6-3	205	5-07-99	1	2	5.60	35	0	2	53	67	37	33	8	11	51	.306	.338	.498	22.1	4.8	231
Cande, Jarrod	R-R	6-2	215	8-16-99	4	4	3.25	19	19	0	105	96	41	38	14	26	109	.241	.290	.398	25.3	6.0	431
Carmichael, Braden	R-L	5-10	186	5-23-00	0	0	0.00	2	0	0	4	3	0	0	0	0	4	.214	.214	.357	28.6	0.0	14
Castillo, Brayan	R-R	6-0	145	9-11-00	2	6	6.21	24	8	0	62	64	48	43	5	46	58	.268	.400	.402	19.6	15.5	296
Chivilli, Angel	R-R	6-2	162	7-28-02	4	9	5.84	50	0	17	57	62	44	37	9	20	65	.274	.353	.456	25.5	7.8	255
Condreay, Joel	L-R	6-3	210	7-05-96	1	0	6.59	13	0	0	14	16	10	10	2	14	16	.308	.441	.500	23.5	20.6	68
Feltner, Ryan	R-R	6-4	190	9-02-96	0	0	3.00	1	1	0	3	3	1	1	0	0	3	.273	.273	.273	27.3	0.0	11
Green, Mason	L-L	6-1	195	2-05-99	1	3	5.52	26	9	0	73	63	46	45	8	48	77	.232	.359	.391	23.3	14.5	331
Halvorsen, Seth	R-R	6-2	225	2-18-00	0	0	3.60	5	0	0	5	6	2	2	1	1	5	.300	.333	.450	23.8	4.8	21
Hernandez, Robinson	R-R	6-0	186	6-11-99	1	0	3.60	1	1	0	5	6	2	2	2	1	4	.300	.333	.600	19.0	4.8	21
Hill, Jaden	R-R	6-4	234	12-22-99	0	9	9.48	16	16	0	44	54	47	46	11	25	57	.295	.401	.557	26.3	11.5	217
Hughes, Gabriel	R-R	6-4	220	8-22-01	4	3	5.50	8	8	0	38	30	24	23	5	15	54	.208	.286	.410	33.5	9.3	161
James, Keegan	R-R	6-3	214	4-01-97	4	1	6.20	25	0	0	45	50	31	31	3	22	37	.287	.379	.437	18.2	10.8	203
Juarez, Victor	R-R	6-0	173	6-19-03	6	6	6.38	20	20	0	92	116	66	65	16	35	94	.314	.385	.520	22.5	8.4	417
Justice, Evan	L-L	6-4	205	7-07-98	1	0	0.00	10	0	1	10	4	0	0	0	5	19	.125	.282	.156	47.5	12.5	40
Kafka, Cullen	R-R	6-4	210	4-16-99	5	4	4.57	22	6	0	67	76	40	34	7	32	56	.288	.375	.432	18.4	10.5	304
Kinley, Tyler	R-R	6-4	220	1-31-91	1	0	6.00	3	0	0	3	3	2	2	2	0	4	.250	.250	.833	33.3	0.0	12
Kostyshock, Jacob	R-R	6-4	175	1-02-98	0	0	3.27	9	0	1	11	9	4	4	0	2	14	.214	.298	.262	29.8	4.3	47
Matthews, Brett	R-R	6-5	219	4-23-98	0	0	6.75	2	0	0	3	2	2	2	0	6	4	.200	.500	.200	25.0	37.5	16
McGowan, Bryce	R-R	6-1	205	3-20-00	3	0	2.04	14	0	1	18	10	4	4	2	9	26	.161	.268	.290	36.6	12.7	71
Mejia, Juan	R-R	6-3	200	7-04-00	2	2	4.81	35	0	1	43	37	32	23	3	23	64	.230	.357	.360	32.2	11.6	199
Palmquist, Carson	L-L	6-3	185	10-17-00	7	2	3.73	15	15	0	70	61	33	29	9	28	106	.238	.331	.398	35.7	9.4	297
Pilar, Anderson	R-R	6-2	210	3-02-98	4	2	3.96	7	3	0	25	19	11	11	2	9	27	.224	.320	.353	27.0	9.0	100
Ramires, Felix	L-L	6-4	175	9-26-99	0	0	8.68	18	0	0	19	26	18	18	6	10	22	.325	.407	.588	24.2	11.0	91
Ras, Tyler	B-R	6-4	205	11-09-99	0	1	5.91	7	0	0	11	12	7	7	1	3	10	.267	.327	.467	20.4	6.1	49
Schmidt, Colten	L-L	6-0	175	11-25-95	0	1	4.63	3	2	0	12	16	10	6	2	2	11	.308	.333	.481	20.4	3.7	54
Shawver, Evan	R-L	6-0	175	9-11-99	2	4	5.94	24	4	0	50	55	36	33	7	34	49	.282	.401	.441	20.7	14.3	237
Summers, Luke	R-R	6-0	215	7-11-98	0	0	16.88	2	0	0	3	5	5	5	1	3	2	.385	.500	.846	12.5	18.8	16
Van Scoyoc, Connor	R-R	6-6	234	11-26-99	1	2	3.33	4	4	0	24	26	11	9	1	5	22	.280	.330	.398	21.2	4.8	104

Fielding

Catcher	PCT	G	PO	A	E	DP	PB
Fulford	.997	34	338	15	1	0	6
Lewis	.991	11	105	3	1	0	2
Ordonez	1.000	14	127	9	0	1	2
Palma	.998	45	394	35	1	3	8
Quijada	.993	32	256	17	2	1	3

First Base	PCT	G	PO	A	E	DP
Bess	.991	15	94	11	1	14
Cordova	1.000	5	27	9	0	2
Kelly	1.000	7	58	6	0	4
Kokoska	.987	56	338	43	5	35
Lewis	.984	41	266	42	5	21
Navarro	1.000	1	1	1	0	0
Quijada	1.000	2	16	4	0	1
Sems	.976	12	74	7	2	10

Second Base	PCT	G	PO	A	E	DP
Amador	1.000	11	14	28	0	7
Baylor	1.000	4	5	10	0	2
Kent	.993	78	110	180	2	40
Lewis	1.000	4	3	5	0	1
MacKenzie	1.000	5	5	13	0	2
Navarro	.857	3	4	2	1	1

	PCT	G	PO	A	E	DP
Perez	.875	2	4	3	1	1
Rodgers	1.000	3	4	3	0	1
Rodriguez	.833	1	3	2	1	1
Sems	.982	16	22	32	1	4
Ward	.980	16	21	29	1	8

Third Base	PCT	G	PO	A	E	DP
Baylor	.692	7	2	7	4	0
Kelly	1.000	6	6	9	0	0
Kent	.500	2	0	1	1	0
Lewis	.857	5	0	6	1	3
Navarro	1.000	2	1	0	0	0
Perez	1.000	3	6	6	0	1

	PCT	G	PO	A	E	DP
Rodriguez	.870	12	3	17	3	0
Sems	.941	48	33	63	6	2
Thompson	.947	56	18	72	5	8

Shortstop	PCT	G	PO	A	E	DP
Amador	.948	43	53	75	7	14
Kent	.955	34	51	76	6	17
Navarro	1.000	5	7	9	0	4
Perez	1.000	6	10	7	0	1
Ritter	.984	46	64	124	3	29
Sems	1.000	1	1	1	0	0

Outfield	PCT	G	PO	A	E	DP
Beck	.982	66	121	2	2	1
Bouchard	.500	3	1	0	1	0
Fernandez	.980	49	92	7	2	0
Guerrero	.982	78	136	4	4	1
Kelly	1.000	8	20	2	0	0
Kokoska	.963	18	23	3	1	0
Martin	1.000	41	75	6	0	1
Montgomery	.990	94	156	5	3	2
Thompson	1.000	1	3	0	0	0
Ward	.982	51	104	2	2	1

FRESNO GRIZZLIES — *LOW CLASS A*

CALIFORNIA LEAGUE

Batting	B-T	Ht.	Wt.	DOB	AVG	OBP	SLG	G	PA	AB	R	H	2B	3B	HR	RBI	BB	HBP	SH	SF	SO	SB	CS	BB%	SO%
Amaral, Daniel	R-R	6-0	190	3-07-97	.301	.392	.429	49	189	163	33	49	6	3	3	23	20	5	0	1	33	27	3	10.6	17.5
Andrews, EJ	R-R	6-1	210	9-28-00	.213	.317	.386	110	404	347	59	74	13	4	13	53	48	6	0	3	127	11	4	11.9	31.4
Baylor, Jamari	R-R	5-10	190	8-25-00	.333	.475	.611	33	139	108	32	36	9	0	7	27	24	6	0	1	37	6	1	17.3	26.6
Betancourt, Bryant	L-R	5-11	170	10-12-03	.244	.325	.327	104	450	394	44	96	19	1	4	57	43	7	1	5	74	2	0	9.6	16.4
Bugarin, Jesus	R-R	5-10	180	12-02-01	.262	.282	.380	113	477	458	60	120	14	5	10	66	11	3	1	4	128	12	7	2.3	26.8
Carrigg, Cole	B-R	6-3	190	5-08-02	.326	.376	.554	23	101	92	19	30	4	4	3	16	7	1	0	1	20	6	1	6.9	19.8
Fernandez, Yanquiel	L-L	6-2	198	1-01-03	.231	.375	.308	3	16	13	3	3	1	0	0	3	3	0	0	0	6	0	0	18.8	37.5
Huff, Kody	R-R	5-10	198	12-11-00	.262	.357	.374	86	340	294	39	77	14	2	5	36	38	6	1	1	73	2	1	11.2	21.5
Jorge, Dyan	R-R	6-3	170	3-18-03	.283	.322	.338	49	215	198	29	56	11	0	0	22	13	0	1	3	35	10	2	6.0	16.3
Karros, Kyle	R-R	6-5	220	7-26-02	.259	.365	.284	22	96	81	15	21	2	0	0	6	12	2	0	1	17	0	0	12.5	17.7
Kelly, Parker	R-R	6-3	220	3-18-99	.235	.352	.357	78	273	230	36	54	13	3	3	23	35	7	0	1	103	5	3	12.8	37.7
Longwell, Aidan	L-L	6-1	205	10-17-01	.295	.340	.341	12	47	44	4	13	2	0	0	6	3	0	0	0	10	0	1	6.4	21.3
Martin, Robby	L-R	6-3	190	8-17-99	.265	.316	.425	52	196	181	24	48	12	1	5	26	14	0	0	1	38	6	2	7.1	19.4
Mendez, Luis	L-R	5-11	157	10-30-02	.208	.347	.251	63	223	183	35	38	6	1	0	15	36	3	1	0	51	7	4	16.1	22.9
Messinger, Skyler	R-R	6-3	220	11-01-98	.258	.364	.475	106	435	364	60	94	19	3	18	78	54	10	1	6	113	7	1	12.4	26.0
Ordonez, Jesus	R-R	5-8	180	12-26-99	.217	.300	.264	36	121	106	13	23	5	0	0	16	11	2	1	1	21	0	0	9.1	17.4
Perez, Andy	L-R	6-3	165	6-03-04	.245	.280	.316	119	502	465	66	114	16	7	1	53	17	8	4	7	74	21	11	3.4	14.7
Perez, Jean	R-R	5-10	178	7-20-02	.183	.223	.296	45	122	115	16	21	4	0	3	10	4	2	1	0	31	3	4	3.3	25.4
Ritter, Ryan	R-R	6-2	200	11-10-00	.305	.405	.606	65	295	246	53	75	14	3	18	58	37	7	1	4	72	6	3	12.5	24.4
Snider, Jake	L-R	6-1	190	5-19-98	.261	.369	.403	112	447	375	82	98	15	10	6	37	55	11	2	4	93	22	2	12.3	20.8
Stilwell, Cole	R-R	6-1	215	2-18-00	.237	.431	.395	12	51	38	4	9	3	0	1	5	13	0	0	0	8	0	0	25.5	15.7

Pitching	B-T	Ht.	Wt.	DOB	W	L	ERA	G	GS	SV	IP	Hits	Runs	ER	HR	BB	SO	AVG	OBP	SLG	SO%	BB%	BF
Adams, Blake	R-R	6-2	215	9-11-00	1	3	2.60	8	8	0	45	38	15	13	0	5	53	.226	.250	.315	30.1	2.8	176
Agnos, Zach	R-R	6-0	210	8-15-00	5	3	2.06	47	0	27	52	40	18	12	4	13	68	.198	.258	.277	30.8	5.9	221
Albright, Mason	L-L	6-0	190	11-26-02	1	0	0.00	1	1	0	5	2	0	0	0	2	9	.118	.211	.118	47.4	10.5	19
Barbosa, Gabriel	R-R	6-0	183	1-22-02	7	6	5.44	22	13	1	94	121	68	57	5	19	82	.312	.350	.446	19.6	4.5	419
Becker, Austin	R-R	6-5	215	9-02-99	2	4	5.83	25	0	2	29	33	21	19	1	13	37	.287	.359	.435	28.0	9.8	132
Coupet, Isaiah	L-L	6-1	190	9-27-02	0	0	0.00	3	0	0	2	1	0	0	0	0	3	.143	.143	.143	42.9	0.0	7
Cox, Jackson	R-R	6-1	185	9-25-03	1	0	7.26	10	9	0	31	39	27	25	2	20	32	.307	.409	.472	21.5	13.4	149
Denton, Cade	R-R	6-3	180	12-28-01	0	0	18.00	4	0	0	5	9	10	10	1	2	5	.375	.464	.583	17.9	7.1	28
Fernandez, Wuardo	R-R	6-1	168	12-14-00	0	0	10.61	11	0	0	9	16	11	11	2	12	14	.364	.509	.591	24.6	21.1	57
Franzen, Caleb	L-L	6-3	200	6-10-01	4	5	4.22	22	21	0	113	121	62	53	9	42	108	.273	.337	.404	22.0	8.5	492
Hernandez, Robinson	R-R	6-0	186	6-11-99	1	0	2.50	6	0	0	18	14	5	5	1	7	16	.209	.280	.358	21.3	9.3	75
Hill, Brady	L-R	6-0	180	11-10-00	2	0	7.62	24	0	0	26	29	22	22	7	13	16	.284	.364	.559	13.6	11.0	118
Hoffman, Tyler	R-R	6-0	182	9-01-99	2	1	6.85	24	0	0	24	21	19	18	2	15	25	.239	.358	.375	22.9	13.8	109
Hyde, Braxton	R-R	6-3	195	6-06-01	3	2	5.22	37	0	0	50	50	32	29	3	19	42	.262	.341	.414	19.0	8.6	221
Madden, Jake	R-R	6-6	185	12-26-01	0	2	7.80	6	6	0	15	18	13	13	4	9	14	.290	.380	.516	19.7	12.7	71
McGowan, Bryce	R-R	6-1	205	3-20-00	0	0	0.68	12	0	2	13	8	2	1	0	6	16	.182	.288	.182	30.8	11.5	52
Pacheco, Alberto	L-L	6-1	176	11-29-02	7	4	5.45	14	14	0	73	90	51	44	4	23	69	.313	.364	.434	21.5	7.2	321
Palermo, Davison	R-R	6-4	200	12-16-99	1	3	4.36	38	0	2	43	33	24	21	4	20	49	.206	.326	.356	25.7	10.5	191
Pilar, Anderson	R-R	6-2	210	3-02-98	1	2	4.91	3	3	0	15	17	8	8	0	7	15	.283	.386	.367	21.4	10.0	70
Prosecky, Michael	L-L	6-3	200	2-28-01	11	7	2.72	21	21	0	109	87	37	33	4	41	125	.217	.299	.282	27.6	9.1	453
Ramires, Felix	L-L	6-4	175	9-26-99	1	0	0.50	25	0	1	36	22	5	2	1	10	41	.180	.252	.213	30.1	7.4	136
Ramos, Javier	R-R	6-6	210	10-15-99	0	0	7.98	12	0	0	15	19	14	13	2	11	17	.311	.455	.410	22.1	14.3	77
Rodriguez, Gabriel	L-L	6-1	193	4-09-99	1	0	9.00	12	0	0	12	10	15	12	2	15	14	.217	.419	.370	22.6	24.2	62
Rolison, Ryan	R-L	6-2	213	7-11-97	0	0	6.00	2	2	0	6	6	4	4	1	3	7	.240	.321	.440	25.0	10.7	28
Sanchez, Sergio	R-R	6-0	180	1-13-01	3	1	3.50	37	1	2	62	46	26	24	3	34	73	.210	.322	.311	28.3	13.2	258
Skipper, Carson	L-L	6-2	211	8-12-99	1	2	3.20	42	0	1	51	56	21	18	4	10	65	.279	.318	.423	30.4	4.7	214
Staine, Connor	R-R	6-4	200	1-12-01	10	5	5.25	21	20	0	94	107	62	55	8	28	93	.282	.337	.403	22.2	6.7	418
Sullivan, Sean	R-L	6-4	190	7-22-02	1	0	0.00	1	0	0	2	0	0	0	0	0	6	.000	.000	.000	100.0	0.0	6
Torres, Carlos	R-R	6-4	240	5-03-01	6	1	3.50	43	0	0	62	63	32	24	5	21	54	.267	.335	.407	20.5	8.0	263
Vargas, Jordy	R-R	6-3	153	11-06-03	6	3	4.22	13	13	0	64	55	35	30	4	24	69	.239	.314	.348	26.1	9.1	264

Fielding

Catcher	PCT	G	PO	A	E	DP	PB
Betancourt	.996	31	244	25	1	2	8
Carrigg	1.000	4	32	5	0	2	1
Huff	.995	82	725	59	4	5	6
Ordonez	.988	28	221	22	3	3	2
Stilwell	1.000	1	5	0	0	0	0

First Base	PCT	G	PO	A	E	DP
Betancourt	.987	43	275	38	4	34
Kelly	.991	49	316	32	3	26
Longwell	1.000	8	68	6	0	5
Messinger	.993	36	254	14	2	28

	PCT	G	PO	A	E	DP
Perez	1.000	1	4	0	0	1
Stilwell	1.000	9	65	2	0	5

Second Base	PCT	G	PO	A	E	DP
Baylor	.958	23	33	58	4	12
Jorge	1.000	11	15	18	0	4
Mendez	.943	55	100	117	13	34
Perez, A	1.000	28	39	50	0	15
Perez, J	.985	21	25	40	1	11
Ritter	.979	11	18	29	1	9

Third Base	PCT	G	PO	A	E	DP
Baylor	1.000	1	1	0	0	0
Karros	.964	20	16	38	2	5
Kelly	1.000	8	1	4	0	0
Messinger	.949	54	33	78	6	8
Perez, A	.898	46	22	84	12	10
Perez, J	.897	19	12	23	4	4

Shortstop	PCT	G	PO	A	E	DP
Carrigg	.967	7	11	18	1	3
Jorge	.916	38	45	97	13	20
Perez, A	.973	42	51	92	4	27
Perez, J	.900	6	2	7	1	2
Ritter	.951	48	67	107	9	19

Outfield	PCT	G	PO	A	E	DP
Amaral	1.000	48	95	4	0	1
Andrews	.976	101	183	5	6	1
Bugarin	.909	105	202	3	9	0
Carrigg	1.000	11	27	1	0	0
Fernandez	1.000	3	6	0	0	0
Kelly	.984	23	42	0	1	0
Martin	.920	45	74	6	7	1
Snider	.496	87	126	5	1	0

ACL ROCKIES — ROOKIE

ARIZONA COMPLEX LEAGUE

Batting	B-T	Ht.	Wt.	DOB	AVG	OBP	SLG	G	PA	AB	R	H	2B	3B	HR	RBI	BB	HBP	SH	SF	SO	SB	CS	BB%	SO%
Amador, Adael	B-R	6-0	160	4-11-03	.389	.500	.778	5	22	18	6	7	1	0	2	9	4	0	0	0	3	0	0	18.2	13.6
Amaral, Daniel	R-R	6-0	190	3-07-97	.258	.405	.355	11	43	31	7	8	3	0	0	7	8	1	1	2	5	8	1	18.6	11.6
Baylor, Jamari	R-R	5-10	190	8-25-00	.333	.600	.333	1	5	3	3	1	0	0	0	0	2	0	0	0	2	0	0	40.0	40.0
Bernabel, Warming	R-R	6-1	180	6-06-02	.333	.389	.636	8	36	33	9	11	4	0	2	8	1	2	0	0	6	0	0	2.8	16.7
Bess, Cuba	L-R	6-2	215	9-29-97	.286	.389	.623	22	95	77	19	22	5	0	7	26	13	2	0	3	25	1	0	13.7	26.3
Bouchard, Sean	R-R	6-3	215	5-16-96	.000	.333	.000	1	3	2	0	0	0	0	0	1	0	1	0	0	0	0	0	0.0	0.0
Carrigg, Cole	B-R	6-3	190	5-08-02	.396	.464	.688	13	57	48	13	19	6	1	2	13	6	1	1	1	13	7	2	10.5	22.8
Castillo, Juan	R-R	6-1	170	1-16-03	.240	.345	.320	24	59	50	10	12	2	1	0	5	5	3	1	0	15	0	0	8.5	25.4
Cordova, Jose	R-R	6-0	180	1-11-00	.286	.333	.357	4	15	14	2	4	1	0	0	3	1	0	0	0	2	1	0	6.7	13.3
Cron, C.J.	R-R	6-4	235	1-05-90	.250	.429	.250	2	7	4	1	1	0	0	0	1	1	1	0	1	0	0	0	14.3	0.0
Cruz, Fadriel	L-R	5-10	170	11-12-00	.276	.402	.448	50	221	181	52	50	3	5	6	39	36	2	2	0	52	18	5	16.3	23.5
Datres, Kyle	R-R	6-0	205	1-05-96	.000	.429	.000	2	7	4	2	0	0	0	0	0	2	1	0	0	3	0	0	28.6	42.9
Diaz, Eddy	R-R	5-10	175	2-14-00	.195	.277	.341	15	48	41	8	8	0	0	2	5	4	1	1	1	10	0	1	8.3	20.8
Fulford, Braxton	R-R	5-10	190	12-09-98	.111	.400	.111	3	15	9	3	1	0	0	0	3	2	3	0	1	1	0	0	13.3	6.7
Garcia, Francisco	R-R	6-0	190	11-10-02	.233	.324	.567	8	34	30	4	7	4	0	2	15	1	3	0	0	13	0	0	2.9	38.2
Gile, Nick	R-R	5-11	210	1-12-99	.223	.353	.455	37	136	112	26	25	7	2	5	22	19	4	0	1	37	2	0	14.0	27.2
Hannah, Jameson	L-L	5-10	185	8-10-97	.483	.568	.724	9	37	29	7	14	4	0	1	6	7	0	0	1	3	2	0	18.9	8.1
Harris, Daniel	R-R	6-0	195	7-21-99	.358	.444	.491	21	63	53	12	19	1	0	2	10	6	3	0	1	13	1	1	9.5	20.6
Hinchman, Jason	R-R	6-3	220	7-19-99	.302	.426	.484	51	195	159	38	48	16	2	3	25	29	6	0	1	47	6	2	14.9	24.1
Hobson, Caleb	R-R	6-1	183	1-24-02	.213	.362	.277	15	59	47	14	10	1	1	0	7	10	1	1	0	16	6	0	16.9	27.1
Jorge, Dyan	R-R	6-3	170	3-18-03	.370	.495	.644	21	94	73	31	27	5	3	3	18	19	0	1	1	12	9	0	20.2	12.8
Karros, Kyle	R-R	6-5	220	7-26-02	.327	.450	.408	14	60	49	15	16	2	1	0	11	10	1	0	0	8	3	0	16.7	13.3
Longwell, Aidan	L-L	6-1	205	10-17-01	.366	.446	.479	18	83	71	12	26	8	0	0	15	9	2	0	1	9	4	0	10.8	10.8
MacIver, Willie	R-R	6-1	205	10-28-96	.359	.537	.513	13	54	39	12	14	4	1	0	10	12	3	0	0	11	6	0	22.2	20.4
MacKenzie, Jake	R-R	5-10	195	5-23-99	.310	.459	.552	14	37	29	12	9	1	0	2	10	7	1	0	0	10	1	0	18.9	27.0
McCabe, Ben	R-R	6-0	185	2-04-00	.111	.273	.167	7	22	18	3	2	1	0	0	3	0	4	0	0	11	0	0	0.0	50.0
Mendez, Luis	L-R	5-11	157	10-30-02	.226	.294	.355	28	102	93	15	21	2	2	2	16	9	0	0	0	28	4	2	8.8	27.5
Meyer, Jake	R-R	6-1	190	3-31-99	.250	.471	.361	20	51	36	9	9	1	0	1	5	12	3	0	0	15	1	0	23.5	29.4
Montano, Daniel	L-R	6-0	204	3-31-99	.148	.361	.148	9	36	27	6	4	0	0	0	2	9	0	0	0	9	0	0	25.0	25.0
Morales, Jonathan	R-R	5-11	200	1-29-95	.000	.000	.000	3	9	8	0	0	0	0	0	1	0	0	0	1	3	0	0	0.0	33.3
Ortiz, Francisco	R-R	6-0	160	9-15-99	.289	.385	.400	16	52	45	10	13	2	0	1	7	4	3	0	0	19	0	0	7.7	36.5
2-team (10-team ACL D-backs Red)					.278	.373	.375	26	84	72	15	20	4	0	1	16	8	3	0	1	22	0	0	9.5	26.2
Palma, Ronaiker	R-R	5-8	180	1-02-00	.357	.400	.357	4	15	14	4	5	0	0	0	1	1	0	0	0	3	0	0	6.7	20.0
Perry, Darius	R-R	6-2	200	5-03-01	.375	.389	.563	6	18	16	8	6	1	1	0	4	0	1	0	1	4	0	0	0.0	22.2
Rodriguez, Aiverson	R-R	6-0	170	4-01-02	.600	.667	.600	4	15	10	4	6	0	0	0	5	4	0	0	1	0	0	0	26.7	0.0
Tena, Felix	R-R	6-0	196	9-27-03	.280	.316	.357	47	193	182	30	51	10	2	0	26	9	1	0	1	36	10	5	4.7	18.7
Tucker, Tevin	R-R	6-0	190	2-10-00	.256	.340	.326	13	50	43	11	11	3	0	0	7	5	1	0	1	14	4	0	10.0	28.0
Wimmer, Braylen	R-R	6-4	200	12-27-00	.383	.453	.596	14	54	47	15	18	5	1	1	5	5	1	1	0	14	2	0	9.3	25.9

Pitching	B-T	Ht.	Wt.	DOB	W	L	ERA	G	GS	SV	IP	Hits	Runs	ER	HR	BB	SO	AVG	OBP	SLG	SO%	BB%	BF
Baumgartner, Collin	L-R	6-6	250	9-26-98	0	0	2.08	4	0	0	4	2	1	1	0	1	4	.133	.188	.133	25.0	6.3	16
Butler, Troy	R-R	6-2	195	3-22-03	0	0	18.00	3	0	0	2	2	4	4	0	5	0	.250	.600	.375	0.0	33.3	15
Carasiti, Matt	R-R	6-2	205	7-23-91	1	0	4.50	2	0	0	2	2	1	1	0	1	4	.250	.333	.375	44.4	11.1	9
Carmichael, Braden	R-L	5-10	186	5-23-00	1	0	0.00	3	0	0	3	3	0	0	0	2	5	.300	.417	.300	41.7	16.7	12
Correa, Yanzel	B-R	6-4	210	12-17-04	0	0	0.00	1	0	0	1	0	0	0	0	1	1	.000	.333	.000	33.3	33.3	3
Coupet, Isaiah	L-L	6-1	190	9-27-02	0	0	0.00	2	0	0	2	0	0	0	0	1	3	.000	.143	.000	42.9	14.3	7
Davis, Noah	R-R	6-2	195	4-22-97	0	0	3.00	1	1	0	3	3	1	1	1	0	6	.250	.250	.583	50.0	0.0	12
Denton, Cade	R-R	6-3	180	12-28-01	0	0	3.60	4	0	1	5	5	2	2	0	1	7	.263	.286	.368	33.3	4.8	21
Emener, Austin	L-L	6-4	210	6-01-02	0	0	4.91	4	0	0	4	3	2	2	0	2	7	.214	.313	.429	43.8	12.5	16
Ethridge, Will	R-R	6-5	240	12-20-97	1	0	4.00	7	1	0	9	9	6	4	0	5	11	.257	.357	.343	26.2	11.9	42
Fernandez, Wuardo	R-R	6-1	168	12-14-00	0	0	2.08	11	0	2	13	8	4	3	0	5	17	.178	.283	.200	32.1	9.4	53
Flesland, Stu	R-L	6-5	207	10-01-00	0	0	2.45	3	0	0	4	2	1	1	0	4	2	.167	.375	.167	12.5	25.0	16
Garcia, Kevin	L-L	6-0	170	11-25-99	0	0	13.50	9	0	1	7	12	13	10	1	10	6	.429	.600	.643	15.0	25.0	40
Halvorsen, Seth	R-R	6-2	225	2-18-00	2	0	0.00	2	0	0	2	3	0	0	0	0	3	.300	.300	.400	30.0	0.0	10
Hammer, Bryson	L-L	6-1	186	10-08-01	0	0	5.06	5	0	0	5	7	3	3	0	2	6	.304	.360	.391	24.0	8.0	25
Handy, Kannon	L-L	6-3	220	6-01-00	0	0	0.00	2	0	0	2	1	0	0	0	0	2	.167	.167	.333	33.3	0.0	6
Hernandez, Robinson	R-R	6-0	186	6-11-99	1	0	0.81	11	3	0	22	10	2	2	0	1	24	.132	.143	.197	31.2	1.3	77
Herrera, Welinton	L-L	6-0	166	4-03-04	2	0	3.27	21	0	1	22	16	8	8	0	15	36	.203	.357	.215	36.7	15.3	98
Hill, Brady	L-R	6-0	180	11-10-00	0	0	0.75	11	0	3	12	2	1	1	0	3	14	.054	.122	.108	34.1	7.3	41

Hoffman, Tyler	R-R	6-0	182	9-01-99	1	1	14.21	8	0	0	6	7	10	10	1	6	6	.280	.419	.520	19.4	19.4	31
Jimenez, Angel	R-R	6-2	190	7-04-03	1	2	3.08	10	9	0	38	35	14	13	3	6	50	.252	.288	.403	34.2	4.1	146
Kaminska, Jace	R-R	6-2	235	12-09-01	0	0	0.00	1	0	0	1	1	0	0	0	0	1	.333	.333	.333	33.3	0.0	3
Kennedy, Nick	R-L	6-1	200	6-20-96	1	0	1.35	7	0	0	7	8	1	1	0	3	9	.286	.355	.321	29.0	9.7	31
Kinley, Tyler	R-R	6-4	220	1-31-91	0	0	40.50	2	2	0	1	5	6	6	0	1	1	.556	.600	.778	10.0	10.0	10
Lackey, Shelby	R-R	6-3	190	7-08-97	0	1	19.64	6	0	0	4	3	8	8	0	10	8	.250	.643	.250	28.6	35.7	28
Luciano, Ismael	R-R	6-0	170	3-04-03	1	1	6.19	8	5	0	16	16	12	11	2	8	13	.258	.347	.468	18.1	11.1	72
Mahoney, Jack	R-R	6-3	205	8-13-01	0	0	9.00	2	0	0	2	3	2	2	1	1	3	.375	.400	.750	30.0	10.0	10
Mann, Hunter	R-R	6-7	225	8-15-01	0	0	0.00	1	0	0	1	1	0	0	0	0	3	.250	.250	.250	75.0	0.0	4
Matthews, Brett	R-R	6-5	219	4-23-98	3	3	4.43	14	3	0	22	16	14	11	4	13	26	.200	.309	.388	27.7	13.8	94
McGowan, Bryce	R-R	6-1	205	3-20-00	0	0	9.00	1	0	0	2	4	2	2	0	0	2	.444	.400	.556	20.0	0.0	10
Mears, Nick	R-R	6-2	200	10-07-96	0	0	0.00	1	1	0	1	1	0	0	0	0	3	.250	.400	.250	60.0	0.0	5
Mena, Bryan	R-R	6-2	185	6-14-04	3	1	5.26	6	6	0	26	28	15	15	0	7	28	.280	.348	.350	25.0	6.3	112
Olivares, Manuel	R-R	5-11	145	12-04-01	5	0	3.70	11	8	0	49	56	25	20	2	13	40	.293	.343	.408	19.1	6.2	209
Perdomo, Alan	R-R	6-4	150	8-24-01	6	4	5.71	24	0	4	35	33	24	22	2	8	35	.248	.315	.398	23.5	5.4	149
Perez, Bryan	R-R	6-2	167	9-08-03	1	0	7.43	10	10	0	36	53	31	30	6	16	37	.335	.411	.551	20.6	8.9	180
Pilar, Anderson	R-R	6-2	210	3-02-98	2	0	0.47	7	3	0	19	14	1	1	0	9	25	.203	.337	.203	30.1	10.8	83
Ramires, Felix	L-L	6-4	175	9-26-99	0	0	0.00	1	0	0	1	0	0	0	0	0	1	.000	.000	.000	50.0	0.0	2
Ramos, Javier	R-R	6-6	210	10-15-99	1	0	2.61	11	0	0	10	7	3	3	0	8	14	.179	.319	.205	29.8	17.0	47
Rodriguez, Gabriel	L-L	6-1	193	4-09-99	1	1	4.38	11	0	0	12	8	6	6	0	13	18	.186	.379	.279	31.0	22.4	58
Schmidt, Colten	L-L	6-0	175	11-25-95	1	0	0.00	2	1	0	5	0	0	0	0	0	5	.000	.000	.000	29.4	0.0	17
Sommers, Jake	R-R	6-2	190	5-05-97	1	0	0.00	5	2	0	5	6	2	0	0	1	5	.273	.304	.273	21.7	4.3	23
Spain, Dylan	R-R	6-6	205	6-21-98	0	0	0.00	1	0	0	1	0	0	0	0	1	1	.000	.250	.000	25.0	25.0	4
Sullivan, Sean	R-L	6-4	190	7-22-02	0	0	0.00	2	0	0	2	0	0	0	0	1	4	.000	.143	.000	57.1	14.3	7
Summers, Luke	R-R	6-0	215	7-11-98	4	1	4.42	19	0	0	18	28	10	9	0	12	22	.368	.456	.566	24.2	13.2	91

Fielding

C: Castillo 23, Meyer 14, MacIver 7, McCabe 6, Perry 6, Ortiz 5, Palma 3, Morales 3, Carrigg 3, Cordova 2, Fulford 2. **1B:** Bess 20, Longwell 16, Hinchman 13, Ortiz 8, Garcia 3, Cron 1. **2B:** Diaz 14, Mendez 14, Tucker 12, MacKenzie 8, Harris 6, Gile 4, Amador 3, Rodriguez 1. **3B:** Gile 31, Karros 14, Bernabel 5, MacKenzie 4, Harris 3, Datres 2, Wimmer 2, Baylor 1, Rodriguez 1. **SS:** Jorge 21, Wimmer 12, Mendez 11, Harris 8, Carrigg 3, Amador 2, Tucker 2. **OF:** Cruz 50, Tena 46, Hinchman 28, Hobson 16, Amaral 11, Montano 8, Hannah 6, Harris 5, Carrigg 4, Cordova 1, MacKenzie 1.

COLORADO ROCKIES

DSL ROCKIES — *ROOKIE*

DOMINICAN SUMMER LEAGUE

Batting	B-T	Ht.	Wt.	DOB	AVG	OBP	SLG	G	PA	AB	R	H	2B	3B	HR	RBI	BB	HBP	SH	SF	SO	SB	CS	BB%	SO%
Alcantara, Elisandro	R-R	6-0	175	10-29-02	.344	.417	.444	29	103	90	25	31	7	1	0	17	10	2	0	1	18	8	0	9.7	17.5
Alvarez, Jjam	R-R	5-11	160	6-03-06	.275	.337	.288	25	89	80	17	22	1	0	0	12	7	1	0	1	26	5	3	7.9	29.2
Arias, Cruzmel	R-R	5-11	176	2-20-04	.246	.317	.304	26	82	69	7	17	4	0	0	11	5	4	0	4	9	0	1	6.1	11.0
Bautista, Erick	R-R	6-2	197	2-18-05	.271	.410	.529	44	178	140	32	38	9	0	9	29	28	7	0	3	62	8	4	15.7	34.8
Bernard, Derek	L-R	6-0	190	8-09-05	.311	.411	.563	42	180	151	32	47	11	3	7	40	26	1	0	2	32	17	3	14.4	17.8
Calaz, Robert	R-R	6-2	202	11-22-05	.325	.423	.561	43	189	157	38	51	12	2	7	29	22	7	0	3	43	6	0	11.6	22.8
Chacon, Adan	L-R	6-1	191	6-24-06	.226	.355	.321	41	172	137	23	31	7	0	2	24	29	1	0	5	40	0	0	16.9	23.3
Ciriaco, Jeremy	R-R	5-10	163	8-15-06	.242	.337	.317	43	190	161	30	39	7	1	1	21	23	1	3	2	31	11	3	12.1	16.3
Cumare, Wuilker	L-R	6-0	182	7-07-06	.177	.311	.274	18	74	62	13	11	4	1	0	6	12	0	0	0	24	4	1	16.2	32.4
Dalis, Wilder	B-R	6-0	172	7-30-06	.245	.339	.277	27	112	94	16	23	3	0	0	8	12	2	3	1	21	11	3	10.7	18.8
De La Cruz, Alessander	R-R	6-1	208	1-02-06	.236	.331	.431	38	142	123	24	29	9	0	5	17	17	1	0	1	48	3	0	12.0	33.8
Felix, Diego	R-R	6-0	160	7-22-06	.149	.295	.276	30	105	87	16	13	3	1	2	9	14	4	0	0	44	7	3	13.3	41.9
Feliz, Angel	L-R	6-1	157	3-02-04	.210	.312	.309	27	93	81	13	17	3	1	1	7	9	3	0	0	29	1	1	9.7	31.2
Freitez, Jesus	R-R	5-11	176	12-19-05	.359	.519	.487	18	55	39	15	14	5	0	0	10	12	2	1	1	10	4	1	21.8	18.2
Gomez, Esneider	R-R	5-11	185	9-18-02	.299	.381	.366	37	156	134	25	40	9	0	0	19	7	12	1	2	19	7	2	4.5	12.2
Guerra, Jorluis	R-R	5-11	165	1-11-04	.262	.324	.377	36	140	122	17	32	2	0	4	20	7	5	4	2	22	1	0	5.0	15.7
Guerra, Jose	B-R	5-11	180	12-18-05	.262	.375	.361	21	72	61	11	16	3	0	1	7	11	0	0	0	10	0	1	15.3	13.9
Hernandez, Roynier	L-R	5-11	180	12-06-04	.339	.445	.406	48	218	180	38	61	8	2	0	35	33	3	0	2	23	6	3	15.1	10.6
HIdalgo, Kelvin	R-R	6-2	166	3-01-05	.310	.406	.574	51	239	197	52	61	8	4	12	54	29	7	0	6	47	14	1	12.1	19.7
Isea, David	R-R	5-11	165	3-25-06	.299	.377	.393	30	122	107	15	32	4	0	2	24	12	2	0	1	22	5	2	9.8	18.0
Kolokie, Aldalay	R-R	6-0	187	8-29-04	.279	.400	.345	48	210	165	41	46	8	0	1	25	26	10	5	4	26	17	6	12.4	12.4
Ledesma, Bairon	R-R	5-9	180	5-03-05	.335	.406	.442	52	245	206	54	69	13	0	3	35	28	0	6	5	27	19	8	11.4	11.0
Lopez, Franklin	R-R	5-9	170	11-19-04	.379	.451	.629	35	143	124	37	47	13	0	6	31	9	8	1	1	19	1	0	6.3	13.3
Paiva, Moises	R-R	5-7	150	3-11-03	.313	.433	.400	33	97	80	20	25	2	1	1	8	14	3	0	0	15	13	2	14.4	15.5
Paredes, Luis	L-L	5-10	170	3-21-04	.138	.282	.276	19	71	58	4	8	2	0	2	10	9	3	0	1	21	0	1	12.7	29.6
Rada, Oswal	R-R	6-1	200	2-17-03	.237	.338	.237	18	69	59	10	14	0	0	0	7	6	3	1	0	15	0	0	8.7	21.7
Reyes, Yeiker	L-R	6-0	175	10-17-05	.301	.431	.367	48	206	166	50	50	9	1	0	19	29	9	2	0	36	33	2	14.1	17.5
Reyes, Yensi	R-R	6-1	189	9-14-03	.205	.362	.337	30	107	83	14	17	5	0	2	11	17	4	1	1	28	3	3	15.9	26.2
Terrero, Gabriel	L-R	6-3	169	12-21-03	.271	.366	.510	51	226	192	35	52	14	4	8	41	27	3	2	2	75	6	7	11.9	33.2
Ugarte, Ronny	L-R	6-3	205	12-10-04	.335	.409	.488	43	186	164	30	55	16	0	3	33	19	2	0	1	28	2	0	10.2	15.1

Pitching	B-T	Ht.	Wt.	DOB	W	L	ERA	G	GS	SV	IP	Hits	Runs	ER	HR	BB	SO	AVG	OBP	SLG	SO%	BB%	BF
Balbino, Gerson	R-R	6-0	167	4-15-05	3	4	6.75	12	3	0	25	36	24	19	6	14	21	.360	.425	.600	17.4	11.6	121
Casilla, Luichi	L-L	6-2	180	12-26-04	1	2	3.32	11	10	0	41	40	22	15	1	17	44	.265	.360	.331	25.1	9.7	175
Cedeno, Keywill	R-R	6-4	204	1-31-05	2	0	2.49	12	9	0	47	34	17	13	3	12	31	.205	.264	.319	17.0	6.6	182
Corpas, Iverson	R-R	6-0	170	1-11-05	0	1	4.05	6	0	1	7	6	7	3	0	7	3	.250	.438	.333	9.4	21.9	32
Cruz, Odarlin	R-R	6-7	188	2-18-05	0	0	6.75	8	0	1	11	17	11	8	2	3	4	.347	.400	.510	7.3	5.5	55
Cruz, Rony	R-R	6-1	196	3-03-04	1	1	6.60	4	4	0	15	17	11	11	1	5	13	.283	.368	.400	19.1	7.4	68
Daniel, Johan	R-R	6-0	172	2-22-05	1	1	5.40	12	0	1	13	14	10	8	0	7	4	.275	.361	.314	6.5	11.3	62

Ferrari, Gian	L-L	6-3	163	4-12-06	1	0	6.59	12	0	0	14	17	13	10	0	12	11	.304	.420	.304	15.9	17.4	69
Flores, Ruver	R-R	6-1	171	3-03-05	0	3	5.74	13	0	1	16	15	10	10	1	17	17	.250	.410	.367	21.8	21.8	78
Galva, Claudio	R-R	6-3	176	10-13-03	3	1	4.46	16	2	1	34	46	21	17	3	9	36	.307	.358	.473	22.1	5.5	163
George, Aneudis	R-R	6-1	172	9-27-03	3	2	4.50	15	0	0	28	34	18	14	5	8	14	.312	.374	.560	11.4	6.5	123
Gomez, Redinson	R-R	6-2	170	7-26-04	3	1	2.56	12	4	2	46	35	16	13	2	9	49	.210	.260	.305	27.1	5.0	181
Herrera, Keider	R-R	5-11	168	1-07-05	2	1	3.44	9	0	0	18	16	9	7	4	5	14	.232	.303	.449	18.4	6.6	76
Herrera, Marcos	R-R	6-2	182	10-11-04	5	0	4.74	11	9	0	44	45	32	23	1	16	38	.263	.337	.351	19.7	8.3	193
Leonardi, Almonte	R-R	6-2	190	3-25-05	0	2	5.50	9	2	0	18	22	15	11	2	14	16	.293	.404	.507	18.0	15.7	89
Medina, Jhon	L-L	6-0	195	1-09-06	3	2	5.00	11	4	0	36	31	28	20	2	18	29	.231	.320	.343	18.7	11.6	155
Milano, Johandry	L-L	6-1	160	2-09-03	2	1	5.33	14	0	1	27	28	17	16	5	5	24	.252	.303	.505	20.0	4.2	120
Moron, Wilny	R-R	6-0	175	12-28-00	1	0	3.51	16	0	2	26	21	16	10	1	7	26	.221	.296	.316	23.9	6.4	109
Ochoa, Nelvis	R-R	5-10	158	1-18-03	6	2	3.38	17	0	3	35	32	19	13	3	8	37	.246	.301	.369	25.5	5.5	145
Ozunz, Sandy	R-R	6-3	177	5-25-06	2	1	4.73	14	5	1	32	30	19	17	3	20	32	.252	.368	.395	22.2	13.9	144
Paulino, Wilmis	R-R	6-0	181	1-16-06	3	5	7.23	11	11	0	42	51	39	34	7	15	35	.295	.378	.491	17.9	7.7	196
Pena, Eliezer	R-R	6-0	167	10-08-05	0	4	7.68	12	10	0	36	35	33	31	5	25	26	.257	.375	.412	15.4	14.8	169
Pichardo, Rodery	R-R	6-0	150	10-24-01	0	0	3.60	5	0	1	5	5	3	2	1	2	3	.294	.409	.529	13.0	8.7	23
Ramirez, Anthony	R-R	6-2	175	8-17-05	2	0	3.09	8	0	1	12	11	4	4	0	4	8	.244	.294	.289	15.7	7.8	51
Romero, Willians	R-R	6-1	190	2-07-05	2	0	10.57	8	0	0	8	7	9	9	0	11	8	.241	.488	.310	18.6	25.6	43
Rudecindo, Isaac	R-R	6-2	210	1-27-01	2	1	8.56	17	0	1	27	35	29	26	5	12	38	.307	.382	.596	28.8	9.1	132
Sanchez, Enger	R-R	6-5	170	5-23-03	1	2	3.48	11	9	0	41	45	23	16	5	15	48	.281	.361	.438	26.7	8.3	180
Sevelen, Kenebell	R-R	6-3	190	8-17-04	0	0	20.25	2	0	0	1	8	8	3	1	3	1	.667	.750	1.083	6.3	18.8	16
Silvestre, Engel	R-R	6-2	230	9-27-05	0	0	2.08	6	5	0	13	12	4	3	1	3	15	.231	.310	.346	25.9	5.2	58
Suarez, Junior	L-L	6-1	195	6-24-05	1	0	4.50	13	0	1	16	15	9	8	0	11	23	.250	.373	.300	30.7	14.7	75
Tejada, Kevin	R-R	6-5	187	5-08-05	3	0	3.23	16	0	0	31	25	15	11	2	10	32	.221	.290	.327	25.6	8.0	125
Tejeda, Luis	R-R	6-2	170	12-13-04	4	3	4.74	11	9	0	49	47	29	26	3	10	43	.254	.309	.368	21.0	4.9	205
Torres, Ervin	L-L	6-0	185	11-03-04	4	2	4.93	11	10	0	46	51	29	25	5	12	49	.279	.337	.421	24.6	6.0	199
Valdez, Yoan	R-R	6-1	187	8-19-05	0	0	6.06	13	0	1	16	22	18	11	2	9	24	.319	.410	.449	28.9	10.8	83
Vargas, Cesar	R-R	6-4	176	12-01-04	0	0	2.70	5	0	1	7	8	2	2	0	1	3	.333	.385	.500	11.5	3.8	26
Vargas, Juan	R-R	6-3	180	10-10-00	1	0	7.50	5	0	0	6	12	7	5	2	4	1	.414	.500	.690	2.9	11.8	34
Villanueva, Bill	L-R	6-2	147	1-20-05	1	1	13.00	6	0	0	9	15	13	13	3	11	6	.405	.540	.757	12.0	22.0	50
Zacarias, Alison	R-R	6-3	200	11-10-05	0	0	6.75	6	0	0	5	2	4	4	1	9	3	.125	.481	.313	11.1	33.3	27

Fielding

C: Lopez 32, Guerra 20, Isea 16, Freitez 16, Rada 16, Arias 13, Gomez 11. **1B:** Chacon 41, Ugarte 37, Terrero 12, Arias 11, Gomez 6, Alvarez 4, Rada 2, Guerra 1. **2B:** Ledesma 42, Hernandez 33, Paiva 16, Alvarez 8, Bernard 6, Guerra 4, Ciriaco 2, Dalis 1. **3B:** Guerra 31, Dalis 22, Gomez 18, HIdalgo 18, Alvarez 11, Paiva 6, Hernandez 5, Arias 2, Terrero 1. **SS:** Ciriaco 39, HIdalgo 33, Felix 19, Hernandez 9, Ledesma 5, Dalis 4. **OF:** Reyes 77, Kolokie 52, Bautista 45, Calaz 38, Terrero 37, De La Cruz 28, Feliz 26, Alcantara 23, Bernard 13, Cumare 12, Paredes 6, Paiva 1.

Detroit Tigers

SEASON SYNOPSIS: The Tigers dominated American League Central rivals, going 35-17 in winning the season series against all four clubs. But the new balanced schedule meant the Tigers had to play 110 games out of the division, so while Detroit improved by 12 wins from 2022 and finished second for the first time since 2016, it wound up with its seventh straight losing season.

HIGH POINT: When the Tigers walked off the White Sox on May 28, they won the series with three of four, improved to 25-26 and got within one game of first-place Minnesota. That wound up being as close to .500 as Detroit would get all season. Another high point: Miguel Cabrera's final weekend, which included his 511th home run Sept. 27 against the Royals, and him taking the field at first base and fielding a ground ball to close his final game.

LOW POINT: Detroit lost nine in a row and 11 of 12 to open June and fall out of contention. Three of the losses came in walk-off fashion, including a grand slam off closer Alex Lange. A three-game sweep in Philadelphia during the losing streak included a walk-off double off Lange by former Tiger Kody Clemens.

NOTABLE ROOKIES: Righthander Reese Olson, a 13th-round pick in 2018 out of a Georgia high school, blossomed into a rotation power arm, going 5-7, 3.99 with 103 strikeouts in 103.2 innings with an average 94.8 mph fastball. Another late pick, 2019 19th-rounder Kerry Carpenter, emerged as a power bat in right field, ranking second to Spencer Torkelson with 20 home runs while batting .278/.340/.471. Reliever Tyler Holton thrived in a multi-inning relief role, posting a 2.11 ERA in 85 innings.

KEY TRANSACTIONS: Detroit was reported to have traded lefthander Eduardo Rodriguez to the Dodgers before Rodriguez invoked his no-trade clause, dealing Detroit's rebuild a blow. An elbow injury felled young building block Riley Greene in September; it previously prompted him to shift to left field, making room in center for rookie Parker Meadows.

DOWN ON THE FARM: The Tigers' farm system is steadily improving both in talent and wins and losses. Four of the five U.S. domestic teams had winning records. Led by Jackson Jobe and Colt Keith, Double-A Erie won its first Eastern League title.

OPENING DAY PAYROLL: $122,235,500 (19th).

PLAYERS OF THE YEAR

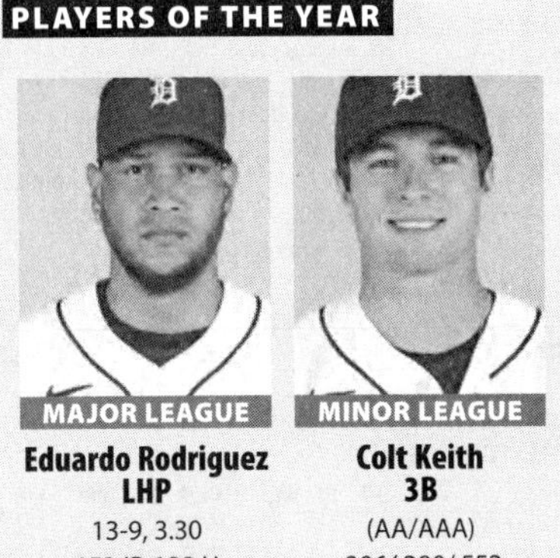

MAJOR LEAGUE	MINOR LEAGUE
Eduardo Rodriguez	**Colt Keith**
LHP	**3B**
13-9, 3.30	(AA/AAA)
153 IP, 128 H	.306/.380/.552
48 BB, 143 SO	38 2B, 27 HR

ORGANIZATION LEADERS

Batting		***Minimum 250 AB**
MAJORS		
* AVG	Riley Greene	.288
* OPS	Kerry Carpenter	.811
HR	Spencer Torkelson	31
RBI	Spencer Torkelson	94
MINORS		
* AVG	Justice Bigbie, W. Mich./Erie/Toledo	.343
* OBP	Justyn Henry-Malloy, Toledo	.417
* SLG	Colt Keith, Erie/Toledo	.552
* OPS	Tyler Nevin, Toledo	.943
R	Seth Stephenson, Lakeland/W. Michigan	95
H	Colt Keith, Erie/Toledo	155
TB	Colt Keith, Erie/Toledo	280
2B	Colt Keith, Erie/Toledo	38
3B	Seth Stephenson, Lakeland/W. Michigan	9
HR	Jace Jung, Western Mich./Erie	28
RBI	Colt Keith, Erie/Toledo	101
BB	Justyn Henry-Malloy, Toledo	110
SO	Izaac Pacheco, West Michigan	160
SB	Seth Stephenson, Lakeland/W. Michigan	70

Pitching		**#Minimum 75 IP**
MAJORS		
W	Eduardo Rodriguez	13
# ERA	Tyler Holton	2.11
SO	Eduardo Rodriguez	143
SV	Alex Lange	26
MINORS		
W	Keider Montero, W. Mich./Erie/Toledo	15
L	Zach Logue, Toledo	10
L	Jack O'Loughlin, W.Mich,/Toledo	10
# ERA	Troy Melton, Lakeland/W. Mich.	2.74
G	Aneurys Zabala, Toledo	53
GS	Keider Montero, W. Mich./Erie/Toledo	26
GS	Brant Hurter, Erie	26
SV	Miguel Diaz, Toledo	14
IP	Keider Montero, W. Mich./Erie/Toledo	127
BB	Jack O'Loughlin, W.Mich,/Toledo	52
# SO	Keider Montero, W. Mich./Erie/Toledo	160
AVG	Lael Lockhart, Erie/Toledo	.209

2023 PERFORMANCE

General Manager: Scott Harris. **Farm Director:** Ryan Garko. **Scouting Director:** Scott Bream.

Class	Team	League	W	L	PCT	Finish	Manager
Majors	Detroit Tigers	American	78	84	.481	10 (15)	A.J. Hinch
Triple-A	Toledo Mud Hens	International	70	78	.473	14 (20)	Anthony Iapoce
Double-A	Erie SeaWolves	Eastern	75	62	.547	3 (12)	Gabe Alvarez
High-A	West Michigan Whitecaps	Midwest	68	62	.523	3 (12)	Brayan Pena
Low-A	Lakeland Flying Tigers	Florida State	70	61	.534	3 (10)	Andrew Graham
Rookie	FCL Tigers	Florida Complex	29	25	.537	6 (15)	Mike Alvarez
Rookie	DSL Tigers 1	Dominican Sum.	25	26	.490	28 (50)	Marcos Yepez
Rookie	DSL Tigers 2	Dominican Sum.	31	23	.574	13 (50)	Sandy Acevedo
Overall 2023 Minor League Record			**368**	**337**	**.522**	**9th (30)**	

ORGANIZATION STATISTICS

DETROIT TIGERS

AMERICAN LEAGUE

Batting	B-T	Ht.	Wt.	DOB	AVG	OBP	SLG	G	PA	AB	R	H	2B	3B	HR	RBI	BB	HBP	SH	SF	SO	SB	CS	BB%	SO%
Baddoo, Akil	L-L	6-1	214	8-16-98	.218	.310	.372	112	357	312	40	68	13	1	11	34	42	0	2	1	89	14	3	11.8	24.9
Baez, Javier	R-R	6-0	190	12-01-92	.222	.267	.325	136	547	510	58	113	18	4	9	59	24	9	0	3	125	12	0	4.4	22.9
Cabrera, Miguel	R-R	6-4	267	4-18-83	.257	.322	.353	98	370	334	21	86	20	0	4	34	31	2	0	3	74	0	0	8.4	20.0
Carpenter, Kerry	L-R	6-2	220	9-02-97	.278	.340	.471	118	459	418	57	116	17	2	20	64	32	8	0	1	115	6	0	7.0	25.1
Diaz, Isan	L-R	5-10	201	5-27-96	.000	.000	.000	2	5	5	0	0	0	0	0	0	0	0	0	0	2	0	0	0.0	40.0
2-team (6 San Francisco)					.042	.115	.042	8	26	24	0	1	0	0	0	1	2	0	0	0	9	0	0	7.7	34.6
Greene, Riley	L-L	6-3	200	9-28-00	.288	.349	.447	99	416	378	51	109	19	4	11	37	35	1	0	2	114	7	0	8.4	27.4
Haase, Eric	R-R	5-10	210	12-18-92	.201	.246	.284	86	282	264	22	53	8	1	4	26	16	0	1	1	78	3	1	5.7	27.7
2-team (3 Cleveland)					.201	.247	.281	89	293	274	22	55	8	1	4	26	17	0	1	1	81	4	1	5.8	27.6
Ibanez, Andy	R-R	5-10	205	4-03-93	.264	.312	.433	114	383	356	42	94	23	2	11	41	24	1	1	1	69	1	0	6.3	18.0
Kelly, Carson	R-R	6-2	212	7-14-94	.173	.271	.269	19	59	52	7	9	2	0	1	7	7	0	0	0	17	0	0	11.9	28.8
2-team (33 Arizona)					.206	.278	.287	52	151	136	13	28	5	0	2	13	14	0	0	1	40	1	0	9.3	26.5
Kreidler, Ryan	R-R	6-4	208	11-12-97	.111	.111	.111	11	18	18	2	2	0	0	0	0	0	0	0	0	7	0	0	0.0	38.9
Lipcius, Andre	R-R	6-0	190	5-22-98	.286	.342	.400	13	38	35	3	10	1	0	1	4	3	0	0	0	8	0	0	7.9	21.1
Marisnick, Jake	R-R	6-4	220	3-30-91	.232	.270	.420	33	75	69	9	16	3	2	2	10	3	1	1	1	20	2	2	4.0	26.7
3-team (9 Chicago White Sox, 4 Los Angeles Dodgers)					.225	.263	.408	42	77	71	10	16	3	2	2	10	3	1	1	1	21	2	2	3.9	27.3
Maton, Nick	L-R	6-2	178	2-18-97	.173	.288	.305	93	293	249	29	43	9	0	8	32	38	3	1	2	73	1	2	13.0	24.9
McKinstry, Zach	L-R	6-0	180	4-29-95	.231	.302	.351	148	518	464	60	107	21	4	9	35	44	5	2	3	113	16	6	8.5	21.8
Meadows, Austin	L-L	6-3	225	5-03-95	.238	.238	.286	6	21	21	0	5	1	0	0	2	0	0	0	0	3	0	0	0.0	14.3
Meadows, Parker	L-R	6-5	205	11-02-99	.232	.331	.368	37	145	125	19	29	4	2	3	13	17	2	0	1	37	8	1	11.7	25.5
Nevin, Tyler	R-R	6-4	225	5-29-97	.200	.306	.316	41	111	95	11	19	3	1	2	10	12	3	0	1	25	0	1	10.8	22.5
Rogers, Jake	R-R	6-1	201	4-18-95	.221	.286	.444	107	365	331	47	73	11	0	21	49	28	3	1	2	118	1	1	7.7	32.3
Schoop, Jonathan	R-R	6-1	247	10-16-91	.213	.278	.272	55	151	136	15	29	8	0	0	7	13	0	0	2	37	0	0	8.6	24.5
Short, Zack	R-R	5-10	180	5-29-95	.204	.292	.339	112	253	221	17	45	9	0	7	33	28	0	3	1	66	5	0	11.1	26.1
Torkelson, Spencer	R-R	6-1	220	8-26-99	.233	.313	.446	159	684	606	88	141	34	1	31	94	67	6	0	5	171	3	0	9.8	25.0
Vierling, Matt	R-R	6-3	205	9-16-96	.261	.329	.388	134	530	479	63	125	21	5	10	44	44	5	1	1	112	6	6	8.3	21.1

Pitching	B-T	Ht.	Wt.	DOB	W	L	ERA	G	GS	SV	IP	Hits	Runs	ER	HR	BB	SO	AVG	OBP	SLG	SO%	BB%	BF
Alexander, Tyler	R-L	6-2	203	7-14-94	2	1	4.50	25	1	0	44	44	25	22	8	5	44	.256	.283	.453	24.3	2.8	181
Boyd, Matthew	L-L	6-3	223	2-02-91	5	5	5.45	15	15	0	71	69	46	43	11	25	73	.250	.317	.424	24.1	8.3	303
Brieske, Beau	R-R	6-3	200	4-04-98	2	3	3.60	25	1	2	35	36	14	14	4	12	31	.259	.316	.410	20.4	7.9	152
Bristo, Braden	R-R	6-0	180	11-01-94	0	0	4.50	2	0	0	4	5	3	2	0	3	1	.294	.400	.294	5.0	15.0	20
Cisnero, Jose	R-R	6-3	258	4-11-89	3	4	5.31	63	0	2	59	63	39	35	10	25	70	.270	.351	.446	26.2	9.4	267
Diaz, Miguel	R-R	6-0	224	11-28-94	1	0	0.64	12	3	0	14	8	1	1	0	5	16	.163	.241	.204	29.6	9.3	54
Englert, Mason	B-R	6-4	206	11-01-99	4	3	5.46	31	1	0	56	67	39	34	12	17	41	.291	.343	.526	16.2	6.7	253
Faedo, Alex	R-R	6-5	225	11-12-95	2	5	4.45	15	12	0	65	48	35	32	12	20	58	.200	.263	.404	22.1	7.6	262
Foley, Jason	R-R	6-4	215	11-01-95	3	3	2.61	70	0	7	69	65	21	20	2	15	55	.251	.293	.340	19.9	5.4	276
Gipson-Long, Sawyer	R-R	6-4	225	12-12-97	1	0	2.70	4	4	0	20	14	7	6	2	8	26	.189	.268	.351	31.7	9.8	82
Hanifee, Brenan	R-R	6-5	215	5-29-98	0	0	5.40	3	0	0	5	8	3	3	1	0	3	.348	.348	.522	13.0	0.0	23
Hill, Garrett	R-R	6-0	185	1-16-96	0	0	9.19	9	0	1	16	19	20	16	4	14	14	.302	.430	.587	17.5	17.5	80
Holton, Tyler	L-L	6-2	200	6-13-96	3	2	2.11	59	1	1	85	56	21	20	9	18	74	.185	.232	.304	22.8	5.6	324
Kelly, Carson	R-R	6-2	212	7-14-94	0	0	13.50	1	0	0	1	4	1	1	1	0	1	.667	.667	1.167	16.7	0.0	6
Lange, Alex	R-R	6-3	202	10-02-95	7	5	3.68	67	0	26	66	43	30	27	6	45	79	.185	.328	.315	27.4	15.6	288
Logue, Zach	L-L	6-0	165	4-23-96	0	0	7.36	3	0	0	11	13	9	9	3	2	10	.277	.306	.511	20.4	4.1	49
Lorenzen, Michael	R-R	6-3	217	1-04-92	5	7	3.58	18	18	0	106	89	44	42	11	27	83	.233	.285	.366	19.9	6.5	418
Manning, Matt	R-R	6-6	195	1-28-98	5	4	3.58	15	15	0	78	60	37	31	11	21	50	.212	.274	.375	15.8	6.6	316
McKinstry, Zach	L-R	6-0	180	4-29-95	0	0	18.00	1	0	0	1	3	2	2	1	0	0	.500	.500	1.167	0.0	0.0	6
Misiewicz, Anthony	R-L	6-1	196	11-01-94	0	0	81.00	1	0	0	0	4	3	3	1	0	0	.800	.800	1.600	0.0	0.0	5
Olson, Reese	R-R	6-1	160	7-31-99	5	7	3.99	21	18	0	104	83	49	46	14	33	103	.215	.277	.373	24.4	7.8	422
Rodriguez, Eduardo	L-L	6-2	231	4-07-93	13	9	3.30	26	26	0	153	128	59	56	15	48	143	.227	.289	.359	23.0	7.7	621
Schoop, Jonathan	R-R	6-1	247	10-16-91	0	0	0.00	1	0	0	1	1	0	0	0	0	1	.200	.200	.200	20.0	0.0	5
Short, Zack	R-R	5-10	180	5-29-95	0	0	6.00	6	0	0	6	12	4	4	0	1	1	.400	.438	.433	3.1	3.1	32
Shreve, Chasen	L-L	6-4	180	7-12-90	1	2	4.79	47	0	0	41	45	24	22	6	12	42	.278	.324	.451	23.3	6.7	180

Pitching	B-T	Ht.	Wt.	DOB	W	L	ERA	G	GS	SV	IP	Hits	Runs	ER	HR	BB	SO	AVG	OBP	SLG	SO%	BB%	BF
Skubal, Tarik	R-L	6-3	240	11-20-96	7	3	2.80	15	15	0	80	58	28	25	4	14	102	.199	.242	.298	32.9	4.5	310
Turnbull, Spencer	R-R	6-3	210	9-18-92	1	4	7.26	7	7	0	31	37	26	25	5	15	24	.291	.379	.488	16.6	10.3	145
Vasquez, Andrew	L-L	6-6	235	9-14-93	0	0	8.31	12	0	0	9	11	9	8	0	9	9	.297	.458	.405	18.4	18.4	49
Vest, Will	R-R	6-0	180	6-06-95	2	1	2.98	48	4	2	48	40	18	16	3	13	56	.216	.268	.324	28.1	6.5	199
Wentz, Joey	L-L	6-5	220	10-06-97	3	13	6.90	25	19	0	106	131	87	81	25	47	98	.295	.362	.532	19.9	9.6	492
White, Brendan	R-R	5-11	185	11-18-98	2	3	5.09	33	2	0	41	40	25	23	4	15	44	.258	.341	.387	24.9	8.5	177
Wingenter, Trey	R-R	6-7	237	4-15-94	1	0	5.82	17	0	0	17	16	11	11	2	7	22	.246	.342	.400	28.9	9.2	76

Fielding

Catcher	PCT	G	PO	A	E	DP	PB
Haase	.994	57	452	12	3	0	0
Kelly	1.000	16	145	10	0	2	1
Rogers	.992	99	793	35	7	3	2

First Base	PCT	G	PO	A	E	DP
Cabrera	1.000	1	1	0	0	0
Ibanez	1.000	4	15	3	0	1
Nevin	.980	8	48	1	1	6
Torkelson	.991	154	1137	89	11	117

Second Base	PCT	G	PO	A	E	DP
Diaz	1.000	2	1	2	0	1
Ibanez	.984	77	106	148	4	43
Kreidler	1.000	3	9	6	0	2
Maton	1.000	30	25	31	0	3
McKinstry	.979	47	52	87	3	15
Schoop	.988	27	29	51	1	8
Short	.986	53	57	81	2	20
Vierling	.000	1	0	0	0	0

Third Base	PCT	G	PO	A	E	DP
Ibanez	.952	16	5	15	1	2
Kreidler	1.000	3	2	5	0	0
Lipcius	.900	11	4	14	2	2
Maton	.911	53	19	63	8	5
McKinstry	.938	52	16	59	5	6
Nevin	.917	14	9	13	2	1
Schoop	.925	24	10	39	4	3
Short	.918	31	15	30	4	1
Vierling	.986	35	18	54	1	5

Shortstop	PCT	G	PO	A	E	DP
Baez	.962	130	153	324	19	70
Kreidler	1.000	3	1	2	0	1
Maton	1.000	4	0	4	0	0
McKinstry	.983	23	25	32	1	5
Schoop	.000	1	0	0	0	0
Short	.975	33	28	51	2	12

Outfield	PCT	G	PO	A	E	DP
Baddoo	.996	106	177	3	2	0
Carpenter	.951	91	158	7	3	1
Greene	.990	91	191	1	5	1
Haase	.984	24	30	1	1	0
Ibanez	.940	21	31	1	2	1
Marisnick	.987	30	76	0	1	0
McKinstry	1.000	62	77	6	0	0
Meadows, A	.500	7	13	0	0	0
Meadows, P	1.000	36	88	0	0	0
Nevin	1.000	8	9	1	0	0
Rogers	.000	1	0	0	0	0
Short	.000	4	0	0	0	0
Vierling	.994	130	228	6	1	0

TOLEDO MUD HENS

TRIPLE-A

INTERNATIONAL LEAGUE

Batting	B-T	Ht.	Wt.	DOB	AVG	OBP	SLG	G	PA	AB	R	H	2B	3B	HR	RBI	BB	HBP	SH	SF	SO	SB	CS	BB%	SO%
Baddoo, Akil	L-L	6-1	214	8-16-98	.275	.388	.475	11	49	40	6	11	3	1	1	7	8	0	0	1	10	2	1	16.3	20.4
Bigbie, Justice	R-R	6-2	200	1-24-99	.275	.345	.392	15	58	51	5	14	3	0	1	8	5	1	0	1	15	0	0	8.6	25.9
Camargo, Johan	B-R	5-11	195	12-13-93	.238	.295	.400	22	88	80	9	19	4	0	3	11	6	1	0	1	15	0	0	6.8	17.0
2-team (15 Omaha)					.263	.348	.460	37	156	137	16	36	6	0	7	19	17	1	0	1	26	0	0	10.9	16.7
Carpenter, Kerry	L-R	6-2	220	9-02-97	.171	.275	.286	9	40	35	4	6	1	0	1	3	5	0	0	0	12	0	0	12.5	30.0
Davis, Brendon	R-R	6-4	185	7-28-97	.178	.288	.363	43	156	135	15	24	10	0	5	14	18	3	0	0	47	1	0	11.5	30.1
Davis, Jonathan	R-R	5-8	190	5-12-92	.258	.336	.516	36	141	124	21	32	9	4	5	20	14	1	0	1	32	5	2	9.9	22.7
Diaz, Isan	L-R	5-10	201	5-27-96	.217	.333	.478	6	27	23	6	5	0	0	2	6	4	0	0	0	5	0	0	14.8	18.5
Dingler, Dillon	R-R	6-3	210	9-17-98	.202	.266	.384	26	109	99	14	20	7	1	3	9	8	1	0	1	34	0	0	7.3	31.2
Gonzalez, Alvaro	B-R	6-0	165	9-16-00	.000	.143	.000	3	7	6	0	0	0	0	0	0	1	0	0	0	4	0	0	14.3	57.1
Greene, Riley	L-L	6-3	200	9-28-00	.500	.500	.833	3	12	12	3	6	1	0	1	3	0	0	0	0	2	0	0	0.0	16.7
Ibanez, Andy	R-R	5-10	205	4-03-93	.297	.418	.609	20	79	64	14	19	5	0	5	16	13	1	0	1	14	2	1	16.5	17.7
Joyce, Corey	R-R	6-0	190	8-19-98	.268	.393	.446	54	206	168	25	45	12	3	4	22	30	6	0	2	56	8	2	14.6	27.2
Keith, Colt	L-R	6-2	211	8-14-01	.287	.369	.521	67	301	261	45	75	20	1	13	51	35	1	0	4	58	1	1	11.6	19.3
Knapp, Andrew	B-R	6-1	189	11-09-91	.253	.337	.397	70	267	237	27	60	12	2	6	25	27	3	0	0	67	3	1	10.1	25.1
Kreidler, Ryan	R-R	6-4	208	11-12-97	.239	.349	.460	49	209	176	31	42	6	0	11	42	28	3	0	2	53	11	4	13.4	25.4
Leonard, Eddys	R-R	5-11	195	11-10-00	.302	.374	.530	40	171	149	30	45	10	0	8	31	17	2	0	3	37	2	1	9.9	21.6
Lipcius, Andre	R-R	6-0	190	5-22-98	.272	.363	.419	97	419	360	53	98	16	2	11	58	52	2	0	5	74	1	1	12.4	17.7
Malloy, Justyn-Henry	R-R	6-1	212	2-19-00	.277	.417	.474	135	611	487	89	135	25	1	23	83	110	10	0	4	152	5	1	18.0	24.9
Maton, Nick	L-R	6-2	178	2-18-97	.293	.414	.457	38	175	140	32	41	12	1	3	27	27	4	1	3	37	3	1	15.4	21.1
McLaughlin, J.D.	R-R	6-2	195	12-28-00	.091	.167	.091	4	12	11	2	1	0	0	0	0	1	0	0	0	6	0	0	8.3	50.0
Meadows, Parker	L-R	6-5	205	11-02-99	.256	.337	.474	113	517	449	78	115	27	7	19	65	57	2	1	8	123	19	2	11.0	23.8
Nevin, Tyler	R-R	6-4	225	5-29-97	.326	.400	.543	87	385	337	63	110	22	3	15	58	38	6	0	4	65	4	0	9.9	16.9
Palacios, Jermaine	R-R	6-0	145	7-19-96	.176	.232	.352	36	138	125	12	22	2	1	6	21	10	0	0	3	43	3	2	7.2	31.2
2-team (16 Omaha)					.183	.233	.372	52	198	180	18	33	5	1	9	29	12	0	1	5	63	3	2	6.1	31.8
Papierski, Michael	B-R	6-2	224	2-26-96	.266	.370	.422	77	305	256	43	68	14	1	8	51	42	3	0	4	65	0	0	13.8	21.3
Perez, Wenceel	B-R	5-11	203	10-30-99	.264	.394	.496	35	160	129	29	34	13	4	3	19	27	2	0	2	29	6	5	16.9	18.1
Rizzo, Joe	L-R	5-9	194	3-31-98	.299	.358	.518	38	151	137	23	41	12	0	6	28	11	2	0	1	28	0	0	7.3	18.5
2-team (11 Jacksonville)					.260	.326	.439	49	191	173	26	45	13	0	6	29	15	2	0	1	40	0	0	7.9	20.9
Sands, Donny	R-R	6-2	190	5-16-96	.225	.318	.353	89	371	320	32	72	24	1	5	36	45	1	0	5	74	1	2	12.1	19.9
Short, Zack	R-R	5-10	180	5-29-95	.195	.340	.427	21	100	82	20	16	4	0	5	12	18	0	0	0	32	1	1	18.0	32.0
Solak, Nick	R-R	5-9	185	1-11-95	.221	.348	.315	54	221	181	26	40	7	2	2	20	33	4	0	3	47	2	1	14.9	21.3
2-team (38 Gwinnett)					.244	.358	.373	92	394	332	49	81	15	2	8	48	50	9	0	3	74	4	3	12.7	18.8
Valente, John	R-R	5-11	190	6-23-95	.236	.323	.382	18	62	55	9	13	1	2	1	4	6	1	0	0	8	1	1	9.7	12.9
Vierling, Matt	R-R	6-3	205	9-16-96	.143	.143	.143	2	7	7	0	1	0	0	0	1	0	0	0	0	2	0	0	0.0	28.6
Walker, Steele	L-L	5-11	209	7-30-96	.115	.179	.154	7	28	26	1	3	1	0	0	2	1	1	0	0	8	0	2	3.6	28.6
Witherspoon, Grant	L-L	6-1	200	9-27-96	.205	.340	.333	35	141	117	15	24	6	0	3	6	22	2	0	0	42	3	0	15.6	29.8

Pitching	B-T	Ht.	Wt.	DOB	W	L	ERA	G	GS	SV	IP	Hits	Runs	ER	HR	BB	SO	AVG	OBP	SLG	SO%	BB%	BF
Bergner, Austin	R-R	6-5	210	5-01-97	1	3	8.34	9	4	0	23	29	24	21	4	15	32	.309	.411	.596	28.6	13.4	112
Brieske, Beau	R-R	6-3	200	4-04-98	0	0	3.18	9	1	0	11	8	4	4	1	6	10	.200	.304	.350	21.7	13.0	46
Bristo, Braden	R-R	6-0	180	11-01-94	2	0	7.19	38	1	1	41	44	34	33	10	29	53	.265	.387	.506	26.6	14.6	199
Calvo, Blair	R-R	6-3	195	2-27-96	4	3	6.95	29	0	0	34	34	26	26	4	34	36	.276	.445	.431	22.0	20.7	164
Castro, Kervin	R-R	6-0	185	2-07-99	0	0	2.30	10	0	1	16	14	5	4	0	9	19	.255	.354	.345	29.2	13.8	65

Clay, Sam	L-L	6-3	238	6-21-93	6	3	5.16	42	1	1	52	52	33	30	8	29	53	.257	.360	.426	22.2	12.1	239
Del Pozo, Miguel	L-L	6-1	205	10-14-92	0	1	6.05	15	1	2	19	17	13	13	3	5	23	.230	.288	.392	28.8	6.3	80
Diaz, Miguel	R-R	6-0	224	11-28-94	2	4	5.05	49	0	14	57	54	36	32	3	26	73	.239	.325	.372	28.6	10.2	255
Elledge, Seth	R-R	6-3	240	5-20-96	0	1	3.86	10	0	0	14	9	6	6	2	7	13	.184	.298	.388	22.8	12.3	57
Englert, Mason	B-R	6-4	206	11-01-99	1	0	7.15	9	0	0	11	16	9	9	4	4	19	.320	.370	.620	35.2	7.4	54
Faedo, Alex	R-R	6-5	225	11-12-95	0	2	3.42	7	7	0	26	20	10	10	4	6	30	.208	.255	.385	29.4	5.9	102
Fernander, Chavez	R-R	6-3	205	7-07-97	1	1	12.91	6	0	0	8	11	11	11	1	10	3	.355	.500	.548	6.8	22.7	44
Fry, Jace	L-L	6-1	209	7-09-93	1	1	4.50	7	0	0	10	8	5	5	0	5	12	.229	.357	.343	28.6	11.9	42
Garcia, Rony	R-R	6-3	200	12-19-97	2	2	8.29	27	2	0	38	44	35	35	8	25	50	.288	.403	.588	26.9	13.4	186
Gipson-Long, Sawyer	R-R	6-4	225	12-12-97	2	3	5.45	8	6	0	35	33	21	21	8	14	50	.244	.333	.459	32.7	9.2	153
Goudeau, Ashton	R-R	6-6	220	7-23-92	2	5	7.42	18	14	0	61	76	55	50	14	31	49	.305	.381	.554	16.8	10.7	291
Guenther, Sean	L-L	5-11	194	12-29-95	2	1	4.88	25	3	0	31	31	19	17	8	9	37	.252	.319	.504	27.2	6.6	136
Hanifee, Brenan	R-R	6-5	215	5-29-98	2	8	4.38	25	13	2	90	103	50	44	11	30	82	.285	.348	.448	20.6	7.5	399
Hembree, Heath	R-R	6-4	220	1-13-89	1	0	3.00	6	0	0	6	6	2	2	0	2	6	.261	.320	.261	24.0	8.0	25
Henderson, Layne	R-R	6-4	200	6-08-96	2	1	5.87	23	0	1	31	29	20	20	5	25	41	.246	.375	.492	28.3	17.2	145
Higginbotham, Jake	L-L	6-0	190	1-11-96	0	0	0.00	1	0	0	1	1	0	0	0	1	2	.200	.429	.200	28.6	14.3	7
Hill, Garrett	R-R	6-0	185	1-16-96	3	2	6.02	26	4	0	46	55	36	31	6	32	64	.302	.422	.478	28.7	14.3	223
Holton, Tyler	L-L	6-2	200	6-13-96	3	0	7.04	4	0	0	8	6	6	6	4	3	7	.207	.303	.621	21.2	9.1	33
Lescher, Billy	R-R	6-4	215	9-17-95	0	0	1.93	4	0	0	5	4	1	1	0	4	3	.222	.391	.389	13.0	17.4	23
Lockhart, Lael	B-L	6-3	225	12-31-97	1	0	3.60	1	1	0	5	6	2	2	0	2	5	.286	.375	.429	20.8	8.3	24
Logue, Zach	L-L	6-0	165	4-23-96	3	10	6.58	27	21	0	90	113	70	66	20	44	85	.306	.384	.547	20.2	10.5	420
Lorenzen, Michael	R-R	6-3	217	1-04-92	0	1	15.43	1	1	0	2	2	4	4	0	3	2	.222	.417	.222	16.7	25.0	12
Magno, Andrew	R-L	5-11	190	4-30-98	0	0	1.50	8	0	0	12	10	2	2	1	9	15	.213	.339	.383	26.8	16.1	56
Manning, Matt	R-R	6-6	195	1-28-98	0	0	0.00	3	3	0	9	8	1	0	0	8	9	.258	.410	.290	23.1	20.5	39
Misiewicz, Anthony	R-L	6-1	196	11-01-94	0	1	13.50	3	0	0	3	5	4	4	0	1	3	.385	.429	.615	21.4	7.1	14
Montero, Keider	R-R	6-1	145	7-06-00	5	2	4.93	8	7	0	42	42	24	23	8	14	47	.258	.330	.491	25.8	7.7	182
O'Loughlin, Jack	L-L	6-5	223	3-14-00	3	7	4.78	18	16	0	87	93	48	46	9	37	79	.278	.357	.436	20.8	9.7	380
Olson, Reese	R-R	6-1	160	7-31-99	2	3	6.38	10	10	0	37	42	28	26	5	22	47	.282	.377	.477	26.9	12.6	175
Rodriguez, Eduardo	L-L	6-2	231	4-07-93	0	0	0.00	1	1	0	4	3	0	0	0	1	4	.200	.250	.267	25.0	6.3	16
Rosenthal, Trevor	R-R	6-2	230	5-29-90	0	0	4.50	2	0	0	2	2	1	1	0	3	1	.286	.500	.286	10.0	30.0	10
Sammons, Bryan	L-L	6-4	235	4-27-95	1	3	5.28	15	13	0	60	69	37	35	12	27	69	.290	.357	.525	25.4	9.9	272
Skubal, Tarik	R-L	6-3	240	11-20-96	0	0	1.86	3	3	0	10	6	4	2	1	3	13	.176	.243	.294	35.1	8.1	37
Turnbull, Spencer	R-R	6-3	210	9-18-92	0	1	6.86	6	6	0	21	30	16	16	2	11	25	.337	.422	.551	24.5	10.8	102
Vasquez, Andrew	L-L	6-6	235	9-14-93	0	1	1.35	7	0	0	7	8	5	1	0	1	9	.308	.379	.385	31.0	3.4	29
Vest, Will	R-R	6-0	180	6-06-95	1	0	8.31	11	1	0	13	11	12	12	5	9	20	.224	.356	.551	33.9	15.3	59
Wentz, Joey	L-L	6-5	220	10-06-97	2	1	4.40	6	6	0	29	32	14	14	3	12	37	.278	.352	.435	28.9	9.4	128
White, Brendan	R-R	5-11	185	11-18-98	3	2	4.14	29	0	0	37	45	19	17	4	11	50	.306	.358	.469	30.9	6.8	162
Wingenter, Trey	R-R	6-7	237	4-15-94	0	0	5.57	22	0	1	21	19	13	13	2	11	27	.244	.341	.410	29.7	12.1	91
Wisler, Matt	R-R	6-3	215	9-12-92	5	2	4.40	39	2	2	47	48	28	23	5	26	53	.265	.359	.436	25.2	12.4	210
Zabala, Aneurys	R-R	6-3	259	12-21-96	7	3	4.25	53	0	5	66	51	36	31	2	49	103	.210	.357	.292	34.3	16.3	300

Fielding

Catcher	PCT	G	PO	A	E	DP	PB
Dingler	.992	22	224	16	2	2	1
Knapp	.997	31	288	21	1	3	4
Papierski	.994	30	306	13	2	2	0
Sands	.997	67	664	34	2	5	4

First Base	PCT	G	PO	A	E	DP
Ibanez	1.000	8	51	3	0	6
Knapp	.994	24	142	14	1	16
Lipcius	1.000	32	234	11	0	21
Maton	1.000	3	17	1	0	4
Nevin	1.000	29	185	14	0	17
Papierski	.989	42	257	19	3	31
Rizzo	1.000	10	53	8	0	5
Sands	1.000	5	27	3	0	2

Second Base	PCT	G	PO	A	E	DP
Camargo	1.000	6	12	12	0	3
Diaz	1.000	3	2	6	0	0
Gonzalez	1.000	1	1	1	0	0
Ibanez	.973	7	17	19	1	5
Joyce	.964	15	19	34	2	5
Keith	.992	35	65	62	1	16
Kreidler	1.000	4	8	5	0	3
Leonard	.950	4	3	16	1	3
Lipcius	.975	30	47	69	3	25
Maton	1.000	5	3	11	0	3
Palacios	1.000	7	7	21	0	4
Perez	.932	14	16	25	3	6
Rizzo	1.000	3	9	7	0	3
Short	1.000	4	7	12	0	4
Valente	.982	15	19	35	1	10

Third Base	PCT	G	PO	A	E	DP
Gonzalez	1.000	2	1	2	0	1
Ibanez	1.000	1	0	1	0	0
Keith	.979	21	12	35	1	3
Kreidler	1.000	4	3	3	0	0
Leonard	.667	2	0	2	1	1
Lipcius	.872	17	6	28	5	1
Malloy	.897	60	38	67	12	6
Maton	.938	7	3	12	1	0
Nevin	.917	18	16	28	4	4
Rizzo	.957	17	13	31	2	4
Valente	1.000	2	2	4	0	0

Shortstop	PCT	G	PO	A	E	DP
Camargo	.959	14	17	30	2	7
Davis	1.000	5	9	10	0	1
Joyce	.966	38	38	77	4	26
Kreidler	.981	28	40	65	2	11
Leonard	.952	17	21	39	3	7
Maton	.969	8	11	20	1	4
Palacios	.933	26	28	56	6	12
Short	.976	12	10	31	1	9

Outfield	PCT	G	PO	A	E	DP
Baddoo	1.000	9	11	0	0	0
Bigbie	.965	14	30	0	1	0
Carpenter	1.000	1	2	0	0	0
Davis, B	.989	34	52	4	1	2
Davis, J	.987	35	68	4	1	3
Greene	.000	1	0	0	0	0
Ibanez	1.000	2	7	0	0	0
Kreidler	1.000	13	38	3	0	0
Leonard	1.000	13	16	0	0	0
Lipcius	.500	14	17	1	0	0
Malloy	.968	44	72	6	2	1
Maton	.977	15	30	1	1	0
McLaughlin	1.000	4	9	1	0	0
Meadows	.997	112	240	6	2	3
Nevin	.957	33	43	3	2	0
Papierski	1.000	1	2	0	0	0
Perez	.975	20	30	1	1	0
Short	1.000	5	9	0	0	0
Solak	.981	47	59	2	2	0
Vierling	1.000	2	5	0	0	0
Walker	1.000	7	15	1	0	1
Witherspoon	.991	31	63	4	1	2

ERIE SEAWOLVES — *DOUBLE-A*

EASTERN LEAGUE

Batting	B-T	Ht.	Wt.	DOB	AVG	OBP	SLG	G	PA	AB	R	H	2B	3B	HR	RBI	BB	HBP	SH	SF	SO	SB	CS	BB%	SO%
Alfonzo, Eliezer	B-R	5-10	155	9-23-99	.333	.429	.833	2	7	6	1	2	0	0	1	2	1	0	0	0	0	1	0	14.3	0.0

Allen, Brady	R-L	6-1	218	9-03-99	.129	.229	.290	8	35	31	3	4	2	0	1	3	4	0	0	0	12	0	0	11.4	34.3
Bigbie, Justice	R-R	6-2	200	1-24-99	.362	.421	.564	63	272	243	51	88	13	0	12	43	22	4	0	2	34	5	1	8.1	12.5
Burgess, Colin	R-R	5-8	195	11-10-00	.125	.125	.125	2	8	8	0	1	0	0	0	2	0	0	0	0	3	0	0	0.0	37.5
Cabrera, Daniel	L-L	5-11	200	9-05-98	.236	.340	.312	63	237	199	25	47	10	1	1	26	32	1	0	3	36	3	1	13.5	15.2
Crouch, Josh	R-R	6-0	200	12-07-98	.173	.259	.288	13	58	52	3	9	3	0	1	6	5	1	0	0	20	0	0	8.6	34.5
Cruz, Trei	B-R	6-1	204	7-05-98	.214	.335	.371	120	538	453	73	97	21	4	14	53	81	2	0	1	127	9	6	15.1	23.6
De La Rosa, Eric	R-R	6-3	186	6-03-97	.000	.214	.000	4	14	11	1	0	0	0	0	0	3	0	0	0	4	2	0	21.4	28.6
Dingler, Dillon	R-R	6-3	210	9-17-98	.253	.372	.462	51	219	182	35	46	11	0	9	41	27	8	0	1	63	3	1	12.3	28.8
Feliciano, Mario	R-R	5-10	200	11-20-98	.221	.279	.271	39	154	140	12	31	7	0	0	12	9	3	0	2	21	0	0	5.8	13.6
Holton, Jake	R-R	6-0	210	3-02-98	.245	.378	.401	111	463	379	60	93	13	2	14	47	68	14	0	2	68	0	1	14.7	14.7
Joyce, Corey	R-R	6-0	190	8-19-98	.147	.306	.198	37	147	116	14	17	3	0	1	13	23	5	0	3	38	2	1	15.6	25.9
Jung, Jace	L-R	6-0	205	10-04-00	.284	.373	.563	47	209	183	28	52	9	0	14	39	23	3	0	0	56	0	0	11.0	26.8
Keith, Colt	L-R	6-2	211	8-14-01	.325	.391	.585	59	276	246	43	80	18	2	14	50	25	3	0	2	63	2	1	9.1	22.8
Malgeri, Ben	R-R	6-1	215	1-12-00	.233	.319	.413	99	389	344	63	80	19	2	13	34	40	4	0	1	118	15	6	10.3	30.3
Meyers, Chris	L-R	6-3	210	4-27-99	.248	.305	.391	70	282	258	32	64	10	0	9	40	15	7	0	2	67	2	1	5.3	23.8
Navigato, Andrew	R-R	5-11	188	5-28-98	.300	.350	.545	58	254	233	38	70	22	1	11	46	16	3	0	2	50	8	7	6.3	19.7
Packard, Bryant	L-R	6-3	200	10-06-97	.000	.125	.000	6	16	14	1	0	0	0	0	0	0	2	0	0	5	0	0	0.0	31.3
Perez, Wenceel	B-R	5-11	203	10-30-99	.271	.353	.375	76	343	299	56	81	9	2	6	28	35	5	0	4	52	19	2	10.2	15.2
Rincones, Diego	R-R	5-11	175	6-14-99	.242	.306	.401	51	206	182	29	44	8	0	7	37	16	3	0	5	30	0	0	7.8	14.6
Rodriguez, Julio E.	R-R	5-11	245	6-11-97	.223	.311	.427	74	296	260	36	58	5	0	16	46	30	4	0	2	85	0	0	10.1	28.7
Rubalcaba, Alonzo	R-R	5-10	210	2-22-00	.071	.133	.071	5	16	14	0	1	0	0	0	1	1	0	0	0	8	0	0	6.3	50.0
Sands, Donny	R-R	6-2	190	5-16-96	.316	.316	.474	4	19	19	2	6	0	0	1	4	0	0	0	0	8	0	0	0.0	42.1
Santana, Luis	R-R	5-6	196	7-20-99	.240	.288	.457	61	236	221	30	53	13	1	11	39	12	3	0	0	50	1	1	5.1	21.2
Serretti, Danny	B-R	6-0	195	5-07-00	.205	.314	.269	49	186	156	15	32	7	0	1	15	25	1	0	3	36	1	1	13.4	19.4
Valente, John	R-R	5-11	190	6-23-95	.250	.250	.250	1	4	4	0	1	0	0	0	0	0	0	0	0	0	0	0	0.0	0.0
Witherspoon, Grant	L-L	6-1	200	9-27-96	.264	.358	.472	38	165	144	23	38	5	2	7	23	20	1	0	0	42	6	5	12.1	25.5
Workman, Gage	B-R	6-4	202	10-24-99	.191	.318	.382	55	214	178	37	34	9	2	7	19	31	3	0	2	83	11	1	14.5	38.8

Pitching	B-T	Ht.	Wt.	DOB	W	L	ERA	G	GS	SV	IP	Hits	Runs	ER	HR	BB	SO	AVG	OBP	SLG	SO%	BB%	BF
Alvarado, Elvis	R-R	6-4	183	2-23-99	0	0	0.00	1	1	0	1	0	0	0	0	0	1	.000	.000	.000	33.3	0.0	3
Bergner, Austin	R-R	6-5	210	5-01-97	6	2	4.41	28	2	2	51	47	29	25	6	26	62	.240	.329	.393	27.4	11.5	226
Bienlien, Michael	R-R	6-3	246	3-19-98	1	1	8.73	23	1	0	33	40	32	32	5	17	37	.296	.381	.467	23.9	11.0	155
Chentouf, Yaya	R-R	5-9	205	6-18-97	2	2	7.98	22	0	0	29	44	27	26	3	20	24	.358	.470	.528	16.1	13.4	149
De Jesus, Angel	R-R	6-4	200	2-13-97	1	4	4.21	32	0	2	36	31	24	17	7	20	45	.228	.325	.434	28.1	12.5	160
Faedo, Alex	R-R	6-5	225	11-12-95	0	0	5.06	1	1	0	5	6	3	3	1	1	8	.273	.304	.409	34.8	4.3	23
Fernander, Chavez	R-R	6-3	205	7-07-97	0	0	16.88	2	0	0	3	4	5	5	1	1	4	.333	.385	.750	30.8	7.7	13
Flores, Wilmer	R-R	6-4	225	2-20-01	5	3	3.90	18	18	0	81	72	36	35	5	32	82	.242	.318	.357	24.3	9.5	337
Gardea, Dario	R-R	6-2	210	1-29-99	2	2	9.39	12	0	0	15	17	19	16	3	14	16	.279	.418	.525	20.3	17.7	79
Gipson-Long, Sawyer	R-R	6-4	225	12-12-97	6	5	3.74	14	13	0	65	51	27	27	12	15	76	.214	.267	.437	29.8	5.9	255
Guenther, Sean	L-L	5-11	194	12-29-95	0	0	1.59	8	0	0	11	9	2	2	1	2	14	.209	.244	.279	31.1	4.4	45
Henderson, Layne	R-R	6-4	200	6-08-96	3	1	2.93	19	0	0	28	21	10	9	1	18	38	.210	.336	.250	30.9	14.6	123
Higginbotham, Jake	L-L	6-0	190	1-11-96	2	1	3.31	35	0	0	52	52	20	19	4	22	46	.265	.344	.378	20.4	9.8	225
Holden, Connor	R-R	6-5	240	6-25-98	0	1	10.13	4	0	0	5	7	6	6	3	3	2	.304	.385	.783	7.7	11.5	26
Holton, Jake	R-R	6-0	210	3-02-98	0	1	13.50	1	0	0	1	1	2	1	0	2	0	.333	.667	.333	0.0	33.3	6
Holub, Blake	R-R	6-6	230	10-23-98	1	3	3.79	30	0	7	40	36	19	17	6	13	44	.252	.319	.413	27.2	8.0	162
Hurter, Brant	L-L	6-6	250	9-06-98	6	7	3.28	26	26	0	118	108	50	43	7	33	133	.242	.307	.348	26.7	6.6	498
Jobe, Jackson	R-R	6-2	190	7-30-02	0	0	0.00	1	1	0	6	4	0	0	0	0	6	.167	.167	.167	25.0	0.0	24
Kirby, Chance	R-R	5-11	165	7-19-95	0	1	5.56	5	0	0	11	10	11	7	3	8	9	.233	.365	.442	17.3	15.4	52
Lescher, Billy	R-R	6-4	215	9-17-95	2	1	8.20	15	0	0	19	23	17	17	5	5	21	.291	.333	.595	25.0	6.0	84
Lockhart, Lael	B-L	6-3	225	12-31-97	5	2	2.69	18	12	0	74	54	26	22	5	32	89	.205	.299	.326	29.5	10.6	302
Madden, Ty	R-R	6-3	215	2-21-00	3	4	3.43	26	25	0	118	101	50	45	16	50	146	.233	.316	.406	29.7	10.2	492
Magno, Andrew	R-L	5-11	190	4-30-98	3	3	2.10	36	0	10	51	34	19	12	1	27	67	.185	.292	.255	31.5	12.7	213
Mattison, Tyler	R-R	6-4	235	9-05-99	2	0	1.62	22	3	4	33	20	9	6	0	18	46	.171	.279	.205	33.8	13.2	136
Michael, Trevin	R-R	6-2	200	9-15-97	0	1	16.20	2	1	0	2	2	3	3	0	6	2	.286	.615	.571	15.4	46.2	13
Montero, Keider	R-R	6-1	145	7-06-00	10	2	4.93	15	15	0	69	73	41	38	7	31	91	.267	.343	.410	29.6	10.1	307
Moreno, Williander	R-R	6-0	160	3-13-99	0	0	20.25	2	0	0	3	10	7	6	0	3	4	.526	.591	.526	18.2	13.6	22
Naughton, Tim	R-R	6-3	195	11-14-95	4	3	4.62	36	3	1	51	48	26	26	5	19	60	.249	.322	.368	28.0	8.9	214
Packard, Bryant	L-R	6-3	200	10-06-97	0	0	9.00	1	0	0	1	2	1	1	1	0	0	.400	.400	1.000	0.0	0.0	5
Petit, RJ	R-R	6-8	300	9-23-99	2	4	3.83	37	1	2	52	62	29	22	6	17	48	.295	.357	.467	20.4	7.2	235
Sammons, Bryan	L-L	6-4	235	4-27-95	2	1	3.63	4	4	0	22	13	10	9	4	11	26	.163	.264	.363	28.6	12.1	91
Smith, Dylan	R-R	6-2	180	5-28-00	0	1	12.71	3	2	0	6	11	9	8	0	5	10r	.393	.485	.464	30.3	15.2	33
Tassin, Bryce	R-R	6-2	209	1-11-97	2	2	4.67	20	1	0	35	42	27	18	3	14	31	.292	.352	.410	19.4	8.8	160
Wolf, Adam	L-L	6-6	215	12-26-96	5	4	3.48	40	7	2	85	69	36	33	5	39	79	.220	.339	.323	21.2	10.5	372

Fielding

Catcher	PCT	G	PO	A	E	DP	PB
Alfonzo	1.000	2	14	0	0	0	0
Burgess	1.000	2	29	1	0	0	0
Crouch	.992	11	117	12	1	2	2
Dingler	.985	40	378	26	6	4	4
Feliciano	.983	20	223	15	4	1	1
Rodriguez	.995	58	543	29	3	2	5
Rubalcaba	.973	5	35	1	1	0	1
Sands	1.000	2	29	1	0	0	0

First Base	PCT	G	PO	A	E	DP
Feliciano	.960	3	24	0	1	3
Holton	.997	89	642	31	2	53
Meyers	1.000	35	239	16	0	24
Santana	.989	13	91	1	1	12

Second Base	PCT	G	PO	A	E	DP
Cruz	.982	14	18	37	1	4
Joyce	1.000	4	3	9	0	4
Jung	.989	40	66	118	2	28
Keith	.964	6	11	16	1	3
Navigato	1.000	5	5	13	0	2
Perez	.949	44	65	101	9	17
Santana	1.000	6	5	17	0	3
Serretti	1.000	10	16	17	0	4
Valente	1.000	1	0	5	0	1
Workman	1.000	8	11	19	0	5

Third Base	PCT	G	PO	A	E	DP
Cruz	.931	21	14	40	4	4
Joyce	1.000	4	3	6	0	1
Keith	.953	41	25	56	4	7
Navigato	1.000	4	4	7	0	1
Santana	.958	35	19	49	3	7
Serretti	.974	22	7	31	1	1
Workman	.919	11	7	27	3	2

Shortstop	PCT	G	PO	A	E	DP
Cruz	.909	35	38	82	12	11
Joyce	.933	25	34	50	6	16
Navigato	.924	37	45	77	10	18
Serretti	.961	16	23	26	2	7
Workman	.959	28	44	73	5	11

Outfield	PCT	G	PO	A	E	DP
Allen	1.000	8	20	0	0	0
Bigbie	.988	53	86	2	1	1
Cabrera	.984	61	93	5	2	0
Cruz	1.000	51	112	2	0	0
De La Rosa	.500	4	4	1	0	0
Feliciano	1.000	9	9	0	0	0
Malgeri	.995	98	199	11	2	3
Meyers	1.000	27	39	2	0	1
Navigato	.928	12	22	1	1	0
Packard	.500	3	2	0	0	0
Perez	.988	23	42	2	1	0
Rincones	1.000	30	48	1	0	1
Santana	1.000	2	3	0	0	0
Witherspoon	.980	39	75	4	2	0
Workman	1.000	6	15	1	0	1

WEST MICHIGAN WHITECAPS — HIGH CLASS A

MIDWEST LEAGUE

Batting	B-T	Ht.	Wt.	DOB	AVG	OBP	SLG	G	PA	AB	R	H	2B	3B	HR	RBI	BB	HBP	SH	SF	SO	SB	CS	BB%	SO%
Alfonzo, Eliezer	B-R	5-10	155	9-23-99	.264	.324	.371	94	395	356	50	94	14	0	8	42	28	5	2	3	28	0	0	7.1	7.1
Allen, Brady	R-L	6-1	218	9-03-99	.264	.377	.485	82	361	303	55	80	18	2	15	47	49	7	0	2	89	4	0	13.6	24.7
2-team (37 Beloit)					.262	.365	.472	119	503	428	72	112	30	3	18	65	62	8	0	5	123	5	1	12.3	1.0
Bastidas, Abel	B-R	6-1	165	11-24-03	.000	.000	.000	2	1	1	0	0	0	0	0	0	0	0	0	0	1	0	0	0.0	100.0
Benitez, Lazaro	R-R	5-9	190	10-15-99	.195	.231	.264	26	91	87	7	17	6	0	0	3	3	1	0	0	24	0	0	3.3	26.4
Bigbie, Justice	R-R	6-2	200	1-24-99	.333	.400	.543	37	155	138	25	46	9	1	6	27	15	1	0	1	28	1	1	9.7	18.1
Burgess, Colin	R-R	5-8	195	11-10-00	.313	.450	.375	9	20	16	4	5	1	0	0	0	3	1	0	0	3	0	0	15.0	15.0
Campos, Roberto	R-R	6-3	200	6-14-03	.257	.313	.395	88	371	339	34	87	22	5	5	53	28	1	0	3	81	4	2	7.5	21.8
Chacon, Esney	R-R	6-0	160	3-17-00	.115	.161	.115	23	57	52	4	6	0	0	0	3	3	0	1	1	18	1	1	5.3	31.6
Crouch, Josh	R-R	6-0	200	12-07-98	.250	.329	.331	72	292	260	19	65	10	1	3	33	25	6	0	1	69	1	0	8.6	23.6
Garcia, Luis	B-R	5-11	170	10-01-00	.171	.340	.244	44	156	123	10	21	3	0	2	9	28	4	0	1	51	4	1	17.9	32.7
Gold, Luke	R-R	6-0	220	10-10-00	.250	.352	.456	36	159	136	27	34	8	1	6	22	14	8	0	1	27	1	0	8.8	17.0
Gonzalez, Alvaro	B-R	6-0	165	9-16-00	.167	.167	.333	2	6	6	1	1	1	0	0	0	0	0	0	0	3	0	0	0.0	50.0
Jenkins, Andrew	R-R	5-11	217	11-03-00	.292	.344	.336	29	123	113	10	33	2	0	1	10	8	1	0	0	35	0	0	6.5	28.5
Johnson, Dom	R-R	5-9	185	3-07-01	.124	.254	.182	39	143	121	16	15	4	0	1	6	16	5	1	0	52	4	2	11.2	36.4
Jung, Jace	L-R	6-0	205	10-04-00	.254	.377	.465	81	366	303	46	77	18	2	14	43	56	5	0	2	83	5	1	15.3	22.7
Kreidler, Ryan	R-R	6-4	208	11-12-97	.176	.263	.235	5	19	17	1	3	1	0	0	2	2	0	0	0	7	0	0	10.5	36.8
Lee, Hao-Yu	R-R	5-9	190	2-03-03	.214	.313	.429	8	32	28	4	6	1	1	1	3	3	1	0	0	9	2	2	9.4	28.1
Lipcius, Andre	R-R	6-0	190	5-22-98	.286	.400	.476	7	25	21	3	6	1	0	1	3	4	0	0	0	5	0	0	16.0	20.0
Malgeri, Ben	R-R	6-1	215	1-12-00	.283	.370	.630	13	54	46	9	13	5	1	3	7	5	2	0	1	12	0	0	9.3	22.2
Mendoza, Carlos	L-R	5-7	165	12-14-99	.257	.395	.304	63	244	191	34	49	7	1	0	16	40	5	6	2	39	8	5	16.4	16.0
Meyers, Chris	L-R	6-3	210	4-27-99	.333	.429	.638	40	163	138	28	46	13	1	9	32	18	6	0	1	28	2	0	11.0	17.2
Murr, Austin	L-L	6-1	218	1-26-99	.242	.315	.389	89	319	285	38	69	17	5	5	37	24	7	0	1	49	9	1	7.5	15.4
Pacheco, Izaac	L-R	6-3	225	11-18-02	.211	.283	.352	119	508	455	54	96	22	3	12	50	47	1	0	5	160	5	2	9.3	31.5
Paulson, Dillon	L-L	6-2	200	6-10-97	.255	.336	.378	54	214	188	24	48	14	0	3	23	23	1	0	2	42	0	0	10.7	19.6
Santana, Luis	R-R	5-6	196	7-20-99	.365	.441	.462	17	59	52	8	19	2	0	1	8	6	1	0	0	11	1	0	10.2	18.6
Serretti, Danny	B-R	6-0	195	5-07-00	.284	.367	.441	53	238	204	35	58	13	2	5	24	26	3	0	4	45	2	4	10.9	18.9
Stephenson, Seth	R-R	5-8	165	1-10-01	.298	.412	.404	14	68	57	11	17	4	1	0	1	5	6	0	0	19	8	2	7.4	27.9
Valencia, Eduardo	R-R	6-1	180	1-25-00	.161	.206	.290	8	34	31	4	5	1	0	1	6	1	1	0	1	6	0	0	2.9	17.6
Walker, Steele	L-L	5-11	209	7-30-96	.262	.324	.377	16	68	61	9	16	2	1	1	11	6	0	0	1	12	0	0	8.8	17.6
Workman, Gage	B-R	6-4	202	10-24-99	.288	.355	.435	45	198	177	36	51	6	1	6	29	17	2	0	1	56	8	2	8.6	28.3

Pitching	B-T	Ht.	Wt.	DOB	W	L	ERA	G	GS	SV	IP	Hits	Runs	ER	HR	BB	SO	AVG	OBP	SLG	SO%	BB%	BF
Alvarado, Elvis	R-R	6-4	183	2-23-99	2	1	4.73	25	0	2	27	28	17	14	5	11	33	.267	.342	.467	27.5	9.2	120
Anderson, Jack	R-R	6-3	197	11-23-99	1	1	4.80	39	0	2	54	59	34	29	8	14	43	.271	.311	.459	18.3	6.0	235
Bienlien, Michael	R-R	6-3	246	3-19-98	0	0	2.74	12	0	0	23	18	7	7	0	12	26	.220	.350	.244	26.0	12.0	100
Brieske, Beau	R-R	6-3	200	4-04-98	0	0	0.00	2	1	0	2	0	0	0	0	1	2	.000	.143	.000	28.6	14.3	7
Brown, Cameron	L-R	6-2	165	5-12-98	0	1	4.63	8	0	1	12	8	7	6	1	9	12	.195	.353	.341	23.5	17.6	51
Burhenn, Garrett	R-R	6-3	215	9-12-99	6	6	4.04	24	18	0	94	98	47	42	7	29	70	.271	.327	.390	17.6	7.3	398
Fernander, Chavez	R-R	6-3	205	7-07-97	2	1	4.62	19	0	3	25	29	13	13	4	11	21	.276	.353	.486	17.6	9.2	119
Flores, Wilmer	R-R	6-4	225	2-20-01	0	1	11.88	3	3	0	8	12	11	11	0	1	8	.343	.395	.400	21.1	2.6	38
Gardea, Dario	R-R	6-2	210	1-29-99	1	5	6.17	25	0	8	35	34	26	24	3	17	40	.248	.346	.394	25.2	10.7	159
Haase, Aaron	R-R	5-8	193	5-24-00	1	1	5.94	10	0	0	17	23	13	11	3	5	18	.329	.359	.543	23.1	6.4	78
Hernandez, Wilkel	R-R	6-3	195	4-13-99	3	8	3.65	26	20	0	106	87	50	43	11	31	97	.220	.292	.357	22.0	7.0	440
Hess, Zack	R-R	6-6	219	2-25-97	1	0	9.00	5	0	0	6	6	6	6	1	3	8	.250	.333	.417	29.6	11.1	27
Holden, Connor	R-R	6-5	240	6-25-98	0	0	4.58	12	0	0	18	13	9	9	1	5	12	.197	.264	.303	16.7	6.9	72
Holub, Blake	R-R	6-6	230	10-23-98	5	1	1.80	18	0	1	25	17	6	5	3	4	32	.187	.227	.319	33.0	4.1	97
Jobe, Jackson	R-R	6-2	190	7-30-02	2	3	3.60	8	8	0	40	39	17	16	7	3	54	.252	.264	.413	33.8	1.9	160
Kirby, Chance	R-R	5-11	165	7-19-95	0	0	40.50	1	0	0	1	3	3	3	0	1	1	.600	.667	1.000	16.7	16.7	6
Marks, Jordan	L-R	6-2	220	4-29-99	1	2	3.86	23	0	1	30	29	20	13	2	8	25	.252	.298	.374	20.0	6.4	125
Mattison, Tyler	R-R	6-4	235	9-05-99	3	1	3.42	19	2	2	26	20	10	10	5	10	45	.215	.288	.430	43.3	9.6	104
Melton, Troy	R-R	6-4	210	12-03-00	3	1	2.48	16	15	0	65	55	19	18	2	18	61	.225	.281	.357	22.8	6.7	267
Michael, Trevin	R-R	6-2	200	9-15-97	5	4	3.43	34	0	5	39	35	19	15	1	14	50	.236	.299	.291	30.1	8.4	166
Montero, Keider	R-R	6-1	145	7-06-00	0	0	2.81	4	4	0	16	10	5	5	1	4	22	.175	.230	.281	36.1	6.6	61
Moreno, Williander	R-R	6-0	160	3-13-99	5	3	5.64	29	14	1	69	92	47	43	11	21	39	.324	.381	.518	12.4	6.7	314
O'Loughlin, Jack	L-L	6-5	223	3-14-00	3	3	2.17	9	9	0	37	36	10	9	0	15	39	.248	.329	.283	23.8	9.1	164

Pena, Carlos	L-L	5-11	160	9-07-98	5	6	3.11	24	21	0	110	95	41	38	8	38	107	.235	.311	.356	23.5	8.4	455
Petit, RJ	R-R	6-8	300	9-23-99	0	0	0.00	5	0	1	5	2	0	0	0	1	8	.118	.167	.118	44.4	5.6	18
Pinales, Erick	R-R	6-2	185	1-27-99	4	2	3.76	35	0	1	38	27	21	16	5	26	41	.190	.320	.338	24.3	15.4	169
Reyes, Angel	R-R	6-2	205	10-17-97	6	3	4.50	34	4	2	56	53	35	28	2	26	45	.244	.343	.346	17.7	10.2	254
Sequeira, Gabriel	L-L	6-0	200	8-18-97	2	0	2.74	45	0	6	49	39	17	15	2	18	57	.215	.306	.320	27.3	8.6	209
Skubal, Tarik	R-L	6-3	240	11-20-96	0	0	0.00	2	2	0	5	3	1	0	0	0	7	.167	.211	.167	36.8	0.0	19
Smith, Dylan	R-R	6-2	180	5-28-00	1	1	3.67	6	6	0	27	31	11	11	3	5	23	.287	.322	.426	19.8	4.3	116
Stofel, Luke	R-R	6-5	235	11-25-01	0	0	27.00	1	0	0	0	0	1	1	0	3	0	.000	.750	.000	0.0	75.0	4
Tassin, Bryce	R-R	6-2	209	1-11-97	1	3	2.59	17	0	0	24	23	14	7	1	6	18	.250	.307	.337	17.6	5.9	102
Tortosa, Cristhian	L-L	6-4	170	10-30-98	5	4	5.58	30	1	0	31	29	22	19	1	26	32	.254	.403	.404	21.5	17.4	149
Turnbull, Spencer	R-R	6-3	210	9-18-92	0	0	3.60	2	2	0	5	4	2	2	1	0	5	.211	.211	.526	26.3	0.0	19

Fielding

Catcher	PCT	G	PO	A	E	DP	PB
Alfonzo	.984	80	729	30	12	4	8
Burgess	1.000	4	14	1	0	0	0
Crouch	.988	41	304	23	4	1	2
Valencia	.987	8	74	2	1	0	1

First Base	PCT	G	PO	A	E	DP
Jenkins	.984	25	165	14	3	13
Lipcius	1.000	1	7	1	0	1
Meyers	1.000	29	231	7	0	22
Murr	1.000	29	203	12	0	18
Paulson	.986	47	329	30	5	32
Santana	1.000	6	25	3	0	2

Second Base	PCT	G	PO	A	E	DP
Bastidas	.000	1	0	0	0	0
Garcia	1.000	5	8	10	0	7
Gold	.938	29	38	52	6	9
Gonzalez	1.000	2	2	5	0	0
Jung	.996	69	94	166	1	34
Kreidler	1.000	1	2	2	0	0
Lee	1.000	5	4	12	0	1
Lipcius	1.000	1	0	2	0	0
Mendoza	.947	20	37	53	5	11
Serretti	1.000	2	3	5	0	1

Third Base	PCT	G	PO	A	E	DP
Garcia	.900	6	6	12	2	2
Gold	1.000	3	5	2	0	0
Lipcius	1.000	2	1	1	0	0
Mendoza	.941	14	7	25	2	1
Pacheco	.926	93	67	171	19	19
Santana	1.000	10	7	15	0	1
Serretti	1.000	3	2	5	0	1
Workman	1.000	1	1	2	0	0

Shortstop	PCT	G	PO	A	E	DP
Bastidas	1.000	1	1	0	0	0
Garcia	.978	29	36	52	2	10
Kreidler	1.000	2	1	2	0	0
Lee	1.000	2	4	6	0	1
Pacheco	.980	13	14	34	1	7
Serretti	.973	46	68	111	5	26
Workman	.980	39	59	91	3	18

Outfield	PCT	G	PO	A	E	DP
Allen	.978	82	166	6	3	2
Benitez	.913	21	36	1	2	0
Bigbie	.915	29	43	1	2	0
Campos	.974	86	168	5	5	2
Chacon	1.000	21	40	1	0	0
Garcia	1.000	1	2	0	0	0
Johnson	.992	40	89	2	1	0
Lipcius	.000	1	0	0	0	0
Malgeri	.976	14	18	0	1	0
Mendoza	.979	27	43	1	1	0
Meyers	.889	3	8	0	1	0
Murr	.989	58	103	3	2	0
Stephenson	1.000	14	36	2	0	0
Walker	1.000	14	20	0	0	0
Workman	1.000	2	5	0	0	0

LAKELAND FLYING TIGERS — *LOW CLASS A*

FLORIDA STATE LEAGUE

Batting	B-T	Ht.	Wt.	DOB	AVG	OBP	SLG	G	PA	AB	R	H	2B	3B	HR	RBI	BB	HBP	SH	SF	SO	SB	CS	BB%	SO%
Anderson, Max	R-R	6-0	195	2-28-02	.289	.345	.445	32	145	128	18	37	12	1	2	21	12	1	0	4	26	2	0	8.3	17.9
Bastidas, Abel	B-R	6-1	165	11-24-03	.216	.291	.312	57	244	218	31	47	13	1	2	18	19	5	0	2	58	0	0	7.8	23.8
Benitez, Lazaro	R-R	5-9	190	10-15-99	.330	.371	.427	27	116	103	9	34	7	0	1	15	8	1	0	4	13	0	0	6.9	11.2
Briceno, Josue	L-R	6-4	200	9-23-04	.293	.396	.439	11	48	41	8	12	6	0	0	1	7	0	0	0	8	0	0	14.6	16.7
Brookman, Archer	R-R	5-11	200	1-08-99	.203	.409	.313	22	88	64	9	13	2	1	1	12	21	2	0	1	20	0	0	23.9	22.7
Cabrera, Daniel	L-L	5-11	200	9-05-98	.263	.563	.316	7	32	19	6	5	1	0	0	1	12	1	0	0	4	2	0	37.5	12.5
Callahan, Brett	L-R	6-0	195	11-02-01	.286	.432	.371	12	46	35	7	10	1	1	0	7	7	2	0	0	7	4	0	15.2	15.2
Campbell, Clayton	R-R	6-1	209	9-11-03	.189	.354	.378	12	48	37	11	7	2	1	1	3	9	1	0	1	16	1	0	18.8	33.3
Clark, Max	L-L	6-1	190	12-21-04	.154	.353	.179	11	51	39	5	6	1	0	0	7	12	0	0	0	15	1	0	23.5	29.4
De La Cruz, Jose	R-R	6-1	216	1-03-02	.243	.341	.397	89	381	325	53	79	14	0	12	51	46	5	0	5	120	2	3	12.1	31.5
Dingler, Dillon	R-R	6-3	210	9-17-98	.395	.509	.767	12	53	43	9	17	4	0	4	8	7	3	0	0	8	3	0	13.2	15.1
Feliciano, Mario	R-R	5-10	200	11-20-98	.154	.214	.269	7	28	26	5	4	3	0	0	2	1	1	0	0	5	0	0	3.6	17.9
Gold, Luke	R-R	6-0	220	10-10-00	.269	.367	.428	59	245	208	32	56	13	1	6	37	25	9	0	3	54	11	1	10.2	22.0
Gonzalez, Alvaro	B-R	6-0	165	9-16-00	.153	.311	.254	23	75	59	12	9	0	0	2	6	12	2	1	1	22	1	0	16.0	29.3
Graham, Peyton	R-R	6-3	185	1-26-01	.232	.339	.355	54	239	203	38	47	11	1	4	29	28	6	0	2	53	15	3	11.7	22.2
Jarvis, Jim	L-R	5-10	185	11-06-00	.260	.344	.356	28	122	104	19	27	7	0	1	24	11	4	0	3	22	6	3	9.0	18.0
Jenkins, Andrew	R-R	5-11	217	11-03-00	.304	.380	.382	51	234	204	36	62	7	3	1	38	23	4	0	3	62	3	1	9.8	26.5
Johnson, Dom	R-R	5-9	185	3-07-01	.271	.367	.401	58	245	207	32	56	9	3	4	33	29	5	0	4	64	14	3	11.8	26.1
Johnson, Tyler	L-L	6-0	220	10-25-99	.172	.324	.259	20	71	58	9	10	2	0	1	3	13	0	0	0	22	0	0	18.3	31.0
Kreidler, Ryan	R-R	6-4	208	11-12-97	.211	.400	.421	5	25	19	7	4	1	0	1	6	6	0	0	0	9	1	0	24.0	36.0
Lee, Bennett	R-R	6-0	208	4-26-02	.200	.444	.217	23	90	60	6	12	1	0	0	7	22	6	0	2	11	1	0	24.4	12.2
McGonigle, Kevin	L-R	5-11	185	8-18-04	.350	.438	.475	12	48	40	7	14	2	0	1	5	7	0	0	1	5	2	2	14.6	10.4
McLaughlin, J.D.	R-R	6-2	195	12-28-00	.190	.328	.299	47	177	147	30	28	8	1	2	15	25	5	0	0	41	12	0	14.1	23.2
Mendoza, Carlos	L-R	5-7	165	12-14-99	.200	.414	.350	6	29	20	3	4	0	0	1	6	8	0	0	1	4	0	1	27.6	13.8
Navigato, Andrew	R-R	5-11	188	5-28-98	.174	.250	.304	11	52	46	5	8	4	1	0	6	4	1	0	1	9	0	1	7.7	17.3
Nieporte, Quincy	R-R	6-0	225	7-29-94	.227	.333	.227	7	27	22	2	5	0	0	0	3	4	0	0	1	6	0	0	14.8	22.2
Peck, John	R-R	6-0	185	7-18-02	.280	.379	.320	8	29	25	6	7	1	0	0	2	3	1	0	0	7	3	0	10.3	24.1
Pelegrin, Carlos	R-R	6-3	180	6-21-00	.239	.322	.374	46	184	163	24	39	8	1	4	25	17	3	1	0	58	6	1	9.2	31.5
Perez, Wenceel	B-R	5-11	203	10-30-99	.381	.409	.524	5	22	21	4	8	3	0	0	1	1	0	0	0	5	1	0	4.5	22.7
Reyes, Adinso	R-R	6-1	195	10-22-01	.208	.273	.366	28	110	101	15	21	5	1	3	11	9	0	0	0	41	1	0	8.2	37.3
Rothenberg, Mike	B-R	6-3	215	10-05-98	.239	.354	.455	69	302	255	36	61	17	1	12	52	41	5	0	1	106	1	1	13.6	35.1
Santana, Cristian	R-R	5-11	165	11-25-03	.156	.365	.312	97	419	308	68	48	12	0	12	42	91	14	0	6	116	6	5	21.7	27.7
Sequera, Manuel	R-R	6-1	170	9-28-02	.207	.283	.357	58	237	213	30	44	11	0	7	35	18	5	0	1	63	3	1	7.6	26.6
Smith, David	B-R	5-11	195	2-20-01	.196	.354	.255	21	66	51	6	10	0	0	1	10	10	3	1	1	14	4	0	15.2	21.2
Stephenson, Seth	R-R	5-8	165	1-10-01	.277	.376	.399	99	437	368	84	102	17	8	4	36	37	24	4	4	89	62	13	8.5	20.4
Tapia, Sergio	R-R	5-10	160	8-24-02	.176	.317	.284	34	124	102	15	18	5	0	2	16	17	4	1	0	21	1	1	13.7	16.9
Turney, Cole	L-L	6-1	215	1-16-99	.333	.412	.533	4	17	15	4	5	1	1	0	0	2	0	0	0	7	0	0	11.8	41.2

Valero, Moises R-R 6-1 185 3-01-02 .220 .280 .339 50 182 168 18 37 6 4 2 17 12 2 0 0 66 2 2 6.6 36.3

Pitching	B-T	Ht.	Wt.	DOB	W	L	ERA	G	GS	SV	IP	Hits	Runs	ER	HR	BB	SO	AVG	OBP	SLG	SO%	BB%	BF
Adametz, Joe	L-L	6-5	190	12-23-99	1	0	0.90	2	2	0	10	5	1	1	1	1	7	.147	.171	.235	19.4	2.8	36
Alba, Max	R-R	6-5	215	7-15-99	6	6	4.07	41	0	7	55	46	28	25	6	25	65	.224	.303	.361	27.8	10.7	234
Alvarado, Elvis	R-R	6-4	183	2-23-99	0	1	8.44	5	1	0	5	7	6	5	0	3	6	.318	.423	.409	23.1	11.5	26
Apker, Garrett	R-R	6-5	195	9-18-99	1	4	7.88	23	6	0	48	56	48	42	8	37	47	.295	.418	.500	20.3	15.9	232
Brown, Cameron	L-R	6-2	165	5-12-98	4	2	4.39	32	0	11	41	37	22	20	3	12	44	.245	.335	.364	25.3	6.9	174
Campos, Ulices	R-R	5-10	170	12-14-01	0	4	8.51	17	9	0	49	74	47	46	7	23	41	.352	.412	.562	17.2	9.7	238
Chalas, Gregoris	R-R	5-10	143	8-12-00	1	0	9.35	8	0	0	9	6	12	9	2	8	9	.207	.419	.448	20.5	18.2	44
Cruz, Jesus	R-R	6-4	185	10-08-00	4	0	2.50	14	0	0	18	15	5	5	0	12	17	.231	.367	.277	21.5	15.2	79
Diaz, Jose	R-R	6-5	200	5-12-00	2	1	6.34	30	0	1	38	29	28	27	3	30	40	.209	.383	.331	22.2	16.7	180
Fields, Colin	R-R	6-2	200	3-18-00	5	0	3.38	14	8	0	45	31	17	17	3	17	51	.194	.293	.275	27.7	9.2	184
Garcia, Pedro	R-R	6-1	190	2-27-02	0	0	0.00	1	0	0	2	1	0	0	0	1	2	.167	.286	.500	28.6	14.3	7
Gonzalez, Alvaro	B-R	6-0	165	9-16-00	0	0	0.00	2	0	0	1	1	0	0	0	0	1	.500	.500	.500	50.0	0.0	2
Green, Max	L-L	6-1	175	5-28-96	1	2	11.77	12	3	0	13	18	17	17	1	11	15	.333	.449	.500	21.7	15.9	69
Gudaitis, Quinn	R-R	6-7	225	4-10-99	5	4	5.26	38	0	0	51	41	35	30	4	40	44	.219	.380	.348	18.4	16.7	239
Guenther, Sean	L-L	5-11	194	12-29-95	0	0	1.13	6	3	0	8	4	1	1	0	1	11	.154	.185	.154	40.7	3.7	27
Haase, Aaron	R-R	5-8	193	5-24-00	0	0	1.23	5	0	2	7	2	1	1	0	1	8	.087	.120	.130	32.0	4.0	25
Hamm, Jaden	R-R	6-1	190	9-05-02	0	0	0.00	4	4	0	11	3	1	0	0	1	11	.081	.105	.081	28.9	2.6	38
Higginbotham, Jake	L-L	6-0	190	1-11-96	1	0	0.00	3	1	0	5	1	0	0	0	1	5	.071	.133	.071	33.3	6.7	15
Hill, Garrett	R-R	6-0	185	1-16-96	0	0	3.60	2	2	0	5	4	2	2	0	3	6	.222	.364	.278	27.3	13.6	22
Holden, Connor	R-R	6-5	240	6-25-98	3	2	3.64	18	0	1	30	28	14	12	0	8	35	.246	.295	.360	28.7	6.6	122
Huizi, Eiker	R-R	6-0	155	9-24-00	3	0	6.75	25	0	0	31	24	25	23	1	20	27	.211	.348	.342	19.6	14.5	138
Ibarra, Edgardo	L-L	6-0	160	6-02-03	2	4	5.00	17	14	0	63	55	40	35	4	48	55	.242	.383	.352	19.5	17.0	282
Jimenez, Marco	R-R	5-11	239	12-06-99	0	2	7.63	12	7	0	31	37	32	26	0	16	32	.282	.371	.382	21.1	10.5	152
Jobe, Jackson	R-R	6-2	190	7-30-02	0	1	2.25	6	6	0	16	14	4	4	2	3	20	.222	.279	.349	29.4	4.4	68
Kirby, Chance	R-R	5-11	165	7-19-95	0	1	6.75	3	2	0	5	9	4	4	1	1	1	.409	.435	.545	4.2	4.2	24
Kohlhepp, Tanner	L-R	6-4	210	5-27-99	2	3	3.42	20	4	0	24	12	14	9	0	25	39	.143	.351	.179	35.1	22.5	111
Marcano, Carlos	R-R	6-2	150	7-08-03	4	5	4.50	22	18	0	100	88	57	50	7	41	78	.237	.326	.371	18.2	9.6	429
Marks, Jordan	L-R	6-2	220	4-29-99	3	0	2.42	15	0	0	22	14	9	6	0	10	18	.182	.281	.234	20.0	11.1	90
Mauloni, Christopher	L-R	6-2	200	6-16-98	1	0	4.15	30	0	0	35	25	21	16	4	33	42	.202	.378	.347	25.6	20.1	164
Melton, Troy	R-R	6-4	210	12-03-00	0	0	3.38	7	7	0	27	26	10	10	3	6	33	.252	.300	.398	30.0	5.5	110
Mendez, Eric	R-R	6-0	175	12-03-99	2	1	3.99	20	0	2	29	26	15	13	4	8	24	.241	.297	.426	20.2	6.7	119
Michael, Trevin	R-R	6-2	200	9-15-97	0	0	1.04	6	0	2	9	2	1	1	0	6	15	.074	.242	.074	45.5	18.2	33
Miller, Jake	L-L	6-2	185	6-27-01	1	2	8.59	9	6	0	29	35	28	28	5	17	33	.299	.415	.462	23.2	12.0	142
Miller, Joe	L-L	5-10	195	3-13-00	2	3	3.93	18	12	0	69	78	38	30	4	31	78	.283	.368	.409	24.5	9.7	318
Nunez, Hendry	R-R	6-4	180	7-22-99	0	1	6.97	7	0	0	10	10	8	8	0	9	5	.270	.417	.378	10.4	18.8	48
Patten, Cole	R-R	6-4	194	8-05-99	1	4	4.70	15	3	0	44	43	27	23	5	14	43	.254	.314	.414	23.1	7.5	186
Perez, Cleiverth	L-L	6-0	211	2-05-00	6	3	4.99	38	1	5	58	51	36	32	2	26	52	.239	.335	.343	20.9	10.4	249
Perez, Franklin	R-R	6-3	197	12-06-97	0	0	12.00	5	0	0	6	9	8	8	1	6	2	.346	.471	.654	5.9	17.6	34
Rodriguez, Erick	R-R	5-10	185	3-21-02	0	1	3.52	6	0	0	8	10	7	3	0	5	6	.303	.385	.485	15.4	12.8	39
Rosenthal, Trevor	R-R	6-2	230	5-29-90	0	0	0.00	1	1	0	1	0	0	0	0	1	0	.000	.333	.000	0.0	33.3	3
Sanchez, Yosber	R-R	6-1	170	5-22-01	1	0	1.69	5	0	0	5	4	1	1	0	3	6	.222	.333	.222	28.6	14.3	21
Valero, Moises	R-R	6-1	185	3-01-02	0	0	0.00	1	0	0	1	2	0	0	0	0	0	.400	.400	.400	0.0	0.0	5
Walker, Matt	L-L	6-3	217	6-15-98	2	0	4.33	6	5	0	27	32	13	13	3	11	19	.296	.358	.444	15.8	9.2	120
Williams, Chris	L-L	6-2	205	3-03-00	6	3	4.93	21	4	0	38	29	25	21	6	31	47	.203	.363	.378	26.3	17.3	179
Wingenter, Trey	R-R	6-7	237	4-15-94	0	1	54.00	2	2	0	1	1	4	4	0	4	2	.333	.714	.333	28.6	57.1	7

Fielding

Catcher	PCT	G	PO	A	E	DP	PB
Briceno	1.000	5	45	3	0	1	1
Brookman	1.000	21	171	6	0	1	1
Dingler	1.000	6	37	2	0	1	1
Feliciano	1.000	4	28	1	0	0	0
Lee	.995	23	198	15	1	1	2
Rothenberg	.995	41	364	38	2	0	5
Tapia	.983	33	259	23	5	0	4
Valero	.984	6	55	5	1	1	1

First Base	PCT	G	PO	A	E	DP
Briceno	1.000	4	44	1	0	4
Brookman	1.000	1	4	0	0	0
Campbell	.971	12	91	8	3	5
Jenkins	.982	43	307	18	6	33
Johnson	.986	20	136	10	2	11
Rothenberg	.987	10	69	9	1	10
Sequera	1.000	6	36	2	0	4
Valero	.993	39	284	12	2	24

Second Base	PCT	G	PO	A	E	DP
Anderson	.992	24	50	70	1	17
Bastidas	.977	9	9	34	1	6
Gold	.972	24	46	57	3	17
Gonzalez	.914	14	24	29	5	4
Graham	.950	3	10	9	1	2
Jarvis	.000	1	0	0	0	0
McGonigle	.900	4	2	7	1	0
Mendoza	1.000	4	9	17	0	3
Navigato	1.000	4	6	10	0	3
Peck	1.000	2	0	6	0	0
Perez	.938	4	7	8	1	1
Reyes	1.000	2	1	5	0	1
Santana	.979	24	35	57	2	14
Sequera	.962	14	16	34	2	2
Smith	.875	4	2	5	1	0

Third Base	PCT	G	PO	A	E	DP
Bastidas	.922	19	18	29	4	3
Gold	.931	31	18	36	4	4
Gonzalez	.750	6	2	4	2	0
Graham	.774	8	9	15	7	2
Jarvis	.900	9	8	10	2	0
Kreidler	1.000	1	1	0	0	0
Mendoza	.667	1	1	1	1	0
Navigato	.833	2	1	4	1	1
Peck	.000	1	0	0	0	0
Reyes	.911	20	11	30	4	7
Santana	.937	35	30	59	6	7

Shortstop	PCT	G	PO	A	E	DP
Bastidas	.960	30	51	68	5	10
Graham	.957	36	49	84	6	13
Jarvis	.982	14	23	32	1	7
Kreidler	1.000	3	5	6	0	2
McGonigle	.933	7	9	19	2	6
Navigato	.917	2	4	7	1	3
Peck	1.000	4	5	8	0	0
Reyes	.700	3	4	3	3	1
Santana	.919	33	44	80	11	18
Sequera	.900	2	4	5	1	1

Outfield	PCT	G	PO	A	E	DP
Benitez	.984	22	40	2	1	0
Cabrera	1.000	3	8	1	0	0
Callahan	1.000	12	18	3	0	1
Clark	1.000	11	24	2	0	0
De La Cruz	.944	73	98	11	5	3
Johnson	.972	54	103	4	3	0
McLaughlin	.990	43	85	4	1	1
Pelegrin	1.000	42	73	6	0	1
Sequera	.984	30	58	2	1	0
Smith	.976	14	22	2	1	1
Stephenson	.984	93	191	9	4	0
Turney	1.000	3	4	0	0	0
Valero	1.000	2	4	0	0	0

FCL TIGERS

ROOKIE

FLORIDA COMPLEX LEAGUE

Batting	B-T	Ht.	Wt.	DOB	AVG	OBP	SLG	G	PA	AB	R	H	2B	3B	HR	RBI	BB	HBP	SH	SF	SO	SB	CS	BB%	SO%
Benitez, Lazaro	R-R	5-9	190	10-15-99	.250	.333	.375	2	9	8	2	2	1	0	0	2	1	0	0	0	2	0	0	11.1	22.2
Briceno, Josue	L-R	6-4	200	9-23-04	.325	.404	.550	44	198	169	40	55	13	2	7	37	23	2	0	4	28	3	1	11.6	14.1
Calderon, Cesar	R-R	6-2	170	11-01-01	.170	.302	.245	20	63	53	5	9	1	0	1	8	8	2	0	0	22	0	0	12.7	34.9
Callahan, Brett	L-R	6-0	195	11-02-01	.389	.511	.528	10	45	36	9	14	2	0	1	9	9	0	0	0	11	5	2	20.0	24.4
Campbell, Clayton	R-R	6-1	209	9-11-03	.284	.416	.514	33	137	109	21	31	16	0	3	25	21	5	0	2	30	4	0	15.3	21.9
Cerkownyk, Brady	R-R	6-0	190	2-02-03	.167	.286	.167	2	7	6	1	1	0	0	0	4	0	1	0	0	1	0	0	0.0	14.3
Clark, Max	L-L	6-1	190	12-21-04	.283	.411	.543	12	56	46	13	13	4	1	2	12	9	1	0	0	10	4	1	16.1	17.9
De La Cruz, Daneurys	R-R	5-10	160	4-27-01	.235	.316	.471	24	77	68	13	16	5	1	3	11	7	1	0	0	28	2	1	9.1	36.4
De Los Santos, Raudy	R-R	5-10	155	3-18-03	.144	.323	.278	37	124	97	25	14	4	3	1	8	24	2	0	1	18	10	7	19.4	14.5
Diaz, Yimmy	B-R	5-10	155	2-19-04	.191	.353	.236	35	139	110	23	21	2	0	1	11	24	4	0	1	27	7	1	17.3	19.4
Fana, Nomar	B-R	5-11	175	9-28-02	.253	.365	.345	33	104	87	16	22	2	0	2	10	15	1	0	1	23	5	1	14.4	22.1
Feliciano, Mario	R-R	5-10	200	11-20-98	.391	.417	.478	6	24	23	5	9	2	0	0	6	0	1	0	0	4	0	0	0.0	16.7
Gil, Samuel	R-R	5-9	165	11-01-04	.298	.406	.404	44	192	161	34	48	7	2	2	18	29	1	0	1	32	7	4	15.1	16.7
Graham, Peyton	R-R	6-3	185	1-26-01	.250	.400	.500	3	5	4	0	1	1	0	0	0	0	1	0	0	1	1	0	0.0	20.0
Hurtado, Ricardo	R-R	5-10	180	5-23-03	.224	.337	.421	23	93	76	11	17	4	1	3	15	9	5	1	2	25	1	0	9.7	26.9
Jarvis, Jim	L-R	5-10	185	11-06-00	.000	.000	.000	1	1	1	0	0	0	0	0	0	0	0	0	0	0	0	0	0.0	0.0
Jenkins, Andrew	R-R	5-11	217	11-03-00	.643	.706	.786	4	17	14	1	9	2	0	0	2	3	0	0	0	3	1	0	17.6	17.6
Johnson, Tyler	L-L	6-0	220	10-25-99	.206	.325	.471	14	40	34	4	7	3	0	2	10	5	1	0	0	17	1	0	12.5	42.5
Kreidler, Ryan	R-R	6-4	208	11-12-97	.100	.250	.200	4	12	10	1	1	1	0	0	1	1	1	0	0	4	0	0	8.3	33.3
Leon, Andri	L-L	6-0	150	2-28-03	.156	.188	.182	25	80	77	7	12	2	0	0	5	3	0	0	0	29	1	2	3.8	36.3
Leonardo, Iverson	L-L	5-11	173	8-21-01	.265	.433	.408	29	127	98	16	26	11	0	1	16	24	5	0	0	43	2	2	18.9	33.9
McGonigle, Kevin	L-R	5-11	185	8-18-04	.273	.467	.333	9	45	33	11	9	2	0	0	1	11	1	0	0	5	6	3	24.4	11.1
Peck, John	R-R	6-0	185	7-18-02	.125	.400	.125	9	35	24	4	3	0	0	0	1	9	2	0	0	6	5	2	25.7	17.1
Pelegrin, Carlos	R-R	6-3	180	6-21-00	.350	.350	.750	5	20	20	3	7	2	0	2	4	0	0	0	0	7	0	0	0.0	35.0
Perez, Reylin	B-R	6-2	160	10-05-04	.152	.270	.257	35	123	105	24	16	1	2	2	15	16	1	1	0	42	8	2	13.0	34.1
Reina, Jose	R-R	6-2	160	2-28-01	.268	.371	.427	26	97	82	12	22	4	3	1	12	13	1	0	1	24	1	3	13.4	24.7
Reyes, Adinso	R-R	6-1	195	10-22-01	.325	.372	.475	11	43	40	9	13	3	0	1	6	3	0	0	0	11	1	2	7.0	25.6
Rothenberg, Mike	B-R	6-3	215	10-05-98	.391	.517	1.304	7	29	23	11	9	0	0	7	14	5	1	0	0	8	0	0	17.2	27.6
Rubalcaba, Alonzo	R-R	5-10	210	2-22-00	.235	.381	.382	12	42	34	6	8	2	0	1	8	7	1	0	0	11	0	0	16.7	26.2
Rucker, Carson	R-R	6-2	195	8-18-04	.242	.390	.364	9	41	33	5	8	1	0	1	9	6	2	0	0	9	4	1	14.6	22.0
Schultz, Austin	R-R	5-9	200	2-21-00	.188	.316	.438	9	19	16	3	3	1	0	1	1	2	1	0	0	9	0	1	10.5	47.4
Sequera, Manuel	R-R	6-1	170	9-28-02	.455	.538	.773	6	26	22	8	10	1	0	2	6	3	1	0	0	4	0	0	11.5	15.4
Smith, David	B-R	5-11	195	2-20-01	.429	.556	.429	3	9	7	3	3	0	0	0	0	1	1	0	0	2	1	0	11.1	22.2
Turney, Cole	L-L	6-1	215	1-16-99	.432	.571	.757	11	49	37	11	16	4	1	2	15	6	6	0	0	12	2	0	12.2	24.5
Valero, Moises	R-R	6-1	185	3-01-02	.455	.500	.773	8	26	22	3	10	2	1	1	6	2	1	0	1	7	1	0	7.7	26.9
Walker, Steele	L-L	5-11	209	7-30-96	.118	.318	.353	5	22	17	3	2	1	0	1	1	5	0	0	0	3	0	0	22.7	13.6

Pitching	B-T	Ht.	Wt.	DOB	W	L	ERA	G	GS	SV	IP	Hits	Runs	ER	HR	BB	SO	AVG	OBP	SLG	SO%	BB%	BF
Adametz, Joe	L-L	6-5	190	12-23-99	3	0	2.92	8	3	0	25	12	8	8	3	12	28	.141	.270	.259	28.0	12.0	100
Apker, Garrett	R-R	6-5	195	9-18-99	0	1	6.35	3	3	0	11	10	9	8	1	7	15	.244	.347	.488	30.6	14.3	49
Boyer, Jorge	L-L	6-4	182	4-15-03	0	0	4.60	11	0	0	16	12	12	8	3	15	16	.207	.378	.448	21.6	20.3	74
Castillo, Rayner	R-R	6-3	180	6-30-04	1	0	7.27	8	4	0	17	20	17	14	2	11	19	.294	.410	.456	22.9	13.3	83
Chalas, Gregoris	R-R	5-10	143	8-12-00	0	1	9.90	11	0	1	10	9	11	11	0	8	8	.250	.412	.333	15.7	15.7	51
Chentouf, Yaya	R-R	5-9	205	6-18-97	1	0	0.00	3	0	0	4	2	0	0	0	1	5	.143	.200	.143	33.3	6.7	15
Cruz, Jesus	R-R	6-4	185	10-08-00	1	2	4.35	6	0	0	10	10	7	5	1	4	13	.250	.319	.375	27.7	8.5	47
Di Monte, Daniele	R-R	6-2	187	2-16-02	0	3	11.49	16	0	0	16	16	22	20	2	22	17	.262	.511	.410	18.5	23.9	92
Diaz, Jatnk	R-R	6-4	215	8-19-04	0	0	0.00	2	0	0	3	3	0	0	0	2	2	.300	.417	.400	16.7	16.7	12
Dunford, Andrew	R-R	6-7	235	1-05-05	0	0	0.00	4	0	1	4	2	0	0	0	2	3	.133	.235	.133	17.6	11.8	17
Evans, Donye	R-R	6-6	220	2-15-02	0	0	13.50	4	0	0	3	7	5	5	1	4	2	.500	.611	.714	10.5	21.1	19
Fields, Colin	R-R	6-2	200	3-18-00	0	0	0.00	1	1	0	3	0	0	0	0	0	6	.000	.100	.000	60.0	0.0	10
Garcia, Pedro	R-R	6-1	190	2-27-02	0	2	5.70	11	8	0	36	43	27	23	8	17	37	.293	.369	.551	21.9	10.1	169
Green, Max	L-L	6-1	175	5-28-96	0	0	9.00	2	0	0	2	2	2	2	1	1	1	.250	.333	.625	11.1	11.1	9
Hamm, Jaden	R-R	6-1	190	9-05-02	0	0	0.00	1	1	0	1	0	0	0	0	0	1	.000	.000	.000	33.3	0.0	3
Herrera, Martin	L-R	6-0	175	9-22-00	5	0	4.80	16	0	1	30	31	16	16	2	13	20	.274	.352	.425	15.6	10.2	128
Hess, Zack	R-R	6-6	219	2-25-97	0	0	4.50	5	0	0	4	5	4	2	0	4	5	.294	.500	.353	20.8	16.7	24
Huizi, Eiker	R-R	6-0	155	9-24-00	0	1	4.66	5	0	1	10	11	10	5	2	10	14	.268	.412	.488	27.5	19.6	51
Jobe, Jackson	R-R	6-2	190	7-30-02	0	0	0.00	1	1	0	2	0	0	0	0	0	4	.000	.000	.000	66.7	0.0	6
Lee, Zack	L-R	6-4	200	12-05-00	0	0	9.00	3	0	0	4	5	4	4	0	1	4	.357	.375	.500	25.0	6.3	16
Lequerica, Carlos	R-R	6-2	195	9-06-00	0	0	5.40	5	0	0	3	3	2	2	0	2	4	.231	.313	.308	25.0	12.5	16
Masloff, Jack	L-L	6-2	185	6-09-00	4	0	4.88	18	0	2	28	30	15	15	6	8	18	.278	.325	.509	15.4	6.8	117
Mendez, Eric	R-R	6-0	175	12-03-99	0	0	0.00	5	0	2	5	2	0	0	0	1	7	.111	.158	.278	36.8	5.3	19
Miller, Jake	L-L	6-2	185	6-27-01	0	0	0.00	3	3	0	6	2	0	0	0	1	9	.105	.150	.105	45.0	5.0	20
Minton, Hayden	L-R	6-4	220	3-14-01	0	0	27.00	2	0	0	1	2	4	4	1	4	2	.286	.583	.857	16.7	33.3	12
Montilla, Henry	R-R	6-1	170	4-12-02	0	1	7.30	5	2	0	12	14	14	10	1	14	12	.304	.515	.478	18.2	21.2	66
Moreno, Edwin	R-R	6-1	170	2-08-03	1	3	7.27	9	6	0	26	23	24	21	2	17	21	.245	.400	.436	17.5	14.2	120
Perez, Franklin	R-R	6-3	197	12-06-97	1	0	3.72	5	0	0	10	10	4	4	1	6	5	.278	.381	.417	11.9	14.3	42
Peters, DJ	R-R	6-5	225	12-12-95	1	0	6.23	17	0	0	22	17	19	15	3	27	24	.213	.447	.350	21.1	23.7	114
Pivaroff, Blake	L-R	6-0	200	6-01-01	0	1	5.06	4	0	1	5	6	3	3	0	3	7	.286	.375	.333	29.2	12.5	24
Rogers, Johnathan	R-R	6-3	215	9-05-04	0	0	27.00	2	0	0	1	0	3	3	0	5	0	.000	.625	.000	0.0	62.5	8
Sanchez, Yosber	R-R	6-1	170	5-22-01	0	0	13.50	2	0	0	2	4	3	3	0	2	3	.444	.545	.444	27.3	18.2	11
Sears, Andrew	L-L	6-3	200	10-30-02	0	0	0.00	1	0	0	1	0	0	0	0	2	1	.000	.400	.000	20.0	40.0	5

Smith, Dylan	R-R	6-2	180	5-28-00	0	0	5.79	3	3	0	5	5	3	3	0	3	5	.263	.364	.316	22.7	13.6	22
Stofel, Luke	R-R	6-5	235	11-25-01	0	1	31.50	3	0	0	2	4	7	7	0	2	3	.400	.500	.400	21.4	14.3	14
Stuka, Ted	R-R	6-7	225	5-13-97	2	3	7.94	15	0	0	17	11	15	15	1	25	19	.196	.459	.321	22.4	29.4	85
Stupp, Cole	R-R	6-4	205	11-10-00	3	3	5.13	10	8	0	40	34	24	23	2	21	39	.222	.358	.307	20.9	11.2	187
Torres, Gabriel	R-R	6-1	160	8-13-03	2	2	6.38	11	9	0	42	46	38	30	2	34	34	.280	.413	.433	16.3	16.3	208
Walker, Matt	L-L	6-3	217	6-15-98	2	1	2.63	5	2	0	14	15	8	4	1	4	13	.268	.317	.429	21.7	6.7	60
Williams, Chris	L-L	6-2	205	3-03-00	2	0	4.22	7	0	0	11	5	5	5	1	7	8	.132	.283	.316	17.4	15.2	46

Fielding

C: Briceno 19, De La Cruz 13, Hurtado 12, Rubalcaba 6, Campbell 5, Rothenberg 3, Cerkownyk 2. **1B:** Campbell 14, Johnson 13, Calderon 11, Briceno 8, Valero 7, Rubalcaba 5, Reyes 3, Hurtado 3, Jenkins 3, Rothenberg 2, De La Cruz 1, Feliciano 1. **2B:** Gil 28, Perez 15, De Los Santos 7, Diaz 5, Sequera 3, Peck 3, McGonigle 2, Smith 2, Graham 1. **3B:** Diaz 22, Campbell 15, Calderon 9, Reyes 5, De Los Santos 4, Peck 3, Perez 3, Rucker 2, Jarvis 1. **SS:** Perez 16, Gil 15, Diaz 9, McGonigle 7, Rucker 6, Peck 2, Kreidler 2, De Los Santos 1, Graham 1. **OF:** Fana 29, Leonardo 28, Reina 26, Leon 24, De Los Santos 23, Clark 12, Callahan 11, Turney 10, Schultz 7, Walker 5, De La Cruz 5, Pelegrin 4, Benitez 2, Feliciano 2.

DSL TIGERS — *ROOKIE*

DOMINICAN SUMMER LEAGUE

Batting	B-T	Ht.	Wt.	DOB	AVG	OBP	SLG	G	PA	AB	R	H	2B	3B	HR	RBI	BB	HBP	SH	SF	SO	SB	CS	BB%	SO%
Berti, Willian	L-L	6-0	160	11-05-05	.243	.386	.345	48	184	148	24	36	5	2	2	22	30	5	0	1	38	2	2	16.3	20.7
Caraballo, Brandy	R-R	5-9	150	9-26-05	.212	.397	.308	28	68	52	12	11	2	0	1	10	8	8	0	0	28	3	3	11.8	41.2
Cruz, Angel	R-R	5-11	165	9-27-01	.314	.387	.507	43	163	140	26	44	9	0	6	28	12	7	0	4	30	7	3	7.4	18.4
De Leon, Jensy	R-R	6-0	175	5-14-04	.208	.337	.312	29	92	77	17	16	3	1	1	13	5	10	0	0	19	2	0	5.4	20.7
Encarnacion, Bryan	B-R	6-1	140	4-20-03	.150	.333	.250	19	51	40	6	6	0	2	0	4	9	2	0	0	24	0	3	17.6	47.1
Estevez, Geury	B-R	6-0	180	2-20-02	.312	.400	.422	51	180	154	28	48	5	3	2	23	20	4	0	2	23	3	0	11.1	12.8
Estrada, Johan	R-R	5-11	170	10-27-05	.184	.344	.224	17	61	49	6	9	2	0	0	2	12	0	0	0	20	2	1	19.7	32.8
Hernandez, Juan	L-R	6-0	160	3-27-06	.292	.410	.375	44	173	144	31	42	9	0	1	15	24	5	0	0	29	6	5	13.9	16.8
Hoyte, Adrian	L-L	5-7	145	1-09-06	.262	.392	.381	19	51	42	7	11	2	0	1	5	8	1	0	0	11	1	3	15.7	21.6
Jimenez, Enrique	B-R	5-10	170	11-03-05	.277	.388	.418	46	170	141	23	39	11	3	1	14	24	3	0	2	30	3	2	14.1	17.6
Lopez, Abelaldo	R-R	6-1	160	9-05-02	.200	.364	.233	27	77	60	12	12	2	0	0	6	16	0	0	1	24	3	3	20.8	31.2
Luna, Wagnel	R-R	6-0	155	12-14-05	.167	.409	.244	39	127	90	18	15	2	1	1	7	33	4	0	0	30	5	2	26.0	23.6
Machado, Jesus	R-R	5-10	152	3-24-03	.270	.401	.349	43	157	126	22	34	5	1	1	15	19	10	0	2	35	10	7	12.1	22.3
Marin, Nelson	R-R	5-11	165	9-29-05	.124	.212	.169	30	99	89	6	11	1	0	1	4	10	0	0	0	39	0	0	10.1	39.4
Martinez, Dany	R-R	5-11	170	6-30-03	.067	.222	.067	8	18	15	3	1	0	0	0	1	2	1	0	0	2	0	0	11.1	11.1
Matos, Delvis	R-R	5-11	165	11-09-04	.161	.206	.210	24	68	62	7	10	1	1	0	13	3	1	0	2	24	2	1	4.4	35.3
Medrano, Abelardo	L-R	6-2	180	1-27-06	.180	.270	.236	29	100	89	6	16	2	0	1	4	9	2	0	0	32	2	2	9.0	32.0
Montilla, Franyerber	B-R	6-0	160	4-15-05	.280	.394	.439	31	127	107	17	30	6	1	3	17	17	3	0	0	22	11	5	13.4	17.3
Ochoa, Jose	R-R	5-9	162	7-25-03	.328	.403	.359	21	72	64	14	21	2	0	0	4	8	0	0	0	19	3	1	11.1	26.4
Orozco, Maikol	R-R	5-11	175	9-09-05	.256	.389	.346	43	167	133	27	34	4	1	2	17	23	8	0	3	29	9	3	13.8	17.4
Osorio, Javier	R-R	6-0	165	3-29-05	.272	.359	.515	33	117	103	24	28	6	2	5	21	11	3	0	0	40	11	2	9.4	34.2
Perea, Randy	R-R	5-11	150	1-21-04	.250	.348	.336	47	136	116	25	29	8	1	0	11	16	2	1	1	47	23	5	11.8	34.6
Perez, Cristian	R-R	5-11	190	8-15-06	.319	.351	.462	29	97	91	17	29	6	2	1	16	2	3	0	1	24	1	0	2.1	24.7
Pinto, Santiago	L-L	5-11	170	2-05-06	.168	.280	.228	37	118	101	16	17	3	0	1	9	12	4	0	1	50	6	3	10.2	42.4
Quezada, Junior	R-R	6-0	165	2-03-05	.222	.313	.283	35	115	99	12	22	1	1	1	14	11	3	0	2	26	6	2	9.6	22.6
Rodriguez, Justin	R-R	5-10	155	3-11-04	.204	.316	.254	48	174	142	16	29	4	0	1	19	25	1	0	6	49	7	2	14.4	28.2
Rojas, Samuel	R-R	5-10	190	11-06-02	.239	.363	.310	25	91	71	13	17	5	0	0	13	12	4	0	4	13	1	1	13.2	14.3
Rondon, Newremberg	R-R	5-11	170	7-10-03	.233	.320	.512	14	50	43	9	10	3	0	3	11	5	1	0	1	10	0	0	10.0	20.0
Salas, Anibal	B-R	5-11	180	9-30-05	.281	.451	.465	42	153	114	32	32	4	1	5	25	33	4	0	2	36	8	3	21.6	23.5
Sanchez, Heison	L-R	6-0	170	9-06-04	.231	.347	.339	38	146	121	24	28	7	3	0	16	16	6	2	1	35	6	2	11.0	24.0
Santana, Manuel	R-R	6-0	175	10-30-04	.034	.152	.034	15	33	29	2	1	0	0	0	2	2	2	0	0	14	0	0	6.1	42.4
Tamara, Martin	R-R	6-0	185	2-05-04	.190	.277	.345	30	94	84	12	16	5	1	2	13	8	2	0	0	31	2	1	8.5	33.0
Watter, Luis	R-R	5-8	150	1-10-03	.325	.407	.405	45	146	126	23	41	4	0	2	18	14	4	1	1	33	9	3	9.6	22.6

Pitching	B-T	Ht.	Wt.	DOB	W	L	ERA	G	GS	SV	IP	Hits	Runs	ER	HR	BB	SO	AVG	OBP	SLG	SO%	BB%	BF
Acosta, Luis	R-R	5-11	185	2-08-02	1	0	3.96	19	0	3	25	26	13	11	2	7	29	.263	.324	.465	26.6	6.4	109
Bastardo, Yeremi	L-L	5-9	160	1-13-02	0	2	2.81	15	0	0	16	8	7	5	1	14	16	.140	.338	.246	21.6	18.9	74
Brete, Jaison	R-R	6-1	160	4-27-01	6	1	1.01	19	1	1	36	25	10	4	2	14	47	.200	.275	.280	33.1	9.9	142
Briceno, Ignacio	L-L	5-11	155	6-04-01	3	1	2.63	18	0	8	27	22	14	8	2	12	30	.220	.339	.310	25.4	10.2	118
Castillo, Luis	R-R	6-0	180	3-19-02	1	0	7.27	11	0	0	9	10	8	7	0	9	12	.303	.442	.394	27.9	20.9	43
Chalas, Ronny	R-R	5-10	162	8-19-02	4	2	2.33	18	0	0	27	19	7	7	1	5	40	.196	.229	.299	38.1	4.8	105
De Los Santos, Ericksson	L-L	6-6	200	3-24-06	0	0	9.00	13	0	0	13	11	14	13	0	21	11	.239	.500	.304	15.3	29.2	72
Florian, Jose	R-R	5-11	155	2-03-04	0	0	14.54	3	0	0	4	5	7	7	1	4	6	.278	.409	.556	27.3	18.2	22
Florido, Antonio	R-R	6-1	175	2-15-05	1	0	8.68	6	2	0	9	13	9	9	2	7	6	.351	.455	.649	13.3	15.6	45
Grant, Frenny	L-L	6-1	170	10-14-03	1	1	2.82	14	3	0	22	12	11	7	0	20	28	.160	.347	.173	28.6	20.4	98
Guacache, Xiomer	R-R	6-3	195	2-11-04	3	0	2.41	12	8	0	41	31	13	11	3	14	40	.203	.269	.307	24.0	8.4	167
Hebbert, Duque	R-R	5-10	170	10-29-01	2	1	4.58	14	8	0	37	37	22	19	2	6	41	.250	.287	.372	26.1	3.8	157
Landaeta, Abraham	R-R	6-2	175	11-29-00	0	4	11.00	7	2	0	9	10	14	11	0	15	9	.270	.491	.351	16.4	27.3	55
Martinez, Jose	R-R	6-2	170	8-27-02	3	0	2.08	11	0	2	22	13	6	5	0	9	12	.176	.274	.230	14.3	10.7	84
Mateo, Andy	R-R	6-4	180	10-19-05	0	0	23.14	3	0	0	2	4	6	6	0	4	4	.400	.533	.600	26.7	26.7	15
Mendez, Wuilberth	R-R	6-3	150	5-29-04	1	3	6.44	11	9	1	36	46	27	26	5	5	28	.305	.333	.450	17.5	3.1	160
Merino, Anderson	L-L	6-4	194	3-06-03	0	1	14.54	7	0	0	4	5	7	7	0	12	8	.313	.600	.313	26.7	40.0	30
Montas, Donal	R-R	6-3	190	5-05-02	1	2	5.35	11	11	0	39	37	27	23	3	18	21	.257	.351	.368	12.4	10.7	169
Moreno, Frank	R-R	6-2	185	10-16-02	2	1	2.92	12	12	0	52	50	21	17	1	15	50	.249	.308	.323	22.6	6.8	221
Mota, Eliseo	R-R	6-2	185	11-07-02	3	4	2.66	11	11	0	44	40	20	13	1	12	37	.240	.304	.311	20.1	6.5	184
Palmero, Diego	R-R	6-4	190	8-04-03	0	5	7.89	13	5	0	22	18	20	19	1	35	20	.247	.517	.384	17.2	30.2	116
Parra, Josbeiker	R-R	6-3	160	2-25-05	0	0	81.00	3	0	0	0	2	4	3	0	6	0	.500	.818	.500	0.0	54.5	11

Paulino, Franklin	R-R	6-3	160	7-24-03	3	3	3.76	10	9	0	41	44	18	17	2	3	29	.273	.291	.360	17.6	1.8	165
Pena, Victor	R-R	6-3	185	3-01-05	2	0	1.26	9	0	0	14	7	4	2	0	6	20	.137	.241	.157	34.5	10.3	58
Petri, Jorger	L-L	5-10	155	11-03-04	2	3	4.08	9	9	0	35	42	22	16	1	11	32	.282	.352	.376	19.4	6.7	165
Ramirez, Wanmer	R-R	6-1	190	1-06-04	0	1	5.00	2	2	0	9	12	5	5	1	0	13	.324	.324	.514	35.1	0.0	37
Ramos, Andres	R-R	5-11	180	3-26-05	1	1	6.52	14	0	0	19	18	22	14	2	19	14	.247	.433	.370	14.4	19.6	97
Rivas, Jose	R-R	5-11	160	12-20-01	3	3	3.74	19	0	2	22	24	10	9	0	8	19	.286	.348	.369	20.7	8.7	92
Rodriguez, Deibi	R-R	6-0	175	12-09-05	1	0	0.00	6	1	0	10	4	1	0	0	5	10	.111	.238	.139	23.8	11.9	42
Rodriguez, Jesus A.	L-L	5-11	145	10-15-03	2	1	9.35	11	0	0	17	16	23	18	1	15	23	.235	.376	.338	27.1	17.6	85
Rodriguez, Moises	R-R	6-2	170	3-03-02	4	2	1.90	12	11	0	43	32	17	9	0	18	38	.200	.283	.213	21.1	10.0	180
Rossel, Leonardo	R-R	6-0	170	12-17-04	0	2	4.40	12	1	2	14	13	11	7	2	7	18	.236	.338	.400	27.7	10.8	65
Ruiz, Juan	R-R	5-11	216	11-03-03	0	0	1.93	4	0	0	5	3	2	1	0	2	7	.167	.250	.167	35.0	10.0	20
Salcedo, Kelvis	R-R	6-0	180	1-23-06	2	0	6.20	14	2	0	25	26	20	17	0	12	32	.257	.359	.356	27.4	10.3	117
Salgado, Keni	R-R	6-2	165	11-18-03	0	3	7.98	13	0	1	15	15	17	13	1	14	13	.254	.408	.390	16.9	18.2	77
Sanchez, Yosber	R-R	6-1	170	5-22-01	1	1	3.22	18	0	3	22	20	9	8	0	14	39	.233	.340	.302	39.0	14.0	100
Valerio, Elvin	R-R	6-5	225	8-29-02	1	0	15.00	3	0	0	3	4	5	5	0	4	4	.333	.500	.333	22.2	22.2	18
Vasquez, Luis	R-R	6-4	180	12-11-04	2	1	1.86	13	0	0	29	27	8	6	0	5	23	.248	.299	.294	19.7	4.3	117

Fielding

C: Jimenez 29, Marin 25, Tamara 25, Rojas 18, Santana 13, Rondon 8, Martinez 7, Estrada 1. **1B:** Estevez 47, Cruz 35, Jimenez 12, Estrada 9, De Leon 5, Rojas 5, Tamara 4, Marin 3, Encarnacion 2, Rodriguez 1. **2B:** Sanchez 36, Orozco 29, Luna 13, Cruz 8, De Leon 8, Montilla 6, Watter 6, Encarnacion 5, Hernandez 2, Estevez 1, Osorio 1. **3B:** Rodriguez 43, Watter 25, Hernandez 13, De Leon 11, Orozco 9, Osorio 8, Encarnacion 5, Cruz 3, Sanchez 1. **SS:** Hernandez 28, Luna 26, Montilla 25, Osorio 23, Encarnacion 9, Orozco 3, Rodriguez 2. **OF:** Perea 46, Machado 40, Salas 35, Berti 34, Perez 28, Quezada 27, Lopez 26, Pinto 25, Medrano 23, Matos 22, Caraballo 19, Ochoa 18, Watter 12, Hoyte 10, Cruz 1.

Houston Astros

SEASON SYNOPSIS: The American League West champions for the sixth straight 162-game season, the Astros reached the AL Championship Series for the seventh straight year. Division and in-state rival Texas denied them a repeat pennant, however, defeating them in a tense seven-game LCS.

HIGH POINT: Houston rode a September roller coaster, mostly losing at home and winning on the road. They needed a big finish to win the division and came through, winning two of three at Seattle before sweeping NL wild-card entrant Arizona to tie the Rangers for the division lead. Houston won the tiebreaker by winning the season series 9-4.

LOW POINT: That regular-season record gave Houston home-field when the Rangers and Astros met in the LCS but meant nothing, as the road team won every game in the series. Jose Altuve's game-winning ninth-inning homer won Game 5, but Houston lost twice at home to lose the series, including an 11-4 rout in Game 7.

NOTABLE ROOKIES: Once again, Houston's maligned farm system produced. Righthander J.P. France fell off in the second half but provided an 11-6, 3.83 mark in 136 innings. That helped offset some of Hunter Brown's struggles (11-13, 5.09), though Brown's FIP was lower and his 178 strikeouts ranked second on the club. C/1B Yainer Diaz (.282/.308/.538) mashed 23 homers as a part-time player, stuck behind veteran Martin Maldonado, especially in the playoffs.

KEY TRANSACTIONS: Dana Brown was hired as GM to replace James Click as owner Jim Crane asserted his control of the front office. When the Mets collapsed, Brown struck, re-acquiring Justin Verlander, who'd left in the offseason as a free agent. The price was fairly steep: lefty-hitting OFs Drew Gilbert, the team's 2022 first-round pick, and Ryan Clifford. 1B Jose Abreu, the club's biggest offseason signee, struggled in the regular season (.680 OPS). But Abreu seemed to find a new gear in the postseason. He hit four home runs and was one of the team's biggest power threats.

DOWN ON THE FARM: The Astros continued run of big league success has led the team to use the farm system in trades to bolster the big league roster. That, along with the Spygate draft penalties have thinned the farm system. Houston finished 25th in organzational winning percentage. Double-A Corpus Christi was the Astros' only full season team to post a winning record.

OPENING DAY PAYROLL: $192,667,233 (10th).

PLAYERS OF THE YEAR

MAJOR LEAGUE

Kyle Tucker
OF
.284/.369/.517
37 2B, 29 HR
30 SB, 112 RBI

MINOR LEAGUE

Joey Loperfido
OF
(HiA/AA/AAA)
.278/.370/.510
27 2B, 25 HR, 27 SB

ORGANIZATION LEADERS

Batting		*Minimum 250 AB
MAJORS		
* AVG	Jose Altuve	.311
* OPS	Yordan Alvarez	.990
HR	Yordan Alvarez	31
RBI	Kyle Tucker	112
MINORS		
* AVG	Will Wagner, Corpus Christi/S. Land	.337
* OBP	Will Wagner, Corpus Christi/S. Land	.420
* SLG	Zach Dezenzo, Asheville/C. Christi	.531
* OPS	Will Wagner, Corpus Christi/S. Land	.938
R	Jacob Melton, Ashevile/Corpus Christi	83
H	Joey Loperfido, Asheville/C. Christi/S. Land	130
TB	Shay Whitcomb, Corpus Christi/S. Land	253
2B	Joey Loperfido, Asheville/C. Christi/S. Land	27
3B	Zach Cole, Fayetteville/Asheville	8
HR	Shay Whitcomb, Corpus Christi/S. Land	35
RBI	Shay Whitcomb, Corpus Christi/S. Land	102
BB	Bligh Madris, Sugar Land	67
SO	Shay Whitcomb, Corpus Christi/S. Land	178
SB	Jackson Loftin, Fayettev./Sugar Land	60

Pitching		#Minimum 75 IP
MAJORS		
W	Framber Valdez	12
# ERA	Framber Valdez	198
SO	Framber Valdez	200
SV	Ryan Pressly	31
MINORS		
W	Julio Robaina, Corpus Christi	10
L	Misael Tamarez, Sugar Land	10
L	Jose Nodal, Fayetteville	10
# ERA	Julio Robaina, Corpus Christi	3.18
G	Enoli Paredes, Sugar Land	52
GS	Rhett Kouba, C. Christi/S.Land	24
GS	Colton Gordon, C. Christi/S.Land	24
SV	Joe Record, Sugar Land	11
IP	Colton Gordon, C. Christi/S.Land	128
BB	Alimber Santa, Fayetteville	74
# SO	Colton Gordon, C. Christi/S.Land	151
AVG	Jose Fleury, Fayetteville	.181

2023 PERFORMANCE

General Manager: Dana Brown. **Farm Director:** Sara Goodrum. **Scouting Director:** Kris Gross.

Class	Team	League	W	L	PCT	Finish	Manager
Majors	Houston Astros	American	90	72	.556	3 (15)	Dusty Baker
Triple-A	Sugar Land Space Cowboys	Pacific Coast	61	89	.407	10 (10)	Mickey Storey
Double-A	Corpus Christi Hooks	Texas	70	68	.507	4 (10)	Dickie Joe Thon
High-A	Asheville Tourists	South Atlantic	51	76	.402	12 (12)	Nate Shaver
Low-A	Fayetteville Woodpeckers	Carolina	60	72	.455	10 (12)	Ricky Rivera
Rookie	FCL Astros	Florida Complex	26	25	.510	9 (15)	Carlos Lugo
Rookie	DSL Astros Blue	Dominican Sum.	29	26	.527	20 (50)	Manuel Alfonsin
Rookie	DSL Astros Orange	Dominican Sum.	35	19	.648	7 (50)	Manny Martinez
Overall 2023 Minor League Record			332	375	.470	25th (30)	

ORGANIZATION STATISTICS

HOUSTON ASTROS

AMERICAN LEAGUE

Batting	B-T	Ht.	Wt.	DOB	AVG	OBP	SLG	G	PA	AB	R	H	2B	3B	HR	RBI	BB	HBP	SH	SF	SO	SB	CS	BB%	SO%
Abreu, Jose	R-R	6-3	235	1-29-87	.237	.296	.383	141	594	540	62	128	23	1	18	90	42	6	0	6	130	0	1	7.1	21.9
Altuve, Jose	R-R	5-6	166	5-06-90	.311	.393	.522	90	410	360	76	112	21	2	17	51	44	5	0	1	71	14	2	10.7	17.3
Alvarez, Yordan	L-R	6-5	225	6-27-97	.293	.407	.583	114	496	410	77	120	24	1	31	97	69	13	0	4	92	0	0	13.9	18.5
Bannon, Rylan	R-R	5-8	180	4-22-96	.000	.000	.000	2	6	6	0	0	0	0	0	0	0	0	0	0	3	0	0	0.0	50.0
Brantley, Michael	L-L	6-2	209	5-15-87	.278	.298	.426	15	57	54	7	15	2	0	2	7	2	0	0	1	2	0	0	3.5	3.5
Bregman, Alex	R-R	6-0	192	3-30-94	.262	.363	.441	161	724	622	103	163	28	4	25	98	92	8	0	2	87	3	1	12.7	12.0
Diaz, Yainer	R-R	6-0	195	9-21-98	.282	.308	.538	104	377	355	51	100	22	0	23	60	11	5	0	6	74	0	0	2.9	19.6
Dubon, Mauricio	R-R	6-0	173	7-19-94	.278	.309	.411	132	492	467	76	130	26	3	10	46	19	3	0	3	70	7	2	3.9	14.2
Hensley, David	R-R	6-6	190	3-28-96	.119	.213	.167	30	94	84	12	10	1	0	1	3	10	0	0	0	35	1	0	10.6	37.2
Julks, Corey	R-R	6-1	185	2-27-96	.245	.297	.352	93	323	298	35	73	14	0	6	33	22	1	0	2	75	15	3	6.8	23.2
Kessinger, Grae	R-R	6-1	204	8-25-97	.200	.289	.325	26	45	40	3	8	2	0	1	1	5	0	0	0	12	0	1	11.1	26.7
Madris, Bligh	L-R	6-0	208	2-29-96	.154	.267	.192	12	30	26	4	4	1	0	0	0	4	0	0	0	7	0	0	13.3	23.3
Maldonado, Martin	R-R	6-0	230	8-16-86	.191	.258	.348	117	407	362	33	69	12	0	15	36	30	3	12	0	139	0	0	7.4	34.2
McCormick, Chas	R-L	6-0	208	4-19-95	.273	.353	.489	115	457	403	59	110	17	2	22	70	40	11	1	2	117	19	6	8.8	25.6
Meyers, Jake	R-L	6-0	200	6-18-96	.227	.296	.382	112	341	309	42	70	16	1	10	33	26	5	0	1	88	5	2	7.6	25.8
Pena, Jeremy	R-R	6-0	202	9-22-97	.263	.324	.381	150	634	577	81	152	32	3	10	52	43	9	1	1	129	13	9	6.8	20.3
Salazar, Cesar	L-R	5-9	185	3-15-96	.111	.158	.111	13	19	18	1	2	0	0	0	0	1	0	0	0	6	0	0	5.3	31.6
Singleton, Jon	L-L	6-0	256	9-18-91	.194	.301	.323	25	73	62	8	12	2	0	2	10	10	0	0	1	12	0	0	13.7	16.4
Tucker, Kyle	L-R	6-4	199	1-17-97	.284	.369	.517	157	674	574	97	163	37	5	29	112	80	3	0	10	92	30	5	11.9	13.6

Pitching	B-T	Ht.	Wt.	DOB	W	L	ERA	G	GS	SV	IP	Hits	Runs	ER	HR	BB	SO	AVG	OBP	SLG	SO%	BB%	BF
Abreu, Bryan	R-R	6-1	225	4-22-97	3	2	1.75	72	0	5	72	44	17	14	6	31	100	.177	.274	.286	34.8	10.8	287
Bielak, Brandon	L-R	6-2	208	4-02-96	5	6	3.83	15	13	0	80	86	43	34	12	36	62	.277	.361	.460	17.6	10.2	353
Blanco, Ronel	R-R	6-0	180	8-31-93	2	1	4.50	17	7	0	52	49	29	26	12	28	52	.251	.350	.462	23.0	12.4	226
Brown, Hunter	R-R	6-2	212	8-29-98	11	13	5.09	31	29	0	156	157	94	88	26	55	178	.262	.332	.456	26.8	8.3	665
Dubin, Shawn	R-R	6-1	171	9-06-95	0	0	7.00	3	1	0	9	12	7	7	1	3	11	.324	.381	.514	26.2	7.1	42
France, J.P.	R-R	6-0	216	4-04-95	11	6	3.83	24	23	0	136	138	64	58	19	47	101	.263	.322	.414	17.4	8.1	581
Gage, Matt	L-L	6-3	265	2-11-93	0	0	2.70	5	0	0	7	6	2	2	1	3	8	.261	.346	.435	29.6	11.1	27
Garcia, Luis	R-R	5-11	244	12-13-96	2	2	4.00	6	6	0	27	25	12	12	3	10	31	.243	.316	.427	27.0	8.7	115
Graveman, Kendall	R-R	6-2	200	12-21-90	2	2	2.42	23	0	0	22	18	7	6	3	16	24	.228	.358	.380	25.0	16.7	96
Javier, Cristian	R-R	6-1	213	3-26-97	10	5	4.56	31	31	0	162	143	85	82	25	62	159	.234	.309	.424	23.1	9.0	687
Kuhnel, Joel	R-R	6-5	290	2-19-95	0	0	4.66	7	0	0	10	10	5	5	2	3	3	.270	.341	.459	7.3	7.3	41
Madris, Bligh	L-R	6-0	208	2-29-96	0	0	9.00	1	0	0	1	1	1	1	1	1	0	.333	.500	1.333	0.0	25.0	4
Maldonado, Martin	R-R	6-0	230	8-16-86	0	0	36.00	1	0	0	1	5	4	4	1	1	0	.714	.700	1.429	0.0	10.0	10
Martinez, Seth	R-R	6-2	200	8-29-94	2	3	5.23	35	0	1	43	45	29	25	5	19	45	.265	.359	.435	23.1	9.7	195
Maton, Phil	R-R	6-2	206	3-25-93	4	3	3.00	68	0	1	66	49	27	22	6	25	74	.207	.304	.333	27.0	9.1	274
Montero, Rafael	R-R	6-0	190	10-17-90	3	3	5.08	68	0	1	67	74	40	38	11	29	79	.279	.356	.479	26.5	9.7	298
Mushinski, Parker	L-L	6-0	218	11-22-95	0	0	5.52	14	0	0	15	19	9	9	5	4	15	.311	.391	.623	21.7	5.8	69
Neris, Hector	R-R	6-2	227	6-14-89	6	3	1.71	71	0	2	68	41	16	13	7	31	77	.174	.277	.292	28.2	11.4	273
Pressly, Ryan	R-R	6-2	206	12-15-88	4	5	3.58	65	0	31	65	54	33	26	8	16	74	.220	.265	.358	27.6	6.0	268
Sousa, Bennett	L-L	6-3	220	4-06-95	0	0	0.00	5	0	0	6	1	0	0	0	0	8	.050	.050	.050	40.0	0.0	20
Stanek, Ryne	R-R	6-4	226	7-26-91	3	1	4.09	55	0	0	51	42	24	23	8	21	51	.221	.300	.389	23.9	9.9	213
Urquidy, Jose	R-R	6-0	217	5-01-95	3	3	5.29	16	10	1	63	65	37	37	11	25	45	.263	.335	.453	16.4	9.1	275
Valdez, Framber	R-L	5-11	239	11-19-93	12	11	3.45	31	31	0	198	166	86	76	19	57	200	.228	.290	.365	24.8	7.1	808
Verlander, Justin	R-R	6-5	235	2-20-83	7	3	3.31	11	11	0	68	62	27	25	9	14	63	.236	.283	.403	22.3	4.9	283

Fielding

Catcher	PCT	G	PO	A	E	DP	PB
Diaz	.986	60	388	24	6	4	0
Maldonado	.994	116	1040	51	7	3	12
Salazar	.955	9	38	4	2	0	0

First Base	PCT	G	PO	A	E	DP
Abreu	.995	134	1017	67	5	106
Diaz	1.000	8	41	4	0	11
Dubon	1.000	2	10	0	0	1
Hensley	1.000	5	21	1	0	4
Kessinger	1.000	5	25	2	0	2
Madris	.944	2	17	0	1	4
Singleton	1.000	14	97	10	0	10

Second Base	PCT	G	PO	A	E	DP
Altuve	.975	87	103	175	7	51
Bannon	.000	1	0	0	0	0
Dubon	.978	79	87	181	6	52
Hensley	.950	9	8	11	1	3
Kessinger	1.000	6	3	5	0	2

HOUSTON ASTROS

Third Base	PCT	G	PO	A	E	DP
Bregman	.963	160	109	281	15	30
Dubon	.000	1	0	0	0	0
Hensley	1.000	1	0	1	0	0
Kessinger	1.000	7	0	4	0	1

Shortstop	PCT	G	PO	A	E	DP
Dubon	.971	9	13	20	1	3
Kessinger	.957	7	7	15	1	6
Pena	.976	150	200	362	14	89

Outfield	PCT	G	PO	A	E	DP
Alvarez	1.000	40	59	2	0	0
Brantley	1.000	10	13	1	0	0
Dubon	.667	40	89	1	0	0
Hensley	1.000	2	1	0	0	0
Julks	.995	70	90	4	1	0
Madris	1.000	1	2	0	0	0
McCormick	.996	138	246	1	1	0
Meyers	.992	107	239	3	4	0
Tucker	.990	153	303	8	3	1

SUGAR LAND SPACE COWBOYS — *TRIPLE-A*

PACIFIC COAST LEAGUE

Batting	B-T	Ht.	Wt.	DOB	AVG	OBP	SLG	G	PA	AB	R	H	2B	3B	HR	RBI	BB	HBP	SH	SF	SO	SB	CS	BB%	SO%
Adolph, Ross	L-R	5-11	190	12-17-96	.230	.347	.426	19	73	61	6	14	3	0	3	6	6	5	1	0	30	0	0	8.2	41.1
Altuve, Jose	R-R	5-6	166	5-06-90	.077	.077	.077	3	13	13	0	1	0	0	0	0	0	0	0	0	2	0	0	0.0	15.4
Alvarez, Yordan	L-R	6-5	225	6-27-97	.333	.455	.444	3	11	9	0	3	1	0	0	2	2	0	0	0	1	0	0	18.2	9.1
Arias, Bryan	R-R	5-10	205	6-06-97	.400	.667	.800	3	9	5	2	2	2	0	0	1	4	0	0	0	1	0	0	44.4	11.1
Bannon, Rylan	R-R	5-8	180	4-22-96	.241	.360	.449	95	408	336	62	81	12	2	18	56	63	3	0	6	90	12	9	15.4	22.1
Berryhill, Luke	R-R	6-0	227	5-28-98	.228	.371	.384	77	307	250	54	57	9	3	8	28	55	2	0	0	104	5	1	17.9	33.9
Brantley, Michael	L-L	6-2	209	5-15-87	.298	.453	.447	16	64	47	7	14	4	0	1	12	15	0	0	2	1	0	0	23.4	1.6
Costes, Marty	R-R	5-9	200	12-18-95	.251	.365	.389	53	197	167	23	42	9	4	2	19	24	6	0	0	36	7	0	12.2	18.3
Dirden, Justin	L-R	6-3	209	7-16-97	.231	.314	.396	84	364	316	39	73	12	5	10	42	37	3	4	4	108	4	3	10.2	29.7
Espinosa, Rolando	R-R	6-0	177	1-05-01	.000	.000	.000	2	5	5	0	0	0	0	0	0	0	0	0	0	2	0	0	0.0	40.0
Hamilton, Quincy	L-L	5-10	190	6-12-98	.223	.333	.438	28	132	112	18	25	3	0	7	18	16	3	0	1	21	2	1	12.1	15.9
Hensley, David	R-R	6-6	190	3-28-96	.220	.365	.356	65	293	236	42	52	10	2	6	36	54	1	0	2	82	9	3	18.4	28.0
Julks, Corey	R-R	6-1	185	2-27-96	.240	.388	.462	27	129	104	26	25	12	1	3	11	24	1	0	0	23	6	1	18.6	17.8
Kessinger, Grae	R-R	6-1	204	8-25-97	.283	.397	.435	54	230	184	37	52	10	0	6	32	35	4	1	6	45	2	1	15.2	19.6
Knapp, Andrew	B-R	6-1	189	11-09-91	.171	.300	.316	23	91	76	9	13	2	0	3	4	11	3	1	0	27	0	0	12.1	29.7
Lee, Korey	R-R	6-2	210	7-25-98	.283	.328	.406	68	302	283	37	80	18	1	5	32	17	2	0	0	75	12	4	5.6	24.8
Leon, Pedro	R-R	5-8	170	5-28-98	.244	.343	.435	128	564	483	74	118	23	3	21	72	63	11	4	3	160	21	7	11.2	28.4
Loftin, Jackson	R-R	6-2	195	5-14-00	.385	.529	.615	4	17	13	5	5	3	0	0	2	4	0	0	0	1	0	0	23.5	5.9
Loperfido, Joey	L-R	6-3	220	5-11-99	.235	.333	.403	32	138	119	15	28	5	0	5	16	16	2	0	1	45	4	1	11.6	32.6
Machado, Dixon	R-R	6-1	190	2-22-92	.230	.369	.356	74	293	239	35	55	7	1	7	33	51	2	0	1	48	1	0	17.4	16.4
Madris, Bligh	L-R	6-0	208	2-29-96	.235	.349	.413	100	456	378	61	89	10	6	15	53	67	2	2	6	115	12	6	14.7	25.2
Matijevic, J.J.	L-R	6-0	206	11-14-95	.244	.329	.441	118	495	435	66	106	26	6	16	76	54	3	0	3	122	8	1	10.9	24.6
McKenna, Alex	R-R	6-0	204	9-06-97	.221	.315	.337	30	108	95	10	21	0	1	3	15	12	1	0	0	36	0	1	11.1	33.3
Perez, Joe	R-R	6-1	198	8-12-99	.255	.328	.399	87	357	318	52	81	12	2	10	47	34	2	0	3	97	3	1	9.5	27.2
Salazar, Cesar	L-R	5-9	185	3-15-96	.191	.362	.272	57	222	173	21	33	8	0	2	16	31	16	1	1	33	3	0	14.0	14.9
Sandle, Michael	R-R	5-8	200	9-21-98	.194	.311	.500	15	46	36	10	7	2	0	3	7	4	3	1	2	11	1	0	8.7	23.9
Singleton, Jon	L-L	6-0	256	9-18-91	.333	.446	.692	33	148	120	27	40	7	0	12	28	26	0	0	2	34	1	0	17.6	23.0
Stubbs, C.J.	R-R	6-3	207	11-12-96	.750	.750	1.000	1	4	4	1	3	1	0	0	0	0	0	0	0	1	0	0	0.0	25.0
Wagner, Will	L-R	5-11	210	7-29-98	.577	.607	.692	6	28	26	3	15	3	0	0	4	2	0	0	0	2	2	0	7.1	7.1
Whitcomb, Shay	R-R	6-1	202	9-28-98	.224	.281	.434	87	392	362	44	81	7	0	23	66	24	5	0	1	122	12	5	6.1	31.1
Wrobleski, Ryan	R-R	6-1	196	2-02-00	.500	.667	.500	1	3	2	1	1	0	0	0	0	1	0	0	0	1	0	0	33.3	33.3

Pitching	B-T	Ht.	Wt.	DOB	W	L	ERA	G	GS	SV	IP	Hits	Runs	ER	HR	BB	SO	AVG	OBP	SLG	SO%	BB%	BF
Allgeyer, Nick	L-L	6-3	225	2-03-96	5	4	6.62	19	6	1	69	76	53	51	14	46	70	.271	.385	.482	20.9	13.7	335
Arrighetti, Spencer	R-R	6-2	186	1-02-00	2	5	4.64	15	13	0	64	49	33	33	7	36	62	.217	.336	.385	23.1	13.4	268
Bielak, Brandon	L-R	6-2	208	4-02-96	1	4	5.24	13	11	0	55	59	35	32	6	19	63	.268	.332	.445	25.8	7.8	244
Blanco, Ronel	R-R	6-0	180	8-31-93	7	4	3.68	15	13	0	73	49	31	30	10	37	81	.188	.289	.337	26.8	12.3	302
Brown, Tyler	R-R	6-4	242	10-02-98	1	1	8.10	5	0	0	7	7	6	6	3	4	7	.259	.344	.704	21.9	12.5	32
Buttrey, Ty	L-R	6-6	240	3-31-93	0	1	5.40	14	0	2	13	11	11	8	2	13	12	.220	.394	.420	18.2	19.7	66
Cobos, Franny	R-R	5-9	195	2-01-01	1	0	18.00	1	0	0	2	7	4	4	1	1	0	.583	.643	1.000	0.0	7.1	14
Conn, Devin	R-R	5-11	169	4-03-97	0	1	10.50	6	0	0	6	6	7	7	0	12	5	.261	.500	.435	13.9	33.3	36
Costes, Marty	R-R	5-9	200	12-18-95	1	0	0.00	1	0	0	1	0	1	0	0	2	0	.000	.500	.000	0.0	50.0	4
Cousins, Jake	R-R	6-4	193	7-14-94	1	0	6.00	15	0	0	15	12	10	10	3	12	18	.222	.382	.444	26.5	17.6	68
Davis, Austin	L-L	6-4	235	2-03-93	0	2	11.22	20	0	0	26	29	35	32	3	38	34	.279	.469	.423	23.1	25.9	147
Dubin, Shawn	R-R	6-1	171	9-06-95	1	5	6.63	20	12	1	56	52	45	41	7	37	60	.246	.373	.460	23.3	14.3	258
Endersby, Jimmy	R-R	6-1	194	1-16-98	4	6	5.61	37	3	0	67	65	47	42	13	43	61	.256	.359	.480	19.9	14.1	306
France, J.P.	R-R	6-0	216	4-04-95	2	1	2.33	5	3	0	19	9	6	5	0	11	26	.136	.260	.197	33.8	14.3	77
Gage, Matt	L-L	6-3	265	2-11-93	1	1	4.58	34	0	0	37	41	20	19	5	20	39	.287	.373	.476	23.4	12.0	167
Garcia, Bryan	R-R	6-1	205	4-19-95	2	4	6.98	15	9	0	49	60	44	38	7	45	39	.300	.433	.500	15.2	17.6	256
Gomez, Cesar	L-R	6-3	195	7-09-98	2	2	5.25	9	0	1	12	14	9	7	2	4	9	.298	.340	.489	17.0	7.5	53
Gordon, Colton	L-L	6-4	225	12-20-98	3	2	4.63	9	6	0	35	39	19	18	8	22	30	.277	.374	.504	18.4	13.5	163
Hansen, Austin	R-R	6-0	204	8-25-96	2	2	6.86	35	6	3	84	103	67	64	18	64	85	.309	.420	.550	21.1	15.9	403
Kouba, Rhett	R-R	6-0	180	9-03-99	1	2	4.50	5	3	0	18	21	14	9	2	14	18	.292	.414	.458	20.7	16.1	87
Kuhnel, Joel	R-R	6-5	290	2-19-95	1	1	5.03	17	0	1	20	26	14	11	2	5	16	.321	.356	.481	18.4	5.7	87
Macuare, Angel	R-R	6-2	250	3-03-00	0	1	5.71	4	3	0	17	19	13	11	5	11	15	.275	.383	.551	18.5	13.6	81
Martinez, Seth	R-R	6-2	200	8-29-94	0	0	2.25	19	0	1	20	19	6	5	1	10	30	.247	.341	.299	34.1	11.4	88
Maton, Phil	R-R	6-2	206	3-25-93	0	0	0.00	1	0	0	1	1	0	0	0	0	3	.250	.250	.250	75.0	0.0	4
McGowin, Kyle	R-R	6-3	202	11-27-91	3	7	7.36	16	9	0	62	62	55	51	14	29	58	.255	.336	.490	21.1	10.5	275
Murray, Jayden	R-R	6-1	190	4-11-97	2	4	8.27	11	8	0	41	58	42	38	8	32	42	.335	.455	.555	19.8	15.1	212
Mushinski, Parker	L-L	6-0	218	11-22-95	3	1	2.84	32	0	0	32	22	11	10	2	11	39	.198	.288	.270	31.2	8.8	125
Paredes, Enoli	R-R	5-11	171	9-28-95	3	4	4.80	52	0	6	54	38	33	29	6	45	66	.198	.349	.359	27.3	18.6	242
Record, Joe	R-R	6-3	232	1-12-95	3	2	3.71	50	0	11	53	42	26	22	2	29	52	.218	.321	.311	23.2	12.9	224

Pitching	B-T	Ht.	Wt.	DOB	W	L	ERA	G	GS	SV	IP	Hits	Runs	ER	HR	BB	SO	AVG	OBP	SLG	SO%	BB%	BF
Ruppenthal, Matt	R-R	6-4	225	10-21-95	4	1	6.64	30	1	0	41	46	39	30	6	28	44	.282	.406	.454	21.8	13.9	202
Sandle, Michael	R-R	5-8	200	9-21-98	0	0	45.00	1	0	0	1	3	5	5	2	2	0	.500	.625	1.667	0.0	25.0	8
Solis, Jairo	R-R	6-2	205	12-22-99	1	4	8.46	18	14	1	62	87	59	58	13	37	50	.335	.419	.596	16.2	12.0	308
Sousa, Bennett	L-L	6-3	220	4-06-95	0	0	0.00	2	0	0	2	0	0	0	0	0	4	.000	.000	.000	66.7	0.0	6
Stanek, Ryne	R-R	6-4	226	7-26-91	1	0	0.00	1	0	0	1	1	0	0	0	0	0	.333	.333	.333	0.0	0.0	3
Tamarez, Misael	R-R	6-1	206	1-16-00	1	10	5.08	26	17	2	101	89	63	57	18	60	100	.235	.340	.433	22.6	13.6	442
Taylor, Blake	L-L	6-3	220	8-17-95	0	2	5.15	35	0	0	37	45	24	21	2	22	25	.310	.399	.434	14.9	13.1	168
Urquidy, Jose	R-R	6-0	217	5-01-95	0	0	3.60	2	2	0	5	5	4	2	0	2	4	.263	.318	.316	18.2	9.1	22
VanWey, Logan	R-R	6-2	205	2-14-99	0	0	20.25	2	0	0	1	2	3	3	0	3	1	.500	.667	.500	11.1	33.3	9
Watkins, Spenser	R-R	6-2	195	8-27-92	1	3	9.74	6	5	0	20	31	23	22	2	14	16	.348	.433	.618	15.4	13.5	104
Whitley, Forrest	R-R	6-7	238	9-15-97	1	2	5.70	8	6	0	30	23	19	19	6	17	32	.205	.336	.438	23.7	12.6	135

Fielding

Catcher	PCT	G	PO	A	E	DP	PB
Berryhill	.985	39	326	11	5	0	4
Knapp	1.000	14	125	3	0	1	3
Lee	.986	53	456	25	7	2	7
Salazar	.994	47	440	33	3	7	3
Stubbs	1.000	1	6	1	0	0	0

First Base	PCT	G	PO	A	E	DP
Arias	1.000	3	18	3	0	4
Berryhill	1.000	17	122	6	0	17
Brantley	1.000	2	10	2	0	2
Hensley	.986	10	65	7	1	9
Kessinger	.923	2	11	1	1	4
Knapp	1.000	5	37	5	0	7
Loperfido	1.000	2	10	0	0	0
Madris	.986	29	194	15	3	23
Matijevic	.998	62	425	42	1	36
Perez	.962	3	21	4	1	3
Singleton	.987	21	137	15	2	17

Second Base	PCT	G	PO	A	E	DP
Altuve	1.000	2	1	3	0	0
Bannon	.965	30	50	61	4	14
Espinosa	1.000	2	1	4	0	1
Hensley	.961	15	24	25	2	8
Kessinger	.967	16	19	39	2	11
Leon	.969	51	85	100	6	32
Loftin	1.000	2	6	3	0	1
Machado	1.000	21	22	54	0	12
Perez	.927	12	12	26	3	7
Salazar	1.000	1	1	1	0	0
Wagner	1.000	1	2	3	0	1
Whitcomb	1.000	5	8	16	0	6

Third Base	PCT	G	PO	A	E	DP
Bannon	.962	55	43	85	5	9
Hensley	.964	29	30	51	3	9
Kessinger	.957	14	6	16	1	2
Machado	1.000	10	12	16	0	1
Perez	.887	26	14	41	7	6
Wagner	.875	4	1	6	1	2
Whitcomb	.932	15	10	31	3	1

Shortstop	PCT	G	PO	A	E	DP
Bannon	.977	10	20	22	1	6
Hensley	.966	10	11	17	1	3
Kessinger	.988	25	37	48	1	13
Loftin	.857	3	2	4	1	1
Machado	.989	42	67	108	2	28
Whitcomb	.963	66	75	157	9	37

Outfield	PCT	G	PO	A	E	DP
Adolph	1.000	14	22	1	0	0
Alvarez	1.000	1	2	0	0	0
Brantley	1.000	11	18	1	0	0
Costes	.994	41	75	4	1	2
Dirden	.984	82	162	2	4	0
Hamilton	1.000	28	62	2	0	1
Hensley	1.000	2	4	0	0	0
Julks	1.000	25	38	2	0	1
Leon	.640	79	146	5	4	1
Loperfido	1.000	29	63	4	0	2
Madris	.986	49	110	5	1	1
Matijevic	.971	34	68	0	2	0
McKenna	.975	25	43	2	2	1
Perez	.972	41	68	3	2	0
Sandle	1.000	13	13	1	0	0

HOUSTON ASTROS

CORPUS CHRISTI HOOKS — *DOUBLE-A*

TEXAS LEAGUE

Batting	B-T	Ht.	Wt.	DOB	AVG	OBP	SLG	G	PA	AB	R	H	2B	3B	HR	RBI	BB	HBP	SH	SF	SO	SB	CS	BB%	SO%
Altuve, Jose	R-R	5-6	166	5-06-90	.111	.111	.111	2	9	9	0	1	0	0	0	0	0	0	0	0	2	0	1	0.0	22.2
Arias, Bryan	R-R	5-10	205	6-06-97	.243	.384	.414	22	86	70	16	17	3	0	3	10	14	2	0	0	18	6	0	16.3	20.9
Aviles, Luis	R-R	6-2	210	3-16-95	.265	.330	.478	72	298	268	43	71	14	2	13	39	21	6	0	2	77	17	7	7.0	25.8
2-team (31 San Antonio)					.243	.309	.423	103	408	366	58	89	17	2	15	47	30	6	3	2	107	26	7	7.4	26.2
Barber, Colin	L-L	5-11	200	12-04-00	.244	.358	.433	79	321	270	42	66	16	1	11	40	45	4	0	2	73	5	2	14.0	22.7
Barefoot, Matthew	R-L	5-11	205	9-20-97	.176	.222	.529	4	18	17	3	3	0	0	2	3	1	0	0	0	9	0	0	5.6	50.0
Brewer, Jordan	R-L	6-0	204	8-01-97	.243	.330	.393	67	283	247	38	60	11	1	8	39	30	3	0	2	73	12	4	10.6	25.8
Corona, Kenedy	R-R	5-10	184	3-21-00	.244	.324	.449	111	491	434	63	106	21	4	20	61	48	5	1	3	127	31	9	9.8	25.9
Correa, J.C.	R-R	5-9	200	9-15-98	.246	.307	.339	100	398	357	50	88	13	1	6	46	33	1	0	7	48	7	2	8.3	12.1
Daniels, Zach	R-R	6-1	220	1-23-99	.278	.348	.469	79	345	309	44	86	20	0	13	50	30	4	0	2	108	22	5	8.7	31.3
Dezenzo, Zach	R-R	6-4	220	5-11-00	.257	.339	.486	63	277	245	42	63	12	1	14	41	26	5	0	1	79	16	0	9.4	28.5
Encarnacion, Luis	R-R	5-8	170	9-25-02	.400	.400	.600	1	5	5	0	2	1	0	0	0	0	0	0	0	1	0	0	0.0	20.0
Encarnacion, Yamal	B-R	5-8	150	9-08-03	.150	.261	.150	7	23	20	2	3	0	0	0	2	1	2	0	0	4	2	0	4.3	17.4
Espinosa, Rolando	R-R	6-0	177	1-05-01	.125	.462	.125	4	13	8	3	1	0	0	0	0	5	0	0	0	5	2	1	38.5	38.5
Gilbert, Drew	L-L	5-9	195	9-27-00	.241	.342	.371	60	264	224	36	54	11	0	6	20	33	2	0	1	46	6	3	12.5	17.4
Hamilton, Quincy	L-L	5-10	190	6-12-98	.268	.361	.445	44	191	164	22	44	11	0	6	32	24	1	0	2	47	4	4	12.6	24.6
Kessinger, Grae	R-R	6-1	204	8-25-97	.286	.375	.286	2	8	7	0	2	0	0	0	3	1	0	0	0	4	0	0	12.5	50.0
Loperfido, Joey	L-R	6-3	220	5-11-99	.296	.392	.548	84	365	314	60	93	20	1	19	57	47	3	0	1	81	20	3	12.9	22.2
McCormick, Chas	R-L	6-0	208	4-19-95	.294	.455	.471	6	22	17	6	5	0	0	1	3	4	1	0	0	3	1	0	18.2	13.6
McKenna, Alex	R-R	6-0	204	9-06-97	.196	.338	.339	16	68	56	9	11	3	1	1	6	11	1	0	0	22	1	1	16.2	32.4
Melton, Jacob	L-L	6-3	208	9-07-00	.250	.304	.558	13	56	52	10	13	1	0	5	13	4	0	0	0	16	5	0	7.1	28.6
Nieves, Hector	L-R	6-3	185	7-08-03	.100	.174	.125	13	46	40	1	4	1	0	0	3	4	0	0	2	18	0	1	8.7	39.1
Santana, Luis	R-R	5-6	196	7-20-99	.226	.250	.355	8	32	31	2	7	1	0	1	5	0	1	0	0	9	1	0	0.0	28.1
Santander, Juan	R-R	6-2	180	12-09-02	.375	.444	.375	4	9	8	2	3	0	0	0	0	1	0	0	0	3	0	0	11.1	33.3
Schreiber, Scott	R-R	6-3	230	10-13-95	.283	.353	.425	29	119	106	10	30	6	0	3	15	10	2	0	1	33	3	0	8.4	27.7
Stevens, Chad	R-R	6-3	215	2-03-99	.220	.333	.397	122	495	418	53	92	19	5	15	60	61	12	0	4	176	23	7	12.3	35.6
Stubbs, C.J.	R-R	6-3	207	11-12-96	.196	.314	.380	95	370	316	60	62	16	0	14	33	42	12	0	0	132	15	5	11.4	35.7
Wagner, Will	L-R	5-11	210	7-29-98	.309	.385	.507	53	234	207	36	64	16	2	7	32	26	0	0	1	47	3	2	11.1	20.1
Whitcomb, Shay	R-R	6-1	202	9-28-98	.273	.340	.545	46	197	176	35	48	12	0	12	36	18	1	0	2	56	8	2	9.1	28.4
Wolforth, Garrett	B-R	6-2	220	10-13-97	.212	.267	.332	59	210	193	22	41	11	0	4	19	13	2	0	2	68	3	0	6.2	32.4

Pitching	B-T	Ht.	Wt.	DOB	W	L	ERA	G	GS	SV	IP	Hits	Runs	ER	HR	BB	SO	AVG	OBP	SLG	SO%	BB%	BF
Arrighetti, Spencer	R-R	6-2	186	1-02-00	7	2	4.15	13	8	0	61	48	28	28	4	23	79	.218	.304	.332	31.2	9.1	253
Bellozo, Valente	R-R	5-10	170	1-04-00	0	1	1.72	4	3	1	16	9	5	3	2	6	12	.170	.250	.321	20.0	10.0	60
Betances, Jose	R-R	6-0	170	10-17-99	0	0	9.00	8	0	0	9	12	10	9	1	12	12	.324	.519	.432	23.1	23.1	52

Blubaugh, A.J.	R-R	6-2	190	7-04-00	0	0	1.26	4	3	0	14	4	2	2	1	8	19	.093	.235	.186	37.3	15.7	51
Brown, Aaron	R-R	6-4	220	3-19-99	5	2	4.30	26	14	2	103	111	59	49	13	36	110	.272	.332	.429	24.4	8.0	450
Brown, Tyler	R-R	6-4	242	10-02-98	5	3	3.12	38	0	3	49	37	22	17	5	26	49	.207	.317	.341	23.4	12.4	209
Chaidez, Adrian	R-R	6-1	180	6-10-99	1	6	6.75	18	6	0	45	38	37	34	6	33	50	.233	.380	.429	23.9	15.8	209
Cobos, Franny	R-R	5-9	195	2-01-01	0	2	5.54	5	1	1	13	17	8	8	1	9	17	.321	.429	.491	27.0	14.3	63
Conn, Devin	R-R	5-11	169	4-03-97	0	1	1.08	5	0	0	8	6	2	1	0	5	6	.222	.382	.333	17.6	14.7	34
De Paula, Brayan	L-L	6-3	225	6-25-99	1	0	0.00	2	0	0	3	0	0	0	0	1	3	.000	.111	.000	33.3	11.1	9
DeLabio, Jacob	R-R	6-5	235	9-18-97	1	0	1.40	21	0	2	26	15	5	4	0	20	28	.167	.318	.222	25.5	18.2	110
Gaither, Ray	R-R	6-4	224	3-04-98	4	1	3.51	30	0	3	33	31	23	13	4	24	36	.233	.354	.361	22.4	14.9	161
Gomez, Cesar	L-R	6-3	195	7-09-98	2	4	7.93	34	0	2	36	53	40	32	6	24	32	.333	.427	.522	17.1	12.8	187
Gordon, Colton	L-L	6-4	225	12-20-98	4	5	3.95	20	18	1	93	75	44	41	9	36	121	.215	.300	.350	30.7	9.1	394
Gusto, Ryan	R-R	6-4	232	3-11-99	5	2	2.93	14	8	1	61	37	22	20	2	25	62	.170	.265	.239	24.9	10.0	249
Henley, Blair	R-R	6-3	190	5-14-97	3	6	5.06	25	17	1	107	104	67	60	8	53	106	.255	.354	.358	22.3	11.1	476
Kouba, Rhett	R-R	6-0	180	9-03-99	7	5	3.27	23	21	0	110	95	48	40	12	23	118	.231	.286	.365	26.2	5.1	451
Macuare, Angel	R-R	6-2	250	3-03-00	1	4	5.31	15	10	2	58	71	38	34	9	17	54	.297	.355	.498	20.6	6.5	262
McDonald, Cole	L-R	6-1	218	3-11-97	2	3	3.94	35	0	7	48	40	25	21	2	21	66	.225	.309	.292	32.2	10.2	205
Melendez, Jaime	L-R	5-8	190	9-26-01	2	0	5.59	3	2	0	10	8	6	6	2	7	8	.222	.341	.444	18.2	15.9	44
Plumlee, Peyton	R-R	6-3	201	2-10-97	1	6	7.66	19	7	3	47	55	43	40	6	28	53	.286	.384	.432	23.7	12.5	224
Robaina, Julio	L-L	5-11	170	3-23-01	10	6	3.18	26	16	0	116	105	46	41	6	48	114	.241	.316	.369	23.2	9.8	492
Ruppenthal, Matt	R-R	6-4	225	10-21-95	0	1	2.84	4	0	0	6	4	2	2	0	3	7	.190	.393	.190	25.0	10.7	28
Sprinkle, Jonathan	R-R	6-6	237	7-08-98	3	3	10.59	26	0	0	26	29	33	31	5	32	32	.274	.476	.472	21.5	21.5	149
Taveras, Diosmerky	R-R	6-5	256	9-23-99	3	3	4.66	21	2	0	56	58	35	29	6	25	58	.270	.357	.423	23.2	10.0	250
Urquidy, Jose	R-R	6-0	217	5-01-95	0	1	5.00	2	2	0	9	10	5	5	0	1	7	.263	.300	.289	17.5	2.5	40
VanWey, Logan	R-R	6-2	205	2-14-99	2	1	3.00	23	0	2	30	21	13	10	5	17	42	.193	.318	.349	32.6	13.2	129
West, Derek	R-R	6-5	257	12-02-96	1	0	5.54	10	0	0	13	11	8	8	1	9	14	.239	.351	.391	24.6	15.8	57

Fielding

Catcher	PCT	G	PO	A	E	DP	PB
Correa	.992	28	237	14	2	0	7
Stubbs	.984	69	658	36	11	5	11
Wolforth	.979	44	443	22	10	2	8

First Base	PCT	G	PO	A	E	DP
Arias	.982	9	49	6	1	6
Aviles	.979	5	42	5	1	5
Brewer	.984	30	177	9	3	17
Correa	.981	24	147	10	3	23
Dezenzo	1.000	4	36	2	0	0
Encarnacion	1.000	1	6	0	0	0
Loperfido	1.000	16	104	12	0	7
Santander	1.000	3	19	1	0	3
Schreiber	.970	19	155	5	5	13
Stubbs	.984	19	112	10	2	15
Wolforth	1.000	11	56	5	0	8

Second Base	PCT	G	PO	A	E	DP
Altuve	1.000	2	2	3	0	0
Arias	1.000	1	1	0	0	0
Aviles	.959	13	27	20	2	4
Correa	.967	38	43	76	4	14
Dezenzo	.667	2	0	2	1	0
Encarnacion	1.000	5	12	11	0	4
Espinosa	1.000	1	1	3	0	1
Kessinger	1.000	1	0	1	0	0
Loperfido	.966	17	26	31	2	5
Nieves	.974	10	21	17	1	7
Santana	1.000	4	6	11	0	4
Stevens	1.000	5	5	14	0	1
Wagner	.985	35	55	76	2	24
Whitcomb	.975	10	16	23	1	10

Third Base	PCT	G	PO	A	E	DP
Aviles	.917	21	18	26	4	1
Correa	.714	4	1	4	2	1
Dezenzo	.915	56	31	77	10	3
Espinosa	1.000	2	2	6	0	1
Nieves	1.000	3	1	3	0	0
Santana	1.000	4	2	3	0	0
Stevens	.974	30	19	56	2	6
Wagner	.944	15	11	23	2	5
Whitcomb	.769	4	1	9	3	2

Shortstop	PCT	G	PO	A	E	DP
Aviles	.919	22	28	40	6	15
Kessinger	1.000	1	3	3	0	0
Stevens	.968	84	109	194	10	42
Whitcomb	.952	31	28	72	5	13

Outfield	PCT	G	PO	A	E	DP
Arias	.957	9	21	1	1	0
Aviles	1.000	9	11	0	0	0
Barber	.977	49	79	1	3	0
Barefoot	.500	2	3	0	0	0
Brewer	.958	28	39	4	1	0
Corona	.951	106	241	12	5	2
Daniels	.997	72	171	4	1	1
Espinosa	.000	1	0	0	0	0
Gilbert	.969	36	88	1	4	1
Hamilton	.990	33	63	2	1	1
Loperfido	.977	45	81	3	2	1
McCormick	1.000	6	7	0	0	0
McKenna	1.000	14	17	0	0	0
Melton	1.000	7	21	0	0	0
Schreiber	1.000	4	14	0	0	0
Stubbs	1.000	3	6	0	0	0
Wolforth	.000	1	0	0	0	0

ASHEVILLE TOURISTS

HIGH CLASS A

SOUTH ATLANTIC LEAGUE

Batting	B-T	Ht.	Wt.	DOB	AVG	OBP	SLG	G	PA	AB	R	H	2B	3B	HR	RBI	BB	HBP	SH	SF	SO	SB	CS	BB%	SO%
Borden, Tim	R-R	6-1	200	9-01-99	.245	.328	.387	100	412	364	45	89	17	1	11	49	24	22	0	2	148	7	3	5.8	35.9
Cerny, Logan	R-R	6-1	185	9-28-99	.221	.297	.380	84	360	321	50	71	10	1	13	42	31	5	0	3	128	20	4	8.6	35.6
Clifford, Ryan	L-L	6-3	200	7-20-03	.271	.356	.547	58	250	214	35	58	11	0	16	46	21	10	0	5	62	1	1	8.4	24.8
2-team (32 Brooklyn)					.242	.345	.486	90	390	331	48	80	15	0	22	66	39	13	0	7	113	2	1	10.0	29.0
Cole, Zach	L-R	6-2	190	8-04-00	.247	.349	.480	41	175	150	31	37	5	3	8	19	21	3	0	1	58	12	4	12.0	33.1
Corona, Kenedy	R-R	5-10	184	3-21-00	.360	.448	.600	6	29	25	7	9	0	0	2	4	4	0	0	0	9	1	1	13.8	31.0
Deming, Austin	R-R	6-0	200	12-21-99	.159	.282	.216	27	103	88	9	14	5	0	0	3	14	1	0	0	34	0	1	13.6	33.0
Dezenzo, Zach	R-R	6-4	220	5-11-00	.407	.474	.628	31	133	113	38	46	11	1	4	20	16	1	0	3	27	6	2	12.0	20.3
Espinosa, Rolando	R-R	6-0	177	1-05-01	.230	.317	.394	53	190	165	27	38	10	1	5	21	22	0	0	2	73	12	6	11.6	38.4
Garcia, John	R-R	6-0	190	9-25-00	.306	.420	.403	24	88	72	10	22	5	1	0	7	8	7	0	1	18	0	1	9.1	20.5
Gilbert, Drew	L-L	5-9	195	9-27-00	.360	.421	.686	21	95	86	21	31	8	1	6	18	6	3	0	0	21	4	0	6.3	22.1
Guilamo, Freddy	R-R	5-11	160	12-10-00	.194	.260	.343	21	73	67	7	13	1	0	3	9	6	0	0	0	32	0	0	8.2	43.8
Kato, Kobe	L-R	6-1	170	3-19-99	.233	.347	.329	82	303	258	38	60	19	0	2	30	42	3	0	0	54	19	4	13.9	17.8
Loperfido, Joey	L-R	6-3	220	5-11-99	.265	.297	.529	8	37	34	4	9	2	2	1	5	2	0	0	1	8	3	0	5.4	21.6
Melton, Jacob	L-L	6-3	208	9-07-00	.244	.338	.453	86	394	344	73	84	16	1	18	42	48	1	0	0	83	41	7	12.2	21.1
Nova, Freudis	R-R	6-0	178	1-12-00	.174	.274	.261	38	157	138	19	24	3	0	3	12	18	1	0	0	44	2	1	11.5	28.0
Palma, Miguel	R-R	5-8	170	1-04-02	.274	.340	.409	61	262	230	29	63	13	0	6	38	23	3	0	6	51	3	1	8.8	19.5
Price, Collin	R-R	6-6	225	11-15-99	.198	.341	.368	58	223	182	19	36	13	0	6	24	37	3	0	1	55	0	1	16.6	24.7

Rodriguez, Nerio	R-R	6-0	230	9-21-99	.111	.200	.333	5	20	18	2	2	1	0	1	5	2	0	0	0	6	0	0	10.0	30.0
Sacco, Tommy	B-R	5-10	195	5-21-99	.225	.354	.382	104	418	346	49	78	16	1	12	47	66	4	0	2	102	16	8	15.8	24.4
Sandle, Michael	R-R	5-8	200	9-21-98	.202	.277	.321	91	357	321	37	65	17	0	7	26	30	4	0	2	96	15	5	8.4	26.9
Whitaker, Tyler	R-R	6-4	190	8-02-02	.203	.301	.406	17	73	64	10	13	4	0	3	4	8	1	0	0	22	2	1	11.0	30.1
Williams, Justin	R-R	6-1	215	6-26-00	.152	.213	.238	73	244	223	23	34	11	1	2	26	17	1	0	3	97	1	1	7.0	39.8
Wrobleski, Ryan	R-R	6-1	196	2-02-00	.241	.289	.371	82	339	315	32	76	18	1	7	56	14	8	0	2	86	15	4	4.1	25.4

Pitching	B-T	Ht.	Wt.	DOB	W	L	ERA	G	GS	SV	IP	Hits	Runs	ER	HR	BB	SO	AVG	OBP	SLG	SO%	BB%	BF
Batista, Edinson	R-R	6-2	210	5-19-02	1	3	10.13	11	7	1	29	40	35	33	9	14	28	.323	.407	.613	19.3	9.7	145
Bellozo, Valente	R-R	5-10	170	1-04-00	3	3	6.18	22	13	3	95	106	68	65	21	26	94	.280	.325	.515	22.8	6.3	413
Betances, Jose	R-R	6-0	170	10-17-99	0	1	8.44	6	0	1	5	8	8	5	1	8	6	.333	.515	.500	18.2	24.2	33
Blubaugh, A.J.	R-R	6-2	190	7-04-00	6	3	4.94	22	9	1	86	85	50	47	10	37	93	.258	.335	.407	25.1	10.0	371
Brockhouse, Walker	R-R	6-4	197	2-22-99	3	0	5.28	25	0	0	29	24	17	17	2	19	37	.229	.354	.343	28.2	14.5	131
Calderon, Carlos	R-R	6-0	210	10-04-01	3	3	8.63	30	3	4	41	56	42	39	5	31	35	.335	.452	.509	16.7	14.8	209
Coats, Jacob	R-R	6-6	235	6-04-98	0	0	16.20	2	0	0	2	4	3	3	0	2	2	.444	.545	.556	18.2	18.2	11
Cobos, Franny	R-R	5-9	195	2-01-01	4	2	4.40	21	0	1	45	43	25	22	2	23	56	.246	.332	.377	27.7	11.4	202
De Paula, Brayan	L-L	6-3	225	6-25-99	3	6	6.30	28	6	1	64	66	50	45	4	47	98	.265	.405	.361	31.4	15.1	312
DeLabio, Jacob	R-R	6-5	235	9-18-97	1	0	0.00	5	0	0	6	4	1	0	0	3	8	.190	.346	.286	30.8	11.5	26
DeVos, Nolan	R-R	6-0	185	8-11-00	4	3	4.27	12	7	0	46	48	22	22	7	23	43	.262	.345	.432	20.9	11.2	206
Ford, Kasey	L-R	6-6	275	1-10-98	0	0	3.86	8	0	0	9	8	5	4	2	7	8	.222	.341	.444	18.2	15.9	44
Garcia, Ronny	R-R	6-3	170	12-02-99	2	2	3.38	29	0	2	35	34	16	13	4	20	40	.268	.362	.425	26.8	13.4	149
Guilfoil, Tyler	R-R	6-4	215	1-19-00	0	3	4.57	5	4	0	22	20	15	11	2	9	32	.241	.316	.373	33.7	9.5	95
Gusto, Ryan	R-R	6-4	232	3-11-99	2	2	6.47	12	6	0	49	58	37	35	11	21	53	.293	.361	.515	24.2	9.6	219
Knorr, Michael	R-R	6-5	245	5-12-00	1	5	4.61	11	8	0	41	39	25	21	8	17	54	.242	.317	.460	30.0	9.4	180
Mancini, Joey	L-R	6-1	195	10-04-00	1	7	7.42	19	10	0	70	94	60	58	8	31	69	.318	.389	.500	20.8	9.3	332
Matthews, Zack	B-R	6-0	205	1-31-99	0	1	13.50	2	0	0	2	5	3	3	0	2	2	.455	.538	.636	15.4	15.4	13
McDonald, Cole	L-R	6-1	218	3-11-97	0	0	0.00	4	0	0	5	4	0	0	0	1	8	.222	.263	.278	42.1	5.3	19
Miley, Deylen	R-R	6-2	220	1-25-98	2	7	5.81	25	13	1	88	87	61	57	14	63	120	.256	.378	.459	29.0	15.2	414
Plumlee, Peyton	R-R	6-3	201	2-10-97	2	0	3.00	3	2	0	12	14	7	4	1	3	19	.275	.327	.412	34.5	5.5	55
Roberts, Max	R-L	6-6	190	7-23-97	6	4	5.67	27	0	1	27	26	21	17	4	18	43	.250	.357	.413	34.1	14.3	126
Rodriguez, Luis Angel	L-L	6-1	190	9-10-99	0	1	3.67	7	4	0	27	16	13	11	1	16	38	.162	.314	.242	31.4	13.2	121
Salgado, Bryant	R-R	6-1	205	3-02-00	0	2	9.31	8	0	0	10	9	12	10	3	11	10	.237	.400	.526	20.0	22.0	50
Santos, Alex	R-R	6-4	208	2-10-02	3	7	6.94	25	12	2	83	100	77	64	17	64	92	.290	.405	.501	21.9	15.2	421
Swanson, Nic	R-R	6-2	180	7-08-99	1	2	4.08	12	10	0	57	49	27	26	11	18	55	.225	.293	.427	23.0	7.5	239
Taveras, Diosmerky	R-R	6-5	256	9-23-99	0	0	4.50	1	0	0	2	1	1	1	0	0	2	.143	.250	.143	25.0	0.0	8
Ullola, Miguel	R-R	6-1	205	6-19-02	3	9	5.86	25	13	0	91	87	67	59	12	63	116	.251	.368	.431	27.7	15.0	419
VanWey, Logan	R-R	6-2	205	2-14-99	0	0	3.71	15	0	1	17	19	7	7	1	10	20	.279	.372	.397	25.6	12.8	78

Fielding

Catcher	PCT	G	PO	A	E	DP	PB
Garcia	.983	10	107	7	2	0	4
Guilamo	.979	10	90	3	2	0	5
Palma	.983	33	336	21	6	1	4
Price	.980	34	310	29	7	0	8
Rodriguez	1.000	3	30	2	0	0	1
Wrobleski	.980	42	419	21	9	6	4

First Base	PCT	G	PO	A	E	DP
Clifford	.971	29	188	13	6	15
Dezenzo	.929	3	12	1	1	1
Garcia	.917	5	20	2	2	0
Guilamo	.947	8	54	0	3	2
Loperfido	1.000	1	6	1	0	0
Palma	.993	19	127	6	1	10
Price	.985	19	125	5	2	7
Rodriguez	1.000	1	4	0	0	0
Williams	1.000	26	137	10	0	8
Wrobleski	.988	25	150	13	2	12

Second Base	PCT	G	PO	A	E	DP
Borden	.965	35	55	82	5	17
Deming	1.000	6	12	6	0	2
Dezenzo	1.000	10	11	28	0	6
Espinosa	.893	10	6	19	3	2
Kato	.938	53	68	112	12	16
Loperfido	.875	4	5	9	2	1
Nova	1.000	3	2	6	0	1
Sacco	1.000	1	0	6	0	0
Williams	1.000	7	7	10	0	2

Third Base	PCT	G	PO	A	E	DP
Borden	.905	38	23	44	7	3
Deming	.917	14	10	23	3	2
Dezenzo	.927	16	19	19	3	2
Espinosa	.926	13	6	19	2	0
Kato	1.000	2	1	2	0	0
Nova	.929	9	2	11	1	0
Sacco	.935	16	18	25	3	4
Whitaker	.700	5	3	4	3	0
Williams	.973	18	14	22	1	2

Shortstop	PCT	G	PO	A	E	DP
Borden	.919	14	17	17	3	5
Espinosa	.909	9	14	26	4	6
Nova	.917	27	25	52	7	7
Sacco	.958	78	88	165	11	26

Outfield	PCT	G	PO	A	E	DP
Cerny	.963	72	129	7	5	3
Clifford	1.000	26	37	2	0	0
Cole	1.000	37	63	4	0	1
Corona	1.000	5	10	0	0	0
Espinosa	1.000	18	25	2	0	0
Garcia	.917	7	10	1	1	0
Gilbert	.980	19	31	0	1	0
Kato	1.000	25	36	2	0	0
Loperfido	1.000	3	5	0	0	0
Melton	.979	67	143	8	4	2
Sandle	.983	82	170	5	2	0
Whitaker	.961	11	17	1	1	0
Williams	1.000	26	25	1	0	1
Wrobleski	1.000	9	14	3	0	1

FAYETTEVILLE WOODPECKERS — *LOW CLASS A*

CAROLINA LEAGUE

Batting	B-T	Ht.	Wt.	DOB	AVG	OBP	SLG	G	PA	AB	R	H	2B	3B	HR	RBI	BB	HBP	SH	SF	SO	SB	CS	BB%	SO%
Baez, Luis	R-R	6-1	205	1-11-04	.239	.324	.413	41	179	155	20	37	13	1	4	23	17	4	0	3	48	0	0	9.5	26.8
Balogh, Ricardo	B-R	6-3	175	7-09-02	.241	.315	.358	89	346	307	37	74	12	3	6	31	33	2	0	4	93	3	0	9.5	26.9
Clifford, Ryan	L-L	6-3	200	7-20-03	.337	.488	.457	25	121	92	22	31	5	0	2	15	25	3	0	1	27	3	1	20.7	22.3
Cole, Zach	L-R	6-2	190	8-04-00	.265	.397	.494	70	312	253	48	67	15	5	11	46	45	12	0	2	97	25	5	14.4	31.1
Cruz, Narbe	R-R	6-3	181	10-01-00	.263	.331	.373	62	260	236	22	62	14	0	4	26	20	4	0	0	50	2	2	7.7	19.2
Daniels, Zach	R-R	6-1	220	1-23-99	.250	.368	.313	5	19	16	2	4	1	0	0	2	2	1	0	0	6	0	0	10.5	31.6
Encarnacion, Luis	R-R	5-8	170	9-25-02	.243	.301	.366	97	402	366	40	89	15	0	10	44	31	1	0	4	82	7	6	7.7	20.4
Encarnacion, Yamal	B-R	5-8	150	9-08-03	.167	.235	.200	9	34	30	2	5	1	0	0	2	3	0	0	1	9	0	0	8.8	26.5
Espinosa, Rolando	R-R	6-0	177	1-05-01	.194	.350	.255	33	123	98	7	19	6	0	0	6	21	3	0	1	41	10	3	17.1	33.3
Ferreras, Pascanel	R-R	5-10	185	11-25-01	.212	.284	.288	29	116	104	11	22	5	0	1	10	8	3	0	1	33	3	3	6.9	28.4

Fisher, Cameron	L-R	6-2	210	6-12-01	.273	.396	.500	31	134	110	16	30	6	2	5	15	22	1	0	1	44	5	0	16.4	32.8
Garcia, John	R-R	6-0	190	9-25-00	.198	.347	.300	73	294	237	34	47	12	0	4	26	36	19	0	2	74	8	5	12.2	25.2
Gaston, Sandro	R-R	6-3	210	12-16-02	.198	.254	.269	86	331	308	26	61	19	0	1	32	22	1	0	0	93	4	2	6.6	28.1
Guillemette, Garret	R-R	6-1	210	9-04-01	.235	.325	.382	28	120	102	15	24	6	0	3	17	9	6	0	3	18	0	0	7.5	15.0
Johnson, Ryan	R-R	6-0	175	12-27-00	.192	.285	.350	34	137	120	12	23	5	1	4	12	12	4	0	1	48	2	1	8.8	35.0
Kato, Kobe	L-R	6-1	170	3-19-99	.667	.800	.833	6	20	12	7	8	2	0	0	1	7	1	0	0	0	3	0	35.0	0.0
Loftin, Jackson	R-R	6-2	195	5-14-00	.207	.323	.315	116	450	381	61	79	14	0	9	45	49	17	0	2	100	60	7	10.9	22.2
Lorenzo, Dauri	B-R	5-9	186	10-29-02	.224	.304	.286	72	273	245	25	55	6	0	3	22	25	3	0	0	58	1	1	9.2	21.2
Machandy, Roilan	R-R	6-0	170	5-18-01	.175	.268	.302	25	71	63	5	11	2	0	2	4	7	1	0	0	27	5	3	9.9	38.0
Matthews, Brice	R-R	6-0	175	3-16-02	.217	.373	.367	33	150	120	22	26	6	0	4	11	24	6	0	0	40	16	3	16.0	26.7
McGowan, Garrett	L-L	6-4	215	4-14-99	.168	.263	.265	46	175	155	12	26	6	0	3	11	18	2	0	0	55	1	0	10.3	31.4
Molina, Leosdany	R-R	6-0	182	1-09-00	.211	.273	.287	96	319	289	36	61	4	0	6	30	23	3	0	4	69	17	3	7.2	21.6
Nieves, Hector	L-R	6-3	185	7-08-03	.308	.438	.769	4	16	13	3	4	0	0	2	3	3	0	0	0	5	0	0	18.8	31.3
Perez, Frank	R-R	6-2	180	12-24-01	.143	.200	.214	22	60	56	3	8	1	0	1	2	2	2	0	0	34	1	0	3.3	56.7
Perez, Luis	R-R	5-10	193	10-24-02	.049	.114	.049	12	44	41	1	2	0	0	0	1	2	1	0	0	17	0	0	4.5	38.6
Santander, Juan	R-R	6-2	180	12-09-02	.297	.333	.378	11	39	37	4	11	0	0	1	6	2	0	0	0	7	1	0	5.1	17.9
Whitaker, Tyler	R-R	6-4	190	8-02-02	.236	.378	.322	57	249	199	30	47	6	1	3	24	38	9	0	3	71	14	4	15.3	28.5
Williams, Jeron	R-R	6-1	180	9-29-00	.211	.375	.211	18	72	57	9	12	0	0	0	3	13	2	0	0	13	9	0	18.1	18.1
Williams, Justin	R-R	6-1	215	6-26-00	.348	.464	.609	6	28	23	5	8	2	2	0	3	5	0	0	0	4	0	0	17.9	14.3
Wrobleski, Ryan	R-R	6-1	196	2-02-00	.214	.389	.500	5	18	14	1	3	1	0	1	3	2	2	0	0	4	0	0	11.1	22.2

Pitching	B-T	Ht.	Wt.	DOB	W	L	ERA	G	GS	SV	IP	Hits	Runs	ER	HR	BB	SO	AVG	OBP	SLG	SO%	BB%	BF
Bloss, Jake	R-R	6-3	205	6-23-01	1	1	2.76	5	4	0	16	14	8	5	0	11	20	.250	.377	.286	29.0	15.9	69
Brockhouse, Walker	R-R	6-4	197	2-22-99	1	0	3.38	5	0	0	5	1	2	2	0	4	7	.063	.250	.063	35.0	20.0	20
Carrasco, Deury	L-R	6-0	182	9-20-99	4	5	2.49	29	0	2	47	36	19	13	0	18	54	.214	.301	.274	27.7	9.2	195
Chirinos, Amilcar	R-R	6-3	200	11-07-01	0	4	4.20	17	10	0	60	60	34	28	3	35	61	.265	.365	.372	22.8	13.1	267
DeVos, Nolan	R-R	6-0	185	8-11-00	2	1	2.24	13	8	0	52	33	14	13	1	27	74	.181	.289	.247	35.1	12.8	211
Dombroski, Trey	R-L	6-5	235	3-13-01	7	9	3.71	26	15	1	119	97	63	49	15	36	148	.216	.276	.388	30.1	7.3	491
Espinosa, Carlos	R-R	6-2	188	8-08-01	4	4	4.53	11	6	0	44	40	27	22	7	22	49	.237	.328	.408	25.1	11.3	195
Fleury, Jose	R-R	6-0	185	3-08-02	4	3	3.65	26	14	3	99	63	42	40	8	48	139	.182	.282	.289	34.9	12.1	398
Foggo, Ian	R-R	6-1	200	6-01-98	4	2	3.86	32	0	4	30	20	15	13	3	26	45	.190	.358	.324	33.3	19.3	135
Ford, Kasey	L-R	6-6	275	1-10-98	2	1	1.88	21	0	3	29	17	6	6	0	15	47	.170	.306	.250	38.8	12.4	121
Garcia, Elvis	R-R	6-0	165	9-24-02	0	0	3.00	2	0	0	6	3	2	2	1	4	5	.150	.292	.300	20.8	16.7	24
Garcia, Ronny	R-R	6-3	170	12-02-99	1	0	0.00	1	0	0	2	1	0	0	0	0	2	.167	.167	.333	33.3	0.0	6
Gillis, Brett	R-R	6-2	215	9-29-99	0	0	0.00	1	0	0	2	1	0	0	0	0	3	.143	.143	.286	42.9	0.0	7
Guedez, Jose	R-R	6-0	169	9-27-01	1	4	4.08	11	5	1	35	29	16	16	0	29	44	.223	.366	.269	27.2	17.9	162
Guilfoil, Tyler	R-R	6-4	215	1-19-00	3	3	2.74	18	9	1	62	42	24	19	2	28	91	.190	.302	.267	35.1	10.8	259
Hunt, Marshall	R-R	6-3	200	7-08-99	0	0	9.53	6	0	0	6	9	8	6	0	7	3	.375	.500	.583	9.4	21.9	32
Knorr, Michael	R-R	6-5	245	5-12-00	2	0	2.60	4	2	0	17	13	6	5	0	7	24	.206	.282	.238	33.8	9.9	71
Mancini, Joey	L-R	6-1	195	10-04-00	1	1	4.01	6	3	0	25	15	11	11	2	6	33	.172	.242	.299	34.0	6.2	97
Matthews, Zack	B-R	6-0	205	1-31-99	1	2	2.45	5	0	0	4	2	4	1	0	0	5	.143	.200	.214	31.3	0.0	16
Mejia, Sandy	R-R	6-0	160	1-03-04	0	0	40.50	1	0	0	1	1	3	3	0	3	2	.250	.571	.250	28.6	42.9	7
Molero, Jeremy	R-R	6-2	170	11-08-99	2	0	0.93	25	0	8	29	12	4	3	0	31	43	.128	.369	.128	32.6	23.5	132
Nodal, Jose	L-L	6-3	195	7-16-02	3	10	6.55	25	11	0	77	83	70	56	6	52	66	.274	.396	.389	17.8	14.0	371
Pecko, Ethan	R-R	6-2	195	8-25-02	0	1	7.50	4	3	0	12	12	12	10	0	9	14	.250	.362	.313	24.1	15.5	58
Perez, Bryan	R-R	5-11	160	4-14-00	0	1	9.00	20	0	0	20	28	23	20	1	15	22	.329	.442	.459	21.2	14.4	104
Rodriguez, Luis Angel	L-L	6-1	190	9-10-99	1	0	1.49	9	4	2	36	20	7	6	1	18	49	.163	.273	.211	34.3	12.6	143
Santa, Alimber	R-R	5-10	163	5-03-03	3	9	5.98	26	14	0	87	86	61	58	5	74	119	.260	.398	.363	28.8	17.9	413
Swanson, Nic	R-R	6-2	180	7-08-99	4	2	2.61	14	7	0	59	42	24	17	2	21	66	.194	.267	.253	27.5	8.8	240
Taylor, Andrew	R-R	6-5	190	9-23-01	4	8	4.61	24	12	1	84	87	52	43	12	43	126	.269	.357	.415	33.8	11.5	373
Temple, Austin	R-R	6-4	180	8-24-99	1	0	2.29	20	0	2	20	11	5	5	1	20	24	.159	.348	.232	27.0	22.5	89
Urias, Manuel	R-R	6-6	200	3-08-01	4	1	4.15	24	5	2	56	44	28	26	7	18	70	.210	.279	.338	30.0	7.7	233

Fielding

Catcher	PCT	G	PO	A	E	DP	PB
Encarnacion	.992	22	223	23	2	3	3
Garcia	.981	39	426	41	9	4	6
Gaston	.974	50	550	48	16	3	10
Guillemette	.972	16	187	20	6	3	5
Santander	.952	4	54	5	3	0	0
Wrobleski	1.000	3	26	1	0	0	0

First Base	PCT	G	PO	A	E	DP
Balogh	.988	42	229	12	3	20
Clifford	1.000	4	26	3	0	1
Cruz	.985	10	64	3	1	4
Encarnacion	.995	33	201	9	1	17
Ferreras	1.000	3	15	1	0	0
Garcia	1.000	1	7	2	0	0
Gaston	.993	19	140	2	1	13
Guillemette	1.000	6	47	0	0	1
Lorenzo	.952	4	20	0	1	0
McGowan	.989	14	84	6	1	9
Molina	1.000	1	1	0	0	0
Santander	1.000	3	19	0	0	1
Williams	.941	2	15	1	1	0
Wrobleski	1.000	2	13	1	0	1

Second Base	PCT	G	PO	A	E	DP
Balogh	1.000	12	28	21	0	6
Cruz	.959	17	26	45	3	7
Encarnacion	.889	3	3	5	1	0
Espinosa	.875	5	3	4	1	1
Ferreras	.982	16	15	39	1	5
Johnson	.982	13	24	31	1	8
Kato	1.000	2	3	5	0	0
Loftin	.974	11	22	16	1	4
Lorenzo	.957	35	45	67	5	6
Molina	.926	20	23	27	4	8
Williams, Je	1.000	6	6	12	0	1
Williams, Ju	1.000	2	5	4	0	1

Third Base	PCT	G	PO	A	E	DP
Balogh	.883	30	16	37	7	5
Cruz	.891	23	11	30	5	2
Espinosa	.250	1	0	1	3	0
Ferreras	.944	7	6	11	1	3
Johnson	.943	14	12	21	2	0
Loftin	1.000	26	17	40	0	5
Lorenzo	.833	4	2	3	1	2
Molina	1.000	2	1	1	0	0
Whitaker	.951	29	14	25	2	1
Williams, Je	.950	8	8	11	1	0
Williams, Ju	1.000	2	0	3	0	0

Shortstop	PCT	G	PO	A	E	DP
Cruz	.933	8	12	16	2	4
Espinosa	.909	3	3	7	1	1
Ferreras	.909	3	3	7	1	0
Johnson	1.000	5	4	8	0	1
Loftin	.932	37	37	72	8	6
Matthews	.922	27	24	47	6	4
Molina	.910	52	41	90	13	15
Williams	1.000	3	1	7	0	1

Outfield	PCT	G	PO	A	E	DP
Baez	.971	37	58	2	3	1
Balogh	.000	1	0	0	0	0
Clifford	.961	19	21	4	1	1

Cole	.904	69	131	6	7	3
Daniels	1.000	5	11	0	0	0
Encarnacion, L	.926	23	24	1	2	0
Encarnacion, Y	.500	7	9	0	0	0
Espinosa	.983	24	38	4	1	0
Fisher	.857	27	26	2	2	0
Garcia	.881	25	30	3	3	0
Kato	1.000	3	1	1	0	0
Loftin	.995	48	82	3	1	2
Machandy	.980	25	34	1	1	1
McGowan	1.000	26	30	2	0	1
Molina	.500	21	30	2	0	0
Nieves	.667	4	8	2	0	1
Perez, F	.982	21	23	5	1	0
Perez, L	.925	10	19	1	2	0
Whitaker	.954	27	48	2	1	0

FCL ASTROS — *ROOKIE*

FLORIDA COMPLEX LEAGUE

Batting	B-T	Ht.	Wt.	DOB	AVG	OBP	SLG	G	PA	AB	R	H	2B	3B	HR	RBI	BB	HBP	SH	SF	SO	SB	CS	BB%	SO%
Arias, Bryan	R-R	5-10	205	6-06-97	.242	.375	.333	9	40	33	5	8	3	0	0	2	5	2	0	0	8	1	0	12.5	20.0
Baez, Luis	R-R	6-1	205	1-11-04	.271	.434	.661	17	76	59	10	16	2	0	7	15	16	1	0	0	14	1	1	21.1	18.4
Barefoot, Matthew	R-L	5-11	205	9-20-97	.273	.429	.545	7	28	22	6	6	3	0	1	4	6	0	0	0	4	1	0	21.4	14.3
Brewer, Jordan	R-L	6-0	204	8-01-97	.067	.263	.133	4	19	15	3	1	1	0	0	0	4	0	0	0	3	0	0	21.1	15.8
Bush, Will	L-R	6-4	230	3-04-04	.304	.500	.522	9	32	23	11	7	2	0	1	7	7	2	0	0	8	0	0	21.9	25.0
Caldera, Fernando	R-R	5-11	170	10-10-02	.283	.387	.453	22	62	53	10	15	3	0	2	8	8	1	0	0	15	1	0	12.9	24.2
Casserilla, Xavier	R-R	6-0	210	5-16-03	.212	.316	.394	10	38	33	10	7	3	0	1	4	5	0	0	0	5	2	1	13.2	13.2
Colon, Rabel	L-R	6-0	175	8-29-03	.163	.285	.268	38	144	123	19	20	4	0	3	16	17	4	0	0	47	9	2	11.8	32.6
Del Rosario, Richel	R-R	6-0	191	2-27-04	.159	.333	.193	33	114	88	11	14	0	0	1	9	18	6	0	2	38	1	4	15.8	33.3
Deming, Austin	R-R	6-0	200	12-21-99	.333	.429	1.000	2	7	6	2	2	1	0	1	1	1	0	0	0	1	0	0	14.3	14.3
Diaz, Victor	R-R	5-10	175	11-25-01	.226	.292	.452	29	106	93	12	21	6	0	5	23	9	1	0	3	27	2	0	8.5	25.5
Encarnacion, Yamal	B-R	5-8	150	9-08-03	.314	.405	.314	12	43	35	8	11	0	0	0	3	5	1	0	1	7	4	2	11.6	16.3
Familia, Daniel	R-R	6-0	203	9-05-02	.222	.382	.481	13	34	27	4	6	2	1	1	4	5	2	0	0	9	0	0	14.7	26.5
Ferreras, Pascanel	R-R	5-10	185	11-25-01	.000	.500	.000	1	2	1	0	0	0	0	0	0	1	0	0	0	0	0	0	50.0	0.0
Fisher, Cameron	L-R	6-2	210	6-12-01	.000	.000	.000	1	3	3	0	0	0	0	0	0	0	0	0	0	1	0	0	0.0	33.3
Gaston, Sandro	R-R	6-3	210	12-16-02	.000	.000	.000	1	1	1	0	0	0	0	0	0	0	0	0	0	0	0	0	0.0	0.0
Gomez, Kenni	L-R	5-11	185	5-14-05	.208	.311	.321	16	61	53	8	11	0	0	2	12	6	2	0	0	12	8	3	9.8	19.7
Gonzalez, Cristian	R-R	6-3	210	10-22-01	.280	.333	.600	7	27	25	6	7	2	0	2	5	2	0	0	0	1	0	0	7.4	3.7
Gonzalez, Richi	R-R	6-2	182	12-29-02	.224	.378	.345	21	74	58	8	13	4	0	1	5	12	3	0	1	17	0	2	16.2	23.0
Guilamo, Freddy	R-R	5-11	160	12-10-00	.571	.667	.857	5	9	7	2	4	2	0	0	3	1	1	0	0	1	0	0	11.1	11.1
Guillemette, Garret	R-R	6-1	210	9-04-01	.000	.000	.000	1	3	3	0	0	0	0	0	0	0	0	0	0	0	0	0	0.0	0.0
Hernandez, Alberto	R-R	6-0	169	2-04-04	.257	.375	.414	40	169	140	23	36	14	1	2	20	24	3	1	1	31	9	2	14.2	18.3
Huezo, Anthony	L-R	6-2	170	11-02-05	.171	.333	.244	12	51	41	10	7	0	0	1	5	9	1	0	0	11	1	0	17.6	21.6
Hurtado, Carlos	R-R	6-0	170	5-18-01	.269	.321	.423	9	28	26	3	7	1	0	1	4	0	2	0	0	5	1	0	0.0	17.9
Jaworsky, Chase	L-R	6-1	170	7-31-04	.281	.395	.281	9	38	32	4	9	0	0	0	2	6	0	0	0	6	0	0	15.8	15.8
Johnson, Ryan	R-R	6-0	175	12-27-00	.500	.600	.500	2	5	4	0	2	0	0	0	0	0	1	0	0	0	0	0	0.0	0.0
Luciano, Waner	R-R	6-1	170	1-13-05	.247	.345	.476	45	194	166	33	41	8	0	10	29	22	4	0	2	36	5	0	11.3	18.6
Machado, Dixon	R-R	6-1	190	2-22-92	.235	.500	.353	7	28	17	3	4	2	0	0	1	8	2	0	1	3	0	0	28.6	10.7
Machandy, Roilan	R-R	6-0	170	5-18-01	.071	.133	.071	4	15	14	2	1	0	0	0	0	0	1	0	0	5	4	0	0.0	33.3
Matthews, Brice	R-R	6-0	175	3-16-02	.000	.167	.000	2	6	5	0	0	0	0	0	0	1	0	0	0	1	2	1	16.7	16.7
Nieves, Hector	L-R	6-3	185	7-08-03	.204	.371	.315	20	70	54	7	11	3	0	1	5	12	3	0	1	16	5	0	17.1	22.9
Nunez, Alejandro	L-R	5-10	179	9-08-04	.259	.390	.356	40	164	135	21	35	10	0	1	17	25	4	0	0	24	16	3	15.2	14.6
Ochoa, Nehomar	R-R	6-4	210	7-31-05	.222	.310	.528	12	42	36	10	8	2	0	3	9	3	2	0	1	7	1	0	7.1	16.7
Palma, Miguel	R-R	5-8	170	1-04-02	.385	.357	.577	7	28	26	5	10	2	0	1	8	0	0	0	2	4	0	0	0.0	14.3
Perez, Frank	R-R	6-2	180	12-24-01	.200	.556	.200	3	9	5	2	1	0	0	0	0	3	1	0	0	3	0	0	33.3	33.3
Santander, Juan	R-R	6-2	180	12-09-02	.239	.345	.479	27	84	71	10	17	5	0	4	16	11	1	0	1	16	1	0	13.1	19.0
Sherwin, Anthony	L-R	5-11	190	6-20-02	.391	.545	.522	9	33	23	8	9	3	0	0	5	9	0	0	1	7	2	1	27.3	21.2
Wagner, Will	L-R	5-11	210	7-29-98	.313	.542	.375	6	25	16	5	5	1	0	0	2	7	1	0	0	1	1	0	28.0	4.0
Whitaker, Tyler	R-R	6-4	190	8-02-02	.333	.429	.583	3	14	12	2	4	0	0	1	1	1	1	0	0	5	0	0	7.1	35.7
Williams, Jeron	R-R	6-1	180	9-29-00	.250	.250	.250	2	4	4	0	1	0	0	0	0	0	0	0	0	0	0	0	0.0	0.0

Pitching	B-T	Ht.	Wt.	DOB	W	L	ERA	G	GS	SV	IP	Hits	Runs	ER	HR	BB	SO	AVG	OBP	SLG	SO%	BB%	BF
Austin, Kelly	R-R	6-0	195	12-17-00	0	0	0.00	1	0	0	0	1	3	3	0	2	0	1.000	1.000	1.000	0.0	66.7	3
Bloss, Jake	R-R	6-3	205	6-23-01	0	0	3.86	2	2	0	2	2	1	1	0	1	3	.222	.300	.222	30.0	10.0	10
Buttrey, Ty	L-R	6-6	240	3-31-93	0	0	0.00	3	3	0	4	1	0	0	0	1	4	.091	.167	.091	33.3	8.3	12
Carrillo, Yefri	R-R	6-2	170	1-13-01	1	0	4.32	8	2	0	17	5	10	8	0	21	15	.088	.358	.123	18.5	25.9	81
Dixon, Joey	R-R	6-2	190	1-01-02	0	0	0.00	1	0	0	1	1	0	0	0	0	0	.250	.250	.250	0.0	0.0	4
Espinosa, Carlos	R-R	6-2	188	8-08-01	0	1	3.46	4	1	0	13	12	7	5	0	4	21	.235	.286	.275	37.5	7.1	56
Garcia, Elvis	R-R	6-0	165	9-24-02	0	3	7.50	6	3	0	18	22	18	15	2	10	17	.286	.368	.455	19.3	11.4	88
Garcia, Heribert	R-R	6-0	220	10-02-99	2	1	6.17	8	2	0	23	18	17	16	4	16	24	.209	.337	.372	23.1	15.4	104
Guedez, Jose	R-R	6-0	169	9-27-01	0	1	7.71	3	3	0	5	2	5	4	0	6	8	.125	.364	.125	36.4	27.3	22
Guilamo, Freddy	R-R	5-11	160	12-10-00	0	0	9.00	1	0	0	1	1	1	1	0	2	1	.250	.571	.250	14.3	28.6	7
Hicks, James	R-R	6-2	190	5-09-01	0	0	1.59	3	2	0	6	5	5	1	0	2	6	.227	.292	.227	25.0	8.3	24
Hurtado, Carlos	R-R	6-0	170	5-18-01	0	0	0.00	1	0	0	1	1	0	0	0	1	2	.250	.400	.500	40.0	20.0	5
Jorge, Roger	R-R	6-1	180	4-03-01	4	0	5.82	10	1	0	22	13	16	14	1	35	23	.186	.455	.343	20.9	31.8	110
Langford, Colby	L-L	6-3	195	4-30-02	1	0	5.06	4	1	0	5	4	3	3	0	4	6	.222	.364	.222	27.3	18.2	22
Macuare, Angel	R-R	6-2	250	3-03-00	0	1	5.06	3	3	0	5	6	3	3	0	0	9	.286	.273	.429	40.9	0.0	22
Martinez, Angelo	R-R	6-1	155	6-17-00	0	2	19.29	11	0	0	7	8	18	15	1	23	9	.296	.636	.519	16.4	41.8	55
Mateo, Carlos	R-R	6-1	164	12-16-03	0	0	5.19	7	1	1	9	8	5	5	2	4	12	.242	.324	.424	32.4	10.8	37
Matthews, Zack	B-R	6-0	205	1-31-99	0	0	19.29	4	1	0	2	4	5	5	0	7	1	.444	.688	.778	6.3	43.8	16
Mejia, Sandy	R-R	6-0	160	1-03-04	2	1	2.17	12	2	2	29	15	7	7	1	10	42	.152	.243	.253	37.8	9.0	111
Mercedes, Abel	R-R	6-1	185	6-29-02	0	3	6.83	11	3	0	29	20	26	22	0	38	49	.194	.428	.223	33.8	26.2	145
Pecko, Ethan	R-R	6-2	195	8-25-02	0	1	3.00	2	1	0	3	4	1	1	0	0	3	.308	.308	.385	23.1	0.0	13
Pena, Alain	R-R	5-11	155	4-10-03	3	1	3.22	11	6	0	36	27	17	13	5	17	32	.203	.301	.361	20.9	11.1	153

Pitching	B-T	Ht.	Wt.	DOB	W	L	ERA	G	GS	SV	IP	Hits	Runs	ER	HR	BB	SO	AVG	OBP	SLG	SO%	BB%	BF
Rodriguez, Raimy	R-R	6-1	185	7-16-05	1	1	5.89	6	1	0	18	13	12	12	1	15	24	.197	.372	.318	27.9	17.4	86
Rosario, Leomar	R-R	6-6	217	6-11-03	1	1	6.32	6	1	0	16	14	11	11	1	16	16	.250	.419	.339	21.3	21.3	75
Sanchez, Wilmy	R-R	5-9	193	12-17-03	2	0	2.43	10	2	0	33	24	9	9	1	20	34	.198	.322	.281	23.8	14.0	143
Santander, Juan	R-R	6-2	180	12-09-02	0	0	0.00	1	0	0	1	0	0	0	0	0	0	.000	.000	.000	0.0	0.0	2
Santos, Yeriel	R-R	6-0	165	11-20-03	2	4	5.35	11	5	0	35	25	26	21	4	30	42	.189	.341	.364	25.6	18.3	164
Soto, Juan	R-R	6-2	209	4-30-03	0	1	8.06	11	3	0	26	28	27	23	3	25	17	.277	.426	.446	13.1	19.2	130
Torres, Alejandro	R-R	6-1	238	4-26-01	0	1	6.75	2	0	0	3	3	2	2	1	1	3	.300	.333	.800	25.0	8.3	12
True, Derek	R-R	6-2	180	4-25-01	0	0	16.20	2	1	0	2	2	3	3	0	2	3	.333	.500	.500	37.5	25.0	8
Vega, Luis	R-R	6-3	165	11-16-01	4	2	4.97	13	1	0	29	25	17	16	2	13	39	.229	.312	.349	31.0	10.3	126
Victorino, Luis	R-R	6-0	167	8-18-02	3	0	4.26	12	0	3	19	14	10	9	0	20	18	.209	.393	.239	20.2	22.5	89

Fielding

C: Caldera 20, Diaz 16, Santander 14, Palma 6, Bush 6, Hurtado 5, Guilamo 4, Guillemette 1. **1B:** Diaz 14, Del Rosario 6, Santander 6, Gonzalez 5, Casserilla 4, Luciano 4, Caldera 3, Arias 2, Brewer 2, Bush 2, Nieves 2, Palma 2, Nunez 1, Wagner 1, Hernandez 1, Hurtado 1. **2B:** Hernandez 15, Nunez 12, Sherwin 7, Encarnacion 6, Nieves 5, Wagner 4, Jaworsky 3, Johnson 1, Luciano 1, Arias 1, Casserilla 1, Del Rosario 1. **3B:** Luciano 27, Del Rosario 6, Hernandez 6, Arias 5, Casserilla 4, Deming 2, Whitaker 2, Williams 1, Machado 1, Wagner 1, Encarnacion 1, Gonzalez 1, Johnson 1. **SS:** Nunez 19, Hernandez 18, Jaworsky 6, Gonzalez 6, Machado 4, Matthews 2, Nieves 1. OF: Colon 36, Del Rosario 21, Baez 14, Gomez 12, Huezo 12, Ochoa 12, Luciano 11, Nieves 11, Familia 9, Nunez 8, Barefoot 7, Encarnacion 5, Gonzalez 3, Machandy 3, Perez 2, Brewer 2, Fisher 1, Whitaker 1.

DSL ASTROS — ROOKIE

DOMINICAN SUMMER LEAGUE

Batting	B-T	Ht.	Wt.	DOB	AVG	OBP	SLG	G	PA	AB	R	H	2B	3B	HR	RBI	BB	HBP	SH	SF	SO	SB	CS	BB%	SO%
Arias, Jose	R-R	5-10	170	11-03-04	.152	.263	.258	28	76	66	12	10	1	0	2	6	8	2	0	0	34	4	2	10.5	44.7
Caldera, Francisco	R-R	6-1	193	3-09-06	.198	.327	.333	30	98	81	12	16	3	1	2	10	15	1	0	1	22	1	0	15.3	22.4
Capellan, Samuel	R-R	5-11	155	1-05-05	.193	.266	.422	25	94	83	9	16	2	4	3	15	6	3	0	2	43	3	0	6.4	45.7
Castro, Daniel	B-R	5-10	190	10-21-03	.188	.359	.250	30	103	80	14	15	3	1	0	10	15	7	0	1	26	6	1	14.6	25.2
Cauro, Carlos	R-R	6-2	184	6-14-05	.313	.444	.521	47	180	144	25	45	12	0	6	25	29	6	0	1	43	1	0	16.1	23.9
Colon, Andy	R-R	6-1	176	1-05-04	.138	.324	.276	35	74	58	14	8	2	0	2	6	14	2	0	0	29	6	3	18.9	39.2
Colon, Luis	B-R	5-8	160	12-02-03	.286	.419	.400	34	129	105	24	30	6	3	0	11	23	1	0	0	17	13	5	17.8	13.2
De Leon, Darwin	R-R	5-9	156	10-31-03	.317	.470	.490	35	134	104	29	33	6	0	4	25	23	7	0	0	21	10	3	17.2	15.7
De Paula, Axell	R-R	5-10	178	10-18-04	.276	.371	.398	39	143	123	24	34	6	0	3	22	10	9	0	1	40	6	3	7.0	28.0
Diaz, Camilo	R-R	6-3	208	9-05-05	.209	.374	.353	48	195	153	29	32	6	2	4	15	41	0	0	1	64	7	2	21.0	32.8
Diaz, Jhon	R-R	6-0	162	3-26-05	.250	.403	.330	45	144	112	23	28	6	0	1	21	20	10	0	2	27	4	6	13.9	18.8
Gonzalez, Cristopfer	R-R	6-5	167	7-20-05	.273	.385	.418	37	131	110	17	30	4	3	2	19	16	4	0	0	25	1	6	12.2	19.1
Lara, Wilton	R-R	5-11	175	1-21-04	.201	.265	.343	44	147	134	22	27	11	1	2	20	8	4	0	1	56	11	1	5.4	38.1
Lebron, Ariel	R-R	5-11	148	5-18-05	.313	.469	.364	35	131	99	14	31	1	2	0	15	13	17	1	1	21	5	6	9.9	16.0
Marcelino, Marco	R-R	5-9	190	10-30-04	.203	.422	.305	24	83	59	8	12	0	0	2	14	16	7	0	1	26	3	4	19.3	31.3
Mujica, Jesus	R-R	5-11	179	9-02-05	.224	.330	.337	32	115	98	16	22	4	2	1	15	12	4	0	1	40	2	6	10.4	34.8
Pereira, Sandro	B-R	5-7	147	9-30-05	.298	.457	.427	43	166	124	30	37	5	4	1	18	17	20	4	1	30	8	3	10.2	18.1
Perez, Eduardo	R-R	6-4	214	7-24-06	.263	.331	.415	34	130	118	13	31	6	0	4	15	7	5	0	0	45	3	0	5.4	34.6
Pratt, Karniel	R-R	5-10	170	1-03-05	.271	.425	.457	44	179	140	34	38	5	3	5	26	34	4	0	1	53	22	5	19.0	29.6
Quesada, Luis	R-R	6-2	193	1-18-05	.247	.398	.438	26	93	73	10	18	3	1	3	8	13	6	0	1	20	1	0	14.0	21.5
Quintana, Roiner	R-R	5-11	157	6-20-05	.293	.408	.390	38	147	123	25	36	4	1	2	17	23	1	0	0	28	10	4	15.6	19.0
Ramirez, German	R-R	6-0	179	7-28-06	.257	.324	.328	48	206	183	23	47	6	2	1	21	15	4	2	2	39	3	4	7.3	18.9
Ramirez, Rafael	R-R	6-1	185	11-09-04	.269	.357	.417	41	126	108	24	29	3	2	3	20	14	2	0	2	27	5	2	11.1	21.4
Robledo, Jose	B-R	5-7	188	9-14-03	.270	.374	.338	45	176	148	33	40	6	2	0	13	22	3	1	1	32	7	4	12.5	18.2
Sanchez, Brayan	R-R	6-0	195	12-19-04	.123	.326	.137	37	96	73	12	9	1	0	0	9	20	2	1	0	30	5	0	20.8	31.3
Sierra, Juan	R-R	6-1	208	12-08-05	.174	.327	.298	41	150	121	21	21	3	0	4	10	25	3	0	1	29	1	1	16.7	19.3
Sosa, Andrews	R-R	5-10	160	1-07-05	.257	.383	.345	41	141	113	21	29	4	0	2	13	23	2	0	3	23	6	4	16.3	16.3
Trujillo, Kedaur	R-R	5-11	188	3-02-04	.252	.359	.473	39	153	131	26	33	5	0	8	26	20	2	0	0	36	6	2	13.1	23.5
Valencia, Esmil	R-R	5-10	182	10-09-05	.262	.346	.388	46	211	183	35	48	9	4	2	24	19	6	0	3	31	11	5	9.0	14.7
Vasquez, Yosweld	R-R	5-9	176	11-08-04	.188	.269	.319	23	78	69	11	13	3	0	2	10	4	4	0	1	9	2	0	5.1	11.5
Villarroel, Jancel	R-R	5-8	176	1-17-05	.313	.435	.491	47	200	163	46	51	14	0	5	29	28	8	0	1	32	6	4	14.0	16.0

Pitching	B-T	Ht.	Wt.	DOB	W	L	ERA	G	GS	SV	IP	Hits	Runs	ER	HR	BB	SO	AVG	OBP	SLG	SO%	BB%	BF
Aguilar, Luis	R-R	5-11	176	4-04-04	3	2	4.84	13	5	0	35	39	21	19	3	13	41	.275	.348	.394	25.9	8.2	158
Aparicio, Antony	R-R	6-2	183	10-18-02	2	1	2.84	13	7	0	32	27	12	10	2	10	40	.225	.285	.300	30.8	7.7	130
Arias, Jose	R-R	5-10	170	11-03-04	1	0	21.00	2	0	0	3	6	7	7	2	3	0	.400	.500	1.000	0.0	16.7	18
Aybar, Angel	R-R	6-3	162	4-28-04	1	1	9.70	11	1	0	21	22	25	23	1	21	18	.278	.422	.468	17.5	20.4	103
Cabrera, Geraldo	R-R	6-1	176	10-07-04	0	2	9.53	9	2	0	11	10	15	12	0	17	10	.222	.438	.267	15.6	26.6	64
Carrera, Jesus	R-R	5-11	160	11-27-04	2	0	3.32	6	3	0	19	6	7	7	0	6	27	.100	.214	.117	38.6	8.6	70
Castellar, Jonaiker	R-R	5-10	141	5-23-02	1	2	4.79	12	7	0	36	30	21	19	6	22	45	.227	.350	.439	28.5	13.9	158
Colon, Luis	B-R	5-8	160	12-02-03	0	0	0.00	1	0	0	0	1	0	0	0	0	1	.500	.500	1.000	50.0	0.0	2
Coronel, Enrique	R-R	6-0	175	8-25-00	1	1	3.71	12	8	0	34	36	15	14	1	9	40	.267	.317	.393	27.6	6.2	145
Cruz, Anthony	R-R	5-11	179	8-19-02	1	1	3.53	14	6	3	43	37	19	17	1	17	50	.240	.322	.344	27.9	9.5	179
De La Cruz, Cristian	R-R	5-11	194	1-16-03	2	2	3.81	15	0	3	26	24	16	11	1	16	22	.247	.351	.330	19.1	13.9	115
De La Cruz, Luis	R-R	6-0	182	8-04-02	3	1	4.81	12	5	0	34	26	18	18	1	20	38	.215	.351	.331	25.7	13.5	148
Diaz, Norbis	R-R	6-0	165	8-10-04	1	3	6.14	9	2	0	15	23	19	10	1	15	19	.343	.464	.507	22.6	17.9	84
Frias, Francisco	R-R	5-11	190	10-15-04	2	1	3.21	10	0	0	14	12	5	5	2	7	19	.222	.323	.407	30.6	11.3	62
Geraldo, Jorge	R-R	6-6	197	12-07-01	2	0	3.86	11	6	1	28	25	12	12	1	22	38	.240	.382	.327	29.0	16.8	131
Gil, Franklin	R-R	5-11	155	1-06-03	2	1	1.42	12	5	1	38	22	8	6	1	8	46	.167	.211	.242	32.4	5.6	142
Gomez, Miguel	R-R	5-11	152	6-12-06	2	1	6.23	12	4	0	26	20	21	18	2	30	28	.213	.417	.340	21.2	22.7	132
Gonzalez, Edwin	R-R	6-2	153	7-19-04	2	4	7.15	12	2	0	23	23	20	18	0	17	22	.267	.422	.337	20.2	15.6	109
Gonzalez, Rafael	R-R	5-11	195	7-18-04	3	1	4.81	13	6	0	43	31	24	23	0	23	53	.199	.323	.295	28.5	12.4	186
Landeta, David	R-R	6-2	244	3-28-03	1	1	5.93	13	2	1	27	32	21	18	2	16	28	.291	.397	.391	21.4	12.2	131

Liriano, Eudy	R-R	5-10	160	5-27-04	5	1	4.94	15	0	2	24	19	15	13	1	14	21	.221	.336	.349	19.6	13.1	107
Maican, Mauricio	R-R	5-10	150	12-28-03	3	4	5.40	12	3	2	25	20	18	15	2	32	43	.225	.426	.326	35.2	26.2	122
Marquez, Pedro	R-R	5-11	172	12-07-01	2	2	6.05	14	1	4	19	21	15	13	1	17	28	.273	.411	.364	29.5	17.9	95
Marte, Julio	R-R	6-5	180	4-27-03	1	1	1.25	13	2	2	36	30	10	5	1	12	49	.231	.301	.300	33.6	8.2	146
Martinez, Jeremy	R-R	6-2	200	6-07-04	2	0	3.49	12	2	0	28	25	16	11	2	18	24	.260	.385	.354	19.5	14.6	123
Martinez, Yefri	R-R	6-0	205	1-26-03	0	3	5.60	13	0	2	18	22	17	11	0	14	15	.297	.429	.351	16.5	15.4	91
Mendez, Abel	R-R	6-4	205	4-04-03	1	0	6.75	12	1	0	17	20	17	13	0	20	19	.286	.463	.357	20.0	21.1	95
Mendoza, Manuel	R-R	6-1	195	8-03-06	1	1	5.27	13	0	0	14	13	13	8	1	15	12	.260	.464	.400	17.1	21.4	70
Mori, Oswald	R-R	6-4	185	6-20-02	1	0	2.63	5	1	1	14	12	5	4	0	8	14	.245	.373	.347	23.7	13.6	59
Mujica, Jesus	R-R	5-11	179	9-02-05	0	0	0.00	1	0	0	0	0	0	0	0	0	0	.000	.000	.000	0.0	0.0	1
Nunez, Juan	R-R	6-0	155	10-13-03	3	0	3.00	15	0	3	24	15	12	8	0	11	27	.183	.313	.268	27.0	11.0	100
Ogando, Joan	R-R	6-1	179	5-23-04	2	0	1.74	9	1	1	10	5	2	2	1	10	10	.156	.372	.313	23.3	23.3	43
Peralta, Engel Daniel	R-R	6-4	190	6-03-04	3	0	5.35	11	4	1	34	37	22	20	6	11	56	.270	.329	.504	37.6	7.4	149
Peralta, Jean	R-R	6-4	185	7-05-03	0	0	0.00	2	1	0	1	0	0	0	0	2	1	.000	.400	.000	20.0	40.0	5
Pichardo, Jank	R-R	6-1	170	8-04-04	0	0	6.28	12	0	0	14	13	10	10	0	8	7	.241	.359	.296	10.9	12.5	64
Presinal, Cristopher	R-R	6-2	156	11-28-04	0	3	6.32	10	3	1	16	11	15	11	2	23	20	.193	.429	.316	23.8	27.4	84
Ramos, Porfirio	R-R	5-10	163	12-03-03	0	0	9.82	8	0	0	7	9	9	8	0	16	6	.409	.610	.500	14.6	39.0	41
Rodriguez, Raimy	R-R	6-1	185	7-16-05	0	1	4.05	4	2	0	13	10	9	6	0	10	22	.196	.328	.235	36.1	16.4	61
Rojas, Cesar	R-R	6-3	162	5-12-02	0	0	0.00	1	0	0	1	1	0	0	0	2	1	.250	.500	.500	16.7	33.3	6
Sanchez, Liz	L-L	5-9	190	4-11-01	0	0	0.00	1	1	0	1	0	0	0	0	2	2	.000	.400	.000	40.0	40.0	5
Sanchez, Yanquiel	L-L	6-3	200	1-28-01	0	1	1.00	9	6	0	18	7	2	2	0	4	24	.117	.172	.150	37.5	6.3	64
Serrano, Jose	R-R	6-2	212	2-14-04	0	0	5.40	3	0	0	3	2	4	2	0	1	4	.143	.200	.143	26.7	6.7	15
Severino, Wander	R-R	6-0	163	10-24-03	3	2	3.58	13	4	0	33	30	19	13	2	20	36	.248	.363	.339	24.7	13.7	146
Silvera, Fernando	L-L	5-11	190	12-08-02	0	0	4.15	3	1	0	4	5	3	2	0	2	1	.313	.389	.375	5.6	11.1	18
Varela, Jose	R-R	6-1	183	10-29-04	5	1	2.49	13	5	1	47	27	16	13	2	24	71	.166	.284	.276	37.4	12.6	190

Fielding

C: Sanchez 31, Sosa 22, Castro 21, Villarroel 19, Trujillo 19, Cauro 18, Vasquez 11, Caldera 10. **1B:** Villarroel 24, Cauro 19, Vasquez 18, Trujillo 15, Sanchez 11, Castro 10, Lara 10, Quesada 9, Caldera 9, Colon 9, Gonzalez 8, Robledo 2, Perez 1. **2B:** Colon 27, Diaz 25, Pereira 22, Capellan 16, Mujica 10, De Leon 9, Sosa 8, Robledo 7, Lara 5, Ramirez 2. **3B:** Ramirez 40, Diaz 28, Mujica 15, De Leon 12, Lara 11, Pereira 11, Robledo 11, Colon 3, Capellan 2, Gonzalez 1. **SS:** Diaz 38, Ramirez 34, Robledo 21, Lara 21, De Leon 4, Colon 1, Mujica 1. **OF:** Pratt 44, Valencia 42, De Paula 39, Quintana 38, Lebron 35, Sierra 33, Gonzalez 26, Perez 24, Arias 23, Colon 23, Marcelino 22, Quesada 12, Ramirez 8.

Kansas City Royals

SEASON SYNOPSIS: Despite new manager Matt Quatraro and J.J. Picollo taking over for Dayton Moore as the new head of baseball operations, the Royals careened to 106 losses, tying the worst mark in franchise history. It's their third 100-loss season since the 2015 World Series championship.

HIGH POINT: Kansas City was frisky down the stretch, going 15-12 in September and October, including 5-1 against the Astros. Bobby Witt Jr. led the way as he wrapped up a 30-homer, 49-steal season. Witt batted .301/.343/.563 with 16 homers after the all-star break, with just 41 strikeouts in 303 plate appearances, as his skills started catching up to his talent.

LOW POINT: The Royals were never in it, but June was a disastrous 6-20 slog that included a 10-game losing streak in which they were outscored 61-26.

NOTABLE ROOKIES: Maikel Garcia, coming off a nine-game cameo in 2022, seized the everyday third base job, stealing 23 bases, posting a .272/.323/.358 slash line and boasting strong Statcast metrics, particularly defensively (98th percentile for range/outs above average) and with some hopeful offensive indicators for the future. Catcher Freddy Fermin was old for a rookie at 28 but showed some pop with nine homers in 217 at-bats before a season-ending right hand fracture. Outfielder Drew Waters also had flashes defensively but struggled offensively (.228/.300/.377).

KEY TRANSACTIONS: Signing veteran reliever Aroldis Chapman as a reclamation project in the offseason paid off when the Royals flipped him to the Rangers on June 30 for lefty Cole Ragans. Texas' 2016 first-round pick, Ragans blossomed, becoming Kansas City's best starter with a 5-2, 2.64 mark, 89 strikeouts in 71 innings and one of the hardest fastballs by a lefty starter, averaging 96.5 mph. Righty Jose Cuas was sent to the Cubs for outfielder Nelson Velazquez, who belted 14 homers in his Kansas City debut. The Royals added to their front office in September, adding Brian Bridges, a former Braves scouting director, to lead their amateur staff.

DOWN ON THE FARM: The Royals' MiLB talent is less than one would expect for a team that has regularly picked at the top of the draft. The team had no Top 100 Prospects for much of 2023 and finished with a .472 overall organizational winning percentage.

OPENING DAY PAYROLL: $92,468,100 (23rd).

PLAYERS OF THE YEAR

MAJOR LEAGUE

Bobby Witt Jr.
SS
.276/.319/.495
28 2B, 11 3B, 30 HR
49 SB, 97 R

MINOR LEAGUE

Mason Barnett
RHP
(HiA/AA)
6-7, 3.30
3.9 BB/9, 10.8 SO/9

ORGANIZATION LEADERS

Batting		*Minimum 250 AB
MAJORS		
* AVG	Bobby Witt Jr.	.276
* OPS	Bobby Witt Jr.	.813
HR	Bobby Witt Jr.	30
RBI	Bobby Witt Jr.	96
MINORS		
* AVG	Samad Taylor, Omaha	.301
* OBP	Samad Taylor, Omaha	.418
* SLG	Angelo Castellano, Omaha	.489
* OPS	Samad Taylor, Omaha	.884
R	Tyler Tolbert, NW Arkansas	95
H	Tyler Tolbert, NW Arkansas	143
TB	Tyler Tolbert, NW Arkansas	217
2B	Peyton Wilson, NW Arkansas	33
3B	Tyler Tolbert, NW Arkansas	10
HR	Jorge Bonifacio, NW Arkansas	22
RBI	Jorge Bonifacio, NW Arkansas	88
BB	Carter Jensen, Quad Cities	92
SO	Brett Squires, Columbia	146
SB	Tyler Tolbert, NW Arkansas	50

Pitching		#Minimum 75 IP
MAJORS		
W	Brady Singer	8
# ERA	Zack Greinke	5.06
SO	Brady Singer	133
SV	Scott Barlow	13
MINORS		
W	Chandler Champlain, Q.Cities/NW Ark.	11
L	Noah Cameron, Q. Cities/NW Ark.	12
# ERA	Mason Barnett, Quad Cities/NW Ark.	3.30
G	Evan Sisk, Omaha	58
GS	Andrew Hoffman, NW Ark./Omaha	27
SV	Anderson Paulino, Quad Cities/NW Ark.	12
IP	Chandler Champlain, Q.Cities/NW Ark.	135
BB	Drew Parrish, NW Ark./Omaha	73
SO	Mason Barnett, Quad Cities/NW Ark.	137
# AVG	Eric Cerantola, Q. Cities/NW Ark.	.198

2023 PERFORMANCE

General Manager: J.J. Picollo. **Farm Director:** Mitch Maier. **Scouting Director:** Danny Ontiveros.

Class	Team	League	W	L	PCT	Finish	Manager
Majors	Kansas City Royals	American	56	106	.346	14 (15)	Matt Quatraro
Triple-A	Omaha Storm Chasers	International	68	77	.469	16 (20)	Mike Jirschele
Double-A	NW Arkansas Naturals	Texas	64	74	.464	10 (10)	Tommy Shields
High-A	Quad Cities River Bandits	Midwest	55	77	.417	12 (12)	Brooks Conrad
Low-A	Columbia Fireflies	Carolina	66	65	.504	8 (12)	Tony Pena
Rookie	ACL Royals	Arizona Complex	31	25	.554	7 (17)	Jesus Azuaje
Rookie	DSL Royals Blue	Dominican Sum.	29	25	.537	18 (50)	Sergio De Luna
Overall 2023 Minor League Record			335	375	.472	24th (30)	

ORGANIZATION STATISTICS

KANSAS CITY ROYALS

AMERICAN LEAGUE

Batting	B-T	Ht.	Wt.	DOB	AVG	OBP	SLG	G	PA	AB	R	H	2B	3B	HR	RBI	BB	HBP	SH	SF	SO	SB	CS	BB%	SO%
Beaty, Matt	L-R	6-0	215	4-28-93	.232	.358	.304	26	67	56	7	13	4	0	0	3	6	5	0	0	12	0	0	9.0	17.9
Blanco, Dairon	R-R	5-11	170	4-26-93	.258	.324	.452	69	138	124	19	32	7	4	3	18	10	2	2	0	33	24	5	7.2	23.9
Bradley, Jackie	L-R	5-10	196	4-19-90	.133	.188	.210	43	113	105	10	14	5	0	1	6	5	2	1	0	29	0	0	4.4	25.7
Cropley, Tyler	R-R	5-8	185	12-10-95	.167	.143	.167	2	7	6	0	1	0	0	0	1	0	0	0	1	2	0	0	0.0	28.6
Dozier, Hunter	R-R	6-4	220	8-22-91	.183	.253	.305	29	91	82	8	15	2	1	2	9	8	0	0	1	29	2	0	8.8	31.9
Duffy, Matt	R-R	6-2	190	1-15-91	.251	.306	.325	79	209	191	17	48	8	0	2	16	12	4	0	2	39	1	0	5.7	18.7
Eaton, Nate	R-R	5-11	185	12-22-96	.075	.125	.075	28	56	53	2	4	0	0	0	1	2	1	0	0	21	3	0	3.6	37.5
Fermin, Freddy	R-R	5-9	200	5-16-95	.281	.321	.461	70	235	217	26	61	10	1	9	32	13	1	1	3	50	0	0	5.5	21.3
Garcia, Maikel	R-R	6-0	145	3-03-00	.272	.323	.358	123	515	464	59	126	20	4	4	50	38	2	1	10	115	23	7	7.4	22.3
Isbel, Kyle	L-R	5-11	190	3-03-97	.240	.282	.380	91	313	292	45	70	22	2	5	34	17	1	1	2	59	7	1	5.4	18.8
Loftin, Nick	R-R	5-11	180	9-25-98	.323	.368	.435	19	68	62	10	20	5	1	0	10	4	1	0	1	12	2	0	5.9	17.6
Lopez, Nicky	L-R	5-11	180	3-13-95	.213	.323	.281	68	190	160	19	34	5	3	0	13	21	5	4	0	30	4	2	11.1	15.8
Massey, Michael	L-R	6-0	190	3-22-98	.229	.274	.381	129	461	428	42	98	18	1	15	55	24	4	1	4	99	6	2	5.2	21.5
Melendez, MJ	L-R	6-1	190	11-29-98	.235	.316	.398	148	602	533	65	125	29	5	16	56	62	3	0	4	170	6	4	10.3	28.2
Olivares, Edward	R-R	6-2	190	3-06-96	.263	.317	.452	107	385	354	47	93	23	4	12	36	22	7	0	2	64	11	5	5.7	16.6
Pasquantino, Vinnie	L-L	6-4	245	10-10-97	.247	.324	.437	61	260	231	24	57	17	0	9	26	25	2	0	1	31	0	0	9.6	11.9
Perez, Salvador	R-R	6-3	255	5-10-90	.255	.292	.422	140	580	538	59	137	21	0	23	80	19	13	0	8	135	0	0	3.3	23.3
Porter, Logan	R-R	6-0	200	7-12-95	.194	.324	.323	11	38	31	4	6	1	0	1	3	5	1	1	0	11	0	0	13.2	28.9
Pratto, Nick	L-L	6-1	215	10-06-98	.232	.307	.353	95	345	306	33	71	16	0	7	35	29	6	0	4	138	1	1	8.4	40.0
Reyes, Franmil	R-R	6-5	265	7-07-95	.186	.231	.288	19	65	59	5	11	0	0	2	7	4	0	0	2	24	0	0	6.2	36.9
Taylor, Samad	R-R	5-8	160	7-11-98	.200	.279	.267	31	69	60	11	12	2	1	0	4	7	0	1	1	22	8	0	10.1	31.9
Velazquez, Nelson	R-R	6-0	190	12-26-98	.233	.299	.579	40	147	133	27	31	4	0	14	28	11	2	0	1	43	0	0	7.5	29.3
Waters, Drew	B-R	6-0	185	12-30-98	.228	.300	.377	98	337	302	40	69	11	5	8	32	27	5	0	3	107	16	5	8.0	31.8
Witt, Bobby	R-R	6-1	200	6-14-00	.276	.319	.495	158	694	641	97	177	28	11	30	96	40	4	1	8	121	49	15	5.8	17.4

Pitching	B-T	Ht.	Wt.	DOB	W	L	ERA	G	GS	SV	IP	Hits	Runs	ER	HR	BB	SO	AVG	OBP	SLG	SO%	BB%	BF
Barlow, Scott	R-R	6-3	210	12-18-92	2	4	5.35	38	0	13	39	38	26	23	3	22	47	.255	.351	.369	26.7	12.5	176
Bowlan, Jonathan	R-R	6-6	240	12-01-96	0	1	3.00	2	1	0	3	5	1	1	1	0	3	.357	.357	.571	21.4	0.0	14
Bubic, Kris	L-L	6-3	225	8-19-97	0	2	3.94	3	3	0	16	19	7	7	1	2	16	.292	.324	.385	23.5	2.9	68
Castillo, Max	R-R	6-2	280	5-04-99	0	1	4.43	7	0	0	20	20	10	10	2	9	10	.267	.364	.427	11.2	10.1	89
Chapman, Aroldis	L-L	6-4	218	2-28-88	4	2	2.45	31	0	2	29	16	10	8	0	20	53	.158	.295	.188	43.4	16.4	122
Clarke, Taylor	R-R	6-4	217	5-13-93	3	6	5.95	58	2	3	59	71	42	39	12	24	65	.303	.371	.513	24.4	9.0	266
Coleman, Dylan	R-R	6-5	230	9-16-96	0	2	8.84	23	1	0	18	18	19	18	3	19	21	.261	.438	.435	21.9	19.8	96
Cox, Austin	L-L	6-4	235	3-28-97	0	1	4.54	24	3	1	36	28	20	18	2	17	33	.220	.315	.339	22.1	11.4	149
Cruz, Steven	R-R	6-7	225	6-15-99	0	0	4.97	10	4	0	13	11	7	7	1	11	15	.220	.371	.400	24.2	17.7	62
Cuas, Jose	R-R	6-3	195	6-28-94	3	0	4.54	45	1	0	42	46	21	21	6	21	52	.277	.370	.452	27.1	10.9	192
Davidson, Tucker	L-L	6-2	215	3-25-96	0	1	5.03	20	1	0	20	20	12	11	4	8	15	.263	.341	.474	17.0	9.1	88
Duffy, Matt	R-R	6-2	190	1-15-91	0	0	4.50	2	0	0	2	3	1	1	1	0	0	.333	.400	.667	0.0	0.0	10
Eaton, Nate	R-R	5-11	185	12-22-96	0	0	0.00	1	0	0	1	2	0	0	0	0	1	.400	.400	.400	20.0	0.0	5
Garrett, Amir	R-L	6-5	239	5-03-92	0	1	3.33	27	0	0	24	22	11	9	4	20	28	.244	.378	.422	25.0	17.9	112
Greinke, Zack	R-R	6-2	200	10-21-83	2	15	5.06	30	27	0	142	158	82	80	25	23	97	.282	.312	.467	16.4	3.9	593
Hearn, Taylor	L-L	6-6	230	8-30-94	0	0	8.22	8	0	0	8	12	7	7	2	2	8	.343	.378	.629	21.6	5.4	37
Heasley, Jonathan	R-R	6-3	225	1-27-97	0	0	7.20	12	0	0	15	17	13	12	5	2	9	.288	.317	.610	14.3	3.2	63
Hernandez, Carlos	R-R	6-4	245	3-11-97	1	10	5.27	67	4	4	70	62	43	41	10	31	77	.233	.313	.425	25.7	10.3	300
Keller, Brad	R-R	6-5	255	7-27-95	3	4	4.57	11	9	0	45	42	26	23	3	45	31	.259	.427	.364	14.7	21.3	211
Kowar, Jackson	R-R	6-5	200	10-04-96	2	0	6.43	23	0	0	28	34	24	20	4	20	29	.293	.401	.457	21.2	14.6	137
Kriske, Brooks	R-R	6-3	190	2-03-94	0	0	4.05	4	0	0	7	3	3	3	2	4	6	.150	.280	.450	24.0	16.0	25
Lyles, Jordan	R-R	6-5	230	10-19-90	6	17	6.28	31	31	0	178	176	130	124	39	45	120	.255	.305	.501	16.0	6.0	748
Lynch, Daniel	L-L	6-6	200	11-17-96	3	4	4.64	9	9	0	52	50	29	27	9	16	34	.245	.300	.426	15.2	7.2	223
Marsh, Alec	R-R	6-2	220	5-14-98	3	9	5.69	17	8	0	74	77	50	47	16	39	85	.266	.369	.524	24.9	11.4	342
Mayers, Mike	R-R	6-2	220	12-06-91	1	2	6.15	6	2	0	26	34	19	18	4	10	17	.315	.370	.491	14.3	8.4	119
McArthur, James	R-R	6-7	230	12-11-96	1	0	4.63	18	2	4	23	20	12	12	2	2	23	.235	.256	.412	25.6	2.2	90
McMillon, John	L-R	6-3	230	1-27-98	0	0	2.25	4	0	0	4	1	1	1	1	0	8	.077	.077	.308	61.5	0.0	13

Ragans, Cole	L-L	6-4	190	12-12-97	5	2	2.64	12	12	0	72	50	23	21	3	27	89	.195	.273	.272	31.1	9.4	286
Singer, Brady	R-R	6-5	215	8-04-96	8	11	5.52	29	29	0	160	182	102	98	20	49	133	.287	.341	.467	18.9	7.0	702
Snider, Collin	R-R	6-4	195	10-10-95	0	0	4.87	20	1	1	20	24	12	11	3	13	11	.296	.389	.469	11.6	13.7	95
Staumont, Josh	R-R	6-3	200	12-21-93	0	0	5.40	21	1	0	20	16	12	12	1	13	24	.219	.352	.288	27.0	14.6	89
Taylor, Josh	L-L	6-5	245	3-02-93	1	3	8.15	17	1	0	18	22	17	16	4	9	26	.306	.373	.542	31.3	10.8	83
Veneziano, Anthony	L-L	6-5	205	9-01-97	0	0	0.00	2	0	0	2	2	2	0	0	2	1	.200	.333	.500	8.3	16.7	12
Wittgren, Nick	R-R	6-2	216	5-29-91	1	0	4.97	27	0	0	29	30	17	16	2	11	18	.263	.344	.404	14.1	8.6	128
Yarbrough, Ryan	R-L	6-5	205	12-31-91	4	5	4.24	14	7	0	51	52	24	24	5	9	29	.265	.316	.378	13.7	4.2	212
Zerpa, Angel	L-L	6-0	220	9-27-99	3	3	4.85	15	3	0	43	46	24	23	7	8	36	.272	.319	.462	19.8	4.4	182

Fielding

Catcher	PCT	G	PO	A	E	DP	PB
Cropley	1.000	2	14	1	0	0	0
Fermin	.982	65	470	24	9	5	5
Melendez	.988	10	80	1	1	0	2
Perez	.999	91	655	25	1	2	2
Porter	.988	11	78	3	1	0	0

First Base	PCT	G	PO	A	E	DP
Beaty	.991	15	97	9	1	13
Dozier	1.000	5	28	3	0	3
Duffy	.977	17	79	6	2	7
Loftin	1.000	8	33	3	0	2
Lopez	1.000	2	6	2	0	1
Melendez	.000	1	0	0	0	0
Pasquantino	.997	44	309	11	1	27
Perez	.994	23	149	14	1	13
Pratto	.993	78	512	28	4	51

Second Base	PCT	G	PO	A	E	DP
Duffy	.946	22	28	42	4	8
Garcia	1.000	4	6	6	0	2
Loftin	1.000	7	8	12	0	6
Lopez	.990	35	39	63	1	11
Massey	.993	118	193	257	3	71
Taylor	.966	12	15	13	1	4

Third Base	PCT	G	PO	A	E	DP
Dozier	.962	17	9	16	1	1
Duffy	.943	31	21	45	4	5
Eaton	.000	1	0	0	0	0
Garcia	.972	104	66	179	7	21
Loftin	1.000	4	1	11	0	2
Lopez	1.000	27	14	51	0	4
Taylor	.000	2	0	0	0	0

Shortstop	PCT	G	PO	A	E	DP
Duffy	.000	1	0	0	0	0
Garcia	.974	14	11	26	1	4
Lopez	1.000	5	9	11	0	4
Witt	.977	149	169	344	12	69

Outfield	PCT	G	PO	A	E	DP
Beaty	1.000	2	1	0	0	0
Blanco	1.000	68	98	4	0	0
Bradley	1.000	45	74	3	0	0
Dozier	.500	7	8	0	0	0
Eaton	.967	23	24	2	1	0
Isbel	.995	89	200	2	1	0
Lopez	1.000	2	3	1	0	0
Melendez	.970	130	244	11	8	1
Olivares	.655	59	88	4	3	1
Pratto	1.000	21	35	3	0	0
Reyes	.500	5	6	0	0	0
Taylor	.500	16	28	0	0	0
Velazquez	.988	29	56	0	1	0
Waters	.985	101	200	7	5	1

OMAHA STORM CHASERS — *TRIPLE-A*

INTERNATIONAL LEAGUE

Batting	B-T	Ht.	Wt.	DOB	AVG	OBP	SLG	G	PA	AB	R	H	2B	3B	HR	RBI	BB	HBP	SH	SF	SO	SB	CS	BB%	SO%
Alexander, CJ	L-R	6-3	215	7-17-96	.220	.280	.423	86	314	286	44	63	17	1	13	34	24	1	0	3	94	4	2	7.6	29.9
Beaty, Matt	L-R	6-0	215	4-28-93	.294	.368	.471	14	57	51	7	15	3	0	2	9	5	1	0	0	6	0	0	8.8	10.5
Blanco, Dairon	R-R	5-11	170	4-26-93	.347	.444	.451	49	208	173	37	60	7	1	3	19	22	10	1	2	35	47	6	10.6	16.8
Bradley, Tucker	L-L	5-9	206	5-06-98	.267	.366	.433	69	250	210	37	56	17	3	4	36	33	1	4	2	52	10	4	13.2	20.8
Briceno, Jose	R-R	6-1	225	9-19-92	.214	.279	.464	34	122	112	15	24	1	0	9	17	8	2	0	0	28	0	0	6.6	23.0
Camargo, Johan	B-R	5-11	195	12-13-93	.298	.412	.544	15	68	57	7	17	2	0	4	8	11	0	0	0	11	0	0	16.2	16.2
2-team (22 Toledo)					.263	.348	.460	37	156	137	16	36	6	0	7	19	17	1	0	1	26	0	0	10.9	16.7
Castellano, Angelo	R-R	5-10	165	1-13-95	.281	.384	.489	107	386	327	54	92	21	1	15	55	53	3	1	2	60	12	4	13.7	15.5
Cropley, Tyler	R-R	5-8	185	12-10-95	.200	.333	.600	2	6	5	0	1	0	1	0	3	1	0	0	0	3	0	0	16.7	50.0
Dungan, Clay	L-R	5-11	190	6-02-96	.273	.386	.365	89	329	271	50	74	14	1	3	30	50	3	0	5	68	16	2	15.2	20.7
Eaton, Nate	R-R	5-11	185	12-22-96	.252	.312	.441	85	367	333	52	84	16	1	15	39	29	1	2	2	85	22	3	7.9	23.2
Emshoff, Kale	R-R	6-2	228	5-02-98	.250	.455	.500	5	11	8	2	2	2	0	0	0	3	0	0	0	3	0	0	27.3	27.3
Fermin, Freddy	R-R	5-9	200	5-16-95	.304	.448	.674	14	58	46	12	14	2	0	5	14	11	1	0	0	9	0	0	19.0	15.5
Garcia, Maikel	R-R	6-0	145	3-03-00	.242	.348	.347	24	112	95	11	23	7	0	1	17	16	0	0	1	22	4	3	14.3	19.6
Gentry, Tyler	R-R	6-0	210	2-01-99	.253	.370	.421	129	572	475	69	120	28	2	16	71	81	10	1	5	127	14	3	14.2	22.2
Hechavarria, Adeiny	R-R	6-0	195	4-15-89	.220	.291	.425	36	141	127	18	28	8	0	6	24	12	1	0	1	32	0	0	8.5	22.7
Hicklen, Brewer	R-R	6-1	220	2-09-96	.233	.338	.451	61	240	206	41	48	15	3	8	29	26	7	0	1	59	15	3	10.8	24.6
2-team (11 Lehigh Valley)					.236	.351	.455	72	286	242	52	57	17	3	10	33	36	7	0	1	70	21	3	12.6	24.5
Isbel, Kyle	L-R	5-11	190	3-03-97	.290	.405	.548	9	37	31	7	9	2	0	2	6	6	0	0	0	6	0	0	16.2	16.2
Jenista, Greyson	L-R	6-2	210	12-07-96	.154	.214	.231	4	14	13	1	2	1	0	0	0	1	0	0	0	6	0	0	7.1	42.9
Loftin, Nick	R-R	5-11	180	9-25-98	.270	.344	.444	82	358	315	41	85	13	0	14	56	34	4	0	5	47	6	4	9.5	13.1
Lopez, Nicky	L-R	5-11	180	3-13-95	.300	.462	.400	3	13	10	1	3	1	0	0	1	3	0	0	0	1	1	0	23.1	7.7
Mann, Devin	R-R	6-2	180	2-11-97	.198	.354	.405	37	164	131	18	26	9	0	6	15	29	3	0	1	50	2	0	17.7	30.5
Massey, Michael	L-R	6-0	190	3-22-98	.182	.250	.273	3	12	11	2	2	1	0	0	0	1	0	0	0	3	0	0	8.3	25.0
McCullough, Morgan	L-R	5-6	180	12-19-97	.286	.375	.500	8	32	28	5	8	1	1	1	6	3	1	0	0	10	1	0	9.4	31.3
Olivares, Edward	R-R	6-2	190	3-06-96	.365	.424	.635	13	59	52	10	19	5	0	3	12	3	3	0	1	11	4	1	5.1	18.6
Palacios, Jermaine	R-R	6-0	145	7-19-96	.200	.220	.418	16	60	55	6	11	3	0	3	8	2	0	1	2	20	0	0	3.3	33.3
2-team (36 Toledo)					.183	.233	.372	52	198	180	18	33	5	1	9	29	12	0	1	5	63	3	2	6.1	31.8
Porter, Logan	R-R	6-0	200	7-12-95	.232	.339	.377	110	448	379	52	88	16	0	13	48	60	4	0	5	113	1	1	13.4	25.2
Pratto, Nick	L-L	6-1	215	10-06-98	.180	.290	.342	31	131	111	14	20	4	1	4	17	16	2	0	2	37	0	0	12.2	28.2
Rave, John	L-L	5-9	185	12-30-97	.236	.326	.376	70	302	263	34	62	14	1	7	38	36	0	1	2	84	4	4	11.9	27.8
Reetz, Jakson	R-R	6-0	205	1-03-96	.274	.349	.526	27	106	95	11	26	12	0	4	15	9	2	0	0	34	1	0	8.5	32.1
Reyes, Franmil	R-R	6-5	265	7-07-95	.200	.278	.467	4	18	15	4	3	1	0	1	4	1	1	0	1	7	0	0	5.6	38.9
2-team (34 Rochester)					.217	.321	.392	38	167	143	22	31	5	1	6	23	21	1	0	2	43	0	0	12.6	25.7
Taylor, Samad	R-R	5-8	160	7-11-98	.301	.418	.466	89	414	335	65	101	23	4	8	55	66	6	0	7	85	43	10	15.9	20.5
Thompson, Bubba	R-R	6-2	197	6-09-98	.259	.313	.410	33	153	139	21	36	7	1	4	17	8	3	3	0	41	11	3	5.2	26.8
Velazquez, Nelson	R-R	6-0	190	12-26-98	.045	.087	.045	6	23	22	1	1	0	0	0	0	1	0	0	0	6	2	0	4.3	26.1
2-team (74 Iowa)					.239	.319	.439	80	353	314	49	75	15	0	16	44	33	4	0	2	103	9	3	9.3	29.2
Wallace, Paxton	R-R	5-10	215	1-06-99	.500	.538	.583	4	13	12	2	6	1	0	0	1	1	0	0	0	5	1	0	7.7	38.5
Waters, Drew	B-R	6-0	185	12-30-98	.327	.397	.635	13	58	52	12	17	6	2	2	6	6	0	0	0	13	2	0	10.3	22.4

Pitching	B-T	Ht.	Wt.	DOB	W	L	ERA	G	GS	SV	IP	Hits	Runs	ER	HR	BB	SO	AVG	OBP	SLG	SO%	BB%	BF
Anderson, Justin	L-R	6-3	230	9-28-92	0	0	0.00	2	0	0	3	3	0	0	0	1	2	.231	.286	.231	14.3	7.1	14
Barlow, Joe	R-R	6-2	210	9-28-95	1	1	7.36	12	1	0	18	29	18	15	6	9	19	.363	.418	.700	20.9	9.9	91
Bowlan, Jonathan	R-R	6-6	240	12-01-96	6	6	5.24	14	12	1	67	72	40	39	12	32	58	.275	.351	.466	19.6	10.8	296
Castellano, Angelo	R-R	5-10	165	1-13-95	0	0	0.00	1	0	0	1	1	0	0	0	1	0	.500	.667	.500	0.0	33.3	3
Castillo, Max	R-R	6-2	280	5-04-99	6	7	4.58	22	21	0	116	117	66	59	31	28	94	.257	.303	.514	19.2	5.7	490
Chamberlain, Christian	L-L	5-10	173	7-20-99	1	2	8.51	26	0	0	24	22	28	23	5	28	35	.239	.427	.478	28.0	22.4	125
Coleman, Dylan	R-R	6-5	230	9-16-96	1	5	4.70	32	0	2	31	20	18	16	3	32	48	.183	.395	.312	32.7	21.8	147
Cox, Austin	L-L	6-4	235	3-28-97	2	1	3.61	12	9	0	47	45	20	19	12	21	39	.263	.349	.538	20.0	10.8	195
Cruz, Steven	R-R	6-7	225	6-15-99	0	1	6.88	14	0	0	17	12	13	13	3	10	22	.200	.319	.367	30.6	13.9	72
Cuas, Jose	R-R	6-3	195	6-28-94	0	0	9.00	1	0	1	1	1	1	1	1	1	2	.250	.400	1.000	40.0	20.0	5
de Geus, Brett	R-R	6-2	190	11-04-97	0	2	11.45	9	0	0	11	21	15	14	2	9	7	.404	.492	.558	11.5	14.8	61
Dipoto, Jonah	R-R	6-1	225	9-03-96	3	2	4.24	36	0	0	40	35	23	19	8	27	47	.236	.376	.419	26.0	14.9	181
Dye, Josh	L-L	6-5	180	9-14-96	0	1	1.80	3	0	0	5	6	2	1	1	0	2	.286	.286	.429	9.5	0.0	21
Garrett, Amir	R-L	6-5	239	5-03-92	0	0	10.13	3	0	0	3	3	3	3	1	5	2	.273	.500	.545	12.5	31.3	16
Hearn, Taylor	L-L	6-6	230	8-30-94	0	0	2.45	12	0	2	15	16	5	4	1	9	22	.281	.388	.368	32.8	13.4	67
Heasley, Jonathan	R-R	6-3	225	1-27-97	2	5	6.85	32	15	1	95	108	72	72	20	45	88	.286	.361	.552	20.5	10.5	429
Hoffmann, Andrew	R-R	6-5	210	2-02-00	3	3	5.45	8	8	0	38	42	25	23	8	16	46	.275	.345	.542	26.9	9.4	171
Keller, Brad	R-R	6-5	255	7-27-95	0	3	15.00	9	2	0	9	11	17	15	1	21	5	.324	.579	.500	8.5	35.6	59
Klein, Will	R-R	6-5	230	11-28-99	1	3	5.66	28	1	3	35	40	23	22	3	25	49	.276	.397	.393	28.2	14.4	174
Kowar, Jackson	R-R	6-5	200	10-04-96	2	5	5.96	30	1	2	45	51	35	30	4	32	49	.288	.408	.429	22.3	14.5	220
Kriske, Brooks	R-R	6-3	190	2-03-94	0	4	5.52	27	0	5	29	30	21	18	5	16	49	.256	.356	.436	36.3	11.9	135
Lynch, Daniel	L-L	6-6	200	11-17-96	2	0	3.15	5	5	0	20	20	7	7	3	4	18	.256	.293	.410	22.0	4.9	82
Marquez, Emilio	L-L	5-8	170	4-28-98	0	0	5.40	1	0	0	2	2	1	1	1	0	1	.333	.333	.833	16.7	0.0	6
Marsh, Alec	R-R	6-2	220	5-14-98	2	0	2.40	3	3	0	15	13	4	4	1	7	19	.232	.318	.304	28.8	10.6	66
Martinez, Marcelo	L-L	6-2	190	8-10-96	1	1	4.29	9	1	0	21	24	10	10	6	5	13	.276	.330	.517	13.8	5.3	94
Mayers, Mike	R-R	6-2	220	12-06-91	3	1	6.80	12	8	0	41	47	31	31	7	17	34	.287	.360	.482	18.2	9.1	187
McArthur, James	R-R	6-7	230	12-11-96	2	1	3.98	23	2	1	41	31	19	18	3	21	57	.201	.309	.292	31.5	11.6	181
Mengden, Daniel	R-R	6-1	215	2-19-93	0	0	7.36	6	3	0	15	19	14	12	0	8	14	.317	.414	.433	20.0	11.4	70
Nunez, Andres	R-R	6-4	240	9-20-95	3	2	6.66	21	0	0	24	28	19	18	1	14	20	.289	.395	.423	17.5	12.3	114
Parrish, Drew	L-L	5-11	200	12-08-97	5	6	7.18	21	18	0	84	97	70	67	24	58	64	.292	.392	.581	16.2	14.7	395
Pennington, Walter	L-L	6-2	205	4-14-98	7	2	3.69	41	1	0	61	52	31	25	5	31	64	.234	.326	.342	24.7	12.0	259
Poteet, Cody	R-R	6-1	190	7-30-94	0	0	0.00	1	1	0	2	0	0	0	0	1	1	.000	.167	.000	16.7	16.7	6
Ragans, Cole	L-L	6-4	190	12-12-97	2	1	4.82	4	4	0	19	18	10	10	1	10	22	.254	.346	.324	27.2	12.3	81
Sisk, Evan	L-L	6-2	209	4-23-97	2	4	6.34	58	3	0	61	68	50	43	6	40	62	.283	.388	.388	21.4	13.8	290
Snider, Collin	R-R	6-4	195	10-10-95	5	1	5.91	39	0	3	43	42	29	28	5	31	42	.258	.384	.436	21.0	15.5	200
Staumont, Josh	R-R	6-3	200	12-21-93	0	0	0.00	4	0	1	4	3	0	0	0	1	7	.200	.250	.333	43.8	6.3	16
Taylor, Josh	L-L	6-5	245	3-02-93	0	0	6.75	5	0	0	5	9	4	4	1	1	5	.375	.400	.625	20.0	4.0	25
Veneziano, Anthony	L-L	6-5	205	9-01-97	5	4	4.22	18	17	0	90	83	44	42	9	43	79	.249	.335	.402	20.6	11.2	383
Weiss, Ryan	R-R	6-4	210	12-10-96	0	1	7.07	12	0	0	14	14	14	11	3	14	15	.259	.459	.537	20.3	18.9	74
Wittgren, Nick	R-R	6-2	216	5-29-91	1	0	1.25	17	0	5	22	12	3	3	0	6	19	.171	.253	.186	24.1	7.6	79
Yarbrough, Ryan	R-L	6-5	205	12-31-91	0	0	1.23	3	3	0	15	9	2	2	1	2	18	.176	.208	.275	34.0	3.8	53
Zerpa, Angel	L-L	6-0	220	9-27-99	0	2	4.73	6	6	0	27	27	14	14	4	13	23	.267	.359	.465	19.7	11.1	117

Fielding

Catcher	PCT	G	PO	A	E	DP	PB
Briceno	.986	33	271	17	4	5	1
Cropley	1.000	2	9	2	0	0	0
Emshoff	1.000	3	16	0	0	0	1
Fermin	.974	12	107	7	3	1	2
Porter	.992	82	690	32	6	3	8
Reetz	.987	24	219	7	3	3	0

First Base	PCT	G	PO	A	E	DP
Alexander	.993	64	398	25	3	55
Beaty	1.000	8	59	3	0	5
Briceno	1.000	1	2	0	0	0
Camargo	1.000	4	16	1	0	1
Castellano	1.000	17	101	14	0	11
Emshoff	1.000	1	4	0	0	0
Jenista	.967	4	27	2	1	1
Loftin	1.000	3	19	0	0	3
Mann	1.000	7	52	6	0	4
Palacios	1.000	5	41	4	0	3
Porter	.994	25	157	12	1	13
Pratto	1.000	25	165	14	0	24
Wallace	1.000	3	20	2	0	2

Second Base	PCT	G	PO	A	E	DP
Camargo	1.000	3	5	6	0	2
Castellano	.957	7	13	9	1	5
Dungan	.992	33	53	72	1	23
Eaton	.905	8	5	14	2	5
Loftin	.967	26	47	69	4	13
Lopez	1.000	1	1	2	0	0
Mann	.959	12	22	25	2	6
Massey	1.000	2	4	6	0	2
McCullough	1.000	6	8	14	0	3
Taylor	.979	58	86	148	5	36

Third Base	PCT	G	PO	A	E	DP
Camargo	.917	7	4	7	1	1
Castellano	.968	13	4	26	1	1
Dungan	.941	25	4	44	3	3
Eaton	.930	18	11	42	4	7
Garcia	.821	10	6	17	5	1
Loftin	.944	47	31	70	6	6
Lopez	1.000	1	1	5	0	1
Mann	.935	16	19	24	3	4
McCullough	1.000	2	1	4	0	0
Palacios	.964	10	7	20	1	3
Taylor	1.000	2	0	4	0	0

Shortstop	PCT	G	PO	A	E	DP
Camargo	.000	1	0	0	0	0
Castellano	.951	71	96	173	14	46
Dungan	.961	25	27	47	3	16
Garcia	.967	14	16	42	2	15
Hechavarria	.968	36	40	82	4	18
Lopez	1.000	1	2	1	0	1
Palacios	1.000	2	2	5	0	1

Outfield	PCT	G	PO	A	E	DP
Alexander	.909	4	10	0	1	0
Blanco	1.000	45	90	4	0	2
Bradley	1.000	51	66	2	0	0
Eaton	.963	48	108	7	3	0
Gentry	.942	116	223	6	2	3
Hicklen	1.000	24	39	3	0	0
Isbel	1.000	8	20	0	0	0
Loftin	1.000	3	2	1	0	0
Mann	1.000	3	3	0	0	0
Olivares	1.000	10	18	2	0	0
Pratto	1.000	3	9	0	0	0
Rave	1.000	62	124	4	0	2
Reyes	1.000	1	0	1	0	0
Taylor	.947	28	48	2	2	0
Thompson	.921	29	72	0	2	0
Velazquez	1.000	5	9	0	0	0
Waters	1.000	13	27	1	0	1

NORTHWEST ARKANSAS NATURALS

DOUBLE-A

TEXAS LEAGUE

Batting	B-T	Ht.	Wt.	DOB	AVG	OBP	SLG	G	PA	AB	R	H	2B	3B	HR	RBI	BB	HBP	SH	SF	SO	SB	CS	BB%	SO%
Bates, Parker	L-R	5-11	205	11-16-97	.222	.293	.276	85	290	257	31	57	7	2	1	23	24	3	3	3	62	8	6	8.3	21.4
Bonifacio, Jorge	R-R	6-0	220	6-04-93	.267	.354	.483	118	508	435	71	116	20	4	22	88	61	3	0	9	101	6	0	12.0	19.9
Bradley, Tucker	L-L	5-9	206	5-06-98	.301	.355	.473	27	107	93	12	28	5	1	3	19	10	0	0	4	24	1	0	9.3	22.4
Briceno, Jose	R-R	6-1	225	9-19-92	.246	.269	.292	15	67	65	3	16	3	0	0	7	2	0	0	0	16	0	0	3.0	23.9
Cropley, Tyler	R-R	5-8	185	12-10-95	.234	.329	.359	43	168	145	17	34	6	0	4	17	19	2	1	1	39	0	1	11.3	23.2
Cross, Gavin	L-L	6-1	210	2-13-01	.000	.167	.000	2	6	5	0	0	0	0	0	0	1	0	0	0	2	0	0	16.7	33.3
Glendinning, Robbie	R-R	6-0	196	10-06-95	.242	.373	.363	26	110	91	6	22	3	1	2	16	18	1	0	0	28	0	1	16.4	25.5
Govern, Jimmy	R-R	5-9	190	12-11-96	.226	.296	.332	63	241	217	33	49	7	2	4	23	15	7	1	1	44	3	1	6.2	18.3
Guzman, Jeison	B-R	6-0	205	10-08-98	.244	.348	.423	64	252	213	32	52	10	2	8	36	30	5	2	2	89	4	3	11.9	35.3
Hayes, Kyle	R-R	6-2	190	10-08-97	.364	.556	.636	6	18	11	6	4	1	1	0	1	5	1	0	1	2	0	0	27.8	11.1
Hernandez, Diego	L-L	6-0	150	11-21-00	.245	.302	.290	60	269	241	30	59	7	2	0	20	16	4	7	1	69	17	3	5.9	25.7
Hernandez, Omar	R-R	5-11	170	12-10-01	.130	.333	.174	9	30	23	1	3	1	0	0	3	6	1	0	0	9	0	1	20.0	30.0
Jenista, Greyson	L-R	6-2	210	12-07-96	.183	.272	.378	23	92	82	9	15	5	1	3	6	9	1	0	0	33	1	0	9.8	35.9
McCullough, Morgan	L-R	5-6	180	12-19-97	.240	.346	.391	78	309	258	40	62	17	2	6	25	36	9	0	6	84	10	3	11.7	27.2
Means, Jake	R-R	6-0	215	4-14-96	.165	.264	.277	69	266	231	23	38	5	0	7	27	28	4	0	2	70	5	2	10.5	26.3
Rave, John	L-L	5-9	185	12-30-97	.275	.379	.430	54	236	200	33	55	10	3	5	24	34	0	1	1	58	6	4	14.4	24.6
Reinheimer, Jack	R-R	6-1	185	7-19-92	.132	.185	.171	26	82	76	10	10	3	0	0	3	4	1	1	0	29	4	0	4.9	35.4
Shrum, Dillan	R-L	5-11	200	3-04-98	.235	.399	.433	95	358	277	47	65	12	2	13	48	54	23	2	2	115	2	2	15.1	32.1
Tolbert, Tyler	R-R	6-0	160	1-27-98	.276	.336	.419	126	574	518	95	143	24	10	10	50	40	8	5	3	127	50	8	7.0	22.1
Town, River	L-R	5-9	181	7-08-99	.111	.357	.111	4	14	9	1	1	0	0	0	1	4	0	0	1	3	1	0	28.6	21.4
Tresh, Luca	R-R	5-11	193	1-11-00	.228	.313	.362	92	380	334	44	76	11	2	10	48	43	0	0	3	72	1	1	11.3	18.9
Valera, Leonel	R-R	6-3	206	7-09-99	.221	.292	.372	25	98	86	8	19	4	3	1	10	6	3	2	1	20	1	1	6.1	20.4
Vaz, Javier	L-R	5-9	151	9-22-00	.304	.391	.429	33	130	112	17	34	4	2	2	12	15	1	2	0	18	4	1	11.5	13.8
Wallace, Cayden	R-R	5-10	205	8-07-01	.236	.300	.362	33	140	127	19	30	5	1	3	20	12	0	0	1	23	3	0	8.6	16.4
Wilson, Peyton	B-R	5-8	180	11-01-99	.286	.366	.411	128	562	489	70	140	33	5	6	65	55	10	1	6	101	19	7	9.8	18.0

Pitching	B-T	Ht.	Wt.	DOB	W	L	ERA	G	GS	SV	IP	Hits	Runs	ER	HR	BB	SO	AVG	OBP	SLG	SO%	BB%	BF
Alcantara, Adrian	R-R	6-1	178	8-29-99	2	0	3.00	5	0	0	9	10	4	3	1	9	9	.294	.455	.471	20.5	20.5	44
Anderson, Justin	L-R	6-3	230	9-28-92	0	2	7.47	10	0	0	16	16	14	13	1	5	20	.276	.343	.431	29.4	7.4	68
Barnett, Mason	R-R	6-0	218	11-07-00	2	1	3.58	7	7	0	33	27	13	13	2	12	43	.218	.292	.347	31.4	8.8	137
Biasi, Dante	L-L	6-0	205	12-04-97	4	4	4.43	36	3	2	69	56	43	34	12	52	77	.222	.361	.413	24.8	16.7	311
Bowlan, Jonathan	R-R	6-6	240	12-01-96	1	5	7.20	10	9	0	35	44	30	28	7	13	47	.301	.366	.514	28.7	7.9	164
Brentz, Jake	L-L	6-1	205	9-14-94	0	0	9.00	1	0	0	1	0	1	1	0	2	2	.000	.400	.000	40.0	40.0	5
Cameron, Noah	L-L	6-3	220	7-17-99	3	10	6.10	17	17	0	72	87	52	49	14	26	74	.297	.361	.522	22.8	8.0	324
Cerantola, Eric	R-R	6-5	225	5-02-00	0	1	1.93	3	2	1	14	9	4	3	0	5	19	.196	.296	.217	35.2	9.3	54
Chamberlain, Christian	L-L	5-10	173	7-20-99	1	2	1.99	20	0	0	32	13	10	7	0	22	49	.120	.294	.148	36.0	16.2	136
Champlain, Chandler	R-R	6-5	220	7-23-99	5	5	3.82	14	14	0	73	64	38	31	11	25	64	.234	.308	.403	21.2	8.3	302
Cruz, Steven	R-R	6-7	225	6-15-99	0	0	2.20	29	0	9	33	20	11	8	1	20	42	.174	.307	.200	30.7	14.6	137
de Geus, Brett	R-R	6-2	190	11-04-97	2	1	2.80	20	2	1	35	34	11	11	3	8	29	.260	.305	.374	20.6	5.7	141
Del Rosario, Yefri	R-R	6-2	180	9-23-99	6	2	3.12	39	0	2	52	38	24	18	4	26	65	.198	.300	.313	28.9	11.6	225
Dipoto, Jonah	R-R	6-1	225	9-03-96	0	0	0.87	7	0	0	10	9	4	1	0	4	13	.231	.333	.231	28.9	8.9	45
Fleming, William	R-R	6-6	220	3-06-99	2	0	4.34	10	8	0	48	49	23	23	6	17	38	.262	.325	.422	18.3	8.2	208
Govern, Jimmy	R-R	5-9	190	12-11-96	0	0	0.00	2	0	0	2	0	0	0	0	0	0	.000	.000	.000	0.0	0.0	6
Guerrero, Tyson	L-L	6-1	188	2-16-99	1	2	6.55	3	3	0	11	10	8	8	2	5	15	.233	.327	.419	30.6	10.2	49
Hoffmann, Andrew	R-R	6-5	210	2-02-00	4	6	5.56	20	19	0	87	95	55	54	12	43	87	.280	.368	.451	22.3	11.0	390
Kaufman, Rylan	L-L	6-4	225	6-23-99	0	3	16.20	4	1	1	7	8	12	12	1	12	7	.320	.526	.640	18.4	31.6	38
Keller, Brad	R-R	6-5	255	7-27-95	2	0	4.15	6	0	0	9	7	4	4	1	4	8	.212	.297	.364	21.6	10.8	37
Klein, Will	R-R	6-5	230	11-28-99	0	2	3.38	21	0	1	29	28	15	11	1	14	44	.250	.338	.339	33.6	10.7	131
Lynch, Daniel	L-L	6-6	200	11-17-96	0	0	7.71	1	1	0	2	4	2	2	1	1	6	.364	.417	.636	50.0	8.3	12
Marquez, Emilio	L-L	5-8	170	4-28-98	1	0	5.63	12	0	0	16	19	14	10	2	8	16	.284	.392	.448	20.3	10.1	79
Marsh, Alec	R-R	6-2	220	5-14-98	3	3	5.32	11	11	0	47	51	31	28	4	24	56	.276	.363	.422	26.4	11.3	212
McClelland, Jackson	R-R	6-5	220	7-19-94	0	0	13.50	4	0	0	5	6	7	7	1	7	4	.300	.481	.600	14.8	25.9	27
McCullough, Morgan	L-R	5-6	180	12-19-97	0	0	0.00	2	0	0	2	0	0	0	0	0	0	.000	.000	.000	0.0	0.0	5
McInvale, Andrew	R-R	6-2	195	11-03-96	1	0	6.23	11	0	1	13	13	9	9	1	10	16	.265	.387	.408	25.8	16.1	62
McMillon, John	L-R	6-3	230	1-27-98	3	2	0.87	15	0	5	21	12	4	2	0	11	30	.171	.284	.257	37.0	13.6	81
Medrano, Ronald	R-R	6-0	170	9-17-95	1	1	5.23	9	6	0	31	34	20	18	3	11	27	.279	.360	.459	19.4	7.9	139
Murdock, Noah	R-R	6-8	205	8-20-98	3	1	5.87	36	1	1	69	62	52	45	4	49	77	.242	.373	.328	24.4	15.6	315
Parrish, Drew	L-L	5-11	200	12-08-97	2	2	4.91	7	6	1	33	33	18	18	8	15	32	.252	.342	.511	21.5	10.1	149
Paulino, Anderson	R-R	6-2	200	9-12-98	2	0	4.32	19	0	5	25	26	13	12	0	9	20	.260	.333	.350	18.0	8.1	111
Pennington, Walter	L-L	6-2	205	4-14-98	0	0	0.00	8	0	1	10	4	0	0	0	4	11	.129	.229	.129	31.4	11.4	35
Sikkema, T.J.	L-L	6-0	221	7-25-98	4	4	5.85	34	0	0	72	61	50	47	11	39	63	.236	.352	.421	19.9	12.3	316
Simonelli, Anthony	R-R	6-2	200	12-23-98	1	0	6.35	9	0	1	11	16	8	8	2	3	14	.333	.389	.583	25.9	5.6	54
Veneziano, Anthony	L-L	6-5	205	9-01-97	5	1	2.13	8	8	0	42	37	10	10	5	5	48	.236	.280	.350	28.4	3.0	169
Wallace, Jacob	R-R	6-1	190	8-13-98	1	5	4.20	49	0	5	49	46	34	23	1	40	57	.241	.382	.335	23.9	16.8	238
Way, Beck	R-R	6-4	200	8-06-99	2	9	6.67	28	17	0	80	78	65	59	10	63	80	.257	.408	.405	20.7	16.3	387
Zerpa, Angel	L-L	6-0	220	9-27-99	0	0	1.13	3	3	0	8	5	1	1	1	3	7	.179	.258	.321	22.6	9.7	31

Fielding

Catcher	PCT	G	PO	A	E	DP	PB
Briceno	.962	11	119	8	5	0	2
Cropley	.992	40	376	12	3	0	3
Hayes	.979	6	46	1	1	0	0
Hernandez	.976	9	75	8	2	0	1
Tresh	.980	77	728	39	16	6	7

First Base	PCT	G	PO	A	E	DP
Glendinning	.984	11	55	5	1	7
Guzman	.984	16	117	6	2	7
Jenista	1.000	1	6	1	0	0
Means	1.000	26	180	13	0	13
Shrum	.994	92	632	52	4	59

Second Base	PCT	G	PO	A	E	DP
Govern	1.000	1	2	0	0	0
Guzman	.667	1	2	0	1	0
McCullough	.983	17	21	38	1	8
Vaz	.944	5	12	5	1	2
Wilson	.967	117	194	281	16	68

Third Base	PCT	G	PO	A	E	DP
Glendinning	.800	3	0	8	2	1
Govern	.965	33	28	54	3	2
Guzman	.867	10	2	24	4	1
McCullough	1.000	28	17	54	0	9
Means	.968	32	25	36	2	7
Valera	1.000	2	0	1	0	0
Wallace	.939	32	24	53	5	2
Wilson	.000	1	0	0	0	0

Shortstop	PCT	G	PO	A	E	DP
Guzman	.800	4	6	2	2	1
McCullough	.909	24	16	54	7	13
Reinheimer	.961	25	26	48	3	8
Tolbert	.968	71	93	179	9	29
Valera	.966	22	29	57	3	12

Outfield	PCT	G	PO	A	E	DP
Bates	.997	90	123	5	1	1
Bonifacio	.996	96	154	4	1	1
Bradley	1.000	18	29	1	0	0
Cross	1.000	2	2	0	0	0
Govern	1.000	19	26	0	0	0
Guzman	.944	13	14	2	1	0
Hernandez	.988	58	122	2	3	1
Jenista	.977	12	23	0	1	0
McCullough	.000	1	0	0	0	0
Means	1.000	1	1	0	0	0
Rave	.881	52	103	4	3	1
Tolbert	1.000	50	102	1	0	0
Town	1.000	5	5	0	0	0
Vaz	.486	26	33	1	1	0
Wilson	1.000	1	1	0	0	0

QUAD CITIES RIVER BANDITS — HIGH CLASS A

MIDWEST LEAGUE

Batting	B-T	Ht.	Wt.	DOB	AVG	OBP	SLG	G	PA	AB	R	H	2B	3B	HR	RBI	BB	HBP	SH	SF	SO	SB	CS	BB%	SO%
Alexander, Jack	R-R	5-10	212	5-30-00	.184	.250	.235	51	197	179	15	33	7	1	0	20	13	3	0	1	56	0	0	6.6	28.4
Bates, Parker	L-R	5-11	205	11-16-97	.200	.333	.320	7	30	25	3	5	0	0	1	1	4	1	0	0	9	1	1	13.3	30.0
Collins, Darryl	L-R	6-0	185	9-16-01	.244	.322	.308	23	87	78	13	19	2	0	1	9	9	0	0	0	12	4	0	10.3	13.8
Cross, Gavin	L-L	6-1	210	2-13-01	.206	.300	.383	94	407	355	49	73	21	3	12	58	42	7	0	3	113	23	3	10.3	27.8
Dickerson, Dustin	R-R	6-1	180	3-28-01	.223	.336	.272	27	122	103	10	23	2	0	1	10	15	3	0	1	21	1	0	12.3	17.2
Dunhurst, Hayden	L-R	5-8	220	9-19-00	.000	.000	.000	1	3	3	0	0	0	0	0	0	0	0	0	0	2	0	0	0.0	66.7
Emshoff, Kale	R-R	6-2	228	5-02-98	.225	.296	.380	89	353	316	35	71	15	2	10	44	29	4	0	2	91	2	1	8.2	25.8
Gonzalez, Herard	B-R	5-9	167	5-16-01	.209	.296	.286	94	376	325	28	68	14	4	1	29	41	1	5	4	92	7	5	10.9	24.5
Hayes, Kyle	R-R	6-2	190	10-08-97	.000	.000	.000	1	4	3	0	0	0	0	0	1	0	0	1	0	1	0	0	0.0	25.0
Hernandez, Diego	L-L	6-0	150	11-21-00	.231	.333	.615	3	15	13	2	3	0	1	1	1	1	1	0	0	4	2	1	6.7	26.7
Hollie, David	R-R	6-1	205	10-25-99	.208	.291	.325	25	86	77	12	16	4	1	1	5	8	1	0	0	34	4	1	9.3	39.5
Jensen, Carter	L-R	6-1	210	7-03-03	.211	.356	.363	116	497	399	61	84	20	4	11	45	92	1	0	5	120	11	1	18.5	24.1
Johnson, Justin	R-R	5-11	185	4-03-00	.202	.296	.239	30	126	109	8	22	4	0	0	8	12	3	1	1	25	4	1	9.5	19.8
Kennedy, Eric	L-R	5-11	203	9-15-99	.225	.360	.366	23	89	71	11	16	2	1	2	7	16	0	0	2	23	2	0	18.0	25.8
Negret, Juan Carlos	R-R	5-9	190	6-19-99	.210	.306	.390	111	464	405	55	85	16	0	19	70	43	14	0	2	125	3	1	9.3	26.9
Newton, Shervyen	B-R	6-3	209	4-24-99	.222	.305	.432	96	366	324	47	72	17	3	15	47	37	2	2	1	119	3	1	10.1	32.5
Pineda, Jack	L-R	5-7	170	8-10-99	.227	.344	.314	62	288	242	42	55	15	0	2	15	41	2	3	0	74	16	3	14.2	25.7
Ramirez, Jean	L-L	5-10	190	10-25-00	.218	.306	.299	22	100	87	15	19	1	0	2	6	9	2	2	0	20	6	3	9.0	20.0
Town, River	L-R	5-9	181	7-08-99	.269	.375	.365	84	357	301	44	81	9	1	6	38	41	12	0	3	55	20	4	11.5	15.4
Valdez, Enrique	L-R	5-11	185	5-15-01	.197	.254	.258	22	71	66	10	13	2	1	0	3	3	2	0	0	36	3	0	4.2	50.7
Vaz, Javier	L-R	5-9	151	9-22-00	.270	.367	.390	86	388	333	49	90	14	4	6	39	49	3	1	2	32	26	2	12.6	8.2
Wallace, Cayden	R-R	5-10	205	8-07-01	.261	.341	.431	97	428	376	56	98	22	6	10	64	42	6	0	4	94	15	6	9.8	22.0
Wallace, Paxton	R-R	5-10	215	1-06-99	.194	.273	.266	42	154	139	9	27	8	1	0	6	13	2	0	0	40	1	3	8.4	26.0

Pitching	B-T	Ht.	Wt.	DOB	W	L	ERA	G	GS	SV	IP	Hits	Runs	ER	HR	BB	SO	AVG	OBP	SLG	SO%	BB%	BF
Alcantara, Adrian	R-R	6-1	178	8-29-99	1	4	5.26	6	6	0	26	25	16	15	3	13	15	.250	.348	.410	13.0	11.3	115
Arias, Wander	R-R	6-4	230	11-03-99	3	4	6.23	45	0	8	65	68	53	45	8	31	76	.270	.359	.421	25.7	10.5	296
Avila, Luinder	R-R	6-3	195	8-21-01	4	7	4.39	22	20	0	109	101	57	53	3	44	102	.248	.336	.339	21.6	9.3	472
Barnett, Mason	R-R	6-0	218	11-07-00	4	6	3.18	16	16	0	82	59	33	29	3	38	94	.203	.306	.279	27.7	11.2	339
Barroso, Luis	R-R	6-3	165	9-07-98	1	3	5.98	19	1	2	41	45	28	27	7	12	19	.278	.330	.500	10.8	6.8	176
Cameron, Noah	L-L	6-3	220	7-17-99	2	2	3.60	7	7	0	35	28	15	14	5	9	58	.215	.282	.392	40.8	6.3	142
Cerantola, Eric	R-R	6-5	225	5-02-00	3	3	4.04	29	2	1	62	46	31	28	3	41	80	.199	.339	.312	28.6	14.6	280
Champlain, Chandler	R-R	6-5	220	7-23-99	6	3	2.74	11	11	0	62	48	20	19	5	18	61	.214	.283	.326	24.7	7.3	247
Fleming, William	R-R	6-6	220	3-06-99	3	2	3.92	13	11	0	60	69	26	26	3	17	53	.292	.351	.407	20.5	6.6	259
Guerrero, Tyson	L-L	6-1	188	2-16-99	2	4	3.63	18	17	0	84	65	37	34	10	29	106	.215	.295	.361	31.0	8.5	342
Harm, Parker	L-L	6-2	208	2-02-97	3	4	5.21	33	0	0	38	28	26	22	2	31	44	.204	.376	.321	24.6	17.3	179
Johnson, Brandon	R-R	6-0	195	6-12-99	6	3	5.04	40	0	2	61	58	41	34	8	34	80	.247	.343	.438	29.1	12.4	275
Kaufman, Rylan	L-L	6-4	225	6-23-99	0	0	1.62	5	3	0	17	11	3	3	0	14	21	.183	.338	.233	28.4	18.9	74
Kudrna, Ben	R-R	6-3	175	1-30-03	1	4	5.36	8	8	0	40	52	25	24	7	15	34	.325	.384	.519	19.2	8.5	177
Marquez, Emilio	L-L	5-8	170	4-28-98	1	0	3.00	9	0	0	15	9	6	5	2	4	24	.167	.237	.333	40.7	6.8	59
McKeehan, Cooper	L-L	6-1	195	3-28-01	2	2	8.78	10	0	0	13	17	17	13	2	12	14	.309	.426	.473	20.6	17.6	68
McMillon, John	L-R	6-3	230	1-27-98	3	1	2.70	13	0	1	20	8	6	6	1	8	40	.119	.221	.209	51.9	10.4	77
Medrano, Ronald	R-R	6-0	170	9-17-95	0	0	5.40	2	1	0	5	5	3	3	0	2	7	.294	.350	.353	33.3	9.5	21
Monke, Caden	L-L	6-3	170	9-02-99	0	0	2.70	3	0	0	3	3	1	1	0	3	4	.250	.400	.333	26.7	20.0	15
Mozzicato, Frank	L-L	6-3	175	6-19-03	0	4	7.12	9	9	0	37	34	33	29	7	33	45	.239	.382	.430	25.3	18.5	178
Noriega, Cruz	R-R	6-1	175	10-01-97	3	3	3.12	20	6	1	66	57	29	23	5	15	56	.227	.279	.335	20.5	5.5	273
Olivarez, Marcus	R-R	6-3	200	9-12-98	0	0	29.25	3	0	0	4	12	13	13	1	6	3	.522	.600	.826	10.0	20.0	30
Panzini, Shane	R-R	6-3	220	10-30-01	0	2	17.05	2	2	0	6	14	13	12	3	5	7	.452	.526	.903	18.4	13.2	38
Paulino, Anderson	R-R	6-2	200	9-12-98	0	2	3.97	27	0	7	34	34	19	15	1	14	35	.260	.349	.328	23.3	9.3	150
Ramsey, Ryan	R-L	6-0	195	1-18-01	1	2	10.67	5	2	0	14	24	18	17	0	10	22	.358	.449	.507	27.8	12.7	79
Sandlin, David	R-R	6-4	215	2-21-01	0	1	4.50	2	2	0	8	6	4	4	1	5	8	.207	.343	.310	22.9	14.3	35

Sears, Ben	R-R	6-5	208	6-15-00	0	1	10.00	5	0	0	9	13	10	10	2	4	6	.351	.419	.568	13.6	9.1	44
Simonelli, Anthony	R-R	6-2	200	12-23-98	2	4	3.29	33	0	4	38	30	17	14	3	12	42	.213	.279	.333	27.1	7.7	155
Wallace, Chase	R-R	6-2	195	11-13-98	0	0	2.00	6	0	0	9	8	3	2	1	3	7	.242	.306	.424	19.4	8.3	36
Wereski, Ben	L-L	6-2	210	10-26-97	3	2	4.05	18	0	0	20	25	10	9	3	7	35	.294	.344	.482	37.6	7.5	93
Willis, Marlin	L-L	6-4	190	6-05-98	0	0	7.84	29	0	0	31	16	29	27	0	44	47	.154	.428	.250	29.6	27.7	159
Zobac, Steven	L-R	6-3	185	10-14-00	1	4	5.31	8	8	0	39	44	26	23	3	12	37	.280	.335	.395	21.8	7.1	170

Fielding

Catcher	PCT	G	PO	A	E	DP	PB
Alexander	.995	40	376	33	2	1	5
Dunhurst	1.000	1	10	1	0	0	0
Emshoff	.980	23	223	16	5	1	1
Hayes	1.000	1	14	1	0	0	0
Jensen	.985	68	649	58	11	2	16

First Base	PCT	G	PO	A	E	DP
Emshoff	.997	44	307	12	1	27
Newton	.990	53	382	30	4	21
Wallace	.993	38	270	11	2	20

Second Base	PCT	G	PO	A	E	DP
Gonzalez	.971	57	79	122	6	18
Johnson	.991	29	51	60	1	16
Newton	1.000	6	5	11	0	1
Valdez	.939	8	16	15	2	4
Vaz	.980	35	55	89	3	16

Third Base	PCT	G	PO	A	E	DP
Gonzalez	.927	14	10	28	3	2
Newton	1.000	15	4	26	0	4
Valdez	.900	11	6	12	2	2
Wallace, C	.949	90	62	143	11	11
Wallace, P	1.000	2	0	1	0	0

Shortstop	PCT	G	PO	A	E	DP
Dickerson	.964	27	52	54	4	13
Newton	.974	22	28	46	2	9
Pineda	.958	62	68	116	8	17
Vaz	.976	21	26	54	2	9

Outfield	PCT	G	PO	A	E	DP
Bates	1.000	7	9	1	0	0
Collins	1.000	22	40	1	0	0
Cross	.995	90	203	7	2	0
Hernandez	1.000	2	5	0	0	0
Hollie	1.000	24	38	0	0	0
Kennedy	1.000	24	47	0	0	0
Negret	.997	96	162	5	1	0
Ramirez	.906	22	47	1	5	0
Town	.993	84	120	4	2	1
Vaz	1.000	30	52	1	0	0
Wallace	.000	1	0	0	0	0

COLUMBIA FIREFLIES

LOW CLASS A

CAROLINA LEAGUE

Batting	B-T	Ht.	Wt.	DOB	AVG	OBP	SLG	G	PA	AB	R	H	2B	3B	HR	RBI	BB	HBP	SH	SF	SO	SB	CS	BB%	SO%
Calderon, Junior	R-R	5-11	205	12-09-01	.160	.282	.266	30	110	94	6	15	3	2	1	5	16	0	0	0	39	3	2	14.5	35.5
Candelario, Wilmin	B-R	6-0	195	9-11-01	.123	.215	.175	26	65	57	6	7	3	0	0	2	6	1	0	1	32	3	1	9.2	49.2
Charles, Austin	R-R	6-4	215	11-13-03	.230	.290	.356	69	296	261	29	60	18	3	3	31	22	3	3	7	73	12	3	7.4	24.7
Dickey, Jared	L-R	6-1	204	3-01-02	.347	.434	.463	28	113	95	18	33	5	3	0	19	12	4	0	2	11	3	0	10.6	9.7
Dunhurst, Hayden	L-R	5-8	220	9-19-00	.178	.237	.311	27	98	90	6	16	4	1	2	12	6	1	1	0	41	0	1	6.1	41.8
Florentino, Omar	B-R	5-9	170	10-26-01	.153	.229	.204	35	111	98	9	15	3	1	0	7	9	1	2	1	30	6	4	8.1	27.0
Hernandez, Omar	R-R	5-11	170	12-10-01	.223	.312	.311	81	333	283	51	63	8	1	5	27	35	4	2	5	52	26	10	10.5	15.6
Hollie, David	R-R	6-1	205	10-25-99	.150	.363	.450	21	80	60	11	9	0	0	6	12	13	7	0	0	26	8	0	16.3	32.5
Leyton, Roger	R-R	5-11	200	2-03-03	.221	.299	.283	82	309	272	27	60	8	0	3	33	22	10	1	4	82	11	4	7.1	26.5
McNair, Brennon	R-R	5-10	185	9-15-02	.191	.314	.293	70	256	215	24	41	6	5	2	15	35	4	1	1	98	19	2	13.7	38.3
Nivens, Spencer	L-R	5-11	185	11-16-01	.184	.336	.276	28	122	98	12	18	3	0	2	7	23	0	0	1	20	7	3	18.9	16.4
Pena, Erick	L-R	6-1	205	2-20-03	.133	.276	.296	75	290	240	26	32	7	1	10	33	47	1	0	2	153	11	6	16.2	52.8
Pire, Enmanuel	R-R	5-10	180	5-18-01	.167	.297	.167	11	37	30	7	5	0	0	0	2	6	0	0	1	6	0	0	16.2	16.2
Ramirez, Jean	L-L	5-10	190	10-25-00	.298	.374	.407	81	342	295	47	88	9	4	5	24	36	1	8	2	85	28	17	10.5	24.9
Roccaforte, Carson	L-L	6-1	195	3-29-02	.257	.377	.356	27	122	101	19	26	6	2	0	12	19	1	0	1	31	11	3	15.6	25.4
Rodriguez, Lizandro	B-R	5-11	180	11-16-02	.235	.325	.347	118	486	426	64	100	17	5	7	44	49	9	0	2	108	18	11	10.1	22.2
Salon, Dionmy	R-R	5-11	215	11-18-01	.230	.330	.288	74	280	243	31	56	8	0	2	18	27	9	1	0	68	3	4	9.6	24.3
Squires, Brett	L-R	6-2	210	2-26-00	.263	.381	.430	122	511	419	65	110	21	2	15	69	66	17	1	5	146	32	8	12.9	28.6
Usher, Levi	L-R	5-11	210	6-25-00	.158	.308	.261	60	227	184	26	29	7	3	2	14	35	6	0	2	86	11	4	15.4	37.9
Vazquez, Daniel	R-R	6-1	150	12-15-03	.223	.330	.288	113	471	400	57	89	15	1	3	43	62	3	4	2	107	32	10	13.2	22.7
Werner, Trevor	R-R	6-3	225	9-03-00	.354	.459	.699	31	135	113	32	40	11	2	8	36	21	1	0	0	31	8	4	15.6	23.0

Pitching	B-T	Ht.	Wt.	DOB	W	L	ERA	G	GS	SV	IP	Hits	Runs	ER	HR	BB	SO	AVG	OBP	SLG	SO%	BB%	BF
Alcantara, Adrian	R-R	6-1	178	8-29-99	0	0	0.00	1	1	0	3	2	0	0	0	0	6	.182	.182	.273	54.5	0.0	11
Anglin, Mack	R-R	6-4	220	7-05-00	1	1	2.29	24	0	0	39	30	15	10	1	27	44	.210	.331	.308	25.6	15.7	172
Arronde, Felix	R-R	6-3	185	4-25-03	1	0	3.72	2	2	0	10	8	8	4	2	6	12	.216	.326	.432	27.9	14.0	43
Diaz, Andres	R-R	6-1	215	7-06-01	0	1	8.10	2	2	0	7	12	7	6	0	3	4	.387	.457	.581	11.4	8.6	35
Hernandez, Ben	R-R	6-2	205	7-01-01	2	3	4.71	9	8	0	42	53	26	22	2	22	26	.312	.388	.424	13.3	11.2	196
Herrera, Eduardo	B-R	5-9	179	1-05-00	7	2	5.02	34	0	3	52	55	33	29	5	34	74	.282	.402	.451	31.0	14.2	239
Isbell, Chase	R-R	6-2	198	9-12-00	0	1	13.50	2	0	0	3	5	7	5	0	4	2	.313	.450	.438	10.0	20.0	20
Kudrna, Ben	R-R	6-3	175	1-30-03	4	3	3.56	14	13	0	68	67	28	27	7	30	70	.257	.333	.387	24.1	10.3	291
Martin, Logan	R-R	6-1	180	7-17-01	0	0	3.60	2	2	0	5	4	2	2	1	2	6	.235	.300	.412	30.0	10.0	20
Martinez, Chazz	L-L	6-3	210	1-06-00	6	8	4.08	39	0	2	64	64	41	29	4	31	86	.252	.334	.350	30.0	10.8	287
McKeehan, Cooper	L-L	6-1	195	3-28-01	8	1	1.08	31	0	11	50	29	10	6	2	10	53	.171	.221	.235	29.3	5.5	181
McMillon, John	L-R	6-3	230	1-27-98	1	0	3.38	9	0	4	11	4	4	4	0	6	21	.108	.233	.135	48.8	14.0	43
Mozzicato, Frank	L-L	6-3	175	6-19-03	2	5	3.04	12	12	0	56	36	21	19	5	34	85	.180	.298	.310	36.2	14.5	235
Novas, Elvis	R-R	6-0	205	9-02-02	0	0	4.09	8	0	0	11	13	5	5	2	6	9	.302	.407	.442	16.7	11.1	54
Olivarez, Marcus	R-R	6-3	200	9-12-98	1	4	6.08	28	0	0	40	45	32	27	5	30	53	.290	.430	.465	27.3	15.5	194
Panzini, Shane	R-R	6-3	220	10-30-01	3	9	4.47	20	20	0	91	90	52	45	8	51	98	.268	.367	.411	24.7	12.9	396
Patteson, Hunter	L-L	6-4	190	4-04-00	0	0	0.00	1	1	0	3	3	0	0	0	0	2	.250	.250	.250	16.7	0.0	12
Ramsey, Ryan	R-L	6-0	195	1-18-01	2	0	0.54	7	7	0	33	17	3	2	0	10	38	.150	.244	.177	29.5	7.8	129
Rayo, Oscar	L-L	6-1	180	1-13-02	5	2	3.15	23	6	2	71	65	32	25	1	12	66	.239	.284	.301	22.8	4.2	289
Regalado, Nicholas	R-R	6-2	215	5-15-02	1	1	2.78	20	0	3	32	29	13	10	0	17	43	.242	.345	.317	30.9	12.2	139
Reyes, Emmanuel	R-R	6-0	180	5-16-04	1	5	4.30	7	7	0	38	39	20	18	4	8	29	.267	.310	.452	18.4	5.1	158
Sandlin, David	R-R	6-4	215	2-21-01	4	1	3.38	12	12	0	59	57	23	22	8	13	79	.259	.298	.432	33.5	5.5	236
Scott, Wesley	R-R	6-1	185	3-02-01	2	2	4.76	24	0	2	34	28	20	18	0	29	40	.222	.395	.262	24.5	17.8	163
Sears, Ben	R-R	6-5	208	6-15-00	3	1	3.21	31	0	9	62	57	27	22	5	9	62	.244	.272	.368	25.2	3.7	246
Solano, Adrian	R-R	6-1	180	10-17-99	0	0	94.50	2	0	0	1	2	7	7	0	8	2	.500	.833	.500	16.7	66.7	12

Pitching	B-T	Ht.	Wt.	DOB	W	L	ERA	G	GS	SV	IP	Hits	Runs	ER	HR	BB	SO	AVG	OBP	SLG	SO%	BB%	BF
Valerio, Samuel	R-R	6-4	230	10-08-01	1	5	5.35	27	3	0	35	26	23	21	3	30	53	.208	.371	.320	33.3	18.9	159
Veliz, Mauricio	R-R	6-2	220	7-17-02	5	6	4.76	22	20	0	98	107	63	52	10	38	68	.273	.341	.408	15.3	8.6	443
Wallace, Chase	R-R	6-2	195	11-13-98	3	1	3.52	21	0	1	31	30	15	12	1	9	35	.254	.328	.339	26.1	6.7	134
Widener, Jacob	R-L	6-7	235	6-15-01	0	0	10.38	4	0	0	4	4	5	5	2	2	8	.235	.480	.588	32.0	8.0	25
Williams, Henry	R-R	6-5	200	9-18-01	2	1	3.38	5	5	0	24	18	10	9	3	13	23	.209	.317	.372	22.8	12.9	101
Zobac, Steven	L-R	6-3	185	10-14-00	1	2	2.09	14	10	0	52	43	15	12	2	12	61	.225	.275	.304	29.9	5.9	204

Fielding

Catcher	PCT	G	PO	A	E	DP	PB
Dunhurst	.980	15	132	12	3	1	2
Hernandez	.987	73	719	63	10	4	4
Pire	1.000	4	26	2	0	0	3
Salon	.981	43	386	28	8	0	12

First Base	PCT	G	PO	A	E	DP
Calderon	.966	19	130	11	5	12
Salon	.918	8	45	0	4	5
Squires	.998	105	740	74	2	70

Second Base	PCT	G	PO	A	E	DP
Candelario	1.000	1	3	5	0	2
Florentino	.962	12	21	29	2	3
McNair	.944	5	8	9	1	1
Rodriguez	.959	114	194	268	20	61

Third Base	PCT	G	PO	A	E	DP
Calderon	.750	3	0	3	1	0
Charles	.938	37	28	62	6	11
Florentino	.921	17	11	24	3	2
McNair	.882	58	39	73	15	5
Werner	.778	20	8	20	8	2

Shortstop	PCT	G	PO	A	E	DP
Charles	.940	19	35	43	5	8
Florentino	1.000	6	9	9	0	2
Vazquez	.963	108	146	247	15	43

Outfield	PCT	G	PO	A	E	DP
Candelario	.984	21	28	0	1	0
Dickey	1.000	25	41	0	0	0
Hollie	1.000	17	22	1	0	0
Leyton	.979	77	108	10	2	1
Nivens	.990	26	53	1	1	0
Pena	.978	73	131	2	3	0
Ramirez	.991	78	110	8	3	1
Roccaforte	1.000	24	48	0	0	0
Squires	1.000	6	8	0	0	0
Usher	.967	55	95	6	3	1

ACL ROYALS

ROOKIE

ARIZONA COMPLEX LEAGUE

Batting	B-T	Ht.	Wt.	DOB	AVG	OBP	SLG	G	PA	AB	R	H	2B	3B	HR	RBI	BB	HBP	SH	SF	SO	SB	CS	BB%	SO%
Advincola, Yeudi	R-R	6-1	170	10-09-01	.188	.316	.250	16	57	48	12	9	1	1	0	1	8	1	0	0	15	5	1	14.0	26.3
Alexander, CJ	L-R	6-3	215	7-17-96	.412	.600	1.235	6	25	17	8	7	2	0	4	15	6	2	0	0	3	0	0	24.0	12.0
Allende, Giullianno	L-L	6-0	165	9-04-03	.226	.347	.310	25	101	84	21	19	4	0	1	16	14	2	0	1	32	10	2	13.9	31.7
Burke, Chris	L-R	5-10	180	8-16-01	.091	.286	.182	5	14	11	1	1	1	0	0	0	3	0	0	0	6	0	0	21.4	42.9
Candelario, Wilmin	B-R	6-0	195	9-11-01	.286	.444	.714	2	9	7	2	2	0	0	1	1	2	0	0	0	4	1	0	22.2	44.4
Cepero, Ryan	R-R	5-10	180	2-11-03	.158	.250	.211	25	88	76	13	12	4	0	0	7	8	2	0	2	27	2	0	9.1	30.7
Charles, Austin	R-R	6-4	215	11-13-03	.455	.455	1.000	2	11	11	5	5	1	1	1	3	0	0	0	0	3	0	0	0.0	27.3
Collins, Darnel	L-L	5-10	200	7-12-04	.172	.232	.299	27	95	87	8	15	3	1	2	15	7	0	0	1	29	2	1	7.4	30.5
De Los Santos, Jaswel	L-R	5-11	185	1-28-02	.130	.310	.174	8	29	23	6	3	1	0	0	0	6	0	0	0	10	3	0	20.7	34.5
Dickerson, Dustin	R-R	6-1	180	3-28-01	.357	.357	.357	4	14	14	2	5	0	0	0	4	0	0	0	0	2	1	0	0.0	14.3
Dickey, Jared	L-R	6-1	204	3-01-02	.182	.357	.364	4	14	11	2	2	0	1	0	1	2	1	0	0	2	1	0	14.3	14.3
Dunhurst, Hayden	L-R	5-8	220	9-19-00	.091	.313	.182	3	16	11	2	1	1	0	0	3	4	0	0	1	5	0	0	25.0	31.3
Figueroa, Derlin	L-R	6-0	163	9-07-03	.571	.659	1.029	11	44	35	14	20	10	0	2	8	9	0	0	0	4	1	2	20.5	9.1
2-team (31 ACL Dodgers)					.328	.452	.555	42	157	128	30	42	14	0	5	29	28	1	0	0	29	6	3	17.8	18.5
Florentino, Omar	B-R	5-9	170	10-26-01	.182	.217	.364	6	23	22	3	4	2	1	0	2	1	0	0	0	6	0	0	4.3	26.1
Guzman, Diego	R-R	5-11	200	9-12-03	.198	.260	.302	31	96	86	10	17	4	1	1	19	8	0	0	2	17	2	2	8.3	17.7
Guzman, Jeison	B-R	6-0	205	10-08-98	.154	.313	.346	7	32	26	4	4	0	1	1	7	4	2	0	0	7	0	0	12.5	21.9
Hernandez, Diego	L-L	6-0	150	11-21-00	.440	.517	.760	6	29	25	7	11	0	1	2	6	3	1	0	0	6	0	1	10.3	20.7
Johnson, Justin	R-R	5-11	185	4-03-00	.375	.444	.500	3	9	8	2	3	1	0	0	0	1	0	0	0	1	0	2	11.1	11.1
Kennedy, Eric	L-R	5-11	203	9-15-99	.444	.667	.556	4	15	9	4	4	1	0	0	0	6	0	0	0	1	0	0	40.0	6.7
Loftin, Nick	R-R	5-11	180	9-25-98	.471	.615	.706	6	26	17	10	8	1	0	1	5	6	2	0	1	4	1	0	23.1	15.4
Lucas, Aldrin	R-R	5-10	165	2-07-03	.301	.463	.411	26	95	73	15	22	5	0	1	12	18	4	0	0	18	5	0	18.9	18.9
Mendez, Jairo	L-L	6-0	155	10-06-02	.292	.355	.500	28	107	96	15	28	5	3	3	17	9	1	0	1	34	4	4	8.4	31.8
Mitchell, Blake	L-R	6-1	192	8-03-04	.147	.423	.176	13	52	34	8	5	1	0	0	3	17	0	0	1	14	1	0	32.7	26.9
Nivens, Spencer	L-R	5-11	185	11-16-01	.313	.353	.563	4	17	16	3	5	4	0	0	1	1	0	0	0	2	1	1	5.9	11.8
Novas, Josi	R-R	6-4	180	2-12-05	.324	.437	.450	35	135	111	26	36	5	0	3	21	23	0	0	1	42	8	3	17.0	31.1
Nuel, Omar	R-R	5-11	210	5-12-03	.321	.369	.440	29	122	109	19	35	10	0	1	22	6	4	0	3	30	10	3	4.9	24.6
Perdomo, Jhonny	R-R	5-10	168	6-09-02	.336	.381	.455	36	148	134	31	45	8	1	2	24	9	2	1	2	29	16	1	6.1	19.6
Pire, Enmanuel	R-R	5-10	180	5-18-01	.279	.377	.395	17	53	43	8	12	2	0	1	9	8	0	0	2	10	0	1	15.1	18.9
Roccaforte, Carson	L-L	6-1	195	3-29-02	.533	.500	.600	4	16	15	3	8	1	0	0	3	0	0	0	1	3	5	0	0.0	18.8
Rushford, Milo	L-L	6-0	185	2-12-04	.333	.441	.541	32	136	111	32	37	8	3	3	21	20	3	0	2	30	9	1	14.7	22.1
Russell, Stone	R-R	6-1	195	6-17-04	.269	.367	.462	9	30	26	6	7	3	1	0	3	4	0	0	0	5	2	1	13.3	16.7
Seijas, Rothaikeg	R-R	5-10	170	7-22-02	.200	.365	.425	15	52	40	5	8	3	0	2	6	10	1	0	1	14	1	1	19.2	26.9
Silva, Gabriel	R-R	5-9	218	12-10-03	.254	.360	.424	34	139	118	18	30	8	0	4	24	16	4	0	1	50	2	2	11.5	36.0
Torres, Erick	R-R	5-10	160	12-20-04	.319	.392	.428	36	160	138	29	44	5	5	0	18	16	2	2	2	20	11	4	10.0	12.5
Town, River	L-R	5-9	181	7-08-99	.125	.462	.500	3	13	8	2	1	0	0	1	2	3	2	0	0	1	1	0	23.1	7.7
Um, Hyungchan	R-R	6-1	190	4-24-04	.220	.305	.320	15	59	50	9	11	2	0	1	5	7	0	0	2	15	1	0	11.9	25.4
Valera, Leonel	R-R	6-3	206	7-09-99	.235	.333	.294	6	21	17	2	4	1	0	0	3	3	0	0	1	6	0	0	14.3	28.6
Werner, Trevor	R-R	6-3	225	9-03-00	.333	.375	.733	4	16	15	4	5	1	1	1	4	1	0	0	0	6	2	0	6.3	37.5

Pitching	B-T	Ht.	Wt.	DOB	W	L	ERA	G	GS	SV	IP	Hits	Runs	ER	HR	BB	SO	AVG	OBP	SLG	SO%	BB%	BF
Anderson, Justin	L-R	6-3	230	9-28-92	3	0	7.64	12	1	0	18	15	16	15	0	14	37	.217	.357	.261	44.0	16.7	84
Anglin, Mack	R-R	6-4	220	7-05-00	1	0	0.00	3	1	0	5	3	0	0	0	2	5	.158	.238	.211	23.8	9.5	21
Arronde, Felix	R-R	6-3	185	4-25-03	1	1	1.85	11	5	0	39	28	12	8	3	15	46	.201	.284	.295	29.7	9.7	155
Bosacker, Ethan	R-R	6-2	210	2-20-01	0	0	10.80	2	0	0	2	4	2	2	0	1	2	.444	.500	.556	20.0	10.0	10
Brentz, Jake	L-L	6-1	205	9-14-94	0	0	0.00	2	1	0	2	1	1	0	0	1	3	.143	.333	.143	33.3	11.1	9
Cepeda, Luis	L-L	6-1	175	10-12-00	1	2	8.27	8	2	0	16	27	18	15	2	4	22	.351	.390	.532	26.5	4.8	83
Diaz, Andres	R-R	6-1	215	7-06-01	1	2	3.66	8	2	0	20	21	11	8	2	5	16	.263	.314	.450	18.6	5.8	86

Pitching	B-T	Ht.	Wt.	DOB	W	L	ERA	G	GS	SV	IP	Hits	Runs	ER	HR	BB	SO	AVG	OBP	SLG	SO%	BB%	BF
Fenlong, Connor	R-R	6-4	225	9-22-99	0	0	6.75	3	1	0	4	4	3	3	0	3	4	.267	.421	.267	21.1	15.8	19
Hansell, Josh	R-R	6-6	215	2-07-02	1	0	3.00	2	0	0	3	3	1	1	0	1	1	.273	.333	.455	8.3	8.3	12
Herbold, Brandon	R-R	6-6	180	8-10-04	1	1	6.46	12	10	0	24	23	17	17	4	7	15	.258	.327	.539	14.9	6.9	101
Hernandez, Ben	R-R	6-2	205	7-01-01	0	3	5.74	5	2	0	16	17	12	10	1	10	10	.262	.377	.446	13.0	13.0	77
Isbell, Chase	R-R	6-2	198	9-12-00	1	0	0.00	2	0	0	3	1	0	0	0	1	7	.111	.200	.111	63.6	9.1	11
Kaufman, Rylan	L-L	6-4	225	6-23-99	0	0	1.59	4	4	0	6	3	2	1	0	4	7	.167	.400	.167	28.0	16.0	25
Keller, Brad	R-R	6-5	255	7-27-95	1	1	16.20	2	1	0	2	3	3	3	0	3	2	.375	.545	.375	18.2	27.3	11
Kirkland, Doug	R-R	5-11	212	12-03-00	1	0	3.86	3	0	0	2	1	3	1	0	4	6	.111	.385	.222	46.2	30.8	13
Marte, Yunior	R-R	6-5	210	9-08-03	0	1	4.14	12	6	0	37	38	18	17	3	11	39	.259	.309	.388	24.1	6.8	162
Martin, Logan	R-R	6-1	180	7-17-01	0	0	0.00	2	0	1	3	1	0	0	0	1	6	.100	.182	.100	54.5	9.1	11
Martinez, Luis	L-L	6-1	180	9-17-03	2	0	9.15	13	0	0	21	28	23	21	3	12	30	.311	.394	.467	28.8	11.5	104
McClelland, Jackson	R-R	6-5	220	7-19-94	1	0	0.00	2	0	0	3	0	0	0	0	0	5	.000	.000	.000	55.6	0.0	9
Mendieta, Augusto	R-R	5-11	190	8-19-04	3	2	8.79	11	1	0	14	20	16	14	2	7	20	.328	.414	.541	28.6	10.0	70
Michel, Ismael	R-R	6-3	175	2-14-02	0	1	10.03	11	0	1	12	12	15	13	1	15	18	.250	.439	.396	27.3	22.7	66
Novas, Elvis	R-R	6-0	205	9-02-02	0	0	10.80	6	0	0	8	15	12	10	1	5	6	.385	.455	.615	13.6	11.4	44
Oliver, Connor	L-L	6-1	170	5-26-01	0	0	0.00	1	0	0	1	2	0	0	0	0	0	.400	.400	.600	0.0	0.0	5
Patteson, Hunter	L-L	6-4	190	4-04-00	0	0	5.28	7	6	0	15	17	11	9	1	3	21	.266	.309	.391	30.9	4.4	68
Picard, Coleman	R-R	6-2	185	10-27-01	0	0	3.00	2	0	0	3	1	1	1	0	3	5	.100	.308	.200	38.5	23.1	13
Polanco, Luis	R-R	6-3	225	8-10-00	3	0	3.54	16	0	8	20	22	10	8	3	6	26	.265	.319	.434	28.6	6.6	91
Presinal, Yimi	R-R	5-11	175	9-18-04	1	2	5.40	12	4	1	35	32	27	21	3	19	47	.244	.348	.435	29.7	12.0	158
Ramsey, Ryan	R-L	6-0	195	1-18-01	0	1	6.75	2	1	0	4	3	3	3	0	3	9	.200	.333	.267	50.0	16.7	18
Reyes, Emmanuel	R-R	6-0	180	5-16-04	3	2	3.38	8	3	0	32	30	15	12	0	8	35	.244	.309	.350	25.7	5.9	136
Rios, Jesus	R-R	6-1	190	12-27-01	0	0	3.86	4	0	0	5	7	2	2	0	4	4	.368	.478	.421	17.4	17.4	23
Rosado, Jarold	R-R	6-3	215	7-13-02	2	2	10.38	15	1	0	26	35	32	30	1	23	35	.318	.442	.473	25.4	16.7	138
Santana, Osiris	R-R	5-11	158	10-11-01	0	1	6.00	14	0	2	21	24	16	14	1	10	19	.282	.354	.412	19.6	10.3	97
Solano, Adrian	R-R	6-1	180	10-17-99	0	1	13.50	4	0	0	3	5	6	5	0	2	6	.333	.412	.400	35.3	11.8	17
Valdez, Richy	R-R	6-1	180	7-29-05	3	1	6.92	10	2	0	26	33	23	20	2	12	31	.306	.400	.417	24.6	9.5	126
Wereski, Ben	L-L	6-2	210	10-26-97	1	0	0.00	2	1	0	2	3	0	0	0	2	2	.300	.417	.400	16.7	16.7	12
Widener, Jacob	R-L	6-7	235	6-15-01	0	0	7.36	3	0	1	4	5	3	3	0	0	3	.294	.294	.412	17.6	0.0	17
Yarbrough, Ryan	R-L	6-5	205	12-31-91	0	1	9.00	1	1	0	3	5	3	3	1	0	2	.357	.357	.857	14.3	0.0	14

Fielding

C: Silva 26, Pire 15, Um 11, Mitchell 8, Burke 2, Dunhurst 1. **1B:** Collins 26, Lucas 25, Figueroa 6, Silva 4, Alexander 4. **2B:** Perdomo 27, Cepero 18, Guzman 10, Florentino 4, Johnson 2, Loftin 1. **3B:** Guzman 22, Perdomo 9, Russell 8, Novas 5, Loftin 4, Advincola 4, Figueroa 4, Werner 3, Valera 2, Florentino 2. **SS:** Novas 30, Advincola 13, Cepero 7, Valera 3, Dickerson 3, Charles 2, Candelario 2, Guzman 1, Johnson 1. **OF:** Torres 36, Allende 26, Mendez 26, Rushford 23, Nuel 21, Seijas 13, Hernandez 6, De Los Santos 6, Dickey 3, Figueroa 3, Guzman 3, Kennedy 3, Nivens 3, Roccaforte 3, Town 3, Silva 1.

DSL ROYALS — *ROOKIE*

DOMINICAN SUMMER LEAGUE

Batting	B-T	Ht.	Wt.	DOB	AVG	OBP	SLG	G	PA	AB	R	H	2B	3B	HR	RBI	BB	HBP	SH	SF	SO	SB	CS	BB%	SO%
Acosta, Angel	L-R	5-9	160	3-02-03	.293	.397	.422	35	141	116	19	34	7	1	2	13	16	6	0	3	20	1	4	11.3	14.2
Bravo, Osman	R-R	5-11	170	6-16-04	.250	.341	.333	22	82	72	8	18	3	0	1	9	8	2	0	0	11	2	0	9.8	13.4
Cabrera, Roni	R-R	6-1	175	7-31-05	.271	.357	.407	22	70	59	10	16	3	1	1	7	7	2	0	2	19	1	1	10.0	27.1
Castro, Jose	R-R	6-3	160	4-21-06	.197	.286	.258	24	79	66	9	13	4	0	0	4	9	0	2	2	20	2	1	11.4	25.3
Chacon, Jose	R-R	6-0	165	11-29-02	.216	.345	.278	35	116	97	13	21	3	0	1	8	15	4	0	0	22	9	1	12.9	19.0
Cruz, Darvin	L-L	5-11	165	11-10-05	.203	.352	.259	44	181	143	18	29	8	0	0	13	34	0	2	2	41	9	3	18.8	22.7
Fernandez, Yosmi	B-R	5-11	165	4-15-04	.220	.423	.268	32	112	82	21	18	1	0	1	9	23	6	1	0	34	3	4	20.5	30.4
German, Manuel	R-R	6-1	220	4-29-05	.228	.281	.307	35	114	101	9	23	2	0	2	10	5	4	0	4	28	0	0	4.4	24.6
Gonzalez, Asbel	R-R	6-2	170	1-02-06	.245	.355	.364	43	173	143	25	35	10	2	1	18	19	7	1	3	26	17	11	11.0	15.0
Gonzalez, Ricson	R-R	6-0	170	6-16-05	.244	.398	.344	34	113	90	15	22	6	0	1	4	16	7	0	0	21	0	1	14.2	18.6
Hernandez, Jorge	L-R	6-0	180	12-20-05	.310	.397	.380	41	152	129	21	40	7	1	0	20	14	6	1	2	29	4	2	9.2	19.1
Lopez, Daniel	L-L	6-2	165	9-14-05	.310	.414	.490	45	174	145	23	45	7	5	3	24	23	4	0	2	40	8	4	13.2	23.0
Medina, Jose	B-R	5-10	185	4-16-05	.229	.356	.275	44	164	131	19	30	4	1	0	12	26	2	1	4	36	0	2	15.9	22.0
Medina, Raimel	R-R	5-11	165	11-15-04	.219	.265	.344	18	68	64	4	14	3	1	1	6	3	1	0	0	11	1	1	4.4	16.2
Mota, Edgar	R-R	6-1	170	12-14-05	.178	.288	.222	17	52	45	4	8	2	0	0	0	5	2	0	0	13	0	0	9.6	25.0
Nova, Charles	R-R	5-10	155	1-15-05	.171	.293	.200	37	123	105	12	18	3	0	0	10	15	3	0	0	18	4	2	12.2	14.6
Olmos, Juan	R-R	6-2	175	11-22-04	.196	.364	.343	34	132	102	19	20	6	0	3	22	23	5	0	2	51	0	1	17.4	38.6
Orasma, Alexander	B-R	6-0	165	11-19-04	.165	.226	.186	33	108	97	8	16	2	0	0	10	7	1	2	1	25	3	2	6.5	23.1
Paulino, Jose	L-L	5-11	165	10-23-05	.220	.346	.280	43	160	132	26	29	3	1	1	17	22	4	1	1	57	8	7	13.8	35.6
Ramirez, Angel	R-R	6-2	190	3-28-05	.240	.379	.300	39	125	100	23	24	6	0	0	11	19	4	1	1	12	5	3	15.2	9.6
Ramirez, Ramon	R-R	6-0	180	6-15-05	.344	.440	.615	41	150	122	26	42	9	0	8	27	21	3	0	4	18	6	4	14.0	12.0
Ramos, Henry	L-L	6-1	175	9-20-04	.227	.301	.375	52	196	176	28	40	9	4	3	14	16	3	0	1	49	11	2	8.2	25.0
Reyes, Omar	L-R	5-11	170	3-03-05	.242	.444	.341	32	126	91	13	22	3	3	0	15	32	2	0	1	16	3	2	25.4	12.7
Roque, Pedro	R-R	5-10	160	12-21-05	.243	.364	.308	37	135	107	19	26	4	0	1	11	20	2	3	3	17	9	3	14.8	12.6
Ruiz, Sandy	R-R	5-10	160	1-24-06	.215	.339	.280	37	127	107	17	23	4	0	1	9	18	2	0	0	36	2	2	14.2	28.3
Ruiz, Tony	R-R	6-3	170	12-08-05	.267	.353	.458	38	150	131	24	35	11	1	4	16	16	2	0	1	54	1	2	10.7	36.0
Santos, Enmanuel	R-R	6-0	185	12-20-05	.238	.307	.352	38	137	122	17	29	8	0	2	19	12	1	0	2	31	8	0	8.8	22.6
Sosa, Ivan	R-R	6-2	180	9-09-04	.157	.240	.303	30	100	89	9	14	4	0	3	10	8	2	0	1	41	3	2	8.0	41.0
Vargas, Yeison	R-R	5-11	155	9-10-03	.206	.313	.289	35	114	97	11	20	1	2	1	7	12	3	2	0	32	5	2	10.5	28.1
Zue, Jhosmmel	R-R	5-11	146	2-05-04	.246	.368	.485	40	163	134	23	33	8	3	6	26	23	4	0	2	49	8	2	14.1	30.1

Pitching	B-T	Ht.	Wt.	DOB	W	L	ERA	G	GS	SV	IP	Hits	Runs	ER	HR	BB	SO	AVG	OBP	SLG	SO%	BB%	BF
Amezquita, Moises	L-L	5-10	160	7-27-04	2	1	3.52	9	4	0	23	26	12	9	5	8	22	.295	.380	.489	22.0	8.0	100
Baez, Dioni	R-R	6-2	185	1-24-03	1	4	7.34	11	6	0	31	28	31	25	6	17	41	.243	.351	.452	30.6	12.7	134
Basora, Andy	R-R	6-3	155	4-13-05	1	2	1.97	12	4	0	32	34	15	7	0	10	27	.268	.340	.354	19.0	7.0	142

Betemit, Wilson	R-R	6-1	170	7-27-03	2	0	2.08	3	0	0	9	7	3	2	1	3	10	.206	.270	.412	27.0	8.1	37
Carmona, Samuel	R-R	6-0	160	12-23-04	0	0	3.00	3	0	1	3	1	1	1	0	2	4	.100	.250	.300	33.3	16.7	12
Castillo, Emilio	L-L	5-10	150	10-18-02	1	3	3.74	13	0	0	22	17	14	9	0	10	30	.210	.302	.210	31.3	10.4	96
Castro, Jeremy	R-R	6-4	190	11-16-02	0	0	3.00	3	0	0	6	4	2	2	1	3	5	.182	.308	.364	19.2	11.5	26
Downs, Lloyd	R-R	6-1	170	4-13-06	2	1	6.00	7	3	0	15	10	11	10	1	17	13	.192	.417	.308	18.1	23.6	72
Espinoza, Weskendry	R-R	6-1	185	3-18-02	1	2	2.45	11	9	0	37	27	13	10	1	15	36	.201	.292	.299	23.2	9.7	155
Franco, Jesus	L-L	6-1	170	3-04-05	1	1	3.86	8	0	0	12	10	10	5	1	10	9	.227	.404	.341	15.8	17.5	57
Gomez, Jhonny	R-R	5-11	180	8-27-02	2	1	2.52	12	2	3	25	20	10	7	2	13	15	.220	.355	.352	13.5	11.7	111
Gonzalez, Carlos	R-R	6-1	150	2-14-06	2	3	6.63	11	0	0	19	26	22	14	5	9	11	.310	.385	.595	11.5	9.4	96
Gutierrez, Jose	R-R	6-1	155	5-24-03	3	1	4.50	6	2	0	16	19	8	8	1	3	17	.292	.352	.385	23.9	4.2	71
Gutierrez, Julio	R-R	6-1	175	3-05-05	1	0	8.76	9	0	1	12	12	16	12	4	17	7	.250	.463	.625	10.3	25.0	68
Guzman, Franquely	R-R	6-3	220	5-12-03	0	2	10.03	9	0	0	12	10	16	13	0	20	16	.227	.500	.295	22.9	28.6	70
Herrera, Jorge	R-R	6-0	160	5-15-03	0	1	5.91	9	5	0	21	22	16	14	2	8	26	.256	.337	.442	26.5	8.2	98
Jimenez, Damian	R-R	6-5	190	9-21-04	0	0	4.09	11	2	2	22	22	11	10	0	12	17	.265	.361	.325	17.5	12.4	97
Jorge, Marwys	R-R	6-4	175	2-15-06	0	2	4.15	11	9	1	30	22	17	14	0	19	28	.210	.364	.276	21.2	14.4	132
Leal, Henson	R-R	6-1	176	9-19-03	1	1	4.13	10	5	0	24	32	15	11	3	9	29	.317	.375	.485	25.9	8.0	112
Leon, Jesus	L-L	6-3	160	5-05-04	2	1	0.93	13	1	2	19	6	7	2	0	8	22	.097	.211	.097	30.1	11.0	73
Lorenzo, Jhoan	R-R	5-11	165	1-12-05	2	2	9.00	12	0	1	17	22	22	17	1	16	10	.328	.505	.493	11.0	17.6	91
Lorenzo, Ricardito	L-L	6-3	200	8-03-03	0	2	10.03	10	0	0	12	14	20	13	1	11	5	.292	.444	.458	7.8	17.2	64
Mendez, Eslahiber	R-R	5-11	160	12-09-03	0	0	17.36	5	1	0	5	9	11	9	0	12	3	.391	.600	.565	8.6	34.3	35
Nova, Fraynel	R-R	6-0	190	5-22-02	2	0	3.04	13	0	4	24	21	9	8	1	5	24	.233	.274	.311	25.3	5.3	95
Oduber, Shawndrick	R-R	6-0	170	12-16-04	0	2	3.06	11	11	0	32	31	13	11	3	8	45	.244	.304	.362	32.4	5.8	139
Oliveira, Jesus	R-R	6-0	160	12-31-04	1	0	0.00	2	0	0	3	0	0	0	0	4	1	.000	.333	.000	8.3	33.3	12
Ozuna, Juan	L-L	5-10	165	10-26-04	1	3	6.91	11	0	0	14	21	21	11	1	10	21	.333	.423	.508	26.6	12.7	79
Pena, Victor	L-L	5-11	165	12-21-02	6	0	0.86	13	0	3	31	20	6	3	1	3	44	.175	.203	.246	37.3	2.5	118
Perez, Yeri	R-R	6-3	180	10-16-04	1	3	3.33	11	7	0	24	20	17	9	1	24	23	.235	.420	.294	20.4	21.2	113
Pineda, Alvaro	R-R	6-2	170	6-30-04	2	1	5.01	11	6	0	32	31	21	18	3	12	26	.238	.322	.369	17.8	8.2	146
Pineda, Wermer	R-R	6-4	171	10-27-02	1	1	3.20	9	0	0	20	14	11	7	0	10	18	.206	.349	.206	21.4	11.9	84
Reyes, Jhon	R-R	6-1	165	5-30-04	0	1	4.05	7	0	2	7	2	4	3	0	4	10	.087	.222	.130	37.0	14.8	27
Rios, Jesus	R-R	6-1	190	12-27-01	0	0	0.00	1	0	0	1	0	0	0	0	1	1	.000	.200	.000	20.0	20.0	5
Rodriguez, Darwin	L-L	6-1	175	7-24-03	1	2	3.65	11	2	0	25	31	12	10	4	8	22	.313	.382	.475	20.0	7.3	110
Rodriguez, David	L-L	5-11	152	9-27-03	1	1	1.84	12	0	2	29	19	7	6	1	3	35	.178	.207	.215	31.5	2.7	111
Rodriguez, Edwin	R-R	6-2	170	8-24-03	2	1	6.14	13	0	2	22	20	20	15	1	19	15	.238	.407	.345	13.9	17.6	108
Rodriguez, Frandy	R-R	5-9	155	1-28-06	0	1	2.45	11	9	0	37	30	12	10	4	5	28	.216	.247	.345	19.2	3.4	146
Rojas, Marvin	R-R	6-3	185	4-10-04	0	0	12.71	7	0	0	6	2	10	8	0	19	3	.125	.568	.125	8.1	51.4	37
Rosario, Julio	R-R	6-1	205	7-12-02	1	4	3.18	12	3	1	28	24	15	10	3	6	20	.229	.281	.419	17.4	5.2	115
Salgado, Edinson	L-L	6-0	150	1-06-05	1	2	7.16	11	1	0	16	14	20	13	0	16	19	.230	.388	.328	23.8	20.0	80
Sanchez, Junior	R-R	6-2	180	2-02-05	1	1	1.38	3	3	0	13	7	4	2	0	6	8	.156	.264	.222	14.8	11.1	54
Sosa, Yenfri	L-L	6-0	170	12-29-03	3	1	0.71	15	0	4	25	17	5	2	0	11	41	.195	.277	.218	40.6	10.9	101
Valdez, Luis	R-R	6-0	170	10-25-04	1	2	3.02	12	12	0	42	32	18	14	2	9	46	.209	.274	.294	27.4	5.4	168
Vicente, Jheremy	R-R	6-1	170	10-01-03	2	1	5.75	9	2	0	20	20	15	13	1	14	16	.253	.365	.316	16.7	14.6	96

Fielding

C: Gonzalez 29, Ramirez 24, Olmos 23, Zue 21, Medina 13, Mota 7, Hernandez 1. **1B:** German 35, Medina 27, Zue 17, Bravo 16, Hernandez 16, Gonzalez 3, Mota 1. **2B:** Vargas 28, Reyes 26, Nova 24, Orasma 19, Chacon 9, Fernandez 8, Acosta 8. **3B:** Ruiz 34, Chacon 26, Hernandez 22, Acosta 20, Orasma 9, Vargas 2, Sosa 1, Castro 1, Fernandez 1. **SS:** Roque 37, Sosa 22, Castro 22, Fernandez 21, Nova 15, Chacon 1, Vargas 1. **OF:** Ramos 52, Cruz 45, Gonzalez 42, Lopez 42, Paulino 42, Ramirez 37, Santos 36, Ruiz 25, Cabrera 22, Medina 11, Orasma 5.

Los Angeles Angels

SEASON SYNOPSIS: Somehow, some way, the Angels had their eighth consecutive losing season with Mike Trout on the roster. Despite Shohei Ohtani turning in another Major League Player of the Year season, the Angels collapsed in the second half, crushed by injuries to stars such as Ohtani and Trout as well as to depth pieces, plus a lack of pitching and, frankly, a lack of luck.

HIGH POINT: Ohtani was brilliant while healthy, shining brightest in a doubleheader at Detroit on July 27. In the first game, he threw a one-hit shutout, striking out eight in a 6-0 victory. In the nightcap, he helped power an 11-4 win with a pair of home runs, numbers 37 and 38, en route to his AL-leading 44 home runs.

LOW POINT: There were too many … Anthony Rendon had another lost season, with the lowlight coming Opening Night when he grabbed the shirt of a heckling fan as he came off the field in Oakland. Trout broke a bone in his hand in early July, missed seven weeks, and tried to come back in late August, playing one game before realizing the pain was too much. He missed the rest of the season. At the end of August, the Angels put six players on waivers, trying to save money.

NOTABLE ROOKIES: The Angels flashed some hope for the future. Catcher Logan O'Hoppe, limited by a left shoulder injury in the first half, returned to hit 14 home runs in 182 at-bats. Shortstop Zach Neto, the club's 2022 first-round pick out of Campbell, leapt to the majors less than a year later, though an oblique strain limited his bat and playing time. 2023 first-rounder Nolan Schanuel jumped to the majors after just 22 games in the minors and reached base in all 29 MLB games, tied for the third-best streak all time.

KEY TRANSACTIONS: GM Perry Minasian tried to go all-in at the trade deadline in a playoff push. Minasian traded two top prospects, catcher Edgar Quero and lefty Ky Bush, to the White Sox for righthanders Lucas Giolito and Reynaldo Lopez. They also traded prospects to Colorado for veterans C.J. Cron, Randal Grichuk and Mike Moustakas, and to the Mets for Eduardo Escobar. But the club punted in late August and lost lefty Matt Moore, righty Dominic Leone, outfielder Hunter Renfroe, Giolito and Lopez on waivers.

DOWN ON THE FARM: As it has been for a decade, the system remains thin, but the team's speedy promotions of top prospects also played a role.

OPENING DAY PAYROLL: $212,228,096 (6th).

PLAYERS OF THE YEAR

MAJOR LEAGUE
Shohei Ohtani
LHP/DH
.304/.412/.654
10-5, 3.14
AL-best 44 HR

MINOR LEAGUE
Nelson Rada
OF
(LoA)
.276/.395/.346
55-for-66 on SBs

ORGANIZATION LEADERS

Batting		*Minimum 250 AB
MAJORS		
* AVG	Shohei Ohtani	.304
* OPS	Shohei Ohtani	1.066
HR	Shohei Ohtani	44
RBI	Shohei Ohtani	95
MINORS		
* AVG	Michael Stefanic, Salt Lake	.365
* OBP	Michael Stefanic, Salt Lake	.463
* SLG	Trey Cabbage, Salt Lake	.596
* OPS	Trey Cabbage, Salt Lake	.975
R	Nelson Rada, Inland Empire	94
H	Michael Stefanic, Salt Lake	139
TB	Trey Cabbage, Salt Lake	249
2B	Orlando Martinez, Rocket City/Salt Lake	27
3B	Jadiel Sanchez, Inland Empire	10
HR	Trey Cabbage, Salt Lake	30
RBI	Trey Cabbage, Salt Lake	89
BB	Kyren Paris, Rocket City	88
SO	Alexander Ramirez, Tri-Cities	170
SB	Nelson Rada, Inland Empire	55

Pitching		#Minimum 75 IP
MAJORS		
W	Shohei Ohtani	10
# ERA	Shohei Ohtani	3.14
SO	Reid Detmers	168
SV	Carlos Estevez	31
MINORS		
W	Jorge Marcheco, I. Empire/Tri-Cities	10
L	Jake Kalish, Salt Lake	11
# ERA	Jorge Marcheco, I. Empire/Tri-Cities	3.55
G	Kelvin Caceres, T-C/Rocket City/S. Lake	52
GS	Jake Kalish, Salt Lake	25
SV	Kenyon Yovan, Rocket City/Salt Lake	10
IP	Jake Kalish, Salt Lake	138
BB	Walbert Urena, Inland Empire	60
SO	Jorge Marcheco, I. Empire/Tri-Cities	124
# AVG	Jorge Marcheco, I. Empire/Tri-Cities	.218

2023 PERFORMANCE

General Manager: Perry Minasian. **Farm Director:** Joey Prebynski. **Scouting Director:** Timothy McIlvaine.

Class	Team	League	W	L	PCT	Finish	Manager
Majors	Los Angeles Angels	American	73	89	.451	12 (15)	Phil Nevin
Triple-A	Salt Lake Bees	Pacific Coast	70	79	.470	6 (10)	Keith Johnson
Double-A	Rocket City Trash Pandas	Southern	58	80	.420	7 (8)	Andy Schatzley
High-A	Tri-City Dust Devils	Northwest	58	72	.446	5 (6)	Jack Howell
Low-A	Inland Empire 66ers	California	68	61	.527	4 (10)	Dave Stapleton
Rookie	ACL Angels	Arizona Complex	26	30	.464	11 (17)	Ever Magallanes
Rookie	DSL Angels	Dominican Sum.	37	18	.673	6 (50)	Hector De La Cruz
Overall 2023 Minor League Record			317	340	.482	21st (30)	

ORGANIZATION STATISTICS

LOS ANGELES ANGELS

AMERICAN LEAGUE

Batting	B-T	Ht.	Wt.	DOB	AVG	OBP	SLG	G	PA	AB	R	H	2B	3B	HR	RBI	BB	HBP	SH	SF	SO	SB	CS	BB%	SO%
Adams, Jordyn	R-R	6-2	181	10-18-99	.128	.125	.128	17	40	39	1	5	0	0	0	1	0	0	0	1	16	1	2	0.0	40.0
Adell, Jo	R-R	6-3	215	4-08-99	.207	.258	.448	17	62	58	7	12	3	1	3	6	4	0	0	0	25	1	0	6.5	40.3
Cabbage, Trey	L-R	6-2	204	5-03-97	.208	.232	.321	22	56	53	5	11	3	0	1	7	2	0	0	1	26	1	1	3.6	46.4
Cron, C.J.	R-R	6-4	235	1-05-90	.200	.259	.260	15	54	50	7	10	0	0	1	5	4	0	0	0	15	0	0	7.4	27.8
Drury, Brandon	R-R	6-2	230	8-21-92	.262	.306	.497	125	523	485	61	127	30	3	26	83	25	8	0	5	136	0	2	4.8	26.0
Escobar, Eduardo	B-R	5-10	193	1-05-89	.219	.259	.303	60	189	178	17	39	3	3	2	15	10	0	0	1	54	0	1	5.3	28.6
Fletcher, David	R-R	5-9	185	5-31-94	.247	.302	.326	33	97	89	7	22	1	0	2	12	7	0	1	0	9	0	0	7.2	9.3
Grichuk, Randal	R-R	6-2	216	8-13-91	.216	.264	.412	54	208	194	25	42	12	1	8	17	11	2	0	1	45	0	0	5.3	21.6
Lamb, Jake	L-R	6-3	215	10-09-90	.216	.259	.353	19	54	51	7	11	1	0	2	5	3	0	0	0	15	0	0	5.6	27.8
Moniak, Mickey	L-R	6-2	195	5-13-98	.280	.307	.495	85	323	311	35	87	21	2	14	45	9	3	0	0	113	6	3	2.8	35.0
Moustakas, Mike	L-R	6-0	225	9-11-88	.236	.256	.371	65	250	237	22	56	8	0	8	31	6	2	0	5	61	0	0	2.4	24.4
Neto, Zach	R-R	6-0	185	1-31-01	.225	.308	.377	84	329	289	38	65	17	0	9	34	20	16	1	3	77	5	1	6.1	23.4
O'Hoppe, Logan	R-R	6-2	185	2-09-00	.236	.296	.500	51	199	182	23	43	6	0	14	29	14	2	0	1	48	0	1	7.0	24.1
Ohtani, Shohei	L-R	6-4	210	7-05-94	.304	.412	.654	135	599	497	102	151	26	8	44	95	91	3	0	3	143	20	6	15.2	23.9
Okey, Chris	R-R	5-11	200	12-29-94	.000	.000	.000	2	2	2	0	0	0	0	0	0	0	0	0	0	2	0	0	0.0	100.0
Padlo, Kevin	R-R	5-11	210	7-15-96	.125	.125	.250	3	8	8	1	1	1	0	0	0	0	0	0	0	0	0	0	0.0	0.0
Paris, Kyren	R-R	6-0	180	11-11-01	.100	.200	.100	15	46	40	4	4	0	0	0	1	4	1	1	0	17	3	0	8.7	37.0
Phillips, Brett	L-R	6-0	195	5-30-94	.175	.268	.333	40	71	63	9	11	1	0	3	6	8	0	0	0	36	3	1	11.3	50.7
Rendon, Anthony	R-R	6-1	200	6-06-90	.236	.361	.318	43	183	148	23	35	6	0	2	22	25	6	0	4	27	2	0	13.7	14.8
Renfroe, Hunter	R-R	6-1	230	1-28-92	.242	.304	.434	126	504	459	56	111	31	0	19	56	39	3	0	3	113	0	0	7.7	22.4
Rengifo, Luis	B-R	5-10	195	2-26-97	.264	.339	.444	126	445	394	55	104	15	4	16	51	41	6	0	4	82	6	4	9.2	18.4
Schanuel, Nolan	L-R	6-3	195	2-14-02	.275	.402	.330	29	132	109	19	30	3	0	1	6	20	3	0	0	19	0	0	15.2	14.4
Soto, Livan	L-R	5-10	160	6-22-00	.222	.417	.222	4	12	9	2	2	0	0	0	0	3	0	0	0	2	0	0	25.0	16.7
Stefanic, Michael	R-R	5-8	180	2-24-96	.290	.380	.355	25	71	62	5	18	2	1	0	6	8	1	0	0	8	0	1	11.3	11.3
Thaiss, Matt	L-R	6-0	215	5-06-95	.214	.319	.340	95	307	262	32	56	6	0	9	31	36	6	0	3	83	2	0	11.7	27.0
Trout, Mike	R-R	6-2	235	8-07-91	.263	.367	.490	82	362	308	54	81	14	1	18	44	45	7	0	2	104	2	0	12.4	28.7
Urshela, Gio	R-R	6-0	215	10-11-91	.299	.329	.374	62	228	214	22	64	8	1	2	24	10	1	0	3	36	3	2	4.4	15.8
Velazquez, Andrew	R-R	5-9	170	7-14-94	.173	.264	.284	54	94	81	12	14	3	0	2	3	10	0	3	0	30	13	3	10.6	31.9
Wallach, Chad	R-R	6-2	246	11-04-91	.197	.259	.376	65	172	157	18	31	5	1	7	15	13	0	2	0	57	0	1	7.6	33.1
Walsh, Jared	L-L	6-0	210	7-30-93	.125	.216	.279	39	116	104	10	13	4	0	4	11	11	1	0	0	45	0	0	9.5	38.8
Ward, Taylor	R-R	6-1	200	12-14-93	.253	.335	.421	97	409	356	60	90	18	0	14	47	39	8	0	6	80	4	2	9.5	19.6

Pitching	B-T	Ht.	Wt.	DOB	W	L	ERA	G	GS	SV	IP	Hits	Runs	ER	HR	BB	SO	AVG	OBP	SLG	SO%	BB%	BF
Anderson, Tyler	L-L	6-2	220	12-30-89	6	6	5.43	27	25	0	141	146	90	85	20	64	119	.266	.346	.455	18.9	10.2	629
Bachman, Sam	R-R	6-1	235	9-30-99	1	2	3.18	11	0	1	17	17	7	6	0	11	14	.262	.377	.292	18.2	14.3	77
Barria, Jaime	R-R	6-1	210	7-18-96	2	6	5.68	34	6	0	82	91	63	52	20	30	62	.277	.340	.512	17.1	8.3	362
Caceres, Kelvin	R-R	6-1	205	1-26-00	0	0	6.75	2	0	0	1	2	1	1	0	2	1	.400	.571	.400	12.5	25.0	8
Canning, Griffin	R-R	6-2	180	5-11-96	7	8	4.32	24	22	0	127	121	62	61	22	36	139	.245	.303	.430	25.9	6.7	536
Daniel, Davis	R-R	6-1	190	6-11-97	1	1	2.19	3	0	0	12	7	3	3	1	9	9	.167	.308	.333	17.3	17.3	52
Davidson, Tucker	L-L	6-2	215	3-25-96	1	1	6.54	18	0	2	32	44	25	23	2	11	31	.331	.388	.481	20.9	7.4	148
Detmers, Reid	L-L	6-2	210	7-08-99	4	10	4.48	28	28	0	149	141	81	74	19	60	168	.248	.332	.401	26.1	9.3	644
Devenski, Chris	R-R	6-3	211	11-13-90	3	2	5.08	29	0	0	34	31	20	19	5	9	33	.244	.295	.394	23.6	6.4	140
Diaz, Jhonathan	L-L	6-0	170	9-13-96	0	0	10.29	4	1	0	7	13	11	8	0	7	4	.419	.524	.581	9.5	16.7	42
Escobar, Eduardo	B-R	5-10	193	1-05-89	0	0	2.45	3	0	0	4	2	2	1	0	1	0	.154	.250	.231	0.0	6.3	16
Estevez, Carlos	R-R	6-6	277	12-28-92	5	5	3.90	63	0	31	62	62	34	27	7	31	78	.254	.350	.381	27.8	11.0	281
Fulmer, Carson	R-R	6-0	210	12-13-93	1	1	2.70	3	1	0	10	6	3	3	1	4	6	.176	.282	.353	15.4	10.3	39
Giolito, Lucas	R-R	6-6	245	7-14-94	1	5	6.89	6	6	0	33	33	28	25	10	15	34	.258	.345	.563	22.8	10.1	149
Herget, Jimmy	R-R	6-3	170	9-09-93	2	4	4.66	29	1	0	29	33	15	15	7	8	26	.282	.339	.547	20.5	6.3	127
Ingram, Kolton	L-L	5-9	170	10-21-96	0	0	8.44	5	0	0	5	8	7	5	2	5	7	.333	.433	.667	23.3	16.7	30
Joyce, Ben	R-R	6-5	225	9-17-00	1	1	5.40	12	0	0	10	9	6	6	1	9	10	.243	.396	.351	20.8	18.8	48
Lamb, Jake	L-R	6-3	215	10-09-90	0	0	0.00	1	0	0	1	1	0	0	0	0	0	.250	.250	.500	0.0	0.0	4
Leone, Dominic	R-R	5-10	215	10-26-91	0	0	5.54	11	0	1	13	15	8	8	2	9	11	.288	.393	.500	18.0	14.8	61
Lopez, Reynaldo	R-R	6-1	225	1-04-94	0	2	2.77	13	0	2	13	12	4	4	1	8	19	.235	.350	.333	31.7	13.3	60
Loup, Aaron	L-L	5-11	210	12-19-87	2	3	6.10	55	0	1	49	65	37	33	6	20	45	.313	.377	.462	19.5	8.7	231

Marte, Jose	R-R	6-3	180	6-14-96	0	0	8.68	10	0	0	9	14	10	9	3	7	7	.359	.438	.667	14.6	14.6	48
Mederos, Victor	R-R	6-2	227	6-08-01	0	0	9.00	3	0	0	3	5	3	3	0	3	3	.417	.529	.417	17.6	17.6	17
Moore, Matt	L-L	6-3	210	6-18-89	4	1	2.66	41	0	0	44	33	14	13	6	12	49	.208	.270	.377	28.0	6.9	175
Moronta, Reyes	R-R	5-10	265	1-06-93	0	0	6.75	2	0	0	1	4	1	1	1	3	2	.500	.636	.875	18.2	27.3	11
Ohtani, Shohei	L-R	6-4	210	7-05-94	10	5	3.14	23	23	0	132	85	50	46	18	55	167	.184	.285	.333	31.5	10.4	531
Phillips, Brett	L-R	6-0	195	5-30-94	0	0	0.00	1	0	0	0	1	0	0	0	1	0	.500	.667	.500	0.0	33.3	3
Quijada, Jose	L-L	5-11	215	11-09-95	0	1	6.00	10	0	4	9	8	7	6	0	3	8	.222	.317	.250	19.5	7.3	41
Reyes, Gerardo	R-R	5-11	195	5-13-93	0	0	7.45	8	0	0	10	11	9	8	2	6	10	.275	.388	.525	20.4	12.2	49
Rosenberg, Kenny	L-L	6-1	195	7-09-95	2	2	3.82	7	3	0	33	35	14	14	3	14	29	.267	.342	.389	19.9	9.6	146
Sandoval, Patrick	L-L	6-3	190	10-18-96	7	13	4.11	28	28	0	145	145	89	66	12	74	128	.256	.344	.374	19.6	11.3	652
Silseth, Chase	R-R	6-0	217	5-18-00	4	1	3.96	16	8	0	52	41	26	23	9	26	56	.212	.312	.399	25.3	11.8	221
Soriano, Jose	R-R	6-3	220	10-20-98	1	3	3.64	38	0	0	42	33	22	17	4	23	56	.214	.342	.325	30.3	12.4	185
Suarez, Jose	L-L	5-10	225	1-03-98	1	3	8.29	11	7	0	34	46	32	31	10	20	28	.324	.409	.592	17.0	12.1	165
Tepera, Ryan	R-R	6-1	195	11-03-87	2	2	7.27	10	0	0	9	15	9	7	2	3	10	.385	.455	.564	21.7	6.5	46
Wantz, Andrew	R-R	6-4	235	10-13-95	2	0	3.89	27	3	0	39	28	18	17	4	15	33	.197	.275	.352	20.6	9.4	160
Warren, Austin	R-R	6-0	170	2-05-96	1	0	5.40	2	0	0	2	2	1	1	1	0	2	.333	.333	.833	33.3	0.0	6
Webb, Jacob	R-R	6-2	210	8-15-93	1	1	3.98	29	0	1	32	23	14	14	6	20	34	.197	.324	.402	24.3	14.3	140
Weiss, Zack	R-R	6-3	210	6-16-92	1	0	5.06	6	0	0	5	6	3	3	2	2	7	.273	.360	.545	28.0	8.0	25

Fielding

Catcher	PCT	G	PO	A	E	DP	PB
O'Hoppe	.995	49	411	10	2	1	3
Okey	.875	2	6	1	1	0	0
Thaiss	.987	82	596	14	8	0	2
Wallach	.996	59	457	16	2	3	4

First Base	PCT	G	PO	A	E	DP
Cabbage	.983	9	53	6	1	6
Cron	.978	14	87	2	2	13
Drury	1.000	47	198	21	0	19
Escobar	1.000	5	26	0	0	2
Lamb	.989	16	82	11	1	9
Moustakas	1.000	26	141	8	0	8
Padlo	1.000	2	13	0	0	0
Renfroe	1.000	5	23	2	0	1
Schanuel	.990	28	177	13	2	20
Thaiss	1.000	3	18	0	0	1
Urshela	.992	22	120	10	1	13
Wallach	1.000	1	1	0	0	0
Walsh	.994	29	161	12	1	26
Ward	1.000	1	1	0	0	0

Second Base	PCT	G	PO	A	E	DP
Drury	.994	92	137	195	2	49
Escobar	1.000	11	4	9	0	0
Fletcher	.976	14	18	23	1	8
Paris	1.000	2	1	0	0	0
Rengifo	.986	65	97	108	3	32
Soto	1.000	2	2	2	0	0
Stefanic	.970	12	20	12	1	5
Urshela	.000	1	0	0	0	0
Velazquez	1.000	10	6	7	0	2

Third Base	PCT	G	PO	A	E	DP
Escobar	.944	36	17	51	4	4
Fletcher	1.000	3	0	4	0	0
Moustakas	.968	40	24	68	3	11
Padlo	1.000	1	0	1	0	0
Rendon	.927	43	39	63	8	6
Rengifo	.958	23	11	35	2	6
Stefanic	.938	8	5	10	1	1
Urshela	.942	37	17	64	5	8

Shortstop	PCT	G	PO	A	E	DP
Fletcher	1.000	18	20	30	0	5
Neto	.979	84	114	205	7	43
Paris	1.000	9	15	22	0	2
Rengifo	.920	37	26	43	6	8
Soto	.900	2	2	7	1	3
Urshela	.966	9	8	20	1	1
Velazquez	.926	39	32	43	6	9

Outfield	PCT	G	PO	A	E	DP
Adams	.956	14	27	0	2	0
Adell	1.000	18	40	0	0	0
Cabbage	.667	11	14	0	0	0
Grichuk	.491	54	101	6	2	2
Moniak	.964	82	168	1	4	0
Paris	1.000	2	3	0	0	0
Phillips	.994	31	66	0	1	0
Renfroe	.978	122	216	8	5	3
Rengifo	.974	21	39	1	1	0
Trout	1.000	79	183	2	0	1
Velazquez	1.000	3	1	0	0	0
Walsh	1.000	9	21	0	0	0
Ward	1.000	93	162	3	0	0

SALT LAKE BEES

TRIPLE-A

PACIFIC COAST LEAGUE

Batting	B-T	Ht.	Wt.	DOB	AVG	OBP	SLG	G	PA	AB	R	H	2B	3B	HR	RBI	BB	HBP	SH	SF	SO	SB	CS	BB%	SO%
Adams, Jordyn	R-R	6-2	181	10-18-99	.267	.351	.465	109	480	415	74	111	25	6	15	67	53	4	2	6	133	44	5	11.0	27.7
Adell, Jo	R-R	6-3	215	4-08-99	.273	.375	.586	74	330	278	62	76	15	0	24	57	40	7	0	3	87	9	1	12.1	26.4
Cabbage, Trey	L-R	6-2	204	5-03-97	.306	.379	.596	107	474	418	83	128	25	3	30	89	45	6	2	3	142	32	3	9.5	30.0
Drury, Brandon	R-R	6-2	230	8-21-92	.182	.231	.455	3	13	11	1	2	0	0	1	2	1	0	0	1	5	1	0	7.7	38.5
Fletcher, David	R-R	5-9	185	5-31-94	.330	.382	.428	85	380	348	57	115	16	3	4	38	27	3	0	2	24	6	2	7.1	6.3
Gomez, Jose	R-R	5-11	175	12-10-96	.184	.205	.184	12	40	38	3	7	0	0	0	0	1	0	1	0	9	1	1	2.5	22.5
Humphreys, Zach	R-R	5-10	195	10-09-97	.259	.351	.381	59	224	189	25	49	15	1	2	30	27	2	2	4	51	7	4	12.1	22.8
Jones, Taylor	R-R	6-5	230	12-06-93	.229	.333	.440	49	204	175	32	40	13	0	8	29	26	2	0	1	47	5	1	12.7	23.0
Lamb, Jake	L-R	6-3	215	10-09-90	.317	.453	.492	34	150	120	21	38	6	0	5	29	26	4	0	0	30	2	0	17.3	20.0
Lopez, Jack	R-R	5-10	160	12-16-92	.277	.333	.476	93	380	347	50	96	18	6	13	74	26	4	2	1	89	10	6	6.8	23.4
Martinez, Orlando	L-L	6-0	185	2-17-98	.245	.307	.374	42	164	147	20	36	10	0	3	15	14	0	1	2	30	2	1	8.5	18.3
Molfetta, Christian	R-R	5-10	195	10-17-96	.129	.206	.129	11	34	31	0	4	0	0	0	1	3	0	0	0	9	0	0	8.8	26.5
Moniak, Mickey	L-R	6-2	195	5-13-98	.308	.355	.585	33	141	130	27	40	2	5	8	23	7	3	0	1	35	2	1	5.0	24.8
Mulrine, Anthony	R-R	6-0	205	3-30-98	.149	.286	.191	20	56	47	6	7	2	0	0	1	7	2	0	0	13	0	0	12.5	23.2
Murphy, Daniel	L-R	6-1	223	4-01-85	.295	.379	.362	38	169	149	24	44	7	0	1	25	20	0	0	0	18	0	0	11.8	10.7
Neto, Zach	R-R	6-0	185	1-31-01	.308	.438	.846	4	16	13	5	4	1	0	2	3	1	2	0	0	4	0	0	6.3	25.0
O'Hoppe, Logan	R-R	6-2	185	2-09-00	.600	.667	.600	2	6	5	3	3	0	0	0	1	1	0	0	0	1	0	0	16.7	16.7
Okey, Chris	R-R	5-11	200	12-29-94	.281	.345	.414	63	235	210	24	59	6	2	6	26	16	5	3	1	48	2	2	6.8	20.4
Oliva, Jared	R-R	6-1	200	11-27-95	.261	.348	.423	92	325	284	48	74	12	5	8	37	31	7	2	0	68	16	6	9.5	20.9
Padlo, Kevin	R-R	5-11	210	7-15-96	.261	.384	.450	92	406	333	61	87	24	0	13	50	67	2	0	4	98	9	4	16.5	24.1
Palmeiro, Preston	L-R	5-10	180	1-22-95	.184	.298	.301	51	161	136	13	25	8	1	2	16	22	1	0	2	34	1	0	13.7	21.1
Phillips, Brett	L-R	6-0	195	5-30-94	.230	.352	.366	66	264	213	37	49	5	3	6	25	42	1	3	5	87	7	3	15.9	33.0
Soto, Livan	L-R	5-10	160	6-22-00	.248	.347	.389	79	350	298	48	74	14	2	8	42	44	3	1	4	83	0	0	12.6	23.7
Stefanic, Michael	R-R	5-8	180	2-24-96	.365	.463	.467	99	455	381	67	139	20	2	5	62	60	11	1	2	33	8	7	13.2	7.3
Velazquez, Andrew	R-R	5-9	170	7-14-94	.203	.337	.392	23	92	74	15	15	3	1	3	7	15	0	3	0	23	7	0	16.3	25.0
Viloria, Meibrys	L-R	5-11	225	2-15-97	.167	.265	.333	10	34	30	4	5	2	0	1	1	4	0	0	0	12	0	0	11.8	35.3
Wallach, Chad	R-R	6-2	246	11-04-91	.361	.442	.556	11	43	36	6	13	1	0	2	8	6	0	0	1	7	1	0	14.0	16.3

Walsh, Jared	L-L	6-0	210	7-30-93	.217	.360	.375	52	225	184	28	40	2	0	9	28	38	3	0	0	78	0	2	16.9	34.7

Pitching	B-T	Ht.	Wt.	DOB	W	L	ERA	G	GS	SV	IP	Hits	Runs	ER	HR	BB	SO	AVG	OBP	SLG	SO%	BB%	BF
Caceres, Kelvin	R-R	6-1	205	1-26-00	1	0	0.90	7	0	1	10	5	1	1	0	5	11	.152	.275	.182	27.5	12.5	40
Daniel, Davis	R-R	6-1	190	6-11-97	0	1	4.50	1	1	0	4	2	2	2	0	7	5	.154	.476	.154	23.8	33.3	21
Dashwood, Jack	L-L	6-6	240	11-17-97	0	1	12.00	1	0	0	3	4	4	4	3	0	4	.286	.286	.929	28.6	0.0	14
Devenski, Chris	R-R	6-3	211	11-13-90	0	0	4.00	7	0	0	9	8	4	4	1	3	9	.242	.297	.455	24.3	8.1	37
Diaz, Jhonathan	L-L	6-0	170	9-13-96	9	2	4.55	38	8	1	87	82	50	44	10	43	79	.253	.344	.420	21.1	11.5	375
Erla, Mason	R-R	6-4	200	8-19-97	0	3	13.50	7	5	0	21	35	35	31	5	14	13	.380	.459	.674	11.9	12.8	109
Fulmer, Carson	R-R	6-0	210	12-13-93	0	2	5.27	12	11	0	41	45	26	24	5	28	33	.288	.402	.481	17.5	14.8	189
Garza, Justin	R-R	5-10	170	3-20-94	0	0	4.32	6	0	2	8	6	4	4	1	4	5	.207	.324	.345	14.7	11.8	34
Hammer, JD	R-R	6-3	202	7-12-94	1	2	6.63	8	7	0	38	50	30	28	5	21	19	.318	.402	.503	10.6	11.7	180
Herget, Jimmy	R-R	6-3	170	9-09-93	1	2	4.68	25	0	1	33	29	17	17	5	13	36	.242	.324	.417	26.5	9.6	136
Hernandez, Aaron	R-R	6-1	170	12-02-96	1	1	7.36	11	0	1	11	8	10	9	2	15	11	.211	.429	.447	19.6	26.8	56
Holder, Jonathan	R-R	6-2	232	6-09-93	1	5	5.40	46	5	2	67	69	46	40	8	40	76	.263	.369	.416	24.5	12.9	310
Ingram, Kolton	L-L	5-9	170	10-21-96	2	3	3.21	22	0	2	34	24	13	12	2	15	39	.203	.299	.271	28.5	10.9	137
Jones, Nick	L-L	6-6	224	1-22-99	2	0	2.08	6	0	0	13	8	3	3	1	10	10	.205	.396	.308	18.9	18.9	53
Kalish, Jake	B-L	6-2	210	7-09-91	9	11	7.19	30	25	0	138	178	114	110	30	55	103	.315	.381	.550	16.2	8.6	637
Kerry, Brett	R-R	6-0	213	4-12-99	2	1	9.72	4	3	0	17	29	18	18	4	9	16	.397	.459	.658	18.6	10.5	86
King, Dylan	R-R	6-3	237	12-05-96	0	0	9.00	1	0	0	1	0	1	1	0	3	0	.000	.750	.000	0.0	60.0	5
Ledo, Luis	R-R	6-4	240	5-28-95	4	3	5.66	24	16	0	76	80	50	48	8	53	62	.270	.382	.395	17.6	15.0	353
Lee, Jake	R-R	6-4	215	6-30-95	1	2	7.17	18	9	0	54	85	51	43	17	20	40	.365	.412	.674	15.6	7.8	256
Lopez, Jack	R-R	5-10	160	12-16-92	0	0	0.00	1	0	0	0	0	0	0	0	0	0	.000	.000	.000	0.0	0.0	1
Marte, Jose	R-R	6-3	180	6-14-96	1	0	4.15	4	0	0	4	1	2	2	1	3	5	.071	.278	.286	27.8	16.7	18
Martinez, Erik	R-R	5-11	193	3-21-96	0	0	4.50	1	0	0	2	1	1	1	1	1	1	.167	.286	.667	14.3	14.3	7
Molfetta, Christian	R-R	5-10	195	10-17-96	0	0	3.86	2	0	0	2	3	1	1	1	3	2	.333	.500	.667	16.7	25.0	12
Moronta, Reyes	R-R	5-10	265	1-06-93	4	2	3.32	34	0	6	41	27	19	15	3	36	52	.189	.350	.308	28.4	19.7	183
Mulrine, Anthony	R-R	6-0	205	3-30-98	0	0	21.60	1	0	0	2	4	4	4	0	1	1	.444	.583	.556	8.3	8.3	12
Palmeiro, Preston	L-R	5-10	180	1-22-95	0	0	4.50	2	0	0	2	3	1	1	0	1	0	.333	.400	.444	0.0	10.0	10
Pina, Robinson	R-R	6-5	225	11-26-98	1	2	7.83	7	4	0	23	33	21	20	3	21	14	.340	.454	.485	11.7	17.5	120
Reyes, Gerardo	R-R	5-11	195	5-13-93	3	5	5.58	36	0	1	40	39	29	25	7	24	56	.247	.348	.468	29.9	12.8	187
Rodriguez, Chris	R-R	6-2	185	7-20-98	0	0	10.80	2	0	0	2	3	2	2	0	3	0	.429	.545	.714	0.0	27.3	11
Romero, Fernando	R-R	6-0	215	12-24-94	0	1	31.50	2	1	0	2	8	7	7	2	6	1	.615	.737	1.231	5.3	31.6	19
Rosenberg, Kenny	L-L	6-1	195	7-09-95	7	7	4.95	20	20	0	100	105	61	55	14	46	120	.268	.349	.439	27.0	10.3	445
Seig, Hayden	R-R	6-5	227	9-10-98	1	1	7.36	2	0	0	7	11	8	6	0	3	6	.344	.400	.469	17.1	8.6	35
Silseth, Chase	R-R	6-0	217	5-18-00	4	1	2.96	11	11	0	46	34	18	15	1	20	49	.210	.303	.296	26.3	10.8	186
Smith, Ryan	L-L	5-11	185	8-13-97	2	2	6.48	14	0	0	25	26	18	18	1	23	18	.277	.421	.383	14.9	19.0	121
Swanda, John	R-R	6-2	193	3-18-99	0	1	11.72	5	5	0	18	30	26	23	2	19	14	.375	.514	.538	13.3	18.1	105
Torres, Eric	L-L	6-0	195	9-22-99	1	2	9.62	26	0	1	34	39	39	36	11	43	42	.289	.481	.563	22.6	23.1	186
Valdez, Cesar	R-R	6-2	225	3-17-85	4	7	6.95	33	16	0	114	163	91	88	21	32	94	.338	.380	.550	17.9	6.1	524
Vieaux, Cam	L-L	6-3	200	12-05-93	4	4	5.23	50	1	1	72	63	43	42	9	36	71	.232	.332	.399	22.6	11.5	314
Wantz, Andrew	R-R	6-4	235	10-13-95	0	0	4.62	22	0	5	25	26	13	13	5	14	29	.268	.360	.474	26.1	12.6	111
Warren, Austin	R-R	6-0	170	2-05-96	1	0	0.00	5	0	1	7	4	0	0	0	3	8	.174	.321	.174	27.6	10.3	29
Webb, Jacob	R-R	6-2	210	8-15-93	1	3	6.75	16	1	1	17	20	14	13	0	12	21	.278	.388	.375	24.4	14.0	86
Weiss, Zack	R-R	6-3	210	6-16-92	2	1	6.03	30	0	2	37	42	25	25	6	24	50	.290	.386	.517	29.2	14.0	171
Yovan, Kenyon	R-R	6-2	221	12-28-97	0	1	10.38	7	0	0	9	9	10	10	2	7	11	.281	.405	.531	26.2	16.7	42

Fielding

Catcher	PCT	G	PO	A	E	DP	PB
Humphreys	.980	53	413	31	9	5	1
Molfetta	1.000	9	74	1	0	1	2
Mulrine	1.000	18	112	12	0	2	3
O'Hoppe	1.000	2	9	0	0	0	0
Okey	.992	58	482	40	4	3	4
Viloria	.988	9	81	2	1	0	1
Wallach	.981	11	96	5	2	1	1

First Base	PCT	G	PO	A	E	DP
Cabbage	.991	58	386	35	4	46
Drury	1.000	1	10	0	0	2
Jones	1.000	10	69	5	0	6
Lamb	1.000	7	56	6	0	5
Mulrine	.000	1	0	0	0	0
Murphy	.994	18	141	12	1	22
Padlo	.995	26	188	16	1	27
Palmeiro	1.000	7	45	3	0	3
Walsh	.988	31	244	8	3	25

Second Base	PCT	G	PO	A	E	DP
Drury	1.000	1	5	2	0	2
Fletcher	.994	35	63	101	1	34
Gomez	1.000	2	2	2	0	0
Lopez	1.000	7	10	22	0	5
Murphy	.958	9	5	18	1	5
Padlo	1.000	3	0	10	0	0
Palmeiro	.981	14	15	37	1	9
Soto	.963	17	33	45	3	16
Stefanic	.974	63	106	154	7	43
Velazquez	1.000	5	7	15	0	2

Third Base	PCT	G	PO	A	E	DP
Gomez	1.000	9	6	21	0	3
Jones	.911	34	20	62	8	12
Lamb	1.000	11	4	19	0	2
Lopez	.987	24	19	58	1	8
Padlo	.894	40	22	71	11	10
Soto	.895	19	13	21	4	2
Stefanic	.957	20	14	30	2	6

Shortstop	PCT	G	PO	A	E	DP
Fletcher	.970	48	60	100	5	23
Gomez	1.000	1	3	2	0	1
Lopez	.965	48	56	109	6	28
Neto	1.000	4	5	10	0	2
Palmeiro	.000	1	0	0	0	0
Soto	.962	38	49	101	6	27
Velazquez	.944	15	23	45	4	10

Outfield	PCT	G	PO	A	E	DP
Adams	.944	110	208	10	12	2
Adell	.986	66	124	2	2	0
Cabbage	.966	25	44	3	3	1
Jones	1.000	1	1	0	0	0
Lopez	1.000	15	24	4	0	1
Martinez	.986	43	76	3	1	0
Moniak	.983	33	62	0	1	0
Oliva	.980	90	152	2	3	1
Palmeiro	1.000	20	26	0	0	0
Phillips	.993	65	132	6	2	1
Velazquez	1.000	4	9	0	0	0
Walsh	.909	6	10	0	1	0

ROCKET CITY TRASH PANDAS — DOUBLE-A

SOUTHERN LEAGUE

Batting	B-T	Ht.	Wt.	DOB	AVG	OBP	SLG	G	PA	AB	R	H	2B	3B	HR	RBI	BB	HBP	SH	SF	SO	SB	CS	BB%	SO%
Aguilar, Ryan	L-L	6-2	168	9-11-94	.169	.313	.231	22	80	65	8	11	1	0	1	9	11	3	0	1	31	2	1	13.8	38.8
Blakely, Werner	L-R	6-3	185	2-21-02	.000	.222	.000	2	9	7	0	0	0	0	0	0	2	0	0	0	5	0	0	22.2	55.6
Calabrese, David	L-R	5-11	160	9-26-02	.194	.309	.345	122	535	458	63	89	18	3	15	48	70	6	1	0	164	14	9	13.1	30.7
Campero, Gustavo	B-R	5-8	183	9-20-97	.000	.167	.000	2	6	4	1	0	0	0	0	1	1	0	0	1	1	0	0	16.7	16.7
DiChiara, Sonny	R-R	6-1	263	7-29-99	.223	.327	.355	77	330	282	34	63	13	0	8	38	38	7	0	3	114	0	0	11.5	34.5
Emmerson, Myles	R-R	5-11	185	5-15-98	.333	.333	.417	4	12	12	2	4	1	0	0	3	0	0	0	0	6	0	0	0.0	50.0
Flint, Tucker	L-L	6-2	215	4-05-01	.233	.358	.395	123	519	433	64	101	23	4	13	63	67	18	0	1	151	4	4	12.9	29.1
Gomez, Jose	R-R	5-11	175	12-10-96	.251	.316	.343	102	378	335	45	84	12	2	5	34	30	4	5	4	86	12	2	7.9	22.8
Humphreys, Zach	R-R	5-10	195	10-09-97	.200	.273	.400	7	22	20	4	4	1	0	1	6	2	0	0	0	5	2	0	9.1	22.7
Jackson, Jeremiah	R-R	6-0	165	3-26-00	.248	.321	.447	82	349	311	46	77	15	1	15	56	33	2	0	3	94	21	7	9.5	26.9
Knowles, D'Shawn	B-R	6-0	181	1-16-01	.240	.318	.333	21	86	75	11	18	3	2	0	5	9	0	1	1	21	12	3	10.5	24.4
Maitan, Kevin	B-R	6-2	190	2-12-00	.192	.300	.256	53	200	172	18	33	8	0	1	15	23	4	0	1	67	0	0	11.5	33.5
Martinez, Orlando	L-L	6-0	185	2-17-98	.267	.325	.445	78	325	292	33	78	17	4	9	55	24	3	1	4	64	6	3	7.4	19.7
Matthews, Gabe	L-R	6-2	232	11-24-97	.241	.397	.367	51	199	158	19	38	5	0	5	22	31	10	0	0	62	1	0	15.6	31.2
McCroskey, Mac	R-R	6-1	180	12-31-99	.225	.324	.256	42	150	129	12	29	2	1	0	18	19	0	2	0	52	1	0	12.7	34.7
Mulrine, Anthony	R-R	6-0	205	3-30-98	.180	.324	.279	22	78	61	5	11	3	0	1	9	9	4	4	0	17	0	0	11.5	21.8
Neto, Zach	R-R	6-0	185	1-31-01	.444	.559	.815	7	34	27	10	12	1	0	3	10	6	1	0	0	8	3	0	17.6	23.5
Paris, Kyren	R-R	6-0	180	11-11-01	.255	.393	.417	113	514	415	79	106	23	1	14	45	88	7	0	2	151	44	5	17.1	29.4
Payne, Tyler	R-R	5-11	210	10-25-92	.313	.369	.472	44	157	144	18	45	11	0	4	26	11	2	0	0	32	0	0	7.0	20.4
Placencia, Adrian	B-R	5-11	173	6-02-03	.170	.237	.226	14	60	53	5	9	0	0	1	4	4	1	1	1	24	0	0	6.7	40.0
Podaras, Straton	R-R	6-1	200	12-09-97	.000	.000	.000	2	3	3	0	0	0	0	0	0	0	0	0	0	0	0	0	0.0	0.0
Quero, Edgar	B-R	5-11	170	4-06-03	.246	.386	.332	70	321	256	40	63	13	0	3	35	55	6	0	4	53	1	2	17.1	16.5
2-team (31 Birmingham)					.255	.387	.351	101	455	368	52	94	17	0	6	57	72	7	0	8	76	1	2	15.8	16.7
Ricciardi, Mariano	L-R	5-7	170	6-29-98	.137	.255	.158	33	110	95	15	13	2	0	0	7	13	2	0	0	21	0	0	11.8	19.1
Schanuel, Nolan	L-R	6-3	195	2-14-02	.333	.474	.467	17	76	60	15	20	3	1	1	12	16	0	0	0	9	1	0	21.1	11.8
Soto, Livan	L-R	5-10	160	6-22-00	.206	.331	.271	31	127	107	18	22	4	0	1	5	19	1	0	0	34	1	1	15.0	26.8
Teodosio, Bryce	R-L	6-3	220	6-18-99	.212	.299	.315	118	419	368	53	78	15	1	7	39	36	11	1	3	141	16	8	8.6	33.7
Vera, Arol	B-R	6-2	213	9-12-02	.286	.300	.411	14	60	56	8	16	1	0	2	8	1	1	0	2	10	2	0	1.7	16.7
Whitefield, Aaron	R-R	6-4	210	9-02-96	.190	.280	.324	37	118	105	15	20	5	0	3	13	12	1	0	0	47	12	2	10.2	39.8

Pitching	B-T	Ht.	Wt.	DOB	W	L	ERA	G	GS	SV	IP	Hits	Runs	ER	HR	BB	SO	AVG	OBP	SLG	SO%	BB%	BF
Aguilar, Ryan	L-L	6-2	168	9-11-94	0	0	0.00	1	0	0	1	0	0	0	0	0	0	.000	.000	.000	0.0	0.0	2
Armstrong, Ivan	R-R	6-5	247	7-27-00	2	4	5.14	43	4	0	70	77	43	40	13	39	76	.280	.377	.458	23.3	12.0	326
Bachman, Sam	R-R	6-1	235	9-30-99	3	2	5.81	6	6	0	26	15	18	17	3	20	29	.163	.331	.304	24.6	16.9	118
Burns, Nathan	R-R	6-1	202	6-01-99	0	2	13.86	14	0	0	12	19	21	19	4	12	13	.352	.485	.611	19.1	17.6	68
Bush, Ky	L-L	6-6	240	11-12-99	1	3	5.88	6	6	0	26	23	19	17	6	14	33	.245	.351	.479	29.7	12.6	111
Caceres, Kelvin	R-R	6-1	205	1-26-00	5	1	5.61	34	0	2	34	30	21	21	3	22	53	.229	.358	.374	33.3	13.8	159
Carter, Alan	R-R	6-3	200	12-16-97	0	0	10.80	5	0	0	8	15	10	10	2	7	6	.405	.489	.622	13.3	15.6	45
Chaney, Chase	R-R	6-1	199	12-16-99	0	0	13.50	1	1	0	2	4	3	3	0	2	1	.444	.545	.556	9.1	18.2	11
Crow, Coleman	R-R	6-0	175	12-30-00	2	0	1.88	4	4	0	24	9	5	5	3	6	31	.114	.176	.266	36.0	7.0	86
Darrell-Hicks, Michael	R-R	6-5	220	11-13-97	0	3	6.00	3	3	0	12	12	9	8	2	5	12	.250	.339	.417	21.4	8.9	56
Dashwood, Jack	L-L	6-6	240	11-17-97	2	0	5.67	18	1	0	27	35	20	17	9	12	30	.315	.384	.604	24.0	9.6	125
Donovan, Dakota	R-R	6-6	238	7-25-97	2	0	8.75	15	0	0	24	31	25	23	2	15	27	.323	.458	.479	22.3	12.4	121
Dufault, Brandon	R-R	6-5	204	10-19-98	1	0	5.66	16	0	0	21	21	13	13	0	19	19	.259	.410	.259	18.1	18.1	105
Erla, Mason	R-R	6-4	200	8-19-97	1	3	5.65	6	6	0	29	32	21	18	5	16	26	.278	.376	.504	19.5	12.0	133
Gomez, Jose	R-R	5-11	175	12-10-96	0	0	6.00	3	0	0	3	5	2	2	1	1	0	.357	.438	.643	0.0	6.3	16
Harding, Houston	L-L	6-1	230	5-22-98	1	0	7.38	17	2	0	46	53	39	38	7	31	46	.290	.396	.454	21.1	14.2	218
Ingram, Kolton	L-L	5-9	170	10-21-96	1	1	2.63	23	0	2	27	17	10	8	1	19	38	.177	.331	.229	32.2	16.1	118
Jones, Nick	L-L	6-6	224	1-22-99	2	1	3.86	22	0	3	28	24	13	12	2	13	37	.233	.325	.330	31.4	11.0	118
Joyce, Ben	R-R	6-5	225	9-17-00	0	1	4.60	14	0	4	16	7	12	8	1	13	24	.135	.357	.250	34.3	18.6	70
Kerry, Brett	R-R	6-0	213	4-12-99	6	4	3.88	23	20	2	118	100	54	51	23	40	106	.226	.290	.430	21.7	8.2	488
Kochanowicz, Jack	L-R	6-7	228	12-22-00	4	5	6.53	16	16	0	70	81	54	51	15	22	55	.290	.360	.527	17.7	7.1	311
Kristofak, Zac	R-R	5-9	189	12-08-97	4	3	4.07	16	6	0	42	34	21	19	3	16	33	.225	.301	.331	19.1	9.2	173
Lee, Jake	R-R	6-4	215	6-30-95	1	2	4.42	17	4	0	39	32	19	19	5	7	38	.224	.261	.357	24.8	4.6	153
Marceaux, Landon	R-R	6-0	199	10-08-99	3	6	4.88	12	12	0	59	72	42	32	7	19	45	.305	.354	.483	17.1	7.2	263
Martinez, Erik	R-R	5-11	193	3-21-96	1	1	4.43	11	1	0	22	23	14	11	1	9	23	.253	.320	.363	22.8	8.9	101
Mederos, Victor	R-R	6-2	227	6-08-01	4	9	5.67	20	20	0	92	93	65	58	21	43	99	.258	.350	.479	23.9	10.4	414
Mulrine, Anthony	R-R	6-0	205	3-30-98	0	0	0.00	1	0	0	1	1	0	0	0	0	0	.250	.400	.250	0.0	0.0	5
Murphy, Luke	R-R	6-5	190	11-05-99	3	3	4.96	44	1	2	49	53	33	27	4	27	62	.275	.363	.389	27.8	12.1	223
Natera, Sammy	L-L	6-4	225	11-06-99	0	1	11.57	2	2	0	7	7	9	9	2	5	10	.250	.382	.571	29.4	14.7	34
Osmond, Bryce	R-R	6-3	183	9-05-00	0	2	9.00	3	3	0	13	15	13	13	4	10	12	.288	.397	.519	19.0	15.9	63
Payne, Tyler	R-R	5-11	210	10-25-92	0	0	0.00	1	0	0	0	0	0	0	0	0	0	.000	.000	.000	0.0	0.0	1
Percival, Cole	R-R	6-5	220	2-26-99	1	5	6.45	10	7	0	45	55	39	32	4	22	39	.299	.383	.424	18.1	10.2	215
Phillips, Dylan	L-L	6-0	220	6-16-99	0	0	1.59	4	0	0	6	3	6	1	0	6	6	.150	.379	.200	20.7	20.7	29
Pina, Robinson	R-R	6-5	225	11-26-98	4	3	3.29	19	7	0	63	45	24	23	2	30	58	.210	.319	.276	22.7	11.7	256
Podaras, Straton	R-R	6-1	200	12-09-97	0	0	54.00	1	0	0	0	1	2	2	0	4	0	.500	.833	.500	0.0	66.7	6
Romero, Fernando	R-R	6-0	215	12-24-94	0	0	6.00	1	0	0	3	5	2	2	0	1	6	.357	.438	.429	37.5	6.3	16
Seig, Hayden	R-R	6-5	227	9-10-98	1	1	2.57	4	0	1	7	4	2	2	1	2	5	.167	.231	.375	19.2	7.7	26
Soriano, Jose	R-R	6-3	220	10-20-98	0	2	4.24	17	2	1	23	18	16	11	1	16	31	.212	.356	.282	29.8	15.4	104
Suarez, Willian	R-R	6-3	209	3-21-98	0	0	7.71	3	0	0	2	4	2	2	1	2	2	.333	.467	.583	13.3	13.3	15
Swanda, John	R-R	6-2	193	3-18-99	0	5	8.91	16	4	0	33	42	36	33	1	25	35	.311	.441	.415	20.6	14.7	170

Pitching	B-T	Ht.	Wt.	DOB	W	L	ERA	G	GS	SV	IP	Hits	Runs	ER	HR	BB	SO	AVG	OBP	SLG	SO%	BB%	BF
Torres, Eric	L-L	6-0	195	9-22-99	0	1	5.14	13	0	1	14	9	9	8	1	15	25	.188	.459	.271	33.8	20.3	74
Yovan, Kenyon	R-R	6-2	221	12-28-97	3	6	4.86	44	0	10	46	39	30	25	8	22	45	.227	.320.	.407	22.7	11.1	198

Fielding

Catcher	PCT	G	PO	A	E	DP	PB
Campero	1.000	1	5	0	0	0	0
Emmerson	1.000	4	50	2	0	0	0
Humphreys	1.000	7	53	1	0	0	0
Mulrine	.984	21	176	10	3	1	2
Payne	.980	43	356	28	8	1	2
Podaras	1.000	1	6	0	0	0	1
Quero	.985	68	610	36	10	3	2

First Base	PCT	G	PO	A	E	DP
Aguilar	1.000	10	71	9	0	7
DiChiara	.997	41	292	16	1	31
Flint	.975	25	145	11	4	14
Maitan	.988	27	158	11	2	14
Matthews	.991	30	195	15	2	19
Schanuel	.990	13	94	6	1	15

Second Base	PCT	G	PO	A	E	DP
Gomez	.985	27	51	80	2	23
Jackson	1.000	21	35	40	0	12
McCroskey	.941	18	15	33	3	12
Paris	.966	32	45	70	4	18
Placencia	.881	11	9	28	5	2
Ricciardi	1.000	26	30	54	0	12
Soto	.956	12	18	25	2	3
Vera	1.000	1	1	1	0	0

Third Base	PCT	G	PO	A	E	DP
Blakely	.500	2	0	2	2	0
Gomez	.968	72	53	100	5	14
Jackson	.970	29	22	42	2	6
Maitan	.949	26	14	42	3	1
McCroskey	.897	16	8	18	3	1
Ricciardi	.800	3	0	4	1	0
Soto	1.000	3	3	5	0	0

Shortstop	PCT	G	PO	A	E	DP
Gomez	.000	1	0	0	0	0
Jackson	.880	11	21	23	6	5
McCroskey	.886	9	11	28	5	2
Neto	.962	7	11	14	1	5
Paris	.956	80	108	195	14	38
Placencia	1.000	2	6	5	0	1
Soto	.948	16	18	37	3	9
Vera	.927	13	21	30	4	5

Outfield	PCT	G	PO	A	E	DP
Aguilar	1.000	4	10	0	0	0
Calabrese	.986	121	226	6	3	2
Campero	1.000	1	1	0	0	0
Flint	.988	81	109	6	2	0
Gomez	1.000	3	6	1	0	0
Jackson	.984	25	46	3	1	1
Knowles	1.000	21	56	2	0	1
Martinez	.978	38	57	6	2	0
Teodosio	.993	115	253	4	4	1
Whitefield	.974	29	39	0	1	0

TRI-CITY DUST DEVILS

HIGH CLASS A

NORTHWEST LEAGUE

Batting	B-T	Ht.	Wt.	DOB	AVG	OBP	SLG	G	PA	AB	R	H	2B	3B	HR	RBI	BB	HBP	SH	SF	SO	SB	CS	BB%	SO%
Blake, Andy	R-R	6-4	195	8-15-00	.235	.325	.397	19	77	68	7	16	2	0	3	10	8	1	0	0	15	3	1	10.4	19.5
Blakely, Werner	L-R	6-3	185	2-21-02	.214	.316	.331	92	374	323	45	69	17	3	5	28	44	5	0	2	137	22	1	11.8	36.6
Bruggeman, Kevin	R-R	5-9	186	7-25-01	.294	.368	.353	7	19	17	3	5	1	0	0	3	2	0	0	0	6	1	0	10.5	31.6
Campero, Gustavo	B-R	5-8	183	9-20-97	.337	.414	.644	62	239	205	41	69	19	4	12	41	22	8	0	4	43	20	4	9.2	18.0
Coutney, Matt	L-R	6-1	230	7-08-99	.272	.333	.382	47	192	173	16	47	8	1	3	17	11	6	0	2	66	0	1	5.7	34.4
Dana, Casey	R-R	6-4	212	5-31-99	.134	.226	.203	61	197	172	15	23	3	0	3	19	17	4	2	2	81	2	1	8.6	41.1
Emmerson, Myles	R-R	5-11	185	5-15-98	.178	.256	.224	65	243	219	27	39	8	1	0	12	23	0	1	0	76	1	0	9.5	31.3
Gregorio, Osmy	R-R	6-2	196	5-27-98	.226	.285	.306	69	273	248	32	56	5	3	3	32	19	2	3	1	57	7	4	7.0	20.9
Hernandez, Ryan	R-R	6-4	233	10-15-98	.154	.262	.269	17	61	52	5	8	3	0	1	7	7	1	0	1	21	0	0	11.5	34.4
Ketchup, Caleb	R-R	5-10	160	1-04-02	.245	.355	.283	16	62	53	7	13	0	1	0	1	7	2	0	0	22	3	1	11.3	35.5
Knowles, D'Shawn	B-R	6-0	181	1-16-01	.251	.323	.360	107	423	375	46	94	21	4	4	35	38	3	5	2	109	18	8	9.0	25.8
Lovelace, Kyle	R-R	5-10	163	8-03-98	.000	.000	.000	3	6	6	0	0	0	0	0	0	0	0	0	0	3	0	0	0.0	50.0
Matthews, Gabe	L-R	6-2	232	11-24-97	.238	.397	.414	56	234	181	29	43	11	0	7	35	44	6	0	3	53	1	1	18.8	22.6
McGillis, Will	R-R	6-3	200	1-16-99	.227	.277	.409	12	47	44	5	10	5	0	1	2	3	0	0	0	13	0	0	6.4	27.7
Pendleton, Caleb	R-R	6-2	185	4-05-02	.213	.245	.234	15	49	47	3	10	1	0	0	1	2	0	0	0	19	0	0	4.1	38.8
Placencia, Adrian	B-R	5-11	173	6-02-03	.218	.354	.336	109	480	390	59	85	15	2	9	46	82	2	3	3	133	24	11	17.1	27.7
Podaras, Straton	R-R	6-1	200	12-09-97	.059	.158	.176	5	19	17	1	1	0	1	0	3	1	1	0	0	9	0	0	5.3	47.4
Ramirez, Alexander	R-R	6-2	229	8-29-02	.247	.296	.352	114	466	429	53	106	23	5	4	44	23	8	3	3	170	23	7	4.9	36.5
Redfield, Joe	L-R	6-2	200	10-18-01	.255	.340	.426	12	53	47	8	12	3	1	1	8	5	1	0	0	10	2	1	9.4	18.9
Rivas, Steven	L-L	6-1	218	6-28-99	.173	.231	.227	35	121	110	6	19	1	1	1	9	8	1	0	2	42	1	1	6.6	34.7
Rodriguez, Gabriel	R-R	6-1	154	9-29-02	.000	.200	.000	4	5	4	0	0	0	0	0	0	1	0	0	0	2	0	0	20.0	40.0
Sepulveda, Christian	R-R	6-5	222	1-05-98	.279	.326	.488	11	46	43	3	12	3	0	2	9	1	2	0	0	7	1	0	2.2	15.2
Stewart, Joe	R-R	6-5	212	5-06-98	.244	.309	.327	119	518	471	57	115	17	5	4	38	37	8	0	2	134	42	8	7.1	25.9
Tinsman, Brendan	R-R	6-2	225	12-06-99	.190	.393	.190	8	28	21	2	4	0	0	0	2	7	0	0	0	10	0	0	25.0	35.7
Vera, Arol	B-R	6-2	213	9-12-02	.231	.287	.297	116	491	438	54	101	16	2	3	60	34	4	7	8	128	10	5	6.9	26.1
Williams, Cam	B-R	5-10	195	2-07-98	.286	.320	.514	18	75	70	6	20	7	0	3	9	2	2	0	1	32	2	2	2.7	42.7

Pitching	B-T	Ht.	Wt.	DOB	W	L	ERA	G	GS	SV	IP	Hits	Runs	ER	HR	BB	SO	AVG	OBP	SLG	SO%	BB%	BF
Albanese, Glenn	R-R	6-7	223	10-22-98	1	0	6.97	7	0	1	10	14	8	8	0	5	12	.326	.408	.419	24.5	10.2	49
Burns, Nathan	R-R	6-1	202	6-01-99	1	0	1.54	19	0	0	23	13	4	4	1	13	32	.165	.292	.228	32.7	13.3	98
Caceres, Kelvin	R-R	6-1	205	1-26-00	0	0	2.45	11	0	5	11	8	4	3	0	5	21	.205	.289	.256	46.7	11.1	45
Chaney, Chase	R-R	6-1	199	12-16-99	7	6	3.63	24	19	0	112	113	54	45	6	34	84	.259	.325	.376	17.4	7.1	482
Christopherson, Will	R-R	6-4	210	8-08-99	0	4	6.75	8	0	0	13	13	11	10	5	4	15	.260	.309	.600	27.3	7.3	55
Dana, Caden	L-R	6-4	215	12-17-03	2	4	4.22	11	11	0	53	45	28	25	3	24	71	.228	.317	.355	31.7	10.7	224
Darrell-Hicks, Michael	R-R	6-5	220	11-13-97	2	4	3.15	13	9	0	54	48	21	19	4	21	59	.232	.316	.333	25.1	8.9	235
Donovan, Dakota	R-R	6-6	238	7-25-97	0	0	0.00	4	0	0	5	2	0	0	0	1	9	.125	.176	.125	52.9	5.9	17
Guzman, Emilker	R-R	5-10	185	2-10-99	3	3	3.75	26	0	1	36	41	23	15	2	20	42	.285	.380	.410	25.3	12.0	166
Harding, Houston	L-L	6-1	230	5-22-98	2	0	1.32	10	0	1	14	7	2	2	2	6	15	.146	.236	.271	27.3	10.9	55
Horvath, Nick	R-L	5-11	200	7-13-96	0	2	4.79	6	5	0	21	22	14	11	1	13	26	.275	.392	.363	26.8	13.4	97
Jones, Nick	L-L	6-6	224	1-22-99	2	3	3.24	22	0	5	25	17	9	9	1	5	30	.193	.253	.273	31.3	5.2	96
Key, Keythel	R-R	6-3	180	10-10-03	0	1	1.04	2	2	0	9	2	1	1	0	7	10	.074	.286	.111	28.6	20.0	35
Killam, Brent	L-L	5-11	190	3-26-98	0	1	13.50	1	0	0	1	4	4	1	0	1	2	.571	.625	.714	25.0	12.5	8
King, Dylan	R-R	6-3	237	12-05-96	1	1	2.70	5	0	0	7	6	2	2	0	4	12	.231	.344	.346	37.5	12.5	32
Kochanowicz, Jack	L-R	6-7	228	12-22-00	1	0	1.52	5	5	0	24	22	7	4	0	3	14	.247	.284	.258	14.6	3.1	96
Marcheco, Jorge	R-R	6-1	185	8-06-02	3	1	1.88	5	5	0	29	22	6	6	4	3	33	.210	.231	.390	30.6	2.8	108
Martinez, Alex	R-R	5-10	170	9-15-02	1	0	3.38	4	0	0	8	4	4	3	0	10	7	.154	.405	.192	18.4	26.3	38

Martinez, Erik	R-R	5-11	193	3-21-96	2	0	1.54	17	0	6	23	14	5	4	0	9	31	.169	.274	.217	32.6	9.5	95
Mayhue, C.J.	R-L	5-11	181	1-22-01	1	1	5.02	5	2	0	14	15	8	8	1	4	9	.263	.311	.386	14.8	6.6	61
Mendez, Haminton	R-R	6-1	177	6-05-04	0	0	13.50	2	0	0	5	6	7	7	1	7	8	.316	.519	.474	29.6	25.9	27
Mondak, Nick	L-L	6-4	203	6-02-98	1	1	5.53	16	1	0	28	40	20	17	6	5	36	.339	.360	.576	28.6	4.0	126
Natera, Sammy	L-L	6-4	225	11-06-99	2	8	4.20	20	20	0	84	71	43	39	12	42	108	.229	.336	.397	29.8	11.6	363
Osmond, Bryce	R-R	6-3	183	9-05-00	4	7	3.55	20	20	0	84	79	44	33	11	37	88	.247	.338	.422	23.9	10.1	368
Percival, Cole	R-R	6-5	220	2-26-99	0	3	4.24	9	8	1	34	35	19	16	1	22	42	.259	.379	.319	26.1	13.7	161
Peters, Andrew	R-R	6-2	191	11-25-98	0	1	11.25	7	0	0	8	8	10	10	3	14	9	.267	.522	.567	19.6	30.4	46
Phansalkar, Roman	R-R	6-1	195	6-02-98	4	3	3.30	27	0	4	44	31	18	16	3	18	39	.197	.292	.293	21.9	10.1	178
Phillips, Dylan	L-L	6-0	220	6-16-99	0	1	6.66	20	0	0	24	26	20	18	0	9	31	.274	.361	.358	28.7	8.3	108
Pina, Robinson	R-R	6-5	225	11-26-98	0	0	0.79	8	0	1	11	4	2	1	0	4	18	.100	.200	.150	40.0	8.9	45
Rivas, Steven	L-L	6-1	218	6-28-99	0	0	0.00	1	0	0	0	0	0	0	0	0	0	.000	.000	.000	0.0	0.0	1
Rivera, Erik	L-L	6-2	200	4-02-01	0	0	0.00	2	2	0	4	4	0	0	0	2	5	.267	.353	.467	29.4	11.8	17
Salvador, Jose	L-L	6-2	170	9-21-99	1	2	6.00	10	3	0	27	27	18	18	7	7	22	.257	.307	.533	19.3	6.1	114
Sanchez, Andre	R-R	5-10	140	2-05-03	0	0	7.20	4	0	0	10	11	9	8	3	5	14	.262	.354	.548	29.2	10.4	48
Sandy, Will	L-L	6-4	210	9-17-99	0	1	15.00	2	0	1	6	11	10	10	1	5	6	.393	.500	.607	17.6	14.7	34
Seig, Hayden	R-R	6-5	227	9-10-98	2	1	3.32	26	0	1	41	39	19	15	1	9	51	.250	.312	.340	29.5	5.2	173
Smith, Jake	R-R	6-4	189	10-04-99	2	1	10.86	29	0	2	32	49	41	39	4	28	37	.348	.472	.532	21.0	15.9	176
Smith, Julian	R-L	6-4	210	6-03-97	1	0	1.32	6	0	0	14	9	2	2	0	3	16	.184	.231	.204	30.8	5.8	52
Southard, Jared	R-R	6-2	220	10-04-00	0	4	8.24	15	0	1	20	29	18	18	2	10	24	.333	.408	.483	24.2	10.1	99
Suarez, Willian	R-R	6-3	209	3-21-98	3	3	3.60	37	0	1	50	35	25	20	7	38	55	.200	.347	.377	25.3	17.5	217
Swanda, John	R-R	6-2	193	3-18-99	4	0	2.31	6	6	0	35	28	9	9	2	4	25	.220	.254	.323	18.7	3.0	134
Thompson, Ben	R-R	6-0	215	1-17-02	1	1	5.00	5	0	1	9	3	6	5	1	8	13	.125	.333	.250	39.4	24.2	33
Tullar, Cameron	R-L	6-2	215	6-30-00	0	1	6.00	5	1	0	9	7	6	6	0	7	11	.219	.381	.281	26.2	16.7	42
Van Scoyoc, Connor	R-R	6-6	234	11-26-99	4	3	2.76	11	11	0	62	43	25	19	6	25	56	.195	.289	.318	22.5	10.0	249

Fielding

Catcher	PCT	G	PO	A	E	DP	PB
Bruggeman	1.000	7	66	1	0	0	1
Campero	.994	33	316	13	2	2	7
Emmerson	.993	65	638	35	5	4	4
Lovelace	1.000	1	1	1	0	0	0
Pendleton	.992	15	119	11	1	2	0
Podaras	.981	5	49	3	1	2	1
Rodriguez	.000	1	0	0	0	0	0
Tinsman	.986	8	70	3	1	0	1

First Base	PCT	G	PO	A	E	DP
Coutney	.991	46	304	27	3	34
Dana	.974	5	34	3	1	3
Hernandez	1.000	5	24	1	0	0
Matthews	.998	53	389	41	1	34
Sepulveda	1.000	6	40	1	0	10
Williams	.993	18	128	7	1	9

Second Base	PCT	G	PO	A	E	DP
Blake	1.000	3	9	6	0	4
Gregorio	.985	18	25	39	1	12
Ketchup	1.000	2	2	5	0	1
Knowles	.000	1	0	0	0	0
McGillis	.967	9	14	15	1	4
Placencia	.974	76	114	182	8	43
Vera	.965	23	39	44	3	13

Third Base	PCT	G	PO	A	E	DP
Blake	.875	3	1	6	1	2
Blakely	.924	79	63	131	16	10
Dana	.829	21	6	28	7	3
Gregorio	.869	20	16	37	8	6
Hernandez	.769	5	4	6	3	0
Ketchup	1.000	3	3	2	0	0
Knowles	.750	1	1	2	1	0
Sepulveda	1.000	2	2	1	0	0

Shortstop	PCT	G	PO	A	E	DP
Blake	.980	11	18	32	1	6
Gregorio	.957	19	25	41	3	6
Ketchup	1.000	8	10	19	0	6
Placencia	.886	11	13	26	5	5
Vera	.964	81	91	201	11	44

Outfield	PCT	G	PO	A	E	DP
Campero	1.000	11	16	0	0	0
Dana	1.000	26	29	0	0	0
Gregorio	.965	12	20	2	1	2
Knowles	.988	103	203	7	6	1
Ramirez	.982	106	188	7	6	2
Redfield	1.000	10	23	0	0	0
Rivas	1.000	21	33	1	0	0
Stewart	.982	112	173	9	3	2

INLAND EMPIRE 66ERS

LOW CLASS A

CALIFORNIA LEAGUE

Batting	B-T	Ht.	Wt.	DOB	AVG	OBP	SLG	G	PA	AB	R	H	2B	3B	HR	RBI	BB	HBP	SH	SF	SO	SB	CS	BB%	SO%
Arocho, Jeremy	B-R	5-10	165	10-06-98	.255	.406	.318	101	388	302	62	77	6	5	1	26	78	1	4	3	59	47	4	20.1	15.2
Burns, Peter	L-R	5-10	195	10-14-99	.033	.250	.033	13	40	30	1	1	0	0	0	2	5	4	0	1	8	0	0	12.5	20.0
Coutney, Matt	L-R	6-1	230	7-08-99	.260	.378	.458	74	320	262	43	68	8	4	12	54	47	6	0	5	87	0	0	14.7	27.2
Flores, Ronaldo	R-R	6-0	175	5-17-02	.266	.316	.377	83	320	297	30	79	19	1	4	28	20	2	0	1	68	1	1	6.3	21.3
Fontenelle, Cole	B-R	6-3	205	3-11-02	.266	.333	.420	38	162	143	22	38	6	2	4	26	13	3	0	3	38	7	3	8.0	23.5
Gill, Starlin	R-R	5-10	150	3-16-00	.182	.308	.182	9	13	11	1	2	0	0	0	2	1	1	0	0	6	1	0	7.7	46.2
Gobbel, Ben	R-R	6-1	190	11-02-99	.267	.361	.412	59	255	221	33	59	11	3	5	27	27	6	0	1	64	14	3	10.6	25.1
Guzman, Denzer	R-R	6-1	180	2-08-04	.239	.309	.371	111	472	426	62	102	21	7	7	52	42	2	0	2	131	8	4	8.9	27.8
Holt, Mason	R-R	5-11	190	10-20-98	.193	.299	.351	30	67	57	8	11	2	2	1	12	6	3	0	1	24	1	1	9.0	35.8
Macias, Johan	B-R	5-9	150	1-06-03	.236	.326	.311	77	324	280	45	66	9	3	2	24	27	11	4	1	65	4	1	8.3	20.1
O'Hoppe, Logan	R-R	6-2	185	2-09-00	.316	.409	.474	6	22	19	4	6	3	0	0	3	3	0	0	0	5	0	0	13.6	22.7
Peabody, Mike	L-R	6-4	206	10-01-98	.230	.317	.364	69	273	239	38	55	8	3	6	32	20	11	2	1	69	10	2	7.3	25.3
Phillips, Dylan	L-L	6-0	220	6-16-99	.195	.298	.268	31	47	41	3	8	0	0	1	3	6	0	0	0	14	0	0	12.8	29.8
Rada, Nelson	L-L	5-10	160	8-24-05	.276	.395	.346	115	540	439	94	121	13	6	2	48	73	16	9	3	98	55	11	13.5	18.1
Reyes, Jose	L-R	6-2	180	9-22-00	.000	.000	.000	1	4	4	0	0	0	0	0	0	0	0	0	0	3	0	0	0.0	75.0
Rios, Alberto	R-R	6-0	203	3-19-02	.181	.269	.315	33	145	127	19	23	4	2	3	18	14	2	0	2	37	7	2	9.7	25.5
Ruiz, Jorge	L-L	5-10	164	6-30-04	.304	.379	.419	73	342	296	49	90	19	3	3	52	28	10	4	4	54	13	4	8.2	15.8
Sanchez, Jadiel	B-R	6-2	185	5-10-01	.297	.378	.475	105	443	381	59	113	15	10	11	66	47	7	1	7	64	7	4	10.6	14.4
Santana, Natanael	R-R	6-3	190	7-27-01	.059	.111	.059	6	18	17	0	1	0	0	0	0	1	0	0	0	12	0	0	5.6	66.7
Schanuel, Nolan	L-R	6-3	195	2-14-02	.833	.778	.833	2	9	6	2	5	0	0	0	2	1	1	0	1	0	0	0	11.1	0.0
Sepulveda, Christian	R-R	6-5	222	1-05-98	.228	.324	.376	42	173	149	26	34	4	3	4	22	11	11	0	2	41	13	3	6.4	23.7
Tinsman, Brendan	R-R	6-2	225	12-06-99	.241	.299	.368	23	97	87	12	21	4	2	1	14	7	1	0	2	29	2	0	7.2	29.9
Torres, Luis	R-R	6-3	210	1-12-04	.172	.293	.203	18	75	64	3	11	2	0	0	7	11	0	0	0	24	0	0	14.7	32.0
Villahermosa, Yeremi	B-R	5-9	150	10-16-02	.175	.298	.175	16	47	40	2	7	0	0	0	1	7	0	0	0	13	0	2	14.9	27.7
Watson, Kevin	L-R	6-1	190	5-25-99	.296	.396	.361	86	351	294	48	87	13	3	0	40	50	2	0	5	62	9	4	14.2	17.7
Williams, Cam	B-R	5-10	195	2-07-98	.247	.300	.644	24	80	73	16	18	4	2	7	16	6	0	0	1	25	4	0	7.5	31.3

Pitching	B-T	Ht.	Wt.	DOB	W	L	ERA	G	GS	SV	IP	Hits	Runs	ER	HR	BB	SO	AVG	OBP	SLG	SO%	BB%	BF
Albright, Mason	L-L	6-0	190	11-26-02	9	4	3.62	15	14	0	80	78	34	32	10	20	86	.248	.293	.414	25.7	6.0	334
Barraza, Chris	R-R	6-0	196	12-03-99	0	1	6.75	8	0	0	9	11	7	7	2	6	11	.314	.415	.543	26.8	14.6	41
Canning, Griffin	R-R	6-2	180	5-11-96	0	1	1.80	1	1	0	5	6	2	1	0	2	10	.300	.364	.400	45.5	9.1	22
Carter, Alan	R-R	6-3	200	12-16-97	2	2	1.77	14	0	2	20	14	9	4	0	11	32	.189	.291	.216	36.8	12.6	87
Clark, Chris	R-R	6-4	195	8-14-01	0	2	4.66	6	6	0	19	22	11	10	1	5	22	.278	.337	.494	25.6	5.8	86
Dana, Caden	L-R	6-4	215	12-17-03	1	1	1.20	3	3	0	15	6	2	2	1	6	18	.120	.228	.200	31.6	10.5	57
Daniel, Davis	R-R	6-1	190	6-11-97	1	1	1.77	4	4	0	20	15	5	4	0	5	28	.200	.250	.307	35.0	6.3	80
Darrell-Hicks, Michael	R-R	6-5	220	11-13-97	3	0	4.22	12	6	1	43	40	21	20	2	9	53	.247	.293	.364	30.5	5.2	174
Devenski, Chris	R-R	6-3	211	11-13-90	0	0	0.00	1	0	0	1	0	0	0	0	0	1	.000	.000	.000	33.3	0.0	3
Franco, Sadrac	R-R	6-0	155	6-04-00	3	4	3.67	29	0	4	42	38	24	17	6	18	42	.242	.331	.420	23.2	9.9	181
Garcia, Leonard	L-L	6-2	165	8-11-03	6	5	5.38	22	20	0	102	97	65	61	8	50	98	.251	.357	.404	21.4	10.9	458
Gieg, Max	R-R	6-5	230	6-08-01	3	2	4.95	31	0	2	40	38	27	22	2	20	49	.253	.341	.367	28.3	11.6	173
Gonzalez, Jenrry	L-L	5-10	185	6-07-01	1	0	2.30	23	0	1	43	39	15	11	3	13	63	.236	.294	.364	34.8	7.2	181
Guanare, Fernando	R-R	6-1	140	6-21-03	3	3	5.48	16	7	0	48	52	30	29	5	23	35	.281	.385	.454	16.1	10.6	218
Hanley, Mo	L-L	6-2	195	7-19-99	0	0	27.00	1	0	0	1	3	4	4	0	3	1	.500	.667	1.000	11.1	33.3	9
Hernandez, Gabriel	R-R	6-1	160	1-22-02	0	0	1.93	3	0	0	5	2	1	1	0	1	5	.133	.176	.133	29.4	5.9	17
Horvath, Nick	R-L	5-11	200	7-13-96	2	0	3.10	10	0	1	20	19	8	7	1	4	19	.247	.280	.364	23.2	4.9	82
Hurtado, Joel	R-R	6-2	180	2-06-01	6	5	5.42	22	10	0	78	78	53	47	2	31	90	.260	.343	.347	26.3	9.1	342
Joyce, Ben	R-R	6-5	225	9-17-00	0	0	0.00	2	0	0	2	1	0	0	0	1	2	.167	.286	.333	28.6	14.3	7
Joyce, Zach	R-R	6-4	225	9-17-00	0	1	2.53	11	0	1	11	9	4	3	0	3	9	.231	.279	.359	20.5	6.8	44
Kendrick, Dalton	L-L	6-6	211	9-26-00	0	1	9.00	5	0	0	5	9	5	5	0	3	5	.429	.500	.429	20.0	12.0	25
Kent, Barrett	R-R	6-4	200	9-29-04	0	0	0.00	1	1	0	4	2	0	0	0	1	5	.143	.250	.214	31.3	6.3	16
Langford, Ryan	R-R	6-0	160	8-31-99	3	3	3.34	31	3	6	62	50	25	23	5	21	59	.211	.281	.342	22.7	8.1	260
Madden, Jake	R-R	6-6	185	12-26-01	2	6	5.46	14	14	0	64	63	43	39	7	39	66	.250	.365	.401	21.9	12.9	302
Marcheco, Jorge	R-R	6-1	185	8-06-02	7	5	4.06	17	17	0	93	77	42	42	11	23	91	.223	.280	.390	24.1	6.1	377
Marte, Jose	R-R	6-3	180	6-14-96	0	0	0.00	4	1	0	5	2	0	0	0	0	8	.118	.118	.176	47.1	0.0	17
Martinez, Erik	R-R	5-11	193	3-21-96	2	1	1.59	9	0	0	17	11	3	3	0	5	28	.183	.269	.250	41.8	7.5	67
Martinez, Quinton	L-L	6-4	190	1-23-99	3	2	4.89	35	0	3	57	43	33	31	6	26	66	.214	.319	.388	27.5	10.8	240
Mayhue, C.J.	R-L	5-11	181	1-22-01	0	0	2.18	10	0	0	21	16	6	5	3	7	15	.213	.289	.347	18.1	8.4	83
Minacci, Camden	R-R	6-3	210	1-14-02	0	0	5.40	7	0	0	8	18	6	5	0	1	10	.450	.465	.525	23.3	2.3	43
Phansalkar, Roman	R-R	6-1	195	6-02-98	2	0	3.21	9	0	0	14	11	5	5	1	10	20	.212	.339	.288	32.3	16.1	62
Phillips, Dylan	L-L	6-0	220	6-16-99	2	2	3.77	18	0	3	31	25	14	13	1	11	45	.217	.305	.348	34.4	8.4	131
Rodriguez, Chris	R-R	6-2	185	7-20-98	0	0	18.00	1	0	0	1	3	2	2	0	0	2	.500	.500	.667	33.3	0.0	6
Seig, Hayden	R-R	6-5	227	9-10-98	2	0	1.13	4	0	0	8	5	1	1	0	2	14	.172	.226	.207	45.2	6.5	31
Southard, Jared	R-R	6-2	220	10-04-00	1	2	3.45	23	0	2	31	23	15	12	1	20	38	.204	.331	.292	27.0	14.2	141
Tepera, Ryan	R-R	6-1	195	11-03-87	0	0	0.00	2	1	0	2	0	0	0	0	0	5	.000	.000	.000	83.3	0.0	6
Timmins, Mark	R-R	6-3	210	5-12-98	0	0	9.00	5	0	0	10	20	10	10	2	2	6	.455	.490	.614	12.2	4.1	49
Urena, Walbert	R-R	6-0	170	1-25-04	4	7	5.66	22	21	0	99	94	66	62	5	60	97	.253	.365	.374	21.7	13.5	446
Zabala, Mario	R-R	6-2	195	5-08-02	0	0	27.00	1	0	0	1	2	2	2	0	2	0	.500	.667	.750	0.0	33.3	6

Fielding

Catcher	PCT	G	PO	A	E	DP	PB
Burns	.980	13	93	5	2	1	1
Flores	.995	83	740	54	4	5	12
O'Hoppe	1.000	3	14	2	0	0	0
Tinsman	.986	22	206	11	3	1	4
Villahermosa	.978	16	123	8	3	0	1
Watson	.968	8	59	2	2	0	3

First Base	PCT	G	PO	A	E	DP
Arocho	.987	19	141	11	2	18
Coutney	.996	72	509	27	2	44
Gobbel	1.000	10	83	3	0	14
Phillips	.944	4	15	2	1	2
Schanuel	1.000	2	16	5	0	2
Sepulveda	.976	5	39	2	1	5
Torres	.993	18	137	4	1	10
Watson	1.000	2	9	4	0	3
Williams	1.000	3	16	0	0	1

Second Base	PCT	G	PO	A	E	DP
Arocho	.993	65	110	170	2	42
Gill	1.000	5	6	8	0	2
Gobbel	1.000	4	5	11	0	2
Holt	.000	2	0	0	0	0
Macias	.995	58	96	125	1	28
Williams	1.000	3	7	6	0	3

Third Base	PCT	G	PO	A	E	DP
Arocho	.976	19	7	34	1	1
Fontenelle	.928	36	21	69	7	9
Gill	.000	1	0	0	0	0
Gobbel	.921	36	18	52	6	4
Sepulveda	.945	37	28	75	6	9
Williams	.846	5	3	8	2	1

Shortstop	PCT	G	PO	A	E	DP
Arocho	1.000	1	1	5	0	0
Guzman	.930	110	99	233	25	54
Macias	.958	19	20	48	3	9

Outfield	PCT	G	PO	A	E	DP
Arocho	1.000	1	2	0	0	0
Holt	1.000	22	44	3	0	2
Peabody	.991	59	102	2	1	1
Rada	.996	115	259	2	1	1
Rios	.979	29	44	2	1	0
Ruiz	.990	76	136	3	3	0
Sanchez	.912	96	134	15	6	4
Santana	1.000	6	12	0	0	0
Watson	.375	2	3	0	2	0
Williams	.000	1	0	0	0	0

ACL ANGELS

ROOKIE

ARIZONA COMPLEX LEAGUE

Batting	B-T	Ht.	Wt.	DOB	AVG	OBP	SLG	G	PA	AB	R	H	2B	3B	HR	RBI	BB	HBP	SH	SF	SO	SB	CS	BB%	SO%
Alfonso, Edgar	B-R	5-9	175	3-27-04	.247	.327	.290	35	108	93	16	23	2	1	0	7	11	0	4	0	27	3	0	10.2	25.0
Bartolero, Caleb	R-R	5-11	175	11-04-99	.294	.429	.353	6	21	17	1	5	1	0	0	3	1	3	0	0	9	1	0	4.8	42.9
Blake, Andy	R-R	6-4	195	8-15-00	.318	.348	.500	6	23	22	4	7	1	0	1	8	1	0	0	0	3	0	1	4.3	13.0
Bruggeman, Kevin	R-R	5-9	186	7-25-01	.250	.250	.750	1	4	4	0	1	0	1	0	1	0	0	0	0	1	0	0	0.0	25.0
Burns, Peter	L-R	5-10	195	10-14-99	1.000	.500	1.000	1	2	1	1	1	0	0	0	1	0	0	0	1	0	0	0	0.0	0.0
De Jesus, Randy	R-R	6-4	210	2-13-05	.249	.310	.331	48	202	181	32	45	9	0	2	26	15	2	0	2	50	4	2	7.4	24.8
Fontenelle, Cole	B-R	6-3	205	3-11-02	.200	.333	.200	3	12	10	2	2	0	0	0	2	1	1	0	0	2	0	0	8.3	16.7
Foster, Rio	R-R	6-3	205	6-18-03	.174	.240	.174	8	25	23	2	4	0	0	0	1	2	0	0	0	10	0	1	8.0	40.0
Garcia, Cristian	B-R	6-1	168	7-26-04	.266	.418	.413	48	184	143	25	38	5	5	2	23	37	2	0	2	42	1	0	20.1	22.8
Gobbel, Ben	R-R	6-1	190	11-02-99	.273	.467	.364	4	15	11	3	3	1	0	0	2	4	0	0	0	3	0	0	26.7	20.0
Hidalgo, Edwin	R-R	5-9	188	8-12-03	.286	.375	.286	5	8	7	2	2	0	0	0	0	1	0	0	0	2	0	0	12.5	25.0
Ketchup, Caleb	R-R	5-10	160	1-04-02	.375	.615	.500	5	14	8	0	3	1	0	0	1	4	1	1	0	3	4	0	28.6	21.4

Laverde, Dario	L-R	5-10	160	2-26-05	.306	.419	.455	43	167	134	23	41	9	4	1	32	28	1	0	4	31	7	3	16.8	18.6
Linares, Jonathan	B-R	6-0	200	4-02-05	.261	.375	.348	16	57	46	9	12	0	2	0	3	5	4	1	1	14	1	0	8.8	24.6
Manon, Junior	L-R	5-10	165	2-06-03	.302	.412	.465	16	51	43	7	13	0	2	1	7	8	0	0	0	17	1	1	15.7	33.3
McCroskey, Mac	R-R	6-1	180	12-31-99	.400	.667	.600	3	9	5	2	2	1	0	0	0	4	0	0	0	1	2	0	44.4	11.1
McGillis, Will	R-R	6-3	200	1-16-99	.378	.525	.644	15	59	45	11	17	7	1	1	14	11	3	0	0	10	2	0	18.6	16.9
Munroe, Kristin	R-R	6-1	175	8-06-04	.196	.281	.373	15	57	51	10	10	1	1	2	8	5	1	0	0	21	1	1	8.8	36.8
Murphy, Daniel	L-R	6-1	223	4-01-85	.143	.143	.143	2	7	7	1	1	0	0	0	1	0	0	0	0	2	0	0	0.0	28.6
Ortega, Jesus	R-R	6-0	170	1-18-01	.310	.434	.429	22	53	42	12	13	3	1	0	5	9	1	0	1	14	0	0	17.0	26.4
Ortiz, Capri	R-R	6-0	150	4-01-05	.273	.374	.345	53	230	194	39	53	8	3	0	22	29	3	3	1	68	30	7	12.6	29.6
Padlo, Kevin	R-R	5-11	210	7-15-96	.214	.267	.357	4	15	14	2	3	2	0	0	1	1	0	0	0	3	0	0	6.7	20.0
Pendleton, Caleb	R-R	6-2	185	4-05-02	.250	.250	.250	1	4	4	0	1	0	0	0	1	0	0	0	0	1	0	0	0.0	25.0
Ramirez, Ramon	L-L	6-2	195	1-30-05	.256	.333	.465	18	48	43	6	11	2	2	1	10	4	1	0	0	17	1	1	8.3	35.4
Redfield, Joe	L-R	6-2	200	10-18-01	.200	.333	.300	3	12	10	1	2	1	0	0	1	1	1	0	0	1	1	1	8.3	8.3
Rios, Alberto	R-R	6-0	203	3-19-02	.200	.333	.200	3	12	10	3	2	0	0	0	1	2	0	0	0	0	1	0	16.7	0.0
Rivero, Eliezer	R-R	6-0	180	3-29-05	.244	.327	.289	14	52	45	8	11	2	0	0	6	4	2	0	1	15	2	0	7.7	28.8
Rodriguez, Luis	R-R	6-1	176	12-22-04	.260	.352	.438	29	92	73	20	19	5	1	2	13	10	2	4	3	21	5	0	10.9	22.8
Rodriguez, Raudi	R-R	6-0	190	7-07-03	.368	.415	.447	12	41	38	6	14	1	1	0	1	3	0	0	0	7	1	0	7.3	17.1
Santana, Natanael	R-R	6-3	190	7-27-01	.239	.369	.370	32	111	92	18	22	2	2	2	11	14	5	0	0	38	5	1	12.6	34.2
Schanuel, Nolan	L-R	6-3	195	2-14-02	.250	.500	.375	3	12	8	3	2	1	0	0	1	4	0	0	0	1	1	0	33.3	8.3
Scull, Anthony	L-L	6-0	165	1-26-04	.300	.377	.453	48	192	170	31	51	7	5	3	30	12	9	0	0	41	10	1	6.3	21.4
Torres, Luis	R-R	6-3	210	1-12-04	.361	.439	.565	29	123	108	21	39	7	3	3	20	13	2	0	0	33	0	0	10.6	26.8
Velazquez, Andrew	R-R	5-9	170	7-14-94	.300	.364	.600	3	11	10	2	3	1	1	0	2	1	0	0	0	4	0	0	9.1	36.4
Villahermosa, Yeremi	B-R	5-9	150	10-16-02	.200	.167	.200	3	7	5	1	1	0	0	0	1	0	0	1	1	1	0	0	0.0	14.3
Wallace, Landon	B-R	6-2	170	2-27-02	.320	.514	.400	10	35	25	5	8	2	0	0	2	6	4	0	0	9	3	1	17.1	25.7
Wimmer, John	R-R	6-1	170	3-21-05	.161	.206	.226	9	34	31	4	5	2	0	0	4	2	0	0	1	17	0	0	5.9	50.0

Pitching	**B-T**	**Ht.**	**Wt.**	**DOB**	**W**	**L**	**ERA**	**G**	**GS**	**SV**	**IP**	**Hits**	**Runs**	**ER**	**HR**	**BB**	**SO**	**AVG**	**OBP**	**SLG**	**SO%**	**BB%**	**BF**
Albanese, Glenn	R-R	6-7	223	10-22-98	0	0	0.00	1	0	0	1	1	0	0	0	0	0	.250	.250	.500	0.0	0.0	4
Bauman, Riley	R-R	6-0	181	8-30-02	0	1	11.25	2	2	0	4	7	6	5	0	2	4	.412	.476	.412	19.0	9.5	21
Britt, Logan	R-R	6-5	222	7-16-00	0	0	22.50	3	0	0	2	5	5	5	0	2	1	.500	.538	.500	7.7	15.4	13
Bush, Ky	L-L	6-6	240	11-12-99	0	1	15.75	2	2	0	4	10	8	7	0	1	9	.435	.458	.565	37.5	4.2	24
Cazorla, Manuel	L-L	6-2	170	1-03-05	1	3	6.06	9	5	0	36	36	24	24	3	15	33	.269	.355	.440	21.0	9.6	157
Charle, Sandi	R-R	6-5	180	9-05-02	0	0	7.36	8	0	0	11	19	13	9	1	8	15	.352	.444	.556	23.8	12.7	63
Choban, Brady	R-R	6-5	240	9-16-00	0	1	54.00	1	0	0	1	4	4	4	0	1	2	.667	.714	.833	28.6	14.3	7
Christopherson, Will	R-R	6-4	210	8-08-99	0	0	0.00	1	0	0	1	0	0	0	0	0	2	.000	.000	.000	66.7	0.0	3
Daniel, Davis	R-R	6-1	190	6-11-97	0	0	1.80	2	2	0	5	4	1	1	0	0	9	.200	.200	.250	45.0	0.0	20
Devenski, Chris	R-R	6-3	211	11-13-90	0	0	1.29	6	6	0	7	7	2	1	0	0	15	.250	.241	.250	51.7	0.0	29
Dowdell, Kevin	L-L	6-1	210	12-03-99	0	0	16.20	4	0	0	3	5	6	6	0	4	2	.357	.545	.357	9.1	18.2	22
Fulmer, Carson	R-R	6-0	210	12-13-93	0	1	2.25	1	1	0	4	3	2	1	1	1	7	.188	.235	.375	41.2	5.9	17
Gockel, Chase	R-R	6-1	195	1-01-00	0	0	30.86	4	0	0	2	2	9	8	1	12	3	.200	.652	.500	13.0	52.2	23
Gomez, Yendy	R-R	6-2	170	12-19-03	2	5	6.55	12	8	0	55	73	46	40	7	19	49	.313	.372	.472	18.8	7.3	261
Hernandez, Gabriel	R-R	6-1	160	1-22-02	1	0	4.00	4	0	0	9	7	4	4	1	3	8	.233	.294	.467	23.5	8.8	34
Kent, Barrett	R-R	6-4	200	9-29-04	1	0	0.00	2	0	0	5	2	0	0	0	3	5	.125	.300	.125	25.0	15.0	20
Key, Keythel	R-R	6-3	180	10-10-03	3	5	4.53	11	8	0	44	39	29	22	3	32	40	.250	.393	.359	20.1	16.1	199
Marte, Jose	R-R	6-3	180	6-14-96	0	0	6.75	3	0	0	3	3	2	2	1	2	4	.273	.385	.545	30.8	15.4	13
Martinez, Alex	R-R	5-10	170	9-15-02	1	2	1.17	16	0	5	23	16	6	3	0	15	35	.195	.327	.207	35.7	15.3	98
Mayhue, C.J.	R-L	5-11	181	1-22-01	2	0	2.35	3	0	0	8	11	6	2	1	5	9	.344	.421	.500	23.7	13.2	38
Mendez, Haminton	R-R	6-1	177	6-05-04	2	1	6.15	7	4	1	26	28	23	18	3	17	12	.262	.370	.364	9.4	13.4	127
Moreno, Darwin	R-R	6-2	175	1-26-02	0	0	15.88	6	0	0	6	10	10	10	0	5	2	.400	.545	.480	6.1	15.2	33
Nunez, Luis	R-R	6-2	175	9-19-01	2	0	10.80	10	0	1	15	24	19	18	1	7	19	.358	.416	.537	24.7	9.1	77
Peters, Andrew	R-R	6-2	191	11-25-98	2	1	6.14	5	0	0	7	3	5	5	0	6	13	.125	.300	.125	43.3	20.0	30
Podaras, Straton	R-R	6-1	200	12-09-97	0	0	10.13	4	0	0	3	3	4	3	1	2	4	.273	.385	.636	30.8	15.4	13
Quintero, Santiago	L-L	6-3	180	4-16-05	1	0	4.94	13	0	0	27	24	21	15	2	22	34	.224	.362	.346	26.2	16.9	130
Rivera, Erik	L-L	6-2	200	4-02-01	0	1	6.75	5	4	0	7	3	5	5	0	13	11	.136	.459	.182	29.7	35.1	37
Romero, Fernando	R-R	6-0	215	12-24-94	0	0	0.00	1	1	0	3	1	0	0	0	2	3	.111	.273	.222	27.3	18.2	11
Sanchez, Andre	R-R	5-10	140	2-05-03	2	2	8.03	11	2	1	25	31	23	22	3	8	22	.307	.354	.545	19.5	7.1	113
Sandy, Will	L-L	6-4	210	9-17-99	1	0	1.29	3	0	0	7	3	1	1	1	1	13	.125	.160	.250	48.1	3.7	27
Segura, Dawry	R-R	6-2	140	8-05-03	3	3	4.69	11	6	0	48	56	35	25	6	12	29	.290	.332	.482	13.9	5.7	209
Sepulveda, Christian	R-R	6-5	222	1-05-98	0	0	0.00	2	0	0	2	2	0	0	0	2	3	.250	.400	.250	30.0	20.0	10
Sifontes, Enderjer	R-R	6-0	135	11-19-02	0	0	9.00	5	1	0	6	10	8	6	0	3	3	.333	.412	.400	8.8	8.8	34
Smith, Julian	R-L	6-4	210	6-03-97	0	2	6.94	7	0	0	12	10	10	9	0	9	17	.244	.373	.317	33.3	17.6	51
Suarez, Jose	L-L	5-10	225	1-03-98	0	0	2.70	2	2	0	3	5	1	1	0	2	4	.333	.412	.400	23.5	11.8	17
Thompson, Ben	R-R	6-0	215	1-17-02	0	0	6.75	4	0	0	4	0	3	3	0	5	8	.000	.333	.000	44.4	27.8	18
Timmins, Mark	R-R	6-3	210	5-12-98	0	0	9.00	3	0	0	4	7	5	4	0	1	4	.389	.450	.500	20.0	5.0	20
Tullar, Cameron	R-L	6-2	215	6-30-00	1	0	2.08	2	0	1	4	4	1	1	0	2	4	.267	.333	.267	22.2	11.1	18
Viloria, Luis	L-L	5-10	150	9-24-03	1	1	3.06	5	2	0	18	14	7	6	1	5	15	.212	.264	.288	20.8	6.9	72
Zabala, Mario	R-R	6-2	195	5-08-02	0	0	0.00	1	0	0	0	1	2	2	0	3	0	1.000	1.000	1.000	0.0	75.0	4

Fielding

C: Laverde 28, Linares 11, Rivero 10, Bartolero 4, Villahermosa 3, Hidalgo 3, Bruggeman 1, Burns 1, Pendleton 1. **1B:** Garcia 27, Torres 24, Ramirez 7, Schanuel 2, Murphy 2. **2B:** Alfonso 23, Rodriguez 22, Ortiz 11, McGillis 7, McCroskey 3, Velazquez 1. **3B:** Garcia 21, Munroe 14, Alfonso 13, Blake 6, Gobbel 4, Padlo 4, Fontenelle 3, McGillis 2. **SS:** Ortiz 43, Wimmer 9, Rodriguez 7, Ketchup 4, Velazquez 2. **OF:** Scull 48, De Jesus 45, Santana 31, Ortega 20, Rodriguez 12, Wallace 10, Manon 8, Foster 7, Redfield 3, Rios 3, Ramirez 1, Munroe 1.

DSL ANGELS

ROOKIE

DOMINICAN SUMMER LEAGUE

Batting	B-T	Ht.	Wt.	DOB	AVG	OBP	SLG	G	PA	AB	R	H	2B	3B	HR	RBI	BB	HBP	SH	SF	SO	SB	CS	BB%	SO%
Bolivar, Eduar	R-R	5-11	180	3-22-06	.300	.350	.391	35	123	110	19	33	7	0	1	18	6	4	0	3	24	5	4	4.9	19.5
Castillo, Byron	R-R	6-0	197	10-07-05	.158	.248	.205	43	165	146	26	23	4	0	1	14	9	9	0	1	49	8	3	5.5	29.7
Castillo, Kevyn	L-L	5-10	170	6-12-05	.371	.478	.548	55	234	186	44	69	10	7	3	35	40	2	2	4	36	23	9	17.1	15.4
Chirinos, Jorge	R-R	6-0	170	5-11-03	.000	.000	.000	1	1	1	0	0	0	0	0	0	0	0	0	0	1	0	0	0.0	100.0
Colina, Optiel	R-R	6-2	180	11-08-05	.176	.419	.235	26	74	51	10	9	1	1	0	2	17	5	0	1	24	5	0	23.0	32.4
Dishmey, Samil	L-R	6-2	175	12-22-05	.294	.395	.333	35	119	102	17	30	1	0	1	8	14	3	0	0	17	6	6	11.8	14.3
Duarte, Athanael	R-R	5-10	165	11-11-04	.311	.363	.417	45	169	151	21	47	7	0	3	25	12	2	1	3	19	9	0	7.1	11.2
Espinal, Edwardo	R-R	6-1	182	11-19-05	.225	.330	.288	22	94	80	12	18	5	0	0	7	9	4	0	1	29	11	1	9.6	30.9
Florentino, Jerson	R-R	5-7	155	10-23-04	.267	.395	.333	25	76	60	16	16	4	0	0	8	12	2	0	2	5	9	2	15.8	6.6
Flores, Juan	R-R	5-10	180	2-13-06	.236	.352	.388	46	197	165	32	39	7	0	6	26	15	15	1	1	25	6	1	7.6	12.7
Hernandez, Luis	R-R	5-8	186	2-10-06	.139	.326	.194	19	46	36	6	5	2	0	0	3	10	0	0	0	13	3	1	21.7	28.3
Marquez, Anyelo	L-R	6-0	166	12-12-05	.231	.324	.327	46	173	147	19	34	8	3	0	17	22	0	0	4	29	8	7	12.7	16.8
Martinez, Bryan	L-R	6-2	170	12-26-05	.206	.341	.235	16	41	34	5	7	1	0	0	3	7	0	0	0	15	3	3	17.1	36.6
Medina, Rafael	R-R	6-2	210	12-07-05	.170	.298	.277	21	57	47	6	8	2	0	1	9	6	3	0	1	24	0	0	10.5	42.1
Morrobel, Felix	B-R	6-0	175	9-24-05	.286	.322	.335	42	171	161	21	46	4	2	0	20	8	1	0	1	13	11	8	4.7	7.6
Patino, Oswaldo	L-R	5-10	160	7-03-06	.304	.513	.375	31	80	56	11	17	2	1	0	9	20	4	0	0	8	2	1	25.0	10.0
Rodriguez, Victor	R-R	5-10	185	1-24-06	.224	.297	.391	48	175	156	27	35	6	4	4	24	11	6	0	2	50	11	6	6.3	28.6
Villaman, Axel	L-R	6-0	200	1-04-05	.205	.340	.333	19	47	39	7	8	2	0	1	7	6	2	0	0	17	1	0	12.8	36.2

Pitching	B-T	Ht.	Wt.	DOB	W	L	ERA	G	GS	SV	IP	Hits	Runs	ER	HR	BB	SO	AVG	OBP	SLG	SO%	BB%	BF
Acosta, Adrian	R-R	6-1	170	5-20-05	2	3	1.17	10	10	0	46	28	12	6	1	22	64	.174	.293	.224	34.0	11.7	188
Anzola, Rolando	R-R	6-2	170	5-31-05	0	1	15.63	8	0	0	6	6	12	11	0	20	9	.240	.587	.360	19.6	43.5	46
Baro, Sadiel	L-L	6-2	177	11-10-04	2	1	3.27	12	11	1	44	41	20	16	0	26	43	.255	.358	.323	22.5	13.6	191
Cabrera, Anel	R-R	6-4	200	2-12-03	4	1	1.25	19	0	2	43	30	12	6	1	11	50	.196	.254	.275	29.6	6.5	169
Castillo, Ruben	R-R	6-1	160	6-18-01	5	1	2.37	18	0	9	30	14	13	8	2	11	46	.133	.222	.210	39.0	9.3	118
Castro, Javiel	R-R	6-3	177	10-15-05	0	0	12.00	5	0	0	6	6	8	8	0	7	5	.286	.469	.286	15.6	21.9	32
Faringthon, Luis	R-R	5-11	187	5-27-03	2	1	7.53	9	0	0	14	20	19	12	2	7	13	.333	.417	.483	18.1	9.7	72
Gomez, Miguel	R-R	6-3	175	1-05-05	0	0	81.00	1	0	0	0	1	4	3	0	2	1	.333	.600	.333	20.0	40.0	5
Gonzalez, Junior	R-R	6-4	210	9-16-05	0	0	13.86	10	1	0	12	14	21	19	1	20	12	.311	.521	.422	16.9	28.2	71
Hernandez, Bryan	R-R	6-1	145	5-25-04	0	0	3.97	10	0	0	11	3	5	5	0	17	15	.086	.407	.086	27.8	31.5	54
Lara, Davidxon	R-R	5-10	165	7-31-06	3	2	2.70	9	9	0	40	38	19	12	2	5	34	.244	.283	.359	20.4	3.0	167
Mendez, Haminton	R-R	6-1	177	6-05-04	3	1	1.64	4	4	0	22	11	4	4	1	5	20	.149	.222	.243	24.7	6.2	81
Monte De Oca, Bryan	R-R	6-3	190	3-22-06	1	2	5.48	12	2	0	23	28	15	14	2	19	20	.311	.436	.478	18.2	17.3	110
Poline, Jesus	R-R	6-3	170	10-22-04	2	1	2.10	14	0	1	26	17	8	6	1	16	23	.191	.314	.270	21.7	15.1	106
Reyes, Yokelvin	L-L	6-1	195	3-29-04	2	1	4.03	14	0	0	22	18	11	10	1	10	29	.214	.327	.321	29.6	10.2	98
Soto, Ubaldo	R-R	6-2	185	7-12-06	4	1	1.64	11	6	2	44	32	15	8	1	23	42	.204	.317	.261	23.0	12.6	183
Texido, Francis	L-L	6-2	180	4-01-05	6	1	2.31	12	12	0	51	36	16	13	3	12	61	.200	.286	.283	30.0	5.9	203
Tirado, Leudy	L-L	5-10	160	9-27-05	1	0	2.89	11	0	1	19	11	8	6	0	15	12	.172	.333	.219	14.8	18.5	81
Valdespina, Edinson	R-R	6-6	190	5-31-04	0	1	0.00	1	0	0	2	3	3	0	0	2	1	.300	.417	.500	8.3	16.7	12

Fielding

C. Flores 39, Medina 16, Bolivar 6. **1B.** Duarte 44, Colina 14, Bolivar 3. **2B.** Marquez 30, Patino 24, Florentino 13. **3B.** Rodriguez 47, Florentino 9, Martinez 2. **SS:** Morrobel 40, Marquez 19, Patino 1. **OF:** Castillo 95, Bolivar 18, Espinal 18, Dishmey 16, Hernandez 15, Villaman 11, Colina 10.

Los Angeles Dodgers

SEASON SYNOPSIS: Clayton Kershaw, Mookie Betts and Freddie Freeman led L.A. to its 10th National League West title in the last 11 seasons, and its fourth consecutive full season with 100 victories. But for the second straight year, the Dodgers lost in the first round of the postseason, swept in three games by the Diamondbacks.

HIGH POINT: The Dodgers put the NL West away with a 24-5 August hot streak that included an 11-game win streak that started during a series win at San Diego. The streak finished with a 1-0 victory to sweep Milwaukee, with Lance Lynn tossing seven scoreless and reserve catcher Austin Barnes hitting a solo shot in the eighth

LOW POINT: The D-backs steamrolled the Dodgers in the Division Series, jumping on Kershaw for six runs in the first inning of the series opener, an 11-2 victory. They didn't have a starter make it through two full innings in 4-2 losses in Games 2 and 3 and hit just .177 for the series, with Betts and Freeman combining to go 1-for-21.

NOTABLE ROOKIES: While his 181 strikeouts ranked as the sixth most among MLB batters, center fielder James Outman was one of the Dodgers' better contributors, playing creditable defense, hitting 23 homers, swiping 16 bags and batting .248/.353/.437 in 567 plate appearances. Righty Bobby Miller struggled in his postseason start but regularly hit 100 mph in the regular season and posted an 11-4, 3.76 mark over 22 starts. Handed the second-base job to open the season, Miguel Vargas couldn't retain it, hitting just .195/.305/.367 and struggling defensively (-7 outs above average). Righty Emmet Sheehan (4-1, 4.92) had ups and downs but did enough to be called upon to relieve Kershaw in the Game 1 debacle, giving up three runs in 3.2 innings.

KEY TRANSACTIONS: Lefthander Julio Urias, a free agent at season's end, left the rotation in a lurch when he was placed on administrative leave in early September following his arrest on a felony domestic violence charge. The loss of Urias, combined with Kershaw's fragility and the absences of righties Walker Buehler (Tommy John surgery recovery), Dustin May (flexor tendon surgery) and Tony Gonsolin (TJ surgery), strained the rotation.

DOWN ON THE FARM: The Dodgers led all organizations in minor league winning percentage (.582). Before promotions struck, the Double-A Tulsa rotation was viewed as one of the best scouts had seen in many years.

OPENING DAY PAYROLL: $222,717,834 (5th).

PLAYERS OF THE YEAR

MAJOR LEAGUE

Mookie Betts
OF/2B
.307/.408/.579
40 2B, 39 HR
126 R, 107 RBI

MINOR LEAGUE

Michael Busch
3B
(AAA)
.323/.413/.618
26 2B, 27 HR, 90 RBI

ORGANIZATION LEADERS

Batting — *Minimum 250 AB

MAJORS

* AVG	Freddie Freeman	.331
* OPS	Mookie Betts	.987
HR	Mookie Betts	39
RBI	Mookie Betts	107

MINORS

* AVG	Gavin Lux, Tulsa, Oklahoma City	.347
* OBP	Connor Joe, Oklahoma City	.426
* SLG	Kyle Garlick, Oklahoma City	.675
* OPS	Kyle Garlick, Oklahoma City	1.057
R	Gavin Lux, Tulsa, Oklahoma City	99
H	Gavin Lux, Tulsa, Oklahoma City	159
TB	Gavin Lux, Tulsa, Oklahoma City	278
2B	Miguel Vargas, Great Lakes, Rancho Cucamonga	38
3B	Jeren Kendall, Rancho Cucamonga	10
HR	Edwin Rios, Oklahoma City	31
RBI	Zach Reks, Tulsa, Oklahoma City	93
BB	Dillon Paulson, Great Lakes, Rancho Cucamonga	82
SO	Donovan Casey, Rancho Cucamonga, Tulsa	174
SB	Brayan Morales, Rancho Cucamonga	35

Pitching — #Minimum 75 IP

MAJORS

W	Clayton Kershaw	13
# ERA	Clayton Kershaw	2.46
SO	Clayton Kershaw	137
SV	Evan Phillips	24

MINORS

W	Alec Gamboa, Tulsa/Okla. City	9
W	Orlando Ortiz-Mayr, G. Lakes/Tulsa	9
L	Orlando Ortiz-Mayr, G. Lakes/Tulsa	9
# ERA	Landon Knack, Tulsa/Okla. City	2.51
G	John Rooney, Tulsa/Okla. City	53
GS	Maddux Bruns, R.Cuca./Great Lakes	26
SV	Wander Suero, Oklahoma City	17
IP	Orlando Ortiz-Mayr, G. Lakes/Tulsa	111
BB	Maddux Bruns, R.Cuca./Great Lakes	67
SO	Kyle Hurt, Tulsa/Oklahoma City	152
# AVG	Maddux Bruns, R.Cuca./Great Lakes	.184

2023 PERFORMANCE

General Manager: Andrew Friedman. **Farm Director:** Will Rhymes. **Scouting Director:** Billy Gasparino.

Class	Team	League	W	L	PCT	Finish	Manager
Majors	Los Angeles Dodgers	National	100	62	.617	2 (15)	Dave Roberts
Triple-A	Oklahoma City Dodgers	Pacific Coast	90	58	.608	1 (10)	Travis Barbary
Double-A	Tulsa Drillers	Texas	65	73	.471	7 (10)	Scott Hennessey
High-A	Great Lakes Loons	Midwest	76	55	.580	2 (12)	Daniel Nava
Low-A	Rancho Cuca. Quakes	California	71	61	.538	3 (10)	John Shoemaker
Rookie	ACL Dodgers	Arizona Complex	34	22	.607	3 (17)	Jair Fernandez
Rookie	DSL LAD Bautista	Dominican Sum.	42	11	.792	1 (50)	Dunior Zerpa
Rookie	DSL LAD Mega	Dominican Sum.	36	17	.679	5 (50)	Hipolito Cordell
Overall 2023 Minor League Record			414	297	.582	1st (30)	

ORGANIZATION STATISTICS

LOS ANGELES DODGERS

NATIONAL LEAGUE

Batting	B-T	Ht.	Wt.	DOB	AVG	OBP	SLG	G	PA	AB	R	H	2B	3B	HR	RBI	BB	HBP	SH	SF	SO	SB	CS	BB%	SO%
Barnes, Austin	R-R	5-10	187	12-28-89	.180	.256	.242	59	200	178	15	32	5	0	2	11	17	2	1	2	43	2	1	8.5	21.5
Betts, Mookie	R-R	5-9	180	10-07-92	.307	.408	.579	152	693	584	126	179	40	1	39	107	96	8	0	5	107	14	3	13.9	15.4
Busch, Michael	L-R	6-1	210	11-09-97	.167	.247	.292	27	81	72	9	12	3	0	2	7	8	0	0	1	27	1	0	9.9	33.3
DeLuca, Jonny	R-R	6-0	200	7-10-98	.262	.311	.429	24	45	42	5	11	1	0	2	6	3	0	0	0	8	1	0	6.7	17.8
Freeman, Freddie	L-R	6-5	220	9-12-89	.331	.410	.567	161	730	637	131	211	59	2	29	102	72	16	0	5	121	23	1	9.9	16.6
Hernandez, Enrique	R-R	5-11	190	8-24-91	.262	.308	.423	54	185	168	19	44	12	0	5	30	12	1	0	4	29	1	0	6.5	15.7
Hernandez, Yonny	B-R	5-9	140	5-04-98	.136	.231	.182	14	27	22	5	3	1	0	0	4	2	1	1	1	8	0	0	7.4	29.6
Heyward, Jason	L-L	6-5	240	8-09-89	.269	.340	.473	124	377	334	56	90	23	0	15	40	34	3	0	3	64	2	2	9.0	17.0
Marisnick, Jake	R-R	6-4	220	3-30-91	.400	.500	.400	4	6	5	0	2	0	0	0	0	0	1	0	0	0	0	1	0.0	0.0
3-team (33 Detroit, 9 Chicao White Sox)					.225	.263	.408	42	77	71	10	16	3	2	2	10	3	1	1	1	21	2	2	3.9	27.3
Martinez, J.D.	R-R	6-3	230	8-21-87	.271	.321	.572	113	479	432	61	117	27	2	33	103	34	2	0	9	149	1	0	7.1	31.1
Miller, Shelby	R-R	6-3	225	10-10-90	.000	.000	.000	36	1	1	0	0	0	0	0	0	0	0	0	0	0	0	0	0.0	0.0
Muncy, Max	L-R	6-0	215	8-25-90	.212	.333	.475	135	579	482	95	102	17	1	36	105	85	6	0	6	153	1	2	14.7	26.4
Outman, James	L-R	6-3	215	5-14-97	.248	.353	.437	151	567	483	86	120	16	3	23	70	68	12	0	4	181	16	3	12.0	31.9
Peralta, David	L-L	6-1	210	8-14-87	.259	.294	.381	133	422	394	47	102	25	1	7	55	20	2	0	6	72	4	1	4.7	17.1
Rojas, Miguel	R-R	6-0	188	2-24-89	.236	.290	.322	125	423	385	49	91	16	1	5	31	26	5	2	5	48	8	3	6.1	11.3
Rosario, Amed	R-R	6-2	190	11-20-95	.256	.301	.408	48	133	125	19	32	6	2	3	18	7	1	0	0	22	6	2	5.3	16.5
Smith, Will	R-R	5-10	195	3-28-95	.261	.359	.438	126	554	464	80	121	21	2	19	76	63	15	0	12	89	3	0	11.4	16.1
Taylor, Chris	R-R	6-1	196	8-29-90	.237	.326	.420	117	384	338	51	80	15	1	15	56	41	4	0	1	125	16	3	10.7	32.6
Thompson, Trayce	R-R	6-3	225	3-15-91	.155	.310	.366	36	87	71	12	11	0	0	5	14	15	1	0	0	37	0	0	17.2	42.5
Vargas, Miguel	R-R	6-3	205	11-17-99	.195	.305	.367	81	304	256	36	50	15	4	7	32	38	4	1	4	61	3	2	12.5	20.1
Williams, Luke	R-R	6-0	186	8-09-96	.100	.100	.100	4	10	10	0	1	0	0	0	0	0	0	0	0	3	1	0	0.0	30.0
2-team (7 Atlanta)					.053	.053	.053	11	19	19	1	1	0	0	0	0	0	0	0	0	7	4	0	0.0	36.8
Wong, Kolten	L-R	5-7	185	10-10-90	.300	.353	.500	20	34	30	4	9	0	0	2	8	2	1	0	1	7	2	1	5.9	20.6
Wynns, Austin	R-R	6-0	190	12-10-90	.182	.250	.273	5	12	11	0	2	1	0	0	2	1	0	0	0	5	0	0	8.3	41.7
2-team (45 Colorado)					.208	.264	.277	51	145	130	11	27	6	0	1	10	9	2	3	1	39	1	0	6.2	26.9

Pitching	B-T	Ht.	Wt.	DOB	W	L	ERA	G	GS	SV	IP	Hits	Runs	ER	HR	BB	SO	AVG	OBP	SLG	SO%	BB%	BF
Almonte, Yency	R-R	6-5	223	6-04-94	3	2	5.06	49	0	0	48	43	30	27	6	24	49	.239	.341	.372	23.6	11.5	208
Bickford, Phil	R-R	6-4	200	7-10-95	2	3	5.14	36	0	0	42	38	27	24	5	26	48	.235	.339	.407	25.3	13.7	190
Brasier, Ryan	R-R	6-0	227	8-26-87	2	0	0.70	39	0	1	39	18	6	3	1	10	38	.140	.203	.194	26.6	7.0	143
Bruihl, Justin	L-L	6-2	215	6-26-97	1	0	4.07	20	0	0	24	24	11	11	2	8	19	.264	.333	.407	18.6	7.8	102
Covey, Dylan	R-R	6-1	215	8-14-91	0	0	4.50	1	0	0	4	5	2	2	2	1	3	.294	.333	.647	16.7	5.6	18
Cyr, Tyler	R-R	6-1	205	5-05-93	0	0	0.00	2	0	0	2	1	0	0	0	0	2	.167	.167	.167	33.3	0.0	6
Ferguson, Caleb	R-L	6-3	226	7-02-96	7	4	3.43	68	7	3	60	64	30	23	4	23	70	.269	.352	.366	25.9	8.5	270
Gonsolin, Tony	R-R	6-3	205	5-14-94	8	5	4.98	20	20	0	103	86	61	57	19	40	82	.226	.307	.415	18.9	9.2	435
Gonzalez, Victor	L-L	6-0	180	11-16-95	3	3	4.01	34	1	0	34	27	15	15	2	10	30	.223	.296	.331	22.2	7.4	135
Graterol, Brusdar	R-R	6-1	265	8-26-98	4	2	1.20	68	1	7	67	53	14	9	3	12	48	.221	.262	.296	18.7	4.7	257
Grove, Michael	R-R	6-3	200	12-18-96	2	3	6.13	18	12	0	69	83	47	47	12	19	73	.296	.348	.500	24.2	6.3	302
Hernandez, Yonny	B-R	5-9	140	5-04-98	0	0	0.00	1	0	0	1	1	0	0	0	0	0	.250	.250	.250	0.0	0.0	4
Hudson, Bryan	L-L	6-8	220	5-08-97	0	0	7.27	6	0	0	9	12	7	7	1	4	7	.316	.386	.447	15.9	9.1	44
Hudson, Daniel	R-R	6-3	215	3-09-87	0	0	0.00	3	0	1	3	2	0	0	0	3	5	.182	.357	.273	35.7	21.4	14
Hurt, Kyle	R-R	6-3	240	5-30-98	0	0	0.00	1	0	0	2	0	0	0	0	0	3	.000	.000	.000	50.0	0.0	6
Jackson, Andre	R-R	6-3	210	5-01-96	0	0	6.62	7	0	2	18	22	13	13	5	3	16	.289	.316	.553	20.3	3.8	79
Kelly, Joe	R-R	6-1	174	6-09-88	1	0	1.74	11	0	0	10	3	3	2	0	6	19	.088	.225	.088	47.5	15.0	40
Kershaw, Clayton	L-L	6-4	225	3-19-88	13	5	2.46	24	24	0	132	100	39	36	19	40	137	.209	.273	.367	26.2	7.6	523
Kolarek, Adam	L-L	6-3	215	1-14-89	0	0	0.00	1	0	0	1	1	0	0	0	0	2	.200	.200	.200	40.0	0.0	5
Lynn, Lance	B-R	6-5	270	5-12-87	7	2	4.36	11	11	0	64	59	33	31	16	22	47	.238	.305	.460	17.2	8.1	273
May, Dustin	R-R	6-6	180	9-06-97	4	1	2.63	9	9	0	48	29	14	14	1	16	34	.173	.251	.250	18.2	8.6	187
Miller, Bobby	L-R	6-5	220	4-05-99	11	4	3.76	22	22	0	124	105	53	52	12	32	119	.226	.283	.364	23.6	6.3	505
Miller, Shelby	R-R	6-3	225	10-10-90	3	0	1.71	36	1	1	42	19	8	8	3	19	42	.135	.247	.241	25.8	11.7	163
Miller, Tyson	R-R	6-5	220	7-29-95	0	0	4.50	2	0	0	4	4	2	2	0	1	3	.286	.333	.286	20.0	6.7	15

Pitching	B-T	Ht.	Wt.	DOB	W	L	ERA	G	GS	SV	IP	Hits	Runs	ER	HR	BB	SO	AVG	OBP	SLG	SO%	BB%	BF
Pepiot, Ryan	R-R	6-3	215	8-21-97	2	1	2.14	8	3	0	42	27	10	10	7	5	38	.179	.220	.364	23.9	3.1	159
Phillips, Evan	R-R	6-2	215	9-11-94	2	4	2.05	62	0	24	61	38	19	14	6	13	66	.177	.233	.302	28.2	5.6	234
Reed, Jake	R-R	6-2	195	9-29-92	0	0	81.00	1	0	0	1	5	6	6	1	1	1	.833	.857	1.500	14.3	14.3	7
Robertson, Nick	R-R	6-6	265	7-16-98	0	1	6.10	9	0	0	10	17	10	7	1	4	13	.370	.420	.565	26.0	8.0	50
Rojas, Miguel	R-R	6-0	188	2-24-89	0	0	6.00	3	0	0	3	3	2	2	0	1	0	.250	.357	.417	0.0	7.1	14
Scott, Tayler	R-R	6-3	185	6-01-92	0	0	9.00	6	0	0	6	6	6	6	0	4	8	.250	.367	.417	26.7	13.3	30
Sheehan, Emmet	R-R	6-5	220	11-15-99	4	1	4.92	13	11	1	60	46	33	33	11	26	64	.210	.294	.416	25.8	10.5	248
Stone, Gavin	R-R	6-1	175	10-15-98	1	1	9.00	8	4	1	31	46	32	31	8	13	22	.338	.401	.603	14.5	8.6	152
Suero, Wander	R-R	6-4	216	9-15-91	1	0	7.88	5	0	0	8	6	7	7	2	5	9	.200	.314	.400	25.7	14.3	35
Syndergaard, Noah	L-R	6-6	242	8-29-92	1	4	7.16	12	12	0	55	71	44	44	12	9	38	.313	.350	.551	15.4	3.7	246
Urias, Julio	L-L	6-0	225	8-12-96	11	8	4.60	21	21	0	117	112	61	60	24	24	117	.252	.296	.482	24.3	5.0	482
Varland, Gus	L-R	6-1	213	11-06-96	1	1	3.09	8	0	0	12	12	6	4	0	8	14	.279	.392	.419	26.9	15.4	52
Vesia, Alex	L-L	6-1	209	4-11-96	2	5	4.35	56	1	1	50	52	27	24	7	17	64	.263	.327	.414	29.5	7.8	217
Williams, Luke	R-R	6-0	186	8-09-96	0	0	0.00	1	0	0	1	0	0	0	0	0	0	.000	.000	.000	0.0	0.0	3
Yarbrough, Ryan	R-L	6-5	205	12-31-91	4	2	4.89	11	2	2	39	44	21	21	8	5	38	.278	.309	.475	23.0	3.0	165

Fielding

Catcher	PCT	G	PO	A	E	DP	PB
Barnes	.994	53	461	6	3	1	3
Smith	.996	111	937	32	4	3	2
Wynns	1.000	5	22	4	0	0	0

First Base	PCT	G	PO	A	E	DP
Busch	1.000	4	11	1	0	2
Freeman	.999	161	1131	128	1	126
Hernandez	1.000	10	22	1	0	2
Heyward	1.000	6	7	2	0	0
Vargas	1.000	5	9	2	0	2

Second Base	PCT	G	PO	A	E	DP
Barnes	.000	1	0	0	0	0
Betts	.991	70	87	136	2	33
Busch	1.000	1	4	2	0	1
Hernandez, E	.967	15	13	16	1	3
Hernandez, Y	1.000	8	6	8	0	3
Rojas	1.000	1	1	3	0	1
Rosario	1.000	36	34	50	0	20
Taylor	.667	3	2	0	1	0
Vargas	.982	78	120	156	5	46
Wong	.957	11	7	15	1	3

Third Base	PCT	G	PO	A	E	DP
Busch	.852	13	7	16	4	3
Hernandez, E	.939	12	7	24	2	4
Hernandez, Y	1.000	3	2	5	0	2
Muncy	.944	124	63	206	16	23
Rojas	1.000	1	1	0	0	0
Taylor	.977	28	10	32	1	0

Shortstop	PCT	G	PO	A	E	DP
Betts	.935	16	16	27	3	4
Hernandez	1.000	10	13	17	0	4
Rojas	.986	121	143	281	6	61
Rosario	.967	16	10	19	1	3
Taylor	.980	31	27	69	2	12
Williams	1.000	4	6	5	0	1

Outfield	PCT	G	PO	A	E	DP
Betts	1.000	107	141	8	0	1
Busch	.000	1	0	0	0	0
DeLuca	.978	24	31	2	1	1
Hernandez	1.000	24	29	0	0	0
Heyward	.981	120	190	1	5	0
Marisnick	1.000	4	1	0	0	0
Martinez	.000	3	0	0	0	0
Outman	.998	158	318	6	2	1
Peralta	.995	130	203	3	2	2
Taylor	.995	62	89	4	1	1
Thompson	1.000	34	42	0	0	0

OKLAHOMA CITY DODGERS

TRIPLE-A

PACIFIC COAST LEAGUE

Batting	B-T	Ht.	Wt.	DOB	AVG	OBP	SLG	G	PA	AB	R	H	2B	3B	HR	RBI	BB	HBP	SH	SF	SO	SB	CS	BB%	SO%
Avans, Drew	L-L	5-9	195	6-13-96	.254	.355	.380	129	596	508	95	129	27	2	11	58	77	5	1	5	132	23	8	12.9	22.1
Barnhart, Tucker	L-R	5-11	192	1-07-91	.227	.370	.273	7	27	22	4	5	1	0	0	1	5	0	0	0	10	0	0	18.5	37.0
Brigman, Bryson	R-R	5-11	180	6-19-95	.292	.388	.402	66	255	219	31	64	9	3	3	33	28	7	0	1	40	6	4	11.0	15.7
Busch, Michael	L-R	6-1	210	11-09-97	.323	.431	.618	98	469	390	85	126	26	4	27	90	65	11	0	3	88	4	0	13.9	18.8
Calhoun, Kole	L-L	5-10	205	10-14-87	.308	.366	.531	35	161	143	22	44	11	3	5	28	14	1	0	3	26	0	0	8.7	16.1
Dahl, David	L-R	6-1	197	4-01-94	.282	.354	.493	54	237	213	33	60	21	0	8	39	23	1	0	0	43	3	0	9.7	18.1
2-team (17 El Paso)					.278	.351	.466	71	313	281	44	78	26	0	9	49	31	1	0	0	50	3	0	9.9	16.0
DeLuca, Jonny	R-R	6-0	200	7-10-98	.306	.397	.548	41	184	157	27	48	13	2	7	35	21	4	0	2	29	3	0	11.4	15.8
DeLuzio, Ben	R-R	6-3	200	8-09-94	.180	.286	.258	25	106	89	13	16	2	1	1	15	12	2	1	2	33	5	2	11.3	31.1
Duggar, Steven	L-R	6-1	187	11-04-93	.242	.360	.410	69	272	227	46	55	11	0	9	38	42	1	0	2	92	5	1	15.4	33.8
Feduccia, Hunter	L-R	6-0	215	6-05-97	.279	.387	.451	90	380	319	61	89	18	2	11	57	58	0	0	3	79	0	0	15.3	20.8
Freitas, David	R-R	6-1	250	3-18-89	.295	.364	.491	29	129	112	17	33	7	0	5	26	12	2	0	3	24	0	0	9.3	18.6
Hernandez, Yonny	B-R	5-9	140	5-04-98	.252	.395	.342	93	407	322	72	81	13	2	4	34	75	4	2	4	81	17	12	18.4	19.9
Jones, Jahmai	R-R	6-0	210	8-04-97	.292	.427	.542	62	263	212	40	62	20	3	9	34	46	4	1	0	55	2	4	17.5	20.9
Mann, Devin	R-R	6-2	180	2-11-97	.307	.402	.541	89	386	329	68	101	33	1	14	71	50	4	0	3	99	2	1	13.0	25.6
Marisnick, Jake	R-R	6-4	220	3-30-91	.292	.280	.542	8	25	24	2	7	3	0	1	6	0	0	0	1	5	0	0	0.0	20.0
Martinez, J.D.	R-R	6-3	230	8-21-87	.125	.222	.250	2	9	8	0	1	1	0	0	3	1	0	0	0	2	0	0	11.1	22.2
Mazeika, Patrick	L-R	6-1	210	10-14-93	.214	.284	.275	52	201	182	19	39	8	0	1	17	16	2	0	1	28	0	0	8.0	13.9
Mercado, Oscar	R-R	6-2	197	12-16-94	.259	.313	.431	15	64	58	11	15	4	0	2	13	4	1	0	1	16	3	1	6.3	25.0
2-team (31 El Paso)					.313	.375	.593	46	202	182	39	57	9	3	12	50	15	3	0	2	45	13	2	7.4	22.3
Pages, Andy	R-R	6-1	212	12-08-00	.000	.250	.000	1	4	3	0	0	0	0	0	0	1	0	0	0	2	0	0	25.0	50.0
Reed, Michael	B-R	6-4	218	4-27-95	.190	.320	.571	8	25	21	6	4	2	0	2	6	3	1	0	0	6	1	0	12.0	24.0
Thompson, Trayce	R-R	6-3	225	3-15-91	.625	.667	1.500	2	9	8	4	5	4	0	1	3	0	1	0	0	1	0	0	0.0	11.1
Valaika, Pat	R-R	6-0	200	9-09-92	.225	.276	.303	25	98	89	9	20	1	0	2	10	7	0	0	2	23	1	0	7.1	23.5
2-team (38 Tacoma)					.233	.321	.362	63	241	210	30	49	7	1	6	36	26	1	0	4	53	2	0	10.8	22.0
Vargas, Miguel	R-R	6-3	205	11-17-99	.288	.407	.479	60	285	236	45	68	15	0	10	43	46	2	0	1	57	8	0	16.1	20.0
Vivas, Jorbit	L-R	5-10	171	3-09-01	.225	.339	.294	26	121	102	16	23	2	1	1	9	15	3	0	1	19	4	1	12.4	15.7
Ward, Ryan	L-R	5-9	200	2-23-98	.234	.324	.424	139	615	538	87	126	27	6	21	95	68	5	0	3	157	12	5	11.1	25.5
Williams, Luke	R-R	6-0	186	8-09-96	.268	.364	.452	42	198	168	31	45	9	2	6	29	24	3	0	3	47	11	2	12.1	23.7
Wong, Kolten	L-R	5-7	185	10-10-90	.538	.571	.923	3	14	13	3	7	2	0	1	6	1	0	0	0	1	0	0	7.1	7.1
Yurchak, Justin	L-R	6-0	204	9-17-96	.260	.372	.393	77	288	242	39	63	12	1	6	41	42	2	0	2	48	1	0	14.6	16.7
Zimmer, Bradley	L-R	6-2	185	11-27-92	.219	.322	.343	31	121	105	18	23	4	0	3	14	13	3	0	0	46	8	1	10.7	38.0

Pitching	B-T	Ht.	Wt.	DOB	W	L	ERA	G	GS	SV	IP	Hits	Runs	ER	HR	BB	SO	AVG	OBP	SLG	SO%	BB%	BF
Andriese, Matt	R-R	6-2	215	8-28-89	8	6	6.05	21	19	0	94	122	76	63	21	25	78	.316	.356	.552	18.6	6.0	419
Avans, Drew	L-L	5-9	195	6-13-96	0	0	0.00	1	0	0	1	1	0	0	0	1	0	.250	.400	.250	0.0	20.0	5

Bettencourt, Trevor	R-R	6-0	195	7-21-94	1	0	7.13	10	0	0	18	19	14	14	1	8	14	.275	.351	.420	18.2	10.4	77
Bickford, Phil	R-R	6-4	200	7-10-95	0	0	0.00	1	0	0	1	0	0	0	0	0	1	.000	.000	.000	33.3	0.0	3
Brasier, Ryan	R-R	6-0	227	8-26-87	1	0	0.00	2	0	0	3	0	0	0	0	0	5	.000	.000	.000	55.6	0.0	9
Bruihl, Justin	L-L	6-2	215	6-26-97	5	2	2.04	15	0	1	18	14	7	4	0	7	17	.209	.293	.269	22.7	9.3	75
Buehler, Walker	R-R	6-2	185	7-28-94	0	0	0.00	1	1	0	2	0	0	0	0	0	2	.000	.000	.000	33.3	0.0	6
Burdi, Zack	R-R	6-3	210	3-09-95	0	0	0.00	4	0	0	5	3	0	0	0	1	8	.188	.222	.250	44.4	5.6	18
Covey, Dylan	R-R	6-1	215	8-14-91	1	0	4.22	7	6	0	32	28	16	15	3	18	28	.228	.331	.333	19.7	12.7	142
Cuevas, William	B-R	6-2	215	10-14-90	2	2	6.14	11	9	0	44	42	30	30	13	20	43	.247	.338	.518	22.1	10.3	195
Curtis, Keegan	R-R	6-0	175	9-30-95	2	2	6.48	20	1	0	33	41	26	24	5	18	26	.301	.388	.485	16.3	11.3	160
Cyr, Tyler	R-R	6-1	205	5-05-93	2	2	6.16	18	0	0	19	20	14	13	3	13	28	.270	.393	.459	31.5	14.6	89
Dodson, Tanner	B-R	6-1	160	5-09-97	0	1	7.50	12	0	0	18	21	15	15	0	14	13	.304	.430	.348	15.1	16.3	86
Erlin, Robbie	R-L	5-11	200	10-08-90	4	2	5.83	17	16	0	79	101	60	51	19	31	65	.312	.375	.571	17.9	8.5	363
Frasso, Nick	R-R	6-5	200	10-18-98	1	2	3.26	4	4	0	19	19	9	7	0	7	13	.257	.345	.324	15.5	8.3	84
Gamboa, Alec	B-L	6-1	205	1-17-97	2	4	4.91	23	3	1	40	36	26	22	3	29	43	.235	.355	.320	23.5	15.8	183
Giles, Ken	R-R	6-3	197	9-20-90	1	0	9.50	19	0	0	18	24	20	19	3	19	28	.316	.459	.553	28.6	19.4	98
Gonsolin, Tony	R-R	6-3	205	5-14-94	0	0	6.00	1	1	0	3	1	2	2	1	2	7	.100	.250	.400	58.3	16.7	12
Gonzalez, Victor	L-L	6-0	180	11-16-95	2	1	5.40	20	0	1	20	16	14	12	0	16	22	.216	.359	.243	23.9	17.4	92
Grove, Michael	R-R	6-3	200	12-18-96	0	0	2.70	5	2	0	13	11	4	4	2	1	22	.212	.226	.365	41.5	1.9	53
Hagenman, Justin	R-R	6-3	205	10-07-96	4	0	2.78	25	5	1	55	48	17	17	10	11	60	.230	.270	.407	27.0	5.0	222
Hernandez, Yonny	B-R	5-9	140	5-04-98	0	0	0.00	1	0	1	1	0	1	0	0	0	0	.000	.000	.000	0.0	0.0	3
Hudson, Bryan	L-L	6-8	220	5-08-97	5	2	2.43	46	8	0	56	47	23	15	3	26	86	.221	.308	.333	35.7	10.8	241
Hudson, Daniel	R-R	6-3	215	3-09-87	1	0	0.00	3	1	0	3	1	0	0	0	0	5	.091	.091	.091	45.5	0.0	11
Hurt, Kyle	R-R	6-3	240	5-30-98	2	1	3.33	7	1	0	27	19	10	10	3	11	42	.198	.284	.333	38.5	10.1	109
Jackson, Andre	R-R	6-3	210	5-01-96	1	1	5.86	11	1	0	28	25	18	18	4	17	31	.245	.350	.412	25.8	14.2	120
Jones, James	L-L	6-3	205	9-24-88	2	1	3.27	15	2	0	22	18	9	8	2	12	15	.234	.333	.338	16.0	12.8	94
Kasowski, Marshall	L-R	6-3	215	3-10-95	0	0	5.79	4	0	0	5	5	4	3	1	4	4	.294	.409	.529	18.2	18.2	22
Knack, Landon	L-R	6-2	220	7-15-97	3	1	2.93	10	10	0	43	44	19	14	6	18	38	.262	.335	.435	20.2	9.6	188
Kolarek, Adam	L-L	6-3	215	1-14-89	0	3	2.40	33	0	1	30	26	10	8	0	17	26	.252	.368	.291	20.5	13.4	127
Miller, Bobby	L-R	6-5	220	4-05-99	1	1	5.65	4	4	0	14	11	13	9	2	6	12	.212	.295	.385	19.7	9.8	61
Miller, Shelby	R-R	6-3	225	10-10-90	0	0	11.25	5	0	0	4	8	5	5	2	2	7	.400	.455	.750	31.8	9.1	22
Miller, Tyson	R-R	6-5	220	7-29-95	2	0	1.69	9	2	1	16	12	4	3	2	4	21	.211	.262	.316	34.4	6.6	61
Montgomery, Mike	L-L	6-5	220	7-01-89	4	4	5.26	18	16	0	77	81	53	45	4	53	68	.267	.386	.383	18.6	14.5	365
Nelson, Jimmy	R-R	6-6	250	6-05-89	1	1	5.00	29	0	0	27	21	16	15	2	31	34	.223	.435	.330	25.8	23.5	132
Pepiot, Ryan	R-R	6-3	215	8-21-97	0	2	3.97	6	6	0	23	21	10	10	4	5	26	.241	.280	.414	28.0	5.4	93
Peto, Robbie	R-R	6-4	225	7-10-98	0	0	27.00	1	1	0	2	5	7	6	1	4	4	.417	.563	.833	25.0	25.0	16
Reed, Jake	R-R	6-2	195	9-29-92	3	1	7.34	29	0	1	34	39	28	28	5	21	31	.287	.410	.463	18.7	12.7	166
Robertson, Nick	R-R	6-6	265	7-16-98	2	0	2.54	27	0	7	28	19	10	8	2	9	42	.184	.250	.272	37.5	8.0	112
Rooney, John	R-L	6-5	215	1-28-97	3	1	3.31	24	1	0	35	27	14	13	4	13	32	.214	.298	.365	22.7	9.2	141
Ryan, River	R-R	6-2	195	8-17-98	0	1	10.29	2	2	0	7	12	10	8	2	2	12	.364	.400	.697	34.3	5.7	35
Scott, Tayler	R-R	6-3	185	6-01-92	3	0	1.37	19	0	2	20	13	3	3	0	10	25	.194	.313	.239	31.3	12.5	80
Sheehan, Emmet	R-R	6-5	220	11-15-99	0	1	5.59	3	1	0	10	4	7	6	2	6	14	.129	.289	.355	36.8	15.8	38
Sherriff, Ryan	L-L	6-1	190	5-25-90	1	0	27.00	2	0	0	2	4	5	5	0	3	3	.444	.615	.444	23.1	23.1	13
Stone, Gavin	R-R	6-1	175	10-15-98	7	4	4.74	21	19	0	101	86	56	53	12	46	120	.226	.309	.375	27.8	10.7	431
Suero, Wander	R-R	6-4	216	9-15-91	6	3	3.26	47	0	17	50	32	21	18	6	23	53	.178	.278	.317	25.9	11.2	205
Syndergaard, Noah	L-R	6-6	242	8-29-92	0	1	5.40	2	2	0	10	10	6	6	1	0	8	.263	.256	.421	20.5	0.0	39
Treinen, Blake	R-R	6-5	225	6-30-88	0	1	20.25	2	0	0	1	2	3	3	0	1	0	.333	.500	.333	0.0	12.5	8
Vanasco, Ricky	R-R	6-3	180	10-13-98	0	0	0.00	5	0	1	5	3	0	0	0	1	6	.167	.211	.167	31.6	5.3	19
Varland, Gus	L-R	6-1	213	11-06-96	2	1	2.16	30	1	2	33	29	12	8	2	8	39	.236	.278	.350	29.3	6.0	133
Vesia, Alex	L-L	6-1	209	4-11-96	1	1	3.38	13	0	0	13	10	6	5	2	6	22	.204	.291	.347	40.0	10.9	55
Washington, Mark	R-R	6-7	205	3-22-96	4	1	3.69	30	2	1	46	40	19	19	6	16	43	.242	.314	.394	22.8	8.5	189
Williams, Kendall	R-R	6-6	205	8-24-00	0	1	7.50	1	1	0	6	6	5	5	2	5	2	.286	.407	.810	7.4	18.5	27

Fielding

Catcher	PCT	G	PO	A	E	DP	PB
Barnhart	.985	7	62	3	1	0	0
Feduccia	.994	86	791	41	5	5	6
Freitas	.967	9	84	4	3	0	0
Mazeika	.994	52	477	23	3	5	2

First Base	PCT	G	PO	A	E	DP
Busch	1.000	7	51	5	0	9
Freitas	.955	12	79	5	4	8
Mann	1.000	20	138	8	0	14
Mazeika	1.000	1	10	1	0	0
Valaika	1.000	12	93	8	0	13
Ward	.984	42	290	15	5	29
Yurchak	.996	62	422	29	2	44

Second Base	PCT	G	PO	A	E	DP
Brigman	1.000	1	1	2	0	0
Busch	.990	26	40	62	1	16
Hernandez	1.000	4	3	5	0	2
Jones	.968	47	71	110	6	29
Mann	.985	17	32	32	1	18
Valaika	1.000	4	4	5	0	0
Vargas	.974	28	43	70	3	22
Vivas	1.000	23	52	59	0	20

Third Base	PCT	G	PO	A	E	DP
Brigman	1.000	1	0	2	0	0
Busch	.920	61	32	117	13	15
Hernandez	.977	33	19	65	2	14
Jones	.000	1	0	0	1	0
Mann	.942	29	15	66	5	2
Valaika	1.000	4	4	1	0	0
Vargas	.936	20	14	30	3	3
Vivas	1.000	2	1	10	0	1
Williams	1.000	1	2	3	0	1

Shortstop	PCT	G	PO	A	E	DP
Brigman	.958	44	41	97	6	22
Hernandez	.947	52	62	134	11	28
Mann	.862	7	10	15	4	3
Valaika	1.000	5	7	10	0	2
Williams	.977	40	49	81	3	23
Wong	1.000	3	0	4	0	1

Outfield	PCT	G	PO	A	E	DP
Avans	.939	120	267	7	9	4
Brigman	.956	20	35	1	2	0
Busch	1.000	2	4	1	0	0
Calhoun	.983	25	59	0	1	0
Dahl	1.000	46	94	4	0	2
DeLuca	1.000	39	81	2	0	1
DeLuzio	.944	23	54	0	2	0
Duggar	.978	46	69	2	2	1
Mann	.909	9	10	0	1	0
Marisnick	1.000	6	2	0	0	0
Mercado	.965	13	27	2	2	1
Pages	1.000	1	2	0	0	0
Reed	1.000	7	16	0	0	0
Thompson	1.000	2	7	0	0	0
Vargas	.900	7	9	0	1	0
Ward	.973	73	105	4	3	1
Williams	1.000	2	1	0	0	0
Yurchak	1.000	5	8	0	0	0
Zimmer	.980	26	39	0	1	0

TULSA DRILLERS — *DOUBLE-A*

TEXAS LEAGUE

Batting	B-T	Ht.	Wt.	DOB	AVG	OBP	SLG	G	PA	AB	R	H	2B	3B	HR	RBI	BB	HBP	SH	SF	SO	SB	CS	BB%	SO%
Alcantara, Ismael	R-R	6-1	165	9-25-98	.275	.338	.353	59	230	207	35	57	5	1	3	20	17	3	2	1	61	9	8	7.4	26.5
Betancourt, Kenneth	R-R	5-8	160	2-05-00	.000	.000	.000	1	3	3	0	0	0	0	0	0	0	0	0	0	1	0	0	0.0	33.3
Brigman, Bryson	R-R	5-11	180	6-19-95	.186	.262	.186	18	65	59	5	11	0	0	0	5	5	1	0	0	9	0	0	7.7	13.8
Cartaya, Diego	R-R	6-3	219	9-07-01	.189	.278	.379	93	403	354	51	67	10	0	19	57	37	8	0	4	117	0	0	9.2	29.0
Chalo, Wladimir	R-R	5-8	197	4-21-00	.214	.292	.238	12	48	42	4	9	1	0	0	4	5	0	0	1	15	0	0	10.4	31.3
DeLuca, Jonny	R-R	6-0	200	7-10-98	.279	.380	.590	32	142	122	29	34	8	0	10	18	14	6	0	0	26	9	1	9.9	18.3
Diaz, Luis Yanel	R-R	5-11	170	9-09-99	.178	.267	.271	30	120	107	13	19	1	0	3	12	11	2	0	0	37	6	2	9.2	30.8
Diaz, Yusniel	R-R	6-1	215	10-07-96	.278	.374	.484	94	406	345	54	96	21	1	16	60	56	0	0	5	78	7	4	13.8	19.2
Dodson, Tanner	B-R	6-1	160	5-09-97	.000	.000	.000	39	1	1	0	0	0	0	0	0	0	0	0	0	1	0	0	0.0	100.0
Gauthier, Austin	R-R	6-0	188	5-07-99	.293	.411	.433	84	392	321	72	94	19	4	6	34	64	3	0	4	54	15	6	16.3	13.8
Hoese, Kody	R-R	6-4	200	7-13-97	.244	.300	.390	98	383	344	34	84	11	3	11	36	26	5	0	8	71	1	0	6.8	18.5
Leonard, Eddys	R-R	5-11	195	11-10-00	.254	.327	.411	92	388	350	37	89	20	1	11	44	29	9	0	0	85	3	3	7.5	21.9
Lewis, Brandon	R-R	6-2	222	10-23-98	.199	.268	.300	93	369	337	33	67	13	0	7	30	28	4	0	0	100	1	0	7.6	27.1
Male, Umar	R-R	5-10	175	5-14-01	.000	.000	.000	1	3	3	0	0	0	0	0	0	0	0	0	0	2	0	0	0.0	66.7
Marte, Hamlet	R-R	5-10	180	2-03-94	.157	.257	.270	30	102	89	13	14	1	0	3	7	11	1	0	0	25	1	0	10.8	24.5
Pages, Andy	R-R	6-1	212	12-08-00	.284	.430	.495	33	142	109	23	31	12	1	3	25	25	5	0	3	32	7	3	17.6	22.5
Ramos, Jose	R-R	6-1	200	1-01-01	.240	.333	.409	113	485	416	55	100	13	0	19	68	54	7	2	6	140	7	2	11.1	28.9
Sheehan, Emmet	R-R	6-5	220	11-15-99	.000	.500	.000	12	2	1	0	0	0	0	0	1	1	0	0	0	1	0	0	50.0	50.0
Stowers, Josh	R-R	6-0	200	2-25-97	.174	.256	.321	86	320	287	34	50	13	1	9	25	26	6	0	1	90	13	3	8.1	28.1
Taylor, Carson	B-R	6-2	205	6-02-99	.221	.310	.369	77	281	249	35	55	5	1	10	26	31	1	0	0	64	1	0	11.0	22.8
Vargas, Imanol	L-R	6-3	215	6-29-98	.251	.357	.463	125	526	447	69	112	29	0	22	90	76	0	0	3	174	0	0	14.4	33.1
Vivas, Jorbit	L-R	5-10	171	3-09-01	.280	.391	.436	109	491	404	82	113	23	2	12	54	54	24	0	6	52	21	4	11.0	10.6

Pitching	B-T	Ht.	Wt.	DOB	W	L	ERA	G	GS	SV	IP	Hits	Runs	ER	HR	BB	SO	AVG	OBP	SLG	SO%	BB%	BF
Acosta, Aldry	R-R	6-4	235	9-07-99	1	3	6.75	20	0	0	25	28	22	19	2	14	13	.280	.390	.410	11.0	11.9	118
Alcantara, Ismael	R-R	6-1	165	9-25-98	0	0	0.00	1	0	0	1	0	0	0	0	1	1	.000	.250	.000	25.0	25.0	4
Bettencourt, Trevor	R-R	6-0	195	7-21-94	4	1	4.87	33	1	0	41	47	25	22	3	19	42	.285	.362	.400	22.6	10.2	186
Cantleberry, Jake	L-L	6-1	180	8-08-97	1	0	6.00	2	0	0	3	2	2	2	1	2	2	.182	.308	.545	15.4	15.4	13
Casparius, Ben	R-R	6-2	215	2-11-99	2	7	6.62	18	13	0	71	73	57	52	15	37	76	.264	.362	.522	23.5	11.5	323
De Paula, Reinaldo	R-R	5-11	177	10-20-98	0	0	7.27	6	0	0	9	12	7	7	0	8	6	.333	.444	.444	13.3	17.8	45
Dodson, Tanner	B-R	6-1	160	5-09-97	5	6	3.91	38	0	0	48	42	23	21	6	29	38	.232	.341	.392	17.7	13.5	215
Fisher, Braydon	R-R	6-4	180	7-26-00	5	4	2.95	42	1	5	61	41	29	20	9	37	82	.188	.308	.358	31.3	14.1	262
Frasso, Nick	R-R	6-5	200	10-18-98	3	4	3.91	21	21	0	74	68	34	32	4	24	94	.242	.314	.352	29.8	7.6	315
Gamboa, Alec	B-L	6-1	205	1-17-97	7	0	2.25	14	0	0	36	17	9	9	2	19	33	.140	.266	.215	23.1	13.3	143
Gowdy, Kevin	R-R	6-4	205	11-16-97	2	1	4.93	31	0	3	38	35	24	21	4	20	41	.243	.345	.361	24.4	11.9	168
Harris, Ben	L-L	6-1	195	2-22-00	2	3	4.88	46	0	2	52	32	32	28	4	48	74	.179	.362	.279	31.4	20.3	236
Hurt, Kyle	R-R	6-3	240	5-30-98	2	3	4.15	19	15	0	65	50	32	30	7	33	110	.207	.312	.369	39.4	11.8	279
Knack, Landon	L-R	6-2	220	7-15-97	2	0	2.20	12	12	0	57	42	18	14	3	12	61	.202	.248	.313	27.4	5.4	223
Knowles, Antonio	R-R	6-1	190	1-15-00	2	2	5.05	34	0	2	41	26	24	23	5	27	43	.187	.337	.360	25.0	15.7	172
Lao, Sauryn	R-R	6-2	182	8-14-99	0	0	10.13	2	0	0	3	4	3	3	1	0	1	.364	.417	.636	8.3	0.0	12
Leasure, Jordan	R-R	6-3	215	8-15-98	2	2	3.09	29	0	9	35	21	12	12	6	16	56	.169	.270	.347	39.7	11.3	141
Little, Jack	L-R	6-4	190	1-10-98	0	1	7.71	20	0	0	19	20	21	16	4	15	18	.270	.383	.500	18.9	15.8	95
Lockhart, Lael	B-L	6-3	225	12-31-97	1	1	11.40	8	0	0	15	22	20	19	4	13	18	.324	.432	.618	22.2	16.0	81
Marte, Hamlet	R-R	5-10	180	2-03-94	0	0	18.00	1	0	0	1	2	2	2	0	1	0	.400	.571	.800	0.0	14.3	7
Nastrini, Nick	R-R	6-3	215	2-18-00	5	3	4.03	17	17	0	74	66	39	33	8	37	85	.232	.328	.396	26.1	11.3	326
Ortiz-Mayr, Orlando	R-R	6-3	195	12-06-97	3	8	5.79	13	11	0	61	65	40	39	9	19	48	.272	.344	.439	17.7	7.0	271
Percival, Cole	R-R	6-5	220	2-26-99	0	0	7.71	5	0	0	5	1	4	4	0	7	5	.071	.435	.071	21.7	30.4	23
Peto, Robbie	R-R	6-4	225	7-10-98	1	1	7.97	12	6	0	35	47	32	31	8	27	33	.315	.425	.550	18.3	15.0	180
Pilarski, Jake	R-R	6-2	215	5-12-98	1	2	6.23	25	0	1	30	36	25	21	3	24	24	.313	.424	.417	16.3	16.3	147
Reyes, Carlo	R-R	6-0	212	7-04-98	0	1	7.06	19	0	0	22	18	18	17	4	18	23	.222	.375	.444	22.1	17.3	104
Rooney, John	R-L	6-5	215	1-28-97	3	2	2.38	29	0	3	34	33	13	9	3	9	37	.262	.329	.397	26.2	6.4	141
Ryan, River	R-R	6-2	195	8-17-98	1	6	3.33	24	22	0	97	78	41	36	8	44	98	.221	.323	.317	23.7	10.7	413
Sheehan, Emmet	R-R	6-5	220	11-15-99	4	1	1.86	12	10	0	53	24	11	11	5	23	88	.131	.246	.235	41.7	10.9	211
Sublette, Ryan	R-R	6-2	190	10-01-98	2	4	6.27	43	1	2	47	38	35	33	6	46	60	.222	.400	.374	26.4	20.3	227
Vanasco, Ricky	R-R	6-3	180	10-13-98	1	4	1.52	20	0	1	24	17	11	4	3	9	36	.189	.267	.322	35.6	8.9	101
Williams, Kendall	R-R	6-6	205	8-24-00	3	3	3.92	8	8	0	39	30	17	17	1	23	33	.207	.326	.303	19.1	13.3	173

Fielding

Catcher	PCT	G	PO	A	E	DP	PB
Cartaya	.988	68	698	46	9	8	8
Chalo	1.000	12	105	6	0	0	3
Marte	.991	26	208	10	2	0	5
Taylor	.980	39	384	11	8	1	9

First Base	PCT	G	PO	A	E	DP
Lewis	.989	49	322	33	4	32
Marte	1.000	3	15	1	0	1
Taylor	1.000	12	72	2	0	4
Vargas	.980	82	558	40	12	40

Second Base	PCT	G	PO	A	E	DP
Betancourt	1.000	1	1	0	0	0
Brigman	.958	5	11	12	1	3
Gauthier	.964	19	33	48	3	13
Hoese	1.000	17	21	51	0	9
Vivas	.979	97	132	233	8	45

Third Base	PCT	G	PO	A	E	DP
Brigman	1.000	1	0	1	0	0
Diaz	.941	7	6	10	1	1
Gauthier	.941	9	4	12	1	0
Hoese	.942	75	56	91	9	11
Lewis	.918	45	34	55	8	4
Vivas	.813	10	5	21	6	1

Shortstop	PCT	G	PO	A	E	DP
Brigman	1.000	3	3	8	0	2
Diaz	.949	20	16	58	4	8
Gauthier	.957	26	32	58	4	10
Leonard	.957	90	112	179	13	37

Outfield	PCT	G	PO	A	E	DP
Alcantara	.960	58	115	11	4	1
Brigman	.500	9	8	0	0	0
DeLuca	1.000	30	48	0	0	0

Diaz, L	.500	4	1	0	0	0
Diaz, Y	.989	67	113	5	2	0
Gauthier	1.000	32	47	0	0	0
Pages	1.000	31	69	1	0	1
Ramos	.957	111	212	1	5	1
Stowers	.938	72	100	6	5	0
Vargas	1.000	25	32	3	0	0

GREAT LAKES LOONS

HIGH CLASS A

MIDWEST LEAGUE

Batting	B-T	Ht.	Wt.	DOB	AVG	OBP	SLG	G	PA	AB	R	H	2B	3B	HR	RBI	BB	HBP	SH	SF	SO	SB	CS	BB%	SO%
Alcantara, Ismael	R-R	6-1	165	9-25-98	.204	.299	.314	46	157	137	20	28	4	1	3	16	16	3	0	1	45	13	1	10.2	28.7
Alleyne, Chris	B-R	5-10	190	11-13-98	.199	.277	.322	103	402	357	47	71	15	4	7	38	33	7	1	4	103	24	8	8.2	25.6
Betancourt, Kenneth	R-R	5-8	160	2-05-00	.252	.296	.307	36	136	127	12	32	4	0	1	13	8	0	1	0	24	6	1	5.9	17.6
Biddison, Nick	R-R	5-10	190	7-30-00	.169	.272	.247	26	103	89	5	15	4	0	1	10	7	6	0	1	36	0	1	6.8	35.0
Diaz, Luis Yanel	R-R	5-11	170	9-09-99	.265	.322	.419	74	287	260	46	69	14	4	6	38	18	5	0	3	86	19	9	6.3	30.0
Dreyer, Jack	R-L	6-2	205	2-27-99	.000	.000	.000	43	4	3	0	0	0	0	0	0	0	0	1	0	1	0	0	0.0	25.0
Fernandez, Yeiner	R-R	5-9	170	9-19-02	.273	.360	.375	99	433	373	47	102	14	3	6	50	47	7	0	6	56	4	2	10.9	12.9
Freeland, Alex	B-R	6-2	200	8-24-01	.240	.345	.362	106	461	392	58	94	17	2	9	57	60	5	0	4	131	31	8	13.0	28.4
Garcia, Yunior	R-R	6-0	198	7-29-01	.272	.320	.430	32	125	114	14	31	3	0	5	17	7	2	0	2	36	0	0	5.6	28.8
Gauthier, Austin	R-R	6-0	188	5-07-99	.365	.487	.568	40	187	148	39	54	10	1	6	25	36	1	0	2	30	4	0	19.3	16.0
Guerra, Luis	R-R	6-1	180	10-04-03	.182	.270	.182	11	37	33	3	6	0	0	0	2	4	0	0	0	6	0	0	10.8	16.2
Hewitt, Max	L-R	6-0	182	9-14-97	.212	.331	.279	35	127	104	13	22	7	0	0	10	19	1	0	3	40	1	1	15.0	31.5
Keith, Damon	R-R	6-3	195	5-28-00	.229	.312	.373	106	439	389	56	89	21	1	11	55	44	4	0	2	146	4	3	10.0	33.3
Lockwood-Powell, Griffin	R-R	6-2	195	2-23-98	.238	.365	.437	98	395	323	53	77	23	1	13	54	60	7	0	5	87	1	1	15.2	22.0
Newell, Chris	L-L	6-3	200	4-23-01	.222	.321	.424	42	184	158	24	35	9	1	7	22	24	0	0	2	58	8	5	13.0	31.5
Puerta, Jorge	R-R	5-11	178	12-05-01	.000	.667	.000	2	3	1	1	0	0	0	0	0	2	0	0	0	0	0	0	66.7	0.0
Rodriguez, Frank	R-R	5-11	197	9-28-01	.163	.231	.291	44	156	141	16	23	6	0	4	19	9	4	0	2	36	0	0	5.8	23.1
Rushing, Dalton	L-R	6-1	220	2-21-01	.228	.404	.452	89	381	290	55	66	18	1	15	53	72	16	0	3	93	1	0	18.9	24.4
Vogel, Jake	R-R	5-11	165	10-12-01	.236	.312	.325	113	421	369	49	87	22	1	3	39	35	9	0	7	109	28	2	8.3	25.9
Young, Taylor	R-R	5-9	170	8-06-98	.246	.375	.363	124	545	443	76	109	21	5	7	55	82	13	0	6	112	56	5	15.0	20.6

Pitching	B-T	Ht.	Wt.	DOB	W	L	ERA	G	GS	SV	IP	Hits	Runs	ER	HR	BB	SO	AVG	OBP	SLG	SO%	BB%	BF
Acosta, Aldry	R-R	6-4	235	9-07-99	2	1	1.65	20	0	2	27	15	7	5	1	7	17	.167	.240	.211	16.8	6.9	101
Bruns, Maddux	L-L	6-2	205	6-20-02	0	7	4.74	20	20	0	76	56	45	40	7	54	93	.205	.351	.352	27.2	15.8	342
Casparius, Ben	R-R	6-2	215	2-11-99	4	0	2.68	8	8	0	37	23	11	11	5	18	44	.173	.272	.331	29.1	11.9	151
Castro, Yon	R-R	6-0	203	5-23-99	4	2	2.27	12	12	0	48	29	13	12	3	15	47	.172	.246	.266	25.1	8.0	187
Choi, Hyun-il	R-R	6-2	215	5-27-00	4	5	3.75	16	13	0	60	63	30	25	6	12	46	.269	.315	.444	18.1	4.7	254
De La Paz, Franklin	L-L	6-2	190	3-29-99	1	0	5.19	32	0	0	35	39	23	20	2	23	37	.291	.410	.366	23.0	14.3	161
De Los Santos, Carlos	R-R	6-2	170	11-18-00	1	0	4.97	34	0	1	38	41	28	21	3	28	42	.273	.389	.380	22.6	15.1	186
De Paula, Reinaldo	R-R	5-11	177	10-20-98	2	2	4.30	38	0	1	44	38	23	21	3	17	53	.226	.323	.321	27.0	8.7	196
Dreyer, Jack	R-L	6-2	205	2-27-99	5	0	2.30	42	0	0	55	32	16	14	1	38	79	.171	.308	.235	34.8	16.7	227
Fisher, Braydon	R-R	6-4	180	7-26-00	1	0	0.00	4	0	0	4	0	0	0	0	0	8	.000	.077	.000	61.5	0.0	13
Heubeck, Peter	R-R	6-3	170	7-22-02	2	2	8.47	6	5	0	17	21	16	16	4	9	16	.304	.380	.536	20.3	11.4	79
Hobbs, Michael	R-R	6-3	215	7-10-99	5	2	3.12	44	0	7	49	34	22	17	5	32	62	.192	.330	.322	28.3	14.6	219
Karros, Jared	R-R	6-7	195	11-16-00	1	0	0.69	3	2	1	13	8	1	1	1	1	11	.174	.208	.261	22.9	2.1	48
Knowles, Antonio	R-R	6-1	190	1-15-00	3	0	1.53	13	0	1	18	11	3	3	2	8	25	.175	.278	.317	34.7	11.1	72
Kopp, Ronan	L-L	6-7	250	7-29-02	0	4	2.99	30	21	1	72	45	26	24	6	50	107	.184	.331	.291	35.8	16.7	299
Lao, Sauryn	R-R	6-2	182	8-14-99	1	0	5.25	9	0	0	12	19	7	7	2	4	15	.373	.421	.529	26.3	7.0	57
Morillo, Juan	R-R	6-1	150	3-19-99	0	2	5.14	29	1	4	28	27	17	16	5	19	38	.248	.359	.422	29.7	14.8	128
Ortiz-Mayr, Orlando	R-R	6-3	195	12-06-97	6	1	3.58	14	2	0	50	43	21	20	0	19	45	.236	.314	.247	21.7	9.2	207
Peto, Robbie	R-R	6-4	225	7-10-98	5	1	5.24	14	1	0	45	46	28	26	5	18	40	.267	.347	.459	20.3	9.1	197
Pilarski, Jake	R-R	6-2	215	5-12-98	0	0	0.71	12	0	9	13	7	2	1	0	6	20	.156	.283	.178	37.7	11.3	53
Ramirez, Adolfo	R-R	6-0	165	6-01-99	3	4	5.98	16	5	0	44	42	33	29	6	30	39	.256	.389	.451	19.1	14.7	204
Robles, Benony	L-L	6-4	185	10-01-00	4	2	3.86	33	1	12	33	19	14	14	3	19	53	.167	.299	.298	38.7	13.9	137
Rosario, Jerming	R-R	6-1	175	5-08-02	7	5	4.70	19	9	0	67	65	35	35	6	33	82	.258	.344	.381	28.4	11.4	289
Smith, Julian	R-L	6-4	210	6-03-97	2	0	3.86	6	0	0	7	3	3	3	0	3	9	.120	.267	.200	30.0	10.0	30
Suarez, Christian	L-L	5-11	160	11-25-00	6	4	3.97	45	0	1	48	54	36	21	5	22	61	.278	.356	.402	27.6	10.0	221
Tyranski, Mitchell	L-L	6-2	215	9-02-97	2	2	3.83	36	1	0	42	33	19	18	5	21	47	.212	.305	.378	26.6	11.9	177
Wepf, Lucas	L-R	6-5	192	12-23-99	0	3	4.68	19	0	1	25	20	13	13	4	14	30	.227	.340	.375	28.3	13.2	106
Williams, Kendall	R-R	6-6	205	8-24-00	1	2	1.99	7	7	0	32	20	9	7	2	10	27	.177	.254	.274	21.4	7.9	126
Wrobleski, Justin	L-L	6-1	194	7-14-00	4	4	2.90	25	23	0	102	93	37	33	6	35	109	.244	.310	.352	26.0	8.3	420
Young, Taylor	R-R	5-9	170	8-06-98	0	0	0.00	1	0	0	1	1	0	0	0	0	1	.250	.250	.250	25.0	0.0	4

Fielding

Catcher	PCT	G	PO	A	E	DP	PB
Fernandez	.984	39	397	28	7	4	9
Hewitt	.949	6	55	1	3	0	1
Lockwood-Powell	1.000	18	138	11	0	1	3
Rodriguez	.987	32	288	23	4	1	3
Rushing	.985	46	425	30	7	1	4

First Base	PCT	G	PO	A	E	DP
Alcantara	.909	2	9	1	1	0
Betancourt	1.000	6	28	1	0	2
Biddison	1.000	1	3	0	0	0
Diaz	.991	14	107	4	1	9
Fernandez	1.000	1	1	0	0	0
Garcia	.949	12	69	5	4	2
Hewitt	1.000	5	20	1	0	1
Lockwood-Powell	.994	69	461	38	3	51
Puerta	1.000	1	4	0	0	0
Rodriguez	1.000	8	46	1	0	9
Rushing	.968	23	146	7	5	11

Second Base	PCT	G	PO	A	E	DP
Alleyne	.667	1	0	2	1	0
Betancourt	1.000	12	19	20	0	3
Fernandez	.983	31	51	62	2	13
Gauthier	.946	9	13	22	2	4
Hewitt	.960	19	30	42	3	11
Young	.992	65	87	152	2	37

Third Base	PCT	G	PO	A	E	DP
Betancourt	.946	16	15	20	2	1
Biddison	1.000	5	4	6	0	1
Diaz	.940	50	38	71	7	7
Fernandez	1.000	3	1	4	0	1

	PCT	G	PO	A	E	DP
Gauthier	.956	23	10	33	2	2
Guerra	.923	7	3	9	1	0
Young	1.000	32	27	39	0	5

Shortstop	PCT	G	PO	A	E	DP
Betancourt	1.000	1	1	1	0	0
Diaz	.900	4	5	4	1	2
Freeland	.964	103	142	208	13	46
Gauthier	1.000	4	5	3	0	2
Young	.969	22	23	39	2	9

Outfield	PCT	G	PO	A	E	DP
Alcantara	1.000	38	64	2	0	1
Alleyne	.979	93	135	5	4	0
Betancourt	1.000	3	5	0	0	0
Biddison	.946	20	31	2	2	0
Diaz	1.000	3	6	0	0	0
Garcia	1.000	8	13	0	0	0
Gauthier	1.000	5	4	0	0	0
Hewitt	1.000	1	1	0	0	0
Keith	.957	88	138	7	9	1
Lockwood-Powell	1.000	2	1	0	0	0
Newell	1.000	36	64	2	0	0
Vogel	.980	112	236	6	5	2
Young	1.000	5	8	0	0	0

RANCHO CUCAMONGA QUAKES

LOW CLASS A

CALIFORNIA LEAGUE

Batting	B-T	Ht.	Wt.	DOB	AVG	OBP	SLG	G	PA	AB	R	H	2B	3B	HR	RBI	BB	HBP	SH	SF	SO	SB	CS	BB%	SO%
Alonso, Juan	R-R	6-0	180	11-03-03	.202	.329	.264	38	155	129	21	26	4	2	0	12	20	5	0	1	60	2	3	12.9	38.7
Betancourt, Kenneth	R-R	5-8	160	2-05-00	.308	.364	.384	65	249	224	34	69	11	0	2	36	19	2	2	2	33	9	1	7.6	13.3
Biddison, Nick	R-R	5-10	190	7-30-00	.240	.336	.368	64	277	242	36	58	4	3	7	29	29	6	0	0	92	5	2	10.5	33.2
Campbell, Dylan	R-R	5-11	205	7-02-02	.205	.225	.231	10	40	39	3	8	1	0	0	3	0	1	0	0	8	2	1	0.0	20.0
Chalo, Wladimir	R-R	5-8	197	4-21-00	.250	.250	.250	2	4	4	1	1	0	0	0	0	0	0	0	0	1	0	0	0.0	25.0
De Paula, Josue	L-L	6-3	185	5-24-05	.284	.396	.372	74	340	282	55	80	15	2	2	40	46	8	0	2	61	14	3	13.5	17.9
Decker, Cameron	B-R	6-1	205	9-22-03	.203	.297	.344	19	74	64	11	13	3	3	0	10	9	0	0	1	23	3	0	12.2	31.1
Diaz, Wilman	R-R	6-2	182	11-15-03	.266	.304	.481	40	168	158	25	42	4	3	8	18	7	2	0	1	66	4	2	4.2	39.3
Doncon, Rayne	R-R	6-2	176	9-22-03	.215	.283	.368	107	473	427	62	92	21	1	14	52	36	6	0	4	103	3	2	7.6	21.8
Dooney, Dayton	R-R	5-10	190	8-21-99	.191	.280	.266	81	314	278	26	53	14	2	1	31	31	4	0	1	113	1	0	9.9	36.0
Galiz, Jesus	R-R	6-0	183	12-19-03	.267	.316	.407	80	330	300	37	80	16	1	8	52	21	3	0	5	74	3	1	6.4	22.4
Gelof, Jake	R-R	6-1	195	2-25-02	.225	.314	.433	30	137	120	23	27	8	1	5	23	16	0	0	1	41	2	1	11.7	29.9
George, Kendall	L-L	5-10	170	10-29-04	.381	.469	.429	12	50	42	13	16	2	0	0	3	6	1	1	0	9	6	2	12.0	18.0
Guerra, Luis	R-R	6-1	180	10-04-03	.260	.302	.380	14	53	50	6	13	6	0	0	6	3	0	0	0	10	0	1	5.7	18.9
Howard, Gaige	L-R	6-2	220	5-22-98	.111	.273	.111	3	11	9	0	1	0	0	0	0	2	0	0	0	5	0	0	18.2	45.5
Izarra, Jose	R-R	6-0	175	3-07-02	.219	.305	.332	108	455	398	57	87	18	3	7	49	41	11	0	5	145	10	3	9.0	31.9
Liranzo, Thayron	B-R	6-3	195	7-05-03	.272	.400	.562	94	418	345	81	94	24	2	24	70	70	3	0	0	112	2	1	16.7	26.8
McLain, Sean	R-R	5-11	170	3-22-01	.182	.250	.318	5	24	22	4	4	0	0	1	2	2	0	0	0	5	0	0	8.3	20.8
Mongelli, Sam	R-R	6-1	185	3-06-01	.241	.389	.310	29	108	87	14	21	3	0	1	9	15	6	0	0	23	4	1	13.9	21.3
Nevin, Kyle	R-R	6-4	200	8-22-01	.312	.388	.473	47	209	186	37	58	11	2	5	21	20	3	0	0	47	3	4	9.6	22.5
Newell, Chris	L-L	6-3	200	4-23-01	.312	.426	.662	41	188	154	41	48	8	2	14	38	32	0	0	2	52	7	2	17.0	27.7
Perez, Jeral	R-R	6-0	179	11-06-04	.238	.407	.333	7	27	21	2	5	2	0	0	2	5	1	0	0	6	0	0	18.5	22.2
Puerta, Jorge	R-R	5-11	178	12-05-01	.256	.363	.335	82	336	281	40	72	16	0	2	33	41	9	0	5	74	2	3	12.2	22.0
Reid, Simon	L-R	6-1	200	4-19-01	.239	.341	.367	31	126	109	11	26	11	0	1	15	15	2	0	0	48	0	0	11.9	38.1
Rodriguez, Frank	R-R	5-11	197	9-28-01	.333	.375	.500	2	8	6	2	2	1	0	0	1	1	0	0	1	0	0	0	12.5	0.0
Rodriguez, Luis	R-R	6-2	175	9-16-02	.275	.354	.393	80	336	295	39	81	16	2	5	42	34	4	0	3	95	11	2	10.1	28.3
Rojas, Miguel	R-R	6-0	188	2-24-89	.333	.429	.833	2	7	6	2	2	0	0	1	2	0	1	0	0	0	0	0	0.0	0.0
Taylor, Chris	R-R	6-1	196	8-29-90	.333	.500	1.333	1	4	3	1	1	0	0	1	1	1	0	0	0	1	0	0	25.0	25.0
Thompson, Jordan	R-R	6-0	175	1-09-02	.270	.329	.297	21	82	74	8	20	2	0	0	7	5	2	0	1	22	4	2	6.1	26.8
Vetrano, Joe	L-L	6-3	220	5-10-02	.270	.354	.357	33	144	126	14	34	3	1	2	24	17	0	0	1	36	0	1	11.8	25.0

Pitching	B-T	Ht.	Wt.	DOB	W	L	ERA	G	GS	SV	IP	Hits	Runs	ER	HR	BB	SO	AVG	OBP	SLG	SO%	BB%	BF
Abad, Dailoui	R-R	6-0	168	5-02-02	0	0	0.00	2	0	0	2	1	0	0	0	1	4	.143	.250	.143	50.0	12.5	8
Bautista, Kelvin	L-L	5-11	155	7-07-99	3	1	5.44	40	0	2	46	49	37	28	1	51	59	.274	.439	.363	24.8	21.4	238
Betancourt, Kenneth	R-R	5-8	160	2-05-00	0	0	0.00	1	0	0	1	1	0	0	0	0	1	.250	.400	.250	20.0	0.0	5
Bruihl, Justin	L-L	6-2	215	6-26-97	0	0	0.00	1	0	0	1	0	0	0	0	0	1	.000	.000	.000	33.3	0.0	3
Bruns, Maddux	L-L	6-2	205	6-20-02	0	0	1.29	6	6	0	21	11	3	3	0	13	33	.149	.284	.189	37.5	14.8	88
Cabrera, Jeisson	R-R	6-2	170	9-05-98	2	1	7.00	16	2	3	18	21	16	14	1	12	30	.292	.411	.375	33.3	13.3	90
Campos, Chris	R-R	5-10	170	8-13-00	5	6	5.06	25	16	0	69	73	42	39	9	30	85	.275	.348	.468	28.3	10.0	300
Castro, Fran	R-R	6-0	175	7-09-00	1	0	7.28	22	0	1	30	38	28	24	4	20	25	.306	.414	.484	16.4	13.2	152
Copen, Patrick	R-R	6-6	220	2-15-02	0	0	0.00	2	2	0	3	2	0	0	0	3	2	.167	.333	.167	13.3	20.0	15
Doolan, Liam	R-R	6-5	230	10-11-98	3	0	3.63	20	0	1	40	32	16	16	1	15	43	.219	.315	.308	25.3	8.8	170
Edwards, Jonathan	R-R	6-6	185	1-26-00	2	3	6.28	34	2	0	43	35	36	30	2	48	46	.213	.406	.311	21.2	22.1	217
Emmett, Gabe	R-R	6-5	175	5-22-01	7	7	5.55	28	14	1	86	79	64	53	11	55	71	.249	.382	.432	18.3	14.2	388
Gonzalez, Jorge	R-R	6-5	203	8-30-02	0	0	6.75	2	0	0	1	0	1	1	0	5	2	.000	.556	.000	22.2	55.6	9
Gutierrez, Roque	R-R	5-9	177	9-07-02	2	4	4.59	16	9	0	49	47	26	25	2	17	54	.251	.330	.364	25.5	8.0	212
Heubeck, Peter	R-R	6-3	170	7-22-02	3	5	5.11	19	19	0	69	55	41	39	7	34	91	.219	.329	.371	30.7	11.5	296
Ibarra, Joel	R-R	6-0	176	7-10-02	6	3	2.64	38	2	1	61	31	20	18	2	49	71	.153	.331	.232	27.4	18.9	259
Jeffrey, Madison	L-R	6-0	190	3-14-00	1	4	6.86	41	3	10	42	40	35	32	0	49	63	.252	.447	.321	28.8	22.4	219
Karros, Jared	R-R	6-7	195	11-16-00	3	4	3.95	19	16	0	71	63	39	31	9	22	75	.236	.295	.412	25.7	7.5	292
Kelly, Joe	R-R	6-1	174	6-09-88	1	0	0.00	2	0	0	2	1	0	0	0	1	0	.200	.333	.200	0.0	16.7	6
Lao, Sauryn	R-R	6-2	182	8-14-99	3	0	2.98	23	1	0	42	37	16	14	3	7	57	.236	.275	.382	33.7	4.1	169
Martin, Payton	R-R	6-0	170	5-19-04	2	1	2.04	14	12	0	40	30	9	9	1	15	48	.213	.293	.270	30.2	9.4	159
Martinez, Carlos	R-R	6-3	190	11-09-01	0	1	8.40	11	0	0	15	12	14	14	4	16	20	.214	.392	.482	26.7	21.3	75
McDaniels, Garrett	L-L	6-2	180	12-15-99	0	1	2.87	13	0	1	16	15	6	5	0	8	19	.250	.348	.350	27.5	11.6	69
Morillo, Juan	R-R	6-1	150	3-19-99	0	0	3.38	6	1	0	5	4	3	2	0	4	10	.200	.333	.250	41.7	16.7	24
Neeck, Brandon	R-L	6-1	190	10-19-99	1	4	7.43	20	0	0	27	33	25	22	2	16	36	.314	.409	.438	28.3	12.6	127
Pinales, Darlin	R-R	6-4	240	8-28-02	3	2	9.86	8	0	0	21	22	25	23	1	31	24	.278	.473	.367	21.4	27.7	112
Ramirez, Kelvin	R-R	6-4	187	6-10-01	4	2	3.92	37	0	3	57	47	33	25	0	31	64	.226	.325	.274	26.2	12.7	244
Reinoso, Livan	R-R	6-1	185	8-27-98	3	1	4.39	38	0	3	66	58	36	32	2	51	83	.239	.380	.350	27.2	16.7	305
Rodriguez, Jose	B-R	6-6	200	7-18-01	0	0	9.00	1	0	0	2	2	2	2	1	0	2	.250	.250	.625	25.0	0.0	8
Romero, Christian	R-R	6-3	195	12-11-02	8	2	3.17	20	10	0	77	60	29	27	10	21	74	.217	.279	.368	24.4	6.9	303

Rosario, Jerming	R-R	6-1	175	5-08-02	1	1	2.88	6	6	0	25	24	10	8	2	7	32	.250	.308	.375	30.8	6.7	104
Ruebeck, Christian	R-R	6-0	185	9-03-00	1	0	5.19	10	0	0	9	7	6	5	0	10	15	.219	.444	.344	33.3	22.2	45
Ruen, Noah	R-R	6-4	190	3-21-03	1	1	2.92	10	1	0	12	10	5	4	0	4	12	.222	.300	.356	24.0	8.0	50
Santana, Waylin	R-R	6-1	155	3-13-03	0	1	3.00	1	1	0	3	4	1	1	0	2	1	.364	.429	.455	7.1	14.3	14
Serunkuma, Ben	R-R	5-10	170	9-19-01	1	0	8.10	2	0	0	3	3	4	3	0	5	7	.231	.444	.231	38.9	27.8	18
Tiburcio, David	R-R	6-2	195	12-29-01	2	0	4.42	10	0	0	18	19	11	9	2	9	11	.275	.358	.449	13.6	11.1	81
Urias, Julio	L-L	6-0	225	8-12-96	0	0	2.25	1	1	0	4	2	1	1	0	1	8	.143	.200	.143	53.3	6.7	15
Valdez, Luis	L-L	6-2	158	7-18-03	0	2	3.12	8	8	0	17	14	6	6	1	14	24	.219	.386	.297	28.9	16.9	83
Wepf, Lucas	L-R	6-5	192	12-23-99	1	2	2.43	22	0	4	33	25	11	9	1	8	58	.207	.258	.289	43.6	6.0	133
Yean, Reynaldo	R-R	6-4	190	1-04-04	1	2	9.00	18	0	1	16	13	20	16	3	16	28	.220	.403	.458	36.4	20.8	77

Fielding

Catcher	PCT	G	PO	A	E	DP	PB
Galiz	.979	52	499	52	12	4	17
Liranzo	.990	53	521	68	6	3	12
Puerta	.981	18	149	7	3	0	11
Reid	.984	17	168	14	3	2	1
Rodriguez	1.000	1	14	0	0	0	0

First Base	PCT	G	PO	A	E	DP
Dooney	.988	73	517	51	7	42
Liranzo	.944	13	94	8	6	8
Nevin	1.000	5	17	1	0	2
Puerta	.991	16	104	12	1	13
Vetrano	.993	32	272	5	2	31

Second Base	PCT	G	PO	A	E	DP
Betancourt	.987	45	52	95	2	22
Biddison	.917	3	4	7	1	2
Diaz	.978	23	34	55	2	15
Doncon	.980	25	29	67	2	9
Dooney	1.000	1	1	1	0	1
Guerra	.900	6	7	11	2	1
Izarra	.990	26	36	65	1	17
McLain	1.000	1	4	3	0	1
Mongelli	.897	7	17	18	4	7
Perez	1.000	5	4	16	0	3
Thompson	.929	2	4	9	1	2

Third Base	PCT	G	PO	A	E	DP
Betancourt	.971	16	15	18	1	2
Biddison	.966	11	8	20	1	4
Diaz	.800	7	1	11	3	2
Doncon	.948	45	24	68	5	9
Gelof	.938	26	15	45	4	4
Guerra	.000	1	0	0	0	0
Izarra	1.000	4	2	6	0	1
Nevin	.913	27	25	38	6	2
Perez	1.000	2	1	0	0	0
Thompson	1.000	1	0	2	0	0

Shortstop	PCT	G	PO	A	E	DP
Betancourt	.900	5	4	5	1	0
Diaz	.857	5	4	8	2	2
Doncon	.975	37	45	70	3	25
Izarra	.965	67	79	144	8	24
McLain	1.000	3	1	8	0	2
Mongelli	.944	4	6	11	1	4
Rojas	1.000	1	0	1	0	0
Taylor	.500	1	1	0	1	0
Thompson	.980	17	16	32	1	16

Outfield	PCT	G	PO	A	E	DP
Alonso	.990	38	70	4	1	0
Betancourt	1.000	3	7	0	0	0
Biddison	.981	53	71	1	2	0
Campbell	1.000	10	26	0	0	0
De Paula	.965	71	88	4	6	1
Decker	.950	17	21	0	1	0
Diaz	.000	1	0	0	0	0
Dooney	1.000	2	3	0	0	0
George	1.000	11	18	0	0	0
Guerra	1.000	8	4	1	0	0
Howard	1.000	3	3	0	0	0
Izarra	1.000	13	23	1	0	1
Mongelli	.986	17	31	0	1	0
Nevin	1.000	18	33	2	0	1
Newell	.500	40	74	2	0	0
Puerta	.989	36	46	2	1	1
Rodriguez	.981	70	102	2	3	0

ACL DODGERS — *ROOKIE*

ARIZONA COMPLEX LEAGUE

Batting	B-T	Ht.	Wt.	DOB	AVG	OBP	SLG	G	PA	AB	R	H	2B	3B	HR	RBI	BB	HBP	SH	SF	SO	SB	CS	BB%	SO%
Albertus, Alexander	R-R	6-1	176	10-27-04	.313	.532	.438	14	47	32	10	10	1	0	1	8	14	1	0	0	4	1	2	29.8	8.5
Alonso, Juan	R-R	6-0	180	11-03-03	.333	.412	.600	5	17	15	3	5	2	1	0	4	0	2	0	0	5	0	1	0.0	29.4
Avila, Carlos	R-R	5-11	180	12-04-03	.000	.200	.000	4	10	8	0	0	0	0	0	0	1	1	0	0	4	0	0	10.0	40.0
Biddison, Nick	R-R	5-10	190	7-30-00	.143	.250	.286	2	8	7	1	1	1	0	0	0	0	1	0	0	4	0	0	0.0	50.0
Campbell, Dylan	R-R	5-11	205	7-02-02	.250	.455	.875	4	11	8	3	2	0	1	1	3	3	0	0	0	2	1	0	27.3	18.2
Decker, Cameron	B-R	6-1	205	9-22-03	.200	.200	.200	2	5	5	0	1	0	0	0	0	0	0	0	0	2	0	0	0.0	40.0
Diaz, Wilman	R-R	6-2	182	11-15-03	.241	.320	.352	28	125	108	20	26	7	1	1	10	10	4	0	3	38	6	3	8.0	30.4
Elkins, Jaron	R-R	6-1	193	11-04-04	.333	.500	.333	1	4	3	2	1	0	0	0	0	0	1	0	0	1	1	0	0.0	25.0
Figueroa, Derlin	L-R	6-0	163	9-07-03	.237	.372	.376	31	113	93	16	22	4	0	3	21	19	1	0	0	25	5	1	16.8	22.1
2-team (11 ACL Royals)					.328	.452	.555	42	157	128	30	42	14	0	5	29	28	1	0	0	29	6	3	17.8	18.5
Garcia, Darol	R-R	5-11	178	9-12-02	.143	.267	.195	31	90	77	14	11	4	0	0	8	11	2	0	0	30	5	0	12.2	33.3
Garcia, Yunior	R-R	6-0	198	7-29-01	.298	.353	.383	13	51	47	6	14	2	1	0	4	3	1	0	0	9	0	0	5.9	17.6
Gelof, Jake	R-R	6-1	195	2-25-02	.231	.412	.692	4	17	13	6	3	1	1	1	4	4	0	0	0	5	2	0	23.5	29.4
George, Kendall	L-L	5-10	170	10-29-04	.362	.451	.414	16	71	58	11	21	3	0	0	7	11	0	0	2	11	11	4	15.5	15.5
Gonzalez, Bryan	R-R	5-10	160	7-15-05	.219	.286	.219	9	35	32	4	7	0	0	0	6	2	1	0	0	7	2	0	5.7	20.0
Guerra, Luis	R-R	6-1	180	10-04-03	.204	.381	.306	16	63	49	8	10	2	0	1	6	13	1	0	0	12	1	0	20.6	19.0
Luna, Jesus	R-R	6-6	165	11-06-00	—	1.000	—	9	1	0	0	0	0	0	0	0	1	0	0	0	0	0	0	100.0	0.0
Male, Umar	R-R	5-10	175	5-14-01	.158	.200	.316	6	20	19	3	3	3	0	0	3	1	0	0	0	11	1	0	5.0	55.0
Martinus, M'shendrick	R-R	6-3	161	2-03-05	.234	.294	.344	49	170	154	29	36	6	1	3	24	13	1	0	2	65	10	1	7.6	38.2
McLain, Sean	R-R	5-11	170	3-22-01	.167	.545	.167	3	11	6	0	1	0	0	0	1	5	0	0	0	5	0	0	45.5	45.5
Meza, Jose	R-R	6-1	160	4-22-03	.287	.464	.408	54	235	174	46	50	7	1	4	27	55	4	0	2	51	3	4	23.4	21.7
Mongelli, Sam	R-R	6-1	185	3-06-01	.286	.500	.286	2	10	7	3	2	0	0	0	3	2	1	0	0	0	0	0	20.0	0.0
Munoz, Samuel	L-R	6-3	190	9-22-04	.273	.338	.412	52	240	216	35	59	10	7	2	32	21	1	0	2	41	9	2	8.8	17.1
Osorio, Oswaldo	L-R	6-1	171	4-12-05	.262	.393	.445	49	201	164	32	43	6	3	6	22	29	7	0	1	54	1	1	14.4	26.9
Perez, Jeral	R-R	6-0	179	11-06-04	.257	.389	.503	53	221	179	33	46	9	1	11	41	36	4	0	2	51	9	2	16.3	23.1
Quiroz, Nelson	B-R	5-8	194	11-05-01	.000	.273	.000	3	11	8	2	0	0	0	0	0	3	0	0	0	2	0	0	27.3	18.2
Reid, Simon	L-R	6-1	200	4-19-01	.143	.294	.357	5	17	14	1	2	0	0	1	3	3	0	0	0	5	0	0	17.6	29.4
Rodrigues, Victor	R-R	6-3	203	9-23-04	.217	.379	.304	17	58	46	8	10	4	0	0	7	12	0	0	0	13	1	1	20.7	22.4
Rojas, Carlos	R-R	6-0	165	7-25-02	.245	.406	.336	38	143	110	19	27	7	0	1	16	28	3	0	2	23	1	0	19.6	16.1
Shelton, Easton	R-R	6-5	225	9-17-05	1.000	1.000	1.333	1	4	3	2	3	1	0	0	3	1	0	0	0	0	0	0	25.0	0.0
Tapia, German	R-R	6-2	170	9-19-03	.500	.500	1.250	1	4	4	2	2	0	0	1	4	0	0	0	0	2	0	0	0.0	50.0
Taylor, Chris	R-R	6-1	196	8-29-90	.500	.667	.500	1	3	2	0	1	0	0	0	0	1	0	0	0	1	0	0	33.3	33.3
Thompson, Jordan	R-R	6-0	175	1-09-02	.250	.333	.375	2	9	8	1	2	1	0	0	1	0	1	0	0	4	0	0	0.0	44.4
Thompson, Trayce	R-R	6-3	225	3-15-91	.167	.167	.167	2	6	6	0	1	0	0	0	1	0	0	0	0	2	0	0	0.0	33.3
Valladares, Jefferson	R-R	6-0	190	5-30-02	.273	.419	.455	22	86	66	16	18	3	0	3	10	11	7	0	2	16	4	0	12.8	18.6

Batting	B-T	Ht.	Wt.	DOB	AVG	OBP	SLG	G	PA	AB	R	H	2B	3B	HR	RBI	BB	HBP	SH	SF	SO	SB	CS	BB%	SO%
Vetrano, Joe	L-L	6-3	220	5-10-02	.167	.500	.167	2	10	6	2	1	0	0	0	0	4	0	0	0	2	0	0	40.0	20.0
Wagner, Logan	B-R	6-1	200	3-09-04	.091	.333	.091	4	15	11	3	1	0	0	0	0	4	0	0	0	5	0	0	26.7	33.3
Wong, Kolten	L-R	5-7	185	10-10-90	.000	.400	.000	2	5	3	0	0	0	0	0	0	1	1	0	0	1	0	0	20.0	20.0

Pitching	B-T	Ht.	Wt.	DOB	W	L	ERA	G	GS	SV	IP	Hits	Runs	ER	HR	BB	SO	AVG	OBP	SLG	SO%	BB%	BF
Abad, Dailoui	R-R	6-0	168	5-02-02	3	1	2.39	22	0	11	26	18	10	7	0	7	33	.188	.255	.250	31.1	6.6	106
Arvizu, Guillermo	L-L	6-4	242	8-28-02	2	0	7.64	14	0	0	18	22	16	15	5	7	27	.293	.361	.547	32.5	8.4	83
Batista, Aldrin	R-R	6-2	185	5-04-03	3	1	3.46	10	7	0	39	33	18	15	1	15	54	.237	.331	.331	33.1	9.2	163
Benua, Alvaro	R-R	6-4	198	1-11-03	1	0	3.58	17	3	0	28	19	12	11	0	29	48	.207	.413	.250	38.1	23.0	126
Brito, Moises	L-L	6-5	215	7-09-02	0	1	9.00	1	1	0	3	5	4	3	0	2	4	.417	.533	.500	26.7	13.3	15
Cabrera, Felix	L-L	6-3	170	4-08-02	2	0	3.81	19	0	0	26	18	16	11	1	17	30	.196	.336	.293	26.3	14.9	114
Copen, Patrick	R-R	6-6	220	2-15-02	0	0	0.00	1	0	0	1	1	0	0	0	0	0	.333	.333	.333	0.0	0.0	3
Cyr, Tyler	R-R	6-1	205	5-05-93	0	0	0.00	1	0	0	1	0	0	0	0	1	0	.000	.250	.000	0.0	25.0	4
Day, Cam	B-R	6-2	195	7-25-02	0	0	3.86	2	1	0	2	1	1	1	1	0	2	.125	.125	.500	25.0	0.0	8
Giles, Ken	R-R	6-3	197	9-20-90	0	0	0.00	2	2	0	2	1	0	0	0	0	4	.167	.167	.167	66.7	0.0	6
Gonzalez, Jorge	R-R	6-5	203	8-30-02	2	2	8.38	15	0	0	19	19	19	18	0	11	35	.241	.355	.329	37.2	11.7	94
Gutierrez, Roque	R-R	5-9	177	9-07-02	0	0	0.00	2	0	0	2	1	0	0	0	0	3	.143	.143	.143	42.9	0.0	7
Hudson, Daniel	R-R	6-3	215	3-09-87	0	0	0.00	5	5	0	5	3	0	0	0	1	8	.200	.250	.333	50.0	6.3	16
Jones, James	L-L	6-3	205	9-24-88	0	1	5.40	5	3	0	5	5	4	3	1	4	9	.250	.385	.450	34.6	15.4	26
Joseph, Luis	R-R	6-4	176	4-22-03	0	0	81.00	1	0	0	0	2	3	3	1	1	1	.667	.800	2.333	20.0	20.0	5
Lewis, Jimmy	R-R	6-6	200	11-02-00	1	1	6.14	11	0	0	15	21	11	10	4	4	12	.339	.397	.565	17.6	5.9	68
Linan, Sean	R-R	6-0	185	11-07-04	0	2	4.54	12	6	0	36	38	24	18	3	11	43	.255	.321	.403	26.1	6.7	165
Lohman, Carter	L-L	6-2	205	12-25-99	1	0	3.38	7	1	0	11	10	4	4	0	3	13	.244	.311	.268	28.9	6.7	45
Luna, Jesus	R-R	6-6	165	11-06-00	1	0	1.46	9	0	0	12	5	2	2	0	7	18	.122	.250	.122	36.7	14.3	49
Martinez, Carlos	R-R	6-3	190	11-09-01	0	1	2.70	3	0	0	3	1	2	1	0	4	8	.091	.412	.091	47.1	23.5	17
Martinez, Maximo	R-R	6-2	185	6-21-04	0	0	4.73	9	5	0	27	21	16	14	0	17	28	.216	.358	.330	23.3	14.2	120
Matos, Alberluis	L-L	6-0	175	9-30-01	4	1	1.93	12	0	0	14	12	5	3	1	9	15	.245	.383	.327	25.0	15.0	60
McDaniels, Garrett	L-L	6-2	180	12-15-99	0	0	0.00	3	0	1	2	2	0	0	0	0	4	.222	.222	.333	44.4	0.0	9
Miller, Shelby	R-R	6-3	225	10-10-90	0	0	0.00	3	3	0	3	2	2	0	0	2	8	.182	.308	.182	61.5	15.4	13
Neeck, Brandon	R-L	6-1	190	10-19-99	0	0	0.00	3	0	2	2	1	0	0	0	1	6	.111	.200	.111	60.0	10.0	10
Nelson, Jimmy	R-R	6-6	250	6-05-89	0	0	0.00	4	2	0	4	1	0	0	0	2	5	.077	.294	.077	29.4	11.8	17
Pinales, Darlin	R-R	6-4	240	8-28-02	3	1	8.31	12	4	0	17	17	19	16	3	14	23	.250	.393	.426	27.4	16.7	84
Reyes, Carlo	R-R	6-0	212	7-04-98	0	0	4.66	8	1	0	10	8	5	5	1	4	12	.235	.316	.382	31.6	10.5	38
Rodriguez, Jose	B-R	6-6	200	7-18-01	3	1	4.76	19	0	0	23	29	12	12	1	3	31	.309	.327	.457	31.6	3.1	98
Ruen, Noah	R-R	6-4	190	3-21-03	0	0	0.00	1	0	0	1	0	0	0	0	0	1	.000	.000	.000	33.3	0.0	3
Santana, Waylin	R-R	6-1	155	3-13-03	2	5	6.42	12	8	0	41	47	33	29	8	18	39	.294	.389	.506	21.0	9.7	186
Santillan, Pedro	R-R	6-4	200	7-07-01	3	1	2.93	18	0	1	15	13	5	5	1	8	19	.236	.348	.364	28.8	12.1	66
Serunkuma, Ben	R-R	5-10	170	9-19-01	0	1	5.23	10	0	0	10	14	7	6	1	5	14	.326	.396	.419	28.6	10.2	49
Tiburcio, David	R-R	6-2	195	12-29-01	0	0	3.97	10	1	0	11	12	10	5	2	8	12	.267	.389	.444	22.2	14.8	54
Treinen, Blake	R-R	6-5	225	6-30-88	0	0	0.00	1	1	0	1	0	0	0	0	0	2	.000	.000	.000	66.7	0.0	3
Vanasco, Ricky	R-R	6-3	180	10-13-98	0	0	0.00	1	1	0	1	0	0	0	0	0	1	.000	.000	.000	33.3	0.0	3
Wallace, Callum	R-R	6-3	190	4-06-04	2	1	11.37	12	1	0	13	12	17	16	5	22	19	.240	.479	.620	26.0	30.1	73
Williams, Kendall	R-R	6-6	205	8-24-00	0	1	12.00	1	0	0	3	5	4	4	0	1	0	.417	.563	.500	0.0	6.3	16
Yean, Reynaldo	R-R	6-4	190	1-04-04	1	0	0.00	7	0	0	8	1	0	0	0	1	16	.037	.071	.037	57.1	3.6	28

Fielding

C: Rojas 37, Rodrigues 11, Reid 5, Valladares 4, Quiroz 3, Avila 3, Male 1. **1B:** Valladares 17, Guerra 15, Rodrigues 10, Figueroa 10, Garcia 10, Avila 1, Biddison 1, Decker 1, Shelton 1, Vetrano 1. **2B:** Osorio 17, Perez 17, Diaz 9, Garcia 6, Gonzalez 5, Albertus 4, Martinus 1, Mongelli 1. **3B:** Perez 20, Osorio 12, Garcia 9, Albertus 6, Martinus 6, Diaz 5, Wagner 4, Gelof 2, Guerra 1. **SS:** Perez 16, Martinus 14, Osorio 11, Diaz 10, Albertus 6, Gonzalez 4, McLain 2, Thompson 2, Wong 2. **OF:** Munoz 57, Meza 52, Martinus 29, Figueroa 24, Garcia 16, Alonso 5, Campbell 4, Valladares 3, George 2, Guerra 1, Male 1, Elkins 1, Biddison 1, Tapia 1, Taylor 1, Thompson 1.

DSL DODGERS

ROOKIE

DOMINICAN SUMMER LEAGUE

Batting	B-T	Ht.	Wt.	DOB	AVG	OBP	SLG	G	PA	AB	R	H	2B	3B	HR	RBI	BB	HBP	SH	SF	SO	SB	CS	BB%	SO%
Acosta, Agustin	L-R	6-2	173	9-07-04	.000	.222	.000	3	9	7	0	0	0	0	0	0	2	0	0	0	5	0	0	22.2	55.6
Albertus, Alexander	R-R	6-1	176	10-27-04	.309	.447	.479	31	123	94	19	29	4	0	4	25	24	2	0	3	15	8	4	19.5	12.2
Angela, Rodmar	L-L	5-9	180	9-20-04	.180	.383	.230	29	81	61	23	11	3	0	0	5	16	4	0	0	11	0	2	19.8	13.6
Barett, Luis	R-R	5-11	165	11-25-03	.181	.322	.267	41	143	116	24	21	4	0	2	20	21	4	0	2	34	4	1	14.7	23.8
Campos, Elio	R-R	5-9	157	1-02-04	.321	.432	.353	51	191	156	41	50	3	1	0	30	29	3	1	2	18	19	3	15.2	9.4
Castaneda, Luis	R-R	5-11	163	2-24-04	.302	.400	.460	27	76	63	10	19	2	1	2	17	8	3	1	1	21	3	2	10.5	27.6
Diaz, Angel	R-R	5-11	180	2-04-04	.353	.457	.586	39	164	133	31	47	10	0	7	33	23	5	0	3	21	2	2	14.0	12.8
Dominguez, Miguel	R-R	6-0	195	2-20-04	.231	.381	.342	39	147	117	33	27	7	0	2	22	24	5	0	1	30	0	2	16.3	20.4
Familia, Railin	R-R	6-0	186	9-15-04	.202	.336	.270	30	110	89	19	18	3	0	1	16	17	2	0	2	34	2	2	15.5	30.9
Gonzalez, Harold	R-R	5-10	175	8-29-06	.240	.410	.272	45	162	125	35	30	4	0	0	17	34	2	1	0	20	9	3	21.0	12.3
Gonzalez, Jose	L-R	6-2	180	1-29-05	.182	.333	.250	32	111	88	17	16	3	0	1	11	20	1	0	2	27	6	3	18.0	24.3
Guerrero, Eduardo	B-R	6-2	165	5-09-05	.259	.332	.377	42	184	162	31	42	12	2	1	23	18	1	0	3	24	4	3	9.8	13.0
Hernandez, Jose	R-R	6-1	145	4-30-03	.290	.404	.534	43	162	131	33	38	12	1	6	30	18	9	1	3	26	5	2	11.1	16.0
Herrera, Javier	B-R	5-10	160	2-09-05	.238	.361	.418	46	147	122	29	29	4	3	4	22	22	2	0	1	38	7	2	15.0	25.9
Johnson, Paris	R-R	6-2	205	3-09-05	.258	.380	.500	25	79	66	15	17	2	1	4	12	12	1	0	0	20	2	1	15.2	25.3
Lantigua, Arnaldo	R-R	6-2	200	12-19-05	.222	.345	.475	29	119	99	18	22	4	0	7	24	18	1	0	1	26	4	2	15.1	21.8
Lasso, Roger	B-R	6-0	180	2-27-04	.337	.514	.446	33	142	101	25	34	7	2	0	23	32	7	0	2	25	0	2	22.5	17.6
Lorenzo, Abel	L-R	6-0	160	8-14-05	.275	.376	.443	44	198	167	36	46	12	2	4	36	24	4	1	2	54	4	5	12.1	27.3
Medina, Elias	R-R	5-10	171	11-09-05	.313	.381	.553	44	176	150	42	47	9	3	7	40	16	4	0	6	37	16	5	9.1	21.0
Medina, Yorfran	R-R	6-4	195	1-25-05	.270	.538	.667	32	106	63	29	17	8	1	5	20	24	16	0	3	22	1	0	22.6	20.8

Mielcarek, Daniel	B-R	6-3	185	12-19-05	.191	.371	.235	24	89	68	14	13	1	1	0	4	18	2	0	1	33	6	4	20.2	37.1
Ortega, Raynerd	R-R	6-1	154	7-08-05	.225	.345	.300	47	194	160	32	36	6	0	2	29	24	7	0	3	30	6	4	12.4	15.5
Pacheco, Orlando	R-R	5-11	175	12-25-04	.235	.438	.324	14	48	34	4	8	3	0	0	3	10	3	0	1	8	2	1	20.8	16.7
Pena, Javier	R-R	6-0	185	9-10-04	.189	.318	.311	28	91	74	10	14	1	1	2	16	11	3	3	0	35	3	2	12.1	38.5
Quintero, Eduardo	R-R	6-0	175	9-16-05	.359	.472	.618	49	212	170	54	61	15	7	5	42	32	7	0	3	34	22	4	15.1	16.0
Ramirez, Raynier	R-R	5-10	185	12-13-04	.265	.403	.513	37	149	117	40	31	9	1	6	25	28	1	0	3	36	2	1	18.8	24.2
Rodrigues, Victor	R-R	6-3	203	9-23-04	.292	.407	.406	30	118	96	22	28	3	1	2	20	19	1	0	2	11	9	4	16.1	9.3
Sanchez, Edwin	R-R	6-3	180	8-02-04	.234	.407	.391	44	168	128	32	30	8	0	4	22	30	8	1	1	33	7	1	17.9	19.6
Torrez, Jose	R-R	6-1	195	10-05-04	.128	.281	.154	29	96	78	8	10	2	0	0	6	12	5	0	1	16	0	0	12.5	16.7
Vargas, Joendry	R-R	6-4	175	11-08-05	.328	.423	.529	48	208	174	47	57	12	1	7	31	30	1	0	3	31	19	5	14.4	14.9

Pitching	B-T	Ht.	Wt.	DOB	W	L	ERA	G	GS	SV	IP	Hits	Runs	ER	HR	BB	SO	AVG	OBP	SLG	SO%	BB%	BF
Adon, Rancer	R-R	6-5	180	8-02-04	0	0	24.30	10	0	0	7	7	20	18	0	25	2	.292	.660	.333	3.8	47.2	53
Bartolozzi, Javier	R-R	6-4	193	4-14-05	0	3	3.66	13	13	0	39	39	24	16	2	11	42	.252	.314	.387	24.9	6.5	169
Batista, Erick	R-R	6-0	186	3-03-04	1	0	2.53	8	2	0	11	4	3	3	0	12	12	.118	.388	.176	24.5	24.5	49
Bonilla, Peter	L-L	6-3	195	12-16-04	6	1	1.41	19	0	0	32	21	6	5	1	20	38	.189	.321	.243	28.4	14.9	134
Brito, Moises	L-L	6-5	215	7-09-02	3	0	2.36	12	11	0	42	22	13	11	2	10	54	.152	.210	.241	34.4	6.4	157
Camacho, Roman	R-R	6-0	194	11-23-04	0	0	0.00	3	0	0	2	3	3	0	0	1	2	.250	.308	.333	15.4	7.7	13
Carias, Luis	R-R	6-4	170	9-30-04	3	0	4.70	17	0	1	23	25	14	12	0	13	15	.291	.388	.395	14.6	12.6	103
Castro, Jeremy	R-R	6-2	180	1-27-05	0	1	7.23	14	0	0	19	29	21	15	2	11	11	.345	.439	.524	11.2	11.2	98
Colon, Ilmerson	L-L	6-2	167	3-10-05	4	1	4.07	16	0	0	24	16	14	11	0	23	34	.188	.389	.212	30.1	20.4	113
Corcho, Marco	R-R	6-2	200	5-02-05	2	1	4.43	18	0	4	22	25	20	11	0	8	29	.260	.317	.344	27.9	7.7	104
Cruz, Angel	R-R	6-1	210	10-12-04	5	0	2.63	18	5	1	38	25	15	11	1	23	56	.184	.319	.243	34.4	14.1	163
Cruz, Nicolas	R-R	5-11	160	4-23-04	1	1	2.86	11	6	0	28	30	14	9	0	8	21	.268	.317	.295	17.1	6.5	123
De La Cruz, Yuliangel	R-R	6-3	158	1-24-05	0	1	6.12	13	11	0	32	39	26	22	2	16	28	.305	.396	.422	18.8	10.7	149
De Los Santos, J.	R-R	6-0	175	9-21-03	0	1	11.25	6	0	0	4	4	9	5	0	10	7	.267	.560	.267	26.9	38.5	26
Estevez, Anderson	R-R	6-2	185	12-12-04	0	0	5.59	5	0	0	10	9	7	6	0	8	11	.257	.409	.286	25.0	18.2	44
Figueredo, Dilan	R-R	6-0	174	3-28-03	5	0	2.12	17	0	1	30	16	9	7	1	12	25	.157	.256	.206	21.4	10.3	117
Fischer, Tim	R-R	6-3	195	9-08-04	0	2	6.84	12	11	0	26	29	21	20	3	19	30	.287	.416	.436	24.0	15.2	125
Geronimo, Domingo	R-R	5-11	150	10-07-04	4	1	2.05	19	0	4	31	22	10	7	0	11	25	.202	.288	.239	20.0	8.8	125
Herder, Jholbran	R-R	6-2	170	11-02-04	0	0	3.24	4	3	0	8	7	3	3	1	3	4	.241	.324	.414	11.8	8.8	34
Hernandez, Jose	R-R	6-1	145	4-30-03	0	0	0.00	1	0	0	1	1	0	0	0	0	0	.200	.200	.200	0.0	0.0	5
Hernandez, Juan	R-R	6-2	187	11-19-02	1	1	9.42	14	0	1	14	8	16	15	2	23	25	.163	.481	.286	31.6	29.1	79
Hernandez, Wilkerson	R-R	6-3	185	9-30-03	1	0	7.36	13	0	0	18	20	15	15	3	16	20	.294	.446	.529	21.7	17.4	92
Herrera, Wuillians	R-R	6-4	183	3-12-04	1	0	4.76	16	0	2	23	23	14	12	0	14	24	.271	.394	.329	23.1	13.5	104
Jerez, Anderson	R-R	5-10	185	7-19-04	4	2	3.10	17	0	0	20	11	12	7	0	22	17	.164	.400	.179	17.9	23.2	95
Jimenez, Jhonny	R-R	6-5	180	11-09-03	6	0	1.44	17	0	1	31	15	6	5	2	13	25	.143	.235	.238	21.0	10.9	119
Leon, Edgar	R-R	6-3	170	12-29-04	0	0	3.73	13	11	0	31	24	16	13	2	17	37	.202	.304	.319	26.8	12.3	138
Liborius, Jecsua	R-R	6-1	190	5-28-05	3	1	4.82	15	0	3	19	24	14	10	1	12	19	.308	.398	.385	20.4	12.9	93
Medrano, Lesther	R-R	6-2	185	3-05-03	0	0	4.66	5	0	0	10	8	5	5	1	2	9	.216	.275	.378	22.5	5.0	40
Montero, Ricardo	R-R	6-6	237	2-17-04	3	1	4.15	16	3	1	26	19	14	12	2	17	20	.194	.331	.296	16.9	14.4	118
Morel, Franderly	L-L	6-2	160	9-12-03	6	0	3.97	18	1	1	34	35	17	15	2	12	30	.263	.331	.376	20.3	8.1	148
Mujica, Roiger	R-R	6-2	180	7-24-05	0	1	40.50	1	1	0	1	3	3	3	0	2	0	.600	.750	1.000	0.0	25.0	8
Nava, Erick	R-R	6-0	190	1-09-05	0	0	21.60	5	0	0	3	4	9	8	0	7	2	.308	.591	.308	9.1	31.8	22
Nieves, Marlon	R-R	6-3	170	6-10-05	1	0	6.43	11	9	0	21	25	16	15	1	21	17	.309	.447	.481	16.3	20.2	104
Omosako, Kinn	R-R	6-4	210	6-24-04	3	1	5.04	18	1	1	30	28	20	17	0	16	30	.237	.331	.347	22.1	11.8	136
Reyes, Yobany	R-R	6-2	195	10-18-04	0	0	0.00	1	0	0	1	1	2	0	0	2	1	.200	.500	.200	12.5	25.0	8
Rivero, Alexander	R-R	6-0	165	1-11-06	0	0	5.63	7	0	1	8	9	6	5	0	5	9	.257	.395	.400	20.9	11.6	43
Romero, Luciano	R-R	6-2	190	1-08-05	2	2	6.00	10	1	0	15	16	14	10	4	14	9	.276	.449	.483	11.5	17.9	78
Sanchez, Samuel	R-R	5-11	150	10-21-05	0	1	7.50	4	4	0	6	9	5	5	1	2	6	.333	.379	.444	20.7	6.9	29
Sevilya, Enrike	R-R	6-3	195	7-27-05	0	0	10.80	4	2	0	3	8	6	4	0	6	4	.471	.640	.706	16.0	24.0	25
Simarra, Yoryi	R-R	6-1	174	11-18-04	4	0	1.38	17	1	3	26	14	5	4	0	18	32	.159	.324	.182	28.8	16.2	111
Tello, Angel	R-R	6-4	165	1-26-04	3	1	1.95	17	0	5	28	17	7	6	1	11	19	.175	.257	.247	17.4	10.1	109
Tillero, Jesus	R-R	6-0	190	5-02-06	0	1	1.47	10	10	0	31	19	10	5	0	6	34	.170	.218	.223	28.6	5.0	119
Ventura, Robinson	R-R	6-1	169	6-28-06	0	0	21.60	5	0	0	3	4	8	8	0	7	2	.308	.591	.462	9.1	31.8	22
Vilchez, Michael	R-R	6-3	180	6-03-04	6	3	3.81	17	0	1	26	23	15	11	1	15	27	.240	.362	.333	23.1	12.8	117

Fielding

C: Dominguez 25, Diaz 22, Torrez 22, Rodrigues 17, Pacheco 14, Pena 12, Familia 4. **1B:** Medina 27, Hernandez 18, Familia 18, Dominguez 13, Diaz 12, Castaneda 9, Rodrigues 9, Gonzalez 8, Pena 7, Lorenzo 5, Torrez 4. **2B:** Ramirez 19, Ortega 17, Campos 14, Guerrero 14, Gonzalez 13, Herrera 11, Castaneda 8, Albertus 8, Medina 6, Mielcarek 5, Hernandez 2, Pena 2, Vargas 1, Angela 1. **3B:** Gonzalez 21, Hernandez 18, Medina 18, Ortega 11, Ramirez 11, Albertus 9, Vargas 8, Campos 7, Herrera 6, Castaneda 1. **SS:** Vargas 28, Guerrero 25, Ortega 15, Herrera 14, Medina 12, Albertus 9, Mielcarek 7, Campos 3, Hernandez 2, Gonzalez 1. **OF:** Sanchez 44, Quintero 42, Barett 41, Lorenzo 34, Gonzalez 31, Angela 28, Campos 27, Johnson 25, Lantigua 25, Lasso 21, Herrera 17, Castaneda 12, Familia 8, Hernandez 5, Acosta 2, Pena 2.

Miami Marlins

SEASON SYNOPSIS: They only scored 666 runs, but the Marlins had a charmed season. Outscored by 57, they went 33-14 in one-run games under first-year manager Skip Schumaker and outlasted a muddled field to snag one of the last two National League wild-card spots, just their fourth berth in 31 seasons as a franchise.

HIGH POINT: Miami had win streaks of six and five games during a 19-8 June that included a sweep of the Red Sox at Fenway Park. Second baseman Luis Arraez led the first win of that series with three hits in a 10-1 victory, lifting him to a .399 average through the season's 80th game as he threatened the .400 mark. Finishing the sweep left the Marlins a season-high 14 games over .500.

LOW POINT: Miami lost five straight series to end August, falling below the .500 mark Aug. 30 in a 3-0 loss to Tampa Bay in front of 9,803 fans at loanDepot Park, spoiling six scoreless, one-hit innings by lefty Jesus Luzardo. They had just four hits and absorbed one of their 14 shutouts en route to ranking 25th in the majors in runs per game (4.11).

NOTABLE ROOKIES: Six-foot-8 righty Eury Perez graduated from top prospect to top pitcher, posting a 3.15 ERA in 19 starts and striking out 108 in 91.1 innings while the Marlins tried to monitor his innings carefully. RHP Bryan Hoeing provided a depth arm with seven starts and 70.2 IP.

KEY TRANSACTIONS: The Marlins acquired Arraez from the Twins in January, trading right-hander Pablo Lopez plus prospects Jose Salas, an infielder, and outfielder Byron Chourio. Arraez became the first batting champ to win the title the next year in the other league. In-season, GM Kim Ng boosted the offense by trading pitching prospect Jake Eder to the White Sox for slugging third baseman Jake Burger while adding DH/1B Josh Bell from the Guardians. Burger and Bell combined for 20 homers while playing 53 games apiece.

DOWN ON THE FARM: The Marlins have shown a talent for developing pitching, as Perez's ascent to the majors in 2023 once again proved, but it continues to struggle to develop position players which has left the system thin in close-to-the-majors hitters. Pensacola was the org's bright spot. The Blue Wahoos went 79-57 (.581) and finished as Southern League runners-up, beating Montgomery in the first round before falling to Tennessee in the championship series.

OPENING DAY PAYROLL: $91,700,000 (24th).

PLAYERS OF THE YEAR

MAJOR LEAGUE

Luis Arraez
2B
.354/.393/.469
71 R, 30 2B
69 RBI

MINOR LEAGUE

Xavier Edwards
OF/2B
(AAA)
.351/.429/.457
52 BB, 30 SO, 80

ORGANIZATION LEADERS

Batting — *Minimum 250 AB

MAJORS		
* AVG	Luis Arraez	.354
* OPS	Luis Arraez	.861
HR	Jorge Soler	36
RBI	Bryan De La Cruz	78
MINORS		
* AVG	Xavier Edwards, Jacksonville	.351
* OBP	Xavier Edwards, Jacksonville	.429
* SLG	Troy Johnston, Pensacola/Jacksonville	.549
* OPS	Troy Johnston, Pensacola/Jacksonville	.947
R	Troy Johnston, Pensacola/Jacksonville	102
H	Javier Sanoja, Jupiter/Beloit	158
TB	Troy Johnston, Pensacola/Jacksonville	281
2B	Troy Johnston, Pensacola/Jacksonville	36
3B	3-tied	8
HR	Jerar Encarnacion, Jacksonville	26
HR	Troy Johnston, Pensacola/Jacksonville	26
RBI	Troy Johnston, Pensacola/Jacksonville	116
BB	Nasim Nunez, Pensacola	87
SO	Jerar Encarnacion, Jacksonville	200
SB	Nasim Nunez, Pensacola	52

Pitching — #Minimum 75 IP

MAJORS		
W	Jesus Luzardo	10
# ERA	Tanner Scott	2.31
SO	Jesus Luzardo	208
SV	A.J. Puk	15
MINORS		
W	Luis Palacios, Beloit/Pens./Jackson.	11
W	Patrick Monteverde, Pensacola/Jacksonv.	11
L	Zach King, Beloit/Pensacola	11
# ERA	Breidy Encarnacion, 4-levels	2.03
G	Jefry Yan, Pensacola/Jacksonville	49
GS	Evan Fitterer, Beloit/Pensacola	26
SV	Evan Taylor, Jupiter	20
IP	Luis Palacios, Beloit/Pens./Jackson.	144
BB	Evan Fitterer, Beloit/Pensacola	84
SO	Patrick Monteverde, Pensacola/Jacksonv.	121
# AVG	Breidy Encarnacion, 4-levels	.178

2023 PERFORMANCE

General Manager: Kim Ng. **Farm Director:** Hector Crespo. **Scouting Director:** DJ Svihlik.

Class	Team	League	W	L	PCT	Finish	Manager
Majors	Miami Marlins	National	84	78	.519	6 (15)	Skip Schumaker
Triple-A	J'ville Jumbo Shrimp	International	70	79	.470	15 (20)	Daren Brown
Double-A	Pensacola Blue Wahoos	Southern	79	57	.581	1 (8)	Kevin Randel
High-A	Beloit Sky Carp	Midwest	56	75	.427	11 (12)	Billy Gardner
Low-A	Jupiter Hammerheads	Florida State	70	62	.530	4 (10)	Nelson Prada
Rookie	FCL Marlins	Florida Complex	27	25	.519	8 (15)	Luis Dorante
Rookie	DSL Marlins	Dominican Sum.	22	30	.423	36 (50)	Carlos Mota
Rookie	DSL Miami	Dominican Sum.	18	35	.340	43 (50)	Oscar Escobar
Overall 2023 Minor League Record			342	363	.485	20th (30)	

ORGANIZATION STATISTICS

MIAMI MARLINS

NATIONAL LEAGUE

Batting	B-T	Ht.	Wt.	DOB	AVG	OBP	SLG	G	PA	AB	R	H	2B	3B	HR	RBI	BB	HBP	SH	SF	SO	SB	CS	BB%	SO%
Amaya, Jacob	R-R	6-0	180	9-03-98	.222	.222	.222	4	9	9	1	2	0	0	0	2	0	0	0	0	1	1	0	0.0	11.1
Arraez, Luis	L-R	5-10	175	4-09-97	.354	.393	.469	147	617	574	71	203	30	3	10	69	35	4	1	3	34	3	2	5.7	5.5
Bell, Josh	B-R	6-4	261	8-14-92	.270	.338	.480	53	224	200	26	54	9	0	11	26	20	1	0	1	53	0	0	8.9	23.7
Berti, Jon	R-R	5-10	190	1-22-90	.294	.344	.405	133	424	388	53	114	16	3	7	33	29	2	2	3	77	16	6	6.8	18.2
Burdick, Peyton	R-R	6-0	205	2-26-97	.182	.270	.333	14	37	33	4	6	2	0	1	2	3	1	0	0	18	1	0	8.1	48.6
Burger, Jake	R-R	6-2	230	4-10-96	.303	.355	.505	53	217	198	27	60	13	0	9	28	10	7	0	2	47	0	0	4.6	21.7
Chisholm, Jazz	L-R	5-11	184	2-01-98	.250	.304	.457	97	383	352	50	88	12	2	19	51	26	2	1	2	118	22	3	6.8	30.8
Cooper, Garrett	R-R	6-5	235	12-25-90	.256	.296	.426	82	324	305	28	78	11	1	13	46	17	1	0	1	97	0	0	5.2	29.9
2-team (51 San Diego)					.251	.305	.419	123	457	422	42	106	18	1	17	61	31	2	0	2	132	0	0	6.8	28.9
Davis, Jonathan	R-R	5-8	190	5-12-92	.244	.307	.378	34	104	90	22	22	4	1	2	10	7	2	2	2	29	1	2	6.7	27.9
De La Cruz, Bryan	R-R	6-2	175	12-16-96	.257	.304	.411	153	626	579	60	149	32	0	19	78	40	1	0	5	142	4	1	6.4	22.7
Edwards, Xavier	B-R	5-10	175	8-09-99	.295	.329	.333	30	84	78	12	23	3	0	0	3	3	1	2	0	14	5	0	3.6	16.7
Fortes, Nick	R-R	5-11	198	11-11-96	.204	.263	.299	108	323	294	33	60	10	0	6	26	17	7	3	2	59	4	2	5.3	18.3
Garcia, Avisail	R-R	6-4	250	6-12-91	.185	.241	.315	37	118	108	8	20	3	1	3	12	6	2	0	0	39	2	0	5.1	33.1
Gurriel, Yuli	R-R	6-0	215	6-09-84	.245	.304	.359	108	329	298	32	73	16	3	4	27	26	1	0	4	44	4	0	7.9	13.4
Hampson, Garrett	R-R	5-11	196	10-10-94	.276	.349	.380	98	252	221	30	61	12	1	3	23	23	3	3	2	67	5	0	9.1	26.6
Myers, Dane	R-R	6-0	205	3-08-96	.269	.286	.358	22	70	67	9	18	3	0	1	9	2	0	0	1	19	1	1	2.9	27.1
Sanchez, Jesus	L-R	6-3	222	10-07-97	.253	.327	.450	125	402	360	43	91	23	3	14	52	38	2	1	1	107	3	1	9.5	26.6
Segura, Jean	R-R	5-10	220	3-17-90	.219	.277	.279	85	326	301	25	66	5	2	3	21	22	2	1	0	47	6	2	6.7	14.4
Soler, Jorge	R-R	6-4	235	2-25-92	.250	.341	.512	137	580	504	77	126	24	0	36	75	66	6	0	4	141	1	0	11.4	24.3
Stallings, Jacob	R-R	6-5	225	12-22-89	.191	.278	.286	89	276	241	22	46	14	0	3	20	27	3	3	2	67	0	0	9.8	24.3
Wendle, Joey	L-R	6-1	195	4-26-90	.212	.248	.306	112	318	297	33	63	16	3	2	20	13	2	3	3	67	7	1	4.1	21.1

Pitching	B-T	Ht.	Wt.	DOB	W	L	ERA	G	GS	SV	IP	Hits	Runs	ER	HR	BB	SO	AVG	OBP	SLG	SO%	BB%	BF
Alcantara, Sandy	R-R	6-5	200	9-07-95	7	12	4.14	28	28	0	185	176	91	85	22	48	151	.251	.302	.391	19.8	6.3	762
Barnes, Matt	R-R	6-4	208	6-17-90	1	0	5.48	24	1	0	21	25	13	13	2	10	20	.284	.364	.386	20.2	10.1	99
Bradley, Archie	R-R	6-4	215	8-10-92	0	0	11.05	4	0	0	7	13	10	9	2	3	7	.371	.436	.657	17.9	7.7	39
Brazoban, Huascar	R-R	6-3	155	10-15-89	5	2	4.14	50	0	0	59	53	28	27	5	31	65	.243	.344	.349	25.3	12.1	257
Cabrera, Edward	R-R	6-5	217	4-13-98	7	7	4.24	22	20	0	100	78	48	47	11	66	118	.215	.341	.355	27.2	15.2	434
Castano, Daniel	L-L	6-3	231	9-17-94	0	0	21.00	2	0	0	3	7	8	7	2	3	4	.412	.500	.882	20.0	15.0	20
Chargois, JT	B-R	6-3	200	12-03-90	1	0	3.61	46	5	1	42	35	17	17	3	18	35	.232	.308	.377	20.1	10.3	174
Cueto, Johnny	R-R	5-11	229	2-15-86	1	4	6.02	13	10	0	52	51	36	35	17	15	39	.256	.317	.543	17.9	6.9	218
De Jesus, Enmanuel	L-L	6-3	190	12-10-96	0	0	11.37	2	0	0	6	9	8	8	0	4	5	.333	.471	.444	14.7	11.8	34
Floro, Dylan	L-R	6-2	203	12-27-90	3	5	4.54	43	0	7	40	48	24	20	2	11	41	.302	.351	.415	24.0	6.4	171
Garcia, Robert	R-L	6-4	225	6-14-96	0	0	0.00	1	0	0	0	1	0	0	0	1	0	.500	.667	.500	0.0	33.3	3
Garrett, Braxton	R-L	6-2	202	8-05-97	9	7	3.66	31	30	0	160	154	68	65	20	29	156	.250	.294	.420	23.7	4.4	659
Gonzalez, Chi Chi	R-R	6-3	210	1-15-92	0	0	7.36	3	0	0	4	7	3	3	1	1	3	.389	.421	.667	15.8	5.3	19
Hartlieb, Geoff	R-R	6-5	240	12-09-93	0	0	2.25	2	0	0	4	2	1	1	1	3	3	.154	.313	.385	18.8	18.8	16
Hoeing, Bryan	R-R	6-6	210	10-19-96	2	3	5.48	33	7	0	71	71	45	43	13	25	53	.259	.322	.504	17.4	8.2	304
Lindgren, Jeff	R-R	6-1	200	9-17-96	0	0	5.14	3	0	0	7	4	4	4	0	4	1	.167	.286	.292	3.6	14.3	28
Lopez, Jorge	R-R	6-3	200	2-10-93	2	0	9.26	12	0	0	12	20	13	12	1	9	8	.400	.475	.540	13.1	14.8	61
Luzardo, Jesus	L-L	6-0	218	9-30-97	10	10	3.58	32	32	0	179	162	79	71	22	55	208	.239	.301	.409	28.1	7.4	741
Moore, Matt	L-L	6-3	210	6-18-89	1	0	0.00	4	0	0	4	4	0	0	0	1	3	.250	.333	.375	16.7	5.6	18
Nardi, Andrew	L-L	6-3	215	8-18-98	8	1	2.67	63	0	3	57	45	18	17	7	21	73	.213	.297	.365	30.8	8.9	237
Nolin, Sean	L-L	6-4	250	12-26-89	0	0	18.00	1	0	0	3	7	6	6	2	2	2	.438	.500	1.000	11.1	11.1	18
Okert, Steven	L-L	6-2	202	7-09-91	3	2	4.45	64	2	0	59	50	31	29	9	24	73	.229	.310	.427	29.6	9.7	247
Perez, Eury	R-R	6-8	220	4-15-03	5	6	3.15	19	19	0	91	72	35	32	15	31	108	.214	.282	.424	28.9	8.3	374
Puk, A.J.	L-L	6-7	248	4-25-95	7	5	3.97	58	0	15	57	54	29	25	10	13	78	.241	.286	.420	32.2	5.4	242
Quezada, Johan	R-R	6-9	255	8-25-94	0	0	40.50	1	0	0	1	1	3	3	0	5	0	.500	.750	1.000	0.0	62.5	8
Robertson, David	R-R	5-11	195	4-09-85	2	4	5.06	22	0	4	21	22	15	12	2	12	30	.262	.361	.393	30.9	12.4	97
Rogers, Trevor	L-L	6-5	217	11-13-97	1	2	4.00	4	4	0	18	16	9	8	2	6	19	.229	.316	.329	24.1	7.6	79
Scott, Tanner	R-L	6-0	235	7-22-94	9	5	2.31	74	0	12	78	53	22	20	3	24	104	.191	.264	.264	33.9	7.8	307
Smeltzer, Devin	R-L	6-3	195	9-07-95	0	1	6.45	9	1	0	22	29	18	16	7	4	16	.315	.370	.609	16.0	4.0	100

Soriano, George	R-R	6-2	210	3-24-99	0	0	3.81	26	1	1	52	46	26	22	6	23	52	.234	.326	.371	22.8	10.1	228
Stallings, Jacob	R-R	6-5	225	12-22-89	0	0	4.50	7	0	0	8	12	4	4	1	0	1	.364	.389	.576	2.8	0.0	36
Weathers, Ryan	R-L	6-1	230	12-17-99	0	2	7.62	3	2	0	13	13	11	11	3	12	14	.277	.417	.596	23.0	19.7	61

Fielding

Catcher	PCT	G	PO	A	E	DP	PB
Fortes	.986	104	826	36	12	2	1
Stallings	.992	82	688	17	6	3	3

First Base	PCT	G	PO	A	E	DP
Arraez	1.000	12	75	2	0	12
Bell	.991	30	199	23	2	17
Cooper	.998	51	392	20	1	41
Gurriel	.997	93	569	32	2	64

Second Base	PCT	G	PO	A	E	DP
Amaya	1.000	1	1	0	0	0
Arraez	.993	134	219	315	4	93
Berti	.962	15	10	15	1	4
Edwards	1.000	24	24	35	0	12
Hampson	1.000	13	11	16	0	4

Third Base	PCT	G	PO	A	E	DP
Berti	.969	41	23	71	3	6
Burger	.952	49	28	92	6	8
Hampson	1.000	5	2	8	0	2
Segura	.954	84	45	163	10	16

Shortstop	PCT	G	PO	A	E	DP
Amaya	1.000	3	0	2	0	0
Berti	.966	64	60	138	7	33
Hampson	.980	30	36	60	2	12
Wendle	.970	107	107	218	10	46

Outfield	PCT	G	PO	A	E	DP
Berti	.485	19	31	1	1	1
Burdick	.667	15	14	0	0	0
Chisholm	.983	95	171	4	3	1
Davis	.667	34	51	0	0	0
De La Cruz	.994	164	277	7	5	3
Edwards	1.000	4	1	0	0	0
Garcia	1.000	34	45	1	0	0
Hampson	.980	57	50	2	2	1
Myers	1.000	21	46	0	0	0
Sanchez	.994	123	190	6	3	1
Soler	1.000	32	42	0	0	0

JACKSONVILLE JUMBO SHRIMP — *TRIPLE-A*

INTERNATIONAL LEAGUE

Batting	B-T	Ht.	Wt.	DOB	AVG	OBP	SLG	G	PA	AB	R	H	2B	3B	HR	RBI	BB	HBP	SH	SF	SO	SB	CS	BB%	SO%
Alfaro, Jorge	R-R	6-3	230	6-11-93	.200	.274	.262	18	73	65	3	13	4	0	0	6	5	2	0	1	17	0	0	6.8	23.3
2-team (43 Worcester)					.288	.345	.450	61	264	240	25	69	17	2	6	36	14	7	0	3	60	4	0	5.3	1.1
Allen, Austin	L-R	6-2	219	1-16-94	.225	.311	.491	91	366	324	49	73	15	1	23	67	36	5	0	1	84	0	0	9.8	23.0
Amaya, Jacob	R-R	6-0	180	9-03-98	.252	.345	.407	128	566	484	85	122	26	2	15	65	70	3	0	9	106	6	2	12.4	18.7
Burdick, Peyton	R-R	6-0	205	2-26-97	.219	.327	.448	114	492	420	63	92	20	2	24	74	57	12	0	3	180	12	2	11.6	36.6
Chavez, Santiago	R-R	5-11	205	8-05-95	.164	.266	.212	53	188	165	20	27	5	0	1	10	20	3	0	0	55	0	0	10.6	29.3
Chisholm, Jazz	L-R	5-11	184	2-01-98	.250	.438	.333	4	16	12	2	3	1	0	0	3	4	0	0	0	1	1	0	25.0	6.3
Conine, Griffin	L-R	6-1	210	7-11-97	.225	.297	.350	23	91	80	8	18	2	1	2	10	9	0	0	2	35	1	0	9.9	38.5
Cooper, Garrett	R-R	6-5	235	12-25-90	.000	.000	.000	1	4	4	0	0	0	0	0	0	0	0	0	0	1	0	0	0.0	25.0
De Goti, Alex	R-R	6-0	192	8-19-94	.133	.278	.333	4	18	15	3	2	0	0	1	4	3	0	0	0	4	0	0	16.7	22.2
2-team (51 St. Paul)					.179	.332	.276	55	193	156	29	28	9	0	2	13	33	3	1	0	52	2	1	17.1	26.9
Edwards, Xavier	B-R	5-10	175	8-09-99	.351	.429	.457	93	433	370	80	130	14	2	7	47	52	2	4	5	30	32	4	12.0	6.9
Encarnacion, Jerar	R-R	6-4	250	10-22-97	.228	.347	.452	122	516	434	63	99	17	1	26	76	78	2	0	2	200	6	2	15.1	38.8
Fletcher-Vance, Cobie	R-R	5-7	190	8-24-97	.214	.333	.321	17	66	56	6	12	3	0	1	7	9	1	0	0	14	0	0	13.6	21.2
Garcia, Avisail	R-R	6-4	250	6-12-91	.259	.375	.667	8	32	27	4	7	2	0	3	6	5	0	0	0	11	0	0	15.6	34.4
Groshans, Jordan	R-R	6-3	200	11-10-99	.243	.339	.330	125	528	460	60	112	20	1	6	60	66	1	0	1	92	0	0	12.5	17.4
Hampson, Garrett	R-R	5-11	196	10-10-94	.348	.412	.435	21	103	92	17	32	6	1	0	5	9	1	1	0	15	6	0	8.7	14.6
Hinojosa, C.J.	R-R	5-10	185	7-15-94	.244	.284	.357	91	360	336	37	82	13	2	7	38	20	0	1	3	59	5	2	5.6	16.4
Johnston, Troy	L-L	6-0	205	6-22-97	.323	.403	.520	51	226	198	31	64	13	1	8	33	20	7	0	1	44	8	1	8.8	19.5
Leblanc, Charles	R-R	6-3	195	6-03-96	.252	.384	.423	94	370	305	49	77	12	2	12	34	61	4	0	0	96	4	1	16.5	25.9
Livesey, Hudson	B-R	6-0	170	8-09-99	.000	.000	.000	2	2	2	0	0	0	0	0	0	0	0	0	0	2	0	0	0.0	100.0
Mangum, Jake	B-L	6-1	179	3-08-96	.298	.346	.425	119	515	473	62	141	29	8	5	52	28	9	0	5	91	16	6	5.4	17.7
McIntosh, Paul	R-R	6-1	220	11-20-97	.230	.333	.380	28	117	100	17	23	0	0	5	13	13	3	0	1	32	0	0	11.1	27.4
Mesa, Victor	R-R	5-11	200	7-20-96	.206	.270	.294	12	37	34	5	7	0	0	1	5	2	1	0	0	5	2	1	5.4	13.5
Miller, Brian	L-R	6-1	196	8-20-95	.241	.324	.322	81	312	270	34	65	10	3	2	30	32	3	3	4	65	18	6	10.3	20.8
Myers, Dane	R-R	6-0	205	3-08-96	.339	.417	.516	51	223	192	43	65	8	1	8	37	23	5	0	3	43	6	2	10.3	19.3
Rizzo, Joe	L-R	5-9	194	3-31-98	.111	.200	.139	11	40	36	3	4	1	0	0	1	4	0	0	0	12	0	0	10.0	30.0
2-team (38 Toledo)					.260	.326	.439	49	191	173	26	45	13	0	6	29	15	2	0	1	40	0	0	7.9	20.9
Sanchez, Jesus	L-R	6-3	222	10-07-97	.250	.308	.500	3	13	12	2	3	0	0	1	2	1	0	0	0	3	0	0	7.7	23.1
Santos, Angeudis	B-R	6-4	168	9-19-01	—	1.000	—	1	1	0	0	0	0	0	0	0	1	0	0	0	0	0	0	100.0	0.0
Wendle, Joey	L-R	6-1	195	4-26-90	.189	.189	.432	8	37	37	5	7	1	1	2	8	0	0	0	0	9	1	0	0.0	24.3

Pitching	B-T	Ht.	Wt.	DOB	W	L	ERA	G	GS	SV	IP	Hits	Runs	ER	HR	BB	SO	AVG	OBP	SLG	SO%	BB%	BF
Alcantara, Sandy	R-R	6-5	200	9-07-95	7	12	4.14	28	28	0	185	176	91	85	22	48	151	.251	.302	.391	19.8	6.3	762
Barnes, Matt	R-R	6-4	208	6-17-90	1	0	5.48	24	1	0	21	25	13	13	2	10	20	.284	.364	.386	20.2	10.1	99
Bradley, Archie	R-R	6-4	215	8-10-92	0	0	11.05	4	0	0	7	13	10	9	2	3	7	.371	.436	.657	17.9	7.7	39
Brazoban, Huascar	R-R	6-3	155	10-15-89	5	2	4.14	50	0	0	59	53	28	27	5	31	65	.243	.344	.349	25.3	12.1	257
Cabrera, Edward	R-R	6-5	217	4-13-98	7	7	4.24	22	20	0	100	78	48	47	11	66	118	.215	.341	.355	27.2	15.2	434
Castano, Daniel	L-L	6-3	231	9-17-94	0	0	21.00	2	0	0	3	7	8	7	2	3	4	.412	.500	.882	20.0	15.0	20
Chargois, JT	B-R	6-3	200	12-03-90	1	0	3.61	46	5	1	42	35	17	17	3	18	35	.232	.308	.377	20.1	10.3	174
Cueto, Johnny	R-R	5-11	229	2-15-86	1	4	6.02	13	10	0	52	51	36	35	17	15	39	.256	.317	.543	17.9	6.9	218
De Jesus, Enmanuel	L-L	6-3	190	12-10-96	0	0	11.37	2	0	0	6	9	8	8	0	4	5	.333	.471	.444	14.7	11.8	34
Floro, Dylan	L-R	6-2	203	12-27-90	3	5	4.54	43	0	7	40	48	24	20	2	11	41	.302	.351	.415	24.0	6.4	171
Garcia, Robert	R-L	6-4	225	6-14-96	0	0	0.00	1	0	0	0	1	0	0	0	1	0	.500	.667	.500	0.0	33.3	3
Garrett, Braxton	R-L	6-2	202	8-05-97	9	7	3.66	31	30	0	160	154	68	65	20	29	156	.250	.294	.420	23.7	4.4	659
Gonzalez, Chi Chi	R-R	6-3	210	1-15-92	0	0	7.36	3	0	0	4	7	3	3	1	1	3	.389	.421	.667	15.8	5.3	19
Hartlieb, Geoff	R-R	6-5	240	12-09-93	0	0	2.25	2	0	0	4	2	1	1	1	3	3	.154	.313	.385	18.8	18.8	16
Hoeing, Bryan	R-R	6-6	210	10-19-96	2	3	5.48	33	7	0	71	71	45	43	13	25	53	.259	.322	.504	17.4	8.2	304
Lindgren, Jeff	R-R	6-1	200	9-17-96	0	0	5.14	3	0	0	7	4	4	4	0	4	1	.167	.286	.292	3.6	14.3	28
Lopez, Jorge	R-R	6-3	200	2-10-93	2	0	9.26	12	0	0	12	20	13	12	1	9	8	.400	.475	.540	13.1	14.8	61
Luzardo, Jesus	L-L	6-0	218	9-30-97	10	10	3.58	32	32	0	179	162	79	71	22	55	208	.239	.301	.409	28.1	7.4	741
Moore, Matt	L-L	6-3	210	6-18-89	1	0	0.00	4	0	0	4	4	0	0	0	1	3	.250	.333	.375	16.7	5.6	18

Nardi, Andrew	L-L	6-3	215	8-18-98	8	1	2.67	63	0	3	57	45	18	17	7	21	73	.213	.297	.365	30.8	8.9	237
Nolin, Sean	L-L	6-4	250	12-26-89	0	0	18.00	1	0	0	3	7	6	6	2	2	2	.438	.500	1.000	11.1	11.1	18
Okert, Steven	L-L	6-2	202	7-09-91	3	2	4.45	64	2	0	59	50	31	29	9	24	73	.229	.310	.427	29.6	9.7	247
Perez, Eury	R-R	6-8	220	4-15-03	5	6	3.15	19	19	0	91	72	35	32	15	31	108	.214	.282	.424	28.9	8.3	374
Puk, A.J.	L-L	6-7	248	4-25-95	7	5	3.97	58	0	15	57	54	29	25	10	13	78	.241	.286	.420	32.2	5.4	242
Quezada, Johan	R-R	6-9	255	8-25-94	0	0	40.50	1	0	0	1	1	3	3	0	5	0	.500	.750	1.000	0.0	62.5	8
Robertson, David	R-R	5-11	195	4-09-85	2	4	5.06	22	0	4	21	22	15	12	2	12	30	.262	.361	.393	30.9	12.4	97
Rogers, Trevor	L-L	6-5	217	11-13-97	1	2	4.00	4	4	0	18	16	9	8	2	6	19	.229	.316	.329	24.1	7.6	79
Scott, Tanner	R-L	6-0	235	7-22-94	9	5	2.31	74	0	12	78	53	22	20	3	24	104	.191	.264	.264	33.9	7.8	307
Smeltzer, Devin	R-L	6-3	195	9-07-95	0	1	6.45	9	1	0	22	29	18	16	7	4	16	.315	.370	.609	16.0	4.0	100
Soriano, George	R-R	6-2	210	3-24-99	0	0	3.81	26	1	1	52	46	26	22	6	23	52	.234	.326	.371	22.8	10.1	228
Stallings, Jacob	R-R	6-5	225	12-22-89	0	0	4.50	7	0	0	8	12	4	4	1	0	1	.364	.389	.576	2.8	0.0	36
Weathers, Ryan	R-L	6-1	230	12-17-99	0	2	7.62	3	2	0	13	13	11	11	3	12	14	.277	.417	.596	23.0	19.7	61

Fielding

Catcher	PCT	G	PO	A	E	DP	PB
Alfaro	1.000	11	91	4	0	1	1
Allen	.995	72	539	26	3	5	5
Chavez	.996	53	414	35	2	4	8
McIntosh	.994	21	172	2	1	0	0

First Base	PCT	G	PO	A	E	DP
Allen	1.000	1	11	0	0	1
Cooper	1.000	1	4	0	0	1
Encarnacion	.979	23	169	15	4	28
Groshans	.994	41	309	22	2	42
Johnston	.986	47	334	23	5	39
Leblanc	.992	18	124	7	1	8
Myers	.989	12	88	6	1	12
Rizzo	1.000	8	51	6	0	5

Second Base	PCT	G	PO	A	E	DP
Amaya	1.000	10	23	15	0	8
Edwards	.982	46	63	105	3	24
Hampson	1.000	6	4	16	0	5
Hinojosa	.975	56	83	155	6	40
Leblanc	.986	35	51	85	2	27

Third Base	PCT	G	PO	A	E	DP
De Goti	1.000	2	3	3	0	0
Edwards	1.000	12	7	28	0	2
Fletcher-Vance	.962	10	11	14	1	5
Groshans	.926	77	48	140	15	13
Hampson	1.000	2	2	2	0	0
Hinojosa	1.000	11	7	12	0	3
Leblanc	.886	31	20	50	9	7
Myers	.882	5	5	10	2	1
Rizzo	1.000	1	1	3	0	1

Shortstop	PCT	G	PO	A	E	DP
Amaya	.968	118	157	269	14	78
De Goti	1.000	1	0	1	0	0
Edwards	.923	4	6	6	1	3
Hampson	.893	5	9	16	3	3
Hinojosa	.984	19	19	41	1	13
Wendle	1.000	6	3	12	0	2

Outfield	PCT	G	PO	A	E	DP
Burdick	.989	94	192	11	3	3
Chisholm	.933	4	13	1	1	1
Conine	.974	23	49	2	1	0
Edwards	1.000	30	60	1	0	0
Encarnacion	.964	73	152	9	6	1
Garcia	1.000	7	13	2	0	2
Hampson	1.000	6	19	0	0	0
Leblanc	1.000	3	3	0	0	0
Mangum	.995	111	272	5	1	0
Mesa	1.000	11	27	0	0	0
Miller	.992	62	108	3	2	1
Myers	.991	29	62	0	1	0
Sanchez	1.000	2	4	1	0	0

PENSACOLA BLUE WAHOOS — *DOUBLE-A*

SOUTHERN LEAGUE

Batting	B-T	Ht.	Wt.	DOB	AVG	OBP	SLG	G	PA	AB	R	H	2B	3B	HR	RBI	BB	HBP	SH	SF	SO	SB	CS	BB%	SO%
Allen, Tanner	L-R	5-11	190	6-05-98	.274	.297	.323	17	64	62	4	17	0	0	1	4	2	0	0	0	10	0	0	3.1	15.6
Banfield, Will	R-R	6-0	215	11-18-99	.258	.302	.472	115	495	458	70	118	25	2	23	76	25	6	1	5	122	3	0	5.1	24.6
Berry, Jacob	B-R	6-0	212	5-05-01	.248	.301	.442	28	123	113	22	28	5	1	5	22	9	0	0	1	26	5	0	7.3	21.1
Bradshaw, Davis	L-R	6-2	175	4-25-98	.290	.353	.355	10	34	31	2	9	0	1	0	0	2	1	0	0	5	0	0	5.9	14.7
Castillo, Kyler	R-R	5-9	185	10-29-97	.286	.333	.286	5	15	14	0	4	0	0	0	0	1	0	0	0	2	1	0	6.7	13.3
Conine, Griffin	L-R	6-1	210	7-11-97	.253	.370	.493	87	353	292	52	74	14	1	18	62	47	9	0	3	120	1	1	13.3	34.0
Devers, Jose	L-R	6-0	174	12-07-99	.276	.352	.421	96	420	373	61	103	21	6	7	46	36	8	2	1	62	5	2	8.6	14.8
Estrada, Jose	R-R	5-8	175	5-05-00	.222	.364	.333	3	11	9	1	2	1	0	0	0	2	0	0	0	3	0	0	18.2	27.3
Fletcher-Vance, Cobie	R-R	5-7	190	8-24-97	.257	.314	.382	41	156	144	19	37	12	0	2	16	9	3	0	0	36	0	0	5.8	23.1
Garcia, Avisail	R-R	6-4	250	6-12-91	.176	.333	.412	5	21	17	4	3	1	0	1	3	3	1	0	0	5	0	0	14.3	23.8
Gonzalez, Norel	L-R	6-1	240	6-26-94	.245	.348	.397	71	276	237	29	58	8	2	8	32	34	4	0	1	61	1	1	12.3	22.1
Hostetler, Bennett	R-R	6-0	195	9-23-97	.249	.371	.481	71	279	233	38	58	12	0	14	42	37	8	1	0	69	5	1	13.3	24.7
Johnston, Troy	L-L	6-0	205	6-22-97	.296	.396	.567	83	374	314	71	93	23	4	18	83	42	12	1	3	64	16	1	11.2	17.1
Marinez, Ynmanol	R-R	5-11	190	4-12-01	.167	.211	.278	5	19	18	2	3	2	0	0	2	1	0	0	0	6	0	0	5.3	31.6
McIntosh, Paul	R-R	6-1	220	11-20-97	.255	.373	.445	38	166	137	24	35	2	0	8	26	23	4	0	2	34	3	2	13.9	20.5
Mercado, Jan	R-R	6-0	200	8-28-99	.353	.450	.588	5	20	17	3	6	1	0	1	7	3	0	0	0	5	0	0	15.0	25.0
Mesa, Victor	L-L	6-0	195	9-08-01	.242	.308	.412	123	533	483	73	117	24	2	18	76	41	6	1	2	122	16	3	7.7	22.9
Mesa, Victor	R-R	5-11	200	7-20-96	.000	.000	.000	1	3	3	1	0	0	0	0	0	0	0	0	0	0	0	0	0.0	0.0
Morissette, Cody	L-R	6-0	175	1-16-00	.223	.282	.399	105	434	391	58	87	17	2	16	52	31	4	2	6	108	3	2	7.1	24.9
Myers, Dane	R-R	6-0	205	3-08-96	.291	.395	.462	49	215	182	34	53	6	2	7	25	27	5	0	1	37	14	1	12.6	17.2
Nunez, Nasim	B-R	5-9	168	8-18-00	.224	.341	.286	125	585	490	84	110	11	2	5	43	87	2	2	4	107	52	7	14.9	18.3
Orr, J.D.	L-L	5-10	185	9-11-96	.197	.347	.226	50	171	137	25	27	2	1	0	10	28	4	1	1	41	13	4	16.4	24.0
Rizzo, Joe	L-R	5-9	194	3-31-98	.228	.298	.362	32	142	127	20	29	8	0	3	21	13	0	0	1	31	1	0	9.2	21.8
Rosario, Dalvy	R-R	6-0	185	7-22-00	.223	.296	.337	62	208	184	30	41	6	0	5	20	16	4	2	2	50	11	4	7.7	24.0
Thompson, Jake	L-R	6-0	207	3-03-98	.271	.379	.417	14	58	48	6	13	1	0	2	9	9	0	0	1	11	0	0	15.5	19.0
Zamora, Joshua	R-R	5-10	190	5-18-99	.300	.349	.450	12	43	40	5	12	3	0	1	5	2	1	0	0	6	1	0	4.7	14.0

Pitching	B-T	Ht.	Wt.	DOB	W	L	ERA	G	GS	SV	IP	Hits	Runs	ER	HR	BB	SO	AVG	OBP	SLG	SO%	BB%	BF
Alcantara, Sandy	R-R	6-5	200	9-07-95	0	0	0.00	1	1	0	4	1	0	0	0	0	4	.077	.077	.077	30.8	0.0	13
Bice, Dylan	L-R	6-5	245	8-17-97	0	3	5.00	20	2	2	27	30	16	15	4	13	16	.280	.352	.449	13.0	10.6	123
Bolanos, Ronald	R-R	6-2	230	8-23-96	3	10	8.63	16	15	0	66	86	68	63	8	48	48	.322	.432	.517	14.5	14.5	331
Bradley, Archie	R-R	6-4	215	8-10-92	0	2	5.47	14	1	1	26	22	16	16	5	11	21	.229	.324	.458	18.9	9.9	111
Brazoban, Huascar	R-R	6-3	155	10-15-89	1	0	10.13	2	0	0	3	5	3	3	0	1	3	.417	.462	.583	23.1	7.7	13
Burgos, Enrique	R-R	6-3	255	11-23-90	1	1	16.20	3	0	0	3	7	8	6	1	3	4	.412	.500	.706	20.0	15.0	20
Cabrera, Edward	R-R	6-5	217	4-13-98	3	1	2.22	5	5	0	28	20	7	7	2	12	30	.202	.292	.293	26.5	10.6	113
Castano, Daniel	L-L	6-3	231	9-17-94	5	2	4.67	17	9	0	62	55	38	32	10	26	58	.235	.310	.419	21.6	9.7	268
Castillo, Jose	L-L	6-6	252	1-10-96	3	1	5.59	14	0	0	19	18	12	12	1	13	26	.254	.375	.408	29.5	14.8	88

Chargois, JT	B-R	6-3	200	12-03-90	0	0	0.00	3	0	0	4	1	0	0	0	1	5	.091	.167	.091	41.7	8.3	12
Charle, Cristian	R-R	6-1	208	6-02-00	0	0	0.00	1	0	0	1	4	4	0	0	1	1	.500	.556	.500	11.1	11.1	9
Cueto, Johnny	R-R	5-11	229	2-15-86	0	0	11.51	5	5	0	23	38	30	29	15	6	13	.376	.427	.881	11.8	5.5	110
De Jesus, Enmanuel	L-L	6-3	190	12-10-96	4	5	4.78	17	16	1	85	92	49	45	9	51	61	.286	.389	.450	15.9	13.3	384
Encarnacion, Breidy	R-R	6-3	185	11-09-00	0	0	10.80	1	0	0	2	2	2	2	1	2	0	.286	.545	1.000	0.0	18.2	11
Enright, Nic	R-R	6-3	205	1-08-97	1	0	3.97	7	0	0	11	11	5	5	2	1	11	.244	.261	.489	23.9	2.2	46
Garcia, Robert	R-L	6-4	225	6-14-96	2	0	2.85	31	1	2	41	33	15	13	4	22	62	.226	.341	.356	35.4	12.6	175
Gonzalez, Chi Chi	R-R	6-3	210	1-15-92	6	9	6.07	24	23	0	122	160	94	82	23	34	71	.318	.366	.535	13.0	6.2	547
Hartlieb, Geoff	R-R	6-5	240	12-09-93	2	6	3.63	35	0	7	45	41	25	18	4	18	46	.237	.316	.347	23.8	9.3	193
Hoeing, Bryan	R-R	6-6	210	10-19-96	1	0	2.35	7	4	0	31	25	10	8	3	4	37	.219	.246	.386	30.8	3.3	120
Leban, Zack	R-R	6-2	235	5-30-96	0	0	5.29	12	0	1	17	6	11	10	0	20	21	.111	.372	.148	26.9	25.6	78
Lindgren, Jeff	R-R	6-1	200	9-17-96	6	6	4.88	22	17	0	87	73	49	47	15	47	59	.231	.335	.443	15.8	12.6	373
Lowe, Collin	R-R	6-4	210	9-11-98	0	1	11.57	2	1	0	5	9	6	6	2	4	3	.429	.520	.810	12.0	16.0	25
Maldonado, Anthony	R-R	6-4	220	2-06-98	7	3	1.76	34	0	9	46	23	11	9	5	21	71	.148	.257	.265	39.4	11.7	180
Monteverde, Patrick	R-L	6-2	200	9-24-97	1	1	15.58	2	2	0	9	15	15	15	4	6	7	.375	.438	.775	14.6	12.5	48
Nance, Tommy	R-R	6-6	235	3-19-91	0	0	4.50	2	0	0	2	3	1	1	0	1	1	.375	.444	.500	11.1	11.1	9
Nardi, Andrew	L-L	6-3	215	8-18-98	0	0	10.80	3	0	0	2	1	2	2	0	3	3	.167	.500	.167	30.0	30.0	10
Nolin, Sean	L-L	6-4	250	12-26-89	1	1	4.37	5	5	0	23	24	12	11	6	7	22	.267	.327	.533	22.4	7.1	98
Okert, Steven	L-L	6-2	202	7-09-91	0	0	0.00	4	0	0	6	4	0	0	0	1	11	.190	.227	.238	50.0	4.5	22
Palacios, Luis	L-L	6-2	160	7-01-00	1	1	5.28	3	3	0	15	16	9	9	6	3	12	.276	.323	.638	19.4	4.8	62
Puckett, Brady	R-R	6-9	250	7-31-95	0	0	10.80	3	0	0	5	6	6	6	1	8	3	.300	.517	.500	10.3	27.6	29
Quezada, Johan	R-R	6-9	255	8-25-94	4	2	4.39	26	0	2	41	43	21	20	5	28	41	.279	.390	.422	21.8	14.9	188
Reynolds, Sean	L-R	6-8	250	4-19-98	2	0	3.50	14	0	3	18	14	8	7	1	7	17	.215	.293	.292	22.7	9.3	75
Roberts, Austin	R-R	6-0	205	7-27-98	1	2	7.18	20	0	0	31	39	26	25	3	20	38	.300	.403	.408	24.7	13.0	154
Rodriguez, Richard	R-R	6-4	220	3-04-90	2	1	4.38	39	0	0	64	63	35	31	5	20	43	.258	.319	.402	15.8	7.3	273
Rogers, Trevor	L-L	6-5	217	11-13-97	1	0	0.00	1	1	0	5	1	0	0	0	1	5	.063	.118	.063	29.4	5.9	17
Rose, Jackson	R-R	6-2	185	4-25-96	1	0	4.91	14	0	1	26	21	17	14	4	16	32	.231	.336	.407	28.1	14.0	114
Simpson, Josh	L-L	6-2	190	8-19-97	1	1	4.19	25	0	0	34	30	19	16	4	23	59	.229	.346	.382	37.6	14.6	157
Smeltzer, Devin	R-L	6-3	195	9-07-95	5	10	6.38	20	20	0	86	99	74	61	20	48	70	.292	.378	.552	17.8	12.2	394
Soriano, George	R-R	6-2	210	3-24-99	1	2	5.33	17	5	0	25	29	16	15	3	14	27	.284	.375	.480	22.3	11.6	121
Stewart, Will	L-L	6-2	190	7-14-97	0	1	4.24	11	0	1	17	18	8	8	0	18	7	.286	.434	.365	8.4	21.7	83
Villalobos, Eli	R-R	6-4	195	6-26-97	0	1	4.43	16	0	1	22	23	12	11	4	25	23	.271	.434	.435	20.4	22.1	113
Walters, Jacob	R-R	6-0	190	3-11-96	0	4	6.95	18	6	0	56	54	44	43	10	42	52	.255	.396	.448	19.6	15.8	265
Weathers, Ryan	R-L	6-1	230	12-17-99	4	0	2.54	7	7	0	39	28	11	11	4	14	38	.209	.282	.343	25.5	9.4	149
Yan, Jefry	L-L	6-3	185	8-17-96	0	2	15.00	6	0	0	6	8	10	10	1	9	11	.308	.514	.500	29.7	24.3	37

Fielding

Catcher	PCT	G	PO	A	E	DP	PB
Banfield	.994	81	771	43	5	3	6
Estrada	1.000	3	29	2	0	0	0
Hostetler	.991	27	223	10	2	2	8
McIntosh	.995	20	192	6	1	2	3
Mercado	.979	5	43	3	1	0	0

First Base	PCT	G	PO	A	E	DP
Berry	1.000	17	130	8	0	10
Hostetler	.990	36	268	17	3	18
Johnston	.988	75	534	52	7	61
Marinez	1.000	2	16	2	0	1
Rizzo	.983	8	52	6	1	4

Second Base	PCT	G	PO	A	E	DP
Devers	.935	34	60	70	9	22
Morissette	.968	73	82	190	9	50
Nunez	.971	29	43	58	3	10
Zamora	1.000	5	0	10	0	2

Third Base	PCT	G	PO	A	E	DP
Berry	.864	9	6	13	3	0
Devers	.939	17	10	36	3	5
Fletcher-Vance	.946	37	34	53	5	8
Hostetler	.923	4	4	8	1	0
Marinez	1.000	3	0	7	0	1
Morissette	.938	25	19	41	4	5
Myers	.889	11	8	16	3	0
Rizzo	.961	22	11	38	2	6
Rosario	.960	9	9	15	1	4
Zamora	.800	3	2	2	1	0

Shortstop	PCT	G	PO	A	E	DP
Devers	.960	35	46	73	5	15
Fletcher-Vance	.909	3	2	8	1	0
Nunez	.965	95	163	228	14	54
Zamora	1.000	4	6	8	0	0

Outfield	PCT	G	PO	A	E	DP
Allen	1.000	18	23	2	0	1
Bradshaw	1.000	9	14	0	0	0
Castillo	1.000	5	8	0	0	0
Conine	.960	87	123	6	6	2
Garcia	.750	3	3	0	1	0
Gonzalez	.985	37	62	4	1	1
McIntosh	1.000	2	4	1	0	1
Mesa	.997	120	276	11	3	1
Myers	.987	38	60	2	1	0
Orr	1.000	47	73	4	0	0
Rosario	.646	50	85	8	3	1
Thompson	1.000	11	16	1	0	0

BELOIT SKY CARP — HIGH CLASS A

MIDWEST LEAGUE

Batting	B-T	Ht.	Wt.	DOB	AVG	OBP	SLG	G	PA	AB	R	H	2B	3B	HR	RBI	BB	HBP	SH	SF	SO	SB	CS	BB%	SO%
Allen, Brady	R-L	6-1	218	9-03-99	.256	.324	.440	37	142	125	17	32	12	1	3	18	13	1	0	3	34	1	1	9.2	23.9
2-team (82 West Michigan)					.262	.365	.472	119	503	428	72	112	30	3	18	65	62	8	0	5	123	5	1	12.3	1.0
Allen, Tanner	L-R	5-11	190	6-05-98	.264	.358	.429	62	266	231	33	61	10	2	8	30	32	2	1	0	39	5	1	12.0	14.7
Barstad, Cameron	L-R	6-1	195	11-29-00	.236	.315	.385	52	181	161	21	38	13	1	3	28	17	2	0	1	55	0	0	9.4	30.4
Berry, Jacob	B-R	6-0	212	5-05-01	.227	.278	.369	79	345	317	28	72	19	7	4	37	16	8	0	4	70	5	1	4.6	20.3
Bradshaw, Davis	L-R	6-2	175	4-25-98	.317	.387	.410	76	301	268	45	85	10	3	3	30	21	10	1	1	54	3	4	7.0	17.9
Caballero, Jorge	R-R	6-0	170	1-10-00	.254	.348	.325	38	132	114	23	29	8	0	0	13	15	2	0	1	45	0	0	11.4	34.1
Cappe, Yiddi	R-R	6-3	175	9-17-02	.220	.250	.308	123	536	509	53	112	26	2	5	53	18	4	0	5	102	18	9	3.4	19.0
Castillo, Kyler	R-R	5-9	185	10-29-97	.327	.393	.442	18	61	52	4	17	4	1	0	6	7	0	0	2	11	0	0	11.5	18.0
Estrada, Jose	R-R	5-8	175	5-05-00	.333	.333	.333	2	6	6	1	2	0	0	0	0	0	0	0	0	1	0	0	0.0	16.7
Fernandez, Andrew	R-R	6-3	196	10-19-98	.125	.176	.313	7	17	16	2	2	0	0	1	2	1	0	0	0	6	0	0	5.9	35.3
Hostetler, Bennett	R-R	6-0	195	9-23-97	.129	.206	.161	9	35	31	3	4	1	0	0	5	1	2	1	0	8	0	0	2.9	22.9
Ignoffo, Ryan	R-R	5-10	215	7-21-00	.304	.360	.391	6	25	23	2	7	2	0	0	1	2	0	0	0	3	1	0	8.0	12.0
Johnson, Osiris	R-R	6-0	198	10-18-00	.248	.311	.390	82	272	246	31	61	11	0	8	34	22	1	2	1	80	6	2	8.1	29.4
Luttrell, Chase	L-L	6-0	200	6-01-00	.143	.191	.206	22	70	63	6	9	4	0	0	4	3	1	2	1	14	0	0	4.3	20.0

Mack, Joe	L-R	6-1	210	12-27-02	.218	.295	.287	120	503	449	46	98	13	0	6	36	42	8	1	3	118	0	0	8.3	23.5
Marinez, Ynmanol	R-R	5-11	190	4-12-01	.199	.272	.309	78	283	256	29	51	14	1	4	27	25	1	0	1	90	0	0	8.8	31.8
Montgomery, Torin	R-R	6-3	230	5-02-01	.214	.304	.282	35	148	131	11	28	6	0	1	12	16	1	0	0	35	1	0	10.8	23.6
Rodriguez, Cristhian	L-R	6-3	160	12-23-01	.145	.217	.210	27	69	62	9	9	1	0	1	6	6	0	0	1	30	0	0	8.7	43.5
Rosario, Dalvy	R-R	6-0	185	7-22-00	.221	.276	.287	53	214	195	25	43	5	1	2	21	15	1	0	3	68	9	3	7.0	31.8
Sanoja, Javier	R-R	5-7	150	9-03-02	.267	.324	.351	30	142	131	10	35	2	0	3	10	10	1	0	0	10	6	6	7.0	7.0
Santos, Angeudis	B-R	6-4	168	9-19-01	.160	.344	.280	19	32	25	10	4	0	0	1	3	7	0	0	0	10	0	0	21.9	31.3
Thompson, Jake	L-R	6-0	207	3-03-98	.279	.386	.516	89	339	287	57	80	14	3	16	44	38	13	0	1	61	6	0	11.2	18.0
Watson, Kahlil	L-R	5-10	178	4-16-03	.206	.337	.362	58	243	199	26	41	10	0	7	22	35	6	0	3	68	14	2	14.4	28.0
2-team (23 Lake County)					.214	.333	.386	81	341	285	41	61	13	0	12	38	43	8	0	5	92	25	3	12.6	27.0
Zamora, Joshua	R-R	5-10	190	5-18-99	.230	.292	.338	92	326	296	36	68	14	0	6	37	20	7	1	2	44	1	0	6.1	13.5
Zubia, Zach	R-R	6-4	230	11-04-97	.279	.415	.451	79	282	226	38	63	9	0	10	34	50	4	0	2	77	0	1	17.7	27.3

Pitching	B-T	Ht.	Wt.	DOB	W	L	ERA	G	GS	SV	IP	Hits	Runs	ER	HR	BB	SO	AVG	OBP	SLG	SO%	BB%	BF
Arias, Luarbert	R-R	6-2	176	12-12-00	2	1	1.93	25	0	1	37	27	11	8	5	12	49	.197	.272	.372	32.5	7.9	151
Bierman, Gabe	R-R	6-2	200	9-03-99	5	4	3.46	19	19	0	91	67	40	35	3	37	68	.204	.292	.317	18.2	9.9	373
Buxton, Ike	R-R	6-3	208	7-18-00	2	2	3.71	7	7	0	34	31	15	14	3	15	23	.235	.318	.333	15.5	10.1	148
Charle, Cristian	R-R	6-1	208	6-02-00	1	4	3.48	14	0	2	21	20	9	8	2	9	20	.263	.341	.461	23.5	10.6	85
Crigger, Kyle	R-R	6-2	180	6-04-99	5	2	4.59	33	0	3	51	59	30	26	5	16	48	.286	.345	.437	21.1	7.0	227
Eckberg, Tyler	R-R	6-4	220	9-04-97	2	1	3.53	39	0	3	64	74	33	25	6	10	60	.291	.316	.457	21.7	3.6	276
Encarnacion, Breidy	R-R	6-3	185	11-09-00	1	0	3.18	20	0	1	34	30	13	12	2	14	42	.233	.306	.395	29.2	9.7	144
Fitterer, Evan	R-R	6-3	192	6-26-00	2	1	2.87	3	3	0	16	10	6	5	1	12	18	.175	.329	.281	25.7	17.1	70
Gibson, Cade	L-L	6-2	195	2-18-98	4	7	5.18	16	13	0	83	92	57	48	9	27	66	.281	.349	.440	18.1	7.4	364
Givin, Matt	R-R	6-3	180	6-17-99	3	0	3.63	26	0	0	40	36	20	16	2	13	34	.240	.315	.367	20.2	7.7	168
Jimenez, Yeuris	R-R	6-3	218	3-23-01	2	2	6.22	40	0	0	55	49	41	38	2	39	56	.237	.373	.348	21.9	15.2	256
Jones, Holt	R-R	6-8	235	5-08-99	0	4	8.78	10	6	0	27	29	27	26	2	22	20	.276	.421	.390	15.0	16.5	133
Jozwiak, Chandler	L-L	6-0	185	2-15-99	1	1	3.07	31	0	8	44	38	16	15	2	11	36	.232	.289	.341	19.9	6.1	181
King, Zach	L-L	6-6	228	4-30-98	5	9	6.35	22	13	0	72	87	54	51	6	39	63	.301	.398	.474	18.3	11.3	344
Mendez, Josan	R-R	6-2	180	7-10-00	0	0	0.00	1	0	0	2	0	0	0	0	1	1	.000	.143	.000	14.3	14.3	7
Mercedes, Jorge	R-R	6-3	185	7-01-00	0	1	40.50	3	0	0	1	3	7	6	0	5	3	.429	.667	.429	25.0	41.7	12
Milbrandt, Karson	R-R	6-2	190	4-21-04	0	3	4.60	11	11	0	43	46	25	22	1	24	41	.274	.364	.381	21.0	12.3	195
Mokma, Chris	R-R	6-4	210	2-11-01	0	1	9.86	14	1	0	21	33	24	23	0	11	19	.355	.417	.527	17.4	10.1	109
Palacios, Luis	L-L	6-2	160	7-01-00	1	1	1.80	3	3	0	20	12	5	4	2	2	17	.167	.197	.264	22.4	2.6	76
Poland, Jared	R-R	6-0	215	1-12-00	5	6	4.94	19	19	0	98	103	61	54	19	31	92	.268	.330	.510	21.9	7.4	421
Pushard, Matt	R-R	6-4	245	10-27-97	1	1	1.21	17	0	6	22	13	6	3	0	5	29	.157	.202	.217	32.6	5.6	89
Rodriguez, Eliezer	L-L	6-1	160	2-17-99	0	0	54.00	2	0	0	2	6	10	10	1	4	2	.545	.667	.909	13.3	26.7	15
Sanchez, Edgar	R-R	6-1	190	8-02-00	1	4	6.38	19	9	0	42	38	37	30	5	29	36	.238	.369	.425	18.1	14.6	199
Sanchez, Franklin	R-R	6-6	183	9-12-00	3	1	6.90	28	0	0	30	30	30	23	3	39	35	.265	.469	.398	21.9	24.4	160
Schrand, Jake	R-R	6-0	180	8-08-99	1	0	6.84	16	1	0	25	31	20	19	3	9	21	.313	.363	.515	18.6	8.0	113
Stewart, Will	L-L	6-2	190	7-14-97	1	0	0.00	2	0	0	3	3	0	0	0	1	0	.333	.400	.333	0.0	10.0	10
White, Josh	R-R	6-1	205	11-24-00	1	7	4.65	15	5	0	31	26	21	16	3	23	21	.226	.364	.348	15.0	16.4	140
Williams, Alex	L-R	6-3	220	10-22-99	2	8	5.06	21	21	0	100	97	57	56	16	35	107	.254	.330	.437	25.0	8.2	428
Wurster, Caleb	L-L	5-11	182	9-21-98	5	4	2.47	35	0	4	55	31	15	15	3	31	72	.168	.303	.266	32.4	14.0	222

Fielding

Catcher	PCT	G	PO	A	E	DP	PB
Barstad	.991	38	296	20	3	0	5
Estrada	1.000	2	18	2	0	0	0
Fernandez	1.000	5	29	3	0	1	0
Hostetler	.983	7	52	6	1	0	1
Mack	.989	85	724	71	9	6	4

First Base	PCT	G	PO	A	E	DP
Berry	1.000	19	136	13	0	20
Hostetler	1.000	1	5	0	0	0
Marinez	.983	23	153	17	3	9
Montgomery	.982	34	243	23	5	23
Rodriguez	1.000	5	4	0	0	0
Thompson	.983	26	154	16	3	23
Zamora	.990	13	90	10	1	8
Zubia	.989	29	167	20	2	11

Second Base	PCT	G	PO	A	E	DP
Cappe	.959	90	149	225	16	49
Ignoffo	.833	3	1	4	1	0
Marinez	1.000	1	1	1	0	1
Rosario	1.000	2	2	2	0	0
Sanoja	.952	5	10	10	1	2
Santos	.857	3	2	4	1	0
Watson	1.000	10	10	19	0	3
Zamora	.991	26	44	65	1	18

Third Base	PCT	G	PO	A	E	DP
Berry	.905	63	46	116	17	6
Marinez	.942	52	34	64	6	8
Rodriguez	.926	12	6	19	2	2
Santos	.000	1	0	0	0	0
Zamora	.935	19	14	29	3	1

Shortstop	PCT	G	PO	A	E	DP
Cappe	.935	35	48	68	8	18
Rodriguez	.927	9	15	23	3	3
Rosario	1.000	2	4	4	0	0
Sanoja	.976	14	20	20	1	6
Watson	.918	46	54	69	11	22
Zamora	.957	37	54	81	6	20

Outfield	PCT	G	PO	A	E	DP
Allen, B	.667	38	81	6	0	1
Allen, T	.980	63	79	1	2	0
Bradshaw	.661	70	113	5	2	1
Caballero	.991	36	65	2	1	0
Castillo	1.000	12	19	0	0	0
Ignoffo	1.000	3	9	0	0	0
Johnson	.656	83	188	8	2	3
Luttrell	.667	22	22	0	0	0
Rosario	.970	52	127	2	4	0
Sanoja	.949	16	35	2	2	2
Santos	1.000	9	12	0	0	0
Thompson	1.000	40	76	7	0	0

JUPITER HAMMERHEADS

LOW CLASS A

FLORIDA STATE LEAGUE

Batting	B-T	Ht.	Wt.	DOB	AVG	OBP	SLG	G	PA	AB	R	H	2B	3B	HR	RBI	BB	HBP	SH	SF	SO	SB	CS	BB%	SO%
Alderman, Kemp	R-R	6-3	265	8-20-02	.205	.286	.316	34	133	117	13	24	8	1	1	15	7	7	0	2	39	4	0	5.3	29.3
Allen, Tanner	L-R	5-11	190	6-05-98	.296	.333	.389	15	57	54	10	16	1	2	0	7	2	1	0	0	10	3	1	3.5	17.5
Barstad, Cameron	L-R	6-1	195	11-29-00	.164	.268	.262	18	71	61	3	10	3	0	1	7	8	1	0	1	27	1	0	11.3	38.0
Bramwell, Spencer	R-R	5-11	220	1-10-99	.190	.314	.310	31	70	58	9	11	4	0	1	4	10	1	0	1	26	1	0	14.3	37.1
Bullard, Tony	R-R	6-4	212	2-17-00	.152	.253	.273	22	76	66	10	10	0	1	2	4	8	1	1	0	16	4	1	10.5	21.1
Caballero, Jorge	R-R	6-0	170	1-10-00	.330	.409	.445	60	247	218	40	72	10	3	3	32	26	3	0	0	47	8	3	10.5	19.0
Castillo, Kyler	R-R	5-9	185	10-29-97	.000	.250	.000	1	4	3	1	0	0	0	0	0	1	0	0	0	1	0	0	25.0	25.0

Chisholm, Jazz	L-R	5-11	184	2-01-98	.500	.667	1.000	1	3	2	0	1	1	0	0	1	1	0	0	0	1	1	0	33.3	33.3
Coley, Mark	R-R	6-2	193	11-22-00	.265	.395	.480	33	122	98	20	26	8	2	3	17	16	5	3	0	36	9	1	13.1	29.5
DeLeo, Jake	R-R	6-2	194	5-30-01	.227	.302	.383	41	159	141	20	32	6	2	4	20	14	2	0	2	41	14	0	8.8	25.8
Fernandez, Andrew	R-R	6-3	196	10-19-98	.175	.242	.188	26	91	80	6	14	1	0	0	8	7	1	0	3	24	0	0	7.7	26.4
Hidalgo, Renny	R-R	5-9	165	9-05-02	.258	.395	.419	13	39	31	8	8	2	0	1	3	7	0	1	0	10	1	0	17.9	25.6
Lewis, Ian	B-R	5-11	177	2-04-03	.225	.304	.333	115	477	423	70	95	19	6	5	44	44	5	3	2	98	33	10	9.2	20.5
Luttrell, Chase	L-L	6-0	200	6-01-00	.244	.313	.385	80	311	275	39	67	16	1	7	40	27	2	4	3	64	8	7	8.7	20.6
McCants, Jordan	L-R	6-0	165	5-21-02	.225	.304	.286	111	483	426	66	96	12	4	2	35	48	2	3	4	131	36	4	9.9	27.1
McIntosh, Paul	R-R	6-1	220	11-20-97	.238	.347	.429	11	49	42	4	10	5	0	1	7	7	0	0	0	19	0	0	14.3	38.8
Mercado, Jan	R-R	6-0	200	8-28-99	.189	.295	.315	36	129	111	14	21	6	1	2	13	15	2	0	1	52	1	1	11.6	40.3
Montgomery, Torin	R-R	6-3	230	5-02-01	.341	.481	.486	63	237	185	36	63	14	2	3	32	42	9	0	1	47	4	3	17.7	19.8
Morissette, Cody	L-R	6-0	175	1-16-00	.118	.237	.176	14	59	51	5	6	0	0	1	2	6	2	0	0	9	1	1	10.2	15.3
Olmstead, Johnny	R-R	6-2	185	7-10-00	.288	.345	.442	14	58	52	8	15	5	0	1	7	4	1	0	1	13	4	1	6.9	22.4
Praytor, Sam	R-R	5-9	205	4-04-99	.170	.244	.305	45	158	141	19	24	7	0	4	14	12	2	2	1	42	1	0	7.6	26.6
Roberts, Brett	R-R	6-0	182	3-12-01	.273	.317	.387	91	373	344	58	94	16	4	5	45	22	2	1	4	77	20	2	5.9	20.6
Rodriguez, Cristhian	L-R	6-3	160	12-23-01	.222	.309	.339	58	195	171	20	38	7	5	1	20	17	5	1	1	58	8	2	8.7	29.7
Sanoja, Javier	R-R	5-7	150	9-03-02	.308	.356	.400	102	434	400	51	123	18	8	1	57	31	0	1	2	32	31	16	7.1	7.4
Santiago, Carlos	B-R	5-11	145	7-24-01	.212	.288	.370	44	163	146	17	31	9	1	4	23	15	1	0	1	38	5	3	9.2	23.3
Spohn, Harrison	R-R	6-1	185	12-03-98	.244	.329	.393	92	353	308	36	75	14	1	10	49	40	1	0	4	76	8	4	11.3	21.5
Vradenburg, Brock	L-R	6-7	230	3-20-02	.236	.368	.291	34	133	110	15	26	3	0	1	10	22	1	0	0	37	3	1	16.5	27.8
Williamson, Noah	R-R	6-3	220	8-23-00	.115	.179	.256	27	84	78	7	9	2	0	3	9	6	0	0	0	52	3	1	7.1	61.9

Pitching	B-T	Ht.	Wt.	DOB	W	L	ERA	G	GS	SV	IP	Hits	Runs	ER	HR	BB	SO	AVG	OBP	SLG	SO%	BB%	BF
Barnes, Matt	R-R	6-4	208	6-17-90	1	0	0.00	2	1	0	3	2	0	0	0	1	2	.222	.300	.222	20.0	10.0	10
Belgrave, Nigel	R-R	6-4	195	5-12-02	2	0	2.16	4	0	0	8	5	2	2	0	7	14	.167	.324	.200	37.8	18.9	37
Bradley, Archie	R-R	6-4	215	8-10-92	0	0	0.00	3	0	0	4	2	0	0	0	0	1	.154	.214	.231	7.1	0.0	14
Buxton, Ike	R-R	6-3	208	7-18-00	4	0	1.62	12	5	0	39	20	9	7	1	25	46	.152	.294	.220	28.8	15.6	160
Chargois, JT	B-R	6-3	200	12-03-90	0	0	1.80	4	0	0	5	3	1	1	0	1	6	.167	.211	.278	31.6	5.3	19
Crigger, Kyle	R-R	6-2	180	6-04-99	1	1	5.02	12	0	2	14	10	9	8	0	4	22	.185	.241	.296	37.3	6.8	59
De Jesus, Enmanuel	L-L	6-3	190	12-10-96	1	0	3.68	2	2	0	7	8	3	3	0	1	9	.267	.290	.300	29.0	3.2	31
De La Cruz, Juan	R-R	6-3	180	3-04-05	1	4	4.57	12	12	0	43	48	30	22	3	32	42	.282	.418	.412	19.7	15.0	213
Eder, Jake	L-L	6-4	215	10-09-98	0	2	4.66	3	3	0	10	10	8	5	0	5	10	.250	.362	.350	21.3	10.6	47
Ekness, Josh	R-R	6-4	225	2-07-02	0	0	2.08	6	0	3	9	4	2	2	0	10	10	.133	.350	.167	25.0	25.0	40
Encarnacion, Breidy	R-R	6-3	185	11-09-00	2	0	0.81	18	0	3	33	14	3	3	0	16	41	.127	.234	.173	31.8	12.4	129
Enright, Nic	R-R	6-3	205	1-08-97	0	0	3.86	2	0	0	5	5	2	2	0	0	7	.250	.250	.300	35.0	0.0	20
Fall, Justin	L-L	6-6	240	6-11-99	2	0	13.50	5	0	0	12	23	23	18	2	11	12	.404	.521	.649	16.9	15.5	71
Gibson, Cade	L-L	6-2	195	2-18-98	2	3	3.12	7	6	0	35	27	12	12	1	10	33	.220	.297	.309	23.9	7.2	138
Gowen, Jack	R-R	6-1	220	10-29-99	0	0	4.91	4	0	0	4	4	2	2	0	4	1	.286	.444	.357	5.6	22.2	18
Hock, Colton	R-R	6-5	230	3-15-96	0	1	54.00	1	0	0	0	2	2	2	0	0	1	.667	.667	.667	33.3	0.0	3
Jones, Holt	R-R	6-8	235	5-08-99	0	0	3.09	7	4	0	23	15	12	8	1	14	30	.183	.320	.293	30.0	14.0	100
Kirschsieper, Cole	R-L	5-11	170	12-27-00	9	6	4.39	24	15	0	105	90	55	51	10	45	91	.232	.320	.379	20.5	10.1	444
Lara, Yeremin	R-R	6-1	160	11-06-98	4	0	2.63	28	0	0	41	27	12	12	3	13	40	.184	.250	.327	25.0	8.1	160
Leon, Maycold	L-L	6-1	160	4-29-02	0	0	19.64	5	0	0	4	9	8	8	1	6	3	.474	.600	.895	12.0	24.0	25
Lowe, Collin	R-R	6-4	210	9-11-98	6	3	3.28	20	11	0	91	86	42	33	5	20	78	.246	.297	.367	20.5	5.3	380
Maldonado, Anthony	R-R	6-4	220	2-06-98	0	0	0.00	3	0	0	4	1	0	0	0	0	7	.077	.077	.154	53.8	0.0	13
McCambley, Zach	L-R	6-2	220	5-04-99	2	0	0.00	3	0	0	4	0	0	0	0	1	5	.000	.071	.000	35.7	7.1	14
Meachem, Xavier	R-R	5-11	210	9-06-02	1	0	1.64	6	0	0	11	8	2	2	1	6	16	.205	.311	.308	35.6	13.3	45
Medina, Manuel	L-L	5-10	140	3-25-02	2	0	4.28	15	0	0	27	27	15	13	4	12	38	.241	.325	.402	30.2	9.5	126
Mendez, Julio	L-L	5-11	180	1-07-05	0	1	27.00	1	1	0	1	5	4	4	0	2	1	.556	.636	.556	9.1	18.2	11
Meyer, Noble	R-R	6-5	185	1-10-05	0	0	3.86	3	3	0	7	9	3	3	0	4	9	.310	.394	.345	26.5	11.8	34
Milbrandt, Karson	R-R	6-2	190	4-21-04	3	3	5.33	12	12	0	52	50	34	31	4	26	52	.251	.336	.392	22.7	11.4	229
Miller, Jacob	R-R	6-2	180	8-10-03	2	4	4.70	14	14	0	59	46	34	31	3	25	50	.213	.297	.319	20.2	10.1	247
Mokma, Chris	R-R	6-4	210	2-11-01	2	2	4.38	15	1	0	25	20	14	12	2	11	36	.213	.306	.309	33.3	10.2	108
Montero, Euri	R-R	6-4	170	3-28-02	2	1	5.40	28	0	3	43	47	31	26	4	22	40	.275	.373	.456	19.9	10.9	201
Nance, Tommy	R-R	6-6	235	3-19-91	0	1	3.38	4	1	0	5	7	2	2	0	1	6	.318	.348	.364	26.1	4.3	23
Nolin, Sean	L-L	6-4	250	12-26-89	0	1	5.06	2	2	0	5	9	3	3	1	2	3	.360	.407	.520	11.1	7.4	27
Polanco, Natanael	R-R	6-1	170	4-24-03	1	0	5.63	5	0	0	8	5	7	5	0	8	6	.185	.436	.370	15.4	20.5	39
Poland, Jared	R-R	6-0	215	1-12-00	1	0	1.69	3	3	0	16	15	4	3	1	4	17	.254	.302	.339	27.0	6.3	63
Pushard, Matt	R-R	6-4	245	10-27-97	0	0	0.00	1	0	1	1	0	0	0	0	0	2	.000	.000	.000	66.7	0.0	3
Reynoso, Juan	R-R	6-0	165	4-04-04	2	5	8.28	13	5	0	29	23	31	27	3	40	39	.219	.439	.333	26.4	27.0	148
Rodriguez, Eliezer	L-L	6-1	160	2-17-99	0	0	3.48	4	1	0	10	8	4	4	1	2	11	.216	.286	.459	26.2	4.8	42
Rogers, Trevor	L-L	6-5	217	11-13-97	0	0	0.00	1	1	0	4	1	0	0	0	1	7	.077	.143	.077	50.0	7.1	14
Salvador, Jose	L-L	6-2	170	9-21-99	1	1	2.63	6	4	0	24	22	8	7	1	7	17	.244	.307	.344	16.8	6.9	101
Sanchez, Edgar	R-R	6-1	190	8-02-00	0	0	1.13	5	0	1	8	4	1	1	0	2	3	.143	.226	.179	9.7	6.5	31
Sanchez, Franklin	R-R	6-6	183	9-12-00	0	0	15.00	3	0	0	3	4	5	5	0	5	5	.364	.611	.455	27.8	27.8	18
Schrand, Jake	R-R	6-0	180	8-08-99	1	1	5.87	7	0	0	8	6	8	5	3	8	8	.222	.389	.630	21.6	21.6	37
Serrano, Jhoniel	R-R	6-2	178	10-17-03	0	4	6.96	10	10	0	32	38	31	25	2	29	32	.288	.431	.439	19.2	17.4	167
Simpson, Josh	L-L	6-2	190	8-19-97	1	0	6.23	3	0	0	4	3	3	3	0	4	7	.200	.368	.200	36.8	21.1	19
Stanavich, Dale	L-L	5-11	175	6-23-99	2	5	3.56	24	0	2	30	28	19	12	1	16	46	.237	.328	.322	34.1	11.9	135
Stevens, Tristan	R-R	6-2	200	12-08-97	3	0	5.71	11	4	0	35	47	22	22	3	11	37	.326	.376	.472	23.4	7.0	158
Taylor, Evan	L-L	6-4	250	12-26-99	2	7	2.18	46	0	20	54	50	22	13	2	21	70	.246	.338	.310	29.7	8.9	236
Tineo, Riskiel	R-R	6-3	190	2-27-03	5	1	3.03	19	0	1	33	32	20	11	4	12	23	.252	.312	.409	16.3	8.5	141
Valencio, Henry	R-R	6-1	170	5-11-99	1	0	8.24	15	0	0	20	16	18	18	1	24	17	.216	.400	.365	17.0	24.0	100
White, Brandon	R-R	6-8	230	11-26-99	0	4	5.30	5	5	0	19	16	11	11	2	7	18	.229	.313	.386	22.5	8.8	80
White, Josh	R-R	6-1	205	11-24-00	1	0	2.38	15	4	5	34	22	10	9	3	11	44	.180	.259	.287	32.4	8.1	136
White, Thomas	L-L	6-5	210	9-29-04	0	1	7.36	2	2	0	4	3	3	3	0	4	5	.214	.389	.357	27.8	22.2	18

Fielding

Catcher	PCT	G	PO	A	E	DP	PB
Barstad	.995	18	176	8	1	0	2
Bramwell	.991	17	96	10	1	0	0
Fernandez	.980	24	225	15	5	4	1
McIntosh	.969	7	57	5	2	0	0
Mercado	.982	35	294	32	6	3	5
Praytor	.989	40	337	25	4	0	2

First Base	PCT	G	PO	A	E	DP
Bramwell	1.000	1	2	0	0	0
Bullard	1.000	6	43	1	0	3
Montgomery	.986	60	450	26	7	35
Rodriguez	.990	33	193	14	2	20
Santiago	.989	12	85	5	1	8
Vradenburg	.976	26	198	7	5	14

Second Base	PCT	G	PO	A	E	DP
Lewis	.944	72	86	133	13	33
McCants	.947	39	54	89	8	20
Morissette	.957	7	13	9	1	4
Sanoja	.970	25	20	44	2	7
Spohn	1.000	1	1	4	0	0

Third Base	PCT	G	PO	A	E	DP
Bullard	.826	10	7	12	4	1
Lewis	.917	33	27	50	7	5
McCants	.927	55	32	69	8	7
Morissette	.857	3	0	6	1	1
Rodriguez	.958	19	15	31	2	1
Sanoja	.750	2	0	3	1	1
Santiago	.929	22	21	31	4	3

Shortstop	PCT	G	PO	A	E	DP
McCants	.933	8	7	21	2	4
Olmstead	.981	14	19	34	1	8
Rodriguez	.867	3	8	5	2	2
Sanoja	.957	20	22	44	3	10
Santiago	1.000	2	2	3	0	0
Spohn	.956	86	105	198	14	38

Outfield	PCT	G	PO	A	E	DP
Alderman	.972	31	43	0	2	0
Allen	.667	11	23	1	0	1
Caballero	.974	56	85	2	2	0
Castillo	1.000	1	1	0	0	0
Chisholm	1.000	1	1	0	0	0
Coley	1.000	28	63	3	0	0
DeLeo	.987	38	58	2	1	0
Hidalgo	1.000	9	10	0	0	0
Luttrell	.994	70	142	3	1	1
Roberts	.992	71	95	2	2	0
Sanoja	.975	65	149	4	4	2
Santiago	1.000	6	8	0	0	0
Williamson	.984	26	37	1	1	0

FCL MARLINS — ROOKIE

FLORIDA COMPLEX LEAGUE

Batting	B-T	Ht.	Wt.	DOB	AVG	OBP	SLG	G	PA	AB	R	H	2B	3B	HR	RBI	BB	HBP	SH	SF	SO	SB	CS	BB%	SO%
Castillo, Kyler	R-R	5-9	185	10-29-97	.200	.200	.400	2	5	5	1	1	1	0	0	0	0	0	0	0	2	0	0	0.0	40.0
DiSpigna, Angelo	L-R	6-6	229	11-02-99	.373	.515	.627	17	68	51	13	19	5	4	0	11	14	2	0	1	12	0	0	20.6	17.6
Estrada, Jose	R-R	5-8	175	5-05-00	.333	.286	.667	2	7	6	1	2	2	0	0	4	0	0	0	1	2	0	0	0.0	28.6
Gerardo, Jose	R-R	6-0	179	6-12-05	.192	.345	.319	49	226	182	40	35	6	1	5	29	37	6	0	1	96	17	5	16.4	42.5
Gonzalez, Danny	R-R	6-0	160	11-26-04	.204	.317	.265	19	60	49	6	10	0	0	1	7	9	0	0	2	16	2	0	15.0	26.7
Henriquez, Julio	R-R	5-11	190	11-04-04	.234	.336	.282	37	144	124	18	29	6	0	0	14	13	6	0	0	20	4	1	9.0	13.9
Hernandez, Jesus	R-R	5-9	150	2-20-04	.262	.403	.381	50	211	168	36	44	9	1	3	26	40	1	0	2	37	10	2	19.0	17.5
Hernandez, Ronald	B-R	5-11	155	10-23-03	.298	.464	.452	31	138	104	27	31	5	1	3	25	32	1	0	1	27	3	0	23.2	19.6
2-team (14 FCL Mets)					.295	.481	.460	45	191	139	33	41	9	1	4	36	47	3	0	2	37	4	1	24.6	19.4
Hidalgo, Renny	R-R	5-9	165	9-05-02	.176	.300	.176	7	20	17	3	3	0	0	0	1	2	1	0	0	5	0	1	10.0	25.0
Ignoffo, Ryan	R-R	5-10	215	7-21-00	.299	.380	.388	19	79	67	10	20	3	0	1	16	10	0	0	2	4	3	1	12.7	5.1
Lane, Carmine	R-R	6-0	200	3-28-01	.345	.500	.379	23	77	58	15	20	2	0	0	4	17	1	0	0	9	0	0	22.1	11.7
Livesey, Hudson	B-R	6-0	170	8-09-99	.333	.500	.333	1	4	3	1	1	0	0	0	0	1	0	0	0	1	0	0	25.0	25.0
Monserrate, Jose	R-R	6-0	176	9-20-04	.259	.400	.259	25	35	27	12	7	0	0	0	6	7	0	0	1	3	4	1	20.0	8.6
Olmstead, Johnny	R-R	6-2	185	7-10-00	.216	.348	.324	12	46	37	7	8	1	0	1	7	5	3	0	1	8	2	1	10.9	17.4
Peguero, Antony	R-R	6-0	175	6-14-05	.224	.311	.282	43	180	156	24	35	5	2	0	21	17	4	0	3	42	6	3	9.4	23.3
Rios, Nestor	R-R	5-9	175	1-04-05	.067	.067	.067	8	15	15	1	1	0	0	0	0	0	0	0	0	9	0	0	0.0	60.0
Rodriguez, Miguel	R-R	6-0	160	11-08-02	.130	.259	.304	7	27	23	4	3	1	0	1	4	4	0	0	0	7	0	0	14.8	25.9
Sanchez, Carlos	B-R	5-9	175	9-20-04	.219	.309	.266	36	149	128	14	28	3	0	1	24	18	0	0	3	21	1	1	12.1	14.1
Sanchez, Junior	L-R	5-10	177	12-18-02	.242	.356	.315	45	179	149	22	36	7	2	0	21	27	0	2	1	20	6	2	15.1	11.2
Santos, Angeudis	B-R	6-4	168	9-19-01	.400	.556	.400	3	9	5	3	2	0	0	0	2	3	0	0	1	0	1	0	33.3	0.0
Simmons, Toby	B-L	5-10	175	12-02-04	.218	.382	.319	39	152	119	31	26	5	2	1	14	27	5	0	1	34	18	1	17.8	22.4
Vargas, Marco	L-R	6-0	170	5-14-05	.283	.457	.442	33	162	120	32	34	11	1	2	19	38	2	0	2	22	8	2	23.5	13.6
2-team (15 FCL Mets)					.269	.438	.401	48	219	167	41	45	14	1	2	24	48	2	0	2	31	10	2	21.9	14.2
Watson, Kahlil	L-R	5-10	178	4-16-03	.333	.333	1.333	2	6	6	2	2	0	0	2	2	0	0	0	0	1	0	0	0.0	16.7
Williamson, Noah	R-R	6-3	220	8-23-00	.300	.417	.350	6	24	20	4	6	1	0	0	5	3	1	0	0	7	1	1	12.5	29.2

Pitching	B-T	Ht.	Wt.	DOB	W	L	ERA	G	GS	SV	IP	Hits	Runs	ER	HR	BB	SO	AVG	OBP	SLG	SO%	BB%	BF
Alegre, Delvis	R-R	6-2	180	2-02-01	0	0	0.00	7	0	1	8	3	0	0	0	1	7	.111	.143	.148	25.0	3.6	28
Barnes, Matt	R-R	6-4	208	6-17-90	0	0	0.00	1	1	0	1	0	0	0	0	1	1	.000	.250	.000	25.0	25.0	4
Belgrave, Nigel	R-R	6-4	195	5-12-02	0	1	6.00	2	0	0	3	1	2	2	0	3	3	.100	.308	.200	23.1	23.1	13
Brooks, Jake	R-R	6-4	202	7-08-01	0	1	11.57	2	0	0	2	3	3	3	0	2	0	.300	.417	.500	0.0	16.7	12
Burguillos, Yoelvis	R-R	6-2	150	9-07-02	1	1	5.14	10	0	1	14	11	11	8	2	10	18	.196	.357	.357	25.7	14.3	70
Cabral, Jhon	R-R	6-1	172	8-09-05	0	2	13.00	9	7	0	18	23	28	26	1	30	3	.348	.554	.470	2.9	29.4	102
Castano, Daniel	L-L	6-3	231	9-17-94	0	0	4.50	2	0	0	2	1	1	1	0	2	2	.143	.333	.286	22.2	22.2	9
Castillo, Walin	R-R	6-3	175	1-02-05	1	1	1.42	9	3	1	32	21	10	5	4	12	26	.189	.289	.333	20.3	9.4	128
Cesar, Luis	L-L	6-3	183	2-24-04	2	1	4.08	11	9	0	40	42	23	18	2	31	41	.271	.399	.361	21.8	16.5	188
De La Cruz, Juan	R-R	6-3	180	3-04-05	1	1	2.00	2	1	0	9	4	3	2	0	6	8	.129	.270	.161	21.6	16.2	37
De La Cruz, Rodolfo	R-R	6-2	193	2-19-04	1	2	11.77	9	0	0	13	13	19	17	0	22	14	.255	.487	.392	18.4	28.9	76
Dishmey, Eliazar	R-R	6-1	175	10-25-04	1	1	6.64	7	3	0	20	19	15	15	3	11	24	.250	.352	.434	26.4	12.1	91
Ekness, Josh	R-R	6-4	225	2-07-02	0	0	40.50	1	0	0	1	3	3	3	0	1	1	.600	.667	1.200	16.7	16.7	6
Fernandez, Jose	R-R	6-1	155	10-16-03	1	0	2.35	12	0	0	23	16	6	6	0	19	24	.203	.364	.228	24.2	19.2	99
Gowen, Jack	R-R	6-1	220	10-29-99	1	1	4.22	7	0	2	11	8	5	5	1	7	14	.216	.356	.351	30.4	15.2	46
Jones, Holt	R-R	6-8	235	5-08-99	1	0	5.79	3	0	0	5	5	3	3	1	2	5	.250	.348	.400	21.7	8.7	23
Lawrence, Colson	R-R	6-5	210	3-03-02	1	0	0.00	2	0	0	3	2	0	0	0	1	3	.200	.273	.200	27.3	9.1	11
Leon, Maycold	L-L	6-1	160	4-29-02	0	0	2.16	7	0	0	8	6	2	2	1	3	6	.207	.281	.379	18.8	9.4	32
Lindsey, Andrew	R-R	6-3	216	11-15-99	0	1	8.31	2	2	0	4	6	4	4	0	1	2	.316	.350	.526	10.0	5.0	20
Maldonado, Nick	R-R	6-1	207	6-12-00	0	0	7.71	2	0	0	2	3	2	2	1	1	2	.300	.364	.600	18.2	9.1	11
Martinez, Liomar	R-R	6-2	165	6-25-05	2	6	9.53	9	7	0	28	40	31	30	6	14	22	.325	.418	.561	15.1	9.6	146
McCambley, Zach	L-R	6-2	220	5-04-99	0	0	0.00	2	1	0	2	0	0	0	0	1	2	.000	.143	.000	28.6	14.3	7
Meachem, Xavier	R-R	5-11	210	9-06-02	0	0	3.86	4	0	0	9	5	4	4	2	6	12	.156	.289	.375	31.6	15.8	38

Pitching	B-T	Ht.	Wt.	DOB	W	L	ERA	G	GS	SV	IP	Hits	Runs	ER	HR	BB	SO	AVG	OBP	SLG	SO%	BB%	BF
Medina, Manuel	L-L	5-10	140	3-25-02	0	0	0.00	2	0	0	3	1	0	0	0	2	2	.125	.300	.125	20.0	20.0	10
Mendez, Julio	L-L	5-11	180	1-07-05	1	0	7.94	3	1	0	6	7	5	5	1	3	9	.280	.379	.440	31.0	10.3	29
Meyer, Noble	R-R	6-5	185	1-10-05	0	1	4.50	2	2	0	4	2	2	2	0	3	6	.143	.294	.143	35.3	17.6	17
Miller, Jacob	R-R	6-2	180	8-10-03	0	0	0.00	2	1	0	5	2	0	0	0	2	5	.143	.250	.143	31.3	12.5	16
Nance, Tommy	R-R	6-6	235	3-19-91	0	0	0.00	2	2	0	2	0	0	0	0	1	3	.000	.167	.000	50.0	16.7	6
Nin, Lester	R-R	6-0	195	11-15-03	2	1	4.74	9	1	0	19	20	13	10	2	9	16	.267	.353	.413	18.8	10.6	85
Nolin, Sean	L-L	6-4	250	12-26-89	0	0	0.00	1	0	0	2	2	0	0	0	0	2	.250	.250	.375	25.0	0.0	8
Olson, Emmett	L-L	6-4	230	5-15-02	0	0	5.40	1	0	0	2	1	1	1	0	1	2	.167	.286	.167	28.6	14.3	7
Polanco, Natanael	R-R	6-1	170	4-24-03	3	0	4.50	12	0	1	12	9	11	6	0	10	9	.214	.357	.262	16.1	17.9	56
Reynoso, Juan	R-R	6-0	165	4-04-04	2	0	8.16	7	1	0	14	19	13	13	0	12	13	.328	.444	.466	18.1	16.7	72
Rodriguez, Eliezer	L-L	6-1	160	2-17-99	0	0	0.00	2	0	0	3	3	2	0	0	3	1	.250	.400	.333	6.7	20.0	15
Sellinger, Jack	R-L	6-2	200	11-20-99	0	1	0.00	4	0	0	3	2	1	0	0	1	3	.200	.273	.500	27.3	9.1	11
Serrano, Jhoniel	R-R	6-2	178	10-17-03	1	0	0.89	5	4	0	20	11	3	2	0	13	19	.162	.337	.221	22.1	15.1	86
Stevens, Tristan	R-R	6-2	200	12-08-97	1	0	0.00	2	0	0	5	3	1	0	0	1	3	.176	.211	.235	15.8	5.3	19
Storm, Justin	L-L	6-7	232	9-12-01	0	0	6.23	4	0	0	4	2	3	3	0	6	4	.154	.435	.154	17.4	26.1	23
Tineo, Riskiel	R-R	6-3	190	2-27-03	1	0	7.94	3	0	0	6	9	6	5	0	2	5	.360	.407	.440	18.5	7.4	27
Tunnell, West	L-R	6-1	195	11-20-93	0	0	3.86	2	0	0	2	2	1	1	0	2	4	.222	.364	.333	36.4	18.2	11
Valencio, Henry	R-R	6-1	170	5-11-99	1	0	1.50	10	0	4	12	7	4	2	0	2	7	.175	.233	.225	15.6	4.4	45
Vaupel, Kevin	R-L	6-1	210	8-03-01	0	0	0.00	1	0	0	1	1	0	0	0	0	1	.333	.333	.333	33.3	0.0	3
Vizcaino, Luis	R-R	6-4	199	7-09-01	1	2	5.08	11	5	0	28	24	16	16	0	20	31	.242	.391	.303	24.2	15.6	128
White, Brandon	R-R	6-8	230	11-26-99	1	1	4.50	5	1	0	10	7	7	5	0	3	8	.184	.262	.289	19.0	7.1	42
White, Thomas	L-L	6-5	210	9-29-04	0	0	0.00	1	0	0	1	0	4	0	0	2	2	.000	.333	.000	33.3	33.3	6
Zabaleta, Jesus	R-R	6-0	150	5-05-04	0	0	3.18	5	0	1	6	3	2	2	1	2	6	.158	.273	.368	27.3	9.1	22

Fielding

C: Sanchez 24, Hernandez 17, Lane 11, Rios 8, Estrada 2, Livesey 1. **1B:** Henriquez 37, DiSpigna 9, Lane 4, Rodriguez 2, Santos 2, Sanchez 1, Hernandez 1. **2B:** Sanchez 45, Vargas 6, Hernandez 1, Ignoffo 1, Olmstead 1. **3B:** Hernandez 31, Ignoffo 10, Rodriguez 5, Lane 4, Olmstead 3, Santos 2. **SS:** Vargas 26, Hernandez 20, Olmstead 8, Watson 2. **OF:** Gerardo 43, Simmons 38, Peguero 36, Gonzalez 19, Monserrate 15, Ignoffo 9, Hidalgo 7, Williamson 6, Castillo 1.

DSL MARLINS — ROOKIE

DOMINICAN SUMMER LEAGUE

Batting	B-T	Ht.	Wt.	DOB	AVG	OBP	SLG	G	PA	AB	R	H	2B	3B	HR	RBI	BB	HBP	SH	SF	SO	SB	CS	BB%	SO%
Abreu, Jesus	R-R	6-1	190	9-15-05	.240	.375	.320	15	64	50	9	12	2	1	0	8	8	4	0	2	14	2	0	12.5	21.9
Almonte, Jeremy	R-R	6-0	170	10-12-05	.227	.298	.293	21	84	75	13	17	2	0	1	8	6	2	0	1	10	0	1	7.1	11.9
Almonte, Khris	R-R	6-1	160	9-06-05	.247	.340	.329	29	97	85	6	21	4	0	1	8	7	5	0	0	25	0	1	7.2	25.8
Altamirano, Greyber	L-R	6-2	145	10-15-04	.261	.362	.420	27	106	88	18	23	4	2	2	17	14	1	1	2	19	4	1	13.2	17.9
Batista, Remington	B-R	5-10	175	1-28-05	.294	.358	.486	33	122	109	23	32	8	5	1	11	9	2	2	0	23	7	3	7.4	18.9
Bello, Adrian	B-R	5-11	165	5-19-06	.218	.304	.336	28	125	110	18	24	6	2	1	14	12	2	0	1	36	0	0	9.6	28.8
Bonifacio, Lisandro	B-R	6-0	155	8-12-05	.191	.349	.234	18	63	47	4	9	2	0	0	6	11	2	0	3	11	5	1	17.5	17.5
Castillo, Rafael	B-R	5-11	160	4-07-06	.190	.397	.224	22	78	58	11	11	2	0	0	5	19	1	0	0	24	3	0	24.4	30.8
Chirinos, Nixon	R-R	6-0	190	10-25-05	.195	.346	.220	13	52	41	8	8	1	0	0	3	6	4	0	1	10	0	0	11.5	19.2
Colina, Oscar	R-R	6-0	150	1-28-04	.388	.552	.490	22	67	49	16	19	3	1	0	11	11	7	0	0	10	5	3	16.4	14.9
Cueto, Derek	R-R	5-10	167	10-26-05	.094	.256	.125	15	39	32	5	3	1	0	0	0	6	1	0	0	12	0	0	15.4	30.8
De La Cruz, Jancory	L-L	6-2	180	2-17-06	.229	.360	.394	49	211	175	27	40	8	3	5	25	35	1	0	0	61	7	2	16.6	28.9
De Los Santos, Kengri	R-R	6-1	179	9-11-04	.000	.000	.000	2	7	7	0	0	0	0	0	0	0	0	0	0	1	0	0	0.0	14.3
Dean, Breyias	R-R	6-2	175	9-01-05	.220	.370	.346	47	200	159	20	35	9	1	3	20	22	17	0	2	59	4	3	11.0	29.5
Felicia, Jayden	B-R	6-0	150	3-14-06	.223	.408	.288	40	184	139	29	31	7	1	0	13	42	2	0	1	45	8	5	22.8	24.5
Feliz, Kendry	R-R	5-11	160	11-17-04	.260	.383	.415	37	149	123	21	32	9	2	2	22	23	2	0	1	28	12	5	15.4	18.8
Gaitor, Daniel	B-R	5-10	170	11-22-05	.218	.354	.365	48	190	156	28	34	9	1	4	22	29	4	0	0	64	11	7	15.3	33.7
Heredia, Osvaldo	L-R	6-2	170	3-07-06	.189	.284	.301	43	162	143	21	27	3	2	3	14	9	10	0	0	45	13	5	5.6	27.8
Ibarra, Adrian	R-R	6-2	175	4-08-06	.286	.337	.379	44	175	161	20	46	10	1	1	25	10	3	0	1	37	9	3	5.7	21.1
Lara, Erick	L-R	6-2	165	6-10-06	.305	.416	.445	34	154	128	21	39	8	2	2	32	23	2	0	1	37	5	1	14.9	24.0
Lopez, Fabian	B-R	6-0	165	9-18-05	.265	.327	.405	49	220	200	28	53	12	2	4	22	16	3	0	1	53	15	5	7.3	24.1
Miller, Janero	B-L	6-2	195	1-10-06	.239	.331	.310	42	131	113	14	27	4	2	0	10	14	2	0	1	56	4	2	10.7	42.7
Mota, Gregory	R-R	6-3	172	12-20-04	.238	.333	.262	13	48	42	6	10	1	0	0	2	5	1	0	0	19	1	0	10.4	39.6
Neymour, Cherif	B-R	5-11	150	3-04-05	.315	.436	.417	34	134	108	24	34	4	2	1	19	19	5	1	1	24	18	1	14.2	17.9
Novoa, Kevin	R-R	5-11	175	8-27-04	.288	.439	.308	18	66	52	14	15	1	0	0	3	11	3	0	0	8	1	0	16.7	12.1
Ortega, Victor	R-R	6-1	200	1-19-04	.261	.474	.304	24	97	69	14	18	3	0	0	9	27	1	0	0	9	3	0	27.8	9.3
Perez, Robert	R-R	6-2	165	4-27-04	.255	.324	.392	50	225	204	36	52	10	0	6	38	18	3	0	0	63	16	2	8.0	28.0
Requena, Alexander	R-R	6-0	175	10-05-05	.292	.433	.375	9	30	24	4	7	2	0	0	1	5	1	0	0	6	0	0	16.7	20.0
Rivera, Jose	B-R	6-0	145	11-17-04	.239	.374	.295	30	107	88	17	21	3	1	0	10	16	3	0	0	17	9	2	15.0	15.9
Rodriguez, Anthony	R-R	6-2	175	9-14-05	.166	.230	.296	44	183	169	22	28	7	0	5	16	11	3	0	0	62	2	1	6.0	33.9
Solano, Yoffry	B-R	5-10	155	11-04-04	.281	.387	.438	17	75	64	10	18	3	2	1	6	8	3	0	0	12	2	1	10.7	16.0
Tailor, Joseph	L-R	5-11	175	6-14-06	.237	.312	.309	42	158	139	20	33	2	1	2	20	13	3	1	2	43	12	2	8.2	27.2
Valor, Andres	R-R	6-3	180	11-08-05	.294	.360	.466	51	228	204	39	60	16	2	5	25	21	1	0	2	55	21	7	9.2	24.1

Pitching	B-T	Ht.	Wt.	DOB	W	L	ERA	G	GS	SV	IP	Hits	Runs	ER	HR	BB	SO	AVG	OBP	SLG	SO%	BB%	BF
Abad, Andelzon	L-L	6-0	155	6-19-04	0	1	18.00	1	0	0	1	1	2	2	0	4	1	.333	.714	.333	14.3	57.1	7
Aponte, Oswaldo	R-R	6-2	185	5-02-06	0	2	4.88	10	8	0	31	29	24	17	1	16	27	.242	.372	.358	18.5	11.0	146
Arellan, Derek	R-R	6-2	175	2-19-06	0	1	9.00	2	2	0	5	7	5	5	1	1	6	.333	.375	.619	25.0	4.2	24
Arias, Josue	L-L	6-2	165	5-05-05	1	5	6.53	11	11	0	41	38	36	30	2	28	52	.247	.372	.331	27.7	14.9	188
Baldiris, Luis	L-L	5-11	150	5-07-04	0	1	5.50	12	0	1	18	25	20	11	1	20	27	.313	.461	.400	26.5	19.6	102
Benitez, Keyner	L-L	6-1	165	5-23-06	2	1	3.74	11	11	0	46	28	20	19	1	26	44	.179	.316	.250	23.4	13.8	188
Campos, Willian	R-R	6-3	175	9-24-04	2	1	7.11	12	0	1	19	22	21	15	2	19	15	.301	.471	.507	14.7	18.6	102

Carpio, Samuel	R-R	6-2	200	5-06-03	1	1	7.36	5	0	0	7	7	7	6	1	7	9	.241	.389	.345	25.0	19.4	36
Castaneda, Rafael	R-R	6-4	165	5-18-04	0	1	5.32	11	0	2	22	30	15	13	2	5	15	.326	.367	.522	15.3	5.1	98
De La Rosa, Fernando	R-R	6-1	155	11-22-05	2	0	6.63	12	0	1	19	17	19	14	1	15	20	.243	.402	.414	21.7	16.3	92
Espinoza, Eiver	R-R	6-6	168	1-11-04	1	3	6.33	13	2	0	27	31	27	19	2	14	35	.274	.356	.442	26.3	10.5	133
Espinoza, Luis	R-R	5-11	150	3-23-05	1	2	2.91	13	0	1	22	16	8	7	1	10	27	.213	.306	.387	31.4	11.6	86
Fernandez, Jarol	L-L	5-11	190	2-14-03	0	0	9.00	1	0	0	2	4	2	2	0	1	0	.400	.455	.600	0.0	9.1	11
Fuente, Johandry	R-R	6-0	185	12-29-02	1	1	6.75	11	0	0	16	12	12	12	0	13	20	.211	.395	.263	26.0	16.9	77
Garcia, Hamlet	R-R	6-2	175	11-23-05	1	3	4.74	11	11	0	44	43	31	23	6	15	41	.262	.335	.463	21.8	8.0	188
Garcia, Julio	R-R	6-0	170	12-28-04	0	3	4.24	13	0	3	17	17	13	8	1	7	14	.246	.325	.420	18.2	9.1	77
Hernandez, Angel	R-R	6-2	194	1-24-04	0	0	4.26	8	0	1	13	9	6	6	1	2	12	.200	.250	.333	25.0	4.2	48
Hernandez, Jeckferxon	R-R	6-3	185	9-18-02	0	1	2.45	10	0	0	11	8	4	3	0	7	13	.200	.319	.225	27.1	14.6	48
Jimenez, Elvin	R-R	6-2	210	3-19-05	0	0	5.40	13	0	1	18	12	11	11	0	17	24	.185	.391	.277	27.6	19.5	87
Mejia, Jeyson	R-R	6-1	170	12-22-05	3	1	7.11	11	0	0	19	26	22	15	5	10	18	.321	.404	.580	19.1	10.6	94
Melo, Bayant	R-R	6-3	165	12-31-04	0	4	12.63	11	11	0	21	18	37	29	1	46	20	.243	.548	.338	15.9	36.5	126
Miller, Janero	B-L	6-2	195	1-10-06	0	6	7.07	10	9	0	28	24	25	22	2	22	22	.231	.385	.365	16.9	16.9	130
Moreta, Franklyn	R-R	6-0	160	1-11-04	1	1	7.71	13	0	2	14	16	17	12	2	7	17	.286	.354	.464	26.2	10.8	65
Morillo, Elier	L-L	5-11	160	10-06-05	1	1	7.09	9	6	0	27	35	22	21	2	13	34	.318	.414	.436	26.6	10.2	128
Ortega, Juan	R-R	6-2	170	6-03-05	1	0	10.80	10	0	0	13	17	18	16	3	14	16	.333	.528	.569	22.2	19.4	72
Palacios, Johan	R-R	6-9	175	12-26-04	1	0	6.48	11	0	0	17	20	13	12	0	12	18	.308	.451	.385	22.0	14.6	82
Perez, Michael	R-R	6-3	160	9-05-02	0	0	4.50	3	0	0	4	4	2	2	0	2	0	.286	.375	.286	0.0	12.5	16
Polanco, Albert	R-R	6-2	174	6-30-05	2	2	5.30	12	6	0	36	37	23	21	2	14	36	.282	.377	.382	23.4	9.1	154
Porfirio, Luis	L-L	6-0	155	11-07-05	0	2	9.00	4	2	0	11	16	12	11	1	13	9	.356	.517	.578	15.0	21.7	60
Ramirez, Luis	R-R	6-3	175	2-19-02	2	2	3.16	12	2	1	31	25	18	11	0	17	32	.221	.346	.274	23.4	12.4	137
Reyes, Bryan	R-R	6-0	150	10-11-05	0	0	3.65	8	0	0	12	10	5	5	1	2	13	.217	.280	.326	26.0	4.0	50
Rodriguez, Darwin	R-R	6-1	180	11-10-04	1	3	9.14	6	5	0	22	26	23	22	2	15	17	.302	.417	.523	16.5	14.6	103
Romero, Luifer	L-L	6-2	160	12-09-04	0	2	6.12	12	5	0	32	39	27	22	4	8	31	.300	.391	.492	20.4	5.3	152
Rueda, Cristian	R-R	6-1	180	1-05-05	2	2	4.18	15	0	3	24	27	13	11	4	7	24	.287	.343	.447	23.5	6.9	102
Salas, Braulio	R-R	6-2	175	11-05-04	0	1	5.46	9	8	0	30	32	24	18	1	16	25	.274	.372	.393	18.2	11.7	137
Santana, Yohanfer	R-R	6-7	200	10-13-05	0	4	7.40	10	7	0	24	22	24	20	3	30	25	.247	.460	.393	20.2	24.2	124
Serrata, Elian	R-R	6-0	160	1-27-02	2	0	2.01	13	0	0	22	16	6	5	1	9	32	.195	.283	.280	34.8	9.8	92
Smith, Brandon	R-R	6-0	165	11-09-05	2	2	3.46	11	0	0	26	22	12	10	2	7	14	.242	.311	.396	13.6	6.8	103
Suriel, Fraylin	R-R	6-1	170	5-21-04	2	0	10.19	14	0	0	18	16	22	20	1	23	17	.242	.447	.364	18.1	24.5	94
Takahashi, Hiroshi	R-R	6-1	170	6-15-06	1	0	14.26	13	0	1	18	31	30	28	5	23	16	.383	.532	.667	14.4	20.7	111
Uriepero, Nicolas	R-R	6-2	209	3-03-05	4	1	6.53	12	0	0	21	33	19	15	3	8	22	.379	.433	.644	22.4	8.2	98
Uzcategui, Jonas	L-L	6-0	155	10-30-04	0	1	12.08	11	0	0	13	7	19	17	0	30	13	.175	.558	.225	16.9	39.0	77
Villegas, Mado	R-R	5-11	165	7-06-03	3	3	4.09	11	0	1	22	22	13	10	1	5	24	.262	.323	.393	25.8	5.4	93

Fielding

C: Bello 24, Ortega 24, Almonte 21, Abreu 15, Chirinos 10, Requena 9, Novoa 7. **1B:** Ibarra 33, Feliz 31, Dean 19, Rodriguez 16, Novoa 10, Mota 4, Cueto 2, De Los Santos 1. **2B:** Tailor 27, Felicia 22, Rivera 15, Castillo 11, Altamirano 9, Lopez 5, Neymour 5, Ibarra 4, Lara 4, Bonifacio 3, Cueto 3, Dean 2, De Los Santos 1. **3B:** Dean 26, Neymour 20, Tailor 15, Solano 14, Altamirano 11, Cueto 10, Castillo 6, Ibarra 6, Bonifacio 5, Rivera 3, Feliz 1. **SS:** Lopez 41, Lara 28, Rivera 13, Bonifacio 10, Felicia 10, Altamirano 6, Castillo 2, Neymour 1. **OF:** De La Cruz 47, Perez 47, Gaitor 46, Valor 46, Heredia 43, Batista 30, Almonte 29, Rodriguez 26, Colina 21, Mota 6, Cueto 1.

Milwaukee Brewers

MILWAUKEE BREWERS

SEASON SYNOPSIS: Milwaukee spent 122 game days in first place and won the National League Central for the third time in the last five full seasons. But for the third time in their last four playoff trips, they failed to win a postseason game, getting swept at home by the Diamondbacks.

HIGH POINT: The division race was tight for much of the season before the Brewers won nine straight in late August, sweeping series at Texas and at home against the Twins and Padres. They scored 64 runs in that streak, sparked by catcher William Contreras, who hit .318/.391/.489 in the second half of the season and hit safely in the eight games he played in during the win streak.

LOW POINT: A chic postseason pick thanks to a strong finish and its pitching, Milwaukee flamed out quickly in October. The first bad news came when starter Brandon Woodruff was pronounced out for the playoffs on Oct. 2 and later needed shoulder surgery, likely to sideline him for all of 2024. Then the Brewers blew a 3-0 lead and left 11 on base in a 6-3 Game 1 loss, before a similar formula (early 2-0 lead, nine LOB) led to a 5-2 elimination in Game 2.

NOTABLE ROOKIES: Brice Turang won the second base job and provided solid defense and speed (his 26 stolen bases ranked second on the club), but he hit just .218 with only 18 extra-base hits. Sal Frelick, a 2021 first-round pick, provided a second-half spark with his defense and bat (.246/.341/.351, 7 SB). Infielder Andruw Monasterio (.259/.330/.348), a minor league free-agent pickup, was a regular starter at third base in the second half. Righty Abner Uribe struck out 39 in 30 innings.

KEY TRANSACTIONS: The Brewers swooped in to add Contreras as part of a three-way off-season trade that sent catcher Sean Murphy from Oakland to Atlanta, while the Brewers gave up speedy outfielder Esteury Ruiz. Milwaukee also got reliever Joel Payamps from Oakland in that deal, and he posted a 2.55 ERA in 70 innings. GM Matt Arnold also was active at the Aug. 1 trade deadline, adding veterans Carlos Santana and Mark Canha to boost the offense.

DOWN ON THE FARM: Outfielder Jackson Chourio remains one of the top prospects in baseball and Jacob Misiorowski has developed into a high-ceiling pitching prospect. Milwaukee's .525 winning percentage was seventh best in baseball.

OPENING DAY PAYROLL: $118,761,987 (20th).

PLAYERS OF THE YEAR

MAJOR LEAGUE

Corbin Burnes
RHP
10-8, 3.39
194 IP, 1.07 WHIP
200 SO

MINOR LEAGUE

Jackson Chourio
OF
(AA/AAA)
.282/.338/.467
26 2B, 22 HR, 44 SB

ORGANIZATION LEADERS

Batting		***Minimum 250 AB**
MAJORS		
* AVG	William Contreras	.289
* OPS	William Contreras	.825
HR	Willy Adames	24
RBI	Willy Adames	80
MINORS		
* AVG	Dylan O'Rae, ACL Brewers/Carolina	.349
* OBP	Dylan O'Rae, ACL Brewers/Carolina	.491
* SLG	Keston Hiura, Nashville	.563
* OPS	Keston Hiura, Nashville	.960
R	Tyler Black, Biloxi/Nashville	105
H	Jackson Chourio, Biloxi	150
TB	Jackson Chourio, Biloxi	248
2B	Abraham Toro, Nashville	36
3B	Tyler Black, Biloxi/Nashville	12
HR	Wes Clarke, Biloxi	26
RBI	Jackson Chourio, Biloxi	91
BB	Wes Clarke, Biloxi	89
SO	Wes Clarke, Biloxi	147
SB	Tyler Black, Biloxi/Nashville	55

Pitching		**#Minimum 75 IP**
MAJORS		
W	Freddy Peralta	12
# ERA	Bryse Wilson	2.58
SO	Freddy Peralta	210
SV	Devin Williams	36
MINORS		
W	Tobias Myers, Biloxi/Nashville	10
L	Christian Mejias, Biloxi	12
# ERA	Ryan Brady, Wisc./Biloxi	2.69
G	Alex Claudio, Nashville	51
GS	3-tied	26
SV	Cam Robinson, Biloxi/Nashville	15
IP	Tobias Myers, Biloxi/Nashville	141
BB	Christian Mejias, Biloxi	58
SO	Tobias Myers, Biloxi/Nashville	175
# AVG	Logan Henderson, Carolina	.165

2023 PERFORMANCE

General Manager: David Stearns. **Farm Director:** Cam Castro. **Scouting Director:** Tod Johnson.

Class	Team	League	W	L	PCT	Finish	Manager
Majors	Milwaukee Brewers	National	92	70	.568	3 (15)	Craig Counsell
Triple-A	Nashville Sounds	International	83	65	.561	4 (20)	Rick Sweet
Double-A	Biloxi Shuckers	Southern	74	63	.540	4 (8)	Mike Guerrero
High-A	Wisconsin Timber Rattlers	Midwest	62	68	.477	8 (12)	Joe Ayrault
Low-A	Carolina Mudcats	Carolina	72	55	.567	2 (12)	Victor Estevez
Rookie	ACL Brewers	Arizona Complex	31	25	.554	5 (17)	Rafael Neda
Rookie	DSL Brewers 1	Dominican Sum.	25	27	.481	30 (50)	Fidel Pena
Rookie	DSL Brewers 2	Dominican Sum.	22	31	.415	38 (50)	Natanael Mejia
Overall 2023 Minor League Record			369	334	.525	7th (30)	

ORGANIZATION STATISTICS

MILWAUKEE BREWERS

NATIONAL LEAGUE

Batting	B-T	Ht.	Wt.	DOB	AVG	OBP	SLG	G	PA	AB	R	H	2B	3B	HR	RBI	BB	HBP	SH	SF	SO	SB	CS	BB%	SO%
Adames, Willy	R-R	6-1	214	9-02-95	.217	.310	.407	149	638	553	73	120	29	2	24	80	71	6	0	6	165	5	3	11.1	25.9
Anderson, Brian	R-R	6-2	215	5-19-93	.226	.310	.368	96	361	318	38	72	12	3	9	40	36	4	0	3	108	1	3	10.0	29.9
Brosseau, Mike	R-R	5-11	203	3-15-94	.205	.256	.397	29	78	73	4	15	2	0	4	8	4	1	0	0	20	0	0	5.1	25.6
Canha, Mark	R-R	6-2	209	2-15-89	.287	.373	.427	50	204	178	23	51	10	0	5	33	17	8	0	1	27	4	1	8.3	13.2
2-team (89 New York Mets)					.262	.359	.400	139	507	435	51	114	25	1	11	62	49	17	0	6	79	11	1	9.7	15.6
Caratini, Victor	B-R	5-11	225	8-17-93	.259	.327	.383	62	226	201	23	52	4	0	7	25	19	3	0	3	45	1	1	8.4	19.9
Contreras, William	R-R	5-11	216	12-24-97	.289	.367	.457	141	611	540	86	156	38	1	17	78	63	5	1	2	126	6	1	10.3	20.6
Donaldson, Josh	R-R	6-1	210	12-08-85	.169	.290	.390	17	69	59	5	10	4	0	3	11	10	0	0	0	18	0	0	14.5	26.1
Frelick, Sal	L-R	5-10	182	4-19-00	.246	.341	.351	57	223	191	29	47	9	1	3	24	28	1	0	3	37	7	0	12.6	16.6
Jones, Jahmai	R-R	6-0	210	8-04-97	.200	.273	.300	7	11	10	2	2	1	0	0	3	1	0	0	0	5	1	0	9.1	45.5
Miller, Owen	R-R	5-11	195	11-15-96	.261	.303	.371	90	314	291	29	76	17	0	5	27	17	2	0	4	61	13	2	5.4	19.4
Mitchell, Garrett	L-R	6-3	224	9-04-98	.246	.315	.446	19	73	65	10	16	2	1	3	7	7	0	0	1	26	1	1	9.6	35.6
Monasterio, Andruw	R-R	5-11	186	5-30-97	.259	.330	.348	92	315	282	38	73	14	1	3	27	28	3	0	2	66	7	2	8.9	21.0
Perkins, Blake	B-R	5-11	197	9-10-96	.217	.325	.350	67	168	143	28	31	7	0	4	20	23	0	2	0	46	5	2	13.7	27.4
Ruf, Darin	R-R	6-2	232	7-28-86	.192	.300	.231	11	30	26	2	5	1	0	0	0	4	0	0	0	7	0	0	13.3	23.3
2-team (9 San Francisco)					.224	.333	.286	20	57	49	3	11	3	0	0	3	8	0	0	0	16	0	0	14.0	28.1
Santana, Carlos	B-R	5-11	215	4-08-86	.249	.314	.459	52	226	205	33	51	8	1	11	33	20	0	0	1	35	0	0	8.8	15.5
2-team (94 Pittsburgh)					.240	.320	.429	146	619	550	78	132	33	1	23	86	65	0	0	4	104	6	0	10.5	16.8
Singleton, Jon	L-L	6-0	256	9-18-91	.103	.188	.138	11	32	29	3	3	1	0	0	2	3	0	0	0	11	0	0	9.4	34.4
Tapia, Raimel	L-L	6-3	175	2-04-94	.173	.267	.288	20	61	52	10	9	0	0	2	3	6	1	1	1	20	2	1	9.8	32.8
Taylor, Tyrone	R-R	6-1	218	1-22-94	.234	.267	.446	81	243	231	36	54	17	1	10	35	8	3	0	1	55	9	0	3.3	22.6
Tellez, Rowdy	L-L	6-4	270	3-16-95	.215	.291	.376	106	351	311	26	67	9	1	13	47	35	0	0	5	86	0	0	10.0	24.5
Toro, Abraham	B-R	6-0	223	12-20-96	.444	.524	.778	9	21	18	4	8	0	0	2	9	2	1	0	0	5	0	0	9.5	23.8
Turang, Brice	L-R	6-0	176	11-21-99	.218	.285	.300	137	448	404	46	88	9	3	6	34	38	1	3	2	94	26	4	8.5	21.0
Urias, Luis	R-R	5-10	202	6-03-97	.145	.299	.236	20	68	55	5	8	2	0	1	5	7	5	0	0	15	0	0	10.3	22.1
Voit, Luke	R-R	6-2	258	2-13-91	.221	.284	.265	22	74	68	5	15	3	0	0	4	4	2	0	0	27	2	0	5.4	36.5
Wiemer, Joey	R-R	6-4	220	2-11-99	.204	.283	.362	132	410	367	48	75	19	0	13	42	36	5	0	2	116	11	4	8.8	28.3
Winker, Jesse	L-L	6-2	230	8-17-93	.199	.320	.247	61	197	166	16	33	5	0	1	23	26	4	0	1	51	0	0	13.2	25.9
Yelich, Christian	L-R	6-3	207	12-05-91	.278	.370	.447	144	632	550	106	153	34	1	19	76	78	3	0	1	140	28	3	12.3	22.2

Pitching	B-T	Ht.	Wt.	DOB	W	L	ERA	G	GS	SV	IP	Hits	Runs	ER	HR	BB	SO	AVG	OBP	SLG	SO%	BB%	BF
Andrews, Clayton	L-L	5-6	160	1-04-97	0	1	27.00	4	0	0	3	10	11	10	3	2	4	.500	.545	1.100	18.2	9.1	22
Boushley, Caleb	R-R	6-3	190	10-01-93	1	0	3.86	1	0	0	2	1	1	1	1	2	5	.125	.300	.500	50.0	20.0	10
Brosseau, Mike	R-R	5-11	203	3-15-94	0	0	3.86	3	0	0	2	1	1	1	1	1	0	.125	.222	.500	0.0	11.1	9
Bukauskas, J.B.	R-R	6-0	208	10-11-96	0	0	0.00	5	0	0	6	4	0	0	0	1	6	.190	.261	.190	26.1	4.3	23
Burnes, Corbin	R-R	6-3	246	10-22-94	10	8	3.39	32	32	0	194	141	77	73	22	66	200	.200	.274	.324	25.5	8.4	784
Bush, Matt	R-R	5-10	193	2-08-86	0	2	9.58	12	0	1	10	11	11	11	5	6	10	.262	.354	.690	20.8	12.5	48
Chafin, Andrew	R-L	6-2	235	6-17-90	1	1	5.82	20	0	0	17	14	13	11	3	10	14	.222	.338	.444	18.9	13.5	74
Claudio, Alex	L-L	6-2	190	1-31-92	0	0	0.00	1	0	0	0	2	0	0	0	0	0	.667	.667	.667	0.0	0.0	3
Cousins, Jake	R-R	6-4	193	7-14-94	0	0	4.82	9	0	0	9	10	5	5	1	10	7	.286	.444	.429	15.6	22.2	45
Guerra, Javy	L-R	6-0	190	9-25-95	0	0	8.64	8	0	0	8	10	8	8	1	9	5	.303	.467	.424	11.1	20.0	45
Houser, Adrian	R-R	6-3	242	2-02-93	8	5	4.12	23	21	0	111	121	56	51	13	34	96	.273	.324	.406	20.0	7.1	481
Junk, Janson	R-R	6-2	202	1-15-96	0	1	4.91	2	1	0	7	8	5	4	1	2	5	.267	.313	.467	15.2	6.1	33
Lauer, Eric	R-L	6-3	209	6-03-95	4	6	6.56	10	9	0	47	54	39	34	16	24	43	.292	.370	.616	20.4	11.4	211
Megill, Trevor	L-R	6-8	250	12-05-93	1	0	3.63	31	2	0	35	35	14	14	2	12	52	.265	.324	.386	35.1	8.1	148
Mejia, J.C.	R-R	6-6	250	8-26-96	1	0	5.56	9	0	0	11	15	7	7	2	3	13	.326	.380	.478	26.0	6.0	50
Miley, Wade	L-L	6-1	220	11-13-86	9	4	3.14	23	23	0	120	99	44	42	16	38	79	.223	.287	.386	16.1	7.8	490
Miller, Tyson	R-R	6-5	220	7-29-95	0	0	5.79	7	0	0	9	9	6	6	2	3	7	.250	.317	.500	17.1	7.3	41
Milner, Hoby	L-L	6-3	184	1-13-91	2	1	1.82	73	0	0	64	49	16	13	5	13	59	.209	.254	.319	23.4	5.2	252
Pannone, Thomas	L-L	6-0	209	4-28-94	0	0	6.75	1	0	0	3	5	2	2	0	1	4	.385	.429	.462	28.6	7.1	14
Payamps, Joel	R-R	6-2	217	4-07-94	7	5	2.55	69	0	3	71	57	24	20	8	17	77	.219	.278	.342	26.8	5.9	287
Peguero, Elvis	R-R	6-5	237	3-20-97	4	5	3.38	59	0	1	61	49	25	23	4	26	54	.222	.313	.303	21.4	10.3	252

Peralta, Freddy	R-R	6-0	196	6-04-96	12	10	3.86	30	30	0	166	131	77	71	26	54	210	.212	.282	.387	30.9	7.9	680
Rea, Colin	R-R	6-5	218	7-01-90	6	6	4.55	26	22	0	125	110	65	63	23	38	110	.235	.296	.434	21.3	7.4	517
Small, Ethan	L-L	6-2	200	2-14-97	0	0	11.25	2	0	1	4	9	5	5	1	2	6	.429	.478	.714	26.1	8.7	23
Sousa, Bennett	L-L	6-3	220	4-06-95	0	0	13.50	2	0	0	3	5	4	4	1	2	2	.417	.500	.667	14.3	14.3	14
Strzelecki, Peter	R-R	6-2	216	10-24-94	3	5	4.54	36	0	0	36	32	18	18	3	10	37	.235	.323	.360	23.7	6.4	156
Teheran, Julio	R-R	6-2	205	1-27-91	3	5	4.40	14	11	0	72	68	36	35	13	13	50	.254	.296	.466	17.4	4.5	288
Tellez, Rowdy	L-L	6-4	270	3-16-95	0	0	0.00	1	0	0	1	1	0	0	0	0	1	.250	.250	.250	25.0	0.0	4
Uribe, Abner	R-R	6-3	225	6-20-00	1	0	1.76	32	0	1	31	16	8	6	0	20	39	.154	.291	.192	30.7	15.7	127
Varland, Gus	L-R	6-1	213	11-06-96	0	0	11.42	8	0	0	9	15	12	11	3	8	6	.357	.471	.619	11.8	15.7	51
Vieira, Thyago	R-R	6-3	265	7-01-93	0	1	0.00	2	0	0	3	0	1	0	0	1	2	.000	.100	.000	20.0	10.0	10
Williams, Devin	R-R	6-2	192	9-21-94	8	3	1.53	61	0	36	59	26	13	10	4	28	87	.129	.238	.218	37.7	12.1	231
Wilson, Bryse	R-R	6-2	267	12-20-97	6	0	2.58	53	0	3	77	60	26	22	9	22	61	.211	.271	.377	19.4	7.0	314
Woodruff, Brandon	L-R	6-4	244	2-10-93	5	1	2.28	11	11	0	67	40	17	17	9	15	74	.172	.229	.322	29.2	5.9	253

Fielding

Catcher	PCT	G	PO	A	E	DP	PB
Caratini	.998	58	482	16	1	2	0
Contreras	.989	108	969	30	11	5	2

First Base	PCT	G	PO	A	E	DP
Brosseau	1.000	4	20	3	0	1
Canha	1.000	5	31	1	0	5
Caratini	1.000	1	6	1	0	0
Miller	.985	35	182	15	3	15
Ruf	1.000	4	10	0	0	0
Santana	.990	50	375	33	4	26
Singleton	.969	5	27	4	1	3
Tellez	.996	76	468	49	2	46
Toro	1.000	2	11	0	0	3
Voit	1.000	11	85	12	0	7

Second Base	PCT	G	PO	A	E	DP
Brosseau	.000	1	0	0	0	0
Jones	1.000	2	0	2	0	0
Miller	.983	42	44	72	2	14
Monasterio	.990	32	40	57	1	19
Turang	.986	119	164	268	6	53
Urias	1.000	11	9	13	0	5

Third Base	PCT	G	PO	A	E	DP
Anderson	.966	70	45	96	5	11
Brosseau	.844	20	3	24	5	2
Donaldson	.975	15	8	31	1	4
Miller	.981	23	12	40	1	2
Monasterio	.960	56	29	91	5	10
Toro	.833	4	0	5	1	0
Urias	.964	11	9	18	1	1

Shortstop	PCT	G	PO	A	E	DP
Adames	.973	147	159	351	14	58
Monasterio	1.000	5	3	8	0	2
Turang	1.000	22	16	27	0	8

Outfield	PCT	G	PO	A	E	DP
Anderson	1.000	39	58	4	0	0
Canha	.967	30	32	0	1	0
Frelick	1.000	71	95	4	0	1
Miller	1.000	9	4	1	0	0
Mitchell	1.000	19	46	0	0	0
Perkins	.994	66	107	5	1	1
Tapia	.667	20	22	0	0	0
Taylor	1.000	89	130	4	0	2
Wiemer	.996	135	287	7	3	1
Winker	.500	6	1	0	0	0
Yelich	.991	122	222	0	2	0

NASHVILLE SOUNDS — *TRIPLE-A*

INTERNATIONALLEAGUE

Batting	B-T	Ht.	Wt.	DOB	AVG	OBP	SLG	G	PA	AB	R	H	2B	3B	HR	RBI	BB	HBP	SH	SF	SO	SB	CS	BB%	SO%
Allen, Greg	B-R	6-0	185	3-15-93	.219	.297	.250	8	37	32	4	7	1	0	0	1	3	1	0	1	7	3	1	8.1	18.9
Alvarez, Eddy	L-R	5-8	178	1-30-90	.283	.397	.473	63	257	205	42	58	14	2	7	31	36	6	5	5	58	16	2	14.0	22.6
2-team (1 Worcester)					.286	.402	.476	64	259	206	42	59	14	2	7	31	37	6	5	5	58	17	2	14.3	22.4
Anderson, Brian	R-R	6-2	215	5-19-93	.250	.400	.250	2	10	8	0	2	0	0	0	0	2	0	0	0	2	0	0	20.0	20.0
Black, Tyler	L-R	5-10	190	7-26-00	.310	.428	.514	39	173	142	35	44	9	4	4	25	27	3	0	1	23	8	3	15.6	13.3
Bolt, Skye	B-R	6-2	194	1-15-94	.257	.359	.367	64	248	210	36	54	10	2	3	23	33	2	0	3	60	3	1	13.3	24.2
Brosseau, Mike	R-R	5-11	203	3-15-94	.164	.205	.329	20	78	73	8	12	0	0	4	10	3	1	0	1	21	0	1	3.8	26.9
Campbell, Noah	B-R	5-11	200	6-06-99	.217	.278	.301	32	90	83	7	18	1	0	2	12	6	1	0	0	22	0	1	6.7	24.4
Chourio, Jackson	R-R	5-11	165	3-11-04	.333	.375	.476	6	24	21	4	7	3	0	0	2	2	0	0	1	1	1	0	8.3	4.2
Collins, Isaac	B-R	5-7	185	7-22-97	.000	.222	.000	3	9	7	0	0	0	0	0	0	2	0	0	0	1	0	0	22.2	11.1
Devanney, Cam	R-R	6-1	195	4-13-97	.271	.362	.461	103	390	336	57	91	27	2	11	47	46	4	0	3	71	6	5	11.8	18.2
Diaz, Brent	R-R	6-1	205	3-22-96	.357	.438	.786	6	16	14	3	5	0	0	2	2	2	0	0	0	3	0	0	12.5	18.8
Donaldson, Josh	R-R	6-1	210	12-08-85	.176	.364	.529	5	22	17	5	3	0	0	2	3	5	0	0	0	4	0	0	22.7	18.2
2-team (3 Scranton/Wilkes-Barre)					.231	.429	.615	8	35	26	9	6	1	0	3	5	9	0	0	0	6	0	0	25.7	17.1
Dorrian, Patrick	L-R	6-2	188	6-26-96	.238	.312	.466	100	407	365	55	87	18	1	21	65	34	6	0	2	127	4	3	8.4	31.2
Frelick, Sal	L-R	5-10	182	4-19-00	.247	.333	.342	40	183	158	25	39	7	1	2	18	19	2	0	1	18	8	4	10.4	9.8
Harrison, Monte	R-R	6-1	218	8-10-95	.208	.277	.316	88	296	269	45	56	12	1	5	23	22	4	0	1	123	18	6	7.4	41.6
Henry, Payton	R-R	6-0	229	6-24-97	.294	.341	.454	65	255	238	32	70	11	0	9	35	12	5	0	0	59	0	1	4.7	23.1
Hiura, Keston	R-R	5-11	208	8-02-96	.308	.395	.565	85	367	315	55	97	12	0	23	77	31	17	0	4	90	0	2	8.4	24.5
Jackson, Alex	R-R	5-11	238	12-25-95	.286	.360	.554	45	189	168	31	48	7	1	12	35	16	4	0	1	48	0	0	8.5	25.4
2-team (14 Durham)					.284	.348	.556	59	248	225	42	64	11	1	16	45	18	4	0	1	62	0	0	7.3	25.0
Jones, Jahmai	R-R	6-0	210	8-04-97	.232	.392	.352	41	182	142	31	33	8	0	3	14	37	1	1	1	42	10	1	20.3	23.1
Miller, Owen	R-R	5-11	195	11-15-96	.283	.336	.472	29	116	106	12	30	8	0	4	17	6	3	0	1	18	1	0	5.2	15.5
Mitchell, Garrett	L-R	6-3	224	9-04-98	.188	.257	.250	8	35	32	3	6	0	1	0	0	2	1	0	0	6	3	0	5.7	17.1
Monasterio, Andruw	R-R	5-11	186	5-30-97	.271	.410	.400	42	178	140	26	38	6	0	4	19	32	3	0	3	29	11	2	18.0	16.3
Naquin, Tyler	L-R	6-1	202	4-24-91	.284	.333	.432	40	160	148	21	42	4	0	6	21	9	2	1	0	45	3	0	5.6	28.1
2-team (28 Charlotte)					.257	.317	.408	68	269	245	31	63	10	0	9	30	19	3	1	1	81	3	0	7.1	30.1
Navarreto, Brian	R-R	6-2	233	12-29-94	.233	.305	.380	78	301	266	33	62	14	2	7	42	27	2	1	3	64	0	0	9.0	21.3
Perkins, Blake	B-R	5-11	197	9-10-96	.308	.396	.500	40	182	156	28	48	14	2	4	17	24	0	0	2	39	5	2	13.2	21.4
Quinn, Roman	B-R	5-10	175	5-14-93	.121	.275	.152	10	41	33	5	4	1	0	0	3	6	1	1	0	11	5	0	14.6	26.8
2-team (15 Columbus)					.149	.326	.194	25	89	67	13	10	3	0	0	9	16	3	3	0	30	7	0	18.0	33.7
Reed, Michael	B-R	6-4	218	4-27-95	.207	.311	.326	29	107	92	10	19	5	0	2	11	14	0	1	0	36	4	1	13.1	33.6
Roller, Chris	R-R	5-11	190	10-08-96	.364	.493	.618	16	69	55	9	20	3	1	3	20	13	1	0	0	15	6	2	18.8	21.7
2-team (92 Columbus)					.247	.399	.449	108	396	312	55	77	16	1	15	67	68	11	0	5	109	19	6	17.2	27.5
Ruf, Darin	R-R	6-2	232	7-28-86	.120	.258	.280	7	31	25	1	3	1	0	1	5	5	0	0	1	10	0	0	16.1	32.3
Singleton, Jon	L-L	6-0	256	9-18-91	.258	.384	.483	49	216	178	23	46	8	1	10	29	37	0	0	1	41	0	1	17.1	19.0
Taylor, Tyrone	R-R	6-1	218	1-22-94	.245	.339	.571	12	56	49	11	12	2	1	4	12	4	3	0	0	12	2	0	7.1	21.4

Tellez, Rowdy	L-L	6-4	270	3-16-95	.226	.294	.387	8	34	31	4	7	2	0	1	5	3	0	0	0	7	0	0	8.8	20.6
Toro, Abraham	B-R	6-0	223	12-20-96	.291	.374	.471	96	414	357	53	104	36	2	8	58	49	2	0	6	73	8	2	11.8	17.6
Turang, Brice	L-R	6-0	176	11-21-99	.298	.365	.561	15	63	57	10	17	6	0	3	15	6	0	0	0	10	2	0	9.5	15.9
Urias, Luis	R-R	5-10	202	6-03-97	.233	.345	.379	29	139	116	20	27	5	0	4	16	19	2	0	2	34	1	1	13.7	24.5
VanMeter, Josh	L-R	5-9	198	3-10-95	.199	.400	.362	46	190	141	31	28	3	1	6	20	46	2	0	1	43	1	1	24.2	22.6
Voit, Luke	R-R	6-2	258	2-13-91	.259	.444	.481	8	36	27	5	7	3	0	1	8	8	1	0	0	9	0	0	22.2	25.0
2-team (37 Syracuse)					.263	.422	.615	45	200	156	35	41	8	1	15	43	39	4	0	1	53	0	0	19.5	26.5
Wiemer, Joey	R-R	6-4	220	2-11-99	.105	.143	.263	5	21	19	3	2	0	0	1	3	1	0	0	1	3	0	0	4.8	14.3
Winker, Jesse	L-L	6-2	230	8-17-93	.286	.462	.500	23	93	70	13	20	3	0	4	7	23	0	0	0	13	0	3	24.7	14.0

Pitching	B-T	Ht.	Wt.	DOB	W	L	ERA	G	GS	SV	IP	Hits	Runs	ER	HR	BB	SO	AVG	OBP	SLG	SO%	BB%	BF
Abad, Fernando	L-L	6-2	235	12-17-85	0	1	7.88	9	0	2	8	15	8	7	2	4	8	.395	.452	.711	19.0	9.5	42
Alexander, Jason	R-R	6-2	227	3-01-93	2	4	5.86	16	8	1	55	73	43	36	5	19	35	.322	.375	.467	13.8	7.5	253
Andrews, Clayton	L-L	5-6	160	1-04-97	6	0	2.53	48	1	5	57	39	18	16	4	31	74	.193	.300	.307	31.1	13.0	238
Ashby, Aaron	R-L	6-1	188	5-24-98	0	1	27.00	2	2	0	2	1	6	5	0	7	1	.167	.615	.167	7.7	53.8	13
Bennett, Nick	L-L	6-4	210	9-01-97	1	0	27.00	1	0	0	1	4	4	3	0	0	1	.500	.556	.500	11.1	0.0	9
Boushley, Caleb	R-R	6-3	190	10-01-93	9	8	5.11	29	26	0	136	136	82	77	18	51	110	.263	.331	.440	18.9	8.8	581
Bukauskas, J.B.	R-R	6-0	208	10-11-96	5	2	2.92	32	0	6	37	35	19	12	2	10	42	.246	.299	.338	26.8	6.4	157
Bush, Matt	R-R	5-10	193	2-08-86	0	0	0.00	6	0	0	5	1	1	0	0	4	6	.063	.250	.063	30.0	20.0	20
Claudio, Alex	L-L	6-2	190	1-31-92	2	2	4.19	51	1	3	43	54	26	20	1	13	26	.310	.362	.385	13.8	6.9	188
Contreras, Luis	R-R	6-1	175	4-29-96	4	2	4.76	26	0	1	45	42	28	24	5	20	61	.240	.323	.400	30.3	10.0	201
Cousins, Jake	R-R	6-4	193	7-14-94	1	2	7.30	13	0	0	12	17	10	10	1	4	22	.321	.379	.434	37.9	6.9	58
Dorrian, Patrick	L-R	6-2	188	6-26-96	0	0	13.50	1	0	0	2	3	3	3	2	3	0	.333	.500	1.111	0.0	25.0	12
Erceg, Lucas	L-R	6-2	214	5-01-95	3	1	6.46	13	0	0	15	14	15	11	3	10	16	.250	.364	.429	23.9	14.9	67
Fernandez, Pedro	R-R	6-0	175	5-25-94	3	3	4.05	21	10	0	67	69	33	30	14	28	57	.267	.343	.492	19.7	9.7	290
Gasser, Robert	L-L	6-0	192	5-31-99	9	1	3.79	26	25	0	135	123	64	57	12	50	166	.236	.318	.372	28.0	8.4	592
Henry, Payton	R-R	6-0	229	6-24-97	0	0	13.50	1	0	0	2	2	3	3	1	2	0	.250	.455	.625	0.0	18.2	11
Herb, Tyler	R-R	6-4	212	4-28-92	1	0	1.93	3	0	0	5	5	1	1	1	0	5	.278	.278	.500	27.8	0.0	18
Houser, Adrian	R-R	6-3	242	2-02-93	0	1	3.07	4	4	0	15	17	5	5	2	5	12	.321	.379	.453	20.7	8.6	58
Jarvis, Justin	R-R	6-2	183	2-20-00	0	2	10.80	3	3	0	12	17	16	14	2	12	11	.354	.468	.604	17.7	19.4	62
Junk, Janson	R-R	6-2	202	1-15-96	7	10	4.18	27	25	0	140	145	77	65	14	44	94	.269	.327	.407	15.8	7.4	594
Lauer, Eric	R-L	6-3	209	6-03-95	3	4	5.15	12	9	0	44	54	33	25	6	23	64	.303	.385	.438	31.1	11.2	206
McKendry, Evan	R-R	6-3	200	2-06-98	4	3	4.93	8	8	0	46	40	25	25	8	18	35	.237	.305	.438	18.4	9.5	190
Meeker, James	R-R	6-4	222	3-22-95	0	0	9.00	2	0	0	4	7	4	4	0	3	1	.389	.478	.556	4.3	13.0	23
Megill, Trevor	L-R	6-8	250	12-05-93	1	0	4.09	11	0	1	11	7	5	5	0	3	18	.175	.267	.200	40.0	6.7	45
Mejia, J.C.	R-R	6-6	250	8-26-96	2	1	3.86	23	0	0	30	25	18	13	2	13	32	.229	.325	.376	25.2	10.2	127
Middendorf, Ryan	L-R	6-6	220	12-22-97	1	0	7.71	10	0	0	12	14	11	10	1	6	14	.286	.397	.469	24.1	10.3	58
Miller, Tyson	R-R	6-5	220	7-29-95	1	0	3.86	15	0	0	26	27	13	11	1	10	27	.281	.345	.396	24.5	9.1	110
Myers, Tobias	R-R	6-1	217	8-05-98	0	0	0.00	2	0	0	3	1	0	0	0	1	7	.100	.182	.100	63.6	9.1	11
Pannone, Thomas	L-L	6-0	209	4-28-94	3	1	2.70	11	9	0	53	45	18	16	5	13	50	.224	.278	.358	23.1	6.0	216
Peguero, Elvis	R-R	6-5	237	3-20-97	2	0	2.45	4	0	0	7	7	2	2	1	2	10	.241	.290	.345	32.3	6.5	31
Rea, Colin	R-R	6-5	218	7-01-90	0	0	2.50	4	4	0	18	16	7	5	1	1	21	.239	.257	.373	30.0	1.4	70
Robinson, Cam	R-R	6-0	205	9-06-99	0	1	6.75	8	0	0	8	11	7	6	0	7	11	.333	.439	.333	26.8	17.1	41
Rodriguez, Carlos F.	R-R	6-0	206	11-27-01	0	0	5.79	1	1	0	5	5	3	3	0	4	6	.313	.435	.313	26.1	17.4	23
Seminaris, Adam	R-L	6-0	191	10-19-98	0	0	15.00	1	1	0	3	7	5	5	1	2	1	.438	.500	.625	5.6	11.1	18
Small, Ethan	L-L	6-2	200	2-14-97	2	4	3.18	38	2	3	51	40	20	18	5	24	61	.212	.304	.354	28.5	11.2	214
Sousa, Bennett	L-L	6-3	220	4-06-95	2	2	4.76	16	0	1	17	15	10	9	2	7	23	.231	.315	.369	31.5	9.6	73
Stock, Robert	L-R	6-1	260	11-21-89	0	3	8.22	11	4	0	23	29	22	21	6	18	19	.319	.456	.604	16.7	15.8	114
Strzelecki, Peter	R-R	6-2	216	10-24-94	0	0	7.04	7	0	1	8	7	7	6	0	4	11	.226	.333	.355	30.6	11.1	36
Teheran, Julio	R-R	6-2	205	1-27-91	2	0	4.40	4	4	0	14	13	8	7	1	6	13	.241	.349	.352	20.6	9.5	63
Thompson, Darrell	L-L	6-4	185	4-27-94	4	3	5.12	39	0	0	46	44	27	26	8	25	57	.257	.361	.450	28.2	12.4	202
Uribe, Abner	R-R	6-3	225	6-20-00	0	0	2.25	7	0	0	8	3	2	2	0	7	13	.107	.306	.143	36.1	19.4	36
Varland, Gus	L-R	6-1	213	11-06-96	0	1	9.82	3	0	0	4	3	4	4	2	4	3	.250	.471	.750	17.6	23.5	17
Vieira, Thyago	R-R	6-3	265	7-01-93	2	2	3.35	33	0	8	38	31	17	14	3	15	51	.223	.304	.345	31.7	9.3	161
Wilson, Justin	L-L	6-2	205	8-18-87	1	0	1.42	7	0	0	6	7	1	1	1	1	6	.280	.308	.400	23.1	3.8	26
Woodruff, Brandon	L-R	6-4	244	2-10-93	0	0	5.79	1	1	0	5	3	3	3	0	2	4	.188	.316	.375	21.1	10.5	19

Fielding

Catcher	PCT	G	PO	A	E	DP	PB
Diaz	1.000	5	42	5	0	1	1
Henry	.989	51	436	31	5	3	4
Jackson	.987	32	289	19	4	2	4
Navarreto	.993	66	562	33	4	5	4

First Base	PCT	G	PO	A	E	DP
Black	.987	9	72	2	1	8
Brosseau	1.000	4	20	1	0	2
Campbell	.966	5	28	0	1	3
Devanney	1.000	8	47	1	0	3
Dorrian	1.000	15	93	4	0	9
Henry	.933	2	13	1	1	1
Hiura	1.000	30	217	14	0	23
Miller	1.000	6	34	0	0	3
Navarreto	.000	1	0	0	0	0
Ruf	1.000	3	21	1	0	1
Singleton	.987	42	277	23	4	34
Tellez	1.000	5	31	1	0	5
Toro	.992	18	112	8	1	11
Voit	1.000	3	19	0	0	1
Winker	1.000	10	65	4	0	6

Second Base	PCT	G	PO	A	E	DP
Alvarez	.969	26	65	59	4	16
Campbell	1.000	4	6	7	0	1
Devanney	.964	14	20	34	2	9
Dorrian	.974	28	51	61	3	20
Hiura	.938	5	8	7	1	2
Jones	.972	10	10	25	1	3
Miller	1.000	7	6	16	0	1
Monasterio	.941	5	4	12	1	1
Toro	.985	20	29	37	1	13
Turang	.966	5	10	18	1	6
Urias	1.000	8	9	15	0	2
VanMeter	.983	25	42	75	2	12

Third Base	PCT	G	PO	A	E	DP
Alvarez	.905	5	7	12	2	0
Anderson	1.000	1	0	4	0	1
Black	.971	28	24	43	2	3
Brosseau	.949	15	10	27	2	5
Devanney	1.000	8	2	9	0	1
Donaldson	1.000	3	3	4	0	1
Dorrian	.957	26	18	48	3	4
Monasterio	1.000	4	6	11	0	1
Toro	.932	49	28	81	8	7
Urias	.946	16	12	23	2	2

Shortstop	PCT	G	PO	A	E	DP
Alvarez	.963	10	9	17	1	0
Devanney	.951	70	82	153	12	35
Dorrian	.933	27	42	70	8	11
Monasterio	.963	33	45	86	5	23
Turang	.935	10	11	32	3	6
Urias	1.000	1	2	2	0	0

Outfield	PCT	G	PO	A	E	DP
Allen	1.000	8	12	0	0	0
Alvarez	.925	20	31	1	3	0
Bolt	.977	61	107	3	3	1
Campbell	1.000	19	18	1	0	0
Chourio	.967	5	16	0	1	0
Collins	1.000	2	4	0	0	0
Frelick	.986	40	87	3	1	2
Harrison	.968	83	155	6	8	2
Hiura	.980	28	46	3	1	1
Jones	.986	31	47	3	1	0
Miller	1.000	20	30	0	0	0
Mitchell	1.000	5	8	0	0	0
Naquin	.667	37	62	3	0	0
Perkins	.972	39	81	5	2	1
Quinn	1.000	9	20	2	0	0
Reed	.977	27	50	1	2	0
Roller	.938	16	34	3	3	0
Taylor	1.000	9	20	3	0	1
VanMeter	1.000	7	9	0	0	0
Wiemer	1.000	4	5	0	0	0
Winker	1.000	4	6	0	0	0

BILOXI SHUCKERS — *DOUBLE-A*

SOUTHERN LEAGUE

Batting	B-T	Ht.	Wt.	DOB	AVG	OBP	SLG	G	PA	AB	R	H	2B	3B	HR	RBI	BB	HBP	SH	SF	SO	SB	CS	BB%	SO%
Black, Tyler	L-R	5-10	190	7-26-00	.273	.411	.513	84	385	308	70	84	16	8	14	48	61	13	0	2	77	47	9	15.8	20.0
Brown, Eric	R-R	5-10	190	12-19-00	.000	.125	.000	5	8	7	1	0	0	0	0	0	1	0	0	0	3	1	0	12.5	37.5
Campbell, Noah	B-R	5-11	200	6-06-99	.255	.394	.431	55	232	188	38	48	9	3	6	28	40	3	1	0	55	6	3	17.2	23.7
Chourio, Jackson	R-R	5-11	165	3-11-04	.280	.336	.467	122	559	510	84	143	23	3	22	89	41	4	0	4	103	43	9	7.3	18.4
Clarke, Wes	R-R	6-0	228	10-13-99	.241	.392	.497	118	503	398	68	96	24	0	26	80	89	12	0	4	147	6	1	17.7	29.2
Collins, Isaac	B-R	5-7	185	7-22-97	.269	.424	.431	93	376	290	67	78	13	2	10	44	75	6	1	4	55	29	9	19.9	14.6
Diaz, Brent	R-R	6-1	205	3-22-96	.308	.438	.423	9	32	26	6	8	3	0	0	5	5	1	0	0	2	0	0	15.6	6.3
Gray Jr., Joe	R-R	6-0	214	3-12-00	.054	.103	.081	10	39	37	3	2	1	0	0	3	1	1	0	0	17	1	0	2.6	43.6
Kahle, Nick	R-R	5-8	210	2-28-98	.169	.329	.356	27	74	59	7	10	2	0	3	17	13	1	1	0	15	0	0	17.6	20.3
Lopez, Jason	R-R	5-9	160	3-16-98	.273	.385	.455	12	26	22	3	6	1	0	1	3	3	1	0	0	7	0	0	11.5	26.9
Lutz, Tristen	R-R	6-1	210	8-22-98	.221	.348	.377	48	187	154	20	34	6	0	6	24	27	4	0	2	65	0	1	14.4	34.8
Martinez, Ernesto	L-L	6-5	250	6-20-99	.245	.355	.349	31	125	106	17	26	5	0	2	14	17	1	0	0	22	3	2	13.6	17.6
Murray, Ethan	R-R	5-10	201	5-13-00	.256	.359	.370	104	413	351	52	90	16	3	6	48	53	4	2	2	93	10	5	12.8	22.5
Quero, Jeferson	R-R	5-11	215	10-08-02	.262	.339	.440	90	381	336	47	88	12	0	16	49	38	3	0	4	68	5	0	10.0	17.8
Rodriguez, Carlos D.	L-L	5-8	186	12-07-00	.291	.359	.367	115	436	392	51	114	21	3	1	43	40	2	1	1	50	14	8	9.2	11.5
Sparks, Lamar	R-R	6-1	170	9-26-98	.253	.364	.421	90	343	292	57	74	16	3	9	47	48	3	0	0	120	19	7	14.0	35.0
Valerio, Felix	R-R	5-5	165	12-26-00	.223	.286	.345	80	290	264	41	59	10	2	6	31	19	5	0	2	54	7	5	6.6	18.6
Warren, Zavier	B-R	5-10	215	1-08-99	.236	.319	.406	105	429	377	57	89	15	2	15	63	45	3	0	4	86	6	3	10.5	20.0
Wilken, Brock	R-R	6-4	225	6-17-02	.217	.280	.565	6	25	23	3	5	2	0	2	8	2	0	0	0	9	0	0	8.0	36.0
Zamora, Freddy	R-R	5-10	190	11-01-98	.255	.352	.361	108	437	377	64	96	17	1	7	51	53	5	0	2	89	17	3	12.1	20.4

Pitching	B-T	Ht.	Wt.	DOB	W	L	ERA	G	GS	SV	IP	Hits	Runs	ER	HR	BB	SO	AVG	OBP	SLG	SO%	BB%	BF
Alexander, Jason	R-R	6-2	227	3-01-93	0	0	15.00	1	1	0	3	8	5	5	0	1	1	.500	.529	.688	5.6	5.6	18
Amaya, Luis	L-L	5-11	160	8-26-98	1	0	5.79	20	0	0	23	24	16	15	2	14	31	.261	.378	.402	27.9	12.6	111
Ashby, Aaron	R-L	6-1	188	5-24-98	0	1	27.00	2	1	0	2	3	5	5	0	2	1	.429	.600	.429	10.0	20.0	10
Baker, Robbie	R-R	6-1	211	1-31-95	3	2	5.96	31	0	0	54	66	36	36	16	20	57	.301	.360	.571	23.6	8.3	242
Bennett, Nick	L-L	6-4	210	9-01-97	3	3	4.08	32	3	0	64	61	34	29	9	25	63	.248	.330	.398	22.7	9.0	277
Bowman, Kaleb	R-R	6-1	195	5-22-97	2	0	7.97	16	0	0	20	26	19	18	4	8	26	.299	.378	.517	26.5	8.2	98
Brady, Ryan	R-R	6-1	185	3-23-99	1	1	2.57	18	0	0	28	29	13	8	0	10	26	.259	.325	.366	21.1	8.1	123
Chirino, Harold	R-R	6-2	173	1-12-98	0	0	0.00	11	0	0	14	7	0	0	0	3	22	.156	.208	.200	45.8	6.3	48
Contreras, Luis	R-R	6-1	175	4-29-96	0	1	4.00	13	0	0	18	16	8	8	2	8	29	.229	.341	.343	35.4	9.8	82
Jarvis, Justin	R-R	6-2	183	2-20-00	6	4	3.33	14	14	0	76	69	31	28	10	26	91	.240	.306	.410	28.6	8.2	318
Kahle, Nick	R-R	5-8	210	2-28-98	0	0	0.00	1	0	0	1	1	0	0	0	0	0	.333	.333	.667	0.0	0.0	3
Knarr, Brandon	R-L	5-10	217	6-02-98	0	2	8.25	5	3	0	12	17	12	11	2	9	19	.321	.419	.566	30.6	14.5	62
Lazar, Max	R-R	6-1	200	6-03-99	0	2	3.86	17	1	1	26	26	15	11	3	10	30	.260	.324	.420	27.0	9.0	111
Lopez, Jason	R-R	5-9	160	3-16-98	0	0	0.00	1	0	0	1	1	0	0	0	0	1	.250	.250	.250	25.0	0.0	4
Meeker, James	R-R	6-4	222	3-22-95	8	4	3.13	34	8	1	89	90	39	31	12	12	80	.258	.292	.413	21.6	3.2	371
Mejias, Christian	R-R	6-0	160	5-19-99	6	12	6.90	27	24	0	121	127	99	93	21	58	123	.266	.356	.483	22.3	10.5	552
Middendorf, Ryan	L-R	6-6	220	12-22-97	3	1	3.74	32	0	2	46	54	24	19	4	12	43	.286	.346	.423	20.6	5.7	209
Miley, Wade	L-L	6-1	220	11-13-86	1	0	0.00	1	1	0	5	4	0	0	0	1	5	.211	.250	.211	25.0	5.0	20
Misiorowski, Jacob	R-R	6-7	190	4-03-02	2	1	5.57	5	5	0	21	17	13	13	2	16	36	.215	.411	.316	33.6	15.0	107
Myers, Tobias	R-R	6-1	217	8-05-98	10	5	5.03	27	26	0	138	129	85	77	30	45	168	.242	.307	.487	28.7	7.7	586
Robinson, Cam	R-R	6-0	205	9-06-99	3	1	5.06	41	0	15	43	47	26	24	6	32	47	.272	.390	.422	22.3	15.2	211
Rodriguez, Carlos F.	R-R	6-0	206	11-27-01	9	6	2.77	25	25	0	124	82	46	38	10	53	152	.183	.281	.276	29.5	10.3	516
Seminaris, Adam	R-L	6-0	191	10-19-98	2	5	5.70	12	12	0	54	60	35	34	5	21	57	.286	.353	.471	24.3	8.9	235
Shook, TJ	R-R	6-4	217	5-29-98	7	5	4.62	25	12	1	97	83	59	50	13	36	107	.229	.312	.394	26.0	8.7	412
Smith, Russell	L-L	6-7	255	9-10-98	1	3	5.11	21	1	0	37	37	22	21	8	18	47	.255	.357	.476	28.0	10.7	168
Smith, Shane	R-R	6-4	235	4-04-00	0	0	0.00	2	0	0	2	1	0	0	0	1	2	.167	.286	.167	28.6	14.3	7
Thompson, Darrell	L-L	6-4	185	4-27-94	1	1	0.68	9	0	1	13	5	2	1	0	4	20	.122	.196	.171	42.6	8.5	47
Uribe, Abner	R-R	6-3	225	6-20-00	1	0	1.80	15	0	7	15	7	4	3	1	9	28	.137	.279	.216	45.9	14.8	61
Vennaro, Zach	R-R	6-6	220	6-03-96	4	3	6.05	41	0	4	42	38	35	28	1	35	47	.241	.408	.323	22.7	16.9	207
Yeager, Justin	L-R	6-4	215	1-20-98	0	0	0.00	3	0	0	2	1	0	0	0	3	2	.125	.364	.125	18.2	27.3	11

Fielding

Catcher	PCT	G	PO	A	E	DP	PB
Clarke	.985	34	330	9	5	2	4
Diaz	1.000	9	63	3	0	0	0
Kahle	.981	26	194	11	4	2	2
Lopez	.986	9	66	3	1	0	0
Quero	.988	74	717	44	9	3	10

First Base	PCT	G	PO	A	E	DP
Black	1.000	7	74	4	0	4
Campbell	.978	8	42	3	1	2
Clarke	.990	43	273	14	3	17
Martinez	.986	27	203	15	3	21
Warren	.989	57	339	33	4	24

Second Base	PCT	G	PO	A	E	DP
Brown	.000	1	0	0	0	0
Campbell	1.000	1	1	2	0	0
Collins	.976	24	29	53	2	7
Murray	1.000	39	61	92	0	18
Valerio	.969	59	74	142	7	23

	PCT	G	PO	A	E	DP
Warren	1.000	1	1	2	0	1
Zamora	.947	19	24	48	4	4

Third Base	PCT	G	PO	A	E	DP
Black	.921	69	48	81	11	6
Collins	.857	4	3	3	1	0
Murray	.976	17	18	22	1	2
Valerio	1.000	3	2	0	0	0
Warren	.943	42	23	60	5	7
Wilken	.867	5	5	8	2	2

Shortstop	PCT	G	PO	A	E	DP
Brown	1.000	2	2	4	0	1
Murray	.930	50	77	96	13	17
Warren	1.000	1	0	2	0	0
Zamora	.946	88	126	188	18	29

Outfield	PCT	G	PO	A	E	DP
Campbell	1.000	30	37	3	0	1
Chourio	.990	111	199	6	4	0
Collins	.663	62	96	3	1	1
Gray Jr.	.967	11	18	2	1	1
Lutz	.986	23	37	0	1	0
Rodriguez	.982	118	187	9	4	0
Sparks	.968	87	150	7	3	2

WISCONSIN TIMBER RATTLERS — *HIGH CLASS A*

MIDWEST LEAGUE

Batting	B-T	Ht.	Wt.	DOB	AVG	OBP	SLG	G	PA	AB	R	H	2B	3B	HR	RBI	BB	HBP	SH	SF	SO	SB	CS	BB%	SO%
Acosta, Jose	B-R	5-10	170	3-20-00	.225	.282	.419	50	178	160	25	36	10	3	5	19	10	3	4	1	45	5	5	5.6	25.3
Adames, Willy	R-R	6-1	214	9-02-95	.333	.556	1.000	2	9	6	3	2	1	0	1	1	3	0	0	0	1	1	0	33.3	11.1
Bello, Micah	R-R	5-10	165	7-21-00	.186	.239	.256	14	46	43	3	8	3	0	0	1	3	0	0	0	15	0	0	6.5	32.6
Boeve, Mike	L-R	6-3	200	5-05-02	.250	.333	.333	19	84	72	11	18	3	0	1	18	10	0	0	2	19	1	0	11.9	22.6
Brown, Eric	R-R	5-10	190	12-19-00	.265	.362	.347	63	287	245	48	65	8	0	4	25	32	7	0	3	48	37	5	11.1	16.7
Chirinos, Jesus	R-R	6-0	165	7-27-01	.177	.282	.339	19	71	62	7	11	4	0	2	5	9	0	0	0	24	1	0	12.7	33.8
Doston, Terence	L-R	5-10	160	9-22-00	.251	.319	.309	63	211	191	28	48	6	1	1	21	16	3	1	0	35	16	3	7.6	16.6
Fernandez, Eduarqui	R-R	6-2	176	11-20-01	.230	.306	.345	50	183	165	23	38	8	1	3	19	16	2	0	0	71	9	2	8.7	38.8
Garcia, Eduardo	R-R	6-1	160	7-10-02	.208	.280	.326	80	329	298	36	62	13	5	4	29	26	4	0	1	106	10	2	7.9	32.2
Gray Jr., Joe	R-R	6-0	214	3-12-00	.249	.305	.378	101	440	402	50	100	17	1	11	57	27	7	0	4	104	16	8	6.1	23.6
Hall, Alex	B-R	5-10	204	6-08-99	.227	.328	.401	78	322	277	41	63	15	0	11	40	39	3	0	1	72	0	0	12.1	22.4
Lara, Luis	B-R	5-7	155	11-17-04	.290	.351	.377	17	79	69	13	20	2	2	0	8	5	2	0	1	15	8	1	6.3	19.0
Martinez, Ernesto	L-L	6-5	250	6-20-99	.267	.341	.444	67	272	243	33	65	11	1	10	30	23	4	0	0	57	13	4	8.5	21.0
Mendez, Hendry	L-L	6-2	175	11-07-03	.236	.307	.326	62	257	233	29	55	8	2	3	25	23	1	0	0	40	0	1	8.9	15.6
Metzinger, Ben	R-R	5-11	195	6-26-99	.226	.344	.321	94	375	318	43	72	15	0	5	45	55	2	0	0	119	1	0	14.7	31.7
Miller, Darrien	L-R	5-10	186	3-10-01	.228	.336	.364	89	372	316	45	72	20	1	7	47	43	10	0	3	76	4	1	11.6	20.4
Moore, Robert	B-R	5-9	170	3-31-02	.233	.321	.361	123	563	490	68	114	33	3	8	62	55	11	2	5	108	26	13	9.8	19.2
Vargas, Jheremy	R-R	5-10	160	5-10-03	.241	.313	.276	18	64	58	7	14	2	0	0	4	6	0	0	0	18	1	1	9.4	28.1
Ward, Je'Von	L-R	6-2	190	10-25-99	.231	.297	.390	78	291	264	38	61	18	0	8	30	24	1	0	1	94	8	3	8.2	32.3
Wilken, Brock	R-R	6-4	225	6-17-02	.289	.427	.438	34	150	121	21	35	6	3	2	15	27	2	0	0	32	3	0	18.0	21.3
Winker, Jesse	L-L	6-2	230	8-17-93	.385	.467	.462	4	15	13	2	5	1	0	0	2	2	0	0	0	2	0	0	13.3	13.3
Wood, Matthew	L-R	5-10	190	3-02-01	.242	.349	.284	83	361	306	28	74	8	1	1	43	47	5	0	3	53	2	1	13.0	14.7

Pitching	B-T	Ht.	Wt.	DOB	W	L	ERA	G	GS	SV	IP	Hits	Runs	ER	HR	BB	SO	AVG	OBP	SLG	SO%	BB%	BF
Amaya, Luis	L-L	5-11	160	8-26-98	2	2	2.41	17	0	2	37	27	10	10	4	9	31	.196	.255	.312	20.7	6.0	150
Ashby, Aaron	R-L	6-1	188	5-24-98	0	1	4.91	3	3	0	4	3	3	2	1	5	5	.214	.421	.500	26.3	26.3	19
Blalock, Bradley	R-R	6-2	200	12-25-00	0	0	5.27	4	4	0	14	13	8	8	3	7	17	.245	.328	.623	27.9	11.5	61
Bowman, Kaleb	R-R	6-1	195	5-22-97	0	1	2.77	13	0	6	13	9	5	4	0	3	15	.200	.260	.244	30.0	6.0	50
Brady, Ryan	R-R	6-1	185	3-23-99	3	3	2.76	19	0	1	49	39	19	15	2	9	46	.218	.268	.302	23.7	4.6	194
Cornielle, Alexander	R-R	6-2	180	8-22-01	1	3	4.55	20	18	0	89	77	47	45	6	34	92	.231	.313	.360	24.4	9.0	377
Cruz, Stiven	R-R	6-2	165	11-14-01	7	6	6.90	24	19	1	90	102	75	69	16	54	74	.287	.388	.503	17.6	12.9	420
Floyd, Taylor	R-R	6-1	185	12-08-97	1	2	3.04	15	0	0	24	16	10	8	2	7	32	.190	.250	.310	34.8	7.6	92
Gardner, Sam	R-R	6-1	205	1-04-97	3	1	2.22	21	0	3	45	34	14	11	3	25	59	.207	.309	.335	30.9	13.1	191
Guerrero, Miguel	R-R	6-5	216	7-15-00	2	1	6.11	14	0	1	28	31	20	19	4	10	24	.282	.347	.491	19.4	8.1	124
Hall, Alex	B-R	5-10	204	6-08-99	0	0	18.00	1	0	0	1	3	2	2	0	0	0	.500	.500	.667	0.0	0.0	6
Hernandez, Joseph	R-R	5-11	150	6-15-00	2	3	4.02	12	10	0	47	34	24	21	4	30	34	.202	.341	.345	16.3	14.4	208
Jimenez, Edwin	R-R	6-3	175	12-12-01	7	5	4.50	21	15	0	102	96	52	51	14	31	93	.247	.306	.443	21.7	7.2	428
Jordan, Brannon	R-R	6-2	190	7-20-98	3	0	3.21	26	0	2	34	31	14	12	3	13	39	.242	.312	.406	27.7	9.2	141
King, Justin	L-L	6-1	215	12-19-97	1	2	2.93	28	0	1	31	23	14	10	1	25	54	.205	.353	.286	38.6	17.9	140
Lazar, Max	R-R	6-1	200	6-03-99	1	3	2.91	16	0	2	43	41	16	14	2	9	43	.250	.290	.390	24.3	5.1	177
Matulovich, Joey	R-R	6-3	208	7-06-97	0	0	8.44	5	0	0	5	7	5	5	0	4	4	.389	.500	.611	18.2	18.2	22
Merkel, Nick	R-R	6-7	255	7-03-98	3	3	3.88	19	0	2	49	41	24	21	5	13	53	.225	.274	.368	26.2	6.4	202
Misiorowski, Jacob	R-R	6-7	190	4-03-02	1	0	1.90	6	6	0	24	15	7	5	0	14	28	.176	.321	.235	26.4	13.2	106
Morales, Karlos	L-L	6-3	170	8-10-99	4	6	4.91	33	0	2	48	39	29	26	3	40	54	.220	.374	.379	24.3	18.0	222
Peterson, Nate	L-L	5-10	180	2-15-00	2	3	4.94	7	7	0	31	32	18	17	6	13	23	.264	.331	.512	16.9	9.6	136
Shears, Tanner	R-R	6-3	205	6-20-99	3	1	1.52	26	0	7	30	14	6	5	2	25	44	.140	.358	.210	32.8	18.7	134
Smith, Russell	L-L	6-7	255	9-10-98	1	2	4.15	8	1	0	17	21	10	8	2	11	27	.288	.388	.438	31.8	12.9	85
Smith, Shane	R-R	6-4	235	4-04-00	3	1	1.37	17	0	6	26	12	5	4	2	10	34	.133	.228	.222	33.7	9.9	101
Teheran, Julio	R-R	6-2	205	1-27-91	0	0	3.00	1	1	0	3	3	1	1	1	0	4	.250	.308	.583	30.8	0.0	13
Varland, Gus	L-R	6-1	213	11-06-96	0	1	13.50	2	0	0	2	4	3	3	0	1	0	.400	.455	.700	0.0	9.1	11
Vassalotti, Michele	R-R	6-2	180	8-02-00	0	0	6.75	24	0	0	35	35	29	26	3	32	42	.255	.421	.423	23.5	17.9	179
Wagoner, Cameron	R-R	6-5	187	6-21-01	6	11	5.67	24	22	0	100	112	71	63	7	38	87	.280	.360	.420	19.2	8.4	454
Woessner, Tyler	R-R	6-4	230	10-26-99	6	7	4.02	24	22	0	121	115	63	54	7	54	112	.247	.324	.357	21.3	10.3	525
Woodruff, Brandon	L-R	6-4	244	2-10-93	0	0	1.29	2	2	0	7	6	1	1	0	0	7	.240	.240	.280	28.0	0.0	25

Fielding

Catcher	PCT	G	PO	A	E	DP	PB
Hall	.988	19	155	7	2	1	2
Miller	.990	59	548	37	6	4	3
Wood	.996	56	504	26	2	2	6

First Base	PCT	G	PO	A	E	DP
Acosta	.750	1	2	1	1	0
Chirinos	.968	12	87	3	3	10
Hall	.980	25	193	8	4	20
Martinez	.986	64	441	35	7	42
Metzinger	.981	29	194	10	4	17
Vargas	1.000	3	21	2	0	2
Winker	1.000	3	11	0	0	0

MILWAUKEE BREWERS

Second Base	PCT	G	PO	A	E	DP
Acosta	.954	38	55	90	7	20
Boeve	.919	10	11	23	3	7
Brown	1.000	6	5	9	0	2
Moore	.969	72	78	174	8	33
Vargas	1.000	9	11	24	0	8

Third Base	PCT	G	PO	A	E	DP
Acosta	1.000	1	0	1	0	0
Boeve	.900	4	3	6	1	0
Garcia	.958	45	39	74	5	8
Metzinger	.956	52	51	79	6	3
Moore	1.000	1	1	2	0	0
Vargas	.923	4	6	6	1	0
Wilken	.941	27	17	47	4	1

Shortstop	PCT	G	PO	A	E	DP
Adames	1.000	1	3	2	0	1
Brown	.946	53	86	125	12	35
Garcia	.977	32	48	78	3	17
Moore	.983	46	67	103	3	23
Vargas	1.000	2	4	4	0	0

Outfield	PCT	G	PO	A	E	DP
Acosta	.750	7	8	0	1	0
Bello	.875	13	17	2	1	0
Doston	.991	57	118	3	1	0
Fernandez	.987	49	105	1	1	1
Gray Jr.	1.000	99	203	9	0	2
Hall	1.000	29	47	4	0	0
Lara	1.000	17	36	0	0	0
Mendez	.887	54	79	4	8	0
Ward	.986	75	150	3	3	1

CAROLINA MUDCATS — *LOW CLASS A*

CAROLINA LEAGUE

Batting	B-T	Ht.	Wt.	DOB	AVG	OBP	SLG	G	PA	AB	R	H	2B	3B	HR	RBI	BB	HBP	SH	SF	SO	SB	CS	BB%	SO%
Adams, Luke	R-R	6-4	210	4-24-04	.233	.400	.401	99	440	339	74	79	18	3	11	54	76	21	0	4	99	30	10	17.3	22.5
Areinamo, Jadher	R-R	5-8	160	11-28-03	.306	.333	.407	103	420	396	52	121	26	1	4	52	17	2	0	5	52	16	5	4.0	12.4
Avina, Jace	R-R	5-11	180	6-06-03	.233	.373	.442	99	399	326	57	76	22	2	14	50	56	17	0	0	118	10	3	14.0	29.6
Baez, Juan	R-R	5-9	175	6-27-05	.233	.265	.333	9	34	30	7	7	3	0	0	6	2	0	0	2	4	2	0	5.9	11.8
Barrios, Gregory	R-R	6-0	180	4-08-04	.232	.283	.302	106	445	410	52	95	20	3	1	37	24	7	0	4	60	32	8	5.4	13.5
Cabrera, Jhonnys	R-R	5-11	150	6-05-02	.069	.182	.103	12	33	29	0	2	1	0	0	0	3	1	0	0	19	0	0	9.1	57.6
Castillo, Luis	L-L	6-0	175	10-11-03	.226	.307	.322	40	166	146	14	33	5	0	3	21	16	2	0	2	46	1	1	9.6	27.7
Chirinos, Jesus	R-R	6-0	165	7-27-01	.291	.438	.460	67	276	213	37	62	13	1	7	34	55	4	0	4	78	2	1	19.9	28.3
Diaz, Blayberg	R-R	5-11	190	1-31-03	.249	.277	.281	52	195	185	17	46	4	1	0	15	7	1	0	2	42	1	1	3.6	21.5
Fernandez, Eduarqui	R-R	6-2	176	11-20-01	.231	.385	.346	17	65	52	11	12	3	0	1	1	12	1	0	0	22	2	2	18.5	33.8
Guilarte, Daniel	R-R	5-11	160	10-29-03	.269	.377	.314	58	265	223	35	60	6	2	0	31	35	5	0	2	66	26	8	13.2	24.9
Hall, Tayden	L-R	6-4	215	1-12-03	.266	.406	.312	49	217	173	27	46	8	0	0	20	40	2	0	2	41	3	3	18.4	18.9
Lara, Luis	B-R	5-7	155	11-17-04	.285	.379	.354	70	318	274	55	78	11	1	2	21	39	3	0	1	46	22	9	12.3	14.5
Low, Quinton	L-R	6-4	215	9-05-02	.207	.324	.345	22	34	29	4	6	1	0	1	3	5	0	0	0	11	0	0	14.7	32.4
Mercado, Reidy	B-R	5-11	153	1-06-01	.162	.197	.221	25	71	68	9	11	4	0	0	5	3	0	0	0	22	8	2	4.2	31.0
Nicasia, Kaylan	B-R	5-11	176	4-10-02	.216	.327	.352	90	342	287	53	62	13	4	6	37	47	3	0	5	105	27	7	13.7	30.7
O'Rae, Dylan	L-R	5-7	160	2-14-04	.330	.439	.375	23	107	88	14	29	4	0	0	8	17	1	0	1	14	16	4	15.9	13.1
Parra, Jesus	R-R	6-2	184	8-30-02	.235	.280	.366	45	164	153	17	36	12	1	2	31	7	3	0	1	56	1	1	4.3	34.1
Perez, Alexander	R-R	5-9	140	3-12-03	.151	.220	.189	21	59	53	2	8	2	0	0	5	4	1	0	1	17	1	0	6.8	28.8
Perez, Hedbert	L-L	5-10	160	4-04-03	.216	.288	.345	63	257	232	27	50	10	1	6	29	22	2	0	1	68	9	3	8.6	26.5
Sibrian, Jose	R-R	5-10	175	10-24-98	.278	.358	.481	61	244	212	28	59	16	0	9	51	18	10	0	3	41	0	0	7.4	16.8
Vargas, Jheremy	R-R	5-10	160	5-10-03	.236	.358	.306	49	187	157	27	37	11	0	0	17	28	2	0	0	33	10	3	15.0	17.6
Wood, Matthew	L-R	5-10	190	3-02-01	.293	.468	.488	25	109	82	13	24	7	0	3	20	26	1	0	0	15	1	0	23.9	13.8

Pitching	B-T	Ht.	Wt.	DOB	W	L	ERA	G	GS	SV	IP	Hits	Runs	ER	HR	BB	SO	AVG	OBP	SLG	SO%	BB%	BF
Aquino, Patricio	R-R	6-0	175	5-01-03	5	3	2.75	21	19	0	88	80	29	27	6	31	86	.244	.325	.351	23.3	8.4	369
Brustoski, Jakob	L-L	6-2	240	3-20-99	0	0	9.00	3	0	0	3	2	3	3	0	4	4	.200	.438	.200	25.0	25.0	16
Cabrera, Jhonnys	R-R	5-11	150	6-05-02	0	0	0.00	1	0	0	0	0	0	0	0	0	0	.000	.000	.000	0.0	0.0	1
Calzadilla, Gerson	R-R	5-11	155	4-05-03	0	0	9.00	2	0	0	6	10	6	6	2	3	2	.370	.438	.667	6.3	9.4	32
Chavez, Jose	R-R	6-2	150	1-09-03	3	0	6.51	17	0	0	28	28	21	20	1	17	32	.259	.370	.389	25.2	13.4	127
Childers, Will	L-R	6-4	210	11-14-00	2	4	5.95	14	8	0	59	64	41	39	7	27	42	.276	.355	.427	16.0	10.3	263
Costello, Chase	R-R	6-4	215	4-13-00	9	4	3.76	28	0	1	65	52	29	27	3	20	53	.225	.300	.316	20.6	7.8	257
Figueroa, Jeferson	R-R	6-0	180	8-22-00	2	1	2.80	27	1	1	45	31	14	14	5	29	51	.194	.328	.319	26.6	15.1	192
Fitzpatrick, Brian	B-L	6-7	230	6-01-00	0	1	4.15	6	4	0	22	20	10	10	0	10	18	.253	.337	.329	19.6	10.9	92
Galindez, Yorman	R-R	6-1	160	2-03-03	2	0	1.50	4	2	0	18	10	3	3	1	7	20	.172	.284	.241	29.9	10.4	67
Guerrero, Miguel	R-R	6-5	216	7-15-00	1	2	2.76	18	0	1	29	19	9	9	2	11	33	.188	.274	.267	29.2	9.7	113
Henderson, Logan	R-R	5-11	194	3-02-02	4	3	2.75	18	18	0	79	50	25	24	8	26	106	.185	.259	.322	35.2	8.6	301
Herrera, Yujanyer	R-R	6-3	175	8-17-03	5	4	4.08	22	11	1	79	70	40	36	3	47	65	.244	.363	.328	18.7	13.5	348
Jimenez, Edwin	R-R	6-3	175	12-12-01	2	0	2.00	4	1	0	18	13	4	4	0	5	23	.213	.265	.262	33.8	7.4	68
Low, Quinton	L-R	6-4	215	9-05-02	1	3	4.68	14	7	0	33	20	18	17	3	29	47	.177	.367	.292	32.0	19.7	147
Maldonado, Aidan	R-R	6-0	170	5-27-00	1	6	6.18	15	8	0	39	52	33	27	1	25	43	.317	.418	.409	22.1	12.8	195
Merkel, Nick	R-R	6-7	255	7-03-98	1	0	3.62	15	0	2	27	22	12	11	4	6	41	.214	.264	.379	37.3	5.5	110
Misiorowski, Jacob	R-R	6-7	190	4-03-02	1	1	3.04	9	9	0	27	10	9	9	0	12	46	.118	.238	.176	45.5	11.9	101
Olguin, Fernando	R-R	5-9	155	3-04-01	0	1	22.50	2	0	0	2	3	5	5	2	3	1	.375	.545	1.125	9.1	27.3	11
Pena, Jeison	R-R	6-1	165	9-14-02	5	2	7.96	36	0	1	46	43	45	41	4	41	51	.249	.412	.370	22.1	17.7	231
Peterson, Nate	L-L	5-10	180	2-15-00	4	1	2.91	12	5	0	43	32	16	14	1	18	55	.203	.293	.285	30.4	9.9	181
Rivero, Jesus	R-R	6-1	175	5-14-03	2	1	3.00	11	4	4	39	23	16	13	1	27	49	.177	.345	.238	29.7	16.4	165
Rodriguez, Yerlin	R-R	6-2	172	3-22-02	1	0	4.00	28	0	11	36	32	20	16	2	21	40	.248	.382	.326	25.5	13.4	157
Root, Bayden	R-R	6-3	235	10-27-98	1	0	0.00	4	0	0	4	2	1	0	0	0	4	.154	.143	.154	28.6	0.0	14
Rudy, Will	R-R	6-1	170	5-07-01	5	3	3.46	18	18	0	81	78	38	31	9	26	69	.257	.328	.406	20.6	7.8	335
Shears, Tanner	R-R	6-3	205	6-20-99	1	1	1.35	15	0	3	20	12	4	3	1	17	33	.171	.348	.271	37.1	19.1	89
Smith, Shane	R-R	6-4	235	4-04-00	4	3	2.59	19	0	4	31	23	10	9	3	10	50	.215	.317	.346	40.3	8.1	124
Vallecillo, Alexander	R-R	6-2	150	7-01-02	2	4	6.17	17	11	0	54	42	38	37	4	32	58	.216	.333	.361	25.1	13.9	231
Wehrle, Tyler	R-R	6-3	220	5-18-00	8	7	4.11	28	1	2	81	76	45	37	5	31	74	.249	.327	.354	21.3	8.9	347
Whiting, Blake	R-R	6-2	180	4-21-99	0	0	0.00	2	0	0	3	0	0	0	0	0	5	.000	.000	.000	55.6	0.0	9

Fielding

Catcher	PCT	G	PO	A	E	DP	PB
Cabrera	1.000	4	26	6	0	0	0
Diaz	.979	49	421	49	10	3	2
Hall	1.000	1	12	0	0	0	3
Sibrian	.993	56	507	56	4	6	6
Wood	.988	20	233	24	3	4	1

First Base	PCT	G	PO	A	E	DP
Adams	.988	11	77	4	1	5
Cabrera	.833	1	4	1	1	0
Chirinos	.987	49	361	23	5	47
Hall	1.000	30	193	10	0	17
Parra	.996	34	232	14	1	22
Vargas	1.000	8	39	0	0	4

Second Base	PCT	G	PO	A	E	DP
Areinamo	.972	59	101	144	7	43
Baez	1.000	1	6	2	0	2
Barrios	.931	16	18	36	4	8
Guilarte	.985	17	33	31	1	7
O'Rae	1.000	8	12	20	0	6
Perez	1.000	14	23	29	0	3
Vargas	1.000	14	19	28	0	8

Third Base	PCT	G	PO	A	E	DP
Adams	.946	75	57	117	10	18
Areinamo	.983	31	15	44	1	4
Baez	.917	6	6	5	1	0
Guilarte	1.000	6	4	11	0	1
Parra	.917	2	2	9	1	1
Perez	.000	1	0	0	0	0
Vargas	.950	10	8	11	1	0

Shortstop	PCT	G	PO	A	E	DP
Areinamo	.974	8	18	20	1	4
Barrios	.979	86	103	217	7	44
Guilarte	.985	33	58	70	2	20
Perez	.000	1	0	0	1	0
Vargas	.857	2	1	5	1	0

Outfield	PCT	G	PO	A	E	DP
Avina	.993	96	163	13	2	5
Castillo	.489	33	44	3	1	2
Fernandez	1.000	17	34	2	0	0
Hall	1.000	3	3	0	0	0
Lara	.994	68	153	7	1	1
Mercado	.967	26	30	4	1	1
Nicasia	.981	85	122	10	3	3
O'Rae	1.000	15	36	1	0	1
Perez, A	1.000	1	1	0	0	0
Perez, H	.995	54	95	2	1	0
Vargas	1.000	8	7	0	0	0

ACL BREWERS

ROOKIE

ARIZONA COMPLEX LEAGUE

Batting	B-T	Ht.	Wt.	DOB	AVG	OBP	SLG	G	PA	AB	R	H	2B	3B	HR	RBI	BB	HBP	SH	SF	SO	SB	CS	BB%	SO%
Adamczewski, Josh	L-R	6-0	190	5-10-05	.000	.125	.000	3	8	7	0	0	0	0	0	0	1	0	0	0	3	0	0	12.5	37.5
Baez, Juan	R-R	5-9	175	6-27-05	.370	.395	.557	48	205	192	39	71	16	4	4	42	8	2	0	3	23	17	2	3.9	11.2
Barrios, Johan	R-R	6-1	180	1-08-05	.228	.338	.276	40	145	123	8	28	3	0	1	12	20	1	0	1	50	4	1	13.8	34.5
Bitonti, Eric	L-R	6-4	205	11-17-05	.179	.333	.410	12	48	39	8	7	1	1	2	9	9	0	0	0	15	0	0	18.8	31.3
Boeve, Mike	L-R	6-3	200	5-05-02	.500	.556	1.000	9	36	30	8	15	3	0	4	12	4	1	0	1	6	0	0	11.1	16.7
Briceno, Miguel	R-R	5-9	155	7-06-03	.313	.348	.361	30	89	83	21	26	4	0	0	10	5	0	0	1	12	3	2	5.6	13.5
Brown, Eric	R-R	5-10	190	12-19-00	.182	.400	.727	4	15	11	5	2	0	0	2	2	3	1	0	0	3	1	0	20.0	20.0
Caballero, Jose	R-R	5-10	140	3-26-03	.100	.270	.133	11	37	30	5	3	1	0	0	0	7	0	0	0	10	2	1	18.9	27.0
Castillo, Luis	L-L	6-0	175	10-11-03	.471	.538	.647	6	26	17	6	8	3	0	0	9	6	0	0	3	4	0	0	23.1	15.4
Fernandez, Eduarqui	R-R	6-2	176	11-20-01	.250	.333	.333	4	15	12	1	3	1	0	0	2	2	0	0	1	3	2	0	13.3	20.0
Frelick, Sal	L-R	5-10	182	4-19-00	.333	.500	.556	3	12	9	4	3	2	0	0	1	3	0	0	0	2	0	0	25.0	16.7
Garcia, Duncan	R-R	6-1	170	10-31-03	.242	.338	.403	19	74	62	11	15	3	2	1	15	7	3	0	2	28	7	2	9.5	37.8
Garcia, Jesus	R-R	5-7	163	10-02-02	.278	.409	.333	14	22	18	4	5	1	0	0	1	3	1	0	0	8	0	0	13.6	36.4
Guilarte, Daniel	R-R	5-11	160	10-29-03	.450	.500	.450	5	22	20	9	9	0	0	0	2	1	1	0	0	2	5	0	4.5	9.1
Guzman, Jonatan	R-R	5-9	155	11-25-03	.233	.254	.317	24	63	60	12	14	2	0	1	9	1	1	0	1	12	3	0	1.6	19.0
Hall, Tayden	L-R	6-4	215	1-12-03	.333	.500	.375	10	36	24	9	8	1	0	0	5	9	1	0	2	4	3	0	25.0	11.1
Hiura, Keston	R-R	5-11	208	8-02-96	.400	.455	.500	3	11	10	1	4	1	0	0	2	1	0	0	0	1	0	0	9.1	9.1
Medina, Luis	L-L	6-2	168	2-24-03	.234	.247	.340	36	97	94	12	22	5	1	1	17	1	1	0	1	17	2	0	1.0	17.5
Mendez, Hendry	L-L	6-2	175	11-07-03	.600	.600	.800	4	15	15	5	9	3	0	0	5	0	0	0	0	0	0	1	0.0	0.0
Mercado, Reidy	B-R	5-11	153	1-06-01	.345	.400	.431	19	65	58	14	20	1	2	0	8	6	0	0	1	12	6	1	9.2	18.5
Norman, Satchell	R-R	5-8	200	7-22-02	.308	.425	.473	30	113	91	17	28	6	0	3	20	19	1	0	2	26	8	3	16.8	23.0
O'Rae, Dylan	L-R	5-7	160	2-14-04	.362	.522	.408	37	178	130	44	47	4	1	0	15	40	6	0	2	23	28	2	22.5	12.9
Ollarve, Jason	L-R	5-9	160	5-20-04	.389	.368	.444	7	19	18	3	7	1	0	0	1	0	0	0	1	3	0	0	0.0	15.8
Ordonez, Edgardo	L-R	5-11	155	9-24-03	.253	.384	.392	26	99	79	15	20	8	0	1	7	18	0	0	2	31	2	2	18.2	31.3
Pastran, Beyker	R-R	5-10	162	4-01-03	.286	.375	.429	5	8	7	0	2	1	0	0	1	1	0	0	0	0	0	0	12.5	0.0
Pereira, Angel	R-R	5-10	176	3-30-05	.155	.331	.273	36	142	110	17	17	2	4	1	15	28	2	0	2	65	7	1	19.7	45.8
Perez, Alexander	R-R	5-9	140	3-12-03	.222	.300	.370	12	30	27	3	6	1	0	1	6	2	1	0	0	4	1	1	6.7	13.3
Perez, Yeison	L-L	5-10	165	1-13-04	.250	.329	.347	39	140	124	18	31	5	2	1	19	12	3	0	1	50	3	2	8.6	35.7
Pratt, Cooper	R-R	6-4	195	8-18-04	.356	.426	.444	12	54	45	9	16	2	1	0	8	5	2	0	2	11	4	0	9.3	20.4
Rodriguez, Alejandro	R-R	5-11	200	12-27-99	.217	.357	.261	9	28	23	2	5	1	0	0	1	4	1	0	0	4	0	0	14.3	14.3
Serrano, Ney	R-R	5-10	150	5-08-04	.167	.292	.200	30	72	60	7	10	2	0	0	8	10	1	0	1	30	2	0	13.9	41.7
Severino, Jhonny	R-R	6-1	185	11-08-04	.250	.288	.583	12	52	48	12	12	2	1	4	10	1	2	0	1	10	5	0	1.9	19.2
Valderrama, Felipe	R-R	5-11	170	7-24-04	.303	.361	.333	19	36	33	6	10	1	0	0	2	2	1	0	0	11	2	0	5.6	30.6
VanMeter, Josh	L-R	5-9	198	3-10-95	.294	.400	.294	5	20	17	3	5	0	0	0	2	3	0	0	0	3	1	0	15.0	15.0
Walling, Reece	L-R	6-5	202	9-22-03	.232	.346	.357	35	133	112	16	26	4	2	2	8	20	0	0	1	47	3	0	15.0	35.3
Wilken, Brock	R-R	6-4	225	6-17-02	.333	.464	.571	7	28	21	3	7	0	1	1	6	4	2	0	1	6	1	0	14.3	21.4

Pitching	B-T	Ht.	Wt.	DOB	W	L	ERA	G	GS	SV	IP	Hits	Runs	ER	HR	BB	SO	AVG	OBP	SLG	SO%	BB%	BF
Alexander, Jason	R-R	6-2	227	3-01-93	0	0	3.86	2	2	0	5	6	2	2	0	1	8	.300	.333	.350	38.1	4.8	21
Austin, Morris	R-R	6-2	215	3-27-00	0	0	7.36	4	0	0	4	2	3	3	0	4	5	.182	.400	.364	33.3	26.7	15
Briceno, Miguel	R-R	5-9	155	7-06-03	0	1	9.00	2	0	0	3	5	4	3	0	1	0	.417	.400	.583	0.0	6.7	15
Calzadilla, Gerson	R-R	5-11	155	4-05-03	4	0	0.98	16	0	4	37	25	8	4	1	10	36	.192	.266	.254	25.0	6.9	144
Carrasco, Cristofher	R-R	5-10	175	12-24-02	2	2	5.32	14	1	1	24	22	16	14	3	22	25	.259	.417	.424	22.9	20.2	109
Chavez, Jose	R-R	6-2	150	1-09-03	0	1	2.08	4	0	2	4	6	2	1	0	0	10	.316	.316	.368	52.6	0.0	19
Corniel, Daniel	R-R	6-0	177	7-07-04	1	1	5.70	11	8	0	36	35	24	23	3	22	48	.263	.373	.368	29.8	13.7	161
Cousins, Jake	R-R	6-4	193	7-14-94	1	0	0.00	1	0	0	1	0	1	0	0	2	3	.000	.400	.000	60.0	40.0	5
Dario, Samuel	R-R	6-3	175	12-23-02	0	0	20.25	4	0	0	3	2	6	6	0	10	5	.222	.619	.222	23.8	47.6	21
De Los Santos, Felipe	R-R	6-0	180	11-29-02	1	1	7.71	10	3	1	26	28	31	22	3	25	31	.269	.425	.452	23.1	18.7	134
Fitzpatrick, Brian	B-L	6-7	230	6-01-00	1	1	12.00	5	3	0	9	11	13	12	2	8	15	.297	.426	.514	31.9	17.0	47
Galindez, Yorman	R-R	6-1	160	2-03-03	1	0	5.02	10	7	0	38	39	29	21	0	25	45	.273	.393	.364	26.0	14.5	173
Hernandez, Joseph	R-R	5-11	150	6-15-00	1	0	4.91	3	1	0	7	6	4	4	1	5	7	.214	.333	.393	21.2	15.2	33
Hunt, K.C.	L-R	6-3	200	7-14-00	0	0	4.15	4	0	0	4	4	2	2	0	2	5	.211	.286	.263	23.8	9.5	21
Jackson, Isaiah	R-R	6-5	185	9-01-01	0	0	6.75	2	0	0	1	2	1	1	0	3	2	.333	.556	.500	22.2	33.3	9
Kuehner, Tate	L-L	6-1	195	2-07-01	0	0	0.00	2	1	0	3	2	0	0	0	1	2	.250	.333	.500	22.2	11.1	9

Pitching	B-T	Ht.	Wt.	DOB	W	L	ERA	G	GS	SV	IP	Hits	Runs	ER	HR	BB	SO	AVG	OBP	SLG	SO%	BB%	BF
Lauer, Eric	R-L	6-3	209	6-03-95	0	0	0.00	1	1	0	1	0	0	0	0	1	2	.000	.333	.000	66.7	33.3	3
Mogollon, Osbriel	L-L	5-10	160	4-01-04	2	3	3.72	11	5	1	39	35	20	16	1	24	43	.229	.333	.301	24.3	13.6	177
Moore, Ryne	R-R	6-4	210	11-27-98	0	2	4.50	9	6	0	18	29	14	9	1	6	6	.363	.416	.438	6.7	6.7	89
Mota, Henrison	R-R	6-3	193	7-04-03	2	1	11.12	13	0	1	23	23	29	28	2	36	35	.264	.504	.402	27.1	27.9	129
Perez, Anthony	R-R	6-3	190	10-28-01	0	2	13.89	13	1	1	12	13	24	18	2	14	16	.265	.478	.469	23.2	20.3	69
Reyes, Anfernny	L-L	6-3	170	2-23-04	3	3	4.85	15	0	1	30	23	20	16	3	15	41	.211	.333	.367	31.8	11.6	129
Rivero, Jesus	R-R	6-1	175	5-14-03	2	0	3.18	3	1	0	11	10	5	4	1	1	19	.238	.273	.405	43.2	2.3	44
Robinson, Edrian	R-R	6-5	170	3-01-02	0	0	7.94	17	2	0	17	15	15	15	1	23	18	.254	.455	.339	20.5	26.1	88
Rodriguez, Brailin	R-R	6-2	185	8-10-02	3	2	8.16	11	3	0	29	42	33	26	4	17	34	.336	.429	.528	23.1	11.6	147
Rodriguez, Manuel	R-R	6-2	175	8-08-05	4	2	4.35	10	5	0	41	41	21	20	8	10	34	.253	.297	.438	19.4	5.7	175
Root, Bayden	R-R	6-3	235	10-27-98	0	0	3.38	3	0	1	3	3	1	1	0	2	3	.273	.385	.455	23.1	15.4	13
Seminaris, Adam	R-L	6-0	191	10-19-98	0	1	3.38	3	3	0	5	9	2	2	0	2	6	.409	.458	.500	25.0	8.3	24
Solano, Darling	R-R	6-1	165	12-25-03	3	1	7.96	10	2	0	26	25	29	23	1	29	19	.263	.474	.400	14.1	21.5	135
Sousa, Bennett	L-L	6-3	220	4-06-95	0	0	0.00	1	0	0	1	1	0	0	0	1	1	.250	.400	.500	20.0	20.0	5
Timmerman, Josh	R-R	6-4	195	8-04-02	0	1	6.00	2	1	0	3	4	2	2	0	0	2	.308	.308	.462	15.4	0.0	13
Whiting, Blake	R-R	6-2	180	4-21-99	0	0	0.00	3	0	0	2	0	0	0	0	0	4	.000	.000	.000	57.1	0.0	7
Wilson, Justin	L-L	6-2	205	8-18-87	0	0	3.00	3	0	0	3	2	1	1	1	0	6	.182	.182	.455	54.5	0.0	11
Yoho, Craig	R-R	6-3	205	10-23-99	0	0	10.13	3	0	0	3	6	3	3	1	1	3	.462	.500	.769	20.0	6.7	15

Fielding

C: Ordonez 22, Norman 21, Valderrama 13, Garcia 7, Rodriguez 6, Ollarve 4, Hall 3. **1B:** Barrios 28, Perez 24, Hall 7, Garcia 4, Pastran 4, Hiura 2. **2B:** O'Rae 25, Guzman 19, Boeve 6, Briceno 4, Perez 4, Pratt 3, Serrano 2, Caballero 2, Adamczewski 2, Baez 2, Pereira 1, Guilarte 1. **3B:** Serrano 22, Baez 16, Barrios 9, Bitonti 7, Severino 6, Wilken 6, VanMeter 4, Briceno 2, Pastran 1. **SS:** Baez 24, Caballero 9, Pratt 9, O'Rae 6, Guilarte 5, Brown 4, Severino 4, Perez 3, Serrano 2, Bitonti 2. **OF:** Medina 34, Walling 34, Pereira 33, Briceno 23, Garcia 19, Mercado 17, Perez 13, O'Rae 6, Castillo 5, Fernandez 4, Frelick 3, Mendez 3, Hiura 1.

DSL BREWERS

ROOKIE

DOMINICAN SUMMER LEAGUE

Batting	B-T	Ht.	Wt.	DOB	AVG	OBP	SLG	G	PA	AB	R	H	2B	3B	HR	RBI	BB	HBP	SH	SF	SO	SB	CS	BB%	SO%
Alastre, Luiyin	B-R	5-10	160	9-27-05	.287	.387	.375	42	163	136	22	39	7	1	1	17	22	2	0	3	18	8	5	13.5	11.0
Aparicio, Argenis	B-R	6-0	180	9-23-05	.187	.274	.227	31	84	75	8	14	3	0	0	5	8	1	0	0	15	3	3	9.5	17.9
Bencosme, Jhon	B-R	5-9	172	2-01-06	.147	.244	.200	30	86	75	7	11	4	0	0	5	7	3	0	1	17	1	0	8.1	19.8
Charles, Eduardo	R-R	5-10	160	4-22-06	.188	.316	.188	6	19	16	0	3	0	0	0	0	3	0	0	0	7	1	1	15.8	36.8
Di Turi, Filippo	B-R	5-11	165	11-09-05	.282	.414	.354	52	222	181	35	51	9	2	0	27	38	3	0	0	32	12	8	17.1	14.4
Ereu, Kevin	R-R	5-10	165	5-24-06	.162	.310	.243	41	168	136	17	22	8	0	1	11	25	5	0	2	42	6	3	14.9	25.0
Espinal, Smarlin	L-L	5-10	175	9-09-05	.171	.277	.220	28	94	82	8	14	2	1	0	10	8	4	0	0	25	3	1	8.5	26.6
Flores, Roderick	R-R	5-9	167	8-24-06	.216	.368	.275	49	212	171	32	37	10	0	0	14	37	4	0	0	62	10	2	17.5	29.2
Garcia, Luis	R-R	5-11	180	1-19-05	.149	.292	.189	24	89	74	9	11	3	0	0	4	11	4	0	0	27	0	0	12.4	30.3
Gomez, Antony	L-L	6-1	175	4-05-06	.193	.376	.229	38	141	109	17	21	0	2	0	13	31	1	0	0	34	8	5	22.0	24.1
Gutierrez, Joan	L-R	5-11	165	10-07-05	.159	.316	.238	38	156	126	24	20	6	2	0	11	27	2	0	0	44	7	3	17.3	28.2
Holguin, Gery	R-R	6-0	160	8-03-05	.235	.350	.383	42	177	149	20	35	11	1	3	24	24	3	0	1	36	5	6	13.6	20.3
Ibarguen, Pedro	R-R	5-10	180	7-02-06	.311	.437	.447	43	167	132	27	41	7	1	3	26	25	7	0	3	32	7	7	15.0	19.2
Igualas, Irving	L-R	6-0	175	7-27-03	.169	.258	.220	23	66	59	8	10	3	0	0	3	6	1	0	0	22	0	0	9.1	33.3
La Torre, Roman	L-R	5-10	160	5-04-05	.184	.255	.204	15	55	49	3	9	1	0	0	3	5	0	0	1	10	1	0	9.1	18.2
Lameda, Luis	B-R	5-10	160	1-17-06	.238	.440	.277	35	141	101	17	24	2	1	0	15	35	3	0	2	20	4	4	24.8	14.2
Lozano, Estefano	R-R	6-0	182	2-07-04	.194	.370	.306	14	46	36	4	7	1	0	1	3	7	3	0	0	9	1	0	15.2	19.6
Martinez, Eric	R-R	6-0	175	4-06-04	.208	.331	.377	41	157	130	23	27	7	0	5	18	21	4	0	2	38	0	0	13.4	24.2
Moreno, Ramon	R-R	5-9	165	10-27-04	.213	.386	.344	39	158	122	25	26	6	2	2	20	32	3	0	1	55	14	3	20.3	34.8
Nadal, Demetrio	R-R	5-7	125	7-03-04	.342	.478	.525	40	157	120	28	41	6	5	2	20	24	10	0	3	19	33	10	15.3	12.1
Oropeza, Brayan	R-R	6-1	175	11-18-03	.278	.339	.333	22	59	54	7	15	3	0	0	6	3	2	0	0	10	0	0	5.1	16.9
Puerta, Danny	L-L	5-8	150	4-01-06	.272	.385	.346	31	96	81	12	22	6	0	0	8	13	2	0	0	19	3	1	13.5	19.8
Rodriguez, Donis	B-R	5-8	150	8-30-05	.075	.200	.075	15	50	40	6	3	0	0	0	4	3	4	0	3	13	5	2	6.0	26.0
Rodriguez, Tyler	R-R	5-10	165	2-08-06	.200	.412	.300	32	97	70	19	14	1	0	2	8	19	7	0	1	14	9	4	19.6	14.4
Rodriguez, Yophery	L-L	6-1	185	12-05-05	.253	.393	.449	52	224	178	34	45	13	2	6	36	41	2	0	3	40	12	7	18.3	17.9
Rojas, Freider	B-R	5-8	155	10-23-05	.193	.324	.246	20	68	57	6	11	1	1	0	2	11	0	0	0	9	1	1	16.2	13.2
Sanchez, Brian	L-R	6-3	170	7-04-04	.297	.414	.446	33	128	101	20	30	7	4	0	19	20	3	0	4	23	8	4	15.6	18.0
Santiesteban, Idalberto	L-L	6-2	175	6-12-04	.273	.366	.295	27	101	88	11	24	2	0	0	6	11	2	0	0	23	12	4	10.9	22.8
Tejada, Ludwin	L-R	5-10	175	5-12-05	.170	.245	.277	20	53	47	5	8	2	0	1	7	4	1	0	1	10	0	0	7.5	18.9
Tovar, Pedro	L-L	6-1	160	6-23-06	.220	.333	.288	36	156	132	18	29	7	1	0	14	20	3	0	1	41	9	3	12.8	26.3
Valera, Fabricio	L-R	6-2	174	9-21-04	.218	.397	.236	19	73	55	12	12	1	0	0	6	15	2	0	1	13	2	2	20.5	17.8
Vasquez, Christopher	R-R	6-4	195	7-09-05	.203	.359	.500	26	92	74	14	15	7	0	5	19	11	7	0	0	36	0	1	12.0	39.1
Walther, Yannic	R-R	6-0	185	4-12-04	.235	.394	.304	32	132	102	12	24	4	0	1	12	26	2	0	2	37	0	1	19.7	28.0

Pitching	B-T	Ht.	Wt.	DOB	W	L	ERA	G	GS	SV	IP	Hits	Runs	ER	HR	BB	SO	AVG	OBP	SLG	SO%	BB%	BF
Aparicio, Argenis	B-R	6-0	180	9-23-05	0	1	6.75	9	0	0	8	11	7	6	1	1	7	.314	.333	.486	18.9	2.7	37
Broca, Jesus	L-L	5-8	174	10-16-03	0	0	3.00	2	2	0	3	3	1	1	0	0	2	.250	.250	.333	16.7	0.0	12
Cabrera, Jesael	R-R	6-0	155	10-22-03	4	1	4.23	12	3	1	38	34	19	18	1	13	23	.241	.304	.326	14.6	8.2	158
Caceres, Justin	R-R	6-1	168	11-13-04	1	4	3.81	15	0	1	28	32	22	12	0	19	26	.278	.401	.374	18.2	13.3	143
Camilo, Oliver	R-R	6-0	153	2-08-06	1	0	11.51	12	3	0	20	21	27	26	3	27	20	.273	.482	.506	17.5	23.7	114
Colmenarez, Gabriel	R-R	6-1	155	3-28-06	3	2	3.11	10	7	0	38	26	19	13	0	15	26	.197	.307	.288	17.0	9.8	153
Cordero, Wilfredo	R-R	6-2	190	9-30-02	0	1	5.06	6	0	0	5	1	5	3	0	11	5	.071	.500	.071	19.2	42.3	26
Cortez, Enniel	R-R	6-0	180	5-01-06	4	1	1.58	11	8	0	46	35	12	8	1	5	49	.208	.244	.315	27.8	2.8	176
Dominguez, David	L-L	6-2	185	11-10-03	3	1	4.50	13	0	0	24	16	16	12	0	24	30	.190	.386	.226	26.1	20.9	115
Flores, Anthony	L-L	5-11	165	10-21-04	1	3	3.22	11	11	0	45	33	19	16	1	16	57	.206	.289	.263	31.7	8.9	180
Flores, Jesus	B-R	6-2	180	3-16-05	0	4	3.80	6	6	0	21	15	11	9	1	8	16	.197	.282	.303	18.8	9.4	85

Florimon, Yonawil	R-R	6-0	150	11-22-02	1	3	4.50	16	0	3	22	21	13	11	0	20	28	.253	.398	.325	25.9	18.5	108
Geraldo, Dencer	R-R	6-1	160	3-05-03	0	0	3.38	2	0	0	3	3	1	1	0	1	2	.273	.333	.364	16.7	8.3	12
Gonzalez, Elias	R-R	6-1	185	10-09-03	1	1	5.28	8	0	0	15	8	12	9	3	12	9	.160	.353	.380	13.2	17.6	68
Guevara, Luis	R-R	6-1	180	6-03-06	5	2	5.56	12	5	0	34	38	25	21	2	11	26	.273	.333	.424	16.9	7.1	154
Hernandez, Melvin	R-R	5-11	139	7-03-06	2	2	2.06	10	7	0	35	32	13	8	1	9	30	.239	.295	.321	20.5	6.2	146
Jimenez, Linbel	R-R	6-5	198	10-26-04	1	1	6.57	10	5	0	25	23	19	18	0	25	25	.261	.433	.341	20.8	20.8	120
Maurera, Carlos	R-R	6-0	180	3-01-05	2	0	3.68	6	1	0	15	8	6	6	0	8	14	.167	.293	.250	24.1	13.8	58
Mena, Nestor	R-R	6-1	154	9-17-04	0	1	4.55	12	0	0	28	32	21	14	2	14	27	.286	.382	.491	20.6	10.7	131
Mendez, Lenin	R-R	6-3	193	9-22-04	2	3	4.73	12	0	2	27	23	17	14	0	17	26	.242	.373	.316	22.0	14.4	118
Meneses, Jose	L-L	6-1	150	3-09-05	2	2	3.63	11	5	1	35	29	18	14	0	26	34	.232	.380	.304	21.3	16.3	160
Oropeza, Brayan	R-R	6-1	175	11-18-03	0	0	27.00	1	0	0	1	3	3	3	2	1	0	.500	.571	1.667	0.0	14.3	7
Perez, Roman	R-R	6-4	180	10-26-00	2	4	6.45	21	0	6	22	25	26	16	0	22	27	.284	.462	.386	22.9	18.6	118
Prado, Eric	R-R	6-0	174	11-11-05	2	1	1.54	11	7	0	41	24	8	7	2	14	37	.175	.257	.241	24.3	9.2	152
Quintana, Pedro	L-L	5-11	165	3-04-04	0	0	3.86	12	0	1	12	8	7	5	1	11	11	.186	.386	.326	19.3	19.3	57
Rivera, Bryan	R-R	6-1	170	6-17-05	2	2	3.57	12	12	0	53	35	21	21	5	24	63	.191	.300	.317	29.6	11.3	213
Rodriguez, Aneuris	R-R	6-3	185	6-14-04	1	2	3.48	11	4	1	41	33	20	16	1	15	47	.213	.285	.265	27.3	8.7	172
Sanchez, Dikember	R-R	5-11	160	2-20-04	0	5	6.49	15	0	3	26	30	22	19	1	16	33	.288	.382	.365	26.6	12.9	124
Sanchez, Saul	R-R	5-11	175	8-08-06	1	4	9.89	14	0	1	24	32	28	26	1	19	23	.308	.424	.471	18.4	15.2	125
Smith, Ranwell	R-R	5-11	140	8-23-05	2	4	4.34	11	4	0	37	40	24	18	1	22	41	.276	.394	.379	23.4	12.6	175
Suarez, Esmir	R-R	6-2	185	9-01-04	3	1	2.80	10	8	0	35	31	14	11	1	12	31	.235	.308	.311	21.2	8.2	146
Tales, Yeferson	R-R	6-1	165	12-06-03	1	2	6.66	11	1	1	26	30	28	19	3	11	27	.283	.382	.434	22.0	8.9	123
Tejada, Ludwin	L-R	5-10	175	5-12-05	0	0	0.00	1	0	0	0	0	0	0	0	0	0	.000	.000	.000	0.0	0.0	1
Yanez, Ismael	R-R	6-0	180	11-09-05	0	0	4.12	7	7	0	20	11	12	9	0	19	26	.169	.393	.215	29.2	21.3	89
Zapata, Johan	R-R	5-11	160	11-10-05	0	0	6.55	8	0	1	11	11	9	8	2	9	8	.268	.423	.439	15.1	17.0	53

Fielding

C: Martinez 33, Walther 23, Rojas 20, Tejada 16, Garcia 14, Oropeza 10, Lozano 5, La Torre 3. **1B:** Puerta 21, Holguin 15, Oropeza 13, La Torre 12, Espinal 12, Bencosme 11, Rodriguez 11, Lozano 9, Walther 8, Tejada 4, Martinez 4, Garcia 1, Igualas 1. **2B:** Flores 17, Bencosme 14, Rodriguez 14, Gutierrez 13, Di Turi 12, Alastre 11, Ereu 10, Ibarguen 8, Lameda 7, Nadal 4, Charles 4. **3B:** Holguin 25, Lameda 25, Rodriguez 16, Alastre 16, Nadal 15, Flores 6, Bencosme 3, Ibarguen 2, Gutierrez 1, Charles 1, Ereu 1. **SS:** Di Turi 31, Ereu 24, Gutierrez 22, Flores 17, Alastre 9, Nadal 6. **OF:** Rodriguez 53, Moreno 39, Gomez 37, Tovar 31, Sanchez 28, Santiesteban 27, Igualas 20, Valera 19, Ibarguen 16, Espinal 16, Vasquez 15, Aparicio 12, Nadal 11, Puerta 9.

Minnesota Twins

SEASON SYNOPSIS: The only American League Central team with a winning record, the Twins won the division for the third time in five seasons, then won their first playoff series since 2002 before losing to the Astros in the AL Division Series.

HIGH POINT: Minnesota had lost 18 straight postseason games since 2004 before Pablo Lopez (5.2 IP, 1 R) and rookie Royce Lewis (2 HR) powered them past Toronto in the first game of the wild-card series. The next day, Sonny Gray tossed five shutout frames and the Twins won 2-0, giving the club its first postseason series victory since knocking off the Moneyball A's in the 2002 Division Series.

LOW POINT: Minnesota led the AL Central for 157 days but fell into an offensive funk in the first half, culminating with a home sweep against Baltimore by a cumulative 24-5 score that dropped them into second place, a half-game behind Cleveland, at the all-star break. Ex-Twin Kyle Gibson tied a career high with 11 strikeouts, emblematic of the Twins setting the all-time MLB single-season record with 1,654 punchouts.

NOTABLE ROOKIES: Lewis, the No. 1 pick in the 2017 draft, hardly played for three seasons due to the 2020 pandemic, a torn right ACL in the winter of 2021 and a repeat torn ACL during his 2022 MLB debut. That rehabilitation, a later oblique strain and a late-September hamstring issue limited him to 58 games, but he hit four grand slams among his 15 homers and ranked third on the team with 52 RBIs. Second baseman Edouard Julien led the club with 64 walks, establishing himself as the leadoff man in a .263/.381/.459 season that included 16 homers. Minnesota native Matt Wallner hit 14 homers in 76 games with a .249/.370/.507 slash line while showcasing one of baseball's best throwing arms.

KEY TRANSACTIONS: Carlos Correa returned to the Twins on a six-year, $200 million deal. Lopez, plus two prospects, arrived in a January trade with the Marlins that shipped 2022 batting champ Luis Arraez to Miami. Lopez won both of his playoff starts; in the regular season he was 11-8, 3.66 in a team-best 194 innings while ranking third in the majors with 234 strikeouts.

DOWN ON THE FARM: Midwest League champion Cedar Rapids was one of the best teams in the minors. The Kernels went 82-50, led by outfielders Kala'i Rosario and Emmanuel Rodriguez and MiLB Manager of the Year Brian Dinkelman.

OPENING DAY PAYROLL: $153,588,740 (17th).

PLAYERS OF THE YEAR

MAJOR LEAGUE

Sonny Gray
RHP
8-8, 2.79
32 GS, 184 IP
154 ERA+, 1.15 WHIP

MINOR LEAGUE

Yunior Severino
3B
(AA/AAA)
.272/.352/.546
35 HR, 84 RBI

ORGANIZATION LEADERS

Batting		*Minimum 250 AB
MAJORS		
* AVG	Donovan Solano	.282
* OPS	Matt Wallner	.877
HR	Max Kepler	24
RBI	Max Kepler	66
MINORS		
* AVG	Andrew Stevenson, St. Paul	.317
* OBP	Andrew Cossetti, Fort Myers/C. Rapids	.426
* SLG	Yunior Severino, Wichita/St. Paul	.546
* OPS	Andrew Cossetti, Fort Myers/C. Rapids	.960
R	Andrew Stevenson, St. Paul	91
H	DaShawn Keirsey, Wichita/St. Paul	144
TB	Yunior Severino, Wichita/St. Paul	255
2B	Brooks Lee, Wichita/St. Paul	39
3B	Emmanuel Rodriguez, Cedar Rapids	9
HR	Yunior Severino, Wichita/St. Paul	35
RBI	Kala'i Rosario, Cedar Rapids	94
BB	Emmanuel Rodriguez, Cedar Rapids	92
SO	Yunior Severino, Wichita/St. Paul	173
SB	Yoyner Fajardo, Wichita	50

Pitching		#Minimum 75 IP
MAJORS		
W	Pablo Lopez	11
W	Joe Ryan	11
# ERA	Sonny Gray	2.79
SO	Pablo Lopez	234
SV	Jhoan Duran	27
MINORS		
W	Pierson Ohl, C.Rapids/Wichita	9
W	Cory Lewis, Fort Myers/C. Rapids	9
L	Travis Adams, Wichita	10
L	Carlos Luna, Wichita/St. Paul	10
# ERA	Cory Lewis, Fort Myers/C. Rapids	2.49
G	Michael Boyle, Wichita/St. Paul	49
GS	Randy Dobnak, St. Paul	26
SV	Miguel Rodriguez, C. Rapids/Wichita	17
IP	Pierson Ohl, C.Rapids/Wichita	127
BB	Randy Dobnak, St. Paul	61
SO	David Festa, Wichita/St. Paul	119
# AVG	Cory Lewis, Fort Myers/C. Rapids	.196

2023 PERFORMANCE

General Manager: Derek Falvey. **Farm Director:** Drew MacPhail. **Scouting Director:** Sean Johnson.

Class	Team	League	W	L	PCT	Finish	Manager
Majors	Minnesota Twins	American	87	75	.537	7 (15)	Rocco Baldelli
Triple-A	St. Paul Saints	International	84	64	.568	3 (20)	Toby Gardenhire
Double-A	Wichita Wind Surge	Texas	64	73	.467	9 (10)	Ramon Borrego
High-A	Cedar Rapids Kernels	Midwest	82	50	.621	1 (12)	Brian Dinkelman
Low-A	Fort Myers Mighty Mussels	Florida State	67	64	.511	5 (10)	Brian Meyer
Rookie	FCL Twins	Florida Complex	25	29	.463	12 (15)	Seth Feldman
Rookie	DSL Twins	Dominican Sum.	14	37	.275	49 (50)	Rafael Martinez
Overall 2023 Minor League Record			336	317	.515	10th (30)	

ORGANIZATION STATISTICS

MINNESOTA TWINS

AMERICAN LEAGUE

Batting	B-T	Ht.	Wt.	DOB	AVG	OBP	SLG	G	PA	AB	R	H	2B	3B	HR	RBI	BB	HBP	SH	SF	SO	SB	CS	BB%	SO%
Buxton, Byron	R-R	6-2	190	12-18-93	.207	.294	.438	85	347	304	49	63	17	1	17	42	35	4	0	4	109	9	0	10.1	31.4
Castro, Willi	B-R	6-1	206	4-24-97	.257	.339	.411	124	409	358	60	92	18	5	9	34	34	12	2	3	99	33	5	8.3	24.2
Correa, Carlos	R-R	6-4	220	9-22-94	.230	.312	.399	135	580	514	60	118	29	2	18	65	59	4	0	3	131	0	0	10.2	22.6
Farmer, Kyle	R-R	6-0	205	8-17-90	.256	.317	.408	120	369	336	49	86	14	2	11	46	23	8	0	2	86	2	4	6.2	23.3
Gallo, Joey	L-R	6-5	250	11-19-93	.177	.301	.440	111	332	282	39	50	9	1	21	40	48	2	0	0	142	1	1	14.5	42.8
Garlick, Kyle	R-R	6-1	210	1-26-92	.179	.233	.429	14	30	28	2	5	1	0	2	4	2	0	0	0	11	0	0	6.7	36.7
Gordon, Nick	L-R	6-0	160	10-24-95	.176	.185	.319	34	93	91	13	16	5	1	2	7	1	0	1	0	11	0	0	1.1	11.8
Jeffers, Ryan	R-R	6-4	235	6-03-97	.276	.369	.490	96	335	286	46	79	15	2	14	43	33	10	4	2	93	3	2	9.9	27.8
Julien, Edouard	L-R	6-0	195	4-30-99	.263	.381	.459	109	408	338	60	89	16	1	16	37	64	2	1	3	128	3	0	15.7	31.4
Kepler, Max	L-L	6-4	225	2-10-93	.260	.332	.484	130	491	438	72	114	22	2	24	66	45	4	0	4	106	1	1	9.2	21.6
Kirilloff, Alex	L-L	6-2	195	11-09-97	.270	.348	.445	88	319	281	35	76	14	1	11	41	28	7	0	3	80	1	0	8.8	25.1
Larnach, Trevor	L-R	6-4	223	2-26-97	.213	.311	.415	58	212	183	26	39	7	3	8	40	27	0	0	2	72	1	1	12.7	34.0
Lewis, Royce	R-R	6-2	200	6-05-99	.309	.372	.548	58	239	217	36	67	7	0	15	52	20	2	0	0	55	6	1	8.4	23.0
Luplow, Jordan	R-R	5-11	195	9-26-93	.206	.315	.349	32	73	63	10	13	3	0	2	4	9	1	0	0	19	2	0	12.3	26.0
2-team (7 Toronto)					.232	.344	.399	90	312	263	40	61	14	0	10	39	39	6	0	4	64	4	1	12.5	20.5
Miranda, Jose	R-R	6-2	210	6-29-98	.211	.263	.303	40	152	142	12	30	4	0	3	13	9	1	0	0	24	0	0	5.9	15.8
Polanco, Jorge	B-R	5-11	208	7-05-93	.255	.335	.454	80	343	302	38	77	18	0	14	48	36	2	0	3	88	4	0	10.5	25.7
Solano, Donovan	R-R	5-8	210	12-17-87	.282	.369	.391	134	450	394	43	111	26	1	5	38	40	15	0	1	100	0	0	8.9	22.2
Stevenson, Andrew	L-L	5-11	191	6-01-94	.189	.250	.216	25	40	37	4	7	1	0	0	1	2	1	0	0	8	4	1	5.0	20.0
Taylor, Michael A.	R-R	6-4	215	3-26-91	.220	.278	.442	129	388	355	48	78	14	1	21	51	26	3	3	1	130	13	1	6.7	33.5
Vazquez, Christian	R-R	5-9	205	8-21-90	.223	.280	.318	102	355	327	34	73	13	0	6	32	25	1	1	1	82	1	0	7.0	23.1
Wallner, Matt	L-R	6-4	220	12-12-97	.249	.370	.507	76	254	213	42	53	11	1	14	41	28	13	0	0	80	2	1	11.0	31.5

Pitching	B-T	Ht.	Wt.	DOB	W	L	ERA	G	GS	SV	IP	Hits	Runs	ER	HR	BB	SO	AVG	OBP	SLG	SO%	BB%	BF
Alcala, Jorge	R-R	6-3	205	7-28-95	0	1	6.23	11	0	0	17	14	13	12	5	10	16	.222	.333	.508	21.3	13.3	75
Balazovic, Jordan	R-R	6-5	215	9-17-98	1	0	4.44	18	0	0	24	26	13	12	5	12	17	.274	.352	.484	15.7	11.1	108
Castro, Willi	B-R	6-1	206	4-24-97	0	0	11.57	3	0	0	2	3	3	3	0	2	0	.375	.455	.375	0.0	18.2	11
De Leon, Jose	R-R	6-0	220	8-07-92	0	1	4.67	12	1	0	17	16	10	9	2	5	17	.250	.314	.359	24.3	7.1	70
Duran, Jhoan	R-R	6-5	230	1-08-98	3	6	2.45	59	0	27	62	46	25	17	6	25	84	.207	.298	.324	32.9	9.8	255
Floro, Dylan	L-R	6-2	203	12-27-90	2	1	5.29	19	0	0	17	22	10	10	1	6	17	.324	.390	.397	22.1	7.8	77
Funderburk, Kody	L-L	6-4	230	11-27-96	2	0	0.75	11	0	0	12	6	1	1	1	5	19	.146	.255	.244	40.4	10.6	47
Gray, Sonny	R-R	5-10	195	11-07-89	8	8	2.79	32	32	0	184	156	59	57	8	55	183	.226	.288	.319	24.3	7.3	754
Headrick, Brent	L-L	6-6	235	12-17-97	3	0	6.31	14	0	1	26	27	18	18	7	10	30	.267	.350	.564	25.6	8.5	117
Jax, Griffin	R-R	6-2	195	11-22-94	6	10	3.86	71	0	4	65	58	30	28	5	19	68	.232	.297	.344	24.8	6.9	274
Keuchel, Dallas	L-L	6-2	205	1-01-88	2	1	5.97	10	6	0	38	45	25	25	3	18	25	.298	.378	.457	14.5	10.5	172
Lopez, Jorge	R-R	6-3	200	2-10-93	4	2	5.09	37	0	3	35	34	22	20	7	11	27	.256	.344	.481	17.4	7.1	155
Lopez, Pablo	L-R	6-4	225	3-07-96	11	8	3.66	32	32	0	194	176	81	79	24	48	234	.238	.292	.385	29.2	6.0	801
Luplow, Jordan	R-R	5-11	195	9-26-93	0	1	13.50	2	0	0	1	1	3	2	1	0	0	.200	.333	.800	0.0	0.0	6
Maeda, Kenta	R-R	6-1	185	4-11-88	6	8	4.23	21	20	0	104	94	50	49	17	28	117	.239	.292	.429	27.3	6.5	428
Mahle, Tyler	R-R	6-3	210	9-29-94	1	2	3.16	5	5	0	26	22	11	9	5	5	28	.227	.265	.423	27.5	4.9	102
Moran, Jovani	L-L	6-1	167	4-24-97	2	2	5.31	43	0	0	42	35	27	25	3	27	48	.226	.341	.342	26.1	14.7	184
Ober, Bailey	R-R	6-9	260	7-12-95	8	6	3.43	26	26	0	144	125	58	55	22	29	146	.232	.279	.403	25.3	5.0	577
Ortega, Oliver	R-R	6-0	165	10-02-96	0	1	4.30	10	0	0	15	11	7	7	2	7	14	.204	.302	.333	22.2	11.1	63
Paddack, Chris	R-R	6-5	217	1-08-96	1	0	5.40	2	0	0	5	6	3	3	1	1	8	.286	.318	.476	36.4	4.5	22
Pagan, Emilio	L-R	6-2	208	5-07-91	5	2	2.99	66	1	1	69	45	26	23	5	21	65	.181	.246	.306	23.8	7.7	273
Rodriguez, Dereck	R-R	6-0	208	6-05-92	0	0	13.50	1	0	0	1	1	1	1	0	1	0	.500	.500	.500	0.0	25.0	4
Ryan, Joe	R-R	6-2	205	6-05-96	11	10	4.51	29	29	0	162	155	83	81	32	34	197	.248	.290	.452	29.3	5.1	672
Sands, Cole	R-R	6-3	215	7-17-97	0	0	3.74	15	0	0	22	20	10	9	4	13	21	.235	.337	.435	21.4	13.3	98
Stewart, Brock	L-R	6-3	220	10-03-91	2	0	0.65	28	0	1	28	19	2	2	1	11	39	.196	.284	.268	35.8	10.1	109
Thielbar, Caleb	R-L	6-0	205	1-31-87	3	1	3.23	36	0	0	31	23	12	11	7	6	36	.204	.244	.451	30.0	5.0	120
Varland, Louie	L-R	6-1	205	12-09-97	4	3	4.63	17	10	0	68	66	35	35	16	17	71	.252	.299	.492	25.1	6.0	283
Winder, Josh	R-R	6-5	210	10-11-96	2	1	4.15	19	0	1	35	35	16	16	3	14	28	.267	.333	.435	19.0	9.5	147
Woods Richardson, Simeon	R-R	6-3	210	9-27-00	0	0	9.64	1	0	0	5	7	5	5	1	3	5	.350	.435	.600	20.8	12.5	24

Fielding

Catcher	PCT	G	PO	A	E	DP	PB
Jeffers	.996	82	675	31	3	4	6
Vazquez	.990	94	895	29	9	10	3

First Base	PCT	G	PO	A	E	DP
Farmer	1.000	4	7	1	0	2
Gallo	1.000	51	265	19	0	27
Julien	1.000	4	17	1	0	0
Kirilloff	.993	75	396	23	3	34
Luplow	1.000	3	14	1	0	1
Miranda	1.000	2	3	0	0	1
Solano	.994	85	466	23	3	40
Vazquez	1.000	7	18	0	0	3

Second Base	PCT	G	PO	A	E	DP
Castro	1.000	10	4	9	0	0
Farmer	1.000	45	30	54	0	18
Gordon	1.000	11	9	21	0	8
Julien	.991	75	80	138	2	22
Polanco	.976	58	70	134	5	22
Solano	1.000	28	17	31	0	8
Vazquez	.000	2	0	0	0	0

Third Base	PCT	G	PO	A	E	DP
Castro	1.000	41	15	49	0	6
Farmer	.955	43	20	43	3	6
Lewis	.955	49	32	73	5	11
Miranda	.940	38	17	62	5	4
Polanco	.963	15	3	23	1	1
Solano	.931	19	4	23	2	2

Shortstop	PCT	G	PO	A	E	DP
Castro	1.000	8	1	10	0	2
Correa	.987	135	166	278	6	56
Farmer	.989	40	32	55	1	9
Gordon	.000	2	0	0	0	0
Lewis	1.000	1	1	1	0	1

Outfield	PCT	G	PO	A	E	DP
Castro	.990	103	128	3	2	1
Farmer	.000	3	0	0	0	0
Gallo	.990	72	89	2	2	1
Garlick	1.000	12	10	0	0	0
Gordon	.986	32	46	0	1	0
Kepler	.996	124	220	3	1	0
Kirilloff	1.000	21	24	0	0	0
Larnach	1.000	64	91	0	0	0
Luplow	.667	25	22	1	0	0
Stevenson	.977	23	23	1	1	0
Taylor	.990	126	289	1	3	0
Wallner	.989	72	97	2	1	0

ST. PAUL SAINTS — *TRIPLE-A*

INTERNATIONAL LEAGUE

Batting	B-T	Ht.	Wt.	DOB	AVG	OBP	SLG	G	PA	AB	R	H	2B	3B	HR	RBI	BB	HBP	SH	SF	SO	SB	CS	BB%	SO%
Bechtold, Andrew	R-R	6-1	185	4-18-96	.257	.335	.464	73	206	183	23	47	14	0	8	27	22	0	0	1	56	0	0	10.7	27.2
Buxton, Byron	R-R	6-2	190	12-18-93	.167	.286	.167	4	14	12	0	2	0	0	0	1	2	0	0	0	5	0	0	14.3	35.7
Camargo, Jair	R-R	5-10	230	7-01-99	.259	.323	.503	90	368	332	56	86	16	1	21	63	29	4	0	3	119	2	1	7.9	32.3
Castro, Willi	B-R	6-1	206	4-24-97	.182	.308	.182	3	13	11	2	2	0	0	0	1	2	0	0	0	5	0	0	15.4	38.5
Celestino, Gilberto	R-L	6-0	170	2-13-99	.243	.392	.389	55	233	185	31	45	11	2	4	31	42	4	1	1	37	4	2	18.0	15.9
Contreras, Mark	L-R	6-0	195	1-24-95	.274	.352	.418	90	381	340	52	93	17	1	10	54	36	5	0	0	99	23	8	9.4	26.0
De Goti, Alex	R-R	6-0	192	8-19-94	.184	.339	.270	51	175	141	26	26	9	0	1	9	30	3	1	0	48	2	1	17.1	27.4
2-team (4 Jacksonville)					.179	.332	.276	55	193	156	29	28	9	0	2	13	33	3	1	0	52	2	1	17.1	26.9
Farmer, Kyle	R-R	6-0	205	8-17-90	.308	.400	.692	4	15	13	4	4	2	0	1	3	2	0	0	0	4	0	0	13.3	26.7
Gallo, Joey	L-R	6-5	250	11-19-93	.172	.265	.414	9	34	29	2	5	1	0	2	6	4	0	0	1	11	0	0	11.8	32.4
Garlick, Kyle	R-R	6-1	210	1-26-92	.242	.346	.450	79	355	298	55	72	18	1	14	65	43	8	0	6	110	2	1	12.1	31.0
Gordon, Nick	L-R	6-0	160	10-24-95	.100	.217	.150	6	23	20	2	2	1	0	0	0	2	1	0	0	7	0	1	8.7	30.4
Gray, Seth	L-R	6-3	205	5-30-98	.250	.250	.250	1	4	4	1	1	0	0	0	0	0	0	0	0	1	0	0	0.0	25.0
Helman, Michael	R-R	5-11	195	5-23-96	.296	.356	.546	27	118	108	22	32	7	1	6	31	7	3	0	0	16	5	1	5.9	13.6
Julien, Edouard	L-R	6-0	195	4-30-99	.293	.435	.496	38	170	133	29	39	12	0	5	22	32	3	0	2	42	3	0	18.8	24.7
Keirsey, DaShawn	L-L	6-0	195	5-13-97	.264	.375	.364	39	152	129	20	34	1	3	2	13	19	4	0	0	31	8	0	12.5	20.4
Kirilloff, Alex	L-L	6-2	195	11-09-97	.369	.438	.662	16	73	65	14	24	4	0	5	18	6	2	0	0	13	2	1	8.2	17.8
Kolozsvary, Mark	R-R	5-7	185	9-04-95	.214	.267	.500	6	15	14	2	3	1	0	1	4	1	0	0	0	5	0	0	6.7	33.3
2-team (20 Norfolk)					.171	.253	.305	26	91	82	11	14	2	0	3	11	6	3	0	0	31	1	0	6.6	34.1
LaMarre, Ryan	R-L	6-1	215	11-21-88	.204	.315	.366	28	108	93	12	19	6	0	3	12	12	3	0	0	33	7	1	11.1	30.6
Larnach, Trevor	L-R	6-4	223	2-26-97	.271	.384	.504	72	323	262	56	71	14	1	15	47	50	3	0	8	90	2	2	15.5	27.9
Lee, Brooks	B-R	5-11	205	2-14-01	.237	.304	.428	38	168	152	20	36	8	3	5	23	15	0	0	1	28	1	0	8.9	16.7
Lewis, Royce	R-R	6-2	200	6-05-99	.356	.412	.778	12	51	45	11	16	1	0	6	13	5	0	0	1	13	3	1	9.8	25.5
Martin, Austin	R-R	6-0	185	3-23-99	.263	.386	.405	59	252	205	33	54	11	0	6	28	36	7	1	3	43	16	4	14.3	17.1
Miranda, Jose	R-R	6-2	210	6-29-98	.255	.326	.360	39	181	161	24	41	6	1	3	23	15	3	0	2	29	2	0	8.3	16.0
Perez, Hernan	R-R	6-1	213	3-26-91	.279	.351	.485	63	231	204	30	57	8	2	10	47	23	1	0	3	48	9	4	10.0	20.8
Polanco, Jorge	B-R	5-11	208	7-05-93	.281	.395	.406	9	38	32	5	9	1	0	1	1	5	1	0	0	10	0	0	13.2	26.3
Prato, Anthony	R-R	5-9	186	5-11-98	.302	.452	.539	72	299	232	53	70	23	1	10	45	59	6	0	2	69	10	4	19.7	23.1
Severino, Yunior	B-R	6-0	189	10-03-99	.233	.320	.511	36	153	133	24	31	2	1	11	22	15	3	0	2	56	0	0	9.8	36.6
Soto, Elliot	R-R	5-9	160	8-21-89	.213	.282	.299	53	184	164	23	35	7	2	1	13	14	2	3	1	59	9	0	7.6	32.1
Stevenson, Andrew	L-L	5-11	191	6-01-94	.317	.394	.522	106	470	416	91	132	23	7	16	57	42	11	1	0	97	44	5	8.9	20.6
Wallner, Matt	L-R	6-4	220	12-12-97	.291	.403	.524	67	305	254	50	74	20	3	11	47	39	10	0	2	87	0	0	12.8	28.5
White, Tyler	R-R	5-11	238	10-29-90	.259	.386	.414	16	70	58	10	15	3	0	2	7	11	1	0	0	13	0	0	15.7	18.6
2-team (12 Syracuse)					.257	.375	.356	28	120	101	14	26	4	0	2	10	18	1	0	0	23	0	0	15.0	19.2
Williams, Chris	R-R	5-11	225	11-23-96	.236	.352	.495	95	376	309	58	73	13	2	21	75	51	8	0	7	122	3	0	13.6	32.4
Wolters, Tony	L-R	5-10	195	6-09-92	.244	.386	.343	57	215	172	25	42	8	0	3	21	36	5	0	2	46	0	1	16.7	21.4
Yake, Ernie	L-R	5-10	175	11-20-97	.286	.359	.571	11	39	35	9	10	4	0	2	5	4	0	0	0	7	1	0	10.3	17.9

Pitching	B-T	Ht.	Wt.	DOB	W	L	ERA	G	GS	SV	IP	Hits	Runs	ER	HR	BB	SO	AVG	OBP	SLG	SO%	BB%	BF
Alcala, Jorge	R-R	6-3	205	7-28-95	2	1	1.17	6	0	0	8	5	1	1	1	4	10	.192	.300	.346	33.3	13.3	30
Balazovic, Jordan	R-R	6-5	215	9-17-98	1	1	5.32	22	3	0	46	47	29	27	5	32	54	.269	.381	.440	25.7	15.2	210
Bechtold, Andrew	R-R	6-1	185	4-18-96	3	1	11.00	20	0	0	18	22	22	22	1	24	16	.333	.505	.515	16.8	25.3	95
Boyle, Michael	R-L	6-3	200	4-12-94	4	3	5.15	30	1	0	37	24	22	21	6	27	37	.182	.327	.356	22.7	16.6	163
Bravo, Jose	R-R	6-3	213	6-10-97	1	0	10.50	3	0	0	6	10	7	7	3	6	6	.357	.471	.857	17.6	17.6	34
Brice, Austin	R-R	6-4	238	6-19-92	3	1	5.54	32	0	0	37	36	26	23	3	18	40	.257	.346	.407	24.5	11.0	163
De Leon, Jose	R-R	6-0	220	8-07-92	0	2	3.62	9	4	1	27	25	13	11	2	12	26	.245	.325	.363	22.2	10.3	117
Dobnak, Randy	R-R	6-1	230	1-17-95	5	9	5.13	31	26	1	126	148	82	72	12	61	115	.295	.376	.445	20.2	10.7	569
Enlow, Blayne	R-R	6-3	170	3-21-99	2	5	7.94	15	12	0	45	53	41	40	10	19	44	.294	.377	.544	21.3	9.2	207
Festa, David	R-R	6-6	185	3-08-00	1	1	2.92	3	3	0	12	10	4	4	1	9	15	.222	.352	.356	27.8	16.7	54
Funderburk, Kody	L-L	6-4	230	11-27-96	4	1	2.60	37	2	5	52	34	15	15	1	21	75	.183	.276	.253	35.7	10.0	210
Headrick, Brent	L-L	6-6	235	12-17-97	4	2	4.68	19	12	0	75	72	42	39	11	26	83	.251	.321	.415	25.9	8.1	321
Henriquez, Ronny	R-R	5-10	155	6-20-00	5	3	5.68	37	0	1	57	54	38	36	6	36	49	.244	.356	.371	18.7	13.7	262
Keuchel, Dallas	L-L	6-2	205	1-01-88	1	0	1.13	6	6	0	32	28	6	4	3	12	28	.233	.303	.333	21.2	9.1	132
Laweryson, Cody	L-R	6-4	205	5-10-98	3	4	4.80	32	4	0	51	52	35	27	11	25	51	.257	.349	.495	22.0	10.8	232

Luna, Carlos	R-R	6-1	208	9-25-96	0	1	18.00	2	1	0	4	10	8	8	2	3	4	.476	.538	.857	15.4	11.5	26
Maeda, Kenta	R-R	6-1	185	4-11-88	0	0	2.03	4	4	0	13	10	3	3	1	5	17	.200	.273	.260	30.9	9.1	55
McMahon, Hunter	R-R	6-3	185	4-09-98	0	1	1.59	7	2	0	11	10	4	2	0	6	7	.233	.320	.302	13.7	11.8	51
Megill, Trevor	L-R	6-8	250	12-05-93	0	0	13.03	7	0	0	10	9	14	14	4	13	16	.243	.431	.622	31.4	25.5	51
Moran, Jovani	L-L	6-1	167	4-24-97	0	0	1.08	6	0	1	8	7	1	1	0	9	8	.233	.410	.267	20.5	23.1	39
Murphy, Patrick	R-R	6-5	211	6-10-95	6	4	3.69	42	4	6	85	83	39	35	7	50	97	.256	.365	.370	25.1	12.9	387
Ober, Bailey	R-R	6-9	260	7-12-95	2	1	2.38	5	5	0	23	16	7	6	1	6	25	.195	.244	.305	27.8	6.7	90
Ortega, Oliver	R-R	6-0	165	10-02-96	3	1	1.82	24	0	5	35	24	11	7	3	10	44	.195	.261	.317	32.6	7.4	135
Paddack, Chris	R-R	6-5	217	1-08-96	0	0	0.00	1	0	0	3	2	0	0	0	1	5	.182	.250	.182	41.7	8.3	12
Peguero, Francis	R-R	6-1	185	8-11-97	0	0	7.20	3	1	0	5	7	7	4	2	4	6	.333	.464	.714	21.4	14.3	28
Rodriguez, Dereck	R-R	6-0	208	6-05-92	2	0	4.66	7	2	0	19	15	12	10	3	10	20	.205	.318	.411	23.5	11.8	85
Ryan, Joe	R-R	6-2	205	6-05-96	0	0	2.25	1	1	0	4	1	1	1	1	2	7	.077	.200	.308	46.7	13.3	15
Sadzeck, Connor	R-R	6-7	235	10-01-91	1	3	5.40	25	2	1	35	40	28	21	6	26	42	.290	.402	.522	24.6	15.2	171
Sanchez, Aaron	R-R	6-4	212	7-01-92	4	4	5.30	18	16	1	73	74	47	43	10	53	57	.270	.401	.438	16.8	15.6	339
Sands, Cole	R-R	6-3	215	7-17-97	0	2	1.47	19	0	4	31	17	6	5	2	10	41	.156	.227	.248	34.5	8.4	119
Scherff, Alex	B-R	6-3	205	2-05-98	0	0	9.53	5	0	0	6	5	7	6	2	7	7	.238	.414	.619	24.1	24.1	29
Schulfer, Austin	R-R	6-2	175	12-22-95	7	3	3.79	41	0	0	57	61	24	24	1	30	51	.281	.372	.373	20.2	11.9	253
Stewart, Brock	L-R	6-3	220	10-03-91	0	0	1.54	10	0	2	12	7	3	2	0	4	22	.171	.261	.293	47.8	8.7	46
Taylor, Curtis	R-R	6-6	235	7-25-95	0	0	0.00	1	0	0	1	2	0	0	0	0	1	.500	.500	.500	25.0	0.0	4
Thielbar, Caleb	R-L	6-0	205	1-31-87	1	0	0.00	4	0	0	4	1	0	0	0	1	5	.077	.143	.077	35.7	7.1	14
Varland, Louie	L-R	6-1	205	12-09-97	7	1	3.97	16	15	0	82	84	48	36	8	26	88	.265	.325	.429	25.1	7.4	351
Winder, Josh	R-R	6-5	210	10-11-96	5	3	6.16	18	0	2	31	39	22	21	5	19	39	.312	.404	.528	26.7	13.0	146
Wolters, Tony	L-R	5-10	195	6-09-92	0	0	0.00	1	0	0	0	1	0	0	0	0	0	.500	.667	1.000	0.0	0.0	3
Woods Richardson, Simeon	R-R	6-3	210	9-27-00	7	6	4.91	24	22	0	114	109	68	62	13	61	96	.253	.345	.422	19.3	12.3	497

Fielding

Catcher	PCT	G	PO	A	E	DP	PB
Camargo	.991	72	621	38	6	5	7
Kolozsvary	.952	6	38	2	2	0	0
Williams	.979	25	220	10	5	1	1
Wolters	.994	51	485	29	3	2	4

First Base	PCT	G	PO	A	E	DP
Bechtold	1.000	9	58	1	0	5
Camargo	1.000	4	20	3	0	0
Gallo	1.000	4	28	4	0	8
Garlick	.996	32	233	22	1	26
Kirilloff	.958	9	61	8	3	6
LaMarre	1.000	4	18	1	0	0
Miranda	.965	8	54	1	2	10
Perez	1.000	4	9	0	0	2
Severino	1.000	15	115	9	0	18
White	.974	10	68	7	2	10
Williams	.998	60	400	40	1	44

Second Base	PCT	G	PO	A	E	DP
Bechtold	1.000	8	11	15	0	5
De Goti	1.000	7	17	16	0	6
Farmer	1.000	1	1	1	0	0
Gordon	1.000	2	1	5	0	1
Helman	1.000	8	13	19	0	8
Julien	.981	34	55	100	3	24
Martin	.987	35	69	80	2	22
Perez	.975	21	30	47	2	12
Polanco	1.000	4	6	9	0	1
Prato	.974	26	41	72	3	17
Severino	1.000	4	5	14	0	4
Soto	1.000	2	1	3	0	0
Wolters	1.000	5	5	13	0	1
Yake	.947	5	6	12	1	4

Third Base	PCT	G	PO	A	E	DP
Bechtold	.963	31	17	35	2	7
Castro	1.000	1	0	4	0	0
De Goti	.944	11	5	12	1	2
Farmer	1.000	1	0	1	0	0
Gray	1.000	1	1	1	0	0
Helman	1.000	5	1	6	0	1
Lee	1.000	6	4	12	0	0
Lewis	.929	7	3	10	1	2
Miranda	.957	27	16	50	3	8
Perez	.966	14	9	19	1	5
Polanco	.875	3	2	5	1	0
Prato	.913	35	27	46	7	3
Severino	1.000	13	11	26	0	1
Soto	1.000	1	0	3	0	0
Yake	.667	1	1	1	1	0

Shortstop	PCT	G	PO	A	E	DP
De Goti	1.000	32	40	63	0	17
Farmer	1.000	1	4	1	0	0
Helman	.913	6	9	12	2	2
Lee	.949	29	39	73	6	21
Lewis	1.000	4	4	8	0	2
Perez	.957	24	26	64	4	18
Prato	1.000	9	7	16	0	0
Soto	.993	50	53	87	1	14
Yake	1.000	5	2	9	0	3

Outfield	PCT	G	PO	A	E	DP
Buxton	1.000	1	1	0	0	0
Castro	1.000	1	1	0	0	0
Celestino	.963	49	72	3	2	1
Contreras	.977	76	136	4	3	1
De Goti	.000	1	0	0	0	0
Gallo	1.000	3	5	0	0	0
Garlick	1.000	28	54	2	0	1
Gordon	.500	3	2	0	0	0
Helman	1.000	7	14	0	0	0
Keirsey	.974	39	73	1	1	0
Kirilloff	1.000	4	5	0	0	0
LaMarre	1.000	22	41	1	0	0
Larnach	.984	50	73	2	1	0
Martin	.985	23	59	2	1	0
Perez	1.000	2	6	1	0	0
Prato	1.000	1	2	0	0	0
Stevenson	.649	96	174	2	5	0
Wallner	.970	53	103	5	5	0

WICHITA WIND SURGE — *DOUBLE-A*

TEXAS LEAGUE

Batting	B-T	Ht.	Wt.	DOB	AVG	OBP	SLG	G	PA	AB	R	H	2B	3B	HR	RBI	BB	HBP	SH	SF	SO	SB	CS	BB%	SO%
Banuelos, David	R-R	6-0	205	10-01-96	.270	.369	.526	48	178	152	24	41	7	1	10	30	21	3	2	0	68	1	0	11.8	38.2
Fajardo, Yoyner	L-R	6-0	179	4-06-99	.305	.375	.446	123	527	469	75	143	23	8	9	53	50	4	1	3	84	50	13	9.5	15.9
Garry, Willie Joe	L-L	6-0	187	5-29-00	.264	.313	.500	34	116	106	14	28	9	2	4	23	7	1	1	1	37	9	1	6.0	31.9
Gray, Seth	L-R	6-3	205	5-30-98	.260	.366	.400	84	333	285	48	74	9	2	9	37	41	7	0	0	108	14	6	12.3	32.4
Helman, Michael	R-R	5-11	195	5-23-96	.227	.250	.409	6	24	22	2	5	1	0	1	5	1	0	0	1	5	0	0	4.2	20.8
Holland, Will	R-R	5-9	181	4-18-98	.197	.300	.306	101	341	294	50	58	11	3	5	35	42	2	1	2	95	30	7	12.3	27.9
Isola, Alex	R-R	5-11	215	7-22-98	.279	.366	.480	110	465	408	66	114	22	0	20	58	50	6	0	1	100	5	2	10.8	21.5
Keirsey, DaShawn	L-L	6-0	195	5-13-97	.305	.363	.488	91	397	361	59	110	17	5	13	48	31	3	0	2	93	31	5	7.8	23.4
Lee, Brooks	B-R	5-11	205	2-14-01	.292	.365	.476	87	399	349	63	102	31	0	11	61	41	2	0	5	63	6	4	10.3	15.8
Lewis, Royce	R-R	6-2	200	6-05-99	.333	.500	.500	2	8	6	3	2	1	0	0	1	1	1	0	0	3	2	0	12.5	37.5
Nigro, Frank	R-R	6-3	200	8-01-97	.111	.273	.111	3	11	9	1	1	0	0	0	0	2	0	0	0	4	0	0	18.2	36.4
Prato, Anthony	R-R	5-9	186	5-11-98	.171	.305	.248	43	156	129	17	22	2	1	2	15	20	5	2	0	35	8	2	12.8	22.4
Ross, Ben	R-R	6-0	180	6-06-01	.226	.306	.226	10	36	31	5	7	0	0	0	4	4	0	0	1	7	2	0	11.1	19.4
Rucker, Jake	R-R	6-0	195	9-14-99	.248	.323	.381	119	476	420	51	104	21	4	9	63	42	7	2	5	123	10	11	8.8	25.8
Sabato, Aaron	R-R	6-2	230	6-04-99	.221	.329	.430	77	319	272	38	60	19	1	12	45	42	3	0	2	103	2	2	13.2	32.3
Schmidt, Kyle	R-R	6-0	205	7-13-97	.250	.333	.250	2	9	8	2	2	0	0	0	1	1	0	0	0	2	0	0	11.1	22.2
Schobel, Tanner	R-R	5-9	170	6-04-01	.226	.329	.305	49	207	177	19	40	6	1	2	18	25	3	0	2	40	3	1	12.1	19.3

Batting	B-T	Ht.	Wt.	DOB	AVG	OBP	SLG	G	PA	AB	R	H	2B	3B	HR	RBI	BB	HBP	SH	SF	SO	SB	CS	BB%	SO%
Severino, Yunior	B-R	6-0	189	10-03-99	.287	.365	.560	84	375	334	56	96	15	2	24	62	36	5	0	0	117	3	4	9.6	31.2
Shuffield, Dalton	R-R	5-10	170	3-31-99	.241	.337	.402	26	101	87	11	21	2	0	4	10	13	0	0	1	28	6	1	12.9	27.7
Smith, Armani	R-R	6-2	215	7-19-98	.202	.287	.292	26	101	89	10	18	2	0	2	8	10	1	0	1	31	2	1	9.9	30.7
Soularie, Alerick	R-R	5-11	175	7-05-99	.231	.356	.409	79	270	225	41	52	5	1	11	33	39	5	0	1	75	22	5	14.4	27.8
Winkel, Pat	L-R	6-0	200	1-27-00	.266	.362	.424	88	356	304	43	81	16	1	10	48	45	3	0	4	86	3	1	12.6	24.2
Yake, Ernie	L-R	5-10	175	11-20-97	.177	.301	.274	24	73	62	9	11	3	0	1	4	10	1	0	0	13	2	2	13.7	17.8

Pitching	B-T	Ht.	Wt.	DOB	W	L	ERA	G	GS	SV	IP	Hits	Runs	ER	HR	BB	SO	AVG	OBP	SLG	SO%	BB%	BF
Adams, Travis	R-R	6-1	197	1-19-00	4	10	5.66	26	25	0	110	118	75	69	16	43	97	.275	.344	.466	20.3	9.0	479
Alcala, Jorge	R-R	6-3	205	7-28-95	0	0	9.00	2	0	0	2	3	2	2	1	1	4	.333	.400	.667	40.0	10.0	10
Banuelos, David	R-R	6-0	205	10-01-96	0	0	94.50	1	0	0	1	6	7	7	4	1	1	.667	.700	2.111	10.0	10.0	10
Beck, Tyler	R-R	6-1	190	11-16-95	3	0	3.06	10	0	0	18	13	6	6	1	9	19	.203	.307	.344	25.3	12.0	75
Bentley, Denny	L-L	6-2	195	5-28-98	3	1	4.36	29	0	0	43	50	22	21	3	18	45	.292	.365	.421	23.4	9.4	192
Boyle, Michael	R-L	6-3	200	4-12-94	2	0	2.63	19	0	1	27	24	8	8	5	9	29	.235	.297	.402	26.1	8.1	111
Bravo, Jose	R-R	6-3	213	6-10-97	3	3	6.28	11	2	0	29	33	26	20	8	10	25	.280	.333	.542	18.8	7.5	133
Brink, Jordan	L-R	6-0	200	3-18-93	1	2	6.00	28	0	5	33	31	22	22	4	21	27	.250	.363	.419	18.2	14.2	148
Cabezas, Andrew	R-R	5-10	175	12-05-96	1	2	4.43	14	0	1	20	25	12	10	5	10	22	.291	.378	.523	22.4	10.2	98
Carr, Jordan	B-L	6-2	210	7-17-97	1	1	6.10	4	1	0	10	14	8	7	2	4	5	.318	.388	.568	10.0	8.0	50
Donato, Chad	R-R	6-0	195	6-03-95	1	7	11.57	13	11	0	42	72	55	54	13	23	36	.377	.447	.654	16.6	10.6	217
Enlow, Blayne	R-R	6-3	170	3-21-99	3	1	3.17	11	10	0	54	48	23	19	6	13	65	.236	.307	.374	28.8	5.8	226
Festa, David	R-R	6-6	185	3-08-00	3	3	4.39	21	19	0	80	76	45	39	8	33	104	.249	.325	.354	30.4	9.6	342
Floyd, Taylor	R-R	6-1	185	12-08-97	2	2	5.97	28	0	0	38	45	26	25	6	19	41	.298	.385	.483	23.4	10.9	175
Funderburk, Kody	L-L	6-4	230	11-27-96	1	0	1.00	5	0	1	9	8	1	1	0	6	14	.235	.350	.235	35.0	15.0	40
German, Osiris	R-R	6-1	170	11-02-98	2	1	5.40	15	0	0	18	24	11	11	1	9	15	.316	.398	.421	17.0	10.2	88
Grace, Regi	L-R	6-2	215	12-10-99	1	3	4.11	27	1	2	50	40	27	23	5	23	53	.216	.319	.351	24.4	10.6	217
Griffith, Owen	R-R	6-1	195	2-06-98	0	0	0.00	1	0	0	0	1	3	3	1	1	0	1.000	1.000	4.000	0.0	33.3	3
Holland, Will	R-R	5-9	181	4-18-98	0	0	16.20	3	0	0	2	4	3	3	2	0	0	.444	.500	1.111	0.0	0.0	10
Luna, Carlos	R-R	6-1	208	9-25-96	2	9	5.87	23	16	0	95	106	69	62	30	24	96	.279	.333	.566	23.2	5.8	414
Mattson, Isaac	R-R	6-2	205	7-14-95	3	1	3.62	21	1	0	32	15	15	13	3	24	42	.138	.312	.248	30.2	17.3	139
McMahon, Hunter	R-R	6-3	185	4-09-98	2	1	6.71	40	0	4	60	65	50	45	9	19	57	.277	.343	.451	21.5	7.2	265
Mooney, Sean	R-R	6-1	200	1-11-98	0	1	8.31	5	2	0	4	5	5	4	2	4	5	.263	.391	.632	21.7	17.4	23
Nordlin, Seth	R-R	6-4	213	9-04-97	0	1	5.67	16	0	0	27	37	17	17	3	12	13	.322	.391	.470	10.2	9.4	128
Nowlin, Jaylen	L-L	6-1	180	1-29-01	3	1	3.82	9	7	0	38	31	21	16	4	22	35	.230	.359	.356	20.2	12.7	173
Ohl, Pierson	R-R	6-1	180	9-10-99	7	3	2.69	16	14	0	87	70	26	26	9	13	74	.217	.251	.351	21.8	3.8	339
Paddack, Chris	R-R	6-5	217	1-08-96	0	1	4.50	1	1	0	4	4	2	2	1	0	6	.267	.267	.467	40.0	0.0	15
Peguero, Francis	R-R	6-1	185	8-11-97	3	4	4.50	31	0	3	40	42	24	20	9	10	34	.261	.310	.491	19.4	5.7	175
Phillips, Alex	R-R	6-4	220	12-16-94	1	0	11.57	4	0	0	5	9	6	6	2	6	2	.429	.556	.810	7.4	22.2	27
Raya, Marco	R-R	6-1	170	8-07-02	0	3	5.28	11	11	0	29	22	19	17	2	14	26	.204	.304	.296	20.8	11.2	125
Rodriguez, Miguel	R-R	6-0	180	2-25-99	3	2	3.95	13	0	3	14	19	14	6	0	4	24	.317	.364	.417	36.4	6.1	66
Rozek, Aaron	L-L	6-2	225	8-20-95	3	3	5.76	26	15	1	86	93	59	55	15	30	81	.276	.342	.472	21.5	8.0	377
Scherff, Alex	B-R	6-3	205	2-05-98	4	2	3.57	39	0	4	53	50	23	21	5	31	66	.244	.345	.385	27.7	13.0	238
Taylor, Curtis	R-R	6-6	235	7-25-95	2	5	3.98	31	1	2	43	37	24	19	3	21	46	.230	.335	.323	24.3	11.1	189

Fielding

Catcher	PCT	G	PO	A	E	DP	PB
Banuelos	.998	44	396	32	1	6	2
Isola	.982	15	106	4	2	0	2
Nigro	.963	3	25	1	1	0	0
Schmidt	1.000	2	20	0	0	0	0
Winkel	.984	79	693	38	12	7	6

First Base	PCT	G	PO	A	E	DP
Gray	.994	25	160	14	1	12
Isola	.989	50	354	20	4	25
Prato	1.000	2	1	0	0	0
Rucker	1.000	21	76	8	0	9
Sabato	.988	55	401	26	5	35

Second Base	PCT	G	PO	A	E	DP
Holland	1.000	12	16	17	0	4
Prato	1.000	17	38	34	0	8
Ross	1.000	1	2	2	0	1
Rucker	.975	52	71	125	5	22
Schobel	.953	33	36	66	5	13
Severino	.957	17	31	35	3	8
Shuffield	.971	10	12	22	1	4
Yake	1.000	6	6	11	0	1

Third Base	PCT	G	PO	A	E	DP
Gray	.943	51	25	90	7	10
Helman	1.000	1	0	2	0	0
Lee	.667	1	2	0	1	0
Lewis	1.000	1	0	1	0	0
Prato	1.000	1	0	2	0	0
Rucker	.898	28	13	31	5	3
Schobel	.938	13	5	10	1	1
Severino	.915	51	33	64	9	3

Shortstop	PCT	G	PO	A	E	DP
Helman	1.000	2	2	6	0	1
Holland	.976	22	34	47	2	10
Lee	.961	82	113	204	13	29
Lewis	1.000	1	3	1	0	0
Prato	.939	8	15	16	2	8
Ross	1.000	9	6	20	0	0
Schobel	1.000	5	6	8	0	0
Yake	.929	15	18	34	4	5

Outfield	PCT	G	PO	A	E	DP
Fajardo	.981	106	196	3	4	0
Garry	.975	34	75	3	2	1
Helman	1.000	1	3	0	0	0
Holland	1.000	64	127	2	0	2
Keirsey	.998	88	189	4	1	0
Prato	1.000	17	27	0	0	0
Rucker	.487	23	35	3	1	1
Shuffield	.984	18	34	0	1	0
Smith	1.000	21	34	2	0	0
Soularie	.988	67	118	4	4	2
Yake	1.000	1	3	0	0	0

CEDAR RAPIDS KERNELS — HIGH CLASS A

MIDWEST LEAGUE

Batting	B-T	Ht.	Wt.	DOB	AVG	OBP	SLG	G	PA	AB	R	H	2B	3B	HR	RBI	BB	HBP	SH	SF	SO	SB	CS	BB%	SO%
Cardenas, Noah	R-R	5-11	195	9-10-99	.272	.397	.382	90	378	309	44	84	23	1	3	38	55	11	0	3	77	9	5	14.6	20.4
Cavaco, Keoni	R-R	6-0	195	6-02-01	.193	.266	.287	59	222	202	24	39	4	0	5	14	18	2	0	0	88	1	0	8.1	39.6
Cossetti, Andrew	R-R	5-10	215	1-31-00	.262	.406	.492	60	249	195	45	51	12	3	9	30	42	8	0	4	54	0	0	16.9	21.7
Fedko, Kyler	R-R	6-1	195	9-21-99	.242	.398	.412	59	211	165	29	40	6	2	6	24	41	3	0	2	39	5	2	19.4	18.5
Garry, Willie Joe	L-L	6-0	187	5-29-00	.216	.294	.358	46	154	134	20	29	8	1	3	15	14	2	1	3	54	10	1	9.1	35.1
Keaschall, Luke	R-R	6-1	190	8-15-02	.313	.353	.563	8	34	32	5	10	2	0	2	6	2	0	0	0	3	1	0	5.9	8.8
Mack, Charles	L-R	5-9	190	11-12-99	.103	.156	.138	9	33	29	0	3	1	0	0	3	2	0	1	1	14	1	0	6.1	42.4
McCusker, Carson	R-R	6-8	250	5-22-98	.237	.293	.566	21	82	76	13	18	4	0	7	18	5	1	0	0	32	0	0	6.1	39.0
Miller, Noah	B-R	5-11	190	11-12-02	.223	.309	.340	120	526	462	71	103	20	5	8	60	58	1	1	4	108	12	3	11.0	20.5

Batting	B-T	Ht.	Wt.	DOB	AVG	OBP	SLG	G	PA	AB	R	H	2B	3B	HR	RBI	BB	HBP	SH	SF	SO	SB	CS	BB%	SO%
Morales, Jeferson	R-R	5-8	170	5-13-99	.262	.375	.452	52	200	168	32	44	10	2	6	22	27	4	0	1	41	6	1	13.5	20.5
Ortega, Jorel	R-R	6-0	194	1-22-01	.233	.326	.410	60	264	227	38	53	12	2	8	36	28	5	0	4	69	10	2	10.6	26.1
Perez, Mikey	R-R	5-11	185	8-24-99	.185	.450	.185	12	40	27	7	5	0	0	0	1	8	5	0	0	6	2	1	20.0	15.0
Rodriguez, Emmanuel	L-L	5-10	210	2-28-03	.240	.400	.463	99	455	354	87	85	13	9	16	55	92	5	0	4	134	20	5	20.2	29.5
Rosario, Kala'i	R-R	6-0	205	7-02-02	.252	.364	.467	118	530	445	71	112	27	3	21	94	75	6	0	4	157	2	2	14.2	29.6
Ross, Ben	R-R	6-0	180	6-06-01	.240	.322	.455	103	457	400	61	96	25	2	19	71	45	6	0	6	116	7	3	9.8	25.4
Salas, Jose	B-R	6-0	191	4-26-03	.190	.265	.272	93	372	331	36	63	13	1	4	33	27	8	2	4	97	22	9	7.3	26.1
Schobel, Tanner	R-R	5-9	170	6-04-01	.288	.366	.493	77	347	302	53	87	10	5	14	61	36	4	0	5	64	9	1	10.4	18.4
Shuffield, Dalton	R-R	5-10	170	3-31-99	.143	.143	.143	3	7	7	1	1	0	0	0	0	0	0	0	0	4	0	0	0.0	57.1
Urbina, Misael	R-R	5-10	190	4-26-02	.180	.289	.282	102	412	355	45	64	18	3	4	40	49	6	0	2	109	6	3	11.9	26.5
Yake, Ernie	L-R	5-10	175	11-20-97	.235	.342	.397	25	79	68	12	16	1	2	2	7	10	1	0	0	9	2	0	12.7	11.4

Pitching	B-T	Ht.	Wt.	DOB	W	L	ERA	G	GS	SV	IP	Hits	Runs	ER	HR	BB	SO	AVG	OBP	SLG	SO%	BB%	BF
Barrington, Malik	R-R	6-2	236	10-08-97	6	2	4.29	39	0	2	65	44	34	31	3	40	80	.195	.321	.314	29.1	14.5	275
Carr, Jordan	B-L	6-2	210	7-17-97	4	2	1.48	18	6	1	61	45	14	10	2	18	61	.205	.285	.265	24.8	7.3	246
Culpepper, C.J.	R-R	6-3	193	11-02-01	2	2	4.99	10	10	0	40	40	25	22	2	16	36	.260	.339	.344	20.2	9.0	178
Dalatri, Gianluca	R-R	6-6	250	4-04-98	1	0	1.17	7	0	1	8	3	2	1	0	3	7	.111	.226	.148	22.6	9.7	31
Grace, Regi	L-R	6-2	215	12-10-99	2	2	1.16	17	0	5	23	12	4	3	0	5	30	.154	.250	.179	33.7	5.6	89
Hicks, Jackson	R-R	6-3	225	2-15-98	0	0	14.14	5	0	1	7	15	11	11	0	3	10	.429	.462	.543	25.6	7.7	39
Hidalgo, Alejandro	R-R	6-1	160	5-22-03	0	5	5.28	21	8	0	58	52	38	34	7	53	57	.239	.389	.390	20.7	19.3	275
Jones, Kyle	L-R	6-1	200	2-07-00	6	6	4.26	22	20	0	99	97	53	47	10	35	89	.255	.316	.379	21.2	8.3	420
Klein, John	R-R	6-5	225	4-22-02	0	0	3.60	1	1	0	5	6	2	2	0	1	4	.300	.364	.450	18.2	4.5	22
Labas, A.J.	R-R	6-3	223	12-08-98	2	1	4.88	18	0	3	24	28	14	13	1	10	17	.292	.358	.354	16.0	9.4	106
Lewis, Cory	R-R	6-5	220	10-09-00	5	1	2.32	13	13	0	62	48	20	16	3	18	63	.211	.265	.298	25.3	7.2	249
MacLeod, Christian	L-L	6-4	227	4-12-00	5	2	4.13	15	14	0	65	67	32	30	7	26	61	.267	.344	.402	21.3	9.1	286
Matthews, Zebby	R-R	6-5	225	5-22-00	4	2	4.59	14	13	0	67	65	35	34	13	10	59	.248	.277	.443	21.5	3.6	274
Morris, Andrew	R-R	6-0	195	9-01-01	5	1	3.28	7	7	0	36	46	15	13	2	8	28	.313	.344	.415	17.8	5.1	157
Mullenbach, Matt	R-R	6-4	195	10-06-96	0	1	7.15	8	0	0	11	20	9	9	4	4	13	.377	.431	.660	22.4	6.9	58
Neuweiler, Charlie	R-R	6-1	205	2-08-99	1	0	5.54	18	0	0	26	23	16	16	4	17	29	.245	.365	.383	25.2	14.8	115
Nowlin, Jaylen	L-L	6-1	180	1-29-01	3	6	4.79	15	13	0	68	69	40	36	11	23	79	.260	.338	.426	26.4	7.7	299
Ohl, Pierson	R-R	6-1	180	9-10-99	2	4	4.69	8	7	0	40	47	24	21	6	5	41	.285	.308	.473	23.8	2.9	172
Paredes, Mike	R-R	5-11	185	7-27-00	7	1	3.14	28	3	2	63	52	26	22	4	20	58	.219	.285	.338	22.1	7.6	262
Prielipp, Connor	L-L	6-2	210	1-10-01	0	0	6.75	1	1	0	4	5	4	3	0	2	3	.294	.368	.412	15.8	10.5	19
Raya, Marco	R-R	6-1	170	8-07-02	0	1	2.94	11	11	0	34	23	14	11	4	8	39	.192	.250	.325	29.5	6.1	132
Rimmel, Niklas	R-R	6-3	200	7-05-99	3	2	3.16	28	0	2	43	32	18	15	2	24	38	.218	.328	.327	21.7	13.7	175
Rodriguez, Miguel	R-R	6-0	180	2-25-99	2	3	2.85	33	0	14	41	32	17	13	2	11	42	.212	.268	.325	25.6	6.7	164
Rodriguez, Orlando	R-R	6-2	195	12-16-95	7	2	2.43	12	5	0	41	35	17	11	4	16	31	.227	.316	.344	17.8	9.2	174
Stankiewicz, John	R-R	6-4	230	9-08-98	7	1	3.11	37	0	4	67	51	24	23	7	15	66	.206	.251	.332	25.1	5.7	263
Swain, Matthew	R-R	6-7	225	8-20-97	2	0	5.53	30	0	1	41	36	28	25	7	21	36	.240	.339	.440	20.6	12.0	175
Velez, Ricardo	R-R	6-1	180	8-21-98	1	1	2.84	3	0	0	6	4	3	2	0	3	7	.174	.321	.217	25.0	10.7	28
Whorff, Jarret	R-R	6-3	195	10-02-98	2	0	4.91	10	0	3	15	16	9	8	2	6	15	.271	.338	.390	23.1	9.2	65
Wilson, John	L-L	6-0	195	7-17-97	2	2	4.01	26	0	1	34	41	15	15	1	13	26	.301	.383	.382	16.9	8.4	154
Yanez, Gabriel	L-L	6-3	168	7-22-99	1	0	6.48	5	0	0	8	8	6	6	0	3	8	.250	.314	.375	22.9	8.6	35

Fielding

Catcher	PCT	G	PO	A	E	DP	PB
Cardenas	.995	69	610	48	3	2	5
Cossetti	.996	29	220	20	1	2	7
Mack	1.000	8	79	6	0	0	3
Morales	.979	27	215	14	5	0	3

First Base	PCT	G	PO	A	E	DP
Cardenas	1.000	9	59	2	0	3
Cavaco	.996	59	430	30	2	33
Cossetti	.991	15	107	9	1	14
Mack	1.000	1	1	1	0	0
Ortega	1.000	18	145	14	0	9
Ross	.996	31	254	8	1	20
Yake	1.000	4	19	2	0	2

Second Base	PCT	G	PO	A	E	DP
Keaschall	.913	5	5	16	2	1
Miller	.978	12	15	30	1	5
Ortega	.984	16	17	46	1	6
Perez	.980	11	19	29	1	5
Salas	.983	55	89	136	4	28
Schobel	.957	25	52	60	5	10
Shuffield	1.000	2	0	5	0	0
Yake	.976	10	15	26	1	6

Third Base	PCT	G	PO	A	E	DP
Keaschall	1.000	1	1	0	0	0
Ortega	.935	23	28	30	4	2
Ross	.914	39	34	51	8	1
Salas	.913	21	13	29	4	2
Schobel	.970	46	38	58	3	5
Yake	1.000	5	5	4	0	1

Shortstop	PCT	G	PO	A	E	DP
Miller	.984	107	144	295	7	54
Ross	.964	12	16	37	2	8
Salas	.911	14	17	24	4	1

Outfield	PCT	G	PO	A	E	DP
Fedko	.951	47	56	2	3	0
Garry	.902	37	82	3	2	1
Keaschall	1.000	2	2	0	0	0
McCusker	.977	15	24	1	1	0
Rodriguez	.976	94	240	7	6	1
Rosario	.991	104	175	14	3	1
Ross	.987	14	36	1	1	0
Urbina	.996	91	154	4	1	0
Yake	1.000	5	9	0	0	0

FORT MYERS MIGHTY MUSSELS — LOW CLASS A

FLORIDA STATE LEAGUE

Batting	B-T	Ht.	Wt.	DOB	AVG	OBP	SLG	G	PA	AB	R	H	2B	3B	HR	RBI	BB	HBP	SH	SF	SO	SB	CS	BB%	SO%
Aguiar, Carlos	L-L	6-2	175	8-28-01	.223	.291	.446	52	206	184	24	41	5	6	8	37	17	2	0	3	65	5	2	8.3	31.6
Baez, Luis	R-R	5-11	170	11-23-00	.174	.296	.196	27	54	46	10	8	1	0	0	2	6	2	0	0	15	3	3	11.1	27.8
Baez, Nate	R-R	5-11	191	5-17-01	.268	.424	.381	29	125	97	18	26	5	0	2	16	25	2	0	1	40	1	0	20.0	32.0
Celestino, Gilberto	R-L	6-0	170	2-13-99	.250	.250	.333	4	12	12	2	3	1	0	0	0	0	0	0	0	5	0	0	0.0	41.7
Centeno, Andres	R-R	6-1	183	10-23-03	.000	.000	.000	2	5	5	0	0	0	0	0	0	0	0	0	0	4	0	0	0.0	80.0
Cespedes, Rubel	L-R	6-0	210	8-29-00	.233	.313	.398	115	476	420	62	98	26	2	13	74	50	1	0	5	101	3	1	10.5	21.2
Cossetti, Andrew	R-R	5-10	215	1-31-00	.330	.462	.607	35	143	112	20	37	11	1	6	33	22	7	0	2	25	1	0	15.4	17.5
Cruz, Rafael	R-R	6-1	166	11-13-03	.206	.270	.372	66	278	253	25	52	14	2	8	38	17	6	0	2	96	1	1	6.1	34.5
De Andrade, Danny	R-R	5-11	173	4-10-04	.244	.354	.396	105	475	394	72	96	21	3	11	67	58	14	0	9	103	20	4	12.2	21.7
Duran, Gregory	L-R	6-2	201	10-08-02	.184	.318	.296	56	217	179	23	33	11	0	3	24	32	4	0	2	63	2	2	14.7	29.0
Florentino, Francis	R-R	6-1	180	10-13-99	.143	.222	.143	4	9	7	1	1	0	0	0	2	1	0	0	1	1	0	0	11.1	11.1

Harry, Jay	L-R	6-0	195	7-18-02	.337	.419	.465	27	117	101	22	34	8	1	1	9	11	4	0	1	8	4	1	9.4	6.8
Helman, Michael	R-R	5-11	195	5-23-96	.421	.542	.684	5	24	19	7	8	3	1	0	4	3	2	0	0	3	3	0	12.5	12.5
Houghton, Maddux	R-R	5-11	190	2-23-99	.216	.331	.341	99	326	273	47	59	14	4	4	36	45	4	0	4	96	24	2	13.8	29.4
Jenkins, Walker	L-R	6-3	205	2-19-05	.392	.446	.608	12	56	51	10	20	2	3	1	10	4	1	0	0	6	2	1	7.1	10.7
Keaschall, Luke	R-R	6-1	190	8-15-02	.292	.426	.472	20	94	72	20	21	8	1	1	9	15	4	0	3	20	8	0	16.0	21.3
Kirilloff, Alex	L-L	6-2	195	11-09-97	.250	.400	.500	4	15	12	2	3	0	0	1	1	3	0	0	0	3	0	0	20.0	20.0
Martin, Austin	R-R	6-0	185	3-23-99	.158	.200	.158	5	20	19	0	3	0	0	0	1	1	0	0	0	2	1	0	5.0	10.0
Martinez, Yohander	R-R	5-10	175	1-08-02	.262	.410	.349	48	161	126	21	33	5	0	2	21	28	5	0	2	35	1	2	17.4	21.7
McCusker, Carson	R-R	6-8	250	5-22-98	.286	.352	.520	25	108	98	15	28	2	0	7	18	10	0	0	0	38	0	0	9.3	35.2
Neuse, Dylan	R-R	5-9	180	12-22-98	.255	.366	.373	79	310	255	34	65	13	4	3	33	45	3	1	6	57	12	5	14.5	18.4
Nigro, Frank	R-R	6-3	200	8-01-97	.067	.243	.100	13	37	30	1	2	1	0	0	0	7	0	0	0	10	1	0	18.9	27.0
Olivar, Ricardo	R-R	5-10	176	8-10-01	.285	.403	.452	100	449	372	75	106	28	2	10	58	59	16	0	2	93	12	1	13.1	20.7
Ortega, Jorel	R-R	6-0	194	1-22-01	.279	.396	.480	60	273	229	46	64	22	3	6	39	41	3	0	0	64	17	5	15.0	23.4
Perez, Hernan	R-R	6-1	213	3-26-91	.235	.417	.294	6	24	17	6	4	1	0	0	1	6	0	0	1	6	2	0	25.0	25.0
Perez, Mikey	R-R	5-11	185	8-24-99	.202	.307	.368	55	190	163	30	33	6	0	7	22	21	4	1	1	54	23	6	11.1	28.4
Polanco, Jorge	B-R	5-11	208	7-05-93	.278	.364	.333	6	22	18	3	5	1	0	0	1	3	0	0	1	6	0	0	13.6	27.3
Sayre, Alec	R-R	5-11	195	10-05-00	.222	.354	.303	84	319	261	51	58	5	2	4	28	52	3	0	3	84	12	3	16.3	26.3
Schmidt, Kyle	R-R	6-0	205	7-13-97	.217	.345	.319	45	165	138	21	30	6	1	2	22	20	7	0	0	27	1	1	12.1	16.4
Shuffield, Dalton	R-R	5-10	170	3-31-99	.261	.390	.396	34	136	111	23	29	5	2	2	17	24	0	0	1	36	11	1	17.6	26.5
Tatum, Dillon	R-R	5-11	220	5-24-00	.173	.358	.263	53	173	133	19	23	7	1	1	15	33	6	0	1	59	1	0	19.1	34.1
Willman, Kamron	R-R	6-1	175	2-25-98	.197	.322	.263	33	90	76	10	15	3	1	0	7	14	0	0	0	28	2	2	15.6	31.1

Pitching	B-T	Ht.	Wt.	DOB	W	L	ERA	G	GS	SV	IP	Hits	Runs	ER	HR	BB	SO	AVG	OBP	SLG	SO%	BB%	BF
Alcala, Jorge	R-R	6-3	205	7-28-95	0	0	0.00	1	0	0	1	0	0	0	0	0	2	.000	.000	.000	66.7	0.0	3
Aria, Develson	L-L	6-0	155	3-20-01	2	6	9.45	25	12	0	47	44	51	49	4	61	57	.244	.454	.361	22.6	24.2	252
Boadas, Miguelangel	R-R	6-1	181	12-07-02	0	2	7.75	11	11	0	36	41	35	31	2	24	35	.277	.410	.405	19.1	13.1	183
Cleto, Tomas	R-R	6-2	206	10-09-00	0	2	4.40	4	4	0	14	17	9	7	1	8	10	.304	.400	.446	15.4	12.3	65
Culpepper, C.J.	R-R	6-3	193	11-02-01	4	3	2.33	11	11	0	46	32	15	12	2	15	53	.196	.268	.239	29.4	8.3	180
Ethridge, Ben	R-R	6-2	190	7-03-01	3	6	2.99	25	13	1	78	59	29	26	4	36	63	.212	.308	.309	19.5	11.1	323
Gabbert, Matt	L-R	6-4	200	6-28-02	3	0	2.13	4	1	0	13	5	3	3	1	4	13	.116	.188	.233	27.1	8.3	48
Hamilton, Xander	L-R	6-3	216	7-07-01	0	0	0.00	3	0	0	5	2	0	0	0	4	9	.118	.318	.118	40.9	18.2	22
Henriquez, Ronny	R-R	5-10	155	6-20-00	0	0	4.91	2	0	0	4	4	2	2	0	3	4	.267	.389	.400	22.2	16.7	18
Hicks, Jackson	R-R	6-3	225	2-15-98	6	1	3.22	36	0	3	50	46	21	18	4	19	65	.241	.316	.361	30.5	8.9	213
Klein, John	R-R	6-5	225	4-22-02	2	1	2.97	6	6	0	30	18	10	10	1	13	30	.170	.279	.245	24.6	10.7	122
Labas, A.J.	R-R	6-3	223	12-08-98	1	2	4.85	20	0	4	30	26	21	16	5	11	30	.230	.313	.363	23.4	8.6	128
Langenberg, Ty	R-R	6-2	190	12-08-01	0	1	5.06	3	0	0	5	7	3	3	0	3	2	.368	.462	.421	7.7	11.5	26
Lavallee, Johnathan	R-R	6-4	240	8-11-99	2	2	7.78	30	0	2	42	48	41	36	6	33	47	.291	.404	.461	23.2	16.3	203
Lee, Jeremy	R-R	5-11	203	9-07-01	0	0	0.00	2	0	0	3	4	0	0	0	3	5	.308	.438	.385	31.3	18.8	16
Lewis, Cory	R-R	6-5	220	10-09-00	4	3	2.75	9	9	0	39	26	17	12	3	15	55	.179	.259	.303	33.7	9.2	163
MacLeod, Christian	L-L	6-4	227	4-12-00	0	0	3.38	2	2	0	5	1	2	2	0	6	8	.056	.292	.056	33.3	25.0	24
Martinez, Yohander	R-R	5-10	175	1-08-02	0	0	11.57	2	0	0	2	4	3	3	1	1	3	.364	.417	.727	25.0	8.3	12
Matthews, Zebby	R-R	6-5	225	5-22-00	3	1	2.56	8	7	0	39	31	15	11	1	5	53	.217	.240	.273	35.3	3.3	150
Mendez, Juan	R-R	6-4	240	10-18-98	2	5	4.89	34	0	1	46	31	26	25	8	31	66	.189	.325	.396	32.4	15.2	204
Mercedes, Juan	R-R	5-10	181	1-07-02	2	1	5.61	8	6	0	26	30	20	16	3	14	21	.294	.387	.431	17.6	11.8	119
Mineo, Ricky	R-R	6-5	225	8-22-00	1	1	5.21	11	0	0	19	14	12	11	2	15	23	.209	.384	.343	26.1	17.0	88
Mooney, Sean	R-R	6-1	200	1-11-98	0	0	0.00	2	0	0	2	0	0	0	0	1	4	.000	.143	.000	57.1	14.3	7
Moreno, Danny	R-R	6-1	180	10-10-99	2	2	5.40	30	0	0	47	49	33	28	4	26	39	.268	.374	.339	17.8	11.9	219
Morris, Andrew	R-R	6-0	195	9-01-01	3	1	2.59	11	10	0	49	40	19	14	2	11	51	.216	.265	.308	25.5	5.5	200
Noble, Jack	R-R	6-2	200	4-02-00	2	2	3.38	10	9	0	51	38	21	19	4	23	43	.211	.321	.339	20.2	10.8	213
Olivares, Jose	R-R	6-1	199	1-18-03	3	4	6.22	21	20	0	85	82	61	59	15	43	83	.251	.340	.468	22.1	11.4	376
Paddack, Chris	R-R	6-5	217	1-08-96	0	0	6.75	1	1	0	3	2	2	2	0	2	4	.200	.333	.200	33.3	16.7	12
Perez, Mikey	R-R	5-11	185	8-24-99	0	0	40.50	2	0	0	1	0	3	3	0	4	0	.000	.667	.000	0.0	66.7	6
Perez, Samuel	L-L	5-11	205	11-29-99	6	2	3.30	35	1	2	63	54	28	23	5	15	63	.228	.278	.338	24.6	5.9	256
Reyes, Wilker	L-L	6-0	170	2-25-02	1	4	5.49	28	3	0	57	67	41	35	4	38	58	.295	.403	.423	21.1	13.8	275
Santos, Nolan	R-R	6-1	205	12-07-00	0	0	4.15	3	0	0	4	3	2	2	0	5	1	.214	.450	.429	5.0	25.0	20
Schmidt, Kyle	R-R	6-0	205	7-13-97	0	0	0.00	1	0	0	0	0	0	0	0	0	0	.000	.000	.000	0.0	0.0	1
Veen, Zach	L-L	6-0	180	4-18-01	5	4	4.32	41	0	5	58	50	34	28	6	26	48	.233	.312	.391	19.0	10.3	252
Velez, Ricardo	R-R	6-1	180	8-21-98	4	1	3.49	19	0	3	28	21	12	11	3	12	36	.202	.294	.337	30.3	10.1	119
Whorff, Jarret	R-R	6-3	195	10-02-98	3	2	2.76	15	5	1	49	35	16	15	2	27	56	.201	.319	.259	27.1	13.0	207
Winder, Josh	R-R	6-5	210	10-11-96	0	1	1.93	3	0	0	5	5	1	1	0	2	7	.263	.333	.368	33.3	9.5	21
Yanez, Gabriel	L-L	6-3	168	7-22-99	3	4	4.56	32	0	2	51	57	31	26	3	11	61	.289	.333	.376	28.5	5.1	214

Fielding

Catcher	PCT	G	PO	A	E	DP	PB
Baez	1.000	16	151	5	0	1	1
Cossetti	.982	18	160	8	3	1	3
Nigro	.987	11	67	8	1	0	1
Olivar	.992	39	354	21	3	1	3
Schmidt	.995	25	178	18	1	4	3
Tatum	.997	40	305	24	1	2	5

First Base	PCT	G	PO	A	E	DP
Baez	1.000	10	77	4	0	7
Cespedes	.991	48	324	21	3	22
Cossetti	1.000	6	43	0	0	0
Duran	.993	43	275	18	2	24
Kirilloff	1.000	2	14	1	0	1
Nigro	1.000	2	4	2	0	0
Perez	1.000	5	17	0	0	1
Schmidt	.986	20	129	7	2	16
Shuffield	.000	1	0	0	0	0
Tatum	1.000	13	75	5	0	2

Second Base	PCT	G	PO	A	E	DP
Cespedes	.981	16	26	27	1	6
Harry	1.000	9	14	26	0	8
Keaschall	.982	16	18	36	1	6
Martin	1.000	1	0	2	0	0
Martinez	.954	34	32	51	4	8
Ortega	.951	17	24	34	3	4
Perez	.974	26	23	53	2	10
Polanco	1.000	5	2	15	0	1
Shuffield	.936	13	11	33	3	5
Willman	.952	20	24	36	3	7

Third Base	PCT	G	PO	A	E	DP
Cespedes	.889	39	25	47	9	10
Cruz	.872	38	22	46	10	4
De Andrade	1.000	1	2	2	0	0
Duran	.000	1	0	0	0	0
Harry	1.000	9	7	8	0	2
Keaschall	.500	1	1	0	1	0
Martinez	.667	2	0	2	1	0

	PCT	G	PO	A	E	DP
Ortega	.929	37	20	45	5	1
Perez, H	1.000	1	1	3	0	1
Perez, M	1.000	7	6	13	0	0
Shuffield	1.000	5	5	4	0	0
Willman	1.000	2	0	1	0	0

Shortstop	PCT	G	PO	A	E	DP
Cruz	.933	14	18	24	3	2
De Andrade	.954	90	116	195	15	45
Harry	1.000	8	9	19	0	2
Helman	1.000	2	3	5	0	0
Ortega	.000	1	0	0	0	0
Perez, H	1.000	3	3	8	0	2
Perez, M	.963	12	4	22	1	1
Willman	.880	8	10	12	3	2

Outfield	PCT	G	PO	A	E	DP
Aguiar	.977	44	62	3	3	0
Baez	.667	19	17	0	0	0
Celestino	.500	4	2	0	0	0
Centeno	1.000	2	2	0	0	0
Duran	.500	16	23	1	0	0
Florentino	.500	3	2	0	0	0
Harry	1.000	2	0	1	0	0
Helman	1.000	2	3	0	0	0
Houghton	.997	93	214	7	2	5
Jenkins	.481	8	24	1	1	1
Keaschall	.000	2	0	0	0	0
Kirilloff	.500	2	1	0	0	0
Martin	1.000	3	7	0	0	0
McCusker	.965	22	27	3	2	0
Neuse	.997	79	158	16	1	3
Olivar	.993	39	69	5	1	1
Perez, H	1.000	1	6	0	0	0
Perez, M	1.000	4	3	1	0	1
Sayre	.974	80	129	4	5	0
Shuffield	.933	16	17	2	1	0
Willman	.000	1	0	0	0	0

FCL TWINS — ROOKIE

FLORIDA COMPLEX LEAGUE

Batting	B-T	Ht.	Wt.	DOB	AVG	OBP	SLG	G	PA	AB	R	H	2B	3B	HR	RBI	BB	HBP	SH	SF	SO	SB	CS	BB%	SO%
Acuna, Bryan	R-R	6-0	176	8-11-05	.185	.327	.227	40	147	119	8	22	2	0	1	14	25	1	0	2	39	4	4	17.0	26.5
Baez, Nate	R-R	5-11	191	5-17-01	.300	.417	.500	3	12	10	2	3	2	0	0	1	2	0	0	0	2	0	0	16.7	16.7
Castro, Wilfri	R-R	5-11	165	3-21-01	.077	.250	.154	6	16	13	3	1	1	0	0	0	2	1	0	0	5	0	0	12.5	31.3
Cavaco, Keoni	R-R	6-0	195	6-02-01	.333	.333	.533	4	16	15	3	5	1	1	0	3	0	0	1	0	5	0	0	0.0	31.3
Centeno, Andres	R-R	6-1	183	10-23-03	.231	.389	.327	35	131	104	16	24	2	1	2	10	24	3	0	0	46	4	2	18.3	35.1
Chourio, Byron	B-R	6-2	171	5-20-05	.262	.415	.298	24	106	84	11	22	3	0	0	11	20	2	0	0	19	4	2	18.9	17.9
Daniel, Omari	R-R	6-0	185	5-04-04	.205	.417	.295	17	60	44	11	9	4	0	0	8	14	2	0	0	12	4	2	23.3	20.0
Duran, Gregory	L-R	6-2	201	10-08-02	.000	.286	.000	2	7	5	0	0	0	0	0	0	2	0	0	0	2	0	0	28.6	28.6
Elvis, Cole	R-R	6-1	215	8-04-99	.188	.333	.250	6	21	16	2	3	1	0	0	2	3	1	0	1	3	0	1	14.3	14.3
Grant, Harold	R-R	5-11	160	10-29-04	.250	.317	.403	36	139	124	17	31	5	1	4	23	12	1	0	2	37	2	1	8.6	26.6
Harry, Jay	L-R	6-0	195	7-18-02	.375	.583	.500	3	12	8	1	3	1	0	0	1	3	1	0	0	0	3	0	25.0	0.0
Hewitt, Duncan	R-R	6-2	215	5-17-98	.000	.100	.000	4	10	9	2	0	0	0	0	0	1	0	0	0	4	0	0	10.0	40.0
Jenkins, Walker	L-R	6-3	205	2-19-05	.333	.390	.537	14	59	54	6	18	3	1	2	12	5	0	0	0	8	4	2	8.5	13.6
Keaschall, Luke	R-R	6-1	190	8-15-02	.143	.500	.143	3	12	7	4	1	0	0	0	0	2	3	0	0	2	2	0	16.7	16.7
Madrigal, Reynaldo	R-R	6-1	174	9-23-03	.067	.333	.133	7	21	15	6	1	1	0	0	0	2	4	0	0	12	4	0	9.5	57.1
Martin, Austin	R-R	6-0	185	3-23-99	.429	.600	.857	3	10	7	2	3	0	0	1	1	2	1	0	0	1	2	0	20.0	10.0
Mercedes, Yasser	R-R	6-2	175	11-16-04	.196	.248	.381	25	105	97	14	19	4	1	4	17	6	1	0	1	23	6	1	5.7	21.9
Michel, Fredy	B-R	5-9	154	7-10-04	.152	.339	.239	22	59	46	12	7	1	0	1	5	8	5	0	0	18	3	0	13.6	30.5
Nigro, Frank	R-R	6-3	200	8-01-97	.171	.310	.314	14	42	35	4	6	2	0	1	2	4	3	0	0	12	0	1	9.5	28.6
Nova, Anderson	L-L	6-0	165	2-14-05	.200	.340	.294	30	103	85	8	17	5	0	1	13	16	2	0	0	32	0	1	15.5	31.1
Ortiz, Jankel	B-R	5-9	170	6-14-04	.177	.320	.304	34	98	79	16	14	2	1	2	5	13	4	1	1	31	2	2	13.3	31.6
Pena, Daniel	R-R	5-11	205	3-09-05	.278	.376	.474	34	117	97	14	27	4	0	5	23	15	2	0	3	14	0	0	12.8	12.0
Pena, Isaac	B-R	5-10	160	12-27-03	.281	.388	.381	44	165	139	28	39	5	3	1	17	24	1	0	1	28	11	0	14.5	17.0
Rivero, Giovanny	B-R	5-10	173	10-19-03	.186	.314	.186	19	51	43	6	8	0	0	0	2	6	2	0	0	12	1	0	11.8	23.5
Rodriguez, Alex	R-R	5-10	205	9-10-98	.000	.111	.000	4	9	8	1	0	0	0	0	0	1	0	0	0	3	0	0	11.1	33.3
Rodriguez, Endy	L-R	5-9	148	6-10-03	.293	.453	.634	16	53	41	7	12	6	1	2	10	10	2	0	0	20	1	1	18.9	37.7
Rodriguez, Jose	R-R	6-2	196	6-10-05	.262	.325	.412	49	209	187	28	49	10	0	6	23	18	1	0	3	41	0	2	8.6	19.6
Ruiz, Poncho	R-R	6-2	210	2-23-02	.107	.188	.143	9	32	28	4	3	1	0	0	1	3	0	0	1	6	0	0	9.4	18.8
Salas, Jose	B-R	6-0	191	4-26-03	.111	.200	.111	2	10	9	2	1	0	0	0	0	1	0	0	0	2	0	0	10.0	20.0
Sayre, Alec	R-R	5-11	195	10-05-00	.077	.250	.077	4	16	13	1	1	0	0	0	1	3	0	0	0	7	1	1	18.8	43.8
Schell, Austin	R-R	5-10	238	2-04-99	.000	.250	.000	1	4	3	0	0	0	0	0	0	1	0	0	0	1	0	0	25.0	25.0
Shuffield, Dalton	R-R	5-10	170	3-31-99	.545	.615	.545	3	13	11	2	6	0	0	0	0	2	0	0	0	1	1	1	15.4	7.7
Vasquez, Amilcar	B-R	5-8	170	12-26-01	.083	.154	.083	4	13	12	0	1	0	0	0	0	1	0	0	0	3	0	0	7.7	23.1
Winokur, Brandon	R-R	6-5	210	12-16-04	.288	.338	.545	17	71	66	14	19	5	0	4	17	4	1	0	0	23	0	1	5.6	32.4

Pitching	B-T	Ht.	Wt.	DOB	W	L	ERA	G	GS	SV	IP	Hits	Runs	ER	HR	BB	SO	AVG	OBP	SLG	SO%	BB%	BF
Banks, Pierce	R-R	6-0	205	3-31-98	2	1	6.14	12	0	0	22	28	17	15	1	11	24	.311	.386	.400	23.8	10.9	101
Bengard, Spencer	R-R	6-4	220	4-19-02	0	0	0.00	2	1	0	2	1	0	0	0	1	3	.143	.250	.143	37.5	12.5	8
Bischoff, Kyle	R-R	6-2	210	7-29-99	3	0	3.18	9	0	1	23	15	10	8	3	9	33	.181	.284	.337	34.7	9.5	95
Bonilla, Julio	R-R	6-3	180	11-15-00	1	0	8.78	8	0	0	13	16	14	13	1	15	11	.286	.444	.393	15.3	20.8	72
Gabbert, Matt	L-R	6-4	200	6-28-02	3	1	4.05	9	3	0	27	32	14	12	1	11	36	.305	.368	.429	30.8	9.4	117
Garcia, Hector	R-R	5-10	190	10-12-01	0	1	13.50	2	0	0	1	4	3	2	1	1	2	.500	.556	.875	22.2	11.1	9
Griffith, Owen	R-R	6-1	195	2-06-98	0	0	1.50	4	0	0	6	5	1	1	0	0	4	.227	.261	.227	17.4	0.0	23
Gutierrez, Carlos	R-R	6-3	180	1-16-00	1	6	6.03	11	3	0	31	39	34	21	6	14	43	.295	.373	.545	28.7	9.3	150
Hamilton, Xander	L-R	6-3	216	7-07-01	0	0	4.50	2	0	0	2	4	1	1	0	0	4	.444	.400	.444	40.0	0.0	10
King, Jacob	R-R	6-4	215	10-02-01	0	0	5.40	2	0	0	2	2	1	1	0	2	1	.333	.500	.333	12.5	25.0	8
Kirby, Devin	R-R	5-10	220	8-10-99	1	0	3.09	3	0	0	12	10	4	4	2	6	17	.238	.333	.381	35.4	12.5	48
Klein, John	R-R	6-5	225	4-22-02	0	3	5.87	6	6	0	23	29	17	15	3	9	27	.305	.396	.505	24.3	8.1	111
Landaeta, Yon	R-R	6-1	170	3-16-00	3	0	4.26	17	0	4	25	21	18	12	2	30	37	.221	.409	.347	29.1	23.6	127
Langenberg, Ty	R-R	6-2	190	12-08-01	0	0	0.00	2	0	0	2	1	1	0	0	1	3	.143	.250	.143	37.5	12.5	8
Lares, Cesar	L-L	6-0	155	7-03-03	0	4	8.13	9	9	0	31	38	30	28	5	8	43	.295	.356	.527	29.5	5.5	146
Lee, Jeremy	R-R	5-11	203	9-07-01	0	0	0.00	1	0	1	1	0	0	0	0	1	1	.000	.250	.000	25.0	25.0	4
Liendo, Bianger	R-R	6-1	175	3-07-04	0	1	3.38	6	1	0	13	6	5	5	0	10	8	.136	.321	.182	14.3	17.9	56
Lopez, Jeferson	R-R	6-1	174	11-22-04	0	1	10.54	9	0	1	14	16	19	16	2	14	12	.291	.451	.455	16.7	19.4	72
Maldonado, Cleiber	L-L	6-1	200	11-20-03	1	0	4.21	11	2	0	26	31	13	12	0	15	21	.295	.388	.352	17.4	12.4	121
Medina, Brayan	R-R	6-1	180	10-06-02	2	2	4.82	9	8	0	37	30	25	20	1	19	24	.216	.327	.317	14.5	11.4	166
Mercedes, Juan	R-R	5-10	181	1-07-02	1	0	1.17	5	0	0	15	8	2	2	0	4	25	.151	.211	.208	43.9	7.0	57
Mitchell, Josh	R-L	6-2	220	9-08-94	0	0	6.00	3	1	0	3	3	2	2	0	1	5	.250	.308	.333	38.5	7.7	13

Pitching	B-T	Ht.	Wt.	DOB	W	L	ERA	G	GS	SV	IP	Hits	Runs	ER	HR	BB	SO	AVG	OBP	SLG	SO%	BB%	BF
Mooney, Sean	R-R	6-1	200	1-11-98	0	0	0.00	2	1	0	2	1	0	0	0	0	4	.143	.143	.429	57.1	0.0	7
Neff, Zach	L-L	6-1	195	3-14-96	0	0	0.00	2	1	0	2	1	0	0	0	0	2	.167	.167	.167	33.3	0.0	6
Noble, Jack	R-R	6-2	200	4-02-00	2	0	1.72	3	3	0	16	12	3	3	0	7	20	.218	.306	.236	32.3	11.3	62
Olivares, Miguel	R-R	6-1	180	9-19-03	1	1	2.19	12	0	2	12	7	4	3	0	11	18	.163	.368	.186	31.6	19.3	57
Phillips, Alex	R-R	6-4	220	12-16-94	0	0	0.00	1	0	0	1	0	0	0	0	0	1	.000	.000	.000	33.3	0.0	3
Prielipp, Connor	L-L	6-2	210	1-10-01	0	0	6.75	1	1	0	3	3	2	2	0	2	4	.300	.417	.400	30.8	15.4	13
Rocha, Liam	R-R	6-3	200	5-08-02	0	0	0.00	2	0	0	2	1	0	0	0	0	1	.143	.143	.143	14.3	0.0	7
Rodriguez, Alex	R-R	5-10	205	9-10-98	0	0	3.00	1	0	0	3	1	1	1	0	5	4	.111	.429	.111	28.6	35.7	14
Santos, Nolan	R-R	6-1	205	12-07-00	0	0	0.00	2	1	0	2	1	0	0	0	1	3	.143	.250	.143	37.5	12.5	8
Sharpe, Zarion	R-L	6-5	207	9-30-98	0	1	4.50	4	2	0	6	6	3	3	1	1	5	.250	.280	.458	20.0	4.0	25
Soriano, Eduardo	R-R	6-1	190	10-04-02	1	2	3.98	6	5	0	20	16	17	9	2	13	17	.213	.348	.307	18.5	14.1	92
Velez, Ricardo	R-R	6-1	180	8-21-98	1	1	0.00	5	0	1	5	4	4	0	0	0	8	.211	.211	.368	42.1	0.0	19
Wosinski, Jacob	R-R	6-8	220	3-09-99	2	4	6.21	12	6	0	33	40	31	23	6	16	42	.288	.379	.468	26.1	9.9	161

Fielding

C: Pena 21, Rivero 16, Nigro 10, Ruiz 8, Castro 4, Vasquez 3, Elvis 2, Baez 2, Hewitt 1, Schell 1, Rodriguez 1. **1B:** Pena 20, Rodriguez 11, Daniel 8, Grant 6, Nigro 4, Ortiz 3, Duran 2, Castro 2, Rivero 1, Elvis 1. **2B:** Acuna 11, Ortiz 11, Grant 10, Michel 9, Pena 6, Rodriguez 5, Keaschall 3, Martin 3, Rivero 2, Shuffield 2, Salas 1. **3B:** Pena 19, Grant 12, Acuna 7, Ortiz 7, Daniel 5, Rodriguez 5, Cavaco 1, Harry 1, Michel 1. **SS:** Acuna 22, Pena 12, Ortiz 9, Winokur 9, Daniel 3, Harry 2, Rodriguez 2, Salas 1, Michel 1. **OF:** Rodriguez 35, Centeno 34, Chourio 24, Mercedes 24, Nova 18, Michel 10, Winokur 7, Madrigal 6, Grant 5, Jenkins 3, Sayre 1.

DSL TWINS — *ROOKIE*

DOMINICAN SUMMER LEAGUE

Batting	B-T	Ht.	Wt.	DOB	AVG	OBP	SLG	G	PA	AB	R	H	2B	3B	HR	RBI	BB	HBP	SH	SF	SO	SB	CS	BB%	SO%
Bass, Jayson	L-R	5-11	165	4-29-06	.308	.406	.378	46	170	143	26	44	5	1	1	16	22	3	0	2	24	12	7	12.9	14.1
Castro, Ariel	L-L	6-2	178	2-17-06	.206	.323	.375	44	189	160	31	33	7	4	4	24	24	4	0	1	63	4	5	12.7	33.3
Chivilli, Hendry	R-R	6-3	165	9-14-05	.173	.278	.284	25	97	81	14	14	1	1	2	8	12	1	0	3	37	4	2	12.4	38.1
Del Valle, Junior	R-R	5-11	173	3-23-04	.306	.378	.389	31	83	72	9	22	3	0	1	13	6	3	1	1	15	7	4	7.2	18.1
Gervis, Denyerbe	B-R	5-8	139	9-05-03	.179	.341	.269	34	85	67	15	12	2	2	0	5	16	1	0	1	16	5	1	18.8	18.8
Hernandez, Juan	R-R	6-1	180	2-11-06	.169	.270	.234	29	89	77	9	13	3	1	0	6	9	2	0	1	20	1	3	10.1	22.5
Herrera, Yilber	B-R	5-11	145	1-15-05	.228	.383	.386	42	149	114	25	26	11	2	1	19	30	1	0	4	31	10	6	20.1	20.8
Lopez, Moises	L-R	6-1	170	5-07-06	.269	.379	.462	46	174	145	27	39	7	3	5	32	22	5	0	2	52	10	1	12.6	29.9
Matos, Ewing	R-R	6-2	180	5-22-06	.242	.308	.359	39	143	128	21	31	8	2	1	15	8	5	0	2	47	5	2	5.6	32.9
Pena, Dameury	R-R	5-10	150	9-01-05	.382	.453	.496	39	139	123	25	47	8	3	0	16	14	2	0	0	9	13	4	10.1	6.5
Pena, Ricardo	R-R	6-0	180	5-30-05	.276	.364	.382	26	88	76	20	21	5	0	1	10	7	4	0	1	14	3	1	8.0	15.9
Peraza, Jesus	R-R	6-0	170	11-08-04	.231	.390	.292	33	82	65	5	15	4	0	0	11	12	5	0	0	17	1	0	14.6	20.7
Roman, Javier	R-R	6-0	155	3-26-03	.283	.374	.414	42	115	99	12	28	7	0	2	19	14	1	0	1	20	0	1	12.2	17.4
Silva, Carlos	R-R	5-10	168	3-01-06	.196	.328	.277	41	134	112	17	22	6	0	1	11	18	4	0	0	28	3	0	13.4	20.9
Trinidad, Angel	R-R	5-11	150	9-06-05	.209	.274	.326	38	95	86	11	18	5	1	1	9	5	3	0	1	21	5	4	5.3	22.1
Zapata, Juan	B-R	5-9	140	12-05-04	.216	.344	.294	31	61	51	9	11	2	1	0	5	10	0	0	0	13	2	3	16.4	21.3

Pitching	B-T	Ht.	Wt.	DOB	W	L	ERA	G	GS	SV	IP	Hits	Runs	ER	HR	BB	SO	AVG	OBP	SLG	SO%	BB%	BF
Abrego, Gerardo	R-R	6-3	190	4-16-01	0	0	6.75	7	1	0	8	12	10	6	1	5	8	.343	.425	.514	20.0	12.5	40
Betancourt, Jose	R-R	6-3	182	12-16-04	0	2	16.20	14	0	0	13	18	26	24	0	25	11	.340	.582	.396	12.0	27.2	92
Bohorquez, Adrian	R-R	6-1	190	3-03-05	0	4	5.25	8	6	0	24	21	20	14	0	18	30	.233	.378	.367	27.0	16.2	111
Cordero, Miguel	R-R	6-1	170	8-15-06	1	2	2.81	9	9	0	42	38	21	13	2	18	46	.242	.326	.318	25.8	10.1	178
Cota, Juan	R-R	6-1	170	6-02-05	2	2	2.73	10	5	0	30	20	15	9	0	7	30	.185	.248	.241	25.6	6.0	117
Crisostomo, Alejandro	R-R	6-5	184	9-11-00	0	0	2.25	7	0	2	8	6	4	2	0	3	10	.214	.313	.286	31.3	9.4	32
De Jesus, Yency	R-R	5-11	170	6-20-02	2	3	4.24	10	4	0	40	30	33	19	5	22	44	.195	.304	.357	23.8	11.9	185
Del Valle, Junior	R-R	5-11	173	3-23-04	0	0	0.00	3	0	0	2	1	0	0	0	0	1	.167	.167	.167	16.7	0.0	6
Dishmey, Christopher	R-R	6-2	200	11-12-00	1	1	7.82	7	0	1	13	14	15	11	1	8	14	.275	.367	.392	23.3	13.3	60
Garcia, Joel	R-R	5-10	165	7-03-04	2	2	4.88	11	2	1	31	32	21	17	2	15	39	.258	.343	.379	27.1	10.4	144
Garcia, Reynel	R-R	6-2	130	4-16-06	0	1	4.58	9	1	0	18	17	11	9	5	10	14	.230	.329	.473	16.5	11.8	85
Hernandez, Cristian	R-R	6-1	185	1-08-05	0	7	11.53	11	7	0	30	43	52	38	2	35	32	.323	.474	.466	18.4	20.1	174
Lugo, Leonardo	R-R	5-11	170	9-11-04	0	5	7.33	10	2	0	27	34	28	22	2	20	22	.304	.451	.402	15.4	14.0	143
Machuca, Eider	R-R	6-2	190	8-11-04	1	0	5.71	12	0	0	17	17	15	11	1	17	26	.246	.404	.377	29.2	19.1	89
Monsalve, Fabian	R-R	6-0	155	3-04-05	0	0	19.64	2	0	0	4	7	10	8	1	7	3	.412	.560	.647	12.0	28.0	25
Ojo, Jose	R-R	6-0	170	5-17-01	2	1	3.43	15	0	1	21	17	10	8	1	15	25	.227	.372	.307	26.6	16.0	94
Paredes, Oscar	R-R	6-0	176	10-02-03	1	0	6.00	12	0	1	15	14	14	10	3	7	12	.237	.328	.458	17.6	10.3	68
Rincon, Luis	R-R	5-11	183	1-13-03	0	0	6.48	8	1	0	8	6	8	6	0	12	11	.194	.444	.226	24.4	26.7	45
Roman, Javier	R-R	6-0	155	3-26-03	0	0	0.00	1	0	0	1	0	0	0	0	0	0	.000	.000	.000	0.0	0.0	3
Rubio, Orlando	R-R	6-0	170	1-03-04	0	0	Inf.	1	1	0	0	1	2	1	0	3	0	1.000	1.000	1.000	0.0	75.0	4
Soriano, Eduardo	R-R	6-1	190	10-04-02	1	2	3.38	6	2	0	21	25	13	8	2	6	29	.275	.327	.396	29.6	6.1	98
Surumuy, Jeicol	R-R	6-3	180	1-09-06	0	1	12.38	6	2	0	8	15	13	11	2	7	9	.385	.460	.564	18.0	14.0	50
Taveras, Ledwin	R-R	6-2	175	3-01-05	0	2	9.82	3	3	0	11	18	14	12	0	4	23	.367	.448	.429	39.7	6.9	58
Vasquez, Jose	R-R	6-4	200	12-12-04	1	2	11.62	11	6	0	26	33	35	34	1	32	26	.317	.507	.385	17.8	21.9	146
Zapata, Juan	B-R	5-9	140	12-05-04	0	0	12.00	1	0	0	3	7	4	4	1	1	0	.467	.471	.667	0.0	5.9	17

Fielding

C: Silva 33, Pena 17, Peraza 13, Roman 11. **1B:** Roman 26, Peraza 19, Del Valle 18, Pena 5. **2B:** Pena 25, Zapata 18, Gervis 16, Herrera 15. **3B:** Lopez 32, Hernandez 19, Gervis 9. **SS:** Herrera 26, Chivilli 23, Zapata 11, Hernandez 4, Gervis 1. **OF:** Bass 46, Castro 45, Matos 40, Trinidad 36, Del Valle 15, Gervis 6.

New York Mets

SEASON SYNOPSIS: The Mets opened the season with the largest payroll in MLB history, more than $350 million. But closer Edwin Diaz blew out a knee in the World Baseball Classic in March, kicking off a season of bad injuries, underperformance and bad vibes, leading owner Steve Cohen to make significant changes throughout the season.

HIGH POINT: New York entered June on a high, sweeping a series against the Phillies May 30-June 1 at Citi Field behind great starts from Japanese rookie Kodai Senga, Carlos Carrasco and Max Scherzer. The Phillies scored three runs all weekend as the Mets improved to 30-27, just four games behind the Braves.

LOW POINT: New York lost nine out of 10 following the Phillies sweep, went 7-19 in June and shifted into seller mode. Scherzer (Rangers) and Justin Verlander (Astros), as well as closer David Robertson (Marlins), and outfielders Mark Canha (Brewers) and Tommy Pham (Diamondbacks) all were sold off in a Mets reboot.

NOTABLE ROOKIES: The Mets had only one notable rookie, but Senga, signed from Japan to a five-year, $75 million deal, lived up to his billing in a 12-7, 2.98 season that included 202 strikeouts in 166 innings. Top prospect Francisco Alvarez had ups and downs but slugged 25 homers and caught 108 games as a 21-year-old, marking himself as a future star. Third baseman Brett Baty, the 2019 first-round pick, had a rougher go of it (.212/.275/.323), as did DH/corner infielder Mark Vientos (.211/.253/.367).

KEY TRANSACTIONS: The Mets were the story of the offseason, losing Jacob deGrom to the Rangers but replacing him by signing Verlander and lefty Jose Quintana. But GM Billy Eppler had to oversee and execute a sell-off in which the Mets paid off parts of their stars' salaries to get better prospects in return, such as Luisangel Acuña from the Rangers and outfielders Drew Gilbert and Ryan Clifford from Houston. Cohen hired former Brewers and Astros executive David Stearns to be president of baseball operations in October,

DOWN ON THE FARM: Shortstop/center fielder Jett Williams was excellent in his first full pro season, showing an advanced batting eye and the speed to cause havoc on the bases. He was the Mets' breakout prospect. While Binghamton had a solid club, St. Lucie was easily the worst team in the Florida State League, finishing 40 games under .500.

OPENING DAY PAYROLL: $353,546,854 (1st)

PLAYERS OF THE YEAR

MAJOR LEAGUE

Francisco Lindor
SS
.254/.336/.470
33 2B, 31 HR
31 SB, 108 R

MINOR LEAGUE

Jett Williams
SS
(LoA/HiA/AA)
.263/.425/.451
45-for-52 on SB, 81 R

ORGANIZATION LEADERS

Batting — *Minimum 250 AB

MAJORS		
* AVG	Brandon Nimmo	.274
* OPS	Brandon Nimmo	.829
HR	Pete Alonso	46
RBI	Francisco Lindor	98
MINORS		
* AVG	Rhylan Thomas, St. Lucie/Brook./Bingh.	.328
* OBP	Jett Williams, St Lucie/Brooklyn/Bingham.	.425
* SLG	Mark Vientos, Syracuse	.612
* OPS	Mark Vientos, Syracuse	.999
R	Jett Williams, St Lucie/Brooklyn/Bingham.	81
H	Ronny Mauricio, Syracuse	143
TB	Ronny Mauricio, Syracuse	248
2B	Ronny Mauricio, Syracuse	30
2B	Brandon McIlwain, Binghamton/Syracuse	30
3B	Jett Williams, St Lucie/Brooklyn/Bingham.	8
HR	Luke Ritter, Binghamton/Syracuse	27
RBI	Ronny Mauricio, Syracuse	71
BB	Jett Williams, St Lucie/Brooklyn/Bingham.	104
SO	Jaylen Palmer, Brooklyn/Bingham./Syrac.	183
SB	Jett Williams, St Lucie/Brooklyn/Bingham.	45

Pitching — #Minimum 75 IP

MAJORS		
W	Kodai Senga	12
# ERA	Kodai Senga	2.98
SO	Kodai Senga	202
SV	David Robertson	14
MINORS		
W	Blade Tidwell, Brooklyn/Bingham.	11
L	4-tied	9
# ERA	Tyler Stuart, Brooklyn/Bingh.	2.20
G	Nate Lavendar, Binghamton/Syracuse	42.00
GS	Mike Vasil, Binghamton/Syracuse	26
SV	3-tied	7
IP	Mike Vasil, Binghamton/Syracuse	124
IP	Dominic Hamel, Binghamton	124
BB	Jordany Ventura, Brooklyn/Bingham.	83
SO	Dominic Hamel, Binghamton	160
# AVG	Christian Scott, St. Lucie/Brook./Bingh.	.199

2023 PERFORMANCE

General Manager: Billy Eppler. **Farm Director:** Kevin Howard. **Scouting Director:** Drew Toussaint.

Class	Team	League	W	L	PCT	Finish	Manager
Majors	New York Mets	National	75	87	.463	12 (15)	Buck Showalter
Triple-A	Syracuse Mets	International	61	85	.418	19 (20)	Dick Scott
Double-A	Binghamton Rumble Ponies	Eastern	74	61	.548	2 (12)	Reid Brignac
High-A	Brooklyn Cyclones	South Atlantic	66	65	.504	7 (12)	Chris Newell
Low-A	St. Lucie Mets	Florida State	44	84	.344	10 (10)	Gilbert Gomez
Rookie	FCL Mets	Florida Complex	32	18	.640	1 (15)	Jay Pecci
Rookie	DSL Mets Blue	Dominican Sum.	26	28	.481	29 (50)	Danny Ortega
Overall 2023 Minor League Record			327	371	.468	26th (30)	

ORGANIZATION STATISTICS

NEW YORK METS

NATIONAL LEAGUE

Batting	B-T	Ht.	Wt.	DOB	AVG	OBP	SLG	G	PA	AB	R	H	2B	3B	HR	RBI	BB	HBP	SH	SF	SO	SB	CS	BB%	SO%
Almonte, Abraham	B-R	5-10	223	6-27-89	.067	.125	.133	8	16	15	1	1	1	0	0	0	1	0	0	0	8	0	0	6.3	50.0
Alonso, Pete	R-R	6-3	245	12-07-94	.217	.318	.504	154	658	568	92	123	21	2	46	118	65	21	0	4	151	4	1	9.9	22.9
Alvarez, Francisco	R-R	5-10	233	11-19-01	.209	.284	.437	123	423	382	51	80	12	0	25	63	34	6	0	1	110	2	0	8.0	26.0
Arauz, Jonathan	B-R	6-0	195	8-03-98	.136	.203	.288	27	66	59	3	8	0	0	3	9	5	0	2	0	18	0	0	7.6	27.3
Baty, Brett	L-R	6-3	210	11-13-99	.212	.275	.323	108	389	353	41	75	12	0	9	34	29	2	1	1	109	2	0	7.5	28.0
Canha, Mark	R-R	6-2	209	2-15-89	.245	.343	.381	89	303	257	28	63	15	1	6	29	32	9	0	5	52	7	0	10.6	17.2
2-team (50 Milwaukee)					.262	.359	.400	139	507	435	51	114	25	1	11	62	49	17	0	6	79	11	1	9.7	15.6
Escobar, Eduardo	B-R	5-10	193	1-05-89	.236	.286	.409	40	120	110	15	26	3	2	4	16	8	0	1	1	24	2	0	6.7	20.0
Guillorme, Luis	L-R	5-10	190	9-27-94	.224	.288	.327	54	120	107	12	24	6	1	1	9	10	0	2	1	28	0	0	8.3	23.3
Lindor, Francisco	B-R	5-11	190	11-14-93	.254	.336	.470	160	687	602	108	153	33	2	31	98	66	12	0	7	137	31	4	9.6	19.9
Locastro, Tim	R-R	6-1	200	7-14-92	.232	.338	.393	43	67	56	13	13	3	0	2	3	3	6	2	0	22	6	0	4.5	32.8
Marte, Starling	R-R	6-1	195	10-09-88	.248	.301	.324	86	341	315	38	78	7	1	5	28	16	8	2	0	69	24	4	4.7	20.2
Mauricio, Ronny	B-R	6-3	166	4-04-01	.248	.296	.347	26	108	101	11	25	4	0	2	9	7	0	0	0	31	7	0	6.5	28.7
McNeil, Jeff	L-R	6-1	195	4-08-92	.270	.333	.378	156	648	585	75	158	25	4	10	55	39	18	3	3	65	10	0	6.0	10.0
Mendick, Danny	R-R	5-10	195	9-28-93	.185	.232	.277	35	69	65	4	12	3	0	1	4	4	0	0	0	15	1	0	5.8	21.7
Narvaez, Omar	L-R	5-11	220	2-10-92	.211	.283	.297	49	146	128	12	27	5	0	2	7	14	0	1	3	27	0	0	9.6	18.5
Nido, Tomas	R-R	6-0	211	4-12-94	.125	.153	.125	22	61	56	5	7	0	0	0	1	2	0	2	1	18	0	0	3.3	29.5
Nimmo, Brandon	L-R	6-3	206	3-27-93	.274	.363	.466	152	682	592	89	162	30	6	24	68	74	11	1	4	146	3	3	10.9	21.4
Ortega, Rafael	L-R	5-11	180	5-15-91	.219	.341	.272	47	136	114	16	25	3	0	1	8	20	1	1	0	33	6	1	14.7	24.3
Perez, Michael	L-R	5-10	195	8-07-92	.500	.500	.625	3	8	8	1	4	1	0	0	0	0	0	0	0	1	0	0	0.0	12.5
Pham, Tommy	R-R	6-1	223	3-08-88	.268	.348	.472	79	264	231	29	62	15	1	10	36	29	1	0	3	56	11	1	11.0	21.2
2-team (50 Arizona)					.256	.333	.446	129	481	426	55	109	27	3	16	68	47	2	0	6	106	22	3	9.8	22.0
Sanchez, Gary	R-R	6-2	230	12-02-92	.167	.143	.167	3	7	6	0	1	0	0	0	1	0	0	0	1	3	0	0	0.0	42.9
2-team (72 San Diego)					.217	.291	.492	75	267	240	33	52	9	0	19	47	21	4	0	2	67	0	0	7.9	25.1
Stewart, DJ	L-R	6-0	210	11-30-93	.244	.333	.506	58	185	160	21	39	9	0	11	26	15	7	1	1	56	1	1	8.1	30.3
Vientos, Mark	R-R	6-4	185	12-11-99	.211	.253	.367	65	233	218	19	46	5	1	9	22	10	3	0	2	71	1	0	4.3	30.5
Vogelbach, Daniel	L-R	6-0	270	12-17-92	.233	.339	.404	104	319	275	33	64	8	0	13	48	42	2	0	0	81	0	0	13.2	25.4

Pitching	B-T	Ht.	Wt.	DOB	W	L	ERA	G	GS	SV	IP	Hits	Runs	ER	HR	BB	SO	AVG	OBP	SLG	SO%	BB%	BF
Bickford, Phil	R-R	6-4	200	7-10-95	3	2	4.62	25	0	1	25	21	14	13	3	13	28	.221	.339	.368	24.6	11.4	114
Brigham, Jeff	R-R	6-0	195	2-16-92	1	3	5.26	37	0	0	38	26	23	22	9	18	42	.191	.306	.419	26.3	11.3	160
Butto, Jose	R-R	6-1	202	3-19-98	1	4	3.64	9	7	0	42	33	17	17	3	23	38	.212	.313	.301	21.2	12.8	179
Carrasco, Carlos	R-R	6-4	224	3-21-87	3	8	6.80	20	20	0	90	115	71	68	18	38	66	.310	.381	.531	15.8	9.1	417
Coonrod, Sam	R-R	6-1	225	9-22-92	0	0	9.45	10	0	0	7	5	7	7	0	8	6	.208	.441	.208	17.6	23.5	34
Curtiss, John	R-R	6-5	220	4-05-93	0	0	4.58	15	0	0	20	17	10	10	3	8	16	.236	.309	.389	19.8	9.9	81
Garrett, Reed	R-R	6-2	195	1-02-93	1	0	5.82	9	0	0	17	15	11	11	3	6	16	.238	.310	.429	22.5	8.5	71
Gott, Trevor	R-R	5-11	185	8-26-92	0	2	4.34	34	0	1	29	30	15	14	2	11	30	.256	.328	.359	22.7	8.3	132
Guillorme, Luis	L-R	5-10	190	9-27-94	0	0	0.00	1	0	0	1	1	0	0	0	0	0	.250	.250	.250	0.0	0.0	4
Hartwig, Grant	R-R	6-5	235	12-18-97	5	2	4.84	28	0	0	35	34	23	19	3	15	30	.250	.348	.390	19.0	9.5	158
Hunter, Tommy	R-R	6-3	250	7-03-86	0	1	6.85	14	0	0	24	28	20	18	6	5	20	.286	.330	.541	18.9	4.7	106
Kay, Anthony	L-L	6-0	225	3-21-95	0	0	5.40	3	0	0	3	1	2	2	1	1	3	.111	.250	.444	25.0	8.3	12
Kolarek, Adam	L-L	6-3	215	1-14-89	0	0	0.00	4	0	0	5	1	0	0	0	1	5	.071	.188	.071	29.4	5.9	17
Leone, Dominic	R-R	5-10	215	10-26-91	1	3	4.40	31	0	0	31	27	15	15	7	11	33	.243	.307	.468	26.0	8.7	127
Lucchesi, Joey	L-L	6-5	225	6-06-93	4	0	2.89	9	9	0	47	44	17	15	4	17	32	.251	.325	.394	16.4	8.7	195
McFarland, T.J.	L-L	6-3	200	6-08-89	0	1	5.40	3	0	0	2	4	2	1	0	1	2	.444	.545	.556	18.2	9.1	11
Megill, Tylor	R-R	6-7	230	7-28-95	9	8	4.70	25	25	0	126	141	76	66	18	58	105	.282	.362	.440	18.5	10.2	567
Mendick, Danny	R-R	5-10	195	9-28-93	0	0	36.00	2	0	0	2	9	8	8	2	0	0	.600	.600	1.200	0.0	0.0	15
Miller, Tyson	R-R	6-5	220	7-29-95	1	0	0.00	1	0	0	2	0	0	0	0	2	0	.000	.250	.000	0.0	25.0	8
Muckenhirn, Zach	L-L	6-0	205	2-27-95	0	0	6.00	3	0	0	6	11	4	4	0	2	3	.407	.452	.556	9.7	6.5	31
Nittoli, Vinny	R-R	6-1	210	11-11-90	0	0	2.45	3	0	0	4	4	1	1	0	0	3	.286	.333	.357	20.0	0.0	15
Nogosek, Stephen	R-R	6-2	205	1-11-95	0	1	5.61	13	0	0	26	28	16	16	6	14	25	.280	.373	.530	21.2	11.9	118
Ottavino, Adam	B-R	6-5	246	11-22-85	1	7	3.21	66	0	12	62	46	24	22	7	29	62	.208	.320	.339	23.8	11.1	261
Peterson, David	L-L	6-6	240	9-03-95	3	8	5.03	27	21	0	111	124	64	62	16	50	128	.287	.367	.456	26.0	10.2	492
Quintana, Jose	R-L	6-1	220	1-24-89	3	6	3.57	13	13	0	76	75	33	30	5	24	60	.260	.314	.363	18.8	7.5	319

Raley, Brooks	L-L	6-3	200	6-29-88	1	2	2.80	66	0	3	55	44	19	17	4	25	61	.217	.319	.330	25.8	10.6	236
Reid-Foley, Sean	R-R	6-3	230	8-30-95	0	1	3.52	8	0	0	8	4	3	3	0	6	16	.148	.294	.185	47.1	17.6	34
Reyes, Denyi	R-R	6-4	255	11-02-96	0	2	7.78	9	3	0	20	25	17	17	3	8	17	.309	.378	.481	18.9	8.9	90
Robertson, David	R-R	5-11	195	4-09-85	4	2	2.05	40	0	14	44	31	13	10	5	13	48	.199	.269	.333	27.9	7.6	172
Santana, Dennis	R-R	6-2	190	4-12-96	1	0	5.91	9	0	0	11	10	7	7	2	7	12	.244	.360	.463	24.0	14.0	50
Scherzer, Max	R-R	6-3	208	7-27-84	9	4	4.01	19	19	0	108	98	49	48	23	30	121	.240	.295	.445	27.3	6.8	444
Senga, Kodai	L-R	6-1	202	1-30-93	12	7	2.98	29	29	0	166	126	60	55	17	77	202	.208	.301	.327	29.1	11.1	694
Smith, Drew	R-R	6-2	190	9-24-93	4	6	4.15	62	0	3	56	50	31	26	7	29	60	.240	.344	.442	24.6	11.9	244
Uceta, Edwin	R-R	6-0	155	1-09-98	0	0	0.00	1	0	0	3	0	0	0	0	2	3	.000	.273	.000	27.3	18.2	11
Verlander, Justin	R-R	6-5	235	2-20-83	6	5	3.15	16	16	0	94	77	36	33	9	31	81	.219	.282	.344	21.0	8.0	386
Walker, Josh	L-L	6-6	225	12-01-94	0	1	8.10	14	0	0	10	12	11	9	2	6	12	.286	.375	.452	25.0	12.5	48
Yacabonis, Jimmy	R-R	6-3	225	3-21-92	2	1	6.59	7	0	0	14	14	10	10	2	6	11	.259	.339	.444	17.7	9.7	62

Fielding

Catcher	PCT	G	PO	A	E	DP	PB
Alvarez	.986	108	870	43	13	3	8
Narvaez	.987	47	355	15	5	3	2
Nido	.987	21	153	3	2	0	1
Perez	1.000	3	11	1	0	0	0
Sanchez	1.000	3	17	0	0	0	1

First Base	PCT	G	PO	A	E	DP
Alonso	.995	144	983	122	6	119
Canha	.989	13	77	12	1	7
McNeil	1.000	1	2	0	0	0
Vientos	.982	10	49	5	1	9

Second Base	PCT	G	PO	A	E	DP
Arauz	.962	7	13	12	1	4
Escobar	1.000	9	11	21	0	8
Guillorme	1.000	29	38	57	0	17
Mauricio	1.000	21	46	52	0	15
McNeil	.992	107	164	196	3	55
Mendick	.979	16	18	29	1	8

Third Base	PCT	G	PO	A	E	DP
Arauz	1.000	15	8	30	0	2
Baty	.956	100	68	149	10	17
Canha	1.000	4	0	1	0	0
Escobar	.958	29	16	52	3	4
Guillorme	.938	14	7	8	1	1
Mauricio	.941	5	4	12	1	0
Mendick	1.000	9	8	10	0	2
Vientos	.932	19	9	32	3	2

Shortstop	PCT	G	PO	A	E	DP
Arauz	1.000	5	3	4	0	1
Escobar	.000	1	0	0	0	0
Guillorme	.867	9	8	5	2	4
Lindor	.981	158	181	396	11	98
Mauricio	1.000	2	0	1	0	0
McNeil	1.000	1	1	0	0	0

Outfield	PCT	G	PO	A	E	DP
Almonte	1.000	2	6	0	0	0
Baty	.000	1	0	0	0	0
Canha	1.000	64	103	3	0	0
Locastro	.933	33	32	1	1	0
Marte	.997	85	155	7	1	1
McNeil	.988	76	115	6	2	2
Mendick	1.000	4	2	0	0	0
Nimmo	.994	146	352	3	4	1
Ortega	1.000	51	76	2	0	0
Pham	.940	58	83	3	3	0
Stewart	.993	48	79	1	1	0

SYRACUSE METS

TRIPLE-A

INTERNATIONAL LEAGUE

Batting	B-T	Ht.	Wt.	DOB	AVG	OBP	SLG	G	PA	AB	R	H	2B	3B	HR	RBI	BB	HBP	SH	SF	SO	SB	CS	BB%	SO%
Almonte, Abraham	B-R	5-10	223	6-27-89	.201	.321	.455	36	159	134	27	27	1	0	11	30	24	0	0	1	41	1	0	15.1	25.8
Alvarez, Francisco	R-R	5-10	233	11-19-01	.250	.368	.688	4	19	16	4	4	1	0	2	4	3	0	0	0	8	1	0	15.8	42.1
Arauz, Jonathan	B-R	6-0	195	8-03-98	.239	.340	.415	100	415	352	59	84	14	3	14	53	55	2	0	6	90	2	0	13.3	21.7
Baty, Brett	L-R	6-3	210	11-13-99	.298	.388	.625	26	121	104	20	31	4	0	10	31	16	0	0	1	29	2	2	13.2	24.0
Berbesi, Cesar	L-R	5-9	160	4-13-00	.400	.500	.600	4	6	5	2	2	1	0	0	1	0	1	0	0	2	0	0	0.0	33.3
Campos, Oscar	R-R	5-10	170	12-08-96	.500	.500	.500	1	5	4	1	2	0	0	0	1	0	0	1	0	0	0	0	0.0	0.0
Cedrola, Lorenzo	R-R	5-8	152	1-12-98	.250	.373	.410	59	229	188	41	47	8	2	6	18	25	12	4	0	27	15	4	10.9	11.8
Cortes, Carlos	L-S	5-7	197	6-30-97	.241	.355	.428	118	442	369	63	89	22	1	15	54	65	3	0	5	89	3	2	14.7	20.1
Davis, Jaylin	R-R	5-11	205	7-01-94	.220	.340	.436	74	309	259	36	57	13	2	13	47	41	7	0	2	91	2	2	13.3	29.4
Estep, Chase	L-R	5-10	200	4-12-00	.357	.400	.500	4	15	14	2	5	2	0	0	3	1	0	0	0	3	0	0	6.7	20.0
Fryman, Branden	R-R	6-1	176	3-16-98	.222	.250	.370	10	30	27	3	6	1	0	1	3	1	0	2	0	9	0	0	3.3	30.0
Gil, Mateo	R-R	6-0	180	7-24-00	.000	.071	.000	4	14	13	0	0	0	0	0	0	1	0	0	0	5	0	0	7.1	35.7
Gomez, Dariel	L-R	6-4	190	7-15-96	.167	.286	.667	3	7	6	1	1	0	0	1	1	1	0	0	0	4	0	0	14.3	57.1
Guillorme, Luis	L-R	5-10	190	9-27-94	.241	.397	.352	16	68	54	9	13	3	0	1	6	13	1	0	0	6	0	0	19.1	8.8
Lee, Khalil	L-L	5-10	170	6-26-98	.185	.299	.323	21	77	65	8	12	6	0	1	7	10	1	0	1	17	2	0	13.0	22.1
Locastro, Tim	R-R	6-1	200	7-14-92	.200	.313	.345	14	66	55	8	11	0	1	2	10	4	5	1	0	13	0	1	6.1	19.7
Mauricio, Ronny	B-R	6-3	166	4-04-01	.292	.346	.506	116	532	490	76	143	30	3	23	71	35	6	0	1	97	24	7	6.6	18.2
McIlwain, Brandon	R-R	6-0	205	5-31-98	.219	.382	.391	43	191	151	26	33	11	0	5	23	34	6	0	0	46	11	1	17.8	24.1
Mena, Jose	R-R	5-10	208	12-22-96	.000	.100	.000	3	10	9	0	0	0	0	0	0	1	0	0	0	3	0	0	10.0	30.0
Mendick, Danny	R-R	5-10	195	9-28-93	.282	.369	.424	91	425	373	62	105	18	1	11	57	46	6	0	0	60	14	2	10.8	14.1
Meyer, Nick	R-R	6-1	200	2-18-97	.217	.309	.309	71	264	230	36	50	3	0	6	26	28	3	2	1	55	6	1	10.6	20.8
Murphy, Tanner	R-R	6-3	199	5-01-98	.292	.320	.417	7	25	24	4	7	3	0	0	2	1	0	0	0	10	0	0	4.0	40.0
Narvaez, Omar	L-R	5-11	220	2-10-92	.200	.333	.267	4	18	15	1	3	1	0	0	2	3	0	0	0	3	0	0	16.7	16.7
Nido, Tomas	R-R	6-0	211	4-12-94	.281	.336	.393	39	146	135	19	38	3	0	4	12	11	0	0	0	27	0	0	7.5	18.5
O'Neill, Matt	R-R	5-10	205	8-20-97	.105	.227	.263	7	22	19	3	2	0	0	1	2	3	0	0	0	9	0	0	13.6	40.9
Ortega, Rafael	L-R	5-11	180	5-15-91	.230	.379	.398	30	140	113	20	26	7	0	4	15	27	0	0	0	23	6	3	19.3	16.4
Palka, Daniel	L-L	6-2	230	10-28-91	.250	.320	.455	23	98	88	11	22	3	0	5	12	8	1	0	0	24	0	0	8.2	24.5
2-team (79 Worcester)					.237	.311	.420102.000412.00037155					88	15	1	17	60	38	2	0	0	96	3	2	9.2	23.3
Palmer, Jaylen	R-R	6-3	208	7-31-00	.250	.380	.594	21	80	64	17	16	4	0	6	17	13	1	1	1	29	3	1	16.3	36.3
Peraza, Jose	R-R	6-0	210	4-30-94	.261	.315	.366	41	147	134	21	35	6	1	2	9	5	6	1	1	28	1	0	3.4	19.0
Perez, Michael	L-R	5-10	195	8-07-92	.204	.309	.352	70	270	230	27	47	7	0	9	27	34	2	1	3	64	0	0	12.6	23.7
Peroza, Jose	R-R	6-1	221	6-15-00	.333	.474	.633	9	38	30	10	10	1	1	2	9	6	2	0	0	8	0	0	15.8	21.1
Ritter, Luke	R-R	5-11	187	2-15-97	.247	.360	.448	64	264	223	32	55	6	0	13	35	37	3	0	1	78	1	0	14.0	29.5
Sanchez, Gary	R-R	6-2	230	12-02-92	.308	.514	.500	8	37	26	3	8	2	0	1	5	9	2	0	0	10	0	0	24.3	27.0
Saunders, Warren	R-R	6-1	205	12-15-98	.000	.000	.000	2	4	4	0	0	0	0	0	0	0	0	0	0	1	0	0	0.0	25.0
Stewart, DJ	L-R	6-0	210	11-30-93	.229	.362	.516	51	229	188	35	43	6	0	16	41	35	5	0	1	46	0	0	15.3	20.1
Suozzi, Joe	R-R	6-2	215	2-28-98	.270	.370	.397	38	146	126	22	34	2	1	4	16	15	5	0	0	33	3	0	10.3	22.6
Vientos, Mark	R-R	6-4	185	12-11-99	.306	.387	.612	61	269	232	38	71	21	1	16	50	29	4	0	4	58	0	0	10.8	21.6
Voit, Luke	R-R	6-2	258	2-13-91	.264	.415	.643	37	164	129	30	34	5	1	14	35	31	3	0	1	44	0	0	18.9	26.8

2-team (8 Nashville)					.263	.422	.615	45	200	156	35	41	8	1	15	43	39	4	0	1	53	0	0	19.5	26.5
White, Tyler	R-R	5-11	238	10-29-90	.256	.360	.279	12	50	43	4	11	1	0	0	3	7	0	0	0	10	0	0	14.0	20.0
2-team (16 St. Paul)2-team (16 St. Paul)						.257	.375	.356	28	120	101	14	26	4	0	2	10	18	1	0	0	23	0	0.0	15.0
Young, Wyatt	L-R	5-6	160	12-05-99	.240	.302	.339	42	192	171	17	41	8	0	3	26	16	1	0	4	34	1	0	8.3	17.7

Pitching	B-T	Ht.	Wt.	DOB	W	L	ERA	G	GS	SV	IP	Hits	Runs	ER	HR	BB	SO	AVG	OBP	SLG	SO%	BB%	BF
Battenfield, Peyton	R-R	6-4	224	8-10-97	1	1	6.00	2	2	0	9	10	6	6	0	6	4	.286	.390	.400	9.8	14.6	41
Brigham, Jeff	R-R	6-0	195	2-16-92	0	1	10.00	10	0	0	9	14	11	10	3	9	6	.400	.532	.743	12.8	19.1	47
Bundy, Dylan	B-R	6-1	225	11-15-92	0	2	10.08	6	6	0	25	42	28	28	12	7	21	.372	.405	.805	17.4	5.8	121
Butto, Jose	R-R	6-1	202	3-19-98	3	7	5.93	19	19	0	91	99	63	60	17	49	82	.278	.370	.483	19.8	11.8	414
Chacin, Jose	R-R	6-4	192	3-25-97	1	1	5.66	10	5	0	35	37	23	22	7	13	28	.272	.344	.529	18.1	8.4	155
Clenney, Nolan	L-R	6-2	200	6-16-96	0	3	6.08	12	0	0	24	21	16	16	3	11	37	.231	.327	.407	35.6	10.6	104
Coonrod, Sam	R-R	6-1	225	9-22-92	0	1	12.91	9	0	1	8	10	12	11	3	10	8	.323	.500	.742	19.0	23.8	42
Courtney, Justin	R-R	6-5	225	7-24-96	0	0	3.00	2	0	0	3	1	1	1	1	1	3	.100	.182	.400	27.3	9.1	11
Curtiss, John	R-R	6-5	220	4-05-93	1	2	7.17	18	0	0	21	26	20	17	6	10	21	.286	.356	.538	20.8	9.9	101
Dibrell, Tony	R-R	6-3	190	11-08-95	1	2	10.86	9	6	1	29	40	36	35	12	24	23	.325	.433	.683	15.3	16.0	150
Elledge, Seth	R-R	6-3	240	5-20-96	0	0	8.49	8	0	0	12	18	11	11	1	8	9	.367	.459	.490	14.8	13.1	61
Garrett, Reed	R-R	6-2	195	1-02-93	0	0	5.68	12	0	0	13	15	11	8	2	9	12	.288	.387	.481	19.4	14.5	62
Griffin, David	R-R	6-0	205	7-16-96	2	5	7.76	13	11	0	53	69	48	46	10	26	41	.311	.392	.559	16.1	10.2	255
Hall, Dylan	R-R	6-5	210	9-07-97	0	0	0.00	2	0	0	3	3	0	0	0	1	1	.231	.286	.308	7.1	7.1	14
Hartwig, Grant	R-R	6-5	235	12-18-97	4	3	5.02	24	0	3	29	35	18	16	3	18	37	.304	.401	.452	27.0	13.1	137
Hernandez, Elieser	R-R	6-1	214	5-03-95	0	0	4.50	2	0	0	2	3	1	1	1	3	2	.333	.500	.667	16.7	25.0	12
Hunter, Tommy	R-R	6-3	250	7-03-86	1	0	0.00	2	0	0	2	1	1	0	0	1	0	.143	.250	.143	0.0	12.5	8
Jarvis, Justin	R-R	6-2	183	2-20-00	0	5	8.04	9	9	0	31	43	33	28	8	22	36	.309	.404	.554	22.4	13.7	161
Jay, Tyler	L-L	6-1	185	4-19-94	0	1	6.00	6	0	0	6	9	5	4	1	0	8	.346	.333	.500	29.6	0.0	27
Kay, Anthony	L-L	6-0	225	3-21-95	2	0	0.00	2	0	0	3	1	0	0	0	1	8	.091	.167	.091	66.7	8.3	12
Kolarek, Adam	L-L	6-3	215	1-14-89	0	0	3.38	6	0	0	5	1	2	2	0	3	8	.059	.238	.059	38.1	14.3	21
Kubichek, Kolby	R-R	6-0	180	11-28-99	0	0	0.00	1	0	0	1	1	0	0	0	0	1	.250	.250	.250	25.0	0.0	4
Lavender, Nathan	L-L	6-2	210	1-20-00	4	3	3.27	35	1	3	44	34	17	16	7	23	67	.209	.325	.393	35.1	12.0	191
Lucchesi, Joey	L-L	6-5	225	6-06-93	6	5	4.74	15	14	0	82	77	46	43	12	39	75	.252	.335	.431	21.4	11.1	350
McFarland, T.J.	L-L	6-3	200	6-08-89	2	2	2.76	23	0	0	33	30	12	10	2	17	37	.242	.331	.379	25.9	11.9	143
Megill, Tylor	R-R	6-7	230	7-28-95	0	3	8.67	6	6	0	27	35	26	26	3	11	14	.321	.390	.514	11.4	8.9	123
Mejia, Humberto	R-R	6-4	244	3-03-97	1	3	6.17	8	8	0	35	39	27	24	11	12	30	.275	.327	.556	19.2	7.7	156
Miller, Tyson	R-R	6-5	220	7-29-95	0	0	13.50	2	0	0	2	3	3	3	1	1	2	.333	.400	.667	20.0	10.0	10
Minnick, Matt	R-L	6-2	210	3-11-96	0	0	0.00	1	0	0	3	1	0	0	0	3	1	.111	.385	.111	7.7	23.1	13
Moreno, Luis	R-R	5-8	170	5-29-99	0	0	2.70	1	1	0	3	3	2	1	0	4	5	.214	.389	.214	27.8	22.2	18
Muckenhirn, Zach	L-L	6-0	205	2-27-95	1	1	0.88	16	1	1	31	21	3	3	1	13	19	.198	.289	.236	15.7	10.7	121
Nittoli, Vinny	R-R	6-1	210	11-11-90	0	1	5.73	19	2	1	22	22	15	14	9	13	25	.265	.361	.602	25.8	13.4	97
Nogosek, Stephen	R-R	6-2	205	1-11-95	0	1	6.75	1	0	0	1	2	1	1	0	1	1	.333	.429	.333	14.3	14.3	7
Nunez, Dedniel	R-R	6-2	180	6-05-96	2	4	6.75	29	0	1	40	50	36	30	8	29	48	.307	.405	.509	24.4	14.7	197
Orze, Eric	R-R	6-4	195	8-21-97	3	4	5.31	39	1	0	61	52	38	36	6	41	81	.229	.349	.388	29.8	15.1	272
Parsons, Hunter	R-R	6-2	215	6-24-97	2	2	5.57	21	0	0	32	32	24	20	5	15	38	.256	.358	.392	25.7	10.1	148
Peterson, David	L-L	6-6	240	9-03-95	1	2	4.86	7	7	0	37	37	23	20	5	23	43	.262	.367	.426	25.9	13.9	166
Quintana, Jose	R-L	6-1	220	1-24-89	0	1	9.00	2	2	0	7	8	7	7	1	6	7	.296	.412	.481	20.6	17.6	34
Reid-Foley, Sean	R-R	6-3	230	8-30-95	0	1	4.96	16	0	1	16	9	9	9	4	10	26	.155	.279	.414	38.2	14.7	68
Reyes, Denyi	R-R	6-4	255	11-02-96	2	3	5.79	20	18	0	92	97	63	59	24	33	72	.266	.330	.544	17.9	8.2	403
Ridings, Stephen	R-R	6-8	220	8-14-95	1	0	4.91	11	0	0	11	6	6	6	0	8	11	.162	.304	.216	23.9	17.4	46
Rossman, Bubby	B-R	6-5	220	6-29-92	1	3	8.18	18	0	0	22	26	23	20	5	17	20	.295	.407	.568	18.5	15.7	108
Santana, Dennis	R-R	6-2	190	4-12-96	5	3	4.91	29	2	5	33	40	21	18	6	20	41	.313	.400	.531	27.0	13.2	152
Thomas, Tyler	R-L	6-1	175	12-22-95	1	0	6.75	9	0	0	12	18	9	9	1	8	11	.360	.459	.500	18.0	13.1	61
Uceta, Edwin	R-R	6-0	155	1-09-98	1	0	1.93	4	0	0	5	2	3	1	1	6	0	.133	.381	.333	0.0	27.3	22
Valverde, Alex	R-R	6-2	185	9-26-96	2	2	7.56	10	9	0	33	45	32	28	7	19	25	.321	.409	.564	15.2	11.6	164
Vasil, Mike	L-R	6-5	225	3-19-00	4	4	5.30	16	16	0	73	70	44	43	10	38	81	.250	.344	.411	24.9	11.7	325
Walker, Josh	L-L	6-6	225	12-01-94	2	2	1.84	21	0	1	29	19	11	6	1	13	40	.181	.283	.238	33.3	10.8	120
Woods, William	R-R	6-3	190	12-29-98	2	1	7.88	27	0	1	38	52	37	33	10	20	41	.323	.398	.578	21.9	10.7	187
Yacabonis, Jimmy	R-R	6-3	225	3-21-92	2	0	3.97	20	0	2	23	15	10	10	2	11	16	.192	.300	.321	17.8	12.2	90

Fielding

Catcher	PCT	G	PO	A	E	DP	PB
Alvarez	.976	4	38	3	1	0	0
Campos	1.000	1	8	1	0	0	0
Mena	.000	1	0	0	0	0	0
Meyer	.993	36	258	20	2	3	1
Narvaez	1.000	4	30	3	0	0	0
Nido	.991	38	336	12	3	3	2
O'Neill	1.000	4	53	1	0	0	0
Perez	.993	66	543	33	4	3	1
Sanchez	.950	5	37	1	2	0	1

First Base	PCT	G	PO	A	E	DP
Cortes	.833	1	3	2	1	1
Gil	1.000	3	21	3	0	1
Gomez	.000	1	0	0	0	0
Mendick	.000	2	0	0	0	0
Meyer	.964	8	51	3	2	6
O'Neill	1.000	1	6	0	0	0
Palka	.990	16	91	6	1	11
Peraza	.987	23	130	18	2	15
Ritter	1.000	17	86	8	0	8
Saunders	1.000	2	11	1	0	2
Stewart	1.000	16	119	2	0	10
Suozzi	1.000	10	50	7	0	4
Vientos	.982	26	148	18	3	17
Voit	.989	26	166	11	2	19
White	1.000	10	71	14	0	10

Second Base	PCT	G	PO	A	E	DP
Arauz	1.000	19	27	30	0	6
Berbesi	1.000	3	2	5	0	1
Guillorme	1.000	3	7	4	0	1
Mauricio	.952	56	109	128	12	36
Mendick	1.000	20	31	57	0	8
Meyer	1.000	6	6	13	0	1
Peraza	1.000	1	4	2	0	1
Peroza	.941	4	8	8	1	1
Ritter	.976	32	50	72	3	16
Young	1.000	8	9	21	0	5

Third Base	PCT	G	PO	A	E	DP
Arauz	1.000	11	6	25	0	5
Baty	.930	23	28	25	4	3
Estep	.875	4	2	5	1	0
Fryman	.857	5	3	3	1	1
Guillorme	1.000	2	1	4	0	0
Mauricio	.857	2	1	5	1	0
Mendick	.905	23	9	29	4	6
Meyer	.947	18	17	19	2	3
Palmer	1.000	10	4	9	0	2
Peraza	1.000	9	3	11	0	0
Peroza	.727	5	1	7	3	1
Ritter	1.000	12	7	18	0	5
Vientos	.950	33	40	55	5	5

Shortstop	PCT	G	PO	A	E	DP
Arauz	.955	60	88	125	10	32
Fryman	1.000	3	4	5	0	0
Guillorme	1.000	11	14	17	0	7
Mauricio	.932	27	39	57	7	14
Mendick	.971	10	11	23	1	3
Peraza	1.000	3	3	4	0	0
Ritter	1.000	1	1	1	0	1
Young	.981	35	33	68	2	9

Outfield	PCT	G	PO	A	E	DP
Almonte	.930	21	36	4	3	0
Berbesi	.000	1	0	0	0	0
Cedrola	.990	59	122	2	3	1
Cortes	.991	86	167	9	5	1
Davis	.983	58	98	2	2	0
Lee	.976	19	35	0	1	0
Locastro	.667	14	35	0	0	0
Mauricio	.935	26	41	2	3	0
McIlwain	.980	43	109	4	3	4
Mendick	1.000	32	54	2	0	1
Meyer	1.000	2	2	0	0	0
Murphy	1.000	6	9	0	0	0
Ortega	.987	30	74	2	1	2
Palka	.000	1	0	0	0	0
Palmer	1.000	12	17	0	0	0
Peraza	.667	2	2	0	1	0
Stewart	.917	24	39	0	1	0
Suozzi	.957	26	40	4	2	1

BINGHAMTON RUMBLE PONIES

DOUBLE-A

EASTERN LEAGUE

Batting	B-T	Ht.	Wt.	DOB	AVG	OBP	SLG	G	PA	AB	R	H	2B	3B	HR	RBI	BB	HBP	SH	SF	SO	SB	CS	BB%	SO%
Acuna, Luisangel	R-R	5-8	181	3-12-02	.243	.317	.304	37	167	148	25	36	3	0	2	12	15	2	0	2	30	15	5	9.0	18.0
Berbesi, Cesar	L-R	5-9	160	4-13-00	.130	.286	.130	8	28	23	4	3	0	0	0	0	5	0	0	0	12	0	1	17.9	42.9
Fryman, Branden	R-R	6-1	176	3-16-98	.225	.258	.351	43	161	151	17	34	7	3	2	11	6	1	2	1	40	4	2	3.7	24.8
Gil, Mateo	R-R	6-0	180	7-24-00	.248	.313	.349	43	167	149	15	37	7	1	2	15	15	0	1	2	44	2	1	9.0	26.3
Gilbert, Drew	L-L	5-9	195	9-27-00	.325	.423	.561	35	154	123	22	40	7	2	6	21	19	4	0	3	30	2	2	12.3	19.5
Gomez, Dariel	L-R	6-4	190	7-15-96	.212	.337	.318	25	101	85	7	18	6	0	1	9	16	0	0	0	38	0	0	15.8	37.6
Guillorme, Luis	L-R	5-10	190	9-27-94	.000	.350	.000	4	20	13	1	0	0	0	0	0	7	0	0	0	5	0	0	35.0	25.0
Jackson, Jeremiah	R-R	6-0	165	3-26-00	.264	.344	.457	37	151	129	15	34	4	0	7	24	15	3	0	4	50	6	2	9.9	33.1
Jordan, Rowdey	B-R	5-10	190	1-27-99	.230	.344	.389	119	509	427	67	98	23	3	13	63	65	12	0	5	116	30	5	12.8	22.8
McIlwain, Brandon	R-R	6-0	205	5-31-98	.260	.342	.394	85	360	315	40	82	19	1	7	47	27	14	0	4	73	9	6	7.5	20.3
Mena, Jose	R-R	5-10	208	12-22-96	.202	.228	.247	25	92	89	1	18	4	0	0	5	2	1	0	0	29	0	0	2.2	31.5
Murphy, Tanner	R-R	6-3	199	5-01-98	.187	.289	.273	44	160	139	18	26	6	0	2	12	18	2	1	0	66	9	0	11.3	41.3
O'Neill, Matt	R-R	5-10	205	8-20-97	.177	.279	.308	60	226	198	22	35	8	0	6	19	28	0	0	0	80	0	0	12.4	35.4
Palmer, Jaylen	R-R	6-3	208	7-31-00	.143	.260	.222	42	146	126	18	18	1	0	3	7	17	3	0	0	62	8	1	11.6	42.5
Parada, Kevin	R-R	5-11	197	8-03-01	.185	.250	.389	14	60	54	4	10	2	0	3	11	4	1	0	1	23	0	0	6.7	38.3
Peroza, Jose	R-R	6-1	221	6-15-00	.246	.337	.410	97	404	349	42	86	25	1	10	50	42	8	0	5	124	4	1	10.4	30.7
Ritter, Luke	R-R	5-11	187	2-15-97	.240	.389	.568	43	186	146	36	35	4	1	14	29	30	7	1	2	59	4	1	16.1	31.7
Rudick, Matt	L-L	5-6	170	7-02-98	.271	.414	.449	61	266	214	45	58	11	0	9	31	46	6	0	0	42	12	1	17.3	15.8
Ruiz, Agustin	L-R	6-2	215	9-23-99	.203	.300	.401	105	423	364	47	74	14	2	18	60	41	12	0	6	134	0	2	9.7	31.7
Saunders, Warren	R-R	6-1	205	12-15-98	.159	.211	.232	20	76	69	4	11	2	0	1	9	5	0	0	2	20	0	0	6.6	26.3
Schwartz, JT	L-R	6-4	215	12-17-99	.302	.383	.437	66	277	245	30	74	17	2	4	49	27	5	0	0	46	4	0	9.7	16.6
Senger, Hayden	R-R	6-1	210	4-03-97	.188	.307	.295	81	309	261	30	49	11	1	5	26	36	10	0	2	95	3	3	11.7	30.7
Suozzi, Joe	R-R	6-2	215	2-28-98	.248	.353	.386	30	119	101	11	25	3	1	3	7	14	3	0	1	39	1	1	11.8	32.8
Thomas, Rhylan	L-L	5-10	170	4-15-00	.353	.431	.392	16	59	51	8	18	2	0	0	2	7	0	1	0	5	2	2	11.9	8.5
Villavicencio, Kevin	R-R	5-9	172	11-24-03	.000	.286	.000	2	7	5	0	0	0	0	0	0	2	0	0	0	3	0	0	28.6	42.9
Williams, Jett	R-R	5-6	175	11-03-03	.227	.308	.273	6	26	22	5	5	1	0	0	2	2	1	0	1	10	1	0	7.7	38.5
Young, Wyatt	L-R	5-6	160	12-05-99	.209	.319	.259	90	377	321	46	67	8	1	2	20	52	1	1	2	81	15	3	13.8	21.5

Pitching	B-T	Ht.	Wt.	DOB	W	L	ERA	G	GS	SV	IP	Hits	Runs	ER	HR	BB	SO	AVG	OBP	SLG	SO%	BB%	BF
Acosta, Daison	R-R	6-2	160	8-24-98	4	3	4.75	29	0	3	36	28	21	19	6	24	39	.214	.344	.397	24.2	14.9	161
Alvarez, Manuel	R-R	6-3	225	9-17-95	1	0	11.25	8	0	0	12	9	15	15	1	15	9	.209	.452	.372	14.5	24.2	62
Brodey, Harris	L-L	6-1	195	12-01-95	0	1	30.86	3	0	0	2	8	8	8	1	3	2	.571	.611	.929	11.1	16.7	18
Carrasco, Carlos	R-R	6-4	224	3-21-87	0	0	1.29	2	2	0	7	5	1	1	0	2	5	.208	.269	.208	19.2	7.7	26
Chacin, Jose	R-R	6-4	192	3-25-97	3	5	5.05	18	16	0	71	68	43	40	18	18	63	.248	.292	.515	21.1	6.0	298
Clenney, Nolan	L-R	6-2	200	6-16-96	1	2	5.36	25	0	2	40	48	28	24	7	18	44	.287	.354	.473	23.3	9.5	189
Colina, Robert	R-R	5-11	175	4-24-01	1	0	6.00	1	0	0	3	4	2	2	1	1	4	.308	.357	.538	28.6	7.1	14
Courtney, Justin	R-R	6-5	225	7-24-96	1	3	5.48	14	0	1	21	18	13	13	7	9	20	.231	.310	.551	22.7	10.2	88
Garcia, Benito	R-R	6-0	165	3-10-00	1	0	0.00	2	1	0	7	2	0	0	0	2	8	.083	.154	.083	30.8	7.7	26
Geber, Jordan	R-R	6-3	205	7-31-99	2	0	0.00	3	1	0	18	14	0	0	0	0	11	.215	.215	.246	16.9	0.0	65
Gervase, Paul	R-R	6-10	230	5-23-00	2	0	3.60	7	0	1	10	5	4	4	1	4	20	.143	.250	.286	50.0	10.0	40
Griffin, David	R-R	6-0	205	7-16-96	2	1	4.55	9	4	0	28	26	17	14	6	10	22	.245	.305	.472	18.6	8.5	118
Hall, Dylan	R-R	6-5	210	9-07-97	0	1	3.04	19	0	4	27	25	11	9	2	11	22	.263	.327	.432	19.8	9.9	111
Hamel, Dominic	R-R	6-2	206	3-02-99	8	6	3.85	26	25	0	124	108	56	53	12	49	160	.230	.305	.370	30.4	9.3	527
Hardy, Brendan	R-R	6-4	170	12-15-99	1	0	2.16	6	0	0	8	9	2	2	1	1	15	.265	.286	.412	42.9	2.9	35
Juarez, Daniel	L-L	5-11	155	9-28-00	1	3	3.27	21	2	0	41	30	18	15	4	12	37	.200	.271	.307	22.2	7.2	167
Kubichek, Kolby	R-R	6-0	180	11-28-99	1	1	3.97	7	0	0	11	8	5	5	1	10	8	.205	.380	.282	16.0	20.0	50
Lancellotti, Joey	R-R	5-11	205	1-15-98	0	1	4.97	6	1	0	13	13	9	7	3	6	11	.265	.345	.490	19.0	10.3	58
Lavender, Nathan	L-L	6-2	210	1-20-00	0	0	1.74	7	0	4	10	5	4	2	0	3	19	.139	.238	.167	45.2	7.1	42
Marceaux, Landon	R-R	6-0	199	10-08-99	0	1	22.50	1	1	0	2	5	5	5	0	1	0	.500	.545	.600	0.0	9.1	11
McLoughlin, Trey	R-R	6-2	210	6-11-99	2	1	3.31	25	0	4	35	30	16	13	4	10	38	.227	.280	.386	26.2	6.9	145
Miller, Troy	R-R	6-4	210	2-13-97	0	1	7.36	1	1	0	4	3	3	3	1	3	4	.231	.353	.462	23.5	17.6	17
Minnick, Matt	R-L	6-2	210	3-11-96	2	0	3.16	20	0	1	26	18	11	9	4	9	24	.198	.282	.385	23.3	8.7	103
Moreno, Luis	R-R	5-8	170	5-29-99	9	6	4.98	25	21	0	119	118	73	66	12	59	117	.260	.349	.407	22.2	11.2	526
Nogosek, Stephen	R-R	6-2	205	1-11-95	0	1	16.20	1	0	0	2	2	3	3	1	3	3	.286	.500	.857	30.0	30.0	10
Nunez, Dedniel	R-R	6-2	180	6-05-96	1	0	2.65	11	0	2	17	14	5	5	1	3	22	.230	.266	.344	34.4	4.7	64
Parsons, Hunter	R-R	6-2	215	6-24-97	3	2	3.80	16	0	1	24	17	11	10	4	12	28	.198	.296	.384	28.6	12.2	98
Raley, Brooks	L-L	6-3	200	6-29-88	0	0	0.00	1	0	0	1	1	0	0	0	0	3	.250	.250	.750	75.0	0.0	4

Ramos, Wilkin	R-R	6-5	165	10-31-00	2	0	1.47	12	0	2	18	10	4	3	0	14	24	.161	.321	.161	30.8	17.9	78
Renteria, Marcel	R-R	5-11	185	9-27-94	1	1	3.54	19	0	1	28	22	13	11	1	14	23	.227	.325	.309	19.7	12.0	117
Santos, Junior	R-R	6-7	244	8-16-01	4	8	5.94	28	15	3	97	119	67	64	10	41	71	.310	.378	.471	16.2	9.3	439
Scott, Christian	R-R	6-4	215	6-15-99	4	3	2.47	12	12	0	62	44	17	17	5	8	77	.198	.243	.320	32.8	3.4	235
Stuart, Tyler	R-R	6-9	250	10-08-99	3	2	3.60	7	7	0	35	34	16	14	4	9	28	.258	.303	.394	19.3	6.2	145
Suarez, Joander	R-R	6-3	223	2-27-00	2	0	0.00	3	3	0	18	3	0	0	0	4	19	.055	.119	.055	32.2	6.8	59
Tavarez, Sammy	R-R	6-7	225	10-20-98	1	1	3.00	13	0	0	18	12	8	6	0	24	25	.197	.425	.279	28.7	27.6	87
Tebrake, Dylan	R-R	6-3	225	7-13-99	1	0	5.40	4	0	0	5	5	3	3	0	5	7	.263	.417	.474	29.2	20.8	24
Thomas, Tyler	R-L	6-1	175	12-22-95	1	0	0.79	15	0	4	23	11	2	2	0	5	30	.147	.207	.160	36.1	6.0	83
Tidwell, Blade	R-R	6-4	207	6-08-01	3	3	4.72	8	8	0	34	32	18	18	6	17	41	.254	.365	.476	27.7	11.5	148
Valverde, Alex	R-R	6-2	185	9-26-96	1	0	2.21	7	2	0	20	9	5	5	1	7	21	.134	.221	.209	27.3	9.1	77
Vasil, Mike	L-R	6-5	225	3-19-00	1	2	3.71	10	10	0	51	35	22	21	8	8	57	.187	.223	.364	28.9	4.1	197
Verlander, Justin	R-R	6-5	235	2-20-83	0	0	0.00	1	1	0	5	2	0	0	0	1	6	.125	.176	.125	35.3	5.9	17
Wilson, Kyle	R-R	6-1	185	9-27-96	1	2	9.22	7	2	0	14	19	14	14	2	7	6	.339	.409	.571	9.1	10.6	66
Woods, William	R-R	6-3	190	12-29-98	2	0	1.80	11	0	6	15	7	3	3	2	5	18	.137	.214	.275	32.1	8.9	56
Yacabonis, Jimmy	R-R	6-3	225	3-21-92	1	0	2.57	4	0	1	7	6	4	2	0	1	5	.240	.296	.280	18.5	3.7	27

Fielding

Catcher	PCT	G	PO	A	E	DP	PB
Mena	.973	6	34	2	1	0	3
O'Neill	.990	51	445	27	5	1	6
Parada	.983	11	113	5	2	0	0
Senger	.996	71	644	34	3	2	6

First Base	PCT	G	PO	A	E	DP
Gil	1.000	10	73	2	0	4
Gomez	.979	21	134	7	3	15
Mena	.986	13	65	4	1	3
Palmer	1.000	9	56	6	0	7
Ritter	1.000	11	78	7	0	10
Saunders	.976	17	110	12	3	17
Schwartz	.997	46	300	23	1	32
Suozzi	.983	15	104	11	2	8

Second Base	PCT	G	PO	A	E	DP
Acuna	1.000	12	20	31	0	6
Berbesi	.941	5	11	5	1	4
Fryman	1.000	1	1	2	0	1
Gil	.333	1	1	0	2	0
Guillorme	1.000	1	1	3	0	0
Jackson	.981	14	21	31	1	10
Jordan	.981	43	54	98	3	24
Peroza	1.000	7	10	12	0	1
Ritter	.975	19	28	49	2	16
Saunders	1.000	1	0	4	0	0
Villavicencio	1.000	1	0	2	0	0
Young	.992	32	44	78	1	16

Third Base	PCT	G	PO	A	E	DP
Fryman	1.000	4	4	7	0	2
Gil	.958	21	17	29	2	2
Guillorme	1.000	1	1	3	0	1
Jackson	.920	8	8	15	2	1
Jordan	1.000	4	2	3	0	0
Palmer	.800	2	0	4	1	1
Peroza	.950	81	55	134	10	8
Ritter	.955	12	8	13	1	0
Saunders	1.000	2	3	5	0	0
Young	1.000	2	0	6	0	2

Shortstop	PCT	G	PO	A	E	DP
Acuna	.974	25	29	47	2	7
Berbesi	.846	3	6	5	2	0
Fryman	.973	37	65	81	4	20
Gil	.778	2	4	3	2	0
Guillorme	1.000	1	3	2	0	3
Jackson	.960	8	10	14	1	2
Peroza	.833	2	4	1	1	1
Villavicencio	1.000	1	1	3	0	0
Williams	.889	4	2	6	1	1
Young	.981	53	69	139	4	35

Outfield	PCT	G	PO	A	E	DP
Gilbert	.967	33	75	2	1	0
Jackson	1.000	4	9	0	0	0
Jordan	.974	65	137	2	3	1
McIlwain	.982	70	136	6	1	2
Murphy	1.000	33	72	1	0	0
Palmer	.993	32	80	2	1	0
Ritter	1.000	1	1	0	0	0
Rudick	.993	53	94	3	1	1
Ruiz	.993	85	134	4	2	1
Schwartz	1.000	12	22	0	0	1
Suozzi	1.000	7	13	0	0	0
Thomas	1.000	16	34	0	0	0
Williams	1.000	2	3	0	0	0

BROOKLYN CYCLONES

HIGH CLASS A

SOUTH ATLANTIC LEAGUE

Batting	B-T	Ht.	Wt.	DOB	AVG	OBP	SLG	G	PA	AB	R	H	2B	3B	HR	RBI	BB	HBP	SH	SF	SO	SB	CS	BB%	SO%
Almonte, Abraham	B-R	5-10	223	6-27-89	.333	.516	.476	8	31	21	5	7	0	0	1	4	9	0	0	1	6	2	0	29.0	19.4
Berbesi, Cesar	L-R	5-9	160	4-13-00	.221	.349	.305	50	186	154	30	34	6	2	1	16	30	1	0	1	64	12	2	16.1	34.4
Campos, Dyron	R-R	5-10	155	12-26-00	.000	.000	.000	1	3	3	0	0	0	0	0	0	0	0	0	0	1	0	0	0.0	33.3
Clifford, Ryan	L-L	6-3	200	7-20-03	.188	.307	.376	32	140	117	13	22	4	0	6	20	18	3	0	2	51	1	0	12.9	36.4
2-team (58 Asheville)					.242	.345	.486	90	390	331	48	80	15	0	22	66	39	13	0	7	113	2	1	10.0	29.0
Consuegra, Stanley	R-R	6-2	167	9-24-00	.232	.294	.489	93	394	358	52	83	15	4	23	63	29	4	0	3	109	6	2	7.4	27.7
De Los Santos, Jefrey	L-R	5-11	154	5-30-03	.250	.400	.250	1	5	4	0	1	0	0	0	0	1	0	0	0	2	1	0	20.0	40.0
De Los Santos, Omar	R-R	6-1	172	8-08-99	.207	.261	.310	98	400	368	47	76	15	1	7	38	20	8	1	3	144	37	13	5.0	36.0
Dominguez, Carlos	R-R	5-11	190	10-11-99	.273	.273	.273	3	11	11	1	3	0	0	0	0	0	0	0	0	4	1	0	0.0	36.4
Estep, Chase	L-R	5-10	200	4-12-00	.219	.289	.315	79	301	270	41	59	13	2	3	33	27	1	0	3	77	5	2	9.0	25.6
Gil, Mateo	R-R	6-0	180	7-24-00	.208	.282	.443	62	234	212	35	44	14	3	10	31	20	2	0	0	56	3	1	8.5	23.9
Guerrera, Justin	R-R	5-9	185	1-11-00	.139	.179	.250	10	40	36	2	5	1	0	1	2	2	0	1	1	24	1	0	5.0	60.0
Guillorme, Luis	L-R	5-10	190	9-27-94	.000	.000	.000	2	6	6	0	0	0	0	0	0	0	0	0	0	3	0	0	0.0	50.0
Kendall, Kevin	L-R	5-10	175	6-25-99	.214	.308	.311	28	121	103	13	22	4	3	0	10	15	0	1	2	34	6	0	12.4	28.1
Lugo, William	R-R	6-2	215	1-02-02	.237	.316	.385	106	437	384	41	91	18	3	11	53	40	7	0	6	92	7	4	9.2	21.1
Malm, Brad	R-R	5-11	185	8-19-99	.100	.250	.100	3	12	10	1	1	0	0	0	0	1	1	0	0	7	1	0	8.3	58.3
Mena, Jose	R-R	5-10	208	12-22-96	.238	.290	.286	20	69	63	5	15	3	0	0	5	5	0	0	1	11	0	0	7.2	15.9
Narvaez, Omar	L-R	5-11	220	2-10-92	.250	.500	.250	2	6	4	2	1	0	0	0	2	2	0	0	0	2	0	0	33.3	33.3
Osborn, Drake	R-R	5-9	190	7-22-98	.179	.259	.359	71	267	234	35	42	9	0	11	35	22	5	1	5	65	0	1	8.2	24.3
Ota, Scott	L-L	5-10	195	8-16-97	.167	.158	.222	7	19	18	0	3	1	0	0	1	0	0	0	1	6	0	0	0.0	31.6
Palmer, Jaylen	R-R	6-3	208	7-31-00	.167	.290	.268	59	238	198	27	33	6	1	4	18	32	4	0	4	92	19	6	13.4	38.7
Parada, Kevin	R-R	5-11	197	8-03-01	.265	.340	.447	87	382	340	44	90	21	4	11	42	30	10	0	2	96	1	2	7.9	25.1
Pregent, Christian	R-R	6-3	215	12-26-00	.143	.231	.190	7	26	21	3	3	1	0	0	2	3	0	0	2	12	0	0	11.5	46.2
Ramirez, Alex	R-R	6-3	170	1-13-03	.221	.310	.317	120	521	457	66	101	21	1	7	53	56	4	0	3	114	21	6	10.7	21.9
Reimer, Jacob	R-R	6-2	205	2-22-04	.203	.354	.278	25	99	79	13	16	3	0	1	8	17	2	0	1	22	0	1	17.2	22.2
Salazar, Eduardo	R-R	6-2	167	12-15-00	.154	.254	.192	17	59	52	1	8	2	0	0	1	6	1	0	0	19	0	0	10.2	32.2
Saunders, Warren	R-R	6-1	205	12-15-98	.139	.184	.139	10	38	36	1	5	0	0	0	2	2	0	0	0	11	0	0	5.3	28.9
Smith, D'Andre	R-R	5-8	180	5-10-01	.237	.321	.353	64	253	224	30	53	15	1	3	17	21	7	0	0	76	8	1	8.3	30.0

Suozzi, Joe	R-R	6-2	215	2-28-98	.283	.339	.343	29	109	99	12	28	6	0	0	11	7	2	0	1	26	3	1	6.4	23.9
Thomas, Rhylan	L-L	5-10	170	4-15-00	.341	.432	.429	39	148	126	19	43	5	0	2	16	19	2	0	1	10	3	8	12.8	6.8
Tilien, Junior	R-R	6-1	168	9-09-02	.228	.299	.386	33	127	114	14	26	9	0	3	15	10	2	0	1	28	1	1	7.9	22.0
Williams, Jett	R-R	5-6	175	11-03-03	.299	.451	.567	36	162	127	25	38	9	2	7	18	33	2	0	0	32	12	1	20.4	19.8

Pitching	B-T	Ht.	Wt.	DOB	W	L	ERA	G	GS	SV	IP	Hits	Runs	ER	HR	BB	SO	AVG	OBP	SLG	SO%	BB%	BF
Alfonseca, Miguel	R-R	6-0	190	2-13-00	0	0	8.44	2	0	0	5	7	5	5	2	2	1	.304	.360	.696	4.0	8.0	25
Ankeney, Eli	L-L	6-0	200	1-10-01	2	3	3.94	21	1	4	32	26	14	14	2	22	37	.228	.345	.377	26.4	15.7	140
Beck, Jace	R-R	6-9	200	6-14-00	6	5	3.73	26	1	0	31	25	22	13	3	30	57	.217	.388	.357	38.5	20.3	148
Brodey, Harris	L-L	6-1	195	12-01-95	1	0	4.67	20	0	2	27	31	18	14	5	20	34	.290	.424	.514	25.8	15.2	132
Colina, Robert	R-R	5-11	175	4-24-01	4	5	3.84	19	8	0	61	62	29	26	5	16	75	.263	.318	.394	29.0	6.2	259
Colon, Jeffrey	R-R	6-1	170	11-09-99	1	4	5.72	17	12	1	61	75	44	39	5	22	54	.296	.361	.462	18.9	7.7	285
Cornielly, Joshua	R-R	6-2	175	1-15-01	2	3	3.71	31	1	1	51	48	26	21	8	17	58	.245	.320	.429	26.4	7.7	220
De La Cruz, Felipe	L-L	6-0	160	5-26-01	2	1	2.65	3	3	0	17	11	6	5	2	5	17	.183	.258	.317	25.8	7.6	66
Foster, Cameron	R-R	6-5	230	3-17-99	4	6	4.20	18	16	0	81	81	44	38	8	31	85	.260	.329	.420	24.6	9.0	346
Garcia, Benito	R-R	6-0	165	3-10-00	3	1	1.18	20	2	2	38	23	7	5	2	4	34	.168	.197	.248	23.9	2.8	142
Garcia, Saul	R-R	6-0	180	6-11-03	1	0	3.46	3	2	0	13	12	6	5	0	4	10	.240	.296	.260	18.5	7.4	54
Geber, Jordan	R-R	6-3	205	7-31-99	3	1	4.59	7	3	0	33	30	17	17	6	9	33	.244	.293	.431	24.4	6.7	135
Gervase, Paul	R-R	6-10	230	5-23-00	2	2	1.72	31	0	6	47	24	13	9	0	38	76	.146	.319	.207	36.4	18.2	209
Gomez, Raimon	R-R	6-2	175	9-06-01	0	0	6.43	3	3	0	7	4	6	5	1	9	12	.174	.424	.348	36.4	27.3	33
Hall, Dylan	R-R	6-5	210	9-07-97	1	2	3.63	15	0	1	22	17	14	9	1	14	35	.198	.314	.279	34.3	13.7	102
Hardy, Brendan	R-R	6-4	170	12-15-99	0	2	1.61	15	0	1	22	12	9	4	0	10	30	.162	.273	.216	33.7	11.2	89
Hernandez, Elieser	R-R	6-1	214	5-03-95	0	1	4.50	3	1	0	4	6	3	2	1	0	6	.333	.316	.556	31.6	0.0	19
Juarez, Daniel	L-L	5-11	155	9-28-00	2	0	0.00	12	0	1	16	5	1	0	0	6	24	.096	.186	.154	40.7	10.2	59
Krauza, Michael	R-R	6-1	200	8-07-97	0	2	8.53	6	0	0	6	8	7	6	0	6	6	.286	.429	.429	17.1	17.1	35
Kubichek, Kolby	R-R	6-0	180	11-28-99	0	1	5.40	20	0	2	27	29	19	16	3	19	21	.282	.417	.466	16.5	15.0	127
Lancellotti, Joey	R-R	5-11	205	1-15-98	0	0	3.65	11	0	1	12	12	8	5	3	1	15	.255	.271	.489	31.3	2.1	48
Lucchesi, Joey	L-L	6-5	225	6-06-93	0	0	1.13	2	2	0	8	5	1	1	0	2	8	.179	.233	.179	26.7	6.7	30
McLoughlin, Trey	R-R	6-2	210	6-11-99	2	2	1.65	10	0	1	16	13	5	3	1	6	26	.213	.275	.279	37.7	8.7	69
Montas, Luis	R-R	6-2	203	9-16-00	1	1	5.68	9	0	0	13	16	12	8	0	3	11	.296	.356	.426	18.6	5.1	59
Ovalles, Layonel	R-R	6-3	216	6-16-03	0	1	3.38	2	2	0	11	14	4	4	0	5	9	.326	.396	.372	18.8	10.4	48
Quintana, Jose	R-L	6-1	220	1-24-89	0	0	2.25	1	1	0	4	2	1	1	1	1	5	.143	.200	.429	33.3	6.7	15
Ramirez, Jawilme	R-R	6-2	170	11-28-01	1	1	5.52	6	6	0	29	34	18	18	4	10	15	.288	.346	.500	11.5	7.7	130
Ramos, Wilkin	R-R	6-5	165	10-31-00	3	2	2.97	21	0	1	39	25	18	13	0	23	43	.184	.315	.199	26.5	14.2	162
Reid-Foley, Sean	R-R	6-3	230	8-30-95	0	0	3.38	3	0	0	3	1	1	1	1	1	3	.111	.200	.444	30.0	10.0	10
Reid, Bailey	R-R	6-2	195	7-03-98	0	1	5.40	7	0	0	8	6	6	5	0	6	10	.207	.395	.241	26.3	15.8	38
Rodriguez, Joe Joe	R-R	6-1	200	10-12-99	0	0	2.79	4	0	1	10	9	3	3	0	2	13	.243	.349	.270	30.2	4.7	43
Rodriguez, Luis	R-R	6-4	175	2-27-03	0	0	13.50	2	0	1	1	3	2	2	0	1	1	.429	.500	.714	12.5	12.5	8
Rodriguez, Manny	R-R	5-10	166	7-04-96	3	3	5.06	22	0	1	32	22	22	18	4	25	26	.188	.351	.350	17.4	16.8	149
Scott, Christian	R-R	6-4	215	6-15-99	1	0	2.28	6	6	0	24	15	6	6	0	4	27	.176	.222	.247	30.0	4.4	90
Stuart, Tyler	R-R	6-9	250	10-08-99	4	0	1.55	14	14	0	76	56	14	13	3	23	84	.204	.272	.288	27.8	7.6	302
Suarez, Joander	R-R	6-3	223	2-27-00	5	9	5.08	21	19	0	90	83	59	51	6	45	118	.240	.342	.350	29.3	11.2	403
Tavarez, Sammy	R-R	6-7	225	10-20-98	0	0	17.28	9	0	0	8	11	18	16	2	15	9	.306	.537	.556	16.4	27.3	55
Tebrake, Dylan	R-R	6-3	225	7-13-99	1	1	2.08	14	1	1	26	15	7	6	0	10	40	.163	.245	.228	39.2	9.8	102
Tidwell, Blade	R-R	6-4	207	6-08-01	8	3	3.09	17	17	0	82	55	32	28	8	46	112	.190	.302	.325	33.0	13.6	339
Ventura, Jordany	R-R	6-0	162	7-06-00	3	2	3.86	10	10	0	49	32	24	21	1	33	46	.186	.330	.256	21.7	15.6	212

Fielding

Catcher	PCT	G	PO	A	E	DP	PB
Mena	1.000	13	105	11	0	1	2
Narvaez	1.000	2	17	1	0	0	0
Osborn	.990	57	560	32	6	3	1
Parada	.989	59	616	43	7	1	7
Pregent	1.000	6	51	3	0	0	1

First Base	PCT	G	PO	A	E	DP
Clifford	1.000	19	127	11	0	14
Estep	.982	34	197	23	4	14
Gil	.995	25	170	19	1	12
Lugo	1.000	11	78	2	0	7
Malm	1.000	3	15	0	0	0
Mena	.947	3	18	0	1	1
Osborn	1.000	2	4	1	0	0
Palmer	1.000	6	36	4	0	4
Reimer	1.000	3	20	0	0	2
Salazar	1.000	8	43	3	0	2
Saunders	.985	8	62	3	1	4
Suozzi	.990	14	97	5	1	6

Second Base	PCT	G	PO	A	E	DP
Berbesi	.981	15	18	35	1	6
De Los Santos	.800	1	2	2	1	2
Estep	.952	20	13	27	2	3
Gil	.963	7	12	14	1	0
Guerrera	.941	9	10	22	2	2
Guillorme	1.000	1	3	5	0	3
Kendall	.984	16	28	34	1	9
Saunders	.833	2	1	4	1	0
Smith	.930	59	76	151	17	23
Tilien	.970	7	11	21	1	5

Third Base	PCT	G	PO	A	E	DP
Estep	.914	23	13	40	5	1
Gil	.935	29	23	35	4	3
Guerrera	1.000	1	3	3	0	1
Guillorme	1.000	1	0	1	0	0
Lugo	.939	47	45	63	7	5
Palmer	.938	11	13	17	2	1
Reimer	.897	18	12	23	4	1
Tilien	.889	4	2	6	1	1

Shortstop	PCT	G	PO	A	E	DP
Berbesi	.991	32	43	64	1	11
Kendall	.958	9	7	16	1	1
Lugo	.963	42	64	65	5	16
Tilien	.892	21	19	39	7	4
Williams	.949	29	30	44	4	16

Outfield	PCT	G	PO	A	E	DP
Almonte	.833	5	3	0	1	0
Campos	.000	1	0	0	0	0
Clifford	1.000	10	22	1	0	0
Consuegra	.980	85	148	11	9	2
De Los Santos	.925	81	130	10	11	2
Dominguez	1.000	1	1	0	0	0
Kendall	1.000	3	5	1	0	0
Ota	1.000	7	11	1	0	0
Palmer	.972	41	61	2	1	0
Ramirez	.659	113	233	11	5	2
Salazar	1.000	5	8	0	0	0
Suozzi	.875	4	5	0	1	0
Thomas	1.000	37	68	2	0	0
Williams	1.000	5	11	2	0	0

ST. LUCIE METS

LOW CLASS A

FLORIDA STATE LEAGUE

Batting	B-T	Ht.	Wt.	DOB	AVG	OBP	SLG	G	PA	AB	R	H	2B	3B	HR	RBI	BB	HBP	SH	SF	SO	SB	CS	BB%	SO%
Almonte, Abraham	B-R	5-10	223	6-27-89	.231	.444	.538	6	18	13	2	3	1	0	1	1	5	0	0	0	6	0	0	27.8	33.3
Campos, Dyron	R-R	5-10	155	12-26-00	.182	.244	.327	52	172	159	22	29	4	2	5	23	7	6	0	0	48	6	1	4.1	27.9
Castillo, Luis	L-R	6-1	180	11-13-01	.135	.256	.297	16	43	37	2	5	0	0	2	4	6	0	0	0	18	1	0	14.0	41.9
Clark, Kellum	L-R	6-4	205	4-21-01	.231	.367	.359	11	49	39	5	9	2	0	1	5	8	1	0	1	14	1	0	16.3	28.6
Consuegra, Stanley	R-R	6-2	167	9-24-00	.091	.167	.182	3	12	11	1	1	1	0	0	0	1	0	0	0	4	0	0	8.3	33.3
Cuevas, Yohairo	L-L	6-3	172	9-16-03	.215	.308	.354	23	91	79	11	17	3	1	2	13	9	2	0	1	24	6	1	9.9	26.4
Davis, Jaylin	R-R	5-11	205	7-01-94	.111	.111	.444	2	9	9	1	1	0	0	1	1	0	0	0	0	4	0	0	0.0	44.4
De Los Santos, Jefrey	L-R	5-11	154	5-30-03	.220	.357	.372	63	267	218	31	48	10	4	5	31	43	4	0	1	73	4	3	16.1	27.3
Dominguez, Carlos	R-R	5-11	190	10-11-99	.211	.306	.374	42	170	147	21	31	5	2	5	25	16	5	0	2	57	4	3	9.4	33.5
Gomez, Dariel	L-R	6-4	190	7-15-96	.429	.600	.857	2	10	7	2	3	0	0	1	1	3	0	0	0	2	0	0	30.0	20.0
Hernandez, Adrian	R-R	5-9	210	2-08-01	.146	.239	.268	14	46	41	3	6	0	1	1	7	5	0	0	0	17	2	0	10.9	37.0
Hernandez, Jose	R-R	5-10	190	5-13-02	.200	.357	.384	41	157	125	23	25	3	1	6	15	25	6	0	1	51	3	0	15.9	32.5
Hernandez, Ronald	B-R	5-11	155	10-23-03	.172	.333	.241	8	39	29	3	5	2	0	0	7	6	2	0	2	13	0	0	15.4	33.3
Lantigua, Andriel	R-R	6-0	190	11-29-03	.143	.333	.143	3	9	7	0	1	0	0	0	0	2	0	0	0	3	0	0	22.2	33.3
Lara, Wilfredo	R-R	5-10	180	4-28-04	.264	.362	.452	99	409	352	54	93	18	3	14	49	50	5	0	2	89	17	6	12.2	21.8
Locastro, Tim	R-R	6-1	200	7-14-92	.067	.176	.133	4	17	15	2	1	1	0	0	0	0	2	0	0	5	1	0	0.0	29.4
Lorusso, Nick	R-R	6-2	212	9-11-00	.169	.250	.270	26	100	89	10	15	7	1	0	10	9	1	0	1	27	2	1	9.0	27.0
Martinez, Yeral	L-R	6-3	220	10-30-02	.239	.328	.399	86	314	276	40	66	13	2	9	42	29	8	0	1	92	12	2	9.2	29.3
McIntosh, Blaine	L-L	6-4	180	6-09-01	.152	.276	.200	40	123	105	13	16	3	1	0	9	17	1	0	0	42	2	4	13.8	34.1
McLean, Nolan	R-R	6-4	214	7-24-01	.111	.308	.111	5	13	9	2	1	0	0	0	1	3	0	0	1	6	0	0	23.1	46.2
Morabito, Nick	R-R	5-11	185	5-07-03	.286	.403	.378	27	120	98	14	28	4	1	1	7	14	6	0	1	27	10	3	11.7	22.5
Mosquera, Diego	R-R	5-9	156	3-14-04	.229	.354	.284	28	130	109	16	25	4	1	0	5	17	4	0	0	31	0	0	13.1	23.8
Nido, Tomas	R-R	6-0	211	4-12-94	.200	.200	.400	4	15	15	2	3	0	0	1	2	0	0	0	0	3	0	0	0.0	20.0
Ota, Scott	L-L	5-10	195	8-16-97	.260	.337	.384	23	83	73	7	19	4	1	1	7	8	1	0	1	8	5	1	9.6	9.6
Parada, Kevin	R-R	5-11	197	8-03-01	.077	.200	.077	4	15	13	2	1	0	0	0	1	2	0	0	0	7	0	0	13.3	46.7
Paz, Karell	B-R	6-0	215	8-11-99	.261	.371	.388	61	224	188	26	49	10	1	4	32	24	10	0	2	50	10	3	10.7	22.3
Peraza, Jose	R-R	6-0	210	4-30-94	.333	.400	.444	2	10	9	3	3	1	0	0	0	0	1	0	0	0	0	0	0.0	0.0
Peroza, Jose	R-R	6-1	221	6-15-00	.100	.308	.100	3	13	10	2	1	0	0	0	2	3	0	0	0	3	0	0	23.1	23.1
Perozo, Vincent	L-R	6-0	170	3-06-03	.226	.322	.380	88	342	297	42	67	18	2	8	46	32	11	0	2	103	1	1	9.4	30.1
Pregent, Christian	R-R	6-3	215	12-26-00	.154	.154	.385	4	13	13	1	2	0	0	1	1	0	0	0	0	7	0	0	0.0	53.8
Reimer, Jacob	R-R	6-2	205	2-22-04	.280	.412	.392	75	311	250	48	70	10	0	6	37	44	14	0	3	61	3	1	14.1	19.6
Salazar, Eduardo	R-R	6-2	167	12-15-00	.238	.297	.345	27	91	84	12	20	6	0	1	9	5	2	0	0	24	0	1	5.5	26.4
Schwartz, JT	L-R	6-4	215	12-17-99	.125	.125	.125	2	8	8	2	1	0	0	0	0	0	0	0	0	3	0	0	0.0	37.5
Thomas, Rhylan	L-L	5-10	170	4-15-00	.303	.370	.434	36	139	122	13	37	9	2	1	9	14	0	1	2	13	2	1	10.1	9.4
Tilien, Junior	R-R	6-1	168	9-09-02	.251	.339	.417	57	242	211	28	53	15	1	6	32	27	2	0	2	42	0	1	11.2	17.4
Vargas, Marco	L-R	6-0	170	5-14-05	.308	.419	.308	6	31	26	5	8	0	0	0	4	5	0	0	0	7	3	2	16.1	22.6
Villalobos, Fernando	L-R	5-11	195	6-24-02	.110	.301	.161	44	153	118	16	13	3	0	1	5	32	1	0	2	58	1	0	20.9	37.9
Villavicencio, Kevin	R-R	5-9	172	11-24-03	.240	.295	.306	102	380	350	43	84	11	3	2	35	24	4	0	2	67	23	7	6.3	17.6
Williams, Jett	R-R	5-6	175	11-03-03	.249	.422	.410	79	346	261	51	65	12	6	6	35	69	12	0	4	76	32	6	19.9	22.0

Pitching	B-T	Ht.	Wt.	DOB	W	L	ERA	G	GS	SV	IP	Hits	Runs	ER	HR	BB	SO	AVG	OBP	SLG	SO%	BB%	BF
Acosta, Daison	R-R	6-2	160	8-24-98	0	0	0.00	1	0	0	2	1	0	0	0	1	1	.167	.375	.167	12.5	12.5	8
Alfonseca, Angel	L-L	5-10	171	1-10-01	0	1	4.26	4	0	0	6	10	3	3	0	6	4	.370	.500	.370	11.8	17.6	34
Alfonseca, Miguel	R-R	6-0	190	2-13-00	1	1	7.39	21	0	2	28	36	24	23	2	15	25	.324	.420	.468	18.1	10.9	138
Alvarez, Manuel	R-R	6-3	225	9-17-95	0	0	13.50	2	0	0	1	2	2	2	0	3	1	.333	.600	.333	10.0	30.0	10
Ankeney, Eli	L-L	6-0	200	1-10-01	1	0	0.00	6	0	0	9	2	1	0	0	2	14	.067	.147	.067	41.2	5.9	34
Atencio, Javier	L-L	6-0	160	11-26-01	1	8	10.40	13	7	0	41	58	51	47	5	33	37	.339	.453	.579	17.5	15.6	212
Bartnicki, Luke	L-L	6-3	220	1-07-00	1	1	7.50	15	0	3	18	13	15	15	1	17	17	.203	.407	.375	19.8	19.8	86
Calderon, Jean	R-R	6-0	220	11-15-00	0	2	6.43	24	0	2	28	25	25	20	1	35	31	.243	.449	.350	21.1	23.8	147
Colina, Robert	R-R	5-11	175	4-24-01	0	0	0.00	1	0	0	4	1	0	0	0	0	3	.083	.083	.083	25.0	0.0	12
Coonrod, Sam	R-R	6-1	225	9-22-92	0	0	0.00	4	2	0	4	1	0	0	0	1	6	.077	.143	.154	42.9	7.1	14
Cuevas, Candido	R-R	6-1	202	4-24-04	2	2	4.56	9	5	0	24	18	18	12	1	17	33	.212	.352	.294	30.6	15.7	108
De La Cruz, Felipe	L-L	6-0	160	5-26-01	3	6	4.68	21	19	0	90	92	56	47	9	41	114	.262	.345	.413	28.7	10.3	397
Escalante, Estarlin	R-R	6-4	235	8-22-03	0	0	81.00	1	0	0	0	0	3	3	0	4	0	.000	.857	.000	0.0	57.1	7
Esterlin, Wilson	R-R	6-3	160	8-17-04	0	1	13.50	3	0	0	6	5	9	9	3	11	6	.263	.548	.789	19.4	35.5	31
Ferrer, Andinson	R-R	6-3	180	5-05-04	0	0	0.00	1	0	0	1	0	0	0	0	1	0	.000	.250	.000	0.0	25.0	4
Foggo, Eric	R-R	6-5	255	7-19-99	0	2	4.70	19	0	3	23	16	14	12	3	20	20	.203	.402	.342	18.5	18.5	108
Garcia, Benito	R-R	6-0	165	3-10-00	1	2	5.63	8	0	0	16	19	12	10	1	5	10	.292	.351	.415	13.5	6.8	74
Garcia, Saul	R-R	6-0	180	6-11-03	5	9	5.35	22	8	2	67	49	40	40	3	48	96	.203	.355	.295	31.9	15.9	301
Geber, Jordan	R-R	6-3	205	7-31-99	0	1	13.50	2	1	0	5	11	8	8	1	1	4	.458	.444	.833	14.8	3.7	27
Gomez, Cristofer	R-R	6-4	222	5-13-03	0	0	0.00	1	0	0	1	0	0	0	0	0	2	.000	.000	.000	66.7	0.0	3
Gomez, Franklin	L-L	6-0	145	7-06-05	0	1	6.75	1	0	0	3	2	3	2	0	1	3	.200	.250	.400	25.0	8.3	12
Gomez, Jose	R-R	6-4	177	1-24-04	0	1	13.50	5	2	0	8	11	13	12	1	7	7	.324	.442	.588	16.3	16.3	43
Gursky, Brian	R-L	6-1	205	2-04-98	0	1	7.11	11	0	1	13	15	14	10	0	12	12	.288	.415	.423	18.2	18.2	66
Hardy, Brendan	R-R	6-4	170	12-15-99	0	0	2.08	3	0	1	4	2	1	1	0	2	9	.143	.250	.286	56.3	12.5	16
Hawkins, Dakota	R-R	6-0	208	3-20-00	0	0	0.00	3	0	0	6	2	0	0	0	0	7	.105	.105	.105	33.3	0.0	21
Henriquez, Ramon	R-R	6-2	180	6-29-99	3	0	2.96	11	0	1	27	23	16	9	1	28	25	.221	.388	.298	18.0	20.1	139
Hernandez, Elieser	R-R	6-1	214	5-03-95	0	0	0.00	3	3	0	3	0	0	0	0	1	4	.000	.091	.000	36.4	9.1	11
Jenkins, Bryce	R-R	5-11	175	4-03-01	0	1	13.50	3	0	0	3	6	5	4	0	3	3	.429	.529	.500	17.6	17.6	17
Johnstone, Elliot	R-R	6-2	203	9-24-98	3	4	6.32	27	0	5	47	48	34	33	6	26	52	.267	.380	.433	24.1	12.0	216
Krauza, Michael	R-R	6-1	200	8-07-97	0	0	0.00	3	0	0	3	1	0	0	0	4	5	.091	.333	.091	33.3	26.7	15

Lancellotti, Joey	R-R	5-11	205	1-15-98	1	0	5.18	14	0	1	24	30	18	14	0	24	29	.291	.434	.379	22.5	18.6	129
Loper, Jimmy	R-R	6-4	215	11-08-99	1	3	3.86	24	0	4	44	40	19	19	0	19	55	.242	.326	.291	29.4	10.2	187
Lopez, Wilson	R-R	6-1	216	7-15-02	0	0	3.38	2	0	0	3	3	1	1	0	3	5	.273	.429	.273	35.7	21.4	14
Louis, Gregori	L-L	6-3	161	10-28-02	0	0	67.50	1	0	0	1	1	5	5	0	3	0	.500	.714	.500	0.0	42.9	7
Marceaux, Landon	R-R	6-0	199	10-08-99	0	2	7.27	3	3	0	9	11	11	7	2	6	7	.289	.386	.526	15.9	13.6	44
McLean, Nolan	R-R	6-4	214	7-24-01	0	0	2.70	2	1	0	3	1	1	1	0	2	2	.100	.250	.100	16.7	16.7	12
Mercedes, Ernesto	R-R	6-2	180	10-14-03	1	1	3.86	3	3	0	9	8	7	4	0	9	13	.235	.422	.265	28.9	20.0	45
Montas, Luis	R-R	6-2	203	9-16-00	1	0	0.00	5	0	0	7	4	0	0	0	1	2	.182	.217	.227	8.7	4.3	23
Morris, Kade	R-R	6-3	170	6-21-02	0	0	3.86	1	1	0	2	1	1	1	0	2	3	.111	.273	.111	27.3	18.2	11
Orellana, Douglas	R-R	6-1	196	5-01-02	4	4	4.53	23	18	1	89	74	51	45	9	50	112	.221	.330	.355	28.4	12.7	395
Ovalles, Layonel	R-R	6-3	216	6-16-03	3	6	4.73	22	18	0	84	68	46	44	10	36	84	.220	.322	.356	23.5	10.1	358
Quintana, Jose	R-L	6-1	220	1-24-89	0	0	0.00	2	1	0	5	4	2	0	0	1	4	.250	.278	.250	22.2	5.6	18
Ramirez, Jawilme	R-R	6-2	170	11-28-01	4	8	4.91	18	6	0	77	81	51	42	9	23	61	.265	.315	.454	18.3	6.9	333
Reid-Foley, Sean	R-R	6-3	230	8-30-95	0	0	0.00	3	2	0	3	1	0	0	0	0	4	.111	.111	.111	44.4	0.0	9
Reid, Bailey	R-R	6-2	195	7-03-98	0	2	8.53	8	0	0	6	5	6	6	0	8	13	.208	.472	.417	36.1	22.2	36
Reyes, Brawny	R-R	6-3	165	3-07-03	1	0	9.00	7	0	0	9	9	9	9	2	6	10	.265	.381	.588	23.8	14.3	42
Ridings, Stephen	R-R	6-8	220	8-14-95	0	0	3.00	3	2	0	3	2	1	1	0	0	3	.200	.200	.300	30.0	0.0	10
Rodriguez, Joe Joe	R-R	6-1	200	10-12-99	2	1	8.55	23	0	1	34	44	36	32	2	27	42	.310	.436	.465	23.2	14.9	181
Rodriguez, Jorge	R-R	6-3	180	12-18-01	0	1	16.88	1	1	0	3	5	6	5	1	2	3	.385	.471	1.000	17.6	11.8	17
Rodriguez, Luis	R-R	6-4	175	2-27-03	0	1	4.30	13	0	2	23	17	13	11	2	10	18	.202	.299	.345	18.6	10.3	97
Rodriguez, Luis	L-L	6-3	190	12-03-02	0	0	1.69	2	1	0	5	2	1	1	0	5	6	.118	.333	.118	25.0	20.8	24
Scott, Christian	R-R	6-4	215	6-15-99	0	1	9.00	1	1	0	2	4	2	2	0	0	3	.400	.400	.400	30.0	0.0	10
Simon, Ben	R-R	5-11	197	3-22-02	0	0	9.64	4	0	0	5	8	9	5	2	2	7	.348	.423	.696	26.9	7.7	26
Tong, Jonah	R-R	6-1	180	6-19-03	0	1	5.40	3	3	0	8	8	7	5	2	9	13	.250	.415	.500	31.7	22.0	41
Uceta, Edwin	R-R	6-0	155	1-09-98	0	0	0.00	2	1	0	2	0	0	0	0	0	1	.000	.000	.000	16.7	0.0	6
Vasquez, Christopher	R-R	6-0	160	3-17-01	1	5	6.39	25	3	1	56	56	44	40	3	44	48	.256	.394	.361	17.5	16.1	274
Ventura, Jordany	R-R	6-0	162	7-06-00	4	3	5.67	15	13	0	54	47	38	34	4	50	60	.237	.408	.364	23.1	19.2	260
Victorino, Omar	R-R	6-2	170	6-09-05	0	1	99.00	2	1	0	1	4	11	11	0	8	0	.667	.867	1.167	0.0	53.3	15
Wenninger, Jack	L-R	6-4	210	3-14-02	0	0	13.50	1	1	0	1	1	2	2	0	2	3	.200	.500	.200	37.5	25.0	8
Wilson, Kyle	R-R	6-1	185	9-27-96	0	0	10.80	1	0	0	2	3	2	2	0	1	1	.375	.444	.375	11.1	11.1	9
Ziegler, Calvin	R-R	6-0	205	10-03-02	0	0	0.00	1	1	0	1	0	0	0	0	0	3	.000	.000	.000	100.0	0.0	3

Fielding

Catcher	PCT	G	PO	A	E	DP	PB
Hernandez, J	.992	14	116	7	1	2	1
Hernandez, R	.962	5	46	4	2	0	0
Lantigua	1.000	3	30	3	0	0	1
Nido	1.000	2	18	3	0	0	0
Parada	.944	2	17	0	1	0	0
Perozo	.992	66	549	40	5	2	14
Pregent	1.000	3	26	1	0	0	0
Villalobos	.988	43	362	33	5	1	11

First Base	PCT	G	PO	A	E	DP
Castillo	1.000	6	27	2	0	2
Cuevas	.986	12	68	5	1	4
De Los Santos	1.000	1	6	0	0	0
Gomez	1.000	1	8	0	0	1
Hernandez	.993	23	141	10	1	15
Lara	1.000	2	1	0	0	0
Lorusso	1.000	1	5	0	0	1
Martinez	.978	60	376	29	9	38
Reimer	.987	12	70	4	1	11
Salazar	.984	18	110	13	2	10
Schwartz	1.000	1	5	0	0	0
Villavicencio	1.000	1	1	0	0	0

Second Base	PCT	G	PO	A	E	DP
Castillo	1.000	4	6	10	0	2
De Los Santos	.966	30	56	58	4	16
Lara	.962	7	10	15	1	1
Mosquera	1.000	7	6	13	0	1
Peraza	1.000	1	0	1	0	0
Tilien	.967	25	39	50	3	7
Vargas	1.000	1	3	4	0	1
Villavicencio	.971	58	99	132	7	30

Third Base	PCT	G	PO	A	E	DP
Castillo	1.000	5	3	2	0	0
Lara	.966	27	11	45	2	7
Lorusso	.905	22	21	36	6	4
Peroza	1.000	2	1	2	0	0
Reimer	.876	53	35	57	13	7
Tilien	.915	21	20	23	4	5
Villavicencio	.933	4	4	10	1	3

Shortstop	PCT	G	PO	A	E	DP
Lara	.667	1	1	1	1	0
Mosquera	.932	21	22	46	5	10
Tilien	.870	6	6	14	3	3
Vargas	.895	5	4	13	2	0
Villavicencio	.971	39	47	86	4	16
Williams	.908	59	78	99	18	24

Outfield	PCT	G	PO	A	E	DP
Almonte	1.000	4	8	0	0	0
Campos	.912	47	54	3	5	0
Clark	1.000	10	15	1	0	0
Consuegra	1.000	1	2	0	0	0
Cuevas	1.000	8	12	0	0	0
Davis	1.000	2	3	0	0	0
De Los Santos	.977	28	31	3	2	0
Dominguez	.993	38	60	6	1	1
Hernandez	.928	12	19	0	3	0
Lara	.990	58	102	3	1	0
Locastro	1.000	3	8	0	0	0
Martinez	.931	15	25	2	2	0
McIntosh	.986	34	57	2	1	2
Morabito	1.000	27	62	4	0	0
Ota	.979	17	20	2	1	1
Paz	.928	57	90	2	2	0
Salazar	1.000	3	2	0	0	0
Schwartz	1.000	1	3	0	0	0
Thomas	.994	37	85	4	1	1
Williams	1.000	14	25	0	0	0

FCL METS — *ROOKIE*

FLORIDA COMPLEX LEAGUE

Batting	B-T	Ht.	Wt.	DOB	AVG	OBP	SLG	G	PA	AB	R	H	2B	3B	HR	RBI	BB	HBP	SH	SF	SO	SB	CS	BB%	SO%
Baez, Jesus	R-R	5-9	180	2-26-05	.210	.306	.333	40	160	138	18	29	9	1	2	17	19	1	0	2	28	5	2	11.9	17.5
Baro, Boston	L-R	6-1	175	8-23-04	.316	.458	.421	7	24	19	4	6	2	0	0	2	5	0	0	0	1	0	0	20.8	4.2
Campos, Dyron	R-R	5-10	155	12-26-00	.200	.333	.250	7	24	20	3	4	1	0	0	2	3	1	0	0	7	2	0	12.5	29.2
Castillo, Luis	L-R	6-1	180	11-13-01	.219	.390	.313	22	41	32	7	7	1	1	0	0	9	0	0	0	9	2	0	22.0	22.0
Cedrola, Lorenzo	R-R	5-8	152	1-12-98	.250	.318	.300	5	22	20	7	5	1	0	0	2	2	0	0	0	3	0	0	9.1	13.6
Clark, Kellum	L-R	6-4	205	4-21-01	.308	.500	.385	11	38	26	14	8	0	1	0	3	10	1	0	1	7	2	0	26.3	18.4
Consuegra, Stanley	R-R	6-2	167	9-24-00	1.000	1.000	1.000	1	3	1	2	1	0	0	0	0	1	1	0	0	0	0	0	33.3	0.0
Cuevas, Yohairo	L-L	6-3	172	9-16-03	.310	.444	.577	23	90	71	13	22	3	2	4	15	18	0	0	1	21	7	1	20.0	23.3
De Leon, Francis	R-R	6-0	201	10-04-03	.174	.345	.174	15	29	23	3	4	0	0	0	1	5	1	0	0	7	7	1	17.2	24.1
De Los Santos, Jefrey	L-R	5-11	154	5-30-03	.409	.462	.591	7	26	22	3	9	4	0	0	7	2	1	0	1	5	1	0	7.7	19.2
Dominguez, Carlos	R-R	5-11	190	10-11-99	.600	.714	1.800	2	7	5	3	3	0	0	2	6	1	1	0	0	1	1	0	14.3	14.3

Ewing, A.J.	L-R	6-0	160	8-10-04	.286	.524	.357	7	21	14	3	4	1	0	0	3	5	2	0	0	6	1	0	23.8	28.6
Fanas, Willy	B-R	6-1	190	1-23-04	.248	.316	.423	39	152	137	20	34	9	3	3	25	14	0	0	1	43	4	1	9.2	28.3
Gomez, Dariel	L-R	6-4	190	7-15-96	.188	.316	.375	6	19	16	2	3	0	0	1	4	3	0	0	0	7	0	0	15.8	36.8
Gomez, Tommy	R-R	5-9	188	4-21-04	.500	.667	.500	3	3	2	2	1	0	0	0	0	1	0	0	0	0	0	0	33.3	0.0
Guance, Manuel	R-R	5-10	150	11-06-03	.083	.214	.083	7	14	12	2	1	0	0	0	0	1	1	0	0	4	0	1	7.1	28.6
Henriquez, Yonatan	B-R	5-10	185	10-12-04	.221	.353	.300	43	173	140	25	31	8	0	1	22	29	1	0	3	34	7	6	16.8	19.7
Hernandez, Ronald	B-R	5-11	155	10-23-03	.286	.509	.486	14	53	35	6	10	4	0	1	11	15	2	0	1	10	1	1	28.3	18.9
Houck, Colin	R-R	6-2	190	9-30-04	.241	.389	.310	9	36	29	6	7	0	1	0	4	7	0	0	0	8	0	1	19.4	22.2
Juan, Simon	R-R	5-11	195	7-13-05	.220	.293	.303	40	147	132	9	29	5	0	2	17	12	2	0	1	39	1	2	8.2	26.5
Lantigua, Andriel	R-R	6-0	190	11-29-03	.257	.429	.314	15	49	35	8	9	2	0	0	6	11	1	0	2	8	0	0	22.4	16.3
Leal, Gregory	R-R	5-9	171	2-14-03	.000	.000	.000	2	2	2	0	0	0	0	0	0	0	0	0	0	2	0	0	0.0	100.0
Locastro, Tim	R-R	6-1	200	7-14-92	1.000	1.000	1.000	1	2	2	1	2	0	0	0	0	0	0	0	0	0	0	0	0.0	0.0
Machado, Fabian	R-R	5-11	180	4-25-03	.120	.405	.160	14	37	25	7	3	1	0	0	3	11	1	0	0	7	0	0	29.7	18.9
McLean, Nolan	R-R	6-4	214	7-24-01	.143	.455	.571	3	11	7	3	1	0	0	1	2	4	0	0	0	5	1	0	36.4	45.5
Mejia, Gerald	B-R	6-0	156	6-14-03	.400	.500	.400	2	6	5	1	2	0	0	0	0	1	0	0	0	2	2	0	16.7	33.3
Mercado, Estarling	L-R	6-0	195	3-06-03	.273	.333	.364	8	12	11	2	3	1	0	0	4	0	1	0	0	4	1	0	0.0	33.3
Morabito, Nick	R-R	5-11	185	5-07-03	.324	.437	.432	30	135	111	22	36	5	2	1	18	20	3	0	1	22	11	1	14.8	16.3
Mosquera, Diego	R-R	5-9	156	3-14-04	.272	.331	.307	31	127	114	18	31	2	1	0	11	9	2	0	2	15	1	3	7.1	11.8
Oviedo, Carlos	R-R	6-1	210	8-20-04	.190	.354	.397	25	79	63	15	12	4	0	3	12	15	1	0	0	20	0	0	19.0	25.3
Peraza, Jose	R-R	6-0	210	4-30-94	.188	.350	.250	6	20	16	2	3	1	0	0	2	1	3	0	0	4	0	0	5.0	20.0
Perera, Yordis	R-R	5-9	215	5-24-02	.175	.209	.250	14	43	40	3	7	0	0	1	6	2	0	0	1	15	0	0	4.7	34.9
Reimer, Jacob	R-R	6-2	205	2-22-04	.429	.444	.857	2	9	7	2	3	0	0	1	4	1	0	0	1	1	0	0	11.1	11.1
Rodriguez, Orangel	L-R	6-0	180	4-01-05	.067	.067	.067	7	15	15	0	1	0	0	0	0	0	0	0	0	6	0	0	0.0	40.0
Rubio, Adrian	B-R	6-2	175	12-10-02	.000	.222	.000	5	9	7	0	0	0	0	0	0	2	0	0	0	3	0	0	22.2	33.3
Rudick, Matt	L-L	5-6	170	7-02-98	.235	.316	.353	6	19	17	2	4	2	0	0	2	2	0	0	0	2	0	0	10.5	10.5
Santana, Eric	B-R	6-0	180	11-02-02	.143	.250	.286	4	8	7	0	1	1	0	0	0	1	0	0	0	3	1	0	12.5	37.5
Sarmiento, Dangelo	R-R	6-0	160	1-04-05	.139	.279	.139	14	43	36	3	5	0	0	0	0	7	0	0	0	12	0	0	16.3	27.9
Schwartz, JT	L-R	6-4	215	12-17-99	.667	.818	.667	4	11	6	2	4	0	0	0	2	5	0	0	0	0	0	0	45.5	0.0
Suero, Christopher	R-R	5-10	205	1-27-04	.281	.422	.469	22	83	64	15	18	1	1	3	9	14	3	0	2	18	3	0	16.9	21.7
Suozzi, Joe	R-R	6-2	215	2-28-98	.500	.714	.750	2	7	4	2	2	1	0	0	0	2	1	0	0	1	1	0	28.6	14.3
Vargas, Marco	L-R	6-0	170	5-14-05	.234	.368	.298	15	57	47	9	11	3	0	0	5	10	0	0	0	9	2	0	17.5	15.8
2-team (33 FCL Marlins)					.269	.438	.401	48	219	167	41	45	14	1	2	24	48	2	0	2	31	10	2	21.9	14.2
Zitella, Jacob	R-R	5-11	195	2-24-05	.167	.286	.222	6	21	18	3	3	1	0	0	0	3	0	0	0	4	0	0	14.3	19.0

Pitching	**B-T**	**Ht.**	**Wt.**	**DOB**	**W**	**L**	**ERA**	**G**	**GS**	**SV**	**IP**	**Hits**	**Runs**	**ER**	**HR**	**BB**	**SO**	**AVG**	**OBP**	**SLG**	**SO%**	**BB%**	**BF**
Alfonseca, Angel	L-L	5-10	171	1-10-01	1	2	5.06	12	0	0	21	19	15	12	0	19	19	.244	.426	.295	17.4	17.4	109
Alvarez, Manuel	R-R	6-3	225	9-17-95	0	1	20.25	2	2	0	1	2	3	3	0	3	1	.400	.556	.800	11.1	33.3	9
Arnaud, Juan	R-R	6-2	164	6-22-03	4	1	4.71	15	0	0	21	12	11	11	2	18	22	.169	.366	.296	23.7	19.4	93
Atencio, Javier	L-L	6-0	160	11-26-01	0	1	5.14	2	2	0	7	6	5	4	1	3	7	.231	.333	.346	23.3	10.0	30
Banks, Brett	L-R	6-3	210	10-03-01	0	0	3.38	3	0	1	3	0	1	1	0	2	3	.000	.222	.000	33.3	22.2	9
Brandon, Connor	R-R	6-3	220	3-26-01	0	1	30.86	3	0	0	2	3	8	8	1	8	1	.375	.737	.750	5.3	42.1	19
Escalante, Estarlin	R-R	6-4	235	8-22-03	1	0	6.75	13	0	1	17	23	15	13	3	17	15	.315	.462	.493	16.1	18.3	93
Esterlin, Wilson	R-R	6-3	160	8-17-04	2	2	4.01	11	8	0	43	30	21	19	5	24	57	.203	.330	.345	31.8	13.4	179
Ferrer, Andinson	R-R	6-3	180	5-05-04	3	2	4.38	11	3	0	37	32	18	18	3	18	42	.227	.331	.355	25.6	11.0	164
Garrido, Rodolfo	R-R	6-1	176	9-23-04	0	0	3.00	3	2	0	9	6	4	3	2	5	6	.188	.297	.406	16.2	13.5	37
Geber, Jordan	R-R	6-3	205	7-31-99	0	0	6.75	3	2	0	5	8	4	4	1	0	6	.348	.348	.565	26.1	0.0	23
Gomez, Cristofer	R-R	6-4	222	5-13-03	2	0	1.04	10	0	2	17	13	4	2	0	8	19	.224	.318	.259	28.8	12.1	66
Gomez, Franklin	L-L	6-0	145	7-06-05	1	0	2.25	1	0	0	4	1	2	1	0	1	7	.071	.125	.214	43.8	6.3	16
Gomez, Jose	R-R	6-4	177	1-24-04	3	0	1.45	9	2	0	19	10	3	3	1	5	25	.147	.227	.235	33.3	6.7	75
Hawkins, Dakota	R-R	6-0	208	3-20-00	0	0	0.00	2	0	0	2	0	0	0	0	2	1	.000	.250	.000	12.5	25.0	8
Henriquez, Ramon	R-R	6-2	180	6-29-99	1	1	5.23	7	0	0	10	14	9	6	1	4	13	.326	.396	.442	27.1	8.3	48
Jenkins, Bryce	R-R	5-11	175	4-03-01	0	0	0.00	2	0	0	1	0	1	0	0	1	1	.000	.286	.000	14.3	14.3	7
Lopez, Wilson	R-R	6-1	216	7-15-02	1	0	3.00	4	1	0	6	4	2	2	0	6	6	.222	.444	.278	22.2	22.2	27
Louis, Gregori	L-L	6-3	161	10-28-02	2	0	3.18	13	0	2	23	16	9	8	3	16	25	.195	.327	.341	25.5	16.3	98
Marceaux, Landon	R-R	6-0	199	10-08-99	0	0	3.18	2	2	0	6	6	5	2	0	2	7	.240	.321	.320	25.0	7.1	28
Mercedes, Ernesto	R-R	6-2	180	10-14-03	1	1	3.00	9	5	0	24	20	10	8	0	15	27	.227	.349	.295	24.8	13.8	109
Mercedes, Pedro	R-R	6-6	230	10-23-01	1	0	1.86	8	0	0	10	7	2	2	0	10	8	.212	.409	.212	18.2	22.7	44
Montas, Luis	R-R	6-2	203	9-16-00	0	0	0.00	2	0	0	2	0	0	0	0	0	2	.000	.000	.000	33.3	0.0	6
Morris, Kade	R-R	6-3	170	6-21-02	0	0	0.00	1	1	0	1	1	1	0	0	0	0	.200	.200	.400	0.0	0.0	5
Oramas, Juan	R-R	6-3	170	7-14-05	0	0	6.75	1	0	0	3	0	2	2	0	0	2	.000	.182	.000	18.2	0.0	11
Palacios, Jonaiker	R-R	6-0	170	5-07-03	3	1	5.56	13	0	5	11	13	17	7	1	6	14	.260	.356	.380	23.3	10.0	60
Peguero, Jeremy	L-L	6-2	175	5-03-02	2	1	7.04	11	0	0	15	16	17	12	0	16	20	.262	.432	.344	24.7	19.8	81
Pena, Herlyn	R-R	6-2	168	9-24-03	1	0	6.57	12	0	0	12	16	11	9	0	7	9	.320	.397	.420	15.3	11.9	59
Reid, Bailey	R-R	6-2	195	7-03-98	0	0	0.00	1	0	0	1	0	0	0	0	1	1	.000	.250	.000	25.0	25.0	4
Reyes, Brawny	R-R	6-3	165	3-07-03	0	0	4.50	6	0	0	6	6	7	3	0	2	5	.240	.321	.360	17.9	7.1	28
Rodriguez, Jorge	R-R	6-3	180	12-18-01	2	0	2.45	7	2	0	22	14	7	6	0	11	28	.173	.295	.210	29.5	11.6	95
Rodriguez, Luis	L-L	6-3	190	12-03-02	0	1	6.75	4	4	0	5	7	4	4	1	2	4	.333	.391	.571	17.4	8.7	23
Rodriguez, Luis	R-R	6-4	175	2-27-03	0	0	0.00	4	0	3	7	0	0	0	0	3	11	.000	.120	.000	44.0	12.0	25
Scotti, Claudio	R-R	6-4	210	7-08-98	0	0	10.13	3	1	0	3	5	3	3	1	2	2	.385	.467	.615	13.3	13.3	15
Simon, Ben	R-R	5-11	197	3-22-02	0	0	0.00	2	0	0	2	1	0	0	0	0	2	.167	.167	.167	33.3	0.0	6
Tong, Jonah	R-R	6-1	180	6-19-03	0	1	6.39	7	5	0	13	9	9	9	1	13	25	.196	.373	.283	42.4	22.0	59
Troesser, Austin	R-R	6-3	189	3-29-02	0	0	0.00	1	1	0	1	0	0	0	0	1	3	.000	.400	.000	60.0	20.0	5
Uceta, Edwin	R-R	6-0	155	1-09-98	0	0	0.00	1	1	0	1	0	0	0	0	0	1	.000	.000	.000	33.3	0.0	3
Victorino, Omar	R-R	6-2	170	6-09-05	0	2	6.41	8	6	0	20	24	23	14	2	20	25	.300	.467	.425	23.4	18.7	107
Wenninger, Jack	L-R	6-4	210	3-14-02	0	0	0.00	1	0	0	1	0	0	0	0	0	1	.000	.000	.000	25.0	0.0	4

Fielding

C: Suero 21, Lantigua 14, Oviedo 12, Hernandez 8, Rodriguez 3, Gomez 1, Leal 1. **1B:** Cuevas 14, Oviedo 14, Perera 10, Castillo 8, Hernandez 4, Zitella 4, Gomez 3, Schwartz 2, Campos 1. **2B:** Baez 13, Mosquera 8, Vargas 6, Henriquez 6, Morabito 5, Sarmiento 5, Ewing 4, Baro 3, Castillo 2, Peraza 2, Rubio 1, De Los Santos 1, Guance 1, Houck 1. **3B:** Henriquez 27, Mosquera 5, Baez 5, Baro 3, Sarmiento 3, Vargas 3, Castillo 2, Guance 2, Peraza 2, Reimer 2, Houck 2, Zitella 1. **SS:** Baez 20, Mosquera 16, Vargas 6, Houck 6, Sarmiento 5, Rubio 4, Guance 3, Baro 1. **OF:** Juan 39, Fanas 34, Morabito 21, De Leon 12, Clark 11, Machado 11, Castillo 9, Cuevas 9, Henriquez 8, Mercado 6, Rudick 5, De Los Santos 4, Cedrola 4, Campos 3, Ewing 3, Santana 3, Mejia 2, Locastro 1, Dominguez 1, Consuegra 1, Schwartz 1, Suozzi 1.

DSL METS — *ROOKIE*

DOMINICAN SUMMER LEAGUE

Batting	B-T	Ht.	Wt.	DOB	AVG	OBP	SLG	G	PA	AB	R	H	2B	3B	HR	RBI	BB	HBP	SH	SF	SO	SB	CS	BB%	SO%
Acosta, Alex	R-R	6-1	187	11-24-05	.214	.294	.214	4	17	14	0	3	0	0	0	3	1	1	0	1	6	0	0	5.9	35.3
Almonte, Jostyn	R-R	5-11	193	5-10-03	.311	.443	.507	45	185	148	32	46	9	1	6	28	29	7	0	1	42	14	4	15.7	22.7
Asencio, Enderson	R-R	6-4	195	3-17-06	.210	.343	.347	50	204	167	24	35	11	0	4	18	26	9	0	2	55	2	1	12.7	27.0
Aular, Jose	R-R	5-11	175	1-02-04	.234	.344	.351	26	90	77	11	18	6	0	1	7	10	3	0	0	15	0	0	11.1	16.7
Baptist, Anthony	L-L	5-11	155	10-17-05	.276	.426	.476	32	136	105	29	29	3	6	2	16	25	4	0	2	29	12	6	18.4	21.3
Camacaro, Samuel	B-R	6-0	179	11-23-03	.278	.346	.322	35	127	115	15	32	5	0	0	14	9	3	0	0	23	8	1	7.1	18.1
Castillo, Lewis	R-R	6-0	163	6-23-03	.303	.385	.378	35	135	119	24	36	9	0	0	12	10	6	0	0	10	4	0	7.4	7.4
Cordero, Daris	R-R	5-11	185	9-02-05	.191	.345	.270	46	174	141	25	27	6	1	1	22	27	6	0	0	62	1	0	15.5	35.6
Cumare, Wuilder	R-R	6-2	185	7-07-06	.192	.377	.250	20	69	52	6	10	1	1	0	5	10	6	0	1	25	1	0	14.5	36.2
De Oleo, Branny	R-R	6-1	156	5-15-05	.313	.403	.476	46	191	166	36	52	12	3	3	25	14	11	0	0	18	6	1	7.3	9.4
Diaz, Reniel	R-R	6-0	160	4-03-06	.181	.294	.345	35	136	116	16	21	5	1	4	13	15	4	0	1	45	5	2	11.0	33.1
Garcia, Keiver	B-R	5-10	145	8-06-06	.219	.390	.271	33	123	96	20	21	5	0	0	6	23	4	0	0	23	9	3	18.7	18.7
Gomez, Vladi	L-R	5-11	150	9-12-05	.181	.335	.303	43	194	155	31	28	6	2	3	20	33	4	0	2	44	14	1	17.0	22.7
Gutierrez, Daiverson	R-R	5-11	206	9-11-05	.186	.321	.244	50	211	172	27	32	4	0	2	22	22	13	0	2	36	2	0	10.4	17.1
Guzman, Randy	R-R	6-4	215	4-19-05	.175	.333	.294	46	177	143	17	25	8	0	3	14	30	4	0	0	59	0	0	16.9	33.3
Hernandez, Julian	R-R	6-0	180	9-24-05	.197	.376	.379	25	85	66	12	13	4	1	2	10	17	2	0	0	30	0	1	20.0	35.3
Larez, Cristopher	R-R	6-1	190	1-10-06	.274	.351	.405	24	97	84	14	23	8	0	1	13	10	1	0	2	29	9	3	10.3	29.9
Marcano, Jose	R-R	6-0	160	5-06-04	.182	.216	.212	15	37	33	3	6	1	0	0	4	2	0	0	2	7	0	0	5.4	18.9
Mata, Yohenny	R-R	6-2	175	6-03-04	.271	.333	.356	20	66	59	11	16	3	1	0	7	5	1	0	1	11	1	0	7.6	16.7
Montano, Arnaldo	R-R	6-0	175	2-03-06	.225	.375	.324	25	88	71	12	16	4	0	1	13	16	1	0	0	23	0	1	18.2	26.1
Perez, Jonathan	L-L	6-1	160	2-27-06	.178	.365	.244	21	63	45	12	8	1	1	0	4	14	1	0	3	17	2	0	22.2	27.0
Pizani, Henry	R-R	6-1	190	6-05-06	.154	.316	.179	28	98	78	9	12	2	0	0	5	13	6	0	1	27	0	0	13.3	27.6
Ramirez, Justin	L-L	6-3	190	2-09-05	.257	.330	.446	52	224	202	23	52	12	4	6	33	17	5	0	0	42	4	4	7.6	18.8
Reyes, Railin	R-R	5-11	170	9-08-04	.160	.364	.253	28	99	75	12	12	1	0	2	12	19	5	0	0	20	6	0	19.2	20.2
Reyes, Rainer	R-R	5-11	190	5-19-03	.268	.379	.464	19	66	56	10	15	6	1	1	11	7	3	0	0	21	2	1	10.6	31.8
Rincon, Heriberto	R-R	6-1	160	2-16-06	.301	.398	.373	48	196	166	32	50	7	1	1	21	23	5	0	2	39	17	3	11.7	19.9
Rodriguez, Jeremy	L-R	6-0	170	7-04-06	.422	.536	.711	13	56	45	13	19	4	3	1	15	11	0	0	0	4	7	1	19.6	7.1
Rosa, Jeffry	R-R	6-1	190	9-11-04	.277	.400	.669	44	182	148	35	41	13	0	15	39	16	15	0	1	46	1	1	8.8	25.3
Ruiz, Leyderman	R-R	6-2	165	12-04-05	.250	.344	.313	34	128	112	23	28	5	1	0	19	11	5	0	0	30	3	3	8.6	23.4
Silva, Daniel	B-R	6-2	200	1-12-05	.286	.412	.500	4	17	14	2	4	0	0	1	4	3	0	0	0	2	0	0	17.6	11.8
Subero, Jose	R-R	6-0	160	3-08-05	.087	.333	.130	10	33	23	5	2	1	0	0	2	8	1	0	1	13	1	2	24.2	39.4
Terrero, Marcos	L-R	5-11	155	11-11-05	.292	.390	.417	17	59	48	10	14	6	0	0	8	9	0	0	2	13	1	0	15.3	22.0
Vargas, Jeisel	R-R	5-7	155	12-02-04	.281	.361	.469	14	36	32	8	9	3	0	1	2	4	0	0	0	9	3	2	11.1	25.0
Zayas, Julio	R-R	5-11	190	2-16-06	.307	.368	.517	49	202	176	34	54	14	1	7	43	15	5	0	5	26	1	1	7.4	12.9

Pitching	B-T	Ht.	Wt.	DOB	W	L	ERA	G	GS	SV	IP	Hits	Runs	ER	HR	BB	SO	AVG	OBP	SLG	SO%	BB%	BF
Alvarez, Luis	R-R	6-5	185	5-05-03	1	0	13.97	10	0	0	10	16	16	15	0	13	10	.356	.516	.400	16.1	21.0	62
Anton, Jesus	R-R	6-3	175	2-17-06	1	1	14.81	10	0	0	10	11	17	17	3	17	12	.275	.524	.575	19.0	27.0	63
Aracena, Wellington	R-R	6-3	180	12-27-04	3	3	3.77	11	10	0	43	33	22	18	3	23	46	.212	.313	.308	25.3	12.6	182
Avendano, Jorge	L-L	6-1	175	9-23-03	0	0	0.00	1	0	0	1	1	0	0	0	1	1	.250	.400	.250	20.0	20.0	5
Barreto, Brayhans	L-L	6-4	185	5-05-01	1	2	4.85	7	3	0	26	30	18	14	2	10	35	.286	.359	.362	29.9	8.5	117
Beltre, Anderson	R-R	6-5	225	9-13-04	2	6	6.97	12	10	1	41	53	36	32	4	20	38	.315	.410	.435	19.5	10.3	195
Brito, Carlos	R-R	6-5	192	2-24-02	0	3	10.07	14	0	2	20	24	26	22	1	22	17	.300	.448	.438	16.2	21.0	105
Cadiz, Yoralbert	R-R	6-1	171	10-24-04	1	0	4.61	12	0	1	14	10	8	7	0	14	9	.213	.422	.277	14.1	21.9	64
Calvo, Osiris	L-L	6-4	195	5-06-04	3	2	3.82	15	0	0	31	27	18	13	5	9	40	.231	.297	.393	31.3	7.0	128
Castro, Edgardo	R-R	6-3	190	12-20-03	0	0	0.00	7	0	1	10	4	2	0	0	9	7	.111	.289	.167	15.6	20.0	45
Ceballos, Luis	R-R	6-4	170	6-13-05	1	2	8.17	11	6	0	25	35	24	23	1	16	22	.324	.423	.528	16.9	12.3	130
Chirinos, Jose	R-R	6-3	170	10-16-04	0	5	4.62	11	11	0	39	40	26	20	1	17	51	.253	.346	.335	27.9	9.3	183
Cornelia, Jamdrick	L-L	6-0	140	11-17-05	0	0	27.00	1	0	0	1	0	2	2	0	4	1	.000	.800	.000	20.0	80.0	5
Cortez, Rogert	L-L	6-1	150	9-15-05	1	0	8.36	8	0	0	14	13	16	13	1	8	22	.241	.358	.333	32.8	11.9	67
Cota, Irving	R-R	5-9	165	2-14-04	4	1	3.66	14	2	0	39	40	22	16	0	9	43	.258	.316	.335	25.1	5.3	171
Crespo, Anthony	R-R	6-0	197	5-04-04	1	0	0.00	3	0	1	3	3	4	0	0	2	3	.214	.389	.357	16.7	11.1	18
Diaz, Franyel	R-R	6-7	208	12-18-04	2	2	3.00	12	10	0	45	35	23	15	1	25	54	.212	.328	.273	27.3	12.6	198
Figuera, Fredayan	R-R	6-0	175	10-05-05	1	0	4.26	7	1	1	13	14	9	6	2	6	10	.286	.373	.449	16.9	10.2	59
Gomez, Franklin	L-L	6-0	145	7-06-05	4	3	2.45	11	9	0	44	34	18	12	0	15	61	.210	.286	.235	33.5	8.2	182
Gomez, Gaspar	R-R	6-5	190	7-07-03	0	0	18.69	3	0	0	4	10	9	9	1	3	3	.455	.571	.682	10.7	10.7	28
Gordillo, Lucas	R-R	6-0	180	7-02-02	2	2	1.21	13	9	0	37	26	13	5	1	21	55	.197	.318	.242	35.0	13.4	157
Jimenez, Jonathan	R-R	6-2	182	3-21-04	0	0	3.86	7	0	1	12	12	5	5	1	7	13	.255	.352	.404	24.1	13.0	54
Lopez, Misael	L-L	6-2	180	4-08-03	2	0	12.74	14	0	0	18	22	25	25	1	20	18	.314	.490	.471	18.8	20.8	96
Lora, Yeudi	R-R	6-2	170	8-25-03	1	1	8.10	8	0	0	13	16	14	12	2	14	19	.302	.451	.434	26.8	19.7	71
Mejias, Miguel	R-R	6-1	150	11-02-04	2	0	5.25	11	1	2	12	7	10	7	0	9	9	.167	.327	.167	17.0	17.0	53
Mercado, Francisco	R-R	6-2	150	12-07-03	0	3	6.14	8	8	0	22	24	19	15	2	13	17	.273	.363	.432	16.7	12.7	102
Mijares, Elwis	R-R	6-0	180	12-29-05	2	2	3.96	18	1	1	39	34	21	17	1	17	47	.234	.321	.303	27.6	10.0	170

Moreta, Edgar	R-R	6-4	192	9-05-03	4	4	3.42	13	13	0	53	42	30	20	3	17	52	.213	.281	.315	24.0	7.8	217
Nunez, Ellian	R-R	6-2	167	12-08-03	1	3	6.27	9	3	0	19	17	18	13	0	16	22	.250	.400	.353	25.6	18.6	86
Nunez, Jhon	R-R	6-4	170	4-19-04	2	2	4.93	14	5	0	38	40	27	21	3	16	29	.261	.347	.392	16.5	9.1	176
Ramirez, Alejandro	R-R	6-2	190	4-21-04	0	3	4.95	15	0	0	20	20	15	11	0	17	30	.250	.408	.288	28.8	16.3	104
Rivera, Cesar	L-L	6-3	190	4-16-05	0	1	4.50	16	1	1	22	19	13	11	0	12	34	.232	.370	.256	34.0	12.0	100
Rodriguez, Arlison	L-L	6-5	220	3-05-03	3	2	3.05	16	3	2	44	41	20	15	3	11	38	.241	.286	.406	20.5	5.9	185
Rodriguez, Christian	R-R	6-0	160	10-12-04	0	0	5.14	10	0	0	14	12	12	8	1	12	16	.214	.371	.339	22.9	17.1	70
Rodriguez, Marcos	L-L	6-3	176	10-28-02	0	0	23.63	4	0	0	5	8	14	14	0	16	2	.400	.641	.450	5.1	41.0	39
Rodriguez, Roberto	L-L	6-2	189	11-05-05	0	0	23.63	5	0	1	3	1	7	7	1	10	3	.125	.611	.500	16.7	55.6	18
Rosario, Wander	R-R	6-7	185	7-06-04	0	0	9.64	5	0	0	5	10	6	5	0	4	3	.417	.533	.542	10.0	13.3	30
Seijas, Freilianderson	R-R	6-1	160	2-10-05	3	2	7.48	16	0	1	22	28	21	18	1	17	21	.318	.455	.523	18.9	15.3	111
Sotillo, Luis	L-L	6-3	176	6-15-05	1	0	8.16	8	2	0	14	15	14	13	2	19	15	.273	.474	.455	19.7	25.0	76
Trinidad, Patricio	R-R	6-4	190	7-22-06	1	2	5.12	15	0	0	19	24	18	11	0	18	16	.312	.455	.338	16.0	18.0	100
Valdez, Krisspy	R-R	6-9	215	11-23-03	0	1	12.71	5	0	0	6	5	9	8	0	7	5	.227	.433	.318	16.7	23.3	30

Fielding

C: Gutierrez 35, Zayas 24, Montano 15, Pizani 13, Hernandez 12, Aular 12, Marcano 5, Silva 2. **1B:** Cordero 17, Aular 13, Pizani 12, Mata 11, Cumare 11, Guzman 10, Asencio 8, Castillo 8, Montano 8, Marcano 6, Zayas 5, Camacaro 5, Hernandez 2, Rosa 1, Silva 1. **2B:** Gomez 18, Garcia 14, Terrero 13, Reyes 12, De Oleo 10, Camacaro 9, Ruiz 9, Subero 7, Vargas 7, Hernandez 6, Mata 3, Cumare 3, Castillo 2, Larez 2, Rodriguez 2, Cordero 1. **3B:** Castillo 24, Cordero 24, Ruiz 13, Camacaro 10, Zayas 10, Reyes 7, Mata 5, Cumare 4, Garcia 4, Gomez 4, Hernandez 3, Vargas 3, Terrero 2, Marcano 1, Subero 1. **SS:** De Oleo 30, Larez 21, Garcia 14, Rodriguez 11, Gomez 10, Camacaro 9, Reyes 8, Ruiz 5, Subero 2, Vargas 2. **OF:** Ramirez 47, Rincon 46, Almonte 44, Rosa 38, Asencio 37, Diaz 31, Guzman 29, Perez 21, Gomez 12, Baptist 12, Reyes 11, Acosta 4, Mata 2, Marcano 1, Ruiz 1, Vargas 1.

New York Yankees

SEASON SYNOPSIS: With preseason expectations as a contender and a $277 million payroll, New York nevertheless had to rally in September to avoid its first losing season since 1992. The 82-80 campaign still meant the Yankees missed the playoffs for the first time since 2016.

HIGH POINT: The Yankees generally played as expected in April and May, with a five-game win streak in May capping a 12-of-15 stretch with a 6-5 walk-off win May 23 against the Orioles. Aaron Judge, fresh off re-signing for nine years and $360 million, homered in the bottom of the ninth off Orioles closer Felix Bautista to tie the game. Judge, who played just 106 games, nonetheless led the Yanks with 37 homers and 75 RBIs.

LOW POINT: New York slipped in June and July, posting losing months, but was on the fringe of playoff contention when a nine-game August losing streak delivered the knockout blow. It was their longest losing streak since 1982, but a win against the Nationals precluded the club's first 10-game losing streak since 1913.

NOTABLE ROOKIES: The Yankees got contributions from plenty of youth. Anthony Volpe won the shortstop job in spring training and shined defensively while posting an inconsistent .209/.283/.383 season, with 21 homers and a team-high 24 stolen bases, as well as 167 strikeouts. Righty Jhony Brito finished fifth on the team with 90 IP and ranked second in victories, going 9-7, 4.28. New York had several top prospects debut in September, but the most celebrated of them, outfielder Jasson Dominguez, had his debut ended by Tommy John surgery.

KEY TRANSACTIONS: Free-agent lefty Carlos Rodon had a disastrous (3-8, 6.85), injury-plagued first season in the Bronx after signing for six years and $162 million. The Yankees finally gave in and released high-priced veterans Josh Donaldson and Aaron Hicks, with Hicks thriving after latching on with Baltimore. Righty Domingo German threw a perfect game against the Athletics on June 28, but had to leave the team in early August to enter alcohol rehabilitation and missed the rest of the season. A slew of waiver-claim/free agent outfielders failed to produce in left field.

DOWN ON THE FARM: In the New York media, the Yankees' farm system is often portrayed as a mess, but reality isn't as ugly as the perception. New York finished fifth in winning percentage and has a very promising group in the lower minors.

OPENING DAY PAYROLL: $276,999,872 (2nd).

PLAYERS OF THE YEAR

MAJOR LEAGUE

Aaron Judge
OF
.267/.406/.613
37 HR in 367 AB
17-for-19 SB

MINOR LEAGUE

Drew Thorpe
RHP
(HiA/AA)
14-2, 2.52
11.8 SO/9, 0.98 WHIP

ORGANIZATION LEADERS

Batting		*Minimum 250 AB
MAJORS		
* AVG	Aaron Judge	.267
* OPS	Aaron Judge	1.019
HR	Aaron Judge	37
RBI	Aaron Judge	75
MINORS		
* AVG	Ben Rice, Tampa/H. Valley/Somers.	.324
* OBP	Ben Rice, Tampa/H. Valley/Somers.	.434
* SLG	Christopher Familia, Tampa/Hud. Valley	.617
* OPS	Ben Rice, Tampa/H. Valley/Somers.	1.048
R	Jared Serna, Tampa/Hudson Valley	90
H	Jared Serna, Tampa/Hudson Valley	144
TB	Jared Serna, Tampa/Hudson Valley	235
2B	Spencer Jones, Hudson Valley/Somerset	29
3B	Alexander Vargas, Hudson Valley	6
HR	Estevan Florial, Scranton/W-B	28
RBI	Andres Chaparro, Scranton/W-B	89
BB	Jasson Dominguez, Somerset/Scranton/W-B	83
SO	Spencer Jones, Hudson Valley/Somerset	155
SB	Spencer Jones, Hudson Valley/Somerset	43

Pitching		#Minimum 75 IP
MAJORS		
W	Gerrit Cole	15
# ERA	Gerrit Cole	2.63
SO	Gerrit Cole	222
SV	Clay Holmes	24
MINORS		
W	Drew Thorpe, H. Valley/Somerset	14
L	Zach Messinger, H. Valley/Somerset	10
L	Baron Stuart, St. Lucie/H. Valley	10
# ERA	Drew Thorpe, H. Valley/Somerset	2.52
G	Aaron McGarity, Scranton/W-B	51
GS	Mitch Spence, Scranton/W-B	29
SV	Greg Weissert, Scranton/W-B	10
IP	Mitch Spence, Scranton/W-B	163
BB	Clayton Beeter, Somerset/Scranton/W-B	75.00
SO	Drew Thorpe, H. Valley/Somerset	182
# AVG	Justin Lange, Tampa/H. Valley	.194

2023 PERFORMANCE

General Manager: Brian Cashman. **Farm Director:** Kevin Reese. **Scouting Director:** Damon Oppenheimer.

Class	Team	League	W	L	PCT	Finish	Manager
Majors	New York Yankees	American	82	80	.506	8 (15)	Aaron Boone
Triple-A	Scranton/WB RailRiders	International	73	75	.493	10 (20)	Shelley Duncan
Double-A	Somerset Patriots	Eastern	84	53	.613	1 (12)	Raul Dominguez
High-A	Hudson Valley Renegades	South Atlantic	70	62	.530	4 (12)	Sergio Santos
Low-A	Tampa Tarpons	Florida State	61	69	.469	8 (10)	Rachel Balkovec
Rookie	FCL Yankees	Florida Complex	33	22	.600	2 (15)	James Cooper
Rookie	DSL NYY Bombers	Dominican Sum.	27	26	.509	25 (50)	Parker Guinn
Rookie	DSL NYY Yankees	Dominican Sum.	33	19	.635	10 (50)	Victor Rey
Overall 2023 Minor League Record			381	326	.539	5th (30)	

ORGANIZATION STATISTICS

NEW YORK YANKEES

AMERICAN LEAGUE

Batting	B-T	Ht.	Wt.	DOB	AVG	OBP	SLG	G	PA	AB	R	H	2B	3B	HR	RBI	BB	HBP	SH	SF	SO	SB	CS	BB%	SO%
Allen, Greg	B-R	6-0	185	3-15-93	.217	.333	.478	22	28	23	6	5	1	1	1	1	2	2	1	0	10	3	1	7.1	35.7
Bader, Harrison	R-R	6-0	210	6-03-94	.240	.278	.365	84	310	288	40	69	11	2	7	37	14	3	1	4	56	17	2	4.5	18.1
Bauers, Jake	L-L	5-11	195	10-06-95	.202	.279	.413	84	272	242	28	49	15	0	12	30	27	0	0	3	95	3	2	9.9	34.9
Cabrera, Oswaldo	B-R	5-11	200	3-01-99	.211	.275	.299	115	330	298	35	63	11	0	5	29	25	2	3	2	72	8	0	7.6	21.8
Calhoun, Willie	L-R	5-8	205	11-04-94	.239	.309	.403	44	149	134	16	32	7	0	5	16	14	0	0	1	20	0	0	9.4	13.4
Cordero, Franchy	L-R	6-3	225	9-02-94	.188	.211	.478	24	71	69	9	13	2	0	6	13	2	0	0	0	25	0	0	2.8	35.2
Dominguez, Jasson	B-R	5-9	190	2-07-03	.258	.303	.677	8	33	31	6	8	1	0	4	7	2	0	0	0	8	1	0	6.1	24.2
Donaldson, Josh	R-R	6-1	210	12-08-85	.142	.225	.434	34	120	106	13	15	1	0	10	15	12	0	0	2	32	0	0	10.0	26.7
Florial, Estevan	L-R	6-1	195	11-25-97	.230	.324	.311	19	71	61	5	14	3	1	0	8	7	2	0	1	20	3	0	9.9	28.2
Hicks, Aaron	B-R	6-1	205	10-02-89	.188	.263	.261	28	76	69	9	13	2	0	1	5	7	0	0	0	20	0	0	9.2	26.3
2-team (65 Baltimore)					.253	.354	.383	93	312	269	44	68	9	1	8	36	42	0	0	1	69	6	0	13.5	22.1
Higashioka, Kyle	R-R	6-1	202	4-20-90	.236	.274	.413	92	260	242	24	57	13	0	10	34	14	0	1	3	74	0	0	5.4	28.5
Judge, Aaron	R-R	6-7	282	4-26-92	.267	.406	.613	106	458	367	79	98	16	0	37	75	88	0	0	3	130	3	1	19.2	28.4
Kiner-Falefa, Isiah	R-R	5-11	190	3-23-95	.242	.306	.340	115	361	326	39	79	12	1	6	37	28	3	1	3	70	14	5	7.8	19.4
LeMahieu, DJ	R-R	6-4	220	7-13-88	.243	.327	.390	136	562	497	55	121	22	3	15	44	60	3	0	2	125	2	2	10.7	22.2
McKinney, Billy	L-L	5-11	205	8-23-94	.227	.320	.406	48	147	128	19	29	3	1	6	14	17	1	0	1	39	1	0	11.6	26.5
Peraza, Oswald	R-R	6-0	200	6-15-00	.191	.267	.272	52	191	173	15	33	8	0	2	14	13	5	0	0	50	4	3	6.8	26.2
Pereira, Everson	R-R	5-11	191	4-10-01	.151	.233	.194	27	103	93	6	14	4	0	0	10	8	2	0	0	40	4	0	7.8	38.8
Rizzo, Anthony	L-L	6-3	240	8-08-89	.244	.328	.378	99	421	373	45	91	14	0	12	41	35	12	0	1	97	0	3	8.3	23.0
Rortvedt, Ben	L-R	5-9	191	9-25-97	.118	.241	.221	32	79	68	6	8	1	0	2	4	11	0	0	0	19	0	0	13.9	24.1
Stanton, Giancarlo	R-R	6-6	245	11-08-89	.191	.275	.420	101	415	371	43	71	13	0	24	60	41	2	0	1	124	0	0	9.9	29.9
Torres, Gleyber	R-R	6-1	205	12-13-96	.273	.347	.453	158	672	596	90	163	28	2	25	68	67	3	0	6	98	13	6	10.0	14.6
Trevino, Jose	R-R	5-10	215	11-28-92	.210	.257	.312	55	168	157	15	33	4	0	4	15	8	2	1	0	22	0	0	4.8	13.1
Volpe, Anthony	R-R	5-9	180	4-28-01	.209	.283	.383	159	601	541	62	113	23	4	21	60	52	5	1	2	167	24	5	8.7	27.8
Wells, Austin	L-R	6-0	220	7-12-99	.229	.257	.486	19	75	70	8	16	6	0	4	13	3	0	0	1	14	0	0	4.0	18.7

Pitching	B-T	Ht.	Wt.	DOB	W	L	ERA	G	GS	SV	IP	Hits	Runs	ER	HR	BB	SO	AVG	OBP	SLG	SO%	BB%	BF
Abreu, Albert	R-R	6-2	190	9-26-95	2	2	4.73	45	0	0	59	52	39	31	9	35	61	.231	.348	.404	22.8	13.1	268
Bowman, Matt	R-R	6-0	185	5-31-91	0	0	9.00	3	0	0	4	6	4	4	1	2	3	.353	.400	.588	15.0	10.0	20
Brewer, Colten	R-R	6-4	222	10-29-92	0	0	4.32	3	0	0	8	6	4	4	3	3	4	.200	.294	.600	11.8	8.8	34
Brito, Jhony	R-R	6-2	210	2-17-98	9	7	4.28	25	13	1	90	82	47	43	14	28	72	.244	.306	.435	19.4	7.5	372
Cole, Gerrit	R-R	6-4	220	9-08-90	15	4	2.63	33	33	0	209	157	64	61	20	48	222	.206	.259	.322	27.0	5.8	821
Cordero, Jimmy	R-R	6-4	245	10-19-91	3	2	3.86	31	1	0	33	25	14	14	2	10	34	.208	.280	.317	25.8	7.6	132
Cortes, Nestor	R-L	5-11	210	12-10-94	5	2	4.97	12	12	0	63	59	36	35	11	20	67	.244	.308	.442	25.2	7.5	266
Donaldson, Josh	R-R	6-1	210	12-08-85	0	0	0.00	1	0	0	1	0	0	0	0	0	0	.000	.000	.000	0.0	0.0	3
Garcia, Deivi	R-R	5-9	163	5-19-99	0	0	1.59	2	0	1	6	4	1	1	1	4	3	.200	.320	.500	12.0	16.0	25
German, Domingo	R-R	6-2	181	8-04-92	5	7	4.56	20	19	0	109	83	61	55	20	34	114	.207	.277	.414	25.7	7.7	444
Gomez, Yoendrys	R-R	6-3	175	10-15-99	0	0	0.00	1	0	0	2	1	0	0	0	0	4	.143	.250	.143	50.0	0.0	8
Hamilton, Ian	R-R	6-1	200	6-16-95	3	2	2.64	39	3	2	58	45	19	17	2	26	69	.215	.310	.297	28.9	10.9	239
Holmes, Clay	R-R	6-5	245	3-27-93	4	4	2.86	66	0	24	63	51	22	20	2	23	71	.218	.294	.291	27.1	8.8	262
Kahnle, Tommy	R-R	6-1	230	8-07-89	1	3	2.66	42	0	2	41	26	14	12	5	19	48	.183	.280	.331	29.1	11.5	165
Kiner-Falefa, Isiah	R-R	5-11	190	3-23-95	0	0	2.25	4	0	0	4	4	1	1	0	0	1	.250	.250	.375	6.3	0.0	16
King, Michael	R-R	6-3	210	5-25-95	4	8	2.75	49	9	6	105	88	35	32	10	32	127	.226	.292	.346	29.5	7.4	431
Krook, Matt	L-L	6-4	225	10-21-94	0	0	24.75	4	0	0	4	8	11	11	1	6	3	.400	.519	.600	11.1	22.2	27
Loaisiga, Jonathan	R-R	5-11	165	11-02-94	0	2	3.06	17	0	0	18	14	7	6	2	1	6	.219	.246	.328	8.7	1.4	69
Marinaccio, Ron	R-R	6-2	205	7-01-95	4	5	3.99	45	0	2	47	35	24	21	6	27	56	.208	.340	.357	27.3	13.2	205
McAllister, Zach	R-R	6-6	240	12-08-87	0	0	10.13	7	0	0	5	9	7	6	2	2	5	.346	.414	.692	17.2	6.9	29
Middleton, Keynan	R-R	6-3	215	9-12-93	0	0	1.88	12	0	0	14	7	3	3	1	7	17	.143	.250	.224	30.4	12.5	56
Misiewicz, Anthony	R-L	6-1	196	11-01-94	1	0	3.38	3	0	0	3	2	3	1	0	3	2	.200	.385	.200	15.4	23.1	13
Montas, Frankie	R-R	6-2	255	3-21-93	1	0	0.00	1	0	0	1	2	0	0	0	1	1	.333	.429	.500	14.3	14.3	7
Peralta, Wandy	L-L	6-0	227	7-27-91	4	2	2.83	63	0	4	54	36	19	17	7	30	51	.190	.319	.323	22.5	13.2	227
Ramirez, Nick	L-L	6-4	232	8-01-89	1	2	2.66	32	0	1	41	41	17	12	1	9	28	.256	.298	.356	16.3	5.2	172

Pitching	B-T	Ht.	Wt.	DOB	W	L	ERA	G	GS	SV	IP	Hits	Runs	ER	HR	BB	SO	AVG	OBP	SLG	SO%	BB%	BF
Rodon, Carlos	L-L	6-2	255	12-10-92	3	8	6.85	14	14	0	64	65	51	49	15	28	64	.261	.340	.498	22.4	9.8	286
Schmidt, Clarke	R-R	6-1	200	2-20-96	9	9	4.64	33	32	0	159	169	91	82	24	46	149	.268	.326	.451	21.5	6.6	694
Severino, Luis	R-R	6-2	218	2-20-94	4	8	6.65	19	18	0	89	113	73	66	23	34	79	.301	.366	.555	18.9	8.2	417
Vasquez, Randy	R-R	6-0	165	11-03-98	2	2	2.87	11	5	0	38	30	12	12	5	18	33	.211	.315	.366	19.9	10.8	166
Weaver, Luke	R-R	6-2	183	8-21-93	1	1	3.38	3	3	0	13	14	5	5	3	3	16	.264	.298	.491	28.1	5.3	57
Weber, Ryan	R-R	6-1	175	8-12-90	1	0	3.14	8	0	1	14	17	5	5	2	1	7	.298	.317	.474	11.7	1.7	60
Weissert, Greg	R-R	6-2	235	2-04-95	0	0	4.05	17	0	0	20	21	9	9	3	8	22	.273	.349	.416	25.3	9.2	87

Fielding

Catcher	PCT	G	PO	A	E	DP	PB
Higashioka	.987	90	663	14	9	1	5
Rortvedt	.991	31	225	6	2	1	1
Trevino	.993	54	411	17	3	2	2
Wells	.994	19	171	3	1	0	0

First Base	PCT	G	PO	A	E	DP
Bauers	1.000	22	144	4	0	14
Cabrera	1.000	1	1	0	0	0
LeMahieu	.995	56	381	32	2	36
McKinney	1.000	1	0	1	0	0
Rizzo	.995	92	656	102	4	58

Second Base	PCT	G	PO	A	E	DP
Cabrera	.917	6	1	10	1	3
Kiner-Falefa	1.000	1	1	0	0	0
LeMahieu	1.000	9	8	17	0	3
Peraza	.977	10	20	22	1	5
Torres	.975	145	234	344	15	80

Third Base	PCT	G	PO	A	E	DP
Cabrera	.972	15	8	27	1	5
Donaldson	.984	23	18	42	1	5
Kiner-Falefa	.963	31	19	59	3	7
LeMahieu	.994	69	35	136	1	12
Peraza	.964	36	18	63	3	5

Shortstop	PCT	G	PO	A	E	DP
Cabrera	.889	5	6	10	2	3
Kiner-Falefa	1.000	1	2	4	0	1
Peraza	1.000	6	10	11	0	1
Volpe	.970	157	186	357	17	63

Outfield	PCT	G	PO	A	E	DP
Allen	1.000	19	18	0	0	0
Bader	.972	83	204	3	6	0
Bauers	.961	56	70	2	3	0
Cabrera	.661	101	118	1	1	1
Calhoun	1.000	12	10	0	0	0
Cordero	1.000	22	34	1	0	0
Dominguez	1.000	8	16	0	0	0
Florial	.976	19	40	0	1	0
Hicks	1.000	26	33	0	0	0
Judge	.995	72	130	2	1	0
Kiner-Falefa	.986	85	154	3	3	0
McKinney	1.000	52	59	1	0	0
Pereira	1.000	27	44	1	0	0
Stanton	1.000	33	47	1	0	1

SCRANTON/WILKES-BARRE RAILRIDERS — *TRIPLE-A*

INTERNATIONAL LEAGUE

Batting	B-T	Ht.	Wt.	DOB	AVG	OBP	SLG	G	PA	AB	R	H	2B	3B	HR	RBI	BB	HBP	SH	SF	SO	SB	CS	BB%	SO%
Allen, Greg	B-R	6-0	185	3-15-93	.231	.333	.462	4	15	13	3	3	0	0	1	3	1	1	0	0	3	0	1	6.7	20.0
2-team (37 Worcester)					.242	.385	.366	49	203	161	32	39	9	1	3	19	25	13	1	3	39	26	2	12.3	19.2
Bader, Harrison	R-R	6-0	210	6-03-94	.105	.190	.105	5	21	19	1	2	0	0	0	0	2	0	0	0	3	1	0	9.5	14.3
Bastidas, Jesus	R-R	5-8	145	9-14-98	.253	.331	.409	101	384	340	49	86	13	2	12	38	29	12	0	3	96	11	4	7.6	25.0
Battle, Kyle	R-R	6-0	190	12-04-97	.250	.400	.375	3	10	8	0	2	1	0	0	0	2	0	0	0	5	1	0	20.0	50.0
Bauers, Jake	L-L	5-11	195	10-06-95	.359	.485	.897	24	97	78	19	28	7	1	11	23	19	0	0	0	16	6	0	19.6	16.5
Breaux, Josh	R-R	6-1	220	10-07-97	.214	.327	.524	12	49	42	7	9	1	0	4	5	5	2	0	0	8	1	0	10.2	16.3
Burt, Max	R-R	6-1	185	8-28-96	.125	.300	.125	7	20	16	1	2	0	0	0	1	4	0	0	0	3	0	0	20.0	15.0
Cabrera, Oswaldo	B-R	5-11	200	3-01-99	.225	.326	.400	10	46	40	7	9	1	0	2	6	5	1	0	0	9	2	1	10.9	19.6
Calhoun, Kole	L-L	5-10	205	10-14-87	.281	.390	.528	23	105	89	24	25	6	2	4	18	13	3	0	0	22	0	0	12.4	21.0
Calhoun, Willie	L-R	5-8	205	11-04-94	.333	.364	.429	5	22	21	1	7	2	0	0	2	1	0	0	0	3	0	0	4.5	13.6
Chaparro, Andres	R-R	6-0	200	5-04-99	.247	.331	.444	137	601	523	82	129	24	2	25	89	65	5	0	8	131	4	0	10.8	21.8
Cordero, Franchy	L-R	6-3	225	9-02-94	.288	.403	.476	82	350	292	53	84	14	1	13	61	53	4	0	1	77	8	1	15.1	22.0
Cowles, Benjamin	R-R	6-0	180	2-15-00	.222	.222	.222	3	9	9	0	2	0	0	0	0	0	0	0	0	5	0	0	0.0	55.6
Difo, Wilmer	B-R	5-10	200	4-02-92	.208	.322	.303	96	336	284	46	59	10	1	5	24	46	3	1	2	69	23	9	13.7	20.5
Dominguez, Jasson	B-R	5-9	190	2-07-03	.419	.514	.581	9	37	31	6	13	3	1	0	10	6	0	0	0	3	3	1	16.2	8.1
Donaldson, Josh	R-R	6-1	210	12-08-85	.333	.538	.778	3	13	9	4	3	1	0	1	2	4	0	0	0	2	0	0	30.8	15.4
2-team (5 Nashville)					.231	.429	.615	8	35	26	9	6	1	0	3	5	9	0	0	0	6	0	0	25.7	17.1
Dunham, Elijah	L-L	5-11	213	5-29-98	.216	.330	.340	69	303	259	37	56	12	1	6	16	39	5	0	0	87	12	4	12.9	28.7
Duran, Edinson	R-R	5-6	180	7-22-02	.000	.000	.000	1	2	2	0	0	0	0	0	0	0	0	0	0	1	0	0	0.0	50.0
Duran, Rodolfo	R-R	5-8	181	2-19-98	.252	.329	.444	62	240	214	22	54	15	1	8	32	22	3	0	1	53	1	0	9.2	22.1
Florial, Estevan	L-R	6-1	195	11-25-97	.284	.380	.565	101	482	409	83	116	23	4	28	79	66	1	0	6	144	25	10	13.7	29.9
Gasper, Mickey	B-R	5-9	205	10-11-95	.191	.295	.265	22	78	68	7	13	2	0	1	4	8	2	0	0	16	2	0	10.3	20.5
Godoy, Jose	L-R	5-11	200	10-13-94	.270	.341	.514	11	41	37	6	10	0	0	3	7	4	0	0	0	8	1	1	9.8	19.5
2-team (25 Norfolk)					.267	.356	.397	36	132	116	19	31	3	0	4	14	15	1	0	0	22	2	1	11.4	16.7
Hermosillo, Michael	R-R	5-10	205	1-17-95	.222	.299	.435	66	234	207	29	46	5	0	13	35	15	9	0	3	55	8	2	6.4	23.5
Lamb, Jake	L-R	6-3	215	10-09-90	.269	.396	.427	51	207	171	27	46	9	0	6	26	32	4	0	0	41	0	0	15.5	19.8
Lockridge, Brandon	R-R	5-11	185	3-14-97	.288	.370	.364	59	211	184	28	53	9	1	1	12	22	2	3	0	52	23	3	10.4	24.6
McKinney, Billy	L-L	5-11	205	8-23-94	.274	.388	.511	40	160	135	20	37	5	0	9	25	22	3	0	0	32	3	1	13.8	20.0
Medina, Nelson	R-R	6-2	175	9-14-00	.156	.191	.200	12	47	45	5	7	0	1	0	2	2	0	0	0	15	2	1	4.3	31.9
Narvaez, Carlos	R-R	5-11	190	11-26-98	.240	.373	.387	84	359	292	41	70	13	0	10	39	57	7	0	3	91	5	1	15.9	25.3
Palensky, Aaron	R-R	5-10	190	9-22-98	.167	.375	.400	9	40	30	6	5	1	0	2	6	8	2	0	0	13	2	2	20.0	32.5
Peraza, Oswald	R-R	6-0	200	6-15-00	.268	.357	.479	63	300	261	48	70	9	2	14	36	29	8	0	2	55	16	4	9.7	18.3
Pereira, Everson	R-R	5-11	191	4-10-01	.312	.386	.551	35	158	138	29	43	7	1	8	33	13	5	0	2	44	4	0	8.2	27.8
Rortvedt, Ben	L-R	5-9	191	9-25-97	.286	.395	.505	29	124	105	19	30	5	0	6	22	16	3	0	0	31	2	0	12.9	25.0
Wells, Austin	L-R	6-0	220	7-12-99	.254	.349	.452	33	146	126	16	32	10	0	5	20	16	3	0	1	34	2	1	11.0	23.3
Westbrook, Jamie	R-R	5-7	193	6-18-95	.294	.400	.496	117	496	411	70	121	20	0	21	65	67	7	0	2	81	6	4	13.5	16.3

Pitching	B-T	Ht.	Wt.	DOB	W	L	ERA	G	GS	SV	IP	Hits	Runs	ER	HR	BB	SO	AVG	OBP	SLG	SO%	BB%	BF
Aguilar, Clay	L-L	6-1	210	3-26-99	1	1	14.29	4	0	0	6	7	12	9	1	4	6	.292	.514	.500	17.1	11.4	35
Barclay, Edgar	L-L	5-10	200	5-25-98	1	3	5.89	10	10	0	44	44	32	29	11	33	49	.253	.376	.483	23.3	15.7	210
Bastidas, Jesus	R-R	5-8	145	9-14-98	0	0	0.00	2	0	0	2	0	0	0	0	0	0	.000	.000	.000	0.0	0.0	5
Beeter, Clayton	R-R	6-2	220	10-09-98	3	5	4.94	15	14	0	71	61	40	39	15	44	89	.227	.339	.461	28.1	13.9	317
Bowman, Matt	R-R	6-0	185	5-31-91	4	1	3.99	49	0	5	59	51	30	26	5	30	58	.232	.328	.368	22.6	11.7	257

Boyle, Sean	R-R	6-1	205	10-29-96	2	3	6.69	9	9	0	35	44	29	26	7	12	36	.301	.389	.541	21.4	7.1	168
Brewer, Colten	R-R	6-4	222	10-29-92	0	0	1.35	15	2	0	20	8	4	3	2	6	23	.116	.208	.203	29.9	7.8	77
Brito, Jhony	R-R	6-2	210	2-17-98	2	2	5.45	7	7	0	36	40	23	22	8	16	33	.270	.345	.466	20.0	9.7	165
Castano, Blas	R-R	5-10	162	9-08-98	0	0	0.00	2	0	0	4	2	0	0	0	0	3	.154	.267	.154	20.0	0.0	15
Difo, Wilmer	B-R	5-10	200	4-02-92	1	0	1.93	5	0	0	5	1	2	1	0	1	2	.071	.118	.143	11.8	5.9	17
Feliz, Michael	R-R	6-4	250	6-28-93	0	0	3.38	13	0	1	13	8	5	5	2	5	15	.167	.259	.313	27.8	9.3	54
Garcia, Deivi	R-R	5-9	163	5-19-99	3	2	5.67	28	1	0	46	49	31	29	9	32	45	.272	.381	.500	20.5	14.6	219
Gomez, Michael	R-R	6-3	210	8-15-96	2	6	5.45	47	0	1	68	65	50	41	7	43	61	.257	.385	.379	19.5	13.7	313
Greene, Zach	R-R	6-1	215	8-29-96	2	1	5.46	21	3	2	28	24	17	17	3	21	24	.233	.370	.417	18.9	16.5	127
Houston, Zac	R-R	6-5	260	11-30-94	3	1	4.67	21	2	0	27	21	18	14	4	17	46	.204	.344	.379	36.8	13.6	125
Howard, Spencer	R-R	6-3	210	7-28-96	0	1	16.88	3	0	0	3	7	6	5	1	0	4	.500	.500	.714	25.0	0.0	16
Kahnle, Tommy	R-R	6-1	230	8-07-89	0	0	0.00	2	0	0	2	1	0	0	0	1	3	.143	.250	.286	37.5	12.5	8
Krook, Matt	L-L	6-4	225	10-21-94	1	1	1.32	27	0	0	34	10	8	5	0	26	55	.090	.271	.108	39.0	18.4	141
Liranzo, Jesus	R-R	6-2	225	3-07-95	0	1	1.29	6	0	1	7	4	3	1	0	7	8	.148	.324	.222	23.5	20.6	34
Loaisiga, Jonathan	R-R	5-11	165	11-02-94	0	0	9.00	2	0	0	2	4	2	2	0	0	3	.400	.400	.500	30.0	0.0	10
Loseke, Barrett	R-R	6-0	170	11-12-96	0	0	2.45	14	0	0	22	15	7	6	4	11	24	.195	.295	.429	27.3	12.5	88
Maciejewski, Josh	R-L	6-3	175	8-14-95	4	1	3.42	16	0	0	24	22	11	9	2	12	18	.244	.358	.367	16.8	11.2	107
Marinaccio, Ron	R-R	6-2	205	7-01-95	0	1	8.80	14	0	1	15	12	16	15	2	18	13	.218	.421	.382	16.9	23.4	77
McAllister, Zach	R-R	6-6	240	12-08-87	1	1	1.62	11	3	0	17	6	3	3	2	4	20	.109	.183	.218	33.3	6.7	60
McGarity, Aaron	R-R	6-3	185	1-31-95	6	4	5.17	51	1	4	70	60	43	40	13	27	72	.229	.322	.431	23.9	9.0	301
Misiewicz, Anthony	R-L	6-1	196	11-01-94	3	1	3.91	19	1	1	25	20	12	11	5	12	30	.215	.302	.430	28.3	11.3	106
Montas, Frankie	R-R	6-2	255	3-21-93	0	0	3.00	2	2	0	3	2	1	1	0	1	4	.182	.250	.273	33.3	8.3	12
Myatt, Tanner	R-R	6-7	220	5-21-98	1	0	0.00	1	0	0	1	1	0	0	0	2	3	.200	.500	.400	37.5	25.0	8
Norwood, James	R-R	6-2	215	12-24-93	0	3	6.56	22	0	2	23	28	21	17	7	17	36	.283	.385	.596	30.8	14.5	117
Ramirez, Nick	L-L	6-4	232	8-01-89	1	0	3.22	18	1	3	22	16	8	8	2	5	21	.200	.247	.313	24.7	5.9	85
Semple, Shawn	R-R	6-1	220	10-09-95	0	2	10.13	3	0	0	3	5	5	3	0	4	1	.417	.588	.583	5.9	23.5	17
Severino, Luis	R-R	6-2	218	2-20-94	0	0	2.70	1	1	0	3	2	1	1	1	1	3	.182	.250	.455	25.0	8.3	12
Snelten, D.J.	L-L	6-6	240	5-29-92	1	3	7.50	30	0	2	36	32	34	30	6	42	48	.242	.430	.439	26.8	23.5	179
Spence, Mitch	R-R	6-1	185	5-06-98	8	8	4.47	29	29	0	163	162	89	81	30	53	153	.254	.317	.440	21.8	7.5	703
Tully, Tanner	L-L	6-2	205	11-30-94	5	5	5.64	19	19	0	91	121	63	57	14	26	77	.318	.365	.526	18.6	6.3	413
Vasquez, Randy	R-R	6-0	165	11-03-98	3	8	4.59	17	17	0	80	78	45	41	10	40	96	.257	.358	.419	26.9	11.2	357
Warren, Will	R-R	6-2	175	6-16-99	7	4	3.61	21	19	0	100	83	50	40	15	47	110	.223	.315	.386	25.6	10.9	430
Weber, Ryan	R-R	6-1	175	8-12-90	3	3	5.77	7	7	0	34	42	22	22	6	6	26	.300	.331	.507	17.6	4.1	148
Weissert, Greg	R-R	6-2	235	2-04-95	5	3	2.90	38	0	10	40	27	18	13	5	17	58	.184	.269	.340	34.3	10.1	169

Fielding

Catcher	PCT	G	PO	A	E	DP	PB
Breaux	1.000	4	53	0	0	1	1
Duran	.989	33	257	14	3	0	3
Gasper	.990	12	92	7	1	0	0
Godoy	1.000	10	93	9	0	0	0
Narvaez	.981	54	491	31	10	1	2
Rortvedt	.983	22	170	8	3	2	3
Wells	.991	22	224	7	2	0	3

First Base	PCT	G	PO	A	E	DP
Bauers	.930	5	33	7	3	3
Breaux	1.000	1	3	0	0	1
Burt	1.000	2	11	0	0	2
Chaparro	.994	60	412	47	3	27
Cordero	.882	3	14	1	2	0
Duran	.975	15	107	10	3	8
Gasper	1.000	7	38	6	0	4
Lamb	.982	24	141	25	3	11
McKinney	.985	23	181	20	3	17
Narvaez	.992	16	107	13	1	13

Second Base	PCT	G	PO	A	E	DP
Bastidas	.986	35	47	89	2	16
Burt	1.000	3	6	9	0	2
Cabrera	1.000	2	3	1	0	0
Difo	.986	35	49	87	2	19
Peraza	1.000	8	17	23	0	4
Westbrook	.969	73	95	189	9	31

Third Base	PCT	G	PO	A	E	DP
Bastidas	.933	8	3	11	1	1
Cabrera	1.000	2	0	2	0	0
Chaparro	.922	70	44	110	13	5
Cowles	1.000	2	1	4	0	0
Difo	.938	14	3	12	1	0
Donaldson	.667	2	0	2	1	0
Lamb	.940	20	14	33	3	4
Peraza	1.000	5	5	5	0	0
Westbrook	.923	35	12	48	5	2

Shortstop	PCT	G	PO	A	E	DP
Bastidas	.963	57	72	135	8	33
Burt	1.000	2	0	4	0	1
Cabrera	.967	6	12	17	1	8
Difo	.956	44	47	83	6	13
Peraza	.949	45	62	88	8	23

Outfield	PCT	G	PO	A	E	DP
Allen	.833	4	5	0	1	0
Bader	1.000	4	7	0	0	0
Battle	1.000	3	2	0	0	0
Bauers	1.000	13	26	0	0	0
Burt	1.000	1	1	0	0	0
Cabrera	1.000	2	2	0	0	0
Calhoun, K	1.000	19	27	2	0	0
Calhoun, W	1.000	4	5	0	0	0
Cordero	.982	59	92	2	3	2
Cowles	.000	1	0	0	0	0
Dominguez	1.000	8	14	1	0	0
Dunham	.975	62	114	4	3	1
Florial	.992	94	189	5	3	3
Hermosillo	.980	61	95	3	3	1
Lockridge	.980	59	124	0	2	0
McKinney	.944	17	23	1	1	0
Medina	.955	12	21	0	1	0
Palensky	1.000	9	19	1	0	1
Pereira	1.000	33	57	0	0	0
Westbrook	1.000	2	4	0	0	0

SOMERSET PATRIOTS

DOUBLE-A

EASTERN LEAGUE

Batting	B-T	Ht.	Wt.	DOB	AVG	OBP	SLG	G	PA	AB	R	H	2B	3B	HR	RBI	BB	HBP	SH	SF	SO	SB	CS	BB%	SO%
Bader, Harrison	R-R	6-0	210	6-03-94	.167	.167	.222	5	18	18	0	3	1	0	0	1	0	0	0	0	5	0	0	0.0	27.8
Bastidas, Jesus	R-R	5-8	145	9-14-98	.228	.380	.439	17	71	57	14	13	3	0	3	7	12	2	0	0	12	1	1	16.9	16.9
Breaux, Josh	R-R	6-1	220	10-07-97	.280	.309	.548	25	97	93	13	26	4	0	7	14	4	0	0	0	24	0	0	4.1	24.7
Burt, Max	R-R	6-1	185	8-28-96	.241	.320	.407	91	347	307	55	74	11	2	12	43	30	7	0	3	95	21	5	8.6	27.4
Calhoun, Willie	L-R	5-8	205	11-04-94	.227	.261	.364	6	23	22	1	5	0	0	1	2	1	0	0	0	2	0	0	4.3	8.7
Crisp, Juan	R-R	6-0	170	5-23-00	.400	.625	.400	3	8	5	2	2	0	0	0	0	3	0	0	0	2	0	0	37.5	25.0
Dominguez, Jasson	B-R	5-9	190	2-07-03	.254	.367	.414	109	507	425	83	108	19	2	15	66	77	1	0	4	130	37	7	15.2	25.6
Donaldson, Josh	R-R	6-1	210	12-08-85	.286	.286	.286	2	7	7	0	2	0	0	0	0	0	0	0	0	0	0	0	0.0	0.0
Dunham, Elijah	L-L	5-11	213	5-29-98	.240	.331	.447	56	251	217	34	52	13	1	10	27	28	3	0	3	64	23	3	11.2	25.5
Durbin, Caleb	R-R	5-6	175	2-22-00	.291	.361	.440	47	194	175	26	51	12	1	4	17	12	7	0	0	9	21	7	6.2	4.6
Gasper, Mickey	B-R	5-9	205	10-11-95	.269	.388	.423	52	188	156	30	42	6	0	6	24	26	5	0	1	27	8	1	13.8	14.4

Hardman, Tyler	R-R	6-2	204	1-27-99	.237	.332	.558	77	331	283	56	67	9	2	26	56	40	3	0	5	110	9	3	12.1	33.2
Jones, Spencer	L-L	6-6	225	5-14-01	.261	.333	.406	17	78	69	9	18	1	0	3	10	7	1	0	1	22	8	3	9.0	28.2
Lockridge, Brandon	R-R	5-11	185	3-14-97	.313	.395	.510	33	114	96	14	30	7	3	2	16	14	1	0	3	22	17	2	12.3	19.3
Narvaez, Carlos	R-R	5-11	190	11-26-98	.235	.350	.451	16	60	51	7	12	5	0	2	5	7	2	0	0	17	1	2	11.7	28.3
Palensky, Aaron	R-R	5-10	190	9-22-98	.183	.327	.383	62	226	180	37	33	10	1	8	28	31	10	0	5	53	11	1	13.7	23.5
Pereira, Everson	R-R	5-11	191	4-10-01	.291	.362	.545	46	185	165	24	48	10	1	10	31	19	0	0	1	54	7	2	10.3	29.2
Perez, Delvin	R-R	6-1	175	11-24-98	.169	.296	.305	19	71	59	10	10	2	0	2	5	9	2	0	1	27	9	1	12.7	38.0
Pita, Matt	R-R	5-8	175	4-21-97	.207	.314	.310	9	35	29	5	6	0	0	1	6	3	2	0	1	7	0	1	8.6	20.0
Ramirez, Agustin	R-R	6-0	210	9-10-01	.211	.273	.313	31	139	128	17	27	7	0	2	11	10	1	0	0	27	3	0	7.2	19.4
Rice, Ben	L-R	6-1	205	2-22-99	.327	.401	.648	48	222	196	40	64	13	1	16	48	21	4	0	1	42	7	3	9.5	18.9
Richardson, Grant	L-L	6-0	210	7-13-99	.340	.426	.642	15	61	53	10	18	1	0	5	11	6	2	0	0	19	5	1	9.8	31.1
Rortvedt, Ben	L-R	5-9	191	9-25-97	.333	.500	.667	1	4	3	1	1	1	0	0	1	0	1	0	0	0	0	0	0.0	0.0
Rosario, Jeisson	L-L	5-11	191	10-22-99	.218	.360	.355	106	429	344	50	75	17	0	10	47	78	1	1	5	127	11	5	18.2	29.6
Rumfield, T.J.	L-R	6-4	225	5-17-00	.219	.320	.438	82	350	297	43	65	14	0	17	55	39	8	0	6	75	8	3	11.1	21.4
Seigler, Anthony	B-S	5-9	200	6-20-99	.166	.333	.263	67	264	205	33	34	5	0	5	27	53	1	0	5	48	7	5	20.1	18.2
Stanton, Giancarlo	R-R	6-6	245	11-08-89	.000	.250	.000	1	4	3	0	0	0	0	0	0	1	0	0	0	0	0	0	25.0	0.0
Sweeney, Trey	L-R	6-2	200	4-24-00	.252	.367	.411	100	472	397	67	100	20	2	13	49	65	8	0	2	90	20	7	13.8	19.1
Torrealba, Eduardo	R-R	5-8	140	3-26-99	.205	.277	.265	44	151	132	20	27	5	0	1	20	13	1	3	2	29	4	1	8.6	19.2
Wagaman, Eric	R-R	6-4	210	8-14-97	.320	.382	.500	35	136	122	20	39	7	0	5	16	12	1	0	1	27	13	3	8.8	19.9
Wells, Austin	L-R	6-0	220	7-12-99	.237	.327	.443	58	263	228	28	54	14	0	11	50	29	3	0	3	60	5	0	11.0	22.8

Pitching	B-T	Ht.	Wt.	DOB	W	L	ERA	G	GS	SV	IP	Hits	Runs	ER	HR	BB	SO	AVG	OBP	SLG	SO%	BB%	BF
Abeyta, Blane	R-R	6-3	185	9-04-98	8	8	5.67	25	23	0	127	130	83	80	18	51	126	.262	.343	.441	22.3	9.0	565
Anderson, Ryan	L-L	6-6	205	9-09-98	3	1	1.01	19	0	1	27	11	4	3	1	12	27	.125	.245	.182	26.5	11.8	102
Barclay, Edgar	L-L	5-10	200	5-25-98	3	1	1.32	11	0	0	34	26	7	5	1	11	51	.213	.276	.279	37.8	8.1	135
Beeter, Clayton	R-R	6-2	220	10-09-98	6	2	2.08	12	12	0	61	44	14	14	3	31	76	.204	.323	.282	29.7	12.1	256
Castano, Blas	R-R	5-10	162	9-08-98	4	3	4.76	17	5	0	45	37	30	24	4	25	42	.220	.345	.339	21.0	12.5	200
Cohen, Harrison	R-R	6-0	190	5-28-99	0	0	0.00	2	0	1	3	0	0	0	0	2	3	.000	.182	.000	27.3	18.2	11
Cortes, Nestor	R-L	5-11	210	12-10-94	0	0	1.42	2	2	0	6	6	1	1	1	1	9	.250	.280	.417	36.0	4.0	25
Dees, Bailey	R-R	6-8	250	2-05-99	1	1	4.29	16	0	2	21	17	11	10	1	12	18	.218	.337	.321	19.4	12.9	93
Diaz, Indigo	R-R	6-5	250	10-14-98	0	1	3.32	14	0	2	19	19	8	7	0	16	25	.264	.398	.347	28.4	18.2	88
Fenter, Gray	R-R	6-0	200	1-25-96	2	2	5.01	10	10	0	41	37	27	23	6	21	51	.233	.319	.415	28.0	11.5	182
Fitts, Richard	R-R	6-3	215	12-17-99	11	5	3.48	27	27	0	153	131	60	59	22	43	163	.227	.283	.383	25.9	6.8	629
Gasper, Mickey	B-R	5-9	205	10-11-95	0	0	0.00	1	0	0	1	0	0	0	0	1	0	.000	.333	.000	0.0	33.3	3
Giacone, Michael	L-L	6-0	175	10-23-96	1	1	2.21	15	0	0	20	14	7	5	1	11	25	.194	.306	.250	29.4	12.9	85
Gomez, Carlos	R-R	6-1	175	6-14-98	2	1	3.86	7	0	0	14	8	6	6	2	9	17	.160	.311	.320	27.9	14.8	61
Gomez, Yoendrys	R-R	6-3	175	10-15-99	0	3	3.58	19	19	0	65	47	28	26	6	37	78	.200	.310	.328	28.5	13.5	274
Hamilton, Ian	R-R	6-1	200	6-16-95	2	1	3.38	3	0	0	3	1	1	1	0	2	4	.111	.273	.222	33.3	16.7	12
Hampton, Chase	R-R	6-2	225	8-07-01	2	2	4.37	11	11	0	60	54	33	29	8	21	68	.240	.302	.409	27.4	8.5	248
Houston, Zac	R-R	6-5	260	11-30-94	0	1	4.02	16	0	2	16	9	7	7	1	11	27	.161	.365	.250	36.5	14.9	74
Jennings, Steven	R-R	6-2	175	11-13-98	3	2	2.87	20	0	1	31	21	13	10	2	12	40	.184	.273	.281	31.0	9.3	129
Kahnle, Tommy	R-R	6-1	230	8-07-89	0	0	9.00	1	0	0	1	1	1	1	0	2	1	.333	.600	.667	20.0	40.0	5
Liranzo, Jesus	R-R	6-2	225	3-07-95	3	1	7.09	20	0	1	27	29	21	21	4	13	35	.271	.361	.449	28.7	10.7	122
Maciejewski, Josh	R-L	6-3	175	8-14-95	1	2	3.06	11	0	1	18	17	8	6	1	4	24	.230	.278	.338	30.4	5.1	79
Maese, Justin	R-R	6-3	190	10-24-96	2	0	7.04	14	0	0	23	25	18	18	5	14	26	.266	.367	.500	23.9	12.8	109
Mauricio, Alex	R-R	6-0	180	9-24-96	2	2	3.14	36	0	5	49	42	18	17	5	19	45	.233	.312	.383	22.0	9.3	205
Messinger, Zach	R-R	6-6	225	10-04-99	0	0	4.15	1	1	0	4	4	2	2	1	1	7	.235	.316	.529	36.8	5.3	19
Munoz, Anderson	R-R	5-8	158	8-04-98	0	1	6.75	4	0	0	4	3	5	3	1	4	1	.214	.389	.643	5.6	22.2	18
Myatt, Tanner	R-R	6-7	220	5-21-98	3	1	2.84	43	0	7	57	31	21	18	4	38	69	.159	.301	.241	28.9	15.9	239
Neely, Jack	R-R	6-8	225	6-05-00	1	2	2.55	11	0	1	18	12	9	5	4	3	26	.182	.217	.364	37.1	4.3	70
Rodon, Carlos	L-L	6-2	255	12-10-92	0	1	1.29	2	2	0	7	2	1	1	0	1	9	.091	.130	.136	39.1	4.3	23
Santos, Lisandro	L-L	6-1	227	7-24-98	2	3	2.65	33	0	0	51	31	25	15	3	34	55	.173	.309	.279	25.2	15.6	218
Sauer, Matt	R-R	6-4	195	1-21-99	6	4	3.42	14	13	0	68	49	27	26	11	29	83	.196	.285	.376	29.5	10.3	281
Semple, Shawn	R-R	6-1	220	10-09-95	2	0	3.24	5	0	0	8	9	4	3	0	1	9	.273	.294	.273	26.5	2.9	34
Severino, Luis	R-R	6-2	218	2-20-94	0	0	5.40	1	1	0	3	6	2	2	0	1	3	.400	.412	.600	17.6	5.9	17
Thorpe, Drew	L-R	6-4	190	10-01-00	4	0	1.48	5	5	0	30	15	5	5	3	5	44	.144	.183	.288	40.0	4.5	110
Warren, Will	R-R	6-2	175	6-16-99	3	0	2.45	6	6	0	29	26	10	8	0	12	39	.239	.314	.284	32.2	9.9	121
Watson, Danny	R-R	6-7	235	10-06-00	4	0	1.64	30	0	5	38	18	8	7	5	16	43	.137	.245	.282	28.5	10.6	151
Wilson, Justin	R-R	6-0	180	9-09-96	3	1	3.86	23	0	2	28	22	13	12	3	18	28	.222	.366	.364	22.8	14.6	123

Fielding

Catcher	PCT	G	PO	A	E	DP	PB
Breaux	1.000	8	83	2	0	0	1
Crisp	1.000	3	18	1	0	0	0
Gasper	.973	7	68	4	2	0	3
Narvaez	.985	12	123	8	2	0	1
Ramirez	.990	18	195	5	2	0	2
Rice	.984	24	239	10	4	1	1
Seigler	.983	28	274	17	5	3	4
Wells	.979	41	406	13	9	1	2

First Base	PCT	G	PO	A	E	DP
Breaux	1.000	5	29	1	0	2
Dunham	1.000	1	2	0	0	0
Gasper	.975	19	107	9	3	11
Ramirez	.926	4	24	1	2	3
Rice	1.000	15	86	10	0	7
Rumfield	.997	76	548	34	2	45
Wagaman	.988	24	154	12	2	16

Second Base	PCT	G	PO	A	E	DP
Bastidas	1.000	3	8	5	0	0
Burt	.989	48	74	108	2	19
Durbin	.991	31	46	60	1	16
Gasper	1.000	16	22	28	0	4
Palensky	1.000	1	3	2	0	0
Perez	.980	12	24	26	1	8
Pita	1.000	7	9	14	0	3
Seigler	.926	15	16	34	4	6
Torrealba	1.000	12	14	18	0	5

Third Base	PCT	G	PO	A	E	DP
Burt	1.000	21	15	33	0	4
Donaldson	1.000	2	1	0	0	0
Durbin	1.000	9	7	15	0	2
Gasper	.000	1	0	0	0	0
Hardman	.892	75	36	113	18	10
Perez	.842	5	2	14	3	1
Torrealba	.985	27	18	47	1	0
Wagaman	1.000	2	1	1	0	0

Shortstop	PCT	G	PO	A	E	DP
Bastidas	1.000	14	20	30	0	8
Burt	1.000	20	13	36	0	7
Durbin	.933	3	6	8	1	1

Perez	.750	1	2	1	1	0
Sweeney	.966	98	95	220	11	41
Torrealba	1.000	4	5	13	0	1

Outfield	PCT	G	PO	A	E	DP
Bader	1.000	5	13	0	0	0
Burt	1.000	1	1	0	0	0
Calhoun	1.000	3	2	0	0	0
Dominguez	.985	101	195	4	3	0
Dunham	1.000	56	110	1	0	0
Jones	.975	15	37	2	1	0
Lockridge	.978	29	62	0	2	0
Palensky	1.000	58	90	1	0	1
Pereira	1.000	42	71	2	0	1
Pita	1.000	2	5	0	0	0
Richardson	1.000	13	25	1	0	0
Rosario	.997	101	165	8	1	3
Seigler	1.000	1	1	0	0	0
Wagaman	1.000	2	1	0	0	0

HUDSON VALLEY RENEGADES

HIGH CLASS A

SOUTH ATLANTIC LEAGUE

Batting	B-T	Ht.	Wt.	DOB	AVG	OBP	SLG	G	PA	AB	R	H	2B	3B	HR	RBI	BB	HBP	SH	SF	SO	SB	CS	BB%	SO%
Battle, Kyle	R-R	6-0	190	12-04-97	.088	.244	.176	15	41	34	6	3	0	0	1	1	6	1	0	0	14	2	0	14.6	34.1
Breaux, Josh	R-R	6-1	220	10-07-97	.204	.271	.278	13	59	54	6	11	1	0	1	3	5	0	0	0	15	0	0	8.5	25.4
Cabrera, Marcos	R-R	6-3	189	10-10-01	.212	.288	.354	65	250	226	22	48	10	2	6	25	23	1	0	0	82	5	2	9.2	32.8
Cowles, Benjamin	R-R	6-0	180	2-15-00	.254	.356	.393	106	444	374	62	95	18	2	10	41	55	8	0	7	122	23	4	12.4	27.5
Crisp, Juan	R-R	6-0	170	5-23-00	.100	.250	.400	6	12	10	1	1	0	0	1	2	2	0	0	0	2	0	0	16.7	16.7
Durbin, Caleb	R-R	5-6	175	2-22-00	.333	.464	.397	22	97	78	20	26	5	0	0	8	14	5	0	0	9	15	1	14.4	9.3
Familia, Christopher	L-L	5-11	170	6-10-00	.264	.332	.472	47	199	178	33	47	4	0	11	32	17	2	0	2	44	0	0	8.5	22.1
Flores, Rafael	R-R	6-4	220	11-07-00	.259	.346	.366	105	434	382	49	99	15	1	8	41	49	2	0	1	108	3	1	11.3	24.9
Gabrielson, Cole	R-R	6-0	185	7-05-00	.265	.359	.412	10	39	34	4	9	2	0	1	5	2	3	0	0	12	1	2	5.1	30.8
Garcia, Anthony	B-R	6-6	204	9-05-00	.191	.312	.350	52	218	183	35	35	6	1	7	26	33	0	0	2	81	4	2	15.1	37.2
Gomez, Antonio	R-R	6-2	210	11-13-01	.236	.291	.326	86	354	322	34	76	18	1	3	33	21	5	0	3	112	1	1	5.9	31.6
Hall, Anthony	L-L	6-1	200	2-09-01	.194	.282	.296	24	111	98	11	19	5	1	1	10	12	0	0	0	28	2	0	10.8	25.2
Henson, Spencer	R-R	6-0	235	11-03-97	.252	.327	.453	82	339	298	50	75	18	0	14	48	26	10	0	5	88	1	2	7.7	26.0
Jones, Spencer	L-L	6-6	225	5-14-01	.268	.337	.450	100	459	411	62	110	28	4	13	56	42	2	0	2	133	35	9	9.2	29.0
Palensky, Aaron	R-R	5-10	190	9-22-98	.352	.434	.744	32	143	125	29	44	9	2	12	34	15	3	0	0	34	10	0	10.5	23.8
Ramirez, Agustin	R-R	6-0	210	9-10-01	.384	.430	.714	27	121	112	21	43	10	0	9	23	8	1	0	0	17	2	0	6.6	14.0
Rice, Ben	L-R	6-1	205	2-22-99	.341	.559	.523	15	68	44	15	15	2	0	2	10	18	5	0	1	10	3	0	26.5	14.7
Richardson, Grant	L-L	6-0	210	7-13-99	.204	.306	.389	77	304	265	36	54	6	2	13	37	34	5	0	0	95	14	2	11.2	31.3
Rodriguez, Jesus	R-R	5-9	182	4-23-02	.356	.464	.533	25	112	90	13	32	5	1	3	20	17	3	0	2	18	6	1	15.2	16.1
Rumfield, T.J.	L-R	6-4	225	5-17-00	.286	.313	.429	4	16	14	2	4	2	0	0	3	1	0	0	1	2	0	0	6.3	12.5
Sanchez, Aldenis	R-R	6-0	165	9-26-98	.225	.300	.352	69	269	236	30	53	10	4	4	32	25	2	0	4	72	14	7	9.3	26.8
Santos, Luis	R-R	5-6	160	1-04-00	.223	.353	.313	42	136	112	14	25	3	2	1	10	21	2	0	1	33	10	4	15.4	24.3
Serna, Jared	R-R	5-6	168	6-01-02	.287	.350	.389	27	120	108	18	31	7	2	0	8	9	2	0	1	15	10	2	7.5	12.5
Torrealba, Eduardo	R-R	5-8	140	3-26-99	.281	.379	.344	42	153	128	17	36	5	0	1	18	18	4	0	3	19	7	1	11.8	12.4
Vargas, Alexander	B-R	5-10	148	10-29-01	.206	.248	.342	103	447	418	56	86	18	6	9	53	24	1	0	4	116	16	6	5.4	26.0
Wegner, Jared	R-R	6-0	220	7-25-99	.254	.343	.424	19	67	59	7	15	4	0	2	6	8	0	0	0	20	1	1	11.9	29.9

Pitching	B-T	Ht.	Wt.	DOB	W	L	ERA	G	GS	SV	IP	Hits	Runs	ER	HR	BB	SO	AVG	OBP	SLG	SO%	BB%	BF
Aguilar, Clay	L-L	6-1	210	3-26-99	3	3	2.25	32	1	2	44	29	13	11	2	24	63	.187	.304	.297	34.1	13.0	185
Anderson, Ryan	L-L	6-6	205	9-09-98	1	3	3.16	18	0	1	31	27	15	11	1	4	37	.233	.278	.310	29.1	3.1	127
Ayers, Cole	R-R	6-3	185	8-17-99	0	1	2.50	11	0	1	18	11	6	5	2	6	22	.180	.261	.344	31.9	8.7	69
Beck, Brendan	R-R	6-2	205	10-06-98	0	1	1.74	9	9	0	31	24	6	6	2	7	35	.214	.267	.339	29.2	5.8	120
Calderon, Yorlin	R-R	6-3	155	8-17-01	0	0	3.38	2	2	0	8	6	4	3	0	3	7	.200	.306	.267	18.9	8.1	37
Carela, Juan	R-R	6-3	186	12-15-01	2	4	3.67	17	16	0	83	65	40	34	7	32	109	.214	.305	.355	31.1	9.1	351
Cohen, Harrison	R-R	6-0	190	5-28-99	3	3	3.86	32	0	1	47	38	22	20	5	24	60	.215	.319	.373	29.1	11.7	206
Cortijo, Harold	R-R	6-2	180	9-29-98	4	1	3.20	12	0	0	20	17	7	7	2	11	25	.230	.345	.351	28.7	12.6	87
Crisp, Juan	R-R	6-0	170	5-23-00	0	1	0.00	1	0	0	1	0	1	0	0	0	0	.000	.250	.000	0.0	0.0	4
Dees, Bailey	R-R	6-8	250	2-05-99	1	1	1.74	26	0	4	41	20	9	8	2	15	59	.143	.248	.200	36.6	9.3	161
Diaz, Indigo	R-R	6-5	250	10-14-98	1	0	5.68	9	0	1	13	12	9	8	4	5	18	.240	.321	.480	32.1	8.9	56
Gomez, Carlos	R-R	6-1	175	6-14-98	3	3	5.33	35	0	2	49	47	32	29	5	31	64	.249	.366	.397	28.6	13.8	224
Gray, Shane	R-R	6-3	215	4-18-00	2	1	7.43	16	0	0	23	29	23	19	5	8	23	.299	.346	.557	21.3	7.4	108
Hampton, Chase	R-R	6-2	225	8-07-01	2	1	2.68	9	9	0	47	31	18	14	5	16	77	.179	.247	.318	40.5	8.4	190
Hermann, Sean	R-R	6-0	160	6-13-03	1	0	1.80	1	1	0	5	6	1	1	0	1	5	.300	.318	.300	22.7	4.5	22
Holloway, Trevor	R-R	6-2	200	6-22-97	0	1	0.00	1	0	0	1	0	1	0	0	0	0	.000	.000	.000	0.0	0.0	4
Lange, Justin	R-R	6-4	220	9-11-01	1	1	5.68	3	3	0	13	12	8	8	0	8	16	.240	.339	.340	27.1	13.6	59
Maciejewski, Josh	R-L	6-3	175	8-14-95	1	0	0.00	3	0	0	4	1	0	0	0	1	4	.071	.133	.071	26.7	6.7	15
Messinger, Zach	R-R	6-6	225	10-04-99	1	10	4.36	21	20	0	97	82	59	47	13	53	113	.225	.335	.409	26.5	12.4	427
Munoz, Anderson	R-R	5-8	158	8-04-98	1	0	0.71	7	0	0	13	2	1	1	0	2	18	.049	.133	.098	40.0	4.4	45
Neely, Jack	R-R	6-8	225	6-05-00	5	3	2.03	31	0	6	49	27	15	11	4	17	74	.160	.243	.272	39.2	9.0	189
Paciorek, Nick	R-R	6-2	195	6-01-98	4	1	2.63	20	0	3	24	16	8	7	1	12	29	.190	.313	.274	29.3	12.1	99
Pestana, Leonardo	R-R	6-4	198	7-30-98	0	0	4.15	5	4	0	13	10	6	6	3	4	16	.217	.294	.478	31.4	7.8	51
Rodon, Carlos	L-L	6-2	255	12-10-92	0	0	0.00	1	1	0	4	1	0	0	0	2	8	.077	.200	.154	53.3	13.3	15
Rodriguez, Osiel	R-R	6-2	210	11-22-01	0	0	0.00	1	0	0	2	3	2	0	0	0	4	.300	.300	.300	40.0	0.0	10
Santana, Enrique	R-R	5-11	190	9-23-97	1	0	8.36	11	0	0	14	14	14	13	3	13	15	.259	.420	.481	21.7	18.8	69
Santos, Luis	R-R	5-6	160	1-04-00	0	0	0.00	2	0	0	2	2	0	0	0	0	0	.250	.250	.250	0.0	0.0	8
Sauer, Matt	R-R	6-4	195	1-21-99	0	0	0.00	1	1	0	2	0	0	0	0	3	5	.000	.333	.000	55.6	33.3	9
Schlittler, Cam	R-R	6-6	210	2-05-01	1	0	4.76	2	2	0	6	9	3	3	0	1	6	.346	.393	.385	21.4	3.6	28
Selvidge, Brock	R-L	6-3	205	8-28-02	4	1	3.58	9	9	0	50	44	22	20	2	14	46	.226	.275	.313	21.7	6.6	212
Stuart, Baron	R-R	6-4	209	7-24-99	2	4	5.26	7	7	0	38	31	22	22	5	20	28	.225	.333	.377	17.2	12.3	163
Thorpe, Drew	L-R	6-4	190	10-01-00	10	2	2.81	18	18	0	109	84	38	34	10	33	138	.215	.275	.346	32.4	7.7	426
Valdez, Joel	L-L	6-4	171	4-28-00	3	7	6.06	25	13	1	79	68	57	53	10	55	81	.235	.387	.388	22.3	15.1	364
Velasquez, Luis	R-R	5-10	155	7-01-01	3	2	2.23	21	0	2	36	21	9	9	2	18	44	.162	.268	.238	29.5	12.1	149
Vinyard, Mason	R-R	6-2	210	6-22-99	2	0	2.97	24	0	1	36	26	13	12	2	19	42	.202	.307	.302	27.8	12.6	151

Pitching	B-T	Ht.	Wt.	DOB	W	L	ERA	G	GS	SV	IP	Hits	Runs	ER	HR	BB	SO	AVG	OBP	SLG	SO%	BB%	BF
Watson, Danny	R-R	6-7	235	10-06-00	3	1	1.48	15	0	0	24	12	6	4	1	9	39	.140	.260	.209	39.0	9.0	100
Yulie, Tyrone	R-R	6-4	180	8-04-01	5	6	4.56	16	16	0	79	60	50	40	13	43	90	.204	.318	.395	25.9	12.4	347

Fielding

Catcher	PCT	G	PO	A	E	DP	PB
Breaux	1.000	6	53	3	0	1	0
Crisp	1.000	4	39	2	0	0	2
Flores	.995	33	354	20	2	1	5
Gomez	.980	60	625	54	14	5	15
Ramirez	.982	16	158	10	3	0	3
Rice	.978	7	88	1	2	0	0
Rodriguez	.960	9	89	7	4	0	2

First Base	PCT	G	PO	A	E	DP
Flores	.998	57	371	31	1	26
Henson	.986	71	469	37	7	37
Rice	1.000	3	12	4	0	1
Rodriguez	1.000	3	21	0	0	3
Rumfield	1.000	2	14	0	0	0

Second Base	PCT	G	PO	A	E	DP
Cowles	.979	46	78	107	4	28
Durbin	.981	16	21	32	1	6
Santos	1.000	34	55	70	0	15
Serna	1.000	13	16	28	0	5
Torrealba	1.000	15	14	28	0	1
Vargas	.969	9	11	20	1	2

Third Base	PCT	G	PO	A	E	DP
Cabrera	.872	64	48	88	20	7
Cowles	.897	31	20	50	8	3
Durbin	.952	6	6	14	1	0
Rodriguez	.800	7	3	13	4	1
Santos	.000	1	0	0	0	0
Torrealba	.971	26	20	46	2	6

Shortstop	PCT	G	PO	A	E	DP
Cowles	.990	30	36	63	1	11
Santos	1.000	2	1	1	0	1
Serna	.963	14	19	33	2	3
Vargas	.948	88	98	178	15	35

Outfield	PCT	G	PO	A	E	DP
Battle	1.000	13	15	0	0	0
Familia	.989	33	52	0	1	0
Gabrielson	1.000	10	24	0	0	0
Garcia	.990	45	70	2	1	2
Hall	1.000	20	24	1	0	0
Jones	.979	86	184	4	4	3
Palensky	1.000	32	42	3	0	2
Richardson	.972	72	113	4	4	1
Rodriguez	.889	5	8	0	1	0
Sanchez	.980	69	108	4	3	2
Wegner	1.000	17	33	3	0	0

TAMPA TARPONS — *LOW CLASS A*

FLORIDA STATE LEAGUE

Batting	B-T	Ht.	Wt.	DOB	AVG	OBP	SLG	G	PA	AB	R	H	2B	3B	HR	RBI	BB	HBP	SH	SF	SO	SB	CS	BB%	SO%
Aguilar, Tayler	L-L	5-10	205	8-15-00	.162	.291	.304	75	302	253	31	41	13	1	7	29	41	6	0	2	108	8	2	13.6	35.8
Allen, Greg	B-R	6-0	185	3-15-93	.500	.571	.500	2	7	6	4	3	0	0	0	0	1	0	0	0	1	2	0	14.3	14.3
Arias, Daury	L-L	5-11	172	8-07-01	.217	.335	.318	103	418	355	52	77	14	2	6	38	58	5	0	0	86	11	1	13.9	20.6
Barrera, Brett	R-R	6-0	217	5-07-01	.151	.227	.189	32	119	106	8	16	2	1	0	10	7	4	0	2	18	1	0	5.9	15.1
Brewer, Beau	R-R	6-1	215	10-28-01	.280	.410	.293	50	195	157	24	44	2	0	0	17	35	1	0	2	12	3	1	17.9	6.2
Castillo, Jackson	L-L	6-0	195	5-02-03	.184	.279	.263	10	43	38	4	7	0	0	1	6	5	0	0	0	16	1	0	11.6	37.2
Chirinos, Roberto	R-R	5-10	172	9-08-00	.240	.321	.280	9	28	25	3	6	1	0	0	1	3	0	0	0	6	1	1	10.7	21.4
Colmenares, Jose	R-R	5-11	173	4-03-02	.244	.410	.564	26	100	78	21	19	4	0	7	19	20	2	0	0	25	2	1	20.0	25.0
Escanio, Brenny	B-R	5-9	145	12-16-02	.224	.335	.296	108	476	398	57	89	10	5	3	36	68	2	0	7	119	21	6	14.3	25.0
Familia, Christopher	L-L	5-11	170	6-10-00	.398	.474	.928	21	95	83	24	33	7	2	11	31	8	4	0	0	17	0	1	8.4	17.9
Gabrielson, Cole	R-R	6-0	185	7-05-00	.176	.250	.275	13	56	51	6	9	3	1	0	7	4	1	0	0	18	2	0	7.1	32.1
Hall, Anthony	L-L	6-1	200	2-09-01	.269	.382	.449	60	272	227	43	61	10	2	9	37	40	3	0	2	61	3	4	14.7	22.4
Jasso, Dylan	R-R	6-3	196	11-30-02	.071	.188	.143	4	16	14	0	1	1	0	0	1	2	0	0	0	1	0	0	12.5	6.3
Lombard, George	R-R	6-3	190	6-02-05	.273	.415	.303	9	41	33	6	9	1	0	0	4	8	0	0	0	10	1	2	19.5	24.4
Martin, Garrett	R-R	6-4	216	6-28-00	.200	.325	.292	18	77	65	5	13	6	0	0	7	8	4	0	0	25	0	0	10.4	32.5
Martinez, Omar	L-R	5-10	192	7-05-01	.251	.367	.445	105	444	371	66	93	16	1	18	71	67	3	0	3	110	8	1	15.1	24.8
Medina, Nelson	R-R	6-2	175	9-14-00	.276	.380	.479	50	192	163	25	45	9	3	6	28	27	1	0	1	58	8	3	14.1	30.2
Mejia, Alan	R-R	6-0	165	7-20-01	.175	.235	.270	17	68	63	4	11	4	1	0	8	5	0	0	0	35	1	2	7.4	51.5
Morales, Coby	L-R	6-3	225	12-05-01	.293	.408	.537	10	49	41	8	12	7	0	1	10	8	0	0	0	15	0	1	16.3	30.6
Moylan, Josh	L-R	6-4	216	7-03-02	.241	.366	.313	24	101	83	14	20	0	0	2	9	16	1	0	1	28	0	0	15.8	27.7
Negueis, Felix	R-R	6-0	200	12-29-00	.104	.281	.172	51	167	134	20	14	3	0	2	11	26	7	0	0	49	3	1	15.6	29.3
Palencia, Manuel	R-R	5-11	175	9-05-02	.314	.368	.314	10	38	35	7	11	0	0	0	4	3	0	0	0	2	0	0	7.9	5.3
Palmer, Jake	L-L	5-9	185	11-19-98	.234	.422	.299	27	102	77	15	18	3	1	0	9	19	6	0	0	6	0	0	18.6	5.9
Perez, Dayro	R-R	5-11	180	1-31-02	.153	.217	.247	22	92	85	7	13	3	1	1	9	6	1	0	0	39	2	1	6.5	42.4
Pita, Matt	R-R	5-8	175	4-21-97	.231	.375	.846	5	16	13	3	3	0	1	2	5	2	1	0	0	3	0	0	12.5	18.8
Ramirez, Agustin	R-R	6-0	210	9-10-01	.245	.384	.397	56	232	184	35	45	7	0	7	35	43	1	0	4	41	7	4	18.5	17.7
Rice, Ben	L-R	6-1	205	2-22-99	.286	.405	.543	10	42	35	7	10	3	0	2	10	5	2	0	0	10	1	0	11.9	23.8
Riggio, Roc	L-R	5-9	180	6-11-02	.193	.395	.228	17	76	57	11	11	2	0	0	9	18	1	0	0	18	3	1	23.7	23.7
Rodriguez, Jesus	R-R	5-9	182	4-23-02	.297	.378	.426	84	348	303	53	90	15	3	6	42	38	3	0	3	52	15	3	10.9	14.9
Rojas, Ronny	B-R	6-0	180	8-23-01	.217	.312	.404	51	186	161	29	35	6	0	8	25	23	0	0	2	62	5	0	12.4	33.3
Romero, Kiko	L-R	5-11	185	9-18-00	.216	.350	.382	27	123	102	15	22	6	1	3	14	20	1	0	0	38	0	0	16.3	30.9
Rortvedt, Ben	L-R	5-9	191	9-25-97	.333	.455	.556	3	11	9	2	3	2	0	0	0	1	1	0	0	1	0	0	9.1	9.1
Salinas, Raimfer	R-R	5-11	175	12-31-00	.000	.000	.000	1	4	4	0	0	0	0	0	1	0	0	0	0	1	0	0	0.0	25.0
Serna, Jared	R-R	5-6	168	6-01-02	.283	.350	.483	95	443	400	72	113	21	1	19	71	40	2	0	1	75	19	6	9.0	16.9
Wegner, Jared	R-R	6-0	220	7-25-99	.250	.250	.333	3	12	12	1	3	1	0	0	2	0	0	0	0	5	0	0	0.0	41.7
Wells, Austin	L-R	6-0	220	7-12-99	.176	.300	.353	5	20	17	2	3	0	0	1	2	3	0	0	0	3	0	0	15.0	15.0

Pitching	B-T	Ht.	Wt.	DOB	W	L	ERA	G	GS	SV	IP	Hits	Runs	ER	HR	BB	SO	AVG	OBP	SLG	SO%	BB%	BF
Arejula, Luis	R-R	6-1	170	2-20-02	1	0	6.30	7	0	1	10	10	8	7	0	6	9	.256	.383	.333	19.1	12.8	47
Ayers, Cole	R-R	6-3	185	8-17-99	2	1	4.08	34	0	4	46	47	25	21	3	17	64	.255	.325	.391	31.1	8.3	206
Bow, Kris	R-R	6-4	225	11-26-00	2	5	10.09	13	5	0	33	39	38	37	3	33	33	.302	.466	.411	19.0	19.0	174
Brian, Will	L-L	5-11	220	4-25-99	0	0	4.26	2	2	0	6	3	3	3	0	10	8	.143	.419	.143	25.8	32.3	31
Bustamante, Alex	R-R	6-3	195	6-22-00	4	0	4.61	41	0	3	57	45	34	29	1	39	65	.220	.389	.322	24.6	14.8	264
Calderon, Yorlin	R-R	6-3	155	8-17-01	6	2	3.07	37	3	1	73	64	28	25	5	23	91	.231	.312	.329	28.7	7.3	317
Cohen, Harrison	R-R	6-0	190	5-28-99	0	0	3.86	2	0	0	2	2	1	1	0	0	4	.222	.222	.222	44.4	0.0	9
Diaz, Yoljeldriz	R-R	5-11	165	7-14-01	0	1	13.50	3	0	0	3	3	4	4	0	5	4	.333	.533	.444	26.7	33.3	15
Fristoe, Jackson	R-R	6-4	210	3-06-01	0	1	3.86	3	3	0	9	5	4	4	0	4	14	.156	.250	.156	37.8	10.8	37
Gabonia, Ocean	R-R	6-1	175	7-31-01	4	0	5.03	36	0	1	54	48	36	30	5	29	49	.240	.345	.390	20.9	12.3	235
Gil, Luis	R-R	6-2	185	6-03-98	0	0	11.25	2	2	0	4	6	5	5	0	3	6	.333	.429	.444	28.6	14.3	21

Gilbert, Geoffrey	L-L	6-0	215	5-03-01	5	3	2.92	38	0	2	49	35	17	16	1	28	58	.202	.309	.283	28.3	13.7	205
Gray, Shane	R-R	6-3	215	4-18-00	2	2	4.26	24	0	0	38	28	21	18	5	15	47	.196	.274	.343	28.7	9.1	164
Harvey, Ryan	R-R	6-3	195	2-08-01	1	2	4.10	7	6	0	26	21	13	12	4	15	19	.219	.327	.365	16.8	13.3	113
Henriquez, Nolberto	R-R	6-4	170	10-16-99	1	1	7.24	10	0	1	14	13	12	11	2	9	5	.265	.419	.469	8.1	14.5	62
Hermann, Sean	R-R	6-0	160	6-13-03	7	6	4.93	22	22	0	108	112	68	59	10	44	86	.272	.357	.408	18.1	9.3	474
Kahnle, Tommy	R-R	6-1	230	8-07-89	0	0	0.00	2	2	0	2	0	0	0	0	0	2	.000	.000	.000	33.3	0.0	6
Keane, Sebastian	R-R	6-3	187	11-02-00	0	2	6.75	2	2	0	5	4	4	4	0	3	8	.211	.400	.263	32.0	12.0	25
Keating, Matt	R-R	6-1	215	12-08-00	5	8	3.58	40	0	2	65	61	32	26	6	37	93	.240	.344	.402	31.5	12.5	295
Lange, Justin	R-R	6-4	220	9-11-01	1	4	4.58	18	18	0	73	50	48	37	8	55	115	.189	.346	.332	34.3	16.4	335
Loaisiga, Jonathan	R-R	5-11	165	11-02-94	1	0	0.00	1	0	0	2	0	0	0	0	0	2	.000	.000	.000	33.3	0.0	6
Merda, Hayden	R-R	6-4	202	3-21-00	3	6	6.21	21	20	0	96	100	74	66	10	57	96	.270	.374	.457	21.8	13.0	440
Morrill, Hueston	R-R	6-0	168	11-27-99	0	1	9.45	5	0	2	7	8	7	7	2	1	6	.286	.310	.607	20.7	3.4	29
Mujica, Pablo	L-L	6-0	180	6-26-01	0	1	3.86	2	1	0	5	5	3	2	0	3	1	.313	.400	.438	4.8	14.3	21
Munoz, Anderson	R-R	5-8	158	8-04-98	0	0	23.14	3	0	0	2	4	7	6	1	6	3	.400	.647	.700	17.6	35.3	17
Pestana, Leonardo	R-R	6-4	198	7-30-98	0	5	6.10	14	14	0	41	44	29	28	7	23	54	.268	.375	.451	28.1	12.0	192
Polimir, Edwar	L-L	5-11	145	11-05-00	0	0	13.50	1	0	0	1	3	3	2	0	4	3	.429	.636	.429	27.3	36.4	11
Ramirez, Manny	R-R	5-11	215	11-21-99	1	0	9.12	24	0	3	26	20	29	26	4	39	35	.217	.482	.391	24.6	27.5	142
Rodriguez, Osiel	R-R	6-2	210	11-22-01	2	0	5.89	13	0	0	18	14	12	12	3	15	23	.212	.376	.424	26.7	17.4	86
Schlittler, Cam	R-R	6-6	210	2-05-01	0	2	5.21	5	5	0	19	23	12	11	3	7	20	.303	.372	.487	23.3	8.1	86
Selvidge, Brock	R-L	6-3	205	8-28-02	4	4	3.38	15	14	0	77	72	34	29	3	21	91	.240	.290	.347	28.0	6.5	325
Semmel, Montana	R-R	6-4	225	1-01-02	4	1	5.31	14	0	0	20	23	16	12	3	5	22	.288	.333	.488	24.4	5.6	90
Stone, Adam	R-R	6-6	220	7-31-01	1	3	7.20	20	0	1	20	24	21	16	2	20	18	.304	.461	.430	17.5	19.4	103
Stuart, Baron	R-R	6-4	209	7-24-99	2	6	4.00	13	11	0	63	60	39	28	7	26	57	.244	.329	.390	20.6	9.4	277
Velasquez, Luis	R-R	5-10	155	7-01-01	0	1	1.05	15	0	0	26	7	5	3	0	15	33	.085	.238	.134	32.7	14.9	101
Vinyard, Mason	R-R	6-2	210	6-22-99	2	1	3.33	14	0	2	24	15	11	9	1	10	32	.183	.277	.305	33.3	10.4	96

Fielding

Catcher	PCT	G	PO	A	E	DP	PB
Martinez	.964	53	487	22	19	1	16
Palencia	.988	10	78	3	1	0	1
Ramirez	.994	46	458	28	3	6	10
Rice	.985	6	61	6	1	1	0
Rodriguez	.971	21	176	26	6	2	5
Rortvedt	1.000	1	2	2	0	0	0
Wells	1.000	3	23	2	0	1	0

First Base	PCT	G	PO	A	E	DP
Brewer	.986	19	133	8	2	14
Jasso	1.000	3	20	0	0	2
Martinez	.989	32	248	10	3	24
Moylan	.994	19	154	11	1	18
Palmer	1.000	4	33	5	0	2
Rodriguez	.957	12	84	4	4	6
Rojas	.988	33	230	13	3	27
Romero	.984	8	53	7	1	7

Second Base	PCT	G	PO	A	E	DP
Barrera	.966	11	10	18	1	4
Brewer	1.000	10	11	26	0	7
Chirinos	1.000	2	1	5	0	1
Colmenares	.985	16	24	43	1	14
Escanio	.950	27	34	79	6	11
Perez	.946	8	11	24	2	4
Riggio	.914	9	11	21	3	3
Rojas	.800	1	1	3	1	0
Serna	.995	47	87	133	1	37

Third Base	PCT	G	PO	A	E	DP
Barrera	.955	12	2	19	1	3
Brewer	.825	20	9	24	7	0
Chirinos	1.000	6	3	10	0	2
Colmenares	1.000	7	6	14	0	3
Escanio	1.000	7	3	9	0	2
Jasso	1.000	1	0	4	0	1
Rodriguez	.919	44	30	83	10	8
Rojas	.853	14	7	22	5	4
Romero	.912	18	10	21	3	3
Serna	.913	5	7	14	2	0

Shortstop	PCT	G	PO	A	E	DP
Chirinos	1.000	1	0	1	0	0
Colmenares	.857	2	2	4	1	0
Escanio	.945	68	98	159	15	42
Lombard	.968	8	8	22	1	6
Perez	.865	11	8	24	5	6
Riggio	.800	3	3	5	2	2
Serna	.940	38	53	89	9	17

Outfield	PCT	G	PO	A	E	DP
Aguilar	1.000	65	83	3	0	3
Allen	.000	2	0	0	0	0
Arias	.970	87	144	2	4	0
Castillo	.667	8	14	0	0	0
Familia	.417	16	14	1	3	0
Gabrielson	.833	12	20	2	1	0
Hall	.958	49	76	3	3	0
Martin	1.000	16	29	1	0	1
Medina	.963	45	95	3	2	0
Mejia	.934	16	27	1	2	1
Morales	1.000	9	19	0	0	0
Negueis	.935	50	69	7	4	1
Palmer	.986	23	39	1	1	0
Pita	1.000	3	2	0	0	0
Rodriguez	1.000	6	11	0	0	0
Salinas	1.000	1	1	0	0	0
Wegner	1.000	3	4	0	0	0

FCL YANKEES

ROOKIE

FLORIDA COMPLEX LEAGUE

Batting	B-T	Ht.	Wt.	DOB	AVG	OBP	SLG	G	PA	AB	R	H	2B	3B	HR	RBI	BB	HBP	SH	SF	SO	SB	CS	BB%	SO%
Arias, Roderick	B-R	6-0	178	9-09-04	.267	.423	.505	27	130	101	32	27	2	2	6	26	27	1	0	1	29	17	6	20.8	22.3
Bonifacio, Mauro	R-R	6-5	252	8-31-01	.200	.368	.267	8	19	15	3	3	1	0	0	2	3	1	0	0	11	0	0	15.8	57.9
Castellano, Enger	R-R	6-0	190	12-02-02	.274	.307	.379	26	101	95	13	26	7	0	1	11	4	1	0	1	23	5	0	4.0	22.8
Castillo, Jackson	L-L	6-0	195	5-02-03	.276	.500	.379	9	42	29	12	8	1	1	0	6	11	2	0	0	10	1	0	26.2	23.8
Cruz, John	L-L	6-3	171	8-29-05	.294	.376	.531	48	202	177	28	52	6	3	10	47	22	2	0	1	44	9	4	10.9	21.8
Delgado, Keiner	B-R	5-7	145	1-05-04	.293	.414	.485	49	239	198	54	58	12	1	8	31	36	5	0	0	31	36	7	15.1	13.0
Duran, Edinson	R-R	5-6	180	7-22-02	.314	.405	.457	32	121	105	24	33	5	2	2	17	9	7	0	0	16	2	0	7.4	13.2
Espino, Kelvin	L-R	6-1	193	12-08-01	.200	.375	.291	20	72	55	7	11	5	0	0	6	16	0	0	1	22	1	0	22.2	30.6
Fleitas, Osmany	R-R	5-9	133	1-07-02	.000	.333	.000	5	3	2	0	0	0	0	0	1	1	0	0	0	0	0	1	33.3	0.0
Gabrielson, Cole	R-R	6-0	185	7-05-00	.333	.500	.867	6	20	15	4	5	0	1	2	5	1	4	0	0	5	0	0	5.0	25.0
Hernandez, Diomedes	R-R	5-11	165	2-06-05	.200	.500	.200	3	8	5	2	1	0	0	0	0	3	0	0	0	0	0	1	37.5	0.0
Jasso, Dylan	R-R	6-3	196	11-30-02	.377	.486	.574	17	74	61	15	23	7	1	1	20	11	2	0	0	5	0	0	14.9	6.8
Lombard, George	R-R	6-3	190	6-02-05	.417	.588	.500	4	17	12	3	5	1	0	0	2	5	0	0	0	2	3	0	29.4	11.8
Mendez, Joel	R-R	6-1	180	1-28-03	.293	.363	.424	29	113	99	15	29	4	3	1	10	11	1	0	2	35	1	0	9.7	31.0
Montero, Hans	R-R	5-9	160	12-25-03	.257	.419	.404	53	234	183	41	47	6	3	5	23	44	7	0	0	48	17	1	18.8	20.5
Montero, Willy	R-R	6-4	202	8-04-04	.331	.389	.436	47	203	181	30	60	9	2	2	43	16	3	0	3	36	5	4	7.9	17.7
Palencia, Manuel	R-R	5-11	175	9-05-02	.271	.354	.314	22	79	70	6	19	3	0	0	6	7	2	0	0	3	0	1	8.9	3.8
Palmer, Jake	L-L	5-9	185	11-19-98	.000	.400	.000	1	5	3	1	0	0	0	0	0	2	0	0	0	1	0	1	40.0	20.0
Perez, Dayro	R-R	5-11	180	1-31-02	.180	.299	.213	28	107	89	15	16	3	0	0	4	12	4	0	2	30	8	2	11.2	28.0
Riggio, Roc	L-R	5-9	180	6-11-02	.188	.381	.188	5	21	16	2	3	0	0	0	0	4	1	0	0	6	0	0	19.0	28.6

Rodriguez, Wilson	L-L	6-1	186	9-10-04	.220	.360	.439	12	50	41	5	9	3	0	2	11	8	1	0	0	13	0	1	16.0	26.0
Rojas, Angel	R-R	5-9	160	11-26-00	—	1.000	—	2	1	0	1	0	0	0	0	0	1	0	0	0	0	0	0	100.0	0.0
Romero, Kiko	L-R	5-11	185	9-18-00	.429	.556	.571	2	9	7	4	3	1	0	0	2	2	0	0	0	3	0	0	22.2	33.3
Sanchez, Edward	R-R	5-11	165	3-28-01	.143	.250	.143	9	16	14	3	2	0	0	0	0	1	1	0	0	4	0	0	6.3	25.0
Sanchez, Juan	L-R	5-11	190	3-21-03	.255	.265	.468	16	49	47	6	12	2	1	2	12	0	1	0	1	8	0	0	0.0	16.3
Serruto, Peter	R-R	6-2	195	3-17-00	.000	.000	.000	1	2	2	0	0	0	0	0	0	0	0	0	0	0	0	0	0.0	0.0
Silverio, Oscar	L-R	5-9	170	10-25-01	.000	.000	.000	1	1	1	0	0	0	0	0	0	0	0	0	0	1	0	0	0.0	100.0
Tejeda, Enmanuel	R-R	5-11	158	12-25-04	.307	.465	.458	50	217	166	37	51	4	3	5	30	44	6	0	1	44	24	6	20.3	20.3
Tiedemann, Josh	R-R	6-2	190	6-09-04	.111	.200	.111	2	10	9	1	1	0	0	0	0	1	0	0	0	3	0	0	10.0	30.0
Wegner, Jared	R-R	6-0	220	7-25-99	.444	.444	1.333	2	9	9	3	4	2	0	2	6	0	0	0	0	0	0	0	0.0	0.0

Pitching	**B-T**	**Ht.**	**Wt.**	**DOB**	**W**	**L**	**ERA**	**G**	**GS**	**SV**	**IP**	**Hits**	**Runs**	**ER**	**HR**	**BB**	**SO**	**AVG**	**OBP**	**SLG**	**SO%**	**BB%**	**BF**
Arejula, Luis	R-R	6-1	170	2-20-02	0	2	2.84	7	0	1	6	7	3	2	0	4	8	.269	.355	.308	25.8	12.9	31
Arias, Chalniel	R-R	6-3	165	9-11-03	0	0	6.23	3	3	0	9	8	6	6	0	8	7	.242	.419	.364	16.3	18.6	43
Beck, Brendan	R-R	6-2	205	10-06-98	0	0	0.00	1	1	0	3	0	0	0	0	0	5	.000	.000	.000	55.6	0.0	9
Bow, Kris	R-R	6-4	225	11-26-00	1	0	2.45	2	0	0	4	1	1	1	0	3	5	.083	.313	.083	31.3	18.8	16
Castellano, Enger	R-R	6-0	190	12-02-02	0	0	0.00	1	0	1	0	1	0	0	0	2	0	.500	.750	1.000	0.0	50.0	4
Diaz, Yoljeldriz	R-R	5-11	165	7-14-01	1	0	0.87	8	0	0	10	5	1	1	0	6	17	.135	.289	.189	37.8	13.3	45
Facundo, Allen	L-L	6-0	171	9-03-02	5	0	2.37	11	2	0	30	20	11	8	0	13	40	.185	.302	.231	31.7	10.3	126
Fleitas, Osmany	R-R	5-9	133	1-07-02	0	0	27.00	2	0	0	2	8	6	6	2	1	1	.533	.563	1.067	6.3	6.3	16
Fristoe, Jackson	R-R	6-4	210	3-06-01	1	3	5.27	10	8	0	27	20	16	16	3	24	31	.206	.379	.320	25.0	19.4	124
Fulgencio, Steven	R-R	6-2	175	10-05-00	1	2	8.04	16	0	1	16	12	18	14	1	14	22	.194	.412	.258	25.6	16.3	86
Garcia, Donys	R-R	6-2	175	2-18-01	2	1	6.75	7	0	0	7	9	8	5	2	7	8	.321	.472	.607	22.2	19.4	36
Greene, Zach	R-R	6-1	215	8-29-96	0	0	5.79	4	1	0	5	5	3	3	2	1	7	.250	.286	.600	33.3	4.8	21
Harvey, Ryan	R-R	6-3	195	2-08-01	0	1	3.72	6	6	0	19	22	9	8	2	7	29	.275	.341	.388	32.6	7.9	89
Henriquez, Nolberto	R-R	6-4	170	10-16-99	0	0	6.35	13	0	0	17	17	18	12	2	6	16	.243	.312	.429	20.8	7.8	77
Keane, Sebastian	R-R	6-3	187	11-02-00	2	0	1.71	18	0	1	26	11	7	5	1	16	35	.126	.296	.195	32.1	14.7	109
Lagrange, Carlos	R-R	6-7	195	5-25-03	0	0	4.97	12	11	0	42	34	25	23	4	24	63	.214	.345	.340	32.5	12.4	194
Lalane, Henry	L-L	6-7	211	5-18-04	1	0	4.57	8	5	0	22	17	12	11	3	4	34	.207	.261	.341	38.6	4.5	88
Luciano, Jordy	R-R	5-10	160	7-22-01	2	4	5.40	12	0	1	25	25	23	15	1	26	29	.245	.405	.343	22.1	19.8	131
Mendoza, Jordarlin	R-R	6-0	175	11-14-03	6	0	4.40	10	0	0	29	16	15	14	2	24	39	.162	.352	.283	30.2	18.6	129
Morrill, Hueston	R-R	6-0	168	11-27-99	1	0	0.00	2	0	0	3	1	1	0	0	1	4	.091	.167	.182	33.3	8.3	12
Mujica, Pablo	L-L	6-0	180	6-26-01	3	4	8.27	10	0	1	21	30	23	19	4	11	15	.326	.415	.500	14.2	10.4	106
Munoz, Anderson	R-R	5-8	158	8-04-98	0	0	6.00	4	0	0	6	5	4	4	0	2	7	.227	.346	.273	26.9	7.7	26
Polimir, Edwar	L-L	5-11	145	11-05-00	4	1	5.19	11	2	0	26	27	16	15	3	18	30	.270	.398	.420	24.4	14.6	123
Pozo, Miguel	L-L	5-11	155	9-09-01	2	1	1.88	13	0	0	24	15	8	5	1	19	26	.176	.340	.224	24.3	17.8	107
Reyzelman, Eric	R-R	6-2	188	6-27-01	1	1	8.22	5	0	1	8	8	7	7	1	3	8	.267	.333	.500	24.2	9.1	33
Rodriguez, Osiel	R-R	6-2	210	11-22-01	0	0	1.59	11	0	1	17	11	3	3	1	5	26	.177	.239	.242	38.8	7.5	67
Rojas, Angel	R-R	5-9	160	11-26-00	0	0	18.00	1	0	0	1	2	2	2	0	1	1	.500	.500	.750	16.7	16.7	6
Sanchez, Edward	R-R	5-11	165	3-28-01	0	0	0.00	1	0	0	1	0	0	0	0	2	0	.000	.400	.000	0.0	40.0	5
Santana, Geralmi	R-R	6-3	173	12-07-00	0	0	33.75	2	0	0	1	4	6	5	0	4	2	.571	.692	.714	15.4	30.8	13
Sauer, Matt	R-R	6-4	195	1-21-99	0	1	4.91	2	2	0	4	2	5	2	1	2	5	.143	.294	.357	29.4	11.8	17
Schlittler, Cam	R-R	6-6	210	2-05-01	0	0	2.95	7	6	0	21	17	10	7	1	13	24	.221	.341	.338	26.4	14.3	91
Semmel, Montana	R-R	6-4	225	1-01-02	0	0	7.50	11	0	1	12	13	10	10	2	7	20	.265	.368	.510	35.1	12.3	57
Serna, Luis	R-R	5-11	162	7-20-04	0	1	4.19	8	8	0	19	17	11	9	2	8	23	.233	.341	.356	27.1	9.4	85

Fielding

C: Duran 32, Palencia 22, Sanchez 6, Hernandez 3, Serruto 1, Silverio 1. **1B:** Castellano 25, Espino 17, Jasso 13, Romero 2. **2B:** Delgado 25, Tejeda 15, Perez 10, Riggio 5, Montero 3, Fleitas 2, Sanchez 1. **3B:** Montero 22, Tejeda 21, Sanchez 5, Jasso 4, Delgado 3, Perez 1, Rojas 1. **SS:** Arias 23, Montero 21, Delgado 11, Lombard 2, Sanchez 1. **OF:** Cruz 47, Montero 46, Mendez 29, Perez 14, Rodriguez 10, Castillo 9, Bonifacio 8, Gabrielson 6, Espino 3, Palmer 2, Wegner 2.

DSL YANKEES — ROOKIE

DOMINICAN SUMMER LEAGUE

Batting	**B-T**	**Ht.**	**Wt.**	**DOB**	**AVG**	**OBP**	**SLG**	**G**	**PA**	**AB**	**R**	**H**	**2B**	**3B**	**HR**	**RBI**	**BB**	**HBP**	**SH**	**SF**	**SO**	**SB**	**CS**	**BB%**	**SO%**
Altagracia, Ramiro	R-R	5-11	180	1-18-04	.273	.353	.406	44	187	165	23	45	6	2	4	19	18	3	0	1	51	8	3	9.6	27.3
Asigen, Niurby	L-L	6-3	180	11-06-04	.186	.346	.267	27	107	86	18	16	4	0	1	8	16	5	0	0	24	1	2	15.0	22.4
Beckles, David	R-R	6-3	215	4-23-04	.267	.451	.400	35	144	105	26	28	8	0	2	22	32	5	0	2	28	4	2	22.2	19.4
Bersing, Gabriel	R-R	6-1	195	10-17-02	.232	.330	.427	25	94	82	16	19	2	1	4	11	12	0	0	0	42	4	0	12.8	44.7
Blanco, Geyber	R-R	5-9	155	6-11-06	.313	.391	.443	37	133	115	21	36	15	0	0	17	9	7	0	2	28	2	1	6.8	21.1
Castillo, Darwin	R-R	5-10	153	2-26-03	.200	.267	.325	16	45	40	7	8	2	0	1	8	1	3	0	1	8	3	2	2.2	17.8
Castro, Jose	R-R	6-2	176	10-04-05	.222	.370	.316	33	146	117	22	26	5	0	2	20	15	13	0	1	49	18	3	10.3	33.6
Coca, Jeison	R-R	5-11	158	11-10-05	.230	.329	.297	22	85	74	12	17	3	1	0	12	11	0	0	0	17	2	0	12.9	20.0
Contreras, Johan	R-R	6-1	218	3-10-05	.200	.389	.260	35	131	100	17	20	6	0	0	16	25	6	0	0	36	1	1	19.1	27.5
Escudero, Luis	B-R	5-8	165	2-09-06	.248	.421	.386	31	133	101	21	25	4	2	2	27	27	4	0	1	25	4	3	20.3	18.8
Ferreira, Johan	R-R	5-11	190	10-05-02	.217	.406	.326	21	64	46	14	10	2	0	1	6	14	2	0	2	24	7	2	21.9	37.5
Frias, Ovandy	R-R	6-0	176	1-12-04	.216	.316	.302	35	133	116	17	25	5	1	1	11	13	4	0	0	62	13	1	9.8	46.6
Gomez, Santiago	R-R	5-11	160	4-05-04	.284	.467	.403	41	184	134	36	38	10	0	2	32	31	17	0	2	33	20	3	16.8	17.9
Gonzalez, Adrian	R-R	6-2	170	3-31-05	.196	.361	.272	32	119	92	18	18	5	1	0	16	19	6	0	2	24	2	2	16.0	20.2
Gonzalez, Josue	R-R	5-9	170	10-30-03	.324	.517	.529	33	147	102	32	33	13	1	2	20	38	5	0	2	21	8	3	25.9	14.3
Herrera, Carlos	R-R	5-10	165	9-01-02	.233	.353	.326	18	51	43	6	10	4	0	0	8	7	1	0	0	15	0	0	13.7	29.4

Imbert, Jhon	R-R	6-1	172	9-01-03	.278	.437	.500	34	142	108	28	30	7	1	5	22	30	2	0	2	40	17	1	21.1	28.2
Javier, Andry	B-R	5-10	160	2-13-04	.299	.465	.429	28	101	77	25	23	5	1	1	17	23	1	0	0	11	10	2	22.8	10.9
Lacruz, Andres	B-R	5-10	158	1-25-05	.245	.430	.333	33	135	102	28	25	4	1	1	18	30	3	0	0	36	19	2	22.2	26.7
Lara, Gabriel	L-L	5-9	165	11-27-05	.267	.401	.411	43	182	146	34	39	7	1	4	29	28	6	0	2	30	18	8	15.4	16.5
Leito, Joshua	R-R	5-10	170	3-20-05	.222	.475	.333	15	40	27	5	6	0	0	1	7	13	0	0	0	8	1	2	32.5	20.0
Martinez, Rafael	R-R	5-10	160	10-23-05	.221	.315	.274	28	111	95	12	21	5	0	0	17	11	3	0	2	23	3	4	9.9	20.7
Matheus, Juan	B-R	5-10	155	4-29-04	.257	.460	.371	10	50	35	13	9	2	1	0	4	14	0	0	1	11	11	3	28.0	22.0
Mayea, Brando	R-R	5-11	175	9-12-05	.276	.382	.400	38	170	145	27	40	7	1	3	18	22	3	0	0	27	22	7	12.9	15.9
Meran, Richard	R-R	6-0	165	6-25-06	.231	.388	.359	13	49	39	8	9	2	0	1	4	8	2	0	0	17	2	3	16.3	34.7
Ogando, Luis	R-R	5-10	175	10-11-03	.352	.446	.541	36	148	122	36	43	11	0	4	28	17	6	0	3	37	13	6	11.5	25.0
Pena, Anthony	R-R	5-10	157	12-27-05	.247	.344	.383	26	93	81	16	20	5	0	2	12	9	3	0	0	34	5	1	9.7	36.6
Perez, Edgleen	R-R	5-10	155	5-25-06	.259	.389	.317	39	175	139	22	36	8	0	0	29	30	2	0	4	31	5	0	17.1	17.7
Pierre, Louis	L-L	6-2	160	9-12-04	.176	.318	.176	6	22	17	1	3	0	0	0	2	4	0	0	1	6	1	0	18.2	27.3
Puello, Luis	R-R	5-11	162	1-22-06	.222	.372	.300	31	113	90	21	20	3	2	0	10	17	5	0	1	28	6	2	15.0	24.8
Ramirez, Abrahan	L-R	5-9	150	10-08-04	.311	.471	.379	35	136	103	36	32	4	0	1	15	31	1	0	1	19	14	3	22.8	14.0
Suarez, Luis	R-R	5-9	143	10-05-04	.212	.333	.342	40	174	146	31	31	5	4	2	25	21	6	0	1	51	22	2	12.1	29.3
Terrero, Gabriel	B-R	5-6	169	9-26-05	.299	.407	.533	37	162	137	33	41	9	1	7	27	22	3	0	0	35	14	6	13.6	21.6
Verde, Kevin	R-R	5-9	160	12-12-05	.258	.316	.433	31	133	120	18	31	9	0	4	26	8	3	0	2	23	8	3	6.0	17.3
Vivas, Edison	R-R	6-0	184	6-03-06	.219	.318	.247	21	85	73	6	16	2	0	0	7	8	3	0	1	23	3	0	9.4	27.1

Pitching	**B-T**	**Ht.**	**Wt.**	**DOB**	**W**	**L**	**ERA**	**G**	**GS**	**SV**	**IP**	**Hits**	**Runs**	**ER**	**HR**	**BB**	**SO**	**AVG**	**OBP**	**SLG**	**SO%**	**BB%**	**BF**
Aguilera, Yedrinson	R-R	5-11	165	9-10-03	0	0	16.88	5	0	0	5	10	11	10	2	4	7	.370	.485	.704	20.6	11.8	34
Alcantara, Stanly	R-R	6-6	187	4-12-04	3	1	3.20	10	1	1	20	16	16	7	0	22	15	.235	.448	.250	15.6	22.9	96
Alejandro, Jerson	R-R	6-6	255	2-23-06	1	4	4.50	10	9	0	36	30	19	18	3	17	36	.224	.325	.328	22.9	10.8	157
Aparicio, Kevin	R-R	6-3	180	1-06-03	1	1	5.19	7	0	0	9	6	6	5	0	6	13	.194	.325	.226	32.5	15.0	40
Arias, Brian	R-R	6-0	177	11-18-03	0	0	3.38	2	2	0	3	3	3	1	0	2	3	.300	.417	.300	25.0	16.7	12
Arias, Chalniel	R-R	6-3	165	9-11-03	1	2	2.37	8	8	0	38	30	17	10	1	9	54	.214	.265	.300	35.3	5.9	153
Bido, Wilfrido	R-R	5-10	170	6-04-04	0	0	7.71	1	1	0	2	0	2	2	0	5	2	.000	.455	.000	18.2	45.5	11
Brinez, Saul	R-R	6-3	170	11-10-04	1	1	11.57	12	0	0	12	15	18	15	0	15	10	.306	.470	.408	15.2	22.7	66
Brito, Dari	R-R	6-1	210	12-15-02	1	0	8.49	9	0	0	12	13	12	11	1	7	11	.325	.423	.525	21.2	13.5	52
Castellanos, Jesus	R-R	5-11	175	1-28-02	2	0	4.50	5	0	0	4	3	2	2	0	3	5	.231	.333	.231	27.8	16.7	18
Chirinos, Michell	R-R	6-2	187	12-09-03	0	1	4.20	12	4	0	30	27	18	14	3	19	28	.250	.374	.426	21.4	14.5	131
Diaz, Keninson	R-R	6-2	180	3-30-04	5	0	2.76	19	0	1	33	26	10	10	3	16	50	.208	.313	.384	34.7	11.1	144
Disla, Ernesto	R-R	6-2	170	3-08-04	0	1	9.69	10	0	2	13	17	17	14	3	10	10	.309	.429	.509	14.3	14.3	70
Feliz, Domingo	R-R	6-1	185	NULL	0	1	7.43	12	0	1	13	9	11	11	1	14	15	.196	.406	.304	23.4	21.9	64
Fernandez, Orvis	R-R	5-11	185	7-14-03	1	0	5.68	9	0	0	25	24	18	16	1	9	22	.258	.373	.355	20.0	8.2	110
Ferreira, Johan	R-R	5-11	190	10-05-02	0	0	7.71	2	0	0	2	6	2	2	0	0	2	.462	.462	.692	15.4	0.0	13
Gomez, Alejandro	R-R	6-4	180	8-03-02	4	3	3.78	12	6	1	48	45	30	20	1	18	48	.245	.327	.332	22.7	8.5	211
Gonzalez, Omar	R-R	6-4	175	7-25-05	0	0	8.18	4	4	0	11	10	11	10	1	11	20	.227	.382	.318	35.7	19.6	56
Guerrero, Daniel	R-R	6-4	204	1-26-04	0	5	6.82	13	8	0	33	46	33	25	3	17	35	.326	.421	.482	21.3	10.4	164
Guzman, Jose	R-R	5-11	185	12-26-01	2	0	5.40	9	0	1	15	7	10	9	1	11	14	.143	.328	.306	21.9	17.2	64
Hampshire, Carlos	R-R	5-9	181	10-11-04	0	1	7.91	6	5	0	19	19	20	17	4	10	20	.250	.374	.500	22.0	11.0	91
Herrera, Carlos	R-R	5-10	165	9-01-02	0	0	11.57	4	0	1	2	1	3	3	0	2	1	.125	.364	.125	9.1	18.2	11
Herrera, Franyer	L-L	6-0	165	5-03-05	1	1	3.38	3	1	0	5	8	3	2	0	3	5	.348	.423	.478	19.2	11.5	26
Jimenez, Richard	R-R	6-0	150	5-16-05	2	0	11.57	7	0	1	9	9	13	12	1	10	8	.243	.408	.324	16.3	20.4	49
Lampson, Joshawn	R-R	6-1	185	6-23-05	0	3	8.77	11	11	0	26	25	32	25	4	24	26	.245	.439	.451	18.7	17.3	139
Luna, Jorge	R-R	6-0	165	11-04-04	1	3	6.45	11	11	0	38	38	28	27	3	27	31	.268	.395	.373	18.0	15.7	172
Marte, Sabier	R-R	6-5	167	2-10-04	2	0	2.43	11	8	0	41	34	14	11	0	13	42	.221	.280	.260	24.9	7.7	169
Martina, Sunayro	R-R	6-3	165	10-09-03	0	3	3.86	12	6	0	28	19	21	12	1	23	34	.188	.374	.248	26.0	17.6	131
Medina, Christopher	R-R	6-1	185	3-21-04	1	0	3.86	12	0	1	14	10	6	6	1	12	10	.196	.349	.314	15.9	19.0	63
Nivar, Rafelin	L-L	5-10	160	10-21-01	2	0	4.73	18	0	0	32	31	24	17	1	14	44	.242	.324	.328	29.7	9.5	148
Paulino, Alexis	R-R	6-0	175	5-05-03	1	1	12.88	10	0	0	22	18	39	31	0	30	25	.240	.500	.347	21.0	25.2	119
Peres, Michael	L-L	6-0	180	9-18-03	1	2	6.75	12	3	0	24	18	20	18	1	29	46	.205	.432	.295	36.8	23.2	125
Quezada, Joshua	R-R	6-2	185	5-04-04	6	0	3.69	11	4	0	46	36	22	19	2	18	48	.214	.307	.310	25.0	9.4	192
Rodriguez, Jose	R-R	5-11	160	1-06-04	0	2	9.00	6	0	1	6	9	13	6	1	10	8	.346	.528	.538	21.6	27.0	37
Rodriguez, Jose Julian	R-R	6-3	170	10-08-03	1	0	1.29	4	0	0	7	4	1	1	0	3	10	.160	.276	.240	34.5	10.3	29
Rodriguez, Pedro	L-L	5-10	145	8-11-02	5	0	1.93	16	0	3	28	17	12	6	0	10	36	.173	.296	.235	31.3	8.7	115
Rosario, Hansel	R-R	6-4	174	8-05-02	5	1	8.16	12	0	0	29	38	33	26	2	23	26	.325	.456	.487	17.4	15.4	149
Salomon, Mariano	R-R	6-3	185	8-05-02	3	3	3.13	11	3	0	46	41	24	16	2	9	60	.229	.278	.318	30.9	4.6	194
Sanchez, Angel	R-R	6-2	185	6-26-01	1	0	1.00	7	0	1	9	7	1	1	1	2	8	.212	.257	.303	22.9	5.7	35
Sosa, Yordanny	R-R	6-2	139	10-12-01	2	3	4.09	16	0	2	22	28	13	10	2	7	27	.298	.359	.457	26.2	6.8	103
Urbano, Luis	L-L	6-2	163	10-01-02	1	0	8.44	14	0	0	16	18	17	15	0	13	25	.277	.422	.446	29.8	15.5	84
Zazueta, Christian	R-R	6-3	163	10-07-04	3	2	3.29	12	12	0	52	41	21	19	6	16	50	.211	.278	.387	23.6	7.5	212

Fielding

C: Perez 32, Gonzalez 29, Contreras 25, Vivas 16, Bersing 11, Herrera 1, Puello 1. **1B:** Ogando 22, Ferreira 17, Imbert 15, Herrera 14, Gonzalez 13, Bersing 13, Contreras 8, Beckles 7, Javier 6. **2B:** Escudero 28, Terrero 24, Ramirez 17, Blanco 10, Martinez 8, Gomez 7, Coca 6, Pena 5, Suarez 5, Leito 3, Castillo 1, Verde 1. **3B:** Gonzalez 19, Verde 13, Pena 12, Frias 11, Gomez 11, Ogando 9, Terrero 8, Suarez 7, Coca 5, Imbert 5, Blanco 4, Martinez 4, Matheus 2, Castillo 2, Javier 2, Leito 2. **SS:** Frias 22, Suarez 22, Verde 17, Gomez 17, Martinez 15, Matheus 7, Pena 7, Coca 5, Ferreira 2, Javier 1, Blanco 1. **OF:** Lara 43, Altagracia 37, Lacruz 35, Mayea 33, Castro 28, Asigen 27, Puello 26, Beckles 25, Javier 18, Ramirez 15, Imbert 13, Blanco 13, Castillo 13, Meran 12, Leito 10, Ogando 3.

Oakland Athletics

SEASON SYNOPSIS: By design, the Athletics flirted with being MLB's worst team all year and set a franchise record with 112 losses to clinch the "worst" spot and most lottery balls for the 2024 draft.

HIGH POINT: Oakland was 12-50 when it embarked on a seven-game win streak in early June—with the first five coming on the road and the last five coming against playoff teams at Milwaukee and against Tampa Bay. This being the 2023 A's, an eight-game losing streak immediately followed.

LOW POINT: The A's were the only MLB club to fall shy of 1 million fans in attendance at 832,352. More than 27,000 showed up for the seventh game of the win streak as a fan-organized "reverse boycott" of owner John Fisher's proposed move of the franchise to Las Vegas, yet to be approved by MLB at press time. A vast majority of those in attendance united in chanting "Sell" during the June 13 game while wearing green "Sell" shirts. But by season's end, there was little doubt that the franchise would eventually move to Las Vegas in the next two to five years.

NOTABLE ROOKIES: Second baseman Zack Gelof was the team's best player after debuting on July 14, posting an .840 OPS while adding 14 home runs and 14 stolen bases. Rule 5 pick Ryan Noda produced while manning first base for most of the season, leading the team with 77 walks while slugging 16 home runs. Center fielder Esteury Ruiz struggled in many aspects but broke the American League rookie stolen base record with 67. Catcher/1B Tyler Soderstrom and righthander Mason Miller, two of the club's top prospects, got their feet wet as well, with Miller hitting 100 mph while Soderstrom (.160, 43 strikeouts) struggled.

KEY TRANSACTIONS: The A's traded two relievers prior to the Aug. 1 deadline. They acquired a high-variance but high-upside arm, righty Joe Boyle, from the Reds for lefty Sam Moll. Righty Shintaro Fujinami, whom they signed in the offseason from Japan for $3 million, was dealt to the Orioles for righty Easton Lucas. They also acquired Bay Area native Lucas Erceg in May from the Brewers for cash; Erceg wound up leading the club's pitchers with 50 appearances.

DOWN ON THE FARM: A big league team this bad should have a better farm system. Oakland finished 28th in organizational winning percentage.The team is thin in impact prospects.

OPENING DAY PAYROLL: $56,895,000 (30th).

PLAYERS OF THE YEAR

MAJOR LEAGUE

Zack Gelof
2B
.267/.337/.504
20 2B, 14 HR
14-for-16 SB

MINOR LEAGUE

Darell Hernaiz
SS
(AA/AAA)
.321/.386/.456
32 2B, 13 SB

ORGANIZATION LEADERS

Batting — *Minimum 250 AB

MAJORS

* AVG	Zack Gelof	.267
* OPS	Zack Gelof	.840
HR	Brent Rooker	30
RBI	Brent Rooker	69

MINORS

* AVG	Darrel Hernaiz, Midland/Las Vegas	.321
* OBP	Jonah Bride, Las Vegas	.432
* SLG	Cody Thomas, Las Vegas	.562
* OPS	Jonah Bride, Las Vegas	.976
R	Max Schuemann, Midland/Las Vegas	97
H	Darrel Hernaiz, Midland/Las Vegas	160
TB	Colby Thomas, Stockton/Lansing	250
2B	Colby Thomas, Stockton/Lansing	39
3B	Cody Thomas, Las Vegas	8
HR	Cody Thomas, Las Vegas	23
RBI	Cody Thomas, Las Vegas	109
BB	Max Schuemann, Midland/Las Vegas	73
SO	Henry Bolte, Stockton	164
SB	Junor Perez, Lansing	41

Pitching — #Minimum 75 IP

MAJORS

W	JP Sears	5
# ERA	Paul Blackburn	4.43
SO	JP Sears	161
SV	Trevor May	21

MINORS

W	Joey Estes, Midland/Las Vegas	9
W	Chase Cohen, Midland/Las Vegas	9
L	Yehizon Sanchez, ACL A's/Stockton/Lansing	12
# ERA	Joey Estes, Midland/Las Vegas	3.74
G	Billy Sullivan, Las Vegas	48
GS	Ryan Cusick, Midland/Las Vegas	24
SV	Tyler Baum, Lansing/Midland	16
IP	Joey Estes, Midland/Las Vegas	137
BB	Ryan Cusick, Midland/Las Vegas	66
SO	James Gonzalez, Stockton/Lansing	135
# AVG	Jose Dicochea, Stockton/Lansing	.197

2023 PERFORMANCE

General Manager: David Forst. **Farm Director:** Ed Sprague. **Scouting Director:** Eric Kubota.

Class	Team	League	W	L	PCT	Finish	Manager
Majors	Oakland Athletics	American	50	112	.309	15 (15)	Mark Kotsay
Triple-A	Las Vegas Aviators	Pacific Coast	75	74	.503	5 (10)	Fran Riordan
Double-A	Midland RockHounds	Texas	70	68	.507	5 (10)	Bobby Crosby
High-A	Lansing Lugnuts	Midwest	60	71	.458	9 (12)	Craig Conklin
Low-A	Stockton Ports	California	50	82	.379	7 (10)	Gregorio Petit
Rookie	ACL Athletics	Arizona Complex	20	36	.357	16 (17)	Adam Rosales
Rookie	DSL Athletics	Dominican Sum.	22	31	.415	37 (50)	Cooper Goldby
Overall 2023 Minor League Record			297	362	.451	28th (30)	

ORGANIZATION STATISTICS

OAKLAND ATHLETICS

AMERICAN LEAGUE

Batting	B-T	Ht.	Wt.	DOB	AVG	OBP	SLG	G	PA	AB	R	H	2B	3B	HR	RBI	BB	HBP	SH	SF	SO	SB	CS	BB%	SO%
Aguilar, Jesus	R-R	6-3	277	6-30-90	.221	.281	.385	36	115	104	8	23	2	0	5	9	8	1	0	1	31	0	0	7.0	27.0
Allen, Nick	R-R	5-8	166	10-08-98	.221	.263	.287	106	329	303	29	67	4	2	4	20	17	1	6	2	52	5	1	5.2	15.8
Bleday, JJ	L-L	6-2	205	11-10-97	.195	.310	.355	82	303	256	35	50	11	0	10	27	42	2	0	3	72	5	1	13.9	23.8
Bride, Jonah	R-R	5-10	200	12-27-95	.170	.286	.205	40	106	88	9	15	3	0	0	7	11	4	1	2	22	0	1	10.4	20.8
Brown, Seth	L-L	6-1	223	7-13-92	.222	.286	.405	112	378	343	33	76	19	1	14	52	30	2	1	2	101	3	1	7.9	26.7
Butler, Lawrence	L-R	6-3	210	7-10-00	.211	.240	.341	42	129	123	10	26	4	0	4	10	4	1	0	1	35	0	0	3.1	27.1
Capel, Conner	L-L	6-1	185	5-19-97	.260	.372	.329	32	86	73	6	19	5	0	0	3	12	1	0	0	25	5	3	14.0	29.1
Diaz, Aledmys	R-R	6-1	195	8-01-90	.229	.280	.337	109	344	315	25	72	20	1	4	24	17	7	1	4	66	1	0	4.9	19.2
Diaz, Jordan	R-R	5-10	175	8-13-00	.221	.273	.364	90	293	272	20	60	9	0	10	27	17	3	0	1	69	0	1	5.8	23.5
Gelof, Zack	R-R	6-2	205	10-19-99	.267	.337	.504	69	300	270	40	72	20	1	14	32	26	3	0	1	82	14	2	8.7	27.3
Kemp, Tony	L-R	5-6	160	10-31-91	.209	.303	.304	124	419	359	42	75	13	3	5	27	44	6	7	3	40	15	4	10.5	9.5
Langeliers, Shea	R-R	6-0	205	11-18-97	.205	.268	.413	135	490	448	52	92	19	4	22	63	34	5	1	2	143	3	2	6.9	29.2
Laureano, Ramon	R-R	5-11	203	7-15-94	.213	.280	.364	64	246	225	24	48	10	3	6	21	17	4	0	0	73	8	0	6.9	29.7
2-team (41 Cleveland)					.224	.305	.371	105	404	361	46	81	18	4	9	35	33	9	0	1	114	12	1	8.2	28.2
Noda, Ryan	L-L	6-3	217	3-30-96	.229	.364	.406	128	495	406	63	93	22	1	16	54	77	10	0	2	170	3	1	15.6	34.3
Perez, Carlos	R-R	5-10	210	10-27-90	.226	.293	.357	68	189	168	17	38	4	0	6	20	13	4	1	3	40	0	0	6.9	21.2
Peterson, Jace	L-R	6-0	215	5-09-90	.221	.313	.324	93	324	281	30	62	7	2	6	28	36	3	1	3	77	11	1	11.1	23.8
Pina, Manny	R-R	6-0	222	6-05-87	.250	.250	.500	4	12	12	1	3	0	0	1	1	0	0	0	0	3	0	0	0.0	25.0
Rooker, Brent	R-R	6-4	225	11-01-94	.246	.329	.488	137	526	463	61	114	20	1	30	69	49	10	0	4	172	4	0	9.3	32.7
Ruiz, Esteury	R-R	6-0	169	2-15-99	.254	.309	.345	132	497	449	47	114	24	1	5	47	20	16	4	1	99	67	13	4.0	19.9
Smith, Kevin	R-R	6-0	190	7-04-96	.185	.220	.326	49	146	135	15	25	4	0	5	11	5	1	5	0	51	1	0	3.4	34.9
Soderstrom, Tyler	L-R	6-1	200	11-24-01	.160	.232	.240	45	138	125	9	20	1	0	3	7	11	1	0	1	43	0	0	8.0	31.2
Thomas, Cody	L-R	6-4	211	10-08-94	.238	.304	.381	19	46	42	1	10	3	0	1	2	4	0	0	0	17	0	0	8.7	37.0
Wade, Tyler	L-R	6-1	188	11-23-94	.255	.309	.314	26	55	51	8	13	1	1	0	2	4	0	0	0	13	4	0	7.3	23.6

Pitching	B-T	Ht.	Wt.	DOB	W	L	ERA	G	GS	SV	IP	Hits	Runs	ER	HR	BB	SO	AVG	OBP	SLG	SO%	BB%	BF
Acevedo, Domingo	R-R	6-7	240	3-06-94	0	0	10.61	9	0	0	9	16	11	11	2	2	7	.381	.404	.738	14.9	4.3	47
Acton, Garrett	L-R	6-2	215	6-15-98	0	0	12.71	6	0	0	6	9	8	8	3	5	5	.346	.469	.846	15.6	15.6	32
Blackburn, Paul	R-R	6-1	196	12-04-93	4	7	4.43	21	20	0	104	117	54	51	11	43	104	.286	.352	.435	22.4	9.3	464
Boyle, Joe	R-R	6-7	240	8-14-99	2	0	1.69	3	3	0	16	8	4	3	1	5	15	.148	.217	.259	25.0	8.3	60
Erceg, Lucas	L-R	6-2	214	5-01-95	4	4	4.75	50	0	0	55	51	33	29	1	36	68	.245	.371	.356	27.1	14.3	251
Estes, Joey	R-R	6-2	190	10-08-01	0	1	7.20	2	2	0	10	12	9	8	4	2	7	.286	.362	.643	14.9	4.3	47
Familia, Jeurys	R-R	6-3	240	10-10-89	0	1	6.39	14	0	2	13	13	12	9	2	13	9	.271	.429	.458	14.1	20.3	64
Felipe, Angel	R-R	6-5	190	8-30-97	1	1	4.20	14	0	0	15	6	7	7	0	13	19	.120	.313	.140	29.7	20.3	64
Fujinami, Shintaro	R-R	6-6	180	4-12-94	5	8	8.57	34	7	0	49	52	48	47	6	30	51	.269	.377	.430	22.1	13.0	231
Garcia, Rico	R-R	5-9	201	1-10-94	0	0	8.31	7	0	0	9	13	8	8	4	5	6	.342	.409	.763	13.6	11.4	44
Harris, Hogan	R-L	6-3	230	12-26-96	3	6	7.14	14	6	0	63	67	51	50	10	28	56	.269	.348	.470	19.7	9.9	284
Jackson, Zach	R-R	6-4	230	12-25-94	2	1	2.50	19	0	1	18	18	7	5	1	10	23	.261	.354	.333	28.8	12.5	80
Jimenez, Dany	R-R	6-1	182	12-23-93	0	2	3.47	25	1	1	23	11	9	9	3	14	21	.143	.269	.286	22.3	14.9	94
Kaprielian, James	R-R	6-3	225	3-02-94	2	6	6.34	14	11	0	61	66	45	43	9	31	57	.274	.367	.452	20.4	11.1	280
Long, Sam	L-L	6-1	185	7-08-95	0	1	5.60	40	1	2	45	49	29	28	5	21	32	.282	.359	.437	16.1	10.6	199
Lovelady, Richard	L-L	6-0	185	7-07-95	0	3	4.63	27	0	0	23	15	13	12	3	10	24	.188	.292	.375	25.0	10.4	96
Lucas, Easton	L-L	6-4	180	9-23-96	0	0	8.10	6	0	0	7	10	6	6	1	4	7	.323	.400	.548	20.0	11.4	35
Martinez, Adrian	R-R	6-2	215	12-10-96	0	2	4.75	22	1	0	55	59	31	29	8	19	47	.278	.344	.448	19.5	7.9	241
May, Trevor	R-R	6-5	240	9-23-89	4	4	3.28	49	0	21	47	35	21	17	4	29	40	.208	.332	.327	19.5	14.1	205
Medina, Luis	R-R	6-1	175	5-03-99	3	10	5.42	23	17	0	110	109	73	66	14	57	106	.255	.352	.440	21.4	11.5	495
Miller, Mason	R-R	6-5	200	8-24-98	0	3	3.78	10	6	0	33	24	15	14	2	16	38	.203	.309	.305	27.3	11.5	139
Moll, Sam	L-L	5-9	190	1-03-92	0	3	4.54	45	1	1	38	34	20	19	1	19	46	.239	.353	.331	27.1	11.2	170
Muller, Kyle	R-L	6-7	250	10-07-97	1	5	7.60	21	13	0	77	112	65	65	16	39	56	.346	.416	.568	15.1	10.5	372
Neal, Zach	R-R	6-3	220	11-09-88	1	1	6.67	14	2	0	27	30	22	20	8	14	25	.280	.374	.589	20.2	11.3	124
Newcomb, Sean	L-L	6-5	255	6-12-93	1	1	3.00	7	2	0	15	8	5	5	1	9	17	.160	.311	.260	27.9	14.8	61
Oller, Adam	R-R	6-4	225	10-17-94	1	1	10.07	9	1	0	20	29	24	22	5	12	13	.341	.416	.576	12.9	11.9	101
Patton, Spencer	R-R	6-1	200	2-20-88	0	0	5.11	12	0	0	12	13	7	7	3	6	7	.277	.345	.574	12.7	10.9	55

Perez, Carlos	R-R	5-10	210	10-27-90	0	0	10.80	2	0	0	2	4	2	2	1	2	0	.500	.600	1.000	0.0	20.0	10
Perez, Francisco	B-L	6-2	227	7-20-97	1	2	5.94	17	1	0	17	17	12	11	0	8	14	.266	.351	.391	18.9	10.8	74
Peterson, Jace	L-R	6-0	215	5-09-90	0	0	9.00	2	0	0	2	3	2	2	1	3	1	.333	.500	.778	8.3	25.0	12
Pruitt, Austin	R-R	5-10	185	8-31-89	2	6	2.98	38	6	0	48	44	18	16	5	12	30	.243	.291	.370	15.3	6.1	196
Rios, Yacksel	R-R	6-3	215	6-27-93	0	0	37.80	3	0	0	2	3	7	7	1	6	2	.375	.643	.750	14.3	42.9	14
Rucinski, Drew	R-R	6-2	190	12-30-88	0	4	9.00	4	4	0	18	27	22	18	5	14	6	.346	.442	.603	6.3	14.7	95
Scott, Tayler	R-R	6-3	185	6-01-92	0	0	3.38	8	1	0	8	11	3	3	2	2	7	.314	.368	.600	18.4	5.3	38
Sears, JP	R-L	5-11	180	2-19-96	5	14	4.54	32	32	0	172	165	90	87	34	53	161	.249	.319	.465	21.9	7.2	735
Smith, Chad	R-R	6-4	200	6-08-95	1	2	6.59	10	0	0	14	15	10	10	2	7	9	.294	.400	.451	15.0	11.7	60
Snead, Kirby	L-L	6-1	218	10-07-94	1	2	4.63	15	0	0	12	14	7	6	1	6	9	.280	.357	.380	16.1	10.7	56
Sweet, Devin	B-R	5-11	183	9-06-96	1	0	10.80	5	0	0	7	8	8	8	3	5	5	.296	.441	.630	14.7	14.7	34
Tarnok, Freddy	R-R	6-3	185	11-24-98	1	1	4.91	5	1	0	15	11	8	8	4	11	14	.204	.338	.500	21.5	16.9	65
Waldichuk, Ken	L-L	6-4	220	1-08-98	4	9	5.36	35	22	1	141	149	93	84	24	71	132	.271	.360	.480	20.7	11.1	639
Watkins, Spenser	R-R	6-2	195	8-27-92	0	1	10.38	1	1	0	4	7	5	5	2	2	4	.368	.429	.842	19.0	9.5	21

Fielding

Catcher	PCT	G	PO	A	E	DP	PB
Langeliers	.990	123	945	47	10	6	7
Perez	.992	31	242	14	2	1	2
Pina	.933	2	14	0	1	0	0
Soderstrom	1.000	15	113	8	0	0	2

First Base	PCT	G	PO	A	E	DP
Aguilar	.984	24	112	10	2	13
Bride	1.000	5	13	2	0	1
Brown	1.000	17	81	4	0	6
Diaz, A	1.000	10	16	0	0	2
Diaz, J	.946	7	34	1	2	1
Noda	.991	119	728	47	7	78
Perez	1.000	15	52	4	0	5
Soderstrom	.981	10	50	3	1	6

Second Base	PCT	G	PO	A	E	DP
Allen	1.000	1	1	0	0	0
Diaz, A	1.000	11	18	17	0	9
Diaz, J	1.000	28	30	44	0	13
Gelof	.989	69	137	141	3	44
Kemp	.980	57	103	96	4	21
Peterson	.986	20	33	38	1	9

Third Base	PCT	G	PO	A	E	DP
Bride	.968	27	19	41	2	8
Diaz, A	.973	40	22	51	2	9
Diaz, J	.918	38	24	43	6	7
Peterson	.977	77	55	113	4	9
Smith	.963	17	5	21	1	1
Wade	1.000	3	0	2	0	0

Shortstop	PCT	G	PO	A	E	DP
Allen	.976	104	120	246	9	41
Diaz	.978	40	33	57	2	7
Smith	.990	34	35	61	1	12
Wade	.981	17	14	39	1	5

Outfield	PCT	G	PO	A	E	DP
Bleday	.987	79	160	4	3	2
Brown	1.000	81	168	3	0	1
Butler	1.000	43	82	1	0	1
Capel	.982	26	42	2	1	0
Diaz	.909	13	10	0	1	0
Kemp	.972	65	101	5	3	1
Laureano	.984	59	144	6	5	3
Noda	.500	9	5	0	0	0
Perez	.000	1	0	0	0	0
Peterson	1.000	1	1	0	0	0
Rooker	.969	60	113	3	4	0
Ruiz	.956	136	294	2	8	0
Thomas	1.000	13	26	0	0	0
Wade	.500	6	2	0	0	0

LAS VEGAS AVIATORS — TRIPLE-A

PACIFIC COAST LEAGUE

Batting	B-T	Ht.	Wt.	DOB	AVG	OBP	SLG	G	PA	AB	R	H	2B	3B	HR	RBI	BB	HBP	SH	SF	SO	SB	CS	BB%	SO%
Allen, Nick	R-R	5-8	166	10-08-98	.333	.420	.519	33	162	135	33	45	14	1	3	18	20	1	5	1	16	13	1	12.3	9.9
Bleday, JJ	L-L	6-2	205	11-10-97	.333	.444	.667	28	133	108	31	36	8	2	8	23	23	0	0	2	18	1	1	17.3	13.5
Bride, Jonah	R-R	5-10	200	12-27-95	.305	.432	.544	73	323	259	60	79	19	2	13	54	56	4	1	3	49	5	2	17.3	15.2
Brooks, Trenton	L-L	5-10	195	7-03-95	.299	.405	.529	94	412	344	78	103	29	1	16	71	57	6	2	3	60	5	0	13.8	14.6
2-team (24 Sacramento)					.286	.402	.516	118	523	430	95	123	31	1	22	90	78	7	3	5	77	7	0	14.9	14.7
Brown, Seth	L-L	6-1	223	7-13-92	.500	.500	.500	1	2	2	0	1	0	0	0	0	0	0	0	0	1	0	0	0.0	50.0
Butler, Lawrence	L-R	6-3	210	7-10-00	.280	.340	.512	22	94	82	14	23	2	1	5	23	8	1	0	3	18	8	0	8.5	19.1
Capel, Conner	L-L	6-1	185	5-19-97	.252	.346	.402	92	391	341	55	86	14	5	9	47	46	3	1	0	84	17	4	11.8	21.5
Cron, Kevin	R-R	6-4	255	2-17-93	.133	.152	.156	10	46	45	4	6	1	0	0	6	1	0	0	0	18	0	0	2.2	39.1
Davidson, Logan	B-R	6-3	185	12-26-97	.264	.333	.375	61	232	208	24	55	12	1	3	31	21	1	1	1	51	4	1	9.1	22.0
Deichmann, Greg	L-R	6-0	205	5-31-95	.261	.318	.484	55	201	184	33	48	10	2	9	30	14	2	0	1	57	9	2	7.0	28.4
Diaz, Jordan	R-R	5-10	175	8-13-00	.308	.351	.506	38	169	156	18	48	13	0	6	31	10	1	0	1	30	0	1	5.9	17.8
Garcia, Dermis	R-R	6-1	200	1-07-98	.263	.359	.532	45	198	171	29	45	8	1	12	29	22	4	0	1	63	3	0	11.1	31.8
Gelof, Zack	R-R	6-2	205	10-19-99	.304	.401	.529	69	308	263	60	80	21	1	12	44	41	2	1	1	86	20	5	13.3	27.9
Harris, Brett	R-R	6-1	208	6-24-98	.271	.347	.419	36	147	129	19	35	7	0	4	14	10	5	3	0	27	4	0	6.8	18.4
Hernaiz, Darell	R-R	5-11	190	8-03-01	.300	.376	.418	60	253	220	44	66	12	1	4	28	24	4	3	2	27	6	2	9.5	10.7
Kennedy, Buddy	R-R	5-9	190	10-05-98	.216	.326	.216	11	46	37	6	8	0	0	0	4	6	1	0	2	13	0	0	13.0	28.3
2-team (90 Reno)				.307	.436	.455	101	463	374	82	115	24	8	5	50	76	9	0	4	81	3		316.4	17.5	
Laureano, Ramon	R-R	5-11	203	7-15-94	.467	.600	.800	5	20	15	5	7	2	0	1	2	4	1	0	0	3	1	0	20.0	15.0
McCann, Kyle	L-R	6-2	217	12-02-97	.270	.351	.474	97	388	344	58	93	17	1	17	57	38	5	0	1	125	3	0	9.8	32.2
Noda, Ryan	L-L	6-3	217	3-30-96	.400	.667	1.200	4	18	10	7	4	2	0	2	5	8	0	0	0	3	0	0	44.4	16.7
Perez, Carlos	R-R	5-10	210	10-27-90	.385	.467	.538	4	15	13	6	5	2	0	0	3	1	1	0	0	0	0	0	6.7	0.0
Pina, Manny	R-R	6-0	222	6-05-87	.324	.395	.559	11	38	34	8	11	2	0	2	8	3	1	0	0	5	0	0	7.9	13.2
Pozo, Yohel	R-R	5-10	201	6-14-97	.306	.338	.523	92	391	369	48	113	26	0	18	81	18	1	0	3	40	2	0	4.6	10.2
Reyes, Pablo	R-R	5-8	175	9-05-93	.257	.385	.351	21	91	74	13	19	2	1	1	10	16	0	0	1	23	3	2	17.6	25.3
Ruiz, Esteury	R-R	6-0	169	2-15-99	.400	.429	.700	5	21	20	4	8	1	1	1	2	1	0	0	0	5	3	0	4.8	23.8
Schuemann, Max	R-R	5-11	186	6-11-97	.277	.402	.429	103	433	350	88	97	18	4	9	43	62	14	3	4	87	20	9	14.3	20.1
Schwartz, Nick	R-R	5-11	190	3-07-01	.167	.286	.333	2	8	6	1	1	1	0	0	1	1	0	1	0	1	0	0	12.5	12.5
Schwarz, JJ	R-R	6-0	205	3-28-96	.217	.321	.261	16	53	46	6	10	2	0	0	2	7	0	0	0	12	0	1	13.2	22.6
Smith, Kevin	R-R	6-0	190	7-04-96	.324	.372	.653	42	183	170	41	55	8	0	16	46	13	0	0	0	49	9	2	7.1	26.8
Soderstrom, Tyler	L-R	6-1	200	11-24-01	.252	.307	.526	77	335	306	49	77	17	2	21	62	25	1	0	3	88	2	0	7.5	26.3
Stevenson, Cal	L-L	5-9	175	9-12-96	.348	.483	.435	7	29	23	7	8	2	0	0	2	6	0	0	0	3	3	0	20.7	10.3
2-team (13 Sacramento)					.222	.356	.292	20	87	72	15	16	2	0	1	3	14	1	0	0	22	5	2	16.1	
Thomas, Cody	L-R	6-4	211	10-08-94	.301	.361	.562	107	477	429	67	129	27	8	23	109	37	6	0	5	97	5	0	7.8	20.3
Wade, Tyler	L-R	6-1	188	11-23-94	.291	.384	.409	91	400	340	68	99	20	1	6	47	47	5	6	1	86	42	9	11.8	21.5

OAKLAND ATHLETICS

Pitching	B-T	Ht.	Wt.	DOB	W	L	ERA	G	GS	SV	IP	Hits	Runs	ER	HR	BB	SO	AVG	OBP	SLG	SO%	BB%	BF
Acevedo, Domingo	R-R	6-7	240	3-06-94	1	0	10.50	6	0	1	6	11	11	7	3	1	6	.355	.375	.742	18.8	3.1	32
Acton, Garrett	L-R	6-2	215	6-15-98	5	2	5.59	21	0	3	29	25	19	18	7	11	33	.223	.290	.464	26.4	8.8	125
Blackburn, Paul	R-R	6-1	196	12-04-93	0	0	7.16	5	5	0	16	26	15	13	3	5	10	.361	.403	.556	13.0	6.5	77
Boyle, Joe	R-R	6-7	240	8-14-99	0	2	2.25	3	3	0	16	8	6	4	1	11	18	.151	.303	.264	27.3	16.7	66
Cohen, Chase	L-R	6-1	183	4-26-97	6	1	6.91	39	0	1	43	47	34	33	5	33	48	.278	.396	.444	23.2	15.9	207
Conley, Bryce	R-R	6-3	200	8-22-94	1	0	6.30	6	0	0	10	11	7	7	2	5	11	.289	.391	.500	23.4	10.6	47
Cron, Kevin	R-R	6-4	255	2-17-93	0	0	18.00	1	0	0	1	4	2	2	1	0	0	.571	.571	1.286	0.0	0.0	7
Cushing, Jack	R-R	6-3	195	12-03-96	0	2	16.55	3	3	0	10	18	20	19	5	4	11	.360	.411	.760	19.6	7.1	56
Cusick, Ryan	R-R	6-6	235	11-12-99	0	1	16.88	1	1	0	3	3	5	5	0	7	2	.300	.611	.400	11.1	38.9	18
Dallas, Micah	R-R	6-2	215	4-14-00	0	1	43.20	1	1	0	2	5	8	8	1	4	3	.500	.643	.900	21.4	28.6	14
Dunshee, Parker	R-R	6-0	215	2-12-95	0	0	18.00	1	0	0	1	2	2	2	1	0	0	.400	.400	1.200	0.0	0.0	5
Eastman, Colton	R-R	6-3	185	8-22-96	0	8	7.26	22	10	0	66	78	69	53	12	41	59	.290	.387	.509	18.6	12.9	317
Estes, Joey	R-R	6-2	190	10-08-01	3	0	5.23	7	6	0	33	32	19	19	10	12	31	.246	.319	.508	21.5	8.3	144
Felipe, Angel	R-R	6-5	190	8-30-97	2	0	1.80	5	0	0	5	2	1	1	0	1	7	.125	.176	.188	41.2	5.9	17
Fishman, Jake	L-L	6-3	195	2-08-95	0	0	24.00	3	0	0	3	9	8	8	1	1	4	.529	.556	.765	22.2	5.6	18
Garcia, Rico	R-R	5-9	201	1-10-94	1	1	3.20	22	0	6	25	17	9	9	3	21	33	.189	.345	.311	29.2	18.6	113
Godley, Zack	R-R	6-3	250	4-21-90	4	2	5.21	12	10	0	57	58	39	33	9	31	57	.266	.367	.459	22.0	12.0	259
Guerra, Deolis	R-R	6-5	245	4-17-89	0	0	11.57	3	0	0	2	3	3	3	0	1	5	.300	.364	.400	45.5	9.1	11
Harris, Hogan	R-L	6-3	230	12-26-96	1	4	6.47	15	14	0	57	60	44	41	12	38	55	.269	.382	.498	20.6	14.2	267
Irvin, Garrett	L-L	6-0	185	2-18-99	0	0	0.00	1	0	0	1	0	0	0	0	1	0	.000	.333	.000	0.0	33.3	3
Jimenez, Dany	R-R	6-1	182	12-23-93	1	0	10.38	9	1	1	9	7	10	10	2	7	14	.219	.375	.406	35.0	17.5	40
Kaprielian, James	R-R	6-3	225	3-02-94	1	0	1.08	2	2	0	8	7	1	1	0	2	7	.226	.273	.258	21.2	6.1	33
Long, Sam	L-L	6-1	185	7-08-95	1	0	3.95	11	0	4	14	14	6	6	0	6	13	.275	.350	.353	21.7	10.0	60
Lucas, Easton	L-L	6-4	180	9-23-96	0	0	5.63	15	0	0	16	28	11	10	3	4	13	.394	.421	.648	17.1	5.3	76
Martinez, Adrian	R-R	6-2	215	12-10-96	0	7	8.45	13	12	0	38	59	40	36	9	21	24	.360	.442	.628	12.6	11.0	191
May, Trevor	R-R	6-5	240	9-23-89	0	0	4.91	4	0	0	4	4	2	2	2	2	2	.267	.353	.733	11.8	11.8	17
Medina, Luis	R-R	6-1	175	5-03-99	0	1	6.48	6	5	0	17	15	13	12	1	16	23	.254	.423	.441	29.1	20.3	79
Miller, Mason	R-R	6-5	200	8-24-98	1	0	0.00	4	4	0	12	3	0	0	0	3	23	.077	.143	.103	54.8	7.1	42
Muller, Kyle	R-L	6-7	250	10-07-97	2	3	7.26	13	13	0	62	79	58	50	12	38	51	.307	.400	.541	16.9	12.6	301
Neal, Zach	R-R	6-3	220	11-09-88	4	2	5.21	18	10	1	74	90	53	43	18	16	54	.288	.330	.524	16.2	4.8	333
Oller, Adam	R-R	6-4	225	10-17-94	4	3	7.11	12	9	0	51	60	42	40	12	24	59	.291	.372	.553	25.2	10.3	234
Patrick, Chad	R-R	6-1	205	8-14-98	0	3	7.89	6	5	0	22	35	20	19	3	15	25	.376	.465	.570	21.7	13.0	115
Patton, Spencer	R-R	6-1	200	2-20-88	4	2	4.66	44	0	5	46	45	25	24	4	23	50	.263	.379	.415	23.8	11.0	210
Peluse, Colin	R-R	6-3	230	6-11-98	1	1	6.78	42	5	2	65	84	50	49	20	38	52	.311	.397	.596	16.5	12.1	315
Perez, Francisco	B-L	6-2	227	7-20-97	4	1	4.86	25	0	1	33	28	19	18	3	19	41	.230	.338	.377	28.9	13.4	142
Pozo, Yohel	R-R	5-10	201	6-14-97	0	0	0.00	3	0	0	3	6	0	0	0	0	2	.400	.400	.400	13.3	0.0	15
Pruitt, Austin	R-R	5-10	185	8-31-89	1	1	2.76	11	0	0	16	13	6	5	2	5	18	.213	.273	.361	27.3	7.6	66
Romero, Miguel	R-R	6-0	202	4-23-94	0	1	6.60	14	0	0	15	15	11	11	2	13	12	.263	.419	.421	16.2	17.6	74
Rucinski, Drew	R-R	6-2	190	12-30-88	1	1	6.52	3	3	0	10	12	9	7	0	5	8	.300	.383	.325	17.0	10.6	47
Ruiz, Norge	R-R	5-10	180	3-15-94	2	2	6.95	38	3	0	45	61	37	35	7	19	32	.318	.377	.464	15.0	8.9	213
Scott, Tayler	R-R	6-3	185	6-01-92	2	0	1.72	14	0	3	16	8	3	3	0	3	17	.154	.196	.173	30.4	5.4	56
Smith, Chad	R-R	6-4	200	6-08-95	1	3	7.53	35	0	4	35	42	33	29	6	30	42	.302	.428	.453	24.3	17.3	173
Snead, Kirby	L-L	6-1	218	10-07-94	2	3	7.59	23	0	0	21	29	21	18	5	16	22	.322	.432	.578	19.5	14.2	113
Sullivan, Billy	R-R	6-2	195	4-16-99	8	2	5.34	48	0	2	57	49	40	34	1	52	54	.236	.401	.284	19.9	19.1	272
Supak, Trey	R-R	6-5	268	5-31-96	2	2	6.33	12	6	0	43	62	36	30	10	16	24	.348	.408	.590	11.9	7.9	202
Sweet, Devin	B-R	5-11	183	9-06-96	0	0	13.50	2	0	0	2	4	3	3	1	0	3	.444	.444	.778	33.3	0.0	9
Tarnok, Freddy	R-R	6-3	185	11-24-98	1	1	1.83	5	5	0	20	12	4	4	2	11	11	.176	.291	.294	13.9	13.9	79
Tomioka, Shohei	R-R	6-0	190	2-29-96	0	1	7.59	8	0	0	11	12	10	9	0	9	8	.293	.420	.390	16.0	18.0	50
Watkins, Spenser	R-R	6-2	195	8-27-92	0	3	6.93	7	5	0	25	30	25	19	6	11	29	.288	.362	.519	25.0	9.5	116
Wieland, Joe	R-R	6-2	205	1-21-90	4	4	8.16	23	1	0	32	44	34	29	9	24	27	.328	.425	.619	16.9	15.0	160
Wilkerson, Aaron	R-R	6-2	230	5-24-89	3	2	6.51	14	6	0	47	61	37	34	12	14	53	.308	.350	.540	24.8	6.5	214
Williams, Garrett	L-L	6-1	200	9-15-94	1	1	5.13	42	1	3	53	41	32	30	1	61	71	.222	.436	.292	27.6	23.7	257

Fielding

Catcher	PCT	G	PO	A	E	DP	PB
McCann	.992	60	505	21	4	3	4
Perez	1.000	2	8	2	0	0	0
Pina	.944	6	33	1	2	0	0
Pozo	.985	49	378	19	6	5	0
Schwartz	.947	2	18	0	1	0	2
Schwarz	1.000	5	36	1	0	0	0
Soderstrom	.988	38	314	17	4	1	4

First Base	PCT	G	PO	A	E	DP
Bride	1.000	2	21	0	0	3
Brooks	.981	14	99	7	2	10
Cron	1.000	7	54	5	0	7
Davidson	.994	39	286	21	2	43
Garcia	.974	29	198	25	6	20
Kennedy	1.000	7	46	3	0	6
McCann	.986	10	65	4	1	17
Noda	1.000	2	14	0	0	0
Pozo	1.000	12	88	6	0	11
Schwarz	1.000	4	35	1	0	3
Soderstrom	.967	28	166	10	6	29

Second Base	PCT	G	PO	A	E	DP
Bride	.970	9	14	18	1	11
Davidson	.981	10	24	27	1	11
Diaz	.875	9	9	12	3	1
Gelof	.975	68	135	172	8	49
Harris	1.000	2	5	8	0	5
Hernaiz	1.000	10	16	24	0	8
Reyes	.974	6	12	26	1	8
Schuemann	1.000	5	10	13	0	3
Smith	1.000	5	9	14	0	6
Wade	.975	28	52	66	3	22

Third Base	PCT	G	PO	A	E	DP
Bride	.945	60	32	106	8	16
Davidson	.880	8	2	20	3	2
Diaz	.714	22	12	13	10	1
Harris	.957	34	21	69	4	7
Hernaiz	1.000	1	0	2	0	0
Kennedy	1.000	2	1	3	0	2
Reyes	.857	5	3	3	1	0
Schuemann	.957	9	6	16	1	1
Smith	.909	4	3	7	1	1
Wade	.952	9	6	14	1	1

Shortstop	PCT	G	PO	A	E	DP
Allen	.943	33	37	78	7	26
Davidson	.947	3	5	13	1	5
Hernaiz	.969	48	67	123	6	37
Reyes	1.000	4	4	5	0	1
Schuemann	1.000	9	8	19	0	3
Smith	.990	29	34	65	1	15
Wade	.948	27	45	65	6	18

Outfield	PCT	G	PO	A	E	DP
Bleday	.961	27	58	3	3	0
Brooks	.995	65	115	2	1	0
Butler	.667	23	36	1	0	0
Capel	.965	91	189	8	7	1

Deichmann	.973	40	71	1	2	1
Laureano	1.000	5	10	0	0	0
Noda	1.000	1	1	0	0	0
Reyes	.833	5	10	0	1	0
Ruiz	.875	4	7	0	1	0
Schuemann	.961	82	143	4	5	1
Stevenson	1.000	7	14	0	0	0
Thomas	.986	94	226	3	4	0
Wade	.954	26	34	3	2	0

MIDLAND ROCKHOUNDS — *DOUBLE-A*

TEXAS LEAGUE

Batting	B-T	Ht.	Wt.	DOB	AVG	OBP	SLG	G	PA	AB	R	H	2B	3B	HR	RBI	BB	HBP	SH	SF	SO	SB	CS	BB%	SO%
Angeles, Euribiel	R-R	5-11	175	5-11-02	.227	.261	.227	6	23	22	3	5	0	0	0	1	1	0	0	0	2	0	0	4.3	8.7
Armenteros, Lazaro	R-R	5-11	182	5-22-99	.248	.380	.464	96	405	330	63	82	19	5	14	72	62	10	0	3	133	10	7	15.3	32.8
Bowman, Cooper	R-R	6-0	205	1-25-00	.262	.358	.435	68	319	271	49	71	17	3	8	38	36	6	3	3	68	35	3	11.3	21.3
Buelvas, Brayan	R-R	5-11	155	6-08-02	.187	.241	.293	20	83	75	13	14	3	1	1	19	5	1	0	2	21	0	0	6.0	25.3
Butler, Jonny	L-R	6-1	200	2-12-99	.288	.380	.475	23	92	80	14	23	3	3	2	10	11	1	0	0	21	6	0	12.0	22.8
Butler, Lawrence	L-R	6-3	210	7-10-00	.285	.352	.465	67	318	284	53	81	17	2	10	47	30	1	0	3	60	13	2	9.4	18.9
Calabuig, Chase	L-L	5-10	185	12-10-95	.329	.393	.523	40	173	155	30	51	12	3	4	20	17	0	0	1	17	1	0	9.8	9.8
Clarke, Denzel	R-R	6-5	220	5-01-00	.261	.381	.496	64	286	234	54	61	11	4	12	43	37	11	0	4	85	11	1	12.9	29.7
Davidson, Logan	B-R	6-3	185	12-26-97	.297	.379	.484	48	206	182	26	54	11	1	7	28	22	2	0	0	56	2	2	10.7	27.2
Deichmann, Greg	L-R	6-0	205	5-31-95	.231	.329	.451	53	225	195	34	45	5	4	10	31	28	1	0	1	66	7	1	12.4	29.3
Eierman, Jeremy	R-R	5-11	205	9-10-96	.188	.295	.305	36	150	128	17	24	6	0	3	6	15	5	1	1	45	4	0	10.0	30.0
Guldberg, Michael	R-R	5-10	171	6-22-99	.220	.272	.323	36	138	127	18	28	5	1	2	16	8	1	1	0	31	3	0	5.8	22.5
Harris, Brett	R-R	6-1	208	6-24-98	.283	.399	.426	69	314	258	44	73	16	3	5	48	40	12	1	3	42	6	1	12.7	13.4
Hernaiz, Darell	R-R	5-11	190	8-03-01	.338	.393	.486	71	308	278	43	94	20	3	5	43	26	0	3	1	48	7	3	8.4	15.6
Masterman, Cameron	R-R	6-2	225	5-05-99	.253	.315	.393	43	165	150	27	38	6	0	5	23	12	2	0	1	53	3	0	7.3	32.1
McGuire, Shane	L-R	5-10	195	4-12-99	.227	.345	.309	98	396	330	44	75	13	1	4	38	55	6	2	3	87	3	2	13.9	22.0
Muncy, Max	R-R	6-1	180	8-25-02	.302	.387	.446	51	233	202	40	61	17	0	4	31	21	7	3	0	54	4	0	9.0	23.2
Schuemann, Max	R-R	5-11	186	6-11-97	.269	.400	.442	13	65	52	9	14	2	2	1	8	11	1	0	1	19	3	0	16.9	29.2
Schwarz, JJ	R-R	6-0	205	3-28-96	.221	.319	.369	60	254	222	24	49	9	0	8	37	31	1	0	0	67	0	1	12.2	26.4
Simoneit, William	R-R	6-3	235	10-14-96	.237	.326	.387	72	289	253	40	60	15	1	7	39	24	10	0	1	79	3	0	8.3	27.3
Susac, Daniel	R-R	6-4	218	5-14-01	.280	.304	.360	13	56	50	2	14	1	0	1	8	2	1	0	3	14	1	0	3.6	25.0
Swift, Drew	R-R	6-0	165	2-15-99	.253	.323	.322	64	292	261	37	66	10	4	0	29	26	1	4	0	73	5	2	8.9	25.0
Trenkle, Caeden	L-L	5-10	179	6-29-01	.247	.311	.331	45	186	166	29	41	6	1	2	15	13	3	0	1	53	2	0	7.0	28.5
Valenzuela, Sahid	B-R	5-7	165	9-16-97	.275	.327	.348	52	199	178	18	49	8	1	1	28	14	1	3	3	29	3	1	7.0	14.6
Winkler, Jack	R-R	6-2	185	11-04-98	.233	.330	.366	46	200	172	28	40	9	1	4	32	21	5	0	2	39	3	2	10.5	19.5
Wright, Joshwan	R-R	5-8	170	11-09-00	.115	.207	.115	8	29	26	2	3	0	0	0	0	2	1	0	0	5	0	0	6.9	17.2
Yamauchi, Casey	R-R	5-9	155	8-08-00	.194	.286	.226	11	35	31	7	6	1	0	0	4	2	2	0	0	5	1	1	5.7	14.3

Pitching	B-T	Ht.	Wt.	DOB	W	L	ERA	G	GS	SV	IP	Hits	Runs	ER	HR	BB	SO	AVG	OBP	SLG	SO%	BB%	BF
Basso, Brady	R-L	6-2	213	10-08-97	2	0	1.89	5	5	0	19	13	5	4	1	4	19	.203	.271	.297	27.1	5.7	70
Baum, Tyler	R-R	6-2	195	1-14-98	1	0	6.88	15	0	5	17	20	17	13	1	11	25	.282	.381	.380	29.8	13.1	84
Beers, Blake	R-R	6-4	215	7-15-98	3	10	7.81	18	17	0	81	98	76	70	16	34	74	.305	.387	.539	19.8	9.1	374
Boyle, Joe	R-R	6-7	240	8-14-99	2	1	2.08	3	3	0	17	12	4	4	0	7	28	.197	.290	.262	40.6	10.1	69
Briggs, Austin	R-L	6-1	205	10-11-95	1	2	4.71	40	0	2	42	37	30	22	2	32	48	.243	.394	.309	24.5	16.3	196
Cohen, Chase	L-R	6-1	183	4-26-97	3	0	2.31	7	0	1	12	8	3	3	0	4	14	.200	.273	.250	31.8	9.1	44
Coker, Calvin	R-R	6-3	174	3-06-96	3	4	3.15	46	0	6	74	76	32	26	4	24	49	.267	.327	.333	15.7	7.7	313
Cushing, Jack	R-R	6-3	195	12-03-96	8	4	4.34	28	18	2	114	116	61	55	18	24	119	.260	.301	.434	24.9	5.0	477
Cusick, Ryan	R-R	6-6	235	11-12-99	5	7	4.77	22	22	0	94	83	50	50	17	57	84	.239	.348	.450	20.7	14.1	405
De La Cruz, Jasseel	R-R	6-1	195	6-26-97	2	0	13.73	18	0	0	20	34	30	30	7	9	19	.382	.447	.742	18.4	8.7	103
Del Rosario, Joelvis	R-R	5-11	170	4-16-01	2	1	7.23	5	4	0	24	34	19	19	6	6	16	.347	.404	.643	14.7	5.5	109
Emanuels, Stevie	R-R	6-5	210	1-30-99	2	0	2.38	6	0	1	11	8	5	3	1	5	16	.190	.286	.310	32.7	10.2	49
Estes, Joey	R-R	6-2	190	10-08-01	6	6	3.28	20	17	0	104	84	43	38	14	31	100	.215	.288	.382	23.3	7.2	430
Feltman, Durbin	R-R	6-0	208	4-18-97	5	1	2.89	21	0	2	37	30	12	12	3	14	40	.217	.295	.326	25.6	9.0	156
Ginn, J.T.	R-R	6-2	200	5-20-99	1	2	8.06	6	6	0	22	27	23	20	2	13	11	.307	.417	.477	10.2	12.0	108
Hall, Charles	R-R	5-10	170	9-06-94	1	1	5.70	16	0	0	30	20	19	19	2	25	27	.194	.353	.301	20.3	18.8	133
Hoglund, Gunnar	L-R	6-4	220	12-17-99	0	0	5.40	1	1	0	5	6	3	3	0	0	5	.300	.300	.300	25.0	0.0	20
Holman, Grant	R-R	6-6	250	5-31-00	0	2	5.85	25	0	3	32	36	21	21	8	11	45	.271	.336	.474	30.8	7.5	146
Howard, Brian	R-R	6-9	213	4-25-95	5	4	4.21	20	0	0	26	28	13	12	1	13	27	.280	.365	.400	23.5	11.3	115
Juan, Jorge	R-R	6-8	200	3-06-99	1	4	5.66	26	0	1	35	29	23	22	3	34	37	.230	.406	.325	21.8	20.0	170
Kubo, Trayson	R-R	6-0	180	9-26-97	0	2	9.13	21	0	1	23	30	25	23	3	20	28	.319	.431	.543	24.1	17.2	116
Leal, David	L-L	6-5	250	4-22-97	7	5	5.44	36	8	1	84	100	51	51	13	22	68	.297	.341	.475	18.3	5.9	372
McGuire, Shane	L-R	5-10	195	4-12-99	0	1	0.00	3	0	0	3	3	1	0	0	1	0	.250	.308	.333	0.0	7.7	13
Miller, Mason	R-R	6-5	200	8-24-98	0	0	4.91	1	1	0	4	2	2	2	2	0	8	.154	.154	.615	61.5	0.0	13
Patrick, Chad	R-R	6-1	205	8-14-98	0	1	8.44	2	2	0	11	21	11	10	6	2	14	.412	.434	.843	26.4	3.8	53
Perez, Francisco	B-L	6-2	227	7-20-97	1	0	2.45	5	0	0	7	6	2	2	1	1	12	.222	.250	.370	42.9	3.6	28
Perkins, Jack	R-R	6-1	220	12-26-99	1	0	5.67	12	11	0	54	70	39	34	2	29	44	.329	.412	.404	17.5	11.5	252
Salinas, Royber	R-R	6-3	205	4-10-01	1	5	5.48	18	16	1	67	59	44	41	9	31	89	.232	.316	.390	30.9	10.8	288
Supak, Trey	R-R	6-5	268	5-31-96	4	0	4.89	25	0	2	42	42	26	23	4	18	38	.250	.335	.399	19.9	9.4	191
Tomioka, Shohei	R-R	6-0	190	2-29-96	2	0	3.02	29	0	2	45	44	19	15	2	26	53	.253	.353	.339	26.4	12.9	201
Walkinshaw, Jake	R-R	6-3	200	7-07-96	1	3	5.94	8	6	0	33	37	26	22	7	13	23	.276	.340	.500	15.6	8.8	147
Weisenburger, Jack	R-R	6-3	220	10-08-97	0	2	3.78	13	1	1	17	11	7	7	1	11	18	.196	.324	.375	26.5	16.2	68
Yamauchi, Casey	R-R	5-9	155	8-08-00	0	0	0.00	1	0	0	1	1	0	0	0	0	2	.250	.250	.500	50.0	0.0	4

Fielding

Catcher	PCT	G	PO	A	E	DP	PB
McGuire	.986	69	572	48	9	4	8
Schwarz	.986	31	272	13	4	0	2
Simoneit	.990	30	282	13	3	4	3
Susac	1.000	9	81	4	0	1	2

First Base	PCT	G	PO	A	E	DP
Butler	1.000	3	28	5	0	0
Calabuig	1.000	5	32	1	0	4
Davidson	.995	25	202	11	1	27
Eierman	.958	8	62	6	3	4

OAKLAND ATHLETICS

First Base	PCT	G	PO	A	E	DP
Masterman	1.000	2	16	0	0	1
McGuire	.993	19	138	11	1	13
Schwarz	.983	16	105	9	2	13
Simoneit	.994	41	298	13	2	29
Winkler	.988	24	161	5	2	10

Second Base	PCT	G	PO	A	E	DP
Bowman	.963	55	103	133	9	37
Davidson	1.000	12	25	39	0	10
Eierman	.960	18	30	42	3	15
Harris	1.000	1	0	1	0	0
Hernaiz	1.000	3	5	4	0	1
Schuemann	1.000	1	1	5	0	0
Swift	1.000	16	25	45	0	8
Valenzuela	.960	25	41	55	4	10
Wright	1.000	2	5	4	0	1
Yamauchi	.978	9	13	31	1	6

Third Base	PCT	G	PO	A	E	DP
Angeles	1.000	5	3	2	0	1
Davidson	.917	10	9	13	2	4
Eierman	1.000	3	2	6	0	1
Harris	.970	63	47	117	5	13
McGuire	1.000	1	1	1	0	0
Swift	.987	35	23	51	1	2
Valenzuela	1.000	1	0	3	0	0
Winkler	.974	19	14	24	1	1
Wright	1.000	5	1	6	0	0

Shortstop	PCT	G	PO	A	E	DP
Angeles	1.000	1	0	3	0	0
Bowman	1.000	5	8	14	0	3
Eierman	.964	7	8	19	1	5
Harris	.833	2	3	2	1	1
Hernaiz	.962	64	61	144	8	29
Muncy	.952	48	62	118	9	25
Schuemann	1.000	1	2	2	0	2
Swift	1.000	13	21	38	0	12

Outfield	PCT	G	PO	A	E	DP
Armenteros	.973	61	102	3	4	1
Bowman	1.000	1	4	0	0	0
Buelvas	1.000	20	39	2	0	0
Butler, J	.977	23	37	1	1	0
Butler, L	1.000	50	127	7	0	3
Calabuig	.988	28	44	0	1	0
Clarke	.953	57	140	2	6	2
Deichmann	.994	33	68	2	1	0
Guldberg	.963	35	52	2	2	1
Masterman	.957	35	56	6	2	1
Schuemann	1.000	10	18	1	0	0
Trenkle	1.000	47	87	5	0	1
Valenzuela	1.000	24	36	2	0	1
Winkler	.000	1	0	0	0	0
Wright	1.000	1	1	1	0	0

LANSING LUGNUTS

MIDWEST LEAGUE

HIGH CLASS A

Batting	B-T	Ht.	Wt.	DOB	AVG	OBP	SLG	G	PA	AB	R	H	2B	3B	HR	RBI	BB	HBP	SH	SF	SO	SB	CS	BB%	SO%
Amaya, Carlos	R-R	5-10	165	12-28-01	.132	.158	.170	17	57	53	3	7	2	0	0	4	1	1	0	2	14	0	0	1.8	24.6
Angeles, Euribiel	R-R	5-11	175	5-11-02	.272	.293	.390	110	415	397	40	108	18	4	7	50	11	2	2	3	56	21	3	2.7	13.5
Armenteros, Lazaro	R-R	5-11	182	5-22-99	.277	.404	.723	14	57	47	12	13	1	1	6	10	7	3	0	0	21	7	5	12.3	36.8
Bautista, Danny	R-R	6-2	185	9-20-00	.271	.314	.340	118	475	435	50	118	17	2	3	46	22	8	2	7	48	22	11	4.6	10.1
Buelvas, Brayan	R-R	5-11	155	6-08-02	.135	.211	.243	32	123	111	6	15	4	1	2	10	9	2	0	1	38	8	2	7.3	30.9
Butler, Jonny	L-R	6-1	200	2-12-99	.238	.326	.463	64	258	227	34	54	9	6	10	33	22	8	0	1	63	19	2	8.5	24.4
Campos, Alexander	R-R	5-10	178	2-20-00	.235	.343	.318	29	99	85	10	20	4	0	1	7	10	4	0	0	24	0	0	10.1	24.2
Elliott, Clark	L-R	6-0	183	9-29-00	.195	.302	.247	67	252	215	31	42	6	1	1	16	28	6	0	3	47	8	0	11.1	18.7
Halter, Colby	L-R	6-1	200	8-24-01	.198	.293	.259	23	92	81	8	16	3	1	0	6	11	0	0	0	31	2	1	12.0	33.7
Lopez, Hansen	R-R	5-9	170	7-03-00	.000	.000	.000	1	3	3	0	0	0	0	0	0	0	0	0	0	2	0	0	0.0	66.7
Milone, Brennan	R-R	6-1	198	5-06-01	.261	.381	.455	52	215	176	31	46	13	0	7	31	33	3	0	3	47	0	0	15.3	21.9
Muncy, Max	R-R	6-1	180	8-25-02	.255	.327	.385	72	312	275	36	70	18	0	6	31	31	0	3	3	92	9	3	9.9	29.5
Perez, Junior	R-R	6-1	165	7-04-01	.237	.320	.392	117	493	434	67	103	27	2	12	45	51	3	3	2	150	41	9	10.3	30.4
Ricciardi, Mariano	L-R	5-7	170	6-29-98	.227	.261	.273	6	23	22	3	5	1	0	0	1	1	0	0	0	2	0	0	4.3	8.7
Rodriguez, CJ	R-R	5-7	200	7-07-00	.185	.260	.270	76	281	248	20	46	13	1	2	30	25	2	0	6	61	0	0	8.9	21.7
Schofield-Sam, T.J.	L-R	6-1	185	6-20-01	.204	.262	.306	44	172	157	21	32	7	0	3	18	7	6	0	2	43	0	1	4.1	25.0
Susac, Daniel	R-R	6-4	218	5-14-01	.303	.373	.437	99	410	366	47	111	18	5	7	54	39	3	0	2	88	8	0	9.5	21.5
Swift, Drew	R-R	6-0	165	2-15-99	.217	.333	.304	6	27	23	3	5	2	0	0	4	4	0	0	0	9	2	1	14.8	33.3
Thomas, Colby	R-R	6-0	190	1-26-01	.290	.333	.516	54	237	217	38	63	15	2	10	33	11	4	1	2	70	11	2	4.6	29.5
Trenkle, Caeden	L-L	5-10	179	6-29-01	.292	.376	.504	32	135	113	24	33	4	1	6	21	14	3	0	3	31	6	2	10.4	23.0
Uhl, Cooper	R-R	5-8	185	10-19-97	.188	.278	.188	6	18	16	2	3	0	0	0	0	2	0	0	0	9	0	0	11.1	50.0
Valenzuela, Sahid	B-R	5-7	165	9-16-97	.262	.294	.291	30	109	103	12	27	3	0	0	6	3	2	0	1	23	0	1	2.8	21.1
Wilson, Jacob	R-R	6-3	190	3-30-02	.318	.378	.455	23	99	88	13	28	9	0	1	8	6	3	1	1	10	4	1	6.1	10.1
Winkler, Jack	R-R	6-2	185	11-04-98	.253	.331	.355	71	300	265	34	67	16	1	3	26	29	3	1	2	65	19	3	9.7	21.7
Wright, Joshwan	R-R	5-8	170	11-09-00	.277	.336	.343	41	155	137	10	38	5	2	0	17	11	2	3	2	23	1	0	7.1	14.8
Yamauchi, Casey	R-R	5-9	155	8-08-00	.667	.750	.778	3	12	9	0	6	1	0	0	1	2	1	0	0	1	3	0	16.7	8.3

Pitching	B-T	Ht.	Wt.	DOB	W	L	ERA	G	GS	SV	IP	Hits	Runs	ER	HR	BB	SO	AVG	OBP	SLG	SO%	BB%	BF
Adamiak, Mark	R-R	6-4	230	12-15-00	0	0	5.40	4	0	0	5	4	3	3	1	2	7	.211	.286	.368	33.3	9.5	21
Anderson, Luke	R-R	6-2	205	8-05-98	2	0	7.36	12	0	1	18	18	17	15	2	22	16	.254	.443	.423	16.5	22.7	97
Basso, Brady	R-L	6-2	213	10-08-97	2	4	2.64	15	12	0	44	34	13	13	4	11	45	.211	.260	.373	26.0	6.4	173
Baum, Tyler	R-R	6-2	195	1-14-98	1	2	1.72	24	0	11	31	15	9	6	1	14	37	.142	.248	.189	30.6	11.6	121
Bautista, Danny	R-R	6-2	185	9-20-00	0	0	72.00	1	0	0	1	6	8	8	3	0	0	.667	.727	1.667	0.0	0.0	11
Beers, Blake	R-R	6-4	215	7-15-98	4	1	2.91	7	4	0	34	28	12	11	2	13	35	.222	.305	.294	24.8	9.2	141
Beller, John	L-L	5-11	175	3-06-99	4	3	4.18	38	0	5	47	44	22	22	4	27	59	.253	.370	.368	28.1	12.9	210
Breault, Hunter	R-R	6-2	228	6-12-99	1	3	8.26	19	0	0	28	48	29	26	4	10	16	.369	.410	.577	11.0	6.9	145
Del Rosario, Joelvis	R-R	5-11	170	4-16-01	3	9	4.82	19	14	0	80	79	44	43	9	31	69	.256	.327	.405	20.2	9.1	342
Dicochea, Jose	R-R	6-3	180	3-21-01	0	3	4.35	13	12	0	50	40	27	24	3	40	41	.230	.381	.356	18.4	17.9	223
Emanuels, Stevie	R-R	6-5	210	1-30-99	0	0	1.44	15	0	4	25	16	4	4	2	10	33	.186	.286	.279	33.7	10.2	98
Fernandez, Christian	R-R	6-2	170	8-11-99	6	4	4.57	30	8	2	83	77	51	42	7	42	89	.245	.346	.401	24.1	11.4	370
Garland, Jake	R-R	6-5	236	9-26-00	4	9	6.51	18	15	0	84	111	65	61	6	28	59	.321	.374	.468	15.5	7.4	380
Gonzalez, James	L-L	6-2	257	9-15-00	2	1	2.18	4	3	0	21	15	5	5	0	11	27	.211	.313	.254	32.1	13.1	84
Hall, Charles	R-R	5-10	170	9-06-94	1	4	3.86	15	0	3	21	21	12	9	2	15	25	.266	.379	.430	26.3	15.8	95
Hoglund, Gunnar	L-R	6-4	220	12-17-99	1	0	1.42	3	3	0	13	5	2	2	0	2	14	.119	.196	.143	30.4	4.3	46
Holman, Grant	R-R	6-6	250	5-31-00	0	0	0.00	7	2	0	9	4	0	0	0	4	13	.129	.229	.129	37.1	11.4	35
Juan, Jorge	R-R	6-8	200	3-06-99	1	0	0.63	9	0	2	14	7	2	1	0	10	28	.137	.279	.157	45.2	16.1	62
Lardner, Mac	R-L	6-4	195	12-29-97	7	0	4.09	31	0	1	62	60	36	28	4	24	61	.251	.317	.364	22.7	8.9	269
Morales, Luis	R-R	6-3	190	9-24-02	0	0	3.52	2	2	0	8	6	3	3	2	3	8	.207	.281	.414	25.0	9.4	32
Myers, Mitch	R-R	6-2	200	1-08-99	3	6	5.35	23	21	0	104	127	73	62	8	36	73	.297	.361	.418	15.3	7.5	478
Nambiar, Kumar	L-L	5-11	188	4-17-98	6	2	3.47	38	1	1	60	50	26	23	6	28	45	.230	.316	.369	18.1	11.3	248
Owen, Jack	L-L	6-2	204	5-26-98	5	1	3.77	30	3	2	62	58	28	26	4	15	53	.245	.285	.342	20.7	5.9	256

Perkins, Jack	R-R	6-1	220	12-26-99	3	3	2.52	10	9	0	54	34	15	15	3	18	49	.182	.262	.299	23.2	8.5	211
Sanchez, Yehizon	R-R	6-2	170	11-16-00	0	1	8.10	4	1	1	13	24	12	12	3	3	12	.375	.403	.656	17.9	4.5	67
Santos, Pedro	R-R	6-4	205	1-07-00	0	2	3.86	15	0	4	21	15	14	9	2	17	31	.195	.351	.299	32.0	17.5	97
Watters, Jacob	R-R	6-4	230	3-03-01	2	9	6.62	22	21	0	84	83	67	62	8	59	94	.254	.374	.367	23.7	14.9	396
Whittlesey, Brock	R-R	6-3	210	2-27-97	2	4	4.41	38	0	1	51	55	28	25	6	22	40	.281	.363	.480	17.7	9.7	226

Fielding

Catcher	PCT	G	PO	A	E	DP	PB
Amaya	.970	13	86	11	3	1	1
Rodriguez	.996	56	459	37	2	9	3
Susac	.986	67	533	22	8	1	5
Uhl	1.000	1	8	0	0	0	0

First Base	PCT	G	PO	A	E	DP
Bautista	.986	71	516	37	8	62
Milone	.992	35	225	16	2	19
Winkler	.983	29	211	20	4	24

Second Base	PCT	G	PO	A	E	DP
Angeles	1.000	37	62	91	0	21
Campos	.931	8	8	19	2	4
Halter	1.000	22	29	59	0	11
Milone	.966	10	5	23	1	4
Ricciardi	.944	4	6	11	1	7
Swift	1.000	6	11	19	0	4
Valenzuela	.991	24	40	67	1	14
Wright	.991	25	33	76	1	19

Third Base	PCT	G	PO	A	E	DP
Amaya	1.000	1	0	2	0	0
Angeles	.915	35	31	55	8	8
Campos	.969	18	14	17	1	0
Schofield-Sam	.922	32	23	48	6	6
Winkler	.933	37	29	69	7	8
Wright	.964	12	11	16	1	1

Shortstop	PCT	G	PO	A	E	DP
Angeles	.977	34	55	71	3	17
Muncy	.969	70	79	175	8	41
Wilson	.968	22	37	53	3	14
Winkler	.947	6	6	12	1	3
Yamauchi	1.000	3	10	5	0	2

Outfield	PCT	G	PO	A	E	DP
Armenteros	.979	8	17	0	1	0
Bautista	.993	40	73	3	1	1
Buelvas	.972	29	68	0	2	0
Butler	.993	55	107	6	1	1
Elliott	.981	61	99	2	2	0
Perez	.973	116	272	14	10	5
Thomas	.989	53	87	3	2	0
Trenkle	1.000	32	59	0	0	0
Valenzuela	1.000	4	6	0	0	0
Wright	1.000	2	4	0	0	0

STOCKTON PORTS

LOW CLASS A

CALIFORNIA LEAGUE

Batting	B-T	Ht.	Wt.	DOB	AVG	OBP	SLG	G	PA	AB	R	H	2B	3B	HR	RBI	BB	HBP	SH	SF	SO	SB	CS	BB%	SO%
Arevalo, Angel	R-R	5-11	160	10-02-03	.186	.278	.229	22	79	70	7	13	1	1	0	7	8	1	0	0	29	3	2	10.1	36.7
Beltran, Nelson	R-R	5-10	160	12-28-01	.116	.238	.170	35	130	112	14	13	6	0	0	4	16	2	0	0	55	0	2	12.3	42.3
Bolte, Henry	R-R	6-3	195	8-04-03	.257	.356	.421	112	491	420	77	108	17	5	14	68	62	5	0	4	164	32	9	12.6	33.4
Brown, Seth	L-L	6-1	223	7-13-92	.364	.417	.364	3	12	11	4	4	0	0	0	0	1	0	0	0	2	0	0	8.3	16.7
Buelvas, Brayan	R-R	5-11	155	6-08-02	.290	.389	.515	54	235	200	36	58	12	3	9	33	31	2	1	1	51	23	2	13.2	21.7
Cooke, Bjay	R-R	6-2	187	3-14-03	.194	.292	.226	97	391	340	31	66	8	0	1	24	44	4	1	2	155	14	7	11.3	39.6
Cox, Jonah	R-R	6-3	190	8-04-01	.264	.325	.373	28	120	110	16	29	2	2	2	10	5	5	0	0	40	14	2	4.2	33.3
Elliott, Clark	L-R	6-0	183	9-29-00	.269	.418	.344	26	122	93	16	25	2	1	1	12	21	5	0	3	20	5	3	17.2	16.4
Escorche, Jose	R-R	5-8	145	4-29-02	.249	.298	.305	67	252	233	37	58	10	0	1	23	15	2	0	2	57	14	4	6.0	22.6
Franco, Carlos	R-R	5-10	150	2-17-03	.252	.316	.285	33	136	123	11	31	1	0	1	18	12	0	0	1	28	0	0	8.8	20.6
Gomez, Mario	L-R	5-10	185	12-30-02	.222	.222	.222	3	9	9	0	2	0	0	0	1	0	0	0	0	4	1	0	0.0	44.4
Laboy, Yeniel	L-R	6-3	196	5-11-04	.195	.317	.266	48	200	169	19	33	6	0	2	14	26	4	1	0	47	3	0	13.0	23.5
Lopez, Hansen	R-R	5-9	170	7-03-00	.125	.300	.125	5	10	8	1	1	0	0	0	1	2	0	0	0	3	0	0	20.0	30.0
Marinez, Luis	R-R	6-1	155	10-11-01	.092	.194	.149	24	98	87	10	8	2	0	1	9	9	2	0	0	48	2	0	9.2	49.0
Masterman, Cameron	R-R	6-2	225	5-05-99	.254	.324	.390	16	68	59	8	15	5	0	1	13	4	3	0	2	19	1	0	5.9	27.9
Milone, Brennan	R-R	6-1	198	5-06-01	.304	.410	.513	62	273	224	42	68	15	1	10	41	39	5	0	5	45	3	1	14.3	16.5
Montero, Darlyn	B-R	6-2	170	5-11-02	.154	.214	.231	13	56	52	5	8	2	1	0	5	4	0	0	0	19	0	0	7.1	33.9
Mujica, Jose	R-R	6-0	164	3-28-01	.214	.276	.309	79	319	285	31	61	7	1	6	39	23	4	0	7	58	2	5	7.2	18.2
Naylor, Myles	R-R	6-2	195	4-15-05	.208	.280	.375	32	132	120	16	25	2	0	6	17	11	1	0	0	52	2	0	8.3	39.4
Pina, Manny	R-R	6-0	222	6-05-87	.300	.417	.700	4	12	10	4	3	1	0	1	2	2	0	0	0	2	0	0	16.7	16.7
Pineda, Pedro	R-R	6-1	170	9-06-03	.224	.310	.300	68	256	223	32	50	7	2	2	14	24	4	4	1	85	19	5	9.4	33.2
Puason, Robert	R-R	6-3	165	9-11-02	.142	.216	.176	51	194	176	13	25	3	0	1	9	11	6	0	1	70	7	2	5.7	36.1
Richards, Kevin	R-R	6-2	160	1-08-00	.273	.333	.295	13	48	44	5	12	1	0	0	2	4	0	0	0	15	1	1	8.3	31.3
Rijo, Elvis	R-R	5-11	165	11-27-03	.149	.226	.149	15	53	47	1	7	0	0	0	4	3	2	0	1	12	0	1	5.7	22.6
Salom, Dereck	R-R	5-10	135	2-22-01	.212	.337	.267	74	312	255	37	54	9	1	1	25	48	3	0	6	60	1	1	15.4	19.2
Schofield-Sam, T.J.	L-R	6-1	185	6-20-01	.273	.337	.410	70	306	271	33	74	22	3	3	37	21	8	0	6	62	3	3	6.9	20.3
Simpson, Will	R-R	6-4	225	8-28-01	.322	.373	.522	29	126	115	18	37	11	0	4	16	10	0	0	1	29	3	1	7.9	23.0
Stevenson, Tommy	R-R	6-4	225	9-13-00	.167	.294	.333	33	143	120	15	20	5	0	5	19	20	2	0	1	54	0	0	14.0	37.8
Thomas, Colby	R-R	6-0	190	1-26-01	.283	.364	.476	72	327	290	49	82	24	4	8	49	26	11	0	0	76	14	4	8.0	23.2
Uhl, Cooper	R-R	5-8	185	10-19-97	.294	.434	.353	46	173	136	23	40	2	0	2	16	32	3	0	2	41	1	0	18.5	23.7

Pitching	B-T	Ht.	Wt.	DOB	W	L	ERA	G	GS	SV	IP	Hits	Runs	ER	HR	BB	SO	AVG	OBP	SLG	SO%	BB%	BF
Blackburn, Paul	R-R	6-1	196	12-04-93	0	0	10.80	1	1	0	2	7	3	2	0	1	0	.636	.615	.727	0.0	7.7	13
Carrasco, Luis	R-R	6-1	180	12-19-01	4	7	4.81	17	15	0	79	97	54	42	4	23	73	.299	.357	.407	20.5	6.5	356
Cerny, Charlie	L-R	6-5	230	9-23-96	3	3	5.92	34	0	0	52	56	46	34	3	42	45	.272	.397	.374	17.9	16.7	252
Cohn, Aaron	R-R	6-0	195	10-30-98	0	3	9.21	24	0	0	28	44	34	29	4	15	19	.364	.431	.603	13.1	10.3	145
Czyz, T.J.	R-R	6-2	175	9-12-00	1	0	8.03	20	2	0	25	34	23	22	5	18	26	.327	.424	.587	20.8	14.4	125
Dallas, Micah	R-R	6-2	215	4-14-00	3	4	6.39	20	4	0	49	67	40	35	6	11	46	.319	.359	.505	20.4	4.9	226
De La Rosa, Franck	R-R	6-8	200	6-09-00	2	0	6.10	15	0	2	21	16	15	14	2	12	23	.203	.323	.342	24.7	12.9	93
Dicochea, Jose	R-R	6-3	180	3-21-01	2	1	3.20	9	7	0	39	23	14	14	3	17	47	.163	.263	.248	29.4	10.6	160
Franco, Carlos	R-R	5-10	150	2-17-03	0	0	0.00	1	0	0	1	0	0	0	0	1	0	.000	.200	.000	0.0	20.0	5
Garland, Jake	R-R	6-5	236	9-26-00	1	2	2.78	6	4	0	32	34	15	10	0	8	31	.266	.314	.367	22.6	5.8	137
Gimenez, Dheygler	R-R	6-2	170	12-03-01	3	2	5.10	14	13	0	65	59	40	37	11	37	60	.237	.358	.438	20.2	12.5	297
Gonzalez, James	L-L	6-2	257	9-15-00	4	8	4.95	20	16	0	87	93	60	48	11	35	108	.262	.332	.420	27.3	8.9	395
Guante, Wander	R-R	6-1	180	6-15-00	3	6	5.25	25	18	0	110	107	73	64	13	53	100	.250	.339	.411	20.4	10.8	490
Guarate, Carlos	R-R	6-2	178	3-30-01	5	5	5.95	36	1	2	65	73	50	43	12	26	58	.278	.347	.471	19.5	8.7	298
Hoglund, Gunnar	L-R	6-4	220	12-17-99	1	5	7.48	12	12	0	43	56	37	36	9	10	27	.313	.349	.547	14.1	5.2	192

Irvin, Garrett	L-L	6-0	185	2-18-99	8	1	2.93	31	0	2	71	54	30	23	7	29	92	.207	.290	.322	31.3	9.9	294
Jackson, Zach	R-R	6-4	230	12-25-94	0	0	9.00	2	0	0	2	2	2	2	2	0	4	.250	.250	1.000	50.0	0.0	8
Lopez, Hansen	R-R	5-9	170	7-03-00	0	0	0.00	1	0	0	1	0	0	0	0	0	1	.000	.000	.000	33.3	0.0	3
Lovelady, Richard	L-L	6-0	185	7-07-95	0	0	9.00	1	0	0	1	1	1	1	1	0	1	.250	.250	1.000	25.0	0.0	4
Manzano, Alejandro	R-R	6-2	165	2-28-02	0	3	11.15	4	3	1	15	29	20	19	3	4	16	.414	.456	.614	20.3	5.1	79
Miller, Mason	R-R	6-5	200	8-24-98	0	0	4.91	2	2	0	4	3	2	2	1	2	4	.231	.333	.538	26.7	13.3	15
Morales, Luis	R-R	6-3	190	9-24-02	0	3	2.20	5	5	0	16	13	8	4	0	8	18	.217	.319	.267	26.1	11.6	69
Pfennigs, Jake	R-R	6-7	215	9-09-99	0	1	3.72	8	4	0	19	9	10	8	1	14	22	.134	.293	.224	26.8	17.1	82
Pontes, Blaze	R-R	6-0	185	1-06-00	0	4	3.23	39	1	11	61	61	26	22	3	22	65	.255	.314	.335	24.5	8.3	265
Reilly, Vince	R-R	5-10	160	6-07-01	0	0	3.86	4	0	0	5	5	2	2	1	2	6	.250	.318	.400	27.3	9.1	22
Rivera, Eduardo	L-L	6-7	237	6-13-03	2	7	5.35	16	12	0	69	67	48	41	3	44	75	.252	.366	.365	23.2	13.6	323
Rodriguez, Franyelson	R-R	6-1	160	5-20-02	2	1	5.03	21	0	1	34	46	23	19	6	8	28	.319	.364	.507	18.1	5.2	155
Sanchez, Yehizon	R-R	6-2	170	11-16-00	1	8	15.53	13	5	0	27	48	47	46	9	19	26	.378	.477	.677	17.2	12.6	151
Santos, Pedro	R-R	6-4	205	1-07-00	2	2	2.73	24	0	6	30	21	16	9	2	18	41	.196	.320	.299	32.0	14.1	128
Sha, Tzu-Chen	R-R	6-2	165	10-15-03	0	1	5.00	7	7	0	27	31	17	15	4	5	15	.284	.322	.450	12.3	4.1	122
Tur, Yunior	R-R	6-6	200	8-09-99	2	2	6.82	19	0	0	32	39	28	24	5	21	47	.298	.400	.466	30.3	13.5	155
Woolfolk, Dallas	R-R	6-2	225	10-30-96	1	3	7.33	37	0	2	50	56	54	41	5	30	47	.272	.379	.398	18.9	12.0	249

Fielding

Catcher	PCT	G	PO	A	E	DP	PB
Franco	.987	26	216	20	3	4	5
Gomez	1.000	3	14	1	0	0	2
Lopez	1.000	4	17	2	0	0	0
Marinez	.968	7	58	3	2	0	5
Mujica	.993	57	518	32	4	4	8
Pina	1.000	1	5	1	0	0	0
Stevenson	1.000	3	21	2	0	0	0
Uhl	.983	41	325	28	6	3	6

First Base	PCT	G	PO	A	E	DP
Laboy	.977	24	165	7	4	14
Marinez	.990	13	92	11	1	9
Masterman	1.000	7	67	2	0	3
Milone	1.000	24	175	14	0	18
Montero	.982	12	103	4	2	8
Mujica	1.000	2	12	2	0	2
Richards	.952	5	38	2	2	2
Schofield-Sam	.974	11	70	6	2	6
Simpson	.994	23	165	13	1	9
Stevenson	.983	14	109	9	2	8
Uhl	.909	1	8	2	1	2

Second Base	PCT	G	PO	A	E	DP
Arevalo	.984	15	22	39	1	8
Cooke	.923	18	28	44	6	6
Escorche	.943	45	64	102	10	23
Milone	.962	19	32	43	3	9
Puason	.880	5	9	13	3	2
Rijo	.943	14	24	26	3	4
Salom	.965	20	30	53	3	10

Third Base	PCT	G	PO	A	E	DP
Cooke	.857	8	5	13	3	0
Escorche	.727	7	1	7	3	0
Laboy	.894	18	14	28	5	4
Milone	.844	10	9	18	5	1
Rijo	.000	1	0	0	1	0
Salom	.904	50	35	87	13	9
Schofield-Sam	.929	46	34	84	9	10

Shortstop	PCT	G	PO	A	E	DP
Cooke	.934	71	123	173	21	31
Escorche	.945	14	18	34	3	8
Naylor	.923	28	43	65	9	11
Puason	.852	19	18	34	9	6
Salom	.857	2	1	5	1	1
Schofield-Sam	1.000	1	1	3	0	2

Outfield	PCT	G	PO	A	E	DP
Arevalo	.929	7	12	1	1	0
Beltran	1.000	32	43	0	0	0
Bolte	.936	103	175	6	6	1
Brown	1.000	2	1	1	0	0
Buelvas	.981	45	99	2	2	0
Cox	.993	24	66	2	1	0
Elliott	.970	19	29	2	1	0
Masterman	.900	6	7	2	1	0
Pineda	.955	65	122	7	7	2
Puason	.953	24	38	3	2	0
Richards	1.000	5	9	1	0	1
Schofield-Sam	.941	14	16	0	1	0
Thomas	.981	64	111	5	3	1

ACL ATHLETICS — *ROOKIE*

ARIZONA COMPLEX LEAGUE

Batting	B-T	Ht.	Wt.	DOB	AVG	OBP	SLG	G	PA	AB	R	H	2B	3B	HR	RBI	BB	HBP	SH	SF	SO	SB	CS	BB%	SO%
Arevalo, Angel	R-R	5-11	160	10-02-03	.191	.372	.327	35	145	110	28	21	5	2	2	10	29	4	0	2	43	8	2	20.0	29.7
Beltran, Nelson	R-R	5-10	160	12-28-01	.299	.429	.403	23	84	67	16	20	2	1	1	10	13	3	0	1	15	6	1	15.5	17.9
Bowman, Cooper	R-R	6-0	205	1-25-00	.250	.400	.333	4	15	12	4	3	1	0	0	2	1	2	0	0	4	3	0	6.7	26.7
Conn, Cole	B-R	6-0	175	7-11-01	.231	.375	.231	10	32	26	3	6	0	0	0	1	5	1	0	0	7	5	1	15.6	21.9
Cox, Jonah	R-R	6-3	190	8-04-01	.421	.560	.579	7	25	19	6	8	1	1	0	5	4	2	0	0	1	6	0	16.0	4.0
Eierman, Jeremy	R-R	5-11	205	9-10-96	.000	.333	.000	1	3	2	0	0	0	0	0	0	1	0	0	0	2	0	0	33.3	66.7
Freitez, Luis	R-R	6-0	180	5-17-03	.200	.319	.263	34	117	95	16	19	2	2	0	13	16	2	1	3	32	2	0	13.7	27.4
Fuentes, Erubiel	R-R	5-8	170	1-15-03	.200	.448	.200	8	29	20	5	4	0	0	0	4	6	3	0	0	8	0	0	20.7	27.6
Gallardo, Moises	R-R	6-0	160	4-23-03	.280	.376	.452	31	109	93	13	26	8	1	2	24	14	1	0	1	34	3	0	12.8	31.2
Garrett, Ray	R-R	5-10	155	3-23-04	.138	.324	.241	15	37	29	5	4	0	0	1	2	8	0	0	0	15	2	1	21.6	40.5
Gomez, Mario	L-R	5-10	185	12-30-02	.272	.405	.480	43	159	125	23	34	11	0	5	34	28	2	0	3	34	3	1	17.6	21.4
Halter, Colby	L-R	6-1	200	8-24-01	.455	.538	.576	11	39	33	7	15	4	0	0	6	5	1	0	0	5	2	0	12.8	12.8
Laboy, Yeniel	L-R	6-3	196	5-11-04	.298	.455	.368	19	77	57	14	17	2	1	0	12	15	3	0	2	10	3	0	19.5	13.0
Lasko, Ryan	R-R	6-0	190	6-24-02	.154	.233	.231	10	30	26	3	4	2	0	0	3	3	0	0	1	5	1	0	10.0	16.7
Lopez, Hansen	R-R	5-9	170	7-03-00	.136	.240	.136	8	25	22	2	3	0	0	0	1	2	1	0	0	8	0	0	8.0	32.0
Machado, Anderson	R-R	6-1	170	10-10-03	.127	.213	.152	30	89	79	7	10	2	0	0	3	8	1	0	1	25	1	0	9.0	28.1
Mann, Luke	L-R	6-2	218	4-13-00	.000	.000	.000	3	6	6	0	0	0	0	0	0	0	0	0	0	2	0	0	0.0	33.3
Marinez, Luis	R-R	6-1	155	10-11-01	.114	.225	.400	14	40	35	7	4	1	0	3	7	4	1	0	0	19	1	0	10.0	47.5
Masterman, Cameron	R-R	6-2	225	5-05-99	.212	.378	.333	10	45	33	8	7	4	0	0	10	9	1	0	2	12	1	0	20.0	26.7
Montero, Darlyn	B-R	6-2	170	5-11-02	.276	.342	.425	48	196	174	38	48	7	5	3	36	15	4	0	3	49	9	0	7.7	25.0
Nankil, Nate	R-R	6-3	185	10-16-02	.189	.259	.245	16	58	53	5	10	3	0	0	7	5	0	0	0	9	1	0	8.6	15.5
Naylor, Myles	R-R	6-2	195	4-15-05	.333	.429	.500	2	7	6	2	2	1	0	0	0	1	0	0	0	3	0	0	14.3	42.9
Ortiz, German	B-R	6-2	195	8-02-04	.217	.358	.259	46	180	143	20	31	6	0	0	14	31	1	2	1	39	3	0	17.2	21.7
Pariguan, Javier	R-R	5-10	160	2-05-04	.175	.329	.302	25	80	63	13	11	5	0	1	4	15	0	1	1	23	0	0	18.8	28.8
Puason, Robert	R-R	6-3	165	9-11-02	.306	.362	.339	17	69	62	9	19	2	0	0	9	6	0	0	1	16	3	3	8.7	23.2
Rijo, Elvis	R-R	5-11	165	11-27-03	.143	.226	.143	19	31	28	2	4	0	0	0	1	3	0	0	0	7	0	1	9.7	22.6
Rivera, Angel	R-R	5-9	175	2-02-03	.208	.368	.245	20	69	53	8	11	2	0	0	6	14	0	1	1	11	0	0	20.3	15.9
Rodriguez, Joseph	R-R	6-1	165	1-04-03	.281	.439	.421	39	157	121	33	34	8	3	1	17	29	6	0	1	47	7	1	18.5	29.9
Rosado, Jamaliel	R-R	6-3	195	8-15-03	.167	.333	.233	22	75	60	14	10	0	2	0	3	14	1	0	0	31	1	0	18.7	41.3
Schwartz, Nick	R-R	5-11	190	3-07-01	.588	.667	.765	6	21	17	5	10	0	0	1	4	3	1	0	0	2	0	0	14.3	9.5

Simpson, Will	R-R	6-4	225	8-28-01	.304	.333	.652	7	24	23	9	7	2	0	2	7	1	0	0	0	5	0	0	4.2	20.8
Swift, Drew	R-R	6-0	165	2-15-99	.200	.500	.333	5	24	15	3	3	2	0	0	4	7	2	0	0	3	2	0	29.2	12.5
Trenkle, Caeden	L-L	5-10	179	6-29-01	.182	.474	.182	5	19	11	5	2	0	0	0	2	3	4	0	1	4	2	1	15.8	21.1
Wilson, Jacob	R-R	6-3	190	3-30-02	.455	.500	.636	3	12	11	4	5	2	0	0	5	0	1	0	0	1	0	0	0.0	8.3
Wright, Joshwan	R-R	5-8	170	11-09-00	.240	.345	.520	7	29	25	5	6	4	0	1	6	3	1	0	0	3	1	0	10.3	10.3
Yamauchi, Casey	R-R	5-9	155	8-08-00	.400	.625	.400	3	8	5	3	2	0	0	0	0	3	0	0	0	0	0	0	37.5	0.0

Pitching	B-T	Ht.	Wt.	DOB	W	L	ERA	G	GS	SV	IP	Hits	Runs	ER	HR	BB	SO	AVG	OBP	SLG	SO%	BB%	BF
Adamiak, Mark	R-R	6-4	230	12-15-00	0	1	10.66	12	0	0	13	18	16	15	2	11	14	.353	.462	.569	21.2	16.7	66
Avant, Corey	R-R	6-4	225	11-06-01	0	1	6.75	3	0	0	4	6	3	3	0	5	3	.400	.550	.467	15.0	25.0	20
Barrera, Diego	L-L	6-0	165	5-05-00	0	0	0.00	2	0	0	2	1	0	0	0	0	2	.143	.143	.143	28.6	0.0	7
Breault, Hunter	R-R	6-2	228	6-12-99	0	0	3.38	3	1	0	3	4	1	1	0	1	4	.333	.385	.583	30.8	7.7	13
Brown, Ryan	R-R	6-2	214	11-02-00	0	0	5.63	5	0	0	8	10	8	5	1	1	4	.303	.343	.455	11.4	2.9	35
Cohn, Aaron	R-R	6-0	195	10-30-98	1	0	3.38	14	0	0	21	19	10	8	3	7	18	.235	.308	.383	19.8	7.7	91
Conley, Bryce	R-R	6-3	200	8-22-94	0	0	0.00	1	1	0	1	1	0	0	0	1	0	.333	.600	.333	0.0	20.0	5
Conover, Drew	R-R	6-5	185	7-27-01	0	0	0.00	1	0	0	1	0	0	0	0	2	2	.000	.500	.000	50.0	50.0	4
Corro, Derek	L-L	5-11	145	11-19-04	1	5	10.17	11	7	0	23	34	33	26	2	28	28	.337	.485	.475	21.2	21.2	132
Cusick, Ryan	R-R	6-6	235	11-12-99	0	0	0.00	1	1	0	3	1	1	0	0	2	5	.100	.250	.100	41.7	16.7	12
Czyz, T.J.	R-R	6-2	175	9-12-00	1	0	3.32	16	0	1	19	13	8	7	1	10	16	.194	.304	.284	20.3	12.7	79
De Jesus, Dairon	R-R	6-3	180	3-27-04	0	2	4.24	19	0	3	23	26	23	11	1	15	36	.280	.374	.452	31.0	12.9	116
De La Cruz, Jasseel	R-R	6-1	195	6-26-97	0	0	5.14	6	2	0	7	7	6	4	0	5	10	.241	.353	.310	28.6	14.3	35
De La Rosa, Franck	R-R	6-8	200	6-09-00	0	0	0.00	3	1	0	3	1	0	0	0	1	5	.111	.273	.111	45.5	9.1	11
Dettmer, Nathan	R-R	6-4	230	4-26-02	0	0	0.00	2	2	0	3	2	0	0	0	1	3	.200	.273	.300	27.3	9.1	11
Emanuels, Stevie	R-R	6-5	210	1-30-99	0	0	5.40	3	0	0	3	3	2	2	0	4	8	.250	.438	.250	50.0	25.0	16
Fishman, Jake	L-L	6-3	195	2-08-95	0	1	2.25	3	1	0	4	4	3	1	0	1	7	.250	.278	.313	38.9	5.6	18
Garza, Roberto	R-R	6-2	175	6-22-02	0	1	9.64	5	1	1	5	11	10	5	1	7	4	.500	.633	.773	13.3	23.3	30
Ginn, J.T.	R-R	6-2	200	5-20-99	0	1	4.15	2	2	0	4	5	3	2	0	3	6	.278	.364	.278	27.3	13.6	22
Gonzalez, Jose	R-R	6-0	160	1-05-02	0	1	5.48	18	0	2	23	20	16	14	1	10	20	.230	.320	.356	19.8	9.9	101
Guerra, Deolis	R-R	6-5	245	4-17-89	0	0	9.00	3	2	0	4	6	4	4	0	1	6	.333	.368	.667	31.6	5.3	19
Hernandez, Camilo	R-R	6-1	190	9-30-03	1	3	4.50	12	2	1	30	36	24	15	0	8	23	.305	.346	.424	17.7	6.2	130
Holman, Grant	R-R	6-6	250	5-31-00	0	0	0.00	3	3	0	3	2	2	0	0	4	2	.200	.400	.200	13.3	26.7	15
Jean, Jefferson	R-R	6-3	170	1-29-05	0	1	6.75	2	2	0	5	9	5	4	1	3	3	.360	.429	.560	10.7	10.7	28
Johnston, Will	L-L	6-3	215	12-12-00	1	0	5.40	4	1	0	7	6	5	4	1	5	6	.250	.379	.458	20.0	16.7	30
Lina, Elvi	R-R	6-2	200	10-17-04	0	1	17.69	14	1	0	10	17	22	19	0	22	12	.370	.586	.500	17.1	31.4	70
Manzano, Alejandro	R-R	6-2	165	2-28-02	3	2	3.76	9	6	0	41	42	27	17	5	10	34	.263	.305	.413	19.5	5.7	174
Morales, Luis	R-R	6-3	190	9-24-02	0	2	6.00	3	3	0	9	10	8	6	0	2	11	.270	.300	.459	27.5	5.0	40
Reisinger, Tom	R-R	6-3	215	3-17-01	0	2	6.00	4	2	0	6	8	6	4	1	2	10	.296	.345	.444	34.5	6.9	29
Restituyo, Brayan	L-L	5-11	160	1-17-02	4	1	5.28	16	0	0	29	28	19	17	3	19	35	.243	.365	.452	25.5	13.9	137
Rodriguez, Franyelson	R-R	6-1	160	5-20-02	0	0	3.18	3	0	0	6	6	4	2	1	0	9	.261	.261	.565	39.1	0.0	23
Saa, Reynaldo	R-R	6-1	175	12-25-04	0	0	22.09	6	2	0	4	6	11	9	0	12	5	.333	.613	.556	16.1	38.7	31
Salinas, Royber	R-R	6-3	205	4-10-01	0	0	4.15	2	2	0	4	6	3	2	0	0	4	.316	.350	.421	20.0	0.0	20
Sanchez, Yehizon	R-R	6-2	170	11-16-00	2	3	5.56	9	4	0	34	39	29	21	2	17	29	.291	.389	.388	18.5	10.8	157
Sarmiento, Carlos	L-L	5-11	145	8-19-03	3	1	5.63	13	0	0	16	24	16	10	2	17	19	.364	.500	.530	22.6	20.2	84
Sha, Tzu-Chen	R-R	6-2	165	10-15-03	2	3	4.01	7	0	0	25	28	12	11	2	3	38	.283	.301	.424	36.9	2.9	103
Silverio, Jesus	R-R	6-2	180	7-15-02	1	3	5.65	12	2	0	37	38	29	23	6	27	29	.271	.402	.464	16.6	15.4	175
Snead, Kirby	L-L	6-1	218	10-07-94	0	1	13.50	2	1	0	2	2	3	3	0	2	2	.250	.400	.375	20.0	20.0	10
Tarnok, Freddy	R-R	6-3	185	11-24-98	0	0	0.00	1	1	0	2	1	0	0	0	1	2	.167	.286	.167	28.6	14.3	7
Tur, Yunior	R-R	6-6	200	8-09-99	0	0	1.59	2	1	0	6	5	5	1	0	3	6	.200	.286	.280	21.4	10.7	28
Weisenburger, Jack	R-R	6-3	220	10-08-97	0	0	2.25	3	2	0	4	5	2	1	0	0	3	.294	.294	.294	17.6	0.0	17

Fielding

C: Pariguan 18, Rivera 14, Conn 10, Gomez 9, Marinez 9, Schwartz 6, Lopez 5. **1B:** Gomez 28, Montero 13, Simpson 7, Machado 7, Laboy 3, Marinez 2, Ortiz 2. **2B:** Ortiz 27, Rijo 10, Halter 9, Garrett 8, Arevalo 7, Bowman 3, Fuentes 3, Yamauchi 3, Swift 2, Wright 1, Machado 1. **3B:** Machado 16, Laboy 13, Ortiz 13, Montero 11, Rijo 4, Wright 4, Fuentes 3, Mann 3, Naylor 1. **SS:** Arevalo 29, Rosado 20, Garrett 4, Rijo 3, Swift 2, Wilson 2, Halter 1, Bowman 1, Eierman 1, Fuentes 1. **OF:** Rodriguez 35, Freitez 34, Gallardo 24, Beltran 19, Montero 19, Nankil 16, Puason 15, Masterman 7, Cox 7, Lasko 7, Ortiz 5, Trenkle 3, Machado 1.

DSL ATHLETICS — ROOKIE

DOMINICAN SUMMER LEAGUE

Batting	B-T	Ht.	Wt.	DOB	AVG	OBP	SLG	G	PA	AB	R	H	2B	3B	HR	RBI	BB	HBP	SH	SF	SO	SB	CS	BB%	SO%
Andrade, Bryan	R-R	6-1	145	2-03-05	.188	.288	.188	29	111	96	10	18	0	0	0	14	11	3	0	1	18	0	0	9.9	16.2
Baldallo, Dayker	L-R	5-10	135	11-29-03	.159	.311	.196	40	132	107	13	17	4	0	0	11	21	3	0	1	30	2	2	15.9	22.7
De La Cruz, Reinaldo	R-R	6-2	170	1-12-06	.193	.310	.247	48	200	166	25	32	3	0	2	16	23	6	3	2	52	12	1	11.5	26.0
De La Paz, Reynaldo	R-R	6-3	190	9-11-05	.246	.386	.351	50	210	171	21	42	14	2	0	17	30	9	0	0	52	2	1	14.3	24.8
Dume, Kevin	L-R	6-5	220	9-19-04	.197	.384	.287	39	159	122	16	24	5	0	2	19	36	1	0	0	49	0	0	22.6	30.8
Duran, Frandy	L-R	6-2	175	9-29-05	.192	.324	.233	41	146	120	15	23	2	0	1	8	19	5	1	1	34	4	0	13.0	23.3
Fernandez, Darling	R-R	6-2	190	12-10-05	.231	.310	.231	10	29	26	1	6	0	0	0	1	3	0	0	0	3	1	1	10.3	10.3
Fernandez, Jesus	R-R	5-11	145	2-14-06	.300	.360	.353	52	229	207	31	62	9	1	0	15	15	5	1	1	14	9	6	6.6	6.1
Gonzalez, Cesar	R-R	6-2	165	1-13-05	.218	.361	.320	44	180	147	25	32	6	0	3	23	27	6	0	0	29	1	2	15.0	16.1
Landaeta, Ramon	R-R	6-2	180	4-19-06	.250	.341	.382	22	88	76	14	19	1	0	3	13	11	0	0	1	27	1	0	12.5	30.7
Lelis, Matheus	R-R	5-9	160	6-12-02	.149	.293	.170	18	58	47	4	7	1	0	0	9	6	4	0	1	15	1	0	10.3	25.9
Lopez, Jeison	R-R	6-1	170	4-06-06	.143	.174	.143	7	24	21	3	3	0	0	0	3	1	0	1	1	10	2	0	4.2	41.7
Natera, Jesus	R-R	5-10	165	7-22-06	.143	.250	.229	16	40	35	2	5	3	0	0	4	5	0	0	0	11	0	1	12.5	27.5
Pacheco, Carlos	R-R	5-10	150	11-01-04	.244	.371	.336	47	160	131	25	32	4	1	2	16	22	5	1	1	38	20	5	13.8	23.8
Superlano, Jesus	R-R	5-11	165	9-20-05	.205	.271	.295	35	133	122	14	25	7	2	0	7	8	3	0	0	38	6	1	6.0	28.6

Yan, Jonatan	R-R	6-0	150	11-01-04	.196	.338	.339	22	69	56	15	11	2	0	2	8	9	3	1	0	17	3	1	13.0	24.6

Pitching	**B-T**	**Ht.**	**Wt.**	**DOB**	**W**	**L**	**ERA**	**G**	**GS**	**SV**	**IP**	**Hits**	**Runs**	**ER**	**HR**	**BB**	**SO**	**AVG**	**OBP**	**SLG**	**SO%**	**BB%**	**BF**
Alvarado, Wilfred	R-R	6-3	190	11-20-05	0	1	5.32	16	0	1	22	23	14	13	0	11	25	.280	.365	.341	25.8	11.3	97
Baldallo, Dayker	L-R	5-10	135	11-29-03	0	0	0.00	2	0	0	3	2	0	0	0	0	1	.222	.222	.333	11.1	0.0	9
Castro, Felix	R-R	6-3	180	2-16-04	0	1	2.75	16	0	6	20	14	6	6	1	8	29	.197	.305	.310	35.4	9.8	82
Chacon, Paul	R-R	6-0	180	9-08-05	2	1	7.00	10	2	0	18	24	16	14	0	11	15	.329	.444	.438	16.7	12.2	90
Cortes, Jonathan	R-R	6-2	200	7-31-04	1	1	16.20	5	2	0	7	17	12	12	2	7	7	.486	.581	.943	16.3	16.3	43
De Los Santos, Eliazar	R-R	6-4	220	8-15-02	0	0	13.50	11	1	0	7	2	12	11	0	20	6	.087	.532	.087	12.8	42.6	47
Fernandez, Richard	R-R	6-1	190	9-22-02	4	2	2.09	11	5	0	47	39	12	11	0	24	47	.231	.340	.266	23.9	12.2	197
Figuereo, Manuel	R-R	6-5	190	10-15-03	1	1	21.09	12	0	0	11	16	28	25	2	20	3	.372	.597	.698	4.2	27.8	72
Guzman, Freilyn	R-R	6-3	160	11-05-05	1	3	7.23	11	5	0	24	25	20	19	1	19	23	.269	.429	.323	19.3	16.0	119
Lopez, Jeison	R-R	6-1	170	4-06-06	0	0	0.00	1	0	0	0	0	0	0	0	0	0	.000	.000	.000	0.0	0.0	1
Marte, Francis	R-R	6-3	180	10-31-05	1	3	3.97	11	4	0	34	26	21	15	1	17	32	.200	.300	.246	21.3	11.3	150
Morales, Luis	R-R	6-3	190	9-24-02	0	0	0.82	4	3	0	11	4	1	1	0	2	16	.108	.154	.108	41.0	5.1	39
Natera, Jesus	R-R	5-10	165	7-22-06	0	0	0.00	1	0	0	1	1	0	0	0	0	2	.200	.200	.200	40.0	0.0	5
Nova, Alvin	R-R	6-4	170	5-05-05	0	0	5.83	11	4	0	29	32	21	19	3	13	30	.281	.379	.456	22.7	9.8	132
Parra, Josnier	R-R	6-1	170	10-15-01	1	3	4.22	15	1	0	32	33	20	15	3	11	33	.270	.353	.443	23.4	7.8	141
Perez, Manuel	R-R	6-2	180	8-29-05	1	2	5.13	10	6	0	33	39	22	19	2	15	41	.289	.384	.452	25.8	9.4	159
Pinto, Jose	R-R	6-1	180	8-04-02	2	0	5.40	10	4	0	27	28	19	16	0	28	13	.272	.440	.388	9.7	20.9	134
Polanco, Brayan	R-R	6-6	180	2-28-05	1	1	16.97	11	0	0	12	11	22	22	0	29	9	.289	.571	.368	12.7	40.8	71
Rangel, Cristhian	R-R	6-1	180	5-20-05	0	2	10.29	9	1	0	7	5	8	8	1	8	4	.200	.459	.400	10.8	21.6	37
Ribeiro, Sulivan	L-L	6-4	218	12-16-03	0	2	9.00	12	0	0	10	14	15	10	2	13	9	.333	.500	.571	16.1	23.2	56
Silva, Yeferson	R-R	6-0	175	6-28-05	3	1	4.82	10	3	0	19	15	12	10	1	24	15	.224	.435	.343	16.3	26.1	92
Troconis, Donny	R-R	6-4	180	10-12-05	2	4	4.09	12	8	0	44	42	29	20	6	15	44	.255	.323	.448	23.5	8.0	187
Urdaneta, Roberto	R-R	6-2	170	9-22-05	2	0	10.80	12	0	0	10	6	13	12	1	17	11	.162	.467	.297	18.3	28.3	60
Veras, Alvin	R-R	6-3	190	11-20-05	0	3	6.92	10	4	0	13	15	10	10	0	8	21	.283	.377	.434	34.4	13.1	61

Fielding

C: Gonzalez 22, Lelis 17, Landaeta 11, Natera 10. **1B:** Dume 37, Baldallo 8, Gonzalez 6, Andrade 3, Duran 1. **2B:** De La Cruz 40, Superlano 7, Fernandez 6, Baldallo 1. **3B:** Superlano 24, Andrade 18, Baldallo 16, Duran 1. **SS:** Fernandez 46, De La Cruz 8, Baldallo 1. **OF:** De La Paz 46, Pacheco 45, Duran 35, Yan 18, Baldallo 11, Fernandez 7, Lopez 6, De La Cruz 2, Natera 1, Lelis 1.

Philadelphia Phillies

SEASON SYNOPSIS: After winning the NL pennant in 2022, the Phillies got off to a slow start, pulled over .500 for keeps in June and barreled into the playoffs with the third-most wins in the league. After eliminating the Braves in the Division Series, though, Philadelphia couldn't finish off the Diamondbacks in the LCS, its offense silenced in the final two games of a seven-game loss.

HIGH POINT: Philadelphia seemed to be in danger of fading away in early June, sitting at 25-32. But the team rolled off 18 wins in 24 games. While the Phillies were never a threat to catch the Braves, they showed from then til the end of the season that they were a team no one would want to face in the postseason, a point they made in eliminating the Braves in the League Division Series.

LOW POINT: The Phillies were outscored 36-11 in a three-game sweep at the hands of the Dodgers in early May. The hope was that would be a wake-up call, but the alarm clock was delayed, as it was another month before the team found its footing.

NOTABLE ROOKIES: Injuries forced the Phillies to speed up center fielder Johan Rojas' timetable, and he provided a boost with his exceptional defense as well as a better-than-expected bat. He hit .302/.342/.430 and earned regular playing time in the postseason. Righthander Orion Kerkering was a late-season callup who had spent time at all four full-season MiLB levels in 2023. He made just three regular season appearances, but

KEY TRANSACTIONS: Shortstop Trea Turner signed a 11-year, $300 mulluon contract in the offseason to join an already loaded roster. He struggled for a while, but boosted by a standing ovation from the normally hardened Phillies' fans, he looked to be his old self down the stretch. His arrival allowed Bryson Stott to slide to second base, where his bat and defense made him one of the league's best. Righthander Michael Lorenzen was added at the trade deadline. He threw a no-hitter on Aug. 9, but then faded and wasn't part of the postseason rotation.

DOWN ON THE FARM: The Phillies were sneaky good in the minors. They have a solid group of pitching prospects led by Mick Abel and outfielder Justin Crawford had an impressive first full season. The Phillies' .553 winning percentage across the minors was second best to only the Dodgers. Low-A Clearwater went 79-50 and finished as Florida State League runners-up. All but one of the seven Phillies' MiLB teams had winning records.

OPENING DAY PAYROLL: $243,009,439 (4th).

PLAYERS OF THE YEAR

MAJOR LEAGUE

Bryce Harper
1B/DH
.293/.401/.499
29 2B, 21 HR
84 R, 72 RBI

MINOR LEAGUE

Orion Kerkering
RHP
(LoA/HiA/AA/AAA)
4-1, 1.51
14 SV, 13.2 SO/9

ORGANIZATION LEADERS

Batting		*Minimum 250 AB
MAJORS		
* AVG	Bryce Harper	.293
* OPS	Bryce Harper	.900
HR	Kyle Schwarber	47
RBI	Nick Castellanos	106
MINORS		
* AVG	Jake Cave, Lehigh Valley	.346
* OBP	Jake Cave, Lehigh Valley	.429
* SLG	Jake Cave, Lehigh Valley	.684
* OPS	Jake Cave, Lehigh Valley	1.113
R	Weston Wilson, Lehigh Valley	90
H	Simon Muzziotti, Lehigh Valley	140
TB	Weston Wilson, Lehigh Valley	237
2B	Matt Kroon, Jersey Shore/Reading/L. Valley	31
2B	Gabriel Rincones, Clearwater/Jersey Shore	31
3B	Justin Crawford, Clearw./Jersey Shore	8
HR	Weston Wilson, Lehigh Valley	31
RBI	Weston Wilson, Lehigh Valley	86
BB	Oliver Dunn, Reading	82
SO	Marcus Lee Sang, Jersey Shore/Reading	163
SB	Emmarion Boyd, Clearwater	56

Pitching		#Minimum 75 IP
MAJORS		
W	Taijuan Walker	15
# ERA	Matt Strahm	3.29
SO	Zack Wheeler	212
SV	Craig Kimbrell	23
MINORS		
W	Jonh Henriquez, Clearwater/J. Shore	14
L	Josh Hendrickson, Reading/L. Valley	9
# ERA	Matt Osterberg, J. Shore/Reading	3.52
G	Taylor Lehman, Reading/L. Valley	50
GS	Nick Nelson, Clear./Read./L. Valley	25
GS	Tyler Phillips, Reading/L. Valley	25
SV	Orion Kerkering, 4-levels	14
IP	David Parkinson, Reading/L. Valley	130
BB	Mick Abel, Reading/L. Valley	65
SO	David Parkinson, Reading/L. Valley	135
# AVG	Mick Abel, Reading/L. Valley	.191

2023 PERFORMANCE

General Manager: Dave Dombrowski. **Farm Director:** Preston Mattingly. **Scouting Director:** Brian Barber.

Class	Team	League	W	L	PCT	Finish	Manager
Majors	Philadelphia Phillies	National	90	72	.556	4 (15)	Rob Thomson
Triple-A	Lehigh Valley IronPigs	International	80	66	.548	6 (20)	Anthony Contreras
Double-A	Reading Fightin Phils	Eastern	59	77	.434	11 (12)	Al Pedrique
High-A	Jersey Shore BlueClaws	South Atlantic	73	58	.557	2 (12)	Greg Brodzinski
Low-A	Clearwater Threshers	Florida State	79	50	.612	1 (10)	Marty Malloy
Rookie	FCL Phillies	Florida Complex	30	25	.545	5 (15)	Shawn Williams
Rookie	DSL Phillies Red	Dominican Sum.	27	26	.509	26 (50)	Nerluis Martinez
Rookie	DSL Phillies White	Dominican Sum.	42	13	.764	3 (50)	Orlando Munoz
Overall 2023 Minor League Record			390	315	.553	2nd (30)	

ORGANIZATION STATISTICS

PHILADELPHIA PHILLIES

NATIONAL LEAGUE

Batting	B-T	Ht.	Wt.	DOB	AVG	OBP	SLG	G	PA	AB	R	H	2B	3B	HR	RBI	BB	HBP	SH	SF	SO	SB	CS	BB%	SO%
Bohm, Alec	R-R	6-5	218	8-03-96	.274	.327	.437	145	611	558	74	153	31	0	20	97	42	5	0	6	94	4	1	6.9	15.4
Castellanos, Nick	R-R	6-4	203	3-04-92	.272	.311	.476	157	671	626	79	170	37	2	29	106	36	3	0	6	185	11	2	5.4	27.6
Castro, Rodolfo	B-R	6-0	205	5-21-99	.100	.156	.100	14	32	30	2	3	0	0	0	2	2	0	0	0	12	0	0	6.3	37.5
2-team (78 Pittsburgh)						.211	.298	.322	92	256	227	21	48	7	0	6	24	23	5	0	1	74	1	4.0	9.0
Cave, Jake	L-L	6-0	200	12-04-92	.212	.272	.348	65	203	184	18	39	8	1	5	21	15	1	1	2	55	3	0	7.4	27.1
Clemens, Kody	L-R	6-1	200	5-15-96	.230	.277	.367	49	148	139	15	32	7	0	4	13	8	1	0	0	40	0	0	5.4	27.0
Ellis, Drew	R-R	6-3	205	12-01-95	.217	.379	.478	12	29	23	4	5	0	0	2	4	6	0	0	0	7	0	1	20.7	24.1
Guthrie, Dalton	R-R	5-11	160	12-23-95	.167	.286	.208	23	28	24	4	4	1	0	0	0	3	1	0	0	7	0	0	10.7	25.0
Hall, Darick	L-R	6-4	232	7-25-95	.167	.196	.241	18	56	54	2	9	1	0	1	3	2	0	0	0	18	0	0	3.6	32.1
Harper, Bryce	L-R	6-3	210	10-16-92	.293	.401	.499	126	546	457	84	134	29	1	21	72	80	5	0	4	119	11	3	14.7	21.8
Harrison, Josh	R-R	5-8	190	7-08-87	.204	.263	.291	41	114	103	8	21	3	0	2	10	3	6	0	2	20	0	0	2.6	17.5
Marsh, Brandon	L-R	6-4	215	12-18-97	.277	.372	.458	133	472	404	58	112	25	6	12	60	59	4	1	4	144	10	2	12.5	30.5
Pache, Cristian	R-R	6-2	215	11-19-98	.238	.319	.417	48	95	84	12	20	7	1	2	11	10	0	1	0	27	2	3	10.5	28.4
Realmuto, J.T.	R-R	6-1	212	3-18-91	.252	.310	.452	135	540	489	70	123	28	5	20	63	35	9	0	5	138	16	5	6.5	25.6
Rojas, Johan	R-R	5-11	165	8-14-00	.302	.342	.430	59	164	149	24	45	9	2	2	23	5	4	6	0	42	14	1	3.0	25.6
Schwarber, Kyle	L-R	6-0	229	3-05-93	.197	.343	.474	160	720	585	108	115	19	1	47	104	126	6	0	3	215	0	2	17.5	29.9
Sosa, Edmundo	R-R	6-0	210	3-06-96	.251	.293	.427	104	300	279	34	70	15	2	10	30	8	9	2	1	74	4	2	2.7	24.7
Stott, Bryson	L-R	6-3	200	10-06-97	.280	.329	.419	151	640	585	78	164	32	2	15	62	39	7	1	8	100	31	3	6.1	15.6
Stubbs, Garrett	L-R	5-10	170	5-26-93	.204	.274	.283	41	125	113	15	23	4	1	1	12	9	2	1	0	29	2	0	7.2	23.2
Turner, Trea	R-R	6-2	185	6-30-93	.266	.320	.459	155	691	639	102	170	35	5	26	76	45	6	0	1	150	30	0	6.5	21.7
Wilson, Weston	R-R	6-3	215	9-11-94	.313	.500	.500	8	22	16	5	5	0	0	1	2	6	0	0	0	5	3	1	27.3	22.7

Pitching	B-T	Ht.	Wt.	DOB	W	L	ERA	G	GS	SV	IP	Hits	Runs	ER	HR	BB	SO	AVG	OBP	SLG	SO%	BB%	BF
Alvarado, Jose	L-L	6-2	245	5-21-95	0	2	1.74	42	0	10	41	30	15	8	3	18	64	.196	.281	.307	37.2	10.5	172
Bellatti, Andrew	R-R	6-1	190	8-05-91	1	0	5.11	27	0	0	25	25	15	14	4	12	25	.250	.327	.440	22.1	10.6	113
Brogdon, Connor	R-R	6-6	205	1-29-95	2	1	4.03	27	1	0	29	29	14	13	5	13	26	.264	.339	.473	20.5	10.2	127
Clemens, Kody	L-R	6-1	200	5-15-96	0	0	3.38	4	0	0	3	4	1	1	0	3	1	.333	.467	.333	6.7	20.0	15
Covey, Dylan	R-R	6-1	215	8-14-91	1	3	3.69	28	1	0	39	43	20	16	3	16	27	.281	.353	.386	15.6	9.2	173
Dominguez, Seranthony	R-R	6-1	225	11-25-94	5	5	3.78	57	0	2	50	48	25	21	7	22	48	.246	.339	.374	21.4	9.8	224
Falter, Bailey	R-L	6-4	175	4-24-97	0	7	5.13	8	7	0	40	50	30	23	7	8	28	.301	.331	.494	16.0	4.6	175
Harrison, Josh	R-R	5-8	190	7-08-87	0	0	27.00	2	0	0	2	8	5	5	0	2	0	.727	.667	.727	0.0	13.3	15
Hoffman, Jeff	R-R	6-5	235	1-08-93	5	2	2.41	54	0	1	52	29	16	14	3	19	69	.158	.244	.257	33.2	9.1	208
Kerkering, Orion	R-R	6-2	204	4-04-01	1	0	3.00	3	0	0	3	3	1	1	0	2	6	.250	.357	.333	42.9	14.3	14
Kimbrel, Craig	R-R	6-0	215	5-28-88	8	6	3.26	71	0	23	69	44	28	25	10	28	94	.181	.273	.337	33.8	10.1	278
Lorenzen, Michael	R-R	6-3	217	1-04-92	4	2	5.51	11	7	1	47	49	32	29	9	20	28	.265	.335	.465	13.6	9.7	206
Marte, Yunior	R-R	6-2	180	2-02-95	1	1	5.03	40	0	2	39	47	27	22	6	17	38	.288	.357	.460	20.9	9.3	182
Moore, McKinley	R-R	6-6	225	8-24-98	0	0	18.90	3	0	0	3	5	7	7	1	5	2	.357	.571	.786	9.5	23.8	21
Nelson, Nick	R-R	6-1	205	12-05-95	1	0	1.69	1	0	0	5	2	1	1	1	2	3	.111	.200	.278	15.0	10.0	20
Nola, Aaron	R-R	6-2	200	6-04-93	12	9	4.46	32	32	0	194	178	105	96	32	45	202	.240	.283	.425	25.5	5.7	793
Ortiz, Luis	R-R	6-3	230	9-22-95	0	0	3.32	14	0	1	19	23	7	7	1	5	16	.311	.354	.446	20.0	6.3	80
Plassmeyer, Michael	L-L	6-2	197	11-05-96	0	1	22.09	1	1	0	4	8	10	9	3	0	4	.400	.478	.900	17.4	0.0	23
Sanchez, Cristopher	L-L	6-1	165	12-12-96	3	5	3.44	19	18	0	99	88	44	38	16	16	96	.235	.271	.421	24.2	4.0	396
Soto, Gregory	L-L	6-1	234	2-11-95	3	4	4.62	69	0	3	60	47	34	31	6	22	65	.210	.284	.335	26.0	8.8	250
Strahm, Matt	R-L	6-2	190	11-12-91	9	5	3.29	56	10	2	88	68	34	32	11	21	108	.213	.263	.375	30.8	6.0	351
Suarez, Ranger	L-L	6-1	217	8-26-95	4	6	4.18	22	22	0	125	129	59	58	13	48	119	.267	.333	.414	22.0	8.9	540
Uelmen, Erich	R-R	6-3	195	5-19-96	0	0	36.00	1	0	0	1	3	4	4	0	2	1	.600	.625	1.000	12.5	25.0	8
Vasquez, Andrew	L-L	6-6	235	9-14-93	2	1	2.27	30	0	0	40	35	12	10	4	14	34	.235	.320	.342	20.0	8.2	170
Walker, Taijuan	R-R	6-4	235	8-13-92	15	6	4.38	31	31	0	173	155	87	84	20	71	138	.238	.320	.397	18.8	9.7	733
Wheeler, Zack	L-R	6-4	195	5-30-90	13	6	3.61	32	32	0	192	168	82	77	20	39	212	.229	.274	.364	26.9	5.0	787

Fielding

Catcher	PCT	G	PO	A	E	DP	PB
Realmuto	.998	133	1190	33	2	8	6
Stubbs	.984	40	294	8	5	5	2

First Base	PCT	G	PO	A	E	DP
Bohm	.990	80	441	40	5	41
Cave	1.000	17	112	4	0	8
Clemens	.996	39	258	25	1	19
Ellis	1.000	6	26	3	0	5
Hall	.974	16	109	5	3	11

	PCT	G	PO	A	E	DP
Harper	.996	36	258	20	1	20
Wilson	1.000	1	5	0	0	0

Second Base	PCT	G	PO	A	E	DP
Castro	.917	4	5	6	1	3
Harrison	.976	11	16	25	1	7
Sosa	1.000	4	5	6	0	1
Stott	.992	149	235	362	5	72
Wilson	.000	1	0	0	0	0

Third Base	PCT	G	PO	A	E	DP
Bohm	.978	90	43	132	4	9
Castro	.900	8	0	9	1	0
Ellis	1.000	4	2	3	0	1
Guthrie	1.000	1	1	0	0	0
Harrison	1.000	16	12	23	0	4
Sosa	.946	82	57	134	11	7
Wilson	1.000	1	0	1	0	0

Shortstop	PCT	G	PO	A	E	DP
Clemens	1.000	1	1	0	0	0
Sosa	1.000	18	22	29	0	9
Turner	.960	153	176	369	23	60

Outfield	PCT	G	PO	A	E	DP
Castellanos	1.000	148	254	10	0	4
Cave	.993	47	61	2	1	1
Clemens	1.000	1	1	0	0	0
Guthrie	.667	21	21	2	0	2
Harrison	.500	8	5	0	0	0
Marsh	.982	144	274	1	5	0
Pache	.986	46	63	2	1	0
Rojas	.986	57	135	3	2	2
Schwarber	.971	103	166	2	5	0
Sosa	.000	1	0	0	0	0
Stubbs	.000	1	0	0	0	0
Wilson	.500	5	2	0	1	0

LEHIGH VALLEY IRONPIGS — TRIPLE-A

INTERNATIONAL LEAGUE

Batting	B T	Ht.	Wt.	DOB	AVG	OBP	SLG	G	PA	AB	R	H	2B	3B	HR	RBI	BB	HBP	SH	SF	SO	SB	CS	BB%	SO%
Cave, Jake	L-L	6-0	200	12-04-92	.346	.429	.684	59	275	237	61	82	30	1	16	49	31	5	0	2	56	2	3	11.3	20.4
Clemens, Kody	L-R	6-1	200	5-15-96	.256	.373	.564	62	279	234	51	60	10	4	18	52	43	1	0	1	58	7	3	15.4	20.8
Ellis, Drew	R-R	6-3	205	12-01-95	.224	.336	.433	70	298	254	41	57	14	0	13	47	40	3	0	1	69	3	0	13.4	23.2
Friscia, Vito	R-R	6-3	225	12-19-96	.263	.383	.500	13	47	38	6	10	0	0	3	6	7	1	0	1	12	0	0	14.9	25.5
Garcia, Aramis	R-R	6-1	228	1-12-93	.251	.295	.523	53	210	195	28	49	11	0	14	44	8	5	0	2	56	3	0	3.8	26.7
Guthrie, Dalton	R-R	5-11	160	12-23-95	.280	.385	.476	22	96	82	11	23	6	2	2	9	11	3	0	0	22	3	2	11.5	22.9
2-team (49 Gwinnett)					.274	.370	.386	71	301	259	32	71	11	3	4	31	31	9	1	1	67	6	3	10.3	22.3
Haley, Jim	R-R	6-1	195	2-23-95	.253	.324	.412	108	410	364	62	92	17	4	11	58	34	6	2	3	94	18	1	8.3	22.9
Hall, Darick	L-R	6-4	232	7-25-95	.311	.395	.545	74	334	286	46	89	11	1	18	57	42	1	0	5	65	0	0	12.6	19.5
Hicklen, Brewer	R-R	6-1	220	2-09-96	.250	.413	.472	11	46	36	11	9	2	0	2	4	10	0	0	0	11	6	0	21.7	23.9
2-team (61 Omaha)					.236	.351	.455	72	286	242	52	57	17	3	10	33	36	7	0	1	70	21	3	12.6	24.5
Hicks, John	R-R	6-2	230	8-31-89	.211	.288	.328	54	206	180	26	38	12	0	3	23	19	2	1	4	56	11	1	9.2	27.2
Kingery, Scott	R-R	5-10	180	4-29-94	.244	.325	.400	117	466	405	68	99	18	3	13	47	48	3	5	5	135	24	1	10.3	29.0
Kroon, Matt	R-R	6-0	195	12-05-96	.381	.467	.698	15	76	63	12	24	7	2	3	13	11	0	1	1	15	4	2	14.5	19.7
Machin, Vimael	L-R	5-11	185	9-25-93	.235	.330	.339	52	213	183	19	43	7	0	4	21	25	2	1	2	35	1	2	11.7	16.4
Marchan, Rafael	B-R	5-9	170	2-25-99	.297	.391	.440	51	207	175	27	52	13	3	2	30	24	5	0	3	20	1	2	11.6	9.7
Marsh, Brandon	L-R	6-4	215	12-18-97	.500	.700	.667	2	10	6	1	3	1	0	0	2	4	0	0	0	1	2	0	40.0	10.0
McDowell, Max	R-R	6-1	208	1-12-94	.300	.300	.400	3	10	10	1	3	1	0	0	4	0	0	0	0	3	0	0	0.0	30.0
2-team (3 Buffalo)					.318	.348	.409	6	23	22	4	7	2	0	0	7	1	0	0	0	6	0	0	4.3	26.1
Muzziotti, Simon	L-L	6-0	175	12-27-98	.296	.358	.404	124	524	473	67	140	22	4	7	61	45	2	1	3	81	26	12	8.6	15.5
Ortiz, Jhailyn	R-R	6-3	215	11-18-98	.269	.381	.481	32	126	104	17	28	5	1	5	11	19	1	0	2	29	1	1	15.1	23.0
Pache, Cristian	R-R	6-2	215	11-19-98	.235	.350	.333	13	60	51	10	12	2	0	1	6	8	1	0	0	13	3	1	13.3	21.7
Peterson, Dustin	R-R	6-1	210	9-10-94	.244	.328	.488	85	348	303	54	74	15	1	19	54	37	3	0	5	85	1	0	10.6	24.4
Podkul, Nick	R-R	6-1	200	4-11-97	.280	.471	.560	8	34	25	9	7	1	0	2	5	5	4	0	0	5	0	0	14.7	14.7
Qsar, Jordan	L-R	6-2	195	12-02-95	.249	.382	.459	76	288	233	43	58	12	2	11	39	48	4	0	3	94	11	2	16.7	32.6
Quiroz, Esteban	L-R	5-4	199	2-17-92	.231	.348	.354	96	388	325	57	75	19	0	7	59	57	3	0	3	62	7	2	14.7	16.0
Stevenson, Cal	L-L	5-9	175	9-12-96	.271	.437	.472	56	202	144	39	39	5	0	8	30	46	2	3	7	45	14	3	22.8	22.3
Wilson, Weston	R-R	6-3	215	9-11-94	.259	.363	.515	125	544	460	90	119	19	3	31	86	75	3	2	4	146	32	6	13.8	26.8

Pitching	B-T	Ht.	Wt.	DOB	W	L	ERA	G	GS	SV	IP	Hits	Runs	ER	HR	BB	SO	AVG	OBP	SLG	SO%	BB%	BF
Abel, Mick	R-R	6-5	190	8-18-01	0	1	3.86	1	1	0	5	5	2	2	0	3	6	.278	.458	.444	25.0	12.5	24
Allgeyer, Nick	L-L	6-3	225	2-03-96	0	1	4.50	4	4	0	12	8	6	6	1	6	15	.182	.308	.295	28.8	11.5	52
Alvarado, Jose	L-L	6-2	245	5-21-95	1	0	0.00	3	0	0	3	2	0	0	0	1	4	.182	.308	.182	30.8	7.7	13
Anderson, Shaun	R-R	6-6	228	10-29-94	4	2	4.85	11	11	0	52	59	30	28	11	15	35	.278	.330	.491	15.2	6.5	231
Barnes, Jacob	R-R	6-2	231	4-14-90	1	0	4.15	11	0	1	13	11	7	6	0	4	12	.234	.283	.340	22.6	7.5	53
Bellatti, Andrew	R-R	6-1	190	8-05-91	1	0	2.42	27	0	6	26	21	7	7	2	14	29	.219	.336	.333	25.7	12.4	113
Bowden, Ben	L-L	6-4	249	10-21-94	6	2	4.64	49	0	5	52	47	31	27	8	32	76	.230	.335	.382	32.2	13.6	236
Brogdon, Connor	R-R	6-6	205	1-29-95	1	1	5.46	26	2	1	28	22	17	17	4	16	34	.216	.323	.402	27.4	12.9	124
Cobb, Trey	R-R	6-1	190	6-24-94	2	1	6.39	34	0	2	31	21	23	22	2	31	33	.196	.400	.355	22.8	21.4	145
Crouse, Hans	L-R	6-4	180	9-15-98	1	3	6.75	16	0	0	20	23	17	15	4	21	26	.288	.441	.500	25.2	20.4	103
Cruz, Jesus	R-R	6-1	230	4-15-95	2	3	5.40	28	2	1	35	38	24	21	4	16	39	.271	.350	.429	24.7	10.1	158
Dominguez, Seranthony	R-R	6-1	225	11-25-94	0	0	0.00	2	0	0	2	1	0	0	0	1	5	.143	.250	.143	62.5	12.5	8
Falter, Bailey	R-L	6-4	175	4-24-97	2	1	4.21	11	11	0	47	45	22	22	7	22	35	.254	.338	.424	17.4	10.9	201
Friscia, Vito	R-R	6-3	225	12-19-96	0	0	0.00	1	0	0	1	1	0	0	0	0	1	.250	.250	.250	25.0	0.0	4
Haley, Jim	R-R	6-1	195	2-23-95	0	0	0.00	1	0	0	0	1	0	0	0	0	0	.500	.500	.500	0.0	0.0	2
Hart, Kyle	L-L	6-5	200	11-23-92	0	0	0.00	1	0	0	1	0	0	0	0	0	1	.000	.000	.000	33.3	0.0	3
Head, Louis	R-R	6-1	180	4-23-90	0	1	10.80	11	0	0	12	10	14	14	4	15	14	.233	.431	.581	24.1	25.9	58
Hendrickson, Josh	L-L	6-4	215	9-18-97	0	0	7.20	3	0	0	10	14	8	8	2	8	14	.341	.451	.488	27.5	15.7	51
Hernandez, Jakob	L-L	6-4	260	5-19-96	1	1	3.52	19	0	1	23	14	9	9	4	13	25	.177	.287	.380	26.6	13.8	94
Hoffman, Jeff	R-R	6-5	235	1-08-93	0	2	7.00	9	0	0	9	5	8	7	1	7	16	.161	.308	.355	41.0	17.9	39
Hutchison, Drew	L-R	6-3	215	8-22-90	4	4	5.62	15	15	0	75	70	49	47	10	46	62	.246	.359	.412	18.3	13.6	338
Jewell, Jake	R-R	6-2	217	5-16-93	1	1	7.66	22	6	0	25	26	22	21	4	14	26	.268	.368	.485	22.8	12.3	114
Kerkering, Orion	R-R	6-2	204	4-04-01	1	0	0.00	1	0	0	1	2	0	0	0	0	1	.400	.400	.400	20.0	0.0	5
Kuhns, Max	R-R	6-2	209	8-11-94	0	0	5.40	1	0	0	2	0	1	1	0	3	1	.000	.500	.000	12.5	37.5	8
Lehman, Taylor	L-L	6-8	240	12-30-95	5	0	4.19	37	0	0	34	25	18	16	3	25	32	.208	.342	.333	21.9	17.1	146
Marte, Yunior	R-R	6-2	180	2-02-95	3	1	1.80	18	0	1	20	12	5	4	1	9	24	.174	.278	.232	30.4	11.4	79
McArthur, James	R-R	6-7	230	12-11-96	0	2	7.31	5	4	0	16	20	13	13	3	7	15	.308	.392	.492	20.0	9.3	75
McGarry, Griff	R-R	6-2	190	6-08-99	0	2	41.54	3	3	0	4	8	20	20	0	14	5	.400	.657	.600	14.3	40.0	35
McGowan, Christian	R-R	6-0	205	3-07-00	0	0	0.00	1	1	0	3	2	0	0	0	3	3	.222	.417	.222	25.0	25.0	12

McKay, Tyler	R-R	6-6	180	8-18-97	2	3	2.67	23	0	2	27	21	11	8	0	19	24	.223	.381	.234	20.2	16.0	119
Moore, McKinley	R-R	6-6	225	8-24-98	2	1	1.38	12	0	0	13	5	4	2	0	17	22	.125	.397	.150	37.9	29.3	58
Morales, Francisco	R-R	6-4	185	10-27-99	0	2	6.75	22	0	2	25	20	19	19	4	26	36	.215	.400	.409	28.8	20.8	125
Nelson, Nick	R-R	6-1	205	12-05-95	7	3	4.35	20	20	0	97	102	48	47	13	42	75	.274	.360	.425	17.7	9.9	423
Ortiz, Luis	R-R	6-3	230	9-22-95	4	1	4.60	33	1	5	45	38	25	23	2	13	45	.230	.310	.333	23.9	6.9	188
Parkinson, David	R-L	6-2	210	12-14-95	0	0	11.25	1	0	0	4	6	5	5	1	3	4	.353	.450	.588	20.0	15.0	20
Perez, Hector	R-R	6-3	223	6-06-96	0	1	3.75	9	0	0	12	5	6	5	0	11	13	.139	.347	.194	25.5	21.6	51
Peterson, Dustin	R-R	6-1	210	9-10-94	0	0	18.00	1	0	0	1	1	2	2	0	3	0	.333	.667	.333	0.0	50.0	6
Phillips, Tyler	R-R	6-5	225	10-27-97	0	2	4.69	9	9	0	40	51	30	21	1	22	30	.315	.398	.395	15.6	11.5	192
Plassmeyer, Michael	L-L	6-2	197	11-05-96	3	4	5.05	16	14	1	68	69	40	38	10	30	74	.263	.342	.477	24.7	10.0	299
Quiroz, Esteban	L-R	5-4	199	2-17-92	0	0	31.50	3	0	0	2	8	7	7	2	3	0	.571	.647	1.071	0.0	17.6	17
Sanchez, Cristopher	L-L	6-1	165	12-12-96	3	2	4.35	10	8	0	50	43	24	24	6	29	44	.229	.344	.372	19.8	13.1	222
Schulze, Brett	R-R	6-2	180	11-24-97	0	1	4.03	15	1	0	22	15	13	10	2	25	27	.197	.413	.342	26.0	24.0	104
Skirrow, Noah	R-R	6-3	215	7-21-98	8	4	5.84	24	14	1	102	126	68	66	19	53	79	.305	.386	.504	16.6	11.2	475
Song, Noah	R-R	6-4	200	5-28-97	1	0	16.20	2	0	0	3	5	6	6	1	4	5	.357	.500	.714	27.8	22.2	18
Stevenson, Cal	L-L	5-9	175	9-12-96	0	0	0.00	1	0	0	1	0	0	0	0	0	0	.000	.000	.000	0.0	0.0	3
Suarez, Ranger	L-L	6-1	217	8-26-95	1	0	1.29	2	2	0	7	4	1	1	0	1	4	.167	.200	.208	16.0	4.0	25
Uelmen, Erich	R-R	6-3	195	5-19-96	1	2	4.02	14	0	1	16	18	9	7	1	8	14	.290	.380	.419	19.7	11.3	71
Vines, Jace	R-R	6-3	215	9-04-94	0	3	8.03	13	0	1	12	21	13	11	1	9	9	.382	.470	.527	13.6	13.6	66
Walker, Jeremy	R-R	6-5	235	6-12-95	6	2	2.90	47	2	0	68	54	25	22	8	31	52	.221	.314	.344	18.6	11.1	280
Zarbnisky, Braden	L-R	6-2	191	12-26-96	2	1	8.62	14	0	0	16	18	16	15	4	10	19	.277	.382	.523	25.0	13.2	76
Zeuch, T.J.	R-R	6-7	245	8-01-95	4	5	5.06	16	15	0	75	81	48	42	8	29	42	.283	.349	.430	13.2	9.1	318

Fielding

Catcher	PCT	G	PO	A	E	DP	PB
Friscia	1.000	7	67	4	0	0	0
Garcia	.985	49	427	22	7	7	4
Hicks	1.000	42	349	23	0	2	6
Marchan	.986	50	381	27	6	4	3
McDowell	1.000	3	18	0	0	0	1

First Base	PCT	G	PO	A	E	DP
Cave	1.000	1	6	1	0	1
Clemens	1.000	7	63	3	0	8
Ellis	.973	3	35	1	1	2
Haley	.990	49	355	23	4	34
Hall	.994	63	466	46	3	60
Hicks	1.000	8	50	5	0	6
Ortiz	1.000	1	9	1	0	1
Podkul	1.000	6	40	4	0	7
Wilson	.982	14	97	14	2	13

Second Base	PCT	G	PO	A	E	DP
Clemens	.983	26	49	64	2	17
Guthrie	1.000	1	1	4	0	1
Haley	.974	36	51	98	4	26
Kingery	1.000	37	52	93	0	27
Machin	1.000	8	5	14	0	2
Quiroz	.968	48	59	125	6	28

Third Base	PCT	G	PO	A	E	DP
Clemens	.895	9	6	11	2	0
Ellis	.959	59	49	92	6	18
Haley	1.000	2	0	2	0	0
Machin	.969	30	19	44	2	1
Quiroz	.982	43	25	87	2	7
Wilson	.923	8	4	8	1	0

Shortstop	PCT	G	PO	A	E	DP
Haley	.915	9	11	32	4	9
Kingery	.982	64	104	166	5	54
Wilson	.985	79	99	163	4	41

Outfield	PCT	G	PO	A	E	DP
Cave	.974	52	127	2	1	1
Clemens	1.000	9	15	1	0	0
Guthrie	.947	21	32	2	2	0
Hicklen	1.000	8	12	0	0	0
Kingery	1.000	18	41	2	0	0
Kroon	1.000	15	33	2	0	1
Marsh	1.000	1	2	0	0	0
Muzziotti	.984	121	218	10	5	2
Ortiz	1.000	16	23	1	0	0
Pache	1.000	8	21	0	0	0
Peterson	.993	61	93	1	1	0
Qsar	1.000	57	90	2	0	0
Stevenson	1.000	56	89	2	0	2
Wilson	1.000	21	27	0	0	0

READING FIGHTIN PHILS — *DOUBLE-A*

EASTERN LEAGUE

Batting	B-T	Ht.	Wt.	DOB	AVG	OBP	SLG	G	PA	AB	R	H	2B	3B	HR	RBI	BB	HBP	SH	SF	SO	SB	CS	BB%	SO%
Cannon, Cam	R-R	5-10	205	10-16-97	.206	.262	.394	46	169	155	18	32	11	0	6	18	12	0	0	1	28	1	0	7.1	16.6
De Freitas, Arturo	R-R	5-10	170	5-28-01	.000	.000	.000	1	3	3	0	0	0	0	0	0	0	0	0	0	2	0	0	0.0	66.7
De La Cruz, Carlos	R-R	6-8	210	10-06-99	.259	.344	.454	129	582	509	80	132	25	1	24	67	54	14	0	5	160	3	0	9.3	27.5
Dunn, Oliver	L-R	5-10	185	9-02-97	.271	.396	.506	119	505	417	65	113	27	4	21	78	82	5	0	1	139	16	5	16.2	27.5
Ellis, Drew	R-R	6-3	205	12-01-95	.257	.409	.600	10	44	35	6	9	3	0	3	8	8	1	0	0	9	0	0	18.2	20.5
Glendinning, Robbie	R-R	6-0	196	10-06-95	.313	.450	.438	5	20	16	1	5	2	0	0	2	4	0	0	0	6	0	0	20.0	30.0
Iser, Herbert	L-R	6-1	210	12-14-97	.229	.308	.371	23	78	70	10	16	1	0	3	8	7	1	0	0	20	0	0	9.0	25.6
Kroon, Matt	R-R	6-0	195	12-05-96	.319	.387	.493	79	344	298	53	95	24	2	8	44	33	5	0	8	66	22	6	9.6	19.2
Lee Sang, Marcus	L-L	5-11	200	1-02-01	.195	.293	.368	25	99	87	9	17	6	0	3	6	11	1	0	0	33	2	1	11.1	33.3
Martin, Casey	R-R	5-9	175	4-07-99	.180	.237	.290	61	236	217	19	39	7	1	5	16	16	1	0	2	87	6	2	6.8	36.9
Martinez, Pedro	B-R	5-9	165	1-28-01	.184	.265	.282	53	181	163	15	30	4	0	4	9	15	3	0	0	57	7	1	8.3	31.5
McDowell, Max	R-R	6-1	208	1-12-94	.224	.366	.319	68	264	210	23	47	2	0	6	26	35	14	1	3	64	0	2	13.3	24.2
Ortiz, Jhailyn	R-R	6-3	215	11-18-98	.210	.293	.345	62	257	229	19	48	7	0	8	34	24	3	0	0	92	0	0	9.3	35.8
Podkul, Nick	R-R	6-1	200	4-11-97	.285	.396	.588	45	197	165	31	47	8	3	12	35	27	4	0	1	41	0	0	13.7	20.8
Radcliff, Baron	L-R	6-4	228	2-09-99	.211	.299	.395	65	251	223	22	47	8	0	11	21	28	0	0	0	97	2	1	11.2	38.6
Rijo, Wendell	R-R	5-9	170	9-04-95	.187	.291	.227	21	86	75	6	14	3	0	0	8	9	2	0	0	27	0	2	10.5	31.4
Roberts, Cody	R-R	6-1	195	6-16-96	.214	.277	.349	72	239	215	33	46	11	0	6	15	16	4	1	3	52	2	2	6.7	21.8
Rojas, Johan	R-R	5-11	165	8-14-00	.306	.361	.484	76	354	320	56	98	20	5	9	45	24	5	2	3	59	30	8	6.8	16.7
Stokes, Madison	R-R	6-2	200	4-25-96	.215	.341	.344	102	431	358	54	77	21	2	7	31	64	5	3	1	119	6	2	14.8	27.6
Tatum, McCarthy	R-R	6-3	210	5-15-96	.246	.331	.362	38	157	138	11	34	10	0	2	18	8	10	0	1	34	3	2	5.1	21.7
Ward, Nick	L-R	5-9	180	10-19-95	.200	.293	.325	21	92	80	10	16	4	0	2	8	10	1	0	1	20	6	0	10.9	21.7
Whitley, Garrett	R-R	6-0	195	3-13-97	.161	.226	.232	15	62	56	6	9	1	0	1	5	4	1	0	1	23	1	0	6.5	37.1
Wilson, Ethan	L-L	6-0	210	11-07-99	.250	.307	.443	114	463	420	52	105	24	3	17	61	31	6	0	6	110	12	7	6.7	23.8
Wingrove, Rixon	L-R	6-4	260	5-23-00	.128	.236	.191	15	55	47	2	6	0	0	1	3	7	0	0	1	19	0	0	12.7	34.5

Pitching	B-T	Ht.	Wt.	DOB	W	L	ERA	G	GS	SV	IP	Hits	Runs	ER	HR	BB	SO	AVG	OBP	SLG	SO%	BB%	BF
Abel, Mick	R-R	6-5	190	8-18-01	5	5	4.14	22	22	0	109	73	53	50	15	62	126	.188	.306	.376	27.5	13.5	458
Alvarado, Jose	L-L	6-2	245	5-21-95	0	1	18.00	1	0	0	1	3	2	2	0	0	0	.500	.500	1.167	0.0	0.0	6
Ash, Konnor	R-R	5-11	191	3-17-99	0	0	54.00	1	0	0	0	1	2	2	0	2	0	.500	.750	1.500	0.0	50.0	4

Baker, Andrew	R-R	6-1	190	3-24-00	0	6	8.12	41	0	1	41	35	41	37	6	48	64	.226	.419	.387	30.5	22.9	210
Crouse, Hans	L-R	6-4	180	9-15-98	0	0	0.00	1	0	0	1	0	0	0	0	1	2	.000	.250	.000	50.0	25.0	4
Francisco, Carlos A	R-R	6-4	220	7-02-99	4	2	5.16	24	0	0	30	24	19	17	2	21	35	.231	.369	.356	26.3	15.8	133
Garnett, Tristan	L-L	6-6	240	3-29-98	1	1	0.68	12	0	1	13	9	4	1	0	4	20	.184	.241	.224	37.0	7.4	54
Haake, Zach	R-R	6-7	220	10-08-96	2	5	5.06	12	11	0	53	52	32	30	6	19	48	.257	.328	.416	20.8	8.2	231
Hendrickson, Josh	L-L	6-4	215	9-18-97	2	9	5.42	21	21	0	98	115	69	59	23	41	77	.290	.369	.528	16.9	9.0	455
Hernandez, Cristian	R-R	6-3	180	9-23-00	4	4	3.66	35	4	0	52	50	26	21	10	24	66	.249	.343	.448	28.7	10.4	230
Iser, Herbert	L-R	6-1	210	12-14-97	0	0	162.00	1	0	0	0	3	6	6	2	3	0	.750	.857	2.250	0.0	42.9	7
Kerkering, Orion	R-R	6-2	204	4-04-01	0	1	2.05	21	0	7	22	19	5	5	2	5	33	.229	.273	.325	37.5	5.7	88
Killgore, Keylan	L-L	6-3	185	9-30-96	3	2	5.20	46	0	0	55	59	40	32	9	28	67	.272	.349	.475	26.8	11.2	250
Kuhns, Max	R-R	6-2	209	8-11-94	1	2	8.07	31	0	3	29	32	29	26	8	24	39	.267	.381	.508	26.5	16.3	147
Lehman, Taylor	L-L	6-8	240	12-30-95	2	0	3.06	13	0	1	18	9	6	6	2	6	17	.153	.254	.339	25.0	8.8	68
Leverett, Adam	L-R	6-4	190	9-19-98	0	6	3.94	35	8	0	64	63	33	28	4	27	52	.265	.347	.387	19.0	9.9	274
Lindow, Ethan	R-L	6-3	180	10-15-98	1	0	5.00	5	3	0	18	16	10	10	4	6	15	.235	.297	.529	20.3	8.1	74
Linginfelter, Zach	L-R	6-5	220	4-10-97	0	1	9.64	14	0	0	14	14	15	15	3	20	13	.259	.467	.500	17.3	26.7	75
Martinez, Jordi	L-L	6-2	185	7-18-00	0	1	3.72	8	0	1	10	10	6	4	0	2	10	.270	.317	.351	24.4	4.9	41
McCollum, Tommy	R-R	6-5	260	6-08-99	1	0	3.86	10	0	1	9	3	4	4	0	9	11	.100	.357	.133	26.2	21.4	42
McGarry, Griff	R-R	6-2	190	6-08-99	1	1	3.13	13	13	0	55	31	23	19	4	36	74	.163	.300	.279	32.0	15.6	231
McKay, Tyler	R-R	6-6	180	8-18-97	2	3	2.54	25	0	6	28	19	11	8	3	10	32	.179	.256	.274	27.4	8.5	117
Moore, McKinley	R-R	6-6	225	8-24-98	0	0	1.42	7	0	0	6	6	1	1	0	5	12	.250	.379	.333	41.4	17.2	29
Nelson, Nick	R-R	6-1	205	12-05-95	0	0	1.38	3	3	0	13	12	3	2	0	1	12	.250	.280	.292	24.0	2.0	50
Ortiz, Jhailyn	R-R	6-3	215	11-18-98	0	0	0.00	1	0	0	1	2	0	0	0	0	0	.500	.500	.750	0.0	0.0	4
Osterberg, Matt	L-L	6-2	200	4-21-99	1	1	3.26	6	6	0	30	26	12	11	3	6	30	.228	.264	.386	24.8	5.0	121
Parkinson, David	R-L	6-2	210	12-14-95	9	5	3.56	24	22	0	126	121	61	50	17	51	131	.249	.324	.406	24.0	9.3	546
Phillips, Tyler	R-R	6-5	225	10-27-97	4	5	5.03	17	16	0	82	84	48	46	12	30	80	.267	.332	.444	22.9	8.6	349
Pipkin, Dominic	R-R	6-4	160	11-05-99	2	2	3.66	18	0	1	20	16	8	8	3	7	23	.222	.300	.389	28.8	8.8	80
Sanchez, Rodolfo	R-R	5-10	165	1-12-00	0	0	0.00	1	0	0	1	1	0	0	0	2	1	.200	.429	.200	14.3	28.6	7
Schultz, Andrew	R-R	6-4	195	7-31-97	1	3	5.97	34	0	0	38	35	30	25	3	30	41	.254	.394	.377	23.3	17.0	176
Schulze, Brett	R-R	6-2	180	11-24-97	5	5	4.41	31	0	6	35	25	18	17	3	16	53	.200	.299	.352	36.6	11.0	145
Seelinger, Matt	R-R	6-3	190	4-19-95	1	1	3.71	21	0	0	27	20	11	11	6	12	28	.213	.296	.447	25.7	11.0	109
Song, Noah	R-R	6-4	200	5-28-97	0	0	6.00	2	0	0	3	3	2	2	0	2	4	.250	.400	.333	26.7	13.3	15
Suarez, Ranger	L-L	6-1	217	8-26-95	0	0	0.00	1	1	0	2	1	0	0	0	1	1	.167	.286	.167	14.3	14.3	7
Thompson, Jake	R-R	6-0	215	9-22-94	0	1	12.86	5	0	0	7	10	13	10	1	9	8	.333	.500	.567	20.0	22.5	40
Uelmen, Erich	R-R	6-3	195	5-19-96	1	0	0.00	1	0	0	1	0	0	0	0	0	1	.000	.000	.000	33.3	0.0	3
Vargas, Victor	R-R	6-1	175	9-03-00	1	3	7.14	6	6	0	29	29	24	23	9	13	12	.264	.349	.573	9.4	10.2	127
Zarbnisky, Braden	L-R	6-2	191	12-26-96	5	1	2.97	30	0	1	39	33	18	13	6	16	47	.224	.303	.388	28.5	9.7	165

Fielding

Catcher	PCT	G	PO	A	E	DP	PB
De Freitas	.929	1	13	0	1	0	0
Iser	.982	17	154	9	3	4	3
McDowell	.992	66	662	43	6	5	9
Roberts	.984	61	468	31	8	2	4

First Base	PCT	G	PO	A	E	DP
De La Cruz	.991	49	334	15	3	27
Ellis	1.000	1	6	0	0	0
Glendinning	.923	2	11	1	1	1
Iser	1.000	1	1	0	0	0
Ortiz	.983	40	260	23	5	27
Podkul	1.000	19	126	13	0	9
Stokes	1.000	5	27	1	0	4
Tatum	1.000	9	67	1	0	6
Wingrove	1.000	13	103	6	0	10

Second Base	PCT	G	PO	A	E	DP
Cannon	.989	27	39	54	1	12
Dunn	.974	92	139	197	9	48
Martinez	.972	8	14	21	1	5
Rijo	1.000	5	9	10	0	3
Stokes	.905	4	4	15	2	3
Tatum	1.000	1	1	0	0	0
Ward	.923	3	5	7	1	4

Third Base	PCT	G	PO	A	E	DP
Cannon	.909	4	3	7	1	4
Dunn	1.000	3	1	3	0	0
Ellis	1.000	5	3	10	0	1
Glendinning	1.000	3	2	5	0	1
Kroon	.908	45	27	62	9	4
Martinez	.980	18	11	38	1	3
Podkul	.974	20	14	24	1	3
Rijo	1.000	3	2	5	0	1
Stokes	.955	15	13	29	2	4
Tatum	.800	8	4	12	4	1
Ward	.929	16	7	32	3	4

Shortstop	PCT	G	PO	A	E	DP
Cannon	.923	9	14	10	2	4
Ellis	1.000	1	1	5	0	1
Martin	.940	58	66	123	12	28
Martinez	.973	27	23	48	2	6
Rijo	.917	4	4	7	1	0
Stokes	.974	38	57	91	4	19
Tatum	.667	1	1	1	1	0
Ward	1.000	1	0	3	0	1

Outfield	PCT	G	PO	A	E	DP
De La Cruz	.988	54	88	0	1	0
Dunn	1.000	2	4	0	0	0
Kroon	.984	31	39	0	1	0
Lee Sang	.667	25	52	2	0	0
Ortiz	.955	13	20	1	1	0
Radcliff	.967	52	74	0	3	0
Roberts	1.000	7	6	0	0	0
Rojas	.975	70	192	5	5	0
Stokes	1.000	37	73	0	0	0
Tatum	1.000	15	28	2	0	0
Whitley	1.000	15	31	1	0	1
Wilson	.984	100	180	9	3	3

JERSEY SHORE BLUECLAWS — *HIGH CLASS A*

SOUTH ATLANTIC LEAGUE

Batting	B-T	Ht.	Wt.	DOB	AVG	OBP	SLG	G	PA	AB	R	H	2B	3B	HR	RBI	BB	HBP	SH	SF	SO	SB	CS	BB%	SO%
Baylor, Jamari	R-R	5-10	190	8-25-00	.172	.333	.172	10	36	29	3	5	0	0	0	1	6	1	0	0	15	0	1	16.7	41.7
Brito, Erick	R-R	5-8	134	5-25-02	.208	.310	.259	65	233	197	26	41	6	2	0	25	21	9	4	2	29	15	5	9.0	12.4
Carr, Jared	L-R	6-0	180	5-24-99	.235	.330	.335	102	380	328	50	77	15	3	4	37	45	3	1	3	98	23	5	11.8	25.8
Crawford, Justin	L-R	6-1	175	1-13-04	.288	.366	.425	18	82	73	20	21	6	2	0	4	7	2	0	0	16	7	1	8.5	19.5
De Freitas, Arturo	R-R	5-10	170	5-28-01	.162	.233	.181	36	116	105	7	17	2	0	0	6	9	1	0	1	39	0	0	7.8	33.6
Fergus, Cade	R-R	6-2	195	8-22-00	.070	.245	.093	14	53	43	6	3	1	0	0	2	8	2	0	0	26	4	2	15.1	49.1
Flores, Wilfredo	L-R	5-8	170	5-14-00	.288	.322	.335	61	202	191	21	55	7	1	0	17	10	0	0	1	33	4	5	5.0	16.3
Garcia, Aramis	R-R	6-1	228	1-12-93	.091	.083	.182	3	12	11	0	1	1	0	0	2	0	0	0	1	5	0	0	0.0	41.7
Kemp, Otto	R-R	5-11	185	9-09-99	.223	.286	.286	31	128	112	14	25	5	1	0	10	8	3	0	3	30	4	3	6.3	23.4
Kroon, Matt	R-R	6-0	195	12-05-96	.200	.333	.400	3	12	10	1	2	0	1	0	1	2	0	0	0	3	0	1	16.7	25.0
Lee Sang, Marcus	L-L	5-11	200	1-02-01	.268	.372	.424	99	436	370	68	99	20	7	8	53	58	5	0	3	130	20	9	13.3	29.8
Lee, Hao-Yu	R-R	5-9	190	2-03-03	.283	.372	.401	64	285	247	35	70	12	1	5	26	29	7	0	2	53	14	3	10.2	18.6

Marchan, Rafael	B-R	5-9	170	2-25-99	.300	.417	.400	3	12	10	1	3	1	0	0	2	2	0	0	0	3	0	0	16.7	25.0
Martin, Casey	R-R	5-9	175	4-07-99	.280	.367	.456	52	208	182	27	51	10	2	6	21	23	2	1	0	51	16	4	11.1	24.5
Minyety, Freylin	R-R	5-7	185	10-22-99	.197	.311	.250	29	90	76	12	15	4	0	0	5	11	2	0	1	14	1	1	12.2	15.6
Moore, Cole	L-R	6-1	211	6-14-99	.176	.341	.353	12	44	34	5	6	3	0	1	3	9	0	0	1	10	0	0	20.5	22.7
Nava, Andrick	B-R	5-10	175	10-06-01	.221	.333	.313	64	246	208	16	46	10	0	3	27	34	2	0	2	45	0	1	13.8	18.3
Pache, Cristian	R-R	6-2	215	11-19-98	.000	.250	.000	2	8	6	1	0	0	0	0	1	2	0	0	0	6	1	0	25.0	75.0
Pineda, Leandro	L-L	6-1	165	6-04-02	.243	.339	.386	107	431	370	52	90	20	3	9	67	48	8	0	5	102	6	2	11.1	23.7
Quirion, Anthony	R-R	6-1	205	10-29-97	.188	.294	.318	52	204	176	20	33	8	0	5	19	20	7	0	1	68	1	2	9.8	33.3
Reyes, Felix	R-R	6-3	195	3-26-01	.257	.282	.343	10	39	35	2	9	0	0	1	6	1	1	0	2	4	0	0	2.6	10.3
Ricketts, Caleb	L-R	6-3	225	5-10-00	.218	.287	.300	44	188	170	21	37	1	2	3	25	15	2	0	1	35	4	2	8.0	18.6
Rincon, Bryan	B-R	5-10	185	2-08-04	.258	.364	.323	18	77	62	13	16	4	0	0	7	9	3	0	3	13	4	4	11.7	16.9
Rincones, Gabriel	L-R	6-3	225	3-03-01	.238	.326	.416	72	319	281	50	67	18	1	10	39	33	4	0	1	79	8	3	10.3	24.8
Schreffler, Troy	R-R	5-11	190	10-27-00	.186	.379	.233	19	58	43	14	8	2	0	0	6	12	2	0	1	15	9	4	20.7	25.9
Simmons, Kendall	R-R	6-0	180	4-11-00	.267	.362	.494	50	213	180	29	48	9	4	8	37	22	7	0	4	55	3	3	10.3	25.8
Viloria, Uziel	B-R	5-9	155	10-06-01	.045	.125	.045	8	24	22	2	1	0	0	0	0	2	0	0	0	14	1	0	8.3	58.3
Ward, Nick	L-R	5-9	180	10-19-95	.270	.392	.371	94	392	318	70	86	8	0	8	50	54	13	2	5	80	22	3	13.8	20.4
Wingrove, Rixon	L-R	6-4	260	5-23-00	.246	.335	.434	101	418	366	47	90	20	2	15	63	41	9	0	2	123	6	3	9.8	29.4

Pitching	B-T	Ht.	Wt.	DOB	W	L	ERA	G	GS	SV	IP	Hits	Runs	ER	HR	BB	SO	AVG	OBP	SLG	SO%	BB%	BF
Aldegheri, Samuel	L-L	6-1	180	9-19-01	1	0	5.63	4	4	0	16	19	10	10	1	5	20	.288	.347	.394	27.8	6.9	72
Antle, Chase	R-R	6-2	215	2-16-97	3	0	3.06	17	1	0	18	10	7	6	1	20	26	.169	.383	.254	32.1	24.7	81
Ash, Konnor	R-R	5-11	191	3-17-99	4	0	2.35	16	1	2	23	16	7	6	0	10	37	.190	.271	.226	38.5	10.4	96
Barber, Albertus	R-R	5-11	190	2-18-96	0	0	7.20	5	0	0	5	5	4	4	0	4	3	.238	.360	.333	12.0	16.0	25
Betancourt, Carlos	R-R	6-1	160	3-27-01	5	3	3.69	39	2	0	78	68	38	32	8	33	92	.229	.311	.374	27.5	9.9	335
Binns, Malik	R-R	6-7	240	1-15-99	1	0	6.04	22	0	0	25	29	28	17	0	23	28	.271	.414	.327	21.1	17.3	133
Cotto, Gabriel	L-L	6-5	175	5-15-00	2	5	6.15	14	11	1	53	53	38	36	5	31	37	.266	.379	.452	15.4	12.9	240
Dallas, Jack	R-R	5-11	200	12-18-98	7	2	2.80	23	0	0	35	24	15	11	1	11	38	.188	.250	.242	27.0	7.8	141
Duplantier, Jon	L-R	6-4	229	7-11-94	0	1	8.38	3	3	0	10	12	10	9	2	5	12	.308	.386	.590	27.3	11.4	44
Fowler, Jordan	L-L	6-3	180	3-09-99	3	3	3.73	15	15	0	70	73	32	29	4	21	50	.273	.324	.375	17.2	7.2	291
Francisco, Carlos A	R-R	6-4	220	7-02-99	2	0	2.93	25	0	5	31	19	12	10	1	11	38	.176	.270	.222	31.1	9.0	122
Garbrick, Alex	R-R	6-1	210	6-04-98	3	0	3.98	14	4	0	20	20	12	9	2	8	23	.253	.337	.380	25.8	9.0	89
Garnett, Tristan	L-L	6-6	240	3-29-98	3	3	2.39	34	0	1	38	25	16	10	2	15	36	.191	.272	.282	23.8	9.9	151
Haake, Zach	R-R	6-7	220	10-08-96	1	0	0.00	1	1	0	5	4	0	0	0	1	6	.222	.263	.222	31.6	5.3	19
Henriquez, Jonh	R-R	6-0	187	10-30-99	0	1	7.11	5	0	0	6	6	6	5	0	8	4	.250	.455	.292	12.1	24.2	33
Jacobsak, Sam	R-R	6-5	200	6-11-98	0	2	6.10	20	3	0	21	15	14	14	2	15	19	.203	.355	.324	20.4	16.1	93
Kerkering, Orion	R-R	6-2	204	4-04-01	2	0	1.77	18	0	3	20	13	4	4	2	6	27	.178	.250	.329	33.8	7.5	80
Kuhns, Max	R-R	6-2	209	8-11-94	0	0	0.00	1	0	0	1	0	0	0	0	0	3	.000	.000	.000	100.0	0.0	3
Lopez, Victor	R-R	6-4	192	9-02-99	0	1	16.88	2	0	0	3	3	5	5	2	4	1	.273	.500	.818	6.3	25.0	16
Marcano, Rafael	L-L	6-1	170	4-20-00	5	6	3.95	23	20	0	93	85	43	41	7	42	97	.248	.332	.397	24.5	10.6	396
Martinez, Jordi	L-L	6-2	185	7-18-00	1	1	3.97	39	0	3	48	44	27	21	4	27	59	.238	.332	.368	27.4	12.6	215
Mayer, Gunner	R-R	6-6	190	7-27-00	3	7	5.47	23	20	0	77	77	51	47	4	54	79	.265	.389	.361	22.1	15.1	357
McCollum, Tommy	R-R	6-5	260	6-08-99	0	0	2.31	34	0	7	35	17	10	9	0	23	56	.143	.287	.202	39.2	16.1	143
McGowan, Christian	R-R	6-0	205	3-07-00	0	0	2.81	5	5	0	16	15	6	5	0	5	17	.259	.328	.293	26.2	7.7	65
Moore, Wesley	L-L	6-2	200	9-05-99	0	1	1.91	25	0	3	28	20	7	6	3	15	40	.194	.311	.291	32.8	12.3	122
Nava, Andrick	B-R	5-10	175	10-06-01	0	0	0.00	2	0	0	1	2	0	0	0	1	0	.400	.500	.400	0.0	16.7	6
Neunborn, Mitch	R-R	6-0	190	6-27-97	3	4	3.38	16	10	0	43	26	16	16	3	14	54	.172	.253	.278	31.8	8.2	170
Osterberg, Matt	L-L	6-2	200	4-21-99	8	5	3.61	18	18	0	92	85	42	37	10	19	76	.244	.289	.391	20.5	5.1	370
Pan, Wen Hui	R-R	6-3	220	9-19-02	0	0	15.00	6	0	0	6	13	10	10	1	5	7	.419	.500	.613	19.4	13.9	36
Plassmeyer, Michael	L-L	6-2	197	11-05-96	0	0	1.13	3	3	0	8	5	1	1	1	1	9	.185	.214	.333	32.1	3.6	28
Ruffcorn, Jason	R-R	6-2	215	7-27-98	4	1	5.01	44	0	2	50	50	32	28	3	22	52	.255	.338	.398	23.1	9.8	225
Russell, Matt	R-R	6-2	190	3-28-99	6	7	5.24	39	0	3	46	47	30	27	2	26	41	.264	.370	.388	19.3	12.3	212
Sanchez, Rodolfo	R-R	5-10	165	1-12-00	3	2	4.94	40	6	2	51	47	31	28	7	29	54	.245	.342	.417	24.0	12.9	225
Vargas, Victor	R-R	6-1	175	9-03-00	0	0	4.91	3	3	0	7	10	4	4	0	3	3	.333	.429	.333	8.6	8.6	35
Vines, Jace	R-R	6-3	215	9-04-94	0	0	0.00	3	0	0	4	3	1	0	0	2	3	.214	.313	.286	18.8	12.5	16
Walling, Andrew	L-L	6-2	220	10-29-99	2	2	3.24	14	0	3	17	9	8	6	0	3	27	.164	.213	.236	44.3	4.9	61
Wynne, Cam	R-R	6-6	220	1-11-99	1	1	2.55	34	1	1	42	29	13	12	5	14	39	.190	.273	.320	22.7	8.1	172

Fielding

Catcher	PCT	G	PO	A	E	DP	PB
De Freitas	.989	34	260	22	3	2	6
Garcia	1.000	3	27	2	0	0	0
Marchan	1.000	3	33	1	0	0	1
Nava	.983	44	388	17	7	1	7
Quirion	.984	25	233	14	4	0	4
Ricketts	.987	30	286	11	4	2	6

First Base	PCT	G	PO	A	E	DP
Baylor	1.000	7	49	2	0	6
Moore	.989	12	78	10	1	12
Nava	1.000	1	7	1	0	0
Quirion	.989	12	82	4	1	4
Reyes	.912	4	31	0	3	1
Ricketts	1.000	2	21	1	0	0
Ward	1.000	13	82	4	0	5
Wingrove	.988	89	622	45	8	56

Second Base	PCT	G	PO	A	E	DP
Brito	1.000	12	21	24	0	5
Flores	.969	16	32	30	2	12
Kemp	1.000	3	5	9	0	3
Lee	.968	48	65	114	6	23
Minyety	.943	11	16	17	2	7
Simmons	.973	31	45	65	3	11
Viloria	.952	5	8	12	1	2
Ward	.984	12	27	33	1	7

Third Base	PCT	G	PO	A	E	DP
Flores	.813	9	1	12	3	1
Kemp	1.000	28	18	62	0	4
Lee	.962	8	5	20	1	3
Minyety	.925	16	6	31	3	0
Reyes	.875	4	2	5	1	1
Simmons	.913	16	9	33	4	3
Viloria	1.000	2	1	3	0	2
Ward	.955	57	38	112	7	6

Shortstop	PCT	G	PO	A	E	DP
Brito	.974	52	58	127	5	21
Lee	1.000	5	4	15	0	2
Martin	.952	51	60	117	9	25
Rincon	.984	18	24	37	1	10
Viloria	1.000	1	0	4	0	1
Ward	1.000	6	2	20	0	1

Outfield	PCT	G	PO	A	E	DP
Carr	.987	100	188	9	3	3
Crawford	.970	17	32	0	1	0
Fergus	1.000	12	20	0	0	0
Flores	.955	22	19	2	1	0
Kroon	.500	2	4	0	0	0
Lee Sang	.975	91	184	10	4	0
Pache	1.000	2	4	0	0	0
Pineda	.991	85	138	3	2	1
Rincones	.967	58	113	6	2	1
Schreffler	.963	16	33	0	1	0

CLEARWATER THRESHERS

LOW CLASS A

FLORIDA STATE LEAGUE

Batting	B-T	Ht.	Wt.	DOB	AVG	OBP	SLG	G	PA	AB	R	H	2B	3B	HR	RBI	BB	HBP	SH	SF	SO	SB	CS	BB%	SO%
Alifano, Matt	R-R	5-11	195	12-31-00	.180	.293	.200	14	59	50	8	9	1	0	0	2	7	1	1	0	20	0	1	11.9	33.9
Anthony, Keaton	R-R	6-4	211	6-24-01	.143	.400	.143	5	20	14	1	2	0	0	0	0	4	2	0	0	3	1	0	20.0	15.0
Arnold, Zach	R-R	6-2	205	6-13-01	.293	.376	.415	22	94	82	15	24	2	1	2	11	10	1	0	0	19	8	0	10.6	20.2
Avila, Kliubert	R-R	5-9	170	5-19-03	.214	.267	.214	4	15	14	2	3	0	0	0	1	1	0	0	0	4	0	0	6.7	26.7
Bergolla, William	L-R	5-11	165	10-20-04	.255	.351	.286	55	228	192	26	49	2	2	0	20	30	0	3	3	17	2	5	13.2	7.5
Boyd, Emaarion	R-R	5-11	177	8-22-03	.262	.366	.324	91	403	343	68	90	8	5	1	36	35	22	1	2	60	56	18	8.7	14.9
Brito, Erick	R-R	5-8	134	5-25-02	.278	.350	.361	44	164	144	21	40	2	2	2	20	15	2	1	2	27	14	3	9.1	16.5
Castillo, Chad	L-R	6-2	225	4-19-00	.246	.330	.419	72	285	248	36	61	10	0	11	37	21	12	0	4	65	4	3	7.4	22.8
Crawford, Justin	L-R	6-1	175	1-13-04	.344	.399	.478	69	308	276	51	95	16	6	3	60	25	2	2	3	53	40	7	8.1	17.2
Dissin, Jordan	R-R	6-3	185	5-29-02	.252	.351	.358	65	263	226	40	57	10	1	4	35	32	3	1	1	83	1	4	12.2	31.6
Farquhar, Trent	L-R	5-8	180	3-12-01	.167	.348	.278	6	24	18	5	3	2	0	0	1	5	0	1	0	4	0	0	20.8	16.7
Fergus, Cade	R-R	6-2	195	8-22-00	.255	.356	.500	74	261	220	48	56	14	2	12	47	29	8	0	4	90	10	1	11.1	34.5
Hall, Darick	L-R	6-4	232	7-25-95	.375	.444	.500	2	9	8	1	3	1	0	0	0	1	0	0	0	0	0	0	11.1	0.0
Heredia, Raylin	R-R	6-0	174	11-10-03	.288	.342	.409	18	73	66	9	19	3	1	1	9	6	0	0	1	23	4	0	8.2	31.5
Kemp, Otto	R-R	5-11	185	9-09-99	.251	.388	.414	78	330	263	57	66	12	5	7	43	49	13	0	5	79	17	4	14.8	23.9
Kotowski, Dakota	R-R	6-4	245	3-26-00	.143	.208	.333	6	24	21	1	3	1	0	1	5	2	0	0	1	10	0	0	8.3	41.7
Leitch, Ryan	R-R	6-0	195	8-26-01	.247	.326	.418	45	178	158	25	39	6	0	7	23	13	6	0	1	55	0	0	7.3	30.9
Marchan, Rafael	B-R	5-9	170	2-25-99	.600	.600	.600	1	5	5	0	3	0	0	0	3	0	0	0	0	0	0	0	0.0	0.0
Mejia, Adony	R-R	5-9	170	6-09-01	.000	.250	.000	1	4	3	1	0	0	0	0	0	1	0	0	0	3	0	0	25.0	75.0
Miller, Aidan	R-R	6-2	210	6-09-04	.216	.341	.297	10	44	37	4	8	1	1	0	0	6	1	0	0	10	4	1	13.6	22.7
Minyety, Freylin	R-R	5-7	185	10-22-99	.310	.374	.356	28	101	87	10	27	4	0	0	14	9	1	1	2	10	4	1	8.9	9.9
Moore, Cole	L-R	6-1	211	6-14-99	.250	.348	.378	47	184	156	25	39	9	1	3	16	25	0	0	3	52	2	1	13.6	28.3
Pache, Cristian	R-R	6-2	215	11-19-98	.273	.467	.273	3	15	11	4	3	0	0	0	0	4	0	0	0	4	0	0	26.7	26.7
Penner, Ty	L-R	6-4	215	5-01-00	.118	.211	.147	10	38	34	3	4	1	0	0	0	3	1	0	0	13	0	0	7.9	34.2
Reyes, Felix	R-R	6-3	195	3-26-01	.264	.310	.416	67	277	250	28	66	9	1	9	62	17	3	0	7	30	6	3	6.1	10.8
Ricketts, Caleb	L-R	6-3	225	5-10-00	.368	.390	.547	23	100	95	16	35	10	2	1	23	3	1	0	1	13	2	2	3.0	13.0
Rincon, Bryan	B-R	5-10	185	2-08-04	.228	.369	.370	81	348	276	49	63	13	1	8	45	59	6	1	6	63	23	10	17.0	18.1
Rincones, Gabriel	L-R	6-3	225	3-03-01	.264	.388	.444	48	214	178	31	47	13	2	5	21	28	8	0	0	55	24	3	13.1	25.7
Rosario, Ricardo	R-R	5-11	160	2-08-03	.236	.336	.348	75	327	276	45	65	6	2	7	39	38	6	3	4	63	29	3	11.6	19.3
Schreffler, Troy	R-R	5-11	190	10-27-00	.289	.392	.479	42	148	121	28	35	1	2	6	24	22	1	0	4	34	11	4	14.9	23.0
Simmons, Kendall	R-R	6-0	180	4-11-00	.000	.333	.000	1	6	4	2	0	0	0	0	0	2	0	0	0	2	0	0	33.3	33.3
Thomas, Jared	L-R	6-0	185	12-03-00	.143	.455	.143	3	11	7	3	1	0	0	0	0	3	1	0	0	2	0	0	27.3	18.2
Viars, Jordan	L-L	6-2	215	7-18-03	.214	.315	.343	83	327	280	43	60	16	1	6	29	27	15	3	2	88	6	3	8.3	26.9
Ware, Bryson	R-R	6-2	193	12-28-00	.188	.269	.362	20	78	69	10	13	3	0	3	7	7	1	0	1	21	2	1	9.0	26.9

Pitching	B-T	Ht.	Wt.	DOB	W	L	ERA	G	GS	SV	IP	Hits	Runs	ER	HR	BB	SO	AVG	OBP	SLG	SO%	BB%	BF
Aldegheri, Samuel	L-L	6-1	180	9-19-01	3	1	3.86	16	15	0	68	59	35	29	8	30	79	.234	.323	.381	27.1	10.3	291
Ash, Konnor	R-R	5-11	191	3-17-99	0	0	3.60	5	0	0	5	5	2	2	0	4	8	.250	.375	.300	33.3	16.7	24
Beckel, Brandon	R-R	6-4	225	10-20-01	0	0	9.00	3	0	0	3	3	3	3	1	2	1	.273	.385	.636	7.7	15.4	13
Bellatti, Andrew	R-R	6-1	190	8-05-91	0	0	0.00	2	0	0	2	1	0	0	0	1	4	.143	.250	.143	50.0	12.5	8
Bortka, Josh	R-R	6-5	225	7-12-99	1	0	3.68	20	0	2	29	12	13	12	2	19	43	.125	.317	.208	34.7	15.3	124
Brown, Cam	R-R	6-3	225	10-15-01	0	1	20.25	2	0	0	1	3	4	3	0	5	1	.500	.727	.667	9.1	45.5	11
Cabrera, Jean	R-R	6-0	145	10-20-01	5	7	4.32	19	13	1	81	108	48	39	3	22	86	.325	.374	.422	24.0	6.1	358
Castellano, Eiberson	R-R	6-3	160	5-09-01	3	2	5.04	22	7	0	50	55	29	28	3	28	58	.276	.380	.377	24.8	12.0	234
Castillo, Starlyn	R-R	6-0	210	2-24-02	0	1	8.76	4	3	0	12	17	14	12	0	11	16	.327	.462	.385	24.6	16.9	65
Cotto, Gabriel	L-L	6-5	175	5-15-00	4	0	2.78	8	7	0	36	26	11	11	3	14	34	.205	.301	.331	23.3	9.6	146
Crouse, Hans	L-R	6-4	180	9-15-98	0	0	0.00	1	0	0	1	0	0	0	0	0	1	.000	.000	.000	33.3	0.0	3
Dallas, Jack	R-R	5-11	200	12-18-98	2	2	0.60	19	0	7	30	25	8	2	0	12	31	.227	.312	.264	24.8	9.6	125
Dillard, Trey	R-R	6-0	195	11-15-98	0	0	40.50	1	0	0	1	0	3	3	0	2	0	.000	.600	.000	0.0	40.0	5
Estanista, Jaydenn	R-R	6-3	180	10-03-01	2	0	8.51	13	1	0	24	26	24	23	3	27	28	.280	.444	.452	22.6	21.8	124
Falter, Bailey	R-L	6-4	175	4-24-97	0	0	0.00	1	1	0	3	1	0	0	0	1	2	.100	.182	.100	18.2	9.1	11
Fausnaught, Braeden	L-L	6-3	235	7-29-99	2	4	4.57	24	7	1	63	54	39	32	4	39	64	.229	.338	.352	22.8	13.9	281
Haake, Zach	R-R	6-7	220	10-08-96	0	1	9.45	2	1	0	7	10	7	7	3	4	6	.345	.441	.655	17.6	11.8	34
Harper, Daniel	R-R	6-4	225	6-01-99	2	1	6.42	23	0	1	34	42	26	24	1	25	27	.313	.411	.455	16.6	15.3	163
Henriquez, Jonh	R-R	6-0	187	10-30-99	14	1	3.21	30	0	3	62	39	30	22	4	36	60	.181	.305	.302	23.4	14.1	256
Jimenez, Estibenzon	R-R	6-1	172	1-25-02	4	8	3.60	21	19	0	90	83	41	36	10	39	78	.245	.335	.416	20.3	10.1	385
Karaffa, Nathan	R-R	6-1	200	1-04-01	0	0	3.72	11	0	1	19	21	12	8	2	13	14	.276	.396	.434	15.4	14.3	91
Kerkering, Orion	R-R	6-2	204	4-04-01	1	0	0.00	9	0	4	10	2	0	0	0	1	18	.061	.114	.061	51.4	2.9	35
Loyd, Hunter	R-R	6-2	205	5-07-00	0	0	1.80	4	1	0	5	4	1	1	0	2	4	.200	.273	.300	18.2	9.1	22
McFarlane, Alex	R-R	6-3	215	6-09-01	0	4	5.72	16	16	0	50	46	32	32	4	38	69	.246	.391	.364	29.6	16.3	233
McGarry, Griff	R-R	6-2	190	6-08-99	0	0	9.00	1	1	0	1	1	1	1	1	0	2	.250	.250	1.000	50.0	0.0	4
McGowan, Christian	R-R	6-0	205	3-07-00	0	1	18.00	1	1	0	2	5	4	4	1	2	2	.455	.538	.909	15.4	15.4	13
Medina, Oswald	R-R	6-0	145	12-02-01	1	1	4.85	3	3	0	13	11	7	7	2	5	9	.234	.308	.447	17.3	9.6	52
Moore, McKinley	R-R	6-6	225	8-24-98	0	0	0.00	1	0	0	1	1	0	0	0	0	3	.250	.250	.250	75.0	0.0	4
Moore, Wesley	L-L	6-2	200	9-05-99	4	0	0.72	17	0	2	25	14	7	2	0	12	39	.157	.283	.202	36.1	11.1	108
Nelson, Nick	R-R	6-1	205	12-05-95	0	0	0.00	2	2	0	5	3	0	0	0	0	5	.176	.176	.235	29.4	0.0	17
Nightingale, Seth	R-R	6-5	224	9-10-99	2	2	4.79	16	0	0	21	17	12	11	1	19	19	.236	.433	.306	19.4	19.4	98
Pan, Wen Hui	R-R	6-3	220	9-19-02	4	1	2.81	27	1	7	58	31	19	18	2	19	81	.154	.241	.219	36.2	8.5	224
Petit, Jonathan	R-R	6-2	174	4-19-01	3	3	5.24	21	17	0	81	79	49	47	10	33	76	.260	.356	.438	21.3	9.2	357
Pipkin, Dominic	R-R	6-4	160	11-05-99	2	0	4.91	3	0	0	4	3	2	2	0	2	4	.231	.333	.231	26.7	13.3	15
Ramirez, Yoniel	R-R	6-0	180	5-27-01	3	0	7.06	15	0	0	22	18	21	17	3	27	25	.225	.452	.388	21.7	23.5	115
Rao, Alex	R-R	6-4	230	10-25-99	0	3	6.00	15	6	0	27	28	20	18	2	14	33	.275	.377	.422	27.0	11.5	122
Ronan, Mason	L-L	6-3	222	3-03-00	0	1	14.54	3	0	1	4	4	7	7	1	8	5	.235	.500	.412	19.2	30.8	26

Segovia, Eduar	R-R	6-0	180	1-10-01	2	1	4.95	14	0	0	20	11	12	11	1	26	29	.162	.414	.206	29.3	26.3	99
Song, Noah	R-R	6-4	200	5-28-97	0	0	1.93	4	0	0	5	4	1	1	0	5	7	.222	.391	.278	30.4	21.7	23
Steward, Casey	R-R	6-5	260	8-02-01	0	0	4.50	3	0	0	4	2	2	2	0	10	3	.154	.522	.231	13.0	43.5	23
Teran, Saul	R-R	6-1	165	3-20-02	0	1	5.00	5	0	0	9	7	5	5	0	3	10	.241	.324	.276	26.3	7.9	38
Thompson, Paxton	R-R	6-1	205	10-05-99	0	0	7.71	4	0	0	5	7	4	4	2	2	8	.350	.391	.800	34.8	8.7	23
Tucker, Braydon	L-R	6-3	205	7-19-99	0	0	3.00	2	0	0	3	3	1	1	0	2	2	.273	.385	.455	15.4	15.4	13
Uelmen, Erich	R-R	6-3	195	5-19-96	0	0	9.00	1	0	0	1	1	1	1	0	0	1	.250	.250	.500	25.0	0.0	4
Velasquez, Giussepe	R-R	6-1	170	4-30-03	1	1	5.40	5	5	0	22	18	13	13	3	11	22	.222	.330	.370	23.4	11.7	94
Ventura, Ezequiel	R-R	6-1	151	6-20-02	1	1	3.00	2	2	0	9	3	3	3	0	5	8	.107	.257	.214	22.9	14.3	35
Vines, Jace	R-R	6-3	215	9-04-94	1	0	0.00	1	0	0	1	0	0	0	0	0	1	.000	.000	.000	33.3	0.0	3
Walling, Andrew	L-L	6-2	220	10-29-99	6	1	3.23	26	0	5	39	29	18	14	4	26	46	.206	.335	.333	27.1	15.3	170
Wilkinson, Danny	L-L	6-0	206	10-19-00	6	0	4.45	34	0	1	57	36	31	28	3	44	106	.177	.336	.276	41.9	17.4	253

Fielding

Catcher	PCT	G	PO	A	E	DP	PB
Avila	1.000	4	39	2	0	0	0
Dissin	.989	62	585	42	7	2	11
Leitch	.998	45	406	30	1	4	4
Marchan	1.000	1	9	1	0	0	0
Mejia	1.000	1	11	4	0	0	0
Ricketts	.987	18	219	16	3	2	4
Thomas	1.000	3	24	1	0	0	0

First Base	PCT	G	PO	A	E	DP
Anthony	.933	4	27	1	2	3
Castillo	.985	48	309	15	5	36
Hall	1.000	1	6	1	0	1
Kotowski	1.000	6	32	2	0	5
Moore	.997	46	279	13	1	30
Reyes	.985	27	195	3	3	20
Ricketts	1.000	3	20	0	0	3

Second Base	PCT	G	PO	A	E	DP
Alifano	.979	14	21	26	1	6
Arnold	1.000	2	3	6	0	1
Bergolla	.985	32	51	78	2	23
Brito	.985	32	58	72	2	20
Farquhar	1.000	6	7	10	0	2
Kemp	.992	30	51	68	1	18
Simmons	1.000	1	3	6	0	2
Ware	.947	14	24	30	3	12

Third Base	PCT	G	PO	A	E	DP
Arnold	.968	12	10	20	1	3
Kemp	.962	49	35	67	4	6
Minyety	.957	28	13	31	2	0
Penner	.947	9	6	12	1	1
Reyes	.960	36	27	45	3	4
Ware	.750	5	2	4	2	0

Shortstop	PCT	G	PO	A	E	DP
Arnold	1.000	7	5	19	0	4
Bergolla	.961	22	30	44	3	15
Brito	.947	12	11	25	2	6
Kemp	1.000	1	0	1	0	0
Miller	.923	9	6	18	2	3
Rincon	.968	80	101	198	10	47

Outfield	PCT	G	PO	A	E	DP
Boyd	.983	83	137	4	3	2
Crawford	.950	60	112	2	6	1
Fergus	.996	67	122	9	1	2
Heredia	.986	18	36	2	1	0
Minyety	1.000	1	0	1	0	0
Pache	1.000	2	3	0	0	0
Rincones	1.000	27	50	1	0	0
Rosario	.989	69	125	5	2	2
Schreffler	.956	42	73	5	5	2
Viars	.905	41	59	4	4	0

FCL PHILLIES — *ROOKIE*

FLORIDA COMPLEX LEAGUE

Batting	B-T	Ht.	Wt.	DOB	AVG	OBP	SLG	G	PA	AB	R	H	2B	3B	HR	RBI	BB	HBP	SH	SF	SO	SB	CS	BB%	SO%
Albrecht, Lou	R-R	6-0	210	11-07-01	.375	.444	.375	5	9	8	0	3	0	0	0	1	1	0	0	0	2	0	0	11.1	22.2
Alifano, Matt	R-R	5-11	195	12-31-00	.267	.389	.467	4	18	15	2	4	3	0	0	1	3	0	0	0	2	0	0	16.7	11.1
Anthony, Keaton	R-R	6-4	211	6-24-01	.379	.486	.621	9	35	29	7	11	1	0	2	9	2	4	0	0	6	0	0	5.7	17.1
Arnold, Zach	R-R	6-2	205	6-13-01	.273	.357	.636	4	14	11	4	3	2	1	0	5	1	1	0	1	2	0	0	7.1	14.3
Avila, Kliubert	R-R	5-9	170	5-19-03	.300	.417	.600	5	12	10	2	3	0	0	1	3	2	0	0	0	3	0	0	16.7	25.0
Bennett, Pierce	R-R	6-1	195	6-28-01	.190	.400	.238	8	30	21	5	4	1	0	0	5	6	2	0	1	3	0	0	20.0	10.0
Cannon, Cam	R-R	5-10	205	10-16-97	.273	.385	.818	3	13	11	3	3	0	0	2	2	2	0	0	0	4	0	0	15.4	30.8
Castillo, Chad	L-R	6-2	225	4-19-00	.273	.273	.636	2	11	11	1	3	1	0	1	3	0	0	0	0	2	0	0	0.0	18.2
Castillo, Starlyn	R-R	6-0	210	2-24-02	.000	.250	.000	13	4	3	0	0	0	0	0	0	1	0	0	0	1	0	0	25.0	25.0
Colmenarez, Jose	R-R	5-9	160	11-24-02	.182	.308	.273	9	13	11	1	2	1	0	0	2	1	1	0	0	4	0	0	7.7	30.8
Farmer, Ezra	L-L	6-0	165	6-10-03	.167	.390	.233	12	41	30	7	5	2	0	0	4	9	2	0	0	13	1	0	22.0	31.7
Farquhar, Trent	L-R	5-8	180	3-12-01	.324	.439	.382	10	41	34	7	11	2	0	0	4	5	2	0	0	4	5	0	12.2	9.8
Flores, Yemal	R-R	5-9	206	11-22-03	.282	.417	.513	14	48	39	9	11	4	1	1	8	8	1	0	0	16	0	2	16.7	33.3
Garcia, Yhoswar	R-R	5-9	150	9-13-01	.235	.300	.324	35	151	136	27	32	7	1	1	22	9	4	1	1	26	11	3	6.0	17.2
Gonzalez, Diego	R-R	5-11	160	6-07-03	.258	.340	.371	30	100	89	19	23	4	0	2	10	10	1	0	0	19	0	0	10.0	19.0
Helmig, Lou	L-R	6-5	198	5-01-03	.149	.293	.298	16	60	47	12	7	2	1	1	6	9	1	2	1	17	2	0	15.0	28.3
Heredia, Raylin	R-R	6-0	174	11-10-03	.326	.415	.532	35	164	141	30	46	9	4	4	25	17	5	0	1	42	7	3	10.4	25.6
Hettiger, Kehden	B-R	6-2	195	5-25-04	.190	.370	.238	10	27	21	5	4	1	0	0	3	6	0	0	0	7	0	1	22.2	25.9
Holgate, Ryan	L-L	6-2	193	6-08-00	.091	.200	.091	7	25	22	0	2	0	0	0	1	3	0	0	0	4	0	0	12.0	16.0
Kotowski, Dakota	R-R	6-4	245	3-26-00	.287	.397	.653	42	179	150	38	43	8	1	15	34	22	6	0	1	50	7	1	12.3	27.9
Lee, Hao-Yu	R-R	5-9	190	2-03-03	.182	.250	.273	3	12	11	1	2	1	0	0	3	1	0	0	0	3	0	0	8.3	25.0
Marin, Junior	R-R	6-2	240	3-15-04	.294	.316	.412	5	19	17	2	5	2	0	0	1	1	0	0	1	4	0	0	5.3	21.1
Martinez, Pedro	B-R	5-9	165	1-28-01	.481	.576	.741	9	33	27	5	13	2	1	1	11	5	1	0	0	5	1	0	15.2	15.2
Mendez, Jorge	R-R	5-10	160	8-01-03	.217	.367	.370	25	60	46	9	10	4	0	1	11	7	5	0	2	1	0	0	11.7	1.7
Miller, Aidan	R-R	6-2	210	6-09-04	.414	.528	.483	10	36	29	6	12	2	0	0	2	6	1	0	0	5	0	0	16.7	13.9
Owusu-Asiedu, Avery	R-R	6-4	230	6-16-03	.217	.327	.348	13	55	46	8	10	3	0	1	14	7	1	0	1	10	2	0	12.7	18.2
Penner, Ty	L-R	6-4	215	5-01-00	.286	.466	.405	14	58	42	9	12	2	0	1	5	13	2	0	1	10	0	0	22.4	17.2
Pertuz, Jackie	L-R	6-0	188	11-01-02	.273	.368	.364	18	38	33	2	9	3	0	0	8	3	2	0	0	11	0	0	7.9	28.9
Quirion, Anthony	R-R	6-1	205	10-29-97	.471	.550	.647	5	20	17	3	8	3	0	0	1	1	2	0	0	2	0	1	5.0	10.0
Radcliff, Baron	L-R	6-4	228	2-09-99	.267	.500	.533	5	22	15	3	4	1	0	1	3	7	0	0	0	5	0	0	31.8	22.7
Ricketts, Caleb	L-R	6-3	225	5-10-00	.222	.364	.333	3	11	9	0	2	1	0	0	2	2	0	0	0	1	0	0	18.2	9.1
Rodriguez, Albert	R-R	6-2	170	12-11-02	.191	.304	.277	24	56	47	10	9	1	0	1	4	7	1	0	1	16	1	2	12.5	28.6
Rondon, Leonardo	B-R	5-7	160	3-10-04	.286	.389	.377	27	92	77	16	22	2	1	1	12	11	2	2	0	11	4	2	12.0	12.0
Saltiban, Devin	R-R	5-10	180	2-14-05	.333	.391	.452	10	46	42	10	14	2	0	1	7	3	1	0	0	7	5	1	6.5	15.2
Sevilla, Jehisbert	R-R	5-11	149	3-21-03	.182	.289	.242	27	76	66	13	12	4	0	0	5	6	4	0	0	13	0	2	7.9	17.1
Shaver, A.J.	R-R	6-2	213	10-08-01	.133	.316	.233	11	38	30	6	4	0	0	1	4	4	4	0	0	16	3	1	10.5	42.1
Simmons, Kendall	R-R	6-0	180	4-11-00	.346	.455	.615	8	33	26	4	9	4	0	1	5	4	2	0	1	6	2	0	12.1	18.2
Sosa, Gustavo	R-R	6-0	203	7-17-01	.239	.311	.418	22	74	67	8	16	3	0	3	13	6	1	0	0	24	1	0	8.1	32.4

Batting	B-T	Ht.	Wt.	DOB	AVG	OBP	SLG	G	PA	AB	R	H	2B	3B	HR	RBI	BB	HBP	SH	SF	SO	SB	CS	BB%	SO%
Soto, Marco	B-R	5-11	145	3-08-04	.252	.315	.339	35	130	115	19	29	7	0	1	13	7	5	0	3	22	0	0	5.4	16.9
Thomas, Jared	L-R	6-0	185	12-03-00	.167	.444	.278	11	27	18	0	3	2	0	0	3	7	2	0	0	6	0	0	25.9	22.2
Tonkel, Gavin	R-R	6-1	180	11-06-02	.326	.408	.535	15	49	43	14	14	3	0	2	8	1	5	0	0	16	1	0	2.0	32.7
Torres, Santiago	R-R	6-1	160	9-20-02	.247	.348	.312	36	112	93	18	23	3	0	1	12	15	1	0	3	32	6	2	13.4	28.6
Vasquez, Randy	L-R	5-11	170	12-16-02	.067	.423	.200	10	27	15	5	1	0	1	0	2	10	0	1	1	7	0	0	37.0	25.9
Walton, TayShaun	R-R	6-3	225	1-29-05	.385	.529	.692	5	17	13	4	5	2	1	0	4	3	1	0	0	6	0	1	17.6	35.3
Ware, Bryson	R-R	6-2	193	12-28-00	.125	.300	.125	5	20	16	4	2	0	0	0	0	3	1	0	0	4	2	0	15.0	20.0

Pitching	B-T	Ht.	Wt.	DOB	W	L	ERA	G	GS	SV	IP	Hits	Runs	ER	HR	BB	SO	AVG	OBP	SLG	SO%	BB%	BF
Alcala, Saul	R-R	6-1	158	11-07-00	1	0	5.66	9	1	0	21	24	14	13	1	14	17	.293	.414	.378	17.2	14.1	99
Ash, Konnor	R-R	5-11	191	3-17-99	0	0	40.50	1	0	0	1	1	3	3	0	2	2	.333	.600	.667	40.0	40.0	5
Beckel, Brandon	R-R	6-4	225	10-20-01	0	0	0.00	1	0	0	1	1	0	0	0	0	1	.250	.250	.250	25.0	0.0	4
Bortka, Josh	R-R	6-5	225	7-12-99	2	0	9.00	8	0	0	8	9	8	8	2	9	13	.265	.432	.529	29.5	20.5	44
Brown, Cam	R-R	6-3	225	10-15-01	0	0	54.00	1	0	0	0	1	2	2	0	3	0	.500	.800	.500	0.0	60.0	5
Castillo, Starlyn	R-R	6-0	210	2-24-02	3	2	5.60	12	6	0	35	38	27	22	2	21	40	.270	.381	.376	23.8	12.5	168
Collins, Ty	L-R	6-3	165	8-29-01	3	0	6.61	10	0	0	16	12	12	12	0	17	13	.211	.408	.263	17.1	22.4	76
Estanista, Jaydenn	R-R	6-3	180	10-03-01	0	0	0.00	1	1	0	1	0	0	0	0	1	2	.000	.250	.000	50.0	25.0	4
Fuenmayor, Javier	R-R	6-2	170	1-20-03	2	1	4.00	11	0	2	18	13	9	8	3	12	17	.200	.342	.400	21.5	15.2	79
Garcia, Eric	R-R	6-5	230	5-12-00	2	2	7.23	15	0	0	19	27	19	15	2	17	24	.342	.470	.481	24.0	17.0	100
Garrett, Drew	R-R	6-6	205	6-20-00	2	1	9.45	12	0	0	13	9	15	14	1	21	15	.209	.463	.279	22.4	31.3	67
Gomez, Luis	R-R	6-1	174	5-14-01	3	3	5.24	19	0	10	22	26	16	13	3	12	17	.302	.388	.558	17.2	12.1	99
Graves, Mavis	L-L	6-6	205	11-20-03	0	4	7.68	11	11	0	34	35	33	29	4	29	45	.273	.423	.438	27.6	17.8	163
Haake, Zach	R-R	6-7	220	10-08-96	0	0	0.00	1	1	0	4	3	0	0	0	2	3	.200	.294	.200	17.6	11.8	17
Hopewell, Chase	R-R	6-4	197	1-23-01	0	0	13.50	2	0	0	2	3	3	3	1	2	4	.333	.455	.667	36.4	18.2	11
Karaffa, Nathan	R-R	6-1	200	1-04-01	1	0	1.88	8	0	0	14	10	4	3	1	8	11	.204	.316	.306	19.0	13.8	58
Loyd, Hunter	R-R	6-2	205	5-07-00	0	0	0.00	2	0	0	1	2	0	0	0	0	1	.400	.400	.400	20.0	0.0	5
McGowan, Christian	R-R	6-0	205	3-07-00	0	0	3.60	2	2	0	5	2	2	2	0	0	6	.118	.167	.176	33.3	0.0	18
Medina, Oswald	R-R	6-0	145	12-02-01	0	1	5.52	4	4	0	15	22	9	9	2	1	15	.338	.358	.492	22.4	1.5	67
Mejia, Daniel	R-R	6-5	164	4-19-02	1	2	3.23	9	7	0	31	23	14	11	1	22	29	.209	.343	.273	21.6	16.4	134
Morales, Francisco	R-R	6-4	185	10-27-99	0	0	4.50	2	0	0	2	2	1	1	0	1	4	.250	.333	.375	44.4	11.1	9
Ortega, Fernando	R-R	6-4	160	10-10-01	0	1	24.30	3	0	0	3	10	10	9	2	5	1	.526	.625	1.000	4.2	20.8	24
Ottenbreit, Micah	R-R	6-4	190	5-07-03	0	0	11.57	2	2	0	2	3	3	3	0	2	0	.333	.538	.556	0.0	15.4	13
Pena, Jose	R-R	6-3	200	7-08-03	3	1	6.68	14	2	1	32	29	25	24	3	32	31	.238	.400	.402	20.0	20.6	155
Pina, Nicoly	R-R	6-3	203	10-08-99	1	1	11.37	11	0	0	13	14	17	16	2	24	16	.304	.560	.457	21.3	32.0	75
Pipkin, Dominic	R-R	6-4	160	11-05-99	0	0	27.00	2	1	0	2	4	5	5	0	1	3	.444	.545	.444	27.3	9.1	11
Querales, Jesus	R-R	6-0	175	2-18-03	0	1	5.25	9	0	0	12	14	7	7	1	8	9	.298	.421	.426	15.8	14.0	57
Ramirez, Yoniel	R-R	6-0	180	5-27-01	0	0	4.30	10	0	0	15	15	8	7	1	9	19	.278	.409	.407	28.8	13.6	66
Rao, Alex	R-R	6-4	230	10-25-99	1	0	0.00	1	0	0	1	0	0	0	0	0	0	.000	.000	.000	0.0	0.0	3
Ronan, Mason	L-L	6-3	222	3-03-00	0	2	17.18	3	0	0	4	5	7	7	0	6	2	.385	.524	.385	9.5	28.6	21
Segura, Enrique	R-R	6-3	175	12-19-04	1	3	6.87	11	10	0	37	32	29	28	4	29	33	.254	.432	.452	19.4	17.1	170
Steward, Casey	R-R	6-5	260	8-02-01	0	0	0.00	2	0	0	2	0	0	0	0	1	2	.000	.143	.000	28.6	14.3	7
Teran, Saul	R-R	6-1	165	3-20-02	1	0	4.01	15	0	3	25	22	12	11	3	8	20	.242	.320	.385	19.4	7.8	103
Thompson, Paxton	R-R	6-1	205	10-05-99	0	0	0.00	1	0	0	1	0	0	0	0	0	2	.000	.000	.000	50.0	0.0	4
Tucker, Braydon	L-R	6-3	205	7-19-99	0	0	13.50	2	1	0	2	3	3	3	0	1	1	.375	.500	.500	10.0	10.0	10
Velasquez, Giussepe	R-R	6-1	170	4-30-03	3	0	1.35	8	2	0	20	11	3	3	2	9	28	.159	.256	.246	35.9	11.5	78
Ventura, Ezequiel	R-R	6-1	151	6-20-02	0	0	5.00	9	4	1	27	27	19	15	4	12	25	.257	.339	.486	21.2	10.2	118
Webster, Chase	R-R	6-4	250	9-12-99	0	0	7.94	4	0	0	6	7	5	5	1	3	3	.368	.458	.632	12.5	12.5	24

Fielding

C: Mendez 23, Pertuz 16, Rondon 14, Thomas 11, Hettiger 10, Colmenarez 8, Avila 5, Albrecht 4, Quirion 4, Sosa 4, Ricketts 3. **1B:** Kotowski 36, Helmig 11, Anthony 6, Castillo 2, Marin 2, Sosa 2, Mendez 1. **2B:** Sevilla 24, Farquhar 9, Bennett 7, Soto 6, Vasquez 4, Simmons 4, Gonzalez 4, Alifano 3, Rondon 3, Lee 2, Ware 1. **3B:** Gonzalez 15, Penner 12, Rondon 8, Vasquez 5, Sosa 4, Soto 4, Ware 3, Sevilla 3, Simmons 2, Helmig 2, Alifano 2, Arnold 2, Farquhar 1. **SS:** Soto 28, Gonzalez 11, Martinez 9, Miller 9, Saltiban 5, Vasquez 2, Cannon 2, Alifano 1, Arnold 1. **OF:** Garcia 33, Heredia 33, Torres 33, Rodriguez 20, Owusu-Asiedu 13, Shaver 11, Flores 11, Tonkel 10, Farmer 10, Walton 5, Radcliff 4, Holgate 3, Marin 1, Bennett 1, Helmig 1.

DSL PHILLIES — *ROOKIE*

DOMINICAN SUMMER LEAGUE

Batting	B-T	Ht.	Wt.	DOB	AVG	OBP	SLG	G	PA	AB	R	H	2B	3B	HR	RBI	BB	HBP	SH	SF	SO	SB	CS	BB%	SO%
Andrade, Dervin	R-R	6-0	200	11-01-03	.200	.282	.214	32	78	70	15	14	1	0	0	1	6	2	0	0	13	2	0	7.7	16.7
Barria, Erick	R-R	5-11	155	1-31-03	.269	.390	.388	37	82	67	14	18	4	2	0	12	13	1	0	1	14	1	0	15.9	17.1
Beltran, Nolan	L-R	6-0	160	1-24-05	.297	.375	.405	32	128	111	23	33	5	2	1	20	15	0	0	2	22	3	4	11.7	17.2
Caba, Starlyn	B-R	5-10	160	12-06-05	.301	.423	.346	38	164	133	29	40	2	2	0	17	28	1	1	1	16	16	6	17.1	9.8
Calderon, Jaeden	R-R	6-1	208	9-17-05	.276	.414	.463	42	152	123	20	34	8	3	3	23	24	5	0	0	34	13	5	15.8	22.4
Cardoza, Victor	R-R	5-11	181	1-19-06	.241	.353	.375	39	133	112	19	27	4	4	1	13	13	7	0	1	34	7	4	9.8	25.6
Carela, Leny	R-R	6-0	170	10-09-04	.264	.343	.333	39	100	87	14	23	4	1	0	15	9	2	1	1	26	7	5	9.0	26.0
Colmenares, Kilwer	B-R	5-8	160	4-26-05	.157	.218	.176	21	55	51	9	8	1	0	0	6	4	0	0	0	12	1	2	7.3	21.8
Escalona, Yhoan	R-R	6-2	185	11-04-05	.232	.346	.348	27	81	69	13	16	5	0	1	6	11	1	0	0	16	0	1	13.6	19.8
Escobar, Aroon	R-R	5-11	180	1-01-05	.209	.343	.300	33	134	110	22	23	7	0	1	24	20	3	0	1	13	13	2	14.9	9.7
Ferrebus, Alirio	R-R	6-2	174	9-12-05	.339	.453	.435	21	75	62	11	21	3	0	1	9	7	6	0	0	15	3	1	9.3	20.0
Gutierrez, Dariam	R-R	6-1	175	1-26-02	.323	.430	.438	37	116	96	28	31	11	0	0	21	13	5	2	0	22	6	0	11.2	19.0
Hernandez, Andres	R-R	6-2	180	3-10-05	.165	.289	.196	36	114	97	7	16	3	0	0	10	14	3	0	0	27	6	4	12.3	23.7
Hernandez, Fernando	R-R	5-11	165	3-30-03	.295	.471	.372	37	104	78	19	23	4	1	0	17	21	5	0	0	17	3	4	20.2	16.3
Jimenez, Manolfi	L-L	6-0	190	11-14-04	.240	.312	.340	45	170	150	20	36	10	1	1	20	15	2	0	3	25	9	6	8.8	14.7
Julio, Jorge	R-R	6-1	182	8-04-06	.171	.383	.257	16	48	35	6	6	3	0	0	3	11	1	1	0	14	2	2	22.9	29.2
Leanez, Jose	R-R	6-0	145	1-13-03	.234	.324	.250	28	74	64	12	15	1	0	0	5	3	6	0	1	15	8	2	4.1	20.3

Manrique, Renair	B-R	6-0	172	2-08-06	.246	.411	.347	40	151	118	21	29	9	0	1	13	25	8	0	0	36	3	2	16.6	23.8
Marchan, Jose	R-R	6-1	187	12-20-05	.266	.366	.329	28	95	79	15	21	5	0	0	7	10	3	1	1	24	8	2	10.5	25.3
Martinez, Jarol	R-R	6-2	150	7-19-03	.272	.375	.348	37	113	92	21	25	5	1	0	16	16	1	1	3	18	5	1	14.2	15.9
Mata, Angel	R-R	6-1	175	1-04-05	.277	.381	.362	44	169	141	20	39	10	1	0	24	22	3	0	2	23	3	4	13.0	13.6
Mendez, Romel	L-L	6-0	160	1-10-05	.214	.362	.333	34	105	84	18	18	5	1	1	9	18	2	0	1	15	5	2	17.1	14.3
Muller, Arquedion	R-R	5-10	170	6-19-04	.154	.371	.231	21	35	26	7	4	2	0	0	4	8	1	0	0	16	8	0	22.9	45.7
Pelegrin, Luis	R-R	5-11	160	2-27-03	.219	.333	.250	30	76	64	8	14	2	0	0	5	6	5	1	0	9	0	2	7.9	11.8
Pena, Jerffson	L-R	6-2	185	12-16-03	.268	.353	.390	46	188	164	27	44	8	3	2	25	15	7	1	1	48	24	3	8.0	25.5
Polanco, Yonkelvin	L-R	5-11	175	7-13-06	.231	.231	.462	5	13	13	2	3	0	0	1	4	0	0	0	0	3	0	1	0.0	23.1
Ramirez, Isaac	B-R	5-10	170	10-07-05	.150	.209	.200	14	43	40	3	6	0	1	0	5	3	0	0	0	20	4	1	7.0	46.5
Ramos, Yoangel	R-R	6-2	165	1-21-04	.247	.382	.288	28	89	73	10	18	3	0	0	8	14	2	0	0	17	4	2	15.7	19.1
Rodriguez, Esterling	L-R	5-11	140	9-08-05	.235	.320	.329	29	97	85	13	20	6	1	0	4	10	1	0	1	16	5	2	10.3	16.5
Rosario, Guillermo	R-R	6-2	190	4-22-05	.264	.402	.319	32	112	91	19	24	5	0	0	11	18	3	0	0	18	2	1	16.1	16.1
Rosario, Neify	R-R	6-0	185	9-25-04	.156	.270	.281	12	37	32	6	5	1	0	1	4	5	0	0	0	13	1	1	13.5	35.1
Rosario, Yemil	R-R	6-2	150	4-12-04	.274	.409	.377	48	186	146	31	40	7	1	2	25	32	4	0	4	47	12	5	17.2	25.3
Silva, Brahian	R-R	5-11	170	12-30-02	.288	.397	.348	31	78	66	5	19	4	0	0	6	6	6	0	0	17	2	2	7.7	21.8
Tabares, Andres	L-L	6-1	165	8-25-05	.174	.357	.186	37	112	86	17	15	1	0	0	10	25	0	0	1	21	7	1	22.3	18.8
Tait, Eduardo	L-R	6-0	175	8-27-06	.333	.400	.517	44	165	147	28	49	12	3	3	36	12	5	0	1	31	4	2	7.3	18.8
Villavicencio, Juan	L-R	5-10	155	11-24-04	.207	.324	.343	49	205	169	40	35	6	4	3	28	26	5	1	4	41	9	5	12.7	20.0

Pitching	B-T	Ht.	Wt.	DOB	W	L	ERA	G	GS	SV	IP	Hits	Runs	ER	HR	BB	SO	AVG	OBP	SLG	SO%	BB%	BF
Alcala, Saul	R-R	6-1	158	11-07-00	0	0	0.00	7	0	2	15	11	2	0	0	3	13	.200	.267	.236	21.7	5.0	60
Amarante, Juan	L-L	5-10	177	4-14-04	0	2	2.86	10	9	1	28	22	11	9	0	18	37	.224	.342	.296	31.6	15.4	117
Andrade, Kleyderve	L-L	5-11	180	12-19-02	5	1	1.76	15	0	3	31	23	7	6	0	12	44	.209	.285	.264	35.8	9.8	123
Avila, Luis	R-R	6-1	170	5-26-03	4	0	2.35	14	0	1	23	21	8	6	0	8	23	.239	.330	.295	23.0	8.0	100
Bata, Eliecer	R-R	6-3	190	3-20-04	1	1	6.55	9	5	0	22	31	19	16	0	8	22	.326	.385	.411	21.2	7.7	104
Blanco, Wilmer	R-R	6-3	170	2-21-04	2	2	2.80	11	10	0	45	31	18	14	1	19	47	.205	.315	.318	26.0	10.5	181
Charles, Jendry	R-R	6-2	190	4-25-02	1	0	5.79	6	0	0	9	7	6	6	1	7	7	.212	.395	.364	16.3	16.3	43
Chirinos, Edwar	L-L	5-10	160	4-20-05	6	2	6.55	16	3	2	34	38	32	25	3	31	37	.286	.428	.421	22.3	18.7	166
De La Cruz, Alexis	R-R	6-6	205	9-20-04	2	2	4.31	10	9	0	31	25	18	15	2	17	43	.223	.351	.339	32.1	12.7	134
De Los Santos, Alexander	R-R	6-1	160	8-23-06	1	0	13.50	3	0	0	3	5	4	4	1	6	3	.417	.611	.667	16.7	33.3	18
Diaz, Cristian	R-R	6-2	180	6-12-05	3	2	2.67	15	0	0	27	19	14	8	0	9	25	.204	.280	.258	23.1	8.3	108
Fernandez, Eduardo	L-L	6-0	170	9-04-04	2	0	4.15	14	0	0	22	15	11	10	2	16	25	.188	.337	.263	25.5	16.3	98
Ferreras, Angel	R-R	6-4	190	3-26-03	1	2	6.75	11	0	1	12	13	11	9	1	9	11	.265	.379	.388	19.0	15.5	58
Fuenmayor, Javier	R-R	6-2	170	1-20-03	1	0	0.90	6	0	4	10	5	2	1	0	3	10	.161	.278	.194	26.3	7.9	38
Garcia, Josbel	R-R	6-0	165	3-30-04	3	2	1.69	14	1	1	32	32	12	6	1	6	15	.262	.301	.344	11.3	4.5	133
Gatier, Claudio	L-L	6-3	180	5-25-02	2	1	3.94	15	2	1	30	22	15	13	0	21	26	.212	.376	.240	19.5	15.8	133
German, Jeffrey	R-R	6-3	175	10-26-04	0	2	4.19	9	8	0	39	29	20	18	0	12	27	.210	.304	.254	17.0	7.5	159
Gonzalez, Luis	R-R	6-0	170	7-15-05	4	1	1.99	11	9	1	50	44	12	11	0	9	38	.242	.287	.330	19.4	4.6	196
Heredia, Joel	R-R	6-6	190	1-15-04	1	4	4.89	11	10	0	35	35	28	19	2	23	33	.269	.422	.362	19.9	13.9	166
Hernandez, Maxwel	R-R	6-2	190	5-14-03	3	0	2.76	10	10	0	46	34	17	14	2	23	40	.201	.301	.290	20.7	11.9	193
Jean, Enderson	R-R	6-3	175	9-21-04	1	1	12.27	6	0	0	7	5	10	10	0	12	5	.217	.475	.348	12.5	30.0	40
Lebron, Gregory	L-L	6-4	220	7-09-04	0	0	0.00	2	0	0	2	3	3	0	0	2	3	.273	.429	.455	21.4	14.3	14
Liranzo, Angel	L-L	6-1	172	8-05-06	5	0	0.89	10	4	0	30	16	3	3	0	8	30	.165	.224	.206	28.0	7.5	107
Martinez, Luis	L-L	6-0	213	12-05-05	1	1	3.97	7	0	0	11	15	9	5	2	8	14	.300	.390	.520	23.7	13.6	59
Mejia, Naoel	R-R	6-5	220	7-05-02	1	3	5.49	11	0	1	20	15	18	12	2	18	23	.217	.387	.377	24.7	19.4	93
Melendez, Juan	R-R	6-3	170	7-19-04	2	1	7.78	13	0	1	20	25	19	17	1	14	20	.301	.410	.494	20.0	14.0	100
Millan, Carlos	R-R	6-2	160	7-19-03	6	0	1.67	14	0	3	27	19	6	5	1	9	32	.196	.278	.258	29.6	8.3	108
Mota, Rainy	R-R	6-1	170	1-26-06	0	0	0.00	2	0	0	1	0	0	0	0	1	1	.000	.167	.000	16.7	16.7	6
Peralta, Adilson	R-R	6-4	175	6-17-03	2	1	3.25	11	10	0	44	46	21	16	1	20	44	.271	.354	.353	22.4	10.2	196
Peralta, Pedro	R-R	5-11	185	7-27-06	0	3	7.20	9	1	0	15	14	15	12	2	13	16	.250	.408	.429	22.5	18.3	71
Pulido, Danyony	R-R	6-1	165	10-19-02	2	1	3.21	11	10	0	42	26	16	15	0	18	51	.179	.300	.248	30.0	10.6	170
Reyes, Pedro	R-R	6-3	175	11-26-02	0	0	1.50	8	6	0	18	8	3	3	1	5	18	.138	.265	.241	26.5	7.4	68
Reyes, Ramon	R-R	6-3	185	2-15-02	1	0	7.31	12	0	0	16	19	15	13	0	15	9	.306	.463	.484	11.0	18.3	82
Robles, Eduardo	R-R	5-9	176	6-27-05	1	1	2.84	10	0	0	19	13	9	6	0	10	12	.188	.296	.203	14.8	12.3	81
Rosario, Raymon	L-L	6-2	198	6-06-05	0	1	7.50	5	1	0	6	5	5	5	0	12	5	.250	.531	.400	15.6	37.5	32
Sosa, John	L-L	6-3	200	2-14-03	2	2	1.91	15	0	1	28	13	8	6	1	26	43	.137	.336	.200	34.1	20.6	126
Ventura, Ezequiel	R-R	6-1	151	6-20-02	3	0	2.19	7	0	2	12	13	3	3	1	4	9	.271	.340	.375	17.0	7.5	53

Fielding

C: Mata 28, Andrade 25, Tait 24, Escalona 18, Silva 17, Rosario 16, Colmenares 6, Ferrebus 5. **1B:** Martinez 26, Hernandez 20, Ramos 16, Silva 10, Mata 10, Barria 10, Calderon 7, Muller 7, Leanez 6, Manrique 6, Pelegrin 5, Ferrebus 3, Andrade 3, Tait 2, Rosario 2, Gutierrez 1, Escalona 1. **2B:** Escobar 28, Manrique 24, Carela 13, Beltran 12, Colmenares 11, Hernandez 10, Barria 9, Rosario 8, Villavicencio 8, Muller 3, Caba 1. **3B:** Hernandez 36, Pelegrin 22, Rosario 19, Barria 14, Manrique 12, Carela 11, Martinez 10, Villavicencio 8, Ramos 4, Escobar 4, Colmenares 2. **SS:** Villavicencio 35, Caba 30, Beltran 21, Rosario 21, Hernandez 12, Pelegrin 3, Carela 3, Ramos 2, Barria 1. **OF:** Pena 44, Jimenez 42, Cardoza 38, Tabares 34, Calderon 32, Gutierrez 31, Mendez 31, Rodriguez 27, Marchan 24, Leanez 22, Julio 15, Ramirez 15, Carela 12, Rosario 8, Polanco 4, Colmenares 1, Barria 1.

Pittsburgh Pirates

SEASON SYNOPSIS: After consecutive 100-loss seasons, the Pirates got off to a blistering start before falling back to fourth place, especially after trading away several veterans. Their 76 victories still represented a 14-game improvement over 2022.

HIGH POINTS: The Buccos swept an April 29 doubleheader at Washington, pushing them to a 20-8 record, with a 16-1 victory in the nightcap serving as an exclamation point. Center fielder Jack Suwinski, who had a streaky season but led the club with 26 home runs, hit one of them in the 16-1 win, a grand slam. He was one of just two Pirates to top 20 home runs.

LOW POINT: The Pirates had a one-game division lead on June 11, but after an off day, they lost 10 straight and 12 of 13, with four of the 12 losses by shutout. Pittsburgh finished 13th in the NL in runs, missing the big bat of shortstop Oneil Cruz, who missed most of the season after suffering a broken left ankle in early April.

NOTABLE ROOKIES: 2B/OF Ji-Hwan Bae carved out a super utility/10th starter role early and showed blazing speed with a team-high 24 stolen bases but a light bat. After falling out of contention, the Pirates turned the team over to rookies, such as catcher Endy Rodriguez, 2021 No. 1 overall pick Henry Davis (now moved to the outfield from catcher), middle infielders Liover Peguero and Nick Gonzales and third baseman Jared Triolo, who had the most offensive success of that group. Rule 5 pick Jose Hernandez stuck as a lefty reliever, while righty Carmen Mlodzinski became the top setup man for closer David Bednar, who finished second in the majors with 39 saves.

KEY TRANSACTIONS: Pittsburgh signed three free agents in the offseason and traded them at the deadline: lefthander Rich Hill (to the Padres) and first basemen Carlos Santana (Brewers) and Ji Man Choi (Padres). The Pirates added a piece through trade as well, acquiring lefthander Bailey Falter in exchange for infielder Rodolfo Castro.

DOWN ON THE FARM: The Pirates' .529 organizational winning percentage was sixth-best in the minors and the organization had solid performances up and down the system. Righthander Paul Skenes' brief MiLB debut after the draft gave a taste of what could be to come in 2023, but the Pirates also got solid work from pitchers like Bubba Chandler and Jared Jones, who both made strides during the season.

OPENING DAY PAYROLL: $73,277,500 (27th).

PLAYERS OF THE YEAR

MAJOR LEAGUE

Ke'Bryan Hayes
3B

.271/.309/.453
31 2B, 15 HR
.984 Field. Pct.

MINOR LEAGUE

Termarr Johnson
2B

(LoA/HiA)
.244/.422/.438
101 BB, 83 R

ORGANIZATION LEADERS

Batting		*Minimum 250 AB
MAJORS		
* AVG	Ke'Bryan Hayes	.271
* OPS	Jack Suwinski	.793
HR	Jack Suwinski	26
RBI	Bryan Reynolds	84
MINORS		
* AVG	Miguel Andujar, Indianapolis	.338
* OBP	Henry Davis, Altoona/Indian.	.454
* SLG	Henry Davis, Altoona/Indian.	.561
* OPS	Henry Davis, Altoona/Indian.	1.015
R	Tres Gonzalez, Bradenton/Greensb.	88
H	Miguel Andujar, Indianapolis	140
TB	Miguel Andujar, Indianapolis	222
2B	Miguel Andujar, Indianapolis	30
3B	Tsung-Che Cheng, Greensb./Altoona	10
HR	Jase Bowen, Greesnb./Altoona	23
RBI	Miguel Andujar, Indianapolis	95
BB	Jesus Castillo, Bradenton	102
SO	Rodolfo Nolasco, Bradenton	152
SB	Jesus Castillo, Bradenton	39

Pitching		#Minimum 75 IP
MAJORS		
W	Mitch Keller	13
# ERA	Mitch Keller	4.21
SO	Mitch Keller	210
SV	David Bednar	39
MINORS		
W	Aaron Shortridge, Altoona/Indian.	12
L	Jared Jones, Altoona/Indian.	9
# ERA	Wilber Dotel, Bradenton	3.09
G	John O'Reilly, Indianapo.	50
GS	Aaron Shortridge, Altoona/Indian.	28
SV	Cy Nielson, Greensboro	10
IP	Aaron Shortridge, Altoona/Indian.	143
BB	Aaron Shortridge, Altoona/Indian.	53
SO	Jared Jones, Altoona/Indian.	146
SO	Thomas Harrington, Bradenton/Greensb.	146
# AVG	J.P. Massey, Bradenton/Greensb.	.207

2023 PERFORMANCE

General Manager: Ben Cherington. **Farm Director:** John Baker. **Scouting Director:** Joe DelliCarri.

Class	Team	League	W	L	PCT	Finish	Manager
Majors	Pittsburgh Pirates	National	76	86	.469	11 (15)	Derek Shelton
Triple-A	Indianapolis Indians	International	70	78	.473	13 (20)	Miguel Perez
Double-A	Altoona Curve	Eastern	67	68	.496	6 (12)	Callix Crabbe
High-A	Greensboro Grasshoppers	South Atlantic	68	61	.527	5 (12)	Robby Hammock
Low-A	Bradenton Marauders	Florida State	76	54	.585	2 (10)	Jonathan Johnston
Rookie	FCL Pirates	Florida Complex	32	23	.582	3 (15)	Jim Horner
Rookie	DSL Pirates Black	Dominican Sum.	17	34	.333	44 (50)	Ethan Goforth
Overall 2023 Minor League Record			371	330	.529	6th (30)	

ORGANIZATION STATISTICS

PITTSBURGH PIRATES

NATIONAL LEAGUE

Batting	B-T	Ht.	Wt.	DOB	AVG	OBP	SLG	G	PA	AB	R	H	2B	3B	HR	RBI	BB	HBP	SH	SF	SO	SB	CS	BB%	SO%
Andujar, Miguel	R-R	6-0	211	3-02-95	.250	.300	.476	30	90	84	9	21	7	0	4	18	6	0	0	0	13	2	0	6.7	14.4
Bae, Ji Hwan	L-R	6-1	185	7-26-99	.231	.296	.311	111	371	334	54	77	17	2	2	32	30	2	3	2	92	24	9	8.1	24.8
Capra, Vinny	R-R	5-8	180	7-07-96	.167	.250	.222	9	21	18	3	3	1	0	0	1	2	0	1	0	5	0	0	9.5	23.8
Castro, Rodolfo	B-R	6-0	205	5-21-99	.228	.317	.355	78	224	197	19	45	7	0	6	22	21	5	0	1	62	1	4	9.4	27.7
2-team (10 Philadelphia)					.211	.298	.322	92	256	227	21	48	7	0	6	24	23	5	0	1	74	1	4	9.0	28.9
Choi, Ji Man	L-R	6-1	260	5-19-91	.205	.224	.507	23	76	73	9	15	4	0	6	11	2	0	0	1	27	0	0	2.6	35.5
2-team (16 San Diego)					.163	.243	.385	39	117	104	12	17	5	0	6	13	10	1	0	2	35	0	0	8.5	29.9
Cruz, Oneil	L-R	6-7	220	10-04-98	.250	.375	.375	9	40	32	7	8	1	0	1	4	7	0	0	1	8	3	0	17.5	20.0
Davis, Henry	R-R	6-0	220	9-21-99	.213	.302	.351	62	255	225	27	48	10	0	7	24	25	4	0	1	69	3	5	9.8	27.1
Delay, Jason	R-R	5-11	200	3-07-95	.251	.319	.347	70	187	167	20	42	11	1	1	18	14	3	2	1	44	0	0	7.5	23.5
Gonzales, Nick	R-R	5-9	195	5-27-99	.209	.268	.348	35	128	115	12	24	8	1	2	13	6	4	1	2	36	0	1	4.7	28.1
Hayes, Ke'Bryan	R-R	5-10	205	1-28-97	.271	.309	.453	124	525	494	65	134	31	7	15	61	28	0	0	3	104	10	6	5.3	19.8
Hedges, Austin	R-R	6-1	223	8-18-92	.180	.237	.230	65	187	161	13	29	5	0	1	14	11	2	9	3	39	1	0	5.9	20.9
Heineman, Tyler	B-R	5-10	190	6-19-91	.111	.200	.111	3	10	9	1	1	0	0	0	0	1	0	0	0	1	1	0	10.0	10.0
Joe, Connor	R-R	6-0	205	8-16-92	.247	.339	.421	133	472	413	63	102	31	4	11	42	50	8	0	1	110	3	5	10.6	23.3
Maggi, Drew	R-R	6-0	192	5-16-89	.333	.333	.500	3	6	6	1	2	1	0	0	1	0	0	0	0	1	0	0	0.0	16.7
Marcano, Tucupita	L-R	6-0	180	9-16-99	.233	.276	.356	75	220	202	16	47	12	2	3	18	10	3	3	2	35	5	2	4.5	15.9
Mathias, Mark	R-R	6-0	200	8-02-94	.231	.355	.269	22	62	52	5	12	2	0	0	4	10	0	0	0	11	3	0	16.1	17.7
2-team (5 San Francisco)					.275	.379	.359	47	154	131	18	36	5	0	2	14	22	0	0	1	31	4	2	14.3	20.1
McCutchen, Andrew	R-R	5-11	195	10-10-86	.256	.378	.397	112	473	390	55	100	19	0	12	43	75	4	0	4	100	11	3	15.9	21.1
Mitchell, Cal	L-L	6-0	205	3-08-99	.000	.200	.000	2	5	4	0	0	0	0	0	0	1	0	0	0	1	0	0	20.0	20.0
Owings, Chris	R-R	5-10	185	8-12-91	.160	.160	.160	11	25	25	0	4	0	0	0	0	0	0	0	0	12	0	0	0.0	48.0
Palacios, Josh	L-R	6-1	200	7-30-95	.239	.279	.413	91	264	247	26	59	9	2	10	40	12	2	2	1	56	5	0	4.5	21.2
Peguero, Liover	R-R	6-0	210	12-31-00	.237	.280	.374	59	213	198	21	47	4	1	7	26	11	1	2	1	67	6	2	5.2	31.5
Reynolds, Bryan	B-R	6-3	205	1-27-95	.263	.330	.460	145	640	574	85	151	31	5	24	84	53	7	0	6	138	12	1	8.3	21.6
Rivas, Alfonso	L-L	5-10	190	9-13-96	.234	.305	.436	40	106	94	6	22	8	1	3	14	7	3	1	1	29	1	0	6.6	27.4
2-team (8 San Diego)					.229	.303	.422	48	123	109	8	25	10	1	3	15	9	3	1	1	36	1	0	7.3	29.3
Rodriguez, Endy	B-R	5-9	170	5-26-00	.220	.284	.328	57	204	186	27	41	7	2	3	13	17	0	0	1	49	0	0	8.3	24.0
Santana, Carlos	B-R	5-11	215	4-08-86	.235	.321	.412	94	393	345	45	81	25	0	12	53	45	0	0	3	69	6	0	11.5	17.6
2-team (52 Milwaukee)					.240	.320	.429	146	619	550	78	132	33	1	23	86	65	0	0	4	104	6	0	10.5	16.8
Smith-Njigba, Canaan	L-R	6-0	230	4-30-99	.125	.216	.219	15	37	32	3	4	1	1	0	5	4	0	0	1	16	1	0	10.8	43.2
Suwinski, Jack	L-L	6-2	215	7-29-98	.224	.339	.454	144	534	447	63	100	21	2	26	74	75	6	0	6	172	13	2	14.0	32.2
Triolo, Jared	R-R	6-3	212	2-08-98	.298	.388	.398	54	209	181	30	54	9	0	3	21	24	3	0	1	63	6	1	11.5	30.1
Williams, Alika	R-R	6-1	180	3-12-99	.198	.270	.248	46	112	101	7	20	5	0	0	6	9	1	1	0	35	0	0	8.0	31.3

Pitching	B-T	Ht.	Wt.	DOB	W	L	ERA	G	GS	SV	IP	Hits	Runs	ER	HR	BB	SO	AVG	OBP	SLG	SO%	BB%	BF
Bednar, David	L-R	6-1	250	10-10-94	3	3	2.00	66	0	39	67	53	22	15	3	21	80	.215	.281	.316	28.9	7.6	277
Bido, Osvaldo	R-R	6-3	175	10-18-95	2	5	5.86	16	9	0	51	55	35	33	4	21	48	.270	.356	.377	20.3	8.9	236
Bolton, Cody	R-R	6-3	230	6-19-98	1	0	6.33	16	0	0	21	30	15	15	3	15	22	.333	.434	.522	20.6	14.0	107
Borucki, Ryan	L-L	6-4	210	3-31-94	4	0	2.45	38	2	0	40	26	11	11	4	4	33	.183	.227	.317	21.7	2.6	152
Contreras, Roansy	R-R	6-0	175	11-07-99	3	7	6.59	19	11	1	68	75	50	50	11	32	55	.282	.360	.466	18.2	10.6	302
Crowe, Wil	R-R	6-2	245	9-09-94	0	1	4.66	5	0	1	10	9	6	5	1	9	9	.243	.404	.405	19.1	19.1	47
De Jong, Chase	L-R	6-4	230	12-29-93	0	0	13.50	6	0	0	11	18	17	17	6	6	7	.367	.433	.837	11.7	10.0	60
De Los Santos, Yerry	R-R	6-2	215	12-12-97	1	1	3.33	22	0	0	24	17	10	9	1	13	18	.193	.298	.295	17.3	12.5	104
Falter, Bailey	R-L	6-4	175	4-24-97	2	2	5.58	10	7	0	40	44	25	25	10	12	32	.275	.326	.513	18.6	7.0	172
Hatch, Thomas	R-R	6-1	195	9-29-94	1	1	4.03	12	2	0	22	23	13	10	2	7	16	.271	.333	.400	17.0	7.4	94
Hernandez, Jose	L-L	5-10	205	12-31-97	1	3	4.97	50	0	0	51	47	30	28	9	22	62	.239	.317	.462	27.8	9.9	223
Hill, Rich	L-L	6-5	221	3-11-80	7	10	4.76	22	22	0	119	129	70	63	15	47	104	.272	.342	.458	19.6	8.9	530
Holderman, Colin	R-R	6-7	240	10-08-95	0	3	3.86	58	0	2	56	55	25	24	4	20	58	.256	.322	.363	24.2	8.3	240
Jackson, Andre	R-R	6-3	210	5-01-96	1	3	4.33	12	7	0	44	30	21	21	6	19	41	.194	.287	.361	23.0	10.7	178
Keller, Mitch	R-R	6-2	220	4-04-96	13	9	4.21	32	32	0	194	187	97	91	25	55	210	.249	.308	.404	25.5	6.7	825
Mlodzinski, Carmen	R-R	6-2	225	2-19-99	3	3	2.25	35	1	1	36	28	14	9	3	18	34	.214	.309	.313	22.4	11.8	152
Moreta, Dauri	R-R	6-2	185	4-15-96	5	2	3.72	55	0	1	58	39	26	24	4	24	76	.187	.276	.330	31.8	10.0	239

Nicolas, Kyle	R-R	6-4	223	2-22-99	0	0	11.81	4	0	0	5	7	7	7	1	4	7	.333	.462	.571	26.9	15.4	26
Ortiz, Luis	R-R	6-2	240	1-27-99	5	5	4.78	18	15	0	87	99	50	46	13	48	59	.288	.373	.448	14.8	12.0	400
Oviedo, Johan	R-R	6-5	245	3-02-98	9	14	4.31	32	32	0	178	161	91	85	19	83	158	.237	.330	.397	20.2	10.6	781
Owings, Chris	R-R	5-10	185	8-12-91	0	0	0.00	1	0	0	1	2	0	0	0	0	0	.333	.333	.333	0.0	0.0	6
Perdomo, Angel	L-L	6-8	265	5-07-94	3	2	3.72	30	0	0	29	21	14	12	3	11	44	.208	.304	.366	37.6	9.4	117
Priester, Quinn	R-R	6-3	210	9-15-00	3	3	7.74	10	8	0	50	58	43	43	12	27	36	.290	.378	.555	15.4	11.5	234
Ramirez, Yohan	R-R	6-4	212	5-06-95	1	0	3.67	26	0	0	34	34	17	14	3	14	31	.260	.374	.344	20.0	9.0	155
Selby, Colin	R-R	6-2	220	10-24-97	2	2	9.00	21	5	0	24	29	24	24	4	15	30	.296	.389	.439	26.3	13.2	114
Stephenson, Robert	R-R	6-3	205	2-24-93	0	3	5.14	18	0	0	14	12	9	8	3	8	17	.231	.328	.442	27.9	13.1	61
Stratton, Hunter	R-R	6-4	225	11-17-96	0	0	2.25	8	0	0	12	9	3	3	2	3	10	.209	.277	.465	21.3	6.4	47
Underwood, Duane	R-R	6-2	225	7-20-94	1	0	5.18	20	0	2	24	24	14	14	3	11	14	.273	.350	.455	14.0	11.0	100
Velasquez, Vince	R-R	6-3	212	6-07-92	4	4	3.86	8	8	0	37	35	16	16	4	14	37	.240	.311	.384	22.8	8.6	162
Zastryzny, Rob	R-L	6-3	205	3-26-92	1	0	4.79	21	1	0	21	24	15	11	1	13	15	.293	.389	.402	15.5	13.4	97

Fielding

Catcher	PCT	G	PO	A	E	DP	PB
Davis	1.000	2	3	0	0	0	0
Delay	.989	68	447	13	5	1	0
Hedges	.987	65	522	8	7	4	1
Heineman	1.000	3	17	0	0	0	0
Rodriguez	.998	52	396	25	1	2	5

First Base	PCT	G	PO	A	E	DP
Choi	1.000	7	50	3	0	5
Joe	.997	53	297	31	1	37
Rivas	.996	39	215	25	1	24
Rodriguez	1.000	2	3	0	0	0
Santana	.994	85	595	70	4	55
Triolo	1.000	7	53	5	0	4

Second Base	PCT	G	PO	A	E	DP
Bae	.964	64	70	116	7	21
Capra	.938	3	7	8	1	1
Castro	.970	41	36	60	3	13
Gonzales	.983	29	53	63	2	18
Marcano	1.000	18	10	18	0	2
Mathias	.940	15	22	25	3	6
Peguero	1.000	33	53	59	0	20
Triolo	1.000	13	24	29	0	10

Third Base	PCT	G	PO	A	E	DP
Capra	1.000	4	1	5	0	1
Castro	.957	9	5	17	1	2
Hayes	.984	122	93	266	6	33
Maggi	1.000	2	0	1	0	0
Marcano	.000	1	0	0	0	0
Triolo	.973	35	30	79	3	6

Shortstop	PCT	G	PO	A	E	DP
Bae	.857	3	2	4	1	0
Castro	.928	31	39	51	7	13
Cruz	.968	9	11	19	1	6
Gonzales	.944	9	4	13	1	1
Marcano	.981	58	60	96	3	18
Owings	1.000	10	11	9	0	5
Peguero	.960	39	39	80	5	15
Williams	.963	45	31	73	4	18

Outfield	PCT	G	PO	A	E	DP
Andujar	1.000	19	34	1	0	0
Bae	.979	62	95	0	2	0
Davis	.937	49	56	3	4	1
Joe	.993	89	124	3	1	0
Mathias	1.000	2	2	0	0	0
McCutchen	1.000	8	19	0	0	0
Mitchell	.000	1	0	0	0	0
Owings	.000	1	0	0	0	0
Palacios	.980	86	112	5	3	2
Reynolds	.968	137	220	1	2	0
Rivas	.000	1	0	0	0	0
Smith-Njigba	1.000	12	18	0	0	0
Suwinski	.999	164	297	2	1	0

INDIANAPOLIS INDIANS — *TRIPLE-A*

INTERNATIONAL LEAGUE

Batting	B-T	Ht.	Wt.	DOB	AVG	OBP	SLG	G	PA	AB	R	H	2B	3B	HR	RBI	BB	HBP	SH	SF	SO	SB	CS	BB%	SO%
Acuna, Francisco	R-R	5-7	150	1-12-00	.286	.286	.429	2	7	7	0	2	1	0	0	0	0	0	0	0	0	0	0	0.0	0.0
Andujar, Miguel	R-R	6-0	211	3-02-95	.338	.404	.536	103	465	414	63	140	30	2	16	86	47	1	0	3	55	5	3	10.1	11.8
Bae, Ji Hwan	L-R	6-1	185	7-26-99	.344	.462	.531	9	39	32	9	11	3	0	1	1	7	0	0	0	10	2	0	17.9	25.6
Bissonette, Josh	R-R	5-11	185	11-01-96	.220	.317	.283	51	184	159	17	35	5	1	1	13	23	0	1	1	34	0	2	12.5	18.5
Capra, Vinny	R-R	5-8	180	7-07-96	.329	.411	.439	49	192	164	30	54	10	1	2	30	24	1	0	3	27	5	1	12.5	14.1
2-team (17 Buffalo)					.289	.402	.383	66	262	218	38	65	13	1	2	35	38	3	0	3	40	6	2	14.5	15.3
Castro, Rodolfo	B-R	6-0	205	5-21-99	.192	.246	.346	12	57	52	7	10	2	0	2	10	3	1	0	1	21	0	0	5.3	36.8
Choi, Ji Man	L-R	6-1	260	5-19-91	.348	.448	.826	6	29	23	7	8	0	1	3	9	5	0	0	1	7	0	0	17.2	24.1
Davis, Henry	R-R	6-0	220	9-21-99	.375	.516	.604	14	63	48	7	18	3	1	2	5	13	1	1	0	13	3	1	20.6	20.6
Delay, Jason	R-R	5-11	200	3-07-95	.357	.419	.500	8	31	28	4	10	4	0	0	5	3	0	0	0	6	1	0	9.7	19.4
Dixon, Brenden	R-R	5-11	205	11-20-00	.300	.364	.600	4	11	10	1	3	0	0	1	4	1	0	0	0	5	0	0	9.1	45.5
Gonzales, Nick	R-R	5-9	195	5-27-99	.281	.379	.507	99	443	377	75	106	27	8	14	49	53	9	0	4	118	4	3	12.0	26.6
Gorski, Matt	R-R	6-2	198	12-22-97	.190	.262	.414	15	65	58	9	11	4	0	3	7	6	0	0	1	15	4	0	9.2	23.1
Hayes, Ke'Bryan	R-R	5-10	205	1-28-97	.111	.333	.111	3	12	9	1	1	0	0	0	0	3	0	0	0	2	0	0	25.0	16.7
Heineman, Tyler	B-R	5-10	190	6-19-91	.333	.478	.667	6	23	18	2	6	1	1	1	6	5	0	0	0	3	0	0	21.7	13.0
2-team (36 Buffalo)					.230	.348	.319	42	165	135	23	31	4	1	2	19	25	1	3	1	35	5	0	15.2	21.2
Hernandez, Luis	R-R	5-10	150	9-06-00	.125	.222	.125	4	9	8	0	1	0	0	0	2	1	0	0	0	3	0	0	11.1	33.3
Koch, Grant	R-R	5-10	195	2-05-97	.255	.318	.391	60	211	192	28	49	9	1	5	23	17	1	0	1	56	0	0	8.1	26.5
Leyba, Domingo	B-R	5-8	205	9-11-95	.257	.343	.410	42	167	144	17	37	5	1	5	15	19	1	1	2	32	0	1	11.4	19.2
Marcano, Tucupita	L-R	6-0	180	9-16-99	.422	.458	.689	11	48	45	8	19	7	1	1	10	3	0	0	0	8	3	0	6.3	16.7
Martin, Mason	L-R	6-0	220	6-02-99	.220	.297	.352	28	101	91	12	20	4	1	2	11	10	0	0	0	31	0	1	9.9	30.7
Mathias, Mark	R-R	6-0	200	8-02-94	.273	.393	.384	31	122	99	14	27	5	0	2	12	18	3	0	2	34	3	0	14.8	27.9
Mitchell, Cal	L-L	6-0	205	3-08-99	.261	.333	.414	78	316	280	46	73	16	0	9	55	29	3	1	3	93	6	2	9.2	29.4
Nunez, Dom	L-R	5-8	212	1-17-95	.119	.224	.186	18	69	59	6	7	1	0	1	1	7	1	2	0	18	0	0	10.1	26.1
2-team (45 Iowa)					.187	.322	.311	63	236	193	35	36	9	0	5	22	36	4	3	0	64	4	0	15.3	27.1
Nunez, Malcom	R-R	6-0	205	3-09-01	.237	.314	.357	67	271	241	30	57	8	0	7	34	19	9	0	2	64	0	2	7.0	23.6
Owings, Chris	R-R	5-10	185	8-12-91	.241	.349	.449	86	371	316	50	76	15	3	15	41	51	2	1	1	106	4	5	13.7	28.6
Palacios, Josh	L-R	6-1	200	7-30-95	.410	.489	.795	20	90	78	19	32	4	1	8	27	11	1	0	0	11	4	1	12.2	12.2
Peguero, Liover	R-R	6-0	210	12-31-00	.259	.333	.556	7	30	27	4	7	0	1	2	5	3	0	0	0	3	2	0	10.0	10.0
Perez, Joe	R-R	6-1	198	8-12-99	.257	.316	.514	9	38	35	4	9	0	0	3	7	3	0	0	0	12	0	1	7.9	31.6
Rodriguez, Endy	B-R	5-9	170	5-26-00	.268	.356	.415	67	315	272	54	73	16	3	6	38	36	3	0	4	47	4	0	11.4	14.9
Shackelford, Aaron	L-R	5-9	215	10-16-96	.223	.344	.406	113	425	355	53	79	17	3	14	52	59	8	0	3	123	8	1	13.9	28.9
Shockley, Dylan	R-R	5-9	195	4-10-97	.000	.000	.000	2	6	6	0	0	0	0	0	0	0	0	0	0	3	0	0	0.0	50.0
Smith-Njigba, Canaan	L-R	6-0	230	4-30-99	.280	.366	.473	105	445	389	57	109	28	1	15	74	53	1	0	2	118	21	5	11.9	26.5
Swaggerty, Travis	L-L	5-10	200	8-19-97	.200	.278	.369	17	72	65	13	13	4	2	1	5	5	2	0	0	19	3	1	6.9	26.4
Triolo, Jared	R-R	6-3	212	2-08-98	.286	.412	.432	53	226	185	39	53	15	3	2	25	39	1	0	1	60	10	3	17.3	26.5

Vilade, Ryan	R-R	6-2	226	2-18-99	.270	.370	.382	122	511	440	64	119	23	4	6	56	64	6	0	1	127	7	4	12.5	24.9
Williams, Alika	R-R	6-1	180	3-12-99	.305	.384	.531	36	148	128	25	39	8	0	7	20	15	2	2	1	22	3	1	10.1	14.9
Young, Chavez	B-R	5-10	200	7-08-97	.195	.336	.356	42	147	118	20	23	6	2	3	22	23	3	1	2	31	13	2	15.6	21.1

Pitching	B-T	Ht.	Wt.	DOB	W	L	ERA	G	GS	SV	IP	Hits	Runs	ER	HR	BB	SO	AVG	OBP	SLG	SO%	BB%	BF
Alldred, Cam	L-L	6-3	205	7-25-96	8	8	5.20	31	17	0	106	99	64	61	16	46	98	.249	.332	.440	21.6	10.2	453
Bido, Osvaldo	R-R	6-3	175	10-18-95	3	4	4.16	19	10	3	63	52	31	29	6	29	65	.224	.321	.379	24.3	10.8	268
Bissonette, Josh	R-R	5-11	185	11-01-96	0	0	0.00	2	0	0	2	0	0	0	0	0	0	.000	.000	.000	0.0	0.0	4
Bolton, Cody	R-R	6-3	230	6-19-98	3	4	3.86	34	2	1	47	39	20	20	2	18	47	.231	.314	.343	24.1	9.2	195
Borucki, Ryan	L-L	6-4	210	3-31-94	1	0	0.00	8	0	0	8	3	0	0	0	6	4	.107	.306	.143	11.1	16.7	36
Burrows, Mike	R-R	6-2	195	11-08-99	0	0	2.70	2	2	0	7	4	2	2	2	2	3	.174	.240	.435	12.0	8.0	25
Case, Brad	R-R	6-6	242	9-13-96	0	0	15.75	3	0	0	4	8	7	7	2	2	2	.444	.524	.833	9.5	9.5	21
Chatwood, Tyler	R-R	5-11	200	12-16-89	0	0	0.00	2	0	0	3	1	0	0	0	2	0	.125	.300	.250	0.0	20.0	10
Contreras, Roansy	R-R	6-0	175	11-07-99	0	0	4.96	8	6	0	33	28	18	18	8	11	30	.233	.306	.475	22.4	8.2	134
Crowe, Wil	R-R	6-2	245	9-09-94	1	1	4.33	14	2	0	27	32	15	13	3	13	30	.291	.363	.482	23.8	10.3	126
De Jong, Chase	L-R	6-4	230	12-29-93	2	2	3.73	24	2	0	31	30	17	13	1	23	30	.259	.373	.353	21.1	16.2	142
De Los Santos, Yerry	R-R	6-2	215	12-12-97	1	5	6.12	23	0	2	25	42	20	17	4	14	28	.372	.442	.549	21.7	10.9	129
Dombkowski, Nick	R-L	6-2	210	8-09-98	0	1	18.00	1	0	0	3	10	6	6	0	0	3	.588	.588	1.000	17.6	0.0	17
Emanuel, Kent	L-L	6-4	225	6-04-92	7	5	6.19	20	13	0	84	110	59	58	13	22	76	.316	.362	.511	20.1	5.8	378
Flowers, J.C.	R-R	6-3	195	5-19-98	2	1	9.39	30	3	0	46	66	50	48	9	39	45	.344	.449	.547	19.1	16.5	236
Hatch, Thomas	R-R	6-1	195	9-29-94	0	0	10.80	1	0	0	2	4	2	2	0	1	2	.444	.500	.444	20.0	10.0	10
Hernandez, Jose	L-L	5-10	205	12-31-97	0	0	3.38	5	2	0	5	2	2	2	1	3	6	.111	.238	.333	28.6	14.3	21
Jackson, Andre	R-R	6-3	210	5-01-96	0	0	3.38	5	3	0	11	6	4	4	1	6	13	.167	.286	.333	30.2	14.0	43
Jones, Jared	L-R	6-1	190	8-06-01	4	5	4.72	16	15	0	82	74	44	43	9	34	99	.240	.321	.390	28.3	9.7	350
Junker, Cameron	R-R	6-5	220	9-03-97	0	0	0.00	1	0	0	2	2	0	0	0	2	5	.250	.400	.250	50.0	20.0	10
Kranick, Max	R-R	6-3	220	7-21-97	0	1	2.76	7	7	0	16	7	5	5	1	6	12	.130	.217	.222	20.0	10.0	60
MacGregor, Travis	R-R	6-4	215	10-15-97	2	2	5.40	27	2	3	43	54	26	26	3	18	39	.303	.383	.455	19.3	8.9	202
Minaya, Juan	R-R	6-4	210	9-18-90	1	1	9.00	12	0	2	11	11	11	11	2	10	14	.239	.386	.435	24.6	17.5	57
Mlodzinski, Carmen	R-R	6-2	225	2-19-99	2	2	3.04	20	0	1	27	26	15	9	2	12	32	.245	.319	.415	26.9	10.1	119
Moreta, Dauri	R-R	6-2	185	4-15-96	0	1	9.39	6	1	1	8	6	8	8	1	9	13	.214	.405	.393	34.2	23.7	38
Nicolas, Kyle	R-R	6-4	223	2-22-99	1	2	6.20	23	6	2	45	42	31	31	8	29	64	.243	.365	.445	30.8	13.9	208
O'Reilly, John	R-R	6-5	225	10-04-95	3	8	5.74	50	2	1	69	90	50	44	9	34	55	.314	.399	.498	16.6	10.2	332
Ogle, Braeden	L-L	6-2	215	7-30-97	0	0	9.00	5	2	0	4	3	4	4	0	8	4	.214	.500	.286	16.7	33.3	24
Ortiz, Luis	R-R	6-2	240	1-27-99	4	4	4.61	13	12	0	57	52	31	29	7	27	54	.236	.321	.414	21.7	10.8	249
Perdomo, Angel	L-L	6-8	265	5-07-94	1	1	3.18	20	0	1	23	13	9	8	2	16	35	.167	.330	.308	36.1	16.5	97
Priester, Quinn	R-R	6-3	210	9-15-00	9	4	4.00	22	20	0	108	97	52	48	6	47	116	.240	.325	.368	25.3	10.2	459
Ramirez, Yohan	R-R	6-4	212	5-06-95	1	1	4.43	18	1	0	22	15	14	11	0	12	32	.192	.330	.269	33.0	12.4	97
Selby, Colin	R-R	6-2	220	10-24-97	0	0	3.86	28	0	6	30	19	13	13	0	22	41	.176	.331	.213	30.8	16.5	133
Shortridge, Aaron	R-R	6-3	215	5-29-97	1	0	1.80	1	1	0	5	1	1	1	0	4	3	.067	.250	.067	15.0	20.0	20
Smith, Caleb	R-L	6-0	207	7-28-91	2	4	6.40	10	9	0	45	40	33	32	7	23	38	.233	.323	.401	19.1	11.6	199
Stephenson, Robert	R-R	6-3	205	2-24-93	0	0	8.10	4	0	0	3	5	3	3	1	5	6	.333	.500	.533	30.0	25.0	20
Stratton, Hunter	R-R	6-4	225	11-17-96	4	4	3.99	47	2	6	56	44	27	25	7	31	74	.219	.324	.363	30.6	12.8	242
Sulser, Beau	R-R	6-2	195	5-05-94	3	1	7.36	8	3	0	26	33	22	21	6	8	16	.303	.353	.550	13.4	6.7	119
Toribio, Noe	R-R	6-2	210	8-25-99	1	0	1.35	2	0	0	7	2	1	1	0	4	4	.100	.250	.100	16.7	16.7	24
Underwood, Duane	R-R	6-2	225	7-20-94	0	5	6.30	15	1	0	20	20	17	14	2	7	13	.263	.352	.368	14.6	7.9	89
Velasquez, Vince	R-R	6-3	212	6-07-92	0	0	0.00	1	1	0	5	4	0	0	0	1	2	.222	.263	.333	10.5	5.3	19
Villalobos, Eli	R-R	6-4	195	6-26-97	1	0	4.15	16	0	0	17	14	11	8	3	15	16	.219	.370	.391	19.8	18.5	81
Zamora, Daniel	L-L	6-3	195	4-15-93	2	1	4.97	27	0	0	29	29	21	16	2	24	32	.259	.411	.384	21.9	16.4	146
Zastryzny, Rob	R-L	6-3	205	3-26-92	0	0	4.41	15	1	1	16	16	8	8	1	1	16	.246	.269	.338	23.9	1.5	67

Fielding

Catcher	PCT	G	PO	A	E	DP	PB
Davis	1.000	5	35	1	0	0	0
Delay	1.000	8	85	5	0	0	0
Heineman	1.000	6	75	1	0	0	0
Hernandez	.952	3	19	1	1	0	0
Koch	.998	58	487	17	1	2	2
Nunez	.988	18	163	5	2	2	1
Rodriguez	.994	54	472	15	3	2	4
Shockley	1.000	2	12	1	0	0	0

First Base	PCT	G	PO	A	E	DP
Andujar	.995	34	193	13	1	20
Choi	1.000	4	33	2	0	5
Gorski	1.000	5	36	1	0	5
Martin	.988	13	77	4	1	7
Nunez	.997	38	304	17	1	33
Rodriguez	1.000	8	50	8	0	5
Shackelford	.993	50	372	27	3	36
Triolo	1.000	3	22	3	0	2
Vilade	1.000	5	25	4	0	2

Second Base	PCT	G	PO	A	E	DP
Bae	1.000	5	6	14	0	3
Bissonette	.971	12	17	16	1	7
Capra	1.000	6	8	15	0	2
Castro	1.000	5	10	15	0	4
Dixon	1.000	2	2	7	0	1
Gonzales	.989	59	95	167	3	42
Leyba	.875	8	7	14	3	2
Marcano	1.000	2	0	3	0	0
Mathias	1.000	8	12	10	0	2
Owings	1.000	7	15	15	0	4
Peguero	1.000	3	9	8	0	4
Shackelford	.939	27	28	49	5	14
Triolo	1.000	9	17	17	0	5
Williams	.970	8	12	20	1	7

Third Base	PCT	G	PO	A	E	DP
Acuna	1.000	2	0	2	0	0
Bissonette	1.000	24	13	37	0	2
Capra	.957	16	11	33	2	4
Dixon	1.000	1	0	1	0	0
Gonzales	.889	14	11	21	4	2
Hayes	1.000	2	0	1	0	0
Leyba	.954	30	21	41	3	5
Marcano	1.000	1	1	3	0	0
Mathias	1.000	4	3	5	0	0
Nunez	.971	15	6	27	1	1
Owings	.962	12	6	19	1	5
Shackelford	1.000	3	1	7	0	0
Triolo	.959	29	20	50	3	3
Vilade	.903	16	9	19	3	2

Shortstop	PCT	G	PO	A	E	DP
Bissonette	1.000	13	12	28	0	6
Capra	.950	23	33	63	5	14
Castro	.917	4	8	14	2	4
Gonzales	.963	25	29	50	3	15
Marcano	.941	7	2	14	1	2
Owings	.964	37	37	71	4	17
Peguero	1.000	4	5	13	0	2
Triolo	.960	16	28	44	3	8
Williams	.958	28	27	64	4	18

Outfield	PCT	G	PO	A	E	DP
Andujar	.993	56	87	8	1	0
Bae	1.000	4	10	0	0	0
Bissonette	1.000	4	5	2	0	0
Davis	1.000	9	18	1	0	0
Gorski	1.000	12	24	0	0	0
Marcano	.667	3	2	0	1	0
Mathias	1.000	13	23	1	0	0
Mitchell	.958	82	111	2	5	2

	PCT	G	PO	A	E	DP
Owings	1.000	34	59	1	0	0
Palacios	.990	20	39	2	1	0
Perez	1.000	6	7	0	0	0

	PCT	G	PO	A	E	DP
Smith-Njigba	.974	115	133	3	4	0
Swaggerty	.656	18	33	1	1	0
Vilade	.995	104	173	5	2	0

	PCT	G	PO	A	E	DP
Young	.911	41	80	2	2	0

ALTOONA CURVE — *DOUBLE-A*

EASTERN LEAGUE

Batting	B-T	Ht.	Wt.	DOB	AVG	OBP	SLG	G	PA	AB	R	H	2B	3B	HR	RBI	BB	HBP	SH	SF	SO	SB	CS	BB%	SO%
Alvarez, Andres	R-R	5-8	175	3-29-97	.215	.285	.345	96	380	339	43	73	18	1	8	35	30	5	1	5	98	4	3	7.9	25.8
Bins, Carter	R-R	5-11	215	10-07-98	.222	.297	.367	25	101	90	12	20	4	0	3	16	8	2	0	1	31	1	1	7.9	30.7
Bowen, Jase	R-R	6-0	190	9-02-00	.219	.242	.438	8	33	32	6	7	3	2	0	7	1	0	0	0	7	2	1	3.0	21.2
Cheng, Tsung-Che	L-R	5-7	154	7-26-01	.251	.304	.352	66	281	247	35	62	11	1	4	25	17	4	8	5	53	13	3	6.0	18.9
Choi, Ji Man	L-R	6-1	260	5-19-91	.250	.400	.375	3	10	8	1	2	1	0	0	0	1	1	0	0	1	0	0	10.0	10.0
Davis, Henry	R-R	6-0	220	9-21-99	.284	.433	.547	41	187	148	25	42	7	1	10	27	32	7	0	0	35	7	3	17.1	18.7
Finol, Claudio	R-R	5-11	171	4-13-00	.236	.329	.350	42	147	123	20	29	5	0	3	12	16	2	4	2	37	4	3	10.9	25.2
Fraizer, Matt	L-R	6-3	220	1-12-98	.252	.326	.357	121	486	437	67	110	16	3	8	50	43	5	1	0	104	21	3	8.8	21.4
Glenn, Jackson	R-R	5-10	205	10-24-97	.274	.329	.443	54	239	219	31	60	13	3	6	30	14	4	2	0	46	4	1	5.9	19.2
Gonzalez, Jacob	R-R	6-4	220	6-26-98	.237	.293	.351	86	338	308	30	73	9	1	8	44	16	10	0	4	60	0	1	4.7	17.8
Gorski, Matt	R-R	6-2	198	12-22-97	.238	.296	.437	93	396	357	56	85	16	2	17	54	27	5	1	6	101	19	4	6.8	25.5
Gutierrez, Abrahan	R-R	6-0	214	10-31-99	.226	.333	.348	33	135	115	11	26	5	0	3	13	16	3	0	1	16	1	1	11.9	11.9
Jarvis, Mike	R-R	5-10	180	5-12-98	.234	.273	.266	28	100	94	10	22	0	0	1	5	5	0	0	0	16	11	0	5.0	16.0
Leyba, Domingo	B-R	5-8	205	9-11-95	.343	.412	.490	30	114	102	12	35	6	0	3	20	12	0	0	0	12	1	0	10.5	10.5
Macias, Fabricio	R-R	6-0	188	3-11-98	.245	.291	.347	15	55	49	4	12	2	0	1	6	4	0	0	2	14	4	1	7.3	25.5
Maggi, Drew	R-R	6-0	192	5-16-89	.181	.257	.220	36	141	127	13	23	5	0	0	10	9	4	1	0	27	4	0	6.4	19.1
Marcos, Norkis	R-R	5-11	170	5-26-01	.115	.179	.115	10	28	26	2	3	0	0	0	0	2	0	0	0	18	2	0	7.1	64.3
Martin, Mason	L-R	6-0	220	6-02-99	.212	.374	.460	69	286	226	34	48	8	0	16	43	52	7	0	1	102	7	4	18.2	35.7
Matthiessen, William	R-R	6-6	230	1-09-98	.146	.253	.171	24	95	82	6	12	2	0	0	6	10	2	0	1	42	0	0	10.5	44.2
Palacios, Josh	L-R	6-1	200	7-30-95	.265	.324	.324	8	37	34	6	9	2	0	0	2	2	1	0	0	2	1	0	5.4	5.4
Peguero, Liover	R-R	6-0	210	12-31-00	.260	.333	.453	69	318	285	50	74	20	1	11	34	32	0	0	1	58	19	3	10.1	18.2
Perez, Joe	R-R	6-1	198	8-12-99	.341	.477	.624	25	107	85	18	29	3	0	7	18	20	2	0	0	24	2	1	18.7	22.4
Sanchez, Lolo	R-R	5-11	186	4-23-99	.227	.332	.320	87	332	278	39	63	11	0	5	25	41	4	7	2	48	6	4	12.3	14.5
Scott, Connor	L-L	6-3	208	10-08-99	.196	.263	.315	74	289	260	28	51	14	4	3	37	25	0	0	4	65	10	4	8.7	22.5
Shockley, Dylan	R-R	5-9	195	4-10-97	.167	.292	.167	36	113	96	12	16	0	0	0	10	14	3	0	0	37	0	0	12.4	32.7
Wilson, Eli	R-R	6-0	190	7-06-98	.262	.297	.443	18	65	61	8	16	2	0	3	7	3	0	1	0	12	1	1	4.6	18.5
Young, Chavez	B-R	5-10	200	7-08-97	.207	.319	.277	60	218	184	15	38	7	0	2	12	25	6	2	1	46	19	7	11.5	21.1

Pitching	B-T	Ht.	Wt.	DOB	W	L	ERA	G	GS	SV	IP	Hits	Runs	ER	HR	BB	SO	AVG	OBP	SLG	SO%	BB%	BF
Ashcraft, Braxton	L-R	6-5	195	10-05-99	0	1	1.35	8	8	0	20	14	6	3	0	5	23	.194	.253	.292	29.1	6.3	79
Bellomy, Bear	R-R	6-3	220	11-29-96	3	0	6.48	12	0	0	17	16	13	12	3	9	16	.246	.355	.492	21.1	11.8	76
Carey, Jack	R-R	6-0	205	9-20-99	0	0	13.50	2	0	0	2	5	3	3	1	1	4	.455	.500	.727	33.3	8.3	12
Case, Brad	R-R	6-6	242	9-13-96	1	2	5.06	14	4	0	27	32	20	15	3	15	25	.294	.383	.413	19.5	11.7	128
Chandler, Bubba	B-R	6-2	200	9-14-02	1	0	0.00	1	1	0	5	1	0	0	0	0	8	.063	.063	.063	50.0	0.0	16
Cruz, Omar	L-L	6-0	210	1-26-99	1	4	3.94	27	1	0	48	39	21	21	2	30	44	.220	.352	.316	20.4	13.9	216
Dombkowski, Nick	R-L	6-2	210	8-09-98	5	6	3.71	33	8	0	85	76	37	35	13	26	58	.233	.292	.399	16.3	7.3	356
Eckelman, Matt	R-R	6-3	285	10-06-93	0	2	8.33	14	2	0	27	30	28	25	3	27	11	.288	.437	.442	8.1	20.0	135
Ford, Grant	R-R	6-1	175	3-11-98	2	1	4.37	19	0	0	23	20	12	11	4	16	19	.244	.394	.415	18.1	15.2	105
Franzua, Geronimo	L-L	6-1	170	9-25-93	2	2	7.08	17	0	1	20	24	17	16	3	7	23	.289	.355	.446	24.2	7.4	95
Garcia, Oliver	R-R	6-3	214	1-08-98	7	3	4.27	41	0	7	46	43	29	22	3	33	50	.247	.386	.374	22.8	15.1	219
Jones, Jared	L-R	6-1	190	8-06-01	1	4	2.23	10	10	0	44	32	11	11	3	16	47	.201	.291	.302	26.3	8.9	179
Junker, Cameron	R-R	6-5	220	9-03-97	4	5	3.25	45	1	2	55	45	25	20	3	29	43	.222	.335	.296	17.8	12.0	242
Linarez, Valentin	R-R	6-5	226	2-14-00	0	0	33.75	2	0	0	1	4	5	5	1	2	2	.500	.636	.875	18.2	18.2	11
MacGregor, Travis	R-R	6-4	215	10-15-97	4	0	1.83	16	1	0	34	29	8	7	3	13	45	.228	.300	.323	32.1	9.3	140
Meis, Justin	R-R	6-2	160	11-23-99	4	3	4.55	29	10	1	83	74	46	42	13	47	77	.239	.343	.419	20.9	12.7	369
Miliano, Michell	R-R	6-3	185	12-22-99	0	1	4.43	11	0	0	20	14	10	10	1	18	12	.192	.348	.274	13.0	19.6	92
Minaya, Juan	R-R	6-4	210	9-18-90	0	2	2.39	22	0	1	26	25	10	7	2	11	27	.250	.348	.350	23.5	9.6	115
Nicolas, Kyle	R-R	6-4	223	2-22-99	3	5	4.36	12	12	0	54	56	34	26	8	23	63	.267	.345	.448	26.4	9.6	239
Ogle, Braeden	L-L	6-2	215	7-30-97	0	0	4.91	29	1	2	33	26	21	18	6	28	36	.220	.375	.432	23.7	18.4	152
Samaniego, Tyler	R-L	6-4	205	1-30-99	2	1	5.51	41	1	6	47	51	31	29	2	23	54	.287	.377	.399	26.0	11.1	208
Shortridge, Aaron	R-R	6-3	215	5-29-97	11	8	5.01	29	27	0	138	157	86	77	19	49	118	.288	.347	.458	19.5	8.1	604
Skenes, Paul	R-R	6-6	235	5-29-02	0	0	13.50	2	2	0	3	4	4	4	0	2	5	.333	.429	.417	35.7	14.3	14
Solometo, Anthony	L-L	6-5	220	12-02-02	2	4	4.35	12	12	0	52	49	27	25	6	14	50	.247	.304	.404	23.0	6.5	217
Sullivan, Sean	R-R	6-1	180	10-02-00	8	4	3.88	24	21	0	114	106	53	49	13	38	97	.245	.312	.382	20.4	8.0	476
Sulser, Beau	R-R	6-2	195	5-05-94	0	1	3.86	4	4	0	14	12	7	6	2	2	12	.222	.263	.463	21.1	3.5	57
Thomas, Tahnaj	R-R	6-4	217	6-16-99	4	2	4.87	36	1	3	44	40	29	24	5	30	26	.252	.388	.377	13.3	15.3	196
Toribio, Noe	R-R	6-2	210	8-25-99	2	3	3.79	34	0	3	57	48	25	24	6	27	68	.226	.333	.358	27.2	10.8	250
Wolf, Jackson	L-L	6-7	205	4-22-99	0	4	4.25	8	8	0	36	32	18	17	5	10	30	.232	.293	.442	19.9	6.6	151

Fielding

Catcher	PCT	G	PO	A	E	DP	PB
Bins	1.000	25	192	12	0	4	3
Davis	.993	30	265	12	2	2	1
Finol	.962	5	22	3	1	0	2
Gutierrez	.992	26	229	7	2	1	2
Shockley	.987	36	273	26	4	5	3
Wilson	.980	18	142	3	3	2	2

First Base	PCT	G	PO	A	E	DP
Bowen	1.000	1	10	3	0	1
Choi	.909	2	9	1	1	0
Gonzalez	.993	53	386	14	3	34
Gorski	1.000	14	64	10	0	8
Martin	.989	51	340	21	4	47
Matthiessen	.986	18	128	12	2	8
Scott	1.000	2	18	0	0	1

Second Base	PCT	G	PO	A	E	DP
Alvarez	.982	31	48	60	2	18
Cheng	.971	14	26	41	2	5
Finol	.972	16	23	46	2	12
Glenn	1.000	20	32	52	0	18
Gorski	1.000	3	5	12	0	3

Jarvis	1.000	10	13	26	0	3
Leyba	1.000	12	11	17	0	4
Maggi	.944	13	17	34	3	9
Marcos	1.000	1	2	2	0	0
Peguero	.957	24	40	48	4	12

Third Base	PCT	G	PO	A	E	DP
Alvarez	.964	28	23	30	2	6
Finol	.906	20	17	31	5	5
Glenn	.969	32	29	65	3	3
Gonzalez	.500	1	1	0	1	0
Jarvis	.923	5	4	8	1	2
Leyba	1.000	18	6	19	0	4
Maggi	.972	22	21	49	2	7

Marcos	.952	7	7	13	1	1
Perez	.895	7	7	10	2	2

Shortstop	PCT	G	PO	A	E	DP
Alvarez	.975	34	46	70	3	14
Cheng	.978	53	63	119	4	28
Finol	.500	2	1	0	1	0
Jarvis	.889	3	4	12	2	1
Peguero	.950	46	64	108	9	29

Outfield	PCT	G	PO	A	E	DP
Alvarez	1.000	4	6	0	0	0
Bowen	1.000	7	21	0	0	0
Davis	.882	7	14	1	2	0
Fraizer	.979	114	264	6	6	2
Gorski	.978	71	154	8	2	2
Jarvis	1.000	7	10	0	0	0
Macias	.950	13	25	4	1	2
Martin	.000	1	0	0	1	0
Matthiessen	1.000	3	3	0	0	0
Palacios	1.000	8	14	1	0	0
Perez	.964	11	27	0	1	0
Sanchez	.987	59	121	7	3	3
Scott	.993	54	108	5	1	0
Young	.988	58	128	13	2	4

GREENSBORO GRASSHOPPERS — HIGH CLASS A

South Atlantic League

Batting	B-T	Ht.	Wt.	DOB	AVG	OBP	SLG	G	PA	AB	R	H	2B	3B	HR	RBI	BB	HBP	SH	SF	SO	SB	CS	BB%	SO%
Acuna, Francisco	R-R	5-7	150	1-12-00	.277	.363	.412	33	137	119	15	33	13	0	1	13	10	6	2	0	22	5	1	7.3	16.1
Basabe, Angel	L-L	5-11	153	12-12-00	.150	.261	.200	6	23	20	3	3	1	0	0	1	3	0	0	0	8	0	0	13.0	34.8
Bowen, Jase	R-R	6-0	190	9-02-00	.257	.333	.469	110	493	435	80	112	15	4	23	88	35	16	3	4	121	24	5	7.1	24.5
Brannigan, Jack	R-R	6-0	190	3-11-01	.299	.382	.605	38	173	147	26	44	7	1	12	37	21	1	0	4	58	7	1	12.1	33.5
Brown, Luke	L-R	5-9	195	3-12-99	.270	.363	.471	64	239	204	42	55	13	2	8	35	25	6	2	2	63	13	5	10.5	26.4
Cheng, Tsung-Che	L-R	5-7	154	7-26-01	.308	.406	.575	57	254	214	45	66	12	9	9	31	35	0	4	0	47	13	9	13.8	18.5
Cimillo, Nick	R-R	6-2	215	2-23-00	.147	.256	.294	19	78	68	9	10	1	0	3	9	9	1	0	0	24	1	0	11.5	30.8
Dixon, Brenden	R-R	5-11	205	11-20-00	.219	.344	.437	65	263	215	36	47	10	2	11	34	39	4	1	4	76	1	3	14.8	28.9
Escotto, Maikol	R-R	5-10	180	6-04-02	.213	.272	.347	89	343	314	49	67	14	2	8	38	22	4	1	2	92	10	5	6.4	26.8
Finol, Claudio	R-R	5-11	171	4-13-00	.250	.250	.250	1	4	4	1	1	0	0	0	0	0	0	0	0	0	0	0	0.0	0.0
Glenn, Jackson	R-R	5-10	205	10-24-97	.299	.380	.474	38	158	137	20	41	6	0	6	30	17	2	0	2	25	3	1	10.8	15.8
Gonzalez, Tres	L-L	5-11	185	10-04-00	.287	.400	.402	94	449	366	73	105	18	0	8	46	65	7	7	4	84	22	8	14.5	18.7
Gutierrez, Abrahan	R-R	6-0	214	10-31-99	.260	.360	.403	20	89	77	10	20	5	0	2	14	10	2	0	0	14	0	0	11.2	15.7
Head, Hudson	L-L	6-0	180	4-08-01	.237	.309	.396	46	188	169	29	40	8	2	5	20	14	4	0	1	51	3	4	7.4	27.1
Hendrie, Wyatt	R-R	5-10	200	2-08-99	.211	.312	.353	62	251	218	42	46	9	2	6	24	29	3	1	0	76	6	2	11.6	30.3
Hernandez, Luis	R-R	5-10	150	9-06-00	.267	.450	.333	6	20	15	4	4	1	0	0	4	4	1	0	0	6	0	0	20.0	30.0
Jarvis, Mike	R-R	5-10	180	5-12-98	.228	.315	.439	61	273	237	53	54	10	5	10	44	25	7	0	4	52	20	1	9.2	19.0
Johnson, Termarr	L-R	5-8	175	6-11-04	.242	.427	.414	30	132	99	26	24	2	0	5	15	29	3	1	0	32	3	0	22.0	24.2
Matthiessen, William	R-R	6-6	230	1-09-98	.245	.328	.445	71	305	265	41	65	13	2	12	52	33	2	0	5	83	1	0	10.8	27.2
Nunez, Malcom	R-R	6-0	205	3-09-01	.313	.450	.625	5	20	16	3	5	2	0	1	7	3	1	0	0	4	0	0	15.0	20.0
Ordonez, Ernny	R-R	6-0	210	1-17-99	.214	.298	.346	50	205	182	24	39	6	0	6	26	20	2	0	1	59	3	0	9.8	28.8
Ross, Shawn	R-R	6-0	185	9-30-99	.203	.324	.467	55	216	182	37	37	6	0	14	33	33	0	0	1	88	0	1	15.3	40.7
Siani, Sammy	L-L	5-10	195	12-14-00	.231	.337	.364	99	398	338	56	78	16	1	9	48	51	4	3	2	126	16	8	12.8	31.7
Sightler, Josiah	L-L	6-3	234	10-19-99	.232	.293	.387	36	157	142	20	33	1	0	7	27	12	1	0	2	45	2	0	7.6	28.7
Swaggerty, Travis	L-L	5-10	200	8-19-97	.333	.600	1.000	1	5	3	1	1	0	1	0	0	2	0	0	0	0	0	0	40.0	0.0
Wilson, Eli	R-R	6-0	190	7-06-98	.230	.353	.416	37	137	113	17	26	7	1	4	20	19	3	1	1	20	2	0	13.9	14.6
Zapata, Wesley	B-R	5-11	152	3-02-04	.143	.143	.143	2	8	7	2	1	0	0	0	0	0	0	1	0	4	0	0	0.0	50.0

Pitching	B-T	Ht.	Wt.	DOB	W	L	ERA	G	GS	SV	IP	Hits	Runs	ER	HR	BB	SO	AVG	OBP	SLG	SO%	BB%	BF
Ashcraft, Braxton	L-R	6-5	195	10-05-99	0	2	3.76	9	9	0	26	29	12	11	4	5	29	.279	.309	.481	26.4	4.5	110
Bosnic, Julian	L-L	6-3	218	12-28-99	1	1	6.35	9	0	2	11	4	8	8	0	11	16	.111	.319	.167	33.3	22.9	48
Carey, Jack	R-R	6-0	205	9-20-99	2	1	4.09	38	2	3	51	52	23	23	4	22	59	.268	.349	.376	27.1	10.1	218
Case, Brad	R-R	6-6	242	9-13-96	1	1	8.78	10	2	0	13	16	14	13	2	17	14	.302	.486	.453	19.2	23.3	73
Chandler, Bubba	B-R	6-2	200	9-14-02	9	4	4.75	24	24	0	106	108	60	56	15	51	120	.265	.359	.419	25.6	10.9	468
Chen, Po-Yu	L-R	6-2	187	10-02-01	5	8	4.44	25	24	0	120	122	65	59	21	43	124	.272	.343	.493	24.5	8.5	506
Deese, Jaycob	R-R	6-1	195	5-30-00	3	3	5.29	32	3	1	68	71	41	40	11	17	65	.272	.321	.479	22.6	5.9	287
Diamond, Derek	R-R	6-2	200	1-04-01	2	2	6.00	9	9	0	45	50	31	30	11	15	34	.284	.345	.540	17.3	7.7	196
Dixon, Brenden	R-R	5-11	205	11-20-00	0	0	0.00	1	0	0	0	1	0	0	0	1	0	.500	.667	1.000	0.0	33.3	3
Florez, Santiago	R-R	6-5	222	5-09-00	5	2	7.08	37	0	0	41	48	37	32	7	24	40	.296	.387	.494	20.9	12.6	191
Ford, Grant	R-R	6-1	175	3-11-98	4	0	3.94	20	0	0	32	17	15	14	4	19	42	.157	.298	.333	32.1	14.5	131
Garcia, Darvin	R-R	6-3	170	4-25-99	2	0	10.13	2	0	0	3	3	3	3	0	5	1	.333	.600	.444	6.7	33.3	15
Harbin, Ryan	R-R	6-4	195	8-06-01	0	2	6.65	14	0	1	22	25	16	16	3	14	24	.294	.406	.482	23.5	13.7	102
Harrington, Thomas	R-R	6-2	185	7-12-01	3	5	3.87	18	18	0	88	86	44	38	11	29	106	.255	.320	.407	28.2	7.7	376
Hofmann, Logan	L-R	5-10	190	11-18-99	1	0	12.27	10	0	0	11	20	18	15	2	11	6	.377	.493	.566	8.8	16.2	68
Irvine, Drew	B-R	6-3	180	12-17-99	1	0	11.37	6	0	0	6	8	10	8	0	10	5	.320	.500	.360	13.9	27.8	36
Kobos, Will	R-R	6-2	180	8-03-97	2	1	1.06	11	0	2	17	4	2	2	0	7	22	.073	.177	.073	35.5	11.3	62
Linarez, Valentin	R-R	6-5	226	2-14-00	1	6	4.70	35	9	2	67	64	43	35	8	37	74	.253	.353	.391	25.1	12.5	295
Loeschorn, Joshua	L-R	6-3	215	3-10-00	2	0	4.13	12	4	0	28	25	15	13	5	7	30	.245	.297	.422	26.8	6.3	112
Massey, J.P.	R-R	6-5	205	4-01-00	2	4	4.65	9	9	0	31	19	20	16	3	23	26	.174	.318	.294	19.7	17.4	132
Mateo, Oliver	R-R	6-2	170	11-07-97	0	0	7.45	11	0	0	10	11	8	8	1	12	15	.289	.481	.447	27.8	22.2	54
Mendoza, Dante	R-R	6-5	186	12-16-98	4	3	3.13	34	0	3	46	39	19	16	1	31	64	.227	.349	.302	30.6	14.8	209
Miliano, Michell	R-R	6-3	185	12-22-99	1	1	3.86	29	0	1	44	39	20	19	3	26	61	.236	.347	.333	31.0	13.2	197
Miller, Mitchell	L-L	6-6	185	6-13-97	3	3	7.22	28	2	1	34	36	27	27	3	21	41	.281	.408	.398	26.1	13.4	157
Nielson, Cy	R-L	6-3	210	2-25-01	4	5	4.44	39	0	10	47	45	32	23	1	21	53	.254	.373	.322	24.9	9.9	213
Ramos, Jorge	R-R	6-0	150	6-05-02	0	0	6.75	2	0	1	5	5	4	4	0	4	5	.250	.360	.400	20.0	16.0	25
Solometo, Anthony	L-L	6-5	220	12-02-02	2	3	2.30	12	12	0	59	43	17	15	2	25	68	.207	.291	.284	29.1	10.7	234

PITTSBURGH PIRATES

Pitching	B-T	Ht.	Wt.	DOB	W	L	ERA	G	GS	SV	IP	Hits	Runs	ER	HR	BB	SO	AVG	OBP	SLG	SO%	BB%	BF
Stevenson, Jake	R-R	6-4	225	3-24-97	2	0	1.85	22	1	0	24	14	5	5	0	18	26	.173	.340	.210	25.2	17.5	103
Thibo, Yunior	R-R	6-4	185	6-24-98	4	1	6.04	23	0	1	22	21	18	15	2	13	17	.253	.370	.373	17.0	13.0	100
Yean, Eddy	R-R	6-1	180	6-25-01	2	3	5.01	40	1	4	50	57	39	28	2	23	44	.292	.362	.385	19.5	10.2	226

Fielding

Catcher	PCT	G	PO	A	E	DP	PB
Cimillo	1.000	1	8	0	0	0	0
Finol	1.000	1	9	0	0	0	0
Gutierrez	.984	13	117	8	2	0	2
Hendrie	.984	61	569	50	10	4	7
Hernandez	.956	6	60	5	3	0	2
Ross	.995	21	177	17	1	0	9
Wilson	.990	33	283	18	3	3	2

First Base	PCT	G	PO	A	E	DP
Bowen	.970	13	93	3	3	10
Cimillo	.985	10	64	3	1	6
Dixon	.986	9	64	9	1	6
Gutierrez	1.000	3	23	2	0	3
Matthiessen	.997	45	331	17	1	37
Nunez	1.000	2	13	1	0	2
Ordonez	.994	26	163	16	1	21
Sightler	.988	25	156	9	2	29

Second Base	PCT	G	PO	A	E	DP
Acuna	.973	8	16	20	1	8
Brannigan	1.000	8	22	20	0	10
Cheng	.990	27	37	58	1	14
Dixon	1.000	1	2	3	0	0
Escotto	.987	42	58	98	2	21
Glenn	1.000	1	1	2	0	0
Jarvis	1.000	16	24	47	0	8
Johnson	.957	30	66	67	6	21
Ross	1.000	6	13	15	0	6

Third Base	PCT	G	PO	A	E	DP
Acuna	.970	15	13	19	1	6
Brannigan	.970	12	11	21	1	3
Dixon	.922	38	26	45	6	8
Glenn	.880	24	13	31	6	2
Jarvis	.980	17	14	35	1	2
Nunez	1.000	1	0	2	0	0
Ordonez	.941	11	8	8	1	1
Ross	.952	14	2	18	1	3
Wilson	.800	2	2	2	1	0
Zapata	1.000	2	2	4	0	1

Shortstop	PCT	G	PO	A	E	DP
Acuna	.946	10	11	24	2	6
Brannigan	.971	18	24	44	2	17
Cheng	.981	31	35	70	2	14
Escotto	.967	53	65	111	6	25
Jarvis	.967	21	33	55	3	14
Ross	1.000	4	2	10	0	4

Outfield	PCT	G	PO	A	E	DP
Basabe	.500	6	7	0	1	0
Bowen	.964	98	193	9	6	1
Brown	1.000	49	82	4	0	2
Gonzalez	.992	91	153	6	2	1
Head	.980	43	92	3	2	0
Jarvis	.938	9	15	0	1	0
Matthiessen	1.000	11	14	0	0	0
Ross	.000	1	0	0	0	0
Siani	.987	90	150	12	3	4
Swaggerty	1.000	1	3	0	0	0

PITTSBURGH PIRATES

BRADENTON MARAUDERS — *LOW CLASS A*

FLORIDA STATE LEAGUE

Batting	B-T	Ht.	Wt.	DOB	AVG	OBP	SLG	G	PA	AB	R	H	2B	3B	HR	RBI	BB	HBP	SH	SF	SO	SB	CS	BB%	SO%
Acuna, Francisco	R-R	5-7	150	1-12-00	.179	.313	.179	17	48	39	3	7	0	0	0	2	7	1	0	1	9	1	0	14.6	18.8
Alfonzo, Omar	L-R	6-1	180	8-03-03	.273	.390	.413	52	182	150	22	41	7	1	4	37	30	0	0	2	46	2	0	16.5	25.3
Bins, Carter	R-R	5-11	215	10-07-98	.000	.250	.000	2	4	3	1	0	0	0	0	0	0	1	0	0	2	0	0	0.0	50.0
Bishop, Braylon	L-L	6-2	193	4-23-03	.111	.273	.111	8	33	27	2	3	0	0	0	1	5	1	0	0	13	0	0	15.2	39.4
Brannigan, Jack	R-R	6-0	190	3-11-01	.253	.398	.451	49	201	162	38	41	7	2	7	17	32	7	0	0	54	17	2	15.9	26.9
Campana, Sergio	R-R	6-0	160	3-29-02	.226	.388	.340	19	67	53	14	12	2	2	0	3	12	2	0	0	24	5	1	17.9	35.8
Castillo, Jesus	B-S	5-10	144	7-12-03	.209	.387	.251	118	506	383	60	80	9	2	1	41	102	13	2	6	95	39	9	20.2	18.8
Cimillo, Nick	R-R	6-2	215	2-23-00	.288	.406	.546	51	197	163	32	47	16	1	8	29	29	4	0	1	43	1	1	14.7	21.8
Custodio, Jauri	R-R	5-9	162	9-21-01	.227	.340	.318	16	53	44	9	10	1	0	1	6	7	1	0	1	13	1	1	13.2	24.5
De Los Santos, Yordany	R-R	6-1	170	2-17-05	.184	.322	.256	38	153	125	20	23	4	1	1	10	22	4	1	1	60	9	3	14.4	39.2
Forrester, Garret	R-R	6-1	208	11-11-01	.278	.552	.278	6	29	18	4	5	0	0	0	3	10	1	0	0	7	0	0	34.5	24.1
Gonzalez, Tres	L-L	5-11	185	10-04-00	.299	.427	.403	19	82	67	15	20	4	0	1	12	15	0	0	0	11	6	0	18.3	13.4
Harrison, Kalae	L-R	5-11	188	6-05-02	.262	.418	.333	18	55	42	6	11	0	0	1	4	11	1	0	1	10	2	0	20.0	18.2
Hendrie, Wyatt	R-R	5-10	200	2-08-99	.200	.328	.291	17	67	55	9	11	2	0	1	8	8	3	0	1	12	2	0	11.9	17.9
Hernandez, Luis	R-R	5-10	150	9-06-00	.211	.360	.263	6	25	19	3	4	1	0	0	4	5	0	0	1	9	0	0	20.0	36.0
Jebb, Mitch	L-R	6-1	185	5-13-02	.297	.382	.398	34	153	128	26	38	6	2	1	13	17	3	1	4	11	11	1	11.1	7.2
Jerez, Juan	R-R	6-1	160	11-28-01	.190	.316	.238	22	76	63	9	12	3	0	0	5	12	0	0	1	22	8	2	15.8	28.9
Johnson, Termarr	L-R	5-8	175	6-11-04	.244	.419	.448	75	330	250	57	61	10	1	13	44	72	5	1	2	88	7	2	21.8	26.7
McAdoo, Charles	R-R	6-2	210	3-06-02	.302	.412	.510	28	114	96	22	29	3	1	5	24	17	1	0	0	22	5	2	14.9	19.3
Miknis, Justin	L-R	6-0	195	9-06-00	.152	.317	.182	11	41	33	3	5	1	0	0	3	8	0	0	0	12	0	0	19.5	29.3
Mitchell, Cal	L-L	6-0	205	3-08-99	.167	.353	.167	4	17	12	2	2	0	0	0	2	4	0	0	1	2	0	0	23.5	11.8
Mojica, Alexander	R-R	6-1	250	8-02-02	.219	.338	.388	56	216	183	24	40	13	0	6	25	29	4	0	0	61	2	1	13.4	28.2
Nadal, Deivis	L-R	6-0	150	2-08-02	.212	.344	.377	101	318	260	51	55	15	2	8	39	48	5	4	1	105	33	4	15.1	33.0
Nolasco, Rodolfo	R-R	5-11	175	9-23-01	.214	.351	.440	102	444	359	59	77	21	0	20	72	71	8	0	6	152	11	3	16.0	34.2
Nunez, Malcom	R-R	6-0	205	3-09-01	.333	.444	.400	4	18	15	2	5	1	0	0	2	3	0	0	0	2	0	0	16.7	11.1
Planchart, Geovanny	R-R	6-1	176	9-17-01	.222	.341	.320	87	317	266	40	59	15	1	3	42	47	2	0	2	69	4	1	14.8	21.8
Polanco, Shalin	L-L	6-0	168	2-06-04	.242	.323	.439	70	303	264	38	64	16	0	12	45	29	4	3	3	87	17	7	9.6	28.7
Rivas, Javier	R-R	6-6	165	9-01-02	.189	.243	.240	54	215	196	16	37	4	0	2	32	13	2	1	3	84	1	0	6.0	39.1
Romero, Rayber	B-R	5-8	155	5-28-02	.081	.292	.135	18	49	37	8	3	0	1	0	1	8	3	1	0	15	1	1	16.3	30.6
Sightler, Josiah	L-L	6-3	234	10-19-99	.516	.563	.891	18	80	64	15	33	6	0	6	24	9	3	0	4	9	0	0	11.3	11.3
Swaggerty, Travis	L-L	5-10	200	8-19-97	.111	.429	.111	4	14	9	2	1	0	0	0	0	5	0	0	0	5	1	0	35.7	35.7
Terrero, Enmanuel	L-L	5-9	160	9-14-02	.266	.368	.409	80	361	308	53	82	8	6	8	36	47	4	0	2	93	21	9	13.0	25.8
Tredaway, Tanner	R-R	6-1	175	8-24-99	.145	.283	.145	24	93	76	10	11	0	0	0	8	13	2	0	1	20	3	0	14.0	21.5
Triolo, Jared	R-R	6-3	212	2-08-98	.438	.500	.688	4	18	16	6	7	4	0	0	4	2	0	0	0	3	0	0	11.1	16.7
Valdez, Esmerlyn	R-R	6-2	181	1-27-04	.250	.348	.400	8	23	20	3	5	1	1	0	4	2	1	0	0	9	0	0	8.7	39.1
White, Lonnie	R-R	6-3	212	12-31-02	.259	.395	.488	44	200	162	36	42	11	1	8	30	32	5	0	1	56	12	1	16.0	28.0

Pitching	B-T	Ht.	Wt.	DOB	W	L	ERA	G	GS	SV	IP	Hits	Runs	ER	HR	BB	SO	AVG	OBP	SLG	SO%	BB%	BF
Ashcraft, Braxton	L-R	6-5	195	10-05-99	0	0	0.00	2	2	0	6	3	0	0	0	1	11	.130	.167	.130	45.8	4.2	24
Barco, Hunter	L-L	6-4	210	12-15-00	0	2	5.06	6	6	0	11	13	7	6	0	4	19	.289	.347	.356	38.8	8.2	49
Bidois, Brandan	R-R	6-2	158	6-21-01	3	0	1.99	22	0	6	23	14	5	5	1	15	42	.173	.327	.284	41.6	14.9	101
Birdsong, Elijah	R-R	6-2	200	10-11-99	2	3	7.02	40	0	8	50	52	49	39	4	30	43	.264	.371	.396	18.1	12.7	237
Bosnic, Julian	L-L	6-3	218	12-28-99	3	2	4.34	27	0	5	46	25	26	22	5	35	60	.164	.342	.289	30.5	17.8	197
Carrion, Danny	R-R	6-3	205	8-12-01	1	0	15.00	6	0	0	6	12	10	10	0	5	5	.414	.514	.655	13.9	13.9	36
Case, Brad	R-R	6-6	242	9-13-96	1	0	3.00	2	0	0	3	3	1	1	0	0	3	.300	.364	.400	27.3	0.0	11

Cederlind, Blake	R-R	6-4	215	1-04-96	1	1	13.50	5	0	0	6	6	9	9	1	6	6	.261	.452	.435	19.4	19.4	31
Chang, Hung-Leng	R-R	6-3	159	10-07-01	2	2	7.46	7	5	0	25	34	27	21	7	12	14	.327	.418	.635	11.5	9.8	122
Chatwood, Tyler	R-R	5-11	200	12-16-89	0	1	4.91	7	1	0	7	3	4	4	1	6	4	.120	.290	.240	12.9	19.4	31
Contreras, Roansy	R-R	6-0	175	11-07-99	0	0	0.00	1	1	0	2	0	0	0	0	0	2	.000	.000	.000	33.3	0.0	6
Cotto, Magdiel	L-L	6-3	225	6-24-02	0	0	5.40	3	0	0	3	2	2	2	0	3	4	.182	.400	.182	26.7	20.0	15
Crowe, Wil	R-R	6-2	245	9-09-94	2	0	0.00	3	1	0	3	2	0	0	0	1	2	.167	.231	.167	15.4	7.7	13
De La Paz, Yoldin	L-L	6-0	165	5-10-02	3	1	5.45	28	0	1	40	41	31	24	2	25	45	.266	.396	.370	24.1	13.4	187
Diamond, Derek	R-R	6-2	200	1-04-01	8	3	3.98	15	12	0	75	77	36	33	5	15	63	.269	.308	.367	20.4	4.9	309
Dotel, Wilber	R-R	6-3	178	9-25-02	7	2	3.09	18	15	0	79	64	37	27	3	44	58	.222	.340	.299	16.8	12.8	345
Emanuel, Kent	L-L	6-4	225	6-04-92	0	0	0.00	1	0	0	1	0	0	0	0	0	2	.000	.000	.000	66.7	0.0	3
Ercolani, Alessandro	R-R	6-2	185	4-20-04	4	5	4.43	17	15	0	65	62	40	32	8	31	66	.257	.343	.432	24.0	11.3	275
Fellows, Drake	L-R	6-5	216	3-06-98	0	1	9.00	10	4	0	11	12	11	11	1	9	12	.279	.404	.395	23.1	17.3	52
Franzua, Geronimo	L-L	6-1	170	9-25-93	1	1	5.87	7	0	0	8	8	7	5	1	0	7	.242	.242	.394	21.2	0.0	33
Fulgencio, Miguel	L-L	6-1	205	1-22-99	0	2	6.75	24	0	1	28	33	28	21	2	22	22	.295	.406	.384	15.8	15.8	139
Garcia, Darvin	R-R	6-3	170	4-25-99	4	2	6.59	35	0	1	42	40	40	31	4	34	37	.245	.392	.405	18.0	16.6	205
Harbin, Ryan	R-R	6-4	195	8-06-01	1	2	0.83	21	0	3	33	19	6	3	1	15	44	.167	.275	.228	33.6	11.5	131
Harrington, Thomas	R-R	6-2	185	7-12-01	4	1	2.77	8	8	0	39	31	12	12	3	12	40	.230	.297	.363	26.7	8.0	150
Hernandez, Luigi	R-R	6-0	185	9-21-03	2	0	3.12	4	0	0	9	2	3	3	0	12	10	.080	.378	.200	26.3	31.6	38
Jerez, Juan	R-R	6-1	160	11-28-01	0	0	0.00	1	0	0	0	0	0	0	0	1	0	.000	.500	.000	0.0	50.0	2
Jimenez, Carlos	R-R	6-2	140	7-14-02	0	0	0.00	2	0	0	3	0	0	0	0	4	8	.000	.333	.000	53.3	26.7	15
Kellington, Owen	L-R	6-3	193	2-05-03	1	3	3.94	23	18	0	80	62	41	35	8	50	90	.215	.328	.372	26.2	14.5	344
Kelly, Antwone	R-R	5-10	183	9-01-03	1	0	2.25	2	0	0	4	2	1	1	0	0	6	.154	.154	.154	46.2	0.0	13
Kennedy, Michael	L-L	6-1	205	11-30-04	0	0	2.08	2	0	0	4	2	1	1	0	6	8	.154	.400	.154	40.0	30.0	20
Kranick, Max	R-R	6-3	220	7-21-97	0	1	10.38	2	2	0	4	4	6	5	1	3	2	.250	.400	.500	10.0	15.0	20
Loeschorn, Joshua	L-R	6-3	215	3-10-00	3	4	3.86	22	0	2	40	26	19	17	3	13	59	.178	.255	.301	36.6	8.1	161
Lomeli, Carlos	R-R	6-2	195	3-19-99	5	2	4.57	26	1	0	41	49	26	21	3	17	46	.293	.366	.413	24.7	9.1	186
Massey, J.P.	R-R	6-5	205	4-01-00	3	3	3.28	11	9	0	49	41	24	18	4	24	57	.230	.335	.337	27.1	11.4	210
Nadal, Deivis	L-R	6-0	150	2-08-02	0	0	54.00	1	0	0	1	2	4	4	0	4	2	.500	.750	1.000	25.0	50.0	8
Perachi, Dominic	L-L	6-4	195	2-27-01	5	0	4.76	22	18	0	91	92	51	48	10	48	96	.267	.366	.414	23.6	11.8	407
Peralta, Luis	L-L	5-11	170	1-06-01	0	3	4.96	23	9	1	53	45	35	29	4	35	67	.228	.353	.330	27.8	14.5	241
Ramos, Jorge	R-R	6-0	150	6-05-02	2	0	3.27	13	0	0	22	22	12	8	2	14	20	.250	.368	.375	18.9	13.2	106
Reilly, Patrick	R-R	6-3	208	10-07-01	2	2	5.91	9	0	1	11	6	7	7	2	8	19	.158	.319	.395	40.4	17.0	47
Sharts, Owen	R-R	6-2	190	11-23-99	1	1	7.33	18	0	1	27	32	24	22	0	23	23	.311	.451	.408	17.3	17.3	133
Skenes, Paul	R-R	6-6	235	5-29-02	0	0	0.00	2	2	0	3	1	0	0	0	0	4	.091	.091	.091	36.4	0.0	11
Thibo, Yunior	R-R	6-4	185	6-24-98	2	2	2.75	14	0	4	20	10	7	6	2	11	17	.149	.266	.254	21.5	13.9	79
Tomkins, Landon	R-R	6-3	200	6-23-00	1	1	4.50	11	0	0	16	17	10	8	1	8	6	.266	.347	.375	8.3	11.1	72
Tredaway, Tanner	R-R	6-1	175	8-24-99	0	0	0.00	1	0	0	1	2	0	0	0	1	0	.500	.600	.500	0.0	20.0	5
Umana, Sergio	R-R	6-0	175	5-21-00	1	0	5.82	10	0	0	17	24	16	11	3	7	8	.329	.417	.507	9.5	8.3	84
Walsh, Mike	R-R	6-2	195	1-17-01	0	0	1.93	9	0	4	9	8	3	2	0	3	11	.250	.342	.250	28.9	7.9	38
Woods, Jaden	L-L	6-2	205	2-01-02	0	1	3.14	10	0	0	14	10	5	5	0	3	21	.196	.241	.235	38.9	5.6	54
Zamora, Daniel	L-L	6-3	195	4-15-93	0	0	0.00	1	1	0	1	1	0	0	0	1	0	.250	.400	.250	0.0	20.0	5

Fielding

Catcher	PCT	G	PO	A	E	DP	PB
Alfonzo	.996	35	228	20	1	2	6
Bins	1.000	2	14	0	0	0	0
Cimillo	1.000	1	1	0	0	0	0
Hendrie	.993	15	133	10	1	0	3
Hernandez	1.000	6	54	4	0	1	2
Miknis	.987	10	73	5	1	2	3
Planchart	.983	78	693	55	13	3	12

First Base	PCT	G	PO	A	E	DP
Alfonzo	.983	15	111	5	2	17
Castillo	.993	36	127	9	1	12
Cimillo	.985	27	184	9	3	20
Hendrie	1.000	2	17	3	0	0
Jerez	.966	13	82	4	3	6
McAdoo	.000	1	0	0	0	0
Mojica	.995	48	350	22	2	46
Nunez	1.000	3	21	0	0	5
Planchart	.978	7	42	2	1	4
Sightler	1.000	5	36	0	0	2
Valdez	.947	7	33	3	2	4

Second Base	PCT	G	PO	A	E	DP
Acuna	1.000	3	6	5	0	1
Brannigan	1.000	3	6	16	0	2
Castillo	.983	27	43	75	2	16
Harrison	.909	6	5	5	1	2
Jebb	.983	18	29	30	1	6
Johnson	.960	57	129	159	12	51
McAdoo	.912	9	8	23	3	5
Nadal	.971	10	17	17	1	2
Romero	.956	15	28	37	3	9

Third Base	PCT	G	PO	A	E	DP
Acuna	.875	6	1	6	1	0
Brannigan	.964	35	25	81	4	14
Castillo	.935	40	27	73	7	13
De Los Santos	.895	15	8	26	4	1
Forrester	.923	6	7	5	1	0
Harrison	.889	12	7	9	2	2
Mojica	.889	4	2	6	1	0
Nadal	.943	32	9	24	2	2
Rivas	.900	6	0	9	1	0
Triolo	.750	3	3	3	2	1

Shortstop	PCT	G	PO	A	E	DP
Acuna	1.000	8	11	25	0	3
Brannigan	1.000	9	4	14	0	2
Castillo	.959	36	51	88	6	23
De Los Santos	.968	25	23	38	2	4
Harrison	1.000	1	2	1	0	0
Jebb	.932	18	15	40	4	8
Johnson	.929	5	4	9	1	1
Rivas	.967	45	56	118	6	31

Outfield	PCT	G	PO	A	E	DP
Bishop	.917	8	12	2	1	1
Campana	.647	19	29	0	1	0
Castillo	.639	12	16	1	1	0
Custodio	1.000	8	7	1	0	0
Gonzalez	1.000	17	29	2	0	0
Jerez	1.000	4	3	0	0	0
McAdoo	1.000	15	20	0	0	0
Mitchell	.667	3	2	0	1	0
Nadal	.961	57	101	7	4	1
Nolasco	.978	87	127	5	4	1
Polanco	.939	62	91	2	4	0
Swaggerty	1.000	3	7	0	0	0
Terrero	.938	72	93	7	7	1
Tredaway	.976	22	28	0	1	0
Valdez	.000	1	0	0	0	0
White	.983	37	59	2	2	1

FCL PIRATES

ROOKIE

FLORIDA COMPLEX LEAGUE

Batting	B-T	Ht.	Wt.	DOB	AVG	OBP	SLG	G	PA	AB	R	H	2B	3B	HR	RBI	BB	HBP	SH	SF	SO	SB	CS	BB%	SO%
Alfonzo, Omar	L-R	6-1	180	8-03-03	.286	.516	.524	8	31	21	5	6	2	0	1	5	9	1	0	0	5	1	1	29.0	16.1
Bins, Carter	R-R	5-11	215	10-07-98	.182	.308	.182	4	13	11	0	2	0	0	0	1	1	1	0	0	2	0	0	7.7	15.4
Bishop, Braylon	L-L	6-2	193	4-23-03	.220	.363	.341	31	113	91	18	20	4	2	1	10	19	2	0	1	29	10	1	16.8	25.7
Campana, Sergio	R-R	6-0	160	3-29-02	.167	.394	.250	9	33	24	9	4	2	0	0	2	7	2	0	0	7	6	0	21.2	21.2
Custodio, Jauri	R-R	5-9	162	9-21-01	.250	.375	.413	25	96	80	16	20	5	4	0	9	12	4	0	0	17	7	2	12.5	17.7
De Los Santos, Yordany	R-R	6-1	170	2-17-05	.328	.397	.463	17	78	67	16	22	6	0	1	15	7	2	0	2	11	13	1	9.0	14.1
Diaz, Kelvin	R-R	6-2	143	10-03-02	.244	.370	.400	36	109	90	17	22	4	2	2	16	16	2	1	0	28	11	1	14.7	25.7
Escalante, Rafael	R-R	5-10	160	9-13-01	.256	.409	.367	34	115	90	22	23	4	0	2	16	23	1	0	1	15	1	1	20.0	13.0
Escalona, Eybert	R-R	5-11	180	10-27-02	.238	.296	.365	21	71	63	6	15	3	1	1	11	3	3	0	2	21	0	0	4.2	29.6
Espinal, Ewry	L-R	6-0	185	12-18-02	.227	.378	.258	23	83	66	15	15	2	0	0	7	15	1	1	0	27	8	1	18.1	32.5
Graham, A.J.	R-R	6-3	180	10-02-02	.200	.429	.200	4	7	5	1	1	0	0	0	1	1	1	0	0	0	0	0	14.3	0.0
Head, Hudson	L-L	6-0	180	4-08-01	.750	.750	.750	1	4	4	3	3	0	0	0	3	0	0	0	0	0	1	0	0.0	0.0
Herman, Jack	R-R	5-10	190	9-30-99	.071	.188	.143	4	16	14	1	1	1	0	0	3	2	0	0	0	1	1	0	12.5	6.3
Jerez, Juan	R-R	6-1	160	11-28-01	.273	.444	.545	14	63	44	16	12	4	1	2	12	14	2	0	3	16	8	2	22.2	25.4
Lopez, John	R-R	5-8	165	10-06-05	.250	.400	.250	3	5	4	0	1	0	0	0	0	0	1	0	0	0	1	0	0.0	0.0
Maguire, Solomon	L-R	5-10	168	3-04-03	.200	.500	.400	3	8	5	3	1	1	0	0	0	3	0	0	0	2	2	0	37.5	25.0
Marcos, Norkis	R-R	5-11	170	5-26-01	.143	.143	.143	2	7	7	1	1	0	0	0	0	0	0	0	0	1	0	0	0.0	14.3
Nunez, Malcom	R-R	6-0	205	3-09-01	.400	.625	.600	2	8	5	1	2	1	0	0	2	3	0	0	0	0	0	0	37.5	0.0
Pena, Jhonson	R-R	5-10	155	8-03-02	.240	.357	.347	41	144	121	27	29	4	3	1	11	18	4	1	0	28	20	2	12.5	19.4
Plaz, Axiel	R-R	5-11	165	8-12-05	.144	.359	.237	33	131	97	18	14	4	1	1	13	21	12	0	1	41	0	1	16.0	31.3
Rivas, Javier	R-R	6-6	165	9-01-02	.285	.362	.400	40	188	165	17	47	11	1	2	31	14	7	0	2	43	7	6	7.4	22.9
Rodriguez, Eddy	R-R	6-0	181	11-05-03	.295	.409	.442	42	159	129	22	38	7	0	4	24	19	8	0	3	26	8	2	11.9	16.4
Romero, Eliecer	R-R	6-0	185	9-08-01	—	—	—	21	0	0	1	0	0	0	0	0	0	0	0	0	0	0	0	—	—
Romero, Rayber	B-R	5-8	155	5-28-02	.300	.417	.300	17	12	10	2	3	0	0	0	1	2	0	0	0	4	0	0	16.7	33.3
Sanchez, Ronny	R-R	6-0	191	7-22-02	.125	.500	.125	9	14	8	1	1	0	0	0	1	5	1	0	0	3	0	0	35.7	21.4
Scherrer, Luke	R-R	6-2	210	12-13-04	.000	.333	.000	4	9	6	1	0	0	0	0	1	1	2	0	0	3	0	0	11.1	33.3
Severino, Jhonny	R-R	6-1	185	11-08-04	.300	.364	.600	3	11	10	3	3	0	0	1	2	1	0	0	0	1	2	0	9.1	9.1
Sightler, Josiah	L-L	6-3	234	10-19-99	.227	.370	.364	6	27	22	7	5	0	0	1	4	4	1	0	0	3	0	0	14.8	11.1
Sosa, Miguel	R-R	5-11	181	12-04-03	.275	.495	.406	34	103	69	23	19	3	0	2	9	30	2	0	2	23	0	1	29.1	22.3
Suero, Estuar	B-R	6-5	180	8-29-05	.217	.379	.326	13	58	46	7	10	0	1	1	6	12	0	0	0	12	2	2	20.7	20.7
Tejeda, Luis	R-R	5-11	170	8-26-02	.133	.409	.133	11	22	15	2	2	0	0	0	1	5	2	0	0	3	1	0	22.7	13.6
Toledo, Jeral	B-R	5-10	135	1-22-03	.306	.413	.479	38	151	121	26	37	9	3	2	21	24	1	1	4	25	11	4	15.9	16.6
Valdez, Esmerlyn	R-R	6-2	181	1-27-04	.312	.377	.518	40	159	141	23	44	9	1	6	32	15	1	0	2	36	3	2	9.4	22.6
White, Lonnie	R-R	6-3	212	12-31-02	.317	.434	.444	17	76	63	13	20	5	0	1	10	11	2	0	0	19	6	2	14.5	25.0
Zapata, Wesley	B-R	5-11	152	3-02-04	.271	.425	.329	32	114	85	22	23	3	1	0	15	25	0	1	3	19	5	2	21.9	16.7

Pitching	B-T	Ht.	Wt.	DOB	W	L	ERA	G	GS	SV	IP	Hits	Runs	ER	HR	BB	SO	AVG	OBP	SLG	SO%	BB%	BF
Alcala, Gilberto	R-R	6-3	175	10-03-02	1	2	4.13	16	1	0	33	21	19	15	2	9	34	.176	.242	.303	25.6	6.8	133
Barco, Hunter	L-L	6-4	210	12-15-00	0	0	1.17	3	2	0	8	4	1	1	0	2	9	.148	.207	.259	31.0	6.9	29
Case, Brad	R-R	6-6	242	9-13-96	0	0	16.20	2	2	0	2	2	3	3	0	2	0	.286	.444	.571	0.0	22.2	9
Chang, Hung-Leng	R-R	6-3	159	10-07-01	2	1	3.20	8	6	1	25	19	12	9	0	12	25	.204	.302	.258	23.6	11.3	106
Cotto, Magdiel	L-L	6-3	225	6-24-02	0	0	0.00	2	0	0	3	4	0	0	0	0	3	.333	.333	.333	25.0	0.0	12
Cruz, Cristopher	R-R	6-2	170	1-06-03	3	2	11.91	10	2	0	11	15	17	15	1	14	8	.300	.470	.520	12.1	21.2	66
De Los Santos, Enmanuel	R-R	6-4	163	10-14-00	1	0	4.22	9	0	0	11	11	8	5	0	8	16	.234	.345	.277	29.1	14.5	55
Fellows, Drake	L-R	6-5	216	3-06-98	0	0	0.00	1	1	0	1	0	0	0	0	2	1	.000	.500	.000	25.0	50.0	4
Franzua, Geronimo	L-L	6-1	170	9-25-93	1	0	4.91	3	1	0	4	5	3	2	0	0	5	.357	.333	.357	33.3	0.0	15
Garces, Jose	R-R	6-2	149	6-09-04	2	0	8.63	10	3	0	24	30	28	23	0	21	17	.319	.476	.436	13.7	16.9	124
Garcia, Roelmy	R-R	6-2	172	4-12-03	4	0	5.03	18	1	0	20	18	15	11	2	21	21	.254	.438	.366	21.9	21.9	96
Grounds, Jackson	R-R	6-1	190	7-13-04	2	0	3.52	12	0	0	15	11	8	6	0	12	16	.212	.391	.308	23.2	17.4	69
Hernandez, Kevison	R-R	6-5	188	7-20-02	0	1	3.25	16	0	0	28	17	12	10	1	26	38	.173	.367	.245	29.7	20.3	128
Hernandez, Luigi	R-R	6-0	185	9-21-03	0	2	5.63	5	4	0	8	7	6	5	0	8	10	.219	.375	.250	25.0	20.0	40
Jimenez, Carlos	R-R	6-2	140	7-14-02	0	0	2.79	5	3	0	10	5	4	3	0	11	13	.152	.404	.182	27.7	23.4	47
Kelly, Antwone	R-R	5-10	183	9-01-03	4	1	2.95	12	4	0	40	35	17	13	0	18	47	.238	.331	.299	27.8	10.7	169
Kennedy, Michael	L-L	6-1	205	11-30-04	2	1	2.13	11	7	0	42	25	10	10	1	19	55	.171	.292	.247	32.2	11.1	171
Kennedy, Tyler	R-R	6-3	223	6-07-02	0	1	21.00	5	0	0	3	5	7	7	2	9	7	.357	.625	.857	29.2	37.5	24
Maldonado, Andy	R-R	6-4	196	7-21-02	2	0	5.56	12	0	0	11	8	8	7	0	16	11	.190	.424	.214	18.6	27.1	59
McMillan, Garrett	L-R	6-4	230	2-10-01	0	0	54.00	1	0	0	0	3	2	2	0	0	0	.600	.600	.600	0.0	0.0	5
Quintanilla, Keneth	R-R	6-0	154	1-21-03	4	2	5.13	18	0	0	33	26	19	19	7	24	38	.211	.351	.423	25.2	15.9	151
Ramos, Jorge	R-R	6-0	150	6-05-02	1	1	2.38	8	0	3	11	5	3	3	1	3	13	.125	.200	.250	28.9	6.7	45
Reed, Carlson	L-R	6-4	200	11-27-02	1	2	2.57	4	2	0	7	7	7	2	0	3	6	.233	.324	.300	17.6	8.8	34
Romero, Eliecer	R-R	6-0	185	9-08-01	0	0	4.22	20	0	3	21	18	14	10	0	17	22	.220	.356	.293	21.8	16.8	101
Shim, Jun-Seok	R-R	6-4	215	4-09-04	0	0	3.38	4	4	0	8	3	3	3	1	3	13	.111	.200	.222	43.3	10.0	30
Silvera, Andres	R-R	6-0	188	7-20-04	0	2	6.87	10	4	0	18	25	18	14	2	12	18	.309	.398	.457	19.4	12.9	93
Skenes, Paul	R-R	6-6	235	5-29-02	0	0	0.00	1	1	0	1	0	0	0	0	0	1	.000	.000	.000	33.3	0.0	3
Stumbo, Peyton	R-R	6-1	200	6-28-02	0	0	1.42	5	0	0	6	4	1	1	0	0	3	.174	.174	.217	13.0	0.0	23
Tejada, Joaquin	R-R	5-11	160	7-16-03	1	0	2.70	19	0	3	27	13	8	8	1	22	30	.151	.342	.221	26.3	19.3	114
Umana, Sergio	R-R	6-0	175	5-21-00	0	1	9.00	2	0	0	3	4	4	3	0	2	3	.308	.400	.385	20.0	13.3	15
Uribe, Isaias	L-L	6-3	172	8-13-02	1	4	3.96	12	7	1	39	40	23	17	2	13	33	.267	.325	.380	19.9	7.8	166

Fielding

C: Escalante 32, Plaz 13, Escalona 8, Alfonzo 6, Bins 4, Scherrer 4, Sosa 4, Lopez 3. **1B:** Espinal 19, Rodriguez 14, Valdez 14, Escalona 8, Sanchez 8, Jerez 3, Alfonzo 2, Diaz 2, Escalante 1, Nunez 1. **2B:** Toledo 34, Zapata 18, Romero 8, Tejeda 3, Graham 2, Pena 2, Rivas 1, Marcos 1, Diaz 1. **3B:** Diaz 19, Zapata 15,

PITTSBURGH PIRATES

Jerez 9, Tejeda 7, De Los Santos 7, Rivas 6, Severino 3, Toledo 1, Marcos 1, Escalante 1. **SS:** Rivas 36, Diaz 14, De Los Santos 10, Toledo 2, Zapata 2. **OF:** Pena 37, Bishop 33, Valdez 27, Custodio 24, Rodriguez 22, Sosa 20, White 17, Suero 10, Campana 9, Herman 3, Jerez 3, Maguire 2, Toledo 2, Espinal 1, Graham 1, Head 1.

DSL PIRATES — *ROOKIE*

DOMINICAN SUMMER LEAGUE

Batting	B-T	Ht.	Wt.	DOB	AVG	OBP	SLG	G	PA	AB	R	H	2B	3B	HR	RBI	BB	HBP	SH	SF	SO	SB	CS	BB%	SO%
Aguiar, Ronny	B-R	5-7	160	4-01-05	.319	.429	.428	47	168	138	22	44	4	4	1	18	23	5	0	2	40	15	6	13.7	23.8
Aquino, Angel	R-R	6-5	207	6-18-05	.185	.252	.210	41	139	124	15	23	3	0	0	11	11	1	0	3	58	3	0	7.9	41.7
Armas, Gustavo	R-R	6-2	175	12-12-03	.161	.390	.214	31	77	56	12	9	1	1	0	7	17	4	0	0	28	2	1	22.1	36.4
Blanco, Tony	R-R	6-6	243	5-14-05	.235	.325	.397	40	157	136	21	32	7	0	5	25	17	2	0	2	59	0	1	10.8	37.6
Brioso, Edwarli	R-R	5-11	161	9-22-04	.179	.243	.221	39	103	95	11	17	4	0	0	7	4	4	0	0	33	7	4	3.9	32.0
Caro, Carlos	R-R	5-11	160	11-04-04	.310	.440	.504	45	159	129	29	40	8	1	5	29	20	10	0	0	33	11	5	12.6	20.8
De La Cruz, Rodolfo	L-L	6-0	160	11-24-03	.121	.326	.273	20	43	33	8	4	0	1	1	8	9	1	0	0	16	4	1	20.9	37.2
De Paula, Robert	R-R	5-11	193	3-23-03	.200	.329	.231	29	82	65	13	13	2	0	0	8	8	6	0	3	21	7	0	9.8	25.6
Escudero, Samuel	R-R	5-9	155	2-27-04	.275	.383	.408	40	141	120	16	33	8	1	2	23	18	3	0	0	18	3	1	12.8	12.8
Gimenez, Yosmar	L-R	6-2	150	5-02-06	.198	.363	.210	33	103	81	12	16	1	0	0	4	19	2	1	0	17	5	6	18.4	16.5
Jauregui, Cristian	B-R	5-11	180	2-09-06	.242	.419	.326	36	124	95	20	23	3	1	1	7	23	6	0	0	30	15	2	18.5	24.2
Machado, Juan	L-R	5-11	145	6-04-03	.291	.483	.441	47	178	127	41	37	3	5	2	24	47	2	0	2	39	29	7	26.4	21.9
Mola, Raymond	R-R	6-2	190	12-01-05	.056	.227	.056	7	22	18	2	1	0	0	0	0	4	0	0	0	7	1	0	18.2	31.8
Morales, Daje	R-R	5-10	155	3-03-05	.178	.345	.280	47	148	118	29	21	5	2	1	10	29	1	0	0	30	14	5	19.6	20.3
Nunez, Lennyn	B-R	5-10	150	8-08-03	.197	.383	.262	34	81	61	12	12	2	1	0	5	11	8	0	1	12	4	2	13.6	14.8
Orelin, Christopher	R-R	5-11	157	1-31-05	.145	.280	.188	28	83	69	10	10	3	0	0	3	13	0	1	0	19	0	1	15.7	22.9
Oviedo, Eduardo	R-R	6-1	169	9-02-04	.299	.389	.488	43	149	127	20	38	7	1	5	25	19	1	0	2	37	15	6	12.8	24.8
Paulino, Isaac	R-R	5-11	160	3-10-05	.175	.333	.316	27	75	57	10	10	6	1	0	6	12	3	0	3	23	3	0	16.0	30.7
Perez, Angel	R-R	5-10	160	9-12-05	.295	.462	.568	33	117	88	17	26	7	1	5	25	24	4	0	1	25	1	0	20.5	21.4
Pimentel, Antonio	L-R	5-10	161	10-02-05	.172	.322	.222	37	121	99	10	17	0	1	1	12	16	6	0	0	23	7	1	13.2	19.0
Ramirez, Richard	R-R	6-0	160	7-03-05	.252	.361	.476	34	122	103	18	26	6	1	5	20	18	0	0	1	26	1	0	14.8	21.3
Rivero, Jonathan	L-R	6-0	191	12-15-05	.152	.308	.190	36	131	105	16	16	1	0	1	9	22	2	1	1	22	0	3	16.8	16.8
Rodriguez, Angel	R-R	6-2	175	10-25-04	.255	.354	.388	36	113	98	17	25	8	1	1	12	11	4	0	0	32	2	2	9.7	28.3
Rodriguez, Miguel	R-R	5-10	152	4-07-06	.261	.395	.319	22	86	69	8	18	2	1	0	11	13	3	0	1	7	4	2	15.1	8.1
Sequera, Joseph	R-R	6-0	185	12-12-05	.236	.337	.333	26	83	72	8	17	4	0	1	8	7	4	0	0	33	1	0	8.4	39.8
Tirado, Carlos	L-R	6-1	187	3-13-05	.236	.376	.354	43	157	127	23	30	7	1	2	17	26	3	0	1	42	1	1	16.6	26.8
Urbina, Fabian	L-R	5-8	175	10-25-01	.274	.400	.435	23	80	62	10	17	4	0	2	16	11	4	0	3	11	1	1	13.8	13.8
Van Der Linden, Joenelly	R-R	5-10	142	7-10-06	.169	.308	.185	25	80	65	6	11	1	0	0	6	11	2	2	0	24	2	3	13.8	30.0
Villafane, Andres	L-L	5-11	175	3-17-06	.133	.333	.167	13	39	30	3	4	1	0	0	1	8	1	0	0	4	1	1	20.5	10.3
Vittini, July	R-R	6-2	190	5-29-03	.215	.381	.338	24	84	65	11	14	2	0	2	9	17	1	0	1	12	0	1	20.2	14.3
Vizcaya, Ruben	R-R	5-9	155	9-30-03	.225	.348	.372	41	155	129	26	29	7	3	2	23	24	1	0	1	38	22	1	15.5	24.5
Zorrilla, John	R-R	6-1	173	5-23-04	.205	.365	.361	32	104	83	15	17	5	1	2	11	20	1	0	0	39	11	1	19.2	37.5

Pitching	B-T	Ht.	Wt.	DOB	W	L	ERA	G	GS	SV	IP	Hits	Runs	ER	HR	BB	SO	AVG	OBP	SLG	SO%	BB%	BF
Almonte, Keuri	L-L	6-2	190	10-16-05	2	1	3.04	16	1	1	27	14	10	9	2	24	30	.163	.360	.244	26.3	21.1	114
Blanco, Hader	L-L	5-11	150	2-14-05	3	0	4.86	17	0	0	33	31	20	18	2	23	27	.252	.380	.366	18.0	15.3	150
Cabreja, Victor	L-L	6-3	180	1-10-02	4	1	2.34	13	4	0	35	20	11	9	1	16	32	.168	.268	.202	23.2	11.6	138
Camacho, Angel	L-L	5-11	150	1-13-04	5	0	2.59	12	0	0	24	17	8	7	1	9	33	.195	.286	.287	33.7	9.2	98
Carreno, Nicolas	L-L	5-10	155	6-09-06	1	2	10.50	12	1	0	12	12	17	14	1	21	17	.267	.500	.400	25.0	30.9	68
Castillo, Carlos	R-R	6-1	165	2-04-06	0	3	1.70	11	11	0	37	25	12	7	0	15	40	.197	.292	.228	27.8	10.4	144
Chiquillo, Diego	L-L	5-11	185	12-09-02	1	0	6.75	8	0	2	11	12	10	8	1	8	13	.279	.404	.349	25.0	15.4	52
Clode, Jesus	R-R	6-2	180	8-28-01	0	0	2.57	6	0	2	14	7	6	4	0	5	8	.140	.267	.180	13.3	8.3	60
De La Paz, Jarlen	L-L	6-4	180	6-04-05	0	0	10.80	12	0	0	15	15	21	18	1	20	20	.273	.506	.436	24.1	24.1	83
Francia, Dariel	R-R	6-2	165	7-23-06	1	1	3.79	13	6	0	36	31	19	15	3	22	46	.233	.348	.368	29.1	13.9	158
Gomez, Ronal	L-L	6-3	140	2-09-06	0	1	108.00	1	1	0	0	2	4	4	0	2	1	.667	.800	1.333	20.0	40.0	5
Gonzalez, Luis C	L-L	6-0	160	11-19-01	1	3	7.53	13	0	1	14	17	15	12	2	11	14	.293	.423	.466	19.7	15.5	71
Hernandez, Yoerys	L-L	6-2	185	9-01-03	3	0	2.63	14	0	2	27	21	8	8	0	8	28	.212	.275	.283	25.7	7.3	109
Joseph, Luis	R-R	6-1	180	6-15-02	3	0	3.80	15	0	2	24	11	11	10	0	18	30	.141	.316	.167	30.6	18.4	98
Linares, Janderson	L-L	6-2	175	10-18-05	0	3	4.60	13	6	0	29	37	18	15	1	17	38	.316	.418	.402	27.0	12.1	141
Lobo, Inmer	L-L	6-1	193	2-12-04	0	0	1.62	8	6	0	17	13	5	3	0	6	17	.210	.279	.226	25.0	8.8	68
Martinez, Dioris	R-R	6-2	185	6-20-06	2	0	4.85	6	1	0	13	10	7	7	0	10	11	.227	.424	.227	18.6	16.9	59
Mateo, Carlos	R-R	6-2	185	10-25-05	1	6	18.75	13	7	0	12	18	28	25	0	30	18	.340	.593	.509	20.9	34.9	86
Matoma, David	R-R	6-0	154	2-02-06	4	0	0.00	9	1	0	17	12	0	0	0	7	14	.211	.297	.246	21.9	10.9	64
Mendez, Greiber	R-R	6-0	150	4-03-04	3	0	1.27	16	1	6	28	22	7	4	1	12	33	.214	.308	.320	28.0	10.2	118
Mendez, Rafael	R-R	6-3	170	8-14-02	6	0	6.65	18	0	5	22	28	20	16	0	19	30	.308	.425	.374	26.3	16.7	114
Ordonez, Dermis	R-R	6-1	170	9-05-04	3	1	7.22	16	3	0	29	29	26	23	0	24	31	.261	.407	.306	22.1	17.1	140
Orelin, Christopher	R-R	5-11	157	1-31-05	0	0	0.00	1	0	0	0	0	0	0	0	0	1	.000	.000	.000	100.0	0.0	1
Osoria, Yojeiry	L-L	6-1	188	1-24-03	1	0	0.71	8	6	1	25	11	4	2	0	9	32	.131	.255	.143	32.7	9.2	98
Oviedo, Adolfo	R-R	6-1	165	11-17-04	3	2	2.60	9	7	0	35	15	11	10	1	27	31	.136	.317	.200	22.3	19.4	139
Paulino, Isaac	R-R	5-11	160	3-10-05	0	0	0.00	1	0	0	0	3	3	0	1	0	0	.600	.600	1.400	0.0	0.0	5
Pichardo, Bladimir	R-R	6-3	193	10-24-05	0	3	3.67	10	8	0	27	16	16	11	1	21	23	.168	.333	.253	18.7	17.1	123
Pierre, Wali	R-R	6-3	180	4-24-03	2	2	6.55	18	0	0	22	30	21	16	1	18	21	.330	.447	.429	18.4	15.8	114
Polanco, Brandison	R-R	6-2	170	8-01-02	0	4	6.75	16	0	0	23	32	23	17	4	12	25	.330	.404	.536	21.7	10.4	115
Regalado, Jose	L-L	6-0	189	6-15-02	3	4	6.45	14	5	0	22	24	23	16	0	26	31	.282	.457	.365	26.7	22.4	116
Reyes, Francis	R-R	6-2	180	6-30-05	0	1	7.59	7	0	0	11	10	12	9	2	9	16	.244	.385	.415	30.8	17.3	52
Rosa, Pitterson	R-R	6-2	178	11-30-04	1	2	6.21	12	11	0	29	28	22	20	1	23	41	.259	.390	.380	30.1	16.9	136
Salazar, Jonathan	R-R	6-3	180	12-22-03	1	0	0.87	8	6	0	21	9	5	2	0	9	23	.129	.256	.157	28.0	11.0	82
Sanchez, Fares	R-R	6-1	170	6-09-04	0	1	6.23	3	0	0	4	7	5	3	0	4	4	.368	.500	.526	16.7	16.7	24

Tejada, Clevari	R-R	6-1	204	9-23-04	1	1	2.30	4	4	0	16	11	6	4	0	3	16	.196	.246	.286	26.2	4.9	61
Torres, Alexis	R-R	6-0	153	3-16-03	2	0	0.95	8	3	0	19	9	3	2	0	11	24	.136	.278	.136	30.4	13.9	79
Urbina, Fabian	L-R	5-8	175	10-25-01	0	0	0.00	1	0	0	1	0	0	0	0	0	0	.000	.000	.000	0.0	0.0	2
Valdez, Jonawel	R-R	6-1	185	3-19-04	0	3	5.56	12	5	0	34	41	28	21	1	16	32	.301	.372	.441	20.5	10.3	156
Valdez, Wilkin	R-R	6-5	210	7-14-01	0	0	27.00	2	0	0	1	1	3	3	0	4	1	.250	.625	.250	12.5	50.0	8
Vittini, July	R-R	6-2	190	5-29-03	0	0	0.00	1	0	0	1	2	0	0	0	1	1	.333	.429	.333	14.3	14.3	7
Zapata, Eduardo	R-R	6-2	160	8-27-03	1	1	12.96	16	0	0	17	24	30	24	1	23	15	.338	.500	.451	15.6	24.0	96

Fielding

C: Ramirez 32, Rivero 19, Vittini 19, Perez 17, Sequera 15, Escudero 6, Urbina 4. **1B:** Tirado 35, Escudero 30, Armas 14, Blanco 13, De Paula 11, Perez 6, Sequera 6, Vittini 3, Paulino 2, Machado 1. **2B:** Aguiar 31, Caro 16, Van Der Linden 16, Brioso 12, Pimentel 11, Machado 10, Paulino 9, Gimenez 8, Morales 4, Urbina 4, Nunez 1, Orelin 1. **3B:** Morales 32, Paulino 16, Orelin 14, Brioso 12, Caro 11, Gimenez 7, Zorrilla 7, Pimentel 6, Urbina 6, Van Der Linden 4, Aguiar 1. **SS:** Pimentel 23, Zorrilla 20, Aguiar 16, Brioso 13, Gimenez 12, Morales 12, Orelin 11, Caro 11, Van Der Linden 4. **OF:** Rodriguez 59, Oviedo 41, Vizcaya 41, Aquino 41, Machado 37, Jauregui 36, Nunez 29, Armas 19, De Paula 19, De La Cruz 17, Villafane 10, Gimenez 7, Tirado 5, Mola 4.

St. Louis Cardinals

ST. LOUIS CARDINALS

SEASON SYNOPSIS: A consensus preseason pick to win the NL Central, the Cardinals never got going, never got hot, never threatened to contend. At 71-91, they posted their first losing season since 2007 and most losses in a season since 1990.

HIGH POINT: The Cardinals showed signs of life in May, going 15-13 for the month and winning four consecutive series. They scored 27 runs in two games, finishing off a sweep at Fenway Park with a 9-1 win thanks to three home runs, then opened a home series by pounding Milwaukee 18-1 behind four homers and seven scoreless innings by Jack Flaherty. He struck out 10 in his best start of the season.

LOW POINT: The Cardinals signed former Cub Willson Contreras to a five-year, $87.5 million deal to take over for retired catcher Yadier Molina, but in the first week of May, they shifted him to DH, and on May 7, club president John Mozeliak clarified to reporters that Contreras was being moved out from behind the plate as the Cardinals tried to stem their poor start. The Cards seemed to be blaming their poor pitching start on Contreras, while Mozeliak called it more of a reset to the club's run prevention.

NOTABLE ROOKIES: Lefty Matthew Liberatore, acquired from the Rays two years ago for Randy Arozarena, failed to secure a rotation spot in his second chance. Outfielder Jordan Walker, the club's No. 1 prospect entering the year, hit 16 homers and showed he was ready offensively but was more mistake-prone than anticipated defensively. DH/OF Alec Burleson had his moments but posted a .691 OPS.

KEY TRANSACTIONS: The Cardinals hoped Flaherty would re-emerge as a healthy ace, but after 20 starts, he was traded to the Orioles. Lefty Jordan Montgomery was the team's best starter before being traded at the deadline to Texas; both deals netted prospects, led by infielder Thomas Saggese from the Rangers. Franchise stalwart Adam Wainwright posted a 7.40 ERA but picked up his 200th career victory in September. He was honored on the season's final day upon his retirement. His last appearance was as a pinch-hitter.

DOWN ON THE FARM: After finishing 30th in overall MiLB winning percentage in 2021, but then climbing to 19th in 2022, the Cardinals slid back to 22nd in 2023, posting a .478 winning percentage. The club's rookie-league teams were a combined 35 games under .500.

OPENING DAY PAYROLL: $175,637,308 (15th).

PLAYERS OF THE YEAR

MAJOR LEAGUE	MINOR LEAGUE
Paul Goldschmidt	**Masyn Winn**
1B	**SS**
.268/.363/.447	(AAA)
31 2B, 25 HR	.288/.359/.474
89 R, 80 RBI	18 HR, 17 SB

ORGANIZATION LEADERS

Batting		*Minimum 250 AB
MAJORS		
* AVG	Brendan Donovan	.284
* OPS	Willson Contreras	.826
HR	Nolan Gorman	27
RBI	Nolan Arenado	93
MINORS		
* AVG	Luken Baker, Memphis	.334
* OBP	Ivan Herrera, Memphis	.451
* SLG	Luken Baker, Memphis	.720
* OPS	Luken Baker, Memphis	1.159
R	Masyn Winn, Memphis	99
H	Victor Scott II, Peoria/Springf.	166
TB	Moises Gomez	235
2B	R.J. Yeager, Peoria/Springf.	30
2B	Chris Rotondo, Palm Beach/Peoria	30
3B	Victor Scott II, Peoria/Springf.	10
HR	Chandler Redmond, Springfield	31
RBI	Chandler Redmond, Springfield	92
BB	Arquimedes Gamboa, Springfield	89
SO	Moises Gomez	180
SB	Victor Scott II, Peoria/Springf.	95
Pitching		#Minimum 75 IP
MAJORS		
W	Miles Mikolas	9
# ERA	Jordan Montgomery	3.42
SO	Miles Mikolas	137
SV	Ryan Helsley	14
MINORS		
W	Michael McGreevy, Ark./Memphis	13
L	Trent Baker, Peoria	9
L	Brycen Mautz, Palm Beach	9
# ERA	Ian Bedell, Peoria	2.44
G	Andre Granillo, Ark./Memphis	53
GS	Michael McGreevy, Ark./Memphis	27
SV	Andre Granillo, Ark./Memphis	14
IP	Michael McGreevy, Ark./Memphis	153
BB	Wilfredo Pereira, Arkansas	53
SO	Pete Hansen, Palm Beach/Memphis	126
# AVG	Max Rajcic, P. Beach/Peoria	.216

2023 PERFORMANCE

General Manager: John Mozeliak. **Farm Director:** Gary LaRocque. **Scouting Director:** Randy Flores.

Class	Team	League	W	L	PCT	Finish	Manager
Majors	St. Louis Cardinals	National	71	91	.438	13 (15)	Oliver Marmol
Triple-A	Memphis Redbirds	International	71	78	.477	11 (20)	Ben Johnson
Double-A	Springfield Cardinals	Texas	72	66	.522	3 (10)	Jose Leger
High-A	Peoria Chiefs	Midwest	69	63	.523	5 (12)	Patrick Anderson
Low-A	Palm Beach Cardinals	Florida State	64	63	.504	6 (10)	Gary Kendall
Rookie	FCL Cardinals	Florida Complex	17	33	.340	14 (15)	Roberto Espinoza
Rookie	DSL Cardinals	Dominican Sum.	17	36	.321	45 (50)	Fray Peniche
Overall 2023 Minor League Record			310	339	.478	22nd (30)	

ORGANIZATION STATISTICS

ST. LOUIS CARDINALS

NATIONAL LEAGUE

Batting	B-T	Ht.	Wt.	DOB	AVG	OBP	SLG	G	PA	AB	R	H	2B	3B	HR	RBI	BB	HBP	SH	SF	SO	SB	CS	BB%	SO%
Arenado, Nolan	R-R	6-2	215	4-16-91	.266	.315	.459	144	612	560	71	149	26	2	26	93	41	3	0	8	101	3	3	6.7	16.5
Baker, Luken	R-R	6-4	280	3-10-97	.209	.313	.314	33	99	86	9	18	3	0	2	10	13	0	0	0	31	0	0	13.1	31.3
Barrera, Tres	R-R	6-0	215	9-15-94	.000	.000	.000	6	2	2	0	0	0	0	0	0	0	0	0	0	0	0	0	0.0	0.0
Burleson, Alec	L-L	6-2	212	11-25-98	.244	.300	.390	107	347	315	34	77	20	1	8	36	23	3	1	2	45	3	1	6.6	13.0
Carlson, Dylan	B-L	6-2	205	10-23-98	.219	.318	.333	76	255	219	27	48	8	1	5	27	26	7	0	3	49	3	0	10.2	19.2
Contreras, Willson	R-R	6-1	225	5-13-92	.264	.358	.467	125	495	428	55	113	27	0	20	67	51	13	1	2	111	6	3	10.3	22.4
DeJong, Paul	R-R	6-0	205	8-02-93	.233	.297	.412	81	306	279	38	65	11	0	13	32	21	5	0	1	87	4	4	6.9	28.4
2-team (18 San Francisco)					.226	.282	.393	99	356	328	40	74	13	0	14	37	21	5	0	2	103	4	4	5.9	28.9
Donovan, Brendan	L-R	6-1	195	1-16-97	.284	.365	.422	95	371	327	48	93	10	1	11	34	33	9	1	1	53	5	1	8.9	14.3
Edman, Tommy	B-R	5-10	180	5-09-95	.248	.307	.399	137	528	479	69	119	25	4	13	47	35	7	3	4	84	27	4	6.6	15.9
Fermin, Jose	R-R	5-9	200	3-29-99	.235	.339	.255	21	61	51	2	12	1	0	0	4	6	2	2	0	8	0	1	9.8	13.1
Goldschmidt, Paul	R-R	6-3	220	9-10-87	.268	.363	.447	154	687	593	89	159	31	0	25	80	87	3	0	3	161	11	2	12.7	23.4
Gorman, Nolan	L-R	6-1	210	5-10-00	.236	.328	.478	119	464	406	59	96	17	0	27	76	53	3	0	2	148	7	2	11.4	31.9
Herrera, Ivan	R-R	5-11	220	6-01-00	.297	.409	.351	13	44	37	6	11	2	0	0	4	5	2	0	0	11	0	0	11.4	25.0
Knizner, Andrew	R-R	6-1	225	2-03-95	.241	.288	.424	70	241	224	30	54	11	0	10	31	12	3	1	1	62	2	0	5.0	25.7
Lopez, Irving	L-R	5-7	175	6-30-95	.000	.000	.000	5	12	11	0	0	0	0	0	1	0	0	0	1	5	0	0	0.0	41.7
Mercado, Oscar	R-R	6-2	197	12-16-94	.290	.313	.387	20	32	31	3	9	3	0	0	5	1	0	0	0	4	2	1	3.1	12.5
Motter, Taylor	R-R	6-1	195	9-18-89	.171	.232	.211	29	82	76	3	13	3	0	0	2	5	1	0	0	31	0	0	6.1	37.8
Nootbaar, Lars	L-R	6-3	210	9-08-97	.261	.367	.418	117	503	426	74	111	23	1	14	46	72	1	1	3	99	11	1	14.3	19.7
O'Neill, Tyler	R-R	5-11	200	6-22-95	.231	.312	.403	72	266	238	27	55	14	0	9	21	28	0	0	0	67	5	0	10.5	25.2
Palacios, Richie	L-R	5-10	180	5-16-97	.258	.307	.516	32	102	93	9	24	6	0	6	16	6	1	1	1	11	2	0	5.9	10.8
Querecuto, Juniel	B-R	5-9	195	9-19-92	.100	.143	.150	9	21	20	2	2	1	0	0	0	1	0	0	0	6	0	0	4.8	28.6
Siani, Michael	L-L	6-1	188	7-16-00	.000	.000	.000	5	5	5	0	0	0	0	0	0	0	0	0	0	1	1	0	0.0	20.0
Wainwright, Adam	R-R	6-7	230	8-30-81	.000	.000	.000	23	2	2	0	0	0	0	0	0	0	0	0	0	1	0	0	0.0	50.0
Walker, Jordan	R-R	6-6	245	5-22-02	.276	.342	.445	117	465	420	51	116	19	2	16	51	37	6	0	2	104	7	4	8.0	22.4
Winn, Masyn	R-R	5-11	180	3-21-02	.172	.230	.238	37	137	122	8	21	2	0	2	12	10	0	2	3	26	2	1	7.3	19.0
Yepez, Juan	R-R	6-1	200	2-19-98	.183	.246	.300	28	65	60	5	11	1	0	2	2	4	1	0	0	20	0	1	6.2	30.8

Pitching	B-T	Ht.	Wt.	DOB	W	L	ERA	G	GS	SV	IP	Hits	Runs	ER	HR	BB	SO	AVG	OBP	SLG	SO%	BB%	BF
Barnes, Jacob	R-R	6-2	231	4-14-90	0	1	5.93	13	0	0	14	18	11	9	1	3	8	.316	.361	.474	13.1	4.9	61
Burleson, Alec	L-L	6-2	212	11-25-98	0	0	21.60	2	0	0	2	8	4	4	1	0	1	.615	.615	.846	7.7	0.0	13
Cabrera, Genesis	L-L	6-2	180	10-10-96	1	1	5.06	32	0	0	32	32	18	18	6	18	38	.258	.352	.460	26.6	12.6	143
Flaherty, Jack	R-R	6-4	225	10-15-95	7	6	4.43	20	20	0	110	116	56	54	10	54	106	.278	.368	.427	21.9	11.1	485
Gallegos, Giovanny	R-R	6-2	215	8-14-91	2	4	4.42	56	0	10	55	54	28	27	11	12	59	.252	.291	.467	25.8	5.2	229
Helsley, Ryan	R-R	6-2	230	7-18-94	3	4	2.45	33	0	14	37	22	11	10	1	17	52	.176	.274	.264	35.6	11.6	146
Hicks, Jordan	R-R	6-2	220	9-06-96	1	6	3.67	40	0	8	42	39	21	17	2	24	59	.244	.349	.338	31.2	12.7	189
Hudson, Dakota	R-R	6-5	215	9-15-94	6	3	4.98	18	12	0	81	88	46	45	9	34	45	.283	.363	.441	12.7	9.6	354
King, John	L-L	6-2	215	9-14-94	1	0	1.45	20	0	0	19	19	3	3	1	6	10	.275	.333	.348	13.2	7.9	76
Lawrence, Casey	R-R	6-0	180	10-28-87	1	0	6.59	15	0	0	27	32	20	20	7	10	20	.299	.364	.589	16.4	8.2	122
Leahy, Kyle	B-R	6-5	200	6-04-97	0	1	21.60	3	0	0	2	4	4	4	1	5	2	.444	.667	1.111	13.3	33.3	15
Liberatore, Matthew	L-L	6-4	200	11-06-99	3	6	5.25	22	11	0	62	66	42	36	5	25	46	.274	.349	.444	16.7	9.1	275
Matz, Steven	R-L	6-2	201	5-29-91	4	7	3.86	25	17	0	105	108	48	45	11	32	98	.263	.320	.405	21.8	7.1	449
Mikolas, Miles	R-R	6-4	230	8-23-88	9	13	4.78	35	35	0	201	226	110	107	26	39	137	.282	.319	.454	15.9	4.5	860
Montgomery, Jordan	L-L	6-6	228	12-27-92	6	9	3.42	21	21	0	121	116	54	46	12	35	108	.250	.306	.414	21.2	6.9	509
Naile, James	R-R	6-4	185	2-08-93	0	0	8.80	10	0	0	15	27	19	15	1	9	7	.380	.450	.479	8.8	11.3	80
Naughton, Packy	R-L	6-2	195	4-16-96	0	0	0.00	4	0	0	5	2	0	0	0	1	5	.125	.176	.188	29.4	5.9	17
Pallante, Andre	R-R	6-0	203	9-18-98	4	1	4.76	62	0	0	68	76	37	36	6	30	43	.286	.362	.414	14.2	9.9	302
Rom, Drew	L-L	6-2	215	12-15-99	1	4	8.02	8	8	0	34	51	34	30	7	19	32	.340	.412	.613	18.8	11.2	170
Romero, JoJo	L-L	5-11	200	9-09-96	4	2	3.68	27	0	3	37	29	17	15	1	10	42	.216	.274	.299	28.6	6.8	147
Stratton, Chris	R-R	6-2	205	8-22-90	1	1	4.19	42	0	1	54	45	28	25	4	17	59	.226	.286	.372	26.7	7.7	221
Suarez, Andrew	L-L	6-0	202	9-11-92	0	0	7.16	13	0	0	28	33	27	22	7	15	17	.287	.369	.557	13.1	11.5	130
Tepera, Ryan	R-R	6-1	195	11-03-87	0	0	9.00	2	0	0	2	3	2	2	1	1	1	.333	.455	.667	9.1	9.1	11
Thompson, Zack	L-L	6-2	215	10-28-97	5	7	4.48	25	9	0	66	69	35	33	8	25	72	.270	.336	.422	25.1	8.7	287
VerHagen, Drew	R-R	6-6	230	10-22-90	5	1	3.98	60	0	0	61	52	30	27	9	26	60	.226	.325	.396	22.4	9.7	268

Name	B-T	Ht.	Wt.	DOB	W	L	ERA	G	GS	SV	IP	Hits	Runs	ER	HR	BB	SO	AVG	OBP	SLG	SO%	BB%	BF
Wainwright, Adam	R-R	6-7	230	8-30-81	5	11	7.40	21	21	0	101	151	89	83	20	41	55	.345	.400	.573	11.4	8.5	484
Woodford, Jake	R-R	6-4	215	10-28-96	2	3	6.23	15	8	0	48	61	34	33	11	22	29	.314	.387	.572	13.1	9.9	222
Zuniga, Guillermo	R-R	6-5	230	10-10-98	0	0	4.50	2	0	0	2	2	1	1	0	0	4	.250	.250	.375	50.0	0.0	8

Fielding

Catcher	PCT	G	PO	A	E	DP	PB
Barrera	1.000	6	12	0	0	0	0
Contreras	.989	97	679	31	8	5	5
Herrera	1.000	13	76	6	0	0	0
Knizner	.998	68	471	21	1	5	3

First Base	PCT	G	PO	A	E	DP
Baker	1.000	12	53	3	0	7
Burleson	1.000	17	115	9	0	8
Donovan	1.000	14	84	7	0	10
Goldschmidt	.998	133	1048	115	2	122
Knizner	1.000	1	1	0	0	0
Motter	1.000	1	2	0	0	0
Querecuto	1.000	2	5	0	0	0

Second Base	PCT	G	PO	A	E	DP
Donovan	.976	34	52	72	3	19
Edman	.986	51	94	122	3	34
Fermin	.976	10	13	28	1	2
Gorman	.984	75	109	195	5	50
Lopez	1.000	2	1	0	0	1
Motter	1.000	14	16	31	0	10
Palacios	1.000	1	2	2	0	1
Querecuto	.917	2	4	7	1	1

Third Base	PCT	G	PO	A	E	DP
Arenado	.973	128	62	264	9	31
Donovan	1.000	6	1	7	0	0
Fermin	.960	8	8	16	1	3
Gorman	.968	18	2	28	1	5
Lopez	.857	3	1	5	1	0
Motter	.947	12	3	15	1	1
Querecuto	1.000	5	4	10	0	1

Shortstop	PCT	G	PO	A	E	DP
DeJong	.990	81	93	196	3	37
Donovan	1.000	1	4	4	0	2
Edman	.977	48	66	143	5	33
Motter	1.000	3	5	4	0	0
Winn	.980	37	54	90	3	25

Outfield	PCT	G	PO	A	E	DP
Burleson	1.000	57	76	5	0	0
Carlson	.996	75	141	1	1	0
Donovan	1.000	30	31	3	0	1
Edman	1.000	50	124	3	0	1
Mercado	.963	19	25	0	2	0
Motter	.000	1	0	0	0	0
Nootbaar	.993	131	268	6	2	2
O'Neill	.989	71	108	5	2	0
Palacios	.968	27	41	2	2	0
Siani	1.000	3	3	0	0	0
Walker	.972	112	188	8	5	0
Yepez	1.000	12	13	1	0	0

MEMPHIS REDBIRDS — TRIPLE-A

INTERNATIONAL LEAGUE

Batting	B-T	Ht.	Wt.	DOB	AVG	OBP	SLG	G	PA	AB	R	H	2B	3B	HR	RBI	BB	HBP	SH	SF	SO	SB	CS	BB%	SO%
Antonini, Aaron	L-R	6-0	200	7-27-98	.206	.391	.382	10	46	34	7	7	1	1	1	9	6	5	0	1	13	1	0	13.0	28.3
Baker, Luken	R-R	6-4	280	3-10-97	.334	.439	.720	84	380	314	71	105	22	0	33	98	59	3	0	4	76	0	0	15.5	20.0
Barrera, Tres	R-R	6-0	215	9-15-94	.213	.306	.343	60	245	216	28	46	7	0	7	33	26	3	0	0	49	1	1	10.6	20.0
Carlson, Dylan	B-L	6-2	205	10-23-98	.333	.500	.444	3	12	9	2	3	1	0	0	1	3	0	0	0	0	0	0	25.0	0.0
DeJong, Paul	R-R	6-0	205	8-02-93	.353	.450	.618	9	40	34	9	12	3	0	2	14	5	1	0	0	12	0	0	12.5	30.0
Dunn, Nick	L-R	5-8	185	1-29-97	.302	.404	.385	51	225	192	28	58	10	0	2	20	32	1	0	0	26	0	0	14.2	11.6
Edman, Tommy	B-R	5-10	180	5-09-95	.250	.250	.250	2	8	8	2	2	0	0	0	1	0	0	0	0	3	0	0	0.0	37.5
Fermin, Jose	R-R	5-9	200	3-29-99	.227	.358	.485	20	81	66	16	15	3	1	4	7	12	2	0	1	5	1	0	14.8	6.2
Gomez, Moises	R-R	5-11	200	8-27-98	.232	.293	.457	131	567	514	77	119	20	3	30	79	39	8	0	6	180	5	1	6.9	31.7
Herrera, Ivan	R-R	5-11	220	6-01-00	.297	.451	.500	83	375	290	66	86	27	1	10	60	75	8	0	2	77	11	2	20.0	20.5
Hurst, Scott	L-R	5-9	175	3-25-96	.133	.278	.133	10	36	30	2	4	0	0	0	2	5	1	0	0	12	4	0	13.9	33.3
Koperniak, Matt	L-R	6-0	200	2-08-98	.275	.353	.431	96	422	371	56	102	12	2	14	67	44	3	0	4	61	9	1	10.4	14.5
Lopez, Irving	L-R	5-7	175	6-30-95	.315	.464	.537	19	69	54	12	17	6	0	2	10	14	1	0	0	12	0	0	20.3	17.4
Mercado, Oscar	R-R	6-2	197	12-16-94	.278	.361	.421	34	145	126	18	35	12	0	2	12	14	3	1	1	28	15	3	9.7	19.3
Moore, Brody	R-R	5-11	183	7-20-00	.000	.000	.000	1	3	3	0	0	0	0	0	0	0	0	0	0	1	0	0	0.0	33.3
Motter, Taylor	R-R	6-1	195	9-18-89	.255	.343	.438	56	236	208	31	53	12	1	8	26	27	1	0	0	59	8	1	11.4	25.0
Nootbaar, Lars	L-R	6-3	210	9-08-97	.467	.500	.933	4	16	15	4	7	1	0	2	5	1	0	0	0	2	0	0	6.3	12.5
O'Neill, Tyler	R-R	5-11	200	6-22-95	.231	.355	.269	8	31	26	4	6	1	0	0	3	5	0	0	0	7	0	0	16.1	22.6
Palacios, Richie	L-R	5-10	180	5-16-97	.299	.418	.459	40	195	157	34	47	10	0	5	29	32	2	1	3	20	3	2	16.4	10.3
2-team (56 Columbus)					.251	.383	.377	96	464	374	76	94	23	0	8	59	73	8	2	7	61	9	6	15.7	13.1
Pinder, Chase	R-R	5-10	185	3-16-96	.265	.401	.417	75	279	223	43	59	16	0	6	34	48	4	2	2	66	8	3	17.2	23.7
Prieto, Cesar	L-R	5-9	175	5-10-99	.270	.314	.387	38	176	163	24	44	5	1	4	20	7	4	1	1	25	2	0	4.0	14.2
2-team (27 Norfolk)					.288	.337	.419	65	291	267	40	77	13	2	6	40	15	5	1	3	35	4	1	5.2	12.0
Querecuto, Juniel	B-R	5-9	195	9-19-92	.269	.343	.418	106	440	390	53	105	15	2	13	57	40	5	3	2	101	12	1	9.1	23.0
Raposo, Nick	R-R	5-10	200	6-03-98	.232	.324	.368	27	108	95	14	22	4	0	3	8	12	1	0	0	16	0	0	11.1	14.8
Robertson, Kramer	R-R	5-10	166	9-20-94	.205	.356	.262	121	510	409	73	84	14	0	3	37	81	16	1	3	115	23	4	15.9	22.5
Robinson, Errol	R-R	5-10	170	10-01-94	.222	.338	.286	39	148	126	12	28	6	1	0	13	21	1	0	0	39	5	2	14.2	26.4
Saggese, Thomas	R-R	5-11	175	4-10-02	.207	.270	.345	13	63	58	9	12	5	0	1	4	3	2	0	0	14	1	0	4.8	22.2
Siani, Michael	L-L	6-1	188	7-16-99	.226	.385	.290	10	39	31	6	7	2	0	0	1	7	1	0	0	8	1	0	17.9	20.5
2-team (108 Louisville)					.225	.345	.345	126	499	414	70	93	17	3	9	48	77	1	3	4	118	24	5	15.4	23.6
Toerner, Justin	L-L	5-9	185	8-11-96	.156	.250	.469	9	36	32	4	5	1	0	3	6	3	1	0	0	12	1	0	8.3	33.3
Walker, Jordan	R-R	6-6	245	5-22-02	.239	.348	.398	29	135	113	14	27	6	0	4	16	16	4	0	2	32	4	0	11.9	23.7
Winn, Masyn	R-R	5-11	180	3-21-02	.288	.359	.474	105	498	445	99	128	15	7	18	61	44	7	0	2	83	17	2	8.8	16.7
Yepez, Juan	R-R	6-1	200	2-19-98	.255	.323	.413	86	384	341	44	87	21	3	9	69	33	4	0	6	73	2	2	8.6	19.0

Pitching	B-T	Ht.	Wt.	DOB	W	L	ERA	G	GS	SV	IP	Hits	Runs	ER	HR	BB	SO	AVG	OBP	SLG	SO%	BB%	BF
Barnes, Jacob	R-R	6-2	231	4-14-90	0	1	1.53	11	0	1	18	12	4	3	1	8	16	.190	.282	.254	22.5	11.3	71
Black, Grant	R-R	6-5	225	7-21-94	2	8	6.61	43	3	0	79	102	65	58	14	48	71	.311	.406	.509	18.5	12.5	383
Cabrera, Genesis	L-L	6-2	180	10-10-96	0	0	0.00	3	0	1	3	1	0	0	0	2	0	.091	.231	.182	0.0	15.4	13
Graceffo, Gordon	R-R	6-4	210	3-17-00	4	3	4.92	21	18	0	86	87	50	47	9	45	81	.261	.347	.420	20.9	11.6	387
Gragg, Logan	R-R	6-5	200	8-08-98	3	0	0.50	4	2	1	18	6	2	1	0	6	12	.105	.203	.123	18.8	9.4	64
Granillo, Andre	R-R	6-4	245	5-12-00	0	0	6.08	9	0	0	13	10	11	9	2	13	17	.196	.369	.353	26.2	20.0	65
Hansen, Pete	R-L	6-2	205	7-28-00	0	0	0.00	1	0	0	1	0	0	0	0	0	0	.000	.000	.000	0.0	0.0	3
Helsley, Ryan	R-R	6-2	230	7-18-94	0	0	0.00	1	0	0	0	1	0	0	0	1	0	.500	.667	1.000	0.0	33.3	3
Hudson, Dakota	R-R	6-5	215	9-15-94	5	4	6.00	11	11	0	48	72	39	32	5	17	39	.355	.409	.542	17.3	7.6	225
Kloffenstein, Adam	R-R	6-5	243	8-25-00	2	1	3.00	9	8	0	39	29	13	13	6	21	35	.209	.333	.388	21.2	12.7	165
Komar, Brandon	R-R	6-0	200	5-08-99	0	1	17.18	1	1	0	4	7	7	7	2	2	5	.368	.429	.737	23.8	9.5	21
Lawrence, Casey	R-R	6-0	180	10-28-87	1	1	5.40	3	3	0	13	17	10	8	3	2	9	.315	.362	.537	15.5	3.4	58
Leahy, Kyle	B-R	6-5	200	6-04-97	5	4	6.26	46	4	0	83	104	66	58	15	39	92	.304	.378	.532	23.8	10.1	386

ST. LOUIS CARDINALS

Liberatore, Matthew	L-L	6-4	200	11-06-99	4	3	4.18	13	13	0	65	58	32	30	8	38	84	.243	.350	.397	29.7	13.4	283
Loutos, Ryan	R-R	6-5	215	1-29-99	2	4	6.40	48	0	1	72	97	54	51	7	39	83	.323	.401	.467	24.1	11.3	344
Martinez, Jose	R-R	6-0	194	4-23-99	0	1	0.00	2	0	1	5	0	1	0	0	5	1	.000	.316	.000	5.0	25.0	20
McGreevy, Michael	L-R	6-4	215	7-08-00	11	6	4.49	24	24	0	134	160	71	67	17	37	107	.291	.338	.445	18.0	6.2	593
Naile, James	R-R	6-4	185	2-08-93	5	3	3.66	31	3	3	59	60	26	24	6	21	66	.267	.340	.382	26.4	8.4	250
Naughton, Packy	R-L	6-2	195	4-16-96	0	0	0.00	1	0	0	0	0	0	0	0	1	0	.000	1.000	.000	0.0	50.0	2
Pallante, Andre	R-R	6-0	203	9-18-98	0	0	2.79	5	0	0	10	5	5	3	0	2	14	.143	.184	.171	36.8	5.3	38
Parsons, Tommy	R-R	6-4	220	9-01-95	1	6	7.30	19	14	0	74	95	66	60	22	31	53	.306	.372	.626	15.4	9.0	344
Roach, Dalton	R-R	6-2	210	4-08-96	1	4	3.77	38	0	5	60	50	29	25	12	23	57	.230	.309	.456	23.1	9.3	247
Robberse, Sem	R-R	6-1	185	10-12-01	2	1	4.84	8	7	0	35	39	21	19	6	24	44	.279	.395	.486	26.2	14.3	168
Rodriguez, Wilking	R-R	6-1	180	3-02-90	0	0	0.00	7	0	0	6	5	3	0	0	2	6	.238	.304	.238	26.1	8.7	23
Rom, Drew	L-L	6-2	215	12-15-99	2	0	0.82	2	2	0	11	2	2	1	1	4	18	.056	.171	.139	43.9	9.8	41
Romero, JoJo	L-L	5-11	200	9-09-96	2	1	3.00	17	0	2	21	19	8	7	3	9	33	.241	.318	.380	37.5	10.2	88
Roycroft, Chris	R-R	6-8	230	6-21-97	5	5	4.83	22	0	1	32	29	22	17	2	25	35	.240	.387	.355	23.3	16.7	150
Sawyer, Logan	R-R	6-5	215	12-29-92	0	0	12.46	6	0	0	4	7	6	6	0	6	2	.389	.542	.389	8.3	25.0	24
Suarez, Andrew	L-L	6-0	202	9-11-92	4	2	4.08	28	3	0	64	70	32	29	6	25	69	.273	.338	.387	24.5	8.9	282
Thomas, Connor	L-L	5-11	173	5-29-98	5	4	5.53	21	17	1	94	134	64	58	10	31	69	.335	.384	.495	15.7	7.0	440
Thompson, Zack	L-L	6-2	215	10-28-97	1	4	8.65	11	9	0	34	42	34	33	5	39	41	.311	.472	.511	22.9	21.8	179
Wainwright, Adam	R-R	6-7	230	8-30-81	1	0	6.35	1	1	0	6	7	4	4	1	1	9	.292	.320	.458	36.0	4.0	25
Walsh, Jake	R-R	6-1	192	7-20-95	2	2	5.28	27	0	4	31	28	21	18	5	23	34	.248	.376	.434	23.9	16.2	142
Whitley, Kodi	R-R	6-3	220	2-21-95	1	5	5.19	32	0	3	43	55	28	25	8	13	48	.314	.359	.531	24.7	6.7	194
Woodford, Jake	R-R	6-4	215	10-28-96	0	2	2.61	7	6	0	21	15	7	6	3	10	23	.195	.311	.351	25.6	11.1	90
Zuniga, Guillermo	R-R	6-5	230	10-10-98	0	2	7.63	29	0	5	31	32	27	26	6	20	37	.262	.377	.549	25.3	13.7	146

Fielding

Catcher	PCT	G	PO	A	E	DP	PB
Antonini	1.000	8	68	1	0	0	1
Barrera	.994	54	452	18	3	3	0
Crooks	.000	1	0	0	0	0	1
Herrera	.991	64	594	35	6	2	5
Raposo	.992	24	216	19	2	5	3

First Base	PCT	G	PO	A	E	DP
Baker	.991	74	609	37	6	75
Barrera	1.000	6	37	2	0	3
Lopez	1.000	2	7	1	0	0
Motter	.984	23	169	16	3	24
Querecuto	1.000	18	106	10	0	15
Yepez	.991	31	191	20	2	21

Second Base	PCT	G	PO	A	E	DP
Dunn	.985	15	25	42	1	13
Fermin	1.000	7	4	23	0	4
Lopez	1.000	4	8	11	0	3
Moore	1.000	1	0	2	0	0
Motter	1.000	3	10	13	0	2
Prieto	.965	22	27	56	3	15
Querecuto	.994	37	56	97	1	30
Robertson	.986	28	61	78	2	30
Saggese	.951	9	19	20	2	2
Winn	.984	26	49	77	2	27

Third Base	PCT	G	PO	A	E	DP
Dunn	.889	22	13	27	5	1
Fermin	1.000	5	4	2	0	1
Lopez	.917	5	3	8	1	2
Motter	.917	16	10	34	4	8
Prieto	.905	12	4	15	2	0
Querecuto	.857	11	5	13	3	2
Robertson	.951	44	31	67	5	5
Robinson	.975	34	23	56	2	4
Saggese	.889	2	4	4	1	1

Shortstop	PCT	G	PO	A	E	DP
DeJong	1.000	7	5	19	0	3
Edman	.750	1	3	0	1	0
Fermin	.947	6	11	25	2	4
Motter	.921	9	14	21	3	7
Querecuto	.983	13	22	35	1	12
Robertson	.982	37	57	106	3	19
Saggese	1.000	2	3	5	0	1
Winn	.982	76	108	225	6	63

Outfield	PCT	G	PO	A	E	DP
Carlson	.500	2	2	1	0	1
Edman	.000	1	0	0	0	0
Gomez	.964	102	132	5	6	0
Hurst	.611	9	11	0	1	0
Koperniak	.992	89	178	3	1	2
Lopez	1.000	3	2	1	0	0
Mercado	.994	33	84	2	1	1
Motter	1.000	1	5	0	0	0
Nootbaar	1.000	3	3	0	0	0
O'Neill	.500	4	6	0	0	0
Palacios	.970	38	97	0	3	0
Pinder	.995	75	152	4	1	0
Querecuto	.986	21	37	1	1	1
Robertson	1.000	3	6	0	0	0
Robinson	.333	4	3	0	0	0
Siani	1.000	10	16	1	0	0
Toerner	1.000	9	21	0	0	0
Walker	1.000	26	53	2	0	0
Yepez	.974	37	42	5	2	0

SPRINGFIELD CARDINALS — DOUBLE-A

TEXAS LEAGUE

Batting	B-T	Ht.	Wt.	DOB	AVG	OBP	SLG	G	PA	AB	R	H	2B	3B	HR	RBI	BB	HBP	SH	SF	SO	SB	CS	BB%	SO%
Alvarez, Jose	R-R	6-1	180	6-04-00	.256	.318	.285	84	309	281	42	72	8	0	0	32	24	2	1	1	54	6	3	7.8	17.5
Antico, Mike	L-R	5-10	200	2-16-98	.265	.350	.447	127	545	476	86	126	23	5	18	72	54	10	2	3	126	52	8	9.9	23.1
Antonini, Aaron	L-R	6-0	200	7-27-98	.255	.336	.451	31	117	102	11	26	5	0	5	25	8	5	1	1	33	2	1	6.8	28.2
Buchberger, Jacob	R-R	6-0	215	10-01-97	.239	.322	.416	117	447	397	67	95	12	2	18	49	44	5	0	1	101	13	5	9.8	22.6
Dunn, Nick	L-R	5-8	185	1-29-97	.332	.420	.483	73	312	265	53	88	15	2	7	40	41	2	0	4	31	2	6	13.1	9.9
Gamboa, Arquimedes	B-R	5-11	190	9-23-97	.243	.372	.366	133	545	448	86	109	18	5	9	70	89	5	0	3	136	25	4	16.3	25.0
Jones, L.J.	R-R	6-0	225	6-27-99	.223	.277	.359	73	279	256	28	57	11	0	8	42	18	2	0	2	49	0	1	6.5	17.6
Koperniak, Matt	L-R	6-0	200	2-08-98	.320	.386	.453	33	145	128	19	41	3	1	4	18	15	0	0	2	27	2	5	10.3	18.6
Lopez, Irving	L-R	5-7	175	6-30-95	.248	.344	.393	78	277	234	29	58	11	1	7	43	29	7	4	3	54	0	0	10.5	19.5
Lott, Todd	R-R	6-3	235	8-22-97	.167	.444	.167	3	9	6	1	1	0	0	0	0	3	0	0	0	1	0	0	33.3	11.1
Mendlinger, Noah	L-R	5-9	180	8-09-00	.299	.422	.393	95	401	321	61	96	16	1	4	49	55	16	5	4	43	5	5	13.7	10.7
Nootbaar, Lars	L-R	6-3	210	9-08-97	.000	.000	.000	1	5	5	0	0	0	0	0	1	0	0	0	0	2	0	0	0.0	40.0
Pages, Pedro	R-R	6-1	234	9-17-98	.267	.362	.443	117	497	424	63	113	23	2	16	72	59	8	0	6	96	3	0	11.9	19.3
Pinder, Chase	R-R	5-10	185	3-16-96	.250	.400	.500	4	15	12	2	3	0	0	1	2	3	0	0	0	2	0	0	20.0	13.3
Raposo, Nick	R-R	5-10	200	6-03-98	.260	.315	.420	13	54	50	8	13	3	1	1	5	4	0	0	0	9	0	0	7.4	16.7
Redmond, Chandler	L-R	6-1	231	1-09-97	.256	.375	.503	132	550	453	88	116	19	0	31	92	81	8	0	5	167	3	2	14.7	30.4
Robinson, Errol	R-R	5-10	170	10-01-94	.233	.301	.295	41	143	129	19	30	2	0	2	13	10	3	0	1	40	4	0	7.0	28.0
Saggese, Thomas	R-R	5-11	175	4-10-02	.331	.403	.662	33	149	130	25	43	7	3	10	29	15	2	0	2	34	3	0	10.1	22.8
2-team (93 Frisco)					.318	.391	.551	126	567	497	92	158	29	6	25	107	49	11	1	9	130	11	2	8.6	22.9
Scott, Victor	L-L	5-10	190	2-12-01	.323	.373	.450	66	310	282	51	91	11	2	7	34	18	6	2	2	45	44	7	5.8	14.5
Stauss, Wade	L-R	6-2	225	4-04-99	.184	.308	.263	28	91	76	10	14	3	0	1	8	8	6	0	1	36	0	0	8.8	39.6
Toerner, Justin	L-L	5-9	185	8-11-96	.160	.325	.275	42	167	131	21	21	4	1	3	13	31	2	1	2	43	3	0	18.6	25.7

Pitching	B-T	Ht.	Wt.	DOB	W	L	ERA	G	GS	SV	IP	Hits	Runs	ER	HR	BB	SO	AVG	OBP	SLG	SO%	BB%	BF
Cornwell, Alex	L-L	6-0	202	5-09-99	2	1	2.70	7	7	0	37	35	14	11	2	8	31	.254	.297	.355	20.9	5.4	148
Escobar, Edgar	R-R	6-1	220	1-20-97	7	2	4.82	25	7	0	65	62	38	35	7	36	55	.258	.357	.433	19.4	12.7	284
Garcia, Roy	R-R	6-0	190	8-28-00	2	2	8.46	18	0	1	22	30	26	21	2	16	27	.319	.434	.468	23.9	14.2	113
Gragg, Logan	R-R	6-5	200	8-08-98	3	7	5.74	23	17	0	107	121	70	68	22	42	90	.286	.363	.499	18.9	8.8	476
Granillo, Andre	R-R	6-4	245	5-12-00	3	4	4.42	44	0	14	55	42	33	27	6	25	72	.209	.294	.333	31.2	10.8	231
Helsley, Ryan	R-R	6-2	230	7-18-94	0	0	9.00	4	0	0	4	7	4	4	1	1	4	.368	.400	.579	20.0	5.0	20
Hence, Tink	R-R	6-1	185	8-06-02	2	5	5.47	12	12	0	54	60	37	33	8	22	53	.283	.354	.472	22.2	9.2	239
Hernandez, Kenny	L-L	6-1	197	6-24-98	7	2	5.96	15	14	0	74	85	52	49	5	32	67	.295	.364	.427	20.4	9.7	329
Komar, Brandon	R-R	6-0	200	5-08-99	4	6	4.62	24	21	0	123	119	66	63	15	44	86	.259	.325	.412	16.8	8.6	511
Lopez, Irving	L-R	5-7	175	6-30-95	0	0	0.00	1	0	0	0	1	0	0	0	0	0	.500	.500	.500	0.0	0.0	2
Loutos, Ryan	R-R	6-5	215	1-29-99	0	1	13.50	2	0	0	1	1	2	2	0	2	1	.250	.571	.250	12.5	25.0	8
Lunn, Connor	R-R	6-3	215	7-08-98	7	7	4.71	25	23	1	130	150	72	68	17	31	111	.290	.329	.478	20.0	5.6	554
Manzo, Edgar	R-R	5-11	181	10-24-00	0	0	0.00	1	0	0	3	1	0	0	0	0	5	.125	.125	.125	55.6	0.0	9
Martinez, Jose	R-R	6-0	194	4-23-99	3	2	5.80	29	1	0	54	64	43	35	7	43	24	.295	.421	.465	9.0	16.0	268
McGreevy, Michael	L-R	6-4	215	7-08-00	2	0	1.45	3	3	0	19	17	4	3	0	1	16	.246	.268	.304	22.5	1.4	71
Pereira, Wilfredo	R-R	6-0	197	4-26-99	10	8	4.97	26	24	0	138	138	84	76	18	53	104	.263	.341	.419	17.6	9.0	591
Pope, Bryan	R-R	6-2	195	1-27-99	2	2	4.22	24	0	0	32	42	23	15	4	14	32	.318	.381	.462	20.6	9.0	155
Ralston, Jack	R-R	6-6	231	8-13-97	0	0	8.31	17	0	2	17	12	16	16	0	20	17	.207	.415	.276	20.7	24.4	82
Roach, Dalton	R-R	6-2	210	4-08-96	0	2	8.71	7	0	0	10	13	10	10	3	6	14	.295	.380	.523	28.0	12.0	50
Roby, Tekoah	R-R	6-1	185	9-18-01	0	0	3.00	4	4	0	12	6	4	4	1	3	19	.146	.205	.293	43.2	6.8	44
Roycroft, Chris	R-R	6-8	230	6-21-97	2	3	8.55	15	0	1	20	28	22	19	1	14	14	.326	.426	.500	13.9	13.9	101
Sawyer, Logan	R-R	6-5	215	12-29-92	5	3	5.21	38	0	7	48	54	29	28	4	17	59	.278	.346	.448	27.4	7.9	215
Shreve, Ryan	R-R	6-6	215	6-23-98	4	4	4.54	44	0	0	71	73	36	36	12	27	63	.264	.328	.435	20.4	8.7	309
Svanson, Matt	R-R	6-5	235	1-31-99	2	0	3.00	15	0	5	21	18	10	7	0	5	25	.243	.313	.297	29.1	5.8	86
Trogrlic-Iverson, Nick	R-R	6-1	175	10-03-97	4	5	4.87	41	0	0	65	69	48	35	7	29	55	.273	.363	.447	18.6	9.8	296
VerHagen, Drew	R-R	6-6	230	10-22-90	0	0	9.00	1	0	0	1	1	1	1	0	0	1	.333	.250	.667	25.0	0.0	4
Wainwright, Adam	R-R	6-7	230	8-30-81	0	0	6.14	2	2	0	7	11	5	5	1	1	4	.344	.364	.625	12.1	3.0	33
Woodford, Jake	R-R	6-4	215	10-28-96	1	0	3.38	3	3	0	8	5	3	3	2	1	11	.172	.200	.414	36.7	3.3	30

Fielding

Catcher	PCT	G	PO	A	E	DP	PB
Alvarez	.966	26	153	17	6	2	3
Antonini	.981	15	101	4	2	0	1
Pages	.992	87	673	64	6	4	4
Raposo	.969	9	86	8	3	0	2
Stauss	1.000	13	71	6	0	1	1

First Base	PCT	G	PO	A	E	DP
Alvarez	1.000	3	5	0	0	0
Buchberger	.000	2	0	0	0	0
Jones	.993	24	134	11	1	15
Redmond	.992	122	888	65	8	89

Second Base	PCT	G	PO	A	E	DP
Dunn	.976	60	90	151	6	42
Gamboa	1.000	1	5	3	0	2
Lopez	.993	35	70	74	1	21
Mendlinger	.969	8	15	16	1	3
Robinson	.967	12	27	31	2	10
Saggese	.964	24	51	56	4	15

Third Base	PCT	G	PO	A	E	DP
Buchberger	.941	97	54	184	15	14
Lopez	.979	15	16	31	1	4
Mendlinger	.959	16	12	35	2	3
Robinson	.893	14	7	18	3	2
Saggese	.960	5	6	18	1	2

Shortstop	PCT	G	PO	A	E	DP
Gamboa	.966	130	191	320	18	63
Lopez	1.000	5	16	15	0	6
Robinson	.905	6	7	12	2	4
Saggese	.857	2	2	4	1	0

Outfield	PCT	G	PO	A	E	DP
Alvarez	.975	56	100	10	2	1
Antico	.984	125	264	3	6	2
Buchberger	1.000	2	2	0	0	0
Jones	.960	20	24	0	1	0
Koperniak	.990	36	43	3	1	0
Lopez	1.000	20	24	0	0	0
Lott	.000	2	0	0	0	0
Mendlinger	.995	73	128	4	1	1
Pinder	1.000	2	4	2	0	0
Robinson	1.000	7	10	3	0	0
Scott	.995	63	187	3	1	0
Toerner	.667	44	77	2	0	0

PEORIA CHIEFS

HIGH CLASS A

MIDWEST LEAGUE

Batting	B-T	Ht.	Wt.	DOB	AVG	OBP	SLG	G	PA	AB	R	H	2B	3B	HR	RBI	BB	HBP	SH	SF	SO	SB	CS	BB%	SO%
Cabell, Elijah	R-R	6-1	223	6-30-99	.109	.246	.145	36	130	110	14	12	1	0	1	6	13	7	0	0	69	2	2	10.0	53.1
Church, Nathan	L-L	5-10	180	7-12-00	.279	.364	.360	119	518	455	65	127	24	2	3	44	46	15	1	1	60	21	12	8.9	11.6
Crooks, Jimmy	L-R	6-1	210	7-19-01	.271	.358	.433	114	477	413	71	112	29	1	12	73	52	6	2	4	101	2	1	10.9	21.2
Francisco, Thomas	L-R	6-0	211	6-26-99	.231	.281	.327	105	389	355	32	82	20	1	4	40	24	3	0	6	63	3	4	6.2	16.2
Hernandez, Francisco	R-R	5-11	190	10-08-99	.215	.268	.325	74	224	209	32	45	8	3	3	18	15	0	0	0	65	8	4	6.7	29.0
Hernandez, Maikel	B-R	6-0	163	2-20-03	.000	.000	.000	2	2	2	0	0	0	0	0	0	0	0	0	0	0	0	0	0.0	0.0
Iadisernia, Alex	L-L	5-10	180	10-11-00	.221	.315	.405	59	254	222	34	49	10	2	9	30	26	5	0	1	62	17	8	10.2	24.4
Kretzschmar, Kade	L-R	6-2	205	6-09-00	.200	.200	.400	3	10	10	2	2	0	1	0	0	0	0	0	0	6	1	0	0.0	60.0
Linarez, Carlos	R-R	6-0	170	10-24-01	.281	.343	.281	11	35	32	4	9	0	0	0	1	3	0	0	0	12	0	0	8.6	34.3
McKeithan, Aaron	R-R	6-1	220	12-13-99	.266	.375	.353	63	256	207	25	55	3	0	5	35	28	13	0	8	33	2	1	10.9	12.9
Mendlinger, Noah	L-R	5-9	180	8-09-00	.250	.446	.400	16	57	40	9	10	1	1	1	6	10	5	1	1	8	2	3	17.5	14.0
Mendoza, Ramon	R-R	5-11	174	8-31-00	.275	.360	.421	72	277	233	33	64	14	1	6	35	30	4	5	5	56	2	3	10.8	20.2
Moore, Brody	R-R	5-11	183	7-20-00	.212	.292	.307	39	154	137	6	29	8	1	1	10	14	2	0	1	36	9	4	9.1	23.4
Moquete, Darlin	R-R	5-8	175	9-19-99	.205	.280	.369	61	223	195	34	40	6	1	8	20	17	4	5	2	47	5	2	7.6	21.1
Reichenborn, Tyler	R-R	5-9	180	7-23-98	.236	.347	.433	55	153	127	17	30	5	1	6	18	20	2	3	1	34	3	3	13.1	22.2
Rivas, Jeremy	R-R	6-0	172	3-04-03	.209	.293	.277	115	453	397	45	83	18	0	3	39	45	4	2	5	101	22	5	9.9	22.3
Rodriguez, Luis	R-R	6-0	175	2-26-00	.165	.224	.227	33	107	97	7	16	4	1	0	9	6	2	0	2	31	0	0	5.6	29.0
Romeri, Patrick	R-R	6-3	195	6-29-01	.206	.229	.353	10	35	34	6	7	2	0	1	2	1	0	0	0	15	0	0	2.9	42.9
Rotondo, Chris	R-R	6-0	200	6-15-99	.277	.398	.489	39	167	137	22	38	12	1	5	28	21	7	1	1	40	10	0	12.6	24.0
Scott, Victor	L-L	5-10	190	2-12-01	.282	.365	.398	66	308	266	44	75	9	8	2	29	28	9	1	4	52	50	7	9.1	16.9
Stauss, Wade	L-R	6-2	225	4-04-99	.500	.500	.500	1	4	4	1	2	0	0	0	0	0	0	0	0	0	0	0	0.0	0.0
Tovalin, Osvaldo	L-R	6-2	225	10-31-99	.239	.290	.357	117	466	431	50	103	24	3	7	62	19	13	0	3	79	8	3	4.1	17.0
Yeager, R.J.	R-R	6-2	200	10-02-98	.283	.356	.446	60	262	233	41	66	12	1	8	27	21	6	1	1	39	12	2	8.0	14.9

Pitching	B-T	Ht.	Wt.	DOB	W	L	ERA	G	GS	SV	IP	Hits	Runs	ER	HR	BB	SO	AVG	OBP	SLG	SO%	BB%	BF
Arias, Benjamin	R-R	6-5	195	11-05-01	0	1	10.80	1	1	0	5	9	6	6	1	2	4	.375	.423	.583	15.4	7.7	26
Baker, Trent	R-R	6-3	243	12-28-98	7	9	3.69	23	22	0	120	110	56	49	11	26	105	.236	.282	.361	21.1	5.2	497
Bedell, Ian	R-R	6-2	214	9-05-99	4	2	2.44	27	19	0	96	76	32	26	7	34	106	.218	.298	.319	27.2	8.7	389
Cornwell, Alex	L-L	6-0	202	5-09-99	5	2	2.94	15	13	0	83	87	33	27	4	15	71	.268	.305	.369	20.6	4.4	344
Garcia, Roy	R-R	6-0	190	8-28-00	5	1	1.88	15	0	4	24	15	7	5	0	7	32	.174	.237	.186	34.4	7.5	93
Gerard, Chris	R-L	5-10	175	11-23-99	0	0	0.00	2	0	0	4	5	4	0	1	0	3	.294	.333	.471	16.7	0.0	18
Hence, Tink	R-R	6-1	185	8-06-02	2	1	2.81	11	11	0	42	34	14	13	4	12	46	.224	.285	.316	27.9	7.3	165
Heredia, Nathanael	L-L	6-3	190	9-10-00	0	1	4.54	23	0	1	38	32	20	19	3	20	26	.237	.362	.341	16.0	12.3	163
Hickey, Matt	L-R	5-11	169	5-11-98	2	4	4.26	27	0	5	44	45	24	21	2	13	35	.265	.344	.376	18.0	6.7	194
Hjerpe, Cooper	L-L	6-3	200	3-16-01	2	3	3.51	10	8	0	41	26	17	16	8	25	51	.183	.322	.387	29.8	14.6	171
King, Joseph	R-R	6-1	194	2-23-01	5	2	3.40	17	1	0	40	41	17	15	4	8	30	.273	.310	.420	19.0	5.1	158
Love, Austin	R-R	6-3	232	1-26-99	0	1	6.23	2	2	0	9	9	6	6	0	3	10	.273	.351	.394	26.3	7.9	38
Manzo, Edgar	R-R	5-11	181	10-24-00	4	3	5.14	30	4	0	70	80	49	40	7	20	49	.289	.347	.433	16.2	6.6	303
Marrero, Andrew	R-R	5-10	196	5-08-00	4	8	4.05	38	0	11	60	45	42	27	9	38	85	.207	.341	.373	31.6	14.1	269
Mills, Zane	R-R	6-4	220	7-04-00	7	6	5.63	23	18	0	93	110	66	58	13	25	65	.293	.339	.489	15.7	6.0	414
Nunez, Edwin	R-R	6-3	185	11-05-01	3	1	3.22	22	0	5	36	33	18	13	4	16	30	.236	.316	.400	19.0	10.1	158
Paniagua, Inohan	R-R	6-1	148	2-06-00	0	3	4.47	11	11	0	44	33	23	22	3	27	41	.208	.342	.308	20.8	13.7	197
Pope, Bryan	R-R	6-2	195	1-27-99	2	1	1.95	15	0	0	32	25	10	7	2	10	38	.212	.279	.288	29.5	7.8	129
Rajcic, Max	R-R	6-0	210	8-03-01	3	3	3.08	11	11	0	61	57	23	21	2	18	55	.251	.315	.317	21.9	7.2	251
Ralston, Jack	R-R	6-6	231	8-13-97	1	1	1.89	13	0	1	19	10	5	4	1	11	31	.156	.286	.234	40.3	14.3	77
Rodriguez, Dionys	L-R	6-0	188	9-03-00	3	4	4.61	30	11	0	80	75	43	41	7	52	59	.248	.364	.384	16.2	14.2	365
Rodriguez, Gustavo J.	R-R	6-3	160	1-08-01	8	4	4.81	38	0	2	67	64	37	36	7	38	70	.250	.352	.414	23.3	12.6	301
Roycroft, Chris	R-R	6-8	230	6-21-97	0	0	3.97	9	0	3	11	8	5	5	0	2	15	.195	.233	.293	34.9	4.7	43
Ruiz, Alfredo	L-L	6-0	200	3-12-00	1	1	4.71	17	0	0	21	21	13	11	1	18	22	.259	.398	.370	21.4	17.5	103
Taveras, Leonardo	R-R	6-5	190	9-07-98	1	1	3.10	11	0	2	20	11	10	7	3	8	38	.153	.274	.306	45.2	9.5	84

Fielding

Catcher	PCT	G	PO	A	E	DP	PB
Crooks	.989	90	772	59	9	4	9
Linarez	1.000	11	68	7	0	0	1
McKeithan	1.000	11	91	3	0	1	1
Rodriguez	.995	25	183	15	1	1	4
Stauss	1.000	1	12	1	0	0	0

First Base	PCT	G	PO	A	E	DP
Francisco	.998	69	492	24	1	44
Hernandez	1.000	1	2	0	0	0
Rodriguez	.979	8	44	3	1	6
Tovalin	.961	8	46	3	2	3
Yeager	.991	52	398	27	4	51

Second Base	PCT	G	PO	A	E	DP
Hernandez	.962	61	99	152	10	39
Mendlinger	.946	9	14	21	2	3
Mendoza	.994	38	58	102	1	16
Moore	.943	24	29	54	5	13
Moquete	.941	3	7	9	1	5
Rivas	1.000	8	9	16	0	4

Third Base	PCT	G	PO	A	E	DP
Mendlinger	.947	7	7	11	1	0
Mendoza	.964	21	22	31	2	4
Tovalin	.933	104	77	145	16	16
Yeager	1.000	9	7	14	0	3

Shortstop	PCT	G	PO	A	E	DP
Mendoza	1.000	11	21	25	0	8
Moore	.941	15	20	28	3	8
Rivas	.957	107	146	272	19	55

Outfield	PCT	G	PO	A	E	DP
Cabell	.952	25	39	1	2	1
Church	.989	113	238	9	4	2
Hernandez	.000	1	0	0	0	0
Iadisernia	.997	59	132	4	1	2
Kretzschmar	.000	1	0	0	0	0
Moquete	.995	46	75	4	1	0
Reichenborn	.954	49	72	1	3	0
Romeri	1.000	9	13	0	0	0
Rotondo	.667	39	76	4	0	1
Scott	.988	66	159	2	2	0
Tovalin	.000	1	0	0	0	0

PALM BEACH CARDINALS

LOW CLASS A

FLORIDA STATE LEAGUE

Batting	B-T	Ht.	Wt.	DOB	AVG	OBP	SLG	G	PA	AB	R	H	2B	3B	HR	RBI	BB	HBP	SH	SF	SO	SB	CS	BB%	SO%
Adkison, Chase	R-R	6-0	205	6-05-00	.333	.367	.381	16	49	42	9	14	2	0	0	7	4	0	0	3	8	0	0	8.2	16.3
Baez, Joshua	R-R	6-3	220	6-28-03	.218	.341	.383	91	358	298	54	65	20	4	7	36	45	12	0	3	122	30	2	12.6	34.1
Bernal, Leonardo	B-R	6-0	200	2-13-04	.265	.381	.362	78	323	268	45	71	15	1	3	44	49	3	0	3	55	4	1	15.2	17.0
Bolivar, Javier	R-R	6-2	170	12-19-02	.125	.258	.196	22	67	56	4	7	1	0	1	3	9	1	1	0	34	0	0	13.4	50.7
Burns, Jake	L-R	6-0	199	2-17-03	.059	.111	.059	8	18	17	1	1	0	0	0	0	1	0	0	0	9	0	0	5.6	50.0
Cho, Won-Bin	L-L	6-1	200	8-20-03	.270	.376	.389	105	452	378	64	102	14	5	7	52	64	4	0	6	98	32	11	14.2	21.7
Cordoba, Jose	R-R	5-11	165	1-03-03	.270	.372	.378	11	44	37	7	10	2	1	0	2	4	2	1	0	7	0	0	9.1	15.9
Cruz, Adanson	R-R	6-0	175	10-06-00	.239	.337	.303	45	166	142	13	34	9	0	0	17	17	5	0	2	40	5	2	10.2	24.1
Curialle, Michael	R-R	6-1	199	6-16-01	.282	.392	.397	110	457	380	66	107	28	5	2	57	51	21	0	5	108	10	7	11.2	23.6
Davis, Chase	L-L	6-1	216	12-05-01	.212	.366	.269	34	131	104	15	22	6	0	0	23	25	1	0	1	34	3	0	19.1	26.0
DeJong, Paul	R-R	6-0	205	8-02-93	.111	.111	.111	3	9	9	1	1	0	0	0	2	0	0	0	0	3	0	0	0.0	33.3
Espinoza, Lizandro	R-R	5-7	158	11-20-02	.184	.272	.290	107	413	359	41	66	15	1	7	47	39	6	5	4	106	13	7	9.4	25.7
Fermin, Jose	R-R	5-9	200	3-29-99	.200	.304	.400	5	23	20	3	4	1	0	1	2	3	0	0	0	0	1	0	13.0	0.0
Fletcher, Tre	R-R	6-0	200	4-30-01	.205	.259	.295	21	86	78	8	16	3	2	0	9	5	1	0	1	40	5	2	5.8	46.5
Friedrick, Ross	L-R	6-4	230	11-26-00	.583	.615	.833	6	13	12	3	7	0	0	1	5	1	0	0	0	0	0	0	7.7	0.0
Harris, Dakota	B-R	6-0	197	2-19-02	.220	.307	.320	31	115	100	15	22	7	0	1	21	8	5	1	1	26	4	0	7.0	22.6
Hernandez, Brandon	L-R	5-11	190	8-21-01	.223	.324	.264	51	172	148	15	33	6	0	0	10	22	0	2	0	42	0	2	12.8	24.4
Hernandez, Sammy	R-R	5-9	185	6-01-04	.212	.350	.303	10	40	33	6	7	0	0	1	7	7	0	0	0	8	0	0	17.5	20.0
Iadisernia, Alex	L-L	5-10	180	10-11-00	.246	.347	.468	52	237	203	38	50	12	3	9	31	28	4	1	1	42	8	0	11.8	17.7
Jobert, Brayden	L-R	6-1	215	11-14-00	.189	.330	.300	32	112	90	16	17	2	1	2	12	15	5	0	2	34	6	1	13.4	30.4
Kretzschmar, Kade	L-R	6-2	205	6-09-00	.333	.457	.453	26	92	75	12	25	4	1	1	11	13	4	0	0	16	3	1	14.1	17.4
Levenson, Zach	R-R	6-2	210	3-06-02	.268	.331	.480	34	139	123	24	33	6	1	6	22	12	1	0	3	32	2	1	8.6	23.0
Linarez, Carlos	R-R	6-0	170	10-24-01	.226	.306	.330	34	122	106	7	24	6	1	1	14	9	4	1	2	36	1	0	7.4	29.5
Mejia, Jonathan	B-R	5-11	185	4-12-05	.107	.242	.143	11	33	28	3	3	1	0	0	2	4	1	0	0	10	1	0	12.1	30.3
Moore, Brody	R-R	5-11	183	7-20-00	.211	.318	.246	15	66	57	6	12	0	1	0	5	9	0	0	0	23	2	0	13.6	34.8
Moquete, Darlin	R-R	5-8	175	9-19-99	.247	.340	.383	24	94	81	11	20	3	1	2	8	11	1	0	1	12	3	2	11.7	12.8
Paige, Trey	L-R	6-0	215	11-09-00	.104	.246	.104	21	61	48	5	5	0	0	0	8	8	2	0	3	15	0	0	13.1	24.6
Richardson, Tre	R-R	5-10	165	12-02-01	.241	.365	.329	26	96	79	16	19	5	1	0	3	14	2	0	1	18	7	1	14.6	18.8

Rotondo, Chris	R-R	6-0	200	6-15-99	.245	.387	.385	77	332	265	55	65	18	5	3	30	50	13	1	3	75	8	0	15.1	22.6
Sullivan, William	L-R	6-3	205	11-25-00	.308	.395	.433	32	119	104	14	32	6	2	1	16	15	0	0	0	24	2	1	12.6	20.2
Tarlow, Graysen	R-R	5-11	190	7-07-01	.200	.390	.333	20	59	45	7	9	3	0	1	10	11	3	0	0	9	0	0	18.6	15.3
Yeager, R.J.	R-R	6-2	200	10-02-98	.296	.392	.471	66	283	240	44	71	18	3	6	38	33	7	0	3	36	5	0	11.7	12.7
Zapata, Jose	R-R	5-11	195	2-14-01	.196	.230	.268	21	61	56	3	11	1	0	1	6	3	0	0	2	29	0	0	4.9	47.5

Pitching	B-T	Ht.	Wt.	DOB	W	L	ERA	G	GS	SV	IP	Hits	Runs	ER	HR	BB	SO	AVG	OBP	SLG	SO%	BB%	BF
Arias, Benjamin	R-R	6-5	195	11-05-01	3	4	4.04	10	8	0	42	38	25	19	7	21	39	.238	.324	.400	21.1	11.4	185
Arnold, Chandler	R-R	6-2	189	11-19-99	0	2	7.23	16	0	0	19	21	17	15	2	24	23	.288	.475	.466	23.0	24.0	100
Bradt, Tyler	R-R	5-11	196	2-11-01	1	1	6.17	11	0	0	12	11	10	8	2	14	8	.250	.433	.455	13.3	23.3	60
Brettell, Michael	R-R	6-3	195	7-13-97	0	1	4.32	6	0	0	8	9	4	4	0	2	5	.290	.368	.387	13.2	5.3	38
Calderon, Augusto	R-R	6-0	190	10-06-00	2	0	5.62	22	0	0	42	34	29	26	3	23	43	.215	.335	.335	22.5	12.0	191
Cuenca, Angel	R-R	6-1	160	7-10-01	3	1	5.47	31	0	1	53	53	34	32	8	18	54	.257	.313	.442	23.8	7.9	227
Davila, Jose	R-R	6-3	177	11-09-02	2	3	5.69	20	10	2	74	81	49	47	2	31	71	.273	.351	.374	21.3	9.3	333
Garcia, Roy	R-R	6-0	190	8-28-00	1	1	2.04	10	0	4	18	15	5	4	1	12	20	.242	.355	.371	26.3	15.8	76
Gastelum, Luis	R-R	6-2	168	9-27-01	1	0	4.00	7	0	0	9	14	8	4	2	1	6	.359	.381	.615	14.0	2.3	43
Gerard, Chris	R-L	5-10	175	11-23-99	2	0	0.00	7	0	0	13	4	0	0	0	5	12	.103	.222	.103	26.7	11.1	45
Gomez, Henry	R-R	6-1	163	10-17-01	1	5	4.91	22	0	3	37	32	26	20	5	21	28	.229	.347	.393	16.7	12.5	168
Hansen, Pete	R-L	6-2	205	7-28-00	11	3	3.12	23	23	0	113	92	39	39	10	39	126	.220	.290	.346	27.1	8.4	465
Hayes, Hunter	R-R	6-1	185	8-05-00	3	3	3.69	20	5	3	61	64	33	25	5	24	48	.270	.338	.397	18.0	9.0	267
Henderson, Ixan	L-L	6-2	180	1-29-02	0	0	0.00	4	0	0	4	1	0	0	0	4	5	.091	.313	.091	31.3	25.0	16
Heredia, Nathanael	L-L	6-3	190	9-10-00	1	0	0.00	2	0	0	3	0	0	0	0	1	2	.000	.125	.000	25.0	12.5	8
Jacobson, Tanner	R-R	6-1	190	1-24-00	4	2	4.19	35	0	5	54	46	31	25	4	28	74	.224	.325	.346	30.8	11.7	240
King, Joseph	R-R	6-1	194	2-23-01	2	3	5.71	19	4	3	52	60	36	33	9	14	51	.288	.332	.476	22.6	6.2	226
Lin, Chen-Wei	R-R	6-7	188	11-22-01	0	3	7.71	4	4	0	12	13	10	10	2	11	17	.271	.407	.458	28.8	18.6	59
Lynch, John	L-L	5-11	190	4-17-01	0	0	13.50	19	0	0	15	27	25	23	0	25	12	.386	.561	.443	12.2	25.5	98
Mautz, Brycen	L-L	6-3	190	7-17-01	4	9	3.98	23	23	0	104	94	54	46	4	45	115	.237	.326	.336	25.2	9.9	456
Nunez, Edwin	R-R	6-3	185	11-05-01	3	3	3.62	19	0	5	27	23	17	11	1	14	35	.219	.317	.333	29.2	11.7	120
Ortega, Wilmer	R-R	6-1	169	4-04-01	1	1	6.35	12	0	0	17	15	16	12	2	13	15	.250	.385	.433	19.2	16.7	78
Rajcic, Max	R-R	6-0	210	8-03-01	6	3	1.89	12	12	0	62	41	14	13	4	9	68	.183	.228	.286	28.6	3.8	238
Rincon, Hancel	R-R	6-2	160	4-28-02	9	6	3.26	24	23	0	133	109	59	48	12	20	97	.219	.260	.343	18.2	3.8	533
Rodriguez, Gustavo J.	R-R	6-3	160	1-08-01	0	0	6.00	2	0	0	3	4	2	2	0	0	5	.308	.308	.538	38.5	0.0	13
Saladin, Darlin	R-R	5-11	150	12-28-02	0	1	9.00	1	0	0	2	2	2	2	0	2	3	.250	.400	.500	30.0	20.0	10
Salas, Gerado	R-R	6-0	189	2-14-03	0	0	8.71	3	2	0	10	15	11	10	1	6	13	.349	.431	.558	25.0	11.5	52
Savacool, Jason	R-R	6-1	210	5-21-02	0	0	9.53	4	0	0	6	3	6	6	2	5	6	.167	.348	.500	26.1	21.7	23
Showalter, Zack	R-R	6-2	195	1-23-04	0	0	0.00	1	0	0	1	0	0	0	0	1	1	.000	.250	.000	25.0	25.0	4
Villanueva, Victor	R-R	6-1	170	3-26-01	1	1	24.30	4	0	0	3	6	9	9	2	4	2	.375	.524	.750	9.5	19.0	21
Winquest, Cade	R-R	6-2	205	4-30-00	3	7	4.87	24	13	0	78	70	47	42	6	35	81	.241	.331	.364	24.2	10.4	335

Fielding

Catcher	PCT	G	PO	A	E	DP	PB
Adkison	.992	16	112	6	1	1	5
Bernal	.991	64	513	50	5	4	7
Burns	1.000	3	4	0	0	0	0
Hernandez	.989	9	85	6	1	1	0
Linarez	1.000	28	210	33	0	1	4
Tarlow	.992	18	122	6	1	1	1
Zapata	1.000	7	27	1	0	0	0

First Base	PCT	G	PO	A	E	DP
Bolivar	1.000	6	31	1	0	3
Burns	.909	2	9	1	1	1
Cruz	.972	16	92	11	3	11
Friedrick	1.000	6	20	0	0	1
Jobert	.992	17	118	3	1	9
Linarez	.974	4	36	2	1	6
Sullivan	.982	28	162	3	3	14
Yeager	.990	62	458	24	5	41

Second Base	PCT	G	PO	A	E	DP
Bolivar	1.000	11	16	30	0	7
Espinoza	.958	28	52	63	5	19
Fermin	1.000	3	2	1	0	0
Hernandez	.972	45	61	114	5	28
Moore	.909	6	6	14	2	1
Moquete	.924	18	28	33	5	6
Paige	1.000	8	8	10	0	2
Richardson	.921	25	26	44	6	7

Third Base	PCT	G	PO	A	E	DP
Bolivar	.667	2	0	2	1	0
Curialle	.930	106	67	131	15	10
Hernandez	.929	6	5	8	1	0
Jobert	.800	5	1	7	2	1
Linarez	.000	1	0	0	0	0
Paige	.967	13	6	23	1	6
Yeager	.833	4	2	3	1	1

Shortstop	PCT	G	PO	A	E	DP
Bolivar	1.000	2	2	7	0	1
DeJong	1.000	1	1	1	0	0
Espinoza	.952	80	142	176	16	36
Fermin	1.000	1	3	3	0	0
Harris	.923	30	32	64	8	13
Mejia	.935	10	11	32	3	4
Moore	.956	8	13	30	2	5

Outfield	PCT	G	PO	A	E	DP
Baez	.975	51	94	4	5	0
Cho	.984	103	177	7	3	2
Cordoba	1.000	10	16	2	0	1
Cruz	.982	30	54	1	2	0
Davis	.972	28	69	0	2	0
Fletcher	.649	21	39	2	2	0
Iadisernia	.938	48	74	2	2	1
Jobert	.944	7	10	0	1	0
Kretzschmar	.500	15	19	0	0	0
Levenson	1.000	28	38	1	0	0
Rotondo	.992	64	145	5	1	2

FCL CARDINALS — *ROOKIE*

FLORIDA COMPLEX LEAGUE

Batting	B-T	Ht.	Wt.	DOB	AVG	OBP	SLG	G	PA	AB	R	H	2B	3B	HR	RBI	BB	HBP	SH	SF	SO	SB	CS	BB%	SO%
Bolivar, Javier	R-R	6-2	170	12-19-02	.000	.333	.000	11	18	11	4	0	0	0	0	2	3	3	0	1	4	2	1	16.7	22.2
Burns, Jake	L-R	6-0	199	2-17-03	.500	.667	.667	4	9	6	1	3	1	0	0	1	3	0	0	0	1	0	0	33.3	11.1
Cabrera, Romtres	R-R	6-0	182	9-13-03	.205	.372	.301	32	94	73	7	15	4	0	1	11	15	5	0	1	28	5	0	16.0	29.8
Cordoba, Jose	R-R	5-11	165	1-03-03	.367	.414	.532	24	87	79	14	29	6	2	1	13	7	0	0	1	15	4	2	8.0	17.2
De La Rosa, Samil	R-R	5-8	175	9-24-03	.250	.403	.339	18	72	56	4	14	2	0	1	8	10	5	0	1	12	2	1	13.9	16.7
Diaz, Fernando	L-R	6-3	185	1-12-02	.133	.212	.233	11	33	30	2	4	0	0	1	4	3	0	0	0	12	0	0	9.1	36.4
Encarnacion, Anyelo	R-R	5-11	164	1-02-04	.205	.333	.339	36	136	112	19	23	5	2	2	14	19	3	1	1	36	6	1	14.0	26.5
Fermin, Jose	R-R	5-9	200	3-29-99	.176	.263	.235	5	19	17	1	3	1	0	0	1	2	0	0	0	3	1	0	10.5	15.8
Grant, Adari	R-R	5-8	163	1-02-04	.237	.395	.320	33	124	97	16	23	6	1	0	6	18	8	0	1	17	3	3	14.5	13.7
Guerrero, Justin	R-R	6-1	195	5-20-03	.244	.352	.422	18	54	45	6	11	2	0	2	7	7	1	0	1	12	1	0	13.0	22.2
Guerrero, Yancel	R-R	6-1	169	4-16-04	.214	.304	.306	31	112	98	21	21	5	2	0	8	8	5	0	1	37	4	1	7.1	33.0
Guzman, Raul	R-R	5-11	180	9-14-02	.208	.418	.417	23	67	48	12	10	1	0	3	6	16	2	0	1	22	2	0	23.9	32.8

Batting	B-T	Ht.	Wt.	DOB	AVG	OBP	SLG	G	PA	AB	R	H	2B	3B	HR	RBI	BB	HBP	SH	SF	SO	SB	CS	BB%	SO%
Heredia, Roblin	L-R	6-0	200	7-22-02	.056	.217	.056	12	23	18	1	1	0	0	0	1	4	0	0	1	9	0	0	17.4	39.1
Hernandez, Maikel	B-R	6-0	163	2-20-03	.268	.411	.321	25	73	56	5	15	3	0	0	7	14	1	0	2	10	0	0	19.2	13.7
Hernandez, Sammy	R-R	5-9	185	6-01-04	.250	.429	.750	6	21	16	4	4	0	1	2	4	5	0	0	0	2	0	0	23.8	9.5
2-team (14 FCL Blue Jays)2-team (14 FCL Blue Jays)					.216	.313	.387	58	228	199	37	43	8	4	6	26	20	8	0	1	51	1	0	8.8	22.4
Loaiza, Alejandro	R-R	5-11	163	12-23-03	.130	.200	.391	14	25	23	3	3	0	0	2	2	2	0	0	0	14	0	0	8.0	56.0
Lott, Todd	R-R	6-3	235	8-22-97	.125	.313	.167	8	32	24	3	3	1	0	0	4	7	0	0	1	4	1	1	21.9	12.5
Mejia, Jonathan	B-R	5-11	185	4-12-05	.173	.331	.288	30	131	104	16	18	0	3	2	8	24	1	0	1	37	7	1	18.3	28.2
Moore, Brody	R-R	5-11	183	7-20-00	.222	.462	.333	3	13	9	3	2	1	0	0	1	4	0	0	0	1	1	1	30.8	7.7
Pino, Luis	R-R	5-10	175	2-07-04	.205	.370	.346	27	100	78	14	16	5	0	2	14	14	7	0	1	31	5	0	14.0	31.0
Ramos, Jeremy	R-R	6-3	173	4-04-03	.159	.275	.341	21	51	44	11	7	2	0	2	4	5	2	0	0	23	3	0	9.8	45.1
Ramos, Yaisel	R-R	6-4	185	2-20-03	.211	.305	.342	37	132	114	13	24	4	1	3	18	13	3	1	1	42	4	1	9.8	31.8
Rodriguez, Luis	R-R	6-1	210	10-07-04	.221	.308	.316	29	107	95	10	21	9	0	0	12	9	3	0	0	32	0	1	8.4	29.9
Suarez, Jose	R-R	6-2	200	8-09-04	.200	.290	.339	33	131	115	18	23	2	1	4	21	12	3	0	1	42	1	2	9.2	32.1
Taveras, Felix	L-R	6-1	186	3-08-03	.302	.402	.427	28	112	96	17	29	5	2	1	16	13	3	0	0	22	3	1	11.6	19.6
Vargas, Miguel	L-L	6-0	176	3-14-04	.123	.283	.198	31	99	81	7	10	3	0	1	9	18	0	0	0	32	2	0	18.2	32.3

Pitching	B-T	Ht.	Wt.	DOB	W	L	ERA	G	GS	SV	IP	Hits	Runs	ER	HR	BB	SO	AVG	OBP	SLG	SO%	BB%	BF
Arias, Benjamin	R-R	6-5	195	11-05-01	1	0	2.84	4	4	0	19	11	6	6	0	4	16	.169	.236	.262	22.2	5.6	72
Arnold, Chandler	R-R	6-2	189	11-19-99	1	2	11.17	7	1	0	10	12	13	12	1	8	8	.316	.426	.500	17.0	17.0	47
Beltre, Alexander	R-L	6-1	169	11-05-02	0	1	2.45	9	3	0	15	12	5	4	2	8	15	.211	.318	.404	22.7	12.1	66
Cervantes, Alejandro	R-R	6-2	189	5-15-01	0	3	11.05	16	0	0	15	16	25	18	1	23	10	.286	.500	.339	11.9	27.4	84
Clemente, Randel	R-R	6-3	173	11-17-01	1	2	4.34	19	0	0	19	13	12	9	0	16	24	.197	.369	.197	28.2	18.8	85
Cuello, Antoni	R-R	6-5	186	11-07-02	2	1	5.63	21	0	2	24	30	18	15	1	18	17	.303	.408	.434	14.2	15.0	120
Dominguez, Yonael	R-R	6-2	175	10-24-01	0	1	11.74	7	1	0	8	13	10	10	2	2	7	.361	.410	.611	17.9	5.1	39
Fabian, Samuel	R-R	6-4	177	5-21-03	0	1	10.00	16	0	1	18	21	25	20	2	24	26	.280	.476	.427	24.8	22.9	105
Gastelum, Luis	R-R	6-2	168	9-27-01	1	2	5.19	11	0	1	17	22	12	10	1	3	20	.297	.333	.405	25.6	3.8	78
Giulianelli, Ettore	R-R	6-3	190	3-30-03	1	1	6.16	15	0	0	19	8	13	13	0	23	34	.123	.360	.154	38.2	25.8	89
Gomez, Henry	R-R	6-1	163	10-17-01	1	0	0.00	1	0	0	2	2	0	0	0	1	3	.250	.333	.375	33.3	11.1	9
Guerrero, Diorys	L-L	6-1	170	2-01-01	0	2	8.10	15	0	0	17	19	16	15	1	18	20	.275	.457	.391	21.7	19.6	92
Jimenez, Ludwin	R-R	6-2	165	8-09-01	0	0	11.81	6	0	0	5	3	7	7	0	6	6	.167	.423	.333	23.1	23.1	26
Kublick, Hunter	R-R	6-4	200	7-01-03	0	0	0.00	1	0	0	1	0	0	0	0	1	0	.000	.333	.000	0.0	33.3	3
Lin, Chen-Wei	R-R	6-7	188	11-22-01	0	0	1.93	2	2	0	5	5	1	1	0	1	4	.278	.333	.333	19.0	4.8	21
Lopez, Bruno	R-R	6-4	220	4-18-02	0	2	9.00	7	0	1	6	7	6	6	0	4	7	.280	.387	.280	22.6	12.9	31
Lynch, John	L-L	5-11	190	4-17-01	0	1	3.12	7	0	0	9	12	6	3	1	3	9	.324	.366	.514	22.0	7.3	41
Martinez, Miguel	R-R	6-0	143	1-26-03	0	0	4.82	16	0	2	19	15	10	10	2	5	24	.214	.286	.329	31.2	6.5	77
Menes, Ruben	R-R	6-3	185	4-17-02	2	1	4.50	5	3	0	12	10	10	6	1	10	11	.217	.368	.391	19.3	17.5	57
Odle, Jacob	R-R	6-5	215	11-30-03	0	0	9.00	2	0	0	2	3	2	2	0	3	2	.375	.583	.375	16.7	25.0	12
Ortega, Wilmer	R-R	6-1	169	4-04-01	0	1	1.64	5	1	0	11	14	6	2	1	1	9	.304	.347	.457	18.4	2.0	49
Paniagua, Inohan	R-R	6-1	148	2-06-00	0	0	0.00	3	3	0	4	3	0	0	0	2	6	.231	.333	.308	40.0	13.3	15
Saladin, Darlin	R-R	5-11	150	12-28-02	2	4	2.85	12	11	0	47	39	16	15	4	21	47	.231	.321	.343	23.9	10.7	197
Salas, Gerado	R-R	6-0	189	2-14-03	2	1	3.21	11	10	0	48	46	25	17	5	16	39	.242	.304	.395	18.8	7.7	207
Sequera, Leonel	R-R	6-0	190	8-06-05	0	1	2.65	5	5	0	17	16	6	5	0	1	15	.250	.262	.266	23.1	1.5	65
Villanueva, Victor	R-R	6-1	170	3-26-01	0	3	7.76	12	6	0	27	27	23	23	0	21	28	.265	.400	.324	22.2	16.7	126
Yanez, Omar	R-R	6-2	190	12-07-02	3	3	5.25	17	0	1	24	31	15	14	1	10	26	.313	.375	.414	23.2	8.9	112

Fielding

C: Rodriguez 22, Hernandez 20, Loaiza 13, Guerrero 11, Heredia 9, Burns 3. **1B:** Vargas 29, Guerrero 10, Hernandez 10, Diaz 8, Bolivar 3, Burns 1, Loaiza 1. **2B:** Grant 27, Encarnacion 15, De La Rosa 8, Guzman 5, Fermin 2, Bolivar 1. **3B:** Guerrero 22, Guzman 17, Bolivar 7, Encarnacion 7, De La Rosa 6. **SS:** Mejia 27, Encarnacion 17, Grant 5, Moore 3, Guzman 2, Fermin 1, Bolivar 1. **OF:** Ramos 57, Suarez 34, Cabrera 29, Pino 23, Cordoba 22, Taveras 9, Lott 5.

DSL CARDINALS — ROOKIE

DOMINICAN SUMMER LEAGUE

Batting	B-T	Ht.	Wt.	DOB	AVG	OBP	SLG	G	PA	AB	R	H	2B	3B	HR	RBI	BB	HBP	SH	SF	SO	SB	CS	BB%	SO%
Almonte, Hancel	R-R	6-1	193	12-06-05	.231	.345	.372	38	143	121	20	28	5	0	4	13	14	7	0	0	50	1	1	9.8	35.0
Arthur, Andru	L-L	6-1	176	11-01-05	.218	.330	.308	28	91	78	13	17	3	2	0	5	9	4	0	0	15	6	1	9.9	16.5
Asprilla, Paulo	R-R	5-8	177	4-28-06	.220	.343	.220	20	71	59	7	13	0	0	0	10	10	1	1	0	19	0	0	14.1	26.8
Atocha, Luis	L-R	6-0	180	12-14-01	.143	.337	.270	22	83	63	6	9	5	0	1	7	13	6	0	1	27	0	1	15.7	32.5
Batista, Arfeni	R-R	6-0	161	9-04-04	.194	.267	.318	43	187	170	23	33	9	0	4	18	14	3	0	0	76	2	0	7.5	40.6
Caraballo, Heriberto	R-R	5-8	191	2-18-05	.241	.318	.310	34	129	116	13	28	6	1	0	9	9	4	0	0	19	0	0	7.0	14.7
Carmona, Carlos	R-R	6-2	190	7-01-04	.200	.200	.200	1	5	5	2	1	0	0	0	0	0	0	0	0	1	0	0	0.0	20.0
Gil, Angel	L-L	6-3	174	12-10-05	.179	.343	.269	27	101	78	8	14	4	0	1	11	16	4	0	1	37	0	0	15.8	36.6
Junco, Yoerny	B-R	5-9	165	11-08-04	.294	.429	.412	5	21	17	4	5	2	0	0	0	4	0	0	0	9	1	2	19.0	42.9
Lopez, Chris	R-R	5-9	175	6-28-05	.138	.239	.172	21	67	58	4	8	2	0	0	1	6	2	0	1	37	0	0	9.0	55.2
Pena, Yordalin	R-R	6-3	177	9-17-04	.263	.341	.410	42	176	156	24	41	9	4	2	16	15	4	0	1	34	7	1	8.5	19.3
Perez, Marcelo	R-R	6-2	181	1-07-04	.176	.327	.235	30	104	85	12	15	2	0	1	5	12	7	0	0	34	0	0	11.5	32.7
Reynoso, Elias	R-R	5-10	158	11-25-03	.172	.398	.259	25	84	58	14	10	2	0	1	8	21	2	1	2	31	6	0	25.0	36.9
Rojas, Daniel	R-R	5-8	151	11-16-05	.241	.318	.321	37	154	137	18	33	5	3	0	16	11	5	0	1	34	7	2	7.1	22.1
Roquez, Fernando	L-R	6-2	181	9-01-05	.234	.387	.363	39	155	124	17	29	4	0	4	17	26	5	0	0	41	2	1	16.8	26.5
Taveras, Bracewell	B-R	6-0	182	6-05-06	.207	.250	.337	43	180	169	22	35	10	0	4	17	7	3	0	1	32	2	0	3.9	17.8
Velasquez, Facundo	B-R	6-2	179	1-16-06	.185	.320	.322	42	175	146	16	27	4	2	4	15	26	3	0	0	66	4	0	14.9	37.7

Pitching	B-T	Ht.	Wt.	DOB	W	L	ERA	G	GS	SV	IP	Hits	Runs	ER	HR	BB	SO	AVG	OBP	SLG	SO%	BB%	BF
Baez, Jarol	R-R	6-1	200	10-21-05	0	1	7.62	12	0	0	13	15	20	11	0	15	15	.283	.444	.415	20.8	20.8	72
Batista, Yadiel	L-L	6-3	170	4-17-04	1	4	3.96	10	9	0	39	42	18	17	2	2	37	.290	.303	.407	24.3	1.3	152
Carrera, Emisael	R-R	6-0	185	2-22-06	3	0	2.08	15	0	2	22	19	9	5	0	11	19	.238	.340	.275	20.2	11.7	94
Chirinos, Junior	R-R	6-3	190	11-18-04	0	0	4.26	4	2	0	6	4	3	3	1	3	7	.174	.269	.304	26.9	11.5	26

Galvez, Jovi	R-R	6-2	223	7-05-04	0	0	11.15	15	0	0	15	15	19	19	0	24	14	.259	.500	.345	16.3	27.9	86
Hernandez, Justin	R-R	6-4	180	4-22-05	0	2	7.65	15	0	2	20	24	24	17	3	20	21	.286	.434	.464	19.8	18.9	106
Herrera, Yordy	L-L	6-2	150	12-02-04	2	1	3.68	17	0	1	29	18	15	12	1	22	36	.191	.356	.277	30.3	18.5	119
Mack, Bernard	L-L	6-3	160	10-24-05	1	0	4.76	15	0	0	17	14	11	9	1	11	23	.219	.351	.328	29.9	14.3	77
Martinez, Guanchi	R-R	6-0	185	8-17-06	0	1	3.86	8	0	0	12	12	5	5	0	6	7	.273	.353	.386	13.7	11.8	51
Moran, Jefferson	R-R	6-1	155	6-04-04	0	4	4.33	9	6	0	27	25	16	13	2	12	28	.263	.372	.389	24.8	10.6	113
Oliver, Ronny	R-R	6-2	155	1-01-04	1	2	4.15	11	6	0	30	30	26	14	1	20	34	.256	.389	.342	22.8	13.4	149
Paulino, Brailyn	R-R	6-0	185	4-26-06	3	3	8.48	16	6	0	29	36	29	27	4	20	28	.308	.442	.521	19.0	13.6	147
Perez, Kener	R-R	6-2	180	10-03-04	0	1	4.91	13	0	1	15	14	11	8	0	11	18	.241	.380	.328	25.4	15.5	71
Ramirez, Keiverson	R-R	6-1	170	4-05-06	1	5	4.31	11	8	0	40	45	22	19	4	8	30	.294	.347	.444	17.6	4.7	170
Rojas, Stiveen	L-L	5-8	136	8-29-06	0	4	2.67	13	3	1	27	24	15	8	1	19	28	.238	.378	.317	22.0	15.0	127
Severino, Juan	R-R	6-0	165	6-06-04	0	4	6.08	15	3	1	27	34	30	18	0	17	31	.293	.393	.397	22.8	12.5	136
Suriel, Jose	R-R	6-3	240	10-09-04	1	1	5.74	13	0	0	16	8	12	10	0	24	27	.148	.439	.204	32.9	29.3	82
Vargas, Giovanni	R-R	6-1	179	3-03-06	1	2	5.50	14	1	1	18	22	15	11	0	11	24	.310	.405	.380	28.2	12.9	85
Ynfante, Nelfy	R-R	6-3	168	2-01-05	3	1	4.50	9	9	0	30	27	17	15	2	11	34	.241	.328	.313	26.6	8.6	128

Fielding

C: Caraballo 19, Lopez 16, Asprilla 16, Atocha 7. **1B:** Caraballo 16, Atocha 15, Perez 12, Roquez 11. **2B:** Taveras 29, Reynoso 24, Junco 2, Rojas 1. **3B:** Rojas 33, Perez 18, Junco 3, Taveras 2. **SS:** Batista 40, Taveras 11, Rojas 3. **OF:** Velasquez 40, Almonte 38, Pena 35, Roquez 27, Arthur 23, Gil 3, Carmona 1.

San Diego Padres

SEASON SYNOPSIS: After opening the season with a payroll north of $248 million—third in MLB—the Padres found that their sum was less than the whole of their parts. A chic preseason World Series pick, they went 2-12 in extra-inning games and 9-23 in one-run games. Despite their +104 run differential, they had to rally to finish above .500.

HIGH POINT: The Padres played as expected in September, winning 20 of their last 27, including a season-best eight in a row at one point, to make a late push at a wild-card spot. Lefthander Blake Snell, a free agent after the season, won four of five starts in the month and didn't allow a run in four of them, part of a stellar 14-9, 2.25 season in which he led the league in walks (99) but also in ERA (2.25), and allowed just 118 hits and fanned 234 in 180 innings.

LOW POINT: The Padres were walked off 12 times. Three came in the last two weeks of June, when San Diego lost nine of 11 to fall to 37-45, 11.5 games back at the end of the month. A pair of walk-offs at the end of August at last-place St. Louis—the latter coming when Tommy Edman homered off normally stalwart closer Josh Hader—drove a stake in their playoff hopes, dropping them to 62-72.

NOTABLE ROOKIES: An expensive, veteran-laden roster got some boosts from rookies in small roles. Most notably, Luis Campusano got his first extended run at catcher and hit .319/.356/.491 with seven homers in 163 at-bats. RHPs Pedro Avila (3.22 ERA in 53 IP) and Matt Waldron (4.35 in 41.1 IP) provided needed rotation depth, with Waldron being the first big leaguer to consistently throw a knuckleball since 2018.

KEY TRANSACTIONS: San Diego won the offseason helping them draw a franchise-record 3,271,554 fans—with the biggest signing being shortstop Xander Bogaerts for 11 years and $280 million during the 2022 Winter Meetings, and Bogaerts performed fine (.285/.350/.440, 19 HR). Free-agent RHP Michael Wacha (14-4, 3.22 in 24 starts) was even better, and May signee Gary Sanchez (19 HR in 260 PA) helped fill a gaping hole behind the plate.

DOWN ON THE FARM: Even as the team keeps trading away prospects, it manages to find more. Catcher Ethan Salas was a 16-year-old spring training sensation who reached Double-A. Robby Snelling was BA's MiLB Pitcher of the Year.

OPENING DAY PAYROLL: $248,995,932 (3rd).

PLAYERS OF THE YEAR

MAJOR LEAGUE

Juan Soto
OF
.275/.410/.519
32 2B, 35 HR
97 R, 109 RBI

MINOR LEAGUE

Robby Snelling
LHP
(LoA/HiA/AA)
11-3, 1.82
10.2 SO/9, 1.12 WHIP

ORGANIZATION LEADERS

Batting		*Minimum 250 AB
MAJORS		
* AVG	Xander Bogaerts	.285
* OPS	Juan Soto	.930
HR	Juan Soto	35
RBI	Juan Soto	109
MINORS		
* AVG	Romeo Sanabria, ACL Padres/L. Elsinore	.341
* OBP	Alfonso Rivas, El Paso	.462
* SLG	Alfonso Rivas, El Paso	.582
* OPS	Alfonso Rivas, El Paso	1.043
R	Jakob Marsee, Fort Wayne/S. Antonio	103
H	Graham Pauley, L. Elsin./F. Wayne/S. Anton.	148
TB	Graham Pauley, L. Elsin./F. Wayne/S. Anton.	259
2B	Marcos Castanon, Fort Wayne/San Antonio	39
3B	Graham Pauley, L. Elsin./F. Wayne/S. Anton.	5
3B	Tyler Robertson, L. Elsin./F. Wayne/S. Anton.	5
HR	Graham Pauley, L. Elsin./F. Wayne/S. Anton.	23
RBI	Graham Pauley, L. Elsin./F. Wayne/S. Anton.	94
BB	Jakob Marsee, Fort Wayne/S. Antonio	98
SO	Samuel Zavala, L. Elsinore/F. Wayne	140
SB	Jakob Marsee, Fort Wayne/S. Antonio	46

Pitching		#Minimum 75 IP
MAJORS		
W	Blake Snell	14
W	Michael Wacha	14
# ERA	Blake Snell	2.25
SO	Blake Snell	234
SV	Josh Hader	33
MINORS		
W	Robby Snelling, L. Els./F. Wayne/S.Ant.	11
L	Matt Waldron, El Paso	10
L	Jay Groome, El Paso	10
# ERA	Robby Snelling, L. Els./F. Wayne/S.Ant.	1.82
G	Eric Hanhold, El Paso	50
GS	Jay Groome, El Paso	30
SV	Cole Paplham, L. Els./F. Wayne/S. Ant.	11
IP	Jay Groome, El Paso	135
BB	Jay Groome, El Paso	112
SO	Jay Groome, El Paso	137
# AVG	Ryan Bergert, F. Wayne/S. Antonio	.202

2023 PERFORMANCE

General Manager: A.J. Preller. **Farm Director:** Ryley Westman. **Scouting Director:** Chris Kemp.

Class	Team	League	W	L	PCT	Finish	Manager
Majors	San Diego Padres	National	82	80	.506	9 (15)	Bob Melvin
Triple-A	El Paso Chihuahuas	Pacific Coast	62	88	.413	9 (10)	Phillip Wellman
Double-A	San Antonio Missions	Texas	70	68	.507	6 (10)	Luke Montz
High-A	Fort Wayne TinCaps	Midwest	69	63	.523	4 (12)	Jon Mathews
Low-A	Lake Elsinore Storm	California	63	66	.488	6 (10)	Pete Zamora
Rookie	ACL Padres	Arizona Complex	30	26	.536	9 (17)	Lukas Ray
Rookie	DSL Padres Brown	Dominican Sum.	16	38	.296	47 (50)	Luis Mendez
Rookie	DSL Padres Gold	Dominican Sum.	37	17	.685	4 (50)	Diego Cedeno
Overall 2023 Minor League Record			347	366	.487	19th (30)	

ORGANIZATION STATISTICS

SAN DIEGO PADRES

NATIONAL LEAGUE

Batting	B-T	Ht.	Wt.	DOB	AVG	OBP	SLG	G	PA	AB	R	H	2B	3B	HR	RBI	BB	HBP	SH	SF	SO	SB	CS	BB%	SO%
Azocar, Jose	R-R	5-11	181	5-11-96	.231	.278	.363	55	102	91	16	21	6	0	2	9	4	2	5	0	24	8	2	3.9	23.5
Batten, Matthew	R-R	5-11	180	6-22-95	.258	.355	.358	43	139	120	19	31	6	0	2	11	17	1	1	0	30	2	2	12.2	21.6
Bogaerts, Xander	R-R	6-2	218	10-01-92	.285	.350	.440	155	665	596	83	170	31	2	19	58	56	7	0	6	110	19	2	8.4	16.5
Campusano, Luis	R-R	5-11	232	9-29-98	.319	.356	.491	49	174	163	27	52	7	0	7	30	7	3	0	1	21	0	0	4.0	12.1
Carpenter, Matt	L-R	6-4	210	11-26-85	.176	.322	.319	76	237	188	18	33	12	0	5	31	41	2	0	5	67	1	0	17.3	28.3
Choi, Ji Man	L-R	6-1	260	5-19-91	.065	.268	.097	16	41	31	3	2	1	0	0	2	8	1	0	1	8	0	0	19.5	19.5
2-team (23 Pittsburgh)					.163	.243	.385	39	117	104	12	17	5	0	6	13	10	1	0	2	35	0	0	8.5	29.9
Cooper, Garrett	R-R	6-5	235	12-25-90	.239	.323	.402	41	133	117	14	28	7	0	4	15	14	1	0	1	35	0	0	10.5	26.3
2-team (82 Miami)					.251	.305	.419	123	457	422	42	106	18	1	17	61	31	2	0	2	132	0	0	6.8	28.9
Cronenworth, Jake	L-R	6-0	187	1-21-94	.229	.312	.378	127	522	458	54	105	24	7	10	48	46	11	1	5	97	6	1	8.8	18.6
Cruz, Nelson	R-R	6-2	230	7-01-80	.245	.283	.399	49	152	143	9	35	5	1	5	23	6	2	0	1	46	1	0	3.9	30.3
Dahl, David	L-R	6-1	197	4-01-94	.111	.111	.444	4	9	9	1	1	0	0	1	1	0	0	0	0	2	0	0	0.0	22.2
Dixon, Brandon	R-R	6-2	215	1-29-92	.203	.244	.329	33	86	79	10	16	4	0	2	9	1	4	0	2	31	1	0	1.2	36.0
Engel, Adam	R-R	6-2	215	12-09-91	.000	.000	.000	5	6	6	0	0	0	0	0	0	0	0	0	0	2	0	1	0.0	33.3
Gamel, Ben	L-L	5-10	180	5-17-92	.200	.200	.267	6	15	15	2	3	1	0	0	2	0	0	0	0	2	0	0	0.0	13.3
Grisham, Trent	L-L	5-11	224	11-01-96	.198	.315	.352	153	555	469	67	93	31	1	13	50	75	5	4	1	154	15	3	13.5	27.7
Kim, Ha-Seong	R-R	5-9	168	10-17-95	.260	.351	.398	152	626	538	84	140	23	0	17	60	75	3	5	5	124	38	9	12.0	19.8
Kohlwey, Taylor	L-L	6-1	200	7-20-94	.154	.154	.154	5	13	13	0	2	0	0	0	0	0	0	0	0	5	0	0	0.0	38.5
Machado, Manny	R-R	6-3	218	7-06-92	.258	.319	.462	138	601	543	75	140	21	0	30	91	50	2	0	6	109	3	2	8.3	18.1
Nola, Austin	R-R	6-0	197	12-28-89	.146	.260	.192	52	154	130	9	19	3	0	1	8	18	2	4	0	31	0	0	11.7	20.1
Odor, Rougned	L-R	5-11	200	2-03-94	.203	.299	.355	59	157	138	21	28	9	0	4	18	17	2	0	0	37	2	1	10.8	23.6
Profar, Jurickson	B-R	6-0	184	2-20-93	.295	.367	.409	14	49	44	4	13	2	0	1	7	5	0	0	0	4	0	0	10.2	8.2
2-team (111 Colorado)					.242	.324	.368	125	521	459	55	111	27	2	9	46	50	6	0	5	90	1	0	9.6	17.3
Rivas, Alfonso	L-L	5-10	190	9-13-96	.200	.294	.333	8	17	15	2	3	2	0	0	1	2	0	0	0	7	0	0	11.8	41.2
2-team (40 Pittsburgh)					.229	.303	.422	48	123	109	8	25	10	1	3	15	9	3	1	1	36	1	0	7.3	29.3
Rosario, Eguy	R-R	5-7	150	8-25-99	.250	.270	.500	11	37	36	6	9	1	1	2	6	1	0	0	0	12	0	0	2.7	32.4
Sanchez, Gary	R-R	6-2	230	12-02-92	.218	.292	.500	72	260	234	33	51	9	0	19	46	21	4	0	1	64	0	0	8.1	24.6
2-team (3 New York Mets)					.217	.291	.492	75	267	240	33	52	9	0	19	47	21	4	0	2	67	0	0	7.9	25.1
Seagle, Chandler	R-R	5-10	190	5-23-96	.000	.000	.000	1	1	1	0	0	0	0	0	0	0	0	0	0	0	0	0	0.0	0.0
Soto, Juan	L-L	6-2	224	10-25-98	.275	.410	.519	162	708	568	97	156	32	1	35	109	132	2	1	5	129	12	5	18.6	18.2
Sullivan, Brett	L-R	6-1	195	2-22-94	.210	.244	.284	33	86	81	7	17	3	0	1	6	4	0	0	1	19	0	0	4.7	22.1
Tatis, Fernando	R-R	6-3	217	1-02-99	.257	.322	.449	141	635	575	91	148	33	1	25	78	53	3	1	3	141	29	4	8.3	22.2

Pitching	B-T	Ht.	Wt.	DOB	W	L	ERA	G	GS	SV	IP	Hits	Runs	ER	HR	BB	SO	AVG	OBP	SLG	SO%	BB%	BF
Avila, Pedro	R-R	5-11	210	1-14-97	2	2	3.22	14	6	0	50	43	23	18	3	25	54	.230	.335	.337	24.5	11.4	220
Barlow, Scott	R-R	6-3	210	12-18-92	0	2	3.07	25	0	0	29	23	13	10	1	12	32	.223	.317	.291	26.0	9.8	123
Carlton, Drew	R-R	6-1	215	9-08-95	2	1	4.35	11	0	0	21	18	12	10	2	6	18	.243	.305	.378	21.2	7.1	85
Castillo, Jose	L-L	6-6	252	1-10-96	0	0	108.00	1	0	0	0	2	4	4	0	2	0	1.000	.833	2.000	0.0	33.3	6
Cosgrove, Tom	L-L	6-2	190	6-14-96	1	2	1.75	54	0	1	51	31	12	10	3	19	44	.173	.270	.246	21.5	9.3	205
Crismatt, Nabil	R-R	6-1	220	12-25-94	0	1	9.82	7	0	0	11	17	12	12	3	7	9	.347	.439	.571	15.8	12.3	57
Darvish, Yu	R-R	6-5	220	8-16-86	8	10	4.56	24	24	0	136	134	71	69	18	43	141	.259	.322	.420	24.6	7.5	574
Dixon, Brandon	R-R	6-2	215	1-29-92	0	0	0.00	1	0	0	1	0	0	0	0	0	0	.000	.000	.000	0.0	0.0	3
Espada, Jose	R-R	6-0	170	2-22-97	0	0	0.00	1	0	0	1	0	0	0	0	2	2	.000	.400	.000	40.0	40.0	5
Garcia, Luis	R-R	6-2	240	1-30-87	2	3	4.07	61	0	0	60	59	30	27	6	24	53	.252	.336	.372	19.9	9.0	267
Hader, Josh	L-L	5-11	180	4-07-94	2	3	1.28	61	0	33	56	32	11	8	3	30	85	.163	.284	.224	36.8	13.0	231
Hernandez, Nick	R-R	6-1	212	12-30-94	0	0	12.00	2	0	0	3	3	4	4	1	4	5	.250	.500	.500	27.8	22.2	18
Hill, Rich	L-L	6-5	221	3-11-80	1	4	8.23	10	5	0	27	36	28	25	8	11	25	.319	.385	.611	19.2	8.5	130
Hill, Tim	R-L	6-4	200	2-10-90	1	4	5.48	48	0	0	44	59	36	27	7	14	26	.331	.395	.511	12.9	6.9	202
Honeywell, Brent	R-R	6-2	195	3-31-95	2	4	4.05	36	0	0	47	44	22	21	8	20	42	.247	.335	.416	20.6	9.8	204
Jacob, Alek	L-R	6-3	190	6-16-98	0	0	0.00	3	0	0	3	0	0	0	0	1	5	.000	.100	.000	50.0	10.0	10
Kerr, Ray	L-L	6-3	185	9-10-94	1	1	4.33	22	0	0	27	25	15	13	5	9	35	.243	.310	.505	30.7	7.9	114
Knehr, Reiss	L-R	6-2	205	11-03-96	0	1	15.88	4	1	0	6	10	10	10	3	5	4	.385	.469	.846	12.5	15.6	32
Lugo, Seth	R-R	6-4	225	11-17-89	8	7	3.57	26	26	0	146	140	62	58	19	36	140	.249	.296	.412	23.2	6.0	604

Martinez, Nick	L-R	6-1	200	8-05-90	6	4	3.43	63	9	1	110	99	45	42	12	40	106	.240	.311	.354	23.0	8.7	461
Morejon, Adrian	L-L	5-11	224	2-27-99	0	0	7.00	8	1	0	9	14	7	7	1	5	8	.368	.442	.553	18.2	11.4	44
Musgrove, Joe	R-R	6-5	230	12-04-92	10	3	3.05	17	17	0	97	90	35	33	10	21	97	.247	.301	.375	24.3	5.3	399
Snell, Blake	L-L	6-4	225	12-04-92	14	9	2.25	32	32	0	180	115	47	45	15	99	234	.181	.293	.286	31.5	13.3	742
Suarez, Robert	R-R	6-2	210	3-01-91	4	3	4.23	26	0	0	28	15	13	13	4	10	24	.155	.231	.299	22.2	9.3	108
Tapia, Domingo	R-R	6-3	263	8-04-91	0	1	3.57	15	0	1	18	13	8	7	2	12	14	.210	.347	.355	18.7	16.0	75
Wacha, Michael	R-R	6-6	215	7-01-91	14	4	3.22	24	24	0	134	113	49	48	15	43	124	.224	.288	.380	22.4	7.8	553
Waldron, Matt	R-R	6-2	185	9-26-96	1	3	4.35	8	6	0	41	39	20	20	9	12	31	.244	.295	.481	17.9	6.9	173
Weathers, Ryan	R-L	6-1	230	12-17-99	1	6	6.25	12	10	0	45	55	33	31	9	17	29	.313	.372	.528	14.8	8.7	196
Wilson, Steven	R-R	6-3	221	8-24-94	1	2	3.91	52	0	0	53	35	23	23	7	27	57	.185	.297	.354	26.0	12.3	219
Wolf, Jackson	L-L	6-7	205	4-22-99	1	0	5.40	1	1	0	5	6	3	3	0	1	1	.286	.318	.333	4.5	4.5	22

Fielding

Catcher	PCT	G	PO	A	E	DP	PB
Campusano	.991	42	318	13	3	0	2
Nola	.997	52	359	21	1	4	1
Sanchez	.995	63	557	39	3	2	4
Sullivan	.982	31	209	13	4	0	2

First Base	PCT	G	PO	A	E	DP
Batten	.968	6	29	1	1	2
Carpenter	1.000	13	68	3	0	10
Choi	1.000	10	67	2	0	5
Cooper	.991	31	202	8	2	14
Cronenworth	.998	106	759	41	2	71
Cruz	1.000	1	1	0	0	0
Dixon	.991	16	102	7	1	11
Odor	.000	1	0	0	0	0
Profar	1.000	5	31	1	0	1
Rivas	1.000	8	37	4	0	6

Second Base	PCT	G	PO	A	E	DP
Batten	1.000	17	21	32	0	7
Cronenworth	.992	35	45	80	1	23
Kim	.991	106	166	269	4	57
Odor	.965	30	36	46	3	13
Profar	1.000	1	1	0	0	0
Rosario	.000	1	0	0	0	0
Tatis	1.000	1	1	1	0	0

Third Base	PCT	G	PO	A	E	DP
Batten	1.000	17	14	26	0	2
Kim	.986	32	19	53	1	5
Machado	.975	105	83	188	7	33
Odor	.933	9	6	8	1	1
Rosario	.967	11	6	23	1	0
Sullivan	1.000	1	0	1	0	0

Shortstop	PCT	G	PO	A	E	DP
Batten	.500	2	1	0	1	0
Bogaerts	.985	146	167	368	8	64
Kim	.966	20	13	44	2	11

Outfield	PCT	G	PO	A	E	DP
Azocar	1.000	47	50	0	0	0
Dahl	1.000	3	7	1	0	1
Dixon	.500	11	19	0	0	0
Engel	.500	4	7	0	0	0
Gamel	.750	4	7	0	2	0
Grisham	.987	153	303	1	4	1
Kohlwey	.500	4	1	0	0	0
Odor	1.000	9	6	0	0	0
Profar	1.000	8	14	0	0	0
Soto	.989	154	254	10	3	2
Tatis	.990	142	283	12	6	1

EL PASO CHIHUAHUAS — *TRIPLE-A*

PACIFIC COAST LEAGUE

Batting	B-T	Ht.	Wt.	DOB	AVG	OBP	SLG	G	PA	AB	R	H	2B	3B	HR	RBI	BB	HBP	SH	SF	SO	SB	CS	BB%	SO%
Azocar, Jose	R-R	5-11	181	5-11-96	.269	.307	.388	49	212	201	31	54	9	0	5	27	9	2	0	0	45	18	5	4.2	21.2
Batten, Matthew	R-R	5-11	180	6-22-95	.235	.341	.399	86	413	353	71	83	20	1	12	50	55	3	0	2	99	27	4	13.3	24.0
Campusano, Luis	R-R	5-11	232	9-29-98	.333	.444	.600	5	18	15	4	5	1	0	1	3	3	0	0	0	3	0	0	16.7	16.7
Cantu, Michael	R-R	6-1	225	8-28-95	.185	.294	.274	40	143	124	16	23	5	0	2	24	18	1	0	0	51	0	0	12.6	35.7
Choi, Ji Man	L-R	6-1	260	5-19-91	.160	.276	.200	7	29	25	1	4	1	0	0	1	4	0	0	0	7	0	0	13.8	24.1
Cruz, Nelson	R-R	6-2	230	7-01-80	.313	.353	.563	4	17	16	2	5	1	0	1	3	0	1	0	0	3	0	0	0.0	17.6
Dahl, David	L-R	6-1	197	4-01-94	.265	.342	.382	17	76	68	11	18	5	0	1	10	8	0	0	0	7	0	0	10.5	9.2
2-team (54 Oklahoma City)					.278	.351	.466	71	313	281	44	78	26	0	9	49	31	1	0	0	50	3	0	9.9	16.0
Dale, Jarryd	R-R	6-2	200	9-11-00	.300	.462	.300	3	13	10	2	3	0	0	0	1	3	0	0	0	4	0	1	23.1	30.8
Didder, Ray-Patrick	R-R	5-9	199	10-01-94	.288	.426	.491	48	202	163	36	47	12	0	7	33	31	8	0	0	45	19	3	15.3	22.3
Dixon, Brandon	R-R	6-2	215	1-29-92	.268	.348	.502	59	273	239	39	64	7	2	15	44	28	3	0	3	85	7	0	10.3	31.1
Dunn, Lucas	R-R	6-0	205	4-30-99	.053	.100	.211	6	20	19	2	1	0	0	1	1	1	0	0	0	5	0	0	5.0	25.0
Engel, Adam	R-R	6-2	215	12-09-91	.170	.262	.358	14	61	53	3	9	4	0	2	8	6	1	0	1	21	3	1	9.8	34.4
2-team (76 Tacoma)					.237	.355	.435	90	376	317	55	75	17	2	14	42	53	5	0	1	116	22	2	14.1	30.9
Gamel, Ben	L-L	5-10	180	5-17-92	.314	.402	.600	18	82	70	14	22	5	0	5	13	11	0	0	1	16	2	3	13.4	19.5
Hollis, Connor	R-R	5-7	170	11-18-94	.600	.778	1.000	2	9	5	3	3	2	0	0	0	4	0	0	0	0	2	0	44.4	0.0
Iglesias, Jose	R-R	5-11	195	1-05-90	.317	.356	.537	28	135	123	22	39	13	1	4	27	9	0	0	3	22	0	1	6.7	16.3
Johnson, Daniel	L-L	5-9	200	7-11-95	.296	.384	.583	28	125	108	21	32	11	1	6	19	13	3	0	1	21	9	2	10.4	16.8
Kohlwey, Taylor	L-L	6-1	200	7-20-94	.276	.390	.437	124	518	428	71	118	29	2	12	73	75	8	0	5	86	15	5	14.5	16.6
Liberato, Luis	L-L	5-11	175	12-18-95	.261	.365	.461	69	276	230	38	60	15	2	9	35	40	0	2	4	64	8	7	14.5	23.2
Lopes, Tim	R-R	5-10	180	6-24-94	.282	.378	.421	121	550	475	88	134	23	2	13	56	72	2	0	1	123	42	8	13.1	22.4
Luis, Carlos	L-R	6-2	160	9-04-99	.304	.333	.391	6	24	23	2	7	2	0	0	1	1	0	0	0	5	0	0	4.2	20.8
McClaughry, Nik	R-R	5-9	159	9-14-99	.500	.667	1.500	1	3	2	0	1	0	1	0	1	1	0	0	0	1	1	0	33.3	33.3
Mendoza, Evan	R-R	6-0	205	6-28-96	.231	.292	.277	17	72	65	11	15	0	0	1	5	6	0	0	1	9	2	0	8.3	12.5
Mercado, Oscar	R-R	6-2	197	12-16-94	.339	.399	.669	31	138	124	28	42	5	3	10	37	11	2	0	1	29	10	1	8.0	21.0
2-team (15 Oklahoma City)					.313	.375	.593	46	202	182	39	57	9	3	12	50	15	3	0	2	45	13	2	7.4	22.3
Nola, Austin	R-R	6-0	197	12-28-89	.185	.267	.222	8	30	27	5	5	1	0	0	2	3	0	0	0	8	0	0	10.0	26.7
Ornelas, Tirso	L-R	6-2	200	3-11-00	.285	.358	.425	55	240	214	34	61	14	2	4	24	23	2	0	1	47	4	2	9.6	19.6
Perez, Jake	R-R	6-0	165	7-05-00	.000	.111	.000	2	9	7	0	0	0	0	0	2	1	0	0	1	6	0	0	11.1	66.7
Plawecki, Kevin	R-R	6-2	208	2-26-91	.276	.333	.439	33	135	123	19	34	9	1	3	21	10	1	0	1	21	0	0	7.4	15.6
2-team (10 Round Rock)					.280	.351	.414	43	175	157	20	44	10	1	3	23	15	2	0	1	32	0	0	8.6	18.3
Profar, Jurickson	B-R	6-0	184	2-20-93	.357	.500	.786	4	20	14	6	5	0	0	2	8	5	0	0	1	2	0	0	25.0	10.0
Quintero, Alison	R-R	5-11	175	4-24-00	.000	.333	.000	1	3	2	1	0	0	0	0	0	1	0	0	0	0	0	0	33.3	0.0
Ravelo, Rangel	R-R	6-0	235	4-24-92	.310	.428	.473	59	258	203	47	63	9	0	8	35	42	5	0	7	36	0	0	16.3	14.0
Rivas, Alfonso	L-L	5-10	190	9-13-96	.332	.462	.582	58	260	208	54	69	19	3	9	40	49	2	0	1	50	8	0	18.8	19.2
Rodriguez, Yorman	R-R	5-8	160	7-23-97	.276	.322	.411	41	178	163	21	45	9	2	3	28	11	1	1	2	23	3	0	6.2	12.9
Rosario, Eguy	R-R	5-7	150	8-25-99	.265	.348	.422	43	187	166	24	44	9	1	5	28	20	1	0	0	39	4	4	10.7	20.9
Sanabria, Jose	R-R	5-10	150	10-30-02	.217	.379	.217	8	29	23	5	5	0	0	0	2	6	0	0	0	8	3	0	20.7	27.6
Schrock, Max	L-R	5-9	185	10-12-94	.289	.352	.453	37	142	128	19	37	10	1	3	22	11	2	0	1	16	2	1	7.7	11.3
Seagle, Chandler	R-R	5-10	190	5-23-96	.233	.270	.367	16	64	60	7	14	2	0	2	8	3	0	1	0	24	1	1	4.7	37.5

Severino, Pedro	R-R	5-11	235	7-20-93	.286	.400	.476	18	75	63	12	18	3	0	3	8	12	0	0	0	10	3	0	16.0	13.3
2-team (46 Tacoma)					.245	.318	.419	64	267	241	43	59	12	0	10	36	25	1	0	0	55	7	0	9.4	20.6
Sullivan, Brett	L-R	6-1	195	2-22-94	.328	.401	.517	61	279	238	45	78	22	1	7	41	32	2	0	7	27	9	3	11.5	9.7
Tatis, Fernando	R-R	6-3	217	1-02-99	.515	.590	1.212	8	39	33	11	17	2	0	7	15	6	0	0	0	3	2	0	15.4	7.7
Tucker, Preston	L-L	6-0	210	7-06-90	.293	.433	.565	55	240	191	47	56	13	3	11	40	43	5	0	1	43	1	0	17.9	17.9
Witte, Jantzen	R-R	6-0	195	1-04-90	.253	.324	.460	106	439	391	62	99	26	2	17	80	39	4	1	4	109	7	5	8.9	24.8

Pitching	B-T	Ht.	Wt.	DOB	W	L	ERA	G	GS	SV	IP	Hits	Runs	ER	HR	BB	SO	AVG	OBP	SLG	SO%	BB%	BF
Avila, Pedro	R-R	5-11	210	1-14-97	1	6	8.57	19	15	0	56	72	56	53	13	31	48	.313	.392	.570	17.8	11.5	270
Baez, Michel	R-R	6-8	220	1-21-96	0	0	7.90	11	0	0	14	12	14	12	4	15	7	.235	.429	.471	10.0	21.4	70
Brooks, Aaron	R-R	6-4	230	4-27-90	4	3	4.95	44	4	0	64	73	38	35	10	20	51	.282	.337	.471	18.1	7.1	282
Cantu, Michael	R-R	6-1	225	8-28-95	0	0	15.43	2	0	0	2	7	4	4	1	0	0	.500	.500	.929	0.0	0.0	14
Carlton, Drew	R-R	6-1	215	9-08-95	2	1	3.00	15	0	0	18	15	8	6	1	5	21	.231	.292	.354	29.2	6.9	72
Castillo, Jose	L-L	6-6	252	1-10-96	1	3	9.82	22	0	2	18	27	20	20	5	11	22	.360	.438	.680	24.4	12.2	90
Cosgrove, Tom	L-L	6-2	190	6-14-96	0	0	0.00	8	0	0	8	0	0	0	0	4	8	.000	.172	.000	27.6	13.8	29
Crismatt, Nabil	R-R	6-1	220	12-25-94	0	0	6.94	9	0	0	12	12	9	9	4	5	11	.261	.340	.565	20.8	9.4	53
Duron, Nick	R-R	6-4	190	1-30-96	0	2	12.91	8	0	0	8	11	12	11	1	10	8	.344	.477	.500	18.2	22.7	44
Espada, Jose	R-R	6-0	170	2-22-97	0	0	2.79	9	2	0	19	17	8	6	2	11	25	.233	.345	.384	28.7	12.6	87
Espinoza, Anderson	R-R	6-0	190	3-09-98	8	9	6.15	28	28	0	132	148	96	90	17	73	117	.285	.381	.480	19.3	12.0	607
Felipe, Angel	R-R	6-5	190	8-30-97	0	2	6.20	25	0	1	25	26	17	17	2	18	39	.257	.380	.376	32.2	14.9	121
Groome, Jay	L-L	6-6	262	8-23-98	4	10	8.55	30	30	0	135	171	133	128	25	112	137	.312	.430	.527	20.5	16.7	669
Hanhold, Eric	R-R	6-5	210	11-01-93	4	2	8.44	50	0	2	53	61	53	50	14	43	61	.292	.415	.541	23.4	16.5	261
Hernandez, Nick	R-R	6-1	212	12-30-94	2	0	4.41	23	0	1	33	26	18	16	3	13	39	.217	.301	.383	28.5	9.5	137
Hill, Tim	R-L	6-4	200	2-10-90	0	0	0.00	1	0	0	1	0	0	0	0	0	1	.000	.000	.000	33.3	0.0	3
Kerr, Ray	L-L	6-3	185	9-10-94	6	0	2.25	36	0	10	36	24	11	9	2	17	42	.189	.283	.283	29.0	11.7	145
Knehr, Reiss	L-R	6-2	205	11-03-96	4	1	3.93	18	1	0	37	32	17	16	5	11	41	.232	.293	.399	27.3	7.3	150
Koenig, Jared	R-L	6-5	235	1-24-94	5	4	5.00	36	1	4	45	61	38	25	8	22	48	.319	.394	.492	21.8	10.0	220
Kopps, Kevin	R-R	6-0	200	3-02-97	0	1	6.89	13	0	1	16	20	14	12	1	12	14	.303	.420	.424	17.3	14.8	81
Leasher, Aaron	L-L	6-3	208	4-28-96	2	3	6.49	19	9	0	51	50	43	37	5	41	42	.262	.391	.424	17.9	17.4	235
Lugo, Moises	R-R	6-1	185	1-20-99	4	3	6.16	46	0	2	50	47	38	34	4	38	69	.242	.379	.407	28.8	15.8	240
Morejon, Adrian	L-L	5-11	224	2-27-99	2	1	6.08	19	2	0	24	29	18	16	3	12	26	.293	.381	.414	23.0	10.6	113
Musgrove, Joe	R-R	6-5	230	12-04-92	0	0	4.15	1	1	0	4	5	3	2	0	1	6	.278	.409	.389	27.3	4.5	22
Otto, Glenn	R-R	6-3	240	3-11-96	0	2	7.94	3	3	0	6	4	11	5	1	13	4	.182	.472	.409	11.1	36.1	36
Pomeranz, Drew	R-L	6-5	246	11-22-88	0	1	30.38	4	0	0	3	8	9	9	1	5	2	.500	.619	.938	9.5	23.8	21
Poppen, Sean	R-R	6-3	210	3-15-94	1	4	6.33	47	1	0	58	79	52	41	3	30	51	.312	.390	.443	17.6	10.3	290
Reynolds, Sean	L-R	6-8	250	4-19-98	0	1	13.50	17	0	0	16	26	28	24	3	27	19	.356	.535	.644	18.8	26.7	101
Sanchez, Angel	R-R	6-1	190	11-28-89	0	2	6.66	24	7	0	53	61	43	39	9	29	55	.282	.369	.472	22.1	11.6	249
Sanchez, Jake	R-R	6-1	205	8-19-89	3	4	5.68	44	0	0	57	60	38	36	9	32	62	.264	.359	.493	23.6	12.2	263
Suarez, Robert	R-R	6-2	210	3-01-91	0	0	16.20	2	0	0	2	4	3	3	0	1	1	.500	.500	.625	10.0	10.0	10
Tapia, Domingo	R-R	6-3	263	8-04-91	1	6	8.22	25	0	0	23	29	25	21	5	21	23	.312	.440	.516	19.7	17.9	117
Teheran, Julio	R-R	6-2	205	1-27-91	4	2	5.63	8	8	0	40	51	26	25	7	16	45	.311	.378	.500	24.3	8.6	185
Wacha, Michael	R-R	6-6	215	7-01-91	0	0	0.00	1	1	0	2	2	0	0	0	3	2	.250	.455	.250	18.2	27.3	11
Waldron, Matt	R-R	6-2	185	9-26-96	2	10	7.31	20	18	0	92	118	79	75	18	30	99	.313	.366	.568	23.8	7.2	416
Watson, Nolan	R-R	6-2	195	1-25-97	1	3	6.39	12	11	0	62	84	48	44	12	29	44	.326	.394	.547	15.1	9.9	292
Weathers, Ryan	R-L	6-1	230	12-17-99	1	2	4.20	8	8	0	41	40	21	19	5	24	52	.261	.365	.431	29.2	13.5	178
Witte, Jantzen	R-R	6-0	195	1-04-90	0	0	18.00	2	0	0	2	5	4	4	1	1	0	.455	.538	.909	0.0	7.7	13

Fielding

Catcher	PCT	G	PO	A	E	DP	PB
Campusano	1.000	4	18	1	0	0	1
Cantu	.997	32	281	11	1	0	4
Nola	.986	8	67	2	1	0	0
Plawecki	.995	20	174	11	1	1	2
Quintero	1.000	1	7	0	0	1	0
Rodriguez	1.000	13	100	7	0	0	5
Seagle	.993	16	120	17	1	2	1
Severino	1.000	16	146	5	0	1	3
Sullivan	.991	48	436	28	4	0	6

First Base	PCT	G	PO	A	E	DP
Cantu	1.000	2	14	0	0	1
Choi	.889	1	8	0	1	0
Dixon	.994	23	162	13	1	23
Gamel	1.000	3	18	4	0	1
Kohlwey	.989	12	82	6	1	9
Luis	1.000	6	51	5	0	2
Plawecki	.923	2	11	1	1	0
Profar	1.000	2	11	1	0	0
Ravelo	.997	42	308	20	1	24
Rivas	.986	47	326	31	5	31
Rodriguez	.875	1	7	0	1	0
Witte	.992	14	117	9	1	12

Second Base	PCT	G	PO	A	E	DP
Batten	.989	20	30	58	1	12
Dale	1.000	3	8	9	0	1
Hollis	1.000	2	4	2	0	0
Iglesias	.960	4	11	13	1	4
Lopes	.976	64	100	147	6	30
McClaughry	1.000	1	1	2	0	1
Rosario	.966	16	27	30	2	5
Sanabria	1.000	5	10	4	0	1
Schrock	.969	34	42	81	4	15
Witte	.943	8	13	20	2	5

Third Base	PCT	G	PO	A	E	DP
Batten	.839	7	5	21	5	4
Dixon	.857	2	2	4	1	1
Dunn	.909	5	2	8	1	1
Iglesias	1.000	2	4	3	0	1
Lopes	.929	17	12	27	3	0
Mendoza	.941	10	8	24	2	3
Rodriguez	.846	8	1	10	2	2
Rosario	.955	21	11	52	3	7
Sanabria	1.000	2	1	4	0	1
Schrock	.000	1	0	0	0	0
Sullivan	1.000	2	2	2	0	0
Witte	.959	77	43	119	7	15

Shortstop	PCT	G	PO	A	E	DP
Batten	.964	56	57	132	7	15
Didder	.968	47	67	114	6	23
Iglesias	.966	21	27	57	3	16
Lopes	.827	15	15	28	9	5
Mendoza	1.000	7	5	25	0	0
Perez	.900	2	3	6	1	2
Rosario	1.000	3	2	4	0	0
Schrock	.000	1	0	0	0	0

Outfield	PCT	G	PO	A	E	DP
Azocar	.993	47	105	4	2	1
Batten	1.000	3	8	0	0	0
Dahl	1.000	15	32	0	0	0
Dixon	1.000	26	46	1	0	0
Engel	.933	11	19	1	1	1
Gamel	.979	16	26	1	1	0
Johnson	.970	28	63	1	2	1
Kohlwey	.971	113	200	8	7	0
Liberato	.979	68	151	9	5	0
Lopes	.928	11	12	0	1	0
Mercado	1.000	29	66	1	0	0
Ornelas	.980	53	97	4	2	1
Profar	1.000	2	5	0	0	0
Rivas	1.000	7	8	0	0	0
Sanabria	.000	1	0	0	0	0
Schrock	1.000	1	1	0	0	0
Tatis	1.000	7	17	2	0	1
Tucker	.979	31	46	1	1	0

SAN ANTONIO MISSIONS

DOUBLE-A

TEXAS LEAGUE

SAN DIEGO PADRES

Batting	B-T	Ht.	Wt.	DOB	AVG	OBP	SLG	G	PA	AB	R	H	2B	3B	HR	RBI	BB	HBP	SH	SF	SO	SB	CS	BB%	SO%
Aviles, Luis	R-R	6-2	210	3-16-95	.184	.252	.276	31	110	98	15	18	3	0	2	8	9	0	3	0	30	9	0	8.2	27.3
2-team (72 Corpus Christi)					.243	.309	.423	103	408	366	58	89	17	2	15	47	30	6	3	2	107	26	7	7.4	26.2
Bell, Brantley	R-R	6-2	185	11-16-94	.232	.287	.354	30	108	99	13	23	9	0	1	12	7	1	0	1	36	6	3	6.5	33.3
Bush, Homer	R-R	6-3	200	10-13-01	.429	.448	.464	8	29	28	2	12	1	0	0	3	1	0	0	0	2	1	1	3.4	6.9
Castanon, Marcos	R-R	6-0	195	3-23-99	.280	.335	.436	54	230	211	24	59	19	1	4	26	18	0	0	1	49	0	0	7.8	21.3
Castellanos, Pedro	R-R	6-3	244	12-11-97	.234	.279	.339	74	315	295	23	69	13	0	6	29	12	7	0	1	64	1	0	3.8	20.3
Cummings, Cole	L-R	6-2	205	6-20-98	.245	.332	.418	84	335	294	43	72	15	0	12	41	30	9	0	1	81	1	0	9.0	24.2
De La Cruz, Michael	B-R	5-9	190	5-15-93	.256	.330	.369	100	408	355	49	91	17	1	7	54	43	0	0	8	67	7	2	10.5	16.4
Didder, Ray-Patrick	R-R	5-9	199	10-01-94	.197	.337	.350	54	190	157	28	31	6	0	6	21	29	4	0	0	52	13	5	15.3	27.4
Farmer, Justin	R-R	6-1	190	12-19-98	.157	.202	.202	29	94	89	10	14	4	0	0	4	4	1	0	0	37	5	3	4.3	39.4
Fernandez, Juan	R-R	5-7	205	3-07-99	.261	.341	.371	102	412	364	49	95	19	0	7	45	36	9	1	2	56	10	5	8.7	13.6
Hollis, Connor	R-R	5-7	170	11-18-94	.240	.338	.335	72	274	233	33	56	9	2	3	20	32	4	2	3	60	13	8	11.7	21.9
Howell, Korry	R-R	6-1	180	9-01-98	.171	.273	.284	63	245	211	31	36	8	2	4	23	23	8	0	3	81	18	4	9.4	33.1
Johnson, Daniel	L-L	5-9	200	7-11-95	.263	.337	.435	98	412	361	58	95	17	3	13	54	40	4	0	7	77	21	6	9.7	18.7
Marsee, Jakob	L-L	6-0	180	6-28-01	.286	.412	.446	16	69	56	12	16	0	0	3	5	11	1	1	0	15	5	0	15.9	21.7
Martorella, Nathan	L-L	6-1	224	2-18-01	.236	.313	.382	23	99	89	12	21	4	0	3	15	9	1	0	0	14	0	0	9.1	14.1
Mendoza, Evan	R-R	6-0	205	6-28-96	.195	.233	.293	11	43	41	2	8	1	0	1	4	2	0	0	0	12	3	0	4.7	27.9
Merrill, Jackson	L-R	6-3	195	4-19-03	.273	.338	.444	46	211	187	26	51	13	2	5	31	18	2	1	3	25	5	1	8.5	11.8
Ona, Jorge	R-R	6-0	235	12-31-96	.218	.301	.391	35	123	110	13	24	10	0	3	12	9	4	0	0	41	2	0	7.3	33.3
Ornelas, Tirso	L-R	6-2	200	3-11-00	.284	.381	.473	72	312	264	38	75	17	0	11	51	44	0	0	4	59	4	4	14.1	18.9
Pauley, Graham	L-R	6-1	200	9-24-00	.321	.375	.556	20	88	81	15	26	10	0	3	12	7	0	0	0	12	2	0	8.0	13.6
Perez, Jake	R-R	6-0	165	7-05-00	.167	.300	.417	9	30	24	7	4	0	0	2	4	4	1	0	1	14	0	0	13.3	46.7
Pichardo, Kervin	R-R	6-0	180	10-15-01	.205	.280	.364	15	51	44	5	9	1	0	2	10	3	2	1	1	14	2	0	5.9	27.5
Quintero, Alison	R-R	5-11	175	4-24-00	.000	.143	.000	2	7	6	0	0	0	0	0	0	1	0	0	0	5	0	0	14.3	71.4
Reyes, Ripken	B-R	5-7	185	4-01-97	.257	.408	.359	119	528	409	82	105	16	4	6	49	56	49	13	1	78	30	7	10.6	14.8
Rodriguez, Yorman	R-R	5-8	160	7-23-97	.179	.195	.333	9	41	39	3	7	0	0	2	6	1	0	0	1	5	0	0	2.4	12.2
Salas, Ethan	L-R	6-2	185	6-01-06	.179	.303	.214	9	33	28	2	5	1	0	0	3	4	1	0	0	8	0	1	12.1	24.2
Seagle, Chandler	R-R	5-10	190	5-23-96	.200	.258	.271	52	187	170	15	34	7	1	1	15	10	4	1	2	55	3	2	5.3	29.4
Valenzuela, Brandon	B-R	6-0	225	10-02-00	.181	.287	.255	27	108	94	10	17	4	0	1	6	13	1	0	0	29	2	0	12.0	26.9
Zabala, Juan	R-R	5-10	190	7-03-99	.191	.233	.279	23	77	68	7	13	6	0	0	6	4	0	4	1	20	0	2	5.2	26.0

Pitching	B-T	Ht.	Wt.	DOB	W	L	ERA	G	GS	SV	IP	Hits	Runs	ER	HR	BB	SO	AVG	OBP	SLG	SO%	BB%	BF
Bachar, Lake	R-R	6-2	219	6-03-95	5	1	2.69	42	0	5	60	52	22	18	4	25	69	.234	.315	.342	27.5	10.0	251
Baez, Michel	R-R	6-8	220	1-21-96	3	1	6.75	18	0	0	23	28	18	17	2	15	21	.311	.422	.511	19.3	13.8	109
Bencomo, Edwuin	R-R	6-2	205	4-14-99	1	0	5.01	12	0	0	23	20	13	13	7	4	15	.225	.281	.494	15.6	4.2	96
Bergert, Ryan	R-R	6-1	210	3-08-00	1	2	2.86	9	8	0	44	32	16	14	1	18	51	.206	.295	.277	28.8	10.2	177
Blanchard, Jason	R-L	6-0	185	6-25-97	1	0	7.36	29	0	0	37	49	33	30	6	19	48	.312	.388	.497	26.1	10.3	184
Bourque, James	R-R	6-4	215	7-09-93	0	1	3.46	11	0	0	13	10	7	5	0	14	18	.213	.413	.298	28.6	22.2	63
Brito, Raul	R-R	6-1	180	5-23-97	5	1	2.68	17	0	0	40	39	14	12	1	19	52	.255	.352	.346	28.7	10.5	181
Camarena, Daniel	L-L	6-0	210	11-09-92	1	7	6.20	25	17	3	70	89	54	48	9	16	54	.309	.351	.483	17.3	5.1	313
Cederlind, Blake	R-R	6-4	215	1-04-96	1	0	10.13	3	0	0	3	2	3	3	0	5	5	.222	.500	.333	31.3	31.3	16
Contreras, Efrain	R-R	5-10	225	1-02-00	6	7	4.92	35	17	4	97	87	59	53	14	49	117	.239	.333	.448	27.8	11.6	421
Espada, Jose	R-R	6-0	170	2-22-97	3	2	2.81	26	7	0	64	47	26	20	5	33	85	.207	.304	.339	32.3	12.5	263
Fernandez, Juan	R-R	5-7	205	3-07-99	0	0	0.00	3	0	0	3	0	0	0	0	0	1	.000	.000	.000	11.1	0.0	9
Gonzalez, Brian	R-L	6-3	230	10-25-95	0	2	6.14	6	3	0	15	15	11	10	2	10	18	.254	.362	.441	26.1	14.5	69
Henry, Henry	R-R	6-4	215	12-17-98	1	3	5.85	24	1	0	32	32	22	21	1	28	25	.281	.414	.333	16.3	18.3	153
Hernandez, Nick	R-R	6-1	212	12-30-94	3	1	3.18	24	0	6	28	22	10	10	1	8	43	.210	.265	.257	37.7	7.0	114
Iriarte, Jairo	R-R	6-2	160	12-15-01	0	1	4.30	13	7	0	29	21	15	14	2	17	51	.198	.325	.283	40.5	13.5	126
Jacob, Alek	L-R	6-3	190	6-16-98	1	0	1.32	18	0	5	27	19	4	4	1	8	32	.192	.266	.263	29.4	7.3	109
Koenig, Jared	R-L	6-5	235	1-24-94	1	0	0.00	12	0	3	14	10	2	0	0	7	22	.200	.293	.220	37.9	12.1	58
Kollar, Jared	R-R	6-0	195	7-24-98	2	2	4.62	12	12	0	51	58	29	26	5	20	34	.283	.354	.405	14.8	8.7	230
Kopps, Kevin	R-R	6-0	200	3-02-97	4	3	2.63	33	0	6	55	55	27	16	2	24	67	.255	.341	.356	27.1	9.7	247
Leasher, Aaron	L-L	6-3	208	4-28-96	1	0	0.73	10	0	0	12	7	1	1	0	11	9	.171	.346	.220	17.3	21.2	52
Lopez, Justin	B-R	6-2	195	5-09-00	3	1	4.60	37	0	4	45	38	24	23	5	29	43	.235	.360	.364	21.7	14.6	198
Mayberry, Seth	R-R	6-3	195	6-22-00	3	4	5.05	31	0	0	41	41	29	23	5	27	54	.258	.381	.396	27.4	13.7	197
Mazur, Adam	R-R	6-2	180	4-20-01	2	3	4.03	12	7	0	38	47	18	17	3	7	43	.301	.329	.436	26.2	4.3	164
Milacki, Bobby	R-R	6-2	210	11-06-96	5	5	4.85	18	5	1	52	55	36	28	14	17	44	.270	.342	.515	19.1	7.4	230
Mosser, Gabe	R-R	6-4	185	6-08-96	1	4	4.97	10	9	0	38	43	26	21	10	15	31	.285	.357	.536	18.5	8.9	168
Paplham, Cole	R-R	6-3	215	3-19-00	0	0	9.00	1	0	0	1	2	1	1	0	0	0	.500	.500	.500	0.0	0.0	4
Pelham, CD	R-L	6-6	238	2-21-95	1	0	12.00	12	0	2	9	10	13	12	1	8	11	.278	.400	.528	24.4	17.8	45
Quezada, Jose	R-R	5-9	165	9-07-95	2	1	4.26	17	0	2	25	22	15	12	2	13	24	.234	.345	.330	21.8	11.8	110
Schlichtholz, Fred	R-L	6-3	215	9-18-95	0	0	2.45	3	0	0	4	2	1	1	0	2	6	.167	.286	.333	40.0	13.3	15
Snelling, Robby	R-L	6-3	210	12-19-03	2	0	1.56	4	4	0	17	12	5	3	1	10	19	.190	.301	.333	26.0	13.7	73
Snider, Duncan	R-R	6-7	235	10-10-97	0	4	5.63	13	11	0	46	48	32	29	5	33	32	.274	.399	.440	15.0	15.4	214
Watson, Nolan	R-R	6-2	195	1-25-97	3	3	4.08	14	12	0	64	60	34	29	7	22	41	.252	.322	.387	15.1	8.1	271
Wolf, Jackson	L-L	6-7	205	4-22-99	8	9	4.08	18	18	0	88	74	44	40	12	22	105	.228	.276	.407	29.8	6.3	352

Fielding

Catcher	PCT	G	PO	A	E	DP	PB
De La Cruz	.995	42	428	12	2	1	2
Fernandez	.970	4	31	1	1	0	0
Quintero	1.000	1	3	0	0	0	0
Rodriguez	.951	4	34	5	2	0	0
Salas	.982	6	53	2	1	0	2
Seagle	.988	50	458	37	6	4	5
Valenzuela	.989	18	158	15	2	1	3
Zabala	.987	20	147	5	2	0	5

First Base	PCT	G	PO	A	E	DP
Aviles	1.000	1	2	0	0	0

	PCT	G	PO	A	E	DP
Bell	1.000	3	14	0	0	0
Castellanos	.987	59	407	40	6	36
Cummings	.989	30	169	7	2	14
De La Cruz	.986	26	190	15	3	31
Fernandez	.974	5	35	2	1	0
Martorella	.980	20	139	9	3	24
Merrill	1.000	1	6	1	0	1
Reyes	1.000	1	6	0	0	0

Second Base	PCT	G	PO	A	E	DP
Aviles	.667	1	2	0	1	0
Bell	1.000	10	12	11	0	6
Castanon	.993	30	59	76	1	22
De La Cruz	.980	21	16	34	1	10
Hollis	1.000	8	12	18	0	5
Mendoza	1.000	2	4	4	0	1
Merrill	.900	2	5	4	1	2
Pauley	1.000	3	6	8	0	2
Perez	.750	2	0	3	1	0
Pichardo	1.000	2	4	2	0	2
Reyes	.983	69	115	167	5	38

Third Base	PCT	G	PO	A	E	DP
Aviles	.947	15	12	24	2	1
Bell	1.000	4	1	3	0	0
Castanon	.895	22	11	23	4	2
De La Cruz	.000	1	0	0	0	0
Didder	1.000	2	1	1	0	1
Fernandez	.876	66	25	81	15	3
Hollis	.972	14	10	25	1	2
Mendoza	.000	1	0	0	0	0
Pauley	.952	14	13	27	2	6
Perez	.909	4	4	6	1	1
Pichardo	1.000	2	6	3	0	0
Reyes	1.000	5	2	2	0	0

Shortstop	PCT	G	PO	A	E	DP
Aviles	.935	13	15	28	3	3
Bell	1.000	2	2	3	0	1
Didder	.975	32	40	75	3	12
Hollis	.979	25	38	56	2	16
Mendoza	.926	8	7	18	2	3
Merrill	.970	31	31	99	4	27
Pichardo	1.000	1	0	2	0	0
Reyes	.947	28	45	62	6	20

Outfield	PCT	G	PO	A	E	DP
Aviles	.800	1	4	0	1	0
Bell	1.000	6	10	0	0	0
Bush	.977	9	22	0	1	0
Castellanos	1.000	7	13	1	0	1
Cummings	1.000	44	74	6	0	0
Didder	1.000	17	27	1	0	0
Farmer	1.000	28	59	1	0	0
Hollis	.968	23	39	1	2	1
Howell	.994	63	136	1	2	0
Johnson	.978	95	181	6	1	2
Marsee	.457	16	32	0	3	0
Martorella	.000	1	0	0	0	0
Merrill	1.000	5	6	1	0	0
Ona	.826	17	18	1	4	0
Ornelas	.882	65	113	3	3	1
Pauley	1.000	4	5	0	0	0
Perez	1.000	3	6	0	0	0
Pichardo	1.000	8	11	2	0	0
Reyes	1.000	23	30	2	0	1

FORT WAYNE TINCAPS — HIGH CLASS A

MIDWEST LEAGUE

Batting	B-T	Ht.	Wt.	DOB	AVG	OBP	SLG	G	PA	AB	R	H	2B	3B	HR	RBI	BB	HBP	SH	SF	SO	SB	CS	BB%	SO%
Bender, Colton	R-R	5-9	195	1-13-99	.207	.327	.321	46	171	140	20	29	5	1	3	14	24	2	3	2	47	2	0	14.0	27.5
Castanon, Marcos	R-R	6-0	195	3-23-99	.287	.352	.491	77	327	289	47	83	20	0	13	58	29	3	0	6	70	1	0	8.9	21.4
Cedeno, Nerwilian	B-R	5-11	175	3-16-02	.220	.299	.382	62	272	241	30	53	12	3	7	34	25	3	0	2	75	6	6	9.2	27.6
Cummings, Cole	L-R	6-2	205	6-20-98	.233	.324	.350	18	68	60	4	14	5	1	0	7	7	1	0	0	21	1	1	10.3	30.9
Dale, Jarryd	R-R	6-2	200	9-11-00	.216	.356	.405	12	45	37	7	8	4	0	1	1	6	2	0	0	17	1	1	13.3	37.8
Doersching, Griffin	R-R	6-4	251	8-12-98	.294	.357	.549	14	57	51	9	15	1	0	4	12	4	1	0	0	23	0	0	7.0	40.4
Dunn, Lucas	R-R	6-0	205	4-30-99	.227	.337	.336	119	479	405	61	92	17	3	7	51	56	13	1	4	122	19	7	11.7	25.5
Fabian, Albert	L-L	6-0	215	12-21-01	.200	.283	.336	41	159	140	17	28	7	0	4	14	16	1	0	2	41	0	0	10.1	25.8
Farmer, Justin	R-R	6-1	190	12-19-98	.233	.328	.340	64	238	206	25	48	11	1	3	28	28	2	0	2	69	13	1	11.8	29.0
Luis, Carlos	L-R	6-2	160	9-04-99	.239	.291	.349	91	358	327	31	78	15	0	7	53	23	3	0	5	75	0	0	6.4	20.9
Marsee, Jakob	L-L	6-0	180	6-28-01	.273	.413	.425	113	499	400	91	109	16	3	13	41	87	10	0	2	82	41	9	17.4	16.4
Martorella, Nathan	L-L	6-1	224	2-18-01	.259	.371	.450	112	483	398	71	103	26	1	16	73	73	3	0	9	87	5	3	15.1	18.0
Mears, Joshua	R-R	6-3	230	2-21-01	.158	.291	.347	62	227	190	30	30	9	0	9	28	29	7	0	1	96	13	5	12.8	42.3
Merrill, Jackson	L-R	6-3	195	4-19-03	.280	.318	.444	68	300	279	50	78	12	2	10	33	17	0	1	3	37	10	3	5.7	12.3
Murphy, Kai	L-L	5-8	173	8-26-00	.204	.255	.280	27	103	93	10	19	4	0	1	7	6	1	1	2	29	1	0	5.8	28.2
Ortiz, Devin	R-R	6-2	215	2-07-99	.094	.231	.125	12	39	32	3	3	1	0	0	1	6	0	0	1	17	0	0	15.4	43.6
Pauley, Graham	L-R	6-1	200	9-24-00	.300	.358	.629	45	187	170	33	51	8	0	16	46	13	3	0	1	41	8	2	7.0	21.9
Pichardo, Kervin	R-R	6-0	180	10-15-01	.267	.387	.410	70	262	217	29	58	7	0	8	33	36	7	0	1	67	6	1	13.7	25.6
Robertson, Tyler	R-R	6-4	200	3-10-00	.343	.375	.552	17	74	67	12	23	2	3	2	7	3	1	2	1	24	5	1	4.1	32.4
Salas, Ethan	L-R	6-2	185	6-01-06	.200	.243	.229	9	37	35	3	7	1	0	0	3	2	0	0	0	10	0	0	5.4	27.0
Valentine, Chase	R-R	5-11	160	4-22-02	.333	.412	.333	6	17	15	0	5	0	0	0	0	2	0	0	0	4	0	1	11.8	23.5
Valenzuela, Brandon	B-R	6-0	225	10-02-00	.279	.372	.456	39	156	136	22	38	10	1	4	15	17	3	0	0	37	0	0	10.9	23.7
Vilar, Anthony	L-R	5-10	190	4-01-99	.232	.321	.358	29	109	95	13	22	3	0	3	9	11	2	0	1	33	0	1	10.1	30.3
Zabala, Juan	R-R	5-10	190	7-03-99	.221	.310	.375	44	157	136	19	30	6	0	5	19	16	2	2	1	40	7	1	10.2	25.5
Zavala, Samuel	L-L	6-1	175	7-15-04	.078	.161	.098	14	56	51	4	4	1	0	0	6	5	0	0	0	19	1	1	8.9	33.9

Pitching	B-T	Ht.	Wt.	DOB	W	L	ERA	G	GS	SV	IP	Hits	Runs	ER	HR	BB	SO	AVG	OBP	SLG	SO%	BB%	BF
Baez, Henry	R-R	6-3	175	10-12-02	0	0	7.20	4	4	0	15	19	12	12	2	7	14	.317	.414	.483	20.0	10.0	70
Baez, Michel	R-R	6-8	220	1-21-96	1	0	6.75	1	0	0	1	2	1	1	1	0	1	.333	.333	1.167	16.7	0.0	6
Bencomo, Edwuin	R-R	6-2	205	4-14-99	2	4	6.85	17	7	0	47	64	41	36	6	11	33	.325	.358	.528	15.6	5.2	212
Bergert, Ryan	R-R	6-1	210	3-08-00	5	2	2.63	14	12	0	62	45	18	18	3	28	75	.202	.295	.314	29.5	11.0	254
Blanchard, Jason	R-L	6-0	185	6-25-97	1	2	2.35	8	0	2	15	15	6	4	1	8	23	.250	.338	.367	33.8	11.8	68
Brito, Raul	R-R	6-1	180	5-23-97	2	0	2.45	10	0	1	22	12	6	6	0	9	26	.167	.259	.194	31.7	11.0	82
Cienfuegos, Miguel	L-L	6-4	195	2-10-97	2	5	3.81	13	11	0	59	51	31	25	7	24	41	.225	.315	.352	16.0	9.3	257
Collett, Keegan	R-R	6-3	215	7-27-98	3	4	4.87	33	2	8	44	39	35	24	4	36	71	.232	.371	.369	33.5	17.0	212
Galindo, Ruben	R-R	6-1	175	1-24-01	0	2	9.39	9	0	0	15	27	16	16	1	5	14	.391	.434	.536	18.4	6.6	76
Geerdes, Will	R-R	6-2	220	3-21-00	1	4	7.06	15	0	3	22	25	20	17	3	12	18	.294	.390	.447	18.0	12.0	100
Geraldo, Jose	R-R	6-3	200	1-30-99	0	0	4.19	28	0	0	34	32	16	16	4	15	33	.250	.336	.398	22.6	10.3	146
Gonzalez, Jesus	L-L	5-10	160	6-12-01	0	1	9.00	1	0	0	3	4	4	3	0	1	7	.308	.400	.462	46.7	6.7	15
Gonzalez, Joan	B-R	6-3	165	5-27-98	1	0	5.21	11	0	0	19	18	12	11	3	10	15	.250	.357	.431	17.9	11.9	84
Hawkins, Garrett	R-R	6-5	230	2-10-00	0	2	3.60	4	4	0	15	17	6	6	2	6	15	.283	.353	.467	22.1	8.8	68
Henry, Henry	R-R	6-4	215	12-17-98	2	1	4.00	10	2	0	18	14	10	8	3	7	12	.209	.293	.358	16.0	9.3	75
Holiday, Aaron	R-R	6-3	205	5-28-00	3	3	4.75	22	0	0	30	26	20	16	2	26	37	.230	.380	.336	26.1	18.3	142
Iriarte, Jairo	R-R	6-2	160	12-15-01	3	3	3.10	14	14	0	61	50	22	21	2	28	77	.224	.326	.332	29.7	10.8	259
Kollar, Jared	R-R	6-0	195	7-24-98	5	0	1.67	9	7	1	38	29	7	7	0	6	35	.210	.247	.268	24.0	4.1	146
Krob, Austin	L-L	6-3	205	9-20-99	5	3	3.03	11	11	0	59	57	26	20	4	21	65	.251	.315	.361	25.6	8.3	254
Lesko, Dylan	R-R	6-2	195	9-07-03	1	1	4.50	3	3	0	12	8	6	6	1	11	20	.190	.358	.310	37.7	20.8	53
Lincoln, Chris	R-R	6-4	175	1-02-98	2	2	4.66	19	0	0	19	16	13	10	2	20	14	.225	.412	.366	14.4	20.6	97

Pitching	B-T	Ht.	Wt.	DOB	W	L	ERA	G	GS	SV	IP	Hits	Runs	ER	HR	BB	SO	AVG	OBP	SLG	SO%	BB%	BF
Lizarraga, Victor	R-R	6-3	180	11-30-03	4	7	4.09	21	21	0	95	85	46	43	5	34	78	.237	.316	.341	19.2	8.4	406
Loewen, Carter	R-R	6-4	240	9-28-98	5	0	2.30	18	0	3	31	26	12	8	2	12	36	.220	.294	.305	26.5	8.8	136
Mazur, Adam	R-R	6-2	180	4-20-01	4	1	2.02	12	11	0	58	50	15	13	2	10	47	.227	.261	.305	20.4	4.3	230
Milacki, Bobby	R-R	6-2	210	11-06-96	3	1	2.32	14	0	2	31	25	10	8	1	12	33	.217	.298	.348	25.2	9.2	131
Morgan, David	R-R	6-0	185	10-26-99	0	0	0.00	3	0	1	4	3	1	0	0	0	4	.188	.188	.188	25.0	0.0	16
Morgan, Tyler	R-R	6-0	200	11-04-00	0	0	5.02	9	1	0	14	10	8	8	2	9	11	.185	.297	.333	17.2	14.1	64
Mundo, Alan	R-R	6-2	170	5-27-00	1	1	10.80	21	0	2	27	32	34	32	2	25	27	.299	.437	.467	20.0	18.5	135
Paplham, Cole	R-R	6-3	215	3-19-00	1	0	1.13	8	0	3	8	4	1	1	1	1	11	.143	.200	.250	36.7	3.3	30
Parra, Reinier	R-R	6-0	155	5-31-01	0	1	108.00	1	0	0	0	4	4	4	0	3	0	1.000	.875	1.000	0.0	37.5	8
Pena, Francis	R-R	6-1	170	1-25-01	0	0	0.00	1	0	0	1	1	0	0	0	1	2	.250	.400	.250	40.0	20.0	5
Rascon, Bodi	L-L	6-5	205	2-03-01	2	4	3.59	17	15	1	63	51	31	25	5	35	63	.219	.332	.356	22.7	12.6	277
Routzahn, Ethan	R-R	6-4	225	3-19-98	3	2	4.66	32	0	1	66	60	40	34	6	24	62	.241	.331	.345	21.6	8.4	287
Smith, Adam	R-R	6-2	180	5-09-00	0	1	5.83	30	0	1	42	46	32	27	3	21	35	.279	.365	.370	18.2	10.9	192
Snelling, Robby	R-L	6-3	210	12-19-03	4	2	2.34	7	7	0	35	31	11	9	1	11	40	.237	.301	.321	27.8	7.6	144
Thwaits, Nick	R-R	6-2	195	6-27-99	3	2	4.58	18	0	3	35	34	20	18	4	19	32	.256	.348	.451	20.1	11.9	159
Varmette, Will	R-R	6-2	195	2-28-03	0	1	0.00	1	0	0	0	3	4	4	0	1	0	1.000	1.000	2.000	0.0	25.0	4
Yost, Eric	R-R	6-1	190	10-15-02	0	1	13.50	1	0	0	1	3	3	2	1	1	2	.375	.444	.750	22.2	11.1	9

Fielding

Catcher	PCT	G	PO	A	E	DP	PB
Bender	.989	33	253	18	3	2	3
Salas	.956	6	42	1	2	0	0
Valenzuela	.994	31	286	22	2	3	7
Vilar	.970	29	270	23	9	4	3
Zabala	1.000	36	297	18	0	0	3

First Base	PCT	G	PO	A	E	DP
Cummings	.986	11	64	4	1	4
Doersching	.980	14	92	6	2	8
Luis	.989	24	156	18	2	10
Martorella	.980	81	571	58	13	47
Ortiz	1.000	3	18	1	0	2
Valenzuela	1.000	1	8	1	0	1

Second Base	PCT	G	PO	A	E	DP
Castanon	1.000	2	4	2	0	2
Cedeno	.950	45	61	110	9	22
Dale	1.000	3	2	4	0	1
Dunn	.973	48	71	107	5	12
Pauley	1.000	12	13	28	0	4
Pichardo	.989	22	28	59	1	13
Valentine	.944	5	8	9	1	2

Third Base	PCT	G	PO	A	E	DP
Castanon	.951	71	44	73	6	5
Dale	1.000	1	1	1	0	0
Dunn	.857	6	3	9	2	0
Luis	.971	20	5	29	1	2
Ortiz	1.000	7	1	10	0	2
Pauley	.984	24	16	47	1	6
Pichardo	.947	6	7	11	1	0

Shortstop	PCT	G	PO	A	E	DP
Cedeno	.957	17	18	48	3	7
Dale	.960	7	8	16	1	2
Merrill	.968	68	97	142	8	29
Pichardo	.938	42	46	90	9	13

Outfield	PCT	G	PO	A	E	DP
Cummings	1.000	4	2	0	0	0
Dunn	.978	66	131	10	3	2
Fabian	.454	15	20	0	2	0
Farmer	.983	66	112	5	3	0
Marsee	.819	113	275	7	9	2
Martorella	.971	21	30	3	1	1
Mears	.983	64	116	6	4	1
Murphy	.979	26	45	0	1	0
Pauley	1.000	6	14	0	0	0
Robertson	.967	17	22	0	1	0
Zavala	.950	14	36	2	2	1

LAKE ELSINORE STORM — *LOW CLASS A*

CALIFORNIA LEAGUE

Batting	B-T	Ht.	Wt.	DOB	AVG	OBP	SLG	G	PA	AB	R	H	2B	3B	HR	RBI	BB	HBP	SH	SF	SO	SB	CS	BB%	SO%
Aquino, Charlis	R-R	6-2	165	11-18-01	.237	.314	.289	78	244	211	31	50	5	0	2	27	22	2	8	1	71	11	6	9.0	29.1
Beshears, Jay	R-R	6-4	215	5-06-02	.229	.283	.314	29	114	105	10	24	4	1	1	13	5	3	0	0	33	1	0	4.4	28.9
Bush, Homer	R-R	6-3	200	10-13-01	.247	.369	.341	24	105	85	16	21	5	0	1	10	12	5	2	1	15	11	1	11.4	14.3
Campbell, Jacob	R-R	6-0	200	5-21-00	.224	.269	.347	14	52	49	4	11	3	0	1	7	3	0	0	0	16	0	1	5.8	30.8
Doersching, Griffin	R-R	6-4	251	8-12-98	.232	.362	.408	93	392	319	52	74	23	0	11	55	63	5	0	5	97	1	1	16.1	24.7
Duarte, Victor	R-R	5-11	170	2-23-01	.230	.354	.304	57	200	161	30	37	7	1	1	26	28	5	0	4	32	4	0	14.0	16.0
Fabian, Albert	L-L	6-0	215	12-21-01	.267	.326	.504	62	264	236	37	63	18	1	12	58	16	7	0	5	50	2	1	6.1	18.9
Head, Dillon	L-L	5-11	180	10-11-04	.241	.311	.333	13	61	54	3	13	1	2	0	3	4	2	0	1	10	1	2	6.6	16.4
Hoffman, Wyatt	R-R	5-9	170	3-16-99	.161	.295	.189	62	222	180	23	29	5	0	0	24	27	8	5	2	61	20	0	12.2	27.5
Karpathios, Braedon	L-L	6-1	186	6-19-03	.181	.410	.267	42	161	116	23	21	6	2	0	10	44	1	0	0	50	2	3	27.3	31.1
Linares, Oswaldo	R-R	5-11	150	4-28-03	.213	.366	.277	49	197	155	24	33	4	0	2	20	36	2	2	1	56	0	0	18.3	28.4
McClaughry, Nik	R-R	5-9	159	9-14-99	.256	.355	.397	27	94	78	10	20	6	1	1	15	8	5	1	2	12	1	1	8.5	12.8
Murphy, Kai	L-L	5-8	173	8-26-00	.287	.361	.435	62	268	237	44	68	15	1	6	31	24	4	2	1	67	11	5	9.0	25.0
Ortiz, Devin	R-R	6-2	215	2-07-99	.266	.380	.324	60	247	207	31	55	9	0	1	31	32	6	2	0	52	4	2	13.0	21.1
Pauley, Graham	L-R	6-1	200	9-24-00	.309	.422	.465	62	276	230	50	71	14	5	4	36	40	5	1	0	40	12	3	14.5	14.5
Robertson, Tyler	R-R	6-4	200	3-10-00	.265	.355	.417	56	266	223	55	59	12	2	6	30	20	13	7	3	65	23	4	7.5	24.4
Salas, Ethan	L-R	6-2	185	6-01-06	.267	.350	.487	48	220	191	35	51	11	2	9	35	24	2	0	3	57	5	2	10.9	25.9
Sanabria, Jose	R-R	5-10	150	10-30-02	.268	.295	.317	13	44	41	5	11	2	0	0	4	2	0	0	1	12	1	0	4.5	27.3
Sanabria, Romeo	L-R	6-2	200	5-02-02	.283	.424	.434	16	67	53	10	15	8	0	0	3	12	1	1	0	15	0	0	17.9	22.4
Valentine, Chase	R-R	5-11	160	4-22-02	.161	.261	.218	38	144	124	11	20	3	2	0	5	15	2	2	1	57	1	2	10.4	39.6
Verdugo, Rosman	R-R	6-0	180	2-02-05	.220	.308	.332	113	472	410	44	90	31	3	3	53	46	8	5	3	124	15	8	9.7	26.3
Vilar, Anthony	L-R	5-10	190	4-01-99	.211	.404	.376	44	179	133	23	28	8	1	4	19	43	1	1	1	53	2	2	24.0	29.6
Vogt, Nick	R-R	6-1	185	8-04-00	.258	.335	.409	79	315	279	45	72	19	1	7	34	28	5	2	1	88	16	4	8.9	27.9
Zavala, Samuel	L-L	6-1	175	7-15-04	.267	.420	.451	101	459	348	83	93	22	0	14	71	89	9	4	9	121	20	6	19.4	26.4

Pitching	B-T	Ht.	Wt.	DOB	W	L	ERA	G	GS	SV	IP	Hits	Runs	ER	HR	BB	SO	AVG	OBP	SLG	SO%	BB%	BF
Baez, Henry	R-R	6-3	175	10-12-02	7	3	3.24	17	14	0	83	68	39	30	3	39	85	.219	.313	.303	23.9	11.0	355
Balboni, Thomas	L-R	6-4	185	7-06-00	2	3	7.17	23	2	0	43	45	36	34	3	18	46	.271	.345	.422	23.7	9.3	194
Boyd, Luke	R-R	6-2	180	11-21-97	1	0	3.00	13	0	0	21	20	11	7	1	7	14	.247	.330	.309	15.4	7.7	91
Campbell, Jacob	R-R	6-0	200	5-21-00	0	0	9.00	1	0	0	1	3	1	1	0	0	1	.500	.571	.833	14.3	0.0	7
Castillo, Wilton	R-R	6-7	190	2-12-00	1	1	9.33	7	3	1	18	28	20	19	4	10	15	.346	.438	.630	15.6	10.4	96
Castro, Manuel	R-R	5-8	180	5-11-02	3	1	3.91	12	5	0	46	43	21	20	3	12	55	.246	.296	.354	29.1	6.3	189
Chacon, Javier	L-L	5-11	190	12-24-02	1	0	2.12	9	0	0	17	9	4	4	0	18	19	.161	.383	.179	23.5	22.2	81
Cienfuegos, Miguel	L-L	6-4	195	2-10-97	1	1	4.50	3	3	0	12	12	6	6	0	4	14	.267	.333	.311	27.5	7.8	51
Eichelberger, Breck	R-R	6-4	195	3-15-00	0	1	7.04	5	4	0	8	6	6	6	2	4	10	.231	.375	.500	31.3	12.5	32

Galindo, Ruben	R-R	6-1	175	1-24-01	2	1	1.02	28	1	6	44	35	5	5	0	12	49	.222	.279	.285	28.3	6.9	173
Geerdes, Will	R-R	6-2	220	3-21-00	2	2	2.97	19	0	4	33	22	11	11	1	14	41	.186	.281	.271	30.4	10.4	135
Gonzalez, Jesus	L-L	5-10	160	6-12-01	1	0	3.12	2	0	0	9	11	5	3	0	0	13	.297	.297	.514	35.1	0.0	37
Gustin, Harry	B-L	6-0	160	5-06-02	0	0	27.00	1	0	0	1	3	2	2	0	1	1	.600	.667	.800	16.7	16.7	6
Haynes, Jagger	L-L	6-3	170	9-20-02	0	3	3.91	11	11	0	25	22	13	11	2	12	29	.234	.327	.298	26.6	11.0	109
Hill, Tim	R-L	6-4	200	2-10-90	0	1	67.50	1	0	0	1	7	6	5	0	0	1	.778	.778	1.111	11.1	0.0	9
Koenig, Ian	L-R	6-2	225	4-10-01	1	1	4.19	6	0	2	19	20	12	9	2	7	24	.247	.315	.407	27.0	7.9	89
Krob, Austin	L-L	6-3	205	9-20-99	0	1	2.34	11	10	0	50	46	21	13	1	22	59	.243	.330	.291	27.3	10.2	216
Lesko, Dylan	R-R	6-2	195	9-07-03	0	3	4.50	5	5	0	16	13	8	8	1	8	23	.228	.338	.351	33.8	11.8	68
Loewen, Carter	R-R	6-4	240	9-28-98	1	2	2.04	16	0	0	18	12	7	4	1	6	22	.190	.257	.270	31.4	8.6	70
Lowe, Isaiah	R-R	6-1	220	5-07-03	0	1	1.59	3	3	0	11	9	5	2	1	4	17	.205	.286	.295	34.7	8.2	49
Lugo, Alejandro	R-R	6-0	165	8-20-02	0	1	3.50	6	0	0	18	17	8	7	2	3	22	.243	.280	.386	29.3	4.0	75
Martinez, Henry	R-R	6-4	190	3-02-04	0	0	12.27	3	3	0	7	8	10	10	2	14	6	.320	.575	.600	14.3	33.3	42
Matos, Dwayne	R-R	6-1	155	11-07-00	2	3	4.85	23	0	0	43	37	24	23	6	18	36	.231	.323	.394	19.4	9.7	186
Mendez, Miguel	R-R	6-2	165	7-01-02	2	3	5.96	15	15	0	54	50	37	36	5	33	50	.240	.356	.385	20.2	13.3	248
Morejon, Adrian	L-L	5-11	224	2-27-99	1	0	7.71	4	2	0	5	5	4	4	1	2	9	.263	.333	.474	42.9	9.5	21
Morgan, David	R-R	6-0	185	10-26-99	4	3	4.24	25	0	0	40	39	19	19	2	13	42	.247	.309	.354	24.0	7.4	175
Mosser, Gabe	R-R	6-4	185	6-08-96	0	1	8.10	1	1	0	3	5	4	3	0	3	3	.333	.444	.467	16.7	16.7	18
Musgrove, Joe	R-R	6-5	230	12-04-92	0	1	7.20	1	1	0	5	6	4	4	0	0	8	.286	.286	.286	38.1	0.0	21
Nedved, Dylan	R-R	6-2	195	4-23-99	5	6	4.94	39	0	1	51	49	35	28	3	19	47	.259	.347	.386	21.3	8.6	221
Nett, Braden	R-R	6-3	185	6-18-02	1	0	4.85	3	2	0	13	11	7	7	0	12	13	.220	.381	.280	20.6	19.0	63
Paplham, Cole	R-R	6-3	215	3-19-00	0	0	4.29	22	0	8	21	17	12	10	0	12	25	.221	.337	.286	27.2	13.0	92
Pelham, CD	R-L	6-6	238	2-21-95	2	1	0.00	4	0	0	4	2	1	0	0	0	5	.133	.133	.133	33.3	0.0	15
Pena, Francis	R-R	6-1	170	1-25-01	1	1	0.51	11	0	0	18	14	3	1	0	2	17	.215	.239	.277	25.0	2.9	68
Pinales, Enmanuel	R-R	6-2	185	4-16-01	3	0	2.87	9	6	0	38	32	12	12	2	11	37	.230	.291	.388	24.3	7.2	152
Pomeranz, Drew	R-L	6-5	246	11-22-88	0	0	0.00	3	2	0	3	0	0	0	0	0	4	.000	.000	.000	44.4	0.0	9
Reyes, Jose Luis	R-R	6-3	190	8-20-02	0	3	3.86	8	7	0	37	37	25	16	3	14	28	.257	.327	.403	17.1	8.5	164
Robinson, Kobe	R-R	6-2	160	3-03-01	6	2	4.01	34	0	1	52	47	27	23	0	25	64	.244	.339	.337	28.3	11.1	226
Ruiz, Xavier	R-R	6-1	180	11-19-02	2	1	9.28	6	0	0	11	11	11	11	1	9	6	.268	.404	.415	11.5	17.3	52
Sanchez, Fernando	L-L	6-0	198	9-13-00	3	7	6.54	25	6	0	76	91	64	55	10	33	82	.293	.380	.466	23.0	9.3	356
Snelling, Robby	R-L	6-3	210	12-19-03	5	1	1.57	11	11	0	52	39	10	9	2	13	59	.211	.261	.314	29.6	6.5	199
Suarez, Robert	R-R	6-2	210	3-01-91	0	0	13.50	1	0	0	1	1	1	1	1	3	0	.500	.800	2.000	0.0	60.0	5
Thwaits, Nick	R-R	6-2	195	6-27-99	0	0	3.70	15	0	0	24	25	13	10	1	11	25	.272	.358	.467	23.4	10.3	107
Vail, Andrew	L-L	6-1	185	8-12-00	0	1	11.08	12	0	0	13	18	19	16	1	14	17	.333	.471	.500	23.9	19.7	71
Varmette, Will	R-R	6-2	195	2-28-03	0	0	1.50	6	0	1	6	4	2	1	1	4	11	.182	.333	.364	40.7	14.8	27
Whiting, Sam	R-R	6-3	220	12-15-00	1	0	2.35	7	0	0	8	5	2	2	1	9	8	.192	.400	.423	22.9	25.7	35
Williams, Henry	R-R	6-5	200	9-18-01	1	5	5.74	12	12	0	42	39	31	27	6	21	40	.250	.352	.423	22.0	11.5	182
Yost, Eric	R-R	6-1	190	10-15-02	1	1	8.18	7	0	1	11	17	11	10	0	1	8	.347	.360	.469	16.0	2.0	50

Fielding

Catcher	PCT	G	PO	A	E	DP	PB
Campbell	.984	7	57	4	1	0	1
Duarte	.990	36	285	15	3	1	8
Linares	.994	35	322	14	2	2	9
Salas	.995	22	186	18	1	0	10
Vilar	.990	37	363	26	4	3	11

First Base	PCT	G	PO	A	E	DP
Beshears	.990	12	90	10	1	6
Doersching	.985	80	568	41	9	50
Duarte	1.000	15	96	6	0	14
Fabian	.967	9	56	3	2	4
Ortiz	1.000	15	77	4	0	4
Sanabria	1.000	6	39	6	0	6

Second Base	PCT	G	PO	A	E	DP
Aquino	.976	48	57	107	4	25
Beshears	.850	5	9	8	3	3
Hoffman	.962	29	53	73	5	23
Linares	1.000	6	7	15	0	2
McClaughry	1.000	9	21	24	0	7
Pauley	1.000	2	2	4	0	1
Sanabria	1.000	1	2	4	0	0
Valentine	.973	21	28	43	2	7
Verdugo	.984	18	30	32	1	10

Third Base	PCT	G	PO	A	E	DP
Aquino	.667	1	1	1	1	0
Beshears	1.000	5	2	2	0	0
Hoffman	.917	24	12	32	4	1
Ortiz	.979	47	27	65	2	6
Pauley	.918	47	35	77	10	10
Sanabria	.909	11	2	18	2	3
Valentine	.500	3	0	1	1	0
Verdugo	.000	1	0	0	1	0

Shortstop	PCT	G	PO	A	E	DP
Aquino	1.000	3	2	7	0	0
Hoffman	.923	10	13	23	3	6
McClaughry	.926	18	20	30	4	7
Valentine	.947	15	17	37	3	7
Verdugo	.937	92	106	206	21	51

Outfield	PCT	G	PO	A	E	DP
Aquino	.981	18	26	0	1	0
Bush	1.000	22	55	0	0	0
Campbell	1.000	3	3	0	0	0
Fabian	.938	30	34	1	1	0
Head	1.000	13	33	0	0	0
Karpathios	.941	36	67	4	5	0
Murphy	.981	60	109	3	3	0
Pauley	1.000	5	6	0	0	0
Robertson	.945	56	94	6	5	0
Vogt	.952	70	133	7	6	1
Zavala	.987	94	193	5	5	0

ACL PADRES

ROOKIE

ARIZONA COMPLEX LEAGUE

Batting	B-T	Ht.	Wt.	DOB	AVG	OBP	SLG	G	PA	AB	R	H	2B	3B	HR	RBI	BB	HBP	SH	SF	SO	SB	CS	BB%	SO%
Beltre, Eddy	R-R	5-11	165	4-16-04	.250	.375	.500	8	24	20	5	5	2	0	1	7	4	0	0	0	9	0	0	16.7	37.5
Beshears, Jay	R-R	6-4	215	5-06-02	.250	.625	.250	2	8	4	4	1	0	0	0	0	2	2	0	0	2	0	0	25.0	25.0
Bush, Homer	R-R	6-3	200	10-13-01	.409	.509	.614	12	53	44	16	18	3	0	2	4	7	2	0	0	7	10	0	13.2	13.2
Camou, Alain	L-R	5-11	150	11-01-03	.287	.380	.369	44	186	157	27	45	13	0	0	23	24	1	2	2	35	2	2	12.9	18.8
Campbell, Jacob	R-R	6-0	200	5-21-00	.308	.333	.462	8	27	26	4	8	1	0	1	6	1	0	0	0	6	5	0	3.7	22.2
Campusano, Luis	R-R	5-11	232	9-29-98	.200	.333	.400	3	12	10	1	2	2	0	0	2	2	0	0	0	1	0	0	16.7	8.3
Cedeno, Nerwilian	B-R	5-11	175	3-16-02	.273	.529	.273	5	17	11	5	3	0	0	0	3	6	0	0	0	6	2	0	35.3	35.3
Choi, B.Y.	L-R	6-3	203	4-30-02	.100	.182	.100	7	22	20	4	2	0	0	0	2	2	0	0	0	13	1	0	9.1	59.1
Coffman, Spence	R-R	6-1	170	1-07-04	.237	.343	.288	21	71	59	9	14	1	1	0	10	10	0	1	1	15	4	0	14.1	21.1
Dale, Jarryd	R-R	6-2	200	9-11-00	.258	.343	.419	9	35	31	5	8	3	1	0	5	4	0	0	0	5	6	0	11.4	14.3
Diaz, Josttin	B-R	6-0	170	5-18-02	.138	.219	.207	9	32	29	3	4	2	0	0	6	3	0	0	0	17	1	1	9.4	53.1
Grant, Donte	L-R	6-0	175	8-29-04	.133	.435	.133	7	23	15	7	2	0	0	0	1	6	2	0	0	5	2	0	26.1	21.7

Head, Dillon	L-L	5-11	180	10-11-04	.294	.413	.471	14	63	51	15	15	4	1	1	8	11	0	0	1	9	3	1	17.5	14.3
Hoffman, Wyatt	R-R	5-9	170	3-16-99	.222	.364	.222	4	11	9	1	2	0	0	0	0	2	0	0	0	3	1	0	18.2	27.3
Hollis, Connor	R-R	5-7	170	11-18-94	.167	.286	.167	2	7	6	1	1	0	0	0	0	1	0	0	0	1	0	0	14.3	14.3
Hollow, Kaden	L-R	6-1	210	3-17-01	.314	.489	.486	16	47	35	8	11	3	0	1	6	11	1	0	0	9	0	1	23.4	19.1
Howell, Korry	R-R	6-1	180	9-01-98	.133	.350	.133	6	20	15	4	2	0	0	0	1	5	0	0	0	5	3	0	25.0	25.0
Karpathios, Braedon	L-L	6-1	186	6-19-03	.361	.512	.525	20	82	61	18	22	6	2	0	12	19	1	0	1	16	4	0	23.2	19.5
King, Lamar	R-R	6-3	215	12-07-03	.324	.440	.397	21	84	68	14	22	1	2	0	10	13	2	0	1	23	5	1	15.5	27.4
Kopack, Addison	R-R	6-2	215	8-06-01	.000	.375	.000	3	8	5	3	0	0	0	0	0	3	0	0	0	3	0	0	37.5	37.5
Linares, Oswaldo	R-R	5-11	150	4-28-03	.325	.557	.600	13	61	40	18	13	5	0	2	10	19	2	0	0	9	2	0	31.1	14.8
Long, Ethan	R-R	6-3	215	5-10-01	.111	.111	.222	3	9	9	0	1	1	0	0	0	0	0	0	0	4	0	0	0.0	44.4
McClaughry, Nik	R-R	5-9	159	9-14-99	.000	.500	.000	2	6	3	1	0	0	0	0	0	3	0	0	0	0	0	0	50.0	0.0
Mendoza, Evan	R-R	6-0	205	6-28-96	.333	.333	.333	3	9	9	2	3	0	0	0	2	0	0	0	0	3	0	0	0.0	33.3
Montesino, Daniel	L-L	6-0	180	2-12-04	.248	.329	.324	42	165	145	24	36	9	1	0	22	15	3	1	1	41	5	1	9.1	24.8
Munoz, Maikol	R-R	6-1	155	10-21-03	.056	.190	.056	7	21	18	2	1	0	0	0	2	2	1	0	0	4	0	0	9.5	19.0
Murillo, Juan	R-R	6-2	180	8-19-02	.299	.368	.474	41	155	137	29	41	9	3	3	29	14	2	0	2	38	6	2	9.0	24.5
Perez, Jake	R-R	6-0	165	7-05-00	.250	.250	.250	6	4	4	3	1	0	0	0	0	0	0	0	0	2	0	0	0.0	50.0
Robertson, Tyler	R-R	6-4	200	3-10-00	.296	.355	.481	9	31	27	4	8	2	0	1	4	2	1	0	1	9	3	0	6.5	29.0
Rodriguez, Carlos	B-R	5-10	155	5-12-03	.289	.384	.361	29	99	83	12	24	1	1	1	19	14	0	0	2	22	3	1	14.1	22.2
Rojas, Yendry	L-R	6-0	185	1-27-05	.222	.382	.296	44	173	135	27	30	3	2	1	17	30	6	0	2	38	9	0	17.3	22.0
Rosario, Eguy	R-R	5-7	150	8-25-99	.714	.750	1.429	2	8	7	3	5	2	0	1	4	1	0	0	0	1	0	1	12.5	12.5
Sanabria, Jose	R-R	5-10	150	10-30-02	.278	.435	.322	40	147	115	26	32	3	1	0	11	31	1	0	0	38	10	6	21.1	25.9
Sanabria, Romeo	L-R	6-2	200	5-02-02	.359	.443	.617	50	203	167	36	60	15	2	8	53	30	0	0	6	48	4	1	14.8	23.6
Schrock, Max	L-R	5-9	185	10-12-94	.273	.529	.545	5	17	11	3	3	0	0	1	2	5	1	0	0	5	0	0	29.4	29.4
Suero, Estuar	B-R	6-5	180	8-29-05	.216	.306	.345	35	160	139	22	30	4	1	4	23	16	3	0	2	49	7	3	10.0	30.6
Valentine, Chase	R-R	5-11	160	4-22-02	.318	.407	.500	12	29	22	3	7	4	0	0	5	4	0	2	1	6	1	2	13.8	20.7
Vincent, Colton	R-R	6-1	182	1-25-00	.083	.154	.167	4	13	12	1	1	1	0	0	0	0	1	0	0	4	0	0	0.0	30.8
Wilson, Ryan	R-R	6-1	195	1-12-02	.143	.200	.357	4	15	14	2	2	0	0	1	2	0	1	0	0	2	0	0	0.0	13.3

Pitching	**B-T**	**Ht.**	**Wt.**	**DOB**	**W**	**L**	**ERA**	**G**	**GS**	**SV**	**IP**	**Hits**	**Runs**	**ER**	**HR**	**BB**	**SO**	**AVG**	**OBP**	**SLG**	**SO%**	**BB%**	**BF**
Addkison, Zac	R-R	6-4	225	6-24-02	0	0	0.00	1	0	0	1	1	0	0	0	0	0	.250	.250	.500	0.0	0.0	4
Baez, Michel	R-R	6-8	220	1-21-96	0	0	0.00	2	1	0	3	2	0	0	0	0	5	.200	.200	.300	50.0	0.0	10
Carlton, Drew	R-R	6-1	215	9-08-95	1	0	0.00	2	1	0	2	3	0	0	0	0	2	.429	.429	.571	28.6	0.0	7
Castillo, Wilton	R-R	6-7	190	2-12-00	1	0	9.69	5	2	0	13	22	14	14	1	5	13	.373	.431	.525	20.0	7.7	65
Cederlind, Blake	R-R	6-4	215	1-04-96	0	0	13.50	2	0	0	2	3	3	3	0	2	2	.375	.500	.500	20.0	20.0	10
Chacon, Javier	L-L	5-11	190	12-24-02	0	0	7.45	6	0	0	10	9	9	8	3	9	10	.257	.391	.571	21.7	19.6	46
Chirinos, Jhosep	R-R	6-4	175	4-17-04	2	3	12.06	14	0	1	16	15	22	21	2	28	33	.250	.511	.483	35.1	29.8	94
Cienfuegos, Miguel	L-L	6-4	195	2-10-97	0	1	5.14	2	2	0	7	9	4	4	0	2	7	.321	.367	.393	23.3	6.7	30
Cosgrove, Tom	L-L	6-2	190	6-14-96	0	0	9.00	1	1	0	1	1	1	1	0	1	2	.250	.400	.500	40.0	20.0	5
Eichelberger, Breck	R-R	6-4	195	3-15-00	0	0	0.00	1	0	0	1	1	0	0	0	1	0	.333	.500	.667	0.0	25.0	4
German, Luis	R-R	6-2	160	10-14-01	1	0	3.38	11	0	0	11	9	5	4	0	14	18	.237	.482	.237	32.1	25.0	56
Gonzalez, Brian	R-L	6-3	230	10-25-95	1	0	0.00	2	1	0	5	2	0	0	0	1	5	.133	.188	.200	31.3	6.3	16
Guerrero, Jordan	R-R	6-5	296	8-01-96	2	0	3.38	6	0	0	5	6	3	2	0	4	7	.286	.400	.381	28.0	16.0	25
Gustin, Harry	B-L	6-0	160	5-06-02	0	0	4.50	2	0	0	2	2	1	1	0	3	2	.250	.455	.375	18.2	27.3	11
Gutierrez, Luis	L-L	6-0	175	7-31-03	2	3	7.65	12	5	0	40	48	38	34	2	24	41	.304	.407	.430	21.6	12.6	190
Leija, Aldo	R-R	6-2	160	6-30-04	0	0	0.00	2	2	0	3	1	0	0	0	1	4	.111	.273	.111	36.4	9.1	11
Lesko, Dylan	R-R	6-2	195	9-07-03	0	1	10.80	4	4	0	5	8	6	6	1	3	9	.381	.458	.619	37.5	12.5	24
Lopez, Jesus	R-R	5-11	175	3-14-06	0	1	17.36	3	0	0	5	8	10	9	1	5	5	.364	.464	.636	17.9	17.9	28
Lowe, Isaiah	R-R	6-1	220	5-07-03	0	0	9.00	1	1	0	1	1	1	1	0	1	1	.250	.400	.250	20.0	20.0	5
Lugo, Alejandro	R-R	6-0	165	8-20-02	1	1	6.67	14	0	0	27	27	23	20	2	20	41	.248	.364	.422	31.8	15.5	129
Martinez, Henry	R-R	6-4	190	3-02-04	2	2	8.54	10	8	1	33	31	33	31	4	34	26	.246	.402	.468	15.9	20.7	164
Mayberry, Seth	R-R	6-3	195	6-22-00	2	0	1.50	4	0	0	6	2	1	1	0	1	7	.100	.143	.200	33.3	4.8	21
Morejon, Adrian	L-L	5-11	224	2-27-99	0	0	0.00	1	1	0	1	0	0	0	0	0	2	.000	.000	.000	66.7	0.0	3
Moreno, Adan	R-R	6-1	185	9-08-04	0	1	6.48	3	0	0	8	10	8	6	2	7	9	.286	.405	.486	21.4	16.7	42
Moreno, Johan	R-R	6-1	180	3-26-03	0	0	7.50	5	0	0	6	10	5	5	0	1	6	.357	.379	.500	20.7	3.4	29
Mosser, Gabe	R-R	6-4	185	6-08-96	2	0	3.00	6	2	0	12	16	8	4	1	2	19	.302	.327	.396	34.5	3.6	55
Mundo, Alan	R-R	6-2	170	5-27-00	0	0	0.00	1	0	0	1	0	0	0	0	1	1	.000	.250	.000	25.0	25.0	4
Nett, Braden	R-R	6-3	185	6-18-02	1	2	4.28	11	9	0	27	17	13	13	0	25	32	.187	.364	.253	26.4	20.7	121
Parra, Reinier	R-R	6-0	155	5-31-01	1	0	4.82	11	0	2	19	22	15	10	0	15	23	.293	.409	.413	24.7	16.1	93
Pelham, CD	R-L	6-6	238	2-21-95	0	0	0.00	1	0	0	1	0	0	0	0	1	0	.000	.250	.000	0.0	25.0	4
Pena, Francis	R-R	6-1	170	1-25-01	1	4	4.50	11	0	0	16	17	20	8	1	7	21	.246	.321	.333	26.9	9.0	78
Pinales, Enmanuel	R-R	6-2	185	4-16-01	1	2	7.15	6	3	0	23	31	19	18	4	8	26	.323	.387	.594	24.5	7.5	106
Qin, Zack	L-L	6-1	198	7-03-05	1	2	5.63	10	5	0	32	33	24	20	2	19	34	.260	.351	.370	22.8	12.8	149
Reyes, Jose Luis	R-R	6-3	190	8-20-02	1	0	8.40	5	2	0	15	26	18	14	2	5	15	.377	.413	.681	20.0	6.7	75
Rosario, Jonney	R-R	5-10	185	7-28-04	3	1	5.08	13	3	2	34	36	21	19	2	16	39	.279	.358	.403	25.8	10.6	151
Ruiz, Xavier	R-R	6-1	180	11-19-02	2	0	3.86	14	0	1	26	24	11	11	1	13	30	.253	.355	.358	27.3	11.8	110
Saba, Elvis	R-R	5-11	180	5-11-00	1	2	4.80	13	0	1	15	16	9	8	1	9	22	.267	.371	.350	31.4	12.9	70
Salazar, Braian	L-L	6-2	165	6-12-05	1	0	3.38	3	0	0	8	4	3	3	1	2	13	.148	.233	.407	43.3	6.7	30
Sanchez, Angel	R-R	6-1	190	11-28-89	0	0	0.00	2	0	0	2	1	0	0	0	0	0	.167	.167	.167	0.0	0.0	6
Snider, Duncan	R-R	6-7	235	10-10-97	0	0	0.00	1	1	0	2	0	0	0	0	2	2	.000	.250	.000	25.0	25.0	8
Suarez, Robert	R-R	6-2	210	3-01-91	0	0	6.75	3	1	0	3	4	3	2	0	1	3	.333	.429	.333	21.4	7.1	14
Varmette, Will	R-R	6-2	195	2-28-03	0	0	21.60	2	1	0	2	4	4	4	0	0	4	.444	.444	.444	44.4	0.0	9
Vela, Noel	L-L	6-1	185	12-21-98	0	0	0.00	1	0	0	1	2	1	0	0	2	0	.667	.800	.667	0.0	40.0	5
Whiting, Sam	R-R	6-3	220	12-15-00	0	0	0.00	1	0	0	1	0	0	0	0	1	2	.000	.200	.000	40.0	20.0	5

Fielding

C: Rodriguez 24, King 12, Hollow 10, Linares 6, Campbell 6, Vincent 3, Kopack 2, Campusano 1. **1B:** Sanabria 44, Montesino 8, Munoz 4, Valentine 2. **2B:** Camou 25, Rojas 11, Valentine 7, Sanabria 5, Coffman 5, Dale 5, Schrock 4, Cedeno 3, Choi 2, Beshears 2. **3B:** Sanabria 26, Camou 21, Hoffman 4, Dale 3, Munoz 2, Perez 2, Rosario 1, Valentine 1, Hollis 1, Choi 1. **SS:** Rojas 33, Coffman 14, Mendoza 3, Valentine 2, Choi 2, McClaughry 2, Sanabria 1, Dale 1, Hollis 1, Camou 1, Cedeno 1. **OF:** Suero 38, Murillo 36, Montesino 31, Karpathios 19, Head 13, Diaz 9, Sanabria 9, Bush 8, Grant 7, Beltre 6, Robertson 6, Howell 2, Long 1, Campbell 1, Vincent 1.

DSL PADRES — ROOKIE

DOMINICAN SUMMER LEAGUE

Batting	B-T	Ht.	Wt.	DOB	AVG	OBP	SLG	G	PA	AB	R	H	2B	3B	HR	RBI	BB	HBP	SH	SF	SO	SB	CS	BB%	SO%
Carrillo, Oliver	R-R	5-11	210	1-19-02	.303	.542	.586	53	225	145	56	44	8	0	11	43	66	12	0	2	45	4	1	29.3	20.0
Castro, Jesus	R-R	5-10	158	7-07-04	.272	.411	.482	38	141	114	31	31	9	0	5	35	26	1	0	0	27	3	0	18.4	19.1
Cedeno, Oliver	B-R	5-10	160	9-10-04	.233	.378	.275	44	149	120	19	28	5	0	0	9	20	8	1	0	10	4	2	13.4	6.7
Chevalier, Nestor	R-R	6-0	165	9-25-04	.239	.401	.321	44	142	109	15	26	3	0	2	16	28	3	0	2	33	5	2	19.7	23.2
Conliffe, Kashon	R-R	5-11	150	7-05-05	.217	.355	.342	44	153	120	27	26	7	1	2	20	26	2	1	4	41	11	2	17.0	26.8
Contreras, Santiago	L-R	6-2	155	8-16-05	.206	.339	.363	34	125	102	25	21	6	2	2	13	13	8	1	1	36	10	1	10.4	28.8
Cordero, Jose	R-R	6-1	165	5-24-03	.203	.380	.371	53	188	143	34	29	8	2	4	25	33	9	1	2	51	15	4	17.6	27.1
Cruz, Gilbert	R-R	5-11	225	5-08-05	.000	.000	.000	2	6	6	0	0	0	0	0	0	0	0	0	0	3	0	0	0.0	50.0
De Leon, Luis	B-R	5-8	155	1-08-06	.293	.482	.350	46	191	140	45	41	4	2	0	24	46	5	0	0	23	19	4	24.1	12.0
Diaz, Ismel	L-R	5-10	170	1-06-06	.227	.383	.267	32	94	75	9	17	3	0	0	8	19	0	0	0	25	1	1	20.2	26.6
Garcia, Alexander	L-R	6-0	170	10-26-05	.243	.320	.320	50	194	169	22	41	7	0	2	25	18	3	0	4	50	6	2	9.3	25.8
Giron, Estiven	R-R	5-11	170	5-25-05	.158	.388	.193	22	80	57	14	9	2	0	0	8	20	2	0	1	19	0	0	25.0	23.8
Hacen, Kevin	R-R	6-2	160	1-30-06	.177	.337	.262	50	205	164	33	29	5	0	3	33	28	12	0	1	50	7	5	13.7	24.4
Hernandez, Alcides	L-R	5-8	160	4-27-05	.313	.476	.313	19	63	48	8	15	0	0	0	6	15	0	0	0	8	4	1	23.8	12.7
Hernandez, Jason	R-R	5-11	160	1-11-06	.191	.296	.426	13	54	47	9	9	2	0	3	8	4	3	0	0	16	1	0	7.4	29.6
Javier, Ismael	B-R	5-8	160	8-27-05	.280	.386	.505	51	216	182	42	51	8	3	9	47	29	3	1	1	37	8	4	13.4	17.1
Marquez, Gustavo	R-R	6-0	160	12-28-04	.208	.376	.289	52	189	149	31	31	6	0	2	24	34	6	0	0	50	13	5	18.0	26.5
Ocopio, Yoiber	R-R	5-10	175	8-24-04	.275	.474	.406	50	193	138	38	38	6	3	2	23	36	17	0	1	29	3	0	18.7	15.0
Perez, Adrian	R-R	5-9	165	10-03-02	.306	.449	.361	38	138	108	16	33	6	0	0	27	28	1	0	1	16	4	1	20.3	11.6
Sanchez, Hugo	L-R	6-0	180	11-06-02	.252	.462	.452	48	198	135	30	34	8	2	5	35	51	5	3	4	45	5	2	25.8	22.7
Santana, William	R-R	5-11	165	10-06-05	.097	.309	.153	32	94	72	11	7	1	0	1	7	15	7	0	0	40	3	2	16.0	42.6
Sierra, Joan	R-R	5-10	175	8-13-06	.186	.333	.288	20	72	59	9	11	3	0	1	6	6	7	0	0	20	0	0	8.3	27.8
Tejeda, Eduarlin	B-R	5-9	150	2-24-05	.429	.467	.571	5	16	14	3	6	2	0	0	2	1	0	1	0	2	1	0	6.3	12.5
Tovar, Yimy	R-R	6-0	160	4-07-06	.316	.412	.474	19	68	57	13	18	3	0	2	16	9	1	0	1	10	2	0	13.2	14.7
Turbi, Emil	B-R	5-8	150	11-26-04	.282	.408	.412	52	216	170	49	48	17	1	1	30	32	7	3	4	46	12	3	14.8	21.3
Valdez, Eric	R-R	6-0	170	9-13-04	.177	.319	.292	40	138	113	16	20	4	0	3	11	16	8	0	1	55	6	5	11.6	39.9
Valdez, Moises	R-R	5-8	165	11-28-05	.260	.378	.310	36	119	100	21	26	1	2	0	12	18	1	0	0	31	4	6	15.1	26.1
Velazquez, Ramses	L-L	6-0	180	10-14-04	.149	.353	.270	54	187	141	26	21	4	2	3	17	41	4	0	1	47	7	2	21.9	25.1

Pitching	B-T	Ht.	Wt.	DOB	W	L	ERA	G	GS	SV	IP	Hits	Runs	ER	HR	BB	SO	AVG	OBP	SLG	SO%	BB%	BF
Acevedo, Josmar	R-R	6-1	170	12-22-03	2	2	10.03	12	8	0	36	39	36	32	6	25	31	.281	.400	.496	18.2	14.7	170
Agramonte, Alexander	R-R	5-11	165	9-23-04	1	5	16.75	14	8	0	45	60	44	24	3	11	34	.309	.357	.428	15.9	5.1	214
Batista, Erick	R-R	6-0	155	9-07-05	0	1	13.36	7	7	0	16	7	12	11	2	22	16	.132	.432	.245	19.8	27.2	81
Carrillo, Oliver	R-R	5-11	210	1-19-02	0	0	0.00	1	0	0	0	0	0	0	0	0	0	.000	.000	.000	0.0	0.0	1
Chavez, Kleiberson	R-R	6-0	195	4-11-05	1	2	6.79	9	3	0	14	24	23	19	2	15	9	.358	.494	.537	10.6	17.6	85
Diaz, Ismel	L-R	5-10	170	1-06-06	0	0	3.00	1	0	0	1	1	3	2	0	4	1	.500	.714	.500	14.3	57.1	7
Garcia, Alexander	L-R	6-0	170	10-26-05	0	0	0.00	1	0	0	1	0	0	0	0	1	0	.000	.200	.000	0.0	20.0	5
Gonzales, Geral	R-R	6-0	170	9-20-02	0	2	5.32	11	0	0	13	11	23	22	1	24	16	.220	.494	.360	20.3	30.4	79
Jose, Bernard	R-R	5-11	160	3-03-03	3	0	16.43	16	2	0	42	33	24	23	1	26	41	.223	.359	.311	22.7	14.4	181
Lazala, Victor	R-R	6-2	175	11-06-02	0	0	30.75	10	0	4	14	6	5	4	1	9	12	.128	.333	.191	19.0	14.3	63
Lopez, Angel	R-R	6-4	195	10-15-03	0	3	6.65	15	6	0	27	32	42	37	0	34	25	.308	.500	.462	16.4	22.4	152
Lopez, Jesus	R-R	5-11	175	3-14-06	1	3	17.55	10	9	0	39	41	22	20	3	15	34	.268	.347	.418	19.7	8.7	173
Mendez, Darlin	R-R	6-1	210	7-19-04	3	2	14.81	18	0	0	26	22	23	16	2	23	27	.229	.394	.396	21.1	18.0	128
Minaya, Johan	R-R	6-1	165	10-22-04	2	2	10.33	12	2	0	31	37	31	27	1	29	32	.298	.440	.379	20.1	18.2	159
Miralles, Maikel	R-R	5-11	160	10-22-04	1	2	15.50	6	1	0	10	12	9	6	2	7	11	.279	.392	.465	21.6	13.7	51
Moreno, Adan	R-R	6-1	185	9-08-04	1	1	22.29	10	10	0	35	34	21	14	0	14	25	.254	.348	.366	16.1	9.0	155
Moreno, Johan	R-R	6-1	180	3-26-03	3	1	35.45	10	10	0	43	31	14	11	1	12	45	.201	.268	.292	26.8	7.1	168
Nava, Rafael	R-R	5-11	155	6-05-05	1	3	6.30	11	5	0	14	20	21	20	1	14	17	.328	.488	.393	21.3	17.5	80
Ojeda, Danny	R-R	6-1	175	10-11-04	1	1	8.55	12	2	0	19	24	22	20	3	18	27	.304	.440	.418	27.0	18.0	100
Olmedo, Kleiber	R-R	6-1	155	8-23-04	2	0	25.80	8	0	1	14	9	5	5	1	6	9	.180	.305	.240	15.3	10.2	59
Ortiz, Anthony	R-R	5-11	150	9-17-02	2	1	10.32	16	0	2	29	30	31	25	4	20	22	.256	.389	.427	15.3	13.9	144
Padilla, Samuel	R-R	6-0	180	8-22-05	0	0	9.60	4	0	0	5	3	5	5	2	5	3	.158	.385	.526	11.5	19.2	26
Parra, Abraham	R-R	6-2	170	12-29-05	1	1	23.40	10	5	0	26	27	11	10	1	8	14	.281	.355	.344	12.6	7.2	111
Pascual, Yovannki	L-L	5-11	185	8-04-02	3	0	28.50	10	8	2	38	32	14	12	1	15	35	.229	.306	.307	22.3	9.6	157
Polanco, Dariel	R-R	5-11	150	9-28-05	1	0	24.00	8	1	0	16	22	12	6	1	6	7	.310	.367	.408	8.9	7.6	79
Prats, Yoniel	R-R	6-0	135	8-10-04	1	3	4.70	14	1	0	16	19	35	30	3	27	16	.311	.532	.525	16.7	28.1	96
Ramirez, Wilmer	L-L	6-3	175	7-22-04	2	5	14.76	13	9	0	41	42	34	25	1	36	44	.271	.415	.329	22.7	18.6	194
Reyes, Jimmy	R-R	5-10	170	11-15-05	2	1	30.33	13	2	0	30	29	15	9	0	15	19	.248	.360	.274	13.7	10.8	139
Rios, Jesus	R-R	6-1	190	12-27-01	6	3	12.69	16	0	2	18	22	15	13	2	10	13	.289	.393	.461	14.4	11.1	90
Sanchez, Hugo	L-R	6-0	180	11-06-02	0	0	0.00	2	0	0	1	0	0	0	0	2	0	.000	.400	.000	0.0	40.0	5
Sanchez, Jeison	R-R	6-0	170	5-12-04	1	3	9.57	14	6	0	39	54	47	37	2	26	30	.331	.437	.454	15.2	13.1	198
Sojo, Santiago	R-R	6-4	185	12-24-00	4	1	18.25	21	0	2	24	29	17	12	2	15	25	.296	.391	.418	21.7	13.0	115
Solano, Leandro	R-R	6-2	160	2-18-05	0	2	4.00	8	0	1	8	9	21	18	0	15	5	.290	.566	.419	9.4	28.3	53
Tejeda, Jefren	L-L	6-1	170	7-24-03	0	0	0.00	2	2	0	4	3	1	0	0	4	4	.214	.389	.357	22.2	22.2	18
Valdez, Miguel	R-R	6-0	170	8-01-03	7	3	13.44	19	1	0	40	39	31	27	4	22	44	.253	.355	.403	24.0	12.0	183
Valenzuela, Jordan	R-R	6-2	190	5-20-05	1	2	8.86	13	0	0	22	20	23	22	1	28	24	.244	.475	.317	19.7	23.0	122

Fielding

C: Ocopio 26, Hernandez 17, Diaz 14, Contreras 7, Cruz 1. **1B:** Garcia 28, Diaz 16, Valdez 16, Ocopio 6, Chevalier 2, Cruz 1, Hernandez 1, Perez 1. **2B:** Valdez 16, Santana 12, Hernandez 11, De Leon 8, Tejeda 4, Sierra 3, Cedeno 3, Ocopio 2. **3B:** Perez 23, Tovar 15, Santana 13, Chevalier 7, Sierra 2, Valdez 2, Hernandez 1. **SS:** Cedeno 39, Valdez 9, De Leon 6, Santana 5, Perez 3, Tovar 1. **OF:** Velazquez 50, Cordero 28, Marquez 27, Valdez 22, Contreras 22, Chevalier 13, Garcia 11, Hernandez 1.

San Francisco Giants

SEASON SYNOPSIS: After missing out on free-agent targets such as Aaron Judge and Carlos Correa in the offseason, the Giants tried once again to platoon and optimize their way to a playoff spot but ultimately didn't have enough talent, finishing below .500 and in fourth place in the National League West.

HIGH POINT: The Giants generally played well in the first half of the season and got hot in the first half of July, reeling off seven straight wins to pull within 1.5 games of the first-place Dodgers. Closer Camilo Doval saved four of the wins, the last an 11-10 victory at Cincinnati. He wasn't needed July 9, when ace Logan Webb threw a 1-0 shutout against the Rockies. Webb wound up leading the league with 216 innings pitched.

LOW POINT: San Francisco's offense collapsed in September, suffering back-to-back shutouts in the middle of a six-game losing streak to open the month and averaging 3.4 runs per game in its final 28 games. The Giants' pitchers also wore down under the weight of having just two starters used in conventional fashion while the rest of the rotation spots were given to openers and starters used in bulk roles.

NOTABLE ROOKIES: The Giants broke in plenty of rookies and ultimately went as rookie catcher Patrick Bailey went; he was 37-for-115 out of the chute (.322) with five homers in his first 33 games, but went 7-for-58 to finish. RHP Tristan Beck and sidewinding RHP Ryan Walker were two key pieces of San Francisco's unique pitching approach. C/OF Blake Sabol (.235/.301/.394), a Rule 5 draft pick, had his moments in the batter's box, less so defensively. Normally a third baseman, Casey Schmitt tried to fill the void at shortstop when Brandon Crawford was hurt but struggled with the role.

KEY TRANSACTIONS: At season's end, team president Farhan Zaidi fired manager Gabe Kapler, but it was Zaidi who'd built a middling roster, with free-agent signees Mitch Haniger and Michael Conforto failing to pay off in their first year and trade-deadline acquisition A.J. Pollock being released in early September.

DOWN ON THE FARM: The Giants aren't swimming in Top 100 Prospects, but they have figured out a way to field respectable MiLB teams. Seven of the Giants eight MiLB teams finished at .500 or better and the team's .544 MiLB winning percentage was 11th best.

OPENING DAY PAYROLL: $187,932,500 (11th).

PLAYERS OF THE YEAR

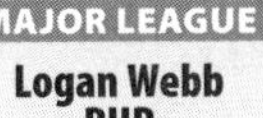

MAJOR LEAGUE

Logan Webb
RHP

11-13, 3.25
33 GS, 216 IP
1.07 WHIP

MINOR LEAGUE

Mason Black
RHP

(AA/AAA)
4-9, 3.71
.219 AVGA, 11.3 SO/9

ORGANIZATION LEADERS

Batting		***Minimum 250 AB**
MAJORS		
* AVG	Wilmer Flores	.284
* OPS	Wilmer Flores	.863
HR	Wilmer Flores	23
RBI	J.D. Davis	69
MINORS		
* AVG	Wade Meckler, Eug./Rich./Sacram.	.371
* OBP	Wade Meckler, Eug./Rich./Sacram.	.456
* SLG	Heliot Ramos, San Jose/Sacramento	.570
* OPS	Wade Meckler, Eug./Rich./Sacram.	.965
R	Grant McCray, Eugene	101.000
H	Carter Howell, San Jose/Eugene	144
TB	Tyler Fitzgerald, Richmond/Sacr.	247
2B	Diego Velasquez, San Jose	32
3B	Carter Howell, San Jose/Eugene	8
HR	Victor Bericoto, Eugene/Richmond	27
RBI	Victor Bericoto, Eugene/Richmond	86
BB	Shane Matheny, Richmond/Sacramento	89
SO	Grant McCray, Eugene	171
SB	Grant McCray, Eugene	52

Pitching		**#Minimum 75 IP**
MAJORS		
W	Logan Webb	11
# ERA	Logan Webb	3.25
SO	Logan Webb	194
SV	Camilo Doval	39
MINORS		
W	Nick Avila, Sacramento	14
L	4-tied	9
# ERA	Wil Jensen, Richmond	2.53
G	Nick Avila, Sacramento	56.00
GS	Mason Black, Richmond/Sacramento	29.00
SV	Erik Miller, Richmond/Sacramento	15
IP	Kai-Wei Teng, Richmond/Sacramento	126.00
BB	Drew Strotman, Sacramento	73
SO	Kai-Wei Teng, Richmond/Sacramento	164
# AVG	Hayden Birdsong, SJ/Eug./Rich.	.199

2023 PERFORMANCE

General Manager: Farhan Zaidi. **Farm Director:** Kyle Haines. **Scouting Director:** Michael Holmes.

Class	Team	League	W	L	PCT	Finish	Manager
Majors	San Francisco Giants	National	79	83	.488	10 (15)	Gabe Kapler
Triple-A	Sacramento River Cats	Pacific Coast	67	82	.450	8 (10)	Dave Brundage
Double-A	Richmond Flying Squirrels	Eastern	74	64	.536	5 (12)	Dennis Pelfrey
High-A	Eugene Emeralds	Northwest	66	66	.500	3 (6)	Carlos Valderrama
Low-A	San Jose Giants	California	68	64	.515	5 (10)	Jeremiah Knackstedt
Rookie	ACL Giants Black	Arizona Complex	33	23	.589	4 (17)	Jose Montilla
Rookie	ACL Giants Orange	Arizona Complex	30	26	.536	8 (17)	Jacob Heyward
Rookie	DSL Giants Black	Dominican Sum.	27	26	.509	24 (50)	Juan Ciriaco
Rookie	DSL Giants Orange	Dominican Sum.	30	23	.566	14 (50)	Drew Martinez
Overall 2023 Minor League Record			395	374	.514	11th (30)	

ORGANIZATION STATISTICS

SAN FRANCISCO GIANTS

NATIONAL LEAGUE

Batting	B-T	Ht.	Wt.	DOB	AVG	OBP	SLG	G	PA	AB	R	H	2B	3B	HR	RBI	BB	HBP	SH	SF	SO	SB	CS	BB%	SO%
Bailey, Patrick	B-R	6-0	210	5-29-99	.233	.285	.359	97	353	326	29	76	18	1	7	48	21	3	2	1	100	1	0	5.9	28.3
Bart, Joey	R-R	6-2	238	12-15-96	.207	.263	.264	30	95	87	9	18	5	0	0	5	3	4	0	1	23	0	0	3.2	24.2
Beaty, Matt	L-R	6-0	215	4-28-93	.200	.200	.200	4	5	5	1	1	0	0	0	1	0	0	0	0	2	0	0	0.0	40.0
Camargo, Johan	B-R	5-11	195	12-13-93	.222	.300	.222	8	20	18	0	4	0	0	0	2	1	1	0	0	4	0	0	5.0	20.0
Conforto, Michael	L-R	6-1	215	3-01-93	.239	.334	.384	125	470	406	58	97	14	0	15	58	53	7	0	4	106	4	0	11.3	22.6
Crawford, Brandon	L-R	6-1	223	1-21-87	.194	.273	.314	94	320	283	31	55	11	1	7	38	28	4	1	4	81	3	0	8.8	25.3
Davis, J.D.	R-R	6-3	218	4-27-93	.248	.325	.413	144	546	480	61	119	23	1	18	69	52	6	0	6	152	1	0	9.5	27.8
DeJong, Paul	R-R	6-0	205	8-02-93	.184	.180	.286	18	50	49	2	9	2	0	1	5	0	0	0	1	16	0	0	0.0	32.0
2-team (81 St. Louis)				.226	.282	.393	99	356	328	40	74	13	0	14	37	21	5	0	2103		4	4	5.9	28.9	
Diaz, Isan	L-R	5-10	201	5-27-96	.053	.143	.053	6	21	19	0	1	0	0	0	1	2	0	0	0	7	0	0	9.5	33.3
Estrada, Thairo	R-R	5-10	185	2-22-96	.271	.315	.416	120	530	495	63	134	26	2	14	49	22	11	0	2	120	23	7	4.2	22.6
Fitzgerald, Tyler	R-R	6-3	205	9-15-97	.219	.265	.469	10	34	32	3	7	2	0	2	5	2	0	0	0	10	2	0	5.9	29.4
Flores, Wilmer	R-R	6-2	213	8-06-91	.284	.355	.509	126	454	405	51	115	22	0	23	60	41	5	0	3	63	0	0	9.0	13.9
Haniger, Mitch	R-R	6-2	214	12-23-90	.209	.266	.365	61	229	211	27	44	13	1	6	28	15	2	0	1	65	1	0	6.6	28.4
Johnson, Bryce	B-R	6-1	195	10-27-95	.163	.229	.256	30	48	43	7	7	1	0	1	3	4	0	0	1	15	3	0	8.3	31.3
Luciano, Marco	R-R	6-1	178	9-10-01	.231	.333	.308	14	45	39	4	9	3	0	0	0	6	0	0	0	17	1	0	13.3	37.8
Mathias, Mark	R-R	6-0	200	8-02-94	.200	.200	.200	5	10	10	1	2	0	0	0	2	0	0	0	0	4	0	0	0.0	40.0
2-team (22 Pittsburgh)					.275	.379	.359	47	154	131	18	36	5	0	2	14	22	0	0	1	31	4	2	14.3	20.1
Matos, Luis	R-R	5-11	160	1-28-02	.250	.319	.342	76	253	228	24	57	13	1	2	14	20	3	2	0	33	3	0	7.9	13.0
Meckler, Wade	L-R	5-10	178	4-21-00	.232	.328	.250	20	64	56	6	13	1	0	0	4	6	2	0	0	25	0	0	9.4	39.1
Pederson, Joc	L-L	6-1	220	4-21-92	.235	.348	.416	121	425	358	59	84	14	3	15	51	57	7	0	3	89	0	0	13.4	20.9
Perez, Roberto	R-R	5-11	220	12-23-88	.133	.235	.133	5	17	15	0	2	0	0	0	1	2	0	0	0	6	0	0	11.8	35.3
Pollock, AJ	R-R	6-1	210	12-05-87	.000	.000	.000	5	6	6	0	0	0	0	0	0	0	0	0	0	2	0	0	0.0	33.3
Ramos, Heliot	R-R	6-1	188	9-07-99	.179	.233	.304	25	60	56	5	10	4	0	1	2	4	0	0	0	20	0	0	6.7	33.3
Ruf, Darin	R-R	6-2	232	7-28-86	.261	.370	.348	9	27	23	1	6	2	0	0	3	4	0	0	0	9	0	0	14.8	33.3
2-team (11 Milwaukee)					.224	.333	.286	20	57	49	3	11	3	0	0	3	8	0	0	0	16	0	0	14.0	28.1
Sabol, Blake	L-R	6-4	225	1-07-98	.235	.301	.394	110	344	310	36	73	10	0	13	44	24	6	2	2	117	4	2	7.0	34.0
Schmitt, Casey	R-R	6-2	215	3-01-99	.206	.255	.324	90	277	253	28	52	15	0	5	30	13	5	3	3	65	2	1	4.7	23.5
Slater, Austin	R-R	6-1	204	12-13-92	.270	.348	.400	89	207	185	24	50	9	0	5	20	20	2	0	0	58	2	2	9.7	28.0
Stevenson, Cal	L-L	5-9	175	9-12-96	.000	.250	.000	6	12	9	1	0	0	0	0	0	3	0	0	0	2	0	0	25.0	16.7
Villar, David	R-R	6-1	215	1-27-97	.145	.236	.315	46	140	124	15	18	6	0	5	12	11	4	0	1	45	1	1	7.9	32.1
Wade, LaMonte	L-L	6-1	205	1-01-94	.256	.373	.417	135	519	429	64	110	14	2	17	45	76	6	4	4	95	2	0	14.6	18.3
Wisely, Brett	L-R	5-10	180	5-08-99	.175	.231	.267	51	131	120	10	21	5	0	2	8	9	0	1	1	40	2	1	6.9	30.5
Wynns, Austin	R-R	6-0	190	12-10-90	.000	.000	.000	1	2	2	0	0	0	0	0	0	0	0	0	0	2	0	0	0.0	100.0
2-team (5 Los Angeles Dodgers)					.208	.264	.277	51	145	130	11	27	6	0	1	10	9	2	3	1	39	1	0	6.2	26.9
Yastrzemski, Mike	L-L	5-10	178	8-23-90	.233	.330	.445	106	381	330	54	77	23	1	15	43	45	3	2	1	99	2	2	11.8	26.0

Pitching	B-T	Ht.	Wt.	DOB	W	L	ERA	G	GS	SV	IP	Hits	Runs	ER	HR	BB	SO	AVG	OBP	SLG	SO%	BB%	BF
Alexander, Scott	L-L	6-2	195	7-10-89	7	3	4.66	55	8	1	48	55	30	25	2	11	31	.282	.324	.369	14.9	5.3	208
Beaty, Matt	L-R	6-0	215	4-28-93	0	0	27.00	1	0	0	1	3	3	3	0	1	1	.500	.571	.833	14.3	14.3	7
Beck, Tristan	R-R	6-4	165	6-24-96	3	3	3.92	33	3	2	85	83	40	37	10	21	68	.252	.300	.388	19.2	5.9	354
Brebbia, John	L-R	6-1	200	5-30-90	3	5	3.99	40	10	0	38	31	21	17	6	14	47	.215	.280	.403	29.2	8.7	161
Cobb, Alex	R-R	6-3	205	10-07-87	7	7	3.87	28	28	0	151	163	69	65	19	37	131	.272	.319	.435	20.3	5.7	646
Crawford, Brandon	L-R	6-1	223	1-21-87	0	0	0.00	1	0	0	1	1	0	0	0	1	0	.250	.400	.250	0.0	20.0	5
DeSclafani, Anthony	R-R	6-2	195	4-18-90	4	8	4.88	19	18	0	100	105	59	54	15	20	79	.271	.311	.456	18.9	4.8	419
Doval, Camilo	R-R	6-2	185	7-04-97	6	6	2.93	69	0	39	68	51	32	22	3	26	87	.209	.304	.287	31.0	9.3	281
Harrison, Kyle	R-L	6-2	200	8-12-01	1	1	4.15	7	7	0	35	29	19	16	8	11	35	.221	.299	.458	23.8	7.5	147
Hjelle, Sean	R-R	6-11	228	5-07-97	2	1	6.52	15	0	0	29	38	25	21	3	13	31	.317	.399	.458	22.3	9.4	139
Jackson, Luke	R-R	6-2	210	8-24-91	2	2	2.97	33	0	0	33	26	14	11	3	15	43	.206	.294	.341	30.1	10.5	143
Junis, Jakob	R-R	6-3	220	9-16-92	4	3	3.87	40	4	1	86	90	42	37	12	21	96	.269	.318	.451	26.2	5.7	367
Llovera, Mauricio	R-R	5-11	224	4-17-96	1	0	1.69	5	0	0	5	4	1	1	1	2	5	.222	.286	.444	23.8	9.5	21
Manaea, Sean	R-L	6-5	245	2-01-92	7	6	4.44	37	10	1	118	104	68	58	14	42	128	.234	.309	.394	25.7	8.4	499

Rogers, Taylor	L-L	6-3	190	12-17-90	6	4	3.83	60	0	2	52	39	27	22	6	25	64	.211	.312	.357	29.6	11.6	216
Rogers, Tyler	R-R	6-3	181	12-17-90	4	5	3.04	68	0	2	74	66	27	25	7	19	60	.236	.289	.368	19.4	6.1	309
Stripling, Ross	R-R	6-1	215	11-23-89	0	5	5.36	22	11	0	89	104	54	53	20	16	70	.287	.320	.497	18.4	4.2	381
Villar, David	R-R	6-1	215	1-27-97	0	0	0.00	1	0	0	1	0	0	0	0	1	0	.000	.333	.000	0.0	33.3	3
Waites, Cole	R-R	6-3	180	6-10-98	0	0	15.43	3	0	0	2	6	5	4	0	2	2	.462	.533	.538	13.3	13.3	15
Walker, Ryan	R-R	6-2	200	11-26-95	5	3	3.23	49	13	1	61	61	25	22	8	24	78	.262	.333	.421	29.7	9.1	263
Webb, Logan	R-R	6-1	220	11-18-96	11	13	3.25	33	33	0	216	201	83	78	20	31	194	.248	.280	.374	22.8	3.6	850
Winn, Keaton	R-R	6-4	238	2-20-98	1	3	4.68	9	5	1	42	36	22	22	6	8	35	.231	.288	.417	20.3	4.7	172
Wisely, Brett	L-R	5-10	180	5-08-99	0	0	9.00	1	0	0	1	1	1	1	1	0	0	.250	.250	1.000	0.0	0.0	4
Wood, Alex	R-L	6-4	215	1-12-91	5	5	4.33	29	12	0	98	98	52	47	9	42	74	.263	.347	.421	17.2	9.8	429

Fielding

Catcher	PCT	G	PO	A	E	DP	PB
Bailey	.984	94	740	50	13	2	8
Bart	.991	30	212	9	2	0	1
Perez	1.000	5	41	1	0	0	0
Sabol	.987	55	371	19	5	1	6
Wynns	1.000	1	8	0	0	0	0

First Base	PCT	G	PO	A	E	DP
Davis	1.000	15	82	5	0	7
Flores	.995	61	412	27	2	38
Pederson	1.000	2	3	0	0	1
Villar	.974	6	36	2	1	5
Wade	.989	116	868	70	10	84

Second Base	PCT	G	PO	A	E	DP
DeJong	1.000	1	1	0	0	0
Diaz	1.000	5	11	18	0	5
Estrada	.989	102	156	304	5	68
Flores	1.000	6	2	3	0	0
Mathias	1.000	5	5	10	0	2
Schmitt	1.000	19	20	51	0	18
Villar	.984	21	29	31	1	6
Wisely	.968	37	43	79	4	17

Third Base	PCT	G	PO	A	E	DP
Camargo	1.000	3	0	3	0	0
Davis	.967	116	58	205	9	14
Diaz	1.000	1	0	2	0	0
Fitzgerald	1.000	3	1	5	0	0
Flores	.848	22	6	33	7	3
Schmitt	.915	35	7	58	6	9
Villar	1.000	17	8	23	0	1

Shortstop	PCT	G	PO	A	E	DP
Camargo	1.000	5	8	11	0	2
Crawford	.964	92	103	223	12	50
DeJong	.963	16	18	34	2	4
Estrada	.957	24	21	45	3	11
Luciano	.978	13	16	29	1	9
Schmitt	.983	42	37	78	2	20
Wisely	.000	1	0	0	0	0

Outfield	PCT	G	PO	A	E	DP
Conforto	.975	114	155	5	2	1
Estrada	1.000	3	2	0	0	0
Fitzgerald	1.000	9	27	0	0	0
Haniger	.987	60	89	1	2	0
Johnson	1.000	30	31	0	0	0
Matos	.989	86	114	4	3	2
Meckler	.984	22	34	0	1	0
Pederson	.956	38	35	0	3	0
Pollock	1.000	5	5	0	0	0
Ramos	.979	26	21	1	1	0
Sabol	.978	43	44	1	1	0
Slater	.986	82	96	2	2	2
Stevenson	1.000	6	12	0	0	0
Wade	.667	23	20	0	0	0
Wisely	.500	19	27	0	0	0
Yastrzemski	.985	124	175	6	1	1

SACRAMENTO RIVER CATS — TRIPLE-A

PACIFIC COAST LEAGUE

Batting	B-T	Ht.	Wt.	DOB	AVG	OBP	SLG	G	PA	AB	R	H	2B	3B	HR	RBI	BB	HBP	SH	SF	SO	SB	CS	BB%	SO%
Alvarez, Armando	R-R	6-0	195	7-14-94	.308	.379	.581	74	298	260	51	80	15	1	18	56	32	1	0	5	47	8	1	10.7	15.8
Bailey, Patrick	B-R	6-0	210	5-29-99	.216	.317	.353	14	60	51	5	11	1	0	2	6	7	1	0	1	15	1	0	11.7	25.0
Bart, Joey	R-R	6-2	238	12-15-96	.248	.357	.393	60	244	206	33	51	12	0	6	28	30	6	0	2	69	1	0	12.3	28.3
Beaty, Matt	L-R	6-0	215	4-28-93	.272	.406	.447	30	129	103	14	28	6	0	4	23	14	10	1	1	24	0	0	10.9	18.6
Brooks, Trenton	L-L	5-10	195	7-03-95	.233	.382	.465	24	111	86	17	20	2	0	6	19	21	1	1	2	17	2	0	18.9	15.3
2-team (94 Las Vegas)					.286	.402	.516	118	523	430	95	123	31	1	22	90	78	7	3	5	77	7	0	14.9	14.7
Camargo, Johan	B-R	5-11	195	12-13-93	.213	.302	.340	14	53	47	5	10	0	0	2	7	6	0	0	0	11	0	0	11.3	20.8
Coulter, Clint	R-R	6-3	225	7-30-93	.243	.332	.403	58	235	206	41	50	15	0	6	39	19	9	0	1	42	4	0	8.1	17.9
Diaz, Isan	L-R	5-10	201	5-27-96	.240	.324	.490	26	108	96	22	23	3	0	7	19	12	0	0	0	38	3	0	11.1	35.2
Estrada, Thairo	R-R	5-10	185	2-22-96	.091	.091	.091	3	11	11	0	1	0	0	0	1	0	0	0	0	3	0	0	0.0	27.3
Fitzgerald, Tyler	R-R	6-3	205	9-15-97	.287	.358	.499	102	466	415	72	119	20	4	20	69	45	2	2	2	111	29	3	9.7	23.8
Genoves, Ricardo	R-R	6-2	190	5-14-99	.218	.317	.343	79	287	248	33	54	13	0	6	34	31	6	0	2	79	0	1	10.8	27.5
Gigliotti, Michael	L-L	6-0	180	2-14-96	.240	.377	.353	75	278	221	36	53	14	1	3	28	46	5	2	4	53	7	2	16.5	19.1
Gonzalez, Luis	L-L	6-1	185	9-10-95	.255	.355	.362	27	110	94	14	24	5	1	1	6	13	2	0	1	20	6	2	11.8	18.2
Guthrie, Dalton	R-R	5-11	160	12-23-95	.275	.310	.375	9	42	40	4	11	4	0	0	1	2	0	0	0	6	1	1	4.8	14.3
Haniger, Mitch	R-R	6-2	214	12-23-90	.167	.286	.367	9	35	30	3	5	0	0	2	3	2	3	0	0	4	0	0	5.7	11.4
Hill, Turner	L-L	5-10	180	4-04-99	.500	.500	.875	2	8	8	2	4	1	1	0	1	0	0	0	0	0	0	0	0.0	0.0
Johnson, Bryce	B-R	6-1	195	10-27-95	.280	.373	.455	66	298	257	48	72	13	4	8	29	34	4	3	0	70	18	4	11.4	23.5
Larsen, Jack	L-L	6-1	195	1-13-95	.100	.280	.150	7	26	20	2	2	1	0	0	0	4	1	1	0	8	0	0	15.4	30.8
2-team (25 Tacoma)					.270	.426	.300	32	129	100	15	27	3	0	0	10	26	2	1	0	32	1	1	20.2	24.8
Luciano, Marco	R-R	6-1	178	9-10-01	.209	.321	.418	18	78	67	10	14	2	0	4	8	10	1	0	0	28	0	0	12.8	35.9
Matheny, Shane	L-R	6-1	205	6-05-96	.221	.362	.302	57	213	172	30	38	3	1	3	19	38	1	0	2	69	9	2	17.8	32.4
Mathias, Mark	R-R	6-0	200	8-02-94	.182	.357	.182	4	14	11	2	2	0	0	0	0	3	0	0	0	3	0	0	21.4	21.4
Matos, Luis	R-R	5-11	160	1-28-02	.353	.404	.626	32	152	139	23	49	7	2	9	22	11	1	1	0	11	6	1	7.2	7.2
Meckler, Wade	L-R	5-10	178	4-21-00	.354	.465	.500	24	102	82	12	29	4	1	2	10	18	0	1	1	20	7	0	17.6	19.6
Nottingham, Jacob	R-R	6-2	220	4-03-95	.262	.360	.415	17	75	65	10	17	4	0	2	9	4	6	0	0	16	1	0	5.3	21.3
2-team (17 Tacoma)					.232	.329	.432	34	143	125	18	29	7	0	6	19	11	7	0	0	35	1	1	7.7	24.5
Pollock, AJ	R-R	6-1	210	12-05-87	.167	.286	.333	2	7	6	0	1	1	0	0	0	1	0	0	0	3	0	0	14.3	42.9
Proctor, Ford	L-R	6-1	195	12-04-96	.230	.358	.335	74	284	230	38	53	6	0	6	29	46	2	2	4	60	3	0	16.2	21.1
Ramos, Heliot	R-R	6-1	188	9-07-99	.300	.382	.546	62	263	227	44	68	14	3	12	45	27	5	1	3	66	9	4	10.3	25.1
Reetz, Jakson	R-R	6-0	205	1-03-96	.227	.338	.486	55	216	185	23	42	7	1	13	42	24	7	0	0	56	3	2	11.1	25.9
Rosario, Dilan	R-R	6-0	185	6-16-01	.429	.556	.429	3	10	7	3	3	0	0	0	1	2	0	1	0	2	0	0	20.0	20.0
Ruf, Darin	R-R	6-2	232	7-28-86	.200	.333	.250	5	24	20	1	4	1	0	0	1	4	0	0	0	6	0	0	16.7	25.0
Sanchez, Gary	R-R	6-2	230	12-02-92	.164	.319	.182	16	69	55	6	9	1	0	0	8	11	2	0	1	19	1	0	15.9	27.5
Schmitt, Casey	R-R	6-2	215	3-01-99	.300	.346	.435	47	217	200	28	60	13	1	4	33	14	1	0	2	44	3	1	6.5	20.3
Slater, Austin	R-R	6-1	204	12-13-92	.333	.417	.524	8	24	21	5	7	1	0	1	6	3	0	0	0	7	1	0	12.5	29.2
Stevenson, Cal	L-L	5-9	175	9-12-96	.163	.293	.224	13	58	49	8	8	0	0	1	1	8	1	0	0	19	2	2	13.8	32.8
2-team (7 Las Vegas)					.222	.356	.292	20	87	72	15	16	2	0	1	3	14	1	0	0	22	5	2	16.1	25.3

Tsutsugo, Yoshi	L-R	6-1	225	11-26-91	.222	.563	.333	4	16	9	3	2	1	0	0	1	6	1	0	0	3	0	0	37.5	18.8
2-team (51 Round Rock)					.247	.396	.427	55	224	178	33	44	10	2	6	34	42	2	0	2	62	2	2	18.8	27.7
Villar, David	R-R	6-1	215	1-27-97	.272	.371	.498	75	334	287	54	78	14	0	17	51	44	2	0	1	89	5	0	13.2	26.6
Walton, Donovan	L-R	5-9	190	5-25-94	.208	.278	.354	31	109	96	10	20	2	0	4	14	10	0	1	2	16	1	2	9.2	14.7
Welker, Colton	R-R	6-0	235	10-09-97	.237	.388	.274	43	170	135	14	32	5	0	0	13	30	4	0	1	36	2	0	17.6	21.2
Wilson, Will	R-R	6-0	184	7-21-98	.234	.304	.408	93	340	299	47	70	13	0	13	47	31	1	5	4	85	2	1	9.1	25.0
Wisely, Brett	L-R	5-10	180	5-08-99	.285	.417	.466	67	280	221	40	63	20	1	6	31	47	5	4	3	64	7	3	16.8	22.9
Wright, Chris	L-L	6-1	205	10-14-98	.500	.500	1.000	41	2	2	0	1	1	0	0	0	0	0	0	0	1	0	0	0.0	50.0
Wynns, Austin	R-R	6-0	190	12-10-90	.154	.267	.462	4	15	13	4	2	1	0	1	2	1	1	0	0	4	0	0	6.7	26.7
Yastrzemski, Mike	L-L	5-10	178	8-23-90	.000	.375	.000	2	8	5	0	0	0	0	0	0	2	1	0	0	4	0	0	25.0	50.0

Pitching	B-T	Ht.	Wt.	DOB	W	L	ERA	G	GS	SV	IP	Hits	Runs	ER	HR	BB	SO	AVG	OBP	SLG	SO%	BB%	BF
Adon, Melvin	L-R	6-3	246	6-09-94	2	6	7.43	32	0	0	40	47	37	33	4	37	50	.297	.441	.437	24.5	18.1	204
Alexander, Scott	L-L	6-2	195	7-10-89	0	0	0.00	1	0	0	1	0	0	0	0	1	1	.000	.250	.000	25.0	25.0	4
Andrews, Tanner	R-R	6-3	220	11-15-95	3	3	5.74	27	2	0	53	61	36	34	6	29	53	.289	.376	.488	21.8	11.9	243
Avila, Nick	R-R	6-4	195	7-25-97	14	0	3.00	56	2	3	72	57	27	24	7	36	64	.220	.317	.375	21.3	12.0	301
Beck, Tristan	R-R	6-4	165	6-24-96	3	3	5.88	9	6	0	26	23	17	17	9	14	26	.242	.345	.600	23.0	12.4	113
Black, Mason	R-R	6-3	230	12-10-99	3	4	3.86	13	13	0	61	53	29	26	9	31	72	.242	.349	.420	27.9	12.0	258
Brebbia, John	L-R	6-1	200	5-30-90	1	0	0.00	2	0	0	2	2	0	0	0	1	4	.222	.300	.222	40.0	10.0	10
Burgos, Raymond	L-L	6-5	170	11-29-98	0	1	5.48	11	1	0	21	22	13	13	4	10	17	.262	.347	.429	17.9	10.5	95
Coulter, Clint	R-R	6-3	225	7-30-93	0	0	0.00	1	0	0	0	0	0	0	0	0	0	.000	.000	.000	0.0	0.0	1
Dabovich, R.J.	R-R	6-3	208	1-11-99	0	0	20.25	4	0	0	3	3	6	6	0	6	3	.300	.563	.400	18.8	37.5	16
Dunshee, Parker	R-R	6-0	215	2-12-95	1	0	3.93	10	4	0	18	15	9	8	4	10	22	.211	.317	.451	26.5	12.0	83
Duron, Nick	R-R	6-4	190	1-30-96	1	1	2.25	6	0	0	8	6	4	2	0	11	9	.214	.425	.250	22.5	27.5	40
Fletcher, Aaron	L-L	6-0	220	2-25-96	0	0	24.00	3	0	0	3	8	8	8	1	7	2	.500	.667	.875	8.3	29.2	24
Frisbee, Matt	R-R	6-5	215	11-18-96	0	0	7.88	5	0	0	8	12	7	7	1	4	7	.364	.421	.545	18.4	10.5	38
Guzman, Jorge	R-R	6-1	246	1-28-96	2	2	3.00	27	0	1	36	30	16	12	2	26	26	.236	.398	.331	16.1	16.1	161
Harrison, Kyle	R-L	6-2	200	8-12-01	1	3	4.66	20	20	0	66	52	36	34	10	48	105	.215	.356	.430	35.6	16.3	295
Helvey, Clay	R-R	6-3	195	2-14-97	0	0	11.57	22	0	1	23	36	30	30	6	26	17	.360	.500	.650	13.3	20.3	128
Hildenberger, Trevor	R-R	6-2	205	12-15-90	0	1	15.88	5	1	0	6	10	12	10	0	9	4	.400	.553	.520	10.5	23.7	38
Hjelle, Sean	R-R	6-11	228	5-07-97	3	7	6.00	22	19	0	93	102	70	62	14	40	70	.283	.366	.467	16.7	9.5	420
Jackson, Luke	R-R	6-2	210	8-24-91	0	0	8.31	5	0	0	4	4	4	4	0	4	8	.235	.409	.294	36.4	18.2	22
Llovera, Mauricio	R-R	5-11	224	4-17-96	1	0	3.92	17	2	1	21	16	9	9	4	6	24	.211	.277	.421	28.6	7.1	84
Long, Sam	L-L	6-1	185	7-08-95	1	0	9.90	4	0	0	10	14	11	11	2	5	7	.326	.388	.535	14.3	10.2	49
Marciano, Joey	L-L	6-5	250	1-11-95	4	5	6.75	31	2	3	43	43	40	32	5	43	51	.253	.413	.441	23.3	19.6	219
McClure, Kade	R-R	6-7	220	2-12-96	2	0	5.79	9	0	0	23	32	16	15	4	11	13	.327	.400	.531	11.8	10.0	110
Miller, Erik	L-L	6-5	240	2-13-98	2	1	2.77	48	0	14	52	27	17	16	2	41	73	.152	.311	.208	32.9	18.5	222
Newcomb, Sean	L-L	6-5	255	6-12-93	0	1	3.16	18	2	0	31	24	12	11	2	20	40	.222	.344	.315	30.5	15.3	131
Nunez, Darien	L-L	6-2	205	3-19-93	0	0	6.43	14	1	0	14	13	10	10	2	17	14	.255	.435	.471	20.3	24.6	69
Rodriguez, Randy	R-R	6-0	166	9-05-99	0	1	5.73	27	0	0	38	32	25	24	3	37	41	.227	.385	.369	22.9	20.7	179
Ross, Joe	R-R	6-4	232	5-21-93	0	0	6.00	3	3	0	6	6	4	4	0	5	5	.286	.407	.429	17.9	17.9	28
Sanchez, Juan	L-L	5-9	165	11-12-00	3	3	4.26	18	0	0	25	19	13	12	2	12	28	.211	.336	.322	25.9	11.1	108
Sanders, Phoenix	R-R	5-10	205	6-05-95	0	1	8.16	13	1	0	14	16	14	13	5	7	12	.276	.354	.638	18.5	10.8	65
Stashak, Cody	R-R	6-2	180	6-04-94	0	1	12.60	5	0	0	5	6	7	7	3	1	4	.286	.348	.857	17.4	4.3	23
Stripling, Ross	R-R	6-1	215	11-23-89	0	0	9.00	1	1	0	1	2	1	1	0	0	1	.400	.400	.600	20.0	0.0	5
Strotman, Drew	R-R	6-3	195	9-03-96	5	7	6.47	32	13	0	97	106	77	70	10	73	96	.276	.402	.438	20.5	15.6	469
Swiney, Nick	R-L	6-3	185	2-12-99	0	2	5.63	26	0	1	40	47	29	25	5	24	30	.299	.386	.471	16.2	13.0	185
Teng, Kai-Wei	R-R	6-4	260	12-01-98	6	5	4.22	17	16	0	79	66	38	37	4	48	96	.231	.357	.360	27.6	13.8	348
Tillo, Daniel	L-L	6-5	215	6-13-96	1	6	9.59	17	4	0	25	28	29	27	2	24	17	.283	.417	.424	13.4	18.9	127
Waites, Cole	R-R	6-3	180	6-10-98	3	4	6.16	32	3	1	31	26	21	21	3	27	32	.224	.368	.379	22.2	18.8	144
Walker, Ryan	R-R	6-2	200	11-26-95	1	0	0.89	15	3	1	20	9	3	2	0	8	23	.138	.243	.200	31.1	10.8	74
Weber, Ty	R-R	6-4	220	3-19-98	0	0	1.80	2	0	1	5	4	1	1	0	1	2	.222	.263	.278	10.5	5.3	19
Winn, Keaton	R-R	6-4	238	2-20-98	0	6	4.81	17	14	0	58	66	34	31	7	26	66	.284	.360	.457	25.1	9.9	263
Wood, Alex	R-L	6-4	215	1-12-91	0	1	2.70	2	2	0	7	9	3	2	0	1	2	.333	.357	.407	7.1	3.6	28
Wright, Chris	L-L	6-1	205	10-14-98	2	2	5.28	40	1	0	46	47	30	27	6	47	65	.264	.419	.438	28.4	20.5	229
Yajure, Miguel	R-R	6-1	215	5-01-98	2	5	5.97	16	13	0	60	63	52	40	9	30	62	.261	.348	.456	22.4	10.8	277

Fielding

Catcher	PCT	G	PO	A	E	DP	PB
Bailey	.984	94	740	50	13	2	8
Bart	.991	30	212	9	2	0	1
Perez	1.000	5	41	1	0	0	0
Sabol	.987	55	371	19	5	1	6
Wynns	1.000	1	8	0	0	0	0

First Base	PCT	G	PO	A	E	DP
Alvarez	.985	35	245	14	4	26
Beaty	.992	19	120	9	1	12
Brooks	.990	14	94	3	1	11
Camargo	1.000	1	5	1	0	1
Coulter	.977	7	36	6	1	7
Genoves	.987	13	71	6	1	5
Matheny	.970	4	27	5	1	8
Nottingham	1.000	7	51	5	0	3
Proctor	1.000	27	160	10	0	21
Ruf	1.000	3	24	4	0	4
Sanchez	1.000	2	10	0	0	3
Tsutsugo	1.000	2	16	0	0	2
Villar	.977	19	120	10	3	15
Welker	.991	19	95	12	1	21

Second Base	PCT	G	PO	A	E	DP
Alvarez	1.000	1	4	2	0	1
Camargo	.889	1	4	4	1	0
Diaz	.956	19	17	48	3	12
Estrada	1.000	2	3	3	0	0
Fitzgerald	1.000	12	27	30	0	13
Luciano	.958	6	10	13	1	5
Matheny	1.000	4	8	6	0	4
Proctor	1.000	11	18	23	0	4
Rosario	1.000	2	2	3	0	0
Schmitt	.947	7	5	13	1	1
Villar	.947	3	9	9	1	5
Walton	.989	22	39	51	1	18
Wilson	.962	47	67	110	7	32
Wisely	.961	24	31	42	3	10

Third Base	PCT	G	PO	A	E	DP
Alvarez	.921	27	16	42	5	5
Camargo	1.000	2	1	1	0	1
Fitzgerald	1.000	7	2	7	0	1
Guthrie	1.000	1	0	2	0	1
Matheny	1.000	6	3	8	0	1
Mathias	1.000	3	4	7	0	1
Proctor	.959	31	14	57	3	7
Schmitt	.938	11	12	18	2	2
Villar	.948	49	26	84	6	7
Welker	1.000	6	1	10	0	0
Wilson	.962	16	4	21	1	5

	PCT	G	PO	A	E	DP
Wisely	.833	3	0	5	1	0

Shortstop	PCT	G	PO	A	E	DP
Camargo	.886	10	7	24	4	2
Diaz	1.000	1	1	4	0	1
Fitzgerald	.976	62	92	157	6	44
Guthrie	1.000	2	7	5	0	2
Luciano	1.000	8	16	15	0	4
Matheny	1.000	2	0	2	0	1
Mathias	1.000	1	1	2	0	0
Proctor	.962	5	9	16	1	8
Schmitt	.992	29	45	82	1	25
Walton	1.000	4	8	11	0	1
Wilson	.961	20	20	53	3	14

	PCT	G	PO	A	E	DP
Wisely	.879	8	10	19	4	5

Outfield	PCT	G	PO	A	E	DP
Beaty	1.000	9	13	0	0	0
Brooks	.469	8	14	1	1	0
Coulter	1.000	41	57	2	0	1
Fitzgerald	1.000	23	47	3	0	1
Gigliotti	.996	66	120	1	1	0
Gonzalez	.961	20	28	0	1	0
Guthrie	.896	6	15	0	2	0
Haniger	.875	5	6	0	1	0
Hill	1.000	3	2	0	0	0
Johnson	.996	69	116	3	1	0
Larsen	1.000	8	8	0	0	0
Marciano	.000	1	0	0	0	0
Matheny	.973	43	69	4	2	2
Matos	.990	32	49	1	1	0
Meckler	1.000	21	32	3	0	2
Pollock	1.000	2	3	0	0	0
Ramos	.972	57	92	3	1	0
Reetz	.982	24	28	0	1	0
Slater	1.000	3	3	0	0	0
Stevenson	.944	13	25	2	1	0
Wilson	1.000	9	9	0	0	0
Wisely	.914	33	59	3	3	1
Wright	.000	1	0	0	0	0

RICHMOND FLYING SQUIRRELS — *DOUBLE-A*

EASTERN LEAGUE

Batting	B-T	Ht.	Wt.	DOB	AVG	OBP	SLG	G	PA	AB	R	H	2B	3B	HR	RBI	BB	HBP	SH	SF	SO	SB	CS	BB%	SO%
Aldrete, Carter	R-R	6-1	205	10-12-97	.223	.282	.384	104	409	372	47	83	21	0	13	51	31	1	1	4	108	2	1	7.6	26.4
Auerbach, Brett	R-R	5-9	185	8-27-98	.153	.211	.190	45	175	163	15	25	3	0	1	14	11	1	0	0	52	6	4	6.3	29.7
Bailey, Patrick	B-R	6-0	210	5-29-99	.333	.400	.481	14	60	54	9	18	2	0	2	10	6	0	0	0	13	2	0	10.0	21.7
Bericoto, Victor	R-R	6-1	155	12-03-01	.237	.292	.478	51	204	186	29	44	10	1	11	31	14	1	2	1	54	0	1	6.9	26.5
Brown, Vaun	R-R	6-0	215	6-23-98	.221	.284	.421	50	208	190	27	42	10	2	8	34	13	4	0	1	78	15	0	6.3	37.5
Cantrelle, Hayden	B-R	5-11	175	11-25-98	.215	.390	.305	99	357	275	54	59	11	1	4	25	66	14	1	1	75	14	1	18.5	21.0
Emery, Robert	R-R	6-0	210	10-22-96	.186	.272	.214	25	83	70	4	13	2	0	0	3	9	0	2	2	26	0	0	10.8	31.3
Fitzgerald, Tyler	R-R	6-3	205	9-15-97	.324	.410	.588	19	78	68	15	22	6	3	2	9	9	1	0	0	22	3	0	11.5	28.2
Gates, Evan	R-R	6-0	210	1-13-98	.000	.000	.000	43	1	1	0	0	0	0	0	0	0	0	0	0	0	0	0	0.0	0.0
Glowenke, Jimmy	R-R	5-10	200	6-05-99	.251	.355	.389	75	289	247	33	62	13	0	7	30	32	8	2	0	61	6	0	11.1	21.1
Luciano, Marco	R-R	6-1	178	9-10-01	.228	.339	.450	56	242	202	32	46	12	0	11	32	36	0	0	4	72	6	0	14.9	29.8
Mahan, Riley	L-R	6-2	220	12-31-95	.193	.226	.398	46	177	166	21	32	8	1	8	28	8	0	0	3	56	2	0	4.5	31.6
Martorano, Brandon	R-R	6-2	198	1-06-98	.190	.323	.307	67	248	205	25	39	4	1	6	20	37	4	0	2	82	2	4	14.9	33.1
Matheny, Shane	L-R	6-1	205	6-05-96	.236	.359	.434	76	324	267	44	63	16	2	11	43	51	2	1	3	84	8	2	15.7	25.9
Matos, Luis	R-R	5-11	160	1-28-02	.304	.398	.443	31	133	115	18	35	7	0	3	16	17	1	0	0	12	9	4	12.8	9.0
Meckler, Wade	L-R	5-10	178	4-21-00	.336	.431	.450	39	174	149	36	50	7	2	2	23	25	0	0	0	29	4	3	14.4	16.7
Munguia, Ismael	L-L	5-10	158	10-19-98	.282	.356	.391	75	335	294	51	83	14	0	6	32	24	11	4	2	45	16	4	7.2	13.4
Myrick, Tyler	R-R	6-0	205	6-25-98	.000	.000	.000	20	1	1	0	0	0	0	0	0	0	0	0	0	1	0	0	0.0	100.0
Roby, Sean	R-R	6-1	215	7-08-98	.182	.232	.284	24	95	88	11	16	3	0	2	7	5	1	0	1	35	0	0	5.3	36.8
Thomas, Andy	L-R	6-1	210	6-17-98	.226	.325	.360	110	448	381	49	86	16	1	11	63	56	3	2	6	107	5	1	12.5	23.9
Tsutsugo, Yoshi	L-R	6-1	225	11-26-91	.311	.436	.578	13	55	45	9	14	0	0	4	10	10	0	0	0	17	1	1	18.2	30.9
Walton, Donovan	L-R	5-9	190	5-25-94	.311	.413	.459	18	76	61	11	19	3	0	2	9	10	2	1	2	9	2	0	13.2	11.8
Whalen, Brady	L-R	6-6	180	1-15-98	.259	.303	.434	38	156	143	19	37	8	1	5	24	8	2	1	2	24	3	0	5.1	15.4
Whiteman, Simon	R-R	5-10	165	1-28-97	.208	.300	.285	73	242	207	25	43	8	1	2	20	28	0	5	2	52	11	1	11.6	21.5
Williams, Carter	L-R	6-3	210	1-14-98	.227	.280	.337	51	186	172	24	39	4	0	5	17	11	2	0	1	42	4	1	5.9	22.6
Wilson, Will	R-R	6-0	184	7-21-98	.215	.276	.354	35	156	144	18	31	3	1	5	19	10	2	0	0	29	2	1	6.4	18.6
Wyatt, Logan	L-R	6-4	230	11-15-97	.257	.339	.442	64	236	206	32	53	11	0	9	34	25	2	0	3	51	1	0	10.6	21.6

Pitching	B-T	Ht.	Wt.	DOB	W	L	ERA	G	GS	SV	IP	Hits	Runs	ER	HR	BB	SO	AVG	OBP	SLG	SO%	BB%	BF
Bertrand, John	L-L	6-3	205	2-08-98	2	3	4.67	11	11	0	52	56	30	27	1	21	39	.284	.351	.381	17.3	9.3	225
Birdsong, Hayden	R-R	6-4	215	8-30-01	0	3	5.48	8	8	0	23	21	18	14	2	13	33	.236	.337	.393	31.7	12.5	104
Bivens, Spencer	R-R	6-5	205	6-28-94	5	4	3.69	27	4	0	78	66	36	32	3	34	72	.231	.326	.325	21.8	10.3	330
Black, Mason	R-R	6-3	230	12-10-99	1	5	3.57	16	16	0	63	45	28	25	7	21	83	.197	.273	.328	32.7	8.3	254
Burgos, Raymond	L-L	6-5	170	11-29-98	5	2	2.17	26	0	2	37	28	14	9	2	15	37	.209	.291	.306	24.3	9.9	152
Cruz, Jose	R-R	6-1	178	5-18-00	0	2	6.66	23	0	4	26	16	21	19	5	31	39	.170	.400	.362	30.0	23.8	130
Delaplane, Sam	R-R	5-11	175	3-27-95	3	2	5.31	12	0	0	20	18	13	12	4	14	21	.234	.362	.429	22.3	14.9	94
Dula, Hunter	L-R	6-1	205	3-08-99	1	0	6.55	7	0	0	11	14	10	8	1	6	11	.304	.396	.457	20.8	11.3	53
Dunshee, Parker	R-R	6-0	215	2-12-95	4	1	2.56	23	1	0	46	35	19	13	4	22	55	.207	.328	.337	27.2	10.9	202
Frisbee, Matt	R-R	6-5	215	11-18-96	6	0	4.54	27	0	0	40	38	23	20	8	15	30	.250	.327	.474	17.5	8.8	171
Gates, Evan	R-R	6-0	210	1-13-98	4	6	4.39	42	0	6	55	64	35	27	3	30	72	.284	.365	.422	27.5	11.5	262
Helvey, Clay	R-R	6-3	195	2-14-97	3	0	6.23	11	0	0	17	15	13	12	3	11	13	.231	.354	.431	16.5	13.9	79
Jensen, Wil	R-R	6-4	180	9-02-97	7	0	2.53	34	4	1	89	75	28	25	10	41	93	.230	.322	.368	24.9	11.0	373
Kempner, William	R-R	6-0	222	6-18-01	0	0	5.40	1	0	0	2	3	1	1	0	2	2	.375	.500	.500	20.0	20.0	10
Madison, Ben	R-R	6-3	205	9-15-97	2	2	3.98	19	0	2	32	19	17	14	3	30	43	.178	.373	.280	29.9	20.8	144
Miller, Erik	L-L	6-5	240	2-13-98	1	0	0.87	6	0	1	10	3	1	1	0	4	15	.094	.194	.156	41.7	11.1	36
Murphy, Ryan	R-R	6-1	190	10-08-99	2	9	4.36	29	27	0	107	102	56	52	15	51	107	.252	.344	.405	23.0	11.0	465
Myrick, Tyler	R-R	6-0	205	6-25-98	2	0	1.44	20	0	6	25	21	7	4	1	9	21	.226	.294	.312	20.6	8.8	102
Olsen, Mat	R-R	5-11	185	7-08-00	2	1	8.53	14	0	0	19	28	19	18	3	4	27	.337	.375	.578	30.7	4.5	88
Rivera, Blake	R-R	6-4	225	1-09-98	2	5	4.93	37	0	2	46	42	30	25	3	41	57	.243	.397	.364	25.8	18.6	221
Rodriguez, Randy	R-R	6-0	166	9-05-99	2	1	2.97	16	0	1	30	19	13	10	1	18	40	.179	.313	.264	31.0	14.0	129
Roupp, Landen	R-R	6-2	205	9-10-98	0	0	1.74	10	10	0	31	22	6	6	1	9	42	.206	.283	.290	35.0	7.5	120
Sanchez, Juan	L-L	5-9	165	11-12-00	6	4	2.39	28	0	3	49	34	16	13	3	20	52	.199	.280	.310	26.7	10.3	195
Seymour, Carson	R-R	6-6	260	12-16-98	5	3	3.99	28	23	0	113	96	58	50	8	43	114	.231	.309	.356	24.5	9.2	466
Stryffeler, Michael	R-R	6-2	210	5-22-96	0	0	4.50	4	0	0	4	3	2	2	0	2	7	.214	.353	.286	41.2	11.8	17
Swiney, Nick	R-L	6-3	185	2-12-99	3	0	1.15	6	0	0	16	9	2	2	1	7	18	.167	.262	.278	29.5	11.5	61
Teng, Kai-Wei	R-R	6-4	260	12-01-98	1	3	4.75	12	12	0	47	38	27	25	4	20	68	.225	.337	.373	33.7	9.9	202
Whisenhunt, Carson	L-L	6-3	209	10-20-00	0	1	3.20	6	6	0	20	16	10	7	1	11	27	.219	.321	.342	32.1	13.1	84

Pitching	B-T	Ht.	Wt.	DOB	W	L	ERA	G	GS	SV	IP	Hits	Runs	ER	HR	BB	SO	AVG	OBP	SLG	SO%	BB%	BF
Wright, Chris	L-L	6-1	205	10-14-98	0	0	0.00	2	0	1	4	2	0	0	0	1	7	.154	.214	.154	50.0	7.1	14
Zwack, Nick	L-L	6-3	230	8-01-98	5	7	6.56	24	16	0	81	93	62	59	14	32	91	.288	.353	.505	24.9	8.8	365

Fielding

Catcher	PCT	G	PO	A	E	DP	PB
Auerbach	.994	17	145	14	1	3	4
Bailey	1.000	9	97	6	0	0	3
Emery	1.000	8	56	4	0	0	3
Martorano	.985	41	382	17	6	0	4
Thomas	.989	74	664	36	8	5	13

First Base	PCT	G	PO	A	E	DP
Aldrete	.980	9	41	7	1	8
Bericoto	1.000	2	9	0	0	0
Emery	.974	6	33	4	1	5
Mahan	.993	39	249	24	2	26
Matheny	1.000	2	4	0	0	1
Roby	1.000	1	7	2	0	1
Thomas	.984	19	117	5	2	13
Whalen	1.000	15	109	8	0	11
Wyatt	.992	54	369	21	3	37

Second Base	PCT	G	PO	A	E	DP
Auerbach	1.000	8	10	20	0	6
Cantrelle	.986	57	89	130	3	36
Glowenk	.979	50	76	113	4	31
Matheny	1.000	5	4	10	0	0
Walton	1.000	8	14	19	0	6
Whiteman	.978	12	15	29	1	3
Wilson	1.000	2	4	5	0	1

Third Base	PCT	G	PO	A	E	DP
Aldrete	.911	49	20	62	8	5
Auerbach	.889	11	11	13	3	0
Cantrelle	.921	30	12	46	5	5
Fitzgerald	.000	1	0	0	1	0
Glowenke	.895	8	6	11	2	1
Matheny	.980	20	13	36	1	4
Roby	1.000	13	6	17	0	2
Whalen	.941	10	2	14	1	0
Whiteman	1.000	6	1	7	0	0

Shortstop	PCT	G	PO	A	E	DP
Cantrelle	1.000	3	3	5	0	1
Fitzgerald	.950	16	20	37	3	13
Glowenke	.939	9	10	21	2	4
Luciano	.956	42	56	95	7	24
Matheny	.951	10	15	24	2	5
Walton	1.000	6	5	10	0	2
Whiteman	.957	23	31	58	4	15
Wilson	.982	32	42	68	2	19

Outfield	PCT	G	PO	A	E	DP
Aldrete	1.000	36	50	2	0	1
Auerbach	1.000	11	15	1	0	1
Bericoto	.960	49	81	5	6	0
Brown	.934	40	76	4	4	1
Cantrelle	1.000	9	16	0	0	0
Mahan	1.000	2	4	0	0	0
Martorano	.667	23	28	0	0	0
Matheny	1.000	43	96	5	0	1
Matos	.972	26	56	1	1	1
Meckler	.973	37	61	2	2	0
Munguia	.974	75	143	3	3	0
Tsutsugo	1.000	7	12	0	0	0
Whalen	.900	8	8	0	1	0
Whiteman	1.000	32	60	1	0	0
Williams	.954	46	74	1	2	0

EUGENE EMERALDS — *HIGH CLASS A*

NORTHWEST LEAGUE

Batting	B-T	Ht.	Wt.	DOB	AVG	OBP	SLG	G	PA	AB	R	H	2B	3B	HR	RBI	BB	HBP	SH	SF	SO	SB	CS	BB%	SO%
Arteaga, Aeverson	R-R	6-1	170	3-16-03	.235	.299	.410	126	546	493	66	116	29	3	17	73	40	7	0	6	132	8	2	7.3	24.2
Auerbach, Brett	R-R	5-9	185	8-27-98	.229	.295	.371	49	193	175	18	40	10	0	5	18	14	3	0	1	56	15	3	7.3	29.0
Bericoto, Victor	R-R	6-1	155	12-03-01	.296	.353	.533	71	309	270	47	80	12	2	16	55	29	0	0	10	60	1	0	9.4	19.4
Brown, Vaun	R-R	6-0	215	6-23-98	.300	.391	.550	5	23	20	2	6	2	0	1	3	2	1	0	0	5	2	0	8.7	21.7
Crawford, Reggie	L-L	6-4	235	12-04-00	.000	.000	.000	7	1	1	0	0	0	0	0	0	0	0	0	0	1	0	0	0.0	100.0
Dues, Damon	L-R	6-0	180	6-21-98	.290	.398	.362	67	250	210	40	61	15	0	0	18	36	2	1	1	52	25	4	14.4	20.8
Dupere, Jared	L-R	5-11	200	1-23-99	.246	.313	.428	93	392	353	48	87	20	4	12	42	29	6	1	2	149	11	2	7.4	38.0
Emery, Robert	R-R	6-0	210	10-22-96	.333	.429	.444	6	21	18	2	6	2	0	0	1	2	1	0	0	4	0	0	9.5	19.0
Gavello, Thomas	L-R	5-10	180	6-06-01	.217	.311	.272	29	106	92	13	20	2	0	1	8	7	6	0	1	38	1	0	6.6	35.8
Glowenke, Jimmy	R-R	5-10	200	6-05-99	.313	.413	.542	26	105	83	17	26	10	0	3	17	13	4	1	4	15	0	0	12.4	14.3
Higgins, Matt	L-R	6-1	215	7-02-99	.204	.289	.327	34	128	113	10	23	5	0	3	10	10	4	0	1	34	1	1	7.8	26.6
Howell, Carter	R-R	6-0	200	2-07-99	.270	.353	.408	80	354	311	50	84	17	4	6	41	38	2	3	0	70	6	3	10.7	19.8
Kachel, Andrew	L-R	6-0	170	12-24-00	.250	.317	.361	11	41	36	2	9	4	0	0	9	4	0	0	1	14	3	0	9.8	34.1
McCray, Grant	L-R	6-2	190	12-07-00	.255	.360	.417	127	584	494	101	126	26	6	14	66	72	12	1	5	171	52	10	12.3	29.3
Meckler, Wade	L-R	5-10	178	4-21-00	.456	.494	.633	20	87	79	14	36	6	1	2	17	6	1	0	1	9	2	1	6.9	10.3
Mora, Edison	R-R	6-2	165	8-13-00	.191	.244	.357	34	123	115	18	22	8	1	3	11	5	3	0	0	43	1	1	4.1	35.0
Morgan, Zach	R-R	6-0	180	3-30-00	.292	.326	.427	26	95	89	12	26	6	0	2	8	5	0	0	1	20	0	0	5.3	21.1
O'Tremba, Tanner	R-R	6-0	212	12-06-99	.242	.306	.333	10	36	33	6	8	1	1	0	4	3	0	0	0	14	1	0	8.3	38.9
Perez, Onil	R-R	6-1	187	9-10-02	.289	.333	.333	13	48	45	4	13	0	1	0	1	3	0	0	0	7	2	2	6.3	14.6
Roby, Sean	R-R	6-1	215	7-08-98	.276	.344	.621	22	96	87	15	24	6	0	8	19	9	0	0	0	27	0	0	9.4	28.1
Rosario, Dilan	R-R	6-0	185	6-16-01	.200	.333	.200	2	6	5	3	1	0	0	0	0	0	1	0	0	1	0	0	0.0	16.7
Santos, Ghordy	B-R	6-1	177	9-02-99	.227	.331	.435	84	303	260	48	59	10	4	12	28	40	1	1	1	112	8	5	13.2	37.0
Sugastey, Adrian	R-R	6-1	210	10-23-02	.298	.333	.423	63	264	248	23	74	15	2	4	40	13	1	0	2	37	1	0	4.9	14.0
Toribio, Luis	L-R	6-1	185	9-28-00	.232	.333	.432	102	412	354	50	82	18	1	17	61	54	1	1	2	112	1	0	13.1	27.2
Walton, Donovan	L-R	5-9	190	5-25-94	.250	.340	.318	12	50	44	7	11	3	0	0	3	4	2	0	0	11	0	0	8.0	22.0
Wielansky, Michael	R-R	6-2	175	3-18-97	.120	.179	.120	7	28	25	3	3	0	0	0	1	0	2	0	1	6	0	1	0.0	21.4
Williams, Carter	L-R	6-3	210	1-14-98	.189	.241	.338	20	79	74	11	14	2	0	3	5	4	1	0	0	22	2	0	5.1	27.8
Wright, Max	L-R	6-3	215	1-08-98	.207	.310	.324	34	129	111	10	23	4	0	3	14	13	4	0	1	34	0	0	10.1	26.4
Wyatt, Logan	L-R	6-4	230	11-15-97	.259	.371	.430	53	229	193	30	50	9	0	8	31	33	2	0	1	52	0	0	14.4	22.7

Pitching	B-T	Ht.	Wt.	DOB	W	L	ERA	G	GS	SV	IP	Hits	Runs	ER	HR	BB	SO	AVG	OBP	SLG	SO%	BB%	BF
Bertrand, John	L-L	6-3	205	2-08-98	5	2	2.92	11	8	0	49	35	18	16	4	12	41	.196	.245	.324	21.4	6.3	192
Birdsong, Hayden	R-R	6-4	215	8-30-01	2	2	3.25	8	7	0	36	24	14	13	4	9	46	.190	.259	.357	33.1	6.5	139
Bivens, Spencer	R-R	6-5	205	6-28-94	3	0	3.60	6	0	0	15	14	6	6	3	4	20	.230	.288	.426	30.3	6.1	66
Blair, Daniel	R-R	6-3	205	4-08-99	1	3	5.58	10	7	0	40	44	26	25	2	16	42	.272	.346	.389	23.1	8.8	182
Castillo, Wilkelma	R-R	6-0	170	1-06-00	0	2	10.57	18	0	1	23	39	30	27	7	16	22	.379	.472	.699	17.7	12.9	124
Choate, Jack	L-L	6-6	249	4-18-01	0	2	2.14	5	4	0	21	21	9	5	0	5	20	.253	.303	.277	22.5	5.6	89
Corry, Seth	L-L	6-2	195	11-03-98	0	0	5.06	3	3	0	5	7	5	3	0	2	9	.292	.357	.333	32.1	7.1	28
Cotter, Cameron	R-R	6-3	220	12-17-98	0	1	1.00	5	0	1	9	9	4	1	0	2	9	.250	.289	.333	23.1	5.1	39
Crawford, Reggie	L-L	6-4	235	12-04-00	0	0	1.13	6	6	0	8	6	2	1	0	6	14	.207	.361	.241	38.9	16.7	36
Cruz, Jose	R-R	6-1	178	5-18-00	0	0	1.45	13	0	1	19	7	4	3	0	7	28	.113	.247	.145	38.4	9.6	73
Delaplane, Sam	R-R	5-11	175	3-27-95	1	0	1.59	7	0	1	11	5	2	2	0	4	19	.139	.256	.194	44.2	9.3	43
Dues, Damon	L-R	6-0	180	6-21-98	0	0	2.70	3	0	0	3	4	1	1	0	0	4	.286	.286	.357	28.6	0.0	14
Dula, Hunter	L-R	6-1	205	3-08-99	4	2	3.14	36	0	8	43	36	17	15	6	19	50	.221	.301	.374	27.3	10.4	183
Gavello, Thomas	L-R	5-10	180	6-06-01	0	0	3.86	3	0	0	2	5	1	1	0	0	0	.455	.455	.818	0.0	0.0	11

Kemlage, Joe	B-L	6-1	220	1-19-99	4	0	6.23	28	0	0	48	62	35	33	6	21	52	.308	.375	.468	23.1	9.3	225
Kempner, William	R-R	6-0	222	6-18-01	3	2	2.91	23	0	0	34	28	15	11	5	13	47	.224	.319	.384	32.6	9.0	144
Kiest, Tanner	R-R	6-3	200	9-16-94	2	3	3.96	25	0	2	39	35	20	17	2	15	52	.235	.307	.329	31.3	9.0	166
Lonsway, Seth	L-L	6-2	210	10-07-98	2	9	5.87	28	17	2	89	101	70	58	9	58	78	.278	.392	.424	17.9	13.3	435
Madison, Ben	R-R	6-3	205	9-15-97	8	1	3.05	22	0	0	38	17	13	13	2	20	62	.131	.250	.246	40.8	13.2	152
McDonald, Trevor	R-R	6-2	200	2-26-01	3	1	0.96	9	8	0	38	24	5	4	1	8	39	.185	.248	.223	27.7	5.7	141
Mikulski, Matt	L-L	6-4	205	5-08-99	4	3	6.75	33	7	0	67	71	59	50	11	54	71	.271	.408	.489	21.3	16.2	334
Morgan, Zach	R-R	6-0	180	3-30-00	0	0	0.00	1	0	0	1	1	0	0	0	0	0	.250	.250	.250	0.0	0.0	4
Morreale, Nick	R-R	6-5	220	7-27-97	6	5	4.36	44	1	2	76	77	43	37	10	22	87	.258	.317	.455	26.4	6.7	329
Myrick, Tyler	R-R	6-0	205	6-25-98	1	2	1.04	26	0	9	26	20	7	3	2	7	25	.213	.267	.298	24.8	6.9	101
Newsome, Ljay	R-R	5-11	210	11-08-96	0	0	0.00	1	0	0	1	1	0	0	0	0	1	.250	.250	.250	25.0	0.0	4
Olsen, Mat	R-R	5-11	185	7-08-00	3	2	3.41	27	0	0	37	27	15	14	2	13	57	.197	.287	.343	36.3	8.3	157
Ragsdale, Carson	R-R	6-8	225	5-25-98	0	1	2.93	7	7	0	28	19	9	9	1	6	42	.190	.270	.290	37.8	5.4	111
Silva, Eric	R-R	6-1	185	10-03-02	2	7	5.92	28	18	0	76	78	51	50	7	39	73	.269	.363	.421	21.3	11.4	342
Sinacola, Nick	L-R	6-2	205	10-29-99	2	5	4.58	23	20	0	88	87	48	45	11	25	100	.255	.316	.437	26.4	6.6	379
Standlee, Brett	R-R	6-4	223	9-14-98	3	4	4.68	39	2	2	75	84	42	39	9	24	72	.281	.334	.452	22.0	7.3	327
Weber, Ty	R-R	6-4	220	3-19-98	3	2	10.08	15	1	1	28	44	31	31	6	12	16	.364	.429	.636	11.3	8.5	141
Whisenhunt, Carson	L-L	6-3	209	10-20-00	1	0	1.42	6	6	0	25	9	4	4	1	8	36	.107	.202	.167	38.3	8.5	94
Wynja, Hayden	L-L	6-9	220	10-14-98	3	4	4.40	10	8	0	43	49	25	21	6	20	47	.288	.368	.482	24.4	10.4	193
Yajure, Miguel	R-R	6-1	215	5-01-98	0	1	8.53	2	2	0	6	10	6	6	1	5	5	.385	.484	.654	16.1	16.1	31

Fielding

Catcher	PCT	G	PO	A	E	DP	PB
Auerbach	.987	8	71	7	1	0	4
Emery	.962	3	25	0	1	0	0
Gavello	.979	6	40	7	1	0	2
Morgan	.995	22	200	15	1	0	3
Perez	.991	12	101	9	1	0	3
Sugastey	.997	58	571	41	2	4	5
Wright	.990	28	279	12	3	2	5

First Base	PCT	G	PO	A	E	DP
Bericoto	1.000	22	165	10	0	9
Higgins	1.000	4	16	0	0	0
Kachel	.984	9	61	2	1	6
Mora	1.000	5	35	3	0	2
Morgan	1.000	2	15	3	0	0
Roby	.986	19	136	8	2	13
Toribio	.992	33	239	19	2	16
Wright	1.000	1	7	0	0	1
Wyatt	.979	43	306	13	7	26

Second Base	PCT	G	PO	A	E	DP
Auerbach	.971	16	30	36	2	8
Dues	.982	30	50	61	2	17
Gavello	.955	5	5	16	1	1
Glowenke	1.000	11	15	34	0	6
Mora	.985	14	24	43	1	8
Rosario	1.000	1	2	0	0	0
Santos	.938	51	70	96	11	16
Walton	1.000	6	12	15	0	3
Wielansky	1.000	3	3	8	0	2

Third Base	PCT	G	PO	A	E	DP
Auerbach	1.000	17	11	32	0	2
Dues	.930	24	4	36	3	1
Gavello	.953	19	16	25	2	1
Glowenke	.944	12	9	25	2	2
Mora	.800	3	3	5	2	0
Toribio	.919	63	24	100	11	6
Wielansky	1.000	2	0	2	0	1

Shortstop	PCT	G	PO	A	E	DP
Arteaga	.963	121	129	288	16	47
Dues	.938	6	4	11	1	1
Glowenke	1.000	2	4	4	0	1
Mora	.000	1	0	0	0	0
Toribio	1.000	1	0	3	0	0
Walton	1.000	4	4	7	0	1
Wielansky	.000	1	0	0	0	0

Outfield	PCT	G	PO	A	E	DP
Auerbach	1.000	6	9	0	0	0
Bericoto	.944	42	58	1	2	0
Brown	.833	5	8	1	1	0
Dues	1.000	1	1	0	0	0
Dupere	.982	78	125	2	3	0
Higgins	1.000	18	22	0	0	0
Howell	.994	74	144	6	2	4
McCray	.965	122	260	11	3	2
Meckler	1.000	19	29	1	0	0
Mora	.909	7	10	0	1	0
O'Tremba	1.000	6	15	0	0	0
Santos	.909	7	10	0	1	0
Williams	.917	18	22	2	1	0

SAN JOSE GIANTS

LOW CLASS A

CALIFORNIA LEAGUE

Batting	B-T	Ht.	Wt.	DOB	AVG	OBP	SLG	G	PA	AB	R	H	2B	3B	HR	RBI	BB	HBP	SH	SF	SO	SB	CS	BB%	SO%
Bandura, Scott	L-R	6-4	190	8-02-01	.241	.364	.405	23	99	79	15	19	5	1	2	13	15	2	0	3	26	3	1	15.2	26.3
Bench, Justin	R-R	6-0	185	8-28-99	.354	.446	.354	13	56	48	13	17	0	0	0	4	4	4	0	0	8	5	0	7.1	14.3
Brown, Vaun	R-R	6-0	215	6-23-98	.412	.500	.529	4	20	17	4	7	2	0	0	1	2	1	0	0	5	3	0	10.0	25.0
Cavanaugh, Drew	B-R	6-0	190	1-27-02	.250	.333	.250	6	24	20	3	5	0	0	0	5	3	0	0	1	7	1	0	12.5	29.2
Crawford, Reggie	L-L	6-4	235	12-04-00	.250	.278	.563	11	18	16	1	4	2	0	1	5	0	1	0	1	4	0	0	0.0	22.2
Diaz, Isan	L-R	5-10	201	5-27-96	.400	.500	.600	1	6	5	2	2	1	0	0	1	1	0	0	0	0	0	0	16.7	0.0
Eldridge, Bryce	L-R	6-7	219	10-20-04	.293	.406	.379	15	69	58	7	17	2	0	1	5	11	0	0	0	18	1	0	15.9	26.1
Foster, Cole	B-R	6-1	193	10-08-01	.230	.306	.390	25	111	100	14	23	4	0	4	15	8	3	0	0	35	2	1	7.2	31.5
Francisco, Javier	R-R	6-1	162	11-11-02	.241	.303	.345	7	33	29	2	7	3	0	0	11	3	0	0	1	8	0	0	9.1	24.2
Frechette, Garrett	L-L	6-3	210	12-31-00	.216	.233	.307	24	90	88	6	19	3	1	1	7	2	0	0	0	25	0	0	2.2	27.8
Gavello, Thomas	L-R	5-10	180	6-06-01	.249	.408	.468	59	263	205	47	51	11	2	10	37	30	26	1	1	70	6	2	11.4	26.6
Higgins, Matt	L-R	6-1	215	7-02-99	.309	.400	.492	64	301	256	50	79	18	1	9	51	33	8	0	3	63	9	2	11.0	20.9
Hill, Turner	L-L	5-10	180	4-04-99	.287	.374	.370	74	347	300	51	86	19	3	0	30	37	6	2	2	31	27	9	10.7	8.9
Hilson, P.J.	R-R	5-10	175	8-25-00	.247	.283	.420	80	307	288	53	71	12	4	10	45	12	4	0	3	54	12	1	3.9	17.6
Howell, Carter	R-R	6-0	200	2-07-99	.337	.398	.500	39	197	178	44	60	9	4	4	18	17	1	1	0	39	8	3	8.6	19.8
Kachel, Andrew	L-R	6-0	170	12-24-00	.289	.376	.437	78	332	284	46	82	20	2	6	49	41	1	0	4	83	7	1	12.3	25.0
McDaniel, Quinn	R-R	5-11	180	9-27-02	.267	.364	.511	13	55	45	11	12	0	1	3	8	8	0	0	2	19	2	1	14.5	34.5
Mora, Edison	R-R	6-2	165	8-13-00	.206	.278	.365	19	72	63	9	13	4	0	2	12	6	1	0	2	25	3	1	8.3	34.7
Morgan, Zach	R-R	6-0	180	3-30-00	.254	.376	.383	59	258	209	36	53	13	1	4	36	43	1	0	5	45	7	1	16.7	17.4
O'Tremba, Tanner	R-R	6-0	212	12-06-99	.271	.404	.438	82	359	292	53	79	21	2	8	50	39	27	0	1	75	17	2	10.9	20.9
Payton, Jack	R-R	5-11	200	8-07-01	.184	.244	.263	10	41	38	6	7	0	0	1	1	2	1	0	0	8	1	0	4.9	19.5
Pederson, Joc	L-L	6-1	220	4-21-92	.000	.000	.000	1	4	3	0	0	0	0	0	1	0	0	0	1	0	0	0	0.0	0.0
Perez, Onil	R-R	6-1	187	9-10-02	.300	.364	.403	62	283	253	46	76	12	4	2	36	23	4	0	3	31	21	2	8.1	11.0
Ramos, Heliot	R-R	6-1	188	9-07-99	.353	.421	.882	5	19	17	2	6	3	0	2	6	2	0	0	0	4	0	1	10.5	21.1
Ramos, Jose	R-R	5-11	143	10-25-02	.211	.308	.311	85	368	318	47	67	16	5	2	38	35	11	1	3	87	29	4	9.5	23.6
Rodriguez, Anthony	B-R	6-2	165	9-20-02	.221	.273	.338	56	238	222	27	49	12	1	4	35	13	3	0	0	84	5	2	5.5	35.3
Rosario, Dilan	R-R	6-0	185	6-16-01	.251	.298	.372	61	225	207	21	52	9	2	4	29	11	4	0	3	65	7	2	4.9	28.9

Santana, Rayner	R-R	6-2	250	8-15-02	.000	.000	.000	1	2	2	0	0	0	0	0	0	0	0	0	0	2	0	0	0.0	100.0
Shliger, Luke	L-R	5-9	180	9-25-01	.298	.403	.351	16	67	57	6	17	3	0	0	6	8	2	0	0	10	1	1	11.9	14.9
Suarez, Alexander	R-R	6-2	200	12-20-01	.245	.310	.353	99	404	363	55	89	11	5	6	39	22	14	1	4	110	22	5	5.4	27.2
Szykowny, Charlie	L-R	6-4	210	6-30-00	.239	.340	.304	12	53	46	4	11	3	0	0	1	5	2	0	0	8	0	1	9.4	15.1
Velasquez, Diego	B-R	6-1	150	10-01-03	.298	.387	.434	111	517	426	76	127	32	1	8	69	56	12	13	10	82	23	6	10.8	15.9
Wishkoski, Justin	R-R	6-3	195	1-19-01	.209	.346	.302	12	52	43	5	9	1	0	1	3	7	2	0	0	5	0	0	13.5	9.6

Pitching	B-T	Ht.	Wt.	DOB	W	L	ERA	G	GS	SV	IP	Hits	Runs	ER	HR	BB	SO	AVG	OBP	SLG	SO%	BB%	BF
Adon, Melvin	L-R	6-3	246	6-09-94	0	1	0.00	6	0	1	10	6	2	0	0	3	12	.171	.237	.200	31.6	7.9	38
Bertrand, John	L-L	6-3	205	2-08-98	4	0	2.65	5	0	0	17	19	6	5	1	2	12	.284	.314	.388	17.1	2.9	70
Birdsong, Hayden	R-R	6-4	215	8-30-01	0	0	2.16	12	10	0	42	34	12	10	0	22	70	.218	.332	.301	38.0	12.0	184
Blair, Daniel	R-R	6-3	205	4-08-99	7	1	2.05	18	0	2	53	38	15	12	4	18	45	.201	.283	.312	21.1	8.5	213
Castillo, Wilkelma	R-R	6-0	170	1-06-00	3	0	3.71	9	0	1	17	16	9	7	4	7	16	.242	.329	.455	21.1	9.2	76
Choate, Jack	L-L	6-6	249	4-18-01	3	1	2.30	13	6	0	47	29	17	12	1	19	67	.173	.275	.214	34.4	9.7	195
Cobb, Alex	R-R	6-3	205	10-07-87	0	0	2.45	1	1	0	4	3	1	1	1	0	9	.214	.214	.429	64.3	0.0	14
Corry, Seth	L-L	6-2	195	11-03-98	0	2	8.16	6	6	0	14	22	13	13	3	8	18	.386	.485	.614	26.5	11.8	68
Cotter, Cameron	R-R	6-3	220	12-17-98	2	0	2.30	17	0	4	31	32	12	8	3	3	31	.252	.271	.362	23.3	2.3	133
Crawford, Reggie	L-L	6-4	235	12-04-00	0	0	4.09	7	7	0	11	9	5	5	3	4	18	.220	.304	.488	39.1	8.7	46
Cumming, Dylan	R-R	6-4	175	5-14-99	7	3	2.93	34	7	6	92	89	33	30	5	36	86	.256	.343	.352	21.7	9.1	397
Delaplane, Sam	R-R	5-11	175	3-27-95	1	2	4.50	13	0	0	14	8	9	7	0	18	27	.163	.388	.245	39.7	26.5	68
Estrella, Mauricio	R-R	6-2	180	4-15-04	0	2	9.27	9	4	0	22	34	27	23	4	17	14	.354	.470	.531	11.8	14.3	119
Garcia, Jorge	R-R	6-0	185	5-10-02	2	3	5.06	14	0	0	27	31	25	15	3	15	26	.292	.386	.453	20.5	11.8	127
Harris, Trent	R-R	6-2	200	1-22-99	1	0	0.00	6	0	0	9	4	1	0	0	2	12	.129	.206	.129	35.3	5.9	34
Hilson, P.J.	R-R	5-10	175	8-25-00	0	0	9.00	2	0	0	3	4	3	3	0	2	2	.308	.438	.462	12.5	12.5	16
Jackson, Luke	R-R	6-2	210	8-24-91	0	0	0.00	1	0	0	1	0	0	0	0	0	0	.000	.000	.000	0.0	0.0	4
Johnson, Marques	R-R	6-2	210	7-04-00	0	1	0.00	11	0	1	18	9	2	0	0	9	20	.145	.254	.145	28.2	12.7	71
Kane, Tom	L-L	6-1	195	10-31-01	0	1	10.29	6	0	0	7	13	8	8	1	3	10	.394	.444	.606	27.8	8.3	36
Kempner, William	R-R	6-0	222	6-18-01	1	3	4.67	14	5	1	27	21	18	14	0	15	29	.208	.333	.287	23.4	12.1	124
Lansville, Cale	R-R	6-1	205	1-06-03	0	0	5.14	3	2	0	7	10	4	4	0	3	11	.313	.371	.344	31.4	8.6	35
Maldonado, Gerelmi	R-R	6-2	170	12-21-03	1	1	4.71	19	16	0	65	52	43	34	5	40	81	.221	.348	.340	28.2	13.9	287
Manzano, Mikell	R-R	6-0	140	11-30-02	0	0	6.08	4	3	0	13	17	10	9	1	6	5	.309	.415	.436	7.7	9.2	65
Medina, Nomar	L-L	6-0	190	11-23-02	6	8	5.19	25	14	2	95	111	71	55	13	46	77	.298	.376	.487	18.0	10.8	427
Mercedes, Manuel	R-R	6-4	190	9-21-02	3	6	3.64	25	21	0	106	111	61	43	2	42	72	.267	.336	.327	15.4	9.0	467
Mora, Miguel	R-R	6-2	187	11-04-01	2	1	13.29	11	0	0	21	23	32	31	4	29	22	.280	.479	.524	18.5	24.4	119
Moreno, Luis	R-R	6-2	174	8-03-98	5	2	4.18	30	0	3	65	63	45	30	5	24	70	.252	.326	.364	25.1	8.6	279
Newcomb, Sean	L-L	6-5	255	6-12-93	1	0	3.00	2	0	0	3	2	1	1	0	0	5	.167	.167	.250	41.7	0.0	12
Newsome, Ljay	R-R	5-11	210	11-08-96	0	0	0.00	1	0	0	2	0	0	0	0	1	3	.000	.167	.000	50.0	16.7	6
Nunez, Darien	L-L	6-2	205	3-19-93	0	0	18.00	1	0	0	1	2	2	2	0	1	1	.400	.500	.400	16.7	16.7	6
Rodriguez, Julio	R-R	6-3	180	2-10-00	3	7	5.97	39	0	2	57	49	50	38	0	33	71	.229	.366	.294	26.5	12.3	268
Rosario, Dilan	R-R	6-0	185	6-16-01	0	0	4.50	4	0	0	4	5	5	2	0	4	1	.313	.409	.438	4.5	18.2	22
Ross, Joe	R-R	6-4	232	5-21-93	0	0	5.14	4	4	0	7	10	5	4	0	3	5	.370	.452	.407	15.2	9.1	33
Simon, Liam	R-R	6-4	220	10-16-00	1	1	3.86	6	2	0	21	18	9	9	1	9	32	.234	.303	.364	36.0	10.1	89
Stripling, Ross	R-R	6-1	215	11-23-89	0	0	4.50	1	1	0	4	4	2	2	0	0	10	.235	.235	.353	58.8	0.0	17
Tucker, Cody	R-R	6-5	210	3-01-99	0	0	3.00	2	0	0	3	2	1	1	0	0	4	.200	.200	.500	40.0	0.0	10
Vinicio, Esmerlin	L-L	6-2	141	1-31-03	4	9	4.91	30	5	0	77	83	54	42	6	42	83	.284	.388	.411	24.1	12.2	344
Vogel, Tyler	R-R	6-0	175	11-16-00	6	7	4.27	39	0	5	65	53	37	31	7	34	89	.220	.321	.373	31.7	12.1	281
Whisenhunt, Carson	L-L	6-3	209	10-20-00	0	0	3.29	4	4	0	14	12	6	5	1	4	20	.231	.298	.346	35.1	7.0	57
Whitman, Joe	L-L	6-3	185	9-17-01	1	0	3.18	3	2	0	6	3	2	2	0	2	9	.158	.273	.158	40.9	9.1	22
Wynja, Hayden	L-L	6-9	220	10-14-98	4	2	3.98	19	8	2	54	44	30	24	6	18	68	.217	.281	.384	29.7	7.9	229
Yajure, Miguel	R-R	6-1	215	5-01-98	0	0	5.00	4	4	0	9	13	6	5	0	3	13	.333	.386	.436	29.5	6.8	44

Fielding

Catcher	PCT	G	PO	A	E	DP	PB
Cavanaugh	.982	5	47	8	1	0	2
Gavello	.966	10	74	10	3	2	7
Morgan	.985	42	416	41	7	0	13
Payton	.963	10	96	9	4	2	3
Perez	.979	50	472	52	11	4	21
Shliger	.973	16	128	15	4	0	4

First Base	PCT	G	PO	A	E	DP
Francisco	1.000	7	65	3	0	10
Frechette	.987	21	148	7	2	26
Higgins	.962	23	150	3	6	12
Kachel	.978	46	325	25	8	35
Mora	1.000	7	37	2	0	7
Morgan	.952	9	74	5	4	4
O'Tremba	.981	5	49	2	1	7
Rosario	.983	18	159	13	3	11
Santana	1.000	1	6	0	0	0
Wishkoski	1.000	5	42	3	0	5

Second Base	PCT	G	PO	A	E	DP
Bench	.875	2	4	3	1	1
Gavello	.970	14	24	41	2	10
Kachel	.926	7	9	16	2	5
McDaniel	.984	11	22	39	1	11
Mora	1.000	1	2	2	0	0
Ramos	1.000	29	53	65	0	19
Rosario	.940	20	29	49	5	15
Velasquez	.977	51	86	131	5	31

Third Base	PCT	G	PO	A	E	DP
Bench	.923	6	5	19	2	1
Diaz	.333	1	0	1	2	0
Gavello	.929	30	18	47	5	9
Kachel	.886	14	11	20	4	2
Mora	1.000	9	5	19	0	5
Rodriguez	.851	42	25	78	18	3
Rosario	.921	17	11	24	3	3
Szykowny	.800	10	5	15	5	2
Wishkoski	1.000	5	3	8	0	2

Shortstop	PCT	G	PO	A	E	DP
Foster	.918	22	31	70	9	19
Ramos	.944	51	80	123	12	32
Rodriguez	.882	7	7	23	4	4
Velasquez	.967	52	67	135	7	32

Outfield	PCT	G	PO	A	E	DP
Bandura	.984	20	37	0	1	0
Brown	1.000	4	15	0	0	0
Eldridge	.867	11	12	1	2	0
Frechette	.000	1	0	0	0	0
Higgins	.991	41	56	3	1	0
Hill	.992	74	123	7	3	0
Hilson	.938	68	121	9	6	1
Howell	1.000	38	75	3	0	1
Mora	1.000	1	2	1	0	1
O'Tremba	.986	62	76	4	2	1
Ramos	1.000	3	5	1	0	0
Suarez	.966	86	135	6	5	2

ACL GIANTS BLACK — ROOKIE

ARIZONA COMPLEX LEAGUE

Batting	B-T	Ht.	Wt.	DOB	AVG	OBP	SLG	G	PA	AB	R	H	2B	3B	HR	RBI	BB	HBP	SH	SF	SO	SB	CS	BB%	SO%
Cardozo, Gustavo	R-R	6-1	160	10-09-03	.152	.233	.212	26	73	66	8	10	2	1	0	6	6	1	0	0	29	0	1	8.2	39.7
Cavanaugh, Drew	B-R	6-0	190	1-27-02	.300	.475	.333	11	40	30	8	9	1	0	0	2	7	3	0	0	10	0	0	17.5	25.0
Diaz, Nomar	R-R	6-1	180	4-15-04	.216	.298	.314	18	57	51	4	11	0	1	1	7	5	1	0	0	16	0	0	8.8	28.1
Dues, Damon	L-R	6-0	180	6-21-98	.273	.492	.364	15	63	44	13	12	1	0	1	3	18	1	0	0	11	6	1	28.6	17.5
Dupere, Jared	L-R	5-11	200	1-23-99	.200	.273	.250	6	22	20	0	4	1	0	0	1	2	0	0	0	11	1	1	9.1	50.0
Foster, Cole	B-R	6-1	193	10-08-01	.333	.355	.700	7	31	30	8	10	2	0	3	8	1	0	0	0	10	0	0	3.2	32.3
Gonzalez, Cesar	R-R	5-11	206	5-08-01	.242	.349	.429	29	106	91	12	22	3	1	4	17	13	2	0	0	32	0	0	12.3	30.2
Gonzalez, Luis	L-L	6-1	185	9-10-95	.167	.286	.167	2	7	6	0	1	0	0	0	1	0	1	0	0	2	0	0	0.0	28.6
2-team (2 Giants Orange)					.182	.308	.273	4	13	11	2	2	1	0	0	1	1	1	0	0	4	0	0	7.7	30.8
Hanchey, Ty	L-R	5-11	175	12-19-99	.750	.600	1.500	1	5	4	2	3	0	0	1	5	0	0	0	1	0	0	0	0.0	0.0
2-team (9 Giants Orange)					.192	.382	.308	10	36	26	5	5	0	0	1	8	8	0	0	2	4	1	0	22.2	11.1
Lewis, Nadir	L-L	6-1	195	11-22-00	.220	.291	.360	14	55	50	7	11	2	1	1	9	4	1	0	0	19	2	0	7.3	34.5
Maduro, Jediael	L-L	6-1	188	12-26-03	.270	.393	.348	35	107	89	15	24	4	0	1	8	15	3	0	0	28	0	0	14.0	26.2
Martorano, Brandon	R-R	6-2	198	1-06-98	.250	.333	.250	2	9	8	1	2	0	0	0	0	1	0	0	0	2	1	0	11.1	22.2
McDaniel, Quinn	R-R	5-11	180	9-27-02	.250	.471	.479	16	70	48	14	12	2	0	3	11	20	1	0	1	16	6	0	28.6	22.9
Morales, Lazaro	R-R	5-11	160	4-16-04	.168	.242	.252	45	133	119	21	20	4	0	2	8	9	3	1	1	38	14	0	6.8	28.6
Ortiz, Jose	R-R	5-10	160	2-13-05	.167	.333	.167	12	31	24	1	4	0	0	0	1	2	4	1	0	10	1	0	6.5	32.3
Pierre, Mauricio	R-R	6-3	180	11-23-03	.143	.208	.143	7	24	21	4	3	0	0	0	1	2	0	0	1	12	0	0	8.3	50.0
2-team (1 Giants Orange)					.208	.269	.208	8	27	24	5	5	0	0	0	1	2	0	0	1	12	0	1	7.4	44.4
Quintas, Cesar	R-R	6-1	175	3-25-03	.372	.506	.473	42	168	129	26	48	10	0	1	17	22	15	0	2	39	3	3	13.1	23.2
Ramos, Jose	R-R	5-11	143	10-25-02	.160	.267	.200	7	30	25	5	4	1	0	0	4	2	2	0	1	9	4	1	6.7	30.0
Rayo, Elian	R-R	6-0	202	3-04-03	.238	.397	.463	49	189	147	37	35	12	0	7	35	34	6	0	2	62	1	1	18.0	32.8
Reckley, Ryan	B-R	5-10	160	9-06-04	.164	.335	.261	45	173	134	28	22	1	0	4	14	33	3	0	3	65	5	0	19.1	37.6
Roby, Sean	R-R	6-1	215	7-08-98	.271	.358	.542	19	67	59	9	16	0	2	4	12	7	1	0	0	24	0	0	10.4	35.8
Sandoval, Eliam	L-L	6-2	175	2-04-04	.238	.350	.376	34	120	101	20	24	5	0	3	14	15	3	0	1	33	2	1	12.5	27.5
Santana, Rayner	R-R	6-2	250	8-15-02	.238	.261	.476	7	23	21	2	5	2	0	1	7	1	0	0	1	8	0	0	4.3	34.8
2-team (13 Giants Orange)					.192	.323	.423	20	65	52	8	10	3	0	3	14	7	3	0	3	22	0	0	10.8	33.8
Szykowny, Charlie	L-R	6-4	210	6-30-00	.250	.391	.462	15	64	52	11	13	3	1	2	11	9	3	0	0	14	1	2	14.1	21.9
Walton, Donovan	L-R	5-9	190	5-25-94	.379	.500	.517	10	36	29	7	11	4	0	0	3	5	2	0	0	5	0	2	13.9	13.9
Whalen, Brady	L-R	6-6	180	1-15-98	.314	.400	.486	10	40	35	8	11	3	0	1	8	4	1	0	0	4	1	0	10.0	10.0
Williamson, Guillermo	L-L	6-1	200	3-16-04	.285	.415	.511	56	229	186	37	53	15	0	9	51	38	4	0	1	67	1	0	16.6	29.3

Pitching	B-T	Ht.	Wt.	DOB	W	L	ERA	G	GS	SV	IP	Hits	Runs	ER	HR	BB	SO	AVG	OBP	SLG	SO%	BB%	BF
Adon, Melvin	L-R	6-3	246	6-09-94	0	0	0.00	4	0	3	8	7	0	0	0	1	7	.241	.267	.241	23.3	3.3	30
2-team (1 Giants Orange)					0	1	13.50	1	0	0	1	1	1	1	0	0	0	.500	.667	.500	0.0	0.0	4
Avendano, Christian	R-R	6-0	168	9-04-03	0	1	4.67	16	0	2	27	20	17	14	0	20	40	.200	.333	.280	32.5	16.3	123
Bermudez, Luis	R-R	6-0	165	6-10-04	2	5	7.13	14	8	1	53	74	47	42	6	28	55	.329	.404	.542	21.5	10.9	256
Bonilla, Jason	R-R	6-0	165	8-30-98	2	0	6.75	12	2	0	24	14	20	18	2	30	23	.171	.424	.293	18.4	24.0	125
Bostick, Josh	R-R	6-4	200	10-20-01	0	0	0.00	3	2	0	3	2	0	0	0	1	6	.182	.250	.182	50.0	8.3	12
Castillo, Wilkelma	R-R	6-0	170	1-06-00	5	0	2.05	9	2	1	22	13	6	5	2	5	32	.169	.226	.286	38.1	6.0	84
Corry, Seth	L-L	6-2	195	11-03-98	0	0	7.36	3	3	0	4	3	3	3	0	2	6	.231	.333	.231	40.0	13.3	15
Flores, Junior	R-R	6-1	170	2-13-02	0	0	0.00	1	1	0	3	2	0	0	0	0	2	.182	.182	.182	18.2	0.0	11
Garcia, Jorge	R-R	6-0	185	5-10-02	2	5	4.61	12	1	2	27	34	19	14	8	6	33	.293	.346	.543	25.8	4.7	128
Harris, Trent	R-R	6-2	200	1-22-99	3	0	0.75	9	0	3	12	9	2	1	0	1	21	.196	.213	.239	44.7	2.1	47
Harrison, Kyle	R-L	6-2	200	8-12-01	0	0	0.00	1	1	0	2	0	0	0	0	0	4	.000	.000	.000	66.7	0.0	6
Helvey, Clay	R-R	6-3	195	2-14-97	2	0	1.04	6	0	1	9	8	1	1	0	5	17	.235	.333	.235	43.6	12.8	39
Herold, Nicolas	L-R	6-6	215	10-05-98	3	1	4.30	9	6	0	38	29	22	18	1	12	50	.213	.286	.324	32.3	7.7	155
Kane, Tom	L-L	6-1	195	10-31-01	2	1	5.93	9	0	2	14	14	10	9	0	4	17	.269	.339	.365	28.8	6.8	59
Kiest, Tanner	R-R	6-3	200	9-16-94	0	0	0.00	1	0	0	1	2	0	0	0	0	1	.500	.500	.500	25.0	0.0	4
Llovera, Mauricio	R-R	5-11	224	4-17-96	0	0	4.50	2	2	0	2	2	1	1	0	0	5	.250	.250	.625	62.5	0.0	8
Maduro, Jediael	L-L	6-1	188	12-26-03	0	0	0.00	1	0	0	1	0	0	0	0	0	1	.000	.000	.000	33.3	0.0	3
Manning, Timmy	L-L	6-2	195	9-10-01	1	0	2.25	3	0	1	4	1	1	1	0	0	5	.077	.143	.077	35.7	0.0	14
Manzano, Mikell	R-R	6-0	140	11-30-02	1	0	6.23	2	0	0	4	4	3	3	2	2	7	.235	.316	.588	36.8	10.5	19
McDonald, Trevor	R-R	6-2	200	2-26-01	0	1	1.04	4	4	0	9	8	5	1	0	2	11	.250	.286	.281	31.4	5.7	35
Mejias, Ubert	R-R	6-3	230	3-24-01	4	3	3.90	14	11	0	62	66	29	27	3	17	56	.268	.326	.415	20.8	6.3	269
Mora, Miguel	R-R	6-2	187	11-04-01	0	0	0.00	1	0	0	1	0	0	0	0	0	0	.000	.000	.000	0.0	0.0	3
Newsome, Ljay	R-R	5-11	210	11-08-96	0	1	2.89	6	1	0	9	7	4	3	1	2	8	.206	.289	.353	21.1	5.3	38
Nunez, Darien	L-L	6-2	205	3-19-93	0	0	0.00	1	0	0	1	0	0	0	0	1	3	.000	.250	.000	75.0	25.0	4
Palencia, Brayan	R-R	5-11	142	1-14-03	0	0	0.00	1	1	0	4	2	0	0	0	1	1	.143	.250	.214	6.3	6.3	16
Perdomo, Cesar	L-L	6-0	170	2-09-02	5	4	5.55	15	5	0	60	81	50	37	4	19	53	.320	.373	.447	19.1	6.8	278
Rodriguez, Michael	L-L	6-5	250	1-08-00	1	1	7.71	3	0	0	2	6	4	2	0	3	2	.462	.588	.462	11.8	17.6	17
Shore, Logan	R-R	6-2	215	12-28-94	0	0	9.00	1	1	0	1	3	1	1	0	0	3	.500	.500	.500	50.0	0.0	6
Silva, Eric	R-R	6-1	185	10-03-02	0	0	5.06	2	2	0	5	7	3	3	0	0	13	.292	.320	.375	52.0	0.0	25
Whitman, Joe	L-L	6-3	185	9-17-01	0	0	0.00	3	3	0	4	1	1	0	0	1	4	.071	.188	.071	25.0	6.3	16

Fielding

C: Gonzalez 25, Diaz 16, Cavanaugh 11, Santana 4, Hanchey 1, Martorano 1. **1B:** Williamson 22, Maduro 17, Whalen 8, Roby 6, Gonzalez 4, Cardozo 2, Santana 2. **2B:** Cardozo 19, Rayo 10, McDaniel 9, Morales 9, Dues 7, Walton 6, Foster 1, Maduro 1. **3B:** Rayo 34, Szykowny 11, Roby 10, Morales 2, Ramos 1, Whalen 1, Cardozo 1. **SS:** Reckley 42, Ramos 5, Foster 4, Dues 2, Morales 2, Walton 1, Cardozo 1, McDaniel 1. **OF:** Quintas 47, Williamson 34, Morales 33, Sandoval 29, Lewis 13, Ortiz 12, Pierre 7, Maduro 7, Dupere 5, Gonzalez 2, Diaz 1, Dues 1, McDaniel 1.

SAN FRANCISCO GIANTS

ACL GIANTS

ROOKIE

ARIZONA COMPLEX LEAGUE

Batting	B-T	Ht.	Wt.	DOB	AVG	OBP	SLG	G	PA	AB	R	H	2B	3B	HR	RBI	BB	HBP	SH	SF	SO	SB	CS	BB%	SO%
Alvarez, Armando	R-R	6-0	195	7-14-94	.357	.419	.464	8	31	28	4	10	3	0	0	2	2	1	0	0	4	1	0	6.5	12.9
Bandura, Scott	L-R	6-4	190	8-02-01	.400	.524	.667	5	21	15	5	6	1	0	1	4	5	0	0	1	6	0	0	23.8	28.6
Bench, Justin	R-R	6-0	185	8-28-99	.370	.466	.587	14	58	46	10	17	5	1	1	13	7	3	0	2	5	1	1	12.1	8.6
Cassiani, Estanlin	L-L	5-11	155	12-30-02	.314	.387	.414	47	191	169	33	53	12	1	1	21	19	2	0	1	29	5	1	9.9	15.2
Castillo, Javier	R-R	6-1	170	11-14-03	.291	.371	.364	34	132	110	21	32	8	0	0	26	12	5	0	5	25	0	0	9.1	18.9
Cumberland, Brett	B-R	5-10	200	6-25-95	.500	.500	.500	1	2	2	1	1	0	0	0	0	0	0	0	0	1	0	0	0.0	50.0
Davidson, Bo	L-R	6-2	205	7-05-02	.286	.397	.469	16	58	49	11	14	4	1	1	7	9	0	0	0	11	0	0	15.5	19.0
Eldridge, Bryce	L-R	6-7	219	10-20-04	.294	.393	.647	16	61	51	8	15	3	0	5	13	9	0	0	1	16	0	0	14.8	26.2
Francisco, Javier	R-R	6-1	162	11-11-02	.280	.442	.542	45	156	118	32	33	10	0	7	25	33	3	0	2	30	2	2	21.2	19.2
Frechette, Garrett	L-L	6-3	210	12-31-00	.282	.393	.437	36	122	103	16	29	7	0	3	12	18	1	0	0	22	0	1	14.8	18.0
Gonzalez, Luis	L-L	6-1	185	9-10-95	.200	.333	.400	2	6	5	2	1	1	0	0	0	1	0	0	0	2	0	0	16.7	33.3
2-team (2 Giants Black)					.182	.308	.273	4	13	11	2	2	1	0	0	1	1	1	0	0	4	0	0	7.7	30.8
Guzman, Ronald	L-L	6-5	235	10-20-94	.000	.200	.000	3	10	8	1	0	0	0	0	0	2	0	0	0	4	0	0	20.0	40.0
Hanchey, Ty	L-R	5-11	175	12-19-99	.091	.323	.091	9	31	22	3	2	0	0	0	3	8	0	0	1	4	1	0	25.8	12.9
2-team (1 Giants Black)					.192	.382	.308	10	36	26	5	5	0	0	1	8	8	0	0	2	4	1	0	22.2	11.1
Laya, Derwin	R-R	6-3	187	9-15-03	.258	.346	.380	48	185	163	26	42	5	0	5	26	17	5	0	0	43	7	3	9.2	23.2
Layer, Abdiel	B-R	6-2	170	8-09-98	.259	.259	.407	8	27	27	4	7	1	0	1	6	0	0	0	0	11	0	0	0.0	40.7
McIntyre, Donovan	L-L	6-2	165	12-10-02	.179	.323	.226	43	131	106	20	19	3	1	0	12	23	0	1	1	43	3	1	17.6	32.8
Munguia, Ismael	L-L	5-10	158	10-19-98	.278	.364	.417	9	44	36	10	10	2	0	1	5	4	2	0	2	5	2	1	9.1	11.4
Payton, Jack	R-R	5-11	200	8-07-01	.400	.483	.480	9	29	25	7	10	2	0	0	11	2	2	0	0	7	1	0	6.9	24.1
Peralta, Ramon	R-R	5-11	165	10-02-03	.266	.409	.437	49	199	158	28	42	12	0	5	35	34	5	1	1	56	5	2	17.1	28.1
Perez, Juan	R-R	6-1	182	9-22-04	.200	.293	.263	25	92	80	12	16	2	0	1	7	9	2	0	1	31	0	0	9.8	33.7
Pierre, Mauricio	R-R	6-3	180	11-23-03	.667	.667	.667	1	3	3	1	2	0	0	0	0	0	0	0	0	0	0	1	0.0	0.0
2-team (7 Giants Black)					.208	.269	.208	8	27	24	5	5	0	0	0	1	2	0	0	1	12	0	1	7.4	44.4
Pomares, Jairo	L-R	6-0	185	8-04-00	.308	.419	.385	9	31	26	4	8	2	0	0	3	5	0	0	0	9	0	0	16.1	29.0
Reyes, Samuel	R-R	6-0	170	1-27-03	.378	.478	.432	17	46	37	11	14	2	0	0	6	7	1	0	1	6	1	0	15.2	13.0
Santana, Rayner	R-R	6-2	250	8-15-02	.161	.333	.387	13	42	31	6	5	1	0	2	7	6	3	0	2	14	0	0	14.3	33.3
2-team (7 Giants Black)					.192	.323	.423	20	65	52	8	10	3	0	3	14	7	3	0	3	22	0	0	10.8	33.8
Sio, Jean Carlos	L-R	6-0	167	4-03-04	.274	.381	.374	52	215	179	35	49	5	2	3	25	31	2	0	3	32	8	2	14.4	14.9
Wielansky, Michael	R-R	6-2	175	3-18-97	.000	.222	.000	3	9	7	1	0	0	0	0	0	2	0	0	0	2	1	0	22.2	22.2
Wishkoski, Justin	R-R	6-3	195	1-19-01	.375	.500	.563	16	60	48	13	18	6	0	1	11	9	3	0	0	1	1	0	15.0	1.7

Pitching	B-T	Ht.	Wt.	DOB	W	L	ERA	G	GS	SV	IP	Hits	Runs	ER	HR	BB	SO	AVG	OBP	SLG	SO%	BB%	BF
Adon, Melvin	L-R	6-3	246	6-09-94	0	1	13.50	1	0	0	1	1	1	1	0	0	0	.500	.667	.500	0.0	0.0	4
2-team (4 Giants Black)					0	0	0.00	4	0	3	8	7	0	0	0	1	7	.241	.267	.241	23.3	3.3	30
Bednar, Will	R-R	6-2	230	6-13-00	1	2	4.22	4	3	0	11	9	7	5	0	7	15	.225	.367	.350	30.6	14.3	49
Bostick, Josh	R-R	6-4	200	10-20-01	0	0	10.80	1	0	0	2	3	2	2	0	1	1	.429	.444	.571	11.1	11.1	9
Brebbia, John	L-R	6-1	200	5-30-90	0	0	0.00	1	1	0	1	0	0	0	0	0	1	.000	.000	.000	33.3	0.0	3
Chires, Samir	R-R	6-0	160	9-17-03	3	3	4.68	13	5	1	50	35	27	26	0	27	47	.194	.303	.256	22.2	12.7	212
Corry, Seth	L-L	6-2	195	11-03-98	0	0	0.00	4	4	0	11	7	0	0	0	6	19	.179	.289	.282	42.2	13.3	45
De La Cruz, Lisander	R-R	6-2	185	8-16-01	4	0	3.46	20	1	3	26	15	14	10	1	24	41	.158	.339	.242	33.9	19.8	121
DeSclafani, Anthony	R-R	6-2	195	4-18-90	0	0	2.25	1	1	0	4	5	1	1	1	0	4	.313	.313	.563	25.0	0.0	16
Estrella, Mauricio	R-R	6-2	180	4-15-04	3	3	6.16	8	4	0	38	50	37	26	5	7	38	.313	.347	.469	22.4	4.1	170
Flores, Junior	R-R	6-1	170	2-13-02	0	1	4.58	18	0	4	35	34	21	18	3	25	37	.248	.370	.365	22.3	15.1	166
Francisco, Javier	R-R	6-1	162	11-11-02	0	1	0.00	1	0	0	0	1	1	0	0	0	0	.500	.667	.500	0.0	0.0	3
Hernandez, Alix	R-R	6-2	155	7-16-04	3	3	4.73	14	5	0	51	35	27	27	6	27	69	.191	.310	.372	31.9	12.5	216
Hillier, Cole	R-R	6-2	205	12-07-00	0	0	2.45	2	0	0	4	2	1	1	0	1	4	.154	.214	.231	28.6	7.1	14
Jackson, Luke	R-R	6-2	210	8-24-91	0	0	0.00	2	1	0	2	0	0	0	0	1	5	.000	.143	.000	71.4	14.3	7
Lansville, Cale	R-R	6-1	205	1-06-03	1	0	2.25	3	1	0	4	6	1	1	1	1	3	.353	.389	.588	16.7	5.6	18
Lee, Chen-Hsun	R-R	6-4	209	1-14-02	0	1	15.19	4	4	0	5	9	9	9	0	3	5	.360	.429	.640	17.9	10.7	28
Lopez, Carlos	L-L	6-0	165	8-31-02	2	4	6.14	10	6	0	37	38	29	25	3	30	35	.266	.402	.406	19.6	16.8	179
Manzano, Mikell	R-R	6-0	140	11-30-02	0	0	0.00	3	3	0	4	4	0	0	0	0	9	.222	.222	.278	50.0	0.0	18
McDonald, Trevor	R-R	6-2	200	2-26-01	0	0	18.00	1	1	0	1	1	2	2	0	1	1	.333	.500	.667	16.7	16.7	6
Molina, Carlos	L-L	6-0	190	2-07-05	4	0	3.90	12	3	0	30	31	14	13	2	11	35	.258	.333	.425	25.9	8.1	135
Mora, Miguel	R-R	6-2	187	11-04-01	4	3	10.86	12	1	1	31	41	41	37	1	35	21	.328	.470	.528	12.4	20.7	169
Newsome, Ljay	R-R	5-11	210	11-08-96	0	0	1.80	3	3	0	5	4	1	1	1	0	10	.222	.222	.444	55.6	0.0	18
Nunez, Darien	L-L	6-2	205	3-19-93	1	0	2.84	5	1	0	6	4	2	2	0	2	10	.182	.250	.273	41.7	8.3	24
Palencia, Brayan	R-R	5-11	142	1-14-03	3	2	6.81	14	2	0	40	49	31	30	5	13	36	.302	.365	.475	19.9	7.2	181
Pineda, Melvin	R-R	5-11	170	5-04-04	0	1	0.00	1	1	0	0	1	4	4	0	3	0	1.000	1.000	1.000	0.0	75.0	4
Rademacher, Shane	R-R	6-3	215	1-30-01	0	0	2.25	2	1	0	4	2	1	1	0	1	5	.143	.200	.214	33.3	6.7	15
Rodriguez, Randy	R-R	6-0	166	9-05-99	0	0	0.00	2	2	0	2	1	1	0	0	2	3	.125	.300	.125	30.0	20.0	10
Ross, Joe	R-R	6-4	232	5-21-93	0	0	0.00	1	0	0	1	1	0	0	0	0	0	.250	.250	.250	0.0	0.0	4
Stripling, Ross	R-R	6-1	215	11-23-89	0	1	4.50	2	2	0	6	7	5	3	0	1	6	.280	.296	.320	22.2	3.7	27
Stryffeler, Michael	R-R	6-2	210	5-22-96	0	0	3.00	3	0	0	3	1	1	1	0	2	2	.143	.300	.143	20.0	20.0	10
Tucker, Cody	R-R	6-5	210	3-01-99	1	0	0.00	3	0	0	4	2	0	0	0	0	6	.133	.133	.267	40.0	0.0	15
Vinicio, Esmerlin	L-L	6-2	141	1-31-03	0	0	1.80	2	0	0	5	6	1	1	0	3	7	.300	.391	.500	30.4	13.0	23

Fielding

C: Castillo 18, Perez 18, Santana 8, Hanchey 8, Payton 7, Cumberland 1. **1B:** Laya 18, Frechette 14, Francisco 12, Castillo 7, Santana 3, Wishkoski 3, Layer 1, Alvarez 1, Guzman 1. **2B:** Sio 20, Peralta 19, Francisco 8, Alvarez 7, Wielansky 3, Layer 2. **3B:** Laya 19, Francisco 14, Wishkoski 11, Bench 10, Layer 4, Sio 2, Peralta 1. **SS:** Peralta 29, Sio 27. **OF:** Cassiani 48, McIntyre 41, Frechette 16, Eldridge 15, Reyes 15, Davidson 14, Munguia 9, Pomares 6, Bandura 5, Bench 4, Francisco 4, Gonzalez 1, Pierre 1.

DSL GIANTS

DOMINICAN SUMMER LEAGUE

Batting	B-T	Ht.	Wt.	DOB	AVG	OBP	SLG	G	PA	AB	R	H	2B	3B	HR	RBI	BB	HBP	SH	SF	SO	SB	CS	BB%	SO%
Alexander, Jesus	L-R	6-2	185	9-04-05	.171	.259	.263	23	85	76	5	13	4	0	1	8	7	2	0	0	18	0	0	8.2	21.2
Arias, Rayner	R-R	6-2	185	4-29-06	.414	.539	.793	16	76	58	19	24	6	2	4	21	15	2	0	1	11	4	2	19.7	14.5
Arosemena, Erick	R-R	6-0	170	4-02-05	.264	.374	.322	36	147	121	18	32	7	0	0	18	15	8	0	3	34	1	2	10.2	23.1
Astudillo, Jose	R-R	5-10	150	2-27-04	.363	.422	.473	25	102	91	25	33	6	2	0	8	8	2	0	1	5	10	1	7.8	4.9
Bautista, Saul	B-R	6-0	145	4-20-04	.203	.300	.329	27	90	79	12	16	3	2	1	7	9	2	0	0	30	1	0	10.0	33.3
Blanco, Miguel	R-R	6-0	155	10-26-05	.231	.302	.325	32	130	117	19	27	3	1	2	6	11	1	0	0	20	5	1	8.5	15.4
Brizuela, Soyger	R-R	5-11	183	12-17-05	.187	.247	.320	23	81	75	6	14	4	0	2	7	5	1	0	0	14	1	0	6.2	17.3
Caldera, Nehomar	L-R	5-11	170	10-03-05	.184	.328	.243	32	125	103	12	19	6	0	0	10	15	7	0	0	30	1	0	12.0	24.0
Camacaro, Keiberg	R-R	5-11	158	8-24-06	.226	.348	.396	47	198	164	30	37	8	4	4	26	23	9	0	2	60	11	6	11.6	30.3
Camacho, Jhosward	B-R	5-10	146	7-09-04	.218	.361	.316	43	169	133	22	29	4	0	3	26	30	2	0	4	35	1	2	17.8	20.7
Concepcion, Carlos	R-R	6-1	189	1-06-06	.291	.368	.436	33	133	117	21	34	5	0	4	23	13	2	0	1	29	3	3	9.8	21.8
De La Rosa, Moises	R-R	6-2	190	11-29-04	.286	.410	.463	45	183	147	36	42	7	2	5	25	26	7	0	3	38	5	3	14.2	20.8
Diaz, Lisbel	R-R	6-2	201	7-19-05	.312	.386	.455	22	88	77	14	24	2	0	3	18	7	3	0	1	10	1	3	8.0	11.4
Ferrer, Brayan	B-R	6-0	170	12-26-03	.260	.370	.386	39	154	127	19	33	12	2	0	22	18	6	0	3	23	1	1	11.7	14.9
Frias, Luis	R-R	5-11	155	8-07-04	.301	.390	.460	41	188	163	38	49	15	1	3	16	17	7	1	0	42	18	5	9.0	22.3
Gonzalez, Anyelo	L-R	5-11	165	9-24-04	.291	.370	.411	43	173	151	26	44	5	2	3	31	15	5	0	2	32	3	2	8.7	18.5
Gonzalez, Diego	B-R	5-11	155	9-22-03	.248	.329	.336	44	170	149	24	37	7	3	0	30	18	1	0	2	26	5	0	10.6	15.3
Gutierrez, Carlos	L-R	5-10	174	8-22-04	.359	.444	.462	22	90	78	18	28	4	2	0	7	11	1	0	0	6	12	0	12.2	6.7
Guzman, Angel	L-L	5-11	170	11-15-05	.257	.392	.450	41	171	140	24	36	11	2	4	26	27	4	0	0	32	6	1	15.8	18.7
Jimenez, Audie	R-R	6-0	151	12-16-04	.200	.295	.247	48	173	150	18	30	4	0	1	10	19	2	0	2	48	1	2	11.0	27.7
Ladera, Oswaldo	R-R	6-2	170	2-14-03	.243	.392	.357	40	148	115	22	28	4	0	3	21	18	12	0	3	38	5	1	12.2	25.7
Lespe, Wueslly	L-R	6-0	165	4-23-03	.221	.432	.274	40	132	95	22	21	2	0	1	19	34	2	0	1	40	4	1	25.8	30.3
Montero, Eduardo	L-R	5-10	150	10-26-03	.204	.309	.333	19	68	54	10	11	5	1	0	11	9	1	0	4	22	0	0	13.2	32.4
Ramirez, Jorge	R-R	5-11	155	3-07-06	.254	.367	.373	22	79	67	9	17	2	0	2	8	11	1	0	0	26	1	1	13.9	32.9
Reynoso, Dario	R-R	5-10	180	3-22-05	.288	.460	.471	31	137	104	30	30	8	1	3	21	30	3	0	0	41	12	0	21.9	29.9
Riera, Dennys	R-R	5-9	165	2-17-05	.207	.294	.309	53	218	188	34	39	10	0	3	26	18	7	0	5	44	4	1	8.3	20.2
Rivas, Yosneiker	L-R	5-10	161	10-06-05	.160	.323	.320	9	31	25	6	4	1	0	1	4	6	0	0	0	1	1	0	19.4	3.2
Rodriguez, Samuel	B-R	5-11	161	10-22-03	.245	.398	.304	36	128	102	18	25	6	0	0	10	25	1	0	0	27	18	4	19.5	21.1
Tandron, Anthony	R-R	6-3	175	11-08-05	.244	.342	.288	45	187	160	28	39	5	1	0	22	23	2	0	2	49	5	6	12.3	26.2
Villegas, Diego	L-L	5-10	170	3-23-04	.297	.420	.396	32	112	91	24	27	7	1	0	13	18	2	0	1	21	1	3	16.1	18.8

Pitching	B-T	Ht.	Wt.	DOB	W	L	ERA	G	GS	SV	IP	Hits	Runs	ER	HR	BB	SO	AVG	OBP	SLG	SO%	BB%	BF
Avendano, Christian	R-R	6-0	168	9-04-03	0	0	9.00	2	0	1	3	4	3	3	0	0	4	.333	.333	.417	33.3	0.0	12
Bello, Jose	R-R	6-1	164	5-29-05	1	2	3.55	9	8	0	33	32	18	13	1	10	39	.248	.312	.333	27.7	7.1	141
Cabello, Brayan	R-R	6-0	155	12-06-03	3	1	6.27	13	7	0	33	43	27	23	2	12	38	.319	.382	.459	25.0	7.9	152
Caldera, Yojanser	R-R	6-0	170	10-12-04	1	3	7.92	12	6	0	31	41	35	27	3	17	22	.323	.430	.488	14.6	11.3	151
Canas, Jilber	R-R	6-2	170	2-22-02	2	2	3.91	18	0	5	23	13	11	10	1	20	20	.167	.340	.244	19.4	19.4	103
Caraballo, Jan	R-R	6-6	181	10-20-03	3	2	4.02	18	0	2	31	29	20	14	0	20	25	.254	.367	.307	18.0	14.4	139
Custodio, Luis	L-L	6-2	184	7-08-04	0	1	0.00	1	0	0	1	1	2	0	0	2	1	.250	.500	.250	16.7	33.3	6
De Frias, Haniel	L-R	6-4	175	10-28-04	2	0	6.23	11	0	1	22	25	15	15	0	13	7	.298	.400	.369	7.0	13.0	100
De Jesus, Larry	R-R	6-1	160	10-19-02	4	0	7.71	15	0	1	19	21	16	16	2	10	14	.276	.396	.474	15.4	11.0	91
De La Torre, Luis	L-L	6-0	188	9-06-03	2	0	7.27	5	0	0	9	5	7	7	0	7	12	.161	.341	.226	29.3	17.1	41
De Leon, Randry	R-R	6-4	201	7-21-05	0	4	8.51	11	9	0	31	28	31	29	4	23	37	.239	.373	.402	26.1	16.2	142
Estrada, Ricardo	L-L	6-0	170	6-25-02	0	1	3.86	2	2	0	7	4	4	3	0	5	3	.148	.281	.185	9.4	15.6	32
Feliz, Ankeily	R-R	6-1	185	6-27-03	1	0	2.14	16	5	1	34	31	10	8	0	15	34	.250	.333	.290	24.1	10.6	141
Franco, Marlon	R-R	6-2	165	9-18-02	1	4	2.68	14	8	0	40	45	16	12	2	7	30	.283	.327	.384	17.5	4.1	171
Gazo, Carlos	R-R	5-11	170	11-29-03	6	0	1.96	9	0	0	18	15	7	4	1	9	8	.221	.321	.324	10.3	11.5	78
Gomez, Carlos	R-R	5-11	165	12-22-04	3	1	2.42	18	0	3	26	24	11	7	0	14	29	.242	.333	.323	25.4	12.3	114
Gonzalez, Jose	R-R	6-1	180	6-15-02	3	1	4.35	14	7	0	41	39	21	20	4	19	40	.260	.339	.393	23.0	10.9	174
Gonzalez, Moises	R-R	6-2	175	10-25-02	2	2	5.91	11	0	0	21	25	18	14	1	5	26	.278	.316	.456	27.4	5.3	95
Grullon, Johnny	L-L	6-0	170	7-04-02	0	0	27.00	2	0	0	1	2	4	3	0	3	2	.400	.625	.600	25.0	37.5	8
Javier, Melvin	R-R	6-5	190	4-25-03	1	3	4.45	21	1	2	30	34	15	15	2	16	21	.298	.397	.412	15.4	11.8	136
Jimenez, Jeison	R-R	6-6	233	9-11-03	0	2	20.86	8	0	0	7	14	17	17	2	14	10	.412	.618	.647	18.2	25.5	55
Lespe, Wueslly	L-R	6-0	165	4-23-03	0	0	0.00	1	0	0	1	0	0	0	0	0	1	.000	.000	.000	33.3	0.0	3
Lopez, Carlos	L-L	6-0	165	8-31-02	1	0	2.19	3	3	0	12	8	6	3	0	2	15	.170	.204	.319	30.6	4.1	49
Lopez, Jesus	R-R	6-2	170	3-03-05	0	4	6.75	12	8	0	33	43	28	25	2	18	17	.323	.413	.444	11.0	11.6	155
Martinez, Jorge	R-R	6-0	161	11-06-01	3	1	1.69	16	0	2	32	20	9	6	1	11	37	.187	.260	.252	29.6	8.8	125
Mejias, Frainer	R-R	6-1	170	1-10-06	2	1	7.62	8	3	0	13	16	12	11	0	12	18	.302	.448	.453	26.9	17.9	67
Molina, Carlos	L-L	6-0	190	2-07-05	1	0	1.38	3	3	0	13	10	3	2	0	2	9	.213	.240	.277	18.0	4.0	50
Moreno, Victor	L-L	6-1	165	1-19-04	1	0	12.86	9	0	0	7	3	10	10	0	19	9	.143	.561	.238	22.0	46.3	41
Morillo, Juan	R-R	5-10	145	11-01-02	0	0	5.14	6	0	0	7	4	5	4	1	6	4	.182	.333	.364	13.3	20.0	30
Mota, Ismael	R-R	6-2	165	8-04-01	1	2	5.14	15	0	4	21	21	14	12	2	20	19	.266	.437	.418	18.3	19.2	104
Narvaez, Brayan	R-R	6-2	175	10-20-04	0	2	3.70	6	6	0	24	25	10	10	2	4	19	.275	.320	.429	19.4	4.1	98
Ochoa, Yonathan	R-R	6-3	175	10-18-02	1	0	9.39	7	0	0	8	7	8	8	1	5	9	.241	.371	.517	25.7	14.3	35
Perez, Alfonso	R-R	6-2	175	8-14-05	2	1	3.80	11	10	0	45	37	26	19	4	15	25	.224	.296	.370	13.4	8.1	186
Ramos, Miguel	R-R	6-1	204	9-05-04	0	0	3.93	12	0	0	18	15	8	8	0	11	15	.221	.346	.324	18.5	13.6	81
Rangel, Carlos	R-R	6-3	175	3-04-04	0	0	5.40	3	3	0	12	16	8	7	0	5	13	.320	.382	.480	23.6	9.1	55
Rengel, Jose	L-L	6-0	168	9-08-05	2	2	4.42	11	11	0	39	28	20	19	1	12	38	.193	.267	.262	23.6	7.5	161
Rodriguez, Johan	R-R	6-0	170	11-12-02	0	2	3.86	12	6	0	28	18	17	12	0	20	21	.188	.342	.219	17.5	16.7	120
Rojas, Jose	R-R	6-1	145	1-02-04	3	1	2.70	14	1	1	37	35	14	11	2	9	22	.257	.313	.382	14.7	6.0	150
Salas, Ken	R-R	6-2	180	7-30-01	3	2	3.97	15	0	4	23	20	10	10	2	12	20	.241	.337	.398	20.8	12.5	96
Sanchez, Angel	R-R	6-1	164	12-20-02	1	0	3.63	14	0	3	17	7	7	7	1	14	15	.127	.310	.200	21.1	19.7	71

Valenzuela, Cristofer	R-R	6-1	170	10-07-01	1	2	6.88	13	0	0	17	20	14	13	0	16	14	.299	.442	.433	16.3	18.6	86

Fielding

C: Gonzalez 34, Brizuela 20, Ramirez 19, Caldera 18, Alexander 12, Ferrer 4, Montero 4. **1B:** Ferrer 34, Gonzalez 30, Camacho 17, Montero 15, Villegas 6, Lespe 5, Alexander 3, Rodriguez 2. **2B:** Rodriguez 28, Riera 21, Jimenez 17, Tandron 17, Reynoso 13, Camacaro 6, Camacho 4, Astudillo 4, Gonzalez 3, Gutierrez 1. **3B:** Lespe 31, Riera 24, Camacho 22, Jimenez 14, Reynoso 11, Astudillo 9, Rodriguez 2. **SS:** Camacaro 43, Tandron 28, Jimenez 18, Reynoso 7, Riera 6, Rivas 6, Rodriguez 2. **OF:** De La Rosa 42, Frias 39, Guzman 39, Ladera 31, Blanco 30, Concepcion 30, Bautista 27, Arosemena 22, Diaz 18, Villegas 18, Gutierrez 16, Arias 15, Gonzalez 14, Astudillo 8, Lespe 3.

Seattle Mariners

SEASON SYNOPSIS: What was supposed to be a step forward after 2022's successul run to the postseason instead proved to be a big disappointment. The Mariners fell one win short of the postseason. With such a thin margin, there are a slew of what could have beens. Robbie Ray made only one start before an elbow injury sidelined him. A nerve issue cost lefthander Marco Gonzales three months. Outfielder Jarred Kelenic missed 45 games after he broke his foot kicking a water cooler.

HIGH POINT: Seattle was 10 games out in the AL West in mid-July and six games back on Aug. 1. But a remarkable 18-4 finish in August meant Seattle entered September in first place in complete control of their own desitny.

LOW POINT: The Mariners lost 15-4 to the Rays on June 30th. That dropped them to 38-42 and capped 9-15 month that proved too much of a hole to climb out of.

NOTABLE ROOKIES: Righthander Bryce Miller and Bryan Woo were the latest arrivals from the Mariners' impressive pitching development pipeline. The two helped cover the loss of Ray, with Miller going 8-7, 4.32 in 25 starts while Woo was 4-5, 4.21 in 18 starts. Righthander Isaiah Campbell was a useful addition to the bullpen. Making his debut in July, Campbell went 4-3, 2.83 in 27 appearances over the second half of the season. Jose Caballero hit .221/.343/.320 while playig three infield positions.

KEY TRANSACTIONS: Seattle added outfielder Teoscar Hernandez in an offseason trade. He hit .258/.305/.435 with 26 home runs while playing 160 games, second best on the team behnd ironman Eugenio Suarez's 162 games played. But for all of Jerry Dipoto's reputation as a wheeler-dealer, the Mariners largely stood pat with the team they had ridden to the playoffs in 2022. This year, that proved to not be enough. Dipoto's comments about winning sustainably did not go over well, and he eventually apologized after saying the goal was to win 54% of the time.

DOWN ON THE FARM: Seattle has shown in recent years that it can consistently make pitchers better. Even after graduating multiple waves of pitchers, Seattle had a .544 MiLB winning percetage. That was best in the American League and third best overall. Righthander Emerson Hancock made it to the majors late in the season, but he marked his full return from Tommy John surgery largely at Double-A Arkansas.

OPENING DAY PAYROLL: $137,119,947 (18th).

PLAYERS OF THE YEAR

MAJOR LEAGUE

Julio Rodriguez
OF
.275/.333/.485
37 2B, 32 HR
103 RBI, 37 SB

MINOR LEAGUE

Cole Young
SS
(LoA/HiA)
.277/.399/.448
34 2B, 9 3B, 22 SB

ORGANIZATION LEADERS

Batting — *Minimum 250 AB

MAJORS		
* AVG	Julio Rodriguez	.275
* OPS	Julio Rodriguez	.818
HR	Julio Rodriguez	32
RBI	Julio Rodriguez	103
MINORS		
* AVG	Lazaro Montes, ACL Mariners/Modesto	.303
* OBP	Lazaro Montes, ACL Mariners/Modesto	.440
* SLG	Lazaro Montes, ACL Mariners/Modesto	.560
* OPS	Lazaro Montes, ACL Mariners/Modesto	1.001
R	Jonatan Clase, Everett/Arkansas	102
H	Zach DeLoach, Tacoma	151
TB	Zach DeLoach, Tacoma	254
2B	Alberto Rodriguez, Everett/Arkansas	38
3B	Cole Young, Modesto/Everett	9
HR	Jake Scheiner, Tacoma	30
RBI	Jake Scheiner, Tacoma	105
BB	Harry Ford, Everett	103
SO	Zach DeLoach, Tacoma	173
SB	Jonatan Clase, Everett/Arkansas	79

Pitching — #Minimum 75 IP

MAJORS		
W	Luis Castillo	14
# ERA	Luis Castillo	3.34
SO	Luis Castillo	219
SV	Paul Sewald	21
MINORS		
W	Tyler Cleveland, Modesto	14
L	Kyle Tyler, Arkansas	11
# ERA	Reid VanScoter, Everett	3.27
G	Riley O'Brien, Tacoma	51
GS	Kyle Tyler, Arkansas	26
SV	Matt Festa, Tacoma	15
IP	Reid VanScoter, Everett	143
BB	Raul Alcantara, Everett	66
SO	Reid VanScoter, Everett	157
# AVG	Raul Alcantara, Everett	.221

2023 PERFORMANCE

General Manager: Jerry Dipoto. **Farm Director:** Justin Toole. **Scouting Director:** Scott Hunter.

Class	Team	League	W	L	PCT	Finish	Manager
Majors	Seattle Mariners	American	88	74	.543	6 (15)	Scott Servais
Triple-A	Tacoma Rainiers	Pacific Coast	77	73	.513	4 (10)	John Russell
Double-A	Arkansas Travelers	Texas	73	65	.529	2 (10)	Mike Freeman
High-A	Everett AquaSox	Northwest	74	58	.561	2 (6)	Ryan Scott
Low-A	Modesto Nuts	California	77	55	.583	2 (10)	Zach Vincej
Rookie	ACL Mariners	Arizona Complex	31	25	.554	6 (17)	Luis Caballero
Rookie	DSL Mariners	Dominican Sum.	27	25	.519	21 (50)	Jose Amancio
Overall 2023 Minor League Record			359	301	.544	3rd (30)	

ORGANIZATION STATISTICS

SEATTLE MARINERS

AMERICAN LEAGUE

Batting	B-T	Ht.	Wt.	DOB	AVG	OBP	SLG	G	PA	AB	R	H	2B	3B	HR	RBI	BB	HBP	SH	SF	SO	SB	CS	BB%	SO%
Caballero, Jose	R-R	5-9	185	8-30-96	.221	.343	.320	104	280	231	37	51	9	1	4	26	28	17	0	4	66	26	3	10.0	23.6
Canzone, Dominic	L-R	5-11	190	8-16-97	.215	.248	.407	44	141	135	19	29	11	0	5	13	6	0	0	0	24	1	0	4.3	17.0
Crawford, J.P.	L-R	6-2	202	1-11-95	.266	.380	.438	145	638	534	94	142	35	0	19	65	94	5	3	2	125	2	0	14.7	19.6
Ford, Mike	L-R	6-0	225	7-04-92	.228	.323	.475	84	251	219	32	50	6	0	16	34	24	7	0	1	81	0	0	9.6	32.3
France, Ty	R-R	5-11	215	7-13-94	.250	.337	.366	158	665	587	79	147	32	0	12	58	43	34	0	1	117	1	0	6.5	17.6
Haggerty, Sam	B-R	5-11	175	5-26-94	.253	.364	.341	52	108	91	13	23	3	1	1	5	15	1	1	0	17	10	1	13.9	15.7
Hernandez, Teoscar	R-R	6-2	215	10-15-92	.258	.305	.435	160	678	625	70	161	29	2	26	93	38	8	0	7	211	7	2	5.6	31.1
Hummel, Cooper	B-R	5-10	198	11-28-94	.087	.192	.130	10	26	23	2	2	1	0	0	0	2	1	0	0	9	1	0	7.7	34.6
Kelenic, Jarred	L-L	6-1	206	7-16-99	.253	.327	.419	105	416	372	44	94	25	2	11	49	41	1	0	2	132	13	5	9.9	31.7
La Stella, Tommy	L-R	5-11	180	1-31-89	.190	.292	.238	12	24	21	2	4	1	0	0	2	3	0	0	0	5	0	0	12.5	20.8
Marlowe, Cade	L-R	6-1	210	6-24-97	.239	.330	.420	34	100	88	14	21	3	2	3	11	12	0	0	0	33	4	2	12.0	33.0
Moore, Dylan	R-R	6-0	205	8-02-92	.207	.303	.428	67	165	145	18	30	9	1	7	19	16	4	0	0	56	7	3	9.7	33.9
Murphy, Tom	R-R	6-1	206	4-03-91	.290	.335	.538	47	159	145	19	42	12	0	8	17	10	1	0	2	44	0	0	6.3	27.7
O'Keefe, Brian	R-R	6-1	210	7-15-93	.105	.190	.211	8	21	19	0	2	2	0	0	2	2	0	0	0	7	0	0	9.5	33.3
Pollock, AJ	R-R	6-1	210	12-05-87	.173	.225	.323	49	138	127	15	22	4	0	5	15	9	0	0	2	30	0	1	6.5	21.7
Raleigh, Cal	B-R	6-3	235	11-26-96	.232	.306	.456	145	569	513	78	119	23	1	30	75	54	1	0	1	158	0	0	9.5	27.8
Rodriguez, Julio	R-R	6-3	228	12-29-00	.275	.333	.485	155	714	654	102	180	37	2	32	103	47	11	0	2	175	37	10	6.6	24.5
Rojas, Josh	L-R	6-1	207	6-30-94	.272	.321	.400	46	134	125	24	34	4	0	4	14	9	0	0	0	30	6	0	6.7	22.4
Suarez, Eugenio	R-R	5-11	213	7-18-91	.232	.323	.391	162	694	598	68	139	29	0	22	96	70	15	0	11	214	2	1	10.1	30.8
Torrens, Luis	R-R	6-0	217	5-02-96	.250	.250	.500	5	8	8	0	2	2	0	0	1	0	0	0	0	1	0	0	0.0	12.5
Trammell, Taylor	L-L	6-2	220	9-13-97	.130	.286	.326	22	56	46	7	6	0	0	3	11	9	1	0	0	22	0	1	16.1	39.3
Wong, Kolten	L-R	5-7	185	10-10-90	.165	.241	.227	67	216	194	21	32	6	0	2	19	16	4	0	2	46	1	1	7.4	21.3

Pitching	B-T	Ht.	Wt.	DOB	W	L	ERA	G	GS	SV	IP	Hits	Runs	ER	HR	BB	SO	AVG	OBP	SLG	SO%	BB%	BF
Adcock, Ty	R-R	6-0	213	2-07-97	0	0	3.45	12	0	0	16	11	7	6	4	0	11	.190	.190	.448	19.0	0.0	58
Bazardo, Eduard	R-R	6-0	190	9-01-95	0	0	2.63	9	0	0	14	9	4	4	2	4	14	.180	.241	.360	25.9	7.4	54
Berroa, Prelander	R-R	5-11	170	4-18-00	0	0	0.00	2	0	0	2	0	0	0	0	3	3	.000	.375	.000	37.5	37.5	8
Brash, Matt	R-R	6-1	173	5-12-98	9	4	3.06	78	0	4	71	65	26	24	3	29	107	.242	.325	.323	34.7	9.4	308
Bukauskas, J.B.	R-R	6-0	208	10-11-96	0	0	9.00	1	0	0	1	2	2	1	0	2	1	.400	.571	.600	14.3	28.6	7
Campbell, Isaiah	R-R	6-4	230	8-15-97	4	1	2.83	27	0	1	29	22	9	9	2	13	33	.210	.300	.314	27.5	10.8	120
Castillo, Diego	R-R	6-3	268	1-18-94	0	0	6.23	8	0	0	9	7	6	6	2	7	7	.212	.366	.424	17.1	17.1	41
Castillo, Luis	R-R	6-2	200	12-12-92	14	9	3.34	33	33	0	197	160	81	73	28	56	219	.218	.276	.395	27.3	7.0	802
Festa, Matt	R-R	6-1	195	3-11-93	0	0	4.00	8	0	0	9	4	4	4	1	12	13	.129	.372	.290	30.2	27.9	43
Flexen, Chris	R-R	6-3	219	7-01-94	0	4	7.71	17	4	0	42	59	36	36	11	19	29	.333	.398	.542	14.8	9.7	196
Ford, Mike	L-R	6-0	225	7-04-92	0	0	18.00	2	0	0	2	5	4	4	2	1	0	.455	.500	1.091	0.0	8.3	12
Gilbert, Logan	R-R	6-6	215	5-05-97	13	7	3.73	32	32	0	191	169	82	79	29	36	189	.233	.270	.409	24.5	4.7	770
Gonzales, Marco	L-L	6-1	205	2-16-92	4	1	5.22	10	10	0	50	55	32	29	5	18	34	.282	.340	.431	15.8	8.4	215
Gott, Trevor	R-R	5-11	185	8-26-92	0	3	4.03	30	0	0	29	33	19	13	2	8	32	.277	.333	.403	24.8	6.2	129
Hancock, Emerson	R-R	6-4	213	5-31-99	0	0	4.50	3	3	0	12	13	6	6	1	3	6	.283	.327	.348	12.2	6.1	49
Kirby, George	R-R	6-4	215	2-04-98	13	10	3.35	31	31	0	191	179	74	71	22	19	172	.246	.270	.395	22.7	2.5	757
Leone, Dominic	R-R	5-10	215	10-26-91	0	0	4.35	9	0	0	10	7	5	5	5	8	10	.184	.340	.632	21.3	17.0	47
McCaughan, Darren	R-R	6-1	200	3-18-96	0	0	5.40	3	0	0	5	7	5	3	1	3	10	.292	.370	.458	37.0	11.1	27
McGee, Easton	R-R	6-6	205	12-26-97	0	0	0.00	1	1	0	7	1	0	0	0	1	2	.048	.091	.095	9.1	4.5	22
Miller, Bryce	R-R	6-2	180	8-23-98	8	7	4.32	25	25	0	131	124	64	63	18	26	119	.248	.293	.427	22.2	4.8	537
Milone, Tommy	L-L	6-0	215	2-16-87	0	1	2.00	2	2	0	9	7	3	2	1	6	3	.212	.325	.303	7.5	15.0	40
Munoz, Andres	R-R	6-2	222	1-16-99	4	7	2.94	52	0	13	49	40	20	16	2	22	67	.217	.318	.304	31.8	10.4	211
Murfee, Penn	R-R	6-2	195	5-02-94	1	2	1.29	16	0	0	14	5	5	2	1	10	16	.109	.281	.196	27.6	17.2	58
Ray, Robbie	L-L	6-2	225	10-01-91	0	1	8.10	1	1	0	3	4	5	3	0	5	3	.308	.474	.385	15.8	26.3	19
Rodriguez, Jose	R-R	6-2	175	8-29-95	0	0	9.00	1	0	0	3	3	3	3	0	1	1	.273	.333	.455	8.3	8.3	12
Ryan, Ryder	R-R	6-2	205	5-11-95	0	0	0.00	1	0	0	1	0	0	0	0	1	2	.000	.250	.000	50.0	25.0	4
Saucedo, Tayler	L-L	6-4	205	6-18-93	3	2	3.59	52	0	1	48	41	20	19	2	23	43	.234	.343	.309	20.8	11.1	207
Sewald, Paul	R-R	6-3	219	5-26-90	3	1	2.93	45	0	21	43	30	15	14	5	14	60	.196	.262	.327	35.5	8.3	169
Speier, Gabe	L-L	5-11	200	4-12-95	2	2	3.79	69	0	1	55	47	24	23	7	11	64	.235	.282	.375	29.6	5.1	216

	B-T	Ht.	Wt.	DOB	W	L	ERA	G	GS	SV	IP	Hits	Runs	ER	HR	BB	SO	AVG	OBP	SLG	SO%	BB%	BF
Sweet, Devin	B-R	5-11	183	9-06-96	0	0	9.00	2	0	0	2	2	2	2	1	1	1	.250	.333	.625	11.1	11.1	9
Then, Juan	R-R	6-1	200	2-07-00	0	0	4.91	9	0	0	11	14	6	6	3	2	5	.304	.333	.543	10.4	4.2	48
Thornton, Trent	R-R	6-0	190	9-30-93	1	2	2.08	23	1	0	26	23	11	6	5	5	21	.235	.272	.459	20.4	4.9	103
Topa, Justin	R-R	6-4	200	3-07-91	5	4	2.61	75	0	3	69	61	26	20	4	18	61	.240	.295	.327	21.9	6.5	279
Weaver, Luke	R-R	6-2	183	8-21-93	0	1	6.08	5	1	0	13	16	9	9	2	3	8	.296	.345	.519	13.8	5.2	58
Woo, Bryan	R-R	6-2	205	1-30-00	4	5	4.21	18	18	0	88	75	44	41	13	31	93	.227	.305	.393	25.1	8.4	371

Fielding

Catcher	PCT	G	PO	A	E	DP	PB
Murphy	.992	41	349	3	3	0	1
O'Keefe	1.000	8	45	1	0	0	0
Raleigh	.991	128	1083	40	10	7	3
Torrens	1.000	2	12	0	0	0	0

First Base	PCT	G	PO	A	E	DP
Ford	1.000	10	43	3	0	3
France	.999	158	1106	104	1	106
Haggerty	.962	4	23	2	1	2
Moore	.833	4	4	1	1	0

Second Base	PCT	G	PO	A	E	DP
Caballero	.983	64	84	152	4	36
Haggerty	1.000	10	6	9	0	3
Moore	.978	23	21	24	1	9
Rojas	.977	43	47	81	3	15
Wong	.987	65	86	139	3	21

Third Base	PCT	G	PO	A	E	DP
Caballero	1.000	9	1	6	0	1
Moore	1.000	1	1	0	0	0
Rojas	.000	1	0	0	1	0
Suarez	.980	159	115	268	8	21

Shortstop	PCT	G	PO	A	E	DP
Caballero	.972	21	23	47	2	14
Crawford	.973	144	160	341	14	62
Moore	.917	9	6	16	2	4

Outfield	PCT	G	PO	A	E	DP
Caballero	.000	1	0	0	0	0
Canzone	.990	35	63	2	1	0
Haggerty	1.000	22	19	1	0	0
Hernandez	.989	135	249	12	3	7
Hummel	.500	2	1	0	0	0
Kelenic	.992	108	183	1	3	0
Marlowe	1.000	30	66	3	0	1
Moore	.972	30	43	0	1	0
Pollock	1.000	23	36	0	0	0
Rodriguez	.994	152	355	3	2	2
Trammell	.500	12	14	0	0	0

TACOMA RAINIERS — TRIPLE-A

PACIFIC COAST LEAGUE

Batting	B-T	Ht.	Wt.	DOB	AVG	OBP	SLG	G	PA	AB	R	H	2B	3B	HR	RBI	BB	HBP	SH	SF	SO	SB	CS	BB%	SO%
Bliss, Ryan	R-R	5-6	165	12-13-99	.251	.356	.466	47	226	191	37	48	7	2	10	35	29	3	1	2	52	20	4	12.8	23.0
2-team (13 Reno)					.239	.339	.441	60	288	247	43	59	9	4	11	39	34	4	1	2	64	25	7	11.8	22.2
Caballero, Jose	R-R	5-9	185	8-30-96	.333	.550	.593	10	40	27	8	9	1	0	2	9	12	1	0	0	4	5	1	30.0	10.0
DeLoach, Zach	L-R	6-0	205	8-18-98	.286	.387	.481	138	623	528	90	151	30	2	23	88	83	7	0	5	173	8	3	13.3	27.8
DeShields, Delino	R-R	5-7	190	8-16-92	.222	.300	.222	12	50	45	7	10	0	0	0	2	5	0	0	0	8	3	2	10.0	16.0
Emery, Robert	R-R	6-0	210	10-22-96	.333	.429	.500	2	7	6	1	2	1	0	0	1	1	0	0	0	2	0	0	14.3	28.6
Engel, Adam	R-R	6-2	215	12-09-91	.250	.371	.451	76	315	264	52	66	13	2	12	34	47	4	0	0	95	19	1	14.9	30.2
2-team (14 El Paso)				.237	.355	.435	90	376	317	55	75	17	2	14	42	53	5	0	1116		22	214.1		30.9	
Ford, Mike	L-R	6-0	225	7-04-92	.302	.427	.605	49	211	172	35	52	11	1	13	56	34	4	0	1	30	2	0	16.1	14.2
Gilliam, Isiah	B-R	6-3	220	7-23-96	.253	.386	.410	24	101	83	8	21	4	0	3	14	15	3	0	0	25	3	2	14.9	24.8
Gregorius, Didi	L-R	6-3	205	2-18-90	.192	.282	.337	25	117	104	18	20	4	1	3	10	9	4	0	0	15	1	0	7.7	12.8
Haggerty, Sam	B-R	5-11	175	5-26-94	.324	.419	.578	47	222	185	41	60	15	4	8	29	29	4	0	4	37	19	2	13.1	16.7
Hernandez, Cesar	B-R	5-10	183	5-23-90	.272	.436	.336	43	164	125	27	34	8	0	0	14	37	0	1	1	34	7	2	22.6	20.7
Hoover, Connor	L-R	5-10	185	7-18-96	.200	.500	.200	3	8	5	1	1	0	0	0	1	3	0	0	0	2	0	0	37.5	25.0
Hummel, Cooper	B-R	5-10	198	11-28-94	.262	.409	.435	104	455	363	71	95	27	6	8	47	82	9	0	1	106	26	6	18.0	23.3
Kelenic, Jarred	L-L	6-1	206	7-16-99	.306	.395	.472	10	43	36	8	11	3	0	1	5	6	0	0	1	11	1	0	14.0	25.6
Kirwer, Tanner	R-R	5-11	185	3-15-96	.115	.200	.115	9	30	26	3	3	0	0	0	1	3	0	0	1	8	2	0	10.0	26.7
Larsen, Jack	L-L	6-1	195	1-13-95	.313	.466	.338	25	103	80	13	25	2	0	0	10	22	1	0	0	24	1	1	21.4	23.3
2-team (7 Sacramento)					.270	.426	.300	32	129	100	15	27	3	0	0	10	26	2	1	0	32	1	1	20.2	24.8
Lavey, Justin	R-R	5-10	205	9-23-97	.500	.750	.500	1	4	2	1	1	0	0	0	0	2	0	0	0	0	0	0	50.0	0.0
Marlowe, Cade	L-R	6-1	210	6-24-97	.257	.338	.443	81	379	334	59	86	17	6	11	52	39	3	0	3	99	29	4	10.3	26.1
Mathias, Mark	R-R	6-0	200	8-02-94	.345	.426	.500	16	68	58	10	20	3	0	2	8	9	0	0	1	13	1	2	13.2	19.1
McCoy, Mason	R-R	5-11	185	3-31-95	.234	.330	.407	87	383	329	53	77	18	3	11	55	45	4	1	4	113	20	1	11.7	29.5
Moore, Dylan	R-R	6-0	205	8-02-92	.200	.333	.240	6	30	25	5	5	1	0	0	4	4	1	0	0	9	1	1	13.3	30.0
Moran, Colin	L-R	6-4	225	10-01-92	.257	.361	.397	40	158	136	19	35	4	0	5	28	19	3	0	0	33	0	0	12.0	20.9
Nottingham, Jacob	R-R	6-2	220	4-03-95	.200	.294	.450	17	68	60	8	12	3	0	4	10	7	1	0	0	19	0	1	10.3	27.9
2-team (17 Sacramento)					.232	.329	.432	34	143	125	18	29	7	0	6	19	11	7	0	0	35	1	1	7.7	24.5
O'Keefe, Brian	R-R	6-1	210	7-15-93	.238	.328	.504	91	403	353	63	84	25	0	23	67	46	2	0	2	99	2	3	11.4	24.6
Salvatore, Mike	R-R	5-9	186	12-27-96	.130	.231	.174	11	26	23	0	3	1	0	0	2	3	0	0	0	4	0	0	11.5	15.4
Scheiner, Jake	R-R	6-1	200	8-13-95	.252	.369	.509	124	553	460	91	116	22	3	30	105	81	7	0	5	134	5	2	14.6	24.2
Severino, Pedro	R-R	5-11	235	7-20-93	.230	.286	.399	46	192	178	31	41	9	0	7	28	13	1	0	0	45	4	0	6.8	23.4
2-team (18 El Paso)				.245	.318	.419	64	267	241	43	59	12	0	10	36	25	1	0	0	55	7	0	9.4	20.6	
Solak, Nick	R-R	5-9	185	1-11-95	.077	.294	.077	4	17	13	2	1	0	0	0	1	3	1	0	0	6	0	1	17.6	35.3
Tenerowicz, Robbie	R-R	5-11	228	1-06-95	.264	.358	.351	47	201	174	27	46	6	0	3	21	18	8	0	1	34	1	1	9.0	16.9
Torrens, Luis	R-R	6-0	217	5-02-96	.200	.238	.350	5	21	20	1	4	0	0	1	2	1	0	0	0	7	0	0	4.8	33.3
Trammell, Taylor	L-L	6-2	220	9-13-97	.268	.390	.530	85	391	317	59	85	20	0	21	63	63	4	1	6	104	17	4	16.1	26.6
Unroe, Riley	B-R	5-11	180	8-03-95	.257	.399	.444	45	179	144	31	37	8	2	5	26	34	0	1	0	37	8	1	19.0	20.7
Valaika, Pat	R-R	6-0	200	9-09-92	.240	.343	.405	38	143	121	21	29	6	1	4	26	19	1	0	2	30	1	0	13.3	21.0
2-team (25 Oklahoma City)					.233	.321	.362	63	241	210	30	49	7	1	6	36	26	1	0	4	53	2	0	10.8	22.0
White, Evan	R-L	6-1	219	4-26-96	.143	.333	.143	2	9	7	1	1	0	0	0	1	1	1	0	0	3	1	0	11.1	33.3
Wong, Kean	L-R	5-9	189	4-17-95	.315	.422	.500	33	109	92	20	29	5	0	4	24	16	1	0	0	19	3	1	14.7	17.4

Pitching	B-T	Ht.	Wt.	DOB	W	L	ERA	G	GS	SV	IP	Hits	Runs	ER	HR	BB	SO	AVG	OBP	SLG	SO%	BB%	BF
Allen, Logan	R-L	6-3	200	5-23-97	5	2	4.66	14	10	0	58	57	30	30	11	28	49	.252	.342	.438	19.1	10.9	257
Bayless, Jarod	R-R	6-4	225	12-29-96	0	0	0.00	2	0	0	2	2	0	0	0	2	2	.286	.500	.429	20.0	20.0	10
Bazardo, Eduard	R-R	6-0	190	9-01-95	1	0	3.86	10	0	0	9	10	4	4	1	5	15	.270	.372	.378	34.9	11.6	43
Bernardino, Brennan	L-L	6-4	180	1-15-92	0	0	12.00	2	0	0	6	13	11	8	2	1	11	.406	.441	.688	32.4	2.9	34
Blackwood, Nolan	R-R	6-5	185	3-16-95	3	4	4.75	36	0	0	47	49	29	25	1	19	35	.275	.343	.388	17.2	9.4	203
Bukauskas, J.B.	R-R	6-0	208	10-11-96	0	0	7.94	4	0	0	6	8	7	5	1	3	7	.308	.379	.538	24.1	10.3	29

SEATTLE MARINERS

Castillo, Diego	R-R	6-3	268	1-18-94	5	5	5.13	43	1	0	47	50	35	27	5	35	50	.273	.399	.443	22.1	15.5	226
Creel, John	L-R	6-5	222	7-01-97	0	0	10.13	2	0	0	3	3	3	3	0	4	3	.300	.533	.300	20.0	26.7	15
Davila, Nick	R-R	6-3	202	11-21-98	1	2	3.86	3	3	0	19	15	10	8	1	5	15	.224	.280	.299	20.0	6.7	75
Davis, Riley	R-R	6-3	200	11-10-98	0	1	10.80	1	1	0	3	4	4	4	0	4	3	.308	.500	.462	16.7	22.2	18
DeLoach, Zach	L-R	6-0	205	8-18-98	0	0	0.00	1	0	0	1	0	0	0	0	2	0	.000	.400	.000	0.0	40.0	5
Dollard, Taylor	R-R	6-3	195	2-17-99	0	2	7.56	3	3	0	8	9	7	7	4	3	8	.273	.333	.758	22.2	8.3	36
Driver, Tyler	R-R	6-2	185	2-04-01	0	0	8.10	2	0	0	3	4	3	3	1	3	2	.333	.500	.667	11.1	16.7	18
Festa, Matt	R-R	6-1	195	3-11-93	1	0	0.53	28	0	15	34	11	5	2	2	16	28	.101	.234	.202	21.9	12.5	128
Gott, Trevor	R-R	5-11	185	8-26-92	0	0	0.00	2	0	0	3	2	0	0	0	1	2	.250	.333	.250	22.2	11.1	9
Hart, Kyle	L-L	6-5	200	11-23-92	4	6	4.58	18	18	0	88	97	49	45	10	35	85	.286	.357	.451	22.1	9.1	385
Hunter, Leon	R-R	6-3	253	3-17-97	0	0	4.50	1	0	0	2	4	1	1	1	1	1	.400	.455	.700	9.1	9.1	11
Jensen, Ryan	R-R	6-0	190	11-23-97	0	1	3.18	13	0	1	11	9	4	4	0	8	12	.214	.340	.262	24.0	16.0	50
Kaminsky, Rob	R-L	6-0	195	9-02-94	2	0	7.52	16	1	0	20	31	17	17	3	8	18	.360	.411	.547	18.9	8.4	95
Kolek, Stephen	R-R	6-3	210	4-18-97	4	2	4.23	44	1	4	62	51	34	29	3	30	65	.224	.322	.298	24.7	11.4	263
Martinez, Bernie	R-R	6-0	195	12-24-96	0	0	7.71	1	1	0	2	3	2	2	1	4	2	.333	.538	.667	15.4	30.8	13
McCaughan, Darren	R-R	6-1	200	3-18-96	7	8	5.83	25	25	0	139	154	98	90	30	44	130	.277	.340	.534	21.2	7.2	613
McGee, Easton	R-R	6-6	205	12-26-97	3	0	3.14	5	5	0	29	26	10	10	1	9	24	.241	.297	.343	20.3	7.6	118
Milone, Tommy	L-L	6-0	215	2-16-87	6	3	5.34	21	21	0	96	92	60	57	22	38	90	.247	.317	.487	21.8	9.2	413
Muckenhirn, Zach	L-L	6-0	205	2-27-95	0	0	6.11	14	0	0	18	19	12	12	4	5	13	.275	.329	.522	17.1	6.6	76
Munoz, Andres	R-R	6-2	222	1-16-99	0	0	0.00	3	0	1	3	0	0	0	0	1	3	.000	.111	.000	33.3	11.1	9
Murfee, Penn	R-R	6-2	195	5-02-94	1	0	0.00	2	0	0	2	0	0	0	0	1	3	.000	.125	.000	37.5	12.5	8
O'Brien, Riley	R-R	6-4	180	2-06-95	2	5	2.29	51	3	15	55	36	19	14	2	31	86	.188	.317	.257	37.7	13.6	228
Oller, Adam	R-R	6-4	225	10-17-94	6	4	5.51	12	12	0	64	72	42	39	13	28	62	.286	.365	.516	21.4	9.7	290
Puckett, A.J.	R-R	6-4	200	5-27-95	0	1	7.36	3	0	0	4	4	3	3	0	4	2	.267	.421	.400	10.5	21.1	19
Rodriguez, Jose	R-R	6-2	175	8-29-95	2	7	7.46	31	13	0	80	112	68	66	18	33	62	.344	.404	.610	16.9	9.0	366
Ryan, Ryder	R-R	6-2	205	5-11-95	4	2	3.76	48	1	2	55	46	24	23	4	22	56	.225	.306	.368	24.3	9.6	230
Sadler, Casey	R-R	6-3	223	7-13-90	1	0	7.63	18	0	0	15	22	13	13	3	5	15	.338	.394	.554	21.1	7.0	71
Saucedo, Tayler	L-L	6-4	205	6-18-93	2	0	0.00	5	0	0	8	2	0	0	0	2	8	.083	.154	.083	30.8	7.7	26
Sheffield, Justus	L-L	5-10	224	5-13-96	0	1	14.04	10	0	0	8	16	17	13	2	11	4	.400	.528	.700	7.5	20.8	53
Stout, Eric	L-L	6-3	205	3-27-93	3	1	4.20	21	4	0	41	39	20	19	3	22	44	.250	.357	.404	24.2	12.1	182
Sweet, Devin	B-R	5-11	183	9-06-96	0	0	2.57	7	0	0	7	6	2	2	2	3	7	.222	.300	.444	23.3	10.0	30
Then, Juan	R-R	6-1	200	2-07-00	2	2	10.21	27	2	0	27	47	34	31	3	22	18	.382	.466	.553	12.2	14.9	148
Thornton, Trent	R-R	6-0	190	9-30-93	0	0	0.00	1	0	0	1	1	0	0	0	0	2	.250	.250	.250	50.0	0.0	4
Topa, Justin	R-R	6-4	200	3-07-91	1	0	3.38	3	0	0	3	2	1	1	0	1	3	.222	.273	.222	27.3	9.1	11
Villarreal, Fred	R-R	5-11	187	4-07-98	1	0	5.40	3	0	0	8	8	5	5	2	4	6	.267	.353	.467	17.1	11.4	35
Wade, Konner	L-R	6-3	195	12-03-91	0	4	8.57	11	11	0	48	81	48	46	11	22	32	.382	.434	.646	13.2	9.1	242
Walden, Marcus	R-R	5-10	198	9-13-88	3	3	5.65	17	14	0	72	86	48	45	11	35	50	.302	.377	.481	15.4	10.8	325
Weiman, Blake	R-L	6-3	210	11-05-95	4	4	5.17	44	0	0	54	59	31	31	13	23	53	.272	.340	.493	22.0	9.5	241
Williams, Taylor	B-R	5-11	185	7-21-91	3	1	7.47	32	0	2	37	43	34	31	4	23	30	.301	.398	.462	17.4	13.4	172
Willrodt, Matt	R-R	6-4	220	10-19-97	0	1	9.00	2	0	0	1	2	2	1	0	2	0	.333	.500	.500	0.0	25.0	8
Wittgren, Nick	R-R	6-2	216	5-29-91	0	1	7.90	12	0	0	14	17	13	12	4	8	10	.309	.412	.600	14.7	11.8	68

Fielding

Catcher	PCT	G	PO	A	E	DP	PB
Emery	1.000	2	9	1	0	0	0
Hummel	.959	12	88	5	4	0	2
Nottingham	.983	16	107	7	2	1	2
O'Keefe	.991	72	619	32	6	3	2
Severino	.981	46	391	25	8	2	6
Torrens	1.000	5	49	4	0	2	1

First Base	PCT	G	PO	A	E	DP
Ford	.984	10	59	3	1	10
Gilliam	1.000	5	40	3	0	6
Gregorius	1.000	1	8	0	0	1
Hummel	.992	54	348	38	3	42
Mathias	1.000	4	38	0	0	5
Moran	.973	10	70	1	2	13
Salvatore	.889	1	7	1	1	0
Scheiner	.984	24	170	11	3	16
Severino	1.000	1	3	0	0	0
Tenerowicz	1.000	29	221	11	0	31
Valaika	1.000	17	128	10	0	17
White	1.000	2	16	2	0	1

Second Base	PCT	G	PO	A	E	DP
Bliss	1.000	6	9	13	0	2
Caballero	1.000	4	5	7	0	3
Gregorius	1.000	6	14	14	0	5
Haggerty	1.000	15	38	31	0	9
Hernandez	.981	25	42	60	2	23
Lavey	1.000	1	2	2	0	1
Mathias	1.000	8	16	28	0	6
McCoy	.971	8	17	17	1	1
Moore	1.000	2	5	7	0	0
Unroe	.990	44	81	122	2	32
Valaika	.969	15	32	30	2	6
Wong	.980	27	40	57	2	22

Third Base	PCT	G	PO	A	E	DP
Caballero	.895	8	3	14	2	1
Gregorius	1.000	1	2	4	0	2
Haggerty	.933	6	7	7	1	1
Hernandez	1.000	6	8	9	0	2
Hoover	1.000	3	2	2	0	1
McCoy	1.000	5	2	11	0	1
Moore	.000	1	0	0	0	0
Moran	.931	24	11	43	4	6
Salvatore	.933	9	3	11	1	0
Scheiner	.946	83	39	119	9	14
Tenerowicz	1.000	12	9	17	0	2
Valaika	.867	6	4	9	2	0

Shortstop	PCT	G	PO	A	E	DP
Bliss	.943	41	57	92	9	28
Gregorius	.949	16	21	54	4	12
Haggerty	1.000	11	16	22	0	5
Hernandez	.947	6	6	12	1	2
McCoy	.986	75	107	236	5	55
Moore	1.000	2	4	6	0	2
Unroe	.000	1	0	0	0	0

Outfield	PCT	G	PO	A	E	DP
DeLoach	.662	123	248	12	3	0
DeShields	.833	11	13	1	2	0
Engel	.995	63	137	6	1	3
Gilliam	.500	11	19	1	0	0
Haggerty	.961	10	25	1	1	0
Hernandez	1.000	5	8	0	0	0
Hummel	.971	37	65	3	2	1
Kelenic	1.000	7	6	0	0	0
Kirwer	1.000	7	13	0	0	0
Larsen	.967	25	48	0	2	0
Marlowe	.957	73	150	5	3	1
Mathias	1.000	2	6	0	0	0
Moore	1.000	1	2	0	0	0
Scheiner	1.000	21	24	2	0	0
Solak	1.000	3	7	0	0	0
Trammell	.975	70	158	1	3	0
Valaika	.000	1	0	0	0	0
Wong	1.000	1	1	0	0	0

ARKANSAS TRAVELERS

DOUBLE-A

TEXAS LEAGUE

Batting	B-T	Ht.	Wt.	DOB	AVG	OBP	SLG	G	PA	AB	R	H	2B	3B	HR	RBI	BB	HBP	SH	SF	SO	SB	CS	BB%	SO%
Anchia, Jake	R-R	5-10	210	3-05-97	.190	.281	.316	68	267	237	32	45	14	2	4	23	24	6	0	0	71	1	0	9.0	26.6
Cabrera, Walking	R-R	6-2	184	8-26-00	.667	.800	.667	1	5	3	2	2	0	0	0	1	2	0	0	0	0	0	0	40.0	0.0
Clase, Jonatan	B-R	5-9	150	5-23-02	.222	.331	.396	108	489	414	79	92	19	7	13	51	64	6	0	5	137	62	11	13.1	28.0
Frick, Patrick	R-R	6-0	200	2-14-97	.275	.325	.333	31	114	102	15	28	6	0	0	9	5	4	0	3	22	2	1	4.4	19.3
Gilliam, Isiah	B-R	6-3	220	7-23-96	.281	.393	.523	98	422	352	70	99	17	1	22	66	62	5	0	3	136	22	5	14.7	32.2
Hoover, Connor	L-R	5-10	185	7-18-96	.197	.320	.344	80	292	244	45	48	7	1	9	35	40	5	1	2	83	8	1	13.7	28.4
Kirwer, Tanner	R-R	5-11	185	3-15-96	.232	.330	.329	58	180	155	33	36	6	0	3	20	19	4	0	1	45	19	3	10.6	25.0
Locklear, Tyler	R-R	6-1	210	11-24-00	.260	.383	.403	22	94	77	11	20	6	1	1	8	11	5	0	1	14	2	0	11.7	14.9
Morgan, Josh	R-R	5-8	190	11-16-95	.226	.303	.372	81	323	288	35	65	13	1	9	41	27	6	0	2	80	2	1	8.4	24.8
Packard, Spencer	L-R	5-10	210	10-12-97	.292	.391	.448	121	550	466	66	136	27	2	14	82	68	11	0	5	86	1	1	12.4	15.6
Perez Jr., Robert	R-R	6-0	170	6-26-00	.242	.321	.416	117	508	450	56	109	22	4	16	62	38	16	0	4	155	2	2	7.5	30.5
Polcovich, Kaden	B-R	5-10	185	2-21-99	.176	.314	.313	40	159	131	23	23	5	2	3	16	26	1	0	1	42	6	2	16.4	26.4
Rivas, Leo	B-R	5-10	150	10-10-97	.255	.411	.347	106	436	329	71	84	11	2	5	47	86	7	5	9	89	50	10	19.7	20.4
Rodriguez, Alberto	L-L	5-10	227	10-06-00	.291	.361	.385	46	202	179	17	52	8	0	3	27	20	1	0	2	51	5	2	9.9	25.2
Rodriguez, Edryn	R-R	5-8	150	4-23-03	.167	.167	.500	2	6	6	0	1	0	1	0	2	0	0	0	0	3	0	0	0.0	50.0
Salvatore, Mike	R-R	5-9	186	12-27-96	.000	.000	.000	1	4	4	0	0	0	0	0	0	0	0	0	0	0	0	0	0.0	0.0
Scheffler, Matt	R-R	6-1	190	2-06-98	.208	.332	.259	67	259	216	27	45	6	1	1	23	33	8	0	2	61	8	2	12.7	23.6
Tenerowicz, Robbie	R-R	5-11	228	1-06-95	.291	.408	.506	87	385	316	62	92	20	0	16	80	44	21	0	4	65	1	2	11.4	16.9
Unroe, Riley	B-R	5-11	180	8-03-95	.244	.346	.358	58	206	176	29	43	5	0	5	25	26	2	1	1	52	11	4	12.6	25.2
Warmoth, Logan	R-R	5-10	195	9-06-95	.239	.350	.358	107	429	360	54	86	17	1	8	45	55	9	0	5	115	28	10	12.8	26.8

Pitching	B-T	Ht.	Wt.	DOB	W	L	ERA	G	GS	SV	IP	Hits	Runs	ER	HR	BB	SO	AVG	OBP	SLG	SO%	BB%	BF
Adcock, Ty	R-R	6-0	213	2-07-97	0	0	2.63	13	0	2	14	8	5	4	1	3	13	.170	.235	.277	25.5	5.9	51
Arias, Dayeison	R-R	6-1	160	1-07-97	0	1	4.62	41	0	0	51	39	27	26	3	37	61	.213	.368	.322	26.4	16.0	231
Benitez, Jorge	L-L	6-2	155	6-02-99	2	3	2.14	40	0	1	59	40	26	14	3	39	74	.190	.336	.270	28.6	15.1	259
Berroa, Prelander	R-R	5-11	170	4-18-00	5	1	2.89	43	5	6	65	45	24	21	2	39	101	.193	.312	.275	36.6	14.1	276
Campbell, Isaiah	R-R	6-4	230	8-15-97	6	0	2.63	23	0	5	24	18	9	7	2	7	27	.205	.263	.307	28.4	7.4	95
Castano, Blas	R-R	5-10	162	9-08-98	1	3	4.30	7	6	0	29	32	14	14	4	10	30	.291	.355	.491	24.8	8.3	121
Driver, Tyler	R-R	6-2	185	2-04-01	0	1	21.86	5	0	0	7	14	17	17	1	9	7	.424	.596	.667	14.3	18.4	49
Flynn, Michael	R-R	6-4	185	8-07-96	0	2	9.00	15	0	0	18	16	20	18	3	9	23	.232	.372	.406	26.7	10.5	86
Haberer, Jake	R-R	6-2	225	2-09-95	1	1	4.21	36	4	0	47	38	22	22	4	27	41	.225	.351	.349	20.3	13.4	202
Hancock, Emerson	R-R	6-4	213	5-31-99	11	5	4.32	20	20	0	98	83	49	47	9	38	107	.230	.313	.374	26.0	9.2	411
Jefferson, Chris	L-R	6-2	200	1-24-97	0	0	0.00	1	0	0	1	0	0	0	0	0	1	.000	.000	.000	50.0	0.0	2
Joyce, Jimmy	R-R	6-2	210	1-13-99	0	3	3.82	7	7	0	31	29	13	13	1	10	29	.250	.320	.345	22.7	7.8	128
Kaminsky, Rob	R-L	6-0	195	9-02-94	4	1	3.00	14	0	0	18	19	10	6	1	2	13	.257	.295	.351	16.7	2.6	78
Kober, Collin	R-R	6-1	185	9-08-94	4	1	5.55	43	1	0	60	61	41	37	10	22	60	.260	.346	.468	22.2	8.1	270
Kolek, Stephen	R-R	6-3	210	4-18-97	2	0	0.00	5	0	0	8	1	0	0	0	2	11	.042	.148	.042	40.7	7.4	27
Kuhn, Travis	R-R	5-10	195	5-20-98	5	3	3.13	49	0	4	55	47	25	19	2	22	51	.237	.320	.298	22.3	9.6	229
Lindow, Ethan	R-L	6-3	180	10-15-98	2	5	4.89	18	14	0	77	85	43	42	14	31	66	.276	.348	.455	19.3	9.1	342
Martinez, Bernie	R-R	6-0	195	12-24-96	1	0	9.00	1	0	0	2	3	2	2	0	0	2	.333	.333	.444	22.2	0.0	9
Mercedes, Juan	R-R	6-2	190	4-03-00	2	1	6.60	12	10	0	46	56	35	34	8	20	40	.296	.375	.519	18.4	9.2	217
Miller, Bryce	R-R	6-2	180	8-23-98	0	2	6.41	4	4	0	20	23	15	14	5	3	18	.280	.306	.573	21.2	3.5	85
Onyshko, Ben	R-L	6-2	205	10-18-96	1	1	5.21	27	3	0	48	46	33	28	4	21	45	.254	.385	.392	19.8	9.3	227
Parisi, Jack	R-R	6-0	215	1-13-99	0	0	4.50	2	0	0	4	3	2	2	1	3	3	.200	.333	.400	16.7	16.7	18
Puckett, A.J.	R-R	6-4	200	5-27-95	6	3	4.35	44	3	0	60	56	31	29	5	25	52	.251	.341	.386	20.0	9.6	260
Saathoff, Allan	R-R	6-1	230	9-18-99	0	3	8.10	9	3	0	20	19	18	18	3	14	21	.253	.376	.400	22.6	15.1	93
Semple, Shawn	R-R	6-1	220	10-09-95	3	8	5.46	17	17	0	91	121	65	55	17	27	56	.323	.369	.523	13.7	6.6	410
Sweet, Devin	B-R	5-11	183	9-06-96	4	1	1.54	27	0	5	35	24	7	6	1	8	47	.190	.243	.246	34.6	5.9	136
Then, Juan	R-R	6-1	200	2-07-00	1	1	5.00	7	0	3	9	10	7	5	1	3	11	.278	.350	.417	27.5	7.5	40
Tyler, Kyle	R-R	6-0	185	12-27-96	7	11	5.60	27	26	0	135	157	93	84	15	58	138	.285	.356	.435	22.3	9.4	619
Valverde, Alex	R-R	6-2	185	9-26-96	2	2	5.68	7	6	0	25	32	16	16	2	16	20	.311	.413	.437	16.5	13.2	121
Willrodt, Matt	R-R	6-4	220	10-19-97	0	0	0.00	1	0	0	2	1	0	0	0	0	3	.143	.143	.143	42.9	0.0	7
Woo, Bryan	R-R	6-2	205	1-30-00	3	2	2.05	9	9	0	44	27	10	10	2	12	59	.174	.256	.232	34.3	7.0	172

Fielding

Catcher	PCT	G	PO	A	E	DP	PB
Anchia	.982	68	623	43	12	6	9
Morgan	1.000	9	73	4	0	0	1
Scheffler	.980	65	546	41	12	2	14

First Base	PCT	G	PO	A	E	DP
Hoover	.986	11	64	4	1	6
Locklear	.993	19	139	9	1	12
Packard	1.000	14	95	7	0	7
Perez Jr.	.992	14	107	10	1	6
Tenerowicz	.994	86	589	34	4	59

Second Base	PCT	G	PO	A	E	DP
Frick	.979	25	34	61	2	14
Hoover	.983	43	84	94	3	24
Polcovich	.975	38	59	94	4	17
Rodriguez	1.000	1	0	1	0	0
Unroe	.991	28	45	68	1	12
Warmoth	1.000	13	35	22	0	9

Third Base	PCT	G	PO	A	E	DP
Frick	1.000	3	2	3	0	0
Hoover	.857	10	6	12	3	0
Morgan	.942	57	38	108	9	11
Rivas	1.000	1	0	1	0	0
Salvatore	.000	1	0	0	1	0
Tenerowicz	.000	1	0	0	0	0
Unroe	.929	13	11	15	2	2
Warmoth	.953	63	33	88	6	6

Shortstop	PCT	G	PO	A	E	DP
Hoover	.983	18	18	39	1	7
Rivas	.972	99	111	206	9	42
Rodriguez	1.000	1	3	3	0	3
Unroe	1.000	2	0	4	0	0
Warmoth	.930	23	37	43	6	11

Outfield	PCT	G	PO	A	E	DP
Cabrera	1.000	1	2	0	0	0
Clase	.989	107	270	2	3	1
Gilliam	1.000	46	72	3	0	0
Hoover	.000	1	0	0	0	0
Kirwer	1.000	53	76	3	0	0
Packard	.995	82	134	3	1	0
Perez Jr.	.973	88	156	4	5	3
Rodriguez	.986	33	68	4	1	1
Unroe	1.000	15	15	0	0	0
Warmoth	.667	11	12	0	0	0

EVERETT AQUASOX — *HIGH CLASS A*

NORTHWEST LEAGUE

Batting	B-T	Ht.	Wt.	DOB	AVG	OBP	SLG	G	PA	AB	R	H	2B	3B	HR	RBI	BB	HBP	SH	SF	SO	SB	CS	BB%	SO%
Barr, Cole	R-R	5-8	195	5-23-98	.048	.167	.190	8	24	21	3	1	0	0	1	2	3	0	0	0	10	1	0	12.5	41.7
Bednar, Randy	R-L	5-8	200	11-30-98	.183	.236	.376	55	212	197	26	36	8	0	10	24	8	6	0	1	73	4	0	3.8	34.4
Cabrera, Walking	R-R	6-2	184	8-26-00	.240	.300	.408	70	293	262	36	63	12	1	10	49	22	3	0	6	85	7	1	7.5	29.0
Clase, Jonatan	B-R	5-9	150	5-23-02	.333	.453	.701	21	106	87	23	29	9	1	7	17	18	1	0	0	28	17	4	17.0	26.4
Crawford, J.P.	L-R	6-2	202	1-11-95	.000	.000	.000	1	3	3	0	0	0	0	0	0	0	0	0	0	1	0	0	0.0	33.3
Davis, Colin	R-R	6-0	190	2-08-99	.214	.291	.329	21	79	70	6	15	5	0	1	7	6	2	0	1	22	2	0	7.6	27.8
Duvall, Ty	L-R	5-11	200	7-11-97	.333	.333	1.333	1	3	3	1	1	0	0	1	1	0	0	0	0	1	0	0	0.0	33.3
Ford, Harry	R-R	5-10	200	2-21-03	.257	.410	.430	118	563	444	89	114	24	4	15	67	103	14	0	2	109	24	8	18.3	19.4
Gonzalez, Gabriel	R-R	5-10	165	1-04-04	.215	.290	.387	43	200	181	27	39	4	0	9	30	13	6	0	0	43	2	0	6.5	21.5
Hood, Josh	R-R	6-2	202	7-21-00	.233	.309	.383	16	68	60	7	14	1	1	2	8	7	0	0	1	18	0	1	10.3	26.5
Knight, Bill	R-R	6-1	195	8-24-99	.227	.333	.432	12	51	44	7	10	0	0	3	7	3	4	0	0	15	4	1	5.9	29.4
Labrada, Victor	L-L	5-9	165	1-16-00	.259	.329	.294	54	226	201	32	52	5	1	0	17	19	3	0	2	46	16	4	8.4	20.4
Locklear, Tyler	R-R	6-1	210	11-24-00	.305	.422	.549	61	275	226	40	69	19	0	12	44	36	11	0	2	60	10	0	13.1	21.8
Miller, Andrew	R-R	6-2	230	9-02-97	.177	.248	.292	27	105	96	13	17	5	0	2	10	7	2	0	0	35	1	0	6.7	33.3
Moore, Dylan	R-R	6-0	205	8-02-92	.300	.500	.300	4	14	10	2	3	0	0	0	1	3	1	0	0	3	1	0	21.4	21.4
Parker, James	R-R	6-1	200	3-26-00	.226	.328	.456	79	302	261	45	59	13	1	15	37	39	1	0	1	117	3	2	12.9	38.7
Rambusch, Blake	R-R	5-8	175	8-31-99	.270	.401	.369	87	300	244	45	66	13	1	3	25	44	10	1	1	70	25	6	14.7	23.3
Ramirez, Ben	L-R	6-1	200	12-02-98	.252	.327	.386	123	534	472	67	119	27	0	12	65	49	6	2	5	143	6	2	9.2	26.8
Rodriguez, Alberto	L-L	5-10	227	10-06-00	.306	.393	.580	72	322	281	61	86	30	7	11	58	31	9	1	0	69	3	1	9.6	21.4
Salvatore, Mike	R-R	5-9	186	12-27-96	.249	.353	.364	53	201	173	22	43	5	3	3	17	26	2	0	0	40	4	1	12.9	19.9
Sanchez, Axel	R-R	5-10	170	12-10-02	.199	.285	.353	72	305	272	33	54	15	3	7	41	26	7	0	0	89	14	4	8.5	29.2
Stock, Erik	R-R	6-0	211	12-30-98	.198	.303	.252	42	152	131	20	26	5	1	0	5	18	2	0	1	32	10	1	11.8	21.1
Welch, Charlie	R-R	5-9	205	2-08-00	.204	.331	.372	35	136	113	17	23	10	0	3	15	22	0	0	1	56	1	0	16.2	41.2
Windish, Hogan	R-R	5-11	222	5-10-99	.270	.372	.506	105	452	385	64	104	17	4	22	84	55	9	0	3	139	10	1	12.2	30.8
Young, Cole	L-R	6-0	180	7-29-03	.292	.404	.479	48	230	192	32	56	14	2	6	23	34	3	0	1	38	5	5	14.8	16.5

Pitching	B-T	Ht.	Wt.	DOB	W	L	ERA	G	GS	SV	IP	Hits	Runs	ER	HR	BB	SO	AVG	OBP	SLG	SO%	BB%	BF
Adcock, Ty	R-R	6-0	213	2-07-97	1	0	0.00	6	0	1	7	1	0	0	0	2	9	.048	.167	.048	37.5	8.3	24
Alcantara, Raul	L-L	6-0	167	1-22-01	5	6	6.35	24	23	0	108	92	85	76	9	66	140	.224	.345	.365	28.2	13.3	496
Alford, Peyton	L-L	6-0	190	8-15-97	4	4	2.83	41	0	6	48	34	19	15	4	21	71	.200	.294	.329	36.4	10.8	195
Bayless, Jarod	R-R	6-4	225	12-29-96	4	3	2.59	33	0	6	42	26	14	12	2	4	50	.181	.229	.306	32.5	2.6	154
Benitez, Jorge	L-L	6-2	155	6-02-99	0	2	0.00	5	0	0	6	2	3	0	0	5	8	.111	.333	.111	30.8	19.2	26
Carlson, Sam	R-R	6-4	195	12-03-98	0	2	5.25	39	1	6	48	38	30	28	3	20	61	.220	.305	.335	30.5	10.0	200
Creel, John	L-R	6-5	222	7-01-97	0	0	9.45	4	0	0	7	8	7	7	2	3	5	.296	.375	.556	15.6	9.4	32
Curvelo, Luis	R-R	6-1	170	10-21-00	3	1	3.78	41	0	0	52	51	26	22	9	16	60	.254	.317	.433	27.1	7.2	221
Davila, Nick	R-R	6-3	202	11-21-98	4	6	4.65	15	13	0	81	91	48	42	11	20	76	.278	.326	.437	21.5	5.6	354
Driver, Tyler	R-R	6-2	185	2-04-01	1	1	12.56	11	0	0	14	24	20	20	4	10	7	.393	.493	.689	9.6	13.7	73
Elliott, Tim	R-R	6-1	200	10-11-97	3	1	4.01	25	0	0	25	28	13	11	4	16	23	.292	.395	.448	20.2	14.0	114
Flynn, Michael	R-R	6-4	185	8-07-96	1	2	4.91	21	0	4	22	18	12	12	2	9	38	.220	.309	.341	40.0	9.5	95
Hill, Kyle	R-R	5-11	200	5-12-97	3	2	2.63	39	0	0	38	32	16	11	3	17	49	.225	.313	.338	30.6	10.6	160
Hunter, Leon	R-R	6-3	253	3-17-97	6	1	2.59	22	0	0	31	18	11	9	4	9	42	.170	.233	.292	36.2	7.8	116
Jackson, Jordan	R-R	6-6	204	10-14-98	0	2	6.75	12	11	0	32	43	24	24	4	13	25	.316	.383	.493	16.2	8.4	154
Jefferson, Chris	L-R	6-2	200	1-24-97	0	0	9.00	1	0	0	1	1	1	1	0	1	0	.250	.400	.250	0.0	20.0	5
Joyce, Jimmy	R-R	6-2	210	1-13-99	2	0	1.60	9	9	0	39	28	10	7	4	10	54	.200	.285	.307	34.0	6.3	159
Kingsbury, Jimmy	R-R	6-1	187	2-13-99	1	2	4.65	31	8	0	60	61	33	31	9	23	63	.263	.353	.453	23.7	8.6	266
Martinez, Bernie	R-R	6-0	195	12-24-96	4	3	6.63	28	8	0	54	69	42	40	8	14	46	.312	.358	.475	19.2	5.8	240
Mercedes, Juan	R-R	6-2	190	4-03-00	1	0	3.43	4	4	0	21	21	8	8	1	5	30	.253	.308	.398	33.0	5.5	91
Morgan, Reid	R-R	6-0	187	3-24-97	2	3	5.51	18	8	0	47	59	34	29	13	13	43	.299	.341	.569	20.3	6.1	212
Nunez, Kelvin	R-R	6-1	170	12-10-99	10	3	5.29	31	4	0	63	68	40	37	10	35	35	.278	.376	.478	12.2	12.2	288
Parker, James	R-R	6-1	200	3-26-00	0	0	0.00	1	0	0	1	0	0	0	0	0	0	.000	.000	.000	0.0	0.0	3
Perez, Marcelo	R-R	5-10	180	11-16-99	0	0	2.70	3	3	0	7	5	2	2	0	4	9	.208	.321	.250	32.1	14.3	28
Quintana, Adrian	R-R	6-0	175	11-20-02	0	0	6.75	1	1	0	4	4	3	3	1	2	5	.250	.333	.563	27.8	11.1	18
Rinehart, Logan	R-R	6-3	185	9-21-97	1	3	2.84	31	0	10	38	28	15	12	4	12	51	.200	.263	.314	33.6	7.9	152
Sadler, Casey	R-R	6-3	223	7-13-90	0	0	6.75	3	0	0	3	2	2	2	1	0	4	.200	.333	.500	33.3	0.0	12
Schaeffer, Brandon	L-L	6-2	195	2-11-00	7	5	4.68	16	14	0	85	92	46	44	10	22	70	.274	.343	.449	18.7	5.9	374
Taylor, Troy	R-R	6-0	195	9-09-01	0	0	0.87	8	0	0	10	5	2	1	0	2	11	.147	.237	.176	28.2	5.1	39
VanScoter, Reid	L-L	6-0	190	11-25-98	10	6	3.27	25	25	0	143	141	60	52	6	35	157	.255	.304	.350	26.0	5.8	605
Welch, Charlie	R-R	5-9	205	2-08-00	0	0	0.00	1	0	0	1	0	0	0	0	0	0	.000	.000	.000	0.0	0.0	3
Willrodt, Matt	R-R	6-4	220	10-19-97	1	0	4.45	23	0	0	28	23	20	14	1	19	36	.219	.357	.324	27.5	14.5	131

Fielding

Catcher	PCT	G	PO	A	E	DP	PB
Duvall	1.000	1	8	0	0	0	0
Ford	.989	78	760	64	9	6	20
Miller	.988	26	221	21	3	3	4
Welch	.993	28	277	20	2	1	9

First Base	PCT	G	PO	A	E	DP
Locklear	.996	58	484	30	2	36
Parker	.991	13	109	0	1	9
Salvatore	1.000	1	1	0	0	0
Stock	.833	1	4	1	1	0
Windish	.994	62	484	26	3	38

Second Base	PCT	G	PO	A	E	DP
Barr	1.000	2	4	2	0	1
Hood	.983	15	21	37	1	8
Parker	.958	12	11	35	2	6
Rambusch	.986	39	59	87	2	16
Salvatore	.992	28	51	72	1	15
Sanchez	1.000	14	26	30	0	6
Windish	.971	25	25	43	2	6
Young	1.000	4	6	9	0	1

Third Base	PCT	G	PO	A	E	DP
Barr	.929	4	4	9	1	1
Parker	.941	11	13	19	2	5
Rambusch	1.000	1	1	2	0	0
Ramirez	.932	119	63	238	22	19
Salvatore	1.000	1	2	2	0	0

Shortstop	PCT	G	PO	A	E	DP
Crawford	1.000	1	2	3	0	0
Moore	1.000	3	0	8	0	0
Parker	.978	25	23	67	2	11

Ramirez	1.000	3	4	4	0	1
Salvatore	1.000	10	11	19	0	1
Sanchez	.920	52	61	112	15	22
Young	.977	44	62	111	4	19

Outfield	PCT	G	PO	A	E	DP
Bednar	.985	56	91	1	1	0
Cabrera	.989	71	111	5	3	2
Clase	.979	20	45	1	1	1
Davis	.956	18	27	3	2	0
Gonzalez	.983	40	52	5	1	0
Knight	.952	12	20	0	1	0
Labrada	1.000	44	65	3	0	1
Rambusch	.959	41	66	4	3	1
Rodriguez	.953	67	98	3	5	0
Salvatore	1.000	7	18	0	0	0
Stock	.988	34	53	3	1	1
Windish	1.000	1	3	0	0	0

MODESTO NUTS — *LOW CLASS A*

CALIFORNIA LEAGUE

Batting	B-T	Ht.	Wt.	DOB	AVG	OBP	SLG	G	PA	AB	R	H	2B	3B	HR	RBI	BB	HBP	SH	SF	SO	SB	CS	BB%	SO%
Arroyo, Michael	R-R	5-8	160	11-03-04	.234	.389	.373	57	265	209	45	49	17	3	2	23	36	18	0	2	53	5	3	13.6	20.0
Batista, Freuddy	R-R	6-0	182	12-12-99	.271	.345	.455	76	328	292	48	79	24	6	6	49	27	7	0	2	84	0	1	8.2	25.6
Cabrera, Walking	R-R	6-2	184	8-26-00	.563	.563	.625	4	16	16	3	9	1	0	0	3	0	0	0	0	3	1	0	0.0	18.8
Davis, Colin	R-R	6-0	190	2-08-99	.252	.323	.446	67	288	258	41	65	18	1	10	37	24	4	0	2	60	12	2	8.3	20.8
Emerson, Colt	L-R	6-0	185	7-20-05	.302	.436	.444	16	79	63	17	19	6	0	1	8	11	4	0	0	14	4	0	13.9	17.7
Gonzalez, Gabriel	R-R	5-10	165	1-04-04	.348	.403	.530	73	335	296	51	103	19	4	9	54	23	9	0	7	46	8	0	6.9	13.7
Guerrero, Arturo	R-R	6-3	165	9-21-00	.214	.267	.357	4	15	14	2	3	2	0	0	2	1	0	0	0	6	0	0	6.7	40.0
Hood, Josh	R-R	6-2	202	7-21-00	.279	.363	.422	98	444	391	71	109	19	2	11	61	49	3	0	1	90	18	3	11.0	20.3
Knight, Bill	R-R	6-1	195	8-24-99	.300	.406	.404	55	252	213	43	64	11	1	3	25	25	13	1	0	60	30	4	9.9	23.8
Lavey, Justin	R-R	5-10	205	9-23-97	.240	.277	.323	24	101	96	8	23	3	1	1	10	4	1	0	0	29	6	1	4.0	28.7
Levins, Tatem	L-R	6-0	206	5-29-99	.286	.358	.476	66	279	248	41	71	18	1	9	55	29	0	0	2	57	0	0	10.4	20.4
Miller, Andrew	R-R	6-2	230	9-02-97	.265	.363	.374	42	182	155	27	41	8	0	3	24	24	1	0	2	48	1	0	13.2	26.4
Moncada, Gabe	L-L	6-2	175	12-17-01	.257	.356	.431	97	424	362	68	93	25	1	12	60	51	7	0	4	112	1	1	12.0	26.4
Montes, Lazaro	L-R	6-3	210	10-22-04	.321	.429	.565	33	156	131	27	42	9	1	7	30	21	4	0	0	39	1	0	13.5	25.0
Peete, Tai	L-R	6-2	193	8-11-05	.242	.299	.387	14	67	62	7	15	3	0	2	14	5	0	0	0	19	3	0	7.5	28.4
Perez, Miguel	R-R	6-1	170	8-21-00	.196	.321	.377	64	240	199	33	39	10	7	4	28	33	5	0	3	99	11	4	13.8	41.3
Perez, Milkar	B-R	5-11	200	10-16-01	.273	.380	.370	94	382	319	44	87	26	1	1	39	50	8	0	5	93	2	0	13.1	24.3
Rodden, Brock	B-R	5-9	170	5-25-00	.319	.376	.465	32	157	144	33	46	11	2	2	20	11	2	0	0	24	1	1	7.0	15.3
Rodriguez, Brett	R-R	5-10	200	5-06-98	.205	.386	.308	40	153	117	22	24	3	0	3	17	29	6	0	1	51	15	3	19.0	33.3
Rodriguez, Edryn	R-R	5-8	150	4-23-03	.128	.185	.156	34	119	109	10	14	3	0	0	12	8	0	0	2	51	3	1	6.7	42.9
Schreck, RJ	L-R	6-1	210	7-12-00	.267	.343	.378	25	102	90	17	24	7	0	1	12	10	1	0	1	11	1	0	9.8	10.8
Smith, Aidan	R-R	6-3	190	7-23-04	.184	.259	.327	14	54	49	11	9	2	1	1	5	4	1	0	0	16	0	0	7.4	29.6
Suisbel, Luis	B-R	6-1	190	5-23-03	.290	.375	.492	31	144	124	26	36	3	2	6	32	12	6	0	2	43	0	0	8.3	29.9
Sundstrom, Jared	R-R	6-3	225	6-21-01	.254	.329	.493	20	79	71	14	18	6	1	3	14	3	5	0	0	17	0	0	3.8	21.5
Washington, Curtis	R-R	6-2	180	5-22-00	.201	.320	.218	57	207	174	23	35	3	0	0	18	25	6	1	1	60	17	4	12.1	29.0
Williamson, Ben	R-R	6-0	190	11-05-00	.229	.289	.343	10	38	35	3	8	2	1	0	6	2	1	0	0	10	1	0	5.3	26.3
Young, Cole	L-R	6-0	180	7-29-03	.267	.396	.429	78	376	303	60	81	20	7	5	39	54	14	0	5	52	17	5	14.4	13.8

Pitching	B-T	Ht.	Wt.	DOB	W	L	ERA	G	GS	SV	IP	Hits	Runs	ER	HR	BB	SO	AVG	OBP	SLG	SO%	BB%	BF
Bayless, Jarod	R-R	6-4	225	12-29-96	0	0	8.44	5	0	1	5	6	5	5	2	1	10	.261	.346	.609	38.5	3.8	26
Bowen, Darren	R-R	6-3	180	2-03-01	4	2	3.88	19	15	0	56	36	27	24	2	25	59	.182	.288	.273	25.7	10.9	230
Burgos, Juan	R-R	6-0	155	12-22-99	1	1	2.53	30	0	7	32	29	13	9	1	17	39	.234	.342	.298	26.7	11.6	146
Cleveland, Tyler	L-R	6-3	185	9-09-99	14	5	3.56	25	20	0	136	129	58	54	10	26	111	.246	.292	.361	19.6	4.6	566
Creel, John	L-R	6-5	222	7-01-97	0	0	1.59	6	0	0	6	5	2	1	0	5	8	.217	.357	.217	28.6	17.9	28
Davila, Nick	R-R	6-3	202	11-21-98	0	1	4.58	4	2	0	18	15	10	9	0	5	18	.227	.278	.318	24.7	6.8	73
Davis, Riley	R-R	6-3	200	11-10-98	8	0	3.57	20	6	0	81	76	36	32	5	30	63	.243	.312	.351	18.0	8.6	350
Evans, Logan	R-R	6-4	215	6-05-01	1	0	0.75	3	3	0	12	7	1	1	0	2	13	.163	.200	.186	28.9	4.4	45
Garabitos, Natanael	R-R	6-0	185	8-04-00	2	3	4.02	39	1	8	40	24	22	18	1	31	54	.175	.337	.241	30.2	17.3	179
Garcia, Brandyn	L-L	6-4	225	5-27-00	0	1	2.57	6	0	2	7	8	3	2	1	2	4	.320	.357	.440	14.3	7.1	28
Gough, Tyler	B-R	6-2	205	8-12-03	1	3	5.70	10	9	0	30	30	19	19	3	15	24	.265	.361	.398	18.0	11.3	133
Hawks, Ryan	R-R	6-2	235	11-24-00	0	0	3.60	4	4	0	10	8	5	4	0	5	12	.216	.326	.216	27.3	11.4	44
Jefferson, Chris	L-R	6-2	200	1-24-97	5	5	6.05	36	0	1	55	61	42	37	4	26	58	.280	.362	.450	22.4	10.0	259
Laws, Holden	L-L	6-2	166	12-08-99	4	4	5.19	36	0	0	52	64	37	30	5	13	66	.298	.349	.465	27.6	5.4	239
Morales, Michael	R-R	6-2	205	8-13-02	5	4	4.53	22	22	0	101	92	60	51	7	40	106	.238	.316	.368	24.4	9.2	435
Parisi, Jack	R-R	6-0	215	1-13-99	0	0	9.45	6	0	0	7	10	8	7	0	4	3	.357	.457	.393	8.6	11.4	35
Peavyhouse, Shaddon	R-R	6-3	205	8-18-98	10	5	4.94	26	23	0	133	132	85	73	10	63	119	.259	.354	.386	19.8	10.5	600
Perez, Brayan	L-L	6-0	170	9-05-00	0	1	4.24	25	1	0	34	35	19	16	2	15	27	.263	.340	.398	17.6	9.8	153
Perez, Marcelo	R-R	5-10	180	11-16-99	3	5	3.44	15	15	0	68	57	29	26	4	20	67	.228	.286	.364	24.4	7.3	275
Raeth, Stefan	L-R	6-1	180	8-31-00	1	2	3.70	40	0	5	49	45	22	20	3	29	54	.245	.362	.342	24.3	13.1	222
Saathoff, Allan	R-R	6-1	230	9-18-99	2	2	7.13	14	0	0	18	20	16	14	1	14	17	.286	.420	.429	19.3	15.9	88
Schaeffer, Brandon	L-L	6-2	195	2-11-00	3	4	3.62	11	11	0	50	40	25	20	1	24	58	.213	.318	.351	26.7	11.1	217
Sosa, Gabriel	R-R	6-2	182	4-17-01	5	2	5.77	32	0	0	39	38	29	25	4	25	40	.255	.396	.383	21.3	13.3	188
Tatiz, Yeury	R-R	6-3	175	11-22-00	1	1	9.17	20	0	0	18	23	22	18	1	20	21	.307	.480	.427	20.4	19.4	103
Taylor, Troy	R-R	6-0	195	9-09-01	1	1	4.11	32	0	3	35	26	23	16	1	19	51	.197	.342	.258	31.7	11.8	161
Tomczak, Anthony	R-R	6-2	200	10-17-00	2	0	3.76	21	0	1	26	26	19	11	0	14	32	.255	.369	.333	26.2	11.5	122
Townsend, Blake	L-L	6-4	220	4-05-01	4	3	3.38	35	0	1	48	40	21	18	1	21	55	.221	.324	.293	26.1	10.0	211

Fielding

Catcher	PCT	G	PO	A	E	DP	PB
Batista	.978	68	620	54	15	4	23
Levins	.993	56	492	39	4	6	9
Miller	.989	9	81	5	1	0	1

First Base	PCT	G	PO	A	E	DP
Lavey	.933	5	23	5	2	1
Miller	.941	2	15	1	1	3
Moncada	.987	84	633	35	9	59
Perez	.975	21	148	9	4	7
Rodriguez	1.000	5	33	3	0	4
Suisbel	.975	18	149	7	4	9

Second Base	PCT	G	PO	A	E	DP
Arroyo	.976	11	11	29	1	4
Emerson	.967	6	7	22	1	4

SEATTLE MARINERS

	PCT	G	PO	A	E	DP
Hood	.923	36	54	66	10	14
Lavey	.973	10	18	18	1	7
Peete	.714	2	2	3	2	1
Rodden	.938	22	33	43	5	8
Rodriguez, B	.982	11	23	31	1	7
Rodriguez, E	.973	30	39	71	3	15
Young	1.000	8	14	25	0	5

Third Base	PCT	G	PO	A	E	DP
Hood	.913	43	28	67	9	6
Lavey	1.000	1	2	3	0	0
Peete	.889	6	4	12	2	2
Perez	.878	59	32	98	18	8
Rodden	.833	9	3	17	4	2
Rodriguez, B	1.000	4	1	2	0	0
Rodriguez, E	.667	3	2	0	1	0
Suisbel	.864	8	4	15	3	1
Williamson	1.000	7	4	12	0	1

Shortstop	PCT	G	PO	A	E	DP
Arroyo	.923	43	49	95	12	13
Emerson	.969	9	10	21	1	5
Hood	.946	10	16	19	2	6
Suisbel	.800	2	3	5	2	1
Young	.947	70	82	167	14	34

Outfield	PCT	G	PO	A	E	DP
Cabrera	.900	4	9	0	1	0
Davis	.987	59	108	3	4	2
Gonzalez	.938	55	88	8	4	2
Guerrero	.667	3	2	0	1	0
Knight	.974	54	123	6	4	1
Miller	.964	16	26	1	1	0
Montes	.984	32	56	4	1	1
Perez	.967	57	103	6	5	0
Rodriguez	.924	19	27	0	2	0
Schreck	.988	24	46	2	1	1
Smith	1.000	13	42	1	0	1
Sundstrom	1.000	19	32	0	0	0
Washington	.972	52	135	1	3	0

ACL MARINERS — ROOKIE

ARIZONA COMPLEX LEAGUE

Batting	B-T	Ht.	Wt.	DOB	AVG	OBP	SLG	G	PA	AB	R	H	2B	3B	HR	RBI	BB	HBP	SH	SF	SO	SB	CS	BB%	SO%
Aguilar, Starlin	L-R	5-11	170	1-26-04	.300	.386	.467	17	70	60	11	18	5	1	1	10	7	2	0	1	17	0	0	10.0	24.3
Arroyo, Michael	R-R	5-8	160	11-03-04	.636	.692	.909	4	13	11	3	7	0	0	1	5	1	1	0	0	1	3	1	7.7	7.7
Barr, Cole	R-R	5-8	195	5-23-98	.280	.507	.600	18	73	50	14	14	4	0	4	13	12	11	0	0	18	6	2	16.4	24.7
Belbin, Jarrod	L-R	6-2	220	6-22-00	.214	.343	.393	14	35	28	6	6	0	1	1	8	6	0	0	1	5	4	2	17.1	14.3
Cabrera, Walking	R-R	6-2	184	8-26-00	.400	.538	.900	4	13	10	5	4	0	1	1	3	2	1	0	0	1	0	0	15.4	7.7
Caguana, Jose	R-R	5-10	175	4-05-02	.286	.344	.491	37	125	112	21	32	4	2	5	15	10	1	0	2	49	5	0	8.0	39.2
Cali, Caleb	R-R	6-3	230	8-20-00	.282	.378	.513	13	45	39	6	11	3	0	2	6	6	0	0	0	13	1	0	13.3	28.9
Charping, Connor	R-R	6-0	210	4-12-99	.268	.434	.341	14	53	41	10	11	0	0	1	10	6	6	0	0	11	10	1	11.3	20.8
Cova, Ricardo	R-R	5-9	145	5-24-04	.330	.425	.440	28	106	91	26	30	7	0	1	11	14	1	0	0	33	17	3	13.2	31.1
Duvall, Ty	L-R	5-11	200	7-11-97	.186	.250	.279	13	48	43	4	8	1	0	1	9	3	1	0	1	12	0	0	6.3	25.0
Emerson, Colt	L-R	6-0	185	7-20-05	.536	.629	.786	8	35	28	10	15	4	0	1	5	6	1	0	0	6	4	0	17.1	17.1
Emery, Robert	R-R	6-0	210	10-22-96	.000	.125	.000	5	8	7	0	0	0	0	0	0	1	0	0	0	4	0	0	12.5	50.0
Feliz, George	R-R	5-10	160	9-21-02	.218	.314	.336	40	137	119	13	26	6	1	2	15	13	4	0	1	54	9	6	9.5	39.4
Fitz-Gerald, Hunter	L-R	6-4	230	12 09 00	.243	.333	.378	12	42	37	2	9	2	0	1	10	5	0	0	0	10	0	0	11.9	23.8
Gonzalez, Junior	R-R	5-8	186	5-10-00	.286	.385	.524	8	26	21	5	6	2	0	1	3	3	1	0	1	9	0	0	11.5	34.6
Guerrero, Arturo	R-R	6-3	165	9-21-00	.233	.346	.407	30	107	86	19	20	6	0	3	25	11	6	0	4	39	4	0	10.3	36.4
Izturis, Cesar	B-R	5-11	145	11-11-99	.271	.363	.471	23	80	70	12	19	6	1	2	8	9	1	0	0	7	1	2	11.3	8.8
Jimenez, Carlos	L-L	5-10	170	2-14-03	.266	.370	.380	45	184	158	34	42	8	2	2	20	22	4	0	0	51	11	3	12.0	27.7
Jones, Carson	L-L	6-2	190	9-29-00	.143	.385	.250	12	39	28	8	4	0	0	1	3	9	2	0	0	10	3	0	23.1	25.6
Knight, Bill	R-R	6-1	195	8-24-99	.200	.200	.200	3	10	10	2	2	0	0	0	0	0	0	0	0	4	2	0	0.0	40.0
Labrada, Victor	L-L	5-9	165	1-16-00	.455	.500	.636	3	12	11	3	5	2	0	0	0	1	0	0	0	3	1	0	8.3	25.0
Lavey, Justin	R-R	5-10	205	9-23-97	.000	.167	.000	2	6	5	0	0	0	0	0	0	1	0	0	0	0	0	0	16.7	0.0
Locklear, Tyler	R-R	6-1	210	11-24-00	.000	.000	.000	2	6	6	0	0	0	0	0	0	0	0	0	0	2	0	0	0.0	33.3
Mendez, Bryant	R-R	5-7	165	9-15-03	.080	.233	.080	10	30	25	4	2	0	0	0	0	4	1	0	0	17	4	0	13.3	56.7
Montes, Lazaro	L-R	6-3	210	10-22-04	.282	.452	.555	37	146	110	31	31	10	1	6	31	33	2	0	1	37	1	2	22.6	25.3
Pagliarini, Charlie	L-R	6-2	210	12-12-00	.263	.344	.561	16	64	57	13	15	5	0	4	13	6	1	0	0	23	3	0	9.4	35.9
Peete, Tai	L-R	6-2	193	8-11-05	.351	.429	.432	10	42	37	4	13	1	1	0	6	5	0	0	0	11	3	1	11.9	26.2
Perez Jr., Robert	R-R	6-0	170	6-26-00	.300	.417	.600	3	12	10	2	3	0	0	1	1	2	0	0	0	3	0	0	16.7	25.0
Polcovich, Kaden	B-R	5-10	185	2-21-99	.200	.429	.400	2	7	5	2	1	1	0	0	0	2	0	0	0	0	1	0	28.6	0.0
Rodden, Brock	B-R	5-9	170	5-25-00	.143	.143	.143	2	7	7	0	1	0	0	0	0	0	0	0	0	2	1	0	0.0	28.6
Rodriguez, Edryn	R-R	5-8	150	4-23-03	.227	.364	.330	32	111	88	15	20	6	0	1	10	15	5	1	2	28	10	1	13.5	25.2
Schreck, RJ	L-R	6-1	210	7-12-00	.143	.250	.571	2	8	7	1	1	0	0	1	1	1	0	0	0	1	0	0	12.5	12.5
Sharp, Jacob	R-R	5-10	190	9-15-01	.143	.250	.143	11	32	28	3	4	0	0	0	4	3	1	0	0	6	1	1	9.4	18.8
Smith, Aidan	R-R	6-3	190	7-23-04	.261	.433	.435	8	30	23	7	6	0	2	0	3	6	1	0	0	8	6	1	20.0	26.7
Suisbel, Luis	B-R	6-1	190	5-23-03	.291	.471	.573	36	140	103	28	30	7	2	6	25	26	10	0	1	39	4	1	18.6	27.9
Sundstrom, Jared	R-R	6-3	225	6-21-01	.000	.167	.000	2	6	4	0	0	0	0	0	1	1	0	0	1	1	0	1	16.7	16.7
Tingelstad, Trent	L-R	5-9	215	6-14-98	.133	.381	.133	11	42	30	3	4	0	0	0	1	12	0	0	0	13	0	0	28.6	31.0
Welch, Charlie	R-R	5-9	205	2-08-00	.333	.667	.667	2	6	3	3	1	1	0	0	0	3	0	0	0	0	0	0	50.0	0.0
Williamson, Ben	R-R	6-0	190	11-05-00	.500	.500	.833	2	6	6	1	3	0	1	0	0	0	0	0	0	2	0	0	0.0	33.3
Zona, Nick	R-R	6-1	200	7-09-99	.290	.450	.323	18	40	31	11	9	1	0	0	5	7	2	0	0	8	6	0	17.5	20.0

Pitching	B-T	Ht.	Wt.	DOB	W	L	ERA	G	GS	SV	IP	Hits	Runs	ER	HR	BB	SO	AVG	OBP	SLG	SO%	BB%	BF
Batcho, Drake	L-L	6-4	215	4-17-00	2	1	7.62	13	0	0	13	9	12	11	0	27	23	.200	.507	.222	31.5	37.0	73
Cardozo, Kristian	R-R	6-2	175	11-10-02	3	2	6.51	11	5	0	37	41	31	27	3	18	40	.279	.353	.442	24.0	10.8	167
Creel, John	L-R	6-5	222	7-01-97	0	0	2.89	6	0	1	9	5	3	3	0	7	13	.161	.333	.226	33.3	17.9	39
Day, Ernie	R-R	6-4	230	10-24-01	1	0	6.75	4	0	0	4	6	3	3	0	3	7	.375	.500	.438	35.0	15.0	20
Dilone, Julio	L-R	6-1	196	3-23-00	1	2	9.00	16	0	0	18	17	19	18	3	19	25	.250	.447	.441	26.6	20.2	94
Driver, Tyler	R-R	6-2	185	2-04-01	2	1	5.03	11	0	1	20	18	12	11	2	10	24	.240	.337	.413	27.9	11.6	86
Emery, Robert	R-R	6-0	210	10-22-96	0	1	54.00	1	0	0	1	4	7	6	1	3	1	.571	.700	1.286	10.0	30.0	10
Evans, Logan	R-R	6-4	215	6-05-01	0	0	0.00	2	2	0	3	3	0	0	0	0	2	.250	.250	.333	16.7	0.0	12
Fajardo, German	R-R	5-11	165	1-29-01	0	0	3.00	4	0	0	3	1	1	1	0	2	5	.100	.250	.100	41.7	16.7	12
Ford, Walter	R-R	6-3	198	12-28-04	0	0	3.57	9	8	0	23	25	12	9	1	10	23	.284	.369	.420	22.3	9.7	103
Garcia, Brandyn	L-L	6-4	225	5-27-00	0	0	0.00	3	0	0	3	0	0	0	0	1	4	.000	.182	.000	36.4	9.1	11
Hawks, Ryan	R-R	6-2	235	11-24-00	0	0	0.00	2	2	0	3	1	0	0	0	0	2	.100	.100	.100	20.0	0.0	10
Izzi, Ashton	R-R	6-3	165	11-18-03	0	2	8.35	9	9	0	18	30	17	17	3	8	13	.361	.419	.566	14.0	8.6	93
Kaminsky, Rob	R-L	6-0	195	9-02-94	0	0	0.00	2	1	0	2	0	0	0	0	1	3	.000	.143	.000	42.9	14.3	7
Lemos, Pedro Da Costa	R-R	6-0	179	5-22-03	1	1	2.55	17	1	4	25	17	9	7	1	11	36	.189	.298	.256	34.6	10.6	104

Lora, Aneury	R-R	6-2	155	3-30-04	1	0	2.70	7	1	0	7	6	2	2	1	1	5	.231	.259	.385	18.5	3.7	27
Medina, Abdiel	R-R	5-11	155	1-20-02	4	1	3.95	10	4	0	43	44	21	19	4	14	30	.270	.361	.399	15.6	7.3	192
Morgan, Reid	R-R	6-0	187	3-24-97	0	0	0.00	1	1	0	1	0	0	0	0	0	0	.000	.000	.000	0.0	0.0	3
Morillo, David	R-R	6-2	168	9-26-01	6	1	1.67	16	1	2	27	19	8	5	1	16	29	.202	.342	.234	24.8	13.7	117
Munoz, Jean	R-R	6-1	155	9-17-02	0	1	6.75	4	2	0	7	6	5	5	0	2	10	.231	.286	.385	35.7	7.1	28
Ouderkirk, Daniel	R-R	6-9	255	3-16-00	2	0	0.00	3	0	0	3	2	0	0	0	1	5	.200	.273	.200	45.5	9.1	11
Ovando, Anyelo	R-R	6-5	222	12-25-00	2	1	2.59	18	1	3	24	15	9	7	0	22	31	.181	.376	.205	28.2	20.0	110
Parisi, Jack	R-R	6-0	215	1-13-99	0	0	5.06	3	0	1	5	2	3	3	1	6	7	.118	.348	.294	30.4	26.1	23
Pinto, Juan	L-L	6-2	165	8-26-04	2	5	15.88	10	5	0	17	26	31	30	2	22	21	.366	.548	.521	20.0	21.0	105
Prins, Connor	R-R	6-2	160	10-04-03	2	2	5.25	10	3	2	24	19	16	14	2	19	24	.216	.369	.364	21.4	17.0	112
Quintana, Adrian	R-R	6-0	175	11-20-02	0	1	4.73	7	4	0	13	9	10	7	0	9	12	.180	.317	.240	20.0	15.0	60
Saathoff, Allan	R-R	6-1	230	9-18-99	1	2	0.90	8	0	3	10	3	2	1	0	2	13	.100	.152	.167	39.4	6.1	33
Sadler, Casey	R-R	6-3	223	7-13-90	0	0	13.50	1	1	0	1	2	1	1	0	1	2	.500	.600	1.000	40.0	20.0	5
Sanchez, Steven	R-R	6-0	160	8-19-03	0	0	3.96	16	2	0	36	43	22	16	3	6	28	.291	.325	.419	17.8	3.8	157
Schomberg, Will	R-R	5-10	170	1-30-01	0	0	10.13	3	0	0	3	2	3	3	0	5	1	.200	.529	.300	5.9	29.4	17
Talavera, Roiber	R-R	6-0	160	3-31-04	0	1	19.06	6	3	0	6	13	13	12	1	6	10	.464	.571	.786	28.6	17.1	35
Tovar, Eduardo	R-R	5-11	165	10-10-03	1	0	6.92	13	0	1	13	9	10	10	0	14	13	.191	.375	.298	19.7	21.2	66

Fielding

C: Caguana 20, Duvall 13, Sharp 10, Charping 9, Gonzalez 8, Emery 4, Welch 2. **1B:** Suisbel 15, Caguana 12, Fitz-Gerald 11, Zona 7, Izturis 6, Cali 4, Belbin 3, Locklear 2, Pagliarini 1, Tingelstad 1. **2B:** Rodriguez 16, Cova 13, Aguilar 9, Mendez 5, Barr 4, Belbin 3, Peete 3, Emerson 2, Feliz 1, Izturis 1, Arroyo 1, Polcovich 1, Rodden 1, Zona 1. **3B:** Pagliarini 13, Suisbel 13, Barr 12, Cali 7, Cova 4, Aguilar 4, Williamson 2, Izturis 1, Lavey 1, Belbin 1, Peete 1. **SS:** Rodriguez 16, Izturis 15, Suisbel 8, Peete 6, Emerson 5, Mendez 4, Arroyo 3, Lavey 1, Rodden 1, Zona 1. **OF:** Feliz 37, Jimenez 37, Guerrero 28, Montes 26, Jones 10, Cova 9, Tingelstad 8, Smith 6, Zona 5, Belbin 4, Cabrera 3, Knight 3, Labrada 2, Izturis 2, Sundstrom 2, Schreck 2, Perez Jr. 1.

DSL MARINERS — *ROOKIE*

DOMINICAN SUMMER LEAGUE

Batting	B-T	Ht.	Wt.	DOB	AVG	OBP	SLG	G	PA	AB	R	H	2B	3B	HR	RBI	BB	HBP	SH	SF	SO	SB	CS	BB%	SO%
Alcantara, Kelvin	L-L	6-0	165	9-15-05	.261	.411	.357	42	146	115	21	30	6	1	1	23	29	1	0	1	23	1	2	19.9	15.8
Beltran, Gustavo	R-R	5-8	145	5-17-05	.185	.292	.259	35	97	81	11	15	3	0	1	11	12	1	1	2	25	2	2	12.4	25.8
Bolivar, Luis	R-R	6-1	160	2-09-04	.171	.298	.215	49	190	158	26	27	7	0	0	14	27	2	1	1	66	9	0	14.2	34.7
Carrasco, Delfry	L-R	5-9	150	6-30-04	.169	.478	.225	42	115	71	19	12	2	1	0	12	35	8	0	1	34	5	1	30.4	29.6
De Andrade, Sebastian	R-R	5-9	165	5-11-06	.269	.355	.361	39	138	119	12	32	5	0	2	21	13	4	0	2	28	0	1	9.4	20.3
De Jesus, Joaan	R-R	5-10	165	6-15-05	.172	.338	.219	29	81	64	8	11	3	0	0	8	15	1	1	0	29	0	2	18.5	35.8
Garcia, Adrian	R-R	5-10	180	5-03-05	.150	.514	.250	13	35	20	7	3	2	0	0	3	12	3	0	0	7	0	2	34.3	20.0
Garcia, Alexander	R-R	5-10	155	10-30-05	.265	.357	.296	35	112	98	19	26	3	0	0	17	12	2	0	0	26	3	0	10.7	23.2
Gonzalez, Carlos	R-R	5-11	175	11-20-03	.280	.418	.441	45	177	143	23	40	11	0	4	23	27	7	0	0	50	0	1	15.3	28.2
Gonzalez, Martin	R-R	5-10	165	9-28-04	.194	.350	.264	41	160	129	17	25	6	0	1	15	25	6	0	0	57	1	0	15.6	35.6
Guilarte, German	R-R	5-10	167	3-06-03	.215	.324	.306	48	173	144	15	31	5	1	2	17	18	7	0	4	47	0	0	10.4	27.2
Gutierrez, Jean C.	R-R	6-1	175	10-25-05	.197	.293	.295	44	150	132	20	26	7	0	2	15	10	8	0	0	49	1	4	6.7	32.7
Martinez, Luis	R-R	5-11	160	8-08-05	—	—	—	11	0	0	1	0	0	0	0	0	0	0	0	0	0	0	0	—	—
Robles, Kay	R-R	6-2	180	3-09-05	.193	.294	.312	38	126	109	20	21	4	0	3	14	7	9	0	1	57	3	1	5.6	45.2
Ventura, Dervy	B-R	5-10	165	1-20-04	.294	.385	.423	53	226	194	36	57	7	6	2	24	27	3	0	2	27	11	6	11.9	11.9

Pitching	B-T	Ht.	Wt.	DOB	W	L	ERA	G	GS	SV	IP	Hits	Runs	ER	HR	BB	SO	AVG	OBP	SLG	SO%	BB%	BF
Barrios, Sebastian	R-R	6-1	165	6-20-04	0	1	5.79	9	0	0	9	8	10	6	0	9	14	.235	.435	.324	30.4	19.6	46
Bello, Yensy	R-R	5-10	180	12-02-02	3	3	3.51	15	0	1	26	20	10	10	0	11	39	.208	.309	.281	35.1	9.9	111
Brito, Lisander	R-R	6-3	175	7-09-02	1	3	2.57	13	0	2	21	18	15	6	0	15	28	.217	.350	.241	27.7	14.9	101
Calderon, William	R-R	6-2	185	8-07-04	0	0	4.50	2	1	0	2	1	1	1	0	2	2	.143	.333	.143	22.2	22.2	9
Diaz, Gleiner	R-R	6-0	170	9-20-03	1	2	2.40	11	9	0	45	30	13	12	0	21	47	.195	.330	.221	25.1	11.2	187
Guevara, Anderson	R-R	5-10	170	11-04-04	1	1	4.63	9	0	0	12	7	10	6	0	13	16	.184	.418	.184	29.1	23.6	55
Jimenez, Federik	R-R	6-0	175	7-27-04	1	1	2.45	10	1	0	11	8	4	3	0	11	20	.200	.396	.275	37.7	20.8	53
Jimenez, Yoryi	R-R	6-1	175	10-28-03	2	0	7.90	10	0	1	14	9	12	12	1	15	14	.184	.394	.306	21.2	22.7	66
Martinez, Jeter	R-R	6-4	180	2-16-06	2	2	1.72	10	8	0	47	17	15	9	1	20	55	.109	.223	.160	30.7	11.2	179
Martinez, Luis	R-R	5-11	160	8-08-05	0	1	5.73	10	0	0	11	9	9	7	1	12	12	.220	.448	.341	20.7	20.7	58
Melenge, Harold	L-L	5-10	170	1-15-02	3	0	1.42	12	8	1	51	38	10	8	1	8	48	.222	.264	.310	26.4	4.4	182
Meza, Kendal	R-R	6-0	160	12-13-05	0	4	12.08	8	1	0	13	16	23	17	2	16	16	.302	.457	.528	22.9	22.9	70
Navarro, Ruddy	R-R	6-1	155	7-21-06	1	0	1.35	5	1	0	7	7	1	1	1	4	12	.259	.355	.407	38.7	12.9	31
Pazos, Francisco	R-R	5-9	200	11-16-05	2	1	7.13	8	6	0	18	23	16	14	0	6	13	.319	.402	.417	15.9	7.3	82
Rodriguez, Erick	R-R	6-1	195	11-07-03	0	0	0.00	3	0	0	3	0	1	0	0	3	1	.000	.308	.000	7.7	23.1	13
Rodriguez, Wuilliams	R-R	6-4	195	2-20-04	2	2	4.38	11	8	0	39	44	25	19	3	15	46	.273	.339	.391	26.0	8.5	177
Romero, Jose	R-R	6-1	160	7-26-04	3	2	2.76	12	4	0	42	31	15	13	3	7	54	.199	.260	.340	32.0	4.1	169
Wilson, Dylan	R-R	6-0	160	12-01-05	0	0	2.20	7	6	0	16	16	7	4	0	9	20	.250	.360	.391	26.7	12.0	75
Yabbour, Joseph	R-R	6-0	175	7-09-03	2	0	3.60	12	0	0	20	13	11	8	0	11	28	.176	.303	.257	31.5	12.4	89
Zerpa, Jose	R-R	6-2	180	10-19-04	3	2	2.70	12	0	1	23	16	9	7	0	8	34	.182	.250	.250	35.4	8.3	96

Fielding

C: De Andrade 20, Guilarte 20, Gonzalez 14, Garcia 11, Robles 1. **1B:** Guilarte 30, Carrasco 16, Gonzalez 11, Beltran 10. **2B:** Ventura 33, De Jesus 16, Garcia 11, Beltran 4. **3B:** Gonzalez 38, De Jesus 11, Carrasco 7, Beltran 6. **SS:** Garcia 23, Ventura 21, Carrasco 12, De Jesus 5, Gonzalez 1. **OF:** Bolivar 51, Gutierrez 45, Alcantara 44, Robles 33, Beltran 6, Ventura 5, Carrasco 4, Gonzalez 1, Martinez 1.

Tampa Bay Rays

SEASON SYNOPSIS: The Rays were baseball's best team for most of the first half of the season, and their 99 wins ranked fourth overall. But rotation injuries and the loss of shortstop Wander Franco in August to an off-field scandal proved too much to overcome, and Texas overwhelmed the Rays in a wild-card series sweep in front of record-low attendance at Tropicana Field.

HIGH POINT: The Rays burst out to a 13-0 start, tying the 1982 Braves and 1987 Brewers for the best marks in modern (1903-) MLB history. Tampa outscored opponents 101-30 and outhomered them 32-6 in the process. The Rays continued to play well and took a 6.5-game lead ahead of second-place Baltimore on June 30, rallying from 4-0 down to score the last 15 runs at Seattle in a 15-4 victory.

LOW POINT: Elbow injuries (requiring season-ending surgeries) to Jeffrey Springs (April), Drew Rasmussen (May) and Shane McClanahan (July) sapped the Rays' pitching depth, though Tampa Bay seemed to be adjusting after an 8-16 July. But an Aug. 12 walk-off win against Cleveland proved to be the last game of the season for Franco; he didn't travel with the club to San Francisco for the following series, and two days later MLB placed him on administrative leave under its joint policy on domestic violence, sexual assault and child abuse as the league investigated his relationships with underage girls.

NOTABLE ROOKIES: Reliever Kevin Kelly led all Rays righthanders with 57 appearances, gave up just two homers and posted a 3.09 ERA. Osleivis Basabe was part of the team's answer for replacing Franco at shortstop, making 18 starts. Curtis Mead became the first Australian position player to play in a big league postseason game and the first Aussie to hit a home run in 12 seasons.

KEY TRANSACTIONS: Kelly was purchased for cash before the season from the Rockies. Righty Zack Littell was a May waiver claim from the Red Sox and bailed out the rotation with 14 starts after making just two in his prior big league career.

DOWN ON THE FARM: The Rays had plenty of MiLB success, but then, that's the norm for them. Tampa Bay's fourth-best .543 organizational winning percentage is the first time they haven't led all of baseball since 2019. Low-A Charleston defended its Carolina League title while Double-A Montgomery and Triple-A Durham earned playoff spots.

OPENING DAY PAYROLL: $73,184,811 (28th).

PLAYERS OF THE YEAR

MAJOR LEAGUE	MINOR LEAGUE
Yandy Diaz	**Junior Caminero**
1B	**3B**
.330/.410/.522	(HiA/AA)
35 2B, 22 HR	.324/.384/.591
95 R, 78 RBI	31 HRs, 94 RBIs

ORGANIZATION LEADERS

Batting		*Minimum 250 AB
MAJORS		
* AVG	Yandy Diaz	.330
* OPS	Yandy Diaz	.932
HR	Isaac Paredes	31
RBI	Isaac Paredes	98
MINORS		
* AVG	Jonathan Aranda, Durham	.339
* OBP	Jonathan Aranda, Durham	.449
* SLG	Jonathan Aranda, Durham	.613
* OPS	Jonathan Aranda, Durham	1.053
R	Austin Shenton, Montg./Durham	102
H	Junior Caminero, B. Green/Montgomery	149
TB	Austin Shenton, Montg./Durham	102
2B	Austin Shenton, Montg./Durham	45
3B	Dru Baker, B. Green/Montgomery	8
HR	Junior Caminero, B. Green/Montgomery	31
RBI	Austin Shenton, Montg./Durham	99
BB	Austin Shenton, Montg./Durham	94
SO	Kameron Misner, Durham	186
SB	Chandler Simpson, Charleston/B. Green	94

Pitching		#Minimum 75 IP
MAJORS		
W	Zach Eflin	16
# ERA	Shane McClanahan	3.29
SO	Zach Eflin	186
SV	Pete Fairbanks	25
MINORS		
W	Trevor Martin, Charleston	10
L	Jonny Cuevas, Charleston	9
# ERA	Jacob Lopez, Mont./Durham	2.68
G	Michael Mercado, Mont./Durham	52
GS	Mason Montgomery, Mont./Durham	29
SV	Javy Guerra, Durham	9
IP	Marcus Johnson, Charleston	130
BB	Yoniel Curet, Charleston/B. Green	73
SO	Yoniel Curet, Charleston/B. Green	144
SO	Mason Montgomery, Mont./Durham	144
# AVG	Yoniel Curet, Charleston/B. Green	.147

2023 PERFORMANCE

General Manager: Erik Neander. **Farm Director:** Jeff McLerran. **Scouting Director:** Chuck Ricci.

Class	Team	League	W	L	PCT	Finish	Manager
Majors	Tampa Bay Rays	American	99	63	.611	2 (15)	Kevin Cash
Triple-A	Durham Bulls	International	88	62	.587	2 (20)	Michael Johns
Double-A	Montgomery Biscuits	Southern	80	58	.580	2 (8)	Morgan Ensberg
High-A	Bowling Green Hot Rods	South Atlantic	69	57	.548	3 (12)	Rafael Valenzuela
Low-A	Charleston RiverDogs	Carolina	66	65	.504	7 (12)	Sean Smedley
Rookie	FCL Rays	Florida Complex	25	29	.463	11 (15)	Frank Maldonado
Rookie	DSL Rays	Dominican Sum.	33	22	.600	11 (50)	Albert Lantigua
Rookie	DSL Tampa Bay	Dominican Sum.	24	31	.436	34 (50)	Henry Lugo
Overall 2023 Minor League Record			385	324	.543	4th (30)	

ORGANIZATION STATISTICS

TAMPA BAY RAYS

AMERICAN LEAGUE

Batting	B-T	Ht.	Wt.	DOB	AVG	OBP	SLG	G	PA	AB	R	H	2B	3B	HR	RBI	BB	HBP	SH	SF	SO	SB	CS	BB%	SO%
Aranda, Jonathan	L-R	6-0	210	5-23-98	.230	.340	.368	34	103	87	13	20	4	1	2	13	13	2	0	1	31	0	0	12.6	30.1
Arozarena, Randy	R-R	5-11	185	2-28-95	.254	.364	.425	151	654	551	95	140	19	3	23	83	80	18	0	5	156	22	10	12.2	23.9
Basabe, Osleivis	R-R	5-11	188	9-13-00	.218	.277	.310	31	94	87	15	19	5	0	1	12	6	1	0	0	25	0	1	6.4	26.6
Bethancourt, Christian	R-R	6-3	205	9-02-91	.225	.254	.381	104	332	315	49	71	16	0	11	33	13	0	1	3	91	1	0	3.9	27.4
Brujan, Vidal	B-R	5-10	180	2-09-98	.171	.241	.197	37	84	76	14	13	2	0	0	6	5	2	1	0	21	3	2	6.0	25.0
Caminero, Junior	R-R	6-1	157	7-05-03	.235	.278	.353	7	36	34	4	8	1	0	1	7	2	0	0	0	8	0	0	5.6	22.2
Diaz, Yandy	R-R	6-2	215	8-08-91	.330	.410	.522	137	600	525	95	173	35	0	22	78	65	8	0	2	94	0	1	10.8	15.7
Franco, Wander	B-R	5-10	189	3-01-01	.281	.344	.475	112	491	442	65	124	23	6	17	58	42	3	0	4	69	30	10	8.6	14.1
Gray, Tristan	L-R	6-1	215	3-22-96	.400	.400	1.000	2	5	5	1	2	0	0	1	1	0	0	0	0	0	0	0	0.0	0.0
Lowe, Brandon	L-R	5-10	185	7-06-94	.231	.328	.443	109	436	377	58	87	15	1	21	68	50	6	0	3	119	7	0	11.5	27.3
Lowe, Josh	L-R	6-4	205	2-02-98	.292	.335	.500	135	501	466	71	136	33	2	20	83	31	1	0	3	124	32	3	6.2	24.8
Margot, Manuel	R-R	5-11	180	9-28-94	.264	.310	.376	99	336	311	39	82	21	1	4	38	18	4	0	3	55	9	3	5.4	16.4
Mead, Curtis	R-R	6-0	171	10-26-00	.253	.326	.349	24	92	83	12	21	3	1	1	5	7	2	0	0	21	0	0	7.6	22.8
Mejia, Francisco	B-R	5-8	188	10-27-95	.227	.258	.400	50	160	150	22	34	11	0	5	19	6	1	1	2	38	0	1	3.8	23.8
Paredes, Isaac	R-R	5-11	213	2-18-99	.250	.352	.488	143	571	492	71	123	24	0	31	98	58	20	0	1	104	1	0	10.2	18.2
Pinto, Rene	R-R	5-10	195	11-02-96	.252	.267	.456	39	105	103	10	26	3	0	6	16	2	0	0	0	34	0	0	1.9	32.4
Raley, Luke	L-R	6-4	235	9-19-94	.249	.333	.490	118	406	357	56	89	23	3	19	49	28	18	1	2	128	14	3	6.9	31.5
Ramirez, Harold	R-R	5-10	232	9-06-94	.313	.353	.460	122	434	400	58	125	19	2	12	68	22	6	0	6	79	5	3	5.1	18.2
Siri, Jose	R-R	6-2	175	7-22-95	.222	.267	.494	101	364	338	58	75	13	2	25	56	20	2	1	3	130	12	3	5.5	35.7
Tapia, Raimel	L-L	6-3	175	2-04-94	.333	.455	.333	5	11	9	4	3	0	0	0	0	2	0	0	0	1	2	0	18.2	9.1
2-team (39 Boston)					.271	.346	.365	44	108	96	18	26	4	1	1	10	11	0	0	0	20	8	1	10.2	18.5
Walls, Taylor	B-R	5-10	185	7-10-96	.201	.305	.333	99	349	303	50	61	12	2	8	36	44	1	1	0	92	22	1	12.6	26.4

Pitching	B-T	Ht.	Wt.	DOB	W	L	ERA	G	GS	SV	IP	Hits	Runs	ER	HR	BB	SO	AVG	OBP	SLG	SO%	BB%	BF
Adam, Jason	R-R	6-3	229	8-04-91	4	2	2.98	56	0	12	54	35	21	18	7	20	69	.181	.288	.342	31.1	9.0	222
Anderson, Chase	R-R	6-1	210	11-30-87	0	0	0.00	2	0	1	5	2	0	0	0	1	2	.118	.167	.118	11.1	5.6	18
Armstrong, Shawn	R-R	6-2	225	9-11-90	1	0	1.38	39	6	0	52	36	12	8	2	11	54	.188	.246	.272	26.1	5.3	207
Beeks, Jalen	L-L	5-11	215	7-10-93	2	3	5.95	30	8	1	42	42	28	28	4	21	47	.251	.335	.383	24.5	10.9	192
Bethancourt, Christian	R-R	6-3	205	9-02-91	0	0	81.00	1	0	0	0	3	3	3	1	0	0	.750	.750	1.750	0.0	0.0	4
Bradley, Taj	R-R	6-2	190	3-20-01	5	8	5.59	23	21	0	105	106	69	65	23	39	129	.255	.317	.495	28.0	8.5	460
Bristo, Braden	R-R	6-0	180	11-01-94	0	0	0.00	1	0	1	3	0	0	0	0	1	4	.000	.100	.000	40.0	10.0	10
Burdi, Zack	R-R	6-3	210	3-09-95	0	0	11.25	3	0	0	4	6	6	5	0	2	5	.353	.400	.588	25.0	10.0	20
Chirinos, Yonny	R-R	6-2	225	12-26-93	4	4	4.02	15	4	0	63	58	30	28	10	20	31	.247	.314	.455	11.8	7.6	262
Civale, Aaron	R-R	6-2	215	6-12-95	2	3	5.36	10	10	0	45	51	27	27	7	11	58	.279	.330	.443	29.3	5.6	198
Cleavinger, Garrett	R-L	6-1	220	4-23-94	1	0	3.00	15	0	0	12	6	5	4	2	6	14	.146	.271	.317	29.2	12.5	48
Criswell, Cooper	R-R	6-6	200	7-24-96	1	1	5.73	10	0	0	33	40	23	21	6	11	27	.296	.364	.496	17.9	7.3	151
Devenski, Chris	R-R	6-3	211	11-13-90	3	2	2.08	9	0	0	9	5	4	2	1	2	9	.167	.212	.333	27.3	6.1	33
Diekman, Jake	R-L	6-4	195	1-21-87	0	1	2.18	50	0	0	45	26	15	11	2	25	53	.166	.283	.236	28.6	13.5	185
Eflin, Zach	R-R	6-6	220	4-08-94	16	8	3.50	31	31	0	178	158	69	69	19	24	186	.235	.264	.379	26.5	3.4	703
Fairbanks, Pete	R-R	6-6	225	12-16-93	2	4	2.58	49	0	25	45	26	14	13	3	20	68	.164	.273	.233	37.0	10.9	184
Faucher, Calvin	R-R	6-1	190	9-22-95	1	1	7.01	17	4	0	26	31	20	20	4	12	25	.290	.367	.458	20.8	10.0	120
Fleming, Josh	L-L	6-2	220	5-18-96	2	0	4.70	12	3	0	52	56	29	27	9	19	25	.281	.339	.467	11.3	8.6	221
Glasnow, Tyler	L-R	6-8	225	8-23-93	10	7	3.53	21	21	0	120	93	52	47	13	37	162	.209	.270	.347	33.4	7.6	485
Guerra, Javy	L-R	6-0	190	9-25-95	0	0	4.09	9	2	0	11	7	5	5	1	13	9	.179	.385	.282	17.3	25.0	52
Hembree, Heath	R-R	6-4	220	1-13-89	0	0	0.00	1	0	0	1	0	0	0	0	1	2	.000	.250	.000	50.0	25.0	4
Kelley, Trevor	R-R	6-2	210	10-20-92	0	1	5.87	10	3	0	15	16	10	10	4	6	11	.262	.348	.541	15.9	8.7	69
Kelly, Kevin	R-R	6-2	200	11-28-97	5	2	3.09	57	0	1	67	53	27	23	2	15	56	.211	.283	.307	20.3	5.4	276
Kittredge, Andrew	R-R	6-1	230	3-17-90	2	0	3.09	14	0	1	12	12	4	4	1	2	10	.255	.300	.383	20.0	4.0	50
LaSorsa, Joe	L-L	6-5	215	4-29-98	0	0	2.08	2	0	0	4	3	1	1	0	3	3	.188	.350	.250	15.0	15.0	20
Littell, Zack	R-R	6-4	220	10-05-95	3	6	3.93	26	14	0	87	91	40	38	13	9	72	.261	.287	.431	19.8	2.5	364
Lopez, Jacob	L-L	6-4	220	3-11-98	1	0	4.38	4	1	1	12	14	7	6	0	2	8	.280	.333	.400	14.8	3.7	54
Lopez, Jose	L-L	6-1	200	2-15-99	0	0	4.50	1	0	0	2	3	1	1	0	1	2	.333	.400	.444	20.0	10.0	10
McClanahan, Shane	L-L	6-1	200	4-28-97	11	2	3.29	21	21	0	115	95	42	42	15	41	121	.222	.290	.388	25.8	8.7	469

Patino, Luis	R-R	6-1	192	10-26-99	0	0	9.00	2	0	0	4	5	4	4	2	2	5	.294	.368	.647	26.3	10.5	19
Perez, Hector	R-R	6-3	223	6-06-96	0	0	27.00	1	0	0	0	3	1	1	0	1	0	.750	.800	.750	0.0	20.0	5
Pinto, Rene	R-R	5-10	195	11-02-96	0	0	45.00	1	0	0	1	5	5	5	3	0	0	.625	.625	1.875	0.0	0.0	8
Poche, Colin	L-L	6-3	225	1-17-94	12	3	2.23	66	0	1	61	42	17	15	4	24	61	.194	.275	.306	24.8	9.8	246
Raley, Luke	L-R	6-4	235	9-19-94	0	0	30.38	2	0	0	3	11	9	9	2	0	1	.579	.579	1.053	5.3	0.0	19
Ramirez, Erasmo	R-R	6-0	220	5-02-90	1	0	6.48	15	2	0	33	46	27	24	7	7	30	.333	.365	.551	20.3	4.7	148
Rasmussen, Drew	R-R	6-1	211	7-27-95	4	2	2.62	8	8	0	45	36	13	13	2	11	47	.221	.273	.294	26.6	6.2	177
Rodriguez, Elvin	R-R	6-3	160	3-31-98	0	0	0.00	1	0	0	3	0	0	0	0	0	5	.000	.000	.000	50.0	0.0	10
Springs, Jeffrey	L-L	6-3	218	9-20-92	2	0	0.56	3	3	0	16	4	1	1	1	4	24	.080	.148	.140	43.6	7.3	55
Stephenson, Robert	R-R	6-3	205	2-24-93	3	1	2.35	42	0	1	38	18	11	10	5	8	60	.138	.187	.300	42.9	5.7	140
Thompson, Ryan	R-R	6-5	210	6-26-92	1	2	6.11	18	0	0	18	14	13	12	2	7	12	.215	.320	.385	15.8	9.2	76

Fielding

Catcher	PCT	G	PO	A	E	DP	PB
Bethancourt	.995	102	844	33	4	3	3
Mejia	.985	50	375	19	6	3	0
Pinto	.997	38	285	16	1	0	5

First Base	PCT	G	PO	A	E	DP
Aranda	.972	11	67	3	2	2
Diaz	.996	118	868	69	4	70
Gray	1.000	1	2	0	0	0
Paredes	1.000	25	104	3	0	8
Raley	.995	35	192	9	1	16
Ramirez	1.000	6	22	1	0	2

Second Base	PCT	G	PO	A	E	DP
Aranda	1.000	4	1	9	0	1
Basabe	1.000	4	2	7	0	0
Brujan	.977	15	12	31	1	9
Caminero	.667	1	2	0	1	0
Lowe	.980	105	158	230	8	51
Mead	1.000	4	3	12	0	1
Paredes	1.000	14	11	21	0	3
Walls	.993	37	54	87	1	23

Third Base	PCT	G	PO	A	E	DP
Aranda	1.000	2	0	1	0	0
Basabe	.714	5	4	1	2	0
Brujan	1.000	4	1	5	0	0
Caminero	1.000	3	2	3	0	1
Diaz	1.000	6	2	3	0	0
Mead	.957	19	12	32	2	2
Paredes	.959	116	69	186	11	17
Walls	.973	39	17	56	2	4

Shortstop	PCT	G	PO	A	E	DP
Basabe	1.000	20	23	37	0	8
Brujan	.786	8	5	6	3	1
Caminero	1.000	2	2	3	0	0
Franco	.979	111	116	310	9	55
Gray	1.000	1	1	3	0	0
Mead	1.000	1	2	2	0	0
Paredes	1.000	1	1	3	0	2
Walls	.954	32	40	63	5	15

Outfield	PCT	G	PO	A	E	DP
Arozarena	1.000	139	245	8	0	1
Basabe	.500	3	1	0	0	0
Brujan	1.000	6	11	0	0	0
Lowe	.996	118	185	5	2	1
Margot	.986	98	170	1	3	0
Raley	1.000	65	107	3	0	1
Ramirez	1.000	14	15	1	0	1
Siri	.991	100	210	2	2	1
Tapia	.500	4	1	0	0	0

DURHAM BULLS — TRIPLE-A

INTERNATIONAL LEAGUE

Batting	B-T	Ht.	Wt.	DOB	AVG	OBP	SLG	G	PA	AB	R	H	2B	3B	HR	RBI	BB	HBP	SH	SF	SO	SB	CS	BB%	SO%
Alvarez, Roberto	R-R	6-0	151	7-28-99	.254	.277	.302	29	65	63	6	16	0	0	1	3	1	1	0	0	18	0	0	1.5	27.7
Aranda, Jonathan	L-R	6-0	210	5-23-98	.339	.449	.613	95	434	357	82	121	23	0	25	81	64	10	0	3	87	2	2	14.7	20.0
Basabe, Osleivis	R-R	5-11	188	9-13-00	.296	.351	.426	94	426	385	45	114	24	7	4	58	31	4	1	5	66	16	6	7.3	15.5
Brujan, Vidal	B-R	5-10	180	2-09-98	.272	.362	.477	59	276	239	41	65	11	4	10	32	31	4	0	2	49	19	14	11.2	17.8
Cardenas, Ruben	R-R	6-0	185	10-10-97	.269	.358	.475	132	550	476	82	128	26	3	22	82	62	7	0	5	145	8	12	11.3	26.4
Dini, Nick	R-R	5-7	190	7-27-93	.198	.355	.371	71	257	202	45	40	8	0	9	29	44	7	0	3	64	6	1	17.1	24.9
Driscoll, Logan	L-R	5-10	195	11-03-97	.265	.342	.412	20	76	68	13	18	4	0	2	15	7	1	0	0	20	0	1	9.2	26.3
Edwards, Evan	L-L	5-11	200	6-21-97	.273	.405	.424	11	42	33	5	9	0	1	1	5	8	0	0	1	12	1	0	19.0	28.6
Gamel, Ben	L-L	5-10	180	5-17-92	.276	.402	.463	59	250	203	37	56	12	1	8	31	42	2	1	2	57	4	1	16.8	22.8
Gray, Tristan	L-R	6-1	215	3-22-96	.235	.312	.485	132	525	468	71	110	25	1	30	98	46	7	1	2	166	2	3	8.8	31.6
Hamilton, Billy	B-R	6-0	160	9-09-90	.300	.391	.300	8	24	20	5	6	0	0	0	0	3	0	1	0	6	5	0	12.5	25.0
2-team (3 Charlotte)					.179	.286	.263	36	113	95	19	17	3	1	1	4	14	1	2	1	35	8	0	12.4	31.0
Hulsizer, Niko	R-R	6-0	225	2-01-97	.212	.338	.403	119	473	392	73	83	22	1	17	63	70	7	0	4	156	7	6	14.8	33.0
Hunt, Blake	R-R	6-3	215	11-10-98	.263	.317	.518	30	126	114	18	30	11	0	6	23	8	2	0	2	23	0	1	6.3	18.3
Infante, Diego	R-R	6-2	178	10-22-99	.187	.219	.253	24	96	91	8	17	3	0	1	13	3	1	0	1	35	2	0	3.1	36.5
Jackson, Alex	R-R	5-11	238	12-25-95	.281	.305	.561	14	59	57	11	16	4	0	4	10	2	0	0	0	14	0	0	3.4	23.7
2-team (45 Nashville)					.284	.348	.556	59	248	225	42	64	11	1	16	45	18	4	0	1	62	0	0	7.3	25.0
Jones, Greg	B-R	6-2	175	3-07-98	.278	.344	.467	51	189	169	32	47	9	1	7	26	15	3	0	2	73	12	4	7.9	38.6
Lopez, Johan	R-R	5-11	167	7-28-00	.241	.425	.241	13	40	29	3	7	0	0	0	3	10	0	0	1	11	1	1	25.0	27.5
Lowe, Brandon	L-R	5-10	185	7-06-94	.214	.353	.357	4	17	14	3	3	2	0	0	1	3	0	0	0	5	0	0	17.6	29.4
Manzardo, Kyle	L-R	6-0	205	7-18-00	.238	.342	.442	73	313	265	33	63	19	1	11	38	42	2	0	4	65	1	1	13.4	20.8
2-team (21 Columbus)					.242	.348	.475	94	405	343	49	83	27	1	17	54	54	2	0	6	79	1	1	13.3	19.5
Margot, Manuel	R-R	5-11	180	9-28-94	.833	.875	1.000	2	8	6	3	5	1	0	0	5	2	0	0	0	0	0	0	25.0	0.0
Mead, Curtis	R-R	6-0	171	10-26-00	.294	.385	.515	61	278	235	41	69	21	2	9	45	35	3	0	5	48	4	2	12.6	17.3
Mejia, Francisco	B-R	5-8	188	10-27-95	.326	.359	.593	20	92	86	13	28	3	1	6	19	4	1	0	1	21	0	0	4.3	22.8
Misner, Kameron	L-L	6-4	218	1-08-98	.226	.363	.458	130	519	421	85	95	25	5	21	58	91	2	1	4	186	21	6	17.5	35.8
Murray, Tanner	R-R	6-1	190	9-03-99	.200	.200	.400	6	20	20	0	4	4	0	0	3	0	0	0	0	6	0	0	0.0	30.0
Pinto, Rene	R-R	5-10	195	11-02-96	.253	.306	.521	37	160	146	25	37	12	0	9	24	10	2	0	2	46	1	0	6.3	28.8
Shenton, Austin	L-R	6-0	205	1-22-98	.301	.432	.603	61	271	219	57	66	24	0	14	50	48	3	0	1	75	0	0	17.7	27.7
Simon, Ronny	B-R	5-7	150	4-17-00	.282	.380	.427	32	137	117	19	33	8	0	3	12	18	1	0	1	28	5	2	13.1	20.4
Siri, Jose	R-R	6-2	175	7-22-95	.125	.125	.250	2	8	8	0	1	1	0	0	1	0	0	0	0	5	0	0	0.0	62.5
Tapia, Raimel	L-L	6-3	175	2-04-94	.269	.371	.413	29	124	104	19	28	3	0	4	11	18	0	0	2	28	7	2	14.5	22.6
Turner, Gionti	R-R	6-2	178	8-17-00	.333	.500	.333	1	4	3	0	1	0	0	0	0	1	0	0	0	1	0	0	25.0	25.0
Walls, Taylor	B-R	5-10	185	7-10-96	.429	.500	.857	2	8	7	3	3	0	0	1	1	1	0	0	0	2	0	0	12.5	25.0
Williams, Carson	R-R	6-1	180	6-25-03	.077	.200	.154	4	15	13	3	1	1	0	0	0	2	0	0	0	6	0	0	13.3	40.0

Pitching	B-T	Ht.	Wt.	DOB	W	L	ERA	G	GS	SV	IP	Hits	Runs	ER	HR	BB	SO	AVG	OBP	SLG	SO%	BB%	BF
Alvarez, Roberto	R-R	6-0	151	7-28-99	0	0	3.24	6	0	0	8	6	3	3	2	3	1	.200	.273	.467	3.0	9.1	33
Armstrong, Shawn	R-R	6-2	225	9-11-90	1	0	2.00	7	0	0	9	2	2	2	1	2	8	.069	.129	.172	25.8	6.5	31
Beeks, Jalen	L-L	5-11	215	7-10-93	2	1	3.86	20	1	0	26	26	11	11	3	9	27	.257	.318	.386	24.5	8.2	110

Bradley, Taj	R-R	6-2	190	3-20-01	2	5	6.45	10	10	0	38	39	28	27	9	20	37	.262	.355	.483	21.5	11.6	172
Brigden, Trevor	L-R	6-3	210	9-20-95	4	4	3.46	44	2	2	78	55	33	30	9	40	95	.192	.298	.329	28.9	12.2	329
Bristo, Braden	R-R	6-0	180	11-01-94	1	2	10.00	6	0	0	9	12	10	10	4	4	10	.324	.372	.730	23.3	9.3	43
Burdi, Zack	R-R	6-3	210	3-09-95	0	0	5.27	9	0	0	14	11	8	8	3	10	13	.229	.367	.458	21.7	16.7	60
Burr, Ryan	R-R	6-4	220	5-28-94	2	1	3.09	18	1	0	23	20	11	8	2	3	23	.225	.250	.371	25.0	3.3	92
Castaneda, Victor	R-R	6-1	185	8-27-98	0	0	6.75	6	0	0	9	10	7	7	1	10	12	.263	.417	.395	25.0	20.8	48
Chirinos, Yonny	R-R	6-2	225	12-26-93	0	1	4.66	5	4	0	19	19	14	10	1	8	17	.247	.326	.338	19.8	9.3	86
Criswell, Cooper	R-R	6-6	200	7-24-96	4	4	3.93	23	17	2	85	87	47	37	8	23	80	.260	.325	.368	21.6	6.2	370
Dacosta, Franklin	L-L	5-11	162	2-27-00	0	0	4.50	1	0	0	2	1	1	1	1	3	2	.167	.444	.667	22.2	33.3	9
Devenski, Chris	R-R	6-3	211	11-13-90	0	0	0.00	1	0	0	1	2	0	0	0	0	0	.400	.500	.400	0.0	0.0	6
Dini, Nick	R-R	5-7	190	7-27-93	1	0	21.00	3	0	0	3	10	8	7	1	4	0	.588	.667	.765	0.0	19.0	21
Doxakis, John	R-L	6-4	215	8-20-98	0	0	27.00	1	0	0	2	4	6	5	2	2	1	.500	.545	1.250	8.3	16.7	12
Fairbanks, Pete	R-R	6-6	225	12-16-93	0	0	13.50	1	0	0	1	1	1	1	0	0	2	.250	.250	.250	50.0	0.0	4
Faucher, Calvin	R-R	6-1	190	9-22-95	0	1	1.04	8	1	0	9	6	2	1	0	7	13	.188	.333	.188	33.3	17.9	39
Fleming, Josh	L-L	6-2	220	5-18-96	1	1	4.35	14	4	0	31	47	21	15	3	8	15	.351	.392	.493	10.4	5.6	144
Garcia, Carlos	R-R	6-3	185	11-28-98	2	3	3.35	18	2	1	38	29	16	14	6	21	39	.207	.321	.379	23.6	12.7	165
Gau, Chris	L-R	6-2	205	2-03-97	0	1	5.14	4	3	0	7	5	4	4	0	6	7	.200	.364	.200	21.2	18.2	33
Glasnow, Tyler	L-R	6-8	225	8-23-93	0	0	0.68	4	4	0	13	8	1	1	1	5	20	.170	.250	.277	38.5	9.6	52
Guerra, Javy	L-R	6-0	190	9-25-95	0	3	4.14	32	0	9	37	31	18	17	4	15	38	.226	.327	.343	23.9	9.4	159
Heller, Ben	R-R	6-3	210	8-05-91	3	2	3.95	18	0	1	27	30	20	12	2	8	34	.270	.359	.423	26.0	6.1	131
Hembree, Heath	R-R	6-4	220	1-13-89	3	1	1.29	8	0	2	7	6	1	1	0	5	8	.231	.344	.269	25.0	15.6	32
Hunley, Sean	R-R	6-4	220	7-05-99	0	3	12.67	5	4	0	16	30	25	23	3	8	10	.400	.460	.640	11.5	9.2	87
Kelley, Trevor	R-R	6-2	210	10-20-92	1	0	5.23	27	3	2	33	38	22	19	7	11	28	.279	.342	.471	18.7	7.3	150
Kittredge, Andrew	R-R	6-1	230	3-17-90	3	1	5.40	12	0	0	13	18	8	8	1	3	9	.316	.361	.456	14.8	4.9	61
LaSorsa, Joe	L-L	6-5	215	4-29-98	2	1	3.86	9	3	0	21	25	10	9	4	8	13	.287	.347	.471	13.7	8.4	95
Littell, Zack	R-R	6-4	220	10-05-95	0	1	18.00	3	0	0	2	4	4	4	1	4	1	.444	.571	.889	7.1	28.6	14
Lopez, Jacob	L-L	6-4	220	3-11-98	4	5	2.72	18	18	0	79	58	30	24	7	47	87	.207	.326	.354	26.0	14.0	335
Lopez, Johan	R-R	5-11	167	7-28-00	0	0	0.00	1	0	0	0	0	0	0	0	0	1	.000	.000	.000	100.0	0.0	1
Lopez, Jose	L-L	6-1	200	2-15-99	2	3	7.89	27	1	2	30	39	28	26	3	19	32	.315	.403	.468	22.2	13.2	144
McKendry, Evan	R-R	6-3	200	2-06-98	8	3	4.00	20	15	0	97	85	47	43	19	28	95	.232	.296	.439	23.5	6.9	405
Mejia, Enmanuel	R-R	5-11	185	12-22-98	1	0	0.77	8	1	0	12	7	1	1	0	7	13	.167	.286	.190	26.5	14.3	49
Mercado, Michael	R-R	6-4	160	4-15-99	2	2	4.99	28	2	2	40	35	23	22	9	21	56	.235	.331	.456	32.6	12.2	172
Molina, Anthony	R-R	6-1	170	1-12-02	3	2	4.37	13	12	0	56	73	33	27	5	18	50	.312	.366	.432	19.7	7.1	254
Montgomery, Mason	L-L	6-2	195	6-17-00	2	0	2.70	4	4	0	17	7	5	5	2	11	13	.127	.304	.255	18.8	15.9	69
Muller, Chris	R-R	6-5	210	4-22-96	1	0	4.95	16	0	1	20	19	13	11	2	11	22	.250	.344	.368	24.4	12.2	90
Patino, Luis	R-R	6-1	192	10-26-99	3	4	6.75	27	6	0	45	49	36	34	10	29	38	.271	.373	.514	17.5	13.4	217
Perez, Hector	R-R	6-3	223	6-06-96	4	0	4.08	33	2	5	53	45	24	24	9	30	69	.232	.352	.418	30.0	13.0	230
Ramirez, Erasmo	R-R	6-0	220	5-02-90	2	1	5.87	9	1	0	23	27	15	15	4	8	29	.293	.347	.533	28.7	7.9	101
Roberson, Josh	R-R	6-3	175	5-12-96	2	1	4.50	31	0	3	36	38	24	18	1	22	43	.270	.380	.362	25.7	13.2	167
Rodriguez, Elvin	R-R	6-3	160	3-31-98	3	3	3.40	10	10	0	45	32	18	17	8	18	48	.198	.279	.377	26.2	9.8	183
Rodriguez, Manuel	R-R	5-11	210	8-06-96	2	0	3.06	15	0	1	18	15	6	6	0	8	24	.231	.329	.262	31.6	10.5	76
Sterner, Justin	R-R	6-1	215	8-29-96	4	0	5.80	23	0	0	36	38	24	23	7	19	42	.273	.354	.489	26.1	11.8	161
Sulser, Cole	R-R	6-1	190	3-12-90	2	0	3.86	12	0	0	19	21	9	8	3	5	19	.269	.329	.423	22.4	5.9	85
Thompson, Ryan	R-R	6-5	210	6-26-92	4	0	3.26	13	0	1	19	12	9	7	0	11	24	.179	.291	.209	30.4	13.9	79
Wiles, Nathan	R-R	6-4	228	7-02-98	7	2	5.94	20	19	0	89	100	63	59	19	27	72	.287	.338	.513	18.8	7.0	383
Zarraga, Alfredo	R-R	5-11	158	11-16-00	0	0	9.00	1	0	0	2	3	2	2	1	1	1	.333	.400	.667	10.0	10.0	10

Fielding

Catcher	PCT	G	PO	A	E	DP	PB
Alvarez	.975	11	76	2	2	0	1
Dini	.984	47	413	9	7	0	2
Driscoll	.985	16	124	9	2	2	0
Hunt	.996	30	248	4	1	1	0
Jackson	.971	10	92	9	3	0	0
Mejia	.969	14	120	7	4	0	0
Pinto	.993	31	275	17	2	2	3

First Base	PCT	G	PO	A	E	DP
Aranda	.987	20	139	9	2	13
Dini	1.000	2	17	0	0	1
Driscoll	1.000	4	30	1	0	2
Edwards	1.000	11	82	4	0	10
Gamel	1.000	15	102	5	0	13
Gray	1.000	6	32	5	0	5
Lopez	.971	5	32	2	1	4
Manzardo	.986	63	439	39	7	50
Shenton	.991	28	196	17	2	22

Second Base	PCT	G	PO	A	E	DP
Aranda	.982	46	90	125	4	35
Basabe	.988	25	41	42	1	12
Brujan	.972	29	51	87	4	18
Gray	1.000	6	6	12	0	1
Lopez	1.000	2	3	2	0	2
Lowe	.917	3	4	7	1	2
Mead	.903	8	9	19	3	6
Murray	1.000	6	9	9	0	1
Simon	.966	30	44	70	4	16
Turner	1.000	1	2	7	0	3

Third Base	PCT	G	PO	A	E	DP
Alvarez	1.000	1	2	1	0	0
Aranda	.783	14	5	13	5	3
Basabe	.983	28	18	41	1	4
Brujan	.929	4	7	6	1	2
Gray	.906	31	17	31	5	2
Lopez	1.000	1	0	2	0	0
Mead	.962	47	32	70	4	9
Shenton	.942	27	11	38	3	3

Shortstop	PCT	G	PO	A	E	DP
Basabe	.945	37	40	80	7	15
Brujan	.964	15	16	38	2	4
Gray	.965	78	107	224	12	59
Jones	.959	15	15	32	2	7
Lopez	1.000	5	8	7	0	5
Simon	1.000	1	0	1	0	0
Walls	1.000	2	4	6	0	0
Williams	1.000	4	5	8	0	4

Outfield	PCT	G	PO	A	E	DP
Brujan	1.000	9	25	2	0	0
Cardenas	.986	110	195	4	2	3
Gamel	.954	29	51	2	2	0
Hamilton	.917	7	11	0	1	0
Hulsizer	.990	104	156	4	3	0
Infante	1.000	18	29	2	0	0
Jones	.969	35	70	0	4	0
Margot	1.000	1	3	0	0	0
Misner	.991	129	321	7	3	2
Siri	1.000	1	5	0	0	0
Tapia	1.000	28	49	1	0	0

MONTGOMERY BISCUITS — *DOUBLE-A*

SOUTHERN LEAGUE

Batting	B-T	Ht.	Wt.	DOB	AVG	OBP	SLG	G	PA	AB	R	H	2B	3B	HR	RBI	BB	HBP	SH	SF	SO	SB	CS	BB%	SO%
Alvarez, Roberto	R-R	6-0	151	7-28-99	.000	.182	.000	3	11	9	1	0	0	0	0	1	1	1	0	0	4	0	0	9.1	36.4
Auer, Mason	R-R	6-1	210	3-01-01	.205	.292	.348	124	511	454	59	93	18	7	11	51	49	7	0	1	184	47	11	9.6	36.0
Baker, Dru	R-R	5-11	205	3-22-00	.287	.346	.417	30	127	115	24	33	6	3	1	15	7	4	0	1	28	11	2	5.5	22.0
Barreat, Elis	R-R	5-9	158	5-22-03	.333	.333	.333	1	3	3	0	1	0	0	0	0	0	0	0	0	1	0	0	0.0	33.3
Battles, Jalen	R-R	6-1	210	12-20-99	.206	.231	.222	19	65	63	7	13	1	0	0	2	2	0	0	0	19	3	2	3.1	29.2
Caminero, Junior	R-R	6-1	157	7-05-03	.309	.373	.548	81	351	314	55	97	9	3	20	62	32	2	0	3	60	3	4	9.1	17.1
Driscoll, Logan	L-R	5-10	195	11-03-97	.263	.329	.415	84	353	316	52	83	14	2	10	43	22	11	0	4	90	4	1	6.2	25.5
Dyer, Matthew	R-R	6-2	185	7-14-98	.222	.293	.361	11	41	36	4	8	2	0	1	7	4	0	0	1	20	0	0	9.8	48.8
Edwards, Evan	L-L	5-11	200	6-21-97	.249	.350	.472	95	357	305	38	76	13	5	15	64	43	6	0	3	116	16	1	12.0	32.5
Hernandez, Heriberto	R-R	5-11	195	12-16-99	.249	.376	.411	118	478	389	64	97	18	3	13	60	76	5	4	4	134	7	2	15.9	28.0
Hunt, Blake	R-R	6-3	215	11-10-98	.250	.342	.455	37	155	132	22	33	9	0	6	18	14	6	0	3	38	2	1	9.0	24.5
Infante, Diego	R-R	6-2	178	10-22-99	.278	.338	.459	72	284	259	42	72	14	0	11	46	22	2	0	1	73	13	5	7.7	25.7
Jones, Greg	B-R	6-2	175	3-07-98	.173	.264	.358	20	92	81	11	14	2	2	3	9	9	1	1	0	36	12	0	9.8	39.1
Lopez, Johan	R-R	5-11	167	7-28-00	.173	.262	.307	22	84	75	10	13	5	1	1	11	8	1	0	0	26	2	0	9.5	31.0
Murray, Tanner	R-R	6-1	190	9-03-99	.256	.345	.438	47	200	176	30	45	13	2	5	26	21	3	0	0	40	0	1	10.5	20.0
Ostberg, Erik	L-R	5-9	225	10-12-95	.213	.278	.404	44	151	136	20	29	11	0	5	20	12	1	0	2	38	2	1	7.9	25.2
Ovalles, Alexander	L-L	6-0	184	10-06-00	.200	.317	.267	32	124	105	17	21	2	1	1	15	18	0	1	0	39	4	0	14.5	31.5
Parra, Jeffry	R-R	5-11	195	1-24-98	.000	.250	.000	1	4	3	0	0	0	0	0	0	0	1	0	0	1	0	0	0.0	25.0
Peters, Tristan	L-R	5-11	180	2-29-00	.275	.361	.421	93	415	363	65	100	22	5	7	46	42	8	0	2	66	14	5	10.1	15.9
Piper, Kenny	R-R	5-9	190	7-12-98	.293	.389	.610	23	95	82	20	24	5	0	7	11	8	5	0	0	28	0	0	8.4	29.5
Seymour, Bobby	L-R	6-4	250	10-07-98	.343	.443	.537	18	79	67	12	23	1	0	4	13	10	2	0	0	17	0	0	12.7	21.5
Shenton, Austin	L-R	6-0	205	1-22-98	.307	.415	.567	73	306	254	45	78	21	0	15	49	46	3	0	3	79	0	0	15.0	25.8
Simon, Ronny	B-R	5-7	150	4-17-00	.240	.323	.391	96	416	363	63	87	17	4	10	44	43	4	1	5	90	26	10	10.3	21.6
Soria, Nate	R-R	5-8	175	11-24-95	.033	.094	.033	12	32	30	2	1	0	0	0	0	2	0	0	0	12	0	0	6.3	37.5
Turner, Gionti	R-R	6-2	178	8-17-00	.225	.310	.283	63	219	191	29	43	5	0	2	13	18	6	2	1	61	10	3	8.2	27.9
Williams, Alika	R-R	6-1	180	3-12-99	.237	.314	.417	42	175	156	21	37	11	1	5	23	15	3	0	1	34	3	1	8.6	19.4
Williams, Carson	R-R	6-1	180	6-25-03	.429	.538	.524	6	26	21	4	9	2	0	0	4	4	1	0	0	5	3	1	15.4	19.2

Pitching	B-T	Ht.	Wt.	DOB	W	L	ERA	G	GS	SV	IP	Hits	Runs	ER	HR	BB	SO	AVG	OBP	SLG	SO%	BB%	BF
Alvarez, Nelson L.	R-R	6-4	220	6-11-98	5	4	4.14	34	0	2	37	28	18	17	2	16	57	.214	.316	.275	37.0	10.4	154
Askew, Keyshawn	L-L	6-4	190	1-05-00	1	0	4.98	11	0	3	22	15	12	12	1	14	26	.192	.351	.256	26.8	14.4	97
Belge, Jeff	L-L	6-5	225	12-04-97	6	1	3.48	41	0	2	52	42	21	20	2	31	74	.213	.319	.305	32.3	13.5	229
Castaneda, Victor	R-R	6-1	185	8-27-98	0	0	3.86	3	0	0	7	6	3	3	2	0	8	.222	.276	.481	27.6	0.0	29
Dacosta, Franklin	L-L	5-11	162	2-27-00	0	1	7.88	8	0	2	16	20	14	14	3	15	17	.313	.444	.484	21.0	18.5	81
Doxakis, John	R-L	6-4	215	8-20-98	8	3	5.47	35	0	0	82	77	56	50	9	42	83	.248	.356	.435	22.4	11.4	370
Garcia, Carlos	R-R	6-3	185	11-28-98	3	1	4.06	20	0	0	38	29	18	17	3	24	49	.220	.352	.348	30.1	14.7	163
Gau, Chris	L-R	6-2	205	2-03-97	5	1	2.09	36	0	5	47	30	12	11	3	15	59	.182	.250	.321	31.9	8.1	185
Harney, Sean	L-R	6-0	190	7-10-98	0	0	5.06	4	0	0	5	4	4	3	1	2	6	.200	.292	.350	25.0	8.3	24
Hunley, Sean	R-R	6-4	220	7-05-99	5	5	3.62	22	22	0	97	90	49	39	13	19	89	.247	.301	.425	22.4	4.8	398
Jimenez, Antonio	L-L	5-11	145	5-06-01	4	0	2.83	25	1	2	48	39	15	15	10	25	51	.223	.320	.440	25.1	12.3	203
LaSorsa, Joe	L-L	6-5	215	4-29-98	0	0	0.00	2	0	0	3	1	0	0	0	0	2	.091	.091	.091	18.2	0.0	11
Lopez, Jacob	L-L	6-4	220	3-11-98	0	0	2.57	8	6	0	28	14	8	8	2	9	45	.144	.231	.237	41.7	8.3	108
Mejia, Enmanuel	R-R	5-11	185	12-22-98	3	3	4.85	33	0	7	39	31	29	21	6	22	61	.207	.320	.380	34.7	12.5	176
Menendez, Antonio	R-R	6-4	215	3-11-99	1	0	2.25	16	0	4	28	15	8	7	1	10	27	.156	.255	.240	24.5	9.1	110
Mercado, Michael	R-R	6-4	160	4-15-99	2	1	4.43	24	0	4	22	13	14	11	3	14	39	.165	.295	.354	40.6	14.6	96
Molina, Anthony	R-R	6-1	170	1-12-02	2	5	4.61	15	15	0	66	72	42	34	8	20	52	.266	.313	.413	17.7	6.8	294
Montgomery, Mason	L-L	6-2	195	6-17-00	5	4	4.18	25	25	0	108	98	55	50	18	49	131	.238	.330	.414	28.0	10.5	468
Munoz, Victor	R-R	6-3	160	12-25-00	8	7	7.49	26	12	0	79	93	66	66	10	33	64	.296	.371	.497	17.7	9.1	361
Ostberg, Erik	L-R	5-9	225	10-12-95	0	0	3.38	4	0	1	3	3	1	1	0	2	4	.273	.429	.364	28.6	14.3	14
Seymour, Ian	L-L	6-0	210	12-13-98	0	0	0.00	1	1	0	5	1	0	0	0	2	4	.071	.188	.143	25.0	12.5	16
Snyder, Jack	R-R	6-2	205	8-04-98	0	0	13.50	1	0	0	1	4	2	2	0	0	2	.500	.500	.875	25.0	0.0	8
Spraker, Graham	R-R	6-2	187	3-19-95	1	0	11.25	9	0	1	8	10	10	10	1	12	17	.294	.478	.500	37.0	26.1	46
Sterner, Justin	R-R	6-1	215	8-29-96	2	1	4.26	11	0	3	19	17	9	9	6	2	29	.246	.278	.507	40.3	2.8	72
Stinson, Graeme	L-L	6-5	250	8-06-97	3	6	5.96	29	2	1	45	43	32	30	5	30	51	.251	.384	.386	24.1	14.2	212
White, Colby	R-R	6-0	190	7-04-98	0	0	0.00	8	0	0	7	4	0	0	0	4	8	.160	.276	.160	27.6	13.8	29
Wicklander, Patrick	R-L	6-1	205	12-31-99	5	2	4.08	23	11	0	82	92	49	37	14	27	69	.285	.341	.471	19.3	7.5	358
Wilcox, Cole	R-R	6-5	232	7-14-99	6	8	5.23	25	25	0	107	95	71	62	14	44	99	.239	.326	.412	21.8	9.7	454
Wiles, Nathan	R-R	6-4	228	7-02-98	1	1	3.00	7	3	0	21	19	7	7	1	2	24	.241	.265	.380	28.9	2.4	83
Workman, Logan	R-R	6-4	215	12-06-98	4	4	4.12	15	15	0	63	67	38	29	7	21	71	.265	.324	.423	25.8	7.6	275
Zarraga, Alfredo	R-R	5-11	158	11-16-00	0	0	0.00	1	0	0	1	1	0	0	0	2	0	.250	.500	.250	0.0	33.3	6

Fielding

Catcher	PCT	G	PO	A	E	DP	PB
Alvarez	1.000	3	27	1	0	1	1
Driscoll	.986	52	506	39	8	3	6
Hunt	.987	33	351	15	5	3	1
Ostberg	.988	25	234	8	3	1	2
Parra	1.000	1	9	2	0	0	0
Piper	.989	21	177	11	2	1	1
Soria	.967	6	28	1	1	0	0

First Base	PCT	G	PO	A	E	DP
Driscoll	.989	11	88	2	1	6
Dyer	1.000	1	6	0	0	2
Edwards	.989	92	589	37	7	43
Murray	1.000	6	46	0	0	4
Ovalles	1.000	6	34	1	0	5
Seymour	.991	14	106	1	1	9
Shenton	.982	9	50	4	1	8

Second Base	PCT	G	PO	A	E	DP
Barreat	.000	1	0	0	0	0
Battles	1.000	4	5	6	0	0
Lopez	1.000	1	1	4	0	0
Murray	.973	26	45	63	3	10
Simon	.965	53	89	103	7	17
Turner	.983	45	73	99	3	27
Williams	.984	17	26	34	1	5

Third Base	PCT	G	PO	A	E	DP
Caminero	.912	63	31	93	12	6
Murray	.952	10	4	16	1	3
Shenton	.941	59	39	57	6	1
Simon	.857	7	3	9	2	1
Turner	.889	3	4	4	1	0

Shortstop	PCT	G	PO	A	E	DP
Battles	.976	15	8	33	1	5
Caminero	.948	20	24	31	3	6
Jones	.961	13	19	30	2	4
Lopez	.915	21	17	48	6	8
Murray	1.000	4	9	10	0	3
Simon	.930	34	41	65	8	13
Turner	.909	5	4	6	1	3
Williams, A	.964	27	31	50	3	7
Williams, C	.909	6	4	16	2	4

Outfield	PCT	G	PO	A	E	DP
Auer	.657	108	250	6	2	0
Baker	1.000	26	50	4	0	1
Driscoll	1.000	8	10	0	0	0
Dyer	1.000	10	13	1	0	0
Hernandez	.972	93	122	7	4	0
Infante	.987	60	97	7	2	2
Jones	.895	7	16	1	2	0
Ovalles	.976	20	34	1	1	0
Peters	.995	81	183	9	1	1
Shenton	1.000	1	1	0	0	0
Turner	.500	11	16	0	0	0

BOWLING GREEN HOT RODS — HIGH CLASS A

SOUTH ATLANTIC LEAGUE

Batting	B-T	Ht.	Wt.	DOB	AVG	OBP	SLG	G	PA	AB	R	H	2B	3B	HR	RBI	BB	HBP	SH	SF	SO	SB	CS	BB%	SO%
Baker, Dru	R-R	5-11	205	3-22-00	.307	.396	.491	90	377	326	58	100	11	5	13	39	40	9	1	1	86	38	3	10.6	22.8
Battles, Jalen	R-R	6-1	210	12-20-99	.232	.316	.344	68	254	224	35	52	5	1	6	31	23	5	1	1	69	3	6	9.1	27.2
Caminero, Junior	R-R	6-1	157	7-05-03	.356	.409	.685	36	159	146	30	52	9	3	11	32	10	3	0	0	40	2	1	6.3	25.2
Dyer, Matthew	R-R	6-2	185	7-14-98	.304	.304	.565	7	23	23	3	7	0	0	2	5	0	0	0	0	6	0	0	0.0	26.1
Fernandez, Mario	R-R	5-11	172	9-28-00	.219	.265	.344	12	36	32	5	7	1	0	1	5	1	1	2	0	11	0	0	2.8	30.6
Haas, Hunter	R-R	6-0	180	4-07-02	.177	.320	.258	19	75	62	10	11	2	0	1	4	11	2	0	0	24	2	0	14.7	32.0
Isaac, Xavier	L-L	6-3	240	12-17-03	.408	.491	.898	12	57	49	13	20	4	1	6	16	8	0	0	0	12	2	0	14.0	21.1
James, Kamren	R-R	6-2	205	5-25-00	.255	.326	.448	61	237	212	39	54	8	3	9	36	17	6	1	1	73	3	1	7.2	30.8
Jones, Brock	L-L	5-11	197	3-28-01	.201	.309	.412	85	372	318	49	64	14	4	15	49	48	3	0	3	123	10	7	12.9	33.1
Keegan, Dominic	R-R	6-0	210	8-01-00	.254	.367	.457	48	207	173	26	44	11	0	8	30	28	4	0	2	42	0	1	13.5	20.3
Manzueta, Oneill	R-R	5-11	190	2-07-01	.173	.274	.222	26	95	81	5	14	1	0	1	7	11	1	0	2	29	0	0	11.6	30.5
Murray, Tanner	R-R	6-1	190	9-03-99	.636	.667	.909	3	12	11	1	7	3	0	0	2	1	0	0	0	3	1	0	8.3	25.0
Parra, Jeffry	R-R	5-11	195	1-24-98	.273	.378	.435	51	180	154	22	42	10	0	5	19	20	6	0	0	39	0	0	11.1	21.7
Piper, Kenny	R-R	5-9	190	7-12-98	.216	.333	.458	70	270	227	36	49	12	2	13	35	29	12	0	2	65	3	1	10.7	24.1
Robertson, Blake	L-R	6-5	200	5-19-01	.278	.375	.424	98	365	316	57	88	13	3	9	42	43	6	0	0	95	1	1	11.8	26.0
Sasaki, Shane	R-R	5-11	165	7-01-00	.301	.375	.465	64	293	256	53	77	15	3	7	39	30	3	0	4	65	12	4	10.2	22.2
Schnell, Nick	L-R	6-1	180	3-27-00	.227	.308	.440	103	391	339	66	77	18	3	16	55	43	0	1	8	135	4	1	11.0	34.5
Seymour, Bobby	L-R	6-4	250	10-07-98	.310	.391	.556	58	248	216	42	67	12	1	13	42	27	3	0	2	71	1	1	10.9	28.6
Simpson, Chandler	L-R	6-2	170	11-18-00	.326	.429	.393	24	106	89	22	29	4	1	0	7	16	0	1	0	9	13	3	15.1	8.5
Soria, Nate	R-R	5-8	175	11-24-95	.243	.417	.270	16	48	37	5	9	1	0	0	5	5	6	0	0	17	0	1	10.4	35.4
Turner, Gionti	R-R	6-2	178	8-17-00	.100	.182	.150	15	46	40	1	4	2	0	0	3	2	2	2	0	13	1	0	4.3	28.3
Vasquez, Willy	R-R	6-2	191	9-06-01	.233	.310	.393	114	472	420	53	98	11	4	16	62	46	2	1	3	109	17	9	9.7	23.1
Williams, Carson	R-R	6-1	180	6-25-03	.254	.351	.506	105	462	401	69	102	18	7	23	77	53	7	0	1	147	17	9	11.5	31.8

Pitching	B-T	Ht.	Wt.	DOB	W	L	ERA	G	GS	SV	IP	Hits	Runs	ER	HR	BB	SO	AVG	OBP	SLG	SO%	BB%	BF
Alvarez, Nelson L.	R-R	6-4	220	6-11-98	2	1	2.30	10	0	2	16	12	6	4	0	6	22	.207	.313	.276	32.8	9.0	67
Askew, Keyshawn	L-L	6-4	190	1-05-00	8	6	3.70	24	9	2	75	58	40	31	6	32	104	.209	.311	.314	32.2	9.9	323
Ayala, Alexander	R-L	6-1	195	11-26-01	0	0	9.00	1	0	0	3	2	3	3	2	2	2	.182	.357	.727	14.3	14.3	14
Cook, Alex	R-R	6-2	220	3-29-01	3	0	1.59	6	0	0	17	9	4	3	0	6	26	.158	.238	.193	41.3	9.5	63
Cortorreal, Aneudy	R-R	6-3	200	12-13-99	2	3	5.77	33	0	0	48	45	35	31	4	46	70	.250	.412	.378	30.0	19.7	233
Curet, Yoniel	R-R	6-2	190	11-03-02	2	0	4.56	6	5	0	24	17	14	12	1	19	33	.200	.367	.259	30.3	17.4	109
Dacosta, Franklin	L-L	5-11	162	2-27-00	1	0	2.31	6	0	1	12	7	4	3	0	3	9	.175	.227	.200	20.5	6.8	44
Dahle, Nate	R-R	6-6	235	10-09-97	0	2	2.82	26	0	3	38	26	12	12	5	10	42	.191	.262	.346	28.2	6.7	149
Davitt, Duncan	R-R	6-3	235	9-23-99	3	4	4.38	18	11	0	62	58	35	30	9	20	73	.245	.309	.388	27.5	7.5	265
Erbe, Haden	R-R	6-3	225	8-13-98	2	2	5.01	25	1	2	41	34	30	23	9	16	63	.218	.309	.410	35.4	9.0	178
Fernandez, Mario	R-R	5-11	172	9-28-00	0	0	13.50	1	0	0	1	1	1	1	1	0	0	.333	.333	1.333	0.0	0.0	3
Galue, Over	R-R	6-2	188	7-31-01	0	1	3.18	3	1	0	6	6	3	2	0	7	2	.286	.483	.333	6.9	24.1	29
Garcia, Roel	R-R	6-4	245	11-21-98	4	8	3.84	20	14	0	80	74	47	34	9	37	80	.250	.339	.419	23.5	10.9	341
Gaston, Sandy	R-R	6-3	200	12-16-01	1	5	7.09	38	7	1	47	43	44	37	7	48	53	.249	.432	.434	23.0	20.9	230
Goss, JJ	R-R	6-3	185	12-25-00	6	6	5.21	22	22	0	95	86	63	55	16	49	90	.244	.340	.439	22.1	12.0	408
Hakanson, Jeff	R-R	6-0	185	8-04-98	2	1	3.80	14	3	0	24	20	10	10	1	7	35	.238	.290	.333	36.8	7.4	95
Halemanu, Cade	R-R	6-4	215	8-09-00	3	1	7.64	7	2	0	18	14	15	15	4	13	16	.219	.375	.438	20.0	16.3	80
Harney, Sean	L-R	6-0	190	7-10-98	3	0	2.81	21	13	0	64	52	22	20	3	22	61	.232	.307	.313	23.6	8.5	258
Jimenez, Antonio	L-L	5-11	145	5-06-01	2	2	5.10	11	1	2	30	33	18	17	2	10	31	.273	.333	.388	23.5	7.6	132
Locey, Tony	R-R	6-3	239	7-29-98	3	0	4.74	16	0	1	19	26	10	10	3	6	17	.325	.372	.475	19.8	7.0	86
Menendez, Antonio	R-R	6-4	215	3-11-99	2	0	4.70	22	1	2	31	24	16	16	0	21	26	.211	.343	.254	19.0	15.3	137
Munoz, Victor	R-R	6-3	160	12-25-00	1	0	0.00	1	0	0	3	1	0	0	0	2	4	.100	.250	.100	33.3	16.7	12
Peoples, Ben	L-R	6-1	175	5-01-01	4	6	4.06	22	22	0	84	76	40	38	7	45	96	.240	.338	.350	26.3	12.3	365
Reifert, Evan	R-R	6-4	190	5-14-99	0	0	6.75	5	0	0	4	0	3	3	0	8	7	.000	.450	.000	35.0	40.0	20
Seymour, Ian	L-L	6-0	210	12-13-98	0	0	2.08	2	2	0	9	4	2	2	1	5	9	.143	.265	.286	26.5	14.7	34
Snyder, Jack	R-R	6-2	205	8-04-98	0	0	0.00	1	0	0	2	0	0	0	0	0	3	.000	.000	.000	50.0	0.0	6
Soria, Nate	R-R	5-8	175	11-24-95	0	0	3.38	3	0	0	3	1	1	1	0	0	1	.111	.111	.222	11.1	0.0	9
Stinson, Graeme	L-L	6-5	250	8-06-97	1	0	3.00	2	0	0	3	3	1	1	0	3	7	.250	.438	.250	43.8	18.8	16
Vernon, Austin	R-R	6-8	265	2-08-99	7	4	6.12	29	6	2	82	79	62	56	14	55	108	.251	.366	.444	28.6	14.6	377
White, Colby	R-R	6-0	190	7-04-98	1	0	3.60	5	0	0	5	4	2	2	0	2	4	.222	.300	.333	20.0	10.0	20
Whitten, Kyle	R-R	6-3	190	9-22-98	1	4	3.19	32	0	7	48	45	23	17	5	18	48	.249	.312	.387	23.4	8.8	205
Wicklander, Patrick	R-L	6-1	205	12-31-99	1	1	3.41	7	7	0	29	31	12	11	3	11	33	.290	.358	.411	26.8	8.9	123
Zarraga, Alfredo	R-R	5-11	158	11-16-00	4	0	2.56	40	0	4	63	50	20	18	6	28	79	.216	.308	.355	29.9	10.6	264

Fielding

Catcher	PCT	G	PO	A	E	DP	PB
Fernandez	1.000	9	78	9	0	0	1
Keegan	1.000	37	380	21	0	1	2
Parra	.992	26	240	14	2	0	5
Piper	.980	49	469	33	10	5	2
Soria	.971	11	93	7	3	1	1

First Base	PCT	G	PO	A	E	DP
Dyer	1.000	1	2	0	0	1
Isaac	.932	9	63	6	5	7
Keegan	1.000	6	35	6	0	2
Parra	.957	8	43	1	2	7
Robertson	.983	67	444	26	8	38
Seymour	.994	42	294	17	2	23

Second Base	PCT	G	PO	A	E	DP
Battles	.980	53	79	121	4	28
Haas	1.000	12	17	33	0	10
James	.986	21	32	37	1	4
Murray	1.000	1	0	2	0	0
Turner	1.000	10	13	29	0	2
Vasquez	.922	37	70	72	12	22

Third Base	PCT	G	PO	A	E	DP
Battles	.957	9	10	12	1	3
Caminero	.873	28	17	45	9	1
Dyer	.667	1	0	2	1	0
James	.947	26	18	36	3	5
Murray	1.000	2	0	1	0	0
Robertson	.000	2	0	0	1	0
Turner	1.000	3	3	1	0	0
Vasquez	.945	60	57	80	8	5

Shortstop	PCT	G	PO	A	E	DP
Battles	1.000	6	5	12	0	2
Caminero	1.000	9	11	15	0	2
Haas	1.000	7	2	13	0	2
Vasquez	1.000	10	11	15	0	1
Williams	.985	100	119	220	5	47

Outfield	PCT	G	PO	A	E	DP
Baker	.988	87	132	9	2	1
Dyer	1.000	5	11	1	0	0
James	1.000	9	15	1	0	0
Jones	.922	75	138	4	2	1
Manzueta	1.000	23	39	1	0	1
Robertson	1.000	12	14	0	0	0
Sasaki	.954	61	98	1	2	0
Schnell	.979	97	135	5	3	1
Simpson	1.000	23	24	3	0	1
Turner	1.000	2	3	0	0	0

CHARLESTON RIVERDOGS — *LOW CLASS A*

CAROLINA LEAGUE

Batting	B-T	Ht.	Wt.	DOB	AVG	OBP	SLG	G	PA	AB	R	H	2B	3B	HR	RBI	BB	HBP	SH	SF	SO	SB	CS	BB%	SO%
Barete, Cristopher	L-L	5-7	155	12-10-01	.252	.318	.318	103	370	330	46	83	12	2	2	33	31	2	5	2	95	25	8	8.4	25.7
Barragan, Edwin	R-R	5-7	158	7-02-03	.209	.329	.284	24	80	67	13	14	2	0	1	7	11	1	1	0	21	1	0	13.8	26.3
Battles, Jalen	R-R	6-1	210	12-20-99	.158	.238	.211	7	21	19	0	3	1	0	0	3	2	0	0	0	8	0	0	9.5	38.1
Broecker, Bryan	R-R	6-2	200	1-26-02	.100	.262	.220	17	61	50	5	5	0	0	2	6	9	2	0	0	23	3	0	14.8	37.7
Castillo, Estanli	R-R	6-3	195	10-07-01	.203	.297	.273	38	145	128	18	26	6	0	1	15	16	1	0	0	46	2	0	11.0	31.7
Cermak, Ryan	R-R	6-0	205	6-02-01	.268	.346	.465	39	160	142	20	38	8	1	6	28	14	3	0	0	36	8	2	8.8	22.5
Colmenarez, Carlos	L-R	5-9	170	11-15-03	.201	.344	.304	83	346	283	42	57	9	1	6	28	52	10	0	1	132	10	11	15.0	38.2
De La Cruz, Willmer	B-R	5-8	168	4-06-03	.217	.250	.348	6	24	23	4	5	1	1	0	0	0	1	0	0	10	0	0	0.0	41.7
Delgado, Enderson	B-R	5-11	184	9-21-04	.103	.257	.172	9	35	29	1	3	2	0	0	1	3	3	0	0	11	0	0	8.6	31.4
Diaz, Jhon	L-L	5-7	160	10-01-02	.235	.321	.379	99	392	340	48	80	19	6	6	45	42	3	3	4	102	14	10	10.7	26.0
Fernandez, Mario	R-R	5-11	172	9-28-00	.139	.162	.167	11	38	36	4	5	1	0	0	3	1	0	1	0	14	0	0	2.6	36.8
Galarraga, Angel	L-R	6-1	178	8-01-02	.135	.220	.216	24	82	74	1	10	3	0	1	3	7	1	0	0	29	0	0	8.5	35.4
Isaac, Xavier	L-L	6-3	240	12-17-03	.266	.380	.462	90	376	312	58	83	16	3	13	56	56	4	0	4	80	10	0	14.9	21.3
James, Kamren	R-R	6-2	205	5-25-00	.204	.305	.336	43	174	152	15	31	6	1	4	18	15	7	0	0	45	4	5	8.6	25.9
Keegan, Dominic	R-R	6-0	210	8-01-00	.315	.402	.475	58	241	200	34	63	9	4	5	35	31	3	0	7	48	2	0	12.9	19.9
Kinney, Cooper	L-R	6-1	200	1-27-03	.274	.341	.393	121	505	456	61	125	24	0	10	61	42	5	0	2	107	3	5	8.3	21.2
Ledbetter, Colton	L-R	6-2	205	11-15-01	.254	.356	.397	18	74	63	11	16	6	0	1	8	10	0	0	0	16	2	2	13.5	21.6
Manzueta, Oneill	R-R	5-11	190	2-07-01	.172	.267	.258	28	105	93	8	16	3	1	1	2	10	2	0	0	42	1	0	9.5	40.0
Martinez, Raudelis	L-R	6-0	180	5-30-02	.210	.326	.286	33	129	105	14	22	2	0	2	18	17	3	0	4	18	3	1	13.2	14.0
Mateo, Angel	R-R	6-2	190	2-13-05	.244	.311	.293	12	45	41	3	10	2	0	0	3	3	1	0	0	14	3	1	6.7	31.1
Meza, Julio	R-R	6-0	165	5-04-99	.288	.336	.448	41	135	125	18	36	7	2	3	14	6	3	0	0	29	0	1	4.4	21.5
Millan, Santiago	R-R	6-2	174	5-27-03	.200	.238	.250	7	21	20	2	4	1	0	0	1	1	0	0	0	9	1	0	4.8	42.9
Morgan, Tre'	L-L	6-1	191	7-16-02	.389	.500	.472	11	44	36	7	14	1	1	0	2	8	0	0	0	2	4	1	18.2	4.5
Peguero, Odalys	B-R	5-9	172	1-25-03	.228	.349	.353	65	261	215	23	49	11	5	2	36	40	2	0	4	52	12	4	15.3	19.9
Simpson, Chandler	L-R	6-2	170	11-18-00	.285	.358	.333	91	397	354	66	101	9	4	0	24	38	2	3	0	35	81	12	9.6	8.8
Spikes, Ryan	R-R	5-8	185	3-13-03	.215	.302	.345	120	501	441	62	95	15	6	10	51	51	5	0	3	154	28	8	10.2	30.7
Taylor, Brayden	L-R	6-1	180	5-22-02	.244	.354	.512	22	96	82	15	20	3	2	5	15	14	0	0	0	31	9	0	14.6	32.3
Turner, Gionti	R-R	6-2	178	8-17-00	.000	.250	.000	1	4	3	0	0	0	0	0	0	1	0	0	0	1	0	0	25.0	25.0

Pitching	B-T	Ht.	Wt.	DOB	W	L	ERA	G	GS	SV	IP	Hits	Runs	ER	HR	BB	SO	AVG	OBP	SLG	SO%	BB%	BF
Ayala, Alexander	R-L	6-1	195	11-26-01	2	5	4.84	22	17	0	71	51	42	38	9	44	57	.199	.331	.348	18.3	14.1	311
Catalina, Neraldo	R-R	6-6	202	6-21-00	1	0	8.53	8	0	0	6	7	7	6	0	7	5	.280	.455	.360	15.2	21.2	33
Christianson, Jake	R-R	6-3	190	10-22-99	4	3	3.48	28	9	2	83	77	35	32	6	30	85	.245	.316	.366	24.2	8.5	351
Cook, Alex	R-R	6-2	220	3-29-01	4	3	3.67	29	0	4	49	35	23	20	7	18	65	.196	.273	.330	32.8	9.1	198
Cuevas, Jonny	R-R	6-3	200	11-20-00	6	9	4.93	25	20	0	102	108	66	56	8	38	74	.281	.348	.435	17.0	8.7	435
Curet, Yoniel	R-R	6-2	190	11-03-02	6	1	2.46	20	17	0	80	34	24	22	1	54	111	.132	.297	.171	34.4	16.7	323
Dahle, Nate	R-R	6-6	235	10-09-97	0	0	0.00	3	0	0	5	6	1	0	0	1	7	.286	.348	.286	30.4	4.3	23
Davitt, Duncan	R-R	6-3	235	9-23-99	2	0	6.87	10	0	1	18	17	17	14	2	6	19	.236	.304	.375	23.8	7.5	80
Gill Hill, Gary	R-R	6-2	160	9-20-04	0	1	7.36	2	2	0	4	5	3	3	0	2	3	.357	.471	.429	17.6	11.8	17
Hakanson, Jeff	R-R	6-0	185	8-04-98	0	1	4.50	16	1	0	26	20	13	13	2	12	39	.208	.306	.333	35.1	10.8	111
Halemanu, Cade	R-R	6-4	215	8-09-00	5	4	2.85	20	2	2	47	35	16	15	3	22	48	.206	.315	.288	24.0	11.0	200
Harney, Sean	L-R	6-0	190	7-10-98	1	0	11.12	4	0	0	6	5	7	7	1	2	9	.227	.320	.409	36.0	8.0	25
Hartman, Jack	R-R	6-3	205	7-13-98	4	3	3.38	43	0	3	53	53	28	20	2	22	61	.264	.336	.353	27.0	9.7	226
Johnson, Marcus	R-R	6-6	200	12-11-00	5	6	3.74	26	24	0	130	130	61	54	12	21	114	.258	.292	.413	21.3	3.9	536
Lancaster, Jackson	L-L	6-1	195	3-22-99	0	2	5.03	17	1	1	20	19	16	11	2	14	24	.241	.362	.367	25.5	14.9	94
Martin, Trevor	R-R	6-5	238	12-15-00	10	5	3.52	25	22	0	110	92	46	43	11	41	131	.227	.305	.370	28.7	9.0	456
Mejia, Samuel	R-R	6-1	160	6-17-02	0	0	5.59	5	0	1	10	10	7	6	2	4	16	.270	.386	.622	35.6	8.9	45
Meza, Julio	R-R	6-0	165	5-04-99	0	0	10.80	3	0	0	3	7	4	4	1	2	1	.438	.474	.750	5.3	10.5	19
Rodriguez, Juan	R-R	6-1	180	8-22-01	1	0	4.91	14	0	0	18	17	14	10	2	9	15	.246	.341	.435	18.3	11.0	82
Rosario, Gerlin	R-R	6-3	211	2-15-02	1	0	1.96	13	0	3	23	24	8	5	2	6	33	.261	.320	.391	33.0	6.0	100
Sansone, Michael	R-L	5-9	195	11-10-99	3	3	3.49	15	0	1	28	26	13	11	3	5	37	.243	.283	.383	32.7	4.4	113
Severino, Kikito	L-L	5-11	145	8-26-01	2	3	6.18	22	5	0	44	52	38	30	4	36	35	.299	.424	.448	16.1	16.5	218
Seymour, Ian	L-L	6-0	210	12-13-98	1	0	1.64	6	6	0	22	12	4	4	1	5	22	.171	.237	.243	28.6	6.5	77

Sommers, Drew	L-L	6-3	250	8-14-00	1	4	2.72	32	0	8	43	48	21	13	4	10	66	.271	.321	.373	34.7	5.3	190
Suarez, Santiago	R-R	6-2	175	1-11-05	1	2	2.29	5	5	0	20	21	9	5	1	3	14	.269	.293	.423	17.1	3.7	82
William, Junior	R-R	6-4	187	3-06-00	4	2	3.69	34	0	3	46	38	24	19	1	39	60	.221	.371	.302	28.0	18.2	214
Wyatt, Matt	R-R	6-4	215	9-26-00	2	8	4.75	35	0	5	55	46	35	29	3	30	59	.230	.339	.315	24.9	12.7	237

Fielding

Catcher	PCT	G	PO	A	E	DP	PB
Broecker	.978	15	126	9	3	0	3
Delgado	.985	6	59	7	1	1	2
Fernandez	.983	11	107	10	2	2	1
Galarraga	.992	16	123	6	1	0	3
Keegan	1.000	43	412	34	0	3	7
Martinez	.983	26	208	23	4	0	5
Meza	.975	19	177	16	5	0	2

First Base	PCT	G	PO	A	E	DP
Delgado	1.000	1	2	0	0	0
Isaac	.978	73	507	28	12	46
James	.950	2	16	3	1	2
Keegan	.974	9	68	6	2	8
Kinney	.992	32	226	9	2	19
Martinez	1.000	2	9	0	0	0
Meza	.989	13	88	4	1	10
Morgan	1.000	5	37	3	0	1

Second Base	PCT	G	PO	A	E	DP
Barragan	.926	6	12	13	2	2
Battles	1.000	1	0	1	0	1
Colmenarez	1.000	13	23	30	0	4
De La Cruz	.933	3	4	10	1	2
James	1.000	1	2	3	0	0
Kinney	.977	66	103	149	6	42
Peguero	.940	20	28	51	5	13
Simpson	.000	1	0	0	0	0
Spikes	.988	27	35	47	1	9

Third Base	PCT	G	PO	A	E	DP
Barragan	.952	16	15	25	2	4
Battles	.750	2	0	3	1	0
Colmenarez	1.000	6	4	14	0	2
De La Cruz	.667	1	1	1	1	0
James	.944	30	21	46	4	6
Peguero	.944	16	11	23	2	0
Spikes	.925	43	28	70	8	8
Taylor	.978	18	13	31	1	5

Shortstop	PCT	G	PO	A	E	DP
Battles	.917	3	5	6	1	2
Colmenarez	.897	63	64	144	24	25
De La Cruz	.857	2	1	5	1	2
Peguero	.915	21	29	36	6	6
Spikes	.949	44	59	91	8	23

Outfield	PCT	G	PO	A	E	DP
Barete	.973	99	171	10	3	3
Barragan	1.000	2	2	0	0	0
Castillo	.812	31	46	1	3	0
Cermak	1.000	34	75	7	0	1
Diaz	.981	88	155	3	3	0
James	1.000	5	9	0	0	0
Ledbetter	1.000	13	29	0	0	0
Manzueta	.933	23	40	2	3	0
Mateo	.925	12	17	0	2	0
Millan	1.000	6	7	1	0	1
Morgan	1.000	4	6	0	0	0
Simpson	1.000	88	138	5	0	2
Turner	.000	1	0	0	0	0

FCL RAYS

ROOKIE

FLORIDA COMPLEX LEAGUE

Batting	B-T	Ht.	Wt.	DOB	AVG	OBP	SLG	G	PA	AB	R	H	2B	3B	HR	RBI	BB	HBP	SH	SF	SO	SB	CS	BB%	SO%
Ariza, Luis	R-R	5-11	155	5-08-04	.281	.333	.406	21	69	64	8	18	5	0	1	8	4	1	0	0	14	0	0	5.8	20.3
Barragan, Edwin	R-R	5-7	158	7-02-03	.091	.355	.091	10	31	22	5	2	0	0	0	1	7	2	0	0	5	1	1	22.6	16.1
Barreat, Elis	R-R	5-9	158	5-22-03	.206	.282	.206	14	39	34	4	7	0	0	0	2	4	0	0	1	7	0	1	10.3	17.9
Broecker, Bryan	R-R	6-2	200	1-26-02	.313	.353	.313	4	17	16	4	5	0	0	0	3	1	0	0	0	2	0	0	5.9	11.8
Brooks, Robert	R-R	5-7	215	11-21-98	.222	.333	.222	9	21	18	1	4	0	0	0	0	3	0	0	0	6	0	0	14.3	28.6
Castillo, Estanli	R-R	6-3	195	10-07-01	.222	.222	.556	2	9	9	1	2	0	0	1	1	0	0	0	0	3	0	0	0.0	33.3
Cermak, Ryan	R-R	6-0	205	6-02-01	.231	.333	.308	4	15	13	2	3	1	0	0	0	1	1	0	0	1	0	0	6.7	6.7
Colmenarez, Carlos	L-R	5-9	170	11-15-03	.333	.417	.429	5	24	21	4	7	2	0	0	5	3	0	0	0	6	0	0	12.5	25.0
De La Cruz, Willmer	B-R	5-8	168	4-06-03	.172	.333	.190	22	76	58	6	10	1	0	0	9	13	2	1	2	18	6	1	17.1	23.7
Delgado, Enderson	B-R	5-11	184	9-21-04	.163	.285	.279	36	151	129	16	21	2	2	3	10	19	3	0	0	36	1	1	12.6	23.8
Galarraga, Angel	L-R	6-1	178	8-01-02	.289	.353	.378	17	51	45	5	13	4	0	0	5	5	0	0	1	8	1	0	9.8	15.7
Gonzalez, Ricardo	B-R	5-11	186	7-06-04	.245	.371	.310	46	186	155	21	38	7	0	1	15	29	2	0	0	35	4	8	15.6	18.8
Haas, Hunter	R-R	6-0	180	4-07-02	.250	.429	.563	5	21	16	2	4	2	0	1	2	5	0	0	0	3	0	1	23.8	14.3
Jimenez, Arison	R-R	5-10	153	11-05-02	.179	.302	.302	41	126	106	14	19	5	1	2	13	16	3	0	1	35	2	1	12.7	27.8
Ledbetter, Colton	L-R	6-2	205	11-15-01	.400	.500	.700	3	12	10	4	4	0	0	1	4	2	0	0	0	1	1	0	16.7	8.3
Lopez, Johan	R-R	5-11	167	7-28-00	.214	.214	.286	4	14	14	1	3	1	0	0	1	0	0	0	0	3	1	0	0.0	21.4
Lowe, Brandon	L-R	5-10	185	7-06-94	.333	.333	.333	1	3	3	0	1	0	0	0	0	0	0	0	0	1	0	0	0.0	33.3
Martinez, Raudelis	L-R	6-0	180	5-30-02	.180	.354	.246	19	79	61	8	11	4	0	0	10	17	0	0	1	10	0	0	21.5	12.7
Mateo, Angel	R-R	6-2	190	2-13-05	.256	.345	.390	48	197	172	31	44	7	2	4	27	14	10	0	1	36	12	0	7.1	18.3
Mead, Curtis	R-R	6-0	171	10-26-00	.167	.214	.250	4	14	12	0	2	1	0	0	4	1	0	0	1	1	0	0	7.1	7.1
Millan, Santiago	R-R	6-2	174	5-27-03	.333	.429	.417	4	14	12	3	4	1	0	0	3	2	0	0	0	5	0	0	14.3	35.7
Morgan, Tre'	L-L	6-1	191	7-16-02	.417	.417	.750	3	12	12	1	5	1	0	1	4	0	0	0	0	1	0	0	0.0	8.3
Murray, Tanner	R-R	6-1	190	9-03-99	.429	.467	.714	4	15	14	4	6	1	0	1	3	1	0	0	0	3	0	0	6.7	20.0
Ovalles, Alexander	L-L	6-0	184	10-06-00	.333	.714	.500	4	14	6	6	2	1	0	0	1	8	0	0	0	1	1	0	57.1	7.1
Paulino, Enzo	L-R	5-11	179	5-25-04	.230	.300	.350	31	110	100	14	23	6	0	2	18	8	2	0	0	24	0	0	7.3	21.8
Peguero, Odalys	B-R	5-9	172	1-25-03	.105	.190	.158	5	21	19	2	2	1	0	0	0	2	0	0	0	6	0	0	9.5	28.6
Pena, Jose	R-R	6-0	185	12-24-02	.333	.455	.333	4	11	9	1	3	0	0	0	3	1	1	0	0	3	1	0	9.1	27.3
Petiyan, Elias	B-R	5-10	160	12-03-01	.171	.310	.200	17	42	35	3	6	1	0	0	0	7	0	0	0	15	0	1	16.7	35.7
Pinto, Rene	R-R	5-10	195	11-02-96	.500	.500	.500	2	6	6	1	3	0	0	0	1	0	0	0	0	1	0	0	0.0	16.7
Piron, Jhonny	R-R	5-10	165	2-06-04	.190	.280	.250	36	132	116	10	22	5	1	0	12	11	4	0	1	34	6	4	8.3	25.8
Polanco, Narciso	L-R	5-10	161	10-28-04	.210	.300	.280	44	180	157	19	33	2	3	1	15	19	2	0	2	35	3	3	10.6	19.4
Rangel, Roylems	R-R	5-8	163	10-17-02	.235	.350	.294	10	20	17	1	4	1	0	0	2	2	1	0	0	6	0	0	10.0	30.0
Rodriguez, Nathanael	R-R	6-0	155	12-06-03	.300	.333	.350	8	21	20	5	6	1	0	0	1	1	0	0	0	8	0	0	4.8	38.1
Salguera, Felix	R-R	6-0	171	3-01-02	.385	.500	.462	5	16	13	3	5	1	0	0	1	2	1	0	0	0	0	0	12.5	0.0
Sanabria, Jose	R-R	6-1	180	2-10-05	.150	.271	.167	19	70	60	5	9	1	0	0	3	9	1	0	0	21	1	2	12.9	30.0
Sandoval, Joshuan	R-R	6-2	215	12-18-97	.200	.261	.400	8	23	20	1	4	1	0	1	2	2	0	0	1	10	0	0	8.7	43.5
Santana, Adrian	B-R	5-11	155	7-18-05	.205	.340	.256	10	47	39	6	8	2	0	0	3	7	1	0	0	9	3	0	14.9	19.1
Sasaki, Shane	R-R	5-11	165	7-01-00	.250	.438	.417	4	16	12	2	3	0	1	0	0	4	0	0	0	4	4	0	25.0	25.0
Seymour, Bobby	L-R	6-4	250	10-07-98	.182	.308	.182	3	13	11	3	2	0	0	0	0	2	0	0	0	4	0	0	15.4	30.8
Shin, Wooyeoul	R-R	6-0	215	12-30-01	.143	.231	.286	7	26	21	4	3	1	1	0	6	3	0	0	2	3	0	0	11.5	11.5
Tamares, Miguel	B-R	5-10	150	9-06-04	.157	.271	.235	13	59	51	8	8	1	0	1	3	7	1	0	0	18	5	0	11.9	30.5
Taylor, Brayden	L-R	6-1	180	5-22-02	.222	.417	.556	3	12	9	4	2	1	1	0	0	3	0	0	0	3	2	0	25.0	25.0
Valera, Victor	B-R	5-9	146	10-15-02	.333	.394	.367	10	33	30	4	10	1	0	0	4	3	0	0	0	6	5	1	9.1	18.2

Pitching	B-T	Ht.	Wt.	DOB	W	L	ERA	G	GS	SV	IP	Hits	Runs	ER	HR	BB	SO	AVG	OBP	SLG	SO%	BB%	BF
Alberto, Alexander	R-R	6-8	190	11-02-01	1	3	5.79	11	3	0	28	13	20	18	0	23	32	.140	.339	.194	26.4	19.0	121
Almonte, Adrian	L-L	6-4	199	3-04-03	0	0	0.00	2	0	0	2	1	0	0	0	4	0	.250	.556	.250	0.0	44.4	9
Arredondo, Baltazar	L-L	6-1	175	1-22-04	0	0	11.25	4	0	0	4	3	5	5	0	7	5	.214	.500	.357	22.7	31.8	22
Barnhart, Hunter	R-R	6-2	205	2-14-02	0	0	3.00	3	1	0	3	2	1	1	0	2	5	.182	.357	.182	35.7	14.3	14
Barrios, Orlando	R-R	6-6	180	8-27-01	0	0	4.73	12	0	2	13	13	13	7	2	7	11	.250	.349	.385	17.5	11.1	63
Boucher, Adam	R-R	6-5	235	10-29-01	1	0	4.50	2	0	0	2	2	1	1	0	3	5	.250	.455	.250	45.5	27.3	11
Castaneda, Victor	R-R	6-1	185	8-27-98	1	0	0.00	3	1	0	4	2	0	0	0	2	6	.154	.267	.154	40.0	13.3	15
Catalina, Neraldo	R-R	6-6	202	6-21-00	1	1	6.75	3	0	0	3	2	2	2	0	1	2	.200	.273	.300	18.2	9.1	11
Chavez, Seth	R-R	6-2	200	10-04-99	0	0	2.45	3	0	0	4	2	1	1	0	3	5	.182	.375	.455	29.4	17.6	17
Cruz, Samuel	R-R	6-3	160	1-09-02	0	0	21.60	2	0	0	2	3	4	4	0	2	2	.375	.500	.375	20.0	20.0	10
De Jesus, Cesar	L-L	6-1	140	9-28-03	1	2	2.88	16	0	1	25	18	14	8	1	23	30	.200	.376	.300	25.4	19.5	118
De La Rosa, Manuel	L-L	6-0	155	4-20-03	2	1	3.14	16	1	1	29	29	17	10	0	22	40	.252	.390	.287	28.4	15.6	141
Fairbanks, Pete	R-R	6-6	225	12-16-93	0	0	0.00	1	1	0	1	0	0	0	0	0	2	.000	.000	.000	66.7	0.0	3
Faucher, Calvin	R-R	6-1	190	9-22-95	0	0	0.00	1	0	0	1	2	1	0	0	1	0	.333	.429	.333	0.0	14.3	7
Fleming, Josh	L-L	6-2	220	5-18-96	0	0	0.00	1	1	0	2	0	0	0	0	0	2	.000	.000	.000	33.3	0.0	6
Florian, Renaldito	R-R	5-11	161	3-26-02	0	0	5.40	11	0	1	15	8	14	9	2	16	13	.154	.361	.269	18.1	22.2	72
Fondtain, T.J.	L-L	6-4	210	2-22-01	0	0	9.00	1	0	0	1	2	1	1	0	0	1	.400	.500	.400	16.7	0.0	6
Fowler, Dalton	L-L	6-7	200	1-07-00	0	0	9.00	2	0	0	3	3	3	3	0	2	7	.250	.400	.333	46.7	13.3	15
Gill Hill, Gary	R-R	6-2	160	9-20-04	1	4	5.30	12	10	0	37	45	25	22	3	17	36	.294	.379	.392	20.7	9.8	174
Gonzalez, Cristhofer	R-R	6-3	166	12-18-04	1	0	6.75	12	0	0	17	18	15	13	3	17	21	.277	.425	.446	24.1	19.5	87
Hernandez, Luis	R-R	6-4	195	4-01-01	2	3	3.81	12	1	1	28	26	16	12	1	17	39	.241	.366	.352	29.8	13.0	131
Hernandez, Maikel	R-R	6-1	184	6-08-05	0	5	5.17	11	9	0	38	54	24	22	2	13	31	.346	.402	.487	17.8	7.5	174
Javier, Sebastian	R-R	6-1	185	12-26-03	0	1	6.23	12	0	1	17	12	18	12	0	24	16	.218	.471	.218	18.8	28.2	85
Kelley, Trevor	R-R	6-2	210	10-20-92	1	0	0.00	1	0	0	1	0	0	0	0	0	1	.000	.000	.000	33.3	0.0	3
Kittredge, Andrew	R-R	6-1	230	3-17-90	0	0	0.00	3	0	0	3	1	0	0	0	0	6	.100	.100	.200	60.0	0.0	10
Lancaster, Jackson	L-L	6-1	195	3-22-99	0	1	1.23	5	0	3	7	4	2	1	0	2	18	.160	.222	.160	66.7	7.4	27
Mejia, Samuel	R-R	6-1	160	6-17-02	4	1	1.46	16	0	3	25	13	6	4	1	4	32	.159	.247	.232	34.4	4.3	93
Muller, Chris	R-R	6-5	210	4-22-96	0	0	0.00	6	0	0	5	2	0	0	0	0	8	.118	.118	.118	47.1	0.0	17
Murphy, Chandler	L-R	6-3	203	12-18-00	0	0	0.00	3	0	0	3	3	0	0	0	3	4	.250	.400	.250	26.7	20.0	15
Nichols, T.J.	R-R	6-5	189	6-24-02	0	0	0.00	3	2	0	5	2	0	0	0	1	4	.118	.167	.118	22.2	5.6	18
Reifert, Evan	R-R	6-4	190	5-14-99	0	0	9.82	4	1	0	4	1	5	4	0	7	5	.091	.545	.091	22.7	31.8	22
Rodriguez, Elvin	R-R	6-3	160	3-31-98	0	0	3.86	1	1	0	2	3	1	1	0	1	5	.273	.333	.273	41.7	8.3	12
Rosario, Gerlin	R-R	6-3	211	2-15-02	2	2	1.96	7	0	0	18	11	5	4	1	7	16	.169	.270	.292	21.6	9.5	74
Sanchez, Ramon	R-R	6-3	160	11-14-01	0	1	2.35	9	0	0	15	9	6	4	1	13	15	.170	.348	.245	21.7	18.8	69
Seymour, Ian	L-L	6-0	210	12-13-98	0	0	1.35	4	4	0	7	4	1	1	0	4	11	.167	.286	.208	39.3	14.3	28
Snelsire, Hayden	R-R	6-1	213	1-16-01	0	0	0.00	3	0	0	3	2	0	0	0	0	2	.200	.200	.200	20.0	0.0	10
Sosa, Jeromy	L-L	6-7	175	2-19-03	1	0	4.50	2	0	0	2	0	1	1	0	5	2	.000	.556	.000	22.2	55.6	9
Stevens, Will	R-R	6-2	210	7-18-01	0	0	9.00	3	0	0	3	4	3	3	0	4	2	.308	.471	.538	11.8	23.5	17
Stevenson, Owen	R-R	6-4	205	9-01-02	0	0	0.00	2	0	0	2	2	0	0	0	2	0	.333	.500	.333	0.0	25.0	8
Suarez, Santiago	R-R	6-2	175	1-11-05	4	0	1.13	10	3	1	40	28	5	5	0	8	38	.199	.242	.270	25.3	5.3	150
Tavarez, Andri	L-L	6-1	165	5-23-03	2	1	8.22	10	0	0	8	12	10	7	2	7	9	.333	.442	.611	20.9	16.3	43
Urbina, Jose	R-R	6-3	180	11-02-05	0	3	5.32	11	8	0	24	23	15	14	4	12	21	.258	.371	.461	20.0	11.4	105
White, Colby	R-R	6-0	190	7-04-98	0	0	1.74	11	5	0	10	3	2	2	0	11	12	.111	.368	.111	31.6	28.9	38
Wild, Owen	R-R	6-2	230	7-30-02	0	0	0.00	1	0	0	1	1	0	0	0	0	2	.250	.250	.250	50.0	0.0	4
Workman, Logan	R-R	6-4	215	12-06-98	0	0	0.00	3	2	0	7	3	0	0	0	1	7	.150	.190	.150	33.3	4.8	21

Fielding

C: Delgado 21, Martinez 11, Ariza 10, Rangel 9, Galarraga 8, Broecker 4, Brooks 3, Salguera 3, Pinto 2, Sandoval 1. **1B:** Paulino 12, Ariza 11, Delgado 9, Martinez 7, Petiyan 5, Sandoval 5, Shin 4, Brooks 2, Morgan 2, Barreat 1, Seymour 1, Rangel 1. **2B:** Polanco 14, Gonzalez 12, Barreat 9, Valera 8, De La Cruz 6, Haas 3, Tamares 3, Peguero 2, Santana 2, Lopez 2, Barragan 2, Colmenarez 1, Murray 1, Rodriguez 1. **3B:** Polanco 14, Gonzalez 12, De La Cruz 11, Rodriguez 6, Barragan 4, Taylor 3, Valera 2, Barreat 2, Mead 2, Peguero 2, Petiyan 1, Murray 1, Lopez 1. **SS:** Gonzalez 22, Polanco 16, Santana 8, Tamares 7, Colmenarez 2, Barragan 1, Haas 1, Lopez 1. **OF:** Mateo 47, Jimenez 40, Piron 36, Paulino 18, Sanabria 15, Petiyan 8, Shin 3, Pena 3, Ledbetter 3, Millan 3, Cermak 3, Ovalles 3, Sasaki 2, Morgan 1, Barragan 1, Barreat 1, Castillo 1.

DSL RAYS — *ROOKIE*

DOMINICAN SUMMER LEAGUE

Batting	B-T	Ht.	Wt.	DOB	AVG	OBP	SLG	G	PA	AB	R	H	2B	3B	HR	RBI	BB	HBP	SH	SF	SO	SB	CS	BB%	SO%
Aybar, Nicandro	B-R	6-1	170	9-08-04	.277	.371	.404	49	222	188	37	52	5	5	3	29	29	1	0	3	33	11	6	13.1	14.9
Blanco, Carlos	L-R	6-0	175	1-23-04	.254	.324	.341	37	139	126	30	32	9	1	0	21	11	2	0	0	29	5	2	7.9	20.9
Chauran, Kleiver	B-R	5-11	165	11-23-05	.253	.370	.335	45	189	158	27	40	8	1	1	17	27	3	0	1	38	7	4	14.3	20.1
Contreras, Jose	R-R	6-1	200	5-05-05	.172	.291	.356	25	103	87	12	15	5	1	3	14	13	2	0	1	35	2	3	12.6	34.0
Cotes, Felix	B-R	5-11	176	8-13-05	.259	.394	.466	19	71	58	18	15	4	1	2	10	13	0	0	0	17	4	1	18.3	23.9
De Sousa, Carlos	R-R	6-1	166	2-24-06	.172	.268	.212	32	112	99	8	17	4	0	0	13	13	0	0	0	42	2	0	11.6	37.5
Frias, Alan	R-R	6-2	206	10-26-05	.164	.330	.301	25	91	73	12	12	2	1	2	11	14	4	0	0	37	4	0	15.4	40.7
Garcia, Yirer	R-R	5-11	165	9-18-05	.227	.360	.286	47	186	154	27	35	2	2	1	14	28	4	0	0	21	5	1	15.1	11.3
Guerrero, Brailer	L-R	6-1	215	6-25-06	.261	.379	.391	7	29	23	3	6	3	0	0	5	4	1	0	1	6	0	1	13.8	20.7
Guillen, Xavier	B-R	5-10	167	9-02-04	.283	.371	.406	36	159	138	24	39	4	5	1	17	17	3	0	1	41	12	5	10.7	25.8
Martinez, Alfonzo	R-R	6-0	180	11-28-05	.207	.345	.234	44	177	145	20	30	4	0	0	10	27	4	0	1	46	14	1	15.3	26.0
Martinez, Larry	R-R	5-11	170	8-06-05	.370	.388	.457	13	49	46	7	17	4	0	0	10	2	0	0	1	5	2	1	4.1	10.2
Monzon, Jose	L-R	6-0	160	11-17-05	.280	.395	.421	46	205	164	30	46	6	1	5	39	35	0	0	6	30	6	3	17.1	14.6
Moreno, Moises	R-R	6-2	169	11-01-05	.206	.321	.284	45	165	141	21	29	7	2	0	6	22	2	0	0	43	3	3	13.3	26.1
Moris, Yohangel	B-R	6-0	160	11-22-05	.167	.300	.256	28	110	90	16	15	4	2	0	7	15	3	0	2	50	7	1	13.6	45.5
Oliver, Jordany	R-R	6-0	160	1-11-05	.207	.304	.233	47	172	150	23	31	2	1	0	7	20	1	1	0	60	11	5	11.6	34.9
Palma, Alberth	R-R	6-0	170	2-02-06	.163	.222	.163	13	55	49	6	8	0	0	0	4	4	0	1	1	9	1	2	7.3	16.4
Peguero, Juanfel	B-R	5-11	142	12-31-04	.236	.339	.286	43	187	161	22	38	6	1	0	21	22	3	0	0	33	15	4	11.8	17.6

Perez, Jhonny	R-R	5-11	195	3-11-05	.151	.233	.233	42	163	146	21	22	3	0	3	16	14	2	0	1	51	6	0	8.6	31.3
Perez, Jose	R-R	5-9	170	3-12-04	.277	.473	.513	50	171	119	31	33	5	7	3	27	42	5	2	3	32	3	4	24.6	18.7
Pulinario, Juan	R-R	5-11	185	4-10-06	.248	.343	.345	46	170	145	27	36	8	0	2	24	18	4	1	2	53	12	0	10.6	31.2
Rodriguez, Alfredo	R-R	5-11	187	9-09-05	.227	.382	.340	33	123	97	16	22	1	2	2	13	21	4	0	1	37	0	2	17.1	30.1
Santana, John	L-R	6-3	176	9-24-05	.227	.356	.533	23	91	75	14	17	5	3	4	15	13	2	1	0	35	2	0	14.3	38.5
Suarez, Wilson	B-R	5-11	183	6-17-05	.247	.378	.329	32	90	73	17	18	3	0	1	9	14	2	0	1	20	4	2	15.6	22.2
Tapia, Roosbert	R-R	6-2	177	6-23-05	.270	.373	.355	42	166	141	29	38	6	3	0	19	22	2	0	1	31	11	0	13.3	18.7
Tea, Railin	B-R	5-9	162	7-20-06	.256	.324	.404	43	173	156	27	40	5	6	2	24	13	3	0	1	34	18	5	7.5	19.7
Tovar, Jose	R-R	5-10	168	11-23-05	.228	.378	.351	37	143	114	15	26	4	2	2	14	24	4	0	1	47	0	1	16.8	32.9
Trinidad, Wilian	L-R	5-8	165	10-06-05	.270	.391	.333	50	230	189	39	51	9	0	1	27	38	1	0	2	46	16	9	16.5	20.0
Vasquez, Neifi	R-R	6-4	173	9-22-03	.245	.336	.432	52	223	192	37	47	14	2	6	31	26	2	0	3	52	14	4	11.7	23.3
Zamudio, Edwin	L-R	6-2	195	9-17-02	.000	.000	.000	18	1	1	0	0	0	0	0	0	0	0	0	0	0	0	0	0.0	0.0

Pitching	**B-T**	**Ht.**	**Wt.**	**DOB**	**W**	**L**	**ERA**	**G**	**GS**	**SV**	**IP**	**Hits**	**Runs**	**ER**	**HR**	**BB**	**SO**	**AVG**	**OBP**	**SLG**	**SO%**	**BB%**	**BF**
Alfonseca, Landany	R-R	6-1	160	3-09-05	1	1	8.36	12	0	1	14	13	17	13	3	26	12	.228	.482	.421	14.1	30.6	85
Bautista, Luis	R-R	6-1	180	10-07-02	1	1	5.32	14	0	1	22	17	13	13	1	18	20	.230	.392	.311	20.6	18.6	97
Benua, Alendry	R-R	5-11	164	8-18-05	2	2	10.07	15	1	1	22	28	27	25	3	13	21	.311	.425	.522	18.6	11.5	113
Berbesi, Alan	R-R	5-3	189	8-20-02	2	0	4.73	7	0	0	13	10	7	7	0	4	12	.213	.275	.234	23.5	7.8	51
Cabral, Ismael	R-R	6-1	194	12-19-03	6	1	4.94	13	0	0	24	22	17	13	1	17	15	.253	.396	.448	13.5	15.3	111
Cabrera, Baldemix	R-R	6-2	191	3-28-03	0	1	2.65	6	5	0	17	16	10	5	2	4	10	.246	.286	.400	14.3	5.7	70
Campos, Alexander	R-R	6-1	190	4-14-03	1	1	1.64	14	0	3	22	18	8	4	2	4	21	.228	.262	.342	25.0	4.8	84
Canizalez, Joel	R-R	6-1	185	9-22-02	0	0	3.90	10	9	0	32	30	18	14	1	12	23	.246	.321	.320	16.8	8.8	137
Castro, Cesar	R-R	6-1	205	7-14-05	0	0	5.56	8	0	0	11	13	9	7	1	8	10	.277	.397	.447	16.9	13.6	59
Clemente, Jharold	R-R	5-10	200	8-05-02	1	2	3.04	8	7	0	24	18	10	8	2	11	26	.209	.320	.349	25.7	10.9	101
De Los Santos, Jhoan	R-R	6-2	170	1-19-05	2	0	3.86	5	1	0	7	6	4	3	0	10	6	.273	.529	.318	17.1	28.6	35
Eusebio, Oliver	R-R	6-0	200	1-05-05	1	3	3.38	17	0	2	27	23	14	10	1	13	22	.230	.319	.300	19.0	11.2	116
Fransua, Victor	R-R	6-1	180	8-13-00	3	2	2.48	18	0	1	29	22	13	8	0	19	31	.210	.320	.248	24.2	14.8	128
Gamez, Alvaro	L-L	6-3	175	2-19-05	0	1	4.10	12	0	0	26	21	15	12	1	15	19	.219	.342	.323	16.7	13.2	114
Garcia, Engert	R-R	5-11	190	4-30-00	3	3	1.58	11	9	0	46	36	16	8	2	8	45	.217	.272	.331	24.9	4.4	181
Hilario, Danny	R-R	6-0	185	9-17-04	2	1	4.38	13	0	2	25	16	12	12	2	16	27	.190	.340	.286	26.2	15.5	103
Infante, Jordi	R-R	6-3	193	10-10-04	0	1	19.44	8	0	0	8	17	18	18	4	10	4	.415	.556	.805	7.4	18.5	54
Jimenez, Jhomber	R-R	6-3	198	12-24-05	1	2	6.83	12	6	0	29	30	26	22	2	20	28	.256	.379	.350	20.0	14.3	140
Juarez, Josue	R-R	6-1	207	5-03-03	1	2	3.76	12	10	0	41	30	21	17	4	14	30	.199	.288	.351	17.6	8.2	170
Laureano, Ismael	R-R	6-0	162	7-02-05	1	0	10.38	14	0	0	17	20	22	20	3	19	10	.303	.462	.470	11.0	20.9	91
Lendof, Javier	R-R	6-0	198	9-20-03	2	0	6.43	11	1	0	14	7	12	10	0	32	15	.163	.532	.233	19.0	40.5	79
Lugo, Yannelbinson	R-R	6-0	166	1-13-04	0	5	5.23	16	6	1	33	43	30	19	1	18	29	.323	.417	.466	18.5	11.5	157
Marte, Alexander	R-R	6-2	200	1-07-01	3	2	8.02	16	0	1	21	26	25	19	4	22	20	.310	.459	.476	17.9	19.6	112
Mateo, Yordi	R-R	6-3	202	3-16-05	1	0	4.50	4	0	0	4	3	2	2	0	6	3	.214	.450	.286	15.0	30.0	20
Medina, Leofanny	R-R	6-4	215	4-14-02	1	1	2.45	10	0	1	15	11	7	4	0	18	20	.204	.403	.241	27.8	25.0	72
Medina, Roberto	L-L	6-1	170	1-19-05	0	3	3.68	11	11	0	37	28	20	15	2	29	53	.209	.365	.299	31.7	17.4	167
Palma, Moises	R-R	6-4	195	9-01-04	4	1	4.40	17	0	0	31	25	20	15	3	14	26	.240	.333	.413	21.0	11.3	124
Primera, Jorman	R-R	6-2	170	12-18-01	1	0	16.88	3	0	0	3	6	5	5	0	0	1	.429	.429	.571	7.1	0.0	14
Radney, Chariel	L-L	6-0	189	3-27-05	0	0	14.54	5	1	0	4	4	8	7	1	5	2	.235	.480	.471	8.0	20.0	25
Ramos, Geudis	L-L	6-1	175	2-16-05	0	0	5.56	7	0	0	11	7	8	7	1	14	15	.171	.414	.293	25.9	24.1	58
Rodriguez, Andy	R-R	6-1	182	7-28-02	1	1	3.60	7	0	3	10	7	4	4	0	7	14	.194	.341	.250	31.8	15.9	44
Rojas, Cesar	R-R	6-3	162	5-12-02	0	0	15.00	4	0	0	3	1	6	5	0	11	1	.100	.591	.100	4.5	50.0	22
Roman, Endry	R-R	6-5	196	7-23-02	2	1	3.21	15	1	1	28	22	11	10	0	12	33	.224	.316	.296	28.9	10.5	114
Russell, Jonathan	R-R	6-1	180	3-14-05	1	2	1.00	11	11	0	36	23	9	4	0	14	34	.184	.278	.224	23.4	9.7	145
Saturria, Michael	R-R	6-4	190	9-01-02	1	1	1.82	18	0	6	30	17	9	6	0	8	50	.172	.248	.232	45.9	7.3	109
Savinon, Starlin	L-L	6-0	182	10-30-04	4	1	7.45	15	0	0	19	19	19	16	2	21	21	.264	.438	.389	21.9	21.9	96
Teus, Yereny	L-L	5-10	157	8-01-03	2	3	2.89	12	10	0	44	32	15	14	1	17	50	.213	.310	.253	28.2	9.6	177
Toscano, Miguel	R-R	6-3	170	5-12-06	0	1	4.97	12	10	0	42	43	26	23	5	15	28	.272	.339	.449	15.6	8.3	180
Valdez, Alexis	R-R	6-3	194	6-02-05	2	1	5.68	14	0	3	19	17	17	12	0	17	31	.227	.396	.253	32.3	17.7	96
Ventura, Wander	R-R	6-2	170	2-26-03	0	3	3.90	10	10	0	28	28	12	12	0	9	21	.264	.358	.340	17.1	7.3	123
Zamudio, Edwin	L-R	6-2	195	9-17-02	4	2	2.54	17	0	4	28	19	14	8	1	11	20	.200	.300	.295	18.2	10.0	110
Zuniga, Keyner	R-R	6-3	165	12-16-05	0	1	5.65	10	1	0	14	10	10	9	1	13	14	.213	.412	.319	20.6	19.1	68

Fielding

C: Tovar 25, Garcia 24, De Sousa 21, Rodriguez 20, Suarez 15, Perez 11, Blanco 7, Martinez 4. **1B:** Perez 53, Tapia 19, Blanco 17, Suarez 16, Martinez 6, Garcia 5, De Sousa 4. **2B:** Tea 41, Trinidad 27, Aybar 15, Monzon 9, Cotes 8, Perez 5, Moris 4, Peguero 3, Palma 2, Guillen 2, Blanco 1, Chauran 1, Suarez 1. **3B:** Chauran 25, Perez 23, Aybar 21, Trinidad 11, Monzon 10, Tapia 9, Peguero 8, Moris 7, Guillen 4, Palma 3, Tea 1, Blanco 1. **SS:** Peguero 36, Monzon 25, Chauran 15, Aybar 12, Trinidad 12, Moris 8, Palma 5, Cotes 5, Perez 1. **OF:** Vasquez 53, Pulinario 48, Oliver 47, Moreno 45, Martinez 43, Guillen 29, Contreras 23, Frias 20, Santana 20, Blanco 16, Guerrero 7, Perez 4, Zamudio 1.

Texas Rangers

TEXAS RANGERS

SEASON SYNOPSIS: A late-season swoon cost the Rangers an AL West division crown and caused plenty of heartburn, but it will all be forgotten now. Thanks to a magical run through the postseason, the Rangers are no longer one of the few remaining MLB teams to never win a World Series. Now, they are the toast of Texas.

HIGH POINT: The Rangers pummeled opponents to jump out to a 40-20 start, but as good as that run was, it won't be remembered nearly as well as the team's excellent October. The Rangers outscored their opponents 97-66 while going 13-4 in the postseason.

LOW POINT: After that 40-20 start, Texas was 50-52 over the final 102 regular season games. The Rangers spent only one day out of first place from Opening Day until mid-August. But a 4-16 stretch dropped the Rangers from first to third. Texas' playoff hopes seemed to take a hit when they lost three of four to Seattle to end the regular season. That allowed Houston to streal the AL West crown.

NOTABLE ROOKIES: Outfielder Evan Carter wasn't called up until Sept. 8, but from the day he arrived until the World Series celebration, he was one of the Rangers' best hitters while also providing exceptional defense. Carter hit 306/.413/.645 in the regular season and .300/.417/.500 in the postseason. Lefthander Cody Bradford had an unremarkable regular season as he swung between the rotation and the bullpen, but he posted a 1.17 ERA over five postseason appearances.

KEY TRANSACTIONS: The offseason addition of Jacob deGrom fizzled as an elbow injury meant he missed almost the entire season. The signing of Nathan Eovaldi had a much bigger immediate payoff. Eovaldi went 12-5, 3.63 in the regular season, but his postseason impact was even bigger. Eovaldi won five of the Rangers' 13 postseason victories. The Rangers traded second baseman Thomas Saggese and righthander Tekoah Roby to the Cardinals in July to add lefthander Jordan Montgomery. He was an astute addition. Montgomery went 4-2, 2.79 after the trade and was the key in Texas' ALCS win over the Astros. Montgomery went 2-0, 1.29 in two starts and a Game 7 ALCS relief appearance.

DOWN ON THE FARM: First rounder Wyatt Langford had one of the best post-draft debuts in years. He hit .360/.480/.677 while reaching Triple-A.

OPENING DAY PAYROLL: $195,869,490 (9th).

PLAYERS OF THE YEAR

MAJOR LEAGUE

Corey Seager
SS
.327/.390/.623
42 2B, 33 HR
88 R, 96 RBI

MINOR LEAGUE

Abimelec Ortiz
1B
(LoA/HiA)
.294/.371/.619
33 HR, 101 RBI

ORGANIZATION LEADERS

Batting		***Minimum 250 AB**
MAJORS		
* AVG	Corey Seager	.327
* OPS	Corey Seager	1.013
HR	Adolis Garcia	38
RBI	Adolis Garcia	107
MINORS		
* AVG	Luisangel Acuna, Frisco	.315
* OBP	J.P. Martinez, Hickory/Frisco/R.Rock	.425
* SLG	Abimelec Ortiz, Down East/Hickory	.619
* OPS	Abimelec Ortiz, Down East/Hickory	.990
R	Elier Hernandez, Round Rock	98
H	Elier Hernandez, Round Rock	165
TB	Elier Hernandez, Round Rock	265
2B	Elier Hernandez, Round Rock	36
3B	Daniel Mateo, Hickory	9
HR	Abimelec Ortiz, Down East/Hickory	33
RBI	Abimelec Ortiz, Down East/Hickory	101
BB	Justin Foscue, Round Rock	85
SO	Aaron Zavala, Frisco	159
SB	Luisangel Acuña, Frisco	42

Pitching		**#Minimum 75 IP**
MAJORS		
W	Nathan Eovaldi	12
# ERA	Nathan Eovaldi	3.63
SO	Andrew Heaney	151
SV	Will Smith	22
MINORS		
W	Grant Wolfram, Frisco/R. Rock	10
L	Nick Krauth, Frisco/R. Rock	12
# ERA	Aidan Curry, D.East/Hickory	2.75
G	Alex Speas, Frisco/R. Rock	49
G	Antonie Kelly, Frisco/R. Rock	49
GS	Robert Dugger, Round Rock	29
SV	Antonie Kelly, Frisco/R. Rock	11
IP	Robert Dugger, Round Rock	146
BB	Cole Winn, Round Rock	79
SO	Robert Dugger, Round Rock	143
# AVG	Aidan Curry, D.East/Hickory	.177

2023 PERFORMANCE

General Manager: Chris Young. **Farm Director:** Josh Bonifay. **Scouting Director:** Kip Fagg.

Class	Team	League	W	L	PCT	Finish	Manager
Majors	Texas Rangers	American	90	72	.556	4 (15)	Bruce Bochy
Triple-A	Round Rock Express	Pacific Coast	89	60	.597	2 (10)	Doug Davis
Double-A	Frisco RoughRiders	Texas	64	73	.467	8 (10)	Carlos Cardoza
High-A	Hickory Crawdads	South Atlantic	70	55	.560	1 (12)	Chad Comer
Low-A	Down East Wood Ducks	Carolina	66	61	.520	3 (12)	Carlos Maldonado
Rookie	ACL Rangers	Arizona Complex	23	33	.411	12 (17)	Guilder Rodriguez
Rookie	DSL Rangers Blue	Dominican Sum.	19	36	.345	42 (50)	Kevin Torres
Rookie	DSL Rangers Red	Dominican Sum.	30	25	.545	17 (50)	Elevys Gonzalez
Overall 2023 Minor League Record			361	343	.513	12th (30)	

ORGANIZATION STATISTICS

TEXAS RANGERS

AMERICAN LEAGUE

Batting	B-T	Ht.	Wt.	DOB	AVG	OBP	SLG	G	PA	AB	R	H	2B	3B	HR	RBI	BB	HBP	SH	SF	SO	SB	CS	BB%	SO%
Carter, Evan	L-R	6-2	190	8-29-02	.306	.413	.645	23	75	62	15	19	4	1	5	12	12	0	0	1	24	3	0	16.0	32.0
Duran, Ezequiel	R-R	5-11	185	5-22-99	.276	.324	.443	122	439	406	55	112	22	2	14	46	23	7	1	2	120	8	4	5.2	27.3
Garcia, Adolis	R-R	6-1	205	3-02-93	.245	.328	.508	148	632	555	108	136	29	0	39	107	65	6	0	6	175	9	1	10.3	27.7
Garver, Mitch	R-R	6-1	220	1-15-91	.270	.370	.500	87	344	296	45	80	11	0	19	50	44	3	0	0	82	0	0	12.8	23.8
Grossman, Robbie	B-L	6-0	209	9-16-89	.238	.340	.394	115	420	353	56	84	23	1	10	49	57	2	0	8	98	1	0	13.6	23.3
Hedges, Austin	R-R	6-1	223	8-18-92	.208	.208	.208	17	25	24	1	5	0	0	0	2	0	0	1	0	8	0	0	0.0	32.0
Heim, Jonah	B-R	6-4	220	6-27-95	.258	.317	.438	131	501	457	61	118	28	0	18	95	40	1	0	3	96	2	0	8.0	19.2
Huff, Sam	R-R	6-4	240	1-14-98	.256	.289	.512	21	45	43	5	11	2	0	3	6	2	0	0	0	17	0	0	4.4	37.8
Jankowski, Travis	L-R	6-2	190	6-15-91	.263	.357	.332	107	287	247	34	65	12	1	1	30	35	2	1	2	42	19	1	12.2	14.6
Jung, Josh	R-R	6-2	214	2-12-98	.266	.315	.467	122	515	478	75	127	25	1	23	70	30	5	0	2	151	1	3	5.8	29.3
Leon, Sandy	B-R	5-10	235	3-13-89	.146	.186	.195	22	44	41	4	6	2	0	0	4	1	1	1	0	20	0	0	2.3	45.5
Lowe, Nathaniel	L-R	6-4	220	7-07-95	.262	.360	.414	161	724	623	89	163	38	3	17	82	93	5	0	3	165	1	0	12.8	22.8
Martinez, J.P.	L-L	5-8	174	3-21-96	.225	.250	.325	17	44	40	7	9	1	0	1	4	2	0	0	2	16	0	0	4.5	36.4
Miller, Brad	L-R	6-2	195	10-18-89	.214	.328	.339	27	67	56	8	12	4	0	1	6	10	0	0	1	11	0	0	14.9	16.4
Ornelas, Jonathan	R-R	6-0	196	5-26-00	.143	.250	.143	8	8	7	2	1	0	0	0	0	0	1	0	0	4	0	0	0.0	50.0
Sborz, Josh	R-R	6-3	215	12-17-93	.000	.000	.000	44	1	1	0	0	0	0	0	0	0	0	0	0	1	0	0	0.0	100.0
Seager, Corey	L-R	6-4	215	4-27-94	.327	.390	.623	119	536	477	88	156	42	0	33	96	49	4	0	6	88	2	1	9.1	16.4
Semien, Marcus	R-R	6-0	195	9-17-90	.276	.348	.478	162	753	670	122	185	40	4	29	100	72	5	0	5	110	14	3	9.6	14.6
Smith, Josh H.	L-R	5-10	172	8-07-97	.185	.304	.328	90	232	195	29	36	8	1	6	15	25	9	2	1	55	1	0	10.8	23.7
Taveras, Leody	B-R	6-2	195	9-08-98	.266	.312	.421	143	554	511	67	136	31	3	14	67	35	1	3	4	117	14	4	6.3	21.1
Thompson, Bubba	R-R	6-2	197	6-09-98	.170	.237	.283	37	60	53	10	9	4	1	0	4	4	1	1	1	16	4	2	6.7	26.7

Pitching	B-T	Ht.	Wt.	DOB	W	L	ERA	G	GS	SV	IP	Hits	Runs	ER	HR	BB	SO	AVG	OBP	SLG	SO%	BB%	BF
Anderson, Grant	R-R	6-0	180	6-21-97	2	1	5.05	26	0	0	36	38	20	20	5	14	30	.277	.344	.431	19.5	9.1	154
Barlow, Joe	R-R	6-2	210	9-28-95	1	1	4.66	13	0	0	10	13	5	5	2	2	6	.310	.341	.500	13.6	4.5	44
Bradford, Cody	L-L	6-4	197	2-22-98	4	3	5.30	20	8	0	56	56	33	33	11	12	51	.259	.296	.500	21.8	5.1	234
Burke, Brock	L-L	6-4	210	8-04-96	5	3	4.37	53	0	0	60	64	32	29	13	9	52	.271	.301	.470	20.8	3.6	250
Chapman, Aroldis	L-L	6-4	218	2-28-88	2	3	3.72	30	0	4	29	21	14	12	4	16	50	.191	.299	.327	39.4	12.6	127
deGrom, Jacob	L-R	6-4	180	6-19-88	2	0	2.67	6	6	0	30	19	11	9	2	4	45	.171	.200	.324	39.1	3.5	115
Dunning, Dane	R-R	6-4	225	12-20-94	12	7	3.70	35	26	0	173	163	73	71	20	55	140	.250	.316	.393	19.4	7.6	722
Eovaldi, Nathan	R-R	6-2	217	2-13-90	12	5	3.63	25	25	0	144	117	59	58	15	47	132	.225	.295	.382	22.9	8.1	577
Gray, Jon	R-R	6-4	225	11-05-91	9	8	4.12	29	29	0	157	149	75	72	22	54	142	.256	.325	.400	21.6	8.2	656
Heaney, Andrew	L-L	6-2	200	6-05-91	10	6	4.15	34	28	0	147	143	74	68	23	60	151	.251	.332	.439	23.6	9.4	641
Hearn, Taylor	L-L	6-6	230	8-30-94	0	0	10.29	4	0	0	7	9	8	8	1	4	7	.300	.382	.400	20.6	11.8	34
Hedges, Austin	R-R	6-1	223	8-18-92	0	0	4.91	4	0	0	4	5	2	2	1	0	1	.333	.375	.600	6.3	0.0	16
Hernandez, Jonathan	R-R	6-3	190	7-06-96	1	2	5.40	33	0	0	32	35	20	19	4	15	34	.280	.370	.432	23.1	10.2	147
Howard, Spencer	R-R	6-3	210	7-28-96	0	0	10.80	3	0	0	3	4	4	4	1	3	2	.286	.444	.500	11.1	16.7	18
Kennedy, Ian	R-R	6-0	210	12-19-84	0	1	7.16	16	0	0	16	16	15	13	4	7	21	.246	.333	.477	28.0	9.3	75
King, John	L-L	6-2	215	9-14-94	1	1	5.79	15	0	0	19	26	12	12	1	4	10	.342	.370	.434	12.3	4.9	81
Latz, Jake	R-L	6-2	185	4-08-96	0	0	0.00	3	0	0	6	1	0	0	0	3	5	.053	.182	.053	22.7	13.6	22
Leclerc, Jose	R-R	6-0	195	12-19-93	0	2	2.68	57	0	4	57	37	19	17	5	28	67	.183	.288	.292	28.8	12.0	233
Leon, Sandy	B-R	5-10	235	3-13-89	0	0	18.00	1	0	0	1	1	2	2	1	0	0	.250	.400	1.000	0.0	0.0	5
Miller, Brad	L-R	6-2	195	10-18-89	0	0	13.50	1	0	0	2	2	3	3	1	2	0	.333	.444	.833	0.0	22.2	9
Montgomery, Jordan	L-L	6-6	228	12-27-92	4	2	2.79	11	11	0	68	61	21	21	6	13	58	.240	.276	.354	21.6	4.9	268
Otto, Glenn	R-R	6-3	240	3-11-96	0	0	10.13	6	0	0	11	14	12	12	6	6	11	.311	.392	.711	21.6	11.8	51
Perez, Martin	L-L	6-0	200	4-04-91	10	4	4.45	35	20	0	142	150	74	70	21	49	93	.274	.336	.441	15.3	8.1	608
Ragans, Cole	L-L	6-4	190	12-12-97	2	3	5.92	17	0	0	24	20	17	16	4	14	24	.225	.330	.393	22.6	13.2	106
Rodriguez, Yerry	R-R	6-2	198	10-15-97	0	1	7.90	13	1	0	14	20	12	12	1	6	15	.339	.394	.508	22.7	9.1	66
Sborz, Josh	R-R	6-3	215	12-17-93	6	7	5.50	44	0	0	52	43	33	32	8	17	66	.219	.285	.383	30.7	7.9	215
Scherzer, Max	R-R	6-3	208	7-27-84	4	2	3.20	8	8	0	45	28	16	16	5	15	53	.174	.249	.311	29.9	8.5	177
Smith, Will	R-L	6-5	255	7-10-89	2	7	4.40	60	0	22	57	44	31	28	5	17	55	.211	.270	.344	24.3	7.5	226
Speas, Alex	R-R	6-3	225	3-04-98	0	2	13.50	3	0	0	2	2	3	3	0	5	4	.286	.583	.286	33.3	41.7	12
Stratton, Chris	R-R	6-2	205	8-22-90	1	0	3.41	22	0	0	29	24	11	11	4	8	22	.229	.282	.362	18.8	6.8	117
White, Owen	R-R	6-3	199	8-09-99	0	1	11.25	2	0	0	4	5	5	5	2	2	4	.313	.389	.688	21.1	10.5	19

Fielding

Catcher	PCT	G	PO	A	E	DP	PB
Garver	.991	28	214	8	2	1	1
Hedges	1.000	15	71	2	0	0	0
Heim	.998	124	938	40	2	8	7
Huff	1.000	10	40	0	0	0	0
Leon	.992	21	117	1	1	0	1

First Base	PCT	G	PO	A	E	DP
Duran	1.000	2	11	0	0	0
Garver	.000	1	0	0	0	0
Huff	1.000	4	3	0	0	1
Lowe	.998	161	1221	106	3	128
Miller	1.000	5	6	1	0	0

Second Base	PCT	G	PO	A	E	DP
Duran	1.000	9	1	3	0	0
Semien	.991	162	270	388	6	109
Smith	1.000	3	1	0	0	0

Third Base	PCT	G	PO	A	E	DP
Duran	.891	22	12	29	5	0
Jung	.988	121	77	258	4	23
Miller	1.000	1	1	0	0	0
Ornelas	1.000	3	0	1	0	0
Smith	.967	25	14	44	2	3

Shortstop	PCT	G	PO	A	E	DP
Duran	.977	37	38	92	3	16
Ornelas	1.000	4	1	0	0	0
Seager	.981	112	139	276	8	69
Smith	.942	33	12	53	4	15

Outfield	PCT	G	PO	A	E	DP
Carter	1.000	24	38	3	0	0
Duran	.487	35	37	1	1	0
Garcia	.961	143	298	11	6	1
Grossman	.972	76	89	1	3	0
Jankowski	1.000	108	135	0	0	0
Martinez	1.000	10	24	0	0	0
Smith	.967	20	26	3	1	2
Taveras	.997	140	357	5	1	0
Thompson	1.000	33	29	0	0	0

ROUND ROCK EXPRESS — *TRIPLE-A*

PACIFIC COAST LEAGUE

Batting	B-T	Ht.	Wt.	DOB	AVG	OBP	SLG	G	PA	AB	R	H	2B	3B	HR	RBI	BB	HBP	SH	SF	SO	SB	CS	BB%	SO%
Arias, Diosbel	R-R	6-2	190	7-21-96	.286	.361	.422	100	397	353	66	101	22	4	6	61	40	2	1	1	116	4	0	10.1	29.2
Bannister, Zion	B-R	6-3	189	9-09-01	.250	.400	.750	1	5	4	1	1	0	1	0	3	1	0	0	0	2	0	1	20.0	40.0
Biggers, Jax	L-R	5-8	175	4-07-97	.308	.400	.359	13	46	39	6	12	2	0	0	9	6	0	1	0	11	0	1	13.0	23.9
Carter, Evan	L-R	6-2	190	8-29-02	.353	.436	.382	8	39	34	8	12	1	0	0	3	4	1	0	0	6	3	1	10.3	15.4
Chavez, Frainyer	B-R	5-8	170	5-24-99	.000	.000	.000	2	3	3	0	0	0	0	0	0	0	0	0	0	1	0	0	0.0	33.3
Crim, Blaine	R-R	5-10	200	6-17-97	.289	.385	.506	133	582	494	89	143	31	5	22	85	71	10	0	7	107	1	0	12.2	18.4
Fabian, Sandro	R-R	5-11	180	3-06-98	.288	.331	.523	117	483	444	67	128	29	3	23	78	23	8	0	5	73	6	2	4.8	15.1
Foscue, Justin	R-R	5-11	205	3-02-99	.266	.394	.468	122	563	462	94	123	31	4	18	84	85	14	0	2	70	14	7	15.1	12.4
Frazier, Clint	R-R	5-11	212	9-06-94	.250	.350	.442	15	60	52	6	13	5	1	1	4	7	1	0	0	18	0	0	11.7	30.0
Garver, Mitch	R-R	6-1	220	1-15-91	.316	.480	.737	6	25	19	7	6	2	0	2	4	6	0	0	0	7	0	0	24.0	28.0
Harris, Dustin	L-R	6-3	185	7-08-99	.273	.382	.455	67	288	242	47	66	11	3	9	31	40	4	0	2	63	17	3	13.9	21.9
Harrison, Josh	R-R	5-8	190	7-08-87	.222	.323	.370	6	31	27	3	6	1	0	1	5	3	1	0	0	9	0	0	9.7	29.0
Hernandez, Elier	R-R	6-3	197	11-21-94	.298	.359	.478	137	612	554	98	165	36	5	18	99	50	5	0	3	126	9	6	8.2	20.6
Huff, Sam	R-R	6-4	240	1-14-98	.298	.399	.548	68	321	272	48	81	17	0	17	67	44	3	0	2	78	0	0	13.7	24.3
Jankowski, Travis	L-R	6-2	190	6-15-91	.300	.417	.400	3	12	10	1	3	1	0	0	2	2	0	0	0	3	0	0	16.7	25.0
Langford, Wyatt	R-R	6-1	225	11-15-01	.368	.538	.526	5	26	19	4	7	3	0	0	1	6	1	0	0	6	3	0	23.1	23.1
Leon, Sandy	B-R	5-10	235	3-13-89	.273	.467	.273	4	15	11	0	3	0	0	0	1	4	0	0	0	3	0	0	26.7	20.0
Martinez, J.P.	L-L	5-8	174	3-21-96	.298	.418	.543	77	353	289	54	86	21	4	14	59	55	6	1	2	81	38	4	15.6	22.9
Miller, Brad	L-R	6-2	195	10-18-89	.222	.300	.481	7	30	27	4	6	1	0	2	3	2	1	0	0	11	0	0	6.7	36.7
Ojeda, Miguel	R-R	6-0	200	6-16-00	.000	.000	.000	1	3	3	0	0	0	0	0	1	0	0	0	0	2	0	0	0.0	66.7
Ornelas, Jonathan	R-R	6-0	196	5-26-00	.253	.368	.359	114	517	434	78	110	18	2	8	52	74	6	1	2	121	15	1	14.3	23.4
Ortega, Rafael	L-R	5-11	180	5-15-91	.226	.333	.381	44	199	168	31	38	11	0	5	26	27	1	1	2	34	8	5	13.6	17.1
Plawecki, Kevin	R-R	6-2	208	2-26-91	.294	.400	.324	10	40	34	1	10	1	0	0	2	5	1	0	0	11	0	0	12.5	27.5
2-team (33 El Paso)					.280	.351	.414	43	175	157	20	44	10	1	3	23	15	2	0	1	32	0	0	8.6	18.3
Procyshen, Jordan	L-R	5-10	185	3-11-93	.247	.367	.356	25	90	73	12	18	5	0	1	12	13	2	0	2	22	0	0	14.4	24.4
Sale, Josh	L-R	5-11	215	7-05-91	.190	.346	.333	15	52	42	10	8	0	0	2	7	9	1	0	0	20	1	0	17.3	38.5
Tanielu, Nick	R-R	5-10	214	9-04-92	.167	.375	.167	2	8	6	0	1	0	0	0	0	2	0	0	0	2	0	0	25.0	25.0
Taveras, Leody	B-R	6-2	195	9-08-98	.500	.600	1.250	1	5	4	2	2	0	0	1	5	1	0	0	0	1	0	0	20.0	20.0
Thompson, Bubba	R-R	6-2	197	6-09-98	.260	.362	.378	32	149	127	28	33	7	1	2	17	19	2	0	1	28	16	2	12.8	18.8
Tsutsugo, Yoshi	L-R	6-1	225	11-26-91	.249	.380	.432	51	208	169	30	42	9	2	6	33	36	1	0	2	59	2	2	17.3	28.4
2-team (4 Sacramento)					.247	.396	.427	55	224	178	33	44	10	2	6	34	42	2	0	2	62	2	2	18.8	27.7
Wendzel, Davis	R-R	5-10	206	5-23-97	.236	.361	.477	124	547	453	84	107	19	0	30	74	77	13	1	3	129	3	3	14.1	23.6
Whatley, Matt	R-R	5-8	200	1-07-96	.203	.289	.322	70	268	236	40	48	10	0	6	25	21	8	2	1	70	5	4	7.8	26.1

Pitching	B-T	Ht.	Wt.	DOB	W	L	ERA	G	GS	SV	IP	Hits	Runs	ER	HR	BB	SO	AVG	OBP	SLG	SO%	BB%	BF
Anderson, Grant	R-R	6-0	180	6-21-97	3	1	3.71	21	2	1	34	26	15	14	5	14	54	.215	.312	.405	38.3	9.9	141
Barlow, Joe	R-R	6-2	210	9-28-95	2	0	4.21	20	0	1	26	25	13	12	4	10	25	.255	.321	.429	22.9	9.2	109
Barnes, Jacob	R-R	6-2	231	4-14-90	0	1	2.21	13	0	1	20	22	13	5	1	10	17	.262	.340	.345	17.5	10.3	97
Bradford, Cody	L-L	6-4	197	2-22-98	9	2	3.63	14	14	0	74	71	33	30	6	16	65	.248	.292	.364	21.3	5.2	305
Bush, Matt	R-R	5-10	193	2-08-86	1	0	2.13	9	2	2	13	8	3	3	2	1	16	.174	.208	.304	33.3	2.1	48
Church, Marc	R-R	6-3	189	3-30-01	7	1	3.48	30	2	2	44	40	19	17	5	28	48	.253	.365	.386	25.0	14.6	192
Cody, Kyle	R-R	6-7	225	8-09-94	5	4	5.90	33	9	0	76	90	53	50	14	28	65	.301	.365	.492	19.4	8.4	335
Colina, Edwar	R-R	5-11	240	5-03-97	4	1	4.65	26	2	1	31	25	18	16	4	20	30	.229	.356	.404	22.6	15.0	133
Duffy, Danny	L-L	6-3	205	12-21-88	0	0	10.38	4	0	0	4	6	5	5	0	8	3	.333	.519	.444	11.1	29.6	27
Dugger, Robert	R-R	6-0	198	7-03-95	7	10	4.31	29	29	0	146	149	79	70	18	60	143	.262	.335	.407	22.6	9.5	632
Dye, Josh	L-L	6-5	180	9-14-96	1	1	7.50	7	1	0	12	16	10	10	1	5	5	.356	.412	.467	9.6	9.6	52
Engler, Scott	R-R	6-4	220	12-12-96	1	0	14.40	9	2	0	10	14	17	16	2	12	13	.333	.481	.571	24.1	22.2	54
Flores, Bernardo	L-L	6-4	190	8-23-95	0	1	7.71	3	1	0	5	4	4	4	0	7	4	.222	.440	.278	16.0	28.0	25
Hearn, Taylor	L-L	6-6	230	8-30-94	2	2	3.66	24	2	0	39	35	19	16	2	24	54	.232	.352	.338	30.2	13.4	179
Hernandez, Jonathan	R-R	6-3	190	7-06-96	1	1	1.13	24	0	2	32	15	5	4	1	21	32	.140	.279	.187	24.8	16.3	129
Howard, Spencer	R-R	6-3	210	7-28-96	1	1	5.40	9	2	0	18	12	11	11	7	7	30	.176	.253	.485	40.0	9.3	75
Jacobsen, Lucas	L-L	6-5	190	7-01-95	3	1	7.40	22	1	0	24	29	22	20	1	20	20	.284	.421	.343	15.9	15.9	126
Kelly, Antoine	L-L	6-5	205	12-05-99	0	0	2.70	6	0	0	7	8	3	2	0	1	10	.296	.345	.333	34.5	3.4	29
Kennedy, Ian	R-R	6-0	210	12-19-84	1	0	3.51	22	0	3	26	20	11	10	5	9	30	.217	.294	.435	29.4	8.8	102
Kent, Zak	R-R	6-3	208	2-24-98	0	1	3.97	10	10	0	34	26	15	15	4	10	34	.205	.271	.354	24.3	7.1	140

King, John	L-L	6-2	215	9-14-94	2	2	3.32	12	3	1	22	28	9	8	1	6	13	.315	.354	.360	13.4	6.2	97
Krauth, Nick	R-R	6-3	170	9-06-99	0	1	10.80	3	2	0	8	12	10	10	4	6	2	.333	.442	.750	4.7	14.0	43
Latz, Jake	R-L	6-2	185	4-08-96	1	4	4.10	46	5	7	64	58	30	29	5	29	87	.251	.341	.394	32.7	10.9	266
Lee, Chase	R-R	6-0	170	8-13-98	3	4	3.98	47	4	4	63	64	33	28	7	28	87	.262	.350	.402	31.0	10.0	281
Leiter, Jack	R-R	6-1	205	4-21-00	0	0	8.10	1	1	0	3	8	3	3	2	2	4	.444	.500	.889	20.0	10.0	20
Leone, Dominic	R-R	5-10	215	10-26-91	2	0	1.59	8	0	2	11	11	2	2	1	2	15	.244	.277	.400	31.9	4.3	47
Littell, Zack	R-R	6-4	220	10-05-95	2	0	2.25	8	0	0	12	9	3	3	1	2	16	.196	.229	.283	33.3	4.2	48
Marvel, James	R-R	6-4	215	9-17-93	1	1	7.88	6	6	0	24	39	23	21	1	12	15	.375	.449	.519	12.7	10.2	118
Mejia, Juan	L-L	5-11	160	1-09-99	0	0	18.00	1	0	0	1	1	2	2	0	4	0	.333	.625	.333	0.0	50.0	8
Nordlin, Seth	R-R	6-4	213	9-04-97	1	1	4.79	5	5	0	21	23	11	11	3	7	10	.291	.348	.494	11.2	7.9	89
Otto, Glenn	R-R	6-3	240	3-11-96	1	1	3.38	10	6	0	29	18	12	11	4	13	39	.176	.277	.314	32.5	10.8	120
Ozuna, Fernery	R-R	5-8	170	11-09-95	4	3	5.73	33	3	0	49	46	33	31	10	28	48	.251	.359	.459	22.1	12.9	217
Palumbo, Joe	L-L	6-0	195	10-26-94	0	0	9.00	3	0	0	2	1	2	2	0	10	0	.143	.647	.143	0.0	58.8	17
Polley, Triston	L-L	6-0	190	12-20-96	1	0	5.63	4	2	0	8	8	5	5	1	4	5	.267	.371	.433	14.3	11.4	35
Ragans, Cole	L-L	6-4	190	12-12-97	0	0	2.79	3	3	0	10	5	3	3	1	6	15	.152	.282	.273	38.5	15.4	39
Robert, Daniel	L-R	6-4	210	8-30-94	1	2	4.40	28	2	0	43	39	27	21	3	23	51	.239	.342	.350	26.4	11.9	193
Rodriguez, Yerry	R-R	6-2	198	10-15-97	3	0	5.03	38	2	8	48	41	35	27	9	26	63	.219	.323	.385	29.0	12.0	217
Rosado, Eury	R-R	6-0	160	11-23-00	0	0	0.00	1	0	0	2	1	0	0	0	1	1	.167	.286	.167	14.3	14.3	7
Sborz, Josh	R-R	6-3	215	12-17-93	0	0	2.25	4	0	0	4	4	1	1	1	0	7	.250	.250	.500	43.8	0.0	16
Slaten, Justin	R-R	6-4	222	9-15-97	1	0	1.08	5	0	0	8	3	1	1	1	4	10	.107	.219	.214	31.3	12.5	32
Speas, Alex	R-R	6-3	225	3-04-98	2	2	5.08	26	1	2	28	21	17	16	2	25	38	.206	.377	.275	29.2	19.2	130
Tepera, Ryan	R-R	6-1	195	11-03-87	5	0	0.00	7	0	0	8	3	0	0	0	3	11	.115	.207	.154	37.9	10.3	29
White, Owen	R-R	6-3	199	8-09-99	2	2	4.99	13	12	0	52	52	34	29	10	32	32	.264	.381	.467	13.5	13.5	237
Winn, Cole	R-R	6-2	190	11-25-99	9	8	7.22	29	13	0	101	114	83	81	17	79	97	.279	.398	.462	19.7	16.0	493
Wolfram, Grant	L-L	6-6	235	12-12-96	0	1	10.80	11	0	0	13	18	16	16	2	10	11	.310	.412	.500	16.2	14.7	68
Zombro, Tyler	R-R	5-10	215	9-02-94	0	0	0.00	2	0	0	3	0	0	0	0	2	2	.000	.273	.000	18.2	18.2	11

Fielding

Catcher	PCT	G	PO	A	E	DP	PB
Garver	1.000	3	18	1	0	0	1
Huff	.997	58	547	33	2	1	6
Leon	1.000	3	31	0	0	0	0
Ojeda	1.000	1	8	1	0	0	0
Plawecki	.982	6	51	3	1	0	1
Procyshen	.978	16	125	6	3	0	0
Whatley	.997	67	620	43	2	3	5

First Base	PCT	G	PO	A	E	DP
Crim	.990	99	625	43	7	90
Foscue	1.000	9	69	11	0	9
Harris	.987	19	138	13	2	13
Miller	1.000	3	17	1	0	0
Tsutsugo	.988	23	153	10	2	19

Second Base	PCT	G	PO	A	E	DP
Arias	.980	50	78	118	4	37
Biggers	.978	9	21	24	1	9
Chavez	1.000	1	2	2	0	1
Foscue	.976	70	122	165	7	41
Harrison	1.000	2	4	2	0	1
Ornelas	.983	15	26	31	1	11
Tanielu	1.000	1	0	1	0	0
Wendzel	.950	4	10	9	1	4

Third Base	PCT	G	PO	A	E	DP
Arias	.942	41	37	60	6	13
Crim	.786	6	2	9	3	0
Foscue	.893	35	16	59	9	7
Harrison	1.000	2	0	4	0	0
Ornelas	1.000	4	2	7	0	1
Tanielu	1.000	1	0	2	0	0
Tsutsugo	.909	13	10	20	3	2
Wendzel	.947	53	33	74	6	11

Shortstop	PCT	G	PO	A	E	DP
Biggers	.750	2	2	1	1	1
Ornelas	.966	85	143	222	13	57
Wendzel	.976	63	100	144	6	45

Outfield	PCT	G	PO	A	E	DP
Bannister	.000	1	0	0	0	0
Carter	1.000	8	12	0	0	0
Fabian	.977	103	189	14	4	2
Frazier	1.000	10	16	1	0	0
Harris	1.000	40	71	0	0	0
Harrison	1.000	2	2	0	0	0
Hernandez	.991	126	238	4	3	0
Jankowski	.500	2	1	0	0	0
Langford	1.000	4	9	0	0	0
Martinez	.990	71	166	5	1	2
Miller	1.000	1	1	0	0	0
Ornelas	1.000	11	19	1	0	0
Ortega	.968	41	79	5	2	2
Sale	1.000	14	13	1	0	0
Taveras	1.000	1	2	0	0	0
Thompson	1.000	31	52	2	0	0

FRISCO ROUGHRIDERS — *DOUBLE-A*

TEXAS LEAGUE

Batting	B-T	Ht.	Wt.	DOB	AVG	OBP	SLG	G	PA	AB	R	H	2B	3B	HR	RBI	BB	HBP	SH	SF	SO	SB	CS	BB%	SO%
Acuna, Luisangel	R-R	5-8	181	3-12-02	.315	.377	.453	84	402	362	68	114	25	2	7	51	37	0	1	2	76	42	5	9.2	18.9
Aponte, Angel	R-R	6-0	170	2-03-00	.250	.250	.625	5	8	8	2	2	0	0	1	1	0	0	0	0	0	0	0	0.0	0.0
Arias, Diosbel	R-R	6-2	190	7-21-96	.256	.360	.581	11	50	43	11	11	2	0	4	8	4	3	0	0	10	0	0	8.0	20.0
Bannister, Zion	B-R	6-3	189	9-09-01	.125	.222	.250	4	9	8	0	1	1	0	0	3	1	0	0	0	2	0	0	11.1	22.2
Biggers, Jax	L-R	5-8	175	4-07-97	.227	.337	.376	101	413	348	53	79	10	3	12	50	56	3	3	3	95	14	5	13.6	23.0
Blackwell, Benjamin	R-R	5-11	185	4-06-99	.250	.250	.250	1	4	4	0	1	0	0	0	1	0	0	0	0	0	0	0	0.0	0.0
Carter, Evan	L-R	6-2	190	8-29-02	.284	.411	.451	97	462	377	68	107	15	6	12	62	74	9	0	2	103	22	10	16.0	22.3
Chavez, Frainyer	B-R	5-8	170	5-24-99	.229	.299	.352	30	118	105	12	24	4	0	3	16	10	1	1	1	24	0	1	8.5	20.3
Easley, Jayce	B-R	5-8	151	8-02-99	.167	.333	.250	5	16	12	3	2	1	0	0	2	3	0	1	0	3	1	1	18.8	18.8
Freeman, Cody	R-R	5-8	180	1-05-01	.000	.000	.000	1	4	4	0	0	0	0	0	0	0	0	0	0	2	0	0	0.0	50.0
Garcia, David	B-R	5-10	201	2-06-00	.197	.340	.270	42	150	122	22	24	3	0	2	15	23	4	0	1	49	1	0	15.3	32.7
Harris, Dustin	L-R	6-3	185	7-08-99	.245	.374	.406	60	278	229	42	56	14	4	5	29	44	4	0	1	65	24	2	15.8	23.4
Hatcher, Josh	L-L	6-2	200	9-03-98	.261	.307	.417	50	200	180	26	47	5	1	7	38	12	2	1	5	51	3	0	6.0	25.5
Hauver, Trevor	L-R	5-11	205	11-20-98	.260	.374	.429	107	471	392	58	102	24	3	12	59	71	3	1	4	135	1	2	15.1	28.7
Hicks, Liam	L-R	5-11	185	6-02-99	.269	.408	.368	77	316	253	30	68	14	1	3	40	49	12	0	2	52	4	0	15.5	16.5
Hurdle, Devin	R-R	6-1	190	6-18-00	.600	.600	.800	1	5	5	1	3	1	0	0	3	0	0	0	0	1	1	0	0.0	20.0
Johnson, Cooper	R-R	6-1	209	4-25-98	.100	.182	.200	5	11	10	1	1	1	0	0	0	1	0	0	0	7	0	0	9.1	63.6
Kapers, Scott	R-R	5-10	198	11-27-96	.210	.303	.343	71	273	233	34	49	14	1	5	29	21	12	2	5	56	0	0	7.7	20.5
Langford, Wyatt	R-R	6-1	225	11-15-01	.405	.519	.762	12	54	42	7	17	3	0	4	10	11	0	0	1	7	1	2	20.4	13.0
Martinez, J.P.	L-L	5-8	174	3-21-96	.182	.400	.273	3	15	11	2	2	1	0	0	0	4	0	0	0	4	0	0	26.7	26.7
Miller, Brad	L-R	6-2	195	10-18-89	.185	.361	.296	8	36	27	3	5	0	0	1	3	8	0	0	1	9	0	0	22.2	25.0
Procyshen, Jordan	L-R	5-10	185	3-11-93	.273	.333	.273	3	13	11	1	3	0	0	0	0	1	0	1	0	2	0	0	7.7	15.4
Rodriguez, Keyber	R-R	5-10	178	10-24-00	.242	.326	.379	41	176	153	31	37	8	2	3	16	18	2	1	2	30	12	3	10.2	17.0

Saggese, Thomas	R-R	5-11	175	4-10-02	.313	.379	.512	93	418	367	67	115	22	3	15	78	34	9	1	7	96	8	2	8.1	23.0
2-team (33 Springfield)					.318	.391	.551	126	567	497	92	158	29	6	25	107	49	11	1	9	130	11	2	8.6	22.9
Sale, Josh	L-R	5-11	215	7-05-91	.160	.300	.320	9	30	25	2	4	1	0	1	3	4	1	0	0	11	0	0	13.3	36.7
Seager, Corey	L-R	6-4	215	4-27-94	.250	.333	.375	3	9	8	1	2	1	0	0	2	1	0	0	0	0	0	0	11.1	0.0
Seise, Chris	R-R	6-1	196	1-06-99	.211	.280	.311	91	358	322	38	68	20	0	4	39	29	3	0	3	122	14	2	8.1	34.1
Strahm, Kellen	R-R	6-0	215	4-25-97	.247	.357	.336	121	517	438	73	108	18	3	5	45	74	2	2	1	115	9	3	14.3	22.2
Tanielu, Nick	R-R	5-10	214	9-04-92	.247	.333	.463	48	186	162	29	40	10	2	7	24	16	6	0	2	45	1	1	8.6	24.2
Taveras, Leody	B-R	6-2	195	9-08-98	.100	.250	.100	3	12	10	1	1	0	0	0	0	2	0	0	0	3	1	0	16.7	25.0
Zavala, Aaron	L-R	6-0	193	6-24-00	.194	.343	.284	95	426	341	47	66	16	0	5	40	72	8	0	5	159	7	3	16.9	37.3

Pitching	B-T	Ht.	Wt.	DOB	W	L	ERA	G	GS	SV	IP	Hits	Runs	ER	HR	BB	SO	AVG	OBP	SLG	SO%	BB%	BF
Acker, Dane	R-R	6-2	189	4-01-99	1	1	2.74	12	12	0	46	33	17	14	4	26	51	.198	.315	.329	25.9	13.2	197
Ahlstrom, Robby	L-L	6-3	195	6-19-99	0	0	3.81	18	0	0	26	22	13	11	1	14	36	.222	.336	.303	31.0	12.1	116
Anderson, Aidan	R-R	6-1	195	6-21-97	1	3	3.81	33	2	1	54	52	27	23	2	21	73	.248	.329	.324	30.7	8.8	238
Anderson, Grant	R-R	6-0	180	6-21-97	1	0	2.70	4	0	0	7	6	2	2	2	1	9	.231	.286	.538	32.1	3.6	28
Birlingmair, Reid	L-R	5-10	210	11-13-96	1	1	2.20	17	0	1	29	27	8	7	3	10	32	.252	.319	.383	26.9	8.4	119
Bremer, Noah	R-R	6-5	206	5-13-96	1	4	6.31	14	13	0	46	50	35	32	7	22	33	.281	.368	.449	16.2	10.8	204
Brewer, Michael	R-R	6-5	215	8-08-00	2	3	6.17	35	0	1	42	43	31	29	7	29	38	.265	.381	.451	19.5	14.9	195
Brosky, Matt	R-R	5-10	190	9-15-99	0	1	15.00	1	1	0	3	6	5	5	2	3	2	.429	.556	.929	11.1	16.7	18
Bueno, Hever	R-R	6-2	179	11-23-94	0	0	4.50	16	0	0	16	12	10	8	0	19	18	.200	.388	.283	22.5	23.8	80
Bush, Matt	R-R	5-10	193	2-08-86	1	0	3.00	15	1	1	18	13	6	6	2	7	22	.203	.278	.375	30.6	9.7	72
Church, Marc	R-R	6-3	189	3-30-01	2	3	4.00	13	0	0	18	14	10	8	2	10	31	.215	.329	.354	40.8	13.2	76
DeVito, Ricky	B-R	6-3	195	8-21-98	0	0	27.00	4	0	0	3	6	10	10	1	8	4	.375	.615	.625	15.4	30.8	26
Duffy, Danny	L-L	6-3	205	12-21-88	2	2	2.30	24	0	0	31	23	9	8	0	21	39	.202	.328	.237	28.3	15.2	138
Funkhouser, Kyle	R-R	6-3	229	3-16-94	0	0	0.00	5	0	0	4	4	0	0	0	3	5	.250	.400	.250	25.0	15.0	20
Garcia, Ryan	R-R	6-0	180	1-24-98	3	9	6.66	26	26	0	99	97	76	73	20	62	110	.263	.367	.482	24.9	14.0	442
Kelly, Antoine	L-L	6-5	205	12-05-99	3	1	1.95	43	0	11	51	37	19	11	4	22	69	.194	.286	.283	31.8	10.1	217
Krauth, Nick	R-R	6-3	170	9-06-99	5	11	6.01	24	22	0	106	122	75	71	12	37	73	.293	.366	.436	15.4	7.8	474
Leclerc, Jose	R-R	6-0	195	12-19-93	0	0	4.50	2	0	0	2	1	1	1	1	0	1	.143	.143	.571	14.3	0.0	7
Leiter, Jack	R-R	6-1	205	4-21-00	2	6	5.07	19	19	0	82	67	48	46	14	47	110	.226	.339	.418	31.3	13.4	351
Manon, Eudrys	R-R	6-1	160	1-16-98	0	0	5.23	19	0	0	21	12	12	12	1	30	22	.171	.438	.243	21.0	28.6	105
Matthews, John	R-R	6-1	190	1-21-98	3	2	8.06	32	1	0	45	46	42	40	4	35	44	.274	.419	.417	19.7	15.7	223
McDowell, Theo	L-R	6-4	175	12-02-98	2	2	8.05	26	0	0	35	41	32	31	7	31	41	.304	.434	.519	24.3	18.3	169
Mejia, Juan	L-L	5-11	160	1-09-99	0	1	6.19	8	1	0	16	20	11	11	3	6	12	.299	.356	.507	16.4	8.2	73
Nordlin, Seth	R-R	6-4	213	9-04-97	2	6	5.92	11	11	0	49	62	36	32	7	9	45	.307	.346	.505	20.9	4.2	215
Polley, Triston	L-L	6-0	190	12-20-96	4	3	5.47	36	0	0	53	58	37	32	5	19	52	.278	.343	.421	22.0	8.1	236
Roby, Tekoah	R-R	6-1	185	9-18-01	2	3	5.05	10	10	0	46	49	28	26	5	12	50	.274	.323	.458	25.6	6.2	195
Rodriguez, Andy	R-R	6-1	165	12-08-98	0	1	18.47	6	0	0	6	11	13	13	3	8	11	.355	.487	.774	28.2	20.5	39
Serrano, Florencio	R-R	6-1	205	2-23-00	1	0	6.00	4	0	0	6	7	4	4	3	2	4	.280	.333	.680	14.8	7.4	27
Slaten, Justin	R-R	6-4	222	9-15-97	4	3	3.16	35	1	2	51	41	21	18	9	16	76	.220	.281	.409	37.4	7.9	203
Smith, Josh	L-L	6-5	205	2-05-97	0	0	0.00	1	0	0	0	2	1	1	0	1	0	1.000	1.000	1.000	0.0	33.3	3
Sparks, Wyatt	R-R	6-2	195	9-27-99	1	1	16.20	3	1	0	5	11	9	9	2	6	1	.440	.548	.720	3.2	19.4	31
Speas, Alex	R-R	6-3	225	3-04-98	3	0	0.64	23	0	2	28	13	7	2	0	13	47	.133	.252	.184	40.9	11.3	115
Starr, Nick	R-R	6-3	225	12-03-96	5	3	5.96	33	0	1	48	51	32	32	7	14	52	.271	.324	.473	25.2	6.8	206
Stephan, Josh	R-R	6-3	185	11-01-01	0	0	4.15	1	1	0	4	5	2	2	0	1	5	.294	.368	.353	26.3	5.3	19
Tanielu, Nick	R-R	5-10	214	9-04-92	0	0	0.00	1	0	0	1	0	0	0	0	0	0	.000	.000	.000	0.0	0.0	2
Vanasco, Ricky	R-R	6-3	180	10-13-98	0	0	23.14	2	2	0	2	4	10	6	0	4	2	.333	.556	.417	11.1	22.2	18
White, Owen	R-R	6-3	199	8-09-99	2	3	3.51	12	12	0	56	40	22	22	5	23	48	.205	.302	.313	21.1	10.1	227
Wolfram, Grant	L-L	6-6	235	12-12-96	10	0	2.02	29	1	1	49	27	12	11	4	14	67	.161	.232	.262	35.8	7.5	187

Fielding

Catcher	PCT	G	PO	A	E	DP	PB
Garcia	.994	36	296	21	2	4	2
Hicks	.997	37	341	17	1	0	4
Johnson	.951	5	37	2	2	0	0
Kapers	.993	68	643	35	5	4	7
Procyshen	1.000	2	20	1	0	0	0

First Base	PCT	G	PO	A	E	DP
Arias	1.000	3	15	0	0	2
Chavez	1.000	4	24	2	0	1
Harris	.989	13	85	7	1	10
Hatcher	.990	43	281	24	3	31
Hauver	.989	26	167	10	2	21
Hicks	1.000	13	93	0	0	10
Miller	1.000	3	22	1	0	3
Sale	.975	5	38	1	1	4
Tanielu	.996	39	239	23	1	26

Second Base	PCT	G	PO	A	E	DP
Acuna	.926	6	8	17	2	6
Arias	1.000	6	11	21	0	6
Bannister	1.000	1	3	3	0	2
Biggers	.996	61	117	164	1	41
Blackwell	1.000	1	2	2	0	0
Chavez	1.000	16	20	31	0	8
Easley	1.000	4	8	9	0	4
Hurdle	1.000	1	2	1	0	0
Saggese	.993	44	52	85	1	19

Third Base	PCT	G	PO	A	E	DP
Arias	.500	1	0	1	1	0
Biggers	.965	32	18	64	3	4
Chavez	.957	10	7	15	1	0
Freeman	.750	1	1	2	1	0
Hauver	1.000	1	0	1	0	0
Miller	1.000	1	0	1	0	0
Saggese	.947	33	18	53	4	5
Seise	.891	52	35	63	12	6
Tanielu	.870	9	8	12	3	0

Shortstop	PCT	G	PO	A	E	DP
Acuna	.977	67	93	158	6	40
Biggers	.889	4	6	10	2	3
Rodriguez	.978	40	44	92	3	19
Saggese	.955	9	17	25	2	6
Seager	1.000	2	1	4	0	1
Seise	.971	19	35	32	2	10

Outfield	PCT	G	PO	A	E	DP
Acuna	.909	4	10	0	1	0
Aponte	.500	3	5	0	0	0
Bannister	1.000	1	3	1	0	0
Biggers	1.000	1	2	0	0	0
Carter	.959	91	199	10	3	2
Harris	.986	40	67	1	1	0
Hatcher	.500	9	12	0	0	0
Hauver	.986	61	89	1	2	0
Langford	1.000	9	22	0	0	0
Martinez	.917	3	10	1	1	1
Miller	.000	1	0	0	0	0
Seise	1.000	11	9	0	0	0
Strahm	.987	111	220	10	4	4
Taveras	1.000	2	3	0	0	0
Zavala	.937	78	101	3	7	0

HICKORY CRAWDADS — HIGH CLASS A

SOUTH ATLANTIC LEAGUE

Batting	B-T	Ht.	Wt.	DOB	AVG	OBP	SLG	G	PA	AB	R	H	2B	3B	HR	RBI	BB	HBP	SH	SF	SO	SB	CS	BB%	SO%
Acosta, Max	R-R	6-1	187	10-29-02	.260	.312	.390	110	473	431	69	112	21	1	11	60	33	2	2	5	100	26	8	7.0	21.1
Aponte, Angel	R-R	6-0	170	2-03-00	.201	.265	.281	48	152	139	15	28	8	0	1	11	10	2	1	0	43	6	2	6.6	28.3
Blackwell, Benjamin	R-R	5-11	185	4-06-99	.290	.355	.406	24	76	69	9	20	2	0	2	10	7	0	0	0	21	4	3	9.2	27.6
Cauley, Cameron	R-R	5-10	170	2-06-03	.248	.336	.424	34	146	125	25	31	7	0	5	24	17	1	0	3	44	14	2	11.6	30.1
Cepeda, Geisel	R-R	6-5	220	1-17-98	.268	.343	.344	97	397	355	42	95	10	1	5	41	34	7	0	1	43	8	7	8.6	10.8
Chavez, Frainyer	B-R	5-8	170	5-24-99	.201	.325	.266	45	170	139	20	28	3	0	2	13	26	1	1	3	44	3	5	15.3	25.9
Cheney, Griffin	R-R	5-11	185	5-21-99	.203	.295	.241	28	95	79	7	16	0	0	1	9	11	1	0	4	28	5	0	11.6	29.5
Easley, Jayce	B-R	5-8	151	8-02-99	.208	.364	.263	83	310	240	39	50	6	2	1	22	53	8	5	4	66	25	4	17.1	21.3
Freeman, Cody	R-R	5-8	180	1-05-01	.236	.304	.403	94	388	347	52	82	18	2	12	55	31	5	0	5	70	6	1	8.0	18.0
Galan, Yosy	R-R	6-4	200	4-25-01	.247	.296	.456	44	169	158	23	39	11	2	6	24	10	1	0	0	60	9	5	5.9	35.5
Hatcher, Josh	L-L	6-2	200	9-03-98	.247	.296	.425	50	199	186	33	46	8	2	7	23	12	1	0	0	57	6	2	6.0	28.6
Hicks, Liam	L-R	5-11	185	6-02-99	.311	.446	.400	15	56	45	5	14	1	0	1	5	10	1	0	0	11	3	0	17.9	19.6
Johnson, Cooper	R-R	6-1	209	4-25-98	.215	.342	.339	42	147	121	22	26	6	0	3	13	21	3	1	1	54	4	1	14.3	36.7
Langford, Wyatt	R-R	6-1	225	11-15-01	.333	.453	.644	24	106	87	22	29	8	2	5	15	18	1	0	0	18	7	1	17.0	17.0
Martinez, J.P.	L-L	5-8	174	3-21-96	.667	.857	1.000	2	7	3	2	2	1	0	0	1	4	0	0	0	0	3	0	57.1	0.0
Mateo, Daniel	R-R	6-1	165	7-03-01	.259	.275	.406	110	452	433	51	112	16	9	10	56	9	3	1	6	102	30	13	2.0	22.6
Mitchell, Tucker	R-R	6-1	210	2-10-01	.258	.352	.440	50	213	182	33	47	4	1	9	37	24	4	0	3	52	2	0	11.3	24.4
Narvaez, Efrenyer	R-R	5-11	155	7-25-02	.063	.167	.250	7	18	16	2	1	0	0	1	1	1	1	0	0	6	0	0	5.6	33.3
Ortiz, Abimelec	L-L	6-0	230	2-22-02	.290	.363	.624	80	333	290	59	84	13	3	26	81	33	4	0	6	90	1	0	9.9	27.0
Osuna, Alejandro	L-L	6-0	185	10-10-02	.259	.381	.385	70	303	247	56	64	14	1	5	35	46	5	1	4	67	16	5	15.2	22.1
Pena, Yenci	R-R	6-2	193	7-13-00	.194	.242	.290	11	34	31	1	6	3	0	0	1	2	0	1	0	9	0	0	5.9	26.5
Piotto, Konner	L-R	5-9	195	1-01-98	.077	.200	.077	4	15	13	0	1	0	0	0	0	1	1	0	0	4	0	0	6.7	26.7
Rodriguez, Keyber	R-R	5-10	178	10-24-00	.262	.316	.355	78	330	301	45	79	13	0	5	31	22	2	4	1	73	20	4	6.7	22.1
Smith, Marcus	L-L	5-11	185	9-11-00	.133	.350	.133	18	60	45	6	6	0	0	0	2	15	0	0	0	27	4	2	25.0	45.0
Walcott, Sebastian	R-R	6-4	190	3-14-06	.154	.313	.231	4	16	13	2	2	1	0	0	2	3	0	0	0	5	0	1	18.8	31.3

Pitching	B-T	Ht.	Wt.	DOB	W	L	ERA	G	GS	SV	IP	Hits	Runs	ER	HR	BB	SO	AVG	OBP	SLG	SO%	BB%	BF
Acker, Dane	R-R	6-2	189	4-01-99	0	0	2.11	6	6	0	21	11	5	5	2	10	25	.147	.264	.267	28.7	11.5	87
Ahlstrom, Robby	L-L	6-3	195	6-19-99	3	1	3.90	22	0	3	32	29	15	14	3	18	43	.246	.345	.373	30.9	12.9	139
Anderson, Aidan	R-R	6-1	195	6-21-97	0	2	5.56	9	0	0	11	10	8	7	1	6	13	.227	.327	.386	25.0	11.5	52
Anderson, Ben	R-R	6-4	200	5-02-98	0	1	9.53	3	1	0	6	7	9	6	0	5	8	.280	.400	.400	26.7	16.7	30
Birlingmair, Reid	L-R	5-10	210	11-13-96	1	1	3.86	8	0	2	12	11	5	5	0	5	15	.250	.327	.318	30.6	10.2	49
Bratt, Mitch	L-L	6-1	190	7-03-03	2	3	3.54	16	16	0	61	60	25	24	6	17	73	.244	.295	.378	27.7	6.4	264
Brewer, Michael	R-R	6-5	215	8-08-00	1	1	2.61	9	0	3	10	14	3	3	0	3	16	.326	.362	.372	33.3	6.3	48
Brosky, Matt	R-R	5-10	190	9-15-99	0	3	9.49	5	2	1	12	19	15	13	2	10	16	.345	.448	.582	23.9	14.9	67
Casanova, Jean	R-R	6-3	181	3-04-97	0	0	0.00	1	0	0	2	1	0	0	0	1	3	.143	.333	.143	33.3	11.1	9
Chavez, Frainyer	B-R	5-8	170	5-24-99	0	0	0.00	1	0	0	1	2	0	0	0	0	0	.667	.667	.667	0.0	0.0	3
Clark, Seth	R-L	6-3	220	11-18-99	4	1	2.53	30	0	4	46	34	14	13	3	25	56	.210	.330	.315	29.2	13.0	192
Collyer, Gavin	R-R	6-1	165	5-12-01	0	7	5.65	30	6	2	51	52	37	32	7	28	58	.269	.381	.446	24.5	11.8	237
Corniell, Jose	R-R	6-3	165	6-22-03	4	2	3.09	13	11	1	58	44	22	20	7	17	63	.208	.274	.363	26.9	7.3	234
Curry, Aidan	R-R	6-5	185	7-05-02	0	0	8.53	2	2	0	6	9	6	6	3	10	5	.346	.528	.731	13.9	27.8	36
DeVito, Ricky	B-R	6-3	195	8-21-98	2	0	5.74	21	0	0	27	23	17	17	3	22	27	.235	.400	.378	21.6	17.6	125
Gessner, Josh	R-R	6-1	205	6-25-00	0	1	14.54	3	2	0	4	5	7	7	1	4	3	.278	.435	.444	13.0	17.4	23
Hoopii-Tuionetoa, Anthony	R-R	6-2	190	8-11-00	0	0	1.54	9	0	2	12	10	2	2	1	4	13	.227	.292	.341	27.1	8.3	48
Kelley, Jackson	R-R	6-0	185	4-26-00	1	1	5.35	26	0	2	35	32	22	21	3	18	52	.244	.344	.366	33.5	11.6	155
Kindreich, Larson	L-L	6-4	210	6-21-99	4	5	5.14	30	13	1	70	52	43	40	7	51	87	.209	.362	.361	27.9	16.3	312
Leath, Jackson	R-R	6-1	192	6-20-99	5	0	1.02	10	0	0	18	4	3	2	0	10	16	.071	.209	.107	23.5	14.7	68
Lockhart, Nick	R-R	6-6	204	2-12-01	1	3	5.02	13	6	0	29	30	17	16	3	16	23	.270	.379	.396	17.4	12.1	132
Manon, Eudrys	R-R	6-1	160	1-16-98	0	0	3.38	7	0	2	8	5	3	3	1	3	12	.172	.250	.345	37.5	9.4	32
Maton, Jacob	R-R	6-1	195	8-22-99	0	0	5.79	5	0	0	9	9	6	6	4	2	9	.257	.297	.686	24.3	5.4	37
Mejia, Juan	L-L	5-11	160	1-09-99	3	0	4.00	13	2	0	36	33	17	16	4	10	34	.241	.291	.394	23.0	6.8	148
Morel, Yohanse	R-R	6-0	170	8-23-00	5	1	2.49	32	2	1	47	34	17	13	3	26	55	.202	.330	.315	27.4	12.9	201
Mraz, Spencer	R-R	6-10	245	5-05-98	2	0	6.69	24	0	1	35	36	27	26	1	29	34	.275	.422	.321	19.7	16.8	173
Rocker, Kumar	R-R	6-5	245	11-22-99	2	2	3.86	6	6	0	28	21	12	12	2	7	42	.202	.252	.327	37.8	6.3	111
Rodriguez, Andy	R-R	6-1	165	12-08-98	4	1	2.66	32	0	4	47	46	18	14	1	20	59	.249	.321	.324	28.2	9.6	209
Santos, Winston	R-R	6-0	160	4-15-02	7	9	6.29	25	23	1	99	117	73	69	19	26	88	.295	.360	.500	19.9	5.9	442
Serrano, Florencio	R-R	6-1	205	2-23-00	1	0	5.32	18	0	0	44	54	28	26	6	16	36	.302	.359	.469	18.2	8.1	198
Sparks, Wyatt	R-R	6-2	195	9-27-99	0	0	8.10	4	0	0	7	9	9	6	1	1	9	.300	.344	.500	28.1	3.1	32
Stephan, Josh	R-R	6-3	185	11-01-01	6	3	2.17	12	11	0	62	38	17	15	8	12	73	.175	.235	.327	31.2	5.1	234
Tejada, Leury	R-R	6-1	160	12-24-99	6	3	4.53	29	2	0	56	54	31	28	5	25	31	.252	.335	.407	12.7	10.2	245
Teodo, Emiliano	R-R	6-1	165	2-14-01	5	3	4.52	18	14	0	62	53	36	31	10	33	84	.231	.337	.410	31.3	12.3	268
Webb, Bradford	R-R	6-3	200	4-20-98	1	1	8.27	11	0	1	21	33	20	19	5	12	22	.355	.444	.591	20.4	11.1	108

Fielding

Catcher	PCT	G	PO	A	E	DP	PB
Freeman	.989	57	526	38	6	3	4
Hicks	1.000	5	50	4	0	0	0
Johnson	.988	40	393	36	5	3	2
Mitchell	.988	17	163	5	2	0	4
Narvaez	.950	6	35	3	2	0	4
Piotto	.977	4	38	5	1	0	0

First Base	PCT	G	PO	A	E	DP
Blackwell	1.000	1	7	0	0	1
Chavez	1.000	3	25	2	0	0
Cheney	1.000	5	18	1	0	0
Easley	1.000	1	7	0	0	1
Hatcher	.993	37	270	18	2	21
Hicks	1.000	3	16	1	0	1
Johnson	1.000	1	1	0	0	1
Mitchell	1.000	15	112	4	0	11
Ortiz	.991	61	414	30	4	43
Pena	.975	6	37	2	1	2

Second Base	PCT	G	PO	A	E	DP
Acosta	.985	17	20	45	1	9
Blackwell	.977	15	16	27	1	6
Cauley	1.000	7	7	13	0	1

TEXAS RANGERS

Chavez	.989	27	38	50	1	11
Cheney	.895	16	21	30	6	5
Easley	.984	46	64	120	3	23
Freeman	1.000	4	8	11	0	1
Rodriguez	1.000	3	2	13	0	0

Third Base	PCT	G	PO	A	E	DP
Blackwell	.842	7	4	12	3	1
Chavez	1.000	13	6	10	0	1
Cheney	.900	9	6	12	2	0
Easley	.930	20	18	35	4	5
Freeman	.977	25	11	31	1	4

Pena	1.000	3	2	3	0	0
Rodriguez	.926	53	37	100	11	4

Shortstop	PCT	G	PO	A	E	DP
Acosta	.957	75	100	165	12	29
Blackwell	1.000	2	0	6	0	1
Cauley	.968	26	33	57	3	11
Chavez	.714	2	2	3	2	0
Rodriguez	.947	24	22	49	4	9

Outfield	PCT	G	PO	A	E	DP
Aponte	.952	45	59	4	1	0
Cepeda	.995	77	130	8	1	2
Easley	.976	18	24	1	1	0
Galan	.919	34	46	0	4	0
Hatcher	1.000	7	8	0	0	0
Langford	1.000	17	31	0	0	0
Martinez	.500	2	1	0	0	0
Mateo	.996	108	247	6	2	1
Ortiz	1.000	4	10	0	0	0
Osuna	.993	61	104	4	2	0
Smith	1.000	17	22	3	0	1

DOWN EAST WOOD DUCKS

LOW CLASS A

CAROLINA LEAGUE

Batting	B-T	Ht.	Wt.	DOB	AVG	OBP	SLG	G	PA	AB	R	H	2B	3B	HR	RBI	BB	HBP	SH	SF	SO	SB	CS	BB%	SO%
Alvarez, Erick	R-R	5-10	150	2-01-05	.189	.295	.243	12	44	37	5	7	2	0	0	2	6	0	0	1	10	1	0	13.6	22.7
Aponte, Angel	R-R	6-0	170	2-03-00	.219	.257	.375	9	35	32	5	7	2	0	1	5	2	0	0	1	11	4	1	5.7	31.4
Bannister, Zion	B-R	6-3	189	9-09-01	.200	.301	.294	49	186	160	20	32	7	1	2	15	18	6	0	2	69	19	3	9.7	37.1
Blackmon, JoJo	L-L	6-0	183	3-31-03	.205	.316	.352	99	388	332	44	68	13	6	8	41	48	6	2	0	146	29	14	12.4	37.6
Calarco, Anthony	L-R	6-3	215	8-21-99	.181	.278	.213	29	108	94	9	17	0	0	1	5	11	2	0	1	37	1	0	10.2	34.3
Cauley, Cameron	R-R	5-10	170	2-06-03	.244	.331	.405	66	275	242	43	59	12	3	7	35	30	2	0	1	89	22	3	10.9	32.4
Cheney, Griffin	R-R	5-11	185	5-21-99	.196	.312	.393	32	125	107	15	21	5	2	4	14	15	3	0	0	46	5	2	12.0	36.8
Cueva, Danyer	L-R	6-1	160	5-27-04	.226	.273	.318	101	411	380	45	86	15	4	4	44	21	5	0	5	137	9	4	5.1	33.3
Espinal, Jeferson	L-L	6-0	180	6-07-02	.063	.167	.063	5	18	16	0	1	0	0	0	0	1	1	0	0	9	1	1	5.6	50.0
Figuereo, Gleider	L-R	6-0	165	6-27-04	.220	.300	.323	107	450	396	51	87	14	0	9	51	42	6	0	6	132	8	3	9.3	29.3
Galan, Yosy	R-R	6-4	200	4-25-01	.229	.333	.492	51	210	179	36	41	9	1	12	34	25	4	0	2	63	10	4	11.9	30.0
Gutierrez, Anthony	R-R	6-3	180	11-25-04	.259	.326	.338	78	325	293	39	76	11	3	2	34	25	5	0	2	72	30	10	7.7	22.2
Hurdle, Devin	R-R	6-1	190	6-18-00	.211	.294	.237	23	86	76	13	16	2	0	0	5	9	0	1	0	26	3	1	10.5	30.2
Mendez, Wady	L-L	6-0	155	10-14-04	.250	.308	.250	4	13	12	0	3	0	0	0	0	1	0	0	0	4	0	1	7.7	30.8
Mesa, Andres	R-R	5-11	170	10-16-02	.191	.265	.316	45	151	136	17	26	5	0	4	15	13	1	0	1	60	6	4	8.6	39.7
Mitchell, Tucker	R-R	6-1	210	2-10-01	.338	.460	.488	24	100	80	18	27	6	0	2	15	12	7	0	1	23	3	1	12.0	23.0
Moller, Ian	R-R	6-0	190	10-26-02	.190	.325	.294	95	394	326	40	62	12	2	6	34	63	3	0	2	112	8	1	16.0	28.4
Moreno, Jesus	R-R	5-11	170	4-16-01	.115	.258	.167	25	93	78	7	9	1	0	1	3	13	2	0	0	43	0	0	14.0	46.2
Morrobel, Yeison	L-L	6-2	170	12-08-03	.273	.384	.313	37	151	128	16	35	2	0	1	13	22	1	0	0	34	12	3	14.6	22.5
Ortiz, Abimelec	L-L	6-0	230	2-22-02	.307	.392	.604	29	121	101	19	31	7	1	7	20	16	0	1	3	36	0	1	13.2	29.8
Pena, Yenci	R-R	6-2	193	7-13-00	.191	.333	.234	15	58	47	4	9	2	0	0	2	9	1	1	0	14	4	1	15.5	24.1
Piotto, Konner	L-R	5-9	195	1-01-98	.255	.354	.345	60	237	200	24	51	9	0	3	28	25	8	0	4	48	7	2	10.5	20.3
Pollard, Chandler	R-R	6-2	173	5-03-04	.200	.429	.400	2	7	5	1	1	1	0	0	0	2	0	0	0	2	1	0	28.6	28.6
Scott, Quincy	R-R	6-4	215	1-15-03	.376	.444	.412	24	99	85	15	32	1	1	0	11	10	2	0	2	28	2	0	10.1	28.3
Specht, Tommy	L-R	6-3	200	6-24-04	.221	.323	.288	61	257	222	25	49	10	1	1	18	32	2	0	1	69	6	2	12.5	26.8
Torres, Marcos	L-L	6-3	163	9-30-04	.108	.195	.108	10	41	37	2	4	0	0	0	1	3	1	0	0	18	0	3	7.3	43.9
Vargas, Echedry	R-R	5-11	170	2-27-05	.500	.500	.500	1	2	2	1	1	0	0	0	0	0	0	0	0	1	0	0	0.0	50.0
Villarroel, Miguel	R-R	6-0	165	12-23-01	.231	.271	.331	68	280	260	32	60	12	1	4	36	12	4	0	4	56	18	0	4.3	20.0

Pitching	B-T	Ht.	Wt.	DOB	W	L	ERA	G	GS	SV	IP	Hits	Runs	ER	HR	BB	SO	AVG	OBP	SLG	SO%	BB%	BF
Bonzagni, Paul	R-R	6-3	195	4-01-02	2	1	2.61	8	0	1	10	8	4	3	1	5	8	.205	.295	.308	18.2	11.4	44
Bormie, Wilian	R-R	6-3	175	2-23-03	0	1	7.56	2	2	0	8	5	7	7	2	6	7	.167	.297	.400	18.9	16.2	37
Brosky, Matt	R-R	5-10	190	9-15-99	1	2	3.96	9	1	0	25	32	22	11	3	6	29	.294	.339	.468	24.4	5.0	119
Chi, Bryan	R-R	6-0	205	3-22-99	2	3	4.11	8	3	0	31	25	20	14	2	10	33	.217	.279	.330	25.6	7.8	129
Clark, Seth	R-L	6-3	220	11-18-99	0	0	0.00	7	1	1	8	6	2	0	0	3	9	.222	.323	.259	29.0	9.7	31
Collyer, Gavin	R-R	6-1	165	5-12-01	0	0	0.00	1	0	0	3	1	0	0	0	1	6	.100	.182	.100	54.5	9.1	11
Corniell, Jose	R-R	6-3	165	6-22-03	4	1	2.70	10	6	1	43	26	15	13	4	14	56	.174	.259	.295	33.7	8.4	166
Curry, Aidan	R-R	6-5	185	7-05-02	6	3	2.30	19	15	0	82	47	24	21	4	29	99	.163	.243	.232	30.8	9.0	321
Davalillo, David	R-R	6-1	175	9-21-02	0	0	1.93	1	1	0	5	4	2	1	0	0	7	.235	.222	.294	38.9	0.0	18
Drake, Kohl	L-L	6-5	220	7-17-00	0	4	7.46	10	2	0	35	47	34	29	4	17	37	.322	.399	.486	22.0	10.1	168
Gessner, Josh	R-R	6-1	205	6-25-00	0	1	2.45	6	3	0	22	9	7	6	1	15	19	.129	.319	.214	20.9	16.5	91
Gonzalez, Jose	R-R	6-3	200	8-05-01	0	0	0.00	1	0	0	0	0	0	0	0	0	1	.000	.000	.000	100.0	0.0	1
Hales, Skylar	R-R	6-4	220	10-24-01	0	1	2.16	5	0	0	8	2	2	2	1	2	7	.077	.143	.192	25.0	7.1	28
Hoopii-Tuionetoa, Anthony	R-R	6-2	190	8-11-00	1	1	7.50	6	0	2	6	4	5	5	3	3	7	.174	.269	.609	26.9	11.5	26
Ireland, Thomas	L-L	6-1	170	6-27-02	1	2	5.79	5	2	0	19	20	13	12	4	8	14	.282	.363	.493	17.5	10.0	80
Kelley, Jackson	R-R	6-0	185	4-26-00	3	1	1.59	12	0	1	17	8	4	3	1	8	25	.143	.262	.196	37.9	12.1	66
Leath, Jackson	R-R	6-1	192	6-20-99	2	2	2.35	25	0	2	31	24	12	8	4	11	34	.209	.278	.348	26.8	8.7	127
Lockhart, Nick	R-R	6-6	204	2-12-01	0	0	1.29	8	0	1	14	8	2	2	1	1	16	.157	.173	.216	30.8	1.9	52
Lopez, Leandro	R-R	6-1	200	6-17-02	2	5	3.32	17	10	0	57	47	36	21	2	38	79	.221	.341	.300	31.0	14.9	255
MacLean, Dylan	R-L	6-4	190	7-12-02	7	5	3.20	23	7	1	76	64	28	27	2	30	75	.225	.302	.320	23.4	9.3	321
Magdaleno, Bryan	L-L	6-1	202	2-22-01	0	1	10.13	6	0	0	5	9	6	6	1	4	7	.360	.467	.520	23.3	13.3	30
Maton, Jacob	R-R	6-1	195	8-22-99	3	0	1.54	14	0	5	23	13	4	4	1	6	33	.160	.218	.222	37.9	6.9	87
McCarty, D.J.	R-R	6-2	145	9-09-02	1	3	3.05	23	12	0	74	58	31	25	1	27	86	.213	.305	.268	27.7	8.7	311
Mendoza, Brayan	L-L	6-0	155	1-19-04	1	3	3.60	17	9	0	50	42	25	20	1	23	48	.228	.322	.321	22.2	10.6	216
Mendoza, Damian	L-R	6-1	175	1-25-01	6	4	4.83	29	0	0	60	68	34	32	9	21	69	.285	.354	.452	25.7	7.8	268
Montalvo, Joseph	B-R	6-2	185	5-04-02	7	2	2.83	22	17	0	95	74	34	30	9	39	107	.211	.300	.331	27.0	9.8	397
Mota, Alberto	R-R	5-11	170	2-17-03	2	2	4.97	23	0	2	25	27	18	14	2	10	41	.273	.342	.414	36.9	9.0	111
Oviedo, Ivan	R-R	6-2	175	10-14-02	1	2	11.17	5	2	0	10	15	13	12	3	8	12	.366	.471	.683	23.5	15.7	51
Porter, Brock	R-R	6-4	208	6-03-03	0	3	2.47	21	21	0	69	39	24	19	1	42	95	.160	.304	.202	32.4	14.3	293

Ramirez, Luis	R-R	6-2	200	4-06-01	1	4	4.03	18	12	1	51	46	25	23	4	16	56	.242	.338	.379	25.5	7.3	220
Rodriguez, Adrian	R-R	6-5	192	5-18-01	3	1	5.08	30	1	9	34	23	27	19	2	32	33	.200	.392	.296	21.6	20.9	153
Rosado, Eury	R-R	6-0	160	11-23-00	1	0	1.86	4	0	0	10	7	2	2	1	5	7	.206	.326	.324	16.3	11.6	43
Serrano, Florencio	R-R	6-1	205	2-23-00	2	0	3.18	3	0	0	6	5	2	2	0	3	7	.238	.333	.381	29.2	12.5	24
Sparks, Wyatt	R-R	6-2	195	9-27-99	4	1	1.88	14	0	1	29	17	7	6	2	7	26	.170	.239	.280	23.9	6.4	109
Valdez, Luis	L-L	6-2	158	7-18-03	0	0	13.50	1	0	0	2	4	3	3	0	1	2	.444	.500	.444	20.0	10.0	10
Widger, C.J.	L-L	6-6	170	5-25-99	2	0	2.45	13	0	0	18	23	5	5	2	2	17	.315	.342	.438	22.4	2.6	76
Wynyard, Kai-Noa	R-R	6-0	176	6-22-02	1	2	2.38	24	0	1	42	29	15	11	1	16	43	.192	.272	.278	25.4	9.5	169

Fielding

Catcher	PCT	G	PO	A	E	DP	PB
Mitchell	.993	12	131	5	1	0	0
Moller	.989	87	839	56	10	7	8
Moreno	1.000	11	112	10	0	2	1
Piotto	1.000	17	170	13	0	1	3

First Base	PCT	G	PO	A	E	DP
Alvarez	1.000	4	27	3	0	3
Bannister	.991	12	100	6	1	7
Calarco	.992	17	118	10	1	13
Cheney	.994	22	169	6	1	4
Mesa	1.000	3	17	2	0	2
Mitchell	.950	4	19	0	1	1
Moreno	1.000	1	6	1	0	0
Ortiz	.974	24	142	9	4	10
Pena	1.000	11	72	1	0	7
Piotto	.990	16	90	10	1	10
Torres	.957	3	22	0	1	2
Villarroel	.990	13	87	10	1	9

Second Base	PCT	G	PO	A	E	DP
Alvarez	1.000	2	6	7	0	2
Cauley	.964	9	13	14	1	1
Cheney	.939	7	17	14	2	3
Cueva	.965	46	66	101	6	24
Figuereo	.714	2	2	3	2	0
Hurdle	.952	20	33	47	4	7
Mesa	.957	23	32	35	3	9
Pollard	1.000	2	3	1	0	0
Villarroel	.976	18	33	47	2	11

Third Base	PCT	G	PO	A	E	DP
Calarco	.800	1	1	3	1	0
Cheney	1.000	3	3	5	0	1
Figuereo	.909	104	67	163	23	15
Mesa	.917	5	3	8	1	1
Pena	.750	2	2	4	2	0
Villarroel	.880	12	6	16	3	1

Shortstop	PCT	G	PO	A	E	DP
Cauley	.930	53	69	118	14	23
Cueva	.933	55	63	118	13	23
Hurdle	.714	3	0	5	2	2
Mesa	.920	5	8	15	2	3
Vargas	.000	1	0	0	0	0
Villarroel	.949	12	12	25	2	3

Outfield	PCT	G	PO	A	E	DP
Alvarez	1.000	5	6	0	0	0
Aponte	.944	7	11	0	1	0
Bannister	.970	29	47	0	2	0
Blackmon	.969	101	193	4	6	0
Espinal	1.000	4	6	0	0	0
Galan	.968	44	59	1	2	0
Gutierrez	.965	73	157	7	6	0
Mendez	.944	4	10	1	1	0
Mesa	1.000	5	8	0	0	0
Morrobel	.990	34	59	6	1	3
Ortiz	.778	5	7	0	2	0
Scott	1.000	19	35	1	0	0
Specht	.974	53	93	4	4	0
Torres	1.000	7	12	0	0	0
Villarroel	.000	2	0	0	0	0

ACL RANGERS — *ROOKIE*

ARIZONA COMPLEX LEAGUE

Batting	B-T	Ht.	Wt.	DOB	AVG	OBP	SLG	G	PA	AB	R	H	2B	3B	HR	RBI	BB	HBP	SH	SF	SO	SB	CS	BB%	SO%
Alvarez, Erick	R-R	5-10	150	2-01-05	.195	.313	.280	25	96	82	10	16	5	1	0	9	12	2	0	0	22	1	2	12.5	22.9
Barroso, Beycker	R-R	5-10	160	1-24-03	.239	.341	.394	21	82	71	9	17	5	0	2	17	8	3	0	0	23	4	0	9.8	28.0
Basabe, Edgar	R-R	6-0	155	4-27-04	.261	.295	.408	44	149	142	23	37	9	3	2	23	7	0	0	0	41	9	2	4.7	27.5
Blackwell, Benjamin	R-R	5-11	185	4-06-99	.125	.222	.125	2	9	8	3	1	0	0	0	0	1	0	0	0	1	0	0	11.1	11.1
Calarco, Anthony	L-R	6-3	215	8-21-99	.125	.222	.125	2	9	8	1	1	0	0	0	1	0	1	0	0	3	0	0	0.0	33.3
Carter, Evan	L-R	6-2	190	8-29-02	.222	.417	.667	3	12	9	3	2	1	0	1	2	3	0	0	0	2	1	0	25.0	16.7
De Jesus, Jose	B-L	6-1	170	1-08-05	.223	.332	.340	50	220	188	29	42	10	3	2	16	29	2	0	1	62	12	6	13.2	28.2
Espinoza, Alfredo	R-R	6-0	160	9-23-04	.308	.317	.333	14	41	39	3	12	1	0	0	6	1	0	0	1	11	0	0	2.4	26.8
Figueroa, Danell	R-R	6-1	205	3-08-04	.190	.382	.310	20	55	42	7	8	2	0	1	5	12	1	0	0	18	0	1	21.8	32.7
Garcia, David	B-R	5-10	201	2-06-00	.412	.600	.588	6	25	17	9	7	1	1	0	3	3	5	0	0	1	2	0	12.0	4.0
Gonzalez, Cristian	R-R	6-0	160	2-14-05	.240	.289	.400	26	83	75	7	18	4	1	2	11	4	2	0	2	26	0	2	4.8	31.3
Gutierrez, Anthony	R-R	6-3	180	11-25-04	.350	.381	.550	6	21	20	4	7	0	2	0	2	1	0	0	0	6	2	1	4.8	28.6
Hurdle, Devin	R-R	6-1	190	6-18-00	.714	.667	1.143	2	9	7	3	5	0	0	1	5	0	1	0	1	1	0	0	0.0	11.1
Langford, Wyatt	R-R	6-1	225	11-15-01	.385	.429	.846	3	14	13	3	5	3	0	1	4	1	0	0	0	3	1	0	7.1	21.4
Lopez, Jesus	L-R	6-1	180	5-24-05	.289	.396	.644	13	53	45	8	13	3	2	3	8	5	3	0	0	13	0	0	9.4	24.5
Martin, Max	L-R	6-1	205	5-05-05	.243	.378	.378	10	45	37	8	9	2	0	1	7	8	0	0	0	11	0	0	17.8	24.4
Mejia, Esteban	R-R	5-11	165	11-03-04	.240	.316	.339	41	137	121	22	29	5	2	1	17	14	0	0	1	34	7	2	10.2	24.8
Mendez, Wady	L-L	6-0	155	10-14-04	.270	.370	.411	45	165	141	21	38	12	1	2	14	21	2	0	1	62	6	5	12.7	37.6
Narvaez, Efrenyer	R-R	5-11	155	7-25-02	.167	.286	.417	5	14	12	2	2	0	0	1	3	2	0	0	0	2	0	0	14.3	14.3
Ojeda, Miguel	R-R	6-0	200	6-16-00	.125	.125	.125	2	8	8	0	1	0	0	0	1	0	0	0	0	2	0	0	0.0	25.0
Pena, Yenci	R-R	6-2	193	7-13-00	.333	.407	.542	9	27	24	7	8	0	1	1	5	3	0	0	0	8	1	0	11.1	29.6
Pollard, Chandler	R-R	6-2	173	5-03-04	.235	.364	.388	51	220	183	43	43	9	5	3	23	24	13	0	0	79	20	2	10.9	35.9
Romero, Josue	R-R	5-9	190	9-19-02	.000	.174	.000	8	23	19	0	0	0	0	0	1	4	0	0	0	10	1	0	17.4	43.5
Scott, Quincy	R-R	6-4	215	1-15-03	.222	.300	.333	2	10	9	1	2	1	0	0	0	1	0	0	0	3	0	0	10.0	30.0
Specht, Tommy	L-R	6-3	200	6-24-04	.100	.182	.100	3	11	10	0	1	0	0	0	0	1	0	0	0	4	0	0	9.1	36.4
Torres, Marcos	L-L	6-3	163	9-30-04	.250	.378	.494	48	201	164	33	41	7	6	7	32	27	8	0	2	48	23	3	13.4	23.9
Vargas, Echedry	R-R	5-11	170	2-27-05	.315	.387	.569	52	222	197	46	62	15	1	11	39	21	3	0	1	54	17	3	9.5	24.3
Villarroel, Miguel	R-R	6-0	165	12-23-01	.250	.250	.250	3	8	8	1	2	0	0	0	3	0	0	0	0	1	0	0	0.0	12.5
Walcott, Sebastian	R-R	6-4	190	3-14-06	.273	.325	.524	35	157	143	26	39	9	3	7	19	10	2	0	2	51	9	5	6.4	32.5

Pitching	B-T	Ht.	Wt.	DOB	W	L	ERA	G	GS	SV	IP	Hits	Runs	ER	HR	BB	SO	AVG	OBP	SLG	SO%	BB%	BF
Agreda, Ismael	R-R	6-0	150	10-08-03	1	3	6.08	11	1	0	24	31	22	16	0	12	28	.298	.381	.346	23.7	10.2	118
Alfonso, Michael	R-R	6-3	205	1-08-03	1	2	13.91	12	0	0	11	28	22	17	2	12	16	.452	.541	.645	21.6	16.2	74
Anderson, Ben	R-R	6-4	200	5-02-98	0	0	1.80	3	3	0	5	3	1	1	0	2	5	.188	.278	.313	27.8	11.1	18
Bautista, Nick	R-R	6-3	200	2-22-02	1	6	6.05	17	0	2	19	22	15	13	1	17	35	.289	.415	.395	37.2	18.1	94
Bonzagni, Paul	R-R	6-3	195	4-01-02	1	0	0.00	1	0	0	1	0	0	0	0	0	2	.000	.000	.000	66.7	0.0	3
Bormie, Wilian	R-R	6-3	175	2-23-03	2	0	3.86	8	5	0	23	17	13	10	3	17	33	.200	.327	.353	31.7	16.3	104
Bremer, Noah	R-R	6-5	206	5-13-96	1	0	7.71	4	0	0	7	9	6	6	2	2	11	.300	.344	.567	34.4	6.3	32
Brito, Biembenido	R-R	6-3	180	2-13-03	0	2	9.23	12	1	0	26	27	35	27	2	27	30	.270	.430	.400	22.1	19.9	136
Bursick-Harrington, Logan	R-R	6-4	185	1-22-01	0	0	18.00	1	0	0	1	1	2	2	1	2	0	.250	.500	1.000	0.0	33.3	6
Casanova, Jean	R-R	6-3	181	3-04-97	0	0	5.79	5	2	0	5	7	3	3	0	4	4	.350	.458	.550	16.7	16.7	24

Chi, Bryan	R-R	6-0	205	3-22-99	1	0	2.50	6	3	1	18	13	5	5	2	3	23	.191	.225	.353	32.4	4.2	71
Cordero, Wilfredo	R-R	6-2	190	9-30-02	0	0	43.20	4	0	1	2	2	8	8	0	8	0	.286	.688	.429	0.0	50.0	16
Curtis, Kolton	B-R	6-4	170	5-05-04	0	0	16.20	6	0	0	7	8	12	12	1	8	11	.286	.459	.429	29.7	21.6	37
Davalillo, David	R-R	6-1	175	9-21-02	1	1	3.71	9	2	0	17	15	8	7	1	4	20	.227	.288	.364	27.4	5.5	73
DeVito, Ricky	B-R	6-3	195	8-21-98	0	0	0.00	2	0	0	2	0	0	0	0	1	1	.000	.125	.000	12.5	12.5	8
Drake, Kohl	L-L	6-5	220	7-17-00	2	1	3.09	4	2	0	12	11	5	4	0	3	18	.250	.306	.295	36.7	6.1	49
Elliott, Evan	R-R	6-3	210	1-10-01	0	0	9.00	3	0	0	3	1	3	3	0	8	4	.111	.556	.111	22.2	44.4	18
Engler, Scott	R-R	6-4	220	12-12-96	0	0	9.00	5	0	0	7	11	7	7	2	2	7	.367	.406	.600	21.9	6.3	32
Figueroa, Danell	R-R	6-1	205	3-08-04	0	0	0.00	2	0	0	1	1	0	0	0	0	1	.333	.333	.333	33.3	0.0	3
Florentino, Dianyer	R-R	6-4	200	1-07-00	1	1	4.91	15	0	1	18	14	22	10	2	20	22	.206	.412	.338	22.7	20.6	97
Gessner, Josh	R-R	6-1	205	6-25-00	0	0	0.00	2	1	0	5	2	0	0	0	0	10	.118	.118	.118	58.8	0.0	17
Gil, Orlando	R-R	6-3	165	9-10-01	0	0	9.31	6	0	0	10	6	10	10	0	13	13	.171	.408	.229	26.5	26.5	49
Gomez, Orceli	R-R	6-5	175	11-23-00	0	0	12.46	5	1	0	4	5	6	6	0	3	3	.294	.429	.471	14.3	14.3	21
Gonzalez, Jose	R-R	6-3	200	8-05-01	2	4	5.40	11	7	0	30	30	22	18	2	11	31	.259	.341	.414	23.5	8.3	132
Hales, Skylar	R-R	6-4	220	10-24-01	0	0	11.57	2	0	0	2	4	3	3	2	0	4	.364	.364	.909	36.4	0.0	11
Hoopii-Tuionetoa, Anthony	R-R	6-2	190	8-11-00	1	0	1.35	4	0	1	7	5	1	1	0	0	5	.192	.192	.192	19.2	0.0	26
Ireland, Thomas	L-L	6-1	170	6-27-02	0	0	1.42	8	5	0	25	19	9	4	1	5	29	.204	.260	.269	29.0	5.0	100
Kent, Zak	R-R	6-3	208	2-24-98	0	0	9.45	3	3	0	7	8	7	7	3	3	9	.296	.355	.630	29.0	9.7	31
Larsen, Kyle	R-R	6-2	240	6-14-03	0	0	0.00	1	1	0	3	3	0	0	0	4	1	.375	.583	.375	8.3	33.3	12
Lobus, Ryan	R-R	6-2	180	9-08-00	0	0	18.00	4	0	0	4	8	8	8	1	4	6	.400	.500	.650	25.0	16.7	24
Magdaleno, Bryan	L-L	6-1	202	2-22-01	1	0	5.84	13	0	1	12	13	8	8	1	4	20	.255	.333	.412	35.1	7.0	57
Matter, Case	R-R	6-2	180	1-16-02	0	0	3.00	3	0	1	3	3	1	1	1	0	4	.273	.273	.545	36.4	0.0	11
Matthews, John	R-R	6-1	190	1-21-98	0	0	0.00	2	0	0	3	1	0	0	0	0	6	.100	.250	.100	50.0	0.0	12
McDowell, Theo	L-R	6-4	175	12-02-98	1	1	5.40	7	0	1	7	7	6	4	0	3	8	.280	.387	.440	25.8	9.7	31
Mejia, Aneudis	R-R	5-11	165	12-13-03	0	3	8.10	11	4	0	20	24	23	18	3	27	31	.296	.478	.543	27.4	23.9	113
Mejia, Esteban	R-R	5-11	165	11-03-04	0	0	0.00	1	0	0	2	1	0	0	0	0	1	.167	.167	.167	16.7	0.0	6
Mejia, Juan	L-L	5-11	160	1-09-99	0	0	5.00	3	2	0	9	13	5	5	2	1	6	.333	.357	.564	14.3	2.4	42
Mendoza, Brayan	L-L	6-0	155	1-19-04	0	0	3.86	1	0	1	2	1	1	1	0	1	6	.125	.300	.125	60.0	10.0	10
Morse, Brendan	R-R	6-3	185	5-24-04	1	0	0.00	2	0	0	2	1	0	0	0	1	1	.167	.286	.167	14.3	14.3	7
Ortega, Teodoro	R-R	6-0	145	3-12-00	0	0	0.00	1	1	0	1	0	0	0	0	0	2	.000	.250	.000	50.0	0.0	4
Oviedo, Ivan	R-R	6-2	175	10-14-02	1	3	5.18	14	3	0	24	21	15	14	3	10	36	.228	.311	.380	34.0	9.4	106
Owen, Andrew	R-R	6-1	185	1-20-02	1	2	14.54	5	1	0	4	7	7	7	1	9	4	.368	.586	.684	13.3	30.0	30
Ozuna, Fernery	R-R	5-8	170	11-09-95	0	0	0.00	2	1	0	2	1	0	0	0	0	6	.125	.125	.125	75.0	0.0	8
Privette, William	R-R	6-6	200	2-01-02	0	1	22.50	3	0	0	2	2	7	5	0	8	2	.250	.625	.250	12.5	50.0	16
Rosado, Eury	R-R	6-0	160	11-23-00	1	1	6.86	10	3	0	21	24	17	16	4	15	27	.289	.427	.506	26.2	14.6	103
Sanchez, Justin	L-L	6-0	183	10-11-03	0	0	4.26	5	0	0	6	6	3	3	1	4	7	.240	.345	.400	24.1	13.8	29
Savage, Luke	R-R	6-1	200	8-10-01	0	0	6.00	3	0	0	3	3	3	2	0	2	4	.250	.357	.333	28.6	14.3	14
Simeon, Victor	R-R	6-2	160	12-04-00	1	1	7.20	8	2	0	15	15	13	12	2	11	17	.273	.408	.400	23.9	15.5	71
Tiger, Izack	R-R	6-2	185	2-08-01	0	0	2.25	3	1	0	4	7	3	1	0	2	4	.438	.500	.563	22.2	11.1	18
Trentadue, Josh	L-L	6-2	185	1-25-02	0	0	0.00	3	0	0	3	1	0	0	0	2	8	.091	.231	.091	61.5	15.4	13
Valdez, Luis	L-L	6-2	158	7-18-03	0	1	4.09	5	1	0	11	10	6	5	1	3	11	.244	.295	.390	25.0	6.8	44
Widger, C.J.	L-L	6-6	170	5-25-99	1	0	0.90	7	0	1	10	7	1	1	0	3	18	.194	.268	.333	43.9	7.3	41

Fielding

C: Barroso 14, Figueroa 13, Lopez 13, Espinoza 10, Garcia 5, Romero 4, Narvaez 3, Ojeda 2. **1B:** Alvarez 16, Mejia 15, Torres 13, Gonzalez 8, Barroso 2, Calarco 2, Espinoza 2, Figueroa 2. **2B:** Vargas 27, Pollard 19, Gonzalez 6, Alvarez 4, Blackwell 2, Hurdle 1. **3B:** Mejia 22, Pollard 10, Gonzalez 9, Vargas 7, Pena 6, Alvarez 5, Villarroel 2, Hurdle 1. **SS:** Pollard 21, Walcott 18, Vargas 17, Gonzalez 1. **OF:** De Jesus 53, Mendez 40, Basabe 34, Torres 33, Martin 10, Gutierrez 5, Langford 2, Carter 2, Scott 2, Specht 2, Gonzalez 1, Alvarez 1.

DSL RANGERS — ROOKIE

DOMINICAN SUMMER LEAGUE

Batting	B-T	Ht.	Wt.	DOB	AVG	OBP	SLG	G	PA	AB	R	H	2B	3B	HR	RBI	BB	HBP	SH	SF	SO	SB	CS	BB%	SO%
Beato, Andy	R-R	5-10	190	11-27-03	.154	.313	.231	9	16	13	2	2	1	0	0	1	2	1	0	0	5	1	0	12.5	31.3
Bruzual, Daniel	R-R	6-0	170	2-01-05	.313	.365	.403	37	159	144	22	45	9	2	0	22	11	2	0	2	35	4	2	6.9	22.0
Cabrera, Roni	R-R	6-1	175	7-31-05	.315	.464	.611	16	69	54	17	17	7	3	1	10	13	2	0	0	7	6	0	18.8	10.1
Cabrera, Yeremi	L-L	5-11	155	7-02-05	.329	.445	.559	46	211	170	49	56	6	6	7	29	33	4	2	2	28	9	6	15.6	13.3
Cuello, Adriel	R-R	6-1	175	12-15-05	.171	.288	.189	37	133	111	20	19	2	0	0	14	10	9	1	2	46	6	2	7.5	34.6
Disla, Arturo	R-R	6-2	240	10-08-00	.274	.416	.468	19	77	62	11	17	3	0	3	12	9	6	0	0	13	0	0	11.7	16.9
Espinoza, Alfredo	R-R	6-0	160	9-23-04	.667	.700	1.111	3	10	9	1	6	2	1	0	3	1	0	0	0	1	1	0	10.0	10.0
Figueroa, Danell	R-R	6-1	205	3-08-04	.333	.400	.333	4	10	9	1	3	0	0	0	0	0	1	0	0	1	0	0	0.0	10.0
Gamez, Jesus	R-R	6-0	190	3-04-03	.267	.306	.472	52	216	195	31	52	13	3	7	38	10	4	0	7	65	11	7	4.6	30.1
Guerrero, Pablo	R-R	6-2	200	7-31-06	.224	.361	.360	36	155	125	23	28	5	0	4	20	23	5	0	2	34	1	4	14.8	21.9
Guzman, Michael	R-R	6-1	165	1-31-06	.247	.384	.359	48	211	170	44	42	3	2	4	30	35	4	0	2	47	13	2	16.6	22.3
Herrera, Angel	L-L	5-11	160	9-16-05	.192	.350	.323	43	163	130	24	25	2	6	1	19	32	0	0	1	33	13	7	19.6	20.2
Lantigua, Hector	R-R	6-0	160	9-16-04	.254	.360	.254	31	76	63	3	16	0	0	0	13	11	0	1	1	17	2	1	14.5	22.4
Lemos, Kleimer	B-R	6-1	175	6-03-05	.218	.292	.363	48	216	193	23	42	5	1	7	37	17	4	0	2	56	5	8	7.9	25.9
Macias, Antonis	B-L	5-11	185	2-01-05	.280	.401	.341	45	197	164	27	46	10	0	0	14	23	10	0	0	45	12	8	11.7	22.8
Marlin, Gedionne	R-R	5-11	165	2-05-04	.233	.311	.333	48	183	159	35	37	7	3	1	21	18	2	0	4	31	10	5	9.8	16.9
Marquez, Luis	R-R	5-10	150	8-31-05	.250	.364	.381	52	212	176	25	44	4	2	5	25	25	7	3	1	37	11	6	11.8	17.5
Mejia, Lisandro	L-R	6-0	150	9-09-05	.175	.330	.266	43	192	154	26	27	7	2	1	17	30	6	1	1	59	13	4	15.6	30.7
Mejias, Sergio	R-R	6-2	185	5-06-06	.077	.368	.231	6	19	13	3	1	0	1	0	1	3	3	0	0	10	0	0	15.8	52.6
Mendoza, Aniel	R-R	6-2	185	9-13-04	.182	.182	.273	5	11	11	1	2	1	0	0	2	0	0	0	0	1	1	1	0.0	9.1
Montero, Neurelin	R-R	5-10	170	5-26-06	.264	.494	.321	21	77	53	11	14	3	0	0	8	19	5	0	0	13	0	2	24.7	16.9
Morel, Braylin	R-R	6-2	180	1-19-06	.344	.417	.644	47	204	180	40	62	17	8	7	43	21	2	0	1	50	2	2	10.3	24.5
Osorio, Hector	L-L	6-0	150	4-06-05	.293	.466	.376	48	223	157	42	46	8	1	1	29	49	9	0	8	26	17	4	22.0	11.7
Pavon, Keiderson	R-R	5-7	140	12-11-03	.222	.373	.294	48	193	153	34	34	9	1	0	24	36	2	0	2	26	13	3	18.7	13.5

Payano, Joselin	R-R	6-1	160	12-28-04	.273	.402	.387	42	184	150	29	41	10	2	1	27	27	6	0	1	38	1	1	14.7	20.7
Rondon, Joswuill	L-L	5-11	165	12-20-05	.227	.342	.325	41	185	154	21	35	7	1	2	16	14	14	1	2	31	10	5	7.6	16.8
Sulbaran, Juan	R-R	5-11	165	10-01-05	.320	.431	.388	32	130	103	19	33	3	2	0	20	17	6	0	4	13	4	1	13.1	10.0
Tavares, Joseph	R-R	6-1	180	9-15-05	.000	.182	.000	3	11	9	1	0	0	0	0	0	1	1	0	0	4	0	0	9.1	36.4
Tineo, Yeferson	B-R	6-0	160	10-10-03	.211	.378	.408	23	90	71	18	15	2	6	0	10	15	4	0	0	22	6	0	16.7	24.4
Tovar, Deward	L-L	5-11	180	4-04-06	.264	.360	.362	47	189	163	29	43	6	2	2	23	24	1	0	1	48	5	3	12.7	25.4
Vargas, Jhocsuanth	R-R	5-11	170	8-31-06	.273	.365	.391	36	126	110	15	30	7	0	2	15	11	5	0	0	19	4	1	8.7	15.1
Walcott, Sebastian	R-R	6-4	190	3-14-06	.161	.381	.323	9	42	31	4	5	3	1	0	3	10	1	0	0	8	3	0	23.8	19.0
Wong, Williams	L-R	5-10	180	10-12-05	.285	.431	.358	39	161	123	18	35	7	1	0	20	32	2	1	3	33	6	3	19.9	20.5

Pitching	**B-T**	**Ht.**	**Wt.**	**DOB**	**W**	**L**	**ERA**	**G**	**GS**	**SV**	**IP**	**Hits**	**Runs**	**ER**	**HR**	**BB**	**SO**	**AVG**	**OBP**	**SLG**	**SO%**	**BB%**	**BF**
Anazco, Angel	L-L	6-3	195	11-17-01	3	2	4.75	18	2	0	36	33	23	19	1	18	59	.241	.352	.307	36.4	11.1	162
Arias, Jordy	R-R	5-11	185	8-04-05	0	4	9.62	13	9	0	24	30	33	26	3	20	26	.303	.440	.475	20.8	16.0	125
Arias, Yeimison	R-R	6-1	165	1-09-05	0	2	6.58	10	5	0	26	28	28	19	3	14	27	.277	.379	.465	21.6	11.2	125
Baptiste, Yefris	L-L	6-2	175	11-23-02	0	0	8.59	10	0	0	15	11	17	14	0	22	25	.208	.462	.245	31.6	27.8	79
Beato, Andy	R-R	5-10	190	11-27-03	0	0	3.38	2	0	0	3	3	1	1	0	1	1	.273	.333	.273	8.3	8.3	12
Belen, Luis	R-R	6-3	185	6-12-04	1	2	5.06	12	0	1	21	29	14	12	4	13	20	.333	.420	.644	20.0	13.0	100
Belisario, Pedro	L-L	6-1	160	12-20-03	0	4	5.73	12	9	1	33	25	25	21	0	31	45	.217	.401	.304	29.4	20.3	153
Burgos, Enyer	R-R	6-0	175	6-15-02	2	2	6.03	16	0	1	31	24	30	21	3	36	43	.202	.417	.345	26.4	22.1	163
Colon, Bawin	R-R	6-3	215	4-14-02	3	2	5.14	15	0	1	21	21	14	12	2	15	27	.256	.392	.427	26.2	14.6	103
Diaz, Jerson	R-R	6-0	175	10-06-04	0	1	10.07	15	0	0	22	24	26	25	2	30	19	.286	.496	.393	15.7	24.8	121
Done, Hayrol	R-R	6-2	175	6-30-03	2	2	4.88	18	0	2	24	21	15	13	3	20	20	.231	.377	.352	17.5	17.5	114
Evangelista, Snarlyn	R-R	6-0	175	2-20-05	0	1	6.66	14	0	0	26	32	21	19	1	11	23	.299	.382	.439	18.7	8.9	123
Florentino, Dianyer	R-R	6-4	200	1-07-00	0	0	0.00	1	0	0	1	0	0	0	0	0	3	.000	.000	.000	75.0	0.0	4
Garcia, Jaiker	R-R	6-4	175	12-23-04	1	2	19.64	7	0	0	7	13	16	16	2	7	5	.394	.523	.727	11.4	15.9	44
Garcia, Luis	L-L	6-4	220	2-18-04	2	1	12.38	6	1	0	8	7	12	11	1	14	9	.241	.500	.345	19.6	30.4	46
Gil, Geral	R-R	6-2	170	3-04-04	0	1	4.85	17	0	0	26	28	20	14	0	13	29	.269	.389	.346	23.0	10.3	126
Gil, Orlando	R-R	6-3	165	9-10-01	1	1	3.65	9	5	1	25	15	11	10	1	11	43	.167	.265	.278	42.2	10.8	102
Heredia, Manuel	R-R	6-2	165	12-13-02	1	4	7.31	12	5	0	32	34	29	26	2	21	31	.268	.409	.354	19.4	13.1	160
Hernandez, Yoniel	R-R	6-2	190	2-18-04	0	0	12.00	3	0	0	3	5	4	4	1	4	2	.417	.588	.667	11.8	23.5	17
Lantigua, Hector	R-R	6-0	160	9-16-04	0	0	4.91	4	0	0	4	5	4	2	0	3	2	.294	.381	.353	9.5	14.3	21
Macias, Antonis	B-L	5-11	185	2-01-05	0	0	0.00	1	0	0	2	1	0	0	0	1	1	.200	.333	.200	16.7	16.7	6
Martinez, Emmanuel	L-L	6-1	170	8-28-03	4	0	2.17	11	7	0	46	28	14	11	0	17	65	.182	.294	.221	35.9	9.4	181
Martinez, Felix	R-R	6-0	180	7-05-02	0	0	10.13	8	0	0	8	4	9	9	0	9	6	.154	.436	.192	15.4	23.1	39
Martinez, Frank	R-R	6-2	165	4-30-02	0	1	10.18	11	2	1	20	28	30	23	1	18	17	.318	.455	.432	15.3	16.2	111
Medina, Angel	R-R	6-1	157	5-21-02	2	0	0.82	6	0	1	11	3	1	1	0	1	13	.086	.135	.114	35.1	2.7	37
Morales, Moises	R-R	6-1	175	2-15-04	0	1	7.20	4	0	0	5	12	8	4	2	3	3	.480	.552	.920	10.3	10.3	29
Munoz, Luimy	R-R	6-2	160	7-28-02	2	2	2.27	11	10	0	36	38	12	9	0	14	40	.270	.340	.326	25.6	9.0	156
Nivar, Jormy	R-R	6-3	170	5-07-03	3	1	3.56	11	1	0	30	27	14	12	1	13	30	.241	.323	.339	23.6	10.2	127
Nunez, German	R-R	6-3	155	5-24-02	4	1	3.16	11	10	0	51	37	20	18	3	22	65	.201	.307	.304	30.5	10.3	213
Nunez, Jorge	R-R	6-3	185	8-19-03	2	0	4.34	20	0	1	29	26	17	14	0	25	19	.255	.420	.363	13.8	18.1	138
Ortiz, Walkin	R-R	6-6	200	12-07-01	0	1	20.25	3	0	0	3	6	6	6	0	3	5	.429	.529	.714	29.4	17.6	17
Parra, Deretd	R-R	6-3	160	6-18-00	3	0	2.67	17	0	1	27	15	13	8	0	20	37	.152	.320	.162	29.6	16.0	125
Paulino, Felix	R-R	6-0	160	6-05-06	0	3	3.94	11	9	0	32	25	16	14	1	15	41	.212	.314	.288	29.9	10.9	137
Pavon, Keiderson	R-R	5-7	140	12-11-03	0	0	81.00	1	0	0	1	4	6	6	1	1	0	.667	.778	1.333	0.0	11.1	9
Peralta, Eddy	R-R	6-2	165	1-27-03	1	3	7.34	13	10	0	31	27	26	25	2	23	47	.241	.410	.384	32.4	15.9	145
Reyes, Ransiel	R-R	6-3	185	8-29-05	0	1	22.24	6	0	0	6	5	15	14	1	17	5	.294	.650	.529	12.5	42.5	40
Rodriguez, Geury	L-L	6-0	155	10-20-04	1	1	2.66	10	1	1	20	17	9	6	0	12	32	.221	.337	.273	34.8	13.0	92
Rubio, Johander	R-R	6-1	185	7-06-06	1	0	10.80	4	2	0	5	3	6	6	0	9	7	.176	.464	.294	25.0	32.1	28
Simeon, Victor	R-R	6-2	160	12-04-00	1	1	6.17	5	4	0	12	12	12	8	2	5	21	.250	.339	.396	37.5	8.9	56
Tabolda, Rafael	R-R	6-4	185	4-06-04	0	2	4.15	14	0	1	22	16	12	10	1	16	28	.203	.366	.291	27.7	15.8	101
Tejada, Danery	R-R	6-0	180	10-21-02	1	3	8.67	18	0	2	27	32	31	26	2	19	35	.317	.422	.515	26.9	14.6	130
Tovar, Jhemiangel	R-R	6-4	195	4-21-03	1	1	8.40	12	0	1	15	18	16	14	0	8	14	.277	.365	.385	18.9	10.8	74
Urbaez, Rayner	R-R	6-0	175	2-13-03	2	2	4.26	12	11	0	38	33	22	18	3	15	57	.231	.317	.364	34.8	9.1	164
Valdez, Jesus	R-R	6-2	175	5-03-01	2	1	4.35	11	0	2	21	23	10	10	1	5	22	.274	.330	.357	24.2	5.5	91
Valverde, Michael	L-L	6-2	211	12-07-02	0	2	9.60	14	1	0	15	19	25	16	2	13	22	.297	.460	.438	25.0	14.8	88
Villavicencio, Adonis	R-R	6-2	200	12-22-00	0	1	7.27	8	0	0	9	13	7	7	1	7	15	.342	.468	.526	31.9	14.9	47
Yunyet, Juan	L-L	6-1	175	12-17-04	3	2	3.65	13	6	0	37	30	18	15	1	15	41	.214	.302	.307	25.5	9.3	161

Fielding

C: Bruzual 33, Sulbaran 27, Vargas 27, Montero 20, Beato 4, Figueroa 4, Espinoza 3, Tavares 2. **1B:** Payano 39, Gamez 24, Disla 19, Marlin 9, Lantigua 7, Macias 7, Cabrera 3, Marquez 3, Vargas 3, Rondon 2, Tavares 1, Mejias 1. **2B:** Wong 23, Marquez 17, Mejia 16, Cuello 16, Pavon 14, Lemos 8, Marlin 7, Lantigua 7, Tineo 5, Mendoza 2. **3B:** Guzman 40, Marlin 30, Marquez 22, Lantigua 10, Pavon 7, Cuello 5, Mendoza 3, Lemos 1, Tineo 1, Wong 1. **SS:** Pavon 25, Mejia 24, Lemos 23, Tineo 15, Cuello 14, Marquez 5, Walcott 5, Lantigua 2, Guzman 1. **OF:** Cabrera 52, Osorio 47, Morel 43, Herrera 43, Macias 40, Rondon 40, Tovar 40, Gamez 25, Guerrero 15, Mejias 4, Pavon 4, Payano 1, Cuello 1, Marlin 1, Lantigua 1.

Toronto Blue Jays

TORONTO BLUE JAYS

SEASON SYNOPSIS: The formula was different, but the results were all too familiar to Blue Jays fans. Toronto won around 90 games for the third straight year, settled for a wild-card spot and exited the postseason after scoring once in two games against the Twins in Minneapolis.

HIGH POINT: Toronto rode the roller coaster in September, getting swept at home in a four-game set by the Rangers before rebounding to win five straight against Boston and at the Yankees. Back-to-back walkoff wins against the Red Sox stood out: A Whit Merrifield 13th-inning RBI single Sept. 16, then Matt Chapman's run-scoring triple in the ninth the next day. The hot streak helped vault the Jays back into a wild-card spot.

LOW POINT: The Rangers sweep was rough. Texas outscored Toronto 35-9 and dropped the Jays 1.5 games back in the wild-card race. George Springer, Bo Bichette and Vladimir Guerrero Jr. combined to go 7-for-44 in the four games, and ace Kevin Gausman didn't make it out of the fourth inning in the finale. That presaged the Jays' struggles in the wild-card series, in which the offense was silenced and Gausman lasted just four innings in Game 1.

NOTABLE ROOKIES: Longtime prospect Nate Pearson got his longest shot in the big leagues, tossing 43 relief innings with a 4.85 ERA. Davis Schneider, a 28th-round pick in the same 2017 draft that produced Pearson, burst on the scene with needed power, hitting eight home runs in 141 plate appearances, but finished September on an 0-for-31 slide.

KEY TRANSACTIONS: Free agent Chris Bassitt, signed for three years, $63 million, turned in a strong season in the rotation. The Blue Jays traded offense for defense prior to the year, signing Kevin Kiermaier to play center field; sending Teoscar Hernandez to the Mariners for pitching depth; and, most significantly, acquiring Daulton Varsho from Arizona for catcher Gabriel Moreno and outfielder Lourdes Gurriel Jr. Collectively, the Blue Jays sought greater run prevention and accomplished that, but the offense backed up.

DOWN ON THE FARM: Infielder Orelvis Martinez had a nice rebound season as he cut his strikeout rate and showed all-around improvements. Lefthander Ricky Tiedemann was generally impressive when he pitched, but he's struggled to stay healthy and show the durability he'll need to be a starter in Toronto.

OPENING DAY PAYROLL: $209,938,983 (7th).

PLAYERS OF THE YEAR

MAJOR LEAGUE
Kevin Gausman
RHP
12-9, 3.16
31 GS, 185 IP
1.18 WHIP, 11.5 SO/9

MINOR LEAGUE
Davis Schneider
2B
(AAA)
.275/.416/.553
21 HR, 21 2B

ORGANIZATION LEADERS

Batting		*Minimum 250 AB
MAJORS		
* AVG	Bo Bichette	.306
* OPS	Brandon Belt	.858
HR	Vladimir Guerrero Jr.	26
RBI	Vladimir Guerrero Jr.	94
MINORS		
* AVG	Ernie Clement, Buffalo	.348
* OBP	Spencer Horwitz, Buffalo	.450
* SLG	Davis Schneider, Buffalo	.553
* OPS	Davis Schneider, Buffalo	.969
R	Rafael Lantigua, Buffalo	101
H	Rafael Lantigua, Buffalo	142
TB	Damiano Palmegiani, N. Hamp./Buffalo	223
2B	Rafael Lantigua, Buffalo	40
3B	Alex De Jesus, Vancouver	7
HR	Orelvis Martinez, N. Hamp./Buffalo	28
RBI	Orelvis Martinez, N. Hamp./Buffalo	94
BB	Rafael Lantigua, Buffalo	98
SO	Damiano Palmegiani, N. Hamp./Buffalo	153
SB	Cam Eden, Buffalo	53

Pitching		#Minimum 75 IP
MAJORS		
W	Kevin Gausman	12
# ERA	Kevin Gausman	3.16
SO	Kevin Gausman	237
SV	Jordan Romano	36
MINORS		
W	Wes Parsons, Dunedin/Buffalo	9
L	Jimmy Robbins, N. Hamp,/Buffalo	8
# ERA	Andrew Bash, N.Hamp./Buffalo	2.52
G	Bradon Eisert, Buffalo	59
GS	Zach Thompson, Dunedin/Buffalo	25
SV	T.J. Brock, Vanc./N. Hamp.	13
IP	Chad Dallas, Vanc./N. Hamp.	123
BB	Michael Dominguez, Vanc./N. Hamp.	72
SO	Chad Dallas, Vanc./N. Hamp.	144
# AVG	Michael Dominguez, Vanc./N.Hamp.	.170

2023 PERFORMANCE

General Manager: Ross Atkins. **Farm Director:** Joe Sclafani. **Scouting Director:** Shane Farrell.

Class	Team	League	W	L	PCT	Finish	Manager
Majors	Toronto Blue Jays	American	89	73	.549	5 (15)	John Schneider
Triple-A	Buffalo Bisons	International	76	72	.514	8 (20)	Casey Candaele
Double-A	NHampshire Fisher Cats	Eastern	62	72	.463	9 (12)	Cesar Martin
High-A	Vancouver Canadians	Northwest	77	54	.588	1 (6)	Brent Lavallee
Low-A	Dunedin Blue Jays	Florida State	62	70	.470	7 (10)	Donnie Murphy
Rookie	FCL Blue Jays	Florida Complex	17	37	.315	15 (15)	Jose Mayorga
Rookie	DSL Blue Jays	Dominican Sum.	28	25	.528	19 (50)	Andy Fermin
Overall 2023 Minor League Record			322	330	.494	17th (30)	

ORGANIZATION STATISTICS

TORONTO BLUE JAYS

AMERICAN LEAGUE

Batting	B-T	Ht.	Wt.	DOB	AVG	OBP	SLG	G	PA	AB	R	H	2B	3B	HR	RBI	BB	HBP	SH	SF	SO	SB	CS	BB%	SO%
Belt, Brandon	L-L	6-3	230	4-20-88	.254	.369	.490	103	404	339	53	86	23	0	19	43	61	2	0	2	141	0	0	15.1	34.9
Bichette, Bo	R-R	6-0	190	3-05-98	.306	.339	.475	135	601	571	69	175	30	3	20	73	27	2	0	1	115	5	3	4.5	19.1
Biggio, Cavan	L-R	6-2	200	4-11-95	.235	.340	.370	111	338	289	54	68	12	0	9	40	40	7	0	2	88	5	2	11.8	26.0
Chapman, Matt	R-R	6-0	215	4-28-93	.240	.330	.424	140	581	509	66	122	39	2	17	54	62	8	0	2	165	4	2	10.7	28.4
Clement, Ernie	R-R	6-0	170	3-22-96	.380	.385	.500	30	52	50	7	19	1	1	1	10	1	0	0	1	4	1	0	1.9	7.7
DeJong, Paul	R-R	6-0	205	8-02-93	.068	.068	.068	13	44	44	1	3	0	0	0	1	0	0	0	0	18	0	0	0.0	40.9
Eden, Cam	R-R	6-1	205	3-31-98	.167	.167	.167	5	6	6	1	1	0	0	0	0	0	0	0	0	2	0	0	0.0	33.3
Espinal, Santiago	R-R	5-10	185	11-13-94	.248	.310	.335	93	254	230	30	57	14	0	2	25	18	3	2	1	36	2	1	7.1	14.2
Guerrero, Vladimir	R-R	6-2	245	3-16-99	.264	.345	.444	156	682	602	78	159	30	0	26	94	67	9	0	4	100	5	3	9.8	14.7
Heineman, Tyler	B-R	5-10	190	6-19-91	.276	.432	.379	19	37	29	4	8	1	1	0	3	7	1	0	0	7	0	0	18.9	18.9
Horwitz, Spencer	L-R	5-10	190	11-14-97	.256	.341	.385	15	44	39	5	10	2	0	1	7	4	1	0	0	12	0	0	9.1	27.3
Jansen, Danny	R-R	6-2	215	4-15-95	.228	.312	.474	86	301	268	38	61	15	0	17	53	23	10	0	0	62	0	0	7.6	20.6
Kiermaier, Kevin	L-R	6-1	210	4-22-90	.265	.322	.419	129	408	370	58	98	21	6	8	36	29	4	1	4	86	14	1	7.1	21.1
Kirk, Alejandro	R-R	5-8	245	11-06-98	.250	.334	.358	123	422	372	34	93	16	0	8	43	42	6	0	2	45	0	0	10.0	10.7
Lukes, Nathan	L-R	5-11	180	7-12-94	.192	.290	.308	29	31	26	4	5	1	1	0	2	4	0	0	1	9	0	0	12.9	29.0
Luplow, Jordan	R-R	5-11	195	9-26-93	.214	.353	.214	7	17	14	1	3	0	0	0	1	3	0	0	0	8	0	0	17.6	47.1
2-team (32 Minnesota)					.232	.344	.399	90	312	263	40	61	14	0	10	39	39	6	0	4	64	4	1	12.5	20.5
McCoy, Mason	R-R	5-11	185	3-31-95	.000	.000	.000	6	1	1	2	0	0	0	0	0	0	0	0	0	1	0	0	0.0	100.0
Merrifield, Whit	R-R	6-1	195	1-24-89	.272	.318	.382	145	592	547	66	149	27	0	11	67	36	3	0	6	101	26	10	6.1	17.1
Schneider, Davis	R-R	5-9	190	1-26-99	.276	.404	.603	35	141	116	23	32	12	1	8	20	21	4	0	0	43	1	0	14.9	30.5
Springer, George	R-R	6-3	220	9-19-89	.258	.327	.405	154	683	613	87	158	25	1	21	72	60	5	0	3	125	20	5	8.8	18.3
Varsho, Daulton	L-R	5-10	207	7-02-96	.220	.285	.389	158	581	527	65	116	23	3	20	61	45	4	1	3	135	16	7	7.7	23.2

Pitching	B-T	Ht.	Wt.	DOB	W	L	ERA	G	GS	SV	IP	Hits	Runs	ER	HR	BB	SO	AVG	OBP	SLG	SO%	BB%	BF
Bass, Anthony	R-R	6-2	205	11-01-87	0	0	4.95	22	0	0	20	19	12	11	3	9	19	.247	.318	.455	21.6	10.2	88
Bassitt, Chris	R-R	6-5	217	2-22-89	16	8	3.60	33	33	0	200	176	88	80	28	59	186	.235	.299	.403	22.5	7.1	826
Berrios, Jose	R-R	6-0	205	5-27-94	11	12	3.65	32	32	0	190	173	82	77	25	52	184	.241	.300	.397	23.5	6.6	782
Cabrera, Genesis	L-L	6-2	180	10-10-96	1	0	2.66	29	0	0	24	17	10	7	2	6	20	.195	.260	.333	20.8	6.3	96
Cimber, Adam	R-R	6-3	195	8-15-90	0	2	7.40	22	0	1	21	25	18	17	6	7	12	.301	.379	.542	12.6	7.4	95
Clement, Ernie	R-R	6-0	170	3-22-96	0	0	9.00	1	0	0	1	3	1	1	0	0	0	.500	.571	.500	0.0	0.0	7
Danner, Hagen	R-R	6-1	215	9-30-98	0	0	0.00	1	0	0	0	0	0	0	0	0	0	.000	.000	.000	0.0	0.0	1
Francis, Bowden	R-R	6-5	220	4-22-96	1	0	1.73	20	0	1	36	22	7	7	5	8	35	.175	.228	.317	25.7	5.9	136
Garcia, Yimi	R-R	6-1	230	8-18-90	3	4	4.09	73	0	3	66	67	35	30	8	15	79	.261	.315	.405	28.0	5.3	282
Gausman, Kevin	L-R	6-2	205	1-06-91	12	9	3.16	31	31	0	185	163	72	65	19	55	237	.233	.291	.379	31.1	7.2	763
Green, Chad	L-R	6-3	215	5-24-91	3	0	5.25	12	0	0	12	12	10	7	1	4	16	.250	.308	.417	30.8	7.7	52
Hatch, Thomas	R-R	6-1	195	9-29-94	0	0	4.26	6	0	0	6	10	5	3	0	5	10	.357	.441	.500	28.6	14.3	35
Hicks, Jordan	R-R	6-2	220	9-06-96	2	3	2.63	25	0	4	24	18	9	7	2	8	22	.207	.281	.322	22.9	8.3	96
Jackson, Jay	R-R	6-1	195	10-27-87	3	1	2.12	25	0	0	30	18	8	7	4	9	27	.171	.243	.314	23.3	7.8	116
Kikuchi, Yusei	L-L	6-0	210	6-17-91	11	6	3.86	32	32	0	168	165	78	72	27	48	181	.255	.311	.426	25.9	6.9	700
Manoah, Alek	R-R	6-6	285	1-09-98	3	9	5.87	19	19	0	87	93	61	57	15	59	79	.269	.388	.460	19.0	14.2	415
Mayza, Tim	L-L	6-3	215	1-15-92	3	1	1.52	69	0	1	53	50	10	9	2	15	53	.251	.302	.342	24.7	7.0	215
Parsons, Wes	R-R	6-5	206	9-06-92	0	1	20.25	1	1	0	4	10	9	9	2	3	3	.455	.538	.773	11.5	11.5	26
Pearson, Nate	R-R	6-6	255	8-20-96	5	2	4.85	35	0	1	43	36	25	23	7	18	43	.226	.313	.409	23.6	9.9	182
Pop, Zach	R-R	6-4	220	9-20-96	1	1	6.59	15	0	0	14	11	11	10	4	6	14	.220	.304	.480	25.0	10.7	56
Richards, Trevor	R-R	6-2	205	5-15-93	2	1	4.95	56	3	0	73	63	41	40	13	35	105	.228	.317	.424	33.3	11.1	315
Romano, Jordan	R-R	6-5	210	4-21-93	5	7	2.90	59	0	36	59	48	20	19	6	24	72	.218	.301	.350	29.0	9.7	248
Ryu, Hyun Jin	R-L	6-3	250	3-25-87	3	3	3.46	11	11	0	52	53	25	20	9	14	38	.257	.306	.447	17.0	6.3	224
Swanson, Erik	R-R	6-3	225	9-04-93	4	2	2.97	69	0	4	67	52	22	22	8	21	75	.217	.280	.358	28.6	8.0	262
Thornton, Trent	R-R	6-0	190	9-30-93	0	0	1.69	4	0	0	5	7	1	1	0	1	5	.333	.364	.333	22.7	4.5	22
White, Mitch	R-R	6-3	210	12-28-94	0	1	7.11	10	0	0	13	15	11	10	2	7	13	.294	.367	.529	21.7	11.7	60

Fielding

Catcher	PCT	G	PO	A	E	DP	PB
Heineman	1.000	17	105	3	0	0	0
Jansen	.990	73	603	20	6	2	1
Kirk	.993	99	829	36	6	3	1

First Base	PCT	G	PO	A	E	DP
Belt	.995	29	197	7	1	16
Biggio	1.000	20	89	4	0	10
Guerrero	.991	121	864	67	8	87
Horwitz	1.000	5	32	4	0	3

Second Base	PCT	G	PO	A	E	DP
Biggio	.993	49	57	84	1	25
Clement	1.000	6	6	3	0	1
Espinal	.953	47	42	81	6	21
Merrifield	.984	84	104	143	4	29
Schneider	1.000	23	27	49	0	10

Third Base	PCT	G	PO	A	E	DP
Biggio	1.000	13	6	12	0	1
Chapman	.968	137	114	253	12	35
Clement	.500	3	0	1	1	0
Espinal	.963	26	16	36	2	2
Schneider	.833	3	1	4	1	0

Shortstop	PCT	G	PO	A	E	DP
Bichette	.980	130	122	265	8	59
Biggio	1.000	1	1	0	0	0
Clement	.958	15	11	35	2	7
DeJong	1.000	13	13	25	0	5
Espinal	.978	16	18	27	1	9
McCoy	1.000	6	0	3	0	1

Outfield	PCT	G	PO	A	E	DP
Biggio	.976	27	40	0	1	0
Eden	1.000	2	2	0	0	0
Kiermaier	.989	127	257	5	3	2
Lukes	1.000	20	11	1	0	0
Luplow	1.000	4	10	0	0	0
Merrifield	.996	87	131	1	1	0
Schneider	1.000	3	3	0	0	0
Springer	1.000	132	261	6	0	1
Varsho	.997	181	312	10	1	2

BUFFALO BISONS — *TRIPLE-A*

INTERNATIONAL LEAGUE

Batting	B-T	Ht.	Wt.	DOB	AVG	OBP	SLG	G	PA	AB	R	H	2B	3B	HR	RBI	BB	HBP	SH	SF	SO	SB	CS	BB%	SO%
Barger, Addison	L-R	6-0	210	11-12-99	.250	.353	.403	88	397	340	53	85	25	0	9	46	52	3	0	2	86	5	3	13.1	21.7
Berman, Stevie	R-R	6-2	225	11-28-94	.253	.378	.341	29	112	91	10	23	2	0	2	12	19	0	1	1	25	0	0	17.0	22.3
Bernard, Wynton	R-R	6-2	195	9-24-90	.271	.360	.393	60	264	229	41	62	19	0	3	31	30	3	0	2	52	15	3	11.4	19.7
Berroa, Steward	B-R	5-9	178	6-05-99	.156	.283	.222	22	54	45	8	7	3	0	0	8	7	1	1	0	13	4	0	13.0	24.1
Bichette, Bo	R-R	6-0	190	3-05-98	.800	.667	1.400	2	6	5	2	4	0	0	1	3	0	0	0	1	0	0	0	0.0	0.0
Brantly, Rob	L-R	6-0	190	7-14-89	.271	.390	.361	46	177	144	22	39	10	0	1	16	18	12	0	3	21	0	0	10.2	11.9
Capra, Vinny	R-R	5-8	180	7-07-96	.167	.357	.222	17	70	54	6	9	3	0	0	5	14	2	0	0	13	1	1	20.0	18.6
2-team (49 Indianapolis)					.289	.402	.385	66	262	218	36	63	13	1	2	35	38	3	0	3	40	6	2	14.5	15.3
Clarke, Phil	L-R	5-11	190	3-24-98	1.000	1.000	1.000	1	1	1	0	1	0	0	0	0	0	0	0	0	0	0	0	0.0	0.0
Clement, Ernie	R-R	6-0	170	3-22-96	.348	.401	.544	72	320	287	57	100	21	1	11	58	26	1	3	3	16	12	2	8.1	5.0
De Los Santos, Luis	R-R	6-1	160	6-09-98	.220	.337	.383	65	255	214	33	47	12	1	7	40	32	7	0	2	54	1	0	12.5	21.2
Eden, Cam	R-R	6-1	205	3-31-98	.257	.354	.333	131	460	393	74	101	19	1	3	48	45	16	1	4	114	53	4	9.8	24.8
Ellison, Karl	R-R	6-0	195	5-23-95	.556	.556	.778	3	9	9	1	5	2	0	0	0	0	0	0	0	1	0	0	0.0	11.1
Ferrer, Jose	R-R	5-11	175	3-01-99	.286	.375	.286	2	8	7	3	2	0	0	0	0	1	0	0	0	3	0	0	12.5	37.5
Heineman, Tyler	B-R	5-10	190	6-19-91	.214	.331	.265	36	142	117	21	25	3	0	1	13	20	1	3	1	32	5	0	14.1	22.5
2-team (6 Indianapolis)					.230	.348	.319	42	165	135	23	31	4	1	2	19	25	1	3	1	35	5	0	15.2	21.2
Horwitz, Spencer	L-R	5-10	190	11-14-97	.337	.450	.495	107	484	392	61	132	30	1	10	72	78	8	0	6	72	9	2	16.1	14.9
Jansen, Danny	R-R	6-2	215	4-15-95	.500	.500	1.125	2	8	8	2	4	2	0	1	1	0	0	0	0	1	0	0	0.0	12.5
Jimenez, Leo	R-R	5-10	215	5-17-01	.190	.338	.238	18	77	63	8	12	3	0	0	3	9	5	0	0	15	0	0	11.7	19.5
Lantigua, Rafael	R-R	5-7	153	4-28-98	.305	.425	.469	129	578	465	101	142	40	0	12	85	98	5	1	9	107	28	9	17.0	18.5
Lopez, Otto	R-R	5-10	185	10-01-98	.258	.313	.343	84	346	318	48	82	9	6	2	35	23	3	1	1	55	13	4	6.6	15.9
Lukes, Nathan	L-R	5-11	180	7-12-94	.366	.423	.530	48	222	202	39	74	16	1	5	32	17	3	0	0	25	3	1	7.7	11.3
Luplow, Jordan	R-R	5-11	195	9-26-93	.239	.341	.438	48	208	176	27	42	11	0	8	31	25	4	0	3	35	2	0	12.0	16.8
Martinez, Orelvis	R-R	5-11	200	11-19-01	.263	.340	.507	55	246	209	37	55	16	1	11	48	26	2	0	7	66	2	0	10.6	26.8
McCoy, Mason	R-R	5-11	185	3-31-95	.170	.288	.239	27	104	88	15	15	3	0	1	10	14	1	0	1	33	5	1	13.5	31.7
McDowell, Max	R-R	6-1	208	1-12-94	.333	.385	.417	3	13	12	3	4	1	0	0	3	1	0	0	0	3	0	0	7.7	23.1
2-team (3 Lehigh Valley)					.318	.348	.409	6	23	22	4	7	2	0	0	7	1	0	0	0	6	0	0	4.3	26.1
Morris, Tanner	L-R	6-0	190	9-13-97	.281	.390	.394	96	411	345	48	97	21	0	6	50	61	2	0	2	81	1	1	14.8	19.7
Palmegiani, Damiano	R-R	6-0	195	1-24-00	.284	.427	.554	20	96	74	13	21	8	0	4	22	15	5	0	2	28	1	0	15.6	29.2
Ritchie, Jamie	R-R	6-2	203	4-09-93	.233	.364	.278	58	214	176	29	41	3	1	1	21	36	1	0	1	39	2	0	16.8	18.2
Schneider, Davis	R-R	5-9	190	1-26-99	.275	.416	.553	87	392	309	61	85	21	1	21	64	72	6	0	5	86	9	3	18.4	21.9
Schwecke, Trevor	R-R	6-1	185	12-18-97	.265	.333	.367	16	55	49	5	13	2	0	1	5	4	1	0	0	20	0	0	7.3	36.4
Talley, LJ	L-R	6-3	203	5-07-97	.219	.332	.332	60	220	187	25	41	7	1	4	27	32	0	0	1	43	5	1	14.5	19.5

Pitching	B-T	Ht.	Wt.	DOB	W	L	ERA	G	GS	SV	IP	Hits	Runs	ER	HR	BB	SO	AVG	OBP	SLG	SO%	BB%	BF
Bard, Luke	R-R	6-3	200	11-13-90	2	1	6.15	16	6	1	26	31	20	18	4	13	29	.295	.398	.457	23.4	10.5	124
Bash, Andrew	R-R	6-0	190	8-01-96	4	1	2.22	13	9	0	49	30	14	12	6	23	38	.183	.289	.366	20.0	12.1	190
Berman, Stevie	R-R	6-2	225	11-28-94	0	0	3.38	3	0	0	3	1	1	1	1	1	0	.100	.182	.400	0.0	9.1	11
Boyer, Ryan	R-R	6-2	225	5-04-97	0	0	27.00	1	0	0	1	1	4	4	1	4	1	.250	.667	1.000	11.1	44.4	9
Burnette, Jimmy	L-L	6-2	205	10-19-98	2	3	10.36	29	0	0	29	30	35	33	4	27	37	.268	.432	.438	25.2	18.4	147
Cimber, Adam	R-R	6-3	195	8-15-90	0	0	4.50	5	0	0	4	9	2	2	1	0	4	.474	.474	.632	21.1	0.0	19
Cooke, Connor	R-R	6-1	203	11-02-99	2	0	4.35	9	0	0	10	6	5	5	1	9	15	.182	.348	.364	32.6	19.6	46
Danner, Hagen	R-R	6-1	215	9-30-98	0	1	3.81	23	1	1	28	20	13	12	8	7	35	.192	.243	.442	31.5	6.3	111
Eisert, Brandon	L-L	6-2	205	1-19-98	4	3	4.17	59	1	2	69	66	35	32	9	25	76	.253	.318	.444	26.2	8.6	290
Fernandez, Julian	R-R	6-6	230	12-05-95	1	0	10.61	7	0	0	9	18	13	11	3	4	5	.383	.431	.723	9.8	7.8	51
Fernandez, Junior	R-R	6-3	215	3-02-97	3	2	5.69	42	0	1	49	58	35	31	9	26	46	.289	.381	.468	19.9	11.3	231
Francis, Bowden	R-R	6-5	220	4-22-96	0	2	2.67	9	7	0	27	28	11	8	6	7	42	.267	.319	.476	37.2	6.2	113
Fraze, Nick	R-R	6-3	180	10-24-97	0	2	10.50	3	1	0	6	8	7	7	1	7	5	.320	.485	.440	15.2	21.2	33
Fry, Paul	L-L	6-0	205	7-26-92	5	3	4.28	47	0	4	55	49	33	26	6	33	65	.234	.341	.359	26.1	13.3	249
Green, Chad	L-R	6-3	215	5-24-91	0	0	2.00	9	0	0	9	8	3	2	1	1	11	.229	.250	.400	30.6	2.8	36
Hatch, Thomas	R-R	6-1	195	9-29-94	4	2	4.40	30	3	1	45	38	25	22	8	21	54	.226	.316	.429	27.8	10.8	194
Hutchison, Drew	L-R	6-3	215	8-22-90	2	2	5.66	9	9	0	35	34	24	22	3	29	31	.260	.389	.389	19.1	17.9	162
Jackson, Jay	R-R	6-1	195	10-27-87	1	3	6.21	25	0	2	29	30	21	20	8	7	43	.263	.317	.509	34.4	5.6	125
Johnston, Kyle	R-R	5-11	218	7-17-96	1	1	5.19	13	3	0	17	15	10	10	3	9	17	.227	.338	.409	22.1	11.7	77

Juenger, Hayden	R-R	6-0	180	8-09-00	5	2	6.33	54	5	2	75	86	54	53	11	39	92	.285	.376	.454	26.4	11.2	348
Klobosits, Gabe	L-R	6-8	254	5-16-95	1	3	4.74	14	1	0	19	17	12	10	3	12	12	.250	.366	.485	14.6	14.6	82
Lawrence, Casey	R-R	6-0	180	10-28-87	3	7	4.67	18	18	0	91	97	55	47	15	29	81	.267	.323	.468	20.5	7.3	396
Mellen, Sean	L-L	6-5	215	2-20-98	0	0	5.68	5	1	0	6	8	4	4	1	4	6	.308	.387	.577	19.4	12.9	31
Parsons, Wes	R-R	6-5	206	9-06-92	9	4	4.52	17	17	0	82	68	44	41	11	45	98	.222	.329	.382	27.5	12.6	356
Peacock, Matt	R-R	6-1	185	2-27-94	1	2	6.46	20	2	2	24	27	18	17	7	17	19	.281	.395	.563	16.7	14.9	114
Pearson, Nate	R-R	6-6	255	8-20-96	0	1	1.74	20	0	2	21	14	4	4	1	15	34	.184	.319	.237	37.4	16.5	91
Ponce, Gabriel	R-R	6-2	205	4-29-99	1	0	2.87	8	4	2	16	10	5	5	3	12	21	.175	.338	.368	29.6	16.9	71
Pop, Zach	R-R	6-4	220	9-20-96	1	2	5.51	31	0	1	33	36	21	20	4	13	32	.277	.345	.446	22.1	9.0	145
Quinones, Luis	R-R	6-0	205	7-02-97	0	1	11.57	3	1	0	7	11	10	9	1	5	6	.355	.432	.516	16.2	13.5	37
Rees, Jackson	R-R	6-4	210	7-30-94	0	3	7.08	20	0	1	20	16	19	16	2	23	27	.219	.412	.370	27.6	23.5	98
Richards, Trevor	R-R	6-2	205	5-15-93	0	0	0.00	1	0	0	1	0	0	0	0	1	1	.000	.333	.000	33.3	33.3	3
Robbins, Jimmy	L-L	6-3	190	12-22-97	0	2	17.55	3	2	0	7	10	14	13	2	12	5	.345	.548	.655	11.9	28.6	42
Romano, Jordan	R-R	6-5	210	4-21-93	0	0	0.00	1	0	0	1	2	0	0	0	0	0	.500	.500	.750	0.0	0.0	4
Ryu, Hyun Jin	R-L	6-3	250	3-25-87	2	0	2.45	2	2	0	11	6	3	3	3	1	10	.162	.184	.405	26.3	2.6	38
Schultz, Paxton	L-R	6-3	205	1-05-98	3	5	5.92	20	11	0	62	67	42	41	11	41	59	.278	.388	.477	20.6	14.3	287
Schwecke, Trevor	R-R	6-1	185	12-18-97	0	0	18.00	1	0	0	1	1	2	2	0	1	0	.250	.500	.250	0.0	16.7	6
Swanson, Erik	R-R	6-3	225	9-04-93	1	0	0.00	1	0	0	1	0	0	0	0	0	1	.000	.000	.000	33.3	0.0	3
Talley, LJ	L-R	6-3	203	5-07-97	0	0	0.00	2	0	0	1	0	0	0	0	0	0	.000	.000	.000	0.0	0.0	3
Thompson, Zach	R-R	6-7	250	10-23-93	6	6	4.61	24	24	0	105	100	56	54	14	48	80	.249	.337	.424	17.4	10.4	460
Thornton, Trent	R-R	6-0	190	9-30-93	5	1	4.18	22	0	0	28	28	20	13	4	18	26	.255	.354	.418	19.8	13.7	131
Tiedemann, Ricky	L-L	6-4	220	8-18-02	0	0	0.00	1	1	0	4	2	1	0	0	2	6	.167	.286	.167	42.9	14.3	14
Watson, Troy	R-R	6-2	180	6-11-97	0	0	0.93	6	0	0	10	4	3	1	0	5	8	.121	.237	.152	21.1	13.2	38
White, Mitch	R-R	6-3	210	12-28-94	1	2	5.50	17	12	0	56	57	36	34	9	30	67	.266	.367	.439	26.7	12.0	251
Wick, Rowan	L-R	6-3	234	11-09-92	0	1	3.86	20	0	5	21	10	11	9	4	10	38	.139	.253	.306	45.8	12.0	83
Wisler, Matt	R-R	6-3	215	9-12-92	2	0	5.17	15	0	0	16	13	10	9	2	4	20	.213	.284	.393	29.9	6.0	67
Zulueta, Yosver	R-R	6-1	190	1-23-98	4	4	4.08	45	7	0	64	53	32	29	1	45	73	.230	.376	.317	25.4	15.7	287

Fielding

Catcher	PCT	G	PO	A	E	DP	PB
Berman	.992	26	250	11	2	2	0
Brantly	.992	40	342	12	3	1	4
Ellison	1.000	2	15	1	0	0	0
Ferrer	1.000	1	9	0	0	0	0
Heineman	.994	35	296	17	2	0	1
Jansen	1.000	2	12	0	0	0	0
McDowell	.946	3	34	1	2	0	1
Ritchie	.996	51	433	15	2	2	7

First Base	PCT	G	PO	A	E	DP
Berman	1.000	1	1	0	0	0
Brantly	1.000	2	25	0	0	2
Clement	1.000	10	54	6	0	6
De Los Santos	.982	25	148	13	3	13
Horwitz	.996	68	471	53	2	53
Morris	1.000	1	1	0	0	0
Palmegiani	1.000	15	98	13	0	14
Schneider	1.000	8	56	6	0	10
Schwecke	1.000	2	16	0	0	2
Talley	.990	27	174	16	2	22

Second Base	PCT	G	PO	A	E	DP
Barger	1.000	2	3	7	0	1
Capra	.929	4	6	7	1	4
Clement	.950	6	8	11	1	4
Horwitz	1.000	3	2	8	0	1
Lantigua	.970	10	14	18	1	4
Lopez	.985	21	23	42	1	11
Martinez	.966	26	53	59	4	20
McCoy	1.000	5	2	15	0	1
Morris	.971	48	62	107	5	20
Schneider	.986	28	59	77	2	27
Schwecke	.000	1	0	0	0	0
Talley	.971	9	13	21	1	4

Third Base	PCT	G	PO	A	E	DP
Barger	.939	20	16	30	3	6
Capra	.833	4	2	3	1	1
Clement	1.000	9	7	16	0	3
De Los Santos	.934	27	14	43	4	5
Lantigua	.943	34	11	39	3	4
Lopez	.800	1	1	3	1	0
Martinez	.950	11	4	15	1	1
McCoy	1.000	6	3	9	0	0
Morris	.961	32	16	57	3	5
Palmegiani	.000	1	0	0	0	0
Schneider	.923	6	2	10	1	0
Schwecke	1.000	1	1	4	0	1
Talley	.949	12	14	23	2	1

Shortstop	PCT	G	PO	A	E	DP
Barger	.941	20	17	47	4	7
Bichette	1.000	1	0	1	0	1
Capra	.833	2	3	2	1	1
Clement	.961	33	52	72	5	22
De Los Santos	.917	3	3	8	1	3
Jimenez	.942	17	18	31	3	6
Lantigua	1.000	24	26	46	0	12
Lopez	.945	31	37	84	7	18
Martinez	.931	9	14	13	2	6
McCoy	1.000	12	10	23	0	7

Outfield	PCT	G	PO	A	E	DP
Barger	.971	33	63	3	2	2
Bernard	.987	54	83	3	1	1
Berroa	.989	19	35	1	1	0
Capra	1.000	4	8	0	0	0
Clement	.500	5	4	0	0	0
Eden	.941	127	239	8	3	2
Horwitz	1.000	24	25	1	0	0
Lantigua	.973	58	80	2	2	0
Lopez	.919	26	42	1	4	0
Lukes	1.000	40	75	2	0	0
Luplow	.994	38	69	3	1	1
McCoy	1.000	3	5	0	0	0
Morris	1.000	1	1	0	0	0
Schneider	.991	34	59	0	1	0
Schwecke	1.000	9	20	0	0	0
Talley	.944	5	9	0	1	0

NEW HAMPSHIRE FISHER CATS — *DOUBLE-A*

EASTERN LEAGUE

Batting	B-T	Ht.	Wt.	DOB	AVG	OBP	SLG	G	PA	AB	R	H	2B	3B	HR	RBI	BB	HBP	SH	SF	SO	SB	CS	BB%	SO%
Arias, Victor	L-L	5-11	150	8-24-03	.091	.091	.091	3	11	11	0	1	0	0	0	1	0	0	0	0	4	1	0	0.0	36.4
Arnold, Bryce	R-R	5-10	175	7-24-01	.152	.200	.182	10	35	33	2	5	1	0	0	1	2	0	0	0	11	1	0	5.7	31.4
Berroa, Steward	B-R	5-9	178	6-05-99	.272	.380	.414	103	396	324	64	88	21	2	7	35	57	2	9	4	106	43	10	14.4	26.8
Britton, Zach	L-R	6-1	200	9-09-98	.218	.427	.309	17	75	55	10	12	2	0	1	4	20	0	0	0	16	3	0	26.7	21.3
Brown, Devonte	R-R	5-9	207	10-15-99	.222	.338	.492	16	74	63	9	14	5	0	4	8	11	0	0	0	24	3	0	14.9	32.4
Clarke, Phil	L-R	5-11	190	3-24-98	.260	.381	.391	69	259	215	38	56	10	0	6	18	33	9	1	0	37	6	0	12.7	14.3
Cook, Zac	L-R	6-0	195	4-29-98	.186	.292	.339	41	140	118	19	22	3	0	5	13	8	10	3	1	53	9	1	5.7	37.9
De Los Santos, Luis	R-R	6-1	160	6-09-98	.256	.318	.385	21	85	78	9	20	7	0	1	11	7	0	0	0	26	3	2	8.2	30.6
Ellison, Karl	R-R	6-0	195	5-23-95	.100	.200	.133	11	35	30	3	3	1	0	0	2	4	0	0	1	10	0	0	11.4	28.6
Espino, Sebastian	R-R	6-3	176	5-29-00	.199	.252	.299	66	244	221	23	44	10	0	4	23	16	1	2	4	97	4	1	6.6	39.8
Ferrer, Jose	R-R	5-11	175	3-01-99	.154	.267	.231	4	15	13	3	2	1	0	0	0	2	0	0	0	8	0	0	13.3	53.3
Hiraldo, Miguel	R-R	5-9	197	9-05-00	.275	.334	.453	89	354	320	41	88	21	0	12	54	26	4	1	3	111	16	5	7.3	31.4
Jimenez, Leo	R-R	5-10	215	5-17-01	.287	.372	.436	76	333	289	54	83	15	2	8	44	32	9	0	3	53	8	2	9.6	15.9
LaRue, Nate	R-R	6-3	217	7-27-01	.000	.000	.000	1	3	3	0	0	0	0	0	0	0	0	0	0	2	0	0	0.0	66.7

Martinez, Orelvis	R-R	5-11	200	11-19-01	.226	.339	.485	70	292	239	33	54	9	1	17	46	41	2	0	4	60	0	0	14.0	20.5
Morris, PK	L-L	5-11	195	11-30-98	.172	.313	.291	45	164	134	18	23	8	1	2	17	28	0	1	1	51	0	0	17.1	31.1
Nunez, Rainer	R-R	6-2	180	12-04-00	.224	.273	.352	78	326	304	26	68	9	0	10	42	21	0	0	1	88	0	0	6.4	27.0
Palmegiani, Damiano	R-R	6-0	195	1-24-00	.249	.351	.463	108	461	393	57	98	25	1	19	71	58	6	0	4	125	6	0	12.6	27.1
Ramirez, Abiezel	B-R	5-10	160	1-26-00	.108	.195	.135	12	41	37	3	4	1	0	0	1	4	0	0	0	20	3	0	9.8	48.8
Rios, Kekai	R-R	5-10	205	6-06-97	.246	.313	.263	17	64	57	7	14	1	0	0	5	5	1	0	1	19	0	0	7.8	29.7
Ritchie, Jamie	R-R	6-2	203	4-09-93	.500	.667	.500	2	6	4	1	2	0	0	0	2	2	0	0	0	0	0	0	33.3	0.0
Robertson, Will	L-L	6-0	215	12-26-97	.245	.323	.488	103	412	363	60	89	25	3	19	57	40	4	0	5	109	9	3	9.7	26.5
Rock, Dylan	R-R	6-0	210	8-21-98	.205	.299	.368	33	134	117	19	24	4	0	5	14	13	3	0	1	44	7	1	9.7	32.8
Roden, Alan	L-R	5-11	215	12-22-99	.310	.421	.460	46	209	174	35	54	6	1	6	27	26	8	0	1	32	9	2	12.4	15.3
Schwecke, Trevor	R-R	6-1	185	12-18-97	.280	.377	.443	71	294	246	43	69	17	1	7	37	34	6	0	3	54	13	2	11.6	18.4
Sosa, Andres	R-R	5-9	210	11-07-97	.228	.322	.339	36	148	127	15	29	11	0	1	11	13	5	2	1	37	2	1	8.8	25.0
Tirotta, Riley	R-R	6-3	195	8-21-98	.213	.327	.373	69	269	225	29	48	8	2	8	32	37	3	0	4	77	7	4	13.8	28.6
Turconi, Michael	L-R	5-10	185	6-24-99	.176	.306	.324	30	121	102	14	18	4	1	3	10	18	1	0	0	27	2	0	14.9	22.3
Wehler, Jeffrey	R-R	6-0	195	1-10-99	.167	.286	.333	3	14	12	3	2	0	1	0	1	2	0	0	0	4	1	1	14.3	28.6

Pitching	B-T	Ht.	Wt.	DOB	W	L	ERA	G	GS	SV	IP	Hits	Runs	ER	HR	BB	SO	AVG	OBP	SLG	SO%	BB%	BF
Bash, Andrew	R-R	6-0	190	8-01-96	1	0	2.88	23	2	0	41	37	14	13	2	24	42	.239	.346	.329	23.1	13.2	182
Brock, T.J.	R-R	6-1	200	8-10-99	2	1	6.68	32	0	9	32	38	27	24	7	14	56	.281	.364	.467	36.4	9.1	154
Burnette, Jimmy	L-L	6-2	205	10-19-98	0	0	2.63	13	0	5	14	10	5	4	0	9	26	.196	.349	.235	41.3	14.3	63
Caracci, Parker	R-R	6-0	205	9-13-96	1	0	2.89	7	0	0	9	5	3	3	1	9	6	.152	.326	.303	14.0	20.9	43
Clifton, Trevor	R-R	6-4	170	5-11-95	1	1	4.50	8	0	1	14	10	7	7	2	7	15	.200	.317	.360	24.6	11.5	61
Concepcion, Jol	R-R	6-5	195	9-17-98	1	1	11.81	4	0	0	5	7	7	7	0	6	7	.318	.484	.364	22.6	19.4	31
Cooke, Connor	R-R	6-1	203	11-02-99	1	2	4.38	20	0	3	25	29	12	12	3	7	46	.282	.333	.466	41.1	6.3	112
Dallas, Chad	R-R	5-11	206	6-26-00	7	3	4.10	18	18	0	97	85	48	44	15	37	107	.234	.311	.409	25.8	8.9	414
Danner, Hagen	R-R	6-1	215	9-30-98	1	1	3.00	8	0	0	9	9	5	3	0	2	16	.257	.297	.257	43.2	5.4	37
Dominguez, Michael	R-R	5-10	175	8-17-00	1	1	4.29	8	8	0	36	22	17	17	11	23	41	.180	.306	.492	27.9	15.6	147
Feldman, Davis	R-R	6-0	195	9-25-97	1	0	0.00	2	0	0	6	0	0	0	0	0	6	.000	.000	.000	30.0	0.0	20
Fluharty, Mason	R-L	6-2	215	8-13-01	2	5	4.25	36	0	4	42	49	23	20	6	18	54	.290	.365	.462	28.0	9.3	193
Fraze, Nick	R-R	6-3	180	10-24-97	2	1	5.13	12	3	0	26	21	18	15	5	17	28	.228	.371	.446	24.1	14.7	116
Hernandez, Adrian	R-R	5-8	190	1-22-00	2	3	4.62	38	0	0	49	35	30	25	5	46	60	.203	.383	.331	26.0	19.9	231
Jones, Joe	R-R	6-5	245	7-22-95	0	2	5.89	14	0	0	18	19	16	12	2	12	21	.264	.386	.403	23.9	13.6	88
Kloffenstein, Adam	R-R	6-5	243	8-25-00	5	5	3.24	17	17	0	89	79	42	32	8	34	105	.236	.317	.370	27.6	8.9	380
Manoah, Alek	R-R	6-6	285	1-09-98	0	0	1.80	1	1	0	5	3	1	1	0	3	10	.188	.350	.188	50.0	15.0	20
Melean, Alejandro	R-R	6-0	175	10-11-00	3	2	4.41	25	6	0	63	63	38	31	8	37	64	.255	.359	.437	22.1	12.8	289
Mellen, Sean	L-L	6-5	215	2-20-98	1	1	0.93	7	0	0	10	3	3	1	0	4	7	.094	.189	.094	18.9	10.8	37
Mendoza, Abdiel	R-R	5-10	160	9-19-98	1	1	3.72	4	4	0	19	15	8	8	3	7	19	.214	.317	.371	23.2	8.5	82
Nunez, Juan	R-R	6-2	185	1-23-96	2	3	3.89	32	0	1	39	21	21	17	2	42	59	.154	.363	.265	32.2	23.0	183
Paulino, Naswell	L-L	5-11	160	4-17-00	0	0	13.50	1	0	0	2	4	3	3	0	2	1	.400	.500	.700	8.3	16.7	12
Pesto, Al	R-R	6-3	210	8-23-96	1	0	3.00	4	0	0	9	9	3	3	2	2	10	.250	.308	.444	25.6	5.1	39
Ponce, Gabriel	R-R	6-2	205	4-29-99	4	4	4.76	30	0	0	45	41	32	24	4	32	61	.238	.365	.401	29.2	15.3	209
Quinones, Luis	R-R	6-0	205	7-02-97	4	5	4.80	28	12	0	86	63	50	46	18	34	104	.198	.282	.415	29.1	9.5	358
Robberse, Sem	R-R	6-1	185	10-12-01	3	5	4.06	18	18	0	89	71	42	40	14	33	86	.213	.288	.386	23.1	8.9	372
Robbins, Jimmy	L-L	6-3	190	12-22-97	5	8	4.67	22	18	0	87	78	48	45	7	54	86	.237	.355	.368	21.9	13.8	392
Schultz, Paxton	L-R	6-3	205	1-05-98	3	3	3.30	10	10	0	46	42	19	17	3	19	54	.236	.308	.331	27.3	9.6	198
Schwecke, Trevor	R-R	6-1	185	12-18-97	0	0	0.00	1	0	0	1	0	0	0	0	0	0	.000	.000	.000	0.0	0.0	3
Stadler, Fitz	R-R	6-9	230	4-02-97	4	0	4.08	23	0	0	29	28	15	13	2	19	34	.262	.385	.393	26.2	14.6	130
Thurman, Grayson	R-R	6-3	205	12-27-98	0	0	4.50	3	0	1	4	3	2	2	1	2	3	.214	.294	.500	17.6	11.8	17
Tiedemann, Ricky	L-L	6-4	220	8-18-02	0	5	5.06	11	11	0	32	28	22	18	1	20	58	.235	.345	.286	39.7	13.7	146
Van Eyk, CJ	R-R	6-1	198	9-15-98	0	2	4.15	4	4	0	13	16	11	6	2	6	7	.308	.383	.423	11.7	10.0	60
Wallace, Trenton	L-L	6-1	200	3-31-99	0	1	6.48	2	2	0	8	11	8	6	0	3	7	.306	.350	.417	17.5	7.5	40
Watson, Troy	R-R	6-2	180	6-11-97	3	6	5.58	37	0	6	50	51	39	31	4	33	46	.263	.363	.376	19.4	13.9	237

Fielding

Catcher	PCT	G	PO	A	E	DP	PB
Britton	1.000	2	23	1	0	1	0
Clarke	.985	69	699	26	11	5	8
Ellison	.989	11	88	3	1	0	2
Ferrer	.946	4	32	3	2	0	1
LaRue	.917	1	10	1	1	0	0
Rios	.988	16	160	3	2	0	1
Ritchie	1.000	2	20	1	0	1	1
Sosa	.983	34	336	20	6	0	12

First Base	PCT	G	PO	A	E	DP
Espino	1.000	2	12	2	0	1
Morris	.991	39	201	17	2	16
Nunez	.980	64	392	46	9	33
Palmegiani	.969	14	86	7	3	12
Schwecke	1.000	17	69	9	0	3
Tirotta	1.000	11	49	2	0	7

Second Base	PCT	G	PO	A	E	DP
Arnold	.800	5	4	8	3	1
Cook	.900	1	3	6	1	2
De Los Santos	1.000	2	3	2	0	0
Espino	1.000	4	4	8	0	3
Hiraldo	.944	75	88	150	14	22
Jimenez	1.000	25	28	40	0	8
Ramirez	1.000	7	3	8	0	0
Schwecke	.975	13	19	20	1	9
Tirotta	.957	8	5	17	1	1
Turconi	1.000	3	4	4	0	0

Third Base	PCT	G	PO	A	E	DP
De Los Santos	1.000	4	4	6	0	2
Martinez	.923	25	17	31	4	4
Palmegiani	.912	70	34	100	13	7
Ramirez	.714	4	4	1	2	1
Schwecke	.867	5	8	5	2	0
Tirotta	.940	25	14	33	3	4
Turconi	.000	1	0	0	0	0
Wehler	.900	3	4	5	1	1

Shortstop	PCT	G	PO	A	E	DP
Arnold	1.000	2	0	4	0	0
De Los Santos	.960	15	18	30	2	7
Espino	1.000	2	4	3	0	0
Jimenez	.928	45	57	84	11	24
Martinez	.888	34	35	60	12	9
Schwecke	.943	18	18	32	3	7
Turconi	.973	22	33	39	2	6

Outfield	PCT	G	PO	A	E	DP
Arias	1.000	3	5	0	0	0
Berroa	.993	103	252	7	3	3
Britton	1.000	9	13	0	0	0
Brown	.955	15	41	1	2	1
Cook	1.000	41	74	2	0	0
Espino	.985	56	89	9	3	2
Morris	1.000	6	12	0	0	0
Robertson	.994	93	148	0	2	0
Rock	1.000	28	54	0	0	0
Roden	.969	43	64	2	1	0
Schwecke	.979	24	38	1	1	0
Tirotta	1.000	7	10	2	0	0

VANCOUVER CANADIANS

HIGH CLASS A

NORTHWEST LEAGUE

TORONTO BLUE JAYS

Batting	B-T	Ht.	Wt.	DOB	AVG	OBP	SLG	G	PA	AB	R	H	2B	3B	HR	RBI	BB	HBP	SH	SF	SO	SB	CS	BB%	SO%
Brown, Dasan	R-R	5-11	185	9-25-01	.218	.309	.315	107	463	403	59	88	12	3	7	39	41	13	1	3	116	26	11	8.9	25.1
Brown, Devonte	R-R	5-9	207	10-15-99	.240	.357	.445	83	339	283	50	68	14	1	14	49	49	4	0	3	98	18	1	14.5	28.9
De Jesus, Alex	R-R	6-1	170	3-22-02	.248	.340	.466	82	344	294	56	73	17	7	11	59	40	4	0	6	91	5	4	11.6	26.5
De La Rosa, Marcos	B-R	5-11	160	1-28-02	.143	.333	.143	2	9	7	1	1	0	0	0	0	2	0	0	0	1	2	0	22.2	11.1
Del Rosario, Angel	R-R	6-0	160	1-11-03	.167	.200	.167	8	25	24	0	4	0	0	0	0	1	0	0	0	10	0	1	4.0	40.0
Doughty, Cade	R-R	6-1	195	3-26-01	.264	.342	.459	102	424	375	61	99	19	0	18	68	35	11	0	3	126	4	2	8.3	29.7
Ellison, Karl	R-R	6-0	195	5-23-95	.225	.295	.250	12	44	40	1	9	1	0	0	4	3	1	0	0	14	0	0	6.8	31.8
Gonzalez, Juan	R-R	5-9	195	2-20-01	.333	.500	.333	1	4	3	0	1	0	0	0	0	1	0	0	0	2	0	0	25.0	50.0
Goodwin, Nick	R-R	6-0	190	9-06-01	.267	.476	.400	5	21	15	3	4	2	0	0	1	5	1	0	0	5	0	1	23.8	23.8
Hernandez, Jommer	R-R	5-11	181	10-20-00	.212	.306	.315	64	232	203	25	43	9	0	4	26	21	7	0	1	73	2	1	9.1	31.5
Kasevich, Josh	R-R	6-1	200	1-17-01	.284	.363	.365	94	383	334	46	95	15	0	4	50	38	6	0	5	41	11	2	9.9	10.7
Lin, Lyle	R-R	6-1	200	6-26-97	.214	.333	.286	28	99	84	12	18	3	0	1	6	10	5	0	0	24	0	0	10.1	24.2
Machado, Estiven	B-R	5-9	170	10-04-02	.187	.285	.251	68	249	219	19	41	9	1	1	25	23	7	0	0	57	8	2	9.2	22.9
Martinez, Gabriel	R-R	5-9	170	7-24-02	.242	.300	.374	109	448	409	58	99	14	2	12	49	31	4	0	3	74	2	2	6.9	16.5
McCarty, Ryan	R-R	5-9	182	4-22-99	.248	.369	.397	38	149	121	17	30	7	1	3	11	20	5	0	3	36	3	2	13.4	24.2
Nunez, Rainer	R-R	6-2	180	12-04-00	.309	.390	.446	37	159	139	27	43	8	1	3	26	16	3	0	1	30	0	0	10.1	18.9
Ramirez, Abiezel	B-R	5-10	160	1-26-00	.143	.143	.143	4	14	14	0	2	0	0	0	1	0	0	0	0	8	0	0	0.0	57.1
Rios, Kekai	R-R	5-10	205	6-06-97	.189	.275	.340	31	120	106	11	20	4	0	4	13	9	4	0	1	34	0	0	7.5	28.3
Roden, Alan	L-R	5-11	215	12-22-99	.321	.437	.459	69	323	268	57	86	23	1	4	41	42	13	0	0	32	15	2	13.0	9.9
Santiago, Glenn	R-R	5-10	165	12-14-00	.308	.379	.577	8	29	26	4	8	2	1	1	11	3	0	0	0	9	0	0	10.3	31.0
Sosa, Andres	R-R	5-9	210	11-07-97	.257	.391	.324	20	92	74	13	19	2	0	1	8	11	6	0	1	12	1	0	12.0	13.0
Spain, Garrett	L-R	5-10	178	9-21-00	.240	.322	.443	91	366	325	44	78	24	3	12	52	35	5	0	1	100	6	5	9.6	27.3
Tirotta, Riley	R-R	6-3	195	8-21-98	.303	.411	.539	27	107	89	18	27	8	2	3	16	15	2	0	1	30	5	1	14.0	28.0
Turconi, Michael	L-R	5-10	185	6-24-99	.299	.418	.486	74	311	251	54	75	18	4	7	41	52	3	0	5	64	3	0	16.7	20.6
Wehler, Jeffrey	R-R	6-0	195	1-10-99	.270	.382	.381	20	76	63	7	17	2	1	1	9	12	0	0	1	21	1	4	15.8	27.6
Williams, Peyton	L-L	6-5	255	9-14-00	.240	.327	.434	35	147	129	21	31	4	0	7	22	13	4	0	1	37	0	0	8.8	25.2

Pitching	B-T	Ht.	Wt.	DOB	W	L	ERA	G	GS	SV	IP	Hits	Runs	ER	HR	BB	SO	AVG	OBP	SLG	SO%	BB%	BF
Benson, Cooper	L-L	6-0	213	8-03-00	7	3	4.04	40	0	2	71	63	49	32	3	48	81	.243	.376	.340	24.9	14.8	325
Boyer, Ryan	R-R	6-2	225	5-04-97	3	0	0.29	22	0	0	31	18	1	1	0	8	39	.171	.250	.229	33.6	6.9	116
Brock, T.J.	R-R	6-1	200	8-10-99	4	0	1.77	15	0	4	20	8	4	4	1	9	31	.119	.244	.209	39.2	11.4	79
Churchill, Ian	L-L	6-2	190	2-28-99	0	0	0.44	15	0	0	20	7	1	1	0	11	24	.104	.268	.119	29.3	13.4	82
Cooke, Connor	R-R	6-1	203	11-02-99	0	0	2.89	9	0	1	9	7	3	3	1	3	19	.194	.256	.306	48.7	7.7	39
Dallas, Chad	R-R	5-11	206	6-26-00	2	0	2.03	5	5	0	27	13	7	6	1	12	37	.146	.255	.225	36.3	11.8	102
Dominguez, Michael	R-R	5-10	175	8-17-00	7	2	3.65	15	15	0	67	38	29	27	6	49	79	.171	.326	.279	28.0	17.4	282
Fluharty, Mason	R-L	6-2	215	8-13-01	1	0	0.59	12	0	1	15	7	2	1	1	5	21	.132	.207	.226	36.2	8.6	58
Gallagher, Pat	R-R	6-0	196	6-30-00	0	0	2.38	3	3	0	11	13	3	3	1	2	12	.271	.300	.438	24.0	4.0	50
Gregory, Hunter	R-R	6-3	215	11-16-98	0	6	4.34	24	11	0	56	54	29	27	5	26	64	.251	.333	.367	25.9	10.5	247
Harrison, Devereaux	R-R	6-0	190	11-08-00	5	5	2.95	26	16	1	95	76	37	31	14	38	88	.225	.306	.396	22.8	9.8	386
Jennings, Ryan	R-R	6-0	190	6-23-99	0	1	2.70	3	3	0	10	9	3	3	1	3	11	.250	.308	.389	28.2	7.7	39
Kelly, Justin	R-R	6-1	195	12-02-98	5	2	1.80	36	0	5	45	39	18	9	5	17	34	.235	.312	.373	17.8	8.9	191
Larkin, Conor	R-R	6-1	205	3-17-99	3	2	4.30	35	0	3	46	33	27	22	2	21	57	.199	.297	.289	29.5	10.9	193
Lin, Lyle	R-R	6-1	200	6-26-97	0	0	0.00	1	0	0	1	0	0	0	0	1	0	.000	.250	.000	0.0	25.0	4
Macko, Adam	L-L	6-0	170	12-30-00	5	5	4.81	20	20	0	86	76	51	46	7	40	106	.239	.335	.340	28.5	10.8	372
Mendez, Leam	L-R	6-2	196	1-21-00	1	0	1.08	3	0	0	8	2	1	1	0	2	9	.074	.138	.111	31.0	6.9	29
Mendoza, Abdiel	R-R	5-10	160	9-19-98	1	2	3.31	22	5	1	52	48	21	19	3	18	49	.247	.321	.361	22.5	8.3	218
Miranda, Kevin	R-R	5-10	178	11-14-98	2	5	4.35	17	13	0	62	75	35	30	6	15	34	.296	.338	.486	12.5	5.5	272
Nunez, Juan	R-R	6-2	185	1-23-96	0	0	3.00	3	0	0	3	3	1	1	0	2	6	.250	.357	.333	42.9	14.3	14
Pardinho, Eric	R-R	5-10	155	1-05-01	2	2	7.15	35	1	0	57	62	46	45	9	31	61	.290	.377	.486	24.0	12.2	254
Paulino, Naswell	L-L	5-11	160	4-17-00	7	4	4.05	37	0	0	53	54	30	24	7	27	49	.255	.346	.392	20.0	11.0	245
Pesto, Al	R-R	6-3	210	8-23-96	0	0	11.57	2	0	0	2	7	3	3	0	1	3	.500	.563	.571	18.8	6.3	16
Ryan, Sam	R-R	6-3	205	9-22-98	5	0	2.76	29	0	0	49	40	19	15	2	19	36	.227	.312	.307	17.7	9.4	203
Sanchez, Rafael	R-R	6-1	215	8-22-99	0	8	5.17	17	17	0	78	96	51	45	10	23	76	.306	.353	.468	22.2	6.7	342
Santos, Dahian	R-R	5-11	160	2-26-03	3	3	3.54	12	12	0	48	30	21	19	5	27	56	.173	.306	.301	27.2	13.1	206
Scott, Braden	R-L	6-3	215	2-06-98	1	0	9.00	8	0	0	8	8	9	8	3	7	11	.258	.415	.613	26.8	17.1	41
Svanson, Matt	R-R	6-5	235	1-31-99	4	1	1.23	24	0	6	29	17	6	4	0	11	36	.165	.252	.184	31.3	9.6	115
Tolhurst, Anders	R-R	6-4	190	9-13-99	4	1	5.40	15	2	0	28	28	18	17	1	10	34	.252	.320	.369	27.2	8.0	125
Wallace, Trenton	L-L	6-1	200	3-31-99	5	2	1.79	8	8	0	40	22	8	8	2	11	47	.155	.224	.254	30.1	7.1	156

Fielding

Catcher	PCT	G	PO	A	E	DP	PB
Ellison	.984	12	117	5	2	0	3
Gonzalez	1.000	1	17	1	0	1	0
Hernandez	.997	64	581	50	2	5	15
Lin	.991	13	98	7	1	0	0
Rios	.992	29	250	12	2	3	5
Sosa	.994	18	153	8	1	2	2

First Base	PCT	G	PO	A	E	DP
Brown	.989	13	83	5	1	8
Lin	1.000	14	86	10	0	7
McCarty	1.000	10	62	3	0	3
Nunez	.995	31	176	5	1	17
Roden	1.000	1	2	0	0	0
Santiago	1.000	2	19	1	0	2
Sosa	1.000	1	9	0	0	2
Tirotta	.989	16	88	1	1	9
Turconi	.983	17	113	6	2	17
Wehler	1.000	4	17	2	0	0
Williams	.991	31	193	26	2	20

Second Base	PCT	G	PO	A	E	DP
Brown	1.000	2	2	4	0	1
Del Rosario	1.000	1	1	1	0	0
Doughty	.974	32	53	60	3	17
Goodwin	.625	3	3	2	3	1
Kasevich	1.000	1	2	2	0	0
Machado	.957	36	54	78	6	19
McCarty	.982	13	20	36	1	8
Ramirez	.889	4	4	4	1	1
Turconi	.963	39	72	85	6	18
Wehler	1.000	4	6	10	0	0

Third Base	PCT	G	PO	A	E	DP
De Jesus	.882	42	21	54	10	9
Doughty	.952	55	45	74	6	10

Kasevich	1.000	13	14	19	0	1
McCarty	1.000	7	4	9	0	1
Tirotta	1.000	6	7	6	0	1
Turconi	1.000	4	2	4	0	1
Wehler	.813	7	5	8	3	0

Shortstop	PCT	G	PO	A	E	DP
De Jesus	.908	29	44	55	10	13
Goodwin	1.000	2	3	2	0	0

Kasevich	.945	69	82	141	13	28
Machado	.936	30	36	66	7	9
Turconi	.933	4	7	7	1	3

Outfield	PCT	G	PO	A	E	DP
Brown, Da	.991	99	228	4	4	4
Brown, De	.925	58	92	6	7	2
De La Rosa	1.000	2	5	0	0	0
Del Rosario	1.000	6	7	0	0	0
Martinez	.991	93	135	6	2	2
Roden	.992	54	94	4	1	1
Santiago	.875	6	11	0	1	0
Spain	.994	77	206	10	3	5
Tirotta	1.000	3	6	0	0	0
Wehler	1.000	2	4	0	0	0

DUNEDIN BLUE JAYS

LOW CLASS A

FLORIDA STATE LEAGUE

Batting	B-T	Ht.	Wt.	DOB	AVG	OBP	SLG	G	PA	AB	R	H	2B	3B	HR	RBI	BB	HBP	SH	SF	SO	SB	CS	BB%	SO%
Aponte, Yhoangel	R-R	5-10	190	2-12-04	.350	.458	.650	6	24	20	4	7	1	1	1	4	4	0	0	0	7	0	0	16.7	29.2
Arias, Victor	L-L	5-11	150	8-24-03	.273	.385	.545	3	13	11	1	3	0	0	1	3	1	1	0	0	0	0	1	7.7	0.0
Arnaez, Jean	R-R	5-9	160	8-22-02	.266	.304	.298	26	102	94	11	25	3	0	0	8	4	2	0	2	17	1	1	3.9	16.7
Arnold, Bryce	R-R	5-10	175	7-24-01	.216	.389	.352	26	113	88	17	19	6	0	2	13	22	3	0	0	19	4	0	19.5	16.8
Barger, Addison	L-R	6-0	210	11-12-99	.273	.429	.273	3	14	11	3	3	0	0	0	1	3	0	0	0	3	0	0	21.4	21.4
Barry, Braden	R-R	6-4	190	2-06-02	.150	.292	.183	16	72	60	11	9	2	0	0	2	10	2	0	0	27	4	0	13.9	37.5
Beltre, Manuel	R-R	5-10	155	6-09-04	.231	.335	.340	98	431	368	67	85	22	0	6	50	48	11	0	3	83	12	2	11.1	19.3
Berman, Stevie	R-R	6-2	225	11-28-94	.000	.200	.000	4	15	12	1	0	0	0	0	0	2	1	0	0	2	0	0	13.3	13.3
Bohrofen, Jace	L-R	6-2	205	10-19-01	.306	.442	.677	17	77	62	17	19	5	0	6	16	15	0	0	0	18	0	0	19.5	23.4
Chirinos, Kendry	R-R	5-11	170	10-06-04	.000	.333	.000	4	15	10	0	0	0	0	0	0	5	0	0	0	5	0	0	33.3	33.3
De Castro, Rikelbin	R-R	5-11	150	1-23-03	.162	.254	.230	44	170	148	17	24	7	0	1	15	18	1	0	2	48	3	2	10.6	28.2
De La Rosa, Marcos	B-R	5-11	160	1-28-02	.125	.208	.167	14	53	48	8	6	0	1	0	1	5	0	0	0	22	5	3	9.4	41.5
Del Rosario, Angel	R-R	6-0	160	1-11-03	.280	.359	.434	57	211	182	38	51	9	2	5	29	18	6	2	3	60	25	9	8.5	28.4
Deschamps, Nicolas	L-R	5-11	180	8-25-02	.170	.341	.248	57	212	165	22	28	4	0	3	17	37	7	1	2	65	3	0	17.5	30.7
Duran, Edward	R-R	5-11	170	5-29-04	.299	.398	.390	24	93	77	11	23	4	0	1	15	13	1	0	2	13	1	0	14.0	14.0
Espinal, Santiago	R-R	5-10	185	11-13-94	.308	.400	.385	4	15	13	2	4	1	0	0	0	2	0	0	0	2	1	0	13.3	13.3
Garcia, Luis	R-R	5-9	160	9-01-03	.214	.343	.214	10	35	28	3	6	0	0	0	3	6	0	0	1	11	3	1	17.1	31.4
Gonzalez, Juan	R-R	5-9	195	2-20-01	.375	.583	.625	3	12	8	1	3	2	0	0	1	2	2	0	0	2	0	0	16.7	16.7
Goodwin, Nick	R-R	6-0	190	9-06-01	.242	.351	.421	26	114	95	20	23	2	3	3	20	9	8	0	2	22	3	1	7.9	19.3
Hernandez, Sammy	R-R	5-9	185	6-01-04	.192	.241	.317	28	112	104	13	20	3	2	2	7	5	2	0	1	27	0	0	4.5	24.1
Hornung, Jackson	R-R	6-2	215	2-06-01	.143	.210	.232	17	62	56	6	8	2	0	1	6	3	2	0	1	20	0	1	4.8	32.3
Masson, J.C.	L-R	6-3	193	8-22-02	.202	.326	.261	38	144	119	13	24	4	0	1	16	22	1	0	2	59	0	1	15.3	41.0
McCarty, Ryan	R-R	5-9	182	4-22-99	.244	.339	.449	59	243	205	32	50	15	3	7	30	28	4	0	5	59	6	2	11.5	24.3
Mesia, Victor	R-R	5-9	175	1-18-03	.216	.322	.314	15	59	51	5	11	0	1	1	9	7	1	0	0	19	1	1	11.9	32.2
Orf, Brennan	L-R	6-3	225	9-06-01	.224	.439	.308	35	148	107	18	24	7	1	0	11	36	5	0	0	39	1	0	24.3	26.4
Pinto, Adrian	R-R	5-6	156	9-22-02	.260	.413	.300	29	129	100	16	26	4	0	0	10	23	3	3	0	25	12	4	17.8	19.4
Ramirez, Abiezel	B-R	5-10	160	1-26-00	.238	.361	.385	40	155	130	21	31	6	2	3	15	23	2	0	0	44	5	1	14.8	28.4
Robertis, Robert	L-L	5-11	188	11-29-02	.185	.282	.232	48	195	168	21	31	3	1	1	12	22	2	0	3	58	1	2	11.3	29.7
Rock, Dylan	R-R	6-0	210	8-21-98	.000	.375	.000	2	8	5	2	0	0	0	0	0	3	0	0	0	3	0	0	37.5	37.5
Rudd, Jaden	L-L	5-10	185	8-16-02	.201	.376	.277	105	426	328	45	66	13	3	2	36	71	22	2	2	109	21	4	16.7	25.6
Salinas, Roque	L-L	5-8	180	11-08-02	.259	.314	.322	104	417	382	54	99	15	3	1	49	21	11	0	3	52	5	1	5.0	12.5
Santiago, Glenn	R-R	5-10	165	12-14-00	.249	.355	.361	74	296	249	34	62	9	2	5	40	38	5	0	4	63	8	1	12.8	21.3
Sosa, Andres	R-R	5-9	210	11-07-97	.200	.429	.300	3	14	10	0	2	1	0	0	1	2	2	0	0	2	0	1	14.3	14.3
Toman, Tucker	B-R	5-11	190	11-12-03	.208	.320	.313	114	503	428	59	89	24	3	5	51	63	9	0	3	135	7	1	12.5	26.8
Wehler, Jeffrey	R-R	6-0	195	1-10-99	.348	.435	.630	27	108	92	19	32	8	3	4	25	14	1	0	1	28	11	3	13.0	25.9
Williams, Peyton	L-L	6-5	255	9-14-00	.274	.370	.476	45	192	164	23	45	10	1	7	35	21	5	0	2	41	3	2	10.9	21.4

Pitching	B-T	Ht.	Wt.	DOB	W	L	ERA	G	GS	SV	IP	Hits	Runs	ER	HR	BB	SO	AVG	OBP	SLG	SO%	BB%	BF
Alcalde, Eliander	R-R	5-9	171	8-09-03	6	8	5.86	23	12	0	74	69	52	48	9	49	65	.249	.364	.437	19.6	14.8	332
Amalfi, Alex	R-R	6-1	185	2-18-01	4	4	3.75	22	5	1	50	41	30	21	2	36	62	.219	.357	.278	27.0	15.7	230
Barriera, Brandon	L-L	6-2	180	3-04-04	0	2	4.42	6	6	0	18	10	10	9	0	8	23	.164	.301	.180	31.5	11.0	73
Bello, Felipe	R-R	6-3	197	2-01-00	0	1	2.61	18	0	0	31	30	12	9	1	11	19	.263	.320	.351	14.8	8.6	128
Bonds, Bo	R-R	5-11	200	1-10-01	0	0	18.00	1	0	0	1	2	2	2	1	0	3	.400	.400	1.200	60.0	0.0	5
Boyer, Ryan	R-R	6-2	225	5-04-97	0	0	7.71	2	0	0	2	4	2	2	0	1	4	.400	.500	.500	33.3	8.3	12
Brewer, Michael	R-R	6-2	185	12-29-98	1	4	6.55	14	0	2	34	29	27	25	5	21	35	.225	.348	.403	22.6	13.5	155
Carter, Irv	R-R	6-4	210	10-09-02	0	7	8.60	13	10	0	38	42	44	36	9	31	30	.271	.412	.503	15.5	16.0	194
Casimiri, Jiorgeny	R-R	6-1	160	7-12-01	1	0	6.75	5	0	0	8	7	6	6	1	7	15	.233	.395	.367	39.5	18.4	38
Chasse, Ryan	L-L	6-3	250	12-11-99	1	1	3.28	15	1	2	25	12	11	9	3	22	17	.156	.362	.299	16.2	21.0	105
Churchill, Ian	L-L	6-2	190	2-28-99	3	0	1.33	16	0	2	20	11	3	3	0	14	28	.162	.313	.176	33.7	16.9	83
Cimber, Adam	R-R	6-3	195	8-15-90	0	0	0.00	1	0	0	1	0	0	0	0	1	1	.000	.333	.000	33.3	33.3	3
Cruz, Darwin	R-R	6-0	190	9-11-01	0	0	15.43	3	0	0	2	2	4	4	2	7	2	.222	.563	.889	12.5	43.8	16
Danner, Hagen	R-R	6-1	215	9-30-98	0	0	4.50	2	0	0	2	1	1	1	0	2	5	.143	.333	.286	55.6	22.2	9
Duran, Edward	R-R	5-11	170	5-29-04	0	0	13.50	1	0	0	1	2	2	1	0	1	1	.500	.571	.500	14.3	14.3	7
Estrada, Lazaro	R-R	5-10	180	4-24-99	2	3	2.83	28	9	4	76	55	30	24	3	26	103	.199	.278	.296	33.3	8.4	309
Feldman, Davis	R-R	6-0	195	9-25-97	2	6	4.47	13	7	0	48	51	29	24	5	26	42	.273	.369	.412	19.4	12.0	217
Francis, Bowden	R-R	6-5	220	4-22-96	0	0	0.00	1	1	0	3	0	0	0	0	0	3	.000	.000	.000	33.3	0.0	9
Gallagher, Pat	R-R	6-0	196	6-30-00	2	5	3.29	11	8	0	52	38	24	19	6	16	63	.204	.273	.339	30.7	7.8	205
Garcia, Winder	R-R	5-10	165	10-11-01	1	0	3.65	9	0	0	12	11	5	5	1	3	7	.250	.292	.364	14.6	6.3	48
Green, Chad	L-R	6-3	215	5-24-91	1	0	0.00	3	1	0	3	2	0	0	0	0	4	.182	.182	.182	36.4	0.0	11
Jennings, Ryan	R-R	6-0	190	6-23-99	2	3	4.36	9	7	0	33	27	17	16	2	14	44	.221	.317	.352	31.7	10.1	139
Johnson, Cobi	R-R	6-4	225	11-06-95	0	0	16.20	2	0	0	2	3	3	3	0	3	0	.429	.545	.714	0.0	27.3	11
Johnston, Kyle	R-R	5-11	218	7-17-96	0	0	11.57	3	0	0	2	2	3	3	0	4	3	.222	.462	.222	23.1	30.8	13

Leon, Keiner	R-R	5-11	190	10-29-03	3	3	4.08	23	0	0	29	26	15	13	4	14	26	.250	.339	.413	21.3	11.5	122
Mendez, Leam	L-R	6-2	196	1-21-00	1	1	2.88	18	0	2	25	20	12	8	4	16	23	.220	.339	.418	21.1	14.7	109
Miranda, Kevin	R-R	5-10	178	11-14-98	1	0	1.11	7	0	1	24	14	5	3	0	3	21	.161	.189	.195	23.3	3.3	90
Mollerus, Josh	R-R	6-3	215	10-06-99	1	0	3.38	11	0	0	13	12	6	5	0	9	17	.235	.350	.353	28.3	15.0	60
Munson, Aaron	L-R	5-10	180	3-15-02	0	0	1.29	4	1	0	7	5	1	1	0	1	5	.200	.231	.280	19.2	3.8	26
Murray, Joey	L-R	6-2	195	9-23-96	0	0	3.86	9	0	1	12	8	5	5	0	12	10	.229	.420	.229	19.6	23.5	51
O'Halloran, Connor	R-L	6-2	190	9-01-02	3	1	6.30	6	1	0	10	8	8	7	1	8	9	.205	.354	.359	18.8	16.7	48
Ohashi, Rafael	R-R	6-1	185	10-08-02	4	6	6.20	22	18	1	94	100	66	65	16	51	77	.287	.383	.484	18.6	12.3	415
Palmer, Trent	R-R	6-1	230	4-02-99	0	0	0.00	2	2	0	4	2	0	0	0	3	5	.133	.316	.133	26.3	15.8	19
Parsons, Wes	R-R	6-5	206	9-06-92	0	0	5.40	1	1	0	3	6	2	2	0	1	2	.400	.438	.467	11.8	5.9	17
Peacock, Matt	R-R	6-1	185	2-27-94	0	0	0.00	1	0	0	1	0	0	0	0	0	3	.000	.000	.000	100.0	0.0	3
Perez Gonzalez, N.	R-R	5-10	159	4-02-01	0	0	3.38	5	0	0	8	7	4	3	1	4	5	.292	.400	.500	16.1	12.9	31
Perez, Kelvin	R-R	6-3	175	9-09-00	2	2	10.22	11	0	0	12	23	20	14	6	4	11	.397	.453	.776	17.2	6.3	64
Pesto, Al	R-R	6-3	210	8-23-96	1	0	8.44	3	0	0	5	7	6	5	1	3	9	.304	.407	.435	33.3	11.1	27
Pierce, Carson	R-R	6-3	215	9-10-01	0	0	4.91	3	1	0	7	8	4	4	0	1	11	.267	.290	.367	35.5	3.2	31
Pop, Zach	R-R	6-4	220	9-20-96	0	0	0.00	3	0	0	3	1	0	0	0	1	2	.100	.250	.200	16.7	8.3	12
Rodning, Brody	R-L	6-1	185	1-14-96	1	0	0.00	4	0	0	4	4	1	0	0	3	5	.235	.409	.235	22.7	13.6	22
Rojas, Kendry	L-L	6-2	190	11-26-02	4	6	3.75	20	15	0	84	71	41	35	8	33	82	.226	.302	.354	23.4	9.4	351
Rojas, Yondrei	R-R	5-10	180	11-22-02	1	3	5.66	14	8	1	49	53	31	31	5	21	42	.272	.350	.415	18.9	9.5	222
Rutkowski, Harry	R-L	6-2	230	4-22-99	5	0	4.05	24	0	1	33	30	17	15	0	25	35	.246	.377	.311	22.7	16.2	154
Ryu, Hyun Jin	R-L	6-3	250	3-25-87	0	0	0.00	1	1	0	4	3	0	0	0	0	1	.214	.214	.286	7.1	0.0	14
Sanchez, J.J.	L-L	5-11	185	9-08-99	0	0	1.80	5	0	0	5	2	1	1	0	3	4	.125	.333	.188	19.0	14.3	21
Sanchez, Rafael	R-R	6-1	215	8-22-99	5	0	2.27	6	6	0	36	27	12	9	3	5	43	.205	.232	.303	30.9	3.6	139
Santiago, Glenn	R-R	5-10	165	12-14-00	0	0	0.00	1	0	0	0	0	0	0	0	0	0	.000	.000	.000	0.0	0.0	1
Sauer, Kelena	R-R	6-3	205	9-26-02	2	1	3.86	12	0	0	14	14	8	6	0	7	19	.255	.339	.364	30.6	11.3	62
Stadler, Fitz	R-R	6-9	230	4-02-97	0	1	3.52	7	0	0	8	5	4	3	0	7	8	.185	.353	.259	23.5	20.6	34
Svanson, Matt	R-R	6-5	235	1-31-99	0	0	0.00	2	0	0	3	2	0	0	0	0	3	.182	.182	.364	27.3	0.0	11
Thompson, Zach	R-R	6-7	250	10-23-93	0	0	0.00	1	1	0	3	2	0	0	0	0	2	.182	.182	.182	18.2	0.0	11
Thurman, Grayson	R-R	6-3	205	12-27-98	1	2	4.80	34	1	6	45	43	27	24	5	24	53	.249	.338	.399	26.4	11.9	201
Tiedemann, Ricky	L-L	6-4	220	8-18-02	0	0	0.00	2	2	0	6	1	0	0	0	1	15	.053	.100	.053	75.0	5.0	20
Tolhurst, Anders	R-R	6-4	190	9-13-99	1	0	8.31	6	0	0	9	6	8	8	1	2	11	.188	.278	.375	30.6	5.6	36
Van Eyk, CJ	R-R	6-1	198	9-15-98	0	0	3.86	6	5	0	19	12	8	8	3	6	22	.182	.247	.364	30.1	8.2	73
Wallace, Trenton	L-L	6-1	200	3-31-99	0	0	0.00	1	1	0	1	0	0	0	0	3	3	.000	.429	.000	42.9	42.9	7
White, Mitch	R-R	6-3	210	12-28-94	0	0	0.00	1	1	0	3	3	1	0	0	0	2	.214	.214	.357	14.3	0.0	14
Yeager, Chay	B-R	5-11	180	9-11-02	0	0	1.35	5	0	0	7	6	1	1	0	1	7	.231	.259	.231	25.9	3.7	27

Fielding

Catcher	PCT	G	PO	A	E	DP	PB
Arnaez	1.000	1	1	0	0	0	0
Berman	1.000	3	13	1	0	0	0
Deschamps	.985	53	490	27	8	1	3
Duran	.989	18	165	10	2	0	3
Gonzalez	1.000	3	22	1	0	0	1
Hernandez	.976	25	214	30	6	2	1
Hornung	1.000	15	105	8	0	1	1
Mesia	.993	15	135	13	1	2	1
Sosa	1.000	3	27	0	0	0	1

First Base	PCT	G	PO	A	E	DP
Arnaez	.979	20	134	6	3	12
Chirinos	1.000	2	18	0	0	1
Duran	1.000	4	20	1	0	2
Hornung	1.000	1	7	1	0	0
McCarty	1.000	15	103	10	0	9
Orf	1.000	25	163	10	0	15
Santiago	.991	33	215	18	2	18
Wehler	1.000	2	5	0	0	1
Williams	.996	34	240	22	1	25

Second Base	PCT	G	PO	A	E	DP
Arnold	.971	20	26	41	2	10
Beltre	.976	23	34	49	2	10
De Castro	.988	24	35	46	1	11
Del Rosario	.967	6	13	16	1	7
Espinal	.938	3	4	11	1	0
Garcia	.957	8	9	13	1	1
Goodwin	1.000	2	4	6	0	1
McCarty	.955	7	8	13	1	3
Pinto	1.000	20	37	45	0	14
Ramirez	.921	18	29	29	5	9
Wehler	1.000	7	9	21	0	6

Third Base	PCT	G	PO	A	E	DP
Del Rosario	.939	10	11	20	2	1
Goodwin	.909	10	6	4	1	0
McCarty	.926	23	13	37	4	6
Ramirez	.824	8	5	9	3	1
Toman	.947	71	46	114	9	15
Wehler	.870	12	9	11	3	1

Shortstop	PCT	G	PO	A	E	DP
Barger	1.000	1	4	5	0	0
Beltre	.969	71	85	162	8	33
De Castro	.939	18	13	33	3	7
Garcia	.875	2	3	4	1	0
Goodwin	.978	10	19	25	1	4
Pinto	1.000	2	0	8	0	1
Toman	.939	30	41	67	7	12

Outfield	PCT	G	PO	A	E	DP
Aponte	1.000	6	11	0	0	0
Arias	1.000	3	3	0	0	0
Barry	.833	15	32	0	1	0
Bohrofen	1.000	15	25	2	0	1
De La Rosa	1.000	15	19	3	0	0
Del Rosario	1.000	35	62	5	0	1
Masson	.940	35	52	3	3	0
Orf	1.000	8	16	1	0	0
Pinto	1.000	4	7	0	0	0
Ramirez	1.000	1	4	0	0	0
Robertis	.993	45	76	3	1	1
Rock	1.000	1	3	0	0	0
Rudd	.970	102	254	6	12	2
Salinas	.996	93	158	9	1	1
Santiago	1.000	34	66	1	0	0

FCL BLUE JAYS — *ROOKIE*

FLORIDA COMPLEX LEAGUE

Batting	B-T	Ht.	Wt.	DOB	AVG	OBP	SLG	G	PA	AB	R	H	2B	3B	HR	RBI	BB	HBP	SH	SF	SO	SB	CS	BB%	SO%
Aponte, Yhoangel	R-R	5-10	190	2-12-04	.231	.344	.462	44	183	156	24	36	10	1	8	27	21	6	0	0	60	4	3	11.5	32.8
Arias, Victor	L-L	5-11	150	8-24-03	.222	.395	.393	41	152	117	19	26	6	1	4	19	30	4	0	1	39	15	1	19.7	25.7
Barger, Addison	L-R	6-0	210	11-12-99	.000	.250	.000	3	8	6	0	0	0	0	0	0	2	0	0	0	1	0	0	25.0	12.5
Barry, Braden	R-R	6-4	190	2-06-02	.214	.313	.643	7	16	14	4	3	0	0	2	5	2	0	0	0	8	0	1	12.5	50.0
Berman, Stevie	R-R	6-2	225	11-28-94	.333	.600	.333	2	5	3	1	1	0	0	0	1	2	0	0	0	1	0	0	40.0	20.0
Bohrofen, Jace	L-R	6-2	205	10-19-01	.267	.450	.467	7	20	15	3	4	0	0	1	2	4	1	0	0	6	1	0	20.0	30.0
Cano, Gregori	L-R	6-0	180	7-18-04	.184	.310	.296	32	116	98	8	18	5	0	2	13	17	1	0	0	33	1	0	14.7	28.4
Chirinos, Kendry	R-R	5-11	170	10-06-04	.198	.435	.260	37	138	96	16	19	0	0	2	16	37	4	0	1	46	2	1	26.8	33.3
De La Rosa, Marcos	B-R	5-11	160	1-28-02	.171	.348	.214	24	89	70	15	12	3	0	0	6	18	1	0	0	25	13	4	20.2	28.1
Duran, Edward	R-R	5-11	170	5-29-04	.340	.459	.460	17	61	50	13	17	3	0	1	8	11	0	0	0	7	0	1	18.0	11.5

Feliz, Cristian	L-L	6-4	190	9-07-02	.196	.348	.393	37	135	107	18	21	3	0	6	16	15	11	0	2	47	3	0	11.1	34.8
Fernandez, Jose	L-R	6-0	150	3-23-05	.114	.295	.143	14	45	35	4	4	1	0	0	2	8	1	1	0	12	0	1	17.8	26.7
Ferrer, Jose	R-R	5-11	175	3-01-99	.125	.300	.125	4	10	8	1	1	0	0	0	2	2	0	0	0	4	0	0	20.0	40.0
Garcia, Endri	R-R	6-0	163	11-09-02	.114	.278	.182	18	54	44	8	5	0	0	1	2	9	1	0	0	13	0	0	16.7	24.1
Garcia, Luis	R-R	5-9	160	9-01-03	.173	.312	.281	44	170	139	23	24	6	3	1	14	24	5	0	2	41	5	4	14.1	24.1
Gimenez, Martin	R-R	6-1	155	2-15-04	.291	.426	.364	25	68	55	7	16	1	0	1	8	10	3	0	0	21	0	1	14.7	30.9
Hernandez, Sammy	R-R	5-9	185	6-01-04	.261	.382	.478	14	55	46	14	12	5	1	1	8	3	6	0	0	14	1	0	5.5	25.5
2-team (6 FCL Cardinals)					.216	.313	.387	58	228	199	37	43	8	4	6	26	20	8	0	1	51	1	0	8.8	22.4
Joseph, Jean	R-R	5-11	160	2-04-05	.213	.352	.303	34	108	89	15	19	5	0	1	10	17	2	0	0	29	6	5	15.7	26.9
LaRue, Nate	R-R	6-3	217	7-27-01	.074	.194	.074	9	31	27	0	2	0	0	0	4	4	0	0	0	11	1	0	12.9	35.5
Luplow, Jordan	R-R	5-11	195	9-26-93	.125	.222	.125	3	9	8	0	1	0	0	0	0	1	0	0	0	2	0	0	11.1	22.2
Masson, J.C.	L-R	6-3	193	8-22-02	.167	.286	.250	4	14	12	2	2	1	0	0	0	2	0	0	0	5	1	0	14.3	35.7
Mesia, Victor	R-R	5-9	175	1-18-03	.136	.174	.182	7	23	22	1	3	1	0	0	1	1	0	0	0	8	1	0	4.3	34.8
Meza, Luis	R-R	5-8	150	9-23-04	.192	.276	.212	19	59	52	4	10	1	0	0	5	3	3	0	0	12	0	0	5.1	20.3
Munoz, Yeuni	R-R	6-1	190	10-04-03	.229	.292	.344	28	106	96	12	22	8	0	1	14	6	3	0	1	40	1	0	5.7	37.7
Nimmala, Arjun	R-R	6-1	170	10-16-05	.200	.500	.320	9	40	25	7	5	1	1	0	3	14	1	0	0	8	1	0	35.0	20.0
Peguero, Jonathan	L-R	5-10	165	7-23-04	.195	.298	.317	18	47	41	5	8	2	0	1	5	6	0	0	0	15	0	0	12.8	31.9
Pinto, Adrian	R-R	5-6	156	9-22-02	.133	.350	.200	6	20	15	2	2	1	0	0	1	4	1	0	0	2	0	0	20.0	10.0
Pizarro, Juan	L-L	5-11	150	1-18-02	.147	.310	.176	15	44	34	4	5	1	0	0	1	7	1	2	0	9	4	1	15.9	20.5
Ramirez, Abiezel	B-R	5-10	160	1-26-00	.571	.667	1.143	2	9	7	4	4	1	0	1	3	2	0	0	0	1	1	0	22.2	11.1
Robertis, Robert	L-L	5-11	188	11-29-02	.179	.314	.214	13	35	28	4	5	1	0	0	2	6	0	0	1	9	0	0	17.1	25.7
Rock, Dylan	R-R	6-0	210	8-21-98	.222	.364	.556	3	11	9	3	2	0	0	1	3	2	0	0	0	1	0	0	18.2	9.1
Shaw, Sam	L-R	5-10	175	2-26-05	.207	.425	.276	9	40	29	4	6	2	0	0	0	10	1	0	0	6	0	2	25.0	15.0
Vasquez, Carlos	L-R	5-8	150	6-04-05	.185	.347	.210	29	102	81	10	15	2	0	0	6	19	1	1	0	20	3	1	18.6	19.6
Williams, Peyton	L-L	6-5	255	9-14-00	.000	.000	.000	2	4	4	0	0	0	0	0	0	0	0	0	0	1	0	0	0.0	25.0

Pitching	**B-T**	**Ht.**	**Wt.**	**DOB**	**W**	**L**	**ERA**	**G**	**GS**	**SV**	**IP**	**Hits**	**Runs**	**ER**	**HR**	**BB**	**SO**	**AVG**	**OBP**	**SLG**	**SO%**	**BB%**	**BF**
Ayala, Cesar	R-R	6-2	180	2-17-03	1	3	7.02	11	10	0	42	45	33	33	9	30	32	.281	.396	.538	16.7	15.6	192
Barriera, Brandon	L-L	6-2	180	3-04-04	0	0	0.00	1	1	0	2	0	0	0	0	1	2	.000	.143	.000	28.6	14.3	7
Bonds, Bo	R-R	5-11	200	1-10-01	0	1	7.71	2	1	0	2	1	2	2	0	2	5	.125	.300	.125	50.0	20.0	10
Brewer, Michael	R-R	6-2	185	12-29-98	0	0	2.57	3	0	0	7	6	3	2	0	4	6	.250	.345	.250	20.7	13.8	29
Caruci, Sergio	R-R	6-2	155	10-12-02	0	1	14.04	6	0	0	8	10	14	13	3	16	9	.294	.510	.647	17.3	30.8	52
Casimiri, Jiorgeny	R-R	6-1	160	7-12-01	1	1	2.50	11	0	4	18	10	7	5	2	7	26	.156	.239	.281	36.6	9.9	71
Castro, Edgar	R-R	6-1	165	2-07-02	0	0	0.00	1	0	0	1	1	0	0	0	0	0	.250	.400	.250	0.0	0.0	5
Fry, Paul	L-L	6-0	205	7-26-92	0	1	9.00	1	1	0	1	2	1	1	0	0	2	.400	.400	.800	40.0	0.0	5
Garcia, Winder	R-R	5-10	165	10-11-01	0	0	3.38	4	1	0	5	3	3	2	0	2	5	.167	.286	.222	23.8	9.5	21
Gregory, Hunter	R-R	6-3	215	11-16-98	0	0	9.00	2	0	0	4	6	4	4	1	0	3	.333	.350	.556	15.0	0.0	20
Guerra, Daniel	R-R	6-6	230	3-13-04	1	3	5.19	9	5	0	35	42	23	20	2	10	35	.294	.350	.392	22.2	6.3	158
Huntzinger, Jerry	R-R	6-2	180	2-15-99	1	1	5.91	10	0	1	11	14	9	7	1	6	15	.292	.414	.438	25.9	10.3	58
Johnson, Cobi	R-R	6-4	225	11-06-95	0	0	6.00	3	1	0	3	2	2	2	0	1	1	.200	.333	.300	8.3	8.3	12
Leon, Keiner	R-R	5-11	190	10-29-03	3	3	8.22	8	0	0	15	21	15	14	2	7	19	.318	.378	.470	25.7	9.5	74
Lucumi, Francisco	R-R	6-2	170	6-14-02	1	0	5.76	14	0	0	25	34	25	16	6	8	22	.309	.367	.545	18.3	6.7	120
Manoah, Alek	R-R	6-6	285	1-09-98	0	1	37.13	1	1	0	3	10	11	11	2	2	3	.556	.600	1.000	15.0	10.0	20
Mendez, Leam	L-R	6-2	196	1-21-00	0	0	0.00	1	0	0	1	0	0	0	0	0	1	.000	.250	.000	25.0	0.0	4
Munson, Aaron	L-R	5-10	180	3-15-02	0	0	0.00	1	0	0	2	1	0	0	0	1	0	.143	.250	.143	0.0	12.5	8
Murray, Joey	L-R	6-2	195	9-23-96	0	1	10.80	4	1	0	3	4	4	4	1	2	2	.286	.375	.643	12.5	12.5	16
Palmer, Trent	R-R	6-1	230	4-02-99	0	0	5.40	2	1	0	3	2	2	2	0	4	3	.182	.400	.182	20.0	26.7	15
Perez, Fernando	R-R	6-3	170	2-12-04	2	2	2.72	11	10	0	50	35	17	15	1	12	57	.198	.272	.277	29.2	6.2	195
Perry, Nolan	R-R	6-2	195	9-02-03	2	3	7.28	9	4	0	38	46	34	31	4	16	51	.286	.356	.447	28.3	8.9	180
Pesto, Al	R-R	6-3	210	8-23-96	1	0	5.06	4	0	0	5	7	3	3	0	0	3	.333	.318	.381	13.6	0.0	22
Pierce, Carson	R-R	6-3	215	9-10-01	0	0	4.50	3	0	0	4	3	5	2	0	5	3	.214	.421	.214	15.8	26.3	19
Ramirez, Julio	R-R	6-0	180	7-29-01	1	2	6.10	15	0	0	21	24	22	14	1	19	16	.293	.434	.390	14.8	17.6	108
Rees, Jackson	R-R	6-4	210	7-30-94	0	0	20.25	2	0	0	1	2	3	3	0	3	3	.333	.556	.500	33.3	33.3	9
Rodning, Brody	R-L	6-1	185	1-14-96	1	0	0.00	4	1	0	5	4	0	0	0	0	7	.222	.222	.333	38.9	0.0	18
Rodriguez, Christopher	R-R	5-10	160	4-21-01	0	4	9.72	12	1	0	25	34	33	27	2	15	21	.315	.423	.509	16.2	11.5	130
Rojas, Yondrei	R-R	5-10	180	11-22-02	0	0	4.91	2	1	0	4	5	3	2	0	1	4	.294	.400	.471	20.0	5.0	20
Ryu, Hyun Jin	R-L	6-3	250	3-25-87	0	0	3.00	1	1	0	3	4	1	1	0	0	5	.308	.308	.538	38.5	0.0	13
Simon, Johan	L-L	6-1	166	7-01-01	1	2	8.36	10	1	1	14	16	13	13	2	8	14	.281	.369	.526	21.5	12.3	65
Stanifer, Gage	R-R	6-3	201	11-18-03	1	4	6.33	11	7	0	43	44	32	30	3	23	47	.263	.358	.389	24.4	11.9	193
Tiedemann, Ricky	L-L	6-4	220	8-18-02	0	0	0.00	1	1	0	2	0	0	0	0	0	3	.000	.000	.000	50.0	0.0	6
Tolhurst, Anders	R-R	6-4	190	9-13-99	0	0	0.00	2	0	0	3	3	0	0	0	0	3	.273	.273	.273	27.3	0.0	11
Van Eyk, CJ	R-R	6-1	198	9-15-98	0	0	0.00	2	2	0	3	1	0	0	0	0	4	.100	.100	.100	40.0	0.0	10
Vasquez, Juanmi	L-L	5-11	140	12-01-03	0	2	10.34	10	1	0	16	28	20	18	5	11	15	.394	.477	.704	17.4	12.8	86
Villasmil, Guillermo	R-R	5-10	160	9-13-02	0	1	9.39	7	0	0	8	11	9	8	1	7	7	.324	.439	.529	17.1	17.1	41
Wallace, Trenton	L-L	6-1	200	3-31-99	0	0	9.00	1	1	0	1	2	1	1	0	0	2	.400	.500	.400	33.3	0.0	6
Ward, Kelsey	L-L	6-2	200	1-07-01	0	0	14.21	4	0	0	6	9	11	10	0	6	6	.346	.485	.500	18.2	18.2	33
Yeager, Chay	B-R	5-11	180	9-11-02	0	1	5.40	1	0	0	2	1	1	1	0	1	1	.167	.286	.167	14.3	14.3	7

Fielding

C: Meza 17, Peguero 17, Hernandez 14, Duran 7, LaRue 6, Mesia 5, Ferrer 2, Berman 2. **1B:** Feliz 36, Duran 10, Chirinos 7, LaRue 3, Williams 2, Cano 2. **2B:** Vasquez 24, Gimenez 17, De La Rosa 15, Garcia 5, Pinto 4, Shaw 3, Ramirez 2, Fernandez 2, Chirinos 1. **3B:** Chirinos 30, Cano 19, De La Rosa 12, Garcia 1. **SS:** Garcia 39, Nimmala 9, Gimenez 8, Barger 2, De La Rosa 2. **OF:** Aponte 37, Arias 37, Joseph 34, Munoz 24, Pizarro 14, Garcia 14, Robertis 12, Shaw 6, De La Rosa 5, Masson 4, Rock 3, Luplow 3, Barry 1, Bohrofen 1.

DSL BLUE JAYS

ROOKIE

DOMINICAN SUMMER LEAGUE

Batting	B-T	Ht.	Wt.	DOB	AVG	OBP	SLG	G	PA	AB	R	H	2B	3B	HR	RBI	BB	HBP	SH	SF	SO	SB	CS	BB%	SO%
Bautista, Jonathan	L-R	6-0	145	10-17-03	.143	.314	.250	11	35	28Ω	4	4	0	0	1	4	7	0	0	0	18	0	0	20.0	51.4
Bonilla, Enmanuel	R-R	6-1	180	1-22-06	.307	.407	.429	50	226	189	41	58	8	3	3	22	27	7	0	3	55	5	5	11.9	24.3
De La Cruz, Faruk	R-R	5-10	145	3-11-05	.199	.295	.247	49	193	166	17	33	8	0	0	21	24	0	0	3	28	1	4	12.4	14.5
Escanio, Aneudi	B-R	5-9	150	11-27-04	.262	.355	.514	35	125	107	22	28	9	6	2	20	13	3	1	1	20	2	2	10.4	16.0
Fernandez, Jose	L-R	6-0	150	3-23-05	.300	.364	.600	3	11	10	1	3	3	0	0	1	1	0	0	0	3	0	0	9.1	27.3
Gaxiola, Aldo	R-R	6-2	187	6-10-06	.246	.365	.328	20	74	61	10	15	2	0	1	8	10	2	0	1	16	3	1	13.5	21.6
Guzman, David	L-L	5-7	160	2-07-06	.292	.403	.390	50	231	195	45	57	11	1	2	26	27	9	0	0	25	8	2	11.7	10.8
Lopez, Edgardo	R-R	6-2	195	1-01-04	.000	.167	.000	10	24	20	2	0	0	0	0	1	3	1	0	0	14	1	0	12.5	58.3
Meza, Adrian	B-R	5-8	155	1-04-05	.274	.410	.303	49	217	175	32	48	5	0	0	16	31	10	0	1	19	13	5	14.3	8.8
Minoso, Maykel	R-R	5-8	170	7-03-05	.278	.368	.315	46	190	162	29	45	6	0	0	26	22	3	0	3	16	1	1	11.6	8.4
Montealto, Jarold	B-R	5-9	170	12-30-05	.279	.402	.412	22	82	68	18	19	2	2	1	10	12	2	0	0	22	1	0	14.6	26.8
Perez, Daniel	L-L	6-2	195	12-09-01	.294	.421	.479	47	205	163	40	48	11	2	5	40	32	5	0	2	40	5	1	15.6	19.5
Ramon, Dariel	R-R	5-7	160	3-17-06	.250	.375	.338	27	96	80	14	20	5	1	0	11	11	5	0	0	25	0	2	11.5	26.0
Romero, Omar	R-R	5-7	155	8-25-05	.196	.388	.235	23	67	51	7	10	2	0	0	4	14	2	0	0	6	2	0	20.9	9.0
Rosas, Juan	R-R	6-0	180	5-05-06	.157	.218	.255	17	55	51	4	8	2	0	1	5	3	1	0	0	16	0	0	5.5	29.1
Tejada, Railin	R-R	5-10	160	2-10-05	.277	.351	.380	50	208	184	27	51	8	4	1	36	19	3	0	2	51	2	2	9.1	24.5

Pitching	B-T	Ht.	Wt.	DOB	W	L	ERA	G	GS	SV	IP	Hits	Runs	ER	HR	BB	SO	AVG	OBP	SLG	SO%	BB%	BF
Acuna, Samuel	R-R	5-10	155	9-13-05	0	0	4.82	4	4	0	9	12	6	5	1	3	12	.308	.357	.410	28.6	7.1	42
Alcazar, Alexis	L-L	5-8	190	10-13-05	0	0	16.62	5	0	0	4	9	8	8	2	3	6	.429	.520	.810	24.0	12.0	25
Barvosa, Andersson	L-L	6-1	198	8-06-05	0	0	13.50	7	0	0	7	11	10	10	0	9	8	.407	.585	.444	19.5	22.0	41
Castro, Gabriel	L-L	6-1	175	11-05-04	0	0	14.73	3	0	0	4	5	6	6	0	8	5	.357	.565	.429	21.7	34.8	23
Colmenares, Samuel	R-R	5-10	187	11-25-04	3	2	3.04	11	11	0	53	34	19	18	2	22	45	.186	.286	.262	21.4	10.5	210
Flores, Eminen	R-R	5-11	160	2-27-03	3	2	4.17	10	10	0	45	45	28	21	4	18	41	.262	.338	.372	21.0	9.2	195
Gomez, Raudy	R-R	5-10	160	11-14-04	2	5	9.77	12	7	0	31	47	39	34	0	17	24	.364	.462	.481	15.4	10.9	156
Gonzalez, Eduar	L-L	5-11	155	5-01-06	2	2	6.00	15	0	2	36	44	25	24	2	16	33	.312	.388	.454	20.4	9.9	162
Guerra, Jorge	R-R	5-11	165	6-06-04	3	2	2.63	14	0	3	24	22	11	7	2	7	17	.237	.314	.366	16.2	6.7	105
Linares, Diego	R-R	6-2	180	9-29-02	0	0	5.14	3	0	0	7	5	4	4	1	2	9	.200	.286	.360	32.1	7.1	28
Meza, Carlos	R-R	6-0	160	11-19-04	5	1	3.28	11	5	0	47	44	18	17	2	10	28	.251	.305	.354	14.7	5.3	190
Munoz, Omar	R-R	5-10	160	9-08-04	4	1	5.84	14	0	2	25	34	19	16	1	11	22	.347	.402	.449	19.6	9.8	112
Omosako, Sann	R-R	6-1	200	12-02-05	1	1	2.61	8	5	0	21	18	9	6	1	3	16	.237	.289	.355	19.3	3.6	83
Ortiz, Julio	R-R	6-3	165	12-30-00	1	1	7.94	5	0	1	6	1	5	5	0	8	7	.056	.370	.056	25.9	29.6	27
Pacheco, Osvaldo	L-L	6-2	178	7-29-05	0	1	5.93	8	1	0	14	14	13	9	0	18	18	.255	.461	.327	23.7	23.7	76
Salcedo, Cawrin	R-R	6-0	172	1-29-04	1	0	10.80	10	0	0	13	18	17	16	2	13	16	.321	.443	.518	22.9	18.6	70
Severino, Lluveres	R-R	6-1	180	8-09-03	0	2	4.50	12	0	3	20	23	11	10	1	4	13	.284	.310	.383	14.9	4.6	87
Toledano, Rodolfo	R-R	6-0	165	2-16-05	0	4	4.32	8	8	0	33	31	20	16	1	11	16	.248	.356	.328	10.7	7.3	150
Torres, Luis	L-L	6-1	165	2-24-05	1	0	3.38	11	0	1	19	9	7	7	0	10	32	.148	.288	.213	43.2	13.5	74
Urena, Franly	R-R	5-8	160	6-08-04	1	1	4.26	13	2	0	19	22	15	9	3	9	15	.282	.374	.449	16.5	9.9	91
Vasquez, Juanmi	L-L	5-11	140	12-01-03	1	0	0.00	3	0	1	7	3	0	0	0	0	12	.130	.130	.130	50.0	0.0	24

Fielding

C: De La Cruz 26, Minoso 18, Rosas 13, Lopez 8. **1B:** Perez 33, De La Cruz 19, Minoso 1. **2B:** Montealto 17, Romero 16, Ramon 13, Minoso 8, Escanio 7. **3B:** Escanio 19, Gaxiola 19, Ramon 10, Romero 7, Meza 3, Minoso 1. **SS:** Meza 47, Montealto 5, Ramon 5, Escanio 1. **OF:** Guzman 50, Tejada 50, Bonilla 49, Escanio 11, Perez 6, Bautista 6.

Washington Nationals

SEASON SYNOPSIS: Not expected to contend when the season began, the Nationals exceeded expectations with a 16-game improvement over their 107-loss debacle in 2022. In the process, they appeared to establish some new franchise stalwarts, such as shortstop CJ Abrams, all-star righthander Josiah Gray and power-speed outfielder Lane Thomas.

HIGH POINT: The Nats started finding a rhythm after the all-star break and won six of eight series during a 17-11 August that included 10 one-run victories, three of them walk-offs. Two came back-to-back Aug. 12-13 against the Athletics, one on a homer by catcher Keibert Ruiz, the other on a six-run comeback capped off by waiver pickup Jeter Downs.

LOW POINT: With the club for sale and in a rebuild, the Nationals got expected news when word leaked that Stephen Strasburg, the No. 1 pick in 2009 and MVP of the 2019 World Series, would retire after three injury-wracked, surgery-filled years. Then the club canceled a scheduled press conference to announce the retirement and released a statement lamenting the news was leaked, then saying the club looked forward to seeing Strasburg in spring training.

NOTABLE ROOKIES: Righthander Jake Irvin, a 2018 fourth-round pick, made 20 starts and looked like a keeper. Stone Garrett, 27, broke through as a regular for the first time in Washington's right-handed-hitting outfield, providing power before a broken left leg ended his season in late August. Homegrown draft picks Jake Alu and Jacob Young had their moments as reserves.

KEY TRANSACTIONS: The Nationals signed Jeimer Candelario to a one-year contract, and his emergence made him one of the top bats available at the trade deadline. Washington dealt him to the Cubs for minor league infielder Kevin Made and lefty D.J. Herz, but held on to other keystones such as Thomas.

DOWN ON THE FARM: Adding first-rounder Dylan Crews to an organization that already had outfielder James Wood gives the team one of the best prospect pairings in the minors. The hope is 2022 first-rounder Elijah Green could join that group as well, but he'll need to improve his contact rate first. Outfielder Robert Hassell had a year that he'd rather forget. Third baseman Brady House had a nice bounce-back year as he showed what he could do when fully healthy.

OPENING DAY PAYROLL: $101,190,153 (22nd).

PLAYERS OF THE YEAR

MAJOR LEAGUE	MINOR LEAGUE
Josiah Gray	**James Wood**
RHP	**OF**
8-13, 3.91	(HiA/AA)
30 GS, 159 IP	.262/.353/.520
80 BB, 143 SO	28 2B, 26 HR

ORGANIZATION LEADERS

Batting		*Minimum 250 AB
MAJORS		
* AVG	Joey Meneses	.275
* OPS	Stone Garrett	.801
HR	Lane Thomas	28
RBI	Joey Meneses	89
MINORS		
* AVG	Blake Rutherford, Harrisb./Rochester	.336
* OBP	Maxwell Romeo, FCL Nats/Fredericks.	.412
* SLG	Blake Rutherford, Harrisb./Rochester	.571
* OPS	Blake Rutherford, Harrisb./Rochester	.964
R	James Wood, Wilm./Harrisburg	80
H	Trey Lipscomb, Wilm./Harrisburg	139
TB	James Wood, Wilm./Harrisburg	246
2B	Trey Lipscomb, Wilm./Harrisburg	29
3B	Daylen Lile, Fredericks./Wilm.	10
HR	James Wood, Wilm./Harrisburg	26
RBI	James Wood, Wilm./Harrisburg	91
BB	Jack Dunn, Harrisburg/Roch.	78
SO	James Wood, Wilm./Harrisburg	173
SB	Johnathon Thomas, Fredericksburg	65

Pitching		#Minimum 75 IP
MAJORS		
W	Patrick Corbin	10
# ERA	Josiah Gray	3.91
SO	MacKenzie Gore	151
SV	Kyle Finnegan	28
MINORS		
W	Alemao Hernandez, Wilm./Harris./Roch.	9
W	Mitchell Parker, Harris./Roch.	9
L	Alex Troop, Harris./Roch.	11
# ERA	Andrew Alvarez, Wilm./Harrisb.	2.99
G	Gerson Moreno, Rochester	59
GS	Mitchell Parker, Harris./Roch.	26
SV	Marquis Grissom Jr., Fredericksburg	11
IP	2-tied	129
BB	Tommy Romero, Rochester	61
BB	Mitchell Parker, Harris./Roch.	61
SO	Mitchell Parker, Harris./Roch.	150
# AVG	Jackson Rutledge, Harrisb./Rochester	.223

2023 PERFORMANCE

General Manager: Mike Rizzo. **Farm Director:** De Jon Watson. **Scouting Director:** Eddie Longosz.

Class	Team	League	W	L	PCT	Finish	Manager
Majors	Washington Nationals	National	71	91	.438	14 (15)	Dave Martinez
Triple-A	Rochester Red Wings	International	66	80	.452	18 (20)	Matthew LeCroy
Double-A	Harrisburg Senators	Eastern	59	77	.434	10 (12)	Delino DeShields
High-A	Wilmington Blue Rocks	South Atlantic	55	75	.423	11 (12)	Mario Lisson
Low-A	Fredericksburg Nationals	Carolina	65	63	.508	6 (12)	Jake Lowery
Rookie	FCL Nationals	Florida Complex	24	25	.490	10 (15)	Luis Ordaz
Rookie	DSL Nationals	Dominican Sum.	11	39	.220	50 (50)	Rafael Ozuna
Overall 2023 Minor League Record			280	359	.438	29th (30)	

ORGANIZATION STATISTICS

WASHINGTON NATIONALS

NATIONAL LEAGUE

Batting	B-T	Ht.	Wt.	DOB	AVG	OBP	SLG	G	PA	AB	R	H	2B	3B	HR	RBI	BB	HBP	SH	SF	SO	SB	CS	BB%	SO%
Abrams, CJ	L-R	6-2	191	10-03-00	.245	.300	.412	151	614	563	83	138	28	6	18	64	32	13	3	3	118	47	4	5.2	19.2
Adams, Riley	R-R	6-4	260	6-26-96	.273	.331	.476	44	158	143	8	39	13	2	4	21	11	2	1	1	45	0	0	7.0	28.5
Alu, Jake	L-R	5-10	186	4-06-97	.226	.282	.289	51	175	159	14	36	2	1	2	16	10	3	1	2	42	5	1	5.7	24.0
Blankenhorn, Travis	L-R	6-0	238	8-03-96	.161	.297	.258	10	37	31	2	5	0	0	1	1	6	0	0	0	6	0	0	16.2	16.2
Call, Alex	R-R	5-11	189	9-27-94	.200	.307	.307	128	439	375	43	75	14	1	8	38	53	6	3	2	78	9	8	12.1	17.8
Candelario, Jeimer	B-R	6-2	222	11-24-93	.258	.342	.481	99	419	368	57	95	30	2	16	53	36	12	0	2	88	6	1	8.6	21.0
2-team (41 Chicago Cubs)					.251	.338	.471	140	576	505	77	127	39	3	22	70	53	13	0	4	127	8	1	9.2	22.0
Chavis, Michael	R-R	5-10	190	8-11-95	.242	.281	.341	48	96	91	16	22	3	0	2	5	5	0	0	0	33	1	0	5.2	34.4
Dickerson, Corey	L-R	6-1	212	5-22-89	.250	.283	.354	50	152	144	12	36	7	1	2	17	7	0	0	1	28	0	1	4.6	18.4
Downs, Jeter	R-R	5-11	197	7-27-98	.400	.667	.400	6	9	5	4	2	0	0	0	1	4	0	0	0	1	2	0	44.4	11.1
Garcia, Luis	L-R	6-2	220	5-16-00	.266	.304	.385	122	482	447	61	119	18	4	9	50	27	0	1	7	60	9	4	5.6	12.4
Garrett, Stone	R-R	6-2	224	11-22-95	.269	.343	.457	89	271	234	40	63	17	0	9	40	26	3	0	5	82	3	1	9.6	30.3
Hill, Derek	R-R	6-2	206	12-30-95	.170	.220	.191	13	50	47	3	8	1	0	0	1	3	0	0	0	11	1	0	6.0	22.0
Kieboom, Carter	R-R	6-2	211	9-03-97	.207	.266	.368	27	94	87	12	18	2	0	4	11	6	1	0	0	27	0	0	6.4	28.7
Meneses, Joey	R-R	6-3	240	5-06-92	.275	.321	.401	154	657	611	71	168	36	1	13	89	38	5	0	3	130	0	0	5.8	19.8
Millas, Drew	B-R	6-0	198	1-15-98	.286	.375	.464	11	33	28	1	8	2	0	1	6	4	0	1	0	5	0	0	12.1	15.2
Robles, Victor	R-R	6-0	194	5-19-97	.299	.385	.364	36	126	107	15	32	5	1	0	8	11	4	4	0	18	8	1	8.7	14.3
Ruiz, Keibert	B-R	6-0	227	7-20-98	.260	.308	.409	136	562	523	55	136	24	0	18	67	31	6	0	2	58	1	1	5.5	10.3
Rutherford, Blake	L-R	6-1	205	5-02-97	.171	.194	.171	16	36	35	4	6	0	0	0	2	1	0	0	0	10	0	0	2.8	27.8
Smith, Dominic	L-L	6-0	224	6-15-95	.254	.326	.366	153	586	527	57	134	21	1	12	46	47	10	0	2	91	1	1	8.0	15.5
Thomas, Lane	R-R	6-0	198	8-23-95	.268	.315	.468	157	682	628	101	168	36	3	28	86	36	11	0	7	176	20	5	5.3	25.8
Vargas, Ildemaro	B-R	6-0	195	7-16-91	.252	.304	.363	86	286	262	32	66	13	2	4	31	19	1	3	1	20	1	1	6.6	7.0
Young, Jacob	R-R	5-11	180	7-27-99	.252	.322	.336	33	121	107	9	27	7	1	0	12	10	1	3	0	22	13	0	8.3	18.2

Pitching	B-T	Ht.	Wt.	DOB	W	L	ERA	G	GS	SV	IP	Hits	Runs	ER	HR	BB	SO	AVG	OBP	SLG	SO%	BB%	BF
Abbott, Cory	R-R	6-2	217	9-20-95	1	2	6.64	22	0	0	39	48	29	29	9	19	40	.306	.388	.516	21.9	10.4	183
Adon, Joan	R-R	6-2	245	8-12-98	2	4	6.45	12	10	0	52	60	37	37	8	24	48	.284	.364	.483	20.0	10.0	240
Banda, Anthony	L-L	6-2	221	8-10-93	0	0	6.43	10	0	0	7	9	5	5	1	5	6	.321	.429	.429	17.1	14.3	35
Corbin, Patrick	L-L	6-4	226	7-19-89	10	15	5.20	32	32	0	180	210	113	104	33	57	124	.293	.344	.481	15.7	7.2	790
Edwards, Carl	R-R	6-3	165	9-03-91	1	3	3.69	32	0	2	32	31	14	13	1	17	24	.250	.345	.355	16.9	12.0	142
Espino, Paolo	R-R	5-10	212	1-10-87	0	0	24.75	3	0	0	4	14	11	11	1	3	3	.583	.607	.792	10.7	10.7	28
Ferrer, Jose A.	L-L	6-1	229	3-03-00	3	0	5.03	39	0	0	34	37	19	19	4	13	25	.289	.359	.422	17.6	9.2	142
Finnegan, Kyle	R-R	6-2	200	9-04-91	7	5	3.76	67	0	28	69	66	33	29	11	24	63	.254	.318	.423	21.9	8.3	288
Garcia, Rico	R-R	5-9	201	1-10-94	0	0	12.00	3	0	0	3	6	4	4	1	1	4	.400	.438	.600	25.0	6.3	16
Garcia, Robert	R-L	6-4	225	6-14-96	2	2	3.69	24	0	0	32	25	16	13	3	11	33	.229	.298	.330	26.6	8.9	124
Gore, MacKenzie	L-L	6-2	192	2-24-99	7	10	4.42	27	27	0	136	134	71	67	27	57	151	.258	.330	.459	25.9	9.8	582
Gray, Josiah	R-R	6-1	210	12-21-97	8	13	3.91	30	30	0	159	152	72	69	22	80	143	.251	.345	.412	20.5	11.5	698
Harris, Hobie	R-R	6-3	212	6-23-93	0	0	5.12	16	0	0	19	21	12	11	2	13	9	.273	.385	.416	9.9	14.3	91
Harvey, Hunter	R-R	6-3	239	12-09-94	4	4	2.82	57	0	10	61	44	21	19	7	13	67	.203	.251	.332	28.5	5.5	235
Irvin, Jake	R-R	6-6	227	2-18-97	3	7	4.61	24	24	0	121	118	66	62	20	54	99	.255	.340	.431	18.7	10.2	530
Kuhl, Chad	R-R	6-3	207	9-10-92	0	4	8.45	16	5	1	38	47	38	36	8	28	31	.313	.419	.567	16.6	15.0	187
LaSorsa, Joe	L-L	6-5	215	4-29-98	1	0	4.76	23	0	0	28	29	15	15	3	6	25	.254	.320	.368	20.0	4.8	125
Machado, Andres	R-R	6-1	232	4-22-93	4	1	5.22	44	0	0	50	53	29	29	12	13	43	.282	.328	.521	20.8	6.3	207
Rainey, Tanner	R-R	6-2	250	12-25-92	0	0	0.00	1	0	0	1	1	0	0	0	1	1	.250	.400	.250	20.0	20.0	5
Ramirez, Erasmo	R-R	6-0	220	5-02-90	2	3	6.33	23	0	0	27	36	20	19	4	6	13	.321	.357	.482	10.3	4.8	126
Rutledge, Jackson	R-R	6-8	251	4-01-99	1	1	6.75	4	4	0	20	24	15	15	4	6	12	.304	.364	.519	13.6	6.8	88
Thomas, Lane	R-R	6-0	198	8-23-95	0	0	27.00	1	0	0	1	3	3	3	1	0	1	.500	.500	1.167	16.7	0.0	6
Thompson, Mason	R-R	6-6	244	2-20-98	4	4	5.50	51	0	1	54	62	35	33	4	22	44	.294	.368	.417	18.3	9.2	240
Vargas, Ildemaro	B-R	6-0	195	7-16-91	0	0	4.50	2	0	0	2	2	1	1	1	1	0	.250	.400	.625	0.0	10.0	10
Ward, Thaddeus	R-R	6-3	204	1-16-97	0	0	6.37	26	0	0	35	29	26	25	7	28	30	.225	.369	.419	18.8	17.5	160
Weems, Jordan	L-R	6-4	212	11-07-92	5	1	3.62	51	0	0	55	38	25	22	9	28	60	.194	.300	.393	25.9	12.1	232
Williams, Trevor	R-R	6-3	231	4-25-92	6	10	5.55	30	30	0	144	178	97	89	34	53	111	.300	.359	.533	16.8	8.0	659
Willingham, Amos	R-R	6-4	217	8-21-98	0	2	6.66	18	0	0	24	35	18	18	8	9	15	.337	.388	.625	12.9	7.8	116

Fielding

Catcher	PCT	G	PO	A	E	DP	PB
Adams	.993	40	293	8	2	1	3
Millas	.985	10	65	2	1	1	0
Ruiz	.991	117	888	36	8	5	8

First Base	PCT	G	PO	A	E	DP
Chavis	1.000	9	20	2	0	5
Meneses	1.000	19	118	9	0	12
Smith	.994	151	1045	143	7	134

Second Base	PCT	G	PO	A	E	DP
Alu	.985	24	30	37	1	9
Chavis	1.000	22	28	53	0	16
Downs	1.000	2	0	1	0	0
Garcia	.983	121	182	276	8	77
Vargas	1.000	18	25	34	0	9

Third Base	PCT	G	PO	A	E	DP
Alu	1.000	5	4	5	0	0
Candelario	.974	96	57	172	6	20
Chavis	1.000	7	3	14	0	1
Kieboom	.957	26	17	28	2	3
Vargas	.960	45	21	75	4	5

Shortstop	PCT	G	PO	A	E	DP
Abrams	.966	151	245	384	22	100
Downs	1.000	4	2	2	0	1
Vargas	.969	15	23	39	2	8

Outfield	PCT	G	PO	A	E	DP
Alu	1.000	27	43	1	0	0
Blankenhorn	1.000	11	17	0	0	0
Call	.999	124	289	4	1	1
Chavis	.000	2	0	0	0	0
Dickerson	.979	44	69	1	3	0
Garrett	.950	89	114	3	2	0
Hill	.972	13	35	0	1	0
Meneses	1.000	1	3	0	0	0
Robles	1.000	36	81	1	0	1
Rutherford	1.000	15	18	0	0	0
Thomas	.993	162	334	18	5	3
Vargas	.500	12	11	0	0	0
Young	.988	32	81	2	1	1

ROCHESTER RED WINGS — *TRIPLE-A*

INTERNATIONAL LEAGUE

Batting	B-T	Ht.	Wt.	DOB	AVG	OBP	SLG	G	PA	AB	R	H	2B	3B	HR	RBI	BB	HBP	SH	SF	SO	SB	CS	BB%	SO%
Adams, Matt	L-R	6-3	263	8-31-88	.246	.296	.430	102	402	374	40	92	18	0	17	53	26	1	0	1	114	0	0	6.5	28.4
Alu, Jake	L-R	5-10	186	4-06-97	.298	.360	.428	74	330	292	46	87	21	1	5	43	29	2	2	5	46	16	3	8.8	13.9
Arcia, Francisco	L-R	5-11	200	9-14-89	.219	.286	.313	11	35	32	5	7	3	0	0	3	2	1	0	0	10	0	0	5.7	28.6
Baker, Darren	L-R	5-10	180	2-11-99	.273	.338	.340	99	448	403	49	110	10	4	3	41	39	1	4	1	76	19	5	8.7	17.0
Barley, Jordy	R-R	5-11	175	12-03-99	.283	.356	.396	23	60	53	12	15	0	0	2	6	6	0	1	0	24	9	2	10.0	40.0
Barreto, Franklin	R-R	5-8	208	2-27-96	.202	.282	.455	29	111	99	17	20	4	0	7	15	9	2	1	0	29	2	0	8.1	26.1
Blankenhorn, Travis	L-R	6-0	238	8-03-96	.262	.360	.517	108	455	393	67	103	27	2	23	75	51	10	0	1	110	0	2	11.2	24.2
Call, Alex	R-R	5-11	189	9-27-94	.275	.388	.425	11	50	40	5	11	3	0	1	3	7	1	1	1	4	3	0	14.0	8.0
Dickerson, Corey	L-R	6-1	212	5-22-89	.200	.273	.300	3	11	10	1	2	1	0	0	0	1	0	0	0	4	0	0	9.1	36.4
Downs, Jeter	R-R	5-11	197	7-27-98	.236	.358	.379	51	193	161	29	38	12	1	3	18	27	4	0	1	47	11	3	14.0	24.4
Dunn, Jack	R-R	6-1	185	9-05-96	.244	.385	.326	65	241	193	33	47	5	1	3	19	41	4	2	1	43	15	3	17.0	17.8
Fox, Lucius	B-R	6-0	182	7-02-97	.200	.286	.200	9	29	25	2	5	0	0	0	1	3	0	1	0	10	0	0	10.3	34.5
Garcia, Luis	L-R	6-2	220	5-16-00	.268	.315	.381	25	108	97	15	26	8	0	1	13	8	0	0	3	13	2	0	7.4	12.0
Garcia, Wilson	B-R	5-10	227	1-11-94	.256	.273	.419	24	88	86	9	22	5	0	3	15	1	1	0	0	17	0	0	1.1	19.3
Garrett, Stone	R-R	6-2	224	11-22-95	.500	.500	.500	2	8	8	2	4	0	0	0	2	0	0	0	0	2	1	0	0.0	25.0
Hernandez, Yadiel	L-R	5-9	185	10-09-87	.205	.225	.256	10	40	39	4	8	2	0	0	4	1	0	0	0	15	0	0	2.5	37.5
Hill, Derek	R-R	6-2	206	12-30-95	.317	.373	.509	83	360	322	65	102	17	6	11	51	29	2	3	4	70	16	4	8.1	19.4
Kieboom, Carter	R-R	6-2	211	9-03-97	.264	.360	.429	34	161	140	24	37	6	1	5	23	19	2	0	0	34	1	1	11.8	21.1
Lindsly, Brady	L-R	6-1	221	3-03-98	.243	.309	.429	21	82	70	10	17	1	0	4	22	7	1	1	3	28	1	0	8.5	34.1
Martin, Richie	R-R	5-11	190	12-22-94	.217	.329	.314	113	425	360	55	78	22	2	3	36	49	12	2	2	103	29	6	11.5	24.2
Mazara, Nomar	L-L	6-4	225	4-26-95	.266	.360	.410	47	203	173	26	46	8	1	5	22	27	0	0	3	40	0	1	13.3	19.7
Mejia, Erick	B-R	5-11	195	11-09-94	.226	.305	.389	71	267	234	34	53	8	3	8	30	27	1	1	4	57	8	1	10.1	21.3
Millas, Drew	B-R	6-0	198	1-15-98	.270	.362	.403	58	229	196	26	53	11	3	3	24	26	4	0	3	33	4	1	11.4	14.4
Noll, Jake	R-R	6-1	213	3-08-94	.247	.305	.418	54	213	194	24	48	15	0	6	30	15	2	0	2	42	0	0	7.0	19.7
Nottingham, Jacob	R-R	6-2	220	4-03-95	.194	.256	.403	19	78	72	7	14	3	0	4	13	4	2	0	0	29	0	0	5.1	37.2
Pinder, Chad	R-R	6-2	210	3-29-92	.218	.306	.309	16	62	55	6	12	2	0	1	4	7	0	0	0	15	0	0	11.3	24.2
2-team (7 Gwinnett)					.256	.319	.395	23	94	86	8	22	3	0	3	7	8	0	0	0	21	0	0	8.5	22.3
Plawecki, Kevin	R-R	6-2	208	2-26-91	.256	.351	.341	24	94	82	8	21	4	0	1	6	11	1	0	0	15	0	0	11.7	16.0
Reyes, Franmil	R-R	6-5	265	7-07-95	.219	.322	.383	34	149	128	18	28	4	1	5	19	20	0	0	1	36	0	0	13.4	24.2
2-team (4 Omaha)					.217	.321	.392	38	167	143	22	31	5	1	6	23	21	1	0	2	43	0	0	12.6	25.7
Robles, Victor	R-R	6-0	194	5-19-97	.364	.500	1.000	4	14	11	5	4	1	0	2	5	3	0	0	0	3	0	0	21.4	21.4
Rutherford, Blake	L-R	6-1	205	5-02-97	.331	.395	.536	42	172	151	16	50	12	2	5	21	15	3	0	3	31	5	1	8.7	18.0
Torrens, Luis	R-R	6-0	217	5-02-96	.258	.311	.470	19	74	66	8	17	5	0	3	13	6	0	0	2	18	0	1	8.1	24.3
Tostado, Frankie	L-L	6-1	205	3-31-98	.254	.333	.408	18	81	71	12	18	3	1	2	9	9	0	0	1	11	1	1	11.1	13.6
Vargas, Ildemaro	B-R	6-0	195	7-16-91	.100	.182	.100	3	11	10	0	1	0	0	0	0	1	0	0	0	2	0	0	9.1	18.2
Vega, Onix	R-R	5-9	200	9-07-98	.204	.290	.222	18	62	54	6	11	1	0	0	3	6	1	0	1	11	0	1	9.7	17.7
Williams, Steven	L-R	6-3	216	2-18-99	.000	.000	.000	2	4	4	0	0	0	0	0	0	0	0	0	0	3	0	0	0.0	75.0
Wilson, Cody	R-R	6-0	200	7-04-96	.213	.291	.294	65	187	160	24	34	7	0	2	13	13	5	8	1	60	13	3	7.0	32.1
Witt, Paul	R-R	5-11	170	10-29-97	.222	.304	.333	8	23	18	1	4	2	0	0	2	2	1	0	2	7	0	0	8.7	30.4
Young, Jacob	R-R	5-11	180	7-27-99	.294	.294	.471	4	17	17	2	5	0	0	1	2	0	0	0	0	2	0	0	0.0	11.8

Pitching	B-T	Ht.	Wt.	DOB	W	L	ERA	G	GS	SV	IP	Hits	Runs	ER	HR	BB	SO	AVG	OBP	SLG	SO%	BB%	BF
Abbott, Cory	R-R	6-2	217	9-20-95	3	4	4.98	13	13	0	56	42	32	31	8	35	69	.209	.326	.388	28.8	14.6	240
Adon, Joan	R-R	6-2	245	8-12-98	3	5	4.62	17	17	0	88	92	51	45	10	40	80	.270	.348	.446	20.7	10.4	386
Baldonado, Alberto	L-L	6-5	270	2-01-93	1	0	3.03	29	0	0	30	23	16	10	2	17	30	.213	.328	.306	23.4	13.3	128
Banda, Anthony	L-L	6-2	221	8-10-93	2	5	7.58	33	10	0	65	84	67	55	9	32	62	.307	.379	.474	19.6	10.1	316
Beck, Tyler	R-R	6-1	190	11-16-95	0	0	18.00	1	0	0	2	6	4	4	1	2	2	.500	.571	.833	14.3	14.3	14
Castro, Anthony	R-R	6-2	191	4-13-95	0	0	135.00	2	0	0	0	3	5	5	0	3	0	.750	.889	.750	0.0	33.3	9
Cate, Tim	L-L	6-0	185	9-30-97	2	1	4.50	27	0	1	24	24	12	12	2	20	24	.273	.407	.398	22.2	18.5	108
Cessa, Luis	R-R	6-0	222	4-25-92	1	3	8.71	16	1	3	21	24	22	20	4	10	23	.286	.364	.524	23.2	10.1	99
Cronin, Matt	L-L	6-2	210	9-20-97	1	1	5.02	14	0	0	14	13	9	8	2	14	13	.250	.403	.462	19.4	20.9	67
Danish, Tyler	R-R	6-0	200	9-12-94	2	2	3.72	26	0	5	29	29	14	12	2	15	20	.264	.359	.391	15.3	11.5	131
Doolittle, Sean	L-L	6-2	218	9-26-86	0	0	9.82	4	0	0	4	5	4	4	2	5	3	.333	.476	.867	14.3	23.8	21
Dunn, Jack	R-R	6-1	185	9-05-96	0	0	6.75	2	0	0	3	6	2	2	0	2	0	.500	.500	.500	0.0	12.5	16
Espino, Paolo	R-R	5-10	212	1-10-87	4	3	4.33	13	13	0	60	58	34	29	10	22	52	.254	.320	.469	20.2	8.6	257

Fernandez, Junior	R-R	6-3	215	3-02-97	0	2	2.79	9	0	1	10	11	5	3	1	6	6	.297	.386	.378	13.6	13.6	44
Ferrer, Jose A.	L-L	6-1	229	3-03-00	4	3	3.83	34	0	0	40	42	22	17	4	20	33	.276	.363	.441	18.4	11.2	179
Garcia, Rico	R-R	5-9	201	1-10-94	1	0	0.00	2	0	0	2	1	0	0	0	0	3	.111	.111	.111	33.3	0.0	9
Harris, Hobie	R-R	6-3	212	6-23-93	2	3	5.57	27	0	1	32	42	27	20	3	19	24	.311	.391	.459	15.2	12.0	158
Hernandez, Alemao	L-L	5-8	187	9-27-99	3	1	4.15	7	7	0	35	40	16	16	7	11	24	.286	.338	.471	15.8	7.2	152
Irvin, Jake	R-R	6-6	227	2-18-97	2	2	5.64	5	5	0	22	23	14	14	3	11	20	.271	.367	.412	20.4	11.2	98
Javier, Odalvi	R-R	6-0	180	9-04-96	0	1	6.75	15	0	0	23	30	22	17	5	21	19	.323	.462	.559	16.0	17.6	119
Kilome, Franklyn	R-R	6-6	175	6-25-95	1	2	19.64	3	2	0	4	9	10	8	1	5	2	.529	.640	.882	8.0	20.0	25
Knowles, Lucas	L-L	6-2	185	3-14-98	0	2	13.50	5	0	0	9	17	13	13	1	6	8	.405	.479	.548	16.7	12.5	48
LaSorsa, Joe	L-L	6-5	215	4-29-98	0	0	4.26	12	0	0	13	16	7	6	1	5	14	.302	.362	.453	24.1	8.6	58
Liranzo, Jesus	R-R	6-2	225	3-07-95	0	1	18.00	2	0	0	2	4	5	4	1	2	3	.444	.500	1.111	25.0	16.7	12
Machado, Andres	R-R	6-1	232	4-22-93	1	0	4.08	24	0	3	29	28	15	13	1	6	35	.250	.300	.393	28.9	5.0	121
Mengden, Daniel	R-R	6-1	215	2-19-93	2	3	7.20	22	3	0	35	48	31	28	5	23	30	.333	.436	.542	17.2	13.2	174
Moreno, Gerson	R-R	6-0	218	9-10-95	7	5	3.14	59	0	10	72	43	29	25	5	50	91	.179	.332	.283	29.8	16.4	305
Mujica, Jose	R-R	6-2	249	6-29-96	2	0	5.92	20	0	0	24	29	17	16	6	9	21	.287	.348	.545	18.8	8.0	112
Munoz, Roddery	R-R	6-2	210	4-14-00	1	3	6.98	12	10	0	39	40	30	30	8	27	41	.265	.376	.470	22.7	14.9	181
Nottingham, Jacob	R-R	6-2	220	4-03-95	0	0	0.00	1	0	0	1	2	0	0	0	0	0	.500	.500	.500	0.0	0.0	4
Parker, Mitchell	L-L	6-4	224	9-27-99	0	1	10.45	3	3	0	10	15	12	12	3	7	18	.326	.415	.543	34.0	13.2	53
Peguero, Joel	R-R	5-11	160	5-05-97	0	2	8.02	15	0	0	21	26	20	19	3	18	13	.313	.430	.494	12.1	16.8	107
Pena, Malvin	R-R	6-2	180	6-24-97	0	0	22.50	1	0	0	2	4	5	5	2	3	0	.400	.538	1.100	0.0	23.1	13
Peralta, Wily	R-R	6-1	261	5-08-89	3	8	6.31	24	24	0	103	106	76	72	13	55	100	.268	.357	.417	21.7	12.0	460
Powell, Holden	R-R	6-0	190	9-09-99	0	0	2.45	2	0	0	4	3	1	1	0	3	2	.273	.429	.455	14.3	21.4	14
Rainey, Tanner	R-R	6-2	250	12-25-92	0	0	3.52	8	0	0	8	7	3	3	1	4	8	.259	.344	.444	25.0	12.5	32
Reyes, Franmil	R-R	6-5	265	7-07-95	0	0	0.00	1	0	0	0	4	7	7	1	3	0	1.000	1.000	2.000	0.0	42.9	7
Reyes, Luis	R-R	6-2	175	9-26-94	5	0	4.35	45	0	0	68	58	41	33	4	47	67	.227	.360	.314	21.4	15.0	313
Ribalta, Orlando	R-R	6-7	245	3-05-98	1	0	0.00	1	0	0	2	1	0	0	0	2	1	.167	.375	.167	12.5	25.0	8
Romero, Tommy	R-R	6-2	222	7-08-97	5	7	5.44	36	10	0	88	86	55	53	11	61	82	.259	.375	.410	20.4	15.2	401
Rutledge, Jackson	R-R	6-8	251	4-01-99	2	3	4.44	11	11	0	51	46	26	25	7	30	44	.250	.369	.424	19.6	13.3	225
Schoff, Tyler	R-R	6-4	220	12-06-98	0	0	27.00	1	0	0	1	4	3	3	0	2	0	.571	.667	1.000	0.0	22.2	9
Sinclair, Jack	R-R	6-4	170	5-03-99	0	0	0.00	1	0	0	1	0	0	0	0	1	3	.000	.250	.000	75.0	25.0	4
Troop, Alex	L-L	6-5	210	7-19-96	0	2	24.75	3	2	0	4	14	14	11	2	4	3	.538	.600	.769	10.0	13.3	30
Urena, Jose	R-R	6-2	208	9-12-91	1	3	6.31	15	15	0	67	80	50	47	16	26	56	.291	.358	.538	18.2	8.4	308
Weems, Jordan	L-R	6-4	212	11-07-92	1	1	3.75	22	0	6	24	13	12	10	2	13	24	.163	.278	.275	24.7	13.4	97
Willingham, Amos	R-R	6-4	217	8-21-98	3	1	2.88	18	0	0	25	23	8	8	1	12	22	.250	.340	.337	20.8	11.3	106
Witt, Paul	R-R	5-11	170	10-29-97	0	0	9.00	3	0	0	4	10	4	4	1	2	0	.500	.522	.750	0.0	8.7	23

Fielding

Catcher	PCT	G	PO	A	E	DP	PB
Arcia	.988	11	76	4	1	2	0
Lindsly	.967	21	202	6	7	2	0
Millas	.993	53	413	25	3	3	2
Nottingham	.981	11	96	5	2	2	2
Plawecki	1.000	24	216	9	0	1	1
Torrens	.985	15	123	8	2	1	2
Vega	.992	16	123	2	1	1	3

First Base	PCT	G	PO	A	E	DP
Adams	.989	62	403	34	5	37
Barreto	1.000	1	3	1	0	1
Blankenhorn	.991	50	304	21	3	29
Dunn	1.000	5	27	0	0	5
Garcia	1.000	4	23	2	0	2
Noll	.993	17	129	9	1	19
Nottingham	.875	2	7	0	1	1
Reyes	1.000	1	1	0	0	1
Torrens	1.000	1	13	0	0	0
Tostado	.978	18	124	10	3	21

Second Base	PCT	G	PO	A	E	DP
Alu	.985	17	22	42	1	8
Baker	.968	63	93	150	8	35
Barley	.974	12	13	25	1	9
Downs	.975	15	30	49	2	15
Fox	1.000	2	2	2	0	2
Garcia	.991	22	46	59	1	14
Martin	1.000	2	1	1	0	1
Mejia	1.000	15	19	43	0	8
Noll	.941	7	15	17	2	5
Witt	.000	1	0	0	0	0

Third Base	PCT	G	PO	A	E	DP
Alu	.959	41	26	67	4	7
Barreto	1.000	5	6	5	0	1
Downs	.892	17	10	23	4	3
Dunn	.963	25	12	40	2	3
Kieboom	.975	29	24	55	2	6
Martin	1.000	2	3	1	0	0
Mejia	.923	25	24	36	5	7
Pinder	.913	10	10	11	2	1
Vargas	.000	1	0	0	0	0
Witt	1.000	2	1	2	0	0

Shortstop	PCT	G	PO	A	E	DP
Alu	1.000	1	0	1	0	0
Barley	.974	9	15	23	1	5
Barreto	.900	2	3	6	1	1
Downs	.984	20	21	41	1	13
Dunn	1.000	2	2	5	0	0
Fox	1.000	6	7	11	0	2
Martin	.976	109	178	261	11	68
Mejia	.920	4	10	13	2	4
Pinder	1.000	1	2	1	0	0

Outfield	PCT	G	PO	A	E	DP
Alu	1.000	14	20	1	0	0
Baker	1.000	33	55	3	0	1
Barreto	.971	23	45	1	2	0
Blankenhorn	.995	60	102	5	1	0
Call	.975	11	20	0	1	0
Dickerson	1.000	2	2	0	0	0
Downs	1.000	1	2	0	0	0
Dunn	1.000	37	63	2	0	1
Garrett	1.000	2	4	0	0	0
Hernandez	1.000	9	14	0	0	0
Hill	.665	81	175	1	1	0
Mazara	.984	43	83	6	3	1
Mejia	.985	27	46	1	1	0
Noll	.788	11	12	0	2	0
Pinder	1.000	5	6	0	0	0
Reyes	.000	1	0	0	0	0
Robles	1.000	3	4	0	0	0
Rutherford	.992	39	70	1	1	0
Vargas	1.000	1	2	0	0	0
Williams	1.000	1	2	0	0	0
Wilson	.987	62	123	4	1	1
Witt	1.000	5	6	1	0	1
Young	1.000	4	7	0	0	0

HARRISBURG SENATORS — *DOUBLE-A*

EASTERN LEAGUE

Batting	B-T	Ht.	Wt.	DOB	AVG	OBP	SLG	G	PA	AB	R	H	2B	3B	HR	RBI	BB	HBP	SH	SF	SO	SB	CS	BB%	SO%
Antuna, Yasel	B-R	6-1	198	10-26-99	.143	.298	.223	34	141	112	10	16	3	0	2	11	25	1	0	3	37	3	2	17.7	26.2
Arruda, J.T.	B-R	5-10	180	10-20-97	.226	.357	.327	114	458	376	49	85	14	3	6	39	74	4	2	2	118	31	8	16.2	25.8
Barley, Jordy	R-R	5-11	175	12-03-99	.000	.000	.000	1	1	1	0	0	0	0	0	0	0	0	0	0	1	0	0	0.0	100.0
Casey, Donovan	R-R	6-2	223	2-23-96	.199	.275	.255	64	258	231	24	46	7	0	2	20	23	2	0	2	83	7	1	8.9	32.2
Cluff, Jackson	L-R	5-11	181	12-03-96	.206	.357	.368	86	311	247	49	51	13	3	7	27	54	5	3	2	85	15	5	17.4	27.3
Connell, Justin	R-R	5-11	185	3-11-99	.167	.259	.208	9	29	24	2	4	1	0	0	1	3	0	2	0	5	0	1	10.3	17.2

Crews, Dylan	R-R	6-0	203	2-26-02	.208	.318	.278	20	85	72	7	15	5	0	0	5	8	4	0	1	19	3	3	9.4	22.4
Dunn, Jack	R-R	6-1	185	9-05-96	.264	.436	.380	48	176	129	32	34	6	0	3	14	37	4	4	2	30	17	3	21.0	17.0
Fox, Lucius	B-R	6-0	182	7-02-97	.164	.246	.230	22	71	61	6	10	1	0	1	4	7	0	2	1	21	0	0	9.9	29.6
Frizzell, Will	L-R	6-3	225	2-21-99	.155	.302	.225	22	86	71	8	11	2	0	1	7	14	1	0	0	31	1	0	16.3	36.0
Gonzales, Jarrett	R-R	5-9	185	3-27-98	.222	.300	.333	4	10	9	2	2	1	0	0	0	0	1	0	0	3	0	0	0.0	30.0
Harris, Trey	R-R	5-9	220	1-15-96	.249	.323	.343	67	260	233	21	58	14	1	2	26	20	6	0	1	58	4	4	7.7	22.3
Hassell, Robert	L-L	6-1	195	8-15-01	.225	.316	.324	106	476	414	54	93	15	1	8	37	52	5	2	3	152	13	5	10.9	31.9
House, Brady	R-R	6-4	215	6-04-03	.324	.358	.475	36	148	139	19	45	8	2	3	12	7	1	0	1	42	1	1	4.7	28.4
Kieboom, Carter	R-R	6-2	211	9-03-97	.250	.438	.250	4	16	12	1	3	0	0	0	1	4	0	0	0	6	1	0	25.0	37.5
Lindsly, Brady	L-R	6-1	221	3-03-98	.229	.342	.313	41	157	131	17	30	5	0	2	11	23	0	2	1	42	3	0	14.6	26.8
Lipscomb, Trey	R-R	6-2	200	6-14-00	.284	.310	.438	80	335	320	40	91	15	2	10	45	12	1	0	2	61	4	3	3.6	18.2
Meregildo, Omar	R-R	5-11	185	8-18-97	.206	.296	.397	18	71	63	4	13	3	0	3	8	7	1	0	0	24	0	0	9.9	33.8
Millas, Drew	B-R	6-0	198	1-15-98	.341	.455	.537	25	99	82	14	28	4	0	4	19	16	1	0	0	16	2	1	16.2	16.2
Morales, Yohandy	R-R	6-4	209	10-09-01	.286	.412	.357	4	17	14	0	4	1	0	0	0	3	0	0	0	2	0	0	17.6	11.8
Perez, Wilmer	R-R	5-10	186	4-16-98	.200	.200	.350	5	20	20	2	4	0	0	1	2	0	0	0	0	3	0	0	0.0	15.0
Pinckney, Andrew	R-R	6-3	205	12-07-00	.235	.235	.235	4	17	17	3	4	0	0	0	0	0	0	0	0	4	1	1	0.0	23.5
Pineda, Israel	R-R	5-11	217	4-03-00	.153	.215	.214	28	107	98	6	15	3	0	1	9	7	1	0	1	34	0	0	6.5	31.8
Rutherford, Blake	L-R	6-1	205	5-02-97	.341	.390	.612	32	141	129	23	44	12	1	7	28	9	2	0	1	25	2	1	6.4	17.7
Sanchez, Jose	R-R	5-11	197	7-12-00	.171	.260	.248	39	147	129	14	22	4	0	2	12	14	2	1	1	33	2	0	9.5	22.4
Stehly, Murphy	R-R	5-10	205	9-27-98	.160	.250	.160	7	28	25	1	4	0	0	0	1	1	2	0	0	6	0	1	3.6	21.4
Tostado, Frankie	L-L	6-1	205	3-31-98	.238	.298	.379	101	419	383	44	91	16	1	12	69	32	2	0	2	70	2	1	7.6	16.7
Upshaw, Armond	B-L	5-10	190	6-20-96	.000	.000	.000	1	2	2	0	0	0	0	0	0	0	0	0	0	1	0	0	0.0	50.0
Valera, Leonel	R-R	6-3	206	7-09-99	.210	.275	.280	57	225	200	20	42	6	1	2	18	15	4	3	3	69	8	3	6.7	30.7
Vega, Onix	R-R	5-9	200	9-07-98	.254	.376	.295	39	149	122	21	31	5	0	0	7	22	3	0	2	29	1	0	14.8	19.5
Wood, James	L-R	6-6	240	9-17-02	.248	.334	.492	87	368	323	48	80	19	3	18	55	39	4	0	2	124	10	2	10.6	33.7
Young, Jacob	R-R	5-11	180	7-27-99	.304	.374	.431	52	231	204	30	62	11	3	3	28	17	7	1	2	37	17	3	7.4	16.0

Pitching	B-T	Ht.	Wt.	DOB	W	L	ERA	G	GS	SV	IP	Hits	Runs	ER	HR	BB	SO	AVG	OBP	SLG	SO%	BB%	BF
Alston, Garvin	R-L	6-4	175	3-12-97	2	4	4.91	44	1	0	59	69	32	32	5	25	45	.297	.370	.435	17.1	9.5	263
Alvarez, Andrew	L-L	6-3	215	6-13-99	0	3	4.50	5	4	0	26	20	14	13	5	11	20	.206	.306	.381	18.0	9.9	111
Beck, Tyler	R-R	6-1	190	11-16-95	2	0	6.75	15	1	0	21	21	17	16	4	14	23	.256	.376	.463	22.8	13.9	101
Carrillo, Gerardo	R-R	6-1	170	9-13-98	0	0	0.00	2	0	0	2	0	0	0	0	2	1	.000	.286	.000	14.3	28.6	7
Casey, Donovan	R-R	6-2	223	2-23-96	0	0	0.00	1	0	0	1	0	0	0	0	0	0	.000	.000	.000	0.0	0.0	3
Cate, Tim	L-L	6-0	185	9-30-97	2	2	3.38	15	0	0	19	15	9	7	2	6	19	.227	.288	.364	26.0	8.2	73
Cuevas, Michael	R-R	6-2	165	6-29-01	4	8	5.53	23	23	0	98	112	69	60	10	45	74	.288	.370	.447	16.8	10.2	440
Doolittle, Sean	L-L	6-2	218	9-26-86	0	1	5.40	3	0	0	3	3	2	2	1	2	4	.250	.357	.667	28.6	14.3	14
Dunn, Jack	R-R	6-1	185	9-05-96	0	0	9.00	1	0	0	1	2	1	1	0	0	0	.500	.500	.500	0.0	0.0	4
Guasch, Richard	R-R	6-4	205	4-10-98	0	0	0.00	4	0	1	6	3	0	0	0	3	7	.158	.273	.211	31.8	13.6	22
Henry, Cole	R-R	6-4	215	7-15-99	0	2	10.31	10	6	0	18	23	21	21	5	13	21	.311	.429	.568	23.1	14.3	91
Hernandez, Alemao	L-L	5-8	187	9-27-99	5	6	3.48	16	14	0	83	93	39	32	11	13	59	.284	.314	.425	16.9	3.7	350
Herrera, Ronald	R-R	5-11	185	5-03-95	0	3	4.81	5	5	0	24	23	16	13	1	7	29	.250	.297	.380	28.7	6.9	101
Herz, DJ	R-L	6-2	175	1-04-01	2	2	2.55	8	8	0	35	20	11	10	1	20	53	.161	.293	.234	36.1	13.6	147
Javier, Odalvi	R-R	6-0	180	9-04-96	2	2	5.79	20	0	1	28	27	18	18	3	19	29	.262	.408	.447	22.3	14.6	130
Knowles, Lucas	L-L	6-2	185	3-14-98	4	2	3.65	25	1	0	44	40	19	18	8	13	43	.244	.306	.433	23.8	7.2	181
Lee, Evan	L-L	6-1	205	6-18-97	0	0	6.45	22	0	0	22	19	16	16	1	26	24	.232	.425	.329	21.2	23.0	113
Luckham, Kyle	R-R	6-2	205	10-01-99	0	0	5.40	1	1	0	5	8	4	3	0	0	6	.348	.348	.391	26.1	0.0	23
Mujica, Jose	R-R	6-2	249	6-29-96	0	0	0.00	1	0	0	1	1	0	0	0	1	1	.500	.667	.500	33.3	33.3	3
Parker, Mitchell	L-L	6-4	224	9-27-99	9	6	4.20	25	23	0	114	100	58	53	10	54	132	.235	.318	.359	27.2	11.1	485
Peguero, Joel	R-R	5-11	160	5-05-97	0	3	2.15	29	0	10	29	30	10	7	1	9	27	.270	.341	.396	21.6	7.2	125
Pena, Malvin	R-R	6-2	180	6-24-97	1	0	2.54	41	0	3	64	45	21	18	5	28	55	.201	.297	.344	21.4	10.9	257
Powell, Holden	R-R	6-0	190	9-09-99	0	0	2.25	3	0	2	4	1	1	1	0	1	4	.071	.188	.071	25.0	6.3	16
Rainey, Tanner	R-R	6-2	250	12-25-92	0	0	0.00	3	1	0	3	1	0	0	0	2	4	.111	.273	.111	36.4	18.2	11
Ribalta, Orlando	R-R	6-7	245	3-05-98	2	1	3.92	17	0	2	21	21	10	9	2	10	19	.259	.341	.395	20.7	10.9	92
Romero, Carlos	R-R	6-6	179	7-15-99	1	1	6.08	10	0	0	13	12	9	9	4	7	12	.235	.328	.569	20.7	12.1	58
Ruotolo, Patrick	R-R	5-10	250	1-16-95	2	3	5.08	21	0	0	28	23	16	16	4	11	30	.217	.294	.377	25.2	9.2	119
Rutledge, Jackson	R-R	6-8	251	4-01-99	6	1	3.16	12	12	0	68	50	25	24	5	25	62	.209	.294	.335	22.8	9.2	272
Saenz, Dustin	L-L	5-11	197	6-02-99	5	5	4.44	15	15	0	73	77	36	36	8	19	42	.282	.332	.429	14.0	6.4	299
Schaller, Reid	R-R	6-3	210	4-02-97	1	4	3.83	32	0	1	47	34	21	20	4	18	57	.206	.302	.339	29.8	9.4	191
Schoff, Tyler	R-R	6-4	220	12-06-98	1	1	3.04	22	0	6	27	23	10	9	2	11	30	.232	.313	.333	26.5	9.7	113
Sinclair, Jack	R-R	6-4	170	5-03-99	2	5	4.12	35	0	1	44	39	22	20	8	25	45	.250	.360	.474	23.8	13.2	189
Thompson, Mason	R-R	6-6	244	2-20-98	0	0	0.00	1	0	0	1	0	0	0	0	0	1	.000	.000	.000	33.3	0.0	3
Troop, Alex	L-L	6-5	210	7-19-96	3	9	4.38	24	18	0	101	92	53	49	15	43	95	.240	.326	.432	21.9	9.9	433
Walters, Nash	R-R	6-5	210	5-18-97	1	1	6.08	10	1	3	13	9	9	9	0	10	14	.196	.351	.348	24.6	17.5	57
Ward, Thaddeus	R-R	6-3	204	1-16-97	0	2	3.60	2	2	0	10	11	7	4	2	1	6	.282	.333	.487	13.6	2.3	44
Willingham, Amos	R-R	6-4	217	8-21-98	2	0	0.00	10	0	5	11	6	1	0	0	1	14	.154	.175	.154	35.0	2.5	40

Fielding

Catcher	PCT	G	PO	A	E	DP	PB
Gonzales	1.000	4	29	4	0	0	1
Lindsly	.995	41	326	36	2	5	2
Millas	.991	24	195	15	2	2	4
Perez	.980	5	46	4	1	1	2
Pineda	.996	26	211	13	1	2	0
Vega	.997	39	321	16	1	4	0

First Base	PCT	G	PO	A	E	DP
Dunn	1.000	10	60	2	0	10
Harris	.983	10	49	8	1	6
Lipscomb	1.000	15	115	8	0	16
Meregildo	.981	9	50	3	1	6
Morales	1.000	2	16	1	0	2
Stehly	1.000	4	33	0	0	1
Tostado	.996	92	677	41	3	64

Second Base	PCT	G	PO	A	E	DP
Arruda	.987	109	202	263	6	76
Cluff	.971	14	28	40	2	11
Dunn	.958	6	7	16	1	1
Lipscomb	.966	8	9	19	1	6
Sanchez	1.000	1	0	3	0	0

Third Base	PCT	G	PO	A	E	DP

WASHINGTON NATIONALS

	PCT	G	PO	A	E	DP
Cluff	.929	7	1	12	1	1
Dunn	.906	15	9	20	3	3
House	.951	35	16	62	4	6
Kieboom	1.000	2	2	6	0	1
Lipscomb	.983	42	32	81	2	12
Meregildo	.813	6	1	12	3	0
Morales	1.000	1	0	2	0	0
Sanchez	.955	33	26	58	4	9
Stehly	1.000	1	2	2	0	0

Shortstop	PCT	G	PO	A	E	DP
Barley	.000	1	0	0	0	0
Cluff	.942	40	59	102	10	29
Dunn	1.000	6	5	13	0	0
Fox	.969	20	22	40	2	7
Lipscomb	1.000	11	16	23	0	5
Sanchez	.938	5	5	10	1	2
Valera	.963	57	61	122	7	25

Outfield	PCT	G	PO	A	E	DP
Antuna	.989	29	52	0	1	0
Casey	.984	53	94	7	2	0
Cluff	.944	20	45	1	1	1
Connell	1.000	8	15	0	0	0
Crews	.667	20	36	0	1	0
Dunn	1.000	8	11	0	0	0
Harris	.964	22	44	1	2	0
Hassell	.981	100	214	5	3	1
Pinckney	.667	4	5	0	0	0
Rutherford	1.000	23	34	0	0	0
Upshaw	1.000	1	1	0	0	0
Wood	.981	77	150	3	3	0
Young	1.000	49	124	8	0	2

WASHINGTON NATIONALS

WILMINGTON BLUE ROCKS

HIGH CLASS A

SOUTH ATLANTIC LEAGUE

Batting	B-T	Ht.	Wt.	DOB	AVG	OBP	SLG	G	PA	AB	R	H	2B	3B	HR	RBI	BB	HBP	SH	SF	SO	SB	CS	BB%	SO%
Alu, Jake	L-R	5-10	186	4-06-97	.200	.294	.267	4	17	15	2	3	1	0	0	0	2	0	0	0	3	1	0	11.8	17.6
Antuna, Yasel	B-R	6-1	198	10-26-99	.221	.312	.294	21	77	68	5	15	3	1	0	8	8	1	0	0	24	3	1	10.4	31.2
Baker, Darren	L-R	5-10	180	2-11-99	.444	.545	.444	5	22	18	1	8	0	0	0	1	4	0	0	0	2	2	0	18.2	9.1
Barley, Jordy	R-R	5-11	175	12-03-99	.228	.297	.350	61	203	180	26	41	9	2	3	16	17	2	1	3	67	22	3	8.4	33.0
Boissiere, Branden	L-L	6-1	205	3-23-00	.240	.313	.318	40	147	129	12	31	7	0	1	15	12	3	0	3	31	0	0	8.2	21.1
Casey, Donovan	R-R	6-2	223	2-23-96	.091	.231	.091	4	13	11	1	1	0	0	0	0	0	2	0	0	1	1	0	0.0	7.7
De La Rosa, Jeremy	L-L	6-0	215	1-16-02	.240	.324	.361	93	383	338	44	81	16	2	7	42	41	2	0	2	129	13	7	10.7	33.7
Diaz, Geraldi	L-R	5-11	205	7-08-00	.081	.183	.129	28	71	62	4	5	0	0	1	7	8	0	0	1	33	0	0	11.3	46.5
Downs, Jeter	R-R	5-11	197	7-27-98	.100	.250	.200	3	12	10	1	1	1	0	0	0	2	0	0	0	7	0	0	16.7	58.3
Emiliani, Leandro	L-L	6-1	180	3-22-00	.179	.231	.313	34	121	112	9	20	6	0	3	17	8	0	0	1	45	0	0	6.6	37.2
Farmer, Caleb	R-R	6-2	205	9-08-99	.185	.269	.305	52	173	151	10	28	6	0	4	15	15	3	2	2	59	0	0	8.7	34.1
Fox, Lucius	B-R	6-0	182	7-02-97	.256	.293	.410	10	41	39	4	10	0	0	2	3	2	0	0	0	11	0	0	4.9	26.8
Frizzell, Will	L-R	6-3	225	2-21-99	.240	.395	.411	76	309	246	43	59	11	2	9	35	54	9	0	0	70	0	0	17.5	22.7
Hill, Derek	R-R	6-2	206	12-30-95	.250	.400	.333	4	15	12	3	3	1	0	0	0	2	1	0	0	0	1	1	13.3	0.0
House, Brady	R-R	6-4	215	6-04-03	.317	.368	.540	16	68	63	11	20	5	0	3	13	3	2	0	0	13	3	0	4.4	19.1
Infante, Sammy	R-R	6-1	185	6-22-01	.254	.324	.429	20	71	63	10	16	5	0	2	6	6	1	0	1	20	1	1	8.5	28.2
Kieboom, Carter	R-R	6-2	211	9-03-97	.188	.316	.375	6	19	16	1	3	0	0	1	1	3	0	0	0	5	0	0	15.8	26.3
Lawson, Cortland	R-R	6-2	200	5-12-00	.247	.272	.312	23	81	77	8	19	3	1	0	7	2	1	0	1	24	0	0	2.5	29.6
Lile, Daylen	L-R	5-11	195	11-30-02	.234	.310	.357	40	171	154	16	36	7	3	2	18	16	1	0	0	41	2	3	9.4	24.0
Lipscomb, Trey	R-R	6-2	200	6-14-00	.251	.311	.387	49	212	191	19	48	14	0	4	27	15	3	0	3	42	6	3	7.1	19.8
Made, Kevin	R-R	5-9	160	9-10-02	.137	.232	.192	22	83	73	5	10	4	0	0	5	9	0	1	0	18	1	0	10.8	21.7
McKenzie, Jared	L-L	6-0	180	5-16-01	.212	.281	.320	105	420	378	39	80	19	2	6	35	29	9	0	4	116	6	6	6.9	27.6
Mejia, Erick	B-R	5-11	195	11-09-94	.333	.486	.481	8	35	27	8	9	1	0	1	4	7	1	0	0	4	0	0	20.0	11.4
Morales, Yohandy	R-R	6-4	209	10-09-01	.314	.400	.443	18	80	70	12	22	5	2	0	14	8	2	0	0	16	0	0	10.0	20.0
Murzi, Ivan	R-R	6-0	165	5-28-01	.000	.250	.000	1	4	3	0	0	0	0	0	0	1	0	0	0	2	0	0	25.0	50.0
Pena, Viandel	B-R	5-7	148	11-22-00	.217	.344	.275	101	419	346	52	75	16	2	0	35	67	1	3	2	88	18	7	16.0	21.0
Perez, Wilmer	R-R	5-10	186	4-16-98	.240	.333	.320	10	30	25	2	6	2	0	0	4	3	1	0	1	3	2	0	10.0	10.0
Pinckney, Andrew	R-R	6-3	205	12-07-00	.324	.446	.412	18	83	68	13	22	1	1	1	4	13	2	0	0	18	3	1	15.7	21.7
Pineda, Israel	R-R	5-11	217	4-03-00	.205	.225	.308	11	40	39	3	8	1	0	1	4	1	0	0	0	10	0	0	2.5	25.0
Rivero, Yoander	R-R	5-9	155	11-22-01	.175	.200	.263	17	62	57	3	10	2	0	1	3	2	0	2	1	22	1	1	3.2	35.5
Sanchez, Jose	R-R	5-11	197	7-12-00	.202	.289	.263	34	128	114	14	23	7	0	0	6	13	1	0	0	28	0	1	10.2	21.9
Shumpert, Nick	R-R	5-9	180	11-11-96	.168	.276	.271	42	123	107	19	18	2	0	3	7	16	0	0	0	47	6	1	13.0	38.2
Stehly, Murphy	R-R	5-10	205	9-27-98	.314	.382	.424	33	131	118	15	37	5	1	2	10	10	3	0	0	26	1	1	7.6	19.8
Suggs, Matt	R-R	5-9	195	5-31-00	.284	.354	.509	33	130	116	19	33	9	1	5	20	8	5	0	1	41	0	0	6.2	31.5
Vega, Onix	R-R	5-9	200	9-07-98	.175	.290	.316	16	69	57	11	10	3	1	1	8	7	3	0	2	7	1	0	10.1	10.1
White, T.J.	B-R	6-2	210	7-23-03	.170	.277	.279	77	286	247	23	42	5	2	6	25	35	2	0	1	104	0	2	12.2	36.4
Williams, Steven	L-R	6-3	216	2-18-99	.000	.300	.000	4	10	7	1	0	0	0	0	0	3	0	0	0	3	0	0	30.0	30.0
Wilson, Cody	R-R	6-0	200	7-04-96	.064	.182	.064	20	55	47	2	3	0	0	0	1	5	2	0	1	27	6	2	9.1	49.1
Wood, James	L-R	6-6	240	9-17-02	.293	.392	.580	42	181	150	32	44	9	5	8	36	26	1	0	4	49	8	1	14.4	27.1
Young, Jacob	R-R	5-11	180	7-27-99	.307	.383	.401	56	248	212	28	65	10	2	2	28	25	3	5	3	31	22	4	10.1	12.5

Pitching	B-T	Ht.	Wt.	DOB	W	L	ERA	G	GS	SV	IP	Hits	Runs	ER	HR	BB	SO	AVG	OBP	SLG	SO%	BB%	BF
Alvarez, Andrew	L-L	6-3	215	6-13-99	7	4	2.61	21	18	0	103	88	38	30	4	32	96	.235	.300	.307	23.1	7.7	415
Bennett, Jake	L-L	6-6	234	12-02-00	0	3	5.57	6	6	0	21	26	15	13	2	8	19	.313	.372	.446	20.2	8.5	94
Caceres, Bryan	R-R	6-1	170	2-19-00	0	6	7.94	13	13	0	51	75	53	45	8	22	43	.344	.414	.564	17.2	8.8	250
Collins, Brendan	R-R	6-4	215	9-10-99	0	0	9.00	1	0	0	1	1	1	1	0	1	1	.333	.400	.667	20.0	20.0	5
Diaz, Dannel	L-L	5-11	185	3-05-97	3	5	4.37	38	3	1	60	46	36	29	5	41	83	.208	.347	.299	31.0	15.3	268
Donovan, Dakota	R-R	6-6	238	7-25-97	1	0	3.74	19	0	0	22	26	11	9	0	11	22	.280	.356	.344	21.2	10.6	104
Doolittle, Sean	L-L	6-2	218	9-26-86	1	0	0.00	1	0	0	1	1	0	0	0	0	2	.250	.250	.500	50.0	0.0	4
Edwards, Carl	R-R	6-3	165	9-03-91	0	0	20.25	2	0	0	1	4	3	3	2	0	0	.500	.500	1.500	0.0	0.0	8
Glavine, Peyton	R-L	5-11	180	3-23-99	0	0	0.00	1	0	0	1	1	0	0	0	0	0	.250	.250	.500	0.0	0.0	4
Gomez, Miguel	R-R	6-3	170	9-10-01	0	0	0.00	2	0	0	3	3	4	0	0	2	2	.231	.333	.308	13.3	13.3	15
Guasch, Richard	R-R	6-4	205	4-10-98	0	0	4.50	8	0	0	10	9	6	5	0	9	10	.237	.367	.342	20.4	18.4	49
Henry, Cole	R-R	6-4	215	7-15-99	0	1	2.25	2	2	0	8	6	2	2	1	3	5	.214	.290	.464	16.1	9.7	31
Hernandez, Alemao	L-L	5-8	187	9-27-99	1	1	9.00	4	0	0	10	14	10	10	1	1	8	.341	.364	.585	18.2	2.3	44
Huff, Chance	R-R	6-4	220	4-19-00	2	4	6.13	28	9	0	84	94	65	57	10	37	57	.286	.357	.465	15.3	9.9	373
Knowles, Lucas	L-L	6-2	185	3-14-98	3	0	1.76	9	1	1	15	10	4	3	1	10	20	.182	.318	.273	29.9	14.9	67
Lara, Andry	R-R	6-4	180	1-06-03	6	8	4.58	23	23	0	98	90	58	50	11	34	66	.241	.313	.410	15.9	8.2	416
Lord, Brad	R-R	6-3	210	2-14-00	1	5	3.56	9	9	0	43	44	24	17	2	10	40	.259	.314	.335	21.3	5.3	188

Luckham, Kyle	R-R	6-2	205	10-01-99	5	7	4.85	25	24	0	124	123	72	67	12	30	100	.252	.302	.413	18.9	5.7	530
Merrill, Matt	R-R	6-4	202	6-11-98	0	1	5.27	9	0	0	14	11	12	8	0	7	20	.234	.345	.340	34.5	12.1	58
Mujica, Jose	R-R	6-2	249	6-29-96	0	0	0.00	2	0	0	2	0	0	0	0	0	5	.000	.000	.000	83.3	0.0	6
Perez, Marlon	L-L	5-10	180	3-16-00	7	1	2.97	36	1	2	70	61	26	23	6	21	88	.235	.295	.388	30.8	7.3	286
Peterson, Todd	R-R	6-5	230	1-22-98	2	6	4.85	42	0	9	56	56	33	30	5	25	44	.260	.340	.409	17.8	10.1	247
Pogue, Nick	R-R	6-5	235	9-13-99	1	1	3.49	16	0	0	28	24	13	11	2	10	25	.229	.297	.371	21.0	8.4	119
Powell, Holden	R-R	6-0	190	9-09-99	2	4	4.43	19	0	6	20	20	15	10	0	16	22	.247	.370	.284	22.0	16.0	100
Ribalta, Orlando	R-R	6-7	245	3-05-98	1	0	4.76	3	0	0	6	2	3	3	0	2	8	.105	.190	.158	38.1	9.5	21
Romero, Carlos	R-R	6-6	179	7-15-99	1	1	6.59	29	0	2	42	45	34	31	5	25	51	.271	.383	.440	26.0	12.8	196
Ruwe, Thomas	R-R	6-9	225	9-09-95	0	2	8.04	16	0	0	16	21	15	14	2	10	20	.328	.421	.469	26.3	13.2	76
Saenz, Dustin	L-L	5-11	197	6-02-99	2	2	1.97	10	8	0	50	38	18	11	2	12	55	.200	.255	.274	27.0	5.9	204
Schoff, Tyler	R-R	6-4	220	12-06-98	4	3	3.38	23	0	4	35	30	15	13	4	9	53	.224	.283	.351	36.6	6.2	145
Sinclair, Jack	R-R	6-4	170	5-03-99	3	2	3.18	12	0	5	17	10	8	6	0	5	17	.172	.269	.190	24.6	7.2	69
Tetreault, Jackson	R-R	6-5	189	6-03-96	0	2	12.71	2	2	0	6	14	10	8	3	2	4	.452	.485	.935	12.1	6.1	33
Theophile, Rodney	R-R	6-5	230	9-16-99	0	3	3.48	10	9	0	41	33	16	16	6	20	39	.223	.331	.385	22.0	11.3	177
Ward, Thaddeus	R-R	6-3	204	1-16-97	0	0	3.38	2	2	0	8	7	3	3	1	3	7	.233	.324	.367	20.6	8.8	34
Yankosky, Tyler	L-R	6-6	225	5-28-98	1	1	8.49	10	0	0	12	18	11	11	3	7	13	.360	.458	.560	22.0	11.9	59
Zinn, Jaren	R-R	6-4	205	8-05-98	1	2	3.65	36	0	0	44	25	20	18	3	38	59	.171	.342	.281	30.4	19.6	194

Fielding

Catcher	PCT	G	PO	A	E	DP	PB
Diaz	.990	28	185	14	2	0	2
Farmer	.993	52	424	21	3	2	5
Murzi	1.000	1	9	1	0	0	1
Perez	.975	9	78	1	2	0	1
Pineda	1.000	9	64	7	0	1	1
Suggs	.992	33	235	20	2	3	3
Vega	1.000	14	117	9	0	0	2
Williams	1.000	1	10	1	0	0	0

First Base	PCT	G	PO	A	E	DP
Boissiere	1.000	39	273	17	0	24
Emiliani	1.000	30	215	14	0	18
Morales	.000	1	0	0	0	0
Sanchez	1.000	1	1	0	0	1
Stehly	.983	6	55	3	1	5
White	.975	63	469	29	13	29

Second Base	PCT	G	PO	A	E	DP
Alu	1.000	2	2	3	0	0
Baker	1.000	3	5	8	0	1
Barley	1.000	1	1	2	0	0
Infante	.940	11	16	31	3	5
Lawson	1.000	7	8	26	0	4
Mejia	1.000	2	1	5	0	0
Pena	.981	92	131	227	7	40
Rivero	1.000	3	7	5	0	2
Sanchez	.929	7	14	12	2	3
Shumpert	1.000	7	8	20	0	4
Stehly	1.000	1	0	2	0	0
Young	1.000	1	1	2	0	0

Third Base	PCT	G	PO	A	E	DP
Alu	1.000	2	1	5	0	0
Fox	.800	2	2	10	3	0
House	1.000	16	11	24	0	1
Infante	1.000	1	1	1	0	0
Kieboom	1.000	4	6	7	0	3
Lawson	1.000	1	1	1	0	0
Lipscomb	.960	46	30	90	5	7
Morales	.925	16	11	26	3	3
Rivero	1.000	3	1	4	0	0
Sanchez	.911	16	12	29	4	3
Shumpert	.875	6	2	12	2	0
Stehly	.946	24	14	39	3	3

Shortstop	PCT	G	PO	A	E	DP
Barley	.928	60	68	125	15	23
Downs	.909	3	5	5	1	0
Fox	.958	6	8	15	1	3
Lawson	.958	13	13	33	2	8
Made	.939	22	29	48	5	13
Mejia	1.000	4	6	12	0	1
Pena	.900	4	3	6	1	0
Rivero	.961	13	13	36	2	5
Sanchez	.902	11	14	32	5	1
Shumpert	.909	7	10	10	2	0

Outfield	PCT	G	PO	A	E	DP
Antuna	1.000	20	32	3	0	1
Baker	.000	1	0	0	0	0
Casey	1.000	3	9	1	0	1
De La Rosa	.984	91	159	7	4	1
Emiliani	.667	4	2	0	1	0
Hill	1.000	4	5	1	0	0
Lile	.992	40	81	1	1	1
McKenzie	.975	95	148	7	4	1
Mejia	1.000	1	1	0	0	0
Pena	1.000	7	14	1	0	0
Pinckney	.984	18	43	0	1	0
Shumpert	.836	21	31	1	4	1
Williams	1.000	3	1	0	0	0
Wilson	1.000	19	44	0	0	0
Wood	.979	36	57	2	2	0
Young	1.000	56	104	5	0	1

FREDERICKSBURG NATIONALS

LOW CLASS A

CAROLINA LEAGUE

Batting	B-T	Ht.	Wt.	DOB	AVG	OBP	SLG	G	PA	AB	R	H	2B	3B	HR	RBI	BB	HBP	SH	SF	SO	SB	CS	BB%	SO%
Boissiere, Branden	L-L	6-1	205	3-23-00	.227	.340	.375	57	212	176	25	40	9	1	5	29	31	1	0	4	41	2	0	14.6	19.3
Brown, Marcus	L-R	6-0	187	9-14-01	.270	.383	.360	28	120	100	14	27	4	1	1	24	15	4	0	1	15	4	2	12.5	12.5
Casey, Donovan	R-R	6-2	223	2-23-96	.133	.350	.200	5	20	15	1	2	1	0	0	4	5	0	0	0	7	1	1	25.0	35.0
Colmenares, Jose	R-R	5-10	165	8-23-02	.111	.273	.111	10	34	27	1	3	0	0	0	1	4	2	1	0	7	0	1	11.8	20.6
Cox, Brenner	L-R	6-3	195	5-11-04	.139	.244	.174	35	133	115	14	16	1	0	1	10	15	1	2	0	58	13	1	11.3	43.6
Crews, Dylan	R-R	6-0	203	2-26-02	.355	.423	.645	14	71	62	16	22	3	0	5	24	6	2	0	1	19	1	3	8.5	26.8
Cruz, Armando	R-R	5-10	160	1-16-04	.190	.266	.251	90	372	331	44	63	9	1	3	33	31	4	4	2	67	7	7	8.3	18.0
De La Cruz, Christopher	L-L	5-11	145	3-29-01	.139	.310	.165	33	102	79	12	11	2	0	0	10	17	3	2	1	16	5	2	16.7	15.7
Diaz, Geraldi	L-R	5-11	205	7-08-00	.200	.400	.400	16	60	45	5	9	1	1	2	5	14	1	0	0	13	1	0	23.3	21.7
Dugas, Gavin	R-R	5-10	204	5-19-00	.160	.364	.280	16	66	50	9	8	0	0	2	5	7	9	0	0	18	1	0	10.6	27.3
Emiliani, Leandro	L-L	6-1	180	3-22-00	.245	.362	.318	35	138	110	15	27	8	0	0	18	20	3	0	5	28	0	0	14.5	20.3
Glasser, Phillip	L-R	6-0	200	12-03-99	.421	.476	.526	5	21	19	5	8	2	0	0	4	2	0	0	0	2	1	0	9.5	9.5
Green, Elijah	R-R	6-3	225	12-04-03	.210	.323	.306	75	332	281	36	59	13	1	4	36	45	3	0	2	139	30	5	13.6	41.9
Hassell, Robert	L-L	6-1	195	8-15-01	.189	.377	.302	15	69	53	12	10	1	1	1	4	16	0	0	0	9	2	0	23.2	13.0
House, Brady	R-R	6-4	215	6-04-03	.297	.369	.500	36	158	138	22	41	8	1	6	22	16	1	0	2	34	5	1	10.1	21.5
Infante, Sammy	R-R	6-1	185	6-22-01	.243	.351	.321	74	317	268	39	65	13	1	2	34	35	11	0	2	80	24	7	11.0	25.2
Klassen, Blake	L-L	6-2	205	9-26-00	.169	.282	.246	19	78	65	7	11	5	0	0	7	10	1	0	2	20	0	2	12.8	25.6
Lawson, Cortland	R-R	6-2	200	5-12-00	.279	.396	.366	54	222	183	35	51	8	4	0	25	29	8	0	2	69	10	2	13.1	31.1
Lile, Daylen	L-R	5-11	195	11-30-02	.291	.381	.510	66	294	251	49	73	20	7	7	48	36	3	0	4	58	21	3	12.2	19.7
McHenry, John	B-R	5-10	190	6-18-01	.220	.367	.280	40	167	132	24	29	2	0	2	20	28	4	0	2	33	5	2	16.8	19.8
Morales, Yohandy	R-R	6-4	209	10-09-01	.390	.448	.571	18	87	77	18	30	10	2	0	17	8	1	0	1	18	1	1	9.2	20.7
Mota, Jorgelys	R-R	6-3	170	6-03-05	.154	.267	.308	7	15	13	3	2	0	1	0	1	1	1	0	0	7	1	0	6.7	46.7
Nunez, Elijah	L-L	5-10	180	12-06-01	.282	.413	.306	24	109	85	20	24	2	0	0	11	21	0	0	3	20	19	3	19.3	18.3
Perez, Wilmer	R-R	5-10	186	4-16-98	.241	.321	.310	34	131	116	17	28	8	0	0	8	7	7	0	1	26	1	0	5.3	19.8
Pettigrew, Zion	R-R	6-1	175	12-20-98	.250	.333	.308	20	60	52	10	13	1	1	0	4	6	1	0	1	14	4	2	10.0	23.3

Pinckney, Andrew	R-R	6-3	205	12-07-00	.329	.402	.534	17	82	73	21	24	6	0	3	15	4	5	0	0	16	6	1	4.9	19.5
Quintana, Roismar	R-R	6-1	175	2-06-03	.255	.349	.346	92	373	321	38	82	11	3	4	41	44	4	0	4	104	0	0	11.8	27.9
Rivero, Yoander	R-R	5-9	155	11-22-01	.196	.348	.250	19	70	56	7	11	3	0	0	2	11	2	1	0	19	1	1	15.7	27.1
Romero, Maxwell	L-R	6-1	218	4-29-01	.266	.420	.429	54	224	177	27	47	8	0	7	29	42	5	0	0	60	1	1	18.8	26.8
Stehly, Murphy	R-R	5-10	205	9-27-98	.394	.482	.493	23	85	71	11	28	7	0	0	15	8	5	0	1	11	7	2	9.4	12.9
Suggs, Matt	R-R	5-9	195	5-31-00	.143	.273	.250	9	34	28	3	4	1	1	0	3	5	0	1	0	16	0	0	14.7	47.1
Thomas, Johnathon	R-R	5-7	175	3-01-00	.226	.342	.297	96	385	323	61	73	11	0	4	30	35	23	2	2	93	65	12	9.1	24.2
Vaquero, Cristhian	B-R	6-3	180	9-13-04	.197	.321	.288	16	78	66	10	13	1	1	1	9	12	0	0	0	18	7	0	15.4	23.1
Williams, Steven	L-R	6-3	216	2-18-99	.000	.333	.000	3	6	4	0	0	0	0	0	1	2	0	0	0	3	0	0	33.3	50.0
Witt, Paul	R-R	5-11	170	10-29-97	.221	.292	.419	60	242	217	35	48	11	1	10	29	20	2	0	1	40	1	1	8.3	16.5

Pitching	B-T	Ht.	Wt.	DOB	W	L	ERA	G	GS	SV	IP	Hits	Runs	ER	HR	BB	SO	AVG	OBP	SLG	SO%	BB%	BF
Abreu, Juan	R-R	6-2	190	6-12-00	2	0	5.24	34	0	0	45	32	26	26	4	40	45	.201	.361	.358	22.3	19.8	202
Agostini, Gabriel	L-L	6-0	160	7-24-04	1	0	0.00	1	0	0	2	3	0	0	0	0	1	.375	.375	.375	12.5	0.0	8
Aldonis, Pablo	L-L	6-1	160	3-21-02	0	2	4.05	5	5	0	20	13	9	9	1	11	21	.186	.301	.257	25.3	13.3	83
Amaral, Austin	R-R	6-0	200	12-04-01	1	1	3.38	4	3	0	8	6	6	3	0	5	13	.194	.306	.226	36.1	13.9	36
Arguelles, Anthony	R-R	5-10	195	8-16-00	0	0	0.00	1	0	0	0	1	0	0	0	0	0	.500	.500	1.000	0.0	0.0	2
Atencio, Jose	R-R	5-11	165	9-18-01	4	4	5.37	18	7	0	57	75	39	34	3	18	63	.311	.371	.411	23.8	6.8	265
Baldo, Merrick	R-R	6-1	200	7-17-00	0	0	1.59	9	0	0	17	15	4	3	0	4	14	.242	.284	.274	20.9	6.0	67
Bennett, Jake	L-L	6-6	234	12-02-00	1	3	1.93	9	9	0	42	34	18	9	2	8	54	.222	.274	.301	32.9	4.9	164
Caceres, Bryan	R-R	6-1	170	2-19-00	3	0	4.80	15	7	0	51	48	32	27	1	29	44	.255	.368	.335	19.3	12.7	228
Ciuffetelli, Christian	R-R	6-2	200	12-27-99	0	2	6.32	13	0	3	16	19	14	11	2	10	20	.279	.372	.441	25.6	12.8	78
Cornelio, Riley	R-R	6-3	195	6-06-00	4	8	4.68	22	22	0	92	108	66	48	4	49	86	.285	.371	.398	19.8	11.3	434
Denaburg, Mason	R-R	6-4	195	8-08-99	4	4	11.64	28	4	0	36	43	55	47	6	49	33	.293	.483	.490	16.0	23.8	206
Diaz, Moises	R-R	6-0	195	4-27-01	2	1	2.78	12	0	2	23	21	11	7	3	9	11	.259	.337	.407	11.8	9.7	93
Doolittle, Sean	L-L	6-2	218	9-26-86	0	1	3.38	3	0	0	3	2	1	1	0	0	4	.200	.200	.200	40.0	0.0	10
Gomez, Miguel	R-R	6-3	170	9-10-01	6	4	6.10	20	0	0	31	39	22	21	4	10	28	.331	.381	.542	20.9	7.5	134
Gonzalez, Pedro	R-R	6-2	225	7-16-00	8	3	4.32	34	0	2	73	81	48	35	5	20	50	.278	.335	.409	15.7	6.3	319
Grissom, Marquis	R-R	6-2	202	7-19-01	4	2	2.18	31	0	11	41	33	12	10	1	13	39	.213	.283	.297	22.5	7.5	173
Hall, Bubba	R-R	6-1	212	4-10-00	4	2	3.51	21	0	1	33	25	16	13	2	13	29	.202	.277	.315	20.6	9.2	141
Henry, Cole	R-R	6-4	215	7-15-99	0	0	0.00	2	2	0	7	4	0	0	0	0	11	.167	.231	.208	42.3	0.0	26
Leon, Jefrem	R-R	6-1	155	9-09-02	0	0	2.25	1	1	0	4	3	1	1	1	1	5	.200	.250	.400	31.3	6.3	16
Lord, Brad	R-R	6-3	210	2-14-00	3	1	4.38	18	8	1	62	67	32	30	2	18	44	.279	.347	.358	16.6	6.8	265
Marquez, Franklin	L-L	6-0	165	12-06-02	5	2	3.60	27	0	0	35	37	23	14	2	37	25	.270	.436	.372	14.0	20.7	179
McHenry, John	B-R	5-10	190	6-18-01	0	0	0.00	2	0	0	2	3	0	0	0	0	0	.375	.375	.500	0.0	0.0	8
Merrill, Matt	R-R	6-4	202	6-11-98	0	0	3.04	16	0	2	24	20	11	8	2	14	39	.217	.339	.359	35.8	12.8	109
Otanez, Johan	R-R	6-1	168	2-19-02	1	0	4.50	2	0	0	2	3	1	1	0	2	4	.333	.500	.444	33.3	16.7	12
Pogue, Nick	R-R	6-5	235	9-13-99	0	0	3.12	6	0	1	9	9	5	3	1	2	6	.257	.333	.400	15.4	5.1	39
Polanco, Bryan	R-R	6-2	190	9-12-01	0	1	4.50	2	2	0	6	6	3	3	2	0	3	.250	.250	.500	12.5	0.0	24
Powell, Holden	R-R	6-0	190	9-09-99	0	1	1.42	5	0	1	6	1	1	1	1	0	5	.050	.050	.200	25.0	0.0	20
Rainey, Tanner	R-R	6-2	250	12-25-92	0	1	27.00	1	1	0	1	3	2	2	0	0	0	.600	.600	.600	0.0	0.0	5
Ribalta, Orlando	R-R	6-7	245	3-05-98	0	0	5.79	4	0	0	5	3	3	3	0	2	5	.188	.278	.313	27.8	11.1	18
Rodriguez, Kevin	R-R	6-1	145	8-13-00	4	1	3.88	38	1	1	70	68	34	30	8	24	74	.260	.332	.385	25.3	8.2	293
Sanchez, Bryan	R-R	6-1	175	8-12-02	1	2	6.42	12	6	0	34	34	28	24	5	27	35	.264	.406	.488	21.2	16.4	165
Schultz, Thomas	R-R	6-6	243	8-03-99	0	2	4.30	9	0	0	15	10	8	7	3	4	15	.192	.271	.385	25.4	6.8	59
Simpson, Jared	L-L	6-4	205	6-28-00	0	0	1.59	9	0	2	11	9	4	2	0	5	17	.205	.286	.227	34.7	10.2	49
Sthele, Travis	R-R	6-0	198	9-21-01	0	0	7.36	4	4	0	11	17	9	9	1	3	6	.354	.377	.625	11.3	5.7	53
Sullivan, Liam	L-L	6-6	255	5-16-02	1	0	5.28	6	5	0	15	11	9	9	2	12	24	.196	.348	.375	34.8	17.4	69
Susana, Jarlin	R-R	6-6	235	3-23-04	1	6	5.14	17	17	0	63	56	42	36	3	40	62	.241	.360	.323	21.8	14.1	284
Tepper, Mikey	L-R	6-0	210	6-02-02	0	2	13.50	4	3	0	9	14	15	14	0	7	10	.341	.460	.366	20.0	14.0	50
Tolman, Erik	L-L	6-2	193	6-03-99	0	2	3.15	6	6	0	20	18	8	7	0	7	17	.234	.306	.299	20.0	8.2	85
Ulloa, Jose	R-R	6-2	200	5-06-99	0	1	15.43	6	0	0	9	17	16	16	1	3	7	.405	.471	.643	13.7	5.9	51
Witt, Paul	R-R	5-11	170	10-29-97	0	0	0.00	2	0	0	1	1	0	0	0	0	0	.200	.200	.200	0.0	0.0	5
Yankosky, Tyler	L-R	6-6	225	5-28-98	1	0	4.15	7	0	3	9	8	4	4	0	4	5	.258	.324	.355	13.5	10.8	37
Young, Luke	R-R	6-3	170	10-31-01	4	4	4.40	26	15	1	94	90	55	46	15	39	107	.254	.337	.465	26.6	9.7	403

Fielding

Catcher	PCT	G	PO	A	E	DP	PB
Colmenares	.977	10	76	8	2	1	1
Diaz	.978	16	119	12	3	1	1
Perez	.984	34	272	33	5	2	3
Romero	.992	54	461	42	4	1	5
Suggs	.978	9	77	10	2	2	4
Williams	1.000	1	7	2	0	0	0
Witt	.989	13	89	3	1	0	2

First Base	PCT	G	PO	A	E	DP
Boissiere	.990	50	370	20	4	40
Emiliani	.979	26	173	15	4	17
Klassen	.984	15	110	11	2	5
Quintana	.983	48	328	17	6	28

Second Base	PCT	G	PO	A	E	DP
Brown	.952	9	7	13	1	3
Cruz	.931	6	9	18	2	4
Dugas	.958	13	20	26	2	4
Glasser	1.000	4	2	5	0	0
Infante	.948	41	46	99	8	15
Lawson	.909	26	42	68	11	19
McHenry	.980	15	16	32	1	11
Pettigrew	.925	10	15	22	3	3
Rivero	.967	8	9	20	1	4

Third Base	PCT	G	PO	A	E	DP
Dugas	.000	1	0	0	0	0
House	.924	36	37	60	8	1
Infante	.900	21	8	28	4	1
McHenry	.935	15	10	19	2	1
Morales	.914	15	13	19	3	1
Mota	.923	6	3	9	1	1
Rivero	.778	9	2	12	4	2
Stehly	.909	16	13	27	4	2
Witt	1.000	12	11	17	0	1

Shortstop	PCT	G	PO	A	E	DP
Brown	.969	17	22	41	2	6
Cruz	.955	84	116	201	15	49
Glasser	1.000	1	3	2	0	1
Lawson	.919	25	42	71	10	12
Rivero	1.000	2	4	5	0	2

Outfield	PCT	G	PO	A	E	DP
Casey	1.000	5	8	0	0	0
Cox	.967	33	53	6	2	1
Crews	1.000	12	46	0	0	0
De La Cruz	.945	31	38	6	5	0
Emiliani	.000	1	0	0	0	0
Green	.991	71	149	7	3	0
Hassell	.883	13	16	1	2	1
Lile	.995	58	113	3	1	0
McHenry	1.000	7	14	0	0	0
Nunez	1.000	22	47	2	0	1

Pinckney	.906	15	27	2	3	0	Thomas	.995	91	182	8	1	2	Williams	.000	2	0	0	0	0
Quintana	.893	24	25	0	3	0	Vaquero	.980	15	30	1	1	0	Witt	1.000	1	1	0	0	0

FCL NATIONALS

ROOKIE

FLORIDA COMPLEX LEAGUE

Batting	B-T	Ht.	Wt.	DOB	AVG	OBP	SLG	G	PA	AB	R	H	2B	3B	HR	RBI	BB	HBP	SH	SF	SO	SB	CS	BB%	SO%
Acosta, Jeisel	R-R	6-0	170	9-04-01	.132	.195	.263	16	41	38	3	5	2	0	1	7	2	1	0	0	13	0	0	4.9	31.7
Antuna, Yasel	B-R	6-1	198	10-26-99	.240	.321	.600	8	28	25	4	6	1	1	2	9	2	1	0	0	3	2	0	7.1	10.7
Baca, Tyler	B-L	5-9	180	5-22-00	.256	.400	.282	18	50	39	9	10	1	0	0	5	8	2	0	1	9	0	0	16.0	18.0
Baker, Darren	L-R	5-10	180	2-11-99	.444	.444	.556	3	9	9	0	4	1	0	0	2	0	0	0	0	1	0	1	0.0	11.1
Brown, Marcus	L-R	6-0	187	9-14-01	.000	.200	.000	2	5	4	0	0	0	0	0	0	0	1	0	0	2	0	1	0.0	40.0
Colmenares, Jose	R-R	5-10	165	8-23-02	.308	.378	.641	12	45	39	6	12	4	0	3	19	4	1	0	1	8	0	0	8.9	17.8
Contreras, Jhoan	R-R	6-1	185	12-26-03	.148	.361	.148	17	36	27	4	4	0	0	0	2	8	1	0	0	8	0	1	22.2	22.2
Cooper, Everett	L-R	6-1	184	7-31-03	.373	.460	.400	28	87	75	18	28	2	0	0	9	9	3	0	0	10	6	3	10.3	11.5
Cox, Brenner	L-R	6-3	195	5-11-04	.147	.312	.213	24	93	75	14	11	1	2	0	7	15	3	0	0	36	4	1	16.1	38.7
Crews, Dylan	R-R	6-0	203	2-26-02	1.000	1.000	1.333	1	3	3	3	3	1	0	0	0	0	0	0	0	0	0	0	0.0	0.0
De La Cruz, Christopher	L-L	5-11	145	3-29-01	.000	.556	.000	2	9	3	2	0	0	0	0	1	5	0	0	1	1	1	0	55.6	11.1
De La Cruz, Edward	R-R	5-11	165	8-27-02	.083	.214	.083	7	14	12	1	1	0	0	0	0	2	0	0	0	4	0	0	14.3	28.6
Diaz, Winder	B-R	6-3	170	9-05-02	.279	.395	.324	25	82	68	9	19	3	0	0	6	11	2	1	0	27	2	2	13.4	32.9
Downs, Jeter	R-R	5-11	197	7-27-98	.111	.500	.111	6	18	9	2	1	0	0	0	2	8	0	0	1	3	0	0	44.4	16.7
Dugas, Gavin	R-R	5-10	204	5-19-00	.500	.600	.750	2	5	4	1	2	1	0	0	0	0	1	0	0	0	0	0	0.0	0.0
Fox, Lucius	B-R	6-0	182	7-02-97	.833	.889	1.000	3	9	6	4	5	1	0	0	2	3	0	0	0	0	1	0	33.3	0.0
Garcia, Juan	R-R	6-0	170	2-17-03	.302	.412	.372	15	51	43	6	13	0	0	1	5	7	1	0	0	12	2	0	13.7	23.5
Geraldo, Angel	R-R	6-1	160	6-14-01	.185	.241	.259	19	58	54	8	10	2	1	0	6	2	2	0	0	7	1	0	3.4	12.1
Glasser, Phillip	L-R	6-0	200	12-03-99	.256	.400	.359	13	50	39	12	10	1	0	1	6	9	1	0	1	4	4	1	18.0	8.0
Green, Elijah	R-R	6-3	225	12-04-03	.318	.483	.591	8	29	22	9	7	1	1	1	3	7	0	0	0	11	1	0	24.1	37.9
Klassen, Blake	L-L	6-2	205	9-26-00	.338	.476	.600	21	84	65	17	22	9	1	2	18	16	2	0	1	7	1	1	19.0	8.3
McHenry, John	B-R	5-10	190	6-18-01	.267	.421	.533	6	19	15	2	4	1	0	1	5	4	0	0	0	1	0	0	21.1	5.3
Mojica, Misael	L-R	6-0	155	12-29-04	.200	.397	.273	23	73	55	15	11	2	1	0	8	17	1	0	0	20	0	1	23.3	27.4
Morales, Yohandy	R-R	6-4	209	10-09-01	.400	.400	.400	2	5	5	0	2	0	0	0	1	0	0	0	0	0	0	0	0.0	0.0
Mota, Jorgelys	R-R	6-3	170	6-03-05	.318	.398	.459	28	98	85	22	27	5	2	1	21	9	3	0	1	31	1	2	9.2	31.6
Murzi, Ivan	R-R	6-0	165	5-28-01	.000	.094	.000	11	33	29	1	0	0	0	0	0	3	0	1	0	13	0	0	9.1	39.4
Nunez, Elijah	L-L	5-10	180	12-06-01	.250	.400	.250	2	5	4	1	1	0	0	0	0	1	0	0	0	0	1	0	20.0	0.0
Ochoa Leyva, Nathaniel	R-R	6-4	215	10-15-03	.290	.371	.366	28	107	93	18	27	3	2	0	9	12	0	2	0	34	2	0	11.2	31.8
Peoples, Nick	B-R	6-5	205	7-24-04	.172	.288	.333	32	104	87	12	15	2	0	4	16	10	5	0	2	44	1	0	9.6	42.3
Pettigrew, Zion	R-R	6-1	175	12-20-98	.313	.436	.469	10	39	32	7	10	2	0	1	5	6	1	0	0	7	4	0	15.4	17.9
Pimentel, Brandon	L-L	6-3	210	6-16-00	.371	.463	.629	10	41	35	8	13	4	1	1	15	4	2	0	0	8	0	0	9.8	19.5
Pinckney, Andrew	R-R	6-3	205	12-07-00	.500	.667	.750	2	6	4	2	2	1	0	0	1	2	0	0	0	0	1	0	33.3	0.0
Pineda, Israel	R-R	5-11	217	4-03-00	.400	.500	1.000	2	6	5	3	2	0	0	1	1	1	0	0	0	1	0	0	16.7	16.7
Ramirez, Enmanuel	R-R	6-1	170	11-05-03	.259	.400	.333	12	35	27	5	7	0	1	0	4	5	2	0	1	4	1	1	14.3	11.4
Romero, Maxwell	L-R	6-1	218	4-29-01	.286	.364	.393	9	33	28	2	8	3	0	0	8	4	0	0	1	9	0	0	12.1	27.3
Santana, Eliesel	R-R	6-2	185	10-02-02	.242	.345	.333	33	116	99	15	24	3	0	2	21	14	2	0	1	25	0	1	12.1	21.6
Snell, Ryan	R-R	5-10	206	4-14-00	.111	.238	.278	7	21	18	5	2	0	0	1	3	3	0	0	0	4	0	0	14.3	19.0
Stehly, Murphy	R-R	5-10	205	9-27-98	.238	.385	.286	7	26	21	5	5	1	0	0	3	4	1	0	0	4	2	1	15.4	15.4
Suggs, Matt	R-R	5-9	195	5-31-00	.222	.200	.556	3	10	9	1	2	0	0	1	3	0	0	0	1	4	0	0	0.0	40.0
Tejeda, Erick	R-R	6-4	162	12-26-01	.194	.286	.194	10	35	31	5	6	0	0	0	1	4	0	0	0	13	0	0	11.4	37.1
Vaquero, Cristhian	B-R	6-3	180	9-13-04	.279	.410	.393	42	182	140	34	39	9	2	1	16	29	5	4	4	35	15	8	15.9	19.2

Pitching	B-T	Ht.	Wt.	DOB	W	L	ERA	G	GS	SV	IP	Hits	Runs	ER	HR	BB	SO	AVG	OBP	SLG	SO%	BB%	BF
Agostini, Gabriel	L-L	6-0	160	7-24-04	2	6	4.53	11	7	0	44	36	25	22	4	19	38	.221	.319	.344	19.9	9.9	191
Arguelles, Anthony	R-R	5-10	195	8-16-00	0	0	0.00	1	0	0	1	1	0	0	0	0	1	.333	.333	.333	33.3	0.0	3
Baldo, Merrick	R-R	6-1	200	7-17-00	0	0	0.00	1	0	0	1	2	0	0	0	0	0	.400	.400	.400	0.0	0.0	5
Bollenbacher, Matthew	R-R	6-1	203	11-09-99	1	0	2.45	3	0	0	4	3	1	1	0	1	1	.231	.286	.231	7.1	7.1	14
Carmona, Josue	L-L	6-3	185	9-03-00	1	2	5.73	12	0	0	11	16	7	7	0	10	14	.364	.474	.477	24.6	17.5	57
Colon, Leodarlyn	R-R	6-4	190	12-01-04	0	1	11.57	10	1	0	9	16	13	12	2	11	6	.390	.527	.634	10.9	20.0	55
Diaz, Moises	R-R	6-0	195	4-27-01	1	1	2.89	11	0	4	19	17	7	6	2	4	19	.224	.263	.329	23.8	5.0	80
Dyson, Tyler	R-R	6-4	220	12-24-97	0	1	13.00	7	0	0	9	7	14	13	0	15	11	.226	.490	.226	22.4	30.6	49
Edwards, Carl	R-R	6-3	165	9-03-91	0	0	40.50	1	0	0	1	3	3	3	0	1	0	.600	.667	1.000	0.0	16.7	6
Fortunato, Marcos	R-R	6-0	175	9-12-03	0	0	10.69	12	0	0	16	12	19	19	2	16	13	.211	.397	.333	16.7	20.5	78
Glavine, Peyton	R-L	5-11	180	3-23-99	0	0	0.00	2	0	0	2	2	0	0	0	1	4	.250	.333	.250	44.4	11.1	9
Gomez, Miguel	R-R	6-3	170	9-10-01	1	2	7.15	7	0	0	11	17	13	9	1	3	10	.347	.397	.449	17.2	5.2	58
Gomez, Niomar	R-R	6-3	173	9-09-98	3	1	8.31	14	0	0	13	17	14	12	2	5	11	.309	.365	.618	17.5	7.9	63
Guasch, Richard	R-R	6-4	205	4-10-98	1	0	4.50	2	1	0	2	2	1	1	0	1	5	.250	.333	.250	55.6	11.1	9
Hall, Bubba	R-R	6-1	212	4-10-00	1	0	4.32	5	0	0	8	7	5	4	1	0	9	.226	.235	.387	26.5	0.0	34
Jimenez, Cristian	R-R	6-2	180	5-16-04	1	0	5.12	12	0	1	19	20	14	11	3	6	20	.256	.318	.462	22.7	6.8	88
Leon, Jefrem	R-R	6-1	155	9-09-02	1	1	5.58	11	8	1	31	37	23	19	4	9	35	.287	.343	.457	24.8	6.4	141
Luis, Andy	L-R	6-0	150	1-14-03	3	3	5.59	13	0	0	19	19	18	12	2	18	16	.257	.400	.365	16.8	18.9	95
Marte, Daniel	R-R	6-0	165	1-14-02	0	0	54.00	1	0	0	0	1	4	2	0	3	1	.333	.714	.667	14.3	42.9	7
Mujica, Jose	R-R	6-2	249	6-29-96	0	0	0.00	1	1	0	1	1	0	0	0	0	0	.333	.333	.333	0.0	0.0	3
Ogando, Adrian	R-R	6-2	190	11-20-03	0	1	10.13	2	2	0	5	11	8	6	1	5	5	.393	.500	.607	14.7	14.7	34
Otanez, Johan	R-R	6-1	168	2-19-02	1	1	25.07	8	1	0	5	8	16	13	1	14	6	.320	.585	.560	14.6	34.1	41
Pogue, Nick	R-R	6-5	235	9-13-99	0	0	0.00	1	0	0	1	0	0	0	0	0	0	.000	.000	.000	0.0	0.0	3
Polanco, Bryan	R-R	6-2	190	9-12-01	3	0	5.63	9	7	0	38	44	29	24	7	16	26	.289	.364	.520	14.8	9.1	176
Powell, Holden	R-R	6-0	190	9-09-99	0	0	4.50	1	0	0	2	1	1	1	0	1	2	.143	.250	.143	25.0	12.5	8

Pitching	B-T	Ht.	Wt.	DOB	W	L	ERA	G	GS	SV	IP	Hits	Runs	ER	HR	BB	SO	AVG	OBP	SLG	SO%	BB%	BF
Rainey, Tanner	R-R	6-2	250	12-25-92	0	0	0.00	1	1	0	1	0	0	0	0	0	1	.000	.000	.000	33.3	0.0	3
Ribalta, Orlando	R-R	6-7	245	3-05-98	0	0	0.00	2	0	0	2	2	1	0	0	0	3	.250	.250	.625	37.5	0.0	8
Sanchez, Camilo	R-R	6-2	164	6-28-03	0	2	7.92	9	7	0	31	36	30	27	4	22	22	.293	.403	.472	14.8	14.8	149
Schultz, Thomas	R-R	6-6	243	8-03-99	0	0	0.00	1	0	0	1	1	0	0	0	1	2	.250	.400	.500	40.0	20.0	5
Sthele, Travis	R-R	6-0	198	9-21-01	0	0	0.00	1	0	0	1	1	0	0	0	1	0	.333	.500	.333	0.0	25.0	4
Sullivan, Liam	L-L	6-6	255	5-16-02	0	0	0.00	1	1	0	1	0	0	0	0	0	1	.000	.000	.000	33.3	0.0	3
Tepper, Mikey	L-R	6-0	210	6-02-02	0	0	2.25	3	0	0	4	1	1	1	0	3	5	.077	.250	.077	31.3	18.8	16
Tolman, Erik	L-L	6-2	193	6-03-99	0	1	1.13	3	3	0	8	5	2	1	0	6	8	.185	.343	.185	22.9	17.1	35
Ulloa, Jose	R-R	6-2	200	5-06-99	1	0	6.53	17	0	2	21	21	15	15	0	17	14	.263	.406	.375	13.9	16.8	101
Ward, Thaddeus	R-R	6-3	204	1-16-97	0	0	3.60	2	2	0	5	4	2	2	0	2	6	.222	.391	.278	26.1	8.7	23
Zapata, Genderson	R-R	6-3	170	6-26-04	3	1	4.81	10	7	0	39	46	27	21	7	13	25	.295	.353	.487	14.5	7.5	173

Fielding

C: Acosta 16, Colmenares 12, Murzi 11, De La Cruz 7, Romero 7, Snell 7, Suggs 3, Pineda 1. **1B:** Klassen 15, Ochoa Leyva 12, Tejeda 10, Contreras 8, Pimentel 8, Santana 2. **2B:** Cooper 21, Mojica 21, Pettigrew 5, McHenry 4, Baker 2, Dugas 2. **3B:** Mota 27, Geraldo 16, Garcia 10, Stehly 5, Contreras 2, Morales 2. **SS:** Diaz 25, Glasser 13, Ochoa Leyva 10, Downs 4, Brown 2, Mojica 2, Fox 1, Geraldo 1. **OF:** Vaquero 43, Peoples 32, Cox 24, Santana 23, Baca 19, Ramirez 12, Green 6, Ochoa Leyva 6, Antuna 5, De La Cruz 2, Nunez 2, Pinckney 2, Crews 1.

DSL NATIONALS — *ROOKIE*

DOMINICAN SUMMER LEAGUE

Batting	B-T	Ht.	Wt.	DOB	AVG	OBP	SLG	G	PA	AB	R	H	2B	3B	HR	RBI	BB	HBP	SH	SF	SO	SB	CS	BB%	SO%
Acevedo, Andy	L-L	6-1	170	11-26-05	.170	.299	.248	47	184	153	22	26	2	2	2	19	25	4	0	2	59	23	11	13.6	32.1
Arias, Luis	R-R	6-0	165	7-19-05	.500	.600	.750	2	5	4	1	2	1	0	0	0	1	0	0	0	0	0	0	20.0	0.0
Batista, Carlos	R-R	6-1	170	11-03-05	.232	.374	.352	43	155	125	26	29	5	2	2	7	27	2	0	1	44	30	9	17.4	28.4
Bautista, Jeremy	R-R	6-0	175	10-20-04	.146	.255	.171	19	47	41	3	6	1	0	0	1	4	2	0	0	12	3	1	8.5	25.5
Cabrera, Manuel	R-R	5-10	155	2-16-06	.155	.281	.216	49	179	148	20	23	6	0	1	16	20	7	1	3	40	8	1	11.2	22.3
Joaquin, Eikel	R-R	5-10	155	11-14-05	.235	.336	.336	45	137	119	14	28	7	1	1	12	18	0	0	0	28	5	2	13.1	20.4
Liriano, Hector	L-R	6-2	180	5-17-06	.232	.295	.268	18	61	56	5	13	2	0	0	3	5	0	0	0	17	2	1	8.2	27.9
Marcano, Agustin	R-R	6-0	160	6-28-06	.143	.263	.224	21	58	49	4	7	2	1	0	0	8	0	1	0	16	2	0	13.8	27.6
Maricuto, Jermaine	L-R	5-10	155	10-07-05	.240	.298	.240	33	105	96	4	23	0	0	0	9	6	2	1	0	15	1	0	5.7	14.3
Obispo, Juan	R-R	6-0	180	5-09-06	.184	.244	.316	28	82	76	8	14	3	2	1	6	2	4	0	0	37	4	1	2.4	45.1
Rivera, Yefri	B-R	5-8	142	2-12-04	.182	.286	.255	24	64	55	7	10	2	1	0	5	7	1	1	0	11	1	0	10.9	17.2
Rosario, Helder	R-R	6-1	165	1-26-05	.171	.270	.237	33	89	76	7	13	2	0	1	11	10	1	0	2	38	5	3	11.2	42.7
Sanchez, Jose	R-R	6-3	180	2-06-06	.190	.227	.190	12	22	21	1	4	0	0	0	1	0	1	0	0	13	1	1	0.0	59.1
Solano, Edwin	R-R	5-11	168	3-14-06	.117	.274	.133	43	159	128	12	15	2	0	0	8	22	6	2	1	44	3	4	13.8	27.7
Soto, Elian	L-R	6-1	182	1-10-06	.182	.281	.232	35	114	99	7	18	5	0	0	5	13	1	0	1	44	0	3	11.4	38.6
Tavares, Carlos	L-L	6-2	190	9-17-05	.256	.364	.328	46	151	125	8	32	4	1	1	20	20	3	0	3	34	3	1	13.2	22.5
Tejeda, Dashyll	R-R	6-0	170	3-16-06	.139	.292	.165	38	96	79	17	11	2	0	0	3	14	3	0	0	26	12	3	14.6	27.1

Pitching	B-T	Ht.	Wt.	DOB	W	L	ERA	G	GS	SV	IP	Hits	Runs	ER	HR	BB	SO	AVG	OBP	SLG	SO%	BB%	BF
Acevedo, Luis	L-L	6-1	170	3-03-04	1	2	6.50	12	0	0	18	18	15	13	1	18	22	.265	.433	.397	24.4	20.0	90
Brito, Jose	R-R	6-1	168	9-19-99	0	1	5.52	10	0	0	15	11	15	9	1	11	20	.186	.314	.254	28.6	15.7	70
Cuevas, Ramon	R-R	6-3	170	8-03-03	2	1	3.44	14	1	0	34	31	13	13	1	11	27	.248	.329	.328	19.3	7.9	140
Familia, Jeffrey	L-L	5-11	160	11-11-05	0	3	8.10	13	0	1	17	19	17	15	3	12	23	.302	.430	.492	29.1	15.2	79
Farias, Victor	R-R	6-2	150	7-17-02	0	4	7.07	12	12	0	28	34	23	22	3	11	32	.304	.386	.473	25.2	8.7	127
Hernandez, Jose	R-R	6-6	200	11-01-03	1	0	27.00	3	0	0	2	5	6	6	0	4	3	.500	.600	.800	20.0	26.7	15
Mariano, Raymond	L-L	6-3	160	8-08-04	0	0	7.20	7	0	0	10	14	10	8	0	11	9	.341	.491	.488	16.4	20.0	55
Martina, Clarence	R-R	6-2	195	12-16-04	1	2	3.52	12	0	0	15	13	7	6	0	10	14	.245	.391	.302	20.0	14.3	70
Moreno, Henry	L-L	6-2	170	11-03-04	0	5	4.70	11	9	0	31	20	20	16	0	28	25	.192	.403	.240	17.4	19.4	144
Moreno, Miguel	R-R	6-1	160	10-28-03	0	1	7.98	10	0	0	15	13	14	13	3	19	11	.265	.478	.531	15.9	27.5	69
Oliveros, Deiver	R-R	6-7	180	6-25-03	0	5	8.14	11	6	0	24	35	30	22	0	12	12	.350	.442	.440	10.0	10.0	120
Pena, Angel	R-R	6-0	190	9-30-04	2	0	3.07	9	0	0	15	11	7	5	1	5	19	.208	.279	.302	31.1	8.2	61
Pena, Wilfry	R-R	6-2	170	4-20-05	1	1	13.50	11	0	0	13	18	20	19	1	14	13	.360	.547	.600	17.3	18.7	75
Perez, Doimil	R-R	6-3	170	11-03-03	0	2	4.45	14	2	1	32	34	21	16	5	18	40	.270	.379	.484	26.1	11.8	153
Portorreal, Leuris	R-R	6-3	160	8-13-05	1	3	4.79	11	11	0	36	39	25	19	2	10	29	.262	.313	.376	17.9	6.2	162
Ramirez, Reilin	R-R	6-2	180	5-19-04	0	2	3.26	14	5	0	30	31	19	11	1	17	27	.250	.347	.298	18.8	11.8	144
Rivas, Gustavo	R-R	6-2	165	11-21-03	0	0	0.00	1	0	0	2	1	0	0	0	1	4	.167	.286	.333	57.1	14.3	7
Rivero, Enyerber	R-R	6-6	175	4-25-05	1	6	7.30	10	4	0	25	32	28	20	2	16	19	.305	.402	.467	15.0	12.6	127
Roman, Angel	L-L	5-11	162	9-24-03	1	1	3.20	15	2	2	39	34	16	14	1	7	32	.230	.275	.297	20.0	4.4	160

Fielding

C: Rosario 28, Marcano 14, Bautista 12, Maricuto 5. **1B:** Tavares 30, Soto 14, Maricuto 10, Bautista 1, Joaquin 1, Tejeda 1. **2B:** Cabrera 26, Joaquin 20, Rivera 10. **3B:** Joaquin 23, Cabrera 22, Marcano 7, Rivera 5, Arias 2. **SS:** Solano 43, Rivera 8, Cabrera 2. **OF:** Acevedo 45, Batista 41, Tejeda 34, Soto 21, Liriano 14, Sanchez 12, Tavares 9, Obispo 3.

MINOR LEAGUES

Players Reach First Ever MiLB CBA in 2023

BY JJ COOPER

The last few years have been brutal for many who work in minor league baseball.

There was the lost 2020 season. There were furloughs, layoffs and payroll cuts that proved to be an off-ramp for a number of longtime minor league front office employees.

On the heels of that came the MLB-mandated reduction of the minor leagues from 160 affiliated ticket-selling teams to 120.

The effects of the coronavirus pandemic didn't end there. When the minors returned in 2021, there were still capacity restrictions for many teams, and there was still a reluctance by some to return to games.

The 2022 season was supposed to be the return to normalcy, but when the year ended, teams across the minors faced a new realm of fears. Attendance across the minors was down 380 fans per game per team compared with 2019, the last year before the pandemic. Some expressed concern that the new sea level for minor league attendance had dipped significantly.

Minor league attendance hasn't really grown since 2007, when a record 43.26 million fans came to games, an average of 4,170 fans per game. While there's no hope that the slimmed-down minor leagues will ever again come close to that 43 million total attendance record, the minors found a nice equilibrium throughout the 2010s. Most years, the average team drew a little more than 4,000 fans per game.

In 2022, the average team drew just 3,910 fans per game. If that were the new normal, it would mean that it had settled in at a level worse than what Minor League Baseball had seen in any year since the start of the 21st century.

Now, a collective sigh of relief can be heard around the minors. Last year appears to be an aberration. This year looks a whole lot more like 2019 than it does 2022.

Across the affiliated minor leagues, attendance increased by 4 percent compared to 2022, giving minor league operators their best year since the coronavirus pandemic wiped out the 2020 season.

Minor League Baseball's 120 ticket-selling clubs drew 32,137,365 fans in announced attendance in 2023. That's up from 30,916,465 fans in 2022, which is a 3.95% increase. On a per-game basis, the average attendance improved to 4,076 fans per game, up from 3,910 fans per game in 2022. That's a 4.25% increase. The discrepancy between total attendance increase and per-game averages was because there were slightly fewer games played in 2023.

Average minor league attendance climbed to 4,076 fans per game in 2023.

JOHN E. MOORE III/GETTY IMAGES

It's not all good news however. Comparing the 120 full-season clubs that remain after the MiLB reorganization to the 120 full-season clubs that existed in the 2010s, attendance remains significantly below where it was before the 2020 MiLB season was cancelled because of the coronavirus pandemic. The worst average attendance for the 120 full-season clubs in the 2010s was 2018, when teams averaged 4,184 fans per game.

In conversations with front office officials with multiple teams, groups returned to the ballpark in 2023 in a way they didn't in 2022. While season-ticket sales and single-game tickets returned to pre-pandemic levels last year, civic groups and corporate outings remained hard to book in 2022.

In 2023 those groups were back.

"This feels the most normal since 2019. We're seeing that group element come back to the ballpark now," Gwinnett Stripers general manager Erin McCormick said. The Stripers finished with their best attendance since 2015.

According to McCormick, in 2022 some groups were still hesitant to come back to the ballpark because of the pandemic. Others said they needed a year of steady revenues before they were able to do staff outings. This year, both those concerns have largely evaporated.

"In 2021, it was a short season; (in) 2022 there were still a lot of unknowns," McCormick said. "Now this is the first year where it's a sigh of relief. We're back. Now we can focus on what we're doing and grow on that."

A New World

Even if you go to minor league baseball games every year, it's easy to miss the subtle changes that have occurred over the span of a couple of decades.

Some differences aren't very subtle. The arrival of a pitch clock at Triple-A in 2015 was hard to miss. The reduction of the ticket-taking, affiliated minor leagues from 160 to 120 teams was a seismic change.

A lot of other changes are a little less apparent. One year's bleachers become next year's party deck. A "bark in the park" joins the promotional schedule.

Any one of these moves is very minor, but they are the tweaks that over the years that transform the experience for players, teams and fans.

Consolidated Ownership

The days of the mom and pop-owned minor league team largely disappeared in the 1990s, replaced by the wealthy owner or ownership group. For the owners who survived the threadbare days of the 1970s and '80s, the chance to sell at increased valuations made it a logical time to get out.

Now, we are seeing another transformation. As part of MLB's takeover of the minor leagues, previous rules that prevented a single ownership group from owning more than one team in any league were eliminated.

That opened the doors for consolidation in a manner that had never been possible. Add the desire for some owners to cash out after losing an entire season to the pandemic in 2020, not to mention the concerns that MLB could push for further reductions in the minors in 2031, and the conditions were set for private equity groups to make big inroads into the minor leagues.

Diamond Baseball Holdings, a group owned by private equity firm SilverLake, owned 15 teams at the start of the 2023 season. By November 2023, they owned 26 MiLB teams. With over 20% of all full-season clubs owned by one group, DBH is easily the largest owner of MiLB clubs in the modern era.

Minor League Baseball has a new logo, which has closer ties to the Major League Baseball logo, but also with MiLB touches

These sales have confirmed that franchise valuations were not diminished by the pandemic or MLB's takeover of the minors.

So far, DBH has run teams much as they were run before, though SilverLake's other business ties provide plenty of additional opportunities to use the stadiums for a plethora of other non-baseball events as well.

Nets Go Down The Lines

MLB had already mandated that protective netting for minor league teams had to stretch beyond the dugouts. Now, teams have to have nets that stretch from foul pole to foul pole. Teams have been encouraged to do so promptly, but it has to be complete by Opening Day 2025.

There were more rules changes brought to the minors in 2023. The automated ball-strike systems (ABS) were tested at every Triple-A park plus the Low-A Florida State League, with teams flipping back and forth between the challenge system tried last year and a strike zone called exclusively by ABS.

Those rules themselves were then tweaked in-season. On Sept. 5, the rules in Triple-A were tweaked. For most of the season the ABS strike zone was set based on percentages of a player's height, which has led to some complaints that the strike zone didn't always best correspond with the "human" strike zone for a hitter. Different players have different body types. One 6-foot-2 player may be very long-legged, while another could have a very long trunk. Under the height-based system, they had the exact same strike zone, even if that meant it started below the knee for one batter and ended well above the belt for another. Those strike zones also did not take into account any aspect of a player's batting stance.

Beginning on Sept. 5, the ABS system used the Hawkeye system's visual tracking to set the Triple-A strike zone. The strike zone was set individually for each player. The system set the bottom of the strike zone at a player's knees. For the top of the zone, the strike zone was set as two baseballs above the midpoint of the measurements of a player's left and right hips. The change aimed to put the top of the zone near the belt-line.

The new rules meant each player's strike zone is uniquely tied to their body and stance rather than a universal formula. The new strike zone was hoped to more closely resemble the strike zone used by human umpires, although the top end is still designed to be lower than the top end of the MLB strike zone.

That lower top end of the zone was intentionally designed into the new Triple-A strike zone to see if it would reduce the number of strikeouts on riding four-seam fastballs on the top of the zone. That change reduced strikeouts by a modest amount, but in doing so it has also upped the walk rate by roughly twice the number of reduced strikeouts.

The new strike zone was expected to return a half inch or so of the reduction in the top of the strike zone (when compared to the MLB zone) but will still have a lower top than the MLB zone.

Pitch Clock Tweaks

In addition to the strike zone adjustment, there were some tweaks to the pitch clock for Triple-A as well. In Septeber, the Triple-A pitch clock was set at 17 seconds between every pitch. In the past, it had been 14 seconds with no one on base and 19 seconds with a runner on base. (In the majors, it's 15 seconds with no one on and 20 seconds with runners on base).

The new 17-second rule was a response to feedback from hitters who said the switch between 15 to 20 seconds depending on baserunners was disruptive to their pre-pitch rhythm.

This was an example of a change that couldn't happen without technology. Without the PitchCom system that allowed catchers and pitchers to communicate without using signs, there would have to be more time allowed with runners on base to allow teams to run through multiple signs to thwart sign stealing. But with PitchCom being used near universally in the majors and Triple-A, that was no longer a factor.

Two other changes were less noticeable to fans and even players. The maximum number of mound visits in a Triple-A game was cut from five to four (with an extra mound visit in the ninth inning allowed if a team has used up its allotment). This appears to be an effort to cut down on the number of times a catcher thwarts a pitch clock violation by calling for a mound visit as the clock ticks to zero.

And pitch clock operators were instructed to start the pitch clock as soon as the pitcher receives a new baseball. In the past, they had been instruct-

ORGANIZATION STANDINGS

Cumulative minor league records for all 30 organizations, with annual winning percentages back to 2018. Beginning in 2021, most organizations have six affiliates.

		2023						
Rk	**MLB Org**	**W**	**L**	**PCT**	**2022**	**2021**	**2019**	**2018**
1.	Dodgers	414	297	.582	.545	.533	.557	.547
2.	Phillies	390	315	.553	.483	.484	.509	.539
3.	Mariners	359	301	.544	.493	.571	.487	.477
4.	Rays	385	324	.543	.576	.623	.564	.604
5.	Yankees	381	326	.539	.548	.595	.518	.493
6.	Pirates	371	330	.529	.517	.537	.526	.485
7.	Brewers	369	334	.525	.516	.497	.494	.507
8.	Rockies	368	337	.522	.549	.546	.482	.488
9.	Tigers	368	337	.522	.522	.480	.462	.498
10.	Twins	336	317	.515	.532	.507	.525	.529
11.	Giants	395	374	.514	.503	.529	.509	.462
12.	Rangers	361	343	.513	.522	.534	.567	.504
13.	Orioles	356	352	.503	.463	.463	.517	.477
14.	Red Sox	352	349	.502	.529	.588	.464	.470
15.	Reds	324	331	.495	.463	.505	.467	.455
16.	Cubs	348	357	.494	.499	.453	.484	.461
17.	Blue Jays	322	330	.494	.479	.525	.496	.527
18.	D-backs	378	394	.490	.469	.443	.552	.533
19.	Padres	347	366	.487	.522	.462	.523	.503
20.	Marlins	342	363	.485	.501	.505	.504	.476
21.	Angels	317	340	.482	.523	.463	.409	.417
22.	Cardinals	310	339	.478	.487	.398	.462	.550
23.	Guardians	335	370	.475	.528	.521	.499	.522
24.	Royals	335	375	.472	.426	.509	.496	.483
25.	Astros	332	375	.470	.457	.484	.529	.562
26.	Mets	327	371	.468	.485	.457	.494	.487
27.	Braves	304	349	.466	.502	.513	.469	.457
28.	Athletics	297	362	.451	.426	.436	.470	.508
29.	Nationals	280	359	.438	.486	.415	.475	.483
30.	White Sox	284	370	.434	.441	.404	.492	.490

POSTSEASON RESULTS

League (Lvl)	Champion	Runner-Up
International (AAA)	Norfolk (BAL)	Durham (TB)
Pacific Coast (AAA)	Oklahoma City (LAD)	Round Rock (TEX)
Eastern (AA)	Erie (DET)	Binghamton (NYM)
Southern (AA)	Tennessee (CHC)	Pensacola (MIA)
Texas (AA)	Amarillo (ARI)	Arkansas (SEA)
Midwest (A+)	Cedar Rapids (MIN)	Great Lakes (LAD)
Northwest (A+)	Vancouver (SEA)	Everett (SEA)
South Atlantic (A+)	Greenville (BOS)	Hudson Valley (NYY)
California (A)	Modesto (SEA)	R. Cucamonga (LAD)
Carolina (A)	Charleston (TB)*	Down East (TEX)
Florida State (A)	Jupiter (MIA)	Clearwater (PHI)
Arizona Complex (R)	Brewers (MIL)	D-backs Red (ARI)
Florida Complex (R)	Braves (ATL)	Yankees (NYY)
Dominican Summer (R)	Dodgers Bautista (LAD)	Pirates Gold (PIT)

* Repeat champion from 2022

DANIEL SHIREY/GETTY IMAGES (HENDERSON)

Holliday Has Proven He's The One

BY J.J. COOPER

PLAYER OF THE YEAR

The draft is not a crapshoot. It's not a random dice roll that determines success or failure. Teams devote thousands of hours from dozens of people to get draft decisions right.

But there is always some luck involved. Sometimes a team picks at the top of a draft with a franchise player available. Other times, there's no franchise player to be picked. Sometimes, teams get it wrong.

Ken Griffey Jr., Chipper Jones, Joe Mauer and Bryce Harper proved to be the type of No. 1 picks that playoff teams are built around.

Other times, Matt Bush, Tim Beckham or Luke Hochevar are drafted first overall.

Just 16 months after being drafted first overall in 2022, Jackson Holliday looks like he belongs with the group of franchise players.

Jackson Holliday

Holliday was the 2022 BA High School Player of the Year heading into the draft before the Orioles drafted him first overall.

A year later he was in Double-A. He finished his first full season at Triple-A Norfolk after blitzing through four levels of the minor leagues in 2023.

Holliday hit .323/.442/.501 and led the minors with 113 runs scored and ranked fifth in both on-base percentage. He walked almost as much as he struck out. He's proven a reliable and solid defender at shortstop and second base. He swiped 24 bases while showing off his plus speed.

And he's impressed by playing with the approach and intelligence of a savvy veteran, even if he's a baby-faced 19-year-old.

"I mean, just look at him. I know he's 19, but he passes as 16," Norfolk manager Buck Britton said, "but the skill set is off the charts."

Holliday's outstanding season, which saw him dominate as a teenager while spending half the season at the upper levels, earned him our Minor League Player of the Year award.

Holliday becomes the second consecutive Orioles player to be named Minor League POY, following shortstop Gunnar Henderson last year. Orioles catcher Matt Wieters previously won in 2008.

Holliday also becomes the fourth player to win both High School and Minor League POY, joining Joe Mauer, Byron Buxton and Bobby Witt Jr.

It was the right choice. The obvious choice.

But it wasn't obvious heading into the draft.

"It's a very, very high stakes game (picking 1-1), because if you happen into a good one, you're going to change your franchise. If you blow it, you're gonna have a lot of people lose a lot of sleep for a long time," Orioles executive vice president and general manager Mike Elias said.

"And you don't have a crystal ball. Sometimes these things look so obvious in hindsight, but I can promise you at the moment, there's no scouting department that doesn't have its doubts about any of these players."

Every other prospective pick at the top of the 2022 draft has failed to come close to what Holliday has done.

Less than two years after being picked first overall, Holliday is the favorite to rank No. 1 on the Top 100 Prospects list next spring. He looks likely to reach the majors in the near future. He gives the Orioles yet another potential franchise player on a team that has been producing them at a furious pace in recent years, including No. 1 overall prospects Rutschman and Henderson. ■

LAST 10 WINNERS

2012: Wil Myers, Northwest Arkansas/Omaha (Royals)
2013: Byron Buxton, Cedar Rapids/Fort Myers (Twins)
2014: Kris Bryant, Iowa (Cubs)
2015: Blake Snell, Charlotte/Montgomery/Durham (Rays)
2016: Yoan Moncada, Salem/Portland (Red Sox)
2017: Ronald Acuña Jr., Florida/Mississippi/Gwinnett (Braves)
2018: Vladimir Guerrero Jr., New Hampshire/Buffalo (Blue Jays)
2019: Gavin Lux, SS, Tulsa/Oklahoma City (Dodgers)
2021: Bobby Witt Jr., SS, NW Arkansas/Omaha (Royals)
2022: Gunnar Henderson, SS, Bowie/Norfolk (Orioles)

Full list: search "Baseball America awards"

MIKE JANES/FOUR SEAM IMAGES

ed to start the clock when the pitcher has the ball and stands on the mound. Some pitchers had come to realize they could delay the pitch clock start by standing somewhere other than the mound when they got a new baseball.

A New Minor League CBA

Just before the 2023 season began, the Minor League Baseball Players Association and Major League Baseball agreed on the first collective bargaining agreement in the history of the minor leagues.

The deal marks the first time in the nearly 125-year history of the "organized" minor leagues that minor league players have played a part in determining their employment conditions.

Under the terms of the agreement, minor league player salaries will be increased dramatically. Players in the complex leagues will go from making a minimum of $4,800 per year to $19,800 a year. The minimum salary for players in Low-A will go from $11,000 to $26,200. High-A salaries will jump from $11,000 to $27,300. Double-A salaries will go from $13,800 to $30,250. Triple-A salaries will increase from $17,500 to $35,800.

Housing standards, especially for players with families, have also been improved in the CBA. And going forward, new signees who sign at 19 or older will be eligible for minor league free agency after six seasons. Previously, all minor league players regardless of age had to play seven seasons before they reached minor league free agency.

After decades of stagnation, the pace of improvement in minor league working conditions in the past few years has been dramatic. A minor league player who signed in 2000 and retired in 2018 would have noticed very little difference in overall working conditions in his career. The per diem for road trips increased slightly, but minimum salaries remained largely unchanged. Minor league players paid for their own food, largely through mandatory clubhouse dues. Housing was the responsibility of the players, even though MLB teams could move a player from city to city with little advance notice.

Comparatively, a minor league player who signed in 2019 has seen more change in the past four years than what occurred in the previous 50 years.

When that player signed in 2019, teams didn't have to pay players during spring training. The minimum salary for a first-year player in the complex leagues was $3,480.

The following year, the entire minor league season was canceled because of the coronavirus pandemic. Before minor league players returned to work in 2021, MLB unilaterally pushed through a reduction of the minor leagues from 160 to 120 teams. With that decision, thousands of minor league players were out of a job.

Tigers first-rounder Max Clark will never play a game under the pre-CBA rules

CLIFF WELCH/ICON SPORTSWIRE VIA GETTY IMAGES

MLB did announce salary increases for the remaining players, banned clubhouse dues and made teams responsible for providing meals for players at the ballpark. A new schedule format also guaranteed one day off per week. Under previous minor league schedules, players sometimes only had one off day per month.

While there were improvements, the memories of 2020 and the reduction of the minor leagues spurred a newfound activism among players. The efforts of Advocates for the Minor Leagues and other groups to raise awareness of poor living conditions helped bring further pressure onto MLB.

In 2022, MLB announced for the first time that parent clubs would be responsible for housing minor league players. Later that year, MLB agreed to settle a class-action lawsuit brought by minor league players for back pay for spring training, extended spring training and other wage violations. And late last year, minor league players voted to organize as a union for the first time. MLB quickly recognized the union, and the two sides began negotiating this CBA.

"Think of where things were just a few years ago," labor attorney and former minor league

Zerjav's Roots Help Club Flourish

BY J.J. COOPER

EXECUTIVE OF THE YEAR

LAST 10 WINNERS

2013: Martie Cordaro, Omaha (Pacific Coast)
2014: Sam Bernabe, Iowa (Pacific Coast)
2015: Dave Oster, Lake Elsinore (California)
2016: Tom Kayser, president, Texas League
2017: Ryan Keur, Daytona (Florida State)
2018: Bob Murphy, Dayton (Midwest)
2019: Don Logan, Las Vegas (Pacific Coast)
2020: Adam Giardino, broadcaster
2021: K.L. Wombacher, president/GM, Hillsboro (Northwest)
2022: Kristin Call, GM, Myrtle Beach (Carolina)

For full list, search "Baseball America awards"

The Timber Rattlers' stadium is renovated and fully compliant with the stricter rules of the Professional Development License standards. And its front office staff of 30 is an excellent mix of team lifers (13 employees have been with the team for 10+ years) and new energy.

All of that seems truly amazing if you rewind to where the Appleton, Wisc. club was in 2020.

The Timber Rattlers were community-owned. That had worked well, but community ownership wasn't designed to handle a pandemic year without baseball. The team needed new ownership. The stadium was owned separately.

And when MLB took over the operation of the minor leagues and cut the number of affiliated ticket-buying teams from 160 to 120, all of that uncertainty arrived at the very moment when the Timber Rattlers were in a beauty pageant to prove they were a team worth keeping in affiliated baseball.

But the Timber Rattlers did have some advantages. A one-time member of the volunteer board who ran the team, Craig Dickman, had interest in buying the team and the stadium. And Dickman was working with Timber Rattlers' president and general manager Rob Zerjav.

Rob Zerjav

So instead of asking the board to trust an outside group to purchase the club, the bid was coming from people with long-time ties to the team. In Zerjav's case, he'd already worked for the Timber Rattlers for 24 years. There was a trust that the club was going to be in good hands.

The purchases were made, Zerjav became the managing partner to add to his titles of president and general Manager, and Wisconsin got a PDL as part of the 120-team reorganized minor leagues.

"A lot of dominos had to fall in the right order in such a quick amount of time, and they did," Zerjav said. "It was relieving to have that domino fall and this one fall. It's been everything we could have hoped for."

As the head of a team that has consistently been a model operation, Zerjav is Baseball America's 2023 Minor League Executive of the Year.

"I got to become an owner of an MiLB team. I never in a million years thought that would happen. To be able to keep our full-time staff intact and compensated and take care of them and their families, that was important. Then it was all about: 'How do we save baseball in Appleton?" Zerjav said.

On his first day as an intern for the club in 1997, Zerjav never imagined he was starting what has proven to be his workplace home for more than a quarter of a century. Much like everything that had to fall in place for affiliated baseball to survive in Appleton, however, Zerjav's career has seen domino after domino fall in the right order.

"Never did I think I'd just stay here. (Working in the minor leagues) is nomadic. Maybe it was God saying 'This is your spot.' Every time I was ready to move on, something opened up here. It was ticket sales. Then it was stadium operations. The GM job opened up when I was 27," he said.

Now, he's helping to ensure that others get those opportunities as well.

"Treat people like you want to be treated," he said. "That's one of the core values we have with the Timber Rattlers. We try to take care of people ... That's the way we try to do business here. We have a great group of people here who continue to grow, and it's even better now." ■

Dinkelman Pushed Kernels To Title

MANAGER OF THE YEAR

LAST 10 WINNERS

2012: Dave Miley, Triple-A Scranton/W-B (Yankees)
2013: Gary DiSarcina, Triple-A Pawtucket (Red Sox)
2014: Mark Johnson, Low-A Kane County (Cubs)
2015: Tony DeFrancesco, Triple-A Fresno (Astros)
2016: Dave Wallace, Double-A Akron (Indians)
2017: Stubby Clapp, Triple-A Memphis (Cardinals)
2018: Drew Saylor, High-A Rancho Cucamonga (Dodgers)
2019: Corey Ragsdale, High-A Down East (Rangers)
2021: Chris Widger, High-A Quad Cities (Royals)
2022: Gil Velazquez, Triple-A Reno (D-backs)
For full list, search "Baseball America awards"

BY PHIL MILLER

Brian Dinkelman had toiled in the Twins organization for 17 years, all but six weeks of it in the minor leagues, without ever winning a championship.

And it showed.

The Cedar Rapids Kernels last September had just fought their way to the franchise's first Midwest League title in almost three decades, the ecstatic players were armed with sparkling cider in a jubilant home clubhouse, poised to drench each other in celebration—and their manager was nowhere to be found.

"Dink kept the players waiting a little bit longer than maybe they were hoping for. He was out on the field, because staff members, stadium personnel and a bunch of fans wanted their pictures taken with him on such a big night. And he obliged them all," Twins farm director Drew MacPhail said. "It shows you what a connection he has with that community. And the players waited for him, which shows you how much respect he has in that clubhouse."

Oh, not just in that small-town Iowa clubhouse, his office for the past seven years. Dinkelman, 40, has earned respect around minor league baseball, having guided the Kernels to winning records and a playoff berth in each of his four seasons as manager and posting a career .574 winning percentage, including an 82-50 record (.621) in 2023 that was the best in the minor leagues. He's also guided 14 players so far on a path that took them to the majors.

MIKE JANES/FOUR SEAM IMAGES

Brian Dinkelman

With a track record like that, the low-key Dinkelman is an easy choice as Baseball America's Minor League Manager of the Year.

"He's so deserving. He handles every challenge you can throw at him," MacPhail said. "This year, he had one of the youngest rosters in the Midwest League, and probably the youngest, least-experienced coaching staff as well. And then to put up the best record in minor league ball, and finish the job with a championship, it was just awesome to watch."

The Twins got to watch Dominican slugger Emmanuel Rodriguez crack 16 homers at the age of 20, pitching prospect Cory Lewis strike out 63 hitters with a 2.32 ERA in 63 innings, and right fielder Kala'i Rosario earn Midwest League MVP honors with 21 homers and an .832 OPS. And they watched Dinkelman help them develop into future major leaguers.

"He has an incredible feel for the game, but he has an incredible feel for their space, too," MacPhail said. "He's not their boss, if that makes sense, he's their leader."

The 40-year-old former second baseman and outfielder established a supportive culture in the clubhouse, and it helped during an inconsistent start to the season. After the first month, the Kernels were still below .500 at 14-15. But they went on a 16-4 run in June, then a 20-7 tear in August.

Dinkelman was assigned to Cedar Rapids in 2016 under Jake Mauer, kept the job when Toby Gardenhire took over in 2018, then succeeded him as manager in 2019.

Four years later, he guided the Kernels to tense victories over Peoria in the semifinals, and Great Lakes in the championship round, both series came down to winner-take-all games.

"I'll never forget it, and these players, that's for sure," Dinkelman said. "I'm not sure I ever expected to manage. But seeing the game from the dugout, absorbing the entire game, I thought managing might be right for me. And it's given me so much." ■

CLASSIFICATION ALL-STARS

TRIPLE-A

Pos	Player, Team (Organization)	Age	AVG	OBP	SLG	PA	H	2B	3B	HR	RBI	BB	SO	SB
C	Ivan Herrera, Memphis (Cardinals)	23	.298	.444	.496	347	81	25	1	9	56	65	69	10
1B	Luken Baker, Memphis (Cardinals)	26	.334	.439	.720	380	105	22	0	33	98	59	76	0
2B	Jonathan Aranda, Durham (Rays)	25	.339	.449	.613	434	121	23	0	25	81	64	87	2
3B	Michael Busch, Oklahoma City (Dodgers)	25	.323	.432	.615	424	114	23	4	24	82	61	80	3
SS	Joey Ortiz, Norfolk (Orioles)	24	.321	.378	.507	389	112	30	4	9	58	32	69	11
OF	Dominic Canzone, Reno (D-backs)	25	.354	.431	.634	304	91	18	3	16	71	39	40	2
OF	Colton Cowser, Norfolk (Orioles)	23	.313	.439	.524	315	79	15	1	12	45	56	80	7
OF	Justyn-Henry Malloy, Toledo (Tigers)	23	.292	.431	.509	548	128	24	1	23	81	100	129	5
DH	Christian Encarnacion-Strand, Louisville (Reds)	23	.331	.405	.637	316	92	21	2	20	62	33	69	2

Pos	Pitcher, Team (Organization)	Age	W	L	ERA	G	GS	IP	H	BB	SO	HR	SO/9	WHIP
SP	Cody Bradford, Round Rock (Rangers)	25	9	2	3.63	14	14	74	71	16	65	6	7.9	1.17
SP	Robert Gasser, Nashville (Brewers)	24	9	1	3.73	24	23	125	109	46	155	11	11.1	1.24
SP	Quinn Priester, Indianapolis (Pirates)	22	8	4	4.13	21	20	102	93	43	106	6	9.3	1.33
SP	Mike Soroka, Gwinnett (Braves)	25	4	4	3.41	17	17	87	65	28	92	6	9.5	1.07
SP	Kai-Wei Teng, Sacramento (Giants)	24	4	4	3.99	13	12	59	48	32	75	3	11.5	1.36
RP	Gerson Moreno, Rochester (Nationals)	27	7	4	2.30	54	0	67	36	44	83	4	11.2	1.20

DOUBLE-A

Pos	Player, Team (Organization)	Age	AVG	OBP	SLG	PA	H	2B	3B	HR	RBI	BB	SO	SB
C	Adrian Del Castillo, Amarillo (D-backs)	23	.273	.386	.505	265	60	13	1	12	45	40	67	2
1B	Coby Mayo, Bowie (Orioles)	21	.307	.424	.603	347	88	30	2	17	44	51	86	4
2B	Thomas Saggese, Frisco/Springfield (TEX/STL)	21	.318	.386	.550	553	154	28	6	24	104	48	129	10
3B	Junior Caminero, Montgomery (Rays)	19	.319	.386	.557	308	87	8	3	17	55	30	54	3
SS	Luisangel Acuña, Frisco/Binghamton (TEX/NYM)	21	.301	.369	.411	529	142	27	2	7	59	51	94	54
OF	Evan Carter, Frisco (Rangers)	20	.284	.411	.451	462	107	15	6	12	62	74	103	22
OF	Jackson Chourio, Biloxi (Brewers)	19	.282	.336	.471	509	131	21	2	21	86	36	97	37
OF	Pete Crow-Armstrong, Tennessee (Cubs)	21	.289	.371	.527	342	86	19	5	14	60	31	82	27
DH	Owen Caissie, Tennessee (Cubs)	20	.285	.396	.523	483	114	28	2	21	78	70	152	6

Pos	Pitcher, Team (Organization)	Age	W	L	ERA	G	GS	IP	H	BB	SO	HR	SO/9	WHIP
SP	Will Dion, Akron (Guardians)	23	2	3	3.03	14	13	68	60	24	70	6	9.2	1.23
SP	Richard Fitts, Somerset (Yankees)	23	9	5	3.40	24	24	135	114	37	143	19	9.5	1.12
SP	Brant Hurter, Erie (Tigers)	24	6	7	3.55	24	24	109	105	29	125	7	10.3	1.23
SP	Carlos Rodriguez, Biloxi (Brewers)	21	8	5	2.75	23	23	111	73	50	141	8	11.4	1.10
SP	Emmet Sheehan, Tulsa (Dodgers)	23	4	1	1.86	12	10	53	24	23	88	5	14.9	0.88
RP	Antoine Kelly, Frisco (Rangers)	23	3	1	1.95	43	0	51	37	22	69	4	12.3	1.16

JOHN E. MOORE III

Before he starred for the Rangers in the MLB postseason, Evan Carter dominated the Texas League.

CLASSIFICATION ALL-STARS

HIGH-A

Pos	Player, Team (Organization)	Age	AVG	OBP	SLG	PA	H	2B	3B	HR	RBI	BB	SO	SB
C	Harry Ford, Everett (Mariners)	20	.257	.412	.432	544	110	22	4	15	65	100	105	24
1B	Abimelec Ortiz, Hickory (Rangers)	21	.290	.352	.613	315	81	12	3	24	76	27	87	1
2B	Jace Jung, West Michigan (Tigers)	22	.254	.377	.465	366	77	18	2	14	43	56	83	5
3B	Tanner Schobel, Cedar Rapids (Twins)	22	.288	.366	.493	347	87	10	5	14	61	36	64	9
SS	Jackson Holliday, Aberdeen (Orioles)	19	.314	.452	.488	259	65	11	5	5	35	50	54	17
OF	Roman Anthony, Greenville (Red Sox)	19	.294	.412	.569	245	60	14	3	12	38	40	75	2
OF	Yanquiel Fernandez, Spokane (Rockies)	20	.319	.354	.605	268	79	14	3	17	64	14	48	1
OF	Alberto Rodriguez, Everett (Mariners)	22	.306	.393	.580	322	86	30	7	11	58	31	69	3
DH	Jordan Beck, Spokane (Rockies)	22	.292	.378	.566	341	86	19	1	20	72	43	71	11

Pos	Pitcher, Team (Organization)	Age	W	L	ERA	G	GS	IP	H	BB	SO	HR	SO/9	WHIP
SP	Julian Aguiar, Dayton (Reds)	22	4	1	1.92	14	14	70	44	24	77	2	9.9	0.97
SP	Chase Petty, Dayton (Reds)	20	0	2	1.95	16	16	60	58	14	61	0	9.2	1.20
SP	Anthony Solometo, Greensboro (Pirates)	20	2	3	2.30	12	12	59	43	25	68	2	10.4	1.16
SP	Tyler Stuart, Brooklyn (Mets)	23	4	0	1.55	14	14	76	56	23	84	3	10.0	1.04
SP	Drew Thorpe, Hudson Valley (Yankees)	22	10	2	2.81	18	18	109	84	33	138	10	11.4	1.07
RP	Logan Rinehart, Everett/Aberdeen (SEA/BAL)	25	2	3	2.03	38	0	53	34	19	69	4	11.6	0.99

LOW-A

Pos	Player, Team (Organization)	Age	AVG	OBP	SLG	PA	H	2B	3B	HR	RBI	BB	SO	SB
C	Samuel Basallo, Delmarva (Orioles)	18	.299	.384	.503	352	92	19	4	12	60	41	73	7
1B	Xavier Isaac, Charleston (Rays)	19	.266	.380	.462	376	83	16	3	13	56	56	80	10
2B	Carlos Jorge, Daytona (Reds)	19	.295	.400	.483	355	88	11	9	9	36	47	70	31
3B	Sal Stewart, Daytona (Reds)	19	.269	.395	.424	387	85	19	0	10	60	66	59	10
SS	Diego Velasquez, San Jose (Giants)	19	.298	.387	.434	517	127	32	1	8	69	56	82	23
OF	Justin Crawford, Clearwater (Phillies)	19	.344	.399	.478	308	95	16	6	3	60	25	53	40
OF	Gabriel Gonzalez, Modesto (Mariners)	19	.348	.403	.530	335	103	19	4	9	54	23	46	8
OF	Samuel Zavala, Lake Elsinore (Padres)	18	.267	.420	.451	459	93	22	0	14	71	89	121	20
DH	Thayron Liranzo, Rancho Cucamonga (Dodgers)	19	.274	.396	.557	399	91	24	2	22	65	64	107	2

Pos	Pitcher, Team (Organization)	Age	W	L	ERA	G	GS	IP	H	BB	SO	HR	SO/9	WHIP
SP	Hayden Birdsong, San Jose (Giants)	21	0	0	2.16	12	10	42	34	22	70	0	15.1	1.34
SP	Aidan Curry, Down East (Rangers)	20	6	3	2.30	19	15	82	47	29	99	4	10.9	0.93
SP	Brock Porter, Down East (Rangers)	20	0	3	2.47	21	21	69	39	42	95	1	12.3	1.17
SP	Max Rajcic, Palm Beach (Cardinals)	21	6	3	1.89	12	12	62	41	9	68	4	9.9	0.81
SP	Robby Snelling, Lake Elsinore (Padres)	19	5	1	1.57	11	11	52	39	13	59	2	10.3	1.01
RP	Wen Hui Pan, Clearwater (Phillies)	20	4	1	2.81	27	1	58	31	19	81	2	12.6	0.87

ROOKIE COMPLEX

Pos	Player, Team (Organization)	Age	AVG	OBP	SLG	PA	H	2B	3B	HR	RBI	BB	SO	SB
C	Josue Briceño, FCL Tigers	18	.325	.404	.550	198	55	13	2	7	37	23	28	3
1B	Adrian Gil, DSL White Sox	17	.340	.481	.517	190	50	11	0	5	33	25	21	5
2B	Echedry Vargas, ACL Rangers	18	.315	.387	.569	222	62	15	1	11	39	21	54	17
3B	Juan Baez, ACL Brewers	18	.370	.395	.557	205	71	16	4	4	42	8	23	17
SS	Ricardo Cabrera, ACL Reds	18	.350	.469	.559	175	50	7	4	5	21	21	35	21
OF	Kevyn Castillo, DSL Angels	18	.371	.478	.548	234	69	10	7	3	35	40	36	23
OF	Jaison Chourio, ACL Guardians	18	.349	.476	.463	189	52	12	1	1	25	38	37	19
OF	Eduardo Quintero, DSL Dodgers	17	.359	.472	.618	212	61	15	7	5	42	32	34	22
DH	Lazaro Montes, ACL Mariners	18	.282	.452	.555	146	31	10	1	6	31	33	37	1

Pos	Pitcher, Team (Organization)	Age	W	L	ERA	G	GS	IP	H	BB	SO	HR	SO/9	WHIP
SP	Jeter Martinez, DSL Mariners	17	2	2	1.72	10	8	47	17	20	55	1	10.5	0.79
SP	Angel Liranzo, DSL Phillies	16	5	0	0.89	10	4	30	16	8	30	0	8.9	0.79
SP	Fernando Perez, FCL Blue Jays	19	2	2	2.72	11	10	50	35	12	57	1	10.3	0.95
SP	Santiago Suarez, FCL Rays	18	4	0	1.13	10	3	40	28	8	38	0	8.6	0.91
SP	Michael Kennedy, FCL Pirates	18	2	1	2.13	11	7	42	25	19	55	1	11.7	1.04
RP	Teofilo Mendez, ACL D-backs	21	4	0	2.25	21	0	36	26	9	50	4	10.9	0.97

MINOR LEAGUE ALL-STARS

Heston Kjerstad hit for average and power at Double-A and Triple-A.

After an injury-slowed 2022, Colt Keith hit .306 with 27 homers and 101 RBIs.

DIAMOND IMAGES (LEFT)/ SCOTT AUDETTE (RIGHT)

FIRST TEAM

Pos	Player, Organization (Levels)	Age	AVG	OBP	SLG	AB	H	HR	RBI	BB	SO	SB
C	Samuel Basallo, Orioles (A, A+, AA)	18	.313	.402	.551	419	131	20	86	61	94	12
1B	Luken Baker, Cardinals (AAA)	26	.334	.439	.720	314	105	33	98	59	76	0
2B	Thomas Saggese, Rangers/Cardinals (AA, AAA)	21	.306	.374	.530	555	170	26	111	52	144	12
3B	Junior Caminero, Rays (A+, AA)	19	.324	.384	.591	460	149	31	94	42	100	5
SS	Jackson Holliday, Orioles (A, A+, AA, AAA)	19	.323	.442	.499	477	154	12	75	101	118	24
OF	Roman Anthony, Red Sox (A,A+, AA)	19	.272	.403	.466	397	108	14	64	86	119	16
OF	Owen Caissie, Cubs (AA)	20	.289	.398	.519	439	127	22	84	76	164	7
OF	Heston Kjerstad, Orioles (AA, AAA)	24	.303	.376	.528	479	145	21	55	42	100	5
DH	Jonathan Aranda, Rays (AAA)	25	.339	.449	.613	357	121	25	81	64	87	2

Pos	Pitcher, Organization (Levels)	Age	W	L	ERA	G	GS	IP	H	BB	SO	WHIP
SP	Robert Gasser, Brewers (AAA)	24	9	1	3.79	26	25	135	123	50	166	1.28
SP	Cade Horton, Cubs (A, A+, AA)	21	4	4	2.65	21	21	88	61	27	117	1.00
SP	Carlos Rodriguez, Brewers (AA, AAA)	21	9	6	2.88	26	26	128	87	57	158	1.12
SP	Robby Snelling, Padres (A, A+, AA)	19	11	3	1.82	22	22	104	82	34	118	1.12
SP	Drew Thorpe, Yankees (A+, AA)	22	14	2	2.52	23	23	139	99	38	182	0.98
RP	Orion Kerkering, Phillies (A, A+, AA, AAA)	22	4	1	1.51	49	0	54	36	12	79	0.89

SECOND TEAM

Pos	Player, Organization (Levels)	Age	AVG	OBP	SLG	AB	H	HR	RBI	BB	SO	SB
C	Thayron Liranzo, Dodgers (A)	19	.272	.400	.562	345	94	24	70	70	112	2
1B	Abimelec Ortiz, Rangers (A, A+)	21	.294	.371	.619	391	115	33	101	49	126	1
2B	Michael Busch, Dodgers (AAA)	25	.323	.431	.618	390	126	27	90	65	88	4
3B	Coby Mayo, Orioles (AA, AAA)	21	.290	.410	.563	504	146	29	99	93	148	5
SS	Jett Williams, Mets (A, A+, AA)	19	.263	.425	.451	410	108	13	55	104	118	45
OF	Justice Bigbie, Tigers (A+, AA, AAA)	24	.343	.405	.537	432	148	19	78	42	77	6
OF	Blake Dunn, Reds (A+, AA)	24	.312	.425	.522	458	143	23	79	62	130	54
OF	Victor Scott II, Cardinals (A+, AA)	22	.303	.369	.425	548	166	9	63	46	97	95
DH	Colt Keith, Tigers (AA, AAA)	21	.306	.380	.552	507	155	27	101	60	121	3

Pos	Pitcher, Organization (Levels)	Age	W	L	ERA	G	GS	IP	H	BB	SO	WHIP
SP	Will Dion, Guardians (A+, AA)	23	6	4	2.39	26	19	117	91	35	129	1.08
SP	Wikelman Gonzalez, Red Sox (A+, AA)	21	9	4	3.96	25	25	111	76	70	168	1.31
SP	Chase Hampton, Yankees (A+, AA)	21	4	3	3.63	20	20	107	85	37	145	1.14
SP	Connor Phillips, Reds (AA, AAA)	22	4	5	3.86	25	24	105	91	57	154	1.41
SP	Tyler Stuart, Mets (A+, AA)	23	7	2	2.20	21	21	111	90	32	112	1.10
RP	Antoine Kelly, Rangers (AA, AAA)	23	3	1	2.04	49	0	57	45	23	79	1.19

Tides Ride New Wave Of Success

TEAM OF THE YEAR

When the 2023 minor league season began, we at Baseball America ranked the Norfolk Tides as the minors' most-talented roster.

With six Top 100 prospects on the Tides Opening Day roster (Grayson Rodriguez, Jordan Westburg, Joey Ortiz, Connor Norby, Colton Cowser and D.L. Hall), Norfolk had more Top 100 talent than all but five MLB teams had in their entire organization.

Prospect talent doesn't always equate to wins and losses. While there was no debate about the potential of the Tides' lineup, that didn't guarantee on-field success. Norfolk, Baseball America's 2023 Minor League Team of the Year, made sure its on-field production was as impressive as its long-term potential.

Coby Mayo

Norfolk won seven of its first eight games. The Tides finished April with a 19-7 record, alone atop the 20-team International League. By June 1, their 38-16 record was the best in the league by 5.5 games. The Tides topped their division for every day of the season.

Rodriguez, Westburg and Hall all moved up to the major leagues, but the replacements were equally impressive. Coby Mayo and Heston Kjerstad became lineup stalwarts. And then in early September, 19-year-old shortstop Jackson Holliday joined the team. Holliday had begun the season in Low A, but he was going to end it trying to help the Tides win an International League and Triple-A Championship.

Even as the names of the players in the lineup kept changing, the winning never stopped. Norfolk finished the year with a .604 winning percentage, which was best in the International League. In the IL championship series, Norfolk lost the opener to the Durham Bulls, but bounced back to outscore Durham 14-2 in the final two games of the series. Mayo homered in both Game Two and Game Three, while Holliday homered in Game Three to give Norfolk its first title since 1983.

The Tides then added one more title. Facing the Pacific Coast League champion Oklahoma City Dodgers, Norfolk fell behind early before a Cowser grand slam gave the Tides the lead. A two-run ninth inning home run by Norby also proved important, as Oklahoma City rallied for four runs in the bottom of the ninth. But Joey Krehbiel struck out Ryan Ward to give the Tides a 7-6 victory and the Triple-A national title.

Adley Rutschman and Gunnar Henderson had given Norfolk fans a glimpse of the Orioles' success to come on their way to the majors, but this year's Tides' team is the first since 2015 to post a winning record.

"I mean, it's been a wild ride, to be honest. But I think once when (GM) Mike (Elias) and them came in, they had a plan. They stuck to their guns, and they've really executed. They've done a really nice job of bringing in not only talented players, but high character players. And you're starting to see that take off now in the big leagues. I think I don't even think they imagined it would happen this fast. But I mean, after last season, you know, kind of you give young talented guys a bunch of confidence. And it's just kind of what you get," said Norfolk manager Buck Britton.

"We've been very fortunate that these guys have really created bonds, even outside of the game. They're really good friends. We have a really good environment in the clubhouse and throughout the organization. And I think there's a sense of responsibility that I have to be the best player I can be." ■

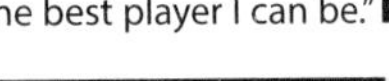

LAST 10 WINNERS

2012: Double-A Springfield Cardinals/Texas (Cardinals)
2013: High-A Daytona Cubs/Florida State (Cubs)
2014: Double-APortland Sea Dogs/Eastern (Red Sox)
2015: Double-A Biloxi Shuckers/Southern (Brewers)
2016: Low-A Rome Braves/South Atlantic (Braves)
2017: Double-A Midland RockHounds/Texas (Athletics)
2018: Low-A Bowling Green Hot Rods/Midwest (Rays)
2019: Double-A Amarillo/Texas (Padres)
2021: Triple-A Durham/International (Rays)
2022: Low-A Charleston/Carolina (Rays)
Full list: search "Baseball America awards"

JULIO AGUILAR/GETTY IMAGES

*Full-season teams only

2023 OVERALL MINOR LEAGUE DEPARTMENT LEADERS

FULL-SEASON TEAM LEADERS

WINS

Norfolk Tides (International)	90
Oklahoma City Dodgers (Pacific Coast)	90
Round Rock Express (Pacific Coast)	89
Durham Bulls (International)	88
Reno Aces (Pacific Coast)	88

LONGEST WINNING STREAK

Modesto Nuts (California)	16
Hickory Crawdads (South Atlantic)	15
Round Rock Express (Pacific Coast)	14
Clearwater Threshers (Florida State)	13
Quad Cities River Bandits (Midwest)	12
Lakeland Flying Tigers (Florida State)	12
Memphis Redbirds (International)	12
Omaha Storm Chasers (International)	11

LOSSES

Charlotte Knights (International)	96
Sugar Land Space Cowboys (Pacific Coast)	89
El Paso Chihuahuas (Pacific Coast)	88
Birmingham Barons (Southern)	87
Syracuse Mets (International)	85

LONGEST LOSING STREAK

Aberdeen IronBirds (South Atlantic)	13
Hickory Crawdads (South Atlantic)	13
Tulsa Drillers (Texas)	12
Birmingham Barons (Southern)	12
Columbus Clippers (International)	11
Omaha Storm Chasers (International)	11
Beloit Sky Carp (Midwest)	11

BATTING AVERAGE

Reno Aces (Pacific Coast)	.303
Las Vegas Aviators (Pacific Coast)	.287
Albuquerque Isotopes (Pacific Coast)	.280
Louisville Bats (International)	.279
El Paso Chihuahuas (Pacific Coast)	.277

RUNS

Reno Aces (Pacific Coast)	1043
Las Vegas Aviators (Pacific Coast)	984
Albuquerque Isotopes (Pacific Coast)	959
El Paso Chihuahuas (Pacific Coast)	935
Tacoma Rainiers (Pacific Coast)	922

HOME RUNS

Durham Bulls (International)	225
Syracuse Mets (International)	222
Las Vegas Aviators (Pacific Coast)	221
Scranton/W-B RailRiders (International)	219
Worcester Red Sox (International)	215

STOLEN BASES

Clearwater Threshers (Florida State)	270
Lynchburg Hillcats (Carolina)	266
Somerset Patriots (Eastern)	256
Columbia Fireflies (Carolina)	252
Fredericksburg Nationals (Carolina)	247

EARNED RUN AVERAGE

Down East Wood Ducks (Carolina)	3.39
Somerset Patriots (Eastern)	3.56
Hudson Valley Renegades (South Atlantic)	3.62
Vancouver Canadians (Northwest)	3.62
Great Lakes Loons (Midwest)	3.73

STRIKEOUTS

Toledo Mud Hens (International)	1470
Fayetteville Woodpeckers (Carolina)	1455
Chattanooga Lookouts (Southern)	1435
Norfolk Tides (International)	1424
Hudson Valley Renegades (South Atlantic)	1420

INDIVIDUAL BATTING

BATTING AVERAGE*

Minimum 378 PA

Michael Stefanic (Salt Lake)	.365
Xavier Edwards (Jacksonville)	.351
Justice Bigbie (West Michigan, Erie, Toledo)	.343
Jonathan Aranda (Durham)	.339
Miguel Andujar (Indianapolis)	.338

RUNS

Jackson Holliday (4 teams)	113
Austin Gauthier (Great Lakes, Tulsa)	111
Ryan Bliss (Amarillo, Reno, Tacoma)	110
Blake Dunn (Dayton, Chattanooga)	107
Phillip Evans (Reno)	107

Thomas Saggese

BEN LUDEMAN

HITS

Thomas Saggese (Frisco, Springfield, Memphis)	170
Victor Scott II (Peoria, Springfield)	166
Elier Hernandez (Round Rock)	165
Ryan Bliss (Amarillo, Reno, Tacoma)	164
Connor Norby (Norfolk)	164

TOP HITTING STREAKS

Elier Hernandez (Round Rock)	26
Josh Hood (Modesto)	26
David Fletcher (Salt Lake)	24
David Freitas (Oklahoma City)	22
Jake Mangum (Jacksonville)	21
Darren Baker (3 teams)	21
Jake Cave (Lehigh Valley)	21
Tirso Ornelas (2 Teams)	21
Jahmai Jones (Oklahoma City)	21

MOST HITS (ONE GAME)

Xavier Edwards (Jacksonville)	6
Bryce Johnson (Sacramento)	6
Korey Lee (Sugar Land)	6
LJ Talley (Buffalo)	6
Colt Keith (Erie)	6
Luis Mieses (Birmingham)	6
Alex Ramirez (Brooklyn)	6
Charles McAdoo (Bradenton)	6
German Ramirez (DSL Astros)	6

TOTAL BASES

Thomas Saggese (Frisco, Springfield, Memphis)	294
Coby Mayo (Bowie, Norfolk)	284
Ryan Bliss (Amarillo, Reno, Tacoma)	283
Troy Johnston (Pensacola, Jacksonville)	281
Colt Keith (Erie, Toledo)	280

EXTRA-BASE HITS

Coby Mayo (Bowie, Norfolk)	77
Austin Shenton (Montgomery, Durham)	74
Colt Keith (Erie, Toledo)	68
Troy Johnston (Pensacola, Jacksonville)	67
Yonathan Perlaza (Iowa)	66
Thomas Saggese (Frisco, Spring., Memphis)	66

DOUBLES

Coby Mayo (Bowie, Norfolk)	45
Austin Shenton (Montgomery, Durham)	45
Devin Mann (Oklahoma City, Omaha)	42
Rafael Lantigua (Buffalo)	40
Connor Norby (Norfolk)	40
Yonathan Perlaza (Iowa)	40

TRIPLES

Tyler Black (Biloxi, Nashville)	12
Edwin Arroyo (Dayton, Chattanooga)	11
Nine players tied	10

HOME RUNS

Yunior Severino (Wichita, St. Paul)	35
Shay Whitcomb (Corpus Christi, Round Rock)	35
Hunter Goodman (Hartford, Albuquerque)	34
Luken Baker (Memphis)	33
Bobby Dalbec (Worcester)	33
Abimelec Ortiz (Down East, Hickory)	33

RUNS BATTED IN

Troy Johnston (Pensacola, Jacksonville)	116
Hunter Goodman (Hartford, Albuquerque)	111
Thomas Saggese (Frisco, Spring., Memphis)	111
Cody Thomas (Las Vegas)	109
Tim Elko (Kannapolis., W-S, Birmingham)	106

MOST RBIs(ONE GAME)

Andy Yerzy (Chattanooga)	9
Alex Hall (Wisconsin)	9
Jhon Imbert (DSL Yankees)	9
15 players tied	8

WALKS

Justyn-Henry Malloy (Toledo)	110
Jett Williams (St. Lucie, Brooklyn, Binghamton)	104
Harry Ford (Everett)	103
Jesus Castillo (Bradenton)	102
Jackson Holliday (4 teams)	101
Termarr Johnson (Bradenton, Greensboro)	101

INTENTIONAL WALKS

Phillip Evans (Reno)	4
Colson Montgomery (ACL, W-S, Birmingham)	4
Imanol Vargas (Tulsa)	4
19 players tied	3

STRIKEOUTS

Jerar Encarnacion (Jacksonville)	200
Ambioris Tavarez (Augusta)	196
Kameron Misner (Durham)	186
Austin Hendrick (Dayton)	185
Mason Auer (Montgomery)	184

STOLEN BASES

Victor Scott II (Peoria, Springfield)	94
Chandler Simpson (Charleston, Bowling Green)	94
Jonathan Clase (Everett, Arkansas)	79
Seth Stephenson (Lakeland, West Michigan)	70
Johnathan Thomas (Fredericksburg)	65

CAUGHT STEALING

Javier Sanoja (Jupiter, Beloit)	22
Jean Ramirez (Columbia, Quad Cities)	20
Ambioris Tavarez (Augusta)	20
Emaarion Boyd (Clearwater)	18
Ryan Bliss (Amarillo, Reno, Tacoma)	15
Jonathan Clase (Everett, Arkansas)	15
Chandler Simpson Charleston, Bowling Green)	15
Seth Stephenson (Lakeland, W. Michigan)	15

ON-BASE PERCENTAGE*

Minimum 378 PA

Jacob Hurtubise (Chattanooga, Louisville)	.479
Michael Stefanic (Salt Lake)	.463
Spencer Horwitz (Buffalo)	.450
Jonathan Aranda (Durham)	.449
Jackson Holliday (4 teams)	.442

SLUGGING PERCENTAGE*

Minimum 378 PA

Luken Baker (Memphis)	.720
Abimelec Ortiz (Down East, Hickory)	.619
Michael Busch (Okla. City)	.618
Jonathan Aranda (Durham)	.613
Trey Cabbage (Salt Lake)	.596

ON-BASE PLUS SLUGGING (OPS)*

Minimum 378 PA

Luken Baker (Memphis)	1.159
Jonathan Aranda (Durham)	1.062
Michael Busch (Oklahoma City)	1.049
Austin Shenton (Montgomery, Durham)	1.007
Abimelec Ortiz (Down East, Hickory)	.990

HIT BY PITCH

Ripken Reyes (San Antonio)	49
Blake Dunn (Dayton, Chattanooga)	32
Thomas Gavello (San Jose, Eugene)	32
Seth Stephenson (Lakeland, West Michigan)	30
Robbie Tenerowicz (Arkansas, Tacoma)	29

SACRIFICE BUNTS

Ripken Reyes (San Antonio)	13
Diego Velasquez (San Jose)	13
Tsung-Che Cheng (Greensboro, Altoona)	12
Steward Berroa (New Hampshire, Buffalo)	10
Jean Ramirez (Columbia, Quad Cities)	10

SACRIFICE FLIES

Maick Collado (Lynchburg)	12
Victor Bericoto (Eugene, Richmond)	11
Jhoneiker Betancourt (Kannapolis)	11
Orelvis Martinez (New Hampshire, Buffalo)	11
Diego Velasquez (San Jose)	10
Arol Vera (Inland Empire, Tri-City, Rocket City)	10
Luke Waddell (Mississippi, Gwinnett)	10

GROUNDED INTO DOUBLE PLAY

Tristin English (Amarillo, Reno)	19
Gabriel Gonzalez (Modesto, Everett)	19
10 players tied	18

BATTING AVERAGE BY POSITION

CATCHERS

Samuel Basallo (Aberdeen, Delmarva, Bowie)	.313
Jesus Rodriguez (Tampa, Hudson Valley)	.310
Michael Turner (Winston-Salem)	.309
Daniel Susac (Lansing, Midland)	.300
Chuckie Robinson (Louisville)	.290

FIRST BASEMEN

Miguel Andujar (Indianapolis)	.338
Spencer Horwitz (Buffalo)	.337
Buddy Kennedy (Reno, Las Vegas)	.307
Troy Johnston (Pensacola, Jacksonville)	.307
Trey Cabbage (Salt Lake)	.306

SECOND BASEMEN

Michael Stefanic (Salt Lake)	.365
Xavier Edwards (Jacksonville)	.351
Jonathan Aranda (Durham)	.339
Cesar Prieto (Bowie, Norfolk, Memphis)	.323
Coco Montes (Albuquerque)	.317

THIRD BASEMEN

Junior Caminero (Bowling Green, Montgomery)	.324
Michael Busch (Oklahoma City)	.323
Nick Dunn (Spring., Memphis)	.319
Phillip Evan (Reno)	.312
Brady House (Fred'burg, Wilmington, Harrisburg)	.312

SHORTSTOPS

Vaughn Grissom (Gwinnett)	.330
Jackson Holliday (4 teams)	.323
Darell Hernaiz (Midland, Las Vegas)	.321
Austin Gauthier (Great Lakes, Tulsa)	.316
Ryan Bliss (Amarillo, Reno, Tacoma)	.304

OUTFIELDERS

Justice Bigbie (West Michigan, Erie, Toledo)	.343
Justin Crawford (Clearwater, Jersey Shore)	.332
Jacob Hurtubise (Chattanooga, Louisville)	.330
Matt Kroon (3 Teams)	.326
Andrew Stevenson (St. Paul)	.317

INDIVIDUAL PITCHING

EARNED RUN AVERAGE*

Minimum 110 IP

Tyler Stuart (Brooklyn, Binghamton)	2.20
WIll Dion (Lake County, Akron)	2.39
Max Rajcic (Palm Beach, Peoria)	2.48
Drew Thorpe (Hudson Valley, Somerset)	2.52
Alex Pham (Aberdeen, Bowie)	2.57

WORST ERA*

Jay Groome (El Paso)	8.55
Jeff Criswell (Albuquerque)	7.51
Sam Benschoter (Charlotte)	7.28
Jake Kalish (Salt Lake)	7.19
Christian Mejias (Biloxi)	6.90

WINS

Keider Montero (West Michigan, Erie, Toledo)	15
Drew Thorpe (Hudson Valley, Somerset)	14
Tyler Cleveland (Modesto)	14
Jonh Henriquez (Clearwater, Jersey Shore)	14
Nick Avila (Sacramento)	14

LOSSES

Alan Rangel (Gwinnett, Mississippi)	16
Matthew Thompson (Birmingham)	15
Garrett Davila (Birmingham, Charlotte)	14
Jackson Wolf (Altoona, San Antonio)	13
6 tied	12

GAMES

Brandon Eisert (Buffalo)	59
Gerson Moreno (Rochester)	59
Ryan Nutof (Louisville)	59
Evan Sisk (Omaha)	58
Nick Avila (Sacramento)	56

GAMES STARTED

Jay Groome (El Paso)	30
Blake Walston (Reno, Salt River)	30
Mason Black (Richmond, Sacramento)	29
Mason Montgomery (Durham, Montgomery)	29
Mitch Spence (Scranton/WB)	29
Robert Dugger (Round Rock)	29

COMPLETE GAMES

German Nunez (DSL Texas)	3
9 tied	2

SHUTOUTS

Angel Bastardo (Greenville, Portland)	2
Ubaldo Soto (DSL Angels)	2
26 tied	1

GAMES FINISHED

Tyler Myrick (Eugene, Richmond)	43
Zach Agnos (Fresno)	41
Billy Seidl (Kannapolis)	41
Wander Suero (Oklahoma City)	41
Evan Taylor (Jupiter, Peoria)	40

HOLDS

Tim Cate (Harrisburg, Rochester)	13
Carson Skipper (Fresno)	13
Michael Hobbs (Great Lakes)	12
Adam Kolarek (3 teams)	12
11 tied	11

SAVES

Zach Agnos (Fresno)	27
Evan Taylor (Jupiter, Peoria)	20
Luis Guerrero (Portland, Worcester)	19
Wander Suero (Oklahoma City)	17
Angel Chivilli (Hartford, Spokane)	17
Miguel Rodriguez (Cedar Rapids, Wichita)	17

INNINGS PITCHED

Mitch Spence (Scranton/WB)	163
Michael McGreevy (Memphis, Springfield)	153
Richard Fitts (Somerset)	153
Blake Walston (Reno, Salt River)	149
Robert Dugger (Round Rock)	146

WALKS

Jay Groome (El Paso)	112
Blake Walston (Reno, Salt River)	93
Joe Boyle (Chattanooga, Las Vegas, Midland)	93
Christian Roa (Chattanooga, Louisville)	91
Matthew Thompson (Birmingham)	85

STRIKEOUTS

Drew Thorpe (Hudson Valley, Somerset)	182
Tobias Myers (Biloxi, Nashville)	175
Cade Povich (Bowie, Norfolk)	171
Christian Roa (Chattanooga, Louisville)	170
Wikelman Gonzalez (Greenville, Portland)	168
Joe Boyle (Chattanooga, Las Vegas, Midland)	168

HITS ALLOWED

Jake Kalish (Salt Lake)	178
Michael McGreevy (Memphis, Springfield)	177
Jay Groome (El Paso)	171
Cesar Valdez (Licey, Salt Lake)	163
Mitch Spence (Scranton/WB)	162

HOME RUNS ALLOWED

Jeff Criswell (Albuquerque)	32
Drew Parrish (NW Arkansas, Omaha)	32
Carlos Luna (St. Paul, Wichita)	32
Max Castillo (Kansas City, Omaha)	31
Josh Rogers (Albuquerque)	31

STRIKEOUTS PER NINE (STARTERS)*

Minimum 100 IP

Wikelman Gonzalez (Greenville, Portland)	13.6
Joe Boyle (Chattanooga, Louisville, Las Vegas)	12.9
Christian Roa (Chattanooga, Louisville)	12.7
Cade Povich (Bowie, Norfolk)	12.2
Blade Tidwell (Brooklyn, Binghamton)	11.9

STRIKEOUTS PER NINE (RELIEVERS)*

Minimum 50 IP

Danny Wilkinson (Clearwater)	16.8
Jefry Yan (Pensacola, Jacksonville)	16.1
John McMillon (Columbia, Quad Cities, NW Ark.)	16.0
Jacob Heatherly (Daytona, Dayton, Chattanooga)	15.5
Paul Gervase (Brooklyn, Binghamton)	15.2

OPPONENT AVERAGE (STARTERS)*

Minimum 100 IP

Yoniel Curet (Charleston, Bowling Green)	.147
Chayce McDermott (Bowie, Norfolk)	.165
Michael Dominguez (Lansing, New Hampshire)	.170
Alex Pham (Aberdeen, Bowie)	.180
Ricardo Yan (Visalia, Hillsboro)	.184

OPPONENT AVERAGE (RELIEVERS)*

Minimum 50 IP

Luis Velasquez (Tampa, Hudson Valley)	.131
Tyler Thornton (Lynchburg, Akron)	.135
John McMillon (Columbia, Quad Cities, NW Ark.)	.137
Danny Watson (Hudson Valley, Somerset)	.138
Anthony Maldonado (Jupiter, Jacksonville)	.141

MOST STRIKEOUTS (ONE GAME)

Andrew Abbott (Chattanooga)	14
Angel Bastardo (Greenville)	14
Yoscar Pimentel (Visalia)	14
9 tied	13

WILD PITCHES

Miguel Mora (ACL Giant, San Jose)	31
Alexis Paulino (DSL Yankees)	30
Seth Lonsway (Eugene)	28
Brayan De Paula (Asheville, Corpus Christi)	27
Angel Lopez (DSL Padres)	24

BALKS

Yorman Gomez (Lynchburg)	12
Blas Castano (Arkansas, Scranton/WB, Somerset)	10
Jhancarlos Lara (Augusta, Rome)	10
Brayan Castillo (Spokane)	9
Sean Hermann (Hudson Valley, Tampa)	9

HIT BATTERS

Ben Onyshko (Arkansas)	20
Kai-Wei Teng (Richmond, Sacramento)	20
Brandon Schaeffer (Everett, Modesto)	19
4 tied	18

GROUNDBALL DOUBLE PLAYS

Robert Dugger (Round Rock)	20
Logan Gragg (Memphis, Springfield)	18
Randy Dobnak (St. Paul)	18
Jake Garland (Lansing,Stockton)	18
4 tied	17

MINOR LEAGUES

INTERNATIONAL LEAGUE TRIPLE-A

Awards selected by Major League Baseball

CHAMPION: Norfolk won its first IL title since 1985 when it defeated Durham two games to one in a best-of-three championship series. The Tides won Game 3 by a score of 7-0 behind four shutout innings from lefthander Cade Povich. All the Orioles' top prospects contributed, from shortstop Jackson Holliday and third baseman Coby Mayo—both hit home runs—to center fielder Colton Cowser (double), left fielder Connor Norby (triple) and second baseman Joey Ortiz (one RBI).

MOST VALUABLE PLAYER: Memphis first baseman Luken Baker tied for the IL lead with 33 home runs and 98 RBIs. The Cardinals' 2018 second-rounder hit .334/.440/.720 in 84 games, earning the 26-year-old three callups to St. Louis.

PITCHER OF THE YEAR: Nashville lefthander Robert Gasser led all Triple-A pitchers with 166 strikeouts and those with at least 100 innings with a 19.6 K-BB%. The 24-year-old Brewers prospect ranked second in the IL with a 3.79 ERA and third with a 1.28 WHIP.

TOP MLB PROSPECT: Memphis shortstop Masyn Winn has the best infield arm in the prospect field. He made his MLB debut in late August and averaged 92.4 mph on his throws, third best among infielders. The 20-year-old Winn hit .288/.359/.474 with 18 homers and 17 steals at Triple-A.

MANAGER OF THE YEAR: Buck Britton guided Norfolk to 90 wins, tied with Oklahoma City for most in the minor leagues.

Masyn Winn

INTERNATIONAL LEAGUE ALL-STARS

Pos	Player	Team	AVG	OPS	HR
C	Ivan Herrera	Memphis	.297	.951	10
1B	Luken Baker	Memphis	.334	1.159	33
2B	Jonathan Aranda	Durham	.339	1.063	25
3B	Justyn-Henry Malloy	Toledo	.277	.890	23
SS	Weston Wilson	Lehigh Valley	.259	.879	31
OF	Estevan Florial	Scranton/WB	.284	.944	28
OF	Colton Cowser	Norfolk	.300	.937	17
OF	Wilyer Abreu	Worcester	.274	.930	22
DH	Christian Encarnacion-Strand	Louisville	.331	1.042	20
UT	Xavier Edwards	Jacksonville	.351	.886	32 SB
Pos	**Pitcher**	**Team**	**G**	**ERA**	**SO**
SP	Robert Gasser	Nashville	26	3.79	166
SP	Quinn Priester	Indianapolis	22	4.00	116
SP	Allan Winans	Gwinnett	23	2.85	113
RP	Anthony Maldonado	Jacksonville	35	1.76	71
RP	Kody Funderburk	St. Paul	37	2.60	75

OVERALL STANDINGS

East Division	W	L	PCT	GB	Manager	Attendance	Avg	Last Penn
Norfolk Tides (Orioles)	90	59	.604	—	Buck Britton	411,429	5,795	2023
Durham Bulls (Rays)	88	62	.587	2.5	Michael Johns	491,753	6,736	2022
Lehigh Valley IronPigs (Phillies)	80	66	.548	8.5	Anthony Contreras	567,322	7,990	Never
Worcester Red Sox (Red Sox)	79	68	.537	10.0	Chad Tracy	519,651	7,424	Never
Buffalo Bisons (Blue Jays)	76	72	.514	13.5	Casey Candaele	487,205	7,165	2004
Scranton/Wilkes-Barre RailRiders (Yankees)	73	75	.493	16.5	Shelley Duncan	336,162	4,944	2016
Jacksonville Jumbo Shrimp (Marlins)	70	79	.470	20.0	Daren Brown	347,723	5,114	Never
Rochester Red Wings (Nationals)	66	80	.452	22.5	Matthew LeCroy	437,561	6,077	1997
Syracuse Mets (Mets)	61	85	.418	27.5	Dick Scott	336,492	5,022	1976
Charlotte Knights (White Sox)	53	96	.356	37.0	Justin Jirschele	498,816	6,833	1999

West Division	W	L	PCT	GB	Manager	Attendance	Avg	Last Penn
St. Paul Saints (Twins)	84	64	.568	—	Toby Gardenhire	460,918	6,492	Never
Nashville Sounds (Brewers)	83	65	.561	1.0	Rick Sweet	556,962	7,736	*2005
Iowa Cubs (Cubs)	82	65	.558	1.5	Marty Pevey	432,246	6,003	Never
Louisville Bats (Reds)	75	73	.507	9.0	Pat Kelly	396,840	5,512	2001
Memphis Redbirds (Cardinals)	71	78	.477	13.5	Ben Johnson	223,751	3,065	*2018
Gwinnett Stripers (Braves)	70	78	.473	14.0	Matt Tuiasosopo	230,801	3,251	Never
Indianapolis Indians (Pirates)	70	78	.473	14.0	Miguel Perez	556,775	7,842	2000
Toledo Mud Hens (Tigers)	70	78	.473	14.0	Anthony Iapoce	447,384	6,214	2006
Omaha Storm Chasers (Royals)	68	77	.469	14.5	Mike Jirschele	304,129	4,166	*2014
Columbus Clippers (Guardians)	68	79	.463	15.5	Andy Tracy	557,131	7,847	2019

* Pacific Coast League title won prior to 2021 minor league realignment

While the International League has divisions, they do not determine the playoff field. The teams with the best first-half and second-half records advance.

Playoffs: Norfolk defeated Durham 2-1 in best-of-3 championship series. Norfolk defeated Oklahoma City in Triple-A Championship Game.

BRIAN WESTERHOLT/FOUR SEAM IMAGES

CLUB BATTING

	AVG	G	AB	R	H	2B	3B	HR	RBI	BB	SO	SB	OBP	SLG
Louisville Bats	.279	148	5047	902	1406	299	35	210	846	732	1345	148	.376	.477
Norfolk Tides	.274	149	5042	876	1384	284	28	201	828	613	1311	110	.360	.462
Buffalo Bisons	.274	148	5009	853	1370	312	15	125	789	775	1139	176	.377	.417
Indianapolis Indians	.269	148	4972	795	1337	281	42	160	760	678	1337	115	.361	.439
Iowa Cubs	.265	147	4888	892	1297	302	29	207	856	729	1385	111	.368	.466
Lehigh Valley IronPigs	.264	146	4866	857	1285	260	31	213	817	697	1268	180	.360	.462
St. Paul Saints	.263	148	4944	875	1302	272	32	206	834	711	1459	158	.364	.456
Durham Bulls	.262	150	5030	881	1320	306	28	225	840	722	1524	124	.359	.469
Memphis Redbirds	.262	149	5093	862	1332	258	23	186	802	714	1227	134	.360	.431
Nashville Sounds	.260	148	4901	796	1273	264	25	183	751	672	1298	129	.355	.436
Scranton/WB RRiders	.259	148	4908	796	1272	228	21	219	741	693	1308	174	.360	.448
Toledo Mud Hens	.258	148	4879	782	1257	289	37	179	759	719	1296	84	.356	.442
Omaha Storm Chasers	.257	145	4851	763	1246	280	24	176	710	671	1273	223	.352	.433
Charlotte Knights	.257	149	4961	674	1273	253	17	144	628	504	1186	85	.330	.402
Jacksonville Jumbo Shrimp	.256	149	5003	751	1280	222	29	160	693	628	1306	124	.344	.408
Rochester Red Wings	.255	146	4893	713	1250	251	29	139	659	547	1214	156	.335	.404
Columbus Clippers	.250	147	4885	808	1222	293	25	176	759	680	1295	111	.349	.428
Gwinnett Stripers	.250	148	4892	725	1223	213	31	134	678	714	1285	190	.350	.388
Syracuse Mets	.249	146	4912	798	1225	224	18	222	764	694	1234	98	.350	.438
Worcester Red Sox	.249	147	4771	834	1189	236	36	215	772	721	1390	197	.355	.449

CLUB PITCHING

	ERA	G	CG	SHO	SV	IP	H	R	ER	HR	BB	SO	AVG
Nashville Sounds	4.48	148	1	9	32	1282	1273	734	638	143	536	1305	.259
Durham Bulls	4.56	150	2	6	34	1315	1285	752	666	188	590	1341	.253
St. Paul Saints	4.59	148	0	2	30	1294	1254	743	660	147	688	1354	.254
Norfolk Tides	4.62	149	2	8	40	1290	1214	724	662	143	676	1424	.246
Scranton/Wilkes-Barre	4.67	148	0	3	33	1284	1185	761	666	199	643	1376	.242
Gwinnett Stripers	4.95	148	3	8	28	1290	1284	779	710	164	612	1269	.261
Buffalo Bisons	5.00	148	0	3	27	1282	1223	787	712	192	685	1376	.250
Worcester Red Sox	5.01	147	1	3	35	1259	1274	786	701	197	647	1269	.260
Indianapolis Indians	5.05	148	1	7	30	1282	1255	774	719	147	646	1317	.255
Lehigh Valley IronPigs	5.07	146	1	7	31	1268	1224	773	714	158	734	1207	.255
Memphis Redbirds	5.09	149	0	7	29	1317	1457	830	744	185	633	1310	.280
Jacksonville Jumbo Shrimp	5.18	149	4	5	31	1287	1301	825	741	195	673	1193	.264
Columbus Clippers	5.32	147	2	7	24	1273	1218	808	753	214	767	1302	.253
Omaha Storm Chasers	5.33	145	0	2	27	1274	1303	821	755	208	695	1282	.265
Iowa Cubs	5.34	147	0	6	34	1270	1220	831	754	173	753	1395	.252
Toledo Mud Hens	5.42	148	0	4	30	1276	1349	829	769	187	665	1470	.270
Rochester Red Wings	5.52	146	1	4	30	1268	1334	872	778	171	731	1195	.272
Syracuse Mets	5.80	146	0	7	21	1261	1344	894	813	232	686	1273	.272
Louisville Bats	6.16	148	0	2	25	1285	1334	945	879	221	793	1182	.269
Charlotte Knights	6.25	149	0	0	27	1272	1412	965	883	216	761	1240	.281

CLUB FIELDING

	PCT	PO	A	E	DP
Louisville	.985	3854	1238	76	156
Gwinnett	.984	3871	1319	82	140
Lehigh Valley	.983	3805	1320	88	145
Indianapolis	.982	3846	1285	94	124
Memphis	.982	3950	1404	99	152
St. Paul	.981	3883	1278	98	137
Iowa	.981	3811	1183	98	119
Columbus	.980	3819	1253	101	130
Omaha	.980	3823	1297	104	136
Jacksonville	.980	3861	1259	106	149

	PCT	PO	A	E	DP
Buffalo	.979	3847	1258	107	131
Rochester	.979	3807	1247	106	130
Toledo	.979	3830	1169	105	119
Charlotte	.979	3815	1258	110	141
Norfolk	.978	3871	1221	112	119
Durham	.978	3947	1232	117	129
Syracuse	.977	3782	1151	114	115
Nashville	.977	3846	1272	120	123
Scranton/Wilkes-Barre	.976	3852	1282	127	97
Worcester	.975	3777	1228	126	120

INDIVIDUAL BATTING

Batter, Club	AVG	G	AB	R	H	2B	3B	HR	RBI	BB	SO	SB
Xavier Edwards, Jacksonville	.351	93	370	80	130	14	2	7	47	52	30	32
Jonathan Aranda, Durham	.339	95	357	82	121	23	0	25	81	64	87	2
Miguel Andujar, Indianapolis	.338	103	414	63	140	30	2	16	86	47	55	5
Spencer Horwitz, Buffalo	.337	107	392	61	132	30	1	10	72	78	72	9
Vaughn Grissom, Gwinnett	.330	102	397	74	131	36	4	8	61	56	66	13
Andrew Stevenson, St. Paul	.317	106	416	91	132	23	7	16	57	42	97	44
Rafael Lantigua, Buffalo	.305	129	465	101	142	40	0	12	85	98	107	28
Samad Taylor, Omaha	.301	89	335	65	101	23	4	8	55	66	85	43
Jake Mangum, Jacksonville	.298	119	473	62	141	29	8	5	52	28	91	16
Osleivis Basabe, Durham	.296	94	385	45	114	24	7	4	58	31	66	16

INDIVIDUAL PITCHING

Pitcher, Club	W	L	ERA	G	GS	CG	SV	IP	H	R	ER	BB	SO
Allan Winans, Gwinnett	9	4	2.85	23	17	1	1	126	101	45	40	36	113
Robert Gasser, Nashville	9	1	3.79	26	25	1	0	135	123	64	57	50	166
Janson Junk, Nashville	7	10	4.18	27	25	0	0	140	145	77	65	44	94
Evan McKendry, Durham, Nashville	12	6	4.30	28	23	1	0	142	125	72	68	46	130
Mitch Spence, Scranton/WB	8	8	4.47	29	29	0	0	163	162	89	81	53	153
Michael McGreevy, Memphis	11	6	4.49	24	24	0	0	134	160	71	67	37	107
Caleb Kilian, Iowa	8	3	4.56	25	24	0	0	120	123	66	61	36	95
Caleb Boushley, Nashville	9	8	5.11	29	26	0	0	136	136	82	77	51	110
Randy Dobnak, St. Paul	5	9	5.13	31	26	0	1	126	148	82	72	61	115
Chi Chi Gonzalez, Jacksonville	6	9	6.07	24	23	0	0	122	160	94	82	34	71

DEPARTMENT LEADERS

BATTING

OBP	Spencer Horwitz, Buffalo	.450
SLG	Luken Baker, Memphis	.720
OPS	Jonathan Aranda, Durham	1.062
R	Connor Norby, Norfolk	104
H	Connor Norby, Norfolk	164
TB	Connor Norby, Norfolk	273
XBH	Yonathan Perlaza, Iowa	66
2B	3 tied	40
3B	Jake Mangum, Jacksonville	8
3B	Nick Gonzales, Indianapolis	8
HR	Bobby Dalbec, Worcester	33
HR	Luken Baker, Memphis	33
RBI	Luken Baker, Memphis	98
RBI	Tristan Gray, Durham	98
SAC	Cody Wilson, Rochester	8
BB	Justyn-Henry Malloy, Toledo	110
HBP	Keston Hiura, Nashville	17
SO	Jerar Encarnacion, Jacksonville	200
SB	David Hamilton, Worcester	57
CS	David Hamilton, Worcester	14

FIELDING

C	PCT	Chuckie Robinson, Louisville	.991
	PO	Chuckie Robinson, Louisville	757
	A	Joe Hudson, Gwinnett	48
	DP	Chuckie Robinson, Louisville	9
	E	Carlos Narvaez, Scranton/WB	10
	CS	Joe Hudson, Gwinnett	28
	SB	Logan Porter, Omaha	80
	PB	Caleb Hamilton, Worcester	9
1B	PCT	No Qualifier	
	PO	Lewin Diaz, Norfolk	631
	A	Kyle Manzardo, Durham	56
	DP	Luken Baker, Memphis	75
	E	Micah Pries, Columbus	8
2B	PCT	Connor Norby, Norfolk	.960
	PO	Raynel Delgado, Columbus	181
	A	Connor Norby, Norfolk	240
	DP	Connor Norby, Norfolk	62
	E	Connor Norby, Norfolk	16
3B	PCT	No Qualifier	
	PO	Yolmer Sanchez, Gwinnett	59
	A	Jordan Groshans, Jacksonville	140
	DP	Drew Ellis, Lehigh Valley	18
	E	Jordan Groshans, Jacksonville	15
SS	PCT	Richie Martin, Rochester	.976
	PO	Richie Martin, Rochester	178
	A	Erik Gonzalez, Charlotte	282
	DP	Erik Gonzalez, Charlotte	78
	DP	Jacob Amaya, Jacksonville	78
	E	Erik Gonzalez, Charlotte	15
OF	PCT	Jake Mangum, Jacksonville	.996
	PO	Kameron Misner, Durham	321
	A	Jhonkensy Noel, Columbus	15
	DP	Brandon McIlwain, Syracuse	4
	E	Monte Harrison, Nashville	8
	E	Richie Palacios, Memphis	8

PITCHING

G	3 tied	59
GS	Mitch Spence, Scranton/WB	29
GF	Alan Busenitz, Louisville	38
GF	Miguel Diaz, Toledo	38
SV	Andrew Politi, Worcester	15
W	Evan McKendry, Durham, Nashville	12
L	Garrett Davila, Charlotte	11
IP	Mitch Spence, Scranton/WB	163
H	Mitch Spence, Scranton/WB	162
R	Chi Chi Gonzalez, Jacksonville	94
ER	Chi Chi Gonzalez, Jacksonville	82
HBP	Robert Gasser, Nashville	15
BB	Drew Hutchison, Buffalo, Lehigh Valley	75
SO	Robert Gasser, Nashville	166
SO/9	Robert Gasser, Nashville	11
BB/9	Michael McGreevy, Memphis	2.5
WP	Francisco Morales, Lehigh Valley	15
Balks	Norwith Gudino, Worcester	4
Balks	Casey Lawrence, Memphis, Buffalo	4
HR	Max Castillo, Omaha	31
BAA	Allan Winans, Gwinnett	.218

PACIFIC COAST LEAGUE TRIPLE-A

Awards selected by Major League Baseball

CHAMPION: Oklahoma City swept Round Rock in two games to win the best-of-three PCL championship series. The Game Two finale was a showcase for two top Dodgers prospects in a 5-2 win. Righthander Gavin Stone struck out 10 in 6.1 innings, allowing two runs on four hits plus two walks. First baseman Michael Busch hit a three-run home run in the fifth inning as part of a 2-for-4 day at the plate.

MOST VALUABLE PLAYER: Dodgers 2019 first-rounder Michael Busch made his MLB debut in 2023 but spent most of his season with Oklahoma City. The 25-year-old led the PCL with a 1.049 OPS as part of a .323/.431/.618 season with 27 home runs and 90 RBIs in 98 games.

PITCHER OF THE YEAR: The Rangers' 2019 sixth-round pick out of Baylor, lefthander Cody Bradford turned in his best pro season in 2023. In 14 starts for Round Rock, he went 9-2 with a 3.63 ERA, striking out 65 and walking 16 in 74.1 innings. His 5.2% walk rate ranked second among Triple-A pitchers with at least 70 innings, which was no mean feat with the unforgiving automated ball-strike system introduced at the level in 2023. The 25-year-old Bradford made his MLB debut by receiving four callups to Texas. He made the Rangers' postseason roster and recorded two scoreless World Series appearances for the champions.

TOP MLB PROSPECT: Michael Busch played primarily first base in college at North Carolina but was drafted as a second baseman. That was his primary pro position until 2023, when he focused on third base at Oklahoma City.

MANAGER OF THE YEAR: PCL managers selected Las Vegas' Fran Riordan as top manager. His Aviators went 75-74 and remained in the playoff hunt late into the season. Riordan has managed in the Athletics system since 2015.

Michael Busch

EDDIE KELLY

PACIFIC COAST LEAGUE ALL-STARS

Pos	Player	Team	AVG	OPS	HR
C	Sam Huff	Round Rock	.298	.947	17
1B	Trey Cabbage	Salt Lake	.306	.975	30
2B	Michael Stefanic	Salt Lake	.365	.930	5
3B	Michael Busch	Oklahoma City	.323	1.049	27
SS	Tyler Fitzgerald	Sacramento	.287	.857	20
OF	Cody Thomas	Las Vegas	.301	.922	23
OF	Dominic Canzone	Reno	.354	1.065	16
OF	Jo Adell	Salt Lake	.273	.961	24
DH	Trenton Brooks	Sacramento	.286	.916	22
UT	Coco Montes	Albuquerque	.317	.951	22
Pos	**Pitcher**	**Team**	**G**	**ERA**	**SO**
SP	Cody Bradford	Round Rock	14	3.63	65
SP	Gavin Stone	Oklahoma City	21	4.74	120
SP	Kyle Harrison	Sacramento	20	4.66	105
SP	Robert Dugger	Round Rock	29	4.31	143
RP	Riley O'Brien	Tacoma	52	2.29	86
RP	Ray Kerr	El Paso	36	2.25	42

OVERALL STANDINGS

East Division	W	L	PCT	GB	Manager	Attendance	Avg	Last Penn
Oklahoma City Dodgers (Dodgers)	90	58	.608	—	Travis Barbary	399,908	5,633	2023
Round Rock Express (Rangers)	89	60	.597	1.5	Doug Davis	411,550	5,561	Never
Albuquerque Isotopes (Rockies)	68	82	.453	23.0	Pedro Lopez	521,521	7,048	1994
El Paso Chihuahuas (Padres)	62	88	.413	29.0	Phillip Wellman	507,907	6,772	2016
Sugar Land Space Cowboys (Astros)	61	89	.407	30.0	Mickey Storey	299,055	4,097	Never
West Division	**W**	**L**	**PCT**	**GB**	**Manager**	**Attendance**	**Avg**	**Last Penn**
Reno Aces (D-backs)	88	62	.587	—	Blake Lalli	372,926	5,040	2022
Tacoma Rainiers (Mariners)	77	73	.513	11.0	John Russell	384,498	5,267	2021
Las Vegas Aviators (Athletics)	75	74	.503	12.5	Fran Riordan	506,047	6,838	1988
Salt Lake Bees (Angels)	70	79	.470	17.5	Keith Johnson	443,494	6,160	1979
Sacramento River Cats (Giants)	67	82	.450	20.5	Dave Brundage	388,246	5,177	2019

While the Pacific Coast League has divisions, they do not determine the playoff field. The teams with the best first-half and second-half records advance.
Playoffs: Oklahoma City defeated Round Rock 2-0 in best-of-3 championship series. Norfolk defeated Oklahoma City in Triple-A Championship Game.

CLUB BATTING

	AVG	G	AB	R	H	2B	3B	HR	RBI	BB	SO	SB	OBP	SLG
Reno Aces	.303	150	5176	1043	1570	302	51	163	984	815	1090	76	.401	.476
Las Vegas Aviators	.287	149	5233	984	1500	319	36	221	933	646	1245	188	.370	.488
Albuquerque Isotopes	.280	150	5244	959	1469	286	52	192	907	689	1378	173	.366	.464
El Paso Chihuahuas	.277	150	5193	935	1439	318	31	191	876	726	1223	212	.369	.461
Salt Lake Bees	.274	149	5040	844	1380	252	40	179	786	670	1298	172	.364	.446
Round Rock Express	.270	149	5104	919	1379	294	35	194	853	733	1290	145	.369	.456
Oklahoma City Dodgers	.269	148	5059	904	1359	306	33	171	854	769	1289	119	.370	.444
Tacoma Rainiers	.260	150	5086	922	1320	274	33	214	879	840	1434	210	.370	.453
Sacramento River Cats	.258	149	5002	817	1290	246	22	189	762	713	1348	142	.358	.429
Sugar Land Space Cowboys	.243	150	5007	787	1217	221	37	189	734	752	1476	127	.348	.415

CLUB PITCHING

	ERA	G	CG	SHO	SV	IP	H	R	ER	HR	BB	SO	AVG
Oklahoma City Dodgers	4.58	148	0	6	38	1314	1247	757	669	166	621	1394	.249
Round Rock Express	4.72	149	0	4	37	1315	1268	763	689	168	675	1377	.253
Tacoma Rainiers	5.33	150	2	5	40	1323	1424	859	784	199	616	1226	.276
Sacramento River Cats	5.39	149	0	2	27	1297	1264	857	777	157	864	1364	.256
Reno Aces	5.79	150	1	3	33	1308	1397	910	841	165	739	1327	.272
Sugar Land Space Cowboys	5.83	150	0	2	30	1311	1328	936	849	200	837	1316	.263
Salt Lake Bees	6.01	149	1	5	28	1295	1441	932	865	197	739	1236	.284
Las Vegas Aviators	6.22	149	0	2	37	1307	1478	1012	903	229	751	1277	.284
Albuquerque Isotopes	6.51	150	0	3	26	1317	1559	1033	952	218	725	1212	.295
El Paso Chihuahuas	6.52	150	0	0	23	1315	1517	1055	952	204	786	1342	.288

CLUB FIELDING

	PCT	PO	A	E	DP
Albuquerque	.983	3950	1453	94	150
Sugar Land	.981	3932	1258	100	134
Round Rock	.981	3944	1279	101	143
Tacoma	.981	3970	1389	104	151
Reno	.981	3925	1285	102	133

	PCT	PO	A	E	DP
Salt Lake	.978	3886	1408	120	149
El Paso	.977	3945	1328	124	108
Oklahoma	.977	3942	1263	125	133
Sacramento	.976	3890	1337	129	155
Las Vegas	.974	3920	1294	141	159

INDIVIDUAL BATTING

Batter, Club	AVG	G	AB	R	H	2B	3B	HR	RBI	BB	SO	SB
Michael Stefanic, Salt Lake	.365	99	381	67	139	20	2	5	62	60	33	8
Michael Busch, Oklahoma City	.323	98	390	85	126	26	4	27	90	65	88	4
Coco Montes, Albuquerque	.317	107	436	96	138	26	5	22	89	59	130	11
Diego Castillo, Reno	.313	124	454	94	142	33	1	3	72	97	79	13
Phillip Evans, Reno	.312	128	481	107	150	24	2	11	88	92	75	2
Buddy Kennedy, Las Vegas/Reno	.307	101	374	82	115	24	8	5	50	76	81	3
Trey Cabbage, Salt Lake	.306	107	418	83	128	25	3	30	89	45	142	32
Cody Thomas, Las Vegas	.301	107	429	67	129	27	8	23	109	37	97	5
Elier Hernandez, Round Rock	.298	137	554	98	165	36	5	18	99	50	126	9
Jimmy Herron, Albuquerque	.296	128	456	106	135	27	4	19	83	69	103	33

INDIVIDUAL PITCHING

Pitcher, Club	W	L	ERA	G	GS	CG	SV	IP	H	R	ER	BB	SO
Robert Dugger, Round Rock	7	10	4.31	29	29	0	0	146	149	79	70	60	143
Blake Walston, Reno	12	6	4.52	30	30	0	0	149	142	81	75	93	104
Darren McCaughan, Tacoma	7	8	5.83	25	25	1	0	139	154	98	90	44	130
Anderson Espinoza, El Paso	8	9	6.15	28	28	0	0	132	148	96	90	73	117
Jake Kalish, Salt Lake	9	11	7.19	30	25	0	0	138	178	114	110	55	103
Jeff Criswell, Albuquerque	5	10	7.51	29	26	0	0	121	140	105	101	71	135
Jay Groome, El Paso	4	10	8.55	30	30	0	0	135	171	133	128	112	137

DEPARTMENT LEADERS

BATTING

OBP	Michael Stefanic, Salt Lake	.463
SLG	Michael Busch, Oklahoma City	.618
OPS	Michael Busch, Oklahoma City	1.049
R	Phillip Evans, Reno	107
H	Elier Hernandez, Round Rock	165
TB	Elier Hernandez, Round Rock	265
XBH	Elier Hernandez, Round Rock	59
2B	Elier Hernandez, Round Rock	36
3B	3 tied	8
HR	3 tied	30
RBI	Cody Thomas, Las Vegas	109
SAC	Tyler Wade, Las Vegas	6
BB	Diego Castillo, Reno	97
HBP	Cesar Salazar, Sugar Land	16
SO	Zach DeLoach, Tacoma	173
SB	Jordyn Adams, Salt Lake	44
CS	Yonny Hernandez, Okla. City	12

FIELDING

C	PO	Hunter Feduccia, Okla. City	791
	A	Matt Whatley, Round Rock	43
	DP	Ricardo Genoves, Sacramento	8
	E	Zach Humphreys, Salt Lake	9
	CS	Matt Whatley, Round Rock	26
	SB	Hunter Feduccia, Okla. City	122
	PB	Pedro Severino, Tacoma	9
1B	PCT	No qualifiers	
	PO	Blaine Crim, Round Rock	625
	A	Blaine Crim, Round Rock	43
	DP	Blaine Crim, Round Rock	90
	E	Blaine Crim, Round Rock	7
2B	PCT	No qualifiers	
	PO	Zack Gelof, Las Vegas	135
	A	Zack Gelof, Las Vegas	172
	DP	Zack Gelof, Las Vegas	49
	E	Zack Gelof, Las Vegas	8
	E	Buddy Kennedy, Las Vegas/Reno	8
3B	PCT	No qualifiers	
	PO	Aaron Schunk, Albuquerque	48
	A	Aaron Schunk, Albuquerque	165
	DP	Aaron Schunk, Albuquerque	20
	E	2 tied	13
SS	PCT		
	PO	Jonathan Ornelas, Round Rock	143
	A	Connor Kaiser, Albuquerque	250
	DP	Connor Kaiser, Albuquerque	62
	E	Jonathan Ornelas, Round Rock	13
OF	PCT	Jimmy Herron, Albuquerque	.991
	PO	Jorge Barrosa, Reno	304
	A	Sandro Fabian, Round Rock	14
	DP	2 tied	4
	E	Jordyn Adams, Salt Lake	12

PITCHING

G	Nick Avila, Sacramento	56
GS	Blake Walston, Reno	30
GS	Jay Groome, El Paso	30
GF	Wander Suero, Okla. City	41
SV	Wander Suero, Okla. City	17
W	Nick Avila, Sacramento	14
L	Jake Kalish, Salt Lake	11
IP	Blake Walston, Reno	149.1
H	Jake Kalish, Salt Lake	178
R	Jay Groome, El Paso	133
ER	Jay Groome, El Paso	128
HBP	Noah Davis, Albuquerque	12
BB	Jay Groome, El Paso	112
SO	Robert Dugger, Round Rock	143
SO/9	Jeff Criswell, Albuquerque	10
BB/9	Darren McCaughan, Tacoma	2.9
WP	Riley Pin, Albuquerque	14
Balks	Jose Rodriguez, Tacoma	4
HR	Jeff Criswell, Albuquerque	32
BAA	Blake Walston, Reno	.254

EASTERN LEAGUE DOUBLE-A

Awards selected by Major League Baseball

CHAMPION: Coming into the season, Erie had not won an EL title in 23 seasons. In fact, the club had reached the league finals only once. That all changed in 2023 when the SeaWolves swept Binghamton in the championship series to bring home the franchise's first title in its 24th season. Erie lefthander Brant Hurter tossed seven shutout innings with seven strikeouts to pick up the win in the deciding Game 2. Tigers 2022 first-rounder Jace Jung went 1-for-5, scored two runs and took part in turning three double plays at second base.

MOST VALUABLE PLAYER: The Orioles went three times over slot value to sign Florida prep third baseman Coby Mayo for $1.75 million in the fourth round of the 2020 draft. That looks like money well spent. Mayo suited up with Bowie in the first half and hit .307/.424/.603 with 17 home runs in 78 games. The 21-year-old moved to Triple-A in mid July and finished with 29 total homers.

PITCHER OF THE YEAR: Righthander Richard Fitts spent the entire season with Somerset and led the EL with 11 wins, 163 strikeouts and a 1.14 WHIP. The 23-year-old's 3.48 ERA ranked third. The Yankees drafted Fitts out of Auburn in the sixth round in 2021.

TOP MLB PROSPECT: Jasson Dominguez was famous in prospect circles before he even signed with the Yankees for $5.1 million in 2019. The 20-year-old Dominican center fielder batted .254/.367/.414 with 15 home runs and 37 stolen bases in 109 games for Somerset, ultimately earning a September callup to New York.

MANAGER OF THE YEAR: Gabe Alvarez has had incredible success in his two seasons managing Erie, going 155-120 (.565). He took the SeaWolves to the EL finals in 2022 and finished the deal with a league championship in 2023.

Jasson Dominguez

RUSTY JONES/FOUR SEAM IMAGES

EASTERN LEAGUE ALL-STARS

Pos	Player	Team	AVG	OPS	HR
C	Nathan Hickey	Portland	.258	.826	15
1B	Carlos De La Cruz	Reading	.259	.798	24
2B	Oliver Dunn	Reading	.271	.902	21
3B	Coby Mayo	Bowie	.307	1.027	17
SS	Leo Jimenez	New Hampshire	.287	.808	8
OF	Jasson Dominguez	Somerset	.254	.781	15
OF	Justice Bigbie	Erie	.362	.985	12
OF	Johnathan Rodriguez	Akron	.289	.876	18
DH	Hunter Goodman	Hartford	.239	.848	25
UT	Colt Keith	Erie	.325	.976	14
Pos	**Pitcher**	**Team**	**G**	**ERA**	**SO**
SP	Richard Fitts	Somerset	27	3.48	163
SP	Brant Hurter	Erie	26	3.28	133
SP	Clayton Beeter	Somerset	12	2.08	76
SP	Christian Scott	Binghamton	12	2.47	77
RP	Luis Guerrero	Portland	43	2.82	59
RP	Andrew Magno	Erie	36	2.10	67

OVERALL STANDINGS

Northeast Division	W	L	PCT	GB	Manager	Attendance	Avg	Last Penn
Somerset Patriots (Yankees)	84	53	.613	—	Raul Dominguez	352,293	5,181	2022
Binghamton Rumble Ponies (Mets)	74	61	.548	9.0	Reid Brignac	206,911	3,183	2014
Portland Sea Dogs (Red Sox)	73	63	.537	10.5	Chad Epperson	403,957	6,121	2006
New Hampshire Fisher Cats (Blue Jays)	62	72	.463	20.5	Cesar Martin	236,809	3,947	2018
Reading Fightin Phils (Phillies)	59	77	.434	24.5	Al Pedrique	384,563	5,916	2001
Hartford Yard Goats (Rockies)	57	76	.429	25.0	Chris Denorfia	402,731	6,293	Never

Southwest Division	W	L	PCT	GB	Manager	Attendance	Avg	Last Penn
Erie SeaWolves (Tigers)	75	62	.547	—	Gabe Alvarez	207,555	3,098	2023
Richmond Flying Squirrels (Giants)	74	64	.536	1.5	Dennis Pelfrey	428,541	6,396	Never
Altoona Curve (Pirates)	67	68	.496	7.0	Callix Crabbe	308,003	4,597	2017
Bowie Baysox (Orioles)	67	70	.489	8.0	Kyle Moore	234,527	3,500	2015
Akron RubberDucks (Guardians)	65	73	.471	10.5	Rouglas Odor	265,938	4,029	2021
Harrisburg Senators (Nationals)	59	77	.434	15.5	Delino DeShields	273,768	4,212	1999

Southwest: Erie defeated Richmond 2-0. **Northeast:** Binghamton defeated Somerset 2-0. **Championship Series:** Erie defeated Binghamton 2-0

CLUB BATTING

	AVG	G	AB	R	H	2B	3B	HR	RBI	BB	SO	SB	OBP	SLG
Portland Sea Dogs	.248	136	4516	708	1119	252	28	135	647	555	1341	231	.335	.406
Erie SeaWolves	.247	137	4575	711	1129	217	19	171	669	564	1179	90	.337	.415
Somerset Patriots	.245	137	4522	749	1106	217	16	197	693	650	1226	256	.346	.430
Bowie Baysox	.242	137	4524	627	1093	219	25	148	580	557	1304	142	.333	.399
Reading Fightin Phils	.240	136	4506	601	1082	229	21	159	566	529	1364	119	.329	.406
N.H. Fisher Cats	.240	134	4307	638	1034	225	16	145	587	560	1305	156	.335	.401
Akron RubberDucks	.237	138	4444	591	1052	218	21	110	544	572	1261	111	.332	.369
Harrisburg Senators	.236	136	4393	571	1038	194	21	100	516	545	1271	148	.327	.358
Altoona Curve	.236	135	4412	594	1040	190	19	122	548	477	1112	163	.319	.370
Richmond Flying Squirrels	.236	138	4472	658	1054	202	17	140	604	552	1236	124	.325	.382
B'ton Rumble Ponies	.230	135	4317	580	991	195	19	120	541	563	1356	131	.329	.367
Hartford Yard Goats	.228	133	4355	580	992	211	18	138	525	501	1243	126	.316	.380

CLUB PITCHING

	ERA	G	CG	SHO	SV	IP	H	R	ER	HR	BB	SO	AVG
Somerset Patriots	3.56	137	1	12	31	1211	954	538	479	127	544	1397	.214
Akron RubberDucks	3.87	138	1	4	35	1192	1019	607	512	138	581	1278	.230
Richmond Flying Squirrels	3.99	138	0	9	29	1192	1041	615	529	111	578	1336	.235
Binghamton Rumble Ponies	4.08	135	1	14	40	1170	1011	580	530	137	468	1216	.233
Portland Sea Dogs	4.10	136	1	8	30	1186	1004	604	541	133	598	1308	.228
Erie SeaWolves	4.12	137	0	10	30	1212	1124	632	555	126	524	1367	.245
Harrisburg Senators	4.21	136	0	8	35	1167	1073	597	546	127	495	1107	.246
NHampshire Fisher Cats	4.26	134	1	6	30	1150	1005	639	545	138	617	1352	.232
Altoona Curve	4.32	135	3	10	26	1176	1104	636	564	133	551	1093	.248
Bowie Baysox	4.36	137	3	9	34	1199	1060	667	581	163	552	1293	.235
Reading Fightin Phils	4.58	136	0	3	29	1181	1064	685	601	166	599	1285	.239
Hartford Yard Goats	5.69	133	4	5	32	1161	1271	808	734	186	518	1166	.278

CLUB FIELDING

	PCT	PO	A	E	DP
Harrisburg	.982	3502	1174	84	123
Binghamton	.981	3512	1094	88	104
Somerset	.980	3633	1060	96	91
Erie	.979	3635	1122	100	104
Portland	.979	3559	1024	99	95
Altoona	.979	3529	1135	102	118
Richmond	.978	3577	1111	104	111
Reading	.977	3542	1073	110	98
Bowie	.976	3596	1013	111	87
Hartford	.975	3484	1091	116	107
Akron	.971	3576	1010	138	99
New Hampshire	.970	3451	944	137	82

INDIVIDUAL BATTING

Batter, Club	AVG	G	AB	R	H	2B	3B	HR	RBI	BB	SO	SB
Matt Kroon, Reading	.319	79	298	53	95	24	2	8	44	33	66	22
Corey Rosier, Portland	.285	104	358	64	102	22	6	7	39	33	86	49
Juan Brito, Akron	.276	87	315	46	87	21	1	10	60	48	63	3
Steward Berroa, New Hampshire	.272	103	324	64	88	21	2	7	35	57	106	43
Oliver Dunn, Reading	.271	119	417	65	113	27	4	21	78	82	139	16
Nick Yorke, Portland	.268	110	444	74	119	25	5	13	61	51	122	18
Carlos De La Cruz, Reading	.259	129	509	80	132	25	1	24	67	54	160	3
Bladimir Restituyo, Hartford	.258	108	430	61	111	20	1	15	55	8	86	17
Chase Meidroth, Portland	.255	91	325	59	83	16	1	7	43	59	78	9
Jasson Domínguez, Somerset	.254	109	425	83	108	19	2	15	66	77	130	37

INDIVIDUAL PITCHING

Pitcher, Club	W	L	ERA	G	GS	CG	SV	IP	H	R	ER	BB	SO
Brant Hurter, Erie	6	7	3.28	26	26	0	0	118	108	50	43	33	133
Ty Madden, Erie	3	4	3.43	26	25	0	0	118	101	50	45	50	146
Richard Fitts, Somerset	11	5	3.48	27	27	0	0	153	131	60	59	43	163
David Parkinson, Reading	9	5	3.56	24	22	0	0	126	121	61	50	51	131
Dominic Hamel, Binghamton	8	6	3.85	26	25	0	0	124	108	56	53	49	160
Sean Sullivan, Altoona	8	4	3.88	24	21	1	0	114	106	53	49	38	97
Connor Gillispie, Bowie	7	4	3.89	27	14	2	2	116	96	55	50	37	99
Carson Seymour, Richmond	5	3	3.99	28	23	0	0	113	96	58	50	43	114
Mitchell Parker, Harrisburg	9	6	4.20	25	23	0	0	114	100	58	53	54	132
Hunter Stanley, Akron	4	11	4.92	26	24	0	0	119	116	76	65	49	108

DEPARTMENT LEADERS

BATTING

OBP	Oliver Dunn, Reading	.396
SLG	Coby Mayo, Bowie	.603
OPS	Oliver Dunn, Reading	.902
R	Jasson Dominguez,Somerset	83
H	Carlos De La Cruz, Reading	132
TB	Carlos De La Cruz, Reading	231
XBH	Oliver Dunn, Reading	52
2B	Coby Mayo, Bowie	30
3B	Corey Rosier, Portland	6
HR	Tyler Hardman, Somerset	26
RBI	Billy Cook, Bowie	81
SAC	Steward Berroa, New Hampshire	9
SAC	Bladimir Restituyo, Hartford	9
BB	Oliver Dunn, Reading	82
HBP	6 tied	14
SO	Carlos De La Cruz, Reading	160
SB	Corey Rosier, Portland	49
CS	Donta' Williams,Bowie	11

FIELDING

C	PO	Drew Romo, Hartford	701
	A	Drew Romo, Hartford	44
	DP	Michael Berglund, Akron	7
	E	Drew Romo, Hartford	14
	CS	Hayden Senger, Binghamton	29
	SB	Drew Romo, Hartford	97
	PB	Andy Thomas, Richmond	13
1B	PCT	Frankie Tostado, Harrisburg	.996
	PO	Grant Lavigne, Hartford	710
	A	Joe Naranjo, Akron	47
	DP	Grant Lavigne, Hartford	71
	E	Grant Lavigne, Hartford	10
	E	Joe Naranjo, Akron	10
2B	PCT	J.T. Arruda, Harrisburg	.987
	PO	J.T. Arruda, Harrisburg	202
	A	J.T. Arruda, Harrisburg	263
	DP	J.T. Arruda, Harrisburg	76
	E	Miguel Hiraldo, New Hampshire	14
3B	PCT	No Qualifier	
	PO	Warming Bernabel, Hartford	56
	A	Jose Peroza, Binghamton	134
	DP	Trey Lipscomb, Harrisburg	12
	E	Tyler Hardman, Somerset	18
SS	PCT	Trey Sweeney, Somerset	.966
	PO	Julio Carreras, Hartford	127
	A	Julio Carreras, Hartford	229
	DP	Julio Carreras, Hartford	43
	E	Julio Carreras, Hartford	19
OF	PCT	Jeisson Rosario, Somerset	.994
	PO	Petey Halpin, Akron	277
	A	Chavez Young, Altoona	13
	DP	Chavez Young, Altoona	4
	E	Johnathan Rodriguez, Akron	8

PITCHING

G	Keylan Killgore, Reading	46
GS	3 tied	27
GF	Luis Guerrero, Portland	34
SV	Luis Guerrero, Portland	18
W	Richard Fitts, Somerset	11
W	Aaron Shortridge, Altoona	11
L	Case Williams, Hartford	11
L	Hunter Stanley, Akron	11
IP	Richard Fitts, Somerset	152.2
H	Aaron Shortridge, Altoona	157
R	Case Williams, Hartford	87
ER	Case Williams, Hartford	80
ER	Blane Abeyta, Somerset	80
HBP	Adam Wolf, Erie	18
BB	Doug Nikhazy, Akron	73
SO	Richard Fitts, Somerset	163
SO/9	Dominic Hamel, Binghamton	11.6
BB/9	Brant Hurter, Erie	2.5
WP	Juan Nunez, New Hampshire	15
Balks	Blas Castano, Somerset	10
HR	Josh Hendrickson, Reading	23
BAA	Connor Gillispie, Bowie	.224

SOUTHERN LEAGUE DOUBLE-A

Awards selected by Major League Baseball

CHAMPION: Tennessee won its first outright SL title—it was named co-champion in 2004—after finishing runner-up in 2022. The Smokies swept Pensacola in two games in the finals to claim the 2023 championship and did so with key contributions from top Cubs prospects. Righthander Cade Horton, drafted seventh overall in 2022, started Game 2 and allowed one run in five innings to pick up the win. Left fielder Kevin Alcantara went 3-for-4 with two doubles. Third baseman BJ Murray Jr. went 1-for-4 with a home run and four RBIs. Right fielder Owen Caissie doubled as part of a 1-for-4 day that included a walk. First baseman Moises Ballesteros and DH Haydn McGeary each collected two hits.

MOST VALUABLE PLAYER: Rays third baseman Junior Caminero joined Montgomery on May 30 and had no trouble adapting to the upper minors or the pre-tacked baseball in use during the first half of the SL season. He hit .309/.373/.548 with 20 home runs in 81 games and earned a Sept. 23 callup to Tampa Bay. While in the minors, Caminero smashed 31 home runs, making him the rare player to reach 30 in his age-19 season.

PITCHER OF THE YEAR: Drafted out of junior college in 2021, Brewers righthander Carlos F. Rodriguez continued his steady climb toward MLB at Biloxi. The 21-year-old led the SL with a 2.77 ERA and .183 opponent average while placing second with 152 strikeouts.

TOP MLB PROSPECT: The SL experimented with a pre-tacked, enhanced-grip baseball in the first half of the season. As a result, whiffs and strikeouts were more prevalent in the first half than the second. Montgomery's Junior Caminero had no trouble with either version of the ball, putting up an .866 OPS in 30 games before the Futures Game and a .941 in 53 games afterward.

MANAGER OF THE YEAR: Pensacola's Kevin Randel had his best season out of four as manager of the Marlins' Double-A affiliate. The Blue Wahoos went 79-57 and reached the league finals.

Junior Caminero

SOUTHERN LEAGUE ALL-STARS

Pos	Player	Team	AVG	OPS	HR
C	Jeferson Quero	Biloxi	.262	.779	16
1B	Troy Johnston	Pensacola	.296	.963	18
2B	Luke Waddell	Mississippi	.290	.798	8
3B	Junior Caminero	Montgomery	.309	.921	20
SS	Kyren Paris	Rocket City	.255	.810	14
OF	Pete Crow-Armstrong	Tennessee	.289	.898	14
OF	Owen Caissie	Tennessee	.289	.917	22
OF	Jackson Chourio	Biloxi	.280	.803	22
DH	Blake Dunn	Chattanooga	.332	.989	15
UT	Tyler Black	Biloxi	.273	.924	14
Pos	**Pitcher**	**Team**	**G**	**ERA**	**SO**
SP	Patrick Monteverde	Pensacola	21	3.32	114
SP	Luis De Avila	Mississippi	25	3.28	125
SP	Carlos F. Rodriguez	Biloxi	25	2.77	152
SP	Connor Phillips	Chattanooga	14	3.34	111
RP	Jefry Yan	Pensacola	43	3.71	91
RP	Luke Little	Tennessee	23	3.12	63

OVERALL STANDINGS

North Division	W	L	PCT	GB	Manager	Attendance	Avg	Last Penn
Tennessee Smokies (Cubs)	75	62	.547	—	Michael Ryan/Kevin Graber	295,603	4,548	2023
Chattanooga Lookouts (Reds)	70	67	.511	5.0	Jose Moreno	228,940	3,417	2017
Rocket City Trash Pandas (Angels)	58	80	.420	17.5	Andy Schatzley	314,306	4,911	Never
Birmingham Barons (White Sox)	51	87	.370	24.5	Lorenzo Bundy	253,232	3,837	2013
South Division	**W**	**L**	**PCT**	**GB**	**Manager**	**Attendance**	**Avg**	**Last Penn**
Montgomery Biscuits (Rays)	80	58	.580	—	Morgan Ensberg	168,751	2,557	2007
Pensacola Blue Wahoos (Marlins)	79	57	.581	—	Kevin Randel	293,581	4,255	2022
Biloxi Shuckers (Brewers)	74	63	.540	5.5	Mike Guerrero	158,586	2,440	Never
Mississippi Braves (Braves)	62	75	.453	17.5	Kanekoa Texeira	162,862	2,545	2021

North: Tennessee def. Chattanooga 2-0. **South:** Pensacola def. Montgomery 2-0. **Championship Series:** Tennessee defeated Pensacola 2-0.

MIKE JANES/FOUR SEAM IMAGES

MINOR LEAGUES

CLUB BATTING

	AVG	G	AB	R	H	2B	3B	HR	RBI	BB	SO	SB	OBP	SLG
Biloxi Shuckers	.255	137	4517	756	1150	212	30	152	695	671	1137	214	.358	.416
Montgomery Biscuits	.251	138	4498	717	1130	221	39	153	653	528	1339	182	.338	.420
Pensacola Blue Wahoos	.250	136	4554	738	1137	205	26	163	682	530	1143	151	.336	.413
Chattanooga Lookouts	.248	137	4527	767	1124	233	40	154	689	584	1329	178	.346	.419
Tennessee Smokies	.243	137	4469	740	1086	244	25	166	687	645	1435	145	.349	.420
Birmingham Barons	.238	138	4594	638	1093	199	10	135	585	538	1284	129	.326	.374
Rocket City Trash Pandas	.232	138	4503	641	1044	200	20	113	586	630	1470	155	.336	.360
Mississippi Braves	.228	137	4410	587	1007	199	21	137	525	585	1450	157	.327	.376

CLUB PITCHING

	ERA	G	CG	SHO	SV	IP	H	R	ER	HR	BB	SO	AVG
Mississippi Braves	3.94	137	0	9	26	1177	1050	595	515	97	548	1297	.236
Pensacola Blue Wahoos	4.23	136	0	8	38	1192	1053	639	560	162	578	1233	.237
Montgomery Biscuits	4.40	138	2	11	37	1186	1073	663	580	145	508	1318	.239
Tennessee Smokies	4.51	137	0	5	30	1188	1051	677	595	141	624	1410	.236
Biloxi Shuckers	4.55	137	1	10	32	1190	1136	683	602	161	492	1361	.247
Chattanooga Lookouts	4.60	137	0	9	32	1189	1042	675	608	142	633	1435	.233
Rocket City Trash Pandas	5.35	138	2	5	28	1192	1165	796	708	168	609	1236	.255
Birmingham Barons	5.62	138	0	1	24	1196	1201	856	747	157	719	1297	.260

CLUB FIELDING

	PCT	PO	A	E	DP
Pensacola	.977	3576	1204	114	112
Montgomery	.976	3557	1012	112	86
Mississippi	.976	3531	1160	116	95
Tennessee	.976	3565	1028	114	114

	PCT	PO	A	E	DP
Chattanooga	.976	3566	1064	116	90
Rocket City	.975	3575	1157	120	106
Biloxi	.974	3570	1073	123	78
Birmingham	.969	3589	1078	147	92

INDIVIDUAL BATTING

Batter, Club	AVG	G	AB	R	H	2B	3B	HR	RBI	BB	SO	SB
Blake Dunn, Chattanooga	.332	77	295	75	98	13	4	15	52	41	84	35
Troy Johnston, Pensacola	.296	83	314	71	93	23	4	18	83	42	64	16
Carlos D. Rodriguez, Biloxi	.291	115	392	51	114	21	3	1	43	40	50	14
Luke Waddell, Mississippi	.290	101	372	57	108	16	1	8	64	65	57	26
Owen Caissie, Tennessee	.289	120	439	77	127	31	2	22	84	76	164	7
Jackson Chourio, Biloxi	.280	122	510	84	143	23	3	22	89	41	103	43
Alex McGarry, Chattanooga	.280	98	371	50	104	19	5	9	60	38	107	14
Jose Devers, Pensacola	.276	96	373	61	103	21	6	7	46	36	62	5
Tristan Peters, Montgomery	.275	93	363	65	100	22	5	7	46	42	66	14
Tyler Black, Biloxi	.273	84	308	70	84	16	8	14	48	61	77	47

INDIVIDUAL PITCHING

Pitcher, Club	W	L	ERA	G	GS	CG	SV	IP	H	R	ER	BB	SO
Carlos F. Rodriguez, Biloxi	9	6	2.77	25	25	0	0	124	82	46	38	53	152
Luis De Avila, Mississippi	6	10	3.28	25	25	0	0	123	99	53	45	61	125
Patrick Monteverde, Pensacola	10	5	3.32	21	21	0	0	114	91	51	42	46	114
Domingo Robles, Mississippi	9	7	3.39	23	22	0	0	119	109	53	45	32	119
Walker Powell, Tennessee	11	6	3.68	25	21	0	0	120	105	57	49	25	109
Brett Kerry, Rocket City	6	4	3.88	23	20	0	2	118	100	54	51	40	106
Cristian Mena, Birmingham	7	6	4.66	23	23	0	0	114	99	64	59	55	136
Alan Rangel, Mississippi	3	15	4.66	23	23	0	0	112	104	62	58	41	128
Matthew Thompson, Birmingham	6	15	4.85	27	27	0	0	124	110	78	67	85	136
Tobias Myers, Biloxi	10	5	5.03	27	26	1	0	138	129	85	77	45	168

DEPARTMENT LEADERS

BATTING

OBP	Isaac Collins, Biloxi	.424
SLG	Troy Johnston, Pensacola	.567
OPS	Troy Johnston, Pensacola	.963
R	Nasim Nunez, Pensacola	84
R	Jackson Chourio, Biloxi	84
H	Jackson Chourio, Biloxi	143
TB	Jackson Chourio, Biloxi	238
XBH	Rece Hinds, Chattanooga	58
2B	BJ Murray, Tennessee	34
3B	Jacob Hurtubise, Chattanooga	10
HR	Wes Clarke, Biloxi	26
RBI	Rece Hinds, Chattanooga	98
SAC	Jose Gomez, Rocket City	5
BB	Wes Clarke, Biloxi	89
HBP	Jacob Hurtubise, Chattanooga	19
SO	Mason Auer, Montgomery	184
SB	Nasim Nunez, Pensacola	52
CS	Cal Conley, Mississippi	13

FIELDING

C PCT	Edgar Quero, Birmingham	.983
PO	Pablo Aliendo, Tennessee	917
A	Pablo Aliendo, Tennessee	58
DP	Pablo Aliendo, Tennessee	7
E	Edgar Quero, Birmingham	16
CS	Edgar Quero, Birmingham	36
SB	Pablo Aliendo, Tennessee	118
PB	2 tied	10
1B PCT	Evan Edwards, Montgomery	.989
PO	Evan Edwards, Montgomery	589
A	Troy Johnston, Pensacola	52
DP	Troy Johnston, Pensacola	61
E	Haydn McGeary, Tennessee	10
2B PCT	No qualifier	
PO	Cal ConleyMississippi	97
A	Cody Morissette, Pensacola	190
DP	Cody Morissette, Pensacola	50
E	4 tied	9
3B PCT	BJ Murray, Tennessee	.959
PO	BJ Murray,Tennessee	64
A	BJ Murray,Tennessee	122
DP	Jose Gomez, Rocket City	14
E	Bryan Ramos, Birmingham	13
SS PCT	Nasim Nunez, Pensacola	.965
PO	Nasim Nunez, Pensacola	163
A	Nasim Nunez, Pensacola	228
DP	Nasim Nunez, Pensacola	54
E	Freddy Zamora, Biloxi	18
OF PCT	Mason Auer, Montgomery	.992
PO	Victor Mesa, Pensacola	271
A	2 tied, Chattanooga	14
DP	Yoelqui Cespedes, Birmingham	5
E	Rece Hinds, Chattanooga	8

PITCHING

GS	Sam Benschoter, Chattanooga	27
GS	Matthew Thompson, Birmingham	27
GF	Jefry Yan, Pensacola	31
SV	Cam Robinson, Biloxi	15
W	Walker Powell, Tennessee	11
L	Alan Rangel, Mississippi	15
L	Matthew Thompson, Birmingham	15
IP	Tobias Myers, Biloxi	137.2
H	Sam Benschoter, Chattanooga	137
R	Sam Benschoter, Chattanooga	102
ER	Sam Benschoter, Chattanooga	100
HBP	Sam Benschoter, Chattanooga	13
BB	Matthew Thompson, Birmingham	85
SO	Tobias Myers, Biloxi	168
SO/9	Carlos F. Rodriguez, Biloxi	11.1
BB/9	Walker Powell, Tennessee	1.9
WP	Matthew Thompson, Birmingham	17
Balks	Christian Mejias, Biloxi	6
Balks	Domingo Robles, Mississippi	6
HR	Tobias Myers, Biloxi	30
HR	Tobias Myers, Biloxi	30
BAA	Carlos F. Rodriguez, Biloxi	.183

TEXAS LEAGUE DOUBLE-A

Awards selected by Major League Baseball

CHAMPION: Amarillo defeated Arkansas two games to one to win its second TL title in the past four seasons. In the deciding Game 3, Sod Poodles righthander Conor Grammes started and pitched four shutout innings with six strikeouts and only one hit allowed. Amarillo won 9-1, with shortstop Camden Duzenack hitting a second-inning grand slam and DH Kristian Robinson going 2-for-3 and with a two-run homer in the fifth inning.

MOST VALUABLE PLAYER: Second baseman Thomas Saggese began the season with Rangers-affiliated Frisco but ended it with Triple-A Memphis in the Cardinals chain. He was a key piece in the trade deadline deal that sent veteran lefthander Jordan Montgomery from St. Louis to Texas. Saggese hit .313/.379/.512 with 15 home runs and eight stolen bases in 93 games for the RoughRiders and led all Double-A players in batting average. He led the TL with 158 hits, 60 extra-base hits, 107 RBIs and a .936 OPS. Texas drafted Saggese in the fifth round in 2020.

PITCHER OF THE YEAR: Corpus Christi righthander Rhett Kouba recorded a 3.27 ERA in 110 innings, striking out 118 and walking 23. The Astros drafted him in the 12th round in 2021 out of Dallas Baptist.

TOP MLB PROSPECT: D-backs top prospect Jordan Lawlar got off to a sluggish start with Amarillo—despite its slugger-friendly environment—but took major strides later in the season, both offensively and defensively. On the season, the 21-year-old hit .263/.366/.474 with 15 homers and 33 steals in 89 games. He was promoted to Triple-A Reno in August and called up to MLB on Sept. 7. Arizona drafted Lawlar sixth overall out of a Dallas high school in 2021.

MANAGER OF THE YEAR: Mike Freeman guided Arkansas to a 73-65 record. The Travelers won 45 games in the first half and had the best Double-A record for a majority of the season.

Jordan Lawlar

EDDIE KELLY

TEXAS LEAGUE ALL-STARS

Pos	Player	Team	AVG	OPS	HR
C	Pedro Pages	Springfield	.267	.805	16
1B	Chandler Redmond	Springfield	.256	.878	31
2B	Thomas Saggese	Frisco/Springfield	.318	.936	25
3B	Yunior Severino	Wichita	.287	.925	24
SS	Jordan Lawlar	Amarillo	.263	.840	15
OF	Joey Loperfido	Corpus Christi	.296	.940	19
OF	Evan Carter	Frisco	.284	.862	12
OF	Caleb Roberts	Amarillo	.278	.905	17
DH	Ryan Bliss	Amarillo	.358	1.008	12
UT	Luisangel Acuña	Frisco	.315	.830	7
Pos	**Pitcher**	**Team**	**G**	**ERA**	**SO**
SP	Emmet Sheehan	Tulsa	12	1.86	88
SP	Pierson Ohl	Wichita	16	2.69	74
SP	Rhett Kouba	Corpus Christi	23	3.27	118
SP	Ryan Gusto	Corpus Christi	14	2.93	62
RP	Prelander Berroa	Arkansas	43	2.89	101
RP	Antoine Kelly	Frisco	43	1.95	69

OVERALL STANDINGS

North Division	W	L	PCT	GB	Manager	Attendance	Avg	Last Penn
Arkansas Travelers (Mariners)	73	65	.529	—	Mike Freeman	307,607	4,591	2008
Springfield Cardinals (Cardinals)	72	66	.522	1.0	Jose Leger	256,947	3,893	2012
Tulsa Drillers (Dodgers)	65	73	.471	8.0	Scott Hennessey	356,002	5,235	2018
Wichita Wind Surge (Twins)	64	73	.467	8.5	Ramon Borrego	322,637	4,676	Never
Northwest Arkansas Naturals (Royals)	64	74	.464	9.0	Tommy Shields	256,552	3,773	2021
South Division	**W**	**L**	**PCT**	**GB**	**Manager**	**Attendance**	**Avg**	**Last Penn**
Amarillo Sod Poodles (D-backs)	77	61	.558	—	Shawn Roof	355,440	5,385	2023
Midland RockHounds (Athletics)	70	68	.507	7.0	Bobby Crosby	233,724	3,387	2017
Corpus Christi Hooks (Astros)	70	68	.507	7.0	Dickie Joe Thon	294,986	4,403	2006
San Antonio Missions (Padres)	70	68	.507	7.0	Luke Montz	284,419	4,183	2013
Frisco RoughRiders (Rangers)	64	73	.467	12.5	Carlos Cardoza	343,606	5,128	2022

North: Arkansas def. Springfield 2-1. **South:** Amarillo def. San Antonio 2-1. **Championship Series:** Amarillo defeated San Antonio 2-1.

CLUB BATTING

	AVG	G	AB	R	H	2B	3B	HR	RBI	BB	SO	SB	OBP	SLG
Amarillo Sod Poodles	.271	138	4707	823	1274	249	33	193	763	500	1314	166	.348	.461
Springfield Cardinals	.263	138	4606	770	1213	194	26	152	709	609	1129	167	.357	.416
Midland RockHounds	.259	138	4712	768	1222	242	44	120	714	572	1272	136	.348	.406
Wichita Wind Surge	.259	137	4599	707	1192	222	32	159	662	574	1320	211	.347	.425
Frisco RoughRiders	.251	137	4612	733	1159	234	31	118	667	680	1334	166	.355	.392
Corpus Christi Hooks	.248	138	4588	710	1140	239	19	184	668	553	1385	213	.336	.429
Arkansas Travelers	.246	138	4505	727	1106	209	26	132	663	650	1307	230	.352	.391
NW Arkansas Naturals	.245	138	4595	658	1128	203	46	110	592	547	1238	146	.334	.382
San Antonio Missions	.241	138	4505	627	1086	230	16	108	569	480	1098	163	.327	.371
Tulsa Drillers	.240	138	4597	678	1102	205	15	164	616	570	1235	101	.332	.398

CLUB PITCHING

	ERA	G	CG	SHO	SV	IP	H	R	ER	HR	BB	SO	AVG
San Antonio Missions	4.27	138	0	8	41	1209	1148	664	574	128	555	1290	.250
Corpus Christi Hooks	4.39	138	0	8	31	1207	1104	676	588	116	572	1315	.241
Tulsa Drillers	4.49	138	0	10	28	1215	1037	682	606	138	661	1379	.229
Arkansas Travelers	4.56	138	0	9	26	1202	1153	679	609	124	517	1230	.251
NW Arkansas Naturals	4.68	138	0	6	37	1213	1131	714	631	133	626	1316	.246
Frisco RoughRiders	4.98	137	0	5	21	1204	1135	733	667	149	606	1335	.249
Springfield Cardinals	5.04	138	2	4	31	1199	1265	752	671	145	493	1060	.273
Midland RockHounds	5.04	138	1	7	31	1208	1225	742	676	156	532	1200	.263
Wichita Wind Surge	5.06	137	0	5	27	1203	1240	756	676	188	487	1209	.264
Amarillo Sod Poodles	5.36	138	0	8	38	1205	1184	803	718	163	686	1298	.257

CLUB FIELDING

	PCT	PO	A	E	DP
Arkansas	.981	3607	1149	94	104
Midland	.980	3624	1233	101	118
Springfield	.979	3598	1265	102	118
Frisco	.979	3613	1149	100	117
Amarillo	.979	3614	1157	104	99
Wichita	.977	3609	1143	113	96
San Antonio	.976	3628	1152	116	117
Tulsa	.976	3644	1127	119	90
Northwest Arkansas	.975	3637	1167	121	97
Corpus Christi	.974	3621	1072	123	106

INDIVIDUAL BATTING

Batter, Club	AVG	G	AB	R	H	2B	3B	HR	RBI	BB	SO	SB
Thomas Saggese, Frisco/Springfield	.318	126	497	92	158	29	6	25	107	49	130	11
Luisangel Acuna, Frisco	.315	84	362	68	114	25	2	7	51	37	76	42
Yoyner Fajardo, Wichita	.305	123	469	75	143	23	8	9	53	50	84	50
DaShawn Keirsey, Wichita	.305	91	361	59	110	17	5	13	48	31	93	31
Noah Mendlinger, Springfield	.299	95	321	61	96	16	1	4	49	55	43	5
Austin Gauthier, Tulsa	.293	84	321	72	94	19	4	6	34	64	54	15
Brooks Lee, Wichita	.292	87	349	63	102	31	0	11	61	41	63	6
Spencer Packard, Arkansas	.292	121	466	66	136	27	2	14	82	68	86	1
Robbie Tenerowicz, Arkansas	.291	87	316	62	92	20	0	16	80	44	65	1
Yunior Severino, Wichita	.287	84	334	56	96	15	2	24	62	36	117	3

INDIVIDUAL PITCHING

Pitcher, Club	W	L	ERA	G	GS	CG	SV	IP	H	R	ER	BB	SO
Julio Robaina, Corpus Christi	10	6	3.18	26	16	0	0	116	105	46	41	48	114
Jack Cushing, Midland	8	4	4.34	28	18	0	2	114	116	61	55	24	119
Jamison Hill, Amarillo	7	6	4.35	26	25	0	0	118	95	60	57	74	104
Brandon Komar, Springfield	4	6	4.62	24	21	2	0	123	119	66	63	44	86
Connor Lunn, Springfield	7	7	4.71	25	23	0	1	130	150	72	68	31	111
Wilfredo Pereira, Springfield	10	8	4.97	26	24	0	0	138	138	84	76	53	104
Luke Albright, Amarillo	8	5	5.46	25	25	0	0	112	118	74	68	69	136
Kyle Tyler, Arkansas	7	11	5.60	27	26	0	0	135	157	93	84	58	138

DEPARTMENT LEADERS

BATTING

OBP	Noah Mendlinger, Springfield	.422
SLG	Yunior Severino, Wichita	.560
OPS	Thomas Saggese, Springfield, Frisco	.936
R	Tyler Tolbert, NW Arkansas	95
H	Thomas Saggese, Springfield, Frisco	158
TB	Thomas Saggese, Springfield, Frisco	274
XBH	Thomas Saggese, Springfield, Frisco	60
2B	Peyton Wilson, NW Arkansas	33
3B	Tyler Tolbert, NW Arkansas	10
HR	Chandler Redmond, Springfield	31
RBI	Thomas Saggese, Springfield, Frisco	107
SAC	Ripken Reyes, San Antonio	13
BB	Arquimedes Gamboa, Springfield	89
HBP	Ripken Reyes, San Antonio	49
SO	Chad Stevens, Corpus Christi	176
SB	Jonatan Clase, Arkansas	62
CS	Yoyner Fajardo, Wichita	13

FIELDING

C PCT	No qualifier	
PO	Luca Tresh, NW Arkansas	728
A	Pedro Pages, Springfield	64
DP	Diego Cartaya, Tulsa	8
E	Luca Tresh, NW Arkansas	16
CS	Pedro Pages, Springfield	47
SB	Luca Tresh, NW Arkansas	143
PB	Matt Scheffler, Arkansas	14
1B PCT	Dillan Shrum, NW Arkansas	.994
PO	Chandler Redmond, Springfield	888
A	Chandler Redmond, Springfield	65
DP	Chandler Redmond, Springfield	89
E	Imanol Vargas, Tulsa	12
2B PCT	Jorbit Vivas, Tulsa	.979
PO	Peyton Wilson, NW Arkansas	194
A	Peyton Wilson, NW Arkansas	281
DP	Peyton Wilson, NW Arkansas	68
E	Peyton Wilson, NW Arkansas	16
3B PCT	Jacob Buchberger, Springfield	.941
PO	Kody Hoese, Tulsa	56
A	Jacob Buchberger, Springfield	184
DP	Jacob Buchberger, Springfield	14
E	2 tied	15
SS PCT	Leo Rivas, Arkansas	.972
PO	Arquimedes Gamboa, Springfield	191
A	Arquimedes Gamboa, Springfield	320
DP	Arquimedes Gamboa, Springfield	63
E	Arquimedes Gamboa, Springfield	18
OF PCT	Daniel Johnson, San Antonio	.995
PO	Jonatan Clase, Arkansas	270
A	Kenedy Corona, Corpus Christi	12
DP	Kellen Strahm, Frisco	4
DP	Neyfy Castillo, Amarillo	4
E	Aaron Zavala, Frisco	7

PITCHING

G	Jacob Wallace, NW Arkansas	49
G	Travis Kuhn, Arkansas	49
GS	Ryan Garcia, Frisco	26
GS	Kyle Tyler, Arkansas	26
GF	Andre Granillo, Springfield	32
SV	Andre Granillo, Springfield	14
W	Emerson Hancock, Arkansas	11
L	Nick Krauth, Frisco	11
L	Kyle Tyler, Arkansas	11
IP	Wilfredo Pereira, Springfield	137.2
H	Kyle Tyler, Arkansas	157
R	Kyle Tyler, Arkansas	93
ER	Kyle Tyler, Arkansas	84
HBP	Ben Onyshko, Arkansas	20
BB	Jamison Hill, Amarillo	74
SO	Kyle Tyler, Arkansas	138
SO/9	Luke Albright, Amarillo	10.9
BB/9	Jack Cushing, Midland	1.9
WP	Kyle Hurt, Tulsa	14
Balks	Orlando Ortiz-Mayr, Tulsa	5
HR	Carlos Luna, Wichita	30
HR	Carlos Luna, Wichita	30
BAA	Jamison Hill, Amarillo	.218

MIDWEST LEAGUE HIGH-A

Awards selected by Major League Baseball

CHAMPION: Cedar Rapids won its first MWL title since 1994 as it defeated Great Lakes two games to one in the championship series. Emmanuel Rodriguez's grand slam proved to be the difference in the deciding game. It was Rodriguez's third home run of the MWL playoffs. Cedar Rapids outscored its opponents by 126 runs during the regular season.

MOST VALUABLE PLAYER: Cedar Rapids outfielder Kala'i Rosario had a breakout season as he led the league with 21 home runs and 94 RBIs while batting .252/.364/.467 in 118 games. He was the Twins' fifth-round pick in 2020 out of high school in Hawaii. The 21-year-old Rosario has long flashed big power, but in 2023 it became a much more consistent part of his game.

PITCHER OF THE YEAR: Peoria righthander Ian Bedell went 4-2, 2.44 in 27 appearances, 19 of them starts, and 96 innings. He struck out 106 while allowing 76 hits and 34 walks. A Cardinals fourth-round pick in 2020 out of Missouri, Bedell started the year in the Chiefs' bullpen before forcing his way into the rotation by striking out 25 of the 49 batters he faced in April.

TOP MLB PROSPECT: Dayton shortstop Edwin Arroyo was acquired by the Reds from the Mariners in the 2022 Luis Castillo trade. He's a smooth and reliable defender who led the MWL in putouts and double plays. Arroyo hit .248/.321/.427 in 119 games and his 10 triples led the league. He swiped 28 bases in 35 tries.

MANAGER OF THE YEAR: BA Minor League Manager of the Year Brian Dinkelman helped lead a very young but promising Cedar Rapids team to the best winning percentage in the full-season minor leagues at .621. The Twins affiliate was 15-15 after 30 games but went 37-20 from July 4 until the end of the season.

Edwin Arroyo

MIKE JANES/FOUR SEAM IMAGES

MIDWEST LEAGUE ALL-STARS

Pos	Player	Team	AVG	OPS	HR
C	Jimmy Crooks	Peoria	.271	.791	13
1B	Nathan Martorella	Fort Wayne	.259	.821	16
2B	Jace Jung	West Michigan	.254	.842	14
3B	Tanner Schobel	Cedar Rapids	.288	.859	14
SS	Edwin Arroyo	Dayton	.248	.748	13
OF	Victor Scott II	Peoria	.282	.763	50 SB
OF	Kala'i Rosario	Cedar Rapids	.252	.831	21
OF	Jakob Marsee	Fort Wayne	.273	.838	13
DH	Emmanuel Rodriguez	Cedar Rapids	.240	.863	16
UT	Taylor Young	Great Lakes	.246	.738	56 SB
Pos	**Pitcher**	**Team**	**G**	**ERA**	**SO**
SP	Ian Bedell	Peoria	27	2.44	120
SP	Julian Aguiar	Dayton	14	1.92	77
SP	Justin Wrobleski	Great Lakes	25	2.90	109
SP	Troy Melton	West Michigan	16	2.48	61
RP	Miguel Rodriguez	Cedar Rapids	33	2.85	42
RP	Frankie Scalzo Jr.	South Bend	35	2.31	64

OVERALL STANDINGS

East Division	W	L	PCT	GB	Manager	Attendance	Avg	Last Penn
Great Lakes Loons (Dodgers)	76	55	.580	—	Daniel Nava	186,080	3,001	2016
Fort Wayne TinCaps (Padres)	69	63	.523	7.5	Jon Mathews	340,038	5,313	2009
West Michigan Whitecaps (Tigers)	68	62	.523	7.5	Brayan Pena	360,999	5,730	2015
Dayton Dragons (Reds)	67	65	.508	9.5	Bryan LaHair	520,433	7,885	Never
Lake County Captains (Guardians)	65	64	.504	10.0	Omir Santos	193,436	3,517	2010
Lansing Lugnuts (Athletics)	60	71	.458	16.0	Craig Conklin	299,449	4,679	2003
West Division	**W**	**L**	**PCT**	**GB**	**Manager**	**Attendance**	**Avg**	**Last Penn**
Cedar Rapids Kernels (Twins)	82	50	.621	—	Brian Dinkelman	161,205	2,480	2023
Peoria Chiefs (Cardinals)	69	63	.523	13.0	Patrick Anderson	158,209	2,472	2002
Wisconsin Timber Rattlers (Brewers)	62	68	.477	19.0	Joe Ayrault	227,119	3,494	2012
South Bend Cubs (Cubs)	57	73	.438	24.0	Lance Rymel	314,591	4,915	2022
Beloit Sky Carp (Marlins)	56	75	.427	25.5	Billy Gardner	104,411	1,606	1995
Quad Cities River Bandits (Royals)	55	77	.417	27.0	Brooks Conrad	173,724	2,632	2021

East: Great Lakes def. Fort Wayne 2-1. **West:** Cedar Rapids def. Peoria 2-1. **Championship Series:** Cedar Rapids defeated Great Lakes 2-0.

MINOR LEAGUES

CLUB BATTING

	AVG	G	AB	R	H	2B	3B	HR	RBI	BB	SO	SB	OBP	SLG
South Bend Cubs	.252	130	4402	621	1110	246	29	91	570	460	1114	157	.330	.383
West Michigan Whitecaps	.252	130	4305	606	1083	225	29	109	550	503	1092	70	.339	.393
Lansing Lugnuts	.250	131	4303	555	1076	216	30	87	508	390	1068	191	.319	.375
Fort Wayne TinCaps	.244	132	4210	641	1028	203	19	136	593	541	1183	140	.337	.398
Peoria Chiefs	.243	132	4346	594	1056	210	29	85	532	439	1009	179	.324	.363
Wisconisin Timber Rattlers	.239	130	4352	602	1038	212	24	87	546	501	1154	162	.325	.358
Beloit Sky Carp	.238	131	4419	566	1051	208	22	92	513	432	1133	76	.314	.357
Great Lakes Loons	.238	131	4251	634	1010	212	25	104	573	583	1235	200	.338	.373
Lake County Captains	.236	129	4123	551	973	203	23	79	500	530	1089	130	.328	.354
Cedar Rapids Kernels	.234	132	4288	694	1003	209	41	137	628	634	1275	125	.340	.398
Dayton Dragons	.231	132	4351	589	1005	200	37	130	542	478	1448	151	.320	.384
Quad Cities River Bandits	.225	132	4329	574	973	195	33	101	526	560	1198	154	.321	.355

CLUB PITCHING

	ERA	G	CG	SHO	SV	IP	H	R	ER	HR	BB	SO	AVG
Great Lakes Loons	3.73	131	0	10	41	1140	947	538	473	98	565	1303	.226
Peoria Chiefs	3.84	132	0	8	34	1160	1061	580	495	104	448	1117	.242
Dayton Dragons	3.89	132	0	6	31	1155	978	580	499	110	527	1205	.228
Cedar Rapids Kernels	3.90	132	1	6	40	1160	1062	569	503	108	437	1133	.242
West Michigan Whitecaps	3.91	130	1	15	36	1126	1057	561	489	99	396	1101	.246
South Bend Cubs	3.96	130	0	7	21	1151	1002	596	506	98	483	1191	.232
Fort Wayne TinCaps	4.16	132	2	8	32	1123	1038	600	519	86	510	1129	.243
Wisconsin Timber Rattlers	4.24	130	0	5	36	1147	1035	605	540	103	526	1177	.239
Lansing Lugnuts	4.47	131	0	4	38	1128	1084	627	560	96	517	1079	.252
Lake County Captains	4.52	129	1	8	32	1095	959	614	550	128	571	1182	.234
Quad Cities River Bandits	4.67	132	0	7	26	1154	1062	668	599	102	545	1282	.243
Beloit Sky Carp	4.70	131	0	7	28	1163	1121	690	608	106	526	1099	.252

CLUB FIELDING

	PCT	PO	A	E	DP
Cedar Rapids	.980	3480	1171	93	89
Quad Cities	.979	3464	1086	96	76
Dayton	.978	3464	1091	102	100
West Michigan	.978	3379	1063	100	97
Lansing	.978	3385	1152	103	117
Wisconsin	.977	3441	1087	105	102
Peoria	.977	3480	1142	108	114
Great Lakes	.977	3421	1022	106	93
Beloit	.974	3491	1161	124	105
Fort Wayne	.974	3369	1083	121	84
Lake County	.972	3284	940	122	79
South Bend	.971	3454	1110	136	103

INDIVIDUAL BATING

Batter, Club	AVG	G	AB	R	H	2B	3B	HR	RBI	BB	SO	SB
Daniel Susac, Lansing	.303	99	366	47	111	18	5	7	54	39	88	8
Ezequiel Pagan, South Bend	.301	97	376	57	113	20	2	5	37	39	66	12
Kevin Alcantara, South Bend	.286	95	371	65	106	25	3	12	66	31	97	15
Nathan Church, Peoria	.279	119	455	65	127	24	2	3	44	46	60	21
Yeiner Fernandez, Great Lakes	.273	99	373	47	102	14	3	6	50	47	56	4
Jakob Marsee, Fort Wayne	.273	113	400	91	109	16	3	13	41	87	82	41
Euribiel Angeles, Lansing	.272	110	397	40	108	18	4	7	50	11	56	21
Noah Cardenas, Cedar Rapids	.272	90	309	44	84	23	1	3	38	55	77	9
Danny Bautista, Lansing	.271	118	435	50	118	17	2	3	46	22	48	22
Jimmy Crooks, Peoria	.271	114	413	71	112	29	1	12	73	52	101	2

INDIVIDUAL PITCHING

Pitcher, Club	W	L	ERA	G	GS	CG	SV	IP	H	R	ER	BB	SO
Carlos Pena, West Michigan	5	6	3.11	24	21	0	0	110	95	41	38	38	107
Wilkel Hernandez, West Michigan	3	8	3.65	26	20	1	0	106	87	50	43	31	97
Trent Baker, Peoria	7	9	3.69	23	22	0	0	120	110	56	49	26	105
Tyler Woessner, Wisconsin	6	7	4.02	24	22	0	0	121	115	63	54	54	112
Connor Noland, South Bend	1	8	4.08	24	23	0	0	108	106	58	49	22	86
Luinder Avila, Quad Cities	4	7	4.39	22	20	0	0	109	101	57	53	44	102
Aaron Davenport, Lake County	6	10	5.73	24	19	1	1	115	109	79	73	65	95

DEPARTMENT LEADERS

BATTING

OBP	Jakob Marsee, Fort Wayne	.413
SLG	Jake Thompson, Beloit	.516
OPS	Emmanuel Rodriguez, Cedar Rapids	.863
R	Jakob Marsee, Fort Wayne	91
H	Nathan Church, Peoria	127
TB	Kala'i Rosario, Cedar Rapids	208
XBH	Brady Allen, Beloit, West Michigan	51
XBH	Kala'i Rosario, Cedar Rapids	51
2B	Austin Callahan, Dayton	34
3B	Edwin Arroyo, Dayton	10
HR	Kala'i Rosario, Cedar Rapids	21
RBI	Kala'i Rosario, Cedar Rapids	94
SAC	Carlos Mendoza, West Michigan	6
BB	Carter Jensen, Quad Cities	92
BB	Emmanuel Rodriguez, Cedar Rapids	92
HBP	Blake Dunn, Dayton	17
SO	Austin Hendrick, Dayton	185
SB	Taylor Young, Great Lakes	56
CS	Robert Moore, Wisconsin	13

FIELDING

C PCT	Jimmy Crooks, Peoria	.989
PO	Jimmy Crooks, Peoria	772
A	Joe Mack, Beloit	71
DP	CJ Rodriguez, Lansing	9
E	Ethan Hearn, South Bend	14
CS	Joe Mack, Beloit	44
SB	Joe Mack, Beloit	125
PB	Carter Jensen, Quad Cities	16
1B PCT		
PO	Nathan Martorella, Fort Wayne	571
A	Nathan Martorella, Fort Wayne	58
DP	Danny Bautista, Lansing	62
E	Nathan Martorella, Fort Wayne	13
2B PCT	Tyler Callihan, Dayton	.972
PO	Yiddi Cappe, Beloit	149
A	Tyler Callihan, Dayton	241
DP	Yiddi Cappe, Beloit	49
E	Yiddi Cappe, Beloit	16
3B PCT	Cayden Wallace, Quad Cities	.949
PO	Osvaldo Tovalin, Peoria	77
A	Izaac Pacheco, West Michigan	171
DP	Izaac Pacheco, West Michigan	19
DP	Austin Callahan, Dayton	19
E	Izaac Pacheco, West Michigan	19
SS PCT	Noah Miller, Cedar Rapids	.984
PO	Edwin Arroyo, Dayton	179
A	Noah Miller, Cedar Rapids	295
DP	Edwin Arroyo, Dayton	60
E	Edwin Arroyo, Dayton	20
OF PCT	Joe Gray Jr., Wisconsin	1.000
PO	Jakob Marsee, Fort Wayne	275
A	Kala'i Rosario, Cedar Rapids	14
A	Junior Perez, Lansing	14
DP	Junior Perez, Lansing	5
E	Junior Perez, Lansing	10

PITCHING

G	3 tied	45
GS	Justin Wrobleski, Great Lakes	23
GS	Connor Noland, South Bend	23
GF	3 tied	27
SV	Miguel Rodriguez, Cedar Rapids	14
W	Gustavo J. Rodriguez, Peoria	8
L	Cameron Wagoner, Wisconsin	11
IP	Tyler Woessner, Wisconsin	121
H	Mitch Myers, Lansing	127
R	Aaron Davenport, Lake County	79
ER	Aaron Davenport, Lake County	73
HBP	Reid Johnston, Lake County	14
BB	Aaron Davenport, Lake County	65
SO	Tyler Woessner, Wisconsin	112
SO/9	Carlos Pena, West Michigan	8.8
BB/9	Connor Noland, South Bend	1.8
WP	Eric Cerantola, Quad Cities	16
Balks	Aaron Davenport, Lake County	8
HR	Jared Poland, Beloit	19
HR	Aaron Davenport, Lake County	19
BAA	Wilkel Hernandez, West Michigan	.220

NORTHWEST LEAGUE HIGH-A

Awards selected by Major League Baseball

CHAMPION: Vancouver defeated Everett three games to one in the NWL championship series. The Canadians shut out the AquaSox twice in the best-of-five series, but also lost a game 10-0. Vancouver finished off the series in emphatic fashion. Right fielder Garrett Spain scored three runs and left fielder Gabriel Martinez had three hits as Vancouver blew out Everett 10-2 in Game Four.

MOST VALUABLE PLAYER: Spokane outfielder Jordan Beck slugged 20 home runs—just two off the league lead—in 79 games before a promotion to Double-A Hartford. The 22-year-old led the NWL with a .566 slugging percentage. Beck was a star for Tennessee in 2022, when the Rockies drafted him in the supplemental first round.

PITCHER OF THE YEAR: These days, few minor league pitchers shoulder a heavy workload. That helped Everett lefthander Reid VanScoter stand out. The 24-year-old led the league with 10 wins, 157 strikeouts, 25 starts, a 3.27 ERA, a 1.23 WHIP and, most importantly, innings. VanScoter's 143.1 innings were 26 more than anyone else in the league. Seattle drafted him in the fifth round out of Coastal Carolina in 2022.

TOP MLB PROSPECT: Spokane shortstop Adael Amador was one of the most difficult hitters to strike out in the Northwest League. The 20-year-old Dominican middle infielder posted more walks (39) than strikeouts (37) and did so while showing he's more than a slap hitter. Amador hit 12 home runs, stole 12 bases and batted .302/.392/.514 in 54 games. He showed he can handle shortstop and second base and looks to be the next in a long line of Rockies middle infield prospects.

MANAGER OF THE YEAR: Everett's Ryan Scott helped develop one of the most talented teams in the league. Catcher Harry Ford and first baseman Tyler Locklear spent the season with the AquaSox, while shortstop Cole Young and outfielder Gabriel Gonzalez joined up in the second half. Everett finished a close second to Vancouver before falling to them in the playoffs.

Adael Amador

PATRICK KROHN/FOUR SEAM IMAGES

NORTHWEST LEAGUE ALL-STARS

Pos	Player	Team	AVG	OPS	HR
C	Harry Ford	Everett	.257	.840	15
1B	Tyler Locklear	Everett	.305	.971	12
2B	Michael Turconi	Vancouver	.299	.904	7
3B	Ivan Melendez	Hillsboro	.270	.945	18
SS	Adael Amador	Spokane	.302	.905	9
OF	Jordan Beck	Spokane	.292	.944	20
OF	Yanquiel Fernandez	Spokane	.319	.959	17
OF	Alberto Rodriguez	Everett	.306	.973	11
DH	Hogan Windish	Everett	.270	.878	22
UT	Sterlin Thompson	Spokane	.323	.919	7
Pos	**Pitcher**	**Team**	**G**	**ERA**	**SO**
SP	Reid VanScoter	Everett	25	3.27	157
SP	Dylan Ray	Hillsboro	22	3.81	123
SP	Yu-Min Lin	Hillsboro	13	3.43	76
SP	Carson Palmquist	Spokane	15	3.73	106
RP	Matt Svanson	Vancouver	24	1.23	36
RP	Tyler Myrick	Eugene	26	1.04	25

OVERALL STANDINGS

Team	W	L	PCT	GB	Manager	Attendance	Avg	Last Penn
Vancouver Canadians (Blue Jays)	77	54	.588	—	Brent Lavallee	297,437	4,876	2023
Everett AquaSox (Mariners)	74	58	.561	3.5	Ryan Scott	140,937	2,237	2010
Eugene Emeralds (Giants)	66	66	.500	11.5	Carlos Valderrrama	145,896	2,316	2022
Spokane Indians (Rockies)	62	67	.481	14.0	Robinson Cancel	249,012	3,953	2008
Tri-City Dust Devils (Angels)	58	72	.446	18.5	Jack Howell	120,444	1,825	Never
Hillsboro Hops (D-backs)	56	76	.424	21.5	Ronnie Gajownik	158,723	2,405	2019

Championship Series: Vancouver defeated Everett 3-1.

CLUB BATTING

	AVG	G	AB	R	H	2B	3B	HR	RBI	BB	SO	SB	OBP	SLG
Spokane Indians	.265	129	4351	710	1151	242	30	126	639	497	1064	198	.354	.421
Eugene Emeralds	.255	132	4431	670	1130	242	30	140	604	488	1308	143	.335	.418
Vancouver Canadians	.251	131	4298	664	1079	217	28	118	627	528	1145	112	.345	.397
Everett AquaSox	.248	132	4429	718	1099	241	30	155	654	592	1342	170	.348	.421
Hillsboro Hops	.233	132	4383	572	1023	188	34	104	514	491	1257	137	.321	.363
Tri-City Dust Devils	.231	130	4223	530	977	189	34	69	471	448	1398	183	.313	.341

CLUB PITCHING

	ERA	G	CG	SHO	SV	IP	H	R	ER	HR	BB	SO	AVG
Vancouver Canadians	3.62	131	1	10	24	1130	953	533	455	96	497	1210	.229
Tri-City Dust Devils	4.03	130	1	10	32	1131	1027	586	506	101	501	1248	.240
Eugene Emeralds	4.41	132	0	7	30	1148	1100	637	563	118	472	1286	.249
Everett AquaSox	4.42	132	1	6	33	1166	1113	646	572	129	428	1278	.250
Hillsboro Hops	4.66	132	0	5	23	1163	1068	713	602	112	639	1280	.243
Spokane Indians	5.40	129	0	2	28	1129	1198	749	677	156	507	1212	.272

CLUB FIELDING

	PCT	PO	A	E	DP
Spokane	.981	3386	1113	87	97
Everett	.978	3498	1217	106	92
Eugene	.977	3445	1121	108	84
Tri-City	.977	3394	1106	108	108
Vancouver	.974	3389	1001	117	102
Hillsboro	.973	3489	1231	129	114

INDIVIDUAL BATTING

Batter, Club	AVG	G	AB	R	H	2B	3B	HR	RBI	BB	SO	SB
Alan Roden, Vancouver	.321	69	268	57	86	23	1	4	41	42	32	15
Josh Kasevich, Vancouver	.284	94	334	46	95	15	0	4	50	38	41	11
Nic Kent, Spokane	.277	112	393	59	109	24	2	11	62	41	69	9
Hogan Windish, Everett	.270	105	385	64	104	17	4	22	84	55	139	10
Cade Doughty, Vancouver	.264	102	375	61	99	19	0	18	68	35	126	4
Wilderd Patino, Hillsboro	.259	99	382	73	99	13	1	5	33	45	126	47
Harry Ford, Everett	.257	118	444	89	114	24	4	15	67	103	109	24
Juan Guerrero, Spokane	.256	112	441	62	113	22	6	6	59	32	70	14
Grant McCray, Eugene	.255	127	494	101	126	26	6	14	66	72	171	52
Ben Ramirez, Everett	.252	123	472	67	119	27	0	12	65	49	143	6

INDIVIDUAL PITCHING

Pitcher, Club	W	L	ERA	G	GS	CG	SV	IP	H	R	ER	BB	SO
Reid VanScoter, Everett	10	6	3.27	25	25	1	0	143	141	60	52	35	157
Chase Chaney, Tri-City	7	6	3.63	24	19	0	0	112	113	54	45	34	84
Spencer Giesting, Hillsboro	7	6	4.00	24	24	0	0	117	100	58	52	71	124
Raul Alcantara, Everett	5	6	6.35	24	23	0	0	108	92	85	76	66	140

DEPARTMENT LEADERS

BATTING

OBP	Harry Ford, Everett	.410
SLG	Jordan Beck, Spokane	.566
OPS	Hogan Windish, Everett	.878
R	Grant McCray, Eugene	101
H	Grant McCray, Eugene	126
TB	Grant McCray, Eugene	206
XBH	Aeverson Arteaga, Eugene	49
2B	Alberto Rodriguez, Everett	30
3B	Alex De Jesus, Vancouver	7
3B	Alberto Rodriguez, Everett	7
HR	Hogan Windish, Everett	22
RBI	Hogan Windish, Everett	84
SAC	Arol VeraTri-City	7
BB	Harry Ford, Everett	103
HBP	Braiden Ward, Spokane	25
SO	Grant McCray, Eugene	171
SB	Grant McCray, Eugene	52
CS	Adrian Placencia, Tri-City	11
CS	Dasan Brown, Vancouver	11

FIELDING

C	PO	Harry Ford, Everett	760
	A	Harry Ford, Everett	64
	DP	Harry Ford, Everett	6
	E	Harry Ford, Everett	9
	CS	Jommer Hernandez, Vancouver	37
	SB	Harry Ford, Everett	101
	PB	Harry Ford, Everett	20
1B	PCT	No qualifiers	
	PO	2 tied	484
	A	Zach Kokoska, Spokane	43
	DP	Shane Muntz, Hillsboro	41
	E	Logan Wyatt, Eugene	7
2B	PCT	No qualifiers	
	PO	Adrian Placencia, Tri-City	114
	A	Adrian Placencia, Tri-City	182
	DP	Adrian Placencia, Tri-City	43
	E	Ghordy Santos, Eugene	11
3B	PCT	Ben Ramirez, Everett	.932
	PO	Ben Ramirez, Everett	63
	PO	Werner Blakely, Tri-City	63
	A	Ben Ramirez, Everett	238
	DP	Ben Ramirez, Everett	19
	E	Ben Ramirez, Everett	22
SS	PCT	Aeverson Arteaga, Eugene	.963
	PO	Aeverson Arteaga, Eugene	129
	A	Aeverson Arteaga, Eugene	288
	DP	Aeverson Arteaga, Eugene	47
	E	Aeverson Arteaga, Eugene	16
OF	PCT	Grant McCray, Eugene	.989
	PO	Grant McCray, Eugene	260
	A	Grant McCray, Eugene	11
	DP	Garrett Spain, Vancouver	5
	E	Devonte Brown, Vancouver	7

PITCHING

G	Angel Chivilli, Spokane	50
GS	Reid VanScoter, Everett	25
GF	Angel Chivilli, Spokane	38
SV	Angel Chivilli, Spokane	17
W	Kelvin Nunez, Everett	10
W	Reid VanScoter, Everett	10
L	Yilber Diaz, Hillsboro	10
IP	Reid VanScoter, Everett	143.1
H	Reid VanScoter, Everett	141
R	Raul Alcantara, Everett	85
ER	Raul Alcantara, Everett	76
HBP	Listher Sosa, Hillsboro	14
HBP	Brandon Schaeffer, Everett	14
BB	Spencer Giesting, Hillsboro	71
SO	Reid VanScoter, Everett	157
SO/9	Raul Alcantara, Everett	11.7
BB/9	Reid VanScoter, Everett	2.2
WP	Seth Lonsway, Eugene	28
Balks	Brayan Castillo, Spokane	9
HR	Victor Juarez, Spokane	16
BAA	Raul Alcantara, Everett	.224

SOUTH ATLANTIC LEAGUE HIGH-A

Awards selected by Major League Baseball

CHAMPION: Greenville swept Hudson Valley in the SAL championship series to win the franchise's second league title—and first since the South Atlantic League moved up a level to High-A in 2021. The Drive won all four playoff games they played, taking the deciding Game 2 of the finals by a score of 7-3. Greenville lefthander Dalton Rogers started and struck out five in three innings, allowing one run. Left fielder Kristian Campbell went 3-for-4 with a three-run homer as the offensive star. Greenville won the first half of the South Division season but backed into the playoffs with a 27-39 second-half record.

MOST VALUABLE PLAYER: Hickory first baseman Abimelec Ortiz hit 26 home runs to lead the league in just 80 games. The Rangers signed the Puerto Rico native as an undrafted free agent after one season of junior college ball in 2021.

PITCHER OF THE YEAR: Yankees 2022 second-round righthander Drew Thorpe led the SAL with 10 wins, a 2.81 ERA, a 1.07 WHIP and finished one shy of the strikeout lead with 138. Promoted to Double-A in mid August, he led the minor leagues with 182 punchouts.

TOP MLB PROSPECT: Aberdeen shortstop Jackson Holliday hit .314/.452/.488 with five home runs and 17 stolen bases in 57 games. That was the lengthiest assignment of the season for the player the Orioles drafted No. 1 overall in 2022. Holliday spent the second half of the season at Double-A and Triple-A, on his way to becoming Minor League Player of the Year as a 19-year-old.

MANAGER OF THE YEAR: Hickory's Chad Comer guided the Crawdads to the league's best winning percentage (.560) despite one of the youngest clubs in the league.

Jackson Holliday

MIKE JANES/FOUR SEAM IMAGES

SOUTH ATLANTIC LEAGUE ALL-STARS

Pos	Player	Team	AVG	OPS	HR
C	Drake Baldwin	Rome	.260	.851	14
1B	Abimelec Ortiz	Hickory	.290	.987	26
2B	Tsung-Che Cheng	Greensboro	.308	.981	9
3B	Blaze Jordan	Greenville	.324	.918	12
SS	Jackson Holliday	Aberdeen	.314	.940	5
OF	Dru Baker	Bowling Green	.307	.887	13
OF	Roman Anthony	Greenville	.294	.981	12
OF	Dylan Beavers	Aberdeen	.273	.832	9
DH	Jase Bowen	Greensboro	.257	.802	23
UT	Carson Williams	Bowling Green	.254	.857	23
Pos	**Pitcher**	**Team**	**G**	**ERA**	**SO**
SP	Drew Thorpe	Hudson Valley	18	2.81	138
SP	Keyshawn Askew	Bowling Green	24	3.70	104
SP	Isaac Coffey	Greenville	11	2.83	83
SP	Josh Stephan	Hickory	12	2.17	73
RP	Jack Neely	Hudson Valley	31	2.03	74
RP	Paul Gervase	Brooklyn	31	1.72	76

OVERALL STANDINGS

North Division	W	L	PCT	GB	Manager	Attendance	Avg	Last Penn
Jersey Shore BlueClaws (Phillies)	73	58	.557	—	Greg Brodzinski	287,602	4,793	2010
Hudson Valley Renegades (Yankees)	70	62	.530	3.5	Sergio Santos	183,649	2,870	Never
Greensboro Grasshoppers (Pirates)	68	61	.527	4.0	Robby Hammock	279,061	4,501	2011
Aberdeen IronBirds (Orioles)	66	63	.512	6.0	Roberto Mercado	141,019	2,203	Never
Brooklyn Cyclones (Mets)	66	65	.504	7.0	Chris Newell	182,875	2,857	Never
Wilmington Blue Rocks (Nationals)	55	75	.423	17.5	Mario Lisson	156,200	2,519	*2019
South Division	**W**	**L**	**PCT**	**GB**	**Manager**	**Attendance**	**Avg**	**Last Penn**
Hickory Crawdads (Rangers)	70	55	.560	—	Chad Comer	112,287	1,841	2015
Bowling Green Hot Rods (Rays)	69	57	.548	1.5	Rafael Valenzuela	155,447	2,507	2022
Rome Braves (Braves)	64	68	.485	9.5	Angel Flores	95,120	1,534	2016
Greenville Drive (Red Sox)	63	69	.477	10.5	Iggy Suarez	303,328	4,973	2023
Winston-Salem Dash (White Sox)	60	66	.476	10.5	Guillermo Quiroz	290,534	4,686	*2003
Asheville Tourists (Astros)	51	76	.402	20.0	Nate Shaver	183,034	3,001	2014

* Carolina League title won prior to 2021 minor league realignment

North: Hudson Valley def. Jersey Shore 2-1. **South:** Greenville def. Hickory 2-0. **Championship Series:** Greenville defeated Hudson Valley 2-0.

MINOR LEAGUES

CLUB BATTING

	AVG	G	AB	R	H	2B	3B	HR	RBI	BB	SO	SB	OBP	SLG
Bowling Green Hot Rods	.259	127	4152	700	1074	185	41	175	642	512	1283	130	.349	.449
Greenville Drive	.259	132	4382	693	1133	249	36	115	618	527	1259	181	.342	.411
Winston-Salem Dash	.254	127	4160	642	1057	200	30	100	565	538	1232	179	.348	.389
Hickory Crawdads	.249	125	4095	640	1020	174	26	118	572	453	1094	202	.329	.391
Hudson Valley Renegades	.249	132	4393	653	1092	211	31	133	585	505	1301	185	.333	.402
Greensboro Grasshoppers	.245	129	4306	764	1057	196	34	170	696	565	1280	155	.341	.425
Jersey Shore BlueClaws	.240	131	4255	633	1022	193	32	86	562	541	1194	173	.336	.361
Asheville Tourists	.235	127	4138	615	972	216	15	136	553	480	1314	180	.324	.393
Rome Braves	.232	132	4244	541	986	200	22	84	495	564	1294	152	.332	.349
Aberdeen IronBirds	.231	129	4159	618	962	210	33	104	546	591	1262	243	.334	.373
Wilmington Blue Rocks	.229	130	4216	531	965	196	30	79	480	508	1287	130	.319	.346
Brooklyn Cyclones	.224	131	4249	578	953	201	27	112	516	477	1296	151	.310	.363

CLUB PITCHING

	ERA	G	CG	SHO	SV	IP	H	R	ER	HR	BB	SO	AVG
Hudson Valley Renegades	3.62	132	1	13	25	1155	887	540	465	111	514	1420	.209
Brooklyn Cyclones	3.74	131	1	11	28	1144	965	571	475	88	546	1326	.226
Aberdeen IronBirds	3.81	129	0	7	29	1120	936	566	474	96	491	1363	.226
Jersey Shore BlueClaws	4.06	131	0	11	36	1143	998	590	515	83	536	1213	.234
Rome Braves	4.09	132	1	9	41	1135	1066	594	516	108	432	1187	.248
Bowling Green Hot Rods	4.30	127	0	11	29	1084	941	598	518	118	557	1254	.234
Wilmington Blue Rocks	4.43	130	1	1	30	1123	1076	654	553	101	463	1104	.251
Hickory Crawdads	4.45	125	0	9	31	1085	1001	589	537	122	502	1203	.244
Greensboro Grasshoppers	4.71	129	0	5	32	1128	1082	666	590	126	562	1231	.255
Greenville Drive	5.02	132	2	10	23	1133	1118	737	632	168	501	1355	.254
Winston-Salem Dash	5.38	127	0	7	21	1091	1069	728	652	131	550	1159	.257
Asheville Tourists	5.74	127	1	0	19	1094	1154	775	698	160	607	1281	.268

CLUB FIELDING

	PCT	PO	A	E	DP
Greensboro	.979	3384	1131	95	128
Hickory	.979	3256	1069	95	87
Jersey Shore	.977	3429	1170	107	91
Bowling Green	.976	3254	1007	103	90
Winston-Salem	.976	3274	1073	109	113
Wilmington	.974	3369	1194	120	89
Hudson Valley	.973	3466	1049	124	80
Rome	.973	3406	1095	125	112
Brooklyn	.971	3433	1026	132	78
Aberdeen	.970	3361	939	135	77
Greenville	.968	3398	982	143	79
Asheville	.967	3282	974	147	68

INDIVIDUAL BATTING

Batter, Club	AVG	G	AB	R	H	2B	3B	HR	RBI	BB	SO	SB
Michael Turner, Winston-Salem	.309	92	304	43	94	26	1	4	41	64	58	0
Dru Baker, Bowling Green	.307	90	326	58	100	11	5	13	39	40	86	38
Tres Gonzalez, Greensboro	.287	94	366	73	105	18	0	8	46	65	84	22
Ignacio Alvarez, Rome	.284	116	419	62	119	24	0	7	66	66	87	16
Blake Robertson, Bowling Green	.278	98	316	57	88	13	3	9	42	43	95	1
Wilfred Veras, Winston-Salem	.277	92	372	52	103	25	1	11	63	20	101	18
Dylan Beavers, Aberdeen	.273	85	311	46	85	26	3	9	48	50	84	22
Nick Ward, Jersey Shore	.270	94	318	70	86	8	0	8	50	54	80	22
Spencer Jones, Hudson Valley	.268	100	411	62	110	28	4	13	56	42	133	35
Geisel Cepeda, Hickory	.268	97	355	42	95	10	1	5	41	34	43	8

INDIVIDUAL PITCHING

Pitcher, Club	W	L	ERA	G	GS	CG	SV	IP	H	R	ER	BB	SO
Drew Thorpe, Hudson Valley	10	2	2.81	18	18	1	0	109	84	38	34	33	138
Juan Carela, Hudson Valley/Winston-Salem	3	7	3.58	23	22	0	0	116	95	58	46	43	136
Po-Yu Chen, Greensboro	5	8	4.44	25	24	0	0	120	122	65	59	43	124
Ian Mejia, Rome	4	11	4.69	23	23	0	0	121	121	71	63	28	110
Bubba Chandler, Greensboro	9	4	4.75	24	24	0	0	106	108	60	56	51	120
Kyle Luckham, Wilmington	5	7	4.85	25	24	1	0	124	123	72	67	30	100

DEPARTMENT LEADERS

BATTING

OBP	Michael Turner, Winston-Salem	.430
SLG	Abimelec Ortiz, Hickory	.624
OPS	Dru Baker, Bowling Green	.887
R	Jase Bowen, Greensboro	80
H	Ignacio Alvarez, Rome	119
TB	Jase Bowen, Greensboro	204
XBH	Carson Williams, Bowling Green	48
2B	Eddinson Paulino, Greenville	28
2B	Spencer Jones, Hudson Valley	28
3B	Daniel Mateo, Hickory	9
3B	Tsung-Che Cheng, Greensboro	9
HR	Abimelec Ortiz, Hickory	26
RBI	Jase Bowen, Greensboro	88
SAC	Tres Gonzalez, Greensboro	7
BB	Kevin Kilpatrick, Rome	68
HBP	Tim Borden, Asheville	22
SO	Wes Kath, Winston-Salem	168
SB	Luis Valdez, Aberdeen	43
CS	3 tied	13

FIELDING

C	PO	Antonio Gomez, Hudson Valley	625
	A	2 tied	54
	DP	2 tied	6
	E	Antonio Gomez, Hudson Valley	14
	CS	Antonio Gomez, Hudson Valley	33
	SB	Kevin Parada, Brooklyn	115
	PB	Antonio Gomez, Hudson Valley	15
1B	PCT	Rixon Wingrove, Jersey Shore	.988
	PO	Rixon Wingrove, Jersey Shore	622
	A	Rixon Wingrove, Jersey Shore	45
	DP	Bryson Horne, Rome	67
	E	T.J. WhiteWilmington	13
2B	PCT	Loidel Chapelli, Winston-Salem	.982
	PO	Loidel Chapelli, Winston-Salem	156
	A	Loidel Chapelli, Winston-Salem	229
	DP	Loidel Chapelli, Winston-Salem	71
	E	D'Andre Smith, Brooklyn	17
3B	PCT	Wes Kath, Winston-Salem	.922
	PO	Wes Kath, Winston-Salem	63
	A	Wes Kath, Winston-Salem	149
	DP	Wes Kath, Winston-Salem	18
	E	Marcos Cabrera, Hudson Valley	20
SS	PCT	Carson Williams, Bowling Green	.985
	PO	Ignacio Alvarez, Rome	144
	A	Ignacio Alvarez, Rome	268
	DP	Ignacio Alvarez, Rome	54
	E	Frederick Bencosme, Aberdeen	16
OF	PCT	Daniel Mateo, Hickory	.992
	PO	Kevin Kilpatrick, Rome	264
	A	Sammy Siani, Greensboro	12
	DP	Sammy Siani, Greensboro	4
	E	Omar De Los Santos, Brooklyn	11

PITCHING

G	Jason Ruffcorn, Jersey Shore	44
GS	3 tied	24
GF	Todd Peterson, Wilmington	26
SV	Cy Nielson, Greensboro	10
W	Drew Thorpe, Hudson Valley	10
L	Ian Mejia, Rome	11
IP	Kyle Luckham, Wilmington	124.1
H	Kyle Luckham, Wilmington	123
R	Juan Daniel Encarnacion, Greenville	85
ER	Juan Daniel Encarnacion, Greenville	70
HBP	Joel Valdez, Hudson Valley	18
BB	Alex Santos, Asheville	64
SO	Angel Bastardo, Greenville	139
SO/9	Drew Thorpe, Hudson Valley	11.4
BB/9	Ian Mejia, Rome	2.1
WP	Brayan De Paula, Asheville	27
Balks	17 tied	3
HR	Juan Daniel Encarnacion, Greenville	22
HR	Juan Daniel Encarnacion, Greenville	22
BAA	Drew Thorpe, Hudson Valley	.215

CALIFORNIA LEAGUE LOW-A

Awards selected by Major League Baseball

CHAMPION: Modesto defeated Rancho Cucamonga two games to none in the Cal League championship series. It was the Nuts' first league title as a Mariners affiliate. Modesto won all four of its playoff games, taking the deciding Game 2 of the finals by a 14-8 tally. Mariners first-round shortstop Colt Emerson was the star, going 4-for-6 with four RBIs and two runs scored. Second baseman Michael Arroyo went 3-for-6 with a triple, three runs and two RBIs, while right fielder Lazaro Montes went 1-for-5 with a run and an RBI.

MOST VALUABLE PLAYER: Fresno shortstop Ryan Ritter hit .305/.405/.606 with 18 home runs in 65 games. Despite being promoted to High-A on July 4, the 22-year-old still finished third in the Cal League in homers. The Rockies drafted Ritter in the fourth round in 2022 out of Kentucky.

PITCHER OF THE YEAR: The Padres liked Reno prep lefthander Robby Snelling so much in the 2022 draft that they nearly selected him 15th overall. Instead, San Diego was able to wait and draft him 39th overall and sign him for $3 million, the equivalent of first-round money. Snelling made an outstanding pro debut in 2023, first with Lake Elsinore, where he went 5-1 with a 1.57 ERA in 11 starts. He struck out 59 and walked 13 in 51.2 innings prior to being promoted to High-A and ultimately Double-A as a 19-year-old.

TOP MLB PROSPECT: Ethan Salas made his pro debut with Lake Elsinore a few days before he turned 17, making him the rare 16-year-old to appear in even a single game in a full-season league. The Padres signed Salas, a lefthanded-hitting catcher, out of Venezuela in January, and he excelled in the Cal League, hitting .267/.350/.487 with nine home runs in 48 games.

MANAGER OF THE YEAR: Steve Soliz guided Fresno to a Cal League-best 78-54 record, though his Grizzlies failed to qualify for the league playoffs because they did not win the North Division in either half of the season.

Ethan Salas

CALIFORNIA LEAGUE ALL-STARS

Pos	Player	Team	AVG	OPS	HR
C	Thayron Liranzo	Rancho Cucamonga	.272	.962	24
1B	Brennan Milone	Stockton	.304	.923	10
2B	Diego Velasquez	San Jose	.298	.821	8
3B	Graham Pauley	Lake Elsinore	.309	.887	4
SS	Ryan Ritter	Fresno	.305	1.011	18
OF	Gabriel Gonzalez	Modesto	.348	.933	9
OF	Samuel Zavala	Lake Elsinore	.267	.871	14
OF	Chris Newell	Rancho Cucamonga	.312	1.088	14
DH	Jadiel Sanchez	Inland Empire	.297	.853	11
UT	Cole Young	Modesto	.267	.825	5
Pos	**Pitcher**	**Team**	**G**	**ERA**	**SO**
SP	Michael Prosecky	Fresno	21	2.72	125
SP	Tyler Cleveland	Modesto	25	3.56	111
SP	Robby Snelling	Lake Elsinore	11	1.57	59
SP	Hayden Birdsong	San Jose	12	2.16	70
RP	Zach Agnos	Fresno	47	2.06	68
RP	Lucas Wepf	Rancho Cucamonga	22	2.43	58

OVERALL STANDINGS

North Division	W	L	PCT	GB	Manager	Attendance	Avg	Last Penn
Fresno Grizzlies (Rockies)	78	54	.591	—	Steve Soliz	277,089	4,198	Never
Modesto Nuts (Mariners)	77	55	.583	1.0	Zach Vincej	83,077	1,259	2023
San Jose Giants (Giants)	68	64	.515	10.0	Jeremiah Knackstedt	124,129	1,881	2021
Stockton Ports (Athletics)	50	82	.379	28.0	Gregorio Petit	117,377	1,778	2008
South Division	**W**	**L**	**PCT**	**GB**	**Manager**	**Attendance**	**Avg**	**Last Penn**
Rancho Cucamonga Quakes (Dodgers)	71	61	.538	—	John Shoemaker	151,082	2,289	2018
Inland Empire 66ers (Angels)	68	61	.527	1.5	Dave Stapleton	139,534	2,147	2013
Lake Elsinore Storm (Padres)	63	66	.488	6.5	Pete Zamora	94,385	1,547	2022
Visalia Rawhide (D-backs)	50	82	.379	21.0	Dee Garner	126,235	1,913	2019

North: Modesto def. San Jose 2-0. **South:** Rancho Cucamonga def. Inland Empire 2-1. **Championship Series:** Modesto defeated R. Cucamonga 2-0.

LARRY GOREN/FOUR SEAM IMAGES

CLUB BATTING

	AVG	G	AB	R	H	2B	3B	HR	RBI	BB	SO	SB	OBP	SLG
San Jose Giants	.266	132	4575	762	1216	251	40	95	667	499	1136	222	.352	.400
Modesto Nuts	.266	132	4540	795	1206	279	43	102	697	571	1247	158	.360	.413
Inland Empire 66ers	.256	129	4305	682	1103	171	61	74	577	551	1100	203	.351	.376
Fresno Grizzlies	.256	132	4495	726	1149	202	47	100	636	498	1164	153	.338	.388
R.C. Quakes	.253	132	4481	706	1134	224	30	111	631	544	1365	97	.342	.391
Lake Elsinore Storm	.244	129	4225	699	1029	241	25	86	620	643	1254	164	.354	.373
Visalia Rawhide	.235	132	4421	606	1040	203	45	83	513	504	1314	160	.321	.358
Stockton Ports	.233	132	4412	611	1030	183	25	82	532	534	1402	168	.325	.342

CLUB PITCHING

	ERA	G	CG	SHO	SV	IP	H	R	ER	HR	BB	SO	AVG
San Jose Giants	4.20	132	0	5	30	1166	1108	694	544	84	547	1276	.250
Inland Empire 66ers	4.29	129	1	7	26	1137	1042	600	542	85	464	1254	.242
Modesto Nuts	4.33	132	0	9	29	1165	1082	658	560	69	511	1189	.243
Lake Elsinore Storm	4.34	129	0	7	25	1131	1060	635	545	75	497	1210	.247
Fresno Grizzlies	4.40	132	0	6	38	1175	1171	659	575	83	444	1237	.259
R.C. Quakes	4.56	132	0	7	31	1164	1020	677	589	82	701	1389	.236
Stockton Ports	5.47	132	0	6	27	1162	1251	838	707	136	535	1171	.270
Visalia Rawhide	5.48	132	0	3	21	1159	1173	826	706	119	645	1256	.261

CLUB FIELDING

	PCT	PO	A	E	DP
Inland Empire	.977	3410	1105	104	108
Rancho Cucamonga	.975	3491	1190	118	106
Fresno	.972	3526	1190	136	114
Lake Elsinore	.970	3394	1134	141	100
Modesto	.964	3494	1169	173	94
Stockton	.962	3487	1183	182	96
Visalia	.962	3477	1203	185	109
San Jose	.962	3498	1278	191	132

INDIVIDUAL BATTING

Batter, Club	AVG	G	AB	R	H	2B	3B	HR	RBI	BB	SO	SB
Gabriel Gonzalez, Modesto	.348	73	296	51	103	19	4	9	54	23	46	8
Diego Velasquez, San Jose	.298	111	426	76	127	32	1	8	69	56	82	23
Jadiel Sanchez, Inland Empire	.297	105	381	59	113	15	10	11	66	47	64	7
Josh Hood, Modesto	.279	98	391	71	109	19	2	11	61	49	90	18
Nelson Rada, Inland Empire	.276	115	439	94	121	13	6	2	48	73	98	55
Milkar Perez, Modesto	.273	94	319	44	87	26	1	1	39	50	93	2
Thayron Liranzo, Rancho Cuca.	.272	94	345	81	94	24	2	24	70	70	112	2
Tanner O'Tremba, San Jose	.271	82	292	53	79	21	2	8	50	39	75	17
Cole Young, Modesto	.267	78	303	60	81	20	7	5	39	54	52	17
Samuel Zavala, Lake Elsinore	.267	101	348	83	93	22	0	14	71	89	121	20

INDIVIDUAL PITCHING

Pitcher, Club	W	L	ERA	G	GS	CG	SV	IP	H	R	ER	BB	SO
Michael Prosecky, Fresno	11	7	2.72	21	21	0	0	109	87	37	33	41	125
Tyler Cleveland, Modesto	14	5	3.56	25	20	0	0	136	129	58	54	26	111
Manuel Mercedes, San Jose	3	6	3.64	25	21	0	0	106	111	61	43	42	72
Caleb Franzen, Fresno	4	5	4.22	22	21	0	0	113	121	62	53	42	108
Shaddon Peavyhouse, Modesto	10	5	4.94	26	23	0	0	133	132	85	73	63	119
Wander Guante, Stockton	3	6	5.25	25	18	0	0	110	107	73	64	53	100

DEPARTMENT LEADERS

BATTING

OBP	Sammy Zavala, Lake Elsinore	.420
SLG	Thayron Liranzo, Rancho Cuca.	.562
OPS	Thayron Liranzo, Rancho Cuca.	.962
R	Nelson Rada, Inland Empire	94
H	Diego Velasquez, San Jose	127
TB	Thayron Liranzo, Rancho Cuca.	194
XBH	Thayron Liranzo, Rancho Cuca.	50
2B	Diego Velasquez, San Jose	32
3B	Jadiel Sanchez, Inland Empire	10
3B	Jake Snider, Fresno	10
HR	Thayron Liranzo, Rancho Cuca.	24
RBI	Skyler Messinger, Fresno	78
SAC	Diego Velasquez, San Jose	13
BB	Samuel Zavala, Lake Elsinore	89
HBP	Tanner O'Tremba, San Jose	27
SO	Henry Bolte, Stockton	164
SB	Nelson Rada, Inland Empire	55
CS	Andy Perez, Fresno	11
CS	Nelson Rada, Inland Empire	11

FIELDING

C	PO	Ronaldo Flores, Inland Empire	740
	A	Thayron Liranzo, Rancho Cuca.	68
	DP	Tatem Levins, Modesto	6
	E	Freuddy Batista, Modesto	15
	CS	Thayron Liranzo, Rancho Cuca.	35
	SB	Thayron Liranzo, Rancho Cuca.	96
	PB	Freuddy Batista, Modesto	23
1B	PO	Gabe Moncada, Modesto	633
	A	Dayton Dooney, Rancho Cuca.	51
	DP	Gabe Moncada, Modesto	59
	E	Griffin Doersching, Lake Elsinore	9
	E	Gabe Moncada, Modesto	9
2B	PO	Jeremy Arocho, Inland Empire	110
	A	Jeremy Arocho, Inland Empire	170
	DP	Jeremy Arocho, Inland Empire	42
	E	Luis Mendez, Fresno	13
	E	Manuel Pena, Visalia	13
3B	PO	Dereck Salom, Stockton	35
	PO	Graham Pauley, Lake Elsinore	35
	A	Milkar Perez, Modesto	98
	DP	3 tied	10
	E	Milkar Perez, Modesto	18
	E	Anthony Rodriguez, San Jose	18
SS	PCT	Rosman Verdugo, Lake Elsinore	.937
	PO	Bjay Cooke, Stockton	123
	A	Denzer Guzman, Inland Empire	233
	DP	Denzer Guzman, Inland Empire	54
	E	Denzer Guzman, Inland Empire	25
OF	PCT	Nelson Rada, Inland Empire	.996
	PO	Nelson Rada, Inland Empire	259
	A	Jadiel Sanchez, Inland Empire	15
	DP	Alvin Guzman, Visalia	4
	DP	Jadiel Sanchez, Inland Empire	4
	E	Alvin Guzman, Visalia	11

PITCHING

G	Josh Swales, Visalia	49
GS	Shaddon Peavyhouse, Modesto	23
GF	Zach Agnos, Fresno	41
SV	Zach Agnos, Fresno	27
W	Tyler Cleveland, Modesto	14
L	Wyatt Wendell, Visalia	10
L	Jacob Steinmetz, Visalia	10
IP	Tyler Cleveland, Modesto	136.1
H	Shaddon Peavyhouse, Modesto	132
R	Shaddon Peavyhouse, Modesto	85
ER	Shaddon Peavyhouse, Modesto	73
HBP	Shaddon Peavyhouse, Modesto	16
HBP	Julio Rodriguez, San Jose	16
BB	Shaddon Peavyhouse, Modesto	63
SO	Michael Prosecky, Fresno	125
SO/9	Michael Prosecky, Fresno	10.3
BB/9	Tyler Cleveland, Modesto	1.7
WP	Shaddon Peavyhouse, Modesto	19
Balks	Alfred Morillo, Visalia	5
Balks	Armando Vasquez, Visalia	5
HR	Wander Guante, Stockton	13
HR	Nomar Medina, San Jose	13
BAA	Michael Prosecky, Fresno	.217

CAROLINA LEAGUE LOW-A

Awards selected by Major League Baseball

CHAMPION: The Charleston RiverDogs completed a three-peat as Carolina League champions by downing Down East in two games in the finals. Charleston won the deciding Game 2 by a score of 7-5, receiving key contributions from top Rays prospects. Third baseman Brayden Taylor (.375 on-base percentage), first baseman Xavier Isaac (.417) and second baseman Cooper Kinney (.500) all scored in the finale and were frequently on base during the playoffs. The RiverDogs had the worst record in the league in the first half but surged to a 39-26 mark in the second.

MOST VALUABLE PLAYER: Delmarva catcher Samuel Basallo didn't let his youth impede his production. As one of just four 18-year-old regulars in the pitcher-friendly Carolina League, he stood out with a .299/.384/.503 batting line that included 12 home runs in 83 games before a promotion to High-A on Aug. 1. Basallo led the league in slugging and placed fourth with 60 RBIs.

PITCHER OF THE YEAR: Unselected in the five-round 2020 draft, righthander Aidan Curry signed with the Rangers out of his Bronx high school. He spent two seasons in Rookie leagues before stepping forward with Down East in 2023. The 21-year-old Curry pitched to a 2.30 ERA with 99 strikeouts and 29 walks in 82 innings.

TOP MLB PROSPECT: Samuel Basallo is the flagship prospect of the Orioles' revitalized international scouting efforts under MLB Executive of the Year Mike Elias. Baltimore signed Basallo out of the Dominican Republic in 2021. He emerged in the Florida Complex League in 2022 and broke out fully in 2023, finishing the year at Double-A.

MANAGER OF THE YEAR: Despite having one of the youngest teams in the league, Victor Estevez led Carolina to a 72-55 record and North Division crown.

Samuel Basallo

CAROLINA LEAGUE ALL-STARS

Pos	Player	Team	AVG	OPS	HR
C	Samuel Basallo	Delmarva	.299	.887	12
1B	Xavier Isaac	Charleston	.266	.842	13
2B	Jadher Areinamo	Carolina	.306	.740	4
3B	Luke Adams	Carolina	.233	.801	11
SS	Jose Devers	Lynchburg	.252	.745	11
OF	Chandler Simpson	Charleston	.285	.691	81 SB
OF	Daylen Lile	Fredericksburg	.291	.891	7
OF	Zach Cole	Fayetteville	.265	.891	11
DH	Tim Elko	Kannapolis	.297	.916	17
UT	Cooper Kinney	Charleston	.274	.734	10
Pos	**Pitcher**	**Team**	**G**	**ERA**	**SO**
SP	Jose Fleury	Fayetteville	26	3.65	139
SP	Brody McCullough	Myrtle Beach	12	2.86	74
SP	Aidan Curry	Down East	19	2.30	99
SP	Tyler Guilfoil	Fayetteville	18	2.74	91
RP	Cooper McKeehan	Columbia	31	1.08	53
RP	Drew Sommers	Charleston	32	2.72	66

OVERALL STANDINGS

North Division	W	L	PCT	GB	Manager	Attendance	Avg	Last Penn
Carolina Mudcats (Brewers)	72	55	.567	—	Victor Estevez	138,299	2,305	Never
Lynchburg Hillcats (Guardians)	67	64	.511	7.0	Jordan Smith	108,725	1,673	2017
Down East Wood Ducks (Rangers)	66	61	.520	6.0	Carlos Maldonado	96,160	1,526	2017
Fredericksburg Nationals (Nationals)	65	63	.508	7.5	Jake Lowery	265,960	4,156	Never
Delmarva Shorebirds (Orioles)	56	74	.431	17.5	Felipe Alou	189,749	3,162	*2000
Salem Red Sox (Red Sox)	55	72	.433	17.0	Liam Carroll	177,083	2,903	2013
South Division	**W**	**L**	**PCT**	**GB**	**Manager**	**Attendance**	**Avg**	**Last Penn**
Myrtle Beach Pelicans (Cubs)	75	55	.577	—	Buddy Bailey	268,600	4,197	2016
Kannapolis Cannon Ballers (White Sox)	67	64	.511	8.5	Pat Leyland	195,500	3,055	*2005
Charleston RiverDogs (Rays)	66	65	.504	9.5	Sean Smedley	270,170	4,288	2023
Columbia Fireflies (Royals)	66	65	.504	9.5	Tony Pena	219,277	3,595	Never
Augusta GreenJackets (Braves)	63	68	.481	12.5	Cody Gabella	260,060	4,195	*2008
Fayetteville Woodpeckers (Astros)	60	72	.455	16.0	Ricky Rivera	187,195	2,971	Never

* South Atlantic League title won prior to 2021 minor league realignment

North: Down East def. Carolina 2-1. **South:** Charleston def. Myrtle Beach 2-1. **Championship Series:** Charleston defeated Down East 2-0

BRIAN WESTERHOLT / FOUR SEAM IMAGES

CLUB BATTING

	AVG	G	AB	R	H	2B	3B	HR	RBI	BB	SO	SB	OBP	SLG
Myrtle Beach Pelicans	.253	130	4292	655	1088	186	26	104	571	477	1090	191	.337	.382
Carolina Mudcats	.250	127	4157	632	1039	220	20	70	548	559	1075	220	.348	.363
Lynchburg Hillcats	.244	131	4294	658	1046	189	40	62	572	625	1083	266	.348	.350
Kannapolis Cannon Ballers	.242	131	4239	645	1024	190	23	95	579	570	1262	121	.340	.364
Delmarva Shorebirds	.241	130	4211	621	1016	203	36	88	531	531	1252	198	.334	.369
Charleston RiverDogs	.240	131	4219	599	1014	179	40	81	516	531	1210	226	.332	.359
Fredericksburg Nationals	.240	128	4179	666	1002	190	29	70	578	608	1198	247	.349	.349
Salem Red Sox	.234	127	4079	573	955	180	37	61	477	523	1153	186	.328	.341
Down East Wood Ducks	.226	127	4063	546	918	160	26	79	481	486	1395	209	.317	.336
Fayetteville Woodpeckers	.226	132	4239	538	956	185	15	90	476	526	1267	200	.325	.340
Columbia Fireflies	.224	131	4074	573	912	162	36	76	465	567	1325	252	.328	.337
Augusta GreenJackets	.217	131	4081	583	885	162	24	91	511	589	1447	203	.325	.335

CLUB PITCHING

	ERA	G	CG	SHO	SV	IP	H	R	ER	HR	BB	SO	AVG
Down East Wood Ducks	3.39	127	1	10	29	1103	886	514	416	79	469	1257	.218
Columbia Fireflies	3.78	131	0	12	37	1129	1042	567	474	83	506	1258	.245
Charleston RiverDogs	3.93	131	1	10	34	1123	995	582	490	90	483	1210	.237
Fayetteville Woodpeckers	3.93	132	0	5	30	1141	922	590	498	77	627	1455	.220
Salem Red Sox	3.99	127	0	9	22	1089	905	612	483	62	597	1194	.226
Carolina Mudcats	4.00	127	0	7	31	1106	919	544	492	78	535	1201	.229
Myrtle Beach Pelicans	4.07	130	0	9	32	1124	880	582	508	52	711	1369	.216
Kannapolis Cannon Ballers	4.38	131	1	9	33	1119	1030	614	545	95	507	1150	.244
Augusta GreenJackets	4.41	131	0	9	39	1118	1028	643	548	97	489	1262	.243
Delmarva Shorebirds	4.54	130	1	7	29	1115	1037	670	563	77	623	1222	.247
Lynchburg Hillcats	4.56	131	0	6	37	1142	1101	678	578	90	506	1098	.250
Fredericksburg Nationals	4.63	128	0	5	31	1113	1110	693	573	87	539	1081	.259

CLUB FIELDING

	PCT	PO	A	E	DP
Carolina Mudcats	.981	3317	1119	87	114
Kannapolis	.975	3357	1151	116	101
Myrtle Beach	.973	3372	1098	125	105
Charleston	.969	3369	1104	144	102
Columbia	.969	3387	1145	147	93
Down East	.968	3309	1025	145	80
Fredericksburg	.966	3339	1159	156	97
Fayetteville	.966	3423	1022	155	81
Lynchburg	.966	3425	1056	157	80
Delmarva	.966	3357	1099	158	103
Augusta	.964	3355	1113	166	85
Salem	.962	3267	1121	173	101

INDIVIDUAL BATTING

Batter, Club	AVG	G	AB	R	H	2B	3B	HR	RBI	BB	SO	SB
Reivaj Garcia, Myrtle Beach	.306	92	366	72	112	21	3	3	41	41	71	21
Jadher Areinamo, Carolina	.306	103	396	52	121	26	1	4	52	17	52	16
Mario Camilletti, Kannapolis	.289	97	339	64	98	23	0	2	60	84	70	0
Chandler Simpson, Charleston	.285	91	354	66	101	9	4	0	24	38	35	81
Wuilfredo Antunez, Lynchburg	.275	89	338	47	93	17	7	6	39	39	72	11
Cooper Kinney, Charleston	.274	121	456	61	125	24	0	10	61	42	107	3
Juan Benjamin, Lynchburg	.271	98	358	53	97	16	1	3	44	49	81	24
Xavier Isaac, Charleston	.266	90	312	58	83	16	3	13	56	56	80	10
Pedro Ramirez, Myrtle Beach	.266	104	354	53	94	19	3	8	54	49	71	17
Rafael Morel, Myrtle Beach	.263	94	334	63	88	10	0	7	30	50	94	16

INDIVIDUAL PITCHING

Pitcher, Club	W	L	ERA	G	GS	CG	SV	IP	H	R	ER	BB	SO
Trevor Martin, Charleston	10	5	3.52	25	22	0	0	110	92	46	43	41	131
Trey Dombroski, Fayetteville	7	9	3.71	26	15	0	1	119	97	63	49	36	148
Marcus Johnson, Charleston	5	6	3.74	26	24	0	0	130	130	61	54	21	114
Austin Peterson, Lynchburg	6	8	4.54	24	24	0	0	117	133	68	59	27	102
Alonzo Richardson, Lynchburg	6	7	4.79	26	24	0	0	124	129	71	66	52	73

DEPARTMENT LEADERS

BATTING

OBP	Mario Camilletti, Kannapolis	.432
SLG	Samuel Basallo, Delmarva	.503
OPS	Xavier Isaac, Charleston	.842
R	Luke Adams, Carolina	74
H	Cooper Kinney, Charleston	125
TB	Brett Squires, Columbia	180
XBH	Jace Avina, Carolina	38
XBH	Brett Squires, Columbia	38
2B	Jadher Areinamo, Carolina	26
3B	3 tied	7
HR	Jeremy Celedonio, Augusta	17
HR	Tim ElkoKannapolis	17
RBI	Brett Squires, Columbia	69
SAC	Jean Ramirez, Columbia	8
BB	Mario Camilletti, Kannapolis	84
HBP	Johnathon Thomas, Fredericksburg	23
SO	Ambioris Tavarez, Augusta	196
SB	Chandler Simpson, Charleston	81
CS	Ambioris Tavarez, Augusta	20

FIELDING

C	PO	Ian Moller, Down East	839
	A	Enderso Lira, Salem	72
	DP	Ian Moller, Down East	7
	E	Sandro Gaston, Fayetteville	16
	E	Enderso Lira, Salem	16
	CS	Nick Clarno, Augusta	52
	SB	Miguel Pabon, Myrtle Beach	122
	PB	Dionmy Salon, Columbia	12
1B	PCT	Brett Squires, Columbia	.998
	PO	Brett Squires, Columbia	740
	A	Brett Squires, Columbia	74
	DP	Brett Squires, Columbia	70
	E	Xavier Isaac, Charleston	12
2B	PCT	Lizandro Rodriguez, Columbia	.959
	PO	Lizandro Rodriguez, Columbia	194
	A	Lizandro Rodriguez, Columbia	268
	DP	Lizandro Rodriguez, Columbia	61
	E	Lizandro Rodriguez, Columbia	20
3B	PCT	Anderson De Los Santos, Delmarva	.911
	PO	Gleider Figuereo, Down East	67
	A	Gleider Figuereo, Down East	163
	DP	Luke Adams, Carolina	18
	E	Gleider Figuereo, Down East	23
SS	PCT	Daniel Vazquez, Columbia	.963
	PO	Daniel Vazquez, Columbia	146
	A	Daniel Vazquez, Columbia	247
	DP	Armando Cruz, Fredericksburg	49
	E	Ambioris Tavarez, Augusta	24
	E	Carlos Colmenarez, Charleston	24
OF	PCT	Chandler Simpson, Charleston	1.000
	PO	JoJo Blackmon, Down East	193
	A	Jace Avina, Carolina	13
	DP	Jace Avina, Carolina	5
	E	4 tied	7

PITCHING

G	Billy Seidl, Kannapolis	47
GS	3 tied	24
GF	Billy Seidl, Kannapolis	41
SV	Billy Seidl, Kannapolis	14
W	3 tied	10
L	3 tied	10
IP	Marcus Johnson, Charleston	130
H	Austin Peterson, Lynchburg	133
R	Alonzo Richardson, Lynchburg	71
ER	Alonzo Richardson, Lynchburg	66
HBP	Billy Seidl, Kannapolis	17
BB	Alimber Santa, Fayetteville	74
SO	Trey Dombroski, Fayetteville	148
SO/9	Trey Dombroski, Fayetteville	11.2
BB/9	Marcus Johnson, Charleston	1.5
WP	Jose Ramirez, Salem	20
Balks	Yorman Gomez, Lynchburg	12
HR	Trey Dombroski, Fayetteville	15
HR	Luke Young, Fredericksburg	15
BAA	Trey Dombrosk, Fayetteville	.216

FLORIDA STATE LEAGUE LOW-A

Awards selected by Major League Baseball

CHAMPION: The Jupiter Hammerheads have been FSL members since 1998 but had never won a league title. That changed in 2023, when Jupiter defeated Clearwater two games to one in the championship series. Jupiter won the deciding Game 3 by a 7-4 score despite recording just three hits in the game. The Hammerheads racked up baserunners via eight walks and three hit batsmen. They scored runs without recording a hit via a sacrifice fly, a bases-loaded walk, a fielder's choice back to the pitcher and a throwing error. Jupiter righthander Jacob Miller started and went four innings, allowing two runs on four hits.

MOST VALUABLE PLAYER: Clearwater center fielder Justin Crawford hit .344/.399/.478 with three home runs and 40 stolen bases in 69 games. The 19-year-old Phillies prospect ranked third in the FSL in steals despite spending only about half the season with the Threshers. Crawford hit .332 overall in 2023, tops among teenagers with at least 350 plate appearances.

PITCHER OF THE YEAR: Righthander Max Rajcic made just 12 starts for Palm Beach, but he made them all count. He recorded a 1.89 ERA in 62 innings to go with 68 strikeouts and just nine walks. The Cardinals drafted Rajcic in the sixth round in 2022 out of UCLA. His overall 2.48 ERA ranked third in the minor leagues.

TOP MLB PROSPECT: The Phillies drafted Justin Crawford 17th overall out of high school in Las Vegas in 2022. He was not only one of the top prospects in his draft class but also the son of four-time all-star Carl Crawford, who like Justin also led with his speed and notched 480 stolen bases in 15-year MLB career.

MANAGER OF THE YEAR: Andrew Graham led Lakeland to a 70-61 mark. The 41-year-old skipper played five seasons in the Tigers' system and has managed Detroit affiliates continuously since 2011, the last four seasons in Lakeland.

Justin Crawford

FLORIDA STATE LEAGUE ALL-STARS

Pos	Player	Team	AVG	OPS	HR
C	Omar Martinez	Tampa	.251	.812	18
1B	Torin Montgomery	Jupiter	.341	.967	3
2B	Termarr Johnson	Bradenton	.244	.867	13
3B	Sal Stewart	Daytona	.269	.819	10
SS	Jared Serna	Tampa	.283	.833	19
OF	Justin Crawford	Clearwater	.344	.877	3
OF	Hector Rodriguez	Daytona	.293	.857	16
OF	Seth Stephenson	Lakeland	.277	.775	62 SB
DH	Ricardo Olivar	Fort Myers	.285	.855	10
UT	Carlos Jorge	Daytona	.295	.883	9
Pos	**Pitcher**	**Team**	**G**	**ERA**	**SO**
SP	Max Rajcic	Palm Beach	12	1.89	68
SP	Pete Hansen	Palm Beach	23	3.12	126
SP	Hancel Rincon	Palm Beach	24	3.26	97
SP	Brock Selvidge	Tampa	15	3.38	91
RP	Wen Hui Pan	Clearwater	27	2.81	81
RP	Evan Taylor	Jupiter	46	2.18	70

OVERALL STANDINGS

East Division	W	L	PCT	GB	Manager	Attendance	Avg	Last Penn
Jupiter Hammerheads (Marlins)	70	62	.530	—	Nelson Prada	35,515	888	2023
Palm Beach Cardinals (Cardinals)	64	63	.504	3.5	Gary Kendall	33,067	870	2017
Daytona Tortugas (Reds)	56	72	.438	12.0	Julio Morillo	93,894	1,514	2011
St. Lucie Mets (Mets)	44	84	.344	24.0	Gilbert Gomez	74,213	1,108	2022

West Division	W	L	PCT	GB	Manager	Attendance	Avg	Last Penn
Clearwater Threshers (Phillies)	79	50	.612	—	Marty Malloy	157,072	2,493	2021
Bradenton Marauders (Pirates)	76	54	.585	3.5	Jonathan Johnston	65,598	1,075	2016
Lakeland Flying Tigers (Tigers)	70	61	.534	10.0	Andrew Graham	38,202	616	2012
Fort Myers Mighty Mussels (Twins)	67	64	.511	13.0	Brian Meyer	108,879	1,675	2018
Dunedin Blue Jays (Blue Jays)	62	70	.470	18.5	Donnie Murphy	31,210	495	2017
Tampa Tarpons (Yankees)	61	69	.469	18.5	Rachel Balkovec	58,150	986	2010

East: Jupiter def. **Palm Beach 2-0. West:** Clearwater def. **Lakeland 2-1. Championship Series:** Jupiter defeated Clearwater 2-1.

TOM DIPACE

MINOR LEAGUES

CLUB BATTING

	AVG	G	AB	R	H	2B	3B	HR	RBI	BB	SO	SB	OBP	SLG
Clearwater Threshers	.257	129	4232	716	1088	176	38	99	633	539	1075	270	.353	.387
Jupiter Hammerheads	.243	132	4192	605	1017	197	44	67	525	465	1123	212	.324	.359
Fort Myers Mighty Mussels	.242	131	4283	720	1038	235	40	103	645	673	1253	173	.355	.388
Palm Beach Cardinals	.241	127	4081	631	985	214	39	64	560	589	1151	155	.348	.360
Daytona Tortugas	.238	128	4141	611	986	219	42	87	546	538	1157	117	.335	.374
Lakeland Flying Tigers	.238	131	4265	719	1013	217	31	94	611	636	1277	171	.349	.369
Tampa Tarpons	.237	130	4238	684	1003	182	27	122	618	678	1174	128	.348	.379
Bradenton Marauders	.236	130	4167	720	983	191	25	117	632	783	1335	222	.365	.378
St. Lucie Mets	.230	128	4022	581	925	180	36	92	513	564	1185	151	.338	.361
Dunedin Blue Jays	.228	132	4198	635	958	192	32	69	551	626	1209	146	.342	.338

CLUB PITCHING

	ERA	G	CG	SHO	SV	IP	H	R	ER	HR	BB	SO	AVG
Jupiter Hammerheads	4.12	132	1	8	41	1115	986	606	511	73	553	1176	.235
Dunedin Blue Jays	4.32	132	2	6	24	1132	982	631	543	108	575	1172	.234
Clearwater Threshers	4.38	129	0	9	36	1123	978	622	546	87	650	1278	.235
Fort Myers Mighty Mussels	4.44	131	2	7	24	1134	993	639	559	96	570	1208	.234
Palm Beach Cardinals	4.44	127	1	6	26	1085	997	618	535	96	472	1085	.241
Bradenton Marauders	4.49	130	0	7	38	1132	1016	683	565	92	621	1191	.240
Daytona Tortugas	4.59	128	0	8	26	1087	970	641	554	87	715	1245	.239
Tampa Tarpons	4.85	130	0	3	23	1126	1018	703	606	99	627	1276	.240
Lakeland Flying Tigers	4.96	131	1	3	31	1139	1045	712	628	90	610	1142	.244
St. Lucie Mets	5.62	128	1	2	30	1067	1011	767	667	86	698	1166	.249

CLUB FIELDING

	PCT	PO	A	E	DP
Clearwater	.979	3368	1048	97	110
Dunedin	.976	3396	1098	112	98
Fort Myers	.973	3402	1097	123	87
Daytona	.973	3262	1004	119	105
Lakeland	.972	3418	1181	133	101
Jupiter	.970	3345	1071	135	96
Bradenton	.969	3395	1250	147	125
Palm Beach	.969	3254	1070	138	96
St. Lucie	.967	3202	993	142	92
Tampa	.967	3377	1149	156	112

INDIVIDUAL BATTING

Batter, Club	AVG	G	AB	R	H	2B	3B	HR	RBI	BB	SO	SB
Javier Sanoja, Jupiter	.308	102	400	51	123	18	8	1	57	31	32	31
Carlos Jorge, Daytona	.295	86	298	70	88	11	9	9	36	47	70	31
Hector Rodriguez, Daytona	.293	101	410	85	120	23	9	16	56	27	84	18
Ricardo Olivar, Fort Myers	.285	100	372	75	106	28	2	10	58	59	93	12
Jared Serna, Tampa	.283	95	400	72	113	21	1	19	71	40	75	19
Michael Curialle, Palm Beach	.282	110	380	66	107	28	5	2	57	51	108	10
Seth Stephenson, Lakeland	.277	99	368	84	102	17	8	4	36	37	89	62
Brett Roberts, Jupiter	.273	91	344	58	94	16	4	5	45	22	77	20
Won-Bin Cho, Palm Beach	.270	105	378	64	102	14	5	7	52	64	98	32
Sal Stewart, Daytona	.269	88	316	55	85	19	0	10	60	66	59	10

INDIVIDUAL PITCHING

Pitcher, Club	W	L	ERA	G	GS	CG	SV	IP	H	R	ER	BB	SO
Pete Hansen, Palm Beach	11	3	3.12	23	23	0	0	113	92	39	39	39	126
Hancel Rincon, Palm Beach	9	6	3.26	24	23	0	0	133	109	59	48	20	97
Sean Hermann, Tampa	7	6	4.93	22	22	0	0	108	112	68	59	44	86

DEPARTMENT LEADERS

BATTING

OBP	Jett Williams, St. Lucie	.422
SLG	Hector Rodriguez, Daytona	.510
OPS	Carlos Jorge, Daytona	.883
R	Hector Rodriguez, Daytona	85
H	Javier Sanoja, Jupiter	123
TB	Hector Rodriguez, Daytona	209
XBH	Hector Rodriguez, Daytona	48
2B	Michael Curialle, Palm Beach	28
2B	Ricardo Olivar, Fort Myers	28
3B	Hector Rodriguez, Daytona	9
3B	Carlos Jorge, Daytona	9
HR	Rodolfo Nolasco, Bradenton	20
RBI	Rubel Cespedes, Fort Myers	74
SAC	Lizandro Espinoza, Palm Beach	5
BB	Jesus Castillo, Bradenton	102
HBP	Seth Stephenson, Lakeland	24
SO	Rodolfo Nolasco, Bradenton	152
SB	Seth Stephenson, Lakeland	62
CS	Emaarion Boyd, Clearwater	18

FIELDING

C PO	Geovanny Planchart, Bradenton	693
A	Geovanny Planchart, Bradenton	55
DP	Agustin Ramirez, Tampa	6
E	Omar Martinez, Tampa	19
CS	Geovanny Planchart, Bradenton	27
SB	Vincent Perozo, St. Lucie	117
PB	Omar Martinez, Tampa	16
1B PCT	No Qualifier	
PO	Yassel Pino, Daytona	560
A	Yassel Pino, Daytona	38
DP	Yassel Pino, Daytona	58
E	Yeral Martinez, St. Lucie	9
2B PCT	No Qualifier	
PO	Termarr Johnson, Bradenton	129
A	Termarr Johnson, Bradenton	159
DP	Termarr Johnson, Bradenton	51
E	Ian Lewis, Jupiter	13
3B PCT	Michael Curialle, Palm Beach	.930
PO	Michael Curialle, Palm Beach	67
A	Michael Curialle, Palm Beach	131
DP	Tucker Toman, Dunedin	15
E	Michael Curialle, Palm Beach	15
SS PCT	Danny De Andrade, Fort Myers	.954
PO	Lizandro Espinoza, Palm Beach	142
A	Bryan Rincon, Clearwater	198
A	Harrison Spohn, Jupiter	198
DP	Bryan Rincon, Clearwater	47
E	Jett Williams, St. Lucie	18
E	Victor Acosta Daytona	18
OF PCT	Roque Salinas, Dunedin	.994
PO	Jaden Rudd, Dunedin	254
A	Dylan Neuse, Fort Myers	16
DP	Maddux Houghton, Fort Myers	5
E	Jaden Rudd, Dunedin	12

PITCHING

G	Evan Taylor, Jupiter	46
GS	3 tied	23
GF	Evan Taylor, Jupiter	40
SV	Evan Taylor, Jupiter	20
W	Jonh Henriquez, Clearwater	14
L	Saul Garcia, St. Lucie	9
L	Brycen Mautz, Palm Beach	9
IP	Hancel Rincon, Palm Beach	132.2
H	Sean Hermann, Tampa	112
R	Hayden Merda, Tampa	74
ER	Hayden Merda, Tampa	66
HBP	Alex Bustamante, Tampa	18
BB	Mason Pelio, Daytona	63
SO	Pete Hansen, Palm Beach	126
SO/9	Pete Hansen, Palm Beach	10.1
BB/9	Hancel Rincon, Palm Beach	1.4
WP	Jean Calderon, St. Lucie	15
Balks	Sean Hermann, Tampa	9
HR	Rafael Ohashi, Dunedin	16
BAA	Hancel Rincon, Palm Beach	.219

ARIZONA COMPLEX LEAGUE

Awards selected by Major League Baseball

CHAMPION: The Brewers defeated D-backs Red by a score of 5-4 in Game 3 of the ACL championship series. Brewers left fielder Miguel Briceno went 3-for-4 with a double and run scored. Righthander Brailin Rodriguez picked up the win with 2.2 innings of relief in which he struck out three and allowed one run on one hit.

MOST VALUABLE PLAYER: The Padres drafted catcher Romeo Sanabria in the 18th round in 2022 out of Indian River JC in Florida. Shifted to first base in 2023, he led the ACL with 53 RBIs, a .617 slugging percentage and a 1.060 OPS. The 21-year-old Sanabria hit .359/.443/.617 with eight home runs and 15 doubles in 50 games, earning an Aug. 22 promotion to Low-A Lake Elsinore.

PITCHER OF THE YEAR: Signed by the Brewers as an 18-year-old out of Venezuela in 2021, righthander Gerson Calzadilla made eight starts that season and the next in Rookie ball. In 2023, he took on a relief-only role and thrived. Calzadilla notched four saves in 16 ACL appearances, going 4-0 and allowing four earned runs (0.98 ERA) in 36.2 innings. He struck out 36 and walked 10, allowing one home run. Calzadilla made two August appearances for Low-A Carolina.

TOP MLB PROSPECT: The Rangers signed Dominican shortstop Echedry Vargas in 2022, and he broke out in a big way a year later. He led the ACL with 27 extra-base hits and tied for the league lead with 11 home runs. The 18-year-old Vargas, who also plays second and third base, batted .315/.387/.569 with 46 runs and 17 stolen bases in 52 games. Promoted to Low-A Down East in late August, he appeared in only one game before suffering a season-ending injury.

MANAGER OF THE YEAR: The Rockies went an ACL-best 40-15 under manager Fred Ocasio. The Rockies led the league with 433 runs scored with a 4.32 ERA that also topped the league. The ACL Rockies' roster skewed old, with the oldest position player group in the league by nearly a year and one of the oldest pitching staffs as well.

ARIZONA COMPLEX LEAGUE ALL-STARS

Pos	Player	Team	AVG	OPS	HR
C	Ronny Hernandez	White Sox	.338	.923	3
1B	Romeo Sanabria	Padres	.359	1.060	8
2B	Echedry Vargas	Rangers	.315	.956	11
3B	Javier Francisco	Giants	.280	.984	7
SS	Juan Baez	Brewers	.370	.952	4
OF	Jaison Chourio	Guardians	.349	.939	1
OF	Derlin Figueroa	Dodgers/Royals	.328	1.007	5
OF	Guillermo Williamson	Giants Black	.285	.926	9
DH	Ricardo Cabrera	Reds	.350	1.028	5
UT	Jeral Perez	Dodgers	.257	.892	11

Echedry Vargas

BILL MITCHELL

Pos	Pitcher	Team	G	ERA	SO
SP	Thomas Ireland	Rangers	8	1.42	29
SP	Felix Arronde	Royals	11	1.85	46
SP	Emmanuel Reyes	Royals	8	3.38	35
SP	Adam Serwinowski	Reds	11	3.62	43
RP	Gerson Calzadilla	Brewers	16	0.98	36
RP	Alex Martinez	Angels	16	1.17	35

OVERALL STANDINGS

Central Division	W	L	PCT	GB	Manager
ACL Brewers Gold	31	25	.554	—	Rafael Neda
ACL Reds	28	28	.500	3.0	Gustavo Molina
ACL Guardians	22	33	.400	8.5	T.J. Rivera
ACL Athletics	20	36	.357	11.0	Adam Rosales
ACL Cubs	18	37	.327	12.5	Nick Lovullo

East Division	W	L	PCT	GB	Manager(s)
ACL Rockies	40	15	.727	—	Fred Ocasio
ACL D-backs Red	34	21	.618	6.0	Jorge Cortes/Jaime Del Valle
ACL Giants Black	33	23	.589	7.5	Jose Montilla
ACL Giants Orange	30	26	.536	10.5	Jacob Heyward
ACL Angels	26	30	.464	14.5	Ever Magallanes
ACL D-backs Black	22	34	.393	18.5	Gift Ngoepe/Jorge Cortes

West Division	W	L	PCT	GB	Manager
ACL Dodgers	34	22	.607	—	Jair Fernandez
ACL Royals	31	25	.554	3.0	Jesus Azuaje
ACL Mariners	31	25	.554	3.0	Luis Caballero
ACL Padres	30	26	.536	4.0	Lukas Ray
ACL Rangers	23	33	.411	11.0	Guilder Rodriguez
ACL White Sox	21	35	.375	13.0	Danny Gonzalez

CLUB BATTING

	AVG	G	AB	R	H	2B	3B	HR	RBI	BB	SO	SB	OBP	SLG
ACL D-backs Red	.299	55	1707	345	511	76	20	28	289	232	406	74	.393	.417
ACL Rockies	.289	55	1745	433	505	103	23	44	351	272	472	96	.398	.450
ACL Brewers	.280	56	1859	357	521	91	22	30	292	266	539	122	.375	.401
ACL Royals	.278	56	1782	371	495	109	22	39	311	269	513	108	.378	.429
ACL Angels	.276	56	1773	333	490	84	36	21	272	253	539	87	.378	.400
ACL Giants Orange	.275	56	1652	325	455	97	6	38	280	274	419	39	.386	.410
ACL Padres	.274	56	1773	372	485	100	18	29	311	322	513	99	.391	.399
ACL Cubs	.270	55	1716	300	463	93	20	29	247	245	498	85	.371	.398
ACL Mariners	.263	56	1645	342	433	92	16	50	280	274	558	121	.386	.430
ACL Guardians	.262	55	1810	377	474	99	28	38	310	317	547	120	.378	.410
ACL Reds	.258	56	1762	385	455	114	20	41	321	328	593	105	.384	.415
ACL Rangers	.254	56	1842	332	468	104	32	49	276	223	602	116	.348	.425
ACL Dodgers	.251	56	1761	341	442	84	18	40	279	322	513	74	.377	.387
ACL D-backs Black	.249	56	1601	256	398	80	19	27	222	224	457	69	.354	.373
ACL Giants Black	.247	56	1619	308	400	78	7	49	264	275	576	49	.374	.395
ACL Athletics	.239	56	1759	345	420	89	18	23	272	324	534	76	.368	.349
ACL White Sox	.237	56	1771	240	420	81	11	23	201	219	536	85	.333	.334

CLUB PITCHING

	ERA	G	CG	SHO	SV	IP	H	R	ER	HR	BB	SO	AVG
ACL Rockies	4.32	55	0	2	12	444	423	235	213	23	196	518	.251
ACL Giants Black	4.36	56	1	3	16	417	419	249	202	29	163	486	.258
ACL Dodgers	4.64	56	0	0	15	460	420	281	237	40	239	607	.242
ACL D-backs Red	4.95	55	1	1	12	427	408	270	235	37	266	469	.251
ACL White Sox	5.07	56	1	3	14	467	465	311	263	37	263	527	.257
ACL Giants Orange	5.25	56	1	3	9	423	405	282	247	29	234	475	.248
ACL Mariners	5.29	56	0	2	18	422	397	282	248	29	266	462	.249
ACL Athletics	5.39	56	0	1	8	454	510	379	272	36	273	483	.281
ACL Royals	5.69	56	0	1	14	459	492	337	290	34	221	552	.268
ACL Brewers	5.78	56	0	0	13	470	476	365	302	39	323	539	.263
ACL Rangers	5.89	56	0	0	11	473	479	374	310	47	301	611	.259
ACL Angels	5.92	56	0	1	9	453	493	356	298	37	252	472	.275
ACL Padres	6.09	56	1	2	8	451	484	356	305	33	296	543	.273
ACL Reds	6.15	56	0	1	10	464	516	381	317	39	277	568	.281
ACL D-backs Black	7.22	56	0	2	11	419	468	389	336	36	308	473	.282
ACL Cubs	7.74	55	0	2	5	434	464	451	373	39	376	487	.275
ACL Guardians	8.11	55	0	1	9	456	516	464	411	34	385	543	.285

CLUB FIELDING

	PCT	PO	A	E	DP
ACL Rockies	.979	1332	459	39	40
ACL Mariners	.966	1267	425	59	48
ACL D-backs Red	.966	1282	461	61	48
ACL Giants Orange	.964	1271	398	63	34
ACL Giants Black	.963	1250	427	64	44
ACL Padres	.963	1352	454	70	38
ACL White Sox	.961	1399	487	76	37
ACL Dodgers	.961	1380	472	75	43
ACL Cubs	.959	1302	435	75	44
ACL Brewers	.959	1410	487	82	58
ACL D-backs Black	.958	1256	424	73	38
ACL Guardians	.958	1369	419	79	44
ACL Angels	.955	1360	496	87	39
ACL Royals	.955	1377	433	85	26
ACL Reds	.955	1391	475	88	36
ACL Rangers	.953	1420	442	92	36
ACL Athletics	.949	1364	475	98	49

INDIVIDUAL BATTING

Batter, Club	AVG	G	AB	R	H	2B	3B	HR	RBI	BB	SO	SB
Cesar Quintas, ACL Giants Black	.372	42	129	26	48	10	0	1	17	22	39	3
Juan Baez, ACL Brewers Gold	.370	48	192	39	71	16	4	4	42	8	23	17
Dylan O'Rae, ACL Brewers Gold	.362	37	130	44	47	4	1	0	15	40	23	28
Romeo Sanabria, ACL Padres	.359	50	167	36	60	15	2	8	53	30	48	4
Jefferson Pena, ACL D-backs Red	.351	43	154	32	54	11	3	1	27	18	43	15
Ricardo Cabrera, ACL Reds	.350	39	143	41	50	7	4	5	21	21	35	21
Jaison Chourio, ACL Guardians	.349	39	149	40	52	12	1	1	25	38	37	19
Ronny Hernandez, ACL White Sox	.338	45	148	20	50	12	1	3	36	22	35	1
Derlin Figueroa, ACL Dodgers/ACL Royals	.328	42	128	30	42	14	0	5	29	28	29	6
Erick Torres, ACL Royals	.319	36	138	29	44	5	5	0	18	16	20	11

INDIVIDUAL PITCHING

Pitcher, Club	W	L	ERA	G	GS	CG	SV	IP	H	R	ER	BB	SO
Manuel Olivares, ACL Rockies	5	0	3.70	11	8	0	0	49	56	25	20	13	40
Gabriel Rodriguez, ACL White Sox	2	1	3.78	14	9	0	1	48	48	22	20	24	61
Ubert Mejias, ACL Giants Black	4	3	3.90	14	11	0	0	62	66	29	27	17	56
Denny Larrondo, ACL D-backs Red	2	0	4.01	12	12	1	0	49	44	23	22	30	54
Ricardo Brizuela, ACL White Sox	3	4	4.62	14	5	1	1	51	51	33	26	16	55
Frankeli Arias, ACL White Sox	3	2	4.67	13	10	0	0	54	55	32	28	23	52
Samir Chires, ACL Giants Orange	3	3	4.68	13	5	0	1	50	35	27	26	27	47
Dawry Segura, ACL Angels	3	3	4.69	11	6	0	0	48	56	35	25	12	29
Alix Hernandez, ACL Giants Orange	3	3	4.73	14	5	1	0	51	35	27	27	27	69
Cesar Perdomo, ACL Giants Black	5	4	5.55	15	5	0	0	60	81	50	37	19	53

DEPARTMENT LEADERS

BATTING

OBP	Dylan O'Rae, ACL Brewers	.522
SLG	Romeo Sanabria, ACL Padres	.617
OPS	Romeo Sanabri, ACL Padres	1.06
R	Fadriel Cruz, ACL Rockies	52
H	Juan BaezACL Brewers Gold	71
TB	Echedry Vargas, ACL Rangers	112
XBH	Echedry Vargas, ACL Rangers	27
2B	Fran Alduey, ACL Guardians	19
3B	Samuel Munoz, ACL Dodgers	7
HR	Jeral Perez, ACL Dodgers	11
HR	Echedry Vargas, ACL Rangers	11
RBI	Romeo Sanabria, ACL Padres	53
SAC	Edgar Alfonso, ACL Angels	4
SAC	Luis Rodriguez, ACL Angels	4
BB	Jose Meza, ACL Dodgers	55
HBP	Cesar Quintas, ACL Giants Black	15
SO	Chandler Pollard, ACL Rangers	79
SB	Capri Ortiz, ACL Angels	30
CS	Capri Ortiz, ACL Angels	7

FIELDING

C PCT	Carlos Rojas, ACL Dodgers	.990
PO	Carlos Rojas, ACL Dodgers	355
A	Carlos Rojas, ACL Dodgers	37
DP	Carlos Rojas, ACL Dodgers	7
E	Javier Pariguan, ACL Athletics	8
CS	Carlos Rojas, ACL Dodgers	17
SB	Adan Sanchez, ACL Cubs	67
PB	Ronny Hernandez, ACL White Sox	12
1B PCT	Romeo Sanabria, ACL Padres	.997
PO	Romeo Sanabria, ACL Padres	275
A	Luis ReyesACL Reds	18
DP	Romeo Sanabria, ACL Padres	28
E	Mario Gomez, ACL Athletics	8
2B PCT	Jose Serrano, ACL Reds	.957
PO	Jose Serrano, ACL Reds	53
A	Jose Serrano, ACL Reds	82
DP	Jose Serrano, ACL Reds	16
DP	Dylan O'Rae, ACL Brewers Gold	16
E	Jose Serrano, ACL Reds	6
E	Adrian Rodriguez, ACL D-backs Red	6
3B PCT	Ruben Santana, ACL D-backs Black	.896
PO	Juan Aparicio, ACL D-backs Black/ACL D-backs Red	24
PO	Elian Rayo, ACL Giants Black	24
A	Elian Rayo, ACL Giants Black	70
DP	Arxy Hernandez, ACL White Sox	11
E	Arxy Hernandez, ACL White Sox	10
E	Ruben Santana, ACL D-backs Black	10
SS PCT	Capri Ortiz, ACL Angels	.947
PO	Ryan Burrowes, ACL White Sox	50
A	Capri Ortiz, ACL Angels	96
DP	Adrian Rodriguez, ACL D-backs Red	20
E	Ryan Reckley, ACL Giants Black	23
OF PCT	5 tied	1.000
PO	Cristian Lopez, ACL D-backs Black	97
A	Cristian Lopez, ACL D-backs Black	9
DP	George Feliz, ACL Mariners	3
E	Esmith Pineda, ACL Reds	7

PITCHING

G	Alan Perdomo, ACL Rockies	24
GS	Denny Larrondo, ACL D-backs Red	12
GF	Dailoui Abad, ACL Dodgers	16
SV	Dailoui Abad, ACL Dodgers	11
W	Alan Perdomo, ACL Rockies	6
W	David Morillo, ACL Mariners	6
L	5 tied	6
IP	Ubert Mejias, ACL Giants Black	62.1
H	Cesar Perdomo, ACL Giants Black	81
R	Mark McLaughlin, ACL White Sox	51
ER	Joneiker Arellano, ACL Reds	45
HBP	Abdiel Medina, ACL Mariners	11
BB	Jose Contreras, ACL Guardians	36
BB	Henrison Mota, ACL Brewers Gold	36
SO	Alix Hernandez, ACL Giants Orange	69
SO/9	Alix Hernandez, ACL Giants Orange	12.1
BB/9	Dawry Segura, ACL Angels	2.25
WP	Frederic Garcia, ACL Guardians	18
WP	Lisander De La Cruz, ACL Giants Orange	18
Balks	2 tied	8
HR	Moises Lira, ACL D-backs Black, ACL D-backs Red	10
BAA	Alix Hernandez, ACL Giants Orange	.191

FLORIDA COMPLEX LEAGUE

Awards selected by Major League Baseball

CHAMPION: The Braves swept the Yankees in the FCL championship series, winning Game 2 by a score of 9-1. In the finale, Braves lefthander Rolando Gutierrez allowed one unearned run in six innings, striking out two and allowing three hits to pick up the win. Shortstop Diego Benitez went 2-for-4 with a triple, a walk, two runs and an RBI. The Yankees led the FCL in runs scored and OPS, but Braves pitchers kept their bats in check, allowing three runs in two games.

MOST VALUABLE PLAYER: Second-year pro Dakota Kotowski, who signed with the Phillies as an undrafted free agent out of Missouri State in 2022, led the FCL with 15 home runs, a .653 slugging percentage and 1.050 OPS. The 23-year-old, righthanded first baseman advanced to Low-A Clearwater on Aug. 22.

PITCHER OF THE YEAR: The Marlins signed righthander Santiago Suarez out of Venezuela in 2022 then dealt him to the Rays that November. In his first season with the Rays, Suarez pitched his way to Low-A Charleston in mid August after dominating the FCL as an 18-year-old. In Rookie ball, he went 4-0, 1.13 in 10 appearances, striking out 38 and walking eight in 39.2 innings.

TOP MLB PROSPECT: The Yankees signed Venezuelan shortstop Keiner Delgado in 2021. Two years later he broke out as a 19-year-old in the FCL, batting .293/.414/.485 with eight home runs in 49 games. Delgado led the league with 54 runs and 36 stolen bases. Primarily a second baseman, he saw time at shortstop and third as well.

MANAGER OF THE YEAR: James Cooper's Yankees squad went 33-22 for the second-best record in the FCL. But the level of talent on his club was second to none, led by shortstop Roderick Arias, second baseman Keiner Delgado, third baseman Enmanuel Tejeda, outfielder John Cruz, lefthander Henry Lalane and righthander Carlos Lagrange. Multiple scouts regarded the 2023 FCL Yankees as one of the more talented Rookie affiliates they had ever evaluated.

Keiner Delgado

MIKE JANES/FOUR SEAM IMAGES

FLORIDA COMPLEX LEAGUE ALL-STARS

Pos	Player	Team	AVG	OPS	HR
C	Josue Briceno	Tigers	.325	.954	7
1B	Dakota Kotowski	Phillies	.287	1.050	15
2B	Keiner Delgado	Yankees	.293	.899	8
SS	Roderick Arias	Yankees	.267	.928	6
3B	Enmanuel Tejeda	Yankees	.307	.923	5
OF	Willy Montero	Yankees	.331	.825	2
OF	Natanael Yuten	Red Sox	.336	.879	3
OF	John Cruz	Yankees	.294	.907	10
DH	Ronald Hernandez	Marlins/Mets	.295	.937	4
UT	Clayton Campbell	Tigers	.284	.930	3

Pos	Pitcher	Team	G	ERA	SO
SP	Santiago Suarez	Rays	10	1.13	38
SP	Giussepe Velasquez	Phillies	8	1.35	28
SP	Fernando Perez	Blue Jays	11	2.72	57
SP	Joe Adametz	Tigers	8	2.92	28
RP	Samuel Mejia	Rays	16	1.46	32
RP	Sebastian Keane	Yankees	18	1.71	35

OVERALL STANDINGS

East Division	W	L	PCT	GB	Manager
FCL Mets	32	18	.640	—	Jay Pecci
FCL Marlins	27	25	.519	6.0	Luis Dorante
FCL Astros Blue	26	25	.510	6.5	Carlos Lugo
FCL Nationals	24	25	.490	7.5	Luis Ordaz
FCL Cardinals	17	33	.340	15.0	Roberto Espinoza

North Division	W	L	PCT	GB	Manager
FCL Yankees	33	22	.600	—	James Cooper
FCL Phillies	30	25	.545	3.0	Shawn Williams
FCL Tigers	29	25	.537	3.5	Mike Alvarez
FCL Blue Jays	17	37	.315	15.5	Jose Mayorga

South Division	W	L	PCT	GB	Manager(s)
FCL Pirates	32	23	.582	—	Jim Horner/Jose Mosquera
FCL Braves	30	24	.556	1.5	Nestor Perez
FCL Red Sox	28	25	.528	3.0	Jimmy Gonzalez/Tom Kotchman
FCL Twins	25	29	.463	6.5	Seth Feldman
FCL Rays	25	29	.463	6.5	Frank Maldonado
FCL Orioles	22	32	.407	9.5	Christian Frias

CLUB BATTING

	AVG	G	AB	R	H	2B	3B	HR	RBI	BB	SO	SB	OBP	SLG
FCL Yankees	.281	55	1807	367	508	84	23	49	321	302	433	129	.397	.434
FCL Red Sox	.266	53	1659	295	441	94	17	27	245	256	466	109	.378	.392
FCL Phillies	.261	55	1799	358	470	105	13	47	301	257	470	61	.373	.412
FCL Tigers	.259	54	1802	363	467	107	17	51	309	304	518	83	.379	.422
FCL Pirates	.259	55	1799	365	466	94	21	32	295	342	471	135	.391	.388
FCL Nationals	.257	49	1481	295	380	67	15	25	250	250	423	53	.376	.373
FCL Marlins	.246	52	1639	327	403	73	14	21	262	324	405	86	.376	.346
FCL Orioles	.245	54	1687	288	414	81	16	40	235	260	452	93	.358	.384
FCL Mets	.244	50	1553	272	379	73	13	26	227	283	403	64	.367	.358
FCL Astros	.237	51	1588	283	377	89	2	53	245	269	399	78	.363	.396
FCL Twins	.230	54	1633	255	375	71	10	37	222	255	474	59	.346	.353
FCL Rays	.221	54	1767	247	391	72	12	21	205	248	451	60	.328	.311
FCL Braves	.220	54	1727	275	380	68	16	19	223	286	523	87	.343	.311
FCL Cardinals	.215	50	1545	232	332	68	15	30	202	255	500	57	.343	.337
FCL Blue Jays	.201	54	1638	255	330	70	7	35	207	319	557	64	.349	.317

CLUB PITCHING

	ERA	G	CG	SHO	SV	IP	H	R	ER	HR	BB	SO	AVG
FCL Rays	3.82	54	0	2	14	474	391	257	201	23	298	531	.226
FCL Pirates	4.22	55	0	2	11	473	390	280	222	23	309	516	.221
FCL Mets	4.32	50	0	3	14	415	344	253	199	29	271	473	.223
FCL Yankees	4.47	55	0	3	9	463	390	288	230	41	286	587	.222
FCL Red Sox	4.56	53	0	0	12	431	388	263	218	29	225	406	.242
FCL Braves	4.69	54	0	2	16	472	429	282	246	35	249	409	.244
FCL Twins	4.80	54	0	3	10	439	432	296	234	37	238	513	.254
FCL Marlins	4.83	52	0	3	11	427	372	270	229	28	287	401	.235
FCL Cardinals	5.18	50	0	4	8	417	410	288	240	26	253	433	.254
FCL Astros	5.30	51	0	2	6	420	328	285	247	29	346	483	.213
FCL Tigers	5.77	54	0	2	9	465	433	345	298	47	322	454	.247
FCL Orioles	5.78	54	0	2	8	442	437	347	284	29	328	462	.255
FCL Phillies	6.01	55	0	2	17	466	459	344	311	46	344	474	.262
FCL Nationals	6.16	49	1	1	8	386	417	313	264	43	224	340	.273
FCL Blue Jays	6.39	54	0	2	6	445	493	366	316	48	230	463	.277

CLUB FIELDING

	PCT	PO	A	E	DP
FCL Tigers	.970	1394	521	60	39
FCL Phillies	.968	1398	534	63	58
FCL Rays	.967	1421	517	66	49
FCL Marlins	.966	1281	458	61	49
FCL Braves	.966	1416	514	68	42
FCL Astros	.963	1259	420	64	39
FCL Pirates	.961	1419	441	76	47
FCL Red Sox	.959	1292	478	75	53
FCL Blue Jays	.958	1335	427	77	39
FCL Orioles	.958	1326	436	78	39
FCL Nationals	.956	1158	393	72	30
FCL Yankees	.955	1388	425	85	30
FCL Mets	.954	1244	396	79	36
FCL Twins	.950	1316	417	91	39
FCL Cardinals	.949	1250	417	90	43

INDIVIDUAL BATTING

Batter, Club	AVG	G	AB	R	H	2B	3B	HR	RBI	BB	SO	SB
Natanael Yuten, FCL Red Sox	.336	38	149	28	50	9	2	3	32	11	36	8
Willy Montero, FCL Yankees	.331	47	181	30	60	9	2	2	43	16	36	5
Raylin Heredia, FCL Phillies	.326	35	141	30	46	9	4	4	25	17	42	7
Josue Briceno, FCL Tigers	.325	44	169	40	55	13	2	7	37	23	28	3
Esmerlyn Valdez, FCL Pirates	.312	40	141	23	44	9	1	6	32	15	36	3
Enmanuel Tejeda, FCL Yankees	.307	50	166	37	51	4	3	5	30	44	44	24
Jeral Toledo, FCL Pirates	.306	38	121	26	37	9	3	2	21	24	25	11
Johanfran Garcia, FCL Red Sox	.302	42	149	21	45	10	2	5	32	19	37	3
Samuel Gil, FCL Tigers	.298	44	161	34	48	7	2	2	18	29	32	7
Ronald Hernandez, FCL Marlins/FCL Mets	.295	45	139	33	41	9	1	4	36	47	37	4

INDIVIDUAL PITCHING

Pitcher, Club	W	L	ERA	G	GS	CG	SV	IP	H	R	ER	BB	SO
Fernando Perez, FCL Blue Jays	2	2	2.72	11	10	0	0	50	35	17	15	12	57
Darlin Saladin, FCL Cardinals	2	4	2.85	12	11	0	0	47	39	16	15	21	47
Gerado Salas, FCL Cardinals	2	1	3.21	11	10	0	0	48	46	25	17	16	39
Rolando Gutierrez, FCL Braves	4	2	4.30	13	8	0	0	52	47	29	25	19	41
Davis Polo, FCL Braves	1	4	4.40	13	9	0	0	45	37	23	22	14	32
Gabriel Agostini, FCL Nationals	2	6	4.53	11	7	0	0	44	36	25	22	19	38

DEPARTMENT LEADERS

BATTING

OPS	Dakota Kotowski, FCL Phillies	1.050
R	Keiner Delgado, FCL Yankees	54
H	Willy Montero, FCL Yankees	60
TB	Dakota Kotowski, FCL Phillies	98
XBH	Dakota Kotowski, FCL Phillies	24
2B	Clayton Campbell, FCL Tigers	16
3B	3 tied	4
HR	Dakota Kotowski, FCL Phillies	15
RBI	John Cruz, FCL Yankees	47
SAC	Cristhian Vaquero, FCL Nationals	4
BB	Marco Vargas, FCL Marlins/FCL Mets	48
HBP	Axiel Plaz, FCL Pirates	12
SO	Jose Gerardo, FCL Marlins	96
SB	Keiner Delgado, FCL Yankees	36
CS	Ricardo Gonzalez, FCL Rays	8
CS	Cristhian Vaquero, FCL Nationals	8

FIELDING

C PO	Edinson Duran, FCL Yankees	306
A	Edinson Duran, FCL Yankees	26
DP	Diego Viloria, FCL Red Sox	3
DP	Jared Thomas, FCL Phillies	3
E	Daniel Pena, FCL Twins	9
CS	Edinson Duran, FCL Yankees	18
SB	Daniel Pena, FCL Twins	54
PB	Yasmil Bucce, FCL Orioles	9
1B PCT	Dakota Kotowski, FCL Phillies	.992
PO	Julio Henriquez, FCL Marlins	266
A	Dakota Kotowski, FCL Phillies	21
DP	Julio Henriquez, FCL Marlins	27
E	Enger Castellano, FCL Yankees	10
2B PCT	Junior Sanchez, FCL Marlins	.984
PO	Junior Sanchez, FCL Marlins	79
A	Junior Sanchez, FCL Marlins	100
DP	Junior Sanchez, FCL Marlins	27
E	Jesus Bae, FCL Mets	7
E	Misael Mojica, FCL Nationals	7
3B PCT	No Qualifier	
PO	Yonatan Henriquez, FCL Mets	25
A	Luis Sanchez, FCL Braves	61
DP	Luis Sanchez, FCL Braves	7
E	Jorgelys Mota, FCL Nationals	10
SS PCT	Javier Rivas, FCL Pirates	.967
PO	Diego Benitez, FCL Braves	65
A	Marvin Alcantara, FCL Red Sox	85
A	Diego Benitez, FCL Braves	85
DP	Javier Rivas, FCL Pirates	22
E	Diego Benitez, FCL Braves	14
OF PCT	2 tied	1.000
PO	Cristhian Vaquero, FCL Nationals	96
A	Kelvin Diaz, FCL Red Sox	9
DP	Douglas Glod, FCL Braves	3
DP	Thomas Sosa, FCL Orioles	3
E	5 tied	6

PITCHING

G	Antoni Cuello, FCL Cardinals	21
G	Harif Frias, FCL Orioles	21
GS	3 tied	11
GF	Luis Gomez, FCL Phillies	17
SV	Luis Gomez, FCL Phillies	10
W	Jordarlin Mendoza, FCL Yankees	6
L	Gabriel Agostini, FCL Nationals	6
L	Carlos Gutierrez, FCL Twins	6
L	Liomar Martinez, FCL Marlins	6
IP	Rolando Gutierrez, FCL Braves	52.1
H	Maikel Hernandez, FCL Rays	54
R	Gabriel Torres, FCL Tigers	38
ER	Cesar Ayala, FCL Blue Jays	33
HBP	Cole Stupp, FCL Tigers	12
HBP	Enrique Segura, FCL Phillies	12
BB	Abel Mercedes, FCL Astros Blue	38
SO	Carlos Lagrange, FCL Yankees	63
SO/9	Fernando Perez,FCL Blue Jays	10.3
BB/9	Fernando Perez, FCL Blue Jays	2.2
WP	Abel Mercedes, FCL Astros Blue	20
Balks	Wilson Esterlin, FCL Mets	6
HR	Cesar Ayala, FCL Blue Jays	9
BAA	Fernando Perez, FCL Blue Jays	.198

ALL-STAR FUTURES GAME

BY GEOFF PONTES

We have singled out the prospects whose tools shined brightest in this year's Futures Game.

BEST PLAYER: Nasim Nunez, SS, Marlins

The infielder came to the plate once and connected for an RBI double that plated three runs. While he's an unlikely hero, Nunez came through in a clutch moment to deliver a death blow to the AL's chances of a comeback.

BEST HITTER: Colt Keith, 3B, Tigers

The Tigers' infielder was one of the hottest hitters in the minor leagues entering the break and he didn't slow down during the Futures Game. Keith connected for a single in the fourth and then walked in the sixth, getting on base twice without making an out.

BEST POWER: Brady House, 3B, Nationals

House showed his ability to impact the baseball before the game in batting practice but also during the game by hitting a 104.2 mph single off of Sem Robberse. This was the hardest hit non-out of the game, and it came during an inning when the National League scored three runs.

BEST PITCHER: Joey Cantillo, LHP, Guardians

Going to a pitcher for five outs in the Futures Game is highly unusual but Cantillo did it in style. His fastball topped out at 97.9 mph, which was his season high, and he generated four of his five whiffs against the pitch. Cantillo used four pitches—his four-seam fastball, slider, changeup and curveball, throwing 24 pitches total. Cantillo came on for Will Klein in the top of the second inning, striking out two and walking one.

BEST FASTBALL: Jacob Misiorowski, RHP, Brewers

Misiorowski's fastball was electric—the Brewers righthander hit 102.4 mph and touched 100 mph 10 times during his inning of work. His fastball generated three whiffs on seven swings and his softest fastball of the game was still harder than all but one fastball (Luis Guerrero 100 mph) by any other pitcher.

BEST BREAKING BALL: David Festa, RHP, Twins

Festa threw his slider four times during his inning of work and generated three whiffs on three swings for a 100% swing rate.

BEST CHANGEUP: Carson Whisenhunt, LHP, Giants

Whisenhunt possesses a truly dominant changeup and the pitch performed as it was supposed to, generating two whiffs on two swings for a 100% whiff rate. Whisenhunt got the No. 2 prospect in baseball, Jackson Holliday, to swing through one.

FUTURES GAME BOX SCORE

NATIONAL LEAGUE 5, AMERICAN LEAGUE 0
JULY 8 IN SEATTLE

AL	AB	R	H	RBI	NL	AB	R	H	RBI
Clase, CF	2	0	0	0	Crow-Armstrong, CF	2	0	0	0
Jones, CF	1	0	0	0	Scott II, PH-DH	2	0	1	0
Mayer, SS	1	0	1	0	Lawlar, SS	2	0	0	0
Holliday, SS	1	0	0	0	Merrill, PH-SS	2	0	0	0
Paris, SS	2	0	0	0	Chourio, LF	4	0	0	0
Kjerstad, RF	2	0	1	0	Wood, RF	1	0	0	0
Gilbert, RF	2	0	1	0	Fernandez, RF	2	1	1	0
Ford, H, C	1	0	0	0	Marte, N, 3B	2	1	0	0
Quero, PH-C	3	0	0	0	House, 3B	1	1	1	0
Butler, L, LF	3	0	0	0	Rodríguez, E, 1B	0	1	0	0
Caminero, 3B	1	0	0	0	Murray Jr., 1B	1	0	0	0
b-Keith, C, PH-3B	1	0	1	0	Quero, C	2	0	1	1
Soderstrom, 1B	2	0	1	0	Rushing, C	0	1	0	0
Malloy, DH	1	0	0	0	Bliss, 2B	1	0	0	0
Yorke, 2B	3	0	1	0	Nuñez, 2B	1	0	1	3
					Crawford, DH-CF	2	0	0	1
Totals	**26**	**0**	**6**	**0**	**Totals**	**25**	**5**	**5**	**5**

NATIONAL LEAGUE	**020**	**003**	**0**	**5**	**5**	**0**
AMERICAN LEAGUE	**000**	**000**	**0**	**0**	**6**	**0**

NL: 2B: Nuñez (1, Zulueta). **TB:** Fernandez; House; Nuñez 2; Quero; Scott II. **RBI**: Crawford (1); Nuñez 3 (3); Quero (1). **Runners left in scoring position, 2 out**: Bliss; Scott II; Chourio; Crow-Armstrong. SF: Crawford. **Team RISP**: 2-for-9. **Team LOB: 5. SB:** Marte, N (1, 3rd base off Klein/Ford, H); Scott II 2 (2, 2nd base off Festa/Quero, 3rd base off Festa/Quero); Nuñez (1, 3rd base off Zulueta/Quero). **PB:** Quero (1). **DP**: (Merrill-Nuñez-Murray Jr.).

AL: 2B: Yorke (1, Schwellenbach). **TB:** Gilbert; Keith, C; Kjerstad; Mayer; Soderstrom; Yorke 2. **Runners left in scoring position, 2 out:** Yorke 3; Gilbert; Ford, H. **GIDP:** Quero. **Team RISP:** 0-for-8. **Team LOB:** 10. **SB:** Mayer (1, 2nd base off Abel/Quero).

AL	IP	H	R	ER	BB	SO	NL	IP	H	R	ER	BB	SO
White	1	0	0	0	0	1	Abel (W)	1	1	0	0	0	2
Klein (L)	0.1	1	2	2	2	0	Hence	1	1	0	0	1	1
Cantillo	1.2	0	0	0	1	2	Whisenhunt	1	1	0	0	0	2
Cannon	1	0	0	0	1	1	Misiorowski	1	1	0	0	0	3
Festa	1	1	0	0	0	1	Schwellenbach	1	1	0	0	0	2
Robberse	0.1	2	2	2	0	1	Massey	1	0	0	0	3	1
Zulueta	0.2	1	1	1	0	2	Vasil	0.1	0	0	0	1	1
Beeter	0.2	0	0	0	0	1	Monteverde	0.2	1	0	0	0	0
Guerrero	0.1	0	0	0	0	1							
Totals	**7**	**5**	**5**	**5**	**4**	**10**	**Totals**	**7**	**6**	**0**	**0**	**5**	**12**

HBP: Rushing (by Zulueta). **Inherited runners-scored**: Monteverde 1-0; Cantillo 2-1; Zulueta 2-2.

Umpires: **HP**: Macon Hammond. **1B**: Willie Traynor. **2B**: Steven Rios Jr. **3B**: Rainiero Valero. **Official Scorer**: Darin Padur. **Weather**: 72 degrees, Clear. Wind: 4 mph, R To L. **First pitch:** 4:11 PM. **T**: 2:12.

MINOR LEAGUE BEST TOOLS

	INTERNATIONAL LEAGUE	PACIFIC COAST LEAGUE	EASTERN LEAGUE	SOUTHERN LEAGUE	TEXAS LEAGUE
Best Batting Prospect	Elly De La Cruz	Michael Busch	Jackson Holliday	Jackson Chourio	Evan Carter
Best Power Prospect	Elly De La Cruz	Jo Adell	James Wood	Owen Caissie	Joey Loperfido
Best Strike-Zone Judgment	Wilyer Abreu	Michael Stefanic	Jasson Dominguez	Tyler Black	Evan Carter
Best Baserunner	Cam Eden	Matthew Batten	Ceddanne Rafaela	Nasim Nunez	Luisangel Acuña
Fastest Baserunner	Elly De La Cruz	Bubba Thompson	Johan Rojas	Mason Auer	Jonatan Clase
Best Pitching Prospect	Gavin Williams	Kyle Harrison	Ricky Tiedemann	Eury Perez	Emmet Sheehan
Best Fastball	Gavin Williams	Kyle Harrison	Ricky Tiedemann	Jacob Misiorowski	Emmet Sheehan
Best Breaking Pitch	Will Warren	J.P. France	Orion Kerkering	Connor Phillips	Prelander Berroa
Best Changeup	Grayson Rodriguez	Gavin Stone	Carson Whisenhunt	Patrick Monteverde	Devin Sweet
Best Control	Mitch Spence	Cody Bradford	Richard Fitts	Sean Hunley	Landon Knack
Best Reliever	Gerson Moreno	Matt Festa	Luis Guerrero	Jefry Yan	Devin Sweet
Best Defensive C	Chuckie Robinson	Korey Lee	Drew Romo	Will Banfield	Pedro Pages
Best Defensive 1B	Spencer Horwitz	Michael Toglia	Grant Lavigne	Haydn McGeary	Robbie Tenerowicz
Best Defensive 2B	Nick Sogard	Michael Stefanic	Nick Yorke	Nasim Nunez	Ryan Bliss
Best Defensive 3B	Jordan Westburg	Aaron Schunk	Chase Meidroth	BJ Murray Jr.	Kody Hoese
Best Defensive SS	Oswald Peraza	Blaze Alexander	Marcelo Mayer	Luis Vazquez	Jordan Lawlar
Best Infield Arm	Elly De La Cruz	Casey Schmitt	Julio Carreras	Nasim Nunez	Luisangel Acuña
Best Defensive OF	Ceddanne Rafaela	Drew Avans	Johan Rojas	Pete Crow-Armstrong	Victor Scott II
Best OF Arm	Wilyer Abreu	Nolan Jones	Matt Gorski	Yoelqui Cespedes	Jose Ramos
Most Exciting Player	Elly De La Cruz	Luis Matos	Jackson Holliday	Jackson Chourio	Jordan Lawlar
Best Manager Prospect	Chad Tracy	Travis Barbary	Callix Crabbe	Kevin Randel	Mike Freeman

	MIDWEST LEAGUE	NORTHWEST LEAGUE	SOUTH ATLANTIC LEAGUE	CALIFORNIA LEAGUE	CAROLINA LEAGUE	FLORIDA STATE LEAGUE
Best Batting Prospect	Jackson Merrill	Sterlin Thompson	Jackson Holliday	Ethan Salas	Samuel Basallo	Termarr Johnson
Best Power Prospect	Nathan Martorella	Yanquiel Fernandez	Abimelec Ortiz	Ryan Ritter	Xavier Isaac	Termarr Johnson
Best Strike-Zone Judgment	Jakob Marsee	Harry Ford	Jackson Holliday	Cole Young	Ahbram Liendo	Jett Williams
Best Baserunner	Victor Scott	Joe Stewart	Jacob Melton	Nelson Rada	Chandler Simpson	Seth Stephenson
Fastest Baserunner	Victor Scott	Jonatan Clase	Luis Valdez	Nelson Rada	Chandler Simpson	Justin Crawford
Best Pitching Prospect	Jacob Misiorowski	Yu-Min Lin	Chase Hampton	Payton Martin	Jacob Misiorowski	Karson Milbrandt
Best Fastball	Zach Maxwell	Yilber Diaz	Bubba Chandler	Livan Reinoso	Jacob Misiorowski	Orion Kerkering
Best Breaking Pitch	Jackson Jobe	Yu-Min Lin	Orion Kerkering	Ricardo Yan	Jacob Misiorowski	Orion Kerkering
Best Changeup	Julian Aguiar	Carson Whisenhunt	Drew Thorpe	Carson Whisenhunt	Jake Bennett	Estibenzon Jimenez
Best Control	Trent Baker	Yu-Min Lin	Drew Thorpe	Mason Albright	Marcus Johnson	Hansel Rincon
Best Reliever	Jake Pilarski	Angel Chivilli	Orion Kerkering	Zach Agnos	Adrian Rodriguez	Orion Kerkering
Best Defensive C	Mat Nelson	Adrian Sugastey	Silas Ardoin	Kody Huff	Jhon Garcia	Logan Tanner
Best Defensive 1B	Ruben Ibarra	Tyler Locklear	Rixon Wingrove	Matt Coutney	Branden Boissiere	Peyton Williams
Best Defensive 2B	Jace Jung	Nic Kent	Tsung-Che Cheng	Diego Velazquez	Jadher Areinamo	Jared Serna
Best Defensive 3B	Dayan Frias	Ben Ramirez	Junior Caminero	Skyler Messinger	Brady House	Jack Brannigan
Best Defensive SS	Edwin Arroyo	Aeverson Arteaga	Marcelo Mayer	Jose Izarra	Gregory Barrios	Bryan Rincon
Best Infield Arm	Yiddi Cappe	Arol Vera	Carson Williams	Jose Fernandez	Cam Cauley	Bryan Rincon
Best Defensive OF	Kevin Alcantara	Grant McCray	James Wood	Nelson Rada	Luis Lara	Justin Crawford
Best Outfield Arm	Emmanuel Rodriguez	Yanquiel Fernandez	Stanley Consuegra	Gabriel Gonzalez	Elijah Green	Cade Fergus
Most Exciting Player	Jackson Merrill	Yanquiel Fernandez	Jackson Holliday	Ethan Salas	Chandler Simpson	Jared Serna
Best Manager Prospect	Daniel Nava	Brent Lavallee	Greg Brodzinski	Jeremiah Knackstedt	Jake Lowery	Andrew Graham

DOMINICAN SUMMER LEAGUE

Awards selected by Major League Baseball

CHAMPION: Dodgers Bautista defeated Pirates Gold 9-5 in the DSL championship game. It was the record ninth title for a Dodgers' DSL affiliate.

MOST VALUABLE PLAYER: Rockies 18-year-old shortstop Kelvin Hidalgo hit .310/.406/.574 with 12 home runs and a league-leading 54 RBIs.

PITCHER OF THE YEAR: Angels 22-year-old reliever Ruben Castillo led the league with nine saves to go with a 2.37 ERA and 0.82 WHIP.

TOP MLB PROSPECT: Rangers 17-year-old outfielder Braylin Morel led the DSL with 32 extra-base hits while batting .344/.417/.644.

MANAGER OF THE YEAR: Dodgers Bautista manager Dunior Zerpa guided his prospect-studded team to a 42-11 record.

DOMINICAN SUMMER LEAGUE ALL-STARS

Pos	Player	Team	AVG	OPS	HR
C	Stiven Flores	White Sox	.391	.933	1
1B	Ronny Ugarte	Rockies	.335	.897	3
2B	Bairon Ledesma	Rockies	.335	.848	3
3B	Starlyn Nunez	Red Sox	.325	.870	4
SS	Kelvin Hidalgo	Rockies	.310	.980	12
OF	Braylin Morel	Rangers	.344	1.061	7
OF	Eduardo Quintero	Dodgers	.359	1.090	5
OF	Oliver Carrillo	Padres	.303	1.128	11
DH	Alfredo Duno	Reds	.303	.944	6
UT	Demetrio Nadal	Brewers	.342	1.003	2
Pos	**Pitcher**	**Team**	**G**	**ERA**	**SO**
SP	Harold Melenge	Mariners	12	1.42	48
SP	Enniel Cortez	Brewers	11	1.58	49
SP	Jesus Palacios	Orioles	11	1.95	60
SP	Adrian Acosta	Angels	10	1.17	64
RP	Victor Pena	Royals	13	0.86	44
RP	Ruben Castillo	Angels	18	2.37	46

DSL CHAMPIONSHIP: DSL Dodgers Bautista def. DSL Pirates Gold

BASEBALL CITY

Team	W	L	PCT	GB
DSL Padres Gold	37	17	.685	—
DSL Orioles Orange	35	19	.648	2.0
DSL White Sox	32	22	.593	5.0
DSL D-backs Black	30	25	.545	7.5
DSL Blue Jays	28	25	.528	8.5
DSL D-backs Red	21	33	.389	16.0
DSL Orioles Black	20	35	.364	17.5
DSL Padres	16	38	.296	21.0

NORTHWEST

Team	W	L	PCT	GB
DSL Astros Orange	35	19	.648	—
DSL Rays	33	22	.600	2.5
DSL Royals Blue	29	25	.537	6.0
DSL Astros Blue	29	26	.527	6.5
DSL Reds	28	26	.519	7.0
DSL Tampa Bay	24	31	.436	11.5
DSL Athletics	22	31	.415	12.5
DSL Royals Gold	22	32	.407	13.0

NORTHEAST

Team	W	L	PCT	GB
DSL Colorado	34	19	.642	—
DSL Yankees	33	19	.635	0.5
DSL Rangers Red	30	25	.545	5.0
DSL Rockies	29	24	.547	5.0
DSL Bombers	27	26	.509	7.0
DSL Mets Blue	26	28	.481	8.5
DSL Mets Orange	24	30	.444	10.5
DSL Marlins	22	30	.423	11.5
DSL Rangers Blue	19	36	.345	16.0
DSL Miami	18	35	.340	16.0

NORTH

Team	W	L	PCT	GB
DSL Dodgers Bautista	42	11	.792	—
DSL Dodgers Mega	36	17	.679	6.0
DSL Brewers 1	25	27	.481	16.5
DSL Guardians Red	25	27	.481	16.5
DSL Guardians Blue	23	20	.434	19.0
DSL Brewers 2	22	31	.415	20.0
DSL Braves	15	36	.294	26.0

SAN PEDRO

Team	W	L	PCT	GB
DSL Pirates Gold	41	12	.774	—
DSL Tigers 2	31	23	.574	10.5
DSL Red Sox Blue	28	26	.519	13.5
DSL Red Sox Red	26	26	.500	14.5
DSL Tigers 1	25	26	.490	15.0
DSL Cubs Red	24	28	.462	16.5
DSL Pirates Black	17	34	.333	23.0
DSL Cubs Blue	17	37	.315	24.5

SOUTH

Team	W	L	PCT	GB
DSL Phillies White	42	13	.764	—
DSL Angels	37	18	.673	5.0
DSL Giants Orange	30	23	.566	11.0
DSL Mariners	27	25	.519	13.5
DSL Phillies Red	27	26	.509	14.0
DSL Giants Black	27	26	.509	14.0
DSL Cardinals	17	36	.321	24.0
DSL Twins	14	37	.275	26.0
DSL Nationals	11	39	.220	28.5

INDIVIDUAL BATTING LEADERS

Player, Team	AVG	G	AB	R	H	2B	3B	HR	RBI	BB	SO	SB
Stiven Flores, White Sox	.391	37	128	15	50	8	0	1	33	15	7	7
Kevyn Castillo, Angels	.371	55	186	44	69	10	7	3	35	40	36	23
Eduardo Quintero, Dodgers Bautista	.359	49	170	54	61	15	7	5	42	32	34	22
Angel Diaz, Dodgers Mega	.353	39	133	31	47	10	0	7	33	23	21	2
Franklin Arias, Red Sox Red	.350	37	137	32	48	9	1	1	15	19	14	3
Yoeilin Cespedes, Red Sox Blue	.346	46	191	37	66	15	4	6	38	14	24	1
Braylin Morel, Rangers	.344	47	180	40	62	17	8	7	43	21	50	2
Demetrio Nadal, Brewers 2	.342	40	120	28	41	6	5	2	20	24	19	33
Adrian Gil, White Sox	.340	45	147	33	50	11	0	5	33	25	21	5
Roynier Hernandez, Colorado	.339	48	180	38	61	8	2	0	35	33	23	6

INDIVIDUAL PITCHING LEADERS

Player, Team	W	L	ERA	G	GS	CG	SV	IP	H	R	ER	BB	SO
Adrian Acosta, Angels	2	3	1.17	10	10	0	0	46	28	12	6	5	22
Harold Melenge, Mariners	3	0	1.42	12	8	0	1	51	38	10	8	2	8
Enniel Cortez, Brewers 1	4	1	1.58	11	8	1	0	46	35	12	8	3	5
Engert Garcia, Tampa Bay	3	3	1.58	11	9	1	0	46	36	16	8	5	8
Jeter Martinez, Seattle	2	2	1.72	10	8	1	0	47	17	15	9	3	20
Jesus Palacios, Orioles Black	3	0	1.95	11	11	0	0	51	37	14	11	5	13
Luis Gonzalez, Phillies Red, Phillies White	4	1	1.99	11	9	0	1	50	44	12	11	3	9
Richard Fernandez, Athletics	4	2	2.09	11	5	0	0	47	39	12	11	4	24
Emmanuel Martinez, Rangers Red	4	0	2.17	11	7	1	0	46	28	14	11	8	17

Excellence That Starts Off The Field

Triple-A

ALBUQUERQUE (PACIFIC COAST)

At an Albuquerque Isotopes game, it's common to hear a mariachi band playing somewhere in the ballpark. The Isotopes joined MiLB in an effort to connect to local Hispanic communities through the Copa de la Diversión.

For a few nights throughout the season, the Isotopes transform into the Mariachis de Nuevo México to honor local communities. For the third time since the program's inception in 2018, the Mariachis were announced the winner of the season-long event series.

The Isotopes work to create authentic and inclusive spaces for all fans every night of the season, even when the team doesn't don the special threads.

On any given day you will see fans cheering, hear the crack of a bat or smell popcorn cooking. However, in a quiet office tucked away inside the ballpark you will see a sign that says "This is someone's first Isotopes game."

John Traub, the vice president and general manager of the Isotopes, keeps these signs up to remind staff of the mission.

"We want to make that first impression as exciting as it was when 20 years ago somebody first gave us a chance (to bring our club here)," said Traub.

Double-A

AMARILLO (TEXAS)

There is something special cooking in Amarillo and not just at the concession stands.

For their consistent investment in the community and innovative new brands, the Amarillo Sod Poodles—or should we say Calf Fries?—are our choice as the 2023 recipients of the Double-A Freitas Award.

For six games throughout the 2023 MiLB season, the Diamondbacks' Double-A affiliate would no longer be the Sod Poodles. Rather, the organization would go by a new alternate identity, the Calf Fries.

The team's alternate identity was a fun way to engage the community and as a nod to a local delicacy. If you are not sure what Calf Fries are, you may know them by another name—Cowboy Caviar, Mountain Tenders or Rocky Mountain Oysters.

Baseball fans not only all over Amarillo, but all over the world loved the brand. In all, the organization sold Calf Fries merchandise to 44 states and 12 countries. Tony Ensor, president and general manager of the Sod Poodles was excited about the alternate identity—that was later named best alternate identity in MiLB this season by the league—but he had no idea how big it would be.

Class A

SOUTH BEND (MIDWEST)

Picture this. You walk into Four Winds Field, home of the South Bend Cubs, and decide to grab a hot dog at the concession stand. Behind the counter, you are greeted by local cheerleaders or members of a non-profit.

The High-A affiliate of the Cubs have a program where local organizations can volunteer to run concessions at a game in exchange for a portion of the sales made.

South Bend is one of a number of MiLB teams that has such a program. It's a way that the team can further cement its bonds with the community. The Concessionaire Program allowed South Bend to donate over $134,000 to local charities.

"It's nice when you can give money back to organizations and give them the opportunity to do the programming that they need to do and also know that they helped us be successful and provide an experience that our fans deserve," South Bend president Joe Hart said.

LAST 10 WINNERS

TRIPLE-A	DOUBLE-A	CLASS A	SHORT-SEASON
2012: Lehigh Valley (International)	**2012:** N-West Arkansas (Texas)	**2012:** Greenville (South Atlantic)	**2010:** Idaho Falls (Pioneer)
2013: Indianapolis (International)	**2013:** Tulsa (Texas)	**2013:** Clearwater (Florida State)	**2011:** Vancouver (Northwest)
2014: Charlotte (International)	**2014:** Montgomery (Southern)	**2014:** West Michigan (Midwest)	**2012:** Billings (Pioneer)
2015: Salt Lake (Pacific Coast)	**2015:** Richmond (Eastern)	**2015:** Myrtle Beach (Carolina)	**2013:** State College (NY-Penn)
2016: Round Rock (Pacific Coast)	**2016:** Pensacola (Southern)	**2016:** San Bernardino (California)	**2014:** Brooklyn (NY-Penn)
2017: Fresno (Pacific Coast)	**2017:** Reading (Eastern)	**2017:** Charleston (South Atlantic)	**2015:** Grand Junction (Pioneer)
2018: Oklahoma City (Pacific Coast)	**2018:** Tennessee (Southern)	**2018:** Winston-Salem (Carolina)	**2016:** Pulaski (Appalachian)
2019: Nashville (Pacific Coast)	**2019:** Tulsa (Texas)	**2019:** Lexington (South Atlantic)	**2017:** Hillsboro (Northwest)
2021: Las Vegas (Pacific Coast)	**2021:** Hartford (Eastern)	**2021:** Greensboro (South Atlantic)	**2018:** Spokane (Northwest)
2022: St. Paul (International)	**2022:** Portland (Eastern)	**2022:** Wisconson (Midwest)	**2019:** Hudson Valley (NY-Penn)

Surprise Wins AFL Again

BRIAN WESTERHOLT/FOUR SEAM IMAGES

Surprise won its second consecutive title and its third since the Saguaros moved to Surprise

BY JOSH NORRIS

For the second straight season, the Surprise Saguaros are Arizona Fall League champions. To keep the trophy, they turned to a combination of prospects—on the mound and in the batter's box—on teams who also play their spring training games in Surprise.

The result was a 6-5 win over a powerful Peoria club at Scottsdale Stadium.

The game was started by a pair of pitchers with a wide range of experience as professionals. The Saguaros called on Royals lefty Angel Zerpa, who has 58.2 innings of big league time and spends his spring training at the Surprise facility, which the Royals share with the Rangers. The Javelinas countered with Padres righty Braden Nett, who was signed in 2022 and has pitched just 13 innings outside of the Arizona Complex League.

Zerpa was a buzzsaw for his three innings, striking out six hitters and allowing just a hit while throwing up three zeroes.

Nett danced in and out of trouble for 3.1 innings but allowed the game's first run when Rangers prospect Liam Hicks—who finished the regular AFL year with a league-best .449 average that included the league's first six-hit game since 2009—slipped a single through the right side.

The Saguaros broke the game open in the fifth inning, when a Will Roberston single, a wild pitch and a two-run single from Abimelec Ortiz led to four runs.

Ortiz's two RBIs served as an appropriate extension of his outstanding regular season, when he slammed 33 home runs and drove in 101 runs between both Class A levels.

Zerpa was relieved by another Royals prospect, righthander Eric Cerantola, who struck out three more hitters over two one-run innings.

Brewers prospect Wes Clarke gave Surprise another jolt in the sixth inning when his double into the left-center field gap put another Saguaros run on the board.

The Saguaros spun shutout innings in the sixth, seventh and eighth innings with Blue Jays righty C.J. Van Eyk and Reds righties Zach Maxwell and Andrew Moore, but things got dicey in the ninth when the Javelinas reprised their resiliency from the semifinal game, when they erased a nine-run deficit to top Scottsdale.

Facing a five-run hole, Peoria got a bases-loaded walk from Marlins prospect and Futures Game MVP Nasim Nunez. The next two hitters—Guardians prospects Chase DeLauter and Kyle Manzardo—notched an RBI groundout and a two-run single to cut Surprise's lead to one and put the go-ahead run at the plate.

Brewers righthander Justin Yeager came into the game and got his lone hitter, Mariners prospect Tyler Locklear to strike out, sealing the game and keeping the trophy with the Saguaros.

STANDINGS

Team	W	L	PCT	GB
Surprise	19	11	.633	-
Peoria	15	14	.517	3.5
Scottsdale	15	14	.517	3.5
Mesa	14	16	.467	5
Salt River	14	16	.467	5
Glendale	12	18	.400	7

INDIVIDUAL BATTING LEADERS

(Minimum 2 Plate Appearances/League Games)

Player, Team	AVG	G	AB	R	H	HR	RBI
Hicks, Liam, Surprise	.449	18	69	20	31	0	12
Triantos, James, Mesa	.417	22	84	18	35	3	15
Marsee, Jakob, Peoria	.391	24	92	25	36	5	20
Durbin, Caleb, Mesa	.353	23	85	18	30	3	12
Dunn, Oliver, Scottsdale	.342	19	73	17	25	2	11
Keegan, Dominic, Peoria	.340	15	53	9	18	3	12
Thompson, Sterlin, Salt River	.338	21	80	15	27	0	13
Montgomery, Benny, Salt River	.333	19	78	16	26	3	14
DeLauter, Chase, Peoria	.299	23	87	19	26	5	27
Ogans, Keshawn, Salt River	.299	17	67	11	20	2	16

INDIVIDUAL PITCHING LEADERS

(Minimum .4 Innings Pitched/League Games)

Player, Team	W	L	ERA	IP	H	BB	SO
Perkins, Jack, Mesa	0	1	0.00	12	9	6	15
Penrod, Zach, Glendale	1	1	1.29	14	9	8	14
Daniel, Davis, Scottsdale	1	0	1.89	19	10	5	25
Ward, Thaddeus, Scottsdale	0	0	2.12	17	9	6	20
Maxwell, Zach, Surprise	0	0	2.19	12	9	9	22
Blubaugh, A.J., Mesa	0	0	2.25	12	11	4	17
Santana, Tyler, Mesa	3	0	2.45	18	11	6	8
Tiedemann, Ricky, Surprise	2	1	2.50	18	12	8	23
Van Eyk, CJ, Surprise	2	1	2.51	14	10	8	14
Carr, Jordan, Glendale	1	1	2.57	21	18	3	14

GLENDALE DESERT DOGS

Name	AVG	AB	R	H	2B	3B	HR	RBI	BB	SO	SB
Fernandez, Yeiner	.289	38	6	11	4	1	1	6	8	5	0
Ramos, Bryan	.267	86	19	23	2	0	4	10	9	19	1
Rosier, Cory	.258	93	14	24	4	2	0	8	13	19	8
Jordan, Rowdey	.255	51	8	13	6	0	0	3	9	19	1
McDonough, Tyler	.254	59	11	15	4	0	2	6	11	17	5
Keith, Damon	.254	71	8	18	4	1	4	5	8	25	0
Burke, Jacobs	.253	91	13	23	5	0	3	14	9	32	5
Schwartz, JT	.247	73	6	18	6	0	2	13	6	20	1
Montgomery, Carson	.244	82	9	20	1	2	3	20	6	27	0
Smith, D'Andre	.235	51	6	12	3	0	1	6	3	13	0
Sabato, Aaron	.215	65	10	14	3	0	7	10	9	27	0
Rosario, Kala'i	.213	89	14	19	3	0	7	16	15	34	3
Parada, Kevin	.186	70	7	13	4	0	3	9	4	29	0
Hickey, Nathan	.182	55	5	10	1	0	0	1	15	24	0
Bonaci, Brainer	.143	7	0	1	0	0	0	0	0	4	0
Cossetti, Andrew	.103	29	4	3	0	0	2	5	6	15	1

Name	W	L	ERA	G	GS	SV	IP	H	BB	SO	AVG
Labas, A.J.	0	0	0.00	4	0	0	4	3	4	5	.214
McLoughlin, Trey	0	0	0.00	9	0	1	9	4	4	8	.133
Clenney, Nolan	0	1	1.00	9	0	0	9	7	4	13	.206
Pilarski, Jake	1	2	1.00	9	0	1	9	9	4	9	.257
Leasure, Jordan	1	0	1.08	8	0	0	8	2	2	13	.074
Kopp, Ronan	0	0	1.13	7	0	0	8	3	6	15	.120
Penrod, Zach	1	1	1.29	4	4	0	14	9	8	14	.184
Sublette, Ryan	0	0	1.93	8	0	0	9	5	8	11	.152
Ellard, Fraser	1	0	2.00	9	0	0	9	8	1	14	.229
Carr, Jordan	1	1	2.57	6	4	0	21	18	3	14	.237
Thomas, Tyler	0	0	3.72	8	0	0	10	7	6	13	.212
Olds, Wyatt	1	0	4.09	8	0	0	11	8	3	12	.205
Veen, Zach	0	0	4.50	7	0	0	8	8	1	5	.250
Williams, Kendall	2	1	5.30	6	5	0	19	17	6	18	.243
Geber, Jordan	1	2	6.00	5	5	0	18	22	3	15	.289
Eder, Jake	1	1	6.11	6	5	0	18	18	15	16	.265
Troye, Christopher	0	0	6.23	8	0	2	9	10	6	11	.278
Hardy, Brendan	0	1	6.35	7	0	0	6	5	5	4	.217
Cepeda, Felix	1	1	6.75	8	0	1	8	11	3	6	.344
Mata, Bryan	0	1	8.00	9	0	0	9	11	2	11	.306
Ethridge, Ben	1	0	8.10	7	1	0	7	7	2	4	.250
Barrington, Malik	0	0	8.53	7	0	0	6	3	7	10	.130
Cousin, Josimar	0	2	8.62	6	4	0	16	25	5	12	.362
Casparius, Ben	0	2	10.43	8	2	0	15	17	9	20	.298
Coffey, Adisyn	0	2	24.00	7	0	0	6	10	11	8	.357

MESA SOLAR SOX

Name	AVG	AB	R	H	2B	3B	HR	RBI	BB	SO	SB
Triantos, James	.417	84	18	35	3	5	3	15	12	15	9
Durbin, Caleb	.353	85	18	30	9	1	3	12	14	7	21
Franklin, Christian	.300	20	3	6	2	0	0	1	1	5	0
Cowles, Benjamin	.290	69	9	20	4	1	4	15	12	24	3
Alcántara, Kevin	.256	86	11	22	7	1	5	23	8	30	3
Corona, Kenedy	.240	25	3	6	2	0	0	4	2	6	2
Dezenzo, Zach	.231	65	12	15	5	0	3	7	8	22	2
Cook, Billy	.222	72	10	16	5	0	4	14	14	28	2
Muncy, Max	.212	85	15	18	5	1	4	16	8	23	8
Bowens, TT	.210	81	15	17	3	1	4	9	11	30	1
Harris, Brett	.192	52	12	10	1	0	0	2	15	16	6
Armenteros, Lazaro	.167	42	8	7	1	0	0	3	12	22	3
Medina, Nelson	.161	31	5	5	1	0	1	6	6	17	1
Rhodes, John	.143	70	11	10	4	0	2	6	8	26	1
Pavolony, Connor	.136	44	3	6	1	0	1	4	6	19	1
Hernandez, Omar	.125	8	0	1	0	0	0	2	0	3	0
Trice, Carter	.125	16	4	2	1	0	1	1	1	10	0
Palma, Miguel	.115	52	3	6	0	0	0	2	4	25	0

Name	W	L	ERA	G	GS	SV	IP	H	BB	SO	AVG
Perkins, Jack	0	1	0.00	10	0	1	12	9	6	15	.209
Weisenburger, Jack	1	0	0.00	3	0	0	2	2	3	2	.250
Gaither, Ray	1	0	1.00	9	0	0	9	6	8	11	.200
Laskey, Adam	0	0	1.00	9	0	0	9	6	2	15	.182
Romero, Jose	0	0	1.69	8	0	0	11	3	8	8	.091
Blubaugh, A.J.	0	0	2.25	6	0	3	12	11	4	17	.239
Santana, Tyler	3	0	2.45	6	2	0	18	11	6	8	.172
Stevens, Kevin	0	0	2.45	9	0	0	7	8	3	10	.286
Emanuels, Stevie	0	0	2.79	10	0	0	10	14	7	19	.326
McGough, Trey	1	1	3.00	7	0	1	9	7	3	12	.194
Baumler, Carter	0	1	4.50	3	2	0	10	11	6	15	.275
Melendez, Jaime	0	1	4.91	2	2	0	4	3	6	3	.273
Vrieling, Trystan	0	1	5.06	5	5	0	11	11	6	15	.262
Kachmar, Chris	0	0	5.40	6	0	0	10	6	5	10	.171
Peek, Zach	1	1	5.63	5	1	0	8	8	4	6	.267
Stuart, Baron	0	0	5.84	5	0	0	12	11	10	10	.250
Sauer, Matt	0	3	5.91	9	0	1	11	8	5	18	.195
Salinas, Royber	2	1	6.16	6	6	0	19	19	12	23	.260
Henriquez, Nolberto	0	0	6.75	8	0	0	7	9	4	4	.333
Guilfoil, Tyler	2	2	6.87	6	6	0	18	16	9	21	.235
Hull, Nick	0	1	7.27	5	4	0	17	22	9	13	.301
Tavera, Carlos	0	0	7.71	5	0	0	5	3	7	7	.176
Tur, Yunior	0	1	8.10	10	0	0	10	12	5	7	.286
Van Loon, Peter	2	2	10.24	5	2	0	10	12	9	15	.300
Ulloa, Miguel	1	0	14.04	7	0	0	8	8	11	6	.258

PEORIA JAVELINAS

Name	AVG	AB	R	H	2B	3B	HR	RBI	BB	SO	SB
Marsee, Jakob	.391	92	25	36	12	1	5	20	21	25	16
Keegan, Dominic	.340	53	9	18	4	0	3	12	10	14	0
DeLauter, Chase	.299	87	19	26	5	0	5	27	14	11	5
Cairo, Christian	.289	38	6	11	0	0	1	9	6	11	2
Locklear, Tyler	.284	74	14	21	5	0	3	16	15	26	1
Manzardo, Kyle	.272	92	19	25	7	1	6	19	9	22	0
Berry, Jacob	.265	68	14	18	4	1	2	7	6	22	0
Sasaki, Shane	.259	81	18	21	2	2	0	9	11	31	13
Nuñez, Nasim	.253	79	13	20	3	0	0	15	13	20	14
Williams, Carson	.246	69	10	17	2	0	0	6	11	30	5
Bliss, Ryan	.239	71	15	17	2	1	0	8	14	21	10
Pauley, Graham	.238	84	14	20	4	0	5	20	4	18	4
Martorella, Nathan	.237	59	8	14	3	0	1	3	7	14	0
McIntosh, Paul	.229	48	11	11	1	0	2	4	6	19	3
Ford, Harry	.174	23	9	4	1	0	3	11	9	8	0

Name	W	L	ERA	G	GS	SV	IP	H	BB	SO	AVG
Bayless, Jarod	1	0	1.17	9	0	1	8	1	3	12	.045
Hanner, Bradley	0	0	1.59	10	0	2	11	10	4	16	.244

Name	W	L	ERA	G	GS	SV	IP	H	BB	SO	AVG
Taylor, Troy	1	0	1.74	9	0	1	10	10	2	12	.256
Sabrowski, Erik	0	0	1.86	9	0	0	10	4	10	16	.125
Webb, Ryan	2	2	4.37	6	6	0	23	16	14	36	.198
Carver, Ross	2	0	4.50	6	5	0	18	16	8	21	.232
Vernon, Austin	0	0	4.50	9	1	0	8	5	5	8	.192
Nett, Braden	1	1	4.67	5	4	0	17	13	10	21	.210
Alford, Peyton	0	0	4.70	8	0	0	8	8	4	9	.276
McCambley, Zach	0	1	5.00	8	0	0	9	6	7	12	.176
Workman, Logan	2	0	5.71	5	4	0	17	23	6	21	.311
Sommers, Drew	0	0	5.79	9	0	0	9	16	6	19	.364
Buxton, Ike	1	1	6.11	5	3	0	18	21	10	19	.292
Wicklander, Patrick	0	2	6.19	7	3	0	16	20	10	17	.303
Miller, Jake	0	0	6.43	8	0	0	7	7	4	6	.250
Bierman, Gabe	2	1	6.75	5	3	0	16	19	10	18	.306
Pena, Francis	0	0	7.36	6	0	0	7	9	4	10	.290
Pinales, Emmanuel	1	0	7.71	8	0	0	12	7	11	13	.175
Stanavich, Dale	1	1	8.22	8	0	0	8	9	5	6	.281
Hunter Jr., Leon	1	2	9.00	8	0	2	8	8	7	12	.250
Mendez, Miguel	0	2	9.95	6	1	0	6	9	5	9	.300
Taylor, Evan	0	0	10.80	6	0	0	5	6	6	8	.286
Erbe, Haden	0	1	11.25	4	0	0	4	5	6	4	.294
Paplham, Cole	0	0	12.15	8	0	0	7	8	5	5	.286

SALT RIVER RAFTERS

Name	AVG	AB	R	H	2B	3B	HR	RBI	BB	SO	SB
Thompson, Sterlin	.338	80	15	27	7	2	0	13	18	24	7
Montgomery, Benny	.333	78	16	26	2	1	3	14	14	27	10
Bins, Carter	.300	40	8	12	4	0	2	6	1	13	1
Ogans, Keshawn	.299	67	11	20	1	0	2	16	4	14	5
Bigbie, Justice	.292	72	10	21	3	0	1	12	10	10	2
Bowen, Jase	.290	100	14	29	5	2	4	19	9	27	6
McCabe, David	.278	72	14	20	6	0	0	8	23	29	1
Vukovich, A.J.	.275	80	10	22	5	0	0	5	4	23	13
Lee, Hao-Yu	.265	49	8	13	2	0	1	9	9	12	1
Romo, Drew	.231	39	11	9	1	2	0	2	8	9	1
Melendez, Ivan	.229	83	12	19	5	1	2	13	10	27	1
Tolve, Tyler	.220	59	8	13	3	1	1	8	3	19	0
Roberts, Caleb	.203	64	11	13	3	0	1	8	17	24	2
Jung, Jace	.200	50	9	10	2	0	1	8	14	19	4
Brannigan, Jack	.177	79	14	14	4	1	4	12	9	35	4

Name	W	L	ERA	G	GS	SV	IP	H	BB	SO	AVG
Walston, Blake	0	0	0.00	1	1	0	3	4	1	4	.333
Barger, Alec	0	0	0.96	8	0	0	9	7	2	13	.212
Mejia, Juan	0	0	2.16	8	0	3	8	6	9	16	.214
Jobe, Jackso	3	1	2.87	4	4	0	16	14	5	19	.233
Montes De Oca, Christian	1	1	3.12	9	0	2	9	12	3	7	.316
Hill, Jaden	0	2	3.18	11	0	0	11	6	4	13	.150
Williams, Case	1	0	3.18	6	6	0	17	12	9	16	.194
Petit, RJ	1	0	3.24	8	0	0	8	7	3	7	.241
Flowers, JC	1	0	3.27	7	1	0	11	6	11	9	.158
Flores, Wilmer	0	0	4.00	6	2	1	18	25	4	22	.338
Dombkowski, Nick	0	0	4.32	8	1	0	8	15	9	8	.417
McSteen, Jake	0	1	4.35	8	0	0	10	7	1	12	.189
Samaniego, Tyler	1	1	4.91	8	0	0	7	8	6	9	.267
Vines, Darius	1	1	5.51	4	4	0	16	15	6	23	.234
Dodd, Dylan	0	1	6.16	4	4	0	19	23	6	20	.291
Rice, Jake	0	1	6.75	9	0	0	8	10	3	13	.323
Junker, Cameron	1	1	7.04	8	0	0	8	11	6	8	.333
Smith, Dylan	0	2	7.29	6	6	0	21	25	12	30	.294
Pope, Austin	1	1	8.64	8	0	2	8	10	6	12	.278
Wilson, Brooks	1	0	9.45	7	0	0	7	6	9	11	.250
Ercolani, Alessandro	1	0	9.82	4	0	0	4	2	11	5	.167
Kohlhepp, Tanner	0	1	10.13	8	0	0	8	11	7	11	.314
McMahon, Chris	1	0	10.38	5	1	0	9	17	4	8	.415
Meza, Carlos	0	2	11.57	8	0	0	7	14	3	10	.400
Halligan, Patrick	0	0	12.27	8	0	0	7	11	5	8	.367

SCOTTSDALE SCORPIONS

Name	AVG	AB	R	H	2B	3B	HR	RBI	BB	SO	SB
Dunn, Oliver	.342	73	17	25	6	4	2	11	15	26	12
Rincones Jr., Gabriel	.293	82	22	24	6	1	2	14	17	28	15
Hassell III, Robert	.290	69	9	20	1	0	1	12	10	21	6
Scott II, Victor	.286	84	19	24	2	0	3	8	12	8	18
Howell, Carter	.273	55	11	15	1	2	3	6	6	19	0
Morgan, Zach	.265	34	4	9	0	0	1	5	6	8	1
Kroon, Matt	.262	61	13	16	2	0	1	15	7	21	5
Ricketts, Caleb	.256	43	5	11	2	0	0	5	4	12	0
Pineda, Israel	.237	59	6	14	2	0	2	12	5	15	0
Rivas, Jeremy	.230	74	13	17	1	1	1	7	7	22	3
Sanchez, Jadiel	.212	52	4	11	2	0	0	5	9	9	0
Lipscomb, Trey	.205	83	10	17	2	0	1	7	1	18	1
Crooks, Jimmy	.186	43	1	8	2	0	0	5	3	10	0
DiChiara, Sonny	.175	57	2	10	0	0	2	11	3	28	0
Placencia, Adrian	.162	68	8	11	1	0	2	7	7	15	3
Crawford, Reggie	.138	58	5	8	2	0	2	8	12	30	0

Name	W	L	ERA	G	GS	SV	IP	H	BB	SO	AVG
Baker, Andrew	0	0	0.00	7	0	1	7	2	6	13	.087
Pipkin, Dominic	0	0	0.00	3	0	0	3	2	1	2	.222
Torres, Eric	0	0	0.00	6	0	0	6	4	7	12	.182
Granillo, Andre	1	0	1.80	8	1	3	10	13	3	14	.310
Daniel, Davis	1	0	1.89	4	4	0	19	10	5	25	.152
Ward, Thaddeus	0	0	2.12	5	2	0	17	9	6	20	.153
Nunez, Edwin	0	1	2.53	8	0	2	11	9	4	6	.231
Sinclair, Jack	3	0	3.12	7	0	1	9	12	4	9	.333
Herz, DJ	1	0	3.71	5	5	0	17	13	9	25	.206
McGowan, Christian	1	1	3.71	4	4	0	17	21	7	12	.304
Ribalta, Orlando	4	1	4.15	8	0	0	9	6	6	6	.207
Hjerpe, Cooper	0	0	4.32	7	0	0	8	5	6	15	.167
Johnson, Marques	0	0	4.50	2	0	0	2	2	0	3	.250
Martinez, Jordi	0	0	4.63	8	0	1	12	9	3	10	.205
Paniagua, Inohan	1	2	4.86	6	1	0	17	13	6	17	.220
Lonsway, Seth	0	0	5.40	5	0	0	10	15	4	13	.349
Choate, Jack	0	1	5.51	6	6	0	16	13	13	21	.217
Roby, Tekoah	1	2	5.93	5	5	0	14	15	6	18	.263
Neunborn, Mitch	1	0	6.00	3	0	0	6	9	1	11	.346
Jones, Nick	0	0	6.48	7	0	0	8	9	4	12	.273
Wynja, Hayden	1	0	7.20	5	0	0	10	6	9	16	.176
Murphy, Luke	0	0	10.80	5	0	0	5	6	5	4	.286
Chaney, Chase	0	3	11.81	6	2	0	16	28	8	14	.389
Powell, Holden	0	2	12.00	7	0	0	9	12	8	9	.333
Bednar, Will	0	1	13.50	6	0	1	5	7	9	8	.304

SURPRISE SAGUAROS

Name	AVG	AB	R	H	2B	3B	HR	RBI	BB	SO	SB
Hicks, Liam	.449	69	20	31	5	0	0	12	16	8	2
Ortiz, Abimelec	.314	35	7	11	1	0	3	9	12	8	0
Clarke, Wes	.297	74	17	22	3	1	5	20	17	27	0
Brown Jr., Eric	.297	91	18	27	7	1	2	15	11	19	8
Robertson, Will	.279	68	13	19	3	1	3	20	19	25	6
Brown, Dasan	.274	73	11	20	4	1	1	9	7	25	4
Loftin, Nick	.273	11	2	3	2	0	0	0	0	1	0
Wilson, Peyton	.272	81	19	22	5	1	2	13	16	19	1
Hurtubise, Jacob	.267	90	21	24	4	0	0	13	16	23	11
Palmegiani, Domiano	.263	80	22	21	5	1	6	21	12	26	1
Cross, Gavin	.222	27	3	6	2	0	0	3	6	8	7
Trautwein, Michael	.217	46	9	10	1	0	3	11	7	18	1
Mendez, Hendry	.216	37	6	8	3	0	0	2	6	10	0
Osuna, Alejandro	.214	14	3	3	0	0	0	1	1	2	0
Alexander, CJ	.213	47	5	10	5	1	3	11	6	16	0
Moller, Ian	.212	33	5	7	2	0	0	1	4	13	0
Cauley, Cam	.186	70	11	13	1	1	4	10	9	35	3
Callahan, Austin	.160	50	5	8	1	1	2	7	1	17	0

Name	W	L	ERA	G	GS	SV	IP	H	BB	SO	AVG
Hoopii-Tuionetoa, Anthony	0	0	0.00	9	0	1	10	4	3	10	.125
Smith, Shane	0	0	0.00	2	0	0	2	2	0	3	.200
Teodo, Emiliano	1	0	0.00	8	0	5	11	3	3	19	.086
Sandridge, Jayvien	0	0	1.42	6	0	0	6	3	2	13	.136
Maxwell, Zach	0	0	2.19	9	0	0	12	9	9	22	.205
Tiedemann, Ricky	2	1	2.50	4	4	0	18	12	8	23	.190
Van Eyk, CJ	2	1	2.51	5	2	0	14	10	8	14	.196
Lynch, Daniel	0	0	3.00	1	1	0	3	4	1	5	.364
Spiers, Carson	4	1	3.00	5	5	0	18	18	1	20	.250
Cerantola, Eric	2	0	3.75	5	1	0	12	12	5	18	.261
Kaufman, Rylan	1	0	4.15	7	0	0	9	7	5	9	.226
King, Justin	0	1	4.26	7	0	0	6	4	3	6	.174
Hubbart, Bryce	0	0	4.91	5	0	1	15	9	8	16	.176
Moore, Andrew	1	0	4.91	7	0	1	7	8	4	7	.296
Slaten, Justin	0	1	4.91	3	0	0	4	1	2	6	.091
Zerpa, Angel	0	0	5.56	5	4	0	11	13	7	14	.289
Seminaris, Adam	2	1	5.87	6	2	0	15	16	5	14	.271
Wallace, Jacob	0	1	6.00	6	0	0	6	6	6	9	.261

Way, Beck	0	0	6.00	6	0	0	6	7	6	7	.292
Yeager, Justin	0	1	6.23	9	0	1	9	8	5	9	.242
Bratt, Mitch	1	0	6.46	6	1	0	15	15	10	17	.254
Kent, Zak	1	2	8.10	5	5	0	17	27	5	23	.360
Hernandez, Joseph	1	0	9.45	5	2	0	13	20	9	13	.333
Sadler, Fitz	0	0	10.29	8	0	0	7	5	8	9	.200
Palmer, Trent	1	1	13.91	6	3	0	11	18	12	12	.360
Larkin, Conor	0	0	19.29	3	0	0	2	7	4	3	.538
Starr, Nick	0	1	5.06	9	0	0	11	11	6	7	.256
Thomas, Tahnaj	0	0	9.64	9	0	0	9	7	9	11	.212
Webb, Nathan	1	0	0.00	6	0	0	6	4	2	6	.190
Wolfram, Grant	1	0	1.86	7	0	0	10	5	2	13	.147

INDEPENDENT LEAGUES

Partner Leagues See Talent Level Climb

BY J.J. COOPER

The talent across the partner leagues (still known to many as independent ball) has never been better.

Thanks to the reduction in the number of teams in affiliated ball, plus the shortened 20-round draft, players who would have been in affiliated ball in the past are now finding themselves in partner leagues.

But it's not just overlooked prospective draftees. Because of stricter roster limits in affiliated ball, players are also being released more quickly in some cases. Those players face a choice of either hanging up their gloves or giving partner leagues a try.

What is odd, however, is that the same qualities that have raised the talent level across the partner leagues have created a more difficult path back to affiliated ball.

In 2021, partner leagues found themelves barely able to hang on to players long enough to fit them for uniforms before they were selling their contracts to affiliated clubs. With teams struggling to find enough arms in a post-pandemic MiLB, it was a seller's market.

At that point, MLB teams were trying to adjust. A number of players didn't come back after the pandemic. Others struggled to stay healthy when they ramped back up.

Partner leagues were happy to become a key part of the pipeline.

Since then, that stream has been reduced to more of a trickle. In 2021, the Atlantic League sold the contracts of 52 players to MLB clubs. In 2022, it was 23 and in 2023 it was 25.

In the past two years, fewer Atlantic League players have gone to affiliated ball than did in 2021 alone.

The American Association sold 74 contracts to affilated ball in 2021. In 2022, it was 18. In 2023, it was five.

What this means for the long term isn't all that clear. MLB is expected to cut 15 players from the affiliated domestic minor league roster limits for 2024.

That will mean another 450 players removed from affiliated ball, many of whom will be an option for partner leagues.

That means the overall talent level of the partner leagues should continue to rise. But the indy leagues have long operated on a symbiotic relationship. They are able to fill their rosters with a never-ending supply of talent because of the opportunituies those players have to find a way to affiliated baseball.

Will the same steady stream of quality players keep coming if the road back to affiliated ball is getting tougher and tougher to navigate?

For some, the answer is yes. There will always be baseball lifers. For the players who won't quit until the jersey is ripped away from them, this will just mean the leagues they play in will be more challenging. The chance to further develop in the partner leagues means an opportunity to keep playing, which will be more than enough.

Others, especially players who have been playing in affiliated ball under the new salary scale that ensures that every affiiated minor leaguer makes $30,000 or more and gets team-provided housing, may find the idea of playing in partner leagues for a significantly reduced salary to be unappealing. Under the old system, the pay disparity between affiliated ball and the partners leagues existed, but it wasn't dramatic. Now it is.

The rise of the training centers also plays a role. For pitchers, the path back to affiliated ball is sometimes navigated by training to add velocity or a new pitch at a facility. Some of those pitchers will then go to a partner league to prove their improvements will carry over into games, but in those stints are often brief.

The partner leagues have successfully navigated the transition to the post-pandemic world.

More than 5.5 million fans attended partner league games in 2023, and the leagues have found that consolidation has given the four largest leagues a reasonably large spread of markets. It's almost guaranteed enough teams to ensure that any of these leagues can weather the loss of one or two struggling clubs. There is a continual churn of markets, but for now it is being done in a sustainable manner.

The partner leagues are in a good place right now, but—as is always true in indy ball—they'll have to work very hard to keep it that way. And the next challenge will likely be just around the corner.

Torres Did It All For Milwaukee Milkmen

In 2022, Bryan Torres did pretty much everything a partner league player could to get noticed and sign a deal with an affiliated club.

The Milwaukee Milkmen's leadoff hitter led the American Association in batting average (.374). He led the league in hits (139). He was among the league leaders in doubles and runs scored while playing multiple up-the-middle defensive positions, including center field, second base and even catcher.

Bryan Torres

No MLB organization called. So what did Torres do? He made sure his next season was even better. The one-time catcher in the Brewers system has blossomed as a center fielder/second baseman for the Milkmen. Torres once again led the league in batting average (.370) and he led the league in on-base percentage (.464). But this time he hit 11 home runs, up from the three he hit in 2022. After stealing 22 bases in 2022, he stole a league-best 71 in 2023. No one else in the league swiped 40.

His speed on the bases helped him score a league-best 94 runs in just 90 games played. He also managed to drive in 67 runs, even though he was primarily a lead-off hitter. He even finished sixth in the league in slugging percentage (.540).

"His mindset was to always be the best player he could be," Milwaukee manager Anthony Barone said. "He didn't get discouraged that he won a batting title and all the achievements in 2022 and didn't get picked up.

"Instead he came back in 2023 and was even better. He added more power and speed to his game. It's constant improvement."

Torres is Baseball America's 2023 Independent/Partner Leagues Player of the Year.

Torres had long reason to hope he could star in Milwaukee. He was signed by the Brewers as an undrafted free agent out of Puerto Rico in 2015. He spent five seasons in the Brewers' organization, but never reached full-season ball with the club. His final season as a Brewer was 2019. He was one of the better hitters on the Pioneer League's Rocky Mountain Vibes that season.

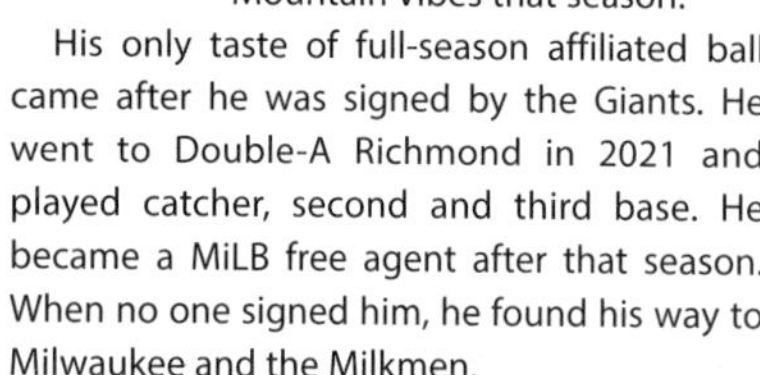

His only taste of full-season affiliated ball came after he was signed by the Giants. He went to Double-A Richmond in 2021 and played catcher, second and third base. He became a MiLB free agent after that season. When no one signed him, he found his way to Milwaukee and the Milkmen.

The Milkmen won't get to see if Torres can defend his back-to-back batting titles. After raising the bar even further in 2023, he did get noticed. The St. Louis Cardinals have signed him, getting him a second shot in affiliated ball.

"His value to the Milkmen was that he brought an intensity to the game that really made us go as a team," Barone said. "He cared about winning ... He set the tone with the way he played. He didn't want to get beat by anybody."

PREVIOUS WINNERS

1996: Darryl Motley, OF, Fargo-Moorhead (Northern)
1997: Mike Meggers, OF, Winnipeg/Duluth (Northern)
1998: Morgan Burkhart, 1B, Richmond (Frontier)
1999: Carmine Cappucio, OF, New Jersey (Northeast)
2000: Anthony Lewis, 1B, Duluth-Superior (Northern)
2001: Mike Warner, OF, Somerset (Atlantic)
2002: Bobby Madritsch, LHP, Winnipeg (Northern)
2003: Jason Shelley, RHP, Rockford (Frontier)
2004: Victor Rodriguez, SS, Somerset (Atlantic)
2005: Eddie Lantigua, 3B, Quebec (Can-Am)
2006: Ian Church, OF, Kalamazoo (Frontier)
2007: Darryl Brinkley, OF, Calgary (Northern)
2008: Patrick Breen, OF, Orange County (Golden)
2009: Greg Porter, OF, Wichita (American Association)
2010: Beau Torbert, OF, Sioux Falls (American Association)
2011: Chris Collabello, 1B, Worcester (Can-Am League)
2012: Blake Gailen, OF, Lancaster (Atlantic)
2013: C.J. Ziegler, 1B, Wichita (American Association)
2014: Balbino Fuenmayor, 1B, Quebec (Can-Am League)
2015: Joe Maloney, OF, Rocland (Can-Am League)
2016: Art Charles, 1B, New Jersey (Can-Am League)
2017: Alonzo Harris, OF, York (Atlantic League)
2018: Jordany Valdespin, INF, Long Island (Atlantic League)
2019: Keon Barnum, 1B, Chicago (American Association)
2021: Adam Brett Walker, OF, Milwaukee (American Association)
2022: Courtney Hawkins, OF, Lexington (Atlantic League)

AMERICAN ASSOCIATION

Brian O'Grady's two-out walk-off RBI single in the botom of the ninth scored Chris Herrmann to hand the Kansas City Monachs their third title in the past five years.

The Monarchs needed just four games to win the best-of-5 series against the Chicago Dogs. The Monarchs outscored their opponents 54-34 in the postseason.

East Division	W	L	PCT	GB
Milwaukee Milkmen *	56	44	.560	-
Chicago Dogs †	56	44	.560	-
Kane County Cougars †	49	51	.490	7
Cleburne Railroaders †	46	54	.460	10
Lake Country DockHounds	46	54	.460	10
Gary SouthShore RailCats	41	58	.414	14.5
West Division	**W**	**L**	**PCT**	**GB**
Kansas City Monarchs *	59	40	.596	-
Sioux City Explorers †	52	48	.520	7.5
Sioux Falls Canaries †	52	48	.520	7.5
Fargo-Moorhead RedHawks †	51	49	.510	8.5
Lincoln Saltdogs	48	52	.480	11.5
Winnipeg Goldeyes	43	57	.430	16.5

*** Clinched division.** † Wild card

PLAYOFFS—Quarterfinals: Sioux City defeated Fargo-Moorhead 2-0; Kansas City defeated Sioux Falls 2-0; Milwaukee defeated Kane County 2-1 and Chicago defeated Cleburne 2-1 in best-of-three series. **Semifinals:** Chicago defeated Milwaukee 2-1 and Kansas City defeated Sioux City 2-1 in best-of-three series. **Finals:** Kansas City defeated Chicago 3-1 in best-of-five series.

ATTENDANCE: Kane County 261,836; Chicago 206,258; Winnipeg 178,393; Fargo-Moorhead 155,331; Lincoln 151,265; Gary SouthShore 148,354; Lake Country 92,914; Milwaukee 85,318; Kansas City 83,608; Sioux Falls 71,924; Cleburne 59,817; Sioux City 54,899.

All-Star Team: C: Chris Hermann, Kansas City. **1B:** Mike Hart, Sioux Falls. **2B:** Brian Torres, Milwaukee. **SS:** Josh Altmann, Chicago. **3B:** Dayson Crooes, Winnipeg. **OF:** Max Murphy, Winnipeg; Hill Alexander, Cleburne; Zach Nehrir, Cleburne. **DH:** Jabari Henry, Sioux Falls. **SP:** Solomon Bates, Sioux City. **RP:** Charlie Hasty, Sioux Falls. **UTIL:** Cam Balego, Milwaukee. **Player of the Year:** Chris Hermann, Kansas City. **Manager of the Year:** Mike Meyer, Sioux Falls. **Rookie of the Year:** Jordan Barth, Sioux Falls.

BATTING LEADERS

Player, Team	AVG	AB	R	H	HR	RBI	SB
Bryan Torres, MKE	.370	359	94	133	11	67	71
Ray Morales, MKE	.360	339	52	122	7	67	3
Chris Herrmann, KC	.355	363	72	129	23	88	2
Dayson Croes, WPG	.351	385	61	135	3	67	5
Ryan Lidge, CHI	.330	349	67	115	9	63	3
Matt Bottcher, CHI	.323	378	68	122	13	55	21
Matt Lloyd, SC	.321	336	70	108	14	61	17
Gio Diaz, GAR	.319	360	75	115	2	33	37
Gavin Collins, KC	.314	239	38	75	10	41	2
Justin Wylie, KC	.309	349	73	108	17	56	16

PITCHING LEADERS

Pitcher, Team	W	L	ERA	IP	H	HR	BB	SO
Kevin McGovern, F-M	9	8	3.11	119	101	7	40	101
Gregory Vasquez, MKE	11	1	3.25	100	94	14	21	62
Ryan Zimmerman, MKE	10	3	3.36	110	87	12	36	100
Westin Muir, KCO	5	3	3.51	100	96	10	47	62
Solomon Bates, SC	10	6	3.57	126	89	12	37	124
Jalen Miller, KC	10	2	3.64	99	75	10	59	78
Tyler Beardsley, KCO	8	6	3.65	111	114	7	41	93
Joey Matulovich, WPG	5	9	3.78	117	101	8	32	121
Austin Drury, SC	5	5	3.79	110	99	7	53	98
Christian Young, MKE		**7**	**63.91**	**94**	**86**	**9**	**30110**	

CHICAGO DOGS

Name	AVG	AB	R	H	HR	RBI	BB	SO	SB
Josh Altmann	.290	373	73	108	26	88	49	74	21
Cody Bohanek	.243	338	51	82	9	41	46	85	16
Matt Bottcher	.323	378	68	122	13	55	24	56	21
Braxton Davidson	.188	16	2	3	1	3	2	8	0
Payton Eeles	.311	151	29	47	3	20	17	25	13
Mike Falsetti	.125	24	3	3	0	3	1	4	0
Caeden Harris	.111	9	1	1	0	0	0	6	0
Nick Heath	.241	241	50	58	4	34	52	63	30
Taylor Jackson	.227	75	8	17	0	4	6	17	3
Ryan Lidge	.330	349	67	115	9	63	46	56	3
Ben Livorsi	.298	104	20	31	7	18	19	25	1
Jesus Lujano	.295	326	38	96	4	35	18	41	15
David Maberry	.297	91	12	27	3	16	8	11	0
Luke Mangieri	.280	332	53	93	17	72	52	68	6
General McArthur	.148	27	5	4	0	2	2	10	3
Brennan Metzger	.210	186	36	39	2	16	38	50	7
Dylan Rosa	.240	200	25	48	6	27	11	75	5
Johnni Turbo	.273	77	14	21	1	15	9	12	7
Donivan Williams	.211	114	17	24	3	13	6	39	1

Name	W	L	ERA	G	SV	IP	H	BB	SO
Cole Aker	1	2	10.43	6	0	15	17	12	8
Joe Cavallaro	3	1	2.26	50	0	68	42	30	94
Jonathan Cheshire	7	3	2.78	41	2	74	65	9	75
Jake Dahlberg	2	3	6.16	6	0	31	42	10	30
Andrew Edwards	1	1	3.82	24	0	31	37	22	38
Austin Faith	1	0	1.50	3	0	12	16	3	11
Nick Green	6	5	4.58	18	0	92	103	30	89
Brenden Heiss	1	0	5.71	15	0	17	19	21	17
Steven Lacey	2	1	3.13	8	0	32	22	13	22
Nolan LaMere	0	0	9.49	11	0	12	14	8	12
Trevor Lane	6	7	5.17	23	0	103	119	38	96
Aiden McIntyre	2	0	4.11	13	0	15	13	7	10
Jake Newberry	2	0	1.82	19	0	25	17	7	29
Ryan O'Reilly	2	8	7.29	13	0	46	57	26	32
Tyler Palm	8	4	4.46	19	0	105	120	36	82
Brian Schlitter	4	2	3.24	46	18	50	55	14	24
D.J. Snelten	2	3	3.33	14	0	24	11	17	40
Johnathon Tripp	2	2	7.20	26	0	45	58	19	50
Bryan Warzek	3	0	2.74	37	3	49	31	26	77
Joe Wieland	1	0	1.76	3	0	15	10	2	24

CLEBURNE RAILROADERS

Name	AVG	AB	R	H	HR	RBI	BB	SO	SB
Hill Alexander	.287	377	78	108	23	70	48	85	14
Bret Boswell	.318	151	34	48	14	43	16	35	2
Blaze Brothers	.231	143	24	33	3	7	21	56	16
Jose Curpa	.212	85	15	18	1	4	16	25	6
Delino DeShields	.291	141	30	41	4	21	21	33	13
John Figueroa	.267	150	17	40	5	34	11	46	3
London Green	.273	11	3	3	0	3	3	4	0
Ryan Hernandez	.303	155	24	47	7	35	12	29	1
Alex Jackson	.223	256	38	57	3	36	24	61	16
Mark Karaviotis	.267	345	58	92	12	59	42	87	1
Brian Klein	.278	360	68	100	4	46	52	56	14
Keshawn Lynch	.212	52	11	11	0	3	10	11	3
Jarel McDade	.273	44	9	12	1	6	2	6	2
Zach Nehrir	.289	405	81	117	15	80	47	67	35
Guillermo Quintana	.277	274	38	76	10	36	35	48	6
Elmer Reyes	.250	224	29	56	6	24	6	41	1
Nik Sanchez	.333	3	0	1	0	0	0	1	0
Jose Sermo	.273	300	63	82	28	77	51	102	10

Name	W	L	ERA	G	SV	IP	H	BB	SO
Miguel Ausua	2	2	6.48	22	0	50	58	30	38
Brendan Bell	1	3	5.20	34	0	45	58	19	29
Luke Boyd	0	0	4.26	11	1	13	13	6	9
Kody Bullard	5	3	8.07	13	0	61	84	37	46
Chandler Casey	3	3	5.06	39	1	59	71	25	46
Joe Corbett	5	4	3.07	34	2	41	27	11	72
Trey Cumbie	2	6	5.36	19	0	50	54	26	57
Austin Fairchild	1	1	5.20	42	1	45	50	32	63
Nick Gardewine	2	3	6.17	24	5	23	22	14	24
Kevin Hilton	7	5	4.49	17	0	106	123	28	52

Name	W	L	ERA	G	SV	IP	H	BB	SO
Kasey Kalich	5	3	3.97	24	1	91	92	32	91
Michael Krauza	1	0	4.50	17	3	18	14	9	24
Michael Mariot	1	1	5.06	5	0	27	29	5	29
Travis Perry	6	8	6.04	20	0	110	130	41	90
Tanner Riley	0	3	3.20	11	0	20	16	7	24
Joe Shaw	1	1	4.26	13	2	13	9	10	13
Riley Smith	3	4	5.73	8	0	44	60	18	25
Johnathon Tripp	1	1	4.55	5	0	28	31	5	26
Michael Wong	0	3	6.11	15	0	35	44	15	25

FARGO-MOORHEAD REDHAWKS

Name	AVG	AB	R	H	HR	RBI	BB	SO	SB
Evan Alexander	.281	370	70	104	9	43	60	95	30
Garrett Alexander	.000	3	0	0	0	0	0	1	0
Manuel Boscan	.278	370	50	103	6	44	36	44	10
Peter Brookshaw	.114	44	7	5	2	8	7	10	1
Sam Dexter	.271	369	43	100	7	47	22	41	11
Jake Dykhoff	.000	1	0	0	0	0	0	0	0
Mike Falsetti	.151	53	10	8	2	5	10	21	1
Matt Goodheart	.286	70	8	20	1	10	12	19	2
Andy Gravdahl	.125	24	3	3	1	4	3	6	1
Jack Hanson	.177	17	3	3	0	0	5	9	0
Ben Livorsi	.156	32	4	5	1	2	7	11	0
BJ Lopez	.209	172	20	36	2	19	30	47	0
Conor Maguire	.125	8	2	1	0	0	1	2	0
Zack Miller	.125	16	0	2	0	3	0	2	0
Nick Novak	.241	282	43	68	8	28	25	76	15
Alec Olund	.281	278	42	78	4	34	33	66	10
Leobaldo Piña	.272	371	61	101	18	65	36	54	2
Correlle Prime	.234	367	39	86	14	51	29	100	1
Conner Richardson	.000	1	0	0	0	0	0	1	0
Scott Schreiber	.284	190	27	54	11	38	14	43	10
John Silviano	.254	130	26	33	5	29	25	45	0
Dillon Thomas	.344	221	49	76	8	35	27	46	9
Donivan Williams	.143	7	0	1	0	0	0	2	1

Name	W	L	ERA	G	SV	IP	H	BB	SO
Reza Aleaziz	2	2	2.70	40	11	43	33	14	38
Garrett Alexander	1	5	4.03	30	2	58	60	30	58
Reid Birlingmair	1	1	2.79	9	7	10	9	4	10
Trey Cumbie	0	3	5.73	10	0	38	38	22	31
Colten Davis	7	0	2.15	9	0	46	29	22	33
Alex DuBord	4	1	4.91	28	2	33	35	21	38
Jake Dykhoff	4	4	5.60	14	0	71	72	32	64
Davis Feldman	3	1	2.42	4	0	26	17	10	29
Edgar García	1	1	5.50	13	0	18	21	7	16
Tyler Grauer	6	4	4.38	20	0	115	123	25	72
Brenden Heiss	1	0	5.40	3	0	10	10	6	11
Conor Maguire	2	0	4.94	11	0	24	20	14	11
Kevin McGovern	9	8	3.11	19	0	119	101	40	101
Kelvan Pilot	1	4	3.68	10	0	44	41	29	33
Correlle Prime	3	8	6.26	17	0	73	65	51	64
Conner Richardson	0	1	4.09	21	1	22	22	13	15
Tanner Riley	2	2	4.45	25	1	30	23	19	33
Tristen Roehrich	0	1	8.41	17	1	31	49	18	26
Bryant Salgado	1	1	13.03	4	0	10	15	16	8
Tasker Strobel	0	2	7.20	10	0	10	15	6	6
John Witkowski	2	0	6.08	10	0	13	17	14	13

GARY SOUTHSHORE RAILCATS

Name	AVG	AB	R	H	HR	RBI	BB	SO	SB
Sam Abbott	.185	27	3	5	1	3	5	19	0
Jacob Bockelie	.177	62	3	11	2	7	6	14	0
Seth Caddell	.171	111	10	19	5	10	13	29	0
LG Castillo	.270	378	39	102	5	49	20	98	5
Jose Contreras	.241	116	16	28	4	11	13	44	7
Will Decker	.288	66	11	19	0	6	10	13	3
Francisco Del Valle	.271	347	55	94	10	58	39	56	5
Gio Díaz	.319	360	75	115	2	33	33	40	37
Marcos Gonzalez	.242	95	10	23	3	11	9	24	0
Thomas Greely	.240	150	16	36	0	14	18	43	5
Marco Hernandez	.189	53	6	10	0	3	5	7	0
Daniel Lingua	.258	318	53	82	5	38	34	48	25
Jesus Marriaga	.281	366	52	103	9	66	32	113	28
Paul Mondesi	.211	19	1	4	0	2	0	3	0
Victor Nova	.197	173	30	34	7	25	41	43	6
Dorssys Paulino	.192	26	5	5	0	0	2	5	0
Tyler Reis	.167	6	1	1	0	0	0	5	0
Miguelangel Sierra	.281	32	1	9	1	5	3	14	0
Emmanuel Tapia	.193	109	17	21	6	15	13	47	0
Jackson Valera	.293	256	23	75	3	45	12	29	2
Michael Woodworth	.245	200	30	49	1	16	19	34	20

Name	W	L	ERA	G	SV	IP	H	BB	SO
Jose Betances	0	4	9.64	13	0	23	24	33	28
Edward Cuello	4	11	5.45	20	0	116	131	39	73
Jack Eisenbarger	2	1	4.85	48	3	52	52	27	54
Chris Erwin	3	4	4.50	13	0	54	53	20	56
Harrison Francis	5	6	4.43	18	0	87	80	46	87
Quincy Jones	0	0	6.59	9	0	14	12	14	17
Matt Leon	1	1	5.18	22	3	24	26	19	38
Ben Miller	0	0	5.40	15	0	20	21	15	22
Oddy Nunez	4	3	4.82	42	0	56	59	30	47
Aaron Phillips	2	3	5.56	43	0	55	68	33	41
Jared Price	1	1	6.87	27	0	37	47	35	34
John Sheaks	6	7	5.22	16	0	90	111	28	64
Joan Valdez	0	5	4.77	37	2	55	55	21	58
Daniel Vitriago	0	2	7.94	6	0	11	17	2	15
Julio Vivas	6	5	5.38	21	0	92	110	35	72
DJ Wilkinson	7	3	2.74	42	12	49	35	24	57

KANE COUNTY COUGARS

Name	AVG	AB	R	H	HR	RBI	BB	SO	SB
Josh Allen	.256	289	49	74	12	43	34	68	11
Olivier Basabe	.293	191	21	56	3	20	14	33	0
T.J. Bennett	.303	152	24	46	6	24	6	40	11
Gio Brusa	.261	115	12	30	3	17	10	35	0
Ashton Creal	.150	20	1	3	0	0	4	10	2
Galli Cribbs	.240	313	39	75	3	29	21	91	12
John Cristino	.125	32	5	4	2	5	4	12	0
Jonah Davis	.253	328	57	83	18	51	39	105	5
Jordan Howard	.115	26	1	3	0	1	3	7	2
Dondrei Hubbard	.120	25	2	3	1	2	3	8	1
Jimmy Kerrigan	.241	253	42	61	11	37	23	59	2
Pete Kozma	.202	198	28	40	0	16	22	29	0
Todd Lott	.269	156	27	42	8	34	10	36	1
Dylan Nolan	.000	4	0	0	0	0	0	3	0
Ernny Ordonez	.279	68	9	19	2	8	6	17	3
J.D. Osborne	.300	140	21	42	3	18	12	32	1
Cornelius Randolph	.279	237	34	66	5	36	33	49	3
Héctor Sánchez	.266	94	9	25	1	18	11	15	1
Harrison Smith	.200	85	9	17	2	6	6	27	1
Cesar Trejo	.192	52	9	10	1	1	9	21	11
Armond Upshaw	.236	344	51	81	9	38	33	104	33
Daniel Wasinger	.238	122	16	29	6	19	18	25	0
Donivan Williams	.329	70	8	23	1	8	10	21	3
Michael Woodworth	.177	51	2	9	0	6	4	5	3

Name	W	L	ERA	G	SV	IP	H	BB	SO
Tyler Beardsley	8	6	3.65	19	0	111	114	41	93
Nick Belzer	1	4	5.14	7	0	35	36	19	17
Daniel Bies	2	2	0.74	39	16	49	43	15	46
C.J. Carter	3	1	3.83	38	0	52	35	23	62
C.J. Eldred	9	5	4.06	21	0	120	122	27	94
Jack Fox	6	8	4.05	17	0	100	104	34	59
Jose Fuentes	2	2	6.75	8	0	27	33	14	14
A.J. Jones	1	3	6.14	24	0	51	55	21	36
Karch Kowalczyk	0	1	3.00	3	0	12	2	9	7
Westin Muir	5	3	3.51	20	0	100	96	47	62
Logan Nissen	3	6	2.82	40	3	45	39	13	42
Ryan Richardson	3	1	4.22	35	0	60	57	21	38
Keith Rogalla	3	4	3.80	42	2	45	41	32	34
Harrison Smith	0	0	5.63	11	1	16	22	7	9
Spencer Van Scoyoc	3	1	7.78	14	2	20	23	20	17
Luke Westphal	0	2	7.82	7	0	25	31	15	33

KANSAS CITY MONARCHS

Name	AVG	AB	R	H	HR	RBI	BB	SO	SB
Micker Adolfo	.301	306	51	92	14	60	28	79	1
Olivier Basabe	.292	72	10	21	4	14	1	12	2

Name	AVG	AB	R	H	HR	RBI	BB	SO	SB
Keon Broxton	.254	130	29	33	6	18	25	38	17
Gio Brusa	.200	5	0	1	0	0	0	2	0
Cam Cannon	.143	28	3	4	0	1	2	6	0
Gavin Collins	.314	239	38	75	10	41	29	27	2
Edwin Díaz	.217	69	11	15	3	11	6	19	1
Johneshwy Fargas	.348	118	26	41	2	15	6	15	19
Allante Hall	.111	18	5	2	1	1	2	10	0
LJ Hatch	.249	326	44	81	4	50	30	66	3
Jan Hernandez	.308	292	51	90	15	63	32	85	3
Odúbel Herrera	.292	233	49	68	4	20	23	34	15
Chris Herrmann	.355	363	72	129	23	88	51	50	2
Peter Maris	.244	78	8	19	2	12	10	20	3
Brian O'Grady	.242	227	29	55	12	39	23	50	6
Jacob Robson	.250	232	52	58	10	31	57	85	23
Dylan Rosa	.260	131	23	34	7	17	17	50	4
Bubby Rossman	.200	5	1	1	0	0	0	2	0
Taylor Snyder	.300	70	9	21	5	14	5	19	0
Aaron Whitefield	.234	107	14	25	0	5	11	23	11
Justin Wylie	.310	349	73	108	17	56	55	63	16
Andy Yerzy	.286	35	5	10	1	4	11	5	0

Name	W	L	ERA	G	SV	IP	H	BB	SO
Beaux Bonvillain	0	0	6.46	19	0	24	32	13	21
Trey Cobb	0	1	7.07	12	0	14	20	5	8
Cody Deason	4	3	4.54	17	0	75	75	46	71
Brandon Finnegan	7	5	4.33	19	0	104	114	34	89
Grant Gavin	6	4	3.88	37	3	51	39	25	78
Ashton Goudeau	2	1	2.57	3	0	14	18	5	15
Zac Grotz	0	0	0.82	2	0	11	13	1	12
Matt Hartman	2	1	4.43	27	2	43	29	17	44
Miller Hogan	2	3	2.75	20	1	56	61	13	48
Trey Jeans	7	0	3.10	35	0	58	56	23	60
Jordan Martinson	5	2	3.16	31	1	57	48	17	69
Zach Matson	6	4	4.33	21	0	98	85	45	90
Jalen Miller	10	2	3.64	18	0	99	75	59	78
Dalton Moats	5	3	4.61	14	0	66	65	26	57
Jeff Singer	0	3	9.64	4	0	14	24	15	11
Alex Valdez	1	2	5.79	28	1	28	35	15	37
Patrick Weigel	1	3	3.86	34	10	35	26	15	30

LAKE COUNTY DOCKHOUNDS

Name	AVG	AB	R	H	HR	RBI	BB	SO	SB
Pat Adams	.257	35	6	9	0	5	5	12	4
Luis Aviles	.333	9	1	3	0	1	1	2	0
Nick Banks	.300	223	35	67	10	43	23	38	5
Brandon Chinea	.000	1	0	0	0	0	0	1	0
Marcus Chiu	.281	356	71	100	18	51	31	89	15
Marek Chlup	.325	126	26	41	9	25	13	43	6
Pat DeMarco	.205	78	9	16	4	10	2	26	1
Casey Dykstra	.000	12	0	0	0	0	1	6	0
Austin Elder	.333	3	0	1	0	0	0	0	0
Juan Graterol	.387	31	4	12	1	5	1	2	0
Jaxx Groshans	.273	231	32	63	7	32	21	58	2
Tyler Hill	.247	85	10	21	2	15	7	33	1
Thomas Jones	.260	304	57	79	14	45	50	89	21
Justin Lavey	.285	123	12	35	3	10	11	31	8
Kevin Maitan	.121	33	3	4	0	3	3	8	0
Michael Marrale	.108	37	5	4	0	2	4	25	0
Omar Meregildo	.207	29	5	6	2	4	5	11	0
Brian Rey	.344	244	46	84	11	45	13	28	10
Matt Rodriguez	.172	29	5	5	2	7	3	11	0
Will Salas	.333	9	1	3	0	1	1	5	0
Cristian Santana	.083	12	0	1	0	1	0	3	0
Steven Sensley	.173	81	12	14	5	14	11	19	1
Aaron Simmons	.206	131	16	27	2	16	10	31	4
Demetrius Sims	.298	353	57	105	9	50	34	97	26
Harrison Smith	.184	49	5	9	2	6	2	20	1
Curtis Terry	.225	151	25	34	16	36	15	29	0
Blake Tiberi	.303	370	69	112	8	33	53	58	10
Sonny Ulliana	.333	6	1	2	0	1	1	3	0
Dustin Woodcock	.230	213	39	49	8	33	32	79	6

Name	W	L	ERA	G	SV	IP	H	BB	SO
Marco Becerril	1	1	9.64	10	0	28	38	17	21
Austin Davis	1	3	4.74	4	0	19	18	11	28
Randall Delgado	5	2	3.88	10	0	60	59	18	61
Austin Faith	1	3	5.98	22	0	47	53	26	44
Conor Fisk	3	6	5.85	14	0	72	82	18	46
Edgar García	0	0	5.59	8	0	10	9	3	4
Alberto Gonzalez	0	0	8.71	9	0	10	8	12	3
Ryan Hartman	1	1	4.34	5	0	19	24	4	14
Nick Herold	4	2	3.38	6	0	37	34	13	43
Juan Hillman	2	2	6.41	9	0	39	48	29	21
Gabriel Jaramillo	1	0	6.85	21	0	24	25	21	20
Brady Kais	1	5	5.14	39	1	35	35	16	31
Franklyn Kilome	1	4	8.38	6	0	29	30	20	29
Matt Mullenbach	3	0	2.61	38	0	38	40	10	27
Tyler Pike	1	1	5.80	7	0	36	41	12	51
Keisy Portorreal	4	0	3.72	28	2	48	37	14	43
David Richardson	2	4	5.22	8	0	40	41	20	40
JJ Santa Cruz	0	2	4.63	9	0	12	6	9	10
Mike Shawaryn	4	9	6.26	18	0	96	120	36	77
Jojanse Torres	4	2	1.98	36	13	36	23	27	55
Augie Voight	6	2	3.95	21	1	84	74	33	61

LINCOLN SALTDOGS

Name	AVG	AB	R	H	HR	RBI	BB	SO	SB
Nick Anderson	.276	322	70	89	20	58	70	61	16
Marshall Awtry	.204	98	15	20	5	18	18	34	0
Drew Devine	.282	393	66	111	7	37	55	78	12
Adam Donachie	.000	3	0	0	0	0	0	0	0
Matt Goodheart	.207	92	7	19	0	8	16	22	0
Carter Hope	.000	1	1	0	0	0	1	1	0
Will Kengor	.220	264	34	58	6	30	52	69	7
Carson Maxwell	.193	57	5	11	0	4	1	22	1
Zack Miller	.140	50	5	7	0	3	7	18	0
Connor Panas	.296	351	70	104	22	59	33	58	12
Yanio Pérez	.299	338	46	101	9	60	26	63	0
Jason Rogers	.300	110	19	33	2	21	29	18	2
Luis Roman	.247	89	14	22	5	12	18	28	1
Luke Roskam	.294	296	47	87	14	62	48	79	4
Nate Samson	.262	382	53	100	7	50	31	19	11
Aaron Takacs	.255	318	39	81	7	43	50	70	7
Cam Touchette	.206	34	3	7	0	3	4	13	0
Zane Zurbrugg	.306	173	32	53	4	21	24	46	12

Name	W	L	ERA	G	SV	IP	H	BB	SO
Abdallah Aris	6	4	4.52	18	0	92	83	55	77
John Bezdicek	5	5	5.98	17	0	84	90	44	72
Walter Borkovich	1	1	2.57	26	1	42	35	25	46
Tanner Brown	4	7	5.78	18	0	81	91	38	78
Devin Conn	2	0	2.11	21	2	21	19	4	23
Matt Cronin	3	6	6.08	37	4	37	36	16	34
R.J. Freure	5	2	2.96	33	2	49	28	37	79
David Holmberg	8	2	4.50	11	0	68	67	16	50
Carter Hope	4	3	4.56	32	3	47	56	11	33
Zach Keenan	4	6	4.98	21	1	108	119	28	81
Nic Laio	0	0	7.88	22	1	40	43	43	45
Steffon Moore	3	2	6.86	36	6	42	41	29	53
Josh Roeder	3	12	5.43	19	0	109	140	25	67
David Zoz	0	2	4.54	35	2	42	49	11	41

MILWAUKEE MILKMEN

Name	AVG	AB	R	H	HR	RBI	BB	SO	SB
Cam Balego	.301	355	68	107	13	63	40	58	9
Gabriel Cancel	.287	370	64	106	13	66	37	92	20
Ashton Creal	.125	8	0	1	0	0	0	2	0
Mike Crouse	.290	169	31	49	6	25	36	54	13
Juan Echevarria	.143	21	1	3	0	1	0	10	0
Miguel Gómez	.296	385	49	114	11	54	23	49	1
Peyton Gray		0	0	0	0	0	1	0	0
Aaron Hill	.249	334	78	83	6	49	51	88	28
Kyle Johnson	.000	1	0	0	0	0	1	1	0
Jack Mahoney	.000	1	1	0	0	0	0	0	0
Rudy Martin	.234	222	32	52	5	25	23	55	21
Kyle Mora	.000	3	0	0	0	0	0	0	0
Roy Morales	.360	339	52	122	7	67	34	37	3
Reggie Pruitt	.234	308	63	72	9	37	45	106	39
Cam Redding	.275	138	19	38	4	30	9	26	2

Bryan Torres	.371	359	94	133	11	67	64	54	71
Drew Ward	.236	267	30	63	7	41	57	78	1
Justin Williams	.225	111	12	25	3	16	13	27	3
Delvin Zinn	.067	15	1	1	0	1	3	7	2

Name	W	L	ERA	G	SV	IP	H	BB	SO
Frankie Bartow	4	6	4.70	27	0	90	108	20	58
Juan Echevarria	4	2	4.04	20	4	82	75	29	65
Jose Fuentes	2	2	7.71	7	0	23	30	8	13
Peyton Gray	1	2	1.38	37	9	39	22	8	64
Nate Hadley	3	8	5.66	41	13	41	48	24	32
Kyle Johnson	0	0	10.24	6	0	10	13	9	9
Jack Mahoney	1	2	3.47	37	0	49	50	17	55
Kyle Mora	7	6	5.09	20	0	111	136	38	69
Trevin Reynolds	2	2	5.40	30	1	32	34	10	42
Hansel Rodriguez	1	0	4.46	33	0	36	40	9	36
Aneuris Rosario	3	3	4.95	37	0	40	39	15	46
Gregori Vasquez	11	1	3.25	21	0	100	94	21	62
Christian Young	7	6	3.91	18	0	94	86	30	110
Ryan Zimmerman	10	3	3.35	20	0	110	87	36	100

SIOUX CITY EXPLORERS

Name	AVG	AB	R	H	HR	RBI	BB	SO	SB
Vince Fernandez	.246	346	56	85	16	62	47	93	20
Wilfredo Gimenez	.277	220	27	61	7	39	18	33	2
Chase Harris	.210	324	53	68	5	29	47	97	26
Kyle Kasser	.278	295	32	82	2	30	35	30	7
Jack Kelly	.216	74	13	16	2	8	20	11	2
Daniel Lingua	.282	39	6	11	0	3	6	9	3
Matt Lloyd	.321	336	70	108	14	61	51	51	17
John Nogowski	.317	123	21	39	4	16	20	9	3
Jake Ortega	.265	242	36	64	4	26	36	57	6
Scott Ota	.311	148	29	46	7	25	15	16	2
Daniel Pérez	.229	253	31	58	9	35	32	53	0
Eury Pérez	.247	73	8	18	2	11	1	7	1
Tyler Rando	.288	198	26	57	2	25	31	37	2
Jake Sanford	.213	141	18	30	2	22	13	28	0
Miguelangel Sierra	.203	246	37	50	4	33	38	98	2
Heitor Tokar	.000	1	0	0	0	0	0	1	0
Delvin Zinn	.211	223	30	47	3	18	20	53	29

Name	W	L	ERA	G	SV	IP	H	BB	SO
Solomon Bates	10	6	3.57	20	0	126	89	37	124
Brandon Brosher	4	1	4.07	44	1	55	51	19	64
Parker Caracci	0	0	0.90	6	0	10	6	3	10
Franklin Dacosta	0	1	5.51	10	0	16	16	11	15
Carlos Diaz	1	4	5.50	31	0	36	33	17	39
Austin Drury	5	5	3.79	20	0	109	99	53	98
Nate Gercken	3	3	5.83	40	0	42	47	25	38
Kent Hasler	4	2	2.17	28	0	37	22	15	59
Brenden Heiss	0	2	8.14	9	0	21	20	27	17
Braunny Muñoz	1	0	6.59	4	0	14	15	8	8
Francys Peguero	2	1	4.24	17	1	40	34	15	34
Sean Rackoski	5	5	2.17	44	20	54	43	19	62
John Sheaks	1	1	3.86	2	0	14	15	2	4
Heitor Tokar	3	4	5.95	23	0	82	98	35	69
Trenton Toplikar	4	2	4.79	12	0	56	60	12	37
Mitchell Verburg	6	4	3.88	15	0	72	63	25	60
Jared Wetherbee	2	4	4.31	13	0	56	57	25	65

SIOUX FALLS CANARIES

Name	AVG	AB	R	H	HR	RBI	BB	SO	SB
Trevor Achenbach	.265	291	50	77	12	50	35	86	9
Jordan Barth	.298	403	59	120	11	66	20	47	16
Shamoy Christopher	.165	164	17	27	5	17	19	46	0
Hunter Clanin	.256	340	51	87	17	67	45	92	19
Carson Clowers	.226	53	6	12	0	3	0	18	8
Welington Dotel	.280	261	29	73	4	40	9	71	27
Logan Eickhoff	.273	44	12	12	0	2	3	10	6
Mike Hart	.302	291	62	88	26	69	45	77	4
Jabari Henry	.265	325	78	86	19	73	89	87	2
Osvaldo Martínez	.277	260	37	72	2	22	28	25	8
Cole Pengilly	.375	16	0	6	0	1	1	8	0
Marshall Rich	.240	75	7	18	0	13	9	21	2
Tyler Ryan	.169	65	5	11	0	3	1	28	0
Spencer Sarringar	.266	64	6	17	2	12	4	19	2
Darnell Sweeney	.283	368	75	104	19	57	59	112	20
Wyatt Ulrich	.283	314	62	89	2	27	35	45	31
Aaron Whitefield	.250	44	10	11	2	9	6	17	7

Name	W	L	ERA	G	SV	IP	H	BB	SO
Bret Barnett	1	0	7.71	10	0	12	10	15	5
Beaux Bonvillain	2	2	5.40	11	0	13	14	7	11
Akeem Bostick	3	4	4.65	15	0	81	75	37	50
Jose Cruz	5	3	5.95	40	3	39	49	19	31
Ty Culbreth	7	5	6.23	19	0	108	132	36	70
Matt Gill	1	0	6.48	9	0	17	22	6	12
Chris Hardin	3	7	6.28	20	0	76	82	43	58
Charlie Hasty	3	3	2.28	44	22	43	44	14	48
Christian Johnson	2	0	6.30	38	1	50	46	19	46
Cole LaLonde	1	0	8.14	17	1	21	26	15	22
Neil Lang	5	8	6.10	21	1	100	107	51	55
Angel Lebron	2	1	7.54	29	1	45	53	38	19
Seth Miller	3	3	5.03	14	0	54	63	19	27
Jerryell Rivera	0	1	9.82	12	1	15	16	19	10
D.J. Sharabi	0	2	6.35	3	0	11	13	10	8
Brady Stover	4	0	2.83	25	0	29	22	24	22
Hayden Thomas	0	1	4.50	14	0	14	10	11	13
Mitchell Walters	8	5	5.02	19	0	95	94	45	92
Colby Wyatt	1	2	6.14	6	0	22	32	10	9

WINNIPEG GOLDEYES

Name	AVG	AB	R	H	HR	RBI	BB	SO	SB
Andy Armstrong	.261	357	51	93	2	32	20	61	4
Jacob Bockelie	.261	142	17	37	7	38	14	32	0
Chris Burgess	.276	185	22	51	5	20	21	54	2
Dayson Croes	.351	385	61	135	3	67	41	36	5
Najee Gaskins	.230	222	35	51	2	18	34	72	9
Hidekel Gonzalez	.233	236	22	55	8	30	12	60	7
Sherman Graves	.128	39	1	5	0	1	5	15	1
Tra Holmes	.190	184	30	35	2	24	21	67	18
Brynn Martinez	.254	284	55	72	3	31	51	41	39
Tommy McCarthy	.189	201	15	38	1	16	24	51	1
Jace Mercer	.250	16	1	4	1	2	0	9	0
Max Murphy	.289	391	66	113	26	84	42	100	1
Andrew Shaps	.079	38	3	3	0	7	5	9	0
Miles Simington	.329	152	25	50	4	21	12	21	5
Jackson Smith	.230	135	19	31	4	12	7	30	1
Keith Torres	.200	140	29	28	4	16	26	43	6
Javeyan Williams	.242	240	37	58	3	22	21	70	11

Name	W	L	ERA	G	SV	IP	H	BB	SO
Samuel Adames	2	4	3.53	37	13	43	45	23	36
Landen Bourassa	11	6	4.62	19	0	109	136	34	64
Chas Cywin	1	3	2.74	28	0	46	34	11	20
Marc-André Habeck	1	2	5.18	18	0	49	60	16	37
Tyler Jandron	2	7	5.67	27	1	79	87	36	72
Nolan LaMere	0	0	5.89	16	0	18	20	10	10
Taylor Lepard	0	0	5.59	13	0	19	25	14	6
Brandon Marklund	0	0	15.53	12	0	13	19	17	9
R.J. Martinez	6	4	4.19	20	0	77	81	35	63
Joey Matulovich	5	9	3.78	20	0	117	101	32	121
Cam Opp	1	4	7.22	21	0	29	41	21	36
Luis Ramirez	8	7	4.73	21	0	120	125	49	86
Travis Seabrooke	6	6	6.30	18	0	86	114	42	68
Josh Vincent	0	3	6.62	19	1	35	40	17	19

ATLANTIC LEAGUE

During the regular season, Lancaster's chances of a title defense often seemed to be slipping away. The Barnstormers were nine games under .500 as late as mid-August, but they finished the regular season by winning their last seven games, drawing them to 37-24 in the second half, which was good enough to win the North's second half.

And once they got there, the suddenly hot Barnstormers were once again in command. They swept Long Island. The finals were more troublesome, as Gastona won the first two games, but Lancaster rallied to win three straight. The clincher saw Brent Teller allow just one run in seven innings while league MVP Andretty Cordero went 3-for-4 with three stolen bases, a run scored and two RBIs in a 7-1 win.

North	W	L	PCT	GB
York	71	54	.568	-
*-Long Island	66	58	.532	4.5
Southern Maryland	64	62	.508	7.5
&Lancaster	62	62	.500	8.5
Staten Island	49	75	.395	21.5
South	**W**	**L**	**PCT**	**GB**
*&-High Point	78	46	.629	-
^Gastonia	79	47	.627	-
Charleston	56	70	.444	23
Spire City	49	74	.398	28.5
Lexington	49	75	.395	29

**First-half champion. & Second-half champion. ^Wild-Card*

Playoffs—Semifinals: Gastonia defeated High Point 3-2 and Lancaster defeated Long Island 3-0 in best-of-five series. **Finals:** Lancaster defeated Gastonia 3-2 in best-of-five series.

Attendance: Long Island Ducks 297,745, Lancaster Barnstormers 242,961, York Revolution 196,968, Southern Maryland Blue Crabs 181,291, Charleston Dirty Birds t146,336, High Point Rockers 116,925, Lexington Counter Clocks 92,806, Gastonia Honey Hunters 91,090, Staten Island Ferry Hawks 68,938, Spire City Ghost Hounds 57,836.

All-Star Team: C - Kole Cottam, Spire City. **1B:** Drew Mendoza, York; Thomas Dillard, Lexington. **2B:** Shed Long, Jr., High Point; Melvin Mercedes, Lancaster**.** **SS:** Angel Aguilar, Staten Island. **3B:** Andretty Cordero, Lancaster. **OF:** Leobaldo Cabrera, Spire City; Dwight Smith, Jr., Charleston; Ben Aklinski, High Point. **DH:** Jose Marmolejos, Spire City. **SP:** Zach Mort, Gastonia. **RP:** Jameson McGrane, High Point; **CL: Ryan** Dull, High Point.

Player of the Year: Andretty Cordero, Lancaster. **Co-pitchers of the Year:** Zach Mort, Gastonia; Nick Raquet, York. **Defensive Player of the Year:** Melvin Mercedes, Lancaster. **Manager of the Year:** Mauro "Goose" Gozzo, Gastonia.

BATTING LEADERS

Player, Team	AVG	AB	R	H	HR	RBI	SB
Drew Mendoza, YOR	.346	428	90	148	15	87	23
Andretty Cordero, LAN	.339	490	83	166	15	116	12
Dwight Smith Jr., CWV	.331	429	95	142	22	64	24
Tomo Otosaka, YOR	.330	373	86	123	2	48	42
Melvin Mercedes, LAN	.328	439	103	144	8	57	34
Angel Aguilar, SI	.324	392	74	127	23	74	18
Wilson Garcia, 2 Teams	.324	392	41	127	14	64	0
Alex Crosby, SMD	.323	362	43	117	8	66	22
Ariel Sandoval, LAN	.323	350	59	113	12	62	23
Alex Dickerson, LI	.314	401	71	126	26	91	00

PITCHING LEADERS

Pitcher, Team	W	L	ERA	IP	H	HR	BB	SO
Danny Wirchansky, CWV	6	5	3.28	121	102	12	42	105
Gunnar Kines, GAS	12	4	3.33	114	104	14	30	110
Jared Lakind, LAN	9	4	3.54	112	95	11	63	99
Nick Raquet, YOR	13	7	3.71	146	129	11	40	133
Christian Capuano, SI	10	4	3.82	118	112	13	46	118
Joe Testa, CWV	9	4	3.93	119	115	12	36	86
Mickey Jannis, HP	14	5	4.01	146	128	19	53	117
Ian Kahaloa, SMD	10	9	4.04	151	127	21	52	143
Robert Stock, LI	9	4	4.40	102	103	9	33	92
Aaron Ochsenbein, LEX	10	7	4.47	107	99	15	35	108

CHARLESTON DIRTY BIRDS

Name	AVG	AB	R	H	HR	RBI	BB	SO	SB
Smith Jr., Dwight	.331	429	95	142	22	64	70	74	24
Perez, Juan Carlos	.282	248	37	70	8	51	25	47	3
Miller, Jalen	.279	344	55	96	12	48	20	62	27
Mehlbauer, Clayton	.274	215	51	59	6	28	35	82	16
Bradley, Bobby	.270	404	70	109	30	81	49	100	3
O'Conner, Justin	.263	293	42	77	12	46	29	85	5
Tejeda, Isaias	.250	124	22	31	4	22	14	24	0
Pérez, Yefri	.241	361	48	87	7	31	30	99	35
Goris, Diego	.231	320	37	74	7	40	18	79	13
Gonzalez, Yovan	.225	173	18	39	4	30	22	33	1
Atiles, Luis	.224	49	4	11	0	2	5	15	1
Nash, Telvin	.219	361	52	79	20	69	48	124	0
Roman, Luis	.218	156	17	34	4	23	14	46	7
Brito, Daniel	.212	33	3	7	0	4	5	9	1
Racusin, Zach	.200	70	9	14	1	9	3	8	1
Bermudez, Jose	.200	150	24	30	0	12	19	52	14
Pugh, Tillman	.188	64	8	12	1	5	2	24	4
Marshall, Montrell	.169	71	8	12	1	6	6	36	0
Bridges, Zachary	.169	124	17	21	3	15	9	51	3
Fuller, Terry	.100	30	2	3	0	0	7	18	3
Ghelfi, Mitch	.074	54	4	4	1	3	7	17	0

Name	W	L	ERA	G	SV	IP	H	BB	SO
Hiraldo, Yaramil	1	0	1.64	11	5	11	6	1	11
Martinez, Joan	0	1	1.69	18	3	16	5	9	14
Hernandez, Arnaldo	1	1	1.80	15	3	15	8	4	16
Bacon, Troy	4	4	2.73	14	0	66	57	21	65
Wirchansky, Danny	6	5	3.28	21	0	121	102	42	105
Bosiokovic, Jacob	4	4	3.35	44	1	43	41	25	58
Gomez, Ricardo	1	4	3.70	48	6	49	45	20	46
Ogando, Cristofer	0	0	3.72	10	0	10	11	5	13
Trabacchi, Nick	0	0	3.75	2	0	12	8	6	15
Testa, Joe	9	4	3.93	25	0	119	115	36	86
Martin, Josh	1	1	4.09	12	0	11	4	16	9
Clark, Ryan	2	3	4.30	48	3	61	60	23	63
Westphal, Luke	1	1	4.38	13	1	12	10	9	16
Adams, Derrick	6	9	5.04	19	0	100	105	48	100
Scheetz, Kit	7	10	5.47	20	0	107	118	43	106
Webb, Colt	4	5	5.67	26	0	102	107	48	80
Suriel, Edison	2	5	6.71	37	2	62	71	35	52
York, Mikey	4	2	6.75	13	0	44	53	28	33
Lopez, Victor	0	1	6.85	16	0	22	30	9	16
Fisher, Jake	0	2	6.88	3	0	17	16	7	9
Jerez, Williams	3	1	7.29	31	0	33	43	13	39
Butler, Eddie	0	2	9.82	3	0	11	15	5	8
Solomon, William	0	0	10.24	5	2	10	19	4	6

GASTONIA HONEY HUNTERS

Name	AVG	AB	R	H	HR	RBI	BB	SO	SB
Franco, Carlos	.374	211	50	79	17	59	47	47	1
Escarra, J.C.	.348	164	40	57	15	41	22	17	1
Moya, Steven	.321	112	24	36	16	41	24	24	0
Reinheimer, Jack	.310	242	62	75	11	29	35	44	30
Jarrett, Zach	.299	452	101	135	25	90	61	104	28
Turbo, Johnni	.289	83	17	24	3	12	4	15	7
Manea, Scott	.274	336	62	92	15	52	60	48	0
Davidson, Braxton	.267	266	59	71	25	78	69	123	3
Curbelo, Luis	.262	359	57	94	13	60	23	91	6
Washington, David	.261	203	38	53	22	51	32	76	3
Freeman, Cole	.254	193	34	49	5	19	12	19	19
Hoover, Jake	.243	144	18	35	3	14	9	40	7
Gonzalez, Pedro	.240	246	36	59	10	35	25	91	6
Sensley, Steven	.239	180	29	43	8	28	21	45	1
Santa, Kevin	.238	323	49	77	4	30	32	35	26
De La Rosa, Eric	.237	198	38	47	11	40	22	75	19
Olmeda, Alexis	.234	128	18	30	6	29	17	54	0
Terry, Curtis	.228	224	31	51	9	29	20	40	0
Butler, Calvin	.207	58	13	12	0	4	2	27	2

Name	W	L	ERA	G	SV	IP	H	BB	SO
Thomas, Tyler	2	1	0.90	15	1	20	14	6	34
Spraker, Graham	0	1	2.08	13	6	13	6	9	15
Daniels, Brett	7	1	2.18	13	0	54	29	20	54
Sammons, Bryan	0	0	2.29	5	0	20	12	5	26
Larson, Grant	0	2	2.53	2	0	11	13	1	8
Walden, Marcus	2	1	2.70	4	0	20	14	2	24
Wells, Nick	0	1	2.90	30	0	31	27	13	37
Kines, Gunnar	12	4	3.33	22	1	114	104	30	110
Fennell, Trent	2	3	3.71	17	0	17	16	11	17
Sanabia, Alex	4	0	3.94	6	0	32	28	2	25
Schultz, Jaime	4	1	4.05	27	9	27	13	19	44
Conroy, Ryan	1	0	4.08	10	0	29	28	5	33
Bugg, Parker	2	1	4.15	14	2	13	10	6	17
McKinney, Ian	4	1	4.24	8	0	47	33	11	53
Blanton, Bryan	3	2	4.43	57	8	61	46	39	78
Mort, Zach	13	3	4.63	25	0	117	109	29	147

	W	L	ERA	G	SV	IP	H	BB	SO
Godley, Zack	5	3	4.79	13	0	71	63	27	86
Romano, Sal	4	5	4.91	28	0	84	93	37	75
Richardson, David	2	3	5.85	19	1	20	18	10	27
Freeman, Sam	2	2	6.06	34	1	36	41	19	41
Westcott, Zac	1	2	6.43	3	0	14	13	4	8
Van Steensel, Todd	1	2	6.48	22	0	25	28	16	18
Williamson, Ryan	1	1	6.91	26	0	57	65	32	51
Gonzalez, Kelvin	3	0	7.83	20	0	33	41	18	31
Gaviglio, Sam	0	2	9.45	5	0	20	22	11	9
Rutkowski, Harry	2	2	9.87	12	0	35	58	27	19
Rodriguez, Orlando	1	1	11.40	5	0	15	19	12	14

HIGH POINT ROCKERS

Name	AVG	AB	R	H	HR	RBI	BB	SO	SB
Russell, Michael	.338	213	48	72	7	28	17	23	13
Latimore, Quincy	.313	128	22	40	8	21	15	34	6
Long Jr., Shed	.307	394	68	121	13	59	52	72	20
Goris, Diego	.298	57	8	17	0	1	2	12	0
Nogowski, John	.297	128	22	38	11	40	23	14	5
Grotjohn, Ryan	.297	384	78	114	14	64	68	74	28
Burt, D.J.	.296	307	64	91	2	32	45	48	32
Taylor, Beau	.291	265	51	77	9	61	42	66	1
Aklinski, Ben	.286	451	114	129	24	102	71	105	31
Wiel, Zander	.276	431	77	119	29	96	38	109	5
Yang, Dai-Kang	.271	340	66	92	10	58	60	94	6
Parreira, Brian	.266	320	41	85	12	56	37	91	1
Martinez, Michael	.249	333	42	83	4	62	18	57	4
Johnson, Joe	.232	56	12	13	2	5	4	16	0
Daly, John	.199	136	31	27	2	12	20	57	15
Tapia, Emmanuel	.190	137	12	26	4	16	24	61	0
Williamson, Cam	.185	27	6	5	1	2	3	6	1

Name	W	L	ERA	G	SV	IP	H	BB	SO
Barraclough, Kyle	1	0	1.00	7	1	18	12	4	17
Braymer, Ben	2	0	1.16	4	0	23	16	4	23
Dull, Ryan	0	1	1.40	46	18	45	24	11	60
McGrane, Jameson	2	0	1.99	44	3	45	30	20	67
Selman, Sam	0	0	2.79	29	0	29	23	21	38
Leibrandt, Brandon	4	3	3.26	12	0	61	50	19	53
Ross, Austin	2	3	3.62	36	0	55	45	23	71
Burton, Sam	0	1	3.86	3	0	14	14	7	8
Cole, A.J.	3	2	3.91	24	1	25	18	7	36
Bedrosian, Cam	3	1	3.94	35	1	32	25	6	54
Jannis, Mickey	14	5	4.01	27	0	146	128	53	117
Rhoades, Jeremy	8	2	4.32	42	0	50	50	23	61
Halbohn, Kyle	2	2	4.33	30	0	35	44	5	25
Manzueta, Jheyson	7	2	4.52	14	0	70	89	30	57
Guerrieri, Taylor	2	1	4.55	30	0	30	26	16	30
Nicolino, Justin	4	1	4.56	9	0	47	47	17	34
Weiss, Ryan	5	3	4.61	9	0	55	62	12	52
Ramírez, Neil	2	3	4.82	10	0	37	31	5	37
Stem, Craig	3	2	6.07	9	0	43	51	14	49
O'Sullivan, Liam	2	2	6.08	9	0	37	50	15	18
Johnson, Joe	0	1	6.19	17	0	32	37	13	21
Solter, Matt	3	2	6.59	6	0	27	35	8	13
Hensley, Bryce	6	1	6.67	39	1	57	70	17	40
Uskali, Neil	1	1	7.04	5	0	23	28	6	12
Atkins, Mitch	1	4	8.13	7	0	28	46	6	23

LANCASTER BARNSTORMERS

Name	AVG	AB	R	H	HR	RBI	BB	SO	SB
Cordero, Andretty	.339	490	83	166	15	116	30	73	12
Garcia, Wilson	.334	350	35	117	13	63	14	24	0
Mercedes, Melvin	.328	439	103	144	8	57	90	62	34
Sandoval, Ariel	.323	350	59	113	12	62	33	47	23
Coca, Yeison	.311	367	75	114	5	42	35	85	37
Carpenter, Joseph	.297	337	56	100	16	62	18	73	5
Peroni, Anthony	.275	80	9	22	1	13	16	15	0
Loehr, Trace	.275	280	49	77	4	37	27	45	8
Sedio, Chad	.274	84	20	23	2	9	10	23	1
Proctor, Chris	.272	158	34	43	4	25	11	34	13
Robinson, Trayvon	.269	294	61	79	9	52	65	92	8
Dunston Jr., Shawon	.261	222	47	58	9	36	33	57	25
Conley, Jack	.237	300	46	71	6	40	31	66	29

	AVG	AB	R	H	HR	RBI	BB	SO	SB
Dugan, Kelly	.191	136	17	26	8	24	13	34	0
Hoover, Jake	.176	188	27	33	0	18	23	65	10

Name	W	L	ERA	G	SV	IP	H	BB	SO
Liranzo, Jesús	0	0	0.90	8	0	10	10	3	18
Duron, Nick	2	0	2.01	23	2	22	15	11	36
Tedesco, Brady	1	1	2.25	2	0	12	13	3	7
Adams, Mike	3	6	3.18	51	12	51	45	19	42
Lakind, Jared	9	4	3.54	23	0	112	95	63	99
Swarmer, Matt	4	1	3.69	7	0	39	30	13	52
Warren, Zach	3	4	3.77	29	0	29	19	21	36
Bain, Jeff	4	2	3.78	9	0	50	48	8	42
Lee, Andrew	3	1	4.25	25	6	30	23	15	40
Marconi, Brian	0	1	4.34	38	1	48	41	34	53
Granitz, Garrett	2	1	4.75	26	0	30	33	14	16
Clarke, Bret	0	5	5.29	39	0	68	72	25	53
Lemoine, Jacob	1	3	5.57	6	0	32	39	11	19
Teller, Brent	11	6	5.69	22	0	125	132	38	102
DiSabatino, Dominic	5	8	5.90	23	1	98	102	49	99
Sittinger, Brandyn	5	7	5.93	31	0	82	86	32	98
Ball, Nile	7	6	6.26	23	0	119	143	56	105
Johnston, Spencer	1	2	6.58	5	0	26	26	5	20
Goodson, Donald	0	0	6.97	8	1	10	10	3	9
LaPorte, Tyler	0	1	7.36	18	0	18	23	11	13
Aker, Cole	0	1	7.47	13	0	16	19	11	11

LEXINGTON COUNTER CLOCKS

Name	AVG	AB	R	H	HR	RBI	BB	SO	SB
Watson, Zach	.309	123	18	38	3	15	4	28	6
Dawson, Ronnie	.282	248	45	70	13	39	26	40	13
Moritz, Andrew	.278	187	27	52	3	22	24	26	12
Brown, Logan	.275	393	41	108	14	57	9	60	0
Owings, Connor	.272	482	75	131	22	92	54	122	15
Encarnacion, JC	.272	486	67	132	17	63	25	132	37
Geraldo, Manuel	.270	174	23	47	2	17	12	34	10
Sanchez, Aldenis	.269	52	7	14	1	8	7	19	1
Valera, Jackson	.268	41	3	11	1	4	1	9	1
Roa, Hector	.263	179	22	47	6	23	10	51	1
Brady, Chris	.260	100	12	26	1	9	9	30	0
Dillard, Thomas	.258	427	83	110	39	100	100	125	8
Ghelfi, Mitch	.252	151	20	38	5	17	13	40	0
Gregorio, Osmy	.249	169	24	42	3	15	5	37	4
Yorgen, Pete	.239	46	5	11	0	2	4	9	0
Avelino, Abiatal	.238	63	5	15	0	6	0	7	5
Tavarez, Jesus	.217	226	26	49	4	15	26	52	3
Broussard, Brandt	.211	294	30	62	1	26	29	51	7
Davis, Zach	.203	123	27	25	0	5	15	26	23
Huma, Josue	.176	142	21	25	0	8	25	28	0
Gitter, Jake	.152	33	4	5	3	3	3	18	1

Name	W	L	ERA	G	SV	IP	H	BB	SO
Feigl, Brady	2	1	2.36	34	0	34	27	8	43
Schilling, Garrett	0	3	3.00	45	18	48	36	10	55
Steele, Joey	2	4	3.61	49	3	62	53	16	98
Henzman, Lincoln	5	4	3.68	36	2	51	45	17	60
Gonzalez, Merandy	3	2	4.31	12	0	56	49	40	46
Ochsenbein, Aaron	10	7	4.47	34	2	107	99	35	108
Corcino, Daniel	1	5	4.91	9	0	40	33	21	26
Martin, Josh	2	0	5.29	14	1	17	18	12	11
Rosa, Raymells	2	3	5.69	41	0	55	54	31	77
Mekkes, Dakota	3	4	5.85	42	0	65	62	38	64
Garcia, Yeudy	5	7	5.89	19	0	96	104	47	81
Ledet, Patrick	4	7	5.94	21	0	80	92	40	57
Eickhoff, Jerad	3	4	6.16	9	0	50	64	20	40
Schmidt, Kaleb	1	1	6.30	2	0	10	6	8	7
Lopez, Victor	0	0	6.62	8	0	18	24	6	15
Kickham, Mike	1	7	7.08	15	0	67	75	44	55
Colon, Steven	0	2	7.12	7	0	30	30	21	25
Burton, Sam	1	0	7.20	3	0	10	14	6	4
Sulbaran, Juan Carlos	1	4	7.23	12	0	37	55	11	25
Salow, Logan	0	2	8.44	15	0	16	22	16	18
Dougherty, Joe	2	2	8.69	30	0	39	56	20	26
Herrera, Alsis	1	4	9.67	22	0	49	75	24	32

LONG ISLAND DUCKS

Name	AVG	AB	R	H	HR	RBI	BB	SO	SB
Castro, Carlos	.354	181	34	64	10	31	9	44	2
Ford, Lew	.340	100	22	34	1	14	8	18	1
Murphy, Daniel	.331	142	20	47	2	19	14	18	3
Dickerson, Alex	.314	401	71	126	26	91	48	77	0
Sisco, Chance	.305	95	24	29	11	33	26	18	0
Wilson, Mike	.303	33	6	10	0	3	3	14	1
Travis, Sam	.303	456	82	138	19	92	43	49	1
De Aza, Alejandro	.298	295	54	88	4	49	43	45	7
Hechavarría, Adeiny	.297	145	29	43	7	34	21	24	2
Tejada, Rubén	.293	266	59	78	6	35	53	35	3
Guerrero, Luis	.286	28	7	8	2	8	3	10	4
Powell, Boog	.285	239	50	68	6	35	34	44	18
Goodwin, Brian	.277	220	50	61	12	38	39	43	13
DeCarlo, Joe	.274	383	60	105	15	71	56	64	2
Lin, Tzu-Wei	.270	152	34	41	7	23	26	36	7
Bell, Brantley	.262	302	53	79	12	66	29	55	22
Guzman, Jonathan	.259	158	18	41	1	22	7	41	5
Ramos, Wilson	.233	150	19	35	3	24	10	18	0
Kelly, Scott	.232	82	15	19	0	6	8	15	6
Caulfield, Philip	.220	82	10	18	0	9	3	16	4
Geraci, Ernie	.207	29	5	6	0	4	3	10	2
Woodcock, Dustin	.195	87	18	17	6	12	10	30	1
Salcedo, Edward	.122	41	1	5	0	5	4	13	2
Taylor, Trent	.118	51	14	6	0	3	7	24	8
Peroni, Anthony	.075	53	4	4	0	2	9	11	0
Sandford, Darian	.036	28	12	1	0	0	2	9	7

Name	W	L	ERA	G	SV	IP	H	BB	SO
Van Gurp, Franklin	1	0	1.85	25	0	24	9	20	36
Jose, Jose	6	2	3.07	54	4	56	52	14	56
Kennedy, Brett	1	0	3.09	3	0	12	16	2	16
Alburquerque, Al	6	1	3.65	50	7	44	49	11	47
Woods Jr., Stephen	7	2	3.77	11	0	60	62	27	60
Pinto, Wladimir	0	1	4.11	8	0	15	9	20	16
Anderson, Jack	1	0	4.24	18	0	17	15	7	18
Stock, Robert	9	4	4.40	16	0	102	103	33	92
Hackimer, Tom	1	0	4.76	20	0	17	8	15	22
Fishman, Jake	2	0	4.82	21	0	19	12	4	19
Tarpley, Stephen	4	5	4.90	14	0	72	75	29	70
Solter, Matt	2	2	5.46	6	0	31	41	16	21
Clarkin, Ian	3	5	5.56	16	0	79	89	35	84
Hayes, Reed	0	0	5.63	22	0	24	21	18	19
Lobstein, Kyle	5	5	5.66	37	0	89	106	42	81
Varela, James	0	0	5.84	6	1	12	14	3	9
Courtney, Justin	0	3	6.19	7	0	16	17	4	18
Alintoff, Justin	2	3	6.25	35	1	81	107	28	54
Iorio, Joe	5	9	6.45	25	0	103	140	34	68
Cepeda, Chris	0	2	7.04	11	0	23	32	9	13
Quackenbush, Kevin	6	3	7.08	40	14	41	49	12	41
Kuzia, Joe	2	3	7.21	40	0	44	61	22	39
Mills, McKenzie	1	1	9.35	6	1	26	38	14	15
Voight, Augie	1	1	9.49	3	0	12	10	9	9
Harkin, Scott	1	3	12.64	4	0	16	28	5	20

SPIRE CITY GHOST HOUNDS

Name	AVG	AB	R	H	HR	RBI	BB	SO	SB
Castro, Starlin	.305	167	26	51	1	24	13	33	2
Read, Raudy	.305	305	42	93	20	53	16	41	0
Marmolejos, José	.303	396	69	120	28	90	61	79	0
Diaz, Eddy	.295	129	18	38	1	10	11	15	23
Cabrera, Leobaldo	.294	466	91	137	34	100	52	122	20
Cottam, Kole	.290	396	65	115	30	75	49	90	3
Brault, Steven	.283	187	30	53	7	27	10	36	4
Dedelow, Craig	.281	406	88	114	26	78	60	132	34
Yorgen, Pete	.273	66	5	18	0	4	3	12	0
Abreu, Osvaldo	.269	312	49	84	13	43	31	53	13
Paredes, Jimmy	.259	293	38	76	18	50	20	70	5
Sierra, Moisés	.253	91	15	23	2	8	13	24	0
Garcia, Wilson	.238	42	6	10	1	1	3	2	0
Twine, Justin	.235	34	3	8	1	2	1	14	2
Becker, Luke	.231	394	77	91	16	41	69	96	9
Kelly, Scott	.224	196	41	44	0	18	18	31	5
Turbo, Johnni	.206	68	10	14	0	3	2	17	4
Johns, Gavin	.197	66	1	13	0	4	1	16	2
Shaw, Chris	.197	76	9	15	3	10	12	26	0

Name	W	L	ERA	G	SV	IP	H	BB	SO
Hernandez, Arnaldo	5	3	2.82	24	2	22	18	9	24
Capellan, Victor	1	2	3.05	19	1	21	18	7	12
Rosscup, Zac	4	4	3.31	22	7	71	62	42	84
Povse, Max	3	3	4.61	25	1	55	58	25	54
Neverauskas, Dovydas	1	2	5.02	26	9	29	21	13	28
Kubiak, David	8	6	5.37	21	0	116	122	34	97
Sosa, Henry	2	2	5.53	5	0	28	30	12	26
Galese, Nick	0	0	5.84	5	0	12	16	6	3
Johnson, Joe	4	4	5.98	44	1	41	48	20	38
Beggs, Dustin	3	13	6.14	24	0	133	174	43	83
Feigl, Brady	1	1	6.28	16	0	14	15	7	20
Medoro, Brendan	2	1	6.98	17	1	30	34	19	20
Lavendier, Winston	2	4	7.04	14	0	69	85	30	36
Fisher, Jake	1	3	7.28	10	0	38	52	18	15
Reitz, Matt	2	1	7.28	11	0	56	79	13	34
Villanueva, Elih	1	7	7.33	14	0	66	80	27	60
Goodson, Donald	1	2	7.82	37	3	38	47	32	57
Kirwan, William	0	0	8.05	11	0	19	29	15	9
Peden, Nate	3	4	8.17	30	0	51	61	24	57
Tiedemann, Tai	0	0	8.25	9	0	12	17	13	6
Tannenbaum, Max	0	1	8.31	14	0	13	18	6	14
Weinberger, Jack	2	5	8.49	40	0	35	38	26	30
Witkowski, John	0	1	9.92	6	0	16	27	8	11
Singer, Jeff	1	2	17.05	16	0	13	17	19	13

STATEN ISLAND FERRYHAWKS

Name	AVG	AB	R	H	HR	RBI	BB	SO	SB
Tsutsugo, Yoshi	.359	39	11	14	7	13	9	16	0
Aguilar, Angel	.324	392	74	127	23	74	35	79	18
Brito, Chris	.317	186	38	59	11	49	21	47	4
Williams, Justin	.314	70	15	22	5	12	8	19	3
Sanchez, Aldenis	.307	114	15	35	0	9	7	17	5
Castro, Luis	.291	361	53	105	15	65	24	68	18
Wehler, Jeffrey	.282	124	20	35	3	13	6	22	12
Elliott, Jack	.273	384	58	105	18	67	34	119	7
Baldwin, Roldani	.272	349	53	95	12	46	23	96	3
Krause, Kevin	.267	266	28	71	7	40	52	39	3
Cespedes, Ricardo	.261	329	64	86	6	29	16	55	25
Santana, Cristian	.255	110	9	28	4	19	7	30	0
Pugh, Brandon	.237	249	39	59	8	28	24	74	35
Johnson, Kolby	.229	35	5	8	0	3	5	6	3
Kueber, Garrett	.226	248	31	56	5	24	36	76	9
Fisher, Noah	.224	85	12	19	2	7	8	33	1
Sparling, Bobby	.200	105	7	21	1	10	8	34	0
Wilson, Mike	.200	115	15	23	5	16	14	68	2
Edelman, Mikey	.193	161	29	31	2	8	9	39	16
Romero, Deibinson	.190	84	6	16	1	12	8	17	0
Jemison, Andrew	.179	28	5	5	1	2	2	6	1
Winaker, Matt	.132	53	3	7	1	7	4	13	0
Racusin, Zach	.128	39	3	5	0	3	2	6	1
Piatnik, Mitch	.085	47	8	4	0	2	3	29	9

Name	W	L	ERA	G	SV	IP	H	BB	SO
Gross, Andrew	1	2	1.50	22	4	24	18	10	24
Ramirez, Williams	2	1	1.71	26	4	26	9	17	49
Kirwan, William	1	1	3.09	20	0	23	22	13	16
Capuano, Christian	10	4	3.82	22	0	118	112	46	118
Hartman, Ryan	6	6	3.93	17	0	89	92	23	64
Payano, Pedro	2	6	3.97	35	8	34	35	22	38
Pineyro, Ivan	6	3	4.14	22	0	96	102	28	58
Remington, Jesse	7	6	5.14	18	0	96	109	53	64
Mitschele, Ryan	0	2	5.76	22	1	30	30	21	36
Peralta, Ofelky	2	4	6.48	12	0	42	44	30	35
Allegretti, Christian	1	3	6.58	28	0	40	40	27	43
Aiello, Vincenzo	0	2	7.12	47	1	61	79	36	62
Quattrocchi, Anthony	0	4	7.69	37	0	55	60	51	34
Katz, Alex	1	2	7.76	22	0	27	28	19	30
DeCarr, Austin	0	6	7.82	6	0	25	27	21	20

Name	W	L	ERA	G	SV	IP	H	BB	SO
Santana, Enrique	1	1	7.84	11	0	10	11	12	6
Loubier, Blake	2	2	8.10	20	0	40	53	33	28
Quinn, Patrick	2	0	8.59	14	1	15	20	15	15
Simpson, Jordan	1	2	8.78	4	0	13	17	11	9
Esposito, John	0	0	9.39	8	0	15	24	7	6
Beardsley, Nick	2	7	9.39	13	0	54	75	46	31
Whitmore, Kelsie	0	0	9.49	13	0	12	23	13	4
Fuller, Jim	0	1	10.22	14	2	12	16	9	13
Skuija, Ethan	0	3	10.88	8	0	22	32	14	23
Byrne, Michael	0	3	11.15	4	0	15	16	21	6
Pazos, James	1	2	11.48	17	0	13	14	13	13

SOUTHERN MARYLAND BLUE CRABS

Name	AVG	AB	R	H	HR	RBI	BB	SO	SB
Kerrigan, Jimmy	.345	145	30	50	13	43	17	28	9
Crosby, Alex	.323	362	43	117	8	66	32	46	22
Wielansky, Michael	.320	97	25	31	8	21	14	16	3
Haug, Ryan	.317	186	28	59	4	38	19	24	3
Lee, Braxton	.292	442	72	129	11	71	62	114	12
Lee, Khalil	.277	303	60	84	15	66	55	81	13
Baca, Michael	.265	378	56	100	1	37	32	75	23
Caulfield, Philip	.263	339	40	89	3	39	29	46	11
Yetsko, Ian	.258	213	36	55	7	25	15	74	10
Kueber, Garrett	.242	33	1	8	0	2	5	11	1
Sundberg, Jack	.239	451	82	108	11	51	92	127	36
Hibbert, Matt	.225	71	19	16	1	5	15	21	3
Rosario, Jose	.221	145	9	32	2	14	8	41	3
Harris, David	.214	154	12	33	3	17	13	51	2
Semones, Fox	.200	60	27	12	0	2	6	31	11
Quiroz, Isaias	.193	274	37	53	17	52	35	117	1
Hobson, K.C.	.185	405	56	75	17	48	69	125	5
Aberouette, Felix	.167	30	4	5	0	3	1	15	1
Deluca, Joe	.139	36	2	5	0	2	5	6	1

Name	W	L	ERA	G	SV	IP	H	BB	SO
Scrubb, Andre	1	2	1.52	26	8	30	18	10	36
Lambson, Mitch	6	0	2.33	8	0	54	45	12	38
Fuller, Jim	0	0	2.66	22	1	24	20	9	26
Rondón, Bruce	2	2	2.77	25	12	26	24	9	31
Pucheu, Jacques	1	2	3.12	34	2	40	34	16	48
Mattson, Isaac	1	1	3.32	18	3	19	12	8	24
Johnston, Spencer	5	3	3.66	11	0	71	66	16	38
Kahaloa, Ian	10	9	4.04	24	0	151	127	52	143
Burch, Jared	3	3	4.40	6	0	29	30	16	19
Estrada, Jesse	1	4	4.71	28	0	63	76	18	36
O'Sullivan, Liam	9	5	4.75	14	0	85	99	21	49
Thompson, Daryl	6	3	4.89	17	0	109	129	9	66
Cabrera, Sandro	3	4	5.18	8	0	49	48	20	31
Briceno, Endrys	1	1	5.28	11	4	15	19	8	24
Mills, McKenzie	3	3	5.33	12	0	52	47	33	35
Dykstra, James	2	2	5.40	21	3	22	22	12	19
Dibrell, Tony	2	8	5.99	13	0	80	69	48	84
Solomon, William	1	1	6.32	13	0	16	28	5	11
Martin, Josh	0	0	6.57	10	0	12	9	14	9
Gilliland, Jacob	1	1	6.57	28	0	38	46	29	32
Uskali, Neil	3	3	7.34	8	0	42	55	22	27
Aker, Cole	0	0	7.94	6	0	11	7	14	7
Rios, Willie	0	3	8.27	15	0	21	33	19	16

YORK REVOLUTION

Name	AVG	AB	R	H	HR	RBI	BB	SO	SB
Mendoza, Drew	.346	428	90	148	15	87	66	80	23
Otosaka, Tomo	.330	373	86	123	2	48	66	66	42
Nuñez, Jhon	.327	254	38	83	11	66	18	57	1
Pantoja, Alexis	.297	219	36	65	1	32	19	34	6
Stokes Jr., Troy	.288	379	67	109	18	77	38	73	27
Giambrone, Trent	.287	450	88	129	22	72	55	90	9
Rhinesmith, Jacob	.282	387	80	109	8	50	47	75	15
Martin, Trey	.282	425	90	120	19	82	56	119	46
Rivero, Alejandro	.272	372	58	101	8	43	29	97	5
Urena, Richard	.269	368	60	99	18	64	25	86	3
January, Ryan	.257	167	40	43	9	37	48	76	0
Rodriguez, Nellie	.253	403	54	102	24	82	70	152	0
Miller, Jalen	.151	53	8	8	0	3	5	11	5

Name	W	L	ERA	G	SV	IP	H	BB	SO
Rogers, Blake	1	0	2.35	15	5	15	10	5	23
Guzman, Emilker	1	0	3.50	18	1	18	15	10	24
Espinal, Carlos	7	3	3.62	22	1	70	61	38	74
Raquet, Nick	13	7	3.71	24	0	146	129	40	133
Woodward, J.P.	1	0	3.76	38	5	38	36	20	37
Cabezas, Andrew	3	4	4.20	13	0	64	72	19	58
Correa, Nelvin	5	4	4.27	47	1	53	49	27	44
Neff, Zach	1	2	4.29	23	3	21	21	10	19
Carter, Will	2	2	4.36	48	5	43	30	33	44
Brittain, Cody	1	0	4.76	3	0	17	19	5	11
McAffer, Will	0	2	4.87	27	0	20	15	14	21
Hintzen, J.T.	10	7	5.21	30	0	121	132	45	111
Vasquez, Pedro	8	4	5.95	19	0	98	118	38	59
Strobel, Tasker	2	2	5.97	34	2	29	43	15	29
Dum, Benjamin	1	0	6.00	19	0	18	23	7	20
Sutera, Tom	9	7	6.10	26	0	125	157	35	100
Gross, Andrew	1	0	6.52	26	1	19	23	12	15
Parker, Nick	0	1	7.58	10	0	19	28	6	17
Martinez, Joan	3	2	7.62	11	0	52	65	15	44
Hull, Denson	1	5	7.74	26	1	43	46	24	37
Capellan, Victor	1	0	8.37	27	8	24	32	15	24

FRONTIER LEAGUE

As one of the Can-Am League teams that joined the Frontier League after the 2019 season, the Quebec Capitales had to wait a long time to actually get to show what they could do.

The 2020 season was wiped out by the pandemic, while the closed U.S.-Canadian border meant they didn't get to play in 2021 either.

But since then, Quebec has been the clas of the league. Quebec won their second title in two tries by knocking off Gateway 3-2 in the championship series.

The championship series was incredibly dramatic. Justin Gideon hit a three-run walk-off home run to win Game 1 for Quebec. Juremi Profar then hit a walk-off home run to win Game 2 for Quebec as well.

Evansville then hit six home runs to win Game 3. Evansville then run Game 4 thanks to a double steal that led to an error that scored two runs in the eighth inning.

Quebec turned down the drama in Game 5 by jumping out to an early lead for a 12-3 win.

West	W	L	PCT	GB
Gateway Grizzlies	59	37	.615	-
Schaumburg Boomers	54	41	.568	4.5
Evansville Otters	52	44	.542	7
Washington Wild Things	47	49	.490	12
Joliet Slammers	46	50	.479	13
Windy City ThunderBolts	43	52	.453	15.5
Florence Y'alls	38	58	.396	21
Lake Erie Crushers	37	59	.385	22
East	**W**	**L**	**PCT**	**GB**
Québec Capitales	60	35	.632	-
New Jersey Jackals	60	35	.632	-
Sussex County Miners	55	40	.579	5
Tri-City ValleyCats	55	40	.579	5
New York Boulders	54	42	.563	6.5
Ottawa Titans	48	48	.500	12.5
Trois-Rivières Aigles	38	57	.400	22

Empire State Greys	18	77	.189	42

Playoffs—Semifinals: Quebec defeated New Jersey 2-1 and Evansville defeated Gateway 2-1 in best-of-3 series. **Finals:** Quebec defeated Evansville 3-2 in best-of-five series.

Attendance: Schaumburg 230,023; Quebec 166,916; New York 151,290; Tri-City 136,231; Joliet 114,901; Florence 111,742; Windy City 98,005; Washington 94,899; Lake Erie 91,501; Gateway 80,453; Ottawa 78,495; Sussex County 72,255; Trois-Rivieres 68,814; New Jersey 36,971..

All-Star Team: C: Rusber Estrada, New Jersey. **1B:** Matthew Warkentin, Joliet. **2B:** Chase Dawson, Schaumburg. **3B:** James Nelson, New Jersey. **SS:** Matt McDermott, New York. **OF:** Josh Rehwaldt, New Jersey; Jairus Richards, Gateway; Anthony Brocato, Washington. **DH:** Keon Barnum, New Jersey. **SP:** Cole Cook, Joliet. **RP:** Frank Moscatiello, Quebec.

Morgan Burkhart MVP Award: James Nelson, 3B, New Jersey. **Brian Tollberg Pitcher of the Year Award:** Cole Cook, SP, Joliet. **Jason Simontacchi Rookie of the Year Award:** Noah Myers, OF, Evansville. **Roger Hanners Manager of the Year Award:** Steve Brook, Gateway. **Darren Bush Coach of the Year Award:** Matt Shepardson, Joliet.

BATTING LEADERS

Player, Team	AVG	AB	R	H	HR	RBI	SB
James Nelson, NJ	.388	363	111	141	30	82	34
Peter Zimmermann, Gate.	.360	258	67	93	21	83	12
Jairus Richards, Gate.	.340	324	82	110	16	56	75
Jamey Smart, Ott.	.334	359	61	120	8	83	3
Andrew Penner, Gate.	.334	380	80	127	8	60	18
Chase Dawson, Schaum.	.332	392	85	130	4	62	50
Craig Massey, Flor.	.328	262	56	86	6	40	8
Edwin Mateo, SC	.323	396	82	128	7	43	39
Noah Myers, Evan.	.322	354	86	114	18	58	41
Nate Scantlin, T-R	.321	374	71	120	6	45	15

PITCHING LEADERS

Pitcher, Team	W	L	ERA	IP	H	HR	BB	SO
Cole Cook, Jol.	12	2	2.23	137	109	4	28	131
Tim Holdgrafer, Evan.	9	5	2.65	122	121	3	20	95
Kobe Foster, Wash.	7	5	2.66	101	86	10	24	94
Collin Sullivan, Gate.	10	5	2.69	110	87	8	35	135
Garrett Christman, WC	8	4	2.75	124	121	4	23	85
Tyler Thornton, SC	7	2	3.57	106	105	7	47	79
Mark Moclair, SC	5	6	3.66	108	87	5	80	105
Jhon Vargas, T-C	8	5	3.73	99	89	9	43	106
Damon Casetta-Stubbs, Ott.	5	5	3.77	105	116	10	37	109
Tucker Smith, T-R	7	8	3.89	113	131	15	15	85

EMPIRE STATE GREYS

Name	AVG	AB	R	H	HR	RBI	BB	SO	SB
Katsuya Arai	.154	26	2	4	0	2	1	8	0
Luis Atiles	.274	190	22	52	2	20	28	34	8
Steve Barmakian	.211	71	9	15	1	6	11	20	1
Eric Callahan	.167	36	3	6	0	4	2	12	0
Cristopher Céspedes	.210	167	19	35	4	27	9	47	0
J.R. DiSarcina	.246	325	36	80	6	33	17	82	3
Walner Espinal	.322	87	7	28	0	8	5	24	0
Manny Garcia	.248	303	34	75	9	50	31	51	9
Mike Gulino	.213	94	14	20	4	13	11	31	0
Josue Herrera	.279	79	9	22	1	11	8	22	0
Quentin Holmes	.232	289	43	67	6	29	25	76	14
Eric Jenkins	.226	297	34	67	5	33	26	100	21
Eddie Niemann	.125	24	3	3	0	2	0	7	0
Jordan Scott	.202	228	31	46	7	29	30	75	8
Josh Sears	.275	331	40	91	16	50	44	101	0
Jaylen Smith	.259	205	28	53	3	17	14	35	18
Jaylin Turner	.219	114	13	25	2	11	17	48	0
Matt Turner	.171	35	2	6	1	4	1	18	0
Zak Whalin	.221	131	17	29	4	11	6	21	2

Name	W	L	ERA	G	SV	IP	H	BB	SO
Mizuki Akatsuka	1	3	7.76	13	0	27	38	14	15
Wes Albert	0	3	4.80	4	0	15	13	10	8
Alejandro Arteaga	0	2	4.80	3	0	15	20	5	18
Michael Barker	4	11	6.88	23	0	107	129	72	74
Tyler Bryant	0	1	4.13	19	0	24	23	10	31
Clarke Davenport	0	3	7.61	21	0	37	44	29	48
Andrew Dietz	0	1	8.75	12	1	24	32	13	17
Carson Ferry	0	1	21.60	12	0	10	16	23	13
Zach Gettys	2	4	7.91	32	0	58	89	25	34
Jhoendri Herrera	0	1	8.27	12	0	21	29	11	23
Nathan Holt	2	3	7.74	32	2	48	63	23	35
Joe LaFiora	0	9	8.50	10	0	54	67	31	27
Matthew Peguero	0	2	4.41	3	0	16	17	13	13
Wilber Pérez	2	2	6.16	15	1	19	14	17	23
Andres Rodriguez	1	11	8.08	16	0	78	100	53	57
Miguel Rondon	1	1	7.63	12	0	15	16	13	13
Garrett Sutton	2	3	6.70	10	0	46	63	14	28
Nick Trabacchi	0	8	5.66	46	2	68	83	30	53
Dawson Young	0	0	7.71	13	0	16	15	15	18

EVANSVILLE OTTERS

Name	AVG	AB	R	H	HR	RBI	BB	SO	SB
Jeffrey Baez	.280	325	49	91	16	67	24	77	17
Aaron Beck	.323	62	11	20	1	4	5	11	0
Austin Bost	.250	72	13	18	2	8	10	17	2
Josh Broughton	.181	72	8	13	3	8	9	18	2
George Callil	.240	246	35	59	5	26	19	71	2
John Dyer	.236	55	7	13	0	6	5	16	0
Justin Felix	.147	68	6	10	0	2	10	37	2
Jake Green	.258	128	18	33	1	10	15	24	1
Gary Mattis	.225	71	7	16	0	5	9	20	7
Noah Myers	.322	354	86	114	18	58	64	88	41
Jacob Olson	.198	91	10	18	3	14	9	14	0
Dakota Phillips	.275	357	58	98	12	74	40	118	1
Kona Quiggle	.268	351	65	94	12	59	55	110	17
Jomar Reyes	.301	365	48	110	7	47	14	60	4
Bryan Rosario	.226	212	35	48	0	25	31	48	51
Ethan Skender	.263	319	55	84	9	53	20	54	22

Name	W	L	ERA	G	SV	IP	H	BB	SO
Jon Beymer	3	1	3.88	38	2	58	56	32	67
Parker Brahms	4	1	2.55	9	0	42	25	12	41
Johan Castillo	1	0	3.60	5	0	15	15	8	15
Kevin Davis	4	2	1.98	41	0	50	23	28	78
Leoni De La Cruz	0	2	3.24	39	0	42	27	21	59
Tim Holdgrafer	9	5	2.65	19	0	122	121	20	95
Hunter Kloke	1	1	5.57	30	0	42	48	22	48
James Krick	3	1	5.26	31	2	50	42	33	47
Jake Polancic	1	5	2.16	32	17	33	21	18	48
Braden Scott	4	1	3.43	8	0	45	26	17	52
Zach Smith	6	9	4.57	20	0	108	100	55	98
Tyler Vail	1	1	1.59	16	0	23	18	11	27
Justin Watland	7	8	6.96	18	0	94	116	53	86

FLORENCE Y'ALLS

Name	AVG	AB	R	H	HR	RBI	BB	SO	SB
Cole Brannen	.247	166	29	41	1	16	34	32	12
Jeremiah Burks	.242	281	35	68	3	29	28	82	13
Harrison DiNicola	.215	288	42	62	5	50	29	53	4
Cooper Edwards	.143	56	4	8	1	5	9	22	1
Brian Fuentes	.284	345	59	98	10	46	52	87	11
Tristin Garcia	.281	146	19	41	1	9	15	21	1
Lane Hoover	.218	174	21	38	0	19	14	28	16
Ed Johnson	.316	133	21	42	1	15	11	23	14
Craig Massey	.328	262	56	86	6	40	41	29	8
Taylor Olmstead	.130	23	1	3	0	1	1	9	1
Sam Plash	.226	53	10	12	3	10	6	29	0
Brennan Price	.304	293	64	89	22	75	68	85	3
Zade Richardson	.284	211	31	60	12	36	26	66	0
Andres Rios	.220	59	11	13	1	11	10	12	3
Nick Wimmers	.258	66	8	17	0	14	8	20	4
Hank Zeisler	.248	117	21	29	1	14	17	27	9
Ray Zuberer	.288	319	62	92	13	67	53	63	43

Name	W	L	ERA	G	SV	IP	H	BB	SO
Evan Brabrand	5	11	6.38	19	0	114	131	46	100
Christian Cosby	0	0	2.63	6	0	14	16	1	13
Nick Ernst	0	1	0.90	9	0	10	6	5	10
Nathan Florence	4	2	3.27	9	0	44	30	30	60
Sean Hughes	0	1	4.85	14	1	13	13	15	9

Name	W	L	ERA	G	SV	IP	H	BB	SO
Rodney Hutchison	1	5	11.62	11	0	26	34	23	14
Jestin Jones	1	1	11.16	9	1	25	36	18	27
Mike Kickham	0	2	9.12	7	0	26	43	11	21
Michael Kirian	1	1	8.02	23	0	34	48	20	33
Kent Klyman	0	2	4.91	30	2	37	44	13	38
Andrew Kramer	0	1	11.45	5	0	11	15	14	7
Edgar Martinez	8	9	5.38	20	0	109	95	69	111
Brandon Mason	2	0	7.63	10	1	15	24	14	14
Brian McKenna	2	4	6.45	22	5	22	25	10	23
Jake McMahill	2	5	4.83	16	0	82	87	41	69
Carter Poiry	4	2	4.38	31	0	62	52	37	47
Aaron Rund	0	1	3.22	11	0	22	20	8	24
Carter Spivey	2	1	3.06	8	0	47	40	16	41
Alex Theis	0	0	14.40	8	0	10	11	16	11
Ross Thompson	1	3	8.15	6	0	18	26	8	17
Ryan Watson	3	3	3.45	8	0	47	45	15	28

GATEWAY GRIZZLIES

Name	AVG	AB	R	H	HR	RBI	BB	SO	SB
Cole Barr	.200	45	7	9	2	6	3	19	1
Cole Brannen	.230	122	23	28	0	10	20	26	19
Abdiel Diaz	.270	226	36	61	4	37	38	38	20
Willie Estrada	.259	162	21	42	6	29	19	37	7
Clint Freeman	.254	299	50	76	11	53	29	56	1
Kyle Gaedele	.286	140	23	40	11	32	12	42	3
Alex Hernandez	.175	183	23	32	4	14	13	73	0
Gabe Holt	.435	191	49	83	4	31	25	10	17
Andrew Penner	.334	380	80	127	8	60	45	69	18
Zach Racusin	.289	159	12	46	1	18	14	24	8
Jairus Richards	.340	324	82	110	16	56	68	70	75
Eric Rivera	.251	307	56	77	5	39	53	56	30
D.J. Stewart	.306	343	53	105	13	77	26	51	25
Mark Vierling	.282	220	49	62	6	39	25	32	8
Peter Zimmermann	.361	258	67	93	21	83	49	58	12

Name	W	L	ERA	G	SV	IP	H	BB	SO
Zach Blankenship	0	1	5.68	11	0	19	20	10	17
Colton Easterwood	2	0	5.47	23	9	25	19	13	35
Brian Eichhorn	0	0	1.74	22	0	21	13	11	36
Nate Garkow	7	2	3.80	40	0	47	38	18	60
Joey Gonzalez	11	7	5.11	19	0	104	117	49	98
Parker Johnson	2	3	5.82	7	0	34	41	9	37
Carson LaRue	5	8	4.57	19	0	106	119	31	96
Josh Lucas	2	2	2.84	21	4	32	21	10	43
Zac Ryan	3	3	5.00	16	0	45	40	23	45
Collin Sullivan	10	5	2.69	19	0	110	87	35	135
Nathanial Tate	1	1	5.06	14	0	32	36	13	28
Trevor Tietz	1	1	2.91	44	1	43	36	18	44
Zac Treece	3	0	3.86	26	0	30	32	7	33
Matt Valin	2	1	5.46	29	0	30	17	35	42
Lukas Veinbergs	9	3	4.54	19	0	103	111	31	90
Alec Whaley	1	1	2.91	55	1	53	39	11	51

JOLIET SLAMMERS

Name	AVG	AB	R	H	HR	RBI	BB	SO	SB
Lane Baremore	.222	234	17	52	2	23	17	63	10
Julian Boyd	.269	26	6	7	0	2	4	11	6
Tyler Depreta-Johnson	.217	313	24	68	1	31	26	42	11
Mike Falsetti	.195	41	2	8	0	3	2	10	0
Christian Fedko	.273	209	31	57	3	29	28	33	8
Matt Feinstein	.206	160	21	33	0	8	26	48	13
J.P. Fullerton	.224	85	11	19	2	10	17	29	1
GJ Hill	.266	248	41	66	15	44	31	92	14
Scott Holzwasser	.159	113	17	18	3	16	17	47	8
Liam McArthur	.309	366	58	113	2	35	55	54	17
Matt McGarry	.205	308	33	63	6	35	32	88	8
Broc Mortensen	.267	120	13	32	2	11	10	42	7
Kyle Novak	.250	24	2	6	0	1	2	3	0
Will Salas	.170	141	16	24	0	11	32	30	6
Phillip Steering	.246	280	42	69	4	29	44	60	18
Tommy Stevenson	.206	63	10	13	5	9	7	23	0
Matt Warkentin	.294	282	52	83	27	64	23	82	1

Name	W	L	ERA	G	SV	IP	H	BB	SO
Cam Aufderheide	3	9	4.96	18	0	94	106	39	67
Chandler Brierley	0	1	5.80	36	0	50	43	36	62
Ricky Castro	4	7	4.07	13	0	80	80	18	85
Cole Cook	12	2	2.23	20	0	137	109	28	131
Andrew Dietz	2	1	2.39	9	1	38	23	18	22
Justin Ferrell	1	3	5.83	6	0	29	25	15	16
David Harrison	3	1	3.25	25	2	28	23	13	28
Tyler Jay	4	3	4.26	20	7	57	48	19	64
Turner Larkins	10	5	4.12	19	0	116	121	32	82
Jared Liebelt	3	0	3.82	32	7	35	29	18	34
Will MacLean	0	1	5.56	8	0	11	6	14	6
Caden O'Brien	1	3	5.24	18	1	22	19	12	38
Ryan O'Reilly	2	7	6.31	9	0	51	64	18	33
Evy Ruibal	1	4	3.72	36	6	36	23	26	43
Brad VanAsdlen	0	1	8.60	24	0	30	35	22	29

LAKE ERIE CRUSHERS

Name	AVG	AB	R	H	HR	RBI	BB	SO	SB
Mike Blanke	.167	24	2	4	1	3	3	5	0
Tyree Bradley	.194	36	4	7	1	4	5	8	0
Vincent Byrd	.324	34	4	11	2	10	4	7	0
Sean Cheely	.217	230	28	50	2	24	18	73	33
Santiago Chirino	.206	107	12	22	1	9	13	5	2
Sam Frontino	.143	84	12	12	0	8	20	33	5
Drue Galassi	.184	98	16	18	6	12	11	36	4
Ellison Hanna	.207	29	3	6	1	3	4	11	2
Jack Harris	.264	322	53	85	9	44	16	104	15
Kenen Irizarry	.239	222	23	53	5	24	24	35	4
Todd Isaacs	.278	255	33	71	3	17	12	66	11
Scout Knotts	.319	91	17	29	2	13	18	25	2
Sean Lawlor	.219	64	7	14	2	7	7	24	3
Collin Mathews	.111	27	4	3	0	2	2	14	1
Jackson Pritchard	.197	132	13	26	3	12	24	54	0
Josh Rego	.240	175	21	42	5	32	11	49	2
Hector Roa	.205	78	7	16	1	11	2	17	0
Gabe Snyder	.211	152	17	32	4	20	15	40	3
Kemuel Thomas-Rivera	.241	137	16	33	5	19	11	50	2
Jiandido Tromp	.241	228	23	55	3	25	26	53	12
Johnny Tuccillo	.194	180	23	35	3	15	17	40	0
Jarrod Watkins	.233	287	31	67	4	26	21	51	4

Name	W	L	ERA	G	SV	IP	H	BB	SO
Perry Bewley	4	0	3.20	37	0	51	47	33	56
Brayden Bonner	1	5	6.00	47	2	51	52	29	28
Stephen Chamblee	3	6	6.66	16	0	72	80	19	50
Sam Curtis	1	2	2.70	18	6	17	16	8	14
Sam Frontino	1	0	3.21	12	0	14	11	11	10
J.D. Hammer	3	3	3.46	19	0	52	37	20	46
Trevor Kuncl	0	6	3.10	48	1	58	41	30	71
Cal McAninch	0	0	5.96	23	0	23	30	9	22
Matt Mulhearn	5	7	4.52	18	0	98	104	38	53
Darrien Ragins	4	5	1.90	39	2	62	41	28	77
Conner Richardson	1	0	8.74	10	0	11	18	5	7
Alexis Rivero	0	2	2.92	12	6	12	10	7	8
Yasel Santana	5	6	4.47	22	1	111	94	57	91
Kyle Seebach	2	3	4.98	11	0	47	58	29	49
Jonaiker Villalobos	2	6	7.96	11	0	52	69	29	44
Ean Walda	0	0	5.40	7	0	10	6	8	5

NEW JERSEY JACKALS

Name	AVG	AB	R	H	HR	RBI	BB	SO	SB
Keon Barnum	.316	304	64	96	30	87	61	82	1
Marcos Castillo	.268	153	22	41	1	18	11	35	7
Phil Ervin	.318	176	38	56	8	38	31	44	14
Rusber Estrada	.308	227	52	70	22	54	31	69	0
Martin Figueroa	.256	168	35	43	5	19	31	22	8
Ti'Quan Forbes	.298	282	63	84	17	45	28	75	16
Jordan Howard	.226	53	7	12	0	5	9	18	4
Alfredo Marte	.311	367	68	114	21	90	38	60	7
Justin Mazzone	.263	118	11	31	1	17	10	21	0
James Nelson	.388	363	111	141	30	82	53	97	34
Josh Rehwaldt	.315	372	98	117	29	90	56	105	18
Nilo Rijo	.218	174	39	38	2	20	46	57	19
Kevin Rolon	.305	105	17	32	5	15	10	29	2
Joe Simone	.231	39	8	9	1	4	5	14	3

Name	AVG	AB	R	H	HR	RBI	BB	SO	SB
Jonathan Soto	.171	41	2	7	0	4	2	13	0
Alex Toral	.274	317	66	87	24	72	67	89	0
Austin White	.219	119	20	26	0	11	19	24	10

Name	W	L	ERA	G	SV	IP	H	BB	SO
Dylan Castaneda	6	4	5.42	18	0	96	101	53	77
Dazon Cole	2	1	4.60	37	3	47	47	29	56
Michael DeSanti	0	0	3.38	16	0	19	10	19	28
Luke Hansen	2	0	6.63	12	0	19	19	14	17
David Lebron	4	1	3.27	9	0	52	47	15	43
Lance Lusk	6	3	5.67	40	5	40	54	13	49
Vin Mazzaro	4	1	3.27	8	0	41	33	10	56
Gleyvin Pineda	4	3	4.95	36	1	36	32	27	42
Jason Pineda	1	0	8.22	10	0	15	16	11	18
Anthony Rodriguez	2	2	6.17	8	0	35	46	16	25
Yuhi Sako	1	0	3.86	22	1	37	40	9	38
Yuichi Shiota	5	2	4.78	22	2	43	46	11	30
Jorge Tavarez	6	1	2.25	7	0	48	35	6	55
Alec Thomas	4	5	6.13	19	0	79	81	59	66
Matt Vogel	2	1	0.97	36	5	37	19	14	51
Cody Whitten	2	2	3.74	36	0	43	34	24	51

NEW YORK BOULDERS

Name	AVG	AB	R	H	HR	RBI	BB	SO	SB
Jimmy Costin	.260	100	12	26	1	13	19	29	0
Joe DeLuca	.229	280	52	64	15	39	49	90	13
Austin Dennis	.226	137	21	31	0	17	13	22	7
Giovanni Garbella	.240	250	51	60	9	46	27	82	13
Gabriel Garcia	.254	342	56	87	9	43	48	72	14
Patrick Kivlehan	.304	345	67	105	23	73	45	67	9
Chris Kwitzer	.301	365	52	110	6	48	28	82	21
Matt McDermott	.312	279	51	87	7	39	26	58	24
Tucker Nathans	.310	364	71	113	15	64	55	69	15
David Vinsky	.280	343	54	96	9	49	54	74	9
Tom Walraven	.260	358	61	93	18	77	47	57	7

Name	W	L	ERA	G	SV	IP	H	BB	SO
Merfy Andrew	0	2	5.79	25	1	28	18	31	33
Brandon Backman	5	3	4.46	17	0	42	32	29	52
Rony Báez	0	1	14.34	4	0	11	15	9	9
Garrett Cooper	5	5	4.62	16	1	86	85	35	64
Aaron Dona	7	3	2.78	21	2	68	55	26	81
Andy Hammond	6	2	5.24	24	0	77	97	23	58
Alec Huertas	3	2	4.96	11	0	53	59	17	37
Tyler Keysor	0	1	6.91	4	0	14	13	7	14
Dawson Lane	6	4	5.07	23	1	55	60	30	44
Weston Lombard	2	1	3.86	8	0	21	17	8	17
Alex Mack	0	0	3.47	9	0	23	23	19	30
Ryan Munoz	4	6	5.28	23	0	77	93	26	55
Zach Schneider	2	2	4.60	34	2	43	49	6	31
Mitchell Senger	3	2	4.46	32	0	34	36	19	33
Dylan Smith	3	3	1.56	35	18	40	23	23	66
July Sosa	4	5	5.63	13	0	64	81	23	56
Aljo Sujak	2	0	3.09	9	0	12	8	13	12
Ryder Yakel	1	0	3.60	23	1	45	43	16	49

OTTAWA TITANS

Name	AVG	AB	R	H	HR	RBI	BB	SO	SB
Brandon Bannon	.176	108	16	19	1	9	18	22	2
Evan Berkey	.257	144	21	37	2	23	10	33	0
Austin Davis	.288	153	23	44	1	12	17	26	19
Jason DiCochea	.280	371	65	104	16	63	26	63	7
Michael Fuhrman	.241	58	12	14	1	8	8	11	1
Mitsuki Fukuda	.145	83	10	12	0	2	12	24	0
Jake Gitter	.155	71	9	11	1	8	15	35	1
Kanta Kobayashi	.208	48	6	10	0	3	4	8	1
Sicnarf Loopstok	.298	238	38	71	8	41	18	47	2
Ivan Marin	.132	38	4	5	0	1	3	8	0
David Mendham	.163	49	4	8	1	6	4	7	1
Kai Moody	.071	28	2	2	0	1	4	11	1
Jake Sanford	.271	107	15	29	2	18	13	17	1
Jamey Smart	.334	359	61	120	8	83	54	64	3
Jacob Talamante	.188	96	15	18	0	5	13	32	3
Joey Terdoslavich	.265	117	14	31	2	16	16	25	0
Justin Thompson	.136	22	1	3	0	3	2	12	0
Jackie Urbaez	.266	237	46	63	5	28	30	50	4
A.J. Wright	.285	355	76	101	14	57	56	91	5
Taylor Wright	.292	298	45	87	9	51	33	62	9

Name	W	L	ERA	G	SV	IP	H	BB	SO
Thomas Bruss	1	1	5.06	32	0	37	41	22	37
Chris Burica	6	4	6.62	34	1	69	103	23	69
Damon Casetta-Stubbs	5	5	3.77	20	0	105	116	37	109
Trevor Clifton	3	1	4.60	23	5	29	28	16	47
Augie Gallardo	2	2	3.48	20	0	21	17	10	25
Grant Larson	8	8	4.29	23	0	122	129	29	94
Nick MacDonald	5	3	7.17	25	1	48	62	21	34
Bryan Peña	4	4	6.26	16	0	73	68	41	71
Erasmo Pinales	5	2	1.50	35	6	36	19	25	39
Andrew Roach	0	1	6.59	9	0	14	14	6	14
Carlos Sano	5	4	5.77	19	0	97	111	47	63
Brooks Walton	1	1	5.63	10	0	40	41	8	32
Zac Westcott	5	9	5.63	22	0	133	168	41	90
Kenny Williams	0	0	7.29	13	0	21	32	10	10
Taylor Wright	0	1	6.00	9	0	12	18	1	10

QUEBEC CAPITALES

Name	AVG	AB	R	H	HR	RBI	BB	SO	SB
Sam Abbott	.200	70	13	14	4	11	29	32	1
Greg Bird	.293	41	4	12	1	4	3	5	0
Tyler Blaum	.225	111	12	25	0	20	16	35	2
Emile Boies	.232	95	14	22	1	15	4	27	0
Elijah Brown	.105	38	11	4	0	4	11	12	11
Ruben Castro	.320	219	48	70	5	26	39	34	8
Kyle Crowl	.278	295	67	82	17	53	50	93	10
Adan Fernandez	.204	54	9	11	1	7	10	16	3
Justin Gideon	.275	346	67	95	22	71	41	87	12
David Glaude	.285	291	46	83	10	63	37	55	17
Jonathan Lacroix	.229	118	13	27	0	8	21	24	5
Marc-Antoine Lebreux	.293	273	57	80	8	36	54	69	14
Bryan Leef	.225	222	40	50	16	44	20	95	4
Juremi Profar	.276	362	50	100	14	55	36	47	2
Ryan Roell	.100	20	1	2	0	1	1	6	0
Tommy Seidl	.219	114	20	25	6	17	12	34	4
Jesmuel Valentín	.323	31	5	10	0	5	5	6	0
Martin Vincelli-Simard	.167	24	3	4	0	3	6	10	0
T.J. White	.254	339	67	86	22	67	42	67	3

Name	W	L	ERA	G	SV	IP	H	BB	SO
Michael Brettell	1	1	7.15	9	0	11	13	6	4
Elliot Carney	1	1	4.40	32	0	45	37	26	70
Chas Cywin	0	2	6.75	5	0	16	21	5	9
Steven Fuentes	9	2	2.35	16	0	92	78	33	57
Harley Gollert	7	0	3.23	10	0	53	53	15	40
Tanner Jesson-Dalton	2	0	5.31	35	0	41	40	35	48
Austin Marozas	3	2	4.66	28	3	29	22	14	24
Frank Moscatiello	7	1	1.86	46	20	48	23	14	78
Kyle Mott	4	2	3.86	36	1	44	45	20	42
Franklin Parra	3	3	4.58	41	5	39	35	22	50
Kenny Pierson	2	1	2.87	43	0	47	49	16	40
Ruben Ramirez	9	2	4.58	20	0	92	93	36	89
Evan Rutckyj	1	0	1.59	20	1	23	20	11	27
Abdiel Saldana	7	2	1.72	20	0	78	60	19	63
Ryan Sandberg	2	8	4.87	16	0	68	68	37	62
Pete Tago	0	2	9.90	6	0	20	28	21	20

SCHAUMBURG BOOMERS

Name	AVG	AB	R	H	HR	RBI	BB	SO	SB
Blake Berry	.283	304	55	86	4	50	56	47	11
Alec Craig	.249	333	68	83	2	40	84	58	32
Chase Dawson	.332	392	85	130	4	62	37	32	50
Kokko Figueiredo	.333	123	22	41	3	29	23	20	4
John Fiorenza	.221	104	14	23	2	12	11	31	0
Kyle Fitzgerald	.230	252	41	58	10	56	27	64	1
Blake Grant-Parks	.302	169	20	51	2	31	17	41	0
Travis Holt	.246	256	33	63	1	27	32	48	8
Gaige Howard	.307	329	74	101	6	49	78	70	25
Zach Huffins	.268	164	25	44	2	19	8	42	8
Brett Milazzo	.300	283	52	85	5	44	42	37	23
Will Prater	.312	221	31	69	1	37	21	40	14

Name	AVG	AB	R	H	HR	RBI	BB	SO	SB
Quentin Selma	.200	130	18	26	6	26	12	38	0
Miles Simington	.250	80	7	20	0	9	5	17	1
Sonny Ulliana	.289	45	7	13	3	13	1	15	0

Name	W	L	ERA	G	SV	IP	H	BB	SO
Merfy Andrew	0	2	4.61	24	1	27	15	29	32
Antonio Frias	3	1	5.05	20	1	68	56	53	94
Aaron Glickstein	5	2	3.20	22	0	90	95	19	63
Austin Gossmann	5	3	6.39	17	0	76	95	42	61
Jackson Hickert	5	4	4.99	19	0	88	76	58	69
Hunter Hoopes	4	3	3.59	8	0	43	36	22	42
Jake Joyce	5	4	3.29	40	5	41	40	24	39
Cristian Lopez	5	3	4.83	35	1	60	54	26	53
Luis Pérez	7	5	4.71	17	0	107	115	33	102
Juan Pichardo	2	1	5.70	13	0	30	27	21	31
Miguel Reyes	3	1	4.32	13	0	42	37	29	26
Kobey Schlotman	6	5	3.55	14	0	79	70	25	58
Kristian Scott	3	1	2.42	38	4	45	28	17	47
Dylan Stutsman	1	3	3.75	37	7	36	29	20	44
Daiveyon Whittle	3	6	6.23	32	10	35	36	25	51
Shumpei Yoshikawa	3	2	4.24	8	0	51	52	14	38

SUSSEX COUNTY MINERS

Name	AVG	AB	R	H	HR	RBI	BB	SO	SB
Jason Agresti	.266	207	26	55	4	30	26	39	0
Oraj Anu	.321	346	52	111	20	69	32	91	2
Willie Escala	.285	340	52	97	4	42	27	74	20
Evan Giordano	.225	80	11	18	3	7	8	21	0
Tony Gomez	.240	175	26	42	1	8	17	41	7
Jawuan Harris	.224	268	44	60	7	36	41	99	28
Johnny Hipsman	.313	134	20	42	3	24	19	36	2
Elvis Lopez	.208	72	6	15	0	7	11	18	1
Edwin Mateo	.323	396	82	128	7	43	39	75	39
Abraham Mow	.236	127	14	30	1	17	16	30	1
Kyle Richards	.206	73	12	15	1	3	7	38	1
Juan Santana	.267	367	49	98	9	65	27	41	10
Gavin Stupienski	.301	349	56	105	17	59	45	81	0
Jackson Valera	.321	28	1	9	1	5	1	4	0
Will Zimmerman	.215	200	40	43	3	20	37	65	27

Name	W	L	ERA	G	SV	IP	H	BB	SO
Freisis Adames	3	0	4.47	19	2	54	51	17	59
Griffin Baker	6	4	4.96	12	0	69	61	23	51
Jimmy Boyce	5	2	2.61	19	1	52	41	7	27
Cole Davis	1	3	4.63	15	1	47	47	32	21
Jack Dellinger	3	2	6.38	17	0	61	56	42	51
Alex Hart	3	6	5.30	10	0	56	63	19	44
Robbie Hitt	4	2	1.26	28	13	29	19	8	38
Jose Ledesma	5	6	4.18	21	0	71	52	34	56
Tyler Luneke	2	2	2.63	21	1	27	26	6	26
Mark Moclair	5	6	3.66	19	0	108	87	80	105
Billy Parsons	5	2	1.50	28	0	36	24	8	34
Mike Reagan	4	2	3.98	10	0	52	49	17	39
Matt Stil	2	1	4.54	24	0	36	24	30	35
Tyler Thornton	7	2	3.57	19	0	106	105	47	79
Ronnie Voacolo	0	1	1.10	30	2	33	15	13	51

TRI-CITY VALLEY CATS

Name	AVG	AB	R	H	HR	RBI	BB	SO	SB
Aaron Altherr	.294	310	64	91	21	70	40	97	8
Connor Bagnieski	.209	43	7	9	0	1	9	10	5
Zach Biermann	.257	331	38	85	11	64	38	65	1
Lamar Briggs	.272	136	26	37	3	22	15	29	6
Josh Broughton	.426	61	15	26	0	4	7	12	8
Oscar Campos	.322	149	30	48	7	29	9	8	1
Cito Culver	.299	375	76	112	12	53	65	83	15
Ciaran Devenney	.188	32	3	6	0	1	1	10	0
Jakob Goldfarb	.293	311	80	91	18	69	45	69	26
Trey Hair	.300	140	25	42	8	33	15	31	7
Jaxon Hallmark	.276	337	67	93	8	40	36	83	33
Cale Jones	.194	36	5	7	0	7	5	14	0
Juan Kelly	.248	299	50	74	8	48	39	58	7
Carson McCusker	.433	157	51	68	17	51	15	27	2
John Mead	.259	116	15	30	6	12	12	35	0
Robbie Merced	.220	118	18	26	5	21	10	28	11
Juan Montes	.203	69	7	14	1	7	9	21	11
Pavin Parks	.224	344	54	77	9	55	62	93	13
Tanner Smith	.289	104	17	30	3	23	4	13	2
Ian Walters	.244	266	49	65	10	51	27	66	1

Name	W	L	ERA	G	SV	IP	H	BB	SO
Angelo Baez	5	8	3.98	19	0	109	111	37	83
Dan Beebe	5	6	4.83	14	0	73	79	23	75
Nick Belzer	4	2	6.41	12	1	59	78	21	36
Garrison Bryant	3	4	6.01	15	0	73	87	27	52
Aaron Ernst	0	1	10.18	15	0	20	25	16	16
Elijah Gill	7	3	6.34	16	0	77	79	53	58
Reymin Guduan	2	2	2.25	21	4	24	24	5	44
Coleman Huntley	1	2	3.15	26	4	34	33	14	35
Tyler Jeans	2	1	5.48	15	0	23	27	6	32
Dwayne Marshall	8	4	6.55	18	0	77	99	45	57
Alex McKenney	0	1	16.55	10	0	10	21	12	10
Caden O'Brien	1	0	5.06	12	0	16	23	5	8
Pavin Parks	1	2	3.80	19	4	21	22	10	22
Tanner Propst	1	3	6.18	30	2	28	24	21	32
Jhon Vargas	8	5	3.73	18	0	99	89	43	106
Rafi Vazquez	4	4	6.18	15	0	71	82	23	51
Greg Veliz	6	2	3.91	40	0	51	39	21	54
Brac Warren	4	3	3.49	25	0	67	51	30	85
Blake Workman	2	0	2.38	19	4	34	26	3	49

TROIS-RIVIÈRES AIGLES

Name	AVG	AB	R	H	HR	RBI	BB	SO	SB
Steve Brown	.287	286	45	82	10	64	31	53	8
Victor Cerny	.297	172	14	51	0	18	9	33	0
Tyler Clark-Chiapparelli	.285	130	22	37	0	18	10	19	4
Dalton Combs	.320	231	44	74	8	44	29	31	8
Brendon Dadson	.264	280	50	74	6	45	59	58	3
Parker DePasquale	.185	27	1	5	0	2	1	7	2
Canice Ejoh	.191	42	8	8	0	2	10	18	2
Brock Ephan	.000	20	2	0	0	2	2	7	0
Chris Fernandez	.044	23	4	1	0	0	3	9	2
Caleb Feuerstake	.250	28	9	7	1	3	7	9	2
Sadler Goodwin	.113	62	6	7	0	3	4	27	0
Óscar Hernández	.242	66	11	16	1	5	7	14	0
Ethan Hunt	.048	21	1	1	0	0	2	8	0
Nolan Machibroda	.245	49	9	12	3	8	4	13	1
Austin Markmann	.241	232	35	56	9	30	25	63	2
Rodrigo Orozco	.295	217	32	64	5	37	32	36	12
L.P. Pelletier	.314	226	42	71	9	28	17	49	12
Ricardo Sanchez	.258	275	38	71	4	41	19	51	4
Nate Scantlin	.321	374	71	120	6	45	27	56	15
Tyler Wilber	.355	124	23	44	2	24	16	18	2
Malik Williams	.302	159	22	48	7	31	8	24	0

Name	W	L	ERA	G	SV	IP	H	BB	SO
Braeden Allemann	0	5	5.98	10	0	41	45	25	49
Brendan Bell	1	1	4.67	32	1	35	32	28	27
Tyler Cornett	3	2	8.16	23	3	29	31	17	36
Gage Feeney	1	2	6.16	16	0	38	38	29	28
Luke Fitton	0	1	8.04	17	0	28	33	24	27
Nick Garcia	6	5	4.91	16	0	73	82	24	42
Blake Garrett	0	2	8.25	3	0	12	16	7	9
Frankie Giuliano	1	2	7.68	42	3	39	50	22	31
Osman Gutierrez	8	4	4.98	21	0	119	110	55	128
Logan Hofmann	0	0	7.24	14	0	14	16	9	12
Rob Klinchock	0	2	14.92	16	0	13	25	11	13
Jacob Kush	2	2	5.94	14	1	50	65	29	36
Tyler Luneke	1	0	3.21	8	0	14	12	6	13
Beau Nichols	0	2	8.25	5	0	12	18	5	11
Sam Poliquin	2	5	7.53	11	0	29	40	18	17
Christian Scafidi	1	2	5.08	20	2	28	27	19	33
Kaleb Schmidt	0	1	3.18	3	0	11	12	18	7
Tucker Smith	7	8	3.89	20	0	113	131	15	85
Jacob Stobart	0	0	6.26	22	0	27	48	16	20
Jesen Therrien	3	2	7.22	15	0	34	39	29	34
Ray Weber	1	6	7.94	9	0	40	58	18	27

WASHINGTON WILD THINGS

Name	AVG	AB	R	H	HR	RBI	BB	SO	SB
Anthony Brocato	.282	341	73	96	28	69	38	94	16
Tommy Caufield	.245	151	16	37	3	26	14	41	4
Robert Chayka	.293	263	44	77	6	43	35	49	23
Carson Clowers	.240	129	14	31	0	9	12	31	17
Jack Cone	.148	27	6	4	0	2	4	3	1
Andrew Czech	.260	300	71	78	21	60	88	94	4
Wes Darvill	.244	127	24	31	4	13	9	30	11
Scotty Dubrule	.286	325	50	93	1	42	56	42	26
Nick Gotta	.285	165	28	47	0	16	24	36	14
Wagner Lagrange	.304	369	63	112	19	69	20	69	10
Caleb McNeely	.323	65	17	21	3	8	6	21	8
Melvin Novoa	.218	211	27	46	7	44	13	49	1
Tristan Peterson	.245	229	31	56	9	35	35	63	2
Harrison Ray	.245	49	10	12	0	3	6	10	8
Tomas Sanchez	.179	28	4	5	1	3	4	10	2
J.C. Santini	.198	157	16	31	4	32	17	40	1
Abraham Sequera	.207	121	22	25	2	5	14	30	4

Name	W	L	ERA	G	SV	IP	H	BB	SO
Anthony Boix	1	1	11.25	11	0	12	21	5	15
Matt Dallas	0	0	8.78	11	0	13	20	7	6
Kobe Foster	7	5	2.66	18	0	101	86	24	94
Dariel Fregio	4	2	3.99	11	0	56	56	18	38
Robert Gonzalez	0	2	12.00	3	0	12	23	6	6
Justin Goossen-Brown	7	1	3.35	31	0	46	36	20	40
Christian James	1	2	2.24	45	0	52	44	28	65
Spencer Johnston	2	4	6.35	6	0	34	41	8	32
Zach Kirby	0	3	2.83	8	0	41	31	13	35
Stephen Knapp	5	0	4.23	25	0	66	70	22	33
Angel Landazuri	0	2	8.27	5	0	16	27	8	13
Greg Loukinen	2	3	12.12	6	0	16	29	12	12
Andrew Mitchell	0	1	6.23	11	1	13	11	6	14
Ray Pacella	0	0	6.17	9	0	12	13	13	10
Arrison Perez	2	4	4.52	31	0	64	79	14	33
Hayden Shenefield	3	6	5.06	17	0	89	106	29	62
Justin Showalter	7	5	5.54	24	0	93	111	22	57
Kyle White	1	0	4.15	13	0	13	14	5	9
Lukas Young	4	2	4.36	39	14	43	41	10	37

WINDY CITY THUNDERBOLTS

Name	AVG	AB	R	H	HR	RBI	BB	SO	SB
Jake Boone	.237	351	42	83	3	31	26	70	25
Paul Coumoulos	.282	302	38	85	4	34	18	58	3
Jordan Hovey	.105	38	3	4	0	3	3	21	2
Peyton Isaacson	.290	341	47	99	5	42	34	87	1
Junior Martina	.247	357	48	88	6	47	23	76	10
Carson Matthews	.188	138	14	26	2	11	7	38	3
Matt Morgan	.182	198	21	36	4	24	17	94	1
Will Riley	.224	192	22	43	0	24	38	42	6
Dan Robinson	.256	242	36	62	0	29	41	52	14
Bren Spillane	.247	288	51	71	16	45	42	94	27
Troy Viola	.220	259	43	57	7	35	8	62	4
Jonathan Waite	.217	129	12	28	4	17	22	37	0
Jordan Wiley	.080	25	1	2	0	0	1	10	0
Micah Yonamine	.264	360	50	95	12	53	29	102	1

Name	W	L	ERA	G	SV	IP	H	BB	SO
Cole Bellair	2	9	8.04	21	0	72	91	50	35
Garrett Christman	8	4	2.75	19	0	124	121	23	85
Cal Djuraskovic	1	2	6.39	30	0	31	38	21	25
Derrick Edington	4	1	1.64	32	5	33	23	24	35
Tyler LaPorte	1	1	0.84	9	0	11	7	8	8
Kenny Mathews	1	6	6.22	10	0	46	70	4	49
Justin Miller	1	2	3.99	43	0	50	41	27	45
Henry Omana	4	0	0.76	6	0	36	17	12	46
Adrien Reese	0	5	6.58	22	0	52	64	22	46
Javier Reynoso	4	1	4.57	12	0	63	65	31	61
Logan Schmitt	7	4	4.34	14	0	83	75	36	74
Sebastian Selway	1	3	2.93	29	0	31	25	18	30
Taylor Sugg	5	8	5.50	18	0	103	110	52	81
Carsie Walker	1	2	7.36	5	0	11	14	5	6

PIONEER LEAGUE

The fourth time was the charm.

The Ogden Raptors had been knocked off in the semifinals in each of the past three seasons, but in 2023, the Raptors outscored their opponents 26-13 in winning their final four playoff games. Ogden claimed its second Pioneer League title, with its other coming in 2017.

Josh Broughton's bases-loaded triple proved the big blow as Ogden clinched the title with a 7-5 win in the decision Game Two of the best-of-three series. It was also Ogden manager Kash Beauchamp's first title since he led the 1998 New Jersey Jackals to a crown.

North	W	L	PCT	GB
*Missoula PaddleHeads	66	29	.695	-
Glacier Range Riders	54	42	.563	12.5
^Billings Mustangs	51	45	.531	15.5
Great Falls Voyagers	35	61	.365	31.5
Idaho Falls Chukars	34	61	.358	32
South	**W**	**L**	**PCT**	**GB**
*Ogden Raptors	50	46	.521	-
Boise Hawks	49	47	.510	1
^Rocky Mountain Vibes	48	47	.505	1.5
Northern Colorado Owlz	46	49	.484	3.5
Grand Junction Jackalopes	45	51	.469	5

**First-half champion. ^Second-half champion.*

Playoffs—Semifinals: Billings defeated Missoula 2-1 and Ogden defeated Rocky Mountain 2-1 in best-of-3 series. **Finals:** Ogden defeated Billings 2-0 in best-of-3 series.

ALL-STAR TEAM: C: John Michael Faile, Billings; **1B:** Joe Johnson, Grand Junction; **2B:** Jaylen Hubbard, Grand Junction; **SS:** Payton Robertson, Northern Colorado; **3B:** Dusty Stroup, Rocky Mountain; **LF:** Jacob Cruce, Grand Junction; **CF:** Reese Alexiades, Ogden; **RF:** Ron Washington Jr., Grand Junction; **DH:** Jacob Barfield, Rocky Mountain; **SP:** Alfredo Villa, Missoula; **SP:** Connor Schultz, Missoula; **RP:** Dan Kubiuk, Ogden; **RP:** Justin Coleman, Glacier Range.

Most Valuable Player: Reese Alexiades, CF, Ogden; **Pitcher of the Year:** Alfredo Villa, Billings; **Reliever of the Year:** Dan Kubiuk, Ogden; **Rookies of the Year:** John Michael Faile, C, Billings and Ron Washington Jr., OF, Grand Junction; **International Player of the Year:** Abdel Guadalupe, OF, Northern Colorado; **Manager of the Year:** Billy Horton, Billings.

Attendance: Ogden Raptors 164,561, Boise Hawks 162,922, Rocky Mountain Vibes 114,041, Billings Mustangs 110,683, Glacier Range Riders 100,661, Idaho Falls Chukars 91,459, Missoula PaddleHeads 90,653, Grand Junction Jackalopes 67,500, Great Falls Voyagers 66,254.

BATTING LEADERS

Player, Team	AVG	AB	R	H	HR	RBI	SB
Jake McMurray, RM	.449	205	51	92	1	50	1
Kamron Willman, Missoula	.427	75	24	32	2	15	1
Brendan Ryan, Billings	.414	116	30	48	4	27	13
Damian Henderson, Ogden	.402	97	30	39	5	16	5
Dondrei Hubbard, Missoula	.395	281	63	111	11	50	17
Sam Olsson, Boise	.389	108	23	42	1	27	2
Xane Washington, GF	.382	275	68	105	4	39	23
Jackson Coutts, N. Colo.	.381	331	76	126	18	89	5
Jake Cruce, GJ	.377	387	78	146	23	96	2
Josh Broughton, Ogden	.376	93	21	35	0	16	0

PITCHING LEADERS

Pitcher, Team	W	L	ERA	IP	H	HR	BB	SO
Alfredo Villa, Missoula	13	1	2.82	109	99	9	35	129
Connor Schultz, Missoula	7	3	3.82	97	87	11	26	91
Justin Kleinsorge, GJ	8	2	4.17	99	108	14	33	113

Noah Barros, GR	9	5	4.58	90	94	10	42	92
Karan Patel, Billings	4	5	5.11	79	87	8	35	69
Brayden Spears, Boise	9	6	5.11	79	75	6	34	69
Izzy Fuentes, Missoula	9	3	5.27	97	116	13	27	72
Pat Maybach, Billings	4	3	5.51	85	95	6	33	70
Jake Mullholland, Ogden	8	1	5.59	76	114	11	30	69
Mark Tindall, N.Colo.	7	3	5.82	87	120	11	36	61

BILLINGS MUSTANGS

Name	AVG	AB	R	H	HR	RBI	BB	SO	SB
Brendan Ryan	.414	116	30	48	4	27	14	11	13
Luis Navarro	.409	22	4	9	0	1	1	4	0
John Michael Faile	.353	201	46	71	21	70	20	58	0
Gabe Wurtz	.344	355	82	122	19	71	35	71	3
Connor Denning	.336	292	77	98	16	65	49	51	16
Mikey Edie	.327	251	49	82	2	39	19	57	14
Taylor Lomack	.322	351	78	113	10	62	33	74	41
Wyatt Crenshaw	.314	51	13	16	4	17	11	14	4
Blake Evans	.302	96	21	29	2	25	7	15	5
Emmanuel Sanchez	.299	117	24	35	1	20	12	20	4
Bryce Donovan	.289	149	31	43	4	13	11	46	6
Alejandro Figueredo	.287	129	33	37	9	38	17	18	0
Brady West	.272	125	21	34	8	26	17	29	1
Luke Fennelly	.270	289	56	78	10	45	25	69	14
Tyler Wilber	.269	145	18	39	1	22	23	24	0
Mitch Moralez	.257	304	58	78	12	44	44	46	7
Jalen Garcia	.235	34	6	8	2	4	5	7	2
Luke Trueman	.226	53	11	12	0	5	1	17	1
Jason Ajamian	.204	54	5	11	0	6	9	17	1
Casey Harford	.195	82	9	16	2	13	3	16	0
Trevor Johnson	.188	32	3	6	1	6	3	7	0
Lance Logsdon	.159	44	3	7	2	6	5	9	0
Antonio Fernandez	.120	25	0	3	0	0	1	5	0

Name	W	L	ERA	G	SV	IP	H	BB	SO
Jacob Stobart	2	1	2.38	6	0	11	11	6	8
Cameron Repetti	6	1	2.43	8	0	37	37	14	20
Cam Tullar	3	1	3.16	9	0	26	29	6	40
Hunter Schilperoort	3	1	3.19	36	8	42	37	14	55
Trevor Jackson	4	3	4.78	28	4	70	68	40	86
Karan Patel	4	5	5.11	16	0	79	87	35	69
Brandon McPherson	3	0	5.23	8	0	33	40	14	24
McLain Harris	3	7	5.51	28	0	65	86	13	60
Pat Maybach	4	3	5.51	16	0	85	95	33	70
Keagan McGinnis	4	2	5.91	31	0	43	43	33	40
Luke Trueman	4	5	5.95	16	0	79	103	25	42
Nate Jenkins	2	2	6.17	36	2	42	58	20	42
Ty Pohlmann	0	0	6.94	7	0	12	12	10	9
Daniel Vitriago	1	1	7.29	5	0	21	24	13	16
Tyler Statler	0	1	8.39	21	6	25	24	26	22
Tristen Hudson	0	0	8.80	11	0	15	23	10	9
Jalen Evans	2	4	9.07	11	0	46	54	38	24
Ethan McRae	2	1	9.69	7	0	26	34	14	17
Jared Kengott	0	4	10.50	10	0	36	51	36	26
Chase Wilkerson	1	0	13.97	8	0	10	14	14	5

BOISE HAWKS

Name	AVG	AB	R	H	HR	RBI	BB	SO	SB
Sam Olsson	.402	97	18	39	0	26	13	11	1
Alex Baeza	.341	258	56	88	14	72	51	54	0
D.J. Poteet	.336	250	61	84	9	52	38	62	15
Derek Maiben	.316	193	25	61	0	31	15	12	3
Trevor Minder	.309	330	62	102	8	61	31	52	5
Kenny Oyama	.297	269	50	80	1	39	30	35	10
Noah Marcelo	.292	96	16	28	0	8	12	28	6
Tyler Jorgensen	.279	362	61	101	3	52	38	64	19
Sean Skelly	.277	195	42	54	10	42	37	59	0
Anthony Walters	.267	258	47	69	12	58	34	86	2
Ray Gil	.266	331	66	88	14	53	42	122	6
Ronnie Allen	.261	153	23	40	6	27	36	56	1
Kole Kaler	.258	334	65	86	4	52	55	71	14
Eddy Arteaga	.250	28	6	7	0	4	7	9	0
Casey Dykstra	.228	123	28	28	6	22	15	52	0
Connor O'Brien	.146	41	9	6	0	1	4	15	1
Rene Mendoza	.087	23	2	2	1	2	2	10	0

Name	W	L	ERA	G	SV	IP	H	BB	SO
Nate Alexander	2	1	3.09	27	9	44	44	14	46
Noah McBride	0	1	3.55	35	2	38	42	22	52
Casey Dykstra	0	1	3.60	15	3	15	7	8	21
Evan Kowalski	2	1	4.38	21	1	37	38	17	40
Brayden Spears	9	6	5.11	16	0	79	75	34	69
Ryley Widell	5	3	5.27	11	0	55	63	28	56
Blake McFadden	1	0	5.28	30	0	29	30	17	29
Gavin Gorrell	4	1	5.49	16	1	57	69	20	54
Alex Smith	5	6	6.60	16	0	90	102	47	55
Kevin Pindel	3	2	6.62	14	0	67	92	23	58
Matt Voelker	7	5	6.78	17	0	81	123	35	42
Matthew Sox	1	5	6.90	12	1	46	55	21	39
Drew Marrufo	2	0	6.91	34	3	43	54	30	33
Ian Oxnevad	1	2	7.50	7	0	30	37	15	22
Mike Peterson	3	2	7.94	19	2	45	73	9	36
Gage O'Brien	1	1	8.31	11	0	13	10	21	23
Luke Malone	2	4	9.00	22	0	38	62	14	28
Andrew Stout	0	2	9.18	4	0	17	23	6	15

GLACIER RANGE RIDERS

Name	AVG	AB	R	H	HR	RBI	BB	SO	SB
Dean Miller	.360	361	86	130	15	80	56	77	29
Christian Kirtley	.320	228	51	73	15	43	35	53	6
Mason Dinesen	.313	310	69	97	7	55	18	77	26
Matt Clayton	.310	271	48	84	13	52	34	44	1
Ben Huber	.309	55	15	17	1	12	10	18	0
Ben Fitzgerald	.306	268	57	82	13	55	29	80	5
Crews Taylor	.303	244	51	74	13	59	46	75	23
Gabe Howell	.299	371	100	111	17	68	65	77	30
Jackson Raper	.299	351	66	105	11	74	42	79	7
Colin Gordon	.291	313	74	91	13	64	38	87	10
Ben McConnell	.279	111	30	31	1	13	18	25	21
Kingston Liniak	.274	325	65	89	20	77	32	80	9
Austin Bates	.265	68	9	18	0	7	3	8	0
Sam Linscott	.259	54	8	14	0	6	3	11	4
Jake MacKenzie	.250	32	7	8	1	5	6	5	1
Nick Lucky	.229	83	13	19	4	17	8	28	2

Name	W	L	ERA	G	SV	IP	H	BB	SO
Lyle Hibbitts	0	0	2.63	12	0	24	17	11	22
Ben Ferrer	1	1	2.65	14	0	17	15	3	19
Justin Coleman	5	0	2.86	41	8	44	33	12	58
Connor Housley	3	1	3.96	29	0	36	38	18	33
Noah Barros	9	5	4.58	22	0	90	94	42	92
John Natoli	3	0	4.78	34	3	38	34	35	35
Nick Zegna	5	4	5.99	15	0	77	101	25	49
Montana Quigley	1	4	6.12	36	2	43	60	14	33
Pat Miner	6	4	6.25	13	0	63	96	15	49
Ryan Cloude	0	0	6.32	31	0	37	50	10	38
Jonathan Clark	5	3	6.79	13	0	57	71	30	49
Jonathan Pintaro	5	6	6.95	21	0	91	114	33	86
Rob Hamby	2	3	7.03	9	0	40	54	20	33
Jack White	3	7	7.04	14	0	61	79	36	69
Luke Dawson	0	1	7.23	18	0	19	21	21	17
Tanner Solomon	2	1	7.41	4	0	17	28	7	12
RJ Robles	0	2	7.46	38	2	35	44	21	33
Joe Kinsky	1	0	7.94	24	0	23	26	26	23
Kevin Kyle	0	2	8.06	9	0	22	36	8	20
Drew Holweger	0	1	8.44	10	0	11	15	7	10
Michael YaSenka	0	1	9.82	10	0	18	24	10	23

GRAND JUNCTION JACKALOPES

Name	AVG	AB	R	H	HR	RBI	BB	SO	SB
Jake Cruce	.377	387	78	146	23	96	41	75	2
Joe Johnson	.370	419	117	155	22	106	64	79	13
Austin Shumaker	.367	79	19	29	0	5	8	20	1
Kokko Figueiredo	.351	151	52	53	9	46	37	27	5
Ron Washington	.350	357	86	125	24	88	54	67	9

Austin Chouinard	.345	145	28	50	6	30	16	37	0
Lavoisier Fisher	.328	67	19	22	3	14	4	13	4
Anthony Ray	.327	223	40	73	5	42	22	38	1
Matt Wong	.324	216	48	70	5	40	27	36	6
Ethan Smith	.321	112	24	36	5	20	10	38	4
Drew Williams	.317	101	22	32	2	13	9	11	2
Jaylen Hubbard	.316	392	94	124	25	117	45	84	11
Andrew Meggs	.313	192	43	60	1	32	23	23	3
Matt Golda	.303	165	37	50	2	27	21	30	3
Alex Nielsen	.300	40	15	12	1	5	3	7	0
Alex Stinnett	.258	89	13	23	2	14	20	24	0
Tyler Sandoval	.252	147	31	37	5	28	26	51	0
Kevin Saenz	.161	31	2	5	0	2	1	13	0
Andrew Brautman	.107	28	4	3	0	1	6	11	2

Name	W	L	ERA	G	SV	IP	H	BB	SO
Justin Kleinsorge	8	2	4.17	18	0	99	108	33	113
Bryan Perez	2	0	4.86	10	0	17	14	25	22
Riyan Rodriguez	1	2	5.20	25	5	28	32	17	26
Ethan McRae	2	0	5.57	5	0	21	25	14	19
Calvin Marley	1	0	6.59	24	6	29	39	19	25
Adam Bloebaum	2	3	6.86	16	0	63	80	25	74
Chris Allen	2	6	6.90	13	0	60	76	33	49
Miguel Cirino	3	2	7.43	15	1	27	32	14	28
Frank Racioppo	3	8	7.58	20	0	95	119	69	67
Keenan Bartlett	2	3	8.76	21	2	62	97	26	52
Tyler Johnson	3	3	8.83	20	0	36	42	25	40
Trey Morrill	4	10	8.90	22	2	86	110	78	107
Connor Barton	2	0	9.49	17	0	25	41	18	13
Diego Jordan	0	1	10.18	20	1	20	31	22	25
Emmanuel Rosario	2	1	10.65	13	1	24	41	16	19
Gaylan Young	1	0	11.62	25	0	26	44	17	26
Jaylen Smith	1	2	13.38	17	0	39	63	38	31
Jimmy Dobrash	1	5	15.85	10	0	31	59	30	24
Ubaldo Romo	1	0	18.21	9	0	14	36	19	11
Connor White	0	0	22.09	8	0	11	17	23	5

GREAT FALLS VOYAGERS

Name	AVG	AB	R	H	HR	RBI	BB	SO	SB
Cristopher De Guzman	.441	59	11	26	0	9	6	13	1
Xane Washington	.382	275	68	105	4	39	17	43	23
Riley Jepson	.374	321	81	120	1	49	54	27	16
Ryan McCarthy	.372	86	29	32	6	25	15	19	4
Jaylyn Williams	.339	304	50	103	12	85	30	54	0
Anthony Herron	.323	235	43	76	7	54	26	49	1
Giovanni DiGiacomo	.312	109	29	34	1	14	23	23	5
Eddie McCabe	.305	226	27	69	4	42	20	31	1
Cal Bocchino	.300	50	15	15	1	5	10	20	6
Jake Malec	.281	164	34	46	0	19	20	41	10
Charley Hesse	.280	225	37	63	7	37	20	67	2
Billy Hancock	.279	154	31	43	4	26	21	45	3
Collin Runge	.279	262	43	73	8	57	33	36	4
Derek Kolbush	.278	108	16	30	2	26	17	21	1
Ryan Peltier	.262	126	18	33	2	19	12	35	3
Chris Coipel	.256	43	3	11	1	9	1	11	0
Beau Dorman	.240	25	4	6	0	3	0	5	0
Langston Ginder	.232	112	25	26	1	13	19	30	5
Matt Richardson	.215	65	14	14	1	6	10	15	1
Jaylen Armstrong	.207	92	23	19	0	13	13	20	9
Greg Ryan	.200	55	11	11	2	9	6	23	2
Dilan Espinal	.194	36	5	7	0	2	4	5	1
Nick Emanuel	.176	131	11	23	0	10	10	38	0

Name	W	L	ERA	G	SV	IP	H	BB	SO
Tommy Snyder	1	1	2.13	7	0	13	14	3	12
Casey Minchey	3	4	4.18	13	0	65	76	9	37
Andrew Garcia	3	3	5.53	32	9	57	51	36	76
G.T. Blackman	3	5	5.80	19	0	64	83	27	47
Brady Held	4	5	5.89	17	0	66	76	28	79
Kelsey Ward	1	2	6.00	10	0	33	38	29	28
Tyler Naumann	3	7	7.16	22	0	93	139	37	70
Brett Lorah	0	2	7.39	11	0	28	46	9	27
Shane Gustafson	1	3	7.65	15	0	42	68	20	31
Breonn Pooler	2	3	7.79	19	2	52	77	21	54
Bo Blessie	0	0	9.31	10	0	10	9	10	15
Jaymon Cervantes	0	3	9.56	5	0	16	23	10	9
Christopher Coipel	1	3	9.89	9	0	24	36	21	23
Collin Runge	1	3	10.01	9	0	30	41	22	11
Payton Harris	3	0	10.16	16	0	28	50	9	27
Joshua Gainer	0	2	11.08	7	0	13	22	8	11
Nik Galatas	0	1	15.55	4	0	11	21	10	6
Bobby Vath	1	2	16.88	10	0	13	34	8	13

IDAHO FALLS CHUKARS

Name	AVG	AB	R	H	HR	RBI	BB	SO	SB
Bryce Brown	.351	225	54	79	3	25	39	58	20
Chris Monroe	.337	101	26	34	4	20	14	25	0
CJ Dunn	.333	135	23	45	6	28	9	37	0
Eduardo Acosta	.323	220	44	71	1	33	34	24	4
Trevor Halsema	.310	345	81	107	6	61	52	71	10
Mark Herron	.302	272	40	82	10	55	18	75	11
Sam Troyer	.301	226	45	68	1	27	26	58	8
Robb Paller	.293	99	25	29	4	20	23	30	2
Tyler Wyatt	.292	267	64	78	14	64	32	49	12
Stephen Cullen	.286	182	30	52	6	36	20	49	1
Brandon Bohning	.272	272	46	74	6	32	23	57	4
Hunter Hudson	.262	183	18	48	0	29	26	50	0
Anthony Frechette	.258	128	19	33	3	16	20	29	2
Mike Kohn	.257	261	47	67	11	69	21	77	0
Jordan Myrow	.257	179	29	46	4	28	16	54	4
Zach May	.232	138	23	32	8	28	26	51	0
Karl Koerper	.150	20	2	3	0	1	1	8	0

Name	W	L	ERA	G	SV	IP	H	BB	SO
Jorge Gonzalez	3	0	4.34	14	0	48	65	14	41
Daniel Silva	5	6	6.12	16	0	97	117	25	65
Brian Williams	3	4	6.46	36	9	39	44	21	39
Armando Valle	1	0	6.89	5	0	16	14	19	13
Jacob Bogacz	1	2	7.02	30	0	33	44	24	34
Dylan Gotto	3	6	8.16	11	0	57	97	20	34
Victor Rodriguez	3	2	8.16	30	0	61	85	34	56
Bryant Bagshaw	0	5	8.73	29	5	56	83	39	36
Robbie Brown	3	0	9.20	28	1	46	73	24	31
Joe Slocum	2	7	9.22	16	0	55	96	22	30
Tom Walker	3	11	10.15	18	0	83	134	54	61
Dusty Baird	1	7	10.24	21	0	61	109	39	53
Tyler Wyatt	0	4	10.36	11	0	33	54	11	35
Jack Zigan	0	0	10.52	19	1	32	50	13	21
Darrien Williams	1	1	10.65	15	0	24	33	23	19
Jack Dicenso	1	5	11.24	14	0	54	84	38	44
Jeff Rotz	1	0	18.00	10	0	14	17	21	5

MISSOULA PADDLEHEADS

Name	AVG	AB	R	H	HR	RBI	BB	SO	SB
Kamron Willman	.427	75	24	32	2	15	10	9	1
Dondrei Hubbard	.395	281	63	111	11	50	23	46	17
Luis Navarro	.351	225	49	79	10	57	44	40	1
Patrick Chung	.348	316	61	110	6	51	22	32	9
Keaton Greenwalt	.345	365	83	126	21	93	35	44	16
Jake Guenther	.344	326	68	112	8	77	50	31	5
Thomas DeBonville	.318	233	49	74	11	47	19	70	8
Josh Elvir	.308	104	27	32	6	23	14	28	2
Jayson Newman-Dodd	.304	69	15	21	7	23	8	11	0
McClain O'Connor	.302	334	90	101	18	73	42	78	30
Reece Yeargain	.300	50	9	15	2	8	4	13	0
Ryan Cash	.296	264	49	78	3	31	26	32	8
Austin Bernard	.291	182	44	53	6	36	36	46	3
Cameron Thompson	.285	316	70	90	10	59	45	62	13
Jared Akins	.281	153	37	43	5	30	14	49	7
Jacob Kline	.278	90	14	25	2	13	4	31	1
Trevor Candelaria	.194	31	8	6	1	4	3	12	2

Name	W	L	ERA	G	SV	IP	H	BB	SO
Ethan Swanson	4	2	2.66	32	0	51	43	28	61
Alfredo Villa	13	1	2.82	18	0	109	99	35	129
Zach Penrod	4	1	2.98	13	2	54	39	32	65
Jestin Jones	1	0	3.75	14	0	24	25	13	21

Name	W	L	ERA	G	SV	IP	H	BB	SO
Connor Schultz	7	3	3.82	18	0	97	87	26	91
Kelvan Pilot	8	1	3.95	9	0	55	54	21	46
Dawson Day	4	2	4.20	9	0	45	47	14	48
John LaRossa	0	0	4.50	34	0	34	27	22	43
Mark Timmins	6	1	4.72	21	0	48	53	13	44
Izzy Fuentes	9	3	5.27	18	0	97	116	27	72
Liu Fuenmayor	4	2	5.45	34	0	33	33	18	39
Mark Simon	1	3	5.63	32	12	32	35	13	46
Karl Blum	0	0	6.41	32	0	27	17	35	41
Austin Dill	3	2	6.80	20	1	45	68	18	54
Mitch Sparks	1	1	6.95	12	0	22	34	2	18

NORTHERN COLORADO OWLZ

Name	AVG	AB	R	H	HR	RBI	BB	SO	SB
Jackson Coutts	.381	331	76	126	18	89	40	52	5
Henry George	.353	348	101	123	16	59	53	36	31
Abdel Guadalupe	.351	333	72	117	17	89	23	39	8
Euro Diaz	.336	286	54	96	2	48	34	64	10
Payton Robertson	.331	320	87	106	11	64	70	70	62
Danny Perez	.326	193	42	63	12	47	43	24	1
Dave Matthews	.325	286	74	93	22	68	53	81	17
Kevin Higgins	.310	87	20	27	2	17	10	17	2
Tim Bouchard	.307	270	43	83	10	53	43	82	9
Brandon Crosby	.300	40	15	12	2	8	7	12	6
Kevin Jimenez	.288	212	41	61	6	30	24	35	11
Nick Michaels	.286	140	29	40	3	28	18	40	4
Josh Glenn	.251	203	36	51	7	39	34	72	3
Jordan Rathbone	.234	141	22	33	6	30	13	49	0
Estevan De La O	.231	134	42	31	3	23	28	46	11
Dakota Popham	.179	67	12	12	1	8	15	22	0

Name	W	L	ERA	G	SV	IP	H	BB	SO
Nathan Draves	0	1	3.03	21	0	36	40	12	35
Carter Linton	3	4	4.86	42	0	50	49	31	66
Cory Wills	3	4	5.14	45	13	49	59	25	65
Mark Tindall	7	3	5.82	21	0	87	120	36	61
Dutch Landis	1	0	6.17	12	0	12	9	12	8
Chase Jessee	2	2	6.33	26	0	81	106	68	85
Will Buraconak	6	4	6.84	17	0	75	89	34	65
Austin Schneider	5	9	7.00	19	0	100	128	46	93
Kris Massey	0	0	7.65	21	0	20	27	17	29
Dalton Ross	2	3	8.60	26	0	30	40	17	27
Jose Diaz	2	4	8.63	24	0	73	106	50	73
Brandon Kaminer	5	4	9.18	15	0	50	68	43	35
Chris Mutter	0	1	9.18	18	0	17	27	17	12
Jacob Walker	2	0	9.76	15	0	40	70	16	24
Luis Florentino	0	1	10.34	15	0	16	18	10	15
CJ Grant-DeBose	0	2	12.64	13	0	16	18	17	15
JC Coronado	0	0	13.50	7	0	10	14	13	8

OGDEN RAPTORS

Name	AVG	AB	R	H	HR	RBI	BB	SO	SB
Damian Henderson	.402	97	30	39	5	16	15	25	5
Jonathan Soto	.391	64	17	25	5	20	8	14	0
Josh Broughton	.376	93	21	35	0	16	7	9	7
Nick Ultsch	.373	343	87	128	7	73	35	67	3
Juan Teixeira	.351	350	63	123	11	74	28	45	7
Cam Phelts	.327	324	72	106	2	56	49	52	40
Reese Alexiades	.326	365	108	119	29	90	73	81	29
Sal Gozzo	.320	197	47	63	4	35	44	39	5
Landen Barns	.314	172	36	54	2	31	12	24	1
Logan Williams	.314	299	53	94	13	72	56	86	6
Rafael Narea	.312	301	59	94	9	55	35	50	8
Dakota Conners	.308	334	63	103	5	69	44	55	7
Coleton Horner	.283	184	36	52	1	26	16	27	1
Dane Tofteland	.248	117	26	29	9	26	13	32	1
Tim Bouchard	.205	39	4	8	0	0	5	14	0
Trevor Rogers	.182	22	4	4	0	2	6	5	0
Brian Dansereau	.159	44	6	7	1	11	7	16	0

Name	W	L	ERA	G	SV	IP	H	BB	SO
Dan Kubiuk	1	0	0.50	35	15	36	26	9	50
Adam Scoggins	1	0	2.92	14	2	12	7	8	18
Isaac Keehn	0	0	4.50	3	1	12	10	7	10
Pablo Arevalo	5	3	5.11	12	0	62	60	22	50
Mitch Stone	4	5	5.27	14	0	67	68	32	81
Matt Hess	3	1	5.34	6	0	32	47	10	16
Jake Mulholland	8	1	5.59	15	0	76	114	30	69
Brock Gilliam	9	6	6.26	18	0	92	117	30	88
Ronny Orta	0	1	6.30	3	0	10	13	4	5
Foster Pace	1	2	6.42	24	0	34	45	13	23
Marshall Shill	2	0	6.70	41	0	47	73	20	43
Ed Baram	3	6	6.88	14	0	54	64	23	40
Brandon McCabe	1	2	7.50	34	2	30	32	27	55
Chase Stratton	1	5	7.79	20	1	54	68	34	60
Riley Ottesen	3	0	8.10	24	0	50	70	27	50
Jon Rice	1	0	8.27	22	0	21	17	38	37
Mason Hoover	0	0	9.28	9	0	11	17	9	11
Jackson Miller	0	3	18.90	3	0	10	18	11	7

ROCKY MOUNTAIN VIBES

Name	AVG	AB	R	H	HR	RBI	BB	SO	SB
Jake McMurray	.449	205	51	92	1	50	29	10	1
Brett Carson	.386	70	28	27	2	18	17	15	7
Jacob Barfield	.357	286	75	102	22	98	44	67	7
Thomas Jeffries	.355	31	8	11	0	2	7	5	2
Stephen Wilmer	.354	130	42	46	10	40	35	44	4
Casey Petersen	.347	190	49	66	6	44	41	50	2
Ethan Lopez	.344	288	79	99	12	66	40	51	5
Dusty Stroup	.343	365	100	125	20	108	68	77	9
Elvis Peralta	.320	303	75	97	6	51	36	89	21
Edmond Americaan	.317	79	14	25	2	15	10	24	2
Brandon Crosby	.314	220	60	69	3	28	34	61	22
Mark Herron	.314	51	12	16	3	16	3	13	2
Brandon Trammell	.310	29	7	9	3	8	5	11	0
CJ Dunn	.303	33	6	10	0	9	5	9	0
Steve Barmakian	.292	137	30	40	4	35	23	26	5
Matt Hogan	.290	152	32	44	10	32	27	46	2
Sonny Ulliana	.270	63	7	17	2	10	10	26	1
Joe Encarnacion	.269	130	21	35	3	35	15	39	0
Milton Smith Jr.	.265	117	27	31	0	9	19	29	10
Brian Dansereau	.261	23	3	6	1	6	7	7	1
Dave Martinez	.236	110	20	26	3	26	20	45	0
Austin Elder	.220	118	28	26	3	20	21	12	0
Brady West	.191	21	3	4	2	2	1	5	0
Carson Maxwell	.158	38	7	6	2	4	6	17	0

Name	W	L	ERA	G	SV	IP	H	BB	SO
Nico Zeglin	3	0	3.03	6	0	30	28	9	39
Sandi Charle	0	0	3.38	11	1	11	10	6	8
Zach Ottinger	5	0	4.95	18	0	64	79	28	36
Carlos Lomeli	0	0	5.54	13	2	13	20	3	10
Blaine Traxel	2	3	5.64	9	0	45	66	13	34
Reed Butz	1	1	5.82	31	1	39	47	22	33
Jack Cunningham	3	3	5.96	48	1	51	72	16	27
Peyton Long	9	4	5.96	19	0	100	127	43	67
Kevin Dickey	1	5	5.97	12	0	38	37	41	22
Christian Day	8	6	7.00	20	0	91	125	39	62
Chris Macca	1	6	7.99	40	3	47	67	35	35
Alexis Cedano	0	2	8.25	12	5	12	18	9	11
Conner Woods	2	3	8.84	11	0	39	53	31	31
Marvin Guzman	4	2	9.41	23	0	51	70	41	60
Dutch Landis	1	0	9.43	16	2	21	28	13	22
Rey Rodriguez	0	0	10.93	14	0	14	18	16	12
Wilber Pérez	0	2	10.95	9	1	12	16	11	9
Ryan Campbell	0	1	11.32	3	0	10	16	10	9
Christian Scafidi	0	2	12.83	7	0	13	20	8	17

PECOS LEAGUE

San Rafael knocked off Tucson to win the 2023 Pecos League crown. The Austin Weirdos finished one of the worst seasons in baseball history, finishing 1-47. They were outscored 737-399.

Pacific	W	L	PCT	GB
San Rafael Pacifics	39	8	.829	--
Monterey Amberjacks	31	18	.632	9

	W	L	PCT	GB
Bakersfield Train Robbers	30	18	.625	9.5
Lancaster Sound Breakers	28	22	.560	12.5
Marysville Drakes	27	23	.540	13.5
Martinez Sturgeon	25	24	.510	15
Vallejo Seaweed	12	37	.244	28
Dublin Leprechauns	4	44	.083	35.5

Mountain	W	L	PCT	GB
Tucson Saguaros	33	13	.717	--
Alpine Cowboys	36	16	.692	--
Trinidad Triggers	30	19	.612	4.5
Garden City Wind	30	20	.600	5
Roswell Invaders	30	23	.566	6.5
Blackwell FlyCatchers	17	25	.404	14
Santa Fe Fuego	17	31	.354	17
Austin Weirdos	1	47	.020	36

Playoffs—First Round: Tucson defeated Garden City 2-0; Trinidad defeated Alpine 2-1; San Rafael defeated Lancaster 2-0 and Bakersfield defeated Monterey 2-1 in best-of-three series. **Semifinals:** Tucson defeated Trinidad 2-0 and San Rafael defeated Bakersfield 2-0 in best-of-three series. **Finals:** San Rafael defeated Tucson 2-1 in best-of-three series.

U.S. PRO BASEBALL LEAGUE

Utica's run as the dominant team in the USPBL continued, as the Unicorns beat Westside 3-1 in the title game. It was Utica's fifth USPBL title and its fourth in the past five years. Matt Colucci was named the postseason MVP. He struck out seven in three scoreless innings of relief.

East Division	W	L	PCT	GB
Eastside Diamond Hoppers	27	22	.523	—
Utica Unicorns	17	26	.395	5.5
West Division	**W**	**L**	**PCT**	**GB**
Westside Woolly Mammoths	27	18	.600	—
Birmingham Bloomfield Beavers	23	24	.477	5.5

Playoffs—Semifinals: Utica defeated Bloomfield and Westside defeated Birmingham. **Finals:** Utica defeated Westside.

All-Star Team:C: Zach Beadle, Mammoths. **1B:** Joe Burke, Hoppers. **2B:** Luis Acevedo, Hoppers. **SS:** Ben Wilcoxson, Beavers. **3B:** Alex Garbacik, Mammoths. **OF:** Chris Davis, Beavers. **OF:** Nick Pastore, Unicorns. **OF:** Burle Dixon, Mammoths. **OF:** Ray Hilbrich, Beavers. **DH:** Malek Bolin, Beavers. **SP:** Ryan Korolden, Hoppers. **SP:** Rhian Mann, Beavers. **SP:** Garrett Martin, Mammoths. **P:** Michael Esposito, **Beavers. P: Christian Stelling, Hoppers. P: Andrew Huffman, Unicorns. UTL: Dre Wiliams-Nelson, Mammoths. UTL: Fox Leum, Mammoths Most Valuable Player:** Ethan Wiskur, Westside. **Pitcher of the Year:** Matt Cronin, Westside.

BATTING LEADERS

Player	Team	AVG	AB	R	H	HR	RBI
Francisco Florentino	WWM	.377	53	9	20	2	12
Raymond Hillbrich	BBB	.343	108	20	37	1	16
Phil Matulia	UU	.327	55	9	18	1	9
Chris Davis	BBB	.325	163	35	53	7	30
Noah Mrcoux	EDH	.318	88	14	28	2	12

PITCHING LEADERS

Player	Team	W	L	ERA	IP	H	BB	SO
Jake Armstrong	BBB	1	2	1.35	47	35	15	32
Andrew Huffman	UU	3	3	2.95	55	31	33	79
Tristan Harvin	UU	5	4	4.19	69	78	24	50
Ryan Korolden	EDH	2	2	4.21	51	44	21	43
Garrett Martin	WWM	6	2	4.35	72	60	31	68

INTERNATIONAL

Japan Edges Team USA For Third WBC Title

CHRISTOPHER PASATIERI

Shohei Ohtani starred on the mound and at the plate as Japan won the WBC

BY KYLE GLASER

MIAMI — It came down to the matchup everyone wanted to see.

Shohei Ohtani vs. Mike Trout. Bottom of the ninth. Two outs. One-run game. World Baseball Classic championship on the line. It was the stuff of childhood dreams, as well as the dreams of millions of baseball fans across the globe. The game's two most talented players, teammates the rest of the year but opponents on this night, facing off for the first championship of their professional careers.

The Angels teammates went back and forth, trading balls and strikes until the count was full. Trout swung hard for the fences, trying to get Team USA back in the game. Ohtani threw 100-plus mph fastballs over and over again, trying to overpower his teammate and friend. It was the game's premier players reaching back for every ounce of ability they had, trying to take the other down and emerge victorious for both them and their teams.

With the count full and the game hanging in the balance, Ohtani took a breath, came set and unleashed one final, furious pitch to beat Trout and lift his country to a title.

Ohtani struck out Trout swinging on a full-count slider for the final out, and Japan beat Team USA, 3-2, to win the 2023 WBC championship game. It is Japan's third WBC championship in five editions of the event and its first since 2009.

Japan went 7-0 in the tournament, joining the Dominican Republic in 2013 as the only teams to go undefeated in a WBC. Ohtani was named MVP after he hit .435 with four doubles, a home run and eight RBIs at the plate and went 2-0, 1.86 on the mound with a save in the championship game.

"I believe," Ohtani said through an interpreter, "this is the best moment in my life."

The battle between Ohtani and Trout lived up to every expectation. Japan led 3-2 going into the top of the ninth when Ohtani emerged from the bullpen and walked slowly to the mound for his first relief appearance since the 2016 postseason

WORLD BASEBALL CLASSIC

STANDINGS

Pool A	W	L	Pool C	W	L
*Cuba	2	2	*Mexico	3	1
*Italy	2	2	*USA	3	1
Netherlands	2	2	Canada	2	2
Panama	2	2	Great Britain	1	3
Chinese Taipei	2	2	Colombia	1	3

Pool B	W	L	Pool D	W	L
*Japan	4	0	*Venezuela	4	0
*Australia	3	1	*Puerto Rico	3	1
Korea	2	2	Dominican Rep.	2	2
Czech Republic	1	3	Israel	1	3
China	0	4	Nicaragua	0	4

Quarterfinals: Cuba defeated Australia 4-3; Japan defeated Australia 9-3; United States defeated Venezuela 9-7 and Mexico defeated Puerto Rico 5-4 in single-game elimination. **Semifinals:** United States defeated Cuba 14-2 and Japan defeated Mexico 6-5 in single-game elimination. **Finals:** Japan defeated United States 3-2.

BATTING LEADERS

PLAYER	TEAM	AVG	AB	R	H	HR	RBI	SB
Choi, Ji Hoon	KOR	.667	3	4	2	0	1	0
O'Neill, Tyler	CAN	.615	13	5	8	0	4	0
Lee, Ji Young	KOR	.600	5	3	3	0	1	0
Park, Hae-Min	KOR	.600	5	3	3	0	0	1
Julien, Edouard	CAN	.538	13	5	7	2	2	1
Adames, Willy	DOM	.500	4	1	2	0	0	0
Alegria, Benjamin	NCA	.500	12	0	6	0	0	0
Candelario, Jeimer	DOM	.500	12	2	6	0	0	0
Kang, Bae-kho	KOR	.500	14	3	7	0	2	0
Kim, Hye-Seong	KOR	.500	2	3	1	0	3	0

PITCHING LEADERS

PLAYER	TEAM	W	L	ERA	IP	H	HR	BB	SO
Arauz, Harold	PAN	1	0	0.00	4.0	2	0	1	3
De León, Jose	PUR	1	0	0.00	5.2	0	0	0	10
Javier, Cristian	DOM	1	0	0.00	4.0	2	0	1	4
Kremer, Dean	ISR	0	0	0.00	4.0	3	0	1	4
Mejía, Humberto	PAN	0	0	0.00	4.0	3	0	3	1
Park, Se Woong	KOR	1	0	0.00	6.0	1	0	0	9
Skirrow, Noah	CAN	1	0	0.00	5.0	2	0	1	5
Sandoval, Patrick	MEX	1	0	1.23	7.1	6	0	3	8
Harvey, Matt	ITA	1	0	1.29	7.0	4	1	1	3
Wu, Che-Yuan	TPE	0	0	1.42	6.1	4	0	2	4

U12 WORLD CUP

FINAL STANDINGS

Team	W	L	Team	W	L
United States	7	2	Mexico	5	3
Taiwan	7	2	Panama	4	4
Venezuela	7	2	Germany	3	5
Japan	6	3	Czech Republic	2	6
South Korea	4	4	Australia	1	7
Dominican Republic	4	4	New Zealand	0	8

Top six teams advanced to Super Round, while other six teams continued in consolation round.

Gold Medal Game: United States defeated Taiwan 10-4.

Bronze Medal Game: Venezuela defeated Japan 9-8.

MVP: Tyler Early (United States).

All-World Team: C: Yosuke Koma (Japan). **1B:** Kengo Wada (Japan). **2B:** Alexandro Ladera (Venezuela). **3B:** Zaylon Johnson (United States). **SS:** Ezequiel Zamora (Venezuela). **LF:** Gavin Gomez (United States). **CF:** Gustavo Talamare (Dominican Republic). **RF:** Tyler Early (United States). **DH:** Keimel Paula (Dominican Republic). **P:** Ya-En Chiu (Taiwan). **RP:** Lei Yeh (Taiwan).

with the Nippon Ham Fighters.

Ohtani started Trout with a slider that missed down for ball one. He came back and blew a 100 mph fastball down the middle past his Angels teammate to even the count. Ohtani unleashed another 100 mph fastball that missed outside for ball two.

Undeterred, Ohtani delivered yet another 100 mph fastball down the middle, and again Trout swung through it to even the count at 2-2.

Then, Ohtani reared back for something extra. He threw another fastball that clocked in at 102 mph, but he yanked it down and away to run the count full.

After throwing four straight fastballs, all 100 mph or harder, Ohtani went back to the slider. He unleashed an 87 mph spinner that started out over the plate and swept toward the outside corner. Trout swung hard and was on time, but to no avail. The pitch dipped out of his bat path at the last second, and the three-time American League MVP caught nothing but air.

Strike three. Game over.

Ohtani, in the battle of the best, had won.

"He won round one," Trout said. " … He's got nasty stuff. He made a good pitch at the end. It's one of those things where you gotta tip your hat to him."

Ohtani let out a primal scream as he stomped off the mound toward his onrushing teammates. He ripped off his glove and threw it toward the plate, and then ripped off his hat and did the same for good measure.

His teammates mobbed him on the mound. The championship celebration began, fittingly, with Ohtani in the middle of it all.

"Earlier in my baseball life, this was one of the things that I wanted to achieve," Ohtani said. " … This really proves that Japanese baseball can beat any team in the world."

When Third Place Is A Win

Great Britain and the Czech Republic each finished in fourth place in Pool C. Only the top two teams in each pool advanced, but those fourth-place finishes were still significant.

By finishing third in its pool, it automatically qualifies for the next World Baseball Classic. The same is true of Israel and Panama. The news is much worse for Taiwan. A participant in every World Baseball Classic so far, Taiwan will have to earn a spot in the next WBC by qualifying. China, Colombia and Nicaragua have also been relegated to the qualifying round.

18U WORLD CUP

STANDINGS

Team	W	L	Team	W	L
Japan	7	2	Panama	4	4
Chinese Taipei	8	1	Mexico	3	5
South Korea	6	3	Czech Republic	3	5
United States	5	4	Australia	3	5
Puerto Rico	5	3	Venezuela	2	6
Netherlands	4	4	Spain	0	8

Format: Top six teams advanced to Super Round, while the other six teams continued in consolation round. **Bronze Medal Game:** Korea defeated United States 4-0. **Gold Medal Game:** Japan defeated Taiwan 2-1.

All-World Team: C: Meng-Chih Hu (Taiwan). **1B:** P.J. Morlando (USA). **2B:** Ren Ogata (Japan). **3B:** Dimas Oda (Panama). **SS:** Manuelle Marin (United States). **LF:** Miquel Willem (Netherlands). **CF:** Ching-Hsien Ko (Taiwan). **RF:** Antonis Macias (Mexico). **DH:** Sang-Jun Lee (South Korea). **P:** Aoi Higashionna (Japan). **RP:** Tae-kyeon Kim (South Korea).

Most Valuable Player: Ren Ogata, (Japan).

A Disappointing Result

USA Baseball's 18U National Team dropped its bronze medal game against South Korea, 4-0, and cemented a fourth-place finish in the 2023 World Baseball Softball Confederation (WBSC) U-18 World Cup, which took place in Taiwan. Japan topped Taiwan in the gold medal game.

The fourth-pace finish is the worst finish for Team USA at the 18U world event since 2010. The result snaps a streak of six consecutive international WBSC events for the 18U team with at least a top two finish, including four consecutive gold medal finishes from 2012 to 2017—capped by one of the most dominant showings ever for an American national team in Thunder Bay, Canada, in 2017.

Team USA went 5-4 in the tournament and failed to medal in the event for the first time in 13 years, going back to the 2010 Junior Baseball World Championship, which was also held in Taiwan.

This was the worst performance by USAs 18U team since a fifth place finish in 2010 when the World Cup was called the Junior Baseball World Championship.

Team USA outscored opponents 29-24, but suffered two shutout losses (once against Taiwan and in the final game against Korea) and ranked fifth out of twelve teams with a 2.44 team ERA and with 29 runs scored.

The Americans had neither the firepower nor the run prevention of each of the top three teams. Gold medal-winning Japan scored 52 runs and had a 1.19 team ERA; silver medal-winning Taiwan scored 48 runs and had a 0.80 team ERA; and bronze medal-winning South Korea scored 37 runs and posted a 1.98 team ERA.

CHRIS CODUTO

Harry Ford and Great Britain guaranteed themselves a spot in the next WBC.

Women's World Cup Field Set

In the first significant international women's baseball competition since the coronavirus pandemic, the Pool A and Pool B qualifiers set the field for next year's Women's World Cup.

Team USA earned the top spot in the Pool A tournament in truly dominating fashion. Team USA outscored its opponents 71-2 while going 5-0. Canada (4-1) and Mexico (3-2) also advanced out of Pool A.

In Pool B, defending World Cup champion Japan, Taiwan and Venezuela all earned spots in the next World Cup. Japan went 5-0, Taiwan was 4-1 and Venezuela was 3-2 in the six-team Pool B field.

Champions League Tournament

For the first time ever, the Baseball Champions League tournament was held in Mexico. The new tournament brought together the 2022 champions of the Mexican League, Cuba's Serie Nacional, the Colombian Professional Baseball League and the U.S.'s American Association.

The Fargo-Moorhead RedHawks, the American Association's representatives won the tournament. The RedHawks went 2-1 in the round-robin portion, and then beat Colombia's Caimanes de Barranquilla 8-0 in the championship game.

Max Murphy homered for the RedHawks in the title game. Tyler Grauer threw six scoreless innings, with relievers Garrett Alexander and Alexander Dubord combined to finish off the shutout.

Puebla Wins a Rare Mexican League Title

For only the second time in the past 50 years, the Puebla Pericos are Mexican League champions after knocking off Laguna thanks in part to a dramatic come-from-behind win in the deciding game of the Serie Del Rey.

Puebla starter Yoimer Camacho was perfect for five innings in the deciding game, but Laguna rallied to take a two run lead into the ninth inning.

But Thomas McIlraith walked two in the ninth, and Danny Ortiz hit a two-run single off reliever Jeff Ibarra to tie the game. Cristhian Adames added the go-ahead RBI single soon after.

Chris Carter was named the Series MVP. He hit .350 with two home runs in the finals.

Puebla finished fourth in the South Division in the regular season and lost their first-round series to Veracruz, but they advanced anyway as the the top team to lose. Given a second chance, Puebla never faced another elimination game, winning 12 of its 17 games from there on out.

By Mexican League standards, offense has returned to some level of normalcy, which is a change from an era of extreme performances.

This was the first time the league failed to have a .400 hitter since before the 2020 pandemic. Kyle Martin's 26 home runs led the league. That would have only been good for seventh-best on the 2022 home run leaderboard.

The league as a whole hit only 1,350 home runs in 2023 (.85 per team per game). That's a 33% reduction from 2022's 2,022 home runs (1.28 per team per game).

STANDINGS

North Division	W	L	PCT	GB
Dos Laredos	50	36	.581	-
Monterrey	50	38	.568	1
Tijuana	50	40	.556	2
Laguna	49	40	.551	2.5
Saltillo	49	40	.551	2.5
Monclova	46	43	.517	5.5
Durango	43	43	.500	7
Guadalajara	42	48	.467	10
Aguascalientes	33	55	.375	18
South Division	**W**	**L**	**PCT**	**GB**
Mexico	55	32	.632	-
Tabasco	46	37	.554	7
Veracruz	48	40	.545	7.5
Puebla	46	40	.535	8.5
Yucatan	47	43	.522	9.5
Quintana Roo	39	51	.433	17.5
Oaxaca	34	53	.391	21
Leon	34	56	.378	22.5
Campeche	31	57	.352	24.5

Playoffs—Wild Card Round: México defeated Quintana Roo 4-2; Veracruz defeated Puebla 4-3; Yucatán defeated Tabasco 4-1; Dos Laredos defeated Monclova 4-0; Laguna defeated Monterrey 4-3 and Tijuana defeated Saltillo 4-1 in best-of-seven series. **Quarterfinals:** Puebla defeated México 4-2; Yucatán defeated Veracruz 4-1; Dos Laredos defeated Monterrey 4-2 and Laguna defeated Tijuana 4-1 in best-of-seven series. **Semifinals:** Laguna defeated Dos Laredos 4-2 and Puebla defeated Yucatan 4-1 in best-of-seven series. **Finals:** Puebla defeated Laguna 4-2 in best-of-seven series.

BATTING LEADERS

Batter, Team	AVG	OBP	SLG	AB	R	H	HR	RBI	SB
Fernando Villegas, SLT	.390	.452	.625	267	47	104	16	58	5
Reynaldo Rodriguez, TIG	.368	.412	.590	307	51	113	16	62	4
Yadir Drake, YUC	.360	.426	.477	333	55	120	6	66	10
Alejandro Mejia, 2 Teams	.359	.397	.562	345	51	124	15	66	0
Julian Ornelas, MEX	.352	.451	.573	349	78	123	14	71	8
Michael Robles, DUR	.350	.409	.468	331	59	116	6	45	16
Eric Filia, 2 Teams	.349	.448	.487	304	62	106	7	40	1
Miguel Guzman, PUE	.346	.391	.411	280	54	97	2	23	11
Jonathan Villar, LAG	.346	.410	.508	309	62	107	11	72	22
Victor Mendoza, MTY	.344	.415	.576	276	37	95	11	73	1
Allen Córdoba, LAG	.338	.421	.444	340	76	115	4	42	18
Nick Torres, LAG	.338	.430	.529	314	77	106	11	61	9
Alberth Martinez, DUR	.336	.419	.533	289	61	97	11	60	1
Japhet Amador, MEX	.335	.406	.532	310	45	104	15	78	2
Yosmany Guerra, 2 Teams	.335	.422	.453	212	38	71	4	33	1
Oswaldo Arcia, 2 Teams	.333	.482	.579	273	64	91	14	60	2
Randy Romero, GDL	.332	.362	.458	319	60	106	5	26	26
Rainel Rosario, SLT	.331	.429	.581	272	51	90	17	49	2
Jasson Atondo, TAB	.331	.378	.418	251	32	83	1	32	7
Leonardo Reginatto, AGS	.330	.384	.438	333	50	110	5	59	7
Carlos Munoz, AGS	.329	.426	.472	252	26	83	9	38	0
Norberto Obeso, YUC	.329	.463	.436	243	51	80	2	21	1
Danry Vasquez, LAR	.328	.428	.520	302	52	99	11	60	3
Gustavo Nunez, VER	.326	.368	.407	356	58	116	4	41	36
Mallex Smith, 2 Teams	.325	.393	.431	246	50	80	2	23	25

PITCHING LEADERS

Player, Team	W	L	ERA	IP	H	HR	BB	SO
Braulio Torres-Perez, TAB	10	3	2.41	78	65	6	28	59
Jake Thompson, YUC	6	3	2.71	90	89	3	36	83
Nivaldo Rodriguez, MTY	5	5	2.76	95	92	6	20	84
Yoimer Camacho, PUE	11	2	3.05	97	94	7	24	75
Ronnie Williams, MEX	4	4	3.24	81	85	3	30	68
Wilmer Rios, MVA	8	5	3.39	98	103	9	13	63
Gabriel Ynoa, PUE	7	3	3.43	105	94	12	26	65
Juan Pablo Oramas, TAB	5	4	3.58	78	70	11	29	78
Raul Carrillo, TIG	8	5	3.66	86	89	5	26	63
Henderson Alvarez, YUC	6	4	3.68	78	92	1	12	38
Brandon Brennan, LAR	11	4	3.69	98	105	10	32	59
Nick Struck, TIJ	5	2	3.71	95	102	11	29	64
Frank Duncan, GDL	5	5	3.74	91	83	9	34	69
Steven Moyers, MEX	10	0	3.77	88	106	7	11	62
Luis Miranda, OAX	5	3	3.89	74	77	7	19	67
Francisco Haro, 2 Teams	4	5	3.95	87	86	8	20	81
Luis Gamez, LAG	6	5	4.01	94	106	9	41	66
Emmanuel Ramirez, MVA	5	6	4.02	87	84	5	28	77
David Reyes, VER	7	7	4.05	100	102	12	34	55
Darel Torres, TIG	6	6	4.10	86	65	11	51	100
Kevin McCarthy, LAR	6	7	4.18	84	91	3	43	47
Aldo Montes, LAG	7	3	4.20	86	82	3	40	67
Jose Pina, VER	7	4	4.23	83	79	10	32	66
Yunesky Maya, 2 Teams	5	2	4.26	82	86	9	23	52
Jose Carlos Medina, AGS	5	3	4.30	73	92	3	13	41

The 'Curse of KFC' Has Been Broken

The long-suffering Hanshin Tigers are suffering no more. Hanshin won its first title in 38 years with 7-1 Game 7 win over Orix in the Japan Series.

Sheldon Neuse hit a three-run home run as part of a four-RBI day to lead the Tigers to the title. He also recorded the final out, setting off a long-awaited celebration. Neuse had also homered against Orix ace Yoshinobu Yamamoto in Game 6.

CHRISTOPHER PASATIERI/GETTY IMAGES

Yoshinobu Yamamoto

The win ends the "Curse of Kentucky Fried Chicken." The supposed hex dates back to 1985, when happy Hanshin fans threw a Colonel Sanders statute into the river in a celebration of the team's Central League pennant.

That 1985 title remained the team's only Japan Series crown until this year. They had previously made it to three Japan Series, but they had fallen short all three times.

It was an emotional year for Hanshin. They also mourned the loss of 28-year-old Shintaro Yokota, who died midseason from brain cancer. He had played for the Tigers in 2016, and tried to return after his cancer went into remission, but he had to retire due to complications from his medical issues. The team brought his uniform onto the field for the Game 7 celebration.

The season was once again notable for the excellence of Orix ace Yamamoto. Yamamoto had played a role in Japan winning the World Baseball Classic in March, and he carried that success into the regular season.

Yamamoto posted the best ERA of his exceptional career, going 16-6, 1.21. He threw a no-hitter for the second time as a pro. He has led the Pacific League in strikeouts and ERA for three consecutive seasons.

Yamamoto won his third consecutive Sawamaru award (the Japanese equivalent of the Cy Young Award). Yamamoto is expected to be posted to the U.S. this offseason. If he leaves, he'll do so with a 1.82 career ERA. After posting a 5.32 ERA as an 18-year-old rookie in 2017, Yamamoto posted an ERA below 3.00 in each of his subsequent six seasons.

Pitching continues to dominate in Japan. Only Five batting quaifiers hit .300 or better this year. Yomiuri's Kazuma Okamoto was the standout slugger, as his 41 home runs led the league by 10 homers.

It was not a particularly impressive year for foreign imports. Yakult's Domingo Santana did hit .300 with solid power, and Neuse had his impressive postseason after a more pedestrian regular season. Gregory Polanco hit 26 home runs for Chiba Lotte.

CENTRAL LEAGUE

Team	W	L	T	PCT	GB
Hanshin Tigers	85	53	5	.616	--
Hiroshima Toyo Carp	74	65	4	.532	11.5
Yokohama DeNA BayStars	74	66	3	.529	12
Yomiuri Giants	71	70	2	.504	15.5
Tokyo Yakult Swallows	57	83	3	.407	29
Chunichi Dragons	56	82	5	.406	29

Playoffs—First round: Hiroshima defeated Yokohama 2-0 in best-of-three series. **Climax Series:** Hanshin defeated Hiroshima 3-0 in best-of-five series. **Japan Series:** Hanshin defeated Orix 4-3 in best-of-seven series.

CENTRAL LEAGUE BATTING QUALIFIERS

Player, Team	AVG	AB	R	H	HR	RBI	SB
Toshiro Miyazaki, BayStars	.326	408	47	133	20	71	1
Ryoma Nishikawa, Carp	.305	416	48	127	9	56	7
Domingo Santana, Swallows	.300	467	52	140	18	66	2
Shugo Maki, BayStars	.293	559	78	164	29	103	2
Yohei Ohshima, Dragons	.289	470	34	136	0	23	6
Yusuke Ohyama, Tigers	.288	513	80	148	19	78	3
Hayato Sakamoto, Giants	.288	403	46	116	22	60	2
Koji Chikamoto, Tigers	.285	501	83	143	8	54	28
Takumu Nakano, Tigers	.285	575	80	164	2	40	20
Takumi Ohshiro, Giants	.281	424	50	119	16	55	0
Yuki Okabayashi, Dragons	.279	584	61	163	3	31	12
Kazuma Okamoto, Giants	.278	503	83	140	41	93	0
Shogo Akiyama, Carp	.274	434	48	119	4	38	8
Seiya Kinami, Tigers	.267	408	41	109	1	41	0
Shogo Sakakura, Carp	.266	395	48	105	12	44	3
Keita Sano, BayStars	.264	560	67	148	13	65	0
Teruaki Sato, Tigers	.263	486	70	128	24	92	7
Taiki Sekine, BayStars	.261	482	69	126	4	31	11
Ryosuke Kikuchi, Carp	.258	442	51	114	5	27	7
Munetaka Murakami, Swallows	.256	496	76	127	31	84	5
Naoki Yoshikawa, Giants	.256	430	47	110	7	36	4
Jose Osuna, Swallows	.253	501	49	127	23	71	2
Seiya Hosokawa, Dragons	.253	518	62	131	24	78	0
Masayuki Kuwahara, BayStars	.252	429	48	108	7	35	3
Takaya Ishikawa, Dragons	.242	434	32	105	13	45	0
Sheldon Neuse, Tigers	.240	475	42	114	9	56	0
Hideki Nagaoka, Swallows	.227	445	43	101	3	35	4

OTHER NORTH AMERICAN HITTERS

Player, Team	AVG	AB	R	H	HR	RBI	SB
Lewis Brinson, Giants	.248	282	25	70	11	35	1
Dayan Viciedo, Dragons	.244	315	20	77	6	23	0
Kenta Bright, Dragons	.241	58	6	14	0	4	2
Orlando Calixte, Dragons	.233	163	13	38	5	13	0
Ryan McBroom, Carp	.221	226	21	50	6	31	1
Matt Davidson, Carp	.210	348	34	73	19	44	0
Zoilo Almonte, Dragons	.189	53	3	10	1	2	0
Aristides Aquino, Dragons	.154	65	2	10	1	6	0

CENTRAL LEAGUE PITCHING LEADERS

Pitcher, Team	W	L	ERA	IP	H	HR	BB	SO
Shoki Murakami, Tigers	10	6	1.75	144	92	9	15	137
Katsuki Azuma, BayStars	16	3	1.98	172	149	14	15	133
Hiroki Tokoda, Carp	11	7	2.19	156	144	13	28	86
Shosei Togo, Giants	12	5	2.38	170	141	14	39	141
Masashi Itoh, Tigers	10	5	2.39	147	120	8	21	91
Yuya Yanagi, Dragons	4	11	2.44	158	126	6	47	105
Hiroto Takahashi, Dragons	7	11	2.53	146	129	6	51	145
Aren Kuri, Carp	8	8	2.53	174	142	8	49	129
Iori Yamasaki, Giants	10	5	2.72	149	119	10	25	106
Shota Imanaga, BayStars	7	4	2.80	148	132	17	24	174
Yasuhiro Ogawa, Swallows	10	8	3.38	144	124	14	33	86
Shinnosuke Ogasawara, Dragons	7	12	3.59	161	153	14	41	134

OTHER NOTABLE PITCHERS

Pitcher, Team	W	L	ERA	IP	H	HR	BB	SO
Raidel Martinez, Dragons	3	1	0.39	47	31	1	4	62
J.B. Wendelken, BayStars	2	2	1.66	60	40	1	22	53
Nik Turley, Carp	7	1	1.74	41	39	1	15	42
Suguru Iwazaki, Tigers	3	3	1.77	56	32	3	14	62
Kazuto Taguchi, Swallows	3	5	1.86	48	39	2	13	55
Akiyoshi Katsuno, Dragons	5	2	2.01	49	33	2	22	49
Kota Nakagawa, Giants	1	4	2.08	43	37	3	9	38
Sotaro Shimauchi, Carp	3	3	2.31	58	50	3	17	64
Kohei Morihara, BayStars	2	1	2.32	43	34	2	11	34
Yuta Iwasada, Tigers	1	0	2.70	43	36	2	12	30
Takuya Yasaki, Carp	4	2	2.81	51	48	5	24	38
Ryoji Kuribayashi, Carp	3	7	2.92	52	42	4	19	51

OTHER NORTH AMERICAN PITCHERS

Pitcher, Team	W	L	ERA	IP	H	HR	BB	SO
Alberto Baldonado, Giants	2	1	1.69	21	15	2	10	21
Kyle Keller, Tigers	1	0	1.71	26	22	1	16	28
Yohander Mendez, Giants	5	5	2.07	87	57	7	33	72
Jeremy Beasley, Tigers	1	2	2.20	41	35	1	13	43
Drew Anderson, Carp	4	1	2.20	45	30	2	17	39
Humberto Mejia, Dragons	3	1	2.23	44	31	3	18	20
Colten Brewer, Tigers	0	1	2.30	11	6	1	6	14
Foster Griffin, Giants	6	5	2.75	121	101	8	29	115
Trevor Bauer, BayStars	10	4	2.76	131	119	14	31	130
Michael Feliz, Dragons	1	0	3.14	14	9	1	11	16
Dillon Peters, Swallows	6	5	3.22	101	99	8	21	66
Cy Sneed, Swallows	7	8	3.67	135	133	15	36	103
Tyler Beede, Giants	0	6	3.99	50	51	5	21	36
Elvin Rodriguez, Swallows	1	5	4.09	33	33	5	13	23
Robert Gsellman, BayStars	3	5	4.45	65	72	6	33	43
Edwin Escobar, BayStars	2	1	4.55	32	28	6	16	30
Robert Corniel, Carp	1	4	5.10	42	46	2	18	23
Raynel Espinal, Swallows	0	0	5.40	5	1	1	5	4

PACIFIC LEAGUE

Team	W	L	T	PCT	GB
ORIX Buffaloes	86	53	4	.619	--
Chiba Lotte Marines	70	68	5	.507	15.5
Fukuoka SoftBank Hawks	71	69	3	.507	15.5
Tohoku Rakuten Golden Eagles	70	71	2	.496	17
Saitama Seibu Lions	65	77	1	.458	22.5
Hokkaido Nippon-Ham Fighters	60	82	1	.423	27.5

Playoffs: First round: Chiba Lotte defeated Fukuoka 2-1 in best-of-three series. **Climax Series:** Orix defeated Chiba Lotte 3-1 in best-of-seven series. **Japan Series:** Hanshin defeated Orix 4-3 in best-of-seven series.

PACIFIC LEAGUE BATTING LEADERS

Player, Team	AVG	AB	R	H	HR	RBI	SB
Yuma Tongu, Buffaloes	.307	401	49	123	16	49	0
Kensuke Kondoh, Hawks	.303	492	75	149	26	87	3
Yuki Yanagita, Hawks	.299	546	57	163	22	85	1
Tomoya Mori, Buffaloes	.294	384	49	113	18	64	4
Go Matsumoto, Fighters	.276	507	51	140	3	30	12
Kotaro Kurebayashi, Buffaloes	.275	443	37	122	8	39	4
Akira Nakamura, Hawks	.274	511	52	140	5	37	0
Hideto Asamura, Eagles	.274	522	64	143	26	78	2
Keita Nakagawa, Buffaloes	.269	506	66	136	12	55	5
Chusei Mannami, Fighters	.265	533	69	141	25	74	2
Ryosuke Tatsumi, Eagles	.263	434	45	114	9	43	13
Shuta Tonosaki, Lions	.260	503	60	131	12	54	26
David Mackinnon, Lions	.259	464	50	120	15	50	1
Hiroto Kobukata, Eagles	.258	477	67	123	5	37	36
Kenta Imamiya, Hawks	.255	427	38	109	9	48	4
Ariel Martinez, Fighters	.246	386	39	95	15	66	0
Yuma Mune, Buffaloes	.245	428	38	105	2	22	1
Gregory Polanco, Marines	.242	447	43	108	26	75	0
Hisanori Yasuda, Marines	.238	416	33	99	9	43	2
Yuki Nomura, Fighters	.236	423	42	100	13	43	4
Koki Yamaguchi, Marines	.235	421	46	99	14	57	0
Shogo Nakamura, Marines	.220	508	61	112	11	48	3

OTHER NORTH AMERICAN HITTERS

Player, Team	AVG	AB	R	H	HR	RBI	SB
Leandro Cedeno, Buffaloes	.244	176	12	43	9	34	0
Maikel Franco, Eagles	.221	312	31	69	12	32	0
Mark Payton, Lions	.215	205	18	44	5	22	1
Arismendy Alcantara, Fighters	.204	113	14	23	4	10	1
Michael Brosseau, Marines	.191	136	9	26	1	11	0
Freddy Galvis, Hawks	.152	33	1	5	0	1	0
Alen Hanson, Fighters	.144	90	9	13	4	9	2
Willians Astudillo, Hawks	.136	44	2	6	1	3	0
Alfredo Despaigne, Hawks	.071	42	0	3	0	0	0
Courtney Hawkins, Hawks	.000	9	0	0	0	1	0

PACIFIC LEAGUE PITCHING LEADERS

Pitcher, Team	W	L	ERA	IP	H	HR	BB	SO
Yoshinobu Yamamoto, Buffaloes	16	6	1.21	164	117	2	28	169
Kona Takahashi, Lions	10	8	2.21	155	123	8	47	120
Hiroya Miyagi, Buffaloes	10	4	2.27	147	107	7	31	122
Kaima Taira, Lions	11	7	2.40	150	115	10	55	153
Takahiro Norimoto, Eagles	8	8	2.61	155	134	7	44	111
Takayuki Katoh, Fighters	7	9	2.87	163	162	14	16	83
Naoyuki Uwasawa, Fighters	9	9	2.96	170	152	14	41	124
Hiromi Itoh, Fighters	7	10	3.46	153	147	11	41	134
Kazuya Ojima, Marines	10	6	3.47	158	143	14	57	114

OTHER NOTABLE PITCHERS

Pitcher, Team	W	L	ERA	IP	H	HR	BB	SO
Yuki Matsui, Eagles	3	2	0.92	49	28	3	6	42
Naoya Masuda, Marines	3	0	0.98	28	11	0	5	37
Yoshihisa Hirano, Buffaloes	3	2	1.13	40	36	1	13	24
Roberto Osuna, Hawks	2	3	1.57	57	38	3	13	72
Seigi Tanaka, Fighters	4	0	1.77	46	22	3	30	52
Tatsushi Masuda, Lions	0	0	1.93	14	6	1	9	13
Soichiro Yamazaki, Buffaloes	2	1	1.95	28	22	1	15	26
Brooks Kriske, Lions	1	1	2.08	52	42	3	18	60
Livan Moinelo, Hawks	1	1	2.08	52	42	3	18	60
Ryosuke Moriwaki, Lions	1	3	2.13	51	49	1	15	41
Taisuke Yamaoka, Buffaloes	2	1	2.30	94	75	4	33	97
Minato Aoyama, Lions	8	3	2.40	49	30	1	20	41
Hirokazu Sawamura, Marines	4	3	2.55	53	46	3	22	29
Luis Perdomo, Marines	2	2	2.68	47	32	5	17	60
Shota Watanabe, Eagles	3	5	2.70	47	37	4	12	42
Katsunori Hirai, Lions	1	5	2.86	50	33	5	12	45
Soichiro Yamazaki, Buffaloes	0	1	2.96	46	32	4	23	34

OTHER NORTH AMERICAN PITCHERS

Pitcher, Team	W	L	ERA	IP	H	HR	BB	SO
James Marvel, Fighters	2	2	2.49	22	21	1	9	12
Jesus Tinoco, Lions	0	3	2.83	35	33	1	20	29
Luis Castillo, Marines	3	3	3.12	49	52	2	3	34
Conner Menez, Fighters	0	2	3.16	26	24	1	14	19
Cristopher Mercedes, Marines	4	8	3.33	116	111	8	36	58
Carter Stewart, Hawks	3	6	3.38	77	70	7	42	67
Cody Ponce, Fighters	4	5	3.66	52	59	3	17	43
Bryan Rodriguez, Fighters	1	7	5.09	35	42	5	20	20
Dietrich Enns, Lions	1	10	5.17	54	53	6	23	30
Joe Gunkel, Hawks	0	1	5.82	17	21	3	5	11
Jharel Cotton, Buffaloes	1	1	5.89	18	24	4	4	22
Jacob Nix, Buffaloes	0	1	10.50	6	7	2	6	5
Darwinzon Hernandez, Hawks	0	0	27.00	1	3	1	1	1
Manny Banuelos, Eagles	0	0	81.00	1	4	0	2	0

KOREA

Twins Win

For LG Twins fans, an extremely long wait is over.

Oh Ji-hwan homered in three straight Korean Series game, setting a record, to earn playoff MVP honors as the Twins won the Korean Series for the first time since 1994. The wins in front of sellout home crowds set off celebrations and pushed LG to slash prices on TVs for celebration sales.

It capped an exceptional season for the Seoul-based team. The Twins easily had the league's best record. It was also a sucessful year for the league as a whole. Attendance topped eight million for the first time since 2018.

US-import Erick Fedde was dominant, leading the league in wins, ERA and strikeouts. Kia's Choi Hyoung-woo broke Lee Seung-Yeop's career RBI record as Choi topped 1,500 RBIs.

STANDINGS & LEADERS

Team	W	L	T	PCT	GB
LG Twins	86	56	2	.606	—
KT Wiz	79	62	3	.560	6.5
SSG Landers	76	65	3	.539	9.5
NC Dinos	75	67	2	.528	11
Doosan Bears	74	68	2	.521	12
Kia Tigers	73	69	2	.514	13
Lotte Giants	68	76	0	.472	19
Samsung Lions	61	82	1	.427	25.5
Hanwha Eagles	58	80	6	.420	26
Kiwoom Heroes	58	83	3	.411	27.5

Playoffs—First Round: Doosan defeated NC Dinos 2-0 in best-of-three series. **Semifinals**: NC Dinos defeated SSG Landers 3-0 in best-of-five semifinals. **Finals:** LG Twins defeat KT Wiz 4-1 in best-of-seven series.

BATTING LEADERS

Player, Team	AVG	PA	R	H	HR	RBI	SB
Ah Seop Son, NC	.339	609	551	187	5	65	14
Ja Wook Koo, SAMSUNG	.336	515	453	152	11	71	12
Hye Seong Kim, KIWOOM	.335	621	556	186	7	57	25
Chang Ki Hong, LG	.332	643	524	174	1	65	23
Guillermo Heredia, SSG	.323	523	473	153	12	76	12
Sun Bin Kim, KIA	.320	473	419	134	0	48	3
Kun Woo Park, NC	.319	533	458	146	12	85	7
Min Woo Park, NC	.316	509	452	143	2	46	26
Austin Dean, LG	.313	583	520	163	23	95	7
Jun Woo Jeon, LOTTE	.312	559	493	154	17	77	92

PITCHING LEADERS

Player, Team	W	L	ERA	IP	H	HR	BB	SO
Erick Fedde, NC	20	6	2.00	180	137	9	35	209
Jin Woo An, KIWOOM	9	7	2.39	151	121	5	38	164
David Buchanan, SAMSUNG	12	8	2.54	188	174	4	43	139
Ariel Jurado, KIWOOM	11	8	2.65	184	164	7	41	147
Raul Alcantara, DOOSAN	13	9	2.67	192	171	16	35	162
Young Pyo Ko, KT	12	7	2.78	175	181	7	19	114
Tae In Won, SAMSUNG	7	7	3.24	150	157	15	34	102
Charlie Barnes, LOTTE	11	10	3.28	170	171	6	56	147
Chan Kyu Im, LG	14	3	3.42	144 2/3	142	10	54	103
Se Woong Park, LOTTE	9	7	3.45	154	145	8	59	129

TAIWAN

Dragons Return To Form

In the first years of the Chinese Professional Baseball League (CPBL), the Wei Chuan Dragons were considered the team to beat.

The Dragons won the first-ever CPBL title in 1990, and then they won it all again in 1997, 1998 and 1999. Then they became one of two teams to withdraw from the league, citing financial troubles.

The Dragons finally returned to the league in 2019 as an expansion club, and this year they completed their return by winning their first title since the 1990s.

Pitcher Jo-Hsi Hsu was named the CPBL Series MVP. He pitched well in Game 1, but it was his seven innings of one-hit ball in Game 6 that stamped his mark on the series. After forcing a Game 7 with that Game 6 win, Wei Chuan starter Drew Gagnon worked six innings to get the win in Game 7.

The first two games of the series were remarkable as well, as Wei Chuan won Game 1 in 14 innings and Rakuten responded by winning Game 2 in 11 innings.

STANDINGS & LEADERS

Team	W	L	T	PCT	GB
Wei Chuan Dragons	62	53	5	.539	
Uni-President 7-Eleven Lions	62	55	3	.530	1
Rakuten Monkeys	60	56	4	.517	2.5
CTBC Brothers	57	58	5	.496	5
Fubon Guardians	48	67	5	.417	14

* First half champion &Second half champion

Finals: Lamigo defeated the UniLions 4-2 in best-of-seven series.

BATTING LEADERS

Player, Team	AVG	OBP	SLG	AB	R	H	HR	RBI	SB
Liang Chia Jung, Monkeys	.338	.400	.507	349	57	118	8	54	0
Lee Tsung Hsien, Guardians	.318	.378	.424	368	47	117	3	41	17
Chen Chieh Hsien, U-Lions	.315	.413	.397	403	70	127	4	49	10
Liao Chien Fu, Monkeys	.313	.388	.522	387	62	121	22	83	0
Chan Tzu Hsien, Brothers	.304	.401	.410	349	40	106	8	48	10
Su Chih Chieh, U-Lions	.300	.391	.447	407	64	122	12	76	9
Liu Ji Hong, Dragons	.291	.343	.450	467	61	136	16	80	6
Chiang Kun Yu, Brothers	.291	.360	.380	395	55	115	5	43	11
Cheng Chin, Monkeys	.290	.368	.338	438	62	127	1	40	14
Li Kai Wei, Dragons	.288	.388	.381	423	64	122	5	40	12

PITCHING LEADERS

Player, Team	W	L	ERA	G	IP	H	BB	SO
Jake Brigham, Dragons	10	6	2.51	22	129	110	41	86
Brock Dykxhoorn, U-Lions	10	7	2.83	25	150	134	39	104
Drew Gagnon, Dragons	13	7	3.00	30	183	168	44	155
Matt Kent, Guardians	5	12	3.23	25	150	160	34	69
José De Paula, Brothers	10	9	3.53	27	173	190	39	139
Huang Tzu Peng, Monkeys	9	10	3.59	24	145	174	44	72
Chen Shih Peng, Guardians	7	9	3.60	22	122	140	28	72

Bologna Grabs Italian Title

UnipolSai Fortitudo Bologna knocked off defending champion San Marino with a sweep in the best-of-7 Italian Baseball Series.

It was Bologna's first title since 2020. Bologna second baseman Ricardo Paolini was named the series MVP. He went 5-for-13 in the series.

FIRST ROUND

Group A	W	L	PCT	GB
Hotsand Macerata	9	1	.900	--
San Marino	9	1	.900	--
Bologna Athletics	4	6	.400	5
Poviglio	4	6	.400	5
Longbridge 2000 Bologna	3	7	.300	6
Padule Baseball Sesto Fiorentino	1	9	.100	8

Group B	W	L	PCT	GB
Parma Climate	10	0	1.000	--
New Black Panthers	7	3	.700	3
Camec Collecchio	4	6	.400	6
Itas Mutua Rovigo	3	7	.300	7
Palfinger Reggio Rays	3	7	.300	7
Navali Cervignano	3	7	.300	7

Group C	W	L	PCT	GB
Unipolsai Fortitudo Bologna	9	1	.900	--
Baseball Godo	7	3	.700	2
Padova	5	5	.500	4
Codogno Baseball '67	4	6	.400	5
Ciemme Ultretorrente Pr	4	6	.400	5
Tecnovap Verona	1	9	.100	8

Group D	W	L	PCT	GB
Nettuno	8	2	.800	--
Big Mat Grosseto	8	2	.800	--
Spirulina Becagli BBC Grosseto	7	3	.700	1
Farma Crocetta	5	5	.500	3
Nettuno 2	2	8	.200	6
Sala Baganza	0	11	.000	8.5

Group E	W	L	PCT	GB
Comcor Modena	8	2	.800	--
Tecnograniti Senago	6	4	.600	2
Ecotherm Brescia	5	5	.500	3
Campidonico Grizzlies Torino	5	5	.500	3
Cagliari	5	5	.500	3
Settimo	1	9	.100	7

SECOND ROUND

Group F	W	L	PCT	GB
Hotsand Macerata	20	2	.909	--
Nettuno 1945	15	9	.625	6
Comcor Modena	9	15	.375	12
New Black Panthers Ronchi Dei Legionari	9	15	.375	12
Baseball Godo	5	17	.227	15

Group G	W	L	PCT	GB
Unipolsai Fortitudo Bologna	17	7	.708	--
San Marino Baseball	17	7	.708	--
Parma Clima	15	9	.625	2
Big Mat Grosseto 1952	10	14	.417	7
Tecnograniti Senago	1	23	.042	16

Group H	W	L	PCT	GB
Cagliari	17	9	.654	--
Platform-Tmc Poviglio	16	10	.615	1
Sultan Allestimenti Navali Cervignano	15	11	.577	2
Padova	13	13	.500	4
Sala Baganza B.C.	7	19	.269	10

Group I	W	L	PCT	GB
Camec Collecchio	16	10	.615	--
Athletics Baseball Bo	14	12	.538	2
Settimo	13	11	.542	2
Codogno Baseball '67	11	15	.423	5
Nettuno 2 B.C.	6	18	.250	9

Group L	W	L	PCT	GB
Spirulina Becagli Bbc Grosseto	21	5	.808	--
Itas Mutua Rovigo	19	7	.731	2
Campidonico Grizzlies Torino	13	10	.565	6.5
Tecnovap Verona	11	13	.458	9
Longbridge 2000 Bologna	8	18	.308	13

Group M	W	L	PCT	GB
Palfinger Reggio Rays	19	7	.731	--
Ciemme Oltretorrente Pr	17	8	.680	1.5
Farma Crocetta	8	18	.308	11
Padule Baseball Sesto Fiorentino	7	19	.269	12
Ecotherm Brescia	4	22	.154	15

PLAYOFFS. Quarterfinals--Grosseto defeats Hotsand 3-2; Parma defeats Nettuno 3-1; Fortitudo Bologna defeats New Black 3-0 and San Marino defeats Modena 3-0 in best-of-5 series. **Semifinals**--San Marino defeats Grosseto 4-0 and Fortitudo Bologna defeats Parma 4-0 in best-of-7 series. **Finals**--Fortitudo Bologna defeats San Marino 4-0 in best-of-7 series.

INDVIDUAL BATTING LEADERS

Player, Team	AVG	AB	R	H	2B	3B	HR	RBI	SB
José Cuesta, Cag	.508	130	45	66	16	2	7	45	14
Gabriele Angioi, Cag	.475	122	49	58	9	3	2	28	17
Humberto Bravo, Rov	.447	132	43	59	7	2	1	20	22
Jorge Luis Barcelan, BBC	.441	102	25	45	9	0	6	31	0
Gabriel Lino, RSM	.430	107	35	46	9	0	12	45	1
Jesus Carrera, Mac	.430	114	31	49	8	2	2	30	4
Kasey Bond, Set	.429	77	19	33	4	7	0	25	3
Kevin Michael, Bol	.421	57	8	24	2	2	0	9	2
Nolberto Viloria, Cro	.396	53	8	21	2	0	1	4	0
Nathanael Batista, RSM	.392	153	42	60	11	1	10	37	9

INDIVIDUAL PITCHING LEADERS

Player	W	L	ERA	IP	H	R	BB	SO
Anderson Martinez, Pad	10	2	0.50	127	63	11	24	207
Raul Rivero, Bol	11	1	1.01	63	37	10	8	65
Manny Correa, Mac	7	1	1.05	43	29	5	6	44
Gabriele Quattrini, Mac	13	0	1.38	91	54	15	23	103
Frank Madan, Reg	9	5	1.38	124	86	26	21	204
Eddy Garcia, Gro	6	3	1.42	63	52	14	20	76
Dimitrios Kourtis, Rsm	9	3	1.44	56	36	16	27	55
Frank Medina, Pov	12	3	1.50	120	71	24	28	155
Hector Rodriguez, Ron	6	4	1.51	71	39	21	39	128
Yoel Suarez, Set	8	8	1.52	124	97	39	21	128

Pirates Rally To Edge Curacao

The Amsterdam Pirates won their seventh Honkbal Hoofdklasse title and their third in the past five years by winning Game 6 and Game 7 in one day as weather forced the two teams to play a deciding doubleheader. Kenny Berkenboch's home run paced Amsterdam to a 5-1 Game 7 win.

STANDINGS

Team	W	L	T	Pts.
Curaçao Neptunus	20	3	1	41
HCAW	20	3	1	41
Amsterdam Pirates	16	7	1	33
RCH-Pinguins	12	11	1	25
Twins Oosterhout	12	11	1	25
DSS/Kinheim	10	14	0	20
Hoofddorp Pioniers	6	17	1	13
Quick Amersfoort	5	19	0	10
UVV	3	19	2	8
Second Round	**W**	**V**	**T**	**Pnt**
Curaçao Neptunus	20	7	0	61
HCAW	14	13	0	49
Amsterdam Pirates	16	11	0	47
RCH Penguins	4	23	0	21

Playoffs—Wild Card: Twins advanced out of bottom tier. **Semifinals:** Curacao deafeated Twins 3-0 and Amsterdam defeated HCAW 3-2 in best-of-five series. **Holland Series:** Amsterdam defeated Curacao 4-3 in best-of-seven series.

INDIVIDUAL BATTING LEADERS

Player, Team	AVG	AB	R	H	2B	3B	HR	RBI	SB
Marnix Ruben, Twi	.376	205	49	77	6	3	0	21	39
Christian Diaz, Nep	.366	224	48	82	10	4	4	47	4
Dwayne Kemp, Nep	.361	252	49	91	13	2	4	48	5
Yurdion Franklin Martie, Twi	.360	161	40	58	4	1	2	34	14
Ibrahin Redan, Qui	.353	116	19	41	10	3	1	29	4
Stijn Van Der Meer, Nep	.344	241	50	83	13	4	0	34	2
Duco Nuijten, Ams	.335	164	26	55	2	0	0	19	6
Jeandro Tromp, Hca	.329	210	39	69	9	1	0	32	8
Delano Selassa, Hca	.325	246	50	80	17	6	5	44	33
John Polonius, Nep	.323	229	45	74	17	1	2	39	13

INDIVIDUAL PITCHING LEADERS

Player, Team	W	L	ERA	IP	H	R	ER	BB	SO
Mathijs Oosterbeek, Dki	4		10.45	40	31	6	2	15	23
Takuya Fukuda, Twi	8		10.74	73	40	11	6	21	83
Lars Huijer, Hca	7		20.81	89	52	11	8	13	85
Juancarlos Sulbaran, Rch	6		11.04	52	25	7	6	10	55
Jelle Van Der Lelie, Ams	7		01.09	66	44	8	8	16	77
Aaron De Groot, Nep	3		21.57	57	36	14	10	17	57
Tom De Blok, Nep	8		01.62	100	63	21	18	36	105
Kaj Timmermans, Hca	8		51.64	115	91	24	21	22	68
Kevin Kelly, Nep	14		22.07	118	67	31	27	38	108
Nelmerson Angela, Ams	10		52.24	132	107	45	33	45	70

European Champions Cup

HCAW was in the midst of yet another solid season in the Dutch Major League, but its biggest memory of 2023 will be winning the European Champions Cup, as it knocked off Italy's Parma, keeping it from a third-straight Champions Cup. It was HCAW's first European Champions Cup title. In the championship game, Victor Draijer, Max Draijer and Shurman Marlin all homered for HCAW. Draijer was named the tournament MVP.

STANDINGS

Rk. Team (Country)	W	L
1. HCAW (NED)	4	1
2. 1949 Parma Baseball Club (ITA)	4	1
3. Amsterdam Pirates (NED)	2	3
4. Bonn Capitals (GER)	2	3
5. Draci Brno (CZE)	3	2
6. Untouchables Paderborn (GER)	2	3
7. SKSB Arrows Ostrava (CZE)	3	2
8. Rouen Huskies (FRA)	0	5

Finals:HCAW defeated Parma 11-4. **Bronze Medal Game:** Amsterdam defeated Bonn 12-6.

European Championship

Spain ensured there was little drama in the European Championship title game, as the club scored five runs in the first on the way to an 11-2 win over Great Britain. Spain's Wander Encarnacion was named the tournament MVP. Didi Gregorious was named the tournament's best defensive player.

STANDINGS

Rk. Team (Country)	W	L
1. Spain	6	0
2. Great Britain	5	1
3. Netherlands	5	1
4. Germany	4	2
5. Czech Republic	4	2
6. Israel	3	3
7. France	3	3
8. Sweden	2	4
9. Italy	4	2
10. Croatia	3	3
11. Belgium	2	4
12. Switzerland	2	4
13. Greece	3	3
14. Ukraine	1	5
15. Austria	1	5
16. Hungary	0	65

Finals:HCAW defeated Parma 11-4. **Bronze Medal Game:** Amsterdam defeated Bonn 12-6.

CUBA

Las Tunas Wins Second Title

For many of the past 45 years, Las Tunas found themselves looking up at pretty much everyone in Serie Nacional. Now, they have turned themselves into a power.

Las Tunas won their first title in 2019. This year, they added a second in convincing fashion. Las Tunas had the best record in the regular season. They had two of the best hitters in the league in Hector Castillo and Yordanys Alarcón and when the postseason arrived, Las Tunas just kept on rolling along. They swept traditional power Industriales in the championship series.

Alarcón homered in the deciding game of the finals. Shortstop Roberto Baldoquin had seven hits in the four games of the finals.

This was the second consecutive season when the Serie Nacional was held in spring and summer, beginning in March and finishing in August.

Replacing the traditional winter Serie Nactional schedule has been a new Cuban Elite League, which includes the top eight teams from Serie Nacional with each team being allowed to add top players from the other teams.

STANDINGS

Team	W	L	PCT	GB
Las Tunas	45	29	.608	-
Santiago de Cuba	43	31	.581	2
Cazadores de Artemisa	41	34	.547	4.5
Gallos de Sancti Spíritus	41	34	.547	4.5
Leones de Industriales	41	34	.547	4.5
Cocodrilos de Matanzas	40	35	.533	5.5
Toros de Camagüey	39	36	.520	6.5
Tigres de Ciego de Ávila	39	36	.520	6.5
Huracanes de Mayabeque	39	36	.520	6.5
Azucareros de Villa Clara	37	38	.493	8.5
Cachorros de Holguín	36	39	.480	9.5
Alazanes de Granma	35	39	.473	10
Piratas de la Isla de la Juventud	35	40	.467	10.5
Vegueros de Pinar del Río	34	40	.459	11
Elefantes de Cienfuegos	27	46	.370	17.5
Indios de Guantánamo	24	49	.329	20.5

Playoffs—Semifinals: Industriales defeated Santiago 4-3 and Las Tunas defeated Matanzas 4-2 in best-of-seven series. **Finals**: Las Tunas defeated Industriales 4-0 in best-of-seven series.

BATTING LEADERS

Player, Team	AVG	AB	R	H	2B	3B	HR	RBI
Héctor Castillo, Las Tunas	.404	213	59	86	9	2	0	27
Yordanys Alarcón, Las Tunas	.402	264	48	106	13	0	6	53
Yoan Moreno, Art.	.379	235	65	89	15	3	2	35
Dayán García, Art.	.377	244	59	92	16	0	15	51
Luís Acosta, Pri.	.370	208	25	77	17	1	2	31
Yoasnier Pérez, Cienfueg.	.365	222	30	81	13	2	4	41
Andrés De La Cruz, Guant.	.364	250	49	91	19	1	5	41
Yosvani Peñalver, Indust.	.363	215	49	78	14	0	3	32
Yordanis Samón, Ca,	.362	221	36	80	24	0	7	65
Alexquemer Sánchez, Gramma	.358	268	50	96	16	3	8	48
Ariel Sánchez, Matanz.	.353	255	61	90	16	2	3	40
Yordan Manduley, Hol	.352	273	40	96	14	3	4	53
José Jiménez, Art.	.352	227	44	80	14	0	8	59
Edilse Silva, Hol	.349	258	41	90	14	1	9	48
Aníbal Medina, Mtz	.348	253	67	88	18	3	3	46
Jonathan Bridón, Cav	.347	251	38	87	19	0	10	58
Osvaldo Abreu, Gramma	.341	220	42	75	7	0	1	19
Yunier Mendoza, SSP	.340	194	23	66	11	0	1	24
Frederich Cepeda, SSP	.339	224	46	76	12	0	13	57
Eduardo Blanco, Matanz.	.338	272	38	92	14	1	2	44
Yudier Rondón, Las Tunas	.337	181	61	38	11	2	4	25
Dennis Laza, May.	.337	249	84	59	18	2	14	74
Osday Silva, Scu.	.336	268	90	41	17	1	18	80
Lázaro Fernández, SSP	.333	237	79	58	15	2	3	31
Yasniel González, May.	.332	229	76	50	16	1	14	64
Yariel Duque, Matanz.	.332	250	83	18	11	0	6	49
Yasiel Santoya, Indust.	.330	227	75	41	18	0	5	52
Yasmani Viera, Isla de la Juv.	.329	216	71	37	14	0	2	31
Raudelín Legrá, May.	.329	246	81	35	9	1	5	43
Rodolexis Moreno, SSP	.327	263	86	61	17	6	3	29
Robert Delgado, Guant.	.325	240	78	42	11	0	7	35
Ariel Hechevarría, Indust.	.324	262	85	52	14	1	6	31
Dasiel Sevila, Scu.	.323	235	76	52	11	3	0	42
Eliseo Rojas, Isla de la Juv.	.321	221	71	49	10	2	2	26
Pavel Quesada, Cienfueg.	.321	168	54	27	14	0	4	21
Luis Rivera, Isla de la Juv.	.320	194	62	27	10	1	6	32
Dainiel López, Art.	.320	222	71	38	7	7	0	20
Osmel Solano, Art.	.318	179	57	26	4	3	0	41
Rangel Ramos, May.	.318	179	57	25	11	2	5	33
Yosvani Alarcón, Las Tunas	.317	252	80	47	9	0	11	64
Lázaro Blanco, Pri.	.316	209	26	66	5	0	4	32
Yoelquis Guibert, Scu.	.316	196	56	62	13	1	7	52
Michel Arteaga, Cav.	.315	216	38	68	7	0	2	27
Alexander Pozo, May.	.315	203	39	64	15	2	2	35
Ernesto Torres, Hol.	.314	245	50	77	14	4	2	30
Luis González, Camag.	.313	262	67	82	22	7	9	55
Moisés Esquerres, Mataz.	.310	248	44	77	15	0	3	39
Carlos De La Tejera, Art.	.307	238	57	73	17	5	3	37
Luis Mateo, Cienfueg.	.306	245	44	75	16	3	1	29
William Saavedra, Pri	.304	191	27	58	7	0	9	35
Alberto Calderón, Indust.	.304	181	31	55	4	4	3	27
José Bring, Isla de la Juv.	.303	218	35	66	7	2	2	26

PITCHING LEADERS

Player, Team	W	L	ERA	IP	H	R	ER	SO	BB
Erly Casanova, Pri	6	5	2.05	88	77	28	20	62	21
Israel Sánchez, Art.	7	2	2.40	79	65	27	21	54	20
José Grandales, SSP	9	3	2.56	91	92	30	26	40	40
Jonathan Carbo, Isla	5	5	2.59	90	84	40	26	60	23
Wilber Reyna, Scu.	6	5	2.63	82	76	32	24	37	26
Javier Mirabal, Villa Clara	6	5	2.64	75	76	26	22	54	26
Yunieski García, Art	7	3	2.69	94	84	30	28	67	14
Dariel Góngora, Camag.	7	5	2.78	107	94	42	33	66	36
Geonel Gutiérrez, Art.	9	3	2.85	92	85	34	29	86	23
Denis Quesada, Matanz.	7	4	3.18	79	82	39	28	40	24
Naykel Cruz, Matanz.	7	2	3.24	83	61	37	30	73	58
Alberto Bisset, Scu	7	2	3.38	99	105	44	37	39	26
Islay Sotolongo, Cienf.	10	4	3.43	97	92	41	37	52	43
Yadián Martínez, May	7	3	3.53	102	115	45	40	48	37
Fernando Betanzo, Ssp	6	4	3.66	79	90	39	32	38	33
Renner Rivero, Matanz.	6	3	3.70	83	90	43	34	72	39
Branlis Rodríguez, Pri	4	4	3.75	74	78	37	31	49	29
Marcos Ortega, Indust.	3	7	4.19	82	75	44	38	49	57
Angel Márquez, Camag.	6	2	4.35	81	77	49	39	69	42
Raidel Alfonso, Villa Clara	5	4	4.57	87	86	47	44	30	40
Wilson Paredes, Hol	4	8	4.98	90	124	63	50	44	37
Albert Valladares, May	5	7	5.25	74	96	50	43	36	34
Raymond Figueredo, Ind	4	6	5.42	75	76	51	45	56	41
Elian Moreno, Art	3	4	6.26	73	94	57	51	45	32
Luis Marrero, Cav	6	6	6.35	79	101	60	56	50	36

Dominican Republic's Jairo Asencio celebrates after recording the final out of the team's 3-0 title game win over Venezuela.

FEDERICO PARRA/AFP VIA GETTY IMAGES

Dominican Republic Wins Its 23rd Caribbean Series Title

Cesar Valdez held Venezuela to three hits in 6.1 scoreless innings and three relievers then finished off the shutout as the Dominican Republic, represented by Licey, edged Venezuela 3-0 in the Caribbean Series title game.

A Kelvin Gutierrez sac fly scored Henry Urrutia in the second inning for what proved to be the deciding run. A Yamaico Navarro RBI single and a Hernan Perez throwing error scored the other two runs.

It was the third time in the past four years that the Dominican Republic has won the Caribbean Series and the country's 23rd Carribean title overall.

Mexico defeated Colombia for third place.

AUSTRALIAN BASEBALL LEAGUE

Northeastern Division	W	L	PCT	GB
Brisbane	30	10	.750	-
Auckland	17	17	.500	10
Canberra	18	19	.486	10.5
Sydney	12	27	.308	17.5

Southwestern Division	W	L	PCT	GB
Adelaide	25	15	.625	-
Perth	23	17	.575	2
Melbourne	15	21	.417	8
Geelong-Korea	13	27	.325	12

Playoffs—Semifinals: Adelaide defeated Auckland 2-1 and Perth defeated Brisbane 2-1 in best-of-three series. **Finals:** Adelaide defeated Perth 2-1 in a best-of-three series.

INDIVIDUAL BATTING LEADERS

Player, Team	AVG	AB	R	H	2B	3B	HR	RBI	BB	SO	SB
Hall, Alex, Per.	.360	139	31	50	11	1	8	37	20	29	0
Bojarski, Ulrich, Per.	.352	145	33	51	10	3	8	35	14	39	4
Ward, Nick, Ade.	.344	157	35	54	10	2	11	23	17	31	4
Quirion, Anthony, Ade.	.338	130	21	44	8	1	5	24	15	20	8
Song, Chan Eui, Gee.	.324	102	18	33	7	0	7	24	9	16	6
Moanaroa, Boss, Can.	.319	119	19	38	6	0	3	11	25	36	1
Bennett, T.J., Bri.	.315	162	36	51	5	0	17	42	12	39	3
Caminero, Junior, Per.	.303	155	33	47	4	1	14	37	15	31	6
Tolbert, Tyler, Bri.	.297	128	32	38	9	1	2	12	23	32	15
Ordonez, Emny, Syd.	.295	139	19	41	7	0	2	19	7	28	6

INDIVIDUAL PITCHING LEADERS

Player, Team	W	L	ERA	G	SV	IP	H	BB	SO	AVG
Fowler, Jordan, Ade.	2	2	1.63	10	0	39	40	11	35	.256
Holland, Sam, Bri.	5	1	2.14	15	0	42	38	7	30	.241
Kines, Gunnar, Per.	4	3	2.86	10	0	57	43	14	61	.213
Gilliam, Brock, Per.	5	1	3.04	10	0	53	56	11	36	.272
Wagoner, Cameron, Bri.	3	1	3.26	10	0	47	33	21	43	.194
Atherton, Tim, Bri.	5	1	3.27	9	0	52	50	9	48	.250
Mincey, Cody, Mel.	1	3	3.35	8	0	40	30	12	25	.205
Murata, Toru, Akl.	1	3	3.35	9	0	43	38	11	36	.236
Weng, Wei-Chun, Akl.	4	1	3.48	9	0	34	30	13	24	.244
Castillo, Starlyn, Ade.	3	3	3.62	10	0	37	34	15	33	.250

DOMINICAN LEAGUE

Team	W	L	PCT	GB
Licey	34	16	.680	-
Aguilas	32	18	.640	2
Gigantes	25	25	.500	9
Estrellas	23	27	.460	11
Escogido	18	32	.360	16
Toros	18	32	.360	16

Playoffs—Round Robin: Licey and Estrellas both go 10-6 to advance as Aquilas and Gigantes each finish at 6-10. **Finals:** Licey defeated Estrellas 4-1 in best-of-seven series.

INDIVIDUAL BATTING LEADERS

Player, Team	AVG	AB	R	H	2B	3B	HR	RBI	BB	SO	SB
Urrutia, Henry, Gig.	.318	148	13	47	10	0	2	21	17	30	0
Tavárez, Aneury, Agu.	.299	137	24	41	7	2	2	17	10	33	11
Mauricio, Ronny, Lic.	.287	188	26	54	15	2	5	31	10	43	10

Nunez, Gustavo, Est.	.279	136	18	38	2	1	0	6	16	13	5
Hernandez, Ramon, Lic.	.279	140	17	39	7	1	4	24	12	29	0
Nunez, Rainer, Est.	.263	137	18	36	4	0	7	20	8	27	0
Polo, Tito, Gig.	.261	138	31	36	6	3	2	13	14	30	16
Tena, Jose, Est.	.259	139	11	36	5	1	2	16	8	32	4
Gutiérrez, Kelvin, Gig.	.246	126	18	31	4	0	4	20	11	33	3
De La Cruz, Bryan, Tor.	.234	124	14	29	7	1	1	9	11	32	1

INDIVIDUAL PITCHING LEADERS

Player, Team	W	L	ERA	G	SV	IP	H	BB	SO	AVG
Maya, Yunesky, Agu.	3	1	1.34	8	0	40	29	12	24	.199
Rogers, Esmil, Lic.	4	2	1.43	11	1	44	31	14	30	.203
Valdez, Cesar, Lic.	6	0	1.51	9	0	54	46	15	37	.231
Hernandez, Carlos, Tor.	1	2	1.60	10	0	45	39	7	39	.227
Mejía, Humberto, Esc.	4	3	2.15	10	0	50	50	3	45	.255
Fernandez, Pedro, Gig.	3	3	2.50	10	0	50	38	10	46	.211
Martinez, Jorge, Gig.	2	3	2.68	9	0	44	34	8	38	.211
Valdez, Phillips, Est.	0	3	3.32	10	0	41	39	12	21	.262
Martinez, Carlos, Agu.	4	3	3.67	10	0	49	50	18	53	.269
Valdes, Raul, Tor.	2	4	3.69	9	0	46	43	24	30	.242

MEXICAN PACIFIC LEAGUE

Team	W	L	PCT	GB
Hermosillo	43	25	.632	-
Los Mochis	41	27	.603	2
Obregon	38	30	.559	5
Guasave	36	32	.529	7
Mazatlan	33	35	.485	10
Monterrey	32	36	.471	11
Mexicali	31	37	.456	12
Navojoa	31	37	.456	12
Jalisco	29	39	.426	14
Culiacan	26	42	.382	17

Playoffs—Quarterfinals: Los Mochis defeated Navojoa 4-1; Hermosillo defeated Mazaltan 4-2; Obregon defeated Mexicali 4-3 and Guasave defeated Monterey 4-3 in best-of-seven series. **Semifinals:** Los Mochis defeated Obregon 4-2 and Guasave defeated Hermosillo 4-2 in best-of-seven series. **Finals:** Los Mochis defeated Guasave 4-2 in a best-of-seven series.

INDIVIDUAL BATTING LEADERS

Player, Team	AVG	AB	R	H	2B	3B	HR	RBI	BB	SO	SB
Valenzuela, Roberto, Mont.	.365	233	40	85	18	0	7	31	43	33	4
Dean, Justin, Mochis	.343	242	37	83	11	7	2	34	34	61	16
Villegas, Fernando, Jalisco	.337	208	28	70	13	5	5	32	18	37	0
Tomás, Yasmany, Moch.	.328	259	33	85	17	0	10	57	25	62	4
Cardona, Jose, Herm.	.313	246	35	77	13	1	1	37	15	24	29
Zazueta, Amadeo, Jalisco	.311	283	29	88	14	2	1	18	9	22	0
Amador, Rodolfo, Mochis	.308	250	31	77	14	0	5	38	16	38	1
Torres, Nick, Herm.	.304	224	38	68	12	2	8	39	29	62	15
Santos, Roel, Herm.	.303	238	33	72	10	6	2	18	20	38	15
Carreon, Alberto, Mont.	.300	227	34	68	9	3	2	24	21	25	3

INDIVIDUAL PITCHING LEADERS

Player, Team	W	L	ERA	G	SV	IP	H	BB	SO	AVG
Miranda, Luis, Moc.	5	1	1.07	12	0	67	40	18	56	.174
Torres-Perez, Braulio, Maz.	4	1	1.49	12	0	54	42	13	46	.215
Rios, Wilmer, Her.	9	2	1.84	13	0	83	68	10	46	.225
Pobereyko, Matt, Gsv.	6	2	2.05	13	0	70	38	36	73	.165
Vera, Eduardo, Mxc.	4	2	2.30	13	0	67	47	17	41	.201
Kinley, Jeff, Gsv.	5	2	2.51	13	0	72	58	23	56	.229
Tellache, Nico, Gsv.	6	3	2.51	12	0	72	71	18	40	.262
Encina, Geno, Gsv.	3	4	2.56	13	0	77	55	23	57	.204
Oramas, Juan, Her.	5	5	2.71	13	0	66	61	22	47	.246
Tellez, Juan, Maz.	7	4	2.87	13	0	63	60	19	41	.256

PUERTO RICAN LEAGUE

Team	W	L	PCT	GB
Caguas	31	19	.620	-
Carolina	28	22	.560	3
Santurce	26	24	.520	5
Mayaguez	26	24	.520	5
Ponce	25	25	.500	6
RA12	14	36	.280	17

Playoffs—Semifinals: Carolina defeated Santurce 4-3 and Mayaguez defeated Caguas 4-2 in best-of-seven series. **Finals:** Mayaguez deafeated Carolina 4-3 in a best-of-seven series.

INDIVIDUAL BATTING LEADERS

Player, Team	AVG	AB	R	H	2B	3B	HR	RBI	BB	SO	SB
Castro, Ruben, Ra12.	.305	131	18	40	4	2	0	8	28	18	2
Rivera, Yadiel, Ra12.	.304	171	14	52	7	0	2	18	7	36	9
Rivera, Emmanuel, May.	.303	142	12	43	5	0	0	14	7	17	2
Blanco, Dairon, Pon.	.301	183	26	55	8	0	1	18	10	27	25
Restituyo, Bladimir, Ra12.	.293	116	12	34	3	2	1	12	0	18	11
Lidge, Ryan, Ra12.	.287	94	9	27	4	0	1	12	9	21	0
Castillo, Rusney, San.	.283	145	9	41	5	0	0	8	13	14	4
Enriquez, Roby, May.	.282	78	13	22	3	0	1	8	8	13	0
Santa, Kevin, Pon.	.281	121	18	34	5	2	0	9	10	15	6
Escarra, J.C., Pon.	.277	159	12	44	14	1	2	25	13	32	0

INDIVIDUAL PITCHING LEADERS

Player, Team	W	L	ERA	G	SV	IP	H	BB	SO	AVG
Hardy, Matt, Cag.	4	1	0.64	25	1	28	20	3	29	.211
Ríos, Yacksel, Cag.	7	0	0.65	24	1	28	17	4	34	.183
Lebron, David, San.	1	0	0.68	7	0	27	10	9	27	.116
Ramirez, Ruben, Ra12.	1	1	0.74	9	0	49	39	15	33	.217
Kasaya, Shunsuke, Car.	3	1	1.00	5	0	27	15	12	28	.161
Echemendia, Pedro, Pon.	2	1	1.16	6	0	31	28	10	18	.250
Rodríguez, Dereck, Cag.	0	1	1.24	10	1	29	17	9	27	.173
Torres, Christian, Cag.	2	0	1.38	25	0	26	16	4	19	.174
De León, Jose, Cag.	2	2	1.51	11	0	48	35	16	60	.207
Francis, Bowden, Cag.	1	2	1.51	9	0	36	19	9	47	.153

VENEZUELAN LEAGUE

Team	W	L	PCT	GB
Caracas	36	19	.655	-
Lara	34	21	.618	2
La Guaira	29	26	.527	7
Magallanes	29	27	.518	7.5
Margarita	26	29	.473	10
Aragua	25	30	.455	11
Caribes	21	34	.382	15
Zulia	21	35	.375	15.5

Playoffs—Round Robin: Caracas (10-6) and La Guaria (9-7) advance out of five-team round-robin play. **Finals:** Caracas defeated La Guaria 4-2 in a best-of-seven series.

INDIVIDUAL BATTING LEADERS

Player, Team	AVG	AB	R	H	2B	3B	HR	RBI	BB	SO	SB
Fermin, Freddy, Car.	.404	166	38	67	13	1	4	28	25	24	2
Martínez, Jose, Ara.	.390	187	23	73	12	0	6	33	22	19	1
Vargas, Ildemaro, Lar.	.342	161	33	55	17	1	1	22	25	12	6
Otosaka, Tomo, Mar.	.333	192	37	64	6	4	0	16	31	17	15
Rodríguez, David, Mar.	.333	192	32	64	12	1	9	36	33	47	0
Rosario, Raniel, Mag.	.333	141	26	47	7	0	8	26	14	25	0
Rondon, Jose, Car.	.330	200	53	66	12	2	11	43	31	48	2
Vasquez, Danry, Lag.	.327	171	32	56	13	0	3	32	38	29	6
Garcia, Maikel, Lag.	.323	201	48	65	13	5	4	33	46	31	10
Arcia, Oswaldo, Car.	.323	124	34	40	9	0	11	44	34	36	1

INDIVIDUAL PITCHING LEADERS

Player, Team	W	L	ERA	G	SV	IP	H	BB	SO	AVG
Sanchez, Mario, Zul.	2	3	2.38	11	0	57	44	7	34	.213
Ramos, David, Mar.	7	1	2.95	19	0	55	57	10	30	.273
Leal, Erick, Mag.	7	2	3.70	12	0	56	43	18	41	.209
Sanchez, Ricardo, Mag.	2	4	4.20	11	0	49	56	12	29	.284
Molina, Nestor, Lar.	3	2	5.40	12	0	53	53	19	29	.262
Diaz, Luis, CAR	2	1	3.36	12	0	56	53	18	36	.249

COLLEGE

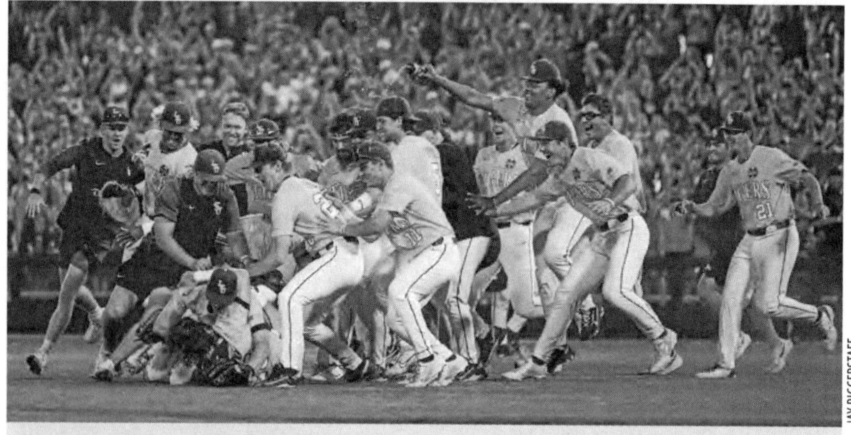

JAY BIGGERSTAFF

Louisiana State won its seventh College World Series title and its first since 2009

LSU Lives Up To Lofty Expectations

BY TEDDY CAHILL

OMAHA—Coach Jay Johnson stood before his team in January, a month before Opening Day and asked the 2023 LSU Tigers a simple question: "What do you want to accomplish?"

The room got quiet. The Tigers were on their way to being the most hyped team in college baseball history. They would be ranked No. 1 in the Preseason Top 25 and had the projected No. 1 overall draft pick on their roster in center fielder Dylan Crews. They were coming off a whirlwind offseason that saw them add All-Americans Paul Skenes and Tommy White through the transfer portal, the No. 1 traditional recruiting class, pitching coach Wes Johnson, who was hired away from the Minnesota Twins, and recruiting coordinator Josh Jordan, the 2018 Assistant Coach of the Year.

One team must be ranked No. 1 in the preseason polls every year. But no preseason No. 1 team had before dealt with the confluence of LSU's superstar talent, the excitement of transactions previously only seen in professional free agency and a No. 1 recruiting class all coming together at one of the sport's bluest bloods.

In that moment, the Tigers had to decide who they were. And it was Crews, the reigning SEC player of the year, who spoke up.

"We want to win a national championship," he said.

"Are you sure?" Johnson asked.

The Tigers were sure. They had all come to LSU with that goal in mind. They had gotten there in different ways. Some, like Crews and first baseman Tre' Morgan, had committed to Paul Mainieri and his staff. Others had committed to Johnson after he took over the program following Mainieri's retirement in 2021. Some had arrived as freshmen. Others came through the transfer portal or from junior college.

But to come to LSU, no matter how you get to Alex Box Stadium, is to commit to excellence. Atop the right field wall stands a full-size billboard called "The Intimidator" that commemorates the Tigers' national championships. A statue of legendary head coach Skip Bertman stands outside the stadium and plaques of the program's All-Americans line the walls of the Box. The expectations and weight of that history are part of the experience.

So, Johnson went about outlining how the Tigers would go from that meeting, a month before Opening Day, to lifting the trophy in Omaha five months later. The plan included things big and small, from having a selfless attitude to a mentality strong enough to withstand the inevitable failure of baseball. It was about how to attack the game in all facets and continually get better.

COACHING CAROUSEL

School	In (Previous Job)	Out (Reason/New Job)
Akron	Bryan Faulds	Tim Donnelly (interim)
Alabama	Rob Vaughn (Maryland head coach)	Brad Bohannon
Boston College	Todd Interdonato (Wofford head coach)	Mike Gambino
Central Florida	Rich Wallace (Florida State assistant coach)	Greg Lovelady
Central Michigan	Jake Sabol (Northwood (Mi.) head coach)	Jordan Bischel
Cincinnati	Jordan Bischel (Central Michigan head coach)	Scott Goggins
Eastern Michigan	Robbie Britt (Charleston (W.V.) head coach)	Eric Roof
Fresno State	Ryan Overland (Fresno State assistant coach)	Mike Batesole (retired)
Georgia	Wes Johnson (LSU assistant coach)	Scott Stricklin
Jacksonville State	Steve Bieser (Missouri head coach)	Jim Case (retired)
Lindenwood	PJ Finigan (Lindenwood assistant coach)	Doug Bietcher
Long Beach State	Bryan Peters (interim)	Eric Valenzuela
Loyola Marymount	Donegal Fergus (UC Santa Barbara assistant coach)	Nathan Choate
Maryland	Matt Swope (Maryland assistant coach)	Rob Vaughn
Maryland-Eastern Shore	Danny Acosta (Iowa Lakes JC head coach)	Brian Hollamon
Massachusetts-Lowell	Nick Barese (Mass.-Lowell assistant coach)	Ken Harring
Memphis	Matt Riser (Southeastern Louisiana head coach)	Kerrick Jackson
Miami	JD Arteaga (Miami assistant coach)	Gino DiMare
Miami (Ohio)	Brian Smiley (Indiana State assistant coach)	Danny Hayden
Mississippi Valley State	CJ Bilbrey	Milton Barney
Missouri	Kerrick Jackson (Memphis head coach)	Steve Bieser
Morehead State	Brady Ward (Morehead State assistant coach)	Mike Aoki
Navy	Chuck Ristano (Florida State assistant coach)	Paul Kostacopoulos (retired)
New Mexico State	Jake Angier (Oregon assistant coach)	Mike Kirby
North Florida	Joe Mercadante (Pittsburgh assistant coach)	Tim Parenton (retired)
Northern Illinois	Ryan Copeland (Illinois-Springfield head coach)	Mike Kunigonis
Northwestern	Ben Greenspan (Michigan assistant coach)	Jim Foster
Northwestern State	Chris Bertrand (Northwestern State assistant coach)	Bobby Barbier
Penn State	Mike Gambino (Boston College head coach)	Rob Cooper
Queens	Jake Hendrick (Austin Peay State assistant coach)	Ross Steedley
Richmond	Mik Aoki (Morehead State head coach)	Tracy Woodson
Saint Mary's	Eric Valenzuela (Long Beach State head coach)	Greg Moore
San Diego State	Shaun Cole (San Diego State assistant coach)	Mark Martinez (retired)
Siena	Alex Jurczynski (Princeton assistant coach)	Tony Rossi (retired)
Southeastern Louisiana	Bobby Barbier (Northwestern State head coach)	Matt Riser
Southern Mississippi	Christian Ostrander (Southern Miss assistant coach)	Scott Berry (retired)
Tarleton State	Fuller Smith (Sam Houston State assistant coach)	Aaron Meade
Washington State	Nathan Choate (Loyola Marymount head coach)	Brian Green
Western Illinois	Terry Davis (Washington State assistant coach)	Tayler Sheriff (interim)
Wichita State	Brian Green (Washington State head coach)	Loren Hibbs (interim)
Wisconsin-Milwaukee	Shaun Wagner (Wis.-Milwaukee assistant coach)	Scott Doffek (retired)
Wofford	JJ Edwards (Wofford assistant coach)	Todd Interdonato

For five months, the Tigers stuck to that plan. It carried them through 12 straight weeks as the top-ranked team in the country. It helped them get past consecutive losing weekends in May against Auburn and Mississippi State to still go into the final day of the regular season with a chance to win the SEC title. It carried them through sweeps in regionals and super regionals to advance to the College World Series for the first time since 2017. In Omaha, it helped them push through the loser's bracket, beating on consecutive nights Tennessee righthander Drew Beam and Wake Forest righthanders Seth Keener and Rhett Lowder, a trio of pitchers with All-American-caliber stuff and moxie.

The Tigers didn't abandon their approach in the finals, either. Righthander Ty Floyd dominated in Game 1, striking out 17 batters in eight innings, and DH Cade Beloso hit a home run in the 11th inning to power LSU to a 4-3 victory. Game 2 didn't go their way at all, as the Gators routed the Tigers, 24-4, setting a CWS record for most runs scored in a game.

By the next day, the Tigers had moved on. There was one game left in the season, one game to win the national championship they had been eyeing all year. Again, the question from Johnson before the game was simple: "Are you in?" This time, knew the Tigers were ready.

LSU didn't hold anything back. After Florida took a quick 2-0 lead in the first inning, LSU responded with six runs in the second, knocking out starter Jac Caglianone. The Tigers never looked back, rolling to an 18-4 rout. Righthander Thatcher Hurd delivered a quality start, holding Florida to two runs on two hits and two walks in six innings, striking out seven. Crews and White both had four-hit nights as the LSU lineup piled up 24 hits and drew eight walks. As badly as

Florida beat LSU in Game 2, the Tigers returned it in the decisive third game of the series.

The game ended with the Tigers dogpiling on the infield of Charles Schwab Field. They were national champions, fulfilling the team's immense promise. They are just the second team in the 21st century to win the national championship after being ranked No. 1 in the Preseason Top 25, joining 2019 Vanderbilt.

"I just can't be more proud of my guys and the way that we came out all year and just competed and fought through adversity," shortstop Jordan Thompson said. "When guys went down, guys stepped up. That just speaks about the character about our team and the way that we just handled our business and own our deal every single day."

"I feel like almost every box was checked off except that national championship box," Crews said. "And we all knew this was going to be our last game here. And to finally say that I'm a national champion, it's the greatest feeling in the world. And I feel all boxes are checked off now."

LSU's national championship is the program's seventh and first since 2009. With the title, LSU passes Texas for sole possession of second place all time. Only Southern California has won more titles and only one of its 12 titles (1998) has come since LSU won its first.

By LSU standards, it's been a relatively long time since that 2009 national championship and its fans were hungry for more. But Johnson said in the two years he's spent in Baton Rouge he's worked to avoid thinking about the weight of that history.

He never shied away from the program's expectations, however.

"I know all that legacy and tradition," he said. "I'm so honored to be part of that. I really wanted it for these guys because they've done everything that I've asked them to do and set the standard better than you could possibly do. And that's why this is important. Not just because we're national champions, but because we've been national champions every day of this thing."

All year, the Tigers played with the sport's biggest target on their backs. They took on all comers and passed just about every test. Crews came into the season regarded as the best player in the

COLLEGE WORLD SERIES CHAMPIONS

Year	Champion	Coach	Record	Runner-Up	Most Outstanding Player
1948	Southern California	Sam Barry	40-12	Yale	None selected
1949	Texas*	Bibb Falk	23-7	Wake Forest	Charles Teague, 2B, Wake Forest
1950	Texas	Bibb Falk	27-6	Washington State	Ray VanCleef, OF, Rutgers
1951	Oklahoma*	Jack Baer	19-9	Tennessee	Sid Hatfield, 1B/P, Tennessee
1952	Holy Cross	Jack Barry	21-3	Missouri	Jim O'Neill, P, Holy Cross
1953	Michigan	Ray Fisher	21-9	Texas	J.L. Smith, P, Texas
1954	Missouri	Hi Simmons	22-4	Rollins	Tom Yewcic, C, Michigan State
1955	Wake Forest	Taylor Sanford	29-7	Western Michigan	Tom Borland, P, Oklahoma State
1956	Minnesota	Dick Siebert	33-9	Arizona	Jerry Thomas, P, Minnesota
1957	California*	George Wolfman	35-10	Penn State	Cal Emery, 1B/P, Penn State
1958	Southern California	Rod Dedeaux	35-7	Missouri	Bill Thom, P, Southern California
1959	Oklahoma State	Toby Greene	27-5	Arizona	Jim Dobson, 3B, Oklahoma State
1960	Minnesota	Dick Siebert	34-7	Southern California	John Erickson, 2B, Minnesota
1961	Southern California*	Rod Dedeaux	43-9	Oklahoma State	Littleton Fowler, P, Oklahoma State
1962	Michigan	Don Lund	31-13	Santa Clara	Bob Garibaldi, P, Santa Clara
1963	Southern California	Rod Dedeaux	37-16	Arizona	Bud Hollowell, C, Southern California
1964	Minnesota	Dick Siebert	31-12	Missouri	Joe Ferris, P, Maine
1965	Arizona State	Bobby Winkles	54-8	Ohio State	Sal Bando, 3B, Arizona State
1966	Ohio State	Marty Karow	27-6	Oklahoma State	Steve Arlin, P, Ohio State
1967	Arizona State	Bobby Winkles	53-12	Houston	Ron Davini, C, Arizona State
1968	Southern California*	Rod Dedeaux	45-14	Southern Illinois	Bill Seinsoth, 1B, Southern California
1969	Arizona State	Bobby Winkles	56-11	Tulsa	John Dolinsek, OF, Arizona State
1970	Southern California	Rod Dedeaux	51-13	Florida State	Gene Ammann, P, Florida State
1971	Southern California	Rod Dedeaux	53-13	Southern Illinois	Jerry Tabb, 1B, Tulsa
1972	Southern California	Rod Dedeaux	50-13	Arizona State	Russ McQueen, P, Southern California
1973	Southern California*	Rod Dedeaux	51-11	Arizona State	Dave Winfield, OF/P, Minnesota
1974	Southern California	Rod Dedeaux	50-20	Miami	George Milke, P, Southern California
1975	Texas	Cliff Gustafson	56-6	South Carolina	Mickey Reichenbach, 1B, Texas
1976	Arizona	Jerry Kindall	56-17	Eastern Michigan	Steve Powers, DH/P, Arizona
1977	Arizona State	Jim Brock	57-12	South Carolina	Bob Horner, 3B, Arizona State
1978	Southern California*	Rod Dedeaux	54-9	Arizona State	Rod Boxberger, P, Southern California
1979	Cal State Fullerton	Augie Garrido	60-14	Arkansas	Tony Hudson, P, Cal State Fullerton
1980	Arizona	Jerry Kindall	45-21	Hawaii	Terry Francona, OF, Arizona
1981	Arizona State	Jim Brock	55-13	Oklahoma State	Stan Holmes, OF, Arizona State
1982	Miami	Ron Fraser	57-18	Wichita State	Dan Smith, P, Miami
1983	Texas	Cliff Gustafson	66-14	Alabama	Calvin Schiraldi, P, Texas

country and went on to repeat as SEC player of the year and win the Golden Spikes Award after hitting .426/.567/.713 with 18 home runs. Skenes took off after transferring from Air Force and focusing exclusively on pitching for the first time in his career. He was named CWS most outstanding player and produced perhaps the best season for a pitcher in the 21st century, going 13-2, 1.69 with an SEC record 209 strikeouts and 20 walks in 122.2 innings. White hit 24 home runs and drove in 105 runs, living up to the incredible expectations after transferring from North Carolina State, where he was the Freshman of the Year in 2022. Beloso, Floyd and Morgan built on their legacies at LSU, while freshmen like Gavin Guidry, Griffin Herring and Jared Jones began to build their own.

LSU has had some incredible teams and players throughout its history. Skenes joins Ben McDonald as the program's greatest pitcher. Crews has a strong case to be the program's greatest hitter. Collectively, the 2023 Tigers will forever be remembered among the program's best.

For Crews, it was a storybook ending to his college career.

"It was a struggle of mine as a kid to be where my feet are," Crews said. "I was always looking ahead, into the future. But when I stepped in the locker room this year and saw all the talent and all the group of guys that we had, I thought, it was my last year, it's so important for me to be where my feet are and enjoy these moments.

"To go out on top a national champion and to cap off my career, it's just an unbelievable feeling."

In Game 3, the Tigers had no problem living in the moment. After the game, as all of Johnson's teams have done after victories, they took a team photo. He does it so that his teams learn to value winning and to emphasize the one-game mindset he asks them to employ.

So, after the dogpile and trophy presentation, the Tigers gathered along the first base line for their standard team picture. Just like the 2023 Tigers, however, this picture is anything but standard. Their smiles are wide, and their new

Year	Champion	Coach	Record	Runner-Up	MOST OUTSTANDING PLAYER
1984	Cal State Fullerton	Augie Garrido	66-20	Texas	John Fishel, OF, Cal State Fullerton
1985	Miami*	Ron Fraser	64-16	Texas	Greg Ellena, DH, Miami
1986	Arizona	Jerry Kindall	49-19	Florida State	Mike Senne, OF, Arizona
1987	Stanford	Mark Marquess	53-17	Oklahoma State	Paul Carey, OF, Stanford
1988	Stanford	Mark Marquess	46-23	Arizona State	Lee Plemel, P, Stanford
1989	Wichita State	Gene Stephenson	68-16	Texas	Greg Brummett, P, Wichita State
1990	Georgia	Steve Webber	52-19	Oklahoma State	Mike Rebhan, P, Georgia
1991	Louisiana State*	Skip Bertman	55-18	Wichita State	Gary Hymel, C, Louisiana State
1992	Pepperdine*	Andy Lopez	48-11	Cal State Fullerton	Phil Nevin, 3B, Cal State Fullerton
1993	Louisiana State	Skip Bertman	53-17	Wichita State	Todd Walker, 2B, Louisiana State
1994	Oklahoma*	Larry Cochell	50-17	Georgia Tech	Chip Glass, OF, Oklahoma
1995	Cal State Fullerton*	Augie Garrido	57-9	Southern California	Mark Kotsay, OF/P, Cal State Fullerton
1996	Louisiana State*	Skip Bertman	52-15	Miami	Pat Burrell, 3B, Miami
1997	Louisiana State*	Skip Bertman	57-13	Alabama	Brandon Larson, SS, Louisiana State
1998	Southern California	Mike Gillespie	49-17	Arizona State	Wes Rachels, 2B, Southern California
1999	Miami*	Jim Morris	50-13	Florida State	Marshall McDougall, 2B, Florida State
2000	Louisiana State*	Skip Bertman	52-17	Stanford	Trey Hodges, P, Louisiana State
2001	Miami*	Jim Morris	53-12	Stanford	Charlton Jimerson, OF, Miami
2002	Texas*	Augie Garrido	57-15	South Carolina	Huston Street, P, Texas
2003	Rice	Wayne Graham	58-12	Stanford	John Hudgins, P, Stanford
2004	Cal State Fullerton	George Horton	47-22	Texas	Jason Windsor, P, Cal State Fullerton
2005	Texas*	Augie Garrido	56-16	Florida	David Maroul, 3B, Texas
2006	Oregon State	Pat Casey	50-16	North Carolina	Jonah Nickerson, P, Oregon State
2007	Oregon State*	Pat Casey	49-18	North Carolina	Jorge Reyes, P, Oregon State
2008	Fresno State	Mike Batesole	47-31	Georgia	Tommy Mendonca, 3B, Fresno State
2009	Louisiana State	Paul Mainieri	56-17	Texas	Jared Mitchell, OF, Louisiana State
2010	South Carolina	Ray Tanner	54-16	UCLA	Jackie Bradley Jr., OF, South Carolina
2011	South Carolina*	Ray Tanner	55-14	Florida	Scott Wingo, 2B, South Carolina
2012	Arizona*	Andy Lopez	48-17	South Carolina	Robert Refsnyder, OF, Arizona
2013	UCLA*	John Savage	49-17	Mississippi State	Adam Plutko, P, UCLA
2014	Vanderbilt	Tim Corbin	51-21	Virginia	Dansby Swanson, 2B, Vanderbilt
2015	Virginia	Brian O'Connor	44-24	Vanderbilt	Josh Sborz, P, Virginia
2016	Coastal Carolina	Gary Gilmore	55-18	Arizona	Andrew Beckwith, P, Coastal Carolina
2017	Florida	Kevin O'Sullivan	52-19	Louisiana State	Alex Faedo, P, Florida
2018	Oregon State	Pat Casey	55-12-1	Arkansas	Adley Rutschman, C, Oregon State
2019	Vanderbilt	Tim Corbin	59-12	Michigan	Kumar Rocker, RHP, Vanderbilt
2020	Canceled due to pandemic				
2021	Mississippi State	Chris Lemonis	50-18	Vanderbilt	Will Bednar, RHP, Mississippi State
2022	Ole Miss	Mike Bianco	42-23	Oklahoma	Dylan DeLucia, RHP, Ole Miss
2023	Louisiana State	Jay Johnson	54-17	Florida	Paul Skenes, RHP, Louisiana State

COLLEGE WORLD SERIES

STANDINGS

Bracket One	W	L
Florida	3	0
TCU	2	2
Oral Roberts	1	2
Virginia	0	2

Bracket Two	W	L
LSU	4	1
Wake Forest	2	2
Tennessee	1	2
Stanford	0	2

CWS FINALS (BEST OF THREE)

June 24: LSU 4, Florida 3
June 25: Florida 24, LSU 4
June 26: LSU 18, Florida 4

ALL-TOURNAMENT TEAM

C: BT Riopelle, Florida. **1B:** Tre' Morgan, LSU. **2B:** Gavin Dugas LSU. **3B:** Tommy White, LSU. **SS:** Josh Rivera, Florida. **OF:** Dylan Crews, LSU; Ty Evans, Florida; Wyatt Langford, Florida. **DH:** Cade Beloso, LSU. **P:** Ty Floyd, LSU; *Paul Skenes, LSU.

**Named Most Outstanding Player.*

BATTING

(Minimum 8 PA)

Player	AVG	R	H	2B	3B	HR	RBI	BB
Maui Ahuna, Tenn.	.462	2	6	1	0	0	1	0
Cole Fontenelle, TCU	.455	3	5	0	0	1	6	6
Logan Maxwell, TCU	.429	0	3	2	0	0	0	2
Carter Graham, Stanford	.429	1	3	2	0	0	1	1
Justin Quinn, ORU	.417	2	5	2	0	0	1	3
Ty Evans, Florida	.400	7	8	2	0	5	9	0
Holden Breeze, ORU	.400	2	4	1	0	0	0	3
Harrison Didawick, Va.	.400	2	2	0	1	0	1	1
Jared Dickey, Tenn.	.385	1	5	0	0	0	1	0
Mac McCroskey, ORU	.385	2	5	0	0	1	2	0

PITCHING

(Minimum 5 IP)

Pitcher	W-L	ERA	G	SV	IP	H	BB	SO
Chase Burns, Tenn.	1-0	0.00	1	0	6	2	0	9
Paul Skenes, LSU	1-0	1.15	2	0	16	7	2	21
Rhett Lowder, WF	0-0	1.46	2	0	12	10	3	12
Nick Parker, Va.	0-0	1.50	1	0	6	4	3	1
Drew Beam, Tenn.	0-1	1.59	1	0	6	6	2	9
Cade Denton, ORU	1-0	1.59	2	0	6	4	4	8
Thatcher Hurd, LSU	2-1	2.25	3	0	12	6	6	13
Kole Klecker, TCU	0-0	2.70	2	0	10	11	2	3
Ben Abeldt, TCU	0-1	2.70	3	1	7	5	1	8
Josh Hartle, WF	0-0	3.00	1	0	6	4	4	9
Ty Floyd, LSU	0-0	3.46	2	0	13	7	5	27

RPI RANKINGS

The Ratings Percentage Index is an important tool used by the NCAA in selecting at-large teams for the 64-team Division I tournament. These were the top 100 finishers for 2019. A team's rank in the final Baseball America Top 25 is indicated in parentheses, and College World Series teams are bolded.

Rk School	Record	Rk School	Record
1. LSU (1)	54-17	**51.** Louisiana	41-24
2. Wake Forest (3)	54-12	**52.** Arizona St.	32-23
3. Florida (2)	54-17	**53.** Kansas St.	35-24
4. Kentucky (19)	40-21	**54.** Arizona	33-26
5. Arkansas (16)	43-18	**55.** Southern Calif.	34-23-1
6. South Carolina (17)	42-21	**56.** UC Santa Barbara	35-20
7. Clemson (15)	44-19	**57.** Wofford	40-19
8. Vanderbilt (14)	42-20	**58.** Notre Dame	30-24
9. Indiana St. (11)	45-17	**59.** Fla. Gulf Coast	42-18
10. Virginia (8)	50-15	**60.** Texas St.	36-23
11. Alabama (18)	43-21	**61.** Florida St.	23-31
12. Tennessee (5)	44-22	**62.** Samford	37-25
13. Campbell (22)	46-15	**63.** Elon	33-22
14. DBU (25)	47-16	**64.** Charlotte	36-28
15. TCU (4)	44-24	**65.** Cal St. Fullerton	32-24
16. Miami (21)	42-21	**66.** UCLA	28-24-1
17. Duke (10)	39-24	**67.** Georgia Tech	30-27
18. Stanford (6)	44-20	**68.** Rutgers	33-23
19. Coastal Carolina (20)	42-21	**69.** Col. of Charleston	36-22
20. Boston College	37-20	**70.** Michigan St.	33-22
21. Texas (9)	42-22	**71.** Grand Canyon	37-21
22. South. Miss (12)	46-20	**72.** Evansville	37-24
23. Okla. St. (23)	41-20	**73.** Cal St. Northridge	34-17
24. North Carolina St.	36-21	**74.** Sam Houston	39-25
25. Connecticut	44-17	**75.** Texas-San Antonio	38-19
26. East Carolina (24)	47-19	**76.** Hawaii	29-20
27. West Virginia	40-20	**77.** Santa Clara	36-20
28. Texas A&M	38-27	**78.** Fla. Atlantic	34-25
29. Auburn	34-23-1	**79.** Ohio St.	31-25
30. Oregon (13)	41-22	**80.** Wright St.	39-23
31. Indiana	43-20	**81.** Pittsburgh	24-31
32. Iowa	40-16	**82.** UC San Diego	34-18
33. North Carolina	36-24	**83.** Missouri St.	33-23
34. Oregon St.	41-20	**84.** California	24-28
35. Northeastern	44-16	**85.** S. Carolina-Up.	38-22
36. Maryland	42-21	**86.** Ole Miss	25-29
37. Texas Tech	41-23	**87.** Long Beach St.	33-22
38. Washington	35-20	**88.** Appal. State	30-25
39. Troy	40-22	**89.** William & Mary	32-25
40. Oklahoma	32-28	**90.** Lipscomb	36-26
41. Georgia	29-27	**91.** Old Dominion	32-23
42. Xavier	39-25	**92.** Army	38-18
43. UNC Wilmington	34-23	**93.** Rider	36-21
44. Louisville	31-24	**94.** Washington St.	28-23
45. Kent St.	40-16	**95.** New Orleans	35-24
46. UC Irvine	38-17	**96.** Illinois	25-27
47. Oral Roberts (7)	52-14	**97.** Liberty	27-31
48. Missouri	30-24	**98.** Georgia St.	31-28
49. Virginia Tech	30-23	**99.** Nebraska	33-23-1
50. Mississippi St.	27-26	**100.** James Madison	31-25

trophy is front and center. This is the moment they planned for five months ago and the one they worked so hard to get to ever since.

SEC Dominance Continues

The CWS championship series between Florida and LSU was an all-SEC affair, the third time in six seasons that the national championship came down to two SEC teams. With LSU winning the title, 2023 marked the fourth straight season and ninth time in 14 seasons that an SEC team won the national championship. At least one SEC team has played for the national championship every year since 2008, except 2016.

While the SEC's success in Omaha has been readily apparent for more than a decade, there was more evidence throughout the season of the conference's overall dominance. The SEC this year broke its own record for number of regional hosts in a season, as it claimed eight of the 16 spots. The conference put 10 teams in the tournament

COLLEGE ALL-AMERICA TEAM

FIRST TEAM

Pos.	Name, School	Year	AVG	OBP	SLG	AB	2B	3B	HR	RBI	BB	K	SB
C	Kyle Teel, Virginia	Jr	.407	.475	.655	258	25	0	13	69	32	36	5
1B	Nolan Schanuel, Florida Atlantic	Jr	.447	.615	.868	197	18	4	19	64	71	14	14
2B	JJ Wetherholt, West Virginia	So	.449	.517	.787	225	24	2	16	60	26	22	36
3B	Tommy White, Louisiana State	So	.374	.432	.725	273	24	0	24	105	23	41	0
SS	Matt Shaw, Maryland	Jr	.341	.445	.697	264	20	1	24	69	43	42	18
OF	Dylan Crews, Louisiana State	Jr	.426	.567	.713	258	16	2	18	70	71	46	6
OF	Wyatt Langford, Florida	Jr	.373	.498	.784	236	28	3	21	57	56	44	9
OF	Alberto Rios, Stanford	Jr	.384	.485	.707	242	24	0	18	73	38	42	5
DH	Jac Caglianone, Florida	So	.323	.389	.738	282	14	2	33	90	17	58	4
UT	Caden Grice, Clemson	Jr	.307	.411	.618	228	15	1	18	68	30	74	4

Pos.	Name, School	Year	W	L	ERA	G	GS	SV	IP	H	BB	SO	AVG
SP	Tanner Hall, Southern Mississippi	Jr	12	4	2.48	18	18	0	112	84	33	124	.207
SP	Josh Hartle, Wake Forest	So	11	2	2.81	18	17	0	102	91	24	140	.237
SP	Rhett Lowder, Wake Forest	Jr	15	0	1.87	19	19	0	120	90	24	143	.208
SP	Paul Skenes, Louisiana State	Jr	13	2	1.69	19	19	0	123	72	20	209	.165
RP	Cade Denton, Oral Roberts	Jr	3	1	1.83	35	0	15	64	48	15	86	.211
RP	Andrew Walters, Miami	Jr	4	0	1.21	28	0	12	45	29	7	72	.179
UT	Caden Grice, Clemson	Jr	8	1	3.35	14	14	0	78	54	33	101	.196

SECOND TEAM

Pos.	Name, School	Year	AVG	OBP	SLG	AB	2B	3B	HR	RBI	BB	K	SB
C	Luke Shliger, Maryland	Jr.	.336	.523	.582	232	24	0	11	52	69	56	14
1B	Nick Kurtz, Wake Forest	So	.353	.527	.784	190	10	0	24	69	63	50	5
2B	Max Anderson, Nebraska	Jr	.414	.461	.770	244	20	2	21	70	20	29	0
3B	Nick Lorusso, Maryland	Sr	.379	.446	.765	264	20	2	26	105	34	46	3
SS	Jacob Wilson, Grand Canyon	Jr	.411	.461	.635	192	17	4	6	61	19	5	8
OF	Charlie Condon, Georgia	Fr	.386	.484	.800	210	10	1	25	67	33	45	0
OF	Ethan Petry, South Carolina	Fr	.376	.471	.733	221	10	0	23	75	33	59	4
OF	Cam Fisher, Charlotte	So	.348	.507	.812	224	14	0	30	66	64	63	10
DH	Brock Wilken, Wake Forest	Jr	.345	.506	.807	238	15	1	31	82	69	58	1
UTL	Payton Tolle, Wichita State	So	.311	.361	.538	212	9	0	13	50	18	53	1

Pos.	Name, School	Year	W	L	ERA	G	GS	SV	IP	H	BB	SO	AVG
SP	Lucas Gordon, Texas	Jr	7	2	2.63	19	17	0	103	85	34	103	.226
SP	Quinn Mathews, Stanford	Sr	10	4	3.75	19	18	0	125	116	40	158	.245
SP	Nico Zeglin, Long Beach State	Sr	8	4	2.00	15	15	0	95	67	27	117	.202
SP	Trey Yesavage, East Carolina	So	7	1	2.61	16	14	1	76	53	23	105	.193
RP	Simon Miller, Texas-San Antonio	Jr	8	1	2.30	27	0	11	70	67	18	81	.246
RP	Tyson Neighbors, Kansas State	So	5	1	1.85	25	0	11	49	22	16	86	.135
UTL	Payton Tolle, Wichita State	So	9	3	4.62	15	14	0	86	81	19	97	.245

THIRD TEAM

Pos.	Name, School	Year	AVG	OBP	SLG	AB	2B	3B	HR	RBI	BB	K	SB
C	Cole Messina, South Carolina	So	.307	.428	.615	231	18	1	17	65	40	48	8
1B	Brock Vradenburg, Michigan State	Jr	.400	.492	.721	215	22	4	13	69	36	34	1
2B	Travis Bazzana, Oregon State	So	.374	.500	.622	238	20	3	11	55	59	47	36
3B	Tommy Troy, Stanford	Jr	.394	.478	.699	249	17	4	17	58	35	42	17
SS	Josh Rivera, Florida	Jr	.348	.447	.617	256	10	1	19	72	46	35	18
OF	Dylan Campbell, Texas	Jr	.339	.436	.603	242	19	3	13	50	39	43	26
OF	Jonah Cox, Oral Roberts	Jr	.412	.470	.646	277	16	8	11	68	30	53	28
OF	Lawson Harrill, Campbell	Jr	.371	.475	.761	213	17	0	22	69	31	63	6
DH	Brayden Taylor, TCU	Jr	.308	.430	.631	260	15	0	23	70	54	60	14

Pos.	Name, School	Year	W	L	ERA	G	GS	SV	IP	H	BB	SO	AVG
SP	Sean Sullivan, Wake Forest	So	5	3	2.45	17	10	3	70	43	21	111	.175
SP	Cade Kuehler, Campbell	Jr	8	1	2.71	13	13	0	73	54	26	91	.199
SP	Andrew Lindsey, Tennessee	Jr	3	4	2.90	21	9	0	71	60	19	73	.225
SP	Hagen Smith, Arkansas	So	8	2	3.64	18	11	2	72	56	42	109	.217
RP	Seth Keener, Wake Forest	Jr	8	2	2.69	23	8	1	70	41	20	94	.169
RP	Fran Oschell, Duke	So	6	0	0.69	22	0	0	39	18	18	66	.133
UTL	TJ Fondtain, San Diego State	Jr	7	4	2.82	15	15	0	93	64	25	99	.192

overall, again matching the record it jointly holds with the ACC. And three SEC teams advanced to Omaha, marking the sixth straight season the conference has had at least three representatives in the CWS.

The all-SEC showdown for the national championship that once seemed novel, is now becoming old hat as the conference pulls further away from the rest of the sport. Perhaps the most impressive testament to the SEC's dominance is that 12 of its 14 members (all but Georgia and Missouri) have hosted a regional in the last three years.

Wake Forest Breaks Through

While Wake Forest fell one win shy of the CWS championship series, losing to LSU, the Demon Deacons still had a historic season. They finished 54-12, set the program record for wins and won their first ACC title since 1963. Their CWS berth was their first since 1955, when they won the national championship.

Wake was the No. 1 overall seed in the NCAA Tournament and rose to No. 1 in the Top 25 for the first time in the 43-year history of the BA rankings.

The Deacs' success in 2023 was historic, but it was not altogether surprising. In the preseason ACC coaches' poll, Wake was picked as the conference's co-favorite with Louisville. It was led by ace Rhett Lowder and slugger Brock Wilken, who were both first round picks in July, as well as first baseman Nick Kurtz, who projects to be a first-round pick in 2024.

Still, the Deacs' rise to the top of the sport in May marked a significant milestone for the program and could be the start of lasting change in the program's trajectory.

Pichardo Is A Trailblazer

On March 17, Olivia Pichardo became the first woman to appear in a Division I baseball game.

She made her debut as a pinch hitter in the ninth inning of Brown's 10-1 loss to Bryant. Facing M.T. Morrissey, she grounded out to first base.

Pichardo said it was a special moment.

"It was a lot of fun and I'm glad that I was able to get something out of my first at-bat," she said. "There probably aren't going to be as much nerves for the rest of my at-bats."

Home Runs Set Record

In 2023, home runs were flying at a rate the college game had never seen before.

There were 25 players in Division I college baseball who averaged 0.39 home runs or more in 2023, equalling or bettering the average per team from 2014.

The home run rate of 1.13 homers per game set the all-time record, breaking the 1.06 home runs per game record set in 1998, which was the final year before the bat standards were changed to begin the BESR (Bat Exit Speed Ratio) era.

Florida's 17 home runs hit during the College World Series equalled the school record set by LSU and Southern California in 1998.

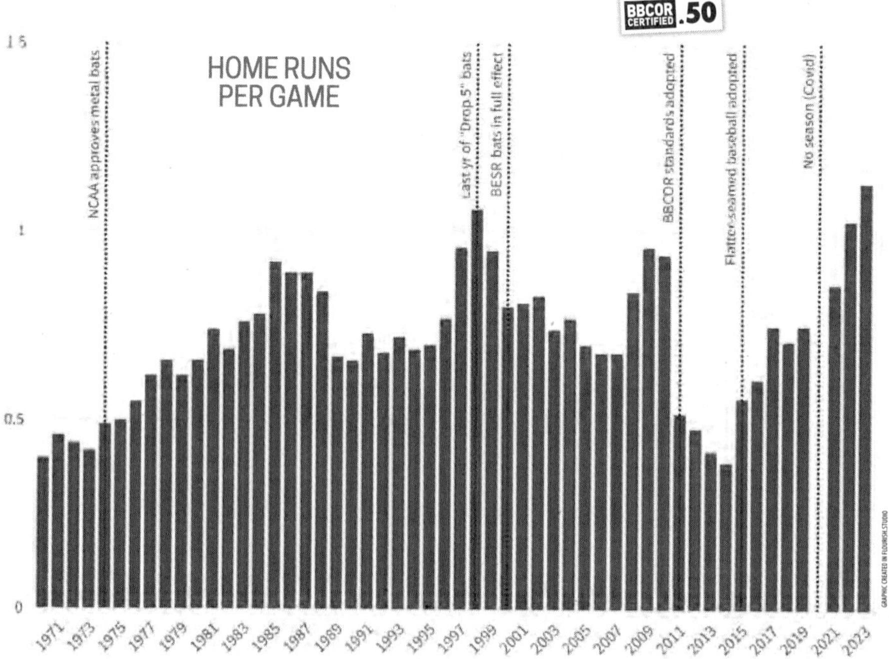

REGIONALS

JUNE 2-5

64 teams, 16 four-team, double-elimination tournaments. Winners advance to super regionals.

WINSTON-SALEM, N.C.

Host: Wake Forest (No. 1 national seed).
Participants: No. 1 Wake Forest (47-10), No. 2 Maryland (41-19), No. 3 Northeastern (44-14), No. 4 George Mason (34-25).
Champion: Wake Forest (3-0).
Runner-up: George Mason (2-2).
Outstanding player: Justin Johnson, Wake Forest.

GAINESVILLE, FLA.

Host: Florida (No. 2 national seed).
Participants: No. 1 Florida (44-14), No. 2 Connecticut (43-15), No. 3 Texas Tech (39-21), No. 4 Florida A&M (29-28).
Champion: Florida (4-1).
Runner-up: Texas Tech (2-2).
Outstanding player: Jac Caglianone, Florida.

FAYETTEVILLE, ARK.

Host: Arkansas (No. 3 national seed).
Participants: No. 1 Arkansas (41-16), No. 2 Texas Christian (37-22), No. 3 Arizona (33-24), No. 4 Santa Clara (35-18).
Champion: Texas Christian (3-0).
Runner-up: Arkansas (2-2).
Outstanding player: N/A.

CLEMSON, S.C.

Host: Clemson (No. 4 national seed).
Participants: No. 1 Clemson (43-17), No. 2 Tennessee (38-19), No. 3 Charlotte (34-26), No. 4 Lipscomb (36-24).
Champion: Tennessee (3-0).
Runner-up: Charlotte (2-2).
Outstanding player: Christian Moore, Tennessee.

BATON ROUGE, LA.

Host: Louisiana State (No. 5 national seed).
Participants: No. 1 Louisiana State (43-15), No. 2 Oregon State (39-18), No. 3 Sam Houston (38-23), No. 4 Tulane (19-40).
Champion: Louisiana State (3-0).
Runner-up: Oregon State (2-2).
Outstanding player: Dylan Crews, Louisiana State.

NASHVILLE

Host: Vanderbilt (No. 6 national seed).
Participants: No. 1 Vanderbilt (41-18), No. 2 Oregon (37-20), No. 3 Xavier (37-23), No. 4 Eastern Illinois (38-19).
Champion: Oregon (3-0).
Runner-up: Xavier (2-2).
Outstanding player: Rikuu Nishida, Oregon.

CHARLOTTESVILLE

Host: Virginia (No. 7 national seed).
Participants: No. 1 Virginia (45-12), No. 2 East Carolina (45-17), No. 3 Oklahoma (31-26), No. 4 Army (38-16).
Champion: Virginia (3-0).
Runner-up: East Carolina (2-2).
Outstanding player: Connelly Early, Virginia.

STANFORD, CALIF.

Host: Stanford (No. 8 national seed).
Participants: No. 1 Stanford (38-16), No. 2 Texas A&M (36-25), No. 3 Cal State Fullerton (31-22), No. 4 San Jose State (31-25).
Champion: Stanford (4-1).
Runner-up: Texas A&M (2-2).
Outstanding player: Tommy Troy, Stanford.

CORAL GABLES, FLA.

Host: Miami (No. 9 national seed).
Participants: No. 1 Miami (40-19), No. 2 Texas (38-20), No. 3 Lousiana (40-22), No. 4 Maine (32-19).
Champion: Texas (3-0).
Runner-up: Miami (2-2).
Outstanding player: Lebarron Johnson Jr., Texas.

CONWAY, S.C.

Host: Coastal Carolina (No. 10 national seed).
Participants: No. 1 Coastal Carolina (39-19), No. 2 Duke (35-21), No. 3 UNC-Wilmington (34-21), No. 4 Rider (35-19).
Champion: Duke (3-1).
Runner-up: Coastal Carolina (3-2).
Outstanding player: MJ Metz, Duke.

STILLWATER, OKLA.

Host: Oklahoma State (No. 11 national seed).
Participants: No. 1 Oklahoma State (41-18), No. 2 Dallas Baptist (45-14), No. 3 Washington (34-18), No. 4 Oral Roberts (46-11).
Champion: Oral Roberts (3-0).
Runner-up: Dallas Baptist (2-2).
Outstanding player: Cade Denton, Oral Roberts.

LEXINGTON, KY.

Host: Kentucky (No. 12 national seed).
Participants: No. 1 Kentucky (36-18), No. 2 West Virginia (39-18), No. 3 Indiana (41-18), No. 4 Ball State (36-21).
Champion: Kentucky (4-1).
Runner-up: Indiana (2-2).
Outstanding player: Devin Burkes, Kentucky.

AUBURN

Host: Auburn (No. 13 national seed).
Participants: No. 1 Auburn (34-21-1), No 2 Southern Miss. (41-17), No. 3 Samford (36-23), No. 4 Penn (32-14).
Champion: Southern Miss. (4-1).
Runner-up: Penn (2-2).
Outstanding player: Dustin Dickerson, Southern Miss.

TERRE HAUTE, IND.

Host: Indiana State (No. 14 national seed).
Participants: No. 1 Indiana State (42-15), No. 2 Iowa (42-14), No. 3 North Carolina (35-22), No. 4 Wright State (39-21).
Champion: Indiana State (3-0).
Runner-up: Iowa (2-2).
Outstanding player: N/A.

COLUMBIA, S.C.

Host: South Carolina (No. 15 national seed).
Participants: No. 1 South Carolina (39-19), No. 2 Campbell (44-13), No. 3 N.C. State (35-19), No. 4 Central Connecticut State (36-12).
Champion: South Carolina (3-0).
Runner-up: Campbell (2-2).
Outstanding player: Gavin Casas, South Carolina.

TUSCALOOSA, ALA.

Host: Alabama (No. 16 national seed).
Participants: No. 1 Alabama (40-19), No 2 Boston College (35-18), No 3 Troy (39-20), No. 4 Nicholls (34-22).
Champion: Alabama (3-0).
Runner-up: Boston College (2-2).
Outstanding player: N/A.

SUPER REGIONALS

JUNE 9-11

16 teams, best-of-three series.
Winners advance to College World Series.

ALABAMA AT WAKE FOREST

Site: Winston-Salem, N.C.
Wake Forest wins 2-0, advances to CWS.

TEXAS AT STANFORD

Site: Stanford, Calif.
Stanford wins 2-1, advances to CWS.

KENTUCKY AT LOUISIANA STATE

Site: Baton Rouge, La.
Louisiana State wins 2-0, advances to CWS.

TENNESSEE AT SOUTHERN MISS.

Site: Hattiesburg, Miss.
Tennessee wins 2-1, advances to CWS.

SOUTH CAROLINA AT FLORIDA

Site: Gainesville, Fla.
Florida wins 2-0, advances to CWS.

DUKE AT VIRGINIA

Site: Charlottesville, Va.
Virginia wins 2-1, advances to CWS.

ORAL ROBERTS AT OREGON

Site: Eugene, Ore.
Oral Roberts wins 2-1, advances to CWS.

INDIANA STATE AT TEXAS CHRISTIAN

Site: Fort Worth, Texas
Texas Christian wins 2-0, advances to CWS.

Skenes Draws Lofty Comps

PLAYER OF THE YEAR

BY TEDDY CAHILL

Paul Skenes didn't want to leave the Air Force Academy a year ago.

He liked being a part of the team, which had won the Mountain West Conference Tournament in 2022 and reached the Austin Regional final, and he had long wanted to serve in the military. But a combination of MLB's draft rules and the Air Force's service requirements led him to transfer so that he could more freely pursue a baseball career.

That led him to Louisiana State, where he spent the year dominating the sport. Skenes finished the year 13-2, 1.69 with 209 strikeouts and 20 walks in 122.2 innings. He led the nation in strikeouts and had more than any college pitcher since Jered Weaver racked up 213 in 2004.

MIKE JANES/FOUR SEAM IMAGES

Paul Skenes

Skenes' sensational season helped lead LSU to its first national championship since 2009 and he was named College World Series Most Outstanding Player after a standout performance in Omaha.

It also pushed him to the top of draft boards, and he was taken No. 1 overall by the Pirates, the first of two LSU players to hear their names called. College coaches and MLB evaluators both agree that they have not been a college pitcher like Skenes since at least Stephen Strasburg in 2009.

For those reasons and more, Skenes is the 2023 Baseball America College Player of the Year. He is just the second player in LSU program history to win the award, fittingly joining Ben McDonald, who won in 1989. McDonald was also the only other player in program history to be drafted first overall.

Coming into the year, Skenes wasn't quite sure what to expect at LSU. He was joining a team and a program with national championship expectations. He was a two-time All-American as a catcher/righthander at Air Force and he knew LSU would be different.

The reality, especially the fans' reception of him, has blown Skenes away.

"It was an awesome opportunity to come here in the first place," he said. "I never thought I'd be receiving the love and all of that that I've gotten from the fans (during the postseason). It's so cool."

Skenes is listed at 6-foot-6, 247 pounds. His physicality stands out on the mound. Until this year, Skenes doubled as a catcher.

At LSU, Skenes focused on pitching for the first time in his baseball career. The results were devastating. His fastball regularly crossed 100 mph. His slider became the best breaking ball in the country. His changeup, a pitch he rarely needed to throw, became a third plus offering. He pitched with above-average command and walked just 1.5 per nine innings, a mark that ranked 16th nationally and first among major-conference pitchers.

PREVIOUS WINNERS

1982: Jeff Ledbetter, OF/LHP Florida St.
1983: Dave Magadan, 1B, Alabama
1984: Oddibe McDowell, OF, Arizona St.
1985: Pete Incaviglia, OF, Oklahoma State
1986: Casey Close, OF, Michigan
1987: Robin Ventura, 3B, Oklahoma State
1988: John Olerund, 1B/LHP, Washington St.
1989: Ben McDonald, RHP, Louisiana State
1990: Mike Kelly, OF, Arizona State
1991: David McCarthy, 1B, Stanford
1992: Phil Nevin, 3B, Cal State Fullerton
1993: Brooks Kieschnick, DH/RHP, Texas
1994: Jason Varitek, C, Georgia Tech
1995: Todd Helton, 1B/LHP, Tennessee
1996: Kris Benson, RHP, Clemson
1997: J.D. Drew, OF, Florida State
1998: Jeff Austin, RHP, Stanford
1999: Jason Jennings, RHP, Baylor
2000: Mark Teixeira, 3B, Georgia Tech
2001: Mark Prior, RHP, S. California
2002: Khalil Greene, SS, Clemson
2003: Rickie Weeks, 2B, Southern
2004: Jered Weaver, RHP, Long Beach St.
2005: Alex Gordon, 3B, Nebraska
2006: Andrew Miller, LHP, North Carolina
2007: David Price, LHP, Vanderbilt
2008: Buster Posey, C/RHP, Florida State
2009: Stephen Strasburg, RHP, San Diego St.
2010: Anthony Rendon, 3B, Rice
2011: Trevor Bauer, RHP, UCLA
2012: Mike Zunino, C, Florida
2013: Kris Bryant, 3B, San Diego
2014: A.J. Reed, 1B/LHP, Kentucky
2015: Andrew Benintendi, OF, Arkansas
2016: Klye Lewis, OF, Mercer
2017: Brendan McKay, LHP/1B, Louisville
2018: Brady Singer, RHP, Florida
2019: Adley Rutschman, C, Oregon State
2021: Kumar Rocker, RHP, Vanderbilt
2022: Ivan Melendez, 1B, Texas

COACH OF THE YEAR

Johnson Meets Incredibly Lofty Expectations

BY TEDDY CAHILL

The buzz around the 2023 LSU Tigers built steadily over the course of last summer. The Tigers were a 40-win team in 2022 and were returning outfielder Dylan Crews, the early favorite to be the first overall pick in the 2023 draft. No one was ever going to overlook them.

Over the course of two months, coach Jay Johnson kept adding piece after piece to the team. All-Americans Paul Skenes and Tommy White transferred in. The Tigers brought in the top-ranked transfer and traditional recruiting classes. Draft-eligible players like Cade Beloso and Ty Floyd decided to return for another season in Baton Rouge. Johnson hired Wes Johnson, then the pitching coach for the Twins, and Josh Jordan, the 2018 Assistant Coach of the Year, to replace Dan Fitzgerald (Kansas) and Jason Kelly (Washington), who had both been hired away to be head coaches.

JAMIE SCHWABEROW/NCAA PHOTOS VIA

Jay Johnson

When the dust settled at the beginning of August and the players began returning to campus, the hype began to explode. LSU was the clear choice as the No. 1 team in the preseason. At the team's preseason banquet, Alex Bregman introduced Johnson and charged him with winning the 2023 national championship. This was what Johnson's success as a recruiter and the built-in lofty standards of one of the sport's biggest brands had wrought.

Having built the monster, Johnson now had to manage it through a challenging five-month season. Many wondered how he could keep everyone happy when there were still just 27 outs a game and nine spots in the batting order to go around. Others questioned how the Tigers would handle the losses that are inevitable in a baseball season, losses that might test the team's bonds and ratchet up the noise in Baton Rouge and beyond.

In the end, the 2023 season was largely drama-free for LSU. The Tigers ranked No. 1 in the first 12 iterations of the Top 25, the longest such streak to start a season in a decade. They lost just two series and had just one losing week—the SEC Tournament. Players were moved in and out of the lineup and the rotation without public complaint. The Tigers stuck together and in Omaha proved just how good they were when they held opponents to six total runs in four must-win games.

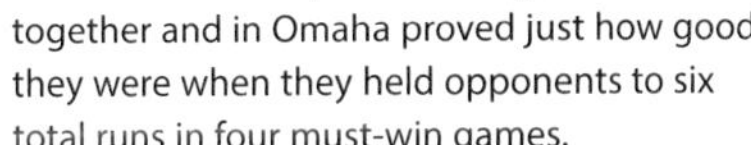

With LSU executing in all phases, it went on to win the national championship, the program's seventh and first since 2009. Johnson is the 2023 Baseball America Coach of the Year. He is the third LSU coach to win the award, joining Skip Bertman (1986 and 1996) and Paul Mainieri (2009). LSU is the first program to have three different men win the award.

PREVIOUS WINNERS

1982: Gene Stephenson, Wichita State
1983: Barry Shollenberger, Alabama
1984: Augie Garrido, Cal State Fullerton
1985: Ron Polk, Mississippi State
1986: Skip Bertman, LSU/Dave Snow, LMU
1987: Mark Marquess, Stanford
1988: Jim Brock, Arizona State
1989: Dave Snow, Long Beach State
1990: Steve Webber, Georgia
1991: Jim Hendry, Creighton
1992: Andy Lopez, Pepperdine
1993: Gene Stephenson, Wichita State
1994: Jim Morris, Miami
1995: Pat Murphy, Arizona State
1996: Skip Bertman, Louisiana State
1997: Jim Wells, Alabama
1998: Pat Murphy, Arizona State
1999: Wayne Graham, Rice
2000: Ray Tanner, South Carolina
2001: Dave Van Horn, Nebraska
2002: Augie Garrido, Texas
2003: George Horton, Cal State Fullerton
2004: David Perno, Georgia
2005: Rick Jones, Tulane
2006: Pat Casey, Oregon State
2007: Dave Serrano, UC Irvine
2008: Mike Fox, North Carolina
2009: Paul Mainieri, Louisiana State
2010: Ray Tanner, South Carolina
2011: Kevin O'Sullivan, Florida
2012: Mike Martin, Florida State
2013: John Savage, UCLA
2014: Tim Corbin, Vanderbilt
2015: Brian O'Connor, Virginia
2016: Jim Schlossnagle, Texas Christian
2017: Dan McDonnell, Louisville
2018: David Pierce, Texas
2019: Mike Martin, Florida State
2021: Chris Lemonis, Mississippi State
2022: Mike Bianco, Mississippi

Condon's Pop Stands Out

FRESHMAN OF THE YEAR

BY TEDDY CAHILL

Charlie Condon is Baseball America's 2023 Freshman of the Year. He hit .386/.484/.800 with 25 home runs in 56 games for Georgia.

Condon led all freshmen in OPS (1.284) and slugging, while tying for the most home runs among freshmen.

Condon's standout season came after he redshirted in 2022, a rarity in today's college baseball world. But Condon credited the decision to sit out his first season in Athens for preparing him for his big breakout. Listed at 6-foot-6, he needed the time to get stronger and work on his swing, improving its consistency so that he could make the most of his significant power.

"Just being able to be around the game was huge," Condon said. "I just watched veteran guys in front of me do their job and see how they went about it. That was big time for me."

BRIAN WESTERHOLT/FOUR SEAM IMAGES

Charlie Condon

His work in Athens, as well as a summer in the Northwoods League, positioned him for a big spring and he delivered. Condon led the SEC in slugging and finished second in batting, behind only LSU's Dylan Crews.

Condon's 25 home runs broke an SEC freshman record, previously held by former Vanderbilt slugging third baseman Pedro Alvarez. Condon homered at least once in every SEC series and showed remarkable consistency throughout the year. He was held hitless in consecutive games just twice all season.

Condon is the second player in program history to be named Freshman of the Year, joining outfielder Ron Wenrich, who in 1986 shared the award with Stanford's Jack McDowell.

PREVIOUS WINNERS

1993: Brett Laxton, RHP, Louisiana State
1994: R.A. Dickey, RHP, Tennessee
1995: Kyle Peterson, RHP, Stanford
1996: Pat Burrell, 3B, Miami
1997: Brian Roberts, SS, North Carolina
1998: Xavier Nady, 2B, California
1999: James Jurries, 2B, Tulane
2000: Kevin Howard, 3B, Miami
2001: Michael Aubrey, OF/LHP, Texas
2002: Stephen Drew, SS, Florida State
2003: Ryan Braun, SS, Miami
2004: Wade LeBlanc, LHP, Alabama
2005: Joe Savery, LHP, Rice
2006: Pedro Alvarez, 3B, Vanderbilt
2007: Dustin Ackley, 1B, North Carolina
2008: Chris Hernandez, LHP, Miami
2009: Anthony Rendon, 3B, Rice
2010: Matt Purke, LHP, Texas Christian
2011: Colin Moran, 3B, North Carolina
2012: Carlos Rodon, LHP, N.C. State
2013: Alex Bregman, SS, Louisiana State
2014: Zack Collins, C, Miami
2015: Brendan McKay, LHP/1B, Louisville
2016: Seth Beer, OF, Clemson
2017: Matt Wallner, OF/RHP, Southern Miss
2018: Kevin Abel, RHP, Oregon State
2019: Kumar Rocker, RHP, Vanderbilt
2021: Jack Leiter, RHP, Vanderbilt
2022: Tommy White, 3B/DH, N.C.. State
Full list of winners can be found at BaseballAmerica.com/Stories/Baseball-America-Awards

FRESHMAN ALL-AMERICA TEAMS

FIRST TEAM

Pos.		AVG	OBP	SLG	AB	2B	3B	HR	RBI	SB
C	Malcolm Moore, Stanford	.311	.386	.564	257	20	0	15	63	3
1B	Anthony Martinez, UC Irvine	.394	.471	.619	231	19	0	11	60	0
2B	Blake Cyr, Miami	.305	.427	.620	200	12	0	17	63	0
3B	Kevin Bazzell, Texas Tech	.348	.452	.572	250	24	1	10	62	2
SS	Anthony Silva, TCU	.330	.416	.471	227	11	0	7	50	17
OF	Cam Cannarella, Clemson	.388	.462	.560	250	16	3	7	47	24
OF	Charlie Condon, Georgia	.386	.484	.800	210	10	1	25	67	0
OF	Ethan Petry, South Carolina	.376	.471	.733	221	10	0	23	75	4
DH	Austin Overn, Southern California	.314	.402	.530	236	11	14	4	38	16
UT	DJ Newman, Bowling Green State	.383	.481	.495	107	5	2	1	11	9

		W	L	ERA	G	SV	IP	H	BB	SO	BAA
SP	Jacob Mayers, Nicholls State	9	1	2.02	15	0	76	44	58	105	.175
SP	Evan Chrest, Jacksonville	8	2	2.58	15	0	91	83	36	98	.249
SP	Kole Klecker, TCU	10	4	3.72	19	0	97	78	30	72	.216
SP	Dominic Fritton, N.C. State	3	4	3.59	17	3	63	50	24	75	.211
RP	Hudson Barrett, UCSB	5	1	1.92	21	6	61	42	32	82	.195
RP	James Tallon, Duke	1	1	1.64	23	12	33	22	11	54	.185
UT	DJ Newman, Bowling Green	3	2	3.49	15	0	28	26	5	33	.250

SECOND TEAM

C: Caden Bodine, Coastal Carolina; **1B:** Jared Jones, LSU; **2B:** Cade Kurland, Florida; **3B:** Colby Shelton, Alabama; **SS:** Wehiwa Aloy, Sacramento State; **OF:** Grant Jay, Dallas Baptist; **OF:** Cam Maldonado, Northeastern; **OF:** Nolan Schubart, Oklahoma State; **DH:** Jace Laviolette, Texas A&M; **SP:** Aiven Cabral, Northeastern; **SP:** Christian Coppola, Rutgers; **SP:** Jack O'Connor, Virginia; **SP:** Justin Mitrovich, Elon; **RP:** Ben Abeldt, TCU; **RP:** AJ Russell, Tennessee; **UT:** Mitch Voit, Michigan.

NCAA DIVISION I LEADERS

HITTING (MINIMUM 140 AT-BATS)

BATTING AVERAGE

Rk.	Player, Team	Class	AVG	OBP	SLG	G	AB	2B	3B	HR	RBI	BB	SO	SB
1	J.J. Wetherholt, West Virginia	So	.449	.517	.787	55	225	24	2	16	60	26	22	36
2	Nolan Schanuel, Fla. Atlantic	Jr	.447	.615	.868	59	197	18	4	19	64	71	14	14
3	Dylan Crews, LSU	Jr	.426	.567	.713	71	258	16	2	18	70	71	46	6
4	Sam Kulasingam, Air Force	Jr	.426	.537	.655	59	235	28	4	6	51	50	24	6
5	Tyler Davis, Sam Houston	Sr	.423	.491	.621	63	253	21	4	7	60	32	31	14
6	Daalen Adderley, Texas Southern	Jr	.421	.541	.624	51	178	16	1	6	42	33	28	16
7	Austin Deming, BYU	Sr	.418	.484	.915	41	165	23	1	19	68	20	29	1
8	Max Anderson, Nebraska	Jr	.414	.461	.770	57	244	20	2	21	70	20	29	0
9	Jonah Cox, Oral Roberts	Jr	.412	.470	.646	66	277	16	8	11	68	30	53	28
10	Jacob Wilson, Grand Canyon	Jr	.411	.461	.635	49	192	17	4	6	61	19	5	8
11	Hunter D'Amato, FDU	Jr	.411	.481	.560	53	207	11	1	6	56	27	25	28
12	Jesse Sherrill, Ga. Southern	Sr	.409	.502	.486	55	220	11	3	0	35	30	25	6
13	Yohandy Morales, Miami (FL)	Jr	.408	.475	.712	61	240	13	0	20	70	30	55	7
14	Kyle Teel, Virginia	Jr	.407	.475	.655	65	258	25	0	13	69	32	36	5
15	Kevin Dubrule, Army West Point	Sr	.405	.454	.617	56	227	19	1	9	68	18	12	2
16	Aidan Longwell, Kent St.	Jr	.404	.478	.652	58	230	23	2	10	75	27	23	5
17	Jeron Williams, Toledo	Jr	.403	.467	.681	55	238	16	4	14	48	22	37	49
18	Sam Mongelli, Sacred Heart	Sr	.402	.495	.743	55	241	16	3	20	54	30	31	22
19	Jayden Kiernan, Utah	Sr	.402	.464	.543	44	184	11	0	5	32	16	16	4
20	Brandon Pimentel, UTRGV	Sr	.402	.486	.710	56	214	9	0	19	73	29	42	10
21	Joe Redfield, Sam Houston	Jr	.402	.485	.683	61	249	19	3	15	56	34	34	15
22	Mike Boeve, Omaha	Jr	.401	.512	.563	47	167	15	0	4	32	32	9	6
23	Victor Figueroa, Mississippi Val.	Fr	.400	.485	.623	52	175	11	2	8	47	25	29	14
23	Brock Vradenburg, Michigan State.	Jr	.400	.492	.721	55	215	22	4	13	69	36	34	1
25	Charlie Pagliarini, Fairfield	Sr	.399	.528	.851	55	208	14	4	24	97	49	68	14
26	Ben Nemivant, Pacific	Sr	.398	.446	.527	48	201	18	1	2	36	13	21	5
27	Javon Hernandez, Jacksonville St.	Jr	.397	.479	.567	56	224	11	3	7	49	33	29	11
28	Griff O'Ferrall, Virginia	So	.396	.453	.495	65	273	20	2	1	42	29	38	16
29	Anthony Martinez, UC Irvine	Fr	.394	.471	.619	55	231	19	0	11	60	25	27	0
30	Tommy Troy, Stanford	Jr	.394	.478	.699	58	249	17	4	17	58	35	42	17
31	Angelo DiSpigna, Georgia Tech	Sr	.393	.509	.667	57	219	12	0	16	58	46	52	8
32	Reed Chumley, Houston Christian	Jr	.392	.458	.722	40	158	19	0	11	36	15	36	1
33	Joey Loynd, Delaware	Jr	.392	.454	.692	59	250	27	3	14	80	29	47	4
34	Ryan Cesarini, Saint Joseph's	So	.392	.470	.618	52	199	17	2	8	56	26	31	12
35	Justin Starke, VMI	Sr	.392	.487	.665	55	212	15	2	13	52	39	44	32
36	Ben Williamson, William & Mary	Sr	.390	.513	.662	55	210	11	5	12	49	40	22	14
37	Nich Klemp, Portland	Sr	.390	.449	.592	51	213	25	0	6	45	17	25	3
38	Nick Iannantone, ETSU	Jr	.389	.468	.554	49	175	14	3	3	27	23	25	2
39	Cam Cannarella, Clemson	Fr	.388	.462	.560	59	250	16	3	7	47	33	39	24
40	Ryan Campos, Arizona St.	So	.388	.503	.594	44	160	7	1	8	24	35	17	4
41	Treyson Hughes, Mercer	So	.387	.504	.604	58	222	15	0	11	52	47	35	9
41	Antonio Valdez, UTSA	Sr	.387	.483	.694	57	222	15	7	13	65	38	39	17
43	Ty Hill, Jackson St.	Sr	.387	.520	.619	52	181	16	4	6	53	50	29	8
44	Ryan Wilson, Davidson	Jr	.387	.533	.737	54	194	17	0	17	54	33	23	8
45	Austin Brinling, North Florida	Jr	.386	.500	.540	52	202	18	2	3	31	36	20	20
46	Charlie Condon, Georgia	Fr	.386	.484	.800	56	210	10	1	25	67	33	45	0
47	Jack Hay, Alabama St.	Jr	.385	.472	.575	56	221	10	1	10	61	36	37	0
48	Alberto Rios, Stanford	Jr	.384	.485	.707	63	242	24	0	18	73	38	42	5
49	Colton Kucera, Northern Ky.	Jr	.384	.500	.488	47	164	13	2	0	29	29	37	7
50	Eddie Micheletti	Sr	.384	.460	.563	55	224	18	2	6	48	28	19	8
51	DJ Newman, Bowling Green	Fr	.383	.481	.495	41	107	5	2	1	11	20	23	9
51	Cameron Sisneros, ETSU	Jr	.383	.472	.692	55	214	18	0	16	59	29	24	3
53	Ryan Galanie, Wofford	Sr	.383	.491	.670	58	230	15	0	17	66	40	39	19
54	Bayram Hot, Marist	Fr	.382	.446	.518	50	191	14	3	2	37	21	28	11
54	Ryan Vogel, Bradley	Jr	.382	.459	.571	48	191	14	2	6	31	22	21	20
56	Lenny Junior Ashby, New Mexico	Jr	.381	.455	.595	51	210	18	0	9	51	26	25	0
57	Johnny Hipsman, Richmond	Sr	.381	.434	.659	54	226	25	1	12	55	22	20	9
58	Justin Murray, Houston	Sr	.379	.422	.598	57	219	11	2	11	58	17	44	20
59	Nick Lorusso, Maryland	Sr	.379	.446	.765	61	264	20	2	26	105	34	46	3
60	Alexander Olivo, Texas Southern	Jr	.379	.498	.706	52	177	17	1	13	69	34	40	3
61	Xane Washington, Nicholls	Sr	.378	.480	.550	57	222	18	4	4	46	32	43	16
62	Kodey Shojinaga, Kansas	Fr	.378	.421	.526	53	196	11	0	6	32	16	25	0
62	Decker Scheffler, Ball St.	Jr	.378	.453	.597	57	196	13	3	8	49	23	23	5
64	Connor Tate, Georgia	Sr	.377	.459	.682	56	220	19	0	16	54	30	45	74
65	Max Ryerson, Georgia St.	Sr	.376	.482	.703	53	202	6	0	20	52	29	51	1
66	Wehiwa Aloy, Sacramento St.	Fr	.376	.427	.662	56	234	15	5	14	46	15	44	2

67	Kristian Campbell, Georgia Tech	So	.376	.484	.549	45	173	16	1	4	24	29	17	4
68	Kemp Alderman, Ole Miss	Jr	.376	.440	.709	54	213	14	0	19	61	26	41	5
69	Ethan Petry, South Carolina	Fr	.376	.471	.733	63	221	10	0	23	75	33	59	4
70	Josh Kross, Eastern Mich.	So	.376	.433	.651	52	229	18	0	15	70	13	26	1
71	Tyler Halstead, Campbell	Sr	.376	.455	.523	58	237	15	4	4	38	24	30	32
72	Grayson Tatrow, Abilene Christian	Sr	.375	.480	.832	58	208	14	3	25	68	43	58	9
73	Ethan Anderson, Virginia	So	.375	.469	.649	65	259	26	0	15	66	42	32	3
74	Sam Brown, Washington St.	So	.374	.481	.674	52	187	19	2	11	58	27	33	5
75	Jack Payton, Louisville	Jr	.374	.472	.642	48	179	10	1	12	41	22	41	8
76	Payton Eeles, Coastal Carolina	Sr	.374	.500	.492	63	246	17	0	4	43	45	34	42
77	Travis Bazzana, Oregon St.	So	.374	.500	.622	61	238	20	3	11	55	59	47	36
78	Tommy White, LSU	So	.374	.432	.725	66	273	24	0	24	105	23	41	0
79	Max Giordano, Niagara	Sr	.374	.481	.741	47	174	12	2	16	54	29	44	10
80	Wyatt Langford, Florida	Jr	.373	.498	.784	64	236	28	3	21	57	56	44	9
81	Devin Hurdle, Omaha	Jr	.373	.425	.547	42	161	9	2	5	29	14	26	4
82	Ty Jackson, Florida A&M	Jr	.373	.473	.520	53	204	8	5	4	30	32	31	9
83	Michael Dattalo, Northwestern St.	Fr	.372	.447	.561	56	223	18	0	8	39	27	20	2
84	Nico Baumbach, Little Rock	So	.372	.453	.643	52	199	10	1	14	52	27	27	3
85	Kyle Walker, Grambling	So	.372	.495	.500	44	156	8	3	2	29	31	27	23
86	Trey Paige, Delaware St.	Jr	.372	.468	.691	48	191	15	2	14	53	34	30	10
87	Daniel Dickinson, Utah Valley	Fr	.372	.441	.592	54	218	19	1	9	42	22	32	10
88	Ali Camarillo, CSUN	So	.371	.421	.611	46	175	15	3	7	44	13	30	1
89	Brock Rodden, Wichita St.	Jr	.371	.474	.701	55	221	18	2	17	64	39	26	12
90	Aaron Mann, St. John's (NY)	Sr	.371	.462	.548	49	186	15	0	6	42	22	36	3
91	Lawson Harrill, Campbell	Jr	.371	.475	.761	58	213	17	0	22	69	31	63	6
91	Tommy Reifler, Binghamton	Jr	.371	.434	.461	49	178	8	1	2	29	20	17	9
93	Kyle DeBarge, Louisiana	So	.371	.448	.546	54	205	15	0	7	38	21	21	18
94	Keith Jones II, New Mexico St.	Jr	.371	.483	.600	47	170	12	0	9	29	35	39	7
95	Ben McCabe, UCF	Sr	.371	.466	.692	59	224	15	0	19	51	17	59	6
96	Chris Conniff, Wagner	Jr	.370	.468	.548	56	219	14	2	7	41	36	40	10
97	Homer Bush Jr., Grand Canyon	Jr	.370	.478	.500	58	238	19	3	2	41	38	27	25
98	Matthew Kurata, CSU Bakersfield	So	.369	.429	.439	42	157	11	0	0	21	11	27	4
99	Spencer Hanson, Kennesaw St.	Sr	.369	.401	.725	42	149	8	0	15	55	11	29	1
100	Dylan Palmer, Hofstra	Fr	.369	.441	.458	46	179	12	2	0	21	20	20	23

ON-BASE PERCENTAGE

Rank	Player, Pos., Team	OBP
1.	Nolan Schanuel, OF, Fla. Atlantic	.615
2.	Dylan Crews, OF, LSU	.567
3.	Daalen Adderley, OF, Texas Southern	.541
4.	Sam Kulasingam, INF, Air Force	.537
5.	Ryan Wilson, INF, Davidson	.533
6.	Charlie Pagliarini, INF, Fairfield	.528
7.	Nick Kurtz, OF, Wake Forest	.527
8.	Nolen Hester, OF, Texas Tech	.525
9.	Luke Shliger, C, Maryland	.523
10.	Ty Hill, UT, Jackson St.	.520

SLUGGING PERCENTAGE

Rank	Player, Pos., Team	SLG
1.	Austin Deming, INF, BYU	.915
2.	Nolan Schanuel, OF, Fla. Atlantic	.868
3.	Charlie Pagliarini, INF, Fairfield	.851
4.	Grayson Tatrow, OF, Abilene Christ.	.832
5.	Cam Fisher, OF, Charlotte	.812
6.	Brock Wilken, INF, Wake Forest	.807
7.	Charlie Condon, 1B, Georgia	.800
8.	J.J. Wetherholt, INF, West Virginia	.787
9.	Nick Kurtz, OF, Wake Forest	.784
10.	Wyatt Langford, UT, Florida	.784

RUNS BATTED IN

Rank	Player, Pos., Team	RBI
1.	Nick Lorusso, 3B, Maryland	105
1.	Tommy White, INF, LSU	105
3.	Charlie Pagliarini, INF, Fairfield	97
4.	Jac Caglianone, UT, Florida	90
4.	Jake Gelof, INF, Virginia	90
6.	Kiko Romero, 1B, Arizona	89
7.	Gavin Kash, INF, Texas Tech	84
8.	Derek Bender, C, Coastal Carolina	83
8.	Edrick Felix, INF, FGCU	83
10.	Brock Wilken, INF, Wake Forest	82

HOME RUNS

Rank	Player, Pos., Team	HR
1.	Jac Caglianone, DH, Florida	33
2.	Brock Wilken, INF, Wake Forest	31
3.	Cam Fisher, OF, Charlotte	30
4.	Shane Lewis, OF, Troy	27
5.	Gavin Kash, INF, Texas Tech	26
5.	Nick Lorusso, 3B, Maryland	26
7.	Charlie Condon, 1B, Georgia	25
7.	Edrick Felix, INF, FGCU	25
7.	Colby Shelton, INF, Alabama	25
7.	Grayson Tatrow, OF, Abilene Christian	25

DOUBLES

Rank	Player, Pos., Team	2B
1.	Wyatt Langford, OF, Florida	28
3.	Joey Loynd, INF, Delaware	27
4.	Ethan Anderson, C, Virginia	26
4.	Josh Leslie, INF, McNeese	26
4.	Carson Roccaforte, OF, Louisiana	26
7.	Johnny Hipsman, OF, Richmond	25
7.	Luke Keaschall, INF, Arizona St.	25
7.	Nich Klemp, C, Portland	25
7.	Kyle Teel, C, Virginia	25

TRIPLES

Rank	Player, Pos., Team	3B
1.	Austin Overn, OF, Southern California	14
2.	Brendan Ryan, OF, A&M-Corpus Christi	9
3.	Jonah Cox, UT, Oral Roberts	8
4.	Brandon Butterworth, INF, W. Carolina	7
4.	Turner Grau, OF, Youngstown St.	7
4.	Mitch Jebb, INF, Michigan St.	7
4.	Josiah Ragsdale, OF, Iona	7
4.	Antonio Valdez, INF, UTSA	7
4.	Mason White, INF, Arizona	7
4.	Tyler Williams, OF, Little Rock	7

STOLEN BASES

Rank	Player, Pos., Team	SB
1.	Jeron Williams, INF, Toledo	49
2.	Payton Eeles, INF, Coastal Carolina	42
3.	Evan Fox, UT, Stony Brook	39
3.	David Smith, INF, UConn	39
5.	Jaylen Armstrong, OF, Southern U.	38
5.	Randy Flores, INF, Alabama St.	38
5.	Jake Rainess, INF, Maine	38
8.	Enrique Bradfield Jr., OF, Vanderbilt	37
8.	Cameron Jones, P, Georgia St.	37
10.	Travis Bazzana, INF, Oregon St.	36
10.	Caleb Hobson, OF, UT Martin	36
10.	Heath Hood, OF, Louisiana	36
10.	J.J. Wetherholt, So., West Virginia	36

RUNS

Rank	Player, Pos., Team	R
1.	Dylan Crews, OF, LSU	100
2.	Luke Shliger, C, Maryland	93
3.	Brock Wilken, INF, Wake Forest	90
4.	Wyatt Langford, UT, Florida	83
5.	Sam Mongelli, INF, Sacred Heart	81
5.	Joe Redfield, OF, Sam Houston	81
7.	Brian Ellis, OF, FGCU	80
7.	Matthew Shaw, INF, Maryland	80
9.	Travis Bazzana, INF, Oregon St.	78
10.	Quinn McDaniel, INF, Maine	77
10.	Brayden Taylor, INF, TCU	77

HITS

Rank	Player, Pos., Team	H
1.	Jonah Cox, UT, Oral Roberts	114
2.	Dylan Crews, OF, LSU	110
3.	Griff O'Ferrall, INF, Virginia	108
4.	Tyler Davis, UT, Sam Houston	107
5.	Kyle Teel, C, Virginia	105
6.	Tommy White, INF, LSU	102

Rank Player, Pos., Team	
7. Max Anderson, INF, Nebraska	101
7. J.J. Wetherholt, INF, West Virginia	101
9. Sam Kulasingam, INF, Air Force	100
9. Nick Lorusso, 3B, Maryland	100
9. Joe Redfield, OF, Sam Houston	100

TOTAL BASES

Rank Player, Pos., Team	TB
1. Jac Caglianone, UT, Florida	208
2. Nick Lorusso, 3B, Maryland	202
3. Tommy White, INF, LSU	198
4. Brock Wilken, INF, Wake Forest	192
5. Max Anderson, INF, Nebraska	188
5. Edrick Felix, INF, FGCU	188
7. Wyatt Langford, UT, Florida	185
8. Dylan Crews, OF, LSU	184
8. Matthew Shaw, INF, Maryland	184
10. Cam Fisher, OF, Charlotte	182
10. Gavin Kash, INF, Texas Tech	182

WALKS

Rank Player, Pos., Team	BB
1. Dylan Crews, OF, LSU	71
1. Nolan Schanuel, OF, Fla. Atlantic	71
3. Luke Shliger, C, Maryland	69
3. Brock Wilken, INF, Wake Forest	69
5. Cam Fisher, OF, Charlotte	64
6. Nick Kurtz, OF, Wake Forest	63
7. Nolen Hester, OF, Texas Tech	61
7. Jack Housinger, INF, Xavier	61
7. Bryce Madron, OF, Oklahoma	61
10. Dan Covino, INF, Delaware	60
10. Quinn McDaniel, INF, Maine	60

TOUGHEST TO STRIKE OUT

Rank Player, Pos., Team	AB/SO
1. Jacob Wilson, INF, Grand Canyon	38.4
2. Garrett Palladino, SS, Alcorn	22.1
3. Kyle Novak, INF, James Madison	21
4. Sammy Diaz, C, Texas-San Anto.	19.9
5. Kevin Dubrule, INF, Army	18.9
6. Mike Boeve, INF, Omaha	18.6
7. Shane Paradine, C, Stony Brook	16.7
8. Ben Jones, INF, Dayton	16.5
9. Rafe Perich, INF, Lehigh	15.5
10. Randy Flores, INF, Alabama St.	15.2

HIT BY PITCH

Rank Player, Pos., Team	HBP
1. Gavin Dugas, INF, LSU	33
1. Connor Dykstra, C, George Mason	33
3. Brooks Coetzee, OF, Notre Dame	31
4. Ryan Wilson, INF, Davidson	30
5. Collin Mathews, OF, Kent St.	26
6. Jackson Gray, OF, Kentucky	25
6. William Sullivan, INF, Troy	25
8. Jacob Lojewski, C, FGCU	24
8. Rhett Rosevear, INF, SE La.	24
8. Luke Shliger, C, Maryland	21

SACRIFICE BUNTS

Rank Player, Pos., Team	SAC
1. Jack Renwick, INF, Wofford	28
2. Blake Covin, OF, Air Force	13
2. Brett Stallings, INF, George Mason	13
2. Bruer Webster, INF, Utah	13
2. Carson Wells, OF, Southern California	13
6. Dylan DeButy, C, Arkansas St.	12
6. Lucas DiLuca, INF, Eastern Ill.	12
6. Brice Martinez, INF, Wofford	12
6. Jatavis Melton, 1B, Jackson St.	12
6. Luke Spillane, OF, UC Irvine	12
6. Marshall Toole, OF, Wofford	12
6. Kade York, INF, UTRGV	12

SACRIFICE FLIES

Rank Player, Pos., Team	SF
1. Jarrod Belbin, UT, Campbell	10
1. Randy Flores, INF, Alabama St.	10
3. Niko Amory, C, Marist	9
3. Johnathan Behm, OF, Saint Peter's	9
3. Anthony Donofrio, OF, Quinnipiac	9
3. Matthew Etzel, OF, Southern Miss.	9
3. R.J. Schreck, OF, Vanderbilt	9
8. 21 tied	8

PITCHING

Rk.	Pitcher, Team	Class	W	L	ERA	G	GS	SV	IP	H	R	ER	BB	SO
1	Jackson Wells, Little Rock	So	7	4	1.65	15	15	0	93	73	27	17	32	80
2	Paul Skenes, LSU	Jr	13	2	1.69	19	19	0	122.2	72	28	23	20	209
3	Grant Rogers, McNeese	Jr	12	1	1.82	15	15	0	103.2	79	24	21	18	88
4	Rhett Lowder, Wake Forest	Jr	15	0	1.87	19	19	0	120.1	90	30	25	24	143
5	Hudson Barrett, UC Santa Barbara	Fr	5	1	1.92	21	4	6	61	42	14	13	32	82
6	Nico Zeglin, Long Beach St.	Sr	8	4	2.00	15	15	0	94.2	67	25	21	27	117
7	Nick Brink, Portland	So	6	0	2.02	14	9	1	58	52	15	13	22	60
8	Jacob Mayers, Nicholls	Fr	9	1	2.02	15	15	0	75.2	44	21	17	58	105
9	Diego Barrera, LMU (CA)	Sr	8	2	2.17	14	14	0	99.2	80	28	24	11	93
10	Isaac Stebens, Oklahoma St.	Jr	4	1	2.24	28	0	6	64.1	49	22	16	24	85
11	Simon Miller, UTSA	Jr	8	1	2.30	27	0	11	70.1	67	27	18	18	81
12	Sean Sullivan, Wake Forest	So	5	3	2.45	17	10	3	69.2	43	25	19	21	111
13	Tanner Hall, Southern Miss.	Jr	12	4	2.48	18	18	0	112.1	84	40	31	33	124
14	Parker Puetz, North Dakota St.	Fr	3	0	2.51	16	10	1	61	43	19	17	17	47
15	Bobby Alcock, Gardner-Webb	Jr	7	3	2.51	14	14	0	89.2	56	32	25	40	106
16	Omar Melendez, Alabama St.	So	12	0	2.52	16	15	0	93	88	30	26	27	96
17	Grant Adler, Wichita St.	Jr	5	4	2.55	14	14	0	77.2	75	36	22	23	75
18	Joseph Whitman, Kent St.	Jr	9	2	2.56	15	15	0	81	63	31	23	29	100
19	Evan Chrest, Jacksonville	Fr	8	2	2.58	15	15	0	90.2	83	32	26	36	98
20	Aiven Cabral, Northeastern	Fr	9	4	2.58	19	16	0	83.2	78	27	24	14	69
21	Jake Bloss, Georgetown	Sr	8	4	2.58	14	13	0	76.2	58	28	22	24	96
22	Trey Yesavage, East Carolina	So	7	1	2.61	16	14	1	76	53	24	22	23	105
23	Lucas Gordon, Texas	Jr	7	2	2.63	19	17	0	102.2	85	33	30	34	103
24	Seth Keener, Wake Forest	Jr	8	2	2.69	23	8	1	70.1	41	24	21	20	94
25	Lucas Mahlstedt, Wofford	So	7	2	2.69	27	0	6	83.2	72	26	25	18	68
26	Shea Sprague, Elon	So	7	3	2.69	15	15	0	90.1	93	35	27	19	82
27	Connor Harrison, Hawaii	Jr	1	5	2.70	25	2	7	53.1	49	20	16	14	43
28	Cade Kuehler, Campbell	Jr	8	1	2.71	13	13	0	73	54	28	22	26	91
29	Dominic Niman, Central Conn. St.	Jr	12	2	2.77	15	15	0	104	86	38	32	26	94
30	Josh Hartle, Wake Forest	So	11	2	2.81	18	17	0	102.1	91	38	32	24	140
31	TJ Fondtain, San Diego St.	Jr	7	4	2.82	15	15	0	92.2	64	37	29	25	99
32	Alex Giroux, Hawaii	So	4	2	2.83	22	6	2	57.1	48	25	18	14	52
33	Tanner Greshman, Army West Point	Jr	5	1	2.90	10	10	0	59	41	21	19	21	56
34	Andrew Lindsey, Tennessee	Jr	3	4	2.90	21	9	0	71.1	60	29	23	19	73
35	Frankie Wright, Wagner	So	5	3	2.90	15	15	0	83.2	76	34	27	21	77
36	Lebarron Johnson Jr., Texas	Jr	8	4	2.91	20	13	1	86.2	73	31	28	38	98
37	Reid Easterly, Yale	Jr	6	3	2.93	13	10	1	73.2	60	28	24	29	56
38	Trennor O'Donnell, Ball St.	Jr	5	4	2.93	16	15	0	92	72	37	30	32	97

39	Luke Johnson, UMBC	Jr	7	1	2.96	14	14	1	79	63	35	26	38	84
40	Jake Combs, Southern Ill.	Jr	3	2	2.97	16	15	0	63.2	60	25	21	18	47
41	Caden Aoki, Southern California	So	4	3	2.98	13	11	0	63.1	59	26	21	20	52
42	Owen Coady, Penn	Sr	5	3	2.98	13	13	0	66.1	49	23	22	43	79
43	Cole Zaffiro, Penn	Jr	6	2	3.00	13	13	0	72	56	31	24	26	80
43	Jesse Barker, Central Ark.	Jr	7	4	3.00	14	14	0	96	85	36	32	22	109
45	Cal McAninch, Toledo	Sr	5	1	3.02	26	0	3	59.2	48	24	20	18	48
46	Michael Stanford, UC Irvine	Sr	7	2	3.06	20	9	1	64.2	63	28	22	15	56
47	Connelly Early, Virginia	Jr	12	3	3.09	19	18	0	87.1	82	35	30	23	100
48	Jacob Cravey, Samford	Jr	9	2	3.10	17	16	1	104.2	83	42	36	40	126
49	Connor Linchey, Saint Mary's (CA)	Sr	5	1	3.11	15	11	1	75.1	64	28	26	15	55
50	Nick Payero, Seton Hall	Sr	5	3	3.12	15	9	0	69.1	60	31	24	22	62
51	Matt Ager, UC Santa Barbara	So	5	4	3.12	15	15	0	92.1	71	35	32	26	115
52	Harry Gustin, Hawaii	So	5	3	3.14	15	14	0	77.1	71	27	27	36	79
53	Ty Abraham, McNeese	Jr	2	2	3.15	25	7	5	68.2	65	26	24	23	75
54	Nate Mitchell, Navy	Sr	6	5	3.16	13	13	0	74	80	35	26	13	50
55	Ryan Dromboski, Penn	So	7	3	3.17	14	13	0	71	51	30	25	35	97
56	Sebastian Gongora, Wright St.	So	10	1	3.17	16	16	0	93.2	79	37	33	33	89
57	Brooks Caple, Lamar University	Jr	5	0	3.19	15	11	0	59.1	51	28	21	16	50
58	Nick Laxner, Eastern Ill.	Sr	5	1	3.21	12	10	0	61.2	63	24	22	7	40
59	Nicholas Wilson, Southern U.	Jr	6	2	3.22	15	13	0	86.2	78	35	31	23	101
60	Angelo Cabral, UTRGV	Jr	10	2	3.22	14	12	1	72.2	64	32	26	22	76
61	Kyler Carmack, Arkansas St.	Fr	5	3	3.23	16	12	0	69.2	63	37	25	37	60
62	Luke Rettig, Lehigh	Sr	6	4	3.24	12	12	0	58.1	43	34	21	21	65
62	Jake Gigliotti, Northeastern	Jr	8	0	3.24	23	8	2	66.2	55	27	24	17	65
64	Brooks Fowler, Oral Roberts	So	9	2	3.26	17	17	0	80	66	31	29	32	78
65	Reese Dutton, USC Upstate	Jr	10	3	3.29	15	15	0	90.1	80	38	33	30	102
66	Austin Amaral, Stetson	Jr	6	3	3.30	15	15	0	76.1	63	32	28	40	82
67	Ryan Delgado, California Baptist	Jr	2	5	3.34	28	2	4	59.1	53	34	22	21	48
68	Will Kinzeler, Southeastern La.	Jr	5	1	3.34	12	12	0	64.2	62	25	24	38	33
69	Caden Grice, Clemson	Jr	8	1	3.35	14	14	0	78	54	35	29	33	101
70	Bennett Flynn, Davidson	Sr	5	1	3.36	20	4	4	56.1	40	26	21	35	82
71	Aidan Tyrell, Notre Dame	Sr	8	3	3.36	16	6	1	69.2	64	36	26	26	59
72	Zach Heaton, DBU	Sr	5	1	3.38	16	16	0	69.1	60	31	26	24	58
73	Chad Gartland, George Mason	So	7	2	3.39	17	13	2	98.1	88	42	37	28	86
74	Kelly Austin, UCLA	Sr	5	4	3.39	17	13	0	82.1	72	39	31	34	104
74	Liam Rocha, California Baptist	Jr	6	1	3.39	17	13	0	82.1	70	43	31	30	103
76	Braden Carmichael, Oklahoma	Sr	7	1	3.39	18	11	0	77	86	39	29	18	62
77	Casey Anderson, Utah Valley	Jr	4	1	3.39	15	8	2	69	63	28	26	25	90
78	Tom Chmielewski, Princeton	Jr	6	6	3.40	13	13	0	76.2	74	38	29	19	73
79	Carson Liggett, Louisville	So	7	2	3.42	14	14	0	71	64	28	27	29	64
80	Nate Knowles, William & Mary	So	5	5	3.43	20	17	0	65.2	52	31	25	30	70
81	Josh Bookbinder, Winthrop	Sr	5	1	3.43	22	0	2	57.2	57	30	22	2	42
82	Mike Ruggieri, Army West Point	Jr	9	2	3.44	15	12	0	73.1	62	37	28	38	61
83	Devin Futrell, Vanderbilt	So	8	3	3.44	16	15	0	83.2	71	38	32	20	72
84	Hunter Viets, Florida A&M	Sr	8	2	3.45	16	16	0	91.1	99	43	35	20	81
85	Cole Mathis, Col. of Charleston	So	5	1	3.45	14	10	1	60	60	27	23	17	52
86	Connor Fenlong, Indiana St.	Sr	11	3	3.45	17	16	0	114.2	93	47	44	31	76
87	Harrison Bodendorf, Hawaii	Fr	5	2	3.45	21	6	5	57.1	52	31	22	27	66
88	Matt Comnos, CSU Bakersfield	Jr	3	6	3.46	15	15	0	83.1	72	44	32	43	80
88	Brandt Thompson, Missouri St.	Jr	6	5	3.46	18	17	0	83.1	87	44	32	27	84
90	Evan Aschenbeck, Texas A&M	Jr	8	1	3.46	26	0	3	65	59	27	25	20	75
91	C.J. Williams, Fla. Atlantic	Jr	3	1	3.47	25	7	3	59.2	50	29	23	33	57
92	James Hicks, South Carolina	Sr	8	1	3.48	25	6	2	67.1	59	29	26	14	56
93	Ethan Bosacker, Xavier	Sr	8	3	3.49	16	16	0	98	82	40	38	29	101
94	Andy Bean, Belmont	Jr	3	6	3.50	13	12	0	72	60	34	28	22	69
95	Sam Armstrong, Old Dominion	Jr	9	4	3.51	15	15	0	77	69	33	30	28	72
96	Joshua Becker, UMass Lowell	Sr	5	3	3.51	15	8	1	59	55	29	23	13	51
97	Nolan Santos, Bethune-Cookman	Jr	7	5	3.51	16	16	0	97.1	80	50	38	35	138
98	Hunter Owen, Vanderbilt	Jr	4	0	3.52	12	12	0	64	52	28	25	17	76
99	Carson Myers, UAB	So	3	5	3.52	14	13	0	71.2	60	30	28	34	70
100	Rich Racobaldo, FDU	Sr	8	2	3.52	14	14	0	79.1	70	36	31	34	79

WINS

Rank Pitcher, Team	W
1. Rhett Lowder, Wake Forest	15
2. Omar Melendez, Alabama St.	12
2. Grant Rogers, McNeese	12
2. Dominic Niman, Central Conn. St.	12
2. Paul Skenes, LSU	12
2. Connelly Early, Virginia	12
2. Tanner Hall, Southern Miss.	12
8. Josh Hartle, Wake Forest	11
8. Connor Fenlong, Indiana St.	11
8. Brandon Mitchell, New Orleans	11
8. Matthew Marchal, Wofford	11

SAVES

Rank Pitcher, Team	SV
1. Mitchell Scott, Kent St.	15
1. Cade Denton, Oral Roberts	15
3. Danny Kirwin, Rider	14
3. Chris Lotito, Jacksonville	14
3. Ben Petschke, Samford	14
6. Joshua Romero, CSUN	13
6. Camden Minacci, Wake Forest	13
6. Brandon Neely, Florida	13
9. 5 tied	12

STRIKEOUTS

Rank	Pitcher, Team	SO
1.	Paul Skenes, LSU	209
2.	Quinn Mathews, Stanford	158
3.	Hurston Waldrep, Florida	156
4.	Rhett Lowder, Wake Forest	143
5.	Josh Hartle, Wake Forest	140
6.	Nolan Santos, Bethune-Cookman	138
7.	Brandon Sproat, Florida	134
8.	Wyatt Hudepohl, Charlotte	129
9.	Jacob Cravey, Samford	126
10.	Tanner Hall, Southern Miss.	124
10.	Juaron Watts-Brown, Oklahoma St.	124

STRIKEOUTS PER NINE

Rank	Pitcher, Team	SO/9
1.	Paul Skenes, LSU	15.33
2.	Sean Sullivan, Wake Forest	14.34
3.	Chase Burns, Tennessee	14.25
4.	Hurston Waldrep, Florida	13.81
5.	Hagen Smith, Arkansas	13.69
6.	Juaron Watts-Brown, Okla. St.	13.55
7.	Matt Duffy, Canisius	13.28
8.	Bennett Flynn, Davidson	13.10
9.	Tyler Bremner, UC S. Barbara	13.01
10.	Trent Sellers, Oregon St.	12.89

FEWEST HITS PER NINE

Rank	Pitcher, Team	H/9
1.	Brody Brecht, Iowa	4.32
2.	Jacob Mayers, Nicholls	5.23
3.	Marcus Morgan, Iowa	5.23
4.	Seth Keener, Wake Forest	5.25
5.	Paul Skenes, LSU	5.28
6.	Sean Sullivan, Wake Forest	5.56
7.	Bobby Alcock, Gardner-Webb	5.62
8.	Ryan DeSanto, Saint Joseph's	5.83
9.	Tommy Vail, Auburn	5.84
10.	Luke Holman, Alabama	6.00

FEWEST WALKS PER NINE

Rank	Pitcher, Team	BB/9
1.	Josh Bookbinder, Winthrop	0.31
2.	Brant Alazaus, Xavier	0.68
3.	Jack Metzger, Dartmouth	0.85
4.	Noah Covington, UMES	0.87
5.	Fynn Chester, Cal St. Fullerton	0.94
6.	Diego Barrera, LMU (CA)	0.99
7.	Nick Laxner, Eastern Ill.	1.02
8.	Michael Dews, Prairie View	1.17
9.	Jack Bowery, Marist	1.33
10.	Cade Feeney, North Dakota St.	1.34

TEAM LEADERS

SCORING

Rank	Team	G	R	R/G
1.	FGCU	60	578	9.6
2.	Campbell	61	587	9.6
3.	Fairfield	55	519	9.4
4.	Coastal Carolina	63	582	9.2
5.	Maryland	63	578	9.2
6.	Wake Forest	66	591	9.0
7.	Virginia	65	582	9.0
8.	LSU	71	634	8.9
9.	Virginia Tech	53	464	8.8
10.	New Mexico	51	441	8.6
11.	Kent St.	58	493	8.5
12.	Alabama St.	59	499	8.5
12.	Arizona	59	499	8.5
12.	Wofford	59	499	8.5
15.	Jackson St.	53	448	8.5
16.	Sam Houston	64	540	8.4
17.	Stanford	64	535	8.4
18.	Columbia	45	376	8.4
19.	Georgia Tech	57	472	8.3
20.	Oklahoma St.	61	505	8.3
21.	DBU	63	520	8.3
22.	Texas Southern	53	437	8.2
23.	Oral Roberts	66	544	8.2
24.	Iowa	60	489	8.2
25.	VMI	55	447	8.1
26.	Texas Tech	64	519	8.1
27.	UC Irvine	55	446	8.1
28.	Northern Ky.	57	461	8.1
29.	Oregon St.	61	492	8.1
30.	Saint Joseph's	53	427	8.1
31.	Grambling	55	442	8.0
32.	Quinnipiac	56	448	8.0
33.	Saint Louis	56	447	8.0
34.	Florida	71	566	8.0
35.	Davidson	54	425	7.9
36.	TCU	68	532	7.8
37.	Old Dominion	55	430	7.8
38.	UConn	61	476	7.8
39.	Georgia St.	59	460	7.8
40.	South Carolina	63	491	7.8
41.	Army West Point	56	435	7.8
42.	New Orleans	60	465	7.8
43.	West Virginia	60	465	7.8
44.	Eastern Mich.	53	409	7.7
45.	Indiana	63	486	7.7
46.	Mercer	58	447	7.7
47.	Ga. Southern	56	431	7.7
48.	Florida A&M	59	453	7.7
49.	Troy	62	476	7.7
50.	Sacred Heart	58	445	7.7

BATTING AVERAGE

Rank	Team	AVG
1.	Alabama St.	.332
2.	Virginia	.332
3.	New Mexico	.329
4.	Georgia Tech	.323
5.	VMI	.322
6.	FGCU	.322
7.	Oral Roberts	.321
8.	Fairfield	.320
9.	Campbell	.318
10.	Stanford	.316

HOME RUNS

Rank	Team	HR
1.	Florida	146
2.	LSU	144
3.	FGCU	142
4.	Maryland	131
5.	Wake Forest	130
6.	Tennessee	126
7.	Campbell	123
8.	Miami (FL)	122
9.	DBU	119
10.	South Carolina	117
10.	Stanford	117

DOUBLES

Rank	Team	2B
1.	Virginia	172
2.	Coastal Carolina	153
3.	Arizona	151
4.	Sam Houston	147
5.	Louisiana	145
5.	Oregon	145
5.	Stanford	145
8.	Oklahoma St.	144
9.	TCU	143
10.	Georgia Tech	142

TRIPLES

Rank	Team	3B
1.	Michigan St.	30
2.	Arizona	29
3.	Southern California	28
3.	UTSA	28
5.	Florida A&M	24
5.	New Mexico	24
5.	Utah Valley	24
8.	A&M-Corpus Christi	23
8.	Delaware	23
8.	Jackson St.	23
8.	UNLV	23

SLUGGING PERCENTAGE

Rank	Team	SLG
1.	FGCU	.592
2.	Campbell	.561
3.	Maryland	.561
4.	New Mexico	.560
5.	LSU	.554
6.	Arizona	.549
7.	Florida	.545
8.	DBU	.540
9.	Fairfield	.540
10.	Stanford	.539

STOLEN BASES

Rank	Team	SB
1.	VMI	192
2.	Louisiana	166
3.	George Mason	164
4.	Mississippi Val.	162
5.	Wofford	153
6.	TCU	141
7.	DBU	134
8.	Campbell	133
8.	Central Mich.	133
8.	Northeastern	133

WALKS

Rank	Team	BB
1.	Wake Forest	424
2.	LSU	413
3.	Texas A&M	405
4.	Maryland	385
5.	South Carolina	380
6.	Oregon St.	373
7.	Texas Tech	367
8.	Central Mich.	362
9.	Charlotte	356
10.	Campbell	351

COLLEGE

PITCHING

EARNED RUN AVERAGE

Rank	Team	ERA
1.	Wake Forest	2.83
2.	Tennessee	3.63
3.	Northeastern	3.75
4.	Virginia	3.81
5.	Indiana St.	3.84
6.	Lamar University	3.96
7.	Oral Roberts	4.03
8.	Penn	4.15
9.	William & Mary	4.17
10.	Texas	4.18
11.	Iowa	4.19
12.	South Carolina	4.19
13.	Kent St.	4.20
14.	UC Santa Barbara	4.20
15.	McNeese	4.26
16.	Alabama	4.26
17.	Vanderbilt	4.27
18.	Duke	4.29
19.	Clemson	4.30
20.	Kentucky	4.33
21.	East Carolina	4.34
22.	Rider	4.39
22.	UC Irvine	4.39
24.	Louisville	4.39
25.	Southern California	4.39
26.	DBU	4.40
27.	Wichita St.	4.41
28.	Long Beach St.	4.41
29.	Army West Point	4.41
30.	NC State	4.42
31.	Seton Hall	4.43
32.	LSU	4.47
33.	UCLA	4.50
34.	West Virginia	4.51
35.	Southern Miss.	4.51
36.	Elon	4.53
37.	Col. of Charleston	4.55
38.	Xavier	4.55
39.	Rutgers	4.55
40.	Santa Clara	4.57
41.	Campbell	4.58
42.	Alabama St.	4.58
43.	Nicholls	4.59
44.	Notre Dame	4.61
45.	Nebraska	4.64
46.	TCU	4.64
47.	North Carolina	4.65
48.	Florida	4.65
49.	Central Mich.	4.70
50.	Oregon St.	4.71

STRIKEOUTS PER NINE

Rank	Team	SO/9
1.	Wake Forest	12.1
2.	LSU	11.7
3.	Tennessee	11.7
4.	Miami (OH)	10.9
5.	Iowa	10.9
6.	Duke	10.8
7.	Oklahoma St.	10.7
8.	Mississippi St.	10.7
9.	Florida	10.6
10.	Penn	10.6

FEWEST WALKS PER NINE

Rank	Team	BB/9
1.	Wofford	2.38
2.	Wake Forest	2.83
3.	Elon	2.86
4.	Tennessee	2.90
5.	UC Irvine	3.11
6.	Indiana St.	3.11
7.	Northeastern	3.14
8.	Virginia	3.19
9.	Loyola Mary.	3.19
10.	New Mexico	3.20

FIELDING

FIELDING PERCENTAGE

Rank	Team	PCT
1.	Oral Roberts	.984
2.	Kentucky	.984
3.	Indiana St.	.983
4.	Creighton	.982
5.	Boston College	.982
6.	Oregon St.	.982
7.	Houston	.982
8.	Louisiana	.982
9.	Arkansas	.981
10.	New Orleans	.981
11.	Georgia	.981
12.	Abilene Christian	.981
13.	Iowa	.981
14.	Vanderbilt	.980
15.	Oklahoma St.	.980
16.	UIC	.980
17.	Binghamton	.979
18.	Virginia Tech	.979
19.	Texas	.979
20.	Ole Miss	.979
21.	Wake Forest	.979
22.	Charlotte	.979
23.	Illinois	.979
24.	Miami (FL)	.979
25.	Toledo	.979
26.	Southern Ill.	.979
27.	Samford	.979
28.	Alabama	.978
29.	VCU	.978
30.	DBU	.978
31.	UAB	.978
32.	Nebraska	.978
33.	TCU	.978
34.	Xavier	.978
35.	Mercer	.978
36.	San Diego	.978
37.	Wofford	.978
38.	East Carolina	.978
39.	Texas A&M	.978
40.	Virginia	.978
41.	Duke	.978
42.	SIUE	.978
43.	Yale	.978
44.	Auburn	.978
45.	Northeastern	.977
46.	Florida	.977
47.	Clemson	.977
48.	Notre Dame	.977
49.	Nicholls	.977
50.	UConn	.977

DOUBLE PLAYS

Rank	Team	DP
1.	Southern Ill.	61
1.	UNC Greensboro	61
3.	Coastal Carolina	58
4.	Eastern Ky.	57
5.	Houston	56
6.	Alabama	54
6.	Arkansas	54
6.	Delaware	54
6.	Rutgers	54
10.	Eastern Ill.	53
10.	Indiana St.	53
10.	New Orleans	53
10.	TCU	53

1. LOUISIANA STATE

Coach: Jay Johnson. **Record:** 54-17

Player, Pos., Year	AVG	OBP	SLG	AB	R	2B	3B	HR	RBI	SB
Crews, Dylan, OF, Jr	.426	.567	.713	258	100	16	2	18	70	6
White, Tommy, INF, So	.374	.432	.725	273	64	24	0	24	105	0
Travinski, Hayden, C, Jr	.356	.465	.692	104	30	5	0	10	30	2
Beloso, Cade, 1B, Sr	.324	.462	.622	185	43	5	1	16	49	2
Morgan, Tre', 1B, Jr	.316	.418	.502	269	66	15	4	9	53	0
Jones, Jared, C, Fr	.304	.426	.640	161	37	12	0	14	45	2
Jobert, Brayden, OF, Jr	.301	.409	.596	193	40	11	2	14	49	4
Dugas, Gavin, INF, Sr	.290	.464	.589	224	74	12	2	17	46	1
Kling, Paxton, OF, Fr	.289	.390	.522	90	29	5	2	4	9	3
Milazzo, Alex, C, Jr	.289	.369	.299	97	21	1	0	0	15	1
Frey, Ethan, C, Fr	.263	.348	.316	19	3	1	0	0	9	0
Thompson, Jordan, INF, Jr	.246	.365	.430	256	50	12	1	11	53	7
Pearson, Josh, OF, So	.226	.393	.387	137	30	4	3	4	27	1
Neal, Brady, C, Fr	.209	.411	.388	67	18	1	1	3	9	0
Nippolt, Ben, INF, Jr	.186	.362	.209	43	9	1	0	0	7	1
Guidry, Gavin, INF, Fr	.143	.333	.143	7	4	0	0	0	1	0
Paul, Mic, OF, Fr	.111	.200	.111	9	5	0	0	0	0	0
Stevenson, Josh, OF, So	.100	.100	.100	10	9	0	0	0	1	0
Merrifield, Jack, INF, Sr	.000	.250	.000	10	2	0	0	0	4	0

Pitcher, Year	W	L	ERA	G	GS	SV	IP	H	BB	SO
Moffett, Aiden, Fr	0	0	0.00	1	0	0	0	0	3	0
Skenes, Paul, Jr	13	2	1.69	19	19	0	123	72	20	209
Edwards, Garrett, Jr	4	0	1.93	10	0	1	23	16	5	27
Shores, Chase, Fr	0	1	1.96	7	4	0	18	15	9	15
Ackenhausen, Nate, Jr	2	1	3.52	17	2	2	31	25	14	36
Guidry, Gavin, Fr	3	0	3.77	23	1	3	29	23	12	42
Herring, Griffin, Fr	5	2	3.93	18	0	2	34	32	19	41
Floyd, Ty, Jr	7	0	4.35	19	17	1	91	70	37	120
Cooper, Riley, Jr	5	3	4.38	32	3	2	62	63	20	63
Hurd, Thatcher, So	8	2	5.68	23	11	3	63	59	40	84
Money, Blake, Jr	1	0	5.97	20	2	0	35	35	12	30
Coleman, Javen, So	1	2	7.07	8	4	0	14	10	16	21
Little, Christian, Jr	2	2	7.79	19	8	2	35	32	29	42
Dutton, Samuel, So	0	0	7.97	19	0	0	20	36	7	21
Hellmers, Will, Jr	0	0	9.00	7	0	0	11	10	9	14
Collins, Bryce, Jr	2	1	9.18	16	0	1	17	16	16	19
Bucknam, Micah, Fr	0	0	11.57	8	0	0	7	8	3	14

2. FLORIDA

Coach: Kevin O'Sullivan. **Record:** 54-17

Player, Pos., Year	AVG	OBP	SLG	AB	R	2B	3B	HR	RBI	SB
Langford, Wyatt, UT, Jr	.373	.498	.784	236	83	28	3	21	57	9
Rivera, Josh, INF, Jr	.348	.447	.617	256	70	10	1	19	72	18
Caglianone, Jac, UT, So	.323	.389	.738	282	74	14	2	33	90	4
Heyman, Luke, C, Fr	.314	.366	.555	191	30	6	2	12	39	1
Kurland, Cade, INF, Fr	.297	.404	.555	263	75	17	0	17	50	4
Fabian, Deric, INF, So	.289	.386	.447	38	9	0	0	2	10	5
Prevesk, Matt, OF, So	.286	.311	.405	42	5	2	0	1	9	0
Shelnut, Tyler, INF, Jr	.277	.371	.474	173	30	13	0	7	28	0
Thomas, Dale, INF, Jr	.250	.429	.438	48	12	4	1	1	4	0
Halter, Colby, INF, Jr	.247	.354	.397	174	29	9	4	3	30	9
Riopelle, BT, C, Sr	.246	.374	.546	240	57	11	2	19	68	5
Evans, Ty, OF, So	.239	.302	.485	163	30	9	2	9	43	2
Robertson, Michael, OF, Fr	.231	.360	.280	186	41	4	1	1	19	11
Schiekofer, Richie, OF, Sr	.189	.259	.264	53	13	1	0	1	5	2
Lastres, Rene, C, So	.188	.278	.312	16	3	0	1	0	3	0
Talbott, Tucker, OF, So	.000	.286	.000	5	5	0	0	0	0	1

Pitcher, Year	W	L	ERA	G	GS	SV	IP	H	BB	SO
Nesbitt, Tyler, So	1	0	2.96	11	3	0	24	27	10	21
Fisher, Cade, Fr	6	0	3.10	27	2	2	49	51	13	48
Abner, Philip, So	3	0	3.16	25	0	3	31	26	19	51
Neely, Brandon, So	2	3	3.58	34	0	13	55	46	22	72
Waldrep, Hurston, Jr	10	3	4.16	19	19	0	102	85	57	156
Slater, Ryan, So	10	1	4.22	27	3	3	60	55	19	48
Caglianone, Jac, So	7	4	4.34	18	18	0	75	51	55	87
Sproat, Brandon, Jr	8	3	4.66	19	19	0	106	87	48	134
Ficarrotta, Nick, So	0	0	4.99	21	0	2	40	46	11	43
Arroyo, Chris, Fr	1	0	5.06	7	0	0	5	2	7	6
Tejeda Jr., Yoel, Fr	2	0	5.56	8	6	0	23	26	12	11
Hartzog, Clete, Jr	1	0	8.53	7	1	0	6	7	6	12
Purnell, Blake, So	2	0	9.28	17	0	0	21	25	17	18
Jameson, Fisher, So	1	3	13.50	11	0	0	13	22	7	15
Ursitti, Anthony, So	0	0	20.25	3	0	0	1	3	1	2
Finnvold, Carsten, So	0	0	36.00	1	0	0	1	3	1	1

3. WAKE FOREST

Coach: Tom Walter. **Record:** 54-12

Player, Pos., Year	AVG	OBP	SLG	AB	R	2B	3B	HR	RBI	SB
Bennett, Pierce, INF, Jr	.353	.431	.523	235	61	19	0	7	65	1
Kurtz, Nick, OF, So	.353	.527	.784	190	76	10	0	24	69	5
Hawke, Tommy, INF, So	.351	.459	.506	271	73	19	1	7	35	14
Wilken, Brock, INF, Jr	.345	.506	.807	238	90	15	1	31	82	1
Johnson, Justin, INF, Sr	.324	.424	.618	238	60	16	3	16	76	7
Lee, Bennett, C, Jr	.303	.435	.472	142	30	3	0	7	34	5
Costello, Lucas, INF, Jr	.288	.402	.429	163	43	9	1	4	24	2
Corona, Danny, INF, So	.285	.360	.609	151	29	10	0	13	45	2
Cecere, Adam, OF, Jr	.284	.430	.574	141	40	11	0	10	37	1
Joye, Kyle, OF, Sr	.282	.391	.538	39	13	4	0	2	10	0
Houston, Marek, 0, Fr	.220	.328	.307	218	38	5	1	4	29	4
Winnay, Jack, INF, Fr	.211	.423	.211	19	5	0	0	0	1	1
Katz, Chris, C, So	.206	.346	.413	63	10	4	0	3	16	0
Noland, Andrew, INF, Fr	.200	.273	.200	10	1	0	0	0	1	0
Cueto, Gio, C, So	.192	.337	.321	78	14	4	0	2	8	0
Reinisch, Jake, INF, Jr	.178	.308	.192	73	8	1	0	0	9	1

Pitcher, Year	W	L	ERA	G	GS	SV	IP	H	BB	SO
Wade, Crawford, Jr	0	0	0.00	2	0	0	4	1	0	4
Andrews, Will, Jr	0	0	0.00	3	0	0	3	0	1	3
Lowder, Rhett, Jr	15	0	1.87	19	19	0	120	90	24	143
Roland, Cole, Sr	2	1	2.05	26	0	2	31	15	14	54
Sullivan, Sean, So	5	3	2.45	17	10	3	70	43	21	111
Massey, Michael, So	3	1	2.59	27	1	1	42	23	16	76
Keener, Seth, Jr	8	2	2.69	23	8	1	70	41	20	94
Minacci, Camden, Jr	0	1	2.78	30	0	13	32	26	10	46
Hartle, Josh, So	11	2	2.81	18	17	0	102	91	24	140
Crum, Derek, Jr	1	0	3.38	19	0	0	16	16	4	14
Walter, Chase, Sr	0	0	3.72	13	0	0	10	5	7	12
Mascolo, Reed, Jr	7	1	3.96	14	11	0	50	49	12	44
Ray, Will, So	1	1	5.40	18	0	0	12	6	9	9
Johnston, Zach, Fr	0	0	6.75	4	0	0	3	3	5	4
Ariola, Joe, Fr	0	0	6.75	17	0	0	13	15	8	17
Shenosky, Ben, Fr	0	0	11.57	6	0	0	5	2	8	8

4. TEXAS CHRISTIAN

Coach: Kirk Saarloos. **Record:** 44-24

Player, Pos., Year	AVG	OBP	SLG	AB	R	2B	3B	HR	RBI	SB
Fontenelle, Cole, INF, Jr	.352	.473	.639	233	66	21	2	14	58	20
Bowen, Karson, C, Fr	.350	.420	.502	217	49	15	0	6	46	9
Silva, Anthony, INF, Fr	.330	.416	.471	227	53	11	0	7	50	17
Richardson, Tre, INF, Jr	.311	.392	.452	270	58	16	2	6	60	25
Taylor, Brayden, INF, Jr	.308	.430	.631	260	77	15	0	23	70	14
Maxwell, Logan, OF, So	.300	.418	.460	100	20	6	2	2	18	4
Nunez, Elijah, OF, Jr	.289	.400	.414	239	59	17	2	3	36	20
Byrne, Kurtis, C, Jr	.285	.343	.487	193	34	9	0	10	48	0
Davis, Austin, OF, Sr	.283	.377	.470	247	48	19	0	9	57	22
Blackledge, Owen, INF, So	.250	.333	.500	4	0	1	0	0	1	0
Boyers, Luke, OF, Jr	.231	.401	.405	173	42	7	1	7	27	7
Duer, Jake, OF, Fr	.231	.333	.231	13	2	0	0	0	1	0
Bishop, David, INF, So	.214	.311	.325	117	20	5	1	2	17	3
Green, Brody, INF, So	.125	.222	.188	16	2	1	0	0	2	0
Ingersoll, Fisher, INF, Fr	.083	.294	.083	12	2	0	0	0	2	0
Speaker, Mason, UT, Jr	.000	.000	.000	1	0	0	0	0	0	0

Pitcher, Year	W	L	ERA	G	GS	SV	IP	H	BB	SO
Feser, Cohen, So	1	0	2.56	20	0	1	32	26	8	28

Pitcher, Year	W	L	ERA	G	GS	SV	IP	H	BB	SO
Hodges, Hunter, Jr	1	0	2.57	13	0	0	14	12	9	14
Wright, Garrett, Jr	3	2	3.41	21	0	5	29	17	16	36
Savage, Luke, Jr	6	4	3.43	18	1	2	39	33	15	27
Abeldt, Ben, Fr	3	4	3.60	32	1	2	55	49	24	71
Klecker, Kole, Fr	10	4	3.72	19	17	0	97	78	30	72
Stoutenborough, Sam, Sr	5	0	4.35	21	10	0	70	73	18	58
Rodriguez, Louis, Fr	2	1	4.53	17	5	3	48	50	12	49
Traeger, Jax, Fr	2	0	4.63	7	0	0	12	14	6	12
Hoover, Chase, Fr	1	1	5.14	13	4	0	35	33	26	34
Brown, Cam, Jr	3	2	5.20	16	12	0	55	40	40	62
Ridings, River, Jr	1	0	5.91	15	0	0	11	12	11	12
Speaker, Mason, Jr	0	0	6.46	14	0	0	15	18	9	17
Sloan, Braeden, Fr	2	3	6.63	11	10	0	38	44	14	28
Vanderhei, Ryan, Jr	4	3	6.75	13	8	0	43	44	25	43
Hackett, Justin, Fr	0	0	11.37	6	0	0	6	12	1	9
Marley, Calvin, So	0	0	81.00	3	0	0	1	2	5	1

5. TENNESSEE

Coach: Tony Vitello. **Record:** 44-22

Player, Pos., Year	AVG	OBP	SLG	AB	R	2B	3B	HR	RBI	SB
Miller, Ryan, C, So	.455	.647	1.364	11	8	1	0	3	9	0
Payne, Ethan, UT, Jr	.333	.467	.500	12	4	2	0	0	3	0
Dickey, Jared, OF, So	.328	.392	.525	244	55	6	3	12	52	7
Ahuna, Maui, INF, Jr	.312	.425	.537	205	43	20	1	8	42	4
Merritt, Griffin, OF, Sr	.311	.392	.648	193	42	11	0	18	48	2
Moore, Christian, INF, So	.304	.444	.603	214	66	13	0	17	50	16
Tears, Kavares, UT, Fr	.304	.379	.518	56	12	6	0	2	11	0
Dreiling, Dylan, OF, Fr	.295	.433	.621	95	20	6	2	7	20	1
Burke, Blake, 1B, So	.280	.369	.527	243	48	6	3	16	43	4
Ensley, Hunter, OF, So	.280	.391	.425	193	37	7	0	7	31	6
Denton, Zane, INF, Sr	.269	.403	.566	212	43	9	3	16	59	1
Scott, Christian, OF, Sr	.266	.396	.461	154	37	7	1	7	34	12
Chapman, Reese, OF, Fr	.263	.417	.579	19	7	0	0	2	7	1
Chambers, Logan, UT, So	.240	.441	.440	25	9	0	1	1	3	0
Booker, Kyle, OF, Jr	.236	.323	.345	55	9	3	0	1	4	2
Taylor, Charlie, C, So	.232	.346	.464	69	16	5	1	3	13	1
Kendro, Jake, INF, Fr	.219	.306	.438	32	6	4	0	1	6	0
Jaslove, Austen, INF, So	.189	.268	.243	37	8	2	0	0	8	1
Stark, Cal, C, Jr	.180	.365	.351	111	19	4	0	5	17	1

Pitcher, Year	W	L	ERA	G	GS	SV	IP	H	BB	SO
Behnke, Andrew, Fr	0	0	0.00	6	0	0	6	2	4	10
Russell, AJ, Fr	2	0	0.89	24	1	0	30	9	7	47
Fanning, Hollis, Jr	0	0	1.26	15	1	0	14	12	3	24
Sechrist, Zander, Jr	0	1	2.05	23	12	0	31	27	5	32
Lindsey, Andrew, Jr	3	4	2.90	21	9	0	71	60	19	73
Combs, Aaron, So	4	0	3.00	26	0	0	21	14	7	39
Connell, Kirby, Sr	1	0	3.52	33	0	0	15	11	4	17
Beam, Drew, So	9	4	3.63	17	17	0	84	88	23	88
Fitzgibbons, Jake, So	2	0	3.75	17	0	0	12	4	10	20
Halvorsen, Seth, Jr	3	3	3.81	25	1	2	52	39	16	52
Burns, Chase, So	5	3	4.25	18	8	2	72	60	22	114
Joyce, Zach, Jr	1	0	4.35	13	0	0	10	9	2	17
Sewell, Camden, Sr	4	0	4.68	15	0	0	25	21	14	32
Dollander, Chase, Jr	7	6	4.75	17	17	0	89	83	30	120
Bimbi, Jacob, Jr	2	0	5.27	15	0	0	14	14	9	22
Jenkins, Bryce, Jr	1	0	5.51	18	0	0	16	13	7	24
Garcia, JJ, Fr	0	0	5.79	4	0	0	5	8	1	7

6. STANFORD

Coach: David Esquer. **Record:** 44-20

Player, Pos., Year	AVG	OBP	SLG	AB	R	2B	3B	HR	RBI	SB
Troy, Tommy, INF, Jr	.394	.478	.699	249	76	17	4	17	58	17
Rios, Alberto, C, Jr	.384	.485	.707	242	69	24	0	18	73	5
Montgomery, Braden, UT, So	.336	.461	.611	244	70	14	1	17	61	6
Park, Eddie, OF, Jr	.333	.412	.475	276	68	19	1	6	47	7
Cobb, Owen, INF, Sr	.324	.368	.471	210	36	7	3	6	32	8
Becerra, Temo, INF, So	.316	.385	.491	57	12	4	0	2	7	1
Graham, Carter, INF, Jr	.315	.390	.558	276	61	22	0	15	77	9
Moore, Malcolm, C, Fr	.311	.386	.564	257	50	20	0	15	63	3
Sapien, Jake, UT, So	.301	.398	.473	93	16	5	1	3	16	0
Bowser, Drew, INF, Jr	.270	.342	.512	244	41	11	3	14	48	1
MacDonald, Cort, OF, Fr	.250	.400	.250	4	1	0	0	0	1	0
Campbell, Saborn, OF, So	.211	.297	.246	57	13	0	1	0	3	4
Saum, Charlie, C, So	.190	.370	.238	21	3	1	0	0	2	0
Hinkelman, Cole, OF, Sr	.188	.350	.375	32	4	0	0	2	10	0
Gargus, Henry, OF, Sr	.136	.208	.273	22	3	0	0	1	3	0
Nati, Jimmy, INF, Fr	.114	.226	.136	44	9	1	0	0	6	0
Haskins, Trevor, INF, So	.083	.154	.208	24	2	0	0	1	4	0
Blair, Brett, OF, So	.000	.000	.000	2	1	0	0	0	0	0

Pitcher, Year	W	L	ERA	G	GS	SV	IP	H	BB	SO
Swartz, Matt, Jr	0	0	0.00	1	0	0	0	1	0	0
Mathews, Quinn, Sr	10	4	3.75	19	18	0	125	116	40	158
Pancer, Brandt, Jr	3	1	4.18	32	1	5	47	50	15	44
Dowd, Drew, Jr	9	3	4.52	32	3	2	66	58	33	88
Dixon, Joey, Jr	7	0	4.73	21	14	0	84	73	43	90
Scott, Matt, Fr	5	5	5.10	24	12	1	67	59	37	62
Bruno, Ryan, Jr	2	2	5.29	30	0	9	34	21	36	56
Lopez, Nicolas, Sr	2	1	7.04	17	2	0	15	16	11	17
Dugan, Nick, Fr	1	0	7.30	24	7	1	62	79	29	63
Uber, Ty, So	1	0	9.86	13	3	0	21	27	20	20
Moore, Trevor, Fr	0	1	10.80	8	1	0	7	9	10	8
Meier, Max, Sr	2	0	11.57	17	0	0	19	29	11	21
O'Harran, Toran, Fr	1	1	11.65	17	1	0	17	21	20	25
Montgomery, Braden, So	1	2	12.21	10	2	0	14	20	11	19

7. ORAL ROBERTS

Coach: Ryan Folmar. **Record:** 52-14

Player, Pos., Year	AVG	OBP	SLG	AB	R	2B	3B	HR	RBI	SB
AWalls, Dawson, C, Fr	1.000	1.000	1.000	1	0	0	0	0	0	0
Cox, Jonah, UT, Jr	.412	.470	.646	277	69	16	8	11	68	28
Lucas, Max, INF, Jr	.364	.391	.455	22	1	2	0	0	2	0
Quinn, Justin, OF, Sr	.355	.432	.518	197	56	11	0	7	40	8
McMurray, Jake, INF, Sr	.326	.420	.449	276	59	14	1	6	47	2
Breeze, Holden, INF, Jr	.320	.410	.444	250	50	13	0	6	42	4
Hogan, Matt, OF, Sr	.320	.460	.662	222	61	13	3	19	72	9
McCroskey, Mac, INF, Sr	.314	.392	.520	271	67	10	2	14	64	17
Brothers, Blaze, INF, Sr	.297	.368	.542	236	64	18	2	12	41	22
Godman, Jacob, C, Sr	.291	.384	.454	196	41	13	2	5	29	3
Stahl, Drew, INF, Jr	.276	.393	.483	232	42	15	0	11	57	5
Thompson, Sam, OF, Jr	.273	.422	.500	66	19	4	1	3	9	0
Blackwell, Ryan, C, Jr	.250	.400	.350	20	4	2	0	0	2	0
Patten, Dalton, UT, So	.250	.400	.625	8	2	0	0	1	3	0
Wipperman, Dylan, INF, So	.250	.250	.250	8	1	0	0	0	0	0
Baumgartner, Preston, OF, Jr	.238	.370	.429	21	2	1	0	1	7	0
Casey, Garrett, C, Jr	.222	.349	.389	36	5	0	0	2	6	0
Ward, Parker, UT, So	.000	.500	.000	1	1	0	0	0	0	1

Pitcher, Year	W	L	ERA	G	GS	SV	IP	H	BB	SO
Denton, Cade, Jr	3	1	1.83	35	0	15	64	48	15	86
Allman, Price, So	0	0	2.08	5	0	0	4	5	2	0
Widener, Jacob, So	2	2	2.90	30	2	1	50	31	21	80
Floyd, Conner, Jr	1	0	3.00	3	0	0	3	1	3	7
Fowler, Brooks, So	9	2	3.26	17	17	0	80	66	32	78
Caravalho, Joshua, So	5	1	3.42	16	10	0	53	47	25	41
Hall, Jakob, So	8	3	3.56	18	18	0	99	93	17	94
Patten, Dalton, So	4	2	4.47	30	0	5	48	29	25	52
Gollert, Harley, Sr	10	2	4.65	18	17	0	91	87	32	94
Isaacs, Caleb, Jr	8	0	5.36	29	0	0	45	50	21	43
Kowalski, Evan, Sr	2	1	5.88	20	2	2	34	37	17	28
Hart, Hudson, Fr	0	0	10.38	5	0	0	4	6	6	4
Roach, Andrew, Sr	0	0	13.50	7	0	0	5	12	3	6
Ronan, Reed, Jr	0	0	27.00	5	0	0	3	7	8	2

8. VIRGINIA

Coach: Brian O'Connor. **Record:** 50-15

Player, Pos., Year	AVG	OBP	SLG	AB	R	2B	3B	HR	RBI	SB
Teel, Kyle, C, Jr	.407	.475	.655	258	67	25	0	13	69	5
O'Ferrall, Griff, INF, So	.396	.453	.495	273	76	20	2	1	42	16
Anderson, Ethan, C, So	.375	.469	.649	259	71	26	0	15	66	3
Hanson, Luke, INF, Fr	.356	.473	.422	45	16	3	0	0	9	0
O'Donnell, Ethan, OF, Jr	.354	.448	.587	254	71	18	1	13	57	18
Courtney, Tommy, OF, Sr	.333	.364	.444	9	1	1	0	0	3	0
Stephan, Anthony, INF, So	.329	.449	.519	158	38	13	1	5	35	4
Gelof, Jake, INF, Jr	.321	.427	.710	252	71	23	3	23	90	3

Player, Pos., Year	AVG	OBP	SLG	AB	R	2B	3B	HR	RBI	SB
Baker, Chris, OF, Sr	.312	.389	.438	32	4	4	0	0	12	0
Saucke, Casey, INF, So	.299	.392	.418	251	50	16	1	4	48	10
Godbout, Henry, INF, Fr	.286	.376	.413	189	37	13	1	3	38	9
Didawick, Harrison, OF, Fr	.252	.366	.428	159	44	6	5	4	34	10
Tuft, Colin, C, So	.234	.368	.298	94	20	3	0	1	17	5
Rubin, Justin, INF, So	.190	.310	.259	58	12	1	0	1	10	1
Reifsnider, Travis, C, Sr	.118	.375	.118	17	4	0	0	0	3	0
Buchanan, Matthew, P, So	.000	.000	.000	1	0	0	0	0	0	0
Hodges, Bradley, P, Fr	.000	.500	.000	1	0	0	0	0	0	0

Pitcher, Year	W	L	ERA	G	GS	SV	IP	H	BB	SO
Greene, Alex, Jr	0	0	0.00	2	0	0	2	1	1	2
Tonas, Angelo, Sr	4	0	2.25	21	0	0	20	20	4	21
Woolfolk, Jay, So	2	1	2.91	30	0	9	34	26	20	38
Blanco, Evan, Fr	1	0	3.04	24	0	0	24	18	10	26
Early, Connelly, Jr	12	3	3.09	19	18	0	87	82	23	100
Edgington, Brian, Sr	9	3	3.57	18	15	0	88	84	23	94
Parker, Nick, Sr	8	0	3.64	16	16	0	82	78	24	79
Jaxel, Kevin, Fr	2	0	3.75	23	0	0	24	26	5	30
McKay, Cullen, Fr	0	0	3.78	10	3	0	17	16	9	26
O'Connor, Jack, Fr	6	3	3.86	19	11	0	65	61	25	64
Berry, Jake, Jr	0	5	3.93	24	1	6	50	42	21	60
Hodges, Bradley, Fr	2	0	4.32	19	1	1	33	35	23	40
Hungate, Chase, Fr	3	0	5.76	16	0	0	25	28	4	21
Hodorovich, Jake, Sr	1	0	6.60	16	0	0	15	20	9	17
Buchanan, Matthew, So	0	0	12.46	5	0	0	4	8	0	4
Mabe, Avery, Jr	0	0	20.25	3	0	0	3	6	2	5

9. TEXAS

Coach: David Pierce. **Record:** 42-22

Player, Pos., Year	AVG	OBP	SLG	AB	R	2B	3B	HR	RBI	SB
Campbell, Dylan, INF, Jr	.339	.436	.603	242	65	19	3	13	50	26
Powell, Peyton, C, Jr	.339	.431	.548	230	52	16	1	10	46	2
Brown, Porter, OF, Jr	.323	.426	.545	235	46	14	1	12	59	11
Thomas, Jared, INF, Fr	.321	.398	.484	215	54	15	4	4	29	10
Carlson, Tanner, INF, Sr	.306	.408	.468	62	17	4	0	2	14	0
Kennedy, Eric, OF, Sr	.306	.378	.588	245	57	14	2	17	47	9
Belyeu, Max, OF, Fr	.300	.333	.350	20	3	1	0	0	2	0
Guillemette, Garrett, C, Jr	.298	.401	.541	218	43	18	1	11	60	0
O'Dowd, Jack, INF, Jr	.284	.353	.441	222	34	13	2	6	37	1
Duplantier, Jayden, INF, Fr	.256	.347	.326	43	12	3	0	0	7	0
Daly, Mitchell, INF, Jr	.231	.323	.403	186	29	9	1	7	22	4
Galvan, Rylan, C, Fr	.226	.356	.405	84	18	1	1	4	19	1
Constantine, Cam, OF, Jr	.200	.346	.400	20	4	1	0	1	2	1
Flores, Jalin, INF, Fr	.175	.293	.311	103	19	2	0	4	23	0
Whitehead, Ace, P, So	.111	.292	.111	18	2	0	0	0	7	3
Hoffart, Preston, C, Jr	.000	.400	.000	2	1	0	0	0	1	0
O'Hara, Cade, INF, Fr	.000	.111	.000	7	1	0	0	0	2	0

Pitcher, Year	W	L	ERA	G	GS	SV	IP	H	BB	SO
ABurke, DJ, Jr	1	0	2.22	15	2	1	24	20	10	17
Duplantier II, Andre, Jr	0	0	2.40	19	0	1	15	17	9	16
Gordon, Lucas, Jr	7	2	2.63	19	17	0	103	85	34	103
Johnson Jr., Lebarron, Jr	8	4	2.91	20	13	1	87	73	38	98
Shaw, David, Fr	2	2	3.09	26	0	1	32	22	14	30
Howard, Cody, Fr	1	0	4.00	8	0	0	9	10	7	12
Whitehead, Ace, So	4	0	4.10	16	4	1	26	31	12	24
Hurley, Charlie, Jr	5	0	4.42	22	5	3	55	48	27	45
Lummus, Chase, Jr	1	1	5.17	11	0	0	16	14	4	12
Morehouse, Zane, Jr	4	3	5.21	28	4	7	57	57	29	60
Minchey, Kobe, Fr	2	1	5.25	9	3	0	12	10	9	13
Sthele, Travis, Jr	3	5	5.75	15	10	1	61	65	31	66
Stuart, Chris, Jr	1	1	7.20	15	0	0	15	11	14	18
Walbridge, Sam, Jr	0	1	8.64	8	0	0	8	11	6	9
Grubbs, Max, Fr	1	0	9.35	8	0	0	9	13	3	6
Witt, Tanner, Jr	2	1	10.97	6	6	0	11	11	8	8
George, Pierce, Fr	0	0	13.50	3	0	0	2	2	4	1
O'Banan, Cameron, So	0	1	40.50	1	0	0	1	2	1	2

10. DUKE

Coach: Chris Pollard. **Record:** 39-24

Player, Pos., Year	AVG	OBP	SLG	AB	R	2B	3B	HR	RBI	SB
Beshears, Jay, UT, Jr	.333	.438	.586	237	58	15	0	15	56	5
Mooney, Alex, INF, So	.315	.434	.504	254	68	20	2	8	38	21
Stone, Alex, C, Jr	.315	.379	.579	254	53	16	0	17	62	0
Albright, Tyler, OF, Fr	.312	.408	.416	154	23	7	0	3	34	4
Santucci, Jonathan, UT, So	.300	.300	.700	10	2	1	0	1	3	0
Metz, MJ, 3B, Sr	.294	.410	.594	197	48	8	0	17	48	2
Fischer, Andrew, P, Fr	.289	.404	.595	173	38	12	4	11	33	1
DiGiacomo, Giovanni, OF, Sr	.268	.389	.411	190	36	9	0	6	36	19
Storm, Luke, INF, Jr	.258	.354	.492	236	54	14	1	13	51	8
Lux, Damon, OF, Sr	.254	.379	.446	213	39	11	0	10	45	10
DiGiacomo, Roman, C, Fr	.250	.500	1.000	4	3	0	0	1	4	0
Obee, Devin, OF, So	.232	.358	.500	56	14	4	1	3	10	0
Knight, Chad, C, Sr	.221	.299	.351	77	13	4	0	2	9	0
Hebble, Cole, INF, Sr	.195	.337	.299	77	12	2	0	2	10	1
Solomon, Josh, C, Sr	.121	.256	.121	33	14	0	0	0	2	3
Yu, Andrew, C, So	.091	.244	.121	33	5	1	0	0	6	1
Israel, Menelik, OF, So	.000	.333	.000	2	0	0	0	0	1	0
Romano, Jimmy, UT, So	.000	.143	.000	6	1	0	0	0	0	0

Pitcher, Year	W	L	ERA	G	GS	SV	IP	H	BB	SO
Oschell III, Fran, So	6	0	0.69	22	0	0	39	18	18	66
Tallon, James, Fr	1	1	1.64	23	0	12	33	22	11	54
Healy, Andrew, Fr	5	1	2.32	19	11	0	43	40	7	45
Thomas, Kassius, Fr	0	0	3.38	6	1	0	5	4	8	11
McRoy, Caleb, Sr	0	0	3.86	3	0	0	2	1	5	5
Beilenson, Charlie, Sr	6	3	3.86	39	0	0	61	56	21	78
Higgins, Ryan, So	3	1	4.04	18	10	0	42	34	15	32
Santucci, Jonathan, So	2	2	4.30	7	7	0	29	27	16	50
Proksch, Owen, Fr	4	3	4.50	33	0	0	42	36	21	44
Weaver, Aidan, Fr	3	3	4.86	24	3	0	33	30	22	36
Gow, Alex, Sr	3	4	4.95	17	17	0	64	54	28	69
Boucher, Adam, Jr	1	0	4.95	29	5	0	40	33	25	59
Nard, Gabriel, Fr	0	1	5.33	22	0	0	27	30	16	22
White, Jason, Sr	2	3	5.85	26	9	0	48	51	20	44
Romano, Jimmy, So	1	1	6.00	16	0	0	12	14	8	13
Beasley, Aaron, Sr	0	0	6.29	23	0	0	24	34	7	29
Hart, Edward, Fr	1	1	7.80	16	0	0	15	22	7	16
Bosley-Smith, Collin, Jr	0	0	9.00	3	0	0	2	1	2	2
Boisvert, David, So	0	0	81.00	1	0	0	0	3	1	0

11. INDIANA STATE

Coach: Mitch Hannahs. **Record:** 45-17

Player, Pos., Year	AVG	OBP	SLG	AB	R	2B	3B	HR	RBI	SB
Watson, Keegan, OF, Sr	.317	.457	.559	145	34	14	0	7	30	1
Pottinger, Adam, OF, Jr	.299	.449	.535	187	51	9	1	11	36	3
Diaz, Randal, INF, So	.297	.372	.502	249	47	15	3	10	36	4
Hernandez, Luis, C, So	.291	.379	.439	223	42	18	0	5	28	4
Gergely, Seth, OF, Sr	.288	.410	.409	198	35	9	0	5	29	10
Krupinski, Dom, INF, Fr	.273	.273	.636	11	3	1	0	1	3	0
Pereira, Jorge, INF, Jr	.267	.333	.333	15	5	1	0	0	6	0
Urdaneta, Josue, INF, Jr	.267	.358	.327	251	44	10	1	1	26	11
Brown, Henry, INF, So	.265	.333	.388	49	6	3	0	1	10	0
Magill, Grant, C, Jr	.262	.332	.354	206	23	13	0	2	38	4
Sears, Mike, INF, Jr	.261	.389	.563	222	46	10	0	19	62	2
Marx, Alex, C, So	.259	.286	.370	27	3	0	0	1	4	0
Hicks, Connor, C, Jr	.250	.294	.500	16	2	1	0	1	4	0
Rivera, Miguel, INF, Sr	.248	.366	.390	141	25	8	0	4	34	4
Stinson, Parker, OF, Jr	.207	.275	.385	135	25	7	1	5	25	1
Kido, Joe, INF, Jr	.182	.282	.212	33	8	1	0	0	8	0
Taylor, Jackson, INF, Jr	.071	.071	.071	14	2	0	0	0	1	0
Fowler, Jace, OF, Fr	.000	.000	.000	1	0	0	0	0	0	0

Pithcer, Year	W	L	ERA	G	GS	SV	IP	H	BB	SO
Holycross, Cameron, Jr	4	1	1.98	16	1	0	36	31	17	34
Davidson, Zach, Jr	4	1	2.50	20	3	2	36	30	16	56
Miller, Lane, Sr	7	0	2.77	11	11	0	62	51	14	38
Fenlong, Connor, Sr	11	3	3.45	17	16	0	115	93	31	76
Gregersen, Simon, Jr	1	1	3.60	15	2	2	25	22	3	23
Edmonson, Cameron, Jr	3	0	3.72	19	2	0	36	34	15	42
Cutts, Brennyn, So	1	3	3.74	18	8	2	43	35	19	44
Spencer, Jared, So	3	2	3.86	25	0	7	37	27	20	51
Jachec, Matt, Jr	7	4	4.05	17	16	1	104	101	17	104
Cortner, Kyle, So	0	0	5.40	9	1	0	8	9	4	4
Patzner, Luke, Jr	0	0	6.14	4	0	1	7	4	5	6
Lybarger, Brayden, Fr	1	1	6.75	4	1	0	7	6	8	8

Pitcher, Year	W	L	ERA	G	GS	SV	IP	H	BB	SO
Pruitt, Jacob, Fr	2	1	7.17	14	1	0	21	26	10	25
Gilley, Cole, Jr	0	0	8.31	6	0	0	9	13	9	10
Moss, Aaron, So	0	0	9.00	5	0	0	5	6	4	6
Hurth, Joey, Jr	0	0	9.53	5	0	0	6	6	1	7

12. SOUTHERN MISSISSIPPI

Coach: Scott Berry. **Record:** 46-20

Player, Pos., Year	AVG	OBP	SLG	AB	R	2B	3B	HR	RBI	SB
Montenegro, Rodrigo, C, Jr.	.375	.507	.433	104	21	6	0	0	16	1
Fowler, Bryce, OF, Fr	.333	.600	.333	3	4	0	0	0	1	1
Dickerson, Dustin, INF, Jr	.328	.419	.552	268	58	21	3	11	52	14
Monistere, Nick, P, Fr	.320	.422	.523	128	29	9	1	5	28	6
Etzel, Matthew, OF, Jr	.317	.381	.472	284	55	17	3	7	51	23
Parker, Tate, OF, Jr	.316	.426	.462	117	19	6	1	3	18	1
Faust, Brady, INF, Jr	.308	.308	.462	13	7	2	0	0	3	3
Wilks, Slade, OF, Jr	.289	.377	.594	249	50	12	2	20	58	1
Paetow, Carson, OF, So	.269	.365	.421	197	34	12	3	4	36	5
Johnson, Blake, C, Sr	.258	.391	.438	128	27	8	0	5	16	0
Lynch, Danny, INF, Sr	.253	.403	.493	225	51	15	0	13	53	0
Sargent, Christopher, 1B, Sr.	.248	.317	.465	254	47	11	1	14	46	4
Ewing, Reece, OF, Sr	.247	.406	.400	170	36	11	0	5	31	1
Robertson, Creek, INF, Fr	.182	.349	.242	66	14	1	0	1	9	0
Lacy, Gabe, INF, Sr	.167	.286	.167	24	2	0	0	0	3	1
Russo, Matthew, INF, Fr	.158	.273	.263	19	2	2	0	0	1	0
Artigues, Casey, INF, Fr	.000	.000	.000	2	2	0	0	0	0	0
Crawford, Graham, C, Jr	.000	.000	.000	8	0	0	0	0	0	0

Pitcher, Year	W	L	ERA	G	GS	SV	IP	H	BB	SO
Armistead, Will, So	2	0	2.09	16	4	2	43	35	16	43
Storm, Justin, Jr	7	2	2.36	29	0	8	46	26	17	72
Hall, Tanner, Jr	12	4	2.48	18	18	0	112	84	33	124
Sivley, Kros, Fr	4	1	3.70	26	1	4	58	61	10	59
Monistere, Nick, Fr	1	0	4.00	9	0	1	9	10	5	10
Oldham, Billy, Jr	8	3	4.21	18	13	1	77	65	23	89
Mazza, Niko, So	5	2	4.34	21	13	2	75	66	46	89
Adams, Matt, Jr	3	2	4.86	15	14	0	63	64	22	72
Dawson, Chandler, Jr	0	0	5.59	13	0	1	19	22	9	15
Adams, Chase, Fr	1	0	6.75	7	0	0	7	6	5	8
Trahan, Luke, Jr	0	0	6.75	10	0	0	12	9	6	10
Middleton, JB, Fr	0	3	8.68	8	1	0	9	10	4	11
Dickerson, Dustin, Jr	0	0	9.00	1	0	0	1	3	0	2
Rhodes, Isaiah, Jr	3	2	10.12	14	0	0	19	22	15	23
Allen, Colby, Fr	0	1	11.57	12	1	0	14	22	4	15
Martin, Tyler, Sr	0	0	12.66	10	1	0	11	11	13	9
Parker, Jackson, Fr	0	0	16.88	4	0	0	3	5	4	2
Townes, Holland, Jr	0	0	27.00	5	0	0	3	3	10	1

13. OREGON

Coach: Mark Wasikowski. **Record:** 41-22

Player, Pos., Year	AVG	OBP	SLG	AB	R	2B	3B	HR	RBI	SB
Smith, Drew, INF, Fr	.365	.430	.552	96	14	5	2	3	18	6
Cowley, Drew, INF, Sr	.341	.425	.631	249	64	22	1	16	70	6
Thompson, Bennett, C, So	.340	.402	.613	106	21	15	1	4	22	2
Shade, Colby, OF, Jr	.336	.422	.523	214	55	16	3	6	31	14
Ceballos, Sabin, INF, Jr	.333	.426	.643	213	48	10	1	18	70	0
Smith, Tanner, OF, Sr	.327	.391	.551	245	50	20	1	11	45	7
Nishida, Rikuu, INF, Jr	.312	.394	.443	253	67	16	1	5	37	25
Jaha, Jackson, INF, Fr	.286	.333	.357	14	3	1	0	0	0	0
Grant, Gavin, INF, Sr	.275	.376	.464	207	39	13	1	8	29	9
Garate, Carter, INF, Fr	.267	.333	.500	30	5	1	0	2	8	0
Aroz, Anson, C, Fr	.265	.324	.382	34	3	1	0	1	7	1
Hellman, Dominic, INF, Fr	.250	.333	.375	32	8	1	0	1	5	0
Cromwick, Josiah, C, Jr	.248	.310	.514	105	16	7	0	7	23	3
Walsh, Jacob, 1B, So	.241	.302	.500	232	36	12	0	16	37	0
Ganus, Tyler, UT, Jr	.222	.364	.222	9	5	0	0	0	0	0
Boettcher, Bryce, OF, Jr	.200	.385	.360	50	12	2	0	2	6	7
Diodati, Owen, OF, Jr	.145	.226	.255	55	3	3	0	1	5	0
Hensley, Tafton, INF, Jr	.000	.000	.000	1	0	0	0	0	0	0
King, Towns, UT, Sr	.000	.077	.000	12	1	0	0	0	0	0
Lytle, Mason, OF, Jr	.000	.167	.000	5	1	0	0	0	0	0
Meggers, Chase, C, Fr	.000	.000	.000	5	0	0	0	0	0	0

Pitcher, Year	W	L	ERA	G	GS	SV	IP	H	BB	SO
Umlandt, Ian, Fr	1	0	2.60	17	0	0	17	21	5	9
Stoffal, Jace, Jr	6	2	2.83	10	10	0	57	37	23	56
Mollerus, Josh, Sr	3	3	3.44	28	0	11	37	27	18	50
Hughes, Jacob, So	0	0	4.15	13	0	0	13	6	22	14
Olson, Logan, Fr	0	0	4.26	8	0	0	6	6	12	6
Grinsell, Grayson, Fr	2	1	4.47	30	3	1	48	41	26	67
Grabmann, Matthew, Fr	1	3	4.60	17	10	0	47	40	30	37
Dallas, Matt, Sr	6	2	5.06	31	0	3	53	43	18	41
Mercado, Logan, Jr	5	1	5.95	21	11	1	82	85	51	78
Spoljaric, Turner, Fr	7	0	6.55	17	8	0	55	71	23	32
Uelmen, Leo, Fr	3	4	7.43	14	10	0	46	57	28	34
Jaha, Jackson, Fr	0	0	7.71	2	0	0	2	2	2	1
Pace, Jackson, Fr	2	4	8.67	15	11	0	46	61	26	26
McShane, Dylan, Fr	1	2	9.00	21	0	0	21	21	12	13
Rogers, Gus, Fr	0	0	40.50	1	0	0	1	4	0	2

14. VANDERBILT

Coach: Tim Corbin. **Record:** 42-20

Player, Pos., Year	AVG	OBP	SLG	AB	R	2B	3B	HR	RBI	SB
Rogers, JD, OF, So	.333	.429	.333	6	3	0	0	0	1	0
Maldonado, Chris, INF, Fr	.310	.411	.542	155	28	12	0	8	32	2
Schreck, R.J., OF, Sr	.306	.454	.588	216	53	15	2	14	59	6
Vastine, Jonathan, INF, So	.287	.355	.448	230	45	18	2	5	34	5
Polk, Matthew, UT, So	.280	.353	.427	150	29	8	1	4	23	4
Bradfield Jr., Enrique, OF, Jr.	.279	.410	.429	233	69	13	2	6	34	37
Noland, Parker, INF, Sr	.277	.367	.455	231	36	12	1	9	39	0
Espinal, Alan, C, Jr	.275	.359	.495	91	20	5	0	5	21	1
Diaz, Davis, INF, So	.263	.376	.415	236	56	7	1	9	57	2
LaNeve, Troy, OF, Sr	.262	.326	.500	42	6	1	0	3	14	0
Austin, RJ, UT, Fr	.257	.351	.390	241	40	11	0	7	43	4
Hewett, Calvin, OF, Jr	.243	.329	.324	74	20	4	1	0	8	11
Bulger, Jack, UT, Jr	.240	.348	.370	154	28	5	0	5	30	3
McKenzie, T.J., INF, Sr	.222	.300	.389	36	5	3	0	1	2	1
Arias, Ivan, INF, Fr	.000	.333	.000	2	0	0	0	0	0	0

Pitcher, Year	W	L	ERA	G	GS	SV	IP	H	BB	SO
Maldonado, Nick, Sr	1	1	1.45	22	0	8	31	14	7	40
Dutkanych IV, Andrew, Fr	1	0	2.84	4	1	0	6	4	9	6
Moore, Grayson, Jr	1	0	3.08	12	2	0	26	20	10	36
Futrell, Devin, So	8	3	3.44	16	15	0	84	71	20	72
Owen, Hunter, Jr	4	0	3.52	12	12	0	64	52	17	76
Anderson, Jack, Sr	2	0	3.97	9	0	0	11	5	13	16
Ginther, Ryan, So	2	1	4.01	21	1	0	34	26	13	34
Schultz, Thomas, Sr	2	2	4.05	21	1	2	33	33	10	37
Carter, Greysen, So	2	1	4.08	13	7	0	29	16	28	23
Holton, Carter, So	4	1	4.11	11	11	0	50	40	24	56
Hliboki, Sam, Sr	3	3	4.88	19	3	0	48	45	12	49
Horn, David, Fr	3	0	5.40	8	0	0	15	11	13	17
Thompson, JD, Fr	2	0	5.73	13	1	0	22	22	13	23
Reilly, Patrick, Jr	5	4	5.77	16	4	0	48	44	30	65
Cunningham , Bryce, So	2	3	6.43	18	4	2	42	35	23	45
Regen, Colton, So	0	0	14.73	4	0	0	4	4	9	5

15. CLEMSON

Coach: Erik Bakich. **Record:** 44-19

Player, Pos. Year	AVG	OBP	SLG	AB	R	2B	3B	HR	RBI	SB
Amick, Billy, INF, So	.413	.464	.772	167	37	17	2	13	63	2
Cannarella, Cam, OF, Fr	.388	.462	.560	250	72	16	3	7	47	24
Taylor, Will, OF, So	.362	.489	.523	218	67	16	2	5	46	11
Ingle, Cooper, UT, Jr	.328	.417	.461	256	60	16	0	6	34	1
Grice, Caden, UT, Jr	.307	.411	.618	228	60	15	1	18	68	4
Blackwell, Benjamin, INF, Sr.	.301	.384	.386	236	36	10	2	2	31	27
Bertram, Riley, INF, Sr	.282	.396	.348	227	38	12	0	1	44	18
Wright, Blake, INF, Jr	.250	.326	.401	232	36	11	0	8	45	7
Hall, Nathan, OF, Fr	.243	.321	.324	74	10	3	0	1	12	3
Crighton, Jack, OF, Fr	.239	.311	.284	67	10	3	0	0	3	4
Fairey, Chad, UT, Jr	.237	.361	.356	59	12	4	0	1	8	1
Abrams, Gavin, OF, So	.231	.394	.462	26	4	1	1	1	4	0
Jarrell, Jacob, C, Fr	.208	.296	.406	101	15	5	0	5	18	1
Olenchuk, Ty, UT, Jr	.200	.200	.200	5	0	0	0	0	1	0
Bissetta, Tristan, OF, Fr	.154	.214	.231	13	0	1	0	0	1	0
Corbitt, Tyler, OF, Sr	.148	.281	.185	27	4	1	0	0	1	0
Starbuck, Mac, INF, Jr	.125	.364	.188	16	2	1	0	0	1	0
Lackey, Lleyton, OF, Fr	.000	.222	.000	7	3	0	0	0	0	0

Pitcher, Year	W	L	ERA	G	GS	SV	IP	H	BB	SO
Garris, Reed, So	4	0	2.12	27	0	0	30	19	13	39
Lindley, Jackson, Sr	3	3	2.73	21	1	2	33	31	14	33
Clayton, Nick, Jr	8	0	3.17	24	0	0	48	35	27	53
Grice, Caden, Jr	8	1	3.35	14	14	0	78	54	33	101
Tallent, Casey, So	1	1	3.43	16	1	1	21	22	10	19
Allen, Joe, Fr	3	0	3.94	17	4	1	30	33	15	33
Olenchuk, Ty, Jr	1	0	3.97	17	1	0	23	27	10	18
Bailey, B.J., Jr	2	2	4.02	17	0	0	16	18	6	20
Ammons, Ryan, Jr	2	0	4.05	13	2	5	20	17	8	26
Smith, Tristan, Fr	0	1	4.55	24	6	4	32	24	25	43
Gordon, Austin, So	2	4	4.61	16	16	0	84	77	22	76
Darden, Ethan, Fr	3	2	5.53	19	12	0	55	60	23	45
Hoffmann, Nick, Jr	3	1	6.58	17	0	1	26	36	9	18
Weiss, Willie, Sr	2	0	7.00	14	0	0	9	11	10	13
Barlow, Billy, So	0	1	8.10	3	1	0	3	6	0	3
Reid, Rocco, So	0	1	8.10	16	2	0	17	24	14	22
Dill, Jay, So	1	1	8.47	11	3	0	17	21	10	18
Dvorsky, Nathan, Fr	1	0	12.00	3	0	0	3	4	3	3

16. ARKANSAS

Coach: Dave Van Horn. **Record:** 43-18

Player, Pos., Year	AVG	OBP	SLG	AB	R	2B	3B	HR	RBI	SB
McLaughlin, Ben, UT, Jr	.346	.442	.487	78	12	3	1	2	14	0
Bohrofen, Jace, OF, Jr	.318	.436	.612	214	54	15	0	16	52	7
Wegner, Jared, OF, Sr	.313	.457	.673	147	46	4	2	15	51	3
Cali, Caleb, INF, Jr	.308	.412	.512	172	38	8	0	9	37	3
Diggs, Kendall, UT, So	.299	.436	.547	201	51	12	1	12	63	1
Josenberger, Tavian, OF, Jr	.286	.414	.490	192	51	9	0	10	33	13
Slavens, Brady, INF, Sr	.277	.340	.488	213	42	14	2	9	42	7
Stovall, Peyton, INF, So	.253	.330	.393	150	30	4	1	5	31	3
Robinett, Reese, INF, Fr	.240	.269	.480	25	7	0	0	2	7	0
Coll, Harold, INF, Jr	.232	.301	.463	82	15	7	0	4	22	1
Bolton, John, INF, Sr	.206	.358	.248	141	32	6	0	0	19	7
Jones, Jayson, INF, Fr	.196	.403	.370	46	12	2	0	2	6	2
Polk, Hudson, C, Jr	.190	.342	.310	58	10	1	0	2	7	0
Grimes, Hunter, UT, Jr	.185	.368	.259	27	9	0	1	0	7	0
Rowland, Parker, C, Jr	.182	.293	.238	143	21	2	0	2	19	0
Neville, Mason, OF, Fr	.111	.250	.148	27	8	1	0	0	2	0

Pitcher, Year	W	L	ERA	G	GS	SV	IP	H	BB	SO
Fitzpatrick, Sean, Fr	0	0	0.00	3	0	0	3	5	2	5
Frank, Koty, Sr	0	0	3.09	6	0	0	12	9	1	9
Tygart, Brady, So	3	1	3.20	10	6	1	25	15	8	31
Smith, Hagen, So	8	2	3.64	18	11	2	72	56	42	109
Carter, Dylan, So	6	0	3.65	16	0	2	37	37	11	26
Hollan, Hunter, Jr	8	2	4.13	17	15	1	81	82	29	74
Wood, Gage, Fr	2	0	4.80	23	0	5	30	21	23	42
McEntire, Will, Jr	8	3	5.07	21	10	2	87	92	29	83
Adcock, Cody, Jr	4	2	5.88	26	8	1	52	47	25	46
Coil, Parker, Fr	0	1	6.55	15	3	1	22	31	9	19
Ledbetter, Austin, So	0	1	7.09	15	0	1	33	50	13	23
Bybee, Ben, Fr	2	1	7.24	15	7	0	27	32	24	29
Morris, Zack, Sr	1	4	7.64	18	1	2	33	39	18	39
Foutch, Christian, Fr	1	0	8.76	14	0	0	12	14	12	9
McLaughlin, Ben, Jr	0	1	16.88	3	0	0	3	5	4	4
Dossett, Cooper, Fr	0	0	21.60	2	0	0	2	2	4	3
Faherty, Jake, So	0	0	40.50	1	0	0	1	0	3	1

17. SOUTH CAROLINA

Coach: Mark Kingston. **Record:** 42-21

Player, Pos., Year	AVG	OBP	SLG	AB	R	2B	3B	HR	RBI	SB
Cromer, David, OF, So	.500	.600	.500	4	0	0	0	0	2	0
Veach, Chris, UT, Jr	.500	.500	.500	4	2	0	0	0	0	0
Petry, Ethan, UT, Fr	.376	.471	.733	221	55	10	0	23	75	4
McGillis, Will, INF, Sr	.313	.469	.798	99	29	4	1	14	30	2
Messina, Cole, C, So	.307	.428	.615	231	62	18	1	17	65	8
Wimmer, Braylen, SS, Sr	.304	.409	.561	214	64	11	1	14	42	13
LeCroy, Talmadge, C, So	.289	.430	.422	180	39	10	1	4	42	0
Casas, Gavin, INF, Jr	.259	.407	.569	216	60	10	0	19	56	0
Braswell, Michael, SS, So	.255	.372	.353	153	21	8	2	1	23	1
Hornung, Carson, OF, So	.248	.464	.393	117	24	5	0	4	27	1
Brewer, Dylan, OF, Sr	.240	.394	.415	171	48	6	0	8	27	11
Denny, Caleb, OF, Jr	.224	.343	.381	147	28	9	1	4	33	9
French, Jonathan, C, Jr	.218	.371	.346	78	12	4	0	2	11	0
Stone, Evan, OF, So	.207	.371	.315	111	30	3	0	3	18	5
Tippett, Will, INF, Fr	.182	.305	.291	110	16	1	1	3	15	4
Madden, Kevin, INF, Sr	.100	.182	.400	10	1	0	0	1	3	0

Pitcher, Year	W	L	ERA	G	GS	SV	IP	H	BB	SO
Jerzembeck, Eli, Fr	0	1	2.84	16	3	0	32	29	6	36
Williamson, Austin, Fr	1	0	3.05	18	0	0	21	16	7	25
Hall, Noah, Sr	5	1	3.29	7	7	0	41	38	9	43
Veach, Chris, Jr	2	1	3.46	20	0	6	26	16	15	32
Hicks, James, Sr	8	1	3.48	25	6	2	67	59	14	56
Proctor, Nick, Sr	5	0	3.86	23	0	1	26	26	7	33
Jones, Eli, So	4	5	3.95	22	6	0	55	55	17	63
Mahoney, Jack, Jr	7	4	4.16	17	17	0	84	86	29	84
Austin, Cade, So	1	0	4.55	23	1	2	30	28	9	38
Becker, Matthew, So	4	3	4.83	18	11	1	54	50	26	71
Phipps, Jackson, Jr	0	0	4.91	9	0	0	7	8	9	11
Thomas, Brett, Sr	0	0	5.14	6	0	0	7	6	9	11
Sanders, Will, Jr	4	4	5.46	14	11	1	63	58	26	77
McCreery, Connor, Fr	0	0	6.00	4	0	0	3	3	4	2
Simpson, Sam, Fr	0	0	6.75	5	1	0	4	3	5	5
Sweatt, Wesley, Sr	0	0	6.75	10	0	0	9	13	3	10
Wheeler, Trey, Fr	0	0	7.71	3	0	0	2	4	2	2
Eskew, Dylan, So	0	1	8.22	5	0	0	8	10	7	6

18. ALABAMA

Coach: Brad Bohanon/Jason Jackson. **Record:** 43-21

Player, Pos., Year	AVG	OBP	SLG	AB	R	2B	3B	HR	RBI	SB
Pinckney, Andrew, OF, Jr	.339	.442	.648	233	55	12	3	18	58	8
Swinney, Mason, INF, Fr	.333	.571	.444	9	3	1	0	0	0	0
Williams, Max, OF, Fr	.320	.452	.440	25	4	3	0	0	7	1
Johnson, Ed, INF, Sr	.315	.426	.455	200	38	8	1	6	42	5
Williamson, Drew, INF, Sr	.304	.411	.519	237	43	6	0	15	59	3
Shelton, Colby, INF, Fr	.300	.419	.729	203	49	10	1	25	51	0
Tamez, Dominic, C, Sr	.289	.376	.445	173	26	10	1	5	35	0
Hodo, Will, INF, So	.280	.411	.420	100	20	2	0	4	21	0
Jarvis, Jim, INF, Sr	.273	.379	.418	249	65	10	4	6	30	9
Eblin, Bryce, INF, Jr	.268	.333	.378	82	16	3	0	2	17	1
Rose, Caden, OF, Jr	.261	.383	.503	153	45	10	0	9	26	9
Guscette, Mac, C, Jr	.260	.345	.479	146	28	5	0	9	34	0
Hamiter, William, OF, Sr	.215	.356	.405	79	20	5	2	2	19	2
Hayslip, Camden, OF, So	.211	.286	.368	19	4	0	0	1	6	0
Portera, Will, C, So	.208	.321	.292	24	9	2	0	0	1	1
West, Jaxson, C, Fr	.185	.371	.333	27	6	1	0	1	5	0
Guardino, Ryan, OF, Sr	.167	.500	.333	6	4	1	0	0	0	0

Pitcher, Year	W	L	ERA	G	GS	SV	IP	H	BB	SO
Leger, Jake, Sr	0	0	0.00	3	0	0	2	2	3	1
Gainey, Brayden, Sr	0	0	2.79	6	1	0	10	10	5	8
Moza, Aidan, So	3	1	3.09	14	0	0	23	18	9	23
Hess, Ben, So	4	0	3.22	7	7	0	36	28	8	49
Banks, Hagan, So	1	1	3.48	16	2	0	34	22	7	37
Hoopes, Hunter, Sr	2	1	3.65	9	0	1	12	10	7	11
Holman, Luke, So	7	4	3.67	16	15	0	81	54	31	87
Quick, Riley, Fr	1	1	3.68	16	0	2	22	21	21	26
Probst, Zane, Jr	2	1	4.08	19	0	0	18	16	13	22
Hitt, Grayson, Jr	3	1	4.19	8	8	0	39	29	25	49
McNairy, Jacob, Sr	7	3	4.35	17	17	0	81	85	22	86
Blatter, Brock, Fr	1	0	4.50	6	0	0	8	7	8	12
Furtado, Hunter, Jr	1	1	4.75	17	2	0	36	31	17	38
McMillan, Garrett, Sr	4	2	4.89	10	9	0	42	38	17	36
Davis II, Alton, Fr	1	2	5.35	25	0	8	34	34	12	32
Ball, Connor, So	1	1	5.40	11	0	0	13	16	4	12
Woods, Kade, Fr	4	1	5.52	17	1	1	29	23	15	38
Myers, Braylon, So	0	1	5.53	17	0	3	28	24	9	22
Reynolds, Jackson, Sr	1	0	5.62	3	2	0	8	11	3	4

19. KENTUCKY

Coach: Nick Mingione. **Record:** 40-21

Player, Pos., Year	AVG	OBP	SLG	AB	R	2B	3B	HR	RBI	SB
Herrera, Patrick, INF, So	.375	.375	.375	8	5	0	0	0	0	0
Gray, Jackson, OF, Sr	.338	.491	.543	219	70	15	6	6	33	19

Gilliam, Hunter, INF, Sr	.324	.414	.551	225	46	13	1	12	71	1
Pitre, Émilien, INF, So	.318	.440	.413	223	51	16	1	1	51	20
Felker, Jase, INF, Sr	.292	.430	.354	192	53	6	3	0	29	21
Burkes, Devin, C, So	.291	.423	.502	223	55	18	1	9	53	9
McCarthy, Nolan, UT, So	.290	.351	.457	138	21	9	1	4	28	1
Waldschmidt, Ryan, INF, So	.290	.427	.445	200	38	14	1	5	37	17
Church, Reuben, INF, Jr	.286	.427	.418	91	18	3	0	3	20	0
Smith, Grant, INF, Sr	.281	.380	.448	192	37	8	0	8	30	2
McCoy, James, INF, Fr	.228	.349	.433	127	23	9	1	5	23	2
Ewell, Kendal, OF, Jr	.189	.333	.216	37	3	1	0	0	1	1
Stanke, Chase, C, Sr	.179	.382	.269	67	11	3	0	1	11	0
Byars, Isaiah, INF, Sr	.111	.167	.148	27	2	1	0	0	2	1
Giles, Ryder, UT, Sr	.000	.000	.000	2	0	0	0	0	0	0

Pitcher, Year	W	L	ERA	G	GS	SV	IP	H	BB	SO
Gannon, Reed, Fr	0	0	0.00	1	0	0	0	0	2	0
McCoy, James, Fr	0	0	0.00	2	0	0	2	2	0	2
Byers, Evan, So	1	0	1.65	24	0	0	16	12	8	14
Moore, Mason, So	4	1	1.80	22	0	4	55	31	30	54
Frieda, Colby, So	0	0	2.57	9	1	0	7	5	7	9
Hagenow, Ryan, Jr	3	1	3.91	20	0	1	25	25	9	34
Giles, Ryder, Sr	1	1	3.93	25	0	1	18	18	4	14
Williams, Darren, Sr	4	2	4.26	17	6	2	63	56	24	61
Lee, Zack, Sr	5	4	4.29	16	15	0	71	67	27	79
Chavez, Seth, Jr	2	1	4.35	12	0	1	10	10	5	15
Nove, Jackson, So	3	0	4.43	18	0	0	22	21	14	26
Martin, Logan, Sr	1	1	4.44	9	8	0	26	20	17	30
Smith, Travis, Fr	4	3	4.84	13	13	0	48	40	26	43
Strickland, Austin, Jr	4	2	5.04	20	3	1	55	48	20	58
Bosma, Tyler, Sr	4	4	5.61	13	13	0	51	55	22	35
Howe, Christian, Fr	1	0	5.62	7	0	0	8	8	6	8
Logue, Seth, Jr	1	0	6.00	13	1	0	15	19	7	18
Cotto, Magdiel, Jr	1	0	6.00	16	0	0	18	18	9	26
Hise, Zach, So	1	1	7.11	10	1	1	13	11	8	11

20. COASTAL CAROLINA

Coach: Gary Gilmore. **Record:** 42-21

Player, Pos., Year	AVG	OBP	SLG	AB	R	2B	3B	HR	RBI	SB
Bodine, Caden, C, Fr	.367	.456	.609	215	65	17	1	11	47	1
Bender, Derek, C, So	.341	.399	.635	252	61	13	2	19	83	2
Beach, Zack, INF, Sr	.321	.458	.613	168	48	10	0	13	56	3
Books, Jake, INF, Fr	.311	.405	.459	61	11	3	0	2	15	1
Barthol, Blake, INF, Fr	.308	.424	.572	159	41	13	4	7	32	4
Lucky, Nick, OF, Sr	.307	.441	.570	228	62	19	1	13	58	19
Born, Chad, OF, So	.297	.406	.459	172	48	10	0	6	36	2
Dooley, Ty, INF, So	.281	.350	.416	178	32	6	0	6	37	3
Brown, Graham, OF, Sr	.278	.377	.573	255	71	24	0	17	71	8
Garrison, Tanner, C, Sr	.275	.396	.588	80	23	7	0	6	20	1
Galason, Anthony, OF, Sr	.267	.410	.333	30	6	2	0	0	11	0
Mihos, Dean, INF, Fr	.246	.338	.348	69	16	7	0	0	15	2
Guangorena, Kameron, C, Sr	.244	.320	.422	45	8	2	0	2	7	0
Pena, Orlando, INF, So	.200	.403	.400	45	11	3	0	2	11	1
Hudson, Chase, INF, Sr	.111	.385	.111	9	4	0	0	0	0	2
Koon, Houston, OF, Jr	.000	.250	.000	3	1	0	0	0	0	0

Pitcher, Year	W	L	ERA	G	GS	SV	IP	H	BB	SO
Bell, Tadan, Fr	0	0	0.00	1	0	0	1	0	2	1
Sharkey, Teddy, Jr	7	2	2.90	27	0	11	50	39	18	74
Doyle, Liam, Fr	3	1	4.15	23	7	1	56	43	20	69
Eikhoff, Riley, So	3	1	4.43	10	6	0	43	39	10	39
Billings, Jack, Sr	4	0	4.63	15	8	0	47	35	27	51
Horn, Darin, So	3	2	5.60	28	1	1	64	66	29	85
Kelly, John, Sr	1	1	6.14	11	1	0	15	20	12	12
Shaffer, Bryce, Jr	5	1	6.27	25	3	1	52	54	31	54
Yablonski, Colin, Jr	2	1	6.50	16	0	0	18	19	15	24
Morrison, Jacob, Fr	6	1	6.55	13	13	0	58	69	21	68
Potok, Matthew, So	3	3	6.75	11	11	0	44	55	14	49
Smith, Will, Jr	4	2	7.71	28	2	0	37	42	31	46
Tyndall, Davis, Sr	0	0	8.24	21	0	0	20	28	15	17
Huesman, Levi, Fr	1	4	9.36	18	8	0	34	51	28	33
Edmondson, Alex, Jr	0	2	13.80	13	3	0	15	14	22	14
McCusker, Josh, Fr	0	0	18.90	4	0	0	3	7	4	4
McBride, Bobby, Jr	0	0	21.00	10	0	0	6	15	10	9

21. MIAMI

Coach: Gino DiMare. **Record:** 42-21

Player, Pos., Year	AVG	OBP	SLG	AB	R	2B	3B	HR	RBI	SB
Torres, Jason, INF, Fr	.472	.500	.861	36	10	3	1	3	11	0
Morales, Yohandy, INF, Jr	.408	.475	.712	240	58	13	0	20	70	7
Kayfus, CJ, INF, Jr	.347	.464	.581	236	61	14	1	13	41	8
Gonzalez, Renzo, OF, So	.322	.385	.414	87	9	2	0	2	11	0
Long, Jacoby, OF, Jr	.312	.413	.500	64	23	3	0	3	9	4
Cyr, Blake, INF, Fr	.305	.427	.620	200	50	12	0	17	63	0
Jones, JD, C, So	.300	.462	.300	10	3	0	0	0	1	0
Pitelli, Dominic, INF, Jr	.294	.380	.525	238	45	14	1	13	54	10
Levenson, Zach, OF, Jr	.292	.397	.554	233	45	17	1	14	45	4
Farrow, Ian, OF, Jr	.291	.385	.555	110	25	4	2	7	21	1
Villegas, Edgardo, OF, So	.264	.419	.430	193	49	9	1	7	27	3
Gomez, Dario, OF, Sr	.254	.317	.316	114	17	4	0	1	13	1
Carrier, Lorenzo, OF, Fr	.253	.326	.520	75	14	4	2	4	20	0
Gutierrez, Gaby, OF, So	.250	.302	.350	40	5	1	0	1	4	0
Perez, Carlos, C, Jr	.210	.316	.473	167	33	3	1	13	31	1
Garcia, Ariel, INF, So	.200	.333	.200	15	0	0	0	0	0	0
Gonzalez Jr., Dorian, INF, So	.193	.305	.330	88	17	3	0	3	15	0
Scanlon, Jack, C, Jr	.140	.315	.256	43	6	2	0	1	5	0
Martin, Kaden, OF, Fr	.000	.000	.000	3	0	0	0	0	0	0

Pitcher, Year	W	L	ERA	G	GS	SV	IP	H	BB	SO
Walters, Andrew, Jr	4	0	1.21	28	0	12	45	29	7	72
Schlesinger, Rafe, So	3	1	3.38	24	0	0	29	31	18	34
Scinta, Chris, Fr	1	1	3.53	27	1	0	36	34	16	38
Ziehl, Gage, So	8	4	4.30	16	16	0	92	92	21	100
Torres, Alejandro, So	4	1	4.62	32	6	2	49	39	16	59
Lequerica, Carlos, Sr	5	1	4.71	30	1	0	42	34	18	49
Ligon, Karson, So	3	2	4.80	10	10	0	51	44	20	37
Walsh, Alex, Fr	0	0	5.40	11	0	0	8	13	6	6
Chestnutt, Ben, Jr	7	0	5.71	25	5	0	63	71	32	53
Walters, Brian, So	0	0	6.75	2	0	0	1	2	1	2
Rosario, Alejandro, Jr	5	6	7.11	18	15	0	75	81	41	91
Gallo, Ronaldo, Jr	2	4	7.55	24	9	0	39	50	18	43
Perez, Sebastian, Fr	0	0	9.26	13	0	0	12	16	5	15
Braendel, Gunther, Fr	0	1	10.45	9	0	0	10	20	5	3

22. CAMPBELL

Coach: Justin Haire. **Record:** 46-15

PLAYER, POS., YEAR	AVG	OBP	SLG	AB	R	2B	3B	HR	RBI	SB
Oster, Jonah, C, Fr	.393	.526	.500	28	6	0	0	1	6	0
Halstead, Tyler, OF, Sr	.376	.455	.523	237	64	15	4	4	38	32
Harrill, Lawson, OF, Jr	.371	.475	.761	213	61	17	0	22	69	6
Mitta, Anthony, INF, Fr	.333	.333	.333	6	3	0	0	0	1	0
Schuldt, Andrew, C, Fr	.333	.432	.333	30	6	0	0	0	4	0
Weller, Max, OF, Jr	.331	.471	.504	121	42	9	0	4	25	9
Thompson, Dalen, INF, So	.328	.429	.391	64	11	2	1	0	15	6
Belbin, Jarrod, UT, Sr	.327	.426	.661	251	75	15	3	21	68	25
Arnold, Bryce, INF, Jr	.321	.412	.638	246	60	19	4	17	65	7
Riley, Chandler, INF, Jr	.309	.493	.441	152	43	6	1	4	25	8
Winters, Drew, OF, Jr	.306	.454	.565	85	19	4	0	6	21	5
Jordan, Logan, C, Jr	.301	.394	.529	206	46	11	0	12	52	1
Knipp, Grant, C, So	.278	.414	.572	180	44	12	1	13	55	9
Pierson, Drake, OF, Sr	.272	.438	.565	184	51	12	0	14	49	3
Howard, Payton, OF, Jr	.271	.429	.357	70	28	1	1	1	11	18
Harris, Trenton, INF, Jr	.242	.405	.442	95	23	5	1	4	21	4
Thompson, Jackson, C, So	.222	.462	.333	9	4	1	0	0	2	0

Pitcher, Year	W	L	ERA	G	GS	SV	IP	H	BB	SO
Roberts, Jackson, Fr	2	0	2.16	17	1	1	33	12	19	35
Kuehler, Cade, Jr	8	1	2.71	13	13	0	73	54	26	91
Adams, Trent, Jr	0	0	3.00	4	0	0	3	1	3	2
Murray, Jake, Jr	4	0	3.18	8	4	0	23	16	9	23
Rund, Aaron, Sr	5	1	3.84	21	0	5	61	54	25	71
Ferguson, George, Sr	0	0	4.05	8	0	0	7	8	4	6
Hartley, Wiley, So	0	0	4.20	11	0	0	15	11	8	16
Cummings, Ty, Jr	6	3	4.31	23	3	3	54	42	23	52
Boxrucker, Cade, Jr	2	1	4.50	18	1	2	42	30	29	56
Loyd, Hunter, Jr	4	4	4.62	15	15	0	72	71	34	69
Daquila, Chance, Jr	9	1	4.85	14	14	0	69	67	24	42
Wright, Brendan, Jr	0	0	5.40	7	0	0	5	6	5	4

Pitcher, Year	W	L	ERA	G	GS	SV	IP	H	BB	SO
O'Brien, Cameron, Jr	4	2	5.54	17	8	0	37	33	21	40
Kangas, Garret, So	0	0	5.79	6	0	0	5	7	2	4
Day, Ernie, Jr	1	1	6.75	14	2	0	21	23	19	28
Wiegman, Jeremy, Jr	1	0	8.66	14	0	0	18	25	14	17
Brown, Peyton, So	0	0	15.75	5	0	0	4	3	5	1
Parrill, Griffin, Sr	0	0	17.18	5	0	0	4	10	3	5
Brown, Daniel, Jr	0	0	54.00	4	0	0	1	0	9	3

23. OKLAHOMA STATE

Coach: Josh Holliday. **Record:** 41-20

Player, Pos., Year	AVG	OBP	SLG	AB	R	2B	3B	HR	RBI	SB
Benge, Carson, UT, Fr	.345	.468	.538	197	59	17	0	7	43	8
Schubart, Nolan, OF, Fr	.338	.451	.667	216	55	20	0	17	74	1
Riggio, Roc, UT, So	.335	.461	.679	224	66	17	3	18	61	7
Brueggemann, Colin, 1B, So	.330	.448	.596	109	29	11	0	6	36	1
Meola, Aidan, INF, So	.330	.368	.568	88	13	7	1	4	18	1
Wulfert, Tyler, INF, Jr	.327	.372	.620	171	40	17	3	9	34	2
Adkison, Chase, C, Jr	.314	.414	.482	191	47	9	1	7	44	4
Mendham, David, INF, Sr	.312	.370	.555	247	52	18	0	14	64	1
Brown, Marcus, INF, Jr	.273	.360	.469	209	40	10	2	9	36	3
McLean, Nolan, UT, Jr	.250	.379	.532	124	31	6	1	9	29	4
Ehrhard, Zach, UT, So	.239	.379	.348	138	36	6	0	3	13	11
Daugherty, Ian, C, So	.235	.381	.353	17	5	2	0	0	1	1
Crull, Jaxson, OF, Jr	.227	.397	.318	44	15	1	0	1	7	5
Sylvester, Beau, UT, Fr	.175	.233	.375	40	5	2	0	2	4	0
Holt, Brennan, INF, Fr	.173	.302	.250	52	11	1	0	1	7	2
Turley, Noah, OF, Jr	.143	.143	.357	14	1	0	0	1	1	0
Smith, Derek, C, Fr	.000	.200	.000	4	0	0	0	0	0	0

Pitcher, Year	W	L	ERA	G	GS	SV	IP	H	BB	SO
Hogue, Brant, Jr	0	0	0.00	3	0	0	1	2	1	0
Stebens, Isaac, Jr	4	1	2.24	28	0	6	64	49	24	85
Reid, Dominick, Fr	0	0	2.25	3	0	0	4	3	4	2
Bogusz, Ryan, Jr	1	1	2.60	9	1	0	17	25	5	11
McLean, Nolan, Jr	1	2	3.30	14	3	6	30	30	17	34
Root, Bayden, Sr	7	1	4.34	20	1	1	37	32	16	40
O'Toole, Evan, Jr	6	1	4.99	22	0	0	40	47	15	28
Watts-Brown, Juaron, So	6	5	5.03	17	15	0	82	68	48	124
Blake, Drew, Fr	1	0	5.46	28	2	0	28	26	15	27
Abram, Ben, Sr	8	3	6.21	18	14	0	71	91	22	76
Hendry, Brian, Sr	2	1	6.63	16	5	0	37	43	14	51
Benge, Carson, Fr	2	2	6.69	10	10	0	35	38	24	35
Keisel, Janzen, So	0	0	7.85	9	4	0	18	15	19	34
Davis, Gabe, Fr	1	2	7.92	22	0	1	25	29	19	40
Taylor, Riley, Sr	0	0	9.00	1	0	0	2	3	1	2
Phillips, Brennan, Fr	2	1	9.69	10	6	0	26	34	12	22
Benzor, Michael, Fr	0	0	9.82	13	0	0	7	15	5	13
Shatwell, Kade, Fr	0	0	10.12	3	0	0	3	4	2	3

24. EAST CAROLINA

Coach: Cliff Godwin. **Record:** 47-19

Player, Pos., Year	AVG	OBP	SLG	AB	R	2B	3B	HR	RBI	SB
Berini, Joey, INF, Jr	.318	.391	.416	214	34	7	1	4	35	3
Wilcoxen, Justin, C, Jr	.318	.384	.538	223	43	20	1	9	49	1
Cunningham, Carter, UT, Jr	.317	.429	.522	186	51	12	1	8	39	5
Starling, Jacob, UT, Jr	.311	.436	.506	241	60	15	1	10	52	19
Moylan, Josh, 1B, Jr	.302	.412	.587	242	55	20	2	15	70	1
Hoover, Lane, OF, Sr	.299	.422	.355	214	60	6	0	2	23	13
Jenkins-Cowart, Jacob, UT, So	.294	.354	.491	214	33	13	1	9	45	2
Johnson, Ryley, OF, Jr	.290	.377	.400	100	22	3	1	2	18	11
Nowak, Luke, OF, So	.288	.398	.370	184	38	9	3	0	33	20
Clonch, Cam, UT, Jr	.276	.418	.494	87	18	7	0	4	15	0
Makarewicz, Alec, UT, Jr	.258	.356	.476	229	44	11	3	11	49	3
McCrystal, Ryan, C, So	.232	.256	.341	82	6	6	0	1	13	0
Murphy, Cam, INF, Jr	.200	.200	.400	5	3	1	0	0	0	0
Williams, Dixon, 2B, Fr	.167	.333	.250	12	4	1	0	0	0	0
Chrismon, Nathan, INF, Fr	.161	.263	.161	31	11	0	0	0	3	8
Rasmussen, Connor, INF, Fr	.111	.158	.111	18	4	0	0	0	1	1
Burgess, Cam, INF, Fr	.000	.250	.000	3	0	0	0	0	0	0

Pitcher, Year	W	L	ERA	G	GS	SV	IP	H	BB	SO
Yesavage, Trey, So	7	1	2.61	16	14	1	76	53	23	105
Beal, Danny, Jr	6	2	2.70	31	0	3	53	38	12	65
Beeker, Merritt, Fr	1	0	3.60	7	0	0	5	4	5	7
Grosz, Josh, Jr	4	2	3.66	16	16	0	76	59	41	79
Saylor, Garrett, Sr	3	0	3.83	21	7	0	54	45	8	57
Lunsford-Shenkman, Wyatt, So	4	2	4.24	28	1	2	51	49	13	49
Ginn, Landon, Jr	6	1	4.67	26	0	2	35	34	11	36
Spivey, Carter, Sr	7	3	4.68	24	10	1	77	85	22	68
Hunter, Jake, So	4	2	4.71	22	4	1	42	35	13	51
Ritchie, Erik, So	2	2	5.01	22	0	0	23	26	17	34
Root, Zach, Fr	3	3	5.53	20	13	1	54	53	27	54
Lumpkin, Willie, Jr	0	0	5.71	15	0	0	17	15	2	16
Winter, Jaden, So	0	0	8.10	10	0	1	10	9	7	15
Bradt, Tyler, Jr	0	1	8.10	18	0	1	17	28	10	23
Little, Jordan, So	0	0	19.29	4	0	0	2	9	1	3
Hodges, Charlie, Jr	0	0	27.00	1	1	0	1	1	2	1

25. DALLAS BAPTIST

Coach: Dan Heefner. **Record:** 47-16

Player, Pos., Year	AVG	OBP	SLG	AB	R	2B	3B	HR	RBI	SB
Kolden, Kodie, INF, Sr	.353	.437	.491	232	57	10	2	6	35	21
Humphreys, Nathan, OF, So	.351	.450	.644	202	58	15	1	14	53	19
Jay, Grant, C, Fr	.319	.445	.755	188	57	17	1	21	62	8
Mann, Ethan, UT, Sr	.319	.444	.695	210	63	15	2	20	80	9
Santos, Miguel, INF, Jr	.313	.363	.558	265	61	18	1	15	63	15
Grady, Jace, OF, Jr	.309	.416	.534	249	58	14	3	12	39	25
Pendergast, Alex, INF, Jr	.297	.350	.486	37	7	1	0	2	12	1
Rombach, Nate, UT, Jr	.288	.355	.455	191	41	11	0	7	35	7
Holder, Jaxon, OF, So	.286	.583	.429	7	3	1	0	0	1	0
Boughton, Noah, INF, Jr	.273	.392	.379	66	9	4	0	1	7	2
Poole, Tom, UT, So	.246	.379	.563	142	35	7	4	10	32	9
Heefner, Luke, INF, So	.243	.341	.359	181	39	10	1	3	23	12
Specht, George, UT, Sr	.228	.319	.422	180	28	12	1	7	39	5
Nerat, Joey, OF, Fr	.091	.091	.364	11	1	0	0	1	2	0
Riley, Ian, OF, Jr	.000	.300	.000	7	3	0	0	0	1	1

Pitcher, Year	W	L	ERA	G	GS	SV	IP	H	BB	SO
Amendt, Kyle, Jr	1	1	1.75	23	0	12	26	16	14	51
Jenkins, Jerrod, Fr	1	0	1.80	4	0	0	5	4	6	8
Russell, Zane, Jr	2	1	2.35	17	1	1	31	17	25	48
Rose, Brady, Jr	7	2	2.93	23	0	1	46	27	23	74
Heaton, Zach, Sr	5	1	3.38	16	16	0	69	60	24	58
Bragg, Braxton, Jr	9	2	4.19	16	16	0	86	94	17	92
Johnson, Ryan, So	8	4	4.43	16	15	0	87	79	22	116
Baker, Alec, Jr	4	0	4.46	24	1	0	40	44	18	40
Beuter, Reece, So	0	0	4.86	15	0	0	17	24	6	15
Hammer, Bryson, So	5	4	5.16	14	8	0	45	44	30	48
Bollenbacher, Matthew, Sr	0	0	5.40	19	3	0	30	36	7	32
DeBerry, Jaron, Jr	3	1	5.71	20	3	1	35	35	15	35
Mackay, Conner, Jr	2	0	7.11	13	0	0	19	21	12	19
Reeves, Cole, Sr	0	0	7.56	10	0	0	8	11	3	6
Tabor, Preston, So	0	0	9.00	6	0	0	6	5	7	5
Smith, Peyton, Fr	0	0	10.80	6	0	0	3	6	3	5
Schott, Tyler, So	0	0	12.00	7	0	0	3	6	0	2
Weigert, Cade, Fr	0	0	21.60	2	0	0	2	2	2	2

CONFERENCE STANDINGS & LEADERS

*NCAA regional teams in bold..

AMERICA EAST CONFERENCE

	Conference W	Conference L	Overall W	Overall L
*Maine	19	5	32	21
UMBC	16	8	30	27
Binghamton	12	12	29	23
Bryant	12	12	26	24
UMass Lowell	11	13	20	35
NJIT	11	13	22	31
UAlbany	3	21	9	34

ALL-CONFERENCE TEAM: SP: Gabe Driscoll, Binghamton; Colin Fitzgerald, Maine; Luke Johnson, UMBC; Aidan Kidd, NJIT. **RP:** Gianni Gambardella, Maine. **C:** Jeremiah Jenkins, Maine. **1B:** Tony Krueger, UMBC. **2B:** Quinn McDaniel, Maine. **3B:** Robert Gallagher, UMass Lowell. **SS:** Jake Rainess, Maine. **OF:** Tommy Reifler, Binghamton; Derek Smith, Bryant; Justin Taylor, UMBC. **DH:** Connor Goodman, Maine. **UTIL:** Will Feil, Albany. **Player of the Year:** Jeremiah Jenkins, Maine. **Pitcher of the Year:** Luke Johnson, UMBC. **Rookie of the Year:** Leewood Molessa, UMBC. **Coach of the Year:** Nick Derba, Maine.

INDIVIDUAL BATTING LEADERS

	AVG	OBP	SLG	AB	2B	3B	HR	RBI	SB
Tommy Reifler, Binghamton	.371	.461	.434	178	8	1	2	29	9
Tony Krueger, UMBC	.367	.500	.438	188	19	0	2	43	2
Jeremiah Jenkins, Maine	.365	.756	.492	197	12	1	21	76	0
Kevin Gsell, Binghamton	.365	.553	.423	197	13	0	8	47	1
Nick Roselli, Binghamton	.357	.592	.441	196	8	4	10	61	4
Quinn McDaniel, Maine	.354	.688	.513	192	14	1	16	45	32
Gustin Jake, Bryant	.348	.583	.448	204	16	4	8	46	4
Justin Taylor, UMBC	.342	.422	.440	199	10	0	2	26	8
Genther, Fritz, UMass Lowell	.324	.555	.419	182	13	1	9	47	9
Jason Bottari, UAlbany	.323	.389	.446	167	3	1	2	19	26
Jake Rainess, Maine	.321	.623	.448	212	14	1	16	47	38
Smith Derek, Bryant	.317	.559	.397	202	15	2	10	44	6
Humphrey, Jacob, UMass Lowell	.317	.523	.421	218	8	5	9	29	33
Devan Bade, Binghamton	.315	.516	.393	184	12	2	7	37	2
Connor Goodman, Maine	.311	.378	.391	209	8	0	2	47	2
Dan Tauken, UAlbany	.311	.508	.378	122	10	1	4	21	1
Christian Easley, UMBC	.307	.450	.388	189	14	2	3	24	28
Siracusa, Gerry, UMass Lowell	.306	.433	.342	180	14	0	3	36	9
Cavan Tully, Binghamton	.305	.457	.433	164	11	1	4	32	5
Will Feil, UAlbany	.301	.509	.449	163	10	0	8	40	4
Will Binder, UAlbany	.300	.411	.371	180	5	0	5	26	2
Leewood Molessa, UMBC	.294	.579	.358	228	15	1	16	66	4
Luke Trythall, UMBC	.294	.466	.376	163	10	0	6	44	0
Zyons Zac, Bryant	.293	.525	.438	99	5	3	4	20	7
Ian Diaz, UMBC	.292	.421	.442	195	11	1	4	34	4

INDIVIDUAL PITCHING LEADERS

	W	L	ERA	GS	SV	IP	H	BB	SO
Luke Johnson, UMBC	7	1	2.96	14	0	79	63	38	84
Becker, Joshua, UMass Lowell	5	3	3.49	8	1	59	55	13	51
Gianni Gambardella, Maine	6	3	3.9	4	2	58	59	15	42
Noah Lewis, Maine	7	1	4.32	13	0	85	63	42	77
Aidan Kidd, NJIT	5	2	4.48	14	0	66	54	34	92
Wichrowski Brett, Bryant	5	3	4.5	7	1	50	49	25	64
Caleb Leys, Maine	5	1	4.94	13	0	71	61	52	72
Gabe Driscoll, Binghamton	7	1	4.98	15	0	78	81	18	66
Thomas Babalis, Binghamton	4	4	5.05	14	0	77	89	33	79
Ryan Fischer, NJIT	4	7	5.16	15	0	91	105	22	74
Colin Fitzgerald, Maine	6	2	5.23	15	0	76	78	42	61
Draper, Matt, UMass Lowell	3	9	5.27	14	0	82	96	30	73
Jayden Shertel, UMBC	5	5	5.71	14	0	76	80	33	51
Joe Georgini, NJIT	3	7	5.85	14	0	68	83	17	30
Turner Ken, Bryant	2	3	5.98	13	0	53	59	19	46
Matt Mariano, UAlbany	2	2	6.75	9	0	49	74	18	36
Ryan Bryggman, Binghamton	4	5	6.98	15	0	68	91	24	49
Cregg Scherrer, UAlbany	0	5	9.07	8	0	45	53	49	53

NICHOLAS FAULKNER

Cliff Godwin and East Carolina won the AAC regular season title

AMERICAN ATHLETIC CONFERENCE

	Conference W	Conference L	Overall W	Overall L
*East Carolina	18	6	47	19
Houston	17	6	36	23
Wichita State	13	10	30	25
UCF	12	12	33	26
Cincinnati	10	14	24	33
Memphis	10	14	29	28
*Tulane	8	16	19	42
South Florida	7	17	21	39

ALL-CONFERENCE TEAM: P: Trey Yesavage, So., East Carolina; Dalton Fowler, Sr., Memphis; Grant Adler, Jr., Wichita State; Clark Candiotti, Jr., Wichita State. **RP:** Dalton Kendrick, Jr., Memphis. **C:** Ben McCabe, R-Sr., UCF. **1B:** Justin Murray, Jr., Houston. **2B:** Brock Rodden, Jr., Wichita State. **SS:** Eric Snow, Fr., South Florida. **3B:** Zach Arnold, Jr., Houston. **OF:** Carter Cunningham, Jr., East Carolina; Bobby Boser, So., South Florida; Drew Brutcher, Jr., South Florida; Chuck Ingram, Jr., Wichita State. **DH:** Andrew Sundean, So., UCF; Jacob Jenkins-Cowart, So., East Carolina. **UTL:** Payton Tolle, So., Wichita State. **Coach of the Year:** Loren Hibbs, Wichita State. **Player of the Year:** Brock Rodden, Jr., 2B, Wichita State. **Pitcher of the Year:** Dalton Fowler, Sr., Memphis. **Newcomer Position Player of the Year:** Justin Murray, Jr., 1B, Houston. **Newcomer Pitcher of the Year:** Grant Adler, Jr., Wichita State. **Defensive Player of the Year:** Eric Snow, Fr., SS, South Florida. **Coach of the Year:** Loren Hibbs, Wichita State.

INDIVIDUAL BATTING LEADERS

	AVG	OBP	SLG	AB	2B	3B	HR	RBI	SB
Murray, Justin, Hou	.379	.422	.598	219	11	2	11	58	20
Rodden, Brock, WSU	.371	.474	.701	221	18	2	17	64	12
Mccabe, Ben, UCF	.371	.466	.692	224	15	0	19	51	6
Arnold, Zach, Hou	.365	.452	.590	222	11	0	13	51	10
Ingram, Chuck, WSU	.362	.437	.579	221	19	1	9	41	16
Snow, Eric, Usf	.343	.418	.526	213	13	1	8	45	6
Sundean, Andrew, UCF	.340	.428	.626	203	10	0	16	54	0
Kohler, Logan, Mem	.330	.404	.574	197	13	1	11	34	9
Boser, Bobby, Usf	.323	.445	.621	195	7	3	15	41	8
Lott, Malachi, Hou	.320	.379	.517	147	12	1	5	33	12
Romano, Nick, UCF	.319	.402	.523	216	12	1	10	41	1
Wilcoxen, Justin, ECU	.318	.384	.538	223	20	1	9	49	1
Berini, Joey, ECU	.318	.391	.416	214	7	1	4	35	3
Cunningham, C., ECU	.317	.429	.522	186	12	1	8	39	5
Betancourt, Rafael, Usf	.317	.340	.470	183	9	2	5	32	0
Millan, Mauricio, WSU	.315	.392	.406	197	15	0	1	26	1
Mcdonald, Kyte, WSU	.313	.395	.463	147	12	2	2	19	21
Tolle, Payton, WSU	.311	.361	.538	212	9	0	13	50	1
Starling, Jacob, ECU	.311	.436	.506	241	15	1	10	52	19
Nickens, Cameron, Hou	.310	.368	.467	184	12	1	5	38	6
Brady Hebert, Tul	.307	.440	.458	192	14	3	3	23	12
Pennington, Garrett, WSU	.307	.372	.560	225	12	0	15	55	11
Brady Marget, Tul	.303	.393	.489	221	12	1	9	31	5
Cantu, Daniel, USF	.302	.399	.557	192	14	1	11	41	3
Moylan, Josh, ECU	.302	.412	.587	242	20	2	15	70	1

INDIVIDUAL PITCHING LEADERS

	W	L	ERA	G	SV	IP	H	BB	SO
Adler, Grant, WSU	5	4	2.55	14	0	78	75	23	75
Yesavage, Trey, ECU	7	1	2.61	16	1	76	53	23	105
Grosz, Josh, ECU	4	2	3.66	16	0	76	59	41	79
Fowler, Dalton, MEM	5	6	4.24	15	0	85	66	43	112
Tolle, Payton, WSU	9	3	4.62	15	0	86	81	19	97
Spivey, Carter, ECU	7	3	4.68	24	1	77	85	22	68
Candiotti, Clark, WSU	7	4	4.87	15	0	78	87	20	82
Cebert, Jack, USF	4	4	5.05	16	0	77	90	21	65
Gomez, Ruddy, UCF	6	3	5.25	15	0	72	83	22	78
Ricky Castro, TUL	4	7	5.44	18	1	86	102	24	86
Warren, David, MEM	5	5	5.57	20	0	73	88	28	64
Marlowe, Jacob, UCF	3	6	5.64	19	0	61	70	12	41
Hopewell, Chase, CIN	2	6	5.79	15	0	65	74	27	52
Dylan Carmouche, TUL	5	9	5.80	17	0	90	104	40	102
Ekness, Josh, HOU	2	4	6.45	21	1	67	67	38	73
Dom Stagliano, UCF	4	5	6.54	19	0	65	79	17	70
Mink, Hunter, USF	6	6	6.75	16	0	73	74	38	82

ATLANTIC COAST CONFERENCE

	Conference		Overall	
Atlantic Division	**W**	**L**	**W**	**L**
*Wake Forest	22	7	54	12
*Clemson	20	10	44	19
*Boston College	16	14	37	20
Notre Dame	15	15	30	24
*NC State	13	16	36	21
Louisville	10	20	31	24
Florida State	9	21	23	31

	Conference		Overall	
Coastal Division	**W**	**L**	**W**	**L**
*Virginia	19	11	50	15
*Miami	18	12	42	21
*Duke	16	13	39	24
*North Carolina	14	14	36	24
Virginia Tech	12	17	30	23
Georgia Tech	12	18	30	27
Pitt	10	18	24	31

ALL-CONFERENCE TEAM: C: Kyle Teel, Virginia, Jr.; 1B: Nick Kurtz, Wake Forest, So.; **2B:** Justin Johnson, Wake Forest, Jr.; **SS:** Alex Mooney, Duke, So.; **SS:** Griff O'Ferrall, Virginia, So.; **3B:** Yohandy Morales, Miami, Jr.; **3B:** Jake Gelof, Virginia, Jr.; **OF:** Ethan O'Donnell, Virginia, Jr.; **OF:** Jack Hurley, Virginia Tech, Jr.; **OF:** Stephen Reid, Georgia Tech, Jr.; **OF:** Cam Cannarella, Clemson, Fr.; **DH/UT:** Billy Amick, Clemson, So.; **SP:** Josh Hartle, Wake Forest, So.; **SP:** Rhett Lowder, Wake Forest, Jr.; **SP:** Sean Sullivan, Wake Forest, So.; **RP:** Andrew Walters, Miami, **So. Player of the Year:** Kyle Teel, Virginia, Jr., **C. Pitcher of the Year:** Rhett Lowder, Wake Forest, Jr., **RHP. Freshman of the Year:** Cam Cannarella, Clemson, Fr., **OF. Defensive Player of the Year:** Vance Honeycutt, North Carolina, So., **OF. Coach of the Year:** Tom Walter, Wake Forest

INDIVIDUAL BATTING LEADERS

	AVG	OBP	SLG	AB	2B	3B	HR	RBI	SB
Billy Amick, Clemson	.413	.464	.772	167	17	2	13	63	2
Yohandy Morales, Miami	.408	.475	.713	240	13	0	20	70	7
Kyle Teel, Virginia	.399	.470	.647	258	25	0	13	69	5
Angelo Dispigna, Georgia Tech	.393	.509	.667	219	12	0	16	58	8
Cam Cannarella, Clemson	.388	.462	.560	250	16	3	7	47	24
Griff O'Ferrall, Virginia	.385	.444	.480	275	19	2	1	41	16
Kristian Campbell, Georgia Tech	.376	.484	.549	173	16	1	4	24	4
Jack Payton, Louisville	.374	.472	.642	179	10	1	12	41	8
Ethan Anderson, Virginia	.366	.466	.650	257	25	0	16	65	0
Jake DeLeo, Georgia Tech	.365	.426	.651	249	23	3	14	52	8
Ethan O'Donnell, Virginia	.365	.459	.611	252	18	1	14	58	18
Will Taylor, Clemson	.362	.489	.523	218	16	2	5	46	11
Pierce Bennett, Wake Forest	.353	.431	.523	235	19	0	7	65	1
Nick Kurtz, Wake Forest	.353	.527	.784	190	10	0	24	69	5
Cannon Peebles, NC State	.352	.456	.697	142	11	1	12	50	0
Tommy Hawke, Wake Forest	.351	.459	.506	271	19	1	7	35	14
CJ Kayfus, Miami	.347	.464	.581	236	14	1	13	41	8
Christian Martin, Virginia Tech	.345	.455	.471	174	7	3	3	26	8
Brock Wilken, Wake Forest	.345	.506	.807	238	15	1	31	82	1
Stephen Reid, Georgia Tech	.344	.430	.621	224	13	2	15	51	0
Garrett Michel, Virginia Tech	.339	.465	.626	171	16	0	11	45	1
James Tibbs III, Florida State	.338	.471	.682	195	14	1	17	43	5
Chris Cannizzaro, Virginia Tech	.337	.397	.570	193	11	2	10	45	2
Anthony Stephan, Virginia	.335	.455	.525	158	13	1	5	35	4
Jay Beshears, Duke	.333	.438	.586	237	15	0	15	56	5
John Giesler, Georgia Tech	.333	.422	.596	156	13	2	8	37	3
Gino Groover, NC State	.332	.430	.546	229	8	1	13	50	2
Christian Knapczyk, Louisville	.331	.455	.408	169	8	1	1	24	19
Jackson Finley, Georgia Tech	.328	.397	.672	198	17	0	17	61	1
Cooper Ingle, Clemson	.328	.417	.461	256	16	0	6	34	1
Jake Gelof, Virginia	.328	.432	.723	253	23	4	23	90	3
Kyle Hess, Pitt	.327	.415	.626	171	9	6	10	42	9
Justin Johnson, Wake Forest	.324	.424	.618	238	16	3	16	76	7
Jaime Ferrer, Florida State	.324	.369	.533	225	22	2	7	42	4
Carson DeMartini, Virginia Tech	.323	.455	.593	189	13	4	10	57	9
Tomas Frick, North Carolina	.322	.408	.571	233	22	0	12	60	0
Jack Hurley, Virginia Tech	.320	.414	.713	178	15	2	17	49	4
Hunter Stokely, North Carolina	.317	.406	.492	199	15	1	6	36	0
Casey Cook, North Carolina	.317	.428	.415	224	11	1	3	23	2
Alex Mooney, Duke	.315	.434	.504	254	20	2	8	38	21
Alex Stone, Duke	.315	.379	.579	254	16	0	17	62	0
Joe Vetrano, Boston College	.315	.407	.671	219	12	0	22	64	3
Barry Walsh, Boston College	.314	.416	.490	194	10	0	8	35	14
Jacoby Long, Miami	.313	.413	.500	64	3	0	3	9	4
Kalae Harrison, NC State	.313	.436	.426	195	10	3	2	31	4
Tyler Albright, Duke	.312	.408	.416	154	7	0	3	34	4
Clay Grady, Virginia Tech	.307	.386	.433	150	5	1	4	34	4
Caden Grice, Clemson	.307	.411	.618	228	15	1	18	68	4
Jackson Van De Brake, N.Carolina	.307	.439	.486	218	15	0	8	48	1
Noah Martinez, Pitt	.306	.442	.558	206	13	0	13	53	2

INDIVIDUAL PITCHING LEADERS

	W	L	ERA	G	SV	IP	H	BB	SO
Rhett Lowder, Wake Forest	15	0	1.87	19	0	120	90	24	143
Sean Sullivan, Wake Forest	5	3	2.45	10	3	70	43	21	111
Seth Keener, Wake Forest	8	2	2.69	8	1	70	41	20	94
Josh Hartle, Wake Forest	10	2	2.81	17	0	102	91	24	140
Connelly Early, Virginia	12	3	3.09	18	0	87	82	23	100
Caden Grice, Clemson	8	1	3.35	14	0	78	54	33	101
Aidan Tyrell, Notre Dame	8	3	3.36	6	1	70	64	26	59
Carson Liggett, Louisville	7	2	3.42	14	0	71	64	29	64
Dominic Fritton, NC State	3	4	3.59	9	3	63	50	24	75
Matt Willadsen, NC State	5	5	3.78	16	0	81	77	31	86

Player	W	L	ERA	G	SV	IP	H	BB	SO
Brian Edginton, Virginia	8	3	3.83	14	0	82	81	21	84
Nick Parker, Virginia	8	0	3.86	17	0	86	84	27	85
Jack O'Connor, Virginia	6	3	3.86	11	0	65	61	25	64
Andrew Armstrong, Florida State	2	3	4.19	2	2	58	55	20	57
Logan Whitaker, NC State	5	3	4.29	15	0	80	77	17	79
Gage Ziehl, Miami	8	4	4.30	16	0	92	92	21	100
Conner Whittaker, Florida State	5	6	4.33	8	0	79	82	19	65
Chris Flynn, Boston College	7	3	4.34	16	0	75	76	34	84
John West, Boston College	5	3	4.50	13	1	68	52	25	71
Ryan Hawks, Louisville	5	3	4.58	14	0	77	88	23	80
Austin Gordon, Clemson	2	4	4.61	16	0	84	77	22	76
Aeden Finateri, Georgia Tech	2	4	4.64	4	2	64	68	17	56
Anthony Arguelles, Virginia Tech	3	1	4.90	13	0	61	55	32	64
Gow, Alex, Duke	3	4	4.95	17	0	64	54	28	69
Jake Knapp, North Carolina	5	4	5.04	16	0	64	67	36	65
Jackson Baumeister, Florida State	5	5	5.09	14	0	69	69	29	95
Blake Hely, Notre Dame	3	3	5.23	15	0	74	70	31	74
Eric Schroeder, Boston College	6	4	5.37	3	0	62	68	17	43
Max Carlson, North Carolina	5	2	5.45	14	1	76	74	32	76
Connor Bovair, North Carolina	4	4	5.57	14	0	73	79	22	57

ATLANTIC SUN CONFERENCE

	Conference		Overall	
	W	L	W	L
*Lipscomb	23	7	36	26
FGCU	20	10	42	18
Stetson	20	10	35	24
Jacksonville State	18	12	27	30
Jacksonville	17	13	34	24
Liberty	16	14	27	31
EKU	15	15	30	30
Austin Peay	15	15	26	32
Kennesaw State	14	16	25	29
Central Arkansas	14	16	23	31
North Florida	13	17	28	27
Queens	9	21	17	38
North Alabama	8	22	14	37
Bellarmine	8	22	13	42

ALL-CONFERENCE TEAM: C: Austin Kelly, Lipscomb, R-So. 1B: Joe Kinker, FGCU, Sr. **2B:** Edrick Felix, FGCU, Jr.; **3B:** Kris Armstrong, Jacksonville, Gr.; **SS:** Logan Thomason, EKU, Sr.; **SS:** Alex Lodise, North Florida, Fr.; **OF:** Brian Ellis, FGCU, Sr.; **OF:** T.J. Reeves, Jax State, Sr.; **OF:** Austin Brinling, North Florida, Jr.; **DH:** Alejandro Figueredo, FGCU, Sr.; **SP:** Jesse Barker, Central Arkansas, Jr.; **SP:** Evan Chrest, Jacksonville, Fr.; **SP:** Logan Van Treeck, Lipscomb, Jr.; **RP:** Chris Lotito, Jacksonville, **R-So. Player of the Year:** Edrick Felix, FGCU. **Defensive Player of the Year:** Logan Thomason, EKU. **Pitcher of the Year:** Logan Van Treeck, Lipscomb. **Freshman of the Year:** Evan Chrest, Jacksonville. **Coach of the Year:** Jeff Forehand, Lipscomb.

INDIVIDUAL BATTING LEADERS

	AVG	OBP	SLG	AB	2B	3B	HR	RBI	SB
Javon Hernandez, Jacks. St.	.397	.479	.567	224	11	3	7	49	11
Austin Brinling, North Florida	.386	.500	.540	202	18	2	3	31	20
Edrick Felix, FGCU	.366	.449	.774	243	22	1	25	83	1
Spencer Hanson, Kennesaw St.	.364	.397	.708	154	8	0	15	56	1
Alejandro Figueredo, FGCU	.361	.461	.693	241	11	0	23	71	0
Joe Kinker, FGCU	.360	.459	.669	236	16	0	19	77	1
Lyle Miller-Green, Austin Peay	.354	.438	.633	237	14	2	16	51	5
Will King, EKU	.348	.428	.635	178	13	1	12	47	1
Mason Maners, Jacksonville St.	.346	.462	.594	217	12	3	12	45	4
Brayden Horton, Liberty	.341	.471	.543	164	13	1	6	40	1
Derrick Jackson, Jacksonville St.	.340	.405	.673	147	16	0	11	37	0
T.J. Reeves, Jacksonville State	.336	.421	.619	226	10	3	16	75	2
Garrett Martin, Austin Peay	.333	.461	.709	165	13	2	15	46	7
Clayton Gray, Austin Peay	.333	.403	.514	249	24	3	5	33	24
Bear Madliak, Jacksonville St.	.330	.389	.490	200	14	0	6	25	3
Alejandro Rodriguez, FGCU	.328	.419	.496	232	14	2	7	50	2
Dylan Byerly, Bellarmine	.325	.381	.416	166	6	0	3	16	10
Kyle Machado, North Alabama	.324	.447	.565	170	14	0	9	44	0
Moran Landon, Stetson	.324	.475	.455	176	11	0	4	34	6
Miguel Larreal, EKU	.323	.437	.471	189	10	0	6	34	9
JJ Sousa, Queens	.322	.404	.454	152	8	0	4	27	3
Aidan Sweatt, North Florida	.320	.418	.424	231	12	0	4	31	16
Jakob Runnels, North Florida	.320	.436	.581	172	3	0	14	57	1
Riley Cheek, Queens	.319	.443	.586	210	18	1	12	40	10
Brayden Eidson, Kennesaw St.	.318	.378	.477	176	10	3	4	26	10
Stephen Wilmer, FGCU	.312	.442	.629	186	7	2	16	52	0
Kane Kepley, Liberty	.310	.457	.432	155	8	4	1	19	17
Trace Willhoite, Lipscomb	.309	.428	.618	220	17	0	17	66	2
Jaylen Guy, Liberty	.309	.359	.434	175	12	2	2	25	22
Cade Reich, North Florida	.309	.389	.500	194	11	4	6	30	13

INDIVIDUAL PITCHING LEADERS

	W	L	ERA	G	SV	IP	H	BB	SO
Evan Chrest, Jacksonville	8	2	2.68	15	0	91	83	36	98
Jesse Barker, Central Arkansas	7	4	3.00	14	0	96	85	22	109
Amaral Austin, Stetson	6	3	3.53	14	0	71	62	37	73
Logan Van Treeck, Lipscomb	8	5	3.67	10	0	88	69	14	108
Bryce Tucker, Lipscomb	7	1	3.97	16	1	93	82	29	98
Garrett Horn, Liberty	5	5	4.09	15	0	66	52	47	87
Noah Thompson, Lipscomb	6	2	4.14	13	0	67	53	24	55
Gonzalez Jonathan, Stetson	8	4	4.18	7	2	71	61	17	89
Braden Osbolt, Kennesaw State	2	2	4.28	13	0	67	77	28	46
Peter Holden, North Florida	4	5	4.45	14	0	87	80	35	84
Nick Zegna, Kennesaw State	4	5	4.57	13	0	63	70	35	57
Tanner Jones, Jacksonville State	7	3	4.67	14	0	79	78	28	84
Blake Wehunt, Kennesaw State	4	4	4.77	14	0	77	87	24	81
Jake Peppers, Jacksonville State	4	4	4.81	9	1	58	52	26	60
Dominick Madonna, N. Florida	8	3	4.95	11	0	84	94	26	51
AJ Causey, Jacksonville State	5	2	5.07	14	0	76	82	23	89
Defabbia Anthony, Stetson	4	4	5.11	6	4	56	68	13	53
Mikey Tepper, Liberty	4	3	5.23	15	0	65	51	46	78
Michael Schuler, EKU	3	2	5.29	10	1	63	74	24	59
Clayton Boroski, North Florida	2	9	5.43	13	0	61	69	22	41

ATLANTIC 10 CONFERENCE

	Conference		Overall	
	W	L	W	L
Saint Joseph's	17	7	28	24
Davidson	15	8	30	24
Saint Louis	15	9	33	23
Dayton	15	9	26	34
Richmond	14	9	27	28
*George Mason	13	10	36	26
Rhode Island	13	11	23	29
George Washington	11	12	21	34
VCU	11	13	25	30
Fordham	7	17	19	36
UMass	6	18	14	35
St. Bonaventure	5	19	8	40

ALL-CONFERENCE TEAM: C: Connor Dykstra, George Mason. **1B:** Cam Redding, Saint Louis. **2B:** Zach Selinger, Fordham. **SS:** Alex Ramirez, Rhode Island. **3B:** Jordan Jaffe, Richmond/Brandon Eike, . **OF:** Ryan Wilson, Davidson; Billy Butler, Rhode Island; Brett Callahan, Saint Joseph's. **DH:** Michael Kohn, George Washington. **P:** Will Schomberg, Davidson; Chad Gartland, George Mason. **RP:** Bennett Flynn, Davidson. **Player of the Year:** Ryan Wilson, Davidson. **Pitcher of the Year:** Chad Gartland, George Mason. **Rookie of the Year:** Jordan Jaffe, Richmond. **Coach of the Year:** Fritz Hamburg, Saint Joseph's.

INDIVIDUAL BATTING LEADERS

Player	AVG	OBP	SLG	AB	2B	3B	HR	RBI	SB
Ryan Cesarini, Saint Joseph's	.392	.470	.618	199	17	2	8	56	12
Ryan Wilson, Davidson	.387	.533	.737	194	17	0	17	54	8
Eddie Micheletti, GW	.384	.460	.563	224	18	2	6	48	8
Johnny Hipsman, Richmond	.381	.434	.659	226	25	1	12	55	9
Luke Zimmerman, St. Joseph's	.370	.436	.560	100	6	2	3	22	5
Smith Cole, Saint Louis	.367	.428	.511	221	15	1	5	35	14
Ben Jones, Dayton	.365	.456	.608	181	13	2	9	33	5
Justin Blumenthal, UMass	.361	.393	.429	133	7	1	0	22	4
Moore Hayden, Saint Louis	.359	.510	.464	153	13	0	1	27	21
AJ Mathis, VCU	.353	.488	.475	204	15	2	2	28	17
Billy Butler, Rhode Island	.349	.396	.636	195	17	0	13	44	6

Player	AVG	OBP	SLG	AB	2B	3B	HR	RBI	SB
Brandon Eike, VCU	.346	.395	.610	231	24	2	11	71	6
Brett Callahan, Saint Joseph's	.344	.435	.615	221	15	6	11	55	14
Nate Thomas, Saint Joseph's	.339	.443	.567	171	7	1	10	53	1
South Trimble, GM	.335	.454	.462	236	17	2	3	38	30
Michael Kohn, GW	.333	.439	.586	198	17	0	11	45	1
Clohisy Patrick, Saint Louis	.332	.438	.546	229	13	3	10	56	24
Sitzman Ethan, Saint Louis	.327	.444	.431	202	9	0	4	43	4
Steve Luttazi, UMass	.327	.415	.460	150	8	0	4	26	0
Nolan Tichy, UMass	.326	.377	.575	193	12	0	12	46	3
Zach Selinger, Fordham	.326	.418	.562	178	6	0	12	40	3
Mikey Kluksa, Richmond	.325	.381	.500	194	9	5	5	35	6
Ryan Weingartner, St. Joseph's	.323	.401	.531	192	10	0	10	36	17
Steve Ditomaso, GW	.322	.373	.433	245	9	3	4	28	18
Jack Putney, St. Bonaventure	.320	.385	.456	169	12	1	3	26	0

INDIVIDUAL PITCHING LEADERS

	W	L	ERA	G	SV	IP	H	BB	SO
Bennett Flynn, Davidson	5	1	3.36	4	4	56	40	35	82
Chad Gartland, George Mason	7	2	3.39	13	2	98	88	28	86
Chris Kahler, GW	4	3	3.57	13	0	86	77	25	79
Will Schomberg, Davidson	7	2	3.98	13	0	66	54	28	68
Ryan Desanto, Saint Joseph's	4	1	3.99	11	0	59	38	31	74
Trystan Levesque, Rhode Island	6	5	4.01	15	0	83	83	19	101
Litman Henry, Saint Louis	6	3	4.32	13	0	77	87	28	54
Esteban Rodriguez, Richmond	5	2	4.32	1	2	67	65	16	81
Domenic Picone, St. Joseph's	5	6	4.50	14	0	70	64	34	74
Logan Koester, GW	6	3	4.62	14	0	90	100	32	53
Ben Shields, George Mason	7	4	4.69	16	1	81	63	36	107
Liam Devine, St. Bonaventure	2	3	4.79	4	5	56	56	30	48
Chaffin Owen, Saint Louis	5	1	4.84	14	0	61	59	30	32
Mark Manfredi, Dayton	3	4	4.99	15	0	79	71	38	96
Weber Jack, Saint Louis	3	2	5.08	0	3	57	71	14	32
Holmes Jackson, Saint Louis	3	2	5.30	14	0	73	77	25	37
Eli Majick, Dayton	5	4	5.32	12	0	66	84	25	53
Will Mccausland, St. Joseph's	5	3	5.42	14	0	75	87	21	68
James Gladden, VCU	5	3	5.43	6	0	61	60	33	45
Teddy Brennan, GW	3	4	5.54	10	0	63	68	38	48

BIG EAST CONFERENCE

	Conference		Overall	
	W	L	W	L
*UConn	15	5	44	17
*Xavier	14	7	39	25
Seton Hall	13	8	31	24
Georgetown	10	10	30	27
Creighton	10	11	25	24
St. John's	8	12	28	25
Villanova	7	13	14	37
Butler	5	16	12	43

ALL-CONFERENCE TEAM: C: Matt DePrey, Xavier, Jr. **1B:** Ben Huber, UConn, Gr. **2B:** Michael Eze, Georgetown, Jr. **SS:** Max Viera, Seton Hall, Jr. **3B:** Dominic Freeberger, UConn, Gr. **DH:** Staus Pokrovsky, Seton Hall, R-Jr. **OF:** Jake Studley, UConn, Gr. **OF:** Ubaldo Lopez, Georgetown, Gr. **OF:** Devin Hack, Seton Hall, R-Jr. **OF:** Andrew Walker, Xavier, Sr. **SP:** Stephen Quigley, UConn, Gr. **SP:** Jake Bloss, Georgetown, Gr. **SP:** Nick Payero, Seton Hall, Gr. **SP:** Brant Alazaus, Xavier, Sr. **RP:** Zach Fogell, UConn, Gr. **Player of the Year:** Dominic Freeberger, UConn. **Pitcher of the Year:** Jake Bloss, Georgetown. **Freshman of the Year:** Joey Urban, Butler. **Coaching Staff of the Year:** Seton Hall, Head coach Rob Sheppard .

INDIVIDUAL BATTING LEADERS

Player	AVG	OBP	SLG	AB	2B	3B	HR	RBI	SB
Aaron Mann, St. John's	.371	.462	.548	186	15	0	6	42	3
Dominic Freeberger, Conn.	.346	.429	.484	246	13	0	7	61	6
Ben Huber, Conn.	.340	.440	.684	209	21	0	17	66	4
Paul Orbon, St. John's	.338	.433	.504	133	11	1	3	33	6
Ubaldo Lopez, Georgetown	.337	.474	.698	199	12	0	20	55	1
Jake Studley, Connecticut	.325	.420	.496	234	12	2	8	57	6
Alex Clyde, Seton Hall	.324	.387	.400	210	5	4	1	28	1
Andrew Walker, Xavier	.323	.406	.492	266	19	1	8	57	30
Max Viera, Seton Hall	.319	.372	.486	216	17	2	5	46	22
Oscar Murray, Seton Hall	.319	.451	.518	166	11	2	6	29	9
Jake Hyde, Georgetown	.318	.390	.605	223	12	2	16	56	3
Hogan Helligso, Creighton	.314	.400	.458	118	9	1	2	19	3
Devin Hack, Seton Hall	.313	.409	.369	198	7	2	0	19	25
Luke Broadhurst, Conn.	.312	.441	.590	205	13	1	14	51	9
Craig Larsen, Villanova	.311	.361	.476	212	14	3	5	44	1
Marty Higgins, St. John's	.310	.369	.462	184	9	2	5	32	3
Matt McCormick, Xavier	.309	.421	.552	223	12	0	14	44	3
David Smith, Connecticut	.304	.429	.464	237	19	2	5	36	39
Jack O'Reilly, Villanova	.303	.409	.503	195	13	1	8	25	7
Sterling Hayes, Creighton	.303	.416	.436	165	16	0	2	28	4
Austin Machado, St. John's	.303	.495	.455	132	8	0	4	31	2
Joseph Urban, Butler	.296	.364	.480	223	17	3	6	35	5

INDIVIDUAL PITCHING LEADERS

	W	L	ERA	G	SV	IP	H	BB	SO
Jake Bloss, Georgetown	8	4	2.58	14	0	77	58	24	96
Nick Payero, Seton Hall	5	3	3.12	15	0	69	60	22	62
Ethan Bosacker, Xavier	8	3	3.49	16	0	98	82	29	101
Ryan Windham, Creighton	5	3	3.82	14	0	75	75	21	60
Brant Alazaus, Xavier	9	3	3.89	17	0	106	91	8	102
Luke Hoskins, Xavier	7	2	4.48	20	0	78	79	18	53
Joe Mascio, St. John's	3	3	4.68	13	0	65	62	26	63
Stephen Quigley, Conn.	4	3	4.83	15	0	76	78	29	74
Sonny Fauci, St. John's	3	2	5.13	14	0	60	62	33	41
Cory Bosecker, Butler	1	8	5.20	14	0	73	71	33	72
Dominic Cancellieri, Creighton	1	3	5.43	14	0	58	70	19	60
Devin Rivera, Villanova	2	7	5.84	14	0	74	79	25	45
Justin Kleinsorge, Creighton	1	4	6.07	14	0	53	54	23	51
Daniel Frontera, Seton Hall	2	3	6.09	14	0	58	67	26	38

BIG SOUTH CONFERENCE

	Conference		Overall	
	W	L	W	L
*Campbell	22	5	46	15
USC Upstate	21	6	38	22
Winthrop	15	12	28	28
Gardner-Webb	15	12	31	25
Charleston Southern	13	14	22	28
UNC Asheville	12	15	26	26
Presbyterian	12	15	21	34
High Point	12	15	20	34
Longwood	11	16	23	31
Radford	2	25	10	45

ALL-CONFERENCE TEAM: C: Grant Knipp, R-Soph., Campbell. **INF:** Jarrod Belbin, R-Sr., Campbell. **INF:** Bryce Arnold, Jr., Campbell. **INF:** Eliot Dix, R-Jr., Longwood. **INF:** Grant Sherrod, Jr., USC Upstate. **OF:** Lawson Harrill, R-Jr., Campbell. **OF:** Robbie Burnett, Soph., UNC Asheville. **OF:** Curtis Robison, R-Sr., Gardner-Webb. **UTL:** Brody Hopkins, Jr., Winthrop. **DH:** Logan Jordan, R-Jr., Campbell. **SP:** Bobby Alcock, R-Soph., Gardner-Webb. **SP:** Cade Kuehler, Jr., Campbell. **SP:** Reese Dutton, Jr., USC Upstate. **RP:** Ty Cummings, Jr., Campbell. **RP:** Aaron Rund, R-Sr., Campbelll. **Player Of The Year:** Lawson Harrill, Campbell. **Pitcher Of The Year:** Bobby Alcock, Gardner-Webb. **Freshman Of The Year:** Jackson Roberts, **Campbell. Coach Of The Year:** Justin Haire, Campbell.

INDIVIDUAL BATTING LEADERS

Player	AVG	OBP	SLG	AB	2B	3B	HR	RBI	SB
Robbie Burnett, UNC Asheville	.379	.486	.759	145	10	3	13	35	11
Tyler Halstead, Campbell	.376	.455	.523	237	15	4	4	38	32
Lawson Harrill, Campbell	.371	.475	.761	213	17	0	22	69	6
Curtis Robison, Gardner-Webb	.362	.460	.528	218	16	4	4	42	20
Brody Fahr, Presbyterian	.361	.452	.510	202	12	3	4	34	5
Jaylin Rae, Charleston So.	.352	.441	.455	176	10	1	2	30	5
Eliot Dix, Longwood	.347	.438	.503	199	13	0	6	32	7
Dylan Bacot, UNC Asheville	.337	.440	.559	202	18	0	9	59	6
Grant Sherrod, USC Upstate	.335	.429	.625	224	14	3	15	66	8
Brett Ahalt, High Point	.333	.403	.540	198	8	0	11	32	13
Max Weller, Campbell	.331	.471	.504	121	9	0	4	25	9
Gregory Ryan, Longwood	.327	.390	.639	202	14	5	13	63	8
Jarrod Belbin, Campbell	.327	.426	.661	251	15	3	21	68	25

SAMUEL LEWIS

Dylan Campbell hit .339 with a .603 slugging percentage for Texas.

	AVG	OBP	SLG	AB	2B	3B	HR	RBI	SB
Kieran Davis, Charleston So.	.327	.419	.548	104	8	0	5	24	2
Troy Hamilton, USC Upstate	.324	.400	.458	179	7	1	5	38	8
Zack Whitacre, Radford	.322	.397	.500	208	12	2	7	33	12
Cael Chatham, High Point	.321	.402	.575	212	15	0	13	43	6
Bryce Arnold, Campbell	.321	.412	.638	246	19	4	17	65	7
Mckinley Erves, Winthrop	.320	.424	.457	197	15	0	4	28	7
Cole Caruso, USC Upstate	.319	.424	.422	232	15	0	3	39	4
Ricky Teel, Winthrop	.315	.359	.365	178	7	1	0	17	4
Kohl Abrams, UNC Asheville	.314	.432	.450	191	10	2	4	26	7
Jace Rinehart, USC Upstate	.310	.396	.535	129	8	0	7	32	3
Jacob Marcos, Gardner-Webb	.309	.390	.339	236	7	0	0	13	11
Chandler Riley, Campbell	.309	.493	.441	152	6	1	4	25	8

INDIVIDUAL PITCHING LEADERS

	W	L	ERA	G	SV	IP	H	BB	SO
Bobby Alcock, Gardner-Webb	7	3	2.51	14	0	90	56	40	106
Cade Kuehler, Campbell	8	1	2.71	13	0	73	54	26	91
Reese Dutton, USC Upstate	10	3	3.29	15	0	90	80	30	102
Aaron Rund, Campbell	5	2	3.84	0	5	61	55	25	71
Ryan Miller, Longwood	4	6	4.08	13	0	68	73	27	55
Henry Proger, USC Upstate	7	5	4.17	13	0	73	70	21	69
Evan Truitt, Charleston Southern	5	7	4.36	4	0	74	74	24	69
Hunter Loyd, Campbell	4	4	4.63	15	0	72	71	34	69
Justin Honeycutt, UNC Asheville	4	2	4.67	6	1	62	56	26	33
Chance Daquila, Campbell	9	1	4.85	14	0	69	67	24	42
Brett Wozniak, High Point	3	2	4.91	10	0	62	74	19	34
Gus Hughes, High Point	6	5	4.98	14	0	81	73	35	90
Logan Berrier, Longwood	2	6	5.24	11	1	57	67	32	57
Chase Matheny, USC Upstate	2	3	5.37	9	1	60	80	20	42
Kaleb Hill, Charleston Southern	3	4	5.37	10	1	54	60	31	59
Clay Edmondson, UNC Asheville	5	3	5.38	13	0	72	81	30	68
Tyler Switalski, Gardner-Webb	8	5	5.60	15	0	80	91	31	80
Mathieu Curtis, USC Upstate	7	2	5.66	13	0	68	75	34	50
Duncan Howard, Presbyterian	4	5	5.68	14	0	82	109	20	59
Ryan Douglas, UNC Asheville	6	1	5.79	14	0	61	70	31	61
Charlie Mcdaniel, Presbyterian	4	8	6.16	15	0	76	98	16	57
Ty Burton, Radford	3	7	6.24	7	0	62	79	12	56
Alex Logusch, Winthrop	1	3	6.63	14	0	58	68	44	76
Dylan Howard, Radford	2	10	6.99	14	0	67	103	14	62
Landon Higgerson, Radford	1	3	7.47	2	1	59	59	38	45

BIG 12 CONFERENCE

	Conference		Overall	
	W	L	W	L
*Texas	15	9	42	22
*Oklahoma State	15	9	41	20
*West Virginia	15	9	40	20
*TCU	13	11	44	24
Kansas State	13	11	35	24
*Texas Tech	12	12	41	23
*Oklahoma	11	13	32	28
Kansas	8	16	25	32
Baylor	6	18	20	35

ALL-CONFERENCE TEAM: C: Garret Guillemette, Texas. **IF:** Roc Riggio, Oklahoma State. **IF:** Brayden Taylor, TCU. **IF:** Gavin Kash, Texas Tech. **IF:** Kevin Bazzell, Texas Tech. **IF:** JJ Wetherholt, West Virginia. **OF:** Nolan Schubart, Oklahoma State. **OF:** Porter Brown, Texas. **OF:** Dylan Campbell, Texas. **DH:** Janson Reeder, Kansas. **UT:** Carson Benge, Oklahoma State. **SP:** Braden Carmichael, Oklahoma. **SP:** Lucas Gordon, Texas. **SP:** Lebarron Johnson Jr., Texas. **SP:** Ben Hampton, West Virginia. **RP:** Tyson Neighbors, Kansas State. **RP:** Carlson Reed, West Virginia. **Player of the Year:** JJ Wetherholt, West Virginia. **Pitcher of the Year:** Lucas Gordon, Texas. **Co-Freshmen of the Year:** Nolan Schubart, Oklahoma State/Kodey Shojinaga, Kansas. **Newcomer of the Year:** Tyler Wulfert, Oklahoma State. **Coach of the Year:** Randy Mazey, West Virginia.

INDIVIDUAL BATTING LEADERS

	AVG	OBP	SLG	AB	2B	3B	HR	RBI	SB
J.J. Wetherholt, West Virginia	.449	.517	.787	225	24	2	16	60	36
Kodey Shojinaga, Kansas	.378	.421	.526	196	11	0	6	32	0
Nolen Hester, Texas Tech	.372	.538	.484	223	19	0	2	39	4
Brady Day, Kansas State	.356	.492	.459	194	9	1	3	26	8
Cole Fontenelle, TCU	.352	.473	.639	233	21	2	14	58	20
Carson Benge, Oklahoma State	.351	.471	.546	194	17	0	7	43	8
Karson Bowen, TCU	.350	.420	.502	217	15	0	6	46	9
Kevin Bazzell, Texas Tech	.344	.449	.563	256	24	1	10	64	2
Roc Riggio, Oklahoma State	.339	.462	.688	221	17	3	18	61	7
Powell Peyton, Texas	.339	.431	.548	230	16	1	10	46	2
Campbell Dylan, Texas	.339	.436	.603	242	19	3	13	50	26
Nolan Schubart, Oklahoma State	.335	.450	.670	212	20	0	17	72	1
Gavin Kash, Texas Tech	.332	.401	.705	268	13	3	27	88	2
Dakota Harris, Oklahoma	.332	.406	.518	193	13	1	7	48	5
Anthony Silva, TCU	.330	.416	.471	227	11	0	7	50	17
Kolby Branch, Baylor	.325	.430	.509	212	17	2	6	41	7
Tyler Wulfert, Oklahoma State	.323	.370	.617	167	16	3	9	31	2
Brown Porter, Texas	.323	.426	.545	235	14	1	12	59	11
Gage Harrelson, Texas Tech	.321	.404	.435	246	15	5	1	45	6
Thomas Jared, Texas	.321	.398	.484	215	15	4	4	29	10
Tevin Tucker, West Virginia	.318	.465	.410	195	9	3	1	23	20
Kendall Pettis, Oklahoma	.317	.437	.398	186	6	3	1	24	18
Chase Adkison, Oklahoma State	.316	.417	.487	187	9	1	7	44	4
Hudson White, Texas Tech	.314	.415	.574	169	11	0	11	54	2
Chase Jans, Kansas	.314	.386	.531	207	13	1	10	50	7
Bryce Madron, Oklahoma	.313	.468	.564	227	15	3	12	51	15
Landon Wallace, West Virginia	.312	.450	.563	199	11	3	11	49	17
David Mendham, Oklahoma State	.311	.368	.553	244	17	0	14	63	1
Tre Richardson, TCU	.311	.392	.452	270	16	2	6	60	25
Hunter Teplanszky, Baylor	.308	.406	.500	172	11	2	6	34	3
Brayden Taylor, TCU	.308	.430	.631	260	15	0	23	70	14
Easton Carmichael, Oklahoma	.308	.350	.483	201	9	4	6	52	4
Kennedy Eric, Texas	.306	.378	.588	245	14	2	17	47	9
Anthony Mackenzie, Oklahoma	.299	.408	.422	251	9	2	6	42	21
Guillemette Garret, Texas	.298	.401	.541	218	18	1	11	60	0
Michael Brooks, Kansas	.298	.392	.505	198	15	1	8	34	2
Hunter Simmons, Baylor	.297	.374	.430	158	7	1	4	34	0
Cash Rugely, Kansas State	.297	.428	.455	202	9	1	7	36	14
Caleb McNeely, West Virginia	.296	.412	.569	216	14	3	13	49	16
Austin Green, Texas Tech	.290	.416	.548	221	14	2	13	60	0

INDIVIDUAL PITCHING LEADERS

	W	L	ERA	GS	SV	IP	H	BB	SO
Isaac Stebens, Oklahoma State	4	1	2.24	0	6	64	49	24	85
Gordon Lucas, Texas	7	2	2.63	17	0	103	85	34	103
Johnson Lebarron, Texas	8	4	2.91	13	1	87	73	38	98
Braden Carmichael, Oklahoma	8	1	3.03	12	0	86	90	18	67
Collin Baumgartner, Kansas	6	1	3.62	15	0	80	82	22	74
Mason Molina, Texas Tech	6	2	3.67	16	0	83	63	35	108
Kole Klecker, TCU	10	4	3.72	17	0	97	78	30	72
Blaine Traxel, West Virginia	7	6	3.86	15	0	105	98	23	77
Sam Stoutenborough, TCU	5	0	4.35	10	0	70	73	18	58
Ben Hampton, West Virginia	5	3	4.45	16	0	85	92	30	66
Thaniel Trumper, Kansas	4	5	4.47	0	2	58	44	28	54
James Hitt, Oklahoma	6	2	4.89	12	0	70	70	23	41
Juaron Watts-Brown, Okla. St.	6	5	5.03	15	0	82	68	48	124
Owen Boerema, Kansas State	7	2	5.06	15	0	85	93	34	95
Ty Ruhl, Kansas State	4	4	5.31	2	3	61	62	22	51
German Fajardo, Kansas State	4	4	5.65	16	0	73	74	37	68
Braxton Douthit, Oklahoma	5	7	6.01	16	0	82	72	61	62
Ben Abram, Oklahoma State	8	3	6.21	14	0	71	91	22	76
Sam Ireland, Kansas	4	7	6.75	14	0	65	73	26	43
Mason Marriott, Baylor	1	7	7.52	14	0	59	72	40	50
Blake Helton, Baylor	1	6	8.35	11	0	55	88	23	51

BIG TEN CONFERENCE

	Conference		Overall	
	W	L	W	L
*Maryland	17	7	42	21
*Indiana	16	8	43	20
*Iowa	15	8	44	16
Nebraska	15	9	33	23
Rutgers	14	10	33	23
Michigan	13	11	28	28
Michigan State	12	12	33	22
Illinois	12	12	25	27
Purdue	11	13	24	29
Minnesota	10	14	18	34
Ohio State	9	15	31	25
Penn State	7	16	25	25
Northwestern	4	20	10	40

ALL-CONFERENCE TEAM: C: Luke Shliger, Jr., Maryland. **1B:** Brock Vradenburg, Jr., Michigan State. **2B:** Max Anderson, Jr., Nebraska. **SS:** Matt Shaw, Jr., Maryland. **3B:** Nick Lorusso, Sr., Maryland. **OF:** Devin Taylor, Fr., Indiana. **OF:** Sam Petersen, So., Iowa. **OF:** Ryan Lasko, Jr., Rutgers. **SP:** Brody Brecht, So., Iowa. **SP:** Connor O'Halloran, Jr., Michigan. **SP:** Christian Coppola, Fr., Rutgers. **RP:** Ryan Kraft, So., Indiana. **DH:** Keaton Anthony, So., Iowa. At-Large: Brice Matthews, Jr., SS, Nebraska. **Player Of The Year:** Matt Shaw, Jr., Maryland. **Pitcher Of The Year:** Connor O'Halloran, Jr., Michigan. **Freshman Of The Year:** Devin Taylor, Fr., Indiana. **Coach Of The Year:** Rob Vaughn, Maryland.

INDIVIDUAL BATTING LEADERS

	AVG	OBP	SLG	AB	2B	3B	HR	RBI	SB
Max Anderson, Nebraska	.414	.461	.770	244	20	2	21	70	0
Brock Vradenburg, Michigan State	.400	.492	.721	215	22	4	13	69	1
Keaton Anthony, Iowa	.389	.505	.701	157	22	0	9	38	1
Nick Lorusso, Maryland	.379	.446	.765	264	20	2	26	105	3
Brice Matthews, Nebraska	.359	.481	.723	206	11	2	20	67	20
Phillip Glasser, Indiana	.357	.444	.515	266	19	1	7	48	14
Brock Tibbitts, Indiana	.357	.447	.585	241	17	4	10	68	1
Brett Bateman, Minnesota	.356	.446	.408	191	10	0	0	12	17
Brennen Dorighi, Iowa	.348	.469	.634	224	19	0	15	67	9
Trent Farquhar, Michigan State	.343	.467	.469	213	19	1	2	35	7
Matt Shaw, Maryland	.341	.445	.697	264	20	1	24	69	18
Mitch Jebb, Michigan State	.337	.438	.495	202	15	7	1	36	14
Luke Shliger, Maryland	.336	.523	.582	232	24	0	11	52	14
Paul Toetz, Purdue	.335	.425	.579	197	14	2	10	53	2
Andy Axelson, Rutgers	.333	.424	.474	114	1	0	5	27	0
Jake Parr, Purdue	.331	.422	.534	163	15	3	4	36	3
Ryan Lasko, Rutgers	.330	.428	.581	227	18	3	11	54	18
Eddie Hacopian, Maryland	.327	.407	.486	251	16	0	8	49	8
Stephen Hrustich, Northwestern	.325	.441	.518	166	12	1	6	31	8
Michael Seegers, Iowa	.322	.428	.449	227	7	5	4	31	17
Sam Petersen, Iowa	.319	.449	.584	166	9	1	11	47	20
Bryan Broecker, Michigan State	.318	.441	.529	170	8	2	8	36	1
Johnny Piacentino, Penn State	.318	.374	.446	157	7	2	3	25	8
Evan Albrecht, Purdue	.316	.365	.375	152	7	1	0	25	13
Tyler Pettorini, Ohio State	.315	.367	.490	149	8	3	4	28	7
Jonathan Kim, Michigan	.315	.373	.473	146	10	2	3	28	5
Evan Sleight, Rutgers	.315	.435	.571	203	14	1	12	44	2
Raider Tello, Iowa	.315	.404	.432	241	14	1	4	50	3
Devin Taylor, Indiana	.315	.430	.650	200	13	3	16	59	1
Brayden Frazier, Iowa	.312	.392	.488	125	10	0	4	29	4
Thomas Bramley, Penn State	.312	.442	.446	186	11	1	4	36	4
Carter Mathison, Indiana	.311	.426	.538	225	15	3	10	49	3
Bobby Marsh, Penn State	.310	.388	.524	145	13	0	6	35	0
Couper Cornblum, Purdue	.310	.385	.386	197	10	1	1	31	26
Camden Janik, Illinois	.308	.435	.514	185	9	1	9	27	1
Ted Burton, Michigan	.306	.421	.574	209	15	1	13	45	4
Cole Evans, Nebraska	.305	.415	.454	141	9	0	4	27	9
Chris Brito, Rutgers	.304	.433	.575	207	14	0	14	55	5
Kevin Ferrer, Northwestern	.303	.365	.455	132	5	0	5	20	0
Boston Merila, Minnesota	.303	.423	.377	175	10	0	1	17	3
Kevin Keister, Maryland	.303	.423	.511	231	16	1	10	51	1
Ryan Moerman, Illinois	.300	.372	.547	190	11	0	12	44	3
Drake Westcott, Illinois	.299	.391	.582	201	3	0	18	47	1
Jack Frank, Michigan State	.299	.418	.456	204	11	0	7	45	19
Jay Harry, Penn State	.299	.376	.463	201	13	1	6	37	6
Josh Kuroda-Grauer, Rutgers	.298	.393	.487	228	15	5	6	32	13
Trevor Cohen, Rutgers	.298	.383	.353	218	7	1	1	34	10
Charlie Fischer, Nebraska	.295	.403	.500	146	5	2	7	36	1
Josh Pyne, Indiana	.295	.357	.445	254	16	2	6	56	3
Henry Kaczmar, Ohio State	.293	.377	.452	208	10	1	7	46	7

INDIVIDUAL PITCHING LEADERS

	W	L	ERA	G	SV	IP	H	BB	SO
Christian Coppola, Rutgers	5	5	3.68	13	66	66	61	27	71
Marcus Morgan, Iowa	5	2	3.72	15	65	65	38	51	72
Brody Brecht, Iowa	5	2	3.74	16	77	77	37	61	109
Jonah Jenkins, Ohio State	6	4	3.81	6	57	57	55	19	44
Andrew Carson, Michigan State	3	4	3.93	6	55	55	59	23	49
Connor O'Halloran, Michigan	8	6	4.11	15	103	103	90	26	110
Jace Kaminska, Nebraska	7	3	4.13	14	72	72	67	15	57
Ty Langenberg, Iowa	6	3	4.15	15	78	78	83	34	86
Jacob Denner, Michigan	3	6	4.16	10	80	80	77	23	82
Nick Powers, Michigan State	5	3	4.21	11	62	62	51	20	41
Jason Savacool, Maryland	9	5	4.22	16	96	96	94	39	95
Luke Sinnard, Indiana	6	3	4.27	16	86	86	83	25	114
Emmett Olson, Nebraska	6	3	4.50	15	82	82	68	30	80
Drew Conover, Rutgers	5	4	4.50	14	68	68	47	45	83
Travis Luensmann, Penn State	6	5	4.50	6	60	60	54	39	59
Kyle Iwinski, Purdue	3	5	4.54	11	69	69	73	19	38
Jack Wenninger, Illinois	6	4	4.59	14	80	80	69	28	76
Jaden Henline, Penn State	5	3	4.70	9	61	61	78	17	35
Gavin Bruni, Ohio State	5	3	4.87	14	57	57	50	42	73
Noah Rennard, Michigan	7	4	4.88	8	66	66	61	26	63
Tucker Novotny, Minnesota	4	5	5.03	14	73	73	69	39	80
Richard Holetz, Minnesota	2	6	5.21	12	76	76	77	23	60
Khal Stephen, Purdue	7	4	5.21	14	76	76	72	30	66
Harrison Cook, Michigan State	5	3	5.40	5	58	58	55	26	40
Jordan Morales, Penn State	3	2	5.50	10	56	56	59	24	53
Nick Dean, Maryland	3	2	5.55	15	75	75	78	32	77
Joseph Dzierwa, Michigan State	6	4	5.69	13	74	74	81	22	60
Jonathan Blackwell, Purdue	5	6	6.22	14	72	72	85	22	58
Riley Gowens, Illinois	2	3	6.30	12	60	60	71	16	75
Matt McClure, Northwestern	1	6	6.71	13	59	59	67	25	38

BIG WEST CONFERENCE

	Conference		Overall	
	W	L	W	L
UC San Diego	21	9	34	18
*Cal State Fullerton	20	10	32	24
CSUN	21	9	35	16
UC Irvine	18	12	37	18

	W	L	W	L
Hawai'i	18	12	29	20
UC Santa Barbara	18	12	35	20
Long Beach State	17	13	33	22
Cal Poly	11	19	21	35
Cal State Bakersfield	9	21	18	34
UC Davis	7	23	17	37
UC Riverside	5	25	11	41

ALL-CONFERENCE TEAM: C: Connor Burns, Jr., Long Beach State. **1B:** Anthony Martinez, Fr., UC Irvine. **2B:** Michael Fuhrman, Sr., UC San Diego. **3B:** Matt Halbach, So., UC San Diego. **SS:** Ali Camarillo, So., CSUN. **OF:** Caden Kendle, Jr., UC Irvine; Nate Nankil, Jr., Cal State Fullerton; Jakob Simons, Jr., CSUN; Jared Sundstrom, R-Jr., UC Santa Barbara. **UTIL:** Collin Villegas, Sr., Cal Poly. **DH:** Ivan Brethowr, So., UC Santa Barbara. **SP:** Matt Ager, So., UC Santa Barbara; Harry Gustin, So., Hawai'i; Nico Zeglin, Gr., Long Beach State. **RP:** Harrison Bodendorf, Fr., Hawai'i; Hudson Barrett, Fr., UC Santa Barbara. **CL:** Izaak Martinez, R-Jr., UC San Diego. **Co-Players of the Year:** Caden Kendle, UC Irvine & Jakob Simons, CSUN. **Pitcher of the Year:** Nico Zeglin, Long Beach State. **Defensive Player of the Year:** Connor Burns, Long Beach State. **Freshman Field Player of the Year:** Anthony Martinez, UC Irvine. **Freshman Pitcher of the Year:** Hudson Barrett, UC Santa Barbara. **Coach of the Year:** Eric Newman, UC San Diego.

INDIVIDUAL BATTING LEADERS

	AVG	OBP	SLG	AB	2B	3B	HR	RBI	SB
Anthony Martinez, UC Irvine	.394	.471	.619	231	19	0	11	60	0
Ali Camarillo, CSUN	.371	.421	.611	175	15	3	7	44	1
Matt Kurata, Cal State Bakers.	.369	.429	.439	157	11	0	0	21	4
Jakob Simons, CSUN	.356	.450	.665	188	14	1	14	48	11
Ryan Fenn, Cal Poly	.344	.390	.405	163	8	1	0	16	9
Cody Hendriks, Cal State Bakers.	.343	.430	.412	102	7	0	0	14	2
Kevin Fitzer, CSUN	.339	.410	.537	177	5	3	8	50	6
Caden Kendle, UC Irvine	.335	.434	.535	230	16	3	8	56	7
Thomas McCaffrey, UC Irvine	.333	.408	.512	129	9	1	4	34	0
Matt Wong, Hawai'i	.330	.404	.563	197	12	2	10	42	0
Caden Connor, Cal State Fullert.	.330	.417	.504	224	20	2	5	45	2
Aaron Casillas, Cal Poly	.329	.369	.394	231	15	0	0	40	1
Anthony Mcfarland, UC Riverside	.329	.402	.399	173	9	0	1	17	2
Patrick Hackworth, UC San Diego	.327	.456	.414	162	9	1	1	15	6
Doyle Kane, UC San Diego	.327	.397	.411	202	14	0	1	39	0
Jacob Igawa, Hawai'i	.324	.377	.451	204	12	1	4	40	3
Jared Sundstrom, UCSB	.322	.399	.672	177	15	1	15	43	11
Aaron Parker, UCSB	.321	.415	.551	187	11	1	10	32	4
Nathan Barraza, CSUN	.319	.359	.429	119	7	0	2	21	4
Jo Oyama, UC Irvine	.319	.418	.500	210	7	5	7	44	14
Jake Steels, Cal Poly	.318	.433	.385	192	5	1	2	27	13
Carter White, Cal State Fullerton	.318	.381	.384	198	11	1	0	22	9
Riley Kapser, Cal State Bakers.	.316	.382	.401	187	11	1	1	22	4
Nate Nankil, Cal State Fullerton	.316	.384	.468	237	21	0	5	39	5
Ryan Stafford, Cal Poly	.313	.393	.500	230	20	1	7	44	4
Alex Gouveia, UC Davis	.313	.345	.462	208	20	1	3	26	7
Jonathon Long, Long Beach St.	.312	.404	.600	215	17	0	15	52	0
Graysen Tarlow, CSUN	.311	.417	.429	177	12	0	3	41	9
Ivan Brethowr, UCSB	.311	.408	.571	177	13	0	11	40	8
Shunsuke Sakaino, CSUN	.310	.428	.374	171	8	0	1	23	8

INDIVIDUAL PITCHING LEADERS

	W	L	ERA	G	SV	IP	H	BB	SO
Hudson Barrett , UCSB	5	1	1.92	4	6	61	42	32	82
Nico Zeglin, Long Beach State	8	4	2.00	15	0	95	67	27	117
Connor Harrison, Hawai'i	1	5	2.70	2	7	53	49	14	43
Alex Giroux, Hawai'i	4	2	2.83	6	2	57	48	14	52
Izaak Martinez, UC San Diego	6	1	2.84	1	9	57	45	16	63
Michael Stanford, UC Irvine	7	2	3.06	9	1	65	63	15	56
Matt Ager, UCSB	5	4	3.12	15	0	92	71	26	115
Harry Gustin, Hawai'i	5	3	3.14	14	0	77	71	36	79
Harrison Bodendorf, Hawai'i	5	2	3.45	6	5	57	52	27	66
Matt Comnos, Cal State Bakers.	3	6	3.46	15	0	83	72	43	80
Evan Yates, Cal State Fullerton	3	2	3.75	15	0	74	83	31	69
Ryan Forcucci, UC San Diego	4	1	3.86	9	0	54	41	21	69
Bryan Green, UC Davis	5	4	4.15	15	0	78	69	32	51
Thomas Bainton, CSUN	7	2	4.18	14	0	84	78	26	63
Fynn Chester, Cal State Fuller.	7	3	4.21	7	1	58	69	6	42

COLONIAL ATHLETIC ASSOCIATION

	Conference		Overall	
	W	L	W	L
*UNC Wilmington	20	8	34	23
Elon	19	9	33	22
*Northeastern	20	10	44	16
Charleston	18	12	36	22
Delaware	17	13	30	29
William & Mary	15	15	32	25
Stony Brook	14	16	23	29
Hofstra	13	15	26	26
N.C. A&T	11	17	19	28
Towson	7	23	19	37
Monmouth	6	22	16	30

ALL-CONFERENCE TEAM: C: Kevin Bruggeman, Sr., Hofstra. **IF:** Jac Croom, Jr., UNCW. **IF:** JJ Freeman, Sr., Delaware. **IF:** Evan Giordano, Gr., Stony Brook. **IF:** Joey Loynd, Jr., Delaware. **IF:** Ben Williamson, Sr., William & Mary. **OF:** Justin Cassella, Jr., Elon. **OF:** Cam Maldonado, Fr., Northeastern. **OF:** Trevor Marsh, Jr., UNCW. **OF:** Mike Sirota, So., Northeastern. **UT:** Evan Fox, Jr., Stony Brook. **DH:** Alex Lane, Sr., Northeastern. **SP:** Aiven Cabral, Fr., Northeastern. **SP:** Ty Good, Sr., Charleston. **SP:** Shea Sprague, So., Elon. **SP:** Zane Taylor, So., UNCW. **RP:** Carter Lovasz, So., William & Mary. **RP:** William Privette, Jr., Charleston. **Player Of The Year:** Ben Williamson, IF, William & Mary. **Pitcher Of The Year:** Ty Good, Charleston. **Defensive Player Of The Year:** Spenser Smith, Northeastern. **Rookie Of The Year:** Cam Maldonado, Northeastern. **Coach Of The Year:** Mike Glavine, Northeastern.

INDIVIDUAL BATTING LEADERS

	AVG	OBP	SLG	AB	2B	3B	HR	RBI	SB
Joey Loynd, Delaware	.392	.454	.692	250	27	3	14	80	4
Ben Williamson, William & Mary	.390	.513	.662	210	11	5	12	49	14
Reyce Curnane, Towson	.376	.475	.697	165	13	2	12	40	3
Parker Haskin, Elon	.369	.460	.595	84	5	1	4	24	1
Dylan Palmer, Hofstra	.369	.441	.464	179	11	3	0	23	23
Tank Yaghoubi, William & Mary	.364	.459	.411	151	5	1	0	20	6
Jac Croom, UNCW	.361	.427	.521	219	12	1	7	34	7
Cam Maldonado, Northeastern	.353	.434	.642	215	13	5	13	45	32
Steve Harrington, Hofstra	.350	.458	.589	163	16	1	7	46	0
Mike Sirota, Northeastern	.346	.472	.678	214	9	4	18	54	19
Danny Crossen, Northeastern	.346	.417	.535	243	14	1	10	46	16
Evan Giordano, Stony Brook	.346	.406	.622	217	19	4	11	54	8
Phil Stahl, Monmouth	.346	.430	.469	162	5	0	5	38	0
Justin Cassella, Elon	.343	.402	.715	172	11	1	17	46	10
Evan Fox, Stony Brook	.333	.429	.534	204	13	2	8	37	39
Tyler Macgregor, Northeastern	.332	.416	.624	229	11	1	18	54	6
Cole Mathis, Charleston	.332	.442	.577	196	19	1	9	51	8
Anthony D'Onofrio, Hofstra	.330	.429	.420	100	6	0	1	17	9
Kevin Bruggeman, Hofstra	.325	.399	.515	200	20	0	6	41	1
Casey Bishop, Towson	.324	.396	.466	204	10	2	5	33	21
Tre Williams, N.C. A&T	.324	.358	.514	148	14	1	4	26	6
Brett Paulsen, Stony Brook	.323	.358	.424	198	12	1	2	38	2
Bryce Greenly, Delaware	.322	.397	.514	208	8	4	8	33	1
Elijah Dickerson, Towson	.321	.382	.439	212	15	2	2	38	1
Cam Dean, Charleston	.321	.407	.375	168	9	0	0	20	7

INDIVIDUAL PITCHING LEADERS

	W	L	ERA	G	SV	IP	H	BB	SO
Aiven Cabral, Northeastern	9	4	2.58	16	0	84	78	14	69
Shea Sprague, Elon	7	3	2.69	15	0	90	93	19	82
Jake Gigliotti, Northeastern	8	0	3.24	8	2	67	55	17	65
Nate Knowles, William & Mary	5	5	3.43	17	0	66	52	30	70
Cole Mathis, Charleston	5	1	3.45	10	1	60	60	17	52
Trey Pooser, Charleston	7	3	3.65	15	0	86	93	25	75
Justin Mitrovich, Elon	7	4	3.68	13	0	64	65	21	66
Zane Taylor, UNCW	7	3	3.72	17	0	87	81	20	60
Tom Mayer, William & Mary	2	3	3.73	4	0	63	59	11	46
Wyatt Scotti, Northeastern	6	4	3.91	15	0	76	75	13	57
Eric Yost, Northeastern	6	1	4.23	15	0	79	91	14	57
Ty Good, Charleston	7	4	4.26	15	0	82	65	44	93
Joey Silan, Delaware	4	2	4.29	7	1	80	83	28	54
Max Simpson, Towson	1	2	4.40	5	2	59	70	16	49
Jacob Shafer, UNCW	7	5	4.62	16	0	88	81	31	55

	W	L	ERA	G	SV	IP	H	BB	SO
Mark Faello, Hofstra	6	7	5.22	12	1	71	86	33	53
Eddie Smink, Stony Brook	3	6	5.25	9	1	62	64	28	52
Josh O'Neill, Stony Brook	6	5	5.30	8	1	75	66	28	68
Ben Fero, Stony Brook	6	4	5.35	13	0	79	79	35	57
Ryan Sprock, Elon	3	3	5.40	14	0	58	71	16	56

CONFERENCE USA

	Conference W	Conference L	Overall W	Overall L
*Dallas Baptist	25	5	47	16
UTSA	21	8	38	19
*Charlotte	17	12	36	28
WKU	16	14	33	26
Florida Atlantic	16	14	34	25
LA Tech	15	15	28	31
MTSU	14	16	27	29
Rice	9	21	21	37
FIU	8	22	21	34
UAB	8	22	17	36

ALL-CONFERENCE TEAM: C: Jorge Corona, Jr., LA Tech. **INF:** Nolan Schanuel, Jr., Florida Atlantic. **INF:** Antonio Valdez, Sr., UTSA. **INF:** Brett Coker, Sr., Middle Tennessee. **INF:** Jackson Ross, Sr., Florida Atlantic. **OF:** Cam Fisher, So., Charlotte. **OF:** Grant Jay, Fr., DBU. **OF:** Alec Sanchez, R-Sr., FIU. **SP:** Ryan Johnson, So., DBU. SP: Parker Smith, So., Rice. **SP:** Wyatt Hudepohl, Jr., Charlotte. **SP:** Jaden Hamm, Jr., Middle Tennessee. **RP:** Simon Miller, Jr., UTSA. RP: Kyle Amendt, R-Jr., DBU. **DH:** Ethan Mann, R-Jr., DBU. **UTIL:** Ethan Bates, Jr., LA Tech. **Player of the Year:** Nolan Schanuel, Florida Atlantic. **Pitcher of the Year:** Simon Miller, UTSA. **Newcomer of the Year:** Ethan Mann, DBU. **Defensive Player of the Year:** Nathan Humphreys, DBU. **Freshman of the Year:** Grant Jay, DBU. Keith LeClair **Coach of the Year:** Dan Heefner, DBU. Assistant **Coach of the Year:** Micah Posey, DBU.

INDIVIDUAL BATTING LEADERS

	AVG	OBP	SLG	AB	2B	3B	HR	RBI	SB
Nolan Schanuel, Florida Atl.	.447	.615	.868	197	18	4	19	64	14
Antonio Valdez, UTSA	.387	.483	.694	222	15	7	13	65	17
Ryne Guida, FIU	.366	.444	.587	213	14	0	11	50	0
Shane Sirdashney, UTSA	.361	.436	.484	155	8	1	3	22	3
Kodie Kolden, Dallas Baptist	.353	.437	.491	232	10	2	6	35	21
Nathan Humphreys, DBU	.351	.450	.644	202	15	1	14	53	19
Cam Fisher, Charlotte	.348	.507	.813	224	14	0	30	66	10
Brett Coker, MTSU	.347	.424	.453	225	10	1	4	35	13
Jackson Ross, Florida Atlantic	.345	.437	.605	238	20	0	14	58	3
Alec Sanchez, FIU	.331	.411	.601	178	7	1	13	35	5
Logan Braunschweig, UAB	.329	.426	.419	167	6	3	1	17	16
JT Mabry, MTSU	.325	.362	.479	234	16	1	6	39	7
Tristin Garcia, WKU	.323	.393	.416	226	21	0	0	36	2
Mike Rosario, FIU	.321	.399	.509	218	10	2	9	33	19
Caleb Hill, UTSA	.319	.388	.525	204	13	4	7	41	11
Ethan Mann, Dallas Baptist	.319	.444	.695	210	15	2	20	80	9
Grant Jay, Dallas Baptist	.319	.445	.755	188	17	1	21	62	8
Leyton Barry, UTSA	.318	.390	.547	236	16	4	10	55	6
Matt King, UTSA	.318	.411	.507	217	11	6	6	58	2
Aidan Gilroy, WKU	.317	.391	.424	205	10	3	2	37	12
Ty Crittenberger, WKU	.314	.400	.454	229	16	2	4	31	20
Miguel Santos, Dallas Baptist	.313	.363	.558	265	18	1	15	63	15
Luke Vinson, MTSU	.311	.384	.383	167	7	1	1	23	12
Drew Reckart, WKU	.311	.434	.464	183	17	1	3	30	3
Taylor Smith, UTSA	.310	.445	.624	197	5	3	17	40	2
Jace Grady, Dallas Baptist	.309	.416	.534	249	14	3	12	39	25
Briggs Rutter, MTSU	.306	.384	.430	193	12	0	4	26	2
Logan Mcleod, LA Tech	.304	.448	.392	194	10	2	1	29	0
Dylan Goldstein, Florida Atl.	.297	.413	.538	236	14	2	13	62	2
Jeremiah Boyd, MTSU	.295	.389	.514	210	7	0	13	50	3

INDIVIDUAL PITCHING LEADERS

	W	L	ERA	G	SV	IP	H	BB	SO
Simon Miller, UTSA	8	1	2.30	0	11	70	67	18	81
Zach Heaton, Dallas Baptist	5	1	3.38	16	0	69	60	24	58
C.J. Williams, Florida Atlantic	2	1	3.47	7	3	60	50	33	57
Carson Myers, UAB	3	5	3.52	13	0	72	60	34	70
Landon Tomkins, LA Tech	6	2	3.52	6	3	77	67	34	75
Dawson Hall, WKU	7	4	3.58	12	0	65	56	24	44
Parker Smith, Rice	2	3	3.58	15	0	88	88	23	82
Braxton Bragg, Dallas Baptist	9	2	4.19	16	0	86	94	17	92
Paxton Thompson, Charlotte	8	2	4.22	4	0	64	56	26	69
Wyatt Hudepohl, Charlotte	7	6	4.27	17	0	105	94	27	129
Devyn Terbrak, WKU	6	4	4.34	15	0	77	89	16	62
Ryan Johnson, Dallas Baptist	8	4	4.43	15	0	87	79	22	116
Lane Diuguid, WKU	2	4	4.52	13	0	66	65	27	51
Blayze Berry, UAB	2	3	4.52	14	0	82	84	22	63
Cameron Hansen, Charlotte	3	1	4.66	12	0	73	64	25	66
Hunter Cooley, Florida Atlantic	7	6	4.66	10	0	85	97	14	77
Jacob Josey, Florida Atlantic	4	5	4.91	13	1	70	89	16	42
Luke Malone, UTSA	6	4	4.99	13	0	92	105	20	77
Ryan Cabarcas, FIU	2	7	5.09	10	1	58	63	25	81
James Sells, MTSU	6	5	5.23	1	5	65	85	19	53

HORIZON LEAGUE

	Conference W	Conference L	Overall W	Overall L
*Wright State	22	8	39	23
Oakland	18	12	29	31
Northern Kentucky	17	13	30	27
Youngstown State	13	16	19	36
Milwaukee	11	18	25	32
Purdue Fort Wayne	8	22	13	43

ALL-CONFERENCE TEAM: C: Sammy Sass, Wright State. **1B:** Braedon Blackford, Purdue Fort Wayne. **2B:** John Odom, Northern Kentucky. **3B:** Aaron Chapman, Milwaukee. **SS:** Noah Fisher, Northern Kentucky. **OF:** Andrew Patrick, Wright State. **OF:** Colton Kucera, Northern Kentucky. **OF:** Jay Luikart, Wright State. DH/Flex: Padraig O'Shaughnessy, Youngstown State. **SP:** Sebastian Gongora, Wright State. **SP:** Clay Brock, Northern Kentucky. **SP:** Jake Shirk, Wright State. **RP:** Brandon Decker, Oakland. **UTIL:** Gehrig Anglin, Wright State. **Player of the Year:** Noah Fisher, Northern Kentucky. **Pitcher of the Year:** Sebastian Gongora, Wright State. **Reliever of the Year:** Brandon Decker, Oakland. **Freshman of the Year:** Matt Thompson, Youngstown **State. Coach of the Year:** Alex Sogard, Wright State.

INDIVIDUAL BATTING LEADERS

	AVG	OBP	SLG	AB	2B	3B	HR	RBI	SB
Kucera Colton , N. Kentucky	.384	.500	.488	164	13	2	0	29	7
Law Trey, Youngstown State	.362	.437	.452	221	17	0	1	29	10
Fisher Noah , N. Kentucky	.343	.502	.716	204	15	2	19	68	4
Andrew Patrick , Wright State	.337	.442	.732	246	23	4	22	66	32
Chapman Aaron, Milwaukee	.335	.406	.493	209	12	0	7	25	10
Simpson Cleary , N. Kentucky	.324	.454	.407	145	10	1	0	25	15
Gehrig Anglin , Wright State	.324	.458	.624	173	16	3	10	53	14
Lia Mcfadden-Ackman , N. Kentucky	.322	.429	.639	208	16	1	16	69	7
Thompson Matt, Youngstown State	.316	.421	.439	171	10	1	3	28	4
Connelly Mark, Milwaukee	.309	.379	.419	217	14	2	2	40	6
Patrick Fultz , Wright State	.308	.393	.438	169	13	0	3	26	6
Lucas Loos , Oakland	.304	.368	.513	115	9	0	5	39	4
Braedon Blackford , Purdue Ft. Wayne	.302	.393	.586	215	17	1	14	61	3
Brandon Nigh , Oakland	.300	.370	.419	210	10	0	5	24	9
Ian Cleary , Oakland	.298	.395	.442	215	17	1	4	43	7
Cade Nelis , Purdue Fort Wayne	.297	.416	.401	212	13	0	3	20	6
Jay Luikart , Wright State	.297	.382	.542	249	16	3	13	47	7
D'Eusiano Steven, Youngst. State	.296	.354	.477	216	21	0	6	47	3
Moss Treyvin , N. Kentucky	.293	.405	.390	164	10	3	0	28	23
Hausser Justin, Milwaukee	.292	.350	.366	161	12	0	0	21	7

INDIVIDUAL PITCHING LEADERS

	W	L	ERA	G	SV	IP	H	BB	SO
Sebastian Gongora, Wright St.	10	1	3.17	16	0	94	79	33	89
Luke Stofel, Wright State	5	6	3.83	14	0	80	79	39	64
Hunter Pidek, Oakland	3	2	4.02	13	0	72	67	15	56
Brandon Decker, Oakland	8	3	4.40	0	5	72	68	36	73
Brock Clay, Northern Kentucky	5	5	4.46	11	1	81	87	18	62
Tristan Haught, Wright State	7	3	4.56	5	4	73	69	15	71
Jake Shirk, Wright State	5	5	4.77	15	0	83	93	14	71
Travis Perry, Youngstown State	5	7	4.79	14	0	73	69	39	61

	W	L	ERA	G	SV	IP	H	BB	SO
Riley Frey, Milwaukee	5	7	4.90	15	0	90	102	38	87
Gerl Ben, Northern Kentucky	6	4	5.12	15	0	84	102	27	74
Echrman Kaden, N. Kentucky	5	3	5.48	15	0	69	76	33	82
Luke Hansel, Milwaukee	6	4	6.04	14	0	67	80	39	66
Braden Gebhardt, Youngstown St.	3	3	6.29	9	1	63	65	41	54
Travis Densmore, Oakland	5	5	6.81	16	0	73	89	35	59
Mac Ayres, Purdue Fort Wayne	3	5	7.03	13	1	64	75	40	59
JD Deany, Purdue Fort Wayne	3	2	7.88	6	1	56	67	36	57
Nick Perez, Youngstown State	1	4	8.79	7	1	70	93	40	61

IVY LEAGUE

	Conference W	Conference L	Overall W	Overall L
*Penn	16	5	34	16
Harvard	15	6	20	24
Princeton	13	8	24	23
Columbia	11	10	23	22
Yale	10	11	17	23
Brown	9	12	12	26
Cornell	8	13	9	26
Dartmouth	2	19	3	38

ALL-CONFERENCE TEAM: C: Jackson Appel, Penn. **1B:** Logan Bravo, Harvard. **2B:** Cole Palis, Penn. **3B:** Wyatt Henseler, Penn. **SS:** Andy Blake, Columbia. **OF:** Scott Bandura, Princeton. **OF:** Derian Morphew, Brown. **OF:** Cole Hage, Columbia. **UTL:** George Cooper, Harvard. **DH:** Mika Petersen, Brown. **SP:** Ryan Dromboski, Penn. **SP:** Tom Chiemelewski, Princeton. **SP:** Cole Zaffiro, Penn. **SP:** Reid Easterly, Yale. **RP:** Callan Fang, Harvard. **Player Of The Year:** Andy Blake, Columbia. **Pitcher Of The Year:** Ryan Dromboski, Penn. **Rookie Of The Year:** Callan Fang, Harvard. **Coach Of The Year:** John Yurkow, Penn.

INDIVIDUAL BATTING LEADERS

	AVG	OBP	SLG	AB	2B	3B	HR	RBI	SB
Andy Blake, Columbia	.366	.429	.644	205	20	2	11	46	13
Scott Bandura, Princeton	.363	.454	.665	182	13	3	12	45	15
Griffin Palfrey, Columbia	.356	.424	.563	174	13	1	7	44	4
Mika Petersen, Brown	.353	.397	.419	136	5	2	0	15	5
Hayden Schott, Columbia	.333	.410	.618	186	16	2	11	31	0
George Cooper, Harvard	.333	.357	.467	135	13	1	1	16	3
Nathan Waugh, Cornell	.330	.423	.573	103	7	0	6	23	0
Cole Hage, Columbia	.328	.436	.555	137	8	1	7	27	10
Wyatt Henseler, Penn	.321	.383	.660	215	17	1	18	63	1
Ben Miller, Penn	.319	.413	.500	204	14	1	7	46	3
Davis Baker, Penn	.316	.396	.497	193	17	3	4	33	7
Derian Morphew, Brown	.314	.401	.497	159	19	2	2	26	8
Jake Bold, Princeton	.313	.400	.450	131	9	0	3	24	2
Cole Palis, Penn	.312	.410	.462	173	9	4	3	31	8
Weston Eberly, Columbia	.309	.435	.552	165	11	1	9	41	3
Elliot Krewson, Dartmouth	.309	.377	.403	149	9	1	1	14	7
Anton Lazits, Columbia	.306	.419	.490	147	12	0	5	27	6
Logan Bravo, Harvard	.304	.400	.509	171	14	0	7	32	2
Hunter Baldwin, Harvard	.303	.374	.455	145	10	3	2	21	9
Jackson Appel, Penn	.300	.389	.467	210	13	5	4	41	0
Seth Dardar, Columbia	.299	.392	.575	134	11	1	8	32	4
DJ Dillehay, Brown	.298	.372	.413	104	4	1	2	21	0
Jake Berger, Harvard	.292	.391	.472	161	11	0	6	32	6
Jarrett Pokrovsky, Penn	.292	.385	.404	171	9	2	2	33	2
Davis Hanson, Yale	.290	.398	.389	131	7	0	2	27	3

INDIVIDUAL PITCHING LEADERS

	W	L	ERA	G	SV	IP	H	BB	SO
Reid Easterly, Yale	6	3	2.93	10	1	74	60	29	56
Owen Coady, Penn	5	3	2.99	13	0	66	49	43	79
Cole Zaffiro, Penn	6	2	3.00	13	0	72	56	26	80
Ryan Dromboski, Penn	7	3	3.17	13	0	71	51	35	97
Tom Chmielewski, Princeton	6	6	3.40	13	0	77	74	19	73
Justin Kim, Princeton	7	3	4.18	0	2	52	50	28	40
Joe Sheets, Columbia	3	4	4.26	12	0	68	90	19	37
Jay Driver, Harvard	3	3	4.41	12	0	67	70	29	69
Bobby Olsen, Brown	3	4	4.44	6	1	47	41	25	56
Colton Shaw, Yale	2	5	4.50	10	0	68	69	28	59
Andy Leon, Columbia	6	3	4.79	12	0	62	65	24	54
Carson Mayfield, Cornell	1	1	4.89	0	2	46	49	12	38
Chris Clark, Harvard	4	4	4.93	12	1	66	61	32	93
Daniel Cohen, Yale	3	5	5.02	5	1	47	45	22	39
Sean Matson, Harvard	3	5	5.02	11	0	61	69	20	59
Dylan Reid, Brown	1	3	5.06	8	0	43	41	27	39
Jacob Faulkner, Princeton	3	2	5.10	0	6	55	60	16	40
Noah Keller, Cornell	2	5	5.37	11	0	52	57	29	50
Spencer Edwards, Cornell	2	4	5.80	4	0	45	42	32	31
Andrew D'Alessio, Princeton	0	5	6.61	6	0	48	63	28	25

METRO ATLANTIC ATHLETIC CONFERENCE

	Conference W	Conference L	Overall W	Overall L
Fairfield	16	5	38	18
*Rider	14	7	36	21
Canisius	16	8	26	25
Quinnipiac	16	8	30	26
Niagara	14	10	24	22
Manhattan	13	11	22	34
Mount St. Mary's	10	14	25	27
Marist	10	14	16	36
Iona	9	15	13	38
Siena	7	17	14	41
Saint Peter's	4	20	9	41

ALL-CONFERENCE TEAM: C: Keegan O'Connor, Jr., Quinnipiac. **1B:** Dylan Vincent, Gr., Canisius. **2B:** Mike Becchetti, Sr., Fairfield. **3B:** Charlie Pagliarini, Sr., Fairfield. **SS:** Noah Lucier, Gr., Fairfield. **OF:** Jackson Strong, So., Canisius. **OF:** Max Giordano, Gr., Niagara. OF: Anthony Donofrio, Sr., Quinnipiac. **P:** Matt Duffy, Jr., Canisius. **P:** Colin McVeigh, Jr., Fairfield. **P:** Kevin Seitter, Sr., Quinnipiac. **DH:** Scott Seeker, Jr., Mount St. Mary's. **UTIL:** Frankie Marinelli, Jr., Manhattan. **Player of the Year:** Charlie Pagliarini, Fairfield. **Pitcher of the Year:** Matt Duffy, Canisius. Relief **Pitcher of the Year:** Danny Kirwin, Rider. **Rookie of the Year:** Bayram Hot, Marist. **Coach of the Year:** John Delaney, Quinnipiac.

INDIVIDUAL BATTING LEADERS

	AVG	OBP	SLG	AB	2B	3B	HR	RBI	SB
Charlie Pagliarini, Fairfield	.393	.524	.839	211	14	4	24	97	14
Bayram Hot, Marist	.382	.446	.518	191	14	3	2	37	11
Max Giordano, Niagara	.374	.481	.741	174	12	2	16	54	10
Matt Bergevin, Fairfield	.366	.470	.591	186	15	0	9	44	5
Noah Lucier, Fairfield	.364	.426	.479	236	14	2	3	45	9
Anthony Donofrio, Quinnipiac	.363	.430	.675	234	17	4	16	65	31
Kyle Maves, Quinnipiac	.358	.440	.457	232	15	4	0	31	32
Jake Field, Iona	.353	.440	.668	187	16	5	11	54	5
Strong Jackson, Canisius	.352	.431	.688	176	10	5	13	49	14
Vincent Dylan, Canisius	.347	.444	.635	167	10	4	10	38	6
Shane Wockley, MSM	.347	.459	.713	150	4	0	17	52	3
Aiden Tierney, MSM	.346	.434	.481	156	10	1	3	21	23
Keegan O'Connor, Quinnipiac	.345	.401	.599	232	16	2	13	60	6
Scott Seeker, MSM	.343	.415	.647	204	18	1	14	40	3
Durocher Pete, Manhattan	.343	.398	.539	230	15	3	8	49	18
Nick Groves, Niagara	.339	.504	.421	171	8	3	0	22	21
Tristan McAlister, MSM	.333	.400	.429	126	4	1	2	16	11
Nick Markantonatos, St. Peter's	.331	.424	.552	172	10	2	8	38	6
Destefano Mike, Canisius	.327	.392	.444	214	15	2	2	48	20
Mike Becchetti, Fairfield	.327	.438	.580	226	16	1	13	54	6
Kelly Corl, Niagara	.326	.383	.451	184	11	0	4	33	12
Matt Bucciero, Fairfield	.326	.445	.517	172	10	4	5	40	8
Anthony Abbatine, St. Peter's	.324	.387	.430	179	8	1	3	30	8

INDIVIDUAL PITCHING LEADERS

	W	L	ERA	G	SV	IP	H	BB	SO
Kevin Seitter, Quinnipiac	8	4	3.58	15	0	88	91	23	79
F. Doelling, Rider	6	2	3.72	15	0	73	74	30	58
Colin McVeigh, Fairfield	8	1	3.93	14	0	76	71	25	76
Duffy Matt, Canisius	6	3	4.13	14	0	81	64	28	119
Zach Cameron, Niagara	3	1	4.34	0	15	48	48	9	53
Cooper Adams, Mount St. Mary's	8	3	4.70	14	0	82	90	20	73
Marcus Cashman, Niagara	3	2	5.13	14	0	60	55	34	57
D. Heine, Rider	4	4	5.30	15	0	73	104	20	50

Player	W	L	ERA	G	SV	IP	H	BB	SO
Mason Ulsh, Quinnipiac	3	2	5.31	7	5	61	65	23	47
Jake Noviello, Fairfield	7	3	5.36	14	0	91	99	31	52
Young Brian, Rider	6	6	5.53	14	0	70	86	27	57
Arlo Marynczak, Siena	5	6	5.73	14	0	82	98	19	86
Tim Blaisdell, Quinnipiac	6	7	5.96	13	0	80	117	16	57
Ryan Bates, Siena	2	7	6.51	14	0	83	104	39	62
Billy Rozakis, Siena	1	8	6.90	8	1	59	77	33	35

MID-AMERICAN CONFERENCE

	Conference		Overall	
	W	L	W	L
Kent State	24	6	42	16
*Ball State	19	11	36	21
Central Michigan	19	11	34	23
Western Michigan	18	11	21	31
Ohio	15	15	19	30
Toledo	14	16	26	29
Bowling Green	13	17	20	30
Miami	13	17	21	35
Eastern Michigan	12	18	27	26
Akron	12	18	21	34
Northern Illinois	5	24	10	43

ALL-CONFERENCE TEAM: C: Justin Miknis, Kent State. **1B:** Aiden Longwell, Kent State. **2B:** Luke Sefcik, Central Michigan. **SS:** Jeron Williams, Toledo. **3B:** Ryan Peltier, Ball State. **OF:** Matt Kirk, Eastern Michigan. **OF:** Collin Mathews, Kent State. **OF:** Decker Scheffler, Ball State. **DH:** DJ Newman, Bowling Green. **SP:** Joe Whitman, Kent State. **SP:** Adam Mrakitsch, Central Michigan. **SP:** Ben Cruikshank, Kent State. **SP:** Kenten Egbert, Miami. **RP:** Mitchell Scott, Kent State. **At-Large:** Josh Kross, Eastern Michigan. **Coach of the Year:** Jeff Duncan, Kent State. **Player of the Year:** Jeron Williams, SS, Toledo. **Pitcher of the Year:** Joe Whitman, LHP, Kent State. **Defensive Player of the Year:** Cooper Weiss, SS, Miami. **Freshman of the Year:** Josh Kross, 1B, Eastern Michigan. Freshman **Pitcher of the Year:** DJ Newman, RHP, Bowling Green.

INDIVIDUAL BATTING LEADERS

Player	AVG	OBP	SLG	AB	2B	3B	HR	RBI	SB
Aidan Longwell, Kent State	.408	.484	.657	233	24	2	10	75	5
Jeron Williams, Toledo	.403	.467	.681	238	16	4	14	48	49
DJ Newman, Bowling Green	.383	.481	.495	107	5	2	1	11	9
Decker Scheffler, Ball State	.378	.453	.597	196	13	3	8	49	5
Josh Kross, Eastern Michigan	.376	.433	.651	229	18	0	15	70	1
Matt Kirk, Eastern Michigan	.358	.459	.679	190	24	2	11	49	6
Collin Mathews, Kent State	.344	.463	.564	218	16	1	10	51	23
Ryan Peltier, Ball State	.338	.418	.629	237	18	3	15	54	12
Alec Patino, Ohio	.325	.421	.550	191	19	0	8	48	2
Billy Adams, Ohio	.324	.361	.373	102	5	0	0	15	6
Kolton Schaller, Kent State	.322	.454	.471	87	4	0	3	25	5
Taylor Hopkins, E. Michigan	.318	.386	.509	214	12	1	9	50	11
Josh Johnson, Kent State	.317	.415	.478	205	16	4	3	30	22
Adam Tellier, Ball State	.316	.394	.515	237	14	3	9	46	12
Justin Miknis, Kent State	.315	.395	.496	238	15	2	8	47	3
Gideon Antle, Ohio	.315	.397	.459	111	8	1	2	16	3
Luke Sefcik, Central Michigan	.315	.408	.432	146	6	1	3	32	13
Garret Pike, Toledo	.314	.398	.623	191	12	1	15	54	12
Parker Lester, Miami	.314	.392	.431	102	9	0	1	16	6
Kyle Gurney, Bowling Green	.313	.439	.475	179	12	1	5	30	5
Garrett Navarra, C. Michigan	.313	.430	.500	176	14	2	5	37	6
Colin Summerhill, N. Illinois	.308	.381	.585	195	17	2	11	54	5
Aaron Harper, N. Illinois	.307	.381	.431	202	10	0	5	41	4
Christian Mitchelle, C. Michigan	.307	.422	.422	192	13	0	3	29	24
Cade Sullivan, W. Michigan	.306	.403	.617	209	9	1	18	59	0

INDIVIDUAL PITCHING LEADERS

Player	W	L	ERA	G	SV	IP	H	BB	SO
Joe Whitman, Kent State	9	2	2.56	15	0	81	63	29	100
Trennor O'Donnell, Ball State	5	4	2.93	15	0	92	72	32	97
Cal McAninch, Toledo	5	1	3.02	0	3	60	48	18	48
Adam Mrakitsch, C. Michigan	8	4	3.59	15	0	93	66	33	80
Connor Oliver, Miami	2	6	3.89	14	0	79	71	46	102
Garrett Navarra, C. Michigan	3	4	3.91	13	1	76	68	29	84
Kenten Egbert, Miami	5	3	3.96	10	0	75	68	29	90
Keegan Batka, C. Michigan	7	3	4.07	15	0	73	76	29	66
Jacob Tate, Ohio	4	1	4.08	3	3	53	50	24	41
Ryan Palmblad, C. Michigan	1	6	4.09	0	10	62	49	22	71
Ben Cruikshank, Kent State	7	1	4.12	15	0	79	61	61	91
Hayden Berg, W. Michigan	1	3	4.47	1	5	52	45	20	48
Sammy Tortorella, Akron	4	5	4.60	17	0	86	88	30	74
Luke Russo, E. Michigan	6	4	4.62	11	2	78	66	25	107
Thomas House, E. Michigan	3	3	4.67	14	1	71	74	52	75
Sam Reed, E. Michigan	3	3	4.80	9	0	60	54	28	51
Gage Schenk, Bowling Green	3	7	4.99	14	0	74	58	29	58
Dane Armbrustmacher, W. Mich.	6	4	5.09	13	0	76	75	37	83
Joe Roth, Akron	2	7	5.15	13	1	73	81	27	42
Brady Miller, W. Michigan	7	4	5.36	15	0	89	100	32	89

MISSOURI VALLEY CONFERENCE

Team	Conference		Overall	
	W	L	W	L
*Indiana State	24	3	45	17
Missouri State	18	9	33	23
Evansville	15	12	37	24
Southern Illinois	15	12	30	27
Murray State	14	13	31	28
UIC	13	14	28	25
Belmont	10	17	27	33
Valparaiso	10	17	20	27
Illinois State	9	18	20	30
Bradley	7	20	16	32

ALL-CONFERENCE TEAM: 1B: Chase Hug, Evansville, 5th **2B:** Kip Fougerousse, Evansville, Jr. **3B:** Charlie Szykowny, UIC, Gr. **SS:** Randal Diaz, Indiana State, So. **C:** Grant Magill, Indiana State, R-Jr. **DH:** Cam Cratic, Missouri State, Gr. **OF:** Spencer Nivens, Missouri State, R-So. **OF:** Eric Roberts, Evansville, Gr. **OF:** Ryan Maka, Valparaiso, So. **OF:** Dustin Mercer, Murray, R-So. **SP:** Matt Jachec, Indiana State, R-Jr. **SP:** Connor Fenlong, Indiana State, R-Sr. **SP:** Brandt Thompson, Missouri State, Jr. **RP:** Jared Spencer, Indiana State, So. **RP:** Garrett Ferguson, Missouri State, Fr. **Player of the Year:** Spencer Nivens, Missouri State. **Pitcher of the Year:** Connor Fenlong, Indiana State. **Coach of the Year:** Mitch Hannahs, Indiana State. **Newcomer of the Year:** Charlie Szykowny, UIC. **Rookie of the Year:** Zack Stewart, Missouri State. **Defensive Player of the Year:** Grant Magill, Indiana State.

INDIVIDUAL BATTING LEADERS

Player	AVG	OBP	SLG	AB	2B	3B	HR	RBI	SB
Ryan Vogel, BRAD	.380	.457	.568	192	14	2	6	31	20
Ryan Maka, VALPO	.345	.428	.525	177	9	1	7	43	3
Spencer Nivens, MOST	.341	.437	.650	226	16	6	14	46	7
Charlie Szykowny, UIC	.335	.426	.655	203	11	3	16	55	2
Nathan Bandy, SIU	.332	.409	.468	205	14	1	4	26	11
Pier-Olivier Boucher, SIU	.331	.411	.614	236	11	4	16	43	19
Dustin Mercer, MUR	.329	.406	.534	249	12	3	11	41	10
Log Delgado, BRAD	.326	.451	.471	138	15	1	1	27	0
Ryan Rodriguez, SIU	.322	.370	.490	239	20	1	6	41	3
AJ Henkle, UIC	.322	.474	.483	118	3	2	4	27	8
Kyle Schmack, VALPO	.322	.461	.579	171	15	1	9	38	11
Luke Lawrence, ILS	.319	.376	.471	119	10	1	2	22	5
Keegan Watson, INS	.317	.457	.559	145	14	0	7	30	1
Auggie Rassmussen, ILS	.315	.399	.571	203	16	3	10	38	25
Chase Hug, UE	.311	.437	.576	238	15	3	14	55	8
Daniel Pacella, ILS	.307	.362	.585	205	9	0	16	56	2
Cam Cratic, MOST	.305	.382	.442	154	3	0	6	22	1
Zack Stewart, MOST	.302	.369	.563	222	18	2	12	61	3
Adam Pottinger, INS	.299	.449	.535	187	9	1	11	36	3
Brennan McCullough, MUR	.299	.385	.496	224	12	4	8	50	15
Nolan Tucker, VALPO	.298	.406	.415	188	8	1	4	24	4
Drew Vogel, MUR	.297	.415	.519	158	14	0	7	46	7
Randal Diaz, INS	.297	.372	.502	249	15	3	10	36	4
Cole Christman, SIU	.295	.374	.511	176	12	1	8	35	3
Eric Roberts, UE	.295	.400	.622	241	10	3	21	58	20

INDIVIDUAL PITCHING LEADERS

	W	L	ERA	G	SV	IP	H	BB	SO
Jake Combs, SIU	3	2	2.97	16	0	64	60	18	47
Connor Fenlong, INS	11	3	3.45	17	0	115	93	31	76
Brandt Thompson, MOST	6	5	3.46	18	0	83	87	27	84
Andy Bean, BEL	3	6	3.50	13	0	72	60	22	69
Jarrett Blunt, UE	5	1	3.64	21	0	64	64	20	65
Bryce Valero, MUR	4	3	4.02	15	1	63	61	30	71
Matt Jachec, INS	7	4	4.05	17	1	104	101	17	104
Hayden Minton, MOST	6	2	4.07	15	0	84	84	27	96
Derek Salata, ILS	5	6	4.08	13	0	75	72	27	88
Bobby Nowak, VALPO	4	5	4.24	17	2	51	42	31	62
Donovan Schultz, UE	6	5	4.31	15	0	77	62	32	63
Nick Smith, UE	5	3	4.63	15	0	84	78	27	72
Noah Edders, BRAD	5	2	4.78	17	0	49	51	39	42
Cade Vernon, MUR	5	6	4.87	16	0	78	86	29	75
Paul Bonzagni, SIU	8	4	4.94	24	3	58	68	28	50
Jacob Pennington, MUR	5	4	5.00	15	0	85	79	29	68
Dominic Baratta, BEL	4	5	5.06	14	0	64	69	32	46
Jordan Bloemer, SIU	4	2	5.31	18	0	63	60	24	59
Brandon Bak, UIC	3	5	5.75	14	0	72	88	26	43
Zak Gould, UIC	6	3	5.77	22	1	64	68	19	38

MOUNTAIN WEST CONFERENCE

	Conference		Overall	
	W	L	W	L
San José State	18	11	31	27
San Diego State	18	11	24	29
Air Force	17	13	28	31
Fresno State	16	14	30	27
New Mexico	13	17	26	25
UNLV	12	18	21	30
Nevada	10	20	20	33

ALL-CONFERENCE TEAM: C: Poncho Ruiz, Jr., San Diego State. **C:** Jacob Sharp, Jr., UNLV. **INF:** Sam Kulasingam, Jr., Air Force. **INF:** Trayden Tamiya, Sr., Air Force. **INF:** Jay Thomason, Jr., Air Force. **INF:** Tommy Hopfe, Jr., Fresno State. **INF:** Reed Spenrath, Jr., New Mexico. **INF:** Theo Hardy, Jr., San José State. **OF:** Cole Carrigg, Jr., San Diego State. **LHP/OF:** TJ Fondtain, Jr., San Diego State. **LHP:** Ixan Henderson, Jr., Fresno State. **RHP:** Kelena Sauer, Jr., San Diego State. **LHP:** Jack White, Sr., San José State. **UTL:** Charles McAdoo, Jr., San José State. **Player of the Year:** Sam Kulasingam, Air Force. **Pitcher of the Year:** TJ Fondtain, San Diego State. **Freshman of the Year:** Murf Gray, Fresno State. **Coaches of the Year:** Mark Martinez, San Diego State; Brad Sanfilippo, San José State.

INDIVIDUAL BATTING LEADERS

	AVG	OBP	SLG	AB	2B	3B	HR	RBI	SB
Sam Kulasingam, Air Force	.426	.537	.655	235	28	4	6	51	6
Lenny Junior Ashby, New Mexico	.381	.455	.595	210	18	0	9	51	0
Braydon Runion, New Mexico	.357	.398	.629	213	23	4	9	56	1
Jay Thomason, Air Force	.344	.439	.722	227	21	1	21	74	6
Jacob Sharp, UNLV	.335	.395	.606	188	13	1	12	48	0
Jake Holland, New Mexico	.333	.371	.633	150	7	1	12	39	0
Trayden Tamiya, Air Force	.329	.365	.434	249	14	3	2	43	3
Theo Hardy, San José State	.329	.426	.449	216	12	4	2	27	3
Charles Mcadoo, San José State	.325	.409	.543	234	19	1	10	47	4
Hunter Dorraugh, San José State	.324	.418	.541	222	18	0	10	45	1
Tommy Hopfe, Fresno State	.321	.379	.592	218	14	3	13	54	4
Jesse Pierce, Nevada	.318	.406	.601	173	12	2	11	36	2
Reed Spenrath, New Mexico	.316	.417	.716	190	11	4	19	65	3
Alex Pimentel, UNLV	.314	.445	.500	172	10	5	4	40	5
Matt Clayton, Nevada	.309	.396	.544	204	18	0	10	38	0
Jeffrey David, New Mexico	.306	.349	.472	193	13	5	3	40	3
Edarian Williams, UNLV	.304	.368	.453	181	12	3	3	27	8
Cole Carrigg, San Diego State	.303	.357	.458	155	8	5	2	27	17
Jack Colette, San José State	.303	.395	.532	218	19	5	7	42	9
Robert Hamchuk, San José State	.300	.361	.472	233	19	0	7	37	0
Dalton Bowling, San José State	.299	.370	.545	224	19	0	12	53	1
Travis Welker, Fresno State	.298	.367	.346	188	7	1	0	19	3
Shaun Montoya, San Diego State	.298	.388	.452	188	15	4	2	15	16
Triston Gray, Fresno State	.297	.338	.495	182	8	2	8	38	0
Deylan Pigford, New Mexico	.297	.389	.503	145	9	3	5	13	8

INDIVIDUAL PITCHING LEADERS

	W	L	ERA	G	SV	IP	H	BB	SO
TJ Fondtain, San Diego State	7	4	2.82	15	0	93	64	25	99
Ixan Henderson, Fresno State	4	4	3.74	15	0	89	80	34	100
Jake Sansing, Air Force	7	4	4.29	11	1	80	90	24	50
Isaac Gallegos, New Mexico	4	2	4.35	12	0	70	69	32	60
Roman Angelo, Fresno State	7	5	4.39	14	1	80	72	36	72
Tristin Lively, New Mexico	6	3	4.42	13	0	77	83	23	62
Micky Thompson, San José State	3	5	4.44	15	0	79	75	41	59
Jonathan Clark, San José State	4	4	5.10	14	0	85	76	54	79
Kade Morris, Nevada	4	7	5.42	14	0	81	96	27	85
Omar Serrano, San Diego State	1	5	5.43	6	1	53	46	21	62
Chris Canada, San Diego State	3	5	5.69	13	0	62	62	29	72
Riley Egloff, New Mexico	7	3	6.05	13	0	74	95	21	67
Josh Sharman, UNLV	7	1	6.05	9	0	58	81	22	44
Peyton Stumbo, Nevada	2	7	6.10	10	0	59	72	32	53
Doyle Gehring, Air Force	4	4	6.32	15	1	74	83	33	63
Jason Doktorczyk, Nevada	3	5	6.45	14	0	75	103	18	71
Noah Beal, UNLV	1	5	6.88	11	0	52	81	15	38
Dylan Rogers, Air Force	2	6	8.51	15	0	68	113	24	46

NORTHEAST CONFERENCE

	Conference		Overall	
	W	L	W	L
*Central Connecticut	25	5	36	14
Wagner	21	9	32	24
FDU	20	10	31	21
Sacred Heart	17	13	28	29
LIU	16	14	19	36
Maryland Eastern Shore	14	16	18	37
Merrimack	14	16	21	30
Coppin State	14	16	21	31
Stonehill	10	20	14	35
Delaware State	8	22	13	35
Norfolk State	6	24	9	42

ALL-CONFERENCE TEAM: C: David Melfi, Sr., Wagner. **1B:** Luke Cantwell, So., FDU. 2B: Chris Conniff, Jr., Wagner. **3B:** Hunter D'Amato, Jr., FDU. **SS:** Sam Mongelli, Sr., Sacred Heart. **OF:** Brantley Cutler, Gr., UMES. **OF:** Justin Jordan, Gr., Sacred Heart. **OF:** Tom Ruscitti, Gr., FDU. **DH:** Carlton Harper, Sr., LIU. **SP:** Alec Huertas, R-Sr., LIU. **SP:** Dominic Niman, Jr., CCSU. **SP:** Rich Racobaldo, Sr., FDU. **RP:** Luke Garofalo, Jr., CCSU. **Player of the Year:** Sam Mongelli, Sacred Heart. **Pitcher of the Year:** Dominic Niman CCSU. **Rookie of the Year:** Frankie Ferrentino, Merrimack. **Coach of the Year:** Charlie Hickey, CCSU.

INDIVIDUAL BATTING LEADERS

	AVG	OBP	SLG	AB	2B	3B	HR	RBI	SB
D'Amato Hunter, FDU	.408	.478	.559	211	12	1	6	56	28
Sam Mongelli, Sacred Heart	.402	.495	.743	241	16	3	20	54	22
Paige Trey, Delaware State	.372	.468	.691	191	15	2	14	53	10
Conniff Chris, Wagner	.364	.468	.535	228	14	2	7	42	10
Kiely Conor, Stonehill	.361	.442	.431	202	9	1	1	23	13
Melfi David, Wagner	.357	.440	.611	221	16	2	12	61	13
Justin Jordan, Sacred Heart	.352	.407	.496	236	13	6	3	36	16
Dionte Brown, Norfolk State	.347	.388	.407	167	4	3	0	24	16
Connor Price, LIU	.341	.422	.514	179	13	0	6	33	7
Jimenez Ramon, Central Conn.	.337	.411	.642	190	17	4	11	55	5
Ryan Donnelly, Sacred Heart	.336	.456	.526	211	10	3	8	50	18
JC Navarro, LIU	.336	.404	.556	214	14	0	11	44	2
Brantley Cutler, Maryland E. Shore	.335	.399	.550	209	16	1	9	49	2
Cantwell Luke, FDU	.331	.490	.709	151	13	1	14	51	6
Carlton Harper, LIU	.330	.387	.440	218	9	0	5	32	6

INDIVIDUAL PITCHING LEADERS

	W	L	ERA	G	SV	IP	H	BB	SO
Niman Dominic, Central Conn.	12	2	2.77	15	0	104	86	26	94
Wright Frankie, Wagner	5	4	3.01	16	0	90	80	22	84
Racobaldo Rich, FDU	8	2	3.52	14	0	79	70	34	79
Friedman Pierce, Stonehill	2	2	3.59	7	0	53	47	25	41
Jake Babuschak, Sacred Heart	6	4	3.65	14	0	81	81	31	70
Hayden Connor, Wagner	10	1	3.92	13	0	83	76	39	79
Evan Nibblett, Maryland E. Sh.	8	4	3.93	15	0	89	95	20	58
Charlie Costello, Sacred Heart	6	2	4.35	1	2	60	55	30	45

Medoro Brendan, FDU	9	0	4.55	1	4	65	63	26	61
Noah Covington, Maryland E. Sh.	4	9	4.81	15	0	103	122	10	75
Butera Justin, Merrimack	3	2	5.16	9	0	68	71	28	36
Jordan Hamberg, Coppin State	4	4	5.19	10	0	52	43	44	70
Marcos Herrand, Coppin State	8	5	5.19	14	0	87	103	36	74
Gillette Cedric, Merrimack	5	3	5.21	9	0	55	56	21	28
Max McCrary, Norfolk State	4	3	5.40	1	0	55	73	20	34

OHIO VALLEY CONFERENCE

	Conference		Overall	
	W	L	W	L
Morehead State	16	7	36	20
Little Rock	14	8	31	23
Southeast Missouri	14	10	26	30
UT Martin	14	10	22	34
*Eastern Illinois	13	11	38	21
Tennessee Tech	10	14	21	34
SIUE	9	15	26	28
Southern Indiana	8	15	17	38
Lindenwood	8	16	13	42

ALL-CONFERENCE TEAM: C: Hayden Gilliland, Tennessee Tech. **1B:** Jackson Feltner, Morehead State. **1B:** John Dyer, Tennessee Tech. **2B:** Skyler Trevino, Little Rock. **SS:** Andrew Fernandez, UT Martin. **3B:** Nico Baumbach, Little Rock. **OF:** Ryley Preece, Morehead State. **OF:** Brennan Orf, SIUE. **OF:** Tyler Williams, Little Rock. **DH:** Roman Kuntz, Morehead State. **UT:** Ryan Ignoffo, Eastern Illinois. **SP:** Jackson Wells, Little Rock. **SP:** Noah Niznik, Southeast Missouri. **SP:** Ky Hampton, Eastern Illinois. **RP:** Zane Robbins, Eastern Illinois. OVC **Player of the Year:** Ryley Preece, Morehead State. **OVC Pitcher of the Year:** Jackson Wells, Little Rock. **OVC Freshman of the Year:** Zach Wager, UT Martin. **OVC Coach of the Year:** Mik Aoki, Morehead State.

INDIVIDUAL BATTING LEADERS

	AVG	OBP	SLG	AB	2B	3B	HR	RBI	SB
Nico Baumbach, Little Rock	.372	.453	.643	199	10	1	14	52	3
Tyler Williams, Little Rock	.363	.411	.596	223	11	7	9	42	23
Brennan Orf, SIUE	.351	.506	.759	191	17	2	19	48	12
Andrew Fernandez, UT Martin	.348	.394	.557	230	21	0	9	53	4
Jackson Feltner, Morehead State	.348	.477	.652	207	15	3	14	47	5
Mac Danford, UT Martin	.347	.388	.613	173	14	1	10	44	3
Luke Pectol, Little Rock	.346	.402	.560	191	14	3	7	36	2
Jacob Ferry, Morehead State	.341	.442	.614	44	3	0	3	10	0
Nicho Jordan, Tennessee Tech	.339	.412	.653	121	9	1	9	25	1
Jared Evans, Eastern Illinois	.339	.453	.565	62	5	0	3	12	0
Ryan Ignoffo, Eastern Illinois	.335	.434	.597	236	13	2	15	60	29
Ryley Preece, Morehead State	.335	.454	.739	218	15	5	21	53	21
Joe Copeland, Lindenwood	.333	.392	.509	171	13	1	5	32	2
Colton Becker, Morehead State	.332	.410	.578	211	17	4	9	51	22
Blaze Bell, UT Martin	.328	.404	.467	195	18	3	1	22	1
Braedyn Brewer, SIUE	.328	.379	.426	61	6	0	0	11	1
John Dyer, Tennessee Tech	.324	.413	.710	207	11	0	23	45	0
Parker Stroh, Southern Indiana	.322	.426	.494	87	6	0	3	19	0
Brady Bunten, SIUE	.322	.392	.528	180	20	1	5	46	1
Tucker Ebest, Southern Indiana	.321	.430	.576	184	9	1	12	53	1
Caleb Hobson, UT Martin	.318	.429	.500	214	9	6	6	39	36
Zac Rice, UT Martin	.317	.390	.547	161	17	1	6	24	12
Alex Seguine, Little Rock	.316	.404	.440	193	10	1	4	32	2
Matthew Klein, SIUE	.316	.350	.368	38	2	0	0	4	0
Dominic Dilello, Eastern Illinois	.314	.455	.400	35	0	0	1	9	1

INDIVIDUAL PITCHING LEADERS

	W	L	ERA	G	SV	IP	H	BB	SO
Jackson Wells, Little Rock	7	4	1.65	15	0	93	73	32	80
Nick Laxner, Eastern Illinois	5	1	3.21	10	0	62	63	7	40
Noah Niznik, Southeast Missouri	6	7	3.99	15	0	86	78	20	85
Tyler Delong, SIUE	5	5	4.25	9	1	66	56	36	77
Haden Dow, Southeast Missouri	4	3	4.55	14	0	63	59	20	51
Grant Herron, Morehead State	5	1	4.59	14	0	65	62	57	74
Ky Hampton, Eastern Illinois	7	2	4.82	17	0	90	110	26	50
Jake Bockenstedt, SIUE	5	6	5.00	15	0	85	80	34	88
Tristan Walton, UT Martin	4	7	5.04	12	1	70	86	36	73
Luke Helton, Morehead State	7	2	5.10	14	0	78	85	30	67
Tyler Conklin, Eastern Illinois	9	6	5.65	15	0	80	87	34	62
John Bakke, Morehead State	6	3	5.74	10	2	64	72	33	60
Eli Brown, Lindenwood	2	7	6.03	14	0	75	85	31	64
Hunter Mann, Tennessee Tech	4	6	6.17	13	1	70	77	31	91
Noah Burkey, Little Rock	2	2	6.19	13	0	57	65	24	29
Seth Petry, UT Martin	3	4	6.42	14	0	67	88	32	50
Jordan Armstrong, UT Martin	4	5	7.47	12	0	63	95	19	42
Teague Conrad, SIUE	4	4	8.25	13	0	64	94	36	48
Preston Salazar, Lindenwood	1	11	8.58	14	0	71	95	38	45

PACIFIC-12 CONFERENCE

	Conference		Overall	
	W	L	W	L
*Stanford	23	7	44	20
*Oregon State	18	12	41	20
*Washington	17	12	35	20
USC	17	13	34	23
*Arizona State	16	13	32	23
Oregon	16	14	41	22
Ucla	12	16	28	24
*Arizona	12	18	33	26
California	12	18	24	28
Washington State	10	19	29	23
Utah	9	20	22	32

ALL-CONFERENCE TEAM: C: Ryan Campos, So., Arizona State. **C:** Darius Perry, Sr., UCLA. **C:** Johnny Tincher, Jr., Washington. **C/1B:** Jayden Kiernan, RS-Sr., Utah. **1B/OF:** Sam Brown, Jr., Washington State. **1B/OF/C:** Kiko Romero, R-So., Arizona. **DH/1B:** Jacob McKeon, SR., Washington State. **DH/INF:** Carter Graham, Jr., Stanford. **INF:** Travis Bazzana, So., Oregon State. **INF:** Sabin Ceballos, Jr., Oregon. **INF:** Cam Clayton, Sor., Washington. **INF:** Drew Cowley, Sr., Oregon. **INF:** Garret Forrester, Jr., Oregon State. **INF:** Duce Gourson, So., UCLA. **INF:** Nik McClaughry, Sr., Stanford. **INF:** Will Simpson, RS-Jr., Washington. **INF:** Tommy Troy, Jr., Stanford. **OF:** Mac Bingham, Jr., Arizona. **OF:** Chase Davis, Jr., Arizona. **OF:** Rodney Green Jr., So., California. **OF:** Luke Keaschall, Jr., Arizona State. **OF:** Kade Kretzschmar, Gr., California. **OF:** Austin Overn, Fr., USC. **OF/C:** Alberto Rios, Jr., Stanford. **OF/RHP:** Braden Montgomery, So., Stanford. **RHP:** Caden Aoki, So., USC. **RHP:** Kelly Austin, Sr., UCLA. **RHP:** Jace Stoffal, Jr., Oregon. **LHP:** Micah Ashman, So., Utah. **LHP:** Ryan Bruno, Jr., Stanford. **LHP:** Stu Flesland III, RS- Jr., Washington. **LHP:** Quinn Mathews, Sr., Stanford. **Player of the Year:** Alberto Rios, Jr., C/OF, Stanford. **Pitcher of the Year:** Quinn Mathews, Stanford. **Freshman of the Year:** Malcolm Moore, Stanford. **Defensive Player of the Year:** Nik McClaughry, Arizona. **Coach of the Year:** David Esquer, Stanford.

INDIVIDUAL BATTING LEADERS

	AVG	OBP	SLG	AB	2B	3B	HR	RBI	SB
Jayden Kiernan, Utah	.402	.464	.543	184	11	0	5	32	4
Tommy Troy, Stanford	.394	.478	.699	249	17	4	17	58	17
Ryan Campos, Arizona State	.388	.503	.594	160	7	1	8	24	4
Alberto Rios, Stanford	.384	.485	.707	242	24	0	18	73	5
Sam Brown, Washington State	.374	.481	.674	187	19	2	11	58	5
Travis Bazzana, Oregon State	.374	.500	.622	238	20	3	11	55	36
Chase Davis, Arizona	.362	.489	.742	221	17	2	21	74	0
Mac Bingham, Arizona	.360	.432	.573	253	20	2	10	51	7
Luke Keaschall, Arizona State	.353	.443	.725	218	25	1	18	58	18
Jonah Advincula, Wash. State	.350	.455	.565	200	20	4	5	33	24
AJ Guerrero, Washington	.345	.439	.518	220	10	2	8	38	0
Kiko Romero, Arizona	.345	.441	.724	232	17	4	21	89	6
Micah McDowell, Oregon State	.342	.427	.509	222	16	0	7	47	15
Jacob McKeon, Wash. State	.341	.444	.556	205	18	1	8	47	6
Drew Cowley, Oregon	.341	.425	.631	249	22	1	16	70	6
Garret Forrester, Oregon State	.341	.485	.522	232	12	0	10	52	3
Elijah Hainline, Wash. State	.337	.430	.615	187	12	2	12	39	10
Colby Shade, Oregon	.336	.422	.523	214	16	3	6	31	14
Braden Montgomery, Stanford	.336	.461	.611	244	14	1	17	61	6
Emilio Corona, Arizona	.336	.369	.691	152	13	4	11	44	3
Will Simpson, Washington	.335	.418	.643	221	12	1	18	58	5
Sabin Ceballos, Oregon	.333	.426	.643	213	10	1	18	70	0
Eddie Park, Stanford	.333	.412	.475	276	19	1	6	47	7
Coby Morales, Washington	.332	.432	.548	217	11	0	12	52	1

	AVG	OBP	SLG	AB	2B	3B	HR	RBI	SB
Tony Bullard, Arizona	.328	.396	.591	198	14	1	12	42	1
Tanner Smith, Oregon	.327	.391	.551	245	20	1	11	45	7
Mason Guerra, Oregon State	.326	.414	.573	218	18	0	12	56	6
Cam Clayton, Washington	.325	.393	.545	246	21	0	11	42	4
Nik McClaughry, Arizona	.325	.429	.467	240	12	5	4	39	7
Owen Cobb, Stanford	.324	.368	.471	210	7	3	6	32	8
Kade Kretzschmar, California	.322	.391	.608	199	14	2	13	36	8
Duce Gourson, UCLA	.319	.438	.515	204	10	0	10	48	8
Jacob Tobias, Arizona State	.317	.404	.546	205	9	4	10	59	1
Caleb Lomavita, California	.316	.367	.612	206	13	0	16	43	9
Carter Graham, Stanford	.315	.390	.558	276	22	0	15	77	9
Luke Hill, Arizona State	.314	.389	.456	204	11	0	6	42	3
Mason White, Arizona	.313	.379	.611	208	18	7	10	35	2
Rikuu Nishida, Oregon	.312	.394	.443	253	16	1	5	37	25
Malcolm Moore, Stanford	.311	.386	.564	257	20	0	15	63	3
Johnny Tincher, Washington	.310	.387	.514	216	14	0	10	42	6

INDIVIDUAL PITCHING LEADERS

	W	L	ERA	G	SV	IP	H	BB	SO
Caden Aoki, USC	4	3	2.98	13	0	63	59	20	52
Kelly Austin, UCLA	5	4	3.39	17	0	82	72	34	104
Quinn Mathews, Stanford	10	4	3.75	19	0	125	116	40	158
Blake Sodersten, USC	4	3	3.82	19	0	68	63	30	72
Paulshawn Pasqualotto, Cal	5	1	4.03	14	0	58	53	33	51
Stu Flesland, Washington	7	2	4.12	16	0	90	89	27	81
Ross Dunn, Arizona State	4	6	4.27	15	0	65	64	44	84
Dakota Hawkins, Washington St.	5	3	4.32	14	0	73	82	27	92
Drew Dowd, Stanford	9	3	4.52	32	2	66	58	33	88
Jacob Kmatz, Oregon State	5	4	4.71	14	0	73	72	26	61
Joey Dixon, Stanford	7	0	4.73	21	0	84	73	43	90
Trent Sellers, Oregon State	7	5	4.86	15	0	74	71	32	106
Matt Scott, Stanford	5	5	5.10	24	1	67	59	37	62
Caden Kaelber, Washington St.	4	5	5.22	20	4	71	76	25	87
Tyler Stromsborg, USC	4	3	5.23	13	0	76	72	25	64
Bradon Zastrow, Arizona	6	5	5.28	17	0	77	97	24	56
Bryson Van Sickle, Utah	3	5	5.59	18	0	68	95	23	68
Jake Brooks, UCLA	6	6	5.64	14	0	75	87	19	77
Jared Engman, Washington	3	5	5.91	16	0	67	70	37	31
Logan Mercado, Oregon	5	1	5.95	21	1	82	85	51	78
Kiefer Lord, Washington	6	5	6.19	15	0	76	86	17	78
Christian Becerra, California	2	5	6.29	18	2	54	78	18	53
Aiden May, Arizona	5	3	6.33	16	0	75	97	33	77
Grant Taylor, Washington State	3	4	6.43	14	0	56	61	37	55
Connor Sullivan, California	2	4	6.96	15	1	53	77	25	38
Khristian Curtis, Arizona State	4	3	7.03	15	0	64	76	35	58
Merit Jones, Utah	2	4	7.65	17	0	60	87	24	49

PATRIOT LEAGUE

	Conference W	Conference L	Overall W	Overall L
*Army	21	4	38	18
Bucknell	14	11	23	23
Navy	14	11	23	27
Lafayette	10	15	15	37
Lehigh	10	15	24	26
Holy Cross	6	19	16	35

ALL-CONFERENCE TEAM: C: Derek Berg, Army, Jr. **1B:** Ross Friedrick, Army, Sr. **2B:** Billy Kender, Bucknell, So. **3B:** Sean Keys, Bucknell, So. **SS:** Kevin Dubrule, Army, Sr. **OF:** Braden Golinski, Army, Jr. **OF:** Grant Voytovich, Bucknell, Jr. **OF:** Peter Ciuffreda, Lafayette, Sr. **OF:** Casey Rother, Lehigh, 5th. **At-Large:** Michael Zarrillo, Lafayette, So. **SP:** Tanner Gresham, Army, Jr. **SP:** Mike Ruggieri, Army, Jr. **SP:** Matthew Ronnebaum, Army, Jr. **SP:** Alex Walsh, Lafayette, Sr. **RP:** Robbie Buecker, Army, Sr. **Player of the Year:** Kevin Dubrule, Army, Sr., SS. **Pitcher of the Year:** Tanner Gresham, Army, Jr., RHP. Defensive Player of the Year: Kevin Dubrule, Army, Sr., SS. Rookie of the Year: Jack Toomey, Holy Cross, Fr., OF. Coach of the Year: Chris Tracz, Army.

INDIVIDUAL BATTING LEADERS

	AVG	OBP	SLG	AB	2B	3B	HR	RBI	SB
Kevin Dubrule, Army	.405	.454	.617	227	19	1	9	68	2
Patrizi Dom, Lehigh	.381	.455	.433	97	5	0	0	14	6
Ross Friedrick, Army	.368	.443	.658	228	15	0	17	59	0
Anthony Sherwin, Bucknell	.362	.486	.567	141	14	3	3	29	3
Chris Klein, Bucknell	.346	.414	.423	78	6	0	0	7	0
Rother Casey, Lehigh	.342	.427	.674	193	17	1	15	64	4
Sean Keys, Bucknell	.339	.444	.679	168	16	1	13	61	3
Alex Smith, Navy	.326	.392	.455	187	12	0	4	24	2
Braden Golinski, Army	.323	.393	.600	220	16	3	13	52	17
Young Tyler, Lehigh	.314	.389	.378	172	8	0	1	25	4
Jack Toomey, Holy Cross	.312	.417	.547	170	19	0	7	36	3
Derek Berg, Army	.312	.392	.558	231	15	3	12	44	12
Kohl Andrew, Lehigh	.309	.407	.593	123	4	2	9	28	6
Perich Rafe, Lehigh	.307	.349	.500	202	19	1	6	47	3
Chris Baillargeon, Holy Cross	.307	.378	.439	114	10	1	1	23	1
Jacob Corson, Bucknell	.304	.462	.532	158	10	1	8	33	1
Gorla Joe, Lehigh	.302	.392	.519	129	7	0	7	18	1
Kyle Lyons, Bucknell	.301	.348	.325	163	4	0	0	12	7
Sean Scanlon, Holy Cross	.297	.461	.506	172	18	0	6	36	3
Sam Ruta, Army	.296	.387	.583	230	17	5	13	58	2

INDIVIDUAL PITCHING LEADERS

	W	L	ERA	G	SV	IP	H	BB	SO
Tanner Gresham, Army	5	1	2.90	10	0	59	41	21	56
Nate Mitchell, Navy	6	5	3.16	13	0	74	80	13	50
Rettig Luke, Lehigh	6	4	3.24	12	0	58	43	21	65
Mike Ruggieri, Army	9	2	3.44	12	0	73	62	38	61
Robbie Buecker, Army	5	4	3.66	8	3	64	61	27	47
Alex Walsh, Lafayette	6	2	3.71	12	0	63	45	42	55
Matthew Shirah, Navy	5	4	3.83	12	0	56	51	19	58
Matthew Ronnebaum, Army	7	4	5.31	14	0	81	94	22	82
Will Greer, Bucknell	3	5	6.09	12	0	65	74	33	39
Chris DiFiore, Bucknell	6	6	7.24	13	0	65	72	33	45
Tyler O'Neill, Bucknell	3	5	8.02	12	0	64	83	29	46

SOUTHEASTERN CONFERENCE

East Division	Conference W	Conference L	Overall W	Overall L
*Florida	20	10	54	17
*Vanderbilt	19	11	42	20
*South Carolina	16	13	42	21
*Tennessee	16	14	44	22
*Kentucky	16	14	40	21
Georgia	11	19	29	27
Missouri	10	20	30	24

West Division	Conference W	Conference L	Overall W	Overall L
*Arkansas	20	10	43	18
*LSU	19	10	54	17
*Auburn	17	13	34	23
*Alabama	16	14	43	21
*Texas A&M	14	16	38	27
Mississippi State	9	21	27	26
Ole Miss	6	24	25	29

ALL-CONFERENCE TEAM: C: Cole Messina, South Carolina. **1B:** Jac Caglianone, Florida. **2B:** Cade Kurland, Florida. **3B:** Tommy White, LSU. **SS:** Josh Rivera, Florida. **OF:** Dylan Crews, LSU. **OF:** Wyatt Langford, Florida. OF: Ethan Petry, South Carolina. **SP:** Paul Skenes, LSU. **SP:** Hagen Smith, Arkansas. **RP:** Brandon Neely, Florida. **DH/UT:** Hunter Hines, Mississippi State. **Player of the Year:** Dylan Crews, LSU. **Pitcher of the Year:** Paul Skenes, LSU. **Freshman of the Year:** Charlie Condon, **Georgia. Coach of the Year:** Dave Van Horn, Arkansas.

INDIVIDUAL BATTING LEADERS

	AVG	OBP	SLG	AB	2B	3B	HR	RBI	SB
Dylan Crews, LSU	.426	.567	.713	258	16	2	18	70	6
Charlie Condon, Georgia	.386	.484	.800	210	10	1	25	66	0
Tommy White, LSU	.377	.435	.729	273	24	0	24	105	0
Kemp Alderman, Ole Miss	.376	.440	.709	213	14	0	19	61	5

	AVG	OBP	SLG	AB	2B	3B	HR	RBI	SB
Ethan Petry, South Carolina	.376	.471	.733	221	10	0	23	75	4
Wyatt Langford, Florida	.373	.498	.784	236	28	3	21	57	8
Connor Tate, Georgia	.364	.454	.661	239	20	0	17	54	7
Jack Moss, Texas A&M	.360	.461	.472	267	16	1	4	39	3
Ike Irish, Auburn	.357	.428	.539	241	24	1	6	50	3
Tommy Seidl, Alabama	.352	.453	.543	199	11	0	9	44	8
Josh Rivera, Florida	.348	.447	.617	256	10	1	19	72	18
Bryson Ware, Auburn	.348	.438	.722	227	11	1	24	64	6
Bobby Peirce, Auburn	.342	.415	.500	184	10	2	5	26	4
Andrew Pinckney, Alabama	.338	.442	.645	234	12	3	18	58	8
Jackson Gray, Kentucky	.338	.491	.543	219	15	6	6	33	19
Cole Foster, Auburn	.336	.432	.571	226	14	0	13	49	5
Jacob Gonzalez, Ole Miss	.327	.435	.564	202	18	0	10	51	0
Jared Dickey, Tennessee	.327	.392	.522	245	6	3	12	52	6
Cade Beloso, LSU	.324	.462	.622	185	5	1	16	49	2
Hunter Gilliam, Kentucky	.323	.412	.549	226	13	1	12	71	1
Hunter Haas, Texas A&M	.323	.445	.502	257	14	1	10	46	7
Jac Caglianone, Florida	.322	.388	.735	283	14	2	33	90	4
Calvin Harris, Ole Miss	.321	.398	.579	209	14	2	12	46	2
Colton Ledbetter, Miss. State	.320	.452	.574	197	12	1	12	52	17
Émilien Pitre, Kentucky	.318	.440	.413	223	16	1	1	51	20
Tre' Morgan, LSU	.316	.418	.502	269	15	4	9	53	0
Ed Johnson, Alabama	.315	.426	.455	200	8	1	6	42	5
Luke Heyman, Florida	.314	.366	.555	191	6	2	12	39	1
Jace Bohrofen, Arkansas	.313	.431	.604	217	15	0	16	52	7
Maui Ahuna, Tennessee	.312	.425	.537	205	20	1	8	42	4

INDIVIDUAL PITCHING LEADERS

	W	L	ERA	G	SV	IP	H	BB	SO
Paul Skenes, LSU	13	2	1.69	19	0	123	72	20	209
Andrew Lindsey, Tennessee	3	4	2.90	21	0	71	60	19	73
Devin Futrell, Vanderbilt	7	3	3.44	16	0	84	71	20	72
James Hicks, South Carolina	8	1	3.51	25	3	67	59	14	56
Hunter Owen, Vanderbilt	4	0	3.52	12	0	64	52	17	76
Drew Beam, Tennessee	9	4	3.63	17	0	84	88	23	88
Hagen Smith, Arkansas	8	2	3.64	18	2	72	56	42	109
Luke Holman, Alabama	7	4	3.67	16	0	81	54	31	87
Tommy Vail, Auburn	5	2	3.76	17	0	69	45	42	81
Hunter Hollan, Arkansas	8	2	4.13	17	1	81	82	29	74
Hurston Waldrep, Florida	8	3	4.16	19	0	102	85	57	156
Chase Burns, Tennessee	5	3	4.25	18	2	72	60	22	114
Darren Williams, Kentucky	4	2	4.26	17	2	63	56	24	61
Jac Caglianone, Florida	7	4	4.34	18	0	75	51	55	87
Ty Floyd, LSU	7	0	4.35	19	1	91	70	37	120
Jacob McNairy, Alabama	7	3	4.35	17	0	81	85	22	86
Jack Mahoney, South Carolina	6	4	4.37	16	0	78	82	25	80
Zack Lee, Kentucky	4	4	4.42	16	0	71	68	27	79
Brandon Sproat, Florida	8	3	4.66	19	0	106	87	48	134
Chase Dollander, Tennessee	7	6	4.75	17	0	89	83	30	120
Will McEntire, Arkansas	8	3	5.07	21	2	87	92	29	83
Chandler Murphy, Missouri	4	5	5.47	14	0	74	68	32	63
Liam Sullivan, Georgia	5	2	5.77	14	0	64	60	33	75
Jack Dougherty, Ole Miss	3	4	6.27	15	2	60	63	22	65
Nathan Dettmer, Texas A&M	1	4	6.32	17	0	73	78	42	65
Xavier Rivas, Ole Miss	5	5	6.35	14	0	68	65	40	89
JT Quinn, Ole Miss	3	4	6.83	17	0	55	62	36	63

SOUTHERN CONFERENCE

	Conference		Overall	
	W	L	W	L
*Samford	15	6	37	25
Mercer	13	8	33	25
Wofford	12	9	40	19
East Tennessee State University	10	11	26	29
VMI	9	11	26	29
UNCG	9	12	25	34
Western Carolina	8	12	21	33
The Citadel	7	14	23	31

ALL-CONFERENCE TEAM: C: Cole Garrett, Jr., VMI. **1B:** Ryan Galanie, Sr., Wofford. **2B:** Jayden Davis, Fr., Samford. **SS:** Pascanel Ferreras, Jr., Western Carolina. **3B:** Justin Starke, R-Jr., VMI. **OF:** Treyson Hughes, So., Mercer. **OF:** Kennedy Jones, So., UNCG. **OF:** Cole Jenkins, Jr., VMI. **DH:** Eric Toth, Gr., Mercer. SP: Nathanial Tate, Sr., ETSU. **SP:** Jacob Cravey, Jr., Samford. **RP:** Lucas Mahlstedt, So., Wofford. **Player of the Year:** Ryan Galanie, Wofford. **Pitcher of the Year:** Jacob Cravey, Samford. **Freshman of the Year:** Lucas Steele, Samford. **Coach of the Year:** Tony David, Samford.

INDIVIDUAL BATTING LEADERS

	AVG	OBP	SLG	AB	2B	3B	HR	RBI	SB
Justin Starke, VMI	.392	.487	.665	212	15	2	13	52	32
Nick Iannantone, ETSU	.389	.468	.554	175	14	3	3	27	2
Treyson Hughes, MER	.387	.504	.604	222	15	0	11	52	9
Cameron Sisneros, ETSU	.383	.472	.692	214	18	0	16	59	3
Ryan Galanie, WOF	.383	.491	.670	230	15	0	17	66	19
Cameron Gill, WOF	.368	.486	.443	174	7	0	2	41	16
Trey Yunger, WOF	.360	.446	.498	225	17	1	4	49	26
Jayden Davis, SAM	.358	.452	.541	229	13	1	9	38	0
Kennedy Jones, UNCG	.357	.445	.598	241	14	1	14	43	5
Brice Martinez, WOF	.352	.458	.418	213	8	3	0	45	16
Cole Garrett, VMI	.350	.437	.630	200	17	0	13	53	5
Cole Jenkins, VMI	.350	.402	.631	206	19	3	11	50	9
Ty Swaim, VMI	.348	.405	.488	244	20	4	2	34	35
Trey Morgan, VMI	.345	.436	.518	220	16	2	6	42	26
Eric Toth, MER	.329	.443	.652	207	7	0	20	53	3
Pascanel Ferreras, WCU	.325	.435	.574	209	16	0	12	53	2
Thomas Rollauer, CIT	.324	.390	.456	204	15	0	4	34	9
Travis Lott, CIT	.321	.454	.465	187	10	1	5	32	2
Cody Miller, ETSU	.318	.402	.400	195	6	2	2	19	10
Zac Morris, VMI	.317	.408	.546	205	13	2	10	49	25

INDIVIDUAL PITCHING LEADERS

	W	L	ERA	G	SV	IP	H	BB	SO
Lucas Mahlstedt, WOF	7	2	2.69	27	6	84	72	18	68
Jacob Cravey, SAM	9	2	3.10	17	1	105	83	40	126
Nathanial Tate, ETSU	9	4	3.56	16	0	94	71	44	97
Cameron Reeves, CIT	7	5	3.56	14	0	81	59	33	68
Sam Swygert, CIT	5	4	4.54	17	0	67	71	28	59
Matthew Marchal, WOF	11	4	4.58	20	1	92	92	22	93
Coulson Buchanan, WOF	5	4	5.22	20	0	91	95	26	91
Colby Stuart, ETSU	1	6	5.45	18	0	66	70	20	48
Nathan Light, VMI	3	3	5.61	16	1	59	69	23	41
Jay Miller, UNCG	2	8	5.76	18	0	75	95	29	44
Jake Wolf, UNCG	4	2	5.77	27	1	73	82	46	40
Brody Westbrooks, SAM	3	4	5.83	17	0	76	94	25	72
Josh Farmer, MER	6	3	5.96	15	0	77	94	15	43
Will Lynch, SAM	5	4	6.09	16	0	78	81	40	65
Landon Smiddy, ETSU	3	7	6.61	17	0	63	86	20	43
Colton Cosper, MER	4	5	6.61	17	0	64	85	24	58
Ryan Lobus, MER	5	4	6.96	17	2	63	68	29	74

SOUTHLAND CONFERENCE

	Conference		Overall	
	W	L	W	L
Nicholls	15	9	34	24
UIW	14	10	28	26
New Orleans	13	11	36	24
Lamar	13	11	32	23
McNeese	12	12	35	23
Northwestern State	12	12	29	27
A&M-Corpus Christi	12	12	24	30
Southeastern	9	14	25	25
HCU	7	16	11	39

ALL-CONFERENCE TEAM: 1B: Edgar Alvarez, Jr., Nicholls. **2B:** Tyler Bischke, Jr., New Orleans. **3B:** Michael Dattalo, Fr., Northwestern State. **SS:** Parker Coddou, Jr., Nicholls. **C:** Ryan Snell, Sr., Lamar. **DH:** Rey Mendoza, Gr., UIW. **OF:** Xane Washington, R-Sr., Nicholls. **OF:** Tristan Moore, Jr., New Orleans. **OF:** Brendan Ryan, Sr., A&M-Corpus Christi. **SP:** Grant Rogers, Jr., McNeese. **SP:** Jacob Mayers, Fr., Nicholls. **SP:** Brandon Mitchell, Sr., New Orleans. **RP:** Steve Hayward, R-Sr., UIW. **UTIL:** Alec Carr, Sr., UIW. **Player of the Year:** Ryan Snell, Lamar. **Hitter of the Year:** Tristan Moore, New Orleans. **Pitcher of the Year:** Grant Rogers, McNeese. **Relief Pitcher of the Year:** Steve Hayward, UIW. **Freshman of the Year:** Jacob Mayers, Nicholls. **Newcomer of the Year:** Rey Mendoza, UIW. Coach of the Year: Mike Silva, Nicholls.

INDIVIDUAL BATTING LEADERS

	AVG	OBP	SLG	AB	2B	3B	HR	RBI	SB
Reed Chumley, HCU	.392	.458	.722	158	19	0	11	36	1
Xane Washington, Nicholls	.378	.480	.550	222	18	4	4	46	16
Michael Dattalo, NW State	.372	.447	.561	223	18	0	8	39	2
Jimmy DeLeon, UIW	.361	.446	.525	202	10	1	7	35	2
Samuel Benjamin, HCU	.354	.426	.634	175	14	1	11	48	7
Brendan Ryan, A&M-CC	.344	.405	.576	224	13	9	7	40	20
Tre Jones, A&M-CCi	.332	.385	.520	196	9	5	6	38	8
Edgar Alvarez, Nicholls	.330	.419	.532	218	17	3	7	39	0
Mitchell Sanford, New Orleans	.324	.398	.512	213	10	3	8	60	6
Garrett Felix, Nicholls	.320	.393	.458	203	17	1	3	31	9
Tanner Wilson, Lamar	.319	.425	.348	138	4	0	0	15	9
Tristan Moore, New Orleans	.318	.393	.650	217	9	3	19	55	3
Jake Haze, Northwestern State	.317	.421	.481	189	15	2	4	42	2
Ryan Snell, Lamar	.317	.412	.654	208	17	1	17	58	2
Max Puls, A&M-CC	.316	.374	.540	187	10	1	10	36	5

INDIVIDUAL PITCHING LEADERS

	W	L	ERA	G	SV	IP	H	BB	SO
Grant Rogers, McNeese	12	1	1.82	15	0	104	79	18	88
Jacob Mayers, Nicholls	9	1	2.02	15	0	76	44	58	105
Ty Abraham, McNeese	2	2	3.15	7	5	69	65	23	75
Brooks Caple, Lamar	5	0	3.19	11	0	59	51	16	50
Will Kinzeler, Southeastern	5	1	3.34	12	0	65	61	38	33
Brandon Mitchell, New Orleans	11	3	3.65	16	0	101	82	28	88
Colin Purcell, A&M-CC	5	6	4.08	13	0	82	83	22	63
Andrew Landry, Southeastern	2	6	4.21	12	0	68	72	27	49
Cal Carver, NW State	7	3	4.38	15	0	86	77	26	77
Jacob Ellis, Lamar	4	5	4.50	15	0	78	69	24	85
Kayden Cassidy, UIW	3	3	4.72	14	0	74	68	41	67
Chase Prestwich, NW State	4	4	5.08	8	2	62	52	27	70
Alex Makarewich, NW State	5	5	5.10	15	0	72	53	44	89
Matthew Watson, A&M-CC	6	5	5.52	14	0	78	84	33	54
Tyler Theriot, Nicholls	3	4	5.52	10	0	62	73	21	42

SOUTHWESTERN ATHLETIC CONFERENCE

East Division	Conference W	Conference L	Overall W	Overall L
Alabama State	26	4	40	16
Bethune-Cookman	20	9	33	27
*Florida A&M	18	12	29	30
Jackson State	13	17	28	24
Mississippi Valley State	7	23	15	37
Alabama A&M	5	24	14	34

West Division	Conference W	Conference L	Overall W	Overall L
Grambling State	22	7	29	24
Texas Southern	17	10	31	22
Southern	17	10	23	27
Prairie View A&M	15	14	20	36
Arkansas-Pine Bluff	10	20	18	32
Alcorn State	6	24	9	39

ALL-CONFERENCE TEAM: C: Ty Hanchey, Florida A&M. **1B:** Keylon Mack, Grambling State. **2B**: Randy Flores, Alabama State. **3B:** Cameron Bufford, Grambling State. **SS:** CJ Castillo, Texas Southern. **DH:** Alexander Olivo, Texas Southern. **OF:** Daalen Adderley, Texas Southern. **OF:** Hylan Hall, Bethune-Cookman. **OF:** Trevor Hatton, Grambling State. **SP:** Omar Melendez, Alabama State. **SP:** Nolan Santos, Bethune-Cookman. **RP:** Joan Gonzalez, Bethune-Cookman. **Coach of the Year:** Jose' Vazquez, Alabama State. **Player/Hitter of the Year:** Daalen Adderley, Texas Southern. **Pitcher of the Year:** Omar Melendez, Alabama State. **Relief Pitcher of the Year:** Joan Gonzalez, Bethune-Cookman. **Freshman of the Year:** Jamal George, Alabama State. **Newcomer of the Year:** Hylan Hall, Bethune-Cookman.

INDIVIDUAL BATTING LEADERS

	AVG	OBP	SLG	AB	2B	3B	HR	RBI	SB
Daalen Adderley, Texas Southern	.426	.541	.623	183	16	1	6	43	17
Victor Figueroa, Mississippi Valley State	.408	.497	.619	147	8	1	7	38	12
Ty Hill, Jackson State	.387	.520	.619	181	16	4	6	53	8
Jack Hay, Alabama State	.385	.472	.575	221	10	1	10	61	0
Alexander Olivo, Texas Southern	.376	.493	.719	178	17	1	14	71	3
Ty Jackson, Florida A&M	.373	.473	.520	204	8	5	4	30	9
Kyle Walker, Grambling State	.373	.495	.513	158	8	4	2	29	23
Ali Lapread, Alabama State	.371	.460	.736	140	10	1	13	39	6
Daniel Bannon, Jackson State	.368	.423	.474	209	14	4	0	36	6
Hylan Hall, Bethune-Cookman	.367	.437	.570	221	18	6	5	54	7
JaKobi Jackson, Arkansas-Pine Bluff	.358	.462	.477	109	10	0	1	18	1
Ian Matos, Alabama State	.355	.482	.595	220	20	3	9	47	4
Ty Hanchey, Florida A&M	.352	.452	.597	216	10	5	11	49	3
CJ Castillo, Texas Southern	.352	.433	.508	199	13	0	6	41	6
Chase Cromer, Texas Southern	.352	.450	.391	128	5	0	0	11	21
Jayden Sloan, Alabama State	.349	.420	.550	149	12	0	6	24	1
Robert Moya, Bethune-Cookman	.348	.454	.604	207	19	2	10	55	0
Trenton Jamison, Alabama State	.342	.406	.516	161	13	0	5	38	10
Marcus Atterberry, Jackson State	.341	.459	.548	126	7	2	5	34	4
Michael Goudeau, Texas Southern	.341	.450	.439	82	8	0	0	19	1

INDIVIDUAL PITCHING LEADERS

	W	L	ERA	GS	SV	IP	H	BB	SO
Omar Melendez, Alabama St.	12	0	2.52	15	0	93	88	27	96
Nicholas Wilson, Southern	6	2	3.22	13	0	87	78	23	101
Nolan Santos, Bethune-Cook	7	5	3.32	17	0	106	85	36	148
Hunter Viets, Florida A&M	8	2	3.45	16	0	91	99	20	81
Ricardo Rivera, Alabama State	10	0	3.58	11	0	65	69	26	66
Abraham Deleon, Texas So.	6	3	3.83	15	1	89	72	37	114
Domenic Martinez, Texas So.	5	3	3.83	10	0	54	53	28	57
Erick Gonzalez, Jackson State	1	3	4.22	0	13	53	51	21	64
Daniel Gaviria, Bethune-Cook.	5	3	4.41	14	0	84	90	19	49
Jorhan LaBoy, Alabama State	2	3	5.12	3	3	70	82	24	58
Christian Womble, Jackson St.	8	2	5.14	14	0	84	81	55	93
Michael Dews, Prairie View	6	7	5.26	14	0	92	121	11	58
Jesse Caver, Jackson State	6	4	5.27	12	0	72	81	36	68
Lorenzo Peterson, Grambling St.	5	3	5.36	17	0	99	105	47	77
Victor Mendoza, Prairie View	4	3	5.40	12	0	70	73	47	43

SUMMIT LEAGUE

	Conference W	Conference L	Overall W	Overall L
*Oral Roberts	23	1	52	14
North Dakota State	16	7	23	30
South Dakota State	13	11	24	28
Omaha	9	14	21	28
Northern Colorado	8	16	11	34
Western Illinois	8	16	12	40
St. Thomas	6	18	10	34

ALL-CONFERENCE TEAM: C: Ryan McDonald, South Dakota St. **1B:** Jake McMurray, Oral Roberts. **2B:** Peter Brookshaw, North Dakota St. **3B:** Mike Boeve, Omaha. **SS:** Devin Hurdle, Omaha. **OF:** Jonah Cox, Oral Roberts. **OF:** Matt Hogan, Oral Roberts. **OF:** Nick Mitchell, Western Illinois. **DH:** Drew Stahl, Oral Roberts. **UT:** Druw Sackett, North Dakota St. SP: Cade Feeney, North Dakota St. **SP:** Jakob Hall, Oral Roberts. **SP:** Tristen Roehrich, North Dakota St. **RP:** Cade Denton, Oral Roberts. **Player of the Year:** Jonah Cox, Oral Roberts. **Pitcher of the Year:** Cade Denton, Oral Roberts. **Newcomer of the Year:** Jonah Cox, Oral Roberts. **Defensive Player of the Year:** Mac McCroskey, Oral Roberts. **Coach of the Year:** Ryan Folmar, Oral Roberts.

INDIVIDUAL BATTING LEADERS

	AVG	OBP	SLG	AB	2B	3B	HR	RBI	SB
Ryan McDonald, South Dakota St.	.417	.575	.929	127	10	2	17	39	11
Jonah Cox, Oral Roberts	.412	.470	.646	277	16	8	11	68	28
Mike Boeve, Omaha	.401	.512	.563	167	15	0	4	32	6
Devin Hurdle, Omaha	.373	.425	.547	161	9	2	5	29	4
Justin Quinn, Oral Roberts	.355	.432	.518	197	11	0	7	40	8
Nick Mitchell, Western Illinois	.354	.454	.568	192	17	6	4	24	8
Jake McMurray, Oral Roberts	.326	.420	.449	276	14	1	6	47	2

	AVG	OBP	SLG	AB	2B	3B	HR	RBI	SB
Dawson Parry, South Dakota St.	.322	.386	.528	199	11	0	10	39	0
James Dunlap, North Dakota St.	.320	.394	.494	178	14	1	5	42	14
Holden Breeze, Oral Roberts	.320	.410	.444	250	13	0	6	42	4
Matt Hogan, Oral Roberts	.320	.460	.662	222	13	3	19	72	9
Jake King, Northern Colorado	.314	.413	.410	156	10	1	1	19	3
Mac McCroskey, Oral Roberts	.314	.392	.520	271	10	2	14	64	17
Cadyn Schwabe, North Dakota St.	.313	.417	.387	217	8	4	0	37	27
Jake Allgeyer, Western Illinois	.310	.391	.421	197	10	0	4	34	1
Hayden Heinze, Northern Colorado	.308	.363	.403	159	10	1	1	18	6
Peter Brookshaw, North Dakota St.	.308	.400	.565	214	14	1	13	40	12
Vujovich, Ben, St. Thomas	.306	.364	.444	160	11	4	1	23	8
Derek Botaletto, Western Illinois	.303	.368	.413	201	11	1	3	31	10
Cam Frederick, Omaha	.301	.372	.459	146	6	1	5	25	8
Caden Wagner, Northern Colorado	.300	.392	.463	160	6	1	6	35	0
Nic Nelson, South Dakota St.	.299	.399	.619	197	9	3	16	52	3
Druw Sackett, North Dakota St.	.298	.402	.558	215	15	1	13	53	9
Blaze Brothers, Oral Roberts	.297	.368	.542	236	18	2	12	41	22
Terrell Huggins, North Dakota St.	.295	.369	.514	183	16	0	8	37	5

INDIVIDUAL PITCHING LEADERS

	W	L	ERA	GS	SV	IP	H	BB	SO
Parker Puetz, North Dakota St.	3	0	2.51	10	1	61	43	17	47
Brooks Fowler, Oral Roberts	9	2	3.26	17	0	80	66	32	78
Jakob Hall, Oral Roberts	8	3	3.56	18	0	99	93	17	94
Tristen Roehrich, N. Dakota St.	5	6	3.91	15	0	81	76	27	83
Jake Goble, South Dakota St.	5	3	4.32	11	0	58	52	19	46
Cade Feeney, North Dakota St.	6	5	4.57	14	0	81	92	12	78
Harley Gollert, Oral Roberts	10	2	4.65	17	0	91	87	32	94
Esch, Evan, St. Thomas	2	3	4.73	7	1	46	40	35	48
Preston Tenney, Omaha	6	6	5.30	14	0	73	65	32	63
Dylan Smith, N. Colorado	5	6	5.33	12	0	74	94	15	47
Jake Armstrong, W. Ilinois	4	6	5.40	14	0	82	95	40	45
Retz, Walker, St. Thomas	2	6	5.57	9	0	52	61	25	55
Murphy Gienger, N. Colorado	2	5	5.93	4	0	58	69	33	76
Tyler Kapraun, Western Illinois	3	7	5.99	12	0	68	79	37	53
Jack Bell, Western Illinois	2	5	6.20	1	6	61	64	26	53
Blake Kunz, South Dakota St.	1	7	6.51	11	0	57	57	38	59
Gartner, Kolby, St. Thomas	1	7	6.60	11	0	60	68	27	46

SUN BELT CONFERENCE

	Conference		Overall	
	W	L	W	L
*Coastal Carolina	23	7	42	21
*Southern Miss	22	8	46	20
*Troy	18	12	40	22
*Louisiana	18	12	41	24
Texas State	17	13	36	23
App State	16	13	30	25
James Madison	15	13	31	25
Georgia State	16	14	30	29
Georgia Southern	16	14	27	29
Old Dominion	15	15	32	23
South Alabama	11	19	23	31
Arkansas State	9	19	20	31
ULM	6	23	17	37
Marshall	5	24	16	36

ALL-CONFERENCE TEAM: C: Caden Bodine, Coastal Carolina. **1B:** Hunter Fitz-Gerald, Old Dominion. **2B:** Jesse Sherrill, Georgia Southern. **SS:** Dustin Dickerson, Southern Miss. **3B:** Caleb Bartolero, Troy. **OF:** CJ Boyd, App State. **OF:** Nick Lucky, Coastal Carolina. **OF:** Shane Lewis, Troy. **UT:** Cameron Jones, Georgia State. **DH:** Derek Bender, Coastal Carolina. P: Xander Hamilton, App State. **P:** Tanner Hall, Southern Miss. P: Grayson Stewart, Troy. **RP:** Teddy Sharkey, Coastal Carolina. **Player of the Year:** Shane Lewis, Troy. Pitcher of the Year: Tanner Hall, Southern Miss. **Newcomer of the Year:** Shane Lewis, Troy. **Freshman of the Year:** Caden Bodine, Coastal Carolina. **Coach of the Year:** Gary Gilmore, Coastal Carolina.

INDIVIDUAL BATTING LEADERS

	AVG	OBP	SLG	AB	2B	3B	HR	RBI	SB
Jesse Sherrill, Georgia Southern	.409	.502	.486	90	11	3	0	35	6
Max Ryerson, Georgia State	.376	.482	.703	76	6	0	20	52	1
Rodrigo Montenegro, S. Miss	.375	.507	.433	39	6	0	0	16	1
CJ Boyd, App State	.374	.410	.721	71	16	1	16	53	11
Payton Eeles, Coastal Carolina	.368	.494	.484	92	17	0	4	43	42
Kyle DeBarge, Louisiana	.365	.440	.538	76	15	0	7	39	18
Caden Bodine, Coastal Carolina	.362	.452	.601	79	17	1	11	47	1
Kyle Novak, James Madison	.357	.443	.467	75	13	2	2	43	9
Heath Hood, Louisiana	.351	.434	.522	86	16	4	6	41	36
Will Turner, South Alabama	.349	.460	.591	75	17	4	9	52	10
Brandon Hager, Arkansas State	.348	.500	.657	63	11	0	15	55	0
Blake Evans, Georgia Southern	.342	.434	.520	69	12	3	6	40	8
Fenwick Trimble, James Mad.	.342	.452	.631	77	22	2	13	52	9
Kyle Edwards, Old Dominion	.341	.379	.659	30	8	1	6	19	12
Derek Bender, Coastal Carolina	.337	.397	.627	86	13	2	19	83	2
Davis Powell, Texas State	.337	.431	.522	62	17	1	5	32	0
Cameron Jones, Georgia State	.336	.458	.431	71	12	1	2	30	37
Xavier Moronta, App State	.335	.437	.456	72	17	0	3	31	5
Hayden Cross, App State	.328	.437	.520	67	14	2	7	47	3
Jack Cone, James Madison	.325	.450	.502	68	20	1	5	29	15
Dustin Dickerson, S. Miss	.323	.416	.548	85	20	3	11	51	14
Nick Monistere, S, Miss	.323	.427	.532	40	9	1	5	28	6
Zack Beach, Coastal Carolina	.321	.458	.613	54	10	0	13	56	3
JoJo Jackson, Georgia State	.319	.437	.595	59	10	1	13	41	8
Carson Roccaforte, Louisiana	.319	.427	.540	75	26	1	8	55	22

INDIVIDUAL PITCHING LEADERS

	W	L	ERA	G	SV	IP	H	BB	SO
Tanner Hall, Southern Miss	12	4	2.48	18	0	112	84	33	124
Kyler Carmack, Arkansas State	5	3	3.23	12	0	70	63	37	60
Sam Armstrong, Old Dominion	9	4	3.51	15	0	77	69	28	72
Grayson Stewart, Troy	9	3	3.65	17	0	91	88	25	94
Ryan Watson, Georgia State	7	2	3.80	15	0	92	85	17	86
Cooper Rawls, Louisiana	10	1	3.88	5	2	67	59	19	53
Billy Oldham, Southern Miss	8	3	4.21	13	1	77	65	23	89
Tony Robie, Texas State	5	4	4.33	12	0	60	59	26	48
Niko Mazza, Southern Miss	5	2	4.34	13	2	75	66	46	89
Zac Addkison, Marshall	3	8	4.60	15	0	72	62	44	72

WEST COAST CONFERENCE

	Conference		Overall	
	W	L	W	L
LMU	21	6	29	24
*Santa Clara	17	10	35	19
San Diego	17	10	24	24
Portland	17	11	31	24
Saint Mary's	14	13	23	28
Gonzaga	14	13	18	34
Brigham Young	13	14	24	28
Pepperdine	8	19	19	30
San Francisco	8	19	18	29
Pacific	6	21	14	35

ALL-CONFERENCE TEAM: Christian Almanza, Saint Mary's. Diego Baqueiro, LMU. Diego Barrera, LMU. Nick Brink, Portland. Mario DeMera, San Francisco. Austin Deming, BYU. Jake Holcroft, Portland. Brian Kalmer, Gonzaga. Nich Klemp, Portland. Connor Linchey, Saint Mary's. Ben Nemivant, Pacific. Angelo Peraza, San Diego. Evan Scavotto, Portland. Zach Toglia, Portland. **Coach of the Year:** Nathan Choate, LMU. **Co-Player of the Year:** Christian Almanza, Saint Mary's. **Co-Player of the Year:** Austin Deming, BYU. **Pitcher of the Year:** Diego Barrera, LMU. **Freshman of the Year:** Khadim Diaw, LMU. **Defensive Player of the Year:** Cole Roberts, LMU.

INDIVIDUAL BATTING LEADERS

	AVG	OBP	SLG	AB	2B	3B	HR	RBI	SB
A Deming, Brigham Young	.418	.484	.915	165	23	1	19	68	1
B Nemivant, Pacific	.398	.446	.527	201	18	1	2	36	5
N Klemp, Portland	.390	.449	.592	213	25	0	6	45	3
C Vest, Brigham Young	.359	.418	.613	181	16	3	8	46	1
B Kalmer, Gonzaga	.358	.454	.682	201	16	2	15	51	1

H Williams III, San Francisco	.352	.426	.577	182	14	0	9	38	22
M DeMera, San Francisco	.348	.427	.440	184	14	0	1	29	9
J Basseer, Pepperdine	.345	.418	.512	168	13	0	5	34	2
J Holcroft, Portland	.343	.404	.508	242	13	3	7	43	14
R Hipwell, Santa Clara	.329	.500	.706	143	12	0	14	39	2
C Cooney, Portland	.329	.399	.479	140	9	0	4	29	6
A Peraza, San Diego	.328	.448	.519	183	11	3	6	31	10
C Gambill, Brigham Young	.325	.412	.644	191	14	1	15	43	3
M O'Hara, Santa Clara	.324	.419	.465	213	12	3	4	39	6
J Decriscio, San Diego	.322	.374	.439	171	9	1	3	18	13
B Knight, Portland	.322	.409	.487	199	21	0	4	43	0
D Brigman, Santa Clara	.321	.419	.475	221	10	3	6	34	13
S Stem, Gonzaga	.317	.354	.470	183	10	3	4	31	2
J Berring, Santa Clara	.315	.416	.419	203	10	4	1	24	16

INDIVIDUAL PITCHING LEADERS

	W	L	ERA	G	SV	IP	H	BB	SO
N Brink, Portland	6	0	2.02	14	1	58	52	22	60
D Barrera, Loyola Marymount	8	2	2.17	14	0	100	80	11	93
C Linchey, Saint Mary's (CA)	5	1	3.11	15	1	75	64	15	55
B Gomez, Santa Clara	6	4	3.66	17	1	59	63	13	57
Z Kirby, Loyola Marymount	5	4	3.84	15	0	82	86	20	89
S Telfer, Pepperdine	4	5	4.15	14	0	64	67	40	71
C Kitchen, Santa Clara	3	2	4.20	17	0	81	67	37	68
J Sashin, San Diego	2	3	4.45	17	0	59	73	27	51
J Barron, San Francisco	4	4	4.54	13	0	71	62	27	59
P Allegro, Portland	7	3	4.98	17	2	78	71	29	79
O Wild, Gonzaga	4	7	5.02	15	0	95	104	31	105
J Feikes, Santa Clara	6	1	5.09	18	1	69	64	22	54
J Gartrell, Portland	5	5	5.17	16	0	78	88	22	66
G Stevens, Pacific	4	7	5.19	15	0	87	102	19	65
A Shew, San Francisco	3	3	5.26	12	0	63	80	15	58
J Rutherford, Gonzaga	4	2	5.33	15	0	76	81	29	72
G Rennie, San Diego	1	3	5.40	13	0	53	67	16	38
M Olsen, Brigham Young	5	3	5.53	17	0	81	91	21	72
B Gillis, Portland	3	3	5.63	16	0	64	59	44	67
O Hackman, Loyola Marymount	4	3	5.71	13	0	65	73	14	40

WESTERN ATHLETIC CONFERENCE

	Conference		Overall	
	W	L	W	L
Grand Canyon	22	7	37	21
*Sam Houston	22	8	39	25
Utah Valley	16	12	34	24
Seattle	17	13	21	32
Abilene Christian	16	14	35	24
UT Arlington	16	14	29	29
UTRGV	15	14	30	26
California Baptist	15	15	28	30
Sacramento State	14	16	30	26
Stephen F. Austin	12	18	22	28
Tarleton State	10	18	26	26
New Mexico State	9	21	14	37
Utah Tech	8	22	13	39

ALL-CONFERENCE TEAM:C: Martin Vincelli-Simard, Sr., Sacramento State. **1B:** Tyler Davis, Sr., Sam Houston. **1B:** Brandon Pimentel, Grad, UTRGV. **2B:** Daniel Dickinson, Fr., Utah Valley. **3B:** Justin Wishkoski, Jr., Sam Houston. **SS:** Jacob Wilson, Jr., Grand Canyon. **OF:** Grayson Tatrow, Sr., Abilene Christian. **OF:** Homer Bush Jr., Jr., Grand Canyon. **OF:** Joe Redfield, Jr., Sam Houston. **DH:** JP Smith, Fr., Sacramento State. **SP:** Liam Rocha, Jr., RHP, California Baptist. **SP:** Daniel Avitia, So., RHP, Grand Canyon. **SP:** Casey Anderson, Jr., RHP, Utah Valley. **RP:** Chandler David, Jr., RHP, Sam Houston. **Player of the Year:** Grayson Tatrow, Abilene Christian. **Pitcher of the Year:** Liam Rocha, California Baptist. **Freshman of the Year:** Wehiwa Aloy, SS, Sacramento State. **Defensive Player of the Year:** Jacob Wilson, Jr., SS, Grand Canyon. **Coach of the Year:** Gregg Wallis, Grand Canyon.

INDIVIDUAL BATTING LEADERS

	AVG	OBP	SLG	AB	2B	3B	HR	RBI	SB
Davis, Tyler, SHSU	.423	.491	.621	253	21	4	7	60	14
Wilson, Jacob, GCU	.411	.461	.635	192	17	4	6	61	8
Pimentel, Brandon, UTRGV	.402	.486	.710	214	9	0	19	73	10
Redfield, Joe, SHSU	.402	.485	.683	249	19	3	15	56	15
Dickinson, Daniel, UVU	.376	.445	.596	218	19	1	9	42	10
Aloy, Wehiwa, SAC	.376	.427	.662	234	15	5	14	46	2
Tatrow, Grayson, ACU	.375	.480	.832	208	14	3	25	68	9
Keith Jones II, NMSU	.371	.483	.600	170	12	0	9	29	7
Bush Jr., Homer, GCU	.370	.478	.500	238	19	3	2	41	25
Yorke, Zach, GCU	.368	.471	.549	204	13	0	8	61	0
Berkley, Garrison, UTA	.365	.457	.519	233	20	2	4	38	7
Morrison, Trace, TSU	.365	.417	.429	170	6	1	1	23	9
Garret Ostrander, CBU	.364	.444	.414	198	7	0	1	24	15
A. Rodgers, SFA	.363	.454	.612	201	18	1	10	43	14
Kleckner, Cole, SU	.361	.456	.383	180	4	0	0	15	8
Britt, Logan, ACU	.354	.408	.591	237	10	5	12	46	33
P. Parker, SFA	.351	.436	.539	154	9	1	6	36	10
Christian Perez, NMSU	.349	.415	.651	166	12	1	12	40	0
C. Loranger, SFA	.343	.413	.460	198	12	1	3	31	7
Vincelli-Simard, M, SAC	.342	.408	.684	196	16	0	17	60	1
Wagner, Jack, TSU	.337	.451	.692	172	8	4	15	56	7
Smith, JP, SAC	.337	.378	.629	175	9	0	14	45	0
Black, Ryan, UTA	.336	.428	.502	223	14	1	7	57	6
Shupe, Hudson, SU	.333	.390	.403	216	11	2	0	28	1
Wishkoski, Justin, SHSU	.332	.414	.552	250	18	2	11	54	16

INDIVIDUAL PITCHING LEADERS

	W	L	ERA	G	SV	IP	H	BB	SO
Cabral, Angelo, UTRGV	10	2	3.22	14	1	72	64	22	76
Ryan Delgado, CBU	2	5	3.34	28	4	59	53	21	48
Liam Rocha, CBU	6	1	3.39	17	0	82	70	30	103
Anderson, Casey, UVU	4	1	3.52	15	2	69	63	26	90
Thornton, Zach, GCU	9	2	3.87	15	0	88	99	18	91
Avitia, Daniel, GCU	7	1	3.92	15	0	82	77	19	81
Aldaz, Jesus, UTRGV	3	3	3.99	13	2	58	45	23	55
Davis, Colten, UTRGV	4	3	4.04	15	0	75	81	23	82
Day, Hunter, TSU	6	2	4.16	13	0	71	77	19	56
Fowlks, Ethan, UVU	4	2	4.17	16	4	58	70	12	47
Eichelberger, Breck, ACU	5	2	4.39	15	0	67	72	35	56
Chronowski, Peter, SU	5	8	4.45	15	0	87	101	19	47
Atkinson, Coltin, SHSU	9	5	4.8	17	0	84	89	29	70
Gerling, Logan, UVU	6	5	5.32	15	0	71	84	13	65
Spencer Bengard, CBU	5	1	5.37	23	1	68	76	18	70
Glaze, Austin, ACU	4	1	5.52	15	0	62	56	25	51
Smith, Blake, SU	4	2	5.54	19	2	65	72	18	62
Beard, Steven, SHSU	8	3	5.78	17	0	85	104	22	58

NCAA DIVISION II

Angelo State (Texas) has been a solid baseball program for years, but it had never won a D-II national title. The Rams easily ended that drought, sweeping through the College World Series undefeated and going 12-1 in the postseason. They toppped Rollins 6-5 in the championship game and finished the season 56-9. It was the Rams' first national title in any men's sport since joining the NCAA.

Aaron Munson picked up the win in the title game by allowing two runs on five hits in 5.1 innings while striking out four. It improved his record to 11-2. He was named the tournament's Most Outstanding Player.

DIVISION II WORLD SERIES

Site: Cary, N.C.
Participants: Augustana (S.D.); Millersville (Pa.); Southern New Hampshire; Indianapolis (Ind.); Rollins (Fla.); North Greenville (S.C.); Angelo State (Texas); Cal State San Bernardino.
Champion: Angelo State (Texas).
Runner-up: Rollins (Fla.).

LEADERS: BATTING AVERAGE

(Minimum 140 at bats)

Rk.	Player, Pos., Team	Class	AVG	OBP	SLG
1.	DJ Van Atten, UT, Southern Nazarene	So.	.470	.562	.923
2.	Tanner Garner, OF, MSU Denver	Sr.	.453	.502	.738
3.	Tim Orr, C, Tiffin	Jr.	.452	.535	.735
4.	Reggie Williams, INF, CSU Pueblo	Sr.	.447	.534	.607
5.	John Nett, OF, St. Cloud St.	Jr.	.444	.527	.625
6.	Jordan Lala, OF, Tampa	Sr.	.443	.566	.537
7.	Dale Francis, Jr., INF, Erskine	So.	.442	.527	.779
8.	Tyson Gingerich, SS, Malone	Sr.	.437	.522	.568
9.	Julian Boyd, OF, Colorado Mesa	Sr.	.436	.529	.762
10.	Alex Epp, INF, William Jewell	Sr.	.435	.561	.663

EARNED RUN AVERAGE

(Minimum 40 innings pitched)

Rk.	Pitcher, Team	Class	W	L	ERA
1.	Kade Bragg, Angelo St.	Sr.	15	1	1.20
2.	Mitch Farris, Wingate	Sr.	11	1	1.21
3.	Jarrett Heilman, Mercyhurst	Sr.	6	2	1.38
4.	Riley O'Sullivan, Concordia U Irvine	Sr.	7	1	1.42
5.	Sam DiGeorge, Le Moyne	Sr.	7	1	1.52
6.	Jake Karaba, Lewis	Sr.	7	2	1.62
7.	Tanner Halvorson, Barton	Sr.	11	2	1.71
8.	Will Hotalen, Alabama Huntsville	Sr.	5	2	1.76
9.	Patrick Gleason, Pace	Sr.	8	2	1.81
10.	Dalton Neuschwander, West Florida	Sr.	10	0	1.87

CATEGORY LEADERS: BATTING

Dept.	Player, Pos., Team	Class	G	Total
OBP	Taj Bates, 3B, Benedict	So.	34	.567
SLG	DJ Van Atten, UT, Southern Nazarene	So.	49	.923
R	Pat Monteith, 3B, North Greenville	Jr.	61	89
	Carson Ogilvie, SS, Lubbock Christian	Jr.	58	89
H	Deshawn Johnson, CSUSB	Sr.	65	101
2B	Ross Smith, OF, MSU Denver	So.	56	31
3B	Damon Burroughs, OF, Southeastern Okla.	Jr.	47	9
	Carson Ogilvie, SS, Lubbock Christian	Jr.	58	9
HR	Luke Napleton, C, Quincy	Jr.	58	29
RBI	Luke Napleton, C, Quincy	Jr.	58	87
SB	Jack Whalen, OF, Seton Hill	Fr.	59	52

CATEGORY LEADERS: PITCHING

Dept.	Pitcher, Team	Class	Total
W	Kade Bragg, Angelo State	Jr.	15
SV	Oscar Rauda, CBUSB	Jr.	14
	Adam Diedrich, Augustana (S.D.)	So.	14
G	Myles Hedgecock, Belmont Abbey	Jr.	31
SO/BB	Brendan Palmer, Bridgeport	Fr.	12.33
SO	Luke Short, St. Edward's	Sr.	130
SO/9	Jake Karaba, Lewis	Sr.	16.06
BB/9	Brendan Palmer, Bridgeport	Jr.	0.57
WHIP	Mitch Farris, Wingate	Sr.	0.62

NCAA Division III

Making their first trip to the Division III World Series, the Lynchburg (Va.) Hornets won it all, topping John Hopkins (Md.) 7-6 in the deciding Game Three of the championship series. It was Lynchburg's first team national title in any sport.

Lynchburg finished the season 48-8. Zack Potts was named the Most Outstanding Player of the CWS. He went 2-0 with a complete game in one start and one earned run allowed in the CWS.

The DIII CWS was held in Eastlake, Ohio for the first time after spending the past several years in Cedar Rapids, Iowa.

DIVISION III WORLD SERIES

Site: Eastlake, Ohio
Participants: Johns Hopkins (Md); Endicott (Mass.); Misericordia (Pa.); Lynchburg (Va.); Salisbury (Md.); Baldwin Wallace (Ohio); Wisconsin-La Crosse; East Texas Baptist.
Champion: Lynchburg (Va.).
Runner-up: John Hopkins (Md.).

LEADERS: BATTING AVERAGE

(Minimum 120 at bats)

RK.	Player, Pos., Team	Class	AVG	OBP	SLG
1.	Justin Fogel, C, Penn St.-Abington	Jr.	.497	.549	.931
2.	Tyler Quade, UT, Mount Aloysius	So.	.496	.564	.812
3.	Ben Watson, OF, Elizabethtown	Sr.	.486	.559	.814
4.	Howie Hatton, OF, Crown (MN)	Sr.	.486	.551	.746
5.	Tyler Warr, 1B, Cairn	So.	.481	.536	.714
6.	Adam Cootway, INF, Wis.-Whitewater	Jr.	.477	.560	.933
7.	Sam Paden, OF, Wis.-Whitewater	So.	.476	.533	.714
8.	Christian Homa, INF, Salve Regina	So.	.472	.538	.667
9.	Colin Solinski, UT, Pitt.-Greensburg	Fr.	.469	.568	.708
10.	Doc Daniels, INF, Wilson	So.	.469	.506	.625

EARNED RUN AVERAGE

Rk.	Pitcher, Team	Class	W	L	ERA
1.	Nathan Mankoski, Pitt.-Greensburg	Fr.	6	1	1.06
2.	Braden Mussat, Kalamazoo	Jr.	7	1	1.22
3.	Wesley Clark, Spalding	Jr.	6	1	1.40
4.	Tyler Reiter, Redlands	Sr.	7	1	1.46
5.	Harrison Boushele, Augustana (IL)	Jr.	8	2	1.47
6.	Liam Alpern, Swarthmore	So.	4	0	1.48
7.	Gabriel Romano, Johns Hopkins	Sr.	11	1	1.56
8.	Brett Sanchez, Belhaven	Jr.	6	2	1.81
9.	Nolan Klocke, Luther	Fr.	4	1	1.83
10.	Maxwell Gitlin, Clark (MA)	Jr.	6	2	1.84

CATEGORY LEADERS: BATTING

Dept.	Player, Pos., Team	Class	G	Total
OBP	Garrett McIlhenney, OF, Misericordia	Sr.	55	.591
SLG	Bobby Pollock, OF, Farmingdale St.	Sr.	34	1.011
R	Garrett McIlhenney, OF, Misericordia	Sr.	55	80
H	Sean Kolenich, INF, Baldwin Wallace	So.	51	95
2B	Tyler Cannon, INF, Rowan	Sr.	48	31
3B	Johannes Haakenson, OF, Concordia Wisconsin	Sr.	39	9
	Alex Richter, 2B, Marietta	So.	43	9
	Sean Tillmon, INF, Concordia Wisconsin	Sr.	39	9
HR	Matthew Cooper, 3B, Johns Hopkins	Sr.	51	25
RBI	Cavan Brady, INF, Wheaton (MA)	Sr.	51	77
SB	Cameron Santerre, OF, Rhode Island Col.	Jr.	43	54

CATEGORY LEADERS: PITCHING

Dept.	Pitcher, Team	Class	Total
W	Zack Potts. Lynchburg	Sr.	13
SV	Jack Bachmore. Lynchburg	Sr.	13
G	Jack Bachmore, Lynchburg	Sr.	29
SO/BB	Timmy Smith. Saint Mary's (MN)	Sr.	14.5
SO	Shaun Gamelin. Rhode Island Col.	Sr.	143
SO/9	Gavin Jacobsen. Bethany Lutheran	So.	15.0
BB/9	Timmy Smith. Saint Mary's (MN)	Sr.	0.33
WHIP	Dylan Beers. Cortland	So.	0.81

NAIA

The Westmont (Calif.) Warriors won their first ever NAIA baseball title, topping host Lewis-Clark (Idaho) State 7-6 in the championship game.

The way Westmont won it was quite unusual. Lewis-Clark had tied the game at six when the Westmont shortstop lost a pop fly in the lights.

But Westmont's Parker O'Neill drew a bases-loaded walk to score Isaac Haws with the winning run.

Lewis-Clark's Isaiah Thomas was named the tournament's Most Valuable Player.

NAIA WORLD SERIES

Site: Lewiston, Idaho.
Participants: 1. Southeastern (Fla.); 2. Georgia Gwinnett; 3. Westmont (Calif.); 4. William Carey (Miss.); 5. Bellevue (Neb.); 6. Cumberlands (Ky.); 7. Taylor (Ind.); 8. Indiana Wesleyan; 9. Lewis-Clark State (Idaho); 10. MidAmerica Nazarene (Kan.).
Champion: Westmont (Calif.).
Runner-up: Lewis-Clark State (Idaho).

LEADERS: BATTING AVERAGE

Rk.	Player, Pos., Team	AVG	OBP	SLG
1.	Cole Turney, OF, Cumberland (Tenn.)	.530	.675	1.311
2.	Korique Rainey, 3B, Morris	.515	.564	.818
3.	Nick Lopez, C, Georgetown (Ky.)	.500	.500	.600
4.	Jhors Gomez, INF, Southwestern Christian	.493	.592	.912
5.	Ivanuel Hernandez, C, Fisher (Mass.)	.485	.537	.788

EARNED RUN AVERAGE

Rk.	Pitcher, Team	W	L	ERA
1.	Tyler Bryant, Ottawa	8	1	1.60
2.	Johnny Blake, Clarke (Iowa)	6	3	1.75
3.	Eli Davis, Oklahoma City	12	2	1.83
4.	Cole Altherr, Embry-Riddle (Ariz.)	3	2	1.89
5.	Alec Martinez, Our Lady of the Lake (Texas)	7	2	1.96

CATEGORY LEADERS: BATTING

Dept.	Player, Pos., Team	G	Total
OBP	Cole Turney, OF, Cumberland	42	.675
SLG	Cole Turney, Cumberland (Tenn.)	42	1.311
HR	Ajay Sczepkowski, OF, Georgia Gwinnett	57	33
RBI	Ajay Sczepkowski, OF, Georgia Gwinnett	57	102
SB	Ryan Major, OF, LSU Shreveport (La.)	52	45

CATEGORY LEADERS: PITCHING

Dept.	Pitcher, Team	Class	Total
W	Jarrett Brannen, Kansas Wesleyan		14
SV	C McFadden, Mount Vernon Nazarene		11
SO	Eli Davis, Oklahoma City		137

NJCAA Division I

Central Florida knocked off Wabash Valley (Ill.) 13-6 to claim its first NJCAA national title. The Patriots came into the tournament as the favorites, as their powerful lineup had earned them the No. 1 seed heading onto the postseason.

Kainen Jorge, Thad Ector and Cole Bullen all homered in the championship game. Central Florida finished the season 56-7.

NJCAA DIVISION I WORLD SERIES

Site: Grand Junction, Colo.
Participants: Andrew (Ga.); Gaston (N.C.); Blinn (Texas); Wabash Valley (Ill.); Johnson County (Kan.); Shelton State (Ala.); Central Florida; Delgado (La.); Weatherford (Texas); Salt Lake (Utah).
Champion: Central Florida.
Runner-up: Wabash Valley.

LEADERS: BATTING AVERAGE

Rk.	Player, Pos., Team	Class	AVG	OBP	SLG
1.	Nicklas Williams, INF, Wabash Valley (Ill.)		.482	.595	.824
2.	Brady Cerkownyk, C, Connors (Okla.) State		.470	.555	.985
3.	Jhanel Bautista, SS, Ranger (Texas)		.470	.516	.667
4.	Tomas Ricny, 3B, Northeastern (Colo.)		.468	.555	.770
5.	Carter Frederick, OF, Snead State (Ala.)		.463	.572	.863

EARNED RUN AVERAGE

Rk.	Pitcher, Team	Class	W	L	ERA
1.	Patrick Steitz, Central Arizona		9	1	1.06
2.	Matt Wilkinson, Central Arizona		10	2	1.07
3.	Ryne Rodriguez, Weatherford		11	0	1.59
4.	Mathias Lacombe, Cochise		5	3	1.74
5.	Jacob Beltran, South Mountain		7	2	1.85

CATEGORY LEADERS: BATTING

Pos., Team		G	Total
OBP	Niklas Williams, INF, Wabash Valley (Ill.)	70	.595
SLG	Brady Cerkownyk, C, Connors (Okla.) State	55	.985
HR	Robin Villeneuve, 1B, Weatherford (Texas)	63	28
RBI	Brady Cerkownyk, C, Connors (Okla.) State	55	107
SB	Jhanel Bautista, SS, Ranger (Texas)	54	56

CATEGORY LEADERS: PITCHING

Dept.	Pitcher, Team	Total
W	Colton Brumley, Southwest Tennessee	13
	Cole Koonce, Johnson County (Tenn.)	13
SV	J.T. Drake, Pima (Ariz.)	15
IP	Roland Marte, Arizona Western	114.2
SO	Brian Holiday, Central Florida	141

NJCAA Division II

In its fifth trip to the NJCAA World Series, Heartland (Ill.) finally got to experience the final celebatory dog pile.

Top-seeded Heartland knocked off Southeastern (Iowa) in the championship game

8-6. Bobby Atkinson homered for Heartlandm while Corey Boyette had three hits, two runs scored and two RBIs.

NJCAA DIVISION II WORLD SERIES

Site: Enid, Okla.
Participants: Heartland (Ill.); Lackawanna (Pa.); Lansing (Mich.); East Central (Miss.); Frederick (Md.); Madison (Wisc.); Southeastern (Iowa); South Arkansas; St. Johns River State (Fla.); Glendale (Ariz.)
Champion: Heartland (Ill.)
Runner-up: Southeastern (Iowa).

LEADERS: BATTING AVERAGE

RK. Player, Pos., Team	Class	AVG	OBP	SLG
1. Sam Antonacci, Heartland (Ill.)		.515	.618	.903
2. Kyle Zaluski, Lakeland (Ohio)		.472	.544	.719
3. Jaden Woolbright, Southern Arkansas Tech		.466	.541	.801
4. Layton Cuvilier, Sussex (N.J.) County		.458	.518	.558
5. Corey Boyette, Heartland (Ill.)		.457	.553	.720

EARNED RUN AVERAGE

Rk. Pitcher, Team	Class	W	L	ERA
1. Cooper Cooksey, Pearl River (Miss.)		9	1	1.32
2. Jerad Berkenpas, Grand Rapids (Mich.)		8	2	1.44
3. Hunter Shaw, Lansing (Mich.)		9	2	1.58
4. Anthony Hausner, Guilford Tech (N.C.)		2	0	1.80
5. Ryan Devanney, Morris (N.J.)		7	1	1.89

CATEGORY LEADERS: BATTING

Dept.	Player, Team	G	Total
OBP	Sam Antonacci, Heartland (Ill.)	62	.618
SLG	Payton Mansfield, John Wood (Ill.)	52	.994
HR	Garrett, Gruell, Murray State (Okla.)	54	27
RBI	Sam Antonacci, Heartland (Ill.)	62	103
SB	Zach Walsh, Lackawanna (Pa.)	53	52

CATEGORY LEADERS: PITCHING

Dept.	Pitcher, Team	Total
W	Casey Perrenoud, Southeastern (Iowa)	12
SV	Nick Scanlon, Kirkwood (Iowa)	12
IP	Connor McBride, St. John's River State (Fla.)	96.1
SO	Colby Langford, Murray State (Okla.)	124

NJCAA Division III

RCSJ Gloucester won its eight NJCAA D-III nastional title with a 15-7 win over Dallas-Eastfield in the title game.

While this the Roadrunners' eight title, it was their first since 2013. It was a second-consecutive runners-up finish for Dallas-Eastfield.

RCSJ Gloucester finished 53-5 and entered the tournament as the top seed. Outfielder Aaron Graber was named the tournament's Most Valuable Player.

NJCAA DIVISION III WORLD SERIES

Site: Greeneville, Tenn.
Participants: Herkimer (N.Y.), Joliet (Ill.); Camp (Va.); Niagara County (N.Y.); Rowan Gloucester (N.J.); Northern Essex (Mass.); St. Cloud Tech (Minn.); Dallas College - Eastfield (Texas).
Champion: Rowan Gloucester.
Runner-up: Dallas College - Eastfield.

LEADERS: BATTING AVERAGE

Rk. Player, Pos., Team	AVG	OBP	SLG
1. Lawrence Bielawski, OF, Allegheny County (Pa.)	.512	.573	.850
2. Matt Deall, INF, Suffolk County (N.Y.)	.512	.577	.583
3. Hayden Setzer, INF, Caldwell Tech (N.C.)	.507	.598	1.053
4. Daziel Cuadrado, SS, Allegheny County (Pa.)	.500	.556	.653
4. Aaron Graeber, CF, RCSJ Gloucester (N.J.)	.500	.566	.897

EARNED RUN AVERAGE

Rk. Pitcher, Team	W	L	ERA
1. Jairo Vazquez, Northern Essex (Mass.)	8	0	0.93
2. Carson Geislinger, St. Cloud Tech (Minn.)	3	0	1.43
3. Anthony Rosario, Nassau (N.Y.)	3	0	1.59
4. Devin Georgetti, Finger Lakes (N.Y.)	5	3	1.64
5. Hunter Vikemyr, Riverland (Minn.)	9	0	1.82

California Junior Colleges

Whatever drama was expected in the California CC Athletic Association championship quickly evaporated as Santa Ana scored 20 runs in the first six innings on its way to a 21-8 win over Saddelback in the title game.

Christian Thompson was 5-for-5 with two doubles for Santa Ana, while Mario Tostado and Mikey Rocha each drove in five runs.

CALIFORNIA CC ATHLETIC ASSOCIATION

Site: Folsom.
Participants: Saddleback, Sierra, Folsom Lake, Santa Ana.
Champion: Santa Ana.
Runner-up: Saddleback.

LEADERS: BATTING AVERAGE

Rk. Player, Pos., Team	AVG	OBP	SLG
1. Will Potter, Mt. San Jacinto	.462	.520	.644
2. Bubba Rocha, Los Medanos	.451	.592	.731
3. Noah Lazuka, Palomar	.448	.533	.679
4. Roberto Gonzalez, Imperial Valley	.447	.550	.642
5. Quincy Scott, Palomar	.438	.522	.648

EARNED RUN AVERAGE

Rk. Pitcher, Team	Class	W	L	ERA
1. David Case, El Camino		6	0	1.09
2. Jaxon Jordan, Moorpark		1	0	1.15
3. Anthony Lopez, Allan Hancock		5	1	1.36
4. Jake Ridding, Cerro Coso		3	0	1.42
5. Danny Veloz, LA Valley		5	3	1.40

COLLEGE SUMMER BASEBALL

USA Baseball's Collegiate National Team annually puts together a roster of the best players in the country during the summer, which provides a great scouting opportunity and preview of the top-of-the-class talent for the upcoming draft class.

The 2022 version of the team was one of the most talented scouts had seen in years. It featured Paul Skenes, Dylan Crews, Wyatt Langford, Jacob Wilson, Rhett Lowder, Kyle Teel, Jacob Gonzalez, Enrique Bradfield Jr. and Brayden Taylor—nine of the top 20 draft picks in July.

The same was not true of Team USA in 2023. That's because the 2024 draft class looks like a down group compared to a historic 2023 group. This group doesn't have the same level of depth or top-end talent as last year's club.

West Virginia second baseman JJ Wetherholt leads the field thanks to his precocious lefthanded bat. There are still plenty of intriguing players on the 2023 College National Team, though each player comes with a few more question marks that will need to be addressed during the fall and next spring season.

Team USA played two five-game series this summer against Taiwan and Japan and went 7-3 overall, sweeping Taiwan in dominating fashion. Team USA outscored Taiwan 46-11 in five games.

Things did not go as well for the Americans against Japan. Team USA lost the opener, but then won the next two games. But Japan then rallied to win the final two games to claime the series 3-2.

Kaito Shimomura held Team USA hitless for five innings in Game Four of a 4-3 win, while four Japanese pitchers combined to hold Team USA to one hit over the final 3.1 innings of a 6-2 Team Japan win in Game Five.

Japan has now won two of its past three friendly series against Team USA's Collegiate National Team. Team USA's last series win against Japan came in 2018.

Bourne Wins Cape Title

"Things continue to evolve in college baseball. A brave new world of eye-popping home run totals, record transfers and NIL money is the new normal. Summer ball—and more specifically the

COLLEGIATE NATIONAL TEAM STATS

Player	Year	School	AVG	OBP	SLG	G	AB	R	H	2B	3B	HR	RBI	BB	SO	SB
Kalelen Culpepper	So.	Kansas State	.471	.526	.853	9	34	8	16	0	2	3	7	3	4	2
Griff O'Ferrall	So.	Virginia	.463	.511	.659	10	41	13	19	3	1	1	9	4	4	3
JJ Wetherholt	So.	West Virginia	.263	.481	.579	8	19	5	5	0	0	2	5	6	1	0
Charlie Condon	Fr.	Georgia	.256	.302	.538	10	39	8	10	2	0	3	11	3	10	1
Jace LaViolette	Fr.	Texas A&M	.250	.314	.438	10	32	7	8	0	0	2	6	3	10	2
Seaver King	So.	Wake Forest	.250	.286	.375	10	32	5	8	0	2	0	5	1	6	0
Ryan Stafford	So.	Cal Poly	.214	.389	.214	6	14	2	3	0	0	0	1	4	2	0
Rodney Green Jr.	So.	California	.211	.318	.368	7	19	2	4	0	0	1	6	2	4	0
Braden Montgomery	So.	Stanford	.200	.250	.400	9	30	4	6	0	0	2	4	2	11	2
Malcolm Moore	Fr.	Stanford	.188	.235	.250	6	16	4	3	1	0	0	0	1	5	0
Jac Caglianone	So.	Florida	.176	.293	.382	10	34	4	6	1	0	2	5	3	10	0
Duce Gourson	So.	UCLA	.154	.313	.154	6	13	3	2	0	0	0	1	3	5	1
Christian Moore	So.	Tennessee	.143	.143	.286	3	7	1	1	1	0	0	1	0	2	0

Pitcher, Pos.	Year	School	W	L	ERA	G	SV	IP	H	R	ER	BB	SO	AVG
Luke Holman	So.	Louisiana State	2	0	0.00	2	0	8	5	0	0	2	15	.172
Brandon Neely	So.	Florida	0	0	0.00	4	1	5	0	0	0	3	9	.000
Ben Abeldt	Fr.	Texas Christian	0	0	0.00	3	0	4	3	2	0	1	6	.188
Fran Oschell III	So.	Duke	1	0	0.00	2	0	4	0	0	0	1	8	.000
Tyson Neighbors	So.	Kansas State	0	0	0.00	4	0	3	3	0	0	1	4	.231
Braden Montgomery	So.	Stanford	0	0	0.00	1	0	1	0	0	0	0	3	.000
Xavier Meachem	So.	NC A&T	0	0	0.00	1	1	0	0	0	0	0	1	.000
Omar Melendez	So.	Alabama State	0	0	0.00	1	0	1	0	0	0	0	1	.000
Trey Yesavage	So,	East Carolina	0	0	1.35	2	0	7	4	1	1	1	5	.174
Hagen Smith	So.	Arkansas	0	1	1.59	3	0	6	2	1	1	1	6	.105
Jay Woolfolk	So.	Virginia	1	0	1.93	4	0	5	2	1	1	0	2	.125
Drew Beam	So.	Tennessee	2	0	2.25	2	0	8	6	2	2	1	7	.222
Ryan Johnson	So,	Dallas Baptist	1	1	3.48	3	0	10	6	4	4	1	11	.294
Matt Ager	So.	UC Santa Barbara	0	0	3.52	3	0	8	6	3	3	1	4	.200
Christian Coppol	Fr.	Rutgers	0	0	4.91	3	0	4	5	5	2	2	1	.200
Carter Holton	So.	Vanderbilt	0	0	5.40	1	0	2	2	1	1	1	3	.286
Michael Massey	So.	Wake Forest	0	0	7.71	4	0	5	3	4	4	4	5	.176
Kyle Robinson	So.	Texas Tech	0	1	8.10	2	0	3	4	5	3	2	0	.267
Nicholas Wilson	Jr.	Southern	0	0	54.00	1	0	.1	3	2	2	1	1	.750

Year indicates 2022-23 class standing

Cape Cod League—has been impacted mightily by the changing dynamics.

In a league and region that is historically resistant to change, the 10 Cape teams have been forced to adapt to the ever-evolving landscape of college sports.

Even before the 2020 pandemic and lost season, the Cape Cod League had already begun morphing into what many called more of a "showcase" league. But when the draft was moved back from early June to mid July in 2021, it changed the nature of summer ball.

With players looking to get one final look from scouts, early Cape Cod League rosters the last three summers have been littered with draft-eligible players. These players are typically juniors and fourth-year players who fall in the day three range of the draft looking for a last-minute bump.

This has allowed for late-arriving players from teams that advanced to the College World Series to get an extra week or two of rest before beginning their summer ball adventures. It's an imperfect cycle, and one that's been further impacted by the transfer portal, as players leave during the summer to take visits and often do not return to the Cape.

It has all led to a transient Cape Cod League, where 50% of rosters will change over two or more times between mid June and early August. Pitching is as scarce as it's ever been, with many pitchers on innings limits.

Despite all this, 2023 was one of the most exciting summers in recent memory with historic home run displays across the league and a strong group of positional talent. The West Division was particularly strong as all four teams that qualified for the playoffs had championship aspirations.

Everything culminated in a classic three-game tilt for the league championship between West Division champion Bourne and East Division champion Orleans.

An explosive game three ended in a second consecutive championship for the Bourne Braves, the first Cape Cod League team to repeat as champions since Yarmouth-Dennis in 2015.

Bourne manager Scott Landers has now won two titles in his two years as the Braves' skipper.

Coastal Carolina's Derek Bender's RBI double and Sam Peterson's RBI single gave Bourne a two-run lead in the deciding Game Three. Bender, the league's No. 3 prospect according to Baeball America, then added a solo home run to add some cushion, and reliever Anthony DeFabbia retired the final 13 batters he faced.

This is the third title in Bourne history, but maybe even more importantly it's the second in two years.

TRACY PROFFITT / FOUR SEAM IMAGES

Wake Forest's Seaver King hit .250 for Team USA.

COLLEGE SUMMER LEAGUES

For players who played for multiple teams: 1: Stats with first team. 2: Stats with second team. 3: Stats with third team. T: combined stats.

COURTESY BEN LILLEY

Jonathan Vastine helped lead Bourne to the Cape Cod League title

CAPE COD LEAGUE

East Division	W	L	T	PTS
Yarmouth-Dennis Red Sox	24	19	.558	--
Orleans Firebirds	24	20	.545	0.5
Harwich Mariners	20	23	.465	4
Brewster Whitecaps	15	27	.357	8.5
Chatham Anglers	15	27	.357	8.5
West Division	**W**	**L**	**T**	**PTS**
Cotuit Kettleers	28	15	.651	--
Hyannis Harbor Hawks	25	17	.595	2.5
Falmouth Commodores	24	18	.571	3.5
Bourne Braves	23	20	.535	5
Wareham Gatemen	15	27	.357	12.5

CHAMPIONSHIP: Bourne Braves defeated Orleans Firebirds, 2-1, in best-of-three championship series.

TOP 50 PROSPECTS:1. Travis Bazzana, 2B, Falmouth (Oregon State). 2. Cameron Smith, 3B, Hyannis (Florida State). 3. Derek Bender, C, Bourne (Coastal Carolina). 4. JJ Wetherholt, 2B, Chatham (West Virginia). 5. Seaver King, 2B/3B, Harwich (Wake Forest). 6. Cole Mathis, 1B/RHP, Cotuit (College of Charleston). 7. Nick McLain, OF, Wareham (Arizona State). 8. Camron Hill, LHP, Cotuit (Georgia Tech). 9. Jo Oyama, 2B, Orleans (UC Irvine). 10. Jonathan Vastine, SS, Bourne (Vanderbilt). 11. Braden Montgomery, OF/RHP, Yarmouth-Dennis (Texas A&M). 12. Matt Halbach, 3B, Orleans (UC San Diego). 13. James Tibbs, OF, Brewster (Florida State). 14. Caden Bodine, C, Bourne (Coastal Carolina). 15. Tristan Smith, LHP, Bourne (Clemson). 16. Cade Obermueller, LHP, Hyannis (Iowa). 17. Caleb Lomavita, C, Cotuit (California). 18. Will Turner, OF, Brewster (South Alabama). 19. Davis Diaz, 3B, Brewster (Vanderbilt). 20. RJ Austin, OF/2B, Yarmouth-Dennis (Vanderbilt). 21. Greysen Carter, RHP, Orleans (Vanderbilt). 22. Derek Clark, LHP, Orleans (West Virginia). 23. Jaime Ferrer, OF, Brewster (Florida State). 24. Hunter Hines, 1B, Yarmouth-Dennis (Mississippi State). 25. Kaeden Kent, 1B/3B, Chatham (Texas A&M). 26. Bryce Eblin, 2B, Bourne (Alabama). 27. Sean Matson, RHP, Orleans (Harvard). 28. Danny Avitia, RHP, Orleans (Grand Canyon). 29. Deric Fabian, SS, Chatham (Auburn). 30. Zach Ehrhard, OF, Hyannis (Oklahoma State). 31. Nick Mitchell, OF, Hyannis (Indiana). 32. Finnegan Wall, RHP, Yarmouth-Dennis (UC Irvine). 33. Jack Penney, 3B, Orleans (Notre Dame). 34. Kaelen Culpepper, 3B, Kansas State). 35. Gavin Turley, OF, Falmouth (Oregon State). 36. Braden Davis, LHP, Falmouth (Oklahoma). 37. Janzen Keisel, RHP, Cotuit (Oklahoma State). 38. Walker Janek, C, Falmouth (Sam Houston State). 39. Bryce Cunningham, RHP, Bourne (Vanderbilt). 40. Zach Yorke, 1B, Hyannis (Grand Canyon). 41. Grant Hussey, 1B, Wareham (West Virginia). 42. Gavin Kilen, SS, Falmouth (Louisville). 43. John Spikerman, OF, Falmouth (Oklahoma). 44. Trevor Haskins, SS, Cotuit (Stanford). 45. Devin Obee, OF, Harwich (Duke). 46. Kade Snell, 1B, Falmouth (Alabama). 47. Garrett Michel, 1B, Bourne (Virginia Tech). 48. Brody Donay, C, Hyannis (Florida). 49. Josh Pearson, OF, Brewster (Louisiana State). 50. Joshua Kuroda-Grauer, 2B, Bourne). Rutgers.

INDIVIDUAL BATTING LEADERS

Player, Team	AVG	AB	R	H	2B	3B	HR	RBI	SB
Travis Bazzana, 2B, FAL	.375	136	33	51	6	2	6	31	14
Derek Bender, BOU	.374	115	22	43	7	1	4	21	18
Bryce Elbin, BOU	.367	120	22	44	3	0	0	20	7
Matt Halbach, ORL	.364	121	22	44	5	2	3	15	0
Jo Oyama, ORL	.360	150	35	54	11	6	5	17	6
Cameron Smith, HYA	.347	167	38	58	12	4	6	26	0
Kaeden Kent, CHA	.329	149	26	49	7	1	2	22	1
RJ Austin, YD	.327	101	22	33	2	0	1	13	5
Cole Mathis, COT	.318	129	28	41	10	1	11	42	0
Tyler MacGregor, FAL	.318	107w	19	34	4	1	2	23	0

INDIVIDUAL PITCHING LEADERS

Player, Team	W	L	ERA	G	SV	IP	H	BB	SO
Camron Hill, COT	3	0	1.09	11	0	33	16	16	45
Daniel Avita, ORL	1	2	1.63	6	0	28	21	14	24

	W	L	ERA	G	SV	IP	H	BB	SO
Derek Clark, ORL	5	1	1.80	12	1	40	31	10	38
Hayden Frank, HYA	0	1	2.67	10	0	30	34	7	25
Smith Pinson, YD	3	1	2.68	7	0	37	28	11	37
Finnegan Wall, YD	2	2	2.91	7	0	34	23	15	38
Cam Schuelke, COT	1	2	3.16	13	1	37	30	16	48
Tom Chmielewski, HAR	1	3	3.21	6	0	28	26	6	23
Jason Doktorczyk, YD	1	2	3.45	8	1	29	28	12	29
Ryan Fischer, BOU	1	1	3.52	8	0	31	32	6	24

BOURNE

Batting	AVG	AB	R	H	2B	3B	HR	RBI	SB
Derek Bender, C	.374	115	22	43	7	1	4	21	18
Bryce Eblin, SS	.367	120	22	44	3	0	0	20	7
Kodey Shojinaga, IF	.326	43	5	14	1	0	0	2	1
Chris Stanfield, CF	.313	32	7	10	0	0	0	6	5
Jonathan Vastine, IF	.306	121	24	37	6	3	1	20	14
Nuu Contrades, 3B	.292	48	10	14	3	0	0	9	4
Sam Petersen, OF	.268	82	12	22	2	0	1	8	15
Hugh Pinkney, C	.263	57	6	15	0	0	0	5	1
Brett Callahan, OF	.250	20	3	5	2	0	0	5	0
Jackson Castillo, CF	.250	40	5	10	2	0	1	7	4
Gage Harrelson, CF	.242	91	14	22	4	0	0	8	11
Cameron Foster, 3B	.235	85	10	20	6	0	0	11	0
Adonys Guzman, C	.231	26	3	6	3	0	0	3	0
Garrett Michel, 1B	.227	110	15	25	4	1	4	16	3
Joey Loynd, IF	.219	32	4	7	3	0	1	4	1
Kendall Diggs, 3B	.214	70	13	15	4	0	0	11	1
Pete Ciuffreda, RF	.213	75	17	16	2	0	1	5	9
Joshua Kuroda-Grauer, 2B	.190	84	13	16	5	0	0	7	8
Andrew Patrick, IF	.167	24	1	4	0	0	1	2	1
Paul Tammaro III, IF	.120	25	3	3	0	0	0	2	4

Pitching	W	L	ERA	G	SV	IP	H	BB	SO
Matthew McShane	0	0	1.40	9	1	19	19	8	25
Tristan Smith	3	0	1.57	6	0	23	10	10	33
Brady Afthim	2	0	1.80	9	1	15	12	7	15
Matt Duffy	0	0	1.88	3	0	14	9	4	16
Kade Grundy	1	0	2.38	4	0	11	8	7	11
Bryce Cunningham	1	1	2.38	5	0	23	24	7	25
Gave Driscoll	2	2	2.49	9	1	25	17	8	27
David Falco	2	0	3.48	5	1	10	10	2	11
Ryan Fischer	1	1	3.52	8	0	31	32	6	24
Ryan Free	1	2	4.40	8	2	14	17	2	17
Logan Evans	0	2	4.50	3	0	14	16	3	12
Max LeBlanc	1	0	4.63	6	0	12	14	4	14
Garrett Horn	0	1	5.00	4	0	18	12	14	22
Henry Weycker	1	0	5.75	7	0	20	22	12	19
Dalton Pence	3	1	6.30	7	1	20	22	12	28
Jack Sullivan	0	2	7.62	8	1	13	21	3	7

BREWSTER

Batting	AVG	AB	R	H	2B	3B	HR	RBI	SB
Trevor Werner, 3B	.343	35	7	12	5	0	1	11	2
Jaime Ferrer, RF	.313	96	21	30	5	0	3	16	2
Hunter DAmato, IF	.304	23	5	7	1	0	0	1	1
James Tibbs, OF	.303	142	17	43	6	0	6	25	3
Joe Stella, C	.300	20	1	6	1	0	0	4	0
Will Turner, CF	.295	95	20	28	2	0	2	16	8
Brock Tibbitts, C	.289	121	16	35	2	0	1	12	1
Davis Diaz, SS	.284	102	14	29	5	0	3	16	4
Ike Irish, C	.283	92	9	26	4	1	0	8	0
Josh Pearson, OF	.277	65	12	18	4	0	3	13	6
Derek Berg, C	.273	22	5	6	1	0	2	4	0
Trevor Austin, 2B	.257	35	4	9	4	0	0	3	2
Patrick Forbes, P	.256	39	5	10	1	0	2	6	0
Michael Robertson, CF	.226	53	6	12	0	0	0	3	7
Dylan Hoy, SS	.211	38	6	8	0	0	0	1	1
Payton Green, SS	.207	87	10	18	2	0	1	8	3
Jared Jones, C	.190	58	5	11	0	0	2	4	0
Mason White, SS	.190	100	10	19	2	2	2	15	1
Dylan Leach, C	.189	74	9	14	1	0	1	5	1
Vincent Cimini, SS	.185	27	4	5	1	0	1	2	0
Jonah Sebring, SS	.107	28	5	3	0	0	0	0	3
Ivan Brethowr, OF	.100	20	4	2	0	0	0	0	0

Pitching	W	L	ERA	G	SV	IP	H	BB	SO
Josh Timmerman	1	1	2.00	6	0	18	5	10	22
Patrick Forbes	1	2	2.60	8	1	17	13	10	20
Brennan Phillips	0	3	3.10	8	0	20	21	13	14
Fisher Jameson	1	1	3.12	6	0	17	14	6	21
Sam Garcia	1	1	3.21	4	0	14	13	3	17
Joey DeChiaro	4	1	3.33	10	0	24	14	7	19
Tyler Mudd	0	1	3.47	9	1	23	23	7	16
Javyn Pimental	0	0	4.15	6	0	26	21	14	22
Austin Gordon	0	1	4.50	3	0	12	12	3	8
Darien Smith	1	0	5.40	4	0	12	11	4	5
Rocco Reid	0	4	5.73	9	0	22	30	10	16
Josh Sanders	3	1	6.52	8	0	19	22	5	15
Brennen Oxford	1	0	6.57	7	1	12	11	9	10
Carson Swilling	0	2	6.60	4	0	15	10	12	10
Jake Marshall	0	1	8.31	4	0	13	17	6	12
Drake Quinn	0	1	8.76	6	0	12	18	11	9
Brendan Lysik	0	2	10.95	7	0	12	18	10	11

CHATHAM

Batting	AVG	AB	R	H	2B	3B	HR	RBI	SB
Deric Fabian, IF	.352	91	22	32	1	0	5	20	3
Carson Benge, OF	.345	29	3	10	0	1	0	4	0
Kaeden Kent, SS	.329	149	26	49	7	1	2	22	1
J.J. Wetherholt, 2B	.321	28	3	9	4	0	1	8	0
Lyle Miller-Green, OF	.310	58	13	18	1	0	3	10	1
Matthew Etzel, CF	.297	37	4	11	1	0	1	8	4
Carter Trice, OF	.292	24	7	7	1	0	2	5	3
Brennan Holt, SS	.278	36	9	10	3	0	0	0	6
Xavier Casserilla, 3B	.258	62	7	16	4	1	1	5	1
Kyson Donahue, SS	.256	86	10	22	4	0	3	10	0
Zach MacDonald, CF	.250	68	15	17	0	0	2	8	4
Tyler Wulfert, 3B	.242	66	7	16	2	0	0	11	0
Bryce Martin-Grudzielanek, SS	.235	68	12	16	5	0	1	10	1
Lane Forsythe, SS	.216	37	6	8	1	0	0	1	0
Sam Antonacci, SS	.216	51	6	11	0	1	0	5	3
Nolan Schubart, OF	.216	116	12	25	6	0	2	16	1
Trace Willhoite, 3B	.200	35	8	7	0	0	3	9	0
Tate Ballestero, C	.174	23	3	4	1	0	0	3	0
Aidan Meola, 3B	.162	74	10	12	2	0	1	3	0
Hudson White, C	.161	62	8	10	3	0	1	5	0
Jayden Melendez, C	.156	32	7	5	0	0	1	2	1
Chris Maldonado, SS	.143	49	6	7	1	0	0	5	0
Kaden Hopson, C	.125	24	1	3	1	0	0	1	1
Janson Reeder, OF	.111	36	2	4	0	0	1	3	3

Pitching	W	L	ERA	G	SV	IP	H	BB	SO
Aiden Jimenez	2	0	1.15	8	1	16	14	2	12
Maxx Yehl	0	0	3.24	9	1	25	27	16	22
Aeden Finateri	0	1	3.60	4	1	10	12	5	9
Jack Seppings	1	1	3.77	5	0	14	13	7	17
Jack Brodsky	0	2	4.80	11	1	15	17	6	22
Carlos Rey	0	1	5.06	4	0	11	10	9	12
Ryan Verdugo	1	1	5.40	5	1	10	13	9	11
Benjamin Peterson	1	0	5.52	5	1	15	12	7	10
Carson Pierce	0	2	6.10	2	0	10	10	4	7
Zander Sechrist	0	0	6.19	7	1	16	20	5	14
Miles Langhorne	0	2	6.35	4	0	11	13	11	15
Liam Paddack	1	1	6.64	9	0	20	13	19	17
Gabe Davis	1	1	6.75	6	0	19	22	9	20
Jack Sokol	1	1	7.02	5	0	17	22	9	18
Tommy Molsky	2	5	7.71	10	0	30	39	13	23
Zach Harris	0	0	8.10	5	0	10	16	3	8
Trey Gibson	1	3	10.24	11	1	29	40	21	27
Hayden Durke	0	2	10.80	4	0	13	17	16	14
Tanner Witt	0	2	11.93	5	0	14	18	9	11

COTUIT

Batting	AVG	AB	R	H	2B	3B	HR	RBI	SB
Brett Bateman, CF	.500	46	6	23	4	0	0	13	5
Sean Keys, 3B	.385	39	6	15	3	0	4	17	0
Trevor Haskins, SS	.364	44	9	16	4	0	3	9	0
Caleb Lomavita, C	.329	85	16	28	5	0	3	17	3
Kalae Harrison, SS	.327	52	10	17	0	0	0	8	1
Jay Harry, SS	.324	37	5	12	5	0	0	6	3
Cole Mathis, P	.318	129	28	41	10	1	11	42	0
Brock Wills, 2B	.289	76	11	22	2	0	0	10	4
Brock Rodden, 2B	.279	43	8	12	2	0	1	3	5
Grant Norris, SS	.271	70	15	19	5	0	4	14	0
James McCoy, IF	.267	86	19	23	7	0	1	12	2
Dylan Johnson, C	.265	34	9	9	1	0	0	4	0
Tanner Thach, 1B	.260	50	10	13	1	1	3	5	1
Carter Mathison, CF	.260	96	20	25	3	0	0	10	5
Emilien Pitre, SS	.242	62	8	15	0	1	1	5	0
Jack Scanlon, C	.238	21	4	5	0	0	1	3	0
Trotter Harlan, IF	.235	34	8	8	1	0	0	3	0
Ryan Galanie, 3B	.232	56	11	13	2	1	4	16	3
Jacob Tobias, 1B	.230	74	9	17	2	0	0	7	2
Cannon Peebles, C	.217	46	4	10	2	0	0	6	2
Trey Yunger, OF	.172	29	8	5	0	0	0	4	1
Teo Banks, CF	.169	71	18	12	1	0	3	10	6
Rodney Green Jr, CF	.161	31	4	5	1	0	1	7	5
Josh Pyne, 3B	.128	39	5	5	1	0	1	5	2
Michael Carico, C	.125	24	5	3	0	0	2	6	0

Pitching	W	L	ERA	G	SV	IP	H	BB	SO
Christopher Kahler	1	0	1.06	4	0	17	7	6	13
Camron Hill	3	0	1.09	11	0	33	16	16	45
Noah Ruen	0	1	1.69	7	3	11	11	0	13
Cullen McKay	2	0	2.53	7	1	11	7	7	6
Chase Hopewell	3	1	2.79	6	1	10	9	4	12
Cam Schuelke	1	2	3.16	13	1	37	30	16	48
Izaak Martinez	2	0	3.48	5	0	10	10	4	7
Jacob Shafer	1	0	3.75	6	1	12	11	3	8
Rafe Schlesinger	1	0	3.86	9	2	19	22	5	20
Janzen Keisel	2	0	4.29	6	0	21	20	10	20
Aidan Hunter	3	0	4.66	6	0	10	13	5	11
Jake Gigliotti	1	2	4.91	7	0	26	29	11	21
Finn McIlroy	1	1	5.27	7	0	14	10	9	7
Cole Mathis	1	1	5.31	9	2	20	25	5	23
Tucker Novotny	0	1	6.55	3	0	11	13	5	14
Brock Peery	0	0	7.43	9	0	13	16	8	16

FALMOUTH

Batting	AVG	AB	R	H	2B	3B	HR	RBI	SB
Jace Laviolette, LF	.381	21	5	8	1	0	0	2	3
Travis Bazzana, 2B	.375	136	33	51	6	2	6	31	14
Kade Snell, 1B	.342	79	12	27	4	1	1	15	2
Tyler MacGregor, 1B	.318	107	19	34	4	1	2	23	0
Sean Darnell, IF	.314	35	5	11	0	0	1	6	0
Joseph Redfield, CF	.308	39	8	12	0	0	0	5	7
Kaleb Hall, 3B	.303	33	7	10	2	0	0	4	2
Gavin Kilen, SS	.302	96	17	29	7	0	0	15	3
Michael Eze, IF	.300	40	11	12	3	0	2	7	1
Will Janek, C	.281	114	22	32	5	1	5	17	7
Tab Tracy, CF	.278	72	13	20	1	0	0	5	3
Barry Walsh, OF	.273	33	4	9	0	0	0	7	1
Kyle DeBarge, SS	.267	101	14	27	3	0	0	15	2
Charlie Condon, 1B	.261	46	3	12	1	0	1	10	1
Luke Heyman, C	.250	56	14	14	2	0	2	9	1
Jordan Spikerman, CF	.238	101	21	24	5	0	2	14	12
Ross Highfill, C	.233	30	8	7	1	0	2	7	4
Gavin Turley, OF	.222	72	15	16	2	2	3	17	4
Christian Martin, 2B	.216	74	13	16	2	0	0	12	5
Nathan Humphreys, CF	.216	97	16	21	4	1	2	15	7
Scott Bandura, CF	.200	20	1	4	0	0	0	2	0

Pitching	W	L	ERA	G	SV	IP	H	BB	SO
Joey Ryan	0	0	0.00	8	3	10	4	2	11
Garrett Coe	0	0	0.92	9	1	20	13	9	18
Shane Telfer	2	0	0.93	3	0	10	5	6	14
Nolan Morr	1	0	1.50	6	1	12	13	1	11
K.C. Hunt	0	0	1.86	5	4	10	8	2	14
Jacob Smith	1	0	2.57	5	0	21	19	12	25
Parker Coil	1	1	2.59	10	2	24	26	5	26
Braden Davis	1	1	2.73	6	0	26	16	17	37
Antoine Jean	1	0	2.79	4	0	10	10	2	9
Evan OToole	2	0	2.79	6	0	19	23	4	11
Mason Barnett	3	0	4.00	6	0	27	32	8	25
Rio Britton	1	1	4.32	6	0	17	12	10	16
AJ Causey	0	1	4.77	3	0	11	8	5	9
Sam Highfill	0	1	5.06	5	0	11	12	3	12
Logan Van Treeck	1	1	5.65	4	0	14	12	6	14
Ryan McCarroll	2	1	5.89	4	0	18	20	6	16
Izack Tiger	0	1	7.30	3	0	12	21	5	15
Carson Montgomery	0	1	8.25	4	0	12	15	10	8

HARWICH

Batting	AVG	AB	R	H	2B	3B	HR	RBI	SB
Seaver King, IF	.424	59	15	25	4	0	1	9	5
Kevin Keister, 2B	.407	27	6	11	2	0	1	7	1
Kevin Karstetter, 3B	.407	27	3	11	1	0	0	6	1
Hunter Fitz-Gerald, 1B	.349	43	8	15	4	0	0	6	0
Talmadge LeCroy, IF	.286	21	3	6	1	0	0	0	1
Elijah Lambros, OF	.286	35	5	10	1	0	0	6	0
Mason Guerra, IF	.276	76	6	21	3	0	1	7	0
Kaelen Culpepper, IF	.270	63	10	17	3	0	0	7	6
Danniel Rivera, SS	.267	60	10	16	5	0	0	6	10
Bryan Arendt, C	.255	94	15	24	4	0	2	12	1
Devin Obee, OF	.250	120	19	30	4	1	5	23	3
Jacob Humphrey, OF	.225	102	23	23	4	1	1	8	15
Kenny Levari, 3B	.217	46	3	10	3	0	0	6	3
Ali Camarillo, SS	.217	143	16	31	5	0	2	15	5
Lorenzo Carrier, OF	.200	65	7	13	3	0	3	12	0
Kennedy Jones, OF	.198	91	11	18	5	1	1	15	0
Matt Scannell, OF	.197	66	9	13	2	0	1	14	5
Andrew Yu, C	.196	56	6	11	1	0	0	3	0
Ethan Anderson, 1B	.195	82	13	16	2	0	2	11	1
Devin Hurdle, SS	.190	21	2	4	0	0	0	1	0
Casey Saucke, OF	.185	54	5	10	3	0	0	5	0

Pitching	W	L	ERA	G	SV	IP	H	BB	SO
Sam Armstrong	1	0	0.00	2	0	10	1	3	13
Andrew Armstrong	1	0	2.31	3	0	12	10	5	17
Sean Hard	1	0	2.35	8	0	23	14	18	31
Christopher Lotito	0	0	2.40	7	0	15	11	12	10
Jake Neuman	1	1	2.46	4	0	11	8	5	12
Collin Caldwell	0	0	2.61	4	0	10	3	10	14
Josh Bostick	1	1	3.00	4	0	18	13	9	21
Tom Chmielewski	1	3	3.21	6	0	28	26	6	23
Zane Probst	1	0	3.45	6	0	16	14	6	14
Aidan Moza	1	1	3.68	5	2	15	11	3	21
Tim Noone	0	0	4.20	4	0	15	17	6	2
Dylan Delvecchio	0	2	4.64	7	0	21	27	10	17
Shea Sprague	0	1	4.85	3	0	13	13	4	11
Domenic Picone	0	3	5.06	5	0	16	16	6	16
Joey Savino	2	2	5.29	5	0	17	20	9	15
Colin Rothermel	0	1	6.30	6	0	20	15	16	23
Reid Easterly	2	2	7.04	4	0	15	20	6	10
Xavier Martinez	0	2	10.66	5	0	13	18	13	11

HYANNIS HARBOR

Batting	AVG	AB	R	H	2B	3B	HR	RBI	SB
Ben Williamson, 3B	.394	33	2	13	4	0	0	5	0
Billy Amick, IF	.368	38	8	14	2	0	2	5	0
Jonathan Gazdar, SS	.361	72	14	26	2	1	0	10	2
Cameron Smith, 3B	.347	167	38	58	12	4	6	26	0
Zach Yorke, 1B	.338	74	13	25	2	0	3	19	0
Mike Sirota, CF	.304	23	5	7	2	0	1	3	2

Batting	AVG	AB	R	H	2B	3B	HR	RBI	SB
Zach Ehrhard, CF	.297	118	24	35	2	0	2	18	11
Brandon Eike, 3B	.275	40	5	11	2	0	1	7	1
Nick Mitchell, CF	.261	111	31	29	4	3	1	10	7
Eric Snow, SS	.257	101	10	26	1	1	1	18	0
Alex Lane, 1B	.246	69	16	17	8	0	0	6	0
Trey Lipsey, CF	.242	95	20	23	1	2	0	11	9
Austin Kelly, C	.241	54	4	13	4	0	0	12	3
Bennett Thompson, C	.238	21	1	5	1	0	0	5	1
Will Taylor, CF	.231	104	15	24	5	0	2	19	6
Brody Donay, C	.229	105	17	24	11	1	4	19	0
Elijah Hainline, SS	.218	87	17	19	3	0	1	7	7
Bradke Lohry, SS	.214	56	6	12	4	1	0	9	4
Aaron Parker, C	.205	39	7	8	1	0	0	2	0

Pitching	W	L	ERA	G	SV	IP	H	BB	SO
Cade Obermueller	2	0	2.12	12	0	17	11	9	30
Thaniel Trumper	2	0	2.46	4	0	11	11	4	7
Hayden Frank	0	1	2.67	10	0	30	34	7	25
Simon Miller	1	0	2.70	4	0	10	9	4	17
Jamie Arnold	1	1	2.95	10	1	18	15	7	21
Ethan Lanthier	1	1	3.00	11	1	18	13	10	25
Carter Lovasz	2	0	3.24	10	0	17	13	5	14
Mason Nichols	1	1	3.46	8	1	26	18	15	15
Kros Sivley	2	1	4.36	11	1	21	22	5	21
Dennis Colleran	4	0	4.85	9	0	13	9	9	18
Jack O'Connor	0	0	5.11	4	0	12	17	7	11
Bradley Hodges	0	1	5.27	5	0	14	17	9	13
Zach Voelker	1	2	5.40	6	0	23	20	15	23
Darin Horn	0	1	5.85	9	1	20	20	8	23
Will Armistead	1	0	7.20	5	0	10	13	6	13
Hiroyuki Yamada	0	1	10.80	6	0	10	21	8	10

ORLEANS

Batting	AVG	AB	R	H	2B	3B	HR	RBI	SB
Justin Rubin, SS	.368	57	10	21	2	0	1	8	2
Matt Halbach, 3B	.364	121	22	44	5	2	3	15	0
Jo Oyama, 2B	.360	150	35	54	11	6	5	17	6
Andy Blake, SS	.350	60	11	21	3	0	1	10	3
Brandon Stahlman, 3B	.296	54	8	16	0	0	0	4	0
Jack Penney, SS	.275	153	26	42	3	1	5	22	0
Eddie Micheletti Jr., RF	.274	146	14	40	9	0	2	22	0
Eddie King, OF	.255	98	24	25	5	0	3	15	8
Johnny Olmstead, 3B	.250	64	9	16	3	0	2	10	1
Austin Overn, OF	.237	38	7	9	1	0	0	1	7
Colin Tuft, C	.224	58	9	13	2	1	2	10	5
Drew Faurot, SS	.221	77	8	17	2	0	0	8	1
Fenwick Trimble, OF	.209	129	14	27	3	1	2	16	4
Henry Hunter, C	.200	60	9	12	1	0	2	9	1
Owen Carapellotti, C	.188	85	8	16	2	0	1	8	0
Jake Hyde, RF	.179	39	1	7	3	0	0	5	0
Jake Casey, OF	.171	70	13	12	2	0	3	8	1

Pitching	W	L	ERA	G	SV	IP	H	BB	SO
Greysen Carter	1	0	0.00	7	0	14	5	9	14
Sean Matson	6	0	0.00	16	5	22	11	3	26
Ryan Rissas	0	0	0.87	5	0	10	9	11	13
Daniel Avitia	1	2	1.63	6	0	28	21	14	24
Chad Gartland	1	0	1.64	3	0	11	9	1	13
Derek Clark	5	1	1.80	12	1	40	31	10	38
Jonathan Gonzalez	2	1	2.53	8	1	21	26	8	24
Jake Peppers	0	0	2.60	4	0	17	14	7	16
Danny Carrion	0	0	3.72	6	1	10	4	6	16
Dylan Jacobs	0	1	3.74	5	0	22	19	8	14
Evan Truitt	1	1	4.60	9	0	29	32	8	21
Riley Frey	1	1	4.61	9	0	14	14	6	15
Ivran Romero	1	1	4.66	5	0	19	19	8	12
Chase Hungate	1	1	6.19	8	1	16	17	5	9
Konner Eaton	2	1	6.62	11	0	18	19	12	17
Sam Hliboki	0	3	7.45	9	0	19	28	10	16

WAREHAM

Batting	AVG	AB	R	H	2B	3B	HR	RBI	SB
Tommy Splaine, C	.390	41	8	16	2	0	0	7	0
Bayram Hot, IF	.350	20	2	7	0	0	0	0	3
Grant Sherrod, 1B	.288	59	8	17	1	0	3	11	2
Garen Caulfield, SS	.283	92	14	26	3	0	1	7	0
Nick McLain, CF	.283	99	17	28	2	0	4	16	5
Grant Hussey, 1B	.276	123	12	34	12	0	4	31	2
David Glancy, CF	.270	63	20	17	2	0	3	13	13
JC Colon, SS	.263	76	13	20	1	0	0	5	4
Sebastian Murillo, SS	.260	77	12	20	1	0	1	13	2
Landon Wallace, CF	.233	30	7	7	1	0	2	3	3
Lawson Harrill, RF	.231	26	4	6	3	0	0	2	1
Dorian Gonzalez, 2B	.231	108	16	25	5	0	0	12	7
Cade Sullivan, 1B	.226	31	4	7	3	0	0	6	0
Bobby Boser, IF	.219	114	18	25	8	0	4	13	2
Michael Brooks, 3B	.204	49	8	10	1	0	1	7	1
Josh Stevenson, CF	.181	94	12	17	5	0	1	12	2
Jedier Hernandez, C	.169	65	6	11	0	0	0	4	0
Zack Stewart, RF	.154	39	7	6	2	0	0	0	0
Ryan Campos, C	.136	22	2	3	0	0	0	3	2
Rene Lastres, C	.119	42	3	5	1	0	1	1	0
Korey Morton, OF	.074	27	4	2	0	0	1	4	2

Pitching	W	L	ERA	G	SV	IP	H	BB	SO
Jackson Reid	2	0	0.93	5	0	10	7	6	11
Daniel Frontera	2	0	1.69	3	0	11	8	6	7
Coleman Picard	1	0	1.93	3	0	14	15	6	13
Mark Manfredi	0	0	2.08	3	0	13	11	4	16
Yoel Tejeda	1	1	2.79	7	0	19	21	10	21
Brett Wozniak	0	0	4.02	4	0	16	21	2	7
James Hepp	1	2	4.95	11	0	20	25	20	16
Riley Eikhoff	1	1	5.04	7	0	25	31	5	21
Will Koger	1	4	5.81	11	1	26	34	11	27
Bryce Shaffer	1	1	5.89	13	1	26	40	13	28
Aidan Major	0	2	6.35	6	0	23	24	11	25
Jonathan Bautista	1	2	6.50	4	0	18	21	10	8
Chase Chatman	0	1	6.75	5	0	12	13	6	4
Brett Wichrowski	1	2	6.94	4	0	12	17	2	10
Jake Faherty	0	1	7.71	13	1	19	16	20	20

YARMOUTH-DENNIS

Batting	AVG	AB	R	H	2B	3B	HR	RBI	SB
Will King, C	.354	65	7	23	1	0	1	16	1
Braden Montgomery, P	.340	53	13	18	4	0	1	12	1
RJ Austin, IF	.327	101	22	33	2	0	1	13	5
Ryan Stafford, C	.312	77	12	24	3	0	1	7	6
Ryan Jackson, SS	.293	58	7	17	2	0	1	9	2
Zander Darby, 3B	.292	113	20	33	4	0	3	15	4
Nathan Archer, CF	.269	52	7	14	0	0	3	9	5
Brady Day, SS	.267	101	11	27	6	0	1	8	4
Hunter Hines, 1B	.265	147	27	39	5	0	13	45	3
Enzo Apodaca, CF	.264	91	14	24	4	0	1	9	1
Max Viera, SS	.264	106	15	28	3	0	0	9	11
Jacob Jenkins-Cowart, CF	.244	41	8	10	0	0	0	1	1
Theo Hardy, SS	.204	54	8	11	1	0	0	3	2
Paxton Kling, OF	.194	36	6	7	1	0	1	2	4
Manny Garza, C	.192	26	3	5	2	0	0	1	0
Jakob Christian, 1B	.179	39	7	7	2	0	1	2	1
Casey Cook, IF	.175	80	12	14	4	0	0	13	2
William Gleed, 3B	.173	98	11	17	2	0	2	18	0
Connor Dykstra, C	.105	38	4	4	0	0	1	3	0

Pitching	W	L	ERA	G	SV	IP	H	BB	SO
Leighton Finley	1	2	0.00	8	4	17	10	5	20
Hector Garcia	1	0	1.84	6	2	15	6	3	23
Jackson Kent	2	1	2.52	6	0	25	23	15	27
Smith Pinson	3	1	2.68	7	0	37	28	11	37
Khal Stephen	2	2	2.73	6	0	26	21	11	27
Finnegan Wall	2	2	2.91	7	0	34	23	15	38
Blake Aita	0	0	3.32	10	1	19	17	11	22
Jason Doktorczyk	1	2	3.45	8	1	29	28	12	29

Landon Beidelschies	2	2	3.63	8	1	22	19	8	31
Micah Bucknam	0	1	3.94	4	0	16	19	3	7
Matt Fernandez	2	1	4.32	5	0	17	16	5	11
Gage Williams	1	0	4.50	3	0	12	13	4	8
Connor O'Hara	0	0	4.86	8	0	17	16	14	16
Nicholas Judice	0	1	5.11	3	0	12	8	11	16
Gavin Bruni	1	2	10.64	4	0	11	17	11	13

ALASKA LEAGUE

	W	L	PCT	GB
Mat Su Miners †	23	16	.590	-
Anchorage Glacier Pilots †	22	18	.550	1.5
Anchorage Bucs †	21	19	.525	2.5
Peninsula Oilers †	18	20	.474	4.5
Chugiak-ER Chinooks	14	25	.359	9

† Clinched playoff

CHAMPIONSHIP: Anchorage Glacier Pilot defeated Mat Su Miners, 3-0, in best-of-three championship series.

INDIVIDUAL BATTING LEADERS

	AVG	AB	R	H	2B	3B	HR	RBI	SB
Jackson, Blake, AGP	.360	111	27	40	11	3	0	19	8
Costello, Nick, OIL	.355	107	23	38	6	1	2	17	10
Lancia, Steven, MIN	.344	90	18	31	8	1	2	15	0
Taguchi, Kan, AGP	.343	67	21	23	5	0	0	9	5
Boedicker, Lex, BUCS	.341	123	27	42	9	6	2	27	8
Harding, Troy, AGP	.319	119	16	38	5	0	3	17	3
Vergara, Alex, MIN	.313	83	21	26	7	2	6	21	4
Lacy, Cade, BUCS	.313	83	19	26	5	0	2	13	7
Helfrick, Leighton, OIL	.313	96	18	30	5	0	0	9	2
Lamb, Andrew, AGP	.305	95	18	29	6	2	1	18	1

INDIVIDUAL PITCHING LEADERS

	W	L	ERA	G	GS	IP	H	BB	SO
Grimm, William, OIL	3	0	0.39	7	2	23	14	7	15
Correa, Ty, OIL	3	1	0.83	7	6	33	27	10	32
Atkins, Tai, AGP	1	1	1.13	10	0	32	24	6	38
Downer, Brandon, MIN	1	1	1.23	4	4	22	16	10	12
Mulamekic, Arnad, OIL	2	0	1.29	5	5	21	13	18	18
Throneberry, Connor, OIL	1	3	1.69	12	2	27	18	17	30
Lyke, Ethan, MIN	4	0	1.81	14	3	45	40	20	33
Whitehead, Ace, MIN	2	1	2.57	5	5	21	18	9	26
Hayes, Mose, OIL	3	1	2.70	9	3	33	25	12	29
Bianchi, Vincent, MIN	3	1	2.70	13	0	23	20	16	25

ATLANTIC COLLEGIATE LEAGUE

Kaiser Division	W	L	PCT	GB
Atlantic Whitecaps	21	10	.677	--
East Coast Sandhogs	21	11	.656	0.5
Old Town Road Patriots	19	12	.613	2
New York Crush	12	17	.414	8
Nassau Collegians	13	10	.565	4
LIB Neptunes	11	13	.458	6.5
Hitters Club Hawkeyes	9	16	.360	9
New York Valor	3	19	.136	13.5
Wolff Division	**W**	**L**	**PCT**	**GB**
Trenton Generals	23	11	.676	--
South Jersey Kings	23	11	.676	--
Bergen Metros	19	11	.633	2
New Brunswick MATRIX	16	12	.571	4
New York Phenoms	13	17	.433	8
Jersey Pilots	11	17	.393	9
Ocean Ospreys	9	20	.310	11.5
Jersey Shore Stallions	7	23	.233	14

CHAMPIONSHIP: Atlantic Whitecaps defeated the Trenton Generals.

CAL RIPKEN COLLEGIATE LEAGUE

SOUTH	W	L	PCT	GB
Alexandria Aces	30	6	.833	--
Metro South County Braves	15	21	.417	15
Southern Maryland Senators	14	22	.389	16
D.C. Grays	14	22	.389	16
NORTH	**W**	**L**	**PCT**	**GB**
Bethesda Big Train	23	13	.639	--
Cropdusters Baseball	22	14	.611	1
SS-T TBolts	14	22	.389	9
Gaithersburg Giants	12	24	.333	115

CHAMPIONSHIP: Bethesda Big Train defeated Alexandria Aces 2-0 in best-of-three series.

INDIVIDUAL BATTING LEADERS

	AVG	AB	R	H	2B	3B	HR	RBI	SB
Miura, Matt, CDB	.388	98	27	38	5	0	0	24	17
Ossenfort, Matt, ACES	.376	101	25	38	8	0	8	35	4
Williams, Dixon, BT	.349	106	32	37	11	1	0	21	18
Hamilton, RJ, ACES	.346	78	29	27	7	0	1	18	21
Heard, Jeffrey, BT	.339	109	23	37	6	1	5	36	11
Sicoli, Matthew, SST	.337	86	24	29	4	1	3	13	11
Nicholson, Tim, ACES	.333	99	37	33	2	0	0	16	16
Zipay, Henry, DC	.333	90	14	30	8	0	0	10	4
Guy, Mikey, SMD	.330	94	11	31	9	0	0	13	5
Taylor, Cory, ACES	.330	109	27	36	8	0	5	25	17

INDIVIDUAL PITCHING LEADERS

	W	L	ERA	G	SV	IP	H	BB	SO
Cassedy, Brandon, BT	3	0	0.64	6	0	28	14	10	32
Barrett, Diego, DC	2	2	1.60	7	0	39	31	10	32
Beck, Josh, CDB	1	0	2.73	7	0	26	20	17	31
Ehly, Anthony, ACES	4	1	3.00	7	0	33	30	15	35
Gray, John, SMD	3	0	3.04	14	1	27	22	9	20
Gutierrez, Jesse, BT	0	1	3.14	7	0	29	31	10	23
Houghtaling, Ethan, ACES	3	0	3.30	6	0	30	26	8	41
Woodbury, Justin, CDB	1	1	3.51	7	0	26	21	9	23
Rishell, Evan, SST	2	0	3.53	6	0	36	37	13	34
Wingenroth, Brandon, SMD	1	2	3.64	7	0	30	25	12	22

CALIFORNIA COLLEGIATE LEAGUE

North Division	W	L	PCT	GB
Santa Barbara Foresters	25	10	.714	--
Arroyo Seco Saints	21	14	.600	4
Orange County Riptide	20	15	.571	5
Conejo Oaks	16	19	.457	9
San Luis Obispo Blues	15	20	.429	10
Academy Barons	8	27	.229	17
South Division	**W**	**L**	**PCT**	**GB**
Healdsburg Prune Packers	26	9	.743	0
Walnut Creek Crawdads	25	10	.714	1
Lincoln Potters	19	15	.559	6.5
Sonoma Stompers	16	19	.457	10
Solano Mudcats	6	29	.171	20

CHAMPIONSHIP: Heraldsburg Prune Packers defeated Arroyo Seco Saints 2-1 in best-of-3 series.

INDIVIDUAL BATTING LEADERS

	AVG	AB	R	H	HR	RBI	BB	SO	SB
Charpiot, C, HPP	.410	83	17	34	3	25	18	7	0
Hamchuk, R, HPP	.403	119	30	48	3	15	11	16	4
Tello, R, AS	.378	90	18	34	1	11	5	16	9
Dorraugh, H, HPP	.375	120	38	45	3	18	21	14	3
Neighbors, K, AB	.357	115	22	41	1	12	23	9	10
Wilson, N, LP	.345	87	16	30	2	23	5	20	0
Burden, J, SS	.344	93	13	32	1	12	13	19	5
Tandy, J, SM	.342	79	18	27	2	14	15	21	0
Nickens, C, HPP	.339	109	26	37	6	24	12	14	1
Belyeu, M, SBF	.333	126	15	42	4	22	16	31	4
Bravo, D, HPP	.333	105	21	35	3	28	4	27	3

INDIVIDUAL PITCHING LEADERS

	W	L	ERA	G	SV	IP	H	BB	SO
Turnquist, C, SBF	4	0	0.55	10	0	33	12	16	45
Fitzpatrick, S, WCC	5	0	1.29	11	0	28	15	4	37
Johnson, F, SLO	2	2	1.50	5	0	30	19	11	19

	W	L	ERA	G	SV	IP	H	BB	SO
Kirrer, J, OCR	0	1	1.82	8	0	35	19	16	32
Herrera, C, AS	2	3	2.00	8	0	36	23	8	35
Gonzales, M, SLO	1	1	2.48	9	0	29	28	11	29
Del Castillo, R, AB	1	0	2.89	5	0	28	25	10	29
Fisher, C, CO	2	1	3.00	8	0	30	29	10	34
Boyce, H, AB	3	3	3.62	9	0	37	34	20	42
Reilly, B, CO	0	4	4.22	7	0	32	33	6	25

COASTAL PLAIN LEAGUE

EAST	W	L	PCT	GB
Morehead City Marlins	32	15	.681	--
Wilmington Sharks	24	21	.533	7
Wilson Tobs	25	23	.521	7.5
Peninsula Pilots	24	24	.500	8.5
Tri-City Chili Peppers	23	23	.500	8.5
Holly Springs Salamanders	23	25	.479	9.5
Florence Flamingos	20	26	.435	11.5
WEST	**W**	**L**	**PCT**	**GB**
Lexington County Blowfish	28	18	.609	--
Forest City Owls	26	20	.565	2
Macon Bacon	24	22	.522	4
Asheboro Zookeepers	20	24	.455	7
Boone Bigfoots	19	26	.422	8.5
Martinsville Mustangs	18	26	.409	9
HP Thomasville HiToms	16	29	.356	11.5

CHAMPIONSHIP: Lexington County defeated Wilmington 2-1 in best-of-three series.

INDIVIDUAL BATTING LEADERS

	AVG	AB	R	H	2B	3B	HR	RBI	SB
Eike, Brandon, TRI	.398	113	27	45	8	0	9	36	0
Dearing, Austin, HPT	.373	134	34	50	14	1	7	29	4
Dunaway, Mason, PEN	.366	131	30	48	8	0	2	26	13
Mershon, Joseph, MHC	.357	129	34	46	9	0	1	24	13
Allen, G., FOR	.357	98	32	35	9	0	4	37	16
Verdung, Will, HPT	.356	101	20	36	7	0	3	15	13
Pendergrass, Dariyan, LEX	.354	127	41	45	9	3	2	23	35
Butcher, Will, FOR	.340	106	17	36	7	1	4	32	3
Kepley, Kane, HPT	.339	121	40	41	8	1	5	27	26
Dorighi, Carter, MAR	.338	145	33	49	8	0	3	23	7
Estrada, Danny, TRI	.331	163	35	54	8	0	8	25	6
Powell, C, WLM	.325	126	20	41	2	0	1	16	10

INDIVIDUAL PITCHING LEADERS

	W	L	ERA	G	SV	IP	H	BB	SO
Moran, Dillon, MAR	3	2	2.82	8	0	38	21	12	55
Montplaisir, Maxwell, MAC	1	1	3.15	9	0	40	27	16	49
Barham, Dalton, PEN	2	0	3.43	14	0	39	31	12	43
Granzow, Cade, WLM	4	4	3.92	12	0	44	37	22	26
Lee, Logan, HYS	2	1	4.31	9	0	40	34	28	30
Ereu, Brian, PEN	3	5	4.35	11	0	50	62	8	45
Bost, Riley, BBF	2	1	5.22	14	0	40	47	26	26
Hunley, Austin, FOR	3	2	5.68	9	0	44	53	12	24
McKissick, Nate, BBF	4	1	5.84	13	0	37	42	20	22
Plummer, Caden, MAR	0	3	6.21	10	0	38	41	24	45

FLORIDA COLLEGIATE SUMMER LEAGUE

	W	L	PCT	GB
Leesburg Lightning	21	12	.636	-
Sanford River Rats	19	13	.594	1.5
Winter Garden Squeeze	17	17	.500	4.5
Winter Park Diamond Dawgs	15	19	.441	6.5
Orlando Snappers	14	19	.424	7
DeLand Suns	13	19	.406	7.5

CHAMPIONSHIP: Leesburg defeated Winter Gardens, 2-1, in best-of-three championship series.

INDIVIDUAL BATTING LEADERS

	AVG	AB	R	H	2B	3B	HR	RBI	SB
Santiago, Gabriel, LL	.372	86	34	32	5	0	0	12	30
Fields, Brandon, WG	.353	51	11	18	2	0	2	13	5
Nunez, Isaac, WP	.345	87	23	30	3	0	2	14	17
Liquori, Jeff, DEL	.344	93	14	32	3	0	4	16	5
Puckett, Stewart, SAN	.344	64	12	22	1	0	3	18	3
Riley, Rohsean, DEL	.333	90	22	30	5	2	1	18	11
Bruno, Chase, DEL	.333	57	7	19	3	0	0	6	2
Young, Michael, WG	.322	87	20	28	2	0	1	17	5
Ballard, Michael, ORL	.319	113	9	36	3	0	2	20	1
Hujsak, Connor, SAN	.319	94	28	30	7	0	5	16	11

INDIVIDUAL PITCHING LEADERS

	W	L	ERA	G	SV	IP	H	BB	SO
Fitzgerald, Riley, LL	4	1	1.90	11	0	24	22	8	12
Burr, Jacob, ORL	4	3	2.02	8	0	49	43	12	50
Perry, Layton, LL	2	2	2.23	8	0	32	30	5	30
Diaz, Victor, ORL	0	0	2.25	12	2	20	10	9	22
Dennis, Brett, ORL	2	2	2.59	5	0	24	18	8	34
Melby, William, SAN	0	2	2.74	8	1	23	10	9	19
Griffith, Anthony, DEL	4	0	2.77	10	1	26	25	12	22
Huskey, Jordan, WG	3	2	2.91	7	0	34	24	16	35
Mills, Jaxon, ORL	2	0	3.20	11	1	25	28	7	16
Chappell, Chase, DEL	3	1	3.68	8	0	29	27	9	20

FUTURES COLLEGIATE LEAGUE

	W	L	PCT	GB
Norwich Sea Unicorns	39	22	.639	-
Vermont Lake Monsters	38	23	.623	1
Worcester Bravehearts	39	24	.619	1
New Britain Bees	35	28	.556	5
Westfield Starfires	31	32	.500	9
Pittsfield Suns	29	32	.475	10
Nashua Silver Knights	24	40	.391	16.5
Brockton Rox	13	47	.217	25.5

CHAMPIONSHIP: Norwich defeated Vermont 2-1 in championship game.

INDIVIDUAL BATTING LEADERS

	AVG	AB	R	H	2B	3B	HR	RBI	SB
Ferrara, Dean, NOR	.422	154	32	65	10	2	0	30	17
Bastunas, Tyler, WOR	.358	212	47	76	8	3	1	34	37
Serce, Nick, WES	.306	183	38	56	10	0	13	41	0
Bucciero, Daniel, WOR	.305	154	25	47	13	2	2	34	3
Caffrey, Kierman, WES	.302	169	27	51	5	1	1	16	5
McDermott, Jack, NSK	.298	171	34	51	9	1	1	24	2
Thorbahn, Jack, WOR	.297	148	25	44	9	0	3	28	2
McNamara, Shane, NSK	.286	192	29	55	13	3	5	44	8
Taylor, Rob, PIT	.281	135	32	38	5	0	3	23	7
Knox, Johnny, NOR	.279	140	26	39	6	0	1	19	14

INDIVIDUAL PITCHING LEADERS

	W	L	ERA	G	SV	IP	H	BB	SO
Ferguson, Francis, VER	6	1	2.25	10	0	52	38	15	50
Bailey, Ryan, WES	3	3	3.18	11	0	51	42	16	59
Lewis, Tim, PIT	3	2	3.81	11	0	54	56	26	41

GREAT LAKES LEAGUE

North Division	W	L	PCT	GB
Muskegon Clippers * †	33	5	.868	--
Lima Locos †	25	13	.658	8
Sandusky Ice Haulers	20	18	.526	13
Royal Oak Leprechauns	17	21	.447	16
Jet Box Baseball Club	13	24	.351	19.5
Michigan Monarchs	11	26	.297	21.5
South Division	**W**	**L**	**PCT**	
Xenia Scouts * †	21	17	.553	--
Hamilton Joes †	21	17	.553	--
Grand Lake Mariners	20	18	.526	1
Richmond Jazz	19	19	.500	2
Cincinnati Steam	18	20	.474	3
S Ohio Copperheads	13	23	.361	7
Licking County Settlers	13	23	.361	7
† Playoff spot				

CHAMPIONSHIP: Lima Locos defeated Xenia Scouts, 2-0, in best-of-three championship series.

INDIVIDUAL BATTING LEADERS

	AVG	AB	R	H	2B	3B	HR	RBI	SB
Piasecki, Aaron, MSC	.344	125	33	43	8	0	0	26	5
Hausner, Anthony, XS	.341	91	16	31	6	0	2	22	2
Robbins, Hayden, GLM	.341	135	26	46	4	1	0	17	15
Cornwell, Colin, MSC	.339	121	23	41	8	1	0	35	9
Sizemore, Michael, HJ	.337	86	27	29	3	1	0	9	20
Ostrander, Connor, SIH	.336	113	25	38	4	3	4	19	10
Walton, Aaron, GLM	.336	113	22	38	8	2	1	22	19
Dupuis, Jack, SOC	.333	75	21	25	2	1	1	9	4
Jaun, William, CS	.333	102	17	34	9	2	3	24	2
Dillon, Drew, RJ	.330	100	25	33	6	2	1	14	19
Vore, B, LCS	.328	116	12	38	3	1	0	19	8
Pollock, L, JBB	.324	111	13	36	6	1	1	16	0

INDIVIDUAL PITCHING LEADERS

	W	L	ERA	G	SV	IP	H	BB	SO
Decker, Jacl, MSC	7	1	1.06	10	0	43	20	8	59
Bultemeier, Justin, GLM	5	0	1.23	7	0	44	22	10	32
Spencer, Bobby, SOC	3	0	1.46	6	0	37	25	9	46
Mitchell, Calvin, CS	3	0	2.03	8	0	31	21	8	37
Layton, Aidan, LCS	2	2	2.56	5	0	32	25	12	30
Gutierrez, Daniel, MSC	6	0	2.60	8	0	35	26	13	37
Rhein, Colin, SOC	3	0	2.65	6	0	34	25	6	49
Hughes, Griffith, XS	3	1	2.81	7	0	32	25	9	30
Thorington, Allan, JBB	2	1	2.81	6	0	32	27	6	27
Mohr, Ethan, SIH	3	1	2.81	6	0	32	26	13	32

HAMPTONS COLLEGIATE LEAGUE

	W	L	T	PTS
Westhampton Aviators	21	11	2	44
Sag Harbor Whalers	19	15	0	38
South Shore Clippers	18	14	2	38
Southampton Breakers	16	17	1	33
Shelter Island Bucks	13	19	2	28
North Fork Ospreys	11	22	1	23

CHAMPIONSHIP: South Shore defeated Westhampton 2-1 in best-of-three championship series.

INDIVIDUAL BATTING LEADERS

	AVG	AB	R	H	2B	3B	HR	RBI	SB
Torres, Matt, WH	.458	59	22	27	6	0	0	19	9
Kiely, Conor, SI	.425	106	19	45	10	0	0	25	14
Keys, Sean, WH	.367	90	33	33	6	0	11	34	2
Larkin, Aidan, SSC	.347	95	21	33	3	0	1	22	8
Acker, Ty, NF	.330	100	19	33	7	2	1	17	8
Suarez, Milo, SAG	.328	61	23	20	4	0	1	20	17
Henshon, Mark, SAG	.319	69	23	22	5	0	1	28	3
Guerra, Ethan, WH	.314	137	28	43	6	0	6	45	10
Franquiz, Kenneth, SH	.313	99	14	31	6	2	0	22	5
Mistone, Luke, WH	.312	93	19	29	3	0	2	13	3
Steinert, Brady, SSC	.302	86	24	26	3	0	0	17	10

INDIVIDUAL PITCHING LEADERS

	W	L	ERA	G	SV	IP	H	BB	SO
Kwiatkowski, Josh, SH	4	1	0.78	6	0	23	25	12	24
Hart, Max, SAG	3	1	1.61	6	0	22	17	8	15
Finn, Bobby, SSC	3	1	2.70	7	0	27	15	24	36
Fortuna, Zach, NF	0	0	2.84	5	0	25	16	20	28
Heiderstadt, Andrew, SSC	1	2	2.86	9	3	22	21	12	10
Bolwell, Garrett, SAG	3	1	3.00	7	0	24	22	13	17
Prough, Eric, SI	3	1	3.29	11	0	27	27	6	25
DiForte, Michael, WH	4	0	3.35	6	0	38	33	20	19
Dooley, Joe, NF	1	2	3.46	5	0	26	29	10	20
Scarry, Myles, SSC	2	2	3.55	6	0	25	28	16	29
Turner, J, WH	5	0	3.58	7	0	33	26	21	38

MINK LEAGUE

North Division	W	L	PCT	GB
St. Joseph Mustangs	29	15	.659	--
Clarinda A's	26	17	.605	2.5
Carroll Merchants	24	20	.545	5
Chillicothe Mudcats	22	22	.500	7
Des Moines Peak Prospects	19	25	.432	10
South Division	**W**	**L**	**PCT**	**GB**
Joplin Outlaws	22	22	.500	--
Jefferson City Renegades	20	24	.455	2
Sedalia Bombers	19	25	.432	3
Nevada Griffons	16	27	.372	5.5

CHAMPIONSHIP: Jefferson City Renegades defeated St. Joseph Mustangs, 2-1, in best-of-three championship series.

INDIVIDUAL BATTING LEADERS

	AVG	AB	R	H	2B	3B	HR	RBI	SB
Michael Alt, Carroll	.428	180	47	77	8	0	0	22	18
Carter Thomas, Des Moines	.367	109	26	40	4	2	0	14	26
Luke Matschiner, Jeff. City	.362	163	50	59	7	0	0	20	41
Nathan Maclaren, Chillic.	.357	84	24	30	5	2	0	15	27
Justin Rivera, Jeff. City	.357	154	22	55	15	0	1	36	0
Junior Barajas, Clarinda	.342	158	31	54	6	1	2	29	5
Kolten Reynolds, Joplin	.336	110	29	37	10	3	3	28	14
Charlie Rogan, Jeff. City	.333	111	28	37	7	0	2	14	4
Aidan Baumann, Jeff. City	.325	114	30	37	4	1	1	24	13
Tanner Sears, Chillic.	.323	99	16	32	12	0	3	31	5

INDIVIDUAL PITCHING LEADERS

	W	L	ERA	G	SV	IP	H	BB	SO
Tucker Starling, Clarinda	6	0	1.31	8	0	48	35	16	36
Antonio Escano, Sedalia	6	1	2.50	15	1	54	39	15	55
Mason Holton, St. Joseph	5	0	2.60	8	0	45	34	16	58
Cullen McBride, Carroll	2	1	2.64	8	0	48	42	9	33
Luke Schmedding, Joplin	3	1	3.44	7	0	37	35	16	32
Michael Infranca, St. Joseph	4	2	3.51	9	0	41	50	10	14
Carter DeGondea, Sedalia	6	2	3.74	12	0	53	56	31	38
Luke Spencer, Clarinda	6	3	3.77	11	0	57	50	17	51
Grant Burson, Sedalia	1	1	3.98	8	0	32	30	11	30
Camden Lutz, St. Joseph	1	0	4.04	12	1	42	37	20	34

NEW ENGLAND COLLEGIATE LEAGUE

Coastal Division	W	L	PCT	GB
Newport Gulls	31	11	.730	--
Mystic Schooners	26	18	.590	6
Ocean State Waves	20	23	.460	11.5
Marthas Vineyard Sharks	18	24	.430	13
North Shore Navigators	18	24	.420	13
West Division	**W**	**L**	**PC**	**GB**
Valley Blue Sox	23	18	.550	--
Bristol Blues	21	18	.530	1
Danbury Westerners	21	22	.480	3
North Adams SteepleCats	13	29	.310	10.5
North Division	**W**	**L**	**PC**	**GB**
Vermont Mountaineers	25	15	.620	--
Sanford Mainers	24	19	.550	2.5
Upper Valley Nighthawks	18	24	.420	8
Keene Swamp Bats	15	28	.340	11.5

CHAMPIONSHIP: Newport defeated Bristol , 2-0, in best-of-three championship series.

NORTHWOODS LEAGUE

Great Lakes East	W	L	PCT	GB
Kalamazoo Growlers	46	24	.657	-
Rockford Rivets	45	27	.625	2
Traverse City Pit Spitters	42	30	.583	5
Kenosha Kingfish	31	41	.431	16
Kokomo Jackrabbits	27	45	.375	20
Battle Creek Battle Jacks	26	46	.361	21
Great Lakes West	**W**	**L**	**PCT**	**GB**
Green Bay Rockers	41	31	.569	-
Wisconsin Rapids Rafters	40	31	.563	0.5
Madison Mallards	39	32	.549	1.5
Wausau Woodchucks	35	37	.486	6
Fond du Lac Dock Spiders	30	42	.417	11
Lakeshore Chinooks	27	44	.380	13.5
Great Plains East	**W**	**L**	**PCT**	**GB**
La Crosse Loggers	40	28	.588	-

	W	L	PCT	GB
Waterloo Bucks	37	31	.544	3
Eau Claire Express	36	31	.537	3.5
Duluth Huskies	36	32	.529	4
Rochester Honkers	32	36	.471	8
Thunder Bay Border Cats	27	41	.397	13
Great Plains West	**W**	**L**	**PCT**	**GB**
Willmar Stingers	51	16	.761	-
St. Cloud Rox	43	25	.632	8.5
Mankato MoonDogs	38	30	.559	13.5
Bismarck Larks	26	41	.388	25
Minnesota Mud Puppies	12	32	.273	27.5
Minot Hot Tots	16	51	.239	35

CHAMPIONSHIP: Green Bay Rockers defeated St. Cloud Rox, 3-2, championship game.

INDIVIDUAL BATTING LEADERS

	AVG	AB	R	H	2B	3B	HR	RBI	SB
Duarte, Joshua, DUL	.398	166	54	66	11	0	1	24	28
Hallquist, Michael, DUL	.355	211	53	75	19	0	15	65	4
Roberts, Kai, MAN	.346	182	55	63	22	2	4	41	39
Ganus, Tyler, KMO	.345	165	24	57	3	1	0	16	17
O'Connell, Dylan, EC	.343	181	46	62	9	0	8	55	18
Pearson, Dalton, WAU	.339	165	45	56	14	1	5	32	17
Good, Elliot, WAT	.337	163	32	55	11	0	3	42	9
Zeigler-Namoa, Ben, LAC	.335	200	46	67	12	1	3	39	12
Byrne, Aidan, WIL	.333	180	44	60	4	1	1	29	19
Ewell, Kendal, GB	.333	165	36	55	14	3	5	29	17
Fitzer, Kevin, WIL	.332	235	73	78	20	0	15	62	34
Strickler, Travis, FDL	.330	209	35	69	8	4	0	19	20
Dirksen, Drey, WIL	.329	170	35	56	11	1	7	45	4
Woodcox, Drew, MOT	.329	161	32	53	14	0	10	40	5
Miyao, Stone, WIL	.324	210	50	68	6	0	2	46	27
Halvorson, Calyn, DUL	.323	198	44	64	14	2	7	52	10
Pepe, Nic, MOT	.321	162	42	52	9	0	1	21	10
Compton, Brandon, DUL	.320	231	55	74	17	0	13	71	5
Herring, Jack, BIS	.320	181	39	58	15	0	7	39	3
Sprock, Ryan, MAD	.320	169	42	54	8	2	8	40	9
Jackson, JoJo, GB	.319	188	33	60	8	2	4	39	12
Regino, Nico, ROC	.316	155	27	49	9	1	3	33	4
Williams, Max, MAN	.316	190	37	60	21	0	5	39	6
Fougerousse, Kip, MAN	.314	210	49	66	15	1	8	37	8
West, Brylan, DUL	.312	157	34	49	12	2	2	38	7

Individual Pitching Leaders

	W	L	ERA	G	SV	IP	H	BB	SO
Horwedel, Eamon, KZO	6	2	2.30	11	0	78	67	11	56
Sanchez, Brett, GB	6	2	3.23	10	0	61	51	10	73
Meeks, Mason, KZO	7	4	3.93	13	0	76	89	10	49
Tsengeg, Amar, FDL	2	6	4.64	13	0	64	63	28	57
Danen, Alec, BIS	4	5	5.82	14	0	56	60	34	25
Roers, Isaac, MIN	1	4	7.41	8	0	38	56	18	26

PERFECT GAME COLLEGIATE LEAGUE

East Division	**W**	**L**	**PCT**	**GB**
Amsterdam Mohawks	36	5	.869	--
Utica Blue Sox	28	13	.683	8
Mohawk Valley DiamondDawgs	26	17	.605	11
Saugerties Stallions	23	17	.573	12.5
Albany Dutchmen	21	20	.512	15
Glens Falls Dragons	14	26	.350	21.5
Boonville Lumberjacks	15	30	.333	23
Watertown Rapids	15	30	.333	23
Oneonta Outlaws	12	32	.273	25.5
West Division	**W**	**LT**	**PCT**	**GB**
Batavia Muckdogs	27	16	.628	--
Elmira Pioneers	27	17	.611	0.5
Jamestown Tarp Skunks	23	18	.560	3
Auburn DoubleDays	23	19	.548	3.5
Niagara Power	22	19	.535	4
Newark Pilots	13	28	.321	13
Geneva Red Wings	12	30	.291	14.5

CHAMPIONSHIP: Amsterdam Mohawks defeated Elmira Pioneers, 2-0, in best-of-three championship series.

PROSPECT LEAGUE

Eastern Conference

Ohio River Valley Division	**W**	**L**	**PCT**	**GB**
Chillicothe Paints	41	17	.707	--
Champion City Kings	29	29	.500	12
Lafayette Aviators	28	29	.491	12.5
Johnstown Mill Rats	24	34	.414	17
Wabash River Division	**W**	**L**	**PCT**	**GB**
Danville Dans	33	23	.589	--
Normal CornBelters	27	30	.474	4.5
Springfield Lucky Horseshoes	25	29	.463	7
REX Baseball	23	33	.411	10

Western Conference

Great River Division	**W**	**L**	**PCT**	**GB**
Clinton LumberKings	33	25	.569	--
Quincy Gems	31	26	.544	1.5
Illinois Valley Pistol Shrimp	27	31	.466	6
Burlington Bees	25	32	.439	7.5
Prairie Land Division	**W**	**L**	**PCT**	**GB**
Cape Catfish	39	18	.684	--
Thrillville Thrillbillies	34	21	.618	4
O'Fallon Hoots	28	30	.483	11.5
Alton River Dragons	20	35	.364	18
Jackson Rockabillys	16	41	.281	231

CHAMPIONSHIP: Chillicothe Paints defeated Quincy Gems, 2-1, in best-of-three championship series.

INDIVIDUAL BATTING LEADERS

	AVG	AB	R	H	2B	3B	HR	RBI	SB
Victor Figueroa, Chill.	.430	151	36	65	9	1	8	50	4
Justin Carinci, Cape	.386	207	51	80	14	4	0	47	26
Brody Chrisman, Cape	.385	179	41	69	17	0	5	55	15
Tim Orr, Chill.	.385	179	61	69	15	5	6	54	13
Cole Kwiatkowski, Chill.	.359	156	45	56	6	3	2	28	17
Tyler Shaneyfelt, Chill.	.355	155	47	55	3	2	1	18	26
Chris Hall, Cape	.351	185	61	65	10	4	0	23	43
Max Holy, Clinton	.350	163	44	57	17	1	2	32	22
Jackson McCoy, Thrillville	.349	149	36	52	5	2	9	38	5
Bryson Arnette, Thrillville	.348	155	30	54	7	2	5	40	2

INDIVIDUAL PITCHING LEADERS

	W	L	ERA	G	SV	IP	H	BB	SO
Jorge Romero, Cape	5	2	1.40	10	0	45	40	12	41
Sebastian Gonzalez, Illinois V.	2	2	2.22	21	7	57	50	18	86
Luke Walter, Chill.	5	2	3.51	10	0	49	32	39	32
Nick Falter, Chill.	4	2	3.60	11	0	55	52	15	56
Dylan Peck, Cape	6	0	3.74	10	0	46	51	14	26
Tyler Fay, Danville	4	3	3.78	10	0	48	39	26	60
Coley Stevens, Lafayette	5	1	3.86	8	0	44	47	13	28
Josh Furtado, Jackson	2	1	4.06	15	0	44	38	26	59
Ryan Daly, Thrillville	3	2	4.55	11	0	55	45	20	73
David Andolina, Illinois Valley	2	1	4.69	14	0	56	47	35	61

SOUTH FLORIDA COLLEGIATE LEAGUE

North Division	**W**	**L**	**PCT**	**GB**
Delray Beach Lightning	22	10	.688	-
Palm Beach Xtreme	22	15	.595	2.5
Boca Raton Lions	15	16	.484	6.5
Boynton Beach Buccaneers	17	19	.472	7
Boca Raton Knights	12	16	.431	8
Delray Beach Wave	2	28	.067	19
South Division	**W**	**L**	**PCT**	**GB**
Pompano Beach Pokers	24	13	.649	-
West Boca Snappers	19	11	.633	1.5
Boca Raton Blazers	19	15	.557	3.5
Coconut Creek Diamond Ducks	11	20	.355	10

CHAMPIONSHIP: Florida Pokers defeated Palm Beach Xtreme, 2-1, in best-of-three championship series.

INDIVIDUAL BATTING LEADERS

	AVG	AB	R	H	2B	3B	HR	RBI	SB
Hall, Kaleb, BCR	.448	67	15	30	8	0	1	11	2
Colon, Justin, PBP	.352	88	20	31	6	3	0	3	15
Porto, Dominic, BRL	.352	71	22	25	2	0	0	6	14
Bellatoni, Gino, BCR	.333	63	22	21	5	0	0	10	0
Knowles, Aijalon, PBX	.313	83	15	26	5	0	0	16	13
Scmid, Andrew, BRL	.310	71	15	22	2	0	2	15	3
Campbell, Alex, DBW	.308	65	4	20	3	0	1	10	1
Delanzo, Joe, BRL	.304	69	14	21	4	0	1	16	3
Riera, Jesus, DBW	.300	70	13	21	6	1	3	12	12
Defazio, Nico, DBL	.282	78	20	22	2	0	0	8	15
McKenna, Chris, BRB	.274	84	21	23	6	1	1	19	10

INDIVIDUAL PITCHING LEADERS

	W	L	ERA	G	SV	IP	H	BB	SO
Rich, Keegan, PBX	2	2	1.99	8	0	32	15	18	37
Greene, Andre, WBS	4	0	2.06	9	0	35	30	12	36
Ferrera, Nick, PBP	3	1	2.56	14	4	46	37	15	50
Robinson, Zack, DBW	1	3	3.33	6	0	24	24	11	24
Rier, Luke, WBS	3	1	3.41	8	0	34	30	12	28
Blake, Eddie, BBB	3	2	3.72	8	0	36	37	11	39
Kinworthy, Gavin, CCD	3	4	3.77	10	0	31	23	18	38
Lampton, Zac, WBS	1	1	3.96	9	1	25	20	14	47
Brassfield, Bryce, BCR	1	1	4.13	8	0	24	27	16	24
Urena, Jeremy, BRL	3	2	4.55	7	0	28	29	9	33

SUNBELT LEAGUE

	W	L	PCT	GB
Gainesville Gol'Diggers	24	9	.727	-
Columbus Chatt-a-Hoots	23	9	.719	0.5
Atlanta Crackers	16	14	.533	6.5
Brookhaven Bucks	16	14	.533	6.5
Chattahoochee Monsters	17	16	.515	7
Atlanta Blues	13	19	.406	10.5
Alpharetta Aviators	10	18	.357	11.5
Waleska Wild Things	4	24	.143	17.5

CHAMPIONSHIP: Gainsville defeated Columbus 2-0 in best-of-3 series.

INDIVIDUAL BATTING LEADERS

	AVG	AB	R	H	2B	3B	HR	RBI	SB
Rose, Matt, GG	.398	98	30	39	5	2	3	13	11
O'Neal, Conner, CC	.386	101	20	39	4	2	4	29	4
Cowan, Evan, BB	.378	82	21	31	3	0	1	12	10
Smith, Braeden, AC	.355	76	17	27	3	0	1	12	3
Stanford, Riley, GG	.346	81	16	28	6	0	2	13	2
Campbell, Scott, AC	.346	104	23	36	7	1	2	19	13
Roddey, Bryce, GG	.338	80	11	27	4	1	1	17	6
Darnell, Robert, CC	.337	86	18	29	7	0	0	15	4
Lester, Parker, CC	.326	89	19	29	6	0	2	15	10
Darden, Noah, BB	.322	87	18	28	1	1	1	6	1

INDIVIDUAL PITCHING LEADERS

	W	L	ERA	G	SV	IP	H	BB	SO
Suppa, Ryan, AC	2	1	0.46	8	8	39	18	12	50
Lynch, Logan, BB	0	1	0.7	14	1	26	15	8	30
Turner, William, CC	6	1	0.99	10	10	45	27	19	55
Roper, Kyle, GG	3	0	2.17	16	1	37	27	12	52
Thornton, Maddox, GG	6	2	2.64	15	0	31	24	6	36
Moore, Eric, CM	2	2	2.68	9	8	40	29	16	37
Munhall, Cole, GG	3	0	2.70	10	9	43	31	22	49
Camp, Tyler, AA	5	1	2.91	12	3	46	31	12	24
Gill, Joey, CC	1	0	3.15	13	7	34	35	15	53
Haskins, Justin, BB	4	1	3.19	12	6	31	32	15	24

VALLEY LEAGUE

	W	L	PCT	GB
Harrisonburg Turks	28	16	.636	--
Charlottesville TomSox	28	16	.636	--
Winchester Royals	27	17	.614	1
Strasburg Express	27	17	.614	1
Woodstock River Bandits	23	21	.523	5
Culpeper Cavaliers	22	22	.500	6
Covington Lumberjacks	22	22	.500	6
Front Royal Cardinals	21	23	.477	7
Purcellville Cannons	20	24	.455	8
New Market Rebels	17	27	.386	11
Staunton Braves	17	27	.386	11
Waynesboro Generals	11	33	.250	17

CHAMPIONSHIP: Harrisonburg Turks defeated Charlottesville TomSox, 2-0, in best-of-three championship series.

WEST COAST LEAGUE

North Division	W	L	PCT	GB
Victoria HarbourCats	38	15	.717	-
Wenatchee AppleSox	37	17	.685	1.5
Bellingham Bells	35	18	.660	3
Kelowna Falcons	31	23	.574	7.5
Nanaimo NightOwls	26	28	.481	12.5
Edmonton Riverhawks	18	36	.333	20.5
Port Angeles Lefties	13	41	.241	25.5
Kamloops NorthPaws	12	40	.231	25.5
South Division	**W**	**L**	**PCT**	**GB**
Corvallis Knights	39	15	.722	-
Cowlitz Black Bears	33	21	.611	6
Ridgefield Raptors	33	21	.611	6
Portland Pickles	28	26	.519	11
Bend Elks	25	29	.463	14
Springfield Drifters	22	32	.407	17
Yakima Valley Pippins	20	34	.370	19
Walla Walla Sweets	20	34	.370	19

CHAMPIONSHIP: Corvallis Knights defeated Victoria HarbourCats in championship game.

INDIVIDUAL BATTING LEADERS

	AVG	AB	R	H	2B	3B	HR	RBI	SB
Parker, Ben, WWS	.366	153	24	56	9	2	2	30	8
Carney, Frankie, WEN	.356	146	44	52	8	1	1	17	11
Shupe, Hudson, VIC	.353	153	35	54	10	2	1	21	10
Tsukada, Jake, RID	.349	186	35	65	11	0	0	32	14
McGill, Jonny, EDM	.335	167	24	56	9	0	0	23	5
Macias, Dallas, VIC	.333	129	27	43	4	0	1	22	14
Espinoza, Aidan, WWS	.331	154	27	51	7	2	2	29	2
Nunez, Roberto, PAL	.330	191	19	63	5	0	2	31	10
DiPaolo, Luca, BEN	.328	122	23	40	17	1	4	22	0
Valdez, Andrew, BEL	.326	181	26	59	10	2	4	29	14

INDIVIDUAL PITCHING LEADERS

	W	L	ERA	G	SV	IP	H	BB	SO
Grote, Tucker, BEN	1	2	1.58	11	0	46	38	15	20
Barrett, Riley, EDM	0	3	1.73	12	1	57	53	8	39
Scheuber, Colby, PAL	0	5	2.16	9	0	50	40	16	31
Knoll, Halen, EDM	5	4	2.20	15	0	74	59	18	52
Harrison, Dallin, EDM	1	4	2.90	11	0	50	34	15	38
Oram, Camden, RID	3	0	3.71	15	3	51	48	21	33
Hangas, Zachary, WWS	4	2	3.88	10	0	53	57	21	30
Spitz, Christian, KAM	2	4	4.22	11	0	43	42	27	26
Vassar, Quincy, WEN	1	2	4.26	9	0	44	40	28	42
Haider, Rylan, SPR	2	4	4.32	12	0	58	67	15	36

HIGH SCHOOL

HIGH SCHOOL

Stoneman Douglas Tops Field For A Third Time

BY JARED MCMASTERS

An acronym graced the back of the Stoneman Douglas High (Parkland, Fla.) practice shirts this year:

INAM.

It stands for, "It's Not About Me", and the Eagles rode that "all for one" spirit all the way to a spotless 29-0 record, a Class 7A Florida state title and a final No. 1 ranking in Baseball America's national poll.

"This was most selfless team I've ever been around," Stoneman Douglas pitching coach Michael Cimilluca said. "No egos."

It worked.

The Eagles were so dominant that they never trailed by more than one run in any game. They also never trailed past the third inning.

Just five teams were able to get one-run leads on Stoneman Douglas: Miami Springs; Park Vista; Monarch; McCarthy; and Spruce Creek in the state semifinals.

Out of Stoneman Douglas' 943 plate appearances this year, it trailed in just 16 of them.

Stoneman Douglas faced teams with a .660 win percentage, yet the Eagles outscored their opponents 248-33. For the second straight year, they won their state final in five innings by virtue of the 10-run rule.

In fact, for the season, Stoneman Douglas hit more homers (35) than it allowed runs (33).

"You shoot for a state title every season, but you never think you will run the table," said Stoneman Douglas' Todd Fitz-Gerald, the first person ever to be named Florida Coach of the Year three consecutive times. "This was a special group."

Indeed. The Eagles have won 51 straight games, the second-longest win streak ever by a Florida baseball team, trailing only Calvary Christian (60). Stoneman Douglas also has the longest active win streak in the nation.

The Eagles have won three straight state titles and have earned BA's National Team of the Year honor three times overall (2016, 2022, 2023).

It's especially noteworthy that the Eagles have accomplished all of this as a public school. In fact, the Eagles are the first Florida public school baseball team to go undefeated since 1945. And they are the only Florida public school baseball team to win three straight state championships.

In addition, Stoneman Douglas allowed zero or one run in 20 of its 29 games. Out of 186 innings pitched, Eagles pitchers allowed more than one run in just five of those frames.

The Eagles pitchers compiled a 0.87 ERA. Their hitters had a collective .342 batting average.

And that's the thing about this Eagles squad: They did everything well.

Just ask their opponents.

"I have to give it to them—they pitched, they hit, they defended, they ran the bases," said Howie Stein, the coach of rival West Broward.

"Their pitchers threw a ton of strikes. Their hitters, when they faced elite arms, they battled long enough to get them out of the game.

"(Stoneman Douglas) played a great schedule. They were battle tested. They were far and away the best team in the state, and they were the best team in the country that I saw."

The Eagles, who won the NHSI title in 2022, were invited back to defend their title, but they were unable to make the trip due to financial concerns.

Still, the Eagles accomplished all that they did despite not having anyone ranked among Baseball America's list of the nation's top 100 high school prospects for the 2023 class.

But don't say the Eagles didn't have a superstar—unless of course you want to pick a fight with Fitz-Gerald.

Stoneman Douglas righthander/outfielder Christian Rodriguez, rated the nation's No. 122 senior, was outstanding this year, earning Fitz-Gerald's fierce loyalty.

Rodriguez went 13-0 with a 0.69 ERA. As a batter, he hit .359 with eight doubles, one triple and six homers in 78 at-bats. He posted a 1.192 OPS.

Not surprisingly, Rodriguez was named the best player in the state—Mr. Florida Baseball.

Fitz-Gerald said Rodriguez's size—6 feet, 195 pounds—is the only thing keeping him from the top of the draft charts.

"Tell me who's better," Fitz-Gerald said of Rodriguez, who has signed with Florida. "He's an absolute bulldog.

"Christian throws 92-95 (mph), and he has more intangibles than any pitcher we faced all

HIGH SCHOOL TOP 50

Rank	School	Record
1	Stoneman Douglas HS, Parkland, Fla.	29-0
2	Barbe HS, Lake Charles, La.	40-1
3	Sinton (Texas) HS	36-2
4	Bishop Gorman HS, Las Vegas	36-2
5	Sickles HS, Tampa	30-2
6	Houston County HS, Warner Robins, Ga.	36-6
7	West Monroe (La.) HS	39-6
8	St. John's HS, Washington, D.C.	30-1
9	Hamilton HS, Chandler, Ariz.	26-5
10	Catholic HS, Baton Rouge, La.	36-3
11	De La Salle HS, Concord, Calif.	27-5
12	New Hanover HS, Wilmington, N.C.	24-3
13	Oxford (Ala.) HS	36-6
14	Calvary Christian HS, Clearwater, Fla.	28-4
15	Bishop Hendricken (R.I.)	21-1
16	Eastlake HS, Sammamish, Wash.	19-2
17	Santa Margarita HS, Rancho Santa Margarita, Calif.	29-7
18	Center Grove HS, Greenwood, Ind.	17-2
19	Valley Christian HS, San Jose, Calif.	31-4
20	Cypress (Texas) Woods HS	37-4
21	Corpus Christi (Texas) Ray HS	33-6
22	Jackson Prep, Flowood, Miss.	27-4
23	North Oconee HS, Bogart, Ga.	33-5
24	Cathedral Prep, Erie, Pa.	21-1
25	Lincoln (Neb.) East HS	31-4
26	Casteel HS, Queen Creek, Ariz.	27-6
27	Archbishop Moeller HS, Cincinnati	29-3
28	Independence HS, Ashburn, Va.	22-1
29	Harlem (Ga.) HS	36-1
30	Loganville (Ga.) HS	33-8
31	Sulphur (La.) HS	37-5
32	Poly Prep, Brooklyn	23-1
33	La Costa Canyon HS, Carlsbad, Calif.	26-7
34	St. Mary's Prep, Orchard Lake, Mich.	11-0
35	Archbishop Spalding HS, Severn, Md.	25-4
36	Farragut HS, Knoxville, Tenn.	36-7
37	Westlake HS, Austin	39-4
38	River Bluff HS, Lexington, S.C.	20-3
39	Cardinal Newman HS, Santa Rosa, Calif.	28-2
40	Franklin HS, Elk Grove, Calif.	30-5
41	Queen Creek (Ariz.) HS	28-8
42	North Marion HS, Citra, Fla.	27-5
43	Liberty (Mo.) North HS	34-7
44	Friendswood (Texas) HS	26-5
45	Sam Houston HS, Lake Charles, La.	33-5
46	Walsh Jesuit HS, Cuyahoga Falls, Ohio	26-3
47	Freedom HS, South Riding, Va.	22-3
48	Blue Valley West HS, Stilwell, Kan.	20-5
49	Catalina Foothills HS, Tucson, Ariz.	27-3
50	Oceanside Collegiate Academy, Mt. Pleasant, S.C.	28-51

year. He has professionalism, a competitive spirit and the ability to take over a game because of his mental toughness.

"He has wide shoulders and is strong as hell. But he's not 6-foot-2. Does that mean he's not good?"

Rodriguez is most certainly good.

For his prep pitching career, Rodriguez went 31-2 with a 1.25 ERA and 312 strikeouts in 191 innings, and he also won a gold medal with Team USA's U-18 National Team this past summer.

In the semifinals against top-rated Japan, Rodriguez inherited a bases-loaded situation, struck out the side without allowing a run while trailing 3-2 and went on to earn the 4-3 win.

"He's a once-every-couple-decades player," Cimilluca said. "No situation fazes him. He gives you everything he has for as long as he can."

Stoneman Douglas' No. 2 starter this year was another Florida recruit—junior righthander Jayden Dubanewicz, who went 11-0, with one save and a 1.17 ERA. He pitched a shutout in the state final.

Junior Gavin Gargiulo, who made eight of his 10 appearances in relief, went 3-0 with a 0.84 ERA and one save. The UCF recruit would start when Stoneman Douglas had three games in one week. Otherwise, he was the Eagles' first choice out of the bullpen.

Sophomore Luke Cherry was Stoneman Douglas' fourth pitcher. He posted a 0.44 ERA with two saves in 11 relief appearances, and he—along with Gargiulo—will likely have a larger role next year.

"We have 11 pitchers, and they all pushed each other and encouraged each other," Cimilluca said. "The thing that made me the happiest all year was that every inning, when our guy walked off the mound, 10 of his fellow pitchers were there to greet him."

Offensively, senior first baseman Matt Ossenfort—who is a Vanderbilt recruit—led the team in homers (10), RBIs (35), slugging percentage (.891) and OPS (1.408).

Ossenfort, who is from South Dakota, missed his freshman season due to the coronavirus pandemic. He missed his next two years after elbow surgery. Finally, his career got on track this year—but only after his father moved to South Florida to give Ossenfort the chance to play at Stoneman Douglas.

Given that Ossenfort was a newcomer to the team and the area, Rodriguez took it upon himself to take his new teammate to dinner in the fall, and they struck up a fast friendship.

"Christian said to me, 'You're from South Dakota. You must have a cowboy hat,' and I did have one in my car," Ossenfort said. "Christian grabbed it and said, 'This has to be a new home run hat,' and that's what happened."

Another Eagles star was junior shortstop Devin Fitz-Gerald, the coach's son. Fitz-Gerald was second on the team in batting average (.410), and he led the starters in on-base percentage (.543).

Fitz-Gerald, a North Carolina State recruit, did not make an error all season, handling 55 chances.

Stoneman Douglas' leadoff batter was junior Alex Rodriguez, a center fielder who has committed to UCF. He hit .385 with a .585 on-base percentage and a 1.115 OPS. He also led the team with 41 runs scored.

HIGH SCHOOL

"When he got on base, it was almost a sure run," Stoneman Douglas hitting coach Will McCrimmon said. "For him, a single is like a triple (due to his team-high 23 steals in 24 tries)."

Junior Niko Benestad, a South Florida recruit, led a deep group of catchers. Benestad hit .351 with four homers and a 1.045 OPS. Sophomore Andrew Freeman, a Louisville recruit, and senior Cayden Freels, a Roanoke (Va.) signee, were the other Eagles catchers.

The other Stoneman Douglas starters included senior second baseman Alex Lazar, a Coker (S.C.) recruit; junior third baseman Rylan Lujo, a Dayton recruit; senior right fielder Dillon Moquin, who signed with Appalachian State; and senior left fielder Jackson Abram, an Adrian (Mich.) College recruit.

Moquin is another example of the selfless mentality for Stoneman Douglas. He waited three years to earn a starting job as he played behind current Florida players Jake Clemente and Chris Arroyo.

But it was worth the wait to be part of such a potent offense.

"The first time through our lineup, a pitcher can get us every once in a while," McCrimmon said. "But the second or third time through, it's hard to hold us down.

"Our hitters will look at charts to see where and what the pitchers are throwing. They will also talk to each other and make really good adjustments together."

After all, "It's Not About Me" with these Stoneman Douglas Eagles.

It's about WWDY—We Will Dominate You.

Boras Classic Winners

The Boras Classic began in 2013 as a tournament to bring together the best California high school teams and determine a de facto state champion. In the 10 years since, the Boras Classic has grown into one of the nation's preeminent high school tournaments and a top destination for evaluators to scout the upcoming draft class.

More than a dozen of the top high school players in this year's draft class participated in the 32-team tournament over the first two weeks of April. Notre Dame (Sherman Oaks) defeated Huntington Beach, 8-6, to win the South Classic. Cardinal Newman (Santa Rosa) beat Bellarmine Prep (San Jose), 8-0, to win the North Classic.

In the Arizona Boras Classic, Phoenix's Bishop Gorman High defeated Phoenix's O'Connor High 7-5 in the championship game.

Huntington Beach Wins NHSI

Over the past decade, teams from California and Florida have generally dominated the National High School Invitational, which is hosted at USA Baseball's complex in Cary, N.C.

But it's more accurate to say that the NHSI has been dominated by a few teams.

In addition to a runners-up finish at the South Boras Classic, Huntington Beach (Calif.) HS won their second National High School Invitational title.

Huntington Beach becomes the third school to win muliple NHSI titles. Between themselves, Mater Dei (Calif.) High and Orange, Calif.'s Orange Lutheran (Calif.) High, the trio has won seven of the 10 titles. Of the 20 teams to play for an NHSI title, 19 have come from California or Florida.

Huntington Beach had to work overtime. San Juan Capistrano's JSerra Catholic HS tied the title game at 1-1 when Charlie Caruso hit a sacrifice fly to score Trent Caraway in the seventh.

Neither team scored in the eighth, but Huntington Beach blew the game open in the ninth. Aidan Espinoza hit a three-run triple. Bradley Navarro added another triple to blow the game open for an 8-1 win.

The Oilers' Tyler Bellerose was named the tournament MVP. Bellerose allowed one run and four hits in nine innings on the mound,.

The entire All-NHSI team included: All-NHSI Team:. Tyler Bellerose (Huntington Beach); Dean Carpentier (Huntington Beach); Trent Caraway (JSerra Catholic); Matthew Champion (JSerra Catholic); Adam Ciccone (Hagerty); Colin Clarke (Santa Margarita); Bradley Gilbert (Aquinas); Aidan Knaak (Bishop Verot); Gunnar Myro (Bishop Gorman); Bryce Nevils (Brother Rice); Gavin Smith (Basha); Ty Starke (St. Xavier); Charley Sturm (Jesuit); Cole Van Essen (Brother Rice); Ralphy Velazquez (Huntington Beach).

AMATEUR/YOUTH CHAMPIONS 2019

ALL-AMERICAN AMATEUR BASEBALL ASSOCIATION (AAABA)

Event	Site	Champion	Runner-up
World Series (21U)	Johnstown, Pa.	Johnstown Mainline Pharmacy	New Orleans Boosters

AMERICAN LEGION BASEBALL

Event	Site	Champion	Runner-up
World Series (19U)	Shelby, N.C.	League City (Texas)	Lincoln (Neb.)

BABE RUTH BASEBALL

Event	Site	Champion	Runner-up
Cal Ripken (10U)	Crown Point, Ind.	Florence Navy All-Stars	Bryant Black Sox
Cal Ripken Major/70 feet	Branson, Mo.	Ohio Valley	Taiwan
14-year-old	Fredericksburg, Va.	Orcutt, Calif.	Eagle Press, Texas
13-15-year-olds	Jamestown, N.Y.	Portland	Norwalk Tides
16-18-year-olds	Cape Giradeau, Mo.	South East Tropics	Alabama

LITTLE LEAGUE BASEBALL

Event	Site	Champion	Runner-up
Little League (11-12)	South Williamsport, Pa.	El Segundo, California	Curacao
Junior League (12-14)	Taylor, Mich.	Taoyuan,, Taiwan	Taylor, Mich.
Senior League (13-16)	Easley, S.C.	Willemstad, Curacao	Cherry Hill, N.J.
Intermediate (50-70)	Livermore, Calif.	Seoul, South Korea	Tampa, Fla.

NATIONAL AMATEUR BASEBALL FEDERATION (NBAF)

Event	Site	Champion	Runner-up
Freshman (12U)	Ramsey, N.J.	Bergen Crush, N.J.	New York Gothams.
Sophomore (14U)	Struthers, Ohio	Astros Falcons, Ohio	Avalanche, Pa.
Junior (16U)	Struthers, Ohio	Creekside Fitness, Ohio	BHM Buckeyes, Ohio
High School (17U)	Clinton, Tenn.	Jackson 96ers, Miss.	Coal Creek Bulls, Tenn.
Senior (18U)	Struthers, Ohio	Whiting Roll-Offs, Ohio	Knightline, Ohio
College (22U)	Sandusky, Ohio	Stark County Terriers, Ohio	SAYO Grays, Tenn.

PERFECT GAME/BCS FINALS

Event	Site	Champion	Runner-up
12U	Southaven, Miss.	SBA Bolts National 12U	Braves Baseball Academy
13U	Fort Myers, Fla.	Birmingham Stars	Team Elite 13U National
14U	Fort Myers, Fla.	Florida Burn	Wow Factor 14U
15U	Fort Myers, Fla.	CBU 2026 Scout Team - James	R3 2026
16U	Fort Myers, Fla.	South Charlotte Panthers	Top Tier Roos American 2025
17U	Fort Myers, Fla.	Original Florida Pokers 17U	USA Prime Scout Team
18U	Fort Myers, Fla.	Nelson Baseball School	Siege Scout Team

PERFECT GAME/WORLD WOOD BAT ASSOCIATION SUMMER CHAMPIONSHIPS

Event	Site	Champion	Runner-up
14U	Marietta, Ga.	Test Black 14U	BPA
15U	Marietta, Ga.	Canes National 15U	Mba 2026 Scout Team
16U	Marietta, Ga.	East Cobb Astros 16u	GBG National 2025
17U	Marietta, Ga..	Power Baseball 2024 Marucci	eXposure 17U National-Church
18U	Marietta, Ga.	USA Prime National/Tigers Scout	Chi Town Cream

PONY BASEBALL

Event	Site	Champion	Runner-up
Pinto 8U	Marion, Ill.	Costa Mesa, Calif.	Tijuana, Mexico
Mustang 9U	Vacaville, Calif.	Tecolote, Calif.	Simi Valley, Calif.
Mustang 10U	Youngsville, La.	Placentia, Calif.	Mexicali, Baja California, Mexico
Bronco 11U	Chesterfield, Va.	Orange, Calif.	Los Mochis, Mexico
Bronco 12U	Laredo, Texas	Edogawa, Japan	Bani, D.R.
Pony 13U	Modesto, Calif.	Monterrey, Mexico	Bel Passi, Calif.
Pony 14U	Washington, Pa.	Edogawa, Japan	Washington County, Pa.
Colt 16U	Marion, Ill.	Southern Illinois	Youngstown, Ohio
Palomino 18U	Laredo, Texas	Youngstown, Ohio	Monterrey, Mexico

REVIVING BASEBALL IN INNER CITIES (RBI)

Event	Site	Champion	Runner-up
Junior (13-15)	Vero Beach, Fla.	Chicago White Sox RBI	Dodgers Dreamteam RBI
Senior (16-18)	Vero Beach, Fla.	Houston Astros RBI	Atlanta Braves Nike RBI

USA BASEBALL

Event	Site	Champion	Runner-up
13U East	Cary, N.C.	Reed Johnson Baseball Academy	SBA 13U National
14U West	Peoria, Ariz.	Cali National Murphy	Next Level Baseball
15U West	Peoria, Ari.	GBG Renegades	Team Utah
15U East	Cary, N.C.	Canes National 15U	Alpha Prime 2026
16U West	Peoria, Ariz.	GBG National 2025	SoCal Birds Orange
17U West	Peoria, Ariz.	Prime	TB SoCal

HIGH SCHOOL

Clark Lives Up To His Lofty Fame

BY RICHARD TORRES

Baseball has had its share of famous high school prospects.

Alex Rodriguez. Bryce Harper. Ken Griffey Jr.

Those teenagers' names were known nationally to fans before they signed their first pro contracts.

Like that impressive trio, Indiana high school outfielder Max Clark was considered a top draft prospect. And it seems like only a matter of time before the 18-year-old Franklin Community High product make himself into a household name.

Clark already has as much social media clout as any prep baseball prospect. He has 600,000-plus ritualistically checking their smartphone notifications across a handful of social media platforms, where his brand thrives. A simple Google search reveals that the hype for Clark is real.

From a Wikipedia page of his own to a YouTube clip of him putting "on a show for his last BP at Perfect Game!" in early June to the biggest of all questions: "Will Max Clark get drafted?"

Now, Clark adds one more Google search result: Baseball America High School Player of the Year.

"Yeah, he's a busy guy," Franklin Community baseball coach Ryan Feyerabend said. "And he handles it all like a pro, good or bad."

Lately, it has been far more good for Clark. The 6-foot-1, 205-pound lefthanded hitter completed a remarkable senior campaign that included a .646 batting average with 33 RBIs, 45 runs scored and six home runs with a state-record 52 walks in 120 plate appearances.

Clark, who is from Franklin, about 20 miles south of Indianapolis, finished his high school career with a .551 average in 216 at-bats. He hit 21 home runs while striking out just 16 times in three seasons.

Scouts assess Clark as having the potential to develop multiple plus tools. He is one of the best pure hitters in the 2023 high school class, with excellent range in center field and speed on the basepaths.

"Out in the social media world, Max is a really big deal," Feyerabend said. "And he is a big deal, but I just kind of see him—and I hate to say he's just another player—but that's kind of how he acts.

"He shows up. He puts his (numbers) up, and asks about the plan and is like, 'Coach, let's go!' "

That work ethic is precisely how Clark rose to prominence. He headed into 2023 as the top prep prospect for the draft and lived up to the hype and scrutiny. North Carolina high school outfielder Walker Jenkins moved ahead of Clark on the draft ranking, but that was not an indictment of Clark so much as an endorsement of Jenkins' hit-plus-power potential.

When he's not crushing long balls during batting practice using a custom 33.25 Pro Maple with his name and "13MC" engraved in its wooden fibers, Clark flashes his personality with necklaces, energetic bat flips, vibrant batting gloves and eye black fashioned into a cross on each cheek that he smears down to his chin, professing his faith.

PLAYER OF THE YEAR

PREVIOUS WINNERS

1992: Preston Wilson, OF/RHP, Bamberg-Ehrhardt (S.C.) HS
1993: Trot Nixon, OF/LHP, New Hanover HS, Wilmington, N.C.
1994: Doug Million, LHP, Sarasota (Fla.) HS
1995: Ben Davis, C, Malvern (Pa.) Prep
1996: Matt White, RHP, Waynesboro Area (Pa.) HS
1997: Darnell McDonald, OF, Cherry Creek HS, Englewood, Colo.
1998: Drew Henson, 3B/RHP, Brighton (Mich.) HS
1999: Josh Hamilton, OF/LHP, Athens Drive HS, Raleigh, N.C.
2000: Matt Harrington, RHP, Palmdale (Calif.) HS
2001: Joe Mauer, C, Cretin-Derham Hall HS, St. Paul, Minn.
2002: Scott Kazmir, LHP, Cypress Falls HS, Houston
2003: Jeff Allison, RHP, Veterans Memorial HS, Peabody, Mass.
2004: Homer Bailey, RHP, LaGrange (Texas) HS
2005: Justin Upton, SS, Great Bridge HS, Chesapeake, Va.
2006: Adrian Cardenas, SS/2B, Mons. Pace HS, Opa Locka, Fla.
2007: Mike Moustakas, SS, Chatsworth (Calif.) HS
2008: Ethan Martin, RHP/3B, Stephens County HS, Toccoa, Ga.
2009: Bryce Harper, C, Las Vegas HS
2010: Kaleb Cowart, RHP/3B, Cook HS, Adel, Ga.
2011: Dylan Bundy, RHP, Owasso (Okla.) HS
2012: Byron Buxton, OF, Appling County HS, Baxley, Ga.
2013: Clint Frazier, OF, Loganville (Ga.) HS
2014: Alex Jackson, OF, Rancho Bernardo (Calif.) HS
2015: Kyle Tucker, OF, Plant HS, Tampa
2016: Mickey Moniak, OF, La Costa Canyon HS, Carlsbad, Calif.
2017: MacKenzie Gore, LHP, Whiteville (N.C.) HS
2018: Cole Winn, RHP, Orange (Calif.) Lutheran HS
2019: Bobby Witt Jr., SS, Colleyville (Texas) Heritage HS
2020: No award given in truncated season
2021: Jackson Jobe, RHP/SS, Heritage Hall HS, Oklahoma City
2022: Jackson Holliday, SS, Stillwater (Okla.) HS

2023 HIGH SCHOOL ALL-AMERICA TEAM

Caraway

Martin

Houck

Clark

Mitchell

Jenkins

Head

Nimmala

Volchko

Eldridge

Meyer

Soto

FIRST TEAM

Pos.	Player, School
C	Blake Mitchell, Sinton (Texas) HS
CI	Trent Caraway, JSerra Catholic HS, San Juan Capistrano, Calif.
CI	Bryce Eldridge, Madison HS, Vienna, Va.
MI	Walker Martin, Eaton (Colo.) HS
MI	Colin Houck, Parkview HS, Lilburn, Ga.
OF	Max Clark, Franklin (Ind.) Community HS
OF	Walker Jenkins, South Brunswick HS, Southport, N.C.
OF	Dillon Head, Homewood-Flossmoor HS, Flossmoor, Ill.
DH	Arjun Nimmala, Strawberry Crest HS, Dover, Fla.

Pos.	Player, School
SP	Noble Meyer, Jesuit HS, Portland, Ore.
SP	Thomas White, Phillips Academy, Andover, Mass.
SP	Charlee Soto, Reborn Christian Academy HS, Kissimmee, Fla.
SP	Travis Sykora, Round Rock (Texas) HS
SP	Joey Volchko, Redwood HS, Visalia, Calif.

Sykora

White

SECOND TEAM

Pos.	Player, School
C	Ralphy Velazquez, Huntington Beach (Calif.) HS
CI	Gavin Grahovac, Villa Park (Calif.) HS
CI	George Wolkow, Downers Grove (Ill.) North HS
MI	Samuel Stafura, Walter Panas HS, Cortlandt Manor, N.Y.
MI	Colt Emerson, Glenn HS, New Concord, Ohio
OF	Johnny Farmelo, Westfield HS, Chantilly, Va.
OF	Kendall George, Atascocita HS, Humble, Texas
OF	Seth Farni, St. Stanislaus Catholic HS, Bay St Louis, Miss.
DH	Kevin McGonigle, Monsignor Bonner HS, Drexel Hill, Pa.

Pos.	Player, School
SP	Josh Knoth, Patchogue-Medford HS, Medford, N.Y.
SP	Cameron Johnson, IMG Academy, Bradenton, Fla.
SP	Paul Wilson, Lakeridge HS, Lake Oswego, Ore.
SP	Jake Brown, Sulpher (La.) HS
SP	Dylan Questad, Waterford (Wisc.) HS

DRAFT

Teams Stick To Script In Loaded Draft

BY CARLOS COLLAZO, KYLE GLASER AND JJ COOPER

SEATTLE — The Pirates had their choice of premium talents with the No. 1 pick in the 2023 draft.

Ultimately, a potential future ace was too good to pass up.

The Pirates selected Louisiana State righthander Paul Skenes with the first overall pick in the 2023 draft on Sunday afternoon at Lumen Field, adding one of the best college pitchers in a decade to their organization.

Skenes, a 6-foot-6, 247-pound righthander, went 13-2, 1.69 with a Southeastern Conference-record 209 strikeouts and 20 walks in 122.2 innings to lead the Tigers to the College World Series championship this spring. He won the CWS Most Outstanding Player Award after allowing two runs in 15.2 innings over two starts in Omaha and was named the 2023 Baseball America College Player of the Year.

"We wanted the player who we thought would help the Pirates win the most games over time," Pirates general manager Ben Cherington said. "That's what we always go back to. We've taken college players three out of four years that I've been here, but it's always focused on the best player. We're excited and thrilled to have Paul join the Pirates."

JAMIE SCHWABEROW

Paul Skenes won a national title as the lead-up to being picked first overall.

A big, physical workhorse with an upper-90s fastball, Skenes drew frequent comparisons to previous college aces Stephen Strasburg and Gerrit Cole, both of whom were selected first overall in their drafts in 2009 and 2011, respec-

FIRST-ROUND BONUS PROGRESSION

After several years of fairly consistent growth of first round bonuses, the money has reached a bit of a plateau in the three years since the covid, five-round draft. In part that stemmed from bonus values remaining static, but with the pandemic now in baseball's rear-view mirror, and new CBA signed and agreed to by MLB and the MLB Players Association, bonuses are once again on the rise.

This year saw a significant jump, as baseball returned to the type of progression that hadn't been seen since before the pandemic.

After the first draft in 1965, first-round bonuses rose by an average of just 0.6 percent annually for the rest of the 1960s and 5.2 percent per year in the 1970s. Bonus inflation picked up in the 1980s, averaging 10.2 percent annually, and soared to 26.9 percent per year in the 1990s.

Below are the annual averages for first-round bonuses since the draft started in 1965. The 1996 total does not include four players who became free agents through a loophole in the draft rules.

Year	Average	Change	Year	Average	Change	Year	Average	Change	Year	Average	Change
1965	$42,516	—	1980	$74,025	8.70%	1995	$918,019	16.10%	2010	$2,220,966	-8.80%
1966	$44,430	4.50%	1981	$78,573	6.10%	1996*	$944,404	2.90%	2011	$2,653,375	19.50%
1967	$42,898	-3.40%	1982	$82,615	5.10%	1997	$1,325,536	40.40%	2012	$2,475,167	-6.70%
1968	$43,850	2.20%	1983	$87,236	5.60%	1998	$1,637,667	23.10%	2013	$2,641,538	6.70%
1969	$43,504	-0.80%	1984	$105,391	20.80%	1999	$1,809,767	10.50%	2014	$2,612,109	-1.10%
1970	$45,230	3.90%	1985	$118,115	12.10%	2000	$1,872,586	3.50%	2015	$2,774,945	6.23%
1971	$45,197	-0.10%	1986	$116,300	-1.60%	2001	$2,154,280	15.00%	2016	$2,897,557	4.42%
1972	$44,952	-0.50%	1987	$128,480	10.50%	2002	$2,106,793	-2.20%	2017	$3,880,723	25.4%
1973	$48,832	8.60%	1988	$142,540	10.90%	2003	$1,765,667	-16.20%	2018	$3,754,123	-3.37%
1974	$53,333	9.20%	1989	$176,008	23.50%	2004	$1,958,448	10.90%	2019	$3,791,729	1.01%
1975	$49.33	-7.50%	1990	$252,577	43.50%	2005	$2,018,000	3.00%	2020	$4,080,307	7.61%
1976	$49,631	0.60%	1991	$365,396	44.70%	2006	$1,933,333	-4.20%	2021	$4,009,424	-1.74%
1977	$48,813	-1.60%	1992	$481,893	31.90%	2007	$2,098,083	8.50%	2022	$4,074,268	1.62%
1978	$67,892	39.10%	1993	$613,037	27.20%	2008	$2,458,714	17.20%	2023	$4,561,460	12.0%
1979	$68,094	0.20%	1994	$790,357	28.90%	2009	$2,434,800	-1.00%			

tively. Skenes led the nation in strikeouts, strikeouts per nine innings (15.33) and WHIP (0.75) and finished second in ERA and innings pitched. His 209 strikeouts were the most of any college pitcher since Long Beach State's Jered Weaver struck out 213 batters in 2004.

"A year ago, two years ago, I never thought it was a possibility to be the first overall pick," Skenes said. "I don't know what I was expecting coming into today, but I'm looking forward to what's to come and hopefully winning a World Series or two in Pittsburgh."

The Lake Forest, Calif. native played his first two seasons at Air Force and starred while playing both ways as a pitcher and catcher/DH. He transferred to LSU for his junior season and focused solely on pitching, leading to his dominant season.

Skenes allowed more than two earned runs just twice all season for LSU and struck out at least 10 batters in 14 of his 19 starts. He saved his best for the biggest moments.

Skenes pitched 7.2 innings with two runs allowed and 12 strikeouts in LSU's CWS opener against Tennessee. He pitched eight scoreless innings with two hits allowed and nine strikeouts in an elimination game against top-seeded Wake Forest to send the Tigers to the CWS finals.

"I think we saw a really good pitcher at the end of the College World Series who has all the weapons to go on and succeed in pro ball but may still have more," Cherington said. "I know he's already thinking about that."

Skenes is the 14th righthanded pitcher to be selected first overall and the first since the Tigers selected Auburn righthander Casey Mize with the first pick in 2018.

Mize, Cole and Strasburg all reached the majors within two years of being drafted, quick ascents that Skenes is expected to follow.

"I think my stuff is big league ready, but to be honest not being in professional baseball yet, there's some stuff I'm going to have to figure out along the way," Skenes said. "My goal is to be in the big leagues as long as possible and as soon as possible, and I'm going to do whatever it takes to accomplish that."

Teammates Go 1-2

The Nationals selected LSU outfielder Dylan Crews with the second overall pick. The selection marked the first time two teammates were taken with the top two picks in the same draft.

"It says that we have the right people and that coach (Jay) Johnson did a good job bringing the right people in to the building," Skenes said. "I think it's going to be a pattern of success for LSU baseball."

Crews hit .426/.567/.713 with 18 home runs and 70 RBI as the Tigers' top hitter and won the Golden Spikes Award. He was a two-time All-American and became the first player to win back-to-back SEC player of the year awards.

"There's a lot of emotions going on right now," Crews said. "I'm so thankful and I can't wait to get going. I know (Washington) is such a great

BONUS SPENDING BY TEAM

The 2023 set a new record for total draft spending, as for the first time the total $350 million spent topped the previous record of $316.5 million spent on draft bonuses in 2019. That's signiifcant as the previous amount covered a 40 round draft while this was the spending over a 20 round draft.

The average team spent $11.67 million in 2023, up from $10.4 million in 2022. The Pirates $17.1 million in bonus spending also set a new individual team record.

The CBA that went into effect in 2012 curtailed spending by instituting harsh penalties for teams that exceeded their bonus pools by more than five percent. It also ended the practice of awarding major league contracts to draftees. But as revenues within the game have increased, so too have the bonus pools MLB allocates to teams for the first 10 rounds. No team has yet been willing to exceed the five percent mark.

The new CBA that added the draft lottery system also included a $25,000 bump in the maximum bonus that teams could spend after the 10th round without counting toward a team's bonus allotment, that led to nearly $5 million in spending in the 2023 draft that would have been beyond the bonus limits in the 2022 draft.

TEAM	2023	2022	2021
Angels	$10,015,225	$8,352,250	$10,722,500
Astros	$8,234,500	$7,972,630	$3,427,500
Athletics	$15,882,600	$9,448,700	$7,196,500
Blue Jays	$7,856,185	$9,536,100	$6,884,200
Braves	$9,988,500	$11,886,600	$7,590,000
Brewers	$12,498,100	$7,572,500	$10,623,400
Cardinals	$7,618,500	$7,744,300	$9,445,000
Cubs	$10,695,000	$11,583,000	$7,748,300
D-backs	$12,055,000	$15,470,200	$11,946,900
Dodgers	$8,583,000	$5,559,990	$5,754,000
Giants	$11,433,525	$6,886,220	$9,213,200
Guardians	$10,221,275	$11,635,000	$8,468,400
Mariners	$13,990,500	$8,421,500	$9,359,600
Marlins	$13,692,400	$11,300,900	$11,257,290
Mets	$9,869,850	$14,716,560	$4,342,900
Nationals	$16,150,000	$12,688,200	$10,106,600
Orioles	$11,414,800	$17,735,600	$12,514,700
Padres	$7,161,600	$11,647,800	$7,763,300
Phillies	$6,761,100	$7,417,100	$9,530,600
Pirates	$17,123,300	$14,543,800	$15,938,700
Rangers	$11,442,900	$10,700,500	$13,362,000
Rays	$12,172,100	$8,511,700	$8,694,800
Red Sox	$11,851,200	$9,204,750	$10,761,900
Reds	$15,321,500	$12,225,800	$13,638,300
Rockies	$13,192,450	$14,338,300	$11,372,200
Royals	$14,002,200	$11,042,000	$12,557,300
Tigers	$17,677,450	$9,221,900	$16,165,700
Twins	$15,245,600	$10,971,500	$8,845,900
White Sox	$10,967,800	$7,557,900	$8,087,000
Yankees	$6,970,900	$7,969,500	$8,089,800
Total	**$350,089,060**	**$313,862,800**	**$291,408,490**
Average	**$11,669,635**	**$10,462,093**	**$9,713,616**

DRAFT

organization with great player development, so I am really looking forward to growing, but I am going to go in there the same person that I am. I'm just ready to grow with these guys."

The Tigers selected Franklin (Ind.) Community High outfielder Max Clark with the third overall pick. Clark won BA's 2023 High School Player of the Year Award after batting .646 with six home runs, 33 RBIs, 45 runs scored and a state-record 52 walks in 120 plate appearances this spring.

"Early on we established a really good personal connection," Clark said. "They visited during the winter at where I work out in the offseason. I didn't know how it was going to go down until the final 10 minutes before I was selected."

The Rangers selected Florida outfielder Wyatt Langford with the fourth overall pick and the Twins drafted South Brunswick (Southport, N.C) High outfielder Walker Jenkins with the fifth overall pick.

As Expected

All year long there was a clear-cut top tier of talent that included five players: Dylan Crews, Paul Skenes, Wyatt Langford, Walker Jenkins and Max Clark.

JAY BIGGERSTAFF

Florida outfielder Wyatt Langford was drafted fourth overall by Texas.

HIGHEST BONUSES EVER

Paul Skenes set a new draft bonus record as his $9.2 million easly topped the previous record of Spencer Torkelson set in 2020.

Player, Pos.	Team, Year (Pick)	Bonus
Paul Skenes, RHP	Pirates, 2023 (No. 1)	$9,200,000
Dylan Crews, OF	Nationals, 2023 (No. 2)	$9,000,000
Spencer Torkelson, 1B	Tigers, 2020 (No. 1)	$8,416,300
Jackson Holliday, SS	Orioles, 2022 (No. 1)	$8,190,000
Druw Jones, OF	D-backs, 2022 (No. 2)	$8,189,400
Adley Rutschman, C	Orioles, 2019 (No. 1)	$8,100,000
Gerrit Cole, RHP	Pirates, 2011 (No. 1)	$8,000,000
Wyatt Langford, OF	Rangers, 2023 (No. 4)	$8,000,000
Jack Leiter, RHP	Rangers, 2021 (No. 2)	$7,922,000
Bobby Witt Jr., SS	Royals, 2019 (No. 2)	$7,787,400
Max Clark, OF	Tigers, 2023 (No. 3)	$7,767,500
Stephen Strasburg, RHP	Nationals, 2009 (No. 1)	*$7,500,000
Bubba Starling, OF	Royals, 2011 (No. 5)	+$7,500,000
Casey Mize, RHP	Tigers, 2018 (No. 1)	$7,500,000
Hunter Greene, RHP/SS	Reds, 2017 (No. 2)	$7,230,000
Andrew Vaughn, 1B	White Sox, 2019 (No. 3)	$7,221,200
Termarr Johnson, SS	Pirates, 2022 (No. 4)	$7,219,000
Walker Jenkins, OF	Twins, 2023 (No. 5)	$7,144,200
Joey Bart, C	Giants, 2018 (No. 2)	$7,025,000
Brendan McKay, 1B/LHP	Rays, 2017 (No. 4)	$7,005,000
Austin Martin, SS	Blue Jays, 2020 (No. 5)	$7,000,825
Kyle Wright, RHP	Braves, 2017 (No. 5)	$7,000,000
Jackson Jobe, RHP	Tigers, 2021 (No. 3)	$6,900,000
Royce Lewis, SS	Twins, 2017 (No. 1)	$6,725,000
Jordan Lawlar, SS	D-backs, 2021 (No. 6)	$6,713,300
Kris Bryant, 3B	Cubs, 2013 (No. 2)	$6,708,400
MacKenzie Gore, LHP	Padres, 2017 (No. 3)	$6,700,000
Max Meyer, RHP	Marlins, 2020 (No. 3)	$6,700,000
JJ Bleday, OF	Marlins, 2019 (No. 4)	$6,670,000
Asa Lacy, LHP	Royals, 2020 (No. 4)	$6,670,000
Marcelo Mayer, SS	Red Sox, 2021 (No. 4)	$6,664,000

**Part of major league contract. +Bonus spread over multiple years under MLB two-sport provisions*

They didn't all go in the exact order of the BA Draft board, but each of the top five players was selected among the top five picks—making the 2023 draft similar to the 2019 class which was notable for its top six group of players: Adley Rutschman, Bobby Witt Jr., Andrew Vaughn, JJ Bleday, CJ Abrams and Riley Greene.

Leading up to the draft there were plenty of rumors about non-top five players entering the mix, particularly with the Rangers and Twins picking at Nos. 4 and 5. However, the teams who were lucky enough to access the elite talent of the draft—and who were lucky enough to pick there after the first-ever draft lottery—didn't play any games and simply took the best available talent.

That seems to be the way the industry operates when there's a standout group at the top of the draft, and that also remained true throughout the first round.

There were few players who were announced who were much of a surprise at all. The Astros taking shortstop Brice Matthews at pick No. 28 was perhaps the biggest "off the board" selection, and he still ranked as the No. 57 player on the BA 500. Hardly a true reach when you consider the history of the draft.

In fact, every player selected among the first 30 picks of the draft ranked inside the top 45

DRAFT

of the BA 500. Only Matthews and No. 99 shortstop Tai Peete, whom the Mariners picked with their third overall selection at No. 30, were ranked lower.

And Matthews might have even been a more surprising name considering some of the pre-draft buzz around Peete entering the day.

Once the anticipation of who the Pirates were taking at No. 1 was resolved, it was mostly a very expected group of players picked in the first. Perhaps that's simply what happens when the industry is picking from one of the best draft classes in years.

NO. 1 OVERALL PICKS

Yr Team: Player, Pos., School	Bonus
1965 Athletics: Rick Monday, OF, Arizona State	$100,000
1966 Mets: Steve Chilcott, C, Antelope Valley HS, Lancaster, Calif.	$75,000
1967 Yankees: Ron Blomberg, 1B, Druid Hills HS, Atlanta	$65,000
1968 Mets: Tim Foli, SS, Notre Dame HS, Sherman Oaks, Calif.	$74,000
1969 Senators: Jeff Burroughs, OF, Centennial HS, Long Beach	$88,000
1970 Padres: Mike Ivie, C, Walker HS, Atlanta	$75,000
1971 White Sox: Danny Goodwin, C, Peoria (Ill.) HS	Did not sign
1972 Padres: Dave Roberts, 3B, Oregon	$70,000
1973 Rangers: David Clyde, LHP, Westchester HS, Texas	*$65,000
1974 Padres: Bill Almon, SS, Brown	*$90,000
1975 Angels: Danny Goodwin, C, Southern	*$125,000
1976 Astros: Floyd Bannister, LHP, Arizona State	$100,000
1977 White Sox: Harold Baines, OF, St. Michaels (Md.) HS	$32,000
1978 Braves: Bob Horner, 3B, Arizona State	*$162,000
1979 Mariners: Al Chambers, 1B, Harris HS, Harrisburg, Pa.	$60,000
1980 Mets: Darryl Strawberry, OF, Crenshaw HS, Los Angeles	$152,500
1981 Mariners: Mike Moore, RHP, Oral Roberts	$100,000
1982 Cubs: Shawon Dunston, SS, Jefferson HS, New York	$135,000
1983 Twins: Tim Belcher, RHP, Mount Vernon Nazarene (Ohio)	Did not sign
1984 Mets: Shawn Abner, OF, Mechanicsburg (Pa.) HS	$150,500
1985 Brewers: B.J. Surhoff, C, North Carolina	$150,000
1986 Pirates: Jeff King, 3B, Arkansas	$180,000
1987 Mariners: Ken Griffey Jr., OF, Moeller HS, Cincinnati	$160,000
1988 Padres: Andy Benes, RHP, Evansville	$235,000
1989 Orioles: Ben McDonald, RHP, Louisiana State	*$350,000
1990 Braves: Chipper Jones, SS, The Bolles School, Jacksonville	$275,000
1991 Yankees: Brien Taylor, LHP, East Carteret HS, Beaufort, N.C.	$1,550,000
1992 Astros: Phil Nevin, 3B, Cal State Fullerton	$700,000
1993 Mariners: Alex Rodriguez, SS, Westminster Christian HS, Miami	*$1,000,000
1994 Mets: Paul Wilson, RHP, Florida State	$1,550,000
1995 Angels: Darin Erstad, OF, Nebraska	$1,575,000
1996 Pirates: Kris Benson, RHP, Clemson	$2,000,000
1997 Tigers: Matt Anderson, RHP, Tigers	$2,505,000
1998 Phillies: Pat Burrell, 3B, Miami	*$3,150,000
1999 Devil Rays: Josh Hamilton, OF, Athens Drive HS, Raleigh	$3,960,000
2000 Marlins: Adrian Gonzalez, 1B, Eastlake HS, Chula Vista, Calif.	$3,000,000
2001 Twins: Joe Mauer, C, Cretin-Derham Hall, St. Paul	$5,150,000
2002 Pirates: Bryan Bullington, RHP, Ball State	$4,000,000
2003 Devil Rays: Delmon Young, OF, Camarillo (Calif.) HS	*$3,700,000
2004 Padres: Matt Bush, SS, Mission Bay HS, San Diego	$3,150,000
2005 D-backs: Justin Upton, SS, Great Bridge HS, Chesapeake, Va.	$6,100,000
2006 Royals: Luke Hochevar, RHP, Fort Worth (American Assoc.)	*$3,500,000
2007 Devil Rays: David Price, LHP, Vanderbilt	*$5,600,000
2008 Rays: Tim Beckham, SS, Griffin (Ga.) HS	$6,150,000
2009 Nationals: Stephen Strasburg, RHP, San Diego State	*$7,500,000
2010 Nationals: Bryce Harper, OF, JC of Southern Nevada	*$6,250,000
2011 Pirates: Gerrit Cole, RHP, UCLA	$8,000,000
2012 Astros: Carlos Correa, SS, Puerto Rico Baseball Acad., Gurabo, P.R.	$4,800,000
2013 Astros: Mark Appel, RHP, Stanford	$6,350,000
2014 Astros: Brady Aiken, LHP, Cathedral Catholic, San Diego	Did not sign
2015 D-backs: Dansby Swanson, SS, Vanderbilt	$6,500,000
2016 Phillies: Mickey Moniak, OF, La Costa Canyon HS, Carlsbad, Calif.	$6,100,000
2017 Twins: Royce Lewis, SS, JSerra Catholic HS, San Juan Capistrano, Calif.	$6,750,000
2018 Tigers: Casey Mize, RHP, Auburn	$7,500,000
2019 Orioles: Adley Rutschman, C, Oregon State	$8,100,000
2020 Tigers: Spencer Torkelson, 3B, Arizona State	$8,416,300
2021 Pirates: Henry Davis, C, Louisville	$6,500,000
2022 Orioles: Jackson Holliday, SS, Stillwater (Okla.) HS	$8,190,000

**Part of major league contract*

Record Year

One of the biggest strengths of the 2023 class was the number of up-the-middle hitters in the class.

On the college and high school sides of the draft, there were plenty of players who had the bats to go in the first round and the defensive profiles to project for extremely well-rounded profiles at valuable spots on the diamond.

There's perhaps no better proxy for that sort of player than shortstops—and there were plenty of shortstops selected in the first round this year.

In fact, according to our partners at Pramana, the 10 shortstops who were taken among the top 28 picks tied 2021 for the most shortstops selected within that range of any draft.

While the depth of offensive talent up the middle was a clear strength of the 2023 class, the college lefthanded demographic was a very notable weakness.

In fact, we wondered earlier this spring whether a college lefthander would be selected in the first round in order to keep alive a 44-year draft streak.

That didn't happen, and the streak is now broken. In fact, not a single lefthanded pitcher of any demographic was taken in the first round, with No. 19 Thomas White being the first southpaw selected in the supplemental first to the Marlins at No. 35.

Another notable pitcher record this year was the fact that Noble Meyer was the only high school pitcher taken in the first round. That is the new record for the fewest number of high school arms in a first round—ever.

The First Draft Lottery

A little less than two hours before the results were announced on MLB Network, Major League Baseball conducted the actual selections for the draft lottery.

Fourteen ping pong balls numbered from 1 to 14 were placed in an airblown lottery machine provided by Smart Play. Smart Play is the same company that also provides lottery devices for the NBA and NHL draft lotteries.

A representative from PriceWaterhouseCoopers was in attendance to observe the procedure. MLB also invited a pool reporter, JJ Cooper of Baseball America, to witness the selections.

The 14 ping pong balls themselves were brought to the event in a carrying case that was sealed. When the time came to conduct the lottery, MLB's John D'Angelo cut the wires that had sealed the case. The balls were then placed in the hopper. D'Angelo also videotaped the announcement of the date and location, while holding a Dec. 6 copy of the San Diego Union-Tribune newspaper to further verify the date.

The balls were then allowed to rotate for 15 seconds, before a button was pressed. That opened the top of the hopper. Every 15 seconds, the button was pressed again, until four balls had been collected. That four-digit code was then checked against a list of all 1,001 possible four-digit combinations. The first ball was 11, the second was eight, the third was 10.

Because the four-digit code would be read in numerical order, that code combination ensured that many teams remained in play for the first pick. If the number one ball came up in any one of the four slots, only the Nationals or Athletics would match that code. If the number two ball was the lowest number to come up in a four-digit code, then only the Athletics, Pirates or Reds could match that code.

But if only higher numbers appeared among the four ping pong balls, the teams with much lower odds would be selected. For instance, there were only two possible combinations by which the Brewers could win a top six pick: 10-11-13-14 or 10-12-13-14.

With no number under eight among the first three, many of the teams with lower odds remained in play. If the final ball had been the 13 or 14, the Red Sox would have picked first. If the final ball was the nine, the Twins would have the No. 1 pick. If the final ball had been the seven, the Angels would have selected first. If the six had come up, it would have been the Marlins. Five would have meant the Rangers would pick first. Four would have meant the Tigers would have the No. 1 selection, and three would have resulted in a Royals No. 1 pick.

The fourth and final ball was a two, which meant the Pirates, the team with the third-worst record, lept into the No. 1 spot, becoming the first winner of the MLB draft lottery.

The second time, the four-digit code was 3-5-1-13, which meant the Nationals picked second. The third pick saw 12-4-13-11 come through the hopper, which meant the Tigers picked third. The fourth time was a Pirates code. Since they had already won the first pick, this was declared null. The next time it was 10-5-8-9. The Rangers picked fourth.

The fifth pick saw 1-5-14-3. Since there was a one in the code, only the Nationals or Athletics could win with this combination. All the A's needed as the fourth ball climbed through the output tube was for that last ball to be greater than five. But when a three popped up, it meant that the code was a Nationals' match. That was

THE BONUS RECORD

Rick Monday, the No. 1 overall pick in baseball's first draft in 1965, signed with the Athletics for $100,000—a figure that no draftee bettered for a decade. The record has been broken many times since, including in 2019, when Adley Rutschman signed with the Orioles as the No. 1 overall pick for $8,100,000. Spencer Torkelson broke the record immediately, signing for $8,416,300 as the No. 1 pick in the 2020 draft with the Tigers. Paul Skenes is now the newest record holder.

The longest bonus record stretch dates back to Todd Demeter, whose $208,000 bonus in 1979 held the mark for nine years until 1988 when Andy Benes topped him with a $235,000 bonus.

The list below represents only cash bonuses and doesn't include guaranteed money from major league deals, college scholarship plans or incentives. It doesn't include draft picks who signed after being granted free agency.

Year	Player, Pos., Club (Round)	Bonus
1965	Rick Monday, OF, Athletics (1)	$100,000
1975	Danny Goodwin, C, Angels (1)	$125,000
1978	Kirk Gibson, OF, Tigers (1)	$150,000
	*Bob Horner, 3B, Braves (1)	$162,000
1979	Todd Demeter, 1B, Yankees (2)	$208,000
1988	Andy Benes, RHP, Padres (1)	$235,000
1989	Tyler Houston, C, Braves (1)	$241,500
	*Ben McDonald, RHP, Orioles (1)	$350,000
	*John Olerud, 1B, Blue Jays (3)	$575,000
1991	Mike Kelly, OF, Braves (1)	$575,000
	Brien Taylor, LHP, Yankees (1)	$1,550,000
1994	Paul Wilson, RHP, Mets (1)	$1,550,000
	Josh Booty, 3B, Marlins (1)	$1,600,000
1996	Kris Benson, RHP, Pirates (1)	$2,000,000
1997	Rick Ankiel, LHP, Cardinals (2)	$2,500,000
	Matt Anderson, RHP, Tigers (1)	$2,505,000
1998	*J.D. Drew, OF, Cardinals (1)	$3,000,000
	*Pat Burrell, 3B, Phillies (1)	$3,150,000
	Mark Mulder, LHP, Athletics (1)	$3,200,000
	Corey Patterson, OF, Cubs (1)	$3,700,000
1999	Josh Hamilton, OF, Devil Rays (1)	$3,960,000
2000	Joe Borchard, OF, White Sox (1)	$5,300,000
2005	Justin Upton, SS, D-backs (1)	$6,100,000
2008	Tim Beckham, SS, Rays (1)	$6,150,000
	Buster Posey, C, Giants (1)	$6,200,000
2009	Donavan Tate, OF, Padres (1)	$6,250,000
	*Stephen Strasburg, RHP, Nationals (1)	$7,500,000
2011	Gerrit Cole, RHP, Pirates (1)	$8,000,000
2019	Adley Rutschman, C, Orioles (1)	$8,100,000
2020	Spencer Torkelson, 3B, Tigers (1)	$8,416,300
2023	Paul Skenes, RHP, Pirates (1)	$9,200,000

**Part of major league contract.*

DRAFT

BONUSES VS. PICK VALUES

Here is a comparison of the top 50 siginging bonuses in the 2023 draft class when compared to the assigned slot values for those picks.

Player, Pos., Team (Round/Overall Pick)	Bonus	Pick Value
1. Paul Skenes, RHP, Louisiana State (1st round/No. 1)	$9,200,000	$9,721,000
2. Dylan Crews, OF, Louisiana State (1st round/No. 2)	$9,000,000	$8,998,500
3. Wyatt Langford, OF, Florida (1st round/No. 4)	$8,000,000	$7,698,000
4. Max Clark, OF, Franklin (Ind.) Community HS (1st round/No. 3)	$7,697,500	$8,341,700
5. Walker Jenkins, OF, South Brunswick HS, Southport, N.C. (1st round/No. 5)	$7,144,200	$7,139,700
6. Chase Dollander, RHP, Tennessee (1st round/No. 9)	$5,716,900	$5,716,900
7. Rhett Lowder, RHP, Wake Forest (1st round/No. 7)	$5,700,000	$6,275,200
8. Jacob Wilson, SS, Grand Canyon (1st round/No. 6)	$5,500,000	$6,634,000
9. Nolan Schanuel, 1B, Florida Atlantic (1st round/No. 11)	$5,253,000	$5,253,000
10. Blake Mitchell, C, Sinton (Texas) HS (1st round/No. 8)	$4,897,500	$5,980,100
11. Matt Shaw, SS, Maryland (1st round/No. 13)	$4,848,500	$4,848,500
12. Noble Meyer, RHP, Jesuit HS, Portland, Ore. (1st round/No. 10)	$4,500,000	$5,475,300
13. Tommy Troy, SS, Stanford (1st round/No. 12)	$4,400,000	$5,043,800
14. Enrique Bradfield, OF, Vanderbilt (1st round/No. 17)	$4,169,700	$4,169,700
15. Thomas White, LHP, Phillips Academy, Andover, Mass. (1st round supp. round/No. 35)	$4,100,000	$2,420,900
16. Kyle Teel, C, Virginia (1st round/No. 14)	$4,000,000	$4,663,100
17. Bryce Eldridge, TWP, James Madison HS (1st round/No. 16)	$3,997,500	$4,326,600
18. Jacob Gonzalez, SS, Ole Miss (1st round/No. 15)	$3,900,000	$4,488,600
19. Brayden Taylor, SS, Texas Christian (1st round/No. 19)	$3,877,600	$3,880,100
20. Colt Emerson, SS, Glenn HS, New Concord, Ohio (1st round/No. 22)	$3,800,000	$3,496,600
21. Chase Davis, OF, Arizona (1st round/No. 21)	$3,618,200	$3,618,200
22. George Lombard, SS, Gulliver Prep HS, Miami (1st round/No. 26)	$3,300,000	$3,065,000
23. Jonny Farmelo, OF, Westfield HS, Chantilly, Va. (1st round/No. 29)	$3,200,000	$2,800,700
24. Brock Wilken, 3B, Wake Forest (1st round/No. 18)	$3,150,000	$4,021,400
25. Aidan Miller, SS, Mitchell HS, New Port Richey, Fla. (1st round/No. 27)	$3,100,000	$2,968,800
26. Arjun Nimmala, SS, Strawberry Crest HS, Dover, Fla. (1st round/No. 20)	$3,000,000	$3,746,000
27. Nazzan Zanetello, SS, Christian Brothers College HS, St. Louis, Mo. (2nd round/No. 50)	$3,000,000	$1,698,000
28. Steven Echavarria, RHP, Millburn (N.J.) HS (3rd round/No. 72)	$3,000,000	$1,005,700
29. Hurston Waldrep, RHP, Florida (1st round/No. 24)	$2,997,500	$3,270,500
30. Walker Martin, SS, Eaton (Colo.) HS (2nd round/No. 52)	$2,997,500	$1,620,800
31. Kevin McGonigle, SS, Monsignor Bonner HS, Drexel Hill, Penn. (1st round supp. round/No. 37)	$2,847,500	$2,309,500
32. Dillon Head, OF, Homewood-Flossmoor HS, Flossmoor, Ill. (1st round/No. 25)	$2,800,000	$3,165,400
33. Blake Wolters, RHP, Mahomet-Seymour HS, Mahomet, Ill. (2nd round/No. 44)	$2,800,000	$1,951,600
34. Colin Houck, SS, Parkview HS, Lilburn, Ga. (1st round supp. round/No. 32)	$2,750,000	$2,607,500
35. Yohandy Morales, 3B, Miami (2nd round/No. 40)	$2,600,000	$2,144,700
36. Travis Sykora, RHP, Round Rock (Texas) HS (3rd round/No. 71)	$2,600,000	$1,021,300
37. Ralphy Velazquez, C, Huntington Beach (Calif.) HS (1st round/No. 23)	$2,500,000	$3,380,900
38. Tai Peete, SS, Trinity Christian HS, Sharpsburg, Ga. (1st round supp. round/No. 30)	$2,500,000	$2,732,500
39. Sammy Stafura, SS, Walter Panas HS, Cortlandt Manor, N.Y. (2nd round/No. 43)	$2,497,500	$1,998,200
40. Charlee Soto, RHP, Reborn Christian Academy HS, Kissimmee, Fla. (1st round supp. round/No. 34)	$2,481,400	$2,481,400
41. Brice Matthews, SS, Nebraska (1st round/No. 28)	$2,478,200	$2,880,700
42. Alexander Clemmey, LHP, Bishop Hendricken HS, Warwick, R.I. (2nd round/No. 58)	$2,300,000	$1,402,600
43. Myles Naylor, 3B, St. Joan of Arc Catholic SS, Mississauga, Ont. (1st round supp. round/No. 39)	$2,202,500	$2,202,500
44. Ty Floyd, RHP, Louisiana State (1st round supp. round/No. 38)	$2,097,500	$2,255,100
45. Adrian Santana, SS, Doral (Fla.) Academy (1st round supp. round/No. 31)	$2,002,950	$2,670,600
46. Josh Knoth, RHP, Patchogue-Medford HS, Medford, N.Y. (1st round supp. round/No. 33)	$2,000,000	$2,543,800
47. Drue Hackenberg, RHP, Virginia Tech (2nd round/No. 59)	$1,997,500	$1,369,300
48. Cole Schoenwetter, RHP, San Marcos HS, Santa Barbara, Calif. (4th round/No. 105)	$1,897,500	$640,300
49. Kendall George, OF, Atascocita HS (1st round supp. round/No. 36)	$1,847,500	$2,362,700
50. Zander Mueth, RHP, Atascocita HS, Humble, Tex. (2nd round supp. round/No. 67)	$1,797,500	$1,128,200
Total	**$188,063,150**	**$185,635,200**

also declared as a null selection.

The second try for the fifth pick saw the code 10-8-13-9. Since there were no low numbers, it meant that a team with lower odds would climb up significantly. The result was the Twins lept from 13th to fifth. Only nine of the 1,001 combinations would result in a top-six Twins pick. This was one of those nine combinations.

The sixth and final pick saw a combination of 10-1-11-12. That was one of the A's 165 different available combinations, ending the team's slide from being one of the three teams with the best odds (16.5%) to the final team to be selected in the lottery.

DRAFT 2023 TOP 100 PICKS

DRAFT

Team, Player, Pos., School	Bonus
1. PIT: Paul Skenes, RHP, Louisiana State	9,200,000
2. WAS: Dylan Crews, OF, Louisiana State	9,000,000
3. DET: Max Clark, OF, Franklin (Ind.) Community HS	7,697,500
4. TEX: Wyatt Langford, OF, Florida	8,000,000
5. MIN: Walker Jenkins, OF, South Brunswick HS, Southport, N.C.	7,144,200
6. OAK: Jacob Wilson, SS, Grand Canyon	5,500,000
7. CIN: Rhett Lowder, RHP, Wake Forest	5,700,000
8. KC: Blake Mitchell, C, Sinton (Texas) HS	4,897,500
9. COL: Chase Dollander, RHP, Tennessee	5,716,900
10. MIA: Noble Meyer, RHP, Jesuit HS, Portland, Ore.	4,500,000
11. LAA: Nolan Schanuel, 1B, Florida Atlantic	5,253,000
12. ARI: Tommy Troy, SS, Stanford	4,400,000
13. CHC: Matt Shaw, SS, Maryland	4,848,500
14. BOS: Kyle Teel, C, Virginia	4,000,000
15. CHW: Jacob Gonzalez, SS, Mississippi	3,900,000
16. SFG: Bryce Eldridge, TWP, Madison HS, Vienna, Va.	3,997,500
17. BAL: Enrique Bradfield, OF, Vanderbilt	4,169,700
18. MIL: Brock Wilken, 3B, Wake Forest	3,150,000
19. TB: Brayden Taylor, SS, Texas Christian	3,877,600
20. TOR: Arjun Nimmala, SS, Strawberry Crest HS, Dover, Fla.	3,000,000
21. STL: Chase Davis, OF, Arizona	3,618,200
22. SEA: Colt Emerson, SS, Glenn HS, New Concord, Ohio	3,800,000
23. CLE: Ralphy Velazquez, C, Huntington Beach (Calif.) HS	2,500,000
24. ATL: Hurston Waldrep, RHP, Florida	2,997,500
25. SDP: Dillon Head, OF, Homewood-Flossmoor HS, Flossmoor, Ill.	2,800,000
26. NYY: George Lombard, SS, Gulliver Prep HS, Miami	3,300,000
27. PHI: Aidan Miller, SS, Mitchell HS, New Port Richey, Fla.	3,100,000
28. HOU: Brice Matthews, SS, Nebraska	2,478,200
29. SEA: Jonny Farmelo, OF, Westfield HS, Chantilly, Va.	3,200,000
30. SEA: Tai Peete, SS, Trinity Christian HS, Sharpsburg, Ga.	2,500,000
31. TB: Adrian Santana, SS, Doral (Fla.) Academy	2,002,950
32. NYM: Colin Houck, SS, Parkview HS, Lilburn, Ga.	2,750,000
33. MIL: Josh Knoth, RHP, Patchogue-Medford HS, Medford, N.Y.	2,000,000
34. MIN: Charlee Soto, RHP, Reborn Christian HS, Kissimmee, Fla.	2,481,400
35. MIA: Thomas White, LHP, Phillips Academy, Andover, Mass.	4,100,000
36. LAD: Kendall George, OF, Atascocita HS, Humble, Tex.	1,847,500
37. DET: Kevin McGonigle, SS, Bonner HS, Drexel Hill, Penn.	2,847,500
38. CIN: Ty Floyd, RHP, Louisiana State	2,097,500
39. OAK: Myles Naylor, 3B, St. Joan of Arc Catholic SS, Mississauga, Ont.	2,202,500
40. WAS: Yohandy Morales, 3B, Miami	2600,000
41. OAK: Ryan Lasko, OF, Rutgers	1,700,000
42. PIT: Mitch Jebb, SS, Michigan State	1,647,500
43. CIN: Sammy Stafura, SS, Walter Panas HS, Cortlandt Manor, N.Y.	2,497,500
44. KC: Blake Wolters, RHP, Mahomet-Seymour HS, Mahomet, Ill.	2,800,000
45. DET: Max Anderson, 2B, Nebraska	1,429,650
46. COL: Sean Sullivan, LHP, Wake Forest	1,700,000
47. MIA: Kemp Alderman, OF, Mississippi	1,400,000
48. ARI: Gino Groover, 3B, North Carolina State	1,783,000
49. MIN: Luke Keaschall, 2B, Arizona State	1,500,000
50. BOS: Nazzan Zanetello, SS, Christian Brothers HS, St. Louis, Mo.	3,000,000
51. CHW: Grant Taylor, RHP, Louisiana State	1,659,800
52. SFG: Walker Martin, SS, Eaton (Colo.) HS	2,997,500
53. BAL: Mac Horvath, OF, North Carolina	1,400,000
54. MIL: Mike Boeve, 3B, Nebraska-Omaha	1,250,000
55. TB: Colton Ledbetter, OF, Mississippi State	1,297,500
56. NYM: Brandon Sproat, RHP, Florida	1,474,500
57. SEA: Ben Williamson, 3B, William & Mary	600,000
58. CLE: Alexander Clemmey, LHP, Bishop Hendricken HS, Warwick, R.I.	2,300,000
59. ATL: Drue Hackenberg, RHP, Virginia Tech	1,997,500
60. LAD: Jake Gelof, 3B, Virginia	1,334,400
61. HOU: Alonzo Tredwell, RHP, UCLA	1,497,500
62. CLE: Andrew Walters, RHP, Miami	955,275
63. BAL: Jackson Baumeister, RHP, Florida State	1,605,100
64. ARI: Caden Grice, LHP, Clemson	1,250,000
65. COL: Cole Carrigg, C, San Diego State	1,300,000
66. KC: Carson Roccaforte, OF, Louisiana-Lafayette	897,500
67. PIT: Zander Mueth, RHP, Belleville Township East HS, Illinois	1,797,500
68. CHC: Jaxon Wiggins, RHP, Arkansas	1,401,500
69. SFG: Joe Whitman, LHP, Kent State	805,575
70. ATL: Cade Kuehler, RHP, Campbell	1,045,000
71. WAS: Travis Sykora, RHP, Round Rock (Texas) HS	2,600,000
72. OAK: Steven Echavarria, RHP, Millburn (N.J.) HS	3,000,000
73. PIT: Garret Forrester, 3B, Oregon State	772,500
74. CIN: Hunter Hollan, LHP, Arkansas	597,500
75. KC: Hiro Wyatt, RHP, Staples HS, Westport, Conn.	1,497,500
76. DET: Paul Wilson, LHP, Lakeridge HS, Lake Oswego, Oregon	1,697,500
77. COL: Jack Mahoney, RHP, South Carolina	925,000
78. MIA: Brock Vradenburg, 1B, Michigan State	916,000
79. LAA: Alberto Rios, 3B, Stanford	847,500
80. ARI: Jack Hurley, OF, Virginia Tech	887,000
81. CHC: Josh Rivera, SS, Florida	725,000
82. MIN: Brandon Winokur, OF, Edison HS, Huntington Beach, Calif.	1,500,000
83. BOS: Antonio Anderson, SS, North Atlanta HS, Ga.	1,500,000
84. CHW: Seth Keener, RHP, Wake Forest	800,000
85. SFG: Cole Foster, SS, Auburn	747,500
86. BAL: Kiefer Lord, RHP, Washington	760,000
87. MIL: Eric Bitonti, SS, Aquinas HS, San Bernardino, Calif.	1,750,000
88. TB: Tre' Morgan, 1B, Louisiana State	781,300
89. TOR: Juaron Watts-Brown, RHP, Oklahoma State	1,002,785
90. STL: Travis Honeyman, OF, Boston College	700,000
91. NYM: Nolan McLean, TWP, Oklahoma State	747,600
92. SEA: Teddy McGraw, RHP, Wake Forest	600,000
93. CLE: C.J. Kayfus, OF, Miami	700,000
94. ATL: Sabin Ceballos, SS, Oregon	597,500
95. LAD: Brady Smith, RHP, Grainger HS, Rutledge, Tenn.	703,000
96. SDP: JD Gonzalez, C, Hernandez HS, Humacao, P.R.	550,000
97. NYY: Kyle Carr, LHP, Palomar (Calif.) JC	692,000
98. PHI: Devin Saltiban, SS, Hilo (Hawaii) HS	602,500
99. HOU: Jake Bloss, RHP, Georgetown	497,500
100. BAL: Tavian Josenberger, OF, Arkansas	603,000

MICHAEL ZAGARIS

The A's selected Grand Canyon shortstop Jacob Wilson with the sixth pick.

2023 CLUB-BY-CLUB SELECTIONS

Order Of Selection In Parentheses | Players Signed In Bold

DRAFT

ARIZONA DIAMONDBACKS (11)

1. Tommy Troy, SS, Stanford
2. Gino Groover, 3B, North Carolina State
2s. Caden Grice, LHP, Clemson
3. Jack Hurley, OF, Virginia Tech
4. Grayson Hitt, LHP, Alabama
5. Kevin Sim, 3B, San Diego
6. Philip Abner, LHP, Florida
7. Ryan Bruno, LHP, Stanford
8. Jackson Feltner, 1B, Morehead State
9. Kyle Amendt, RHP, Dallas Baptist
10. Zane Russell, RHP, Dallas Baptist
11. Casey Anderson, RHP, Utah Valley
12. Sam Knowlton, RHP,South Alabama
13. Hayden Durke, RHP, Rice
14. Jake Fitzgibbons, LHP, Tennessee
15. Rio Britton, LHP, North Carolina State
16. Matthew Linskey, RHP, Rice
17. Carlos Rey, LHP, Nova Southeastern (Fla.)
18. Alec Baker, RHP, Dallas Baptist
19. Wyatt Crenshaw, 2B, Arizona State
20. Dominic Voegele, RHP, Columbia (Ill.) HS

ATLANTA BRAVES (25)

1. Hurston Waldrep, RHP, Florida
2. Drue Hackenberg, RHP, Virginia Tech
2s. Cade Kuehler, RHP, Campbell
3. Sabin Ceballos, SS, Oregon
4. Garrett Baumann, RHP, Hagerty HS
5. Isaiah Drake, OF, North Atlanta HS
6. Lucas Braun, RHP, Cal State Northridge
7. Justin Long, RHP, Rice
8. Cory Wall, RHP, William & Mary
9. Riley Gowens, RHP, Illinois
10. Pier-Olivier Boucher, OF, Southern Illinois–Carbondale
11. Jace Grady, OF, Dallas Baptist
12. Brady Day, 2B, Kansas State
13. Will Verdung, 3B, Itawamba (Miss.) JC
14. Mitch Farris, LHP, Wingate (N.C.)
15. David Rodriguez, RHP, San Joaquin Delta (Calif.) JC
16. Isaac Gallegos, RHP, New Mexico
17. Kade Kern, OF, Ohio State
18. Cam Magee, SS, Washington State
19. Riley Frey, LHP, Milwaukee
20. Will King, C, Eastern Kentucky

BALTIMORE ORIOLES (17)

1. Enrique Bradfield, OF, Vanderbilt
2. Mac Horvath, OF, North Carolina
2s. Jackson Baumeister, RHP, Florida State
3. Kiefer Lord, RHP, Washington
3. Tavian Josenberger, OF, Arkansas
4. Levi Wells, RHP, Texas State
5. Jake Cunningham, OF, UNC Charlotte
6. Jacob Cravey, RHP, Samford
7. Teddy Sharkey, RHP, Coastal Carolina
8. Braxton Bragg, RHP, Dallas Baptist
9. Zach Fruit, RHP, Troy
10. Matthew Etzel, OF, Southern Mississippi
11. Nestor German, RHP, Seattle
12. Blake Money, RHP, LSU
13. Riley Cooper, LHP, LSU
14. Michael Forret, RHP, State JC of Florida
15. Qrey Lott, OF, Lowndes HS, Valdosta, Ga.

MITCHELL LAYTON

Vanderbilt's Enrique Bradfield was Baltimore's No. 1 pick.

16. Cole Urman, C, Cal State Fullerton
17. Zane Barnhart, RHP, Hillsdale (Mich.) College
18. Tanner Witt, RHP, Texas
19. Kollin Ritchie, SS, Atoka (Okla.) HS
20. Jalen Vasquez, SS, North Greenville (S.C).

BOSTON RED SOX (14)

1. Kyle Teel, C, Virginia
2. Nazzan Zanetello, SS, Christian Brothers HS, St. Louis
3. Antonio Anderson, SS, North Atlanta HS
4. Matthew Duffy, RHP, Canisius
4s. Kristian Campbell, SS, Georgia Tech
4s. Justin Riemer, SS, Wright State
5. Connelly Early, LHP, Virginia
6. CJ Weins, RHP, Western Kentucky
7. Caden Rose, OF, Alabama
8. Trennor O'Donnell, RHP, Ball State
9. Blake Wehunt, RHP, Kennesaw State
10. Ryan Ammons, LHP, Clemson
11. Nelson Taylor, OF, Polk State (Fla.) JC
12. Max Carlson, RHP, North Carolina
13. Cade Feeney, RHP, North Dakota State
14. Joseph Ingrassia, LHP, Cal State Fullerton
15. Phoenix Call, SS, Calabasas (Calif.) HS
16. Isaac Stebens, RHP, Oklahoma State
17. Dylan Schlaegel, OF, Legacy HS, Mansfield, Texas
18. Zach Fogell, LHP, Connecticut
19. Stanley Tucker, OF, Texas A&M
20. Robert Orloski, RHP, Middleton (Idaho.) HS

CHICAGO CUBS (12)

1. Matt Shaw, SS, Maryland
2s. Jaxon Wiggins, RHP, Arkansas
3. Josh Rivera, SS, Florida
4. Will Sanders, RHP, South Carolina
5. Michael Carico, C, Davidson
6. Alfonsin Rosario, OF, P27 Academy, Lexington, S.C.
7. Yahil Melendez, SS, B You Academy, Caguas, P.R.
8. Brett Bateman, OF, Minnesota
9. Jonathan Long, 1B, Long Beach State
10. Luis Martinez-Gomez, RHP, Temple JC
11. Zyhir Hope, OF, Colonial Forge HS, Stafford, Va.
12. Carter Trice, 2B, North Carolina State
13. Sam Armstrong, RHP, Old Dominion
14. Grayson Moore, RHP, Vanderbilt
15. Ty Johnson, RHP, Ball State
16. Daniel Brown, LHP, Campbell
17. Ethan Flanagan, LHP, UCLA
18. Brian Kalmer, 3B, Gonzaga
19. Nick Dean, RHP, Maryland
20. Drew Bowser, 3B, Stanford

CHICAGO WHITE SOX (15)

1. Jacob Gonzalez, SS, Ole Miss
2. Grant Taylor, RHP, LSU
3. Seth Keener, RHP, Wake Forest
4. Calvin Harris, C, Ole Miss
5. Christian Oppor, LHP, Gulf Coast (Fla.) JC
6. Lucas Gordon, LHP, Texas
7. George Wolkow, OF, Downers Grove (Ill.) North HS
8. Eddie Park, OF, Stanford
9. Jake Peppers, RHP, Jacksonville State
10. Zach Franklin, RHP, Missouri
11. Rikuu Nishida, 2B, Oregon
12. Mathias LaCombe, RHP, Cochise (Ariz.) JC
13. Ryan Galanie, 3B, Wofford
14. Edrick Felix, 2B, Florida Gulf Coast
15. Carlton Perkins, RHP, Cowley County (Kan.) CC
16. Weston Eberly, C, Columbia
17. Mikey Kane, IF, Oregon State
18. Anthony Imhoff, LHP, Pima (Ariz.) CC
19. Caden Connor, OF, Cal State Fullerton
20. Garrett Wright, RHP, TCU

CINCINNATI REDS (4)

1. Rhett Lowder, RHP, Wake Forest
1s. Ty Floyd, RHP, LSU
2. Sammy Stafura, SS, Walter Panas HS
3. Hunter Hollan, LHP, Arkansas
4. Cole Schoenwetter, RHP, San Marcos HS, Santa Barbara, Calif.
5. Connor Burns, C, Long Beach State
6. Ethan O'Donnell, OF, Virginia
7. Dominic Pitelli, SS, Miami
8. Carter Graham, 1B, Stanford
9. Logan Van Treeck, LHP, Lipscomb
10. Graham Osman, LHP, Long Beach State
11. Jack Moss, 1B, Texas A&M
12. Simon Miller, RHP, Texas-San Antonio
13. Cody Adcock, RHP, Arkansas
14. Kyle Henley, OF, Denmark HS, Alpharetta, Ga.
15. Dylan Simmons, RHP, Pittsburgh
16. Bernard Moon, SS, Redan HS, Stone Mountain, Ga.
17. JeanPierre Ortiz, TWP, Chipola (Fla.) JC
18. Drew Pestka, RHP, John A. Logan (Ill.) JC
19. Herick Hernandez, LHP, Miami Dade (Fla.) JC
20. Gabe Gaeckle, RHP, Aptos (Calif.) HS

JAY BIGGERSTAFF

Wake Forest's Rhett Lowder was the Reds' first pick in the 2023 draft.

DRAFT

CLEVELAND GUARDIANS (24)

1. Ralphy Velazquez, C, Huntington Beach (Calif.) HS
2. Alexander Clemmey, LHP, Bishop Hendricken HS, Warwick, R.I.
2s. Andrew Walters, RHP, Miami
3. C.J. Kayfus, OF, Miami
4. Cooper Ingle, C, Clemson
5. Christian Knapczyk, SS, Louisville
6. Tommy Hawke, OF, Wake Forest
7. Alex Mooney, SS, Duke
8. Jonah Advincula, OF, Washington State
9. Jay Driver, RHP, Harvard
10. Matthew Wilkinson, LHP, Central Arizona JC
11. Johnny Tincher, C, Washington
12. Keegan Zinn, RHP, Lake Minneola (Fla.) HS
13. Jacob Bresnahan, LHP, Sumner (Wash.) HS
14. Zane Morehouse, RHP, Texas
15. Kyle Scott, RHP, Lackawanna (Pa.) JC
16. Jeffrey Heuer, RHP, Georgia Home Education HS, Brooks, Ga.
17. Barrett Riebock, OF, Paris (Texas) JC
18. Matt Jachec, RHP, Indiana State
19. Josh Harlow, RHP, Mercer
20. Ryan Marohn, LHP, Freedom HS, Woodbridge, Va.

COLORADO ROCKIES (8)

1. Chase Dollander, RHP, Tennessee
2. Sean Sullivan, LHP, Wake Forest
2s. Cole Carrigg, C, San Diego State
3. Jack Mahoney, RHP, South Carolina
4. Isaiah Coupet, LHP, Ohio State
5. Kyle Karros, 3B, UCLA
6. Cade Denton, RHP, Oral Roberts
7. Seth Halvorsen, RHP, Tennessee
8. Braylen Wimmer, 2B, South Carolina
9. Ben McCabe, C, Central Florida
10. Jace Kaminska, RHP, Nebraska
11. Stu Flesland, LHP, Washington
12. Bryson Hammer, LHP, Dallas Baptist
13. Caleb Hobson, OF, Tennessee Martin
14. Hunter Mann, RHP, Tennessee Tech
15. Darius Perry, C, UCLA
16. Austin Emener, LHP, East Tennessee State
17. Aidan Longwell, 1B, Kent State
18. Yanzel Correa, RHP, International Baseball Academy, Ceiba, P.R.
19. Kannon Handy, LHP, Colorado Mesa
20. Troy Butler, RHP, Herkimer County (N.Y.) JC

DETROIT TIGERS (6)

1. Max Clark, OF, Franklin (Ind.) Community HS

1s. Kevin McGonigle, SS, Monsignor Bonner HS, Drexel, Pa.
2. Max Anderson, 2B, Nebraska
3. Paul Wilson, LHP, Lakeridge (Ore.) HS
4. Carson Rucker, 3B, Goodpasture Christian HS, Madison, Tenn.
5. Jaden Hamm, RHP, Middle Tennessee State
6. Bennett Lee, C, Wake Forest
7. John Peck, SS, Pepperdine
8. Jatnk Diaz, RHP, Hazleton (Pa.) Area HS
9. Hayden Minton, RHP, Missouri State
10. Andrew Sears, LHP, Connecticut
11. Jim Jarvis, SS, Alabama
12. Andrew Dunford, RHP, Houston County HS, Warner Robins, Ga.
13. Brett Callahan, OF, Saint Joseph's
14. David Smith, 2B, Connecticut
15. Brady Cerkownyk, C, Connors State (Okla.) JC
16. Donye Evans, RHP, UNC Charlotte
17. Bradley Stewart, LHP, Cooper City (Fla.) HS
18. Ethan Farris, 3B, Cypress (Texas) Woods HS
19. Blake Pivaroff, RHP, Arizona State
20. Johnathan Rogers, RHP, Tupelo (Miss.) HS

HOUSTON ASTROS (30)

1. Brice Matthews, SS, Nebraska
2. Alonzo Tredwell, RHP, UCLA
3. Jake Bloss, RHP, Georgetown
4. Cameron Fisher, OF, UNC Charlotte
5. Chase Jaworsky, SS, Rock Canyon HS, Highland Ranch, Colo.
6. Ethan Pecko, RHP, Towson
7. Joey Dixon, RHP, Stanford
8. Ryan Johnson, 2B, Pepperdine
9. Jeron Williams, SS, Toledo
10. Austin Deming, 3B, Howard (Texas) JC
11. Nehomar Ochoa, OF, Galena Park (Texas) HS
12. Anthony Huezo, OF, Etiwanda (Calf.) HS
13. James Hicks, RHP, South Carolina
14. Jackson Nezuh, RHP, Louisiana Lafayette
15. Garret Guillemette, C, Texas
16. Will Bush, C, Tyler (Texas) JC
17. Colby Langford, LHP, Murray State (Okla.) JC
18. Derek True, RHP, Cal Poly
19. Andrew Duncan, OF, A3 Academy, Tampa, Fla.
20. Pascanel Ferreras, SS, Western Carolina

KANSAS CITY ROYALS (5)

1. Blake Mitchell, C, Sinton (Texas) HS
2. Blake Wolters, RHP, Mahomet-Seymour HS, Mahomet, Il..
2s. Carson Roccaforte, OF, Louisiana Lafayette
3. Hiro Wyatt, RHP, Staples HS, Westport, Conn.
4. Hunter Owen, LHP, Vanderbilt
5. Spencer Nivens, OF, Missouri State
6. Coleman Picard, RHP, Bryant
7. Trevor Werner, TWP, Texas A&M
8. Dustin Dickerson, SS, Southern Mississippi
9. Jacob Widener, LHP, Oral Roberts
10. Justin Johnson, SS, Wake Forest
11. Jared Dickey, OF, Tennessee
12. Logan Martin, RHP, Kentucky
13. Ethan Bosacker, RHP, Xavier
14. Mason Miller, LHP, Florida Gulf Coast
15. Chase Isbell, RHP, Auburn
16. Josh Hansell, RHP, Arizona State
17. Connor Oliver, LHP, Miami
18. Stone Russell, C, IMG Academy, Bradenton, Fla.
19. Donovan LaSalle, OF, Barbe HS, Lake Charles, La.
20. Blake Wilson, SS, Santa Margarita Catholic HS, Rancho Santa Margarita, Calif.

BRACE HEMMELGARN

The Angels' Nolan Schanuel became the first 2023 draftee to reach the majors.

LOS ANGELES ANGELS (10)

1. Nolan Schanuel, 1B, Florida Atlantic
3. Alberto Rios, 3B, Stanford
4. Joe Redfield, OF, Sam Houston
5. Chris Clark, RHP, Harvard
6. Camden Minacci, RHP, Wake Forest
7. Cole Fontenelle, 3B, TCU
8. Barrett Kent, RHP, Pottsboro (Texas) HS
9. Chase Gockel, RHP, Quincy (Ill.) University
10. Chris Barraza, RHP, Arizona
11. John Wimmer, SS, Rock Hill (S.C.) HS
12. Sam Brown, 1B, Washington State
13. Riley Bauman, RHP, Abilene Christian
14. Zach Joyce, RHP, Tennessee
15. Caleb Ketchup, SS, Lipscomb
16. Rio Foster, OF, Florence-Darlington (S.C.) JC
17. Logan Britt, RHP, Abilene Christian
18. Dalton Kendrick, LHP, Memphis
19. Raudi Rodriguez, OF, Georgia Premier Academy, Statesboro, Ga.
20. Mac McCroskey, SS, Oral Roberts

LOS ANGELES DODGERS (26)

1. Kendall George, OF, Atascocita HS, Humble, Texas
2. Jake Gelof, 3B, Virginia
3. Brady Smith, RHP, Grainger HS, Rutledge, Tenn.
4. Wyatt Crowell, LHP, Florida State
4s. Dylan Campbell, OF, Texas
4s. Eriq Swan, RHP, Middle Tennessee State
5. Joe Vetrano, 1B, Boston College

6. Bryan Gonzalez, SS, Carlos Beltran Baseball Academy, Florida, P.R.
7. Patrick Copen, RHP, Marshall
8. Jaron Elkins, OF, Goodpasture Christian HS, Madison, Tenn.
9. Ryan Brown, RHP, Ball State
10. Sam Mongelli, SS, Sacred Heart
11. Carson Hobbs, RHP, Samford
12. Noah Ruen, RHP, Tyler (Texas) JC
13. Alex Makarewich, RHP, Northwestern State
14. Jaxon Jelkin, RHP, South Mountain (Ariz.) JC
15. Jordan Thompson, SS, LSU
16. Javen Coleman, LHP, LSU
17. Luke Fox, LHP, Duke
18. Sterling Patick, LHP, South Hills HS, West Covina, Calif.
19. Spencer Green, RHP, Richland HS
20. David Uiagalelei, RHP, Oregon State

MIAMI MARLINS (9)

1. Noble Meyer, RHP, Jesuit HS, Portland, Ore.
1s. Thomas White, LHP, Phillips Academy, Andover, Mass.
2. Kemp Alderman, OF, Ole Miss
3. Brock Vradenburg, 1B, Michigan State
4. Emmett Olson, LHP, Nebraska
5. Andrew Lindsey, RHP, Tennessee
6. Jake DeLeo, OF, Georgia Tech
7. Justin Storm, LHP, Southern Mississippi
8. Nick Maldonado, RHP, Vanderbilt
9. Colby Shade, OF, Oregon
10. Xavier Meachem, RHP, North Carolina A&T
11. Jake Brooks, RHP, UCLA
12. Josh Ekness, RHP, Houston
13. Colson Lawrence, OF, South Alabama
14. Jack Sellinger, LHP, UNLV
15. Nigel Belgrave, RHP, Maryland
16. Kevin Vaupel, LHP, Seton Hill
17. Mark Coley, OF, Rhode Island
18. Tristan Dietrich, LHP, Owen J. Roberts HS, Pottstown, Pa.
19. Johnny Olmstead, 3B, Southern California
20. Ryan Ignoffo, TWP, Eastern Illinois

MILWAUKEE BREWERS (18)

1. Brock Wilken, 3B, Wake Forest
1s. Josh Knoth, RHP, Patchogue Medford HS, Medford, N.Y.
2. Mike Boeve, 3B, Nebraska-Omaha
3. Eric Bitonti, SS, Aquinas HS, San Bernardino, Calif.
4. Jason Woodward, RHP, Florida Gulf Coast
5. Ryan Birchard, RHP, Niagara County (N.Y.) JC
6. Cooper Pratt, SS, Magnolia Heights HS, Senatobia, Miss.
7. Tate Kuehner, LHP, Louisville
8. Craig Yoho, RHP, Indiana
9. Mark Manfredi, LHP, Dayton
10. Morris Austin, RHP, Houston Christian
11. Bishop Letson, RHP, Floyd Central HS, Floyd Knobs, Ind.
12. Bjorn Johnson, LHP, Lincoln HS, Tacoma, Wash.
13. Brett Wichrowski, RHP, Bryant
14. Hayden Robinson, RHP, Berwick (La.) HS
15. Josh Adamczewski, SS, Lake Central HS
16. Josh Timmerman, RHP, Ohio State
17. Jacob Gholston, RHP, Flower Mound (Texas) HS
18. Dylan Watts, RHP, Tacoma (Wash.) JC
19. Isaac Morton, RHP, Spring Lake Park (Minn.) HS
20. Justin Chambers, LHP, Basha HS, Chandler, Ariz.

MINNESOTA TWINS (13)

1. Walker Jenkins, OF, South Brunswick HS, Southport, N.C.
1s. Charlee Soto, RHP, Reborn Christian HS, Kissimmee, Fla.
2. Luke Keaschall, 2B, Arizona State
3. Brandon Winokur, OF, Edison HS, Fresno, Calif.
4. Tanner Hall, RHP, Southern Mississippi
5. Dylan Questad, RHP, Waterford (Wisc.) HS
6. Jay Harry, SS, Penn State
7. Nolan Santos, RHP, Bethune-Cookman
8. Jace Stoffal, RHP, Oregon
9. Jack Dougherty, RHP, Ole Miss
10. Ross Dunn, LHP, Arizona State
11. Ty Langenberg, RHP, Iowa
12. Paulshawn Pasqualotto, RHP, California
13. Jeremy Lee, RHP, South Alabama
14. Xander Hamilton, RHP, Appalachian State
15. Spencer Bengard, RHP, California Baptist
16. Anthony Silvas, RHP, Riverside (Calif.) CC
17. Kade Bragg, LHP, Angelo State
18. Hector Garcia, RHP, Hope International (Calif.)
19. Sam Parker, 1B, Kennesaw Mountain HS, Kennesaw, Ga.
20. Ashton Larson, OF, Saint Thomas Aquinas HS, Overland Park, Kan.

NEW YORK METS (22)

1. Colin Houck, SS, Parkview HS, Lilburn, Ga.
2. Brandon Sproat, RHP, Florida
3. Nolan McLean, 3B/RHP, Oklahoma State
3. Kade Morris, RHP, Nevada
4. Wyatt Hudepohl, RHP, UNC Charlotte
4s. A.J. Ewing, SS, Springboro (Ohio) HS
4s. Austin Troesser, RHP, Missouri
5. Zach Thornton, LHP, Grand Canyon
6. Jack Wenninger, RHP, Illinois
7. Noah Hall, RHP, South Carolina
8. Boston Baro, SS, Capistrano Valley HS, Mission Viejo, Calif.
9. Nick Lorusso, 3B, Maryland
10. Christian Pregent, C, Stetson
11. Brett Banks, RHP, UNC Wilmington
12. Brady Kirtner, RHP, Virginia Tech
13. Ben Simon, RHP, Elon
14. John Valle, RHP, Jefferson HS, Tampa, Fla.
15. Justin Lawson, RHP, North Carolina State
16. Jacob Zitella, 3B, St Charles (Ill.) East HS
17. Bryce Jenkins, RHP, Tennessee
18. Gavyn Jones, LHP, White Oak (Texas) HS
19. Christian Little, RHP, LSU
20. Kellum Clark, OF, Mississippi State

NEW YORK YANKEES (28)

1. George Lombard Jr., SS, Gulliver Prep HS, Miami
3. Kyle Carr, LHP, Palomar (Calif.) JC
4. Roc Riggio, 2B, Oklahoma State
6. Cade Smith, RHP, Mississippi State
7. Kiko Romero, 1B, Arizona
8. Nicholas Judice, RHP, Louisiana-Monroe
9. Jared Wegner, OF, Arkansas
10. Brian Hendry, RHP, Oklahoma State
11. Josh Grosz, RHP, East Carolina
12. Brady Rose, LHP, Dallas Baptist
13. Josh Tiedemann, TWP, Hamilton HS, Chandler, Ariz.
14. Danny Flatt, RHP, P27 Academy, Lexington, S.C.
15. Tomas Frick, C, North Carolina
16. Andrew Landry, RHP, Southeastern Louisiana
17. Wilson Rodriguez, OF, Academia Presbiteriana HS, Carolina, P.R.
18. Coby Morales, OF, Washington
19. Cade Austin, RHP, South Carolina
20. Bryce Warrecker, RHP, Cal Poly

OAKLAND ATHLETICS (2)

1. Jacob Wilson, SS, Grand Canyon
1s. Myles Naylor, 3B, St Joan Of Arc Catholic SS, Mississauga, Ont.

DRAFT

2. Ryan Lasko, OF, Rutgers
3. Steven Echavarria, RHP, Millburn (N.J.) HS
4. Cole Miller, RHP, Newbury Park (Calif.) HS
5. Nathan Dettmer, RHP, Texas A&M
6. Jonah Cox, OF, Oral Roberts
7. Nate Nankil, OF, Cal State Fullerton
8. Jackson Finley, RHP, Georgia Tech
9. Corey Avant, RHP, Wingate
10. Tom Reisinger, RHP, East Stroudsburg (Pa.)
11. Drew Conover, RHP, Rutgers
12. Cole Conn, C, Illinois–Chicago
13. Will Johnston, LHP, Texas A&M
14. Luke Mann, 3B, Missouri
15. Will Simpson, OF, Washington
16. Ryan Brown, RHP, Oregon State
17. Colby Halter, 2B, Florida
18. Derrick Tarpley, OF, Brownsville (Pa.) Area HS
19. Derek Salata, RHP, Illinois State
20. Diego Barrera, LHP, Loyola Marymount

PHILADELPHIA PHILLIES (29)

1. Aidan Miller, SS, J.W. Mitchell HS, New Port Richey, Fla.
3. Devin Saltiban, SS, Hilo (Hawaii) HS
4. TayShaun Walton, OF, IMG Academy, Bradenton, Fla.
6. George Klassen, RHP, Minnesota
7. Jacob Eddington, RHP, Missouri State
8. Bryson Ware, 3B, Auburn
9. Avery Owusu-Asiedu, OF, Southern Illinois–Edwardsville
10. Cam Brown, RHP, TCU
11. Kehden Hettiger, C, Sierra Canyon HS, Chatsworth, Calif.
12. Brandon Beckel, RHP, Texas Tech
13. Marty Gair, RHP, Florida Southwestern JC
14. Zach Arnold, SS, Houston
15. Jared Thomas, C, Loyola Marymount
16. Luke Russo, RHP, Eastern Michigan
17. A.J. Shaver, OF, Florida Southwestern JC
18. Ethan Chenault, RHP, UNC Wilmington
19. Casey Steward, RHP, Washburn (Kan.)
20. Pierce Bennett, 2B, Wake Forest

PITTSBURGH PIRATES (3)

1. Paul Skenes, RHP, LSU
2. Mitch Jebb, SS, Michigan State
2s. Zander Mueth, RHP, Belleville (Ill.) East HS
3. Garret Forrester, 3B, Oregon State
4. Carlson Reed, RHP, West Virginia
5. Patrick Reilly, RHP, Vanderbilt
6. Hunter Furtado, LHP, Alabama
7. Jaden Woods, LHP, Georgia
8. Austin Strickland, RHP, Kentucky
9. Danny Carrion, RHP, California-Davis
10. Landon Tomkins, RHP, Louisiana Tech
11. Magdiel Cotto, LHP, Kentucky
12. Khristian Curtis, RHP, Arizona State
13. Charles McAdoo, 2B, San Jose State
14. Garrett McMillan, RHP, Alabama
15. John Lopez, C, Puerto Rico Baseball Academy, Gurabo, P.R.
16. Justin Miknis, C, Kent State
17. Daniel Cuvet, 3B, ESB Academy, Pembroke Pines, Fla.
18. Kalae Harrison, SS, North Carolina State
19. Tyler Kennedy, RHP, Florida Southwestern JC
20. Peyton Stumbo, RHP, Nevada

SAN DIEGO PADRES (27)

1. Dillon Head, OF, Homewood Flossmoor HS, Flossmoor, Ill.
3. JD Gonzalez, C, Anita Otero Hernandez HS, Humacao, P.R.
4. Homer Bush, OF, Grand Canyon
6. Jay Beshears, 2B, Duke
7. Tucker Musgrove, TWP, Mobile
8. Kannon Kemp, RHP, Weatherford (Texas) HS
9. Ryan Wilson, OF, Davidson
10. Nik McClaughry, SS, Arizona
11. Carson Montgomery, RHP, Florida State
12. Blake Dickerson, LHP, Ocean Lakes HS, Virginia Beach, Va.
13. Dane Lais, RHP, Oregon City (Ore.) HS
14. Tyler Morgan, RHP, Abilene Christian
15. Zac Addkison, RHP, Marshall
16. Sam Whiting, RHP, UC Santa Barbara
17. Eric Yost, RHP, Northeastern
18. Harry Gustin, LHP, Hawaii
19. Adler Cecil, LHP, Temecula Valley HS, Temecula, Calif.
20. B.Y. Choi, SS, New Mexico Military Institute

SAN FRANCISCO GIANTS (16)

1. Bryce Eldridge, TWP, James Madison HS
2. Walker Martin, SS, Eaton (Colo.) HS
2s. Joe Whitman, LHP, Kent State
3. Cole Foster, SS, Auburn
4. Maui Ahuna, SS, Tennessee
5. Quinn McDaniel, 2B, Maine
6. Luke Shliger, C, Maryland
7. Scott Bandura, OF, Princeton
8. Josh Bostick, RHP, Grayson (Texas) JC
9. Charlie Szykowny, 3B, Illinois–Chicago
10. Ryan Vanderhei, RHP, TCU
11. Jack Payton, C, Louisville
12. Timmy Manning, LHP, Arizona State
13. Jose Ortiz, OF, Leadership Christian Academy, Guaynabo, P.R.
14. Cale Lansville, RHP, San Jacinto (Texas) JC
15. Dylan Carmouche, LHP, Tulane
16. Justin Wishkoski, 3B, Sam Houston
17. Drew Cavanaugh, C, Florida Southern
18. Michael Rodriguez, LHP, North Greenville (S.C.)
19. Tom Kane, LHP, Maryland
20. Nadir Lewis, OF, Princeton

SEATTLE MARINERS (23)

1. Colt Emerson, SS, John Glenn HS, New Concord, Ohio
1s. Jonny Farmelo, OF, Westfield HS, Chantilly, Va.
1s. Tai Peete, SS, Trinity Christian HS, Sharpsburg, Ga.
2. Ben Williamson, 3B, William & Mary
3. Teddy McGraw, RHP, Wake Forest
4. Aidan Smith, OF, Lovejoy HS, Lucas, Texas
5. Brock Rodden, SS, Wichita State
6. Brody Hopkins, RHP, Winthrop
7. Ty Cummings, RHP, Campbell
8. Ryan Hawks, RHP, Louisville
9. RJ Schreck, OF, Vanderbilt
10. Jared Sundstrom, OF, UC Santa Barbara
11. Brandyn Garcia, LHP, Texas A&M
12. Logan Evans, RHP, Pittsburgh
13. Elijah Dale, RHP, Illinois State
14. Ernie Day, RHP, Campbell
15. Carson Jones, OF, Virginia Tech
16. Caleb Cali, 3B, Arkansas
17. Jacob Sharp, C, UNLV
18. Daniel Ouderkirk, RHP, Penn State
19. Charlie Pagliarini, 3B, Fairfield
20. William Watson, RHP, San Joaquin Delta (Calif.) JC

ST. LOUIS CARDINALS (21)

1. Chase Davis, OF, Arizona
3. Travis Honeyman, OF, Boston College
4. Quinn Mathews, LHP, Stanford

SAMUEL LEWIS

Florida's Wyatt Langford has already made it to Triple-A for the Rangers.

5. Zach Levenson, OF, Miami
6. Jason Savacool, RHP, Maryland
7. Charles Harrison, RHP, UCLA
8. Ixan Henderson, LHP, Fresno State
9. Christian Worley, RHP, Virginia Tech
10. Caden Kendle, OF, California-Irvine
11. Dakota Harris, SS, Oklahoma
12. Brayden Jobert, OF, LSU
13. William Sullivan, 1B, Troy
14. Jacob Odle, RHP, Orange Coast (Calif.) JC
15. Tre Richardson, SS, TCU
16. Tyler Bradt, RHP, East Carolina
17. Trey Paige, 3B, Delaware State
18. Hunter Kublick, RHP, Umpqua (Ore.) JC
19. Graysen Tarlow, C, Cal State Northridge
20. Cameron Johnson, LHP, IMG Academy, Bradenton, Fla.

TAMPA BAY RAYS (19)

1. Brayden Taylor, SS, TCU
1s. Adrian Santana, SS, Doral (Fla.) Academy
2. Colton Ledbetter, OF, Mississippi State
3. Tre' Morgan, 1B, LSU
4. Hunter Haas, SS, Texas A&M
5. Trevor Harrison, RHP, J.W. Mitchell HS, New Port Richey, Fla.
6. T.J. Nichols, RHP, Arizona
7. Owen Wild, RHP, Gonzaga
8. Drew Dowd, LHP, Stanford
9. Dalton Fowler, LHP, Memphis
10. Adam Boucher, RHP, Duke
11. Garrett Edwards, RHP, LSU
12. Chandler Murphy, RHP, Missouri
13. Bryan Broecker, C, Michigan State
14. T.J. Fondtain, OF, San Diego State
15. Will Stevens, RHP, Tarleton State
16. Wooyeoul Shin, 1B, Miami Dade JC
17. Hayden Snelsire, RHP, Randolph-Macon (Va.)
18. Jeremy Pilon, LHP, Ecole Secondaire Du Chene-Bleu, Pincourt, QC
19. Owen Stevenson, RHP, Arizona State
20. Max Stanley, RHP, Douglas County HS, Castle Rock, Colo.

TEXAS RANGERS (7)

1. Wyatt Langford, OF, Florida
4. Skylar Hales, RHP, Santa Clara
5. Alejandro Rosario, RHP, Miami
6. Caden Scarborough, RHP, Harmony (Fla.) HS
7. Izack Tiger, RHP, Butler County (Kan.) JC
8. Julian Brock, C, Louisiana Lafayette
9. Quincy Scott, OF, Palomar (Calif.) JC
10. Case Matter, RHP, Washington
11. Max Martin, OF, Southridge HS, Kennewick, Wash.
12. Paul Bonzagni, RHP, Southern Illinois–Carbondale
13. William Privette, RHP, College Of Charleston
14. Josh Trentadue, LHP, JC Of Southern Idaho
15. Michael Trausch, LHP, Central Arizona JC
16. Jake Brown, LHP, Sulphur (La.) HS
17. Kamdyn Perry, RHP, Bishop Gorman HS, Las Vegas
18. Brendan Morse, RHP, Niagara County (N.Y.) JC
19. Elijah Ickes, OF, Kamehameha HS, Honolulu, Hawaii
20. Laif Palmer, RHP, Golden (Colo.) HS

TORONTO BLUE JAYS (20)

1. Arjun Nimmala, SS, Strawberry Crest HS, Dover, Fla.
3. Juaron Watts-Brown, RHP, Oklahoma State
4. Landen Maroudis, RHP, Calvary Christian HS, Clearwater, Fla.
5. Connor O'Halloran, LHP, Michigan
6. Jace Bohrofen, OF, Arkansas
7. Nick Goodwin, SS, Kansas State
8. Braden Barry, OF, West Virginia
9. Sam Shaw, OF, Lambrick Park SS, Victoria, B.C.
10. Josh Mollerus, RHP, Oregon
11. Grant Rogers, RHP, Mcneese State
12. Chay Yeager, RHP, Pasco Hernando (La.) JC
13. Brennan Orf, OF, Southern Illinois–Edwardsville
14. Joe Vogatsky, RHP, James Madison
15. Kelena Sauer, RHP, San Diego State
16. Jackson Hornung, C, Skidmore (N.Y.)
17. Sam Kulasingam, 1B, Air Force
18. Chase Brunson, OF, San Clemente (Calif.) HS
19. Aaron Munson, RHP, Angelo State
20. Kai Peterson, LHP, Sierra (Calif.) JC

WASHINGTON NATIONALS (1)

1. Dylan Crews, OF, LSU
2. Yohandy Morales, 3B, Miami
3. Travis Sykora, RHP, Round Rock (Texas) HS
4. Andrew Pinckney, OF, Alabama
5. Marcus Brown, SS, Oklahoma State
6. Gavin Dugas, 2B, LSU
7. Ryan Snell, C, Lamar
8. Jared Simpson, LHP, Iowa
9. Thomas Schultz, RHP, Vanderbilt
10. Phillip Glasser, SS, Indiana
11. Gavin Adams, RHP, Indian River (Fla.) JC
12. Travis Sthele, RHP, Texas
13. Liam Sullivan, LHP, Georgia
14. Elijah Nunez, OF, TCU
15. Mikey Tepper, RHP, Liberty
16. Austin Amaral, RHP, Stetson
17. Merrick Baldo, RHP, Loyola Marymount
18. Nate Rombach, C, Dallas Baptist
19. James Ellwanger, RHP, Magnolia (Texas) West HS
20. Isaac Ayon, RHP, Oregon

APPENDIX

OBITUARIES

Jesus Alou, a key member of the first wave of Dominican players to break into the majors, died March 10. He was 80.

He was the youngest of the trio of Alou brothers to make it to the majors. At a time when the number of Latino players in MLB could be counted on fingers and toes, Alou was in many ways a trailblazer, but he also was following a path that had been cleared in years prior.

After all, his oldest brother Felipe and his older brother Matty had preceded Jesus with the Giants. All three were signed by Chick Genovese. The trio of Alous formed the outfield for Escogido in the winter Dominican League, and they all played together for the Giants in 1963. That was the only year the three got to play together, because Felipe was traded to the Braves after the season.

Jesus' name created discomfort for the media in San Francisco, who had a fear of being perceived as sacrilegious. Where there were many efforts to use a nickname, Jesus stuck to his desire to be called by his name and eventually the media relented.

Jesus Alou could always hit for average, but his aggressiveness was his weakness. He never walked more than 21 times in any season, which explains his career .280/.305/.353 slash line. Alou had a six-hit game in 1964, making him one of now 117 players to achieve that feat in a nine-inning game.

Alou was part of the Athletics' World Series champion teams in 1973 and '74. He played 1,380 games over a 15-year MLB career.

LOUIS REQUENA/MLB VIA GETTY IMAGES

Vida Blue was named as the American League MVP in 1971

Sal Bando was one of the best players on the last team to win three consecutive World Series. A sixth-round pick of the Athletics in the first-ever draft in 1965 out of Arizona State, Bando became the club's everyday third baseman during its final year in Kansas City in 1967.

By 1969 he was an all-star who hit a career-best 31 home runs. Bando finished second in American League MVP voting in 1971 and was an AL all-star in 1972, '73 and '74 as the A's won the World Series each year.

Like the rest of Oakland's stars, including Hall of Famers Reggie Jackson, Catfish Hunter and Rollie Fingers, Bando left the club following the advent of free agency.

In Bando's case, it was truly an escape because he had feuded regularly with A's owner Charlie Finley. Bando spent the final five years of his career, 1977 to '81, with the Brewers, though his power had begun to wane by that point.

Bando hit 242 career home runs. He received MVP votes in seven seasons. After his playing career ended, he served as the Brewers' general manager from late 1991 to 1999.

Bando's Brewers teams did not have much success, though Milwaukee did win 92 games in 1992. That was the only winning record they recorded during his tenure.

Bando died on Jan. 20, 2023 after what his family described as a five-year battle with cancer. He was 78.

On a team filled with stars, **Vida Blue** was truly a force of nature.

Blue's 1971 season set the Athletics on their path to dominate baseball for the next five seasons. First, a 21-year-old Blue announced himself to the baseball world by going 24-8, 1.82 with 301 strikeouts 312 innings in 1971.

It was the kind of season that is nearly impossible to match today. Blue led the American League in ERA, shutouts (eight) and strikeout rate (8.7 per nine innings), making him the overwhelming choice not only for the AL Cy Young Award but

APPENDIX

also for MVP.

Oakland won 101 games and the American League West in 1971 to make the franchise's first postseason appearance in 40 years. Connie Mack's 1931 Philadelphia club had been the last A's playoff team.

In 1972, the A's won their first of three consecutive World Series titles with Blue a part of a rotation that also featured Catfish Hunter, Blue Moon Odom and Ken Holtzman.

Blue remained one of the better pitchers in baseball for most of the 1970s. A's owner Charlie Finley tried twice to sell his contract to other teams, only to have MLB commissioner Bowie Kuhn halt the trades. He was one of the last stars remaining in 1977 as Oakland's once loaded roster was dismantled by the arrival of free agency.

Eventually, Blue was traded to the Giants, where he spent four seasons from 1977 to 1981. After two years with the Royals, he was one of a number of players suspended for cocaine use. He returned for two more seasons after his year-long suspension in 1984.

Blue remained on the Hall of Fame ballot for four years, receiving 8.7% of votes in his peak year of 1993.

A six-time all-star, Blue finished his career with 209 wins, 161 losses and a 3.27 career ERA. He is the all-time Oakland leader with 1,315 strikeouts. Blue died on May 6, 2023. He was 73.

Sonny Bowers, a longtime scout with four organizations, died Jan. 21. He was 75. Bowers had played minor league ball with the Senators and Rangers and then became a coach at Baylor. But his passion and skills in scouting led to jobs with the MLB Scouting Bureau, Pirates, Red Sox, Braves and Phillies. He worked for the Phillies for two decades, retiring in 2015. He was inducted into the Texas Scouts Association Hall of Fame in 2010.

Tom Browning was largely a pitcher known for durability and reliability than dominating stuff, but every once in a while, he could dominate.

Browning threw just the third perfect game in National League history in 1988 against the eventual-champion Dodgers.

Browning led the NL in games started in four different seasons and averaged 235 innings a season from 1985 to 1991. He was a key part of the Reds' World Series championship team in 1990.

Browning threw all but 10 of his 1,921 MLB innings with the Reds, finishing his career in 1995 with the Royals. He went 123-90, 3.94 for his career. He died on Dec. 19, 2022. He was 62.

Bill Campbell had a stretch in the mid 1970s when he was one of the best relievers in the game. He led the American League with 31 saves in 1977 in his first year with the Red Sox.

But it was his final season with the Twins in 1976 that deserves to be remembered. Campbell led the league with 78 appearances as he went 17-5 and threw 167.2 innings while working exclusively as a reliever. He saved 20 games. Campbell died on Jan. 6. He was 74.

Jim Caple had the knack for finding a different slant to a story than the masses.

It was a trait that was apparent when he was a longtime baseball writer for ESPN.com's Page 2, when he covered the Twins for the St. Paul Pioneer Press for more than a decade, and when he was one of the first employees of Baseball America in the 1980s.

Caple was battling ALS and dementia at the time of his passing. He died on Oct. 1. He was 61.

Pat Corrales had a nine-year big league career as a backup catcher, but that proved to be just the prelude to a life in the game. Corrales got his most consistent playing time in 1965 as a rookie, but even then it was just 207 plate appearances. He quickly was pegged as a backup. He was traded to the Cardinals to be Tim McCarver's backup in 1965 and spent four seasons as Johnny Bench's backup in Cincinnati from 1968 to 1972. Corrales' MLB playing career ended in 1973. He was hired as the Rangers' third base coach in 1976.

Two years later, he became the first manager of Mexican-American descent when he was tabbed for the job when Billy Hunter was fired with one game to go in the season. Corrales led the Rangers to a winning record in 1979 but was fired after the 1980 season. He managed a season and a half for the Phillies in 1982 and '83 and then five and a half seasons with Cleveland from 1983 to '87.

He then became a coach for the Braves, working with former high school rival and friend Bobby Cox. He coached for the Braves for 17 seasons from 1990 to 2006 and for the Nationals afterward. He died on Aug. 27, 2023. He was 82.

Over a lifetime of work, longtime minor league general manager **John Dittrich** truly did it all. He ran teams at all levels of the minors, from the independent leagues and Rookie ball to Class

A, Double-A, Triple-A and the major leagues. Everywhere he went, Dittrich connected with the community. He was one of the baseball lifers who came up through the minors at a time when making personal connections was one of the few ways to thrive during the years when operating a minor league team was often a shoestring operation.

Dittrich was the first GM for the Fargo-Moorhead RedHawks, which quickly became one of the more successful independent league teams in the 1990s. He also worked for five years for the Rangers in their front office. Dittrich died on July 19, 203. He was 73.

Nate Colbert's career was brief, but for a stretch in the early 1970s the Padres first baseman was one of the most feared power hitters in the game.

Originally signed by the Cardinals, Colbert was selected by the Astros in the 1965 Rule 5 draft. The Rule 5 draft rules at the time made first-year players eligible in large numbers in an attempt to tamp down signing bonuses.

Colbert got just seven plate appearances while sitting on Houston's bench in 1966. He didn't get back to the majors again until 1968, and then was picked by the Padres in the expansion draft after that season.

In San Diego, Colbert became a star. He hit 24 home runs in the Padres' inaugural season of 1969 and averaged 30 homers a season for his first five years with the club. He was a three-time all-star and tied Stan Musial's record when he hit five home runs in a doubleheader.

Colbert's career was soon derailed by a degenerative back injury. He hit 149 home runs by the end of his age-27 season but hit just 24 more in three more seasons before retiring in 1976.

Colbert died on Jan. 5, 2023. He was 76.

As a catcher, **Harry Dunlop** had the best seat in the house for one of the best pitching performances of all time. He was the catcher when Bristol righthander Ron Necciai struck out 27 batters in a no-hitter in the Appalachian League on May 13, 1952.

Dunlop inadvertently helped Necciai reach 27 strikeouts. He failed to block strike three against one batter, allowing him to reach, and he dropped a foul popup that gave Necciai a chance to finish the batter off with a strikeout instead.

That was one of Dunlop's first games as a pro, but in May of that year he ended up catching three no-hitters for Bristol. Necciai's follow-up to his 27-strikeout game saw him strike out 24 while throwing a two-hitter.

Dunlop was a minor league manager who won nearly 900 games. He also was a major league coach with five different teams. His final stint came with the Marlins in 2005.

Dunlop was 89 when he died on Nov. 17, 2022.

Dave Elder, a righthander who pitched in the Cleveland bullpen in 2003 and '04, died Jan. 31. He was 47. Elder was a fourth-round pick of the Rangers out of Georgia Tech in 1997. He was traded to Cleveland for John Rocker in 2001.

The list of the most significant minor league team owners of the past 50 years is incomplete without **David Elmore** near the top. The founder of the Elmore Sports Group, he was the owner of numerous minor league teams over the years as well as hockey, football and soccer teams.

Elmore's time as an MiLB owner stretched over multiple decades. He was long one of the top minor league decision-makers. He served on the MiLB board of trustees and the Pacific Coast League's executive committee.

The Elmore Sports Group owned at different times the Eugene Emeralds, Birmingham Barons, Colorado Springs Sky Sox, Idaho Falls Chukars, Lynchburg Hillcats, Inland Empire 66ers and San Antonio Missions.

Elmore was elected to the PCL and Texas League Halls of Fame and was honored as the "King of Baseball" at the 2016 Winter Meetings.

Elmore died on June 7, 2023. He was 88.

George Frazier, a major league pitcher and long-time MLB broadcaster, died on June 19, 2023. He was 68.

Frazier pitched on two College World Series teams at Oklahoma in 1975 and 1976. He broke into the majors with the Cardinals in 1978, but in the early 1980s he found his footing with the Yankees as a durable and reliable righthanded reliever.

Frazier pitched in three games in the 1981 World Series, losing all three to tie a World Series record. He made it back to the World Series six seasons later with the 1987 Twins, this time winning a ring in his final season in the majors.

After his 10-year MLB career had concluded, Frazier became a broadcaster. As a color commentator, Frazier broadcast Rockies games from 1998 to 2015.

OBITUARIES

Alex Herrera, a lefthander who made 12 appearances with Cleveland as a reliever in 2002 and 2003, died Feb. 16. He was 43. Herrera had last played in the affiliated minors in 2006 with Triple-A Toledo, but he played for nearly another decade with appearances in Italy and the Venezuelan League.

Rick Hummel covered the Cardinals and the major leagues for more than half a century. Hummel first worked as the Cardinals' beat writer for the St. Louis Post-Dispatch for 24 years, from 1978 through 2001. He then became the Post-Dispatch's national baseball columnist.

Hummel covered 42 consecutive All-Star Games and 35 World Series. He was the 2006 honoree for the BBWAA career excellence award, which is displayed at the Hall of Fame. While he retired at the end of the 2022 season, he made a trip to spring training again this year and wrote some freelance pieces.

Hummel died on May 20, 2023. He was 77.

Longtime scout **Dan Huston** died unexpectedly in his sleep at his home in Redmond, Ore., on July 18, 2023. He was 63.

Huston was an area scout for more than 30 years for the Astros, Reds, Padres and Brewers. He spent most of his career scouting the Pacific Northwest before finishing as the Brewers' area scout for Central and Southern California from 2009 to 2019. He signed two-time American League stolen base champion Brian Hunter and current major leaguers Mitch Haniger, Tyrone Taylor and Clayton Andrews, among others.

"As a baseball scout, he worked tirelessly for his boys, for his guys," his widow Debbie said. "The guys who he felt had that talent—and he had the eye to spot the talent and he knew it—he fought so hard for them to be drafted where they should have been, where they needed to be in those draft sessions. He worked so diligently for them. He fought so hard for them."

Mike Ivie reached the major leagues young, played in parts of 11 seasons and once hit 27 home runs in a season while playing half his games in San Francisco's Candlestick Park.

Ivie also was the No. 1 pick in the 1970 draft by the Padres as a high school catcher from Atlanta. He had a powerful righthanded bat and, according to Hall of Fame catcher Johnny Bench, the softest hands behind the plate.

Padres scouting director Bob Fontaine Sr. is quoted in BA's Ultimate Draft Book as saying that Ivie "could have caught at the major league level the day we signed him. He was the best kid catcher I ever had seen, and I haven't seen anyone better since."

The trouble for Ivie was that early in his pro career he developed a mental block about throwing the ball back to the pitcher and did not live up to expectations. He resisted playing the position that made him the first overall pick and did not play catcher regularly above the Class A California League.

When Ivie reached San Diego for good as a 22-year-old in 1975 he was primarily a first baseman. He started just five games at catcher in the big leagues, four of them during a six-game cup of coffee with the Padres in 1971.

Ivie produced at a league-average rate for the Padres from 1975 to 1977. A trade to the Giants in 1978 set the stage for his best MLB run. Ivie produced a 126 OPS+ with the Giants in 1978 and 1979, in the latter season belting 27 homers with 89 RBIs.

Ivie died July 21, 2023 in North Augusta, S.C. He was 70.

Carl Kline, a photographer for Baseball America for many years, died Feb. 16, 2023. He was 74.

Kline served in the Air Force from 1966 to '72 as a reconnaissance photographer. That photography bug never left him, and he merged it with his deep love of baseball.

Kline shot photos for BA for many years, and his work was featured on a number of magazine covers. Even more importantly, he had a knack for making connections with people, whether fans, players or coaches, whenever he was at the ballpark.

Pete Koegel, a catcher/corner infielder who spent parts of three seasons in the majors in the early 1970s, died Feb. 4, 2023. He was 75. Koegel made his MLB debut with the Brewers during their inaugural season in 1970. He was then traded to the Phillies during the 1971 season. His longest stint in the majors came with Philadelphia in 1972.

Ron Labinski, one of the most influential stadium architects of all time, died Jan. 1, 2023. He was 85.

Labinski was the designer of many stadiums, but his work as the creator of Oriole Park at Camden

LOUIS REQUENA/MLB VIA GETTY IMAGES

Tim McCarver had an excellent career as a player, and an even better one as a broadcaster

Yards in Baltimore is his lasting legacy. By creating a ballpark that managed to both be modern but with design touches from an earlier age of stadiums, he ushered in a trend that has lasted in ballpark construction in the ensuing three decades.

Although he was listed at 5-foot-10, 170 pounds, nearly every contemporary reference about **Hobie Landrith** referred to him as short.

He was often also described as being a light hitter, but the catcher was also always described as smart, which helps explain how he managed to put together a 14-year major league career from 1950-63 despite being a career .233 hitter with just 34 home runs in 772 games.

Landrith broke into the majors in 1950 with the Reds for a brief cup of coffee. He didn't find firmer footing until 1953, when he became a regular backup catcher. That was the role he largely filled for the rest of his career.

Landrith topped 300 plate appearances just twice in 14 years, but he kept finding landing spots, suiting up for the Reds, Giants, Orioles, Cardinals, Senators, Mets and Cubs.

Landrith died on April 6, 2023. He was 93.

Ted Lerner, the owner of the Washington Nationals for almost the entirety of their history, died on Feb. 12, 2023. He was 97.

The Nationals relocated to Washington, D.C. while still owned by Major League Baseball, but MLB's intent was to sell the former Montreal Expos franchise to an ownership group, preferably one with strong ties to the city.

Lerner fit that perfectly. He was a Washington Senators fan growing up, and his purchase ensured the long-term return of baseball to D.C. Under Lerner, the Nationals opened Nationals Park in 2008 and won a World Series in 2019.

Tim McCarver was one of the most successful catchers of the 1960s and a big reason the Cardinals won the World Series in 1964 and '67 and won the National League pennant in '68.

But his legacy as a broadcaster is such that it's easy to construct an argument that when he was playing baseball, he was only setting the stage for his true calling.

McCarver didn't make the Hall of Fame as a player, but he was the 2012 Ford Frick Award recipient, the award given at the Hall of Fame for the best broadcasters in the business. He called a record 24 World Series as a broadcaster and was a master of first-guessing, where he would explain his thought process of what a manager should do in-game before the result was known. Whether right or wrong, he helped the fan think through the strategic or tactical decisions in real time.

McCarver made his MLB debut in 1959 as a 17-year-old. That short eight-game stint, plus his six games with the Phillies in 1980 as a soon-to-retire 38-year-old made him one of the few players who could say he played in the majors in four different decades.

McCarver never hit .300 or 15 home runs in any season, but the lefthanded hitter was among the steadier offensive performers as a catcher in his era. He hit .295/.369/.452 with 14 home runs and 26 doubles in 1967 in his best year at the plate. That year he finished second in NL MVP balloting and was an all-star for one of the two times in his career.

But McCarver will be more remembered as a catcher who caught two of the all-time greats. He was behind the plate for all 21 World Series games the Cardinals played in the '60s. He caught Bob Gibson when Gibson was at the peak of his powers, and then he was the catcher who helped Steve Carlton mature into the best pitcher of the 1970s. McCarver and Carlton were separated when McCarver was traded to the Phillies after the 1969 season, but Carlton was then traded to Philadelphia as well, reuniting the two.

McCarver died on Feb. 16, 2023. He was 81.

Roman Mejias, considered one of the best players in Cuba in the 1950s and a nine-year MLB veteran, died Feb. 23, 2023. He was 97.

Mejias was already 26 when George Sisler scouted and signed him in 1953, but the Pirates announced him as a much younger 19-year-old. The speed with which he was pushed through the system makes more sense in this light.

Mejias put together a 55-game hitting streak for Waco in 1954 which still ranks as one of the longest in minor league history.

Mejias made his MLB debut in 1955 as a 29-year-old, but he was announced to be 21. He was a part-time player for the Pirates from 1957 to '59 and had cups of coffee in 1960 and '61.

But being picked by the Astros in the expansion draft gave Mejias a chance to show what he could do in 1962. He hit .286/.326/.445 with 24 home runs that year.

For 24 years, **John Odell** brought history to life for thousands of baseball fans. In his role as curator of history and research for the National Baseball Hall of Fame, Odell worked to turn the Hall's many artifacts into cohesive exhibits and stories to connect with the Hall's visitors.

Recently, he put together the "Viva Baseball" exhibit that examined the impact of Latino players with more than 150 exhibits and multimedia presentations. Odell died on July 17, 2023. He was 62

Luis Ortiz, a 20-year-old lefthander who was an active member of the Orioles' minor league system, died of cancer on March 11.

Ortiz signed with the Orioles in 2019, which meant his debut was delayed until 2021 because of the coronavirus pandemic. He made his pro debut in 2021, pitching in the Florida Complex League. After being diagnosed with cancer, he missed the entire 2022 season.

Albie Pearson, one of the shortest regulars in MLB history and the 1958 American League Rookie of the Year, died Feb. 21, 2023. He was 88. Pearson hit .275/.354/.358 for the Washington Senators as a rookie in 1958. Despite that impressive debut, Pearson didn't find his footing for a full-time job again until the 1961 Angels picked him from the Orioles in the expansion draft.

Pearson spent five years as a regular with the Angels. He led the league with 115 runs scored in 1962 and earned an all-star spot in 1963, when he hit .304/.402/.398 with six home runs and 17 stolen bases in 154 games.

Joe Pepitone, a three-time all-star for the Yankees in the 1960s and 12-year big league veteran, died March 13, 2023. He was 82.

Pepitone won three Gold Gloves at first base, and was a key regular on the Yankees' 1963 and '64 American League pennant- winners. The lefthanded hitter made the AL all-star team both seasons and averaged 28 homers and 94 RBIs while hitting .261/.292/.433. Pepitone's aggressiveness at the plate helped him hit 25 or more home runs five times, but he also had four seasons with a sub-.300 on-base percentage and finished his with a .301 mark.

Pepitone hit 166 home runs for the Yankees, and then also played for the Astros, Cubs and Braves. He retired after the 1973 season.

Gaylord Perry was the best spitballer the game has ever seen.

That's not hyperbole, and it's not rumor. There's no need to resort to innuendo when talking about Perry and his array of "illegal" pitches. He called his shot. And he did so with nearly half of his career still ahead of him.

In his autobiography "Me and the Spitter," published in 1974, Perry admitted that he had been throwing a spitball since 1964. Not coincidentally, Perry's career as a successful big league pitcher began in 1964.

Perry actually threw the spitball only from 1964 to 1967. A rules change forbidding pitchers from going to their mouth on the mound meant he had to adjust and throw greaseballs and use a variety of other foreign substances in the future.

He was the first pitcher to win a Cy Young Award in both the National and American leagues. He went 314-265 with a 3.11 ERA. He was the 15th pitcher ever to reach 300 wins when he reached the plateau in 1983. He is one of 10 pitchers to win at least 300 games and strike out at least 3,000 batters. Perry's 5,350 innings is sixth-highest total of all time.

Perry's success and durability earned him passage to the Hall of Fame in 1991. Perry died on Dec. 1, 2022. He was 84.

Jim Poole was one of the best relievers in Georgia Tech history, which set the stage for an 11-year MLB career as a reliable and durable lefthanded reliever.

As is often the case with relievers, Poole rarely spent too many seasons in any one place. A Dodgers draft pick, he debuted with Los Angeles in 1990, but that was the first of eight MLB teams for which he played.

His most famous season was 1995, when he was one of the key relievers in the American League pennant-winning Cleveland bullpen. Poole died on Oct. 6, 2023 from complications from ALS. He was 57.

Jim Price was the Tigers' backup catcher from 1967 to 1971. In that role, he got very comfortable hanging out in the dugout, which would serve him well later in life.

Price topped 200 plate appearances in a season only once, in 1969. He was the backup catcher on the Tigers' 1968 World Series champions, though he got just two PAs in the World Series.

Price decided to retire after the 1971 season, even though he was just turning 30. He found he had a talent for broadcasting and eventually became a fixture on Tigers broadcasts.

Price spent 31 years as a Tigers broadcaster, spending much of that time working with Ernie Harwell on the radio. He never retired and was still part of the Tigers' broadcast team in 2023.

Price passed away on Aug. 7. 2023. He was 81.

Mike Radcliff was a scout's scout.

Considered an exceptional evaluator, Radcliff was involved in the acquisition of generations of Twins players as one of the guiding forces in Minnesota's front office for more than three decades. Radcliff died on Feb. 3. He was 66.

Radcliff became the Twins' scouting director in 1993. He was promoted to vice president of player personnel in 2007. For much of that time he was in charge of both the Twins' drafts as well as the organization's international scouting.

Radcliff's hands were all over the Twins' rosters of the past 30 years. His first draft as scouting director was in 1993, when he picked Arkansas high school outfielder Torii Hunter in the first round. The next year, A.J. Pierzynski highlighted another solid draft. Doug Mientkiewicz was picked a year later, and Jacque Jones was part of the 1996 draft class.

Justin Morneau was drafted in 1999 and Joe Mauer was the No. 1 overall pick in 2001. That was a controversial pick at the time, because Southern California righthander Mark Prior was available in the same draft, but Radcliff's choice of the hometown Mauer proved to be wise.

Under his leadership, the Twins international scouting department produced Jorge Polanco, Max Kepler and others.

Radcliff was diagnosed with pancreatic cancer in 2019 but continued to scout and participate in Twins discussions as much as he was able.

Sometimes a man and a moment come together so perfectly that they will forever be inescapably intertwined.

When the Orioles headed to the World Series in 1970, third baseman **Brooks Robinson** was already an 11-time all-star, just weeks away from winning his 11th Gold Glove. He had been the 1964 American League MVP.

If the 1970 World Series had never occurred, Robinson would be a Hall of Famer. He was one of the best players of the 1960s and '70s.

Robinson's performance during the 1970 World Series is something that was so special, so transcendent, that baseball fans who weren't even born in 1970 can immediately picture Robinson diving at a ball hit down the third base line, his momentum taking him into foul territory to make a seemingly impossible play.

Robinson hit .429 (9-for-21) with two home runs and six RBIs over the five games as the Orioles won their second World Series in five seasons. But it was his defense in that series that has to be remembered.

OBITUARIES

SPX/DIAMOND IMAGES VIA GETTY IMAGES

Brooks Robinson may be the greatest defensive third baseman of all time.

Robinson ranged far to his right to field and then threw out Lee May in the sixth inning of Game 1. He quashed a potential rally in Game 3 by turning a double play on a Tony Perez ground ball. He caught a seemingly uncatchable foul ball off Johnny Bench's bat in the ninth inning of Game 5. Two outs later, he threw out Pat Corrales on a grounder to end the series. The announcement that Robinson was World Series MVP was one of the most obvious choices of all-time.

Robinson's career was too great to be summed up by one series, but it was a perfect embodiment of his greatness. His defense remains the gold standard for third basemen, as his 16 Gold Gloves can attest. He leads all third basemen in history in assists and double plays.

He also made 18 all-star appearances, racked up 2,848 hits, hit 268 home runs and drove in 1,357 runs. Robinson died on Sept. 26, 2023. He was 86 years old.

Ted Savage played for eight MLB teams in nine years from 1962 to '71 as a speedy outfielder who could capably handle center field. Unfortunately for his career development, he never hit enough to establish himself as a regular. He hit .233/.334/.361 over his MLB career but still managed to get into 642 games. He worked for the Cardinals, for whom he played from 1965 to '67, in community relations for years and was key to the establishment of a Reviving Baseball in Inner Cities (RBI) program in St. Louis. Savage died on Jan. 15. 2023. He was 85.

Mike Shannon's entire nine-year playing career was spent with the Cardinals, but his legacy with the franchise had really only just begun when he played his last game for St. Louis in 1970.

Shannon accepted a job with the Cardinals to work in promotion and sales. In 1972, he moved to the broadcast booth, serving as the color commentator alongside future Frick Award broadcaster Jack Buck.

Shannon became the Cardinals' primary play-by-play announcer when Buck retired. He worked Cardinals games from 1972 to 2021, marking 50 seasons as a broadcaster.

As a player, Shannon was an outfielder early in his career, but he moved to third base mid-career in 1967. His best season was 1968, when he hit .266 with 15 home runs and 79 RBIs and finished seventh in National League MVP voting. Shannon died on April 29, 2023. He was 83.

Ron Tompkins, a reliever who made 40 appearances with the Kansas City Athletics and Cubs, died Feb. 3. He was 78. Tompkins went 0-2, 4.08 in 35 appearances with the Cubs in 1971.

Frank Thomas was one of the more consistent power hitters of the 1950s as an outfielder/third baseman with the Pirates. He then became one of the few players worth watching on the expansion Mets in 1962. Thomas hit 286 home runs over

16 seasons as he played for seven different MLB teams. He hit 30 or more homers three times and made three all-star teams. Thomas died on Jan. 16, 2023. He was 93.

Lee Tinsley, an Athletics 1987 first-round pick who spent five years in the majors as an outfielder with the Red Sox, Mariners and Phillies, died Jan. 12, 2023. He was 53. After his playing career ended, Tinsley worked as a hitting, baserunning and outfield coach in the minors and major leagues

John Tumminia, who died on Dec. 4, 2022 at 70 years old, was a member of the White Sox's scouting department from 1987 until his retirement in 2020 and helped reshape the direction of the franchise during the frenzied winter of 2017. His evaluations in the preceding season were key to Chicago's acquisitions of Lucas Giolito, Reynaldo Lopez and Dane Dunning from the Nationals as well as Yoan Moncada and Michael Kopech from the Red Sox in respective deals for outfielder Adam Eaton and Chris Sale.

More than any acquisition or evaluation, Tumminia—who was the father-in-law of Pirates general manager Ben Cherington—was most proud of his charity, Baseball Miracles, which aimed to bring the game to places it would not otherwise reach. With the help of his friends and colleagues, Tumminia and the Baseball Miracles crew would collect bats, gloves, balls and other equipment and put on clinics for kids in Mexico City, Puerto Rico and Ireland, as well as the United States.

Sandy Valdespino had a lengthy career as a backup outfielder, playing for six different MLB teams over seven seasons. Valdespino hit .230/.286/.295 over his career. He died on Feb. 26, 2023. He was 83

Dave Wills, a play-by-play broadcaster for the Rays for 18 years, died on March 5, 2023. Wills had broadcast the Rays spring training game the day before.

Wills had worked on the White Sox radio crew for 11 years before he came to the Rays. He joined the Rays in 2005, which means that he was part of the soundtrack to all the Rays' biggest moments, including trips to the World Series in 2008 and 2020.

A first baseman-turned-knuckleballer, **Tim Wakefield** went 8-1, 2.15 in 13 starts as a rookie to help the Pirates to the National League Championship Series, where he won both of his starts with complete games.

SPORTING NEWS VIA GETTY IMAGES

Tim Wakefield was a member of multiple Red Sox World Series teams.

And then, as quickly as he'd become a star, he seemed to lose the feel for his knuckleball. He was shelled in Pittsburgh in 1993, demoted to the minors in 1994 and released in April 1995.

It was actually only the start of his career.

The Red Sox signed him, beginning what would become a 17-year career that carved out a spot in Boston sports history. Wakefield went 16-8, 2.95 for the Red Sox in 1995, finishing third in the Cy Young Award voting as Boston returned to the playoffs for the first time since 1990.

That was Wakefield's best season in Boston statistically, but he became a reliable fixture. He made at least 17 starts for the Red Sox in every season from 1995 to 2011, and he was respected as a clubhouse leader. Wakefield was part of the 2004 World Series championship team that ended the Red Sox franchise's multi-generational title drought, and he was still there in 2007 when the Red Sox won again.

Wakefield's final win came on Sept. 13, 2011. By that point he was 45. That final win was his 200th.

STATISTICS INDEX